D0604471

PAGE ONE

PAGE ONE

Major Events 1920-1975 as Presented in

The New York Times

REFERENCE

ARNO PRESS
A New York Times Company
New York · 1975

Library of Congress Cataloging in Publication Data
Main entry under title:

Page One: major events, 1920-1975, as presented in the
    New York Times.

    1. History, Modern—20th century—Sources. I. New
York Times.
D411.P25   1975   909.82   75-7589
ISBN 0-405-06645-7

The New York Times

229 WEST 43 STREET
NEW YORK, N.Y. 10036

ARTHUR OCHS SULZBERGER
PRESIDENT AND PUBLISHER

May 1, 1975

A newspaper is a mirror. Each day it reflects
some segment of the world's activities, be it the joy of
victory in sports or the agony of defeat in war.

Millions of nameless men and women have
lived on this earth since what was to be lasting peace was
signed into effect in 1920. Some have captured the spotlight for a brief moment thrilling us with their exploits as
they flew the Atlantic or walked upon the moon. Others,
like Lenin, left a heritage that continues to affect all of
our lives deeply.

In the succeeding pages the Editors have
captured a tableau of modern history as seen through the
eyes of the reporters and editors of The New York Times.
This is history at its most intimate -- for it only happened
yesterday.

Contents

1920 - 1929

The New York Times.

VOL. LXIX...No. 22,632.   •••   NEW YORK, SUNDAY, JANUARY 11, 1920. In Eleven Parts, Including Picture and Magazine Sections (Rotogravure) and Book Sections.   FIVE CENTS | In Greater New York | Elsewhere TEN CENTS

PEACE SIGNED IN PARIS AND THE TREATY IS NOW IN FORCE; WILSON TO SUMMON FIRST LEAGUE MEETING FOR FRIDAY; LODGE REBUFFS KENDRICK COMPROMISE PROPOSALS

SWEET DEFENDS ASSEMBLY'S ACTION AGAINST SOCIALISTS

Speaker Writes in Reply to Hughes and Condemns Attitude of Socialist Party.

PROMISES A SQUARE DEAL

Republican State Committee Ignores Subject—Major Mills's Protest Sidetracked.

CITY LEADERS ANGERED

Up-State Members Stand with Sweet—Text of the Speaker's Letter.

Speaker Thaddeus C. Sweet of the Assembly last night replied to the letter of Charles E. Hughes condemning the Speaker and the Assembly for suspending the five Socialist Assemblymen-elect at the opening session of the Legislature last Wednesday.

The letter was sent and made public by the Speaker after he had been in protracted conference at the Republican Club and the Murray Hill Hotel with Senator Clayton R. Lusk, who has been investigating seditious activities; Attorney General Charles D. Newton of Albany, counsel of the Lusk committee; Archibald E. Stevenson, J. Henry Walters, President Pro Tem. of the Senate, and other Republican leaders.

A meeting of the Republican State Committee had brought Republican leaders from all parts of the State to this city, and that Mr. Hughes's letter had set many of them thinking and had thoroughly angered Speaker Sweet and his friends was quite evident. It was clear that a majority of the up-State leaders sided with Sweet, while with only one notable exception leaders in this city and prominent party men were vexed and disturbed as they pondered the possibility that the Assembly's action might react unfavorably in this Presidential and Gubernatorial year.

No mention was made of the Socialist at the State Committee meeting, which was attended by Sweet and many Assemblymen. Major Ogden L. Mills went to the meeting with a proxy and a prepared speech, ready to vent wrath, which he voiced freely to friends.

A dozen Republican leaders, among them Senator Walters, labored with Major Mills before the meeting began, and after it had been called to order. Major Mills was earnestly requested by Walters to join him in the billiard room. In the meantime Chairman Glynn rushed through with the routine committee proceedings and by the time Major Mills and Senator Walters were through talking the meeting had ended.

The proposition which contemplates the right of a majority to exclude a minority because of political beliefs, is revolutionary and as serious a threat to representative Government as can be found in our entire history," said Major Mills after the meeting. "In fact, I do not think anything like it has been attempted since the British Parliament expelled Wilkes back in the eighteenth century. I recommend to Speaker Sweet a thorough perusal of the Letters of 'Junius.'"

Speaker Sweet refused to answer questions of reporters but said he would write a letter in reply to Mr. Hughes. The Speaker's letter follows:

Speaker Sweet's Letter.

"New York, Jan. 10, 1920.

"Hon. Charles E. Hughes.

"My dear Judge Hughes I notice in today's columns of the press that you communicated to the your views upon the action of the Assembly in the adoption of the resolution suspending the right of the five Socialists to seats in that body pending an investigation of the charges that they are unfit to occupy a seat in the Assembly of the State of New York. It seems from your communication that you have assumed that the action of the Assembly was in the nature of expulsion. If you read carefully and consider fully the language of the resolution adopted you would see that the resolution provides as follows: Therefore, be it resolved, that the said framing the five Socialist members be denied seats in this Assembly pending the determination of their qualifications and eligibility to their respective seats."

"You should bear clearly in mind that no attack is made upon the views of the Assemblymen-elect in question, however opposed they may be in theory to the institutions of the United States and this State. The question presented squarely is whether the different organizations of which they are members and which they seek to represent in the Legislature advocate methods and employ tactics to bring about the overturn

Continued on Page Twenty-one.

D'Annunzio May Stake Out Rome-Tokio Air Race Course

LONDON, Jan. 10.—A Caproni airplane left Rome yesterday to make a route to be covered in the Rome to Tokio flight which is being arranged and financed by the Italian Government, according to a Central News dispatch from Rome, under date of Friday. The plane was said to have reached Avlona last night and to have departed immediately for Salonlki.

Three more planes engaged in the same work are scheduled to leave Rome in ten days, and it is reported that Gabriele d'Annunzio, who made an aviation record during the war and now is in command of insurgent forces at Fiume, will be in charge of this contingent.

HOUSE AGAIN DENIES BERGER HIS SEAT

Refuses by Vote of 328 to 6 to Admit Milwaukee Socialist to Membership.

MANN OPPOSES REJECTION

Berger Reiterates Opposition to War—Promptly Renominated at Milwaukee.

Special to The New York Times.

WASHINGTON, Jan. 10.—Victor L. Berger of Milwaukee, re-elected to Congress on the Socialist ticket from the Fifth Wisconsin District, was today, for the second time within two months, refused a seat in the House of Representatives. The vote was 328 to 6, taken after Representative James R. Mann of Illinois, formerly Republican leader of the House, and a supporter of the McLemore resolution, had led a fight in Berger's behalf. Those voting in the negative were Representatives Mann and Voigt of Wisconsin, the latter the only member of the House who had voted for Berger, when he was first refused a seat, and Harrold of Oklahoma, Republicans, and Sisson of Mississippi, Sherwood of Ohio, and Griffin of New York, Democrats. Representative Sabath of Illinois, Democrat, voted "present."

The issue came before the House upon a resolution offered by Representative Dallinger of Massachusetts, who chaired the Committee that "That Victor L. Berger is hereby declared not entitled to a seat in the Sixty-sixth Congress as a Representative from the Fifth Wisconsin District and the House declines to permit him to take the oath and qualify as a Representative."

Convicted under the Espionage act and sentenced for twenty years' imprisonment, Mr. Berger presented today the credentials of his re-election last month. When the House assembled Mr. Berger walked down the aisle from the cloakroom and seated himself in the second row, immediately under the Speaker's rostrum, in the Republican side. He appeared to be very nervous during the one-hour debate in which he was decorated as a "traitor and a friend of Germany." He chewed his gray mustache and moved uneasily. But when a Wisconsin member said that he had not recanted his disloyal doctrines, but continued preaching them, Mr. Berger was noticed to nod approval.

Berger Says He Will Run Again.

Following the action of the House, Mr. Berger gave out a statement in which he announced that he would again seek re-election, and that "he held the same position that he did during the war"—opposition to war and recruiting which brought about his conviction under the Espionage act.

Anticipating disorder, special officers were stationed in the galleries, but while there was intense feeling against some of the utterances made in behalf of Mr. Berger, the only disapproval came from the House itself which hissed one or two points and demanded that the vote be taken after half of the one hour apportioned to debate had been consumed.

As the champion of Mr. Berger, the former Republican leader of the House, Mr. Mann, opposed the resolution, which was approved by Mr. Mondell, the present leader of the House, and the other responsible House leaders.

"Mr. Berger," said Mr. Mann, "has been elected anew to the House by a majority of those who vote in his district, and to me the question is whether we shall magnify into an invasion the representative form of government where people who desire changes in the fundamental or other laws of the land shall have the right to be represented on the floor of this House, even though they cannot be fully represented."

"Has it come to the point that a man who believes certain things cannot be heard? His people, his constituents, desire him to represent them. It is not our duty to select a representative from

Continued on Page Seven.

GLASS URGES LOAN OF $150,000,000 TO STARVING EUROPE

Says America Alone Can Avert Anarchy in Austria, Poland and Armenia.

ASKS USE OF WHEAT FUND

Part of $1,000,000,000 Could Be Directed to Establish Credits, He Tells Committee.

AUSTRIA SEES END IN MONTH

Is Ready to Mortgage Her Forests and Customs for Food—300,000 Hungry in Armenia.

Special to The New York Times.

WASHINGTON, Jan. 10.—Secretary Glass, in a letter sent to the Ways and Means Committee today, appealed for an appropriation of $150,000,000 to aid the starving inhabitants of Poland, Armenia and Austria, giving a vivid picture of the distressing situation existing in these countries. Norman Davis, Assistant Secretary of the Treasury, presented additional details of conditions which, he said, must be remedied to prevent actual starvation and the spread of Bolshevism. He read to the committee excerpts from private reports received from American agents which bore out his statements.

Secretary Glass, appreciating the opposition to extending direct financial aid to the war-torn countries, recommended that the assistance go through the grain corporation, which could use the fund of nearly $1,000,000,000 to extend aid through credits or gifts where necessary. This recommendation seemed to meet with the approval of the committee, which will probably authorize the Grain Corporation to expend $150,000,000 of its fund in aid of these countries.

The fund and food would be divided as follows: Armenia, 7,500 tons of flour and other necessities at a cost of $500,000 monthly; Austria, $100,000,000, with a probable reduction to $70,000,000 due to assistance by Great Britain; Poland, 300,000 tons of grain at a cost of $50,000,000; other parts of Europe, $25,000,000.

Norman Davis told the committee that this country must continue to supply food to these three countries until the next harvest. Austria and Poland, he said, could furnish satisfactory security for food furnished them, but in the case of Armenia the aid must be in the nature of charity as that country is without funds or means of establishing credits. Food is also needed in parts of Italy, Hungary and Czechoslovakia, he said.

"The United States has a surplus of food and is the only nation that can prevent the famine," added Mr. Davis. "Great Britain is prepared to cooperate to the full extent of its ability, which probably will be mainly in supplying ships to transport the supplies, as Great Britain, France, and Italy already have let Austria $65,000,000.

Would Mortgage Natural Resources.

"The condition in Austria is so desperate that she is willing to mortgage her forests, the tobacco monopoly, the water power facilities, and even the collection of customs, to obtain food. The Treasury does not believe that customs should be taken because it would cause great delay to economic rehabilitation. Vienna has 2,500,000 people, and it is probable that many of these will have to leave because the surrounding country, since the separation of Hungary, will not support them. Poland deserves help because she is rendering great service to the world fighting the Bolsheviki."

Secretary Glass in his letter summarizes conditions in the respective countries as follows:

"POLAND—According to the best information obtainable, the minimum grain requirement necessary to carry Poland until its next harvest, and which cannot be filled anywhere but in the United States, is 300,000 tons. This deficiency is due to a partial failure of the wheat crop and to a lack of living under a hand-to-mouth regime, which can be remedied only by a steady flow of imports from the only available surplus stocks of food, namely, those in the United States.

"The potato crop, which is the staple food of the poorer classes, has been destroyed by frosts to the extent of 20 per cent. In many districts, as it is impossible properly to care for potatoes in transit. Due to delays in transportation, Poland has been unable to procure clothing, with the result that during the past five years practically all clothing has been worn out and has not yet been replaced. The food situation in Poland is so serious that the European Children's

Continued on Page Twenty.

Reports China and Japan Negotiating on Shantung

SAN FRANCISCO, Jan. 10.—Japan and China have started negotiations on the question of the restoration of Shantung to China, according to a cable dispatch received today from Tokio by the New World, a Japanese newspaper.

SWINDLED CLERGY, WIDOW CONFESSES

Mrs. May J. Bennett, in Tombs, Says "Divine Psychologist" Dominated Her.

WAS A MISSIONARY LEADER

Church, Social and Political Circles of Washington Heights Her Principal Field.

Blaming her downfall upon the influence of a "divine psychologist" who "dominated" her, Mrs. May Jennings Bennett, a handsome, distinguished-looking widow, confessed in the Tombs last night that she had swindled various persons out of large sums of money and that clergymen had been her chief victims.

Mrs. Bennett, one of the Vice-Presidents of the Women's Foreign Missionary Society of the New York Presbytery, and last year its Corresponding Secretary, made her confession to a newspaper man in the presence of the Tombs Warden and said that, after fleeing her bail, she had surrendered herself in the hope that the court would show her mercy and that she would be allowed her liberty that she might work to repay her victims.

Among those she victimized, she told, was a Paulist Father upon whom she prevailed to write a letter to Assistant District Attorney Alfred J. Talley after she had convinced him she had been badly treated. Once the priest had been won over Mrs. Bennett borrowed $200 from him.

Discussing the influence the "divine psychologist" wielded over her, Mrs. Bennett begged that her cult should not be confused with Christian Science, "which is all right."

She recalled how she was arraigned in the West Side Court last June on a charge of grand larceny, how after she had been indicted she was arraigned in General Sessions, where the case was postponed after it was learned there were three other indictments against her and, despite the urgings of several clergymen, who later proved to have been among her victims, her bail was raised to $3,500. She told of running away and of the bail furnished for her by a surety company being forfeited when she failed to appear when her case was called again last December. Then, reverting to the man upon whom she sought to cast the blame, she said:

"I met a man who advertised a sort of 'new thought.' He told me when I went to him that he could make people prosperous. I told him I wanted to be wealthy. I paid him more than $1,000 at different times and he always told me to go right ahead with my schemes and he was with me, that he would pray for their success. I was under a sort of hypnotic influence; I knew what I was doing was not just right, but had not the power to resist.

"Finally, when I was indicted for grand larceny, I realized that I had been in a terrible dream and that this man, who was or called himself a, 'divine psychologist,' had exercised a power for evil and not for good over me. I went to him to help me. He refused to aid me and appeared to be scared to death. I woke up then. I knew I had not been in my right mind."

While she was conversing at her swindling. Mrs. Bennett lived luxuriously at Bretton Hall, a fashionable family hotel, was known in church and charitable parties and entertained generously. She dressed expensively, was a woman of fashion and, in part through her church connections, gained entrée to many fashionable homes.

Under the auspices of a church she gave a "charitable affair," ostensibly for the Red Cross in which she used the names of Collin H. Woodward, a Republican leader in upper Manhattan, and ex-Representative William S. Bennet. The receipts were said to have been large, but nothing remained for the Red Cross when the affair was over.

The charges thus far brought against Mrs. Bennett aggregate in the amount by her alleged swindles $7,000, but the sums Counting is in her confession, would indicate that she had got more. Mrs. Bennett admitted last night that her "chain of victims" comprised a single rooming house.

REPORT OF GERMAN OVERTHROW DENIED; STRIKE SPREADING

Berlin Dispatch Declares Accounts Given by Travelers Are Untrue.

RAILROAD TIEUP IS WORSE

Communists Are Charged with Promoting It for Their Own Political Ends.

CENTRES IN RUHR DISTRICT

Not Even Food Trains Are Moved There—10,000 Berlin Clerks Walk Out of Insurance Offices.

LONDON, Jan. 10.—Reports reached here early today by way of Brussels that the German Government had been overthrown, but these were later denied by an Amsterdam dispatch quoting Berlin advices received this evening. This dispatch reads:

"The report that the German Government has been overthrown is untrue, according to a dispatch received here from Berlin."

Until this dispatch was received there had been no light on the reports, storms having interrupted telegraphic and telephonic communications with Germany since Thursday.

It was reported that the Socialists were masters of the situation and that a general strike had been declared throughout the territory not under allied occupation.

Serious Strike Trouble in Germany.

BERLIN, Jan. 9.—The situation created by the railroad strike became worse yesterday, especially in the Ruhr district, where there were additions to the ranks of the strikers.

The committee of Social Democratic railway men have charged the Communists with responsibility for the strike, alleging that while it is ostensibly an economic movement it is in reality a political measure intended to accomplish the introduction of an industrial council system on the Communist plan.

The Independent Socialists and Communists are held to be responsible for further walkouts in the Essen, Elberfeld, and Munster districts. In the Ruhr district it was impossible to move even emergency food trains. At Düsseldorf a gas and electricity shutdown is threatened owing to the lack of coal. The situation at Dortmund and Dresden clerks are expected to join in the strike. Labor Ministry mediators are arranging for negotiations with the clerks.

At Dortmund a secret strike vote has resulted overwhelmingly in the affirmative.

Ten thousand Berlin insurance clerks struck yesterday, representing seventy-five companies. The employers claim that the walkout is not justifiable, as the Magdeburg, Frankfort-on-Main, Potsdam, Stuttgart, and Dresden clerks are expected to join in the strike. Labor Ministry mediators are arranging for negotiations with the clerks.

WOULD SEIZE WEALTH ABROAD

Erzberger Proposes Entente Have German Fortunes in Switzerland.

BERLIN, Jan. 9.—Speaking in the Reichstag in the biweek district of Württemberg last night, Matthias Erzberger, Vice-Chancellor and Minister of Finance, declared that he proposed to conclude a treaty with Switzerland enabling the recovery of German capital smuggled into that country in 1919. Should the measure fail of its objective, Herr Erzberger asserted he would authorize the Entente to seize such fortunes and credit them to the indemnity to be paid by Germany.

Herr Erzberger has advertised for 2,000 additional rooms to accommodate the staff which he says will be required to locate German capital. He has announced additional taxing measures will be submitted to the Reichstag shortly.

KING GEORGE HOPES NEW ERA HAS DAWNED

Prays People of British Empire May Forever Live at Peace with Themselves and with All Men.

LONDON, Jan. 10.—Replying to a loyal message from the citizens of London on the occasion of the ratification of peace, the King has telegraphed the Lord Mayor of London as follows:

"With all my heart I reciprocate their hopes and fervently pray that, please God, this day may be the beginning of a new era, in which the people of the British Empire may forever live at peace with themselves and with all men."

REPORT OF GERMAN OVERTHROW DENIED

Supreme Council Prompt to Launch the League; Leon Bourgeois to Preside at the First Session

By EDWIN L. JAMES.
Copyright, 1920, by The New York Times Company.
Special Cable to The New York Times.

PARIS, Jan. 10.—The first meeting of the Council of the League of Nations will be opened in Paris at 10:30 o'clock on the morning of Friday, Jan. 16.

This date was set by Premiers Clemenceau, Lloyd George, and Nitti, sitting with the Supreme Council today, and was at once cabled to President Wilson in order that he might issue immediately the formal call for the historic meeting in accordance with the duty placed upon the powers concerned to have their delegates in Paris on the day set. They will gather at the French Foreign Office, where, it is understood, President Wilson's call will be read and the business of the Council started.

England, France, Italy, Japan, Spain, Belgium, and Brazil will be the nations composing the Supreme Council of the League. Leon Bourgeois, representing France, will preside at the first meeting. "here will be two addresses, one by M. Bourgeois and the other by Earl Curzon, representing Great Britain. It was proposed that this gathering be made a big ceremonial event, but the suggestion was vetoed by both Mr. Lloyd George and M. Clemenceau. "No, we won't need any music," added the "Tiger."

It has not been determined whether the Council will meet on the 16th and keep on meeting until it gets its machinery under way. That, however, will be determined before the first meeting takes place. A great deal of quiet preliminary work has been done in outlining the program for the Council prior to the first meeting of the League Assembly, and it is the desire of England to have this work started at once. France, while recognizing the need of haste, rather favors delaying important action until America shall have joined or shown that it will be a long time before she acts.

In other words, if the League is made an issue of the next Presidential election, the League work must go ahead before that time. If there is any chance of early ratification by the Senate, France prefers to wait for the United States.

LODGE SKEPTICAL OF DEMOCRATS' PLAN

Demands Proof of Substantial Party Support Before He Will Discuss It.

COMPROMISE SPIRIT GROWS

Neither Side Anxious to Take Up President's Challenge of Appeal to People.

Special to The New York Times.

WASHINGTON, Jan. 10.—Senator Lodge today furnished the climax to a second day of unusual activity in behalf of a treaty compromise by demanding a showdown from Democratic Senators on reservations proposed as the basis of compromise.

Mr. Lodge sent word to Senators McKellar and Kendrick, coauthors of the recently submitted Democratic reservations, that unless they could present assurances of substantial Democratic support for their proposals further than a compromise upon this basis was useless. Senators with whom Senator Lodge discussed the matter said that the Republican leader had called upon the Democrats to decide whom they would follow—whether President Wilson, insisting upon interpretations as the limit of concession, or Mr. Bryan, counseling ratification upon any basis found practicable, even though that involved Democratic surrender to the Lodge forces.

In spite of Mr. Lodge's position, practically everything that took place today with reference to the Peace Treaty deadlock indicated that President Wilson's warning that he would call for a "great and solemn referendum" of the American people on the treaty if the League of Nations covenant was modified other than by "interpretations" has had the effect of stimulating rather than retarding efforts at compromise between the two opposing groups of Senators. William J. Bryan's appeal for compromise does not figure in the negotiations. His attitude in the situation is looked upon as negligible.

Still Hope for Harmony.

To say that the divergent views of President Wilson and Mr. Bryan have "killed" the treaty and the accompanying covenant is to go beyond the reasonable expectations born of the renewed attempt to harmonize differences between the Senate groups. Friends of the treaty, a good many of whom may also be classed as friends of the President, have by no means given up hope that harmony may result from what earnest devotees of the League by the "comparatively few" heretofore, they declare, sufficient to bring about an agreement as at the present time which, in the words of Article XI, "threaten to disturb international peace or the good understanding between nations upon which peace depends."

"There is the Russian situation, economic chaos in many European countries and controversies left unsettled by the peace conference, and defects in the Peace Treaty itself and particularly its financial provisions. All these matters within the sphere of action of the League.

"In our opinion it is the duty of the League of Nations Union to formulate a policy of its own based on an urge it upon the Governments, but it would be premature today to lay down that policy in detail.

"Certain points, however, such as the

Continued on Page Two.

PEACE MADE WITHOUT POMP

Simplicity Marks Protocol Signing and Exchange of Ratifications.

LERSNER EXPRESSES JOY

Declares Germany's Determination to "Go to the Limit" in Fulfilling Terms.

GIVES WARNING TO ENTENTE

"Gravest Consequences" Foreseen if War Culprits Are Extradited.

By EDWIN L. JAMES.
Copyright, 1920, by The New York Times Company.
Special Cable to The New York Times.

PARIS, Jan. 10.—The Allies and Germany are at peace. The world war ended formally this afternoon, when representatives of the Powers which had approved the Versailles Treaty deposited their certificates of ratification and signed the procès-verbal which put the treaty into effect. The United States took no part in the proceedings.

Simplicity marked the ceremony in the Clock Hall of the French Ministry of Foreign Affairs, where the final act of the great struggle was staged. Fourteen allied and associated powers on the one hand and Germany on the other made peace and are again friendly nations.

The allied Premiers and Foreign Ministers gathered around the long green-covered tables, upon which were drawn by the Secretary Dutasta, and Herr von Simson, Germany's representative, at a separate small table. They arose one by one as they were designated by the master of ceremonies and affixed their signatures to the procès-verbal spread upon a panel in the middle of the long chamber. There was nothing of the dramatic in the actual proceeding. It was dramatic only in its great significance.

Before the ceremony the representatives of England, France, Italy and Japan and the two German envoys in the office of the French Foreign Minister, and the Germans had signed the protocol binding their nation to pay for the sinking of a German fleet in Scapa Flow and to carry out its unfulfilled terms of the armistice. That done, the Premiers and the Germans were escorted to the Clock Room, where were gathered the diplomats of nearly all the nations of the world for, besides those signing, other invited statesmen should be present.

The first report that the treaty had been actually ratified in Paris reached London a little after 6 P. M. But for the bell-ringing, there is a good deal of public interest, and some papers give first place in their news columns to the labor situation at home. For legal reasons the persons in this country who will be presumed to continue a little longer, and it will be terminated by an Order in Council.

People Must Back League, Says Cecil.

LONDON, Jan. 10. (Associated Press).—Whether the League of Nations is to be the real thing or an imposture depends upon the attitude of the people, in the opinion of Lord Robert Cecil, who, as Chairman of the Executive Committee of the League of Nations Union, issued the following statement today:

"The Peace Treaty come into force today, and with it the League of Nations. We, of the League of Nations, welcome its advent, but we must not think that we have all accomplished our ends.

"The League exists, but what is it to be? Is it to be the real thing or an imposture? Are we going to make it an efficient instrument of peace, or is it to become a meaningless addition to the cumbersome forms of old-fashioned diplomacy?

"All depends upon the attitude of the peoples, and, not the least, of the British people. Are they going to show themselves worthy of this great opportunity or not? If they are, there is no time to be lost, for there is much to be done. Reverence for the limitation of armaments must be worked out, terms of the mandate must be settled and mandatories appointed, an international court of justice must be established.

"Beyond these and other duties directly imposed upon the League by the covenant, may result from what earnest devotees of the League by the circumstances at the present time, which, in the words of Article XI, 'threaten to disturb international peace or the good understanding between nations upon which peace depends.'

"There is the Russian situation, economic chaos in many European countries and controversies left unsettled by the peace conference, and defects in the Peace Treaty itself and particularly its financial provisions. All these matters within the sphere of action of the League.

"In our opinion it is the duty of the League of Nations Union to formulate a policy of its own based on an urge it upon the Governments, but it would be premature today to lay down that policy in detail.

"Certain points, however, such as the

Continued on Page Two.

BELLS OF LONDON PEAL FOR PEACE

But News of the Treaty Ratification Stirs Little Popular Interest.

CECIL APPEALS FOR LEAGUE

Reiterates His Declaration in Favor of the Early Admission of Former Enemy Powers.

Copyright, 1920, by The New York Times Company.
Special Cable to The New York Times.

LONDON, Jan. 10.—The London church bells this evening have been pealing in celebration of the conclusion of peace with Germany and the official coming into existence of the League of Nations.

The first report that the treaty had been actually ratified in Paris reached London a little after 6 P. M. But for the bell-ringing, there is a good deal of public interest, and some papers give first place in their news columns to the labor situation at home. For legal reasons the persons in this country who will be presumed to continue a little longer, and it will be terminated by an Order in Council.

Declares That Peace Is Restored.

The protocol between the allied and associated powers and Germany has been signed. The ratifications of the treaty with Germany have been deposited. From this moment the treaty enters into effect. It will be received in all its terms."

That was all. The diplomats filed out of Europe-was at peace."

The absence of Ambassador Wallace, representing the United States, was a distinct disappointment to the French statesmen. They had invited all the diplomats and hoped that Mr. Wallace would attend. A formal invitation was received last night by Mr. Wallace from Premier Clemenceau, who had insisted that he attend. The American Ambassador waited until a late hour for instructions from Washington. When none arrived he returned his invitation to M. Clemenceau.

It was the sixteen minutes before 5 o'clock when M. Lloyd George signed. Ten minutes later all had signed.

Then a letter from the Supreme Council, presiding Germany that the Allies would reduce from 400,000 tons to 275,000 tons their demand for maritime equipment to pay for the Scapa Flow sinking was handed to Baron von Lersner.

Although the United States did not of course sign the procès-verbal, which put the treaty into effect. The procès-verbal of the ratification of the Treaty of Peace signed at Versailles June 28, 1919.

Between the United States of America and the Empire, France, Italy,

"All the News That's Fit to Print."

The New York Times.

THE WEATHER
Rain and colder today; Thursday, fair; southwest and northwest winds.
For full weather report see Page 17.

VOL. LXIX...No. 22,698 ..... NEW YORK, WEDNESDAY, MARCH 17, 1920. TWO CENTS | Metropolitan District 50 Mile Radius | THREE CENTS Within 200 Miles | FOUR CENTS Elsewhere

KAPP QUITS REVOLT 'IN FAVOR OF EBERT'; CRUISER FIRES ON KIEL, 500 REPORTED KILLED; LENROOT PROPOSES NEW ARTICLE X. POLICY

2,500,000 QUARTS OF MILK KEPT FROM CITY, SAYS SWANN

Asserts Somebody Is Holding It Because It Might Decrease Price to Consumer.

HORTON ASKED TO EXPLAIN

Sheffield Farms Head Admits Urging Cut in Production to Aid Farmers.

COULD NOT SELL IT ALL

Concedes That Daily Surplus, if Shipped Here, Would Bring Down Retail Cost.

A daily surplus of 2,500,000 quarts of milk is produced by the dairy farmers in the New York territory, according to information given to District Attorney Swann by Loton Horton, President of the Sheffield Farms Company, Inc., and its council, George W. Alger, at a hearing before the District Attorney yesterday afternoon. This is 300,000 quarts more than the normal average daily consumption. A decrease in the price of milk and the letting in of unlimited quantities would not increase the consumption more than 7 per cent, according to the representatives of the distributing firm.

"The fact stands out," said District Attorney Swann at the close of the hearing, "that there are 2,500,000 quarts of milk ready to come into this city and somebody is holding it because that might cause a decrease in the price to the consumer."

"That's not true," retorted Mr. Horton.

Mr. Swann said he had been given, in a report which had been made by an investigator of the Federal Fair Price Commission in which it was stated that "Lewis Riggs told me that his tenant, James Muldoland, had told him that he had been notified by the manager for Sheffield Farms Company at Dry Adkins-ville that if he bought any more cows, or increased the production of milk, Sheffield Farms would take no more deliveries from him."

"It looks to me," Mr. Swann pointed out passages in a report which had been made by an investigator of the Federal Fair Price Commission in which it was stated that "Lewis Riggs told me that his tenant, James Muldoland, had told him that he had been notified by the manager for Sheffield Farms Company at Dry Adkinsville that if he bought any more cows, or increased the production of milk, Sheffield Farms would take no more deliveries from him."

"It looks to me," Mr. Swann continued, "as if the distributors will not receive the additional milk because it would reduce the price distributors can charge the consumers."

Swann Asked for Explanation.

The conference was the result of the posting of a notice by the Sheffield Farms Company at its Franklinville plant, advising the farmers to decrease the production of milk. Mr. Swann invited Mr. Horton to come to his office and give him his explanation of the posting. This meeting was executive, but those present were reporters later. Mr. Swann said he had not been able to find any violation of the law by the company in posting the notice. The price of milk will be reduced April 1, Mr. Alger said, as it is the beginning of the flush season. Milk prices begin to go downward at this time every year, it was said.

Present at the conference were James B. Stafford and Frank J. Wilson of the Federal Fair Price Commission in New York State, Mr. Horton, Mr. Alger and Mr. Swann.

Mr. Horton explained that the notice to reduce production was sent out by the younger members of the Directorate of the company, and while he was not personally consulted about it beforehand, he saw no objection to it. He and Mr. Alger urged upon Mr. Swann that it was the logical, sound thing to do economically, to which Mr. Swann replied:

"My contention is that if it isn't illegal it should be made so. It is a very close question whether it is illegal or not. We are looking up the law."

The public, Mr. Horton said, is not prepared to absorb the increased supply, and it probably would result in a reduced price to the consumer. In reply to a question from Mr. Swann as to whether the reduced price would cause the public to consume the additional supply, Mr. Horton said his investigations convinced him that the consumption would not be increased more than 7 per cent.

Willing to Make a Wager.

"Oh, New York would very quickly consume a great deal more if the price came down," was Mr. Swann's rejoinder. Mr. Horton replied that if the three cents a quart the consumption would not increase more than 7 per cent. He offered to make a wager with the District Attorney on this.

Mr. Alger then told of the situation, which, he said, confronts the distributing

Continued on Page Three.

"APHRODITE," Last 2 Weeks. Biggest Sensation in N. Y. Mats. Wed., Sat. 50c to $2. Century Thea. Eve. 8:15.—Advt.

Allies' Answer to Wilson on Russia Asks His Ideas

Copyright, 1920, by The New York Times Co. Special Cable to The New York Times.

PARIS, March 16.—The Allied Governments have agreed on a reply to President Wilson's note on Russia. It will probably be dispatched tomorrow.

In their reply the Allies agree with the President that it is desirable that the Allies act in accord with the United States in arranging to resume commerce with Russia, and they express their desire to obtain fully the ideas of Washington on the subject. But they tell the President that March 20, suggested by him as a date for a conference on the matter, is too soon.

For several days there has been more or less semi-official talk that the course of the President was delaying the Russian negotiations.

SENATE COMMITTEE WILL HEAR COLBY

Nominee for Secretary of State Accepts Request to Attend Meeting Tomorrow.

TO ANSWER PARSONS' STORY

Crane's Nomination for Minister to China Is Favorably Reported.

Special to The New York Times.

WASHINGTON, March 16.—Bainbridge Colby has been asked by the Senate Foreign Relations Committee to appear before it on Thursday and has accepted the invitation. The committee is considering Mr. Colby's nomination to be Secretary of State.

The nominee was first asked to appear today at the same time that Herbert Parsons, member of the Republican National Committee from New York, was a witness. Democratic members of the committee, who had been told the nature of Mr. Parsons's testimony beforehand, wished Mr. Colby to hear it and to have an opportunity to reply to it at once, but Mr. Colby was unable to attend today's session.

No information was given out concerning Mr. Parsons's story, though a circumstantial version has been current in Senate lobbies for several days. This version includes reference to a lawsuit and a New York Judge.

After hearing Mr. Parsons committee members said indications were that the Colby nomination would be before them for some time. Mr. Colby may request that witnesses be called to substantiate his version of certain matters to which the committee's attention has been called. Senators said they would give Mr. Colby the fullest opportunity to make any statement he wished or to present any facts he thought pertinent either in person or through others.

It is understood that the committee is dealing now with matters entirely distinct from those which it took up when hearing earlier witnesses with respect to the nomination. The new phase of the inquiry, it is said, has reduced Mr. Colby's chances of confirmation.

Considerable surprise was shown in the Senate today when Senator Lodge reported from the committee favorably the nomination of Charles R. Crane to be United States Minister to China. It was expected that an objection by Senator Knox and possibly by other Senators, would result in an unfavorable report, or at least in holding up the nomination for some time. But when the committee took up the Crane nomination today Senator Knox said he did not wish to stand in the way of other Senators acting as they saw fit, and, without debate, the favorable report was ordered.

There may be some discussion in the Senate, however, before Mr. Crane is confirmed. Some Senators are likely to recall Mr. Crane's former appointment, while Senator Knox was Secretary of State, and his utterances while en route to his post, which resulted in his summary recall.

Gen. Wood Gets Two Months' Leave; To Tour Every State Having Primaries

Special to The New York Times.

WASHINGTON, March 16.—Upon his own application, Major Gen. Leonard Wood has received from the Secretary of War two months' leave of absence from military duties. The leave will begin on March 29. General Wood will employ the leave period in a speechmaking tour in the interest of his campaign for the Republican nomination for President.

According to reliable information it is the intention of General Wood to make a tour of every State which holds a primary for the election of delegates to the Republican National Convention. Secretary Baker was asked today whether General Wood would be permitted to wear citizen's dress during the period of his leave. He said that no application of that sort had been received from General Wood, but if it were made it would be granted.

The application for leave was made by General Wood through regular military channels and was granted promptly. Under the law which permits an officer of the Army to have thirty days'

FALL MALL ROUNDS, famous cigarette new in shape of ball.—Advt.

HOOVER OPPOSED OUR JOINING BOARDS TO ENFORCE PEACE

Wrote Wilson in Paris Last April We Should Avoid Allies' Snarls.

WOULD BREED FRICTION

And Force Us Into False Relationships as Part of a European Alliance.

WOULD AFFECT THE LEAGUE

Our Part, He Held, Was to Avoid Taking Sides and Lend Whole World Our Strength.

Special to The New York Times.

PHILADELPHIA, Pa., March 16.—The Public Ledger will publish tomorrow a special dispatch from Washington containing an important letter which Herbert Hoover addressed to President Wilson at the Paris Peace Conference on April 11, 1919.

The object of the letter was to utter a protest and a warning against the continuance of American membership in the various commissions provided for by the Treaty of Versailles. In it Mr. Hoover declared, in effect, that if the United States participated in the commissions the inevitable result would be the involving of the country into incalculable military and economic adventures. This, he said he was convinced, would be contrary to the wishes, as it would violate the traditions, of the American people. He asserted that America's safe associate in the war were bent on forcing our co-operation for purposes of their own, and urged the President to defeat these aspirations.

Only by detaching itself from palpable European and Asiatic machinations, Mr. Hoover argued, could the United States perform its part in converting the League of Nations into a "strong and independent court of appeal that will have authority." Otherwise the League would "simply become a few neutrals grating an armed alliance."

The concluding portion of the letter is shown at this time as almost a prophetic dip into the future.

"I have the feeling," he wrote, "that revolution in Europe is by no means over," and then he admonished President Wilson against "tying America into an alliance we have never undertaken."

Mr. Hoover's letter is as follows:
"Dear Mr. President:

"Your economic group has had before it the question whether the United States should continue membership in the various commissions set up under the Peace Treaty. I should like to lay before you my own views on this subject.

"I feel strongly that any continuation of the United States in such an allied relationship can only lead to vast difficulty and would militate against the efficiency of the League of Nations. My reasons are as follows:

"1. These commissions are primarily devoted to the enforcement of reparation and other conditions imposed upon the Central Empires. As the United States is not calling for any matter of reparation for defeating the enemy we should not welcome because it was to the belief of the group that 'the managers were trying to put something over on the club members.'

"2. To give moral and political support to the allied Governments in measures generally for their benefit. It cannot be conceived that in the prostrate condition of the enemy that the Allies will require any physical assistance to

Continued on Page Four.

DELPARK SOFT COLLARS Worn by well-dressed men.—Advt.

Full Field Equipment Issued to American Army on Rhine

COBLENZ, March 16.—The American Army of Occupation, numbering 18,000 men, is receiving full field equipment under orders issued before the German revolution.

There have been no movements, however, to reinforce any positions, or any military activities except those concerned with policing the occupied territory.

The total allied forces along the Rhine are estimated at slightly more than 100,000 men.

WOMEN HEADS QUIT UNIVERSITY CLUB

Former Mrs. Grover Cleveland, Other Officers and Members of Committees Resign.

RESENT RECENT CRITICISM

Trouble Started, Says Statement, by Dissatisfied Minority Over Move to Raise Dues.

Headed by former President, Mrs. J. Preston, Jr., formerly Mrs. Grover Cleveland, practically all officers and members of the various committees of the Women's University Club, 106 East Fifty-second Street, has handed in their resignations, to become effective immediately following the annual meeting, April 24. The officers, in a statement they have issued to the 1,200 members of the club, explain that they have been actuated by a "lack of confidence" and particularly by the bitter attack made upon the management" at the club meeting held March 6.

Lack of confidence in the administrative members of the club, according to one statement of the officers yesterday, is entertained only by a minority. They said the criticism of the club's officers dates back several years, but that criticism of their Board of Managers, in line with similar organizations, proposed an increase in the membership dues amounting to $5, which they said was necessary to meet the increase in expenditures.

This increase, it was said, was opposed by "dissatisfied" members, on the ground that the club's finances showed a surplus at the end of the year. This surplus, they maintained, should not have been allowed to accumulate, but should have been used for increasing the comforts of the members of the club. These same "dissatisfied" members also opposed to the statement of the Board of Managers, and opposed the club's efforts to raise funds with which to remit an ambulance to France and carry on other activities on behalf of the members during the war.

Will Decline Renomination.

Mrs. Preston would not discuss affairs of the club, and referred all questions to Mrs. William Henry Hays, 270 Park Avenue. Mrs. Hays said officers and committee members who have resigned would not consent to renomination at the annual meeting.

"The immediate cause of all these resignations," says the announcement of the Board of Managers to the members, "was the bitter attack made upon the management at the club meeting held March 6. Apparently, the principal reason for defeating the motion to increase the dues was the extreme inefficiency of the Board of Managers, the House and Finance Committees. This was only one of similar attacks and accusations of inefficiency made at other meetings and circulated throughout the club by a group of dissatisfied members.

"For some years past the situation of some of these members has made it difficult to secure or keep the services of many valuable members of the club on committees, and has also caused trouble among the employes. For two Winters, at least, closed meetings have been held by this group, attacking the management of the club. These meetings have advertised as open club meetings, but members of the Board of Managers were not told that they were not welcome because it was the belief of the group that 'the managers were trying to put something over on the club members.'

Continued on Page Three.

SIX (6) BELL-ANS in a little HOT water for INDIGESTION. Quick relief.—Advt.

NEW RESERVATION OFFERED

Draft Warns of "Grave Concern" if European Peace Is Threatened.

HAS REPUBLICAN BACKING

Aim Is to Win Votes for Ratification, but Democrats' Stand Is Uncertain.

BRYAN ENTERS FIGHT TODAY

Irish and Korean Recognition Proposed—Kenyon Rebukes Attacks on Britain.

WASHINGTON, March 16.—A general declaration of international policy, under which the United States would view with "grave concern" any future upheaval threatening the peace and freedom of Europe, were drawn up by Republican Senate leaders today and presented as a new reservation to the Peace Treaty.

Intended to replace the more definite pledges of Article X, the new reservation is to be pressed in the Senate as the furthest step which the Republican leaders are willing to take toward the abandonment of American isolation and participation in European conflicts. The reservation reads:

It shall be the declared policy of this Government that, the freedom and peace of Europe being again threatened by any power or combination of powers, the United States will regard such a situation with grave concern, and will consider what, if any, action it will take in the premises.

Senator Lenroot of Wisconsin drafted the reservation in consultation with other Republican leaders, and introduced it in the Senate at the end of a day of debate on the Irish question, which delayed action and blocked the plan to set a day for a final vote on treaty ratification. It was generally predicted tonight, however, that discussion of the remaining issues of the treaty controversy would soon spend itself, and that the ratification roll call would come on Friday or Saturday.

Lenroot Predicts Adoption of Plan.

Mr. Lenroot said tonight without qualification that his new reservation would be adopted. He explained that the reservation was based upon a reservation by Senator Knox of somewhat similar tenor offered last year when the treaty was under discussion in the Senate, and was intended to carry out a policy of isolation under my reservation," said Senator Lenroot.

The Lodge reservation to Article X, adopted recently, relieves the United States from any obligation under Article X, and provides that no action shall be taken in any matter embraced in that article unless Congress shall so declare. Under the qualification contained in the Lenroot reservation the United States Government is committed to take cognizance of any situation that threatens the freedom or peace of Europe by considering what, "if any," action should be taken.

Aim to Win Votes for Treaty.

Not many Democrats had had an opportunity tonight to study the new Republican proposal, and it was uncertain how much support it would command from that side of the Chamber. Some Senators predicted, however, that it might have the effect of softening the assurance of those who oppose the Republican Article X. reservation, and might win over enough Democratic votes to ratify the treaty.

The words "grave concern," one Senator pointed out, usually carry deep significance in international usage and frequently have been employed to describe an attitude contemplating action. Supporters of the reservation declare that in his moral effect such a declaration would be a powerful deterrent should any nation again threaten to imperil Europe as Germany did.

It is expected that it will be argued that the reservation, while not an immediate direct support to the struggling new nations of Europe and would be reassuring to France, whose defensive treaty with this country still awaits ratification here and faces a bitter fight if it is called up for action.

Continued on Page Three.

FOR INDIGESTION—SIX (6) BELL-ANS in a little HOT water. Quick relief.—Advt.

Kapp's Undertaking Only a "Political Boyish Trick," Says Dutch Correspondent, Telephoning From Berlin

THE HAGUE, March 16 (Associated Press).—The Berlin correspondent of The Nieuwe Rotterdamsche Courant telephoned a message to his paper last night. Communication was severed before he finished. He said:

"Germany is a rudderless ship. Kapp's undertaking proves increasingly to be not an achievement, but a political boyish trick. The new Government is seeking on all sides for support, but realizes that support is nowhere to be found. If the situation were not so serious, one——"

At this point communication ceased. When it was established again the correspondent proceeded:

"——one could see the humorous side of this operetta revolution.

"Kapp supported his efforts to win over the Independents by proposing to form a Cabinet embracing the extremest Left to the farthest Right, but this naive plan naturally miscarried. The new Government seems to have allowed the right moment for action to pass and now is endeavoring to seek a safe issue through negotiations with the old régime."

KAPP APPEALED TO HINDENBURG

Both Field Marshal and Helfferich Refused Their Support, London Hears.

LUDENDORFF ALSO SOUNDED

Resignation of Chancellor Was Demanded by Imperial Office for Distributing Cereals.

LONDON, March 16.—The position of the Kapp Government became critical when Field Marshal von Hindenburg and former Minister of Finance Helfferich refused to way of Administration to a dispatch to the Exchange Telegraph from Berlin by way of Amsterdam.

The same source of information said that a council of the new Cabinet held last night was attended by General Ludendorff, former Quartermaster General of the German Army and Hindenburg's close associate in the war.

The Imperial office for the distribution of cereals had issued an ultimatum demanding the resignation of Chancellor Kapp within twenty-four hours, it was added.

Premier Bauer and Minister of Defense Noske of the Ebert Government were inclined to negotiate with the Kapp régime, but Foreign Minister Müller was against any compromise, according to a Berlin dispatch to The Evening News. In connection with the proposed agreement, the Berlin troops were demanding that Noske be named as Minister of Defense by a General of the dispatch said.

It was pointed out by Mr. Lenroot as representing the Taft reservation on Article X. to the bi-partisan conference of Senators and again in the Senate, gave to it the construction that it did not require the United States to assume any obligation to consider any matter that arose under the terms of the article. Mr. Lenroot said that his reservation carried out Senator Walsh's conception called the Taft reservation. "We do not declare a policy of isolation under my reservation," said Senator Lenroot.

The national strike on the German railways was set to begin this morning, said a message to the Exchange Telegraph Company from Berlin filed on Monday. The railwaymen's officials had declared themselves in solidarity with the workingmen of the country. The railwaymen's Central Committee was moving from place to place, fearing arrest by officials of the Kapp Government.

The boatmen and dockers on the Rhine struck in protest against the coup of the Kapp Government, according to a dispatch to The London Times from Antwerp.

An Antwerp message to The Evening News said a fleet of airplanes had left Berlin to scatter pamphlets for the new Government.

Workingmen are reported to have proclaimed a "Council Republic" at Essen and in the Ruhr district.

BAVARIAN CABINET OUT.

Heinrich Mueller, a Democrat, Asked to Form New Government.

BERLIN, March 15.—Advices from Munich say that Heinrich Ernst Mueller of Meltingen, a Democrat, has entrusted today with the task of forming a new Government.

MUNICH, March 16.—The Diet held a brief session this afternoon in order to receive the resignation of the Government. President Schmidt read the commander-in-chief:

"The Superior Command gives the fullest guarantee that the overthrow of the Diet is planned neither for today nor for a later date by any part whatsoever of the garrison of Munich."

FOR INDIGESTION—SIX (6) BELL-ANS in a little HOT water.—Advt.

"ADAM AND EVA," Longacre Theatre, in New York. Longacre Theatre.—Advt.

KIEL BOMBARDED; REPORT 500 KILLED

Cruiser Eckernforde, Controlled by the Kapp Government, Rakes City Streets.

59 DEAD IN DRESDEN FIGHT

Thirty Slain at Harburg. More Than Twenty at Leipsic—Conflicts in Berlin Suburbs.

Copyright, 1920, by The New York Times Company.

Special Cable to The New York Times.

COPENHAGEN, March 16.—A telegram from Kiel reports that the town has been bombarded by the cruiser Eckernförde, which was at the disposal of the new Government.

The cruiser fired through the streets from the harbor, killing some 500 persons and demolishing a number of buildings.

LONDON, March 16 (Associated Press).—Four hundred persons are reported to have been killed and many persons wounded in a bombardment of Kiel by the German cruiser Eckernförde, says a Central News despatch from Copenhagen, quoting the Ekstrabladet's Kiel correspondent.

The dispatch adds that some quarters of the town were destroyed by the bombardment. The cruiser is said to have directed its fire especially against the quarters of the workmen who are opposed to the Kapp Government.

In addition to the report of the bombardment of Kiel, detailed reports have been received of severe fighting. The Daily Mail's Berlin correspondent, under date of Monday, says that the Communists seized the arsenal and six officers, a number of soldiers being killed. Later a motor brigade supporting the Kapp Government retook the arsenal, where about two hundred are reported to have been killed.

A dispatch to the Central News from Berlin, says that reports have been received from Dresden that the Kapp troops, after severe fighting, dislodged the workingmen's guard from the telegraph office in Dresden. The dispatch adds that it is stated fifty-nine persons were killed and more than 200 wounded.

Armored cars manned by regular troops drove up to the Postplatz to turn the workmen's guard out of the buildings. The regular troops are reported to have advanced in large numbers. Thirty persons were killed, including some women and children, in renewed fighting in Harburg, Prussia, six miles south of Hamburg between citizen guards and Baltic troops, advices from Hamburg received in Copenhagen state. Among the killed was Captain Berch, commanding the Baltic troops.

In a demonstration at Leipsic yesterday troops fired on a crowd killing more than twenty persons and wounding about sixty, says the Copenhagen correspondent of the Central News. Eighteen meetings of Communists and Independent Socialists were held at Leipsic and a general strike was proclaimed in that city. After the meetings had been dismissed, street fighting took place and two street car conductors, were killed. When this news reached other workers all street car employes left their posts, leaving the cars where they stood.

The centre of Leipsic has been entirely cordoned off by troops.

Fifteen persons are reported to have been killed and many wounded in fighting at the municipal offices in the southwestern outskirts of Berlin.

At Charlottenburg, a western suburb of Berlin, four persons are said to have been killed and six wounded.

Several persons are reported to have been killed or wounded at Breslau.

HINDENBURG OPPOSED KAPP

Advised His Withdrawal, As Did Groener, Prussian War Minister.

FINANCIAL PRESSURE USED

Soldiers' Pay Held Up—Ministers and Officials Refused to Take Kapp's Orders.

STRIKE POTENT IN RESULT

Has Spread Widely Throughout Germany and Been Very Effective.

LONDON, March 17.—Chancellor von Kapp, head of the Government at Berlin, has resigned in favor of President Ebert, says the Berlin correspondent of The London Times, under date of Tuesday evening. Efforts to form a Kapp Ministry have been abandoned.

BERLIN, March 16 (Associated Press).—The revolution led by Kapp had virtually reached the end of its resources, so far as concerned himself as head of the revolutionary movement, is evidenced by the fact that he is said to have been ready to retire since Saturday, but was persuaded by Colonel Bauer, leader of the Royalist Party, and Major Gen. Ludendorff to remain.

Kapp Regime Impossible, Groener Said.

General Groener, the Prussian War Minister, the Frankfurter Zeitung asserts, telegraphed to Field Marshal von Hindenburg that in his opinion the Kapp-von Lüttwitz Government was an impossible one, whether from the point of view of home or foreign affairs.

General Groener is also credited with having sent a message to President Ebert offering to act as mediator between him and von Hindenburg with a view to restoring constitutionalism.

Von Hindenburg, the dispatches say, advised Kapp to withdraw from his position, if Cologne dispatches are to be believed, and advised President Ebert to call for new elections.

President Ebert's firm grip on administrative affairs in Berlin is indicated by the fact that the Imperial Finance Minister, by his orders, refused to turn over the money necessary for the payment of the troops, demanded by the revolutionary Chancellor, and the Under Secretaries of the Ministries as well as other officials absolutely refused to take their orders from the Kapp Government. Some of them have quit Berlin. Ebert had declared that the honoring of Kapp's financial demands would be treated as treason.

The general strike proclaimed, not only in Berlin but throughout Germany, is more pronounced today than ever, with the result that thousands are feeling the pinch of hunger and the Socialist and labor leaders are urging that this weapon be used in its full force in behalf of the Constitutionalists.

Capital punishment was decreed by Major Gen. von Lüttwitz for those committing strikes or exercising passive resistance in any vital service. This decree was declared to be effective after 4 o'clock this afternoon.

Sixty Reported Killed in Berlin.

Already it has been estimated that sixty were killed in yesterday's fighting, although this figure is semi-officially denied. There were fresh collisions today in the neighborhood of Potsdamerplatz.

Serious Demonstrations at Coburg.

THE HAGUE, March 16 (Associated Press).—The Handelsblad's Berlin correspondent sums up conditions in various towns of Germany as follows:

Quiet prevails in Coburg and Gotha.

At Essen and East Prussia are quiet, but in favor of the new Government. In many other towns there is a general strike; among these are Munich, Hanover and Hamburg. In Hamburg, however, the gas, water and electrical services are in operation.

Serious demonstrations by the Socialists, Independents and Communists

"All the News That's
Fit to Print."

The New York Times.

THE WEATHER
Snow or rain today; Sunday, fair
and slightly warmer; increasing shifting winds.
For full weather report see Page 15.

VOL. LXIX...No. 22,701.

NEW YORK, SATURDAY, MARCH 20, 1920.

TWO CENTS Metropolitan District | THREE CENTS Within 200 Miles | FOUR CENTS Elsewhere

SENATE DEFEATS TREATY, VOTE 49 TO 35; ORDERS IT RETURNED TO THE PRESIDENT; GERMAN DISORDERS GROW, HUNDREDS SLAIN

RED ARMY CAPTURES ESSEN

City Surrenders After Violent Fighting with 300 Reported Slain.

HUNDREDS DEAD IN LEIPSIC

In Kiel the Losses Are Put at 1,000—Ruhr District Aflame With Bolshevism.

EBERT APPEALS TO ALLIES

Workers in Saxony Demand a Soviet Congress—Berlin Has Scores Killed in Clashes.

BERLIN, March 19.—Essen surrendered this afternoon to armed workmen after violent fighting in which it is estimated that 300 persons were killed.

The street fighting at Kiel only ended this evening, after great damage was caused by mortars. It is believed the number of victims in the disorders there was very great.

It is reported that the Communists have occupied five railroad stations to the east of Berlin, and that troops are being rushed thither in armored cars.

STUTTGART, March 19 (Associated Press).—The Ruhr district is aflame with Bolshevism, according to official reports.

Essen has been taken by a Red army and General von Watter's local troops are awaiting reinforcements.

Tewings is said now to be under control of Government troops.

HAMBURG, March 19.—Government troops in the station here were disarmed this morning without bloodshed and sailors hoisted the white flag over the cruisers Schwartzburg, Regensburg and Kolberg.

The captain of the Wittlesbach committed suicide by shooting.

LEIPSIC, March 19 (Associated Press).—Although an agreement had been reached on Wednesday night between leaders of the workmen and the military authorities for a peaceful settlement of the prevailing situation, the workers yesterday rejected the agreement and fighting was resumed.

Major Gen. Pilack, commanding the city, late yesterday brought a Reichswehr brigade into the city to reduce the hard-pressed volunteers, and ordered a reinforced state of siege. Fighting continued throughout the day and is into the night, workmen everywhere making barricades. In the course of the afternoon a military airplane dropped bombs on Johannisplatz; another airplane was shot down by the workmen.

The General Post Office, railroad station, Town Hall and other public buildings are still in the hands of the volunteer forces.

Losses in the fighting are said to be extremely heavy, and rumors of hundreds killed and wounded in various parts of the city are met on every hand.

1,000 Reported Killed in Kiel.

COBLENZ, March 19 (Associated Press).—Unconfirmed reports received here are to the effect that 1,000 persons have been killed at Kiel. It is said the situation there is grave.

The Communists are reported to be gaining headway in Saxony and Westphalia. A Soviet republic has been proclaimed at Gera.

In the Ruhr Basin the Majority Socialists have given an order to end the strike, but it is doubted if the order is obeyed by the Communists, who continue masters of the situation at Bochum, Dortmund and Gelsenkirchen. On the other hand the Communists have been badly beaten at Solingen and Elberfeld, where they put 5,000 men in line.

LONDON, March 19.—Private advices from Paris state that the Ebert Government has asked the Allies to permit it to send German troops to put down Bolshevism in parts of the neutral zone which was established by the Peace Treaty and in which the Germans were not to have troops.

There is no intimation what action the Allies will take in this matter.

President Ebert believes that military action is necessary to save the south of the country from the Reds.

COPENHAGEN, March 19.—A despatch from Munich, Bavaria, dated Thursday, says Premier von Kahn, in addressing the Landtag on events in Nuremberg, said detachments of some 1,200 revolutionary sailors fired on a detachment of regulars from windows of houses, wounding several pedestrians. In the afternoon a large crowd tried to storm the police station, and twenty-

Continued on Page Three.

Police Trail Kaiser in Walks, Only a Few Steps Removed

AMERONGEN, March 19 (Associated Press).—Evidence that an extremely close guard has been placed by the Dutch Government on former Emperor William was obtained today.

Police officers were detailed to follow him, a few steps in the rear, as he walks about the garden of the Bentinck castle here.

THE HAGUE, March 19 (Associated Press).—It is believed that the former Crown Prince Frederick William was asked today to give a pledge to his father not to mix in German politics and to consent to definite internment.

Secretary General Kan of the Dutch Government went to Wieringen today and conferred with Frederick William and Burgomaster Pereboom.

The anti-militarist and anarchist societies of Holland have arranged a demonstration in Amsterdam March 30 to protest against the continued residence of the Hohenzollern family in Holland.

JUNKER FAREWELL A BERLIN TRAGEDY

Terrible Scenes in Heart of the City When Baltic Troops Fired Into Crowds.

MOB STORMED THE ADLON

Handkerchief Waved from a Window to Departing Soldiers Caused Catastrophe.

By GEORGE RENWICK.
Copyright, 1920, by The New York Times Company.
Special Cable to The New York Times.

BERLIN, March 19.—As the Junker army evacuated Berlin this afternoon a tragic encounter took place at the corner of Wilhelmstrasse and Unter den Linden in front of the Adlon Hotel. A vast crowd had assembled in Unter den Linden to see Kapp's beaten force leave the city. At about 4:30 o'clock the masses of people who had been under hot articulate became somewhat threatening in their demeanor and numerous salvos were fired into the air by the soldiers. This sent the crowd rushing backward for a while, but it soon gathered again. A more subdued mood watched the troops tramp out of Wilhelmstrasse across the Pariserplatz and through the Brandenburg Gate.

It was just a few minutes before 5 o'clock when the tragic incident occurred. Some one, it is said, senselessly enough, waved a handkerchief from an upper window of the hotel. This rather angered the crowd, a section of which rushed the entrance and made its way into the hall of the hotel. Some damage was done there but the people were perhaps no more than 5 seconds before the detectives to arrest him and to order him into the street. As they left the building some soldiers near at hand, evidently under the impression that the crowd was about to rush the outgoing troops, opened fire. Most of the shots went in the air but a number were fired into the crowd.

Panic Among the Masses.

The scene which followed was a terrible one. I witnessed it from a window overlooking Wilhelmstrasse and Unter den Linden. The people on Unter den Linden and thickly packed on both sides of the street were suddenly reduced and transferred to patrol last Wednesday. These two policemen, according to a member of the District Attorney's staff, was

Continued on Page Three.

INDICT A. D. PORTER, ENRIGHT'S DEPUTY, IN VICE INQUIRY

Grand Jurors Act on Sleuths' Story of Capture with Woman in Raid.

SAY HE FORBADE ARRESTS

Neglect of Duty Is the Formal Charge—Official Protests His Innocence.

TWO ACCUSERS SHIFTED

Sent to Uniformed Duty After Talking with Assistant District Attorney.

Third Deputy Police Commissioner Augustus Drum Porter was indicted yesterday by the regular Grand Jury for neglect of duty on the testimony of three detectives, who said that they arrested him and an unidentified woman in an apartment in West Ninety-sixth Street in a raid on March 12, 1919, but released them when the man produced credentials and ordered them to drop the matter.

Police Commissioner Enright promptly suspended Porter when notified of his indictment. A bench warrant issued for Porter did not reach him, but Frank Hendrick of 120 Broadway, his lawyer, promised to produce him in court at 9 o'clock this morning. Through his lawyer Porter said that he was entirely innocent and the victim of "a frame-up."

You remember how Assistant District Attorney Smith was making wholesale raids during the war," Mr. Hendrick added. "He was ready then to arrest the whole town. Well, about the same kind of thing is going on today. All sorts of wild charges are being made for the purpose of making a sensation. Mr. Porter is absolutely innocent of the charge against him and will speedily prove it. He did not even know what he was accused of when I first talked to him today. If he was guilty of the things charged by these policemen he would be a lunatic, not a criminal. Commissioner Porter has been in charge of the police trials at Police Headquarters and that has made him a shining mark. He is not arrested as an individual but as a unit in a movement or drive in the District Attorney's office."

Neglect of duty by a public official is punishable by a maximum of three years in prison and a fine of $500. The specific charge against the Third Deputy is that in the circumstances in which he was alleged to have been found by the detectives it became his duty to order the detectives to arrest him and to his alleged companion, and that he not only neglected to do this but gave orders of opposite tenor.

Accusers Recently Transferred.

The indictment was returned at 7:30 P. M., immediately after the Grand Jury had heard the three detectives making the charges—Detectives Hilbert Wheelwright, Frederick Berger and Matthew J. Cushing, who were attached to the Special Service Squad of Inspector Thomas V. McDonald at the time, the arrest was made. After working on Inspector McDonald's staff for two years Wheelwright and Berger were suddenly reduced and transferred to patrol last Wednesday. These two policemen, according to a member of the District Attorney's staff, was

Continued on Page Nine.

Japan Spurs Shantung Parley; Ready for Big Concessions

TOKIO, March 19 (Associated Press).—It is understood here that the Government has instructed Yukichi Obata, the Japanese Minister at Peking, to begin negotiations immediately for a speedy settlement of the Shantung question, as the views of the Japanese and Chinese Commissioners appointed to investigate have been found to concur in the main points, and Japan is ready to make large concessions toward an amicable solution.

SAN FRANCISCO, March 19.—The National Assembly of China, sitting in Peking, is reviewing a request from the Japanese Minister at Peking for opening negotiations for a settlement of the Shantung question, according to a despatch dated March 17, to the Sai Gai Yat Bo, the Chinese World, a daily newspaper here.

STANDARD OIL GETS $25,000,000 LEASE

Welles Building Gives Company Control of Broadway Frontage of 528 Feet.

HOLDINGS NOW $12,000,000

Corporation Has Biggest Plot in Downtown District—E. E. Smathers the Seller.

In probably the largest leasing transaction ever closed in the history of New York the Standard Oil Company of New York acquired yesterday from E. E. Smathers the Welles Building at 14 to 20 Broadway for a term of ninety-nine years at a net rental of $250,000 a year, indicating a rental for the term of approximately $25,000,000. The lessee will pay the taxes and all other carrying charges. The magnitude of the transaction may even eclipse the recently reported lease by J. P. Morgan & Co. of the Mills Building, at 11 Broad Street, which was taken for a term of eighty-four years at a figure not yet announced.

The Welles Building is nine stories in height covering a plot at Broadway frontage of 89.5 feet, running back 136.5 feet, with an "L" measuring 115.6 feet to 7 Beaver Street, where it has a frontage of 51.7 feet. The building surrounds the northeast corner of Broadway and Beaver Street, occupied by the home of the New York Produce Exchange Bank, a twelve-story building, on plot 73.7 by 32.8, and two five-story structures on Beaver Street, owned by George F. Lockwood.

Bank Property Sold.

The bank property was sold yesterday to an unnamed buyer, rumored to be the Standard Oil Company, official announcement being made that the Board of Directors of the bank had leased for a term of years, quarters in the new Cunard Building, under construction at 25 Broadway. The bank will remain in its present quarters until May, 1921.

Last month the twenty-story office building at 32 Broadway was reported sold to the Standard Oil Company by the Lower Broadway Realty Company. The structure occupies a plot with a frontage of 116.3 feet on Broadway, running through to New Street, whose the frontage is 115 feet. To the north of this building is the low Standard Arcade Building, also owned by the Standard Oil Company and also having a New Street frontage. Negotiations are reported pending for the sale of this Hudson Building at 32.8, and the building at 42, and it is probable that the Standard Oil Company intends to add this property to its large holdings at this point.

Biggest Broadway Frontage.

Closing of these deals will give the oil company control of the largest Broadway frontage in the city, beginning at Beaver Street and running north 528.10 feet. The only properties in the block bounded by Broadway, Beaver, New and Exchange Place not owned by the company will be the nine-story company "still by" Exchange Court, a twelve-story structure at 52 Broadway, corner of Exchange Place, and the seven-story Lisbon Building at the northern corner of New and Beaver Streets. The Standard Oil Company holdings in the block will aggregate in value to $17,000,000.

No information was obtainable yesterday regarding the use to which the enormous site would be put. It is held, however, by real estate men generally, that the site will be available for improvement by the company which owns it, as the entire downtown district.

Mr. Smathers, the seller, has figured within recent weeks in some of the biggest transactions of the year. Last week he paid $650,000 for the Lyric

Continued on Page Two.

MAYOR OF CORK IS SHOT DEAD BY MASKED MEN

Assassins Escape in Automobile After Killing Executive in His Residence.

VICTIM A SINN FEINER

London Government Takes Special Precautions to Prevent an Easter Uprising.

MESSAGE BY DE VALERA

Cables Dublin Suggesting a "Te Deum" in All Irish Churches for Senate's Reservation.

LONDON, Saturday, March 20.—Thomas MacGurin, Lord Mayor of Cork, was shot dead at 1 o'clock this morning.

The revolver was fired by masked persons whose identity is unknown. They entered his residence, and after firing the shot, escaped in an automobile.

Half a dozen men knocked at the door of the home of the Lord Mayor, Mrs. MacGurin opened the door and the men rushed in.

Some of them held her while others ran upstairs to the Mayor's bedroom. They took him to the landing and shot him in the chest. They then fled in haste.

Mrs. MacGurin telephoned immediately for a doctor and a priest. The Mayor died soon after the arrival of the priest.

Mayor MacGurin, who was a prominent Sinn Feiner, was interned after the Easter rebellion.

The latest previous outrage in the Cork district was perpetrated on the night of March 11, when Constable Scully was shot at Glenmire. Two soldiers and several civilians were killed by gangs in the same vicinity the day before.

Twenty-seven police and Government employes had been assassinated in Ireland since Jan. 1, 1919, according to an announcement made in Commons on Thursday by the Chief Secretary for Ireland.

LONDON, Saturday, March 20.—The Government is taking special precautions against possible outbreaks in Ireland on Easter Monday, according to The Daily Mail, which asserts that the authorities have known for some time that the Sinn Fein has considered the possibility of armed risings and drawn up its plans.

"It is not believed, however," the newspaper adds, "that the movement is sufficiently supported to be really formidable, although it is possible there may be sporadic outbreaks in certain districts.

"Precautions also have been taken at Glasgow, where the Sinn Feiners boast the possession of arms and ammunition and threaten a disturbance at Easter Monday. It is rumored that the prospective trouble in Manchester and Liverpool is not expected to materialize."

Referring to the notification given by Allen Clement Edwards, Liberal, to The London Times of his intention to ask the Premier on Monday whether the Government is informed of risings planned for Easter Monday and an announcement from Germany, The Daily Mail declares that no arms from Germany have been seized and that the Government is convinced Germany is in no manner implicated in any Sinn Fein plot.

LONDON, March 19.—Serious statements regarding the continued operations of the republican army in Ireland were made in the Divisional Court here today when the question was raised as to the power to retain Irishmen in prison without trial under the Defense of the Realm Act, which was a war measure.

The Attorney General, upholding the regulation, said that any illegal republican army had continued its preparations with the avowed object of establishing a republic, and he declared that the present state of Ireland was due to the

Continued on Page Two.

Lodge Is Willing to Take Treaty Into Campaign; Hitchcock Glad That Reservations Are Nullified

Special to The New York Times.

WASHINGTON, March 19.—After the adjournment of the Senate tonight Senator Lodge, leader of the Republican majority, said:

"The treaty is gone. It has been rejected by the Senate and sent back to the President. If the President chooses to return it to the Senate it will have to go through the same process as before. If it goes to the Foreign Relations Committee it will be treated as new business. If the President desires to make a campaign issue on the treaty the Republicans are willing to meet that issue."

Senator Hitchcock, leader of the Democratic minority, said:

"I am glad that there was not a vote for ratification which carried the Lodge reservations, but the result was about what I expected. The treaty is now before the President and if there is to be further action he must take the initiative."

BRYAN SAYS PEOPLE WILL SAVE TREATY

Believes Public Sentiment Will Compel Senate to Accept League of Nations Also.

ATTACKS PARTY LEADERS

Unofficial State Convention Not Representative on Liquor Issue, He Says.

Belief that defeat of the Peace Treaty in the Senate is not final, and that the sentiment of the American people will force the Senate to ratify the compact and permit the entrance of the United States into the League of Nations, was expressed last night by William J. Bryan in a speech at a dinner in honor of his sixtieth birthday at the Aldine Club, 200 Fifth Avenue.

Before discussing the treaty Mr. Bryan had talked forcibly on prohibition and had approved the assertion of Samuel Seabury, the toastmaster, that the declaration of the recent Democratic State Convention favoring the repeal of the prohibition amendment misrepresented the Democratic Party. Mr. Bryan declared that prohibition was here to stay, and that no group of Eastern Democratic leaders would be able to commit the Democratic Party to a policy of opposition.

Mr. Bryan's assertion that the American people would see to it that the Peace Treaty was ratified came with rather dramatic suddenness at the end of his speech. He stated that he believed the constitutional provision, requiring the vote of two-thirds of the Senate to ratify a treaty, should be changed, so that merely a majority was required.

"If a majority has a right to take this country into war a majority ought to have a right to take the country out of war," said Mr. Bryan. "I think that the controversy over the treaty precipitated by Senate Knox's resolution declaring that a state of peace exists between the United States and Germany, the President is practically certain to ignore it. He holds that this is an act constitutionally vested in the Executive and that no action by Congress can compel him to follow any other course than that which he chooses.

There is a general conviction in administration circles that the President should act at once to end the anomalous condition of affairs that exist between the United States Government and the nations against which it declared war. He will be advised that negotiations for a peace should be entered into at once with Germany, Austria, and Hungary, and at the same time the United States should begin exchange with his Allies to obtain their assent to the protection of the rights guaranteed the United States in the treaties with the governments with which it was at war.

"I believe that our boys can do more for peace by their influence now than 2,000,000 of them in arms can do a year from now. I think that the world needs us and that, if we refuse to do our duty and enter the League of Nations and if we are foolish enough to permit conditions in Europe to continue there will be a new war over there. Who can say whether the sparks kindled by such a conflagration might not cross the Atlantic?"

Mr. Bryan asserted that there had been unnecessary stress upon Article X, which he said would never be invoked unless the moral force, contained in the rest of the covenant of the League of Nations failed. He stated that he believed that the provisions for a declaration of war, the abolition of secret treaties and the encouragement to disarmament, contained in the covenant, alone justify the League. "If the world's back is broken by war expenses," he said, "if we now go to work and build up great armies and navies, the result will be nothing but bankruptcy.

Mr. Bryan thinks that the American people will be willing to spend

Continued on Page Two.

AMERICA ISOLATED WITHOUT TREATY

Its Defeat, Washington Feels, Will Add to Our Unpopularity Abroad.

STILL TECHNICALLY AT WAR

Hope Expressed That Wilson Will Take Steps to Re-establish Relations.

Special to The New York Times.

WASHINGTON, March 19.—In its international aspects the rejection of the Versailles Treaty by the Senate leaves the United States in an awkward position. America's isolation is now a reality. Not only is this Government now a member of the world league, designed to prevent future conflicts between nations, but it is also still at war with Germany.

Following this action, Senator Robinson of Arkansas, a Democrat, moved to reconsider the vote by which ratification failed. A strict parliamentary battle followed, in which the Republican mild reservationists joined the Democrats in a ruling by Senator Cummins, who was in the chair, and refusal of the mild reservationists to co-operate further with the Democrats unless they were assured that the second vote on the treaty would be taken at once, cut short Mr. Robinson's efforts.

The Senate adjourned to meet again Monday, after the treaty had been ordered to be returned to the President. As that will have been done by Monday, any motion to reconsider cannot be made again, Senator Lodge said after the voting, because the Senate cannot reconsider action on a question over which it has no longer relinquished control.

What President Wilson will do now is problematical. No intimation is obtainable at the White House concerning the rejection of the treaty.

On the resolution of ratification fourteen more Democrats voted to approve the treaty with the Lodge reservation than on the resolution of last November, when four months ago. On Nov. 19, when the Senate rejected the Lodge ratifying resolution by 41 to 51, but seven Democratic Senators voted to ratify: Gore, Myers, Pomerene, Shields, Smith of Georgia and Walsh of Massachusetts.

Today the following Democrats joined the seven: Ashurst, Beckham, Chamberlain, Fletcher, Henderson, Kendrick, King, Nugent, Phelan, Pittman, Ransdell, Smith, Trammell and Wolcott.

The roll call upon the Lodge resolution of ratification was as follows:

Twelve Senators were absent or not voting. As a two-thirds vote was necessary to ratify, pairs were grouped in the ratio of two for ratification to one against. Senator Penrose, Republican, of Pennsylvania, was paired against ratification with Senators Hardwick, Republican, of Ohio and Nelson, Republican, of Minnesota, who were for ratification. Senator Hale, Republican, of New Mexico was paired against ratification with Senators Newberry, Republi-

---

LACK 7 VOTES TO RATIFY

28 Republicans and 21 Democrats Support Lodge Reservations.

23 DEMOCRATS OPPOSE

12 Republicans Also Against Resolution—Reconsideration Is Blocked.

PEACE DECLARATION URGED

Knox Move Waits Until Monday —Senators Look to Wilson for Next Step.

Special to The New York Times.

WASHINGTON, March 19.—The Senate this evening, for a second time, refused to ratify the treaty of peace with Germany, and sent it back to President Wilson.

By a vote of 49 to 35, seven short of the necessary two-thirds of the members present, the Senate rejected the Lodge resolution of ratification.

It then adopted a resolution, proposed by Senator Lodge, to return the treaty to the President, advising him formally that the Senate had failed to advise and consent to its ratification.

The resolution reads:

"That the Secretary of the Senate be instructed to return to the President the Treaty of Peace with Germany signed at Versailles on the twenty-eighth day of June, 1919, and respectfully inform the President that the Senate has failed to ratify said treaty, being unable to obtain the constitutional majority required therefor."

Continued on Page Two.

Duchess of Marlborough Takes First Step Toward Divorce After Years of Separation

Copyright, 1920, by The New York Times Company.
Special Cable to The New York Times.

LONDON, March 19.—A petition for restitution of conjugal rights brought by Consuelo Spencer Churchill, Duchess of Marlborough, against her husband, the Duke of Marlborough, will be heard by the President of the Divorce Division on Monday afternoon.

The suit for restitution of conjugal rights, in the case of a woman, is usually a preliminary to divorce proceedings. If the court grants her an order for such restitution and the husband refuses to obey, it is possible for the wife to establish legal desertion. This will entitle her to a judicial separation or, coupled with proof of misconduct, to a divorce.

During many years there has been much talk about matrimonial differences in this ducal household. In 1906 a private agreement to separate was arrived at by the Duke and Duchess, and it became known that this agreement was reached as a result of the intervention of King Edward.

When the Duchess, who was Miss Consuelo Vanderbilt, came to England from New York twenty-five years ago, she was welcomed into English society with open arms, and soon earned the good graces of the royal family. At the christening of their eldest son, the Marquess of Blandford, who was recently hurried to the Hon. Mary Cadogan, niece of the Earl of Cadogan, King Edward, then Prince of Wales, acted as godfather, and Queen Victoria sent a telegram of congratulation.

The second son of the Duke and Duchess is Lord Ivor Churchill.

The Duchess is probably one of the cleverest and most intelligent society women of the day. In 1916 she was elected to the London County Council as a progressive member for Southwark. The Duke, whose family dates back to the reign of Edward IV, is the owner of more than 20,000 acres and the splendid old palace of Blenheim. In 1917 the Duke was appointed Parliamentary Secretary of the Board of Agriculture, a post which he resigned a year later.

3

The New York Times.

VOL. LXIX...No. 22,717   NEW YORK, MONDAY, APRIL 5, 1920.   TWO CENTS Metropolitan District | THREE CENTS Within 200 Miles | FOUR CENTS Elsewhere

FRANCE TO ENTER GERMANY AND SEIZE FOUR CITIES BECAUSE GERMANS HAVE SENT TROOPS TO RUHR BASIN WHERE THEY HAVE ROUTED RED BANDS IN PITCHED BATTLE

IRISH START WAVE OF INCENDIARISM BURNING TAX LISTS

Fires in Seventeen Government Offices in Many Cities—No Concerted Uprising.

35 ATTACKS ON BARRACKS

Spare Families of Police—Four Men Are Shot, One by Soldiers Whom He Resisted.

CUT WIRES NORTH, SOUTH

Authorities Say New Tax Assessments Will Be Made—Arrest Ten Sinn Feiners.

Copyright, 1920, by The New York Times Company.
Special Cable to THE NEW YORK TIMES.

DUBLIN, April 4.—Fires broke out in a number of Dublin offices last night belonging to Inspectors, Surveyors and Collectors of Income Tax. In all cases much damage was done and records were destroyed.

It is reported that similar burnings have taken place all over Ireland. One Custom House is said to have been burned to the ground. In others the persons who entered and carried out the destruction were armed and held up the caretakers. The reason is obvious.

There is no indication of the reported Easter rising.

The first of the fires which occurred in Dublin was detected at 9 o'clock, and for five hours the fire brigade was busily engaged suppressing the outbreaks. Four of the fires were in Dawson Street, and the raiders gained entrance to the block of offices in which that of the Surveyor of Taxes was situated by holding up the caretaker with revolvers. They then ran upstairs to the tax office and set it alight, using petrol to feed the flames. Extensive damage was done to books and records.

While the fire brigade was quelling the outbreak there further fires were reported to them in the block of offices across the street. In each case the flames obtained a strong grip on the premises, and contents which were not destroyed by fire were damaged by smoke and water.

Beresford Place was the scene of the next outbreak to which the brigade was called, and it was later summoned to Marlborough Street. It was then an hour after midnight, and this last of the series was the fiercest of all. The office was completely destroyed, the floor burned through and the premises beneath damaged.

In County Donegal, at 11 o'clock, fifty armed and masked men raided the house of Maria Patten at Kenneden, near Ballyshannon. Her two brothers were staying with her, and the raiders bound them, and covering Miss Patten with a revolver thoroughly searched the premises for documents. They removed gun books and also took away a gun and ammunition.

In another case four masked and armed men called at the lodgings of the local excise officer and demanded his income tax papers and arms. He had none of the latter, but he was bundled over all over into his income-tax books.

Will Make New Assessment.

These incidents are typical of others that are being enacted throughout Ireland under protection of the darkness. No arrests have been made.

On inquiry at Dublin Castle this afternoon information was given out that no car reports of raids on seventeen offices had been received, among the places affected being Cork, Clifden, Clonmel, Ballina (in County Mayo) and Ballinahinch (in County Down).

"If the object is to destroy the machinery for collection of the income tax," said an official, "it certainly will fail and will only cause inconvenience to individuals from whom the tax has already been collected. A reassessment can be made where records have been destroyed and it will be the task of the individual to prove that the demand has been paid.

In addition to raids on income tax offices, huts and barracks vacated by the constabulary have been attacked, and in many cases totally destroyed. Clearly forty such attacks were carried out, two-thirds being directed against the families of the police officers were still living, although the men had been withdrawn because the buildings were too isolated or not suitable for defense. The raiders, who in some districts numbered 150, heavily armed and carrying bombs and explosives, warned the occupants of their intentions and gave them a small margin of

Continued on Page Three.

Chicago Tribune Asks Public To Borrow it, Not to Buy It

Special to The New York Times.

CHICAGO, April 4.— The Chicago Tribune in its first editorial this morning said:

"Don't buy the Tribune—borrow it. The Tribune may seem to be standing on its head, but it is forced to ask people not to buy it. It wants to keep every one of its readers and gain new ones, but it cannot sell them all the paper. The paper shortage makes it impossible to do so.

"If two families would use one Tribune we could keep the orders and they could have the Tribune. We want the readers; they evidently want the Tribune. Better days some day, but just now borrow and don't buy the Tribune."

PLAN A VAST STRIKE TO 'SAVE 8-HOUR DAY'

Marine Workers Demand Nation-Wide Call to 6,000,000 Union Workers.

GOMPERS'S HELP SOUGHT

Railroads' Manager Declares Harbor Conditions Are Improving Steadily

A general strike of the 6,000,000 union workers in the country against what is termed "a conspiracy on the part of employers to do away with the eight-hour day " is being agitated in this city. It was learned yesterday, as an outgrowth of the strike of harbor workers begun last week.

Leaders in the Marine Workers' Affiliation admitted yesterday that the nation-wide strike was being urged with the object of getting assurances from employers that the eight-hour day would not be jeopardized. The plans, it was said, were being submitted to Samuel Gompers, head of the American Federation of Labor. Although their primary purpose is to gain aid for the striking harbor workers, who charge that the Erie Railroad, in hiring seven of its lighters to a former employee of the company was merely evading the Escha-cummins eight-hour law, there is a broader object of forcing ironclad agreements requiring longer hours from every employer in the country.

While the union leaders were planning yesterday to force this drastic action to help them win the strike against the railroads here, the transportation officials were working to clear up the congestion wrought by four days of the strike, and to restore normal schedules today, when the influx of commodities will cause the first real test of the harbor service under strike conditions. Although a statement by J. J. Mantell, Chairman of the Managers Association, asserted that the ferries, with exceptions, were running regularly, it also showed that less than 25 per cent. of the tugs were now in operation. A large part of the traffic is being diverted by way of Poughkeepsie, and quantities of goods are being brought over on the ferries, but this method will prove adequate to move all of the food supply in its normal flow remains to be seen.

Seek Gompers's Co-operation.

The plan for a nation-wide strike was discussed by Thomas R. Healey, President of the Marine Workers' Affiliation, Captain William A. Maher, Vice President of the organization, and President of the Masters, Mates and Pilots; James H. Stanton, head of the Port and Terminal Workers, and F. Paul Vaccarelli, business agent of the Harbor Boatmen's Union. Mr. Gompers will be asked to submit the plan to labor unions throughout the country.

There are, it is estimated, 6,000,000 trades union members in the country, of which 4,000,000 are members of the American Federation of Labor. The harbormen believe that if they present to all the workers information they say

Continued on Page Eight.

Clinton Convicts Turned Into Magnets by Botulinus Germ in Canned Salmon

Special to The New York Times.

ALBANY, April 4.—Dr. John B. Ranson, in a report which he sent to Charles F. Rattigan, Superintendent of Prisons, today, declared that thirty-two convicts of Clinton prison at Dannemora had been turned into human magnets as the result of a peculiar poisoning that had been baffling medical scientists for the last week or more. Dr. Ranson is the prison physician, and he called to his assistance in determining the mysterious ailment of the prisoners Dr. G. W. Lamson and Dr. J. N. Roseman of the Preventive Medicine Department of Harvard, and Dr. Olaf Olsen, Food and Drug Inspector of the Federal Department of Agriculture.

They found that whenever any of the men touched steel sparks would fly and their finger tips would violently vibrate the filaments of electric bulbs. They traced the trouble to what is termed the deadly botulinus germ, which they believe came from canned salmon served to the men about two weeks ago. While knowing that this germ generates electricity, they are unable to understand how it turns the victims into human electrodes.

Two of the men died from the disease. Sixteen are not so improved that the hospital, but the others are still surcharged with electricity and their vision is impaired.

CRUCIAL PRIMARY TODAY IN MICHIGAN; RESULT UNCERTAIN

Wood's Friends Expect Him to Win by 30,000, but Johnson Is Strong in the Cities.

BLIZZARD MAY CUT VOTE

Labor Fears for Its High Wages and Expects Johnson to Help Keep Them Up

OTHER STATES AFFECTED

A Wood Victory Likely to Insure Ohio—Hoover Men Active; Talk of a "Surprise."

Special to The New York Times.

DETROIT, April 4.—The most important primary election in the history of Michigan politics will be held tomorrow, with leaders of both Wood and Johnson forces making vigorous claims of victory.

The Lowden backers, though less assured in their manner, are claiming privately an even chance for their candidate. The Hoover men assert that it is purely sentimental that it abrogates the authority of the Administration in that the Republicans themselves are not satisfied that Congress has the authority to end war and that the move is intended to embarrass the President and furnish political capital in the coming campaign.

Anxious to End War Restrictions.

While some of the more important Democratic leaders take this view, others say there is such a demand for peace and an adjustment of business to pre-war conditions that they cannot afford to place themselves in a position of opposing legislation which will end the sixty-odd wartime restrictions imposed upon business and trade. That part of the resolution which would abolish the war regulations, it is fair to say, has strong support, and, if not bound up in the resolution, which proposes to end war with Germany by the raising of an economic barrier if Germany does not agree to the resolution within forty-five days, would be accepted by both houses without a particular division almost.

Democrats opposing the resolution say that if it should become effective and Germany refused to carry out its part the United States would be placed in an unenviable position economically. They assert that if Germany did not accept the peace suggestions, and an economic barrier was raised at the end of forty-five days, all the trade between Germany and the United States would be ended to the advantage of France and England.

"This objection is discounted by Republicans, who say that their "inside" information is that Germany would gladly accept any reasonable peace treaty with the United States. In fact, that sentiment in Germany favors a separate peace treaty with the United States.

That danger lies ahead of the United States if a separate peace treaty is made with Germany is the opinion of those familiar with the German mind and the German style of diplomacy. It can be said that Republican Senators largely favor the ratification of the Peace Treaty with the reservations rather than any peace that might be negotiated as the result of a joint resolution of Congress, which would bar the United States out of a league of nations and perhaps destroy for all time any hope of a league of nations plan being worked out by the great powers, including the United States.

Hint of Compromise to Wilson.

There is some reason to believe that President Wilson, who has taken no action on the treaty since its second defeat, may return it with an offer of acceptable compromise before the Senate is called upon to act upon the joint peace resolution.

There is talk of a Democratic caucus of the House this week which will decide

Continued on Page Three.

Report British War Threat Forced Turkish Cabinet Out.

CONSTANTINOPLE, April 4.— The Cabinet of Sali Pasha, which resigned on March 26, went out because of pressure brought upon the Government for the surrender of Colonel Rawlinson, British control officer at Erzerum, and Captain Forbes, control officer at Amasia, according to reports current here. Both officers were seized by the Nationalists, and it was rumored that the British had threatened to resume war against Turkey unless they were surrendered.

DEMOCRATS ASSAIL PEACE RESOLUTION

Administration Members of the House Are Almost a Unit in Opposing It.

HINT OF RETURNING TREATY

President, It Is Suggested, May Resubmit It with an Offer of Compromise.

Special to The New York Times.

WASHINGTON, April 4.—Almost solid Democratic opposition has developed in the House against the adoption of the joint resolution to declare war with Germany at an end. It will be considered next Thursday, two years and two days since the declaration of war.

This opposition is based chiefly on the belief that the resolution is unconstitutional in that it abrogates the authority of the Administration to negotiate peace with sovereign powers. Another objection raised by friends of the Administration in the House is that it was conceived, they say, as a legislative manoeuvre to force the President to act upon the Peace Treaty itself, and also to show to the country that a Republican Congress intended to go as far as possible to effect peace, even though the President would not compromise and accept the reservations to the Peace Treaty favored by a majority of the Senate.

TROOPS CLEAR DUISBURG

Machine Gun and Artillery Fire Drives Rebels Through the Streets.

ORDER IS RESTORED THERE

Military Forces to Withdraw When Civil Authorities Have Re-Established Control.

NO FURTHER ADVANCE MADE

Not Intended to Occupy Essen and Duesseldorf at Present —Quiet Reported There.

DUISBURG, Rhenish Prussia, April 4 (Associated Press).—Easter brought real peace to Duisburg. After heavy fighting the Government troops which reached here early yesterday when combing the industrial district to the south around Wanheim and the woods toward Mülheim, where the scattered Reds are believed to have fled. How far south and east the troops will go depends on how the Reds act.

It is not intended to proceed to Essen or Düsseldorf unless there are unexpected developments.

Military control will be maintained here only until the authorities are satisfied of the stability of civilian administration.

One of the most frequent comments regarding the disturbances at Duisburg is the earnest assurance that the fighting Reds were not natives, but aliens.

April 3 (by Courier to Düsseldorf).—Reichswehr troops marched into the Duisburg region today and cleared out the radical element of the Red Army in pitched battles in the streets.

Machine-gun and rifle bullets swept the business district like a driving rain, artillery threw solid shot and shrapnel, and hand grenades were tossed. There was house-to-house fighting in some quarters. Four citizens were killed and a number were injured.

A shot was killed on the Belgian side of the Rhine, and a Belgian soldier was shot in the hand. The Reichswehr and Red casualties, it is officially announced, were light.

The Reichswehr came to Duisburg in two contingents, the 62d Regiment marching south from West Hemad and Dinslaken into Ruhrort, and the remainder, under General Kabisch, landing in east of Duisburg. The contingents arrived simultaneously at 3 o'clock in the afternoon.

A detachment of police undertook to search houses for resisting Reds, while the Government artillery took up a position north of the old gates of Duisburg, from which spot it placed shots where the Reds were gathered, principally in the high school grounds.

The first shots between the Kabisch forces and the Reds were fired in Kaiserberg, on the eastern edge of the city. Fighting soon followed in the downtown streets of Duisburg, the Reichswehr advancing from corner to corner, driving the Reds before them. The Reds fought in small groups, and many times only three or four manning a machine gun, supplementing its fire with rifles.

The heaviest firing was in Sonnewald Street. The Reichswehr entered the street at the north end from an open square with machine guns, cleared out at range of fifty yards.

The sweeping fire of both sides shivered half the store windows. The gutters were piled high with glass so pulverized that it resembled piles of drifted shaved ice when the shopkeepers later in the evening swept the sidewalks to the accompaniment of machine-gun fire which still was heard as a driving rain of machine gun fire.

Millerand Rejects New German Declaration Defending Troop Movement to Ruhr Basin

Copyright, 1920, by The New York Times Company.
Special Cable to THE NEW YORK TIMES.

PARIS, April 4.—Herr Goeppert, Chancellor of the German Embassy, called on Premier Millerand late today and handed him two copies of a note, one addressed to him as President of the Peace Conference and the other as French Premier.

In this note the German Government stated that it was acting only to restore order and that the French attached entirely too much importance to its action.

Millerand replied that such was not his opinion.

TROOPS PRESSING HARD ON REBELS

Now Approaching the Populous Industrial District Where Reds Are Numerous.

EBERT CHANGES HIS POLICY

Repression to be Used Against the Spartacides in the West— Saxony Is Still Terrorized.

By LEONARD SPRAY.

Copyright, 1920, by The New York Times Company.
By Wireless to THE NEW YORK TIMES.

MUENSTER, April 4.—Day by day the front of the German Government forces approaches from the northern countryside the populous districts of industrial Westphalia which are, for the most part, still in the hands of the Red Army.

I have spent the whole day in the midst of the Bavarian division which are pushing away forward southward from Hamm, thirty miles north of Münster, in an endeavor to restore lawful conditions and clear the country of armed Spartacides.

It was not easy to find this scene of civil combat, and the best indication was the "sound of the guns."

"Where is the front?" I asked of a Major commanding a Bavarian regiment.

"There," he replied, pointing across the field to where dimly visible over the figures of peasants tilling the ground were small groups of soldiers crouching beside machine guns in the ditches or under hedges with a battery of supporting field artillery mounted in a farmyard. "In that windmill over there," he added, is a nest of Spartacides and our airplanes have spotted them. Watch for the smoke. They are going back, but we never know where they may spring up."

Then the Major went for a Lieutenant and instructs him to show me "the front" exactly as it is.

This front comprises nothing more dramatic than lonely country road. There are no trenches and no dugouts. All one has is a close view of these groups of crouching soldiers of which glimpses were caught from a distance a few minutes earlier. They are immobile most of the time, only now and then firing a machine gun round when an officer sees through field glasses signs of movements a long way across the fields.

"I am afraid it is not very exciting!" questions the guide, I agree, and with a smile on his round, fresh, Bavarian face he says:

"But it's war all the same, and a much jollier sort of war than the other business."

But the next moment he remembers what it means, and he adds: "But it is terrible all the same—our own country, against our own fellow-countrymen." His smile vanishes, and his face becomes a mask of tragedy.

FRANCE'S ACTION DISAPPROVED HERE

United States Government Not Yet Advised of Intention to Occupy More Rhine Cities.

MOVE THOUGHT UNJUSTIFIED

Belief in Washington French Are Taking Advantage of Situation to Enter Frankfort.

Special to The New York Times.

WASHINGTON, April 4.—No notification has yet been given by the French Government to the American Government relative to the military measures it plans to pursue under its announced " policy of coercion " against Germany, and which is interpreted as meaning that the French intend to send troops to occupy Frankfort and other cities on the right bank of the Rhine. It is not expected here that France will notify the American Government until the French military machine is ready to move.

Premier Millerand and the French Government are thoroughly aware of the attitude of the American Government relative to the sending of such troops as can be considered necessary by the German Government into the Ruhr district for the sole purpose of putting down Communist disturbances, and as the Paris Government knows that the American Government is not in sympathy with its attitude in opposition to the entry of German troops into the Ruhr district, it is not likely that the French Government will seek the views of Washington any further before acting alone in the policy of coercion.

There is no sympathy in Washington political circles for the attitude of the French Government in the present situation, and the understanding here is that the British Government entertains the same views respecting the Ruhr problem as does the American Government.

The Washington view of the action of the French Government in deciding to adopt its policy of coercion to the extent of sending troops into the region of Frankfort and elsewhere on the Rhine's right bank must be interpreted as being all a part of the present French wave of hysteria over the fear of German aggression. On the other hand the present German Government has not acted very tactfully in the Ruhr controversy, and this has still further served to inflame French fears. There is believed, however, to be no doubt that if the situation in the Ruhr district growing out of the Communist revolt were such as to threaten ominous developments that would contribute to the Red menace east of the Rhine, no harm would be occasioned by the occupation of the Ruhr district by German Government troops merely for that purpose, and this has been the view of the American and British Governments.

The French Government leaders have been what might be described in the vernacular as "rattled" over the failure of the project for an Anglo-Franco-American treaty of alliance. This treaty not become effective in England's part unless the American Senate ratifies the treaty. This is the treaty under which it was proposed that the United States and England should rally to the support of France in the event that support of France should rally to the support of France in the event that any attempt be made against her.

In view of the failure of ratification of this defensive treaty, the French leaders are acting on the theory that they have a menace to meet and that they are alone in facing that menace. It was feelings such as this that gave rise to former Premier Barthou's recent attack in the Chamber of Deputies on Premier Lloyd George of Great Britain, in which Barthou declared that France was left standing alone facing Germany, as the country toward which Germany must prepare her revenge.

The French, it is learned, have always been anxious to occupy Frankfort and are even anxious to occupy Darmstadt. It is the concern of the present situation that gives rise to the strong feeling here that the French are taking advantage of the present situation to make plans for crossing the Rhine and occupying Frankfort, although that is quite contrary to the views of both the United States and of the British Government, which are that such an action on

Continued on Page Two.

FRENCH TROOPS TO ADVANCE

Frankfort, Darmstadt, Homburg and Hanau to be Occupied at Once.

CALLED COERCIVE MEASURE

Allies Invited to Join Movement, but France Will Move Alone on Foch's Advice.

STRONG DEMAND FOR ACTION

Press Accuses Germany of Deceit — Withdrawal When Germans Leave Ruhr.

By EDWIN L. JAMES.

Copyright, 1920, by The New York Times Company.
Special Cable to THE NEW YORK TIMES.

PARIS, April 4.—The French Government has decided to occupy with French troops the German cities of Frankfort, Darmstadt, Homburg and Hanau and their vicinity on the right bank of the Rhine in reprisal for the invasion of the Ruhr Basin in the neutral zone by German Government troops in violation of the Versailles Treaty and as a guarantee of their withdrawal.

It is stated semi-officially tonight that the occupation may be expected at any time.

Premier Millerand has notified the allied and associated Governments of this decision and asked them to take part in the operation, but, it is stated, the French Government will not wait for the Allies to deliberate, and is quite prepared to act alone if necessary.

Two Divisions Reported Ready.

The French War Office, on the advice of Marshal Foch, is said to have ordered General Dégoutte, commanding the French Army on the Rhine, last night to prepare at once two divisions to move at a moment's notice. Whether that order has been given yet is a guarded secret.

It was widely reported in Paris tonight that Frankfort had already been occupied. While the War Office refuses to make any statement, this announcement is perhaps premature. It appears, however, that most any prompt, if not immediate, action by the German Government, and obedience by the troops now marching into the Ruhr basin can prevent the French moving forward. It is generally believed the order will be given tomorrow.

In the meantime the French Foreign Office reports German troops moving forward rapidly in the Ruhr district, and that the workers are massing to give battle in front of Düsseldorf.

It is evident the Germans are trying to hurry and get the best of the armed workers before the French act so that they can state they will withdraw, and therefore there is no need of a French advance. But while there is always a chance of settlement, in view of the confessed double dealing of the Germans and in view of the state of French public opinion, it appears altogether likely that the French are going to extend their occupation in a heroic effort to convince Germany that the French intend to enforce the Peace Treaty.

Text of the French Statement.

The French Foreign Office this afternoon issued this statement:

"The military measures which the French Government plans have for their sole object the forcing of Germany to respect Articles 42 to 44 of the Peace Treaty, which forbid the presence of German troops in the zone fifty kilometers east of the Rhine. They are, therefore, exclusively measures of coercion."

It would be difficult to exaggerate the effect the situation has on French public opinion. The duplicity of the German Government in sending troops into the Ruhr district has aroused France and put the whole country behind Premier Millerand to such an extent that were he to back down now there is little question he would cease quickly to be Premier.

What has stirred France is that

Continued on Page Two.

4

Section 1

"All the News That's Fit to Print."

The New York Times.

THE WEATHER
Generally fair today and Monday,
except possible local thunder
showers.
For full weather report see Page 22.

Section 1

VOL. LXIX...No. 22,786   NEW YORK, SUNDAY, JUNE 13, 1920.—In Nine Parts. Including Rotogravure Picture Section and Book Section.   FIVE CENTS In Manhattan, Bronx, and Brooklyn. Elsewhere TEN CENTS

HARDING NOMINATED FOR PRESIDENT ON THE TENTH BALLOT AT CHICAGO; COOLIDGE CHOSEN FOR VICE PRESIDENT

The New York Times
"All the News That's Fit to Print."
PUBLISHED EVERY DAY IN THE YEAR
BY THE NEW YORK TIMES COMPANY.

NEW YORK, SUNDAY, JUNE 13, 1920.

THE NOMINATION OF HARDING.

Upon a platform that has produced general dissatisfaction, the Chicago convention presents a candidate whose nomination will be received with astonishment and dismay by the party whose suffrages he invites. Warren G. Harding is a very respectable Ohio politician of the second class. He has never been a leader of men or a director of policies. For years a protégé of Foraker, he rose to a subordinate office by favor of "Boss" Cox of Cincinnati. Beaten by Judson Harmon in the contest for the Governorship in 1910, he has never shown independent strength in his own State save when he was named for Senator in 1914, having a majority of a little more than 100,000 over his Democratic competitor; and outside of Ohio he has only such strength as he now derives from his place at the head of the Republican ticket. Senator Harding's record at Washington has been faint and colorless. He was an undistinguished and indistinguishable unit in the ruck of Republican Senators who obediently followed Mr. Lodge in the twistings and turnings of that statesman's foray upon the Treaty and the Covenant.

The nomination of Harding, for whose counterpart we must go back to Franklin Pierce if we would seek a President who measures down to his political stature, is the fine and perfect flower of the cowardice and imbecility of the Senatorial cabal that charged itself with the management of the Republican Convention, against whose control Governor Beckman so vehemently protested. Rejecting Leonard Wood, probably the strongest candidate with the people the party could have chosen, because they knew he would never be dictated to by them, they favored Governor Lowden until Borah served upon them his notice of a veto of that nomination. Borah was commanding and truculent because he knew that he had to deal with a group of white-livered and incompetent politicians. If Republican leadership had not fallen into the hands of pigmies the chief men at Chicago would have told Borah not to be hanged, just as upon the issue of the League they would have defied Johnson to 'do his worst.' But they ran like a frightened flock, surrendered everything, even with his own reservations.

What has befallen the Republican Party of the early days, the party of sixty years ago, when it was possessed of moral purposes, or of forty and thirty years ago, when it could still profess to have them and find believers?

Where are its leaders that can be compared to Morrill, Seward, Hale, Platt of Connecticut, Oliver P. Morton, Sumner, Blaine, Conkling and a dozen others who rose to high places in the party councils? And, if the question be not too unfeeling, where and what are its principles, if any it have? Party control, exercised by a group of Senators, is divided between Lodge on the one hand and Borah and Johnson on the other. None of them, none of their accomplices in party degradation, would have come within hailing distance of the foremost rank of party chiefs in the brilliant days of Republicanism. And for principles, they have only hatred for Mr. Wilson and a ravening hunger for the offices.

Governor Coolidge for Vice President really shines by comparison with the head of the ticket. He at least is a man of achievement, he is known to the party and to the nation. As the police force of Boston went on strike he showed himself to be a man. He met that menace to the public safety with courage and determination, and the nation rang with praise of him. It is fortunate that not a word is to be said against the character of either candidate. They are irreproachable. But that does not compensate for the lack of achievement, for the colorlessness of the candidate for first place, or for the manner in which his nomination was brought about. It will be felt and said everywhere that the Democrats at San Francisco have received from their opponents at Chicago the gift of a splendid opportunity.

HOW THE CONVENTION DID IT

Delegates Had Word Early That Leaders Were for Harding.

RECESS HASTENED CHANGE

Two Ballots Taken After Reassembling Brought Ohio Man's Nomination.

PENNSYLVANIA CLINCHED IT

Big Block of New York Votes Also Helped to Decide the Struggle.

Special to The New York Times.

CHICAGO, June 12.—The afternoon session of the Republican National Convention on its fifth day, which reached a climax in the nomination for the Presidency of Senator Warren G. Harding of Ohio, was more like a rehearsal than a star performance in the great national political drama.

Not a single time-honored device was neglected in the effort to give the performance a touch of spontaneity, a dash of surprise and setting of overwhelming approval. But the convention had "gone dead" about 2 o'clock this morning when it was first learned that conferences of Senators and other party leaders had chosen the Harding way out of the deadlock dilemma. And all the efforts of G. O. P. pulmotor—lacking as it did any modern and novel attachments—to revive it failed.

Just as the limp, wet, worn men balloting in the pit waited until they were sure the tide was running strong, so did the throng of spectators wait to make very sure.

Harding Boom Starts Early.

The suddenly reviving Harding boom started at the morning session. From that moment to the end it was a process of very slow and orderly rising enthusiasm to which Harding arrived at getting a hot and tedious job done contributed no mean element.

None of the stampede tricks of time-honored reliability worked this time. The crowd and the delegates in their separate ways seemed deliberately to prepare themselves for the finale.

As soon as it was recognized in high places that Senator Harding was to be the victor, the proper sort of stage management was set in motion. The galleries, in which were many of Mayor William Hale Thompson's supporters, who were Johnson men out of antagonism to Lowden and Wood, were glad enough to lend themselves to the task of furnishing an appropriate setting for the drama. But with all the stage management and all the willingness of the crowd to do what was expected to the best of its ability when the switching of its delegations made it a certainty, as the ninth ballot was being tallied, that Senator Harding was to be the nominee, and later, when the tenth ended the fight remaining speck of suspense, the performance lacked great enthusiasm.

Victory Outburst Soon Over.

Perhaps two-thirds of the delegates got to their feet. Maybe a hundred climbed on chairs. A few women waved damp handkerchiefs in a valiant effort to add the orthodox feminine touch to the first national convention in which they had participated.

But there was no frenzy, no hatsmashing, no parading worthy of the name, and so little cheering that three minutes after the nomination was announced those on their feet, including virtually every one of the spectators of the Coliseum, were standing listlessly.

It is a safe assertion that if Senator Lodge had elected to pound once with the cumbersome gavel, which looked to have been destined originally to be a potato masher, the hall would have been hushed in an instant.

Announced Lowden by Mistake.

There was just one touch of humor—though the costless, sopping delegates didn't see it in that way. In announcing that Senator Harding had the necessary majority the Secretary inadvertently used the name of Lowden instead of that of the successful candidate. There was a howl of protest and very manifestly even the Lowden men didn't think the mistake was funny.

Senator Lodge made the formal announcement that the Ohio Senator had become the party choice in a tired voice that reflected the weariness in his pale cheeks and dark-ringed eyes. He didn't penetrate through the remnants of the din that the real, genuine Harding men were struggling desperately to accelerate into at least the semblance of a great reception.

Senator McCormick of Illinois then strode to a point of strategic advantage under the mechanical amplifying device.

Continued on Page Four.

WADSWORTH THREW NEW YORKERS' VOTE

Delivered 68 to Harding on Last Ballot, Acting with Senate Leaders.

20 REMAINED UNBOSSED

Organization Men Assert That They Alone Prevented Wood's Nomination.

Special to The New York Times.

CHICAGO, June 12.—The delegates from New York kept up a show of independence until the last hour of today's convention session, but then, when orders were given by the leaders of the organization, sixty-eight responded to the lash and voted for Harding. Their choice lay elsewhere, but they followed instructions. That was more trouble than the organization leaders needed, yet they could have obtained several additional delegates had they been necessary. After Harding's nomination was assured these delegates were not asked to make the sacrifice.

Among the unbossed delegates who stood out on the final ballot were six Wood men, Robert L. Bacon of the First District, Henry L. Stimson of the Sixteenth District, George Henry Payne, alternate for George Z. Medalie of the Twenty-second District, and Lansing G. Hoskins and John Taber of the Thirty-sixth District. They voted for Wood throughout and refused to yield to the wishes of Barnes, Wadsworth and the other leaders.

In the same class was Fiorella H. LaGuardia, President of the New York Board of Aldermen. His choice was Lenroot, and he voted for him to the last.

Other delegates who were not called upon to support Harding were two who favored Butler—Miss Katherine Hackett, alternate from Butler's district, and William Brice Thompson, one of

Continued on Page Three.

REPUBLICAN NOMINEE FOR PRESIDENT
SENATOR WARREN G. HARDING
OF OHIO

JOHNSON IS SILENT ON HARDING VICTORY

But Intimates He May Have Something to Say Today on Combination.

THANKS HIS SUPPORTERS

Says There Is No Rancor and That Their Hands Are Clean— Borah Also Refuses Comment.

Special to The New York Times.

CHICAGO, June 12.—Senator Hiram W. Johnson, a deeply disappointed man, refused to comment tonight upon the nomination of Senator Harding, but, according to his close friends and associates, he will not bolt the Republican nominee.

Mr. Johnson was approached during the noon recess of the convention by emissaries from the Harding camp with an offer to nominate him for Vice President. He is said to have turned down the offer very testily and to have said that he was after the Presidency, not the Vice Presidency. His remarks, however, are said to have indicated that he will support Senator Harding.

The news that the Vice Presidential nomination had been offered to Mr. Johnson was in line with the report, after the adoption of the foreign relations plank, that he (Johnson) could have almost anything he wanted in the convention except the nomination for President. His friends said tonight that he would make a statement concerning Senator Harding's nomination tomorrow.

When Johnson stepped before the "Battalion of Death" at his headquarters tonight to bid them good-bye he was greeted with "For He's a Jolly Good Fellow." The crowd sang lustily and with no signs of depression. When the demonstration had died down Johnson said:

"There are no tears to be shed. There is no rancor. We come out of this fight

Continued on Page Three.

---

4 NAMED FOR SECOND PLACE

But Tired Delegates Turn To Coolidge and First Ballot Is Decisive.

LENROOT NEXT IN FAVOR

Votes Cast Also for Johnson, Allen, Anderson, Pritchard and Gronna.

DELEGATES EAGER TO LEAVE

Adjourned at 7:30 P. M., Many Leaving the Hall Before Roll Call Was Ended.

Special to The New York Times.

CHICAGO, June 12.—Governor Calvin Coolidge of Massachusetts was nominated for the Vice Presidency by the Republican Convention tonight by an overwhelming vote on the first ballot. The nomination was immediately made unanimous.

As soon as the Presidential nomination had been made, the call for Vice Presidential nominations was made by Chairman Lodge.

Medill McCormick went to the speakers' stand, and in a short address nominated Senator Lenroot of Wisconsin for the Vice Presidency. There were cheers and hisses, and the suggestion that Senator Lenroot be the running mate of Harding didn't seem at first to captivate the audience.

Lenroot's nomination was seconded by A. T. Hert, National Committeeman for Kentucky; Senator Calder for New York and ex-Governor Herrick for Ohio.

The Chairman of the Oregon delegation placed in nomination Governor Calvin Coolidge of Massachusetts, and the Kansas delegation nominated Governor Henry J. Allen of Kansas. The convention presented a scene of disorder while various delegations were endeavoring to make themselves heard to second the nomination. Massachusetts started a demonstration for its Governor. The Virginia delegation presented the name of Colonel Henry J. Anderson of Virginia for the post, in the hope that the Republicans would turn to the South for second place on the ticket.

The most enthusiastic demonstration was for Coolidge. The delegates were weary by the hard day's work behind them, and the nomination for the Vice Presidency did not seem to give much of a thrill. Those who attempted to make seconding addresses received scant attention. It was evident that what all was to get away. In fact, many left the hall before the balloting began.

Coolidge had a runaway for the Vice Presidential nomination as soon as the balloting began. The big Eastern States, Massachusetts, New York and Pennsylvania, were lined up solidly for him, and he also got a heavy vote in the Middle West.

When Wisconsin was polled it cast two votes for Lenroot and twenty-four for Senator Gronna of North Dakota. Coolidge gained a lead so rapidly that the result was soon a foregone conclusion. When it became obvious that Coolidge would win the States down on the roll call followed the lead of the others.

The vote was:

Vote for Vice President.

State.	Coolidge.	Lenroot.	Allen.	Gronna.	Anderson.	Johnson.	Pritchard.	Not voting.
Alabama.	14		6		12			
Arizona.	6							
Arkansas.	13	13						
California.	22							2
Colorado.	12							
Conn.	14							
Delaware.	6							
Florida.	8	8						
Georgia.	17	9						
Idaho.	8							
Illinois.	58	26	13			18		
Indiana.	27	31½	3		4½	1		
Iowa.	26							
Kansas.	2		18					
Kentucky.	26	24						
Louisiana.	12							
Maine.	12							
Maryland.	16							
Mass.	35							
Michigan.	30							
Minnesota.	24							
Mississippi.	12							
Missouri.	36							
Montana.	8							
Nebraska.	16							
Nevada.	6							
N. Hamp.	8							
N. Jersey.	28							
N. Mexico.	6							
New York.	88					21		
N. Carolina.	22						5	
N. Dakota.	10				10			
Ohio.								48
Oklahoma.	20		10			10		
Oregon.	10							
Penn'a.	76							
R. Island.	10							
S. Carolina.	11							
S. Dakota.	10							
Tennessee.	20							
Texas.	23							
Utah.	8							
Vermont.	8							
Virginia.	15				15			
Washington.	14							
West Va.	16							
Wisconsin.	2	2		24				
Wyoming.	6							
Alaska.	2							
Dist. of C.	2							
Hawaii.	2							
Philippines.	2							
Porto Rico.	2							

Total......674 674½ 146¼ 69½ 28 25½ 11 24
Illinois 1.
Not voting—Hawaii 2.
Total vote 984

Continued on Page Four.

REPUBLICAN NOMINEE FOR VICE PRESIDENT
GOVERNOR CALVIN COOLIDGE
OF MASSACHUSETTS

HARDING DECLARES HE IS 'VERY HAPPY'

Proud to Receive "This Great Honor from the Republican Party."

COOLIDGE ACCEPTS PLACE

Taft, Hughes, Hoover and Others Congratulate Head of Ticket.

Special to The New York Times.

CHICAGO, June 12.—Senator Harding, General Wood and Governor Lowden were in rooms adjoining the Coliseum during the final balloting today. They were in different parts of the Coliseum Annex. The result of each ballot was delivered to them by messengers.

It was a bulletin flash for a press association that gave Mr. Harding the thrill of his life. It read:

"Harding nominated!"

When the news was given to the first editor ever nominated by the Republican Party for President he did not lose his equanimity. He said he was "very happy."

Later he said:

"I am very proud, as any American would be, to receive this great honor from the Republican Party. I am not unmindful of the obligations and responsibilities that come with it."

Manager Prophets Harmony.

Henry M. Daugherty, national manager for Senator Harding, made the following statement for the Senator tonight:

"On behalf of the Republicans of Ohio, and especially on behalf of Senator Harding, his family and friends, I desire to express to Republicans of the country, men and women, our deep gratitude for the confidence expressed in this wonderful man by nominating him as the candidate of the party for the Presidency.

"We entered this campaign with considerable reluctance because Senator Harding did not desire to make a high-powered organization campaign for the Presidency. Our plan, as is now well known, was carried out, whereby we conducted rather a modest campaign and left the selection to the Republicans of the country without too much pressure.

"We have throughout the campaign had the highest respect for opposition candidates and for their supporters. At no time have we made any attacks upon any candidate or any candidate's supporters, and Senator Harding will receive the support no doubt of every man and woman in the country who desires to vote the Republican ticket. The ticket will be elected overwhelmingly in November."

Harding Receives Correspondents.

With his accustomed simplicity of manner Senator Harding received the newspaper correspondents tonight on the fifth floor of the Hotel La Salle, in a hall adjoining a room in which he was a number of old friends, including Will H. Hays, just re-elected Chairman of the Republican National Committee, who will direct the Harding campaign. The Senator made it plain that he recognized the full responsibilities

Continued on Page Four.

PROPHESIED HOW HARDING WOULD WIN

Daugherty, His Campaign Manager, Said Fifteen Tired Men Would Put Him Over.

SENATE "JUNTA" MADE DEAL

Attended All Conferences Behind Scenes and Blocked Move to Let Wood Bolster Forces.

Special to The New York Times.

CHICAGO, June 12.—At the proper time after Republican National Convention meets some fifteen men, bleary eyed with loss of sleep and perspiring profusely with the excessive heat, will sit down in seclusion around a big table. I will be with them and will present the name of Senator Harding to them, and before we get through they will put him over."

This prediction, substantially as written here, was made by Harry K. Daugherty, campaign manager for Senator Warren G. Harding, Ohio, shortly before the Presidential primaries were held in that State. Daugherty afterward entered the primaries as a candidate for delegate at large, pledged to support Senator Harding. He was beaten but the utterance which led the Republican voters in his own State to oppose him in their unfolding events at the national convention gave him a prophetic measure.

The sweltering crowd which sat down to luncheon this morning gazed on the usual picture of a national convention bent on getting through with its business of nominating a candidate for the President of the United States and preparing to go back home. That picture may have appeared to many of the onlookers as one fraught with unusual interest and importance, but the history of this final day of Republican Convention was really made behind the scenes and very much after the fashion suggested in Daugherty's statement.

Two days ago Senator Harding's fight was looked upon as a forlorn hope by practically every trained political observer at the convention. In fact, up to the very moment the convention took its adjournment last night his prospects were not regarded as rosy. As recently as last night Senator Harding himself could not have entertained much hope of a successful issue. Over a few minutes before midnight he filed with the Secretary of State at Columbus, Ohio, the necessary papers to qualify him as a candidate for re-election to his present position in the United States Senate.

Conferences Held Friday Night.

The conference at which steps were taken to break the deadlock and steering the convention toward Harding was begun soon after it finished its big day's job yesterday. During the night the conferees divided into several small groups, which kept in communication with each other by members interviewing, in two Chicago clubs and at the Blackstone and the Congress Hotels.

While the convention was sitting today a dozen or so leaders met on the re-

Continued on Page Four.

ARRANGED DURING RECESS

Deal for Harding Goes Through When Lowden Frees Delegates.

BIG GAIN ON NINTH BALLOT

When the New York Delegates Swing to Him the Shouting Begins.

URGED AT NIGHT COUNCILS

But Leaders in the Race Refused to Yield at That Time— Later the Break Came.

Special to The New York Times.

CHICAGO, June 12.—Senator Warren G. Harding of Marion, Ohio, was nominated for President of the United States by the Republican Party represented by its delegates assembled in national convention at the Coliseum this evening. Calvin Coolidge, Governor of Massachusetts, was nominated for Vice President.

The nomination of the Presidential candidate came on the tenth ballot. In the ninth ballot the whole trend of the convention sentiment was toward Harding. When New York, with its heavy representation, with a show of reluctance, cast its vote for Harding, everything was over except the shouting—and the shouting began immediately.

Senator Harding's mastery of the difficulties of a complex situation that did not begin to clear until last evening. After four ineffective ballots yesterday the convention had adjourned until this morning. Four additional ballots in the forenoon and early afternoon of today had developed Harding strength, but General Leonard Wood and Governor Frank O. Lowden had remained in the lead. A recess was taken for two hours, and during that short period combinations were formed that made Harding's nomination certain.

The real stampede of delegates to Harding began when Governor Lowden, abandoning his intention to address the convention, issued instead a formal announcement that his delegates were released from their pledges to him.

Interesting and even thrilling, as the open proceedings in the convention were, behind the scenes, of which most of the convention knew nothing, had their dramatic side. The nomination of the candidate for President was arranged in conferences in Washington weeks ago that the convention would get into a deadlock over candidates that would necessitate a combination arranged by a comparatively few of the party's dominating spirits was fulfilled to the letter.

Johnson's Strength Disintegrated.

Johnson's strength in the convention, never very potent, had begun to disintegrate this morning, under the influence of the understanding that the delegates saw the choice of the leaders represented by the Senate group. All along it had been taken for granted that when Johnson saw that he could not be nominated he would ask his supporters to go to Knox. In conferences in which Johnson took part last night, however, he failed to intimate that he was willing to abandon his candidacy, and no effort was made to persuade him.

In the two-hour recess this afternoon pressure seems to have been brought upon Johnson to throw his influence to Knox or some other aspirant for the Presidential honor. It is the understanding that at this juncture Johnson indicated that he was not satisfied with Knox's views on taxation, and perhaps on other public questions. So Johnson failed to place his indorsement on the Knox boom.

Senator Borah entered this afternoon conference of the conservative group of Senators and asked them to consider Knox. He was asked if he came from Senator Johnson. Borah answered that he acted only for himself. Thereupon various objections to Mr. Knox as a Presidential candidate were raised. He was too old. It was said that he was not in good health. He had voter against woman suffrage and for prohibition. He was from a State that did not need a favorite son at the head of the Presidential ticket to keep it in the Republican Party. And the Knox boom died then and there.

Thought Out of the Race.

Harding gained the Presidential nomination within twenty-four hours after he was looked upon as out of the race. He had made a poor showing in convention balloting yesterday and just before midnight last night papers had been filed at Columbus entering his name as candidate for re-election to the United States Senate.

These papers had been prepared in advance and were left with friends in Columbus to show whether or not to file was up to

Continued on Page Four.

Lowden Defends Release of Delegates; Hert Says Wood Would Have Won Otherwise

CHICAGO, June 12.—Fear of a deadlock which he believed would prove detrimental to his party caused Governor Lowden to release his delegates on the convention floor at today's session, according to a statement made by him tonight. Governor Lowden said:

"After the eighth ballot, when I received a plurality of all votes cast, it was represented to me that the deadlock were becoming restive under the delay. Fearing a protracted deadlock, which I believed would have been detrimental to the interests of the country, I decided to release all delegates and advised them to use their best judgment as to whom they should support. I have great confidence in the ability and character of the successful candidate, shall support him with all heartiness and believe the ticket will be elected. The Republican Party has not had such an opportunity for service in half a century.

"For the friendship formed during this campaign and for the loyal support of so many fine patriotic men and women I shall never cease to be grateful."

Asked if he believed Lowden had reached the height of his strength on the eighth ballot, Hert said:

"It is my judgment that Wood would have been nominated had Lowden stayed in the fight.

"All the News That's Fit to Print."

The New York Times.

THE WEATHER
Thunder showers today and probably Thursday; moderate to fresh south winds.
For weather report see next to last page.

VOL. LXIX...No. 22,810   •••   NEW YORK, WEDNESDAY, JULY 7, 1920.   TWO CENTS In Greater New York | THREE CENTS Within 200 Miles | FOUR CENTS Elsewhere

DEMOCRATIC TICKET IS COX AND ROOSEVELT; NEW YORKER UNOPPOSED AS RUNNING MATE; BRYAN IS SAD, BUT OTHER LEADERS REJOICE

LLOYD GEORGE PINS GERMANY DOWN AT SPA MEETING

In Dramatic Scene He Demands Yes or No Answer on Disarmament Question.

HERR FEHRENBACH WEEPS

Offers His Chances of Salvation as Pledge He Speaks for an Unrevengeful People.

TOLD TALK IS VALUELESS

Must Present to Conference Today a Definite Statement—Poles' Plead for Aid Is Refused.

By EDWIN L. JAMES.
Copyright, 1920, by The New York Times Company.
Special Cable to The New York Times.

SPA, July 6.—The Spa conference, with all its possibilities, hangs in the balance tonight. The Allies have served an ultimatum on Germany to present tomorrow a definite statement of how it proposes to meet the treaty disarmament terms or the conference will at once be discontinued.

The meeting today, when the Germans tried to drive the Allies backward from their firm stand on disarmament, was dramatic in the extreme. Premier Lloyd George spoke for the Allies magnificent style. He met the German arguments and did not budge an inch. No less dramatic was the Pan-German, Fehrenbach, trying to tell the Allies that Germany had no revenge, but only wished to aid to all men in her heart.

Human drama indeed seldom reaches the grandeur of the situation this episode presented—one statesman speaking for millions of free people for the woe of the war and the other part as surely for the minority, the Prussianism which was defeated. Tears flowed down Fehrenbach's face as after he had offered that chances of eternal rest as a pledge that he spoke for a gentle Germany and for a no more value, and that her days of revenge were ended. He said Germans would now say whether or not they intended to disarm or all negotiations would be broken off.

Marshal Foch First to Arrive.

Yesterday when the Germans first met the Allies they tried to dodge the disarmament question, but were told they could not. The conference was adjourned until Defense Minister Gessler and General von Seeckt could reach Spa. They arrived today and the conference was set for 4:30. Marshal Foch, with a smile on his face and cap on his ear, reached the Villa Fraineuse at 4 o'clock. Various delegations arrived at 4:30, and two minutes later the Germans came. Von Seeckt, with a staff of half a dozen, made a handsome showing.

The conference was opened by M. Delacroix asking what was the view to the Allies, notes on disarmament.

Herr Gessler replied, saying that Germany had done her best to carry out the treaty provisions, but had serious internal troubles. He said the Reichswehr had been reduced to 200,000 men and the navy to the treaty terms. He then sought sympathy by painting a picture of the scarcity of food. Concluding his plea, he asserted that Germany was "overheated," and "it is impossible in the present state of unrest to reduce the army to 100,000 men."

Premier Lloyd George interposed: "Is that a declaration that the German Government does not intend to fulfill the terms of the treaty?"

"No," was the reply, "but we ask for special consideration for conditions which have arisen since the armistice."

Lloyd George retorted:

"We don't need explanations of the past. We are concerned for the future."

He said Herr Gessler had not spoken of what Germany intended to do, but only that Germany had not fulfilled the treaty.

Here the Defense Minister sat down. Foreign Minister Simons, remarking that Gessler had not clearly explained himself, said Germany intended eventually to reduce the army, but could not at present, but she asked for time.

Premiers Hold Private Conference.

At this juncture Lloyd George asked for an adjournment.

While every one else took tea, the Germans and allied diplomats and Generals leaving together. Lloyd George, Millerand and Delacroix held a private conference.

After the resumption of the session Lloyd George declared that Germany did not seem to realize the gap between the treaty terms and the execution of the treaty. The treaty, he said, left to 1,000 machine guns. Germany still had 200,000 men, 20,000 machine guns and ...

Continued on Page Eleven.

SEE (6) BELL-ANS in a Little HOT Water for INDIGESTION. Quick relief.—Advt.

Gompers Glad Cox Was Named; Calls Him Clean and Fair

Special to The New York Times.

CHICAGO, July 6.—Samuel Gompers, President of the American Federation of Labor, who was in Chicago for a few hours today, expressed his pleasure at the action of the Democratic National Convention in nominating Governor Cox.

"He is a good, clean, fair man," said Mr. Gompers. "He was the logical candidate. Palmer's candidacy, though, was ridiculous. He never had a chance. Those Cox delegates would have stuck if they deadlocked the convention all Summer."

Mr. Gompers had been to San Francisco with a delegation interested in the labor plank in the Democratic platform, and which will discuss the labor planks of both parties and place its views before the public.

GOV. COX ACCEPTS; MAY TOUR COUNTRY

He Intimates to Convention Chairman That He Favors a Wide Campaign.

PLEASED WITH ROOSEVELT

The Governor Calls Him a Strong Running Mate—Visits His Mother's Grave.

DAYTON, Ohio, July 6.—In a telegram to the Democratic National Convention accepting the Presidential nomination and thanking the delegates for their support Governor James M. Cox today intimated that he is going to make an intensive speaking campaign in every State.

Following is the text of the telegram:

"Hon. Joseph E. Robinson, Chairman, Democratic Convention, San Francisco, Cal.:

"Let me thank you for your felicitous message. I shall accept the standard from the Democracy of America, conscious not only of the honor but the great responsibility conferred.

"As Providence gives to me strength and vision, my firm resolve will be to justify the confidence which has been officially expressed.

"The shrine of government is in the communities of the land near to the homes that have given service and sacrifice. To them we will carry our cause with the assurance that the faith shall be kept and that the institutions for a free people are always sufficient to the needs of the, if they are loyal to the causes which we pledged.

"Please convey to the delegates of the convention my grateful acknowledgments.   JAMES M. COX."

The message to the convention was timed so that it would reach San Francisco shortly before the convention reconvened to nominate a Vice Presidential candidate.

It followed a message from Senator Robinson, permanent chairman of the convention, unofficially informing the Governor of his nomination and congratulating him.

Governor Cox also sent a reply to the greetings received earlier in the day from Senator Harding, the Republican Presidential nominee. His telegram to Senator Harding read:

"I accept your message as an evidence of the fraternal inquire which has always characterized the craft to which you and I belong. I heartily reciprocate the felicitous spirit which you have expressed."

Congratulations from Governor Cox tonight expressed his approval of Franklin D. Roosevelt as his running mate in the coming election.

A telegram of congratulation sent by Governor Cox to Mr. Roosevelt late this afternoon said:

"Please accept my earnest congratulations. I am very delighted that we are associated together in the contest."

In discussing Mr. Roosevelt, Governor Cox characterized him as a very vigorous, upstanding, courageous and progressive Democrat.

"Mr. Roosevelt's speech before the National Committee in Chicago last Winter made a very strong impression," said Governor Cox. "He spoke in Dayton on Americanization, and his address at that time was very favorably commented

Continued on Page Three.

FALL MALL ROUNDS, famous cigarette, round in shape—plain ends.—Advt.

FEW TO WITNESS THE CLIMAX

Final Convention Thrills Staged Before Only 800 Spectators.

DETAILS OF COX LANDSLIDE

Colorado's Switch Marked the Moment When the Ohioan's Victory Became Assured.

TEXAS HEADED COX PARADE

McAdoo's Stanchest Supporters Carried Lone Star Standard to Strains of "Ohio! Ohio!"

Special to The New York Times.

SAN FRANCISCO, July 6.—There are in San Francisco today somewhat more than 9,000 angry people. Their rage is not at all lessened by the fact that they have nobody but themselves to be angry at, nor because they have no real reason to blame themselves, but still they are angry. They are 9,000 people who either held tickets for last night's session and didn't go, having heard what a deadly bore the long day session had been to all who participated in it or looked at it, or who went to the night session, concluded that it would be merely another chapter of the Democratic deadlock and went before the delegates got out of the trenches and nominated James M. Cox for President of the United States.

The last half hour of that session was packed with drama, sparkling with thrills. It led up to a culmination of excited enthusiasm such as would have been impossible in the limp and exhausted Republican Convention which obeyed orders and nominated Harding in order to get out of Chicago before Sunday—an outburst which surpassed anything previously seen in the Democratic Convention, even on the day of the great debate between W. Bourke Cockran and William Jennings Bryan. The presence of 300 women delegates didn't seem to lower the temperature at all; they not only did not shut off excitement, but they helped a good deal in creating it.

The excitement did not really begin till the fortieth ballot, when the Pennsylvanians, who had given Palmer their complimentary vote on the thirty-ninth despite his withdrawal, divided according to their own preferences. The delegation had to be polled, a long and tiring interlude, but when the poll was complete it was found that McAdoo had gathered in the bulk of the residuary estate. For half an hour or so the McAdoo managers were hopeful, despite the fact that the breakup of the Palmer bloc had put Cox ahead once more.

As for the newspaper men, the supporters of the dark horses, and the few spectators who had stayed on after it had become apparent that the withdrawal of Palmer was not going to start an instantaneous landslide, they were dismayed and sore of heart. It looked as if nobody would be nominated at the night session, and everything would be left over to another day of the monotonous and exhausting struggle between two deadlocked candidates.

But the forty-first ballot quieted the expectations of the McAdoo forces. Despite Pennsylvania, McAdoo had gained seven and Cox had lost seven. With the forty-second ballot Cox took a big leap forward, getting 540 votes to McAdoo's 427. This was the highest point yet reached by any candidate, and all over the hall people began to sit up and pinch themselves into wakefulness. Something might happen yet.

Here the McAdoo people threw in their reserves and tried to force an overnight adjournment. The Cox leaders stood out against it, and the house was with them. A ballot or two earlier the convention might have passed such a motion, while the galleries and the press section would have voted for it unanimously.

Hopes of Late Stayers Revived.

But things had changed now. Something might happen. The spectators who had stayed on for five hours hoping for some excitement, and who didn't have tickets for Tuesday's session, quivered with the hope that they were going to see something that the nine thousand deserters had missed. Delegates who when the triangular deadlock had apparently transformed itself into a dead-

Continued on Page Two.

FOR INDIGESTION—SIX (6) BELL-ANS in a little HOT Water, quick relief.—Advt.

JAMES M. COX,
DEMOCRATIC NOMINEE FOR PRESIDENT.

Ruger
Photo Harris & Ewing

BRENNAN NOW RANKS AS A PARTY LEADER

Conceded Title as Result of His Successful Fight Against McAdoo.

PUT THROUGH COMBINATION

Illinois Man Credited with Holding Anti-McAdoo Forces in Line to the End.

Special to The New York Times.

SAN FRANCISCO, July 6.—For fully half an hour after the Democratic National Convention had nominated James M. Cox for President and taken a recess early this morning, a rotund, middle-aged little man, with a beatific smile on his face, sat quietly in one of the seats assigned to the Illinois delegation. He was a picture of whole-hearted satisfaction.

The galleries had cleared of the few hundreds who remained into the early hours to join in the demonstration for Cox. All except a handful of the thousand or more delegates had left the hall, worn out. The last of the newspaper correspondents were deserting the press stands, and still the thick-set, smiling man remained. A few friends stepped up to shake hands and offer congratulations. His smile developed into a laugh of utter contentment.

The thick-set little man, who resembles a McManus cartoon of "Father" in a kindly mood, overlooking a beautiful park, while the street crowds were happy and the delegates were breathing relief, the Nebraskan showed himself sad and depressed today, a broken hearted patriot. He did not hesitate to express his feeling and indicated that he knew not what his attitude would be toward the Democratic ticket or politics in general.

After discussing the action of the convention and its long drawn-out proceeding, Mr. Bryan remarked:

"My heart is in the grave with our cause. It must pause until it comes back to me."

"Do you interpret Governor Cox's nomination as a complete victory for the 'wets'?" was asked by one of the interviewers.

"It cannot be interpreted in any other way," was his reply.

"Do you mean that you will hesitate and pause and try to disinter your heart before you decide what you will do regarding the ticket?"

"Just that," was the reply of the peerless one.

"The convention consumed more than the usual time in reaching a decision," he continued, "and the voters now have about four months to decide. I shall use some of that time, to paraphrase a well known excuse, for hesitation.

"I regard the action of the convention in nominating Cox as a very serious mistake, in that it opened the door for the nomination of a wet candidate. I need not repeat what I have said before in regard to the evasion of other issues. I do not wish to discuss my future plans, but the public cannot overlook the importance of selecting a Senate and a

Continued on Page Three.

BRYAN IN DESPAIR OVER HIS DEFEAT

"My Heart Is in the Grave with Our Cause," He Says as Convention Ends.

UNCERTAIN OF HIS FUTURE

He Will "Hesitate," He Asserts, but Democrats Fear He Will Join Prohibition Party.

Special to The New York Times.

SAN FRANCISCO, July 6.—William Jennings Bryan, eliminated as a factor and influence in Democratic politics, and smarting under defeat on his dry plank, coupled with the nomination of Cox, whom he characterizes as a "wet," may go into retirement from Democratic activity or get behind the not yet ended prohibition movement.

In the quiet of his own rooms at the St. Francis Hotel, overlooking a beautiful park, while the street crowds were happy and the delegates were breathing relief, the Nebraskan showed himself sad and depressed today, a broken hearted patriot.

UNANIMOUS FOR ROOSEVELT

Other Candidates for Vice President Withdrawn Without Vote.

GOV. COX WAS CONSULTED

Approved the Choice After Murphy, Brennan and Others Had Agreed.

SMITH SWAYS CONVENTION

New York Governor's Speech for Roosevelt Puts End to Other Booms.

Special to The New York Times.

SAN FRANCISCO, July 6.—Franklin D. Roosevelt of New York, Assistant Secretary of the Navy, was chosen by acclamation by the Democratic National Convention today as the party's candidate for Vice President. The convention, which had been in session since June 28 and had been deadlocked up to the forty-fourth ballot on the selection of a Presidential nominee, chose Mr. Roosevelt in a few minutes.

The question of selecting a Vice Presidential candidate had not consumed much of the time or thought of the leaders here, but with the Presidential nomination out of the way, it was taken up for serious discussion for the first time early this morning. First of all, the leaders got in communication with Governor Cox over the long-distance telephone at his home, in Dayton, Ohio. His advice as to a running mate was asked. He wanted to know who was in the field. When the list was given, he was also informed that Mr. Roosevelt was acceptable to the leaders, and he gave his approval.

Mr. Roosevelt was selected after the names of seven other candidates had been presented to the delegates. When it became apparent that the powers that be had made a decision there was a scramble to get on the band wagon and make the selection unanimous.

The list of other aspirants included David R. Francis of Missouri, ex-Ambassador to Russia; Maj. Gen. L. D. Tyson of Tennessee, Governor Samuel D. Stewart of Montana, ex-Governor James H. Hawley of Idaho, Joseph S. Davies of Wisconsin, T. T. Vaughan of Oregon and Edward L. Doheny of California.

Rush to Withdraw Names.

When these candidates or their representatives got the drift of the Roosevelt sentiment, one after the other mounted the platform and either withdrew their own names or had them withdrawn. Several other embryo candidates were not even presented to the convention. Ex-Senator James Hamilton Lewis of Illinois refused to have his name offered.

Charles F. Murphy of New York, George E. Brennan of Illinois and E. H. Moore of Ohio, leaders of the Cox forces, had united on Roosevelt before the convention was called to order. From delegation to delegation the word was passed that Roosevelt had been agreed upon, and that it was merely a waste of time to proceed with the presentation of other names. But a surge of oratory was waiting to be let loose, and the convention managers, having nothing else to do for a few hours, thought it well to let the speakers have their chance.

It remained for Governor Alfred E. Smith of New York to give the quietus to all the other booms. He mounted the platform, amid the plaudits of the delegates, and in a vigorous speech seconded the nomination of Mr. Roosevelt. The scramble for the Roosevelt band wagon immediately followed and for the next fifteen minutes every representative was busy nullifying what had been said a few minutes before.

At 3:15 o'clock it was suggested that the nomination of Mr. Roosevelt be made unanimous, and the convention by a viva voce vote ratified that proposal. The convention then wound up in a laugh of utter contentment.

The reading of the telegram from Governor Cox accepting the Presidential nomination aroused the delegates from their lethargy. A delegate from each State asked a standard to march around the hall while the band played "He Rambled." After the circle of the room had been made a dozen times and the delegates had given cheers, in which the galleries took no part, the demonstration was over and quietly subsided. In their march around the hall a number of the delegates carried children on their shoulders.

The next speaker was Richard Seeley Bull, Senator of Washington, who seconded by Miss Alice Reynolds of Utah and Senator Key Pittman of Nevada.

Arizona yielded to Arkansas and Arkansas yielded to Montana, with the result that Senator Walsh of that State named Governor Stewart of Montana. Governor Stewart's nomination was seconded by Miss Alice Reynolds of Utah and Senator Key Pittman of Nevada. The Independent Democrats of the West, Senator Pittman said, needed Governor Stewart on the ticket.

L. A. Hanly of California presented

FRANKLIN D. ROOSEVELT,
DEMOCRATIC NOMINEE FOR VICE PRESIDENT.

vention to order at 12:45 P. M. After prayer had been offered, the preliminaries were hurried through with. The men and women members of the new National Committee were formally chosen. W. W. Farley of New York moved that the list be adopted by the convention and it was unanimously done.

Gavin McNab of California moved that the doors of the convention be thrown open to the public and any one allowed to come in, but it was not necessary. For the police had already seen to that. A resolution was adopted praising the local Police Department for the manner in which it had handled the convention crowds.

The thanks of the convention were also tendered to Temporary Chairman Cummings, Permanent Chairman Robinson and the other officers for the manner in which they had discharged their duties.

Mrs. George Bass of the women's Executive Committee was called to order. When she had her representatives and of the convention for her work among the women Democrats. The California women were thanked for their hospitality.

Mr. McNab wanted to keep the delegates longer in San Francisco, and offered a resolution that the convention take an adjournment, but a chorus of disapproval almost rent the roof. Put to a vote, the resolution was immediately lost.

Enthusiasm for F. D. Roosevelt.

Franklin D. Roosevelt was next placed in nomination by Timothy J. Ansberry, a former Congressman from Ohio, who sat in the convention as a delegate from the District of Columbia. The presentation of his name aroused the first genuine cheer. New York gave him a hearty send-off. The nomination was seconded by Judge K. U. M. Jackson of Kansas, and by Walter Myers of Indiana.

Former Senator Nugent of Idaho placed in nomination "Idaho's grand old Democrat," former Governor James H. Hawley. "There were no seconding speeches for him.

Speech of Governor Smith.

Governor Smith said in part:

"I very keenly appreciate the fact that we have had a long and tiresome session. Like most of the rest of you, I am keenly anxious to see other parts of the United States as much as we all appreciate the wonderful hospitality of California.

"For more than a week the eyes of the country and all the world have been on the Democratic Convention. We can fell well satisfied that so far as the platform and candidate are concerned, we have not disappointed the hopes and aspirations of humanity. We have given to the rank and file of the American people a clear and unequivocal program of Democratic doctrine and Democratic beliefs, standing forth in sharp contrast to the platform adopted by the Republicans at Chicago, in which every principle had to be a compromise to satisfy the whims of the delegates.

"When the Republican Convention was over, I met a Republican friend whom who said to me 'Al, it makes me think of picking up a fish in cold weather. We have asked Chicago to adopt the Lodge-Penrose theory that the Government exists for the benefit of special groups and that the Constitution and statute law stand for the protection of money and property.' And I suggested that theory we put forward a Democratic belief that America is made up of men, women and children and that what concerns their health and welfare is a concern of Government.

"No man trifles to a greater extent the principle set forth in our platform than the candidate of our party. Governor Cox of Ohio. New York puts back to the East with a candidate and a platform that she can make a square stand-up fight on. Democracy has the greatest chance at any time in my politi-

"All the News That's Fit to Print."

The New York Times.

THE WEATHER

Fair and colder today; Thursday fair; strong southwest to west winds.

For full weather report see Page 13.

VOL. LXX...No. 22,929. ... NEW YORK, WEDNESDAY, NOVEMBER 3, 1920. TWO CENTS In Greater New York | THREE CENTS Within 200 Miles | FOUR CENTS Elsewhere

HARDING WINS; MILLION LEAD HERE; BIG REPUBLICAN GAINS IN CONGRESS; MILLER LEADS SMITH FOR GOVERNOR

MILLER BY 57,000

But Democrats Refuse to Concede Governor's Defeat.

SMITH'S SURPRISING RUN

In Some Up-State Strongholds He Surpassed His Former Vote.

WINS EVERY CITY BOROUGH

Strongest in Manhattan, but Could Not Overcome Miller's Up-State Lead.

75,000 VICTORY, GLYNN SAYS

Republicans Here Accuse Tammany of Holding Back City Returns.

WADSWORTH IS ELECTED

Plurality Betters Miller's, but is Far Behind That on Presidential Ticket.

NEW YORK—Voted for Presidential Electors, United States Senator, Congressmen, Governor and other State officials and on an amendment to the Constitution. Vote in 1916: Democratic, 759,426; Republican, 868,471.
Polls closed at 6 P. M.

After a neck-and-neck race all evening ex-Judge Nathan L. Miller defeated Alfred E. Smith, his Democratic opponent, for the Governorship on the latest returns by about 57,000 plurality. Despite the big Harding landslide, it seemed probable for some time that Governor Smith would be able to pull through, but his returns from rural Republican districts overcame a record vote for him in New York City.

The Democratic managers refused, however, to give up hope, and early this morning still claimed the election of Mr. Smith. The Governor did not put forth any claim himself, asserting that he preferred to wait until remote up-State districts had been heard from. The Democratic leaders based their hopes for final success upon the fact that his returns showed that the Governor had increased his average majority in each election district in the city from 115 to 118 votes. They did not take into account, however, that Mr. Miller had also increased his average in up-State districts from 75 to 83.

If the present ratios are maintained, ex-Judge Miller will have an up-State lead of 379,735, while Governor Smith's plurality in New York City will be 322,-494, giving the Republican candidate a plurality in the entire State of 57,231. Republican leaders claimed the election of Mr. Miller by approximately 75,000. Democratic leaders said Smith's plurality would be around 40,000.

Smith Led at First

Early reports all evening showed the Tammany Governor in the lead, but when reports from rural Republican strongholds came in Mr. Miller's vote picked up considerably and showed him well into the lead. At the same time Smith's vote in outlying districts in New York City did not keep pace with the huge vote he received in other parts of the city, and the indications were that ex-Judge Miller would be elected by a small plurality.

Some of the members of the Republican County Committee shortly before midnight made the charge that election returns were being held up in Tammany districts until Mr. Miller's full strength had been counted. The First, Third and Fourth Assembly Districts, in lower Manhattan, where Tammany's strength is greatest, were among those mentioned at Republican county headquarters.

Deputy Attorney General Berger, accompanied by several members of the committee set out for the polling places in the districts to learn the true state of affairs.

Wadsworth Elected.

United States Senator James W. Wadsworth, Jr., although running behind Senator Harding did not have any difficulty in defeating his Democratic

Continued on Page Four.

CITY'S VOTE GOES TO HARDING AND SMITH

For Republican President by 443,000 and Democratic Governor by 325,000.

SEPARATE BALLOTS HELPED

But Some Charges Heard That Tammany Traded Votes—Socialists Make Gains.

New York City, in yesterday's election, gave its vote overwhelmingly to Senator Warren G. Harding, Republican candidate for President; to Calvin Coolidge, Republican candidate for Vice President, and to Alfred E. Smith, Democratic candidate for Governor.

Senator Harding carried every Assembly District in the Greater City with one exception—the First Assembly District, which is Governor Smith's home district. This gave Cox a plurality of about 490 votes.

In the minor contests the Republicans made some gains, although these were nothing like what might have been expected from the overwhelming sweep made by the Presidential ticket.

This result was greatly facilitated by the three ballots instituted by the Board of Elections, one for the Presidency, one for the State ticket (which also included the Congressional candidates), and one for the constitutional amendment and bonus proposal. The separation made ticket splitting easy, and the voters took full advantage of it.

Harding's victory in the city was overwhelming. At 2 A. M. today, on the returns then available, the plurality of the Republican candidate for the Presidency in the city was indicated as about 443,000.

Manhattan gave a Republican Presidential plurality of about 136,000; the Bronx, 62,000; Brooklyn, 177,000; Queens, 61,000, and Richmond, 7,000.

Striking Support of Smith.

But on the State ticket it was quite a different story. The same hour that found Harding victorious by 443,000 in the normally Democratic city of New York, showed Alfred E. Smith, Democrat, leading Judge Nathan Miller, his

Continued on Page Three.

OHIO FOR HARDING; 400,000 PLURALITY IS NOW ESTIMATED

Republicans Ahead in Nearly All the Large Cities of the State.

BIG LEAD IN CINCINNATI

Harding's Margin in Hamilton County Believed to be 20,000.

VICTORY IN CLEVELAND

Cuyahoga County About Two to One—Sweep in Toledo Also.

OHIO—Voted for Presidential Electors, United States Senator, Congressmen, Governor and other State officials. Vote in 1916: Democratic, 604,161; Republican, 516,755.
Polls closed at 5.30 P. M. (6.30 P. M. New York time).

COLUMBUS, Ohio, Nov. 2.—Returns from 2,987 precincts out of a total of 7,145 in the State give Harding 499,355, Cox 336,352.

If this ratio is maintained, the indications are that Senator Harding will carry Ohio by more than 400,000 plurality. Under instructions from State officials county election boards counted Presidential returns first. This made returns on the State ticket and the United States Senatorship unusually slow. Many scratched ballots were voted on the State ticket.

Returns from 128 precincts out of the Governorship race show Davis (D.), 15,699; Donahey (D.), 10,833.

Returns from 68 precincts for United States Senator give Willis (R.), 6,341; Julian (D.), 4,734.

Senator Harding has probably carried every large city in the State from which normally the Democrats get their majorities. In some instances his pluralities have been tremendous. He is running even in Columbus, and may have carried it.

Many of the country districts are holding up to normal for Governor Cox. In some instances he is making slight gains there.

Chairman Clark claims the election of the Republican State ticket, including Harry L. Davis for Governor, by 100,000, while Chairman Durbin claims the election of A. V. Donahey (Dem.) for Governor by at least 50,000.

The vote in Cuyahoga County, including Cleveland, is running about two to one for Harding. Indicating the sentiment in Northern Ohio. Four years ago Wilson carried the county two to one. Seventy-eight precincts out of 571 in the city of Cleveland gave Harding 13,840, Cox 7,957. In Cuyahoga County, outside of Cleveland, nine precincts out of 133 give Harding 2,826, Cox 830.

Hamilton County, in which Cincinnati is situated, will give 20,000 plurality for Harding. The first twenty-two precincts to re-

Continued on Page Three.

United States Senators Elected.

REPUBLICANS, 20.	DEMOCRATS, 14.
S. Shortridge, Calif.	O. W. Underwood, Ala.
S. D. Nicholson, Col.	J. T. Heflin, Ala.
F. R. Gooding, Idaho.	M. A. Smith, Ariz.
W. B. McKinley, Ill.	T. H. Caraway, Ark.
J. E. Watson, Ind.	D. U. Fletcher, Fla.
A. B. Cummins, Iowa.	T. E. Watson, Ga.
C. Curtis, Kan.	J. C. W. Beckham, Ky.
O. E. Weller, Md.	E. S. Broussard, La.
G. H. Moses, N. H.	C. B. Henderson, Nev.
J. W. Wadsworth, Jr., N. Y.	L. S. Overman, N. C.
E. F. Ladd, N. Dakota.	S. Ferris, Okla.
F. B. Willis, Ohio.	G. E. Chamberlain, Ore.
B. Penrose, Pa.	E. D. Smith, S. C
P. Norbeck, S. Dakota.	C. Glass, Va.
R. Smoot, Utah.	
W. P. Dillingham, Vt.	
W. L. Jones, Wash.	
I. L. Lenroot, Wis.	

INDIANA IS SWEPT BY REPUBLICANS

Early Returns Indicate That Harding Will Carry State by Upward of 200,000.

WATSON LEADING TAGGART

He Trails Ticket, but on Basis of Returns His Election Is Expected by 185,000 Plurality.

INDIANA—Voted for Presidential Electors, United States Senator, Congressmen, Governor and other State officials. Vote in 1916: Democratic, 334,063; Republican, 341,005.
Polls closed at 6 P. M. (7 P. M. New York time.)

Special to The New York Times.

INDIANAPOLIS, Ind., Nov. 2.—Late returns coming in from the rural districts have piled up the Harding pluralities in the state with every indication pointing that the Republican landslide will be the largest in the history of Indiana. It was estimated late tonight that Cox will be defeated by at least 200,000 votes. The former Republican plurality record for Indiana in a Presidential race was held by Roosevelt with 93,000.

Harding's plurality in Chicago is apparently larger than any ever given a Republican candidate by the city. It exceeds the famous 147,477 which Mayor Thompson got in 1915.

In 1996 of 5,720 Illinois precincts, returns received up to a late hour tonight Harding and Coolidge have carried Illinois by a plurality of more than 800,000. At this hour Harding has an indicated plurality of 331,990 in Chicago. His plurality down State is estimated to be not less than 314,000.

Special to The New York Times.

CHICAGO, Nov. 2.—Upon the basis of returns received up to a late hour tonight Harding and Coolidge have carried Illinois by a plurality of more than 800,000. At this hour Harding has an indicated plurality of 331,990 in Chicago. His plurality down State is estimated to be not less than 314,000.

Continued on Page Three.

ILLINOIS TREBLES REPUBLICAN VOTE

Returns Indicate Harding Has More Than 800,000 Plurality in the State.

McKINLEY CHOSEN SENATOR

Governor, State Officers and Entire Delegation to Congress Probably Republican.

ILLINOIS—Voted for Presidential Electors, United States Senator, Congressmen, Governor and other State officials and on an amendment to the Constitution. Vote in 1916: Democratic, 950,229; Republican, 1,152,549.
Polls closed at 5 P. M. (6 P. M. New York time.)

CHICAGO, Nov. 2.—Upon the basis of returns received up to a late hour tonight Harding and Coolidge have carried Illinois by a plurality of more than 800,000. At this hour Harding has an indicated plurality of 331,990 in Chicago. His plurality down State is estimated to be not less than 314,000.

The Republican sweep apparently is even stronger than in 1904, when Roosevelt carried Cook County by 128,000, the women not voting then. Four years ago Hughes carried the county by 56,000 over Wilson, but Harding's lead over Cox is more than five times greater.

By 1 o'clock it was estimated that 60 per cent. of the 884,000 registered voters had visited the polls. During the afternoon they kept swarming in, and closing time saw many still waiting in line. Early returns indicate about 825,000 votes were cast in Chicago. The plurality

Continued on Page Three.

CONGRESS HEAVILY REPUBLICAN, GAINS IN BOTH HOUSES

Party Will Have a Majority of 12 in the Senate and 113 in the House.

54 REPUBLICAN SENATORS

House Stands: Republicans 274, Democrats 158, Independents 2, Drys 1

IRRECONCILABLES ELECTED

Brandegee in Connecticut and Moses in New Hampshire Returned.

President Harding will have a Republican Congress to support his policies in the first two years at least of his Administration. Returns received up until the time this edition of THE TIMES goes to press show that the party which will have triumphed at the polls yesterday will have increased majorities in both Houses, with that in the House approaching 300.

Returns in the elections for Senators and Representatives are meager from some important States, but the trend of voting in those States in the Presidential and Gubernatorial contests indicates the probable result as far as the Senate is concerned. The returns received indicate that the two houses in the next Congress will stand as follows:

Senate—Republicans, 54; Democrats, 42.
House—Republicans, 274; Democrats, 158; Independents, 2; Prohibitionist, 1.

This gives the Republicans a majority of 12 in the Senate and a majority of 113 in the House. The present Republican majority in the Senate is 2 and in the House 39.

Senator Moses of New Hampshire and Senator Brandegee of Connecticut, both Republicans of the irreconcilable treaty group in the Senate, were strongly opposed on account of their opposition to the League of Nations, but have carried their States by substantial majorities. Senator Brandegee also had the opposition of many women on account of his effort to prevent the ratification of the Nineteenth Amendment.

Phelan Loses California.

Samuel Shortridge, Republican, who supported Senator Hiram Johnson's irreconcilable opposition to the League of Nations, appears to have been elected to the Senate, defeating Senator James D. Phelan, Democrat, a firm friend of the Wilson Administration. Senator James E. Watson, Republican, has been re-elected from Indiana, defeating ex-Senator Thomas Taggart, Democrat. Returns from Iowa are not nearly complete, but they indicate that in the opposition of organizations of farmers and laborers and a great many Re-

Continued on Page Four.

Electoral Vote.

HARDING.

California	13
Colorado	6
Connecticut	7
Delaware	3
Illinois	29
Indiana	15
Idaho	4
Iowa	13
Kansas	10
Maine	6
Maryland	8
Massachusetts	18
Michigan	15
Minnesota	12
Missouri	18
Montana	4
Nebraska	8
Nevada	3
New Hampshire	4
New Jersey	14
New York	45
Ohio	24
Oregon	5
Pennsylvania	38
Rhode Island	5
South Dakota	5
Utah	4
Vermont	4
Washington	7
West Virginia	8
Wisconsin	13
Wyoming	3
Total	**371**

COX.

Alabama	12
Arkansas	9
Florida	6
Georgia	14
Kentucky	13
Louisiana	10
Mississippi	10
New Mexico	3
North Carolina	12
Oklahoma	10
South Carolina	9
Tennessee	12
Texas	20
Virginia	12
Total	**152**

Doubtful or Insufficiently Reported

Arizona	3
North Dakota	5
Total	**8**

Total number of votes in Electoral College, 531; necessary to a choice, 266.

PRESIDENT HEARD FIRST VOTES ONLY

He Retired at 9 o'Clock, His Physician Leaving the White House Earlier.

NO COMMENT ON RETURNS

Wilson at Afternoon Cabinet Meeting Expressed Confidence in Success of League.

Special to The New York Times.

WASHINGTON, Nov. 2.—Although messages to the White House tonight brought the news that Harding was leading in very nearly all the doubtful localities the attitude seemed to be all right and conceals nothing until the actual result was ascertained. The experience of four years ago appeared to hold out a lesson which 9 o'clock and this course for the White House circle.

No public expressions of any kind were made. The atmosphere lacked the gloom usually associated with the news of a reversal. Visitors to the White House found the Secretaries and other members of the staff in perfect good humor.

President Wilson heard bulletins until about 9 o'clock, and this being his usual bed hour, he retired, so it was said. Admiral Cary T. Grayson, his personal physician, left the White House for his home about 8.30 o'clock. This fact seemed to set aside theories that the President would be in a nervous condition if he realized that Senator Harding was far ahead in the Presidential race.
Joseph P. Tumulty, Private Secretary

Continued on Page Four.

State Pluralities.

FOR PRESIDENT.

REPUBLICAN.

California	500,000
Connecticut	100,000
Colorado	40,000
Delaware	5,000
Idaho	25,000
Illinois	800,000
Indiana	200,000
Iowa	200,000
Kansas	200,000
Maine	75,000
Maryland	20,000
Massachusetts	300,000
Michigan	400,000
Minnesota	100,000
Missouri	40,000
Montana	50,000
Nebraska	100,000
New Hampshire	30,000
Nevada	4,000
New Jersey	200,000
New York	1,000,000
Ohio	400,000
Oregon	5,000
Pennsylvania	750,000
Rhode Island	50,000
South Dakota	80,000
Utah	30,000
Vermont	45,000
Washington	150,000
West Virginia	50,000
Wisconsin	300,000
Wyoming	8,000

DEMOCRATIC.

Alabama	70,000
Arkansas	100,000
Florida	
Georgia	
Kentucky	20,000
Louisiana	
Mississippi	
New Mexico	
North Carolina	60,000
Oklahoma	7,500
South Carolina	
Tennessee	40,000
Texas	50,000
Virginia	75,000

DOUBTFUL.

Arizona	
North Dakota	

GIGANTIC MAJORITIES

Pennsylvania, 750,000; Illinois, 800,000; Ohio, 400,000.

MAY BE 6,000,000 IN ALL

More Than 370 Electoral Votes Won by Harding and Coolidge.

BIG GAINS IN THE WEST

Indiana, Wisconsin, Michigan, Iowa, Kansas, Nebraska and California Won.

NEW JERSEY BY 200,000

Maine, with 75,000, Beats the Plurality She Gave in September.

SOLID SOUTH UNBROKEN

Unless Late Figures Change Tennessee—Cox May Lose All Western States.

By majorities unprecedented in American politics, Warren G. Harding was elected President and Calvin Coolidge Vice President yesterday on Senator Harding's fifty-fifth birthday. Though the addition of women to the electorate might have been expected to make the margins of successful candidates somewhat larger than in past years, it would hardly account for any such unheard-of majorities as were rolled up yesterday. From coast to coast records were broken.

Harding's total pluralities in the States he carries may run well over 5,000,000 and it may get plurality over this may be 6,000,000. This surpasses by 2,500,000 the previous record, which was that of Theodore Roosevelt's victory over Alton B. Parker.

The highest State plurality ever previously recorded, Roosevelt's margin of 500,000 over Parker in Pennsylvania in 1904, was surpassed by at least four States yesterday. New York State went for Harding by nearly 1,100,000; Pennsylvania gave him a plurality of 750,000; Illinois gave him 800,000; California, which went for Wilson four years ago by a majority of 2,900, gave Harding a plurality of perhaps 500,000 over Cox; Ohio, the home State of both candidates, went for Harding by 400,000.

At 4 o'clock this morning it seemed that Harding's majority on electoral votes would equal or surpass the record-breaking landslide by which Roosevelt beat Alton B. Parker.

Cox held the solid South, and Kentucky and perhaps Oklahoma among the border States, but West Virginia and Missouri had apparently gone for Harding, as they went for Roosevelt in 1904. New Mexico, however, seems to be due to inadequate reports; the probability is that they are all for Harding.

All over the country the Harding pluralities broke records. Boston, which has been consistently Democratic in recent years, except in 1896, when McKinley carried it over Bryan, allowed the effect of the drift of the Irish vote by giving Harding a plurality of more than 20,000.

New York City, where, over even more surprising. The city went for Taft in 1908 by less than 16,000; it seems to have given Harding a plurality of more than 443,000. Buffalo gave Harding a plurality of 46,247.

The effect of the Harding sweep showed everywhere. Though the Southern States stood fast, Harding had carried two wards in Atlanta and two Louisiana parishes. In the Middle West, Indiana went Republican, and gave him more than 200,000 plurality; Iowa about the same; Michigan nearly 400,000; Wisconsin nearly 300,000.

MAP SHOWING HOW THE STATES VOTED

KEY

- DEMOCRATIC
- REPUBLICAN
- DOUBTFUL or Insufficiently Reported

FIGURES IN CIRCLES INDICATE NUMBER OF ELECTORAL VOTES

"All the News That's
Fit to Print."

The New York Times.

THE WEATHER
Generally fair today and Friday;
moderate, shifting winds.
For full weather report see Page 15.

VOL. LXX....No. 23,105.   NEW YORK, THURSDAY, APRIL 28, 1921.   TWO CENTS In Greater New York | THREE CENTS Within 200 Miles | FOUR CENTS Elsewhere

GERMAN OFFER REJECTED, ALLIES PRESENT BILL FOR 132 BILLIONS;
FORMALLY HANDED TO GERMAN AGENT IN PARIS LAST NIGHT;
HUGHES AWAITS NOTICE OF ALLIED ATTITUDE ON BERLIN NOTE

BONE DRY STATE IN SIXTY DAYS, CHANDLER'S ORDER

Superintendent of State Police Tells His Troopers Two Months Is the Limit.

THEY MAKE FIRST RAIDS

Seize Liquor Worth $30,000 in Saloons in Westchester and Oneida Counties.

MILLER TO AVOID CONFLICT

Governor Opposes Enforcement by State Authorities Where They Conflict With Federal Agents.

Special to The New York Times.

ALBANY, April 27.—Major George F. Chandler, Superintendent of the State Police, began today a drive to make the entire territory in his jurisdiction bone dry within two months. The force with which he expects to do this consists of 232 State troopers, of whom approximately 100 are tied up at the present time by strike duty in this city, Troy and its neighborhood.

The first raids, made early today, netted $30,000 worth of contraband liquor, taken in raids on one saloon on the outskirts of White Plains, Westchester County and two in Oneida County.

Major Chandler said today that every county in the State, outside of counties comprised within the boundaries of New York City and some up-State counties which are provided with large cities, which are provided at some with the illicit liquor traffic, would be a battleground and under constant attack until the illicit liquor traffic within the counties has been driven into hiding for the purpose of Major Chandler's enforcement plan, which contemplates making dry some fifty communities every week from now until his purpose has been achieved.

"We are going to wipe out the illicit liquor traffic which have been flourishing on the outskirts of small towns up-State," said Major Chandler.

"My men are going along about this business in a systematic way which cannot fail but bring the result we are aiming at. We are going to get the illegal possessed liquor. We are going to get the men who sell it and the men who buy and drink it. Town country will be under constant surveillance by my men from the fact that they will pay a business visit to at least one saloon on the average of about once in every fifty counties every week from now on. Bootlegging, moonshining, blind tigers and all traffic in liquor in the territory covered by the State police will be entirely wiped out."

Governor Miller was asked this afternoon to comment on the statement of Major Chandler and to say whether he had inspired the constabulary crusade against the illicit traffic in liquor.

"Major Chandler is charged with the duty of enforcing the laws that come within his jurisdiction," said the Governor. "I haven't especially talked with him on this subject. I have entire confidence that he will observe and enforce the law. That is his business."

The Governor made it plain in an interview this afternoon that he would not favor any plan of enforcing the Federal Prohibition Amendment by State officials that would bring them into direct conflict with Federal officers engaged in the same pursuit. The Governor believes that duplication of effort and conflict of authority would be ruinous and bring about the collapse of the campaign now launched by local authorities throughout the State under the Mullan-Gage act against the illicit traffic in liquor.

"As a general proposition," the Governor was asked, "doesn't the State as an aid to the Federal agents in suppressing the traffic in liquor rather than to the Federal Government as an aid of the State?"

"Of course," the Governor replied, "the very purpose of the State act was to make a law that already worked on the Federal statute books enforcible by local peace officers throughout the State, thus localizing responsibility.

The question was prompted by the fact that Federal enforcement agents had raided some saloons in Albany over the head of the local authorities.

"If a raid is made over the heads of local authorities by Federal agents would you say that this fact laid the local authorities open to censure?" was asked.

"That may or may not be, depending upon the facts," the Governor replied.

"The raids are not necessarily made over their heads. The Federal law is the supreme law, and you would have to have more facts than I have here that Federal officials had made raids."

"Would you consider raids by Federal agents as evidence that there had been dereliction of duty on the part of local authorities?"

"I would not think it was evidence of

Continued on Page Three.

Proposes a 2½-Cent Coin To Bear Roosevelt's Likeness

WASHINGTON, April 27.—Coinage of a 2½-cent piece, bearing the likeness of Theodore Roosevelt, with the date of his birth and death, is provided for in a bill introduced today by Representative Appleby, Republican, of New Jersey.

The proposed limit of the coin as legal tender would be 40 cents and it would be big enough to distinguish it from the one-cent piece.

HOPE TO ESCAPE TIE-UP OF SHIPS

Both Sides Agree to Make One More Effort Tomorrow to Avert Strike.

SAYS WAGES MUST BE CUT

Benson Tells Conferees Shipping Board Holds Reduction of 15 Per Cent. Is Imperative.

Special to The New York Times.

WASHINGTON, April 27.—While no agreement as to wage reductions and working conditions was reached at the conference of marine workers and ship operators, held here today at the call of Admiral W. S. Benson, Chairman of the United States Shipping Board, hope still is held that a compromise may come which will avert a serious tie-up in New York Harbor on May 1.

This hope is based largely on an announcement made by Andrew Furuseth, President of the International Seamen's Union, that he had a final proposition to make, the details of which he did not wish to discuss at this time. Admiral Benson then called a second conference to be held here on Friday morning.

Admiral Benson laid before the workers and employers at today's conference the policy to which the Government will adhere as an operator of ships. Its basic principles are a decrease in wages of 15 per cent., the elimination of overtime charges and refusal to recognize the "closed shop" as applied to the shipping industry. In calling the second conference, he said, it was for those who wished to attend for a fair and just consideration of the problem. There who held back, he added, must take the consequences.

"The belief here today was that the private ship operators, who had sought a much larger cut in wages, would accept the governmental policy, including the 15 per cent. wage decrease.

As to the workers, it was the belief that all of the labor organizations, with the possible exception of the engineers, finally would accept the Government's proposition. It is possible that the engineers may be brought into line, although their representatives here were in a very warlike frame of mind. It was reported that leaders of some of the organizations of workers believed that the present depression in the shipping industry made this a poor time to strike.

Benson Takes Firm Stand.

The information concerning the exchanges was spread on the records during the reassemblage of Frederick H. Loehrs, assistant to Mr. Ainsworth. Ainsworth was asked to "step down" after he refused to waive immunity. Loehrs also refused, but he was permitted to go on. Ainsworth remained in the room as at the direction of Mr. Untermyer.

Mr. Untermyer is being assisted in the open-price accusation phase of the inquiry by former Assemblyman George H. Brennan of Brooklyn.

Loehrs said that Ainsworth was Secretary of thirteen exchanges, but that only nine manufactured articles used in housing. The non-housing exchanges include cotton goods, naphthalene and ammonia.

It was brought out that the various firms were known by code numbers, "not for secrecy" but "for brevity," and that keys to the names of the firms in each association were in the hands of the "members of the association." The reports sent to the members bore no firm names, only the code numbers.

The reports were sent out on colored charts, which were all colors of the rainbow and a few more, including "canary, salmon and goldenrod."

Counsel Change Minutes.

Loehrs said there were about 150 concerns in the nine combinations. He was questioned concerning the minutes of the meetings of the various associations and said that the proceedings were sent to counsel, but denied that the latter had cut certain things expunged from the records. He admitted that counsel suggested changes in the minutes occasionally.

He told of the system whereby some of the members reported day by day the names of customers to whom they sold goods, the date of the sale, character of shipment, price and other details so that by the end of the day a member might know what his competitor's business for the previous day amounted

Continued on Page Seven.

BIG RING CONTROLS ALL HOUSE FIXTURES; LIKE HETTRICK PLAN

Lockwood Committee Hears of Nine Combinations Doing Hundreds of Millions Yearly.

SECRETARY $50,000 A YEAR

Members Informed Minutely of Prices by System of Colored Charts.

MORE REVELATIONS DUE

Untermyer Says 60 Combinations Grip Everything, "From Boilers to Door-Knobs."

The Lockwood committee yesterday disclosed the existence of nine combinations of national manufacturers of appliances used in buildings doing an annual business of several hundred millions of dollars organized in so-called "open-price" associations, maintaining "elaborate systems of price reporting by which competitors were fully informed as to each other's business.

It is the contention of Samuel Untermyer, counsel for the committee, that almost every item that enters into the construction of a house in the centre of a combination of manufacturers who fix and maintain prices by agreement, refusal to recognize the "closed shop" as applied to the shipping industry. The inquiry yesterday revealed that the nine open-price associations, organized in a Hettrick-like manner, and known as exchange, manufacture gas ranges, water meters, pipe fittings, valves, range boilers, sandpaper and sandcloth, steel window sashes, steel lockers, steel shelving, tubular plumbing goods, brass and copper fittings.

The nine combinations of manufacturers operate through a central clearing house at 522 Fifth Avenue, which is in charge of a professional secretary, Albert A. Ainsworth, receiving about $50,000 a year. The manufacturers spend about $200,000 a year in maintaining the 15 representatives of Clark McKercher, formerly an Assistant United States Attorney General, who is counsel.

Exchanges Served by Ainsworth.

The exchanges represented by Mr. Ainsworth embrace some of the largest concerns in the country. The combinations are as follows: The American Brass and Copper Statistical Exchange, the Meter Manufacturers Exchange, the Pipe Fitting and Valve Exchange, the Range Boiler Exchange, the Abrasive Paper and Cloth Manufacturers' Exchange, the Steel Sash Manufacturers' Exchange, the Steel Locker and Shelving Manufacturers' Exchange, the Tubular Plumbing Goods and Tank Filling Exchange and the National Gas Appliance Manufacturers' Exchange.

The information concerning the exchanges was spread on the records during the reassemblage of Frederick H. Loehrs, assistant to Mr. Ainsworth. Ainsworth was asked to "step down" after he refused to waive immunity.

Continued on Page Two.

WASHINGTON WANTS LIGHT

Not Even France's Refusal to Accept Berlin Plan Is Yet Received.

OFFICIALS KEEP SILENCE

Great Care Is Taken Not to Give Any Idea of Our Own View of Proposals.

MEANWHILE REPLY WAITS

Capital Feels That Britain Alone Can Prevent Invasion of the Ruhr Now.

French Rejection of Offer Is Announced in Paris

PARIS, April 27 (Associated Press).—Jean Jules Jusserand, French Ambassador to the United States, has been informed by the French Government that the German reparations proposals, as transmitted to the Washington Government, are absolutely unacceptable.

The French point of view is that these proposals, instead of making any advance toward a satisfactory settlement of the reparations question, are rather a step backward.

WASHINGTON, April 27.—An Associated Press dispatch from Paris this evening announced that instructions had gone forward to Ambassador Jusserand to inform the United States that the German proposition" were unacceptable to France. It was assumed that M. Jusserand would make this known officially to Mr. Hughes tomorrow.

Special to The New York Times.

WASHINGTON, April 27.—No formal move has been made by the United States Government in connection with the new German proposals on the reparations question, submitted to the Allied through the American Commissioner at Berlin and the State Department. To say that exchanges on the subject are at a standstill would give a wrong impression, but officially this Government has taken no step that would justify any prediction of its ultimate course.

Informally, Secretary Hughes has brought the German note to the attention of the Ambassadors of France, Great Britain, Italy, Belgium and Japan, who would have communicated with their Governments. Whatever advices they have received here has been communicated to Mr. Hughes in a most informal way. Late this afternoon it was stated in an official quarter that no communication, formal or informal, had come from any allied Government in regard to the Berlin proposals.

The Government knows that the terms of the German proposals are entirely unsatisfactory to France, which is recognized as having superior claims to consideration. But despite press advices here today, stating that the French Government had forwarded instructions to M. Jusserand here, declaring the Berlin suggestions unacceptable and thus confirming the special cable dispatch from Paris, published in The New York Times this morning, no communication of the sort has been received here. The same is true in respect to other allied Governments.

It is suggested, on the one hand, that the instructions sent to M. Jusserand have been delayed in transmission. But official did not hesitate to acknowledge today that the communication as received here, was identical in all respects with the text of the German note which had been cabled to The New York Times text from Paris last night. It was said by some of those who had seen both that even differences that are usual in transmission of the same text done by two different persons were not apparent.

So that portion of Washington outside of the few connected with the Government and the allied Embassies who are interested, has at least for the moment refrained from drawing conclusions as to what the Germans had proposed.

It is expected that the allied Governments, in considering the German proposals, will treat as one element in the equation the Hughes note to Germany.

Continued on Page Two.

German Offer Unacceptable, Belgian Official Circles Say

BRUSSELS, April 27.—The German counter-proposals with regard to reparations were declared in political circles here today to be entirely unacceptable.

It was pointed out the new proposals did not differ materially from those submitted by the Germans at the London Conference.

ENGLAND ASKS FOR EXPLANATIONS

German Proposals Found Too Ambiguous to Permit of Definite Judgment.

CONDEMNED BY THE PRESS

Scheme Seen to Involve Allies in Further Interminable Debate—Rejection Foreshadowed.

Copyright, 1921, by The New York Times Company.

Special Cable to The New York Times.

LONDON, Thursday, April 28.—The German note is too ambiguous in the view of official circles here to form a definite opinion about. The Government cannot take new reparation negotiations with Germany on the basis of Dr. Simons's propositions sent to the United States. It will maintain the greatest reserve about the matter.

As a matter of fact when the Cabinet met yesterday morning it had heard nothing from Washington and had no official copy of the German proposals before it, but merely a version it had received from Berlin.

Then about the most important point of all, the amount of reparations, there is doubt.

The Germans offer 50,000,000,000 gold marks, or if payment is made by annual installments, 200,000,000,000, but they do not state over how many years these payments would be distributed or at what rate they are to be discounted. The Paris demand of 226,000,000,000, spread over forty-two years, and discounted at 5, 6 and 5 per cent. might not be so far away from the Berlin offer if the conditions of the latter were much the same, but until these conditions are known it is held here to be utterly useless to institute comparison.

"It is difficult for a layman," said an expert to The New York Times correspondent, "to appreciate what a tremendous difference, when you are dealing with enormous sums to be paid over a long period of years, the rate of interest charged and the number of installments required, make. The old story of how a sharper cheated a farmer over showing his horse by inducing him to pay a penny for the first nail, two-pence for the second, and so on, illustrates how things may affect payment, and the Germans must define their offer clearly before we can consider it."

Other Points Obscure.

Then the Government will need full explanation of other points in the German note. What does Berlin mean by "international loan established," or such a basis that it will be possible to reach an extremely high subscription figure"? What does it mean by abolition of the system of sanctions and an agreement that "the present basis of German proposition is not further reduced"? Does this last mean that Germany is to retain the whole of Silesia in spite of the result of the plebiscite?

Innumerable questions of this sort need answering with regard to the conditions Dr. Simons has tacked on to his offer of cash, and until they are elucidated the British Government considers it useless to enter into a detailed discussion of the proposals.

The ambiguity of the note is, in the view of last night's Evening News, the real reason why it was dispatched to Washington.

"The wording of the offer is so vague," it says, "that, it opens up opportunities for interminable discussion. That is just what Germany wants. She is out for delay, for while she talks she does not pay—the paying is done by the Allies. Apparently Germany has set to learn that it is for the Allies to make conditions. If she persists in that attitude she will have to be undeceived."

The Westminster Gazette considers the German terms are not intended to be more than a good basis for further negotiating. It says:

"Germany makes a gesture of willingness to do the utmost that she conceives to be possible. It is for the Allies to examine the offer and if possible to obtain more. The French Government and the French press vie with one another in declaring the offer totally unacceptable. Of course it is if the test be the destruction which Germany has done, but that by common consent is outside the capacity of any one country to pay. The real test, however, is not what Germany can pay provided she has the will to pay. That is a matter for examination and discussion."

The Westminster Gazette considers the new offer is, in essential respects, an

Continued on Page Two.

OFFER DEAD, FRENCH HOLD

Public Opinion Strongly Supports Government's Rejection.

PLEASED WITH OUR PART

Chamber Ready for Action—Payment of Billion Marks by May 1 Might Delay Invasion.

FIND JOKERS IN PROPOSALS

Analyses of the Offer and Conditions Reject Both as Beyond Discussion.

By EDWIN L. JAMES.

Copyright, 1921, by The New York Times Company.

By Wireless to The New York Times.

PARIS, April 27.—Official Paris took it for granted today that the German proposals of April 24 would not be forwarded to Washington to the Allies and that they were dead letters.

The French press strongly backs the Government in its declination to undertake new reparation negotiations with Germany on the basis of Dr. Simons's propositions sent to the United States. It has taken steps to obtain fuller information of how the Germans intend to offer, and until that has been received it will maintain the greatest reserve about the matter.

All of the afternoon newspapers carry a semiofficial note beginning: "The Government of the United States has not transmitted and will not transmit to the allied Governments the German propositions."

French diplomats are very pleased with the graceful manner in which Secretary Hughes permitted the Paris Government to place a veto on the German proposals and thus halt them. It is understood here that as soon as he got the proposals Mr. Hughes gave M. Jusserand the opportunity to point out that they did not measure up to what France demanded. M. Jusserand added to Paris this fact, and last night Paris confirmed its opposition.

No official statement is made as to what France's position may be on any new proposals from Germany, but those proposals will have to go further, much further, than the latest proposals if the French Chamber is to accept them.

The French Chamber is set for action. Probably the only action by Germany now to prevent occupation of the Ruhr the first part of next month is to turn over 1,000,000,000 gold marks cash before May 1.

If this explanation is a long analysis of the German proposals, and finds the note full of jokers, including a purpose to get all of Silesia and of tearing up the sanctions plan of the Treaty of Versailles. It concludes thus:

"This analysis makes comment useless. Very inferior to the accord of Paris, lacking in precision as to their real value, accompanied by demands which would destroy the treaty and deprive the Allies of all their guarantees, the German propositions cannot form the basis of discussion. They justify fully the firm language M. Briand used yesterday before the Chamber and they only make more intense in all France the willingness to have the German group proceed to reason."

The Journal des Débats says it is superfluous to consider these proposals which may be new to Washington, but finds the note full of jokers, including a purpose to get all of Silesia and of folishness like the Allies have been backing from Germany for more than a year.

The Temps tonight publishes a long analysis of the German proposals, and finds them full of jokers, including a purpose to get all of Silesia and of tearing up the sanctions plan of the Treaty of Versailles. It concludes thus.

May Be Federal Inquiry.

The information from Berlin that Secretary Hughes had informed the German Government that the United States could not present the proposals to the Allies was stated without qualification, and it gives rise to the suspicion that somebody has been trying to make the German Government believe that Mr. Hughes's name or attributing to him views that he never sanctioned, for which he would have to pay.

Thus on Jan. 29, the Supreme Council sent a note to the President of the German delegation in which Articles 1 and 2, fixing the Indemnity, or reparations, and describing the manner of payment, read as follows:

For the purpose of satisfying the obligations imposed upon her by Articles 231 and 232 of the Treaty of Versailles, Germany shall, irrespective of the war which Belgium has borrowed from the Allied and Associated Governments up to Nov. 11, 1918, together with interest at the rate of 5 per cent. on such sums:"

Continued on Page Two.

German Blunder Delayed Cabling of Note to Hughes

BERLIN, April 27 (Associated Press).—Clerical blundering in the main telegraph office in Berlin caused a delay of twelve hours in the transmission of the German counter-proposals on reparations to Washington. The American mission here filed the last section of the note at 10 o'clock Sunday night, and the cause of the delay was only located when acknowledgment of receipt of the message came from Washington Tuesday morning, indicating that the note had been an unduly long time in transit.

The night shift at the telegraph office apparently failed to recognize the diplomatic nature of the message and treated it as a routine dispatch.

The English rendering of the original note supplied to the American mission by the Foreign Office not only reveals an imperfect translation, but contains faulty reproduction of the German terms.

HUGHES'S NAME IS MISUSED IN BERLIN

Suggestion for Modification Not His—Did It Come from Unofficial Intruders?

SECRETARY SENT NO WORD

It Is Also Pointed Out That British Inquiries May Have Been Erroneously Attributed to Him.

Special to The New York Times.

WASHINGTON, April 27.—The disclosure today that the United States Government had not communicated with the German Government concerning the latest reparations proposals was in doubt to apply to the statement from Berlin that American suggestions for a modification of the German terms had been received by the German Government.

This statement is attributed in some quarters to confusion with action taken by the British Government. A press dispatch from London saying that the British Government had requested its representatives in Berlin to enquire informally regarding the German reparations offer for the purpose of clearing ambiguity as to the terms of years in which payments would be made under the offer was confirmed in official advices received here. If this explanation is correct, it was the British Government, therefore, and not the American Government, that communicated with the German Government concerning the German proposals. This action of the British Government may be significant of a willingness of Great Britain to give careful consideration to the German offer, but there is no official sanction for such an inference.

Propaganda Active.

At the same time it is possible that the understanding given currency in Berlin that the United States had suggested that it could not transmit the German proposals in their ambiguity to the Allies and had borrowed from the activities of Americans in Berlin who have been acting indirectly arose from the activities of Americans in Berlin who have been rendering to have the German group as undesirable to have the German proposals were unsatisfactory.

The amount of 132,000,000,000 gold marks as the total damages for which reparation is due from Germany fixed by the Reparation Commission represents what would be demanded of Germany, if she were able to pay in full and liquidate the debt today. It may therefore only be compared with the present cash value of the Allies' proposals made at Paris on Jan. 29, which made provision for 132,000,000,000 gold marks, if the debt were estimated at from 60,000,000,000 to 84,000,000,000 gold marks, if the 132,000,000,000 gold marks demanded, payment of which was to be completed in forty-two years, were discounted at once, with the cash value of the German counter-proposal made at London, Feb. 28-March 8, estimated at 30,000,000,000 gold marks, and with the present value of Germany's latest offer, 50,000,000,000 gold marks.

Annex 1, of Part VIII, referred to by the commission, defines in ten paragraphs the various ways in which compensation is to be demanded, and the ways in which the compensation is to be satisfied—material damage to persons and property of the Allies, and various costs including the aid given prisoners of war in Germany and the support of their families.

As it was clearly known that Germany could not possibly meet the total damages to be assessed against her by the Reparation Commission, the Supreme Council approved the suggestion from other point of view, to determine just what Germany should pay, but what Germany could pay.

Thus on Jan. 29, the Supreme Council sent a note to the President of the German delegation in which Articles 1 and 2, fixing the Indemnity, or reparations, and describing the manner of payment, read as follows:

Continued on Page Two.

GERMANS GET FULL BILL

Reparation Commission Fixes Total Claims of the Allies.

LESS THAN WAS EXPECTED

Commission Finishes Its Work Three Days Ahead of Date Set in the Treaty.

EXCEEDS PARIS DEMAND

But Compares With 50,000,000,000 Marks Offered by Germany in Full Settlement.

By EDWIN L. JAMES.

Copyright, 1921, by The New York Times Company.

Special Cable to The New York Times.

PARIS, April 27.—This evening at 9 o'clock the Reparation Commission summoned to the presence Dr. von Oertzen, head of the German Commission on Reparation, who replaces Herr Bergmann, and officially informed him of the sum which Germany owes in reparation for damage done in the war. The total figure is 132,000,000,000 gold marks. This figure is considerably below what had been forecast. Details of how it has been arrived at are not yet available, but will be communicated to the German Commission tomorrow in writing.

Even as late as this afternoon the Reparation Commission members were uncertain when they would be able to fix the total, but by night and day work in the last month they have arrived at the end of this part of their labors, three full days before the date of May 1 fixed by the treaty.

After the meeting with Dr. von Oertzen the following communiqué was issued:

"The Reparation Commission, in pursuance of the stipulations of Article 233, Treaty of Versailles, has decided unanimously to fix at 132,000,000,000 gold marks the amount of damages for which reparation is due by Germany in terms of Article 233, second paragraph, and Annex 1 of Part VIII. of said treaty.

"In fixing this amount the Reparation Commission has effected the necessary deductions from the amount of the figures in respect of all payments in which payments would be made under the offer and it confirmed in official advices received here. If this explanation is correct, it was the British Government, therefore, and not the American Government, that communicated with the German Government concerning the German proposals. The figure of 132,000,000,000 gold marks was the amount above which the sum in respect of further obligation incumbent on Germany."

"The commission has not included in the above amount the sum in respect of further obligation incumbent on Germany by virtue of the third paragraph of Article 232 to 'make reimbursements of all sums which Belgium has borrowed from the Allied and Associated Governments up to Nov. 11, 1918, together with interest at the rate of 5 per cent. on such sums.'"

The amount of 132,000,000,000 gold marks as the total damages for which reparation is due from Germany fixed by the Reparation Commission represents what would be demanded of Germany, if she were able to pay in full and liquidate the debt today.

Continued on Page Two.

The New York Times.

THE WEATHER
Generally fair and warmer today; Monday, cloudy, probably thunder showers; southwesterly winds.
For full weather report see Page 19.
Section 1

VOL. LXX....No. 23,171. ••• NEW YORK, SUNDAY, JULY 3, 1921. In Eight Parts, Including Rotogravure Picture Section, Book and Magazine Section.

FIVE CENTS In Manhattan, Bronx, and Brooklyn, Elsewhere TEN CENTS

DEMPSEY KNOCKS OUT CARPENTIER IN THE FOURTH ROUND; CHALLENGER BREAKS HIS THUMB AGAINST CHAMPION'S JAW; RECORD CROWD OF 90,000 ORDERLY AND WELL HANDLED

HARDING ENDS WAR; SIGNS PEACE DECREE AT SENATOR'S HOME

Thirty Persons Witness Momentous Act in Frelinghuysen Living Room at Raritan.

DROPS BLOT ON SIGNATURE

Joint Resolution of Congress Made Effective at 4:10 P. M., Daylight Saving Time.

TEXT OF THE RESOLUTION

Steel Pen Used to Be Given to Representative Porter, Author of Historic Document.

Special to The New York Times.

RARITAN, N. J., July 2.—War with Germany actually is at an end, by Congressional declaration and Executive signature on American soil.

At 4:10 P. M., local daylight saving time, in the living room of "The Hill," Senator Joseph S. Frelinghuysen's home here, President Harding placed his signature to the Porter joint Congressional resolution declaring peace with Germany and Austria, just two years and four days after the ill-fated Treaty of Versailles was signed.

President Harding Asks, 'Was It a Good Fight?'

RARITAN, N. J., July 2.—President Harding showed little interest when informed today that Jack Dempsey had defeated Georges Carpentier, French challenger, by a knockout in the fourth round.

"Was it a good fight?" he asked of newspaper men when told the result.

He made no further comment and changed the conversation into other channels.

CROWD EARLY AT GATES

Thousands Wait Through Morning Hours for Opening of Arena

POLICE IN PERFECT CONTROL

Handle Entrance and Exit of Huge Throng Without Difficulty —1,000 Firemen on Guard.

CHEER NOTABLES ON ENTRY

Spectators Eat Lunches in Streets — Bootleggers and Crooks Noticeably Absent.

Dempsey's First Thought Is Telegram to His Mother

Jack Dempsey's first thought as he came victorious from the ring was of his mother. He took a pencil and wrote her the following telegram:

Mrs. C. Dempsey, 8,572 South State St., Salt Lake City, Utah.

Dear Mother: Won in the fourth round. Received your wire. Will be home soon as possible. Love and kisses. JACK.

COBB FIGHTS IT OVER AGAIN

Calls Carpentier Soul of the Fray, Dempsey the Body.

ALL WHO'S BALLYHOO THERE

Arts, Science, Drama, Politics, Bar, Bench and Commerce Are Represented.

BOYLE'S 30 ACRES FERTILE

If There Is No New War, He Thinks Jack Will Be Best Fighter for a While.

By IRVIN S. COBB

Dempsey Says He Won Just as He Thought He Would; Carpentier Asserts He Staked His All in the Second

"Carpentier is a good, game fellow, but I think I've got it in him," Jack Dempsey remarked as he entered his dressing room after defending his title. "The champion was as happy as a schoolboy as he ran from the ring."

DEMPSEY PROVES PROWESS

Forces Carpentier Down With Incessant Rain of Terrific Blows.

TWICE FLOORS OPPONENT

But Frenchman Is Courageous After First Knockdown and Fights Until Knocked Out.

NO "ACCIDENTAL CHAMPION"

Great Throng That Gave Louder Cheer for Georges at Start Acclaims Jack at the End.

WIFE AND MOTHER BOTH TAKE POISON

Women Go to Hotel Commodore, Swallow Mercury, and Elder One Phones Physician.

FOUND CLASPING BABY SHOE

Young Woman Was Worried Because Husband Took Child to His Mother—Both May Die.

REFORMERS DEMAND ARREST OF DEMPSEY

Police Refuse Without Warrant, and They Fail to Get Plea Before Any Judge.

NEW MOVE EXPECTED TODAY

Assault and Battery Charged in Complaint—Not So "Brutal" as They Anticipated.

CARPENTIER BROKE HIS THUMB IN FIGHT

He Also Sprained His Right Wrist on Dempsey's Jaw in Second Round.

NOT OFFERED AS EXCUSE

Carpentier Cables to Wife That He Is Uninjured and Was Beaten Fairly.

BLOW TO THE JAW ENDS THE CONTEST

Story of the Fight by Rounds Shows the Superiority of Dempsey.

ONLY ONCE IN DISTRESS

Carpentier Showed Well in Second Round, but After That Was Beaten Down.

Give Notice of Coming Marriage of Col. Balsan To Consuelo, Duchess of Marlborough

Copyright, 1921, by The New York Times Company.
Special Cable to The New York Times.

LONDON, July 2.—Notice has been given at the Westminster Registry office in Covent Garden of the marriage of Consuelo, Duchess of Marlborough, and Colonel Jacques Balsan.

Continued on Page Fifteen.

Continued on Page Five.

The New York Times.

THE WEATHER

Local showers today; Sunday fair; little change in temperature; moderate south and west winds.

For weather report see next to last page.

VOL. LXX....No. 23,177.   NEW YORK, SATURDAY, JULY 9, 1921.   TWO CENTS In Greater New York | THREE CENTS Within 200 Miles | FOUR CENTS Elsewhere

TRUCE IN IRELAND DECLARED, TO BEGIN ON MONDAY AT NOON; DE VALERA AGREES TO MEET LLOYD GEORGE ON PEACE TERMS; DUBLIN CROWDS CHEER BRITISH COMMANDER AND UNIONISTS

FRANCE CALLS BACK MISSION IN ANGER AT LEIPSIC TRIALS

Holds That German Verdicts on Men Accused of War Crimes Are a Mockery.

THREAT OF ALLIED TRIBUNAL

Paris Is Expected to Demand the Handing Over of Offenders Under the Treaty.

BERLIN JARRED BY MOVE

Professes to Suspect a French Design to Continue the Military Occupation.

Copyright, 1921, by The New York Times Company.
Special Cable to The New York Times.

PARIS, July 8.—On the ground that the German trials of German war criminals are a mockery the French Government has withdrawn its mission to the Leipsic court, thus washing its hands of the procedure, and has notified the allied Governments of its action.

It is understood that the French Government will ask the Allies to return to the Treaty plan and demand that Germany hand over the accused men for trial by allied tribunals. It is not the purpose of the French Government to obtain the trial of some six or seven hundred accused Germans, but it believes that at least four or five prominent offenders should be punished for the sake of principle.

This move by the French Government was taken after the acquittal at General Stenger, accused by the French of having given an order to take no prisoners, and after insults to the French mission at Leipsic. Thus the German Government apologized for the French delegates being spat upon, the French Government believes that the procedure has reached a stage where it can no longer recognize it. Practically all the men accused by the British were freed, one test case presented by the Belgians resulted in an acquittal and the same program appears to be followed with respect to those whom the French accuse.

It is the attitude of the French Government that the Allies' treaty rights with respect to war criminals remain intact and that the German trials represented merely an opportunity given to the Germans to right the wrongs which their fighting men committed. The French say that the trials have become the trials of allied witnesses rather than of the accused Germans and that the time has come to call a halt. As the Temps says, France is going to show Germany that Germans like Stenger are expensive luxuries.

It appears unfortunate for the tranquillity of the world at large that Franco-German relations, which were so much bettered by the progress in the reparations settlement, should now become strained again. No matter how peacefully disposed he might be personally, Premier Briand is under practical compulsion to do something to meet the popular wave of indignation caused by the acquittal by the German court of Germans accused of war crimes against the French and already convicted in the court of French opinion.

The Temps tonight reviews the whole question of the war criminals. It recalls how on Dec. 25, 1919, the German Government offered to try the accused men; how on July 9 of last year the Allies agreed at Spa to help the German prosecutors gather evidence in allied countries. The Temps concludes that no attention should be paid further to the procedure at Leipsic and that the Allies should at once take steps.

"The Allies' hands are free," it says, " and they must convince the Germans that crime is a bad business and that General à la Stenger will cost the German people dearly."

The Journal des Débats says tonight that after the acquittal of Stenger the French Government could no longer have anything to do with the Leipsic trials.

"What is serious in this business," says the paper, " is that in the face of the whole world Germany should through the comedy of Leipsic give such exhibition of pan-Germanism. The manner in which she started the war and the theory of contract. By the manner in which she conducted the war she overturned all that civilization had done to limit the effects of...

"BALLY," Met. To-Day. Mac. at $2.50. Big run. Hayfield Production—Marlowe Miller, Long Run, at New Amsterdam Theater—Advt.

Continued on Page Two.

President and Mrs. Harding Observe 30th Anniversary

WASHINGTON, July 8.—President and Mrs. Harding are planning a week-end cruise down the Potomac on the Presidential yacht Mayflower if public affairs will permit Mr. Harding to get away from the capital tomorrow. They do not expect to go ashore.

Today was the thirtieth anniversary of the marriage of President and Mrs. Harding, but they had no formal observance. They were married at the same house in Marion from which the front porch campaign was conducted last year.

At the White House it was stated that nothing was known there of the reported intention of the President to attend the funeral of the World War soldiers in New York Sunday.

BARRICADED MANIAC TAKES LIFE IN FIGHT

Man Crazed With Drink Drove Wife From Home, Then Fought Bloomfield Police.

SHOTS KEPT ATTACKERS OFF

Firemen Failed to Subdue Pole With High-Pressure Stream Turned Into Shack.

Special to The New York Times.

BLOOMFIELD, N. J., July 8.—After turning a little one-story, two-room building on the outskirts of this place into an improvised fort, and defending himself for more than an hour against the attack of policemen and firemen who tried to capture him alive, John Grubach, a Polish laborer, turned his pistol upon himself and committed suicide this afternoon.

During the fight the man fired twelve shots at the police and firemen, but failed to hit any of them. In the early part of the affray one of the policemen fired a shot at the barricaded man, but then ceased firing, and tried to subdue him by turning a high pressure stream of water from a fire hose through a window.

The man apparently was crazed with drink and the desire for money and more liquor. The building in which he made his stand was at 458 Broad street, where his wife, Caroline Grubach, had been living with her 8-months-old baby girl. It was a wooden, flat-roofed, weather-beaten structure, about eight feet on the street and twenty-five feet deep.

In the front is a tiny dry goods and notion shop by which the wife had been supporting herself and child since the husband deserted her several months ago. In the rear is an equally small room, which the woman and child had used as their only living quarters.

Going to Kill Somebody.

The man, who had previously threatened his wife and demanded money of her, started for her home early yesterday afternoon with the apparent intention of shooting her if she did not give him money. Persons who saw him on the way said that he was drunk and brandished a pistol.

Frank Kuttelman, the wife's landlord, met the crazed man on the way to the store, and observed the weapon.

"Let me take that gun," said Kuttelman. "You don't want to get into any more trouble."

"Keep out of this," replied the Pole, cursing Kuttelman. "It's none of your business. I'm going to shoot somebody today."

Kuttelman let the man proceed, but called to the women in the store. Peering out of the window, the wife caught a glimpse of her husband coming down the street. Then she picked up her baby and ran out of the back door, leaving behind a pocketbook containing several...

Continued on Page Five.

HEAT FINDS VICTIMS FROM SEASHORE TO THE ROCKIES

High Humidity Increases Suffering and Many Deaths Are Reported.

DROWNINGS ARE NUMEROUS

One Man Seeking Relief on Roof Rolls Off When Asleep and Is Killed.

TEMPERATURE HERE 89

Thousands Sleep on Sand at the Beaches and on Park Benches— Showers Promised.

From the Atlantic Coast to the Rocky Mountains the country sweltered and sweated yesterday in the grip of a torrid wave, accompanied by high humidity that caused widespread suffering and many deaths.

Chicago reported eight heat deaths and Syracuse five, and from Buffalo, Pittsburgh and Detroit came records of a mounting list of fatalities in which little children were most numerous among the victims.

Even Canada baked under a merciless sun. Quebec, known as a refuge for overheated New Yorkers, had an official high temperature of 98—the hottest in its recorded weather history. Remote parts of this country found things even more sizzling than they were in New York. In Arizona and the interior of Colorado, for example, the temperature went well over 100.

Late afternoon thunderstorms and local showers brought relief in areas which had suffered constantly for days. New York with its environs suffered fewer fatalities than many other parts of the country. Only one death within the city limits was due to drowning and there was none from the direct results of the heat, though one or two were attributed to it indirectly. Several drownings were reported from nearby places, while the bodies of a number of victims of the heat the last few days were recovered.

Highest Temperature Here 89.

The highest local temperature was 89, at 4 o'clock yesterday afternoon. At 11 o'clock last night it was 7 degrees cooler, but didn't seem so, except when a fitful breeze stirred, because the humidity had risen 10 degrees, to 67. At 8 o'clock in the morning with the temperature only 74, the humidity was 84, and suffering was intense.

Local showers and possibly thunder storms are expected to cool things hereabouts today and Sunday, and moderate south to southwest winds were forecasted to aid in the cooling process.

Local beach resorts yesterday had crowds that grew almost to holiday proportions, and last night many thousands, fleeing the stifling atmosphere of apartments and tenements, made their beds on the sands, drowsed on park benches, imperilled their lives on roofs, scattered themselves over the grass of squares and playgrounds or sought refuge on the piers, which were thrown open as an emergency measure when Mayor Hylan issued this order:

Otto B. Shulhof, Esq., Chairman Mayor's Committee on Recreation and Playgrounds, 126 Madison Avenue.

Dear Sir: Beginning tonight, and continuing throughout the hot weather, all piers in every part of the city are to remain open all night. President Gallatin of the Park Board and the Dock Commissioner have been requested to see that this is done. The Police Commissioner has also been asked to have a sufficient number of policemen in attendance at all hours on all piers

Continued on Page Five.

Former Kaiser Objects To Paying Dutch Taxes

Copyright, 1921, by The New York Times Co.
Special Cable to The New York Times.

DOORN, Holland, July 8.—The Municipal Council of Doorn is discussing the vigorous protest lodged by William Hohenzollern against the tax levied by the local authorities. The ex-Kaiser maintains that they have no right whatever to tax him, as he did not come willingly to Holland, and is held practically a prisoner, and is therefore not liable to taxes as if he were a free citizen. William has also protested against the income tax.

The majority of the council, however, takes the view that the ex-Kaiser came as a free agent to Holland and himself chose Doorn as his place of residence and that therefore his protest should be disregarded and measures must be taken to secure the payment of his taxes. The ex-Crown Prince, however, is held to be exempt from taxation.

TWO CHILDREN GONE IN THIRD KIDNAPPING

Friendly Neighbors in Cape May Missing With Boy and Girl After Month's Acquaintance.

SAID TO BE FATHER'S AGENTS

No Trace of Men Who Seized Baby at Pompton Lakes or of Mrs. Mayo and Child.

The third kidnapping of children within a week as a result of the separation of parents was reported yesterday in Cape May, N. J., where two children of Mrs. Robert Emmett Woodland were taken away by a man and a woman who had been acting for her husband, from whom she has been separated a year and a half.

The children were Jack, 3½ years old, and Margaret, 2 years old. They attracted the attention of a Mr. and Mrs. Henry James, who went to live at the Sunnyside Villa, near Mrs. Woodland's home, about a month ago. Because of the interest the Jameses displayed in the children, Mrs. Woodland became friendly with them. She often permitted the couple to take the children to the beach, and sometimes James would stay at Mrs. Woodland's home to care for the two women went to the movies.

The mother learned after their disappearance that Captain Howard Smith of Schellenger's Landing had taken the couple and another man to Lewes, Del., aboard his yacht and that the children were with them, she said. The driver of the James's description led Mrs. Woodland to believe that he was her husband. She also believes Mr. James to have been her husband's younger brother, whom she had seen but once some time ago.

Mr. and Mrs. James took the children to the beach on Thursday, and when they did not return at lunch time Mrs. Woodland went to Sunnyside Villa, only to find that the Jameses had packed up and left without notifying Mrs. Woodland. William Bennett, the manager, Chief of Police Jefferson Gibson of Cape May was told what had happened, and through Prosecutor Eugene Cole warnings were sent to the police of cities in the East and the South to be on the lookout for the kidnappers.

Get Letter From Atlanta.

After Mrs. Woodland found that the children were gone she remembered that the Jameses had received registered letters from Atlanta, Ga., where her husband has been working for the Terminal Railroad.

A desire for ransom may be one of the reasons for the kidnapping, as Mrs. Woodland is the niece of John Wilbraham, formerly a wealthy Philadelphia manufacturer, who lives in Cape May and who was fond of the children. Mr. James and his wife would have settled $20,000 on each of them recently, and it was said that the kidnappers had learned of this and might have planned with the father to get possession of the children and hold them for a reward. The police believed that the kidnappers would buy children somewhere in Delaware or Maryland for a time and that no attempt would be made at present to take them to the Atlanta police.

An attempt was made to kidnap the children a year ago when Mrs. Woodland was in Tampa, Fla., and she thought at that time that her husband was trying to get possession of them. He is in Atlanta, Ga., and Mrs. Woodland left for there last night in the hope of being able to trace the children and obtain them through the aid of the Atlanta police.

Both the children were large for their age. The boy's left eye is brown and the right eye hazel color. He was dressed in a black and white striped suit with a sailor hat. The girl was dressed in a white suit embroidered with flowers, and wore brown socks. She has a birthmark on the left side of her neck in the back.

No trace was found yesterday of the four men who kidnapped nine-month-old...

Continued on Page Three.

DRAMATIC SCENES IN DUBLIN

General Macready, in Full Uniform, Gets Ovation From Crowds

SALUTES IRISH VOLUNTEERS

People Pray Outside the Mansion House, While De Valera Holds His Council.

WAIT HOURS FOR THE NEWS

When De Valera's Reply to the London Invitation Is Given Out, They Disperse Quietly.

Copyright, 1921, by The New York Times Company.
Special Cable to The New York Times.

DUBLIN, July 8.—Just at the stroke of 11 today the four Southern Unionists, Midleton, Woods, Jameson and Dockrell, sat down in the Mansion House at Dublin with de Valera and Griffith, President and Vice President of Sinn Fein, to discuss ways and means of an agreement on the Irish problem preparatory to the London conference. The interval since Monday was occupied by momentous events, the most important being the presence of General Smuts, and the people's hearts were buoyed up to an extraordinary pitch of hopefulness that reason and reasonableness will prevail in the historic conference.

This was amply manifest today by a very much larger gathering of anxious Irishmen and Irishwomen who assembled in front of the Mansion House to greet those whom they rightly regard as the holders of their destiny. De Valera was first to appear, in a taxicab, and he got a rousing cheer. Griffith, on foot, was next, and met with equal cordiality. With all this the lightheartedness of Monday gave place to deep anxiety, which was most manifest during the waiting moments. Shortly before the appointed hour, however, a wave of cheers swept through the crowds, heralding the arrival of the Southern Unionist delegates. Among the first of these to enter the meeting room was Lord Midleton, immediately followed by Sir Robert Woods and Andrew Jameson, Sir Maurice Dockrell arriving later. Notwithstanding all hints since Monday, General Smuts and the Northern Premier were absent, and their absence was noted with grave disappointment.

It is again an instance of the people's hopes for success that many knelt on the gravel and prayed for the success of the deliberations. It was striking testimony to the faith in the leaders who sat in private around a table within the building. Even the singing of patriotic songs was not as enthusiastic as on Monday, so gravely did some regard this day's proceedings.

At 1 o'clock the Lord Mayor appeared and was rushed upon for news, but he would say nothing. Then there was again an adjournment till 4 o'clock, and as the Unionists were passing out for lunch Lord Midleton consoled the multitude by saying "We are coming back at 4 o'clock."

It transpired that messages of good-speed were received from America. James J. Phelan, a Boston banker, cabled fervent hope that the way to lasting peace would be found, as he believed the time was opportune.

When the delegates returned at 4 o'clock it was plain that there was awful seriousness in the deliberations, as each seemed determined to go through with the far-reaching attempt at a settlement of the age-long problem.

At 6 o'clock General Macready arrived as if summoned to the conference. His appearance, dramatic as it was, was a signal for a remarkable demonstration. Met by the Lord Mayor, the distinguished soldier saluted. He himself was saluted by the officer in charge of the Republican volunteers and in soldierly fashion acknowledged the salute amid enthusiastic cheers of the expectant multitude.

Macready, who was in uniform, remained fifty minutes, and on leaving was again cheered. He walked through a long avenue of people kept orderly by volunteers and, head erect with military bearing, entered an automobile. Macready returned to the Mansion House at 7:45, driving through a differently atmosphered city than he has experienced for a long time. He was again loudly cheered.

General Macready remained five minutes and left with the Southern Unionists.

The conference started at 8 o'clock. An hour later the letter of de Valera to Lloyd George was made public. The crowds outside the Mansion House melted away in perfect order and apparent relief.

Continued on Page Two.

Text of De Valera's Letter to Lloyd George; Official Announcement of Truce on Monday

Special Cable to The New York Times.

LONDON, July 8.—The text of the letter sent today to Premier Lloyd George by Eamon de Valera follows:

Sir: The desire you expressed on the part of the British Government to end the centuries of conflict between the peoples of these two islands and to establish relations of neighborly harmony is the genuine desire of the people of Ireland.

I have consulted with my colleagues and received the views of the representatives of the minority of our nation in regard to the invitation you have sent me. In reply I desire to say that I am ready to meet and discuss with you on what basis such a conference as that proposed can reasonably hope to achieve the object desired.

EAMON DE VALERA.

The official wording of the statement issued from Downing Street with reference to a truce was as follows:

In accordance with the Prime Minister's offer and Mr. de Valera's reply, arrangements are being made for hostilities to cease from Monday next, July 11, at noon.

DR. BUTLER TO MEET EMPIRE PREMIERS

Is Invited by Mr. Lloyd George to Spend Week-End With Them at Chequers.

DISCUSSES BRITISH POLICY

Convinced Its Guiding Principle Is Close Accord with America —Freedom of Seas Vital.

Copyright, 1921, by The New York Times Company.
Special Cable to The New York Times.

LONDON, July 8.—Dr. Nicholas Murray Butler of Columbia University and Mrs. and Miss Butler were to have gone to the Continent tomorrow, but THE NEW YORK TIMES correspondent learns from an official source that Prime Minister Lloyd George today sent to Dr. Butler an invitation to pass the week-end with him at Chequers, the country seat destined for the use of British Premiers by Lord Lee. Among Mr. Lloyd George's other guests will be all the Prime Ministers of the dominions who are attending the imperial conference.

It will be remembered that some time ago reports were circulated that Dr. Butler had been invited to address the dominion Premiers at their conference here. In that form the statement was obviously incorrect, for American citizens could have no part in the British imperial conference. As THE NEW YORK TIMES editorially said on June 21 last: "No spokesman for the United States is to be present at the conference. Yet it is plain from the beginning that American interests are in the minds of all the Premiers. Unrepresented and unheard, this country will be a factor in the most important agreements reached."

The invitation extended to Dr. Butler may, on further consideration of course been of an unofficial kind, but they probably have been all the more intimate and penetrative on that account. Speaking to THE NEW YORK TIMES representative today, Dr. Butler said:

"It is quite plain to me that the vital principle of British foreign policy following the war is close accord with the United States and complete trust in the American Government. Great Britain has not the faintest notion of naval rivalry with us. She is an island, and sees freely open to commerce are as necessary to her food supply and her economic life as our transcontinental railways are. This is the basic fact to be reckoned with. In agreeing to limit naval armaments she must make sure that the seas are kept free about war break out anywhere, and in this Great Britain's situation become the same as our own.

"For the American people to be led into huge naval expenditure now is unspeakably foolish. Militarism is as dead as secAtism, which is saying a good deal. The time has come for common-sense to displace both. Common sense dictates scientifically complete military organization that can be quickly and almost automatically expanded to meet an emergency and a naval force or fleet cruisers and destroyers to meet those situations which imperfect human nature makes always possible.

"There is plainly much perplexity here as to the Anglo-Japanese treaty and its renewal. I often hear the question asked, What possible purpose can the treaty serve now? Conditions have wholly changed since 1904. There is good support for the suggestion that the treaty should be denounced a year hence and an agreement up to the problems and policies of the Pacific be entered into by Great Britain, Canada, Australia, Japan, China and the United States become the same as our own.

"The element in Belfast and the Republicans who, I am convinced, do not understand each other, and for that reason I do not look for much from the conference. The Irish people, it is true, because they do not like the people who have been opposed for 700 years, but they mistrust England, too, with reason. I do hope, however, that some lasting benefit may result..."

Continued on Page Two.

IRISH HERE PLEASED OVER MONDAY TRUCE

But They Distrust Lloyd George and Expect Little of a Conference.

STILL HOPE FOR REPUBLIC

Count on de Valera to Demand Full Autonomy — Some Fear Compromise.

News of the coming conferences between Premier Lloyd George and Eamon de Valera wrought different reactions upon the various phases of Irish-American opinion here last night. Many preferred to await the outcome of the conferences before discussing the possibilities; others viewed the news with mistrust, but all apparently were glad that a truce had been declared effective Monday.

Those who discussed the reports last night were certain that de Valera, appearing at the London conference as the President of the Irish Republic, would insist upon the recognition of the Irish Republic as a basis of peace. The Irish Republicans, or those who have held out for the Irish Republic, regarded any conference with Lloyd George as one of the participants with disfavor.

Supreme Court Justice Daniel F. Cohalan, head of the Friends of Irish Freedom, was not in the city and his opinion, representative of a group of American citizens of Irish blood who split with de Valera, could not be obtained.

This group has suspected that de Valera, as a conservative, might accept something short of an Irish Republic, such as dominion rule, in order to obtain peace.

Mgr. James W. Power, an ardent Irish Republican, said the proposed conferences in Ireland did not appear ready to get together, although conferences might be held looking toward a solution of the problem.

Distrusts Lloyd George.

"I haven't much confidence in Lloyd George," Mgr. Power said, "and therefore I do not look for any definite results from the proposed conference. Prejudice in Belfast against the Sinn Fein seems to be too strong to permit of de Valera and those conferring together at this time. The Irish Republicans seem to be very much in the majority in Ireland and I am sure they if the English Government approached the situation frankly—with a view to permitting the republic—neither side would be dissatisfied with the results.

"The Irish of the south are satisfied that their demands are just and legitimate—they want a republic, and will not be satisfied with anything else. They would be willing to give England every possible guarantee of protection. They would never permit Ireland to be employed as the base of a power hostile to England, for example, because they are religious people and would not violate their pledges.

"On the other hand, they would be just as devoted as Australia, Canada or any other of the Dominions of Great Britain. I do not believe the conference which de Valera has proposed to attend will bring lasting peace to Ireland, because I do not think the English Government, at this time, will make any definite guarantee of independence to Ireland such as de Valera demands...

Continued on Page Two.

TO MEET PREMIER FIRST

De Valera Asks to Discuss Basis of Proposed Conference

TRUCE COUNTED A BIG GAIN

Suggested by Lloyd George to Lord Midleton, It Is Agreed To by Republicans.

PEACE HOPES NOW BRIGHT

Ulster Expected to Be Called in After British Ministers Have Smoothed the Way.

Copyright, 1921, by The New York Times Company.
Special Cable to The New York Times.

LONDON, July 8.—Eamon de Valera, replying today to Premier Lloyd George's invitation to a conference of Irish and British representatives in London, agrees to meet Mr. Lloyd George to discuss "on what basis such a conference as that proposed can reasonably hope to achieve the object desired." was stated in authoritative quarters tonight to indicate that the Sinn Fein representatives will have a meeting with British Cabinet representatives before Ulster representatives are called into the conference. It is believed this will smooth the path of the conference and it would not imply any reluctance on the part of Sir James Craig to confer as soon as the preliminaries had been arranged between de Valera and Lloyd George.

Before de Valera's letter was made public the Irish Bulletin issued the following note:

"President de Valera informed the conference of the terms in which he proposed to reply to the British Premier's invitation. At the previous session of the conference the President expressed the view that it would be impossible to conduct negotiations with any hope of achieving satisfactory results if there is bloodshed and violence in Ireland. A letter to Lord Midleton from Mr. Lloyd George was read concurring in this view and indicating the willingness of the British Government to consent to a suspension of active operations on both sides. It is expected that an announcement of a truce to take effect not later than from Monday next will be made early tomorrow."

Premier Suggested a Truce.

Thus it was revealed that when Lord Midleton returned to Ireland after seeing Lloyd George, he took back with him a letter from the Prime Minister in reference to a truce. It had been thought that a truce would be difficult of arrangement and that if an agreement of some kind were reached it would have to be in the nature of a tacit understanding.

The text of the letter in which Lord Midleton took with him to Ireland follows:

London, July 7, 1921.

Dear Lord Midleton: In reference to the conversation I had with you this morning, the Government fully realizes that it would be impossible to conduct negotiations with any hope of achieving satisfactory results if there is bloodshed and violence in Ireland. It would disturb the atmosphere and make the attainment of peace difficult.

As soon as we hear that Mr. de Valera is prepared to enter into a conference with the British Government and to give instructions to those under his control to cease from all acts of violence, we should give instructions to the troops and to the police to suspend active operations against those who are engaged in this unfortunate conflict.

Yours sincerely, D. LLOYD GEORGE.

News of the truce being arrived at in Ireland came as the most auspicious fact that has grown out of the negotiations begun last Monday. It was regarded as the salient, concrete gain of the situation both here and in Dublin. The abstention of Sir James Craig and the other Northern Premier from the peace negotiations on to a new plane of hopefulness and reality. Hitherto hopes had rested rather in the balance. But it is a sign that the negotiations will continue, but it is thought to furnish clear evidence that some basis on which it appears to be possible to carry on negotiations with a hope of eventual success has been discovered. That de Valera has ceased demanding a republic is here taken for granted, for no British Government, it is thought, could agree to a truce which implied a possible ultimate recognition of an Irish Republic. The Unionists who were invited to the conference by de Valera understood to have made that point quite clearly—has the sake; they would go out of their way to please him.

Continued on Page Two.

Alien Residents, Arriving in First Cabin, Detained Under New Immigration Law

G. F. Earle, representative in New York, at 5 Bridge Street, since 1900, of the grain firm of Sanday & Co., who returned yesterday with his wife and daughter from England on the Royal Mail Steam Packet Oropesa, was the first alien resident arriving as a first cabin passenger in the port to be held on board under the new interpretation of the Immigration Restriction act.

Until Thursday, July 7, the immigration Inspectors had been permitting aliens arriving in the first or second cabin to land if they were residents in the United States or intended to live in the country. The latest orders, received from Washington Thursday morning, say that all aliens, irrespective of station or class, on board must be detained to await orders from the Secretary of Labor. Only aliens who declared that they had come on a short visit or were among those representing mercantile...

...1866, when he returned to England and stayed there five years. He had his son born in Plainfield, N. J., where his daughter Louise, who accompanied him, was born. As an American citizen she was permitted to go ashore, but decided to remain with her parents.

Her father said he had been in England three months on business and to see his relatives. The immigration officials said they could do nothing until orders were received of Ellis Island for their release.

Mrs. M. Denekamp, another first cabin passenger on the liner, who lives in East Fifty-eighth Street, returned from a trip to Europe and was met at the pier by her husband, but was not permitted to land, as he is a Hollander. Among the other cabin passengers held on board were five Poles, returned on eleven Germans.

Captain H. A. Le Brecht of the Oropesa said that on June 30 his operator caught by a wireless message from the Shipping Board freighter Chattanooga, which said that half her boilers were out of commission. The Oropesa would have been disabled, 150 miles away, but Captain Le Brecht received another message that the disabled vessel was being towed into Halifax by the freighter Hutchinson.

...in New York in 1886 and remained until

ELKSHORN, TENN, AVE, ATLANTIC CITY, BEST MODERATE PRICED HOTEL—Advt.

Continued on Page Two.

The New York Times.

THE WEATHER.
Rain and colder today; Sunday fair; fresh to strong northwest winds.
Temperature Yesterday—Max., 48; Min., 32.
☞ For weather report see next to last page.

VOL. LXXI....No. 23,303.　　　•••　　　NEW YORK, SATURDAY, NOVEMBER 12, 1921.　　　TWO CENTS In Greater New York | THREE CENTS Within 200 Miles | FOUR CENTS Elsewhere

OUR UNKNOWN WARRIOR BURIED, THE WORLD HONORING HIM; HARDING PLEADS FOR A BAN BY CIVILIZATION ON WAR; DELEGATES ENTER ARMS PARLEY TODAY IN HOPEFUL SPIRIT

ULSTER REJECTS PROPOSED TERMS; DRAFTS NEW ONES

Finds Fundamental Principles Involved Which Are Impossible of Attainment at Present.

WANTS THESE WITHDRAWN

Will "Indicate More Practicable Means" of Obtaining Peace Without Infringing Her Rights.

NEXT MOVE IS UNCERTAIN

British Cabinet Is Expected to Meet Today to Study Reply and to Consider Action.

Copyright, 1921, by The New York Times Company.
Special Cable to THE NEW YORK TIMES.

LONDON, Nov. 11.—Ulster replied this afternoon to the British Government's draft suggestions looking to a settlement of the Irish question, with what on its face appears to be a definite rejection of the proposals. There is, however, an intimation that the Ulster Cabinet will indicate other and more practicable means for securing peace without infringing on Ulster's rights.

Sir James Craig and his colleagues take the position that "certain fundamental principles are involved in the suggestions which make their acceptance conditions are impossible of attainment," and that "no useful purpose would be served by holding formal consultation between his Majesty's Government and the Government of Northern Ireland until such suggestions are withdrawn from the subjects to be discussed."

The public is waiting for further developments and elucidations. Ulster's reply today is, of course, a decided setback for the negotiations along the lines laid out by Premier Lloyd George after J's conference with the Sinn Fein delegates, and there is said to be grave disappointment in Ministerial circles, but progress along those lines had not been expected with much confidence outside of those circles.

The Ulster Cabinet's main objection to the proposed scheme for settlement is the All-Irish Parliament, and it is an objection that goes to the root of that scheme. It is looked upon as possible that the proposition may be brought back again in discussion of the linkage with the Council of Ireland under the present Home Rule act and the possibility of giving Dominion status to that body. That was the point from which the conference with the Sinn Fein began.

The British Cabinet is expected to meet tomorrow morning to consider the reply which Sir James Craig sent to the Prime Minister, and then to decide whether a meeting of the Irish conference committee should be called to discuss the new position, or whether there should be further communications first with the Ulster Cabinet.

Ulsteries Issue Communique.

LONDON, Nov. 11 (Associated Press).—The Ulster Cabinet rejected today the Government's plan for a settlement of the Irish question, on the ground that it contained fundamental principles which make existing conditions were impossible of attainment. The Ulster Ministers, however, are putting forward counter-proposals. A communique issued by the Northern Ireland Cabinet suggests that the Government should consider these counter-proposals before the proposed meeting of the British and Ulster Cabinets.

The text of the communique said:

"The suggestions put forward by the Imperial Government were received last night and were considered. The Ulster Cabinet is drawing up a detailed reply, which it is hoped to forward shortly.

"As, however, certain fundamental principles are involved in the suggestions, which make existing circumstances are impossible of attainment, Sir James Craig, with the unanimous approval of his colleagues, has informed the Prime Minister that no useful purpose would be served by holding a formal consultation between his Majesty's Government and the Government of Northern Ireland until certain suggestions in the Government's proposals are withdrawn."

The formal reply of the Ulster Cabinet will indicate other and more practicable means of securing peace without infringing upon the rights of Ulster.

The Ulster Cabinet Ministers were summoned here recently by Sir James Craig to consider the Government's proposals, and they met this forenoon to discuss the plan for a settlement of the Irish question which was contained in a statement from the British Ministry. This, as noted in the communique, was received last night and was considered to be in the form of certain definite suggestions for a scheme, in which Ulster

Continued on Page Four.

Boy Scouts to Gather Corn For Armenia in Iowa Fields

DES MOINES, Iowa, Nov. 11.—Thousands of Boy Scouts will sweep Iowa tomorrow to gather corn for famine relief in the Near East. Farmers will co-operate, by permitting the boys to go into the fields and haul limited quantities from standing corn.

Free storage services, milling and transportation have been arranged and it will be sent immediately to the famine regions of Armenia.

JOHN M'CORMACK BUYS HALS PAINTING

Singer Pays $150,000 for "Portrait of a Man"—Now on Its Way to America.

SALE IS CONFIRMED HERE

Many Other Pictures Coming— Sir Joseph Duveen Denies "The Blue Boy" Has Been Sold.

John McCormack has paid $150,000 for the "Portrait of a Man" by Frans Hals, and the picture is now on its way to this country, after its removal from the collection of Count Maurice Zamoyski, the Polish Ambassador to France. The report of the purchase was printed in The American Art News and confirmed at the Reinhardt Galleries, but denied for Mr. McCormack in the transaction.

Many other great paintings are on their way to this country, and art dealers predict that the present art season will bring back the pre-war days of large deals in famed pictures. The total of paintings bought abroad this year runs into millions of dollars, and it is predicted that the Winter months will see many more important sales.

Art dealers here were interested yesterday in the report from London that the purchaser of "The Blue Boy," by Gainsborough, was Henry E. Huntington, but Sir Joseph Duveen denied last night that any deal for the picture had been consummated. Sir Joseph repeated that the picture had been bought by Duveen Brothers with no client in mind and that it would not be brought to this country for several months. It is to be exhibited in the National Galleries in London. Another picture bought by the Duveens is "The Tragic Muse," by Sir Joshua Reynolds.

Another important purchase reported this season was that of two Rembrandts for $750,000, for the collection of Joseph Widener. Many other smaller purchases have been reported.

The Hals painting is rated as one of the gems of the Zamoyski art collection, and formerly was in the Blue Palace in Warsaw, which Count Zamoyski turned over to the American Government for use as a legation.

"This 'Portrait of a Man' belongs to the latest and most-sought-after period of Hals art," said The American Art News, "when the master almost abandoned the use of positive color in favor of a scheme of black and white and flesh color, which offered no impediments to the flesh tones. Another work and in the consummate power of his handling the great Dutchmen stands second, if second, to Velasquez alone.

"The subject of this picture is an elderly man verging on old age. The face is alight with youthful spirit. He appears to be a substantial citizen, but albeit a man with a sense of humor and a disposition that enabled him to enjoy life. He is represented at three-quarters length, with a fine head, surmounted by a black hat, slightly turned to the right. He has gray whiskers and a mustache. The white flat lace collar makes such a note against the black coat as the black loved. One hand is gloved, while the other holds the limp glove just taken off."

Special Cable to THE NEW YORK TIMES.

LONDON, Nov. 11.—No confirmation has been received by the Duveens in London of the reported purchase of "The Blue Boy" by H. E. Huntington. It had been said by Sir Joseph Duveen a short time ago, on the revelation of the identity of its purchaser.

Harvey Sees Tolerance Supplanting Force, He Tells London Armistice Day Diners

LONDON, Nov. 11 (Associated Press).—"Today signalizes the joining of the distracted peoples of the world a way to peace and happiness, which constitutes their priceless heritage from the Maker of the universe. A memorial to our own patriot dead, a harbinger of hope for all the living—such is the true purport of this our holy day," declared Colonel George Harvey, United States Ambassador to Great Britain, in an Armistice Day address here tonight.

The occasion of his commemorative discourse was a dinner to him and Mrs. Harvey given by the English-speaking Union. It was presided over by Captain Frederick H. Guest, Air Secretary, and attended by a distinguished Anglo-American assemblage.

In addition, Ambassador Harvey alluded to President Harding's proclamation making the day a national holiday, and pointed out the coincidence of the day's falling on the three-hundred and first anniversary of the arrival of the Mayflower.

"On one bank of the Potomac," he said, "in the sacred soil of Arlington Cemetery, the body of our Unknown Soldier was lowered reverently to rest. On the other side of that historic river, in the capital, for the first time in history are gathered the foremost statesmen from the uttermost parts of the earth in a common determination to find for the distracted peoples of the world a way to peace and happiness, which constitutes their priceless heritage from the Maker of the universe. A memorial to our own patriot dead, a harbinger of hope for all the living—such is the true purport of this our holy day."

Ambassador Harvey asked rhetorically if history must be forever merely a narration of warfare.

"The strength of a country is not measured by armies and navies," he declared. "A schoolteacher at a crossroads is more potent ultimately than a dreadnought on the seas. One little church on a hill is worth a score of regiments. Tolerance has supplanted the antithesis as an actual force. A peculiar responsibility devolves 'pon our two peoples to call only to man but to enhance the now, better, higher power among men.

"Mutual respect, confidence and tolerance—these are the essentials of that genius for co-operation which has already won for our Christian President the hearts of our own people; and a destiny, I believe, to fetch the English-speaking race into a harmonious relationship to nearly perfect that all mankind will realize in the near future that there is more power and glory in 'Lead, Kindly Light' than in all the fighting anthems of the world."

INJUNCTION STRIPS MILKMEN OF POWER TO HARASS DEALERS

Forbids 12,000 Union Members to Use Violence, Intimidation or Persuasion.

TRIED TO WRECK 4 PLANTS

Tampered With Machines, Threw Away Parts, Left Pasteurizers in Shape to Affect Milk.

SWEEPING COURT ORDER

Prohibits Crowds, Appeals to Consumers or False Reports in Five Boroughs and Westchester.

One of the most sweeping injunctions ever obtained in connection with labor troubles in the metropolitan district has been granted to members of the New York Milk Conference Board. It became effective yesterday, restraining officers and members of the milk wagon drivers' union from violence, interference or intimidation in the five boroughs of New York and in Westchester County.

The injunction enjoined the union from the further conduct of the strike by any of the usual methods and practically rendered it powerless to continue the fight of 12,000 wagon drivers and station employes, which has hampered the milk supply of New York for almost two weeks. Although the order, obtained from Supreme Court Justice Charles H. Kelby in Brooklyn, was temporary, counsel for the Milk Board will ask that it be made permanent on Monday, when the union leaders have been summoned to answer the complaint. The unions have obtained counsel and will begin their fight to prevent the distributors from making the order permanent.

The injunction restrained the strikers from "picketing in any way the depots, places of business or routes of any of the plaintiffs or any point where 'two or their employes are receiving or distributing milk," and it also restrained them from "spying on the operations of the plaintiffs or any of their customers or employes."

Attempts to Damage Plants.

In an affidavit asking the injunction, Loton Horton, President of the Sheffield Farms Company, said that upward of fifty carloads of perishable milk had been abandoned by the strikers at the railway terminals on Oct. 31, and attempts made to wreck the company's four pasteurizing plants.

"Immediately upon the commencement of the strike on Oct. 31," he said, "the company found that its pasteurizing machinery had been dislocated, the screws had been taken out of the milk bottle fillers, the temperature regulators in the pasteurizers had been tampered with in each of the four plants, so that the quality of the milk would have been affected, if this had not been discovered; the locks had been changed to prevent the opening of the store doors to prevent the company from entering same. In countless other ways efforts had been made to so leave our business that the complete cessation would cripple this industry.

"Eighteen hundred horses in fourteen stables were left with only three loyal men to tend to their needs."

Frank Zollner, Superintendent of the Sheffield pasteurizing plant at 1,380 Fulton Street, Brooklyn, in a sworn statement said that the collection books and records of 161 drivers had been thrown into a sewer by strikers.

Benjamin D. White, a director of the Orange County Milk Association, swore that a union delegate had called him on

Continued on Page Nine.

Gandhi Exhorts Hindus To Remove Lawrence Statue

LAHORE, British India, Nov. 11.—Mohandas K. Gandhi, the Indian Nationalist leader, today urged a large gathering here to remove the statue of Lord Lawrence which stands in the city. Gandhi exhorted his audience to undertake the task "even at the risk of imprisonment or death." Beneath the statue is the inscription, "Will you be governed by the pen or by the sword?"

Lord Lawrence distinguished himself in putting down the Sepoy mutiny in India. He also served as Governor-General from 1863 to 1869.

TROLLEY SMASHED BY WILD FIRE TRUCK

Driver Loses Control and Big Machine Hits Car Head-On —Four Men Hurt.

FIREMAN IS LIKELY TO DIE

Three-Ton Motor Truck Hits Auto on Manhattan Bridge, Injuring Two Persons.

Four men were injured when a fire truck ran wild and crashed head-on into a surface car containing twenty passengers at First Avenue and Eighty-fifth Street about 6:30 o'clock last night. The fright and excitement among the passengers as the heavy truck rammed the front vestibule of the car was intense, but policemen and firemen calmed the passengers.

One of the injured may die. He is Michael McNamara, fire patrolman, 31 years old, of 2,950 Third Avenue, who was thrown from the truck to the street. Dr. Dunn of Reception Hospital, who responded to an ambulance call, found that McNamara's head was hurt, two ribs were broken and he had other injuries. The fireman was taken to the City Hospital on Blackwell's Island. The others hurt were Edwin Cox, fire patrolman, 29 years old, of 124 East 120th Street, and two passengers of the surface car—Eugene Orthelm, 28 years old, of 238 East Ninety-fourth Street, and Charles Brettenbach, 39 years old, of 407 East Eighty-fifth Street, who continued their journey after Dr. Dunn had bandaged their cuts and bruises.

The truck, which was going at high speed, was so badly damaged that it could not continue its trip in answer to a fire alarm at First Avenue and Eightieth Street. The truck was Fire Patrol No. 4, William T. Clark, fire patrolman, of 28 La Salle Street, said the police he could not explain how the machine got out of his control. He said it suddenly swerved and he could not avert the collision. The surface car was discharging passengers at the time of the accident. Arthur E. and Walter S. Duane, brothers, of 332 Crescent Street, Brooklyn, who sat in front, were injured.

"Now, the supreme condition in order that the equilibrium of the world may be re-established and in order that the countries more severely stricken by the war may rise and recover, is that their economy be fixed. That is why all our efforts must be directed toward creating political guarantees for the lasting maintenance of peace.

"This is the fundamental point of our Italian policy, and it is for this reason that Italy accepted with full heart the invitation of President Harding and is ready through our delegation here to give all possible contribution to the conference in order to obtain concrete results such as to create in the world that atmosphere of peace which constitutes today its supreme need."

Japanese Predict Success.

Japanese official statement: "Japan approaches this great meeting of the nations confident that the conference will succeed. We are undertaking this work in the knowledge that although there may be faults of detail in our position it is in general a just one, and in the belief that all the nations will content themselves with facts, as we shall do, and devote themselves to unprejudiced examination of the facts. A sure foundation will be laid for an international agreement that will make for armament limitation a simple matter.

"All the nations of the world, with their war moods still sore, are clamoring for peace. And, though some of those wounds are of the flesh, there are equally deep economic wounds.

"Japan, in common with all other countries, is demanding relief from the armament burden that threatens to strangle her industrial development. Our delegation, therefore, is here prepared to bare the Japanese situation completely and to join the other nations in any just policy that may remove misunderstanding and in any program of arms limitation that assures our national security.

"We are aware of our position and ready to let it speak for itself in the conference. We want the world to learn our position from the conference itself and to make its own judgment."

British Express Co-operation.

British Empire Delegation: "The stately and impressive symbolism of America's mourning for her sons and daughters dead in the cause of liberty has deeply moved the hearts of their British comrades in the great war. It

Continued on Page Seven.

LEADERS HAIL CONFERENCE

Briand Sees No Reason to Prevent Results in a Few Weeks.

JAPANESE PREDICT SUCCESS

Millerand and Curzon Send Messages of Encouragement to Washington.

POPE TO GIVE FULL SUPPORT

Delegates Pleased With Harding's Arlington Speech— American Group Confers.

WASHINGTON, Nov. 11 (Associated Press).—With the eyes of all the world fixed hopefully upon them the accredited spokesmen of the powers will meet in Washington tomorrow to try to find a way to ease the heavy burden of armaments.

In the historic heart great Britain, France, Italy, Japan and the United States, a group which, acting together, can turn the whole tide of civilization into new channels, will be pledged a solemn and determined co-operation. In addition, China, Belgium, Portugal and the Netherlands, invited because of their vital interests in the problems and crucial problems of the Far East, will sit in the conference to help solve the circle of those who are to strive for the new day of international relationship.

Expressions from the principal delegations on the eve of the assembly were:

—M. Briand, French Prime Minister: "We enter the conference in an earnest spirit to assist in reaching a common understanding that shall give peace of mind to the world instead of an armed peace. I see no reason why a few weeks hence we should not be separating after having defined how the interests of one have become the interests of all. France wishes to arrive at an accord that will create an atmosphere of peace, in which the nations may work in complete security."

Italy Wants Peace Guarantees.

Senator Schanzer, head of the Italian delegation: "The world emerges from an immense catastrophe and needs to find again the equilibrium. The war broke the economic unity of the world. The enormous financial sacrifices which the war imposed on the peoples exhausted their force of resistance and a great difference in their economic conditions and in the value of their money have become the interests of all, and now the almost impossible may only commence among them.

President Harding's Plea for Barring War From the Stage of Righteous Civilization

From President Harding's Speech at Arlington.

The loftiest tribute we can bestow today—the heroically earned tribute—fashioned in deliberate conviction, out of unclouded thought, neither shadowed by remorse nor made vain by fancies, is the commitment of this Republic to an advancement never made before. If American achievement is a cherished pride at home, if our unselfishness among nations in all we wish it to be, and ours is a helpful example in the world, then let us give of our influence and strength, yea, of our aspirations and convictions, to put mankind on a little higher plane, exulting and exalting, with war's distressing and depressing tragedies barred from the stage of righteous civilization.

There have been a thousand defenses justly and patriotically made; a thousand offenses which reason and righteousness ought to have stayed. Let us beseech all men to join us in seeking the rule under which reason and righteousness shall prevail.

Standing today on hallowed ground, conscious that all America has halted to share in the tribute of heart, and mind, and soul to this fellow-American, and knowing that the world is noting this expression of the Republic's mindfulness, it is fitting to say that his sacrifice, and that of the millions dead, shall not be vain. There must be, there shall be, the commanding voice of a conscious civilization against armed warfare.

HOST IN MADISON SQ. HONORS THE DEAD

Fifteen Thousand Guests of the Legion in the Garden, as Many More Outside.

FOLLOW HARDING'S VOICE

The President's Words at Arlington Clearly Heard—50,000 Parade—Thousands Pray.

President Harding's voice rang out in loud and distinct tones to a crowd of 30,000 guests of the American Legion in Madison Square Garden and to Madison Square yesterday, as he delivered his address at Arlington Cemetery in Washington over the grave of the unknown soldier.

Over the amplifying telephone also came the crisp notes of the bugle, the playing of the band, the singing of the quartet and brief words by Admiral Beatty, Marshal Foch, General Diaz and other foreign soldiers, as they laid medals on the casket of the unknown soldier.

Except for a slight blurring of deep sounds and the occasional re-echoing of the rolled "r," the telephone news reproduced with sharpness and clearness. Not a word of the address of President Harding was lost on any part of the crowd. Thousands, including many of the gold star mothers who filled a large section, were in tears, as the President in touching words told how many American families, whose sons were buried when they fell, might hope that unknown soldier was their boy.

A great parade on Fifth Avenue of the Veterans of the Foreign Wars of the United States and the silent prayer of two minutes were the chief of the many other observances of Armistice Day. Every division that fought in the war was represented among the 50,000 who marched, while several hundred thousand spectators applauded from the sidewalks on Fifth Avenue.

Two Minutes of Silent Prayer.

The subways, elevated railroads and surface traffic stopped at 12 o'clock, and business of all kinds was suspended for two minutes of prayer. Groups on the streets paused in all parts of the city, bared their heads and remained in prayer for two minutes. Church bells rang out in some sections to remind them that the time set apart for this observance was arrived. Railroad trains stopped for two minutes on all the Eastern railroads. The Grand Central Terminal was turned into a cathedral a few minutes before noon, when a New York Central employe, formerly a bugler with the Twenty-seventh Division, sounded his bugle from the east balcony of the concourse. Thousands in the building remained with bowed heads for two minutes.

Nearly 1,000 veterans, gold star mothers, a large delegation of wounded and crippled soldiers, representative of 300 American Legion posts, veterans of the Grand Army of the Republic and other organizations and the general public took the 13,000 seats in Madison Square Garden long before the opening of the services, and a great crowd gathered in front of the Garden and in Madison Square, where powerful electric megaphones also trumpeted the vibrant tones of President Harding's address. The voices and the music, arriving over the telephone, were fixed up by an ordinary desk concealed behind the speaker's platform. It penetrated with uniform distinctness to the parts of the audio torium remote from the speaker's platform.

In the open air the President's voice swept over the crowd in Madison Square. The voice seemed to come from the chest of a giant. Words which were thrown against the square to Broadway way in one direction and across to Twenty-third Street on the other, George Whitefield, the eighteenth century evangelist, who is said to have been the possessor of the most powerful voice in history.

OVATION FOR WILSON IN LINE AND AT HOME

Crowds That Watch in Silence as Parade Moves By, Cheer as ex-President Passes.

PILGRIMAGE TO HIS HOUSE

Thousands in Demonstration Lasting an Hour Move Him to Express Thanks.

Special to The New York Times.

WASHINGTON, Nov. 11.—With the last dull boom from the guns which counted off minute after minute of the hours that passed while a nation paid grateful nation paid solemn tribute to the nameless soldier dead through one of their number, and when silence had succeeded eulogy and prayer about the grave at Arlington where his remains had been eased to the final rest, thousands of the throng which had taken part in those ceremonies turned their thoughts to another "soldier of the World War" who, though among the number of the living, had been grievously stricken while engaged in heroic endeavor to realize the supreme object of that great conflict.

The home in S Street, where Woodrow Wilson took up his abode when he moved from the White House, became the objective of a remarkable pilgrimage, and the scene of a demonstration which will live long in the memory of those who witnessed it. On occasion marked up in spontaneous warmth and genuine feeling what it lacked in ceremonial formality. Both Mr. and Mrs. Wilson, who shared with her husband the tribute so lovingly bestowed, seemed moved to the verge of happy tears as their names were joined in the acclaim of those pilgrims. On the eve of the Conference for the Limitation of Armament, an outstanding feature of the demonstration was the unmistakable manner in which the multitude petitioned and applauded from the sidewalks on Fifth Avenue.

Except for a slight blurring of deep sounds, the home in S Street, where Woodrow Wilson took up his abode when he moved from the White House, became the objective. Mr. Wilson seemed to sense this feeling and to exult in the fact that the multitude had come to him in that mood. He was acclaimed not once but repeatedly as "the greatest man on earth." When some one in the crowd proposed three cheers for the limitation of armament, his lips were formed in the words. He waved his tall silk hat for several moments with more vim than any one would have thought him capable.

While the demonstration, which was of an hour's duration, was in progress, Mr. and Mrs. Wilson enjoyed views from their home, and, standing on the front steps, the former President received from the hands of children a wreath of flowers which admirers large bunches of flowers. He shook hands with three badly crippled soldiers from the Walter Reed Hospital, who were seated in a motor car parked in front of the Wilson residence. He also shook hands with a score or more children from schools in the city and in Baltimore with whom some persons who had been concealed behind the speaker's platform.

At one time as the demonstration was nearing its close a great hush fell upon the multitude. It was expected that the former President, whose official utterance has been rare during the life of the present year would speak again in public for the first time since he retired as Chief Magistrate of the nation. After a fashion this expectation was fulfilled, but only in a very small portion of the

Continued on Page Two.

SOLEMN JOURNEY OF DEAD

Ceremonial Procession In Which Nation's Leaders Walk Stirs Capital.

HARDING SOUNDS HIGH NOTE

His Appeal Against War Impresses Great Audience at Arlington.

NATIONS DECORATE WARRIOR

And His Body With Wreaths of War Mothers Is Lowered to Last Resting Place.

Special to The New York Times.

WASHINGTON, Nov. 11.—America buried with honors today the body of that boy whose very namelessness symbolized 50,000 others who had given their lives for America on the field of battle in the World War.

Surrounded by the pomp of state, with none of them too great to bow in homage, this dead boy's funeral was still no pageant, no spectacular drama, no worldly show. It was more a benediction, a spiritual something whose very realities were less pageant than the thoughts they conjured.

Washington has witnessed many notable ceremonials, but never one like this. Its people saw the bodies of Lincoln and Garfield borne along the broad streets, and under cover of darkness, through a drizzling rain, had watched the solemn progress of that procession which followed dead McKinley to the White House. There were tears of joy, but most of those who shed them were carried away by the emotion of the symbolism of patriotism which this unknown American embodied.

Taken from that central spot in the Capitol's rotunda where before this only the bodies of Presidents had lain in state, and where it had been designed to place the body of George Washington, this fighting boy whose coffined figure stood for sacrifice to honor and patriotism was followed to his body's final resting place by statesmen, law-makers, and soldiers of many lands; and many others, led by the President of the United States, all walking for part of the solemn journey close to the funeral caisson.

At Arlington, the nation's military Valhalla, in low Virginia hills which form a background for the capital city, the Unknown Warrior was placed in a marble sarcophagus, designed to be a national shrine like that under the Arc de Triomphe in Paris, where an unknown po'lu's body rests, and Westminster Abbey, where Britain's Unknown lies.

The place of burial is a lawn with grass still green overlooking the Potomac and the city beyond, the white dome of the Capitol and the tall shaft of the Washington Monument standing out conspicuously among the mass of buildings.

Guard of Many Lands at Bier.

The burial services were conducted under the guard of the flag-draped caisson that bore the unknown's name through the world.

President Harding watched the final scene with uncovered head. Near him was ex-President Taft, now Chief Justice of the United States, stalwart and alert, in the vigor of health.

Ex-President Woodrow Wilson was not there as he had planned to be, but he rode in the funeral procession through the streets of Washington as far as the White House and received an ovation all along the route.

The crowds along the line of march were imbued with the solemnity of the occasion and showed an appreciation of the funeral spirit. But when they saw the stricken man who had been Commander-in-Chief of the forces which the Unknown Warrior fought they broke into cheers.

It was apparent that the sight of Wilson, his once strong body broken by ill-health, his intense zeal to permit his marching with the other great men who honored the Unknown catacon on foot, was a grim reminder that he had made an outstanding figure in the events of the conflict which today's ceremonial typified.

Foch, Marshal of France, stood beside the sarcophagus, also. Near by General Pershing, head of America's war army, alert and handsome, the personification of soldierly appearance, watched the scene. Aristide Briand, Premier of France, sturdy as the Breton fisher folk from whom he came, was there; and with him Réné Viviani, whose fire, eloquence and oratory are famous. Admiral Lord Beatty, chief of the British naval warriors, was another to whom this scene must have brought memories of the World War.

Diaz, Generalissimo of the Italian Armies, and hailed by his people as the hero of the Piave; General Baron Jacques, whom Belgium honors as the saviour of the Yser; General Armando Diaz, the Earl of Cavan, who commanded the British forces in Italy; American Generals who led armies, corps and divisions in France; Admirals of the American Navy, and a host of others stood near the unknown's grave.

Arthur J. Balfour, once Prime Minister of England, looking strangely unfamiliar in civilian uniform, appeared for the first time since the declaration of naval service. Was there in the place of Mr. Lloyd George, the present head of the British Government.

Kikujiro, Prince of Japan, part of the military Shogunate, watched closely the solemn ceremonial, which had all the elements of appeal to the Oriental imagination.

Secretary Hughes was in the foreground

Continued on Page Two.

"All the News That's
Fit to Print."

The New York Times.

THE WEATHER.
Fair today; Thursday warmer, probably rain; moderate variable winds.
Temperature Yesterday—Max. 51; Min. 40.
For weather report see next to last page.

VOL. LXXI....No. 23,307.   NEW YORK, WEDNESDAY, NOVEMBER 16, 1921.   TWO CENTS In Greater New York | THREE CENTS Within 200 Miles | FOUR CENTS Elsewhere

BRITAIN AND JAPAN ACCEPT NAVAL PLAN AMID CHEERS; FAR EAST ISSUE UP TODAY; JAPAN WANTS MANCHURIA OPEN; LODGE MAY NEGOTIATE TO END ANGLO-JAPANESE ALLIANCE

TRACTION HEARINGS BEGIN OVER PROTEST; HYLAN ORDERS FIGHT

Commission Rejects City's Plea for Delay Until Legislature Can Act on Law.

PROCEDURE IS OUTLINED

Evidence Will Show Fares Have Increased and Service Decreased, Says McAneny.

WOULD RESTORE 5c FARE

Also Keep It Indefinitely—Four Witnesses Examined—Shearn Tells Evaluation Plan.

Despite the plea of Mayor Hylan that hearings on the traction situation be delayed until after the Legislature had reconsidered the transit law of 1921, the Transit Commission yesterday began examination into the validity of the valuation plan. "it is not only to restore an actual 5-cent fare but to keep the fare indefinitely at 5 cents."

[body text continues, partially illegible]

Continued on Page Six.

KEW GARDENS INN.

Reparations Default Report Denied by German Officials

BERLIN, Nov. 15 (Associated Press).—The report that Germany has notified the Allies that she will be unable to meet the next reparations instalment was emphatically denied tonight in official German quarters.

A similar denial was made in Entente diplomatic circles, which are in close touch with the negotiations now proceeding with the Reparations Commission.

MRS. ENRIGHT LOSES $3,000 IN JEWELRY

Police Commissioner's Wife Misses Rings and Gems After Brooklyn Shopping Tour.

REPORT 'NOT FOR THE PRESS'

Slip to Police Stations So Noted —Chamois Bag Was Pinned to Mrs. Enright's Clothing.

Mrs. Richard E. Enright, wife of the Police Commissioner, lost $3,000 worth of jewels, including her wedding ring, while shopping with a Brooklyn crowd on Fulton Street, Brooklyn, on Monday afternoon.

Police Notified at Once.

DRUG RAID IN THEATRE.

Three Alleged Peddlers Arrested in Bowery Film Show.

Special Deputy Commissioner Dr. Carleton Simon, head of the police Narcotic Squad, sent detectives into a Bowery moving picture theatre yesterday afternoon and placed three alleged drug peddlers under arrest in the balcony.

BRIAND TO PICTURE DANGER

Will Set Forth to America Why France Cannot Reduce Her Army.

EXCEPT WITH GUARANTEES

He Will Quote German Documents to Prove the Fatherland Still France's Foe.

NAVAL ACCORD WITH ITALY

But Agreement of the Delegations Goes No Further, Declares French Premier.

By EDWIN L. JAMES.
Special to The New York Times.

WASHINGTON, Nov. 15.—Premier Briand of France expects to present at a plenary session of the conference, probably on Friday, the case of his country with regard to the reduction of land armament.

Talked Naval Agreement Only.

"May Be No Proposal to Cut Armies."

WASHINGTON, Nov. 15 (Associated Press).—As France is the nation with the largest army, Premier Briand pointed out today, it was appropriate for her to take that question up, but neither at the conference nor in any other quarter is there a suggestion that any such sweeping proposal for the reduction of armies is to be expected at the naval plan put forward by the United States.

Continued on Page Three.

Cost of Army Supplies Cut $22,515,941 in Last Quarter

WASHINGTON, Nov. 15.—A difference of $22,516,941 is shown in the cost report of the Quartermaster General of the army for supplies, clothing, food and other quartermaster properties bought for the quarter ended Sept. 30, 1921, and the same period of last year. The report was said by army officers today to reflect for the first time in official records the reduced cost of supplying the smaller army of 132,000 men as compared with that of about 200,000 in 1920.

Another difference of $4,301,306 is shown in the net cost of operation of the quartermaster depots for the same periods. For the quarter ended September last the cost was only $3,213,189, against $7,514,496 in 1920.

BRITAIN WOULD END ALL SUBMARINES

Failing That, She Wants Fewer Allowed, More Small Craft, New Replacement Method.

JAPAN SEEKS BIGGER RATIO

A Permanent Tonnage of About 67 Per Cent. of Her Rivals' Total Is Her Idea.

By EDWIN L. JAMES.
Special to The New York Times.

WASHINGTON, Nov. 15.—Considerable light was thrown on today's plenary session of the armament conference upon the modifications which will be sought to the American plan for naval limitation.

Balfour Willing to Ban Submarines.

Continued on Page Three.

LODGE MAY SOUND BALFOUR

British Treaty With Tokio Considered Inimical to Our Interests.

REGARD FOR TOKIO FEELINGS

British Want Arrangement Satisfactory to Japan—Expected to Quit Wei-hai-wei.

TODAY'S SESSION SECRET

Conference to Consider Far East in Committee of Whole—Hughes Proposal Awaited.

By RICHARD V. OULAHAN.
Special to The New York Times.

WASHINGTON, Nov. 15.—Exploding international bombshells is not to be followed by Secretary Hughes as a common practice.

Lodge May Help to End Alliance.

British Defer to Japanese Feelings.

Continued on Page Three.

Takahashi Calls Conference Epoch-Making; Says Japan Welcomes Armament Relief

TOKIO, Nov. 15 (Associated Press).—"I am confident that the Washington conference will be epoch-making in the realization of peace and good-will on earth by diminishing, if not removing, causes of distrust and suspicion among nations," said Baron Korekiyo Takahashi, the new Premier, to The Associated Press today.

"The burden of armaments," the Premier continued, "tends to a waste of energy and destruction of purposes and is a curse of the times. Japan's finance feels the pain of the burden of armament as keenly as the other powers. Nothing would be more welcome than relief from this burden through a mutual understanding between the nations based on the principle of equality and fairness.

"The outlay for national defense should be reduced to the minimum necessary for national security. Japan's naval expenditures have been considerably cut down in the budget of 1922-23.

"The success of the Washington conference must be considered to depend on the degree of sincerity on the part of those participating in it, and Japan will be second to none in this respect.

"My fervent prayer is that the meeting in Washington may be successful in insuring lasting peace. This effected, President Harding will be entitled to the gratitude of the world, not only contemporaneous but for generations to come."

Here Is Japan's Far East Program; Shidehara May Present It Today

Integrity of China and Withdrawal From Shantung—Open Door Also but Recognition of Her Special Trade Needs Because Raw Material Supply Is Vital.

Special to The New York Times.

WASHINGTON, Nov. 15.—Japan has a well-defined program for consideration by the Washington conference on the effort to arrive at an international agreement on Pacific and Far Eastern questions.

[body text continues with numbered points]

11. The maintenance of the status quo in the Dairen leased territory and of the Japanese leased zone along the South Manchuria Railway.

12. Less concern over the renewal of the Anglo-Japanese alliance, which is not regarded as being so vitally necessary in view of the pronounced tendency of the Washington conference toward an agreement for sweeping reduction of naval armaments of the three leading naval powers.

13. Solution of the Yap question and the problem of trans-Pacific communication on a basis satisfactory to the United States and Japan and with the endorsement of the other Governments interested in Pacific communications.

Want Conditions Improved.

STIRRING CONFERENCE SCENE

British Willingness to Scrap Half Her Fleet Told by Balfour

BROAD PLAN IS ACCLAIMED

Would Go Further on Submarines Than Hughes—Favors Bringing In Other Powers.

KATO GIVES JAPAN'S ASSENT

Will Suggest Modifications Later —France and Italy Also Agree "in Principle."

By EDWIN L. JAMES.
Special to The New York Times.

WASHINGTON, Nov. 15.—Today a chapter in the history of the world was finished and a new one has begun.

A white-haired man, his shoulders bowed as if weighed down by the responsibility he bore, stood with folded arms within the walls which held the armament conference and declared in the name of Great Britain the abandonment of her traditional policy of supremacy on the sea and her willingness to accept a status of naval equality with another nation—the United States of America.

To Lay Cards on the Table.

Big Implications of the Decision.

The New York Times.

THE WEATHER
Fair today and Thursday; no change in temperature; north winds.
Temperature yesterday—Max., 40; min., 30.
For full weather report see Page 23.

VOL. LXXI....No. 23,328. ... NEW YORK, WEDNESDAY, DECEMBER 7, 1921.

TWO CENTS In Greater New York | THREE CENTS Within 200 Miles | FOUR CENTS Elsewhere

IRELAND TO BE A FREE STATE WITHIN THE BRITISH EMPIRE; AGREEMENT SIGNED GIVING HER A STATUS LIKE CANADA'S; ULSTER CAN STAY OUT; PARLIAMENT CALLED TO RATIFY

HARDING PROPOSES FLEXIBLE TARIFF AND LABOR REGULATION

Asks Congress to Extend the Powers of the Present Tariff Commission.

WOULD FUND FOREIGN DEBT

Will Not Denounce Trade Treaties and Wants Merchant Marine Act Changed.

AGAINST TAX-EXEMPT BONDS

Many Arms Conference Delegates in Throng Which Listens to President's Address to Congress.

Special to The New York Times.

WASHINGTON, Dec. 6.—In an address which President Harding pointed out was not only a message to the Congress but to the people of the entire country he made an appeal today for the united support of his party in the accomplishment of legislation that he considers vital to the peace, prosperity and security not only of the United States but of the world. Senators and Representatives of both parties agreed that it was a very frank expression of the views and hopes of the Chief Executive. In much that he said the President won the outspoken approval of the Democrats as well as the Republicans.

The full text of the message is published on Page 8.

Not since the war days has a more representative audience listened to an address by a President on the opening of Congress. Occupying seats of honor directly in front of the rostrum on the floor of the House were state men of Europe and the Orient who are representing their respective countries at the Conference for Limitation of Armament. They were an intensely interested body of men who, observing the strictest decorum, did not join in the applause that continually interrupted the delivery of the address.

Behind the diplomats and foreign delegations were grouped the members of the Senate and House, Secretary Hughes and the other members of the Cabinet being in the first row of seats in the House reservation. There were just two uniformed personages on the floor, one was General Pershing and the other his aid, Major Quekemeyer.

Text of Agreement to Establish the Irish Free State

LONDON, Dec. 6 (Associated Press.)—The text of the agreement signed this morning by the British Government and the Irish representatives follows:

Article I.—Ireland shall have the same constitutional status in the community of nations known as the British Empire as the Dominion of Canada, the Commonwealth of Australia, the Dominion of New Zealand and the Union of South Africa, with a Parliament having powers to make laws for peace and order and good government in Ireland, and an executive responsible to that Parliament, and shall be styled and known as the Irish Free State.

Article II.—Subject to provisions hereinafter set out, the position of the Irish Free State in relation to the Imperial Parliament, the Government and otherwise shall be that of the Dominion of Canada, and the law, practice and constitutional usage governing the relationship of the Crown or representative of the Crown and the Imperial Parliament to the Dominion of Canada shall govern their relationship to the Irish Free State.

Article III.—A representative of the Crown in Ireland shall be appointed in like manner as the Governor General of Canada and in accordance with the practice observed in making such appointments.

Article IV.—The oath to be taken by the members of the Parliament of the Irish Free State shall be in the following form:

"I do solemnly swear true faith and allegiance to the Constitution of the Irish Free State as by law established, and that I will be faithful to his Majesty King George V., and his heirs and successors by law, in virtue of the common citizenship of Ireland with Great Britain and her adherence to and membership of the group of nations forming the British Commonwealth of Nations."

Article V.—The Irish Free State shall assume liability for service of the public debt of the United Kingdom as existing at the date thereof and toward the payment of war pensions as existing on that date in such proportion as may be fair and equitable, having regard for any just claims on the part of Ireland by way of set-off or counter-claim, the amount of such sums being determined, in default of agreement, by the arbitration of one or more independent persons being citizens of the British Empire.

Article VI.—Until an arrangement has been made between the British and Irish Governments whereby the Irish Free State undertakes her own coastal defense, defense by sea of Great Britain and Ireland shall be undertaken by his Majesty's imperial forces, but this shall not prevent the construction or maintenance by the Government of the Irish Free State of such vessels as are necessary for the protection of the revenue or the fisheries. The foregoing provisions of this article shall be reviewed at a conference of representatives of the British and Irish Governments to be held at the expiration of five years from the date hereof with a view to the undertaking by Ireland of a share in her own coastal defense.

Article VII.—The Government of the Irish Free State shall afford to his Majesty's imperial forces (a) in time of peace such harbor and other facilities as are indicated in the annex hereto, or such other facilities as may from time to time be agreed between the British Government and the Government of the Irish Free State, and (b) in time of war or of strained relations with a foreign power such harbor and other facilities as the British Government may require for the purposes of such defense, as aforesaid.

Article VIII.—With a view to securing observance of the principle of international limitation of armaments, if the Government of the Irish Free State establishes and maintains a military defense force, the establishment thereof shall not exceed in size such proportion of the military establishments maintained in Great Britain as that which the population of Ireland bears to the population of Great Britain.

Article IX.—The ports of Great Britain and the Irish Free State shall be freely open to the ships of the other country on the payment of the customary port and other dues.

Article X.—The Government of the Irish Free State agrees to pay fair compensation, on terms not less favorable than those accorded by the Act of 1920, to Judges, officials, members of the police forces and other public servants who are discharged by it or who retire in consequence of the change of government effected in pursuance of the hereof paragraph.

Provided that this agreement shall not apply to members of the auxiliary police force or persons recruited in Great Britain for the Royal Irish Constabulary during the two years next preceding the date hereof. The British Government will assume responsibility for such compensation or pensions as may be payable to any of these excepted persons.

Article XI.—Until the expiration of one month from the passing of the Act of Parliament for the ratification of this instrument, the powers of the Parliament and Government of the Irish Free State shall not be exercisable as respects Northern Ireland, and the provisions of the Government of Ireland Act of 1920 shall, so far as they relate to Northern Ireland, remain of full force and effect, and no election shall be held for the return of members to serve in the Parliament of the Irish Free State for the constituencies of Northern Ireland unless a resolution is passed by both houses of Parliament of Northern Ireland in favor of holding such elections before the end of said month.

Article XII.—If before the expiration of said month an address is presented to his Majesty by both houses of Parliament of Northern Ireland to that effect, the powers of the Parliament and Government of the Irish Free State shall no longer extend to Northern Ireland, and the provisions of the Government of Ireland Act of 1920 (including those relating to the Council of Ireland), so far as they relate to Northern Ireland, continue to be of full force and effect, and this instrument shall have effect, subject to the necessary modifications.

Provided, that if such an address is so presented, a commission consisting of three persons, one to be appointed by the Government of the Irish Free State, one to be appointed by the Government of Northern Ireland, and one, who shall be Chairman, to be appointed by the British Government, shall determine in accordance with the wishes of the inhabitants, so far as may be compatible with economic and geographic conditions, the boundaries between Northern Ireland and the rest of Ireland, and for the purposes of the Government of Ireland Act of 1920, and of this instrument the boundary of Northern Ireland shall be such as may be determined by such commission.

Article XIII.—For the purpose of the last foregoing article the powers of the Parliament of Southern Ireland under the Government of Ireland Act of 1920, to elect members of the Council of Ireland, shall, after the Parliament of the Irish Free State is constituted, be exercised by that Parliament.

Article XIV.—After the expiration of each month, as mentioned in Article XII. hereof is presented, the Parliament of the Government of Northern Ireland shall continue to exercise as respects Northern Ireland the powers conferred upon them by the Government of Ireland Act of 1920, but the Parliament of the Government of the Irish Free State shall in Northern Ireland have in relation to matters, in respect of which the Parliament of Northern Ireland has not the power to make laws under that act (including matters which, under said act, are within the jurisdiction of the Council of Ireland), the same powers as in the rest of Ireland, subject to such other provisions as may be agreed to in the manner hereinafter appearing.

Article XV.—At any time after the date hereof the Government of Northern Ireland and the Provisional Government of Southern Ireland, hereinafter constituted, may meet for the purpose of discussing provisions, subject to which the last of the foregoing article is to operate in the event of no such address as is therein mentioned being presented, and those provisions may include: (a) Safeguards with regard to patronage in Northern Ireland; (b) safeguards with regard to the collection of revenue in Northern Ireland; (c) safeguards with regard to import and export duties affecting the trade and industry of Northern Ireland; (d) safeguards for the minorities in Northern Ireland; (e) settlement of financial relations between Northern Ireland and the Irish Free State; (f) establishment and powers of a local militia in Northern Ireland and the relation of the defense forces of the Irish Free State and of Northern Ireland, respectively, and if at any such meeting provisions are agreed to, the same shall have effect as if they were included among the provisions subject to which the powers of Parliament and of the Government

of the Irish Free State are to be exercisable in Northern Ireland under Article XIV. hereof.

Article XVI.—Neither the Parliament of the Irish Free State nor the Parliament of Northern Ireland shall make any law so as either directly or indirectly to endow any religion or prohibit or restrict the free exercise thereof or give any preference or impose any disability on the account of religious belief or religious status, or affect prejudicially the right of any child to attend school receiving public money without attending the religious instruction of the school, or make any discrimination as respects State aid between schools under the management of the different religious denominations, or divert from any religious denomination or any educational institution any of its property except for public utility purposes and on the payment of compensation.

Article XVII.—By way of provisional arrangement for the administration of Southern Ireland during the interval which must elapse between the date hereof and the constitution of a Parliament and a Government of the Irish Free State in accordance therewith, steps shall be taken forthwith for summoning a meeting of the Members of Parliament elected for the constituencies in Southern Ireland since the passing of the Government of Ireland act in 1920 and for constituting a Provisional Government, and the British Government shall take steps necessary to transfer to such Provisional Government the powers and machinery requisite for the discharge of its duties, provided that every member of such Provisional Government shall have signified in writing his or her acceptance of this instrument. But this arrangement shall not continue in force beyond the expiration of twelve months from the date hereof.

Article XVIII.—This instrument shall be submitted forthwith by his Majesty's Government for the approval of Parliament and by the Irish signatories to a meeting summoned for the purpose of members elected to sit in the House of Commons of Southern Ireland, and, if approved, it shall be ratified by the necessary legislation.

Signed on behalf of the British delegation:

LLOYD GEORGE. WORTHINGTON-EVANS.
AUSTEN CHAMBERLAIN. GORDON HEWART.
BIRKENHEAD. HAMAR GREENWOOD.
WINSTON CHURCHILL.

On behalf of the Irish delegation:
ART O' GRIOBHTHA (ARTHUR GRIFFITH)
MICHAEL O. O. SILEAIN (MICHAEL COLLINS).
RIOBARD BARTUN (ROBERT C. BARTON).
E. S. DUGAN (EAMON J. DUGGAN)
SEORSA GHABGAIN UI DHUBHTHAIGH (GEORGE GAVAN DUFFY)

Dated the 6th day of December, 1921.

ANNEX.

An annex is attached to the treaty. Clause 1 specifies that Admiralty property and rights at the dockyard port of Berehaven are to remain as at present date and the harbor defenses and facilities for coastal defense by air at Queenstown, Belfast, Lough and Loughswilly to remain under British care, provision also being made for oil, fuel and storage.

Clause 2 provides that a convention shall be made between the two Governments, to give effect to the following conditions: That submarine cables shall not be landed or wireless stations for communication with places outside of Ireland established, except by agreement with the British Government, that existing cable rights and wireless concessions shall not be withdrawn except by agreement with the British Government, and that the British Government shall be entitled to land additional submarine cables or establish additional wireless stations for communication with places outside of Ireland, that lighthouses, buoys, beacons, &c., shall be maintained by the Irish Free State or other bodies concerned, but shall not be removed or added to except by agreement with the British Government, that war signal stations shall be closed down and left in charge of care and maintenance parties, the Government of the Irish Free State being offered the option of taking them over and working them for commercial purposes, subject to Admiralty inspection, and guaranteeing the upkeep of existing telegraphic communication therewith.

Clause 3 provides that a convention shall be made between the two Governments for the regulation of civil communication by air.

Continued on Page Nine.

'IRISH FREE STATE' CREATED

All of Ireland Outside of Ulster to Have Dominion Rule.

ULSTER CANNOT STOP IT

Redrawing of Her Frontiers to Follow if She Finally Refuses to Join.

NAVAL RIGHTS RESERVED

Control of Finances, Land Forces and Powers of Council of Ireland Given to New State.

Copyright, 1921, by The New York Times Company. Special Cable to The New York Times.

LONDON, Dec. 6.—Ireland shall have the same constitutional status in the community of nations known as the British Empire as the Dominion of Canada, the Commonwealth of Australia, the Dominion of New Zealand and the Union of South Africa, with a Parliament having powers to make laws for the peace and order and good government of Ireland and an Executive responsible to that Parliament, and shall be styled and known as the Irish Free State.

Such is the first article of the "treaty" between Great Britain and Ireland which was signed some minutes after 2 o'clock this morning on behalf of Great Britain by Lloyd George, Austen Chamberlain, Lord Birkenhead, Winston Churchill, Sir L. Worthington-Evans, Sir Hamar Greenwood and Sir Gordon Hewart, and on behalf of Ireland by Arthur Griffith, Michael Collins, Robert Barton, E. J. Duggan and Gavan Duffy.

The signatures were affixed to the document in that historic room of 10 Downing Street on whose walls hang the portraits of the greatest British Premiers of the past and of one American, George Washington, the Father of His Country.

It was that same room, Lord Birkenhead pointed out today, which witnessed the fateful and melancholy discussions that preceded the final recognition on the part of the statesmen of the country that the American colonies were lost. It was that room, said the Chancellor of the Exchequer, in which the anxieties, uncertainties and vicissitudes of the war met with daily affliction, that yesterday was entered upon, in my judgment, a new phase which promises, after all these bitter centuries and generations, that at last an era may dawn which will enable us, of our day and generation, to say that we have not achieved less in settlement here at our own doors of the issue which seems, but to not, domestic than we achieved in the fields of arms when we preserved the security and existence of these Islands from the greatest menace that assailed them since the Napoleonic period."

ULSTER RESERVED; DUBLIN REJOICES

Craig Cabinet Begins Sessions to Consider the Terms of the Agreement.

NORTH DISLIKES THE OATH

But Waits to See if Sinn Fein is Really Friendly—Dail's Acceptance Predicted.

Special Cable to The New York Times.

BELFAST, Dec. 6.—News that the settlement had been achieved between the British Government and the Sinn Fein delegates caused some surprise in the North, but particularly in view of De Valera's declaration at Galway in regard to allegiance. The disposition of Ulster people is not to enter upon any hasty criticism or comment, but to wait until the terms are revealed. Should the position of Ulster be safeguarded and recognized position within the British Empire there will be a general feeling of satisfaction in the north that the strife in Ireland has been brought to an end.

A specially convened meeting of the Ulster Cabinet was held today. After considering the terms for two and a half hours the Cabinet adjourned for further consideration until tomorrow.

Colonel Spender, Secretary to the Northern Cabinet, was asked for the Cabinet's first reaction of the terms of settlement. He said they were somewhat puzzled and were anxious to have certain points cleared up. Colonel Spender added that if the proposed changes in area affected any great tract of territory or meant any great disturbance of population they would not be acceptable to Ulster. He understood, however, that they really meant small adjustments along the frontier.

Asked if the form of oath was acceptable, Colonel Spender said that the Ulster people did not like it, but if it were acceptable to the British people (not the south) he regarded with suspicion the fact that the Sinn Feiners were not prepared to take the ordinary

Continued on Page Two.

B. R. T. DIVIDENDS PAID DAY OF RECEIVERSHIP

Checks for $236,250 Mailed by Operating Company Just Before Garrison Took Charge.

HECTIC HOLIDAY FOR HEDLEY

Got $1,000,000 on New Year's Eve to Stave Off the Failure of Interborough.

Stories of quick shifts of millions between holding companies and subsidiaries in both the Interborough and Brooklyn Rapid Transit systems on the eve of receiverships were told in the Transit Commission's hearing yesterday. The works are building.

German Explosion Kills 100, Sets Dynamite Works Afire

BERLIN, Dec. 6 (Associated Press.)—It is reported that 100 persons lost their lives here as the result of the explosion of an oil tank in the Nobel Dynamite Works at Saarlouis, Rhenish Prussia. The works are burning.

America Will Enter No Alliance; Three More Chinese Advisers Out

No Treaty on Far East Likely, but a Less Formal Agreement—Project Shaping Slowly.

By EDWIN L. JAMES.
Special to The New York Times.

WASHINGTON, Dec. 6.—Whatever plans are being worked out for an international treaty, protocol, resolution, agreement, or understanding among three, four, five, six, seven, eight or nine powers to establish a Far Eastern policy do not now form a proper subject for public consideration, according to the official view of the American delegation to the armament conference.

Attaches of Delegation Resign in Protest Against 'Negative Results' of Conference.

Special to The New York Times.

WASHINGTON, Dec. 6.—As a protest against "negative results" of the conference concerning China's aspirations, three additional attaches of the Chinese delegation to the Washington conference, two of them superior advisers, today tendered their resignations.

Carson Sees for Britain Day of 'Abject Humiliation'

Special Cable to The New York Times.

LONDON, Dec. 7.—The Morning Post says that after reading the terms of the Irish agreement the comment of Lord Carson, former Ulster leader, was:

"I never thought I should live to see a day of such abject humiliation for Great Britain."

CANADIAN ELECTION LIBERAL LANDSLIDE

Premier Meighen Loses His Seat and His Protection Policy Is Repudiated.

OTTAWA, Dec. 6.—Premier Meighen was defeated in his home constituency, Portage La Prairie, Manitoba, in the Canadian general election today. His opponent was Harry Leader, Progressive.

SAYS UNION ABUSES RAISE BUILDING COST

Witness Tells Lockwood Committee of Expenses Piled Up by Labor Inefficiency.

The Lockwood committee opened a new phase of its housing inquiry late yesterday afternoon by examining witnesses in an endeavor to learn to what extent housing construction was loaded with high costs due to the inefficiency of labor.

The New York Times.

THE WEATHER

Unsettled today, probably light snow; Wednesday cloudy.
Temperature yesterday—Max., 45; min., 31.
For full weather report see Page 34.

VOL. LXXI....No. 23,334.   NEW YORK, TUESDAY, DECEMBER 13, 1921.   TWO CENTS In Greater New York | THREE CENTS Within 200 Miles | FOUR CENTS Elsewhere

YAP AGREEMENT MADE, JAPAN CONCEDES US LEAGUE RIGHTS; NAVY SETTLEMENT NEAR; 4-POWER TREATY TO BE SIGNED TODAY; BORAH ATTACKS IT IN THE SENATE AS AN ARMED ALLIANCE

DE VALERA DENIES HONOR REQUIRES TERMS BE RATIFIED

He Declares Plenipotentiaries Were Sent on Understanding Dail Would Act.

CROWDS FLOCK TO DUBLIN

Many Now Think That the Issue Should Be Submitted to a Plebiscite.

CRAIG REPORTS TO ULSTER

He Declares, It is Said, That Lloyd George's Attitude is: "There is the Treaty, and it Stands."

Copyright, 1921, by The New York Times Company.
By cable to The New York Times.

DUBLIN, Dec. 12.—Eamon de Valera issued a further statement today on question of ratification. It reads: "I have been asked whether the honor of Ireland is not involved in the ratification of the agreement arrived at. The honor of Ireland is not involved. The plenipotentiaries were sent on the distinct understanding that any agreement they made was subject to ratification by the Dail Eireann and by the country and would be rejected by the Dail Eireann if it did not commend itself to the nation."

Legion Head Sees Harding; Predicts Bonus Legislation

Special to The New York Times.

WASHINGTON, Dec. 12.—Hanford MacNider, National Commander of the American Legion, had a fifteen-minute conference with President Harding this morning, and as he left the White House he predicted that the present session of Congress would pass bonus legislation.

PRINCE BOYCOTTED IN ALLAHABAD VISIT

Whole Native Population Deserts the Streets at His Arrival in the City.

600 AGITATORS ARRESTED

Chairman of Allahabad Council Gets Jail Sentence—Many Imprisoned in Calcutta.

90 DRY AGENTS RAID BROADWAY RESORTS AND A VILLAGE HOTEL

Thomas Healy's, Cafe de Paris, the Little Club and the Hotel Lafayette Visited.

THIRTEEN PRISONERS TAKEN

Raided Premises Searched and Liquors Alleged to Have Been Found in All.

PROTECTION BOAST A CLUE

Raiders, Posing as Western Men Seeking a Good Time, Win Confidence of Proprietors.

Ninety prohibition enforcement agents, some of them disguised as cabaret frequenters and others as longshoremen, shortly before last midnight descended on the Hotel Lafayette.

British Minority Laborites Ask Harding to Free Debs

LONDON, Dec. 12.—The Independent Labor Party has sent a cablegram to President Harding pleading for the immediate release of Eugene Debs and other political prisoners.

MARKETS IN A WHIRL AS EXCHANGES RISE

Continued Upswing Causes Scramble by Dealers in World's Money Centres.

STERLING TOUCHES $4.24½

Variety of Reasons Given for the Extreme Advances—Commodity Markets Unsettled.

An upswing in the exchanges of the principal European countries, which started toward the latter part of last week, continued yesterday and carried sterling up 6⅝ cents.

SPIRITED SENATE DEBATE

Reed, Robinson, Stanley and Watson, of Georgia, Support Borah.

POINDEXTER BACKS TREATY

Kellogg Also Defends It—Idaho Member Wants Submarines and Poison Gas Forbidden.

PLEDGE LIKENED TO ART. X.

Long Discussion Now in Prospect, but Ratification Is Still Predicted.

Special to The New York Times.

WASHINGTON, Dec. 12.—The Conference for the Limitation of Armament and the four-power treaty were the subjects of an unexpected and spirited debate in the Senate this afternoon.

"Brilliant Success," Says Viviani in Farewell; British Delegation Plans to Sail on Dec. 31

WASHINGTON, Dec. 12 (Associated Press).—The Washington conference "is a brilliant success," M. Viviani, head of the French delegation, said tonight in a farewell conference with newspaper correspondents in anticipation of his departure tomorrow for New York, from where he will sail for Paris on Wednesday.

EQUALITY IN YAP GRANTED

We Recognize Mandate Rights of Japan in Pacific Islands.

COVENANT IS PARALLELED

Accord Reached With Tokio Insures Us Rights Equal to Any League Member.

PLAN WILL BE EXTENDED

Deals With Britain on South Pacific and With Other Mandatories Are Forecast.

By EDWIN L. JAMES.
Special to The New York Times.

WASHINGTON, Dec. 12.—The Administration resurrected today another page of the covenant of the League of Nations to obtain for the United States the rights and privileges of League membership in the mandated territories held by Japan in the North Pacific Ocean.

FOUR-POWER TREATY TO BE SIGNED TODAY

Yap Agreement, Which Was a Condition of Our Assent, May Also Be Signed.

CONFERENCE END LOOMS UP

Large Results Counted On by Our Delegates With the Further Agreements Expected.

Special to The New York Times.

WASHINGTON, Dec. 12.—The four-power treaty between the United States, France and Japan and the British Empire, relative to insular possessions and dominions in the region of the Pacific, will be formally signed at 11 A. M. tomorrow in the Diplomatic Room at the State Department.

EXTEND NAVAL RATIO TO FRANCE AND ITALY

Basis of 5-5-3-3-3 Is Studied for Inclusion in Quintuple Limitation Compact.

ORGANIZE NEW COMMITTEE

Heads of Five Delegations and Experts Are Grouped to Expedite Agreement.

Special to The New York Times.

WASHINGTON, Dec. 12.—The program of the Conference for Limitation of Naval Armaments had reached the point where the major problem of ratio has been provisionally decided on—a basis of relative strength of 5-5-3-3-3 for the navies of the United States, the British Empire, Japan, France and Italy.

25 Hurt, 1 Missing, in Acid Blast And Fire at Former German Plant

Twenty-three persons were injured, six of them seriously, and one person was missing last night as a result of an explosion and fire yesterday afternoon at the Heyden Chemical Works, Monroe Street and River Road, Garfield, N. J.

Two Thousand Women in Leaderless Mob Storm Kansas Mine and Attack Workers

Special to The New York Times.

PITTSBURG, Kan., Dec. 12.—The striking several miners on their way to the mine today barred the exit from the Kansas mining field today.

Section 1

"All the News That's Fit to Print."

The New York Times.

THE WEATHER
Fair today; Monday, unsettled, warmer; southeast winds.
Temperature yesterday—Max. 36; min. 26.
For full weather report see Page 22.

Section 1

VOL. LXXI....No. 23,360.   •••   NEW YORK, SUNDAY, JANUARY 8, 1922. In Ten Parts, including Rotogravure Picture Section, Book and Magazine Section.   FIVE CENTS In Manhattan, Bronx and Brooklyn | Elsewhere TEN CENTS

DAIL EIREANN VOTES 64 TO 57 TO ACCEPT IRISH FREE STATE; DE VALERA SAYS HE WILL RESIGN; DUBLIN WILD WITH JOY; WASHINGTON ADOPTS GAS BAN; PREMIERS SUMMON GERMANS

40,000 POLICE FORM DRAGNET IN HARLEM NEGRO MURDER HUNT

Entire Metropolitan District Is Aroused in the Search for Detective's Slayer.

FORCE GOES SLEEPLESS

Search of Houses in Montclair and in San Juan Section Here Is Vain.

SUSPECT'S BROTHER AIDS

Description of Slayer With Scarred Face Sent Broadcast—Detectives Are Confident.

"Hold every scar-faced negro as a suspect" was the message flashed yesterday by the police of this city to approximately 40,000 detectives, policemen, sheriffs and deputy sheriffs in the metropolitan district in the hunt for Luther Boddy, the youthful negro who on Thursday evening last shot and killed Detective Sergeants Francis J. M. Buckley and William A. Miller within 200 feet of the West 135th Street Station, in the heart of Harlem's negro colony.

It's doubtful if the police of this and surrounding cities ever evinced more determination to capture a criminal. Hundreds of negroes answering the police description of Boddy were this time intercepted in the course of the day, and, though in every instance the man was proved not to be the murderer, the police quest did not abate in the slightest. The murderer of the two detectives must be apprehended, whether he was brought in dead or alive, was the word passed out by the detectives in charge of the manhunt.

The police of the surrounding communities expressed the same determination to capture Boddy as did the close associates of the slain detectives in the West 135th Street Station. Concrete evidence of this determination was illustrated yesterday in the alacrity with which hundreds of detectives and policemen responded to what proved to be false alarms.

Many False Clues.

The police were kept on the jump last night answering false reports of the hiding place of the negro. Shortly after 10 o'clock somebody telephoned to Police Headquarters in Jersey City that the slayer was being concealed by negro tenants of the house at 12 Bishop Street, in the negro colony.

Thirty policemen from nearby stations were rushed to the house. Smoke was pouring from Blodman's apartments. The police suspected a ruse to allow Boddy to escape, but on entering, they found an overturned oil lamp had set fire to a mattress. No trace of Boddy was found.

At about the same time the police of the West Sixty-eighth Street station received a telephone message from a man who said he saw Boddy jump out of a taxicab a few minutes before and enter the premises at 38 West Sixty-second Street. Sergeant Velstedt and twenty detectives and policemen went to the house but that also proved to be a false report.

Alarm Brings Quick Response.

Shortly before dawn a negro ex-convict in the San Juan district told a policeman that he saw Boddy enter a house in West Sixty-second Street between Amsterdam and West End Avenues. The policeman jumped to a police signal box and within three minutes detectives and reserves were on their way from the West Seventy-seventh Street, West Sixty-eighth Street and West 100th Street Stations, and an additional contingent of policemen were hurried to the scene in plain clothes hurried to the scene in automobiles from the West 135th Street Station.

The policeman who telephoned the alarm hardly had taken up a position in front of the house when the first batch of policemen and detectives arrived from the West Sixty-third Street station. The detective took charge of the hunt for Boddy and within a few minutes policemen were stationed on the roofs, in the yards and at the entrance to the three tenements occupied by negroes, at 240, 242 and 244 West Sixty-second Street. A solid wall of policemen was thrown around the whole block and every possible avenue of escape was barred.

Every policeman had his pistol in his hand ready for instant use. The detectives were forming in three groups to enter each of the houses when Detective Sergeant William Boyle and James B. Mahoney, associates of the slain detectives in their battle against the criminal element in the Harlem district, appeared. These detectives knew Boddy and they took charge of the arrangements for the capture of the murderer.

The three groups of detectives, most of them armed with two pistols, simul-

Continued on Page Twenty-one.

FINSBURG, N. C.—
Then Pullman, Penn. 2:05 P.M.—Advt.
Surprise of Motordom—the Big Six. A Thru Floor, the Comparison.—Advt.

Allies Criticise Teaching In Rhineland Schools

COBLENZ, Jan. 7.—The Allied High Commission has decided that the German schools of the Rhineland are giving instruction to the children in a manner which violates the spirit of the Weimar constitution, the new German fundamental law, which provides for instruction "toward the reconciliation of peoples," and that therefore the method of instruction is inimical to peace. A committee to take up the matter has been named by the commission.

MRS. STILLMAN WIRES DEFIANCE TO BANKER

"I Hurl My Gauntlet at Your Feet," Says First Message Sent Since He Sued.

MAY REST AT GRANDE ANSE

Hearing on Husband's Appeal Set for Friday—Anne, Sailing, Kisses Guy Good-Bye.

Special to The New York Times.

LA TUQUE, Que., Jan. 7.—Mrs. Anne Urquhart Stillman communicated with James A. Stillman today for the first time since the banker brought his suit to divorce her and disown Guy Stillman. She sent this telegram:

James A. Stillman, 55 Wall Street,
New York City:

Today, standing in the snow of Canada, I know what you tried to do to me, and from the north I hurl my gauntlet at your feet. Gold against courage. James, I am ready for you.
ANNE U. STILLMAN.

The message was sent shortly after Mrs. Stillman definitely learned that at least a month, probably two, must pass before she would again have an opportunity to bring her defense into court.

Tonight, effecting one of the quick changes of mind that have been the rule on the trip, due to shifting conditions, Mrs. Stillman said she would leave here Monday for her lodge at Grande Anse, thirty-five miles down the St. Maurice River from La Tuque. She will rest there for two days and will then continue down the river by sled to Grandes Iles and from there into Montreal, if John E. Mack, guardian ad litem for Guy Stillman, and John J. Brennan, defense counsel, answer Mrs. Stillman's request for a conference on Thursday in Montreal.

May Rest at Grande Anse.

If, however, the attorneys notify her that they will be unable to come to Canada at this time, Mrs. Stillman and she would return to Grande Anse and stay there until the hearings were again scheduled for Montreal. Due the intention of Mr. Stillman's lawyer to prevent from Supreme Court Justice Morschauer's award of $7,500 expense money, the wait for the next hearings may keep Mrs. Stillman at her lodge until late in March.

Mrs. Stillman arrived at La Tuque shortly after 11 o'clock last night. She found that Messrs. Mack and Brennan had not telegraphed her a reply as to the proceedings for the expense allowance. Before leaving Three Rivers she read in a newspaper that Cornelius J. Sullivan, of Mr. Stillman had a report on the proceedings, but she was not settled on Sunday. Her first concern, therefore, was to endeavor to get in touch with her lawyers.

There is no long distance telephone service from La Tuque and Mrs. Stillman was forced to depend on the telegraph. This service had been reinforced by assignment of a telegraph inspector and a direct wire was put through to Yonkers and to Poughkeepsie.

Tired by Wearisome Trip.

Philip J. O'Brien, the lawyer, sent messages over the wire and relayed "bulletins" to Mrs. Stillman, establishing by this means a speed record for telegraphing in this section, Mrs. Stillman ascertained that the hearings had been put off indefinitely.

With this news, Mrs. Stillman turned in at 2 o'clock this morning, "completely played out." The trip from Three Rivers had been wearisome, with three shifts of trains and two long waits in half-built railroad stations that

Continued on Page Twenty-one.

Eight Moonshine Stills Explode in Two Fires; Five Firemen Seriously Burned; One May Die

Eight stills in full operation exploded in Brooklyn last night in one building, and five firemen fighting the blaze resulting from the first explosion were burned, one probably mortally. All the men were taken to hospitals for treatment.

Shortly before midnight a loud report was heard in the basement of a newly constructed two-story brick house at 3658 Eighth Street, Benson hurst, followed closely by two more detonations. Neighbors were routed from their beds and saw flames shooting out of the basement. When the firemen arrived they found the house deserted, but the fire was burning fiercely. Rocco Corfale and his wife, who, the police learned, occupied the first story of the house, had disappeared, apparently in haste, and had been located early this morning. After the firemen entered the basement four stills in an adjoining room blew up, throwing the firemen to the floor and enveloping them in flames. Other firemen rushed to the rescue.

found Battalion Chief Eugene McKenna of 8,619 Idge Boulevard, Brooklyn, and four others seriously burned.

Chief McKenna was burned on the face, hands and neck. The other injured firemen were Lieutenant Martin J. Kane, of 496 Seventh Street, burns of the face and hands; Frank Magrino, of 420 Bay Ridge Avenue, burns on face, hands and body; George Harris, of 217 Sixty-eighth Street, burns on body and face, and Richard Campion, of 160 Twelfth Street, Brooklyn. Campion was taken to Coney Island Hospital, where his condition was said to be very serious.

Earlier in the evening a still exploded on the first floor of 128 Forty-first Street, Brooklyn. The fire which resulted did but little damage. The police said they found four five-gallon cans of mash and two revolvers in the upper part of the house. The owner was holding fifty gallons of mash on a gas stove when the explosion occurred. The owner of the house, said to be owned by August Cable, of 498 Fifth Avenue, Brooklyn.

ROOT PROPOSAL AGREED TO

But British and French See Only Moral Value in Anti-Gas Declaration.

AIRCRAFT REPORT OFFERED

Tells Difficulty of Limiting War Use and Suggests Reference to Larger Conference.

BALFOUR ANXIOUS FOR END

Tells Committee He Lacks Power to Consider Wide Declarations on World Law.

By EDWIN L. JAMES.
Special to The New York Times.

WASHINGTON, Jan. 7.—The American resolution, declaring against the use of gas in warfare, binding the five great powers to prohibit its use between themselves and inviting all other civilized nations to join in withholding this weapon, was passed today by the Naval Limitation Committee of the armament conference.

The discussion in committee showed clearly that no nation would throw away its gas masks as a result of the passage of the resolution. British and French said that the passage of such a declaration, without sanctions, would not permit them to lessen their plans to be ready for the use of gas by another power. As one diplomat expressed it, "the resolution means that in the next war each of us promises to wait until the other fellow uses gas before we do."

At today's meeting the conference took a significant turn. After having stood behind the American delegation in its fight for naval limitation and for the four-power treaty to permit of the ending of the Anglo-Japanese alliance and for the limitation of the use of submarines, so dangerous for England, the British delegation let it be known that they thought the conference had accomplished about all it could.

In connection with a long report by conference experts on the agenda proposal as to the limitation of the use of aircraft in war, the British thought that the conclusion of the report which was that the matter should be left for a larger conference was about right. As for the American proposal to rewrite some international laws, Mr. Balfour said that the powers of the British delegation did not permit it to go into such a task.

Foreigners Want to Go Home.

All the foreign delegations, in fact, are now in favor of ending the conference quickly. Mr. Balfour has booked passage for the 14th, and the French for the 18th. This does not promise well for those plans which mean infinitely more to them than the things left on the agenda of the Washington conference, and, if early adjournment here means any damage to the Hughes program, it is likely that damage will be done.

Henceforth it is a question of how long Mr. Hughes can hold the conference together to discuss his proposals. He can probably keep it going another two weeks. The naval treaty will be ready Tuesday or Wednesday, but the nine-power Far Eastern treaty, if it materializes, is yet to be put into shape, and the Japanese and Chinese have not settled the Shantung issue. From now on Mr. Hughes has a fundamental group of conferees on his hands.

At the opening of today's session, Prince Tokugawa said good-bye to the conference. He left this afternoon on his way to Tokio.

Chairman Hughes put before the committee as the first business the resolution, drafted by Mr. Root, to ban gas warfare. Immediately M. Sarraut, head of the French delegation, was on his feet, "I rise to express my full and frank adherence to Mr. Root's resolution," he said. France detested the use of gas begun by the Germans, he declared, and he thought that the conference powers might set a good example.

With this Mr. Stillman turned him henceforth put that the expense had shown the impossibility of controlling the ability of any nation, which wished, to produce poison gas, since the same machinery was used for peace time requisite.

M. Sarraut, however, did not think the

Continued on Page Seventeen.

Says Harvey Helped Frame The Cannes Resolution

PARIS, Jan. 7.—Ambassador Harvey's participation in the modification of the original text of Premier Lloyd George's resolution yesterday, whereby, the Cannes correspondent of the Temps says, "from a mute observer Mr. Harvey became an active listener and then a collaborator," is placed in the foreground of the newspaper's description of Friday's proceedings of the Supreme Council at Cannes. This participation, the correspondent adds, resulted in the invitation to the United States to take part in the Genoa economic conference.

"It is not likely," in the correspondent's opinion, "that this invitation was issued without assurance beforehand that it would be accepted and without Mr. Harvey having so informed the allied Premiers before the opening of the meeting."

LITVINOFF SNEERS AT AMERICA'S GIFT

Would Have Valued It More if We Hadn't Deprived Russia of Twice as Much.

RED FANATICISM STILL HOT

Bewildered at the Prospect of Sitting at a Council Table With Accursed Capitalists.

By WALTER DURANTY.
Copyright, 1922, by The New York Times Company.
Special Cable to THE NEW YORK TIMES.

MOSCOW, Jan. 6.—The possibility of real American participation in the Washington conference does not interest the rest of the world when we see that the first consequence of the Washington conference may be the invasion of Russian territory by a Japanese army. It looks to us as if any "settlement," accomplished in Washington would consist of carte blanche to Japan to start land-grabbing at our expense.

This statement, made to me by Maxim Litvinoff today, throws much light upon the outlook of the Soviet Government, especially coming from Litvinoff, who is the most "Western-minded" of the Soviet leaders and who is almost certain to figure prominently in any negotiations that may develop between Russia and other States.

Litvinoff, with all his shrewdness—and Lyman Brown bears witness that at Riga he was shrewd enough—typifies the weakness as well as the strength of Soviet diplomacy. Though he professes with the rest of his colleagues faith, realism in home and foreign politics, he cannot get away from his revolutionary training and traditions. After four years of the purist anomaly before him, a pariah's distrust, a pariah's expectation of the kicks that must accompany even half peace. Thus Litvinoff said:

"We greatly appreciate America's gift of $20,000,000 worth of grain, but we would have appreciated it more if we had not had fully $30,000,000 or $40,000,000 in the last two years in consequence of America's veto against Russian gold. Through that veto Scandinavian, French and British bankers were able to hold us up for that amount."

Psychoanalysts find in that statement evidence of the persecution complex—the Russian dog has received such a bad name that he has learned to look for the hangman's noose, even in the hand offering food. Maxim Litvinoff or other sealots of the communist international should speak as not surprising; but from a more broad-minded as Litvinoff the words have a deeper meaning. They illustrate the very real and present difficulty confronting the Soviet Government just at present, up the sleeve. Can he make the different estimates which led nowhere because of different estimates of what Germany can pay in cash and in kind, he launched the suggestion that the Germans should be summoned and asked what they were prepared to do.

The difficulty is this: Soviet diplomacy has hitherto been warlike diplomacy. It has aimed to achieve—chiefly through propaganda in the bosom of enemy nations. Now it is called upon to undertake friendly diplomacy across a council table, and it is bewildered. The weapon of internal propaganda against which the Soviet representatives must face the rest of the world—no longer as a declared enemy—in the diplomatic poker game in which victory rewards skill at cards, not with guns and knives.

The Russians have cards enough—Baku oil is not the least of them, to say nothing of the Donetz mineral basin, the hidden wealth of the Urals, the vast forests of the north and the limitless plains of Siberia. Against America, Japan is the card to be played; against England, America. This they know, but for the moment they are nervous about their skill in playing, and their hands reach nervously back to the empty holster.

It may be suggested that Litvinoff was simply disingenuous; that he was trying to put such an interpretation on events as to bring Russia to the table in the position of the injured party, with good big grievances to set against the foreign complaints of unpaid debts and injured nationals. It is also true that Litvinoff's intelligence to suggest he is not so capable of disingenuousness as any other diplomat, but the facts in the case will not allow this explanation here.

For it is a fact that the Soviet leaders and revolutionaries are steeped in the revolutionary tradition of hostility to the rest of the capitalist world. It is a fact that the Soviet Government, which is supposed to be just fanatics in the science of propaganda, has done nothing to improve its point of view upon the foreign cow; spondents here, instead of giving out information tinged with the color they desire, in the case of France, England and Italy, they give out none. To our Litvinoff at all, I was forced to spend a week in his company before I could overcome Russian suspicion of a stranger. Even at the show, the quickest nation to sum up men, with definite appeals and delays.

Continued on Page Eighteen.

GERMANS TO HEAR NEW PLAN

Conferees Wrangle on Proposal of Modifying Reparation Payments.

BRITAIN MAY GUARD FRANCE

Report at Cannes She May Guarantee Security if Germany Attacks Ally.

TURKISH ISSUE TACKLED

Premiers and Foreign Ministers Begin Discussion of Treaty Signed With Nationalists.

Copyright, 1922, by The New York Times Company.
Special Cable to THE NEW YORK TIMES.

CANNES, Jan. 7.—After a whole day of wrangling between experts and Ministers and the suggestion of half a dozen ways out of their difficulties, the Supreme Council this evening decided to summon German representatives to Paris, from where, if necessary, they can be called later to Cannes.

A suggestion that they come straight to Cannes was made by Mr. Lloyd George and formally opposed by M. Briand. As a compromise the suggestion was made by M. Theunys, the Belgian Premier, that Chancellor Wirth be invited to send delegates to Paris to hold themselves in readiness in case they were needed for consultation.

The whole day was wasted in proposals and counterproposals between the experts. The Belgians stuck firmly throughout the morning to their claim for priority payment and the French sat on the fence, in fact, if not in speech, and made no serious effort to swing them to the British compromise proposal. In the afternoon the Belgians gave way a little but maintained that instead of a half billion gold marks, which is the British estimate of what Germany can and should pay this year, $600,000,000 should be demanded.

Negotiations Break Down.

By 4 o'clock the deadlock had become obvious, but Mr. Lloyd George urged that a new attempt be made and a report on progress submitted to the Supreme Council at 7 o'clock at the Yacht Club.

This new attempt at a settlement leads, however, no further than previous ones and when the experts' report was turned in at 7 o'clock the Supreme Council was faced with a position for which some entirely new remedy had to be found.

This course was the one adopted and the following telegram was sent to Chancellor Wirth:

"The Supreme Council will doubtless need to hear your representatives next week between the 8th and 16th of January, in that case, in order to save time, it suggests that your representatives have the necessary powers to answer a summons from the council.

"The question over which the deadlock has been reached is entirely one of German capacity to pay. The Belgians in-

Continued on Page Eighteen.

De Valera Asks Treaty Foes to Meet Him Today; He Ignores Collins's Overture to Maintain Order

DUBLIN, Jan. 7 (Associated Press).—On the announcement of the vote in the Dail Eireann tonight Eamon de Valera immediately rose and declared that the Irish people had established a republic, and that until the Irish people in a regular manner disestablished the republic, it constitutionally went on. This would be a sovereign body in the nation, to which the nation looked for supreme government. It was the executive until the people disestablished.

Nobody was disposed to challenge this proposition, for the general opinion all along had been that during the transition period Ireland must keep her representative Assembly until the treaty was converted into an act of Parliament and gave them an opportunity to erect a Legislature of the Free State to replace the Dail.

Michael Collins in quiet tones followed de Valera. He said he did not regard the result in any spirit of triumph. The matter that the men representing the Dail, who would be responsible for taking over from the British Government control of the Irish Administration, should get a fair chance. In every country what mattered most was public order, and he appealed to the other side to appoint a joint committee of both sides to carry on the government. (This was greeted with cheers.) Mr. Collins declared that President de Valera held the same place in his heart as ever.

Then followed a violent speech by Mary MacSwiney.

Mr. de Valera rose again, supposedly to reply to Mr. Collins's overture. However, he took no notice of it, and merely appealed to all his own supporters in the Dail to meet him at the Mansion House tomorrow afternoon at 1 o'clock.

This evidently hurt Mr. Collins very much, but he quietly said:

"If the visible presence of myself and my colleagues is so distasteful, there might at any rate be some accommodation between the parties for the purpose of public order."

Minister Burgess immediately retorted:

"I will take care that the discipline of the army is preserved."

The future control of the Irish Republican Party is tonight the subject of anxious speculation, as Charles Burgess, who strongly opposed the treaty, is the Minister of Defense.

HARDING CONSIDERS GENOA INVITATION

Chance of Change of Policy Toward Participation in Affairs of Europe Is Seen.

DECISION EXPECTED SOON

Active Delegates May Take Place of "Observer" of Previous Conferences.

By EDWIN L. JAMES.
Special to The New York Times.

WASHINGTON, Jan. 7.—The possibility of real American participation in the Genoa Economic Conference loomed up today when it was stated officially that the Government soon will decide its policy" with regard to the invitation of the Allied Supreme Council which reached the State Department this morning from Ambassador Harvey in Cannes.

Heretofore, the policy of the Administration toward the European conferences has been that of limiting American participation to the presence of an "unofficial observer." That the Government is now to consider again its policy toward a European conference was taken today as meaning there was at least a chance of a change in policy. There are two questions for the State Department to consider. The first, and the most important, is: Will the United States, Europe and the world be benefited by American participation in a serious manner? The second question to be answered is: Can the United States go into a conference to which the Government of Soviet Russia is a party?

It is understood that President Harding and Secretary of State Hughes will consider the allied invitation on Monday or Tuesday and that subsequently the matter will be thoroughly gone into at a Cabinet meeting next week.

President Harding's Attitude.

Ten days ago it was made known at the White House that President Harding's attitude toward an economic conference to deal primarily with the condition of Europe was that this Government would not try to lead Europe what it should do, but that if Europe had a promising plan to offer, America would "come in." It is also known that recent developments in Russia have interested both the White House and the State Department as indicating a possible real change in the policies and practices of the Moscow Government.

It is believed that both President Harding and Secretary Hughes have come to realize what has long been apparent to European observers at closer range. A European observer at closer range, that the system of having this country represented in international conferences by an "unofficial observer" is a joke, and a poor joke at that. Our observers are often referred to in a not pleasant way by European diplomats as "the professional note-takers."

The invitation to our Government has been kept open because Europe wished to close no path to eventual co-operation by America in solving the ills that we American helped to fight. But the practical benefits of the presence of American delegates who act as well and at their end of the table, without the awe or authority to give one word upon the substance of discussion, have been nil. All that these "unofficial observers" have been able to say, in response to the will of the whole nation directly along the lines of what has been pressed during our tour through previous years in August.

"The Irish people's verdict is in keep-

Continued on Page Eighteen.

PROMISE SUPPORT TO IRISH MINORITY

"Friends of Irish Freedom" Propose to Aid Faction That Will Keep Up the Struggle.

OTHERS WELCOME PEACE

Kennelly Says Those Interested in Ireland Should Now Help to Revitalize the Country.

Widely different opinions were expressed yesterday on the ratification of the treaty creating an Irish Free State by organizations and individuals who have been active in this country in the movement for Irish freedom. Disappointment and congratulation were both expressed, while some looked upon the present step as a temporary resting place in the movement for complete independence for Ireland.

The following statement was issued by the Friends of Irish Freedom through Diarmuid Lynch, the National Secretary:

"If the published dispatch from the so-called treaty has been approved by a vote of 64 to 57 be correct, I desire upon behalf of the Friends of Irish Freedom to state officially that the position of this organization is as follows: Expressly disavowing the intention to interfere with or dictate the decisions of the people of Ireland as to the form of government under which they may live, we within, as American citizens, our unalienable faith in the republican institutions of liberty as established in the United States. Our belief remains unchanged and unshakeable in the blessings to accrue from the establishment in all lands of forms of government modeled upon the Government of the United States. We pledge to such republican party in Ireland as may carry forward the traditional struggle for liberty a continuance in full measure of that hearty support which we have given in the past. Our position as thus expressed was unanimously endorsed by 2,570 delegates in convention less than a month ago.

"Even if the Irish Republic be now abandoned by a majority of the present spokesmen for the Irish people, we, of Irish blood, refuse to accept for our kin a position of slavery to any other race on earth."

Should Now Help Irish Revival.

Bryan L. Kennelly, President of Bryan L. Kennelly, Inc., and Vice President of the Harriman National Bank, said:

"I am glad the Irish people have spoken as they have and made the Irish Free State at last a reality. This alone knew what they wanted and what was best for them, and now that they have spoken the world must accept their decision as final and one to be generally commended. The action of the Dail Eireann in ratifying the peace treaty with the British Government met with overwhelming weight of public opinion in Ireland. The clergy, as well as the great majority of the Irish people, through their associations, societies, clubs and business and social organizations, concluded that the past signal advantages to be gained by the members of the Irish Cabinet in London should be upheld, and their open declarations that the present form of the county of definite expression of the will of the whole nation directly along the lines of what has been pressed during our tour through previous years in August.

"The Irish people's verdict is in keep-

Continued on Page Eighteen.

DRAMATIC SCENE IN DAIL

After Vote de Valera Calls for Republic and Then Breaks Down.

CROWDS CHEER OUTSIDE

Ratification Follows Day of Intense Excitement and Heated Controversy.

BURGESS ASSAILS COLLINS

Griffith Defends Treaty in Closing Speech—Majority Is Greater Than Expected.

Copyright, 1922, by The New York Times Company.
DUBLIN, Jan. 7.—The Dail Eireann ratified the peace treaty tonight by a majority of seven, the vote being 64 for and 57 against. Eamon de Valera, immediately the result was known, said it was his duty to resign as President of the Irish Republic, but there is doubt whether he did so formally or merely to offer the resignation later. In this he called a meeting of his supporters for tomorrow.

The last hours of the debate were made memorable by a bitter attack on Michael Collins by Charles Burgess (Cathal Brugha). He attacked Collins's military record and insisted that he had no better claim to his reputation than mere newspaper notoriety.

The vote in favor of the treaty was received with ringing cheers, but it was taken by de Valera as proof of his complete defeat. He broke down as he tried to speak and many of his supporters were seen in tears.

Grave fears are felt as to the consequences of a split in the Sinn Fein ranks, and Michael Collins immediately took steps to meet the situation. He called for the appointment of a joint committee representing both parties to make arrangements for setting up a Provisional Government.

Charles Burgess undertook, as Minister of Defense, to preserve the discipline of the Irish Republican Army.

Great scenes of rejoicing were witnessed in the streets of Dublin as soon as the result of the Dail's deliberations was known.

Already the news of the acceptance of the treaty had then by some means been flashed to the waiting crowds outside and great cheers arose from them, but in the Chamber itself there was at the moment little in the way of a demonstration.

De Valera rose immediately and said:

"It will be, of course, my duty to resign but I don't know if I will do it just now. But I have to say to the country and to the world that the Irish people have established a republic. A vote of Dail is simply approval; the republic can only be disestablished by the Irish people. Therefore until the Irish people in regular manner disestablish it this republican constitution goes on.

"Whatever arrangements are made, this is the supreme sovereign body in the nation. This is the body to which the nation looks for its supreme Government, and it must remain, no matter who is the Executive, until the Irish nation has disestablished it."

Collins Urges Conciliation.

Collins urged that it was not a matter of question of politics, and he pleaded for the appointment of a united committee with representatives of both parties in the House, so that they could take over the machinery of government. He ended by saying:

"The President has the same position in my heart as he always had."

Miss MacSwiney made another bitter speech in which she characterized the decision "a betrayal worse than Castlereagh." There could be no union, she said, between the representatives of the Irish Republic and the British Government.

"Should We Help Irish Revival." The action was appeared to ignore Mr. Collins's appeal in regard to the setting up of a joint committee, but stated instead that he would preserve order and who had supported him to meet him at Mansion House tomorrow afternoon.

Collins said an understanding might be reached by which they could preserve the present order in the country. He did not know if they were to go a different way or not, but they ought to agree to that at any rate over the week-end.

De Valera rose with an ashen face, his hands trembling with the desk before him. "I will make this my last word," he began. "We have had a glorious record of four years—"

Then he stopped; his words choked him and he broke down completely. He was a pathetic figure as he almost fell back into his seat and covered his eyes with his hands. Many of the President's supporters gave way to their feelings.

Almost immediately from the back of the room some member of the public rose and in a voice which was audible in the Chamber called for cheers for the Valera and the republic, which was quickly responded to. When the cheering had died down, Griffith said:

"So far as I am concerned I will see that discipline is kept in the army and that the relations between us are kept friendly."

The Dail adjourned until 11 o'clock on Monday morning.

Meanwhile the first of the leaders who have taken the University Hall, on next door to

Continued on Page Eighteen.

The New York Times.

THE WEATHER
Cloudy today; Monday, clear and
colder; fresh west winds.
Temperature Yesterday—Max., 36; min., 29.
For full weather report see Page 23.

Section
1

VOL. LXXI....No. 23,374.   NEW YORK, SUNDAY, JANUARY 22, 1922. In Nine Parts, Including Rotogravure Picture Section, Book and Magazine Section.   FIVE CENTS In Manhattan, Bronx and Brooklyn; TEN CENTS Elsewhere

POPE BENEDICT XV. PASSES AWAY EARLY THIS MORNING; LINGERS HOURS AFTER WORLD GETS REPORT OF DEATH; TRIBUTES PAID TO THE PONTIFF BY MEN OF ALL RELIGIONS

LLOYD GEORGE ASKS NATIONS TO RESOLVE ON PEACE AT GENOA

Premier Declares International Conferences Alone Can Restore Confidence.

HITS AT POINCARE'S STAND

Those Who Fear Conferences Are Those Unwilling to Face Realities, He Says.

FULL TEXT OF THE SPEECH

Implies Strong Hope for American Co-operation and Warns Against Party Strife.

Copyright, 1922, by The New York Times Company.
Special Cable to THE NEW YORK TIMES.

LONDON, Jan. 21.—Prime Minister Lloyd George looks to the Genoa conference to carry the world another stage forward in the paths of peace and recuperation after the war if the United States of America will attend and help to complete the good work done by the Washington conference.

Although he was most guarded in his expression of his views, it was obvious to most of those who listened to the remarkable speech he made at Central Hall, Westminster, today, when he wound up the proceedings of the new Liberal Council convention held there, that he counts upon America. He did not say that without America nothing worth while would be accomplished at Genoa, but his whole speech by implication did convey the idea that unless the United States does take a hand there progress at Genoa may be distressingly slow and limited.

He spoke as an optimist struggling hard against adversity. All his emphasis was laid on the necessity of world peace and his conviction that this could be found only through the means of international conferences. His references to the Washington conference, to Mr. Balfour's share in it and to the advantages of an understanding with the United States were made carefully from

The problem which confronted the world, he said, was the restoration of international confidence in every country. Washington had done much to clear away the atmosphere of suspicion. Genoa, he believed, would remove other doubts and fears. Though he did not say it in so many words, he made it clear that his hopes lay in the English-speaking races.

He let his fancy play a little as he spoke of old hatreds, old feuds and old distrusts which complicate European problems and then he almost dramatically gave his experience of how conferences could solve them as with hands weighing the balance from side to side he pictured the weight of argument.

With arm slowly raised he illustrated the approach to agreement and with a blow of the right fist on the palm of the left hand he exclaimed:

"In the end reason prevails. When you are in conference you see that the men who will bring you face to face with realities, and it is those who never face realities who dislike conferences."

Although the British Premier's speech had to deal with many points of purely domestic politics, Lloyd George obviously regarded them as secondary and subsidiary to his main theme, world reconstruction. Even his appeal for the continuance of the coalition Government in this country was based on the argument that the dominant issue of British domestic politics was need of peace in the world.

"There is one great stable country," he declared with a flash of national pride. "That is Great Britain. Do not deprive the world of the full advantages of the power and prestige of this great body by shattering them upon wretched party feeling."

Lloyd George spoke directly in reply to a resolution congratulating the Government on the Irish settlement.

The full text of the Premier's speech is given below.

FULL TEXT OF LLOYD GEORGE'S SPEECH.

I congratulate the promoters of these meetings upon the finest gathering we have seen. (Laughter and cheers.) The Liberals who stood in the nation's need for national unity. A resolution has been moved and seconded of congratulation upon a task which if not altogether accomplished is well-nigh accomplished. Congratulations are given to myself and my colleagues on the result of our labors.

The first thing I have to say is that those congratulations have been directed to the wrong address. They ought to have been sent not to those who did it but to those who talked about it. (Laughter and cheers.) But never did it when they had the chance. It is a fact that we conducted long, difficult and delicate negotiations. It is true that we carried them to a success. But it is true we did most serious decisions and freed grave responsibilities than others, and notably refer to my Unionist colleagues.

Continued on Page Eighteen.

FLORIDA—SEABOARD FLORIDA LIMITED—4:20 P. M., P. R. R. Solid Pullman with Club and Observation Car. Superior Dining Car Service. 143 W.,—Adv.

Freighter Sinking at Sea; Rush to Save Her Crew

BOSTON, Jan. 21.—The new Norwegian steamship Mod, New York for An. erp, Bremen and Hamburg, is sinking in mid-ocean according to radiograms received ere today. The steamer Centennial State reported that all the Mod's lif°cats and her propeller were gone, and that the steamer George Washin.ton was going to her aid. The Mod left New York on Jan. 13, she is a vessel of 2,707 tons and available records indicate that she is a freighter. Her position as given in the wireless messages is about 1,200 miles east of Halifax.

The Mod left New York on Jan. 13, she is a vessel of 2,707 tons and available records indicate that she is a freighter. Her position as given in the wireless messages is about 1,200 miles east of Halifax.

The Mod left New York on Jan. 13, at latitude 46:15 north, longitude 41:10 west.

STORM IN FRANCE OVER GEN. PETAIN

Poincare Sharply Criticised for Appointing Him to Post in War Ministry.

CHAMBER TO DISCUSS IT

Nationalists Not Anxious for American Participation at Genoa.

Copyright, 1922, by The New York Times Company.

PARIS, Jan. 21.—Premier Poincaré's first experimental act in appointing Marshal Pétain to what is in effect not only the office of Inspector General of the Army but a position in the Ministry of War has been during the last few days one of the subjects of most controversy in all the program of the Government.

The Socialists attacked it at once as an indication of the militaristic intentions of the new Premier. Even in the general opinion it was regarded as an unwise step, however fully qualified for the post the Marshal might be and however little attention there might be from his former powers.

Then in the Chamber during the debate on Thursday André Lefèvre, himself a former Minister of War, and always one of the hottest advocates of more complete disarmament of Germany, suddenly refused his support to the Government on the ground of this termination. In a sharp speech he attacked the new appointment of Marshal Pétain as likely to take the army from civilian control and place it in the hands of its military leaders, and by the support he received it became at once apparent that even amid the enthusiasm for the Poincaré administration the Chamber was reserving its full judgment by actions in committing the country to any militarist program. M. Maginot, the new War Minister, who formerly was Minister of Pensions, at once replied to M. Lefèvre, but his reply was so feeble that Poincaré had to intervene and promise that the matter would be fully debated at the first convenient opportunity.

In the two days that have elapsed opinion has visibly hardened and the first symptoms have appeared of opposition to the Government within the Chamber itself. Two important groups of radicals and radical Socialists, led by M. Klotz, the former Minister, have sent a letter to the Premier informing him that they wish the debate to be fixed at early as possible and in which they characterize Pétain's appointment as "an act contrary to the principle of constitutional responsibility and to republican doctrine."

If the Premier persists in maintaining the appointment in face of the opposition which it has aroused the incident may easily become a vital issue, and though Marshal Pétain's popularity and respect for his military and his ability are deep and sincere in the country, there is little doubt that tremendous pressure could easily be brought on the question.

If Premier Poincaré has finished drafting his outline of the preliminary conditions for a Franco-British compact and the terms of the compact itself as he would like to see it. This draft is to be handed to the British Government through the French Ambassador in London, and presumably the reply will be sent by similar channels.

In the new project France is believed to have repeated the request which Briand made a ground for British intervention, and further to have asked that the treaty be operative for a longer term than ten years.

According to the formula announced in the Premier's ministerial declaration of "a treaty between equals," Poincaré is seeking to have the treaty made reciprocal so as to avoid the suggestion that France is a protected country. Just how he purposes to do this is, however, being kept secret, and even those who are most enthusiastic for "equality," profess their fear that England will not accept easily a guarantee which will appear to carry with it approval of France's military upkeep, and much less will she accept any hard and fast stipulation as to the number of army corps which she must supply in case that afternoon.

COLLINS AND CRAIG AGREE ON BOUNDARY AT LONDON MEETING

Terms Give Hope of Peaceable Settlement of Differences of Ulster and South Ireland.

THEY CALL OFF BOYCOTTS

Decide to Devise Better System Than Council of Ireland to Handle Their Relations.

WILL TAKE UP AMNESTY

Ulster Officials Calls News "Best We Have Had, and the Most Cheering."

LONDON, Jan. 21 (Associated Press).—The Irish situation took an unexpected turn today with the announcement that Michael Collins, head of the Irish Provisional Government, and Sir James Craig, Premier of Ulster, had arrived at a mutual agreement, which finds its promise of a peaceable settlement between the North and the South. It was all the more surprising in view of the fact that Mr. Collins had only left Dublin last night to enter into consultations with Sir James this morning.

In addition to the arrangements made to settle the boundary question, it was decided to cease forthwith mutual boycotts. What is considered of vast importance is the decision to devise a better system than the Council of Ireland, as provided in the 1920 act, to deal with problems affecting the whole of Ireland. The terms of the agreement are substantially as follows:

1. The boundary commission, as outlined in the Anglo-Irish treaty, to be altered. The Governments of the Irish Free State and of Northern Ireland are to appoint one representative each to report to Mr. Collins and Sir James, who will mutually agree on behalf of their respective Governments regarding the future boundaries between the two.

2. Without prejudice to future consideration by his Government of the question of tariffs, Mr. Collins undertakes that the Belfast boycott will be discontinued immediately, and Sir James undertakes to facilitate in every possible way the return of Catholic workmen—without tests—to the shipyards, and whenever trade revival enables the firms concerned to absorb the present unemployed workmen. In the meantime a system of relief on a large scale is being arranged to tide over the period of distress.

3. Representatives of both Governments are to unite in facilitating a settlement of the railway dispute.

4. The Governments are to endeavor to devise a more suitable system than the Council of Ireland for dealing with problems affecting all Ireland.

5. A further meeting will be held at a subsequent date in Ireland between the signatories to this agreement to discuss the question of amnesty for persons who have been imprisoned since the operation of the truce.

Ulster Official Is Hopeful.

BELFAST, Jan. 21 (Associated Press).—John Milne Barbour, who is Sir James Craig's Deputy Finance Minister, described the news of the agreement between Michael Collins and Sir James as "the best we have had yet and the most cheering." He thought it eminently desirable that the north and south combine in the interest of the common country so long as the autonomy of Ulster is reserved.

The general feeling here is that the agreement is an outcome of Mr. Collins's desire to protect the Free State in the coming elections against the menace of a possible combination of Republicans and Communists, as there are many of the latter in the Transport Workers' Union. The Ulster Premier, on his part, is anxious for peace within the six-county borders.

The Ulster Unionists naturally will welcome the raising of the boycott, as apprehensive of trouble with the shipyard workers on the restoration of Catholic workmen expelled in July, 1920, after the murder of Colonel Smyth in Cork. There has been a heavy increase of unemployment in the shipyards in the last year, and it is considered definitely certain that the Protestant workmen will insist that their co-legionists be given priority in the filling of jobs.

Lord Pirrie holds the same view with regard to the situation as does the Ulster Premier, but believes that it will be a long time before the bitterness engendered by the shootings and bombings on both sides vanishes. Matters, however, he thinks, would be facilitated if the British Government were prepared to finance a large relief scheme in the Ulster Labor Ministry has been sorely tried by the unemployment problem.

Takes Over Dublin City Hall.

DUBLIN, Jan. 21.—The administration of the Dublin City Hall was handed over today by the British military authorities.

Senate Agrees to Take Up Foreign Debt Refunding Monday

WASHINGTON, Jan. 21.—The Senate late today cleared the way for consideration next Monday of the Allied Debt Funding bill. Adjourning over Sunday, the Senate made the bill its privileged business. A long contest is regarded assured prir ¦pally over a Democratic amendment to require semi-annual interest payments and to require foreign bonds paying not less than 5 per cent. The Genoa Economic Conference and many questions relating to the armament conference are expected to be discussed in connection with the measure.

ARREST 'TEX' RICKARD ON A GIRL'S CHARGE

Boxing Promoter Is Accused of Inviting 15-Year-Old Child to 47th Street House.

HE HINTS AT AN ENEMY PLOT

Alleged Victim's 11 and 12 Year Old Companions Give Evidence to Children's Society.

"Tex" Rickard, lessee and manager of Madison Square Garden and the most conspicuous prize-fight promoter in the country, was arrested yesterday on charges involving a 15-year-old girl. This girl, together with two others, aged 11 and 12 years respectively, have told the Society for the Prevention of Cruelty to Children, to the District Attorney's office, and to the police a story of association that began one night last August at Rickard's swimming pool in Madison Square Garden and ended last Saturday night when two of the girls, afraid to go home, sought shelter at Bellevue Hospital.

According to the girls' statements, Rickard made their acquaintance when they went to swim in the Garden pool, and invited them to visit his offices in the tower. The girls say that Rickard gave them money and offered them wine. Later, the girls say, they visited him in private quarters at 20 and 24 West Forty-seventh Street.

Rickard, who is about 50 years old, denied the accusations and pleaded not guilty when he w.: arraigned in the West ... Court yesterday morning. He went to court with his wife and lawyers and said he had heard he was wanted. Magistrate George W. Simpson held him in $1,000 bail for examination Wednesday on a charge of criminal assault. The men.

McGuiness Offers Apology.

"Comisky told Mr. Dineen that McGuiness then expressed regret that they had fought over the old grudge and, walking up to Soden with his right hand extended, said:

"'Well, Jack, let's forget it. We were old schoolmates together.'"

Soden shook hands with McGuiness, Comisky added, and said:

"'Let bygones be bygones.'"

McGuiness then took a position beside the policeman at the bar, according to Comisky, and Soden suddenly wheeled around on him with his pistol. As McGuiness backed away, the witness said, the policeman shot him in the abdomen, the chest and the right arm.

With the first shot the onlookers fled to the street, Comisky said. Policeman Soden followed.

A policeman, who had been standing a block away, ran into the barroom and found McGuiness dying on the floor. Asked who had shot him, McGuiness refused to reply. He was taken to St. Vincent's Hospital, where questioned him. He persisted in his refusal to answer questions, and the only information he gave was his name and his address—528 West Seventeenth Street.

McGuiness was in the hospital about three hours when Detective Sergeant William Quinn and James McGuiE... to tell who shot him. McGuiness, the detective said, impatiently turned his head aside and mumbled the name of a cabaret singer who knew nothing about the shooting.

Witness Tells of Shooting.

In the meantime detectives had arrested Comisky as a material witness. Comisky told Captain Fay that Soden had fired the shots, and the Captain, accompanied by several detectives, went to the policeman's home, where they found him seated with his wife and two children. They asked him if he was in the Ninth Avenue saloon at the time of the shooting, and they told Mr. Dineen. He refused to make a statement. Captain Fay then examined the policeman's pistol. Five fully loaded, but had been cleaned recently.

Soden was arrested and taken to the hospital in the hope that McGuiness might be able to identify him, but a few minutes before their arrival McGuiness died. Soden then was taken to the West Thirtieth Street Station, where the policeman said he was scheduled to go on duty at his regular station at midnight—two hours before—but had reported sick to the Lieutenant at the station over the telephone.

A police surgeon was summoned to examine whether Soden was drunk and said Captain Fay the policeman was "fit for duty."

Meanwhile Mr. Dineen had endeavored to get a statement from the prisoner, who refused to speak until he had conferred with his lawyer, James J. Mayer of 119 West Tenth Street.

Soden was locked in a cell at the station with S A. M., when he was taken to the Detective Bureau to be questioned and finger printed. The police "line-up" of criminals was gone up, but the prisoner was not shown to the assembled detectives.

After Soden was arraigned, Mr. Dineen reported the shooting to District Attorney Barton. He said Michael O'Brien, the bartender in the saloon, told Mr. Soden,

Continued on Page Seventeen.

DON'T SUFFER FROM INDIGESTION. BELL-ANS GIVE QUICK RELIEF.—Adv.

EX-CONVICT SLAIN; POLICEMAN IS HELD FOR THE KILLING

Victim Shot Down in Dispute Said to Have Grown Out of Boyhood Enmity.

DYING, HE PROTECTS SLAYER

Refuses to Say Who Wounded Him, but Witness Names Patrolman Soden.

OFFICER ARRESTED IN HOME

Pistol Shows Recent Cleaning, but He Is Held About Tragedy—Prompt Trial Promised.

John R. Soden, a mounted policeman attached to the Glendale Station, Queens, was held yesterday without bail for examination next Friday on suspicion of having shot and mortally wounded John McGuiness, an ex-convict, the night before in a drunken brawl in the saloon at 66 Ninth Avenue. He was arraigned before Magistrate Joseph E. Corrigan in Jefferson Market Court.

Soden is 32 years old and has been a member of the force for eleven years. He was arrested four hours after the shooting in his home, at 8 Bethune Street, a short distance from the saloon, by Captain Thomas Fay, head of the Lower West Side Detective Bureau. He refused to make any statement to Captain Fay or Benedict D. Dineen, Assistant District Attorney, who began an investigation shortly before McGuiness died in St. Vincent's Hospital.

Assistant District Attorney said four or five men were in the saloon when the shooting occurred, but the police had found only one of them. This witness, Philip Comisky of 411 West Thirtieth Street, told Mr. Dineen the shooting followed an altercation growing out of ill feeling that had existed between Policeman Soden and McGuiness from their boyhood.

The girls were in civilian clothes, is six feet one inch tall and weighs 190 pounds. He had struck McGuiness a blow as they were standing at the bar, and the men fought for five minutes, he said. McGuiness, who was two years younger than the policeman, was getting the better of the fight, Comisky said, when onlookers separated the men.

World Is Misled by Premature Report of Death; Berlin Started Rumor, Cardinal's Aid Spread It

LONDON, Jan. 22.—All London went to bed last night in the belief that the Pope had died in the afternoon. The report appears to have been circulated throughout Europe and was accepted by church and civil officials as true. The German Reichstag suspended proceedings, while President Loebe delivered a eulogy on the Pope.

All the London evening papers published extra editions, announcing the death of the Pontiff, and the first editions of the Sunday papers, sent to the Provinces, contained the report.

The report of the Pope's death here emanated from Cardinal Bourne's residence. A member of the Cardinal's staff notified all the English press agencies before 6 P. M. that the Cardinal had received official news of the Pope's death, and confirmed this to all by special inquiries. Bells were tolled at Westminster and the Southwark Catholic Cathedral, and an announcement of the death was made from the pulpit of the latter church, followed by a requiem mass.

Late at night the Cardinal's chief secretary informed the news agencies that the information communicated to them, that the Cardinal had received an official report of the Pope's death, was incorrect. It was impossible to obtain an explanation of ¨he mistake.

The first report of the death of the Pope apparently came from Reuter's News Agency. An Associated Press dispatch from London (not timed there but issued in New York at 12:35 P. M. said:

"A Berlin dispatch to Reuter's this afternoon says word has been received there that Pope Benedict is dead."

At 1:32 P. M. this Associated Press dispatch from Paris was issued here:

"A Berlin dispatch to the Havas Agency quotes the Wolff Bureau as saying Pope Benedict died at 5:13 o'clock this afternoon, Rome time."

The Cardinal Bourne message to which the above London dispatch refers was issued at London at 6:55 P. M. (1:55 P. M. New York time). It read:

"Cardinal Bourne, Archbishop of Westminster, stated this evening he had been officially notified by telegraph from Rome that Pope Benedict was dead."

At 7:49 P. M. this Reuter's dispatch from Rome was issued by the Associated Press:

"Pope Benedict died late today."

The time when this message was filed at Rome was not given. A statement issued last night by the Associated Press said:

"Urgent messages, asking for definite information direct from Rome, brought replies from London that the Italian telegraphic system had been in a state of chaos for more than a year and that undoubtedly the wires were overburdened with hundreds of messages regarding the Pope; that this morning messages were coming late in the afternoon, and that doubtless official Vatican messages were being given precedence over press dispatches."

ADOPT PLAN TO LIST ALL CHINA TREATIES

Conferees Extensively Amend Hughes Resolution, but Principle Remains.

JAPANESE GAIN A POINT

Agreements Made by Nationals Apart From Government Need Not Be Notified.

By EDWIN L. JAMES.
Special to The New York Times.

WASHINGTON, Jan. 21.—The Far Eastern Committee of the Washington conference today adopted the Hughes resolution providing for the public listing of commitments under which rights in China are obtained. The resolution as adopted, however, has been amended to such a degree that it is far from the original resolution, though important changes have been made. The amendments come through the action of the Japanese, the original resolution was altered to place on China the task of publishing°agreements with the nationals of the powers with relation to other than public utilities.

The Hughes plan, as adopted, is in four parts. The first lays down that the powers other than China shall file all treaties or other formal documents with relation to China, and that all future treaties shall be notified generally sixty days after their making. Part two says that the powers shall file all commitments between their nationals and China, or with any other agreements with any outside Governments, or, as possible, where they deal with public utilities. The third part obliges China to notify all treaties or other agreements with any outside Governments, or the nationals of any other Government. Part four provides for inviting other powers to adhere to the arrangement.

Most of the treaties with China have been published, however, it is thought that the operation of the listing arrangement will bring some new ones to light. The provision for filing future treaties exists already in Article 18 of the Covenant of the League.

The Resolution as Adopted.

Here is the text of the Hughes resolution:

The powers represented in this conference, considering it desirable that publicity with respect to all matters affecting the political and other international obligations of China and of the several powers in relation to China, are agreed as follows:

The several powers other than China will, at their earliest convenience, file with the Secretariat General of the conference for transmission to the participating powers a list of all treaties, conventions, exchanges of notes or other international agreements which they may have with China, or with any other power or powers in relation to China, which they deem to be still in force and operative, which they may desire to rely. In case citations will be given to any official or other publication in which the document may be found. In any case in which the document may not have been published, a copy of the text or, if in the original language or languages will be filed with the Secretariat General of the conference.

Every treaty or other international agreement of the character described which may be concluded hereafter shall be notified by the Governments concerned within sixty days of its conclusion to or adverse to this signatory or adherent to this agreement.

The several powers other than China will file with the Secretariat General of the conference all their earliest convenience for transmission to the participating powers as possible, as is nearly complete as may be possible, of all those contracts between their nationals, of the one part, and the

Continued on Page Twenty.

MEN OF ALL FAITHS EULOGIZE THE POPE

Protestants Unite With Catholics in Praise of His Great Service to Humanity.

HAYES PAYS HIGH TRIBUTE

"Among the Church's Greatest Pontiffs," Says Archbishop—Bishop Manning's Tribute.

Expressions of sympathy and sorrow on learning of the death of Pope Benedict XV. were given yesterday by officials and prominent citizens as well as church dignitaries throughout the city.

An early report of the Pope's death, which proved to be unfounded, stirred church circles and brought forth many eulogies. When the report of his death was confirmed there were many more such expressions. Orders were given for the draping in purple and black of many church edifices, and announcements of masses for today were made.

Archbishop Patrick J. Hayes made the following statement before the end was announced:

"His death would be a loss not only to the church of which he is the supreme shepherd, but also to the entire world that is longing for peace and stability.

"His services during the war were of the highest order—services which he gave to all mankind, irrespective of race, nation or religion. His thought was to love humanity, and while he did his spirit of love and justice and conscientious neutrality.

"His ministry and influence are needed now in the restoration of order and the stabilizing of the terrified social forces and powers that are crying out of the depths of men's sorrowing and distressed souls for a better and a juster world."

Mayor Hylan issued this statement:

"The death of Pope Benedict XV. is a severe loss to religion and one that will be universally lamented. He was an eminent ecclesiastic and a Pontiff who sought to create a real brotherhood of man. I feel a keen and deep, personal sorrow in his death, for his utterances have been a never-ending source of inspiration to me. His memory will ever be cherished not only at the altars of his own Church, but in the heart of every man regardless of his creed."

Tributes by Protestant Clergymen.

The Right Rev. William T. Manning, Episcopal Bishop of New York, said:

"The death of his Holiness Pope Benedict XV. is a matter of concern to the whole Christian world. All Christians will feel deep sympathy with the Roman Catholic Church in their great loss. The Rev. Caleb R. Stetson, Rector of Trinity Episcopal Church, said:

"The whole Christian world is touched by the death of the Pope, for he is at the head of the largest body of Christian people in the world. Benedict XV. has been known throughout his life as a man devoted to the service of his Church, and one whose interest in latter years as Chief Pastor of the Roman Communion has extended to all parts of the world. His interest in this country was marked, and his expressions of sympathy were warm. My sympathy

Continued on Page Four.

END AT 6 A. M., ROME TIME

Hope Was Given Up Early Yesterday After Two Sinking Spells

BUT HIS STRENGTH REVIVED

Clear-Minded Most of the Time and Full of Affection for Those Around Him.

CROWDS AROUND VATICAN

Messages From the Great of Many Lands Are Received by Gasparri.

ROME, Sunday, Jan. 22 (Associated Press).—Pope Benedict XV. died at 6 o'clock this morning (midnight, New York time).

The end had been expected for several hours. The attending physicians, Cardinal Gasparri and other members of the Pope's household were present at the bedside.

From midnight all hope had been abandoned, and at 2 o'clock Dr. Battistini announced that the Pope could not live longer than four hours at the maximum.

At 3 o'clock this morning Dr. Cherubini, Cardinal Giorgi and the Pope's nephew were gathered around the bedside, the end seemingly being near.

The Pope appeared then to be in considerable distress. His extremities were already becoming cold.

At one lucid period late at night the Pope asked to partake of nourishment. He then instructed the major domo to make him in time for mass, to be celebrated at 5:30 in the morning in his chapel adjoining the bedroom.

Great Power of Resistance.

There had been moments during Saturday when it was feared the end had come, but stimulants revived the Pontiff, and his natural powers of resistance carried him through the turning point temporarily. The Holy Father seemed to cling to life, as did Pope Pius X. in 1914, when the final outcome was in doubt for many hours.

Dr. Battistini, the chief attending physician, visited the patient several times during the night. Each time he said that any minute might see the conclusion of the long hours of suffering through which Benedict XV. had passed in his fight for life.

The last announcement of the evening was that the Pope was sinking late and sure.

"A catastrophe is imminent," the Holy Father is getting worse and worse. We must be prepared for the inevitable.

The Cardinal's face was downcast and sad. He spoke in quiet tones, with deep emotion, making features with his hands.

After the publication of the latest bulletin, Cardinal Giorgi, Mgr. Migone, Father Basil and Dr. Battistini, remained by the bedside. After a time the doctor told his Holiness that the doctors were praying for the peace of the world, to which the Pope replied:

"I would willingly offer my life for the peace of the world." He then turned on his side and lay watching those near him.

Hope Revived, Only to Fade.

Yesterday was a day of great uncertainty and deep anxiety among those who watched and prayed at the Vatican. Virtually all hope of the Pope's recovery was abandoned in the early hours of yesterday morning, and as the hours passed the wonder grew at the recuperative powers of the Holy Father, which enabled him to pass periods of comparative restfulness and strength. It was this changing condition that inspired hope at one moment only to give rise to rumors of death at another.

It was thought that if the Pope passed safely through Friday night he would

"All the News That's Fit to Print."

The New York Times.

THE WEATHER
Rain today, rising temperature;
Thursday rain; east to south winds.
For weather report see next to last page.

VOL. LXXI....No. 23,405.   NEW YORK, WEDNESDAY, FEBRUARY 22, 1922.   TWO CENTS In Greater New York | THREE CENTS Within 200 Miles | FOUR CENTS Elsewhere

GIANT ARMY DIRIGIBLE WRECKED; 34 DEAD, 11 ARE SAVED; VICTIMS PERISH WHEN ROMA BURSTS INTO FLAMES AFTER FALL; COLLAPSE OF RUDDER CAUSES TRAGEDY ON SHORT TRIAL FLIGHT

FOUR-POWER TREATY WILL BE REPORTED WITH RESERVATION

Brandegee's Modification of the Compact Favored by Senate Committee.

HARDING AND LODGE AGREE

Legal or Moral Obligation to Defend Rights of Other Nations in Pacific Excluded.

MAY BE REPORTED TODAY

Committee Will Choose Between Brandegee's Reservation and a Milder Substitute by Pomerene.

Special to The New York Times.

WASHINGTON, Feb. 21.—The Four-Power Treaty, with a reservation which will stipulate that the United States assumes no "legal or moral" obligation to maintain the rights of other nations signatory to the compact, and that any adjustment or agreement, arrived at under the provisions of Articles I. or II., shall not be binding on this Government unless approved by Congress, will probably be reported out of the Committee on Foreign Relations in the next few days.

It is possible, members of the Committee said tonight, that the treaty may be in the Senate before adjournment tomorrow afternoon.

The reservation, which, it is said, Senator Lodge has accepted, and which the President has agreed to interpose no objection to, if by so doing the situation will be, as one member of the committee expressed it, "eased up," was introduced in committee by Senator Brandegee of Connecticut, one of the original League of Nations "irreconcilables." The reservation has not been approved in the committee, although it is understood that it, or some other reservation along similar lines, will command probably twelve of the sixteen votes in the committee.

The Brandegee resolution, as submitted to the Committee today, reads:

The Senate advises and consents, subject to the following reservation which is to be made a part of the Instrument of Ratification, to wit:

The United States understands that it assumes no obligation, "other legal or moral, to maintain the rights, in relation to the insular possessions of the United States, it "eased up," adjustment or understanding under Articles I. or II. by which the United States is to be bound in any way and that there is no obligation either legal or moral to give such consent.

Pomerene Substitute Favored.

The Brandegee reservation would probably have been approved today had not Senator Pomerene, one of the Democratic members, offered a substitute which is intended to "soften" the language of the reservation drafted by the Senator from Connecticut. The Pomerene suggestion was favorably received by several of the members, and the lines indicated in the Brandegee draft in that it may be the reservation which the committee will report to the Senate.

The Pomerene reservation, which will be offered in committee tomorrow morning, is very short, and has nothing in it about "legal or moral" obligations, although in the opinion of some Senators it is just as sweeping as the Brandegee draft, in that Congress receives the right to veto any agreement or adjustment that may be reached by the representatives of the signatory nations.

It is understood, however, that the adjustment provided for under Article I. and the understanding contemplated under Article II. shall be subject to the consent of the United States.

According to reliable information emanating from the Committee on Foreign Relations, the following Senators will vote for a reservation along the lines indicated in the Brandegee and Pomerene drafts: Lodge, Brandegee, Johnson, Moses, McCormick and Wadsworth of the majority, and Hitchcock, Swanson, Pomerene, Pittman and Shields of the minority membership. Senators McCumber, New and Kellogg, Republicans, and Williams, Democrat, are understood to oppose reservations of any kind.

Senator Pomerene agrees with the President's interpretation of the Four-Power Treaty and does not think a reservation necessary, but, realizing that a reservation appears certain of adoption, is attempting to order the reservation, if possible, less objectionable.

The Brandegee reservation has been submitted to President Harding. The President is said to have informed the Senators who conferred with him on the matter that while he is of the opinion that the treaty should be ratified without reservation of any kind, he will

Continued on Page Four.

Hughes, Mellon, Hoover, Smoot, Burton, Named on Foreign Debt Commission

Special to The New York Times.

WASHINGTON, Feb. 21.—Nominations for the Foreign Debt Funding Commission were sent by President Harding to the Senate today.

In addition to Secretary Mellon, whose appointment was expressly stipulated by the Funding bill signed by the President last week, the nominees are Secretary Hughes, Secretary Hoover, Senator Reed Smoot of Utah and Representative Theodore Burton of Ohio.

Upon this commission will rest the duty of working out satisfactory arrangements for funding foreign debts amounting to more than $11,000,000,000. Initial steps in the negotiations will be taken through diplomatic channels, it was indicated at the White House.

it is expected that Secretary Hughes will undertake these soon after returning from his Bermuda vacation the first of March.

Although there is the possibility that one or more members of the commission may be sent to Europe, it was said by Administration officials today that virtually all of the negotiations will be attempted through diplomatic channels in Washington. It has been stated at the Treasury Department that the funding operations will be taken up with each country in order of the size of their loans from this country. This would place the British negotiations first, followed by the French, Italian and Belgian.

MELLON BACKS UP HARDING ON BONUS

Again Warns Ways and Means Committee That Treasury Cannot Stand the Outlay.

SALES TAX ONLY SOLUTION

Senator Calder Announces in Speech Here He Will Refuse to Vote for Bonus.

Special to The New York Times.

WASHINGTON, Feb. 21.—Secretary Mellon, appearing before the Ways and Means subcommittee considering bonus legislation today, reiterated his opposition to such legislation because of the condition of the Treasury. He agreed with the President, however, that, if bonus legislation were to be passed, the only way to raise the revenue without embarrassing the Government and injuring business was through a sales tax.

Mr. Mellon was asked to appear before the committee to discuss the advantages and disadvantages of different forms of a sales tax. The conference was held in executive session. He said that he was so much opposed to a bill without any provision for revenue as he was against a measure which fixed the money by the eight-point taxation scheme recently advanced by the committee or by Treasury certificates.

Experts of the Treasury who were with Mr. Mellon said that a final retail tax would be objectionable in that it would be hard to collect and would be obnoxious to the consumer. They urged that if a sales tax were adopted it be placed upon manufactured articles or on a sales tax. The committee was told that each point would be

2 to 4 Per cent. Tax Favored.

The proposal which seemed to meet with the most favor of the committee was that placing a 2 to 4 per cent. upon specific commodities from the manufacturers or jobbers. All iron and steel manufactured products would have a fixed tax, and so the tax would be imposed all along the line. In some instances it would be 2 per cent., and the maximum would not exceed 4 per cent. Under such a plan, taxes would not be imposed on food products and some articles of every-day household consumption. This tax, it is estimated, would raise $30,000,000 annually.

The manufacturers' tax of 1 per cent. advocated by Senator Smoot did not appear to have much support in the committee. This tax, Treasury experts estimated, would yield $250,000,000 annually.

The subcommittee is not seriously considering any form of taxation other than a sales tax. The hearings have not progressed far enough to indicate just what form the sales tax will take, but it can be said upon authority that the committee intends to report a bonus bill carrying a sales tax provision.

Opposition to a sales tax is increasing so rapidly as to make it doubtful whether sufficient votes can be obtained in the Rules Committee for a special rule in

Continued on Page Nine.

Lloyd George Going to Paris For Conference With Poincare

Copyright, 1922, by The New York Times Company.
Special Cable to The New York Times.

LONDON, Feb. 21.—There is good authority for stating that Premier Lloyd George intends to go to Paris on Saturday to confer with Premier Poincaré on various matters affecting the relations between France and Great Britain in particular the question of the Genoa conference.

SINN FEIN BLOCKS SPLIT OF LEADERS

Insistence of Delegates Forces de Valera and Griffith to Seek a Compromise.

NO VOTE ON THE TREATY

Parish Priests Take the Lead in Demanding Long Delay Before Elections Are Held.

Copyright, 1922, by The New York Times Company.
Special Cable to The New York Times.

DUBLIN, Feb. 21.—For the first time since their historic duel in the Dail, Arthur Griffith and Eamon de Valera met on a public platform in the Mansion House today. In a sense they were there to resume the conflict, but on this occasion the issue was as to which side should capture the organization of Sinn Fein in view of the imminent election on the treaty. Nearly 3,000 delegates from all parts of the country were present to take part in the struggle. It was a remarkable gathering of gray-bearded and young men in the green uniform of the Volunteers and others who limped in on crutches, casualties of the late war, with a sprinkling of parish priests and not a few women, some of them in mourning.

After the dispute had been stated again by de Valera and Griffith, by degrees the feeling to preserve the organization of Sinn Fein against the threatened split became general and a parish priest raised a storm of cheers by suggesting that both de Valera's resolution to stand by the Republic and Griffith's amendment, which would recognize the Free State, should be cancelled. Another priest urged that the treaty and anti-treaty parties should establish their own electoral machinery and leave the Sinn Fein organization as a weapon to enforce the strict adherence of the British Government to the spirit and letter of the treaty in the framing of the Irish Constitution.

The Convention was finally adjourned until tomorrow morning to give the leaders of the opposing forces an opportunity of conferring with a view to evolving a basis whereby the convention could be adjourned for a period without division.

De Valera took the chair nearly half an hour late. Wearing a heavy brown frieze overcoat, he stroke through the Hall, which thousands of cigarettes and pipes were already rendering dim and

Continued on Page Three.

List of the Dead and Survivors In the Wreck of the Big Dirigible

THE DEAD.

Major JOHN G. THORNELL, Air Service; Langley Field.
Major WALTER W. VAUTSMEIER, Coast Artillery Corps; assigned to Air Service; Rockwell Field, Cal.
Captain DALE MABRY, Air Service; Langley Field.
Captain GEORGE D. WATTS, Infantry; assigned to Air Service; Ross Field, Cal.
Captain ALLEN T. McFARLAND, Air Service; McCook Field, Ohio.
Captain FREDERICK B. DURRSCHMIDT.
Lieutenant JOHN R. HALL.
Lieutenant WALLACE C. BURNS.
Lieutenant WILLIAM E. RILEY.
Lieutenant CLIFFORD E. SMYTHE.
Lieutenant WALLACE C. CUMMINGS.
Lieutenant AMBROSE V. CLINTON.
Lieutenant HAROLD K. HINE.

Major JOHN D. REARDON, wife, Mrs. Reardon, 300 Elm Street, Washington, D. C.
Sergeant WALTER J. REED; father, William J. Reed, Scarsdale, N. Y.
Lieutenant CLARENCE H. WELCH; father, W. V. Welch, Papillon, Neb.
Lieutenant BYRON T. BURT Jr.
Sergeant VIRDON T. PEEK; father, Howard Peek, 2,304 Lafayette Avenue, Terre Haute, Ind.
Sergeant HARRY A. CHAPMAN.

Master Sergeant ROGER B. McNALLY.
Master Sergeant MURRAY.
Sergeant LEE M. HARRIS.
Sergeant LEWIS HILLIARD.
Sergeant MYRON G. FIELD.
Sergeant THOMAS YARBOROUGH.
Sergeant BILLY RYAN.
Sergeant VIRGIL C. HOFFMAN.
Sergeant SHUMAKER.
Sergeant HOLMES.
Master Sergeant HOMER GARBY.
Sergeant HEVERDON.
Private KINSTON.
Private THOMAS M. BLAKELEY.
Private THOMPSON.
Private MARION HILL.
Civilian STRYKER.
Civilian HANSON.
Civilian O'LAUGHLIN.
Civilian MERRIMAN.
Civilian SCHULENBERGER.

THE SURVIVORS.

mother, Mrs. J. H. Ward, 1,626 Frederick Avenue, St. Joseph, Mo.
Sergeant JOSEPH M. BIEDENBACH; father, John Biedenbach, 111 East Market Street, Akron, Ohio.
Corporal ALBERT FLORES.
Civilian WALTER A. McNAIR, Bureau of Standards, Washington, D. C.
Civilian CHARLES DWORACK, McCook Field, Ohio.
Civilian RAY HURLEY, National Advisory Committee on Aeronautics.

Survivor Says Roma Often Sailed With a Tilt

NORFOLK, Va., Feb. 21.—One of the survivors of today's disaster said that the Roma often sailed with a slight tilt, and that he paid little attention to the initial lift of the tail of the ship until he heard a man yell that the craft refused to respond to the helm. Then came the crash.

WASHINGTON WAITS FOR A FULL REPORT

General Patrick Flies to Scene to Take Charge of Army Investigation.

AIR MEN NOT DISCOURAGED

Effect of the Disaster on the Future of Military Aviation Is Doubtful.

Special to The New York Times.

WASHINGTON, Feb. 21.—According to information reaching the War Department today from Langley Field, Virginia, the home station of the dirigible Roma, something went wrong with the box-kite elevating planes at the stern of the giant airship, which are used for vertical control, the pilots in charge were unable to keep the nose of the dirigible in the air and it plunged into a high-voltage electric cable, which ignited the hydrogen inside the great gas bag simultaneously with the collapse of the craft.

The capacity of the Roma is 1,100,000 cubic feet and the flames from the ignition of its great cargo of gas not only rendered it impossible for the officers and other passengers, pinned within the wreckage, to escape, but made it difficult to identify the bodies of those taken later from the wreckage.

The Roma left Langley Field base at 1:20 o'clock this afternoon for its initial test flight with newly installed Liberty motors. The big airship had manoeuvred over Hampton Roads and was approaching the Hampton Roads Naval Base, when something went wrong with the vertical steering planes. It was impossible, according to the stories of survivors, to keep the nose of the Roma in the air. The Roma, heading downward, its nose struck the charged land cable carrying 2,300 volts of electricity, the craft collapsed and was destroyed by the explosion and fire that followed.

The accident occurred at 2:19 o'clock. There were forty-five passengers on board, according to information given headquarters of the Army Air Service in Washington tonight by officers making verbal report by long distance telephone from headquarters at Langley Field. This preliminary oral report stated that there were eleven survivors, that thirty-four were missing—all regarded as having lost their lives—that the injured had been taken to the hospital of the Public Health Service, near Norfolk, and that all the bodies had not been recovered. This report stated that the only body recovered that had been identified up to 8 o'clock tonight was that of First Lieut. William E. Riley.

Continued on Page Two.

INJURED SURVIVORS TELL OF DISASTER

Officers Coolly Remained at Their Posts of Duty Until the Roma Struck.

EXPLOSION FOLLOWED FALL

Flames, Eating Fabric, Opened a Way for Some Imprisoned Men to Escape.

Special to The New York Times.

NORFOLK, Va., Feb. 21.—In the greatest disaster that ever befell American military aeronautics, thirty-four men died this afternoon when the army dirigible airship Roma plunged a thousand feet and crashed to earth in flames near the Hampton Roads army base. Only eleven of the forty-five men aboard with her were saved, and some of them were terribly hurt. Three were slightly injured.

The breaking of the rudder with its vertical controls, affixed in box-kite fashion to the stern, is believed to have been the original cause of the disaster. Its more horrible phase came just as the stricken craft plummeted into the earth. The metal-clad cases struck high-tension electric power wires, and with a flash and a roar the airship was fired from stem to stern.

Only those whose fortunate positions in the car enabled them to take the desperate hazard of a leap before the flames ran with lightning speed through the gas bag, more than two New York City blocks long, had much chance for their lives. The thirty-three who couldn't jump died. An officer broke his neck in a dive to earth and was dead before he could be got to a hospital.

Captain Dale Mabry, commandant of the Roma and principal pilot, died with his hands on the wheel. He stuck to his post to the last. The clothes were found burned from his body and the flesh from his fingers, but the fingers still grasped the wheel of the aircraft.

Many Officers Among Dead.

The crushed, misshapen mass that thudded onto the field was a funeral pyre of such intense heat that the agonies of those who were not killed in the crash must have been mercifully brief. The bodies were burned beyond recognition and the slow work of listing the aviators had carried in their pockets. That list when it was completed showed that two Majors, four Captains and seven lieutenants were among the dead. Horrified watchers, some of them veterans of gallant affairs abroad, rushed toward the blazing wreckage. Blistering heat halted them in their tracks. Some had associates among the ill-fated crew, others were actuated by all the traditional daring of the service—but those walls of heat were beyond human penetration. Not until three fire departments, mobilized at breakneck speed, had exhausted their chemicals and the twisted aluminum metal work was losing its red glow could any one approach. Then there remained only the gruesome job of extricating charred bodies.

The fire burned in the wreckage nearly five hours and it was not until 7 o'clock that it was entirely extinguished and the service men could penetrate far enough to take out all the bodies. The work of examining the débris was officially shortly after 9 o'clock tonight, with the total number of dead officially placed at thirty-four.

Things might have been different had the Roma's gas bag, with its cubical capacity of 1,100,000 feet, not been filled with hydrogen. Non-inflammable helium was the levitating gas used when the Roma, which was bought from the Italians, was planned to send the ship—the largest semi-rigid airship in the world—on a flying cruise over the country to demonstrate her fitness to cross the Atlantic. In her bag had been the whole available supply of helium in the United States. Flying officials wanted that for the Spring journey, so they pumped it into tanks and substituted hydrogen.

Trip to Test Liberty Motors.

The occasion for today's flight that was to prove so tremendous a blow to lighter-than-air flying was a desire to test the Liberty motors which had been installed to replace the Italian motors, which had proven poorly in the cold that marked the brief trial flight last December.

In charge of Captain Dale Mabry, with full complement of officers and men and a few civilian guests, the huge craft went aloft from Langley Field at 1:30 o'clock in the afternoon. It was just forty-nine minutes later that she lay in ruins, with most of those who had gone up in gay holiday mood dead in the wreckage.

The whole story was compressed into the last minute or so in that

HITS HIGH TENSION WIRES

Hydrogen Ignites in Norfolk Flight and Flames Sweep Huge Structure.

FEW SAVED BY LEAPING

One Lieutenant Breaks Neck In Jump—Other Victims Buried in Wreckage.

SAFE HELIUM GAS REMOVED

Rescuers Baffled by Intense Heat—Commander Mabry Stuck to Wheel Till Death Came.

THE DIRIGIBLE ROMA, 410 FEET LONG, BUILT BY ITALY FOR THE UNITED STATES, BURNED AT NORFOLK YESTERDAY.

STRIKERS SHOT DOWN IN PAWTUCKET RIOT

Police Fire on Mob Fighting to Bar Textile Workers From Mills.

ONE KILLED, SEVEN INJURED

Troops Rushed From Providence Now on Guard—Other Strike Centres Quiet.

PROVIDENCE, R. I., Feb. 21.—A fatal early-morning riot in Pawtucket, the establishment of National Guard units in three troublesome strike centres and a meeting of the State Board of Mediation and Conciliation here were the day's outstanding developments in the textile situation in Rhode Island.

The Pawtucket riot in which one strike sympathizer was killed, two critically wounded and five less seriously hurt by riot gun fire when a crowd came to grips with the police at the Jenckes Spinning Company plant, led to the immediate dispatch of four coast artillery companies to the Blackstone Valley city from Providence. The Woonsocket and East Greenwich companies went under mobilization orders tonight. Their ultimate destination is believed to be Pawtucket.

With the exception of the disturbance at Pawtucket, quiet prevailed throughout the Blackstone and Pawtuxet Valleys today. At Pontiac and Natick, where trouble was experienced yesterday, two troops of cavalry and a coast artillery company were in complete control.

When the troops arrived at Pawtucket they found only guard duty awaiting them, as the strike sympathizers quieted down immediately after their encounter with the police.

Tonight soldiers guarded the Jenckes mills, the plant of the J. & P. Coates company and the Tamanack mill as a precaution against possible disorders tomorrow. The mills expect to operate on the holiday.

The Board of Mediation and Conciliation, appointed to hear both sides of the strike controversy with a view to arriving at a settlement, declined to make public its progress today. A statement issued after the meeting said:

"In view of the occurrences today in the mill sections of Rhode Island, the board of mediation feels that it should

Continued on Page Two.

BOTH HOUSES PASS PORT PROJECT BILL

Democrats Fail in Effort to Have Hylan Appoint Two Commissioners.

MILLER WILL APPROVE

Senator Straus Breaks Away From Party, Calling Plan Essential to Cheap Food Supply.

Special to The New York Times.

ALBANY, Feb. 21.—Defeating all amendments offered by the opposition, the Senate and Assembly after long debate today, passed Governor Miller's Port Authority bill by very large majorities. The vote in the Senate was 37 to 11 and in the Assembly 97 to 47.

Only on Republican Senator, Smith of Richmond, voted against the bill. One Democratic Senator, Nathan Straus Jr. of New York, and four Democratic Assemblymen voted with the Republicans in support of the measure. The four Democratic Assemblymen were G. T. Cross of Sullivan, Samuel I. Rosenman of New York County, Wallace H. Sidney of Schoharie and Frank J. Taylor of Kings County.

Both in the Senate and Assembly an effort was made by the leaders of the Democratic minority, Senator Walker and Assemblyman Donohue, to have the bill providing for appointment by the Board of Estimate of two members out of the three on the Port Authority Commission from this State taken from the Finance Committee in the upper house and the Committee on Ways and Means in the lower house for debate and final disposition in the open. In both houses the motion was voted down, in the Senate by a vote of 34 to 14 and in the Assembly by a vote of 49 to 52.

In the upper house Senator Smith of Richmond offered a series of amendments substituting lines leading over Staten Island for the proposed Greenville-Bay Ridge tunnel, which under the Port Authority plan has provided for as the principal connecting link between the New Jersey terminals and the Long Island and side of the harbor. These were defeated also, by a vote of 34 to 14.

The bill now goes to Governor Miller.

Continued on Page Two.

"All the News That's Fit to Print."

The New York Times.

THE WEATHER
Rain today; Sunday fair; strong northwest winds.
Temperature yesterday—Max., 45; min., 36.
For weather report see next to last page.

VOL. LXXI....No. 23,422.   ***   NEW YORK, SATURDAY, MARCH 11, 1922.   TWO CENTS In Greater New York | THREE CENTS Within 200 Miles | FOUR CENTS Elsewhere

WILL DROP ELEVATED OR ACCEPT RECEIVER, INTERBORO DECIDES

New Contract Freeing Subway of $7,600,000 Annual Rent the Alternative.

OWNERS PLAN COURT FIGHT

Interborough Also Wants $30,000,000 for Third Tracks and the New Power Houses.

TO OPPOSE BETTER SERVICE

Ready to Quit if Transit Board Compels Improvements Which Eat Up Present Savings.

The Interborough Rapid Transit Company has refused to make any further payments due on its lease of the elevated lines owned by the Manhattan Railway Company. It has asked the latter company to make a new agreement which would shift from the Interborough payments of $7,600,000 a year, save it from the responsibility of the deficits on the elevated lines, and yield in return annual interest payments on betterments aggregating between $1,000,000 and $2,000,000 a year.

In this way the Interborough has answered the question, frequently asked, as to what adjustment could be made in the matter of the lease so far as it concerned the consolidation plan of the Transit Commission.

The Interborough is prepared to consent to the appointment of a receiver for its property if it fails to obtain relief from the payments to the Manhattan Company or if the Transit Commission insists upon enforcing expensive orders directing the company to increase its service to the point of absorbing the savings derived from the present restriction of service.

This new development has been known to the commission for some time and it was suggested that the knowledge was responsible for the amendment to the Public Service Commission law introduced in the Legislature at the instance of the commission. The amendment directly bearing on the situation provides that the present service of the elevated lines shall not be disturbed in any way, even if separated from the Interborough system.

Rental a Heavy Burden.

Under the terms of the lease between the two companies the Interborough is pledged to pay the Manhattan Company 7 per cent. on a valuation of $80,000,000 for the use of the elevated, it has further to meet all fixed charges and interest on bonds aggregating $2,400,000 a year. These payments, it has been asserted, are responsible for the financial condition of the Interborough and one of the principal reasons why the company has been compelled to pinch service on its subway system, pass interest payments on securities, and delay payments for necessary material.

The new agreement between the Interborough and Manhattan companies, suggested by the former, provides that the Manhattan Company shall pay the Interborough $20,000,000 for the third tracks and power houses built by the Interborough. The plan also requires the Manhattan Company to pay the interest due on this money, to adjust the payments of interest on bonds of the lines of Interest fixed when it was obtained; to relieve the Interborough from all payments of any kind named in the present lease, and to operate the lines independently of any relationship between the two companies save that ordered by State authorities.

Such a plan would leave the Interborough in possession of the new extensions, valued by the company at approximately $77,000,000. These extensions are considered of small moment in the transit system of the city, for the reason that they run in territory where the traffic is not heavy. They were built with an eye to future growth and in the hope that some day they would yield substantial profits.

All of Extensions Short.

One of these extensions is from 155th Street, the original terminal of the Ninth Avenue line, which is owned by the Manhattan Company, to Jerome Avenue, a distance of about three-quarters of a mile. It joins the Jerome Avenue line, which is part of the subway system. Another extension runs from the station of the Third Avenue line at Fordham Road near 190th Street to Gun Hill Road and thence to White Plains Road, about one mile and three-quarters. The third extension is from the Second Avenue line at Fifty-seventh Street across Queensboro Bridge to Queensboro Plaza, where it joins rapid transit lines to Astoria and Corona, about one mile and a quarter.

It is the opinion of the Interborough that these extensions can be operated without loss, because of the belief that the railroad law of the State would compel the Transit Commission to fix a fare to cover operating losses. The commission, under present management of the Public Service Commission could compel the company to operate these bits of road at a loss is considered unreasonable by the company's lawyers. The Interborough law, it was said, would compel the company to carry passengers free because they had paid a fare to the Manhattan Company, or compel the Manhattan Company to carry free passengers who had paid fares to the Interborough. There would have to be a fare for a ride on the lines of the two companies, it was explained, which would not be operated at a loss, and litigation

Continued on Page Fourteen.

University Course to Make Bellhops and Head Waiters

BOSTON, March 10.—Bellhops and head waiters de luxe are to be turned out by Boston University. Seventy-five men have signed for a six weeks course for college men who want to earn money during their vacation.

The course, which is to start at the university next week, will show the young men how to become any sort of hotel official. It will be given by the vocational department of the College of Business Administration.

RUM RUNNER KILLS BOOTLEGGER IN BOAT

Man Aboard the Imatra Opens Fire on Motor Craft After Dispute.

WOMAN LEADS GUN FIGHT

Wounds Detective in Fusillade Preceding Capture of $10,000 in Whisky.

An alleged bootlegger was killed in a motor boat off a Brooklyn pier last night in a controversy over several cases of liquor which one of the crew of the tramp steamer Imatra had bargained to sell to five young men who came alongside the vessel in a small power craft. A man charged with the shooting was arrested and was found in the motor boat were taken into custody. The other two are being searched for by the police.

The dead man was George Rauch, 26, of 154 South Fourth Street, Brooklyn, who was one of the five in the motor boat which was to transport the liquor, which had been smuggled into this country. Charged with shooting him, Albert Fosberg, 32, chief engineer of the steamer Imatra, was locked up at the Butler Street Police Station in Brooklyn.

The four men in the motor boat with Rauch, according to the police, were Samuel Kirnsky, 807 Mariner Street, Woodhaven, L. I.; Benjamin Raphael, 642 Henry Street, Manhattan, and his two brothers, Lester and Moe Raphael, 155 Henry Street, Manhattan.

Party Comes for Liquor.

According to the story told to the police by Benjamin Raphael and Kirnsky, the party first visited the steamer in the afternoon, making arrangements to purchase several cases of whisky, which were to be taken off last night. In accordance with this arrangement, the party drew alongside the steamer at 7 o'clock in the 30-foot motor boat Harding. The men first said they didn't get its whisky, but later admitted that they got two cases, for which they said they paid $180.

Fosberg, who is charged with homicide in connection with the death of Rauch, tells a different story. He said the men came aboard the steamer and took off two cases, promising to return to the ship and get additional cases and then pay for the whole. Instead of climbing back aboard the vessel, Fosberg said, the men started the boat's motor and drew away.

At sight of the men getting away with the whisky, Fosberg said, he ran back into his room and got a revolver. He said, according to the police, he fired only one shot at the motor boat. That shot took effect in Rauch's chest, causing his death, the police said.

The motor boat continued on to the foot of Montague Street, half a mile away, and the Poplar Street Police Station was notified. Rauch was taken off the boat a "I was late" pronounced dead by Dr. Thompson of the Long Island Hospital.

After leaving the dead man in charge of Benjamin Raphael and Kirnsky, the two other members of the party sped away in the boat. The police said the prisoners admitted later that the boat carried two cases of whisky, and to land at East Houston Street. The police in Manhattan were notified to look out for the boat.

Benjamin Raphael and Kirnsky are said to have told the police, after admitting that they had actually got whisky, that they paid the third mate, Brynolt Garje, $70, and the first mate, whose name they didn't know, $80.

Fifteen Shots Fired in Fight.

A pistol fight between alleged bootleggers and two detectives in which fifteen shots were fired and at least one person, a detective, was wounded, followed a raid yesterday afternoon on a house at the Chariton Street. The house is believed by the police to be the terminus of this city of a gang of rum smugglers operating by automobile between this

Continued on Page Three.

Plan to Cut Europe's Armies in Half Submitted to League by Commission

By EDWIN L. JAMES.
Copyright, 1922, by The New York Times Company.
By Wireless to The New York Times.

PARIS, March 10.—A temporary mixed commission of the League of Nations Assembly has transmitted to the Governments which are members of the League a draft plan for European armament limitation modeled on the Washington naval reduction treaty. The members have been asked to notify the commission how the allotments of troops compare with their ideas of their needs for national defense. Of course, the plan, which was drafted in accord with instructions of the last League Assembly, last September, is only in a formative state. The commission will meet once again on July 15 and continue work on a scheme to be presented to the third session of the League, which meets in Geneva in September.

The League commission's plan, which was presented at a recent meeting by Lord Esher, representing England, embraces all European countries except the Central Powers, whose armies are limited by the peace treaties, and Russia. The unit taken is 10,000 men. There would be the following allotment of units: Belgium, 2; Czechoslovakia, 3; Denmark, 2; France, 6; Great Britain, 3; Holland, 3; Norway, 2; Poland, 4;

Portugal, 1; Rumania, 3; Sweden, 2; Spain, 3; Switzerland, 2.

This would mean forty-six units, or a total of 1,380,000 soldiers for Europe, which would be a reduction of about 50 per cent. under the present armies.

General Argument also has under consideration another plan to apply the ratios of the Washington naval treaties to the armies of the league members not parties to the Washington agreement.

The weakest point of the League plan is the absence of Russia from the plan. Russia not being a member of the League, the commission naturally could not lay down the idea of her army. It is the intention of the League members to try to get Russia into limitation negotiations and some statesmen hope to raise the matter at Genoa.

As the plan stands it will meet the opposition of France. France's probable reply to it will be a demand that the League be given some sort of Federal force to make it to insure observance of the terms of any such limitation agreement. The plan was tentatively adopted at the conclusion of two weeks ago but was kept secret at the time.

Aguinaldo Coming Here.

Filipino General Accepts Invitation of Spanish War Veterans

MANILA, P. I., March 10.—General Emilio Aguinaldo has accepted an invitation to be the guest of the Spanish American War veterans at their annual convention in Los Angeles next Summer. It will be his first visit to the United States.

General Aguinaldo will be the honorary chairman of the Filipino mission, which is expected to sail for the United States late in April to lay before President Harding claims of the Filipinos for independence.

FORD'S 'FREEZE-OUT' OF RAIL PARTNERS BLOCKED BY I. C. C.

Small Stockholders of D., T. & I. Defeat Alleged Scheme to Get Rid of Them.

PREVENT LEASE OF ROAD

Commission Sustains Their Contention That It Is Against Public Interest.

WILL KEEP THEIR SHARES

Proposed Lessee Was a Company Owned Entirely by Members of the Ford Family.

Henry Ford, who urged the railroads of the country to "get rid of the unproductive stockholders," has been blocked by the Interstate Commerce Commission in an alleged attempt to "get rid of" the minority stockholders in the Detroit, Toledo & Ironton Railroad Company, Mr. Ford's interesting railroad adventure.

Notice of the decision against Henry Ford was received yesterday in a registered letter from the Interstate Commerce Commission at Washington by Alexander L. Strouse, of Frank, Weil & Strouse, 187 Madison Avenue, counsel for some of the small stockholders.

Leon Tanenbaum and Benjamin M. Strauss of this city and several others, who charged that Mr. Ford was trying to "freeze them out," remain as active associates, though on a small scale, in the automobile manufacturer's railroad enterprise. These men have refused offers of several times the market value of the stock and have represented themselves as determined to remain business colleagues of Mr. Ford, in spite of his newspaper campaign against Jews. The holdings of the minority interests are less than 2 per cent. of the total.

Stockholders' Contention.

The minority stockholders in their proceedings before the Interstate Commerce Commission alleged that Ford had tried to destroy their rights in the D., T. & I. by leasing the property to a company owned exclusively by the Ford family. They opposed the lease as being against public interest and being purely a device to deprive the small stockholders of any influence or share of profit in the enterprise. The decision of the Interstate Commerce Commission upholding the minority stockholders against Ford and denying permission to make the lease was rendered on Tuesday of last week.

"The proceedings had created widespread interest, especially among small holders of stock in different railroads, because of Ford's denunciation of what he called 'unproductive stockholders.' He had asserted in interviews that the future of the railroads was imperilled by the necessity of paying large dividends to them. Dividends, according to the 'productive stockholders,' who were defined by him as employees of the road, persons active in the management and others who continued to contribute actively to its success.

"The lease transferring everything of value from the old company to the new would have left the minority stockholders, according to their contention, holding a 2 per cent. interest in the hollow shell of the old company and an interest at all in the new. They alleged that they were victims of a plan by Ford to translate his railroad theories into practice.

Mr. Ford's Statements.

During the course of the litigation, interviews and statements by Ford, telling what he would do if the Pennsylvania or New York Central were turned over to him, were held to have an interesting bearing on the legal merits of the case, as showing what was going on in Mr. Ford's mind at the time he sought to engineer the alleged "freeze-out" lease. Mr. Strouse made application for permission to cross-examine Ford.

One of the statements of Mr. Ford, ridiculing arguments as to the necessity of protecting the rights of widows and orphans by safeguarding stock from railroad manipulation, was printed by Henry Ford in his weekly. Commerce as an authorized interview. In it Mr. Ford urged the policy of "getting

To Draw a Panel of 300.

Their program contemplates the drawing of a panel of 300 citizens. Nominations are to be submitted by the organizations on the joint committee representing the theatrical organizations on the one side, and the Better Public Shows Movement and the City Administration on the other. Each group will be permitted to nominate 150 candidates for the panel, the qualifications for which will be chiefly good citizenship and common sense," according to Mr. Pollock.

"If a complaint against a given theatrical production is received by the city officials," said Mr. Pollock, "they may call for a jury of twelve to be selected from the panel above described, as representing the theatre on the one side and the public on the other. Each will have one week in which to make the change. Then the jury will review the case, in which case, that case officials. First, they must decide whether any part of the production is objectionable from the point of view of public morals. Second, the play as a whole objectionable." A vote of 9 to 3 constitutes a verdict. If the jury decides that a manager must readjust his play, he will have one week in which to make the change. Then the jury will review the play. If the jury decides that the play shall be taken off and that there shall be no appeal to the courts. This agreement is to be included in every contract made by the theatre with both dramatists and actors.

"We agree with the public," said Mr. Pollock. "The theatre must be a decent one."

Germans to Clear Buildings Of All Monarchical Insignia

BERLIN, March 10 (Associated Press).—All insignia of monarchical Germany must be removed from public buildings, Minister of the Interior Adolf Koester today told the Reichstag. He added that the Government had decided to fix a definite period within which this decision would be carried out.

Exceptions will be made, he said, only where these emblems have been structurally incorporated in buildings where their removal would destroy the architectural value and effect.

All paintings, busts and statues in Government offices must also be removed if their retention is incompatible with the Republican régime. This order will chiefly apply to portraits of former Emperor William, although Herr Koester said exceptions might be made if their removal destroyed the "artistic and historical unity" of the interior decorations.

JURIES OF CITIZENS TO BAR BAD PLAYS

Conference of Actors, Dramatists, Managers and Vice Crusaders Fixes Details.

TO AVOID POLITICAL CENSOR

Theatrical Contracts to Stipulate That They Must Obey Jury's Findings.

The organization of a voluntary jury system, designed to eliminate indecent plays and thereby make unnecessary a political censorship of the stage, was launched late yesterday afternoon at a meeting of dramatists, managers and producers, actors and vice crusaders at the American Dramatists' Society, 148 West Forty-fifth Street.

An important feature of the proposed jury system is the insertion of a clause in all future contracts between dramatists and producers and between actors and producers that they will abide by the decisions of the jury.

Those attending the meeting were informed that Mayor Hylan's approval of the undertaking had been given in an informal manner. Early next week a committee will endeavor to see the Mayor and obtain his formal approval.

Many Interests Represented.

The details of the jury system were worked out at a meeting representing the Authors League of America, through Jesse Lynch Williams, President; Channing Pollock, Vice President, and Le Roy, Scott, Chairman of the Executive Committee; its subsidiary, the American Dramatists, represented by Owen Davis, Eugene Buck and George Creel; the Actors' Equity Association, represented by John Emerson, President; Frank Gillmore, Executive Secretary, and John W. Cope of the Equity's council; the Producing Managers' Association, represented by William A. Brady; Charles Coburn and Winthrop Ames; the Better Public Shows Movement, represented by John S. Sumner, head of the Society for the Prevention of Commercialized Vice; Edward J. McGuire and A. G. Boyle of the Y. M. C. A.; Mrs. Herbert J. Glover of the Welfare Board of the Protestant Episcopal Church; Mrs. Marian Tucker and Cranston Brereton and Mrs. Coffin of the Drama League.

"These people believe that a political censorship is impossible without destroying all that is finest in what affects," explained Channing Pollock, spokesman for a committee delegated to give out the facts concerning the meeting after its adjournment. "They believe that the theatre is not in a bad way. However, they agree that there are four or five bad plays and that there is a tendency to produce other plays without which the theatre would be better off."

SENATOR STANFIELD, THE 'WOOL KING,' ACCUSED OF FRAUD.

Idaho National Bank Charges That He Formed a Company to Defraud His Creditors.

HURT BY DROP IN SHEEP

Had Just Bought 400,000—Attempt to Set Aside His Transfer of Real Estate.

THREATENS LIBEL ACTIONS

But Idaho Commissioner Defies Him and Asks Why He Doesn't Pay Farmers What He Owes.

Special to The New York Times.

PORTLAND, Ore., March 10.—Robert Nelson Stanfield, the "wool king" and United States Senator from Oregon, elected in 1920 over former Senator Chamberlain, is in difficulties and is rushing home from Washington to save what he can out of property imperiled by the drop in the prices of wool and sheep.

Prayer that a deed of conveyance of real estate made by Stanfield through the R. N. Stanfield Company be set aside is made in an action filed in the Circuit Court today by the First National Bank of Weiser, Idaho, against Stanfield, the R. N. Stanfield Company and the Columbia Basin Wool Warehouse Company.

Claims for about $75,000 against Stanfield on notes for money loaned him during the last year or two are advanced.

"I am prepared to make sensational disclosures if this matter is pushed. I made the reports with regard to the financial condition of the R. N. Stanfield Company," he said, "designed to hinder, delay and defraud his creditors." When the deed of conveyance was made out, the complaint sets forth, the Wool Warehouse Company assumed the obligation of payment for a mortgage of $200,000. The complaint asks that the value of the warehouse lien on the real estate be adjudicated and that the plaintiff's rights be determined.

The complaint states that several large judgments against the defendant have been secured in various courts of Oregon and in Boise, Idaho.

Miles Cannon, Commissioner of Agriculture, announced today that he would welcome suit against him for criminal libel, threatened by Senator Stanfield. The Capital News this week printed a special dispatch from Washington to the effect that Senator Stanfield had instructed several sheep companies in Idaho and Oregon to start libel suits against Commissioner Cannon because of a published statement by Commissioner Cannon that Stanfield had failed to pay for hay and feed furnished in the Spring of 1921 and that many claims have been filed with the department.

Senator Stanfield also advised the managers of his companies to consult attorneys concerning possible action against Cannon on the ground of criminal libel, the dispatch said. When this dispatch was called to the attention of Commissioner Cannon he said:

"The Department of Justice is about to investigate all cases reported to it where a producer of agricultural or products or live stocks have suffered loss in the marketing of his products or has failed to receive a fair and just reasonable compensation by reason of fraud, injustice, extortion, manipulation or profiteering on the part of others.

On Feb. 11 Commissioner Cannon telegraphed to Senator Stanfield at Washington as follows:

"Please write me immediately whether there are any legal or moral reasons why your sheep companies operating in the State of Idaho should not pay farmers for hay sold and delivered in the Spring of 1921. Quick answer required."

It is known that Mr. Stanfield's losses of wool and sheep have been enormous. In many cases sheep were bought at $14 and when the bottom dropped out of the market, during the final days, in the morgue in which undesirable measures are consigned if they have not already been left there.

It will probably be necessary when the bills finally are reported by the Senate Cities Committee that Senator Lockwood to ask that they be immediately advanced to final reading when they can be read and acted on. One auditary objection will prevent this, for bills can be advanced in this fashion only by unanimous consent.

The petition sent to Chairman Gibbs of the Cities Committee read as follows:

"We, the undersigned members of the Cities Committee, respectfully request that you report promptly for the consideration of the Senate, the bills introduced by the Joint Legislative Committee on Housing."

"Very truly yours,
  "CHARLES C. LOCKWOOD, of Portland, Ore., was born at Umatilla County, Ore., July 9, 1877; educated in the public schools and State normal schools of Oregon; engaged in the live stock industry, handling America's largest product of wool and mutton; also engaged in banking, particularly in the financing of livestock producers; elected three terms in the Oregon State Legislature; one term as Speaker of the House of Representatives; married Miss Barbara Stanfield, who is now 17 years of age; nominated as Republican candidate for the United States Senate over the present incumbent, Senator Gibbs and United States Senator Nov. 7, 1920, receiving an 10,500 votes."

"The five did not constitute a quorum, so we had no right to take action on the

Continued on Page Three.

GANDHI ARRESTED ON CHARGE OF SEDITION; LONDON REPORTS INDIA QUIET THUS FAR; LORD DERBY TO TAKE MONTAGU'S PLACE

Martial Law After Day of Terror in the Rand; Strikers Kill a Manager and Ten of Police

JOHANNESBURG, Union of South Africa, March 10 (Associated Press).— Bold moves by the striking miners, accompanied by fierce fighting between strikers, commandos and police, made the day one of terror in the Rand. Martial law eventually was proclaimed.

Manager Brodigan of the Brakpan mine, the centre of much of the day's fighting, and two special constables were captured and taken out on the veldt and shot. Seven special constables protecting the mine were killed. The strikers also captured twenty-seven policemen at Newlands, west of Johannesburg, where spirited fighting occurred, according to this account.

At Fordsburg one man of a commando, or force of burghers, was killed and thirteen members of the commando and four policemen were wounded. The sound of artillery firing at Fordsburg was audible here.

With the proclamation of martial law, and the seizure of the Rand's headquarters, where all documents were confiscated, the populace felt a sense of relief. The Ministers of Justice and Defense have issued a statement denying reports of a contemplated native rising in the Rand. They assert there is no disposition on the part of the

natives to give trouble. Meanwhile military units are enrolling with remarkable speed and a citizens' protection league is being formed to run public services.

Firing started at Benoni early this morning. Street fighting followed, both sides suffering casualties. Many pedestrians were hit. For two hours the ground between the market square and the workers' hall was a battle area. Then the police formed with the object of surrounding the hall. There was continuous sniping and three persons fell dead, one of them a policeman.

ARREST IS MADE QUIETLY

Leader Taken Into Custody on Order of Government at Delhi.

NEW PLOTS WERE REVEALED

British Opinion Strongly Urged Seizure of Gandhi, First Ordered Last Month.

LORD DERBY TO TAKE OFFICE

Montagu Speaks Today at Cambridge—Resignation of Viceroy Regarded as Inevitable.

BOMBAY, March 10 (Associated Press).—India's non-co-operationist leader, Mohandas K. Gandhi, has been arrested at Ahmedabad, 310 miles north of Bombay. He is charged with sedition.

Copyright, 1922, by The New York Times Company.
Special Cable to The New York Times.

LONDON, March 10.—The announcement by the India Office late tonight that a telegram had been received stating that Gandhi had been arrested and adding there had been no trouble so far follows upon Delhi reports that the Indian Government had decided upon his arrest for today.

London newspapers have been urging that this step should be taken for weeks, and Montagu's statement in the Commons on Feb. 14 that the order for Gandhi's arrest actually had been issued the week before and then cancelled led to charges, as one paper puts it this morning, of "vacillation, hesitation and lack of consistent steadiness" against the Indian and Home Governments.

Montagu on Feb. 14 told the House of Commons that the Government of India had been informed that it in their judgment Gandhi's arrest became necessary they would receive the wholehearted support of the Imperial Government.

"Last week the official order for his arrest was actually issued," he said, "but since then there has been a dramatic change in the situation, Gandhi and his colleagues having decided not to pursue the policy of civil disobedience, volunteer processions or other illegal activities."

In view of this development the Government of India was holding its hand.

Publication of the Indian Government's demands and the resignation of the Ministry have been followed by further sensational disclosures of widespread activities of Indian seditionists and in view of insistent demands of English newspapers it was felt the Indian Government could not longer delay action against Gandhi.

Copyright, 1922, by The New York Times Company.
Special Cable to The New York Times.

LONDON, March 11.—Several political correspondents this morning mention the prediction made in some quarters yesterday that Lord Reading's resignation would shortly be announced.

In that case the Duke of Devonshire is said to be the likely successor.

BIG HOUSING BILL NOW SURE TO PASS

Machold Announces Support of Metropolitan $100,000,000 Building Fund Measure.

LOCKWOOD IS ACCUSED

Absence From Hearing Said to Have Endangered Other Bills—He Denies It.

Special to The New York Times.

ALBANY, March 10.—As the result of developments at the Capitol today the passage in both branches of the Legislature of the Lockwood committee's bill which would enable the Metropolitan Life Insurance Company to devote $100,000,000 of its investable funds to housing relief in New York City seems assured.

The prospect is also that both Senate and Assembly will act favorably on five other measures already on the calendar of the Senate which are intended for the relief and rent and housing.

The financial part of the Lockwood committee's program, however, has been placed in jeopardy through the conduct of Senator Lockwood himself, which has greatly puzzled his colleagues in the Senate. After serving notice that he would move to discharge the Cities Committee from further consideration of those of his committee's bills not already reported, and after filing with Senator Gibbs, Chairman of the Cities Committee, a petition in which seven other members of that committee joined him, demanding that the bills be reported promptly, Senator Lockwood departed for New York City and was not in attendance when the committee met to take action on his bills.

Under the circumstances no action could be taken. At an earlier stage of the session the loss of time would not necessarily prove fatal. But final adjournment is only a week away and little time is available for consideration of those of his committee's bills not already reported.

OUR RHINE CLAIM IS NOT ALLOWED

Finance Ministers Continue the Division of German Payments Among Allied Powers.

BOYDEN ASKS $241,000,000

Question Will Go to Governments Upon Whom Washington Is in a Position to Use Pressure.

By EDWIN L. JAMES.
Copyright, 1922, by The New York Times Company.
Special Cable to The New York Times.

PARIS, March 10.—The Washington Government today asked the Finance Ministers of the allied nations engaged in a conference here for dividing up German payments to the Reparation Commission for a settlement of the claim of $241,000,000 of the American Government for the cost of the American Army of Occupation. The allied Ministers did not comply, but by subsequent action presented a direct refusal to grant the American demand.

The American communication was in the form of a statement by Roland W. Boyden, American member of the Reparation Commission, who is sitting in the allied Finance Ministers' meeting. Although the official communiqué makes no mention of the matter, it is understood ".r. Boyden recalled that America's treaty rights reserved for America the benefits she would enjoy under the Versailles Treaty; that the Versailles Treaty provided that costs of the armies of occupation was a first charge on German payments of prior validity to general reparations; that the Allies having practically paid themselves for their occupation costs, the $241,000,000 due America should be paid before any allotment was made for general reparations.

To grant the American demand the allied Ministers, after having advised sums to meet the French, English and Belgian army occupation costs, would have to assign funds to meet the American claim. What the Finance Ministers did was to complete the division of the 1921 payment and then provide for the allocation of the 1922 payments by Germany, which action included allocation of funds to meet the claims of France and Great Britain for the expense of occupation between now and the next payments is due. No provision was made for meeting the American demand, nor will any be made before the end of the Ministers' conference tomorrow, it was stated tonight officially.

Say We Should Collect Our Own.

The attitude of the Finance Ministers is in accord with that of their Governments, which is that America, having a separate treaty with Germany, should collect direct from Germany. It is always possible the allied Governments may find delicate reasons for changing this attitude, but as the matter stands at present the Allies do not feel that they should collect for America.

The American action is important because for the first time it raises the issue of the validity of the Berlin treaty; that is, it raises the question whether it is a first mortgage, ranking with the Versailles treaty, or a second mortgage ranking after it. It is true the Berlin treaty, in its text, reserves for America under the Versailles treaty. But that reserving is done by America and Germany, without the consent of the Allies, who under the Versailles treaty, according to the European interpretation, already held a first mortgage on all German resources.

It was the expectation of the allied nations that following the signing of the Berlin treaty Washington would negotiate with them to substitute recognition of America's rights. This was pointed out in the Paris dispatches of The New York Times last September, which dispatches brought forth a statement from Washington that no such negotiations were contemplated. Because the allied nations owe America immense sums of money and America can bring pressure

Continued on Page Two.

"All the News That's Fit to Print."

The New York Times.

THE WEATHER
Fair and cold today and Sunday;
northwest winds.
Temperature yesterday—Max., 35; min., 12.
For weather report see last to last page.

VOL. LXXII....No. 23,765. ••• NEW YORK, SATURDAY, FEBRUARY 17, 1923. TWO CENTS In Greater New York | THREE CENTS Within 500 Miles | FOUR CENTS Elsewhere

ESSEN IS COWED AFTER WOUNDING OF TWO SOLDIERS

Fight in Beer Hall Causes the French to Turn Out a Stronger Military Display.

CITY NOW WITHOUT POLICE

Chief Arrested, Men Disarmed and Records Seized — Frequent Clashes Elsewhere.

JAIL FOR 2 BURGOMASTERS

Electric Plant Director Is Fined 5,000,000 Marks—Berlin Supplies Funds for Strikers.

Copyright, 1923, by The New York Times Company.
Special Cable to THE NEW YORK TIMES.

DUESSELDORF, Feb. 16.—Every day is adding more and more to the casualty list of the Ruhr occupation.

Last evening in a beer hall at Essen two French soldiers were slightly, and the German policeman gravely, wounded.

At Gunkenrath a French sentinel fired on and killed a German workman who was trespassing on the railroad track.

At several points last evening sentries and posts fired shots as warnings and with every rifle discharged the tension is growing.

The affair at Essen was the most important as affecting the situation in the town. It began, as trouble may at any time begin, trivially enough. Eight French soldiers and two Belgians went into the beer house and called for drinks about 9:30 in the evening. As usual the landlord refused to serve them and the soldiers, as has become their habit, began to draw beer themselves. In protest the landlord called in the German policeman on duty at the door and, according to all accounts of both the Germans and the French, this policeman entered excitedly with his revolver in his hand crying "Hands up!"

At once the affair which had been a burlesque became serious. The French soldiers instead of obeying such a peremptory order began to draw their revolvers. Then the German fired. Before he could be overpowered he had wounded two men slightly and it was not till he fell with a bullet through his body that he stopped firing.

Attracted by the noise the German police patrol entered at that moment and prevented further fighting.

Police Headquarters Raided.

Today the affair had an aftermath. With armored cars and machine guns a detachment of French troops rode through the town and wheeled sharply into the police barracks before it was well known what was intended. They arrested the chief of police, disarmed every man in the station and took possession of all records.

Everywhere throughout town patrols have been moving about all day, and as if in warning to the nationalist trouble makers, the French are displaying their strength.

Yesterday the town was silent, depressed and suspicious. Today it is cowed. The French have the whip hand and even the most ardent nationalist sees the utter futility of further fighting.

All through the province the measures of the French for repressing organized resistance and propaganda are increasing in severity. Once half the newspapers in the Ruhr have now been suspended—for one cause or another, police took no minute, being arrested in batches, and with every new batch the penalty is being increased.

To aid this tightening up the Germans are making as yet no new move. The telephones of Düsseldorf, Essen and several other places are still suspended.

At Bochum the municipal employes today struck for four hours as a protest against the arrests which have been made in the town and against the requisitioning of automobiles. The only return to work was at Duisburg, where the tramway employes have been granted a 110 per cent. increase in wages at a time when the mark is nearly double.

Yesterday for the first time the effect of the export prohibition order became apparent. As fewer freight trains are leaving the district fewer are coming in, and from 700 the number of coal and ore cars fell to about 40. If that falling off continues a food shortage, which always threatened, may become a reality, and both the French and Germans are doing their utmost to deal with the situation when it arises, each with the hope that their efforts will rally the masses to their support. The German organizing storage and distribution centres as if to urge, and at the same time the French are accumulating all the food they can in the district. The number of military trains has been largely increased and food is being brought from France for in excess of what is needed by the troops.

To counter all this effort to obtain and maintain supplies the workers themselves have now nearly completed their arrangements for payment of workers forced out of employment by the prohibition of exports. The plan proposed is twofold to stand a loss but to small firms the Government, through the Employers' Association and the Reichsbank, is prepared to give aid the hole call is needed. The total wages bill which it is estimated will have to be met is something like 30,000,000 gold marks a month, and the Government, which is prepared to pay any sum to workers in order to support resistance to the French. So far there have, however, been little or no closing down, and except at the coalpits where little or nothing is being done except for repairs and local consumption work, the Ruhr seems almost normal.

Quick Retaliation by French.

ESSEN, Feb. 16 (Associated Press)—Following the wounding of two French soldiers by German security police in a café brawl last night, Essen was the

Continued on Page Three.

BILLIE BURKE in Booth Tarkington's sparkling comedy, "Rose Briar." Empire Theatre. Popular Price Mat.—Advt.

---

89 M. P.'s Ask Harding's Aid; 'One Hope of Saving Europe'

Copyright, 1923, by The New York Times Co.
By Wireless to The New York Times.

LONDON, Feb. 16.—Signed by eighty-nine Labor and Co-operative members of the British Parliament, the following cablegram was sent to President Harding today:

"America with Britain unwittingly made France's present destructive action possible. We appeal for American co-operation today as the one hope of saving Europe."

Among those who have signed the message are Arthur Henderson, George Lansbury, R. E. Buxton and John Hodge.

ANDERSON ENRICHED BY REALTY TRADING, IS STORY TO PECORA

Prosecutor Quotes Him as Saying $24,700 Came, in Currency, From Deals.

CONTRADICTS HIS AFFIDAVIT

Report to Anti-Saloon Directors in 1919 That Money Came From Loans Is Recalled.

GRAND JURY MOVE HINTED

Inquiry Will Be Pressed " In Some Other Way," Brackett Is Warned in Letter.

In a letter to ex-Senator Edgar T. Brackett, counsel for William H. Anderson, State Superintendent of the Anti-Saloon League, Acting District Attorney Ferdinand Pecora yesterday indicated that unless Mr. Anderson answered questions relating to the source and expenditure of the publicity fund of $24,700, he would take Grand Jury action. Mr. Pecora's letter was in reply to a reiteration by Mr. Brackett that Mr. Anderson should not submit replies to questions pertaining to the fund, details of which Mr. Anderson professes to have withheld from the Board of Directors of the League.

Intimating that he questioned the accuracy of statements made by Mr. Anderson, Mr. Pecora disclosed that Mr. Anderson had asserted he had obtained the money through realty investments negotiated by a friend at a time when he was earning $4,000 a year as an official of the League in Maryland. Mr. Pecora quoted Mr. Anderson as saying that the profits were in excess of $24,700, the sum which he alleged he had loaned the League here for its work when the necessary expenditures exceeded the income. Mr. Pecora pointed out that Mr. Anderson was unable to give the location of any of the realty and declined to divulge the name of his investor friend. Mr. Anderson told the Acting District Attorney that he had received the profits in currency, which he placed in his safe rather than in a bank, according to the letter to Senator Brackett.

Text of Pecora's Letter.

Mr. Pecora's letter follows:
Feb. 16, 1923.
Hon. Edgar T. Brackett, 120 Broadway, New York City.
Dear Senator Brackett:

Much as I regret your adherence to your advice to Mr. Anderson to refuse to answer certain questions which I have asked him as to the sources from which he obtained the sum of $24,700.00, which he claims to have expended on behalf of the Anti-Saloon League during the years 1913 and 1914, and details of such expenditure, I recognize fully your unquestioned right to advise him as his counsel in such manner as you may deem to be in accordance with his own interests.

You express the view that it would seem grotesque to base any prosecution of Mr. Anderson on the facts which have been shown. You also recognize that the ascertainment of the sources from which Mr. Anderson obtained the $24,700, and the methods by which he expended the same, properly come within the scope of the inquiry which this office is making in so far as light may be shed on the question as to whether the representations which Mr. Anderson made to the Directors of the league in connection therewith are true or false.

In connection with his expenditure of $24,000, Mr. Anderson has declared that the monies paid out by him to currency from time to time to certain persons whose identities he will not disclose; that these payments were made for publicity work on behalf of the league; that he has no vouchers or written records of any kind which would show the respective dates and specific amounts of such payments, and that he cannot from memory give a single copy or piece of printed matter that was used in such publicity work; that all of said monies came from his personal means which he did not keep in any bank or other such depositary, but which he kept in a safe in the office of his respective headquarters of the league in the State of Maryland and New York; and that he made such expenditures upon his own initiative and judgment and without the having consulted the Board of Directors of the league in New York with regard to them.

Tried to Trace Money.

In view of the unusual circumstances under which, according to his own statements, Mr. Anderson made

Continued on Page Six.

$500,000 GEM THEFT SUSPECT ARRESTED

"Marshall" Held as Leader of Gang That Robbed Mrs. Schoellkopf at Drinking Party.

CAUGHT ON MONTREAL TRAIN

Another Arrest Here Said to Have Furnished Clue—Companion Also in Custody.

Inspector John D. Coughlin at Police Headquarters last night announced that the detectives had arrested the debonair "Marshall," alleged leader of the gang that robbed Mrs. Irene Schoellkopf of $500,000 worth of jewelry in an apartment at 64 West Fifty-second street early on the morning of Jan. 1, had been arrested yesterday on a train between Schenectady and Troy. The arrest was made by Detective Daily, Horan and Buckley of Inspector Coughlin's staff. They caught "Marshall" when he was attempting to return from Montreal and took him to a house at 75 Lancaster Street, Albany, which he said was his home, to look for the stolen jewels. The detectives reported to inspector Coughlin by telephone from the Lancaster Street house that they had not found the booty.

The man alleged to be "Marshall" was traveling under the name of M. D. Riddiugh, according to Inspector Coughlin. His real name is Matthew Darius Biddiugh. The police say that he is an ex-convict, and that he is known to the police all over the country under the aliases of R. H. Matthews, R. H. Harrison and John F. Derby. According to the police, his photograph is No. 17,555 in the Rogues' Gallery at San Francisco, and he has been arrested many times, and convicted several times.

Inspector Coughlin said the man was wanted in Los Angeles and San Francisco on the charge of passing worthless checks.

Search of the records at Police Headquarters last night showed that "Marshall" had been arrested for passing a worthless check at the Yale Club in New York City in 1917, but had got off with a suspended sentence.

"Marshall," when arrested, said he was 75 years old and gave his occupation as traveling salesman and actor. Under the name of Biddiugh, Inspector Coughlin said, the man had had some success as a moving picture actor, appearing in Universal photoplays. By a coincidence, the last film in which he is known to have appeared was called "Wanted at Headquarters," in which he played a "heavy" part—in other words played a movie villain. This was in 1919.

Companion Also Arrested.

The detectives arrested with "Marshall," a man who identified himself as George F. Daley of 83 Clinton Street, Albany. As far as known, Daley had no connection with the Schoellkopf case, but the police are holding him to investigate why he was traveling with "Marshall." Daley had been in the vicinity of Broadway and 52d Street.

The arrest of "Marshall" and Daley followed a few hours after Horan, one of the detectives who made these arrests, had locked up a man named Charles Curtis in Sheriff Horan and his partner, Detective Owens, have been detached from all other duty to work exclusively on the Schoellkopf case for several weeks. In the line-up at Police Headquarters yesterday morning, Horan and Owens recognized Curtis, who had been arrested as a suspect in another case, as a man they had been looking for as a friend of one of "Marshall's" alleged confederates in the gem theft.

Curtis was released from the charge on which he was first held, but Horan immediately rearrested him on the charge of suspicion of burglary in another jewel theft—the robbery of Mrs. Lillian Myers of $50,000 worth of jewels in her apartment at 200 West Forty-ninth Street on July 21 last. Curtis is believed to have given the information on which Horan and the detective formation on which Horan and the detectives.

Continued on Page Two.

Idaho Assembly Bars Japanese From Leasing Any Land There

BOISE, Idaho, Feb. 16.—The Assembly of the Legislature, by a vote of 54 to 6, today passed a measure to prohibit the leasing of lands in the State to Japanese. The measure, according to its author, Representative Gillis, while aimed primarily at the Japanese, is applicable to all aliens.

Speaking to the Assembly, Representative Gillis said he feared an influx of Japanese and other aliens to Idaho through refusal of the Federal Government to re-lease land now occupied in Washington, and because of other States passing anti-leasing laws.

ENGINEER AMBUSHED AND SLAIN AT DOOR

Earl Remington of Los Angeles, Who Made Planes in War, Is Found Dead in Driveway.

WIFE ASLEEP IN THE HOUSE

Victim, Shot as He Stepped From Automobile, Met Death He Had Feared.

LOS ANGELES, Feb. 16.—Earl Remington, wealthy electrical engineer, found dead from gunshot wounds in the yard of his home here early today, had lived in fear of death for the last week, according to his wife, who was so prostrated with grief that she could not be seen until late today.

Two persons took active parts in the slaying of Remington, according to police conclusions announced late tonight. Mrs. Remington said her husband had been acting strangely and showed extreme nervousness. Noises outside the house, particularly at night, seemed to distress him, she said. Remington had offered their home, which is in an exclusive residential district, for sale, the while drawn when the Republicans had never to permit any stranger to enter the house.

Although Remington interpreted in his wife yesterday that he was going to their ranch near Chino and would not return until late, it has been established, according to the police, that he did not go to the ranch.

Detectives are attempting to trace his movements yesterday in the hope of finding some clue to the slaying. They stated they had found two friends of the dead man who said they saw him at 5 o'clock yesterday afternoon.

That Remington was slain by some one having a grudge against him is the opinion expressed by the detectives.

Whether an attempted burglary of the office of the safe company of which Remington was the head, on Oct. 15, 1922, had anything to do with the engineer's death also is being investigated. Two of the company's safes were broken into, according to a report, but nothing of value was taken. The police are working on the theory that papers may have been taken at that time which were used later in a blackmailing plot against Remington.

Remington evidently was murdered at about last midnight. A dozen neighbors heard the fatal shot, and his wife lay sleeping within a few feet of him; but the body was not found until 6 o'clock this morning, when Charity Dawson, a negro maid, started downstairs to light the gas heating plant of the house at 1,409 South St. Andrews Street, a fashionable neighborhood.

There was a trail of blood on the driveway and a riddled leather portfolio which Remington had carried. The maid called Mrs. Remington, and the whole neighborhood was soon aroused by their screams.

Remington left his offices early in the afternoon for a trip to his Chino ranch. He was not seen thereafter by either employee or family until his body was found. He rang up his wife at 3:30 P. M. and told her he was going to Chino, according to the maid.

Remington, the police believe, drew up in his Ford coupé at the order of his house, perhaps at the order of his assailant. He stepped around to the back of the car, shifting the leather portfolio now high, now low, in front of his body in an effort to shield himself.

There was a loud report, perhaps two. One charge from the shotgun tore its way to the engineer's heart. As he staggered away from the machine he fell on his back, arms spread out.

Mrs. Remington, according to the maid, did not hear the report of the gun. As her husband lay dying she was about to step into a bedroom in the north-east corner of the house, directly above the driveway. From her window she could have seen her husband dying as he struggled.

Neighbors playing cards heard the shots but thought they were automobile engines backfiring, or tires exploding. If the Remington dog had not been chloroformed for rabies about two weeks ago, the engineer might still be alive, according to the maid. She believes the dog might have awakened the family. Remington had no children.

"The motive may have been robbery; it may have been revenge," said Detective Sergeant Cline after talking with Mrs. Remington.

Remington was Vice President of the International Electric Protective Association, and had a wide reputation as a safe and bank designer.

Aviation was his profession and he was adept at stunt flying. During the war he organized and was general manager of an aviation company here.

SENATE APPROVES BRITISH DEBT BILL; FINAL VOTE, 70-13

46 Republicans, 24 Democrats Favor It—Borah Among the Four Republicans Opposed.

BITTER DEBATE TO FINISH

Many Assail "British Victory," but Glass Wins Applause by Recalling Allies' Sacrifices.

ONLY ONE AMENDMENT

Settlements With Other Allies Must Have Congress Approval—Bill Now Goes to Conference.

Special to The New York Times.

WASHINGTON, Feb. 16.—The Senate passed the British Debt Refunding bill tonight by a vote of 70 to 13, forty-six Republicans and twenty-four Democrats voting to ratify the settlement as agreed to by the Debt Funding Commission, while nine Democrats and four Republicans were recorded in favor of repudiating the settlement.

The final roll-call vote was ordered at 7:29 o'clock tonight. The Administration victory was much more impressive than had been anticipated. It having been predicted that between fifteen and twenty Senators would oppose the bill when the vote on passage was reached.

The measure passed with only one amendment—that proposed by Senator Robinson of Arkansas, which gives to Congress the right to pass on settlements that may be arrived at in the future with other allied nations. An amendment to equalize the interest rates and require Great Britain to pay the same interest as the United States itself pays on the loan was defeated, 41 to 21.

It is expected that the House will promptly accept the Robinson amendment and that the bill will be in the hands of the President early next week.

All efforts to amend the bill with the purpose of reducing interest rates or in other important particulars were signally defeated. An amendment proposed by Senator Harris of Georgia, which authorizes the appointment of three Democrats on the Funding Commission, would undoubtedly have carried, but was withdrawn when the Republicans promised to give this matter early consideration when it is presented to the Senate in the form of an independent bill. The Republicans appear as anxious as some of the Democrats to have the minority share the responsibility of adjusting the more than $11,000,000,000 debt now due this country by its former associates in the European war.

Sharp Debate Continued All Day.

Eight lively hours preceded the passage of the bill. At times the debate was spirited to the point of bitterness, but the clean-cut Administration victory was never in doubt. The defeat of the Hitchcock amendment to maintain the high tax rates paid by this Government and a speech by Senator Glass of Virginia broke the back of the opposition. The impassioned plea of the Virginia Senator for favorable action and his fervid defense of Great Britain came near the close of the long day. When Senator Glass concluded it appeared for a minute or two as if the session might have to suspend while Senators, Republicans as well as Democrats, pressed forward to shake his hand and congratulate him.

The leaders of the opposition were La Follette, Reed of Missouri, McKellar, Heflin, Trammell and Norris, while Smoot, Lenroot, Glass and Underwood commanded the defending forces. La Follette made the longest of all the speeches, a carefully prepared utterance in which he denounced Secretary Mellon, ridiculed the President and assailed the majority membership of the Finance Committee for what he charged was the work of an unwarranted haste in rushing the bill to a final vote.

The last day arguments of the opposition were based principally on the claim that the United States, in agreeing to fix the interest Great Britain will pay at 3 per cent. for the first ten and 3½ per cent. for the remaining fifty-two years, had, in fact, cancelled what they claimed was approximately $500,000,000 of the interest charges.

Opening the debate, Senator La Follette recalled the White House dinner of a year ago, which was attended, among others, by J. Pierpont Morgan, Charles H. Sabin and Secretary Mellon, all of them, declared the Wisconsin Senator, of the international banking group.

Continued on Page Five.

TUT-ANKH-AMEN'S INNER TOMB IS OPENED, REVEALING UNDREAMED OF SPLENDORS, STILL UNTOUCHED AFTER 3,400 YEARS

KING TUT-ANKH-AMEN,
wearing the crown and royal vestments, as he appeared to his contemporaries. From a multi-colored decoration on the walls of the tomb of Huy, his Viceroy, discovered some years ago near the tomb of the King.
Courtesy Metropolitan Museum of Art.

KING IN NEST OF SHRINES

Series of Ornate Covers Enclose Pharaoh's Sarcophagus.

WHOLE FILLS LARGE ROOM

Mortuary Chamber Opens Into Another Room, Crowded With Great Treasure.

EXPLORERS ARE DAZZLED

Wealth of Objects of Historic and Artistic Interest Exceeds All Their Wildest Visions.

The Times (London) World Copyright, by Arrangement with the Earl of Carnarvon.
Copyright, 1923, by The New York Times Company.
Special Cable to THE NEW YORK TIMES.

LUXOR, Egypt, Feb. 16.—This has been, perhaps, the most extraordinary day in the whole history of Egyptian excavation. Whatever any one may have guessed or imagined of the secret of Tut-ankh-Amen's tomb, they surely cannot have dreamed the truth as now revealed.

The entrance today was made into the sealed chamber of the tomb of Tut-ankh-Amen, and yet another door opened beyond that. No eye have yet seen the King, but to practical certainty we know that he lies there close at hand in all his original state, undisturbed.

Moreover, in addition to the great treasure which the tomb has already yielded, today has brought to light a new wealth of objects of artistic, historical, and even intrinsic value which is bewildering.

It is such a hoard as the sanguine excavator can hardly have pictured, even in visions in his sleep, even as Lord Carnarvon and Mr. Carter's discovery in a class by itself and above all previous finds.

Official Opening Sunday.

Though the official opening of the sealed mortuary chamber of the tomb has been fixed for Sunday, it was obviously impossible to postpone until then the actual work of breaking in the entrance. This was a job involving some hours of work, because it had to be done with the greatest care, so as to keep intact as many of the seals as possible, and also to avoid injury to any of the objects on the other side which might be caused by the falling of material dislodged.

All this could not be done on Sunday while the official guests were kept waiting in the singularly expectant atmosphere of the tomb, so an agreement was made with the Egyptian authorities by which the actual breaking through of the wall should be done in their presence today.

Consequently, Howard Carter was very busy inside the tomb all morning with Professor Breasted and Dr. Alan Gardiner, whose assistance has been invaluable from the beginning of the work of examining and deciphering and copying inscriptions of all kinds. They had finished by noon, and the tomb was closed till after luncheon, at which Lord Carnarvon, Mr. Carter and Lady Evelyn Herbert entertained all those invited to be present today.

Official Story of Inner Tomb.

It was after 1 o'clock when the official party entered the tomb, and the operation was begun which was to result in such astounding discoveries, of which I am able to give the following authoritative description:

Today between the hours of 1 and 3 in the afternoon the culminating moment in the discovery of Tut-ankh-Amen's tomb took place when Lord Carnarvon and Howard Carter opened the inner sealed doorway in the presence of Lady Evelyn Herbert, Abdel Hamid Suliman Pasha, Under Secretary of State for Public Works; Pierre Lacau, Director General of the Antiquities Department; Sir William Garstin, Sir Charles Cust, Mr. Lythgoe, the curator of the New York; Mr. Winlock, Director of the

---

GOV. REILY RESIGNS PORTO RICO OFFICE

Tells President Ill Health Forbids Him to Resume Executive Duties.

HAD BEEN LONG UNDER FIRE

Offended by His Inaugural Address, Unionists Made Many Charges Against Him.

WASHINGTON, Feb. 16 (Associated Press).—The resignation of E. Mont Reily as Governor of Porto Rico was received at the White House today and, following that, no announcement was made concerning it, although there was every indication that it would be accepted.

The text of the cablegram of resignation, as made public at the White House, follows:

Hon. Warren G. Harding, President of the United States:

On account of very serious injury while in the States, my trip to Porto Rico prostrated me, and I have been confined to my bed since, not being able to resume my official duties. My physicians inform me it will be several months before I can recover and resume my duties, and I do not feel that the great demonstration tendered me on my return, and shows that the work of your Administration in Porto Rico has not been in vain, but have based my resignation on that. It was a complete vindication of our American policies instituted in the islands two years ago.

A delegation composed of men of all political parties called on my Secretary yesterday, requesting that I withhold my resignation until you could be communicated with. I have not-withstanding my resignation was irrevocable. Ninety per cent. of the people of the Island are for you and the things you stand for, and are pleading that no backward step be taken in Porto Rico, and I am

Continued on Page Five.

GOETHALS DEMANDS COAL FOR UP-STATE

"We Want Action, Not Conferences," He Says in Message to Federal Fuel Distributer.

SEIZURE IS THREATENED

Insists Shipments to Canada Be Diverted—People Will Get Coal, He Asserts.

General George W. Goethals, State Fuel Administrator, serving notice on the Federal Fuel Distributer that "we want action, not conferences" for the relief of suffering localities in Northern New York, suggested in two telegrams yesterday immediate authorization by the Federal officials of drastic relief measures.

Diversion to up-State towns of coal now moving to Canada, priority of New York shipments over shipments to Canada, and seizure of cars en route to Canada were some of the measures suggested.

"The people in that part of the State are going to get coal," General Goethals asserted in making public the telegrams. "I am awaiting action from Washington on the telegrams. In case I don't get it, I am not saying what I am going to do."

The seizure of one car of coal consigned to Canada for use of the Saratoga Springs Hospital was authorized yesterday by the shipper, John F. Birmingham, President of the Lackawanna Coal Company. General Goethals called this to the attention of P. B. Waddell, Federal Fuel Distributer, in one of his telegrams and asked why the Government could not requisition the Delaware & Hudson Railroad "to supply our needs."

Reports from Mr. Killmer to the State Fuel Administration offices yesterday were that people up-State were "on the point of taking coal off the tracks." The people were ready "to take the law in their own hands," he stated and added that "no juries in the afflicted communities would ever vote for conviction."

Predictions of epidemics from influenza and pneumonia unless coal arrived at some of the up-State points today were made by Mr. Killmer.

General Goethals told reporters that priority must be given both to all the emergency shipment of 20,000 tons, which is required immediately, and to future supply regular allotments. Schools at many points in the Saratoga district have been closed for lack of fuel, reports to the State Fuel Administration said. Two schools in Corinth have been closed, and unless some coal arrives before Monday, or the school authorities can get some wood, the high school also will close. The school at Schuylerville was ordered closed yesterday for an indefinite period because of the lack of fuel.

Louis Cohen, a landlord of 324 West 152d Street, near Eighth Avenue, was arrested yesterday for failing to supply sufficient heat and hot water to the house at 722 West 146th Street. Probation officers reported that the building was badly in need of repairs. Window panes were out and doors were loose, they said, and the temperature recently had been several degrees below the legal minimum.

Mr. Bertha Becker, who owns a building at 824 West 151st Street, was fined $250 on a similar charge in Special Sessions.

Won't Stop Coal to Canada.

WASHINGTON, Feb. 16.—The proposal for an embargo on anthracite exports, especially to Canada, has been canvassed by officials and definitely abandoned. It was said today at the White House.

In the view of high Government officials an embargo would have but little real effect on the coal shortage which is being experienced in sections of New York and New England.

Doctor and Chauffeur Killed When Train Wrecks Ambulance at Jersey Grade Crossing

A fatal grade crossing accident occurred last evening at Hackensack, N. J., where a train running forty miles an hour, on the Erie Railroad, smashed into an ambulance, crushing a hospital interne and a chauffeur to death. James Reape, 38 years old, of 30 Nassau Street, Brooklyn, the chauffeur, was crossing until he was close to it. The crossing gates should have been lowered, but were not. John Burke of Pearl River, N. Y., the gate tender, said the gates were frozen and out of commission. According to Burke, he stood in the middle of the road and swung a red lantern, but the ambulance driver did not heed. Burke was arrested on a technical charge of manslaughter.

Dr. Nishawitz lost his life in the performance of his duty, as he was answering a call to take a sick woman to the hospital from her home on Hudson Street, Hackensack. After the accident a second ambulance was sent for the woman, but the delay had been fatal and she was dead on its arrival.

The accident occurred about 5:50 P. M. at the Essex Street crossing. The train was a Haverstraw express, carrying commuters from New York.

Owing to a sharp curve south of Essex Street, the engineer could not see the crossing until he was close to it. The crossing gates should have been lowered, but were not.

Dr. Michael P. Nishawitz, 25, of 830 Kelly Street, the Bronx, an interne at the Hackensack General Hospital, was mortally injured. His skull was fractured and his left leg and right arm were cut off. He died in the hospital half an hour after the accident.

Dr. Nishawitz was a graduate of De Witt Clinton High School and the Long Island College Hospital.

WHEN YOU THINK OF WRITING Think of Whiting.—Advt.

ZIEGFELD FOLLIES—POP. PRICE MAT. TODAY. New Amsterdam Theatre.—Advt.

BELL-ANS WILL RELIEVE YOUR Indigestion.—Advt.

Harding Threatens to Cut Shipping Fleet Unless Congress Passes the Subsidy Bill

WASHINGTON, Feb. 16.—The Administration Shipping bill was restored tonight to its former place as the regular business of the Senate, after having been laid aside since early in the week to allow consideration of the British debt settlement legislation. This was done on motion of Senator Jones of Washington after advocates of the measure had demonstrated their superior strength by voting down, 38 to 30, a motion by Senator Robinson of Arkansas to adjourn.

The vote on adjournment was not regarded as an accurate test of the strength of the forces supporting and opposing the shipping bill, as several Senators on both sides were absent.

Opposition of the shipping measure was expected, when the Senate resumes tomorrow, to counter with a proposal to lay the bill aside again in favor of the Capper "Truth-in-Fabrics bill, and it was considered probable that a test vote on the merchant marine legislation may result.

Although the future of the subsidy bill in the Senate has not been clearly indicated in the face of claims and counter-claims on its possibility of its passage, it was said at the White House today that President Harding would not call a special session of Congress to consider the merchant marine situation if the Shipping bill should fail.

Mr. Harding was said to feel that the necessity for action looking to a solution of the shipping problem had been clearly demonstrated, and to have reached the decision that if the Shipping bill is not enacted the Government will proceed at once to take such steps as may be possible in a very great degree the present losses of the Government's Fleet.

Detailed reports on the operation of shipping Board vessels, showing net losses on individual voyages running as high as $100,000, have been submitted to the President and his advisers, it was said, and the consensus of opinion was that the necessary economics which would follow the return of the shipping to private ownership.

EMPLOYERS—Don't be intimidated. Hire strong, husky men. Phone 1706 Beekley.—Advt.

Charge Hawaiian Coolie Labor Plot

Special to The New York Times.

WASHINGTON, Feb. 16.—Charges were made today by the Executive Council of the American Federation of Labor that for two years there had been an immigrant agitation for the importation of 80,000 Chinese coolies into the Hawaiian Islands, where they would placed under bond making them "debt slaves" for five years or less if they became rebellious. The council instructed the Federation's legislative representatives to do all in their power to prevent any enactment of laws that would in any degree open the gates to this character of immigration.

"All the News That's Fit to Print."

The New York Times.

EXTRA
6 A.M.
THE WEATHER: Fair Today.

VOL. LXXII....No. 23,932.   ····   NEW YORK, FRIDAY, AUGUST 3, 1923.   TWO CENTS In Greater New York | THREE CENTS Within 200 Miles | FOUR CENTS Elsewhere

PRESIDENT HARDING DIES SUDDENLY; STROKE OF APOPLEXY AT 7:30 P. M.; CALVIN COOLIDGE IS PRESIDENT

COOLIDGE TAKES THE OATH OF OFFICE

His Father, Who Is a Notary Public, Administers It After Form Is Found By Him in His Library.

ANNOUNCES HE WILL FOLLOW THE HARDING POLICIES

Wants All Who Aided Harding to Remain in Office—Roused After Midnight to Be Told the News of the President's Death.

Statement by President Coolidge

Special to The New York Times.

PLYMOUTH, Vt., Aug. 3.—President Calvin Coolidge issued the following statement early this morning:

Reports have reached me, which I fear are correct, that President Harding is gone. The world has lost a great and good man. I mourn his loss. He was my chief and my friend.

It will be my purpose to carry out the policies which he has begun for the service of the American people and for meeting their responsibilities wherever they may arise.

For this purpose I shall seek the co-operation of all those who have been associated with the President during his term of office.

Those who have given their efforts to assist him I wish to remain in the office that they may assist me. I have faith that God will direct the destinies of our nation.

It is my intention to remain here until I can secure the correct form for the oath of office, which will be administered to me by my father, who is a notary public, if that will meet the necessary requirement. I expect to leave for Washington during the day.

CALVIN COOLIDGE.

Takes the Oath of Office.

PLYMOUTH, Vt. (Friday) Aug. 3.—Calvin Coolidge took the oath of office as President of the United States at 2:47, Eastern Standard Time, this morning (3:47 New York time). The oath was administered by his father, John C. Coolidge, who found the text in a book in his library, after having expected to wait until it was received from Washington.

The taking of the oath was a simple and solmn scene. Those who gathered in the living room of the Coolidge rome at Plymouth Notch, besides the President and his father, were Mrs. Coolidge, L. L. Lane, President of the Railway Mail Association of New England; Congressman Porter H. Dale, of Vermont; Joseph H. Fountain, editor of the Springfield Reporter, and Erwin C. Geisser, Mr. Coolidge's Assistant Secretary.

As the elder Mr. Coolidge read the oath Mrs. Coolidge looked on with wet eyes. As the end was reached, President Coolidge, raising his right hand, said in a low, clear voice:

"I do, so help me God."

A moment later the group dissolved, and President and Mrs. Coolidge retired.

Special to The New York Times.

PLYMOUTH, Vt., Friday, Aug. 3.—Calvin Coolidge received the news of the death of President Harding and of his own elevation to the Presidency at ten minutes before 1 o'clock this morning, Daylight Saving Time.

Mr. Coolidge received the first news of President Harding's death from telegrams signed by George C. Christian, the late President's secretary, and from THE NEW YORK TIMES, whose telegram reached him at the same moment.

These telegrams were brought to the Coolidge home at Plymouth Notch by W. A. Perkins of Bridgewater, who owns the telephone line running from Bridgewater to Plymouth. About five minutes later the newspaper men arrived in from Ludlow.

The following telegram was sent to Mrs. Harding:

Plymouth, Vt., Aug. 3, 1923.

Mrs. Warren G. Harding,
San Francisco, Cal.

We offer you our deepest sympathy. May God bless you and keep you.
CALVIN COOLIDGE.
GRACE COOLIDGE.

The following telegrams announcing the death of President Harding.

Continued on Page Five.

CALVIN COOLIDGE
Thirtieth President of the United States by the Death of President Harding.

WARREN GAMALIEL HARDING
Twenty-ninth President of the United States, Who Died Yesterday in San Francisco.

Public Men Voice Tributes To Harding's Worth and Record

Hughes Says He Was a Brave and Strong Leader—Marshall Calls Him a Great Human American—Honored as Martyr to His Duty—Sympathy Goes Out to Mrs. Harding.

Special to The New York Times.

WASHINGTON, Friday, Aug. 3.—Politics was forgotten in community by public men in Washington when informed of the death of President Harding. On account of the late hour at which the news was received it was difficult to reach officials.

Secretary Hughes, who came to his office in the State Department at an early hour this morning, was shaken by the news.

"No words can express," he said, "the grief into which we are plunged by this calamity. The nation has suffered an irreparable loss. A quiet, brave, strong leader has fallen, overborne by the burden he was carrying.

"He was not only an able and faithful public servant but one of nature's noblemen. A true hearted, generous spirit, he has left with the people for whom he came in contact with the President I knew him as a kindly gentleman and a true friend."

Says He Had People's Affection.

Senator Walsh of Massachusetts, Chairman of the Democratic Senatorial Campaign Committee, said:

"The President's death is a terrible shock, coming as it does so soon after it was believed that he was on the way to speedy recovery. His death will be mourned in every corner of the land by every class.

"Few Presidents have had a stronger grip upon the affections of our people. His dignity, simplicity, sincerity and graciousness won the hearts of all. His personality, however, did not alone account for his great popularity. He had won a place in our history among the most worthy of those who have occupied the Presidency.

"His views were statesmanlike and the honor of our nation was safe and secure in his hands. The nation has lost a noble man, and a sound and safe leader."

Roosevelt Tells of Sacrifice.

Colonel Theodore Roosevelt, Acting Secretary of the Navy in the absence of Secretary Denby, said:

"Words cannot express my grief at the death of my chief, President Harding. It is idle to say that his death is a calamity for the United States, for every one knows it. He gave his life to the service of our country as truly as any one in our history."

Senator Walsh of Massachusetts, said:

"This is a tribute from a man who did not agree with his political principles, but it is not necessary to agree with his political principles in order to admire the integrity, patriotism and high-mindedness of a man. That is the thing that as the years go by the people will realize that Mr. Harding tried to serve his country well."

Loss to the World, Says New.

Postmaster General New at his home when the news of President Harding's death was flashed to him from San Francisco.

"I am simply overwhelmed," he said. "There are times when a man can not express his grief. This is one of them. The passing of President Harding is a

President's Death Shocks Capital, Which Had Expected Recovery

News Telephoned to Executive Clerk From San Francisco—Effort Made to Reach Coolidge in Vermont—Only Two Members of Cabinet in Washington.

Special to The New York Times.

WASHINGTON, Friday, Aug. 3.—News of the death of President Harding not only greatly shocked official and Washington but took the capital completely by surprise.

It was the sixth time in the history of the nation that the city had been brought face to face with the death of a President, but the shocking word which received under circumstances wholly different from those surrounding the death of any former President.

The only high officials of the Harding Administration in Washington are Secretary of State Hughes and Postmaster General New. All the other members of the Cabinet are out of the city, and two of them, Secretaries Mellon and Davis, are in Europe, while most of the others, with the exception of Secretaries Weeks and Denby, are in the Far West.

Calvin Coolidge, until last night Vice President, and who will immediately be sworn in as the next President of the United States, is likewise absent from Washington, but it has occurred several times in American annals that Vice Presidents have been absent from the capital on occasions of deaths of former Presidents.

When last heard from, Mr. Coolidge was at Plymouth, Vt. A message notifying him of the death of Mr. Harding was direct from San Francisco communications.

The White House was advised late tonight was sent direct to all other members of the Cabinet not now in San Francisco and to personal friends of the President.

Rudolph Forster, Executive Clerk at the White House, was communicated with direct from San Francisco shortly before midnight by long distance telephone. He talked with Mr. Smithers, the ranking member of the White House executive force in San Francisco in the absence of Mr. Christian who had gone to Los Angeles. Mr. Smithers confirmed the death of the President and informed Mr. Forster that messages were being sent from their homes to call newsboys and automobiles stopped their machines to buy the ink-wet sheets. Newsboys ceased crying extras in Executive Avenue and Pennsylvania Avenue, the two streets leading to the White House on the west and north at midnight, the crisis coming clearly into the Executive Offices.

Dancing Steps at the Hotels.

At the big hotels dancing was immediately stopped and a hush and gloom settled over the crowds who slowly began to leave. Extras were on the streets fairly early and residents read the news.

Mr. Hughes is the ranking member of the Administration now in Washington, so that he will take such steps as are necessary in the present situation.

It will also be the duty of the Secretary of State to notify the members of the Diplomatic Corps, who will in turn officially cable their Governments that Mr. Harding is dead.

No plans have or can be made immediately for the swearing in of Mr. Coolidge as President. It is not necessary for him to take the oath from a member of the United States Supreme Court. Another Judge or other officer qualified to administer an oath can act in that capacity. Even a Justice of the Peace back in Vermont, where Mr. Coolidge was last known to be located, can administer the oath.

The first knowledge the White House had of the President's death came from the Rev. Dr. Freeman Anderson, assistant pastor of the Calvary Baptist Church, which President Harding attended. He telephoned to the Executive Mansion and the message was received by E. C. Goss, one of the White House police force, who was one of the few men on duty at that time of the night, as the President had been away since June 29.

In turn Patrolman Goss telephoned to Mr. Forster and once summoned the entire White House force. One of the first to arrive was Isaac Hoover of years older under at the mansion, and who has known many Presidents intimately, and Joseph Murphy, assistant chief of the Secret Service.

Pedestrians who passed the White House at midnight saw a rush of the President's death stirred that the iron gates on Pennsylvania Avenue were shut and locked, something which has been known since the advent of the Harding regime. It was explained, however, that the gates have been shut every night at 8 o'clock since the extensive repairs to the house and grounds have been going on.

Mr. Hoover, who has charge of the renovation of the White House, said at midnight that the mansion could be put in order in two days. In fact, preparations had been made to do this ever since the first news of the President's illness was received in Washington. At any time that notification was sent here that the President was to leave San Francisco the house could have been put in readiness for his reception. Workmen will begin at once this morning arranging the furniture and placing the draperies as usual.

When the news was communicated to William H. Beck, private secretary to the Secretary of State, at midnight, he started by automobile for the State Department to notify Mr. Hughes.

Continued on Page Four.

Continued on Page Five.

DEATH STROKE CAME WITHOUT WARNING

Mrs. Harding Was Reading to Her Husband When First Sign Appeared —She Ran for Doctor

BUT NOTHING COULD BE DONE TO REVIVE PATIENT

News of Tragic End Shocks Everybody, Coming After Day Said to Have Been the Best Since His Illness Began a Week Ago.

Special to The New York Times.

SAN FRANCISCO, Aug. 2.—President Harding died at 7:30 o'clock tonight [11:30 o'clock New York time] of a stroke of apoplexy.

The end came suddenly while Mrs. Harding was reading to him from the evening newspaper, and after what had been called the best day he had since the beginning of his illness exactly one week ago.

A shudder ran through the President's frame and he collapsed.

Mrs. Harding and the two nurses in the sick room knew the end had come, and Mrs. Harding rushed out of the room and asked for Dr. Boone and the others to "come quick."

Dr. Boone and Brig. Gen. Sawyer reached the President before he passed away, but were not able to avert the inevitable.

This formal announcement following soon after told the story of the tragic end:

"The President died at 7:30 P. M. Mrs. Harding and the two nurses, Miss Ruth Powderly and Miss Sue Drusser, were in the room at the time. Mrs. Harding was reading to the President, when, utterly without warning, a slight shudder passed through his frame; he collapsed, and all recognized that the end had come. A stroke of apoplexy was the cause of his death.

"Within a few moments all of the President's official party had been summoned."

Shocking in Its Suddenness.

Nothing could have been a more shocking surprise. Shortly before the President's sudden collapse General Sawyer had been telling newspaper men that Mr. Harding had had the best day since he became seriously ill. He said that the President had definitely entered upon the stage of convalescence and that everything went to show that Mr. Harding was on the road to ultimate recovery.

The members of the official party had no warning that the President was in danger. They, like the newspaper men, had been assured that a fatal termination of the President's illness was a thing not likely and with good care he would be able to recover health and strength. Most of the members of the official party at dinner when the news came. George B. Christian Jr., secretary to the President and his devoted friend, was in Los Angeles with Mrs. Christian. He had gone there at the President's solicitation to read at a gathering of the Knights Templar tonight an address which the President had prepared in the expectation that he would deliver it in person. Mr. Christian had declined to leave San Francisco and was positively assured by the President's physicians that there was no likelihood of any set-back in the President's condition.

The newspaper men had an engagement with General Sawyer for 8 o'clock. He was to tell them of how the President was progressing toward recovery. In view of what he had said on prior occasions during the day and statements in two official bulletins, the newspaper men had every expectation that they would be able to record that Mr. Harding was one step nearer the goal of recovery.

"There will be a bulletin," said one of the White House messengers gathered in the corridor of the Presidential suite. In a few minutes copies of the bulletin on thin white paper were handed to the waiting reporters. Instead of informing them that the President's condition continued to improve, it gave them the astounding information that he was dead.

Mrs. Harding Is Brave to the End.

First reports that Mrs. Harding had collapsed were denied. The official version indicates that she was calm throughout her husband's last illness. She has been extremely courageous and by her manner and words helped him when he was of suffering intensely and was apprehensive of a fatal termination. The official account says:

"Mrs. Harding, who from the beginning of the President's illness had expressed confidence in his recovery, did not break down. On the other hand, she continued, as from the beginning, the bravest member of the group.

"When it was realized that the President had actually passed away, she turned to those in the room, whose concern had turned to her, and said, 'I am not going to break down.'"

Mrs. Harding was seated by the bedside when at 7:10 o'clock the President suddenly collapsed. His breathing, which had been quick ever since the illness overtook him, suddenly became spasmodic. Mrs. Harding, leaving the two nurses to take whatever steps they could in the emergency, ran to the door of the Presidential suite.

"Dr. Boone!" she called, as she ran part way into the almost deserted corridor. A Secret Service operative was seated about twenty feet down the hall. She hurriedly told the Secret Service man that the President had had a sudden and severe relapse and begged the detective to try to locate Dr. Boone or any of the other physicians.

The Secret Service man took up the search for the physicians, while

Continued on Page Five.

"All the News That's
Fit to Print."

The New York Times.

THE WEATHER
Fair today; unsettled tomorrow;
gentle southerly winds.
Temperature yesterday—Max. 84, Min., 69.
☞For weather report see last page.

VOL. LXXII....No. 23,965.   •••   NEW YORK, WEDNESDAY, SEPTEMBER 5, 1923.   TWO CENTS In Greater | THREE CENTS | FOUR CENTS

JAPANESE DEATH TOLL MAY REACH 300,000;
EARTH STILL ROCKS BUT FIRES ARE WANING;
AMERICA IS RAISING MILLIONS FOR RELIEF

GREEKS OFFER PLAN FOR LEAGUE INQUIRY INTO JANINA CRIMES

Want Geneva to Direct Investigation—Will Post 50,000,000 Lire Guarantee.

ASSEMBLY SNUBS ITALIANS

Elections to Committees Result in Their Exclusion From Posts of Honor.

MUSSOLINI RENEWS THREAT

Rome Cabinet Approves Resolution to Quit League If It Intervenes.

Copyright, 1923, by The New York Times Company.
Special Cable to THE NEW YORK TIMES.

GENEVA, Sept. 4.—Nicholas Politis, delegate of the Greek Government, today proposed to the Council of the League of Nations that in the settlement of the dispute between his country and Italy the Council should appoint one or more neutral representatives.

1. To superintend in Greece the judicial inquiry already begun by the Greek authorities and also the trial of those held responsible for the murder of the Italian officers of the Albanian Boundary Commission.

2. To assist in the work of a commission, the appointment of which has been proposed by the Greek Government, through the Council of Ambassadors, to investigate, both in Albania and in Greece, the circumstances which preceded and accompanied the crime.

3. That the Council should instruct a commission composed of three high judicial authorities—one Greek, one Italian and one neutral (for example, the President of the Swiss Federal Tribunal or the President of the Permanent Court of International Justice—to meet as soon as possible in Geneva to settle the amount of indemnities which it is just that Greece should pay the families of the victims.

4. That the Council should agree that the Greek Government forthwith deposit in a Swiss bank 50,000,000 lire as a guarantee for the immediate payment of whatever indemnities may be decided upon.

Discussion Put Off Till Today.

These proposals were made at a meeting of the Council held this evening at the Secretariat of the League, in the course of which Signor Salandra, head of the Italian delegation, announced a postponement of the discussion of the Greco-Italian incident until Signor Giurati, his associate, should have returned from Rome with new instructions.

M. Politis was arguing that no sovereign nation could accept dictation as to the nature of the punishment to be inflicted upon its nationals when Signor Salandra interrupted him.

His attitude was most friendly, and it was with a smile that he expostulated that he could not consent to allow the Greek delegate to embark on a controversy in the course of the discussion of a simple question whether the Council should grant a postponement.

"If M. Politis is allowed to continue, I shall have to reply," he said.

The common sense of this attitude and the politeness of the Italian delegate toward his Greek colleague won general approval, and Lord Robert Cecil suggested that M. Politis should have an opportunity to submit in writing any new proposals he had to make.

M. Politis then retired from the room and at the end of half an hour brought back the suggestions already noted in this dispatch. In the circumstances they could not be immediately taken up by the Council and Lord Robert moved that the discussion of them should be withheld until tomorrow's meeting, when the Council would be in possession of full information as to the Italian attitude.

The attitude of the small nations was strongly shown this morning when Signor Scialoja, who has been President of the Committee on Legal Questions for the last two years and expected to have that honor again conferred upon his country and himself, was defeated. Dr. Motta of Switzerland being elected. The Presidencies of all the committees were given to representatives of small nations.

1A. the election of six Vice Presidents of the Assembly at the formal morning session of the body, Lord Robert Cecil and Viscount Ishii headed the ballot with forty-two votes each, Gabriel Hanotaux of France coming third with thirty-five. The other three Vice Presidents elected were Count De Cicmeno, Dr. Forloud of Venezuela and M. Pusta of Esthonia. Italy did not win a single place of honor among the Assembly leaders.

Desire Repudiating League's Authority.

GENEVA, Sept. 4 (Associated Press).—A member of the Italian delegation to the League of Nations today authorized the League Secretariat to deny that Italy had ever officially repudiated the competency of the League to handle the Greco-Italian dispute.

"We are awaiting the return of Major Giurati from Rome, and then we will

Continued on Page Ten.

HOTEL ST. GEORGE—Brooklyn's Largest. Now showing historic Fall leasing and low summer rates. (Clark St.) Subway Sta. la.—Advt.

Dirigible ZR-1 Makes Perfect Test Flight; 15,000 Cheer Huge Craft Made at Lakehurst

Special to The New York Times.

LAKEHURST, N. J., Sept. 4.—Exceeding the expectations of its builders, the United States Navy dirigible ZR-1 made its maiden flight this afternoon from the Lakehurst air station, where ten months ago construction was started.

Cheered by 15,000 persons, the dirigible, a "made in America" product, rose gracefully, and, after circling the field, took an easterly course to Toms River. Returning to the field at dusk after a flight on an hour, the dirigible made a perfect landing at the station and "went to bed " in its immense hangar.

From the first preparations this morning toward releasing the ZR-1 until after the dirigible had been safely returned to its hangar, the day was replete with interesting events for naval officials. Commander Frank R. McCrary, skipper of the craft, received favorable weather reports from Washington early in the afternoon, and last word instructions to the twenty-two men in the crew were issued by Captain Anton Heinen, German Zeppelin authority, who has been consultant to the navy in the construction of the craft.

A force of 320 marines and enlisted men marched to their posts as guide-rope holders, and 100 civilian employes gathered at the entrance of the hangar and aid in guiding the dirigible to the centre of the field.

When entry man was in his place Commander Weyerbacher gave the order, "Start walking," and the small army of men began hauling the ZR-1 from the hangar.

One of those who made the flight was Norman O. Walker, the only American who survived the ZR-2 crash in England. He said that the dirigible seemed to him to be a much better craft.

Captain Heinen then climbed into the pilot gondola, and a moment later the order was shouted, " Let's go."

Propelled by four of the six motors, the dirigible rose to a height of about 1,000 feet, when the pilot started to circle the field. Later the big craft began its real flight, and at a height of 1,200 feet, in full view of the crowd, it soared away in perfect control.

Soon this radio message was received by Admiral Moffett: "In twenty minutes of flying all going well."

Signals in electrically illuminated signboards placed flat on the ground aided in the landing, which was made without a hitch upon an immense stretch of red and white bunting, on which a searchlight was turned.

"The flight was highly satisfactory," said Commander McCrary. "The craft steered exceedingly well, although we did not carry out any tests of severity on the initial trip. We only opened up the motors to half speed, and they functioned entirely to our satisfaction. The ship proceeded smoothly and evenly, as evidenced by the fact that Lieutenant Bauch, one of the passengers, and an enlisted man were able to walk on the roadway on top of the gas bag."

"There are a few minor changes we will have to make before the ZR-1 can set out again. We plan a series of test flights, the second probably the latter part of next week."

Rear Admiral Moffett was enthusiastic over the results of the trial trip.

"One of those who made the flight was Norman O. Walker, the only American who survived the ZR-2 crash in England. He said that the dirigible seemed to him to be a much better craft.

DEMOTTE KILLED IN GUN ACCIDENT

International Art Dealer Shot Dead While on Hunting Expedition in France.

NEWS KEPT SECRET A DAY

Involved in Charges of Extensive Art Frauds, He Was Preparing to Push Suit Here.

Copyright, 1923, by The New York Times Company.
Special Cable to THE NEW YORK TIMES.

PARIS, Sept. 4.—George J. Demotte, art dealer of Paris and New York, was killed yesterday while hunting. His companion, Otto Wenger, dropped his gun, which was struck in the shoulder and neck, the jugular vein being severed. Death was almost instantaneous.

The hunting season opened on Saturday, and the art dealer on that day with a party of friends went to the Department of Loir-et-Cher, where he owned property. The accident occurred at the conclusion of the day's hunt, when Wenger was unloading the gun. When he saw his host drop dying to the ground Wenger tried to commit suicide. Other members of the party interfered in time, however, to prevent this.

For unknown reasons the news of the tragic death was kept secret till late this afternoon. Then it became known a rumor about Paris, and the last evening papers tonight carried a brief notice about it.

Demotte was perhaps the world's greatest dealer in statuary, though he did not confine his business to that branch of art. He had sold numerous pieces to the Louvre in Paris and the Metropolitan Museum in New York and to wealthy collectors, both in France and America.

Recently he had been involved in legal processes over the value of a number of his sales. Recently he accused the Paris dealer, Sir Joseph Duveen, of conspiring to drive him out of business, and brought suit for half a million dollars against him for his contrary judgment on a piece of alleged Limoges enamel which had been bought by the Dreicer firm, but not paid for, and for remarks alleged to have been made by Duveen about him in connection with this matter.

The case was overshadowed, however, by the sudden controversy raised in Paris as to the authenticity of objects sold by Demotte to both the Louvre and the Metropolitan, as well as to a number of private collectors. The charges were made specific by a number of critics, including one who claimed to have heard Demotte's boast as to the restoration of statues for American trade. Jean Vigouroux, former manager of Demotte's New York store, corroborated the charge, specifying some half-dozen "fakes " in the Metropolitan. Vigorous, moreover, would under indictment on a charge of retaining illegal commissions on sales, and Demotte made counter-charges that the entire affair was brought up to injure his character.

Despite this defense persons interested in the Louvre continued to press the charges, and a complaint was lodged with the Prosecutor of the Seine. An investigation followed which certain Louvre pieces were restored to an extent to make them valueless as specimens of sculpture of the period they represented. This evidence was turned over to the Prosecutor of the Seine only a few weeks ago, and the next step to be taken in the case had not yet been made public.

Two other serious cases arose from the controversy. One was the revelation that a statue sold by Demotte to a

Continued on Page Seven.

Ziegfeld Follies, Pop. Prices Mat. Today. New Summer Edition New Globe Theatre.—Advt.

COAL PEACE BASIS NOW SEEMS NEAR

Indications Are That $5 Minimum for Day Men Would Satisfy Miners.

MAY DROP OTHER DEMANDS

Lewis Confers With Leaders in Preparation for Conference Today.

Special to The New York Times.

HARRISBURG, Sept. 4.—If the representatives of the anthracite operators agree to grant to day miners a minimum of $5 a day the suspension of work which began Sept. 1 will be lifted and 158,000 miners will return to work. This basis for the settlement of the strike was indicated today on good authority in advance of the meeting tomorrow between Governor Pinchot and the disputants.

Governor Pinchot has asked the operators to give a 10 per cent. wage increase to the contract men. They demanded 20 per cent., but are willing to take half. The day workers, now receiving between $4.20 and $5.60 a day, have signified their unwillingness to take an increase of between 42 and 56 cents a day, as suggested by the Governor. They want a minimum of $5 a day.

A minimum of $5 a day for day men would mean an increase of 80 cents a day. There are 40,000 day workers, and they have signified that the comparatively slight paid contract miner as large a percentage increase as they received would further widen the disparity between the wages of the two classes.

Other Demands Offset Each Other.

A minimum of $5 a day for day men. A 10 per cent. increase for contract workers, would, it was estimated, increase the price of coal $1 a ton at the mines.

With the wage question out of the way there would be two questions left, the check-off and arbitration. The miners have been insistent on the check-off, and the operators just as firmly refused to grant it. The operators demand that the miners agree to a form of permanent arbitration that shall guarantee uninterrupted production during the pendency of wage disputes.

Following a conference between President Coolidge and James L. Fieser, Acting Chairman of the American Red Cross, it was announced that the society immediately will call upon the American people for a fund of at least $5,000,000, of which New York City has been asked to raise $1,000,000. The plan for the relief campaign were worked out in a conference between Mr. Fieser, Secretary of Commerce Hoover, Assistant Secretary of the Treasury Wadsworth, and Masanae Hanihara, the Japanese Ambassador.

Late this afternoon the quotas for the six national Red Cross divisions were announced. They show that while the fund is fixed at $5,000,000 the quotas assigned amount to $5,250,000. The quotas are based on

Continued on Page Four.

RED CROSS ASKS $5,000,000

Sets Its 3,600 American Chapters at Work at Once.

RELIEF SHIPS DUE TODAY

Six Naval Vessels Carrying Supplies Are Nearing Yokohama.

FOOD RUSHED FROM MANILA

Army Transports, Loaded to Capacity, Sail Within 24 Hours.

Prince Regent and Emperor Give $55,000,000 for Relief

SAN FRANCISCO, Sept. 4 (Associated Press).—Relief work in Japan was furthered today by several large donations. The Prince Regent gave $50,000,000 for relief; the Emperor gave $5,000,000 from the Privy Exchequer, and the Government donated $4,500,000.

In Kobe $17,500 was raised for the sufferers in ten minutes.

The vessels in Yokohama harbor have given refuge to 5,000 persons.

From Shanghai it was reported that rioting had broken out in the destroyed cities and that by police were arming citizens to aid in maintaining order.

Special to The New York Times.

WASHINGTON, Sept. 4.—The Government of the United States is giving its time and attention almost exclusively to the work of extending in full measure all possible assistance to the stricken people of Japan. This was the official statement that came this afternoon from the White House, where the President is personally directing the relief activities of the Government.

The speed with which the United States is acting to bring succor to the Japanese can be appreciated when it is stated that the army transports Meiggs and Merritt, each carrying a capacity cargo of relief supplies, are expected to sail from Manila within the next twelve hours, or within twenty-four hours after the order directing their dispatch to Japan was cabled to Governor General Wood.

Dr. J. Bentley Squier Sails From Kobe To Aid Relief Measures at Yokohama

Copyright, 1923, by The New York Times Company.
Special Cable to THE NEW YORK TIMES.

KYOTO, Japan, Sept. 4.—Dr. J. Bentley Squier of New York has sailed from Kobe on the foreign relief ship West Orowa, bound for Yokohama to engage in relief work there. Dr. Squier's family remain at the Miyako Hotel here.

Dr. Squier and Mrs. Squier and their son and daughter were visiting in Japan from a tour in China when the Japanese earthquake occurred. They had intended to sail from Shanghai on the Canadian Pa-

Continued on Page Eight.

Islands of Bonin Group Reported Vanished, Together With Mismia Island and Its Volcano

Copyright, 1923, by The New York Times Company.
Special Cable to THE NEW YORK TIMES.

PEKING, Sept. 4.—Numerous villages along the coast of the Japanese Peninsula south of Yokohama, where many foreigners were spending the Summer, were washed away by the tidal wave that followed the earthquake.

There is no news from the Bonin Islands and it is feared they have sunk into the sea.

Nothing can be seen of Mismia Island, the volcano on which was reported on Monday to be in violent eruption, and it is believed to have disappeared.

Copyright, 1923, by The New York Times Company.
Special Cable to THE NEW YORK TIMES.

LONDON, Sept. 4.—The Bonin Islands, called by the Japanese Ogasawarajima, which are reported to have disappeared, were about twenty in number, though only ten were of appreciable size. They lay about 500 miles from the mainland of Japan on a line which would run almost due south from Yokohama or southeast from Nagasaki.

Until 1861 their few inhabitants had somewhat vaguely considered themselves as a British colony, but in that year the British Government recognized Japan's right of possession. Since then the handful of Europeans and Polynesian half-breeds had been outnumbered by Japanese colonists.

Regular steamship communication had been established and a modern system of administration introduced. Exploitation of the islands' resources—valuable timber and agricultural produce—had provided employment for the population, about 5,000.

AMBASSADOR SAFE, U. S. CONSUL DEAD

Woods and Staff Escape When Explosions Deluged the Doomed Embassy Is Destroyed—Mr. and Mrs. Kirjassoff Killed.

FOREIGN CASUALTIES HEAVY

State Department Trying to Get News of Americans— All Capitals Anxious.

Special to The New York Times.

WASHINGTON, Sept. 4.—The first direct message from American representatives in Japan to the State Department today brought the news of the safety of Ambassador Cyrus E. Woods and all members of his staff in the embassy at Tokio, and the death of Max D. Kirjassoff, the United States Consul at Yokohama, and his wife.

The American Embassy at Tokio and all other embassies were destroyed, presumably by fire, which it is believed accounts for the safety of those connected with the American Embassy.

Ambassador Woods sent an undated dispatch from Iwaki telling of the safety of himself and staff. It reads:

"Embassy buildings totally destroyed, but no one in embassy injured. Food situation is very acute. Send rations at once from Philippines."

John K. Davis, the American Consul at Shanghai, in a dispatch to the State Department told of the death of Mr. and Mrs. Kirjassoff and reported that there was no information about a number of Americans, among them Representative Ackerman of New Jersey.

Mr. Davis said that his information came by radio from the master of the President Jefferson, of the Admiral Line at Yokohama, to the officials of that line in Shanghai. His message to the State Department reads:

"Yokohama completely wiped out

Continued on Page Three.

BURSTING OIL TANKS SET YOKOHAMA AFIRE

Explosions Deluged the Doomed City With Flames That Spread Death.

TOKIO BRIDGES COLLAPSE

Thousands of Victims Go Down With Them to Death—Not a House Undamaged.

Copyright, 1923, by The New York Times Company.
Special Cable to THE NEW YORK TIMES.

PEKING, Sept. 4.—The latest news received here by way of the Tomioka wireless station, 150 miles northeast of Tokio, indicates that the catastrophe in Japan equals the worst apprehensions.

In Yokohama the Government oil tanks exploded and the whole city was set on fire. The deaths alone there are still estimated at 100,000.

All bridges across the river in Tokio, which were densely crowded with refugees from the fire, collapsed during the later earthquake shocks and many thousands were drowned or killed by the fall.

All newspaper offices in Tokio have been destroyed except those of the Nichi Nichi, Miyako and Hochi, and in all of these their machines are damaged so that publication of all newspapers is totally suspended. The University Hospital was destroyed and more than 700 patients perished.

All the hill suburbs of northern Yokohama have been destroyed by earthquakes and fire, and there seems to be no reason to doubt that the foreign quarter on the bluff has suffered a similar fate.

All wards of Tokio have been damaged, but parts of Shiba, Hongo, Kojimachi, Ushicome, Yotsuya and Aoyama wards escaped, though the fire was spreading in Aoyama ward yesterday morning.

Out of about fifty very large buildings in the Marunouchi district only half a dozen are still standing, including the House of Representatives.

Steel-Framed Structures Gone.

The Supreme Court, Imperial Hotel and Central Station, great steel-framed structures recently erected, have been destroyed, either by fire or by the earthquake. This point is of enormous importance to Japan, because, if they were destroyed by the earthquake, buildings of this character will have to be eschewed in the future and this will greatly restrict the country's manufacturing capacity.

The banks burned include the Bank of Japan, Mitsui, Tokai, Yasuda and the Third Bank.

Buildings destroyed in Tokio include the Chinese Legation, French and Italian Embassies, Nicolai and

Continued on Page Three.

DEVASTATION COVERS HUNDREDS OF MILES

At Least Five Big Cities Have Been Almost Wiped Out—Millions Are Starving or Dying of Exposure.

THOUSANDS OF MADDENED PEOPLE LEAP INTO RIVER

The Sumida in Tokio Is Clogged With Bodies— Shocks and Explosions Continue—Five Billion Dollars Needed for Reconstruction.

OSAKA, Japan, Sept. 4 (Associated Press).—So vast an area of Japan has been devastated by the greatest earthquake in the history of this country that it will be long before the actual loss of life is known. The most reliable estimates of the dead up to the present are from 200,000 to 320,000.

The newspaper Osaka Asahi estimates the earthquake dead at 320,000, which includes 150,000 dead in Tokio, 100,000 in Yokohama and 60,000 in Yokosuka. [Other dispatches estimate the casualties as high as 500,000.]

Tokio and Yokohama, with surrounding towns, which formed the centre of the disturbances, are almost completely in ruins. For two days Tokio was swept by flames, and, apart from the loss of life caused directly through the falling of buildings, thousands must have perished in their attempts to make their way through the fire zones and other thousands through exhaustion.

Yokohama, Tokio's busy port, is a city destroyed. Probably more destruction has been wrought there than in the capital itself, for its great docks were torn asunder, its shipping wrecked, its public buildings and homes levelled to the earth.

All advices received here indicate a succession of earth disturbances in that area, extending from many miles inland and to the north, and everywhere the first destructive forces were augmented by explosions, the bursting of water mains, the overflow of rivers and the terrible overpowering rush of tidal waves.

New Islands Arise From the Ocean.

Details of geographical changes are lacking, but it is reported that new islands have been forced up from the bed of the ocean, while whole sections have disappeared. Rivers are said to have changed their courses and volcanoes are erupting in various districts.

The disaster spared none who stood in its path. Many members of noble families have perished, but thus far the only notable foreign resident in the list of killed is the American Consul at Yokohama, Max D. Kirjassoff, who, with his wife, is believed to have been buried in the ruins of the consulate.

The American Ambassador, Cyrus E. Woods, and all the members of the embassy at Tokio are known to be safe, but many of the diplomatic representatives of other nations have not been accounted for, nor has any word been received of their fate.

Word is received that the fires in Tokio burned out on Monday night, but at the same time couriers carry appeals for food supplies and medical supplies and assistance for the hundreds of thousands of homeless refugees who, unless succored speedily, cannot survive.

For the moment all efforts are being devoted, first, to ascertaining the extent of Japan's vast losses, both in citizens and foreign residents, and material damage to its cities, and, secondly, to rushing all assistance in every form to the stricken districts.

There has been no time yet for a summing up of the terrible consequences of the earthquake nor for the preparation of a list of the prominent dead Japanese or foreign residents.

The warships of many foreign nations are on the seas already bringing assistance, which fact serves to give encouragement to the Government and the people in their greatest calamity.

Explosion at Hakone Hot Springs.

A great explosion has occurred at Owakidini, in Hakone, one of the hot springs of Japan, located about fifty miles from Tokio.

Earthquake shocks continue at intervals around Kawaguchi, which is on the only railway open out of Tokio.

The shock of yesterday morning, followed by fire, wiped out Kawaguchi.

Reports from eyewitnesses at Hakone say the earthquake left no houses standing at Miyanoshita, the fashionable mountain resort forty-five miles south of Tokio. The Fujiya Hotel was among the buildings destroyed.

In Tokio, the Ichigaya prison was threatened by fire and about 1,500 prisoners were freed. They included Toshihiko Saki, the Communist leader, and other Communists.

Troops of the Fourteenth Division at Utsunomiya and Thirteenth Division at Takata were marching toward Tokio today.

Following the earthquake horrors many of the refugees died from extreme heat and exposure, according to eye-

"All the News That's Fit to Print."

The New York Times.

THE WEATHER
Warmer and cloudy today; to-morrow, fair and colder.
Temperature yesterday—Max., 27; min., 4.
☞For weather report see Page 19.

VOL. LXXIII....No. 24,105.   •••   NEW YORK, WEDNESDAY, JANUARY 23, 1924.   TWO CENTS In Greater New York | THREE CENTS Within 200 Miles | FOUR CENTS Elsewhere.

LENIN DIES OF CEREBRAL HEMORRHAGE; MOSCOW THRONGS OVERCOME WITH GRIEF; TROTSKY DEPARTS ILL, RADEK IN DISFAVOR

SOVIET CONGRESS IN TEARS

Mass Hysteria Only Averted by a Leader's Brusque Intervention.

BODY WILL LIE IN STATE

Is to Be Taken to Moscow Today From Village Where Premier Passed Away.

KREMLIN WALL HIS TOMB

Washington Expects No Immediate Change in the Policy of the Russian Government.

By WALTER DURANTY.
Copyright, 1924, by The New York Times Company.
By Wireless to The New York Times.

MOSCOW, Jan. 22.—Nikolai Lenin died last night at 6:50 o'clock. The immediate cause of death was paralysis of the respiratory centres due to a cerebral hemorrhage.

For some time optimistic reports had been current as to the effects of a previous lesion gradually cleared up, but Lenin's nearest friends, realizing the progress of the relentless malady, tried vainly to hope against hope.

At 11:20 o'clock this morning President Kalinin briefly opened the session of the All-Russian Soviet Congress and requested every one to stand. He had not slept all night and tears were streaming down his haggard face. A sudden wave of emotion—not a sound, but a strange stir—passed over the audience, none of whom knew what had happened. The music started to play the Soviet funeral march, but was instantly hushed as Kalinin murmured brokenly:

"I bring you terrible news about our dear comrade, Vladimir Ilyitch." [Nikolai Lenin was his party name.]

High up in the gallery a woman uttered a low, wailing cry that was followed by a burst of sobs.

Kalinin Breaks the News.

"Yesterday," faltered Kalinin, "yesterday, he suffered a further stroke of paralysis and—" There was a long pause as if the speaker were unable to nerve himself to pronounce the fatal word; then, with an effort which shook his whole body, it came—"died."

The emotional Slav temperament reacted immediately. From all over the huge opera house came sobs and wailing, not loud nor shrill, but pitifully mournful, spreading and increasing. Kalinin could not speak. Its tried vainly to hope for silence with his hands and for one appalling moment a dreadful outbreak of mass hysteria seemed certain. A tenth of a second later it could not have been averted, but Tomskidze, Secretary of the Russian Federal Union of the Powerful railway frame and with hand and voice demanded calm. Then Kalinin, standing, read out the official bulletin.

"Jan. 21 the condition of Vladimir Ilyitch suddenly underwent sharp aggravation. At 5:30 P. M. his breathing was interrupted and he lost consciousness. At 6:50 Vladimir Ilyitch died from paralysis of the respiratory centres.

"Dated 3:25 A. M., Jan. 22.
"Signed:
"Drs. OHUNK [Lenin's personal physician and chief of the Moscow Health Department, who gave Lenin first treatment when wounded Aug. 30, 1918.]
"SEMIRKO [a close personal friend of Lenin, and Minister of the Health Department.]
"FOERSTER,
"GETIE,
"OSIPOF,
"TEWSISTATOF.

"We propose," continued Kalinin, "that the twenty-first day of January henceforth be set aside as a day of national mourning." By a tragic coincidence today—Jan. 9, old style, is similar Bolshevist holiday in memory of Father Gapon's petitioners, massacred of the Czar's troops in the courtyard of the Winter Palace on "Bloody Sunday," 1905.

"Do you agree?" questioned Kalinin. A confused sound, half sob, half sigh, was the only assent.

Whole Congress Gives Way to Grief.

Kalinin tried to tell the funeral arrangements, but broke down completely. Kamenef and Zinovief, equally unnerved, and other members of the Presiding Committee had laid their heads on the table and cried like children. Even the daredevil Cossack leader Budyenny was weeping unrestrainedly, while the delegates in the body of the theatre stood motionless, sobbing, with tears coursing down their cheeks.

Finally Lashevitch, a member of the Central Executive Committee of the Communist Party and of the Siberian Revolutionary Committee, stepped to the speakers' rostrum. His strong, square body in khaki uniform with dull red facings radiated calm as in a firm voice he announced that the Presiding Committee and a group of senior delegates in the Congress would go tomorrow by special train to the village of Gorky, where

Continued on Page Three.

AUGUSTA SPECIAL. Compartment, Drawing Room Cars, Daily for Augusta, Aiken, Asheville. Golf and all outdoor sports. Ideal climate. Reservations Southern Ry. System, 162 W. 42d St., Tel. 2206.—Advt.

EXPERTS PROPOSE GERMAN GOLD BANK

It Would Be Absolutely Independent and Under International Control.

SCHACHT URGES MEASURE

Dawes Committee Will Go to Berlin on Monday to Discuss Proposal There.

Copyright, 1924, by The New York Times Company.
Special Cable to The New York Times.

PARIS, Jan. 22.—Its first decisive step toward accomplishing the task which has been set it of reorganizing German finance and showing a way of balancing the budget was taken today by the Expert Committee studying the problem under the Chairmanship of General Charles G. Dawes. In a communiqué issued this afternoon the committee announced that it had reached the opinion that an independent gold bank under international control was the first essential to any plan for securing the budget equilibrium and stable currency in Germany.

This opinion, it is emphasized, was a unanimous one, and though the French have been largely instrumental in forwarding the suggestion, their claim to more credit than any other delegates of the five nationalities composing the committee.

Influenced by Schacht.

To the confirmation of opinion in the minds of the committeemen, Dr. Schacht, President of the Reichsbank, by his replies to the questionnaire submitted to him yesterday and answered yesterday, added considerable influence. As yet the plans for creation of such a bank are not fully elaborated, but the committee, working under high pressure, has given Dr. Schacht a two-and-a-half-mile drive to Berlin for Jan. 30, when it proposes to discuss with him a definite plan.

The communiqué issued this evening by the committee read as follows:

"The committee of experts during its sittings up till now has been chiefly devoting its time to investigate the reasons for the depreciation of German currency and balancing the budget has reached the opinion that an independent gold bank should be established, partly by mobilizing some part of the five reserves of gold and foreign currencies which may exist in the hands of German nationals and which at present discharge no economic function, and partly by co-operation of foreign capital, in their view such a step will form part of the ultimate plan to secure future budget equilibrium and stable currency.

"The committee in its connection think some feature of the plan outlined before them yesterday by Dr. Schacht will prove in due course to be very useful and they were glad to have the full and complete oral advantage of his views as part of the whole field of possible or alternative action to be reviewed.

"The President of the committee has heretofore emphasized the need of allied unification in the program. The committee is convinced that foreign co-operation in the management of such a bank is similarly desirable for its ultimate success.

"The committee, in view of necessary prompt decision and action, has advised Dr. Schacht that it will discuss its definite plan in Berlin on Wednesday, Jan. 30."

As usual the members of the committee today showed the greatest reserve

Continued on Page Six.

FLORIDA WEST COAST LIMITED 2:30 P. M. Daily—De Luxe Train to all West Coast Resorts. (No extra fare.) Penn-Sea board, 152 W. 42d St. Tel. Bryant 5415.—Advt.

Captain of Tacoma and Two Radio Men Lose Their Lives in Vera Cruz Storm

Special to The New York Times.

WASHINGTON, Jan. 22.—Wireless messages from official sources tonight report that Captain Herbert G. Sparrow of the wrecked cruiser Tacoma and two radio operators have lost their lives in a severe hurricane outside Vera Cruz Harbor.

The State Department received this dispatch late tonight from Consul Wood at Vera Cruz by Navy wireless:

"Vera Cruz, Jan. 22, 1924.
"Secretary of State,
"Washington.

"I am profoundly distressed to announce the death of Captain of the U. S. S. Tacoma and also of two wireless operators through an accident on board her during a norther, while in the performance of duty. Particulars will follow.
"WOOD, American Consul.

The first intimation that the Tacoma had figured in another tragedy reached Washington early in the evening, when Señor Alvares del Castillo, diplomatic agent of the revolutionary faction, received this radio message from Adolfo la Huerta:

"By orders of the supreme chief, the midst of a furious hurricane, our small naval transports steamed out of

The news of the tragedy was received in Washington with deep sorrow, for Captain Sparrow was a splendid type of the seasoned naval officer.

The Tacoma was sent to Vera Cruz to establish cable communications. She tried to make the breakwater at Vera Cruz at dawn one morning but was cast off by a "norther" and thrown on Blanquilla reef.

Most of her men were sent to the beach at Vera Cruz, to be picked up later by the Richmond, on board which they are at Tampico. Captain Sparrow, six officers and forty-eight sailors remained on the Tacoma.

The King acted on the advice, and before Mr. Baldwin had left the palace Mr. Macdonald had arrived, with J. R. Clynes and J. H. Thomas.

Captain Sparrow was an Ohioan, member of the Naval Academy of 1895. He had seen fifteen years of service at sea.

DECLARES ANDERSON FORCED HIM TO SPLIT PART OF HIS 'DRY' PAY

Chief Accuser of Anti-Saloon League Official Then Admits Trying to Sell Exposure.

DENIES HE TRIED BLACKMAIL

Defense Links Witness With Brewers and Wet Organization at Forgery Trial.

Light on the financial arrangements of the Anti-Saloon League of New York State was contributed by O. Bertsall Phillips, former collector for the league, who was the chief witness yesterday at the trial of William H. Anderson, State Superintendent of the league, on a charge of forgery, before Supreme Court Justice Tompkins and a jury. In turn, the defense launched an attack on the personal character of Phillips.

According to Phillips, he entered into a contract with Superintendent Anderson whereby he was to get commissions on all moneys he collected for the league's propaganda of the league. This contract, according to the witness, stipulated that he was to get 20 per cent. on the first $25,000 he obtained yearly, and 10 per cent. on all money over that figure.

In the course of his direct examination by Chief Assistant District Attorney Pecora, Phillips charged that Anderson had forced him to split "fifty-fifty" on all collection commissions in excess of $10,000. As the witness told it, Anderson declared that his own salary was only $10,000 a year and that no employe of the league was to get more than he.

Taking over the witness for cross-examination, former Governor Charles S. Whitman, leader of the defense, pounced away unmercifully at Phillips. He asked by the British and Dominion Parliaments, but with the possible exception of Canada, where the King's Government is in a nominal minority, there is thought to be no likelihood of an upset of the verdicts already given.

British governmental authorities are now satisfied that the treaty, as revised, will not conflict in any way with the American Constitution. Apprehension had originally existed that the treaty's proposal to allow British ships to carry liquor stores within the three-mile limit might not square with the Eighteenth Amendment, and the British Government was chary of extending the privilege of right of search to an hour's steaming from shore until it was certain that it would receive due quid pro quo.

As stated in official circles, the signing of the treaty will not affect in any way the complaints already filed by the London Government regarding the seizure of British vessels outside the three-mile limit. The Government will continue to seek a solution of the point of law involved in these cases, and will make compensation for its subjects concerned.

LABOR TAKES OFFICE, FULFILLING ANCIENT BRITISH CEREMONIES

Macdonald Kisses the King's Hand in Accepting Commission to Head Government.

THREE PEERS IN CABINET

New Premier Takes Foreign Office Also and Will Base His Policy on League.

By EDWIN L. JAMES.
Copyright, 1924, by The New York Times Company.
Special Cable to The New York Times.

LONDON, Jan. 22.—In the historic setting of Buckingham Palace, replete with the symbolism of British monarchy of more than a thousand years, King George today entrusted to a leader of workingmen the chief post in the government of the British Empire.

Events moved swiftly from the moment when Premier Baldwin visited the King this morning and placed the resignation of his Ministry; defeated last night in the House of Commons, in the hands of the King. Mr. Baldwin recommended to the King that he should send for James Ramsay Macdonald, leader of the opposition and head of the Parliamentary Labor Party, as his successor.

Mr. Macdonald accepted the commission, kissed the King's hand according to custom, and the first Socialist Labor Government in the British Isles came at once into being.

The New Ministry.

The new Ministry was announced as follows:

Prime Minister, First Lord of the Treasury and Secretary of State for Foreign Affairs—James Ramsay Macdonald.
Lord Privy Seal and Leader of the House of Commons—John Robert Clynes.
Lord Chancellor—The Viscount Haldane.
Chancellor of the Exchequer—Philip Snowden.
Secretary of State for Home Affairs—Arthur Henderson.
Secretary of State for the Colonies—J. H. Thomas.
Secretary of State for War—Stephen Walsh.
Air Minister—Brig. Gen. Christopher Thomson.
First Lord of the Admiralty—The Viscount Chelmsford.
President of the Board of Trade—Sidney Webb.
Minister of Health—John Wheatley.
Minister of Agriculture—Noel Buxton.
Secretary of State for Scotland—William Adamson.
President of the Board of Education—C. P. Trevelyan.
Minister of Labor—Thomas Shaw.
Postmaster General—Vernon Hartshorn.
Chancellor for the Duchy of Lancaster—Colonel Josiah Wedgwood.
Commissioner of Works—F. W. Jowett.

Three Laborites Visit the King.

A pacifist, known as an idealist, Mr. Macdonald showed today that he could be practical and swift. With his Cabinet already committed, it is expected that the old and new Ministers will exchange the seals of office tomorrow at noon, after which Labor will be in power.

Parliament adjourned today until Feb. 12, which leaves the new Prime Minister three weeks to prepare to meet the House of Commons.

After last night's vote, Mr. Baldwin met the end of the Baldwin Government. Mr. Baldwin called together his Cabinet at 10 o'clock to receive the resignations of his various Ministers. Then he left No. 10 Downing Street by a back door to walk to Buckingham Palace; to escape a group of photographers he hailed a passing taxi, which took him to the King's presence. His audience lasted about half an hour.

When Mr. Macdonald met his party leaders at the House of Commons he announced that the King had sent for him, and after conducting his business he left for Buckingham Palace.

Continued on Page Four.

COOLIDGE SENDS WATCHER TO OIL HEARING; DAUGHERTY IS ALREADY INVESTIGATING; ASK SINCLAIR TO RETURN, FALL RECALLED

Sinclair Declares Oil Inquiry Is 'Politics'; Denies Paying Fall for Teapot Dome Lease

Copyright, 1924, by The New York Times Company.
Special Cable to The New York Times.

PLYMOUTH, Eng., Jan. 22.—Harry F. Sinclair was on board the liner Paris, which arrived at Plymouth this afternoon from New York. He was accompanied by Mrs. Sinclair and Mr. Day, Vice President of the Sinclair Oil Company. He did not land at Plymouth, but proceeded to Havre. His name appeared on the supplementary passenger list.

"My trip to Europe," said Mr. Sinclair, "has nothing to do with avoiding being called to give testimony before the committee that has been sitting for the last three or four months. I expect to stay four or five weeks in Europe, and upon my return I shall be perfectly willing to testify again if it is wished. I have already given testimony four or five times, and I was excused.

"There was nothing secret or mysterious about my leaving New York. It was public. Every one knew I was in New York and that I was leaving for Europe. There were forty photographers there when I left.

"I absolutely deny all statements or suggestions that I have brought away documents or papers relating to the case. It is perfectly ridiculous, all these statements that I paid Mr. Fall this money for the lease. I absolutely deny it."

"The entire situation," Mr. Sinclair added, "is a political move and a case of American politics."

WON'T CONFER AGAIN ON ST. MARK'S RITES

Bishop Manning Stands on His Edict Against the New Practices.

RECTOR DEMANDS A JURY

Vestry Backs Up His Request That Services Be Judged by 50 Clergy and Laymen.

The differences between Dr. William Norman Guthrie, rector of St. Mark's-in-the-Bouwerie and Bishop William T. Manning of the Protestant Episcopal Diocese of New York over Dr. Guthrie's eurythmic rituals and "pagan" services reached a climax yesterday.

Dr. Guthrie, his wardens and vestry made it known that the Bishop had refused to meet them again in conference, although on their previous meeting at Synod Hall five weeks ago it had been understood that such a step would be taken.

Dr. Guthrie and the vestry made public two letters which are now in the hands of Bishop Manning. The first is Dr. Guthrie's defense and explanation of his position in view of the Bishop's objection to a further conference. The second sets forth the stand of the wardens and vestry on the same point. Dr. Guthrie says in his letter to the Bishop:

Bishop William T. Manning said last night that he had received both Dr. Guthrie's letter and the communication from the wardens and vestry of St. Mark's, but had not had an opportunity to read them. When a summary of their contents was outlined, including Dr. Guthrie's proposal that the eurythmic rituals and "pagan" services should be judged by fifty representative clergymen and laymen of the Protestant Episcopal Church, the Bishop said that he had no comment to make.

"You officially summoned me on the thirteenth of December, demanding, besides, the presence of all my vestry. You did not open our conference with any inquiry into my work, but greatly surprised us by reading a previously prepared arraignment charging me with disloyalty to the Church of a most serious character, calculated to undermine my vestry from their rector. We respectfully answered you to the effect that your arrangement, and your consequent requests, were not founded on fact but upon newspaper headlines, and on irresponsible, because anonymous, testimony.

Indictment Not Pressed.

"Now this indictment, charging me with disloyalty to the Church, was not pressed by you; but you urged the residual complaint that I had conducted my work in complete disregard of the good name and honor of the Protestant Episcopal Church; and your evidence, was that my work had been of such a nature, after which Easter will be in power.

You yourself proposed that we adjourn our conference over the Christmas holidays for thirty days, to consider both sides and discover what common ground there might be between us. We agreed to keep the nature of our conference confidential until the next conference, and especially your request, though you consented to my consulting my fellow-clergy, with the understanding that they should be warned against any authority. On my return home, after dinner, I was promptly notified over the telephone by representatives of the press that your

See New York Times on the 17th December published, therefore, our formal declaration that such information had not reached the press through any channel open to us, and that it was so apparent to you, from the fact that our efforts had resented the at first proposed publication of these requests because of the

TAKE BELL-ANS AFTER MEALS. Relieves Indigestion. Amazing benefit.—Advt.

VETO THREATENED ON A HIGH SURTAX

President Stands Inflexibly for Secretary Mellon's 25 Per Cent. Rate.

COMPROMISERS UNMOVED

House Committee Decides to Act on Indirect Taxes First and Surtax Last.

Special to The New York Times.

WASHINGTON, Jan. 22.—President Coolidge is taking an active personal interest in the developments in the Teapot Dome oil lease hearings before the Senate's special investigating committee. He has ordered the Department of Justice to have an observer at the hearings to watch for any evidence of wrongdoing, and Attorney General Daugherty has been instructed to start action at once if evidence justifying prosecution of any person is presented. Mr. Daugherty declared today that any violation of the law would be prosecuted, "no matter who the person is."

"That's all that can be done now—observe the evidence brought out at the hearing and prepare for action when the Government has enough evidence to make the law."

In asserting this position it was made clear that the President wanted it understood that the Administration was not making any accusations against any one or expressing any opinion as to the investigation.

The spokesman for the President indicated that Mr. Coolidge did not wish to indicate when and in what way the Government would proceed, on the ground that to do so would embarrass the Department of Justice in its present inquiry.

In addition to the White House announcement that the President had instructed the Department of Justice to follow the testimony before the committee, other circles that if fraud were committed in the making of the oil leases they would be canceled, and action started civilly and criminally against any person guilty of wrongdoing in connection with the transfer of the Government properties to oil corporations.

The opinion was expressed by a White House spokesman that all that could be done with dignity and in order had been done and that the President when he ordered the Department of Justice to send an observer to the hearing "to see what evidence might disclose as to possible rumors." These rumors dealt with the allegation that a Government official had received money from a corporation interested in the lease.

Sinclair and Fall Summoned.

The Senate Committee today authorized E. T. Stanford, counsel for Harry Sinclair, to obtain his presence without delay and the production of the books of the Hyva Corporation, which marketed the stock of the company formed to handle the Teapot Dome lease.

Subpoena was also issued for Secretary Fall to appear and answer the testimony of Archie Roosevelt that given by the Sinclair organization. E. W. Neely, one of the counsel for Sinclair, is whom were issued 33,000 shares of the Sinclair Corporation's stock, also has been subpoenaed. Senator Lenroot stated that the committee would probably hear E. L. Doheny to testify later. Mr. Doheny is reported on his way back from New Orleans.

Mr. Fall is expected to appear on Thursday, to which day the committee adjourned.

Senator Caraway served notice today that he will move tomorrow to discharge the Committee on Public Lands from further consideration of the resolution he introduced calling for cancellation of the Teapot Dome lease. This motion, if adopted, would bring the oil lease matter before the Senate for a vote by the whole Senate.

PRESIDENT READY TO ACT

Spokesman Indicates Coolidge Has His Eyes on Developments.

INQUIRY TO BE PRESSED

Senate Committee Wants Fall to Explain Archie Roosevelt's Story.

SINCLAIR'S BOOKS SOUGHT

Mysterious Memorandum Appears of Fall's Ranch Purchase—No Clue to Author.

NIKOLAI LENIN (VLADIMIR ILYITCH ULIANOV).
A sketch made from life for The New York Times by Oscar Cesare in Moscow, November, 1922, and autographed by Lenin.

BRITAIN ACCEPTS THE LIQUOR TREATY

Document Is Approved by All of the Dominions and Hughes Is Notified.

GEDDES MAY SIGN TODAY

Washington Makes Preliminary Proposals for Similar Compacts to Other Powers.

Copyright, 1924, by The New York Times Company.
Special Cable to The New York Times.

LONDON, Jan. 22.—The Anglo-American liquor running treaty is ready for the signatures. All the British Dominions have approved it and the British Ambassador at Washington has been asked to notify the United States State Department that Britain is prepared to sign.

The treaty, of course, must be ratified

FLORIDA WEST COAST RESORTS VIA PENN.-ATLANTIC COAST LINE. Complete schedule. Information at 1266 Broadway.—Advt.

The New York Times.

THE WEATHER

Rain today or tonight and tomorrow; no change in temperature.
Temperature yesterday—Max., 46; Min., 34.
For weather report see next to last page.

VOL. LXXIII....No. 24,117.   ***   NEW YORK, MONDAY, FEBRUARY 4, 1924.   TWO CENTS In Greater New York | THREE CENTS Within 200 Miles | FOUR CENTS Elsewhere

WOODROW WILSON PASSES AWAY IN SLEEP; END COMES AT 11:15 A.M.; NATION SORROWS AND TRIBUTES ARE VOICED IN ALL LANDS

OIL INQUIRY PAUSES IN HONOR OF WILSON; GREGORY RETIRES

Today's Session is Suspended and Committee May Not Resume Till After Funeral.

SENATE SANCTION AWAITED

Testimony Will Be Postponed Pending Action on Fall's Challenge of Authority.

GREGORY EXPLAINS POSITION

Writes President He Had Been Unaware of Doheny's Share in Paying Fee.

Special to The New York Times.

WASHINGTON, Feb. 3.—The death of former President Wilson may delay for several days the Congressional activities in connection with the Naval Reserve oil lease scandals.

It had been the intention of Senator Lenroot, Chairman of the Public Lands Committee, to place before the Senate tomorrow the points made by former Secretary Albert B. Fall on Saturday in refusing to answer questions, and to ask for additional power to proceed with the investigation, if that was considered necessary.

But it now develops that the Senate will adjourn immediately tomorrow out of respect to the memory of Mr. Wilson, thus providing no opportunity for consideration of the oil scandals. It is possible that there may be a session of the Senate on Tuesday, at which action will be taken, but the opinion expressed tonight was that all developments might be held back until after the funeral of the former President.

Former Secretary Fall has been subpoenaed to appear before the investigating committee again on Tuesday morning, but this feature of the proceedings probably will also be postponed.

Long Legal Battle in Prospect.

Mr. Fall is remaining in seclusion and his legal advisers are apparently confident that the courts will uphold his right to refuse to testify on the ground that he might incriminate himself. There have been reports that the committee, after obtaining additional power from Congress, would place Fall in custody, if he persisted in defying it, but these are not confirmed. It is probable that a long legal battle will be witnessed, the committee in the meantime going ahead with other phases of the inquiry.

During the delay, however, the auditing experts retained by the committee will continue their examination of the books of brokerage firms which have been subpoenaed by the committee in an effort to establish whether any persons prominent in the official life of Washington who may have had advance information profited by the rise in the value of Sinclair Consolidated Securities following the announcement of the leasing of Teapot Dome Reserve to Sinclair.

Thomas Watts Gregory, Attorney General in the Wilson Administration, formally withdrew as special counsel in the oil cases today in a letter sent to President Coolidge which was given out at the White House.

Mr. Gregory made the point that while he had talked on the long distance telephone with the President on Tuesday night, he had not accepted the appointment as that time and had simply agreed to come on to Washington and discuss the proposition. He also stated that he had not recalled at that time that he ever received any money paid out by Doheny.

While the President has made no formal announcement, it was generally accepted tonight that he would appoint former Senator Atlee Pomerene as counsel representing the Democratic Party. It was indicated at the White House that the President desired to talk over it with Senator Walsh, and also would wait until the joint resolution adopted in Congress last week was placed before him.

Silas Strawn, selected as the Republican member of counsel, had a long conference today with Mr. Pomerene about the oil cases, and they said afterward that they had made a good start on the preparation of the case. It is believed that the remote connection of Mr. Strawn's law firm with the Texas Oil Company will not prevent his confirmation by the Senate. In this connection Mr. Strawn said:

"For about ten years, I think, my firm has collected bills for the Texas Company and obtained locations for their filling stations in the Chicago territory. These are matters handled by the young men of our firm and I never have had anything to do with them. My firm never has handled any of the corporate business of the Texas or any other oil

Congress to Adjourn Today After Tributes to Wilson

WASHINGTON, Feb. 3.—Congress will pay its tribute tomorrow to Woodrow Wilson.

On convening at noon, both the House and Senate will adjourn out of respect for his memory.

In the House, Representative Longworth, the Republican leader, will give official notification of Mr. Wilson's death, and after a brief eulogy will yield the floor to Representative Garrett, the Democratic leader, who will deliver a eulogy.

In the Senate, Mr. Robinson, the Democratic leader, will deliver an address. Both houses will resume business Tuesday.

EUROPE IS STIRRED BY WILSON'S DEATH

Lloyd George Calls Him Glorious Failure Who Sacrificed His Life for His Ideal.

CECIL PAYS HIM TRIBUTE

France, Italy and Other Allied Capitals Recall His Services in Winning the War.

Special Cable to The New York Times.

LONDON, Feb. 3.—In common with most of the allied statesmen of Europe and other personalities whom destiny summoned to fill leading rôles in the World War, former Premier Lloyd George sees in Woodrow Wilson an idealist who stood out as perhaps the most remarkable figure of that tremendous cataclysm.

In an interview which THE NEW YORK TIMES correspondent had with him today at his new home at Churt, Surrey, concerning the passing of Mr. Wilson, Mr. Lloyd George said:

"Woodrow Wilson was a very great man, and, like all great men, had his defects, but these will be quickly forgotten in the magnitude of his life work. True he was a failure, but a glorious failure. He failed as Jesus Christ failed, and, like Christ, sacrificed his life in pursuance of his noble ideal.

"He was just as much a victim of the great war as any soldier who died in the trenches. Like his health in the endeavor to create a better and happier existence for the people of the whole world, and I am sure that the failure of his altruistic inspirations hastened his tragic end.

"It will perhaps be a generation before the greatness of Woodrow Wilson will be appreciated at its real value by his countrymen and the tragedy which closed his life will bring before the world the unselfishness of his ambitions as nothing else could. Like the tragedy which made for our great martyred Lincoln a permanent place in the hearts of the American people—even of those who disagreed with him, as was made very apparent to me in my recent visit to the Southern States—the sad death of this great Statesman, this great American, will indelibly stamp his name among those at the very top of your history.

Had Violent Likes and Dislikes.

"Like Theodore Roosevelt, Mr. Wilson had violent likes and dislikes, and for this, as always is the penalty of greatness, he was violently criticised. I believe I may say that never have I seen such vicious, cruel vituperation as was heaped upon him at home and in many a man in like position in history and it hurt him terribly.

"Criticism cut him like a knife. Had been a lifelong politician he could have overlooked these attacks. Thirty years or so of political life makes one invulnerable, I know. But Wilson's character was such, he was of such fine stuff, that he was immensely sensitive to this public abuse and he suffered more than others would have done. I have no doubt that this helped to bring on his illness.

"Besides, he was a tireless worker. I remember when we were in Paris I would see lights in his room at all hours of the night as he worked at his League idea. The rest of us found time for golf and we took our Sundays off, but Wilson, in his zeal, worked incessantly. Only those who were there and witnessed it can realize the efforts he expended.

His Personality Grew Upon One.

"He was a man whose personality grew upon one. When I first met him here in England I did not understand him, nor did Clemenceau in Paris; but when you spend every day for five months with a man you have opportunity to become well acquainted with him, and when it was over I had learned to appreciate his great gifts and to like very much personally, and I remember Clemenceau at the time telling me his feelings were similar.

"Yes, Woodrow Wilson was a very good fellow, and I shall mourn his passing. I had the pleasure of spending a

Continued on Page Four.

COOLIDGE ANNOUNCES DEATH

In Formal Proclamation He Calls the Nation to Mourn.

HE LAUDS WILSON'S WORK

With Mrs. Coolidge, He Drives From Church to S Street House and Leaves Cards.

FLAGS ORDERED LOWERED

Will Stay at Half-Staff 30 Days —Government Offices to Close —Receptions Canceled.

Special to The New York Times.

WASHINGTON, Feb. 3.—The death of Woodrow Wilson was formally announced to the people of the nation late this afternoon by a proclamation issued from the White House by President Coolidge, in which he paid high tribute to the war President, and directed that flags on the White House and Government buildings be half-staffed for a period of thirty days.

When the text of the proclamation was made public, the further statement was authorized at the White House that President Coolidge had directed that orders be issued closing all Government departments on the day of Mr. Wilson's funeral. Flags will fly at half-mast on war ships, at military posts and on all American diplomatic and consular Government offices abroad.

President Coolidge's proclamation pays high tribute to the life and services of Mr. Wilson, saying that it brings "to many of us" a sense of profound personal bereavement.

Official Social Functions Canceled.

All official social functions—including the brilliant State reception scheduled for the White House on Thursday—have been canceled.

In ordering the flags on Government buildings half-staffed, and arranging for the issuance of orders for closing Government buildings on the day of the funeral, President Coolidge followed the customary procedure. The President feels that the Government, over which Mr. Wilson presided during eight of the most important years in American history, should in every way act in testimony of the respect in which the memory of so great and distinguished a President is held.

President and Mrs. Coolidge were in their pew in the First Congregational Church, at the corner of Tenth and G Streets, when they first heard of the death of the former President. In that church, in common with many others, announcement of the death was made during the services, at the close of which the pastor, the Rev. Jason Noble Pierce, made a special prayer in view of the occasion.

After the close of the service the Coolidges were driven directly to the Wilson home. The big White House car swept into the drive before the Wilson house at 12:25 o'clock, one hour and ten minutes after the death of the ex-President. The door of the car was opened by a Secret Service man, while another stood outside it and between the car and the spectators.

Although a few of the callers at the Wilson home had stayed in their cars and sent in cards by a footman, both the President and Mrs. Coolidge alighted. The President got out first, assisting Mrs. Coolidge. They walked up the flight of three steps to the door. It happened to be open, because two other callers had rung the bell just as the President's car stopped.

Coolidge Hands Cards to the Butler.

Mr. Coolidge himself handed cards to the negro butler, who received them on a silver tray. They re-entered their car, but its long wheelbase was too much for the narrow arc of the Wilson driveway, and the chauffeur was obliged to back and start twice before he could get started for the street.

The President's car started east over the S Street hill and was followed by the car in which the Secret Service men rode.

The President wore a silk hat and a black overcoat with silk lapels. Mrs. Coolidge was dressed in brown, with hat to match. Both were grave, and during their stop at the Wilson house neither was observed to speak a word.

Perhaps half an hour after the Presidential visit C. Bascom Slemp, Secretary to Mr. Coolidge, arrived alone in his car. He entered the house and remained ten or fifteen minutes. When he emerged, Mr. Slemp said that, in addition to offering his personal condolences as a Virginian and an acquaintance of the family, he had come from the President to tell the members of the Wilson household that the Government was desirous of learning its wishes in respect to funeral arrangements and that anything they desired would be done. Mr. Slemp said he had talked to Joseph Wilson, the former President's brother, and John Randolph Bolling, Mr. Wilson's secretary. They told him that funeral plans had not been discussed, but it was agreed that as soon as any decision was reached Mr. Slemp would be informed.

WOODROW WILSON

President Coolidge's Proclamation

By the President of the United States of America.

A Proclamation

To the People of the United States:

The death of Woodrow Wilson, President of the United States from March 4, 1913, to March 4, 1921, which occurred at 11:15 o'clock today at his home at Washington, District of Columbia, deprives the country of a most distinguished citizen, and is an event which causes universal and genuine sorrow. To many of us it brings the sense of a profound personal bereavement.

His early profession as a lawyer was abandoned to enter academic life. In this chosen field he attained the highest rank as an educator, and has left his impress upon the intellectual thought of the country.

From the Presidency of Princeton University he was called by his fellow citizens to be the Chief Executive of the State of New Jersey. The duties of this high office he so conducted as to win the confidence of the people of the United States, who twice elected him to the Chief Magistracy of the Republic.

As President of the United States he was moved by an earnest desire to promote the best interests of the country as he conceived them. His acts were prompted by high motives and his sincerity of purpose cannot be questioned. He led the nation through the terrific struggle of the World War with a lofty idealism which never failed him. He gave utterance to the aspiration of humanity with an eloquence which held the attention of all the earth and made America a new and enlarged influence in the destiny of mankind.

In testimony of the respect in which his memory is held by the Government and the people of the United States, I do hereby direct that the flags of the White House and of the several departmental buildings be displayed at half-staff for a period of thirty days, and that suitable military and naval honors, under orders of the Secretary of War and of the Secretary of the Navy, be rendered on the day of the funeral.

Done at the City of Washington this Third Day of February, in the Year of Our Lord One Thousand Nine Hundred and Twenty-Four, and of the Independence of the United States of America the One Hundred and Forty-Eighth.

By the President: CALVIN COOLIDGE.

CHARLES EVANS HUGHES, Secretary of State.

WAR PRESIDENT'S END CAME PEACEFULLY

His Life Ebbed Away While He Slept and His Heart Action Became Fainter Until It Finally Ceased.

WIFE AT THE DYING MAN'S BEDSIDE UNTIL THE END

Her Name Was the Last Word to Pass His Lips and His Last Sentence Was 'I Am Ready,' Spoken Friday.

Special to The New York Times.

WASHINGTON, Feb. 3.—Woodrow Wilson, twenty-eighth President of the United States, a commanding world figure and chief advocate of the League of Nations, is dead. He died at 11:15 o'clock this morning, after being unconscious for nearly twelve hours.

Mrs. Wilson, Miss Margaret Wilson, Joseph Wilson, a brother, and Admiral Grayson, his physician, were at the bedside.

Just before death the war President opened his eyes. His wife and daughter spoke to him, but he did not respond. Ten minutes later he passed quietly away. No word was uttered.

All day yesterday and last night he had been sinking rapidly, his pulse becoming fainter and fainter, until finally it ceased to beat. His "broken machinery" had collapsed.

Washington and the nation were prepared for death. The morning papers had carried the news that he had been "profoundly prostrated." The waiting groups, numbering many hundreds, outside of the Wilson home were silent when Admiral Grayson, five minutes after his patient and friend had expired, opened the door and made the announcement.

Text of the Death Bulletin.

Dr. Grayson read the following statement:

11:20 A. M., Feb. 3, 1924.

Mr. Wilson died at 11:15 o'clock this morning. His heart action became feebler and feebler, and the heart muscle was so fatigued that it refused to act any longer. The end came peacefully. The remote causes of death lie in his ill-health, which began more than four years ago, namely, arteriosclerosis and hemiplegia. The immediate cause of death was exhaustion following a digestive disturbance which began in the early part of last week, but did not reach an acute stage until the early morning hours of Feb. 1.

CARY T. GRAYSON.

Arteriosclerosis is a thickening and hardening of the walls of the arteries, and hemiplegia is a paralysis of one side of the body, the limbs on that side losing the power of voluntary motion. Mr. Wilson's left side was so stricken, the outward manifestation being the helpless drop of his left arm and the dragging of the left foot.

Died While Wife Held His Hand.

Mr. Wilson died in a room on the third floor of his home, where for so many months, since his retirement, he sat and looked over Washington, the scene of his greatest achievement. He expired on a large four-poster bed, a replica of the Lincoln bed in the White House.

Mr. Wilson's last word was "Edith," his wife's name. In a faint voice he called for her yesterday afternoon when she had left his bedside for a moment.

His last sentence was spoken on Friday, when he said:

"I am a broken piece of machinery. When the machinery is broken——I am ready."

Mrs. Wilson held his right hand as his life slowly ebbed away. Admiral Grayson remained in the death room for a few minutes and then went down stairs leaving Mrs. Wilson and Margaret at the bedside.

There had been signs during the morning that the end was a matter of minutes. The first bulletin issued by Dr. Grayson at 8:55 o'clock said:

"Mr. Wilson is unconscious and his pulse is very weak."

His 10:30 o'clock bulletin said:

"After a quiet night Mr. Wilson is very low and the end may be expected any time."

When, therefore, Dr. Grayson appeared on the steps of the house at 11:20 it was realized that he was probably there to announce the end.

Dr. Grayson Deeply Moved.

GRAYSON DESCRIBES SCENE AT DEATHBED

War President, He Says, Grew Weaker and Weaker Until He Calmly Passed Away.

ONCE CONSCIOUS AT NIGHT

Then He Relapsed Into Virtual Coma, From Which He Did Not Emerge.

Special to The New York Times.

WASHINGTON, Feb. 3.—Woodrow Wilson's death was peaceful, a gradual fading away of life after a long period of unconsciousness, according to Admiral Cary T. Grayson, who was his physician in the days of his strength and vigor at the White House and now was in almost constant attendance upon him since his tragic breakdown more than four years ago.

Mr. Wilson's last spoken word was "Edith," the name of his wife, uttered in a faint whisper late yesterday afternoon, when Mrs. Wilson had left the sick room temporarily. Mrs. Wilson, sent for by Admiral Grayson, returned almost immediately. She remained in the room thereafter until the end, sitting in a chair at the bedside and holding his husband's hand for the greater part of the time.

Mr. Wilson's last completely phrased sentence, so far as Admiral Grayson could recall, was his remark on Friday about the broken machine and the expression of his readiness to go. "I am a broken piece of machinery," he said. "When the machinery is broken—I am ready to go."

The last message to be received by Mr. Wilson from any one outside his immediate family was from Senator Glass of Virginia, Senator Glass, close friend of Mr. Wilson and a strong supporter of his policies, asked Admiral Grayson to give "the Chief" his love. Admiral Grayson did so early Saturday

Dr. Grayson was making a strong effort to keep himself under control. In his hand he held some of the yellow slips on which the bulletins were typewritten. He came toward the newspaper men, who quickly gathered about him near the steps of the house.

"The end came at 11:15," he said in a low tone.

Immediately there was a commotion in the crowd as the newspaper men assigned to flash the news of death which would speed all over the world, broke through their comrades and rushed off.

The crowd across the street, now grown to large proportions, surged forward in an effort to hear Dr. Grayson, but the police lines held and there was nothing for them to do but to listen with strained attention.

Meanwhile Dr. Grayson had begun to read the bulletin. This was the climax of the emotional strain he had been under, and it was only with difficulty that he could force himself to go ahead.

He read slowly. His voice trembled, but did not break. But as he read, very slowly, tears kept rolling down his cheeks and he used his handkerchief.

This action, more than what they could hear, showed the spectators across the street that he was actually announcing Mr. Wilson's death. Here and there in the crowd men began to take off their hats. Soon almost all were uncovered. The women stood with lowered heads, many of them weeping.

Finally, Dr. Grayson finished reading the bulletin. The newspaper men expressed a few words of sympathy and then hurried off to send the detailed news. Dr. Grayson was left standing with only one or two before him.

The physician and friend of the former President, who has been the only link between the sick room and the outside world, was asked whether, now that Mr. Wilson was dead, he would not give a detailed account of his last hours. He demurred, saying he did not believe there was anything more to be added to what had been said.

He was urged to undertake the task as a duty to the memory of his friend and patient. On this ground he assented. He said he would take an automobile ride for the purpose of resting, and that during its course he

Continued on Page Two.

"All the News That's Fit to Print."

The New York Times.

THE WEATHER
Partly cloudy and warmer today; tomorrow probably showers.
Temperature Yesterday—Max. 60; Min. 54.
For weather report see next to last page.

VOL. LXXIII....No. 24,247.   ••••   NEW YORK, FRIDAY, JUNE 13, 1924.   TWO CENTS In Greater New York | THREE CENTS Within 200 Miles | FOUR CENTS Elsewhere

COOLIDGE AND DAWES NOMINATED; GENERAL IS NAMED FOR SECOND PLACE AFTER LOWDEN, CHOSEN, REFUSES IT

EXPLOSIONS KILL 48 ON U. S. S. MISSISSIPPI; NEW BLAST FEARED

Firing Crew Wiped Out When Back-Fire Sets Off Store of Powder in Turret.

PASSENGER SHIP IN DANGER

14-Inch Gun Is Discharged in San Pedro Harbor, Shell Causing Panic on the Yale.

THIRD GUN STILL LOADED

After Landing Dead and Injured, Dreadnought Puts Back to Sea for Safety.

Special to The New York Times.

LOS ANGELES, Cal., June 12.—Three officers and forty-five enlisted men are known to have been killed, nine others probably fatally injured, and a score more hurt in various degrees in an explosion in a gun turret on the U. S. S. Mississippi, off San Pedro Harbor this afternoon.

There were two separate blasts—the first was that of 1,800 pounds of powder and a charge of a fourteen-inch rifle. The second came as the dreadnought dropped anchor near the hospital ship Relief in the harbor proper; the charge in the second great rifle in the Turret exploding, the shell was hurled out to sea, missing the outgoing liner Yale by a few hundred feet and creating a panic among its passengers.

The battleships Mississippi, Tennessee, Idaho and California, comprising a division under the command of Rear Admiral William V. Pratt, left Los Angeles Harbor today for the San Clemente drill grounds for secret practice.

Part of this consisted in concentrated fire by the Mississippi, Idaho and Tennessee against a giant target to be towed by the California.

According to the reports of men on the other ships, the three dreadnoughts were lined up. In the far distance, a tiny speck showed the California.

In gun turret No. 2, situated above and slightly abaft of gun turret No. 1, forward of the ship, were the eighty-odd men comprising the gun crews for guns Nos. 4, 5 and 6.

Part of these eighty-odd were stationed at the guns themselves; the remainder of the crews were occupied in the handling rooms and in the twin tunnels leading from the ammunition stores. In command of the turret was Lieutenant Thomas Edward Zellars, of Long Beach, Cal., was killed, as were Ensigns Marcus Erwin, J. J. Levasseur and James McCrea, the last two being observers from the U. S. S. New Mexico detailed to witness the target practice. The command was kept in a low speck showed the California.

The monster shells were brought from the ammunition stores by their mechanical carriers, lifted and shoved home in the gun barrels. Then came the great sacks of powder, 450 pounds of it in each sack, and four sacks in each charge of each gun. The three guns were loaded, and four sacks of the explosives still lay on the floor.

Gun Breech Not Closed.

The breeches in guns 5 and 6 swung slowly shut and tightly locked. In gun 4 the breech likewise swung toward closure, but something jammed. And in that moment when the breech hung slightly open, some one—no one knows who that some one was—gave the command to turn on the electrical current detonated the explosive in gun 4. The charge exploded. The eighty-odd men trapped in a steel cage designed to withstand the mightiest blow of an enemy fleet, were burned and crushed and mangled and gassed. Those within the turret proper were instantly killed.

The four sacks of powder still on the floor ignited in the mighty blast—and the armor-plated roof of the turret dissolved into fragments.

In the handling rooms those closest to the door were instantly killed; those further away are in the list of the injured. The fireproof doors to the ammunition tunnels were blown from their hinges; the trap-doors leading to the handling rooms were totally destroyed.

Ensign Levasseur out of the corner of one eye had caught sight of that open gun-breech when the command to fire had been given. He unhesitatingly dove forty feet from the steel deck, where he was standing, down the shaft of the endless chain powder bucket. He was cut and bruised but is still alive. Ensign Erwin, by whom he was standing, was instantly killed.

All this had been expected. There was no excitement almost at the run. Why. But in at least two respects this morning's session showed a tendency to a change of long settled habits of American politics. The conventional "demonstration" for President Coolidge, following the speech in which he was nominated, was not stretched out to the fantastic and artificial length that has been common in past conventions. It stopped after thirteen minutes, although it was two minutes later before all the delegates were in their seats.

Nominating Speech a "Sales Talk."

And the speech which had provoked it, the speech in which Dr. Marion Leroy Burton, President of the University of Michigan, placed President Coolidge in nomination, was of a type wholly new to national conventions and not unfamiliar in the commercial-cultural life of the United States. It was a sales talk, and a good sales talk at that. From some viewpoints it might be open to criticism, but it was perfectly adapted to the object for which it was intended.

The full text of Dr. Burton's speech is printed on page 6.

Dr. Burton is not a delegate. He was appointed by President Coolidge himself to deliver the official adherence of the candidate—for that is what it was, not an address to a convention already wrapped up, sealed and delivered for Coolidge, but an advertisement to the country of the personality and virtues of the head of the Republican ticket.

When the roll of States was called for nominations for the Presidency, Alabama, head of the list, yielded to Massachusetts. President Coolidge's home State, and Governor Channing Cox of Massachusetts moved that Dr. Burton "be accorded the privilege of nominating the candidate of Massachusetts."

That was in accordance with the sacred ritual of American State politics—that the candidate must not be named until the very end of the nominating speech, when his identity is disclosed suddenly to a surprised convention. It seems to be felt that if the name be spoken during the performance of the rites the omens will be inauspicious.

But a moment later Chairman Mondell incautiously let slip the President's name, and Dr. Burton broke with tradition and told the audience right away whom he was going to nominate.

Burton—his manner today suggests that he would feel insulted by continuing the use of his academic title—Burton looks no more like a college President than he does like a politician. Tall—taller than Coolidge—almost as red-headed as Coolidge, smooth faced and brisk and snappy, he can accurately be described only by those hackneyed terms "clean-cut" and "full of pep." He looks like a real estate agent and he talked today like a real estate agent selling a building lot in a suburban home development to an unwilling but a hypnotized and unresisting purchaser.

He talked for fifty-odd minutes. He talked far less than he finished in that time a speech that an ordinary orator would have lingered over for an hour and a quarter.

He omitted two sections of his prepared speech, those dealing with economy, a topic already much overdone in this convention, and capital and labor. Even so, it was no very long, unusually long for a nominating speech, but he talked so fast and played with it that the time never seemed to drag.

Continued on Page Eight.

BURTON NAMES COOLIDGE

Professor Breaks Traditions and Talks Out Like a Modern Salesman.

POPULARIZES HIS VIRTUES

And Carries Audience With Him All the Way With Homely Metaphors.

JEERS AGAIN FOR WISCONSIN

But Only Laughter Greets the South Dakota Vote for Hiram Johnson.

Special to The New York Times.

CLEVELAND, Ohio, June 12.—Calvin Coolidge was nominated for the Presidency at 1:57 o'clock this afternoon on the first ballot taken in the Republican National Convention.

He received 1,065 of the 1,109 votes. Robert Marion La Follette got 34—28 of the 29 from Wisconsin and six of the 13 from North Dakota, and six of Hiram Johnson got 10 of the 13 votes from South Dakota.

As usual, the galleries received every mention of La Follette's name, and the report of the votes cast for him, with jeers and hisses, but they had only laughter for the name of Hiram Johnson.

When the count of the ballot had been announced, S. X. Way of South Dakota, moved that the nomination be made unanimous, and Thomas Scott of Wisconsin, who cast that State's only vote for Coolidge, seconded the motion. When Chairman Frank W. Mondell put it to a viva voce vote everybody shouted "Aye," but the recalcitrant handful of La Follette men in Wisconsin, and North Dakota, and Mr. Mondell announced that "with the exception of a very few voices," Coolidge had been nominated by acclamation.

REPUBLICAN NOMINEE FOR PRESIDENT.
CALVIN COOLIDGE
OF MASSACHUSETTS.

COOLIDGE IS SILENT ON HIS NOMINATION

President Feels He Can Express His Appreciation Best in His Acceptance Speech.

GETS NEWS AT LUNCHEON

Talks With Borah Before Convention Meets, and Then Listens to Its Proceedings.

Special to The New York Times.

WASHINGTON, June 12.—The White House was silent on the nomination of former Governor Lowden for Vice President, and equally uncommunicative after word was flashed to Washington that Mr. Lowden had announced his declination.

President Coolidge, it was stated by his spokesmen at the White House, was maintaining his attitude of "hands off" with respect to the selection of a running mate, and had not during the day communicated any preference to Mr. Butler or any other person in the convention city.

Nor would the President comment on his own nomination by the convention. Edward Clark, his personal secretary, in answer to inquiries by newspaper correspondents, stated that the President had requested him to say there would be no statement coming from the White House.

Mr. Coolidge intimated to friends several days ago that what he had to say in the way of appreciation could be most fittingly said when the Notification Committee arrives with the formal information of the action of the National Convention. On that occasion he will read a carefully prepared acceptance speech.

At Lunch When Nominated.

The President was at lunch at the White House when the vote of the convention was conveyed to him by Isaac Hoover, chief usher at the White House. It is reported to have nodded his acknowledgment of these tidings and resumed his meal.

President Coolidge spent practically all of the time the convention was in session "listening in" upon the convention proceedings over his radio set. Consequently he had up-to-the-minute information as to the progress of the open proceedings, and through his secretary he obtained information as to what was going on behind the scenes at Cleveland.

The President did not go to his executive office during the afternoon because he has been successful beyond their fondest expectations.

Tonight while the convention was in recess preparatory to a new start in the selection of a running mate for Mr. Coolidge, Mr. Butler, in his capacity of campaign manager for President Coolidge, was being "knocked" by score and gloomy delegates, impatient to get away, in the headquarters of practically every delegation, excepting that of the La Follette group from Wisconsin.

They said they were much displeased at Mr. Butler and the members of the Cabinet who have been participating in his councils for more perfect cooperation

Continued on Page Two.

LA FOLLETTE GROUP PREDICTS DEFEAT

Declare Blunders of Butler and Cabinet Advisers Have Beaten Coolidge.

PRAISE LEADERS' STRATEGY

Say Voters Are Alienated From Regulars and Prepare for Third Party Convention.

Special to The New York Times.

CLEVELAND, June 12.—At what one of their number referred to as "the end of a perfect day," the La Follette delegates from Wisconsin tonight are busy making hotel reservations in preparation for their attendance at what they term the "second Cleveland convention," scheduled to convene on July 4 for the purpose of nominating Senator La Follette for President of the United States on a third party ticket, which they hope, and seem to believe, will prove an insurmountable obstacle in the way of a Republican victory.

Robert M. La Follette Jr., son of the Wisconsin Senator and Chairman of the Central Republican Committee of Wisconsin, said tonight, that in his opinion nothing could save the candidate's nomination at the "first" Cleveland convention from defeat.

Blunders on the part of the Coolidge managers, a group of Cabinet members who have operated under the supervision of William M. Butler, Republican National Committeeman from Massachusetts, in connection with the selection of a candidate for second place on the ticket, in the opinion of the La Follette men, has shattered what slender hope there ever was of Republican success in the national election this year.

The younger La Follette has been in frequent communication with his father throughout the day. The successive moves of the La Follette delegates since they arrived at the convention, there is every reason to believe, have been in pursuance of strategy dictated by the Wisconsin Senator himself with a view to putting the convention and the party of which nominally he is an exalted member "in wrong" with the voters.

The consensus among the La Follette delegates tonight is that this purpose has been successful beyond their fondest expectations.

Feeling against him has been growing on the part of leading party workers, especially members of the National Committee, ever since they began gathering in Cleveland. He was charged with being dictatorial, with paying no attention to the counsel of veterans in party affairs, and generally with attempting to use his authority as President Coolidge's agent in a way detrimental

Continued on Page Seven.

REVOLT PUTS DAWES OVER

Old Timers Resent Butler's Domination of the Convention.

HE ASKED FIRST FOR KENYON

Regulars Named Lowden Instead and Then He Switched to Hoover.

DISAFFECTION SPREADING

Talk of Asking Coolidge to Select Another Man to Conduct Campaign.

By RICHARD V. OULAHAN.
Special to The New York Times.

CLEVELAND, June 12.—The Republican National Convention completed its work tonight and adjourned sine die after having chosen Calvin Coolidge of Massachusetts as its candidate for President and General Charles G. Dawes of Illinois as its candidate for Vice President.

Three sessions of the convention were held on the concluding day. The night session was made necessary by an extraordinary situation produced by the refusal of former Governor Frank O. Lowden of Illinois to accept the party's candidacy for Vice President after the convention had conferred that honor on him.

Mr. Lowden had been chosen on the second ballot taken at the afternoon, or second session. Messages from him refusing to accept the nomination, written in advance, were produced after some of Lowden's friends had sought to prevent their being presented.

This remarkable state of affairs compelled a recess to give the party leaders an opportunity to lead the party out of the maze in which it found itself. At the night session this situation was remedied by undoing the nomination of Mr. Lowden and proceeding to ballot again for a candidate for Vice President. On the first ballot at the night session, its third ballot on a candidate for Vice President, victory went to the supporters of General Dawes.

Convention Revolts on Butler.

While only a gesture of protest was made against choosing President Coolidge to head the Republican national ticket in the campaign of 1924, the effort to nominate the candidate for Vice President put a rally in the Republican ointment and threatened to produce serious differences within the party management. Lack of harmony is already apparent among those who are charged with the conduct of the Presidential campaign this year.

The futile nomination of Mr. Lowden was in part the outcome of an abortive, inept effort to stall Senator William E. Borah of Idaho for second place on the national ticket.

At an early hour this morning William M. Butler, political manager for President Coolidge, had made known that President Coolidge desired that Senator Borah should be the Vice Presidential nominee, and that Mr. Butler had already announced that Mr. Borah would accept. The Borah boom collapsed when Mr. Borah positively refused to accept the honor.

Mr. Butler countered on the disappearance of Mr. Borah from the Vice Presidential picture by offering Judge William S. Kenyon of Iowa. Leading men of the party who made wry faces when they were asked to support Judge Kenyon, whom they regarded as a near radical and not too loyal to the Republican cause, demanded a request direct from the White House that they put Judge Kenyon in second place on the National ticket. President Coolidge declined to comply with the request.

After that the leaders felt free to make their own choice of a Vice Presidential candidate. Out of their attitude in this connection came the nomination of former Governor Lowden and brought about the embarrassing situation with which the party was confronted when the convention assembled this evening for its third session.

The embarrassment was remedied, as far as straightening out the physical difficulties of the tangle was concerned, by the acceptance of Mr. Lowden's declination and the subsequent nomination of General Dawes.

But the Vice Presidential muss had another and more important phase than appeared from surface indications. Mr. Lowden's nomination marked a revolt against the domination of Mr. Butler as Dictator.

Access Butler as Dictator.

There seems to be no doubt that Mr. Butler and the members of the Cabinet who have been participating in his councils for more perfect cooperation

Continued on Page Five.

REPUBLICAN NOMINEE FOR VICE PRESIDENT.
CHARLES G. DAWES
OF ILLINOIS.

BITTER FIGHT SPLITS NEW YORK GROUP

Wadsworth and Hayward Factions Engage in War of Words at Secret Conference.

EFFECT ON CAMPAIGN SEEN

"Old Guard" and Progressives Line Up in Opposition Through the Whole State Organization.

Special to The New York Times.

CLEVELAND, June 12.—A split that may have far-reaching consequences in the New York State fight this Fall developed in the New York delegation this afternoon just before the convention opened to nominate a Vice President. Seventy-seven of the delegates held a secret conference at their headquarters in the Cleveland hotel and the so-called Old Guard element, led by Senator Wadsworth, sought to take control. Mr. Wadsworth was denounced for trying to wreck the party and the meeting ended in great bitterness.

Wadsworth, National Committeeman Charles D. Hilles and Representative Ogden L. Mills stood together against the demand of the so-called Progressive element that a Western candidate with progressive ideas be selected for Vice President. The Progressives united on Judge Kenyon of Iowa, but Wadsworth and his followers declared he would never do, because he was not conservative enough and was not even a regular organization Republican. They declared him a follower of La Follette and not in sympathy with President Coolidge.

State Senator Frederick M. Davenport of Oneida led the Kenyon faction, and several delegates made fiery speeches sustaining his choice. One speaker declared that Kenyon had been acceptable to two Republican Presidents, Harding and Coolidge, the former having made him a Federal Judge, and therefore should be acceptable to the convention. On the vote which followed, Kenyon received 23 votes and Burton 54. There were ten absentees.

Hayward Supports Kenyon.

Colonel William Hayward, United States District Attorney for the Southern District of New York, whose candidacy for the Republican nomination for Governor is being vigorously opposed by Senator Wadsworth, aided with Davenport and advocated the selection of Kenyon. The delegates who are opposing Federal positions in the State stood behind Wadsworth. The vote showed a split in the organization extending throughout the State and it is not healed before the Fall campaign.

Continued on Page Seven.

DAWES WINS ON 3D BALLOT

Gets 682½ to 234½ for Hoover on Opening of Night Session.

CONVENTION THEN ADJOURNS

Lowden, Chosen First With Ovation Rivalling President's, Refuses to Accept.

KENYON AND BURTON STRONG

They Shared Lead on Early Ballots, With Watson, Dawes and Others.

By ELMER DAVIS.
Special to The New York Times.

PUBLIC HALL, CLEVELAND, Ohio, June 12.—The Republican National Convention of 1924 adjourned at 10:35 tonight, Eastern Standard Time, having renominated President Calvin Coolidge and placed Brig. Gen. Charles G. Dawes of Illinois on the ticket with him as a candidate for Vice President.

The last day of the convention, the only one that had decently comfortable weather, the only one that saw the auditorium filled with spectators, was also the busiest and most entertaining of the three days of sessions.

The nomination of President Coolidge at the morning session, by 1,065 votes to 34 for Senator Robert M. La Follette and 10 for Senator Hiram Johnson, had, of course, long been expected; but the selection of a Vice President developed quite a struggle. Some of the struggling was done by gentlemen who would not be Vice President and much more of it was done by gentlemen who would not be Vice President under any circumstances and objected to being drafted. General Dawes was nominated on the first ballot tonight, at the last of the day's three sessions, receiving 682½ votes, as against 234½ for Herbert Hoover, Secretary of Commerce, and 73 for Judge William S. Kenyon and a few scattering. It was the second time former Governor Frank O. Lowden of Illinois had been nominated despite his frequently expressed refusal to be a candidate, and it took two or three more refusals before the convention took him at his word.

Hoover Was Butler's Choice.

General Dawes was second choice, but Mr. Hoover, whom the convention finally picked by William M. Butler, President Coolidge's campaign manager, and he was defeated by Dawes, not because the delegates had anything against Hoover, but because they had a great deal against Dawes. With him tonight also was another brother, Beman G. Dawes of Columbus. He had repeatedly refused to let himself be considered for the Vice Presidential nomination.

President Coolidge and Vice President Dawes have ruled this convention in everything—in the selection of the Vice-President, and the discontent against their domination, which has been loudly expressed in words all week, finally blossomed out into action today. The delegates couldn't be at Coolidge, nor the Coolidge platform, but they could and did beat whatever Vice-Presidential candidate was unfortunate enough to have Mr. Butler's approval. They beat one this afternoon and they beat another tonight. And neither of these was Butler's first choice, or even his fourth or fifth choice.

All the work the Administration forces have been trying to find somebody to take the Vice Presidential nomination. Borah refused, Kenyon was cold, Lowden refused; when the convention finally started balloting for a Vice President in its second session of the day Butler had been forced to recognize that though Judge Kenyon had been placed in nomination he stood small chance of being selected as the candidate of the party. In that situation Mr. Butler was forced reluctantly to give his consent to the nomination of Representative Theodore E. Burton, Temporary Chairman of the convention, who is a Clevelander, and has, besides the support of Ohio, that of most of the leaders in the Eastern industrial States.

But the convention had a mind of its own and power to take action of its own—the Vice Presidency.

Half a dozen other candidates had been placed in nomination at the afternoon session, among them ex-Governor Lowden. The President had repeatedly refused to let himself be considered for that nomination, then made this announcement from his friends that he wouldn't take it; but he was nominated again and on the second ballot he was chosen as the Vice Presidential candidate. At the end of the roll call on the ballot he had only 412 votes, as against 286 for Burton, 555 being necessary for a choice; but there was a rush of States to change their votes before another roll call, and when Illinois and Pennsylvania got Lowden over.

Lowden's Refusal Causes a Snarl.

Then it was learned that Lowden, foreseeing something of the sort, had given notice in advance that he would not run, and when the convention a sealed letter, to be read in case he were nominated, absolutely refusing it to be a candidate. The letter was read and William M. Butler began to cheer up. I was just past seven and by this time

DAWES PROMPTLY ACCEPTS NOMINATION

Issues Statement at Old Home in Marietta, Saying He Is "Very Grateful."

COOLIDGE CONGRATULATES

Promptly Sends Message to Running Mate—Lowden Pleased With Choice.

MARIETTA, Ohio, June 12 (Associated Press).—Brig. Gen. Charles G. Dawes, who is at the home of his sister, Mrs. A. Beach, here, said tonight:

"I accept the nomination for the Vice Presidency. I deeply appreciate the honor conferred."

The Republican Convention was taking the roll-call on the Vice Presidency, Brig. Gen. Dawes was "listening in" surrounded by two brothers with their families and friends.

When The Associated Press notified him of his nomination, General Dawes was already aware of it.

"Charley," said his brother, Henry M. Dawes, Controller of the Currency, "it's up to you again."

General Dawes came to Marietta, his native town, on Monday to attend the fortieth annual reunion of his class in Marietta College, where he was graduated in 1884.

Coolidge Congratulates Dawes.

Special to The New York Times.

WASHINGTON, June 12.—President Coolidge sent this telegram to General Dawes late this evening:

"It will be a pleasure to be associated with you in the public service. Best wishes to you and Mrs. Dawes, in which Mrs. Coolidge joins.
"CALVIN COOLIDGE."

The President wrote this in longhand and sent it by Edward B. Clark, his personal secretary, from the main part of the White House, where he had been listening in by radio, to the telegraph room of the Executive office, to be sent immediately to General Dawes.

Herbert Hoover sent the following telegram to General Dawes:
Charles G. Dawes, Chicago, Ill.
I am more than happy at your selection and the assurance of your being again drafted to public service. The country is to be congratulated.
HERBERT HOOVER.

Lowden Much Pleased.

OREGON, Ill., June 12 (Associated Press).—Frank O. Lowden, former Governor of Illinois, who tonight was nomi-

Continued on Page Seven.

The New York Times.

THE WEATHER

Partly cloudy today; tomorrow, probably thunder showers. Temperature yesterday—Max., 70; Min., 62.
For weather report see next to last page.

VOL. LXXIII....No. 24,262.   NEW YORK, SATURDAY, JUNE 28, 1924.   TWO CENTS In Greater New York | THREE CENTS Within 200 Miles | FOUR CENTS Elsewhere

---

RUHR THROWN OPEN TO 210,000 EXILES BY FRENCH AMNESTY

Jail Sentences Also Are to Be Suspended or Reviewed by Herriot's Order.

BERLIN PROPOSAL REFUSED

Premier Won't Let Rail Tax Receipts Be Diverted From Bond Interest Payments.

MARX REPLIES TO ALLIES

Note on Resumption of Military Control Said in Berlin to Be Unconditional Acceptance.

By EDWIN L. JAMES.
Copyright, 1924, by The New York Times Company.
Special Cable to The New York Times.

PARIS, June 27.—Premier Herriot has instructed General Degoutte, commanding the Franco-Belgian forces occupying the Ruhr, to permit with few exceptions the return to the industrial region of all Germans expelled since the beginning of the occupation in January of last year.

While the exact number affected is not known because their families were sent out with all Germans against whom expulsion orders were issued, it is understood the new order will permit the return to their homes of about 210,000 persons. The only exceptions are those expelled for serious non-political crimes, whose number is small. M. Herriot has previously authorized the return of 60,000 Germans expelled from Rhineland territory exclusive of the Ruhr.

It is further announced that the sentences on all Germans condemned to prison for taking part in the passive resistance program without criminal violence will be suspended and that persons convicted for crimes of violence will have their cases reviewed for the purpose of exercising the largest measure of clemency.

This measure is quite in accord with M. Herriot's position that exploitation of the Ruhr should now be given up in favor of putting into operation the Dawes plan, and that regardless of the merits of the expulsion of those who in no use prolonging their deportation. There is some criticism of the Premier's measure before putting into operation the experts' plan, on the ground that he could have used permission to do the expelled Germans's return as a card in the coming negotiations with the Germans.

Coincident with the announcement of this move, it has been made known that M. Herriot sent a note to Berlin rejecting the German proposals in regard to the Ruhr Micum accords. These proposals were made two days before M. Herriot became Premier, and stated that the Germans could not have the agreements for deliveries by the Ruhr industrialists unless the French agreed that the 290,000,000 gold marks railroad tax planned by the Dawes report should be used to repay the railroad tax. Inasmuch as the Dawes plan intended the railroad tax to meet the interest charges on an issue of bonds to be delivered to the Allies, it was perfectly apparent that the German demand amounted to an effort to reduce the amount Germany would have to pay under the experts' system.

In rejecting this proposal M. Herriot said France and Belgium wished the resumption of deliveries on the basis until the Dawes plan went into effect.

While the issue of military supervision will probably go into the interallied conference which opens July 16 the French wish to have the Micum accords kept out of the conference for the reason that the British do not recognize the legality of the Ruhr occupation and it would be embarrassing to have the Ruhr situation considered in London under such conditions.

BERLIN SAID TO AGREE TO MILITARY INQUIRY

Reply to Ambassadors' Demands Being Sent to Premier Herriot by Courier.

By T. R. YBARRA.
Copyright, 1924, by The New York Times Company.
Special Cable to The New York Times.

BERLIN, June 27.—The German Government's answer agreeing to resumption of allied military investigation into the alleged warlike preparations in Germany will be dispatched from here tonight. The Government heads arrived at an agreement regarding the tenor of the note Wednesday, since when slight changes have been made in the original text outlined.

The note will not be telegraphed, but taken direct to Paris by courier, who will hand it personally to Premier Herriot, who is exofficio Chairman of the Conference of Ambassadors, which sent the allied demand for resumption of military control, to which Germany is now replying.

The reply covers five typewritten pages, taking up the question with consummate care.

Continued on Page Seven.

Convention Disturbs Cabinet; Coolidge Shuts Off the Radio

Special to The New York Times.

WASHINGTON, June 27.—Democratic noise over the radio disturbed the Cabinet meeting at the White House so much today that the receiving set was shut down while President Coolidge and his lieutenants held their session.

In the afternoon, however, the machine was turned on again and yells of "Ray for Al!" piercing cries of "Mac'll do!" and blasting music from the band in Madison Square Garden filled the corridors of the executive offices.

TO FLY BY NIGHT WITH PACIFIC MAIL

New Transcontinental Postal Airplane Service to Start Next Tuesday.

3,000 MILES IN 35 HOURS

Special Letter Boxes Here for the Air Mail—40 Pilots to Operate in Relays.

New red, white and blue mail boxes will be placed in the business sections of the city next Monday to serve New Yorkers who wish to have letters delivered in San Francisco within thirty-six hours. They are the new air mail letter boxes and serve to announce the inauguration of a new transcontinental postal airplane service.

The air carriers will begin their daily flights on Tuesday. This is an auspicious event, not circus or spectacular flying, but the beginning of the operation of a through air mail service 365 days in the year, through Summer heat and Winter storms, flying through the entire night as well as by day.

Tuesday at 11 A. M. the first winged pony express will hop off from Hazelhurst Field, Long Island, carrying mail for the Golden Gate, 3,000 miles away. According to schedule the mail should arrive in San Francisco at 5:45 on the afternoon of the following day. The mail planes will leave the Pacific Coast for the Atlantic daily at 4 A. M. with mail due to arrive here 32 hours later.

To Illuminate the Heavens.

By night the highways of the heavens will be illuminated to guide the pilots as they fly over twelve States, making thirteen regular stops. Arrangements have been made with the rail mails so that offices not located on the air mail route may dispatch mail matter to connect therewith. For example: Philadelphia may dispatch to Los Angeles, by rail to New York or Cleveland, thence by air to San Francisco; thence by rail to Los Angeles.

The regular stops on the air mail route from New York are Bellefonte, Cleveland, Bryan, Chicago, Iowa City, Omaha, North Platte, Cheyenne, Rawlins, Rock Springs, Salt Lake City, Elko, Reno and San Francisco.

Any mailable matter will be carried by airplane, including sealed parcels not exceeding fifty pounds in weight and not exceeding forty-eight inches in length and girth combined, if postage is paid at the rate of 8 cents an ounce for each zone or part zone in which mail is carried by plane. The rate of postage to San Francisco is 24 cents. Attached to all of the air mail letter-boxes is a map showing the air-highway across the continent and giving information regarding rates of postage between the various stops. Mail is placed in letter-boxes about three hours before 11 o'clock in the morning, when the plane leaves for the West.

Special airplane stamps are not required. Any stamp good for postage may be used. Also, it is not necessary to post mailable material in the special air mail boxes. The new boxes are merely a convenience for those who wish to post letters at the last minute. All mail for airplane dispatch should be prominently marked "Via Air Mail."

Air Mail Boxes Here.

The new boxes are located at Times Square, General Post Office lobby, Pennsylvania Station, Fifth Avenue and Thirty-fourth Street, City Hall, Grand Central Station, Broadway and Wall Street, Broadway and Twenty-third Street and Fifth Avenue and Forty-second Street.

Mr. James H. Bartlett, Acting Postmaster General; Superintendent Peter A. McGurty and a large number of Post Office officials will be present at Hazelhurst Field at 11 A. M. Tuesday when the first flight will be made. With a higher velocity than the winds that blew in Madison Square Garden from 11:40 yesterday morning till nearly 6 o'clock last night, but the Democratic wind was considerably larger in this State. We will bear witness to the beginning of a new epoch in the history of the Postal

Continued on Page Eight.

Octogenarian Runaway Gets His Wish; Wanted All His Life to See a Convention

James John Brady, the 82-year-old Civil War veteran who ran away from Mrs. Florence Grey's boarding house in Vincennes, Ind., last Sunday and came to New York on money he had saved from his pension because he wanted to attend a Democratic National Convention and see the Brooklyn Bridge before he died, realized one of his ambitions yesterday. If it doesn't rain, he will realize the other today.

From 10:30 A. M. until nearly 4:30 in the afternoon Brady sat in the "centre of the space reserved for spectators on the floor of Madison Square Garden. Charles A. Greathouse, member of the Democratic National Committee from Indiana, sent the runaway an Alternate's ticket after reading in The Times that Brady had appeared penniless and exhausted at the Travelers' Aid Society, 144 East Forty-fourth Street, after vainly attempting to get a convention ticket at the Indiana headquarters at the Hotel McAlpin.

Although Brady, who was born in Fourteenth Street, but hasn't been in New York since he left here as a lad of 14, protested that he couldn't possibly get lost, one of the Travelers' Aid Society workers went with him to the Garden.

Brady went to bed early to make ready for today's program. At 10:30 o'clock, unless the weather prevents, he will be taken across the Brooklyn Bridge in an automobile by William Crockett, architect of the Travelers' Aid Society building.

When Louise Closser Hale, who also comes from Indiana, heard of Brady's presence in New York, she sent him tickets to "Expressing Willie," in which he is appearing at the Forty-eighth Street Theatre. Brady attended the performance Thursday night. Yesterday Mrs. Grey, the runaway's landlady, meets this Constitutional provision. To the casual observer, she might seem to be below the age limit and therefore ineligible.

"It simply cannot be true," she exclaimed, "but it certainly is nice for all these good friends of mine to consider me worthy of such a compliment. Of course, I know it is just a delightful tribute. There isn't a chance in the world of my being nominated. Just the same I appreciate it very, very much."

KLAN ISSUE OVERSHADOWS ALL ON EVE OF BALLOTING; PLANK SPLITS PLATFORM MAKERS, M'ADOO WINS ON LEAGUE; LAST NOMINEES ARE IN, UNDERWOOD AND DAVIS STRONGER

LAST NOMINEES IN FIELD

Call of the States Ends With Sixteen Candidates Named.

MANY SECONDING SPEECHES

John W. Davis, Glass, Cox, Silzer, C. W. Bryan and Brown Added to the Long List.

WOMEN LEAD IN ORATORY

They Stir Up Weary Delegates and Start Real Demonstrations.

Today's Official Program

FIFTH SESSION.

Following is the official program for today's session of the Democratic Convention:

Convention called to order by the Hon. Thomas J. Walsh, Permanent Chairman, at 9:30 A. M., Daylight Saving Time.

Invocation by the Rev. John Roach Straton of Calvary Baptist Church of New York.

Report of Committee on Resolutions.

Roll-call of States for vote on President.

Adjournment.

By ELMER DAVIS.

The Democrats are through at last with making nominations for the Presidential nomination. They devoted six hours and a quarter yesterday to the last necessary but painful task, finishing up a work that had been begun on Wednesday afternoon and carried forward through most of Thursday's sessions.

According to the ethnographic record, only about 40,000 or 50,000 words were spoken yesterday, but anybody who had to sit through it all would be willing to swear that there were at least 40,000,000.

The convention is supposed to resume its operations at 9:30 o'clock this morning, though it will probably start late, as usual. The adoption of the platform, probably after considerable argument, is the first thing in the order of business. Before the day is over the balloting for the Presidency may begin.

Six new Presidential candidates were placed before the convention yesterday. Ohio nominated James M. Cox; Nebraska, Governor Charles W. Bryan; New Hampshire, Governor Fred W. Brown; New Jersey, Governor George S. Silzer; Virginia, Senator Carter Glass, and West Virginia, John W. Davis.

This makes sixteen candidates presented altogether: Oscar W. Underwood, Joseph T. Robinson and Alfred E. Smith, who were nominated on Wednesday, and Alfred E. Smith, Willard Saulsbury, David Franklin Houston, Samuel M. Ralston, Jonathan M. Davis, Albert C. Ritchie and Woodbridge N. Ferris on Thursday.

If you don't see your favorite among the beladed sixteen, don't worry. A lot of other people will be voted for on the first ballot, and later. Quite possibly the eventual nominee of this convention will be somebody who has not been formally placed in nomination at all.

But the nominations were not half of it yesterday. There were also secondsing speeches. Mr. McAdoo was seconded seven times, Governor Smith four times, and Senator Underwood once. This makes their total score: McAdoo 11, Smith 7 and Underwood 2, for all of them had been extensively seconded on Thursday. Messrs. Silzer, Ritchie, Davis, Glass and Brown also were seconded yesterday.

The big wind accompanying the thunderstorm of Wednesday evening had a higher velocity than the winds that blew in Madison Square Garden from 11:40 yesterday morning till nearly 6 o'clock last night.

Continued on Page Three.

© Campbell Studio.

THE FIRST WOMAN TO BE PLACED IN NOMINATION FOR THE VICE PRESIDENCY.

Mrs. Leroy Springs, National Committeewoman From South Carolina, Whose Name Will Be Put Forward by That Delegation.

TO PRESENT WOMAN FOR VICE PRESIDENT

Mrs. Leroy Springs of South Carolina to Be First of Her Sex Put in Nomination.

SENATOR WHEELER O. K.'S IT

Says Comely and Brilliant Southerner Would Improve Situation in the Senate.

Mrs. Leroy Springs of Lancaster, S. C., is to be the first woman in American history to be placed in nomination for the Vice Presidency.

Those behind the move do not expect that she will be nominated—that is not the end they have in mind. They simply believe that this woman—generally conceded to be one of the most brilliant as well as one of the handsomest in the convention—is entitled to a fine compliment.

Mrs. Springs caught the fancy of the convention from the start and when it was suggested that she preside over the Committee on Credentials there was a chorus of unanimous ayes.

And Mrs. Springs handled her committee like a veteran, winning the plaudits of her colleagues not only for the ability she showed but for the courtesy and fairness of her every act.

The decision of friends of Mrs. Springs to place her in nomination for Vice President was conveyed to the press section by a member of the South Carolina delegation.

"We have," he said, "the leading woman Democrat of the South in this delegation of ours and we have decided when our name is reached in the roll of States to offer her as a candidate for the Vice Presidential nomination. While she probably will not go over the line a winner she will at least, we are sure, receive a rousing compliment such as has been accorded to few women in our history."

Mrs. Springs was taken completely by surprise when told of the plan. Not a hint of what was going on had been permitted to reach her. She refused to believe the report was accurate.

'DARK HORSES' BUSY ON TRACK STRATEGY

All Decide to Canter Under Wraps in Early Balloting, Waiting for Break.

RALSTON TALK STRONGER

Supporters of All Candidates Find Encouragement in Acclaim Which Delegates Gave Names.

With fourteen "dark horses" entered in the race for the Democratic Presidential nomination and waiting to be off when the convention, possibly today, starts balloting on candidates, from "Tom" Taggart's entry, United States Senator Ralston of Indiana, continued strong last night.

According to those actively identified with the Ralston boom, he grew in strength throughout yesterday, a day most of the leaders, great and small, spent at the Garden sitting with their respective delegations, listening to nominating speeches and trying to gauge sentiment for the several candidates through the degree of enthusiasm with which their names were received. Scores of conferences, held while the speechmaking was in progress, convinced the friends of the Hoosier candidate—and with Governor Smith and William G. McAdoo out of the way, a drift toward him would set in very promptly.

Pending their expected declaration, it was stated last night, it is possible that Senator Ralston may be found drifting along with his thirty Hoosier votes and little or nothing more recorded in his favor. Those active in his support are anxious to avoid during the early balloting any unusual showing of strength which might arouse antagonism in the camps of other "dark horses." They are intent on shaping their strategy so that the potential strength of their candidate will be disclosed when the crucial stage of the struggle is reached and not before. They profess to be confident that from that time on he will continue to show gains on each successive ballot.

Unite on Early Strategy.

Mr. Taggart has been actively engaged in establishing among promoters of lesser booms a modus vivendi which he believes will endure throughout the early part of the battle.

The strategy to be pursued by the leaders behind the standards of the fourteen candidates is this:

Each, including favorite sons to whom delegations from one State are more or less loosely committed, will bend every effort toward holding on to his own delegates during the early stage of the balloting, neither attempting to

Continued on Page Five.

KLAN HOLDS UP PLATFORM

Committtee in Session Early This Morning Over Question.

34 TO 20 FOR NAMING KLAN

McAdoo League Plan, Calling for a Referendum, Is Adopted by Vote of 34 to 16.

BAKER CONTINUES STRUGGLE

He May Take 1920 Plank to the Convention—Child Labor Plank Turned Down.

The McAdoo forces triumphed in the Resolutions Committee yesterday when by a vote of 32 to 16 the committee adopted the McAdoo policy on the League of Nations, with a plank declaring approval of the League but making adherence to it dependent upon a referendum of the people.

With the League plank adopted, the committee proceeded to take up the Ku Klux Klan plank. A poll indicated that 34 members of the committee favored a plank which did not mention the Klan by name, while 20 were for a plank which should denounce the organization specifically.

Three planks with respect to the Ku Klux Klan were presented. That which omitted the name of the Invisible Empire was prepared by William J. Bryan. That naming the Klan was the prejudice of the anti-Klan forces in general.

There was, however, an additional plank presented from Alabama, the home State of Oscar W. Underwood.

The Composite Klan Plank.

The composite plank of the opponents of the Klan reads:

We condemn political secret societies of all kinds as opposed to the exercise of free government and contrary to the spirit, if not the letter, of the Constitution. No member of such society can justly claim to be a disciple of Thomas Jefferson.

We therefore pledge the Democratic Party to the efforts of the Ku Klux Klan or any similar organization that interferes with political freedom or religious liberty, or which engenders racial prejudices.

It declares, further, that a religious test cannot be required for any office of trust in the Government, and that no church should be the effort to arouse religious dissension.

The Bryan plank, which leaves out any specific mention of the Klan, reaffirms the devotion of the Democratic Party to the fundamental principles contained in the Constitution, providing for the free exercise of religion, freedom of speech, freedom of the press and the right of the people to free assembly.

The third, or so-called Alabama plank, is long, reviewing the history of organizations of that character and making specific reference to the "Know-Nothings."

It declares that the Democratic Party openly opposed the "Know-Nothings." There from adopted by the Republican Convention is acceptable to the organized workers affiliated with the Committee for Progressive Political Action.

"The insistent among the great mass of organized wage earners is overwhelmingly for McAdoo, and, in the judgment of those same leaders, he must be the nominee if these leaders are to go to the Convention for Progressive Political Action on a platform of principles which the committee was engaged in drafting last night.

Continued on Page Two.

---

16 Candidates for President Now Before the Convention

When the roll-call of States was completed yesterday sixteen candidates for the Presidency had been nominated by the Democratic National Convention. Among the nominees are five United States Senators and the Governors of six States. Here is the list, in order of the candidates' respective States:

Senator O. W. Underwood..Alabama
Senator J. T. Robinson......Arkansas
William Gibbs McAdoo....California
Ex-Senator W. Saulsbury..Delaware
Senator Samuel M. Ralston...Indiana
Governor Jonathan M. Davis..Kansas
Governor Albert C. Ritchie.Maryland
Governor W. N. Ferris.....Michigan
Governor Chas. W. Bryan..Nebraska
Governor F. H. Brown.N. Hampshire
Governor G. S. Silzer....New Jersey
Governor Alfred E. Smith..New York
David Franois Houston......Texas
Ex-Governor James M. Cox....Ohio
Senator Carter Glass.......Virginia
John W. Davis.........West Virginia

RAIL LABOR CHIEFS STAND BY M'ADOO

Statement Signed by Forty Officials Declares Organized Workers Are For Him.

MAKE THIRD-PARTY THREAT

Gompers and Holland Repudiate Inclusion of Federation and State Workers.

Forty officials of railway labor unions who are working for the nomination of William G. McAdoo issued a statement through his headquarters yesterday saying that organized labor was overwhelmingly for him.

The statement was received with surprise among the 350 labor leaders in New York, and Samuel Gompers, who is Chairman of organized labor's Non-Partisan Committee, made the following comment:

"No one has the right to speak for the American Federation of Labor.

"The political situation so far as the labor vote is concerned is without parallel. There is no precedent for it in our political history. There are here today more than forty representatives of leading labor organizations, including those of railroad labor, working day and night for the support of Mr. McAdoo's candidacy. These men are all here because of their own convictions, supported by the rank and file of their organizations.

"The statement among the great mass of organized wage earners is overwhelmingly for McAdoo, and, in the judgment of those same leaders, he must be the nominee if these leaders are to go to the Convention for Progressive Political Action on it at Cleveland and vote against the placing of an independent candidate in the field.

"They have the necessary votes to prevent the successful launching of an independent movement. There is no other available Democratic candidate to whom the workingmen will give the same unqualified support. Neither the Republican Party nominee nor the platform adopted by the Republican Convention is acceptable to the organized workers affiliated with the Committee for Progressive Political Action.

"If Wall Street, the Democratic bosses and the representatives of big business wish to divorce these workers from the Democratic Party in the present campaign they will continue their opposition to Mr. McAdoo. They do not realize the state of mind of labor and of the masses of the people for a truly progressive candidate.

"The present activities of some of the Democratic bosses can be likened to nothing more clearly than to the fiddling of Nero while Rome burned."

The statement was signed by Timothy Shea, Assistant President of the Brotherhood of Locomotive Engineers and Firemen; A. O. Wharton, member of the Federal Labor Board; B. M. Jewell, President of the Railroad Employes Department of the A. F. of L.; J. A. Franklin, President of the Brotherhood of Boilermakers and Iron Shipbuilders; J. O. Lehmon, President of the Railway Telegraphers and E. Millmen, Vice President of the Maintenance of Way Employes.

At the Hotel Aberdeen headquarters of the Federation surprise was expressed that the railway men should have issued a statement on behalf of organized labor. It was pointed out that organized labor officially has no candidate, that its policy with respect to candidates is non-partisan, and that if the candidate is to its liking it will support him whoever he may be. At the same time it was said that the railway unions would be expected to support whatever candidate was nominated if he were agreeable to the representatives of the mass of organized labor.

Federation representatives believe that the platform will strike a truly progressive note with regard to those planks in which labor is interested. This include an unqualified demand for joint action on the Federal Child Labor amendment; a restoration of the Railroad Labor Board section of the Esch-Cummins act and a clear-cut attack on the abuse of the injunction in industrial disputes.

It was reported yesterday that in-

Continued on Page Five.

STORM OVER KLAN MENACING

Leaders Expect Lively Contest Today on the Convention Floor.

SERIOUS SCHISM IS FEARED

McAdoo Proposal for Klan Compromise Is Promptly Rejected by Smith.

CANDIDATES MORE ACTIVE

Delegates Appraise Dark Horses With a View to Second Choice in Case of Deadlock.

By RICHARD V. OULAHAN.

No more confused party situation could possibly exist than that which confronted the Democratic National Convention when it adjourned at 6 o'clock last evening until 9:30 o'clock this morning.

The Ku Klux Klan issue is the centre of the whirligig of uncertainty in which the Democratic Party finds itself involved after its convention has been in session for four days without having accomplished anything of a definite or forward character. The Klan question shadows everything, even the important matter of choosing the party's candidate for President.

A cloud no bigger than a man's hand when leading Democrats and party workers began assembling in New York last week for the party's quadrennial gathering, the Ku Klux problem has blackened the entire Democratic sky and promises a storm that may play havoc with party interests during the political campaign of 1924.

Today the convention's Committee on Resolutions, its members overworked, drowsy from lack of sleep, overwrought, will bring into the convention the platform of principles which the committee was engaged in drafting last night. At least the expectation was that the platform would be presented.

Nothing known of the proceedings behind the closed doors of the room in the Madison Square Hotel, opposite the Garden, in which the Committee on Resolutions has been holding its sessions, justified the contention of optimistic leading Democrats that there was a prospect of a unanimous agreement on a Ku Klux Klan plank which would enable the convention to dispose of this awkward embarrassment without exposing to the country a serious schism ominous of the preservation of party solidarity in the months preceding the Presidential election.

Sessions to Go Into Next Week.

The issue of the confusion on one fact stands out clearly. That is that the Democratic Convention will go over into next week. How long its duration will be, nobody knows. It threatens to be the longest national gathering in the party's history. With that meticulous regard for the sensibilities of voters who believe in keeping holy the Sabbath day, there will be an adjournment from this evening until Monday morning.

What today will bring forth in the historic interior of Madison Square Garden is as much a matter of speculation as everything else involving the convention other than an extension of the convention's sessions into next week.

The whole day may be devoted to discussing the platform, with assurance of a battle royal between the McAdoo and the anti-McAdoo forces over the question of condemning the Ku Klux Klan by name. It is possible—barely possible—that before the convention takes the weekend adjournment on Saturday night balloting on a choice of a Presidential aspirant will be in progress without any definite result.

Sunday promises to be a day of conferences among leaders with a view to determining upon a way to lead the party out of the mass in which it finds itself through the foremost position given the question of religious liberty.

Last night it was the understanding that such conferences will be held. They probably will comprise three groups, each meeting separately, but with one group seeking to serve in a mediatory and conciliatory capacity. A group composed of leading men—and perhaps including some women—will make an effort to bring into harmony the diverse views of the McAdoos and the anti-McAdoos over the Klan. These arbiters are certain to have a difficult task in the conditions that now prevail, in which old party chiefs, veterans of many political conventions, cool and collected in most circumstances, are showing a tendency to see red.

Candidates Are Still Active.

Meanwhile, the matter of choosing the Democratic candidate for President to oppose Calvin Coolidge has been shoved into what seems to be a secondary place. But proponents of the selection of Presidential aspirants think that have not lost sight of it.

While there appears to be a rather general feeling that no light on the Presidential situation is possible while the Ku Klux issue remains unsettled, undercurrents are at work that affect the matter of a Presidential choice.

The situation with reference to candidates underwent no perceptible change yesterday other than that there was a tendency in the tendencies at the closing of balloting.

Continued on Page Five.

"All the News That's Fit to Print."

The New York Times.

THE WEATHER
Showers today; tomorrow, fair and slightly cooler; westerly winds.
Temperature yesterday—Max. 82, min. 65.
For weather report see Page 2.

VOL. LXXIII...No. 24,274.   · · ·   NEW YORK, THURSDAY, JULY 10, 1924.   TWO CENTS In Greater New York | THREE CENTS Within 200 Miles | FOUR CENTS Elsewhere

DEMOCRATS NOMINATE DAVIS AND C. W. BRYAN; FORMER, ACCLAIMED, CALLS PARTY TO BATTLE; SMITH PROMISES TO WORK HARD FOR THE TICKET

DEMOCRATS FILL THEIR TICKET

Choose Davis and Bryan After Another Day of Balloting.

CHOICE OF DAVIS UNANIMOUS

Convention Adopts Taggart Motion With a Shout While a Stampede Is On.

HE HAD MADE STEADY GAINS

Beginning the Day With 203½ Votes, He Advanced as Meredith and Others Slumped.

By RICHARD V. OULAHAN.

Rising superior to the intra-party differences that have marked its session in New York, the Democratic National Convention yesterday, with impressive unanimity, ended its deadlock by choosing John W. Davis of West Virginia as its candidate for President.

At 2:30 o'clock this morning, in a session that was begun at 8:30 o'clock last night, while shouts of protest came from many delegates, the convention followed this action by choosing Governor Charles W. Bryan of Nebraska as its candidate for Vice President. With that done the convention at 2:25 o'clock adjourned sine die, thus ending one of the longest and most momentous national party gatherings ever held in America.

Governor Bryan's selection was a great surprise. His name had not been placed formally before the convention. He was picked for second place on the ticket at a midnight conference between Mr. Davis and other party leaders during a recess, and when the convention reassembled at 1:15 o'clock this morning word was passed that this was satisfactory to the new party leader.

William Jennings Bryan was active in the effort to have his brother named for Vice President, although he had declared his hostility to Mr. Davis's candidacy and had threatened to attack him in a speech before the convention.

One Ballot on Vice President.

Only one ballot was taken on the choice of a Vice Presidential candidate, with more than a dozen persons, including one woman, voted for. Before the result of the ballot, which was inconclusive, was announced State delegations began to change their votes, and the swing to Bryan was on.

New York gave Bryan his ninety votes on the first roll-call. Connecticut, Kentucky, Virginia, Texas, Ohio and Oklahoma went to him as fast as the Chairman of the delegations could be recognized. Then Gavin McNab of California moved that Governor Bryan be nominated by acclamation. Booing came from the floor and galleries and the protests were so many and so loud that Mr. McNab withdrew his motion.

But in the end Governor Bryan was chosen to be the partner of Mr. Davis on the Democratic National ticket. He received 738 votes or seven more than the necessary two-thirds majority. Announcement of his selection was received with cheers, jeers and hisses.

Immediately following the selection of Mr. Davis for the Presidential candidate at the first two sessions held yesterday a dramatic effort was made to give the Vice Presidential nomination to Senator Thomas J. Walsh of Montana by acclamation. The hard work of the overwhelming desire of shouting delegates to commander him for second place.

Walsh Declines the Honor.

At last night's session a letter was read in which Senator Walsh declined in advance the honor the convention sought to thrust upon him and took himself definitely out of consideration. Edwin T. Meredith of Iowa, former Secretary of Agriculture, had been the choice of William G. McAdoo after Mr. McAdoo's retirement from the contest appeared to be most in the minds of delegates for a running mate to Mr. Davis. But McAdoo did not desire to be so honored and no formal announcement that he did not desire to be so honored was made to the convention.

Shortly before midnight Mr. Davis was escorted to the platform in Madison Square Garden and got a rousing reception. He spoke easily and gracefully and in a clear voice. Mr. Davis caught the fancy of his audience in a way to bring loud laughter when he said no one could claim that this convention acted in haste and without deliberation. Laying down the creed of the Democratic Party, with "honesty in government" as its first tenet, Mr. Davis brought applause from his hearers when he said in this phase a keynote of the campaign.

Continued on Page Seven.

JOHN WILLIAM DAVIS
OF WEST VIRGINIA,
Democratic Candidate for President.

DAVIS IS PUT OVER IN WILD STAMPEDE

Weary Delegates Jump for Band Wagon and Then All Join Big Demonstration.

IT IS WEST VIRGINIA'S DAY

Convention Pays Tribute to the Men and the State That Gave It the New Leader.

By ELMER DAVIS.

The Democrats have finally nominated and gone home. John W. Davis was selected as the Presidential candidate yesterday afternoon, on the 103d ballot. At 2:25 o'clock this morning Governor Charles W. Bryan of Nebraska was nominated as Vice President.

The fierce tension had been relaxed by the long days of fruitless balloting. The two men in this convention who have inspired the bitterest ecstasies of love and hate had been driven out of the running after a struggle that had endured too long, so there was not the frenzied joy springing from the release of pent-up feeling such as greeted the nomination of James M. Cox in San Francisco four years ago. The delegates had fought each other to a standstill and themselves to exhaustion. They had no spirit left for the revival that should have come with the dismissal of the two leading candidates, the settlement by treaty of that endless war, and the turning toward more productive effort.

There were cheers for Davis as State after State piled up its ballot on his rising total, there was a demonstration when his nomination was finally confirmed by acclamation at the end of the 103d ballot; but it was less a demonstration for Davis, or even for the Democratic Party, than for West Virginia, the Cinderella, among the States, come into her own.

It Was West Virginia's Day.

As West Virginia's day, it was successful. As the great climactic festival of a confident party pushing on to the hope of victory, it was not. Too many personal and sectional and partisan hatreds have been fought out in this convention. If the spirit of this convention is a key to the spirit in which the party will fight the campaign, Mr. Davis has a hard life ahead of him. But he can always cherish the comforting thought that he gave West Virginia her great day among the States.

This convention has a gift for making fire on its negativing climactic moment. The withdrawal of Smith and McAdoo ought to have opened a chance for enthusiasm for repair, some sense of emotion. The Southern McAdoo States, always cold to the proposition that they support either Senator Walsh of Montana or Edwin T. Meredith of Iowa, were...

Continued on Page Nine.

WIFE FIRST TO TELL DAVIS HE HAD WON

Nominee Was Having a Quiet Smoke While She Listened In on the Radio

AT HOME OF FRANK L. POLK

Reporters, Camera Men and Personal Callers Soon Brought an End to His Solitude.

John W. Davis sat alone, smoking, in the reception room of the home of his close friend and legal associate, Frank L. Polk, at 6 East Sixty-eighth Street, when he received the news of his nomination for the Presidency yesterday afternoon. It was called to him by Mrs. Davis, who, with Mrs. Polk, had been listening in on the radio. Running from the sitting room on the second floor to the head of the stairs Mrs. Davis cried: "You've won—you're nominated!"

Mr. Davis put down his cigar, sprang up the stairs to greet Mrs. Davis, embraced her and—just smiled.

Within a few minutes the inevitable rush of friends and supporters to congratulate Mr. Davis began. The street quickly filled with visitors' automobiles, newspaper men, movie cameras and reporters and personal callers. And Mr. Davis's re-entry into public life was well under way.

When the newspaper men arrived Mr. Davis greeted them in the hallway of the Polk home. Mr. Polk had arrived by that time and at once took up the task of reinforcing Mr. Davis in his stand against the reportorial onslaught.

Greets Reporters Cordially.

Mr. Davis greeted the reporters cordially. He singled out those he knew and chatted with them personally. He apparently was willing to attempt to answer the questions which were being fired at him from all sides, but Mr. Polk warded off some which were considered irrelevant or premature and they went unanswered. One of these was the query as to how the candidate "squared" his position on the League of Nations (Mr. Davis having been an ardent supporter of President Wilson and his League proposals) with the Democratic platform's declaration on the League. Mr. Polk "ruled out" this question as "unfair at this time."

Mr. Davis told the newspaper men that his views on all public issues which might not be fully known would be set forth in his speech of acceptance. Later the reporters received from Mr. Polk a prepared statement from Mr. Davis. (The text of this statement is printed elsewhere.)

Although Mr. McAdoo did not withdraw in his letter, but merely announced that he released his delegates, the latter had all the effect of a withdrawal. The McAdoo forces, which had held together so long and so firmly, disintegrated rapidly. The Southern McAdoo States, always cold to the proposition that they support either Senator Walsh...

Continued on Page Eight.

"There Can Be No Compromise With Reaction,"
Says Davis in First Statement After Nomination

John W. Davis, the Democratic Presidential nominee, gave out the following statement last night:

The history of national conventions may be searched in vain for one which has excelled this in freedom or frankness of discussion, or whose actions have been more clearly the result of the unfettered wishes of the assembled delegates. The resolution and endurance they have exhibited is but proof of their sense of the solemn responsibilities to the country under which they acted and of the supreme vitality of democracy.

I cannot but feel deeply sensible of the honor done by the convention and am even more conscious of the weighty obligations that have fallen to me by its deliberate and unanimous choice. Not least of these is the duty to put before the country, as clearly as my powers permit, the Democratic creed and the Democratic policy as the convention has declared them.

That this creed and this policy will receive the militant support of all those who call themselves by the Democratic name I do not doubt for an instant. I shall hope to rally to their aid that great body of liberal, progressive and independent thought which believes that "progress is motion, Government is action," which detests privilege in whatever form and which does not wish the American people or their Government to stand still or retreat from the midst of a changing world.

There can be no compromise with reaction. Liberal principles must and will prevail. This is the mandate of the hour and I shall obey it.

DAVIS GETS BY WIRE CONGRATULATIONS OF SMITH AND M'ADOO

Governor Announces That He Will Aid in Campaign if the Nominee Desires.

McADOO IS GOING ABROAD

With Family, He Will Spend Several Weeks in Europe—Discord Among His Workers.

Among the hundreds of persons in all walks of life who sent their congratulations to John W. Davis following his nomination for the Presidency by the Democrats yesterday were Governor Alfred E. Smith and William Gibbs McAdoo, the leading candidates through many ballots for the place.

Governor Smith sent this telegram to Mr. Davis:

Hon. John W. Davis, care Frank L. Polk, 6 East Sixty-eighth Street, New York City.

Sincere congratulations and best wishes for success and my promise of hearty support.

ALFRED E. SMITH.

The Governor said he would not make a long statement because he expected to go before the convention at the night session and "say a few things." The Governor did say, however, that in selecting Mr. Davis he thought the convention made a good choice. He said he considered Mr. Davis to be of Presidential size and that he would make a great campaign. The Governor added that he would heartily support the ticket and do anything the nominee desired him to do. He said he expected to make speeches, either in New York State or throughout the country.

New McAdoo Boom Ended.

Surrounded by a group of his supporters, part of whom were still willing to go down fighting, Mr. McAdoo sat in a room of Suite 30J of the Madison Square Hotel early yesterday morning and saw the collapse of his six-year campaign for the Democratic nomination.

It was 1 o'clock when Mr. McAdoo acquiesced in the demand of some of his supporters that he withdraw in the interest of party harmony after a last desperate drive for him had failed. This decision was reached in the absence of Judge David Ladd Rockwell, Mr. McAdoo's campaign manager, who was making a fight for him on the floor.

A long discussion followed when Judge Rockwell was sent for and told of the situation. It was largely this discussion and failure of the McAdoo leaders to agree on a second choice candidate that delayed, until after 3 A. M., the sending of Mr. McAdoo's letter, releasing his delegates, to Senator Walsh, Chairman of the convention.

Continued on Page Two.

LEADERS ACCLAIM CHOICE OF DAVIS; SEE PARTY UNITED

"Shows Democrats Have Feet on the Ground," Says Former Governor Cox.

DANIELS PAYS TRIBUTE

Brennan of Illinois and Moore of Ohio See Breaches Healed—Bryan Pledges Support.

The nomination of John W. Davis as Democratic candidate for President was received yesterday with general acclaim by the party leaders and Democrats of prominence. Among those commenting were the following, who said:

William Jennings Bryan (who the other day omitted from his list of candidates meeting his approval the name of John W. Davis)—"You can say that I shall support the ticket. That is all—for the present."

James M. Cox, former Governor of Ohio—"It is an instance of the party nominating one of the most conspicuously able men of his generation, and it is an evidence of the fact that notwithstanding some of the most controverted questions this convention the Democratic Party, in the last analysis, had its feet on the ground. The country has proved these it as available it has demonstrated its intellectual courage and honesty."

"Biggest and Brainiest Available."

George E. Brennan, Democratic leader of Illinois—"We are more than pleased with the nomination of John W. Davis. We are delighted. The hard work of weeks has been rewarded. We now present to the voters as our candidate the biggest and brainiest man available for the honor. Behind him is arrayed the entire Democratic Party, united for the campaign as it was united in the tremendous enthusiasm that broke forth when Mr. Davis's nomination became assured. We look forward to an unbroken continuance of this good feeling around and Democrats, right up to the day of election. That was one thing, the election of Mr. Davis."

Edmund H. Moore, Democratic leader of Ohio—"John W. Davis is the biggest man who has run for President, with the possible exception of Wilson, since 1876."

Josephus Daniels—"I think they nominated a man whom the whole country recognizes as a great man in learning, in character, and one who measures up to the position of President. He stands for independence and equality and illustrates how a man of ambition and poise can reach the heights. He has illustrated his ability for public service as legislator in West Virginia, in the House of Congress as Solicitor General and as an Ambassador. He is a great American."

Franklin D. Roosevelt—"In John W. Davis the Democratic Party has found a candidate of whom it can be proud and the voters of the country a man on whom they can unite with confidence that he will make a President worthy of the voters of the country. A young man personal friend of mine, have found him to be a man of great intellect, clear thinking and high progressive ideals. Mr. Davis will have my heartiest support and I intend...

Continued on Page Two.

CHARLES W. BRYAN
OF NEBRASKA,
Democratic Candidate for Vice President.

Davis and Smith Are Cheered In Speeches at the Night Session

Presidential Candidate Appeals for Party Harmony and Gives Creed as Honesty in Government—Governor Pledges Full Support to Ticket.

John W. Davis, the Democratic candidate for President, and Governor Alfred E. Smith addressed the Democratic National Convention last night.

Both had rousing receptions. Mr. Davis when he appealed for party harmony and said that the Democratic creed was "honesty in Government" and "public office is a public trust," and Mr. Smith when he declared that he was ready to take off his coat and vest to fight for the ticket headed by Mr. Davis.

His speech was as follows:

"Mr. Chairman, ladies and gentlemen of the Convention: The most solemn announcement which can be made to any American is the information that he has been elected President of the United States. [Cries of "Good," "Pardon me, that is good!"] And second only to that message in weight and dignity is the information that he has been chosen by one of the great parties of the United States to lead their forces in the national campaign. [Applause.] You will not be surprised, then, if I say to you at this moment, grateful as I am for this great honor, I think even more of the burdens and the duties you have given me to bear and to perform. But I take heart of grace, and I realize that whatever may be said of the wisdom of your selection, no one, I think, in all this land will contend that this convention has acted in haste and without deliberation. [Laughter and applause.]

"And I take comfort again when I look at the banners that are erected throughout this hall, and reflect that the signs of all these States and Territories are not the emblem of a phantom army, but that they represent millions of Democrats all over this broad land ready to do as they have been for 60 years—to do battle for the cause of liberty and freedom. [Applause.] We are a national party, and in every State and Territory whose banner rests upon this floor we do battle and we win our party victory; and if we are a national party it must be, as I think, because we profess a truly national creed.

"The great principles of the Democratic Party: Honesty in Government [applause]; all public office is a public trust [applause]; equal rights to all men [applause]; fair and equal privilege to come [applause]; and equal taxation; an open door of opportunity to the humblest citizen in all the land [applause]; loyalty at home, courage and honor and helpfulness abroad. [Applause.]

"These principles are as sacred to the American of the East as they are to the American of the West, as highly revered by the American of the North as they are by the American of the South [applause], and in the name of this truly national creed, this truly and national party, it is ready again to do battle with all those who challenge this crucial any part of it. [Applause.] On this platform all progressives, in this country can stand; to this banner all liberals can rally, and in the cause all Democrats can-aye, more, all Democrats will unite. [Applause.]

"As a more or less interested bystander I can not be ignorant of the fact that this convention has had in the debates and the differences, and in the truly Democratic fashion has fought out its conflicts of opinion, and all these things, disturbing as they may have seemed at the moment, were but the thunderstorm that has cleared the clouds away and left shining on us the sun of coming victory and success. [Applause.]

"It may be, and I think when I am duly advised of your mandate it will be, my duty to speak further on these and kindred themes. I shall, therefore, add no more at this moment than to express my appreciation of the great honor you have done me, and my confident belief that I shall lead in this campaign a united and militant and a victorious party. [Long and extended applause.]

The Governor's Address.

Governor Smith's speech was as follows:

"Mr. Chairman: Not being familiar with the rules of the convention, I am the least bit afraid that any applause may be taken out of my time [laughter] and I will therefore very respectfully request you refrain from applause until I finish.

"I feel that it would be senseless, if not entirely useless, for me to extend any word of welcome to the delegates and their friends from the different States who are here gathered, because I think that the great City of New York has made about as complete a job as could be made of the business of extending a welcome to our friends from various sections of the country.

"If you have been annoyed in any way by the various people with whom you have come in contact, in their zeal to explain to you why in their opinion I was the greatest man in the world, over-look it. [Applause.]

"For the first time in a very great many years the Democratic Convention has been held in this city, although it is conceded that New York is the greatest city in the world, and that it is the very centre and the very heart, not only of this country, but practically of all the world. Naturally, we felt very proud. We felt particularly proud to have the convention come into this State at a time when we were able to point to a record of progress in this State under Democratic administration which cannot be equaled by any State in the Union. [Applause.]

Continued on Page Four.

BRYAN PICKED BY LEADERS

Daniels Suggests Him When Group Confers With John W. Davis.

ALL FACTIONS AGREEABLE

Head of Ticket Accepts Choice of Bryan's Brother as Running Mate.

SETTLED ON FIRST BALLOT

After 24 Candidates Are Voted On Host of States Swing Over to Bryan.

Governor Charles W. Bryan of Nebraska, brother of William J. Bryan, was nominated for Vice President on the first ballot, with a vote of 738, after a sweeping number of changes were recorded from the original votes of the States. The announcement of his nomination came at 2:30 A. M.

The convention adjourned sine die at 2:30 A. M. on motion of Senator Key of Utah.

A resolution was passed in the last moments providing that the Permanent Chairman, Senator Thomas J. Walsh, be appointed Chairman of the committee to notify J. W. Davis of his nomination for President and that Senator Harrison be Chairman of the committee to notify Bryan of his selection for Vice President.

The totals on the ballot for the principal candidates were announced as follows:

Governor C. W. Bryan	738
Major George Berry	219¼
Bennett Clark	42
Mrs. Leroy Springs	18
Colonel Alvin Owsley	28
Governor George S. Silzer	10
Mayor John F. Hylan	3
Governor Jonathan M. Davis	1

The nomination of Governor Bryan for second place was the direct result of a conference held by leaders with John W. Davis. The Presidential nominee, at the Manhattan Club, between 12 and 1 o'clock this morning when the convention was in recess, pending consideration on a candidate. More than a dozen men had been put in nomination, besides Mrs. Leroy Springs.

The meeting was held in Governor Smith's rooms. Every one deferred to Davis as to whom he would suggest, and the nominee said that he had no choice in the matter and was there merely to hear the suggestions.

Besides Mr. Davis and Governor Smith there were present Joseph F. Guffey of Pennsylvania; George E. Brennan of Illinois, Mayor Hague of Jersey City, Josephus Daniels, Frank L. Polk, the manager of the Davis pre-convention campaign; Isidore Dockweiler of California, J. Bruce Kremer of Montana, Gavin McNab of California, ex-Governor Stuart of Montana and Thomas Taggart of Indiana.

Governor Smith was asked whom he favored and he replied that he thought the nominee's own preference, but he indicated he should be Governor Silzer of New Jersey. He said he was willing to accede to the judgment of the others. It was recalled, however, that Mr. Baker had already refused the nomination.

Senator Walsh then brought into a side conference and was pressed to take the nomination. He said that his refusal was final and he left the conference early.

Josephus Daniels then proposed Governor Bryan. This was agreeable to the McAdoo's while the Smith element made no objection. It was argued that his selection would tend to bring together all the warring factions of the party and that he would be the ideal candidate to run with Mr. Davis.

The advice of Mr. Davis was asked regarding the Bryan choice and he declared that the selection in his opinion was an excellent one.

"If you have been annoyed in any way that William J. Bryan had asked a delegate from Maryland to pit his brother in nomination for the Vice Presidency. This delegate, however, did not desire to do anything which was not agreeable to the leaders and he declined to roll-call of States.

The conference had taken up the full hour of the recess and immediately broke up when Mr. Bryan's name had been agreed upon. The party left the Club and Mr. Davis returned to the home of Mr. Polk, where he spent the night.

The convention started on the roll-call of States for second ballot at night.

Several States passed and others declared their choice candidates with 323 votes, George E. Berry, Mayor Hylan of New York, Le Roy Spring of South Carolina, Mrs. Leroy Springs of South Carolina, and others.

There seemed about half wasbusy lobbying. It seemed that the convention as a whole watched on vote to vote, waiting until some State would set the ball rolling. It came as pretty near doing it on the first breaks. It was New York that put the question of the State, but when it came to the credit of the Bryan and Davis vote at Memorial Hospital at Liberty Park, on Friday, the delegations for the soldiers were sent...

Continued on Page Four.

The New York Times.

EXTRA 5 A.M.
THE WEATHER—Fair today.

VOL. LXXIV....No. 24,392. . . . . NEW YORK, WEDNESDAY, NOVEMBER 5, 1924. TWO CENTS in Greater New York | THREE CENTS Within 100 Miles | FOUR CENTS Elsewhere

COOLIDGE WINS, 357 TO DAVIS'S 136; LA FOLLETTE CARRIES WISCONSIN; SMITH BEATS ROOSEVELT BY 140,000

CITY ELECTS SMITH

Big Manhattan and Bronx Vote Wins for Governor.

UP-STATE STRONGLY G. O. P.

Roosevelt Carries Buffalo and Several Large Industrial Centres.

BROOKLYN GOES TO SMITH

Kings County Gives Him 152,000 Plurality, Although Coolidge Carries It by 80,000.

LEGISLATURE REPUBLICAN

Democrats Lose Control of Senate and Their Numbers in Assembly Are Reduced.

SOME OFFICES IN DOUBT

Whole Smith Ticket May Not Be Elected—Vote for the Socialist Nominee, Thomas, Is Small.

Overcoming a Republican Presidential sweep that reached nearly a million plurality, Alfred E. Smith was re-elected Governor of New York in yesterday's election, defeating his Republican opponent, Colonel Theodore Roosevelt, by an estimated plurality of 140,000.

GOVERNORS ELECTED.

REPUBLICAN.

Connecticut......Hiram Bingham
Delaware......Robert P. Robinson
Illinois......Len Small*
Idaho......Charles C. Moore*
Indiana......Ed Jackson
Iowa......John Hammill
Kansas......Ben S. Paulen
Massachusetts......Alvan T. Fuller
Michigan......Alex J. Groesbeck
Nebraska......Adam McMullen
New Hampshire..John G. Winant
Rhode Island......Aram J. Pothier
South Dakota....Carl Gunderson
Vermont......Franklin K. Billings
Washington......Roland H. Hartley
West Virginia......Howard M. Gore
Wisconsin......John J. Blaine*

DEMOCRATIC.

Florida......Jonn W. Martin
Georgia......Clifford Walker*
New York......Alfred E. Smith*
North Carolina....A. W. McLean
South Carolina....T. G. McLeod
Tennessee......Austin Peay*
Texas...Mrs. Miriam A. Ferguson
*Re-elected.

COOLIDGE AND SMITH CARRY THIS CITY

The President's Plurality About 130,000 and the Governor's About 500,000.

LA FOLLETTE VOTE 250,000

Coolidge Wins in Every Borough—Democrats Elect All Local Officers.

New York City gave its vote at yesterday's election to Calvin Coolidge, Republican nominee for President, and Charles G. Dawes, Republican nominee for Vice President, and at the same time rolled up a record plurality for Governor Alfred E. Smith, electing him Chief Executive of New York State for the third time.

MRS. FERGUSON WINS 2 TO 1 IN TEXAS RACE FOR GOVERNORSHIP

Incomplete Returns Indicate That She Will Have a Majority of 225,000 Over Republican.

RUNS BEHIND IN CITIES

But the Big Majorities in the Rural Districts Carry Her to Victory.

LARGE KLAN VOTE IS CAST

Party Lines Are Ignored as Ku Klux Vote for Republican, While Negroes Vote for Democrat.

Special to The New York Times.
AUSTIN, Texas, Nov. 4.—Returns from the rural districts of Texas coming in late this evening show that Mrs. Miriam A. Ferguson will probably receive a majority of about 225,000 votes over Dr. George C. Butte, Republican for Governor.

United States Senators Elected

REPUBLICANS—18.

Colorado......*L. C. Phipps
Colorado......†Rice W. Means
Delaware......T. C. du Pont
Idaho......*William E. Borah
Illinois......*C. S. Deneen
Kansas......*Arthur Capper
Kentucky......F. M. Sackett
Massachusetts....*F. H. Gillett
Michigan......*James Couzens
Nebraska......*G. W. Norris
New Hampshire..*H. W. Keyes
New Jersey......*W. E. Edge
Oklahoma......*W. B. Pine
Oregon......*C. L. McNary
Rhode Island....*J. H. Metcalf
South Dakota....W. H. McMaster
West Virginia....*Guy D. Goff
Wyoming......*F. E. Warren

DEMOCRATS—10.

Alabama......*J. T. Heflin
Arkansas......*J. T. Robinson
Georgia......*W. J. Harris
Louisiana......*J. E. Ransdell
Mississippi......*Pat Harrison
North Carolina..*F. M. Simmons
South Carolina....C. L. Blease
Tennessee......*L. D. Tyson
Texas......*M. Sheppard
Virginia......*Carter Glass

*Re-elected.
†Elected for short term to fill vacancy in present Senate.
‡Elected for both short and long terms.

LEGISLATURE AGAIN SOLIDLY REPUBLICAN

Party Recovers Control of the Senate, With a Probable Majority of Four.

STRONGER IN THE ASSEMBLY

J. A. McGinnies of Chautauqua Is Slated for Speaker—One Woman Elected.

Returns from the legislative elections throughout New York State yesterday showed that the Republicans had recaptured control of the State Senate, and increased the Republican majorities in both branches of the State Legislature.

COOLIDGE AND EDGE WINNERS IN JERSEY

Record Vote Gives President Plurality Which Is Estimated at 350,000.

MRS. NORTON IS ELECTED

First Woman in Congress From the East—Tunnel Bond Issue Adopted.

New Jersey, breaking all previous records in the one day's vote, gave huge pluralities to Coolidge and Senator Edge, and increased the Republican majorities in both branches of the State Legislature.

THIRD PARTY POLLS 4,000,000 VOTES IN WHOLE COUNTRY

Showing in Electoral College Far Behind Strength in Popular Support:

CARRIED ONLY WISCONSIN

Mid-West Deserted the Senator but Industrial Districts in Cities Helped Him.

COLLAPSE IN CALIFORNIA

But the Senator Ran Second in That State, the Dakotas, Minnesota, Montana and Nevada.

Returns from the Eastern and Southern States, and a few States in the West, showed that the Progressive Party movement, headed by Senator Robert M. La Follette of Wisconsin, fell far short of the expectations of its leaders.

Electoral Vote

COOLIDGE.

California	13
Colorado	6
Connecticut	7
Delaware	3
Idaho	4
Illinois	29
Indiana	15
Iowa	13
Kansas	10
Kentucky	13
Maine	6
Maryland	8
Massachusetts	18
Michigan	15
Missouri	18
Nebraska	8
New Hampshire	4
New Jersey	14
New York	45
North Dakota	5
Ohio	24
Oregon	5
Pennsylvania	38
Rhode Island	5
South Dakota	5
Vermont	4
Washington	7
West Virginia	8
Wyoming	3
Total	**357**

DAVIS.

Alabama	12
Arkansas	9
Florida	6
Georgia	14
Louisiana	10
Mississippi	10
North Carolina	12
Oklahoma	10
Tennessee	12
Texas	20
Virginia	12
Total	**136**

LA FOLLETTE

Wisconsin	13
Total	**13**

DOUBTFUL

Arizona	3
Minnesota	12
Montana	4
Nevada	3
New Mexico	3
Total	**25**

Total number of votes in Electoral College, 531; necessary to a choice, 266.

NEW YORK BY 900,000

Coolidge's Plurality in This State Little Below Harding's

DAVIS GETS THE SOUTH ONLY

La Follette Apparently Only His Own State, but Large Industrial Vote

CALIFORNIA FOR COOLIDGE

Doubtful States of the Far West Lean to the President as Returns Increase.

DAVIS LOSES WEST VIRGINIA

Refused at Late Hour to Concede Defeat and Hoped for Upset From the West.

BRYAN'S STATE TO COOLIDGE

Plurality of 50,000 in Nebraska for the President Indicated in Latest Dispatches.

Calvin Coolidge has been elected President of the United States in a victory of impressive proportions.

REPUBLICANS MAKE GAINS IN CONGRESS

Retain Control of Senate and May Increase House Majority to 50.

BROOKHART LIKELY TO LOSE

Stanley of Kentucky and Walsh of Massachusetts, Democratic Senators, Apparently Beaten.

La Follette Wins Koenig's Home District; Coolidge Captures Davis's and Olvany's

Senator La Follette carried the home election district of Samuel S. Koenig, Manhattan Republican leader, with a vote of 236 to 159 for Coolidge and 102 for Davis.

State Pluralities Rolled Up by Coolidge.

The following table shows President Coolidge's estimated pluralities on the returns so far received from the States given by him:

California	*300,000	New Jersey	350,000
Colorado	70,000	North Dakota	*50,000
Connecticut	80,000	Ohio	500,000
Illinois	750,000	Pennsylvania	1,100,000
Indiana	200,000	Rhode Island	46,000
Iowa	*325,000	South Dakota	*45,000
Kansas	250,000	Utah	45,000
Maine	80,000	Washington	100,000
Maryland	25,000	West Virginia	38,000
Massachusetts	250,000		
Michigan	400,000		

*Over La Follette.

Section 1

"All the News That's Fit to Print"

The New York Times.

THE WEATHER
Partly cloudy, much colder today; fair tomorrow, continued cold. Temperature yesterday—Max. 47, min. 41.
☞For weather report see Section 10, Page 7.

Section 1

VOL. LXXIV....No. 24,431.   ····   NEW YORK, SUNDAY, DECEMBER 14, 1924.   FIVE CENTS In Manhattan. Bronx and Brooklyn TEN CENTS

SAMUEL GOMPERS DIES IN SAN ANTONIO, BLESSING 'OUR GREAT INSTITUTIONS;' NATION MOURNS THE GREAT LABOR CHIEF

END COMES ON HOME SOIL

His Last Wish Granted, He Cheers Sorrowing Labor Colleagues.

STATE HONORS ARE OFFERED

Funeral Train, With Body in Bronze Casket, Starts for Washington and New York.

FUNERAL HERE THURSDAY

Body Will Lie in State in Two Cities—Burial at Sleepy Hollow.

SAN ANTONIO, Texas, Dec. 13 (Associated Press).—Samuel Gompers, for more than forty years President and active leader of the American Federation of Labor, died here this morning after a futile but gallant fight against the weaknesses that come with age and general disorders, from which he had suffered for many months. Mr. Gompers was 74 years old. He died upon American soil, realizing his last hope.

Since Saturday a week ago, when the fatal illness came upon him in Mexico City, where he had gone to attend the convention of the Pan-American Federation of Labor, Mr. Gompers's life was all but despaired of by labor leaders and friends who had accompanied him on this last trip of his career. Fighting death valiantly, but with a greatly weakened heart, due to the rigors of the Mexican trip and the higher altitudes there, he was placed aboard a special train and rushed to the United States, arriving in San Antonio last night.

The labor chieftain died surrounded by his comrades, many of whom had fought beside him, shoulder to shoulder, for a generation in behalf of the economic principles he expounded.

The end came in a hotel room here after his arrival from Mexico City. His last words were spoken to his nurse about an hour before he died—a prayer for the American people and American institutions. Realizing that he was losing the battle so stubbornly fought, he turned to her and whispered:

"Nurse, this is the end. God bless our American institutions. May they grow better day by day."

Shortly before he lapsed into the unconsciousness which presaged the end, President Gompers gave a few simple directions for his funeral and bade a few life-long friends farewell.

Body Borne on Gun Carriage.

Tonight the body of the labor chieftain, sleeping in a massive bronze casket similar to that in which President Harding was laid to rest, was started on its long journey to the nation's capital, accompanied by his friends and associates. The funeral train left at 11:07. There were no services at the mortuary where the body reposed today.

A cosmopolitan throng all day long filed past the body, and tonight the city paid its respects to the stricken labor leader as his body was borne to the station for the beginning of its last journey, mounted on an artillery caisson, surrounded by a military escort and accompanied by delegations representing the city and the labor organizations here.

Up almost to the hour of departure, the crowds thronged about the little frame house that had been turned into a mortuary.

As the hour approached for the start of the cortege to the Missouri, Kansas & T. train waited at the station for their noted passenger and for the labor officials who had been Mr. Gompers's closest councilors in life and were now his chief mourners in death.

The rear observation coach was made ready to receive the casket, while members of the labor group were to occupy a sleeping car just ahead. Two beds were placed in the funeral car, near the casket, for the labor officials, who will act as the watch and guard on the journey. Plans were made to have at least two comrades of the dead leader watch at all times.

Members of the Executive Council of the Federation have been requested by telegraph to board the train at points on the route nearest their homes, so that the full council may award the fallen President to his home in Washington.

Sixteen stops are listed on the train's itinerary as it goes to Washington. The first stop will be at Fort Worth.

Continued on Page Twenty-six.

DUNCAN IS LIKELY TO SUCCEED GOMPERS

Vice President of Federation Will Probably Be Named for Office Thursday.

COMMITTEE TO MEET THEN

New Executive's Term Will Hardly Extend Beyond Next October's Convention.

A successor to Samuel Gompers as President of the American Federation of Labor will be chosen at a meeting of the Executive Council, probably next Thursday in New York, following the funeral.

Present indications are that the successor will be James Duncan, First Vice President and former President of the Granite Cutters' Union. Other contenders, in the order of possibility, are Matthew Woll, Sixth Vice President, and for fifteen years head of the Photo Engravers' Union; William Green, Third Vice President, who is Treasurer of the United Mine Workers, and T. A. Rickert, President of the United Garment Workers.

It is believed that had he been able to designate his successor Mr. Gompers would have named Matthew Woll, who in recent years was the confidant of the labor chief.

It is not thought in labor circles that an immediate successor to Mr. Gompers will be difficult for the Executive Council to choose. Whoever he is, it is likely that he will not remain in office longer than the convention of the Federation next October in Atlantic City.

Short Term Expected.

The contending factions in the Federation virtually will make it impossible for the immediate successor of Mr. Gompers to remain long on the uncertain seat provided for him. Those who say that Mr. Duncan probably will be chosen are of the opinion that, because of his age, Mr. Duncan will not aspire to continue in office after October. In deference, therefore, to his contributions to the labor movement, and also because of his lifelong friendship for the late leader, it is considered more than likely that he will be chosen.

The Acting President of the A. F. of L. today is Frank Morrison, its Secretary. The Constitution provides that in case of a vacancy in the office of President the Secretary shall perform its duties until his successor is chosen.

"In that event," the constitution says, "it shall be the duty of the Secretary to jointly with his fellow officers of the Executive Council call the executive council for the purpose of electing a President to fill said vacancy."

As the members of the Executive Council have been away from their homes for a month, the first opportunity for them to meet and name a successor will be the day of the funeral. Although, as one labor leader put it, "a bag of peanuts thrown into the

Continued on Page Twenty-six.

WOULD BAN BRINDELL 100 MILES FROM CITY

Untermyer Proposes a Geographical Limit on Labor Leader After Release.

WANTS HIM OUT OF UNIONS

Lawyer Renews Attack on Parole Board and Suggests Restrictions on Freedom.

Special to The New York Times.

OSSINING, Dec. 13.—Samuel Untermyer, who convicted lawyer Robert P. Brindell, grafting labor leader, wrote the State Board of Parole today condemning its methods and suggesting how Brindell be curbed when he is let out of prison on Dec. 26.

Several letters and telegrams exchanged between Mr. Untermyer, as Special Attorney General in the Brindell case, and members of the Parole Board, were made public today for the first time.

Mr. Untermyer recommends the following plan of restricting Brindell:

"First, that until the expiration of the maximum term of the sentence Brindell should take up his residence not less than 100 miles from the City of New York, or

"Second, that his parole be conditioned on his being and remaining during that term, directly or indirectly, disassociated from employment by interest in or relations with any labor union."

Mr. Untermyer's correspondence also discloses he wrote to Governor Smith last Summer recommending he be released then, because his sons contended their mother was seriously ill, but assumed that Brindell would be kept out of the labor unions.

Continued on Page Twenty-four.

Sharp Border Patrol and Bad Weather Cuts Christmas Supply of Canadian Liquor Here

OGDENSBURG, N. Y., Dec. 13 (Associated Press).—The word has gone out from points along the northern boundary of the State that downState residents and those living in metropolitan New York will have to be content with a limited amount of holiday liquor from the Northland this year. The movement of "refreshments" across the Northland New York line has been slow and is inadequate to supply the demand, customs and prohibition forces say.

The reason is declared to be the united efforts of augmented forces of customs agents and border patrolmen. The weather, causing bad roads and storms on the lakes, aided the Government forces.

Blizzards and storms such as raged today on Lake Ontario have been prevalent for some time, thus causing the marine rum-runners much trouble. Since held off later than usual, also, and there was much warm weather, rendering the roads deep and soggy. Many a liquor-laden car has been mired but long enough to permit troopers or prohibition agents to capture rum-runners and their cargoes.

The main highways across the line have been so closely guarded recently that the smugglers have been forced to seek the old, out of the way roads, hence lengthening their journeys. According to prohibition agents, any highgrade liquors that reach New York this holiday season will have crossed the line by the marine route.

Prohibition agents also say that January will witness the most intensive drive against liquor smuggling ever attempted in this region. It will be directed against the rum-running that has the border patrol leading the attack. Approximately 1,000 barrels of liquor have been taken by the customs men since July 1 in Northern New York, along with about 400 automobiles. In addition, more than 21,000 worth of drugs has been seized. About 500 arrests are being made for smuggling charges have been made in this period.

Ralston Urges Democrats to Get Together; Asserts Party Will Live Despite Leaders

CHICAGO, Dec. 13 (Associated Press).—Senator Samuel M. Ralston of Indiana, who withdrew his name from the Democratic National Convention in New York last July when he appeared far in the lead for the Presidential nomination, in a public statement made here today, called upon Democrats to "pull themselves together, marshal their forces" and carry on.

Senator Ralston came to the city to speak before the annual dinner of the Indiana Society of Chicago.

In calling for new leadership in the ranks of democracy, the Senator said:

"As to the future of the Democratic Party, I have no doubt. It will live.

"It will live, not because of many of its present so-called leaders, but in spite of them. If they were all to meet and unitedly resolve that the party of Jefferson, of Jackson, of Cleveland and of

Wilson should cease to be, their resolution would add strength and hope to that party.

"I can see that the Democratic Party can be crippled from within, but it cannot be killed, even from within.

"When the rule of democracy fails in this country chaos in the affairs of Government will, in my judgment, soon prevail everywhere; and it is my sincere belief that the life-giving force of American democracy has its source in the basic principles of the Democratic Party; and while they may be blurred for a time, they cannot be extinguished nor can Government remain virile.

"It is therefore the patriotic duty of Democrats the country over to pull themselves together and marshal their forces, for the party will, where prevailing wrongs are uprooted, be just to all the people."

$110,000,000 A YEAR TO KEEP NAVY RATIO URGED BY WILBUR

That Amount Is Needed for New Ships Annually for Twenty Years, He Says.

COMMITTEE DENIES ALARM

Says Our Prestige Is Not Waning—Reports Out Supply Bill of $290,485,578.

Special to The New York Times.

WASHINGTON, Dec. 13.—America should spend $110,000,000 annually for the next twenty years on new construction for the navy, if its fleets are to be maintained on an equality with Great Britain's in all its branches, and, in regard to Japan's, thus carrying out the 5-5-3 ratio, Secretary Wilbur testified recently before the House Subcommittee on Naval Appropriations.

Secretary Wilbur's testimony became public today when the Naval Appropriation bill was reported to the House by the Appropriations Committee. The measure carries a total of $290,485,578, or only $938,350 less than recommended by the budget. While the sum allowed by the Appropriations Committee is not much below the budget it is $14,299,562 less than was approved for the current fiscal year.

The Secretary insisted to the subcommittee, however, that the modernization program recently approved was necessary to place the navy on a parity with Great Britain's, and that continuing appropriations were essential to keep the fleet up to standard.

Secretary Wilbur's Building Estimate.

"The cost of building and replacements required for the next twenty years to build up and maintain the same ratio in all combatant ships and aircraft, as is provided in the treaty for capital ships (5-5-3) and based on the present strength of the treaty powers' navies, built, building and authorized (unless there is some further limitation of armament), will, if promptly made, average about $92,000,000 per annum for ships and about $18,000,000 for aircraft, a total $110,000,000," Secretary Wilbur said.

When asked by the subcommittee about the eighteen battleships which this country possesses, the Secretary said:

"All the ships are in condition to fight tomorrow, and the Florida could, with the limitations that I referred to."

The Secretary's allusion was to the needed repairs on the Florida, which have been authorized by Congress in the modernization bill just passed.

"There are repairs which we class as urgent," he said, "and the repairs

Continued on Page Twenty-six.

NATION'S DRYS SEEK TO COMPEL FEDERAL INQUIRY IN JERSEY

Attorney General Stone Has Been Asked to Detail Special Bootleg Investigator.

POLITICS ENTER SITUATION

Leaders Fear That "Rum Bottle May Replace Teapot as Emblem of Graft."

All the influence that the organized prohibition forces of the country can muster will be brought to bear on Attorney General Stone, it was learned yesterday, to induce him to send a special Assistant Attorney General to New Jersey to assume charge of the investigation and prosecution of the bootleg disclosures. Twelve men already have been indicted by the Hudson County Grand Jury as a result of charges of wholesale bribing of officials and politicians to furnish protection for the landing of millions of dollars' worth of liquor.

Political considerations also have become factors in the revelations, and it was said in Newark last night that "politicians fear the rum bottle may take the place of the teapot as an emblem of graft."

May Appeal to President.

If Attorney General Stone declines to accede to the request, already placed before him by Samuel Wilmer, Assistant Superintendent of the Anti-Saloon League of New Jersey, the matter, it was said here last night, would be taken directly to President Coolidge. It was argued that one appeal has already been made by the Anti-Saloon forces in this matter to the Attorney General and that there will be a second appeal to put the situation more strongly before Mr. Wilson.

"If Attorney General Stone declines to accede to the request," said Mr. Wilmer yesterday, "if Attorney General Stone and Mrs. Mabel Willebrandt, Assistant Attorney General, will commission a special Attorney General to work here, we will turn up enough evidence to rock the country. I have strongly recommended that kind of action, but what I communicated to the Attorney General must be kept private until I get a reply."

Wilson May Be Called Off.

Mr. Wilmer's comment last night was: "I wouldn't be surprised if I were called off by Washington, but I haven't heard anything yet."

Senator Edge, in Washington, announced his intention to see the Attorney General tomorrow to learn exactly how Mr. Winne stood with the Department of Justice and whether there was a basis for recent reports that Mr. Winne's resignation would be welcomed because of wet sympathies.

"I believe that Winne is thoroughly honest and able," Senator Edge said. "I have every reason to hold him in the highest esteem and I believe he is as conscientious as any official in the public service.

"I think it is time to resent the assumption of superior virtue by the Anti-Saloon League and similar people in view of the actions of their own appointees.

"It is pretty nearly time they were made to answer for the character of the persons they have put in office. I well realize that I cannot give a blanket insurance policy on all of my own appointments, but I am sick and tired of hearing these people proclaim that they are the only honest people in New Jersey.

Federal Jury to Get Evidence.

Despite his doubt that he would be permitted by Washington to continue prosecutions, Mr. Winne was busily engaged yesterday with preparations for presenting all the evidence that has come into his possession to the Federal Grand Jury next Tuesday. He spent most of the day, he said, in framing the indictments which will be asked for. Al-

Continued on Page Eighteen.

THE LATE SAMUEL GOMPERS, President of the American Federation of Labor.

CANADIAN COURT ORDERS H. S. OSLER TO TELL INVESTIGATORS FROM THIS GOVERNMENT OF FALL'S CONNECTION WITH SINCLAIR DEAL

WITNESS IS NOW IN AFRICA

Formed a Trading Company for Sinclair and Paid Profits in Liberty Bonds.

$2,000,000 IN ONE DEAL

Judge Calls Company a "Fake" and Sweeps Away Objections to Testifying.

OTHER WITNESSES ABROAD

O'Neil and Blackmer in France—Teapot Dome Trial Off Awaiting Their Testimony.

EX.SEC.ALBERT B. FALL   HARRY SINCLAIR

J. E. O'NEIL   H. M. BLACKMER

PRINCIPAL FIGURES IN THE GOVERNMENT'S ATTEMPT IN CANADA TO TRACE SINCLAIR PAYMENT IN LIBERTY BONDS TO ALBERT B. FALL.

Special to The New York Times.

TORONTO, Dec. 13.—Justice Riddell of the Supreme Court of Ontario handed down a sweeping decision today in connection with the Teapot Dome case in the United States.

He directs Henry Smith Osler, former President of the defunct Continental Trading Company, Ltd., to appear before United States Consul Shantz and commissioner and answer questions put to him by Newton C. Rowell and S. G. McMillan of Toronto, counsel for the United States Government, who are endeavoring to trace $90,000 worth of Liberty bonds alleged to have been paid Albert B. Fall, former American Secretary of the Interior, in the form of a dividend.

For several months Mr. Osler, who is a King's Counselor, has fought against giving testimony. He and other witnesses who previously had appeared for examination refused to answer certain questions, whereupon the present motion was made to commit them for contempt of court. Mr. Osler claimed the privileges of attorney and client in the matter, but two high court judges here had already decided that he must give the information.

There are big difficulties, however, in the way of getting an immediate answer to the questions. One is an appeal to the Appellate Division of the Supreme Court and the other is that Mr. Osler is away with a large party of friends hunting elephants in the interior of Africa and will not be back for some time. Nothing is said in the judgment as to any urgent necessity for his return.

The other day when the case was up in court Wallace Nesbit, a former Judge of the Supreme Court of Canada, entered into a conspiracy to defraud the United States by bringing about the lease of the Teapot Dome property.

DE FORD TO AID CITY IN TRANSIT INQUIRY

He Will Assist Edmund L. Mooney in Representing Transportation Board.

FIRST SESSION TOMORROW

No Indication Given as to Probable Procedure—Hylan to Start Subway Work on Heights.

The City Administration's array of counsel for the transit investigation, which will begin tomorrow morning at 10:30 before Justice John V. McAvoy in the large meeting room of the New York City Bar Association, received further additions yesterday when William A. De Ford, the only lawyer member of the commission, to attend the hearings as its official representative. Mr. De Ford will be assisted by a Secretary, John F. X. McGhey, who is a lawyer.

The selection of Mr. De Ford, who was formerly an attorney for William Randolph Hearst, was announced after a conference of the members of the Board of Transportation, at which John H. Delaney, Chairman, Daniel L. Ryan, Mr. De Ford, Edmund L. Mooney, special counsel of the board, and William G. Fullen, its counsel, attended. It was explained that the selection of Mr. De Ford to attend the hearings was entirely because he was a lawyer, and had no other significance.

In addition to Mr. De Ford and Mr. McGhey the lawyers who are expected to attend the opening hearing before Justice McAvoy as legal representatives of some branch of the City Government are:

Max D. Steuer and Harry A. Gordon, special counsel to the Board of Estimate; Edmund L. Mooney, special counsel to the Board of Transportation; Corporation Counsel George P. Nicholson and Louis Lande, Special Assistant Corporation Counsel in the transit inquiry. The Transit Commission will be represented by former Justice Clarence J. Shearn, its special counsel.

Calder Denies Seeing Smith.

Mr. Delaney denied a report that he had been to Albany to see Governor Smith in relation to the coming inquiry. Mr. Delaney has been credited with having brought about a change of attitude on the part of the City Administration.

In the absence of any information from Justice McAvoy or Henry L. Sherman, his counsel, the officials interested in the inquiry indulged in considerable speculation concerning the matters likely to be considered first. The belief at the office of both the Transit Commission and the Board of Transportation was that the first day's program would depend largely upon the time Justice McAvoy might allow to counsel, and that it was quite likely that a start would be made at the first session on the part of the City Administration.

Continued on Page Eighteen.

MILLS URGES FUSION AT 'VICTORY' DINNER

Tells Republicans Hylanism Can Be Beaten Only by Aid of Independents.

SOUNDS PARTY RALLY CRY

Snell Says G. O. P. Here Must Mend Its Ways—Wadsworth Wants More Liberalism.

A rallying cry for next year's Mayoralty contest was sounded by Representative Ogden L. Mills and other speakers at the Victory Dinner given last night at the National Republican Club in the celebration of the successful party candidates in the recent State campaign. Representative Mills said that if the Republican city organizations would stand together and make a winning appeal to the independents, Hylanism would become a thing of the past in New York City.

Mr. Mills boldly opposed some of the most influential leaders in the Republican State organization who would have the Republicans "go it alone" in the coming campaign. He believed Tammany could be defeated and Hylanism wiped out only by a concerted appeal to Republicans and independents combined. He stood for fusion. He warned against opportunism that might mislead his party into attempting "the same kind of appeal" to the voters as the Tammany opposition and said that to win the Republicans must appeal to the conscience and intellect of the electorate.

Snell Wields the Gavel.

Former United States Senator William M. Calder, as President of the National Republican Club, wielded the gavel when the after-dinner oratory commenced. Seated with him at the speakers' table were Senator Wadsworth, Charles B. Hilles, Vice Chairman of the Republican National Committee; Colonel Theodore Roosevelt, defeated Republican candidate for Governor; Mrs. Florence E. S. Knapp, Secretary of State-elect; Representative Mills, Seymour Lowman, Lieut. Governor-elect, and Representative Bertrand H. Snell, Chairman of the Rules Committee of the House of Representatives.

At a long table running at right angles with the speakers' table sat a majority of the other successful candidates for State offices and seats in Congress.

Senator Calder in his introductory remarks ascribed the defeat of Colonel Roosevelt mainly to the Republican stand against modification of the Volstead law. The Colonel said that in view of the victory won by all the other candidates on the State ticket, he felt reconciled to his own defeat, inasmuch as he realized that the Republican Party leaders had done all in their power to uphold him in his contest with his popular Democratic opponent.

Representative Mills prefaced his speech with a reference to the Republican organizations in New York, which have been criticized by party leaders up-State as a result of the big plurality rolled up by Governor Smith here. While admitting that the party was not as efficient as it might be in New York City, he declared the up-State Republicans were in part responsible for the condition

Continued on Page Twenty-three.

"All the News That's Fit to Print."

The New York Times.

THE WEATHER
Fair and cooler today; tomorrow, fair; fresh northwest winds.
Temperature yesterday—Max., 70; min., 54.
☞For weather report see Page 23.

VOL. LXXIV....No. 24,565.

NEW YORK, MONDAY, APRIL 27, 1925.

TWO CENTS In Greater New York | THREE CENTS Within 200 Miles | FOUR CENTS Elsewhere in the U. S.

REAL FIGHT ON HYLAN FOR RENOMINATION EXPECTED THIS WEEK

Smith Will Be in Town and Tammany Conferences May Settle Mayor's Fate.

SOME LEADERS FOR HIM

McCooey's Continued Silence Starts Reports That He May Withhold His Support.

SOMERS IS A POSSIBILITY

President of the Brooklyn Chamber of Commerce Added to List of Candidates.

Paris to New York Flight By French Plane Is Planned

Copyright, 1925, by The New York Times Co.
Special Cable to THE NEW YORK TIMES.

PARIS, April 26.—There is being built secretly in Paris a large hydroplane with which it is hoped to fly without stopping 4,000 miles between Paris and New York.

This machine is being constructed on orders of the French navy according to its own plans. It will have a motor of 550 horse-power and will carry 6,000 liters of gasoline. The first trials will take place in June and the flight will be attempted during the Summer.

French aviation headquarters admit the machine is being made, but refuse to reveal any details beyond those given above.

COPPERHEAD BITES GIRL ON SNAKE HUNT

Venom Enters Veins, but First Aid and Serum Apparently Prevent Harm.

INCIDENT AMUSES VICTIM

Officer in Reptile Study Club, Miss Condon Keeps Serpents as Pets in Her Home.

1,909 MURDERS HERE IN LAST 7 YEARS, ARON REPORT SAYS

Republican Publicity Chairman Adds That Only 231 Slayers Have Been Convicted.

INCREASE OF 40 PER CENT.

There Were 333 Homicides Last Year Compared With 240 Reported in 1918.

POLICE ARE CRITICIZED

Statements of Hylan and Enright That Crimes of Violence Are Decreasing Are Denied.

VON HINDENBURG IS ELECTED PRESIDENT OF GERMANY; BEATS MARX, REPUBLICAN LEADER, BY 887,000 VOTES; TWO KILLED AND MANY INJURED IN RIOTING AT POLLS

WASHINGTON UNPERTURBED

General View Is That It Means No Sudden Shift in Berlin Policy.

OFFICIALS ARE SILENT

Question of Effect of Election on American Loans and Dawes Plan Is Discussed.

NO REACTION, SAYS LANSING

Borah Likewise Expresses Optimism—Swanson Is Not So Confident.

Hindenburg's Statement On Dawes Plan Fulfillment

Field Marshal von Hindenburg, President-elect of Germany, stated his views on the fulfillment of the Dawes program by Germany in an interview with the Associated Press correspondent at Hanover on April 20. Von Hindenburg said:

"Whether the obligations under the Dawes report are capable of fulfillment will become evident only after a certain period of time, since, as you know, the burdens imposed will steadily increase for years.

"We, of course, will not be able to fulfill the conditions unless the foreign powers participating in the pact evince political and economic loyalty."

GERARD SEES DANGER FROM HINDENBURG

Ex-Envoy to Berlin Says Election Means Return to Monarchism and Militarism.

GERMANS HERE HOPEFUL

They Predict Unity and Peace —Blow to Red Influence and Treaty Protest Discerned.

FIELD MARSHAL VON HINDENBURG
First German to Be Elected President by Popular Vote.

HINDENBURG IS IDOL OF GERMAN PEOPLE

Victory Over Russians Raised Him From Obscurity to Place of War Chief.

CALLED WOTAN AND THOR

He Insisted His Candidacy for Presidency Had No Partisan Character.

CLASHES REPORTED ALL OVER GERMANY

In Berlin Two Men Are Mortally Injured and Scores Hurt in Fighting Between Gangs.

TWO KILLED IN KARLSRUHE

Silesian Nationalists Besiege Police Headquarters After a Series of Encounters.

REPUBLICAN BLOC BEATEN

Marx Gets 13,752,000 Votes to 14,639,000 for Hindenburg.

30,000,000 BALLOTS CAST

Feverish Excitement Prevails as Early Returns Favor One, Then the Other Candidate.

WOMEN SUPPORT MARSHAL

They With Previous Stay-at-Homes Are Believed to Have Swung the Election.

Latest Official Election Totals.

BERLIN, April 27 (Associated Press).—The official provisional figures of the Presidential election follow:

Von Hindenburg	14,639,399
Marx	13,752,640
Thaelmann	1,931,091
Votes declared invalid	21,919
Total	30,345,560

Fleet Has "Seized" Hawaiian Flying Fields Umpires of the War Manoeuvres Decide

HONOLULU, April 26 (Associated Press).—The umpires in the army-navy manoeuvres here issued a communiqué at 9 o'clock this morning saying that the attacking "Blue" fleet has "seized" the flying field of the "Black," or defending forces, on the islands of Molokai, Lanai and Maui last night.

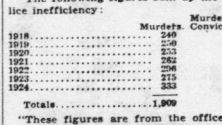

The New York Times.

THE WEATHER

Showers today and tomorrow; fresh south and southwest winds. Temperature yesterday—Max., 72; min., 63.

☞For weather report see Page 22.

VOL. LXXIV....No. 24,651. ... NEW YORK, WEDNESDAY, JULY 22, 1925.

TWO CENTS In Greater New York | THREE CENTS Within 200 Miles | FOUR CENTS Elsewhere in the U. S.

LONG STEP TO PEACE IS SEEN BY BRITAIN IN GERMANY'S REPLY

Chamberlain to Consider With Briand Chances of a Parley in August.

WANTS COMPACT PRESSED

Meanwhile the French Think There Are Traps in the Berlin Note.

GERMANS LOOKING TO US

They Want Americans Made Members of the Arbitration Tribunal.

By EDWIN L. JAMES.

Copyright, 1925, by The New York Times Company.
By Wireless to THE NEW YORK TIMES.

LONDON, July 21.—The British Government regards the German security note as a distinct step toward making the Rhine peace compact. While less favorable than London had hoped Dr. Stresemann's communication is seen as opening the way to early negotiations.

Here one finds the belief that some of the most troublesome passages in the German Foreign Ministry's note were written for home consumption, especially the section relating to article XVI. of the Covenant of the League. Excluding the action of the League Council notifying Germany that no special conditions could attend her entry, it is thought here that Dr. Stresemann knows this part of the note will fail knowledge that it was doomed to failure but in the hope of mollifying opposition in the Reich.

As the British see it, the last paragraph of the note is the most important one, in which Berlin says: "On essential points a significant rapprochement of the views of the two sides has already taken place," and in which the German Government hopes for a settlement of outstanding differences and expresses a wish for speedier discussions. That, the British say, really sums up what the Reich's note means, namely, that the matter should be gone ahead with.

Party Goes South on Yacht To See Dredging by Beebe

The Vanadis, the yacht of Harrison Williams, 60 Broadway, left New York early yesterday morning for Cape Hatteras, where William Beebe and the New York Zoological Society Expedition on the Arcturus are expected Friday afternoon.

A party of friends of Mr. Williams are on board the Vanadis, and George Palmer Putnam, William Beebe's publisher, left New York by rail yesterday morning to join the party at Cape May at the invitation of Mr. Williams.

Beebe, returning from the Sargasso Sea, has notified the New York Zoological Society that he is on his way back to New York and will stop at a designated place off Hatteras to travel and dredge. This point will be the rendezvous of the Arcturus and the Vanadis.

The Vanadis will also accompany the Arcturus on its return to New York on Saturday. Mr. Williams is chief patron of the zoological society's expedition.

MOB CLUBS DEPUTY, FOE OF THE FASCISTI

Giovanni Amendola, Leader of Aventine Opposition, Is Attacked on Country Road.

BOOED OUT OF MONTECATINI

Assault Follows Siege of Hotel, Peace Truce and Flight From Town of Water Cures.

Copyright, 1925, by The New York Times Company.
By Wireless to THE NEW YORK TIMES.

ROME, July 21.—Deputy Giovanni Amendola, perhaps the most important leader of the Aventine opposition to the Fascist regime, was attacked and clubbed by unidentified persons presumed to have been Fascisti, while fleeing by motor car toward Pistola from Montecatini, where a Fascist crowd, after besieging him in his hotel for several hours, eventually booed and hissed him out of town.

Deputy Amendola suffered several bruises and superficial wounds on various parts of the body, and will have to remain twenty days in a hospital, it was said at Pistola, where he went for first aid. He was later brought to Rome by rail accompanied by members of the Fascist railroad police, who guarded him from further attacks.

About half way between Montecatini and Pistola, Signor Amendola's motor car was obliged to halt by two other motor cars drawn up across the road. As soon as Amendola had passed about fifteen or more individuals who had been hiding behind the hedge sprang up and rushed at the Opposition leader, striking at him with sticks they carried. They then re-entered their motor cars and headed toward Montecatini at a rapid pace.

Amendola, though bleeding from several cuts, was not seriously wounded and the car drove on to Pistola.

Search All London for Wisconsin Professor; He Had $3,000 and Family Suspects Foul Play

Copyright, 1925, by The New York Times Company.
Special Cable to THE NEW YORK TIMES.

LONDON, July 21.—Joseph Victor Collins, Professor of Mathematics at Wisconsin University and candidate in 1910 for the United States Senate, is missing in London and foul play is suspected by his wife and daughter.

Scotland Yard circulated a description and photographs of the missing man, and detectives spent yesterday combing London and hospitals in carrying out a systematic search for him.

Once during the day it was believed he was found and his daughter was called to St. George's Hospital and endured the ordeal of inspecting a suicide's body. It wasn't that of her father.

ALL POLICE BELOW 14TH ST. JOIN HUNT FOR A MISSING BOY

Comb East Side Tenements Aided by Forty Detectives for Robert Peries.

ABANDON DROWNING THEORY

Marine Division Fails to Find Clue in River—Lad Seen by Man at 5 P. M. on Sunday.

LITTLE GIRL ALSO SAW HIM

Says She Played With Him but Can Tell No More—Sewers and Intakes to Be Searched Today.

Forty detectives from lower east side precincts and all the uniformed patrolmen between the Battery and Fourteenth Street, on the east side, were brought into the hunt yesterday for Robert Peries, 4 years and 6 months old, who disappeared last Sunday after he had left his home at 272 East Third Street to visit a relative at 55 Ridge Street.

Buck M'Neil, Saver of 40 Lives, Gets First Honors on Tablet

"Buck" McNeill, the Battery Dock Master, who has saved more than forty persons from drowning off the sea wall at Battery Park, will be the first "Honor Man" to have his name engraved on a tablet to be placed in the office of Dock Commissioner Cosgrove, it was announced yesterday.

The tablet will be a memorial to the late Charles F. Murphy, who served as Dock Commissioner from 1898 to 1902. It will be presented by Charles F. Murphy, a nephew of the Tammany leader. Annually a Dock Department "Honor Man" will have his name engraved on the tablet. McNeill will also be presented with a medal by members of the department. He already has more than three dozen medals for saving life.

COAL STRIKE THREAT IS WIRED TO HOOVER

Miners' Official Warns of General Tie-Up Over West Virginia Wage Fight.

SEEKS ROCKEFELLER AID

Charges Assaults by Armed Guards—Anthracite Conferees Make Little Headway.

Special to The New York Times.

ATLANTIC CITY, N. J., July 21.—While the anthracite operators and miners spent an afternoon in fruitless bickering over a new wage agreement, representatives of the bituminous coal miners here today drew up plans for an intensive campaign against soft coal operators in Northern West Virginia. Van A. Bittner, chief representative of the United Mine Workers in that territory, sent an identical telegram to Secretary of Commerce Hoover and Secretary of Labor Davis denouncing the Bethlehem Mines Corporation, a subsidiary of the Bethlehem Steel Corporation, and the Consolidation Coal Company for their alleged violation of the Jacksonville agreement.

HYLAN REFUSES BAIT TO GO ON BENCH AND QUIT MAYOR'S RACE

Foes Realize Need for Keeping Him on Ticket to Block Third-Party Plan.

McCOOEY CALLS LEADERS

Brooklyn Chief Confers With Olvany, but Both Refuse to Tell What Was Said.

HEARST EMISSARY ACTIVE

Meeting of Borough Leaders on Mayoralty Situation Is Put Off Until Next Week.

In a final attempt to avert an open break and keep him in line for the ticket, Democrats who do not believe Mayor Hylan could make a winning fight for a third term, yesterday sent friendly emissaries to the Mayor, who now are bringing all their persuasive powers to bear with a view to inducing him to quit the Mayoralty race and accept a nomination from the Supreme Court for the Second Judicial District.

Up to last night virtually none of the anti-Hylan forces had not been able to budge Mayor Hylan from his determination to make a fight for the Mayoralty again.

SCOPES GUILTY, FINED $100, SCORES LAW; BENEDICTION ENDS TRIAL, APPEAL STARTS; DARROW ANSWERS NINE BRYAN QUESTIONS

Both Sides Speed Procedure for Scopes Appeal; Defense Cost $25,000, With Lawyers Serving Free

Special to The New York Times.

KNOXVILLE, Tenn., July 21.—With the conviction of John Thomas Scopes, attorneys for the defense at Dayton began at once to formulate their plans for the appeal. The case will come before the Supreme Court when that tribunal sits in Knoxville in September. Attorneys for both sides today agreed to expedite the appeal procedure in order to assure a hearing of the issues at that session.

Clarence Darrow, chief of the defense staff, is expected to argue the case before the Supreme Court here. Frank Spurlock, prominent attorney of Chattanooga, assisting the defense, will also plead for Mr. Scopes, being well versed in the peculiarities of Tennessee law. John R. Neal of Knoxville also is expected to take an important part in the appeal proceedings.

For the State, Attorney General Stewart and Ben G. McKenzie doubtless will carry the burden.

The defense's appeal will consist of two main points: First, that the Anti-Evolution law is unconstitutional; second, that even though the law were valid, Mr. Scopes did not violate it, and that the defense was prohibited from proving this at the Dayton trial.

DAYTON, Tenn., July 21 (AP).—A misdemeanor case carrying a penalty to the guilty offender a fine of $100 and costs of the trial brought an expenditure to the defenders of John Thomas Scopes of about $25,000.

The actual court costs are estimated at well over $300, or more than treble the fine assessed.

The greatest expense of the trial was that of bringing expert witnesses, who were not allowed to testify. Defense counsel estimated that cost to be $20,000 to $25,000.

Attorneys on both sides bore their own expenses and served without fees.

In addition several hundred dollars was paid out by the county in preparing the Court House for the trial.

FINAL SCENES DRAMATIC

Defense Suddenly Decides to Make No Plea and Accept Conviction.

BRYAN IS DISAPPOINTED

Loses Chance to Examine Darrow and His Long-Prepared Speech Is Undelivered.

HIS EVIDENCE IS EXPUNGED

Differences Forgotten in the End as All Concerned Exchange Felicitations.

Special to The New York Times.

DAYTON, Tenn., July 21.—The trial of John Thomas Scopes for teaching evolution in Tennessee, which Clarence Darrow characterized as "the first case of its kind since we stopped trying people for witchcraft," is over. Mr. Scopes was found guilty and fined $100, and his counsel will appeal to the Supreme Court of Tennessee for reversal of the verdict. The case was shifted from Dayton to Knoxville, where the case will probably come up on the first Monday in September.

But the end of the trial did not end the battle on evolution, for not long after its conclusion William Jennings Bryan opened fire on Clarence Darrow with a strong statement and a list of nine questions on the basic principles of the Christian religion. To these Mr. Darrow replied and added a statement explaining Mr. Bryan's "rabies." Dudley Field Malone also contributed a statement predicting ultimate victory for evolution and repeating that Mr. Bryan ran away from the fight.

The end of the trial came as unexpectedly as everything else in this trial, in which nothing has happened according to schedule except the opening of court each morning with prayer.

G. G. HAVEN A SUICIDE, DUE TO ILL HEALTH

Banker and Opera Patron Shoots Himself After Vain Struggle to Recover.

FRIEND DISCOVERS BODY

Dr. E. Eliot Finds Him Dead in His Room While Wife Is Away Shopping.

George Griswold Haven, senior member of the banking firm of Strong, Sturgis & Co. of 11 Wall Street and President of the Metropolitan Opera and Real Estate Company, which controls the Metropolitan Opera House, committed suicide by shooting himself through the head with a revolver at his residence, 6 East Fifty-third Street, yesterday morning.

Mr. Haven, who was 59 years old, had been suffering from a nervous disorder for eighteen months. His mind was clear, but for a year and a half he had been inactive in business and had rested and traveled, seeking to regain his health.

BONAPARTE GIVES PROPERTY TO WIFE

Great-Grandnephew of the Emperor Signs Away All but $5,000 a Year.

AGREEMENT ENDS HER SUIT

Referee Files Report and Recommends That Leon Jacobs, Lawyer, Get $5,000 Fee.

The details of the settlement of the banking firm of Jerome Napoleon Bonaparte, great-grandnephew of the Emperor, against his wife, Blanche Bonaparte, to set aside an agreement transferring all of his property to her, became known in the Supreme Court yesterday, when a report was filed by Emanuel B. Cohen, appointed referee to determine the amount of the fee to be paid to Leon H. Jacobs, who acted as attorney for Mr. Bonaparte. The referee recommends that the fee be fixed at $5,000, although counsel for Mrs. Bonaparte contended that $200 should be enough.

Girl, Saved by Dog, Shoots Her Assailant; Negro Again Shot by Posse Before Capture

Special to The New York Times.

NEW BRUNSWICK, N. J., July 21.—Shot twice, once by Miss Barbara Long, who lives with her brother Nicholas on a farm near the Lincoln Highway a few miles from here, and a second time by one of a posse which pursued him through the fields after he is alleged to have attacked Miss Long, Jess Williams, a negro, was arrested today on a charge of atrocious assault. After his wounds had been treated at the Middlesex General Hospital he was taken to the New Brunswick Jail.

Miss Long was saved from serious injury by the intervention of a large shepherd dog which made the negro take to his heels through the fields. The negro begged for food, and as Miss Long handed it to him he sprang at her.

Continued on Page Five.

Continued on Page Four.

Continued on Page Six.

Continued on Page Fourteen.

Continued on Page Three.

Continued on Page Ten.

Continued on Page Eight.

The New York Times.

THE WEATHER
Fair and slightly warmer today; to-morrow warmer; easterly winds.
Temperature yesterday: Max., 57; Min., 39.
For weather report see Page 54.

VOL. LXXV....No. 24,938. ... NEW YORK, WEDNESDAY, MAY 5, 1926. TWO CENTS in Greater New York | THREE CENTS Within 200 Miles | FOUR CENTS Elsewhere in the U. S.

BRITISH INDUSTRY CRIPPLED BY NATION-WIDE STRIKE; MILLIONS WALK TO WORK IN HUGE LONDON TRAFFIC JAM; SOME RIOTING IN SLUM AREAS, COUNTRY GENERALLY CALM

BRITAIN TO AID FIGHT ON LIQUOR SMUGGLING FROM THE BAHAMAS

Concedes in Note to Kellogg the Right of Cutters to Enter Waters for a Year.

TO WAR ON RUM-RUNNERS

Government Agrees to Prosecute Ship Captains Who Violate the Customs Act.

KELLOGG ACCEPTS OFFER

He Will Send Delegates to London to Confer on Cooperation in Prohibition Enforcement.

Special to The New York Times.

WASHINGTON, May 4 (P).—Rum smuggling from the Bahamas to the United States seems likely to receive a heavy blow through concessions just made by Great Britain, revealed today by Secretary Kellogg, in administrative measures which the British Government is prepared to adopt to assist this country in its efforts to prevent the smuggling of liquor from the seas.

Cutters of the Coast Guard service will have permission, under the cooperative concessions, to enter British territorial waters at Gun Cay and island contiguous thereto in Bahama waters without strict compliance with British Admiralty regulations governing visits of foreign vessels to British overseas ports.

At the same time the British Government will take all necessary administrative action to prosecute masters of British vessels for infraction of the British Customs act when reasonable grounds of suspicion are available to believe them guilty of making false declarations in regard to destinations.

Restrictions to Last a Year.

These corporate arrangements are to continue under the arrangement already made for one year, at the end of which period they may be renewed, from time to time, for similar periods. The measures which the British Government has notified Secretary Kellogg it is prepared to take do not constitute what would be technically a binding engagement, but represent a spontaneous and voluntary offer on the part of Great Britain to assist in the enforcement of American prohibition laws and prevent rum-running from British possessions.

This step is one of the most notable in the way of international cooperation and indicates the close accord now existing between the British and the United States and Britain. Its results of the liquor smuggling industry is likely to be marked and will interfere materially with the use of the Bahamas as a source of supply.

In the interest of closer cooperation the British Government has invited the United States to send representatives to London for discussion with the competent British authorities, to learn what are the latter's powers and limitations and acquaint them with the nature of the information and assistance the United States authorities are in a position to supply. This conference will be held immediately, during the present month.

The American delegation will leave the United States on May 22 and is due to reach London on May 28. While the composition of the delegates has not been officially made known it is understood it will include General Lincoln C. Andrews, Assistant Secretary in charge of prohibition enforcement; Rear Admiral Frederick C. Billard, Commandant of the Coast Guard Service, and William R. Vallance, Assistant Solicitor of the State Department.

Hold Visit Will Prove Accord.

The British Government is of the opinion that such a visit would materially contribute toward a full understanding and the efficient execution of the offer of cooperation which it asks the Government to accept as proof of the desire of the British Government to give such assistance as it is possible to give in the circumstances in connection with the plans of the American Government for intensive warfare against West Indian rum-runners.

The State Department made public today an "aide memoire" on the subject, dated March 27, the result of a conference held Dec. 2 last, in which the British Ambassador, Sir Esme Howard, participated with representatives of the Department of State, the United States Treasury and the Department of Justice, and Secretary Kellogg's reply.

Instances are cited in the British Note where the British authorities already have taken action to limit control smuggling, as in the case of this Government Berrett. This ship was loaded at Antwerp for Halifax with a cargo of whisky. The ship was held up at Dover and her cargo unloaded.

Text of the British Note.

The following is the text of the aide:
British Embassy,
Washington, D. C.,
March 27, 1926.
Aide Memoire.
His Majesty's Government had already for some months been devoted

Continued on Page Eleven.

All British Sports Hard Hit By Lack of Transportation

LONDON, May 4 (P).—Sport of all kinds has been hard hit in Great Britain by the general strike because of interference with transportation.

The stewards of the Jockey Club and the National Hunt Committee have decided to abandon horse racing for the present. Their decision applies to all meets, excepting that at Chester, where the cup race will be run tomorrow as scheduled.

"Chester is the oldest race course in the country, being the same ground on which the Romans once held their foot races.

The international soccer games among teams from England, Belgium and France, scheduled for May 8 and 12, have been abandoned, as well as all cricket and tennis meets.

The golfers, however, were still carrying on today to a certain extent.

GEORGE F. PEABODY ADOPTS A DAUGHTER

Banker Gives His Name to Mrs. Marjorie Waite, His Aid in Charity Enterprises.

PRAISES HER HELP TO HIM

Intimates She Eventually May Be Head of Philanthropies in His Wife's Memory.

Special to The New York Times.

LONDON, May 4.—Although the general strike is everything the union leaders expected, it has been answered by a tremendous rally of Britain's inarticulate millions to the defense of the Constitution, according to J. C. C. Davidson, Parliamentary Secretary to the Admiralty, who is in charge of the Government's news bureau and is the manager of "The British Gazette," to be issued tomorrow morning.

George Foster Peabody, retired banker and philanthropist, adopted yesterday as his daughter Mrs. Marjorie Knappen Waite, a widow, 36 years old, who for the last five years has been closely associated with Mr. Peabody in his philanthropic enterprises.

The adoption papers were signed at Ballston Spa, the county seat of Saratoga County, where Mr. Peabody makes his home, by Surrogate George Tusk. Mr. Peabody confirmed the announcement on his arrival at the Harvard Club last night. He came to the city to attend the funeral today of the late Oscar S. Straus, his boyhood friend.

Mr. Peabody said Mrs. Waite was a "very able woman" and had been very helpful in carrying on the work instituted in memory of his wife, the late Mrs. Katrina Trask Peabody, formerly of Saratoga Springs.

He also intimated that the legal adoption of Mrs. Waite would mean that in the event of his death the philanthropic affairs in which he was interested would remain in the hands of a person who was thoroughly conversant with them and who would handle them with sympathy and understanding.

Aid in Charity Work.

Mrs. Waite, whose husband died about two years ago, is a graduate of the University of Minnesota. Her brother, Theodore M. Knappen, is Vice President of the American Lumber Association, Washington, D. C. Mrs. Waite was formerly a member of the Faculty of the Hollywood School for Girls in Los Angeles. On her arrival here about seven years ago she took the position of secretary of the Knox School for Girls at Cooperstown, in which Mr. Peabody is interested. About five years ago she became associated with Mr. Peabody in the organization of a community center for working girls at Saratoga Springs, where Mr. Peabody has made his home since his retirement from active business. This proved so successful that Mr. Peabody arranged for Mrs. Waite to establish a Summer school at Saratoga for working women of the city. This institution provided rest and education for a selected number of young women and girls. Mr. Peabody's philanthropies in Saratoga are grouped under the name of the Katrina Trask Alliance, of which Mrs. Waite is the executive secretary.

Mr. Peabody, who is in his seventy-fourth year, for many years has been an outstanding figure in financial, philanthropic, educational and political circles. He was a member of the banking firm of Spencer Trask & Co., 25 Broad Street, and twenty years ago retired from active participation in the firm's affairs to devote his entire time to educational and philanthropic matters.

Close Friend of Wilson.

He was Treasurer of the National Democratic Committee in 1904 and was a close friend of the late President Woodrow Wilson. When the Federal Reserve law went into effect in 1914, Mr. Peabody was appointed by President Wilson to the office of Vice Chairman and Director of the Federal Reserve Board of New York.

He displayed considerable interest in the reclamation by the State of natural springs in and around Saratoga and served as Chairman of the Reser

CHATTANOOGA, NOTED SCENIC CENtre, has mishievous climate. Average temperature 84.8 degrees.—Advt.

VOLUNTEERS RALLY TO AID

Thousands in All Parts of the Country Flock to Recruiting Stations.

FEW TRAINS ARE RUNNING

Grimsby Clerks Refuse to Quit —Private Concern Lends Its Employes to Railways.

CHEMICAL WORKERS BACK

Nottingham Transport Strikers Volunteer to Work and Get Back Old Jobs.

Copyright, 1926, by The New York Times Company.
By Wireless to The New York Times.

LONDON, May 4.—Although the general strike is everything the union leaders expected, it has been answered by a tremendous rally of Britain's inarticulate millions to the defense of the Constitution, according to J. C. C. Davidson, Parliamentary Secretary to the Admiralty, who is in charge of the Government's news bureau and is the manager of "The British Gazette," to be issued tomorrow morning.

In Stepney, a section of London, the employers of the municipal power plant acceded to the union, demands that no electric current be supplied from sunset to sunrise. This is due to the fact that the majority of the Stepney Common Council are Socialists.

The Government is taking measures to deal with this dereliction, which Mr. Davidson had declared had only injured the sick in hospitals.

Hundreds of seamen on leave from foreign service returned to duty today and naval reservists, though not called out, also reported for duty, he said.

Chemical Strikers Reported Back.

Reports from the District Commissioners were most reassuring, stated Mr. Davidson. That leaders of the striking miners in Northumberland had guaranteed today that there would be no interference with food and transport, was one report. Another was that 10,000 chemical workers in Cheshire returned to work this morning, despite a strike order.

Trucks are practically plentiful and traffic in London today was almost the heaviest in history.

The strike is proceeding good-temperedly in most sections of the country, said Mr. Davidson. That leaders of the Commissioner's office to assist the Government and were assigned to their old jobs.

The Emergency Committee declares the situation is entirely satisfactory and that thousands of people continue to volunteer for special service. Crowds of people were gathered today at the recruiting offices in the neighborhood of the Government buildings, waiting in turn to enlist in the special services.

Another reassuring report came from Grimsby, where the Union of Railway Clerks decided to refuse to strike and to withdraw from the Association of Unions.

One business concern today supplied thirty locomotive engineers and a number of other skilled workers to the railroads.

The situation at all the electric power plants, except that at Stepney, was good tonight.

The Board of Trade today authorized an increase of two pence per quart in the price of milk.

LONDON STOCKS ARE EASIER.

Financial Section Carries on Business With Skeleton Staffs.

LONDON, May 4 (P).—The financial section of London started what business there was to do on an hour or so late today owing to the congested roads, which delayed the staffs on the way to their offices. Even so noon many banks and insurance houses worked only skeleton personnels working.

The Stock Exchange was occupied only with the current settlement, which will be concluded tomorrow, and there was talk of closing after that date if the strike continued.

New business was generally meagre and the prices, where quoted, were easier.

LIVERPOOL, May 4 (P).—The Cotton Exchange, it was announced today, will hereafter open at 11 o'clock, one hour later than usual, during the strike, and will remain closed on Saturdays.

BOSTON ALL THE WAY BY WATER via Cape Cod Canal every evening. Connections at Boston for Maine, New Hampshire, etc. Fall River Line. Reservations, Pier 14, North River, foot of Murray St., N. R. R. I. Leach, Passenger Dept.—Advt.

'It's a Mere Curtain-Raiser,' Soviet View of British Strike

Copyright, 1926, by The New York Times Co.
By Wireless to The New York Times.

BERLIN, May 4.—"It's a mere curtain-raiser," a high official at the Soviet embassy here said of the British general strike tonight. "We don't consider English labor's action revolutionary, but believe it will stimulate the movement toward world revolution in general and overthrow English capitalism in particular."

HOUGHTON REPORTS BRITISH PUBLIC FIRM

Ambassador Says Parleys May Be Renewed in Three Days or a Long Conflict Is Coming.

COOLIDGE WATCHES CRISIS

He Sees No Analogy to Labor Conditions Here and Doubts Serious Effect on Our Trade.

Special to The New York Times.

WASHINGTON, May 4.—Government officials and labor leaders in Washington were deeply concerned today over the general strike in Britain.

Through the Departments of State, Commerce and Labor President Coolidge is keeping a close watch on the situation, recognizing the importance of our trade with Great Britain and the possible influence of a prolonged conflict on various phases of American industry.

Confidential reports are being received by Secretary Kellogg from Ambassador Houghton at London, and by Secretary Hoover from our commercial agents in various parts of the United Kingdom.

The President indicated to callers today his belief that the situation that now confronts the British nation will not have serious effect upon American commerce because foodstuffs, which constitute a large percentage of American exports to the United Kingdom, are understood to be excluded from the transportation embargo by the labor leaders.

There may be some loss of cotton exports, but there is no certainty, according to the President's advices, that the labor leaders will exclude raw materials to the injury of industries not involved in the sympathetic strike. President Coolidge, it was added at the White House, is unable to find any analogy between labor conditions in Great Britain and those in the United States.

Reports Made to the Cabinet.

Secretary of Labor Davis, on the basis of a conference with John L. Lewis, President of the United Mine Workers, reported to President Coolidge today that conditions in the American coal industry were satisfactory. Mr. Lewis refused to comment on the British strike.

One of the messages received by Secretary Kellogg from Ambassador Houghton today, dated London, May 4, said:

"The general strike began at midnight and will probably involve from two to three million members of unions embracing mines, railroad engineers, transports, iron and steel, paper and printing and electrical trades.

"The railway and postal services are partially maintained but uncertain. The London underground railways and the principal omnibus lines are not running. Taxis have been partially affected.

"The people as a whole seem to take the situation stoically and are going quietly about their business.

"Many persons have enrolled as volunteers to maintain services and to act as special constables. The army and navy leaves have been stopped.

"It is impossible to say whether the effect of this situation will be to force a renewal of negotiations within two or three days or will lead to a prolonged conflict."

Quick Settlement Expected.

Although high officials here indicated today their full recognition of the extreme gravity of the situation confronting the British nation, they felt that it would be quite improper, and certainly not helpful at this time, for them to comment publicly on the strike. Despite the seriousness of the situation, however, the opinion prevailed privately among certain high officials that a path out of the woods would be found and that British leaders would be able to breast the crisis and effect an immediate settlement without a prolonged conflict.

Should efforts in that direction succeed, the effect upon American commerce would be slight. Only in case that there is a prolonged general strike, and British trade and industry are thrown into a condition of paralysis, it is fully recognized, despite the optimistic opinions expressed in some quarters since from the White House, that American export trade to the United Kingdom will be seriously affected.

Anxiety Over Trade With Britain.

One official pointed out today that the present value of our trade with the United Kingdom is close to $25,000,000

Continued on Page Four.

LIVELY SCENES IN LONDON

Every Conceivable Kind of Vehicle Pressed Into Transportation Service.

STREET CROWDING TERRIFIC

Impatient Suburbanites Abandon Conveyances and Hurry Afoot to Work.

CROWDS IN GOOD HUMOR

Most Theatres Open at Night, but Are Little Patronized— Suburbs Are Quiet.

By ERNEST MARSHALL.
Copyright, 1926, by The New York Times Company.
By Wireless to The New York Times.

LONDON, May 4.—On this, the first day of the general strike, London is taking matters with what the French writers call characteristic British phlegm.

In the ordinary physiognomy of the metropolis there is no very marked alteration. People appear to be going about their business, and in some cases about their pleasures, much as usual. Bakers' boys and milkmen delivered their ordinary supplies to houses in not only the West End but throughout the outlying districts at regular hours, and exchanged their customary quips with cooks and housemaids as if they had not a care in the world. Of course, everybody asked everybody else about the strike, and it was almost a case of hot ominous quot sententiae.

Spirit of Cheerful Courage.

Possibly the most striking aspect of the moment was the spirit of cheerful courage in which the difficult situation was accepted as something not far removed from a necessary evil. The milkman assured you he would be there on time every morning and the baker had no fears of shortage in his deliveries.

Among the community at large there has been no evidence of panic. There has been no rush to get in supplies, such as showed itself in a certain section during the days of the war before rationing was put in force. After the difficulties of transporting workers to the city and the West End from suburbs had been very successfully coped with, traffic arrangements seemed to become almost normal. This was, of course, more apparent than real, for the underground railways and tubes were closed and trams and omnibuses, whose men are controlled by unions, were not running.

Private initiative, however, had filled the gaps thus created with surprising success. Fleets of charabancs sailed gayly through the main thoroughfares and omnibuses, owned by private firms and individuals who had been latterly striving to break the virtual monopoly of the "combine," the head of which is Lord Ashfield—the Albert Stanley of other days in the United States—and there were taxicabs galore. For some years the problem facing the railroads has been the growing competition of the motorcar and its big brother, the charabanc. The latter are seizing their golden opportunity now, and doubtless adding to their resources for even keener competition with the railroads when these come again into operation.

Tickers Centre of Attraction in Clubs.

In the clubs around about the luncheon hour one saw little or nothing different from ordinary times. There were bigger groups of people gathered round the tickers, for those useful instruments were almost the only medium for dissemination of news. But most comments one heard were calm and composed, though, as Premier Baldwin said yesterday, there are few light hearts in England today; there is no lack of courage and no abandonment of hope.

If it were possible to convey the dominant impression of the moment in a few words, it might be said that what is most deeply regretted is that this should have come at a time when the skies seemed to be clearing. There is less fear of direct results of the strike than of the indirect losses and the burdens which will be the outcome. One British administrator, whose name is known throughout the empire, assessed those indirect consequences as likely to put England back for a period of five years.

Among subsidiary incidents of the situation the chief topics of discussion were reports that the Government had taken over The Morning Post's facilities for news purposes and that a warrant had been issued generally condemned on first approval. In the one case it was argued that whatever need the Government might have of printing presses and offices for the issue of the special bulletins and gazettes which it is intended to distribute, recourse should have been had to some newspaper office other than the organ which is so closely identified with the "diehards" among the coal owners.

In the form in which they first gained currency the reports were to

Continued on Page Two.

Prince of Wales Races Back to London in an Airplane, Cutting Short Vacation at French Seaside Resort

LONDON, May 4 (AP).—The Prince of Wales, after a flying trip from Le Bourget, France, to Croydon, England, which occupied two hours and a half, came to London by motor, arriving at his home in St. James's Palace at 9 o'clock tonight.

He was cheery and alert and looked very fit, indicating he has quite recovered from his recent operation. The airplane on which he traveled from Le Bourget to Croydon was escorted by another light machine.

The Prince went to Buckingham Palace and dined with the King and Queen. He had nothing to say about his flight except that it was uneventful. It was not his first air voyage.

The Princess Mary, Viscountess Lascelles, undismayed by the dense traffic, made her way in a limousine through Piccadilly to the Shaftesbury Theatre for a performance in aid of the Children's Hospital, of which she is patroness.

REICH MINERS COOL ON AIDING BRITISH

They Feel That Their Help Would Not Assist Strikers to Win Their Battle.

UNIONS TO VOTE ON ATTITUDE

British Tie-Up Is Not Expected to Aid German Coal Exports Materially Abroad.

By LINCOLN EYRE.
Copyright, 1926, by The New York Times Company.
By Wireless to The New York Times.

BERLIN, May 4.—The German mining unions as a whole do not desire to participate in the British general strike. They were required to do today about any attempt to prevent coal being exported to Britain would be an act of sabotage against the transport tariff agreement. Communists in the Ruhr have asked their party members to lay down their tools, but none has responded.

Appeals have been made to the German miners to keep on working, since by striking they could not further the chances of the British workers winning their conflict, and a strike would merely increase the present unemployment crisis.

On the other hand, Germany, it is held, cannot expect much relief through possible coal shipments to Britain, as 1,000,000 tons monthly, which is the maximum that could be exported, would merely decrease the surplus of 10,000,000 tons now lying in coal dumps without helping the miners.

Though the "old union," which is one of the largest and is affiliated with the British unions and in constant touch with the British situation through the strike leaders there, has promised aid to them in effecting the solidarity of the strike, the Catholic Miners' Union, which is equally strong, but is not affiliated with the British unions, states it will keep its hands off.

What the German mine owners and miners both wish to see in the outcome of the present strike is the abolition of the British subsidy precedent, which is held to be responsible for Germany's having to export coal at $1.25 a ton in order to compete abroad. "Who is to blame for the strike does not concern us," said The Tag today; "What is important for Germany is the fact that the Brussels conventions put us face to face with a new problem regarding the possible actions of our miners."

The paper adds: "It does not appear that Premier Baldwin's defeat would be desirable for the Fatherland. It would cost us much in State authority and national power."

The Vossische Zeitung says:

"It is of especial significance whether the present labor strife in England will open the eyes of Englishmen to the fact that their subsidy policy is antiquated and unendurable. If the strike shows that the English must agree to a round-table conference with the Continental industries, it will be a right step. Otherwise it is unimportant whether the Government or labor wins."

Financial circles point out that the small sums that may be gained by the coal export will be lost through the corresponding lowering of Britain's buying power in German markets.

Meeting of Federation Called.

BERLIN, May 4 (P).—The General Federation of Trade Unions has summoned its Executive Board to assemble tomorrow to decide on the course to be followed with regard to the British strike.

According to a leading officer of the Federation, this course naturally is dependent upon whether the Amsterdam International Federation of Trade Unions will urge as the general course of action for all its affiliated bodies.

M. Oudegeest, Secretary of the International Federation of Trade Unions, embracing the unions of twenty-three countries, announced in Amsterdam last night that the Federation would strongly support the British Trade Unions Congress.

German official circles seemed to comment on the strike, believing that to do so would be unjustified meddling in British affairs.

The uproar the German Miners' Federation's promise to aid the British, contending that during the Ruhr occupa

EAT RAISINS AFTER MEALS

GOVERNMENT ISSUES A DAILY IN LONDON

Put Out From Morning Post Office, It Mingles 'Zoo Notes' With Strike News.

LONDON TIMES A LEAFLET

Carried in Automobiles Throughout Provinces—Daily Express Also Appears in Miniature.

Copyright, 1926, by The New York Times Company.
Special Cable to The New York Times.

LONDON, Wednesday, May 5.—After a momentous day in London's appetite for news there was approaching the ravenous stage, today's issue of the lone Government emergency sheet, The British Gazette, finally appeared at 11 o'clock last night with "Zoo Notes," "Brooding Lovebirds" and "Lizards With Beards" among the headlines over the tidbits it set before the news-hungry Londoners. There was much more, of course, in solemn vein in this sheet—entire columns about the strike. But the fact remains that the Zoo columns stuck out from among the other items like a sore thumb and caused surprised and delighted chuckles from those who eagerly clutched the lone news sheet as it came hot from the presses.

The British Gazette was published despite the strikers' threats that they would prevent its appearance. As it was delayed hour after hour the impression strengthened that the strikers would make good their threats. But the doughty Gazette appeared, nevertheless. The Government had set its heart on getting it out in the teeth of the strikers. Winston Churchill himself, the Chancellor of the Exchequer, was at The Morning Post office this afternoon, whence the sheet was issued, to see that nothing went wrong with it.

The Gazette consists of four pages. Two of them are blank. Printing appears only on the first and the fourth. This, it is explained, is to make it possible to post the paper on walls and in windows, where those who run may read. The price for those buying it is 1 penny. It will doubtless become a landmark in the history of British journalism.

On the first page is an article headed "First Day of the Great Strike—Not So Complete as Hoped by Its Promoters."

In a Hopeful Vein.

"Reports from all parts of the country," says The Gazette's first article, "indicate that satisfactory arrangements have been set up for the distribution of essential foodstuffs. Volunteers came forward in large numbers in London and all important provincial centres."

The rest of the sheet is in the same hopeful vein. The Government anti-strike measures are described at length and a tone of confidence in the ultimate success of the anti-strike elements is upflagging throughout. The Gazette also prints prominently news of the arrest of the Communist Member of Parliament Saklatvala.

Then come the incongruous "Zoo Notes."

"Great interest is being taken in the expected arrival at the Zoo of a white elephant from Burma," chronicles The British Gazette gravely. "It is stated that the new arrival will not provide rides for children visitors to the Gardens."

Further Zoo items are to the effect that there soon will be a family of baby lovebirds in the parrot house; also that "a pair of Nyassa lovebirds have built a charming nest of stripped bark and tiny twigs." The hen bird, it is further stated, "has laid three eggs." As for the lizards with beards, the Government's anti-strike emergency organ solemnly declares that twelve of these strange reptiles have just arrived from Australia.

London Times a Leaflet.

The London Times was able to keep up continuity of publication by the production of a leaflet eight inches by thirteen inches in size, compared with the usual twenty-eight page issue. This abbreviated edition, which was printed by the multigraph process, required no large fleet of motor vans for its

Continued on Page Four.

BOTH SIDES STAND FIRM

No Signs of Peace and Plans Are Being Made for a Long Fight.

UNION LEADERS JUBILANT

They Assert the Walkout Exceeds Expectations and Is Steadily Spreading.

BALDWIN CALLS ON THE KING

Public Opinion Tends Toward the Government in Its Efforts to Maintain Law and Order.

By T. R. YBARRA.
Copyright, 1926, by The New York Times Company.
Special Cable to The New York Times.

LONDON, Wednesday, May 5.—For twenty-four hours Great Britain has been in the grip of the stupendous general strike without a sign of weakening among the strikers, or among the employers, backed by the Government, bent on breaking the resistance of the millions of striking workers. There is no talk yet of further negotiations or steps tending toward conciliation. Both sides are full of fight, full of confidence.

Neither is saying much. Both are silently and grimly engaged in strengthening their positions in preparing for a possibly long and bitter struggle.

So far violence has been conspicuous by its absence. The strikers in general have obeyed the exhortations of their leaders to refrain from disorder. Tonight there was some incipient rioting in the workers' quarters in East London, such as I observed around the East India Docks. Motor cars coming into the district were overturned by strikers in an ugly mood, and some were set afire.

The police were forced to charge the disturbers of the peace in some cases. They used their clubs in these charges and had some difficulty in restoring order. But they restored it.

Baldwin Reports to the King.

King George received Premier Baldwin at Buckingham Palace during the day and heard from his lips a full report of the latest happenings in this, the greatest industrial crisis in history.

Late in the afternoon the Prince of Wales, who cut short his stay at Biarritz as soon as the grave news from England reached him, arrived by airplane from Paris.

From strike headquarters come reports indicating that the strike leaders are well satisfied with the progress of the strike thus far. They declare that the stoppage of work meets their most sanguine expectations, and that the response to the strike order was most encouraging. They also say the strike is spreading to the "second line of defense"—unions not specifically called out on the first general strike summons.

At the moment of writing the London newspapers are hoping to issue editions today, but they are still uncertain. The trouble is not so much with printing the paper, even a mere skeleton sheet, as with circulating it.

Crowds Storm Newspapers.

Around The London Times Building, outside the windows of The New York Times office, groups of strikers collected tonight and hung around for hours obviously seeking to interfere with any attempt to distribute today's London Times. The same is true of other newspaper offices in and around Fleet Street.

At 11 o'clock the Government's makeshift newspaper, "The British Gazette," was published at The Morning Post office. It was issued despite threats from the strikers that they would never let it appear. The Daily Herald, the extremist Labor organ, is not expected to appear today.

Throughout the day both sides stood firm. While the strike leaders urged their men to refuse to work and abstain from violence the Government displayed immense activity in perfecting its emergency measures. As no time during the day was there serious talk of further negotiations. For the present at least each side is apparently willing to carry the fight much further.

Strikers Are Resentful.

Among the strikers there is considerable resentment because of the feeling that the Government's efforts to mediate between the coal owners and the miners leaned too strongly toward the former. This resentment is in many sections of the British public before the outbreak of the general strike—among some in fact who sup

The New York Times.

THE WEATHER
Cloudy and warmer, probably show-
ers, today; tomorrow showers.
Temperature yesterday—Max., 84; min., 42.
☞For weather report see Page 40.

VOL. LXXV....No. 24,943. ....

NEW YORK, MONDAY, MAY 10, 1926.

TWO CENTS in Greater | THREE CENTS | FIVE CENTS
New York | Within 200 Miles | Elsewhere in the U. S.

BYRD FLIES TO NORTH POLE AND BACK; ROUND TRIP FROM KINGS BAY IN 15 HRS. 51 MIN.; CIRCLES TOP OF THE WORLD SEVERAL TIMES

BALDWIN STRATEGY IS WINNING STRIKE FOR GOVERNMENT

Aggressive Action Keeps Vital Services Going as Unions Balk at "Trump Cards."

THOMAS'S TALK SIGNIFICANT

Both Sides Spend a Quiet Sunday, While London Sees Another Food Convoy.

FOOD PRICES KEPT DOWN

Only Rise Allowed Is for Milk— Incoming Cargoes Are Unloaded and Distributed.

By T. R. YBARRA.

Copyright, 1926, by The New York Times Company.
Special Cable to The New York Times.

LONDON, May 9.—The essence of strategy is robbing the enemy of his freedom of action. If that axiom be transferred from the domain of warfare to that of strikes it must be admitted tonight that so far the British Government, led by Premier Baldwin, has robbed leaders of Britain's great general strike of their freedom of action.

At the close of the sixth day of this gigantic industrial struggle it becomes increasingly apparent that even if the British Government has not won the game yet it has consistently forced the play.

From the very outset of the great strike, at midnight last Monday, most of the aggressiveness recorded has been contributed by those seeking to crush the strike. Each day brings increased railway service. Each day shows a more efficient organization of the Government's emergency food distributing services. Each day has shown a bigger enrollment of volunteers in every branch of strike breaking. Each day has shown hesitation on the part of the strikers to play their trump cards.

They have not tried to smash the great foe: distributor organization of the Government. They have not called it the "second line of defense" and the "third line of defense." Will they? That is the question, asked in a constantly growing tone of skepticism by those who have lived through these first six days of one of the greatest industrial crises in the history of the world.

Thomas Adds to Skepticism.

Tonight this skepticism received decided impetus from J. H. Thomas, the noted labor leader, who has been consistently against extremist measures in the fight to obtain a panacea for British labor grievances. Speaking at Hammersmith, a London suburb, Mr. Thomas made statements which, as befits the moderate without infuriating the extremist, partook largely of the nature of those "weasel words" which so infuriated the late Theodore Roosevelt in the heyday of his acrimonious political combats.

Nevertheless, stripping the speech of all its diplomatic "I don't want to displease anybody" quality, there shone in it statements which clearly imply that the general strike is not going exactly as its instigators hoped and that, therefore, Moderates like Mr. Thomas are beginning to hope that the dawn of conciliation is approaching. The most striking statement in Thomas's speech is:

"If the people who talk about a fight to a finish carried it out in that sense the country would not be worth having at the end of it."

"I have never despaired and I do not disguise now that I have never been in favor of the principle of the general strike," said Mr. Thomas. "No one will disagree, however, that the fundamental principle of trade unionism is not only the right for men and women to organize, but the essential part of that legal right is collective bargaining. The workers have no right to say to the employers, 'You must negotiate under the threat of a strike, but it is equally right and just that the workers should not be asked to carry on negotiations under the threat of a lockout.'

"From the start I deliberately went in to get peace. Let there be no mistake about that, and in spite of all that has been said I repeat that it is the duty of both sides to keep the door open."

Extols Workers' Solidarity.

"The response to the appeal of the Trades Union Congress has been the most wonderful, the most marvelous demonstration of solidarity the world has ever seen and has staggered your opponents.

"All attempts to raise the constitutional issue are not only wrong, but

Continued on Page Five.

Chattanooga, headquarters for cheap hydro-electric power, 270,000 actually developed.—Advt.

Strikers Urged 'to Stick to It' If 'Further Steps' Are Needed

LONDON, May 9 (Æ).—C. T. Cramp, President of the National Union of Railwaymen, addressing a strikers' meeting in London today, warned that it might be necessary "to take further steps" to gain that for which they were fighting. He said:

"We have entered this fight as railwaymen because we realize that if the miners' standards of living is depressed below the present level, it would not be long before the remainder of the organized workers would find themselves in the same position."

If it were necessary to take further steps to uphold the things which they now required, he asked his hearers to "stick to it," remarking:

"If I am going into a scrap I prefer to scrap with both hands and not with one tied behind my back."

BALFOUR DENOUNCES REVOLUTION INTENT

He Calls Upon Britons to Save "the Civilization of Which They Are the Trustees."

SAYS NATION FACES RUIN

Declares Success of the Revolt Would Put a Minority of Extremists in Power.

Copyright, 1926, by The New York Times Company.
By Wireless to The New York Times.

LONDON, May 9.—The Earl of Balfour declares the general strike to be an attempt at revolution "which would bring ruin, swift, complete and irresistible upon this country," in a statement upon the industrial conflict which appears in tonight's issue of The British Gazette, the official Government organ.

"From such a fate," concludes Lord Balfour, "may the courage and resolution of our countrymen save the civilization of which they are the trustees."

Lord Balfour's Statement.

The text of Lord Balfour's statement follows:

"Two hundred and thirty-eight years have passed since a revolution occurred in this country, whose object was to secure the supremacy of parliamentary government and the traditional liberties of our people. Through eight generations it has proved successful.

"But we are now threatened, it seems, with a revolution of a very different kind, and it behooves us anxiously to consider what would be its ultimate results were it, unhappily, to succeed.

"Its methods are being practiced before our eyes; they are directed to the people of food, transport, employment and a free press. The convenience of civilized life, which long have been counted among its necessities, are in some cases to be immensely diminished, in others to be brought to an end.

"Personal security is to be threatened: industry is to be seriously hampered even when it is not wholly stopped. Willing workers are to be kept in idleness; anxious purchasers are to be kept in want; perishable food is to rot in port. All the wheels of social life are to be clogged.

"Such are the methods of the revolutionary movement. What, then, are its objects?

"The nominal object is to maintain unchanged existing conditions of the miners' remuneration as regards hours of work and rates of pay. Now, there is no man who does not heartily share this desire; but neither is there any man who has read the real mine report, who thinks it can be available under existing conditions.

"Were the revolution to succeed tomorrow, the country would suffer, but the miner would not gain.

"No revolution in Great Britain, however triumphant, is going to diminish the cost of getting coal. A revolution in Government, extensive bootlegging and a widespread use of the still in the home, the wets assert in their brief. Women and children are drinking today, there is an army of rum-runners and moonshiners, demand alcohol can be easily renatured and prohibition has been an utter failure from a temperance standpoint, the brief adds.

"The example of Canada, which sells liquor under Government regulation, is contrasted with conditions in the United States where the public morale has been broken, the modificationists assert.

"Reopening of Hearing Unlikely.

In spite of the strenuous nature of the plea for a reopening of the hearings, the request of the wets probably will go unheeded. The Senate subcommittee is 4 to 1 dry, Senator Reed of Missouri, being the only modification on it.

So arid is the committee that there also seems to be no chance that it will favorably report any of the bills which would authorize a modification

Continued on Page Twelve.

BOSTON ALL THE WAY BY WATER
via Cape Cod Canal every evening
6 and 7 P. M. from or Boston New England States. See 8 S. page or phone
Eastern S. S. Lines, Inc., Barclay 0700.

WETS NOW DEMAND SENATORS SUMMON GARY, ROCKEFELLER

In Brief Filed Today With the Committee They Call for Noted Drys' Testimony.

AIM OF GIFTS CHALLENGED

End of Anti-Trust Prosecution Is Charged When 'Big Business' Allied With Prohibition.

WAYNE WHEELER ATTACKED

Subpoenas Are Urged for Counsel of Anti-Saloon League and the Congress Members in Its Pay.

Special to The New York Times.

WASHINGTON, May 9.—A demand that the Senate Judiciary Committee reopen its prohibition hearings and subpoena Wayne B. Wheeler, John D. Rockefeller Jr., Judge Elbert H. Gary and others and ask them to disclose the sources of the great sums expended by the Anti-Saloon League, is made in a brief which will be filed tomorrow by the wets.

Denouncing Mr. Wheeler for not "keeping his word" to appear as a witness at the recent hearings, the brief declares the anti-prohibitionists wish to question him about the $35,000,000 he has asserted was used by the drys in their fight for the Eighteenth Amendment.

The wets assert that Mr. Wheeler should be forced to tell about contributions by Mr. Rockefeller, Judge Gary and other captains of industry and also "as to the significance of the strange phenomenon that after the alliance of the Anti-Saloon League and the big business to keep up a continuous ferment or smoke screen over prohibition, anti-trust prosecutions suddenly ceased."

Members of the House and Senate who have admitted that they are on the League's payroll should also be summoned, as well as Dr. Ernest H. Cherrington of the World League Against Alcohol, who like Mr. Wheeler, escaped cross-examination by Senator Reed, the wets insist.

"Let us have the whole story of prohibition propaganda and prohibition politics as well aste sordid story of prohibition itself," the brief states.

Attack Cited on Reformers.

There is a review of the testimony given at the hearings, but it is upon Mr. Wheeler that the fire is centred. Declaring that prohibition is costing the United States $500,000,000 annually in direct enforcement and loss of revenue, the wets contend that this is too heavy a price, "even to keep the liquor-soaked volatile enough in the open forum but silent as a clam when it comes to testifying under oath before this commission of high-minded religious and industrial organizations, and as a matter of fact a parasite upon misguided religious and industrial organizations, and as a supra-Government in his own divine right."

Mrs. Ella Boole, President of the Women's Christian Temperance Union, is severely criticized for refusing to reply to questions as to whether it would be better to sell mild alcoholic beverages in the open or to allow them to be made at home in the presence of children.

Dr. E. C. Dinwiddie, while described as a man who has earned his living in the cause of prohibition, is complimented as "the highest type of professional dry."

Prohibition has brought in its wake increased drunkenness, secret drinking, deaths from alcoholism, corruption in Government, extensive bootlegging and a widespread use of the still in the home, the wets assert in their brief. Women and children are drinking today, there is an army of rum-runners and moonshiners, demand alcohol can be easily renatured and prohibition has been an utter failure from a temperance standpoint, the brief adds.

Only 147 Workless in Paris, Says French Labor Minister

TOURS, France, May 9 (Æ).—There are only 147 unemployed persons in Paris, whereas London before the strike there had 800,000 and Berlin 450,000, Minister of Labor Durafour said at a banquet inaugurating the Tours exposition week.

France's birth rate, the Minister asserted, hardly varied from 1913 figures of 192 births for each 10,000 of population, whereas German statistics for the same units of population were 283 in 1913 and 200 in 1926. England, he said, shows 238 in 1913 and 186 in 1926.

"We have done this by organizing against infant mortality," the Minister affirmed, "which, although 13 per cent. before the war, had fallen to 9 per cent. in 1925. Therefore we must not despair. Our percentages of births equal Germany's and surpass England's."

NO TRACE OF WARD; FAMILY IS ALARMED

Brother, Fearing Foul Play, Asks Police to Broadcast Alarm for Missing Man.

SEARCH ON IN THREE STATES

Trenton Police Suspect Ruse in Abandoning His Car—Race Tracks to Be Watched.

The police began a search for Walter S. Ward yesterday at the request of his brother, Ralph D. Ward, who reported his disappearance to the Missing Persons Bureau at Police Headquarters. Mr. Ward said that his brother, who was acquitted three years ago of the murder of Clarence M. Peters, had not been seen or heard from since last Wednesday and that his family feared foul play.

Captain John Ayres, in command of the Missing Persons Bureau, broadcast a confidential alarm for Ward, with his description, among all the police stations in the metropolitan district. Detectives working on the case said last night that they had no clue to Ward's whereabouts, and had no idea whether he had been killed or had disappeared for some reason known only to himself.

No Clue in Abandoned Car.

Ward's automobile was found in Trenton, N. J., last Friday morning, with the windshield broken and a large stone on the front seat. There was neither anything in the car nor any witness to clear up the mysterious circumstances under which the machine had been abandoned.

Ralph Ward told Captain Ayres that at the time his brother disappeared he had been on a business trip to Baltimore and was on his way back or was driving to Baltimore when the car was abandoned.

To reporters who called at his home, 1,010 Fifth Avenue, at Eighty-second Street, Ralph Ward said:

"Walter went to Baltimore early in the week, but came back to New York and was seen here on Wednesday. He went away again in his car and was to have returned home again on Thursday. But we have not seen him since Wednesday."

Thinks It Was Second Trip.

"Was he going to Baltimore on his second trip?"

"I believe so," replied his brother.

"On business?"

"Presumably."

"Have you any clue to what has become of him?"

"Absolutely none," said the brother. "We have no idea what has become of him or where he is."

"Do you think that violence is indicated?"

"Yes, that is the only possible explanation."

Ralph Ward said that the family intended to investigate to see whether Walter might have had an enemy who could have had a motive for attacking him.

At Walter Ward's home, 30 West Seventieth Street, it was said that the missing man's wife was too ill to see reporters. A physician was in attendance on her yesterday morning. Ralph Ward said the police and reporters that his sister-in-law had been "prostrated" by her husband's disappearance.

George S. Ward, former head of a bakery chain company, and father of Walter and Ralph Ward, has been in the South for some time but is expected back soon, it was said at the home. The Ward family is said to have engaged private detectives to search for

Continued on Page Ten.

BERYL HALLEY, America's Most Perfect Beauty, now with the revue hit, "Bunk," at the Broadhurst Theatre, 2 shows in 1.—Advt.

TAKE SELL-ANS AFTER MEALS for Perfect Digestion.—Advt.

PEARY'S OBSERVATIONS ARE CONFIRMED

Flight Is Favored by Sunlight and the Absence of Fog; Sun Compass Functions Perfectly

LEAK DEVELOPS IN PLANE'S OIL SYSTEM NEAR POLE

But Byrd Insists on Going On, Overruling Pilot Bennett—Commander's Nose and Fingers Frozen in Zero Temperature

By WILLIAM BIRD.

The New York Times Correspondent With the Byrd Expedition.
Copyright, 1926, by The New York Times Company and The St. Louis Post-Dispatch.
By Wireless to The New York Times.

KINGS BAY, Spitzbergen, May 9.—America's claim to the North Pole was cinched tonight when, after a flight of fifteen hours and fifty-one minutes, Commander Richard E. Byrd and Floyd Bennett, his pilot, returned to announce that they had flown to the Pole, circling it several times and verifying Admiral Peary's observations completely.

They were favored by continued sunlight, and there was never the slightest fog, enabling Commander Byrd to use his sun compass and bubble sextant and obtain the most accurate observations possible. There were three magnetic compasses in the plane, but all of them deviated eccentrically after reaching high latitudes. Bennett declared that when he was piloting the magnetic compasses were wholly useless and would swing almost a quarter turn, returning very slowly.

Take Turns in Piloting.

Without the sunlight, navigation would have been almost impossible. Bennett and Commander Byrd alternated in the piloting, Bennett refilling the gasoline containers while the Commander piloted and navigated.

Commander Byrd found that the Bumstead sun compass worked perfectly, even when held in the hand, so when he was in the pilot's seat he held the control stick in one hand while he got his direction from the sun compass held in the other.

When they were within sixty miles of the Pole the oil system of the right-hand motor began leaking badly and it seemed necessary to choose between proceeding with two motors or attempting a landing to make repairs.

Bennett For Landing, Byrd Refuses.

In the neighborhood of the Pole numerous stretches of smooth ice were visible and a landing was favored by Bennett, but Commander Byrd, remembering his difficulties in starting at Kings Bay, vetoed this proposal.

Both agreed, however, to continue the flight to the Pole even if they went on with only two motors. To their surprise, the right-hand motor continued to work effectively, despite the ruptured oil tank, and when the Fokker returned to Kings Bay all three motors were hitting perfectly.

Chantier's Men Embrace Fliers.

The Josephine Ford, after making three circles over Kings Bay, landed at the take-off runway and taxied to her original starting position.

Commander Byrd and Bennett hurried a mile and a half to the shore, where a motor boat rushed them to the Chantier. The crew aboard her went wild with joy, waving flags and their caps. Many of the crew completely broke down with emotion, and with tears streaming from their eyes embraced the fliers.

Commander Byrd's nose and several fingers were frozen while he was taking observations in zero temperature (Fahrenheit) above the North Pole, but treatment was speedily restored circulation, and the Commander is all right now.

At 3 o'clock this morning, Greenwich Time [11 P. M. Sunday, New York Daylight Saving Time], the Norwegian radio station at Stavanger reported that heavy static was interfering with further transmission of The New York Times dispatches from Spitzbergen. These dispatches will be published tomorrow. Commander Byrd's story will be told in New York exclusively in The New York Times.

First News of Byrd's Great Feat As It Reached The New York Times

Whole Population of Kings Bay, Including the Members of the Amundsen-Ellsworth Party, Out to Welcome the Aviator

From Staff Correspondents of The New York Times.
Copyright, 1926, by The New York Times Co. and The St. Louis Post-Dispatch.
By Wireless to The New York Times.

KINGS BAY, Spitzbergen, Sunday, May 9, 6 P. M. Greenwich Time (2 P. M. New York Time). — Lieut. Commander Richard E. Byrd, U. S. N., leader of the Byrd Polar Expedition, returned from his flight to the North Pole in the airplane Josephine Ford at 4:20 this afternoon, Greenwich Time (12:20 P. M. New York Daylight Time). The Commander reached the North Pole. He started at 12:50 o'clock this morning, Greenwich Time (8:50 P. M. Saturday, New York Time), which is full daylight at this time of the year in the Arctic, so that his flying time on the dash to the Pole and back was fifteen hours and a half hours.

Some error in the wireless transmission of these figures is possible, according to later dispatches to The Times, which state that the commander's total flying time was 15.3 hours, 51 minutes. The elapsed time here indicated. It is, however, possible that the hour 4:20, recorded as marking the commander's return, was the moment at which the returning plane was sighted.]

The Josephine Ford had as its pilot on the trip Floyd G. Bennett, the American pilot of the Byrd Expedition.

The two were welcomed on their return by Captain Roald Amundsen, Lincoln Ellsworth and the entire crew of the airship Norge, now awaiting her chance to fly over the North Pole from Spitzbergen to Alaska, and the entire Summer population of Kings Bay, all of whom had been asleep when the airplane took off fifteen hours previously.

LIEUT. COMMANDER RICHARD E. BYRD, U. S. N.
The American Naval Aviator Who Flew Yesterday to the North Pole and Back.

BLYTHE

Coolidge Sends 'Heartiest Congratulations'; Glad That Flight Was Made by an American

Special to The New York Times.

WASHINGTON, May 9.—President Coolidge received the first details of Commander Byrd's successful flight to the Pole from a radio message sent by The New York Times to the Mayflower, which is cruising tonight in the lower Potomac River.

The message, sent by the Washington Bureau soon after 5 o'clock, furnished the President with all the details known at that time. In reply he radioed:

"Thanks for your message."

Later Mr. Coolidge sent by radio the following comment:

The President sends his heartiest congratulations to Commander Byrd on the report that he has flown to the North Pole. It is a matter of great satisfaction that this record has been made by an American.

The fact that the flight seems to have been accomplished without mishap demonstrates the high development of the art in this country. That it was made by a man trained in the American Navy is a great satisfaction.

CALVIN COOLIDGE.

It is well known that the President was very anxious that the flight should be made, and, although there had been some adverse criticism of the proposal, Mr. Coolidge gave his approval to the plans.

BYRD FAMILY PROUD OF FLIER'S SUCCESS

Governor of Virginia Declares His Brother Never Would Give Up—Mother Rejoices.

Special to The New York Times.

RICHMOND, Va., May 9—Richmond received its first information of the successful polar flight of Lieut. Commander Richard Evelyn Byrd about 3 o'clock this afternoon, a message saying the flier had "returned safely" was received by Governor Harry F. Byrd by telephone. The flier's mother, Mrs. Richard Evelyn Byrd, was at the executive mansion when the message was received.

"I am tremendously gratified," Governor Byrd said, "and proud to hear of my brother's success in reaching the Pole."

"Dick has always been so lucky all his life that he believes he will come through, even though ninety-nine of a hundred chances might be plainly against him. I am proud of him. He has always been our adventurous fellow, as we somewhat relieved, though proud, that he has made the flight. If he had not, and believed there was a ghost of a chance to do so, he would try again as soon as possible."

This one day of the year dedicated to mothers, the message flashed across the frozen miles, brought happiness and comfort to Virginia's "first mother," Mrs. Richard Evelyn Byrd.

The New York Times.

VOL. LXXV....No. 24,945. ..... NEW YORK, WEDNESDAY, MAY 12, 1926. TWO CENTS *In New York* | THREE CENTS *Within 200 Miles* | FOUR CENTS *Elsewhere in the U. S.*

THE NORGE FLIES OVER NORTH POLE AT 1 A. M.; REPORTS HER FEAT TO TIMES BY WIRELESS; GOING ON OVER ARCTIC WASTES TO ALASKA

EFFORTS FOR PEACE ACTIVE IN LONDON; BOTH SIDES SILENT

Baldwin Waits Until a Late Hour for an Important Message From the Unions.

EXPECTED THIS FORENOON

Strike Leaders in Session Most of Day and Night, With Mac-Donald Exploring Situation.

MORE MEN ARE CALLED OUT

Meanwhile the Government Reports Still Further Progress in Maintaining Services.

By T. R. YBARRA.

Copyright, 1926, by The New York Times Company
Special Cable to THE NEW YORK TIMES.

LONDON, Wednesday, May 12.— Though the Government and the strikers can need to face each other in full battle formation throughout yesterday, the eighth day of Britain's great general strike, there were signs that the dove of peace was hovering somewhere in the immediate neighborhood. Up to a late hour last night, however, nobody had quite located the bird. Many insisted, nevertheless, that they had distinctly heard the soft whirring of its wings.

They stuck to their assertion despite the declaration in last night's British Worker, the strikers' official organ, that today more workers will join the great strike—the molders and shipyard workers, members of the Amalgamated Engineering Unions and the General Engineering Unions. The strikers' organ also said that instead of "dribbling back to work," according to the Government's statement, the workers are "standing like a rock and more are coming out."

There were also two statements in the official Government communiqué last night which did not partake of the generally rosy hue pervading the bulk of the official statements. One was: "There is as yet little sign of a general collapse of the strike." The other was the admission that the Trades Union Council "is believed to be making efforts to call out certain trades still at work."

Peace Rumors Still Persist.

But these and other similar reports current during the eighth day of the strike could not down the rumors of imminent peace.

The General Council of the Trades Union Council was met last night at strike headquarters to "explore the position with a view to leaving no door shut that could be opened." The meeting was attended by Ramsay MacDonald and J. H. Thomas, who came from Parliament for the purpose. After the meeting had over, in session for some hours Mr. MacDonald and Mr. Thomas hastily returned to the Commons, their arrival giving rise to the hope they might have something to announce. They found, however, that the Commons had concluded its sitting.

They went back to the meeting, which lasted until 1.35 o'clock this morning. No announcement was made at its conclusion, but it is understood that there was a spirited discussion between Mr. MacDonald, Mr. Thomas and other members of the Parliamentary Labor Party who are moderate in their views and Ernest Bevin and other leaders of more extreme opinion.

One of those stated to have been active during the day in the interests of conciliation was Ramsay Mac Donald. One of the most influential of labor chiefs, in addition to visiting the strikers' executive and the General Council of the Trades Union Congress today, MacDonald sent the following message to The British Independent, a mimeographed miniature newspaper run by university students:

"I welcome most heartily your efforts for conciliation. This dispute ought never to have happened, and had the problem in the dispute been handled with ordinary care and common sense there would have been neither a lockout nor a strike.

"On one thing I can give the nation confident assurance. The general strike in support of the miners was never meant as and even now is not a strike against Parliament, the Government or the Constitution. For purely war propaganda purposes the Government says it is.

"Good-will and calm may prevail in the end, and calm heads will in the end prevail. We could be working literally night and day that may be soon.

It was certainly apparent during the day that something was going on beneath the surface, that it was somehow...

Continued on Page Five.

BOSTON ALL THE WAY BY WATER
via Cape Cod Canal every evening. Connections at Boston for Maine, Nova Scotia and New Brunswick. Res. B 3 p.m. or phone Hancock 5 S Lines, Inc. Barclay 5100—Advt.

TAKE NO LESS AFTER MEALS
for English Digestion.—Advt.

RAIL LABOR BILL PASSED BY SENATE

By 69 to 13 the Upper Branch Accepts the House Measure Without Amendment.

HARD FIGHT FOR CHANGES

Curtis Fails to Get Commerce Board Power Over Wages— Coolidge's Approval Expected.

Special to The New York Times.

WASHINGTON, May 11.—The bill to abolish the Railroad Labor Board and permit railways and their employees to settle disputes over wages and working conditions by mutual agreement was passed by the Senate by a vote of 69 to 13 late this afternoon. As the Senate approved the bill in identically the same form it passed the House no conference will be necessary and the bill will become law when the President affixes his signature.

Before the Senate passed the bill it was stated at the White House that it was not an Administration measure. The President, it was said, was interested in it to the extent that he believed it would work well because a majority of the railroad managers and employees favored it. But it was also understood that he did not entirely approve the bill as passed, he having suggested that it be amended so as to protect the public interest.

The detailed vote follows:

FOR THE BILL—69.

Republicans—39.

Borah,	Howell,	Robinson
Butler,	Johnson,	(Ind.),
Cameron,	Jones (Wash.),	Sackett,
Couzens,	LaFollette,	Schall,
Cummins,	Lenroot,	Shortridge,
Dale,	McMaster,	Smoot,
Deneen,	McNary,	Stanfield,
Edge,	Means,	Wadsworth,
Ernst,	Metcalf,	Warren,
Fess,	Norris,	Watson,
Frazier,	Nye,	Weller,
Gillett,	Oddie,	Willis.
Gooding,	Pine,	
Harreld,	Reed (Pa.)	

Democrats—29.

Ashurst,	Glass,	Sheppard,
Blease,	Harris,	Simmons,
Bratton,	Heflin,	Steck,
Broussard,	Jones (N. M.)	Stephens,
Bruce,	Kendrick,	Swanson,
Copeland,	McKellar,	Trammell,
Dill,	Mayfield,	Tyson,
Edwards,	Neely,	Walsh,
George,	Overman,	Wheeler.
Gerry,	Pittman,	

Farmer-Laborite—1.

| Shipstead. | | |

AGAINST THE BILL—13.

Republicans—9.

Bingham,	Keyes,	Norbeck,
Curtis,	McLean,	Phipps,
Hale,	Moses,	Williams.

Democrats—4.

| Bayard, | Robinson | Underwood. |
| Randsell, | (Ark.), | |

Provisions of the Measure.

The bill, which was agreed upon last year by most of the railway executives and heads of the four brotherhoods, and which the President endorsed in principle in his message to Congress, provides:

1. That the railroads and employees shall establish adjustment boards to arrange disputes.

2. That the President may appoint, with the consent of the Senate, a board of mediation of five persons, none of whom has a pecuniary interest on either side, to intervene when the adjustment boards fail.

3. That boards of arbitration shall be created when both parties consent to arbitration.

4. That when the above methods fail the Board of Mediation shall notify the President, who may appoint an emergency board to investigate and report to him within thirty days. For thirty days after the report has been made there shall be no change in the situation.

Continued on Page Twelve.

Union Pacific's New Fifth Avenue Office.
On Fifth Avenue at 41st. Phone Lexington 2450. Downtown office, 236 Broadway. Phone Worth 1717. Information and reservations everywhere West.—Advt.

The finest aux produits de France furnished in Paris Parisian Fournish—

FIRST MESSAGE EVER RECEIVED FROM THE NORTH POLE

By FREDRIK RAMM.
New York Times Correspondent Aboard the Norge.

Copyright, 1926, by The New York Times Company and The St. Louis Globe Democrat.
By Wireless to The New York Times.

NORTH POLE, Wednesday, May 12, 1 A. M. (on Board the Dirigible Airship Norge)--We reached the North Pole at 1 A. M. today, and lowered flags for Amundsen, Ellsworth, and Nobile.

LATER, 3.30 A. M.--Lowering the three flags, Norwegian, American and Italian, when the Norge was over the North Pole, was the greatest of all events of this flight. Riiser-Larsen's observations showed that we were over the Pole. The Norge descended and speed was reduced, when the flags were lowered over the wastes whose edges gleamed like gold in the pale sunlight, breaking through the fog which surrounded us.

Roald Amundsen first lowered the Norwegian flag. Then Ellsworth the Stars and Stripes; finally Nobile the Italian flag.

* The airship's 1 A. M. time (Norwegian time), was 8 o'clock on Tuesday night, New York daylight time.

PROGRESS OF THE NORGE AND HER PROJECTED ROUTE ONWARD TO ALASKA

Here is shown the route covered, according to the last wireless reports from the Amundsen-Ellsworth-Nobile airship Norge, which sailed from Kings Bay, Spitzbergen, at 10 o'clock yesterday morning, Norwegian time (5 A. M. New York daylight time) to fly over the North Pole, and her probable course onward toward her ultimate destination, Nome, Alaska. The hours given in the hollow squares on the map show the position of the Norge at the times stated. The figures are Norwegian time, which is five hours ahead of New York daylight time. The thick black line shows the course the airship has already covered; double line shows her probable future course to Nome. Dotted lines show the routes taken to the Pole by Lieut. Commander Peary in 1909 by dogsled, and by Lieut. Commander Byrd by airplane on Sunday last.

Norge Sails Straight Into the Golden Glow of the Morning Sun, A Silver Creature of the Air, Moving With Grace and Quiet Dignity

Kings Bay Cheers and Weeps as the Giant Dirigible Starts Down the Fjord Accompanied by Commander Byrd and Bennett in Their Polar Airplane, a Striking Contrast in Arctic Exploration—Colonel Nobile Says That the Wind Is His Only Concern—Expedition May Spend Sixty Hours on the Trip to Alaska.

By RUSSELL D. OWEN.
Staff Correspondent of The New York Times.

Copyright, 1926, by The New York Times Company and The St. Louis Globe-Democrat.
By Wireless to THE NEW YORK TIMES.

KINGS BAY, Spitzbergen, May 11.—At 9 o'clock this morning, Greenwich time, or 5 A. M. New York time, the Norge, of the Amundsen-Ellsworth-Nobile expedition, started for Point Barrow, Alaska.

Straight into the morning sun, a tiny speck soon lost in the golden glow of the north, the dirigible disappeared on her journey across the Pole and into the unknown wilderness of the Arctic.

The giant airship, like a silver creature of the air, rose slowly and gracefully from the hands that held her and with her motors humming sailed swiftly down the fjord, following the path Commander Byrd had taken in his spurt to the Pole. She turned over across the bay and rose over Cape Mitre. Then her black silhouette was lost in the sun.

There was rush and swift action to Commander Byrd's departure and his quick take-off, but the Norge's departure was tremendously impressive because of the ponderous grace and quiet dignity of the great ship, lifting her immense burden from the ground and sailing into the unknown like a liner of the air. There were power, endurance and swiftness all embodied in her action.

Cheers and Tears at Departure.

Those below the floating fabric raised their hats in the air or flung up their arms in farewell, some cheering and a few

Continued on Page Two.

moved to tears by the tenseness of the moment which saw their comrades departing on the greatest Arctic feat ever attempted. The air voyagers will spend at least sixty hours in Arctic regions never seen by man and at the end face the greatest hazard, when they may be forced to land the dirigible without assistance from the ground, something never done before.

All the day before Kings Bay was in a fever of preparation, the men of the expedition assembling equipment, packing provisions and small things for comfort, and making sure that nothing was overlooked. Mechanics swarmed over the dirigible, grooming her as though she were a race horse. Every bolt, stay, control wire and girder was gone over carefully. The full tanks were minutely examined, all pipes were overhauled and all instruments tested.

The big motors raced as they received their final turnovers, the immense green curtain near the end of the hangar billowing out in the gale created by the propellers. The new motor was put in splendid condition. Commander Gottwaldt tinkered over the wireless, making sure that the batteries and all the connections were in good condition, for on his direction-finder much depends.

Crew Spurts at Tasks.

There had been uncertainty all day as to the time of departure, but late at night it was announced that the start would

Continued on Page Two.

NORGE SAILS OVER VAST ICE DESERT

Start Made From Kings Bay at 9 A. M. Greenwich Time and Course Is Laid Due North

VOYAGERS SEE POLAR BEARS AND SEALS BELOW

Gentle Wind, Clear Skies and Temperature A Few Degrees Above Zero Accompany Fliers on First Reach to Pole.

By FREDRIK RAMM.

New York Times Correspondent Aboard the Norge.
Copyright, 1926, by The New York Times Company and The St. Louis Globe-Democrat.
By Wireless to The New York Times.

ON BOARD THE DIRIGIBLE NORGE, KINGS BAY, Spitzbergen, May 11.—The airship Norge, carrying the Amundsen-Ellsworth-Nobile expedition on its flight across the Pole to Nome, Alaska, started today at 10 A. M. Norwegian time (9 A. M. Greenwich Time, 5 A. M. New York Time).

Make 66 Miles an Hour at Start.

ON BOARD THE DIRIGIBLE NORGE, Flying Poleward, May 11, 11:40 A. M. Norwegian Time (10:40 A. M. Greenwich time, 6:40 New York Time).—We are north of Danes Island, 80 degrees latitude, 9 east longitude. The weather is bright, with the lightest breeze from the south-southeast. The temperature is minus 7 degrees centigrade (19 degrees above zero, Fahrenheit). Our altitude is 425 meters (1,394 feet) and our speed is 107 kilometers (66 miles) an hour. The edge of the ice pack is a few kilometers north of Danes Island. We have sighted seals on the ice. Our motors are running perfectly and we are not feeling cold.

[Later] We are now in latitude 81.12. Our speed is 100 kilometers [62 miles] an hour. The weather is bright with a light easterly breeze. The temperature is minus 10 degrees centigrade (14 degrees above zero, Fahrenheit) and our altitude is 530 meters (1,732 feet).

Espy Polar Bears on Ice.

ON BOARD THE DIRIGIBLE NORGE, Flying Poleward, May 11, 2 P. M., Norwegian Time (1 P. M. Greenwich Time, 9 A. M. New York Time).—We are now in latitude 82.30, longitude 9 east. Our altitude is 560 meters (1,836 feet). The temperature is minus 9 degrees centigrade (15.8 degrees above zero, Fahrenheit). The weather stays clear, with a light southeasterly breeze.

In the sea some lanes are covered with new ice. All the time we have used the left and back motors. Lieutenant Riiser-Larsen has been navigating, assisted by Captain Gottwaldt. Ellsworth has been measuring the atmospheric electricity. Our better speed is due to our new altitude, where the conditions are more favorable.

We have now lost all sight of land and the ice changes the whole aspect. We see several great polar bears and can discern white fish in the small openings in the ice. One meteorological report from the Stavanger radio promises that fine weather will continue far on the other side of the Pole.

All of us are naturally in the highest spirits. We are now eating our first meal and discussing how to celebrate Ellsworth's forty-sixth birthday tomorrow.

View of Ice Desert Most Beautiful.

ON BOARD THE DIRIGIBLE NORGE, Flying Poleward, May 11, 5:15 P. M. Norwegian Time (4:15 Greenwich Time, 12:15 New York Time).—We are now in 85 degrees north latitude 10 east longitude, and heading directly north at a speed of 87 kilometers and a height of 610 meters. A gentle south wind is blowing and the weather is clear. The temperature is minus 12 degrees centigrade (9.8 degrees above zero Fahrenheit) and the barometer stands at 727 millimeters.

We have now flown over the ice a long time. Despite our great height we can clearly see how the ice is cracking and screwing.

The low temperature has as yet had no effect on us. The whole view of this desert of ice is indescribable and most beautiful.

All are well.

Speed North Under Clear Sky.

ON BOARD THE DIRIGIBLE NORGE, Flying Poleward, May 11, 6:30 P. M. Norwegian Time.—We are now in 86 degrees of latitude, 10 degrees east longitude. Our course is due north and our speed is 92 kilometers (57 miles) an hour. A light south-southwest breeze is blowing and the skies are entirely clear. The temperature is minus 12 degrees centigrade (9.8 degrees above zero Fahrenheit) and the barometer stands at 727 millimeters. Weather reports, which are constantly being received, continue to be favorable. The left engine has been stopped and all instruments tested. All are well.

The Pole Four Hours Ahead.

ON BOARD THE DIRIGIBLE NORGE, Flying Poleward, May 11, 8:25 P. M. Norwegian Time.—We are now at 87 d

"All the News That's Fit to Print."

The New York Times.

THE WEATHER

Showers today; tomorrow rain; slight change in temperature.
Temperature yesterday—Max., 74; Min., 65.
For weather report see Page 38.

VOL. LXXV....No. 25,023. ••••

NEW YORK, THURSDAY, JULY 29, 1926.

TWO CENTS in Greater | THREE CENTS | FOUR CENTS
New York | Within 200 Miles | Elsewhere in the U.S.

MEXICAN WOMEN START TRADE BOYCOTT; MULTITUDES FLOCKING TO THE CHURCHES; CALLES' STAND BACKED BY LEGISLATORS

STORE SALES CUT IN HALF

But Government Is Firm —Mayors Ordered to Take Over Churches.

LAY SERVICES AUTHORIZED

Arrival of Americans Invited by Calles to Report on Situation Is Resented.

CLASH WITH LABOR FEARED

Dawn Finds Thousands on Way to Guadalupe Shrine, Which They Enter on Their Knees.

Copyright, 1926, by The New York Times Company.
Special Cable to The New York Times.

MEXICO CITY, July 28.—Enforcement of the economic boycott by the Catholic women of Mexico City as a protest against the Government's religious regulations has already cut in half the normal sales of the large stores in the capital. Managers declared today that if the boycott is carried out their business will suffer grievously.

Catholic women have abandoned the use of gayly colored clothes and are wearing black dresses with large black shawls covering their heads.

Crowds continue to flood the churches and from the large number of children brought here for baptism it seems as if the entire population of the small towns near Mexico City has decided to bring the children to Sagrario here instead of to their own town churches.

From advance reports, the demonstrations to be held on Friday night in all the Catholic churches will be the greatest ever seen in the Republic of Mexico. Special services known as the Services of Sorrow, will be conducted in all the churches throughout Mexican territory.

Trouble Feared at Labor Parade.

Church officials, in a statement addressed to the Catholic people, say they have not authorized any street demonstration, as they wish to avoid trouble. A group of Catholics had planned to hold a mammoth parade as a sign of protest against the recent religious laws, but, out of respect to the wishes of Archbishop Mora y del Rio, the parade has been postponed.

It is feared that trouble will occur in Mexico City on Sunday, when the Confederation of Labor intends to hold a demonstration to show its adherence to the Government's religious policy. Many Catholics are also members of the unions, and it is believed that, unless strong police and military forces are posted in the streets, the labor demonstration will cause many fights and possibly create a much more serious situation. Military and police forces will patrol the streets and escort the paraders.

New Legislators Back Calles.

It is said that certain Masonic bodies will also join the labor parade. One of their leaders states that all Socialists and their sympathizers will join in the manifestation in order to show the people of Mexico City that the Socialists, radicals and labor unions are in accord with the policy of President Calles.

A group of Congressmen which is still waiting to present their credentials following the recent elections in order to obtain their seats in Congress has sent a telegram to President Calles declaring that the Labor group in Congress supports his stand on the religious question, through which, they say, political enemies of the Government are seeking to destroy the Government's efforts toward reconstruction. "The Labor bloc," the telegram said, "upholds the Constitution and the ideas expressed by you."

A group of Congressmen, in another telegram to President Calles, asserts that the revolutionary socialistic bloc is solidly behind him in his energetic attitude on the religious question.

Reports from Puebla state that a commission has arrived there from Mexico City and ordered all churches closed immediately, in spite of the protests of the Catholics.

Americans Will Study Situation.

A group of American writers and ministers arrived in Mexico City today, headed by Dr. Alva Taylor. Dr. Sidney Gulick and Joseph Todd, a circular announcing their arrival states that Dr. Taylor is head of the National Service Commission and editor of The Christian Century, a weekly journal characterized as the most influential Protestant religious review published in the United States.

Dr. Taylor was associated with the committee named by the Inter-Church World Movement to investigate the

Continued on Page Two.

Catholic Women Plead With Senora Calles To Get President to Revoke Religious Laws

Copyright, 1926, by The New York Times Company.
Special Cable to The New York Times.

MEXICO CITY, July 28.—A touching appeal has been addressed by women of the Catholic Society of Orizaba to Senora Calles, wife of the President, as follows:

The mothers of the society of which I am President send to you cordial greetings and this time, when I wish to make known to you the views of my companions. Sad, very sad, indeed, is the news which grieves the hearts of Mexican mothers; sad, indeed, for persons of our strong religious convictions and unshakeable faith.

Since the day when we opened our eyes to the light, Mexicans have been Catholics. We have been nurtured on Catholic ideas and grown up with them. They must be good, since for mothers, fathers, husbands, brothers and sisters these ideas have served as a compass and a helm.

Intolerance in religious matters disturbs us. We fear the consequences. Fearful of the trouble that may come now, we look to the past and see that the world's most terrible wars have sometimes arisen over religion.

We purpose to permit you to hear the echoes of the voices of the mothers of Mexico. We believe firmly that our letter is a reflection of that impetuous light which flashes from the hearts of good mothers, obedient daughters and faithful wives. We know that there is not one Catholic woman in Mexico who does not think as we do, because we were all educated according to the same principles.

Why is our religion so bitterly attacked? What end is being sought in this onslaught on the religion which defends women, which lifts her up to a higher moral level, which places her by the side of the man she loves as a companion and not as a slave?

We love Mexico, love her welfare, happiness, progress and peace. We are optimistic; we believe this crisis will pass because you, Señora, will speak, speak plainly, as the First Lady of the Land should speak.

History teaches us that in a time of crisis a woman always arises who with valor defends her country, placing high its banner, as Judith, Joan del Arco, Isabel de Castilla and Josefa Ortiz de Dominguez.

You, Señora, can transform the actual state of affairs, if you wish, through love and sweetness. It is true that a woman has a great influence in the home when she is simple, charitable and loving. Man, made rude, more egotistical, feels the power of a woman.

The association over which I preside believes in your help, as you are a Mexican and, naturally, should love Mexico, for the mission of woman is to love, love, love.

Your husband, President Calles, will not listen to our entreaties, but he will listen to you, the companion of his life, the mother of his children.

We ask only tolerance, equity and justice. We are Catholics. No one can take this talk away. All our country is Catholic, all its children.

You command; you have in your hands the sceptre which allows woman to reign through her purity, beauty and womanly temperament. Your husband will listen; he will do what you request.

We do not wish others to say that Mexicans are uncultured, that we are a nation that cannot pronounce the name of your husband without fear. We hope to pronounce it with charity and love.

GUADALUPE ORTEGA.

POINCARE SHELVES DEBT AGREEMENTS

Will Not Submit American and British Deals to Parliament Until Fall Session.

TO SEEK CONCESSION HERE

'Safeguard' Letter, Similar to That Obtained From Britain, Is Said to Be His Aim.

By EDWIN L. JAMES.
Copyright, 1926, by The New York Times Company.
Special Cable to The New York Times.

PARIS, July 28.—The French Government has apparently postponed indefinitely any effort to obtain ratification of the Berenger-Mellon agreement and hopes to get new concessions. It will not submit either the Washington or London debt accords to Parliament before the vacation period and this means that they will not be considered by the French Parliament in any event before next Fall.

In response to a question from a member of the Chamber Finance Committee today, M. Poincaré replied:

"France will pay to the limit of her capacity."

Pressed for specifications the Premier said he did not intend to ask approval of either the Berenger-Mellon or Caillaux-Churchill agreement before the Parliamentary vacation.

Inasmuch as it had been M. Poincaré's intention to submit these agreements to Parliament without recommendation, it is evident that he has made some change in his position.

It is understood tonight to be the purpose of the Premier to try and obtain from Washington an accompanying letter similar to that attached to the Caillaux-Churchill accord stating that in the event of German reparations payments under the Dawes Plan falling below 50 per cent. of the expected normal England would agree to a reconsideration of the terms of the debt settlement.

This decision of the new French Government to allow the debt settlement with America to slide for the time being may cause some surprise in the United States, especially in view of the fact that the Briand-Caillaux Government had decided to forego any chance of improving the Washington agreement as an essential part of the Government's financial program, based on the experts' report prime provision which was obtaining foreign credits.

But here one must look at M. Caillaux's financial plan was builded on the proposed stabilization of the franc through the aid of credits which could be obtained only after ratification of the debt accords.

M. Poincaré's Policy Different.

M. Poincaré has a different policy. Not only does he not seek to stabilize

Continued on Page Four.

'DREAM BABY' WINS RIGHTS IN PEERAGE

British Court Definitely Decides the Russell Boy's Title to Ampthill Succession.

ENDS £40,000 DIVORCE SUIT

Decree Granted to Husband Had Been Annulled by House of Lords Tribunal.

Copyright, 1926, by The New York Times Company.
By Wireless to The New York Times.

LONDON, July 28.—The final chapter of a long legal story was concluded today when Geoffrey Russell, 4½ years old, was pronounced the lawful child of the Hon. John Hugo Russell—and heir—and his rights in the Ampthill peerage were thus established.

The proceedings, which were taken under the Legitimacy Declaration act, brought the Russell marital affairs before the courts for the fifth time. Mrs. Christabel Russell's fight on behalf of her own reputation and for her son began in 1922, and has cost $300,000.

After defeating her husband's appeal through the boy's maternal grandmother, who had been appointed guardian by the courts, for a formal declaration that her son was the legitimate offspring of her marriage with the Hon. John Hugo Russell.

Final Evidence Is Heard.

Today's proceedings were brief and formal. It was represented to Justice Swift that since the child was born, Oct. 18, 1921, the father had not contributed anything to the support of either his son or wife. Mr. Dorothy Shaw gave evidence that she had been a servant with the Russells in Curzon Street, that they had occupied adjoining bedrooms and had often broken-fasted together in the wife's bedroom.

Court on the ground that the marriage was certified too late to be legally submitted. Justice Proskauer of the Supreme Court on the ground that other legal questions might be involved into which he had not examined.

Justice Swift then gave judgment that the petitioner, Geoffrey Denis Erskine Russell, was the lawful child of his parents and son of John Hugo and Christabel Hulme Russell.

Mrs. Russell on hearing the words which marked the final success of her four years' struggle shook her mother's hand and smilingly received the congratulations of her friends. She then passed unconcerned through the curious crowds that had gathered outside the court to await the result. Her composure was as perfect as it had been during all the sensational proceedings which made the Russell case célèbre.

The domestic affairs of Lord Ampthill's son and heir first came before the courts in 1922, when he sued his wife for divorce, alleging that he was not the father of the boy Geoffrey. He asserted in his evidence that his relations with his wife had never been those of a husband.

Evidence was adduced by counsel

Continued on Page Seven.

Moving Images Sent by Wire or Wireless By Professor Belin Before Paris Experts

Copyright, 1926, by The New York Times Company.
Special Cable to The New York Times.

PARIS, July 28.—At Malmaison today, in the presence of General Ferrie, head of the French Military Telegraph, and Professor Fabre of Sorbonne, experiments were made which were hailed as establishing the discovery of a method of television which, it is asserted, results in instantaneous transmission of moving images by wire or wireless.

The demonstration marked a step in the extended research by Professor Belin, discoverer of a means of transmission of photographs by wireless, and Professor Hallwach, chief of experiments in the Radium Institute.

The scientists succeeded in transmitting from one end of the laboratory to the other images of a moving finger as well as of several small objects moved before the ending apparatus. Professor Belin and his partner are confident that within a few months they will have solved satisfactorily the problems of television, so that at one end of a telephone the subscriber will be able to see the person to whom he is talking.

The method used is a combination of mechanics and electricity based on the use of electrons which permit the transmission of images or parts of images in a time shorter than the duration of a retinal impression, which is the sixteenth part of a second. In sending a photoelectric cell instantly transforms the luminous intensity of the ray into electrical intensity, and at the receiving end a jet of electrons spraying into a vacuum controlled by these impulses gives an inverse reproduction.

The sending instrument has two mirrors rotating on a perpendicular axis at differing rates of speed which help decompose the image to be sent into very small lines which are transmitted by wire or wireless through receiving electrons onto a phosphorescent screen which, by white, gray and black paints, reproduce the image being sent.

In today's experiments the images were only jet black and white, it being explained that the only process being used was that of interruption. It was explained that by intensification shading could be given to images reproduced.

TAMMANY TO TEST 5-CENT FARE ISSUE BY BALLOT IN FALL

Would Take It Out of Politics by Putting It Directly Before the City's Voters.

NOW FRAMING THE QUESTION

Olvany Says Passage of Craig Bill by City Assembly Makes Action Mandatory.

With the State campaign drawing near, Tammany is taking steps to eliminate the five-cent fare as a possible partisan issue. Tammany leader George W. Olvany announced yesterday that the Tammany Law Committee had given an opinion that the so-called Craig Five-Cent Fare Referendum bill passed by the Municipal Assembly last year too late to go on the ballot in the form of a question to the voters required approval at the polls before it could become effective. He was asked if it would be submitted at the general election this year.

"I understand that Corporation Counsel Nicholson is even now framing the question to be printed on the ballot," Mr. Olvany replied. "The question must be verified step by step by the City Clerk, and certain legal forms must be gone through, including some advertising. The machinery is now in motion to make sure that the matter is placed before the voters in this city in November."

Says Officials Must Act.

Mr. Olvany said that the passage to the Municipal Assembly of the bill made it mandatory upon city officials concerned in the procedure necessary for its submission to do their part.

"Any public official failing to do that, in my opinion, would be derelict in his duty," Mr. Olvany said. "If the referendum is approved by the people, the five-cent fare should become a fixture until such time in the future as the people of this city shall express their willingness to pay more for a ride."

The text of a new section of the New York City Charter provided for in the Craig bill follows:

Section 243d—It shall be unlawful for the Board of Estimate and Apportionment to adopt any resolution authorizing, or purporting to authorize the adoption of any contract or franchise for the operation of any subway or rapid transit railway or street railway in the City of New York, the purpose of which is to increase the fare of 5 cents now provided by law, or which grants to any operating company any preferential or bonus, or subsidy, or releases it from any of its obligations to render the service to the public required by any contract or franchise whatsoever.

The Board of Estimate and Apportionment is hereby forbidden to consider any resolution having any such purpose or effect unless and until the proposal for the adoption of any such resolution shall have been first submitted to the people of the city upon a referendum and approved by the affirmative vote of a majority of the qualified voters of such city, such referendum to be held at the first general election after there has been filed with the City Clerk at least ninety days prior thereto a petition signed and acknowledged by qualified voters in such city in number equal to at least 15 per cent of the total number of votes cast for Governor at the last Gubernatorial election in such city.

Rejoined by Courts.

The bill was passed by the Municipal Assembly on Sept. 17 last year and on the same date was certified by City Clerk Cruise. When the Board of Elections took steps to have the referendum question printed on the ballot an injunction was sought and was applied by Justice Proskauer of the Supreme Court on the ground that the measure was certified too late to be legally submitted. Justice Proskauer indicated tonight that other legal questions might be involved into which he had not examined.

The provision in the Craig bill which requires popular approval of any proposal for a change in the fare or rapid transit lines before it can be given effect by the Board of Estimate and the further requirement that such proceedings must be initiated through petitions carrying signatures of qualified voters equal in number to at least 15 per cent. of the total vote cast for Governor within the city at the last preceding election, is regarded by political observers as practically a bar against any such action.

The vote for Governor in 1924 was 1,644,696. Fifteen per cent. of the total, or 236,702 voters in the city, would be required to sign a petition necessary for submission of any such proposal in the future should the Craig bill be approved at the coming election.

Continued on Page Six.

30 CRIMES FASTENED ON WEEPING GUNMEN—MURDER SUSPECTED

Oberst Gang Beg Mercy From Accusers Who Identify Them in Ten Hold-Ups.

CONFESS TO 20 OTHERS

Police Say "Worst Is Yet to Come for Them" When Killings Are Investigated.

Thirty robberies were fastened yesterday on the Oberst gang, founded up the night before. They condensed twenty and were identified in ten others.

It was a day of whirlwind disaster for the gangsters, a day that closed with a strong probability that some or all of them will face first-degree murder charges before the case is over. It was a day, too, that dragged the erstwhile lead men into a group of whimpering youths begging for the mercy they had never shown.

The police lost no time and spared no energy in making the most of their sensational capture of Tuesday night and the District Attorneys of two counties were busy helping them, with the result that the five men in custody and a fugitive ex-convict were already under indictment by night for the $2,000 Roosevelt Hospital robbery, with more to come.

Cry as They Are Identified.

The prisoners, caught originally as the perpetrators of a Bronx bank hold-up, were viewed by their victims in any "line-up" in the Detective Bureau at Police Headquarters and became completely unnerved. They wept like babies, detectives said, when in one player of the Sungie-Sills grocery firm in West Thirteenth Street tentatively identified one as a participant in a robbery there on June 12, in which a girl stenographer and a visiting salesman were shot and killed. They shuddered that they never had shot any one in any of their crimes.

They shed more tears in St. John's Hospital, Long Island City, when Probationary Patrolman James Broderick identified another of the gang as the man who shot him on Aug. 18 in the frustrated hold-up of the Left candy factory there, and they cried again when the girl telephone operator in the factory identified another as one of the gunmen who had invaded the office of the firm before the probationary patrolman interrupted the escape of the gang.

Red-eyed and sagging, the robbers pleaded with Inspector Coughlin, head of the Detective Division, and Acting Captain Henry Bruckman of the North Bronx Detective Branch to save them from being identified as murderers, but their imploring met with curt statements that "the worst is yet to come for you fellows, because we find that murders and shootings perpetrated by you in hold-ups will want to be pinned on you."

Near Sing Sing Waits for Them.

When they were lodged in cells in the Bronx County Jail last night they were told that before the end of two weeks it was expected that all of them would be in Sing Sing under long sentences unless some or all of them face murder charges.

The day began with a dramatic scene in Inspector Coughlin's office when the prisoners, Bernard Frankel, alias Frenchie; Leo Mackey, alias Stein; Philip Oberst, alias Duffy, leader of the gang; John Ward, alias Kerrigan, and Peter Mahoney, alias Brown, chauffeur on the hold-up expeditions, were brought in shackled together for their first line-up.

Pacing the inspector's desk and with a background of detectives, the robbers dropped their eyes as the first witness, Helen Mackey, a bookkeeper in the Sungie-Sills grocery house, stepped into the room. The girl walked in front of the gang, eyeing each prisoner critically. Then standing off from Frankel she looked at him intently for a minute.

Placing her hand on one of his shoulders, Miss Mackey said: "This man resembles the one who held a gun in his hand near the office in which I was employed on the day Miss Josephine da Fiore our stenographer, and Samuel Winterbottom, a salesman, were shot and killed in the payroll robbery."

They Quail and Weep.

Frankel trembled. It was obvious that his under confederates spun knowing any feeling of rivalry betrayed against him. "Please don't say that I killed anybody," pleaded Frankel, holding out

When they approach the Wedding Clock of Whiting.—Advt.

Continued on Page Three.

STATE ARRESTS MRS. FRANCES S. HALL FOR MURDER OF HUSBAND AND SINGER; DRAMATIC TURN IN 4-YEAR-OLD MYSTERY

Miss Gates of New York Arrested in Paris On Charge of Shoplifting From Big Store

Copyright, 1926, by The New York Times Company.
Special Cable to The New York Times.

PARIS, July 28.—A pretty American girl, who said she was Louisa Gates, daughter of a New York Judge, was arrested in a Paris department store today, charged with shoplifting.

At the police station the store detectives told the Magistrate that they saw her put some gloves into her blouse and that when they searched her they found other articles, including a small picture frame.

They said that she explained, "I am quite ready to pay," and offered them $200 and a diamond ring said to be worth more than $1,000.

In court she said:

"I am an American girl from New York and my name is Louisa Gates.
My father is a Judge and my brother is a lawyer."

She complained bitterly of the search to which she was subjected.

Soon after a representative of the American Consulate called at the court and the girl was paroled in his custody after promising to return when summoned to face the charge of theft.

As far as could be learned last night the American Consulate was nonplussed. The New York City or New York State Bar Directory lists only four attorneys named Gates in the State. Merrill E. Gates, the only one reached last night, said that he had no relative named Louisa Gates.

ILLINOIS FUND RISES TO $971,603 TOTAL

Senators Bare $10,000 More Given by Insull, Making $193,734 in All.

BARRETT SPENT $175,000

Insists, However, That His Group Put Up Mainly for County Offices.

Special to The New York Times.

CHICAGO, July 28.—The million-dollar mark was in sight as the Reed committee ceased its third day of delving into the money spent in the Illinois primary in April, when Frank L. Smith won the Republican Senatorial nomination over Senator William B. McKinley. By nightfall the committee had developed the following expenditures:

Frank L. Smith, accounted about	
William B. McKinley, defeated candidate	$252,547
Len Small	$259,035
Samuel Insull	$193,734
Propaganda by Samuel Insull against the World Court	$13,124
Crowe-Barrett fund for campaign work	175,000
Mrs. Medill McCormick for foreign language campaign advertising	100,000
McKinley's billing	50,000
Total	$971,603

Driving in through the mystic mazes of Chicago politics the committee learned that Samuel Insull, public utilities man, had given the Crowe-Barrett group $10,000, making his total contribution only $10,000 to the group opposing Senator McKinley, but $10,000 to the Deneen group his candidate, Colonel Smith; $15,000 to Mr. Brennan, who is to oppose Colonel Smith in November, and $125,000 to Colonel Smith himself. In addition, he handed out $32,726 for propaganda against the World Court, a gift which manifestly aided Colonel Smith and damaged Mr. McKinley's campaign.

At every angle of the investigation the power and influence of the Chicago traction companies have been hinted at, sometimes darkly, sometimes broadly. Senator Reed is trying hard to find out if animosity between McKinley on one side and the Commonwealth Edison Company, and Senator McKinley, a large stockholder in the Illinois Power & Light Co., was not the real factor in the fight against Senator McKinley and the fight for Colonel Smith, who headed the thesis Commerce Commission, controlling all the traction companies of this State.

Groan Questioned on Franchises.

Henry L. Green, Senator McKinley's personal attorney, and Edward H. Wright, a negro member of the Illinois Commerce Commission, were asked searching questions today about the part the traction influence played in the primary and in Illinois politics. Senator Reed made no concealment of a charge that Mr. Insull sought to influence the commission to renew Chicago street-car franchises at a time when Colonel Smith was seeking the Republican nomination.

But Mr. Green, a frank witness, admitted knowing any feeling of rivalry between McKinley and Insull, while Wright, a truculent witness, denied any theories of the kind. Nothing to substantiate this was brought forward, but Representative M. A. Michaelson correctly was brought out.

Senators Reed and La Follette, the only committee members here, worked rapidly during the two sessions, but the ramifications of local politics puzzled them greatly. When Mr. Green said, "Plenty I can't understand Chicago politics." Senator Reed smiled and said heartily, "Well, neither can I."

Practically all the McKinley expenditure was accounted for by Mr. Green, who detailed sums of $226,000, leaving only about $64,000 and he could not tell how that was spent. He told the story of the Crowe-Barrett fund deserting Senator McKinley, although the Senator was prepared to contribute. The committee was covered in $2,364 hours in the air. The cost of operating the flying machine, it is in the infancy of commercial aviation, Mr. Green said, astounded him by endorsing Colonel Smith as Senator McKinley.

"We thought that was a mistake."

Continued on Page Three.

FORDS PLAN TO CUT COST OF AIRPLANES

Edsel Tells Coolidge That Commercial Aviation Can Be Made Profitable.

EXPECTS MASS PRODUCTION

All-Metal, 3-Engine Machines Can Then Be Made Cheaper for Business.

Special to The New York Times.

PAUL SMITH'S, N. Y., July 28.—Edsel Ford, of the automobile manufacturing family, detailed to President Coolidge the program made by the Ford Motor Company in the development of commercial aviation. Engines and planes that are sound and efficient are being evolved, he declared, and he expects a wide development of commercial flying to result in such a demand for them as to make their production in large quantities necessary and profitable.

Mr. Ford told the President that their program, slowly being worked out, does not contemplate entrance into air service, but that the production of machines so cheaply that they can be operated at a profit in the populous centres for passenger and freight transportation. He looks for such strides in the country in making airplanes safe and cheap as to make the American people a nation of flyers. He does not believe, however, that air routes will displace railroads, but that they will radiate into every large centre as emergency carriers.

Favors Multiple-Engined Planes.

The advantage of the three-engine monoplane they are producing, he said in an interview after his conference with the President, is that all three engines are started to lift the load, and after the machine is in the air they may be throttled down or two of them stopped.

"Multiple engines make flying safer and the life of the plane longer," he added. "It is not likely that all engines would become impaired at one time, and with one engine in commission a forced landing can be made within an area of 1,000 feet.

"I believe that the future development of flying machines lies with multiple-engined ships of the all-metal type."

Asked the cost of the all-metal three-engine monoplane which his firm has developed Mr. Ford said that the present cost $27,000.

"After the first 100 machines are manufactured," he declared, "we hope to be able to reduce that cost 25 per cent. and the unit cost will be greatly reduced as the production is further increased."

This plane, he explained, has a sixty-eight-foot spread, weighs 4,000 pounds and its carrying capacity in ton. Its radius can be increased if the load is reduced and might safely be estimated at 2,500 miles.

"Is it your purpose to develop commercial aviation?" he was asked.

Hopes to Make Planes Profitable.

"No; our interest is chiefly in the manufacture of planes and we have no plans for an extension of our present routes between Chicago, Detroit and Cleveland," he replied. "These air routes were established chiefly as an experiment, but we are using them to carry emergency parts of automobiles between our plant; and Chicago and Cleveland. We hope to produce a plane that will be so cheap as to make air service profitable without Government aid. At the present time air routes cannot be made to pay unless they have mail service to produce their returns from private sources. We hope to put a machine in the air that will be so economical as to make commercial aviation a pleasure craft."

The air routes maintained by the Ford concern started 1,492 flights up to July 17, of which 1,467 were completed, an efficiency of 98.3 per cent. The failures, he said, were caused about equally by engine trouble and by bad weather, a total of 286,000 miles was covered in 2,364 hours in the air. The cost of operating the flying machine, is in the infancy of commercial aviation, Mr. Ford said. To this is due in fact that it has not received much encouragement here until

Continued on Page Four.

ARREST MADE AT MIDNIGHT

Widow Awakened in Her Home and Lodged in Somerset Jail.

WILL MAKE NO STATEMENT

Says That She Must Know on What Evidence the Warrant Is Based.

CASE RECENTLY REOPENED

Somerset County Prosecutor Swears to Warrant, Keeping Nature of Evidence Secret.

Mrs. Frances Stevens Hall, widow of the Rev. Edward W. Hall, pastor of the Protestant Episcopal Church of St. John the Evangelist in New Brunswick, N. J., who was shot and killed with Mrs. Eleanor Mills, choir singer in his church, on the morning of Sept. 14, 1922, was arrested shortly before midnight last night in her home in New Brunswick, charged with the murder of her husband and Mrs. Mills.

Mrs. Hall was taken into custody by Captain John J. Lamb of the New Jersey State Police, on a warrant issued by Justice of the Peace William R. Sutphin of Somerville. Accompanying Captain Lamb were Captain Harry W. Walsh and Detective Sergeant Richard Burke of the Jersey City police.

Prosecutor Makes Charge.

The warrant on which the arrest was made, had been sworn out by Prosecutor Francis Bergen of Somerset County on the borderline of which, on the afternoon of Saturday, Sept. 16, the bodies of the clergyman and the choir singer, the wife of the sexton of his church, were found under a crab apple tree.

It is understood that the warrant was issued after a conference in the afternoon between Captain Lamb, who had been working with him on new leads in the murder mystery for the last week, the authorities of Somerset and Middlesex Counties, in the latter of which Mrs. Hall was arrested, and Supreme Court Justice Charles W. Parker in the Justice's chambers at Morristown.

Defendant Is Jailed.

Following her arrest Mrs. Hall was hurried in an automobile to the office of Prosecutor Bergen in Somerville, where she was questioned for some time. She invariably answered by saying:

"I shall make no statements until I have learned what this murder charge is based on."

Shortly after 2 o'clock this morning she was taken to the Somerset County Jail in Somerville. Prosecutor Bergen announced that no details would be revealed as to the developments of the recent investigation which led up to the formal murder charges.

Captain Lamb, who was a sergeant of the New Jersey State Constabulary was one of a group of State Troopers assigned to investigate the Hall-Mills murder mystery after the authorities of New Jersey placed and we have no plans for an extension of our present routes between Chicago, Detroit and Cleveland, the new investigation of the Hall's home, in the new Brunswick. By County Detective Joseph Hanlon of Prosecutor Bergen's staff. Hanlon was Sheriff of Somerset County when the murders were committed.

Captain Lamb held the warrant in his hand as he pushed the electric door button on the porch of the Hall home, after he and the other officers had alighted in the circular driveway in front of the house from two automobiles at 11:40 P. M.

Mrs. Hall Awakened.

Mrs. Hall was asleep upstairs when the bell rang. One of the servants opened the door and the officers passed into the foyer. They were told to inform Mrs. Hall that three of the detectives who had backed of the cordon formed a part of the house, while awaiting Mrs. Hall's disposition.

"Willie" Stevens, brother of the widow, was the first of the family

Continued on Page Four.

The New York Times.

THE WEATHER
Thundershowers today, cooler at night; tomorrow fair.
Temperatures yesterday—Max., 79; min., 67.
For weather report see Page 25.

VOL. LXXV....No. 25,032.   ••••   NEW YORK, SATURDAY, AUGUST 7, 1926.   TWO CENTS In Greater | THREE CENTS | FOUR CENTS
New York | Within 200 Miles | Elsewhere in the U. S.

PLANT'S 'HEARTBEAT' THRILLS SCIENTISTS AT OXFORD MEETING

Hindu Savant Causes Further Sensation by Showing 'Blood' of Plant Flowing.

AUDIENCE SITS ABSORBED

Watches With Rapt Attention as Lecturer Submits Snapdragon to Death Struggle.

WIDE RANGE OF DISCUSSION

Papers on Education, Penal System, Labor and Electricity Read Before British Association.

Copyright, 1926, by The New York Times Company.
Special Cable to THE NEW YORK TIMES.

OXFORD, Aug. 6.—Rarely in all its history of nearly a hundred years of scientific achievement has the British Association for the Advancement of Science witnessed a more remarkable scene than this afternoon's, when Sir Jagadis Chandra Bose, the Hindu savant, demonstrated to an audience listening with absorbed interest the experiments by which he says he has proved that plants live lives akin to the lives of human beings.

Using instruments of almost incredible delicacy, one of which he had never exhibited before in public, the Oriental scientist showed his spectators the "heart" of a plant "beating" and the "blood" of a plant "flowing" in a manner which, according to him (and his audience was more than inclined to believe it), was far more similar to the phenomena connected with human life than science was willing to admit.

After explaining his theories by actual experiment, Sir Jagadis declared that present scientific conceptions of plant life were erroneous. If his theories are applied, he said, would be the elimination of the vivisection of animals as an aid to scientific investigation.

Program Again Diverse.

The remarkable revelations of the Hindu savant formed only one of the many items on the program of the third session of the British Association at Oxford this afternoon. As was the case yesterday, the program was most diverse, allowing opportunity for experts in various provinces of science to have their innings and advance their views.

Among those men who read papers before sections of the association to-day were Professor J. Graham Kerr, who predicted this time if education continues in its now accepted grooves; Dr. James Drever, who spoke on the penal system; Sir Lynden Macassey, who suggested a cure for the present day "strike fever"; Sir Thomas Holland, who attacked the neglect of civic training in our education, and Sir John F. C. Snell, who discussed the future of electricity.

These and others invariably the results of their long and painstaking study on audiences listening as raptly as never to lose a syllable.

Shows Plants Have "Hearts."

Sensational revelations of Sir Jagadis Chandra Bose concerning the "heartbeats" of plants were followed with breathless interest by his Oxford audience.

It was known that he had brought to Oxford extraordinarily delicate instruments with which he seeks to prove the existence in plants of life closely resembling that of human beings, including one instrument which he never before has shown in public.

Hence both sexes of the audience were on tiptoe with eager anticipation when the world-renowned Hindu scientist appeared this afternoon in the lecture hall.

Before entering he had plucked at random an ordinary snapdragon and with this he made his experiment.

Placing the snapdragon in a tiny tray amid an awe-inspiring array of bottles and instruments, he showed how his apparatus recorded, by a series of continuous lines, the action of the beating "heart" of the plant, the lines being transcribed on a sensitized plate.

Then, to prove that it was indeed a heart he had under observation, he moved the plant slightly to another tray containing bromide. The plant immediately dropped and the "writing" changed perceptibly. Then he moved it into a tray containing musk, which immediately revived it.

He made further experiments with cobra poison and strychnine, obtaining even more startling results, which he declared proved that the nervous reactions of plants are stimulated by drugs exactly as in the case of human beings.

Measures Sap Pressure of Plants.

The hitherto unknown instrument revealed by Sir Jagadis today was designed by him for recording and measuring the rate of movement of sap or "blood" in plants and studying how it is modified by the action of drugs which affect the circulation of the life force.

When the circulation of the sap is stimulated by a drug, the recorder showed an upcurve, and when a depressant was used the struggle between the forces of life and death was clearly visible to the absorbed spectators.

They saw the development of a crisis

Continued on Page Six.

Lord Grey Advises British To Keep Their Walking Legs

EPSOM, England, Aug. 6 (AP).—"Keep your legs" was the advice Viscount Grey of Fallodon recently gave to the boys of Epsom College. He warned them against giving up walking and riding bicycles because the means of communication have been so much improved, and said even a middle-aged man is better for walking twenty miles a day or riding fifty on a wheel.

Viscount Grey is doubtful whether all the modern mechanical contrivances which have become part of everyday life are of benefit to humanity and warned his audience against neglecting their minds and bodies because mechanical genius has devised ways of amusing persons without requiring them to make any effort on their own behalf.

FIVE WARRANTS OUT IN HALL-MILLS CASE, BUT ARE NOT SERVED

State to Keep Check on Former Servants, Mrs. Russell and Gorsline.

SIX ARE QUESTIONED AGAIN

Rector's Intrigue Was Known to Many, Maid Says—Denies Call to Mrs. Hall on Murder Night.

HURRY IN BURIAL ALLEGED

Dr. Long Declares Undertaker Seemed in Desperate Rush—Mrs. Riehl Gets Permit to Leave State.

Six witnesses told Assistant Attorney General Alexander Simpson yesterday what they knew about the Hall-Mills case, and the prosecutor and the State's troopers, finally in agreement on this phase of the revived investigation, reported that five warrants had been obtained, but would be held unserved.

The examination of the witnesses was conducted at Somerville, N. J. The stories heard included that of Barbara Tough, former maid in the Hall household. She denied that she telephoned to Mrs. Frances Stevens Hall, now at liberty in $15,000 bail charged with the slaying of her husband, the Rev. Dr. Edward W. Hall, and Mrs. Eleanor R. Mills shortly before the clergyman and his choir leader were shot to death four years ago near New Brunswick, N. J.

Tells of Gossip in Parish.

The former servant, however, did add to the voluminous history of the case. She told Senator Simpson, according to his version of her narrative, that the intimacy of Mrs. Mills and the rector was "common knowledge," a fact that all of those who were questioned have denied. Miss Tough, a slow-spoken but emphatic Scotswoman, doubted whether Mrs. Hall knew about it.

The other witnesses examined were Dr. William H. Long, Somerset County physician; Mrs. Maria Gildea, who was cook for the Hall family; Mrs. Minna Clarke, organist of Dr. Hall's church, who was erroneously reported "missing," and Raymond Schneider, a youth, who found the bodies and who was sentenced to the Rahway Reformatory after he had falsely charged a New Brunswick youth, Clifford Hayes, with the double murder.

The warrants included one for Ralph V. Gorsline, vestryman of the Church of St. John the Evangelist. All the warrants were merely for material witnesses except Gorsline's. This warrant charged him as an "accessory after the fact." The documents were obtained, it was explained, for service only if the persons named showed a disposition to leave the State. None of the witnesses has shown any such disposition.

Others Named in Warrants.

Others named in the warrants were Mrs. Nellie Lo Russell, negress, who discredited the story of the State's chief witness to date, Mrs. Jane Gibson, the "pig woman"; Barbara Tough, Tumulty and Mrs. Gildea. It was made clear that nobody would be arrested and that the issuance of the warrants was merely a precautionary step.

The Assistant Attorney General motored from his office in Jersey City to the State Troopers' headquarters in Main Street, Somerville, at noon. He left after he had received a telephone call informing him that troopers had brought in several witnesses to be questioned. Miss Tough came to the headquarters voluntarily, and so did Mrs. Clarke. The latter explained that she had shuttered her home in New Brunswick in order to shield herself against intrusion, and that she had never been "missing."

The questioning of the witnesses lasted from about 2 o'clock until 7 o'clock last night. Mrs. Gildea, Schneider and Tumulty were the last witnesses to be questioned, the examination in their case being conducted by Major Mark O. Kimberling and Captain John J. Lamb, the prosecutor having returned to Jersey City. In his absence the State Troopers declined to give out the substance of what Mrs. Gildea, Schneider and the chauffeur had to offer.

Simpson Quotes Witnesses.

In substance, Senator Simpson gave as the examination of Miss Tough.

Continued on Page Four.

American Girl Rescues Another At Lausanne, but Refuses Name

Copyright, 1926, by The New York Times Co.
By Wireless to THE NEW YORK TIMES.

GENEVA, Aug. 6.—A young American girl on a holiday was walking alone along the shore of Lac de Joux, near Lausanne, yesterday, when she saw a small boat containing a young man and a girl overturn.

The man, who could not swim, was hanging to the keel, shouting for help, but the girl had disappeared in the water. Without hesitating, the American girl swam out to the spot and brought the girl to the shore, where she was soon recovered, while a man in a boat rescued the other victim.

The American girl when asked for her name said that it did not matter. The plucky, modest girl then amilingly nodded good-bye to a small crowd and walked away amidst the cheers of "Bravo, l'Americaine."

LONG CHASE ABROAD LANDS BANK THIEVES

Two Men Wanted in Robbery of $109,000 Snared After Hunt Through Seven Countries.

SHOE TREES ARE SOLE CLUE

Reveal Names of Fugitives Who Are Brought Back on Liner— Pair to Be Sent to Coast.

With the arrival here yesterday of the Berengaria two young Poles ended a ten months' holiday at the expense of a couple of San Francisco banks and there was brought to a close a true detective story containing elements such as movies are made of and emphasizing the relentless persistence of surety investigators.

The young man, brothers, are charged with having stolen $109,000 in securities. They are Ludwig and Julius Busch, respectively 33 and 29 years old, and they came to this country in 1924. But for a pair of shoe trees—articles which are not known ever to have figured prominently in any detective story—the two would still be at liberty.

The two were traced and brought back to this country by Samuel MacCubbin, head of the investigation and claims department of the Fidelity and Deposit Company of Baltimore, which has an office in this city at 85 Liberty Street, and bonds bank employes. The romantic story of the Busch brothers was told yesterday by Vincent Cullen, Vice President of the company, and pieced out by MacCubbin, the detective, when the ship arrived.

Both Get Bank Jobs.

Coming to the land of the free in search of riches, the two young men arrived in San Francisco in July, 1924, and one, Julius, went to work for the Bank of Italy, while Ludwig got a job with the Anglo-California Trust Company. Neither was bonded individually, but each bank carried a blanket policy with the Fidelity and Deposit Company covering defalcations.

Suddenly, in October, 1925, both young men disappeared. At the time not much was thought of their going, but when a check of their books was made in January it was found that securities valued at about $109,000 had disappeared from the Bank of Italy. Investigation disclosed that one bewildered, apparently, had taken the securities piecemeal, then through the brother employed in the other bank.

The San Francisco police could find no trace of the two, but did find that the Buschs had abandoned certain belongings in their lodgings at 1,927 Jackson Street. From all articles of clothing and everything else, however, marks of possible identification had been carefully removed.

MacCubbin started on the case in March, the fugitives having a lead on him then of five and a half months. Diligent work, according to Mr. Cullen, resulted in MacCubbin's finding that at some time or other the two men shipped some baggage to Montreal. According to Mr. Cullen, the trail was completely lost. MacCubbin, even with the aid of the Montreal police, being unable to find any trace of the two men. MacCubbin even went to the extent of poring over hotel registers for many months back, but to no purpose. So he returned to San Francisco.

The Telltale Shoe Trees.

Going thoroughly through the effects of the two men again, MacCubbin made a very careful examination of the

Continued on Page Four.

KEHOE FOUND GUILTY OF MILK CONSPIRACY; IS LOCKED IN TOMBS

Jury Out 6 Hours, 12 Minutes; Judge Refuses to Continue Defendant's $10,000 Bail.

AUG. 12 SET FOR SENTENCE

Maximum Penalty Three Years' Imprisonment, Together With $500 Fine.

LAWYER PROMISES APPEALS

Mrs. Kehoe Hysterical at Verdict— Conviction a Warning, Health Commissioner Says.

Three weeks to a day after he had been placed on trial, William H. Kehoe, formerly Assistant Corporation Counsel, was found guilty last night of conspiracy in the bootleg cream graft scandal. After deliberating six hours and twelve minutes, the jury returned its verdict before Judge Max S. Levine in General Sessions at 10:07 P. M.

Kehoe was taken to the Tombs and locked in a cell after the Court had denied the application of Michael M. Edelstein, his counsel, for the continuance of the $10,000 bail under which he has been at liberty since his indictment. Aug. 12 was named as the date for his sentence.

Kehoe and his wife were chatting together in the corridor outside the court room when word was received that the jury was ready to report. Both had looked for a disagreement because of the length of time which the jury had been out. Mrs. Kehoe remained outside as her husband entered and stood at the bar. He gave a glance of swift appraisement at the faces of the jurymen as they filed in and his own face went white.

When the verdict was announced Kehoe leaned heavily forward on the railing with both hands clutching it. He swayed slightly and sought to steady himself. His pedigree was given in a voice little above a whisper. He was 40 years old, he said; born in the United States, lived at 191st Street and Woodall Avenue, Hollis, Queens; was a lawyer, married and of temperate habits.

Wife Informed of Verdict.

A relative who was seated near the door stepped out of the court room and approached Mrs. Kehoe, who had been informed of the verdict. Mrs. Kehoe became hysterical and her cries could be heard through the building. She was calmed somewhat later and led from the building without seeing her husband before he was taken to the Tombs.

After the verdict had been rendered Edward L. Purves of 54 West 108th Street, Juror No. 9, thanked Judge Levine in behalf of the jury for the consideration shown by the Court. Kehoe was convicted of conspiracy to do an act injurious to the public health, or for the perversion or obstruction of justice, or of the due administration of the laws. It is a misdemeanor punishable by an indeterminate sentence in the penitentiary, the maximum of which is three years, or by a fine of $500, or both.

Mr. Edelstein said no move could be made to obtain Kehoe's release until after his sentence was pronounced. A certificate of reasonable doubt will then be sought and an attempt made to obtain his admission to bail. The case will be fought through the highest courts, Mr. Edelstein said.

Warning, Says Harris.

In commenting on the result of the trial last night Dr. Louis I. Harris, Health Commissioner, said:

"The hands of the guardians of the lives of the children, the sick and all others in the community have been strengthened by this verdict, and it may properly be interpreted as the utterance of a warning by representatives of the citizens of the community that the people of this city will not tolerate a corrupt act that endangers the welfare of any of our people.

"If Mr. Pecora's address to the jury and his appeal for the protection of the public health were studied by every citizen, it would create a sentiment that would insure against a repetition of the scandalous conditions revealed at this trial. Mr. Pecora's address was a brilliant presentation of the basis of public health service."

It was 2:35 P. M. when Judge Levine finished his charge and the jury retired. Kehoe, his coat removed because of the heat, paced back and forth in the gallery about the central rotunda of the Criminal Courts Building. Mrs. Kehoe clinging to his arm.

Mr. Pecora told the jury that he had no apology to make for the character of Doner or Harry Dansiger, his chief

Continued on Page Eleven.

GERTRUDE EDERLE SWIMS THE CHANNEL IN RECORD TIME OF 14 HOURS 31 MINUTES; AMERICAN IS FIRST WOMAN TO CROSS

"It Had to Be Done, I Did It," Says Miss Ederle; Twice Spurned Burgess's Advice to Give Up

By ALEC RUTHERFORD,
British Expert on Channel Swimming.

Copyright, 1926, by The New York Times Company.
Special Cable to THE NEW YORK TIMES.

DOVER, England, Aug. 6.—During the wait on the tug in Dover Harbor and the journey to the hotel after the Channel triumph, I had an opportunity of chatting with Miss Ederle, her father and the rest of the party. Miss Ederle said:

"I just knew if it could be done, it had to be done, and I did it."

Her father said he was never sure until the finish. He was very proud that his daughter had performed the feat, whose achievement he attributed largely to her splendid persistence.

Burgess told me that twice during the swim he wanted Miss Ederle to give up the water—the first time at noon and the second time at 6 o'clock. It was her father and sister who would not let her come out, he said.

Anyway, Gertrude herself refused and repeatedly declared she had no intention of giving up. She said:

"I am doing it for mummy."

This was in reference to a series of wireless messages urging her to go on sent by her mother in New York during the swim. They were read to Gertrude while she was in the water.

I gather that Gertrude achieved her victory by a margin of only ten minutes. Had she not reached the favorable flood tide when she did she could never have got over.

During the latter half of the swim an amusing dialogue took place between "Pop" Ederle and his daughter. "Pop" continually roared over the side of the boat:

"Trudie, don't forget you won't get that roadster unless you get over."

Gertrude always responded:

"Pop, I will have that roadster."

Aboard the tug on the way back to Dover she constantly reminded her father that the roadster was to be got immediately. After her bath at the hotel when I asked what she was going to do next, she said:

"I shall go to bed and sleep all day. I want it. I am so tired."

I understand she is to return to France tomorrow, then go on to Germany to see her father's people and then go back to Paris to buy some 'nice clothes' and presents for 'Mum.'"

She will return to America on the Berengaria on Aug. 21.

CHEERED AT BRITISH SHORE

She Lands Smiling at Kingsdown After Hard Battle From Gris-Nez.

CONQUERS WIND, RAIN, TIDE

Fights for Three Desperate Hours Off English Coast Still Favoring Current Aids.

BONFIRES LIGHT LAST DASH

Searchlights Also Sweep From Shore as New York Girl Comes In With Strokes Still Strong.

By T. R. YBARRA.

Copyright, 1926, by The New York Times Company.
Special Cable to THE NEW YORK TIMES.

DOVER, Aug. 6.—Gertrude Ederle, the plucky little New York girl, swam across the English Channel today in 14 hours 31 minutes, thus winning not only the honor of being the first woman to accomplish this feat but breaking by a goodly margin the best record made by a male cross-Channel swimmer.

The speediest cross-Channel swim made before today was that of the Italian swimmer, Sebastian Tirabocchi, who swam from France to England in 16 hours 23 minutes.

Gertrude Ederle's successful swim came fifty-one years after the Channel was first conquered by an English swimmer, Captain Matthew Webb. In 1911, the Channel was crossed by another Englishman, T. W. Burgess, who now has achieved the added glory of having trained the young American girl and of having guided her today from start to finish of her magnificent swim.

Fought to Beach Favoring Current.

Miss Ederle plunged into the water this morning at 7:09 o'clock at Cape Gris-Nez, France. Gris-Nez at Kingsdown, near Deal, England, at 9:40 o'clock this evening. For three desperate hours she fought the ebb and flow of the tide, with the British shores looming temptingly before her yet apparently hopelessly out of reach. But she gritted her teeth and stuck to it, putting every ounce of strength and will power into her strokes.

She knew that if she could only stick it out a favorable turn in the tide might let her reach the coveted shore. Instead of making for Shakespeare Cliff or St. Margaret's Bay, as swimmers usually do, Gertrude made toward Deal. And at last the favoring current for which she was praying swept her toward the cliffs of England.

English Cheers Greet Smiling Victor.

Soon after 9 o'clock tonight she was off Kingsdown. Just before 10 o'clock she emerged from the water and walked ashore. Delight at her victory had effaced all memory of the terrible hours through which she had passed.

As she came on to the beach she was happy and smiling. And the crowd who had rushed to Kingsdown from all directions at the news that the game little American was struggling toward the English shore surged around her in a frenzy of enthusiasm and sent up cheer after cheer of delirious joy.

Miss Ederle had hardly reached the shore before she was hustled into a rowboat which whisked her off to the tug which had accompanied her across the Channel.

During the last few hours of her record-breaking swim, Gertrude Ederle had to buck the wickedest possible combination of obstacles. The sea was rough, the tide was running strongly against her and a stinging spray was hurled into her face as she swam doggedly forward. It was a fine piece of headwork which enabled her to take advantage of the "voering current and reach Kingsdown Beach.

EXPERT'S STORY OF SWIM.

By ALEC RUTHERFORD,
British Expert on Channel Swimming.

Copyright, 1926, by The New York Times Company.
Special Cable to THE NEW YORK TIMES.

DOVER, Aug. 6.—Gertrude Ederle, the nineteen-year-old New York champion girl swimmer, is one of the pluckiest swimmers that ever attempted the huge task of swimming the English Channel. I watched this pretty, tiny atom of humanity in her red bathing dress and skull cap, with goggles like a motorist's, battle for fourteen hours today against the merciless elements.

At 6:30 this evening she was facing the white cliffs of Dover, only six miles away from England. She was watching the Whitney farm cause persons in charge there to establish a guard to protect 300 blooded horses and a score of foals. Farmers in the neighborhood are apprehensive also of their stock, but even more so of their children.

Continued on Page Three.

HANDS OFF MEXICO, IS COOLIDGE POLICY

He Holds That There Has Been No Cause for Action in Religious Struggle.

NO MOVE ON SOVIET DEBT

President Talks of Fall Campaigns With Tilson—Wades Brook and Lands Trout.

Special to The New York Times.

PLYMOUTH, Vt., Aug. 6.—President Coolidge is watching with great concern the struggle between the Government of Mexico and the Catholic Church, but has not been advised of any developments in Mexico which would justify American intervention, as suggested yesterday by the Supreme Council of the Knights of Columbus at its convention in Philadelphia. The President's policy in the struggle is hands off.

Since coming here the President has not been in touch with the State Department, and, has not been informed of any violation of treaty rights or of violations to American citizens or property rights which would justify any action by the United States in the present domestic problem in Mexico, a problem which has deeply affected Catholics and others in this country.

Sitting on the piazza of his old homestead this afternoon after a day devoted to fishing and cable on 'relatives, Mr. Coolidge gave his views upon foreign questions that have become acute since he began his vacation. The fight between the Government of Mexico and other matters concerning American rights have formed the subject of an inquiry by President Coolidge in the last two weeks. He has kept in close touch with reports from Mexico, but it was said here authoritatively that nothing had occurred there that would warrant drastic action by this Government.

No Violence Reported to Him.

While President Coolidge may not accept the action of the Mexican Government as one tending to create a friendly sentiment in the United States, because of the religious issue involved, he has not received word that ports of violence against Americans there as the result of the contention. However, he has decided that American rights must be rigidly upheld. The President will act on the protests of the Knights of Columbus and other organizations only if American rights or American property are violated as a result of the conflict.

The Administration policy toward Mexico, which has been one of patience respecting the land and oil laws, would be no more aggressive than at present. It was made clear here today, if treaty rights or the rights of American citizens in that country are violated. President Coolidge is anxious to help that-Government, as evidenced in the negotiations on the land and oil laws concerning American rights between Church and State was in progress. His patience, it was apparent today, might become exhausted if American rights are not upheld in the present situation.

Concerned with foreign relations as deeply as with domestic affairs, President Coolidge reasserted today the American position in regard to Soviet Russia, as the result of a report that the Soviet Government desires to settle the Russian debt to the United States. He holds that all that the President regime in Russia had to do toward that end was to revoke the ordinance by which it repudiated its debts to the United States. He had not heard that this had been done or that the Soviet Government desired to send agents here to confer on the debt settlement.

Tilson Presents Political Affairs.

President Coolidge had the political situation presented to him in detail today by Representative Tilson of Connecticut, the Republican House leader, who will be in charge of headquarters in New York for the Republican Senate and House campaigns. Offices there will be opened on Aug. 15. Stopping off on his way to his Summer home at Lake Sunapee, Mr. Tilson, accompanied by Mrs. Tilson, had luncheon with the President and Mrs. Coolidge. He told the President that conditions were improving steadily for the Republican Party and that there no longer appeared to be any free from murder or common thieving. Two days ago he was brought to the Palais de Justice in Paris in a Black Maria, similar to that from which the fictional Arsene Lupin escaped by lifting the floor boards.

Reme's method was not so crude. He reached the Palais de Justice with a dozen other offenders, but instead of sitting on the bench with those who were conducted in an antechamber, he went to the bench where there were a number of genuine delinquents waiting to be questioned.

Continued on Page Two.

MAYOR PICKS KELBY FOR HEALTH INQUIRY

Ex-Justice Will Investigate Conditions in Department as Special Counsel.

TO TAKE UP MILK GRAFT

Centralization of Inquiry in All Boroughs Planned to Help in Prosecutions.

Mayor Walker authorized yesterday the announcement that Charles H. Kelby, former Justice of the Appellate Division of the Supreme Court, Second Department, had accepted appointment as special counsel to take charge of conditions in the affairs of the Board of Health.

The announcement was made by Charles F. Kerrigan, assistant to the Mayor, after a talk over the telephone with Mayor Walker at Dixville Notch, N. H. Judge Kelby, it was learned, will have charge of a general investigation of conditions in the Health Department and will carry on in each of the five boroughs the inquiry into milk graft, which has already resulted in several indictments, with a view to submitting evidence to the District Attorneys in the several counties.

Judge Kelby has held conferences with Health Commissioner Louis I. Harris and said he considered it in the public interest to have the whole situation in the Health Department thoroughly investigated and submitted to the prosecuting authorities for action.

The appointment of Judge Kelby, who is a Republican and a law associate of former Controller Charles L. Craig, with offices at 18 Broadway, was the city administration's answer to the demand of the Citizens Union and others, for an investigation of the milk situation by the Attorney General on the ground that an attempt was being made to protect those higher up in milk graft. Governor Smith, it has been said, has been reluctant to put the investigation into the hands of Attorney General Albert Ottinger, a Republican and a candidate for Republican nomination for Governor, and believes that this would inject the inquiry too much into the politics out of the inquiry.

Centralizes the Inquiry.

Mayor Walker, it was said, decided that the centralization of the investigation, which was the chief argument advanced in support of an investigation by the Attorney General, would be obtained by the appointment of Judge Kelby.

The announcement of the selection of Judge Kelby, who will rank as a special aid to the Corporation Counsel, was made at the Mayor's office, read:

"Mayor Walker and Commissioner Harris have agreed that the investigation collected by the Health Commissioner should be reviewed by a lawyer of high standing who would be able to sift the evidence and prepare cases for prosecution by the District Attorneys in the five counties of the City of New York. Judge Kelby has been assured of the cooperation of all the District Attorneys in Manhattan, the Bronx, Brooklyn, Queens and Richmond.

"Working with Commissioner Harris it is felt special counsel will be able to develop cases, reinforce those where there are missing links in the chain of

Continued on Page Two.

HUNT JERSEY WOODS FOR ROVING LEOPARD

Scores of Volunteers Aid Posse in Search for Escaped Cat as Fear for Children Spreads.

DOGS PUT ON ITS TRAIL

Animal Reported Seen Twice, but It Eludes Hunters—Reward for Capture Raised to $500.

Special to The New York Times.

RED BANK, N. J., Aug. 6.—In the glare of automobile headlights a posse of State troopers, Monmouth County detectives and farmers, armed with high power rifles and pistols, scoured the woodland covers on and near the Brookdale farm of Lewis J. Thompson near Lincroft until midnight tonight for the full-grown Indian leopard that escaped yesterday from Oliver W. Holton's Twinbrook zoo at Middletown.

The search tonight was trying to pick up the trail, the posse explored the woods and brush land, using flashlights when beyond the beams of the automobile lights. But when the search was given up at midnight the leopard was still at large. It was said that the hunt would be resumed and continued until the animal was found.

Mr. Holton, who offered a reward of $50 yesterday for the capture of the animal dead or alive, increased the offer today to $500, and it was agreed that no effort was to be made to capture the leopard alive, due to a fear that some one might be injured or killed.

The excitement of the hunt increased this afternoon when Charles H. Kelby, who is a Republican and a law associate of the animal reported seen twice, but it eludes several hundred of volunteers for the hunt. The search was centred around the Brookdale farm during the day after Jerrard Vaughan, a watchman at the Harry Payne Whitney breeding farm, reported that he believed he had seen the leopard fleeing from a dog near a barn early in the morning. Abram Lower, superintendent of Mr. Holton's zoo, hurried to the farm and positively identified tracks in a nearby cornfield and a clump of woods as those of the fugitive animal.

The reward and the fear sprang over the countryside that the roving animal might attack a child brought scores of volunteers to the hunt. The circle of men became smaller the tension increased and a sudden burst of shots in the wood sent all members of the posse in that direction. They were keenly disappointed to find the shots had been fired by jokers in the posse.

The reported presence of the leopard near the Whitney farm caused persons in charge there to establish a guard to protect 300 blooded horses and a score of foals. Farmers in the neighborhood are apprehensive also of their stock, but even more so of their children.

Margaret Ellison, eight-year-old daughter of a farmer on the Nut Swamp Road, was believed to have seen the leopard last night near her home. It was skulking along the edge of a wood.

The girl ran home, telling of the "big white dog with yellow spots on it" that she had seen. Earlier her father reached the spot the animal had been seen.

Late in the afternoon Superintendent Lower expressed the belief that the leopard was cornered and would break through within a short time.

"We found footmarks along the edge of the cornfield and around rabbit burrows," he said. "We traced them into tracks leading from the woods and I think the leopard is in there and that we have a good chance of getting it tonight."

The leopard was one of two the Middletown zoo from Singapore, India.

"The Eel," Noted Paris Criminal, Escapes By Underground Tunnels, Posing as Inspector

Copyright, 1926, by The New York Times Company.
Special Cable to THE NEW YORK TIMES.

PARIS, Aug. 6.—In the case of Georges Reme, known as "The Eel," it seems that something like a "master criminal" really does exist.

Reme is wanted for numerous crimes and felonies and may be characterized as a "con man," his career so far being free from murder or common thieving. Two days ago he was brought to the Palais de Justice in Paris in a Black Maria, similar to that from which the fictional Arsene Lupin escaped by lifting the floor boards.

Reme's method was not so crude. He reached the Palais de Justice with a dozen other offenders, but instead of sitting on the bench with those who were conducted in an antechamber, he went to the bench where there were a number of genuine delinquents waiting to be questioned.

When one of these was called Reme took him by the arm, having concealed him under the bench, and marched him out of the room.

Then taking a number of typewritten letters from his pocket, he went into the underground passage which leads from the Juvenile Court and walked coolly to the end of the tunnel, where a policeman challenged him. "I am a secret service inspector," he said, without batting an eyelash, and with a sure step and apparently complete familiarity with his surroundings he passed through the intricate base of hallways to the outer door, where he passed the guard and went to the street.

Then his trail was lost, but a black automobile which had been noticed hovering about was discovered to have disappeared.

Continued on Page Two.

The New York Times.

THE WEATHER

Showers today; tomorrow fair, slight change in temperature.
Temperature Yesterday—Max. 73; Min. 63.
☞For weather report see Page 42.

VOL. LXXV....No. 25,049.   NEW YORK, TUESDAY, AUGUST 24, 1926.   TWO CENTS In Greater New York | THREE CENTS Within 200 Miles | FOUR CENTS elsewhere in the U. S.

PEACE HOPE FADES AS MEXICAN BISHOPS REJECT COMPROMISE

Prelates Refuse to Negotiate Further Till Calles Suspends Religious Regulations.

WON'T RESUME SERVICES

Boycott Will Continue to Be Pressed, Says Bishop Diaz, as Catholics' Legal Right.

DOUBLE-DEALING CHARGED

President Is Accused of Altering the Episcopate's Statement and Shifting on Registry of Priests.

Copyright, 1926, by The New York Times Company.
Special Cable to THE NEW YORK TIMES.

MEXICO CITY, Aug. 23.—Unless the Mexican Government suspends all regulations of the penal code affecting religion and the penal code for the registration of the priests, the Episcopate will not continue negotiations for an adjustment of the controversy between the Church and the State.

This position was taken by the prelates today when they rejected the formula for a compromise advanced in the conference of their delegates with President Calles last Saturday night.

The President, they said at the time, had assured them that the registration of the priests was entirely administrative in purpose, but later they discovered that he gave out a statement to a newspaper saying that returning priests would be "subject to the laws." The Bishops also charged that the statement which they issued after the conference, at the President's request, had been altered in its wording at the Chapultepec Palace.

As a result of the breakdown in negotiations, the Episcopate has dropped its tentatively considered project for resuming services in the churches.

Episcopate Decides to Fight On.

The Episcopate held a meeting tonight and unanimously decided to carry out the orders first issued when the Calles decrees were published, suspending all church services. It was decided that further conferences were useless as the prelates were convinced that the present Government was playing for time and was unwilling to suspend the penal regulations and the order requiring the registration of priests.

The bishops are confident that four weeks more of the boycott will bring the Government to terms, as Catholics in all parts of the republic report that the whole country is showing the effects.

Bishop Diaz Explains Situation.

Bishop Pascual Diaz of the State of Tabasco, who as Secretary of the Episcopate is the spokesman of the Church in Mexico, explained to THE NEW YORK TIMES correspondent today the reasons for the conference with President Calles and the significance of the result.

Moved by a desire to place themselves on record as having protested against the religious regulations in person to President Calles, he said, a committee of the episcopate, comprising Archbishop Leopoldo Ruiz y Flores of Michoacan and Bishop Diaz, readily accepted the invitations extended by Eduardo Mestre to meet the President. Bishop Diaz added that the episcopate always had been ready and anxious to accept mediation in a form that would satisfy the Catholics and would permit the renewal of religious worship.

The members of the episcopate were consulted, and after a discussion it was agreed that Archbishop Ruiz and Bishop Diaz should explain to President Calles the exact position of the Church and, if possible, arrive at a conclusion that would permit the faithful to use the churches and at the same time settle once for all the difficulties under which the Catholic Church had been working for many years. It was believed that though pain always had been ready and anxious to accept mediation in a form that would satisfy the Catholics and would permit the renewal of religious worship the Catholic countries would be placed before the Chief Magistrate in such a form that an agreement would soon be reached.

Calles's Power to Act at Issue.

When ushered into the presence of the President in the Chapultepec Palace, Bishop Diaz found him in unusually good humor. During the conversation, which lasted for two and a half hours, no decision was reached, both sides continued firm in their positions.

Archbishop Ruiz, representing the Church side of the problem, told the President that if Señor Calles, in the exercise of his extraordinary powers which were granted by Congress sat through which he issued the penal decree and the order for all priests to register, would suspend the regulations, the prelates would immediately reopen the churches, resume services and use their personal influence with the faithful to end the present agitation.

President Calles in reply said that he personally could not use these same powers, as Congress would be in session within the next few days.

Bishop Diaz then pointed out that as Congress did not meet until Sept. 6 President Calles still enjoyed the usage of these privileges and that it was an easy matter for the President to suspend the regulations until Congress could find time to study the question and through the proper legal channels amend the articles to which the majority of Mexicans objected.

Dependence on Rome's Consent.

Bishop Diaz further informed the President that unless the church service could not be resumed, at least until consent

Continued on Page Four.

Callizo, French Flier, Rises 41,811 Feet, World's Record

BUC, Versailles, France, Aug. 23 (AP).—M. Callizo is reported to have broken the world's altitude record today, reaching a height of 12,800 metres (41,811 feet). The record had stood at 12,066 metres (39,576 feet) a mark made by the same aviator. Callizo took off at the airdrome at 5 o'clock this afternoon and landed at Le Bourget two hours and twenty-five minutes later.

His instruments will be officially tested by the Air Ministry tomorrow, but experts here are confident that the record will stand. The mark he set is approximately eight miles.

Lieutenant John A. Macready holds the American altitude record, 38,704 feet, made on Jan. 19. He attempted to break Callizo's record March 13, but reached only 37,575 feet.

PANGALOS CAUGHT; PRISONER IN ATHENS

Destroyer on Which He Was Fleeing Quit When Threatened With Destruction.

TWO AIDS ARE ALSO TAKEN

Attempt to Hide in Wireless Turret Has Brought Ridicule on Former Dictator.

Copyright, 1926, by The New York Times Company.
Special Cable to THE NEW YORK TIMES.

ATHENS, Greece, Aug. 23.—The destroyer Leon, which has been seized by the new Condylis regime to prevent the escape of General Pangalos, deposed President, found the destroyer Pergamos, on which he was fleeing, surrendered. The crew of the Pergamos intended to surprise the Leon by using hand grenades until they saw from the first fusillade that resistance was impossible.

General Pangalos was found hiding on board in spite of the commander's denials. The warships returned about 6:30 o'clock this morning. Pangalos is now confined under close guard in the military hospital here. General Condylis, leader of the revolution, addressed a popular demonstration yesterday which was called to celebrate the suppression of General Pangalos's "tyrannical rule." He was repeatedly interrupted by the crowd, which demanded immediate formation of a coalition Government and announcement of a general election. This General Condylis promised to do. He declared that those who had been responsible for the tyranny now suppressed must be held fully responsible or their action and that their punishment was a duty to the nation.

Demand Punishment as Example.

A similar demonstration held in Saloniki demanded that the army return to its work and that exemplary punishment be meted to those responsible for the Pangalos Government as an example for posterity and as the end of all dictatorship.

General Condylis today called a conference of party leaders to discuss formation of a new coalition Cabinet, but it probably will not be held until tomorrow, to give the parties time for discussion.

Admiral Conduriotis was expected to return this evening to take up his duties as President of the republic.

General Pangalos will be put on trial before the High Court of Justice with the other deposed Ministers. While a prisoner on board the Pergamos he was interviewed by Representative Eleftherios Typos, who once supported him. Pangalos expressed sorrow and surprise because his former friends and supporters had betrayed him and encompassed his downfall. He said he had had definite plans to bring about normal conditions and to announce holding elections. He said he had a clear conscience and had done his duty

Continued on Page Five.

HALL SUSPECTS STAY IN JAIL AS BAIL PLEA IS SHIFTED BY COURT

Justice Gummere Refuses to Act, Holding Case Is One for Justice Parker.

HEARING LIKELY THURSDAY

Two Now Balk at Signing Their Testimony, but Revisions Won't Be Allowed.

ONE TOLD OF FINDING CLUB

Charlotte Mills Said to Have Given New Clue—More Evidence in Abeyance, Beggars Says.

Henry de la Bruyere Carpender and Willie Stevens, who are charged with the murder of the Rev. Dr. Edward W. Hall and Mrs. Eleanor R. Mills four years ago near New Brunswick, N. J., did not win freedom on bail yesterday. Chief Justice William S. Gummere, before whom application was made in Newark, refused to act. He said that his colleague, Supreme Court Justice Charles W. Parker, whose judicial district includes the place of the crime, had volunteered to cut short his vacation in order to hear the bail application.

Justice Parker is at Northeast Harbor, Me. Robert H. McCarter, counsel for the accused men, who have been in jail twelve days, telephoned and telegraphed to the Justice, seeking a date for a hearing. Senator Alexander Simpson, in charge of the Hall-Mills investigation, did likewise.

At Northeast Harbor, Me., it was said last night that Justice Parker had started back.

The hearing before Justice Parker probably will be held in Somerville on Thursday, according to the understanding last night of Mr. McCarter.

Court Hearing in Newark.

Application to the Chief Justice was made in the Newark Court House. After several routine motions in other litigation had been disposed of, but before all the motions awaiting ruling had been presented, Senator Simpson, who brought up the Hall-Mills case.

"If the Court pleases," he said, "I am here in response to a telegram signed Robert H. McCarter. I had no formal notice of motion and I am wondering whether they are going to make a motion. I have had no formal notice and I have been sitting here for an hour waiting for themto make the application.

"This is a criminal matte and I understood that your Honor would hear criminal matters in the borough of the litigated motions. So I would like to know whether they are going to make the motion."

Former Attorney General McCarter, leader of the defense, was obviously surprised by the action of the special prosecutor. He explained to the Chief Justice that he had been merely awaiting the convenience of the Court.

"What is your application?" said the Chief Justice.

"Our application is to admit to bail Mr. Henry Carpender and Mr. William C. Stevens, who are incarcerated in the Somerset County Jail because of the murder indictment on Sept. 16, 1922."

Asks Why They Come to Him.

"Why do you make the application to me?" asked the Court.

"Because Justice Parker, who sits in that circuit, is away and will not return until September, I understand, and also because Judge Cleary, the local Judge, has no jurisdiction to hear such an application."

Justice Gummere paused, and then said:

"I heard an application some two weeks ago to release Mrs Hall on bail, probably connected with the same crime, according to the theory of this case, but I had no knowledge of the application going to be made until it was made.

"Justice Parker, having observed in the newspapers—there has been some little notoriety given to this case in the newspapers now and then—revised telling me that if at any time before his normal period of return any matter

Continued on Page Eight.

Vault Built to Withstand Mobs and Bombs To Hold State's $200,000,000 in New Building

Special to The New York Times.

ALBANY, Aug. 23.—A most modern vault for holding $200,000,000 in cash and gilt-edged securities owned by the State will be built in the new twenty-six-story office building which the State is to erect just west of the Capitol. In case of fire it can be flooded with water. Three shifts of guards it would be the safest vault that human ingenuity could devise. It will contain alarms connected with sirens outside the building and also with Albany Police Headquarters and the bankers' protective system.

Plans for the vault are being drawn by the State Architect's force. Its proposed location is being kept a secret and the specifications and details of the construction are confidential. The entrance approximately 50 by 50

On Wednesday Governor Smith and members of the State Building Commission will open bids for the wrecking of the buildings that now occupy the site where the new office building is to be built. By Jan. 1 next it is proposed to have the site cleared, test borings completed and the final program for construction ready for presentation to the Legislature.

Departments of the State Government that now have large sums on hand or hold large blocks of securities hire strong boxes at the local banks, but win the new building is ready and all State departments are housed under one roof this will not be necessary.

While the State carries no insurance, the new vault will be so designed and built that it would take the lowest insurance rate. It will be fire and burglar proof and as near drill proof as it can be made, and will offer the greatest resistance to bombs and explosives or to mob attack.

The walls, floors and roof will be of finest concrete forty-eight inches in thickness, reinforced by an armor mat of high grade cold-drawn steel fabric. The doors will be of the circular type, two feet in thickness, with a time lock opened and closed with a concealed electric engine.

The day gate will be of hardened steel, equipped with a spring-bolt cylinder lock. A corridor will run all around it and mirrors will enable guards to see all sides. Three shifts of armed guards will be on duty every minute of the day and night. The expectation is that they will be former service men, former policemen and detectives.

Only accredited representatives of State departments will have access to the vault, and they will be triply identified by photographs, signature and fingerprints. State troopers, it is expected, will provide additional guards. Small vaults will be built into the structure for the use of departments in the Controller's, Banking and Insurance.

---
*When you think of Writing
Think of Whiting.
Whiting Paper Company.—Advt.*

Berry Ousts Two Chief Aids, Tammany Men; General Shake-Up of His Office Forecast

A general shake-up of the higher officials of the city's Finance Department was forecast yesterday when it became known that Deputy Controller John J. Sullivan and Hans P. Freece, chief of the Bureau of Law and Adjustment, had resigned at the request of Controller Charles W. Berry. Both are residents of Manhattan and Tammany men. The salary of the Deputy Controller is $10,000 a year and that of the place held by Mr. Freece $7,500.

"There is no scandal of any sort," General Berry said. "We had many differences of opinion regarding the conduct of the department. That is all. I thought that it would be better to release the two officials and fill their places with appointees with whom I can work in harmony."

Another Finance Department official who is prominent in Tammany denied that the requests for the resignations of the two men were aimed at Tammany or was due to the recent differences between the Controller and Mayor Walker over transit and bus policies.

Mr. Sullivan entered the employ of the Finance Department in 1924. He was chief of the Law and Adjustment Bureau until last January, when he was promoted to Deputy Controller by General Berry on recommendation of Tammany. The Law and Adjustment Bureau is considered one of the most important in the department. It handles negligence claims against the city and the claims of contractors, these claims amounting to millions of dollars annually.

General Berry said he was not ready to announce the successors to Messrs. Sullivan and Freece. Robert B. Jordan of 133 Cambridge Place has been put in Mr. Freece's place and it was said he might obtain a permanent appointment.

U. S. TO PAY FOR TIPS TRAPPING RUM BOATS

Clause of Tariff Act Allowing Percentage of Proceeds Up to $50,000 Is Invoked.

NEW SQUADS PATROL RIVERS

Forty Customs Inspectors on Prohibition Duty in Three Eight-Hour Shifts.

The Federal Government is prepared to pay tipsters for information leading to the seizure of rum boats. This was announced yesterday by Deputy Surveyor of Customs John McGill, who is in charge of the new harbor patrol of forty customs inspectors who were sworn in on Saturday as prohibition agents in General Lincoln C. Andrews's latest drive to dry up New York.

These inspector-agents who began patrolling the East, North and Harlem Rivers yesterday in three converted rum-runners which they will confiscate, the arrival of eight specially built speed boats ordered from Detroit, to attain their customs rank, although they are on the payroll of the prohibition department, and with it the right of search and seizure.

The patrol will work in three shifts of eight hours each and will devote its attention principally to attempts to land liquor from liners. While customs officials said yesterday that they were satisfied that no legitimate steamship company was helping in the work of unloading liquor at this port, they said a good sized rum fleet was being carried on by individual firemen and other men of the crews of various vessels. Already several seizures of considerable size have been made, the liquor in such cases usually being hidden beneath coal in the bunkers of liners. "And we will get more," Mr. McGill said yesterday.

Rewards Under Tariff Act.

In announcing that the Government was prepared to reward persons giving information leading to the seizure of rum boats, Mr. McGill said a similar practice had long been in effect in regard to gems and other things being smuggled into the country. The clause in the Tariff act of 1922 makes provision for such things, he said, and he quoted Section 619 under the heading "Awards and Compensations," which reads:

"Any person not an officer of the United States who detects or seizes any vessel, vehicle, merchandise or baggage subject to seizure and forfeiture under the customs laws and reports the same to an officer of the customs or who furnishes to any District Attorney, to the Secretary of the Treasury, or to any customs officer original information concerning any fraud upon the customs revenue, or a violation of the customs laws perpetrated or contemplated, which detection or information enables to a recovery of any duties withheld, or of any fine, penalty or forfeiture incurred, may be awarded and paid by the Secretary of the Treasury a compensation of 25 per centum of a net amount recovered, but not to exceed $50,000, which shall be paid out of the moneys appropriated for that purpose. For the purpose of this section any amount recovered under a bail bond shall be deemed a recovery of a fine incurred."

Old Rum-Runner in Use.

Among the converted rum-runners doing service with the new patrol is the Cigarette, formerly one of the fastest craft of the craft carrying liquor into this port. The auxiliary schooner U. S. Customs 417 is doing duty as mother ship for the new fleet and will serve as headquarters and repair base.

United States Attorney William A. De Groot in Brooklyn filed padlock proceedings yesterday for violation of the Volstead act against five former saloons and two restaurants. The saloons are at 2,902 Fort Hamilton Parkway, 1,420 Neck Road, 2,117 Utica avenue, 172 Troy avenue and 178 Richards Street. The restaurants are at 2,937 West Eighth Street, Coney Island, and 170 Hamilton Avenue.

Jean Schulman, 19 years old, a blond typist of 996 Herkimer Street, Brooklyn, was yesterday arraigned in the United States District Court in Brooklyn and charged with selling a quart of home-made liquor to Patrolman Nicholas Gaffney for $1 on July 19. She pleaded guilty and was fined $200, which her mother paid. Gaffney said he made the arrest after he had received complaints that the tailor shop owned by Miss Schulman's father was a "speakeasy."

Continued on Page Nine.

DEMANDS $45,000,000 IN ALUMINUM SUIT

G. D. Haskell Names Directors and J. B. Duke's Executors in Anti-Trust Action.

R. B. MELLON A DEFENDANT

Deal With Duke to Bar Plaintiff and Keep American Co. as a Monopoly Is Charged.

A suit for $45,000,000 against the Aluminum Company of America of Pittsburgh, seven members of its directorate and the executors of the late James B. Duke was filed here yesterday in the United States District Court by George D. Haskell of Springfield, Mass., President and director of the Bausch Machine and Tool Company.

Mr. Haskell alleges that the Aluminum Company of America now owns or controls substantially all the deposits of bauxite, the ore from which aluminum is manufactured, in this country, and that it also owns or controls large deposits in foreign countries.

He further charges that the defendant company has for many years maintained, and now maintains, a monopoly in trade and commerce in crude or semi-finished aluminum in the United States and that it is operating in restraint of trade in violation of the Sherman Anti-Trust law.

Agreement With Duke.

The bill of complaint sets forth that the plaintiff entered into an agreement with the late James B. Duke in 1924 by which they were to undertake the manufacture of aluminum in competition with the Aluminum Company of America.

Prior to this time, the complaint states, Mr. Duke had about completed a water-power development on the Saguenay River in the Province of Quebec. The plant cost $40,000,000 and generated 600,000 horsepower per annum.

The plaintiff says that for many years he had been preparing to enter into the manufacture and sale of aluminum and had ascertained facts regarding the existence of bauxite deposits in foreign countries which had not been acquired by the Aluminum Company of America. Mr. Duke's Saguenay River development and began negotiations with him for sufficient water power for a proposed enterprise.

Mr. Duke, the plaintiff says, was then offering the water power of his development at $12 per horsepower per annum, "a rate at which commercial production of aluminum and its importation and sale in and among the several States of the United States in competition with the defendant Aluminum Company of America was not only possible but carried with it a suggestion of great profits."

While these negotiations were being carried on, the plaintiff says, Mr. Duke was advised of the use the plaintiff planned to make of the water power and all the material facts with regard to the plaintiff's undertaking in the manufacture of aluminum.

Planned Saguenay Plant.

"Thereupon," the complaint says, "as the result of negotiations, an agreement was reached between the plaintiff and said James B. Duke that they should jointly undertake the establishment of an aluminum manufacturing business on the Saguenay River; the said James B. Duke to furnish said enterprise the water power and to assist in financing the enterprise; the plaintiff, on the other hand, to contribute to the joint enterprise his knowledge of the aluminum business, its processes of manufacture, location and availability of bauxite beds, and other facts which had resulted from the plaintiff's study of several years.

"The business itself, the object of their joint undertaking, was to be the manufacture of aluminum and its sale in commerce among the States of the United States and with foreign nations, and in competition with the Aluminum Company of America.

"In pursuance of said joint venture and as instrumentality in carrying it out, said James B. Duke caused the organization of the Quebec Development Company, Ltd., to be organized with a capital stock temporarily fixed at $1,000,000."

The complaint then says that the plaintiff at all times fulfilled his

Continued on Page Two.

VALENTINO PASSES WITH NO KIN AT SIDE; THRONGS IN STREET

Three Doctors and Two Nurses See "Film's Greatest Lover" Die After Long Coma.

MANAGER WEEPS IN HALL

Crowds Blocking Traffic, Held Back by Police Reserves, Rush to Funeral Church.

ASSOCIATES PAY TRIBUTES

Actor Dead at 31 Left Little of Huge Earnings—Arrangements for Funeral Yet Unmade.

Rudolph Valentino, motion picture actor, died at 12:10 o'clock yesterday at the Polyclinic Hospital where he had undergone a double operation for acute appendicitis and gastric ulcers on Aug. 15. He was thirty-one. His youthfulness and rugged constitution aided him in making a valiant fight even after his five doctors had given up hope. Peritonitis and septic endocarditis, an affection of the heart tissues, were the immediate causes of death.

When the end came, the street in front of the Polyclinic Hospital was blocked by thousands of the actor's admirers and the curious, awaiting the latest bulletins from his bedside. The hospital switchboard was swamped by endless calls from persons anxious for the latest news.

Valentino lost consciousness several hours before he died. Shortly before the end came, a priest was called and administered the last rites of the Roman Catholic Church.

Last Words Gave Cheer.

The actor closed his thoughts against death, almost to the end. His last rational words were spoken to Joseph M. Schenck, Chairman of the Board of Directors of the United Artists Corporation, who was at his bedside at 4 A. M.

"Don't worry, Chief," said Valentino. "I will be all right."

"Valentino smiled and said: 'I am looking forward to going fishing with you next month. I hope you have plenty of fishing rods. I'll see you in California.'"

Valentino said he felt no fortune from his very large earnings. Mr. Schenck said upon Valentino, said that the actor never gave up his thoughts of a vacation, so sure was he that he would conquer the complications which followed the operation.

"He passed peacefully," said Dr. Meeker. "He was asleep. He was going. At 2:30 this morning, he turned to me and said cheerily:

"'Doctor, do you know the greatest thing I am looking forward to?'

"'What is it?' I asked.

No Relatives at His Side.

Despite the fact that Valentino had been cited as an illustration of the fact that "all the world loves a lover," he died alone save for his three doctors and two nurses. His brother and sister are in Europe. His first wife, Jean Acker, remained in New York in order to be in constant communication with the sick bed, but was not at the hospital when Valentino died. His second wife, the former Natacha Rambova, is in Europe.

Pola Negri, who recently had been reported engaged to the actor, is in California. By long distance telephone she had made many inquiries concerning his condition. Her last call to the Polyclinic Hospital was at 4:25 A. M. yesterday. She tried to get the actor's manager, S. George Ullman, and failing in that, tried to communicate with others near Valentino for the latest information concerning him.

Unnerved by his long and patient vigil, Mr. Ullman was unable to remain in the anteroom before the end came. He had not slept for four nights and four days. He stood just outside the door so as to be near Valentino while the actor's life ebbed away. Mr. Ullman broke down when he was informed that Valentino was dead. Doctors ordered him to bed. Before withdrawing, he expressed appreciation of the solicitude shown for Valentino. He said:

"Mr. Valentino was greatly cheered during his last days by the thousands of messages sent him by his friends and motion picture admirers, and while he was too weak to read all of them, it was a great comfort to him

Continued on Page Two.

Friend Says Valentino Had Premonition of Dying Young

LOS ANGELES, Cal., Aug. 23 (AP).—Rudolph Valentino, who died today in New York, had a premonition of an early death and welcomed it in preference to living to a decrepit old age, it was revealed here today by John W. Considine, producer of his pictures.

Considine said: "Valentino several times remarked to me, 'I shall die young. I know it, and I shall not be sorry. I would hate to live to be an old man.'

"Valentino's prophecy has been fulfilled, but it has been a terrific blow to his friends. I found Rudolph a man of great courage and unquenchable spirit. He will be greatly missed."

COURT FINDING HALTS VOTE MACHINES HERE

Their Use in Fall Elections Is Doubtful, Knapp Contract Being Held Illegal.

ONLY HOPE LIES IN APPEAL

Justice Crain Finds Secretary of State Violated Charter in Acting as City's Agent.

Unless a decision by Supreme Court Justice Crain, handed down yesterday, is reversed by the higher courts before the November election, no voting machines paid for by the city's funds will be used here during the Fall balloting. This is the result of a ruling that the contract made by Secretary of State Florence E. S. Knapp, in behalf of the city, with the Automatic Registering Company of Jamestown, N. Y., is in violation of the city charter and constitutes a waste of city funds.

Justice Crain grants an injunction in the suit of Adolph Hill, a taxpayer, who alleged waste of city funds amounting to about $200 on each machine because of the manner in which the contract was let. The Court upholds this contention and finds that under the requirements for the purchase of city property the machines could have been bought for less money.

City's Opposition Lethargic.

Although the question was taken before the court in the guise of a taxpayer's action and it was made evident that it was in behalf of the Shoup Voting Machine Company, an unsuccessful bidder on the voting machine contract, who asserted that the terms were so drawn that only the Automatic Company's machine fulfilled the requirements, the members of the Tammany City Administration involved were not active in opposing it. Controller Berry, as disbursing officer of the city's funds, was made a main defendant with the Secretary of State, but, the argument before Justice Crain was presented by Deputy Attorney General Obermier in behalf of the Secretary of State.

Temporary Victory for City.

The result of the suit is a temporary victory for the city officials in opposing action by the State Legislature to compel the installation of voting machines in New York City. The bill requiring the city to buy and use them was passed four years ago, and contained a provision that if the city officials did not act the Secretary of State had authority to do so.

During the Hylan régime Commissioner of Accounts Hirshfield declared that the cost of the Jamestown machines was excessive by $200, and the Administration refused to buy.

Justice Crain's decision is based upon his findings that, although the Legislature succeeded in one respect in circumventing the New York City charter in empowering the Secretary of State to buy supplies for the city by making ineffective the charter provisions as to the purchase of "patriotic articles," the lawmakers failed to overcome other requirements as to making contracts for city supplies. Justice Crain accordingly said:

"It is conceded that the provisions of the charter were ignored by the Secretary of State in the making of the contract. She did that which the applicable charter provisions did not permit her to do, and omitted to do that which the applicable charter provisions required her to do. Her action was illegal and it will incidentally involve an outlay of money in excess of that which the city would have been called upon to make had the charter provisions been followed.

"The Secretary of State's motives for doing what she did are not involved

Continued on Page Two.

Berlins Plan Start for New York Tonight By Train, Mrs. Berlin Dreading Motor Ride

Special to The New York Times.

ALEXANDRIA BAY, N. Y., Aug. 23.—Irving Berlin, composer of jazz music, and Mrs. Berlin, the former Ellin Mackay, daughter of Clarence Mackay, who are sojourning in St. Lawrence Park, the guest of Mr. and Mrs. Max Winslow of New York, passed a quiet day. It is understood that they expect to leave by train tomorrow night for New York, taking a sleeper at Watertown or Syracuse. They motored to Alexandria Bay from Quebec. Mrs. Berlin, remained indoors today, but Mr. Berlin, with Mrs. Max Winslow, with his free indulgence of a game of golf on the Municipal Links, and went shopping in the village. Mr. Berlin, wearing white flannels and a silk shirt, turned in at the neck, said:

"We had a wonderful trip over on the ship. We are seeking now a rest and a little vacation. I am at peace with the world and I hope everybody is as happy as we are. We only want a chance to be happy and to be left alone."

Mr. Berlin said he had to get back to Broadway soon to begin work on a new musical glee. Mrs. Berlin is so weary from the long motor ride from Quebec that they shrink from the journey by motor to New York.

At Mr. Mackay's apartment at 29 West Forty-sixth Street it was said yesterday that no word had been received from him, and at the music publishing house the same information was given.

REPUBLICAN CHIEFS WILL CONFER TODAY ON GOVERNORSHIP

Wadsworth, Koenig and Morris to Discuss Candidates at Meeting in Saratoga.

KOENIG CONSULTS COOLIDGE

County Chairman Lays the New York Political Situation Before the President.

CROPSEY MEN RENEW HOPE

Leaders at Work Up-State to Win Convention Delegates Who Will Be "Harmonious."

Special to The New York Times.

PAUL SMITH'S, N. Y., Aug. 23.—Samuel S. Koenig, Chairman of the New York County Republican Committee, conferred with President Coolidge today on State politics, but their discussion did not result in determining who should be the party nominee for Governor this Fall.

Mr. Koenig left this afternoon for Saratoga, where he will meet tomorrow Senator Wadsworth and Chairman Morris of the Republican State Committee. The conference of these party leaders is expected to lead to more positive results on the Governorship.

The conferences held here with President Coolidge have been intended only to demonstrate that the President is vitally interested in the New York State affairs, and to help soften, if possible, the opposition of the drys, among whom the President is strong.

Cropsey and Hilles Lead List.

After today's conference between the President and Mr. Koenig Supreme Court Justice Charles J. Cropsey and Charles D. Hilles appeared to be leading the list from which the nominee for Governor will be selected. It was indicated that Justice Cropsey seemed to satisfy more sections of the State than others who had been considered, and that he would be acceptable to the party leaders if he agreed to enter the race.

In his half-hour conference with the President, who is greatly interested in the New York situation because of its national politics involved, Mr. Koenig told him that the Republicans would gain four members of Congress in Greater New York and the party would control the next delegation from the State.

Mr. Koenig also assured Mr. Coolidge that prosperity was going to be an issue favoring Senator Wadsworth's re-election, assuring him support from Democratic politicians, and who, asserted that the terms were so drawn that only the Automatic State Republican drys.

Mr. Coolidge is not interfering in any way in the New York politics, Mr. Koenig made it clear after the conference, but is interested in seeing that the Republicans increase their hold in Congress and retain the Wadsworth seat in the Senate. He will make no speeches in New York and do nothing to aid the party here, except what he may do before the November election in the way of a general statement on the trend of politics.

Mr. Koenig declined to commit himself on the Governorship, but admitted that Justice Cropsey seemed to be coming to the front. He said he felt that Cropsey, Attorney General Ottinger or Charles D. Hilles would make a strong stand-bearer in the State fight.

As to what the candidate would represent between the wets and drys, Mr. Koenig declared he would not be a wet.

Suggests Campaign Issues.

The candidate for Governor will be the creature of his own making, whatever may be the extravagance of the Smith Administration and the splendid record the Republican Legislature made last year," he said.

"The wet issue will figure only incidentally, but still as a live and vital question. There will be other economic matters that are going to appeal to the voters and, as the situation now stands, the Republicans enter the field with excellent chances.

"As for Senator Wadsworth, he will present the business prosperity brought about by the Republican Administration and stand on the accomplishments of his party. His chief appeal will not be modification of the Volstead amendment, but that and more far-reaching issues.

"I see no reason to feel that Mr. Wadsworth will be defeated. He is going to get a large vote in New York, much larger than the normal Republican vote. It will come from Democrats and ought to be large enough to overbalance his losses to the dry candidate for the Senate. There are thousands of dry Republicans, Democrats and independents who will fight for him to sustain the National Administration; then, too, the referendum will figure largely against the Republican Party on State issues.

"The Republicans will not wage their campaign on the sole issue of prohibition. Senator Wadsworth will discuss national issues, and the candidate for Governor will stress the failures of the Smith Administration and the work done by the last Legislature.

Won't Be "Tool of the Drys."

"This is the first campaign in years that the Republican organization has not had to carry the load of being the tool of the drys. The agitation against Senator Wadsworth up-State is going to help him in New York City. The more the drys declare they are going to beat him, the greater his strength will become among the wets, with a consequent weakening of the Democratic candidate for the Senate.

"The Republican will not wage their campaign on the sole issue of prohibition. Senator Wadsworth and the candidate for Governor will stress the failures of the Smith Administration and the work done by the last Legislature.

"If there is a well organized movement under way to defeat Representative LaGuardia of New York,

Continued on Page Two.

The New York Times.

THE WEATHER
Showers today and tonight, followed by clearing and cooler tomorrow.
Temperatures yesterday—Max. 70, min. 62.
For weather report see Page 46.

VOL. LXXVI....No. 25,080. ....

NEW YORK, FRIDAY, SEPTEMBER 24, 1926.

TWO CENTS In Greater New York | THREE CENTS Within 200 Miles | FOUR CENTS Elsewhere in the U. S.

TUNNEY WINS CHAMPIONSHIP, BEATS DEMPSEY IN 10 ROUNDS; OUTFIGHTS RIVAL ALL THE WAY, DECISION NEVER IN DOUBT; 135,000 PAY MORE THAN $2,000,000 TO SEE BOUT IN THE RAIN

FLORIDA CONSCRIPTS ALL ITS UNEMPLOYED TO CLEAR WRECKAGE

Police, Militia and Legion Round Up Men in Streets and Set Them to Work.

CALL ISSUED FOR LABORERS

Miami Wants 25,000 Men and Hollywood and Fort Lauderdale 2,000 Each.

LOSS PUT AT $165,000,000

Known Dead Now 365, With 1,100 Injured, 500 Seriously—Fight on Disease Goes On.

By WARREN IRVIN
Staff Correspondent of The New York Times.

MIAMI, Fla., Sept. 23.—Conscription of all unemployed persons to aid in clearing away wreckage and to speed the work of rehabilitating the Florida storm-swept area was adopted everywhere in that area today. Militiamen and police, aided by several hundred members of the American Legion who have been specially deputized, patrolled all streets and highways, apprehending all persons who could not show that they were employed and putting them immediately to work.

At the same time the city of Miami sent out a call for 25,000 laborers, and officials of Hollywood and Fort Lauderdale announced that they would employ 2,000 laborers in each city.

Mayor E. C. Romfh of Miami predicted this afternoon that within sixty days every trace of the storm's ravages will have been removed from Miami and the city will be as prosperous as ever.

Death Lists Called Inadequate.

Many here believe that the death list lacks scores of names of persons killed. A local newspaper man declared today that he made a check-up of bodies in the city and temporary morgues last Monday, at which time there were 175, but orders were given, he said, to bury the dead as quickly as possible, and many bodies were buried or shipped North for burial without any record being kept of them.

Even now it is almost impossible to get definite information as to the number of dead. The Police Department in Miami keeps no record of dead or injured and persons who inquire there are directed to the newspaper offices for information. Bodies are being taken to half a dozen different undertaking establishments and the only means of keeping a record is by constant checking up at undertaking establishments.

At Miami Beach the situation is still worse. No record was kept there for several days but yesterday the Publicity Director of the Chamber of Commerce was instructed to compile a list of dead and injured.

Hollywood and Fort Lauderdale are the only cities in which accurate records have been kept from the start.

Four new cases of typhoid at Davie, a village of 300 population five miles west of Fort Lauderdale, were reported today and caused health authorities to order the village evacuated. Water there is still several feet deep in spots.

Doctor News to Patients.

One doctor who was on duty thirty hours for seventy-two hours was compelled to row to a house in which a woman and three children were marooned. He said the demand for medicine liquor in the stricken area has caused the warehouse in Miami jail, where seized liquors are kept, to be emptied for the first time since this city became the bootleg distributing point for Florida.

In other sections, such as Hollywood, the police were sent out to raid all speakeasies and bootleg places, with orders to bring in seized liquors. For lack of a storm of protest arose from the church people when word got out that the doctors were using liquor for medicine.

The same doctor at Davie who rowed out to the home of the marooned woman was reported for "drunkenness," because a woman there said an smelled liquor on his breath, and in another case when he prescribed liquor for a woman who had been exposed to the wind and rain for several hours the woman's husband threatened to shoot him if "he dared give my wife a drop of liquor."

A flotilla of destroyers arrived today from the navy base at Charleston, bringing all the anti-typhoid serum available in that district. This amounted to several thousand units.

While City Health Officer Claxton of Miami reported an adequate supply on hand today, health officials at Miami Beach said they needed about 3,000 more units of anti-typhoid serum and about 500 units of anti-tetanus serum. Nearly 10,000 persons have been vaccinated in the Miami area.

One case of tetanus developed yesterday in Miami Beach and two in Hollywood. All available tetanus serums

Continued on Page Eleven.

North Carolinians Weave Homespun Suit for Walker

North Carolina mountaineers, reputed by novelists to be a hard-drinking and generally rough lot, are now sitting peacefully in their hillside homes spinning a new suit for Mayor Walker.

The addition to the Mayor's wardrobe will be made of gray homespun and will be presented to him by citizens of Asheville, who arrive on the "Land of the Sky" special train on Oct. 6 on a booster tour. The color will be gray—chosen by the Mayor himself.

When the delegation reaches the city it will go directly to the City Hall, where, with appropriate ceremony, the suit will be presented.

GENEVA CONFERENCE ADOPTS COURT PLAN

Right of Powers to Withdraw Approval of American Reservations Is Recommended.

NEW PROTOCOL NEXT STEP

United States Will Be Invited to Help Draft It—President's Action in Doub

Copyright, 1926, by The New York Times Company.
By Wireless to The New York Times.

GENEVA, Sept. 23.—With a single modification, the conference of signatories of the statute of the Permanent Court of International Justice adopted unanimously the conclusions concerning the American reservations which were presented this morning by its committee.

These conclusions were incorporated in "the final act of the conference," which was submitted for signatures.

The single modification concerned the fourth American reservation. The first part of the reservation provided for the withdrawal by the United States of adherence. The committee, to assure equality of treatment to all members, made the provision that the signatory States acting together and by not less than two-thirds majority should have a corresponding right to withdraw consent to the American reservations.

Modified by New Zealander.

On the proposal of Sir Francis Bell of New Zealand this provision was modified so as to extend only to the second paragraph of Reservation 4—by which statute the Court could not be amended without the consent of the United States—and Reservation 5 dealing with advisory opinions. The modification was made after a long debate in which it was agreed that any difficulties which might arise would be confined to the provisions covered by these reservations.

As it stands adopted, a decision by a two-thirds vote against the last points of the American reservations would not in any manner affect America's membership in the Court but only her prerogatives. The United States remains a full member, participating in the election of the Judges, paying her share of Court expenses and possessing the right to withdraw from the Court.

This modification followed a long series of compromises made between national dignity and resentment at the American demands on the one hand and the general desire to extend the influence and jurisdiction of the Permanent Court on the other. The effort made to meet the American demands was stressed by the President tonight in disavowing the conference.

The American reservations, he said, quoting Sir George Foster of Canada, comprised a legislative act by a State outside the League and Court and it would be very easy to say "no." But the conference had considered the difficulties were there to be overcome and nothing had been left undone to give satisfaction to the United States and assure her participation in the Permanent Court.

As to the fate of the conference's work nobody could know what this would be. But the spirit and manner in which the work had been done had proved in obvious manner its sincere desire to find a solution. The only thing that remained to be done was for the Governments to hasten their replies to the United States Government.

This part mentioned by the President and which had been evident on the part of the great majority of the delegations persisted in the debates today, though Canada and Sweden stood out against giving the United States more than equality.

Sir Francis Bell at the opening of the reading of the committee's conclusions this morning asked that all the provisions for withdrawal be dropped. This was not the personal demand of a delegate, he said, but a motion by a Government signatory of the statute of the Court. His Government wanted to see the United States come into the Court and stay in it.

Question of Samoa Raised.

Western Samoa, which was now under the flag of New Zealand, was

Continued on Page Sixteen.

CROWD ARRIVES SMOOTHLY

Throngs Ushered Into Philadelphia Stadium Without Confusion.

MANY NOTABLES ATTEND

Governors of Six States and Mayor Walker Among Long List of Officials.

OVER 75,000 FROM HERE

Trains Alone Carry That Number and Others Make the Trip by Automobile.

Special to The New York Times.

PHILADELPHIA, Sept. 23.—One hundred and thirty-five thousand persons, the largest crowd which ever attended a sports event in America, let out a roar when the referee placed the heavyweight crown on the head of Gene Tunney, which must have made the old Liberty Bell in Independence Hall quiver once more.

As the battle began and the heavyweights set to exchanging their jarring blows which rang with a "plop" audibly many rows back of the ring, they followed it with a roaring enthusiasm that only the greatest prize-fight crowd in history could produce.

From Stroudsburg, Pa., where Tunney trained for the three weeks, to Philadelphia the challenger took the shortest route. He winged above the silvery course of the Delaware River, winding through the Pocono Mountains, and landed at the navy yard in plenty of time to weigh in before the astonished eyes of the Pennsylvania State Boxing Commission.

Shortly before the main bout it was announced that the stadium had been completely sold out, breaking both attendance and receipt records. The paid admissions exceeded 130,000 and the gate receipts were over the two-million mark.

In addition to the paid admissions there were unpaid admissions amounting to $50,000 money value. Tex Rickard announced that he had purposely understated the crowd expected in order not to discourage possible last-minute purchasers of seats.

Crowd Is Well Handled.

Old-timers at the ringside who had seen every big fight since Fitzsimmons defeated Corbett said it was the most perfectly handled bout they had ever seen, for the huge concourse was ushered into the stadium without confusion.

The crowd, which had been cheering the preliminary fighters as they mauled each other to while away the spectators' time, broke into their first frenzy when Gene Tunney appeared in the path alongside the ring and began climbing up. The cheering was continuous from the moment he appeared. It broke into a single great outburst of yells, with shrill whistles from the thousands of lips sharpening it, as he entered the ring and went to his corner, smiling. In the ovation for Tunney there was perhaps a note of sympathy.

Dempsey entered a moment after Tunney, and another great roar went up. Plain began falling but nobody seemed to notice it, least of all the fighters as they squared away and the blows began to fly.

They were yelling madly for Gene as he began swinging into the champion with a force they had not dreamed the young challenger possessed. And when the first round ended with Tunney so unmistakably in the lead there was a minute of sheer delirium.

Women Shout Dismay.

They were at it again, and the voices of the women spectators now and again sounded out over all the frame of Tunney staggered under the blows of the infuriated champion. There were feminine shouts of dismay as well when Tunney shot a hard one at Dempsey.

As the fight settled down into a give and take and the surprise at Tunney's showing waned, the cries of encouragement and warning became an intermittent hum, punctuated by shouts as the blows landed or missed. The crowd was watching for the fine points now.

As one of the thinly padded flats struck its target of flesh with a whack a concerted groan went through the rows of onlookers.

"There was the nose," the crowd yelled as one of Gene's uppercuts brought blood on Dempsey's right cheek. "That fancy nose is a goner. Hit that and he's through."

The fourth round passed and the fifth began. The clamor of the crowd quieted a little, for it gave place to admiration that Tunney had lasted so long. The crowd was yelling for a good man with the same formula Tunney pushed Dempsey into the ropes.

Dempsey was fighting an unexpectedly good man and the crowd was with his enemy. Then the sixth round began, the round which had been set by the experts as the last one possible for Tunney to fight. The crowd was busing as Tunney went confidently from his corner.

A sigh of relief swept the stadium as Tunney emerged from it shaken but still strong, and there was a burst of applause as he took his seat. The old-time fight followers wagged their heads. "It's not the same old Dempsey," they said.

"He missed his chance right there," said somebody as Dempsey drove with all his dreadful strength at a point in space which Tunney had just left. "If that had landed we'd been on our way home."

And then a burst of women's cries

Continued on Page Three.

Dempsey's Share $850,000; Tunney to Receive $200,000

Special to The New York Times.

PHILADELPHIA, Sept. 23.—The receipts of the Dempsey-Tunney fight tonight were in excess of $2,000,000. On the basis of $2,000,000, the receipts were divided as follows:

Dempsey	$850,000
Tunney	$200,000
Federal Tax	$200,000
State	$100,000
Sesquicentennial	$200,000
Preliminary fights	$40,000
Tex Rickard, promoter	$410,000

AIRPLANE CARRIES TUNNEY TO SCENE

Challenger Is First to Make Way to Heavyweight Title Bout Through Air.

RISK DEPLORED BY MANY

Tunney, However, Is Calm Throughout—Calls Flying Least Trying on Nerves.

Special to The New York Times.

PHILADELPHIA, Sept. 23.—Not content with the prospect of facing Dempsey and destiny, Gene Tunney had to defy death, too. For the first time in the history of heavyweight championships, the challenger flew forth to the field of battle in an airplane.

From Stroudsburg, Pa., where Tunney trained for the three weeks, to Philadelphia the challenger took the shortest route. He winged above the silvery course of the Delaware River, winding through the Pocono Mountains, and landed at the navy yard in plenty of time to weigh in before the astonished eyes of the Pennsylvania State Boxing Commission.

Challenger Disdains Danger.

The utter distain Tunney displayed for the battle at hand, with the golden goal for which he has striven seven years in the balance, was unusual in itself. He disregarded entirely the fact that a tremendous gate, the greatest financial success in the history of sports, depended upon his appearance in the ring at the proper time. He laughed at the suggestion of danger which he was tempting. He continued in the same unperturbed, undisturbed, confident mood he had displayed from the start.

When the news spread that the challenger had taken to the air with the chance of his life only a few hours away there was a general outcry of disapproval. But there was no opportunity in which to make the challenger change his course. He had decided on his means of travel a week before and he kept it secret from every one, including his manager, Billy Gibson, and Tex Rickard.

The challenger slept late on his morning of destiny, facing the beckoning call of opportunity with the calmness of a child. He arose at 8 o'clock and relished a special breakfast at the Glen Brook Country Club in Stroudsburg, specially prepared by George Ransberry, his private chef. When he came forth into the misty morning he greeted the small crowd waiting to bid him farewell and godspeed in his quest for the coveted crown with the announcement that he was going to fly to Philadelphia.

Cheer Sends Him on Way.

There was gasps of amazement, and after a moment of surprised silence a cheer broke forth from the little knot of well-wishers.

Morton, the race driver, was waiting for the challenger with the motor running in a high-powered Duesenberg. Tunney climbed in beside the driver's seat and was speeded to the Shawnee Country Club at Buckwood Inn, about five miles away. There Jones and his Oriole awaited the coming of the precious passenger.

On arriving at the Buckwood Inn Gene was greeted by Reggie Worthington.

"Where's Casey?" asked the challenger.

"Oh, he's out playing golf," Worthington informed him.

"Say, I might play a couple of holes myself before I leave," Gene suggested in his matter-of-fact way, still calm and unexcited.

However, it was decided that the aerial expedition had better get under way, and Casey Jones was summoned from a bunker. He went over to a near-by shed and in a short time taxied out in a blood red sky chariot. Gene walked over to the third tee on the golf course, accompanied by a few friends and a few strangers who had been playing golf but had deserted their game on hearing that the challenger...

Continued on Page Two.

TUNNEY ALWAYS MASTER

Challenger Bewilders His Opponent With His Speed, Accuracy.

AGGRESSIVE IN ALL ROUNDS

Sends Rain of Whiplike Lefts Which Champion Cannot Avoid.

OUTCOME IS A SURPRISE

Dempsey Lacks All Evidence of His Old Aggressiveness—Victor Is Acclaimed.

By JAMES P. DAWSON.
Special to The New York Times.

RINGSIDE, SESQUICENTENNIAL STADIUM, Philadelphia, Sept. 23.—Gene Tunney is the new world's heavyweight champion. The ex-marine fought like a marine here tonight in the Sesquicentennial Stadium, when he carried off the decision over Jack Dempsey, once known as the Manassa Mauler and the ring's man-killer, in a ten-round bout which saw the first passing of a heavyweight championship title on a decision.

Through every round of the ten, Tunney battered and pounded Dempsey. He rained rights on the tottering champion's jaw and he bewildered Dempsey with his speed and the accuracy of a whip-like left hand which Dempsey could not evade. When the decision was announced, the crowd let loose a roar of acclaim for "the man of destiny," who had conquered the man-killer, and the countryside sent the roar echoing back.

Confidence Aids Tunney.

The transfer of the title, the ascension of Tunney to the pinnacle in boxing, surprised the majority of those who witnessed the fight and experienced followers of boxing form. It surprised everybody, almost, but Tunney, whose confidence, more than anything else, perhaps, carried him on to a height which the vast majority thought unattainable for him.

He was complete master, from first bell to last. He out-boxed and he out-fought Dempsey at every turn. Where it had been expected that Tunney would break and run before the vicious attack of Dempsey, the tiger man, Tunney, the fighting marine, not only failed to back up, but he went forward all the time with the instinct of the true leatherneck and hammered Dempsey in a driving attack which brooked no restraining effort on the part of the champion.

There was no question of the victor at the finish. There was no question of disapproval. But there was no opportunity in which to make the challenger change his course. He had decided on his means of travel a week before and he kept it secret from every one, including his manager, Billy Gibson, and Tex Rickard.

The challenger slept late on the morning of destiny, facing the beckoning call of opportunity with the calmness of a child. All the evidences of the old Dempsey were merely that; only faint evidences, indications, unexpressive flashes save for their expression of futility of helpless hopelessness, of utter ineffectiveness.

They fought this battle in the rain, a driving, torrential downpour which started when the men entered the ring and which increased in fury as the fight progressed. The ring was flooded, the spectators drenched and the gladiators were drenched, but as the fury of the storm increased so did the fighting of Tunney, and Dempsey had nothing with which to meet this Marine attack.

Knockdown Is Lacking.

It was a disappointing transfer of a heavyweight title in one respect. The battle did not end in a knockout. Indeed, through its ten rounds the struggle held not even a knock down; but aside from the fact that Tunney is a weak hitter in the sense that he is not a finishing or destructive hitter.

For the first time in the history of the old Dempsey fighting school. But the New York lad is a cunning hitter, a cruel, tantalizing, tormenting puncher and a cool, unruffled boxer at all times. He did about everything else to Dempsey but knock the defending champion down and out. He battered Dempsey to a pulp, until the beaten champion at the finish was a close resemblance to the giant Jess Willard, whom Dempsey pounded and hammered into a helpless hulk out on the shores of Maumee Bay seven years ago when he won the title. For the first time in Dempsey's career

Continued on Page Two.

GENE TUNNEY, THE NEW CHAMPION
Times Wide World Photo.

Champion Tunney Praises the Loser; "I Have No Alibis," Asserts Dempsey

Special to The New York Times.

SESQUICENTENNIAL STADIUM, PHILADELPHIA, Sept. 23.—The following statements were made after the bout tonight:

By GENE TUNNEY.

Dempsey fought like the great champion that he was. He has the kick of a mule in his fists and the heart of a lion in his breast. I never fought a harder socker nor do I hope to meet one. Dempsey fought like a gentleman and never took an unfair advantage in the ring. Once or twice he may have hit me a little low, but always it was by accident. He never meant it.

"I'm sorry," he always said following anything close to a foul blow. When the gong rang at the end of the fight he threw his arm over my shoulder and said: "Great fight, Gene; you won." I don't care what they may say about him he is certainly a man in the ring. The hardest blows I felt were two socks on the Adam's apple. That's why I'm so hoarse. I have no plans for the future, but am content to rest a while with the ambition I have nourished for seven years at last realized. The marines, you know, are always first to fight, and last to leave. No matter how heavy the going may be you will always find them there in the ring.

By JACK DEMPSEY.

I have no alibis to offer. I lost to a good man, an American—a man who speaks the English language. I have no alibis.

Story of the Fight by Rounds

Special to The New York Times.

RINGSIDE, SESQUICENTENNIAL STADIUM, PHILADELPHIA, Sept. 23.—The round by round detail of the Tunney-Dempsey bout tonight follows:

First Round.

Dempsey was attired in blue trunks and Tunney in purple. Dempsey looked rather thin as he stepped forward for a consultation.

As the round started Dempsey, with a scowl on his face, rushed out and drove Tunney to his own corner. Dempsey again rushed. Jack sent a terrific left to the jaw. Dempsey kept rushing for the jaw but missed. Gene stood up straight and jabbed lefts and rights to Jack's jaw. Gene put over a heavy right to the head and wrestled Jack back to the ropes. Tunney swung a hard right to Dempsey's chin. Dempsey weaved in again and Tunney was short with a right. They boxed in the centre of the ring for a moment, then Tunney missed a right for the head, but ripped two rights to the jaw. Dempsey jabbed Tunney away, but Gene jabbed again and sent a heavy right to the chin. In a terrific exchange Tunney showered left and right swings to Dempsey's jaw and Dempsey was groggy. Gene's only mark in the exchange was a bleeding mouth.

Between rounds Dempsey appeared very tired and his seconds worked hard over him.

Second Round.

Dempsey rushed over to Tunney's corner, trying to get his man. Dempsey swung his right to the jaw, but Tunney got out of the way. The old Tunney was in bad shape, but he continued to jab Jack away with a left. Jack's right was out with one of these lefts. Dempsey went in and sent two lefts to the jaw. Dempsey came through with a right to the body and drove Tunney to his corner. Jack drove Gene to a neutral corner and punished him about the head. Tunney sent two lefts to Jack's head. They wrestled across the ring, Dempsey pounding the body. Gene sent short rights and lefts to the

Third Round.

Dempsey came out slowly for the third and they met in the middle of the ring. Jack tried a terrific right for the jaw but missed. Gene stood up and jabbed Jack in mid-ring. He graced the chain-men's jaw and then landed a good right to Jack's jaw. Tunney jumped away and speared cleverly. Jack jumped over boring in. Jack came in only to be sent back to the ropes with rights and lefts to the jaw. Tunney sent another left to the head, but Jack punished him heavily in the body in return. As Jack came in Tunney ripped lefts and rights to the body at the bell.

Fourth Round.

Dempsey came out with a terrific rush and with a wild right aen; Tunney was almost over the ropes. Tunney was in bad shape, but he continued to jab Jack away with a left. Jack's was out with one of these lefts. Dempsey went in and sent two lefts to the jaw. Dempsey came through with a right to the body and drove Tunney to his corner. Jack drove Gene to a neutral corner and punished him about the head. Tunney sent two lefts to Jack's head. They wrestled across the ring, Dempsey pounding the body. Gene sent a heavy right to Jack's head and swung a heavy right to Jack's jaw. Dempsey was in bad shape and

Continued on Page Three.

VICTORY IS POPULAR ONE

Ex-Marine Gets Ovation as He Enters Ring—Crowd 'Boos' Foe.

BIGGEST IN SPORT HISTORY

Rickard's Luck Turns, However, and Distinguished Gathering Is Thoroughly Drenched.

DEMPSEY'S NOSE SUFFERS

Rebuilt for Movies, It Is Target of Challenger as He Piles Up Points for Victory.

By ELMER DAVIS.

RINGSIDE, SESQUICENTENNIAL STADIUM, PHILADELPHIA, Sept. 23.—While the rain poured down on the greatest crowd that ever saw a sporting event, Gene Tunney beat Jack Dempsey, and captured the world's heavyweight championship in a ten-round fight here tonight.

The champion, in the phrase of one of the ringside critics, won his title by a synthetic nose. It was by steady pounding away at the built-in black which Dempsey acquired a couple of years ago that Tunney piled up a heavy fighter from Greenwich Village could stand up and take it.

Though the experts and the gamblers thought, up to a minute before the fight, about 90 per cent. of the 130,000 people who saw the encounter were for Tunney. There was an uproarious cheer when the challenger entered the ring. He wore the scarlet trimmed blue dressing gown, with the Marine Corps emblem on the back, which was presented to him by old comrades of the Marine Corps. He climbed through the ropes at 9:30, and stood up to let the crowd see him.

Two minutes later the champion of the world came in. There was a scattering round of applause as he entered the ring, but when the proverbial Rickard luck had held, even against the weather. Though it rained in Philadelphia early this morning and heaps of dark clouds obscured the sky at nightfall, when the crowd began to gather in the stadium, the rain held off.

A dozen fight programs had rained on New York since the Summer, but it looked as if Rickard, with the biggest fight of the past three years and the biggest fight crowd and biggest gate of all time, was going to get away untouched.

Five preliminary bouts had gone on and the ring had been cleared for the entrance of the principals to the big event when the rain began at last. The amplifier announces the relayed Joe Griffo's statements to the farthest edges of the huge stadium had just announced three or four times that all persons in the audience were requested to keep their seats.

Suddenly all over the huge U-shaped cup of the permanent amphitheatre and the broad wooden expanse of the temporary seats, people stood up by thousands struggling into rain coats. Then they sat down again, grimly determined to stay to the finish, whatever the weather.

At the end, when the bleeding champion and the eager challenger were exchanging wallops before the bell, the ring was splashed and puddled, the crowd was drowned out, but everybody but Dempsey and his friends was happy.

All the predictions and expectations about this fight were upset. Dempsey had hoped to finish his opponent in one punch and expected to do it within seven

The comparatively few last ditch supporters who expected Tunney to win

Continued on Page Three.

The New York Times.

VOL. LXXVI....No. 25,262. ★★★★

NEW YORK, FRIDAY, MARCH 25, 1927.

TWO CENTS In Greater New York | THREE CENTS Within 200 Miles | FOUR CENTS Elsewhere in the U.S.

AMERICANS AND BRITISH KILLED IN ATTACKS AT NANKING; WARSHIPS THEN SHELL CITY AND RESCUE SOME FOREIGNERS; ALLIED COMMANDERS SERVE ULTIMATUM; ALL CHINA AFLAME

DEAF TO LAST APPEAL REPUBLICANS KILL SMITH POWER BILLS

He Promises Veto in Special Message Asking That Decision Be Left to People.

BAUMES FENCE BILL DIES

Pistol Measure Is Saved After Defeat—Tammany Members Less Hostile.

CHARGES ROUSE ASSEMBLY

Host of Acts Are Passed as Noon Today Is Set for Final Adjournment.

Special to The New York Times.

ALBANY, March 24.—In a final drive to clear their calendars preparatory to final adjournment tomorrow noon, the Senate and Assembly labored all day, disposing of approximately 250 bills, of which less than a dozen were defeated.

Among the notable measures that were passed were the constitutional amendment providing for the creation of the Executive budget system in the State, a Smith program proposal adopted in the Senate, and the Friedsam bill providing for State contributions aggregating $16,500,000 for the common schools throughout the State, with a little more than $10,000,000 of the total going to New York City, approved in the Assembly.

The Senate amended the Assembly resolution, which in its original form called for final adjournment on March 18 so as to provide for adjournment sine die at noon tomorrow. The resolution was sent back to the Assembly for approval of the amendment, but up to the time of adjournment this evening the lower house had not concurred. There is no doubt, however, that the curtain will fall over the 1927 session some time tomorrow.

Smith Power Bill Defeated.

Defeat in the Assembly of the Governor's Power Authority bill and his measure providing for a referendum on water power in the election this year and passage of the Republican Water Power bill by a party vote in the lower house, in concurrence with the Senate, which has already approved the bill, were other outstanding features of the day.

The action on the Governor's bill was taken despite an urgent appeal made by the Chief Executive in a special message that the Legislature pass the referendum bill and let the voters determine whether the State or private interests should develop the hydroelectric resources of the State. The Governor will veto the Republican power bill.

Discussion of Baumes anti-crime bills in the Assembly provoked a bitter and prolonged debate, which ended in a second defeat for the so-called "fence" bill, which would legalize testimony by a thief against receivers of goods he had stolen. Considerable progress was made on legislation of this series, however, eight measures being passed. One, the so-called "Pistol bill," was snatched from defeat after it had been beaten.

Measures Passed by Both Houses.

Measures upon which favorable action was taken today and in which both houses have concurred include:

The executive budget constitutional amendment.

The constitutional amendment providing for an increase to $25,000 in the Governor's salary and increases for Lieutenant Governor and lawmakers; the tri-State Delaware River compact.

Bills Passed by Senate.

New York City Grade Crossing Elimination bill.

Hickey bill to discourage child marriages.

Westchester Charter.

Bill to license operators at milk-gathering stations.

Lease of Ward Island in part by New York City to be used for establishment of a sewage disposal plant.

Passed by the Assembly.

Friedsam bill appropriating $16,500,000 for additional State aid to public schools.

Republic water power bill providing for a commission to investigate and recommend a State development policy.

Measures Defeated.

Governor Smith's power authority and water power referendum bills.

The Baumes series bill to legalize testimony of thiefs against receivers of stolen goods.

Democratic resolution proposing an amendment to the Constitution which would permit the State to sell or cede the Barge Canal to the Federal Government.

Continued on Page Four.

---

14 Big Atlantic Liners Race For Spring Tourist Rush Here

Copyright, 1927, by The New York Times Co.
By Wireless to The New York Times.

LONDON, March 24.—The pick of the great Atlantic liners are racing to catch the Spring tide of American tourists headed for Europe. Fourteen of the vessels sailing between New York and English ports will be on the high seas almost at the same time during the next ten days.

The Majestic and the France sailed westward yesterday. The President Roosevelt and the Antonia will sail tomorrow. The Berengaria, Washington, Ascania, Cedric, Aurania and Minnewaska will sail on Saturday. Closely following will be the Leviathan, Homeric, Lancastria, New York and Mauretania.

SAPIRO CUTS OUT 54 OF ALLEGED LIBELS

Court Tentatively Accepts New Basis of Suit, Refusing Long Recess to Study It.

LAWYERS BATTLE OVER IT

Defense Suggests a Mistrial—Court Bars Questions on Ford Ordering Attacks on Jews.

From a Staff Correspondent of The New York Times.

DETROIT, March 24.—The Aaron Ford libel trial produced several developments today. The first was Aaron Sapiro's elimination of 54 of the 141 libels he had alleged against Henry Ford and the Dearborn Publishing Company. The second was the vain attempt of the plaintiff to show that Mr. Ford motivated an attack on Mr. Sapiro as part of a general onslaught aimed at his race.

The alleged libels which went out of the case were dropped in the amended declaration which William H. Gallagher, counsel for Mr. Sapiro, handed to Federal Judge Fred M. Raymond. The declaration, which sets forth the grounds upon which the suit is based, was criticised by the Court several days ago. In the opinion of Mr. Gallagher, the form submitted today simplified and consolidated his case. Senator James A. Reed and others of the Ford counsel regarded the elimination as a victory.

When the document was tendered Stewart Hanley, who has been most active on the Ford firing line, demanded time in which to study it. He said that the cursory examination he had given it persuaded him that the new declaration altered the whole case. It was possible, he said, although he had no thought of recourse to such a procedure, that the new form might necessitate a mistrial. Mr. Gallagher minimized the importance which the defense attached to the new declaration.

Editorial Is Deleted.

One of the alleged libels which Mr. Sapiro took out voluntarily dealt with an editorial in The Dearborn Independent, published after the series containing the alleged libels, in which the Chicago attorney was accused of unprofessional conduct and pictured as a "cheat" and "fraud" and "grafter" and "faker" and "mountebank." Mr. Gallagher said Mr. Sapiro was not mentioned in the editorial and, further, it was not part of the series which he contends were anti-Jewish. Mr. Hanley countered by saying that the defense had been ready to prove the truth of the editorial, and that the concluding paragraph of the editorial had named Mr. Sapiro.

Mr. Hanley asked that the trial be adjourned to Monday so that he and his associates could readjust their lines of defense, if necessary. Mr. Gallagher opposed that. Judge Raymond, who observed that there had been little "visible progress" in the case, although many issues had been clarified which would result in progress later, settled the matter by adjourning from 10 A. M. to 2 P. M. He then said that he would accept the amended declaration tentatively.

The Court explained that he provisionally accepted the document so that the taking of testimony by William J. Cameron, editor of The Independent, could go on. He gave tentative approval to all of the declaration except one clause. He struck that out. This paragraph sought to establish that the periodical, by earlier attacks on Mr. Sapiro's coreligionists, had made the word "Jew" a word of contumely, hate and opprobrium in the minds of The Independent's 800,000 readers.

Amended Basis Taken Up First.

The matter of amended basis of suit was the first order of the session when court convened at 9:30 A. M. Judge Raymond had indicated that he felt the document was insufficient in some of its counts, mixing certain single phrases lifted from their context, had been cited as libels. Mr. Gallagher and his associates, Judge Robert F. Marx and Walter F. Lynch, had been revising it since the Judge indicated his opinion. As Mr. Gallagher

Continued on Page Twenty-four.

POISONED WHISKY IN SNYDER HOME BARES EARLY PLOT

Scheme That Failed Revealed by Gray and Chemist Finds Bichloride of Mercury.

NO TRACE IN VICTIM'S BODY

Dr. Gettler Says 20 Tablets Must Have Been Used—To Seek Other Drugs Today.

TRIAL IS SET FOR APRIL 11

Newcombe Would Try Both at Once and Will Ask Death Penalty—Woman Protests Her Innocence.

To check up a statement made by Henry Judd Gray that Mrs. Ruth Brown Snyder had tried to poison her husband some time before the murder last Sunday morning, the police took a bottle of whisky from the Snyder cellarette yesterday to Dr. Alexander O. Gettler, city toxicologist, at Bellevue Hospital.

"There were several bottles in the cellarette, but the chemist was asked to analyze only the one which had been described by Gray as containing the poison, said to be bichloride of mercury.

As soon as the Snyder whisky bottle was handed to him with the explanation, Dr. Gettler heated up a shining copper wire, dipped it in hydrochloric acid and thrust it in the whisky.

This is the ordinary quick test for bichloride of mercury. If it is present, the mercury deposits on the copper in minute globules. Usually a microscope has to be used to detect the deposit.

After leaving the copper wires in the whisky for half an hour, Dr. Gettler removed it.

Wire Thickly Coated.

"Great Scott," he exclaimed. The copper wire seemed to be silverplated. There was no need of using the microscope, so thickly was the wire coated with quicksilver (mercury).

"Enough bichloride of mercury was put into that bottle of whisky to kill any man who took one good drink of it," said Dr. Gettler.

Four other copper wires were then heated and dipped into hydrochloric acid. One was inserted into the stomach contents of the murdered man. The others were placed in contact separately with grain, kidney and liver tissue.

After half an hour they were removed. Their appearance was still that of ordinary copper wire. Each wire was examined under the microscope. No globules of quicksilver were found.

"This shows that Snyder had not touched the poisoned whisky recently," said Dr. Gettler. "It has nothing to do with his death. It is possible that he might have tasted the liquor at some time in the past. Mercury, however, remains in the system for some time. We would find traces in the organs probably for two months if he had swallowed any of the whisky with mercury in it."

Dr. Gettler did not have an opportunity yesterday to measure the quicksilver quantitatively, but the evidence of the thickly coated wire made it certain that a large quantity of bichloride of mercury had been used.

"Possibly twenty tablets or more were dissolved in it," said Dr. Gettler. It is probable that the poisoner or poisoners overshot the mark in putting so many mercury tablets in the whisky as to give it a noticeable taste. Whether he was suspicious of the flavor

Continued on Page Nine.

Soviet Warned on Propaganda Hurting Stage as Church Rival

MOSCOW, March 24 (P).—Mikhail Tomsky, Chairman of the All-Russian Council of Trade Unions, has warned the Soviet authorities that theatres in Russian villages and towns will not keep the people from the churches unless something more than propaganda is offered to entertain audiences.

"Performances in our playhouses must be artistic, esthetic creations, designed to appeal to the taste and pocketbooks of the workers," he declares. "They must be more than propaganda vehicles."

TONGMEN KILL NINE AS WAR FLARES ANEW

Two Chinese Slain in Brooklyn Restaurant While 250 Are Dining There.

KILLINGS OCCUR IN 6 CITIES

27 Bullets Fired Into Man at Newark—Banton Warns He Will Start Deportations.

Chinese tong warfare flared anew yesterday over the eastern part of the United States after a peace of two years between the On Leong Tong and the Hip Sing Tong, and last night nine Chinese had been killed and two wounded in six different cities. The police arrested forty-five.

In Chicago one man was killed early yesterday morning in a crowded restaurant. In Newark a Chinese from Boston was riddled with bullets in the early morning. Cleveland and Pittsburgh each had one murder during the early hours of the day and in Pittsburgh a second Chinese was wounded.

In New York's Chinatown there was an air of fear and mystery yesterday morning and there were an unusual number of uniformed patrolmen and detectives. There were more police than Chinese on the three streets of Chinatown. On the "bloody angle" of Doyers and Pell Streets a single uniformed policeman remained alone most of the day.

Tongmen Out of Sight.

The ornate building of the On Leong Tong on Mott Street was deserted and the leaders of that organization congregate elsewhere. The Hip Sings gathered at 15 Pell Street in a room behind a darkened laundry. The once quiet alley between Pell and Mott Streets was again drawn, and few if any Chinese turned from one street into the other.

Two years ago, almost to the day, the two tongs signed a peace pact. It was hailed with relief by the police and with rejoicing by the Chinese. It was to last "for all time" it was said, though the skeptical who knew the nature of the two tongs and grave doubts. The success of one tong means the decay of the other. Each is jealous, suspicious and watchful of the other.

According to the reports yesterday in Chinatown, the renewal of the warfare was started by the shooting in Chicago of Dan Chin Pock, found shot to death in a gambling house in Chicago's Chinatown. Chin, the gray goss, belonged to the On Leong Tong. A few months ago he resigned and joined the Hip Sings. Recently he reversed the process, going back to the On Leongs. The Hip Sings called him a spy and a traitor. He died in Tom Jack's Chinese gambling house Wednesday night, and by morning Hip Sings had been killed in Brooklyn, Newark and elsewhere, another On Leong man was dead in Pittsburgh and a large part of

Continued on Page Three.

WASHINGTON ACTS QUICKLY

Orders More Cruisers to China and Gives Admiral Fullest Backing.

GRAVE MESSAGES RECEIVED

Nanking Incident and Unrest Elsewhere Taken Seriously by Officials.

NO LIGHT ON CASUALTIES

Admiral Hough Simply Reports Some Americans Were Slain on Socony Hill.

Special to The New York Times.

WASHINGTON, March 24.—News of the serious incident at Nanking reached Washington early today, when Admiral Charles S. Williams, Commander-in-Chief of the Asiatic Fleet, reported that a "number" of American civilians had been killed and wounded in an attack by Cantonese troops on Socony Hill in that city.

Rear Admiral Harry H. Hough, ranking American naval officer at Nanking, said in his official report. "It is feared that the number of dead is large."

Admiral Hough and the British ranking naval officer on the cruiser Emerald then served an ultimatum on the Chinese General, demanding:

First—The immediate protection of all foreigners and foreign property.

Second—The reporting on board of the Cantonese General in command at Nanking before 11 o'clock the night of March 24 (Chinese time) to negotiate respecting the outrages committed.

Third—That all foreigners must be brought to the bund under escort by 10 o'clock the morning of March 25 (Chinese time), which is 9 o'clock New York time tonight.

If the demands of this ultimatum were not complied with, Admiral Hough reported to Admiral Williams, Nanking would be treated as a military area. This meant, according to naval officials today that Nanking could no longer have immunity from enemy attack under the protection of international law, accorded to unfortified cities.

President Coolidge and the Government at Washington, shocked at the sudden turn of events at Nanking, intend to back up Admiral Williams and Hough "100 per cent." Secretary Wilbur asserted this afternoon.

"Admiral Williams," Mr. Wilbur added, "has full authority to use all the forces under his command at his discretion for the protection of American lives and property. That I have probably said before, but I wish to reiterate it now. He has been given from time to time all the forces he has requested."

At Admiral Williams's request three cruisers were ordered at once from Honolulu to join his forces.

No fresh instructions were sent to the Admiral because he needed none, having, from the beginning, been clothed with the widest authority to act in any emergency threatening the lives of Americans in China.

Late tonight Admiral Williams sent word that the destroyers Perry, Ford and Pillsbury were proceeding to Nanking from Manila. In addition other destroyers, not yet designated, have been ordered from Manila to Swatow, Amoy and Foochow, one destroyer to each port.

Williams's Report in Summary.

The Navy Department issued this summary of the messages from Admiral Williams, which also contains the text of the report from Admiral Hough:

Foreigners on Socony Hill were attacked. British cruiser Emerald and the United States destroyers Noa and Preston shelled the area around the hill to protect the foreigners, opening fire about 3:30 P. M. Landing forces were sent to attempt the rescue of foreigners from the hill. The commander of the Yangtze patrol force, Rear Admiral H. H. Hough, U. S. N., arrived in the U. S. S. Isabel at 6:30 P. M. and the following dispatch has been received from him through Admiral C. S. Williams, U. S. N., commander-in-chief of the Asiatic fleet, who has forwarded the entire dispatch to the Navy Department:

"At 5 P. M. the Preston and the Noa ceased heavy gun fire and the cruiser Emerald sent a landing force to a wall under the Standard Oil house, while the Emerald covered with shrapnel and the Noa and the Preston cleared the bund and far shore of snipers by firing from the ships.

"The landing forces successfully brought off all the foreigners from the Standard Oil house, including the American Consul and his family and all American naval personnel.

Continued on Page Two.

Calls on Gov. Smith to Give His Views On Allegiance to His Church or State

A statement from Governor Alfred E. Smith setting forth his views regarding the jurisdiction of the Roman Catholic Church, of which he is a member, is asked by Charles C. Marshall, a lawyer of this city, in an open letter to the Governor published in the April number of The Atlantic Monthly. The Governor is asked to state what would be his views in case of possible conflict regarding jurisdiction between the Church and the American Government.

Saying that letters of various Popes made it clear that the Church holds that it has divine ecclesiastical power and that, while it concedes secular power to the State, it remains the judge in its own opinion as to what constitutes secular power, Mr. Marshall contends that the Roman Catholic who hesitates to challenge the peace and safety of the State? Nothing will be of greater satisfaction to those of your fellow-citizens who hesitate to their endorsement of your candidacy because of religious issues involved than a disclaimer by you of the convictions here imputed or such an exposition by others of the questions here presented as may justly turn public opinion in your favor.

cites the recent annulment of the Marlborough marriage as a case in point. Mr. Marshall also cites the beatification in 1886 of John Felton, an Englishman, who was convicted of treason in 1570. Felton's offense, three centuries and a half ago, was the posting on the walls of London of the decree to Pope Pius V deposing Queen Elizabeth.

"The honors paid him were rendered 300 years after his treasonable act," Mr. Marshall says, "according to the letter in the city. There lies their sinister import. They are no part of the medieval milieu; they belong to the modern world and must have judgment not by medieval but by modern standards.

"Is the record of the Roman Catholic Church in England, sir, in your opinion, consistent with the peace and safety of the State?

More British Troops at Shanghai And Foreign Defenses There Hold

American Marines, Used Only in Emergency, Chafe for More Active Part—Cantonese Split—Pledges to Restore Order Unfulfilled.

By FREDERICK MOORE.

Copyright, 1927, by The New York Times Company.
Special Cable to The New York Times.

SHANGHAI, March 24. — Some Americans here are complaining of the inactivities of the American marines and have started a circular letter, to which foreigners other than the British are readily affixing their signatures, thanking the British for protecting their lives and properties. Ever since their arrival the marines have been anxious to land and participate in the preparations for the defense, but have been restrained aboard their vessels and have not placed a single sandbag or a single reel of barbed wire in position. Finally, when a state of emergency was declared, they came ashore as soon as possible, but six hours after the British and French were in position.

They were then permitted only patrol duty, not even police service. They were not permitted to search for Chinese suspects and not permitted to break up menacing gatherings. Consequently they only paraded the streets in the safer interior sections of the city.

This was commented on as not being adequate defense of American lives and property and neither did they nor civilian Americans profess that it was.

American volunteer soldiers and policemen did not serve under American command. Both of these contingents gladly accepted dangerous orders from the British police chief and commanding officer.

Marines Anxious for Action.

The marines themselves are anxious for more active duty. They themselves point out that had the British not held the lines they would have been required to shoot down many Chinese, civilians as well as soldiers, inside the settlement and would have been looted and burned out. They would have been unable to keep the slaughter to a minimum.

Yesterday the marines at the request of the British twice sent detachments, a score of men with two machine guns, into the defenses, immediately withdrawing them in each case after the emergency terminated. In neither case, nor at any other time, have they fired a shot.

I tell this only to contradict exaggerated reports that may have gone to the United States.

Shoot Only in Last Extremity.

The marines have been fully instructed, like the British, not to fire except in the last extremity. I, myself, standing behind a Durham battalion machine gunner in a sandbagged emplacement, witnessed the self-control of the British. An unofficered group, of whom forty were defeated Northerners, with guns and pistols in hand, seemed to charge across the open space. The machine gunner aimed, but held fire till the defeated Northerners were within twenty-five feet of him. The Shantungese

Denies Handicapping Marines.

Special to The New York Times.

WASHINGTON, March 24.—Positive denial that American marines at Shanghai are in any way handicapped by orders from Washington was obtained tonight from officials in authority when their attention was called to the reported complaint of

Continued on Page Two.

Reports Conflict on Americans Left in Nanking; Shanghai Hears of Negotiations for Release

By The Associated Press.

SHANGHAI, Friday, March 25.—Conflicting messages early this morning from the City of Nanking, where a number of foreigners, including Americans, were killed and wounded by Cantonese shelling yesterday, left the fate of a portion of the American community there in doubt.

Prior to yesterday's shelling of Socony Hill, which resulted in counterfire by British and American warships, it was known that 155 Americans, consisting of 90 men, 45 women and 20 children, were ashore. Some of those remained, despite the landing of a rescue party made up of American and British forces, who succeeded in removing most of the foreigners.

Other messages from Nanking this morning, however, told of further rescue efforts, which resulted in the rescue and evacuation of all the remaining foreigners, only after further casualties, including some Americans. These messages reported that British and American landing parties approached Socony Hill under renewed fire from the Cantonese, but ultimately rescued all the foreigners.

Nevertheless reports received from Nanking at 5 A. M. said that the fate of 155 Americans was still unknown. There were some Britishers also ashore and the Anglo-American authorities were attempting to negotiate with the Cantonese to effect the rescue of the remaining foreigners without further bloodshed, such as occurred yesterday.

The Americans ashore at Nanking are those who failed to reach the Socony compound. It is believed that they remained at mission centres which are widely separated within Nanking walls. All who reached the Socony compound were believed to have been brought out.

JOINT FORCES ARE LANDED

Parties From Ships Fight Way to Socony Hill to Reach Nationals.

CHINESE FIRE ON RESCUERS

Cantonese Sympathizers Attack Foreign Consuls, Drive Them Out and Loot Offices.

ANTI-FOREIGN SPIRIT GROWS

Our Consul General Appeals Again to Americans in Interior to Go to Shanghai.

By FREDERICK MOORE.

Copyright, 1927, by The New York Times Company.
Special Cable to The New York Times.

SHANGHAI, March 24.—In view of the news from Nanking, Hankow, Wuhu and other Yangtze River and neighboring coast ports, all showing that the Nationalists' success at Shanghai has emboldened them to further assaults upon foreigners, American Consul General Clarence E. Gauss is broadcasting tonight signals summoning all Americans in Shanghai immediately for refuge.

It is evident that Bolshevist propaganda has succeeded in its effort to inflame the Chinese and to embolden them against the foreigners, and, as one success follows another, it is impossible to foresee the conclusion.

Today one of the first acts of the Nationalists entering captured Nanking was to assault the British, American and Japanese Consuls, as well as other foreigners. Only a partial number of these escaped through the courageous dash of a joint British-American naval landing force. There were 45 women, 20 children and 90 men, totaling 155 Americans, left in an unknown fate, besides other foreigners, whose numbers are unobtainable.

No Word of New Attempt.

A series of brief naval wireless messages to the British, American and Japanese warships stationed here told the tale, but said nothing about another effort to relieve the surrounded foreigners tomorrow.

The Nanking news has been daily becoming more serious. Pieced together the story is approximately as follows:

For several days the Northerners, with little fighting, have been falling back upon Nanking, because it is the crossing place to the railway leading back to Shantung. Without the customary warning to civilians, the Southerners, following them, shelled the city.

There were not enough vessels for the Shantungese to recross the river, and they were compelled to fight or surrender to possible decapitation. Consequently the city, inside and outside the walls, became a battleground. The Northerners pillaged at will, but did not attack the foreigners. The incoming Nationalists, however, did not hesitate to attack the consulates today. They killed a Briton, Dr. Smith; wounded the British Consul, Giles, and drove American Consul Davis with his wife and his children from the American Consulate.

A small group of foreigners accompanied by a few American sailors who were protecting the consulate sought safety in the Standard Oil compound immediately inside the city walls, at a point a few miles from the river, but they were unable to escape.

Warships Open Fire.

Evidently the sailors signalled the American destroyers Noa and Preston and the British cruiser Emerald, which created a barrage of shells around the Standard Oil compound, to keep off the assailants, simultaneously landing a joint American and British force, which, it is believed, crossed sunken creek and moat, finally getting the foreigners down over the city walls and retrieving them, one by one. Altogether it was several miles back and forth to the destroyers.

It reported erroneously yesterday that the American destroyers had left for Shanghai with their 145 American refugee women and chil-

---

The New York Times.

THE WEATHER
Generally fair today and tomorrow; moderate to fresh southerly winds.
Temperature yesterday—Max., 60; Min., 52.
For weather report see Page 31.

Section 1

VOL. LXXVI....No. 25,320. ● ● ●   NEW YORK, SUNDAY, MAY 22, 1927.   *Including Rotogravure Picture Section in three parts; Section and Book Sections in Rotogravure*   FIVE CENTS *In Manhattan* Bronx and Brooklyn *Elsewhere* TEN CENTS

LINDBERGH DOES IT! TO PARIS IN 33½ HOURS; FLIES 1,000 MILES THROUGH SNOW AND SLEET; CHEERING FRENCH CARRY HIM OFF FIELD

COULD HAVE GONE 500 MILES FARTHER

Gasoline for at Least That Much More

Flew at Times From 10 Feet to 10,000 Feet Above Water.

ATE ONLY ONE AND A HALF OF HIS FIVE SANDWICHES

Fell Asleep at Times but Quickly Awoke—Glimpses of His Adventure in Brief Interview at the Embassy.

LINDBERGH'S OWN STORY TOMORROW.

Captain Charles A. Lindbergh was too exhausted after his arrival in Paris late last night to do more than indicate, as told below, his experiences during his flight. After he awakes today, he will narrate the full story of his remarkable exploit for readers of Monday's New York Times.

By CARLYLE MACDONALD.
Copyright, 1927, by The New York Times Company.
Special Cable to THE NEW YORK TIMES.

PARIS, Sunday, May 22.—Captain Lindbergh was discovered at the American Embassy at 2:30 o'clock this morning. Attired in a pair of Ambassador Herrick's pajamas, he sat on the edge of a bed and talked of his flight. At the last moment Ambassador Herrick had canceled the plans of the reception committee and, by unanimous consent, took the flier to the embassy in the Place d'Iena.

A staff of American doctors who had arrived at Le Bourget Field early to minister to an "exhausted" aviator found instead a bright-eyed, smiling youth who refused to be examined.

"Oh, don't bother; I am all right," he said.

"I'd like to have a bath and a glass of milk. I would feel better," Lindbergh replied when the Ambassador asked him what he would like to have.

A bath was drawn immediately and in less than five minutes the youth had disrobed in one of the embassy guest rooms, taken his bath and was out again drinking a bottle of milk and eating a roll.

"No Use Worrying," He Tells Envoy.

"There is no use worrying about me, Mr. Ambassador," Lindbergh insisted when Mr. Herrick and members of the embassy staff wanted him to be examined by doctors and then go to bed immediately.

It was apparent that the young man was too full of his experiences to want sleep and he sat on the bed and chatted with the Ambassador, his son and daughter-in-law.

By this time a corps of frantic newspaper men who had been madly chasing the flier, following one false scent after another, had finally tracked him to the embassy. In a body they descended upon the Ambassador, who received them in the salon and informed them that he had just left Lindbergh with strict instructions to go to sleep.

As Mr. Herrick was talking with the reporters his son-in-law came downstairs and said that Lindbergh had rung and announced that he did not care to go to sleep just yet and that he would be glad to see the newspaper men for a few minutes. A cheer went up from the group who dashed by Mr. Herrick and rushed upstairs.

Expected Trouble Over Newfoundland.

In the blue and gold room, with a soft light glowing, sat the conqueror of the Atlantic. He immediately stood up and held out his hands to greet his callers. THE NEW YORK TIMES correspondent being first to greet him.

"Sit down, please," urged every one with one voice, but Lindbergh only smiled again his famous boyish smile and said:

"It's almost as easy to stand up as it is to sit down."

Questions were fired at him from all sides about his trip across the ocean, but Lindbergh seemed to dismiss them all with nonchalant answers.

"I expected trouble over Newfoundland because I had been warned that the situation there was unfavorable. But I got over that hazard with no trouble whatsoever."

Sleet and Snow for 1,000 Miles.

"However, it wasn't easy going. I had sleet and snow for over 1,000 miles. Sometimes it was too high to fly over and sometimes too low to fly under, so I just had to go through it as best I could.

"I flew as low as 10 feet in some places and as high as 10,000 in others. I passed no ships in the daytime, but at night I saw the lights of several ships, the night being bright and clear."

Everyone then wanted to know if the flier was most sleepy on the voyage.

"I didn't really get what you might call downright sleepy," he said, "but I think I sort of nodded several times. In fact, I could have flown half that distance again. I had enough fuel

Continued on Page Ten.

MAP OF LINDBERGH'S TRANSATLANTIC ROUTE, SHOWING THE SPEED OF HIS TRIP.

LEVINE ABANDONS BELLANCA FLIGHT

Venture Given Up as Designer Splits With Him—Plane Narrowly Escapes Burning.

BYRD'S CRAFT IS NAMED

Lindbergh Cheered at Ceremony—Commander, Now Last in Field, Waits on Weather.

Through no fault of his own, Clarence D. Chamberlin, who with Bert Acosta established a world's non-stop flying record a few weeks ago, will not fly the record-breaking monoplane in an attempt to establish a second New York-Paris non-stop flight.

G. M. Bellanca, designer of the plane, and Charles S. Levine of the Columbia Aircraft Company, owner of the ship, came to the parting of the ways last night and the designer finally severed his connection with the promoter. Then Levine issued a statement that the proposed flight, which has been talked of for weeks, was off.

The statement said:

"Due to the crowning blow of Mr. Bellanca's resignation, the plane will be placed in the hangar. Mr. Bellanca's resignation causes us to abandon plans for the New York-Paris flight for the present."

At the very moment that the statement was issued the plane was near the runway at Roosevelt Field with gas tanks filled and oil and equipment aboard ready for the start for Paris.

Plane Threatened by Fire.

A few minutes later, as it was being wheeled off, preparatory to being housed for the night, it narrowly escaped being destroyed by fire. When the word came to the field that the flight was definitely off mechanics were ordered to empty one gasoline tank to lighten the machine. The gasoline spilled on the ground and while the ship was being towed away a careless spectator threw the stub of a lighted cigarette down.

In an instant there was a terrific flare and a dense burst of smoke as the gasoline blazed up.

"The Bellanca's gone," was the cry that rose from thousands of spectators who had gathered at the field.

Word was flashed to the army air station at Mitchel Field that there had been an accident and ambulances and fire-fighting apparatus were sent across the road. An ambulance from the Nassau County Hospital at Mineola was also sent to Roosevelt Field, as well as fire apparatus from Mineola.

The plane, however, was beyond the danger line and was not injured.

It had been announced that the Columbia would take off at 8 o'clock and Chamberlin was in his flying clothes ready to climb into the cockpit with the unnamed pilot who was to have accompanied him on the trip.

With the elimination of the Bellanca monoplane, only Lieut.

Continued on Page Four.

CAPTAIN CHARLES A. LINDBERGH,
Who Flew Alone Across the Atlantic, New York to Paris, in Thirty-three and One-half Hours.

Times Wide World Photo.

New York Stages Big Celebration After Hours of Anxious Waiting

Harbor Craft, Factories, Fire Sirens and Radio Carry Message of the Flier's Victory Throughout the City—Theatres Halt While Audiences Cheer.

New York bubbled all day yesterday with excitement and expectancy, first yearning for word of Captain Lindbergh, then half-doubting, gaining confidence as the afternoon progressed and finally acclaiming the victory of the young aviator with street demonstrations where the crowds were thickest, in which the ancient phrase, "I told you so," was often repeated. It was evident during the day that New York had confidence in the lad from the West.

On the streets and elsewhere Lindbergh was the one topic of conversation the whole day long. In the subway, on the elevated, in trains and cars, motion-picture houses, theatres, wherever a few had gathered, or even where one man could find another to talk to, one heard "Lindbergh — Lindbergh — Lindbergh."

And such expressions as this:

"He'll make it, all right."

"Some baby!"

"Well, if he's hit Ireland, he's safe anyway."

"He's away ahead of his time."

"What's the difference in time between here and there, anyway!"

She said it with an air which signified: "I don't mean maybe." A surprising number of persons insisted that the difference in time was three hours.

Early in the day, even before there was any good reason why there should be definite news, the interest of the people was demonstrated in two ways. At every news stand there were little groups scanning the headlines and buying newspapers. In every newspaper office the switchboards were literally swamped with inquiries. It was not sufficient that the operator said there was no word, or, later, that Lindbergh's plane had been seen over Ireland. The inquirers wanted specific information:

"Well, when will you get the first news?" they asked. And later:

"If he's over Ireland how long will it be before he gets to Paris?"

"Is he all right?"

The questions that were asked, considering that no news could possibly come direct from Captain Lindbergh before he landed, were as surprising as the guesses at the difference in time.

The Times Gets 10,000 Phone Calls.

The telephone inquiries came from all sorts of people and all directions. Not a few rang up THE TIMES office and apologetically explained that they were on golf links or elsewhere at a distance, and hence could not

Continued on Page Three.

LINDBERGH TRIUMPH THRILLS COOLIDGE

President Cables Praise to "Heroic Flier" and Concern for Nungesser and Coli.

CAPITAL THROBS WITH JOY

Kellogg, New, MacNider, Patrick and Many More Join in Paying Tribute to Daring Youth.

Special to The New York Times.

WASHINGTON, May 21.—The triumph of Captain Charles A. Lindbergh in flying from New York to Paris without a stop created a tremendous sensation in the national capital and found immediate response in a host of official messages congratulating the daring aviator upon his achievement.

President Coolidge expressed his admiration in a message transmitted through Ambassador Herrick in Paris for delivery to the young flier in person.

With a single possible exception, this city has never been more thrilled since the armistice, when Woodrow Wilson mingled with noisy thousands in celebrating the end of the war. The exception was when Walter Johnson arose from apparent defeat and won the deciding world series baseball game in 1924.

"The American people," the President said, "rejoice with me at the brilliant termination of your heroic flight. The first non-stop flight of a lone aviator across the Atlantic crowns the record of American aviation, and in bringing the greetings of the American people to France you likewise carry the assurance of our continued anxiety concerning their fate."

Secretary Kellogg, in a message similarly transmitted, said:

"I heartily congratulate you on the success of your great adventure in accomplishing a non-stop flight from New York to Paris. It is a great step in the advancement of aviation. Every one in the United States is proud of your accomplishment."

Knew Lindbergh as a Boy.

In a statement issued here Mr. Kellogg referred to his personal friendship for Lindbergh, whom he has known for years through the young man's late father, a Representative in Congress from the Secretary's home State of Minnesota.

"News has just reached me," Mr. Kellogg said, "of the success of Lindbergh in completing his flight from New York to Paris. It is an achievement of which every American can justly be proud. I have known Lindbergh since he was a boy and rejoice at this culmination of his ambitions, which could only have been gained by scientific knowledge, superb courage and physique and sterling character. Our rejoicing in Lindbergh's success, however, is tempered by our continued ignorance of the fate of Nungesser and Coli, whose courage and valor have now been equaled, but never be surpassed."

Hanford MacNider, Acting Secre-

Continued on Page Three.

CROWD ROARS THUNDEROUS WELCOME

Breaks Through Lines of Soldiers and Police and Surging to Plane Lifts Weary Flier from His Cockpit

AVIATORS RESCUE HIM FROM FRENZIED MOB OF 25,000

Paris Boulevards Ring With Celebration After Day and Night Watch—American Flag Is Called For and Wildly Acclaimed.

By EDWIN L. JAMES.
Copyright, 1927, by The New York Times Company.
Special Cable to THE NEW YORK TIMES.

PARIS, May 21.—Lindbergh did it. Twenty minutes after 10 o'clock tonight suddenly and softly there slipped out of the darkness a gray-white airplane as 25,000 pairs of eyes strained toward it. At 10:24 the Spirit of St. Louis landed and lines of soldiers, ranks of policemen and stout steel fences went down before a mad rush as irresistible as the tides of the ocean.

"Well," smiled Lindbergh, as the little white monoplane came to a halt in the middle of the field and the first vanguard reached the plane. Lindbergh made a move to jump out. Twenty hands reached for him and lifted him out as if he were a baby. Several thousands in a minute were around the plane. Thousands more broke the barriers of iron rails round the field, cheering wildly.

Lifted From His Cockpit.

As he was lifted to the ground Lindbergh was pale and, with his hair unkempt, he looked completely worn out. He had strength enough, however, to smile, and waved his hand to the crowd. Soldiers with fixed bayonets were unable to keep back the crowd.

United States Ambassador Herrick was among the first to welcome and congratulate the hero.

A NEW YORK TIMES man was one of the first to reach the machine after its graceful descent to the field. Those first to arrive at the plane had a picture that will live in their minds for the rest of their lives. His cap off, his famous locks falling in disarray around his eyes, "Lucky Lindy" sat peering out over the rim of the little cockpit of his machine.

Dramatic Scene at the Field.

It was high drama. Picture the scene. Twenty to twenty-five thousand people were massed on the east side of Le Bourget air field. Some of them had been there six and seven hours.

Off to the left the giant phare lighthouse of Mount Valerien flashed its guiding light 300 miles into the air. Closer on the left Le Bourget Lighthouse twinkled, and off to the right another giant revolving phare sent its beams high into the heavens.

Big arc lights on all sides with enormous electric glares were flooding the landing field. From time to time rockets rose and burst in varied lights over the field.

Seven thirty, the hour announced for the arrival, had come and gone. Then 8 o'clock came, and no Lindbergh; at 9 o'clock the sun had set but then came reports that Lindbergh had been seen over Cork. Then he had been seen over Valentia in Ireland and then over Plymouth.

Suddenly a message spread like lightning, the aviator had been seen over Cherbourg. However, remembering the messages telling of Captain Nungesser's flight, the crowd was skeptical.

"One chance in a thousand!" "Oh, he cannot do it without navigating instruments!" "It's a pity, because he was a brave boy." Pessimism had spread over the great throng by 10 o'clock.

The stars came out and a chill wind blew.

Watchers Are Twice Disappointed.

Suddenly the field lights flooded their glares onto the landing ground and there came the roar of an airplane's motor. The crowd was still, then began a cheer, but two minutes later the landing glares went dark for the searchlight had identified the plane and it was not Captain Lindbergh's.

Stamping their feet in the cold, the crowd waited patiently. It seemed quite apparent that nearly every one was willing to wait all night, hoping against hope.

Suddenly—it was 10:16 o'clock—another motor roared over the heads of the crowd. In the sky one caught a glimpse of a white gray plane, and for an instant heard the sound of one. Then it dimmed, and the idea spread that it was yet another disappointment.

Again landing lights glared and almost by the time they had flooded the field the gray-white plane had lighted on the far side nearly half a mile from the crowd. It seemed to stop almost as it hit the ground, so gently did it land.

And then occurred a scene which almost passed description. Two companies of soldiers with fixed bayonets and the Le Bourget field police, reinforced by Paris agents, had held the crowd in good order. But as the lights showed the plane

The New York Times.

THE WEATHER
Cloudy today, showers tonight or tomorrow; moderate winds.
Temperature yesterday—Max. 78, min. 64.
For weather report see Page 46.

VOL. LXXVI....NO. 25,393.   NEW YORK, WEDNESDAY, AUGUST 3, 1927.   TWO CENTS in Greater New York | THREE CENTS Within 200 Miles | FOUR CENTS Elsewhere in the U.S.

COOLIDGE DOES NOT CHOOSE TO RUN IN 1928; STARTLES PARTY WITH 12-WORD MESSAGE; SOME DOUBTERS, OTHERS SEE FIELD OPEN

NEW SACCO TRIAL INDICATED AS STEP FULLER WILL TAKE

Governor Is Expected to Call for Reprieve of Men and Action by the Legislature.

POLITICAL ISSUE IS RAISED

Move Would Be 'Expedient,' but Observers Say Executive Feels It Is Right.

PAIR ENTER DEATH HOUSE

Newly Found Vanzetti Alibi Is Presented as Fuller Interviews Last Witnesses.

From a Staff Correspondent of The New York Times.

BOSTON, Aug. 2.—Nicola Sacco and Bartolomeo Vanzetti will die in the electric chair on the date set. Neither will they be pardoned. Further reprieve pending steps by the Massachusetts Legislature looking to a new trial was indicated at the State House tonight as the solution of the historic case of the Italian radicals, which Governor Fuller will place before the Executive Council tomorrow, the defense was more cheerful than it has been since the Governor's investigation began.

This optimism is not shared by Sacco, whose mind is weakening on the eighteenth day of his hunger strike at Charlestown State Prison. Vanzetti is feeling better and partaking of a little food. He is buoyed up by the news that his sister has sailed from France and is due here on Aug. 10. That is the day set for the execution under the terms of the sentence of the two men.

Every sign today pointed to the fact that Governor Fuller, despite his exhaustive and exhausting inquiry, had not made up his mind on certain phases of the case of the men convicted for the murder of a paymaster and his guard on April 15, 1920.

Interviews Last of Witnesses.

This afternoon Governor Fuller saw the last of the long line of witnesses who have filed into his office for three months, and he then closed the inquiry. He continued his work on the case after lunch away from his office at o'clock. When he returned he gave every indication of being in a comfortable frame of mind.

At 9:10 tonight Sacco and Vanzetti and Celestino Madeiros, facing execution for another murder, whose case is linked with that of the two radicals by his "confession" seeking to exonerate them, were transferred from the Cherry Hill section of the State Prison to the death house, about 100 yards away. The transfer was effected without incident. The removal of the men has no significance, being a routine procedure. Men condemned to die in the electric chair are, according to law, removed to the death house ten days before execution.

Until a few days ago those at the State House who have followed the Governor's inquiry, as well as members of the Sacco-Vanzetti Defense Committee, felt that the result would be clear cut and uncompromising. The defense hoped for an outright pardon. State House sources were of the opinion that the Governor would take no action and permit the death penalty to be imposed.

The tide apparently turned with the latest visit of Superior Court Judge Webster Thayer, who presided at the joint trial as well as at the previous trial of Vanzetti, convicted of an attempted hold-up and sentenced to from twelve to fifteen years. Judge Thayer, who refused the eight applications for a new trial in his report.

The stress placed on the meeting of the Council tomorrow is emphasized by the Defense Committee as a certain sign that the Governor could not have made up his mind to send the men to the electric chair. There are eight Councilors from widely separated parts of the State and their bearing on the case is apparent from the following provision in the State Constitution:

"The power of pardoning offenses, except such as persons may be convicted of before the Senate by an impeachment of the House, shall be in the Governor, by and with the advice of the Council.

Since receiving the idea of a further reprieve and action by the Legis-

Continued on Page Fourteen.

Sept. 19 to Be French Holiday In Honor of American Legion

Copyright, 1927, by The New York Times Company.
Special Cable to The New York Times.

PARIS, Aug. 2.—A law proclaiming Monday, Sept. 19, as a French national holiday this year in honor of the American Legionaires returning to celebrate the tenth anniversary of their entry in the World War was promulgated in the Journal Officiel today.

In this same bill the sum of 3,760,000 francs is allocated to the Minister of Foreign Affairs for expenditures for the entertainment of the American veterans on their visit here.

The announcement declares it to be a joy and an honor for the Government and the French populace to receive the members of the American Legion, who remain an "unshakable base of friendship for France in the United States."

JAPANESE OFFER NEW NAVAL PLAN

Suggestion That May Save Conference Is Wired to Washington and London.

MAINTAINS STATUS QUO

But Gives America and Japan Chance to Catch Up With Britain on Cruisers.

By WYTHE WILLIAMS.
Copyright, 1927, by The New York Times Company.
Special Cable to The New York Times.

GENEVA, Aug. 2.—The plenary session of the tripower naval conference is still set for Thursday, and Ambassador Gibson is expected to attempt the seemingly hopeless task of obtaining a naval limitations treaty acceptable to the United States.

The delegates today were still busy suggesting new compromises, which for the most part are merely old plans re-dressed. They gave it up after lunch and decided they might as well play golf. It is still evident, though, that all the delegations—particularly a portion of the American one—are anxious to avoid adjournment of the conference at almost any cost.

It is not generally clear just what is the newest proposal—at one time labeled Japanese and at another Japano-American—because sometimes the official spokesmen said there were no proposals and at others admitted there were, until interest slackened as the mystery grew. It is evident that they were sized up by Allen Dulles, the legal adviser of the American delegation, who thought they might lead to something being arranged. Thus they assumed a semi-American character.

Mr. Dulles, who recently resigned from the State Department to rejoin a New York law firm, was re-engaged especially for this conference. His most distinguished relative is Robert Lansing, ex-Secretary of State, whom he resembles in his pacific ambition to become a treaty maker rather than a contrivance breaker.

Meanwhile the unconsulted American navy experts are viewing the civilian members of the delegation askance, fearful that something of the same effect on the navy as the Treaty of Washington. They are anxiously counting the hours from now until the plenary session. Then if Ambassador Gibson takes the floor and brings the conference to an end they will breathe freely, but not until then.

The only delegates taking the situation placidly and unconcernedly and not indulging in gossip are the British.

Tonight the Japanese delegation gave a full dress dinner in honor of the former Crown Prince of Korea. It was followed by a dance and a midnight supper.

New Plan Submitted by Japanese.

By The Associated Press.

GENEVA, Aug. 2.—The Japanese statesmen today presented to Hugh S. Gibson, chief American representative, a compromise formula on the cruiser problem which has menaced the Tripartite Naval Conference with failure. In handing their formula to the Ambassador, Viscount Ishii and his associates remarked that it was "just an idea."

Despite this new move it was said responsible quarters tonight that the spectre of failure—failure which, as a prospect, has saddened the minds of many countries—should not yet be deemed definitely avoided. Yet, from the American standpoint at least, the Japanese plan to save the conference is said to appear

Continued on Page Six.

PARTY HERE IS AMAZED

State Organization in Consternation at Coolidge Statement.

IS FINAL, HILLES THINKS

Leaders Expect Effort to Force Renomination by a Popular Demand.

DR. BUTLER LAUDS ACTION

Says President Has Done Wise and Patriotic Act—Ex-Senator Butler Is Silent.

New York State Republicans, with very few exceptions, were thunderstruck yesterday by President Coolidge's announcement regarding his candidacy for another term.

Neither former Senator William M. Butler of Massachusetts, Chairman of the Republican National Committee, who happened to be in the city, nor Charles D. Hilles, the Vice Chairman, had any advance notice of the President's intention. Senator Butler was the President's personal choice for National Chairman and managed his 1924 campaign. Mr. Hilles is considered particularly close to the President and is consulted by him on all matters affecting New York State, and the fact that the President's statement came to them as a surprise indicates the degree of astonishment felt by Republicans here generally.

Hilles Sees Withdrawal.

Mr. Hilles declared that President Coolidge had made his statement without reservation and believes that his withdrawal is to be final unless some emergency should confront the country in 1928. He said:

"The President's laconic statement was entirely unexpected, and I regret his action. He is a singularly self-reliant man. I believe he took his own counsel until the decision was announced. He is a man of candor and sincerity, and I think he made the statement without reservation. Except that if an emergency should confront the country in 1928, and it should clearly be a duty to run, he will be free to do so. Otherwise I think he intends this to be final.

"He has had the satisfaction of knowing that he would have been renominated by an overwhelming majority.

"I think the President was considerate in announcing his renunciation now. It gives us ten months in which to prepare for the nomination of his successor. I do not agree with those who think he will lose a strategic advantage with the next Congress. He will cease to be a target for partisan attack. Members of his own party who have withheld their support as well as those of the opposition party will now have a kindlier feeling for him and an appreciation of the great service he has rendered."

By the leaders of the State party organization, President Coolidge's renomination and re-election were regarded as virtually certain. With few exceptions, the local Republican leaders accepted the President's statement as final and at its face value, although it was said that a movement would undoubtedly develop to take advantage of the phraseology of his statement that he did "not choose to be a candidate," and seek to bring about his renomination by popular demand.

Think Field Now Wide Open.

The general feeling among those New York Republican leaders who could be found in or near the city, was that the President's statement had left the field wide open for the Republican Presidential nomination in 1928, and that strong movements for former Governor Frank O. Lowden, of Illinois, and Herbert Hoover, Secretary of Commerce, were certain to develop in this State.

The one Republican of prominence who did not feel surprised at the President's announcement was Dr. Nicholas Murray Butler, president of Columbia University, who returned earlier in the day from a trip to Europe. Dr. Butler predicted last February that President Coolidge would not violate the third term tradition by becoming a candidate for renomination, and the attitude of opposition to a third term brought at that time a great deal of criticism from members of the State party organization, who had based all their plans on the probability of President Coolidge's renomination.

Dr. Butler's Statement.

Asked to comment on the President's statement, Dr. Butler said:

"As a personal friend and a political supporter of President Coolidge, although without knowledge of his purpose, I have taken it for granted, as I stated in an address to my friends and neighbors of the

Continued on Page Two.

Smith Is Silent on Coolidge, But Democrats See His Gain

President Coolidge's statement that he did "not choose to be a candidate for renomination" was met with silence by leading Democrats here yesterday.

"I have no comment to make," said Governor Smith, a leading aspirant for the Democratic Presidential nomination, said at the Hotel Biltmore.

George W. Olvany, leader of Tammany, and Mayor Walker also declined to comment.

The speculation among Democrats was mostly over how the President's statement might affect Governor Smith's chances of nomination for and election to the Presidency. The general offhand opinion was that it would have no material effect on his chance for the nomination, but probably would increase his chance for election.

COOLIDGE'S ACTION PLEASES CORN BELT

Iowa Leaders in Farm Legislation Agitation Think It Will Aid Their Cause.

BOOM IN LOWDEN'S STOCK

His Supporters Think Greatest Obstacle to His Candidacy Has Been Removed.

Special to The New York Times.

DES MOINES, Iowa, Aug. 2.—Iowa's first concern tonight over the announcement of President Coolidge that he does not choose to run for President in 1928 was for the effect of the President's statement on the Middle West's fight for farm relief legislation.

Leaders in the farm agitation were almost unanimous in their belief that the President's action was a victory, or at least a material aid, for the cause of agriculture. Comment also concerned itself largely with the effect of the Coolidge statement on the candidacy of Frank O. Lowden, which has been the chief concern of many of the State's political leaders.

Those who thought first of the bearing of the statement on another term for President Coolidge generally complimented the President on his "courageous act" in taking a stand against breaking the third term tradition.

State Chairman for Lowden.

Perhaps the most significant development in Iowa was the statement of Willis L. Stern, Republican State Chairman, that "this State will doubtless be united for Frank O. Lowden, as all Iowa holds him in high esteem." The statement was interpreted as placing the State party organization back of the Lowden candidacy.

Ex-Governor Lowden's most ardent supporters hailed the Coolidge withdrawal as removing the most serious obstacle to his candidacy, namely the ability of the President to obtain renomination. Organization leaders who have had nothing against Mr. Lowden but who have to stay on the Coolidge reservation may not be disposed to advocate some other candidate against Mr. Lowden, it was pointed out.

Some observers, however, held that the Lowden movement made no gain by the Coolidge statement because the withdrawal of the President had left the Lowden forces without an object against which to direct their attack. This attitude was reflected in the declaration of Frank J. Lund, head of the Iowa Lowden for President League, who predicted that "the East will have another candidate of the same type."

Too Soon to Discuss, Says Hoover.

PALO ALTO, Cal., Aug. 2.—Herbert Hoover, Secretary of Commerce, said tonight that he had nothing to say for the present as to President Coolidge's announcement. "I have no comment to make," the Secretary said. "It is too soon to discuss it. I must think over the President's announcement."

Finality, Borah Thinks.

By Telegraph to the Editor of The New York Times.

BOISE, Idaho, Aug. 2.—The President could have been renominated by simply remaining silent. His election seemed reasonably certain. His announcement, therefore, that he does not desire to be a candidate in 1928 must be regarded as the result of a profound conviction and as a finality. Naturally, other candidates will be brought out, but it will be a

Continued on Page Five.

LEADERS ARE CAUTIOUS

Vice President Dawes Says Public Will Regret the Decision.

LONGWORTH KEEPS SILENT

Ex-Governor Lowden Repeats That No One Can Run Away From the Presidency.

HOOVER TO "THINK IT OVER"

Borah Accepts Announcement as Final—West Did It, Says Brookhart.

President Coolidge's sudden announcement that he did "not choose to be a candidate for renomination in 1928" was manifestly as much a surprise to those who have been mentioned as probable aspirants for the nomination at the next Republican National Convention as to any one else, judging from their expressions as told in the press.

When asked to comment on Mr. Coolidge's declaration Frank O. Lowden would only say that no one could run away from the Presidency. Vice President Charles G. Dawes at first refused to comment on the President's statement, but later issued a statement of his own, which in effect accepted the President's statement as final on the question of his candidacy for renomination. Senator Hiram Johnson of California characterized the President's statement as "astonishing." Speaker Nicholas Longworth of the House of Representatives, who is visiting in San Francisco, declined to comment. Secretary Hoover's views are not available.

Mr. Dawes Voices Regrets.

CHICAGO, Aug. 2.—Vice President Charles G. Dawes said in a statement here tonight:

"President Coolidge enjoys the confidence and respect of the American people, and his decision will be received with regret by millions of his countrymen."

Ex-Governor Lowden's Comment.

Special to The New York Times.

ALEXANDRIA BAY, N. Y., Aug. 2.—Concerning the announcement made today by President Coolidge on 1928, former Governor Frank O. Lowden of Illinois who, with his family is visiting here, issued the following statement to which he would add nothing: "I have no statement to make beyond the one already made to different delegations calling upon me. That statement was in substance, that I know of no man in all our history who has run away from the Presidency."

Longworth Too Surprised to Talk.

Special to The New York Times.

SAN FRANCISCO, Cal., Aug. 2.—Two of the outstanding possibilities for the Republican nomination for the Presidency were in San Francisco today.

Herbert Hoover, Secretary of Commerce, was at the Bohemian Grove when the message came from the President.

Nicholas Longworth, Speaker of the House of Representatives, received the news from the President's Sunnyer home while attending a luncheon given in his honor at the San Francisco Commercial Club. He declared that he was too surprised to say anything.

"I may have something to say later on," he remarked.

Senator Hiram Johnson admitted that when he first heard of the President's statement he was too astonished to talk. He said:

"If the statement as reported is true, the best Republican Convention will be a grand free-for-all, a regular Donnybrook Fair."

Want Smoot to Discuss.

Senator Smoot, however, would not hazard a guess as to what the party convention would do in the face of the President's declaration. It was too early to make any guesses in that respect, he explained, and then added:

"My opinion is that the American people would like to have Mr. Coolidge for President again, but that is just my personal opinion.

"There is no disposition here to discuss Senator Smoot's construction that the President's announcement would not bar Mr. Coolidge from accepting another Republican nomination if it should be bestowed upon him by the national convention. At the same time, it was contended by most of those present tonight, this phase of the subject that Mr. Coolidge has served notice, that no

Continued on Page Three.

A Recent Studio Portrait. Copyright, Harris & Ewing.
CALVIN COOLIDGE.
"I Do Not Choose to Run for President in Nineteen Twenty-eight."

Washington Sees 1928 Field Open; Some Talk of Drafting Coolidge

Hoover, Lowden, Dawes, Longworth, Borah and Norris Are Listed as the Chief of Those Whose Presidential Aspirations Will Now Take Active Form.

By RICHARD V. OULAHAN.
Special to The New York Times.

WASHINGTON, Aug. 2.—It was a real sensation of the infinitesimal segment of political Washington which the hot weather has not driven away, the announcement of President Coolidge at his Summer home in South Dakota that he did not "choose" to run for President in 1928. With it was dovetailed the element of complete surprise.

While some of those concerned or interested in party politics have been expressing the opinion that Mr. Coolidge would decline to be considered as a candidate for another nomination, their number is negligible in comparison with those who were of the opinion that he would be the Republican nominee next year. Besides, nobody expected the President to show his hand at this early date, more than ten months prior to the assembling of the Republican National Convention.

Two Features of Comment.

In the comment which followed the President's terse declaration at Rapid City there were two conspicuous features. One was the speculative slant of whether the President meant it to be understood that in no circumstances would he accept a nomination for another Presidential term. The other was the apparent evidence, cumulative over a period of many months and accentuated by what was learned today, that Mr. Coolidge did not consult close political friends or party leaders with reference to his spectacular statement.

There is reason to believe that he never discussed with any member of the Cabinet the matter of becoming a candidate for President in 1928, with the possible exception of Secretary Hoover, "of whom later," as the compilers of genealogical records say.

Very generally opinion among political observers was that Mr. Coolidge intended his announcement to mean that he had taken himself out of the running. The argument was advanced that a man occupying the high position of President of the United States could not afford, if for no other reason than that of dignity, to make a declaration of such an important character that would be open to the accusation of deception or intentional dubiousness.

A notable exception to this view was the construction placed on the President's announcement by such a conspicuous Republican as Senator Smoot of Utah.

"I construe the statement to mean," said Senator Smoot, "that if the Republican convention nominates him again he will accept the nomination. It does not bar him from running again in such an event."

Want Coolidge, Smoot Thinks.

Senator Smoot, however, would not hazard a guess as to what the party convention would do in the face of the President's declaration. It was too early to make any guesses in that respect, he explained, and then added:

"My opinion is that the American people would like to have Mr. Coolidge for President again, but that is just my personal opinion.

"There is no disposition here to discuss Senator Smoot's construction that the President's announcement would not bar Mr. Coolidge from accepting another Republican nomination.

Discussion of Hoover.

One of Washington's first reactions to the surprise sprung upon the country by Mr. Coolidge was the conviction that Herbert Hoover will be considered as conspicuous in the running for next year's Republican Presidential nomination. Among many political observers the belief prevails that to the country he appears as a national hero. His most recent public service in the administration of relief measures in the flooded areas of the South has given to him a renewed prominence which has served to recall his masterful handling of Belgian and Russian relief and other work for humanity and his direction of the food administration during the World War.

The doubt exists in the minds of those who follow party political tendencies that Mr. Hoover will now be brought forward as a candidate for the Presidential nomination.

A widespread opinion exists in political quarters that his aspirations will have the moral support of President Coolidge. A knowledge of the President's mental processes and habits leads to the conviction that he will not make a declaration in favor of any particular candidate for the nomination, but will find means of having the word passed that Hoover is his favorite against the candidatorial field.

The recent unexplained incident arising from Mr. Coolidge's vacation tarry assertion that if Mr. Kellogg should retire from the office of Secretary of State Mr. Hoover would not be appointed to succeed him, may lend to the evidence that the President is not particularly cordial toward his Secretary of Commerce, but, in the face of it, the sympathetic good attitude of the President are expected to aid Mr. Hoover's hat as it is cast into the ring.

Will Spur Lowden Boomers.

It goes without saying that the announcement from Rapid City will be followed by increased activities on the part of those who have put Frank O. Lowden forward as their choice for the Republican Presidential nomination.

Mr. Lowden is primarily the favorite of the advanced farm aid advocates and has been regarded as the candidate of those party leaders chiefly in the Middle West, who resented Mr. Coolidge's attitude toward their Congressional demands for agricultural relief, a resentment that found expression when the President vetoed the McNary-Haugen bill.

As it has been seen by politicians, Mr. Lowden's boom is a protest against what the President's critical term "Coolidgeism." In that light it has been construed by the President's friends, and it will be a

Continued on Page Three.

PRESIDENT ACTED ALONE

His Close Friends Were Unaware of His Stand on Another Term.

CALLS IN NEWSPAPER MEN

President Hands Out Typed Slip in School Room, and Declines to Comment.

DRAMATIC SURPRISE STAGED

Statement Is Issued on the Eve of Coolidge's Fourth Anniversary as President.

From a Staff Correspondent of The New York Times.

RAPID CITY, S. D., Aug. 2.—President Coolidge today dramatically and unexpectedly, and without consultation with friends, issued the following statement to the correspondents here:

"I do not choose to run for President in nineteen twenty-eight."

This brief statement was written by him on a slip of paper at 9:52 A. M. and later transcribed by stenographers to a slip of paper five inches by two inches. The year was put in words, not figures, and so made a twelve-word statement.

The President had doubled the slips twice and held fifteen of them in his right hand, from which he gave them to the newspaper correspondents, who had been notified to return to his office at noon for a statement. This notice to the correspondents was given at the end of the regular Tuesday morning press conference, in which he had discussed the Geneva conference before the public.

The long line of correspondents filed past the President and gasped with surprise as they read the words on the slips of paper. The President was solemn and composed as he gave out the announcement of his desire not to stand for renomination.

"Is there any other comment?" he was asked.

"None," he replied.

The door closed as the correspondents and the secretaries departed, leaving Mr. Coolidge alone for fifteen minutes to consider the effect of his decision.

Stages Dramatic Surprise.

The startling political statement was made "under circumstances simple and dramatic. It came on the eve of the fourth anniversary of the day Mr. Coolidge took the oath of office as President of the United States, by the light of the kerosene lamp in his boyhood home at Plymouth, Vt.

Today's decision in the Black Hills was reached without consultation with friends or advisers, and his associates here say that it effectively takes Mr. Coolidge out of the Presidential race in 1928.

While the word "choose" is subject to popular qualification and reservation, the impression obtained here from the President's associates is that it was selected as properly presenting the President's mind and as expressing completely the President's attitude toward another term.

To avoid saying that he is not a candidate, and what he does say may leave the situation open in the minds of some of his supporters and others, but, according to the views of those close to him here, President Coolidge has closed the doors of the White House to himself after March 4, 1929.

There may be a more definite and final utterance from him, but it is regarded here as doubtful. It is expected here, with the passage of the entrance of Secretary Hoover, Speaker Longworth, Vice President Dawes and the renewed activity of former Governor Lowden to gain the delegates in the coming Republican primaries.

It is believed here that the President will say nothing more and will not expected to allow his Administration to be used in the promotion of the candidacy of any others who have been mentioned for the nomination.

His now famous announcement takes the place alongside that of his message to Congress, in which he favored the granting of a bonus. It also referred to the line of his announcement, as followed the first step in his political career which ended in his becoming

At the close of the legislative ses-

The New York Times.

THE WEATHER
Fair and slightly warmer today and tomorrow; moderate winds.
Temperature yesterday—Max. 71, min. 56.
For weather report see Page 42.

VOL. LXXVI....No. 25.394. ....   NEW YORK, THURSDAY, AUGUST 4, 1927.   TWO CENTS In Greater New York | THREE CENTS Within 200 Miles | FOUR CENTS Elsewhere in the U. S.

SACCO AND VANZETTI GUILTY, SAYS FULLER, AND MUST DIE; BAY STATE GOVERNOR UPHOLDS JURY, CALLS TRIAL FAIR; HIS BOARD UNANIMOUS, EXECUTION OF PAIR SET FOR AUG. 10

MESSAGES OF REGRET FLOOD COOLIDGE; STRONG DESIRE TO DRAFT HIM SHOWN AS DEBATE OVER STATEMENT GOES ON

PRESIDENT KEEPS SILENT

His Associates Declare He Issued His Statement As a Final Word.

SEEMS IN A HAPPIER MOOD

He Spends an Hour in His Office Reading Telegrams, Then Returns to Lodge.

EXPECT LATER STATEMENT

Politicians at Rapid City See Coolidge Forced by Primaries to Clarify His Stand.

From a Staff Correspondent of The New York Times.

RAPID CITY, S. D., Aug. 3.—President Coolidge, having announced that he does not choose to run for President in 1928, finds himself flooded with telegrams urging him again to lead the Republican Party.

These messages, which have poured in upon him here in the Black Hills, are most complimentary and make clear to him that he has the esteem of a great following. A large proportion of the telegrams seek to prevail upon Mr. Coolidge to accept the nomination if it should come to him after his new announcement, couched in somewhat indefinite language.

The dispatches not only have come from all parts of this country, but there are scores of cable messages from Americans traveling abroad, insisting that the present situation calls for President Coolidge to permit himself to be renominated by the Republican Party.

Some messages told the President that he had made himself one of the greatest men in recent times by virtually refusing what they declared was certain re-election as President, and going down in history as the man who has longest held that office.

It would be a calamity to the nation, declared some of the messages if Mr. Coolidge should eliminate himself from the race and plunge the country into an uncertain contest for the Presidency, with what was stated as the possibility of radical change in governmental policies that have made the nation strong and prosperous.

Many Talk of Drafting Coolidge.

The nation, judged by these messages that tonight are being digested by the President in his distant lodge in the hills, does not accept as final or conclusive the terse and cryptic statement that the President prepared without consultation and then personally distributed to the press yesterday in his office in the school building.

Apparently a great many people, including many of the dominant Republican leaders, do not believe the statement effectively eliminates President Coolidge from the race. They all construe the announcement as expressing his state of mind and not his actual determination not to accept the nomination if in the face of it the Republican Party should cast aside President Coolidge's apparent personal desires and nominate him next year.

The trend of sentiment reflected in the messages coming here is that the admirers inclined to draft Mr. Coolidge and actually show him that there is a real call from the people, a call that rises above his wishes, and disregards the so-called third term talk that he has fully made up his mind to retire at the end of his term in 1929.

In the opinion of some observers here who have analyzed the messages and read the interviews given in the country, it is necessary for the President to be more definite. It is stated, however, that some move, such as the entrance of a member of his Cabinet in the race, would show that he has fully made up his mind to retire at the end of his term in 1929.

The messages received here indicate that only Mr. Coolidge's refusal to permit his name to be entered in the first primaries to be held in New Hampshire and North Dakota next March will satisfy his supporters and others of the finality of his announcement. In the last twenty-four hours the Summer White House wires have brought in reports of a great national party readjusting its entire campaign procedure, the fixed opinion of many voters altered and their views as to the strongest candidate of the Republican Party can select rendered uncertain. The wires also

Continued on Page Five.

Hoover Declares He Hopes President Will Run Again

PALO ALTO, Cal., Aug. 3 (P).—Herbert Hoover, Secretary of Commerce, commenting today on President Coolidge's announcement that he did not choose to be a candidate for re-election in 1928, said:

"I regret the suggestion in the President's statement.

"However, I still believe as I stated in Chicago two weeks ago, that President Coolidge should be renominated and re-elected."

BULL MARKET JARRED BY COOLIDGE STAND

Fifty Representative Stocks Decline—Most of Losses Are Regained in Buying Rally.

2,767,170 SHARES SOLD

Trading Next to Heaviest of the Year—Clamor From Exchange Reaches the Street.

By RICHARD V. OULAHAN.
Special to The New York Times.

WASHINGTON, Aug. 3.—On this, the day following President Coolidge's laconic announcement, "I do not choose to run for President in 1928," Washington's chief reaction is that the President owes to the country a clearer explanation of what his declaration was meant to convey.

This feeling is accentuated by editorial comment throughout the Union, showing there is widespread mystification as to the President's intention with reference to next year's Presidential nomination.

It is easily conceivable that without clarification of his statement the President will lay himself open to the accusation of having made a deceptive utterance. Only a frank explanation from him personally can overcome this accusatory tendency, if a cross-section of Washington opinion is well founded.

Pretty generally the Washington view is that Mr. Coolidge's purpose was to notify the electorate and especially Republican workers, that he was out of the running. Put in another way, he took the method employed to serve notice that he was not to be considered as a candidate for this party's nomination.

Has High Regard for Dignities.

No man occupying his position, it is held, can afford to practice deception on the nation, and in this connection it may be added that no President has had a higher regard for the dignities which invest the office. Without ostentatious show, he has adhered to the little ceremonials which carry out the idea of dignity. Despite his parading in cowboy regalia, it is the observation of those who have been brought into close contact with him that he looks upon the Presidential office with too much respect to permit him to bring it into even the semblance of the disrepute that might attach to it through any method of deception or questionable practice by its incumbent.

But in the face of all this, the mystification continues. Those who adhere to the belief that Mr. Coolidge intended the country to understand that he would retire from the Presidency at the end of the term of office in March, 1929, insist that the President said all that was necessary in the circumstances; it is apparent that they cannot justify their confidence in that conviction by any positive expression in the brief words which Mr. Coolidge employed in yesterday's statement at Rapid City.

The bolt from the Black Hills caught the market off balance. In the first place, the market had been hit. In a long period of readjustment, which were mainly perpendicular during July and thus far in August, were in part, at least, of their promising definitely that the President in no circumstances would permit his name to be presented to the Republican National Convention next June.

A considerable number of them are relating the interpretation that Mr. Coolidge has withdrawn from the party contest. There is no mystery about this. The generality of party regulars, and even a large segment of those party men inclined to be spotty in their regularity, have assumed that Mr. Coolidge would be nominated for President next year.

Thompson Declines Comment.

William G. Thompson, attorney for the condemned men, shortly after 6 P. M. planning to return to his office in the Tremont Building to await the news of the Governor's decision, being informed that the decision would not be announced until 9:30 P. M., no later to decide—

Continued on Page Four.

CAPITAL DESIRES LIGHT

Thinks President Should Remove All Doubt as to His Intent.

ACCEPTS HIS WITHDRAWAL

But Fears Accusation of Deception Might Follow Lack of Clearer Explanation.

MUCH TALK OF CANDIDATES

Lowden Held Formidable—Hoover Needs Positive Assurance of Coolidge Withdrawal.

Wall Street's "Coolidge bull market" was jarred to its foundations yesterday morning by the President's cryptic announcement that he does not choose to be a candidate for re-election in 1928. There was a pell-mell scramble to sell stocks and opening prices were from 2 to 15¾ points lower than the previous day's close. Then banking institutions, individual operators, pool managers and bargain hunters rushed to the market's rescue with such a volume of buying orders that the decline of stocks was turned to a rally within a brief thirty minutes.

The demonstration of the market's inherent strength and its vigorous rallying power was even more impressive than the selling which had taken place, which was mainly of the panic-stricken, save-my-profit type characteristic of the small trader.

It was the general impression, in banking parlors and brokerage offices, after the close that most stocks had given a good account of themselves. It was a characteristic of the market, and an outstanding one, too, that the trading was most orderly. There were many wide swings, to be sure, and some hurried ones, but the market at all times—even in the hectic fifteen minutes of the first hour when the selling was heaviest—had an outward calm which inspired confidence in it and probably brought in many buying orders.

Market Caught Off Balance.

The sudden injection of an awkward and unsettling political situation into a bull market which has been built upon a basis of general business prosperity, individual corporate expansion, generally good earnings, easy money conditions and the probability of an upswing in operations in basic industries this Fall was the new element which prompted many stockholders to "sell at the market." The President's announcement had not reached Wall Street until 2:15 P. M. the previous day, too late for any market reaction to it, and nervous groups had gathered in brokerage offices after the close, trying to guess what would happen when trading was resumed in the morning.

Continued on Page Four.

Berlin Talks to Buenos Aires By 7,000-Mile Radio Telephone

Copyright, 1927, by The New York Times Co.
By Wireless to The New York Times.

BERLIN, Aug. 3.—Official tests of a radio telephone service between Berlin and Buenos Aires were carried out tonight, representatives of the various departments of the German Government sending greetings to Argentina. The voices carried over the distance of practically 7,000 miles clearly, a cable from Buenos Aires reported.

Since the South American capital was equipped with only a receiving apparatus, the greetings of the Argentine Government had to be sent via cable. Experiments with short-wave transmitters have been conducted over a long period. Tonight's success has led to a decision to build a number of sets of this type and it is hoped that regular wireless telephone service will be opened to the public by January.

NAVAL PARLEY FAILS; FINAL MEETING SET FOR THIS AFTERNOON

Cruiser Difficulty, the Crux of Geneva Conference, Brings Break-Down.

JAPAN'S PLAN FRUITLESS

Gibson Says There Would Be No Advantage in Treaty on 'Authorized' British Program.

By The Associated Press.

GENEVA, Aug. 3.—The tripartite naval conference reached a deadlock tonight, it was stated in authoritative American circles, and the last session is planned for tomorrow. This statement was confirmed later by the Japanese delegation.

It was stated that the delegates had mutually and sorrowfully agreed that no compact could be reached at this time to limit further the naval armaments of Great Britain, the United States and Japan.

This announcement was made after tonight's meeting of the plenipotentiaries to consider the Japanese compromise proposals. The hour of the final session was set for 3 o'clock tomorrow afternoon.

British Not Quite Clear on Plan.

When the private meeting of the delegates opened at the villa of Hugh R. Wilson, American Minister to Switzerland, with Ambassador Hugh S. Gibson, chief American delegate, presiding, the Japanese proposal was immediately brought up for discussion.

W. C. Bridgeman, First Lord of the Admiralty and chief British representative, and his colleague, Viscount Cecil of Chelwood (all accounts of the meeting agree here) were not quite clear as to whether the Japanese compromise could be acceptable to them.

This compromise virtually meant a naval holiday for Great Britain until the United States could catch up with her in new construction. The British delegates, however, indicated that the compromise were acceptable to both the United States and Japan, more time would be required to look into it.

In the Japanese plan the word "authorized" was employed to emphasize that Great Britain and Japan would finish only their authorized cruiser program.

Gibson-Bridgeman Exchange.

Mr. Gibson asked Mr. Bridgeman what he understood this word to signify, adding:

"Does it mean approved and authorized?"

Viscount Cecil answered that it meant "authorized."

After further dueling, Mr. Gibson asked:

"Does it mean the Birkenhead plan?"

Mr. Bridgeman is understood to have answered "Yes."

"Then that means 683,000 tons for Great Britain by 1931," said Mr. Gibson.

Mr. Gibson added that this was higher than the United States could possibly go and that it would mean that America must build up to that figure.

Mr. Bridgeman's reply was that the British did not wish to press the terms of total tonnage.

Mr. Gibson insisted that the United States could build only up to 400,000

When the villa of Hugh Wilson, Time of Wiping……

Continued on Page Three.

NEWS STUNS THE DEFENSE

Decision Is 'Unbelievably Brutal,' Says Statement by the Committee.

WILL CONTINUE THE FIGHT

Asks Millions Throughout the World to Join in Last Desperate Protest.

PATROLS PUT NEAR PRISON

Guard Is Thrown Around the Hotel Where Governor Fuller Spends the Night.

From a Staff Correspondent of The New York Times.

BOSTON, Thursday, Aug. 4.—Gardner Jackson, Chairman of the Sacco-Vanzetti Defense Committee, issued the following statement at 1:15 o'clock this morning:

"The decision of the Governor was delivered at such a late hour that proper answer cannot be prepared to it before morning. The decision is unbelievably brutal in its partisanship, and even more brutal in the omission of facts—not only facts brought out in the course of the case, like the frame-up of expert testimony as shown by the Proctor affidavit, but also facts of the most overwhelming significance established behind closed doors, both before the Advisory Committee and the Governor.

"Inasmuch as the committee and the Governor must justify themselves by reason, and not by partisan fiat, these facts must be disclosed in their entirety. It is a solemn truth that one cannot know the demonstrated facts of the case from the Governor's statement.

"The days separating Sacco and Vanzetti from the electric chair are few, but the defense committee will continue to fight for justice for these two men. Our faith in their innocence is unshaken. We call upon the millions of people throughout the world who have supported them to come forward and join us in this last desperate effort to stay the hand of the judicial hangman."

All through yesterday the defense headquarters of Sacco and Vanzetti housed anxious men and women. A spirit of optimism reigned. Smiles were quick to wreathe the faces of all with the entrance of another visitor. None thought of supper.

As 8 o'clock in the evening drew near, faces appeared drawn and white. What few smiles there were were ostensibly forced. What little there was anything ring of the telephone all eyes were turned on Mary Donovan, Recording Secretary of the Defense Committee, as she picked up the receiver.

Committee in Despair.

At 9:20 word was telephoned that the Governor had left the State House and that the decision would be announced at 10 o'clock.

"God save the Commonwealth of Massachusetts!" were the first words that greeted the announcement of Governor Fuller's decision as it was received here over the telephone from the State House.

The words were expressed by Aldino Felicani, of whose finances doubters by having a committee conduct an investigation entirely independent of my own, their report to be made to me and to be of help in reaching correct conclusions.

A wave of despair swept over the defenders of the forty people assembled there. Some of them had spent each evening of the last few years in the office, working to free the two men.

No Crowd at Headquarters.

To Miss Donovan fell the lot of going to Mrs. Sacco and breaking the news. Mrs. Sacco remained at the tidings stoically and would make no comment.

The absence of crowds around defense headquarters was a surprise. In a closely populated Italian section, it was thought that the streets would be filled during the evening with a large surge of plain-clothes men was stationed in and about the section. Not more than a handful at any time were at the entrance all during the evening.

After the decision had reached the defense office, a battery of photographers gathered at the entrance flashing pictures of the men and women leaving, their heavy and lagging steps eloquently displaying their frame of mind and spirits.

Continued on Page Two.

Crowds Awaited the Governor's Decision; Fuller's Homes and Other Buildings Guarded

BOSTON, Aug. 3 (AP).—Throngs in the streets in front of the newspaper bulletin boards tonight attested to the wide interest in the Sacco-Vanzetti case. The watchers, who included many women, waited quietly for several hours for the word to come of Governor Fuller's decision. A sprinkling of patrolmen paced the sidewalks where the crowds were the largest.

A detail of patrolmen was assigned to the vicinity of the Phillips house of the Massachusetts General Hospital, where Mrs. Fuller was at the bedside of her son, who is recovering from an operation for appendicitis. Another detail patroled the vicinity of the Ritz-Carlton Hotel in the early part of the evening when the Governor was there.

The Governor's city home in Beacon Street, his Summer home at Rye Beach, N. H.; the State prison, the County Courthouse and jail here and the county jail in Plymouth, Vanzetti's home, also were closely guarded.

Full Text of Gov. Fuller's Decision, Ending Long Fight of Prisoners

He Sketches the Crime of Which Sacco and Vanzetti Were Accused, Reviews the Trial in Detail and Concludes by Declaring the Verdict Right and the Men Guilty as Charged.

From a Staff Correspondent of The New York Times.

STATE HOUSE, Boston, Mass., Aug. 3.—Following is the complete text of the official decision of Governor Fuller in the case of Sacco and Vanzetti:

Decision of Governor Alvan T. Fuller in the matter of the appeal of Bartolomeo Vanzetti and Nicola Sacco from the sentence of death imposed under the laws of the Commonwealth:

On April 15, 1920, a paymaster and his guard were held up, robbed and brutally murdered at Braintree, Mass. On May 15, 1920, Nicola Sacco and Bartolomeo Vanzetti were arrested; they were later tried and found guilty of the murder. The verdict was followed by seven motions for a new trial and two appeals to the Supreme Court of the Commonwealth, all of which were heard and later denied. Prior to the trial of the two men in this case Vanzetti had been arrested, tried and convicted of an attempted hold-up on Dec. 24, 1919, at Bridgewater, Mass., and sentenced to fifteen years' imprisonment.

The appeal to the Governor was presented by counsel for the accused on May 3 of the present year. This was my first official connection with the case.

This appeal, presented to me in accordance with the provision in the Constitution of our Commonwealth, has been considered without intent on my part to sustain the courts if I became convinced that an error had been committed or that the trial had been unfair to the accused.

Saw Doubts in Minds of Many.

I realized at the outset that there were many sober-minded and conscientious men and women who were genuinely troubled about the guilt or innocence of the accused and the fairness of their trial. It seemed to me I ought to attempt to set the minds of such people at rest if it could be done; but I realized that with all I could do personally to find out the truth, some people might well in the end doubt the correctness of any conclusion that I, or in fact any other one man, might reach. I believed that I could best reassure these honest and conduct of the jury and others, I find no evidence to support this allegation. I find the jurors were thoroughly honest men and that they were reluctant to find these men guilty, but were forced to do so by the evidence.

I can see no warrant for the assertion that the jury trial was unfair.

The charge of the Judge was satisfactory to the counsel for the accused, and no exceptions were taken to it. The Supreme Judicial Court for the Commonwealth has considered each of the more than 250 exceptions taken during the course of the trial as counsel for the accused chose to appeal, and overruled them all, thus establishing that the proceedings were without legal flaw.

Sees Trial Fairly Conducted.

I have read the record and examined many witnesses and the jurymen to see from a layman's standpoint whether the trial was fairly conducted. I am convinced that it was.

The next question is whether newly discovered evidence is of sufficient merit to warrant a new trial.

After the verdict against these men, their counsel filed and argued before Judge Thayer seven distinct supplementary motions for a new trial, six of them on the ground of newly discovered evidence. All of which were denied.

I have examined all of these motions and read the affidavits in support of them to see whether they presented any valid reason for granting the accused men a new trial. I am convinced that they do not and that I have concluded that the presiding Judge

Continued on Page Two.

DECISION LATE AT NIGHT

State Executive Backs the Original Verdict in Famous Case.

POSITIVE IN CONVICTION

Three Questions Involved in the Case as He Sees It, and He Answers Them Fully.

PRISONERS NOT YET TOLD

Warden Decides It Inadvisable to Inform Them of Doom Until Today.

From a Staff Correspondent of The New York Times.

BOSTON, Aug. 3.—That Nicola Sacco and Bartolomeo Vanzetti were guilty of the payroll murders and robbery at South Braintree on April 15, 1920, for which they have been condemned to die during the week of Aug. 10, was the decision of Governor Alvan T. Fuller, made public at 11:30 o'clock tonight at the State House.

Governor Fuller declared there was no sufficient reason for executive intervention; that there was no justifiable reason for granting a new trial, as the Dedham trial was conducted fairly and without prejudice by Judge Webster Thayer.

The Governor completely exonerated the Judge and jury against charges of unfairness; held that there was no valid reason for a new trial on the basis of newly discovered evidence; discarded the confession of Celestino Madeiros, who swore that, while he took part in the South Braintree murders and hold-up, Sacco and Vanzetti were not implicated; and pointed out that the advisory committee designated by him was unanimous of his opinion.

The committee consisted of President A. Lawrence Lowell of Harvard University; President Samuel W. Stratton of the Massachusetts Institute of Technology, and former Judge of Probate Robert Grant.

Warden to Tell Men Today.

Warden Hendry of Charlestown State Prison received the news of Governor Fuller's decision almost as soon as it was given out at the State House. He said he would not convey it to the condemned men until tomorrow, after their second night in the death house.

The decision is expected to speed up world-wide protests on behalf of the two anarchists, whose sympathizers have kept up a continuous agitation for seven years.

The decision made public tonight was perhaps the most carefully guarded secret concerning an appeal in a criminal case that has ever been locked in the bosom of a Chief Executive. Yesterday, an authoritative source in the official family of Governor Fuller stated that the Governor would neither and the men to the electric chair nor would he allow them to go scot free.

The statement was made with emphasis and apparently out of full knowledge of the Governor's decision. There was no equivocation, no "ifs, buts or ands." This gave rise at the eleventh hour to the apparently well-authenticated report that a reprieve under certain conditions would be the solution.

Now that the Governor has decided to allow the law to take its course, it will not be necessary for him to consult with the State Executive Council. That body was to have held a regular meeting at noon today and was requested to hold over until tomorrow. This was interpreted by the defense as a hopeful sign, as consultation with the council meant to them anything but the death sentence.

Governor Defines His Inquiry.

The inquiry of the Governor was concerned, as he explained in his decision, with these questions:

"Was the jury fair?"

"Were the accused entitled to a new trial?"

"Are they guilty or not guilty?"

He declared that the eleven living members of the jury were of the opinion that the men had a fair trial.

Discussing the allegations of prejudice against Judge Webster Thayer, Governor Fuller cleared the presiding Judge and said he saw no evidence of prejudice in his conduct of the trial.

The Governor's decision had been awaited by throngs in the Boston streets, a tense situation existing as they waited for hours while copies

Continued on Page Two.

"All the News That's
Fit to Print."

The New York Times.

THE WEATHER
Cloudy with probable showers to-
day; tomorrow partly cloudy.
Temperature Yesterday—Max. 72; Min. 63.
For weather report see Page 50.

VOL. LXXVI....No. 25,413.   NEW YORK, TUESDAY, AUGUST 23, 1927.   TWO CENTS in Greater | THREE CENTS | FOUR CENTS

SACCO AND VANZETTI PUT TO DEATH EARLY THIS MORNING; GOVERNOR FULLER REJECTS LAST-MINUTE PLEAS FOR DELAY AFTER A DAY OF LEGAL MOVES AND DEMONSTRATIONS

COOLIDGE PERCHES GOVERNMENT'S SEAT ON PEAK IN ROCKIES

He Reaches Yellowstone Park and Begins at Once His Sight-Seeing Trips.

VISITS CAMP ROOSEVELT

President Passes First Night in a Cottage Surrounded by Snow-Clad Mountains.

CROWDS EXTEND GREETINGS

Mrs. Coolidge and John Share in Ovations at Stations Where Special Train Halted.

From a Staff Correspondent of The New York Times.

MAMMOTH HOT SPRINGS, Yellowstone Park, Wyo., Aug. 22.—The seat of Government tonight is established on a high peak in the Rockies, the furthermost point west to which it has ever gone, in the majestic scenery of Yellowstone Park. With the arrival of President and Mrs. Coolidge into the national playground through the Gardiner entrance the Presidential flag was unfurled over a gray rambling cottage, the home of H. W. Child, President of the Yellowstone Park Transportation Company.

Here for night the President will remain but in the next four days he will pass each night in a different place as he travels over the park. The Presidential special train reached Gardiner in a Summer rainstorm. The mountain tops were covered with snow and through the clouds the sun was shining, presenting a rainbow that added to the first view the President and Mrs. Coolidge had of the national playground. A large station crowd followed the President's party through the five miles to the cottage, where hundreds had gathered to greet the visitors.

In less than three quarters of an hour Mr. and Mrs. Coolidge set out on their first automobile tour of Camp Roosevelt, where they saw the greatest collection of wild game in the United States.

Five-Hour Auto Trip.

As the Presidential party started out on their afternoon auto trip the 'louds disappeared, and the President and Mrs. Coolidge had sunshine throughout a five-hour journey through the northern end of the park. Their trip took them over forty-four miles to Camp Roosevelt, along the small canyon road to Tower Falls and to the petrified tree. H. M. Albright, superintendent of the park, rode in the President's car, in which were the President, Mrs. Coolidge and John. He explained the scenery, delivering a most informative lecture, so the President said later. His recital held the attention of the President, who sat in silence for most of the trip, thrilled by the panoramic scenes unfolded to him at every turn of the road.

The park now is at the height of its beauty, the mountainsides are green, the roads brilliant in early Fall wild flowers and mining life astir as the cold nights approach.

The President not only saw most of Camp Roosevelt, but antelopes jumping from the crags in Gallatin Range and deer feeding in the pools that indent the lowlands not far from the present Summer White House, opposite the Mammoth Hot Springs Hotel.

On the way to Camp Roosevelt the first Rangers had to cut away a tree that the high wind had blown across the road. All along the route motors bearing the licenses of distant States and park buses drove aside to give the President right of way, cheering the President as he passed. The drives seemed throngs with travelers. Nearly 10,000 are estimated now to be within the park area.

Camp Roosevelt was built in 1906 to commemorate President Roosevelt's trip to the park in 1903 in company with John Burroughs. There Colonel Roosevelt pitched his camp, fished for many days and studied the wild life so abundant in this region. Today hundreds of tourists' tents, supplied with many modern comforts, surround the lodge.

Another bear and three cubs and frolicked about undisturbed by the visitors. President and Mrs. Coolidge and John stood in the background watching them. This gave the movie men a good setting and the first real picture of the President's day in the park.

Visitors Grouped in Song.

On the porch were assembled a bevy of pretty girls and young men, known as the "Savages," composed of college students in the park. They formed a solid mass through which the President

Continued on Page Fifteen.

Continued on Page Fifteen.

Coins Word 'Avigation' For Directing of Aircraft

Special to The New York Times.

WASHINGTON, Aug. 22.—The suggestion that the word 'avigation' be used in connection with aeronautics has been made by Lieutenant Lester J. Maitland, who piloted an army plane in the first successful non-stop flight from California to Hawaii. The idea has found favor with officers of the Navy Bureau of Aeronautics.

Lieutenant Maitland suggested that "we use the term 'avigation' for the directing or operating of aircraft from one place to another."

The combination of the Latin roots avi (to fly) and agere (to move) is not only etymologically correct, the bureau officers argued, but the word will serve to differentiate navigation and avigation, very different arts. It is not too much to believe, officers said, "that in years to come a skilled navigator may be entirely useless in an airplane, while 'avigators' will be in great demand for long-distance commercial flying."

WILBUR PREDICTS STUNT FLIGHT CURB

Naval Secretary Says Federal Law Must Stop Loss of Life as in Pacific Race.

TAKES STAND WITH EBERLE

Navy Extends Search for Dole Fliers by Two Days, but Has No Clues.

By The Associated Press.

SAN FRANCISCO, Cal., Aug. 22.—The navy ships and planes searched under an extended "zero hour." Secretary of the Navy Curtis D. Wilbur, a San Francisco visitor, and officials in Washington agreed today that some Federal move must be made to prevent a recurrence of the disasters that have befallen the Dole air race entrants in the Golden Eagle, the Miss Doran and the Golden Eagle.

Admiral Eberle, Acting Secretary of the Navy, in Washington, predicted the enactment by Congress of a law to prohibit long-distance airplane "stunt flights" except under rigid conditions.

At the same time Admiral Eberle ordered the forty naval vessels searching the Pacific for the missing fliers to continue their efforts until Thursday. The original plans were that the search should officially terminate tomorrow night, a week from the date of the start of the Miss Doran and the Golden Eagle.

The extension was made as the result of the disappearance of the Dallas Spirit, piloted by Captain William Erwin of Dallas, Texas, and navigated by A. H. Eichwaldt of Hayward, Cal., which apparently dived into the sea nearly 700 miles west of San Francisco on Friday night after flashing an S O S call on its radio.

Secretary Wilbur was quoted as agreeing that "some step must be taken by the Federal Government to prevent future loss of lives in long-distance stunt flights."

He declined to comment on Admiral Eberle's prediction. He said that the President had some power in this respect, but added he was not sure that this was sufficient to cover the situation.

He declared it was inevitable that some action would be taken "to prevent needless loss of life."

Wide Hunt Lowers Hope for Erwin.

That navy men conducting the hunt for the missing men in the Dallas Spirit held little hope for their rescue was reflected by Lieut. Commander William C. Toose of the destroyer Hazelwood, who said:

"I do not think there is one chance in a thousand that the Dallas Spirit will ever be found. The Hazelwood, in command of Commander E. D. Connor, covered an area of 4,200 square miles about a point where she gave us her last position and by that space there was not a piece of flotsam—not even an oil spot."

The destroyers Hazelwood, Hull, Kidder, Farenholt and Corry were in San Francisco reconnoitering their lard ers and refueling, preparatory to proceeding back out to sea to rejoin the airplane carrier Langley, some 600 miles offshore. The Langley has been dispatching observation planes over as wide area for some purpose.

Reports from Honolulu bore no more hope. The Associated Press correspondent at the island headquarters declared that "another day

Continued on Page Twelve.

Continued on Page Twelve.

WALKER JOKES WITH BEEFEATER GUIDE IN TOWER OF LONDON

Thinks He Could Find Use for Headsman's Block in New York.

RECEIVES STATE WELCOME

Rides With Mrs. Walker From Station to Hotel in Lord Mayor's Gilded Coach.

TENEMENTS IMPRESS HIM

As Guest of Lord Mayor He Sees Greyhounds Race—Leaves for Berlin Today.

Copyright, 1927, by The New York Times Company.
Special Cable to The New York Times.

LONDON, Aug. 22.—Mayor Walker's last day in London was a busy one. He visited the Tower of London, received a delegation of advertising men, inspected model tenements and after a quiet dinner at his hotel attended the greyhound races at White City tonight as the guest of the Lord Mayor of London. Mayor and Mrs. Walker plan to leave tomorrow morning at 8:30 for Berlin, where they are due to arrive Wednesday evening at 8 o'clock.

The Mayor on arriving from Dublin on the boat train just after 8'clock this morning found, although he had not expected it to meet him, the state coach of the Lord Mayor of London waiting at the railroad station. The coach, an ornate, gilt encrusted affair, with two coachmen on the box and two footmen behind, was drawn by a span of beautifully groomed horses.

At the invitation of the Lord Mayor's representative who met them the Mayor and Mrs. Walker entered it and were driven to their hotel.

Immediately after breakfast the Mayor announced that he wanted to see the Tower of London. Mrs. Walker had planned a shopping tour and could not accompany him. The Mayor's secretary telephoned the Governor of the Tower and made an appointment for 11:30.

Mayor Walker was greeted on his arrival by the Governor, who appointed a stalwart "Beefeater" to conduct him through the Tower. The route led through the Bloody Tower down dark, winding stairs to dungeons, execution rooms of the past, gibbets and all manner of terrifying relics until the Mayor faced the execution block.

The Beefeater pointed to the block and began droning the names of those who perished on it. Mayor Walker stepped forward, the better to examine the block.

"A pretty nifty chin-rest those fellows had," he murmured. "It's nice to inspect close up things you missed. But say," he continued, addressing himself to the Beefeater, "I'd like to see this thing working. Can you arrange it?"

The Beefeater apparently didn't see this humor of the Mayor's remark He continued explaining that the block was once used as a summary answer to political opponents.

"Then a demonstration's over," observed the Mayor. "I can provide you material from New York."

"There are marks which make it look as if the axeman missed and got into the rough," he said.

As the party left the execution chamber the Mayor remarked:

"And, no one ever asked for an encore."

Wanted to Meet Gog and Magog.

With the faintest trace of a smile Mayor Walker suggested to the guide that he would like to meet Gog and Magog, the giants whose statues he

Continued on Page Ten.

Continued on Page Ten.

Society Gets Old Irving Home For Centre of Patriotic Work

The old home of Washington Irving at Seventeenth Street and Irving Place became the property of the National Society of Patriotic Builders of America yesterday when, in the living room, Mrs. William Cumming Story, President of the society, received the title from Algernon S. Bell, the former owner.

The dwelling will be the headquarters of the society. It was selected because it was a type consistent with the aims of the society, which, according to Mrs. Story, are "to preserve historic places, support the Constitution and maintain old American ideals."

Mrs. Story said the society would engage in propaganda for the dissemination of American ideals and culture, asserting that there are "many who come to this country and live and yet remain ignorant of American customs and ideals."

MRS. CHAPLIN WINS DIVORCE AND $825,000

She Gets $625,000 for Herself and $200,000 in Trust for the Two Children.

SUIT BASED ON CRUELTY

Actor Is Not in Los Angeles Court to Hear Her and Friends Tell of Alleged Neglect.

Special to The New York Times.

LOS ANGELES, Aug. 22.—Mrs. Lita Grey Chaplin received an interlocutory decree of divorce from Charles Spencer Chaplin, custody of their two small children and $825,000 in Superior Court today. The film comedian did not appear in court. A year must elapse before a final decree is granted.

When the case was called before Judge Walter Guerin, Edwin T. McMurray, uncle of the plaintiff and chief of her counsel, announced the terms of the property settlement under which Mrs. Chaplin is to receive $625,000, said to be in cash, and $200,000 in trust for the children.

Coming to a sudden and undramatic conclusion, the divorce action, based on charges of cruelty and neglect, was devoid of sensation at its quiet ending, very little different from routine cases. All charges referring to premarital relations of the couple made in the complaint were left out by the Judge, who stated that such evidence might be introduced later through testimony, but nothing further was offered.

Chaplin's chief attorney, Gavin McNab, asked the Court to dismiss the comedian's cross-complaint, asserting that his client agreed to the settlement "as an indication of the love of a father for his children, with a desire to keep the taint of scandal from their names."

Only a few sensation-hunters attended the trial, in contrast to the crowds which usually haunt the courts when film colony divorces are on the docket. They were marks which Mrs. Chaplin testify that her husband had taken her out twice during the first two months of their married life, and then only for the sake of appearances, and that he never came home before 1 o'clock in the morning. Denying that she entertained with his career, she declared that she hardly ever saw him at all.

The witness described alleged incidents immediately prior to the

Continued on Page Eight.

Continued on Page Eight.

FULLER HEARS PETITIONERS

Governor Is Under Steady Pressure Until the Final Hour.

WOMEN LAST TO APPEAL

Mrs. Sacco and Miss Vanzetti Leave Him and at 11:03 P. M. He Gives Decision.

DEFENSE TRIED EVERY PLEA

Stone, Taft, Holmes and Other Federal as Well as State Judges Refused to Act.

From a Staff Correspondent of The New York Times.

BOSTON, Aug. 22.—Governor Fuller, at the end of a day marked by rapid and continuous action of the defense for Nicola Sacco and Bartolomeo Vanzetti, told Michael A. Musmanno of defense counsel at 11:03 o'clock tonight that he would not interfere in the execution.

The Governor made his decision after a series of extraordinary events. Counsel for the men, augmented by new and distinguished arrivals from New York and Washington, made eight ineffectual attempts to obtain a stay in the Federal courts and in the Superior and Supreme Court of Massachusetts.

Chief Justice William Howard Taft refused to cross the border from his Summer home in Canada to act on the case. He referred the lawyers to another effort to get Justice Oliver Wendell Holmes proved futile and other Federal and State Judges likewise declined to take jurisdiction.

A final and dramatic appeal by Mrs. Rose Sacco and Luigi Vanzetti to Governor Fuller at the State House tonight preceded the refusal of the Governor to take any further action to stay the carrying out of the death penalty.

Women Make Family Appeal.

Mrs. Sacco and Miss Vanzetti remained with the Governor for an hour and a half at the State House. In the presence of present and past counsel and State officials, the women begged for a respite. Mrs. Sacco appealed to the Governor as the father of children. She urged her motherhood as an argument that justice could weigh with him.

Miss Vanzetti begged for mercy on behalf of her brother. She urged the Governor to act at once and his name would be blessed. She gave Governor Fuller a message from her brother, saying:

"Some day you will realize my innocence."

To both pleas, Governor Fuller replied:

"I am sorry. My duties are outlined by law."

The women had appeared at the State House at 9:06 P. M. and were at once ushered before the Governor. They left his office at 10:35 P. M. Their eyes were dry. They had wept almost all day and they were hardly of tears at the end.

Effort Is Made to the End.

Among those who pressed into the Governor's office until the last hour before the execution were Francis Fisher Kane, former United States attorney in Philadelphia; State Attorney General Arthur K. Reading, William G. Thompson and Herbert B. Ehrmann, former counsel for the men; Gardner Jackson and Aldini Felicani, members of the Sacco-Vanzetti Defense Committee, and Mr. Musmanno.

The Governor remained at his office until the executives were reported to the executives. He had continued to hear the importunities of defense counsel until nearly midnight.

A few minutes before the time for executions the Governor said good-bye to Mr. Thompson, who had defended Sacco and Vanzetti for many years. When he left Mr. Thompson said:

"Briefly, I outlined to the Governor against the important aspect of the case and did what I considered my duty to my former clients, because, despite the fact that I will draw from the case, I believe them innocent and they did not have a fair trial."

Fuller Receives Editor's Plea.

Governor Fuller reached his office at the State House at 11:40 A. M. from his Summer residence at Rye when about 11 o'clock there

Continued on Page Two.

Continued on Page Two.

Four Final Legal Pleas Made to the Governor That Failed to Delay Execution of Death Sentence

From a Staff Correspondent of The New York Times.

BOSTON, Aug. 22.—Four final appeals to Governor Fuller for delay in the execution of the death sentences on Sacco and Vanzetti were based on the following grounds:

1. Willingness of the Department of Justice to open its files to the Commonwealth authorities.

2. The official docketing of the appeal for a writ of certiorari in the United States Supreme Court, which could not be acted on by the court until October.

3. A specific request from Arthur D. Hill, chief defense attorney, to allow alienists to examine Sacco and Vanzetti.

4. A request from Mr. Hill, dated last Friday, to delay until the matter of the Supreme Court and the Department of Justice files had been cleared up.

Governor Fuller, after a full day's consideration of these pleas, announced that he would take no further action.

CITY CROWDS SILENT ON NEWS OF DEATHS

Sacco Sympathizers Disperse After Many Protest Meetings Earlier in Night.

POLICE DOUBLY VIGILANT

Force Guards All Vital Points, While Warren and Inspectors Stay on Duty All Night.

From a Staff Correspondent of The New York Times.

BOSTON, Aug. 22.—Governor Fuller, at the end of a day marked by rapid and continuous silence by their sympathizers here, who had assembled at various points in the city last night to follow the events in the case to the end. Realizing that their protests had been of no avail, the sympathizers broke up into groups and headed for their homes when the final word came. Some booed as they moved off, but there was no real disorder.

Interest in the fate of the two men was keen throughout the city. Newspaper offices were called by thousands seeking the latest development. Telephone operators of THE NEW YORK TIMES handled 1,755 calls for information from early evening to 1:15 A. M. Crowds gathered in the midtown section for the newspaper giving the details of the carrying out of the sentence.

Although there had been no reports of disorder up to an early hour this morning, the police guard on hand, prominent persons and public and semi-public buildings became doubly vigilant and Police Commissioner Warren announced that he would remain at headquarters throughout the night.

5,000 Wait in Streets.

A crowd of approximately 5,000 persons had stood patiently through the hours leading to the execution outside the offices of The Daily Worker at 30 Union Square East. Brief bulletins told of the approach of the death hour and of demonstrations staged throughout the world. Now and then a cheer would go up at announcement of a foreign protest. A bulletin telling how Sacco's wife and the sister of Vanzetti had arranged to plead with Governor Fuller was received in silence.

As the hour of death grew near the crowd knew that all hope had fled and even the murmur of conversations was stilled. When the final announcement was made to the thousands in the square the murmur of exclamations, blended into one noise, leaped up again, but soon died away. Reinforcements of police had been hurried down to support several hundred patrolmen, under command of Captain William H. Ward, who had controlled the fringes of the meeting. But the reinforcements were not needed.

Motorcycle Police Ride By.

At 12:25 A.M., a sign was put up in a second floor window of the newspaper building warning the crowd that the end was nearing. Just at that moment fourteen motorcycle policemen, with sirens screeching, rushed down Fourth Avenue, dashed through the square and continued down without a halt. The advance of the motorcycle detachment caused an uneasy stir in the crowd, many apparently thinking that the meeting was about to be dispersed.

A few minutes after the detachment had roared its way by a sign appeared in the window. It read:

"Sacco murdered."

From a news from women were heard and here and there some one raised the cry of "Shame." Then the crowd, however, remained curiously undemonstrative. Another sign soon hit the window:

"Vanzetti murdered."

Again the crowd stirred uneasily, but soon again remained silent. Police Go Into Action at Noon.

The police were first called into action in connection with Sacco and Vanzetti today at noon when the

Continued on Page Four.

Continued on Page Four.

BOSTON BESIEGED; SCORES ARRESTED

Thousands Watch Squad After Squad of Sacco Picketers March Into Police Hands.

CHEERS AND JEERS MINGLE

Advances on State House Last Till Bail Gives Out—Night Move on Bunker Hill Fails.

From a Staff Correspondent of The New York Times.

BOSTON, Aug. 22.—Boston, most of whose citizens went calmly about their business twelve days ago when the execution of Nicola Sacco and Bartolomeo Vanzetti was stayed until midnight tonight, lost its indifference today and thousands stood in perspiring masses, blackening the northwest corner of Boston Common, while group after group of picketers, displaying placards and waving banners, were arrested by the police. The number arrested before the State House alone exceeded 150.

A lull came in the picketing at nightfall when bail funds were exhausted, but it started up again at 11 o'clock when two more arrests were made at the State House and two out of sixteen picketers were arrested on Main Street, Charlestown, near the prison.

The first two were Paula Holliday, arrested for the third time in two days, and Frank Shay, actor, author and bookseller, both coming from Provincetown. They staged a small-scale demonstration in the glare of searchlights, from the State House roof and every promptly picked up and jailed. Miss Holliday exclaimed as she was picked up, "Is Justice Dead?" slicker.

The two in Charlestown, near the prison, were the other fourteen who had been marching up and down with banners and placards for twenty minutes mingled with the crowd of curious and escaped.

Police Stop March on Bunker Hill.

Immediately afterward police were dispatched to stop a procession of 300 sympathizers marching from the Defense Committee's headquarters in Salem Street out to the Bunker Hill Monument in Charlestown, a distance of nearly two miles. This was the suggestion of Miss Ruth Hale, who suggested a silent demonstration after a session of prayers had been offered on the ground that Sacco and Vanzetti were atheists and would resent being prayed over.

The marchers reached City Square, Charlestown, 90 in all, barred the way. Mounted men charged. No one was seriously hurt. Nine were arrested.

Although there had been no outbreak of violence until the Charlestown explode, Beacon Street, Tremont Street, the Common and Ruthford Avenue near the State Prison in Charlestown gave the picture of a town captured and placed under martial law. Police in uniforms and plain clothes, aboard on horses and motorcycles, and still others packed into automobiles, were everywhere in evidence.

On the streets approaching the prison and the State House every officer was required to take his self elsewhere.

Members of the State Constabulary from all parts of Massachusetts arrived in Boston in two and three motor cars, and many of them were sent to Charlestown, where the total force of 108 were concentrated.

In addition to them and the regular police, squads of railroad and other private patrolmen were drafted, and the about the city. Surrounding the State House alone 250 were on duty of the vicinity of the prison in several watchtowers were assigned to the vicinity of the prison.

Police Into Action in the Morning.

The witnesses gathered in the Warden's office an hour before midnight. They were instructed as to procedure.

W. E. Playfair of The Associated Press was the only reporter permitted to attend the execution, as the State law designated one representative of the press as a witness. His assignment was handed to him six years ago after Sacco and Vanzetti had been convicted in Dedham for the murder of William Parmenter and Alessandro Berardelli.

At 11:30 all but the official witnesses were asked to leave the Warden's office. Led by Warden Henry the official witnesses walked toward the entrance of the prison. By two or three minutes after 12 they were shut in the prison and a key grated in the lock. Just then Mr. Playfair, breathlessly.

"Funny, Warden," he said, touching Mr. Hendry on the arm, "a last

Continued on Page Two.

Continued on Page Two.

WALK TO DEATH CALMLY

Sacco Cries 'Long Live Anarchy'; Vanzetti Insists on His Innocence.

WARDEN CAN ONLY WHISPER

Much Affected as the Long-Delayed Execution Is Carried Out.

MADEIROS FIRST TO DIE

Machine Guns Bristle, Searchlights Glare During Execution—Crowds Kept Far From Prison.

From a Staff Correspondent of The New York Times.

CHARLESTOWN STATE PRISON, Mass., Tuesday, Aug. 23.—Nicola Sacco and Bartolomeo Vanzetti died in the electric chair early this morning, carrying out the sentence imposed on them for the South Braintree murders of April 15, 1920.

Sacco marched to the death chair at 12:11 and was pronounced lifeless at 12:19.

Vanzetti entered the execution room at 12:20 and was declared dead at 12:26.

To the last they protested their innocence, and the efforts of many who believed them guiltless proved futile, although they fought a legal and extra legal battle unprecedented in the history of American jurisprudence.

With them died Celestino F. Madeiros, the young Portuguese, who on seven respites won the "confessed" that he was present at the time of the South Braintree murder and that Sacco and Vanzetti were not with him. He died for the murder of a bank cashier.

The six years' legal battle on behalf of the condemned men was still on as they were walking to the chair and after the current had been applied, for a lawyer was on the way by airplane to ask Federal Judge George W. Anderson in Williamstown for a writ of habeas corpus.

The first two were Paula Holliday, arrested for the third time in two days, and Frank Shay, actor, author and bookseller, both coming from Provincetown.

Sacco cried, "Long live anarchy," as the prison guards strapped him into the chair and applied the electrodes. He added a plea that his family be cared for.

Vanzetti at the last made a short address, declaring his innocence.

Madeiros walked to the chair in a semi-stupor caused by overeating. He shrugged his shoulders and made no farewell statement.

Warden William H. Hendry was almost overcome by the execution of the men, especially that of Vanzetti, who shook his hand warmly and thanked him for all his kindnesses. He was barely able to pronounce above a whisper, the solemn formula required by law:

"Under the law I now pronounce you dead, the sentence of the court having been legally carried out."

The words were not heard by the official witnesses.

After Governor Fuller had refused counsel for the condemned radicals that he could take no action, their attorney, Michael A. Musmanno, made a dash to the prison in an automobile and tried to make sober call on Sacco and Vanzetti, but Warden Hendry refused, as the legal witnesses were just about to pass into the execution chamber.

The Witnesses Gather.

The witnesses gathered in the Warden's office an hour before midnight. They were instructed as to the procedure.

Continued on Page Two.

Continued on Page Two.

Dawes Declares He Is Not a Candidate, Declining Young America Union's Support

Special to The New York Times.

CINCINNATI, Aug. 22.—Vice President Dawes has informed Douglas Atkinson, League Advocate of the Young America Union, a secret nonsectarian political organization, that he is not a candidate for the nomination.

Mr. Atkinson received Mr. Dawes's reply at his home here today to a letter sent on behalf of the Young America Union pledging support to Mr. Dawes if he should run. The Vice President wrote as follows:

"I wish you to accept my thanks for your letter and the clipping which you enclosed. Also for your kindly words. They are all much appreciated. I am, however, not a candidate for the nomination."

The strategy of the campaign which would like to put Mr. Dawes were he ready to run, is to have the support of the young citizens of the country in civic clubs and to awaken in them a civic pride which it is hoped will be all the natural issues of the day. The union now has chapters in Cincinnati, Co-

Special to The New York Times.

WASHINGTON, Aug. 22.—The statement by Vice President Dawes in his letter to Mr. Atkinson that he was not a candidate for the nomination for the Presidency, is viewed by political leaders who are in Washington as merely a reiteration of the position he is said to have taken when approached by others who have sought to sound him out.

The Vice President, it is understood, has not only told friends that he is not seeking the nomination, but has indicated that he would not undertake it himself. It will draw from the case, I believe them innocent and they did not have a fair trial."

lumbus, Youngstown, Cleveland and other large cities in Ohio and is organizing them in other States.

When the candidate Dawes would like to put Mr. Dawes were he ready to run, is to have the support of the young citizens of the country in civic clubs and to awaken in them a civic pride.

The New York Times.

THE WEATHER
Fair today and tomorrow, not much change in temperature.
Temperature yesterday—Max., 68; min., 52.
☞For weather report see Page 54.

VOL. LXXVII....No. 25,444.   NEW YORK, FRIDAY, SEPTEMBER 23, 1927.   TWO CENTS In Greater New York | THREE CENTS Within 200 Miles | FOUR CENTS Elsewhere in the U. S.

GENE TUNNEY KEEPS TITLE BY DECISION AFTER 10 ROUNDS; DEMPSEY INSISTS FOE WAS OUT IN 7TH, AND WILL APPEAL; 150,000 SEE CHICAGO FIGHT, MILLIONS LISTEN ON RADIO

LEGIONAIRES ELECT SPAFFORD AS CHIEF, ENDING CONVENTION

New York Man is Unanimous Choice for National Commander.

GETS OVATION AT SESSION

Veterans in Paris Approve the Stand of Administration at the Geneva Naval Parley.

PASS MITCHELL'S AIR PLAN

Project for Further Immigration Ban Is Tabled—Bissell of New York Heads '40 and 8.'

Copyright, 1927, by The New York Times Company.
Special Cable to The New York Times.

PARIS, Sept. 22.—The convention in France of the American Legion, so long planned and so long heralded, is now history.

The "greatest ever," as the convention is now known to the Legionaires, came to a close this afternoon in a typical burst of fireworks with the election of the new National Commander and other Legion officials. Edward Elwell Spafford of New York City was the man selected for the Legion's highest honor, and he was chosen unanimously, no other name being even offered to the delegates.

It was the choice, which represented the wishes of Legion men from all parts of the country, as he was nominated by the North Carolina delegation and the nomination was seconded by Washington, was announced, the convention broke into pandemonium.

Paris had never before witnessed such a scene. The Legionaires started shouting and honking horns, while canes rapped applause like the sputter of machine guns.

Mr. Spafford was escorted to the platform amid the blare of bugles, the shrill of fife and the thunder of the drums of the band of the Buffalo Post, which went "over the top" into the press box so as to be nearer the centre of activities, scattering the astonished newspaper men.

Nearly Mobbed in Congratulations.

Immediately a seething ocean of Legionaires was trying to shake his hands, thump his back and congratulate him in any way, form and manner as it swirled around him. He climbed onto the speaker's box, which was almost the only island of safety, but it was fully ten minutes before the noise was sufficiently quieted to allow him to make a short speech of acceptance and thanks.

It was a fitting way in which to end the spectacular convention, for it was marked by the same combination of seriousness of purpose and uproarious good humor and enthusiasm which so impressed the Paris populace in the big parade of last Monday. America's unmistakable such a scene. The Legionaires is now a French by-word.

It was also the right spirit in which to close the proceedings, as it wiped out any ill feeling which may have been aroused by the vehement discussions which marked the attempts to map out the Legion's policies in the earlier hours of the session.

As the nominations for the Legion commanders were made the good-natured gayety. The well-known cry of "Never heard of it!" rang out again and again as the various State delegations were called on. But the greatest opportunity for the now renowned humorous sally of the former soldiers came when, on a point of order, a delegate from the Redwood State said, "California yields to Florida."

"What's that?" was heard from every corner of the enormous room amid general laughter, while the Florida delegate cried, "Louder!" and was greeted with cheers.

Election of Vice Commanders.

The five National Vice Commanders chosen represented all sections of the country. They are Troy D. Loftus of Washington, Paul B. Counts of North Carolina, Daniel W. Spurlock of Louisiana, J. M. Henry of Minnesota and Ralph T. O'Neill of Kansas.

The Rev. Gill Robb Wilson was elected National Chaplain. He comes from Trenton, N. J., and was formerly an aviator in the Lafayette Escadrille.

The session was called to order at 9 o'clock in the morning and 'asted, without recess, until nearly 4 in the afternoon. Almost its first official act was to confer on Count Dejean, head of the American Division in the French Department of Foreign Affairs, the distinguished service cross of the Legion in recognition of his valuable services for Legion, to which he was assigned by Foreign Minister Briand to aid in putting

Continued on Page Two.

These are glorious days at Briarcliff Lodge, Briarcliff Manor, N. Y., in the near-by hills. Horseback-riding, golf, dancing—al-fresco features.—Call Briarcliff 1610.—Advt.

Stinson and Schilling Forced Down and Out Of New York to Spokane Non-Stop Air Derby

From a Staff Correspondent of The New York Times.

FELTS FIELD. SPOKANE, Wash., Sept. 22.—The non-stop race from New York to Spokane came to a definite end today when Eddie Stinson was forced down by engine trouble at Missoula, Mont., and C. A. (Duke) Schiller came down at Billings, Mont.

Stinson would have won the race if he had been flying over country where he could have made a landing at any time. When the intake and exhaust valves on one cylinder of his motor went out. he flew around for several hours, trying to get altitude enough to go on with sufficient gliding distance to make a safe landing.

But he could not .get up high enough, and after four or five hours went down at the landing field at Missoula. The field is only 200 miles from Spokane and the time he spent flying in circles would have been sufficient for him to get here. But it was too risky and he wisely quit. Stinson came in with R. E. Dake

in a Waco, the last entry in Class A to arrive. He picked Stinson up as a passenger. Stinson has become a philosopher in his attitude toward long-distance flying. "Sometimes you make it and sometimes you don't," is his motto.

"We had good weather most of the way," he said, "although there was some rain and fog over Michigan. We kept to a great circle course which took us through the centre of Lake Erie and over the other lakes. A good part of the time we were out of sight of land. It got dark while we were over Michigan and dawn found us over North Dakota. I think we kept to our course fairly well all the time until I began circling around after engine trouble developed."

There was much disappointment among the 30,000 people at the field, who had been waiting all day for the non-stop fliers to arrive. The enthusiastic crowd, which cheers every pilot who arrives as if he were a favorite son, gave a rousing reception to Stinson.

INDIANAPOLIS MAYOR QUICKLY CONVICTED

Duvall Faces 30 Days in Jail, $1,000 Fine and 4-Year Bar From Office for Corruption.

TAKES VERDICT IN SILENCE

Bitterness Marks Closing Pleas, Defense Laying Charges to a "Malicious Press."

Special to The New York Times.

INDIANAPOLIS, Sept. 22.—Mayor John L. Duvall was found guilty of violation of the Corrupt Practices act in the Marion County Criminal Court tonight. The penalty is thirty days in the Marion County jail and a fine of $1,000.

The verdict, reported by the jury at 8 o'clock after three hours' deliberation, makes Mayor Duvall ineligible to hold public office for four years after the date of the crime.

Duvall was pale when the verdict was read and his only comment was: "I have nothing to say."

Under the Corrupt Practices act Duvall was specifically charged with promising William H. Armitage, a politician, the privilege of naming three members of the City Administration in exchange for a cash consideration and support in the 1925 mayoralty campaign. The same Grand Jury which acted upon results of a year's inquiry into alleged political corruption in Indiana also indicted Governor Ed Jackson on a charge of attempting to bribe former Governor Warren T. McCray.

Final Pleas Stir Courtroom.

Ralph Inman, defense counsel, and William H. Remy, Marion County Prosecutor, this afternoon held the packed courtroom spellbound during their pleas which at times became so bitter that the audience gasped.

The crowd got so worked up that once. when work upon a new elevator shaft in the courthouse loosened plaster and showered it through an aperture into the courtroom, half a hundred spectators sprang to their feet in alarm.

Mr. Remy demanded that the jury send Duvall behind the bars for violating the Corrupt Practices act. Mr. Inman denounced the prosecution of Duvall as the result of acts of a malicious press and demanded that the press be "driven out of town."

With Mr. Remy's argument climaxing about 4:20 and Special Judge Cassius C. Shirley taking about half an hour for instructions, the case went to the jury at about 5 P. M.

Mr. Inman fired implacable of ridicule at the State attorneys and the chief State witness, William H. Armitage, and Mr. Remy spent about half of his time in reply.

Answering Mr. Inman's charge that the prosecution of Duvall was a matter of political hatred, Mr. Remy pounded upon the railing of the jury box and declared:

"As long as I am in office this fight against political corruption is going to continue and I pledge myself to the jury and to all the people here that this case will not be the end."

Hurling invectives at the prosecution attorneys and the prosecution witnesses, Mr. Inman charged that he was the victim of "a sinister influence in Indianapolis which must be satisfied and should be driven out—a malicious press."

"John Duvall isn't the first Indianapolis man made to suffer and defend himself solely because he was unfortunate enough to run and be elected to office," he declared.

In his attack on William H. Freeman and William H. Armitage, the State's chief witnesses, Mr. Inman accused Freeman of "willful, corrupt and deliberate" perjury in part of his testimony.

"It is significant that Armitage never talked before his brother was sentenced to jail," he said. "You could tell by the look in his eyes he would tell any kind of a story to save his brother from going to prison for three months."

Defense Denounces the Press.

Mr. Inman declared that Duvall was the victim of "a sinister influence in Indianapolis which must be satisfied and should be driven out—a malicious press."

DARING FLIER, NUMB, AVOIDS CRASH IN CITY

Steve Lacey, on Western Dash, Dazed by Fumes as Gasoline Swirls About His Feet.

MOTOR SPUTTERED AN HOUR

He Fails to Dump Fuel, Fights Back to Field, Lands Safely and Falls Unconscious.

Special to The New York Times.

ROOSEVELT FIELD, L. I., Sept. 22.—A courageous pilot with a sputtering engine fought for an hour to keep his plane under control over New York City and the surrounding area yesterday afternoon, while gasoline swirled four inches deep around his feet and sent up fumes which numbed his hands and his brain. Battling these obstacles, he brought the plane down on the field here and fell over unconscious.

The pilot was Steve Lacey, who had tried so desperately to take part in the non-stop race to the Pacific against C. S. (Duke) Schiller and Eddie Stinson. With his navigator, Louis A. Yancey, he had worked most of the night repairing his blue and silver biplane Air King, which had lost its tail skid in an unsuccessful effort to take off yesterday.

Today, though the New York-Spokane air derby limit was past and he could not hope to share in the non-stop prize money, he took off again in an endeavor to make good his promise to fly westward "just for fun." The ill luck which balked him yesterday dogged him today. He and Yancey got away perfectly at 12:52 P. M. and soon disappeared from sight. In a few minutes they reappeared and came down with their heavily laden plane, making a perfect landing at 100 miles an hour. Their engine was not functioning properly. It was tuned again and readjusted and up they soared once more.

Then came the mishap unique in aviation, which almost cost both men their lives and only for their heroism would have sent a plane loaded with hundreds of gallons of gasoline roaring in flames into the streets of New York.

Misfortune threatened them from the start of their last flight. It was 2:21 P. M. The Wright Whirlwind motor apparently was functioning perfectly again as Lacey gave the ship the gun and it rolled along the ground. It was running beautifully at 2,000 feet from the starting point

Continued on Page Three.

Pope Pius Sends $100,000 to Flood Sufferers; Bishops in Mississippi Area to Distribute It

Pope Pius XI has contributed $100,-000 to the relief of the flood sufferers in the Mississippi Valley. The gift was made public here yesterday by the Right Rev. Dr. Edmond A. Walsh, vice-president of Georgetown University and President of the Catholic Near East Welfare Association. Dr. Walsh was Director-General of Papal Relief during the post-war famines in Europe.

The Pope's intention to help victims of the flood was first made known by the Pontiff during a recent visit of Dr. Walsh to the Vatican. Dr. Walsh went to Rome to report on the activities of the new association. Joseph P. Moore, General Secretary of the association, was also present when the Pope first spoke of his intention to make the donation.

Dr. Walsh was designated by the Pontiff to bring the gift to America and present it to the hierarchy of the United States. This he did last week in Washington at the annual meeting of the archbishops and bishops in the Catholic University of America.

"My Maryland," Johnson's Thos.—One pint out of a 39 Florida bottle—$1.20 A.M. Dally—Baseboard, 142 W. 42d St. Tel. Wis.4271.—Advt.

was made by Cardinal O'Connell of Boston, Chairman of the meeting. A Committee of Bishops from the flood area was formed immediately. On the committee are:

The Most Rev. John W. Shaw, Archbishop of New Orleans; the Right Rev. John B. Morris, Bishop of Little Rock, Ark.; the Right Rev. Cornelius Van de Ven, Bishop of Alexandria, La.; the Right Rev. Jules V. Jeanmard, Bishop of Lafayette, La.; the Right Rev. Richard O. Gerow, Bishop of Natchez, Miss.

The committee is now drawing up recommendations for the most economical and practical disposal of the money.

"As head of the Catholic Church, Pope Pius desired to do something personal in addition to the help already sent to the stricken areas by the various dioceses in the United States," said Dr. Walsh yesterday at his headquarters, 480 Lexington Avenue. "The only regret of his Holiness was that he could not send more."

THE SOUTHERNER.—One night out to all Florida points—7:30 A.M. Dally—Seaboard, 142 W. 42d St. Tel. Wis.4271.—Advt.

TREND TOWARD SMITH PLAIN IN FAR WEST AS LEADERS GATHER

Indications Point to First Raising of His Banner at Ogden (Utah) Conference.

11 STATES REPRESENTED

Iowa Democrats at Own Request, Join Gathering, Which Begins Deliberations Today.

TARIFF IS ON THE AGENDA

Most Available Presidential Candidate and Two-thirds Rule Also Topics.

From a Staff Correspondent of The New York Times.

OGDEN, Utah, Sept. 22.—Democrats in the intermountain States, who went to the Democratic National Convention in 1924 for the most part as enthusiastic supporters of William Gibbs McAdoo, are swinging to Governor Alfred E. Smith of New York. There are indications that at a conference which will begin here tomorrow for the discussion of problems vital to the party they will raise the Smith banner and start the first organized movement in the nation to further the Presidential aspirations of New York's Chief Executive, who, as he did in 1924, will enter next year's Democratic national conclave as the favorite son of his party in the Empire State.

At the Hotel Bigelow, where the conference will be held, fifty rooms have been reserve for prospective conferees, and it is probable that fully that many will attend. Nearly all of those who are expected to answer the roll-call when the meeting is called to order at 10 o'clock tomorrow morning are prominent elements of Mr. McAdoo. Almost without exception, too, they are at least politically dry, as are the Democratic organizations in the several States which will be represented at the gathering.

Prominent Conferees.

At least two Democratic National Committeemen who wield considerable influence in party councils have accepted invitations to the conference. They are Isidore B. Dockweiler of California and James H. Moyle of Utah. Today, unexpectedly and to the great delight of those who have taken the initiative in calling the conference, there was added to the number of prominent participants Delbert M. Draper of Salt Lake City. Mr. Draper, formerly of the Central Committee, and, it is said here, a real power in the party organization in this State. Another spokesman for Utah will be J. W. Stringfellow, Secretary of the organization in Salt Lake City, which supplies approximately one-half of the votes cast in the State. He is openly for Governor Smith for President.

Fred W. Johnson of Rock Springs, Wyo., and former State Senator Joseph Chez of Utah, to whose initiative, in party months the Democrats in these Far Western States owe their opportunity to come together to discuss party problems, said today that it should be clearly understood that no one will be asked at the conference to offer the delegation from his own State to Governor Smith next year.

Purpose of the Meeting.

It is admitted, in fact, that grave doubt exists whether any of the conferees would be in a position to make

Continued on Page Twenty.

GREATEST RING SPECTACLE

Crowd Pays $2,800,000 to Watch Contest at Soldier Field.

THRONG IN SEATS EARLY

Largest Boxing Assemblage in History Handled Smoothly by Police and Ushers.

MANY NOTABLES PRESENT

Senators, Governors and Business Leaders Rub Elbows With Obscure Sport Fans.

By JAMES R. HARRISON.

Special to The New York Times.

CHICAGO, Sept. 22.—Out of the welter and turmoil and clamor of the "fight of the ages" one clear fact stands out—that tonight Tex Rickard unveiled the most beautiful picture in the history of sports here or elsewhere.

One hundred and fifty thousand persons watched in the darkness—the greatest of all boxing crowds by about 35,000. It would fill more than two Yankee Stadiums and almost two Yale Bowls; it would pack the Polo Grounds to capacity and leave 100,000 on the outside.

The total receipts were put at $2,800,000.

Governors and Mayors and United States Senators and millionaires lent the right tone to the occasion and millions listened to the story of the fight as it went out "on the air."

Yet the facts and figures do not seem particularly important as compared to the sheer beauty of a picture that only an artist could paint. This may or may not have been "the fight of the ages," but it most certainly was the "sight of the ages."

The veil of darkness over it all; the rippling sea of humanity stretching out as far as the eye could see; the Doric columns of Soldier Field glowing a soft white along the upper battlements of the arena; and finally the ring itself, where two men fought it out with their fists in a pool of white light—these were the high spots of an unforgettable spectacle.

Impressive in Its Vastness.

It was a picture that should have been seen from the air, from the cockpit of an airplane, where the lights and shadows and the blacks and whites of the panorama could have been viewed in their proper perspective.

The ingredients of the picture were striking. A long, low oval stadium of classic lines, filled to its utmost rim. A gently sloping bank of humanity that seemed to stretch to the horizon, and in the centre of the canvas a twenty-foot ring bathed in the fierce light that beats about a throne.

The vastness of the spectacle was its most impressive quality. It filled the eye and staggered the senses. We have seen the Yale Bowl jammed with people, and last November we saw the same Soldier Field at the Army-Navy game, but this was the crowd of crowds and the spectacle of spectacles, lacking only the natural beauty of Poughkeepsie and New London.

Even though he did not sell all of his 163,000 seats, Rickard reached a long cherished goal in his career as an impresario. The 90,000 of Boyle's Thirty Acres and the 115,000 of the Sesquicentennial were left far behind as Chicago and its influx of fight fans poured through the portals of this sports temple.

There they sat, shoulder to shoulder, from the ring up to the top row where American flags rippled in a brisk western wind. Not that the stadium was full. The cheaper $5 seats, a few city blocks to the north and south, were sparsely settled, proving that you may lead a boxing fan to water but you can't make him drink.

This will probably stand as the record crowd of ring history, because people will sit only as far away from the scene of activities. And tonight Rickard reached the limit in distances. His $5 patrons were 700 or more feet from the ring, while the Yankee Stadium would locate them somewhere beyond the centre field fence.

Some Bring Radio Sets.

Time was when a fight fan could buy almost any seat and see the proceedings with the naked eye. But no more. As the citizens flocked through the gates half of them were armed with binoculars, opera glasses and telescopes. Here and there one could see some shrewd lads who had brought portable radios with them. They were the $5 boys, who were going to listen even if they did not

The committee was the fair and warmer, for that was a perfect forecast. The fans brought light coats with them, but they were hardly necessary, especially around the ring, where the heat of the bright lights was very noticeable.

The afternoon was gray and overcast and twilight showed a drab, threatening sky and mist which foreshadowed

Continued on Page Eighteen.

GENE TUNNEY, STILL THE CHAMPION.

DEMPSEY TO APPEAL DECISION ON FIGHT

He Says Tunney Was Down for 14 or 15 Seconds in the Seventh Round.

TIMEKEEPER CITES RULE

And Boxing Commissioner Says the Point Was Explained Before Bout Started.

Special to The New York Times.

CHICAGO, Sept. 22.—Jack Dempsey and his manager, Leo Flynn, announced tonight that they intend to appeal to the Illinois Boxing Commission to reverse the decision of the referee and two judges allowing Gene Tunney to retain his world's heavyweight title.

"Intentionally or otherwise, I was robbed of the championship," Dempsey said in his dressing room after the bout. "In the seventh round Tunney was down for a count of fourteen or fifteen. Every stopwatch around the ring caught the time as about fifteen seconds, and the inefficiency of the referee or the timekeeper or both deprived me of the fight.

"Everybody knows I am not a whiner. When Tunney beat me last year I admitted that he was the better man that night. I am not an alibi artist, but I know down in my soul that I knocked Tunney out tonight, and, what's more, chased him all around the ring and should have won on points at least."

There they sat, shoulder to shoulder, from the ring up to the top row where American flags rippled in a brisk western wind. Not that the stadium was full. The cheaper $5 seats, a few city blocks to the north and south, were sparsely settled, proving that you may lead a boxing fan to water but you can't make him drink.

"Tunney was cleanly knocked out for the count of fifteen in the seventh round. Look at that watch here. It has stopped on the figure fifteen. I have not found a watch yet that got the count under ten. I'm not saying the referee was dishonest. I'm saying that he was inefficient, and it amounts to the same thing as far as we are concerned.

"He failed to take up the timekeeper's count at the start—didn't take it up until the timekeeper had got to four or five. This is the biggest injustice I have ever seen in a ring. Leaving aside the knockout in the seventh round, Jack knocked him down again in the ninth and chased him all around the ring. Why didn't Tunney come out and fight like a champion? Dempsey clearly won on points.

"You can say this for me. Dempsey will fight Tunney any time and any place and knock him out."

Dempsey Wants Another Fight.

"Will I fight but again?" echoed Dempsey. "You bet your life. I beat Tunney tonight and I will beat him again any time he wants to get into the same ring with me. I am not ready to retire, by a long shot—not when they hand me a decision like that tonight.

There was plenty of high dudgeon in the Dempsey dressing room

Continued on Page Eighteen.

STORY OF THE FIGHT TOLD BLOW BY BLOW

Detailed Description of Tunney-Dempsey Bout From the Ringside.

BOTH FIGHTERS AGGRESSIVE

Bout Is Marked by Lively Exchanges—Dempsey Hangs On at the End.

Special to The New York Times.

RINGSIDE, SOLDIER FIELD, CHICAGO, Sept. 22.—The detail of the Tunney-Dempsey bout, which was fought here tonight, follows, round by round:

First Round.

Dempsey rushed Tunney, who sidestepped, and Dempsey again swung a left and clinched and Tunney hooked a left. Tunney hit a right to face an the clinch. Referee pulled them apart. Tunney flashed left to Dempsey's face. Dempsey bobbed and weaved and jabbed to Tunney's face. Tunney came in with a right to Dempsey's jaw. Tunney twice jabbed with lefts to the face and they clinched. Tunney followed with a right to Dempsey's jaw and then dodged away from Dempsey's left hook. Gene looked to Dempsey's body. Gene again got Jack against the ropes and dealt Tunney a left to the head and face.

In a masterful exhibition of boxing Tunney was evading the attack of his heavier rival and was countering cleanly, superbly, skillfully, accurately the whole for half of the round or so.

Second Round.

Tunney jabbed a left to face. Dempsey sent one to chest. They clinched and Tunney held Dempsey's arm. Dempsey put a straight left to jaw, backing Dempsey to the ropes. Dempsey missed a right to the jaw as Dempsey ducked and then Tunney drove a right to the head. Dempsey hooked a left to the head and pounded the body when Tunney left himself open. Tunney drove two rights to the head and clinched. Tunney crossed a right to the jaw and another clinch followed. Tunney put a left to the body and Tunney a left to the face and clinched. Tunney drove two rights to Dempsey's head. Dempsey put a left to Tunney's face and another to the body.

Third Round.

They danced about at start of the third and Gene led with a right as Dempsey hooked three lefts to the body. Gene started a right hook to Jack's body, but stopped the blow short as they clinched. Tunney rushed Dempsey and landed with short lefts. Jack drove away with Gene's body. The blows being perilously close to the belt line. They got in at close quarters and Dempsey again hit a few and Jack hooked "Low" to the referee. Dempsey was short with a left and then Tunney missed a short right and Tunney danced away from a short left. Gene missed a left and came in at close quarters to hook at Dempsey.

Continued on Page Eighteen.

FIGHT FAST AND FURIOUS

On Verge of Knockout in Seventh Round Tunney Comes Back Strong.

FLOORS DEMPSEY IN EIGHTH

Referee and Judges Unanimous in Their Verdict for the Champion.

DISPUTE ON KNOCKDOWN

Challenger Went to Wrong Corner and Thus Delayed Count on Tunney for Few Seconds.

By JAMES P. DAWSON.
Special to The New York Times.

RINGSIDE, SOLDIER FIELD, CHICAGO, Sept. 22.—His refusal to observe the boxing rules of the Illinois State Athletic Commission, or his ignorance of the rules, or both, cost Jack Dempsey the chance to regain the world's heavyweight championship here tonight in the ring at Soldier Field.

By the same token this disregard of rules of ring warfare, or this surprising ignorance, saved the title for Gene Tunney, the fighting ex-marine, who has been king of the ring for just a year.

The bout ended with Tunney getting the decision, and the vast majority of the staggering assemblage of 150,000 people, who paid, it is estimated, $2,800,000 to see this great sport spectacle, approved the verdict.

The decision was given by Referee Dave Barry and Judges George Lytton, wealthy department store owner, and Commodore Sheldon Clark, of the Sinclair Oil Company. It was announced as a unanimous decision, but this could not be verified in the excitement attending the finish of the battle. But it should have been unanimous according to all methods of reasoning and boxing scoring, for Tunney won seven of the ten rounds, losing only the third, sixth and seventh, in the last of which, Dempsey made his great mistake. It is known that Judge Lytton voted for Tunney.

Dempsey's Furious Plunge.

In that seventh round Dempsey was being peppered and buffeted about on the end of Tunney's left jabs and hooks and sharp though light right crosses, as he had been in every preceding round, with the exception of the third.

Then Dempsey, plunging in recklessly, charging full-tilt, furiously and with utter contempt for the blows of the champion, since he had tasted of Tunney's best previously, suddenly landed a long, wicked left to the jaw with the power of old. This he followed with a right to the jaw, the old "iron mike" as deadly as ever, and quickly drove another left hook to the jaw, under which Tunney toppled like a falling tree, hitting the canvas with a solid thud near Dempsey's corner, his hand reaching blindly for a helping rope which somehow or other refused to be within clutching distance.

Count Begun and Halted.

The knockdown brought the knockdown timekeeper, Paul Beeler, to his feet automatically, watch in hand, eyes glued to the ticking seconds and he bawled "one" before he looked upon the scene in the ring.

There he saw Dempsey in his own corner, directly above the prostrate, brain-numbed Tunney, sitting there looking foolishly serious, his hand finally resting on the middle ring strand. Beeler's count stopped.

Referee Barry never started one.

It is the referee's duty to see to it that a boxer scoring a knockdown goes to the corner farthest from his fallen foe and it is the duty of the knockdown timekeeper

Continued on Page Eighteen.

"All the News That's Fit to Print."

The New York Times.

THE WEATHER
Partly cloudy and continued cold today and tomorrow; west winds.
Temperature yesterday—Max. 32, Min. 24.
☞For weather report see Page 47.

VOL. LXXVII....No. 25,531.   ★ ★ ★   NEW YORK, MONDAY, DECEMBER 19, 1927.   TWO CENTS In Greater New York | THREE CENTS Within 200 Miles | FOUR CENTS Elsewhere in the U. S.

SIX MEN FOUND ALIVE IN TORPEDO ROOM OF SUNKEN S-4; TAP PATHETIC PLEA 'HOW LONG WILL YOU BE?' TO DIVER; NAVY BATTLES AGAINST TIME TO LIFT SHATTERED CRAFT

AMITY WITH MEXICO IS BROUGHT CLOSER BY LINDBERGH VISIT

Mexico City Hears President Calles Will Go to Havana to Meet Coolidge.

TOTTERING STOCKS RISE

Confidence in Efforts of Ambassador Morrow and the Flier Revives Business.

POPULAR FEELING CHANGING

Parading Workers Cheer Lindbergh and Morrow—Aviator Sees a Bullfight, but Is Silent.

By RUSSELL OWEN.
Staff Correspondent of The New York Times.
Copyright, 1927, by The New York Times Company. All Rights Reserved.
By Wireless to The New York Times.

MEXICO CITY, Dec. 18.—The visit of Colonel Charles A. Lindbergh to Mexico already has brought about some remarkable results, political, economic and social. He has acted as a clarifying agent in a slowly enveloping situation. Not even the our Ambassador Morrow, who paved the way, probably expected anything so immediately valuable to an accord between the two nations.

Out of the dramatic interest in Colonel Lindbergh, who seems determined to make men of alien race forget their difference in a common admiration of a splendid manhood, has come a definite advance toward a solution of the so-called Mexican problem.

The most significant of the movements in that direction are the reports that President Calles will go to Havana to meet President Coolidge at the Pan-American Congress.

Just what might come of such a meeting in the form of a better economic and social understanding between the two countries men grown old and discouraged in Mexican affairs do not dream of predicting.

Mexico Eager for Amity.

All they know is that with Calles apparently seated firmly in power, with a prospect of comparative internal peace in Mexico and with a wave of sentiment breaking down the barriers between the United States and Mexico, there might come from a meeting of the two Chief Executives an understanding of which the consequences could not be estimated.

Mexico is tired of fighting. Mexico wants peace and a better degree of prosperity. There are those who believe this lies in a very distant future. But at the same time, under the stir of the emotional reaction of Mexico to Colonel Lindbergh's visit and the honest, commonsense work of Ambassador Morrow, there are many who see a new opportunity for Mexico, both financial and social.

Morrow in Leading Rôle.

As a factor in bringing about this situation Ambassador Morrow has played a leading rôle. He has used diplomacy in Mexico on a new basis, treating those with whom he has dealt as men of their word who wished the best for their country. If he differed with them, he tried to see their point of view, to find some point of mutual agreement. The result has been remarkable, and it is not stretching the truth to say that Ambassador Morrow is one of the most popular men in Mexico.

Slowly there has penetrated to the minds of the Mexican people a suspicion that the gringo is not the national enemy of Mexico. Ambassador Morrow's unfailing courtesy—his tact, his willingness to go personally to members of the Mexican Government instead of writing notes to them, his refusal to be anything but frank—has brought about the feeling which led today to thousands being carried in a parade of workmen, the workmen who have been called Bolsheviki, a banner with the inscription, "Morrow is an honest man."

Lindbergh Crystallizes Situation.

This tendency to change the Mexican attitude toward America and its representatives was still inchoate when Colonel Lindbergh arrived. When this frank, simple and courageous representative of America dropped over the wings of his famous plane, Mexico was swept by a wave of pro-Americanism which is difficult to realize, even in the midst of it. There is something about this young aviator, a magnificent simplifi-

Continued on Page Six.

"NEW YORK-FLORIDA LIMITED"—9.40 P. M. Daily. Jacksonville next morning. Coast Line at West Palm Beach, Tampa, Sarasota, St. Petersburg Stations next noon. C. of G. 143 West 42d St. Tel. Wis. 5457.—Advt.

Lindbergh Praises Skill of Riders and Ropers Who Perform for Him

Calls Labor Parade in His Honor Expression of Friendliness for the United States—Not Certain How He Should Wear Gift Cape.

By Colonel CHARLES A. LINDBERGH.
Copyright, 1927, in the United States, Canada, Mexico, Cuba, Central and South America, Europe and the British Dominions by The New York Times Company. All rights reserved.
By Mexican War Department Wireless Direct to The New York Times.

MEXICO CITY, Dec. 18.—This has been another of these wonderful Mexican days. There seems to be no end of them. And I have seen two of the sports of Mexico under a perfect sky and brilliant sun.

The exhibition of roping and riding at the Rancho de Charros was one of the finest things of the kind I have ever seen. Then came the review of members of the Mexican Labor Unions at the National Palace, which was a gratifying expression of friendliness toward the United States.

Receives Cape From Matador.

The much debated bull fight came in the afternoon. I received a beautiful cape here, presented by José Ortiz, one of the matadors. The workmanship on it is different from anything of the kind I have ever seen and it is one of the best nationalistic gifts I have had.

I am not quite certain yet how I should wear it, but Señor Ortiz placed it over my shoulders and I suppose that is the way it should be worn.

Last night I had the first opportunity of seeing some of the country around Mexico City from an automobile in which we drove out some way toward Puebla over a wide and smooth road.

The road went up through the mountains, from which there was a splendid view of Mexico City and the valley. I should think this would be a great tourist centre.

Sees Chance for Hotels.

It is one of the most picturesque places on the continent, easy of access and with a delightful climate. If a few hotels were built on these hills, with golf courses laid out near them, so that it would be possible to stay in the country, it should be one of the most attractive places in North America.

This valley has a romantic history and contains the remains of the old Aztec and Toltec civilizations, which were the oldest north of the Isthmus. The Toltecs and Mayas people were cultured peoples whose ruins are among the most interesting in the world. I am looking forward to a visit to the famous pyramids, where I may see what is believed to be the ruins of the Toltec city.

Tourists Would Bring Air Lines.

It is hard to believe now that this whole valley was originally a huge lake, with little islands in it on which the ancient cities were built. It must have been a beautiful spot in those days, even more so than now, although Mexico City is one of the most delightful I have ever visited.

If tourists would come to Mexico in greater numbers it should be possible to build up air lines which would make it much more accessible. The United States is now two days away by railroad, but it would be only a few hours by airplane. Flying in multi-motored planes is as safe as travelling by rail and in the next few years there should be developed a series of airlines to connect all this part of the continent and extend to South America.

YOUTH ARRESTED IN CHILD SLAYING AT LOS ANGELES

Doctor's Son, a University Man, Held as Suspect in Kidnapping of Marion Parker.

ANOTHER TAKEN IN NEVADA

Clues Found in Suitcase, Abandoned Auto and Tailor's Story of Bloody Coat.

$50,000 REWARD POSTED

Volunteers Raise the Fund and Join Full Police Force in Wide Hunt for Murder Gang.

By The Associated Press.

LOS ANGELES, Dec. 18.—The police late today arrested a suspect in the Marian Parker murder case whose name they refused to divulge.

Officers stated, however, that the prisoner was a man of 25 years, the son of a Los Angeles doctor, a military school and university man and known in the past to have committed offenses against young girls.

The police had earlier declared they had fingerprints of the man wanted which would convict him if captured. These prints were taken from the ransom letters and the originals of the filed telegrams.

Police Describe Type of Guilty Man.

Police investigators here point out definite qualifications which mark the slayer and which are applied to all suspects taken into custody.

Aside from his physical appearance, which is fairly well known from testimony by several who saw him, and his fingerprints taken from his letters, he is, say the officers, keen-minded, well-educated, egotistic, particularly in believing that he has a master criminal mind.

He has some knowledge of anatomy, as evidenced in the dissection of Marian Parker's body. He has a smattering of education in Greek, but only a smattering, for while he used Greek characters in spelling the word "death" in some of his messages to his little victim's father, he used two of them wrongly.

Also, say the police investigators, he had full information on residents in the neighborhood of the Parker home and was thoroughly acquainted with the district.

They point out as well that his admonition to Parker to seek "aid from God and not from man," combined with the ability to destroy innocence as he destroyed it, place him in the category of the mentally warped and the degenerate.

It may be, investigators declare, that the girl's slayer in penning his letters and telegrams to Parker patterned them after the scholarly style of Leopold and Loeb, Chicago's youthful slayers.

Acting on information which they said came from a confidential source a squad of Los Angeles officers tonight descended on Tijuana, across the Mexican border from San Diego, and began combing the dives there for a clue to the killing.

Doubtful on Las Vegas Suspect.

LAS VEGAS, Nev., Dec. 18 (P).—Lewis D. Wyatt was taken from the Red Feather stage here tonight by Los Angeles detectives seeking the kidnapper and slayer of Marian Parker.

He was held for questioning in the Clark County Jail here. His photographs and fingerprints will be rushed to Los Angeles by plane tomorrow. Wyatt, said the California officers, was too stocky to correctly answer

Continued on Page Four.

SEWER CHARGES GO TO CONNOLLY TODAY

Scudder Also Expected to Fix Time and Place, Probably Jan. 3 in Queens Court House.

TWO-FOLD DEFENSE LIKELY

Friends Say Borough President Will Attack Motives of His Accusers and Uphold Costs.

Supreme Court Justice Townsend Scudder, who has been designated by Governor Smith to hear the charges of official misconduct against Borough President Maurice E. Connolly of Queens, is expected to have a copy of the charges served upon Mr. Connolly today, together with notification of the time and place of the hearings.

The law provides that the accused shall have at least eight days in which to prepare his answer after the charges are served upon him. As Christmas Day will intervene, Governor Smith has suggested that Justice Scudder give Mr. Connolly ten days to prepare his answer. This would bring the time as close to New Year's Day that it is believed Justice Scudder may not fix the time any earlier than Jan. 3. The Queens County Court House in Long Island City, where Justice Scudder tried the Snyder-Gray murder case, is regarded as the most likely location for the hearings. It is provided by law that the inquiry shall be held within the county where the accused lives.

Justice Scudder, having spent Saturday in Utica to attend a meeting of the trustees of the Masonic Home there—he is a past Grand Master of the Grand Lodge of Masons for New York State—returned to New York yesterday. He went to his home at Glen Head, L. I., in Nassau County, which he left last night for the Hamilton Club, Brooklyn, where he stays while occupying the bench in Brooklyn or Queens. He made no announcement regarding his plans for the inquiry, and, so far as known, has not yet selected a special counsel to assist him.

Steuer Still Undecided.

Max D. Steuer, criminal lawyer, whom Connolly is said to act as his counsel at the Scudder inquiry, said yesterday that he had not yet been able to say whether he could accept the retainer. He explained that he had been unable to communicate with three opposing attorneys in three suits in which he is to appear next month, in his effort to persuade them to agree to postponements so that he can accept the Connolly case.

One case, he went on, was in the State courts and had been peremptorily

Continued on Page Eight.

City Watches in Vain for Newest Comet; Skjellerup Body Expected by Christmas

The latest visitor from space to make the acquaintance of the solar system, the Skjellerup Comet, which has been making progress in a northerly direction ever since it was discovered by an amateur astronomer of Melbourne, Australia, on Dec. 3, was still invisible to New Yorkers at 5:30 Saturday afternoon. It had been announced in some quarters on Friday that the next day would mark the new comet's appearance over the local horizon.

Dr. Clyde Fisher, curator of astronomy at the American Museum of Natural History, has been looking for it at 5:30 o'clock, just after the sun has set.

"I couldn't pick it up," he said on Saturday. Yesterday he was not at the Museum.

Dr. Harold Jacoby of Columbia University said he thought the comet was "just below the horizon," he said.

"When an object is below the horizon," he said, "you just plain can't see it."

He said that it was barely possible that the comet would be visible tonight at 5:30, or by Christmas, anyway.

He said that as the comet moves to the sun that a brilliant sunset would obscure it, even if it were above the horizon. It was discovered by F. J. Skjellerup, and since Dec. 3 it has been seen by persons in Argentina, Chile, Jamaica and other places near the Equator. It is very bright, according to reports from the Southern Hemisphere.

The comet is generally thought to be a new visitor, although there is a bare possibility, according to Dr. Fisher, that it may turn out to be one that was "discovered" many years ago. It will take close observation to be certain on this point, he said.

WHERE SIX MEN STILL LIVE IN SUNKEN SUBMARINE.
Diagram Shows the Various Compartments in a Submarine of the Type of the S-4. The Forward One, or Torpedo Room, Is Where the Only Known Survivors Have Answered Signals From the Submerged Craft. The Other Compartments in Order Are: Battery Room, Where the Crew's Quarters Are; Control Room, Directly Under the Conning Tower; Engine Room and Motor or Stern Torpedo Room.
P. & A. Photo.

Simon Lake Suggests Way To Rescue Men of the S-4

MILFORD, Conn., Dec. 18 (P).—Simon Lake, inventor of the even keel type of submarine, told what he thought was the only possible manner of rescuing members of the crew of the S-4 who are alive within its sunken shell.

Mr. Lake said that as long as an air line was pumping air into the submarine the only feasible plan for taking out the men would be for divers to cut a hole through the plate at the bottom of the submerged boat and enter with diving suits or helmets for the survivors.

The water would be kept out of the boat by means of air pressure pumped from above. Pressure of forty-five pounds to the square inch, making an air pressure equal to the water pressure at that depth, would allow the diver to enter with his helmets or suits. Members of the submarine's crew could put on the suits and be pulled to the surface when they came out of the submarine.

CAPITAL DUBIOUS ON MANY RESCUES

Crushing of Submarine's Hull Points to Loss of Life in Some Compartments.

SPEED NOW CHIEF FACTOR

Officials Have Full Confidence in Forces Engaged in the Rescue Operations.

Special to The New York Times.

WASHINGTON, Dec. 18.—News that at least six men were still alive in the sunken S-4 was sent to the Navy Department early this evening by Rear Admiral Frank Brumby, who is in charge of the rescue operations off the tip of Cape Cod. He stated that the information had come from the locked room by means of hammer knocks executed in the Morse code against the side of the submarine. The rescue party in this manner asked questions of and received responses from some of the six who survive. There was no evidence so far, he reported that any one was alive in the submarine other than the six in the torpedo room.

Rear Admiral Brumby's message read:

Blowing [air] from the Falcon to the tanks. Air now being hooked up to torpedo compartment.

Following messages sent and received from and to S-4:

First question: Is gas bad?
Answer: "No, but the air, how long will you be now?"

Second question: "How many are there?"
Answer: "There are six; please hurry. Will you be long now?"
Answer: "We are doing everything possible."

These messages were by hammer knocks in the Morse code.

No evidence so far that any one is alive anywhere but in the torpedo room.

Admiral Hughes, chief of naval operations, who had been on duty in the Navy Department since 7 o'clock this morning, working on rescue measures, telephoned the message to Secretary Wilbur as soon as it was received.

The Secretary was informed that submarine S-4 was being used in pumping air into the S-4 and that still another submarine, the S-3, has been ordered from Portsmouth, N. H. to the scene.

Previous to this word a dispatch came from Provincetown stating that divers had heard taps from within the submarine in response to their signals.

These sounds came from the torpedo room, which is just forward of the battery room which was shaped to bear the impact of the collision. Aft of the battery compartment, the order named, are the control, engine and motor rooms.

Hope is held here that members of the S-4's personnel may be still alive in the engine and motor rooms but none that were caught in the control and battery compartments have survived.

The afternoon dispatch which came from Rear Admiral Brumby read:

Divers have examined hull and found large hole starboard side 5 feet forward of gun, and in to about centre line. Knocks on torpedo room were answered.

No answers from engine and motor rooms due to tangled wires on deck.

Divers now securing salvage air line.

Navy Department officials believe the divers will find a way to establish full communication with the men in the engine and motor rooms if any still are living in those compartments. The failure to receive signals from the two central sections of the boat—the control and battery rooms—caused no surprise to those familiar with the submarine's construction, their conjecture being that

Continued on Page Two.

AIR IS BAD, VICTIMS SAY

Faint Sound Once Heard Aft in Vessel, Diver Thought.

BATTERY ROOM CRUSHED

Three to Twelve Men Met Certain Death There, Captain King Declares.

AIR PUMPED INTO TANKS

Rescue Crews Try to Up-End Ill-Fated Craft While Waiting for Pontoons.

From a Staff Correspondent of The New York Times.

PROVINCETOWN, Mass., Dec. 18.—At least six men are alive tonight in the sunken hull of the submarine S-4, which was rammed outside the harbor here yesterday by a Coast Guard boat and went to the bottom with some forty-odd men aboard.

This announcement was made tonight by Rear Admiral Frank Brumby, directing the efforts to bring the disabled craft to the surface and save the lives of the members of the crew. Admiral Brumby based his statement on a report received from a diver who went down 101 feet to the mudbank on which the submarine rests, to converse in code with those inside a forward compartment by hammering on the side of the steel hull.

"How long will you be?" was the pathetic message tapped out by the imprisoned men. The diver answered that everything possible was being done.

"Is the gas bad?" the diver asked.

"No, but the air," was the reply from inside the hull.

"How many are you?" was slowly tapped out with the diver's hammer. "Six," was the response. "Please hurry."

Catches Signals From Inside.

It was just about twenty-four hours after the S-4 was rammed and sunk by the Coast Guard destroyer Paulding a mile outside the harbor that the diver, a crack navy expert, working far beneath the surface of a turbulent sea, caught the signals from inside the forward compartment.

The diver reported to Admiral Brumby that the living men who responded to his signals were in the forward part of the submerged vessel. He also brought up an account of heavy damage to the battery room and to the stern of the ship.

This report of the damage to the S-4, which went down after a collision with the Coast Guard boat while running, caused Captain Ernest K. King, submarine rescue specialist, to declare that at least three out of four of the crew had been killed in the battery room, which might have been a dozen or more men there, he said.

But with Rear Admiral Brumby affirming that some men were surely alive in the torpedo room forward, Captain King joined him in declaring he would do everything possible with the fleet of rescue ships here to save the lives of those who might be still fighting for existence.

Describes Damage to Craft.

Thomas Eadie, a diver whose rank is that of chief torpedo-man, went down at 3:13 P. M. He did not converse until 4:20, when he made a hurried report to Captain King and Rear Admiral Brumby.

Eadie said he was certain that the men alive were in the torpedo room. He told of his examination and of receiving signals in reply.

Heartened by what he heard, he said, he began to explore. As he made his way carefully toward the stern he saw the signs of the severe damage done to the submarine in the crash. The conning tower, he declared, was ripped apart.

Closer examination revealed that a hole had been pierced in the battery chamber. Eadie said that this hole had apparently been caused by the prow of the Paulding. Further toward the stern the damage seemed even greater.

The diver told of getting tangled in the wreckage of the superstructure that obstructed the muddy water and of finding it hazardous to proceed. Despite the danger he pushed his way toward the craft, resuming his hammering and his listening.

Heard Sound in Rear Room.

Once, Eadie said, he thought he heard a signal from inside a rear compartment, and he said he thought that what he heard indicated more life in the stern of the boat. Eadie went back to his examination of the submarine. The battery compartment hole was on the starboard side. It was not so sure though that this was the case.

When Captain King asked the significance of Eadie's discoveries, he said:

"We are certain that men are alive aboard the submarine and we are going to do our best to bring them out safely."

The damage is apparently serious.

BEQUESTS FROM ALL SOUGHT BY COLUMBIA

Dr. Butler in Report Asserts University Merits Mention in Every Citizen's Will.

Columbia University has earned the right to be remembered by some provision in every will that is drawn in New York City because of its service to the community, according to Dr. Nicholas Murray Butler, President of the university, in his 1927 annual report to the Board of Trustees. The report, made public yesterday, again declares that Columbia University "is underscapitalized by some $60,000,000" for the successful discharge of its present obligations.

"The lack of sufficient physical equipment for the present proper functioning of the university as President Butler's report," "is glaring and almost impossible to explain satisfactorily to students, to visiting scholars and to the public."

$3,498,380 Gifts in 1927.

The report says that Columbia's total gifts in 1927, including those to Barnard and Teachers Colleges and are $3,498,380.20; that since 1890 gifts to Columbia University have aggregated $71,588,763.64, and that the combined resources of those institutions as of Dec. 30, 1927, were $114,153,749.87, and their budget appropriations were $12,005,670.66. Columbia's teaching staff numbers 2,210, against 2,092 in 1926.

"It is tiresome to repeat this fact, but, as was shown in detail in the last annual report, the university is undercapitalized by some $60,000,000 for the successful and satisfactory discharge of its present public obligations," says the report. "It cannot possibly be put in funds with which to meet the great demands unless the citizens of New York and of the nation, feeling their moral responsibility for the continuance and prosperity of the great institutions that lead and serve the intellectual life and that organize and promote scientific advance, make constant and large benefactions from the fortunes with which they are so richly blessed."

Continued on Page Nine.

DOUBT ELIGIBILITY OF HOOVER IN 1928

Some Senators Raise Question of His Having Been Resident of Country 14 Years.

Special to The New York Times.

WASHINGTON, Dec. 18.—The question of Secretary Hoover's eligibility to the Presidency under the provision of "fourteen years a resident within the United States" is being seriously raised by Senatorial circles. It is being contended that Mr. Hoover must have been a resident within the United States for fourteen years previous to induction into the Presidency, and the question is being raised as to whether he has been a resident for that length of time.

One of the prominent Republican members of the Senate in discussing Mr. Hoover's eligibility under the fourteen-year clause has been seriously raised among some members of the Senate.

"I have no doubt myself that the Constitutional provision means that a man to be eligible for the Presidency must have been a resident within the United States for fourteen years before entering the White House. I do not think it means fourteen years inclusive of early life in the United States.

The Senator in question declined to discuss the matter, he said, because he was not aware of the fact as to the residence of Mr. Hoover here and abroad. The Constitutional provision, found in Paragraph 4, Section 1 of Article II, reads:

"No person except a natural born citizen or a citizen of the United States at the time of the adoption of this Constitution shall be eligible to the office of President; neither shall any person be eligible to that office who shall not have attained to the age of thirty-five years and been fourteen years a resident within the United States."

If Mr. Hoover were nominated and elected in 1928 he would be sworn into office March 4, 1929. Those who argue that "fourteen years a resident within the United States," as used in the Constitution, means fourteen years immediately prior to induction into office contend that Mr. Hoover must show that he has been a "resident within the United States" ever since March 4, 1915. If that be true, then it is pointed out, the question is raised as to whether Mr. Hoover was a "resident within the United States" during the fourteen years from March 4, 1915, to March 4, 1929.

"The time should now have come when Mr. Hoover must show that he has been

Continued on Page Thirteen.

HOPE TO SAVE MEN BY TILTING THE S-4

Experts Here Say Craft May Be Up-Ended to Surface By Air Pumped In.

With her hull smashed amidships, her control room a wreck, and with her forward compartment apparently watertight, according to the report of Diver Eadie, naval men here last night saw some hope of saving a part of the crew locked in the sunken submarine S-4 off Provincetown.

With the sweeper Falcon's powerful compressors forcing air into forward ballast tanks and the Bushnell and the S-8 standing by with more air compressors ready to feed into the manifolds on the Falcon, it is hoped that enough buoyancy can be added to the "eyeless craft to "up-end" her bow first. Then the engineers say, as was the case in the rescue of the crew of the S-51 in 1920, drills grinding steadily through the thick armor plate might cut the passage for the escape of the entrapped men.

When navy men heard that the control room had been crashed through by the prow of the Coast Guard destroyer Paulding they shook their heads. The diver reported the hole in her as larger than the gash in the S-51; and although later Eadie reported that men were alive in the torpedo compartment, the long, cone shaped room that tapers toward a point and ends, so far as human life is concerned, against the bulkhead rear, they held little hope for those to the rear of that point.

The control room is the heart of the submarine. All the main valves for the ballast tanks operate from there, the engine and motor controls, the diving planes and the rising planes. About a dozen men were probably on duty at several of these controls. Just forward of this compartment is the battery room, where are located the men's sleeping quarters and the ward room for the officers.

None one had a chance to escape either forward or aft into the engine room from the control. If men are alive, what happened is this, naval men say: Some one with presence of mind closed the water-tight door between the torpedo room and the battery room and shot home the heavy steel "dogs" that fasten the door. Then the trapped men retreated for-

Continued on Page Two.

"All the News That's
Fit to Print."

The New York Times.

THE WEATHER
Showers today, probably tomorrow;
not much change in temperature.
Temperature yesterday—Max. 80, Min. 70.
For weather report see Page 45.

Copyright, 1928, by The New York Times Company.

VOL. LXXVII....No. 25,714.   •••   NEW YORK, TUESDAY, JUNE 19, 1928.   TWO CENTS in Greater New York | THREE CENTS Within 200 Miles | FOUR CENTS Elsewhere in the U. S.

AMELIA EARHART FLIES ATLANTIC, FIRST WOMAN TO DO IT;
TELLS HER OWN STORY OF PERILOUS 21-HOUR TRIP TO WALES;
RADIO QUIT AND THEY FLEW BLIND OVER INVISIBLE OCEAN

RITCHIE WITHDRAWS IN FAVOR OF SMITH, URGING PARTY UNITY

New Yorker's Nomination Will Assure Democratic Victory, He Asserts.

DIRECTS APPEAL TO SOUTH

Smith as President Would Restore Popular Government, Maryland Executive Says.

TURNS OVER HIS DELEGATES

Sees Struggle of 1924 Avoided at Houston—Reed Still in Race, Backer Declares.

special to The New York Times.

BALTIMORE, June 18.—Governor Albert C. Ritchie tonight withdrew as a candidate for the Democratic Presidential nomination, with the announcement that he would instruct the Maryland delegation to cast its sixteen votes at the National Convention at Houston next week for Governor Smith of New York.

In a formal statement, Governor Ritchie urged the Democratic Party to unite behind Governor Smith. The New York Executive, he declared, was "fitted by experience, character and ability to assume the leadership" of the party and had the best chance to win in the November election.

"His record is a guarantee that with him as President, honesty in Government would take the place of corruption in Government," he said of Governor Smith.

Governor Ritchie expressed his gratitude that Maryland had advanced his own name for the Presidential nomination. "The great majority of the Democrats of the country," he said, "are ready to back Governor Smith, however, he said, and he felt a responsibility to the party so to declare himself.

Makes Special Plea to South.

Mr. Ritchie directed his plea in behalf of Governor Smith particularly to the South. The national situation demanded, and pointed to, the success of the Democratic Party as the champion of self-government and popular self-rule, principles which led the South through the Democratic Party had saved to the nation, he asserted.

He, "as a son of the South," had fought enthusiastically for these principles. As an American and as a Democrat, he now urged a "united and unbroken front" by the party to assure its success next Fall.

"Every Democrat should subordinate himself to this higher call for party unity," he said. "In nominating this action, I do so without any ulterior motive whatsoever. It emanates from a profound sense of duty to the nation and to the Democratic Party, with which the country's well-being is inseparably bound up."

Governor Ritchie's Statement.

The following is Governor Ritchie's statement in full:

"I am profoundly convinced that no consideration of self or of personal advancement on any one's part should be allowed to stand for one moment in the way of the success of the Democratic Party, which is the natural champion of self-government and popular self-rule.

These principles are challenging the attention of the country today as they have not done for years. To them I have dedicated such political effort as I am able to exert. Faith in them saved the South during the dark days of reconstruction and made possible a reunited and happy nation; and as a son of the South I have brought to the struggle for these principles the enthusiasm and the loyalty which came to me from ancestors who were ready to die, and some of whom did die, for the cause in which they believed.

As a Democrat I have regarded this struggle as a duty, and as an American I believe that the dictates of patriotism require the re-establishment of those principles in our national life.

That my own State should think me worthy to be the standard-bearer of the Democratic Party is a distinction for which I never can sufficiently express my gratitude, nor as I adequately express it to my friends elsewhere in the country.

Continued on Page Ten.

President of Porto Rican Senate Stabbed And Badly Hurt by a Maniac Anarchist

Wireless to The New York Times.

SAN JUAN, Porto Rico, June 18.—Antonio Barcelo, President of the Porto Rican Senate, was stabbed with a chisel at the close of a welcoming demonstration at City Hall today and probably owes his life to the fact that he is fat.

The chisel made a four-inch wound, then was deflected by a rib.

Justo Matos, 35 years old and believed to be demented, who attempted the assassination with the unusual instrument, was himself shot through the abdomen by an unidentified bystander after police, they say, actually had him in custody. The condition of Matos is considered critical.

In their efforts to protect Matos police were unable to detect who had shot him.

The assault on Señor Barcelo took place at the close of a noisy welcome while hundreds of persons surged about him with greetings. Señor Barcelo was just returning home from New York where Columbia University gave him an honorary degree of Doctor of Laws and President Butler had referred to him as "captain of his island people."

By The Associated Press.

SAN JUAN, Porto Rico, June 18.—Señor Barcelo tonight was in a hospital undergoing treatment for his wound. Matos is in prison, heavily guarded to protect him from an outraged populace.

A huge crowd met Señor Barcelo at the docks and escorted him to the Plaza, where on a balcony overlooking the promenade he addressed them.

It was while he was speaking that Matos edged through the crowd, pushed his way onto the low balcony and wielded his chisel. The crowd apparently did not comprehend what had happened. There was a shot from somewhere and Matos was seen to fall, writhing in pain, on the street level, where police took charge of him.

At the hospital, where Señor Barcelo was taken, doctors declined to state whether the wound was likely to prove fatal.

The motive for Matos's action is not known. Some in the crowd who noticed him before his deed said he remarked he was ill, and then added that he could kill ten Porto Ricans willingly.

The stabbing itself, perhaps by coincidence, followed the statement in Señor Barcelo's speech that he was not a member of any political party or faction but a Porto Rican, and was proud of the honor accorded him by Columbia University not so much for his own sake as that it went to a citizen of his country.

La Democratica, Señor Barcelo's newspaper, this afternoon said Matos had visited their office and the Barcelo home for a week asking when the legislator would return here. Other afternoon papers refer to him as a "Socialist fanatic," and one calls him a "confessed anarchist."

SMITH SUPPORTERS SEE A QUICK VICTORY

Hope Ritchie's Withdrawal in Favor of Governor Will Be Followed by Others.

AIDES START FOR HOUSTON

Van Namee, Sure of Success, Says "Steam-Roller" Methods Will Not Be Used.

With George R. Van Namee, manager of Governor Smith's preconvention campaign for the Democratic nomination, speeding toward Houston to open headquarters in the Hotel Rice, Smith supporters here were jubilant last night at the announcement by Governor Ritchie of Maryland that he would advise the sixteen delegates from that State to cast their votes for New York's Governor on the first ballot.

Mr. Van Namee predicted, just as he boarded the train at Grand Central Station yesterday noon, that Governor Smith would be nominated on "an early ballot." The more optimistic Smith supporters contended last night that the first ballot would show a strength of 704 votes, or 29 1-3 short of the number required for nomination. The house was expressed that Governor Ritchie's action might swing other State delegations into line before the voting starts at Houston, in which event Governor Smith might be nominated on the first ballot.

Rules Out "Steam-Roller" Plan.

While declining to name the ballot on which he believed Governor Smith would be nominated, Mr. Van Namee declared that with 650 delegates already instructed and many others known to favor the Smith candidacy, his nomination was practically assured. The Smith forces, Mr. Van Namee declared, would not attempt any "steam-roller" methods at Houston and would seek in no way to prevent any candidate from presenting his claims to the nomination. The Smith forces, he added, are concerned with promoting party harmony.

With Mr. Van Namee were Mrs. Van Namee, Howard Cullman of the Port of New York Authority and George C. Norton, Norman E. Mack, Democratic National Committee—

Continued on Page Nine.

12 INJURED BY BOMB 'PLANTED' IN DETROIT

County Building Shaken, Windows Shattered and Hundreds Panic-Stricken.

'PURPLE' GANG SUSPECTED

Darrow Attending Court Case Is Jarred—Jokes With Judge About Blast.

Special to The New York Times.

DETROIT, June 18.—A devastating blast which injured twelve county employes, two seriously, shattered dozens of panes of glass and rocked the Wayne County Building to its foundation this afternoon is believed by police to have been another attempt at intimidation of the courts by sympathizers with the "Purple" gang, nine members of which are now on trial on charges of conspiracy to extort.

"The dynamite bomb evidently was intended for the Municipal Courts Building, where the 'Purples' are on trial," Police Inspector John T. Doyle of the First Precinct declared, "but as usual in such cases some stranger was hired to plant the bomb and probably mistook the county building for the City Courts building.

"It is a miracle no one was killed. The bomb was a powerful one. If it had exploded in the confined space of the rest room instead of in the courtyard I believe it would have wrecked the building and killed many persons."

The explosion occurred at about 2:50 o'clock. The bomb was left in the men's room on the first floor and was found by Frank Stolpa, a constable, who tossed it into the areaway in the centre of the building and was trying to extinguish it with water when it exploded.

One May Lose an Eye.

Stolpa and Arthur Vercruisse, another constable, who also helped in the efforts to extinguish the bomb, were struck in the face by flying glass and bits of iron from the bomb and taken to Receiving Hospital for treatment. Vercruisse, according to the physicians, may lose the sight of his right eye.

About 100 men and women clerks,

Continued on Page Fourteen.

Keel Laid for Biggest Ship, 1,000 Feet Long; 60,000-Ton 'Oceanic' to Cost $30,000,000

Wireless to The New York Times.

LONDON, June 18.—The biggest ship in the world was begun today at Harland & Wolff's shipyards in Belfast, when the keel was laid for a giant White Star liner to cost $30,000,000. She will be more than 1,000 feet long, with a beam of 100 feet and tonnage of about 60,000.

The ship will not be ready for sail ing until 1932, and experts have yet to decide what type of machinery will be installed in her.

When the new ship is added to the White Star fleet she will be the Oceanic. The six largest steamships in service at the present time, all in the Atlantic trade, are:

The Leviathan of the United States Lines, 59,957 gross tonnage, 907 feet long and 100 feet 3 inches beam.

The Majestic of the White Star Line, claimed by some to be the largest liner afloat, on the basis of the builder and designer's pre-war measurements, which are 56,581 gross tons, 915 feet 5 inches long and 100 feet 1 inch beam.

The Cunarder Berengaria, 52,226 gross tonnage, 883 feet 5 inches long and 98 feet 3 inches beam.

The White Star Olympic, 46,439 gross tonnage, 882 feet 5 inches long, 92 feet 5 inches beam.

The Cunarder Aquitania, 45,647 gross tonnage, 868 feet 7 inches long and 97 feet beam.

The new French liner Ile de France, 43,500 gross tonnage, 797 feet 8 inches long and 91 feet 8 inches beam.

NOBILE VAINLY HAILS FLIERS CIRCLING OVER BUT NOT SEEING HIM

General Radios Base Ship That Rescue Planes Were Over Stranded Men an Hour.

SECOND FLIGHT ALSO FAILS

This Time Italia Castaways Sight One of Planes Piloted by Riiser-Larsen and Holm.

SAVOIA REACHES KINGS BAY

Big Italian Seaplane Ready for Dash North — French and Swedish Craft on Way.

By The Associated Press.

ROME, June 18.—The two Norwegian fliers, Captain Riiser-Larsen and Lieutenant Luetzow Holm, today made a second unsuccessful attempt to find General Umberto Nobile and the party with him near the ice-floes off Spitsbergen. They returned to the ice-breaker Braganza without having sighted the marooned men.

Nobile, however, informed the base ship Citta di Milano by wireless that he had seen one of the planes fly within two kilometers of him.

Snow Hides Frantic Signals.

Copyright, 1928, by The Associated Press.

KINGS BAY, Spitsbergen, June 18.—High overhead yesterday General Nobile saw two seaplanes sent to rescue him and his five comrades from the Arctic ice-floes, but frantic efforts to signal them below failed, and, after an hour's reconnaissance above, the craft were seen to disappear in the grim Arctic horizon, flying back toward Spitsbergen.

This news came to the base-ship Citta di Milano by wireless from the stranded Italia commander. For days has been awaiting on slowly moving floe ice sight of some one from the outside world who might aid in returning him and his mates on the Italia to civilization and home.

Sunday they thought their days of watching perhaps over. But they failed to count on the trickiness of the snow with visibility, and when help had passed them by their situation was if anything more difficult than before.

Good Visibility of No Avail.

The two seaplanes were those piloted by Captain Riiser-Larsen and Lieutenant Leutzow Holm, the Norwegian fliers. Both set out early Sunday and took a course over Beverly Sound, North Cape and Cape Platen, keeping at a height of from 750 to 900 feet. Both planes carried provisions and clothes for the stranded men.

Visibility was good, but when they returned to Spitsbergen they had not seen a trace of the Italia's commander and the remnant of his crew or of the silk tent he had painted red to aid them. This despite the fact that messages from General Nobile indicated that they had remained above him and in the vicinity for more than an hour.

Today Captain Riiser-Larsen and Lieutenant Holm set out for further reconnaissance, intending, if there were to be variations at all in their course, to keep between their route yesterday and the coast of Northeast Land.

No Chance to Land Amid Ice.

The fliers, on returning yesterday, said that in the area where the fliers are supposed to be they found the ice much too rough for landing. They said that the ice floes were opened, considerably, that the cracks and openings were still too narrow for landing attempts by the seaplanes. They were such, however, as to foster progress by the ice breakers.

In his message to the Citta di Milano conveying the tragic irony of the situation, General Nobile, to aid further searches, gave his present position as 88.33 north and 17.12 east. This would put him about five miles to the east of Foyn Island.

Savoia's Arrival Raises Hopes.

The hydro-airplane Savoia-55, piloted by Major Maddalena, arrived here at 10:45 o'clock tonight. She was the first of the four big seaplanes en route to Spitsbergen to reach the Northern base.

Fine weather was in evidence as the big machine settled in the harbor. Her arrival and the news that at least two others of large cargo and passenger capacity were en route, raised hopes of the watchers here who for weeks have been trying to get into direct touch with General Nobile and the other survivors of the Italia.

It was a bit uncertain as to whether

Continued on Page Six.

Washington, N. J., wants five industries. Good labor conditions, honest government.—Or Lack. R. R. Address Borough Clerk.—Advt.

When you think of Writing
Think of Whiting.—Advt.

Dine delightfully on The Night Line for only $1.50. Call Walker 2213.—Advt.

Photo copyrighted by G. P. Putnam.
FIRST WOMAN TO FLY THE ATLANTIC.
Amelia Earhart, Co-pilot of the Airplane Friendship, Photographed in Boston, Just Before She Started on Her Great Adventure.

Eager Crowds Imperil Miss Earhart As They Welcome Fliers at Burry Port

Police Aid Weary Trio to Battle Way to Refuge in Zinc Works—
Friends Fly From Southampton to Greet Them and
Hear Story of Their Adventures.

By ALLEN RAYMOND.

Copyright, 1928, in the United States, Canada, Mexico, South America, Europe and the British Dominions by The New York Times Company.

Special Cable to The New York Times.

BURRY PORT, Carmarthenshire, South Wales, June 18.—The first woman to cross the Atlantic successfully by air, Miss Amelia Earhart, Boston settlement worker, alighted in the seaplane Friendship here this morning on the broad expanse of Loughor estuary, after a flight of 20 hours and 40 minutes elapsed time from Trepassey.

Few persons saw the gilt-winged Fokker monoplane descend on the Welsh coast, but this evening, when friends rushing from Southampton brought Miss Earhart ashore, she was the recipient of so enthusiastic a reception by the 2,000 inhabitants of this town that it seemed for a few minutes as if she would not outlive her triumph.

Eager Crowds Imperil Aviatrix.

The arrival of the Friendship was the greatest event this remote district has had since the end of the World War when the town's boys came home. Miss Earhart was nearly crushed by the anxiety of the crowd of men, women and children to touch the hem of her flying suit, get her autograph on a slip of paper, wring her hand and congratulate her upon her triumphant passage over the Atlantic.

The High Sheriff of Carmarthenshire, who had rowed out to greet her; the town's three policemen and a couple of friends had to form a ring with locked arms about the latest popular heroine and literally to fight their way a hundred yards from the shore to the office of the local zinc works, where they found shelter back of locked doors.

"You must remember," the local Police-Chief said apologetically, "that our people never saw anything to compare with this. I advise you to remain here until we get extra police."

The Friendship's crew was marooned within the walls of the Frickers Metal Company an hour and a half before police reinforcements arrived and cleared a way to two motor cars to take them to a distant hotel where rest, food and sleep could be obtained after their arduous journey.

Poor Visibility Forced Landing.

Poor visibility forced the plane to come down on the Welsh coast after the first tentative objective—Valentia, Ireland—had been left far behind, but the possible goal of Southampton not yet reached.

Except for the first hour over the Atlantic after leaving the rugged shores of Newfoundland, the fliers never saw sea or land until they had winged their way to the Eastern Irish coast. They flew through fog, rain and snow most of the time, fighting for altitude and clearer weather, but they came fast with the wind behind of twenty to thirty miles per hour speeding them on.

They probably had plenty of gasoline left, when they descended, to reach Southampton—seventy-five gallons—but were struggling in the midst of dense fog and knew they were somewhere off the southern coast of Britain. With their object attained—that of making Miss Earhart the first woman to complete a transatlantic crossing—they decided to take no further risks.

They will go on to Southampton tomorrow.

Stultz and Gordon Elated.

The full story of the flight has yet to be told. The two airmen, Stultz and Gordon, who had the major responsibility and labor of getting the Friendship safely across the ocean, were soon fast asleep after battling their way to Burry Port. Both ejaculated their joy at their success and chuckled together over the moments in mid-ocean when they seemed dubious of the outcome.

Miss Earhart, who came through her experience in fine condition and

Continued on Page Two.

FOUGHT RAIN, FOG AND SNOW ALL THE WAY

Miss Earhart Says Motors Spat and Gas Ran Low, But She Had Neither Fear Nor Doubt of Success.

PASSED OVER IRELAND WITHOUT EVEN SEEING IT

Wind Aided Plane—Girl Credits Feat to Stultz and Gordon—She Flew Because It Would Have Been 'Too Inartistic to Refuse.'

By AMELIA EARHART.

Copyright, 1928, in the United States, Canada, Mexico, South America, Europe and the British Dominions by The New York Times Company.

Special Cable to The New York Times.

BURRY PORT, Carmarthenshire, South Wales, June 18.—I have arrived and I am happy—naturally.

Why did I do it? When one is offered such a tremendous adventure it would be too inartistic to refuse it. I have been a flier for years. I had planned to spend my vacation flying. I knew the moment this chance came to me that if I turned it down I would never forgive myself.

My trip across the Atlantic aboard the airplane Friendship was all I had imagined it to be as pleasure, and much more, though pretty uncomfortable at times. This is my first trip to England, and it is rather funny dropping in by airplane. Nevertheless I hope to make the trip again some day and make it in the same way by air. What I wanted to demonstrate in this flight was that this type of travel was comparatively safe and ought to be developed.

Gives Great Credit to Companions.

I was a passenger on the journey—just a passenger. Everything that was done to bring us across was done by Wilmer Stultz and "Slim" Gordan. Any praise I can give them they ought to have. You can't pile it on too thick.

Transoceanic flying has to be done by pilots who can fly by instruments alone. I am afraid that some accidents which marred past flights have been caused by pilots not too sure of instrument flying.

Despite the fact that the weather reports promised us fine visibility and fair weather, we had fog, rain and even snow practically all the way across. We only had clear weather for one hour out of the twenty-two we were on the way.

The reason we came down here was because we could not see anything. We had just about enough gasoline left, we reckoned, to make Southampton, but we did not dare attempt it because we were flying blind and we knew we had come across. We will go on there tomorrow.

Calls Waiting the Worst Part.

To go back to the beginning, the hardest strain of all this flight in a way was the waiting at Trepassey. The flight, of course, was a climax piled on top of this worry. That is what made it so tiring. But we had been trying so much to take off at Trepassey that all I can remember thinking of when we took off was that at last we were on the way. I was not really sure till we had flown for half an hour along the coast and headed against the open sea, because I knew that if everything was not all right Bill would go back.

When we started there was such a burst of spray that the outside motors started cutting out. I was afraid we had made another false start, but the motors picked up again, and although they stammered once in a while on the flight when coated with snow, I never had a moment of real trepidation about them and never doubted that we should arrive.

I did not do much. I did not handle the controls once, although I have had more than 500 hours' solo flying and once held the women's altitude record. When Bill Stultz left the controls to work the radio "Slim" let them.

Thought of Fishing in Newfoundland.

We got two messages from ships on the way, and when I found out what ships they were I did a lot of thinking and jotted down a lot of notes about my feelings, which I hope to expand some day, perhaps.

Leaving the American coast, it was beautiful weather. The jagged coastline beneath us had a grandeur one never forgets, and passing over Newfoundland one could see lots of lakes where they told me there were good trout. I hope to fish there some time.

Beneath us the water was wonderful greens and blues, and everything was serene, though, of course the first thing we did was to start looking for the fog which we knew would meet us off Newfoundland. The first hour over the open sea was the only time we saw it. We did not even see land, although we passed right over it, but when we knew we were over Southern England we could not establish any landmarks and our radio had quit us. We do not know yet how it got out of order, but it was all right when Bill worked it last night and no good when he tried it this morning.

Marvelous Colors in the Clouds.

Last night was gorgeous. The billows of fog shot with pink seemed like a vast sunlit desert, and even when night came, there was an interesting color effect. There was the glow of

"All the News That's Fit to Print."

The New York Times.

LATE EDITION
5:30 A.M.
WEATHER—Fair today; cloudy tomorrow.

Copyright, 1928, by The New York Times Company.

VOL. LXXVIII....No. 25,855. ✶ ✶ ✶ ✶ NEW YORK, WEDNESDAY, NOVEMBER 7, 1928. TWO CENTS In Greater New York | THREE CENTS Within 200 Miles | FOUR CENTS Elsewhere in the U.S.

HOOVER WINS 407 TO 69; DOUBTFUL 55; SMITH LOSES STATE; SOUTH BROKEN; ROOSEVELT IS ELECTED GOVERNOR

HOOVER CARRIES ILLINOIS, SWEEPING IN THE STATE TICKET

Smith Wins in Chicago, but His Republican Rival Gets Big Down-State Vote.

IOWA STRONG FOR HOOVER

Nebraska Puts Republican in Lead and His Victory Seems Certain.

MICHIGAN ALSO REPUBLICAN

Hoover Sweeps Ohio by a Big Majority—Entire State Ticket Elected.

Special to The New York Times.

CHICAGO, Nov. 6.—Illinois went Republican today. Herbert Hoover and the State ticket, headed by Louis L. Emmerson, candidate for Governor, and Otis F. Glenn, nominee for United States Senator, won by such large figures in down-State territory that close battles over some of the places in Cook County were eliminated.

Although he apparently lost Chicago to Governor Smith, incomplete returns indicated that Hoover had carried Cook County, which was counted upon by the Democrats as certain for their entire ticket.

The figures received as this is written forecast a Smith victory in Chicago by about 40,000 and informal reports from the suburbs of the county promised a Republican lead of 73,000.

The vote of 3,208 precincts out of 6,942, including 1,816 from Cook County, gave Hoover 741,167; Smith 694,811. The Republican nominee for President apparently won the State by about 400,000.

Emmerson and his fellow candidates for State executive office apparently felt considerably behind Hoover both in Cook County and down-State, but all apparently were safe on the face of the incomplete figures.

Close Race for Senatorship.

The closest race of all was that for United States Senator which the first reports indicated might be a neck and neck race because of the way that Anton J. Cermak, the "wet" Democrat ran ahead of Governor Smith in Chicago. The first big batch of city precincts to be heard from promised him a Chicago lead of from 250,000 to 275,000.

It was thought that Glenn might not be able to overcome this in the down-State territory because the figures on the Governorship which accompanied it seemed to indicate that Emmerson would carry down-State by quite that big a margin. But when the outside counties began to report the returns forecast a margin for Glenn outside Chicago in excess of 350,000.

Cermak was the only Democrat who seemed ahead of his national ticket in Chicago. Floyd E. Thompson, Democratic gubernatorial entry, was allowed by his party to trail Governor Smith and also Thomas J. Courtney, nominee for Attorney General against Oscar E. Carlstrom, the Republican who now holds that office.

The returns on these offices were far ahead of those for the rest of the offices on the State ticket, but Hoover's lead and the leads of Glenn, Emmerson and Carlstrom were taken as proof that all the Republican entries had carried the State.

On incomplete returns Judge William J. Lindsay, Democrat, was leading Judge John A. Swanson, Republican, for State's Attorney, the centre of the battle over Cook County's offices.

In the battle over lucrative berths on the Board of Review, Thomas D. Nash, Democrat, is leading Edward I. Litsinger, Republican.

Much Splitting of Votes.

Scattering precinct figures from all the wards indicate a day of prodigious vote splitting.

The Crowe-Thompsons whetted their axes for the Dineen Republican candidates, and vice versa. Indications are that if Judge Lindsay maintains his early lead, the entire Democratic ticket may win. Figures on other candidates are slow. The race between the Crowe-Thompson machine was caught in another avalanche, similar to the one that struck it in the popular uprising at the April primaries. In the fight for precious townships, where the Crowe-Thompson

Continued on Page Four.

BAY STATE IS CLOSE, WITH SMITH AHEAD

Walsh, Democrat, Re-elected to Senate and Cole Is in Front for Governor.

SMITH WINS RHODE ISLAND

But State Ticket Goes Republican—Other New England States for Hoover.

Special to The New York Times.

BOSTON, Mass., Nov. 7.—At 4:30 o'clock this morning, after one of the liveliest election nights ever known in Massachusetts, and when it appeared that the plurality for Herbert Hoover had swept the State, there was a possibility that Herbert Hoover, though trailing Governor Smith, might receive the eighteen electoral votes of this State.

At the same time there was a probability that the final returns would show Frank G. Allen winner of the Gubernatorial contest over his Democratic opponent, General Charles H. Cole, despite the latter's lead.

Senator David D. Walsh, Democrat, running 10,000 votes ahead of Governor Smith, was clearly re-elected over Benjamin Loring Young, Republican.

Smith Carries Textile Cities.

From early in the evening, when Hoover had built up a substantial lead, the returns from Boston and some textile centres pulled him down and pushed Smith out in front.

Then followed a see-saw, with Smith slowly forging ahead in the early morning hours, largely as a result of 10,000-vote margins which were given to him in Fall River and Lowell, 4,000 in New Bedford, 5,000 in Salem, 1,000 in Holyoke, and lesser votes in other cities.

For President, 952 precincts out of the 1,805 in the State gave Hoover 405,126, Smith 426,509.

For Governor, 848 precincts, including 300 of the 539 in Boston, gave Allen (R.) 346,495, Cole (D.) 351,082.

For Senator, 848 precincts gave Young (R.) 312,656, Walsh (D.) 331,002.

Unofficial Boston figures for 310 precincts out of 539 gave the Crowe-Thompson

Continued on Page Two.

NEW JERSEY GIVES REPUBLICAN SLATE A HEAVY MAJORITY

Incomplete Figures for State Show Hoover Leads Smith by 116,944.

LARSON AHEAD OF DILL

Victory for Republican by 166,340 Is Indicated in Gubernatorial Race.

KEAN BEATING EDWARDS

Strong Republican Showing Is a Damaging Blow to Prestige of Hague as Leader.

Herbert Hoover's indicated plurality in New Jersey was 309,420 early this morning when the tabulation of returns from 1,102 of the 2,920 districts gave Hoover 303,792 and Smith 186,848. In the metropolitan district of New Jersey the Republican and Democratic candidates ran a close race.

In Essex County, which includes Newark, tabulation of the vote in 150 of the 481 districts showed that it stood, Hoover, 39,122; Smith, 21,810.

Hamilton F. Kean was leading Senator Edward I. Edwards, Democrat, by 91,021 in 1,102 districts and his indicated plurality was 239,440.

Larson in the Lead.

In the Gubernatorial contest the returns from 1,102 districts gave Larson 269,391 and Dill 205,692, giving Larson, Republican, a lead of 166,340.

In 75 of 506 districts in Hudson County, the stronghold of Mayor Frank Hague, the vote was: Hoover 9,106, Smith, 18,302, Kean 10,204, Edwards 18,896, Larson 10,302, Dill 18,107.

Increasing Republican pluralities reported from the counties of Southern New Jersey were not offset by expected Democratic gains in the metropolitan area.

Republican candidates for Congress were leading their opponents in all counties except Hudson, and Republican candidates for the Assembly were reported generally in the lead in all but counties which are now represented in the Assembly by Democrats.

While the Republicans of Camden County were celebrating the success of their State and national tickets there, State Senator Joseph H. Forsyth was reported to be dying from influenza at his home at Haddonfield. He was stricken several days ago. He was elected in 1926 for three years.

Reports from Trenton were to the effect that a plurality of from 150,000 to 200,000 for Hoover was indicated by the early returns. According to The Associated Press fifty-six districts out of 2,920 in strongly Republican territory gave Hoover a lead of 5,456 over Smith. The vote was Hoover 9,078 and Smith 3,622.

Forty-five districts reported in the United States Senatorial and Gubernatorial races. These gave Kean, Republican, 7,080; Senator Edwards, Democrat, 2,217. The Governorship figures were William L. Dill, Democrat, 3,580; Morgan F. Larson, Republican, 5,989.

The indicated heavy pluralities of the Republican candidates for United States Senator and Governor were regarded as a damaging blow to the prestige of Mayor Hague, Vice Chairman of the Democratic National Committee, whose Democratic stronghold in Hudson has been sufficiently disappointing to the Republican tidal in other sections of New Jersey and put Democratic candidates for the Governor's Mansion and the Senate.

Continued on Page Eighteen.

Gov. Smith's Message to Mr. Hoover

Governor Smith sent the following telegram just after midnight to his successful rival:

Hon. Herbert Hoover,
Palo Alto, Cal.:

I congratulate you heartily on your victory, and extend to you my sincere good wishes for your health and happiness and for the success of your Administration.

ALFRED E. SMITH.

Electoral Vote

HOOVER.

Arizona	3	Nevada	3
California	13	New Hampshire	4
Colorado	6	New Jersey	14
Connecticut	7	New Mexico	3
Delaware	3	New York	45
Florida	6	Ohio	24
Idaho	4	Oklahoma	10
Illinois	29	Oregon	5
Indiana	15	Pennsylvania	38
Iowa	13	South Dakota	5
Kansas	10	Tennessee	12
Kentucky	13	Utah	4
Maine	6	Vermont	4
Maryland	8	Virginia	12
Michigan	15	Washington	7
Minnesota	12	West Virginia	8
Missouri	18	Wisconsin	13
Montana	4	Wyoming	3
Nebraska	8	Total	407

SMITH.

Alabama	12	Mississippi	10
Arkansas	9	Rhode Island	5
Georgia	14	South Carolina	9
Louisiana	10	Total	69

DOUBTFUL.

Massachusetts	18	Texas	20
North Carolina	12	Total	55
North Dakota	5		

Total number of votes in Electoral College, 531; necessary to a choice, 266.

HOOVER BREAKS THE SOLID SOUTH

He Carries Virginia and Probably Florida and North Carolina—Leads in Texas Also.

Special to The New York Times.

RICHMOND, Va., Nov. 6.—Herbert Hoover has carried the Old Dominion. Mr. Hoover, or about 88,000 less than the plurality he received over Theodore Roosevelt in 1924, which was the largest plurality the city gave him in any of his Gubernatorial campaigns.

With only 28 out of the 3,493 election districts of the city missing, Smith had 1,106,534 against 680,074 for Hoover, a plurality of 426,450. Norman Thomas, Socialist candidate, received less than 50,000 in the city.

Franklin D. Roosevelt, Democratic candidate for Governor, ran behind Smith in the city. With 90 districts missing, Roosevelt had 1,087,418 against 699,441 for his Republican opponent, Attorney General Albert Ottinger, a plurality of 387,977.

Herbert H. Lehman, Democratic candidate for Lieutenant Governor, and United States Senator Royal S. Copeland, Democratic candidate for re-election to the Senate, ran ahead of their ticket in the city.

With 193 districts missing, Lehman received 1,106,088 votes, against 614,241 for Mr. Lockwood, his Republican opponent, a plurality of 491,847.

With 668 districts missing, Copeland had 953,401 to 498,899 for Alanson B. Houghton, former Ambassador to Germany and Great Britain, the Republican candidate, a plurality of 459,702 for Copeland.

Albert Conway, Democratic candidate for Attorney General, and Maurice S. Tremaine, Democratic candidate for re-election as State Controller, also ran ahead of British in the city. With 582 districts missing, Conway had 1,029,890 votes, against 564,488 for Hamilton Ward, Republican, a plurality of 466,134. With 569 districts missing, Tremaine led with 1,056,027, against 528,520 for

Continued on Page Seven.

CITY GIVES SMITH 430,000 MAJORITY

Incomplete Count Also Indicates Like Lead for Roosevelt for Governor.

Governor Smith carried New York City by about 430,000 plurality over Mr. Hoover, or about 88,000 less than the plurality he received over Theodore Roosevelt in 1924, which was the largest plurality the city gave him in any of his Gubernatorial campaigns.

With only 28 out of the 3,493 election districts of the city missing, Smith had 1,106,534 against 680,074 for Hoover, a plurality of 426,450. Norman Thomas, Socialist candidate, received less than 50,000 in the city.

Franklin D. Roosevelt, Democratic candidate for Governor, ran behind Smith in the city. With 90 districts missing, Roosevelt had 1,087,418 against 699,441 for his Republican opponent, Attorney General Albert Ottinger, a plurality of 387,977.

Herbert H. Lehman, Democratic candidate for Lieutenant Governor, and United States Senator Royal S. Copeland, Democratic candidate for re-election to the Senate, ran ahead of their ticket in the city.

Lehman Has Big Lead.

With 193 districts missing, Lehman received 1,106,088 votes, against 614,241 for Mr. Lockwood, his Republican opponent, a plurality of 491,847.

With 668 districts missing, Copeland had 953,401 to 498,899 for Alanson B. Houghton, former Ambassador to Germany and Great Britain, the Republican candidate, a plurality of 459,702 for Copeland.

Albert Conway, Democratic candidate for Attorney General, and Maurice S. Tremaine, Democratic candidate for re-election as State Controller, also ran ahead in the city. With 582 districts missing, Conway had 1,029,890 votes, against 564,488 for Hamilton Ward, Republican, a plurality of 466,134. With 569 districts missing, Tremaine led with 1,056,027, against 528,520 for

Continued on Page Seven.

U.S. Senators Elected

REPUBLICAN—18

California .... *H. W. Johnson
Connecticut ...... ‡F. C. Walcott
Delaware...John G. Townsend Jr.
Idaho .... §John Thomas
Illinois .... §Otis F. Glenn
Indiana .... *A. R. Robinson
Maine .... ‡Frederick Hale
Maryland.. ‡P. L. Goldsborough
Michigan..... ‡A. H. Vanderberg
Nebraska..... *Robert B. Howell
New Jersey.. ‡Hamilton F. Kean
North Dakota .. *Lynn J. Frazier
Ohio .... Simeon D. Fess
Ohio .... §T. E. Burton
Pennsylvania.. *David A. Reed
Rhode Island... §Felix Hebert
Vermont ...... *Frank L. Greene
Wisconsin.. *R. M. La Follette Jr.

DEMOCRATS—9

Arizona .... *Henry F. Ashurst
Florida ...... *Park Trammell
Massachusetts.. *David I. Walsh
Mississippi..... *H. D. Stephens
New York ...... *R. S. Copeland
Tennessee ... *Kenneth McKellar
Texas .... *Tom Connally
Virginia...... *William H. King
Virginia....... *C. A. Swanson

FARMER-LABORITE—1

Minnesota .... *Henrik Shipstead

IN DOUBT—7

Missouri | New Mexico
Montana | Washington
Nevada | West Virginia
| Wyoming

*Re-elected for full term ending March 3, 1935.
†Elected for both long and short terms.
‡Re-elected Sept. 10, 1928, for full term ending March 3, 1935.
§Elected for short term ending March 3, 1935.

ROOSEVELT IS VICTOR BY SLIM PLURALITY; COPELAND ALSO WINS

Democratic Nominee Captures State Governorship by Margin Indicated to Be 40,000.

SENATOR IN BY 56,000

Re-elected Over Houghton After Running Up Lead of 523,000 in the City.

LEAVES SMITH FAR BEHIND

Polls 90,000 More Votes Than the Governor—Lehman, Conway and Tremaine Leading.

Franklin D. Roosevelt, Democrat, defeated Attorney General Albert Ottinger, Republican, for the Governorship of New York State, on the basis of returns from 7,778 election districts out of the 8,267 in the State. A plurality of about 40,000 for Mr. Roosevelt was indicated on these figures, and it is possible that this plurality might be cut somewhat by the returns from the missing districts but not enough to give Mr. Ottinger the State.

Senator Royal S. Copeland, candidate for re-election on the Democratic ticket, apparently had won over former Ambassador Alanson B. Houghton by an indicated plurality of about 56,000. Senator Copeland ran surprisingly well in New York City, where his plurality seems likely to reach 523,000, or about 90,000 more than the plurality received by Governor Smith, heretofore regarded as the strongest candidate in the city, personally.

The victories for Mr. Roosevelt and Senator Copeland went some distance toward assuring the local Democrats for Governor Smith's defeat. Governor Smith's indicated plurality in New York City was about 430,000, and his defeat in the State by about 125,000 was indicated.

Roosevelt Lead 63,566.

Mr. Roosevelt had an actual lead of 63,566, with 549 out of the 8,267 election districts in the State missing, the vote being Roosevelt 2,073,372 and Ottinger 1,954,754.

Outside New York State, 4,298 election districts out of 4,774 gave Roosevelt 929,953 and Ottinger 1,297,002, an actual plurality of 327,049 and an indicated up-State plurality for Ottinger of 367,589.

In New York City 3,400 out of 3,392 election districts gave Roosevelt 1,093,369 and Ottinger 667,782, an actual plurality of 395,617 and an indicated plurality of 405,188.

Mr. Roosevelt ran ahead of Governor Smith in virtually every county up-State, while Mr. Ottinger ran into the Democratic vote somewhat in New York City, but not as much as expected.

Senator Copeland's run in New York City was surprising. In 3,144 out of the 3,493 election districts in the city he received 1,032,043 and Houghton 561,539, an actual plurality of 471,509 and an indicated plurality of 523,560.

To offset this tremendous plurality, seemingly the largest ever received in the city by any candidate, Mr. Houghton in 3,545 out of 4,774 up-State election districts received 1,086,464 to 713,173 for Senator Copeland. This is an actual plurality of 386,291 and an indicated plurality of 467,852 for Mr. Houghton Up-State.

The delay in the returns from about a thousand up-State districts led Mr. Roosevelt to charge early this morning that there were indications which led him to suspect fraud up-State. He announced that Edward S. Dore, Chairman of the Law Committee of the Democratic State Committee, would leave for up-State this morning with a hundred lawyers ready to relief or prevent any fraud which might be attempted.

"Owing to the extreme delay with which about 1,000 districts up-State are sending in election returns, the Democratic State Committee has become convinced that fraud is being committed in an attempt to elect Ottinger as Governor of the State of New York," Mr. Roosevelt said.

"Accordingly, Mr. Dore, the Godfrey Sacu and Maurice Bloch, minority leader of the Assembly, are leaving New York City on the Empire State Express late (Wednesday) morning for up-State cities, together with a staff of 100 lawyers to uncover such frauds as have been com-

Continued on Page Two.

HOOVER CARRIES NEW YORK BY 125,000

Republican Nominee Captures New Jersey. Takes Wisconsin; Breaks Solid South, Winning Virginia, Florida

GAINING IN NORTH CAROLINA AND BAY STATE

Most of Farm Belt in Republican Column in Record-Breaking Vote—Kentucky, Missouri and Tennessee Lost to Democrats

Voting in unprecedented numbers, a myriad of American citizens yesterday chose Herbert Hoover of California for President of the United States and Charles Curtis of Kansas for Vice President.

How pronounced is the victory of these candidates of the Republican Party over their Democratic competitors, Governor Alfred E. Smith of New York, nominee for President, and Joseph T. Robinson of Arkansas, the Vice Presidential nominee, cannot be determined until the stupendous task of counting 40,000,000 or more votes is completed, but a Republican landslide took place at the polls, and it will be reflected in a heavy Hoover-Curtis majority of the 531 ballots in the Electoral College.

400 Electoral Votes for Hoover

Mr. Hoover is assured of more than 400 electoral votes. It is probable that his majority will increase as further returns are received. He has broken the traditionally Democratic Solid South. He has carried Virginia and returns from Florida indicate that he has won in that State. His tally in the Electoral College may go as high as 444 votes if North Carolina, North Dakota and Texas, which are very close, are added to his strength, or even to the stupendous total of 462, if the count now proceeding is in Massachusetts turns in his favor.

Such an outcome would give Mr. Hoover a majority of 397 electoral votes over Governor Smith. It is already apparent that no Presidential candidate of any major party has ever been beaten as badly as Governor Smith, with the exception of William H. Taft, who polled only 8 votes in the Electoral College in his contest for re-election against Woodrow Wilson and Theodore Roosevelt.

According to the latest returns received from Massachusetts, North Carolina, North Dakota and Texas, these States are still in the doubtful column either by reason of inadequate returns or on account of the closeness of contests as the count proceeds, and while Governor Smith may be shown to have carried some of them, his tally of electoral votes may not exceed seventy.

New York Spells Smith's Doom.

Governor Smith's hope of victory began to fade within a few hours after the polls closed in New York State when it was indicated that he had carried New York City, his great stronghold, by less than 450,000, which was much short of the estimate of his managers. As returns began to roll in from up-State it became apparent that the Hoover plurality in that strong Republican area would materially overcome the showing for Governor Smith in New York City, with the prospect that the Republican nominee would carry the State by a lead in the neighborhood of 125,000.

With New York's forty-five electoral votes placed in the Hoover column it became merely a matter of waiting until the full returns determined what the Republican candidates' majority will be in the Electoral College. The tremendous onsweep of the Hoover following was emphasized when State after State in which the Democrats had placed hope of victory went over into the Republican camp.

New Jersey was to be the Republican national ticket by a heavy majority. Maryland followed suit. Late returns that Hoover also took Missouri. Of other border States, he captured Kentucky and Oklahoma. Minnesota, which the Smith management was also hopeful of carrying on account of the defection among Republican voters because of Mr. Hoover's attitude on the McNary-Haugen bill, gave him a heavy plurality.

Smith Strong Only in South.

As for Governor Smith, there is no assurance that he has carried any State outside of the South. With the results in Florida and Texas still in doubt he seems to be certain of having carried only Alabama, Georgia, Louisiana, Mississippi and South Carolina. In the early morning hours late returns had Hoover forging ahead even in North Carolina. Tennessee was conceded to the Republican candidate.

His victories in Alabama and North Carolina are a set back for Senator J. Thomas Heflin and Senator Furnifold M. Simmons, who deserted their party allegiances to oppose him, Simmons on the ground of Governor Smith's anti-prohibition policy and Senator Heflin for the openly avowed reason that Governor Smith was a Catholic.

In the early morning hours returns from Wisconsin indicated that the portion of the State outside of Milwaukee had voted so heavily for Hoover that Smith's lead in the metropolis made famous by beer had been overcome and that the State's thirteen electoral votes would be added to the steadily mounting Hoover column.

It was after 4 o'clock this morning before virtually complete returns from Rhode Island showed that Smith had carried Rhode Island, the only State outside the Solid South that can with certainty be placed to his credit. He seems to have carried it by a small majority, probably not exceeding 2,000.

Maine, New Hampshire, Vermont and Connecticut joined the Republican procession. At an early hour this morning the prospect was that where the eighteen electoral votes of Massachusetts would go could not be made certain until late today.

Republican Congress Assured.

The victory for the Republican national ticket is accompanied by the assurance that, as President, Mr. Hoover will have the support of a Congress controlled by those of his own faith. While returns are incomplete, the indications are that the Republican majority in the House of Representatives

"All the News That's Fit to Print."

The New York Times.

THE WEATHER
Cloudy and continued cold today; tomorrow fair and warmer.
Temperature yesterday—Max. 59 min. 47.

Copyright, 1929, by The New York Times Company.

VOL. LXXIX....No. 26,207.   ****   NEW YORK, FRIDAY, OCTOBER 25, 1929.   TWO CENTS In Greater | THREE CENTS | FOUR CENTS Elsewhere

GRUNDY SAYS LOBBY IS NEEDED TO UPHOLD PARTY TARIFF VOWS

Pennsylvanian at Senate Inquiry Asserts Hoover Platform Demands the Rates in Bill.

TELLS OF CAMPAIGN FUNDS

Veteran Lobbyist Active in Raising $600,000 in 1924 and $1,000,000 Last Year.

HITS AT SENATE COALITION

Borah Assailed as Having Reversed Himself From Stand Taken in Campaign.

Special to The New York Times.

WASHINGTON, Oct. 24.—Joseph R. Grundy, head of the Pennsylvania Manufacturers' Association and a conspicuous figure for years in the Republican organization of that State, told the Senate Lobby Investigating Committee today that the rates in the pending tariff bill had been adopted in accordance with pledges in the Kansas City platform upon which Herbert Hoover made his successful run for the Presidency. The witness declared that 23,000,000 voters had endorsed the protective principle, and that if the consumers had wanted lower tariff duties they would have shown it by electing Alfred E. Smith to the Presidency.

Mr. Grundy has been identified with "tariff lobbies" since 1897, and frankly said so, insisting that only by alert watchfulness on the part of those concerned could "protected" interests get the kind of legislation that they needed at the hands of Congress.

A big crowd was in attendance to hear the testimony of Mr. Grundy, whose appearance was awaited with interest, by reason of his close association with Pennsylvania manufacturers and the old Penrose machine in that State.

Raised Funds for Campaigns.

Mr. Grundy was examined at the outset upon the part that he had taken in raising funds for the national campaigns of 1924 and 1928 in raising funds for the Republican organization. The ways and means committee of the Pennsylvania Republican State Committee, he stated, had collected $600,000 to further the Coolidge cause in 1924 and last year, with Mr. Hoover at the head of the party ticket, it obtained contributions of about $1,000,000.

The witness testified that at the beginning of the present fight over the tariff he had set up an office in this city and that in the direction of his campaign to uphold the protective principle, he had expended $20,000 out of his own pocket.

This money had been used, he said, in preparing literature for dissemination to the press and in assembling statistical material for manufacturers. He agreed to submit an itemized statement of disbursements.

The name of James Francis Burke, an aide in Mr. Hoover's office during the campaign last year, was brought into the discussion by Senator Walsh of the committee. Mr. Grundy gave the names of several men with whom he had conferred during the Senate Finance Committee's consideration of the tariff bill. Mr. Walsh asked if Mr. Burke was one of them. The witness replied in the affirmative.

"Where did you see Mr. Burke?" asked Senator Walsh.

"At the White House on a number of occasions," was the reply.

"When you went to see him did you go in to the White House?"

"Oh, no—I'd the witness. "I saw him at other places."

Witness Attacks Coalition.

In a statement which the committee refused to permit Mr. Grundy to read, but which was attached to the record, the witness hit squarely at the Republican-Democratic coalition now fighting the Finance Committee bill in the Senate. Four of the members of the Lobby Committee, Senators Caraway and Walsh, Democrats, and Senators Borah and Blaine, Republicans, are identified with the coalition.

Mr. Grundy was particularly pointed in his references to Senator Borah, who was a member of the resolutions committee of the Kansas City convention, and, as such, he endorsed the tariff plank promising "revision wherever necessary."

He quoted from a speech made by Mr. Borah in the Boston arena on Nov. 2, in which the Idaho Senator urged his hearers to keep the "tariff policy in the hands of those who have believed in it from the beginning" by electing Mr. Hoover to the Presidency. Mr. Grundy contrasted Senator Borah's campaign speeches on the tariff with his present course in opposing the present committee bill.

Charges Borah With Shifting.

"What influences have caused the esteemed Senator from Idaho to completely reverse himself within a period of a few months; what changes of mind have prompted him

Continued on Page Twenty-five.

Plane Lost in Channel Gale; 5 Aboard Fail to Reach Paris

Special Cable to The New York Times.

LONDON, Oct. 24.—The English Channel was being swept by searchlights tonight in a hunt for three British airmen and two passengers who left Croydon airdrome in a new three-engined airplane to fly to East Africa.

A sixty-mile-an-hour gale was raging over the Channel when the airplane crossed the cliffs near Dover and disappeared into a mist.

The airplane, intended for passenger service in Kenya Colony, was piloted by Captain Campbell Black and carried G. D. Fletcher, an East African journalist, and R. Rowthorne as passengers.

Owing to low visibility and bumpy conditions the airplane returned once to Croydon and dropped another passenger who preferred to travel on the surface.

HUMBERT ESCAPES ANTI-FASCISTI'S SHOT AT BRUSSELS TOMB

Student Slips as He Tries to Assassinate the Italian Crown Prince.

HEIR CONTINUES PROGRAM

He Places Wreath on Unknown Soldier's Grave and Reviews Guard of Honor.

CROWD MOBS ASSAILANT

Italian Came From Paris to Kill Prince During Celebration of Royal Betrothal.

Special Cable to The New York Times.

BRUSSELS, Oct. 24.—Within a few hours of the official announcement of his engagement to Princess Marie José and only a few feet from the tomb of Belgium's unknown soldier, an attempt was made this morning to assassinate Prince Humbert, heir to the Italian throne.

A young Italian law student, Fernando di Rosa, who had come to Brussels from Paris expressly to kill the Prince, confessed that he fired a revolver at him from a distance of 30 yards. Fortunately the assassin slipped just as he fired and the shot went wide.

Prince Humbert had wished, as his first act in the country of his future bride, to lay a wreath on the tomb of the Unknown Soldier. His engagement to the Princess being official, an elaborate ceremony had been arranged. There was a big crowd in the square around the Colonne du Congrès and two companies of infantry were lined up with their flags and the flag of the Italian veterans.

Gendarme Fells Assailant.

All the official world had gathered, including Burgomaster Max, General Kestens, the Italian Ambassador, Marquis Durazzo and the Minister of War, Count de Broqueville, when the Prince arrived at 9:30 o'clock. The band was playing the Italian national anthem as he stepped from his automobile and started toward the tomb. For an instant Prince Humbert stopped to talk to Count de Broqueville.

At that moment a young man was seen running quickly through the police cordon toward the Prince. As he ran he fired. There was another flash and the bark of a shot. Leaping forward a Belgian gendarme beat down the young assassin's arm with his sword and felled him before he could fire again.

Prince Humbert heard the shot and saw the scuffle but scarcely turned his head.

When the crowd realized what had happened there was a great outburst of cheering. Those near the would-be assassin attacked and nearly lynched him before he could be rescued by the police.

Prince Completes Program.

The whole incident lasted only two minutes, there being scarcely time to complete the playing of the national anthem. At once, with slow and dignified steps, the Prince walked toward the tomb of the Unknown Soldier carrying a large horseshoe wreath of laurel leaves bound with blue ribbon on which was embossed the arms of the House of Savoy.

Every one except the Prince himself was in an intense state of excitement and nervousness. The assassin might not have been alone. Perhaps another attempt would be made. The suggestion was whispered that the ceremony should be cut short, but the Prince insisted on reviewing the guard of honor and he walked down the lines with the Italian Ambassador, Count de Broqueville and Burgomaster Max, who all kept as close to him as etiquette would permit, the three forming a kind of bodyguard.

Meanwhile the police had been fighting for five minutes with the crowd to prevent the assailant from being lynched. He was so bruised in the scuffle as to be all but unconscious. When he reached the police station, however, he had recovered sufficiently to be able to give his name and to declare that he alone was responsible and had been actuated by his hatred of Fascism, which he said was killing his country.

Firer of Shot a Socialist.

Di Rosa is 21 years of age and was born in Milan. He had only a passport, and continued his studies there. He came, two days ago, to Antwerp with a false Swiss passport and waited there for the Prince's visit to Brussels. Dressed as a tourist, it was not difficult for di Rosa to get near the royal party at this morning's ceremony and if he had not slipped on the edge of the curb of a street refuge as he ran toward the Prince, it is almost certain that he would have succeeded in his crime.

Di Rosa declared he was a Socialist and a member of the Second International. He said he fired the second more sighted a fleeting body. A lifeboat was lowered and a drowned seaman was lifted aboard.

Charges Borah With Shifting.

JURY IN FALL TRIAL LOCKED UP FOR NIGHT

No Word Comes After 11½ Hours' Deliberations of 8 Men, 4 Women in Bribe Case.

DEFENDANT STAYS ABED

Exceptions Were Taken by the Ex-Secretary's Counsel to the Judge's Charge.

Special to The New York Times.

WASHINGTON, Oct. 24.—The jury trying the case of Albert B. Fall, former Secretary of the Interior, who is charged with accepting a bribe of $100,000 from Edward L. Doheny, was locked up for the night at 11 o'clock tonight. It had deliberated since 11:30 o'clock in the morning without reporting a verdict. Court was recessed until 10 o'clock tomorrow morning.

In all the hours that had elapsed since the jury began its deliberations not one word had leaked from the jury room as to how the eight men and four women of the jury stood. There were all kinds of rumors about the court corridors, but there was not the least authority for any of them.

The former Secretary of the Interior returned to his hotel as soon as the jury left the court room. He had the court's consent to remain there until a verdict was reached. Mr. Fall made no comment or any kind after the case went to the jury. The silence that has been his policy since the oil cases started more than six years ago was maintained to the end.

Mr. Fall, it was understood, remained in bed while the jury deliberated.

Takes Exceptions to Judge's Charge.

Friends of the defendant admitted frankly that they were not overpleased with Justice Hitz's charge. That this was also the attitude of Mr. Fall's lawyers was indicated by the fact that Frank J. Hogan, chief counsel for Fall, entered ten exceptions to specific parts of the charge and a general exception to the complete utterance. Government counsel said they were entirely satisfied with the charge.

In the court room was jammed to the doors during the delivery of the charge. Time and again Fall looked at his lawyers, and to some persons in the court room it looked as though he were making a silent appeal to Mr. Hogan to interrupt the charge with objections to the interpretation of the law as expounded by Justice Hitz.

Justice Hitz told the jury to leave sympathy out of the case so far as they were concerned. Clemency, he added, was for the judge or the President to exercise.

The "sunshine of New Mexico," to which Mr. Hogan had asked the jury to return Fall, was not evidence declared Justice Hitz.

Judge Speaks Hour and a Quarter.

The charge of Justice Hitz, to which the defense took ten specific exceptions and one general exception to the whole charge, required an hour and fifteen minutes to deliver. With the exception of the written prayers for instruction, submitted by the government and by the defense, Justice Hitz addressed the jury without notes or manuscript of any kind.

Frank T. Hogan, chief counsel for Fall, was kept busy from the moment the justice began his own part of the charge until the end, writing objection to the instructions. When Justice Hitz declared that the trial jurors should decide the facts in the case while the judge passes on the law, Mr. Hogan presented his specific objections ready the moment the charge was concluded.

"Mr. Fall is charged here with bribery," said Justice Hitz. "And the charge of bribery, as used in this case, is the betrayal of a public trust by a public officer. It is not charged with having defrauded the government of the United States. He is not charged with having betrayed his trust as Secretary of the Interior in that, on a certain day, he received certain moneys from

Continued on Page Twenty-two.

Load-Speaker Can Be Nuisance; McAdoo Advises Magistrates

The opinion that a radio loudspeaker under certain conditions, may be classed as a nuisance was expressed by Chief Magistrate William McAdoo in a letter sent to the forty-six magistrates of the five boroughs yesterday. His letter declared:

"As you know, there is a widespread complaint all over the city by people who are annoyed and kept from sleeping by the loud-speaking radios in apartments, tenement houses and other buildings. Many complaints come to this office urging me to ask you gentlemen to treat these cases seriously.

"The person who starts a loudspeaker under conditions where it is found to annoy and disturb other people and keep them from proper rest, in my opinion, is guilty of a disorderly act, and where it is persistent and annoys a considerable number of people, he or she can be charged under Section 1,530 with maintaining a nuisance."

TESTIFIES HE HANDED $10,000 TO WARDER

Dell' Osso Asserts Former State Banking Head Counted Alleged Bribe in Home.

SENT BY FERRARI, HE SAYS

Memorandum on Withdrawal of Cash From City Trust Is Held From Jury Temporarily.

Gennaro Dell' Osso testified yesterday that he handed $10,000 "in large bills" to Frank H. Warder when the latter was State Superintendent of Banks. Dell' Osso, key witness for the State at Mr. Warder's trial for bribery, said he took the money to Mr. Warder's home in Brooklyn at the direction of Francesco M. Ferrari, president of the City Trust Company.

The prosecutor presented evidence tracing the withdrawal of the money from the Atlantic Avenue branch of the City Trust Company in Brooklyn, its delivery to Mr. Ferrari, president. At his sickbed in his home in Brooklyn and its transfer by Ferrari to Dell' Osso, his brother-in-law.

Hiram C. Todd, special assistant district attorney, told Dell' Osso to relate what happened on Sept. 21, 1928, the day the witness said he received the money.

"He called me up there and gave me $10,000 in an envelope," Dell' Osso testified. At this point James L. Cuff, Warder's attorney, objected to the witness telling what Ferrari had said to him. Justice Tompkins sustained Mr. Cuff.

"What did you do then?" Mr. Todd asked.

"I put the money in my pocket," said Dell' Osso.

"After you received the money what did you do with it?"

"I took it in the night time to Mr. Frank Warder's house."

He related how he had gone to work at the Park Row building of which he was superintendent at 9 o'clock, taking the subway to 116th Street and Broadway and finally arriving at Warder's door. Mr. Warder not immobile as Dell' Osso continued:

"Frank Warder will come and open the door. I says, 'I want see Mr. Warder, I got something for him.' He came, I gave him the envelope, he opened the envelope, counted the money, put him in his pocket and asks me, 'What did Mr. Ferrari say?' and I says, 'He says best regards to everybody.'" Dell' Osso testified that he had met Warder at the Hightstown (N. J.) farm of Ferrari and at Ferrari's home in Bay Ridge, Brooklyn.

The cross-examination of Dell' Osso was brief compared to that of other State witnesses. Mr. Cuff had

Continued on Page Two.

Missing Lake Ferry Sank With Crew of 57; Four Bodies Found; All Hands Believed Lost

Special to The New York Times.

CHICAGO, Oct. 24.—All indications tonight pointed to the loss of fifty-seven lives when the car ferry Milwaukee sank Tuesday night in Lake Michigan.

The Milwaukee was definitely given up for lost today, after another ship reported it had recovered the missing ferry's pilot house and two bodies wearing its life belts. A watch found on one of the bodies had stopped at 8:30, indicating that the Milwaukee went down about that time Tuesday night, seven hours after leaving Milwaukee.

The steamship Steel Chemist, a freighter out of Three Rivers, Quebec, was half way between Racine and Kenosha at noon today when the second mate sighted a floating body. A lifeboat was lowered and a drowned seaman was lifted aboard.

Captain Brown flashed a notice to the Grand Trunk car ferry office at Milwaukee. The message was intercepted by the Coast Guard station at Racine, Wis., the same station which on Tuesday night had vainly attempted to catch the sinking ferry's last S O S.

About 8:25 P. M. Tuesday, when the Milwaukee was about to founder, A. W. Pfeiffer, a Racine insurance salesman, was spinning his dials to pick up a Louisville program. His receiver suddenly cut in on the Morse code and Pfeiffer, who was a naval radio operator in wartime, tuned in. The message was an S O S. Pfeiffer telephoned the Coast Guard station at Racine. The Coast Guard cutter operator tuned in, but could hear nothing. Pfeiffer went back to his radio and deciphered three words, "Water up to"... Then silence.

Two other bodies of the Milwaukee's crew were found by other steamships. They were half way between Racine and Kenosha.

Twenty-three officers and seamen of the stranded steamer Maple Court of the Canada Steamship Lines were rescued by the Coast Guard cutter Semloole early today after the ship had been hard aground for 48 hours on a reef at Cockburn Island, Lake Huron.

After taking off the Maple Court's crew, the Coast Guard cutter proceeded to Gravel Island to stand by the car carrier William B Pifley, whose crew refused to abandon ship.

WORST STOCK CRASH STEMMED BY BANKS; 12,894,650-SHARE DAY SWAMPS MARKET; LEADERS CONFER, FIND CONDITIONS SOUND

FINANCIERS EASE TENSION

Five Wall Street Bankers Hold Two Meetings at Morgan Office.

CALL BREAK 'TECHNICAL'

Lamont Lays It to 'Air Holes'—Says Low Prices Do Not Depict Situation Fairly.

FINDS MARGINS BEING MET

Sees Market 'Susceptible of Betterment'—Mitchell, Potter, Wiggin, Prosser at Talks.

Wall Street gave credit yesterday to its banking leaders for arresting the decline on the New York Stock Exchange at a time when the stock market was being overwhelmed by selling orders. The instances at which the steps were taken that reversed the market's trend was hurriedly called at the offices of J. P. Morgan & Co.

The five bankers who met at the headquarters of the famous private banking house at noon yesterday and again at 4:30 P. M., following the meeting of the board of the Federal Reserve Bank of New York, were:

CHARLES E. MITCHELL, chairman of the National City Bank.

ALBERT H. WIGGIN, chairman of the Chase National Bank.

WILLIAM POTTER, president of the Guaranty Trust Company.

SEWARD PROSSER, chairman of the Bankers Trust Company.

THOMAS W. LAMONT, senior partner of the Morgan firm.

Exclusive of the vast wealth of the house of Morgan this group of bankers represented more than $6,000,000,000 of massed banking resources.

Meeting Eases Tenseness.

As the word went out in Wall Street that these financiers had met the air of tense anxiety in the financial district was relieved. Almost at once the word was passed around the floor of the Stock Exchange that "they" were going to support stock prices and the down-rush of security quotations was halted. Outside the offices of the Morgan firm, at Broad and Wall Streets, a crowd quickly gathered, and on the steps of the Subtreasury Building opposite news-paper photographers and motion picture men took their stand.

After the conference Mr. Lamont spoke to reporters. The meeting of the bankers, he said, had been held largely to exchange information on the stock market situation and an plan of concerted action to support the stock market had been agreed upon.

"There has been a little distress selling on the Stock Exchange," Mr. Lamont said, "and we have had a meeting of the heads of several financial institutions to discuss the situation.

"We have found that there are no houses in difficulty and reports from brokers indicate that margins are being maintained satisfactorily." Mr. Lamont stated that the group

Continued on Page Two.

Wall Street Optimistic After Stormy Day; Clerical Work May Force Holiday Tomorrow

Confidence in the soundness of the stock market structure, notwithstanding the upheaval of the last few days, was voiced last night by bankers and other financial leaders. Sentiment as expressed by the heads of some of the largest banking institutions and by industrial executives as well was distinctly cheerful and the feeling was general that the worst had been seen. Wall Street ended the day in an optimistic frame of mind.

The opinion of brokers was unanimous that the selling had got out of hand not because of any inherent weakness in the market but because the public had become alarmed over the steady liquidation of the last few weeks. Over their private wires these brokers counseled their customers against further thoughtless selling at sacrifice prices.

Charles E. Mitchell, chairman of the National City Bank, declared that fundamentals remained unimpaired after the declines of the last few days. "I am still of the opinion," he added, "that this reaction has badly overrun itself."

Lewis L. Pierson, chairman of the board of the Irving Trust Company, issued last night the following statement:

"Severe disturbances in the stock market are nothing new in American experience. The pendulum always swings widely and it would seem as though the long-expected break should bring about an equilibrium.

"The position of the Federal Reserve Banks is unusually strong and the borrowings of member banks are moderate.

"Considering the record-breaking earnings in many industries, we may well remember that whenever fundamental values are lost sight of by the unthinking majority it is time for courage on the part of those investors who have a real sense of basic worth."

Because the clerical facilities of brokerage houses were overtaxed as a result of the recent phenomenally heavy trading, an agitation was started yesterday in favor of a suspension of trading on the New York Stock Exchange tomorrow.

It is thought possible that the governing committee will take action today, without waiting for a petition from the membership. In many brokerage houses the posting of books has fallen far behind and some relief will have to be afforded, according to brokers, unless the market quiets down shortly.

BIG DROP IN WHEAT; PIT IN A TURMOIL

Break of 12 Cents a Bushel to New Season Low and 8-Cent Rally Mark Wild Trading.

STOCKS TUMBLE IN CHICAGO

Selling Swamps Exchange in 1,200,000-Share Day—Part of Big Losses Recovered.

Special to The New York Times.

CHICAGO, Oct. 24.—Fortunes in paper values were wiped out for mid-Western investors and speculators today as prices for grain and securities on the Chicago Board of Trade and the Chicago Stock Exchange, reacting to the selling wave in Wall Street, recorded sensational declines. Amid wild scenes in the wheat pit, quotations for all deliveries at the close were from 4½ to 5¾ cents a bushel under the final prices of Wednesday, when a depreciation of 4 cents a bushel laid the basis for today's unprecedented peace-time grain market.

On the Chicago Stock Exchange the heavy selling shattered records both for volume of sales and the severity of the day's average decline.

1,200,000-Share Turnover.

For the first time in the history of the local stock market more than 1,000,000 shares changed hands—1,200,000 shares, and prices of stocks in about nine cases in ten closed from $5 to $30 a share.

The big Chicago banks came to the aid of the distressed stock market, the heads of these institutions expressing the opinion that selling had become panicky. A statement by the chief downtown institutions led to an estimate that many millions of dollars were made available.

There never has been such a wheat market as that of today outside of wartimes. There prevailed among the brokers in the pit and excitement ran high in La Salle Street brokerage offices as grain quotations dropped 12 cents a bushel in a short period. At one time 7-cent drops in about as many minutes were registered in Chicago and Winnipeg.

December wheat broke from $1.34¾ to $1.13½, with a rally around 4 cents, being 11 cents off last week's prices.

In Winnipeg December wheat broke from $1.37½ to $1.25, but rallied to close at $1.32¾, a net loss of 6 cents a bushel. May wheat broke from $1.45 to $1.31 and was $1.35¼, at the close. Liverpool prices at the last were off 3¾ cents.

A message from Winnipeg reported that a well-known Chicago grain speculator had sold 10,000,000 bushels of wheat there, scattering it among the trade. In Chicago millions of bushels were unloaded indiscriminately. Many orders to sell 500,000 bushels came into the pit during the first three hours of trading.

It was common gossip around the Board of Trade that New York speculators and Arthur W. Cutten, who have been credited with taking the heaviest longs for several months, were changing their holdings here and in Winnipeg and at the door of unsound technical conditions.

TREASURY OFFICIALS BLAME SPECULATION

Drastic Market Decline Found Not Due to Any Basic Business Weakness.

STILL PLAN TAX REDUCTION

Reserve Board Meets Twice in Day and Keeps in Constant Touch With Markets Here.

Special to The New York Times.

WASHINGTON, Oct. 24.—After two extended meetings, over the second of which Secretary Mellon presided, the Federal Reserve Board late today decided that the avalanche of selling on the New York stock market today had not resulted in a situation serious enough to call for any immediate formal declaration. While the tremendous liquidation was at its height there were indications that the board would make an announcement, but such action was withheld when the closing hour on the Exchange showed a part recovery of values.

Throughout the day, however, there were scenes of unusual activity about the offices of the board in the Treasury Building and members were requested to keep constantly in touch with developments.

After the afternoon meeting, which lasted from about 3:30 until 5 o'clock, Mr. Lamont said, "and we have had inquiries with the statement that there was nothing to say, except that the bill rate in New York had been reduced to 5 per cent. No action was taken in regard to the New York bank's 6 per cent rediscount rate.

Secretary Mellon also refused to make any formal comment.

Brokers' Loans Show Decline.

While the board was meeting in the afternoon the report of brokers' loans made by New York member banks was issued, showing a decline of $167,000,000 to a total of $6,634,000,000, as compared with $6,801,000,000 one week ago. This report covered the loans up to the close of the market Tuesday night, and represented only a part of the drop which must have occurred as a result of the liquidation yesterday and today.

In advising December heavy broke from $1.37¾ to $1.25, but rallied to close at $1.32¾, a net loss of 6 cents a bushel. May wheat broke from $1.45 to $1.31 and was $1.35¼, at the close.

At the final meeting of the board at 10:46 A. M. before the selling had gained full force, and continued

Continued on Page Four.

LOSSES RECOVERED IN PART

Upward Trend Starts With 200,000-Share Order for Steel.

TICKERS LAG FOUR HOURS

Thousands of Accounts Wiped Out, With Traders in Dark as to Events on Exchange.

SALES ON CURB 6,337,415

Prices on Markets in Other Cities Also Slump and Rally —Wheat Values Hard Hit.

The most disastrous decline in the biggest and broadest stock market of history rocked the financial district yesterday. In the very midst of the collapse five of the country's most influential bankers hurried to the office of J. P. Morgan & Co. and after a brief conference gave out word that they believe the foundations of the market to be sound, that the market smash had been caused by technical rather than fundamental considerations, and that many sound stocks are selling too low.

Suddenly the market turned about, on buying orders thrown into the pivotal issues, and before the final quotations were tapped out, four hours and eight minutes after the 3 o'clock bell, most stocks had regained a measurable part of their losses.

Losses at Close Not Excessive.

The break was one of the widest in the market's history, although the losses at the close were not particularly large, many having been recouped by the afternoon rally.

It carried down with it speculators, big and little, in every part of the country, wiping out thousands of accounts. It is probable that if the stockholders of the country's foremost corporations had not been calmed by the attitude of leading bankers and the subsequent rally, the business of the country would have been seriously affected. Doubtless business will feel the effects of the drastic stock shake-out, and this is expected to hit the luxuries most severely.

Thousands Sacrifice Holdings.

The total losses cannot be accurately calculated, because of the large number of markets and the thousands of securities not listed on any exchange. However, they were staggering, running into billions of dollars. Fear struck the big speculators and little investors, big investors and little ones. Thousands of them threw their holdings into the whirling Stock Exchange pit for what they would bring. Losses were tremendous and thousands of prosperous brokerage and bank accounts, some built up through a long period of years, were completely wrecked in the strange debacle, due to a combination of circumstances, but accelerated into a crash by fear.

The ticker service maintained by the New York Stock Exchange and the New York Curb Exchange proved pitifully inadequate for the task of recording history's biggest market. By 10:30 o'clock the Exchange ticker had fallen 15 minutes behind and that of the Curb Exchange 18 minutes; by 11:30 this was stretched to 24 minutes for the Exchange and 47 for the Curb; at 1 o'clock they were 92 minutes late; by 2 o'clock, 131 minutes late for the Exchange and 118 for the Curb ticker, and by 3:30 the Exchange quotation was some 167 minutes late and the Curb tickers 130 minutes behind. The New York Stock Exchange tickers did not complete the task of printing the market until 8½ minutes past 7 o'clock last night, while the Curb tickers finished at 5:34.

Financial District in Confusion.

Under these circumstances the trickles and spreads of 10, 20 and at times 30 points along the tape prices and those on the floor of the

The New York Times.

Copyright, 1929, by The New York Times Company.

THE WEATHER

Cloudy, probably rain today and tomorrow; warmer tomorrow.

Temperatures yesterday—Max. 56, min. 44.

VOL. LXXIX....No. 26,212. **** | NEW YORK, WEDNESDAY, OCTOBER 30, 1929. | TWO CENTS In Greater New York | THREE CENTS Within 200 Miles | FOUR CENTS Else-where Except 9th and 8th Postal Zones.

GRUNDY FOR CURBING 'BACKWARD STATES' ON THE TARIFF BILL

Veteran Republican Lobbyist Tells Senate Inquiry the West Needs "Silencing."

PENNSYLVANIA KNOWS BEST

"Unfortunate," He Holds, That the Constitution Gives Equal Voice to States in Senate.

BATTLES INVESTIGATORS

He Assails Borah—Would "Hate to Tell" His Opinion of Wisconsin.

Special to The New York Times.

WASHINGTON, Oct. 29.—Joseph R. Grundy, president of the Pennsylvania Manufacturers' Association, told the Senate Lobby Committee today that certain "backward" States of the West, through their Senators, had been altogether "too vocal" in the consideration of the current tariff bill, and that some method should be found to "silence" them at times when legislation affecting the economic welfare of the United States is under way.

Mr. Grundy declared it "unfortunate" that the framers of the Constitution had seen fit to grant to the States equal rights and representation in the Senate, and the effect of the arrangement was to give sections slow in developing their resources an equal voice in legislation directly involving such great reservoirs of wealth and taxation as Pennsylvania. Mr. Grundy was recalled today for cross-examination on testimony he gave before the lobby committee on Oct. 24. Last week Mr. Grundy and the Senate investigating committee clashed strongly and well, and that session was decorous and orderly in contrast with today, when the witness and his questioners appeared to be antagonistic from the outset.

Criticizes Senator Walsh.

On one stage Mr. Grundy sharply described a series of questions put by Senator Walsh of Montana as "impertinent." There were frequent references to the Vare case, to the party service which Mr. Grundy performed in the collection of Republican campaign funds, and to the relations of the witness with public men and his activities here as a part of the tariff lobby.

At times the hearing resembled a hot political debate, in which the five members of the committee were arrayed against the witness. Mr. Grundy was once reproved by Senator Caraway of Wisconsin, a member of the committee, for alleged evasion, and Mr. Blaine exclaimed heatedly:

"Look me squarely in the eye and answer my question."

The hearing was marked by frequent spats between Mr. Grundy and Senators Borah, Caraway and Walsh, and in one interchange with the witnesses Mr. Borah denied emphatically a statement that he had opposed the debenture plan at the Kansas City convention.

Chairman Caraway repeatedly indicated that the witness was not frank with the committee and that, while his counsel sought to aid him to "sidestep," eventually the investigators would get what they were after.

Hit at "Most Vocal" States.

Mr. Grundy was impelled to enter into a discussion of his belief that "backward Western States" should be silenced on the tariff by questions asked by Senator Walsh. The Senator's examination submitted to the committee a week ago, in which Mr. Grundy asserted that if "volume of voice" in the Senate were proportioned to population, productive power or the total contributed toward the national upkeep, some of those States "which are now most vocal would need amplifiers to make their whispers heard."

Mr. Grundy also had declared that "such States as Arizona, South Dakota, Idaho and Mississippi, do not pay enough toward the upkeep of the government to cover the costs of collection." As a result of Mr. Grundy's examination, Mr. Grundy finally included Arkansas and Montana in his list of "backward" States, thus bringing in three of them having representation on the lobby committee.

"You have not mentioned Wisconsin in your list," suggested Senator Walsh. "What do you think about that State?"

"What I think about Wisconsin I'd hate to tell you," replied the witness. This evoked an outburst of laughter in the audience, in which the committee joined.

Favors a Few Concessions.

Mr. Grundy again caused laughter when he said that he would permit the "backward" States, through their Senators, to have their say on questions affecting "Junior Red Cross" work and outdoor relief," but that, generally speaking, they should be required to "hold their peace" on

Continued on Page Eighteen.

IT'S A SAFE TAXI IF IT'S A Raxant 1000 Yellow Taxi.—Advt.

Van Opel, Rocket Flier, Weds Woman Pilot Who Advised Him

Wireless to The New York Times.

BERLIN, Oct. 29.—Fritz von Opel, the first to fly a rocket plane, and who intends to sail for New York the beginning of November to study and work at General Motors plants, was married on Saturday to Frau Schulz, née Loewenstein, the former wife of a Wiesbaden actor. For many months she has been von Opel's professional adviser on aviation and she herself is one of Germany's six woman pilots, flying her Handley Page plane with the greatest skill.

Frau von Opel, who is also a daring automobilist, is handsome, slender and blonde. When the airman landed safely from his rocket flight she was the first to congratulate him, shedding tears of joy. She will accompany him to the United States.

COALITION FIGHTING MOVE TO KILL TARIFF

Will Try to Force Through Bill, While Reed Favors Ending Session Nov. 15.

WATSON QUITTING CAPITAL

Departure for Florida Tomorrow for Health Leaves Jones as Republican Senate Leader.

Special to The New York Times.

WASHINGTON, Oct. 29.—Faced by Old Guard Republican willingness to leave the Smoot-Hawley tariff bill to its fate, the Democratic-Progressive coalition was today more determined than ever to drive the bill through the Senate and force the conservatives to accept it in a completely rewritten form.

Coalition strategy was centred upon fixing on the Old Guard leaders any responsibility for abandonment of the remodeled bill with the Simmons-Norris flexible provisions and the farm debenture plan. To those old-line Republican who are now ready to desert the measure, the coalition applied the unflattering comparison of "rats and a sinking ship."

The administration Republicans refused to be stirred by such criticism. Senator Reed of Pennsylvania reiterated his conviction that the bill would not emerge from the conference. Senator Moses announced that he would vote against the bill in the Senate, before it ever went to conference. The Republicans were so dismayed that they even seriously considered a motion to adjourn the Senate about the middle of November until the regular session starts on Dec. 2.

To add to their disorganization it was revealed that Senator Watson, Republican floor leader, would leave for Florida on Thursday to rebuild his shattered health.

McNary to Act as Aide.

Old Guard lieutenants hurriedly announced that Senator Jones of Washington, assistant leader, would take charge in Mr. Watson's absence, aided by Senator McNary of Oregon, who is popular with all Senate factions, has a fine record as a conciliator and more influence than most regular Republicans with the farming public.

When it was first announced that Senator Watson was going to Florida, reports spread that his illness was so serious that he might never return to the Senate as floor leader. His friends, however, denied this. They admitted that he was an ill man and needed a complete rest for a time, but asserted that he would return to assume his duties.

There was some assumption that Mr. McNary would be made temporary leader, because Senator Jones had not sufficiently recovered from the effects of a recent operation, but Mr. Jones assured Old Guard members that he felt capable of taking over the task.

While pessimistic, Senator Watson, who is dropping work by his physician's orders, would not admit that the outlook for passing the tariff bill at the special session was absolutely hopeless. He did not share the view that the session might as well be adjourned, which Senator Reed may propose for about Nov. 15. Instead, Mr. Watson will work until his departure to bring about "some sort of agreement for some sort of bill," basing this plea on the idea that the coalition must consider increases on industrial as well as agricultural rates.

Says Action Would Aid Business.

"It would have a quieting effect on business to pass the tariff bill," asserted Senator Watson. "Tariff bills are always the occasion of some unrest, though this bill has caused less agitation than usual because a Republican tariff is to be superimposed on a Republican tariff and everybody knows that if this bill fails the country would continue to be prosperous.

"It is true that there ought to be changes in agricultural rates to meet new conditions, but it is equally true

Continued on Page Fourteen.

KAHN REFUSES POST IN SENATE CAMPAIGN; CALLS CHOICE UNWISE

He Writes to Moses to Withhold His Name for Treasurer Due to 'Divided Reception.'

WAS RELUCTANT, HE SAYS

Recalls He Told Senator of His Stand, but Yielded as a Duty to His Party.

HOLDS VIEWS CONFIRMED

Declares He Is a Wall St. Man but a Liberal in Politics—Friends See Him Put in False Light.

Otto H. Kahn in a letter to Senator George H. Moses of New Hampshire, chairman of the Republican Senatorial Campaign Committee, made public yesterday, declined the post of treasurer of that committee because of the "divided reception" which the announcement of his designation as treasurer had met.

Announcement of the selection of Mr. Kahn was made by Senator Moses at the dinner given last Thursday evening at the University Club here by Jeremiah Milbank for Claudius H. Huston, the new chairman of the Republican National Committee. Publication of this announcement, together with the report that speakers at the dinner attacked the members of the Progressive Republican group in the Senate, brought protests from some of these Senators against the selection of Mr. Kahn.

Mr. Kahn in his letter to Senator Moses declared that, while a Wall Street man, he was a liberal in politics. He said some of the interpretations placed on his designation were erroneous, but added that the way it had been received justified his earlier feeling that he was not the right man for the position. No formal action for the appointment of a treasurer of the Senatorial committee has yet been taken, and Mr. Kahn requested Senator Moses not to present his name to the committee.

Mr. Kahn's Letter.

Mr. Kahn's letter follows:

My dear Senator:

When you did me the honor to ask me to act as treasurer of the Republican Senatorial Campaign Committee I told you that I feared your kindly sentiment toward me, springing from a long friendship, was swaying your judgment, that I felt sure that I was not the right man for the position, that, moreover, I was overwhelmed with demands upon my time and energies and that I hoped very much you would not persist in your request.

You argued to the contrary and, among other things, pointed to the fact that, while a Wall Street man, I was known to be, as indeed I am, a liberal in politics. You repeated your invitation when I had the pleasure of seeing you at Mr. Milbank's dinner last Thursday.

I thereupon stated that, though my views were unchanged—I felt that if we want effective party government, such as our political system requires, every citizen should be willing to make good his profession of party allegiance by submitting to being drafted, within the limits of reason and possibility, and that if the leaders of the party to which I belong demanded of me a service which did not conflict with my other duties and responsibilities I was not at liberty to refuse, however reluctant I was to accept.

You regarded this answer as tantamount to an acceptance in principle, as you were perfectly justified in doing, and at what was supposed and intended to be a strictly private dinner, you made informal reference to that acceptance.

Sees His Doubts Confirmed.

But the divided reception with which the announcement of a separate treasurer for your committee and of my designation as such treasurer has met, however erroneous some of the interpretations placed thereon, appears to have confirmed the validity of the doubts which I ventured to express when you offered that position to me, and to justify me in concluding to abstain from occupying it.

I understand that no formal action has been taken as yet by the National Republican Senatorial committee concerning the appointment of a treasurer, and I am making free to write these lines to request that you will please refrain from bringing my name before the committee for appointment to the treasurership.

Believe me, dear Senator,

Very faithfully yours,

OTTO H. KAHN.

Hon. George H. Moses, The Senate, Washington, D. C.

Influential Republicans expressed regret that Mr. Kahn had decided not to take the post of treasurer of the Republican Senatorial committee. It was recalled that he had

Continued on Page Fourteen.

PINEHURST, N. C.—Golf an income crop. Leave field N.Y. Special Carolina Special now open, party limit 12. Tues. N.Y. 6:15 P.M.—Advt.

Newark Man, 4 Feet 10, Says He Was Smallest in A. E. F.

WASHINGTON, Oct. 29 (AP).—Nicholas Casale of Newark, N. J., wants to be known as the smallest man who went to France with the American Expeditionary Forces.

He has appealed to Representative Hartley of Kearny to establish that fact. Casale recently secured an affidavit from the Veterans' Bureau certifying that he was 4 feet 10 inches tall and weighed 106 pounds when he enlisted. The bureau has refused to declare him the "smallest man," saying it would require months of labor to scan the record of every man who served with the A. E. F.

It was not explained how Casale secured enlistment when the minimum requirements are 5 feet and 110 pounds.

MISSING AIRLINER BROUGHT IN SAFELY

Pilot Lands Western Express Ship at Albuquerque After Being Forced Down.

WOULD NOT RISK STORM

Passengers Tell of Cold Night in Deserted Ranch House as Snow Swirled Round.

Special to The New York Times.

ALBUQUERQUE, N. M., Oct. 29.—Lost for more than twenty-four hours while marooned on a bleak New Mexico mesa, Western Air Express tri-motored liner 113 escaped today from the snow-swept stretch where it was forced down Monday and landed here with its crew of three and two passengers, chilled but safe.

Caught in a blinding swirl of snow Monday at 10:15 A. M., the plane was forced down near Trechado, seventy-five miles southeast of Gallup, N. M. The crew and passengers found refuge in an abandoned ranch house.

The passengers are Dr. A. W. Ward of San Francisco and W. E. Merz of Mount Vernon, N. Y. The crew includes James E. Doles, chief pilot, of Los Angeles; Allan C. Barrie, co-pilot, of Burbank, Cal., and R. L. Britton, steward, of Los Angeles.

Employes of the airport and pilots of two planes waiting for the weather to clear to resume the search for the 113 stood amazed as the big craft glided along the runway. They rushed out to the plane and as the group of men who had been given up for dead stepped out the plane danced around them, clapped them on the back and hugged them in delight.

Wild Night of Anxiety.

Despite their fatigue, Dr. Ward and Mr. Merz were lighthearted and stepped jauntily from the plane. They regretted only the loss of time but joined in praise of Pilot Doles for his skillful maneuvering to save the ship in the storm when further progress could not be risked.

They told of a harrowing night which followed the forced landing, of tramping through snow to find shelter, of sleeping on an old bed spring covered with seat cushions from the plane and of shivering in intense cold while they took turns in keeping up a fire.

"A half frozen rabbit and a rabbit's foot brought us good luck," Dr. Ward said.

"The half-frozen rabbit had been captured in the bushes by co-pilot Barrie. The rabbit's foot was worn by steward Britton. He had bought it the day the T. A. T. plane City of San Francisco crashed."

Suddenly Enveloped by Storm.

"We left Holbrook, flying east," Doles said, "and were about one hour out when we had to dodge a storm. I nosed her down towards St. John's. Suddenly the storm seemed to break over us all at once, and a landing became a necessity. I found a small spot, and it

Continued on Page Three.

Navy Paymaster Leads Way to $47,000 Loot, Dug Up by Night in Washington Chicken Yard

Special to The New York Times.

WASHINGTON, Oct. 29.—Led by Lieutenant Charles Musil, a navy paymaster accused of embezzling $54,600, naval authorities, in a search late at night, recently uncovered $47,000 of the loot buried in a chicken yard in Southeast Washington on the grounds of the Home of the Aged and Infirm.

When Lieutenant Musil voluntarily surrendered himself, on Oct. 14, to the naval authorities at New York, after having disappeared on Sept. 28 from his post as paymaster for Destroyer Division 40 at Charleston, S. C., he is said to have turned over $1,500 to Captain C. T. Owens, commanding the receiving ship Seattle.

This leaves $6,100 unaccounted for and navy officers, in announcing today the discovery in the chicken yard, said they were trying to locate

the rest of the money, although they had scant hope of success.

According to the story told to the officers by Lieutenant Musil, he came here directly from Charleston and buried the money in the yard of his former home. He then left for Chicago, where he bought some stock, and went to Detroit and into Canada. From there he proceeded to New York, where he became conscience-stricken and gave himself up.

He was held at the Brooklyn Navy Yard, but when he told his story of the buried money he was brought here to direct the search for it. He now awaiting general court-martial on specifications involving embezzlement.

Lieutenant Musil was born in Illinois in 1892, entered the navy twenty years ago and was commissioned in 1921. He has a wife and 9-year-old son in New York City.

VOTE FOR PETER J. McCOY, Supreme Court, Republican-Fusion.—Advt.

STOCKS COLLAPSE IN 16,410,030-SHARE DAY, BUT RALLY AT CLOSE CHEERS BROKERS; BANKERS OPTIMISTIC, TO CONTINUE AID

LEADERS SEE FEAR WANING

Point to 'Lifting Spells' in Trading as Sign of Buying Activity.

GROUP MEETS TWICE IN DAY

But Resources Are Unable to Stem Selling Tide—Lamont Reassures Investors.

HOPE SEEN IN MARGIN CUTS

Banks Reduce Requirements to 25 Per Cent—Sentiment in Wall St. More Cheerful.

Resources of the banking group which was organized last Thursday to stabilize conditions in the stock market were utilized yesterday to break the force of the terrific flood of selling which accompanied the biggest day, from the point of view of volume, ever experienced on the New York Stock Exchange.

Despite the drastic decline, sentiment in Wall Street last night was more cheerful than it has been on any day since the torrent of selling got under way. Periodic "lifting spells" which developed between intervals of extreme weakness were cited by bankers at the close of the market, as testifying to the presence of investment buying. The public is in some measure regaining its senses and the unreasoning fear which has prompted the sacrifice of securities for any price they would bring is at length subsiding.

While even the tremendous buying power of the banking group was unable to turn the tide of selling in yesterday's market, the group did not relax its concern over the situation on the Exchange. Two meetings were held during the day, one at noon and one at 4:30 P. M., the latter lasting until 6:30 P. M.

Will Continue Support.

After the evening meeting Thomas W. Lamont of J. P. Morgan & Co. spoke to reporters.

"I want to take occasion," Mr. Lamont said, "to explain again, as heretofore, that the banking group was organized to offer certain support in the market and to act as far as possible as somewhat of a stabilizing factor.

"It was not the intention of the group to attempt to maintain prices, but to maintain a free market; in other words, to correct the condition that prevailed last Thursday.

"The group has continued and will continue in a cooperative way to support the market and has not been a seller of stocks."

The statement was issued at the request of reporters to quiet rumors which had been abroad that the banking group had been selling stocks instead of supporting them.

These rumors were, of course, without foundation, for the group is known to have purchased heavily in directions where the force of its buying power would be most effective in stemming demoralization. It was really reported that in many instances when no bids could be obtained on the floor for large blocks of stock forced on the market the group had supplied the necessary bids and in other instances had acted as a stabilizing influence upon the list as a whole.

At the noon meeting of the group Owen D. Young, chairman of the General Electric Company, director of the Federal Reserve Bank of New York and head of the Young committee on reparations which recently developed the Young plan, joined the

Continued on Page Three.

---

240 Issues Lose $15,894,818,894 in Month; Slump in Full Exchange List Vastly Larger

The drastic effects of Wall Street's October bear market is shown by valuation tables prepared last night by THE NEW YORK TIMES, which place the decline in the market value of 240 representative issues on the New York Stock Exchange at $15,894,818,894 during the period from Oct. 1 to yesterday's closing. Since there are 1,279 issues listed on the New York Stock Exchange, the total depreciation for the month is estimated at between two and three times the loss for the 240 issues covered by THE TIMES table.

Among the losses of the various groups comprising the 240 stocks in THE TIMES valuation table were the following:

Group.	Number of Stocks.	Decline in Value.
Railroads	25	$1,128,686,488
Public utilities	29	5,135,734,327
Motors	25	1,689,840,902
Oils	22	1,332,617,778
Coppers	13	824,403,820
Chemicals	9	1,621,697,897

The official figures of the New York Stock Exchange showed that the total market value of its listed securities on Oct. 1 was $87,073,630,423. The decline in the 240 representative issues therefore cut more than one-sixth from the total value of the listed securities. Most of this loss was inflicted by the wholesale liquidation of the last week.

U. S. STEEL TO PAY $1 EXTRA DIVIDEND

American Can Votes the Same and Raises Annual Rate From $3 to $4.

BIG GAIN IN STEEL INCOME

Earnings for Nine Months Are $15.82 a Share, Against $8.17 a Year Ago.

Two leading industrial companies yesterday declared extra dividends of $1 a share on the common stock, as a result of their earnings through the Summer months. The companies were the United States Steel Corporation and the American Can Company, whose interests touch every section of the country. This action caused the Wall Street district to accept the extra dividends as final proof of the prosperity of the country, despite the breaks which have occurred in the stock market.

While the directors of neither of the companies referred to present conditions in the stock market as a reason for taking the extra dividend action at this time, the opinion was expressed that the directors chose this time to declare the extras as reflecting their belief in the fundamental soundness of industry.

Directors of the American Can Company, in addition to declaring the $1 extra disbursement, also increased the regular dividend rate on the common stock from $3 a year to $4 a year, committing themselves to this payment for the future.

The United States Steel directors contented themselves with announcing that earnings for the first nine months of this year were nearly double those of the same period for 1928, namely, $15.82 a share on the common stock outstanding, compared with $8.17 for the nine months of 1928.

Steel Surplus Up $22,909,447.

Earnings of the United States Steel Corporation for the three months ended on Sept. 30 were reported as $72,000,666, equivalent to $5.57 a share on the common stock outstanding, and the extra dividend makes the disbursements for the quarter less than half of the actual earnings. The operation for the three months, after the preferred and common stock dividends, including the extra dividend, increased the surplus of the company by $22,909,447.

September was the lowest for the three months which enter into the quarterly earnings. The amount reported for this month was $21,794,450, which compares with $25,298,085 in August and $24,917,157 for July. The total earnings for the quarter after deducting all expenses incident to operations, including those for ordinary repairs and maintenance of plants, taxes, including the reserve for Federal income taxes, and the interest on bonds of subsidiary companies, amounted to $70,173,713. Allowances for depreciation, depletion and obsolescence took away another $16,819,998, leaving the net income for the three months at $53,364,320. The interest for the quarter on the bonds of the company outstanding amounted to $1,778,970, and the payment of the 1¾ per cent dividends on the preferred stock amounted to $6,304,919.

Extra Due to Rise in Earnings.

The official statement issued by the company after the meeting of the directors read as follows:

"The United States Steel Corporation's earnings for the first nine

Continued on Page Six.

RESERVE BOARD FINDS ACTION UNNECESSARY

Six-Hour Session Brings No Change in the New York Rediscount Rate.

OFFICIALS ARE OPTIMISTIC

Mellon Also Attends Cabinet Meeting, but Declines to Discuss Developments.

Special to The New York Times.

WASHINGTON, Oct. 29.—The further decline in stock market prices today passed without expressed apprehension on the part of Federal officials. The situation was watched intently by the Federal Reserve Board, which held a continuous session from 10 A. M. until 4 P. M., with Secretary Mellon in attendance. Secretary Mellon, as ex-officio chairman of the board, attended the early part of the meeting before going to the White House for the Cabinet meeting. It could not be learned whether the market situation was discussed by the President and the Cabinet.

At 2:30 P. M. Mr. Mellon returned to the Reserve Board meeting, and remained until near its close. During the day he had conferred with Under-Secretary Ogden L. Mills and Roy A. Young, Governor of the Reserve Board. After the board adjourned, neither Secretary Mellon nor Mr. Young would even intimate the nature or scope of the discussions.

The Federal Reserve Board was studying the financial problems facing the country as the result of another violent stock fluctuation that most of its members did not leave the board room for luncheon.

Board Reviews Credit Situation.

Members of the board, while admitting that the market situation was interesting and of serious character, declared at the end of the day that there was no change which called upon the board for action relative to credits.

There was a report that the board reviewed the credit situation to determine whether the time had come to lower the rediscount rate to ease credit for business ventures. The board has hesitated to act on the rediscount rate during the stock market decline, fearing that lowered rates might be employed to bolster up the market. The board's policy is not to aid in speculation, but it feels that the rediscount rate should be lowered to stimulate business when it is apparent that such action would not be considered as assistance to speculative loans.

Mr. Young said there was no change in financial conditions which the board thought called for the taking of action.

Cut in Discount Rate Expected.

It is thought the question of lowering rediscount rates may come before the Federal Reserve Board shortly. The Boston Federal Reserve Bank directors will meet tomorrow and the New York directors on Thursday. It is possible that one of these banks may suggest a lowering of the rates.

Some observers believe that a reduction in rediscount rates might have a strong psychological effect not only upon business but the market as well. There was no official indication that such a move was imminent, although some observers thought such action might come if suggested by the New York bank directors, since the rate there is 6 per cent as against 5 per cent in other regions. Some thought the New York rediscount rate might be reduced to 5 per cent soon.

Today's session of the board was the longest since the financial flurry

Continued on Page Six.

CLOSING RALLY VIGOROUS

Leading Issues Regain From 4 to 14 Points in 15 Minutes.

INVESTMENT TRUSTS BUY

Large Blocks Thrown on Market at Opening Start Third Break of Week.

BIG TRADERS HARDEST HIT

Bankers Believe Liquidation Now Has Run Its Course and Advise Purchases.

Stock prices virtually collapsed yesterday, swept downward with gigantic losses in the most disastrous trading day in the stock market's history. Billions of dollars in open market values were wiped out as prices crumbled under the pressure of liquidation of securities which had to be sold at any price.

There was an impressive rally just at the close, which brought many leading stocks back from 4 to 14 points from their lowest points of the day.

Trading on the New York Stock Exchange aggregated 16,410,030 shares; on the Curb, 7,096,300 shares were dealt in. Both totals far exceeded any previous day's dealings. From every point of view, in the extent of losses sustained, in total turnover, in the number of speculators wiped out, the day was the most disastrous in Wall Street's history. Hysteria swept the country and stocks went overboard for just what they would bring at forced sales.

Efforts to estimate yesterday's market losses in dollars are futile because of the vast number of securities quoted over the counter and on out-of-town exchanges on which no calculations are possible. However, it was estimated that 880 issues on the New York Stock Exchange, last between $8,000,000,000 and $9,000,000,000 yesterday. Added to that loss is to be reckoned the depreciation on issues on the Curb Market, in the over the counter market and on other exchanges.

Two Extra Dividends Declared.

There were two cheerful notes, however, which sounded through the pall of gloom which overhung the financial centres of the country. One was the brisk rally of stocks at the close, on tremendous buying by those who believe that prices have sunk too low. The other was that the liquidation has been so violent, as well as widespread, that many bankers, brokers and industrial leaders expressed the belief last night that it now has run its course.

A further note of optimism in the soundness of fundamental conditions was sounded by the directors of the United States Steel Corporation and the American Can Company, each of which declared an extra dividend of $1 a share at their late afternoon meetings.

Banking support, which would have been impressive and successful under ordinary circumstances, was swept violently aside, as block after block of stock, tremendous in proportions, deluged the market. Bid prices placed by bankers, industrial leaders and brokers trying to halt the decline were crashed through violently, their orders were filled, and quotations plunged downward in a day of disorganization, confusion and financial impotence.

Change Is Expected Today.

That there will be a change today seemed likely from statements made last night by financial and business leaders. Organized support will be accorded to the market from the start, it is believed, but there are striking their all on the country's leading securities are placing a great deal of confidence, too, in the expectation that there will be an overnight change in sentiment; that the counsel of cool heads will prevail and that the mob psychology which has been so largely responsible for the market's debacle will be broken.

The fact that the leading stocks were able to rally in the last fifteen minutes of trading yesterday was considered a good omen, especially as the weakest period of the day had developed just prior to that time and the minimum prices for the day had then been established. It was a quick run-up which followed the announcement that the American Can directors had declared an extra dividend of $1. The advances in leading stocks in this last fifteen minute period represented a measurable staggering back from the lows. American Can gained 10; United States Steel common, 7; General Electric, 12; New York Central, 8; American Telephone, 9½; Chrysler Motors, 5½; Montgomery Ward, 6½, and Johns Man-

---

808 TONS OF MARBLE ADORN PALAIS de la Mediterranee (Casino), Nice.—Advt.

Mixer of misera! Club Style. Always demand Abbott's Bitters.—Advt.

POPULARITY OF BRILLO CLEANSER. Over 200,000,000 packages sold.—Advt.

Popular Price Mat. today, Eddie Cantor in Whoopee." New Amsterdam Theatre.—Advt.

Section 1

"All the News That's Fit to Print."

The New York Times.

Copyright. 1929, by The New York Times Company.

THE WEATHER
Mostly cloudy today and tomorrow; warmer tomorrow.
Temperatures yesterday—Max. 39, min. 29.
☞U. S. Weather Forecast—Page 11, Section 12.

Section 1

VOL. LXXIX....No. 26,237.   ★ ★ ★   NEW YORK, SUNDAY, NOVEMBER 24, 1929.

including Rotogravure Picture Section in four parts, Magazine and Book Sections in Rotogravure   FIVE CENTS In Manhattan | Elsewhere TEN CENTS Bronx and Brooklyn | Except in 7th and 8th Postal Zones

HOOVER ASKS THE 48 GOVERNORS TO HELP HIS PROGRAM BY SPEEDING PUBLIC WORKS, KEEPING EMPLOYMENT AT A HIGH LEVEL

WANTS STATES CANVASSED

The President Requests a Report on the Outlays Possible for Year.

LAMONT WILL COOPERATE

Commerce Secretary to Work With State, County and Municipal Officials.

5,000 MESSAGES BACK PLANS

Arizona Governor Pledges Aid—Philadelphia and St. Paul Will Expend $100,000,000.

By RICHARD V. OULAHAN
Special to The New York Times.

WASHINGTON, Nov. 23.—The outstanding development today in President Hoover's endeavors to bring about the cooperation of all interests, governmental and private, in forestalling a recession in business because of the recent stock market decline was an appeal sent to the Governors of the forty-eight States by the President, asking them to follow the example of the Federal Government in preparing to speed up necessary construction work, thus absorbing any unemployment and contributing to the maintenance of the nation's consuming power.

Mr. Hoover said in his message that he had asked for the collective action of industry in the expansion of construction activities and stabilization of wages, adding that he felt one of the largest factors that could be brought to bear to supplement the efforts of private interests was the "energetic yet prudent pursuit of public works by the Federal Government and State, municipal and county authorities."

Requests Official Canvass.

The Federal Government, the President said, was prepared to exert itself to the utmost "within its own province," and he desired the cooperation of the State, municipal and county authorities in a like endeavor. He suggested that it would be helpful if road, street, public building and other work could be speeded up to aid in giving additional employment.

The President asked the Governors to have an official canvass made and to send to him a report as to the volume of expenditure that could prudently be arranged in their States in the next twelve months. He informed them that he had asked Secretary of Commerce Lamont to cooperate with the Governors.

The Federal Government's contribution to the program of expanding construction work, will ask Congress to grant an additional $175,000,000 for public buildings, of which $500,000,000 is to be spent outside the District of Columbia and $75,000,000 in the District. It will also seek, if that prove practical, to extend road construction work to which the government contributes, that phase of the effort coming under the Department of Agriculture.

It is the hope of the administration that cooperation of the Federal Government and the States in large building programs and the efforts to be put forth by private industries toward business expansion will aid unjustified fears of a trade depression.

The Proposed Council.

The most definite constructive step expected from the series of conferences held by President Hoover this week with men foremost in trade, finance, industry and labor, is the formation of a council of representative business leaders which "should assume the responsibility for the mobilization of the industrial and commercial agencies," to quote the President, to bring about cooperation in keeping the country's production, trade and commerce on an even keel and prevent a loss of business confidence such as was threatened when Mr. Hoover took his initial steps to stem the tide.

The creation of such a council has been a dream of forward-looking industrialists and others who, like the President, have made a close study of the tremendous advances made by the United States in an economic way. Such a body flows naturally from the study made by the Committee on Recent Economic Changes whose formation was the outgrowth of the President's conferences on unemployment held in Washington in the Harding Administration under the chairmanship of Mr. Hoover, who was then Secretary of Commerce.

Just what will be the scope, character and particular functions of the proposed council will probably be at least partly determined at the meet-

Continued on Page Two.

DEPARTMENT STORES FORCED TO ADD HELP

Increases in Payrolls Made to Meet Huge Holiday Trade in Spite of Stock Slump.

MACY'S SEES NEW RECORD

Altman, Arnold Constable, Wanamaker, Lord & Taylor, Bloomingdale's, Gimbels Gain.

New York City department store owners were virtually unanimous in reporting yesterday that despite the stock market crash they were enjoying a large volume of business and that they were swelling payrolls in anticipation of an increase in holiday trade compared with that of last year. Their statements concerning conditions of employment and sales were in answer to reports, emanating presumably from Wall Street, that the department stores have been laying off employes by the hundreds because of a slump in business.

Percy S. Straus, vice president of R. H. Macy & Co., Inc., said:

"The best judgment that I can bring to bear leads me to the conclusion that as the stock market panic has set thus far seriously interfered with business there is no prospect that it will. I am basing the opinion on my knowledge of conditions at Macy's, and Macy's, catering as it does to a fair cross-section of the city's population, should, I think, be an adequate basis for judgment. I therefore give you the following facts:

"Each month this year sales have been better than those of the corresponding month last year, and November is also showing good increases. As a matter of fact, at the present moment—late Saturday afternoon—indications are that this very day will prove to be a record one.

"As is our custom, we budget our entire business by departments at the beginning of each season. The budget set for this Fall as to numbers of employes has been maintained without interruption, and we thus maintained. At present we have 12,022 employes, representing an increase of 2,041 over the corresponding day last year. The only discharges made were for reasons other than for business conditions. Furthermore, during the current week we employed 650 additional persons. Of course, it has been necessary to augment other facilities to meet conditions requiring the increased number of employes, such as additional motors for delivery, added selling space, improved methods of change-making, elevator replacements, and rearrangements resulting in greater ease of circulation in the building.

"Although conditions are not identical in our three affiliated stores—L. Bamberger & Co. of Newark, N. J., the Lasalle & Koch Company of Toledo, Ohio, and the Davison-Paxon Company of Atlanta, Ga.—none of them has found it necessary to de-

Continued on Page Three.

BARNES ASSURES BUSINESS ADVANCE

Chamber Head, Disclosing Magnitude of Projects Told to Hoover, Hails Cooperation.

STRESSES 'LOGIC OF FACTS'

He Relies on 'Collective Common Sense' to Sustain Industrial Activity, Now Forging Ahead.

Special to The New York Times.

WASHINGTON, Nov. 23.—Julius H. Barnes, chairman of the board of the Chamber of Commerce of the United States, declared tonight that President Hoover had decided to create an executive committee from the Industrial and trade association groups to cooperate with government agencies in the "expansion of construction and maintenance of employment," in a radio speech tonight revealed for the first time the actual reports on present business conditions and the outlook which were made to the President by the industrial chiefs who met at the White House on Thursday.

The speech was made over a twenty-three station network of the National Broadcasting Company's system. Mr. Barnes was introduced by Merle Thorpe, editor of The Nation's Business, a publication of the Chamber.

After reviewing the reports to the President, Mr. Barnes said:

"I again repeat that the basic element needed to maintain our high level of business activity, to preserve employment, to continue wages and earnings, is the element of collective common sense, orderly conduct of every day living, guided by both prudence and courage."

Reassuring Factors Cited.

Reports of business heads to the President's conference, Mr. Barnes said, should dispel the fears that existed that the country was running into a period of great depression. Retail stores reported, he said, the usual employment for the period of the year, mail-order houses were going along in a normal way and the "distribution of automobiles is normal for this period of the year."

The telephone industry will expend over $700,000,000 next year, Walter Gifford, president of the American Telephone and Telegraph Company, told the conference, Mr. Barnes declared.

He quoted Walter Teagle, president of the Standard Oil Company of New Jersey, as stating that the oil industry was becoming stabilized. The steel industry, he said, announced that it expected to supply 300,000,000 tons of steel in new construction and industrial improvements, Matthew Sloan, president of the New York Edison Company, promised expansion in public utility improvements.

These reports, among others, were cited by Mr. Barnes as evidences of confidence in business progress and

Continued on Page Two.

City Gets Snow Flurry and Freezing Weather; Eight Die in South in Widespread Cold Wave

New York was visited yesterday with the coldest temperature of the season thus far, and with its second snowfall. The snow came in brief flurries during the day, too slight to register on the Weather Bureau's instruments. It was more noticeable, however, than the first snow of the season, which consisted of a few random flakes on Oct. 17.

The mercury, starting from its lowest point of 29 above zero at 5:29 A. M., hovered around the freezing point all day, rising to 39 at 6 P. M., the highest point of the day. It was a cheerless day under a dead gray sky.

The prospects for today, however, are for slightly warmer weather. New York enjoyed a mild day in comparison with most of the rest of the country, for the northwest which bore the cold snap veered around the city.

New England and the Southern States, together with much of up-State New York, suffered the most. Many States in the South are blanketed with snow, ice and sleet. Dispatches to The Associated Press

gave a death list of eight persons in the South as a result of the unseasonable cold wave. Six of the deaths were in Arkansas. Three men in that State were killed in automobile accidents resulting from the storm, one child died of exposure, a trolley car operator was killed slipping from the sleet-encrusted roof of his car, and an aged woman died from burns in a overheated stove. Two men were killed on the slippery streets of Richmond, Va. Four passengers were injured in the overturning of a bus near Greensboro, N. C.

Temperatures below zero were recorded in Western Massachusetts, New Hampshire, Vermont and Maine, dropping at some of the points to five below.

In Northern New York, under a bright sun, also had zero and subzero temperatures, with light snow and frost whitening the Adirondacks.

Storm warnings against a northeast gale were set yesterday from the Virginia Capes to the tip of Cape Cod.

M'MANUS TO OFFER ALIBI AS DEFENSE; TO PICK NEW JUROR

Several Witnesses to Testify He Was Not in Room When Rothstein Was Shot.

JUROR, ILL, TO BE EXCUSED

Both Sides Agree to Release Riker and to Replace Him From Special Panel of 50.

George A. McManus will set up an alibi as part of his rebuttal of the charge that he murdered Arnold Rothstein, it was learned yesterday, as a decision was reached to excuse the juror who reported illness, choose another and proceed with the trial in the Criminal Courts Building tomorrow morning.

The defendant expects to be able to account for his whereabouts during the two hours preceding midnight of Nov. 4, 1928, it was said, and will call several witnesses to support his contention. They will testify that McManus was not in Room 349 of the Park Central Hotel at the time that Rothstein was wounded. The defendant will concede, it was reported, that he had hired the room under an assumed name to shield his bookmaking activities.

A vigorous fight by the defense against the State's contention that it has the murder weapon was indicated. Albert M. Hamilton, a small arms expert, began yesterday his tests of the pistol. He found that the barrel of the Colt .38 calibre revolver was not the one in the weapon when it left the Colt plant. The external finish differed from the usual nickeling, and the inside of the barrel had been crudely made. Mr. Hamilton, however, admitted that his tests had not gone far enough as yet to hazard an opinion as to how long the substitute barrel had been in place.

Agree to Excuse Ailing Juror.

The decision to excuse Eugene A. Riker of 211 West Twenty-first Street, the juror who reported illness after adjournment of the trial on Friday, was made after the prosecution, represented by Assistant District Attorney George N. Brothers and the defense attorney, James D. C. Murray, had agreed. Riker, it was reported, is on the verge of a nervous breakdown.

Mr. Murray, the Assistant District Attorney and the presiding judge,

Continued on Page Sixteen.

ROOSEVELT PLEADS FOR REAWAKENING OF CIVIC CONSCIENCE

Points to Irondequoit Inquiry Failure in Asking "What Has Become of Public Morals?"

ALSO CITES WESTCHESTER

Lauds Budget Decision in City Club Address—Sees Power Company Leaders.

Governor Roosevelt told members of the City Club and their guests yesterday at a luncheon given in his honor that he had been "becoming identified with power activities." He did not disclose the identity of the conferees, nor would he say what had occurred at the conference.

As a preface to this plea, Governor Roosevelt recited the experiences of Supreme Court Justice Stephen Callaghan, whom he had sent to Rochester earlier in the year to preside at the Supreme Court's investigation of charges against public officials in the town of Irondequoit. The Governor declared that he had Justice Callaghan's word and the word of District Attorney Guy B. Moore of Erie County that the ends of justice had been defeated by the "fixing" of three successive juries.

Delayed by Power Conference.

The Governor was an hour late in arriving at the luncheon. He explained that he had been detained by an important conference on water power development with "some gentlemen identified with power activities." He did not disclose the identity of the conferees, nor would he say what had occurred at the conference.

It is understood, however, that those with whom the Governor conferred had represented the United Corporation, a Morgan holding concern.

The conference was only one of several the Governor has held recently with spokesmen for various groups interested in water power development, purely preliminary in character. He indicated that other conferences would follow after his return from Warm Springs, Ga., where he went yesterday for a ten days' stay.

Since statements emanating from members of the Morgan firm have indicated that the door is not closed, in so far as they are concerned, to cooperation with the State in power development projects, the Governor is anxious to make the most of his opportunity, especially as he is eager to present to next year's law making body some plan for development under State auspices but what point a way in his message for making against their properties for the improvements. However, the cost was later assessed against the property owners, he said. There was every appearance of connivance between the promoters and public officials.

"I sent Justice Callaghan up there to see if anybody ought to go to jail," the Governor said. "There were three trials. On the first the jury acted ten to two for conviction. At each of the other two the jury

Continued on Page Twenty-four.

Harvard Defeats Yale, 10-6 Notre Dame and Fordham Win

Harvard triumphed over Yale at Cambridge yesterday, 10 to 6, in their forty-eighth annual football encounter before a crowd of 59,000. Albie Booth's kicks were blocked by the Crimson time and again, but his pass to Ellis brought the lone Yale touchdown.

At New York, Fordham blanked Bucknell, 14 to 0, closing its season undefeated. New York University disposed of Rutgers, 20 to 7.

In the Middle West, Notre Dame maintained its unbeaten standing by defeating Northwestern, 26 to 6, and Chicago won from University of Washington, 26 to 6. Nebraska won the Big Six title for the second consecutive year by beating the Kansas Aggies, 16 to 6.

It defeated Ohio Wesleyan, 29 to 6, Navy halted West Virginia Wesleyan, 30 to 6, and Lehigh was victor over Lafayette, 13 to 12.

In the Far West, Stanford defeated the California Bears, 21 to 6.

The complete details of these and other games will be found in the sports section.

CLEMENCEAU, 'FATHER OF VICTORY,' DIES; PASSES AWAY AT 88 AFTER HOURS IN COMA; WORLD JOINS FRANCE IN MOURNING LOSS

Associated Press Photo.
GEORGES CLEMENCEAU.

VITALITY AMAZED DOCTORS

Valiant Fight Had Stirred Friends and Old Foes to Sympathy.

MET DEATH WITHOUT PAIN

Bishop, Old Literary Friend, Visited Unconscious Man After Pleading for Admission.

STATE FUNERAL OPPOSED

'Tiger's' Testament Said to Ask Simple Burial Near His Father in Vendée Plot.

By P. J. PHILIP.
Special Cable to The New York Times.

PARIS, Sunday, Nov. 24.—Georges Clemenceau is dead.

The veteran statesman passed away at 1:55 this morning [8:55 P. M. Saturday, New York Time] after lingering for hours in a comatose state, with intervals of seeming consciousness.

The valiant fight of the "Father of Victory" had stirred both friends and old foes to sympathy. Earlier in the night reports had spread in Paris that the veteran statesman had died, and these were flashed by news bureaus to all sections of the world, only to be contradicted a moment later.

Died Early in Morning.

At midnight the great heart of the fighting statesman, which alone kept him alive all day while his body lay inert, gave signs of collapse. Two hours later it had ceased to beat. Tired in body, but with mind and spirit breaking the spells of unconsciousness at times, he went to his rest.

He did not suffer on the last day of his long life. He had no more pain. Sometimes his eyes opened, and one of the doctors was convinced that he remained fully conscious until this afternoon. Most of the day he spent in sleep. It was almost the first day of his life that he had not been fully awake and active from before dawn until evening.

For those who watched it was as though they awaited something inevitable, yet feared. Ever since Friday, when uraemia had spread through his system, only death could be expected. It was by a miracle of strength that life clung to the body. The heart alone refused to yield until it had no more functions to perform.

Oxygen Administered.

In the last few hours oxygen was administered, but it was with no hope or desire to prolong life. It was only to relieve any final pain and prevent choking.

It was at 1:55, according to official announcement, that death came in the depth of the night. As the heart grew more feeble the doctors were summoned back, and they scarcely expected to find him still alive. There was majestic deliberateness in his going.

In the last chapter of his book, "Demosthenes," which is in the nature of an autobiography, he wrote: "Call that man happy—for it is the lot of all to suffer—who has suffered for a noble cause, and grieve for him who, having sought nothing outside himself, has known nothing but the cinders of life, of egoism vainly consumed."

The words might serve for his own epitaph.

Only three persons were in the sickroom when M. Clemenceau died, his friend and executor, François Pietri; the nun, Sister Theoneste, and his grandson, Dr. René Jacquemaire.

To M. Pietri yesterday he spoke for the last time, asking in some bewilderment, "What has happened, Pietri?" as though he had just wakened out of sleep.

"You have had an attack," his friend replied.

"This time it will be a long one," the old Tiger murmured, and he never spoke again.

Wanted Quick Burial.

M. Clemenceau's wishes were that his chauffeur, François Drabant, should drive immediately on his death down to the Vendée, to prepare his grave, and that he should be buried as quickly as possible. He had hoped that death would come to him when no one would know about it until it was over.

It was more than sentiment which caused the wish that his body should rest in his native province of Vendée. His former lieutenant, now Premier

STRIKERS CUT OFF AIR, IMPERIL 3 IN CAISSON

As Water Rushes In on Bridge-Workers, Engineer Fights His Way to Their Rescue.

LADDER DROPPED TO THEM

Two Beaten by Strikers After Climbing 65 Feet to Safety—24 Arrested at Kearny, N. J.

Thirty compressed-air workers, members of Local 67 of New Jersey, who were discharged last Thursday when a strike was started on the State highway bridge over the Hackensack River at Kearny, attacked the new gang of workers, members of Local 2, New York City, yesterday and were subdued only after police reserves arrived.

The attackers, swarming onto a caisson where three men were working 65 feet below the river level, broke the compressed air pipe, causing water and river mud to rush in. The trapped workmen shouted for help, and John Moyer, the engineer, after having temporarily stopped the break in the pipe, fought off the invaders and managed to drop a ladder down the caisson hold.

The three chambered up, not much faster than the water was rushing upward, and fell exhausted, only to be attacked by the strikers, who beat them with 18-inch steel bolts. The engineer and his friends had been routed, but Moyer, rushing to the engine room, drew his pistol and threatened to shoot if any of the strikers advanced.

Two Rushed to Hospital.

One of the three men who climbed up from the caisson—James Withers—had "escaped in the general mêlée, but the two others were so badly injured that they were rushed to the City Hospital in Jersey City in an ambulance.

The injured are:
LOUIS MAYS, 120 West 130th Street, Manhattan.
ROBERT HAMILTON, 25 DeBevoise Place, Brooklyn.

In the meantime the police had been informed of the fight and reserves, under Captain Cornelius Barrett, arrived in time to stop further trouble.

Twenty-four men, including five alleged ringleaders, were arrested and later arraigned before Police Judge Anthony Casale. The five alleged ringleaders were held in bail of $5,000 each for action by the Hudson County grand jury on charges of atrocious assault and battery. The nineteen others were convicted of malicious mischief and fined $25 each by the judge, who had got up from a sick-bed to hold court.

Engineer Fights Way to Rescue.

Moyer, the engineer, who lives at 29 Mertz Avenue, Belleville, N. J.,

Continued on Page Twenty-two.

ALL CHINA ALARMED AS RUSSIANS INVADE

Manchurian Troops Fall Back Demoralized While Red Army Steadily Moves on Hailar.

NANKING POWERLESS TO AID

With Chiang Involved in Civil War and Treasury Bankrupt Mukden Must' Fight Alone.

By HALLETT ABEND.
Special Cable to The New York Times.

SHANGHAI, Nov. 23.—With a temporary lull on the Honan-Hupeh and Canton area fronts, or a censorship so rigid that information is not obtainable, the flood of disastrous news from Manchuria, where Russians with the aid of Mongols have overrun all of Northwestern Heilungkiang well eastward toward Hailar, has shocked many Chinese circles from complacency to the realization that while the government totters on the verge of bankruptcy China's soil is actually being won by hated foreign invaders.

It has been officially announced that President Chiang Kai-shek and his staff left Honan for Nanking and from thence are likely to proceed to Canton, where the Fiftieth Division has been ordered to join the Third and Eighth, already sent South.

Government spokesmen declare that this means complete victory for Nanking in Honan and Hupeh, the government leaving the remnants of the rebels to be eliminated by General Yen Hsi-shan, who, it is asserted, has promised to dispatch troops to aid Nanking. But this claim is viewed askance here because it was often heard before last month and always proved to be groundless propaganda.

Rebel spokesmen declare that the departure of General Chiang for Nanking and thence south means the abandonment of the campaign north of the Yangtze and an attempt to hold the country solid south of the river.

Desperate efforts are made to raise money in Hankow. Warehouses, docks and foreign firms have been repeatedly visited by illegal tax-gatherers and several Chinese employes spirited away. The foreign firms have thus far refused payment of any new levies. Meanwhile serious situation in the hands of the various Consuls.

Official Manchurian statements charge that Russians have massacred hundreds of civilians, at the instance of the Chinese by discouraging and breakdown in the morale of the Chinese defensive forces with the "disappearance" of whole brigades.

Prepare for Retreat.

TOKIO, Nov. 23 (P).—A Harbin dispatch to the Asahi Shimbun today quoted a Tsitsihar dispatch from Chinese military headquarters on the Western Manchurian frontier were

Continued on Page Nine.

The New York Times.

Copyright, 1929, by The New York Times Company.

VOL. LXXIX....No. 26,243.   ★★★★   NEW YORK, SATURDAY, NOVEMBER 30, 1929.   TWO CENTS in Greater | THREE CENTS | FOUR CENTS Elsewhere New York | Within 100 Miles | Except 7th and 8th Postal Zone

THE WEATHER

Fair and continued cold today; tomorrow cloudy and warmer. Temperatures yesterday—Max. 30, min. 20.

☛ U. S. Weather Bureau—For details See Page 29.

BYRD SAFELY FLIES TO SOUTH POLE AND BACK, LOOKING OVER 'ALMOST LIMITLESS PLATEAU'; DROPS FOOD, LIGHTENS SHIP ON PERILOUS TRIP

WOMAN HEARD CRASH IN HOTEL AT THE TIME ROTHSTEIN WAS SHOT

Says She Saw Man With Angry or Agonized Look Near McManus's Room.

UNCERTAIN ON HIS IDENTITY

Mrs. M. A. Putnam, "Surprise" Witness for State, Attacked by the Defense.

RAYMOND TELLS OF BIG BET

Testifies He Won $40,000 From Rothstein on One Card—Admits That They Had a Quarrel.

A fragile woman with gray hair, but a schoolgirl complexion, took the stand yesterday in the Criminal Courts Building to aid the State in its effort to convict George A. McManus of the murder of Arnold Rothstein. In clear tones she identified herself as Mrs. Marian A. Putnam of Asheville, N. C., chief of the surprise witnesses for the prosecution.

Loosening the gray squirrel collar of a broadtail fur coat, she said that she had been a guest at the Park Central Hotel on the night of Nov. 4, 1928, when Rothstein received a bullet wound which caused his death two days later. She added that she had registered at the hotel on Oct. 30.

Assistant District Attorney George N. Brothers, urbane in manner and soothing of voice, asked her to tell what she had heard and seen that night. Mrs. Putnam turned her thin face toward the jurymen and folded her hands, asparkle with four diamond rings. Quietly she told how she had heard a "crash" and had seen a man walking down a corridor on the third floor, leading from Room 349, part of a suite hired by McManus.

Saw Agony or Anger in Face.

She had looked at the man's face. "It bore the imprint of agony or anger. He had his hands clasped over his abdomen as he followed her down the carpeted passageway. Mrs. Putnam said she locked the door of her room and said nothing about the episode even the following morning, when she learned of the shooting.

On through the events of the evening Mr. Brothers led the witness. She told a straightforward story under the prosecutor's questioning and now and then a faint smile curved her tight lips. Mrs. Putnam told the court that the prosecution had failed to carry out its promise to show that the game gave McManus the motive for the murder. Judge Nott refused to grant the motion.

Mr. Putnam admitted that she had been registered at the Park

Continued on Page Fourteen.

Byrd Lands Radio Amateurs For Help in Message Relays

LOS ANGELES, Nov. 29 (AP).—A congratulatory message sent by Commander Richard E. Byrd just before the start of his flight over the South Pole, was read today at the convention of the Pacific division of the American Radio Relay League.

The message, received by B. E. Sandham, Los Angeles amateur short wave radio operator, read:

"Greetings from Little America to the radio amateurs of the Pacific division, Am glad for this opportunity to acknowledge the big debt our North and South Pole expeditions owe to the amateur radio operators.

"I wish to thank them for their helpfulness and to express my admiration of the high sense of honor they show in handling messages.

"It is radio that has made this expedition possible.

"Cordial good wishes in which all of Little America join.

"RICHARD BYRD."

WINTER GRIPS NATION; MERCURY AT 20 HERE

Icy Blast Sweeping Out of the Northwest Kills 9, Spreads Damage, Blocks Shipping.

BLIZZARDS RAGE IN WEST

One Frozen to Death in New York and No Let-Up in the Frigid Wave is Seen.

Winter came howling out of the northwest and the Arctic wastes yesterday, bringing blizzards to the Western States and Canada, hampering shipping on the Great Lakes, lashing the West, the Middle West, the East and many Southern States in the grip of sub-freezing temperatures.

It was the frigid season's first general offensive, and it scattered death, suffering and property damage widely. While River, Ontario, which usually claims the distinction of recording low temperatures, shared with Thief River Falls, Minn., first place on the icy list yesterday, both communities recording 26 below zero. At least eight persons died in the North Central States as a result of the sudden zero snap, according to the Associated Press. New York City added one death to the list. ears were felt for driving a blizzard over the Minnesota woods. Near the cradle of Winter, where a 30-mile gale was driving a blizzard over the Saskatchewan Lakes, the fate of fifty fishermen, pushing northward on a 50-mile trip, was in doubt. The fishermen had been gone for three days.

Cold to Continue Here Today.

New York had an uncomfortable sample of Winter, and last night the local Weather Bureau gave practically no hope of a let-up today in the cold temperature.

This city felt its lowest temperature of the season at 10 o'clock last night when the thermometer registered 20 degrees above zero, 12 below freezing. Noon the maximum temperature at 9:30 A. M. was only 30 degrees, or 2 below freezing. The average temperature for the day was 26 degrees, compared with a normal Nov. 29 reading of 39. The coldest Nov. 29 on record occurred in 1872 when the thermometer registered 15 degrees.

The cold here was aggravated by a biting northwest wind, blowing at thirty-eight miles an hour. The city's firemen were put to their first severe test of the season in what was a busy "fire" day. Between the Bronx and Brooklyn. Up to 9 o'clock last night the number of fires for the day totaled thirty in Manhattan, in the Bronx and forty-three in Brooklyn.

Fair Weather Forecast.

Although the barometer in the New York Weather Bureau was rising last night, indicating fair weather for today, the cold snap will continue, according to the official forecaster, and the thousands of football spectators who will swarm into the Yankee Stadium for the Army-Notre Dame game this afternoon will have to wear their warmest clothes and wraps.

"Fresh northeast winds and continued cold" was the prediction for today. At the Weather Bureau it was even considered possible that today might be a little colder than yesterday.

A woman on Staten Island was New York's addition to the list of victims of the cold. She was Mrs. Gladys Todd, 53 years old, who was found dead in the back yard of her home, at 4 Schrenkheisen Place, Mar-

Continued on Page Twelve.

FIRST MESSAGE EVER SENT FROM THE SOUTH POLE

By Commander Richard E. Byrd

Copyright, 1929, by The New York Times Company and The St. Louis Post-Dispatch. All Rights for Publication Reserved Throughout the World.

WIRELESS TO THE NEW YORK TIMES.

ABOARD AIRPLANE FLOYD BENNETT, in flight, 1:55 P. M. Greenwich mean time [8:55 A. M. New York time], Friday, Nov. 29.—My calculations indicate that we have reached the vicinity of the South Pole, flying high for a survey The airplane is in good shape, crew all well. Will soon turn north. We can see an almost limitless polar plateau. Our departure from the Pole was at 1:25 P. M.

BYRD

The difference in the times mentioned in this dispatch, that is between 1:55 P. M. in the date line and 1:25 P. M., given by the Commander as that of his departure from the South Pole, is probably accounted for by the lapse between the writing of the dispatch by the Commander and its coding and sending by the wireless operator, Harold I. June. Greenwich time is five hours ahead of New York time and twelve hours ahead of time at Little America.

The Commander's last sentence was evidently added after he began to fly away from the Pole; the first part written before he left there.

CAPITAL DISPLAYS KEENEST INTEREST

President, Waiting News, Is the First in Washington to Hear of Byrd's Success.

OFFICIALS LAUD FLIGHT

Admiral Hughes Says the Commander is a Worthy Successor to Admiral Wilkes.

Special to The New York Times.

WASHINGTON, Nov. 29.—President Hoover, who had stayed anxiously all day for word of the progress of the daring flight to the South Pole, was the first person of the official family, outside of the staff of THE NEW YORK TIMES bureau, to learn of the successful flight of Commander Byrd to the South Pole and back to Little America.

The word was flashed to the White House tonight from the Washington Bureau of THE NEW YORK TIMES. It was transmitted to the President before dinner by Secretary Walter H. Newton.

All day the President had asked for word of the progress of the flight and late in the afternoon had indicated his deep interest. When the news was taken to him, the President expressed his delight over the successful outcome.

Official Washington expressed the most intense relief and the greatest delight at the successful termination of the flight.

Admiral Charles F. Hughes, Acting Secretary of the Navy, was among the first to be informed.

"We are greatly pleased at the success of Commander Byrd's flight," he said. "He is a worthy successor of Admiral Wilkes, the American naval officer who first discovered the Antarctic Continent."

Earlier in the day Admiral Hughes had said:

"The Navy Department is intensely interested and, knowing Commander Byrd, we are thoroughly confident that he will return successfully."

Davison Congratulates Expedition.

F. Trubee Davison, Assistant Secretary of War for Aeronautics, declared the success of the flight demonstrated again the value of aircraft.

"The flight of Commander Byrd and his brave companions at the South Pole," he said, "is another epic in the annals of the achievements of heavier-than-air craft and prove once again the value of the airplane in exploration of unknown areas where distances can be traveled in hours which under ordinary forms of transportation would require weeks and months. On behalf of the War Department and the Army Air Corps, I wish to congratulate the Byrd Antarctic Expedition. Their achievement will be lauded by Americans the world over."

Mr. C. Clarence M. Young, the Assistant Secretary of Commerce for Aeronautics, declared the Byrd flight was simply another demonstration of the "limitless purposes which aviation can serve."

"The flight to the South Pole and back was surely a major accomplish-

Continued on Page Three.

President Sends His Congratulations to Byrd, Saying Spirit of Great Adventure Still Lives

Special to The New York Times.

WASHINGTON, Nov. 29.—After being informed tonight of Commander Byrd's successful flight to the South Pole and back to the base at Little America, President Hoover gave to THE NEW YORK TIMES the following message of congratulations on behalf of himself and the American people, to be transmitted by radio to Commander Byrd:

Commander Richard E. Byrd, Little America:

I know that I speak for the American people when I express their universal pleasure at your successful flight over the South Pole. We are proud of your courage and your leadership. We are glad of proof that the spirit of great adventure still lives. Our thoughts of appreciation include also your companions in the flight and your colleagues, whose careful and devoted preparation have contributed to your great success.

HERBERT HOOVER.

BYRD'S FEAT STIRS ENTHUSIASM HERE

Victorious Flight Hailed With Tributes to Commander's Daring and Foresight.

With the reception of news from Little America of the return of Commander Byrd and his companions from their flight over the South Pole, explorers, aviators, aeronautical designers and builders whose names are known throughout the world of aviation and scores of others offered their congratulations to the Commander and expressed their enthusiasm over the success of his efforts. Some of these comments follow:

Anthony H. G. Fokker, designer of the plane in which Commander Byrd crossed the Atlantic—I didn't he has made another great contribution to scientific advancement and world knowledge. The American flag will certainly look great down there. I know I speak for the people of this city when I say that we rejoice with him and his intrepid companions in this epoch-making exploit. We will await his return to New York with impatience, so that the city can give him the welcome he so richly deserves. New York City has honored Commander Byrd before. It is glad that in honor him again, for it feels that in a very real sense he has done generally until later.

Mayor Walker—That's marvelous news. I can sum up the way I feel about it in a single sentence. I knew Dick Byrd would do it. He has made another great contribution to scientific advancement and world knowledge.

"I was in Washington when we heard Dick had hopped off," he said. "My son Tom drove up there to get me when I phoned him and we went back to Winchester to wait for it. The NEW YORK TIMES called me about 4 o'clock but said they would not release the news generally until later.

"Dick had sent me a Thanksgiving radio message a few hours before they hopped off. 'We are off.' We were very uneasy, but I was not so happy in my life as when we heard he had landed safely back at Little America. We really were quite uneasy during the flight and felt more hazardous than anything he ever tried. Nobody knew anything much about Antarctica.

"When Tom heard Dick had gone over safely he said he was tremen-

Continued on Page Four.

BYRD'S FAMILY GETS NEWS OF FLIGHT

Virginia Governor at Capitol Gets News and Mother Hears It at Winchester.

Special to The New York Times.

RICHMOND, Va., Nov. 29.—Although he knew that his brother, Commander Richard Evelyn Byrd, intended to hop to the South Pole "about this time of the year," Governor Harry F. Byrd and no one else in the family or any one else had known exactly what day the plane Floyd Bennett would leave the base.

Commander Byrd's mother, Mrs. Richard E. Byrd Sr., and Thomas Byrd, his brother, received news of the successful flight at their home in Winchester.

Governor Byrd flew to Richmond late today from Norfolk to get news of his brother. He had been at Chapel Hill for the Virginia-Carolina football game on Thanksgiving Day and stopped in the capital to be the guest of Governor O. Max Gardner of North Carolina. Accompanying Governor Byrd in another plane was Colonel Willard D. Newbill of his staff.

From the Executive Mansion the Governor relayed news of the flight to his mother at Winchester.

When Commander Byrd duplicated his top of the world feat by flying over the South Pole at the very bosom of the world his mother, thought it "glorious" and was "thrilled to death," she said tonight.

Continued on Page Two.

CROSSES GLACIER PASS AT 11,500 FEET

Commander Takes Chance and Plane Roars Upward Amid Swirling Drift Out Through Gorge to Tableland

FLYING TIME FOR THE WHOLE CIRCUIT ABOUT 18 HOURS

With Two New Ranges Discovered, the Four Air Argonauts, Guided by Chief, Turn Back to Wild Welcome at Base Camp.

By RUSSELL OWEN

Copyright, 1929, by The New York Times Company and The St. Louis Post-Dispatch. All rights for publication reserved throughout the world.

Wireless to THE NEW YORK TIMES.

LITTLE AMERICA, Antarctica, Nov. 29.—Conqueror of two Poles by air, Commander Richard E. Byrd flew into camp at 10:10 o'clock this morning, having been gone eighteen hours and fifty-nine minutes. An hour of this time was spent at the mountain base refueling.

The first man to fly over the North and South Poles and the only man to fly over the South Pole stepped from his plane and was swept up on the arms of the men in camp who for more than an hour had been anxiously watching the southern horizon for a sight of the plane.

Deaf from the roar of the motors, tired from the continual strain of the flight and the long period of navigation under difficulties, Commander Byrd was still smiling and happy. He had reached the South Pole after as hazardous and as difficult a flight as has ever been made in an airplane, tossed by gusts of wind, climbing desperately up the slopes of glaciers a few hundred feet above the surface.

Radiant Airmen Borne in Triumph.

His companions on the flight tumbled out stiff and weary also, but so happy that they forgot their cramped muscles. They were also tossed aloft, pounded on the back and carried to the entrance of the mess hall.

Bernt Balchen, the calm-eyed pilot who first met Commander Byrd in Spitzbergen and who was with him on the transatlantic flight, came out first. There was a little smudge of soot under the nose, but the infectious smile which has endeared him to those who know him, was radiant.

He was carried away and then came Harold June who, between intervals of helping Balchen and attending to fuel tanks and lines and taking pictures, found time to send the radio bulletins which told of the plane's progress.

And after him Captain Ashley McKinley lifted from the doorway, beaming like the Cheshire cat because his surveying camera had done its work all the way.

Dumped Food of Forty-five Days, But Not Fuel.

Men crowded about them eager for the story of what they had been through, catching fragments of sentences. It had evidently been a terrific battle to get up through the mountains to the Plateau.

"We had to dump a month and a half of food to do it," said Commander Byrd. "I am glad it wasn't gas. It was nip and tuck all the way."

"Yes," chuckled Balchen. "Do you remember when we were sliding around those knolls picking the wind currents to help us there wasn't more than 300 feet under us at times? We were just staggering along, with drift and clouds and all sorts of things around us."

When the plane approached the mountains on the way south, Commander Byrd picked out the Livingston Glacier, a large glacier somewhat to the west of the Axel Heiberg Glacier, as the best passageway.

Swooping Upward Through Swirling Drift.

The high mountains shut them in all around as they forced their way upward; Balchen, conserving his fuel to the utmost, coaxing his engines, picking the up-currents of air as best he could to help the plane ride upward.

Clouds swirled about them at times, puff-balls of mist driven down the glacier; drift scurried beneath them; it was a wicked place for an airplane to be, hemmed in by the wall of the towering peaks on either side.

This was the time when they had to lighten ship and Byrd, looking around for what could best be spared, decided to dump some food. There was a dump valve in the fuselage tank, but he had determined to go through and did not know what winds he might face at the top of the glacier. So food was thrown overboard, scattered over the ridged and broken surface of the Livingston Glacier.

"It is an awful looking place," Commander Byrd said.

Over the "Hump" and Vast Panorama Unfolds.

They finally reached the hump at an elevation of 11,500 feet, as indicated by the barograph, although it might have been a little more, because of the difference in pressure inland.

But there was little space under the staggering plane, buffeted by the winds that eddied through the gigantic gorge. Once at the top, Balchen could level off for a time and then gain altitude.

Then there came into view slowly the long sweep of mountains of the Queen Maud Range, stretching to the southeast, and the magnificent panorama of the entire bulwark of mountains along the edge of the Polar Plateau.

Beheld Tinted Slopes of Myriad Mountains.

"It was the most magnificent sight I have ever seen," Commander Byrd said. "I never dreamed there were so many mountains in the world. They shone under the sun, wonderfully tinted with color, and in the southeast a bank of clouds hung over the mountains, making a scene that I shall never forget."

Over the plateau the Commander set his course for the pole. They had had a beam wind all the way in to the mountains which

---

BRITISH APPLAUD FLIGHT AS TRIUMPH

Thrill Over Byrd's Feat Puts Polar Land Dispute in the Background.

NEWS EAGERLY AWAITED

German Press and People Followed Commander's Course With Keen Interest.

Special Cable to THE NEW YORK TIMES.

LONDON, Saturday, Nov. 30.—Great Britain watched Commander Byrd's progress over the Antarctic wastes to the South Pole and his return as a magnificent adventure, and what claims he may make to any rich coal or mineral deposits over which he has flown or staked with the American flag is an issue that is exciting no comment here.

Even the publication by New York newspapers of a summary of the British Government's year-old note concerning sovereignty over the Antarctic lands, which was read here as clearly indicating that the United States does not intend to abandon its claims based on earlier discoveries by American explorers, was not allowed to distract attention from Commander Byrd's performance or to cause a controversy almost on the eve of the five-power naval parley in London.

Hailed as Byrd Triumph.

The Daily Chronicle outstripped its London rivals this morning by alone printing a full account of Commander Byrd's "South Pole" flight, as transmitted to it by THE NEW YORK TIMES and associated newspapers. The remainder of the London newspapers were able in their final editions to announce only the bare fact of Commander Byrd's return to his base on the Ross ice shelf, at 10:10 o'clock London time last night, the leading newspapers of the world were able to reproduce the story of the exploit.

It has not escaped notice that scientific development, from the short-wave radio to the finer details of aircraft construction, have been pressed into use on this occasion. Scientists, aviators and public men on every hand are expressing admiration for Commander Byrd's initiative and courage in carrying out successfully a flight which for scientific results may stand alone.

Commander Byrd had been flying over twelve hours before the British

Continued on Page Four.

1930 - 1939

The New York Times.

THE WEATHER
Showers and cooler today; tomorrow fair.
Temperatures yesterday—Max. 84, min 70.
[For details see Page 44.]

Copyright, 1930, by The New York Times Company.

VOL. LXXIX....No. 26,520. *****+ NEW YORK, WEDNESDAY, SEPTEMBER 3, 1930. TWO CENTS In Greater New York | THREE CENTS Within 300 Miles | FOUR CENTS Elsewhere Except 7th and 8th Postal Zones

COSTE DOES IT IN 37 HOURS, 18½ MINUTES!
FIRST TO MAKE PARIS-NEW YORK FLIGHT;
HOOVER, LINDBERGH AND BYRD HAIL FEAT

HEARST IS EXPELLED ON VISIT TO FRANCE FOR 'HOSTILE' ACTION

Government Says Move Was Taken Because of Use of Secret Naval Pact.

NOTE PUBLISHED IN 1928

Tardieu Reported to Have Fixed Ban Aug. 9 After American's Talk to German Press.

ORDER IS OBEYED QUICKLY

Paper Owner Asserts in London He Told French He Would "Save" Nation by Going at Once.

Wireless to THE NEW YORK TIMES.
LONDON, Sept. 2.—Somewhat of a sensation was caused in London today when it was learned that William Randolph Hearst, American newspaper proprietor, who arrived here last night from Paris, had been expelled from France because of the publication of the memorandum on the secret Anglo-French naval pact two years ago in Hearst newspapers.

Mr. Hearst arrived in Paris yesterday morning from the Italian lake district and went to the Hotel Crillon, where he received the expulsion order. He was told the French Cabinet had decided to expel him because his newspapers were "hostile" to France.

Not Molested Month Ago.

Yesterday was not the first time Mr. Hearst had returned to France since the episode of the secret document. He spent some days in Paris a month or so ago on the way to Germany and was not molested then.

When Mr. Hearst reached London last night he told no one, not even his own representatives who met him at the station, of his expulsion and sudden departure from France. It was learned only this morning when a news agency telephoned to him hotel asking for a statement, after which the American publisher was bombarded by reporters and photographers.

Later today Mr. Hearst, who is remaining in London for a while before going to his 800-year-old castle in Glamorgan, South Wales, issued a statement to the press here in which he defended publication of the secret document because it "upset some international applecarts."

Text of Hearst Statement.

Mr. Hearst's statement follows:—

I have no complaint to make. The officials were extremely polite. They said I was an enemy of France and a danger in their midst. They made me feel quite important.

They said I could stay a little while longer if I desired; that they would take a chance on nothing disastrous happening to the republic.

But I told them I did not want to take the responsibility of endangering the great French nation; that America had saved it once during the war and I would save it again by leaving.

Furthermore it was like the man who was told he was going blind and who said he did not mind as he had seen everything anyhow.

Then I asked Mr. Tardieu's emissary to express to Mr. Tardieu my immense admiration at his amazing alertness in protecting France from the peril of invasion, and parted with quite friendly politeness.

It was a little bit foolish but extremely French.

The reason for the strained relations—to use the proper diplomatic term—was the publication of the secret Anglo-French treaty two years ago by the Hearst newspapers, which upset some international applecarts but informed the American people, and of course that being the reason, the French Government was entirely right in levelling its attack at me, and quite wrong in its action toward Mr. Horan, who was only my agent.

I think however, that the general attitude of the Hearst press in opposing the entrance of the United States into the League of Nations

Continued on Page Twenty.

Air and Rail Lines Here Open A Consolidated Ticket Office

Airlines consolidated ticket office was opened yesterday in the lobby of the Hotel Roosevelt by the Airlines Traffic Association. The office will sell tickets for air and air-rail trips on eighteen lines radiating out of the city.

The association opened a similar cooperative ticket bureau in Chicago two years ago with privilege to sell rides on thirty-two lines throughout the country. More such offices will be opened in airplane centres throughout the country soon.

Colonel L. H. Brittin, president of the association, and other officers were present at the formal opening.

HOOVER LAUDS COSTE FOR 'GLORIOUS' FLIGHT

In Cable to Doumergue, the President Calls Exploit of the French Airmen Brilliant.

LINDBERGH HAILS SUCCESS

Own Feat Surpassed, He Says —Byrd, Kimball and Aviation Leaders Add Their Praise.

Special to The New York Times.
WASHINGTON, Sept. 2.—The successful transatlantic flight of Captain Coste and M. Bellonte, which was a cause of general rejoicing here where interest in the daring Frenchmen had superseded all other interests.

Word that the fliers had landed was the signal for the dispatch of congratulatory messages by ranking officials of the government, while others informally expressed their gratification at the successful crossing of the Atlantic with words of high praise for the French aviators.

President Hoover, in a message to President Doumergue of France, declared that by the flight France "has established a glorious record." His message follows:

Sept. 2, 1930.
His Excellency Gaston Doumergue, President of the French Republic, Paris, France.

I join with the people of the American nation in rejoicing over the brilliant exploit of your distinguished aviators, Captain Dieudonné Coste and M. Maurice Bellonte, in successfully completing for the first time in history a nonstop flight from France to the United States.

France has established a glorious record. I hope that in the future many others of your citizens will come to us in this manner.

I extend to your Excellency and to the people of France my heartiest congratulations.

HERBERT HOOVER.

Message to French People.

The State Department at the same time requested Ambassador Edge at Paris to extend to the Minister for Foreign Affairs, and through him to the people of France, the heartiest congratulations of the United States Government on the magnificent flight.

The department's congratulations to the fliers were contained in a message to Captain Coste from Green Hackworth, solicitor of the State Department, and in the absence of higher officials, the acting Secretary of State.

This message read as follows:
Sept. 2, 1930.
Captain Dieudonné Coste, Curtiss-Wright Airport, Valley Stream, Long Island.

Personally, and on behalf of the people of this country, I extend to you and Maurice Bellonte our heartiest congratulations upon your magnificent flight and safe arrival. The same splendid courage and undaunted spirit that inspired Nungesser and Coli have at last been rewarded.

GREEN HACKWORTH.

Among other officials who informally voiced their congratulations was Major Gen. J. E. Fechet, chief of the Army Air Corps, who said:

"I consider it a very marvelous flight and wish to congratulate them."

Navy Heads Add Greetings.

Secretary of the Navy Adams sent the following message to Captain Coste:

"The American Navy extends its congratulations to you and your companion, Maurice Bellonte, on the successful completion of the Paris to New York flight in an airplane. Your courageous feat has aroused the admiration of every of

Continued on Page Three.

COSTE'S OWN STORY TELLS OF FLYING THROUGH MIST

Like Floating Through a Hazy Dream for Hours and Hours—Felt Lucky After Conquering Three Storms Over Atlantic.

ONCE DRIVEN 100 MILES OFF THEIR COURSE

Knew That the Battle Was Over When They Sighted Land at 6 A. M., but Got Into a 'Tight Place' Between Steep Cliffs of a River.

By CAPTAIN DIEUDONNE COSTE.
Copyright, 1930, in North and South America, by The New York Times Company. All rights reserved.

When we took off from Paris the day before yesterday we knew it was the greatest moment in our lives. It was the culmination of three years of hard effort, not unmixed with many heartbreaking disappointments. If we had not left at that particular minute we might well have faced three more years of delay before accomplishing the first flight from a city of the Old World to the greatest city in the New World.

There were many exciting moments during our trip, and at times I could not be sure from one minute to the next—now that it is all over—which was the greatest thrill. I think, however, that that came after we first sighted the coast of North America. As you know, the coast of Nova Scotia is full of bends and turns, fills and rivers, promontories and little gulfs.

Followed the Winding Coast.

When we reached the coast we were determined not to lose sight of it again. In order to keep it in view we had to follow all these devious turns and that was a job. At the same time we had another problem. The sky was overcast, it was raining and we had to fly below these rain clouds. Sometimes they were extremely low, which made it necessary for us to fly as close to the water as ten meters.

We came to one bend and turned it; we flew on, skirting a precipice. Suddenly there loomed up out of the mist another precipice on our port side. We were caught between the steep banks of a river—what river, I do not know. It was a tight place.

Bellonte was at the controls at that time and he had to think fast. Fortunately, having flown thousands of miles, the ship was light. Bellonte gave her the gas and shot upward.

Decided to Fly by Instrument.

It is not pleasant to think how close we came to those cruel, jagged rocks. We went up fairly high and began to fly steadily by instrument. Some time passed before the clouds and the rain cleared somewhat and then we were over what I believe was the Atlantic off the coast of Maine. We came down a little later through a new bank of fog and headed down the coast until we were over a large city.

We were so interested in trying to determine what city it was that it never occurred to us that this was the first great city we had passed since leaving Paris. Only a few minutes later we passed another city, and now there was no doubt. We identified it as Boston. We continued the flight without further incident before landing at Valley Stream.

The tremendous load of fuel required for this flight, in which we expected to buck prevailing unfavorable winds, gave us the first real thrill of the voyage. Would the ship lift off the ground? That was our great concern. We had 5,200 litres of gasoline on board.

Storms Ahead Cause Concern.

But this great fear passed in a few moments and we found new cause for concern with each passing moment. There were storms ahead. We would have to push our over-weighted ship through them. We ran into the first of these disturbances off the Irish coast. The second gave us some trying moments, not long afterward, over the ocean, but fortunately we were able to escape the worst of it. The third—and probably the worst of all—was the storm we encountered over Nova Scotia.

That it occurred only yesterday morning seems impossible just at this moment. So many things seem to have happened since, that that storm seems remote—something that happened long, long ago.

Driven 100 Miles Off Course.

We had to find the best route to Nova Scotia, and that in short order, if we were to avoid the hazards that faced the Bremen when it ran into fog and storm of a similar nature and was forced down hundreds of miles from its goal.

In seeking to avoid this storm we were obliged to fly 100 miles out of our way to the south. We did not find land, as we had expected, so we turned northward again, flying another 100 miles. Time was swiftly passing. Each minute meant the loss of more of our precious fuel. Again we turned.

It occurred to us that three is a lucky number. We had faced three storms—were we now to be defeated? We were sure that we would not be.

Land Sighted in Early Morning.

After three hours of searching we computed that we must be very near the coast of Nova Scotia. At 3 A. M. (French time)—for we had not changed our clock—we sighted land. At the same moment it became obvious that the winds were abating. Naturally we were very happy—very happy. The only thing that could stop us now, we thought, would be failure of our motor.

It had carried us already from France to North America and we knew that it would not fail us now. We had perfect confidence in its stanch heart and that confidence was justified. The motor was wonderful. It did all that we had hoped it would.

Weather conditions, on the whole, were very favorable—at least the winds were on our side. On the other hand, almost the entire route was clouded over and we went hour after hour over that watery waste through a thick white mist. We could not see what lay ahead, below or above. It was like floating in a dream. There was something unreal about it—unreal and awesome. We were two, but we seemed so all alone.

Up and Down to Find Clear Way.

Most of the time I was at the controls, and there was plenty to keep my mind busy. There was no time for dreaming. Constantly I had to shift my course to find a way out of the haze. Sometimes we dropped the plane down to less than 300 feet from the waves. At other times we were up to 2,500 feet. We seldom went above that mark, and never very much above it.

But we had our reward. Although my mind was taken up with the

Continued on Page Three.

Associated Press Photo.
FRENCH FLIER IN HIS HOUR OF TRIUMPH!
Conqueror of Atlantic Carried Off the Field on the Shoulders of His Admirers on His Safe Arrival From Paris.

ALL PARIS ACCLAIMS TRIUMPH BY COSTE

News of Safe Landing Here Shouted Joyfully by Great Throngs in Streets.

FELT CERTAIN OF SUCCESS

Real Demonstration Deferred Until Homecoming of the Two Fliers.

By P. J. PHILIP.
Special Cable to THE NEW YORK TIMES.
PARIS, Sept. 2.—"Vive Coste!" "Vive Bellonte!" "Vive la France!" All over Paris these cries have roused the midnight hours. There is no one in the city who does not know safely from Paris to New York by air; crossed between breakfast time on one day and supper time on the next.

"They have done it," has been called by every street, and every one knew who "they" were and what they had done. And so to bed, with immense, tremendous happiness, contentment and pride.

From Curtiss Field to the Place de la Concorde came the voice of Graham McNamee: "He's taxiing down the field!" The rest was interrupted by the clamor of those who did not understand. Then a French voice broke in: "Coste has landed!"

It was that way that Paris learned that the great adventure of east-to-west crossing of the Atlantic had been accomplished, that Nungesser and Coli and so many others had been avenged, that Lindbergh's great flight had been complemented and that the link between Paris and New York had been forged on both sides by air.

By tremendous handclapping Captain Coste was acclaimed, and there were those who knew who "they" were and what they had done. It was certain, could hold the crowd of those who all day had been asking. "Where are they now; when will they arrive?"

Crowd Sure of Success.

There never was any doubt in the one's mind all day—not in that of Mme. Coste or of Mme. Bellonte; not in that of taxi drivers, who would ask their fares for the latest news; not in that of concierges, who exchanged their views with passers-by. It was a day of most extraordinary

Continued on Page Four.

10,000 STORM FIELD TO WELCOME FLIERS

Coste Cuts Whirling Propeller as Police Lines Snap and the Throngs Rush Plane.

WELCOMERS SHOVED ASIDE

Glare of Torches Lights Wild Greeting as Pilots Are Carried in Triumph From Field.

Special to The New York Times.
CURTISS FIELD, L. I., Sept. 2.—As the red biplane of Captain Dieudonné Coste and Maurice Bellonte swung out of the northeast at dusk and circled low over the Curtiss Airport here a cheer of welcome roared from the throats of 10,000 persons massed in rows behind a wire fence and strung out in a long line in front of the field's six hangars.

A large part of the crowd had waited all afternoon through a heavy rainstorm and, tho gh most of the spectators were held behind the fence and got no more than a fleeting glimpse of the red plane, they were as vociferous in their welcome as if they had been a part of the crowd that helped to carry the two fliers off the field in triumph.

Crowd Breaks Police Lines.

As the plane glided to a graceful landing and started to taxi toward the grand stand on the west side of the field, the crowd inside the fence broke through the police lines and ran shouting and dodging policemen toward the craft. Coste, realizing the danger of the whirling propeller, cut the switch, and the metal blade swung slowly to a stop. A score of policemen and mechanics joined hands, and forming a circle about the plane, tried with scant success to hold back the crowd. At least seventy-five persons broke through the cordon and swarmed about the plane. Coste, looking hot and tired, stepped out of the plane into a seething mob, which kissed him, pummeled him, wrung his hands and all but knocked him from his feet.

"Splendid!" "Magnifique!" "Felicitations!" French as well as American voices screamed. French girls embraced the fliers, kissing them time and again, and Frenchmen followed suit. An announcer for the National Broadcasting Company, holding a microphone high above his head, was lost in the struggling throng, and gasped in the microphone:

"We seem to be having a little difficulty here at Valley Stream."

Elinor Smith, girl aviator, was in the midst of the crowd, but did not get a chance to greet the fliers until later.

A delegation of French war veterans, carrying the French tricolor and the American flag, struggled inside the police cordon, but had but

Continued on Page Two.

FLIERS LAND AT 7:12½ P. M. TO WILD CHEERS OF 10,000

Scarlet Plane Alights Smoothly at Goal With Enough Fuel for Three Hours More—Airmen, Speechless, Watch the Mad Scene of Welcome.

LINDBERGH, HIS VISIT RETURNED, HAILS COSTE

'A Great Flight,' He Says, Gripping Hand of Ace Amid Tumult at Curtiss Field—France Hears the Fliers on Radio—They Will Fly On to Texas.

By JOSEPH SHAPLEN.
Special to The New York Times.
CURTISS FIELD, L. I., Sept. 2.—Captain Dieudonné Coste and his co-pilot, Maurice Bellonte, completed tonight the first direct flight from Paris to New York when they landed at the Curtiss airport at 7:12:30 P. M., after a journey of 37 hours 18 minutes 30 seconds. They covered 6,500 kilometers, or about 4,100 miles, and when they landed had 100 gallons of gasoline left, sufficient for nearly three hours more of flying.

Their achievement marked the first non-stop crossing from Europe to the American metropolis. What others have tried to do and failed Captain Coste and M. Bellonte accomplished. In doing so they triumphed magnificently over the elements which sent Nungesser and Coli, the first two Frenchmen to try the westward trip, to death, and took their revenge upon Neptune for the loss of other valiant aviators who sought to achieve the westward flight.

Colonel Charles A. Lindbergh's time for the eastward crossing was better. It took him only thirty-three hours and a half to fly from Roosevelt Field to Le Bourget to pay the visit which Coste and Bellonte repaid tonight. The Spirit of St. Louis rose from earth and started on its historic flight at 7:52 A. M., May 20, 1927. Lindbergh brought it to earth just outside of Paris at 10:24 Continental Time (5:24 P. M., New York Time), on May 21.

Ten thousand throats yelled a wild greeting to the two French masters of the air as their airplane, the scarlet, enigmatic Question Mark, bearing upon her sides the written record of a dozen odysseys of the sky, came down smoothly and gracefully on the east side of the field and taxied rapidly toward the hangars on the west side. Here among the first to greet Captain Coste and M. Bellonte was Colonel Lindbergh, whose visit to Paris had now been repaid.

"Great Flight," Colonel Lindbergh Declares.

"It's a great flight," was the enthusiastic comment of Colonel Lindbergh after he had finally managed, with the assistance of policemen, to make his way to the French airmen, following their rescue from the cheering crowds, whose enthusiasm exceeded all bounds. Never before in the history of aviation in this country, according to veterans of the air, have any flying men received the reception accorded tonight to Captain Coste and his companion.

Soon after the Question Mark landed, the fliers were informed that Colonel W. E. Easterwood of Dallas, Texas, had offered $25,000 to Captain Coste and M. Bellonte if they would fly their ship to Dallas. Captain Coste said he would be glad to make the trip because it would give him an opportunity for a cross-country flight, and said he would probably take off Thursday morning, after the plane has been tuned up and tightened.

Asked if he had any plans for the future, which might include a trip around the world via the poles, as one interviewer suggested, Captain Coste replied he had no plans beyond the flight to Dallas.

It was 7:10 P. M. when the Question Mark, easily distinguished by her color and peculiar design, appeared in the sky over the airport, escorted by three Curtiss fledglings from the Naval Reserve aviation field here and flanked by a score of other airplanes which had taken off shortly before to extend a welcome to the French fliers.

After circling the field, the Question Mark came down, making a perfect landing. Veering quickly in the direction of the hangars the French victors of the Atlantic raced toward the wings, obviously anxious to avoid the onrush of the crowds. But in vain. The moment Captain Coste and M. Bellonte raised their heads out of the cockpit and stepped over the fuselage they were picked up on the shoulders of several of their compatriots and carried to Hangar 2, while a small army of policemen struggled desperately to protect them against what seemed imminent injury from the ever-increasing pressure of the throng of admirers. "Vive la France," "Vive Coste et Bellonte," came the resounding, ever-mounting cries from the hundreds of Frenchmen who formed a prominent part of the surging crowds.

Police Battle Crowds in Great Rush of Welcome.

Above the unrestrained, joyous clamor of voices the boom of a hundred flashlights accompanied the triumphant procession across the field to the hangar, where the police hoped they could isolate the fliers. Here the police had to fight a veritable battle to get Coste and Bellonte to safety, but even in the hangar they found no refuge, for before the police and airport employes could close and bolt the rolling doors hundreds forced their way in, besieging the fliers, eager to shake their hands, unmindful of the danger in getting as close as possible to the airmen. With their faces dripping perspiration, their backs against a wall, Coste and Bellonte stood speechless for nearly ten minutes, wondering what would be the end of this mad scene which appeared beyond the powers of the police to master, until, in phalanx formation, the guards rushed the crowd back far enough to clear an exit.

With the greatest difficulty, Coste and Bellonte were finally rushed to a room upstairs, to which only a small group of their friends, members of the Nassau County and the Mayor's reception committees and representatives of the French Government made their way in the vain hope of getting a few words with the airmen.

Lindbergh Greets Fliers Returning His Visit.

Here, too, came Colonel Lindbergh, smiling with joy at the success of the flight and rushing forward to congratulate first Coste and then Bellonte.

Captain Coste's eyes flashed as he grasped the hand of the young man who more than any one else had captured the imagination of the world by his solo flight to Le Bourget, the starting point of the Question Mark.

Firmly the two heroes of the air shook hands as thousands outside, standing in the glare of scores of magnesium flares, broke into the wildest outburst of cheering that marked the arrival.

"Comment ça va?" asked Captain Coste.

"I congratulate you, I congratulate you," said Colonel Lindbergh, again pressing the Frenchman's hand and apparently so overcome by

51

"All the News That's Fit to Print."

The New York Times.

THE WEATHER
Fair and continued cool today and tomorrow.
Temperature yesterday—Max.: 64; Min., 53.
☞ Weather Forecast—For details see Page 30.

Copyright, 1930, by The New York Times Company.

VOL. LXXX....No. 26,744. ★ ★ ★ ★ NEW YORK, WEDNESDAY, OCTOBER 1, 1930. TWO CENTS In Greater New York | THREE CENTS | FOUR CENTS Elsewhere Within 200 Miles | Through 7th and 8th Postal Zones

HINDENBURG BACKS DICTATORSHIP PLANS FOR FISCAL REFORM

Approves Threat to Reichstag to Force Approval of Cabinet's Emergency Program.

LOAN TO BE FIRST STEP

Wage Cuts and Other Savings Would Be Put Off Until Next April.

HITLER WARNS PRESIDENT

Fascist Hints That Revolt Would Follow Indefinite Closing of German Parliament.

Special Cable to THE NEW YORK TIMES.
BERLIN, Sept. 30.—Chancellor Bruening announced today his program of financial reforms on which he is determined to combat the Reichstag even to the extent of creating a dictatorship. He also let it be known that President von Hindenburg had approved every item and was ready to back the government in its threat to the Reichstag.

The Bruening program is drastic in some of its projected curtailments of expenditures.

To become a fact it requires the passage of a large number of enabling bills, which are certain to meet determined opposition from one or another Reichstag party.

Plans to Put Off Clash.

The best talking point so far as getting the program through the Reichstag is concerned is the fact that Parliament will for the moment be called on only to authorize the floating of another loan, while all the unpleasant pills the body is going to be asked to swallow are designed for the new budget, and will not have to be taken before April 1, 1931. This is designed to put off the day when the situation must be faced squarely until after the Winter.

It is never difficult to get the Reichstag to authorize loans, and the only other immediate feature of the program, an increase in the unemployment insurance premium by 2 per cent to 6½ per cent, will be promulgated Oct. 4 under Article XLVIII before the Reichstag, which convenes on Oct. 13, has a chance to say anything.

The government expects a deficit for the year ending March 31, 1931, of $185,000,000 to $225,000,000. This has been caused by a $75,000,000 rise in unemployment insurance and by anticipated falling off in tax receipts of $110,000,000 to $150,000,000, resulting from poor business conditions, too high taxes, or both.

Nothing is said, however, about $60,000,000 deficits remaining from previous years. The present deficit is briefly disposed of in the new prospectus by saying it will be covered by special funds during the three years beginning next April.

Borrowings Are Anticipated.

The government is trying to float a $150,000,000 loan and it is assumed the difference will also be met by a loan. It is presumed in some quarters that the appearance of this comprehensive program was timed to strengthen the market for new government borrowing.

Then the government turns to its plans for the future. The new budget is to be cut by $250,000,000, about what the reduction in tax receipts is expected to amount to. It does not mention where the sums are to be obtained for funding the new loans within three years.

The chief items by which the $250,000,000 is to be saved are salary cuts of 20 per cent for the President, Ministers and Reichstag members, cuts of 6 per cent for civil service employes and corresponding wage reductions for the Reichswehr and State railway workers. These cuts are estimated to amount to $50,000,000.

There is a reduction in various ministerial budgets of $75,000,000, a saving on unemployment doles through the new increase in the fee of $88,000,000 and an increase in the tobacco tax, which is to bring in increased tax, of $40,000,000. The salary cuts begin next April. The civil service employes already have suffered a 5 per cent salary cut for this year. The constructive side of the plan urges the introduction of a bill authorizing the simplifying of the structure of the tax collection organization. This organization is found to eat up 4½ per cent of receipts, while British tax collection costs only 2 per cent. The national property tax, real estate tax and tax on incomes under $2,000 will be based in a single tax.

Small farmers and small commercial undertakings will be relieved of turnover taxes which have been found not worth the trouble of collecting. Forcing the same rigid economy, the Reich will hereafter take a hand in the drawing of State budgets and will undertake a thorough...

Continued on Page Ten.

King Feisal to Fly Own Plane; Orders an Air Force for Iraq

Wireless to THE NEW YORK TIMES.
ALEXANDRIA, Egypt, Sept. 30.—Iraq will soon have its own air force, King Feisal announced today after flying from Abukir to Amman with a Royal Air Force escort to visit the Emir Abdullah.

Airplanes, King Feisal said, are essential to Iraq, both for defense and communications, and early next year eight machines will leave England in the hands of Iraqi pilots to form the nucleus of the air force, which by 1934 is to comprise three squadrons. The personnel is now in training and conscription will be introduced. The King has purchased a plane, which he proposes to fly himself to interest his people in aviation.

The Anglo-Iraq treaty, according to Feisal, will be submitted to the Iraq Parliament in November.

"I am sure it will pass," he added. "The treaty is the last step of independent Iraq for the liberation of other Arab countries."

BRIAND HITS AT FOES TRYING TO OUST HIM

Acts Quickly at Geneva to Save Peace Policy as Nationalists Open Fight in Paris.

CURTIUS PLEDGES HIS AID

Answers Appeal for German Moderation—Reich Fears Loss of Briand.

By CLARENCE K. STREIT.
Special Cable to THE NEW YORK TIMES.
GENEVA, Sept. 30.—With telegrams from Paris warning him that Raymond Poincaré and the Nationalist French press, believing that the German elections had proved the failure of his policy of reconciliation with Germany, were working to overthrow him, Foreign Minister Briand of France arose in the League of Nations Assembly today in a supreme defense of his policy of reconciliation.

It is never difficult to get the platform in a supreme test and Briand spoke before a large and enthusiastic audience.

The Germans had received the same telegrams, and even the representatives of the Hugenberg Nationalists were plainly worried by the prospect of M. Briand being overthrown. Dr. Curtius mounted the platform to reply, with a choice of fortifying his own weak position by an easy appeal to the nationalism that might overthrow M. Briand or of helping M. Briand by his moderation. He chose to lean backward toward moderation and agreed with M. Briand that the only thing to do was to work together.

"We must do the utmost at home to prevent trouble," he said in effect, "but we must be able to count on your help."

The German Nationalists knew tonight were openly praising Dr. Curtius for his moderation. The French here seemed agreed that M. Briand had succeeded in his delicate task of strengthening his own position without weakening that of Dr. Curtius.

Repercussions Uncertain.

It remains to be seen what the repercussions will be in Paris and Berlin, far removed from the atmosphere of Geneva, for it was to them, on whom the future depends, that M. Briand and Dr. Curtius were speaking tonight. At Geneva, at least, the atmosphere seems both clearer and lighter.

The peg on which the speeches were hung was disarmament, but the board also approved the ap...

Continued on Page Four.

Students Fight Police in Streets of Havana; 12 Wounded in Anti-Machado Demonstration

Special Cable to THE NEW YORK TIMES.
HAVANA, Sept. 30.—The discovery by secret police several days ago of an alleged plot between students of the National University and other elements, among them Communist agitators, to promote a city-wide movement of protest against the administration of President Machado resulted in a clash between students and police this morning in which four students and two policemen were seriously injured and at least six others wounded. Three and forty-one students were arrested.

Dr. José Martinez Prieto, acting dean of the university, estimated to night there were 600 students and 150 policemen in the clash. The students were armed with bottles, stones and sticks, while the police made use of their nightsticks and revolvers in an attempt to stop the students from holding a meeting and parade.

The protest by the students was to begin at a meeting in the park facing the university, where they were to assemble and march to the home of Enrique José Varona, considered Cuba's greatest philosopher, whose recent declarations opposing present political methods in Cuba have caused wide comment.

The first move of the State Department today was to express doubt that the American embassy in Havana had ordered an investigation of the incident. Department officials said they knew of no authority granted the embassy under which such an inquiry could or would be ordered.

WASHINGTON, Sept. 30 (P).—The State Department awaited tonight a complete report on the students' outbreak in Havana, officials speculated on the possible ramifications of the anti-government demonstration. The news caused surprise among department officials, for throughout the past six weeks the department has been careful in every instance to emphasize its belief that the situation in Cuba was no cause for alarm.

DAHL HEADS I. R. T., WITH FULL POWER TO PUSH UNIFICATION

Election as Chairman Opens Way for City to Deal With One Spokesman for All Lines.

HE SUCCEEDS BERWIND

Chosen to Direct Executive Committee to Which Walsh, Hayden and Wiggin Are Named.

HEDLEY AGAIN PRESIDENT

Walker Hails Action as Hopeful, but Untermyer Sees Possible Danger in Move.

By electing Gerhard M. Dahl, chairman of the B. M. T. directorate, to head its own board and authorizing him to negotiate with the city and Transit Commission for rapid transit unification the Interborough Rapid Transit Company yesterday opened the way for public officials to achieve a comprehensive unification by dealing with a single representative of all privately operated rapid transit lines.

Mr. Dahl was unanimously elected to his new post at the first meeting of the new Interborough board after it had received the resignation of Edward J. Berwind as chairman. Mr. Berwind, who retained his post as a director, suggested Mr. Dahl as his successor, in view of the overwhelming majority of stockholders' votes cast for Mr. Dahl, Albert H. Wiggin and Charles H. Hayden at the annual meeting on Sept. 24 when they were elected directors of the company.

The directors also chose Mr. Dahl to head their executive committee. That the future policy of the Interborough will be largely shaped by directors committed to the principle of rapid transit unification was assured by the election of Mr. Hayden and Mr. Wiggin, also directors of the B. M. T., as executive committee members. Frank P. Walsh, recently elected public director, was also named a member of the executive committee, assuring the city and Transit Commission of a voice in the inner councils of the company.

Strong Bank Representation.

It was regarded as significant in transit and financial circles that Messrs. Dahl, Wiggin and Hayden are also directors of the Chase National Bank, financial sponsors for the B. M. T., and that Frederick H. Ecker, another member of the executive committee; Frank L. Polk, one of the three voting trustees, and Thomas I. Parkinson, director, are also directors of the same bank. It is believed that the Chase National Bank will play an important part in the financing which will be required should a plan for unification of Interborough, B. M. T. and city lines be worked out.

An outline of such a comprehensive unification plan has already been discussed at conferences between Messrs. Dahl and Samuel Untermyer, special counsel for the Transit Commission. As a result of yesterday's election it is expected that representatives of the Board of Transportation and Transit Commission will soon participate officially in future conferences with Mr. Dahl.

Besides the individuals already mentioned the directors elected the following as members of the executive committee: Frank Hedley, Samuel W. Reyburn and William Roberts. Mr. Hedley was re-elected as president and general manager of the company and Earl E. Starbard and H. M. Fisher as vice president and secretary, respectively.

Continued on Page Three.

Japan Accepts London Pact; Emperor to Ratify This Week

By The Associated Press.
TOKYO, Wednesday, Oct. 1.—The Privy Council, in plenary session at the Imperial Palace in the presence of Emperor Hirohito, unconditionally approved the London Naval Treaty today and was advised the Emperor would ratify it. This removes the last obstacle in the way of Japan's ratification of the treaty. Formal fixation of the Emperor's seal, completing the ratification process, is expected tomorrow or Friday.

Japan is the last of the three major adherents to the London treaty to ratify it, the United States and Great Britain having done so during the Summer.

France and Italy signed the treaty, but their rôle was more or less that of witnesses, as their navies were not affected and they merely agreed to continue negotiations for an accord.

STOCK PRICES BREAK; SISTO & CO. SUSPENDED

313 Issues Reach New Lows for Year in Heaviest Trading Since June 18.

SLIGHT RALLY AT CLOSE

Brokers, Temporarily Unable to Meet Obligations, May Be Able to Work Out Troubles.

In the heaviest day of trading since June 18, stock prices declined to new low levels for 1930 yesterday, with transactions totaling 4,496,980 shares. During the general decline, 313 issues established new low records for the year and 690 issues were traded in, constituting the broadest market since June 19. Public liquidation and short selling were joint factors in the decline.

The market's break was aggravated by the announcement early in the afternoon that the Stock Exchange firm of J. A. Sisto & Co., one of the best known financial houses in Wall Street, had admitted its insolvency and had been suspended from membership in the Exchange. Announcement of the suspension was made from the rostrum of the Exchange at 1:30 o'clock in the afternoon by Richard Whitney, president of the Exchange.

While these unfavorable conditions appeared in the day's trading, a compilation of dividends disbursed in September showed that these payments amounted to $475,074,394, against $447,689,154 in the preceding month and $399,391,264 in September, 1929. It showed also that each month this year the dividend payments have been greater than in the corresponding month of last year.

Another development which attracted much attention in Wall Street was the announcement by several leading savings banks of a reduction in the interest rate on deposits from 4½ per cent to 4 per cent during the three-month beginning today.

The settlement in the stock market was most pronounced in a small list of stocks with which the Sisto firm had been identified. These stocks, as well as the general market, rallied somewhat later, and closed above the lowest levels of the day.

Commodity Markets Weak.

Persistent weakness in the commodity markets was one of the unsettling influences. While wheat prices advanced, a long list of other commodities, including copper, cotton, rubber and sugar, declined to the lowest levels in many years.

Although bearish rumors were in more than usual evidence, trading was orderly.

The combined stock price averages compiled by THE NEW YORK TIMES showed a decline of $2.17 to $177.65, the lowest level reached this year. Industrial averages declined $3.23 to $249.38. Railroad averages recently made new lows for the year, but they held above this level yesterday.

TUTTLE CHALLENGES ROOSEVELT TO FORCE A FULL CITY INQUIRY

In Opening Campaign Here He Asks Governor to Push Hunt No Matter Where It Leads.

SEES EXECUTIVE EVASIVE

Wants to Know Why as Head of Party He Did Not Order Curry and Aides to Waive Immunity.

SILENT ON PROHIBITION

Lauds Republican Legislative Record—Warmly Received by Brooklyn Audience.

The text of Mr. Tuttle's speech opening his campaign here is printed on page 23.

Charles H. Tuttle, making his initial appearance before New York City voters in the rôle of Republican Gubernatorial candidate, challenged Governor Roosevelt last night to force the investigations of New York City scandals along all the trails to the end, no matter where the trails lead, or who may be hurt.

He asked the Governor, as the titular leader of the Democratic party in the State, why he had not directed Tammany leader John F. Curry and the district leaders to waive immunity before the grand jury investigating the Ewald case, characterizing the Governor's letter to Mayor Walker as a "half-way" measure.

Mr. Tuttle spoke before a large and enthusiastic audience at Kismet Temple, in Brooklyn. Prolonged cheering greeted Mr. Tuttle's closing remarks that he believed the issue to be exactly as he defined it last Friday. "Are we to have a Governor who is bigger than Tammany Hall, or are we not?"

Greeted by Demonstration.

When Mr. Tuttle stepped on the platform he was greeted by a demonstration that lasted fifteen minutes, five minutes of cheering and ten minutes devoted to a parade of delegations through the hall that resembled the scene at the convention at which he was nominated.

Mr. Tuttle began by pointing to the accomplishments of the Republican Legislature, claiming credit for appropriations for new hospitals and prison construction, adoption of a farm relief program and welfare legislation.

He promised during the campaign to discuss unemployment, public utilities, taxation, promotion of industry, care of the poor and encouragement of agriculture. He did not mention the prohibition issue or the repeal plank in the Republican State platform in his prepared speech.

Switching early in the speech to the corruption issue, and not departing from it during the remainder of his talk, Mr. Tuttle declared that "no solutions of the State's problems are possible unless first we have and maintain clean and honest government."

He declared that for months the Governor had been in the dilemma of choosing between being for Tammany Hall or against Tammany Hall. The Governor, he declared, and reminded the audience that years ago, when a member of the State Legislature, Governor Roosevelt had no difficulty in throwing down a challenge to Tammany. Now, when he needed its support in election, the situation was different, Mr. Tuttle said.

Weapon Too Weak, He Holds.

He recited the list of scandals, and declared that when the Governor finally had to intervene, because of...

Continued on Page Twenty-three.

Hoover Will Open the World Series Today; Four Speeches Scheduled in Next 7 Days

Special to The New York Times.
WASHINGTON, Sept. 30.—President Hoover will leave Washington tomorrow to witness the opening game of the world series at Philadelphia and will then go to Cleveland, where he will deliver the first of four speeches on Thursday the first of four speeches scheduled to be made in seven days.

His Cleveland speech will be delivered to the annual meeting of the American Bankers' Association. The President will return to Washington immediately afterward. In Boston on Monday he will address the American Legion in the morning and the American Federation of Labor the same afternoon.

The fourth address will be made on Oct. 7 at the celebration of the 150th anniversary of the Battle of Kings Mountain, in South Carolina. Although the background for three of these speeches will be political, the White House denies that any political significance attaches to Mr. Hoover's appearances. Democratic spokesmen also denied that the President is "mixing" in the campaign as met by statements that his speeches will have no political tinge and that his sole purpose is to outline some major problems of his administration.

It is stated that the President has done comparatively little traveling since he assumed office and that he desires to make closer contacts with the people.

A large party will go with Mr. Hoover to Philadelphia, including Secretaries Hyde, Hurley Wilbur and Postmaster General Brown.

After the game Mr. Hoover's train will leave for Cleveland, where he will arrive before noon the next day. Mr. Hoover, who is in Indianapolis attending the annual meeting of the Girl Scout executive committee, will join her husband in the afternoon.

The President will return to Washington Oct 5.

President Hoover's addresses to the Bankers Association, the American Legion and at Kings Mountain battlefield will be broadcast over nation-wide radio chains.

ROOSEVELT NOMINATED BY ACCLAMATION, CHALLENGES TUTTLE ON STATE DRY LAW; SMITH SAYS PARTY WILL OUST GRAFTERS

SPEECHES STIR DEMOCRATS

Roosevelt Asks Tuttle if He Would Sign a State Enforcement Act.

SMITH RECEIVES OVATION

Nominating Governor, He Calls Republican Charges False and Misleading.

BENNETT LAW POST CHOICE

Convention, at Final Session, Hears Executive and Lieut. Gov. Lehman Lauded.

The speech of former Governor Smith renominating Governor Roosevelt and the latter's acceptance will be found in full on pages 22 and 23.

RENOMINATED BY ACCLAMATION.
Times Wide World Photo.
Governor Franklin D. Roosevelt, Who Again Heads the State Democratic Ticket, Chosen at Syracuse Yesterday.

By W. A. WARN.
Special to The New York Times.
SYRACUSE, N. Y., Sept. 30.—To the tune of ringing cheers and applause and in the midst of an impressive demonstration of enthusiasm, Governor Franklin D. Roosevelt today was renominated for a second term by the Democratic State Convention. His name was presented by former Governor Alfred E. Smith in a stirring address that brought the convention to its feet. The complete ticket nominated was as follows:

*For Governor—*Franklin D. Roosevelt of Hyde Park renominated.

*For Lieutenant Governor—*Herbert H. Lehman of New York City renominated.

*For Controller—*Morris D. Tremaine of Buffalo renominated.

*For Attorney General—*John J. Bennett Jr. of Brooklyn.

*For Associate Justice, Court of Appeals—*Cuthbert W. Pound of Lockport renominated.

In his speech, the most important public address of political import he has delivered since his defeat for the Presidency in 1928, former Governor Smith actually fired the opening gun of the Democratic State campaign. With typical directness and vigor and to the accompaniment of laughter and applause, he analyzed the various charges on which the Republicans at their State convention last week brought indictments against the Democratic administration at Albany. He denounced them as false and misleading.

Governor Roosevelt, after the business of the convention had been completed, appeared before the delegates to acknowledge the honor that had been conferred upon him, and took up the onslaught on the Republicans where ex-Governor Smith had left off.

Counter Challenge to Tuttle.

The Governor recalled the statement of Charles H. Tuttle in accepting the Republican Gubernatorial nomination that there would be only one issue in the coming campaign, namely, that created by recent disclosures concerning the judiciary in New York City and the refusal of John F. Curry, Tammany Hall, and several district leaders to waive immunity and give testimony before the grand jury.

Mr. Roosevelt served notice that he would force the fight on a number of other issues, and began by challenging the Republican nominee to say whether, in the event of his election, he would sign or veto a State enforcement act should the Legislature pass one.

Governor Roosevelt issued a statement regretting Mr. Bray's retirement.

"More than six months ago Chairman Bray told me that because of the pressure of his business affairs he would be unable even to consider the possibility of being a candidate for re-election as State chairman," the Governor said.

"He has repeated this to me today, much to my regret, and I have expressed to him the hope he would alter his decision. On his finally stepping out until after election day, His work for the Democratic party throughout the State has been of the highest order and the most successful leadership. He has been a splendid worker and a loyal friend."

Mr. Farley, who will resign as chairman of the State Boxing Commission, but not immediately, will return to New York at once to prepare for the campaign.

The Democratic State Committee already has opened headquarters at the Biltmore Hotel in New York City for the re-election of Governor Roosevelt.

Former Governor Smith did not evade attacks made in the Republican...

Continued on Page Twenty-two.

MRS. HEALY DEFIANT; GETS SIX-DAY GRACE

Tammany Leader's Wife Must Then Tell of Ewald Loan or Face Jail Sentence.

HALED TO COURT 5 TIMES

Mayor Prepares to Compel All Tammany Officeholders to Waive Immunity.

A determined and silent woman blocked the efforts of the special grand jury to learn yesterday what became of the $10,000 which former Magistrate George F. Ewald is alleged to have paid to her husband, Martin J. Healy, a Tammany district leader, for his appointment.

Mrs. Healy's refusal to answer questions about her bank account, even in the face of a citation for contempt, provided a colorful interlude in the judiciary investigations while the grand jury awaited a decision on an extension of the powers of Attorney General Hamilton Ward.

As the Tammany district leaders who last week refused to waive immunity were boarding trains at Syracuse after cheering the renomination of Governor Roosevelt to return and postpone and weak that choice, he declared, and reminded the audience that years ago, when a member of the State Legislature, Governor Roosevelt had no difficulty in throwing down a challenge to Tammany. Now, when he needed its support in election, the situation was different, Mr. Tuttle said.

Supreme Court Justice Philip J. McCook, before whom she had been five times in succession yesterday by Special Prosecutor Hiram C. Todd, declared that when the Governor finally had to intervene, because of when Mrs. Healy was told to return.

Continued on Page Eighteen.

J. A. FARLEY HEADS STATE COMMITTEE

Succeeds Bray as Democratic Chairman, Following Contest Behind the Scenes.

BRAY QUITS GRACEFULLY

Roosevelt Tells Regret at His Retirement—Farley Will Resign State Boxing Post.

Special to The New York Times.
SYRACUSE, N. Y., Sept. 30.—James A. Farley of Manhattan, chairman of the State Boxing Commission, today was elected chairman of the Democratic State Committee to succeed M. William Bray of Utica. Mr. Farley had been secretary of the committee since 1928.

George W. Harder of Albany was elected secretary to succeed Mr. Farley. The other officers were re-elected as follows:

Vice chairman, Mrs. Caroline P. O'Day of Westchester treasurer, Edward E. Perkins of Dutchess; assistant secretary, Miss Harriet May Mills, Onondaga; sergeant-at-arms, John J. McGlynn of New York.

The election of Mr. Farley was the culmination of nearly a year of effort to displace Mr. Bray, and followed a contest behind the scenes by a group of up-State leaders from the less populous counties to have Mr. Bray.

Mr. Bray, a lawyer, said he had wished for a long time to be relieved of his political duties and to return to his personal business. He extolled Mr. Farley and said he intended to do everything he could to help the new State chairman to elect the entire State ticket.

"All the News That's Fit to Print."

The New York Times.

THE WEATHER
Cloudy, with probably occasional rain today; tomorrow fair, colder.
Temperature Yesterday—Max. 56; Min. 44.

Copyright, 1930, by The New York Times Company.

VOL. LXXX....No. 26,583.   ★★★★★   NEW YORK, WEDNESDAY, NOVEMBER 5, 1930.   TWO CENTS In Greater New York | THREE CENTS Within 200 Miles | FOUR CENTS Elsewhere Except 7th and 8th Postal Zones

DEMOCRATIC LANDSLIDE SWEEPS COUNTRY; REPUBLICANS MAY LOSE CONGRESS CONTROL; ROOSEVELT WINNER BY MORE THAN 700,000

WETS GAIN IN HOUSE

Win 32 Seats and Lose None; Hold Senate Places.

AIDED BY ILLINOIS SWEEP

Also Helped by Victory of Bulkley in Ohio— Drys Win in Places.

THREE REFERENDA GO WET

Repeal Proposals Are Carried in Rhode Island, Illinois and Massachusetts.

Forces favoring repeal of the Eighteenth Amendment and liquor laws scored gains in the Congressional elections throughout the country yesterday, adding to these victories substantial majorities in favor of repeal referenda in Illinois, Rhode Island and Massachusetts.

On the basis of returns late last night, the so-called "wet bloc" in the House had picked up thirty new votes to add to the ninety-one which the most optimistic of the wets count in the present House.

The Senate wets had picked up several new names, of such imminence as Morrow of New Jersey, Lewis of Illinois and Bulkley of Ohio, but were battling to hold the number of eighteen in the present make-up of the Senate, because of retirements of sitting wet members from States where only dry candidates sought their seats.

Marcus Coolidge of Massachusetts was running well ahead of his dry opponent, William M. Butler, overcoming a substantial lead early in the night.

Results of Referenda.

Wet candidates were carrying with them wet referenda in every State where they were offered. In Illinois the vote went decidedly in favor of repeal of the Eighteenth Amendment. Three proposals, one for repeal of the amendment, another for modification of the Volstead act and the other proposing repeal of the State enforcement act, all carried with good majorities, with the heaviest vote and the heaviest majority recorded on the first question.

Rhode Island registered a vote of more than 2 to 1 in favor of repeal. The vote in Massachusetts was on repeal of the State enforcement act and a majority in favor of the referendum was gaining in size as Marcus Coolidge increased his lead over the dry Butler.

In his landslide in Illinois Mr. Lewis evidently had swept a number of wet Democrats into office, and in Ohio the victory of Mr. Bulkley carried with it an increase in the wet representation of that State in the lower house by at least three. At least two wet gains in the House went with the Morrow victory in New Jersey, and seven apparently had been recorded in Pennsylvania, despite the victories of dry Senate and Gubernatorial candidates.

Many Dry Victories Recorded.

The wets had not actually lost a seat in either house on the face of returns up until early this morning, although dry victories had been scored in a number of States, including three in the South where prohibition figured conspicuously as an issue in the campaign.

The whole delegation in Connecticut, including Representative John Q. Tilson, Hoover spokesman and Republican leader in the House, will be listed among the wets in the next Congress. The only seat in doubt was in the First District, where C. W. Seymour, dry Republican, was pitted with A. Longergan, wet Democrat. Mr. Longergan led on the reports last night.

Four wet gains in New Jersey, including S. H. Person, who will occupy the seat held by Grant M. Hudson, former State Superintendent of the Anti-Saloon

Continued on Page Seven.

U. S. SENATORS ELECTED

REPUBLICANS—13.
Delaware......*D. O. Hastings
Idaho........*William E. Borah
Iowa.........†L. J. Dickinson
Kansas.......†Arthur Capper
Maine........*W. H. White Jr.
Michigan.....*James Couzens
Nebraska.....*George W. Norris
New Hampshire.*Henry W. Keyes
New Jersey...†Dwight W. Morrow
Oregon.......*Charles L. McNary
Pennsylvania.‡James J. Davis
Rhode Island.*J. H. Metcalf
Wyoming......†Robert D. Cary

DEMOCRATS—20.
Alabama......†J. H. Bankhead
Arkansas.....*J. T. Robinson
Colorado.....†E. P. Costigan
Georgia......*William J. Harris
Illinois.....†J. H. Lewis
Louisiana....*Huey P. Long
Massachusetts.†M. A. Coolidge
Minnesota....*Einar Hoidale
Mississippi..*Pat Harrison
Montana......*Thomas J. Walsh
New Mexico...*S. G. Bratton
North Carolina.†Josiah W. Bailey
Ohio.........‡Robert J. Bulkley
Oklahoma.....‡Thomas P. Gore
South Carolina.†James F. Byrnes
Tennessee....*William E. Brock
Tennessee....†Cordell Hull
Texas........*Morris Sheppard
Virginia.....*Carter Glass
West Virginia.†M. M. Neely

IN DOUBT—3.
Kansas
Kentucky
South Dakota

*Re-elected for full term ending March 3, 1937. †Elected for full term ending March 3, 1937. ‡Elected Nov. 3, 1930 for full term ending March 3, 1937. *Elected for short term ending March 3, 1931. *Elected for short term ending March 3, 1931.

LEWIS, DEMOCRAT, SWEEPS ILLINOIS

Out-and-Out Wet Piles Up 2 to 1 Lead Over Mrs. McCormick, Republican, for Senate.

AHEAD 3 TO 1 IN CHICAGO

Victor Breaks Even or Better in Strong Republican Counties Down-State.

Special to The New York Times.

CHICAGO, Nov. 4.—James Hamilton Lewis, Democrat, and an out-and-out wet, won in a landslide over Representative Ruth Hanna McCormick, Republican and "provisionally wet," in today's election of a Senator from Illinois.

After a campaign in which the Democrats stressed prohibition and prosperity, something of a seismic upheaval struck the rock-ribbed Republican State—the home of Lincoln, the first Republican President—and ex-Senator Lewis's plurality seems likely to approach 700,000. The politicians rate it the greatest blow against national prohibition thus far struck.

Incomplete returns at midnight indicated that the Democrats gained three Congressional seats from Cook County districts, two and possibly three seats down-State, and the two places as members of Congress-at-Large. Correspondingly, the complexion of the Illinois delegation to Washington had been changed by wet gains of eight or nine seats.

Figures from nearly half of the State show Mr. Lewis far in the lead both in Cook County, which includes Chicago, and down-State.

Goes Into Lead Down-State.

In Chicago he was running three to one ahead of Mrs. McCormick, the count indicating that his Chicago plurality will be around 425,000.

Mr. Lewis had 365,982 votes in 1,675 out of 3,009 city precincts; 15,400 in 80 other Cook County precincts, or 256,558 in 1,609 down-State precincts, or a total of 637,940 in 3,394 out of 7,109 precincts in the whole State. His plurality over these returns was 351,676 over Mrs. McCormick, whose vote was 126,724 in Cook County and 286,264 in the 3,394 precincts from all parts of the State. In the same number of districts, Mrs. Lottie Holman O'Neill, Independent Dry, polled 30,448 votes.

Mrs. McCormick seemed likely to

Continued on Page Two.

MORROW WINS EASILY

Majority of 100,000 In Jersey Senate Race Indicated.

PARTY LOSES IN HOUSE

Democrats Leading in Six Districts Nominally Republican.

TWO BOND ISSUES WINNING

Legislature Safely Republican —Anti-Prohibitionists Score Heavily.

Dwight W. Morrow, former Ambassador to Mexico, was leading by a wide margin his two Democratic opponents in his race for both the full and short terms for United States Senator from New Jersey early this morning as the returns were coming in from the 3,321 election districts. Voters in 2,052 districts gave Mr. Morrow 322,014 and Alexander D. Simpson, former State Senator from Hudson County, 227,837.

E. Bertram Mott, chairman of the Republican State Committee, said early this morning a conservative estimate of Mr. Morrow's majority would be 100,000. Republican leaders before the election had predicted a majority of 200,000.

Tabulation of returns from 729 districts showed that Mr. Morrow was leading Miss Thelma Parkinson, Smith College Graduate, in the race for the short term or vacancy caused by the resignation of Walter E. Edge to become Ambassador to France, by a vote of 108,972 to 65,524.

Returns from 1,090 out of 3,321 election districts showed two of the $100,000,000 bond issue proposals winning and one losing as follows: Highways, 83,653 against, 78,740 for; water supply, 78,343 against, 88,442 for, and institutional rehabilitation, 80,105 against and 84,956 for.

Democrats were leading in six districts for the House of Representatives in six districts nominally Republican, and that the State Legislature was overwhelmingly Republican.

Mr. Simpson, as candidate for the full term, and Miss Parkinson, as candidate for the short term, polled a surprisingly heavy vote in the early returns although they ran ahead in only three counties, Hudson, Democratic stronghold; Mercer and Middlesex. The Democrats were greatly encouraged by the early returns giving Mr. Simpson and Miss Parkinson leads in half a dozen counties. The leads for the Democratic candidates were accounted for by the fact that they came from industrial centres.

While Mercer, a strongly Republican county, gave Mr. Simpson and Miss Parkinson substantial leads in the early returns, the Republicans expected to see those margins dwindle with the tabulation of returns outside Trenton. The strength of the Democrats in Trenton is said to have been due to the unemployment problem which has been acute there for months.

Representative Mary T. Norton, vice chairman of the Democratic State Committee, conceded the election of Mr. Morrow at 1:25 o'clock this morning.

"Senator Simpson and Miss Thelma Parkinson waged an aggressive and clean battle," said Mrs. Norton. "The opposing forces, wealth and great publicity, supporting fine personality, were hard to overcome and the inevitable resulted. I wish Mr. Morrow every success."

Mrs. Norton Re-elected.

Mrs. Norton was re-elected to the House of Representatives from the Twelfth Congressional District. Fred A. Hartley, Republican, who defeated Paul Moore, Democrat, two years

Continued on Page Five.

Roosevelt Appraises Victory As Expression of Confidence

Governor Franklin D. Roosevelt, speaking over the radio after his re-election had been conceded last night, interpreted the vote he received as one of confidence.

"I want to say a few words to the people of this State tonight," he declared over stations WEAF and WJZ. "I am overwhelmed with gratitude for the vote of confidence you have given to my administration.

"I can only say that in the next two years I will bring all my ability to serve all of the citizens, regardless of party and regardless of locality, in the interest of a program of honest government."

NEW ENGLAND HIT BY DEMOCRATIC WAVE

Massachusetts Elects M. A. Coolidge, Wet, for Senator, and Ely for Governor.

CROSS WINS IN CONNECTICUT

Former Yale Dean Surprises by Victory—Metcalf Rhode Island Winner.

New England Results.

New England Democrats were victorious in two States. Their candidates for United States Senator and Governor, Marcus A. Coolidge and Joseph B. Ely, won in Massachusetts and their nominee for Governor of Connecticut, former Dean Wilbur L. Cross of Yale, was elected. The Republicans carried Rhode Island, New Hampshire and Vermont.

Special to The New York Times.

BOSTON, Nov. 4.—Democratic sweep in today's election which, while not extending into the Congressional fight in the sixteen districts, carried a wet Democrat into the United States Senatorship and the Governorship, by decisive margins.

With about two-thirds of the vote counted, it is estimated that former Senator William M. Butler, dry Republican candidate for the Senate, will be defeated by about 75,000 votes by Marcus A. Coolidge, the Democratic candidate. The same returns indicated the defeat of Governor Frank G. Allen, Republican, by 25,000 votes at the hands of Joseph P. Ely, Democrat.

The vote of 1,070 precincts out of the 1,850 in the State gave:

For Governor—Allen, 345,894; Ely, 365,630.

For Senator—Butler, 319,241; Coolidge, 389,432.

State Dry Act Repeal Carried.

At the same time it was indicated that the referendum for repeal of the "baby volstead act," as the State prohibition enforcement law is known, would be carried by more than 200,000.

The vote on the question from 886 precincts, exclusive of Boston, stood: For repeal, 304,951; against repeal, 186,550.

Led by Boston, the cities of the Commonwealth were largely instrumental in piling up the winning Democratic majority. The Boston vote alone, it was estimated, would have

Continued on Page Nine.

TUTTLE IS SWAMPED

Governor's Record Plurality Amazes His Own Party.

CARRIES TICKET WITH HIM

Lehman and Tremaine Re-elected—Bennett Also Victorious.

UP-STATE FOR ROOSEVELT

Sweep Exceeds Smith's Largest Plurality of 385,338—Lieutenant Governor Wins Easily.

Tables of the city and State votes on Pages 10 and 11.

In a Democratic landslide of unprecedented proportions, Governor Franklin D. Roosevelt was re-elected yesterday by a plurality of approximately 730,000 over Charles H. Tuttle, Republican nominee.

In his overwhelming victory, Governor Roosevelt carried with him Lieut. Gov. Herbert H. Lehman, Controller Morris S. Tremaine and John J. Bennett Jr., candidate for Attorney General, who also obtained large pluralities in New York City but ran far behind the Governor up-State.

Carroll carried Yates County over both Tuttle and Roosevelt and his vote cut heavily into the usual Republican vote in many up-State counties.

556,868 Plurality in City.

New York City gave Governor Roosevelt 556,868 plurality. The vote in the city for Governor was: Roosevelt, 926,665; Tuttle, 369,797; Louis Waldman, Socialist, 86,329, and Carroll, 5,885.

With 168 up-State election districts missing, 4,816 districts out of 4,976 gave Roosevelt, 826,662; Tuttle, 659,-163; Carroll, 158,323, an actual plurality for Roosevelt of 167,499 and an indicated up-State plurality of 174,160 and an indicated plurality in the entire State of 730,925. The up-State vote for Roosevelt in these 4,816 districts exceeded the combined vote for Tuttle and Carroll by 10,461.

Carroll's up-State vote was 158,322.

The tremendous vote for Governor Roosevelt was regarded as increasing greatly his chance for the Democratic nomination for President in 1932, for which he is known to be an aspirant. In rolling up his plurality, Governor Roosevelt reached a mark never before attained by any other candidate for State office. His plurality of 556,868 in New York City would have been a record if it had not been exceeded by the city plurality of Lieut. Gov. Lehman, which was 607,067.

The largest plurality ever received in the State by Alfred E. Smith and

Continued on Page Three.

Times Wide World Photo.
OVERWHELMINGLY RE-ELECTED.
Governor Franklin D. Roosevelt, Who, With His Entire Ticket, Is Returned to Office by a Record Plurality.

REPUBLICANS RETAIN CONTROL AT ALBANY

Hold Assembly by a Reduced Margin—Advantage in the Senate Cut to One Seat.

UP-STATE WETS VICTORIOUS

Drys Who Promised to Defeat Them Fail—Hofstadter Elected by 227 Votes.

Despite the landslide which resulted in the re-election of Governor Roosevelt by a towering majority, the Republicans will continue in control of both branches of the Legislature.

Late returns from the legislative elections give the Republicans continued control of both the Senate and Assembly, barring upsets on revised returns in some districts where the vote was close.

Final election returns received early this morning show that the Republicans failed to hold their own in the Senate elections. The 1931 Senate, accordingly, will be composed of twenty-six Republicans and twenty-five Democrats.

The Democrats made heavy inroads on the Republicans through the Assembly elections. In the present Assembly the Republicans hold eighty-six seats and the Democrats sixty-four. In the 1931 Assembly the Republicans will have eighty votes and the Democrats seventy, a gain of six votes for the Democrats and a corresponding loss for the Republicans.

The vote necessary to pass a bill in the Senate is twenty-six and in the Assembly seventy-six.

New York City thus will have only one Republican representative in the Senate and only two in the Assembly. In the present Assembly there are four Republican Assemblymen, all from Manhattan. In the 1931 Assembly there will be one from Manhattan, Abbot Lowe Moffat of the Fifteenth, and one from Brooklyn, Robert K. Story Jr. of the Seventeenth Kings District.

Mrs. Pratt Wins Close Race.

The Democratic landslide carried into office nearly all of the party's local candidates, such strong Republican candidates as Representative Ruth B. Pratt, Representative F. H. La Guardia and State Senator Samuel H. Hofstadter narrowly escaping defeat. The only upset was in Brooklyn where Robert K. Storey Jr., Republican, won against his Democratic rival for an Assembly seat. This was counterbalanced by the victory of D. H. Stephens, Democrat, who was elected to the Assembly in the Nineteenth Manhattan District.

This district, incidentally, is the one in which Martin J. Healy is Democratic leader. Mr. Healy is one of the central figures in the judiciary scandals upon which Mr. Tuttle largely based his fruitless campaign.

The election was one of the quietest in years, there being but few disturbances at the polling places. From the moment that the returns began to come in it was evident that the issue of judicial corruption and alleged bartering of judicial office would have no effect upon the Roosevelt vote. Nor did the driving rain which fell throughout the day keep

Continued on Page Four.

CITY GIVES GOVERNOR GREATEST PLURALITY

Has Margin of 556,868 as Graft Issue Fails Tuttle—Lehman Leads His Ticket.

MRS. PRATT WINS BY 651

La Guardia Victorious—Miller Elected Judge, Alger Loses— Bond Issue Carries.

Governor Roosevelt carried the city yesterday by the unprecedented plurality of 556,868 votes over his Republican rival, Charles H. Tuttle. His associates on the ticket also piled up huge pluralities over Republican opponents, that of Lieut. Gov. Lehman reaching the mark of 607,067.

The city's vote for Governor was:
Roosevelt 926,665
Tuttle 369,797
Waldman 86,329
Carroll 5,885

Governor Roosevelt's tremendous plurality, although far above the pre-election estimates of John P. Curry and other Democratic leaders, did not arouse the enthusiasm which has greeted the news of large pluralities in the past years. The early estimates were regarded as extremely conservative, the Democratic leaders having somewhat discounted the more optimistic reports which came from the district leaders.

Continued on Page Three.

STILL LEAD IN SENATE

But Republican Hold on House Hangs on Belated Returns.

SEE PRESAGE FOR 1932

Democrats Are Victorious in Nearly All the Chief Battles.

PINCHOT BEATS HEMPHILL

Election of Bulkley, a Wet, as Senator in Ohio Seems Indicated.

By RICHARD V. OULAHAN.

A distinct Democratic sweep, suggesting a landslide for that party, extended across the country in yesterday's elections, held in all the forty-eight States except Maine. While the outcome of a number of contests for important public offices is still in doubt, the Democrats were victorious in most of the outstanding battles from which definite returns have been received.

The general trend of these returns up to the time this edition of THE NEW YORK TIMES went to press furnished encouraging evidence to Democracy's leaders that the sentiment expressed at the polls throughout a widespread area presaged victory for their Presidential candidate in the elections of 1932.

Democratic Governors were elected in New York, Connecticut, Massachusetts, Rhode Island and Ohio, and in States normally Republican. In such States as Kansas, Minnesota, Nebraska, Oregon and Wyoming, where the Republicans win more often than not, the result is in doubt on account of the strong trend of Democratic sentiment.

Senate Lead Slender.

Judging by the latest returns, there is a bare chance that the nominal Republican majority in the Senate will be overthrown, although the prospect is that the Republicans may still have a slight excess of members over the Democrats. It is possible, however, that the next Senate will be a tie politically.

Democratic Senators have been elected in place of Republicans in Colorado, Minnesota, Ohio, Oklahoma, West Virginia and Massachusetts, and the chances favor a victory for the Republican Senatorial candidate in South Dakota. Only one Republican Senatorial aspirant has triumphed over a sitting Democratic Senator. This happened in Iowa.

In line with the general Democratic swing, the return showed that candidates of that party have cut heavily into the big Republican majority in the House of Representatives with a fair prospect that the Democrats will get control, though the actual outcome remains in doubt.

Based on the latest returns, the Senate line-up appears to be 45 Democrats, 47 Republicans and 1 Farmer-Laborite, with 3 contests doubtful. This line-up concedes the election of Hoidale, Democrat, over Senator Schall, Republican, in Minnesota.

Heavy Gains in House.

Heavy gains were made by the Democrats in the contest for 431 seats in the House of Representatives, but whether these will be sufficient to wipe out the present Republican majority is uncertain, with returns incomplete from approximately seventeen districts.

Results of Latest Figures.

Counting nine vacant seats which had been held by Republicans, the majority of that party in the present House is 103. The latest definite election returns give the Republicans 189 seats, the Democrats 200 and the Farmer-Labor party 1, with 44 in the doubtful column and 1 Independent Republican.

The Democrats have 105 members

Heflin Is Beaten in Alabama by Nearly 2 to 1; Democrats Defeat All Candidates on His Ticket

Special to The New York Times.

BIRMINGHAM, Ala., Nov. 4.—J. Thomas Heflin, senior Senator from Alabama, was defeated by the Democrats of the State today for his defection from the party in the 1928 Presidential election. With three-fourths of the vote counted, John H. Bankhead, his opponent, was leading by 46,607 votes out of a total of 211,627. The vote stood 128,817 for Bankhead and 82,810 for Heflin.

Senator Heflin was re-nominated for United States Senator and Hugh Merrill, for Lieutenant Governor, were routed in the same commanding lead over Hugh Locke and Dempsey Powell, "Jeffersonian" candidates running on the same ticket with Senator Heflin.

In a statement to The Montgomery Advertiser tonight Senator Heflin charged "fraud and corruption" in the election and said he would demand an investigation by the Senate Committee on Elections.

"While early returns indicate the vote is going against me, within two hours I will be 100,000 votes ahead."

Boxes which went overwhelmingly for Hoover in the 1928 election went just as strongly for the Democratic nominees today.

No serious political issues other than the election other than whether Alabama would remain in the Democratic column or would become an active two-party State.

"All the News That's Fit to Print."

The New York Times.

LATE CITY EDITION
THE WEATHER—Fair today and tomorrow; not much change in temperature.
Temperature yesterday—Max. 66, min. 47.
U. S. Weather Forecast—For details see Page 30.

Copyright, 1931, by The New York Times Company.

VOL. LXXX....No. 26,744.   ★ ★ ★ ★ ★   NEW YORK, WEDNESDAY, APRIL 15, 1931.   TWO CENTS In Greater New York | THREE CENTS Within 200 Miles | FOUR CENTS Elsewhere Except 7th and 8th Postal Zones

GOVERNOR REQUESTS MINUTES ON CRAIN; QUICK DECISION SEEN

Critics of Prosecutor Predict Early Action—Albany Denies Move Is Significant.

PATHE HEARING ON MONDAY

Seabury Moves to Wind Up the Inquiry May 1—Rothstein Case Is Taken Up.

KLEIN DATA TO PROSECUTOR

Harvey Rebuffed in Plea for Bribe Evidence—Hofstadter Summons Legislative Committee.

Developments yesterday in the investigations into city affairs were:

Governor Roosevelt called upon Samuel Seabury for the minutes of the public hearings on rackets in the removal proceedings against District Attorney Crain.

State Senator Hofstadter called a meeting of the legislative inquiry committee to be held here on Monday.

Controller Berry refused to give Borough President Harvey the transcript of evidence against Irving Klein, borough highway superintendent, to be used at a public hearing on bribery charge would be sent directly to the Queens District Attorney.

GOVERNOR ACTS ON CRAIN.

Governor Roosevelt wrote to Commissioner Samuel Seabury requesting a copy of the minutes of the public hearings in the removal proceedings against District Attorney Crain. The Governor took this step twenty-four hours after the elderly prosecutor confessed helplessness against racketeers, who, he said, infest the business structure of the city.

The Governor's letter, made public in Albany before it was issued to Mr. Seabury, caused considerable surprise, because it had been understood that the commissioner would make no report until he had concluded his investigation of the City Club's charges against Mr. Crain.

Considerable speculation arose immediately regarding the significance of the Governor's action. Critics of the District Attorney, pointing out that the Governor has power to remove Mr. Crain at any stage of the proceedings, were inclined to the belief that the Governor was anticipating a request from some civic body for immediate action.

Persons close to the Governor, however, insisted that his action was predicated only upon a desire to keep informed of the progress of the inquiry he set in motion in order to be able to act promptly when Mr. Seabury filed his report. The latter seemed to bear out this belief, for in it the Governor expressed the desire "to keep up with the matter currently."

Text of Governor's Letter.

The letter follows:
April 13, 1931.
My dear Judge Seabury:

If it is not inconsistent with the progress of your work as Commissioner representing the Governor in the matter of the District Attorney in New York, I would appreciate your sending me the copy of the minutes of the public hearings held up to the present time, and also of other public hearings as they may occur.

This will enable me to keep up with the matter currently.

Very truly yours,
FRANKLIN D. ROOSEVELT.

Crain Had Attacked Governor.

In closing his defense to the first phase of the charges against him—the allegation that he was lax in prosecuting racketeers in Fulton market, Mr. Crain said he would be able to function more effectively if he were not subjected to "attacks from the rear." Part of his helplessness against racketeers, he attributed to Governor Roosevelt's failure to request the Legislature in a special message to grant him the power to issue compulsory subpoenas and examine witnesses under oath.

Overshadowing all this, however, was Mr. Crain's admission that racketeers were virtually immune from punishment so far as he and the police were concerned, and his declaration that in his opinion the evidence of racketeering in Fulton Market adduced by John Kirkland Clark, counsel to Mr. Seabury, was not sufficient to warrant a resubmission of the case to a new grand jury.

Although the public hearings have been adjourned until next Monday, the private examination of witnesses

Continued on Page Twenty-seven.

Crowded Hours of a Busy Day In President Hoover's Life

Special to The New York Times.
WASHINGTON, April 14.—With two addresses, ten innings of an exciting American League game, a Cabinet meeting and a dinner tonight, President Hoover spent one of his busiest days since he entered the White House.

Here is the schedule of the chief events:

8:00 A. M.—Rises.
8:30 A. M.—Medicine ball.
8:45 A. M.—Breakfast.
9:30-10:15 A. M.—Brief conferences with callers.
11:00 A. M.—Cabinet meeting.
12:00 M.—Receives delegation of tourists.
12:30 P. M.—Speech at Pan-American Day celebration.
1:00 P. M.—Luncheon.
3:30 P. M.—Attends opening American League baseball game.
4:30 P. M.—Speaks by radio from White House to Tuskegee celebration.
8:00 P. M.—Dinner with Secretary of the Navy and Mrs. Adams.
11:00 P. M.—Retires.

The usual noon conference with newspaper men was omitted because of the other demands on the President's time.

BETHLEHEM BONUS GETS 72% OF PROXIES

Management Apparently Wins Approval for System That Paid Grace $1,625,753 in Year.

SCHWAB PARRIES CRITICS

Holds Practice Is an Incentive, and Says Board Voted Him $250,000 in 1930.

The Bethlehem Steel Corporation's bonus plan, under which officers received approximately $36,000,000 in fourteen years and which is being fought in the courts by a minority group, was apparently ratified overwhelmingly yesterday at the annual meeting of the stockholders in Newark.

While a restraining order by Vice Chancellor Backes in Trenton prohibited the stockholders from announcing the result of their vote or recording it pending a determination of the minority stockholders' suit, the management announced that it was voting proxies representing 72 per cent of the outstanding common and preferred stock of the Bethlehem Steel Corporation. So it was assumed that the management had won approval of the bonus system, which in one year added to the $12,000 salary of Eugene G. Grace, president, the sum of $1,625,753.

Schwab Backs System.

Responsibility for the bonus system of the corporation was assumed by Charles M. Schwab, chairman, who maintained that the additional sum to the management was not a "gratuity," which would be an insult, but rather "part payment" by the corporation for services.

With rapier-like swiftness the veteran chairman of Bethlehem parried thrusts so skillfully that even his opponents sometimes joined in the applause that greeted his repartee and his sallies.

His black eyes flashing and a smile of sureness playing around his lips, Mr. Schwab had a ready answer for William H. Gilman, director of the Jefferson County National Bank of Watertown, when he wanted to know why Mr. Grace, with his huge bonus, should have received for his services in the comparatively small body of stockholders of the corporation more than the President of the United States gets for his services to the people of the country.

"I appreciate your sincerity," said Mr. Schwab. "I only object to your comparison of Grace's salary to the President's. The United States Government is not a business enterprise, but I would give five times $75,000 a year to be President of the United States."

At one point of his address Mr. Schwab said that the bonus system as he had originated it for Bethlehem was designed not so much as a reward as an "incentive." He said that he had placed Mr. Grace "upon a pedestal," so that he would have to live up to his high position for the good of the corporation.

He asserted that he had learned the lesson of large rewards to produce large returns from his old employer and mentor, the late Andrew Carnegie, who said that it was necessary to make even the best big and act big to accomplish big things.

Mr. Schwab disclosed that for the first seven years after he organized Bethlehem Steel Corporation he had not only backed the undertaking with his entire fortune, as he later did through many crises, but that he had served as its head without compensation. He was answering the question he had heard people often ask: "What does C. M. get out of it?"

"I have been the highest paid man in the United States for a good many years," said Mr. Schwab. "Some years my compensation was in

Continued on Page Twenty.

4 AMERICANS KILLED IN SANDINO ADVANCE; WARSHIP LANDS MEN

Three Missing as Nicaraguan Rebels Near Puerto Cabezas After Jungle Skirmishes.

HEAVIER LOSSES FEARED

Fruit Company Hears Eleven Americans and Some British Employes Were Slain.

8 REBELS KILLED BY GUARD

25 Marines Board Gunboat Again When Patrols Return From Clash —300 Americans in Town.

Special to The New York Times.
WASHINGTON, April 14.—According to a report from the gunboat Asheville of the Special Service Squadron, which arrived this morning at Puerto Cabezas on the east coast of Nicaragua, preliminary skirmishes between rebel groups under Augusto Sandino, advancing toward the town, and National Guardsmen have in the past twenty-four hours resulted in four Americans being killed and three missing.

Their names were not given except for that of a Moravian missionary named Briggenser, who was said to have been killed at Musias. Other reports said six unnamed foreigners had been killed.

As rebel groups under Sandino, Pedron and Blandon moved through the jungle by way of the Coco River and the Pis-Pis Trail with threats to reach Puerto Cabezas "dead or alive," National Guard reinforcements also moved down the Coco River, the preliminary skirmishes resulting.

Gunboat Lands Men.

The fact that Sandino and his chieftains, who have long operated in the Northwestern Provinces of Nicaragua, were transferring their operations to the east coast, with Puerto Cabezas as their objective, thereby precipitating another serious problem for the government of President Moncada and the American naval forces and marines, was disclosed in reports received by the Navy Department today and made public by the State Department.

Simultaneously it was announced that the Asheville had arrived this morning at Puerto Cabezas from Panama and immediately landed forces which will remain until the Nicaraguan National Guard has arrived in sufficient strength to meet the emergency. Then the bluejackets and marines will be withdrawn and such Americans of the 300 in Puerto Cabezas and vicinity as desire to leave will be evacuated. These Americans are employes of the Standard Fruit and Steamship Company, which owns the Bragman's Bluff Lumber Company.

A disquieting circumstance is that rebels have interposed themselves between the National Guard detachment in the jungle and Puerto Cabezas.

Lieutenant Clyde Roy Darrah of the marines, who is in command of a detachment of the Guard, on contrary to unofficial reports yesterday, is alive but at last reports was surrounded by seventy-five rebels under Blandon.

Statement Issued.

The situation as outlined by the State Department today in the following statement:

"The commander of the Asheville, now at Puerto Cabezas, reports that all the Guards except one officer and a few men have left Puerto Cabezas in operations against the ban-

Continued on Page Fifteen.

Fire Wrecks the Bluecher Palace in Berlin; Just Bought for $1,800,000 for Our Embassy

Special Cable to The New York Times.
BERLIN, Wednesday, April 15.—The famous Bluecher Palace on Unter den Linden, which was recently bought by the United States for its embassy, was almost completely destroyed by fire during the night. The fire was under control early this morning.

BERLIN, April 14 (AP).—The right wing of the three-story Bluecher Palace was ablaze when the firemen arrived. Additional alarms emptied the firehouses and almost every piece of apparatus in the city was called out.

Despairing of saving the palace, firemen concentrated on saving nearby buildings.

The offices of the United States Commercial Attaché, which have been located in the palace for several months, were completely destroyed, but there were no known casualties.

The Bluecher Palace, one of the most imposing buildings in the heart of Berlin, was acquired by the American Government on Dec. 10 for about $1,800,000, after negotiations

with a Berlin real estate company that began last June, the real estate company acting in the transaction for Prince Bluecher, great-great-grandson of the Bluecher of Waterloo.

The Palace, adjoining the Brandenburger Gate, had about 120 rooms and occupied 65,000 square feet. Built in the eighteenth century, it was one of the historical landmarks in the German capital. The palace was presented to Marshal Bluecher, the "Marshal Vorwärts" of fame, by King Frederick William III in gratitude for his services in the defeat of Napoleon at Waterloo.

The palace figured prominently in the social life of the German capital under the Hohenzollerns, but after the World War it was converted into an office building.

At the time of the sale to the United States it was announced that the leases held by various tenants would not expire until the end of this year and that, with considerable remodeling to be done, the palace would not be ready for occupancy by our embassy until the middle of 1932.

Utah Woman Is First Chosen To the Presbyterian Assembly

Special to The New York Times.
PHILADELPHIA, April 14.—Election of Mrs. B. J. Silliman of Green River, Utah, as a commissioner to the Pennsylvania General Assembly was reported today to Presbyterian headquarters here.

Mrs. Silliman, a ruling elder from the Presbytery of Southern Utah, thus becomes the first woman in the United States to be recorded as a commissioner in the highest court of the denomination. Last year's General Assembly made women eligible to the ministry.

The General Assembly has a total membership of about 960, equally divided between ministers and ruling elders.

PAN-AMERICAN AMITY HAILED BY PRESIDENT

All Major Differences Will Be Settled by Conciliation and Arbitration, He Says.

TIES FOSTER AGREEMENT

Address Opens First Celebration of Pan-American Day Amid Banners of 21 Nations.

Special to The New York Times.
WASHINGTON, April 14.—The time is not far away when every major difference between the American republics will be settled by the orderly processes of conciliation and arbitration, President Hoover declared today at the first celebration of Pan-American Day. Speaking at the auditorium of the Pan American Union, the President was acclaimed by the diplomatic staffs of all the American republics, by official Washington and scores of others.

It was an inspiring sight within and without. Outside the flags of all the American republics stretched to the breeze. Throngs about were hundreds, unable to get into the building, who waited to witness the arrival and departure of the President. Because of the cherry blossoms in Potomac Park, Washington is crowded with visitors from all parts of the country.

At a ceremony in the gardens of the union, the standards of the twenty-one nations of the Pan American Union were presented to schools and colleges located in and near Washington. The presentation was made by the governing board of the union.

Appeals for Understanding.

The President took peace and good-will among the Americas as the theme of his address. He referred to his visit to many of the Central and South American nations when he was President-elect in 1928. That tour of the sister republics, he declared, had made a deep and lasting impression on him. His tour convinced that the twenty-one nations of the union have everything to gain by "keeping in close touch with one another and by developing that spirit of mutual confidence which has its roots in a reciprocal understanding of national aims and aspirations."

"The spirit of mutual helpfulness," the President added, "is the cornerstone of true Pan-Americanism."

It was near the close of his address that President Hoover pictured the bright future of the Americans—one of mediation, conciliation and arbitration, the full significance of which, he said, is not always realized. He pleaded for an unswerving determination to make the union of the American republics, as now expressed in the Pan American Union, an example to all the other nations of the world.

Secretary of State Stimson echoed the words of the President and said that the nations of the Western

Continued on Page Eighteen.

KING ALFONSO QUITS, SPAIN A REPUBLIC; ALCALA ZAMORA IS FIRST PRESIDENT; NATION ORDERLY UNDER MARTIAL LAW

BRITAIN TO WELCOME EXILE

Alfonso Is Regarded as Member of English Royal Family.

HIS WIFE IS KING'S COUSIN

Much of the Huge Fortune of Deposed Monarch Said to Be Safe in London.

REPUBLICANS TO QUIT PARIS

Members of New Cabinet Pack Belongings to Rush to Madrid —They See Huge Task.

By FERDINAND KUHN Jr.
Special Cable to The New York Times.
LONDON, April 14.—The royal family and the people of Britain are preparing tonight to receive Alfonso of Spain as the latest of royal exiles to find refuge on British soil.

The last of the Bourbons will, however, be an exile with a difference. Unlike Manoel of Portugal and George of Greece—two former kings who are now living in England—Alfonso is a member of the British royal family through his marriage to King George's first cousin. Although the plans are indefinite, there is every reason to believe Alfonso and his English queen will live here with the rank not only of former monarchs but of British royalties as well.

Royal Invitation Likely.

It is expected that King George and Queen Mary will first invite Alfonso to Windsor Castle, where he has been a frequent visitor and where he is enrolled as a voter in the town. Later he is expected to make a home of the imposing Spanish embassy on Belgrave Square where that most royal of all Ambassadors, Marqués de Merry del Val, today shut himself in against visitors in his grief at the fall of the throne.

No London house is better fitted to be a king's than the Belgrave Square mansion, only a few doors away from the equally stately home of Prince and Princess Arthur of Connaught. Alfonso and King George have been occasional guests there. As soon as it is decided that ex-King Alfonso is coming to Britain it is expected Marqués de Merry Del Val will offer the house to the fallen monarch, whose most devoted friend he has been for years.

British Royalty Concerned.

The British royal family was deeply concerned today by the news from Spain. A few weeks ago, when Alfonso left London, the King and Queen paid him the unusual tribute of going to the railroad station to see him off. Since the war years, when Alfonso alienated the affection of the British royal family by his German sympathies, there has been a complete transformation in the relations between the royal relatives in London.

For a few years after the armistice Alfonso seldom visited Buckingham Palace and stayed at Claridge's Hotel. Now, however, his popularity at the palace is greater than ever and the sympathetic help of the British royal family surely will be extended to him in his exile here.

Although Alfonso has lost his throne, he still has a huge fortune. With a prudent eye for eventualities he has been quietly transferring securities and valuables outside of Spain, it is reported here, and much of the private wealth of the royal family has thus been safeguarded. Those who know him intimately say his private fortune is one of the largest in Europe. Much of this wealth, derived largely from investments in Spain, is now believed to be in England.

He has great business and financial ability and is known to have speculated profitably in almost every big

Continued on Page Three.

KING ALFONSO XIII.
Photo by Van Dyck.

WASHINGTON ENVOY OF SPAIN TO RESIGN

Diplomatic Circles Fear Era of Chaos—State Department Awaits Official Report.

BIG CREDIT NOT WITHDRAWN

$60,000,000 Loan to Bank of Spain May Still Be Used, Say New York Financiers.

Special to The New York Times.
WASHINGTON, April 14.—The Spanish Embassy was stunned by the abdication of King Alfonso XIII today. Although, in the absence of any official information from Madrid, it declined to make any statement, there appeared to be no doubt that Señor Don Alejandro Padilla y Bell, who has been Ambassador since Oct. 11, 1926, would resign.

The Ambassador felt the blow keenly today. Until as late as this afternoon he believed everything was quiet and that the throne was in no danger. The King's loss of his throne will be even more heartbreaking to the veteran diplomat than the fact that he is to be succeeded by a Republican as Ambassador. No one, not even Alfonso himself, has been a stauncher Monarchist than Marqués de Merry Del Val, whose brother was Papal Secretary of State for years and who has equally notable career as dean of London's diplomatic corps.

Ambassador Irwin B. Laughlin cabled from Madrid that King Alfonso had turned the government over to Niceto Alcala Zamora, Republican leader and Provisional President, and that Ministers for the Provisional Government had been named. He said that the King, with the royal family, was expected to leave Spain immediately.

Ambassador Laughlin said considerable excitement in Madrid attended the overturn of the government, but no violence of any consequence.

Although American officials would not discuss possibilities, in diplomatic circles fear was expressed that a period of disorder and even of chaos might result, should the authority of the army and the Church break down. Spaniards, it was asserted, are individualists, but a stable order has been maintained through the centrifugal force of the monarchy, with the army and the Church assisting.

Huge Credit Not Affected.

The status of the $60,000,000 eighteen-month credit extended last month to the Bank of Spain by an international banking group is not affected by the recent political developments in that country in the opinion of bankers who participated in the American portion of the credit. Pending a clearer view of the rapidly moving situation in Spain, no definite statement on the subject could be obtained yesterday from the offices of J. P. Morgan & Co. or the other American banks which sub-

Continued on Page Three.

CATALONIA TO STAY IN SPAIN AS STATE

Separatists Decide on Move After Announcing They Would Be Independent.

ROYALISTS YIELD EASILY

Colonel Macia Takes City Hall Without Resistance and Begins Emptying Jails.

By The Associated Press.
BARCELONA, Wednesday, April 15.—Francisco Macia, Provisional President of the Catalonian Republic, issued a declaration early today that Alfonso drew up and signed a proclamation to be issued tomorrow morning. It is neither an abdication nor a renunciation of the throne, as was first announced, but in effect a statement that the King is leaving Spain for the present to avoid bloodshed while the provisional Republican Government holds elections to decide what the country wants. There is no doubt that tonight's demonstrations show the country wants a republic at the moment.

Monarch Clung to Throne.

With the aid of Melquiades Alvarez, the chief of the Constitutionalist party, Alfonso drew up and signed a proclamation to be issued tomorrow morning. It is neither an abdication nor a renunciation of the throne, as was first announced, but in effect a statement that the King is leaving Spain for the present to avoid bloodshed while the provisional Republican Government holds elections to decide what the country wants. There is no doubt that tonight's demonstrations show the country wants a republic at the moment.

Ousted Royalist Mayor.

Special Cable to The New York Times.
BARCELONA, April 14.—A Catalan Republic has been proclaimed.

The Municipal Councilors elected on Sunday took possession of the Hotel de Ville today and Colonel Francisco Macia, the Republican leader, took over the government of the province. The Municipal Council and the Provincial Council immediately proclaimed a Catalan Republic.

Colonel Macia is leader of the Catalan separatist movement. In 1927 he proclaimed a Catalan Republic from the Pyrenees and then was arrested by French authorities.

The military authorities of the Fortress Mont Julich have released a number of military prisoners who had been arrested for their Republican leanings. A popular demonstration followed their release, more than 3,000 persons forming a procession and escorting the liberated prisoners to the town hall.

Complete orders reigns thus far, although the carrying of Republican flags through the streets led to one or two minor skirmishes. The royal forces of Barcelona have put themselves under the orders of Colonel Macia. All public buildings are flying Republican flags alongside the Catalan colors, and it is generally hoped here that Colonel Macia will succeed in obtaining the chief points of his program—the political liberty of Catalonia, which would become a federal unit of the Spanish Republic.

No Resistance to Coup.

BARCELONA, April 14 (AP).—While thousands cheered for the republic and the end of the monarchy, Colonel Macia took possession of the City Hall today without force of arms and proclaimed the existence of a Spanish republic.

With the plaza packed with a shouting multitude, Colonel Macia, who was elected an Alderman in the Republican victories Sunday, came to the balcony and announced that

Continued on Page Four.

MONARCH SAILS ON CRUISER

Crown Prince Is With Him —Queen and Others to Go From Madrid Today.

KING BALKED AT ABDICATION

Left to Avert Bloodshed When Revolt Threatened, but Still Claimed Throne.

MOVE REGARDED AS FINAL

New Rulers Plan New Constitution, but Won't Hold Plebiscite on Monarchy.

By FRANK L. KLUCKHOHN.
MADRID, April 14.—King Alfonso XIII, the last of the Bourbons, yielded his throne today and Spain became a republic.

The monarchy, which had stood proudly for fifteen centuries with only one brief intermission, was toppled over in a few breathless hours this afternoon without a drop of bloodshed. The Republican Government, headed by Niceto Alcala Zamora as first President, is installed peacefully in Madrid and the Republican flag is flying everywhere in the country.

Through the blackness of this moonless night Alfonso, accompanied only by the Duke of Miranda, his majordomo and two Civil Guards, it is understood, is speeding toward Cartagena, where he will board a ship for Marseilles. The King left the palace by the garden gate and got out of Madrid before any one was aware of it.

An attempt was made to cloak the fact that he had left the palace and his destination is being kept as secret as possible. It was regarded as dangerous to allow him to go by way of Portugal because of the political disturbances there and equally dangerous for him to travel through Northern Spain, which has shown itself so unmistakably hostile.

Monarch Clung to Throne.

With the aid of Melquiades Alvarez, the chief of the Constitutionalist party, Alfonso drew up and signed a proclamation to be issued tomorrow morning. It is neither an abdication nor a renunciation of the throne, as was first announced, but in effect a statement that the King is leaving Spain for the present to avoid bloodshed while the provisional Republican Government holds elections to decide what the country wants. There is no doubt that tonight's demonstrations show the country wants a republic at the moment.

The passing of the most brilliant court left in Europe was typical of Republican simplicity. Miguel Maura walked into the office of the Minister of the Interior and said:

"There is no precedent for what I am going to do, so I shall merely say that I am taking control of this office."

With the other members of the government he immediately went into the Under-Secretary's office and waited while Señor Alcala Zamora signed the amnesty decree.

Government Gives Its Program.

The Provisional Government held a prolonged meeting tonight and started drawing up its program. Afterward it was announced that until a Cortes (Parliament) could be convoked it would proceed by decree.

In the next sentence was the first indication that Spain is not to have any further chance to revise her opinion as to the kind of government she wants. The Cortes, the government' announcement reads, will not discuss the question of monarchy or republic, but will merely draw up a new constitution for Spain.

The government then went on to declare it would begin an inquiry into why the Parliament of 1923 was dissolved to make way for the directorate and of all subsequent happenings. It will open an investigation into determine responsibilities.

The government makes public its decision to support the right of freedom of worship and belief. It will, it promises, do everything to protect personal liberty. It further declares that personal property in the land being guaranteed by law, there can be no expropriation except for public purposes. With regard, however, to the condition of the masses of the

Continued on Page Two.

The New York Times.

Copyright, 1931, by The New York Times Company.

VOL. LXXXI....No. 26,903. ★★★★+ NEW YORK, MONDAY, SEPTEMBER 21, 1931. TWO CENTS In New York City | THREE CENTS Within 200 Miles | FOUR CENTS Except 7th and 8th Postal Zones

NANKING WILL INVOKE KELLOGG PEACE PACT; NEW FIGHTING FEARED

Foreign Minister of China Says League Also Will Be Told of Japanese Acts.

MANCHURIANS PLAN BATTLE

Kirin Troops Expected to Attack Japanese Garrison—Harbin Reported Tense.

SOVIET TROOPS AT BORDER

Foreign Observers at Mukden Hold Japanese Military Deliberately Caused Incident.

By HALLETT ABEND.

Wireless to The New York Times.

NANKING, Sept. 20.—"Appropriate steps are being taken to apprise the League of Nations and the powers signatory to the Kellogg pact of the unwarranted actions of Japanese troops," C. T. Wang, Foreign Minister of the Nanking Government, declared in a statement this morning concerning the lodging of vigorous protests by the Nanking Government with the Japanese Government. Mr. Wang continued:

"The National Government is greatly exercised over the situation caused by the unprovoked attack of Japanese troops on Mukden and other cities in three eastern provinces."

Says Chinese Did Not Resist.

Mr. Wang's statement makes no reference to the Japanese charge that Chinese soldiers tried to damage the South Manchuria Railway north of Mukden, but says Japanese troops fired on Chinese soldiers encamped at Peitaying, that the Chinese withdrew without resisting and that the Japanese disarmed the Chinese and set the buildings afire.

Mr. Wang charges that simultaneously the Japanese bombarded the arsenal and the Peitaying camp, but while the arsenal was not damaged the camp's mortar depot was destroyed. The Nanking Foreign Minister also charges the Japanese fired upon and occupied all Chinese police stations inside and immediately outside Mukden and disarmed the policemen, seizes the wireless station, forcibly occupied all government offices and interrupted all electrical communications.

The Japanese Consulate at Nanking announces the transmission last night to Tokyo of the formal protest of the Nanking Foreign Office in regard to the occupation of Mukden by Japanese troops and a formal request that they immediately evacuate the city.

It is officially announced that seventy-one Chinese soldiers were killed in the clash incident to the occupation of Mukden. The number of Chinese wounded is not known. No civilians were killed. The total of the Japanese casualties was one soldier killed and two wounded.

Japanese officially stress the assertion that the magnitude of the incident was due to the extreme nervousness and tension existing in the Mukden area as a result of a long series of minor clashes and growing feeling on both sides of uneasiness and hostility, which resulted in the Japanese commanders taking the bit in their teeth and quickly extending the zone of operations without the knowledge or approval of the higher command.

More Fighting Expected.

Wireless to The New York Times.

MUKDEN, Sept. 20.—More fighting was expected tonight between Japanese and Chinese between Dairen and the Mukden area at those points where Chinese soldiers are quartered along the South Manchuria Railway zone. Now everything is peaceful everywhere, with the Japanese in control.

Chinese are looting in the international section of Mukden, which area in ordinary times is under Chinese control. The Japanese are taking steps to protect the area. Foreign opinion here is that the Japanese military were angry because the Nakamura affair was about to be closed diplomatically, so, according to all foreign observers here, the outbreak on Friday night was premeditated. A Japanese statement says:

"We were always prepared for an emergency, but we were surprised on the night of Sept. 18, when Chinese tried to blow up the South Manchuria Railway tracks and set off a Japanese garrison. The occupation in various cities and towns was necessary to protect everybody. The incident is unfortunate."

This morning Frank Sugden, a British subject, an engineer of the Peiping-Mukden Railway workshop, attempted to go to his office, which

Continued on Page Eight.

PERRIER. Imported French Sparkling Water. Now obtainable Everywhere.—Advt.

Byrd's Old Supply Ship Sails To Load Labrador Lime Shells

By The Canadian Press.

ST. JOHN'S, N. F., Sept. 20.—Carrying out plans of a company, financed largely by Newfoundland capital, to develop the natural resources of Labrador, the steamer Eleanor Bolling sailed yesterday with fifty men and necessary machinery to take marine shell from Hamilton Inlet.

The Eleanor Bolling, once supply ship of the Byrd Antarctic expedition, is one of several vessels chartered to convey cargoes to St. John's, where equipment for screening the product and preparing it for market has been installed.

The sun-bleached shell deposits, which have lain on the foreshore of Hamilton Inlet for ages, are said to be almost 100 per cent lime, valuable for poultry feeding and horticultural purposes. First shipments are expected early in October.

WALKER BACK TODAY, BUT WANTS NO 'FUSS'

Elaborate Reception Vetoed— He Will Stay Aboard Ship Until It Reaches Pier.

HE PHILOSOPHIZES ON LINER

One 'Must Laugh on the Stage of Politics No Matter What the Sadness Within,' He Remarks.

Having been widely fêted, dined and honored in Europe, Mayor Walker will return to New York today on the North German Lloyd liner Bremen, on which he sailed for a month's "rest cure" in Germany on Aug. 4.

His return, in so far as reception plans and organized welcome are concerned, will be quiet. Charles F. Kerrigan, Assistant Mayor, said yesterday. Mr. Kerrigan, Thomas F. McAndrews, the Mayor's secretary, and Police Commissioner Mulrooney will go down the harbor in a revenue cutter and board the Bremen at Quarantine.

The receiving tug Macom, the city's official craft for the reception of distinguished visitors and homecomers, will not be used. Mayor Walker will remain aboard the Bremen until she docks at Pier 4 at the foot of Fifty-eighth Street, Brooklyn, probably between 8 and 9 P. M.

May Speak Over Radio.

There he will be met by Mrs. Walker and probably by a group of friends and city officials and he will go from the pier to his home at 6 St. Luke's Place. Mr. Kerrigan said there had been some talk of having the Mayor make a short statement over the radio from the pier. While no definite plans have been made, he felt that if the microphone were installed on the pier the Mayor would make a short speech.

In the Mayor's party and returning with him are Dudley Field Malone, former Collector of the Port of New York, and Dr. William Schroeder Jr., chairman of the Department of Sanitation and the Mayor's personal physician.

It was the Mayor's own wish that his homecoming be without "fuss" or noisy reception. Plans had been made for a demonstration, with a parade, a luncheon for dinner and other details, but the Mayor, by long-distance telephone from London, was understood to have vetoed it.

It is understood that his decision was influenced by the many receptions, dinners and celebrations with which he was met in Germany, creating a spirit more festive than restful, which followed him through Europe.

Feted in Many Cities.

After a short stop in Southampton on Aug. 10 the Mayor landed in Bremen the following day and was the guest at a reception in his honor. The next day he proceeded to Berlin, where he spent several days. While there he visited the Baroness von Huenefeld, mother of the late Baron von Huenefeld, who crossed the Atlantic Ocean in the plane Bremen in 1929.

Among the German watering places he visited were Carlsbad and Marienbad. He went to Pilsen, Budapest, Vienna, Cannes, Monaco and Monte Carlo, everywhere seeking rest and finding that his mere presence prevented it. In Paris he was entertained at luncheon by President Doumer of France and was made a Commander of the Legion of Honor. In London he was the luncheon guest of Premier Ramsay MacDonald.

In Berlin he made a tour of the night resorts within a few hours after his arrival. The next day he was the luncheon guest of the Carl Schurz Association, and the next night, over a radio hook-up by which he was heard in Europe and the United States, he made a speech in praise of the spirit of determination to pre-

Continued on Page Five.

PRESIDENT DEPARTS TO ADDRESS LEGION AT DETROIT ON BONUS

He Boards Special Train at Martinsburg, W. Va., After Day at Rapidan Camp.

TO WARN OF HEAVY COST

Washington Thinks He May Touch Also on Economic Situation in Europe.

LEGION COMMANDER FIRM

O'Neil Warns Against Cash-Payment Demands and Hints Danger in Prohibition Stand.

From a Staff Correspondent of The New York Times.

MARTINSBURG, W. Va., Sept. 20.—President Hoover left here on a special train at 8:30 o'clock this evening for Detroit where he will deliver an address tomorrow before the national convention of the American Legion.

The President spent the day at his Rapidan camp in Virginia working on his address, which he will deliver at noon tomorrow, but it was not completed when he left here. There were showers throughout the day, and the President remained indoors most of the time.

The President motored from his Rapidan camp to Martinsburg through Sherryville and Winchester. The last twenty-five miles of the trip were made at the slow speed of twenty-two miles an hour so that the President would arrive just before his train was scheduled to leave. As a result, a long line of automobiles which were not permitted by Secret Service men to pass the President's car trailed after it, and there was a wild blowing of horns.

At Martinsburg about 2,000 people were on hand to greet the President and he was called upon for a speech. He waved his hat, but would not make an address.

Accompanying the President are Captain Train and Colonel Hodges, his naval and military aides, and Secretaries Joslin and Richey, Governor Leslie of Indiana and Mrs. Leslie, who were his guests at the camp, will also accompany the President as far as Indianapolis.

Capital Speculates on Speech.

Special to The New York Times.

WASHINGTON, Sept. 20.—With President Hoover on his way to Detroit tonight to address the national convention of the American Legion tomorrow, speculation continues here as to whether there were several compelling motives for the President's sudden decision to attend the convention, after he had made it plain only a few days previously that he would be unable to do so.

There is unanimity of opinion that the President's chief purpose is to set the great power and authority of his influence which comes from his high office against the movements that are gaining public importance other than the bonus, with a rather widespread inclination to surmise that he would take occasion to sketch economic and financial conditions abroad with their effect on the United States.

Those best informed as to the Administration's attitude

Continued on Page Four.

Most Severe Quake Since 1924 Rocks Tokyo; Slipping of Strata Alarms Indiana and Ohio

Special Cable to The New York Times.

TOKYO, Monday, Sept. 21.—The worst earthquake since January, 1924, rocked Tokyo houses violently at 11:53 A. M. today, causing much alarm but apparently little damage. A second and milder shock occurred at 11:58 A. M.

Special to The New York Times.

CINCINNATI, Ohio, Sept. 20.—Earthquake shocks rocked Cincinnati and the surrounding territory shortly after 6 o'clock last night. The shocks were general, reports coming in from every part of Cincinnati—its suburbs. They were felt extensively on the Kentucky side of the river and in a number of up-State, Indiana and Kentucky cities.

No damage was reported here although large buildings were rocked on their foundations, some as much as three inches.

In Mount Adams some residents

became alarmed and rushed into their cellars.

The exact time of the tremors was variously reported from 6:06 to 6:10 o'clock. The shocks, half a dozen or more, lasted less than a minute.

CHICAGO, Sept. 20 (AP).—The earth's surface in parts of Indiana and Ohio did a little readjusting of its own today, but beyond momentarily frightening a few residents, damage was slight.

The disturbance, according to Federal geologists here, was caused by the slipping of strata under the earth's surface.

SIDNEY, Ohio, Sept. 20 (AP).—The Methodist and Lutheran churches, the high school and virtually every house in the village of Anna, Shelby County, were damaged badly by the earthquake today. Authorities said the total damage would exceed $10,000.

NEW YORK BANKERS CONFER

See No Need for Drastic Action — Investments in London Moderate.

RECENT LOANS PROTECTED

Federal Reserve Can Demand Gold—Morgan Credit Payable in Dollars.

EFFECT ON PRICES FEARED

Britain's Action Also Expected to Have Repercussions on World Credit Situation.

American security markets will not follow the lead of the London Stock Exchange, but will be open for business as usual today. No emergency has developed here to warrant any action similar to that in the foreign countries, it was stated authoritatively last night.

New York bankers held informal conferences here yesterday, at which the new London crisis was discussed, but no concerted action seemed to them to be called for, it was said. The bankers were in communication with British banking authorities by transatlantic telephone.

According to a competent authority, the short-term balances of American banks in London do not exceed $50,000,000, while Great Britain's external obligations in this country, exclusive of the $125,000,000 credit recently granted by the Federal Reserve banks to the Bank of England and the $200,000,000 private banking credit to the British Treasury, do not exceed $500,700,000.

No further supporting measures will be taken to defend the pound sterling at this time, it was stated. The private banking credit which was opened on Aug. 28 last, while not yet actually used up, will be exhausted shortly with the taking up of forward commitments made by British banking authorities in their recent attempts to bolster the pound.

Banker Sums Up Situation.

The British financial difficulties, as they are understood here, were summed up last night by an important international banker as follows:

The emergency measures taken by the British Government to check the heavy outflow of gold from London will undoubtedly occasion widespread surprise here, although the steps to be taken are by no means unprecedented. During the early days of the Great War, it will be recalled, Great Britain suspended the Bank Act temporarily, and in 1920 sterling went as low as an exchange value of $3.20 as against parity of about $4.86¾. It was not until 1925 that the country returned officially to a gold basis.

The terms of the announcement by the British authorities make it clear that the suspension of gold payments by the Bank of England is a temporary measure and in no way affects the obligation of the British Government to meet in gold such obligations as it may have outstanding in foreign currencies. Undoubtedly the government had a

Continued on Page Two.

GREAT BRITAIN SUSPENDS GOLD PAYMENTS TODAY; CLOSES STOCK EXCHANGE, DISCOUNT RATE UP TO 6%; GERMAN BOERSES SHUT, STOCK MARKET HERE OPEN

The British Government's Statement

Special Cable to The New York Times.

LONDON, Sept. 20.—This is the statement issued by the government tonight, announcing suspension of the law requiring that the Bank of England sell gold at a fixed price:

His Majesty's Government have decided after consultation with the Bank of England that it has become necessary to suspend for the time being the operation of Subsection 2, Section 1, of the gold standard act of 1925, which requires the Bank to sell gold at a fixed price.

A bill for this purpose will be introduced immediately, and it is the intention of His Majesty's Government to ask Parliament to pass it through all stages Monday, the 21st of September. In the meantime, the Bank of England has been authorized to proceed accordingly in anticipation of the action of Parliament.

The reasons which led to this decision are as follows:

Since the middle of July, funds amounting to more than £200,000,000 (about $1,000,000,00) have been withdrawn from the London market. The withdrawals have been met partly from gold and foreign currency held by the Bank of England, partly from proceeds of a credit of £50,000,000 (about $250,000,000), which shortly matures, secured by the Bank of England from New York and Paris and partly from proceeds of French and American credits amounting to £80,000,000 (about $400,000,000) recently obtained by the government.

During the last few days withdrawals of foreign balances have accelerated so sharply that His Majesty's Government felt that they were bound to take the above action.

This decision will, of course, not affect the obligations of His Majesty's Government or of the Bank of England which are payable in foreign currencies.

Gold holdings of the Bank of England amount to some £130,000,000 (about $650,000,000) and, having regard to contingencies which may have to be met, it is inadvisable to allow this reserve to be further reduced.

There will be no interruption of ordinary banking business. Banks will be opened as usual for the convenience of their customers, and there is no reason why sterling transactions should be affected in any way.

It has been arranged that the Stock Exchange shall not be opened on Monday, the day on which Parliament is passing the necessary legislation. This will not, however, interfere with the business of current settlement on the Stock Exchange, which will be carried through as usual.

His Majesty's Government have no reason to believe that the present difficulties are due to any substantial extent to the export of capital by British nationals. Undoubtedly the bulk of withdrawals has been for foreign accounts.

They desire, however, to repeat emphatically the warning given by the Chancellor of the Exchequer that any British citizen who increases the strain on exchanges by purchasing foreign securities himself, or is assisting others to do so, is deliberately adding to the country's difficulties.

The banks have undertaken to cooperate in restricting purchases by British citizens of foreign exchange except those required for the actual needs of trade or for meeting contracts, and should further measures prove to be advisable his Majesty's Government will not hesitate to take them.

His Majesty's Government have arrived at their decision with the greatest reluctance. But during the last few days international financial markets have become demoralized and were liquidating their sterling assets regardless of their intrinsic worth. In the circumstances there was no alternative but to protect the financial position of this country by the only means at our disposal.

His Majesty's Government are securing a balanced budget and the internal position of the country is sound. This position must be maintained. It is one thing to go off the gold standard with an unbalanced budget and uncontrolled inflation. It is quite another thing to take this measure, not because of internal financial difficulties but because of excessive withdrawals of borrowed capital.

The ultimate resources of this country are enormous and there is no doubt that the present exchange difficulties will prove only temporary.

Gold Standard Subsection to Be Suspended.

Subsection 2 of the British Gold Standard act of 1925, which is to be suspended, reads as follows:

The Bank of England shall be bound to sell to any person who makes demand in that behalf at the head office of the Bank during office hours of the Bank, and pay the purchase price in any legal tender, gold bullion at the price of £3 17s 10½d per ounce troy of gold of the standard of fineness prescribed for gold coin by the coinage act of 1870, but only in the form of bars containing approximately 400 ounces troy of fine gold.

EVENTUAL BENEFITS SEEN BY WASHINGTON

British Move Is Held Likely to Affect War Debts—Hoover Informed on Friday.

Special to The New York Times.

WASHINGTON, Sept. 20.—While government officials were unwilling to discuss formally the British financial crisis because of the delicacy of the situation, the announcement by the British government did not come as a surprise, as word had been received here as early as Friday that some drastic step was in contemplation.

While informally some experts referred to the present situation as the most serious since the world war, there was also expressed the opinion that as a long range proposition any move by Great Britain to put her financial house in order would have a salutary effect on world economic affairs.

It was reported here tonight that the White House dinner Friday evening attended by President Hoover and Secretaries Stimson, Mellon and Lamont was arranged after the President first obtained definite information of the step which Britain was contemplating.

Situation Thoroughly Discussed.

It is now understood that there was a thorough discussion at the dinner of the situation as it might affect financial interests of this country and that consideration also was given as to whether this government might be able to do anything to aid the British in facing the financial crisis. None of the officials has made known just what conclusions were reached at the dinner.

Whether the course to be followed by Great Britain would result in the ultimate revaluation of the pound sterling was a matter of considerable conjecture. In some quarters the belief was held that Great Britain would be compelled in the end to go on an "adjusted gold basis" which would in effect mean a stabilization of the pound at a lower level. One official also felt that Great Britain would find it difficult to keep her foreign obligations on a gold basis and handle her domestic financial affairs on another basis.

That any adjustments which Great Britain must make would require a

Continued on Page Two.

Canada "Proposes to Maintain" Gold Standard, Premier Says

By The Associated Press.

OTTAWA, Ont., Sept. 20.—R. B. Bennett, Prime Minister and Acting Minister of Finance, said tonight that Canada proposed to maintain the gold standard.

"What Great Britain may do is for the government of Great Britain to determine," said Mr. Bennett. "As for Canada, we propose to maintain the gold standard."

The Prime Minister added that he had nothing further to say on the matter.

GERMANY TO CLOSE ALL BOERSES TODAY

To Keep Them Shut Indefinitely if Need Be — Reichsbank Protected by Credit Truce.

By GUIDO ENDERIS.

Special Cable to The New York Times.

BERLIN, Sept. 20.—The news that the Bank of England had announced the suspension of gold payments, effective tomorrow, struck Berlin banking and Boerse circles as a bolt from the blue and left leading financiers completely nonplused as to its possible repercussions on the German financial situation.

It was uniformly asserted, however, that the Reichsbank's position was not affected as it was amply protected for the time being through the ratification of the "standstill" agreement on short-term credits.

Pending further developments in London, the German Boerses will remain closed tomorrow and, if necessary, indefinitely thereafter, in keeping with the conclusions reached late today between bank and Boerse leaders and official quarters, as it was commonly feared that the shock resulting from London's procedure would have a devastating reaction upon the German stock markets.

A preponderant number of Berlin bankers incline to the view that the London move will result in a run on the banks closed tomorrow and, if necessary, indefinitely thereafter, in keeping with the conclusions reached late today between bank and Boerse leaders and official quarters, as it was commonly feared that the shock resulting from London's procedure would have a devastating reaction upon the German stock markets.

A preponderant number of Berlin bankers incline to the view that the London move will result in a run on the Bank of England's action was an S O S to all capitalistic countries, warning them that the existing currency system was in imminent danger and that the present dislocation

Continued on Page Two.

PARLIAMENT TO BACK MOVE

Cabinet Is Unanimous in Decision to End the Drain on Gold.

KING TO SIGN BILL TONIGHT.

London Hopes Drastic Measure Will Not Be Necessary More Than Six Months.

MacDONALD EXPLAINS STEP.

Government Says Withdrawals of Funds Since July Forced Its Action.

By CHARLES A. SELDEN.

Special Cable to The New York Times.

LONDON, Sept. 20.—Great Britain will go off the gold standard tomorrow. Legislation amending the existing financial laws to that effect will be rushed through Parliament in the course of the day and will receive the King's royal assent tomorrow night.

To accomplish this, the new National Government, which is responsible for this drastic step, is assured of the necessary majority in the House of Commons to pass the measure through all its Parliamentary stages in one sitting. The House of Lords, which ordinarily does not sit on Mondays, has been summoned for an emergency session to take the required concurrent action.

Bank of England Approves.

A unanimous decision to abandon the gold standard was reached at an emergency session of Premier MacDonald's Cabinet today after consultation with the Bank of England, which agreed it was the only thing to do.

The Bank of England will raise the discount rate to 6 per cent from 4½ per cent.

The London Stock Exchange and all provincial exchanges will be closed for the day.

Although there is no suggestion in the government statement as to how long this state of affairs will continue the official announcement implies it will be only temporary by saying the suspension is "for the time being."

The expectation, or at least the hope, is that it will last only six months in which that period the country manages to balance its international trade as well as its budget.

It was hoped this shock to British government finance would be averted by the chance in government a month ago with the subsequent achievement of balancing the budget and cutting down government expenses, but it is evident now that the change was too long delayed.

Blow Was Long Impending.

The present blow has been impending a long time. Now that it has fallen, the situation is explained as due both to international and domestic causes. The foreign factors involved, according to the British appraisal of the situation, have been the hoarding of gold by the United States and France and the recent drain on sterling because of the financial difficulties of other countries.

Diminished confidence in the stability of the pound was also too far to be entirely corrected by the recent change in government and by the effect of big loans from New York and Paris. The recent "pay cut mutiny" in the British navy also was one of the ruinous causes of the cumulative effect, which is today's decision to abandon the gold standard.

Also England put a terrific strain on herself six years ago by returning to the gold standard as part of her post-war financial policy and by her whole attitude toward the payment of her war debts. Of all countries on this side of the Atlantic which participated in the war, England is the only one which has not cut the value of its currency. Great Britain alone returned to the pre-war gold parity of its currency while France divided the franc by five.

Plus all the international strain, England has been attempting to carry on at the same time a most expensive experiment in socialism, which, with its enormous cost of unemployment insurance, caused the downfall of the Labor Government just a month ago.

Although the British public do not

Continued on Page Two.

GENEVA IS SHOCKED BY CRISIS IN LONDON

High French Official There Says Paris and America Must Aid the Pound.

By CLARENCE K. STREIT.

Special Cable to The New York Times.

GENEVA, Sept. 20.—The news that the Bank of England tomorrow will go off the gold standard and that the London Stock Exchange will not open came as a shock to the few in Geneva who learned of it late tonight.

"If ever there was a time when the United States and France needed to work together it is now," was the incisive comment of a high French official. "Together we can and must support the pound sterling."

Told of reports from Basle that the British development probably meant the loss in value of sterling by a third, Frenchmen here expressed surprise bordering on consternation and obviously felt every effort ought to be made to avoid this.

It was stressed in the French delegation to the League of Nations that Minister of Finance Flandin had gone last night to Paris, where he had been conversing with officers of the Bank of England. The results of the conversations were not known in the delegation, but M. Flandin was expected back here tomorrow. Whether this meant that a move through Geneva was likely now was unwilling to predict.

In the British delegation the gravity of the situation was indicated by the tenor of voices where it was not indicated by the words used. The British stressed that their financial expert, Sir Arthur Salter, did not believe the situation would really turn out as tragically as laymen assumed to fear.

Though admitting that in such unprecedented matters incalculable factors may play a deciding role, the British seemed inclined to think that "in view of the nervousness of foreigners, who are withdrawing their money from London," the trouble had come to a head sooner than it would otherwise and that it was better that it came sooner than later. Hope was somewhat warmly expressed that everything would be all right in a few days if every one kept his head.

The reports that Sir Arthur Salter

Continued on Page Two.

The New York Times.

Copyright, 1932, by The New York Times Company.

VOL. LXXXI....No. 27,066. ★★★★★ + NEW YORK, WEDNESDAY, MARCH 2, 1932. TWO CENTS In New York City | THREE CENTS Within 200 Miles | FOUR CENTS Elsewhere Except 7th and 8th Postal Zones

JAPANESE ROUTING CHINESE IN FIERCE SHANGHAI BATTLE; DEATH TOLL EXCEEDS 2,000

WHOLE CHINESE LINE FLEES

Pressure From North of Fresh Japanese Troops Forces Quick Move.

PURSUERS LEFT BEHIND

Tachang, Miaoshin and Chapei Fall Before Advance Made Behind Smoke Screen.

TRUCE EXPECTED AT ONCE

Chinese Are Stunned by Sudden Blow—Say Retreat Meets Terms of Japanese.

By HALLETT ABEND
Wireless to THE NEW YORK TIMES.

SHANGHAI, Wednesday, March 2.—The Chinese were routed this morning by the Japanese in the most sanguinary battle since the World War.

The Japanese killed and wounded before 10 o'clock admittedly exceeded 350. Yesterday's advance in this region totaled two kilometers (more than a mile) and the Japanese losses up to midnight officially were admitted to be slightly in excess of 300 killed and wounded, while the bodies of 1,800 Chinese soldiers were discovered this morning on the ground won yesterday.

Brief reports from General Kenkichi Ueda's headquarters report that the Chinese retreat is degenerating into an utter, panicky rout and the rapid Japanese advance is finding difficulty in maintaining contact with the fast fleeing Chinese soldiers.

The pall of smoke from burning Chinese villages and towns was thickening over Shanghai. Immense exultation was manifested in Japanese circles and in those stunned by the suddenness and magnitude of the military disaster. The Japanese captured Tachang at 12:30 today.

Chinese in Pell Mell Retreat.

Early this afternoon the Japanese forces were rapidly approaching from beyond Taching and the Chinese were in pellmell retreat. There was great confusion at Nantao, where Chinese soldiers were attempting to evacuate in railway trains for Hangchow.

The Nineteenth Route Army which has voluntarily withdrawn from Chapei, is abandoning other fronts and concentrating at Chenju, according to official oral notification by the secretary of Mayor Wu Te-chen to United States Consul General Edwin S. Cunningham in his capacity as senior consul.

This withdrawal, the official notification said, also means the evacuation of all Chinese soldiers from Nantao and Lunghua, but Mr. Cunningham was assured there was near 2,000 regular police and 500 picked volunteers already have taken over the maintenance of law and order. It is understood that Chinese will not attempt to hold Chapei, declaring "that is dependent upon the Japanese."

Truce Expected Soon.

Presumably the crumpling of the Nineteenth Route Army will be quickly followed by the signing of a truce and by further retirement of the Chinese forces, since Chenju is inside the twenty-kilometer zone which the Japanese insist must be evacuated.

Between 7:30 and 10 o'clock this morning the Japanese had pushed forward to within two kilometers of Tachang. A vast area was being bombed and shelled with unparalleled intensity and the region was dimmed with smoke from huge conflagrations.

The Chinese began the day's hostilities by using two batteries of big guns, firing from Chapei into the Japanese naval headquarters area in Hongkew Park, where many large fires are now burning. For an hour and a half the Chinese batteries kept the city rocking and the roar of their detonations made sleep impossible. The Japanese had made exceedingly important gains at 10 o'clock when they took Tachang, although the terrain is even more difficult than around Kiangwan, with a multitude of vertical banked creeks and sloughs.

Continued on Page Twelve.

Settlement Stores Reopen And Shoppers Flock to Them

Special Cable to THE NEW YORK TIMES.

SHANGHAI, Wednesday, March 2.—Acting upon the request of General Tsai Ting-chai three of the largest Chinese-owned department stores on the Nanking Road of the International Settlement reopened today and many smaller stores and shops followed suit. This action contributed largely to a return to approximate normalcy in general business conditions.

SHANGHAI, March 1 (P).—Stores and offices in the International Settlement reopened today and bargain hunters turned out in droves.

The three big department stores were crowded with shoppers, but the service staff was considerably depleted. Many of the clerks used to live in Chapei and Hongkew and nobody knows where they are now.

JAPAN WILL OFFER NEW TRUCE TERMS

Accepts League Proposal for Armistice at Shanghai With Reservations.

CHINA AFFIRMS AGREEMENT

Plans for Special Assembly at Geneva Tomorrow Await Outcome of Negotiations.

By CLARENCE K. STREIT.
Special Cable to THE NEW YORK TIMES.

GENEVA, March 1.—Naotake Sato this evening gave Joseph Paul-Boncour, President of the League Council, Tokyo's definite acceptance of the latter's so-called "President's plan" for a Shanghai truce and a round-table discussion. Mr. Sato added that the "details"—which is to say, the truce—were to be worked out in Shanghai. Later he confirmed his oral communication in a brief note.

The note merely said Japan was "happy to accept the plan the President has submitted. It mentioned none of the reservations which Mr. Sato gave M. Paul-Boncour orally regarding the details of the truce to be settled on the spot, apparently because Japan thought the terms of the "President's plan" included such reservations.

At any rate, these reservations not merely still stand, but it is understood Mr. Sato explained to M. Paul-Boncour that Japan, instead of accepting Admiral Kelly's armistice terms, was making a counter-proposal.

The United States delegation preferred to reserve comment on Tokyo's reply.

Diplomatic Move Seen.

There is a suspicion in Chinese and Soviet circles that, if Japan does really accept the truce terms, she will then try to win through diplomacy what she failed to win on the battlefield by seeking to have the boundaries of the International Settlement at Shanghai extended to include some districts largely populated by Japanese. There is nothing, certainly, in either the "President's plan" or Mr. Sato's declaration yesterday to prevent such a maneuvre, for they bar merely any concession or move which exclusively favors the Japanese.

The wording of the second point of the president's plan" and the whole of Mr. Sato's declaration, especially the third point, appear to some to be designed to facilitate such a plan by their references to strengthening the international character of the Settlement.

The Chinese appear to regard the United States as the only one in the group on which they can count not to take advantage of the present situation to try to block China's old fight on the whole question of extraterritoriality.

New Settlement Status Hinted.

There is this some significant, although still vague, talk of the need of improving the status of the Shanghai International Settlement and possibly of putting it under League jurisdiction, like Danzig.

Although the skepticism here is pointed chiefly toward Japan, some are skeptical too of the Chinese Government being able to keep its troops up to the terms of the armistice.

Pending definite developments with regard to the armistice and the

Continued on Page Thirteen.

145 in House Force Vote on Dry Law Test; Texan, Last Signer, Rolls Up in Wheelchair

WASHINGTON, March 1.—An outright vote on whether the House shall consider a proposal to return liquor control to the States was assured today when the necessary 145 members had signed a petition to cite the Judiciary Committee for discharge from further study of the measure.

The vote probably will be taken on March 14, the first "discharge" day on the calendar.

The wets hailed it as the greatest day since prohibition when the last signature necessary was obtained soon after noon. The 145th member affixing his signature was Representative Mansfield, Texas Democrat. Mr. Mansfield, who is crippled, rolled up to the desk in his wheel chair, while Representative Blanton, Democrat, of Texas, a militant dry, was on his feet chiding the wets for their "failure" to get the required signatures.

The House was set into an uproar when at that moment it was found that Mr. Mansfield, from Mr. Blanton's own State, had made the "wet failure" a literal "howling success." Some observers were quick to remark that March 2 is the Independence Day of Texas, the anniversary of its Declaration of Independence from Mexico.

Representative La Guardia of New York, a wet, was taking Mr. Blanton to task for his remarks when the news was broadcast that Mr. Mansfield had signed.

"Any time that this House has the experience of seeing the distinguished gentleman from Texas (Mr. Blanton) get unduly excited," Mr. La

Continued on Page Two.

SALES TAX ACCEPTED BY ADMINISTRATION, MILLS ANNOUNCES

Secretary Pledges Cooperation on New Bill Despite Changes in Treasury Plan.

$625,000,000 NOW IS GOAL

Basis for Manufacturers' Levy Is Widened as Subcommittee Completes Draft.

Special to THE NEW YORK TIMES.

WASHINGTON, March 1.—Acceptance by the administration of the new tax measure, including a general sales tax applicable to practically every manufacturing industry in the country, was assured today by Secretary Mills.

Mr. Mills told a Ways and Means subcommittee that, even though the original treasury plan had been changed at nearly every major point, the administration would cooperate to the fullest extent in setting in motion and administering the new tax increases.

The subcommittee completed the new tax bill, excepting one or two minor administrative features, this afternoon.

The manufacturers' tax provisions, as agreed on, exempt only a few articles, chiefly commodities for the "poor man's breakfast table" and his daily paper, and the farmer's products, his magazines and periodicals.

The final meeting of the subcommittee resulted in a decision to recommend an even wider base for the manufacturers' levy. Yesterday the subcommittee tentatively agreed to frame the tax so as to produce around $550,000,000 in additional revenue. Today it decided to extend the scope so as to produce $625,000,000.

The additions to the sales tax base were understood to have been made by adding commodities which were being held "in reserve" for special excises.

Members of the subcommittee declined to discuss details, but it was the prevailing idea that gasoline and industrial alcohol had been included in their definition of "manufactured products."

If this is true, gasoline and industrial alcohol would be subject to the 2 per cent general tax instead of the special excise of one cent a gallon as proposed originally.

Agree on Excess Levies.

Final decision on the special excise levies was reached today. Committeemen likewise declined to discuss these, holding that to mention them would be to let loose an "avalanche" of protests on members of Congress. Other excises most prominently discussed in the discussions of the measure were a 5 to 10 per cent consumers' levy on electric energy and illuminating gas; a tax on oil, with a differential upward on oil imports, and an increase of 3 cents a share on stock transfers.

The bill probably will be presented to the full Ways and Means Committee tomorrow afternoon and may be offered to the House for action by Saturday night, according to Representative Crisp of Georgia, acting chairman.

Actual passage in the House by the end of next week is the confident hope of authors of the measure.

Representative Crisp, fatigued from his strenuous work on the bill, was buoyed in spirit today with the hope that it might even be introduced in the House tomorrow. He will offer the measure as soon as the Ways and Means Committee has agreed to it. It will then be referred back to the committee, which immediately will go through the routine of making a formal report.

Being a revenue bill, it will have priority in the House and, according to Mr. Crisp, he will call up 13 soon as possible for action. He mentioned next Tuesday as a

Continued on Page Four.

SENATE BODY ACTS FOR BROAD INQUIRY ON SHORT SELLING

Banking Committee Will Go Beyond Hoover Idea in Stock Exchange Investigation.

EFFECTS ON TRADE SOUGHT

Subcommittee Named to Go Into Long and Short Sales and Interstate Phase.

Special to THE NEW YORK TIMES.

WASHINGTON, March 1.—An investigation of the New York Stock Exchange was recommended today by the Senate Banking and Currency Committee. The investigation, headed by Senator Walcott, Republican, of Connecticut, immediately began drafting a resolution requesting authority for such an investigation from the Senate.

This subcommittee was instructed by the full committee to include in the resolution authorizations covering studies of both long and short selling, the effect of speculation on interstate commerce, the use of interstate communications systems by speculators and the value of a proposed stock transfer tax as a check on speculation.

This decision went far beyond the action believed to have been requested by President Hoover Friday when he called Senator Walcott to the White House for a conference on "bear raiding." No intimation of an investigation of trading other than short selling has come from the White House.

The subcommittee was chosen after an executive session, during which the committee members argued the constitutional right of the Senate to investigate the Stock Exchange.

The full committee finally agreed generally that such authority does exist, and the subcommittee, charged with considering this point in more detail, reached the same conclusion late this afternoon.

Regulation Not Contemplated Now.

Leading members of the full committee, including Senator Walcott, indicated that no regulatory measures affecting the Stock Exchange is contemplated at this time. The committee feels that if we can by investigation persuade the Stock Exchange to draw such regulations as will abolish bear raids, bull raids and dangerous pool operations, then we will have done the country good service.

"There is not a man on that committee who wants the Stock Exchange abolished. But we want to see what abuses exist. There is so much talk about the Exchange, and we are just as anxious to clear the Stock Exchange of any unwarranted misrepresentations as we are to uncover abuses in security dealings."

The subcommittee was appointed by Senator Norbeck, Republican, of North Dakota, chairman of the full committee, who named Senators Steiwer, Republican, of Oregon, and Bulkley, Democrat, of Ohio, to serve with Senator Walcott.

What sides were taken by committee members on the question of constitutionality was not revealed, but Senator Norbeck said that eventually "almost every member agreed there is authority under some provision or other." The principal point at issue was whether the Stock Exchange could be considered as engaging in interstate commerce or whether its business should be considered as confined to New York.

The committee's executive session

Continued on Page Thirteen.

LINDBERGH BABY KIDNAPPED FROM HOME OF PARENTS ON FARM NEAR PRINCETON; TAKEN FROM HIS CRIB; WIDE SEARCH ON

FOUR STATES JOIN HUNT

Wire Systems Flash Out Alarm on First Word of Kidnapping.

NEW YORK CAR IS SOUGHT

Roads Are Scoured for Pair Said to Have Inquired Way to the Lindbergh Home.

AUTOS STOPPED ON ROAD

Hunt Here Is Led by Mulrooney—Underworld Haunts Visited in Scores of Cities.

The Baby's Description.

HOPEWELL, N. J., Wednesday, March 2 (P).—A chubby, golden-haired boy closely resembling his famous father—that is the description given Charles Augustus Lindbergh Jr.

He is 20 months old, has blue eyes, curly hair, fair complexion. He is about normal size for a child his age. He has just begun to toddle and is learning to talk.

At 10:40 o'clock last night Colonel Charles A. Lindbergh telephoned the New Jersey State Police headquarters at Trenton that his son had been kidnapped from the Lindbergh home to Hopewell, N. J. Within ten minutes every communication method of modern science had been utilized to broadcast the alarm and to mobilize the police systems of four States and scores of communities in the search.

Colonel Lindbergh had scarcely poured out his tale when the vast machinery of cooperating police systems began to function. While one man was calling the State police barracks at Lambertville, N. J., ten miles from Hopewell, on the telephone, another was writing out this message to be flashed over the police teletype system:

"Colonel Lindbergh's baby kidnapped from Lindbergh home at Hopewell between 7:30 and 10 P. M., Boy, 19 months, dressed in sleeping suit. Search all cars."

Pair in Stolen Car Hunted.

Shortly before 1 o'clock this morning the Princeton Police Department sent over the network of wires the first message containing anything approaching a definite clue. It read as follows:

"Information received that two men in blue or black sedan bearing New York license plates stopped a man working on highway and asked to be directed to the Lindbergh home in Hopewell."

Relayed to every outpost, this message gave the searchers their first indication of the possible description of the kidnappers' car. It was so vague, however, that they did not permit it to stop them from questioning the occupants of cars of other descriptions.

As the first alarm was being typed out, the telephone connection with the Lambertville barracks had been established and Lieutenant Arthur Keaten, in command of that post, had been informed of the situation. With every man who could be spared, he started at once for Hopewell.

Upon their arrival Corporal Joseph Wolf, at Lieutenant Keaten's direction, telephoned back confirmation of the kidnapping, but he was not at that time able to add further details to the few which had been furnished by Colonel Lindbergh.

Meanwhile police detectives were sent on the rounds of known underworld haunts to see if they could pick up any clues as to the identity of the kidnappers.

Window Found Open.

An open window in the nursery of the Lindbergh home at Hopewell indicated how the kidnappers had gained entrance to the house. A close watch has been kept on the baby since it was born. No parent apparently no member of the family dreamed of the possibility of a kidnapping and no one remained in the nursery last night after the nurse had placed the child in his crib and made sure he was asleep.

The small force under Lieutenant Keaten at once began a careful search of the woody areas surrounding the Lindbergh home, on the possibility of uncovering some clue to the

Continued on Page Three.

The Lindbergh baby photographed a year ago. Left to right are Mrs. Dwight W. Morrow, the baby's grandmother; Mrs. Charles Cutter Long, the great-grandmother; Charles Augustus Lindbergh Jr., and Mrs. Charles A. Lindbergh, his mother.

KIDNAPPING OF BABY SPEEDS FEDERAL LAW

Demand in Capital for Statute Providing Death Penalty Expected to Increase.

OFFICIALS HINDERED NOW

Can Act in Almost Any Other Interstate Crime—Patterson Assails "Filthy Act."

Special to THE NEW YORK TIMES.

WASHINGTON, Wednesday, March 2.—Immediate pressure for early passage of the measure making kidnapping a Federal offense is held certain to be the result of the kidnapping of Colonel Lindbergh's son.

Senator Patterson of Missouri recently introduced a bill to this effect. It provides a death penalty. The measure would give authority to the government when the kidnapped person is removed from one State to another. The bill was approved unanimously two weeks ago by the Senate Judiciary Committee and its supporters are confident that it will be adopted by the Senate.

A companion bill introduced by Representative Cochran of Missouri, chairman of the Committee on Expenditures, has been before the Judiciary Committee in that branch for about ten days. The hearings were scheduled for completion soon and the pretests, before this morning's news, were for a favorable report.

Patterson Denounces Crime.

"It is a shock to me to hear of this outrage," said Mr. Patterson this morning when informed by THE NEW YORK TIMES. "I hope the child will soon be returned to its parents. This filthy act will add to the urgent need for the needed legislation, and I am sorry it will not be retroactive, so that the Lindbergh kidnappers can be dealt with by the Federal Government."

On Jan. 23 a telephone message was received by Senator Patterson from Chicago to the effect that there was a plot to kidnap General Charles G. Dawes, who had just been appointed president of the Reconstruction Finance Corporation. Mr. Patterson then said that this information came from a newspaper correspondent. It created excitement in official circles, although the General refused to take it seriously. However, it spurred the efforts of those behind the legislation.

Action Urged in Chicago.

As a result, when the House Judiciary Committee began hearings, Colonel Isham Randolph of Chicago, head of the "Secret Six" of that city, and former Representative Cleveland A. Newton of St. Louis came to Washington to urge early action. Mr. Newton gave the following list of kidnappings which he said had

Continued on Page Three.

FATHER SEARCHES GROUNDS FOR CHILD

Lindbergh and Troopers Hunt With Flashlights for Clues on Big Estate.

NEWS ROUSES COUNTRYSIDE

Hundreds of Autos Rush to Home in Lonely Woodland, Clogging Narrow Road.

Copyrighted, 1932, by The Associated Press.

HOPEWELL, N. J., Wednesday, March 2.—Charles Augustus Lindbergh Jr., 20-month-old son of the flying Colonel, was kidnapped last night from his nursery in the Lindbergh country home near here. The child, clad in a blue sleeping robe, was put to bed at the usual hour, 7:30 P. M. At about 10 P. M. someone peered into the nursery. The child was gone.

Beneath the nursery window, footprints showed in the soft earth. These indicated that the kidnappers, moving with such stealth that no one heard no sound, had removed their shoes before climbing a ladder to the window. The trail of the shoeless footprints was followed by The Associated Press reporter to the rutted lane, where police believe a waiting car was parked. Feminine footprints, as well as those of a man, were found.

Sixty feet away in rocky ground at the edge of a wood the nurse and Chief Williamson found a makeshift ladder. Its rungs were caked with mud. Colonel Lindbergh could not say whether it belonged on the premises. He thought it might have been left there by the builders while the house was being constructed during his flight to the Orient last Summer with Mrs. Lindbergh.

The searchers had no difficulty in following the footprints across the muddy ground. A second set of tracks joined them near the edge of the woods. They were much smaller. The two officers thought they might be those of a woman.

The search was interrupted by the arrival of a detachment of State troopers sent from the barracks at Lambertville and the hunt began anew. The tracks were followed to the main highway, about half a mile from the house, where they disappeared. The kidnappers evidently had entered an automobile at this point.

Lindbergh Aids Search.

Carrying a flashlight, Colonel Lindbergh stayed with the search in party until long after midnight. Once or twice he returned to the house, but he declined to discuss the kidnapping with newspapermen. Instead, he referred them to Major Schoeffel of the State Police, who told the story in detail.

"I hope you boys will help me,"

Continued on Page Three.

CHILD STOLEN IN EVENING

At 10 P. M. Nurse Finds Boy, 20 Months Old, Gone, in Nightrobe.

FOOTPRINTS IN THE ROOM

Muddy Trail Leads to Ladder in Wood and Half Mile to Highway, Where Car Waited.

WOMAN BELIEVED INVOLVED

Parents, Distraught, Guarded in Home—Police Deny Report of Ransom Note.

Charles Augustus Lindbergh Jr., 20-month-old son of Colonel and Mrs. Charles A. Lindbergh, was kidnapped between 8:30 and 10 o'clock last night from his crib in the nursery on the second floor of his parents' home at Hopewell, near Princeton, N. J.

Apparently the kidnapping was carried out either while Colonel and Mrs. Lindbergh were at dinner, or soon afterward. The baby's nurse, Miss Betty Gow, visited the nursery about 8:30 o'clock and found everything in order there. When she returned at 10 o'clock, however, the crib was empty.

Muddy footprints that trailed across the floor from the crib to an open window bore mute testimony as to how the baby had disappeared. "The baby's been kidnapped!" she shouted. Colonel Lindbergh raced to the nursery, followed closely by his wife. Mrs. Lindbergh recalled that earlier in the day she had tried to fasten a screen on the window that had been opened and had been unable to do so.

Satisfied that there was no mistake and that the baby actually was gone, Colonel Lindbergh telephoned Chief of Police Charles Williamson at Hopewell. Williamson drove to the house accompanied by another officer. Outside the door they met the Colonel. He was barehaded, and wearing an old black leather jacket such as he frequently wears on his flights.

Footprints Under Window.

Briefly he told Williamson what had occurred. The Chief telephoned first to State Police Headquarters at Trenton. Then his fellow officer and the Colonel began searching the grounds. Beneath the nursery window there was marks where a ladder had stood and the footprints of one person. There were no shoe print marks on the moccasins.

The kidnapper, apparently, had worn socks or moccasins.

Continued on Page Three.

"All the News That's Fit to Print."

The New York Times.

LATE CITY EDITION

WEATHER—Cloudy, probably rain today; tomorrow fair and warmer. Temperatures Yesterday—Max., 60; Min., 46.

Copyright, 1932, by The New York Times Company.

VOL. LXXXI....No. 27,138. ****+ NEW YORK, FRIDAY, MAY 13, 1932. TWO CENTS In New York City | THREE CENTS Within 200 Miles | FOUR CENTS Elsewhere Except 7th and 8th Postal Zone

WALKER GOT $26,535 BONDS FROM J. A. SISTO AS 'GIFT,' TAXI FINANCIER TESTIFIES

PROFIT IN A STOCK DEAL

Control Board Advocate Bought Shares to Aid Mayor, He Swears.

McKEON WAS INTERMEDIARY

Friend of Walker Says He Took Envelope to City Hall and Handed It Over in Auto.

HASTINGS GOT CAB PROFITS

Terminal Company Hired Him at $18,000 a Year, Seabury Is Told—Unpaid Loans Bared.

J. A. Sisto, who had a hand in financing the Parmelee Transportation Company, gave Mayor Walker bonds worth $26,535.51 before the Municipal Assembly passed the Mayor's bill creating a Board of Taxicab Control, the broker testified yesterday before the Hofstadter committee.

Both Mr. Sisto and John J. McKeon, who delivered the bonds to Mayor Walker in a sealed envelope in the Winter of 1929, demanded that the investigating committee cloak them with immunity before they would say a word about the matter.

Taxi Company Hired Hastings.

Just before Samuel Seabury, chief counsel to the committee, sprang this surprise, B. M. Seymour, vice president and general manager of the Terminal Cab Company, admitted that his company had paid $26,183 in salary to State Senator John A. Hastings, the Mayor's friend.

Colonel George W. Mixter of the firm of Day & Zimmerman testified that it was the Brooklyn Senator who got his company the job of making a traffic survey of New York in 1928. As a result of that survey, the witness said, Mayor Walker appointed a committee, with Frank P. Walsh as chairman, to study the problem of taxicab control.

That committee, of which Colonel Mixter was a member, reported in September, 1930, recommending a board of control, designed eventually to put the city's taxicab industry on a single-franchise basis, which was what the big companies wanted and the independents dreaded. Throughout the entire period of study, Colonel Mixter said, Senator Hastings was in frequent touch with Day & Zimmerman and the taxicab committee. He looked upon the Brooklyn Senator as the "Mayor's messenger or go-between."

More Hastings Loans Bared.

Senator Hastings had been under fire all day as Mr. Seabury sought to show that he had borrowed heavily from companies with which the three backers of the Jamaica Central Railways, an applicant for a Queens bus franchise, were associated, while that company's application was pending in the Board of Estimate.

Park A. Rowley, president of the Manhattan Company, admitted that Hastings had borrowed $7,500 and had not repaid it. William M. Greve, president of New York Investors, was the victim of a $25,000 "touch," which he said he would make good himself. H. P. Williams, chairman of the executive committee of the New York Title and Mortgage Company, admitted that loan agencies had forced him to recommend that Senator Hastings be excused from making good a collateral bond on a $350,000 mortgage because it was cheaper than to resort to litigation.

Throughout the whole proceeding, members of the Democratic minority, especially Assemblyman Louis A. Cuvillier, fought to protect the "dignity of the Senate," as represented in the person of the member from Kings County. Senator Samuel Hofstadter, chairman of the committee, repeatedly overruled their objections to the testimony, and it reached the point where the spectators were laughing every time Assemblyman Cuvillier addressed the chair.

But the court room was gravely sedate and silent, and even the minority dropped their fire of objections, when Mr. Sisto, a slim, grayhaired man, dressed as carefully as the Mayor himself, took the stand and unfolded his story.

He began by refusing to waive immunity.

Continued on Page Twelve.

MARSHALL HOUSE and THE EMERSON and Cottages, York Harbor, Maine. On the ocean, surf, salt bathing; concrete. Elevator. Fire sprinklers.—Advt.

Seabury Has a Prior Right To Explanation, Mayor Says

When Mayor Walker was informed at City Hall of the testimony of J. A. Sisto before the Hofstadter committee he broke in and said:

"I received $26,000 in bonds as the profit from that transaction—is that it?"

Informed that his statement was substantially correct, the Mayor parried questions with:

"Well, now, don't you think that Judge Seabury has a prior right to the answer to that question? I have nothing to say about it now, but it will be answered when Judge Seabury asks about it."

METROPOLITAN LISTS NEW AMERICAN OPERA

"Emperor Jones," Gruenberg's Setting of O'Neill Play, to Be Given in Berlin Also.

TIBBETT WILL SING ROLE

14th Native Work Under Gatti Regime Will Be Produced Early in Coming Season.

The Metropolitan Opera Association will present next season a new American opera, "Emperor Jones," based on Eugene O'Neill's play, by the American composer Louis Gruenberg, it became known yesterday.

The libretto has been prepared by Mr. Gruenberg himself. When he sent Mr. O'Neill a copy of his adaptation, the playwright replied that it had been admirably prepared so that the dramatic qualities and flavor of the work were preserved.

Lawrence Tibbett will enact the part of Jones and Tullio Serafin will conduct. No decision has been made by the Metropolitan as to the date of the presentation, but it is believed that it will be early in the season. Erich Kleiber, general music director of the Berlin Staatsoper, one of the largest opera companies in Europe, has already announced that he will produce the opera in Berlin this Fall. It appears, therefore, that Berlin and New York will vie for the right to give the work its world premiere.

Tom-Tom Used in Score.

Mr. Gruenberg has written the opera in two acts. He has made use, naturally, of the beat of the tom-tom which pursues Jones through the drama. This drum beat, which gradually accelerates in the opera, ceases only in certain brief scenes. These are during the visions and hallucinations which haunt Jones as he flees through the forest.

The work calls for a unique arrangement of the stage. The chorus of pursuing Negroes is grouped out of sight of the audience, below and in front of the stage flooring. At first only crossing hands and arms are seen above it. Then, as the pursuit of Jones draws nearer to its quarry, the bodies of the pursuers gradually emerge as they stalk and triumph gather in volume.

The hallucinations of Jones—of the murdered crap player, of the sheriff whom Jones has killed, and of the auction block—are shown on small raised stages, to indicate that they are figments of the Negro's imagination.

Finally, Jones is seen, a nearly naked savage, seated on the ground with his fellows, swaying in terror as the medicine man leaps on the stage and indicates him as the tribe's victim. At the end the body of the fugitive, who shoots himself with the silver bullet, is carried by the tribesmen into the forest. Choruses of savage exultation are heard dying away in the distance.

Music Moves Swiftly.

To this drama Gruenberg has written what appears to be swift and pungent music. The principal moment of lyrical expansion is his prayer for the Lord's aid in his plight, which is in the general character, but not in slavish imitation, of a Negro spiritual. The score is also reflective of passing incident and gesture on the stage. Each one of the scenes of hallucination has its special musical counterpart. Toward the end, with an immense crescendo and acceleration, several pairs of drums are employed to intensely stirring effect. The opera takes about one hour to perform.

When Erich Kleiber opened the opening season of the recent New

Continued on Page Nine.

Hoover Urges 3-Point Relief Plan Of $1,500,000,000 to Use as Loans

Senate Leaders Are Asked to Put the Proposal Before Colleagues—Finance Corporation Would Help States Handle Jobless and Advance Money for Spurring Business.

By ARTHUR KROCK
Special to The New York Times.

WASHINGTON, May 12.—President Hoover today asked Senators Robinson of Arkansas and Watson, the Democratic and Republican leaders of the Senate, to propose to their colleagues a three-point Federal relief program to stimulate private business in reproductive enterprises, to advance money for self-liquidating projects in States and municipalities, to ameliorate agricultural distress and to loan to States—but not municipalities—money for the relief of unemployed citizens.

The President's plan can be achieved simply by extending the powers and financial resources of the Reconstruction Finance Corporation. It involves no new government borrowings; it does not disturb the processes of budget balancing; it contemplates no bond issues for non-reproductive public works, as was proposed by New York financiers. If Congress will pass an amendment to the act establishing the Reconstruction Finance Corporation, the relief measures can be instituted.

The President's plan provides:

1. That the corporation be authorized to issue an additional $1,500,000,000 in debentures, of the proceeds from which $300,000,000 is to be loaned to States for general relief measures; $40,000,000 for export agricultural aid, and the remaining $1,160,000,000 loaned to private business for reproductive enterprises, assured by contracts.

2. That State bonds and securities which cannot otherwise be floated be purchased by the corporation when the proceeds of these bonds and securities are to be used for unemployment relief.

3. That the corporation be authorized to loan funds for self-liquidating projects such as toll bridges, tunnels and so forth.

It provides that private business planning reproductive enterprises for which credit cannot be obtained from the banks shall but put on a loaning basis with the corporation, a plan originally proposed by Mr. Hoover when the corporation was created, but rejected by Congress.

Senator Robinson, after a morning conference with the President, called a meeting of Democrats after the Senate adjourned this afternoon and outlined the President's idea. It was favorably received.

Senator Watson talked to a number of Republicans and reported progress with the idea. Speaker Garner and Minority Leader Snell were also consulted, and tonight Republican members of the Senate Committee on Banking and Currency were called to

Continued on Page Eleven.

TAX BILL'S TARIFFS ASSAILED IN REPORT BY MINORITY GROUP

Their Elimination From Senate Measure Is Demanded and 'Logrolling' Is Condemned.

GAIN IN REVENUE DOUBTED

Imposts on Oil, Lumber, Copper and Coal Will Mean Embargo, Opponents Assert.

Special to The New York Times.

WASHINGTON, May 12.—Five Democratic members of the Senate Finance Committee opened a fight on the tariff features of the billion-dollar tax bill today in a minority report demanding elimination of the duties on coal, oil, copper and lumber and condemning the "log-rolling" by which, they said, the items were inserted.

Consideration of the measure, expected today, was delayed by further debate on the Glass banking bill. When it appeared that the Glass measure could not be disposed of, even within another day, Republican leaders asked that it be sidetracked to give right of way to the tax bill.

Senator Glass gave rather reluctant consent, explaining that he long since had found it wise "not to go up against a buzz saw."

Senator Smoot will open discussion of the tax bill tomorrow. He had finished preparation tonight of a compromise measure recommending the compromise measure as the prime step toward business recovery through the guarantee of governmental credit.

Senate leaders at the same time completed plans for a series of night sessions next week, by which it is hoped to complete the revenue measure well before June 10, the date tentatively set for adjournment.

Minority Questions Efficacy.

The minority tax bill report was signed by Senators Harrison, George, Walsh of Massachusetts, Costigan and Hull. Democratic members of the Finance Committee whose names were not attached were Senators Barkley of Kentucky, who voted in committee for the coal tariff; Connally of Texas and Gore of Oklahoma, who favored the duty on oil, and King of Utah, who stood for the copper tariff.

The report questioned whether the duties would result in additional revenues, cited adverse decisions on some of the items by the Tariff Commission and predicted that in many cases the consumer would be a sufferer.

The "log-rolling" methods, it said, would be odious even in a general tariff measure. But to resort to "trades, exchanges of votes and on-again, off-again" practices, the minority charges, such as were used in writing the tariff items into an emergency revenue measure, was held by the Democrats to be "an exhibition that will raise serious questions in the public mind concerning the capacity of representative government to function promptly

Continued on Page Thirteen.

NEW RELIEF GROUP WITH SMITH AT HEAD NAMED BY WALKER

Merged Bureaus on Jobs and Home Aid Have $5,000,000 to Use Until Aug. 1.

UNITY OF EFFORT IS OBJECT

Leading Lawyers, Bankers and Welfare Officials to Begin Tasks on June 1.

Members of the Emergency Work and Relief Administration, formed by a consolidation of the Home Relief Bureau and the Emergency Work Commission, who will assume their tasks on June 1, were notified of their appointments yesterday by Mayor Walker.

The new committee will consist of the following:

ALFRED E. SMITH, Empire State Building.

FRANK L. POLK, lawyer, former Under Secretary of State, 15 Broad Street.

LAWSON PURDY, executive director, Charity Organization Society, 105 East Twenty-second Street.

GEORGE V. McLAUGHLIN, president Brooklyn Trust Company, 177 Montague Street, Brooklyn.

JOHN A. STEPHENS, Thompson Starrett Company, 245 East Twenty-third Street.

SOLOMON LOWENSTEIN, executive director, Federation for Support Jewish Philanthropic Societies 71 West Forty-seventh Street.

FRANK J. TAYLOR, Commissioner of Public Welfare.

MARY L. GIBBONS, Catholic Charities, 10 East Thirty-fourth Street.

WILLIAM EWING, J. P. Morgan & Co., 23 Wall Street.

VICTOR F. RIDDER, president, New York State Board of Social Welfare, 22 North William Street.

WILLIAM J. HODSON, executive director, Welfare Council, 122 East Twenty-second Street.

S. SLOAN COLT, president, Bankers Trust Company, 16 Wall Street.

WILLIAM H. MATTHEWS, Association for Improving the Condition of the Poor; director, work bureau of the Gibson committee, 105 East Twenty-third Street.

JOSEPH J. BAKER, director, Brooklyn Federation of Jewish Charities, 554 First Street.

RALPH WOLF, president, Board of Jewish Social Service, 34 Pine Street.

Coordination of Efforts.

The purpose of the joint committee will be to eliminate the duplication of investigations, obtain a closer cohesion of all public relief under moneys appropriated by the city and to plan for the performance of public work other than by contract. It will also be the task of the committee to select the most beneficial method of assigning those in need to work relief or home relief.

The committee will have $5,000,000 at its disposal from June 1 to Aug. 1. Mayor Walker announced that he was pleased that so many members of the Emergency Work Commission had agreed to continue with the new organization. Cornelius N. Bliss, chairman of the Emergency Work Commission, whose term began in October, 1931, will relinquish his work on June 1.

Because of the urgent need that still persists among thousands of New York's unemployed for clothing and food the clothing relief and food relief activities of the Emergency Unemployment Relief Committee will continue indefinitely instead of being discontinued as had been planned, it

Continued on Page Eleven.

LINDBERGH BABY FOUND DEAD NEAR HOME; MURDERED SOON AFTER THE KIDNAPPING 72 DAYS AGO AND LEFT LYING IN WOODS

POLICE INTENSIFY HUNT

Curtis, Norfolk Agent, and Condon, Who Paid Ransom, at Hopewell.

TO AID PROSECUTOR TODAY

Schwarzkopf Says Restraints Designed to Safeguard Baby Now Can Be Thrown Off.

A GROUP UNDER SUSPICION

Gov. Moore Pledges Relentless Hunt—Mulrooney Also Promises Full Aid.

Dr. J. F. Condon, the Bronx lecturer who acted as intermediary in the futile payment by Colonel Lindbergh of $50,000 ransom for his son, and John H. Curtis, the Norfolk boat builder, who also has been conducting negotiations, arrived at Hopewell for questioning by the police early this morning. They were scheduled to go to the prosecutor's office in Mercer County later today.

They arrived at the Lindbergh home shortly before 2 o'clock this morning and were at once closeted with the police. A few minutes before their arrival Colonel H. Norman Schwarzkopf, commanding the New Jersey State Police, made this announcement:

"Dr. Condon and Mr. Curtis will be at these headquarters in a few minutes for questioning in connection with this case and they will be turned over by the police authorities at this point to the prosecuting authorities tomorrow morning."

May Have Secret Data.

It is believed that the two intermediaries may have confidential information about the kidnappers which they are now ready to turn over to the authorities.

With this announcement the head of the New Jersey State Police indicated that the hunt for the murderers would be pursued with the aid of State, New York City and Federal authorities, throwing off the restraint that hitherto had hampered the police effort. It was disclosed further by the New Jersey authorities that immediate steps are being taken to arrest a group of persons suspected of kidnapping the Lindbergh baby.

The police started their search immediately with a close though apparently unpromising examination of the place where the body was found. "No footprints were found in the vicinity of where the baby's body was located," said Colonel Schwarzkopf in a statement early this morning. "This whole territory was thoroughly scoured by investigators from this office, even to the extent of scraping the surface of the ground around where the body was found and putting it all in containers and bringing it to these headquarters for the purpose of test and analysis."

Moore Pledges Every Effort.

Governor A. Harry Moore of New Jersey promised that everything possible would be done to "get the murderers" and announced that he expected to confer today with Colonel Schwarzkopf, head of the New Jersey State police. Meanwhile a grand jury investigation of all the Bronx incidents in the case was predicted last night by an aide of the Bronx District Attorney, Charles B. McLaughlin.

President John Grier Hibben of Princeton University called upon the law-enforcement forces of the country to unite in their hunt for the criminals, in a statement issued after he visited the Lindbergh home with Mrs. Almon told last night.

"A national systematic effort must be made right away," he said. "The authorities have been holding off from the beginning in the fear that their actions must cause the death of the child. Now that is over. The forces of law in the country must unite to get the persons who have done this thing."

Schwarzkopf's Statement.

Colonel Schwarzkopf made clear his course in regard to the hunt in an earlier statement, as follows:

"As long as there was a possibility of the baby being alive, the police have been acting with a certain amount of suppressed activity in order not to interfere with any negotiations that might result in the safe return of the baby.

"Now that the body of the baby

Continued on Page Three.

WHERE KIDNAPPERS LEFT SLAIN BABY.

SYMPATHY POURS IN FROM ALL THE WORLD

Grief and Horror Evidenced in Capital Where Hoovers Request Lindbergh News.

ORTIZ RUBIO IS SADDENED

Messages Sent From Mexico City—Inquiries Made From London to Gov. Moore.

Widespread sympathy for the bereaved parents and relatives of Charles A. Lindbergh Jr. and the American people was expressed in messages that poured into the Lindbergh home at Hopewell, N. J., last night from various parts of the world. Officials and civilians who had hastened to join the international search for the kidnappers when the abduction became known sought to assuage the feelings they knew would follow in the wake of the announcement.

The grief and horror with which the nation received the final answer that immediate steps are being taken to arrest a group of persons suspected of kidnapping the Lindbergh baby, was in Washington, where the report reached the President and Mrs. Hoover among the first. Attaches at the White House, The Associated Press announced, immediately got in touch with the New Jersey authorities to obtain official information.

"I am deeply moved," Vice President Curtis said. "They have my deepest sympathy, and my most heartfelt condolences go out to the bereaved mother and Colonel Lindbergh and to their families in their sorrow." Mr. Curtis exclaimed with feeling: "It is a most shocking thing."

Unofficial like official Washington was horrified at the news and few persons were able to express their feelings about the tragedy. Captain Emory S. Land, cousin of Colonel Lindbergh, could only declare: "Anything I could say would be futile."

Committee Meeting Halts.

The shocked surprise with which Washington officials, many of them personal friends of the aviator, received the information was exemplified when the meeting of the Democratic steering committee of the Senate broke up on receipt of the latest announcement of the discovery at 6:45 o'clock.

The fifteen Senators present, including Senator Wagner of New York, dropped a momentous question under consideration to express their regrets and seek further details of the development.

"I have never heard more shocking news," Senator Wagner declared.

"It is too awful to talk about," Senator Norris of Nebraska said, and Senator Norbeck of South Dakota called the discovery "most tragic," adding: "My most heartfelt sympathy goes out to Colonel and Mrs. Lindbergh."

"The world is shocked at the enormity of the crime," Senator Walcott of Connecticut said.

Mrs. Evalyn Walsh McLean, wife of Edward B. McLean, who has put forth great effort and expended upward of $100,000 in an attempt to find the baby, refused to be quoted, but was said by her attorney to be deeply shocked and grieved. He said

Continued on Page Two.

COLONEL BELIEVED ON A YACHT AT SEA

Reported Somewhere Off Block Island on Search for the Kidnappers.

INFORMED OF BABY'S DEATH

Departed May 4 With Norfolk Aides on Mission That Had Seemed Promising.

Colonel Lindbergh was believed to have been on a yacht, somewhere off Block Island, when the body of his son was discovered yesterday. He had been there searching for the kidnappers of his son. There was no question that he had heard of the finding of the body, for Colonel H. Norman Schwarzkopf said that he had been notified, and one of the men with him—telephoning to Norfolk—said that the news had been received.

Colonel Lindbergh set out from Norfolk on May 4, on board the yacht Marcon, owned by Charles H. Consolvo of Baltimore. With him were John H. Curtis, Norfolk boat builder and one of the trio of negotiators from that city; Edwin A. Bruce of Elmira, N. Y., and Lieutenant George L. Richard, a naval flier. The Marcon cruised up and down the coast near Norfolk until last Saturday, when the men transferred to another boat, which headed out to sea.

Lieutenant Richard Telephones.

The telephone message last night was from Lieutenant Richard to Mrs. Curtis, and was merely "Mr. Curtis is well, and we have heard the news." She could not say from where he had telephoned, nor did she know definitely whether Colonel Lindbergh was still on board. But the Rev. H. Dobson Peacock, one of the other Norfolk negotiators, said that "as far as I know" he was. The second yacht carrying them was generally supposed to have headed directly for Block Island.

When the Marcon sailed from Norfolk it was reported to be going to keep a rendezvous with the kidnappers of Colonel Lindbergh's son, who, according to an unverified rumor at that time, were said be on a foreign ship beyond the twelve-mile limit. Colonel Lindbergh boarded the yacht while in Chesapeake Bay, but bad weather kept the vessel from going out for two days.

The yacht has been running along the Atlantic Coast, it was said, searching for the other ship. Colonel Lindbergh, during the time he was on board, kept watch with the other members of the crew, sleeping in his clothes, always on the lookout for a sign of the second ship. The name of the yacht to which he transferred is not known, nor is its destination. It went straight to sea, however, as soon as he boarded it.

The Norfolk quest had been one of the most promising since the case began. Three prominent citizens of that city were involved, all of them certain that they had been in touch with the kidnappers. They were, besides Mr. Curtis, Rear Admiral Guy H. Burrage, retired, and the Rev. Mr. Peacock. Convinced that they were in communication with the wanted men, they paid Colonel Lind-

Continued on Page Four.

BODY MILE FROM HOPEWELL

Discovered by Chance Near Centre of Wide Search for Child.

HALF-COVERED BY LEAVES

Skull Fractures Caused Death—Body and Clothing Are Identified by Nurse.

MOTHER IS BRAVE AT NEWS

Neighbors Had Complained That Hunt in Vicinity Had Not Been Thorough.

The baby son of Colonel Charles A. Lindbergh was found dead yesterday afternoon. The child had been murdered.

The body, lying face down in a depression and partly covered with dead leaves and wind-blown debris, was discovered by a Negro truck driver, in a patch of woods in the Sourland Mountains less than five miles from the Lindbergh home near Hopewell, N. J.

The discovery was made by accident at 3:15 yesterday afternoon when the driver, walking into the woods from the road, found what he thought was a child's foot sticking out of the ground and notified the police. The identification followed quickly and the official announcement of the Lindbergh baby's fate was made at the Lindbergh home at 6:45 P. M.

The child evidently had been killed soon after he was stolen from his crib in the nursery on the night of March 1. Whether he had been killed with calculating purpose by criminals who found it advantageous to them to get rid of the child, or whether he had been thrown there by kidnappers fleeing in a panic, was not determined last night.

Two Fractures of Skull.

The body showed the marks of two fractures of the skull, one on the left side and the other on the right. The latter was a hole a half-inch in diameter. It was not definitely established whether this was a bullet hole or the result of a blow with a blunt instrument, but since no bullet was found the authorities were inclined to the belief that it was the latter.

The manner in which the baby died was officially stated as follows:

"The diagnosis of the cause of death is a fractured skull due to external violence.

"Unquestionably it was a brutal murder," said Dr. Charles H. Mitchell, county physician of Mercer County, last night, after he had completed an autopsy.

The condition of the body indicated that the child has been dead at least two months—the kidnapping occurred seventy-two days ago yesterday—and there was a strong possibility that he had been killed on the very night of the kidnapping.

Mother Bearing Up Well.

Mrs. Lindbergh and her mother, Mrs. Dwight W. Morrow, were at home when the body was found, but were in complete seclusion.

Despite the shock of the discovery, Mrs. Lindbergh was bearing up courageously, as she has from the beginning, it was learned last night. Colonel Lindbergh, who has been away much of the time in recent weeks making fruitless journeys in an attempt to make contact with the kidnappers, was not at home when the discovery was made. Colonel H. Norman Schwarzkopf, commanding the New Jersey State police, said that Colonel Lindbergh had been informed of his baby's death, however, and was on his way home. He did not disclose where the Colonel was.

Positive identification of the baby's body was furnished last night by Betty Gow, the nursemaid, about whom so much interest in the case

Continued on Page Three.

C & C PALE DRY.—Always the ginger ale of the fastidious.—And, of course, no bottle deposit requirement. At 26 Warehouses. C & C Mfrs. Cantrell & Cochrane, Ltd.—Advt.

"All the News That's Fit to Print."

The New York Times.

LATE CITY EDITION
POSTSCRIPT
WEATHER—Possibly showers today; tomorrow fair and warmer.
Temperature Yesterday—Max. 85; Min. 64.

Copyright, 1932, by The New York Times Company.

VOL. LXXXI....No. 27,173.   ****+   NEW YORK, FRIDAY, JUNE 17, 1932.   TWO CENTS In New York | THREE CENTS | FOUR CENTS Elsewhere

HOOVER, CURTIS RENAMED ON FIRST BALLOTS; DRY-WET PLANK IS DEFENDED BY STIMSON

LAUSANNE TO OFFER REPARATIONS TRUCE TILL FINAL SOLUTION

Britain and France Agree on Plan to Be Put to Reich at Closed Session Today.

IDEA IS TO SATISFY PAPEN

Proposal Can Be Interpreted Fairly in Germany as Virtual End to War Debts.

M'DONALD ASKS BOLDNESS

In Opening Speech He Holds Out Hope That We May Cooperate in Solving Economic Problems.

By FREDERICK T. BIRCHALL
Wireless to THE NEW YORK TIMES.

LAUSANNE, June 16.—To a private plenary meeting of the Lausanne conference tomorrow will be presented a memorandum to which Great Britain and France have already agreed, extending the suspension of all reparations payments, including the French unconditional annuities under the Young Plan, until a final settlement can be worked out.

The idea behind this move is that it will give Chancellor von Papen of Germany something to take home that can be fairly interpreted as a practical ending of reparation payments and therefore something to talk about in the German elections. A second advantage of the step is that it removes from the Lausanne conference the curse of having to work in a hurry before payments by Germany should begin again on July 2.

Third, it is believed it will satisfy French opinion as preparing the way for a larger consideration of the entire economic problem, for which Prime Minister MacDonald appealed in his opening speech today.

Not Moratorium Extension.

It is to be noted that this proposal is not for an "extension of the moratorium," which would bring in the matter of United States debts. It is rather for a continuation of the European status quo and therefore in full accord with the purpose of this conference. Germany, however, would not be obligated to pay indemnities to the Bank for International Settlements on the next instalments, due July 2, of non-postponable reparations due since then a year, France, which under the present arrangement are returned to Germany in the form of railway bonds redeemable in ten years. Thereby will be removed the metaphorical sword overhanging Chancellor von Papen's head. Yet, at the same time, the end of reparations is not formally acknowledged, which satisfies Premier Herriot of France.

Should the proposal prove acceptable tomorrow it will be in fact a success for the method of temporizing as against the clean-cut method of cancellation which Germany came here to demand. On that point Lieut. Col. von Papen is still to be heard from, but the friendliness toward him manifested by frequent visits from M. Herriot and Mr. MacDonald may not be without reward.

Pending the complete economic discussion and final settlement that Mr. MacDonald envisages, the work of exploration and liquidation, if the proposal carries, will be continued by technicians and experts. Thus the conference will in effect have fulfilled some of the expectations based on it as a preparatory movement toward a real world adjustment.

MacDonald Sounds Keynote.

By P. J. PHILIP.
Wireless to THE NEW YORK TIMES.

LAUSANNE, June 16.— Elected unanimously as president of the Lausanne conference, Prime Minister Ramsay MacDonald in a speech that strongly set forth the principles that must be established began the work of trying to get Europe to put its financial house in order.

He mentioned the United States twice, both times to emphasize her unity with the rest of the world. But there was no mention, and from that we may conclude, that there will be no mention of Europe's debts to the United States. That is another problem to be settled at some other time.

Continued on Page Four.

Without Benefit of Congress—Henry Hazlitt, in July Scribner's Magazine.—Advt.

12-Year Sentence on American In Assault Protested to Spain

Special to THE NEW YORK TIMES.

WASHINGTON, June 16.—United States Consular officers at Malaga and Seville, Spain, have intervened with the military authorities in behalf of John C. Wiley of Inglewood, Cal., who has been sentenced by a military tribunal to twelve years' imprisonment, with recommendation for commutation, on charges of assaulting a carabinero in Malaga on March 10.

The carabinero is said to have suffered a broken nose and to have been incapacitated for duty for nineteen days.

The State Department said today that the case would come up for review soon and the American officials had been promised that it would be submitted to the Premier. The consuls contend that the sentence was out of all proportion to the offense and have urged commutation or deportation.

CHILE OVERTHROWS REGIME AS TOO RED

Army Storms Palace and Captures General Grove as His Guards Quit Him.

DAVILA'S FRIENDS IN POWER

Mobs Fight in Streets as Planes Circle Overhead, Dropping Flares.

Special Cable to THE NEW YORK TIMES.

SANTIAGO, Chile, Friday, June 17.—Colonel Marmaduque Grove was overthrown early today as provisional head of the Chilean Government, according to a manifesto by army leaders who launched a counter-revolt against him last night.

Troops opposed to communism surrounded the government palace and demanded Colonel Grove's surrender by midnight. An earlier manifesto signed by General Agustin Moreno on behalf of all garrisons of the army said if he did not yield by that time, planes and troops would bombard the palace if necessary to obtain control of the government.

Colonel Grove replied that he would do rather than surrender. Shortly after midnight troops began attacking the palace and soon afterward it was announced by the counter-revolutionists that their drive had been successful.

At an early hour the army leaders had not yet named the new junta to take over the government, but it was assumed that Carlos G. Davila, who, because of his moderate views, was driven out of the junta dominated by Colonel Grove, would be a member.

Coup a Climax of Communism.

Both manifestos declared the counter-revolt was intended to prevent the establishment of communistic practices and to carry forward the socialistic program enunciated by the junta which seized power from former President Juan Esteban Montero on June 4.

Early last evening rebellious troops began marching on the palace and surrounded it, forcing a loyal guard of carabineers. Soon after the midnight attack began, it was observed that the members of the Presidential guard were quietly abandoning their arms and slipping out of the courtyard and palace. When the surrender of the men was practically complete General Moreno announced the success of the counter-revolt.

Earlier there had been considerable disorder in the city, with mobs parading and shouting for and against Colonel Grove.

The rising was made necessary, according to the counter-revolutionists, by the failure of Colonel Grove to keep promises made before the revolution of June 4 and by his encouragement of Communism. The new regime, it was declared, has the support of the entire army, will put down Communism with a firm hand and will maintain order throughout the country.

Colonel Grove Captured.

SANTIAGO, Chile, Friday, June 17 (P).—Colonel Marmaduque Grove, leading member of the new Socialist junta that deposed President Montero twelve days ago, was captured early today in a counter-revolutionary overthrow of his régime.

When the troops first approached the palace several officers got past the guards and demanded the surrender of General Grove, who re-

Continued on Page Three.

BONUS BILL REPORTED ADVERSELY, 14 TO 2; CAMP MORALE SAGS

Break-Up Starts After Senate Delays Action Till Today and Defeat Appears Likely.

CRUCIAL PERIOD AT HAND

Officials Believe Jobless Men Will Roam Nation in Bands, Hungry and Penniless.

TEMPER OF MEN ON EDGE

Former Leader Flares at the Police, Saying Veterans Are Going to Quit "Soft-Pedaling."

From a Staff Correspondent.
Special to THE NEW YORK TIMES.

WASHINGTON, June 16.—The Senate vote on the Patman bill for the payment of $2,400,000,000 to World War veterans, which was passed by the House yesterday and was scheduled for action by the upper body today, was deferred until tomorrow after the Finance Committee had reported it adversely following a swift consideration this morning.

Late this afternoon Senator Smoot, chairman of the Finance Committee, gave formal notice that the bonus bill would be taken up as soon as the Senate met tomorrow morning. Opponents of the measure say that it will be defeated in the Senate, and even should it unexpectedly succeed, its veto by President Hoover is assured. Its friends admit that it could not possibly be passed over his veto.

Just before the Senate recessed today Senator Watson obtained unanimous consent to have the bonus made unfinished business. He remarked that he hoped for a final vote tomorrow, and said that if this did not materialize there would be ample time for discussion anyway.

With today's developments the morale of the bonus assemblage began marching on the palace and gan almost visibly to sag. The unexpected delay, the adverse report of the committee and the growing expectation of defeat began to weigh heavily on the thousands of destitute ex-service men encamped here, and the movement of the veterans homeward, only a trickle thus far, was notably increased.

Officials believed that the beginning of the long-expected break-up of the camp was at hand, and would begin in earnest after the Senate vote.

Officials Plan Evacuation.

Hence they began planning for what they concede is the most dangerous period of the bonus army's existence—the period in which the men will start roving about the country as isolated bands of unemployed, without funds, without food and without the discipline to which they submitted voluntarily when they thought there was a chance of achieving their objective.

The two proposals which were before the Republican National Convention take similar action, the constitutional steps toward this momentous change will be well under way.

"There has been so much misunderstanding on the subject that it is well to analyze carefully the nature of what has been done. In the first place, both parties, in the convention last evening, advocated an amendment to the Constitution requiring a new amendment to accomplish such a repeal.

"The two proposals which were before the Republican National Convention last evening differed only as to the form which the new amendment should take.

Basis of the Majority Plank.

"In the second place, both propositions were clear and explicit, and the difference between them was fundamental and easily understood. The newspaper criticism that the majority plank was a straddle is quite unfounded. It is definite and perfectly logical. It is well founded in law and fact.

"Let us see what this fundamental difference between the two proposals was, and the reason for that difference. One proposal was an important demand to abrogate the entire work of the past thirteen years under the prohibition amendment, and to confess it to be an entire failure; to do away with all direct power on the part of the Federal Government in regard to the liquor traffic, and to leave the situation in respect to liquor as it was before 1919.

"This proposal was tantamount to asserting that everything which we have done during these years was useless or evil, that we should confess it to be a great and complete failure and go back and start over again.

"Right here it is well to remind you of what is frequently forgotten; namely, that the Eighteenth Amendment did not come out of thin air

Continued on Page Two.

DENIES IT IS A 'STRADDLE'

Secretary, Over Radio, Says Liquor Plan Is 'Definite and Logical.'

'FAITH' WITH PEOPLE KEPT

'Real Gains' Under Dry Law Must Be 'Disentangled From Evils Incurred,' He Holds.

THE ADMINISTRATION REPLY

Mr. Stimson's Address Is First Move to Justify the Party's Stand to Country.

Special to THE NEW YORK TIMES.

CHICAGO, June 16.—Defending the prohibition plank in the Republican platform, Secretary of State Stimson declared over the radio tonight that instead of being a "straddle," the proposed method of dealing with the prohibition problem was "consistent, definite, logical and wellfounded in law and fact."

Secretary Stimson was speaking over a nation-wide radio hook-up of the National Broadcasting Company and this was the first move on the part of the administration to justify the party's stand before the country.

Asserting that the Eighteenth Amendment represented in its adoption the hopes of millions of American wives and mothers, he added:

"To ruthlessly destroy such a faith by indiscriminately condemning an effort like the Eighteenth Amendment, instead of taking the trouble to disentangle the real gains that have been accomplished from the evils which have been incurred, would be an act of social folly and national wrong."

MR. STIMSON'S ADDRESS.

Secretary Stimson's address was as follows:

"My friends of the radio audience: At their meeting last night the members of the Republican National Convention took a momentous step in the direction of American constitutional history. By a vote of 7,153 they have unanimously recommended to submit to the voters of this country a proposal to change the Eighteenth Amendment.

"They divided by a vote of 681 to 472 as to the form of the proposed change which should be submitted. But they were unanimous in recommending the submission of a proposal to change. Should the Democratic party in its approaching convention take similar action, the constitutional steps toward this momentous change will be well under way.

HOOVER LAYS PLANS FOR COMING FIGHT

His First Move Is Selection of Everett Sanders to Be Head of Committee.

SPEAKING TOURS UNLIKELY

Friends of Executive Expect Him to Direct Much of Fight From His Camp on the Rapidan.

Special to THE NEW YORK TIMES.

WASHINGTON, June 16.—Gratified by the outcome of the Republican convention, President Hoover began preparations this afternoon for the campaign for his re-election.

His first move, after sending a message of appreciation for his renomination, was to let the national convention know that he preferred the election of Everett Sanders of Indiana as chairman of the committee.

Mr. Sanders is a former Representative, was secretary to President Coolidge and is experienced in national politics and national campaigns. Since 1929 he has been practicing law here and in Chicago.

The new chairman and the executive committee of the national committee are expected to come here shortly and map out campaign plans. No definite word escaped from the White House on the question today, but it was predicted by Mr. Hoover's close political advisers that he would conduct the campaign from here and make relatively few speeches. It was pointed out that this would be in accordance with past custom when Presidents standing for re-election have attended to the duties of their high office and not engaged in far-flung campaign trips or many speeches.

Trip to California Suggested.

There is some talk among friends of the President of his going to California by warship through the Panama Canal to keep an engagement tentatively set for him to open the Olympic Games at Los Angeles late in July. This would permit a campaign trip back across the country.

Close friends of the President, however, declared that practically any chance of his going to California for notification ceremonies at his Palo Alto home had disappeared, due to the pressure of public business and the efforts he is making to combat the economic depression.

The ceremonies notifying him of the nomination will be somewhere on the south portico of the White House. President Coolidge, it was recalled, delivered his acceptance speech in 1924 at a night meeting in Memorial Continental Hall.

In any event the Rapidan camp will be the scene of important campaign activities, since the President intends to spend week-ends there during the Summer as often as possible.

Continued on Page Fourteen.

AGAIN THE REPUBLICAN STANDARD BEARERS

Harris & Ewing Photo.   Harris & Ewing Photo.
HERBERT HOOVER.   CHARLES CURTIS.

Ballot for President

Special to THE NEW YORK TIMES.

CHICAGO, June 16.—The vote of the Republican National Convention by which President Hoover was renominated here today was as follows:

State.	Delegates	France.	Coolidge.	Dawes.	Blaine.	Hoover.
Alabama	19					19
Arizona	9					9
Arkansas	11					11
California	47					47
Colorado	15					15
Connecticut	19					19
Delaware	9					9
Florida	16					16
Georgia	16					16
Idaho	11					11
Illinois	61					61
Indiana	33			2½		
Iowa	25					25
Kansas	21					21
Kentucky	25					25
Louisiana	12					12
Maine	13					13
Maryland	16					16
Massachusetts	34					34
Michigan	44					44
Minnesota	27					27
Mississippi	11					11
Missouri	33					33
Montana	11					11
Nebraska	17					17
Nevada	9					9
N. Hampshire	11					11
New Jersey	35					35
New Mexico	9					9
New York	97					97
N. Carolina	26					26
N. Dakota	15				13	
Ohio	55					55
Oklahoma	25					25
Oregon	13					13
Pennsylvania	75					75
Rhode Island	13					13
S. Carolina	10					10
S. Dakota	13					13
Tennessee	24					24
Texas	49					49
Utah	11					11
Vermont	11					11
Virginia	25					25
Washington	19					19
W. Virginia	19					19
Wisconsin	29					
Wyoming	9					9
Alaska	2					2
Dist. of Col.	2					2
Hawaii	2					2
Philippines	2					2
Puerto Rico	2					2
Total	1,154	4½	1	13	13	1,126½

*Three not voting.
†One absent.

CHEER HOOVER 27 MINUTES

Delegates Give 1,126 1-2 Votes on First Ballot, 634 1-4 to Curtis.

NEW YORK FOR HARBORD

France Ejected From Rostrum —Coolidge's Name Fails to Stir Convention.

HOOVER VICTORY COMPLETE

Administration Had 200 Votes in Reserve—Convention Ends After Nominations.

By ARTHUR KROCK.
Special to THE NEW YORK TIMES.

CHICAGO, June 16.—Under the disclosed domination of the President, the Republican national convention in its closing session today renominated Herbert Hoover and gave a grudging but clear majority to Charles Curtis of Kansas, renominated as the party candidate for Vice President.

Mr. Hoover received 1,126½ votes on the first ballot, his nomination immediately thereafter being made unanimous. Mr. Curtis, the beneficiary of a last-minute switch of Pennsylvania's 75 votes from its Republican State Chairman, General Edward Martin, to the Vice President, had a first ballot majority of 55%, with a total of 634¼. His nomination also was made unanimous. Until Pennsylvania responded to the administration goad, Mr. Curtis lacked 19½ votes of the sum required for his renomination.

It has been twenty years since the obvious will of a Republican National Committee has been so emphatically and publicly subordinated to a President's program. In 1912, as today, both President and Vice President were renominated, the only time in its history that the Republican party has repeated this ticket.

But then Theodore Roosevelt bolted the convention and formed the Bull Moose party, badly defeating the regular Republicans under William H. Taft in the election and assuring the victory of the Democratic ticket headed by Woodrow Wilson.

No Prospect of a Bolt.

So far as the political elements of the Republican party are concerned, there were no prospects of a bolt as the result of the defeat of the repeal plank last night and the renomination of Mr. Curtis today. The only menacing element was the insurgency of the New York delegation. Today its members cast ninety-five of their ninety-seven votes for General J. G. Harbord for Vice President, ignoring the plain warning which lay in the fact that the two New Yorkers who voted for Mr. Curtis were the Secretary of State, Henry L. Stimson, and the Secretary of the Treasury, Ogden L. Mills.

Last night the New Yorkers cast seventy-six of their votes for the Bingham repeal plank. The administration, which made that struggle the test of its control, had only twenty-one votes. Had not Charles D. Hilles, the national committeeman, declined to aid the State chairman, W. Kingsland Macy, in his effort to supplant Representative Ruth B. Pratt as national committee woman, this steadfast friend of the President would have been defeated.

The church drys, and those who are dry before they are Republican or Democratic, will not be heard from until they meet in national conclave in August, when they have examined the prohibition plank which the Democrats will adopt in Chicago the week after next.

It may be that then, as they did against James W. Wadsworth Jr. and Charles H. Tuttle, they will put independent New York State and National tickets in the field. Should this happen, the effect of that action, joined to the demonstrated dissatisfaction with Mr. Hoover's program of New York's regular Republicans, may be as disastrous to the national Republican candidates as was Colonel Roosevelt's third-party movement twenty years ago.

For days before this convention opened, and for the first day of the session, administration leaders maintained the strategic fiction that the delegates were to "work their will" on all points. In every respect save

Continued on Page Thirteen.

CURTIS VICTORY WON AGAINST FIELD OF 12

Snell, Harbord, Alvin Fuller, Replogle and MacNider Were Put in Nomination.

PENNSYLVANIA TURNS TIDE

Suddenly Gives 75 to Kansan— Foes Unable to Muster Behind One Candidate.

By L. C. SPEERS.
Special to THE NEW YORK TIMES.

CHICAGO, June 16.—Charles Curtis of Kansas won renomination as the Republican Vice Presidential candidate, but it was not an easy victory, and save for the fact that Pennsylvania swung its seventy-five votes to him after the roll-call of the States was concluded, he would have been 19½ ballots short of the majority necessary for nomination.

The anti-Curtis elements in the convention fought to the last, but were unable to concentrate on any one candidate. With General Charles G. Dawes standing as their candidate, they were apparently every justification for their boast they had Mr. Curtis stopped, but with the Illinoisan out of the picture the backbone of the opposition was broken.

Six nominations were made for Vice President, and thirteen names, all told, were on the tally sheet when the roll-call was completed. One of them was that of Senator Couzens of Michigan, who received two of the eleven "Progressive" votes in the Wisconsin delegation. The fact that Mr. Couzens was born in Canada, and therefore ineligible, did not deter the La Follettes from allotting him a share of their honorary vote.

Three ex-soldiers constituted the main opposition to the renomination of Mr. Curtis—Hanford MacNider of Iowa, former National Commander of the American Legion; Major Gen. James G. Harbord of New York, chief of staff of the A. E. F., and General Edward Martin, chairman of the Republican State Committee of Pennsylvania.

Six Placed in Nomination.

Mrs. Edward Everett Gann, sister of the Vice President, was on the firing line to the end. She was tired and smiling when Pennsylvania withdrew the name of General Martin and cast its seventy-five votes for her brother, which assured his renomination on the first ballot.

The six nominations placed before the convention were those of Mr. Curtis, former Governor Alvin E. Fuller of Massachusetts, Mr. MacNider, J. Leonard Replogle of Florida, Representative Bertrand Snell of New York, the permanent chairman of the convention, and General Harbord.

Those who in addition to these were named in the voting that followed were Mr. Dawes, Judge Wilson S. Kenyon of the United States Circuit Court of Appeals, Senator Couzens, Secretary Hurley of Oklahoma, David Ingalls, Republican

Continued on Page Thirteen.

REPUBLICAN PRESS SPLIT ON 'WET PLANK'

Many Papers Hold That It Is a 'Meaningless Evasion'— Others See Notable Step.

Editorial comment of Republican and independent newspapers over the nation differs on the merits of the prohibition plank in the Republican platform, telegraphed excerpts of editorials to THE NEW YORK TIMES indicated last night, with the wet papers bitter at what they called a "straddle."

In New York, The Sun declared that out of the "mountain of minds at Chicago comes a ridiculous mouse." The evident purpose of its authors "was to be obscure, and they have succeeded."

The Post, also Republican, headed its editorial "A moral failure at Chicago," and The World-Telegram, wet and independent, agreed with numerous other newspapers in calling the plank a "meaningless evasion."

The Herald Tribune, wet and Republican, declared that "in some paradise for politicians may yet be devised a compromise more inclusive than the wet-moist-dry plank. * * * To date it has no rival." It added that the "great compromisers of Chicago can retire for a long rest, assured of the hearty disapproval of every one with an honest conviction on the subject."

The Chicago Tribune, Republican,

Continued on Page Fifteen.

IT'S A FINE DAY—Always the thing of the famous—and, of course, no bottle deposit required. 10 oz. Magnums—12½ oz. 50c. Size. Cantrell & Cochrane, Ltd.—Advt.

"All the News That's Fit to Print."

The New York Times.

LATE CITY EDITION
WEATHER—Clearing and cooler today; tomorrow fair.
Temperature Yesterday—Max. 81; Min. 70.

Copyright, 1932, by The New York Times Company.

VOL. LXXXI....No. 27,188.   ++ * * * *   NEW YORK, SATURDAY, JULY 2, 1932.   TWO CENTS In New York City | THREE CENTS Within 200 Miles | FOUR CENTS Elsewhere Except 7th and 8th Postal Zones

ROOSEVELT NOMINATED ON FOURTH BALLOT; GARNER EXPECTED TO BE HIS RUNNING MATE; GOVERNOR WILL FLY TO CONVENTION TODAY

CONFEREES REACH RELIEF COMPROMISE UPON $2,100,000,000

Use Parts of Both Wagner and Garner Bills in Report to Reach Congress Tuesday.

BOND ISSUES ARE BARRED

$1,500,000,000 Provided for R. F. C. Loans—$300,000,000 Available for Public Works.

GRANTS TO STATES SPLIT

$200,000,000 Allowed, According to Population—$100,000,000 on a Basis of Need.

Text of Secretary Mills's review of government finances, page 2.

Special to The New York Times.

WASHINGTON, July 1.—Agreement on relief legislation, the most important subject before Congress, was reached by the conferees tonight just after the Senate and House recessed until Tuesday, when they will take up the conference report.

Compromising between the Wagner and Garner bills, each involving about $2,300,000,000, the conferees drew up a program of $2,100,000,000 divided as follows:

$1,500,000,000 for loans by the Reconstruction Finance Corporation to public and private enterprises, but only to the latter where money is unavailable elsewhere.

$300,000,000 for construction of public works, this money not to be financed by bond issues, but by the Treasury.

$200,000,000 for direct loans to the States on a basis of population.

$100,000,000 for direct loans to the States on a basis of need.

Points of Difference in Bills.

For a week the conferees have been struggling to adjust the administration's viewpoint, as well as differences between the Wagner and Garner bills, as follows:

Wagner Bill—$1,500,000,000 for loans by the Reconstruction Finance Corporation to self-liquidating enterprises of a public character; $300,000,000 for public works, financed by bond issues; $200,000,000 for loans to the States on a population basis.

Garner Bill—$1,000,000,000 for loans by the Reconstruction Finance Corporation to public and private enterprises; $1,190,000,000 for public works financed by bond issues; $100,000,000 for a Presidential emergency fund.

The administration vigorously opposed bond issues, demanded that private business as well as self-liquidating public enterprises be allowed to obtain loans from the Reconstruction Finance Corporation and desired that the loans to States be granted on a need instead of a population basis.

Character and Purpose of Loans.

Announcing the agreement by the conferees, Senator Norbeck explained that the parts of the Garner bill regarding Reconstruction Finance Corporation loans had been accepted with certain restrictions and suitable safeguards.

He said the loans to private enterprises could be made only when it was impossible to obtain money from other sources, and that the loans could be granted for only four purposes—"agriculture, industry, commerce and employment."

Loans to municipalities would be permitted, he said, only for future needs and not to settle debts already contracted. He said that this meant that no loans would be granted for long-due payment of school teachers, as in Chicago, but might be allowed to continue employment of the teachers and other city employes.

The loans could also be made for public works and to the small as well as the large merchant, the Senator stated, but in all cases they would have to be adequately secured.

"Ann Vickers," The new novel by Sinclair Lewis, begins in the August Redbook Magazine.—Advt.

Continued on Page Five.

The Fourth and Decisive Ballot

CHICAGO, July 1.—The detailed vote on the fourth ballot of the Democratic National Convention nominating Franklin D. Roosevelt for President follows:

STATE	Total Vote.	Roosevelt	Smith	Garner	Ritchie	Baker	Reed	Traylor	White	Byrd
24 Alabama	24									
6 Arizona	6									
18 Arkansas	18									
44 California	44									
12 Colorado	12									
16 Connecticut	16		16							
6 Delaware	6									
14 Florida	14									
28 Georgia	28									
8 Idaho	8									
58 Illinois	58									
30 Indiana	30									
26 Iowa	26									
20 Kansas	20									
26 Kentucky	26									
20 Louisiana	20									
12 Maine	12									
16 Maryland	16									
36 Mass'chus'ts	36		36							
38 Michigan	38									
24 Minnesota	24									
20 Mississippi	20									
36 Missouri	36									
8 Montana	8									
16 Nebraska	16									
6 Nevada	6									
8 N. Ham'shire	8									
32 New Jersey	32		32							
6 New Mexico	6									
94 New York	94	31	63							
26 No. Carolina	26									
10 No. Dakota	10									
52 Ohio	29	17		2					3	
22 Oklahoma	22									
10 Oregon	10									
76 Pennsylv'a	49	14½			1½	5½				
10 Rhode Isl.	10		10							
18 So. Carolina	18									
10 So. Dakota	10									
24 Tennessee	24									
46 Texas	46			46						
8 Utah	8									
8 Vermont	8									
24 Virginia	24									
16 Washington	16									
16 West Va.	16									
24 Wisconsin	24	2								
6 Wyoming	6									
6 Alaska	6									
6 Dist. of Col.	6									
6 Hawaii	6									
6 Philippines.	6									
6 Puerto Rico.	6									
6 Canal Zone.	6									
2 Virgin Islds.	2									
1,154. Totals	945		190½			3½	5½			

*Five 1½ votes not cast.
Ohio cast one vote for Cox.

MADDEN MUST GO TO PRISON AGAIN

High Court Holds He and Three Others Still Under Parole, Upsetting Levy Ruling.

The police are looking for Owen Madden, former convict, and three of his associates, former Sing Sing inmates.

The search began yesterday when the Appellate Division of the Supreme Court unanimously reversed the decision of Supreme Court Justice Aaron J. Levy, who sustained a writ of habeas corpus last April freeing the four ex-convicts from the custody of the State Parole Board. Madden and his companions, Jeremiah J. Sullivan, Terrence Reilly, alias Thomas Robinson, and Gustave Guillaume, alias Little Frenchy, are wanted for violation of parole.

Justice Levy, in sustaining the writ releasing Madden, had ruled that Madden was arrested on flimsy and highly technical grounds and that Madden had been discharged from parole in 1929. He also held that Madden's arrest "was an attempt to convict under color of law for wrongs which cannot be brought home to him by competent evidence." He ruled that the other three had also been discharged from parole.

Dispute Levy's Findings.

The five Justices of the Appellate Division, Presiding Justice Finch and Justices Martin, Townley, McAvoy and Merrill, in their review of the proceedings before Justice Levy, commented: "No evidence, either documentary or otherwise, of the

Continued on Page Three.

BINGHAM OFFERS SENATE BEER TEST

Puts 4 Per Cent Beverage Plan Into Rider for Home Loan Bank Bill—Wets Count on 49 Votes.

Special to The New York Times.

WASHINGTON, July 1.—A test in the Senate on modification of the Volstead act seemed likely when Senator Bingham today offered a proposal to legalize beer of 2.2 per cent alcoholic content by weight, or 4 per cent by volume, as an amendment to the Home Loan Bank bill.

He announced that he would not press for a vote on his amendment until the Democratic Senators returned from Chicago, where their party convention has gone on record for immediate liberalization of the Volstead act. The Senate recessed tonight until Tuesday, when the Home Loan Bank bill will come up again.

Through his rider to the bill, the Connecticut Republican hopes to force a House vote also on the proposals.

Prohibition leaders in that body recently made a point of order against another vote on modification as an independent proposal, but wets now consider that attaching the Bingham plan to the Home Loan Bank bill will overcome parliamentary objection.

Conflicting Views of Prospects.

Wet leaders in the Senate drew up tentative polls on their prospects if a vote can be had on the Bingham scheme. Their computations, manifestly speculative, indicated a hope

Continued on Page Nine.

HE IS 'READY FOR ACTION'

Plane Starts With Him at 8 A. M. for Chicago to Open Campaign.

WIFE AND BOYS GOING, TOO

On Way Governor Will Work on Speech Accepting His Party's Nomination.

EXPECTS TO MEET SMITH

Addressing 1,000 Neighbors on Lawn, He Predicts Harmony and Certain Victory.

By JAMES A. KIERAN.
Special to The New York Times.

ALBANY, N. Y., Saturday, July 2.—Wreathed in smiles, Governor Roosevelt sat in his armchair in the Executive Mansion early this morning, jubilant at his nomination and all ready with plans for an intensive campaign to win his way to the White House.

With his wife, his sons and close friends around him, he had heard a short time before the balloting that chose him as the candidate of the Democratic party for the Presidency as it came from the radio in the corner of the room.

Then, as he received newspaper correspondents, he heard coming back over the radio from Chicago the message he had sent telling of his prospective appearance before the convention today, together with the announcement that a meeting of the national committee had been requested for tonight at the Congress Hotel to launch the campaign.

"We are ready for action," the Governor said.

Joyous Night in Mansion.

All through the evening the Executive Mansion, where four years ago Alfred E. Smith received the news of his nomination at Houston, had an atmosphere of suppressed elation. It had been intimated that Texas and California might come to the Roosevelt banner, but nothing was certain.

Just before the radio broadcast started the definite news was circulated and as members of the Governor's family and his aides hurried about the mansion they clearly showed their joy.

Throughout the broadcast the Governor sat in the workroom on the south side with his small party which included Supreme Court Justice Samuel I. Rosenman and Mrs. Rosenman, Miss Marguerite Lehand and Miss Grace Tully, his private secretaries; Detective "Gus" Gennerich, his New York City bodyguard, and several others.

When the doors were finally opened and the Governor officially became the candidate of his party, he was quick to extend the olive branch to Alfred E. Smith.

"Do you expect to see Governor Smith soon?" he was asked.

"I certainly hope so," said the Executive, smiling.

Family to Fly With Him.

"I haven't any particular statement," said the Governor. "I sent it to Chicago and there it is coming back now. The speech tomorrow will be the official notification so that we can save the expense of bringing people here from all over the country later.

"I am going to leave at 8 o'clock in the morning by airplane and expect to reach Chicago by about 2:30 our time. I am going to do some final work on the speech on the trip out.

"Mrs. Roosevelt will go along, and my two boys, Elliott and John. That's four. Then Miss Lehand, Miss Tully, Sergeant Earl Miller and Gus Gennerich and"——

Here he paused and turned toward Justice Rosenman, who has been his constant companion for a week.

"And Sam, will he go?" interjected Mrs. Rosenman. The Justices had previously indicated that he did not intend to make the trip.

"Sure he'll go," said the Governor. The Justice laughed.

"We expect to have a good trip," said the Governor. Then he went on to banter with some of the correspondents whom he has known for some time, posing for a photograph

Continued on Page Four.

The Democratic Nominee

FRANKLIN DELANO ROOSEVELT.
© New York Times Studio Photo.

GARNER WITHDRAWS, AIDING ROOSEVELT

'Politics Is Funny,' the Speaker Philosophizes as He Reveals His Decision.

PLACE ON TICKET IS SEEN

Capital Democrats Look Upon Texan as Logical Nominee for Vice Presidency.

Special to The New York Times.

WASHINGTON, July 1.—Speaker Garner, until this evening a stubborn candidate for the Democratic nomination for the Presidency, telephoned orders to Representative Rayburn and William G. McAdoo, his campaign managers, tonight to release the California and Texas delegations pledged to his support.

He ordered them to be released in favor of Governor Roosevelt, heightening, in the opinion of the capital, the chances of Mr. Roosevelt for winning the nomination.

The Speaker's action is viewed here as making himself Governor Roosevelt's logical running mate.

His announcement of withdrawal from the Presidential race was made to The New York Times shortly before 8 o'clock tonight.

Long past his customary bedtime, Mr. Garner was on the roof garden of the hotel where he makes his home. He was alone and apparently unrecognized by others seeking relief from the heat.

"Do you intend to make the nominee?" he was asked.

"I have no comment to make," Mr. Garner replied.

"You've gone to Roosevelt?" a reporter asked him.

"That's right, son," the Speaker replied. "And that is all I am going to say to you."

His cigar glowed against the night. For a moment there, the reporter, he replied:

"I'm a little older than you are, son. And politics is funny——

"You may become the first man in the——

Continued on Page Five.

SMITH HEARS NEWS IN GRIM SILENCE

Refuses Comment on Rival's Victory—Friends Say He May Not Support Ticket.

By The Associated Press.

CHICAGO, July 1.—Alfred E. Smith, sitting in his hotel headquarters facing a radio and a poster urging "Smith for President," heard, without formal comment, tonight the nomination of Governor Roosevelt.

"Do you intend to support the nominee?" he was asked.

"I have no comment to make," Mr. Smith replied, chewing vigorously at a cigar. Then he turned back to the radio and resumed his grim silence.

Mr. Smith's associates and political backers said they did not believe he would support the Democratic ticket in November.

An expression of bitter sadness came to the face of the "Happy Warrior of 1928" as soon as William G. McAdoo began to announce the switch of California's votes. There was a change in that expression only once during the rest of the evening, when Connecticut's vote for Smith sounded an outburst of cheering. He smiled slightly for the moment.

The outcome of the convention tonight came as a complete surprise to the New York Governor, for the arrest of the switch and its ultimate

Continued on Page Six.

Democratic Nominee's Name Is Pronounced "Rose-velt"

By The Associated Press.

ALBANY, N. Y., July 1.—The Democratic Presidential nominee pronounces his name "Rose-velt" in two syllables and with a long "o," instead of the way it looks as if it should be pronounced.

The name Roosevelt came over with the old Dutch patroons, and in the Dutch language double o is pronounced as a single long "o."

15,000 IN STADIUM FOR CLIMAX SCENE

Galleries Unaware as Ballot Began That Garner Action Made Outcome Certain.

WALKER SILENT ON RESULT

He Lets Curry Acknowledge for Tammany Its Defeat in Overwhelming Vote.

From a Staff Correspondent.

CHICAGO, July 1.—Fifteen thousand persons who crowded the Stadium for the Democratic convention session tonight expecting drama were not disappointed in the spectacle they saw when Franklin D. Roosevelt was nominated, amid the cheers of delegates and the groans and boos from those in the galleries.

It was more than ordinary drama when William G. McAdoo, whose nomination Alfred E. Smith blocked at the Madison Square Garden convention in New York City, went to the platform to announce that California and Texas would give ninety votes for Roosevelt, making the latter's nomination certain and preventing Mr. Smith from continuing any longer at this convention the blocking role he filled in 1924.

With the local sentiment, so revealed by the gallery demonstrations, bitterly opposed to Mr. Roosevelt, the roll-call was attended with great disorder caused by interruptions from the galleries.

As State after State recorded their support for Roosevelt, the men and women in the galleries raved their disapproval and resentment and cheered wildly at the announcement of the votes which stayed with Mr. Smith.

While the Smith states stuck by their candidate, the support of favorite sons disintegrated.

As Missouri broke in

Continued on Page Four.

ROOSEVELT VOTE IS 945

Smith His Nearest Rival, With 190 1-2 as Four States Stick to End.

McADOO BREAKS DEADLOCK

Casts California's 44 Amid Wild Demonstration After Garner Releases Texans.

RITCHIE MEN FALL IN LINE

Tammany Holds Aloof—Cermak Forced to Appeal to the Booing Galleries.

By ARTHUR KROCK.
Special to The New York Times.

CHICAGO, July 1.—California and Texas, which came to Chicago pledged to Speaker John N. Garner, broke the deadlock on the Presidential nomination in the Democratic National Convention on the fourth ballot tonight by casting their ninety votes for Governor Franklin D. Roosevelt of New York.

This started a bandwagon rush, in which only New York—the nominee's home State—Massachusetts, Rhode Island, New Jersey and Connecticut declined to join, and Mr. Roosevelt was elected by a vote of 945, the convention's two-thirds requirement being 769 1-3. His nearest rival, Alfred E. Smith, received 190½ votes, the four States named sticking to him to the last.

Roosevelt to Fly to Chicago.

Governor Roosevelt, as soon as he heard of his success, sent a message which the permanent chairman, Senator Thomas J. Walsh of Montana read to the convention. The Governor announced that he will be here tomorrow, coming by airplane from Albany, to receive his formal notification, thus avoiding the expense of a more formal and distant ceremony.

The national committee will also be reorganized under the eye of the nominee tomorrow with his convention manager, James A. Farley of Chicago, led by Senator Walsh, with bands and speeches, is to be made of the notification ceremonies.

Senator Walsh, the permanent chairman, sent the following telegram to Governor Roosevelt:

"The convention extends its greetings and assurance of fealty to our nominee and welcomes the news that he will be here with us tomorrow."

William G. McAdoo, former Secretary of the Treasury, was the voice of Mr. Roosevelt's destiny. When the name of California was called by the reading clerk he took the platform to explain the change of the vote in the Western States. The news of the impending action had spread throughout the delegates.

But the galleries had not heard about it and, when they sensed what was happening, the boos and yells with which they expressed their anger over the defeat of Alfred E. Smith required the efforts of Mayor Anthony J. Cermak of Chicago, whose presence was demanded by Permanent Chairman Thomas J. Walsh, to restore a measure of quiet.

McAdoo Speaks for West.

Mr. McAdoo said that California had not come to Chicago to deadlock the convention, that Democracy had suffered enough, as in 1924 when he himself had almost pulled a majority, by such methods. He said that the opinion of the West, in which Speaker Garner joined, was that Democrats should find Republicans against one another.

He did not say what has been known here for several days, that William Randolph Hearst, the great influence in the California delegation and who "discovered" the qualification of Mr. Garner as a candidate, pressed the shift to Mr. Roosevelt because he feared that a deadlock might produce Newton D. Baker or another candidate whose international policies is not in agreement. Mr. Hearst also is a believer in majority rule and the Texas-California contingent swung to the nominee's candidate, thus ending the 1928 role in 1924.

Throughout a feverish day in

Continued on Page Four.

The New York Times.

Copyright, 1932, by The New York Times Company.

VOL. LXXXI....No. 27,215.   Entered as Second-Class Matter, Postoffice, New York, N. Y.   NEW YORK, FRIDAY, JULY 29, 1932.   * * * * + TWO CENTS In New York City | THREE CENTS Within 200 Miles | FOUR CENTS Elsewhere Except in 7th and 8th Postal Zones

LATE CITY EDITION
WEATHER—Thunder showers and cooler today; tomorrow fair.
Temperatures Yesterday—Max., 86; Min., 69.

WALKER REPLY A DENIAL OF ALL SEABURY CHARGES; CALLS 10 OF 15 OUTLAWED

GOVERNOR TO ACT QUICKLY

Turns Answer Over to His Advisers—New Move Expected in Week.

POLITICAL PLOT IS CHARGED

Mayor Says He Is the Victim of a Campaign of Calumny to Aid Hoover Regime.

DEFENDS EQUITABLE DEALS

Declares Men Who Gave Him Cash Got No Favors—Denies Sherwood Was Agent.

The text of Mayor's reply to Gov. Roosevelt, Pages 6, 7 and 8.

Terming himself the victim of political misrepresentation, and insisting that his entire official life would bear the closest scrutiny, Mayor Walker filed with Governor Roosevelt yesterday his answer to the removal charges pending against him as the result of allegations first made by Samuel Seabury, counsel to the Hofstadter committee.

The Mayor's answer, a 27,000-word document, contained specific denials of wrongdoing in connection with the Equitable Bus franchise, the receipt of securities from brokerage firms interested in taxicab legislation, the "beneficences" of Paul Block, publisher, or the huge bank accounts of Russell T. Sherwood, missing accountant. The document came from the printers yesterday forenoon, and was given at once to Thomas F. McAndrews, the Mayor's secretary, who carried it by train to the Governor at Albany.

Mr. Roosevelt, after scrutinizing it briefly, released the reply for publication. A conference between the Governor and his two legal advisers, Martin Conboy of New York and John E. Mack of Poughkeepsie, will probably be held in the near future. It was indicated, to determine the next step in the removal case that, it is held, cannot but affect the political fortunes of Mr. Roosevelt as the Democratic Presidential nominee.

Seabury Is Denounced.

In form the Mayor's answer consisted of an attack upon Mr. Seabury and the Hofstadter committee, before which the evidence against the Mayor was developed, followed by a point-by-point reply to the allegations made by Mr. Seabury and subsequently embodied in charges filed with the Governor by William Jay Schieffelin, head of the New York Committee of One Thousand.

Two appendices contained an answer to the separate and supplementary charges filed by James E. Finegan, Brooklyn Democrat, and legal citations and details on financial transactions covered in the main body of the answer.

Most of the legal citations were to support the Mayor's assertion that ten of the fifteen allegations advanced by Mr. Seabury related to a previous term in office, and therefore could not be made the basis of action at present by the Governor. The answer, moreover, also replied in detail to these allegations.

Mayor Walker did not mention Mr. Seabury's statement that Mr. Walker had a "metallic receptacles" in his home, where he put cash received in stock and bond deals, nor did he mention the "unnamed person" said to have received payments from both the Mayor and from Sherwood.

The payments to the unnamed person were stressed at committee hearings as tending to prove a connection between the bank accounts of Sherwood and the Mayor. Mr. Walker in his reply denied Sherwood was his financial agent.

Calls Inquiry Political Plot.

The Mayor declared that the Hofstadter committee was organized and Mr. Seabury retained as counsel "to carry out a deliberate plan of calumny" in the hope of discrediting the Democratic administration of New York City. He accused Mr. Seabury of conducting a "manhunt," and declared the counsel would have fixed upon any Democratic Mayor of New York as a victim, in order to divert attention from the shortcomings of the Hoover Administration.

Continued on Page Eight.

Walker Hastens to Saranac; Gets Word Brother Is Worse

Mayor Walker left on a midnight train for Saranac Lake last night, after he had received a call at City Hall informing him that the condition of his brother, George F. Walker, had taken a sudden turn for the worse.

The brother, the youngest of the three Walker brothers, has been a patient at a Saranac sanitarium for several months, and in the past few days his condition has been a source of worry to the Mayor. A request had been made at City Hall, however, that no publicity be given to the illness of the Mayor's brother, until developments forced it.

George Walker is 48 years old, is married, and has two children. He is in the insurance business, and is a member of the firm of Hughes & Walker of 27 William Street.

COOLIDGE EXPECTED TO AID HOOVER DRIVE

Sanders to Spend Week-End at Former President's Vermont Home for Political Talk.

NO EASTERN MANAGER YET

Senator Hebert Is Likely to Be Named to Run Campaign in This Section.

By CHARLES A. SELDEN.
Special to The New York Times.

OTTAWA, July 28.—The probability that former President Calvin Coolidge will aid President Hoover in his campaign for re-election was indicated yesterday when Everett Sanders, chairman of the Republican National Committee, said that he would visit Mr. Coolidge Saturday and Sunday at the Coolidge homestead at Plymouth Notch, Vt., and expected to discuss the political situation with him.

Mr. Sanders, who was secretary to Mr. Coolidge when he was President, declined to be definite, because the invitation to visit his former chief came before he had been elected national chairman.

"I have no doubt he will take some part in the campaign," Mr. Sanders said, when asked if he expected Mr. Coolidge to make some campaign speeches for the President.

Mr. Sanders said that there had been no selection yet of an Eastern campaign manager and indicated that the choice was between Senator Felix Hebert of Rhode Island and Earl S. Kinsley, national committeeman from Vermont. From other sources it was learned that Senator Hebert probably would be named. Should Senator Hebert not be named for this post he will be the Eastern campaign manager for the Republican Senatorial Committee, Mr. Sanders said.

Mr. Sanders also indicated that General Edward Martin, who was under consideration for Eastern campaign manager, had found his duties as Pennsylvania too exacting to take on additional responsibility. General Martin, besides being active in military affairs, is the Pennsylvania State treasurer and chairman of the Republican State Committee.

Mr. Sanders had a luncheon conference with W. Kingsland Macy, New York State Republican chairman, and earlier in the day conferred with Charles D. Hilles, national committeeman, and former Governor Henry J. Allen of Kansas, publicity director of the national committee.

Asked to make a prediction on New York State, Mr. Sanders said:

"I am very confident that the President will be re-elected, but I do not wish to discuss his chance of carrying the different States."

One point of difficulty in the Republican campaign situation in this State has been cleared up by the recent visit to Washington of Mr. Macy and conferences here with Mr. Sanders, as a result of which it has been decided that the Republican State Committee will be in complete charge of the campaign in this State and that there will be no Hoover campaign committee as there was in 1928.

Sought to Supersede Macy.

Members of the so-called Hooverite group in this State suggested the re-establishment of the Hoover campaign committee and some members of the group went so far as to make suggestions which, if adopted, virtually would have put the officers of the proposed Hoover campaign committee in charge of the campaign and...

Continued on Page Thirteen.

Thousands Crowding Into Los Angeles For Opening of Olympic Games Tomorrow

By ALLISON DANZIG.

LOS ANGELES, July 28.—The biggest migration to California since the Forty-niners wrote an imperishable story of man's courage in braving the perils of the unknown has made Los Angeles the cosmopolitan capital of the world.

Not for a peck of gold at the end of the covered wagon trail has this world exodus to the jewel city of Southern California taken place, but for the tenth revival of the Olympic Games, which begin here on Saturday, with approximately 2,000 representatives of thirty-eight countries competing in an athletic plant that dwarfs the imagination, along with the coliseums and stadiums of the ancient Greeks and Romans.

Already, with the spectacular grand opening parade forty-eight hours away, there are thousands of visitors encamped in Los Angeles and its environs.

By railroad, plane, ship and motor car they continue to pour into the city and no one knows what sagas of enterprise and fortitude are being written on the national highways by athletic zealots who have seized upon the most desperately dilapidated means of conveyance to bring them to the games.

Los Angeles, festooned and bedecked with flags, streamers and banners of welcome to all within its domain, is assimilating this tremendous influx of people in the same ample fashion that it has prepared, over a period of nine years, to stage this tremendous athletic carnival, the first Olympiad to be held in this country since 1904.

With its enormous hotel capacity, it is well prepared to accommodate the great burden of humanity resting within its confines and thus far there is no overcrowding or dearth of reservations.

So far as it has been possible to ascertain, there has been no mark-up in the rates for rooms, nor have prices in the restaurants or else-

Continued on Page Nineteen.

BRITAIN ASKS EMPIRE FOR MORE PURCHASES TO BALANCE HER AID

Baldwin Says United Kingdom Imports Exceeded Exports by £95,700,000 in 1930.

RHODESIA FILES DEMAND

British In Drive at Ottawa to Capture United States Sales of Machinery in Canada.

The text of Britain's trade statement is on Page 10.

By CHARLES A. SELDEN.
Special to The New York Times.

OTTAWA, July 28.—Two more cards were placed face up on the Imperial Economic Conference table today when Stanley Baldwin, leader of the British delegation, presented a statement plainly intimating to the dominions that in his opinion they were lagging behind the United Kingdom in the mutual exchange of trade benefits and that H. W. Moffatt, spokesman for Southern Rhodesia, filed a request that Britain help his country by buying more of its cattle.

The statement of the United Kingdom contained neither threat nor promise of what Great Britain would or would not do after the dominions have agreed upon what they can or cannot do for the mother country. It confined itself to what the United Kingdom already had done for the rest of the empire and showed by figures that she was buying from them annually £100,000,000 worth of goods in excess of what they were buying from her.

Advantages Are Contrasted.

Mr. Baldwin called attention to the fact that practically all of the dominion products were admitted to the ports of Great Britain free of duty, whereas British exports to the dominions bear only the benefit of preferences. Although the preferences are much better than nothing, Mr. Baldwin considers them far less of a boon than free entry. He spoke particularly of the fact that even preferences may be based on tariffs so high that they restrict imports.

He did not refer to the fact, fully and painfully realized at Ottawa by all the dominion delegations, that after Nov. 15 the United Kingdom may deprive them of all the benefits of free entry which the empire countries now enjoy by simply applying to them the new British tariff act. That is England's trump card at the conference, which she may play to get from the dominions the trade concessions and preferences she thinks are just and fair. Although no threats were made today nor even hinted, the British statement added nothing to the harmony of the conference and no doubt the dominions considered it as a rebuke, which they all think undeserved in spite of the figures that support it.

Denies Witholding Assistance.

Perhaps Stanley M. Bruce, head of the Australian delegation, felt personally rebuked. He told the conference the other day that Great Britain had been tardy in recognition of all the preferences the dominions had given her. No doubt Mr. Baldwin had that remark definitely in mind today when he said:

"Any suggestion that the United Kingdom has been backward in developing or assisting dominion trade or that the concessions on the side of the dominions have not been fully reciprocated, both in the letter and...

Continued on Page Ten.

HERRIOT PROTESTS SCHLEICHER SPEECH; EDITORS ATTACK IT

Premier Summons Germany's Envoy to Tell Him Arms Talk Disturbs France.

CITES HIS FRIENDLY POLICY

Description of French Stand as "Hypocritical" Results in Bitter Resentment.

By P. J. PHILIP.
Wireless to The New York Times.

PARIS, July 28.—Premier Edouard Herriot summoned the German Ambassador, Dr. Leopold von Hoesch, to the Quai d'Orsay today to explain to him vigorously that the French people are considerably disturbed by the terms of Lieut. Gen. Kurt von Schleicher's radio speech Tuesday evening, in which he gave notice that Germany would arm, if necessary, contrary to the provisions of the Versailles treaty, and also attacked France.

M. Herriot's protest was the second of the Reich Government has received in two days, for Ambassador André François-Poncet called at the Wilhelmstrasse in Berlin yesterday to make formal denial of some statements made by the German Defense Minister.

In the Paris press the substance of General von Schleicher's statement is the subject of strong comment today, but all their editorial tanks into position, unlimbered their gas bombs and gave the thousands of veterans massed there thirty minutes in which to evacuate. They then sat down waiting for the order to be obeyed.

The spirit of the veterans seemed broken. Leaderless and aghast at the failure of their confident prediction that no soldier would go into action against them, they moved their women and children out of the camp and prepared to leave themselves.

General MacArthur and his staff followed the first troop of cavalry into the field at Anacostia through a road leading off from the bridge. Several veterans, as they heard the troops approach, set fire to improvised huts. The glow from the

Continued on Page Three.

Stocks Rise Again in Year's Heaviest Trading; 2,735,635 Shares Sold, Leaders Up 1 to 4 Points

Invigorated by fresh optimism, the security markets made another broad advance yesterday. The day's transactions on stocks on the New York Stock Exchange totaled 2,735,635 shares, which represented the heaviest trading since Dec. 18 of last year. The net gains in market leaders ranged from 1 to 4 points, while there were scattered advances of 6 points or more.

In the bond market the net gains were widest among domestic corporation issues, running from 3 to 10 points in the conspicuously strong favorites. The extreme gain of 10 points occurred in Schulco 6½s, due 1946, Series B. United States Steel 5s advanced maximum gain of 6 points; Atlantic Coast Line issues advanced as much as 7 points and Bethlehem Steel 5s of 1936 rose 4¾ points. Dealings in bonds were the heaviest in a month.

Aside from a further demonstration of strength in commodities, the development which contributed most to the cheerfulness in Wall Street was a spectacular rise of the dollar in terms of foreign currencies which reflected the further reinforcement of the gold position of the United States. Sterling fell 2¾ cents, while the French franc was off 7-16 point. All the other Continental currencies except the mark, which was unchanged, lost ground.

The upswing in stock prices was most striking in the forenoon. Profit-taking at midday and in the last hour reduced the early gains to some extent, but final prices showed substantial net appreciation in the average. For instance, Allied Chemical was up 2 points on the day; American Telephone, the market leader, closed with a net gain of 4¾ points after falling more than a point from its high; Santa Fe preferred was up ¾ point after falling 2 points from its high.

Bank stocks again advanced vigorously, the bid price of First National showing a gain of 25 points and that of the Fifth Avenue 40 points.

TROOPS DRIVE VETERANS FROM CAPITAL; FIRE CAMPS THERE AND AT ANACOSTIA; 1 KILLED, SCORES HURT IN DAY OF STRIFE

ANACOSTIA CAMP NO MORE

Troops Move Into Last Bonus Army Refuge as Flames Start.

AND FINISH DESTRUCTION

Marchers Stream Away, Some in Broken-Down Autos, Some Trudging Afoot.

FEW KNEW WHITHER TO GO

At Midnight the Former Home of 20,000 of Bonus Army Is Held by the Military.

Special to The New York Times.

WASHINGTON, July 28.—Flames rose high above the desolate Anacostia flats at midnight tonight and a pitiful stream of refugee veterans of the World War walked out of their home of the past two months, going they knew not where.

Cavalry stood guard at all the bridges leading across the river to the camp and thousands of onlookers gazed across the river at what had been the teeming residence of 20,000 persons.

The veterans were leaving at the behest of the military forces of the government, summoned by the President after collisions between the bonus marchers and the police. Some were departing in broken-down automobiles; some, on foot, dragged listlessly in search of new quarters.

Flames were raging in the camp. Many of the tents, numbering 2,100 and mostly belonging to the army, were ablaze and the infantry was busy trying to salvage as many as possible.

A heavy barrage of tear gas, laid down by the troops, penetrated to the houses for blocks around, and residents were forced to close their doors and windows in spite of the sweltering heat.

Had Thirty Minutes to Evacuate.

It was soon after 9 o'clock tonight that the troops, headed by General MacArthur, surrounded the main camp of the Bonus Expeditionary Force at Anacostia, wheeled their

Continued on Page Three.

Text of Hoover's Statement on Call for Troops To Put an End to Bonus Rioting in the Capital

Special to The New York Times.

WASHINGTON, July 28.—The text of President Hoover's statement explaining his action in calling out troops to combat the bonus rioters is as follows:

For some days police authorities and Treasury officials have been endeavoring to persuade the so-called bonus marchers to evacuate certain buildings which they were occupying without permission.

These buildings were on sites where government construction is in progress and their demolition was necessary in order to extend employment in the district and to carry forward the government's construction program.

This morning the occupants of these buildings were notified to evacuate and at the request of the police did evacuate the buildings concerned. Thereafter, however, several thousand men from different camps marched in and attacked the police with brickbats and otherwise injuring several policemen, one probably fatally.

I have received the attached letter from the Commissioners of the District of Columbia, stating that they can no longer preserve law and order in the district.

In order to put an end to this rioting and defiance of civil authority, I have asked the army to assist the District authorities to restore order.

Congress made provision for the return home of the so-called bonus marchers, who have for many weeks been given every opportunity of free assembly, free speech and free petition to the Congress. Some 5,000 took advantage of this arrangement and have returned to their homes. An examination of a large number of names discloses the fact that a considerable part of those remaining are not veterans; many are Communists and persons with criminal records.

The veterans amongst these numbers are no doubt unaware of the character of their companions and are being led into violence which no government can tolerate.

I have asked the Attorney General to investigate the whole incident and to cooperate with the District civil authorities in such measures against leaders and rioters as may be necessary.

[The text of the letter from the District Commissioners to the President is printed elsewhere.]

BOMBS AND SABRES WIN CAPITAL BATTLE

Cavalry, Infantry and Tanks, Advancing as Gas Spreads, Swiftly Drive Veterans.

SHACKS BURN BEHIND THEM

Bayonets Clear the Section of Squatters, Who Are Ringed Finally by 1,500 Soldiers.

Special to The New York Times.

WASHINGTON, July 28.—The Federal troops came out today and cleared Washington proper of the members of the Bonus Expeditionary Force. The cantonments, the "forts" in the unused Federal buildings, the huts that the men themselves had built, were evacuated by the veterans when they found themselves faced with tear-gas bombs, bayonets and tanks.

The regulars had the equipment to do the job, the equipment that the Capitol Police had lacked and they had the orders to do it. The irregulars of the bonus army had only their stubborn sullenness in most cases and bricks, rocks and epithets in others and the fight did not last long.

Down Pennsylvania Avenue at 4:30 this afternoon the regulars came, cavalry leading the way, and after them the tanks, the machine-gunners and the infantry. For them the objective was the "fort" of the B. E. F. in the skeletonized building at Third Street.

There was a wait for maybe half an hour while the army officers talked it over with the police and the bonus marchers shouted defiance. They wanted action, and they got it.

Steady Sweep Down Avenue.

Twenty steel-helmeted soldiers led the way, with revolvers in their hands, and others advanced until about 200 were in position in front of the "bonus fort." Then the mounted men joined. They rode down street, clearing the path with their sabers, striking those within reach with the flat of the blades.

The action was precise, well executed from a military standpoint, but not pretty to the thoughtful in the crowd. There were those who resented a military attack and were not knocked at the horses; there were those who scrambled for safety and those who tried to rescue their meager belongings from the fort.

Inch by inch, foot by foot, they were forced down Pennsylvania Avenue as the soldiers headed them toward Anacostia camp. They left in their path those who had been knocked over, and one passive resider, who sat down and waited unscathed while the storm blew over his head. The success of the movement, the

Continued on Page Three.

B.E.F. TO CARRY ON, WATERS DECLARES

Men Will Organize Elsewhere if Driven From Capital, Commander Says.

WHITE HOUSE IS ASSAILED

'Political Interests' Cost a Life, He Charges, Admitting He Has Lost Control.

By The Associated Press.

WASHINGTON, July 28.—Walter W. Waters, titular commander of the "Bonus Expeditionary Force," declared tonight that "no matter what may happen from now on, the B. E. F. will carry on."

"If driven from Washington, it will organize elsewhere and continue the fight for justice for the veterans and the common people of the United States," he said in a statement. "We have gone too far now to quit."

The Waters declaration, telephoned to newspaper offices, included the assertion that a life was sacrificed "to serve the political interests of the administration."

The one-time dictator of the bonus army watched from the sidelines while the men who formerly paid him allegiance swept completely out of his control.

Before Federal troops arrived to push former service men off their encampments in front of a cloud of tear gas, "Commander" Waters threw up his hands in a gesture of defeat. He said frankly that he no longer had any control over the men.

Accompanied by a handful of his organized adherents, Waters viewed from the sidewalks about the trouble-ridden area the swiftly breaking developments, which resulted in the death of a war veteran.

Just before arrival of the troops, he went to a small restaurant on Pennsylvania Avenue for a cup of coffee.

Asked about the day's happenings he replied:

"The men not completely out of control. There was nothing and is nothing I can do to control them."

In his statement later he said:

"Every drop of blood shed today or that may be shed in days to come as the result of today's events can be laid directly on the threshold of the White House.

"The B. E. F. had been organized on strictly American lines of respect for law and order and is pledged to uphold American institutions.

"They were under strictest orders to conduct themselves in orderly manner in the event of attempted eviction.

"The men got out of control. There was nothing and there is nothing that I can do to control them," he said.

With the bonus army in the city

Continued on Page Two.

HOOVER ORDERS EVICTION

Blaming Reds, He Asserts Bonus Camps Included Many Criminals.

QUICK ACTION BY SOLDIERS

Eject Squatters After Police Fall and Then Burn Camps In and Near Capital.

BONUS ARMY SCATTERED

Demoralized by Soldiers' Gas Attack, Remnants Are Left Leaderless and Helpless.

Special to The New York Times.

WASHINGTON, July 28.—Amidst scenes reminiscent of the mopping-up of a town in the World War, Federal troops late today drove the army of bonus seekers from the shanty village near Pennsylvania Avenue in which the veterans had been entrenched for two months. Earlier in the day the police had fought and lost a battle there which resulted in the death of one veteran, possibly fatal injuries to a policeman and a long list of other casualties, many of them serious.

Ordered to the scene by President Hoover after the District of Columbia authorities confessed defeat, detachments of infantry, cavalry, machine-gun and tank crews laid down an effective tear-gas barrage which disorganized the bonus-seekers, and then set fire to the shacks and tents left behind by the veterans on the government land near Third and Pennsylvania Avenues, scene of the earlier clash with the police.

Begin to Clear Anacostia.

After the disputed area near the Capitol had been cleared, the troops moved late in the evening on Camp Marks, on the Anacostia River, the bonus army's principal encampment. At 10 o'clock this evening infantry-men with drawn bayonets advanced into the camp, driving the crowd before them with tear gas bombs. Then they applied the torch to the shacks in which the veterans lived.

Troops shortly afterward halted at the main bonus camp in response to what General Perry L. Miles, commanding the soldiers, said was a Presidential order. Theodore G. Joslin, the President's secretary, later denied positively that the President had issued any such order, and word came from the camp that the troops would resume operations within an hour.

At 11:15 P. M. the first troop of cavalry had moved into the disordered camp, now a mass of flames as the bonus-seeking veterans set fire to their own miserable shacks. At midnight practically all the veterans had left the place.

War that the soldiers would use tear gas, the veterans had arranged to evacuate the 600 women and children earlier.

The normal population of Camp Marks was augmented by more than 2,000 veterans who had been evicted from other camps, bringing the total male population to 7,000.

Troops Avoid Bloodshed.

Soon after the khaki-clad regulars descended on the various camps along Pennsylvania Avenue this afternoon the bonus seekers were straggling sullenly away from the ominous blue mist of the tear gas, leaderless and apparently demoralized, seeking shelter in other open places scattered afar through the city. A few of them were from minor bruises, but on the whole the Federal troops had conducted their offensive without bloodshed. The veteran who was killed in the earlier clash with the police was identified tonight as William Hushka of Chicago.

The day's disturbances were blamed on the radical element among the bonus-seekers. Walter W. Waters, the young veteran from Oregon who led the unsuccessful bonus march to Washington, disclaimed responsibility for his followers' part in resisting the first eviction order of the police. Waters announced tonight that he was "through."

"The men got out of control."

Continued on Page Two.

"All the News That's Fit to Print."

The New York Times.

5 A.M. Edition
WEATHER—Rain today; tomorrow fair and colder.
Temperatures Yesterday—Max. 56; Min. 56.

VOL. LXXXII....No. 27,318.

Entered as Second-Class Matter,
Postoffice, New York, N. Y.

NEW YORK, WEDNESDAY, NOVEMBER 9, 1932.

*****

TWO CENTS In New York City | THREE CENTS Within 200 Miles | FOUR CENTS Elsewhere Except in 7th and 8th Postal Zones

Copyright, 1932, by The New York Times Company.

ROOSEVELT WINNER IN LANDSLIDE!
DEMOCRATS CONTROL WET CONGRESS;
LEHMAN GOVERNOR, O'BRIEN MAYOR

BIG VOTE FOR M'KEE

O'Brien Is 245,464 Behind Ticket as Protests Rise

BUT FINAL LEAD IS 616,736

Pounds Concedes Defeat Early, Saying 'Day of Miracles Is Past.'

McKEE TOTAL IS 137,538

Thousands of "Write-In" Votes Are Wasted as Backers Fail to Record Choice Properly.

HILLQUIT POLLS 248,425

Gets Greatest Vote in History of City for a Socialist—Runs Far Ahead of Party.

Surrogate John P. O'Brien, Tammany's candidate, was elected Mayor of New York yesterday, but overshadowing his victory, which was a foregone conclusion, was the tremendous "write-in" vote cast for Acting Mayor Joseph V. McKee.

Final returns from the city showed Judge O'Brien to have received a plurality of 616,736 over his nearest opponent, Lewis H. Pounds, Republican. Judge O'Brien's vote was 1,055,768, Mr. Pounds polled 439,032, and Morris Hillquit, Socialist, polled the highest vote ever given a candidate of his party in the city by receiving 248,425 votes.

Vote Listed by Boroughs.

By boroughs, the totals were as follows:

	O'Brien	Pounds	Hillquit
Manhattan	309,256	113,775	39,398
Bronx	161,145	48,284	67,949
Brooklyn	428,527	155,478	112,740
Queens	176,227	105,451	23,831
Richmond	30,131	16,511	2,517
City total	1,055,768	439,032	248,425

The vote for Mr. McKee, put early this morning at 137,538, actually was far more than that, if ballots in which the voters had abbreviated his name, or used initials, or spelled it wrongly, were counted.

The vote was unprecedented, particularly as the use of voting machines made it much more difficult for a name to be written in than on the old paper ballots.

Judge O'Brien had a clear majority of 215,000 votes over the combined vote of Pounds, Hillquit and McKee, but the McKee ballots cast aside as void would have reduced this, it was pointed out last night.

The vote for Mr. McKee by boroughs was as follows:

Manhattan, 26,336, with ten election districts missing.
Bronx, 24,453, complete.
Brooklyn, 43,527, complete.
Queens, 36,303, complete.
Richmond, 6,790, complete.
City total, 137,529.

The vote for Mr. McKee was made without any campaign on his part, and in the face of his own disavowal of the movement, kept him in the political picture as a candidate to be reckoned with for the full four-year term, to be voted on in 1933.

The term for which Judge O'Brien was elected starts on Jan. 1, 1933, and ends on Jan. 1, 1934.

The vote for Mr. O'Brien indicated he ran 381,263 votes behind Governor Roosevelt in the city, in actual votes cast, though his plurality was only 245,464 smaller than that given the Presidential candidate.

Mr. Pounds conceded Mr. O'Brien's victory as early as 9:30 in the evening, and he sent the latter a telegram of congratulation.

He said later he could have been elected only by a miracle, and that the days of miracles were past. Mr. McKee, receiving election returns at the Park Lane, also sent a short

Continued on Page Seven.

FOR LOW COST FALL HOLIDAY
Monterey Hotel-On Beach-Asbury Park.—Adv.

THE GOVERNOR-ELECT.

© New York Times Studio.
Colonel Herbert H. Lehman.

JUDGES IN 'DEAL' WIN; PROTEST VOTE HEAVY

Steuer and Hofstadter Elected With Lydon and Leary to Supreme Court Bench.

290,000 FOR INDEPENDENTS

Bar Leaders Elated by Big Count for Deutsch and Alger—Call It 'Warning to Bosses.'

City Court Justice Aron Steuer and State Senator Samuel H. Hofstadter were elected yesterday over their independent opponents. Bernard S. Deutsch and George W. Alger, by a vote of about 2 to 1.

The protest vote against the so-called deal by which Senator Hofstadter and Justice Steuer received bipartisan nominations for two of four vacancies on the Supreme Court bench in the first judicial district exceeded all expectations, but it was not enough to upset the combined strength of the Republican and Democratic organizations.

Justice Richard P. Lydon, who was nominated by both major parties for re-election, and Municipal Court Justice Timothy A. Leary, who had the Democratic nomination for the fourth vacancy on the bench, were elected with comfortable margins. Municipal Court Justice George L. Genung, who had the Republican nomination, trailed far behind the independent candidates.

Since Justice Lydon's re-election was virtually uncontested, his totals were not computed in the early returns. Of the other, Justice Steuer and Judge Leary were running slightly ahead of Senator Hofstadter, whose lead was large enough, however, to preclude the possibility of his being overtaken by Mr. Deutsch, his nearest rival.

The complete returns for the entire first judicial district, comprising the boroughs of Manhattan and the Bronx, follow:

Steuer	565,405
Leary	547,112
Lydon	544,032
Hofstadter	293,125
Deutsch	287,167
Genung	205,222

The totals recorded for the judiciary candidates in Manhattan follow:

Steuer	367,295
Hofstadter	357,430
Leary	331,442
Deutsch	147,886
Alger	145,546
Genung	138,304

Final returns from the Bronx, where the independent candidates ran strongest, showed the following totals:

Leary	215,670
Steuer	198,110
Hofstadter	186,402
Alger	143,539
Genung	86,918

The independent candidates did not

Continued on Page Twelve.

STATE VICTORY SOLID

Lehman Gets Record Party Plurality of 887,000.

WAGNER CLOSE TO HIM

National Ticket Has Margin of 615,000—Full Slate Is Elected.

RELIEF BONDS ARE VOTED

Republicans Have Narrow Edge Up-State—Hill Admits 'Protest' Defeated Them.

By JAMES A. HAGERTY.

Lieut. Gov. Herbert H. Lehman, Democratic nominee for Governor, defeated Colonel William J. Donovan, Republican, yesterday, in the Democratic whirlwind that swept New York State, by a plurality of about 887,000, a record for a Democratic candidate in this State.

Governor Franklin D. Roosevelt and Speaker John N. Garner, the Democratic candidates for President and Vice President, carried the State by a plurality of about 615,000, as against Governor Roosevelt's heretofore record Democratic plurality of 725,000, which he received as candidate for re-election to the Governorship two years ago.

With Governor Roosevelt and Colonel Lehman were swept into office the other Democratic candidates on the State-wide ticket, United States Senator Robert F. Wagner, candidate for re-election, M. William Bray, for Lieutenant Governor; State Controller Morris S. Tremaine, Attorney General John J. Bennett Jr. and the two candidates for Representatives-at-Large, Elmer E. Studley and John Fitzgibbons.

Colonel Lehman led Governor Roosevelt by 88,279 in actual votes cast in New York City and also led the Governor in many cities and counties up-State. His indicated plurality exceeded that of Governor Roosevelt by more than 250,000, but exceeded the indicated plurality for Senator Wagner by only about 35,000.

Returns on the proposition and proposed constitutional amendment were slow in coming in, but a large majority for the proposal to issue $30,000,000 in bonds for unemployment relief was indicated, and scattering returns indicated that the constitutional amendment to throw open the forest reserve to the development of recreational facilities had been beaten.

The vote for President and State-wide candidates follows:

FOR PRESIDENT.

New York City, complete—Roosevelt, Democrat, 1,437,231; Hoover, Republican, 575,031; Thomas, Socialist, 120,486; actual plurality for Roosevelt, 862,200.

Up-State, 431 election districts missing—Roosevelt, 1,022,121; Hoover, 1,254,032; actual plurality for Hoover, 231,911; indicated plurality for Hoover, 247,107; indicated plurality for Roosevelt in the entire State, 615,093.

FOR GOVERNOR.

New York City, complete—Lehman, Democrat, 1,525,510; Donovan, Republican, 542,492; plurality for Lehman, 983,018.

Up-State, 561 election districts missing—Lehman, 1,056,088; Donovan, 1,141,735; actual plurality for Donovan, 85,647; indicated plurality for Donovan, 95,817.

Indicated plurality for Lehman in the entire State, 887,201.

FOR UNITED STATES SENATOR.

New York City, complete—Wagner, Dem., 1,438,343; Medalie, Rep., 517,733; plurality for Wagner, 920,610.

Up-State, 1,301 districts missing—Wagner, 915,699; Medalie, 964,418;

Continued on Page Five.

THE TAMIAMI—Fast New One Night Out
Train to all Florida from Penn Sta. 10:20
A. M. Daily. Thru Sleepers. Atlantic Coast
Line. & W. 40th St. Tel. LAc. 4-7090.—Advt.

The President's Message To the President-Elect

From a Staff Correspondent.
PALO ALTO, Cal., Nov. 8.—President Hoover conceded his defeat for re-election at 9:17 o'clock tonight, Pacific Time, and dispatched this telegram of congratulations to Governor Roosevelt:

Palo Alto, Cal.,
Nov. 8, 1932.
The Hon. Franklin D. Roosevelt,
Biltmore Hotel,
New York, N. Y.

I congratulate you on the opportunity that has come to you to be of service to the country and I wish for you a most successful administration. In the common purpose of all of us I shall dedicate myself to every helpful effort.

HERBERT HOOVER.

Governor Roosevelt had not received President Hoover's message when he left for his home shortly before 2 o'clock this morning. Pending its receipt he said he preferred not to make reply or comment on the message.

DEMOCRATS CONTROL STATE SENATE, 26-25

Republican Margin in Assembly of 6 Votes Is Reduced to 2 —Lose by 4 Up-State.

ALSO TWO SENATE SEATS

Moffatt Is Re-elected, While Hastings and Dr. Love Are Defeated in City Race.

The slender working majority of two votes by which the Republicans control the present State Senate was swept away in yesterday's Democratic landslide. The next Senate will be made up of 25 Republicans and 26 Democrats, giving the Democrats a majority of one. The present Senate has 27 Republican and 25 Democratic members. Twenty-six votes are required to pass a bill in that branch of the Legislature.

In the Assembly, where 76 votes are required to control legislation, the Republican majority of six is cut down to two in the 1933 Legislature. The Republicans won 77 seats and the Democrats 73 at yesterday's elections for the Assembly.

The Democrats won four Assembly districts north of the Bronx away from the Republicans, one district in Monroe County, one district in Oneida and two in Sullivan and Schoharie counties. The Republicans, however, reduced the up-State Democratic gains by recapturing from them Schuyler county in the southern tier, where last year they succeeded in electing their candidate for the Lower House.

Post Is Defeated.

The Republicans also managed to strengthen their New York City representation by electing Herbert Brownell Jr. in the Tenth (Manhattan) District. This was the district where Langdon W. Post, Democratic incumbent was turned down by Tammany for supporting legislation to broaden the powers and continue the Hofstadter Committee and ran as an independent, polling 5,053 votes. Mr. Brownell defeated his Tammany opponent by a scant plurality of 307 votes. He received 5,907 votes, Sylva La Chappelle, the Democrat, 5,600.

The Democrats gained two Senate districts up-State, the Thirty-first, made up of Rensselaer County, and the Thirty-sixth, made up of Oneida. In the Thirty-fourth, composed of St. Lawrence and Franklin Counties, Warren T. Thayer, the present Republican incumbent, managed to win again after a hard fight.

The New York City Republicans will have three representatives in the Legislature, Senator-elect George Blumberg, who won by a plurality of approximately 500 over Senator John A. Hastings, Democratic incumbent in the Seventh Senatorial

Continued on Page Six.

OVERTURN IN SENATE

Bingham, Watson, Moses and Smoot Are Defeated.

DEMOCRATIC MAJORITY 12

Party Adds to Control in House—May Rule Both Branches This Winter.

LA GUARDIA LOSES SEAT

Mrs. Pratt Defeated, Wadsworth Wins—Texas Sends Garner Back to the House.

The Democratic wave of victory yesterday gave that party complete control of Congress and in its onrush carried down to defeat the four Republican leaders of the Senate. Senator Smoot of Utah, Republican dean of the Senate and chairman of the powerful Finance Committee; Senator Watson of Indiana, floor leader; Senator Moses, president pro tempore and Senator Jones of Washington, chairman of the Appropriations Committee, all were relegated to the ranks of "lame ducks." No such upset has occurred in recent history.

While returns early this morning showed the new Senate will be Democratic by a majority of twelve and the House overwhelmingly Democratic, there was a possibility that in the session of the old Congress convening on Dec. 5, the Democrats will achieve a slender control of the whole body.

Changes in Coming Session.

They now have a majority of one in the House, in the old Congress that still is to hold a "lame-duck" session; in the Senate the numbers were evened with the defeat of Senator Barbour of New Jersey for the short term beginning next month, and there was, early this morning, an even chance that Colorado would elect Walter Walker, a Democrat, also for the short term. In that event the Senate in December would stand: Democrats 49, Republicans 46, Farmer-Labor 1.

On the basis of incomplete returns the new Senate stood at Democrats 54, Republicans 34, Farmer-Labor 1, and seven States still in doubt.

The next Congress not only will be Democratic; it will be wet. New York Republicans fared especially ill in the election, which saw Representative La Guardia, fiery "liberal" Republican who led a bloc that controlled the House temporarily in the last session, defeated by J. J. Lanzetta, Democrat. Representative Ruth Pratt also failed of re-election.

Moses Loses in Close Race.

Of the most prominent Republicans who were unseated, Senator Watson went down first, conceding his defeat by Frederick Van Nuys, Democrat.

Senator Moses ran nip and tuck with Fred H. Brown, Democrat, until after midnight in the poll of ballots, when returns from Manchester, N. H., spelled his certain defeat.

Senator Smoot was defeated by Professor E. D. Thomas and Mr. Jones by Homer T. Bone. Both of the victors were Democrats. Senator Jones, who is better known as the author of the "five-and-ten" law than for his important committee chairmanship, was defeated coincident with adoption of a State referendum in Washington repealing that State's prohibition law.

An important Republican defeat in the House was that of Representative Haugen of Iowa, co-author of the McNary-Haugen bill, who went down before F. Bierman, Democrat.

McAdoo Wins Seat.

William Gibbs McAdoo, Democratic Secretary of the Treasury, who was credited with switching the Democratic National Convention to Franklin D. Roosevelt through

Continued on Page Eight.

THE PRESIDENT-ELECT.

© New York Times Studio.
Franklin D. Roosevelt.

The Electoral Vote

ROOSEVELT 448.

Alabama	11	Nebraska	7
Arizona	3	Nevada	3
Arkansas	9	New Jersey	16
California	22	New Mexico	3
Colorado	6	New York	47
Florida	7	North Carolina	13
Georgia	14	North Dakota	4
Idaho	4	Ohio	26
Illinois	29	Oklahoma	11
Indiana	14	Rhode Island	4
Iowa	11	South Carolina	8
Kansas	9	South Dakota	4
Kentucky	11	Tennessee	11
Louisiana	10	Texas	23
Maryland	8	Utah	4
Massachusetts	17	Virginia	11
Minnesota	11	Washington	8
Mississippi	9	West Virginia	8
Missouri	15	Wisconsin	12
Montana	4	Wyoming	3

HOOVER 59.

Connecticut	8	New Hampshire	4
Delaware	3	Pennsylvania	36
Maine	5	Vermont	3

DOUBTFUL 24.

| Michigan | 19 | Oregon | 5 |

Votes in Electoral College, 531; needed to elect, 266.

Wets in Control in Both Houses, But Short of Two-Thirds in Senate

Modification of Volstead Act Appears Certain, and House Has Easy Majority for Repeal, but Upper Chamber Support Is Uncertain on Basis of Returns

Complete control of the next Congress by forces opposed to Federal prohibition was one of the results which came with the political upheaval that took place with yesterday's election.

With full returns from the major portion of the country and definite trends established in the remainder, it appeared certain that those demanding a change in the dry laws would hold between fifty and fifty-five seats in the Senate and 300 or more in the House of Representatives.

Up until an early hour this morning, only nineteen outspoken drys had been returned definitely to the House, while twenty-four prohibitionists, most of whom did not come up for re-election this year, remained among the Senators. Around 200 House seats were still in doubt, and several Senators and re-elected Representatives were still undecided on the question.

The House was sure of the necessary two-thirds for repeal, as early this morning the anti-prohibitionists had already captured 292 seats; the

Continued on Page Six.

SWEEP IS NATIONAL

Democrats Carry 40 States, Electoral Votes 448.

SIX STATES FOR HOOVER

He Loses New York, New Jersey, Bay State, Indiana and Ohio.

DEMOCRATS WIN SENATE

Necessary Majority for Repeal of the Volstead Act in Prospect.

RECORD NATIONAL VOTE

Hoover Felicitates Rival and Promises 'Every Helpful Effort for Common Purpose.'

Roosevelt Statement.

President-elect Roosevelt gave the following statement to THE NEW YORK TIMES early this morning:

"While I am grateful with all my heart for this expression of the confidence of my fellow-Americans, I realize keenly the responsibility I shall assume and I mean to serve with my utmost capacity the interest of the nation.

"The people could not have arrived at this result if they had not been informed properly of my views by an independent press, and I value particularly the high service of THE NEW YORK TIMES in its reporting of my speeches and in its enlightened comment."

By ARTHUR KROCK.

A political cataclysm, unprecedented in the nation's history and produced by three years of depression, thrust President Herbert Hoover and the Republican power from control of the government yesterday, elected Governor Franklin Delano Roosevelt President of the United States, provided the Democrats with a large majority in Congress and gave them administration of the affairs of many States of the Union.

Fifteen minutes after midnight, Eastern Standard Time, The Associated Press flashed from Palo Alto this line: "Hoover concedes defeat."

It was then fifteen minutes after nine in California, and the President had been in his residence on the Leland Stanford campus only a few hours, arriving with expressed confidence of victory.

A few minutes after the flash from Palo Alto of the text of Mr. Hoover's message of congratulation to his successful opponent was received by THE NEW YORK TIMES, though it was delayed in direct transmission to the President-elect. After offering his felicitations to Governor Roosevelt on his "opportunity to be of service to the country," and extending wishes for success, the President "dedicated" himself to "every possible helpful effort * * * in the common purpose of us all."

This language strengthened the belief of those who expect that the relations between the victor and the vanquished, in view of the exigent condition of the country, may soon confer in an effort to arrive at a mutual program of stabilization during the period between now

Continued on Page Eight.

"All the News That's Fit to Print."

The New York Times.

LATE CITY EDITION

POSTCRIPT

WEATHER—Fair today; tomorrow cloudy, warmer, probably rain
Temperature Yesterday—Max., 42; Min., 37.

Copyright, 1933, by The New York Times Company.

VOL. LXXXII....No. 27,417.

Entered as Second-Class Matter.
Postoffice, New York, N. Y.

NEW YORK, THURSDAY, FEBRUARY 16, 1933.

TWO CENTS In New York City. | THREE CENTS Within 200 Miles | FOUR CENTS Elsewhere Except In 7th and 8th Postal Zones

ASSASSIN FIRES INTO ROOSEVELT PARTY AT MIAMI; PRESIDENT-ELECT UNINJURED; MAYOR CERMAK AND 4 OTHERS WOUNDED

REPEAL VOTE TODAY SET IN THE SENATE; FILIBUSTER BROKEN

Wets Win in Test Ballots as Blaine Plan Is Stripped of Protective Clauses.

ROBINSON LEADS FIGHT

Borah Backs Him on Removing the Anti-Saloon Section, Voted Out 33-32.

STATE LIQUOR PLAN OUT

Commission Proposes to Bar the Saloon—Limit on Places to Sell Beer.

Report of the State Liquor Control Commission is on Page 15.

Special to THE NEW YORK TIMES.

WASHINGTON, Feb. 15.—The Senate today stripped the Blaine prohibition resolution to practically "naked" repeal and agreed to vote on the measure at 3 P. M. tomorrow.

Senator Robinson, the Democratic leader, who led the fight to simplify the resolution, predicted that the Senate would furnish the necessary two-thirds majority for adoption on the morrow.

He expressed confidence, too, that the resolution as amended tonight would be acceptable to Speaker Garner and other House leaders, who announced at the outset that the House would be allowed to vote only on the Democratic repeal plan as advocated in the last campaign.

Every prediction was that the vote tomorrow would be extremely close. Senator McNary, assistant Republican leader, described the resolution as "teetering," with the possibility of going one way or the other. He would make no forecast. Wet leaders, scanning the votes of today, were very hopeful as to the outcome tomorrow. They had succeeded in breaking the filibuster started by the drys to prevent a vote.

Coincidental with the agreement to vote tomorrow, the Senate, by a vote of 33 to 32, struck the so-called anti-saloon provisions from the Blaine resolution and, on a ballot of 45 to 15, decreed that ratification should be by conventions in the several States instead of Legislatures.

Passage in House Predicted.

A deciding vote on the amendment, proposed by Senator Robinson, to strike out the anti-saloon section, was cast by Senator Borah, long a dry stalwart. He held it was impossible for the government properly to exercise any supervisior over saloons once the Eighteenth Amendment was repealed.

As the resolution stood tonight, its proposal was only one degree removed from outright repeal. It carried a clause directing a federal protection of dry States which the Garner repeal resolution, submitted at the outset of the session, did not contain but which was not sufficiently controversial to bring a deadlock between the two branches.

The resolution as it emerged was believed to have a better chance of passage in the House than the proposal submitted by Speaker Garner the first day of Congress. The Speaker's resolution failed by only six votes of obtaining the necessary two-thirds majority, and it was pointed out tonight that the six votes from Senator Robinson's own State, which were cast in the negative at that time, were sufficient to change the tide should repeal be proposed anew to the House.

It was recalled, too, that Senator Robinson was opposed to the Garner resolution, whereas his espousal at this time of the Democratic platform plan was responsible for much of the weight given to the revival of the repeal movement.

The dry filibuster against the Blaine resolution broke up in the Senate today when wets and drys announced

Continued on Page Fourteen.

PINEHURST, N. C.—Enjoy sun-warmed, pine-scented spring days at famous golf resort. Inquire N. Y. Office (Hotel Bogle), Wickersham 2-2677.—Advt.

Illinois Senate Passes Bills For Repeal of Prohibition Laws

By The Associated Press.

SPRINGFIELD, Ill., Feb. 15.—The State Senate today passed two prohibition repeal measures and sent them to the House for further action.

The vote on the repeal measures, which had been delayed because of Governor Henry Horner's insistence that regulatory acts should be provided first, was preceded by promises in the debate that they would not be signed until the regulatory bills also had been adopted.

The two bills would remove from the statute books State prohibition and the search and seizure acts.

A measure designed to authorize banking holidays was introduced in the House. Under its terms, the Governor would be empowered to declare a holiday for the State and Mayors authorized to do so for municipalities.

BOY GANG CHIEF, 15, ADMITS KILLING 'FOE'

Says He Stabbed Queens Lad, 12, for "Lying" About Him and Vowed to "Get" Him.

VICTIM MISSING 2 WEEKS

Found Bound in Closet of a Vacant House to Which Killer Had Lured Him by Ruse.

Bound, gagged and stabbed through the heart, the body of 12-year-old William Bender, who disappeared Jan. 31, was found yesterday in a closet in one of a row of partly-built dwellings, less than two blocks from his home at 6 Bergen Landing Road, Richmond Hill Circle, Queens. He had been dead for at least two weeks.

Nine hours after the body was found, Harry Murch, 15-year-old leader of a juvenile gang, confessed that he had murdered the Bender boy. Murch and his chum, John Miller, 10, who was with him when he was committed, were picked up by the police yesterday afternoon. For more than five hours, despite persistent questioning by officials of the Police Department and the District Attorney's office, they calmly denied all knowledge of the crime. Then finally they broke down.

"I did it," Murch is said to have declared. "Bender lied about me. He told the whole neighborhood that I had hit Mr. Peterson on the head with a monkey wrench. I said I'd get him and I did."

He is to be arraigned today in children's court, Jamaica, on a charge of homicide.

Tells of Meeting Victim.

Murch said that on the afternoon of Jan. 31 he and Miller had met Bender outside the latter's home.

"I told him," Murch said, "that I was going to stick up a peanut peddler and that if he'd come over to the houses in Mauretania Avenue with me I'd show him how I was going to do it. He came along all right. But he seemed a bit suspicious.

"So I tied up Miller first. Then I untied Miller and tied up Bender. As soon as I had him where I wanted him I took out my knife and stabbed him in the heart."

Miller corroborated Murch's story. Afterward, the boys said, they fled from the house and agreed to say nothing to any one. The knife which Murch used for the crime, they said, was taken from the kitchen of his home.

The clue that broke the case was a small piece of gingham cloth that had been used to gag the dead boy. The fact that Murch had threatened to "get Bender" was well known in the neighborhood, and soon after the body was discovered detectives went to the home of Murch's parents, Mr. and Mrs. Charles Murch, in Philbert Avenue, just a short distance from the home of the Bender boy.

In the Murch garage the detectives found other pieces of gingham of exactly the same quality and pattern as that which had been used for the gag. Young Murch and Miller were immediately taken into custody.

The body of the missing boy was

Continued on Page Ten.

TAX RATE OF $2.40 SEEN AS VALUATIONS DROP $1,195,006,742

Sexton Estimates a 19-Point Reduction to the Lowest Basic Levy Since 1920.

REALTY BURDEN EASED

Assessment Totals Cut in All Boroughs—Personalty Less, Franchise Values Rise.

ALDERMEN VOTE BUDGET

Adopt $518,427,972 Document Without Change—Mayor Denies Pleas on Sergeants-at-Arms.

Final adoption of the revised 1933 budget at a total of 18 per cent below that of the 1932 budget and announcement of a cut of $1,195,006,742 in assessed valuations of city real estate, personal property and franchises provided yesterday a substantial basis for belief that the basic tax rate this year will be appreciably lower than the 1932 rate of $2.59 per $100 of assessed valuation.

For the first time in the city's history the total of assessed valuations is lower than in a preceding year. Valuations placed upon franchises for tax purposes were increased in every borough this year. Valuations on real estate showed decreases in every borough, while in the Bronx alone the valuations on personal estate showed a rise. The total valuations for all boroughs in 1932 was $19,977,077,315. For 1933 the final valuations aggregate $18,782,070,573.

The Board of Aldermen adopted a final budget of $518,427,972.16, the same total recently approved by the Board of Estimate. This figure shows a decrease of $112,933,325.81 from the total budget for 1932, which was $631,386,297.97. The budget now goes to Mayor O'Brien for his signature. It must be filed with Controller Berry by Feb. 25.

Nineteen-Point Tax Drop Seen.

James J. Sexton, president of the Department of Taxes and Assessments, said that he was certain the basic tax rate would show a decided drop. He expressed the belief that the rate would not exceed $2.40, a drop of nineteen points.

Deputy Controller Frank J. Prial, in the absence of the Controller, said that no accurate estimate of the rate could be made before the amount of the city's general fund for reduction of taxation is known. The general fund, the budget and the final total of assessed valuation are the three factors used in computing the basic rate. Borough tax rates are added to the basic rate to pay for local improvements. Mr. Prial said that the amount of the general fund would depend

Continued on Page Nine.

Cermak in Critical Condition at Hospital; "Glad It Was I, Not You," He Tells Roosevelt

Special to THE NEW YORK TIMES.

MIAMI, Thursday, Feb. 16.—Mayor Cermak was shot in the right side, just below the ribs, and is in a critical condition at Jackson Memorial Hospital. An X-ray showed the bullet lodged in the back of the abdomen.

An emergency operation was considered at 12:30 A. M. and plans were made to undertake it at once. A short time later physicians put off the operation.

When President-elect Roosevelt called to see Mayor Cermak at the hospital the Mayor turned his head and smiled faintly, saying:

"I'm glad it was I, instead of you. The country needs you very badly. You should not take any more such chances as you took tonight."

The President-elect replied:

"The country needs you, too, too. I can only express my deepest regrets. I have decided not to leave tonight and will return to see you in the morning."

A bulletin on Mayor Cermak's condition, issued at 2 A. M., said:

"Pulse, 88; temperature, 98.6; respiration, 24. His condition is regarded as dangerous, but not immediately critical. The bullet evidently traversed the diaphragm and margin of the liver and lodged in the body of the eleventh dorsal vertebra. Surgical intervention is deemed unwise unless his condition becomes worse."

The bulletin was signed by Dr. John W. Snyder, Dr. Thomas H. Hynson and Dr. 7 S. Nichol. Dr. Snyder is in charge, and at the hospital this morning he said:

"Mrs. Gill and Mayor Cermak have more than a fifty-fifty chance to recover."

James B. Bowler, Chicago City

SERIOUSLY WOUNDED.

Times Wide World Photo.
Mayor Anton J. Cermak of Chicago.

WOMAN DIVERTED AIM OF ASSASSIN

100-Pound Wife of Miami Doctor Tells How She Forced Up Man's Arm.

HELD ON DURING SHOOTING

Gun Had Been Pointed "Right at Mr. Roosevelt," She Relates.

By Telephone to THE NEW YORK TIMES.

MIAMI, Fla., Feb. 15.—Mrs. Lillian Cross, 48 years old, and weighing only 100 pounds, probably saved the life of the President-elect tonight when she forced the would-be assassin's shooting arm upward and caused the bullets to go high.

"He was aiming right at the President," said Mrs. Cross. "I saw him. That's why I caught his arm and forced the gun up. I said to myself, all in a flash, 'Oh! He's going to kill the President!'"

Mrs. Cross said that she was not frightened when she saw the weapon. Her only thought was for Mr. Roosevelt.

"I didn't begin to get nervous at all until it was all over," she related after she reached her home at 1,089 Northwest Second Street.

"I drove to the park tonight with my husband, Dr. W. F. Cross (he's a physician and surgeon here) and with my friend, Mrs. Willis McCrary of Atlanta, Ga. My husband got a seat somewhere in the back of the crowd, but Mrs. McCrary and I found seats right up front, by the guard rail they'd put up.

"President Roosevelt was only about fifteen feet away from us. He finished his speech and got down from the back of the automobile—an open car it was—and had settled in the back seat. I stood up on the bench on which I'd been sit-

Continued on Page Three.

WASHINGTON IS STUNNED

Hoover Wires Roosevelt; Rejoicing That He Was Not Wounded.

ASKS NEWS OF CERMAK

Senators Express Gratitude President-Elect Escaped Madman's Shots.

RISK TO PRESIDENT SEEN

Determination Is Voiced That Life of His Successor Be Safeguarded by All Means.

Special to THE NEW YORK TIMES.

WASHINGTON, Feb. 15.—The nation's capital was deeply shocked tonight on hearing of the attempt on the life of President-elect Roosevelt.

From President Hoover to the lowliest citizen the reaction was instant that the country cast every safeguard around the President-elect.

President Hoover himself struck the keynote when he said:

"I am deeply shocked at the news. It is a dastardly act."

Hoover's Message to Roosevelt.

At the same time the President sent a telegram to Mr. Roosevelt which read:

"Together with every citizen I rejoice that you have not been injured. I shall be grateful to you for news of Mayor Cermak's condition."

Official and unofficial Washington was stunned at the first reports of what appeared to be an attempt on the life of the man who within less than three weeks will become Chief Executive. Newspaper extras were on the street almost immediately, and citizens sat close to their radios, receiving the latest news flashes. General relief was expressed that Mr. Roosevelt escaped injury.

Comment of Leaders.

Speaker Garner said:

"I am gratified beyond words that the President-elect is uninjured and that he will assume the administration of the Government of the United States, which is desired by the American people as expressed in the overwhelming result of the November elections."

Secretary Mills said:

"I am thankful that our next President escaped injury and that the act of a misguided or crazy individual will not deprive the American people of their chosen leader."

"Of course, I am overjoyed that the President-elect escaped," said Senator Byrnes, one of Mr. Roosevelt's closest advisers, "but I deplore profoundly that such a thing could happen. It's awful!"

Senator Robinson of Arkansas, Senate minority leader, said:

"Assuming that the shots were fired at Mr. Roosevelt, it should be understood that this is the United States, not Russia. No fanatic, crank or revolutionist, or any number of them will be permitted to prevent the orderly transfer of power in the government of the United States."

Thinks Assailant Deranged.

"How dreadful, and how fortunate he did not hit!" said Senator Lewis of Illinois. "I do not know what to say except that it was a deplorable thing. I do hope it was not attempted out of ill will. It must have been the result of a deranged mind; certainly no one in his right mind would attempt such a thing. If, as appears possible, the shots were actually fired at Mayor Cermak, it undoubtedly was some member of the old lawless element in Chicago with a fancied grievance against the Mayor."

Chief Moran of the Secret Service, ill at his home here, received a report late this evening from Joseph E. Murphy, Assistant Chief, from the hospital in Miami where Mayor Cermak had been taken. Commenting on the shooting, Senator Shipstead said:

"This unfortunate incident shows the risk the President and the President-elect of the United States are subject to. There are always cranks in the country. Every citi-

Continued on Page Three.

ESCAPES ASSASSIN'S BULLETS.

New York Times Studio Photo.
President-Elect Franklin D. Roosevelt.

GUNMAN LAYS ACT TO BODY 'TORMENT'

Joe Zingara, Hackensack Bricklayer, Says Pain Made Him 'Hate All Presidents.'

DESCRIBED AS ANARCHIST

Man Who Fired at Roosevelt Says He Once Tried in Italy to Kill King Victor Emmanuel.

By Telephone to THE NEW YORK TIMES.

MIAMI, Feb. 15.—Surrounded by detectives and high police officials, the man who shot at President-elect Roosevelt tonight gave his name as Joe Zingara of New York and related, in spasms of words during questioning at Police Headquarters, how "constant torment from a stomach operation" had impelled him to attempt the life of the President-elect.

Zingara, a short, stocky man of about 35, a brick mason who came to Miami two months ago from Hackensack, N. J., betrayed by his manner even in the rational portions of his statement the warped mentality which resulted in his deed tonight.

In an almost boastful tone, he declared that he had attempted the life of King Victor Emmanuel of Italy ten years ago. That failed, he said, for the same reason as his attempt tonight—"there was too big a crowd."

He admitted he had no personal grievance against Mr. Roosevelt. "No, I had none," he swept away questions of that nature.

Nor could the police discover that he had any personal grievance against the King of Italy. But he hated "rich and powerful persons," he said with a hiss, and they were figures, he indicated, for his wrath.

"I Don't Like Presidents."

"I like Roosevelt personally, but I don't like Presidents," he replied when asked if he didn't like the President-elect. He intended to kill him, he said, "and I would be glad if I had killed the President-elect." He did not like Presidents because "rich men send their children to schools."

He said this was because "when I was a young man, rich men's sons went to school while I worked in a brick factory in Italy and burned myself."

Zingara indicated a scar on his stomach which he said was the result of the burn.

He was seized with the idea of trying to kill the President-elect only two days ago, he declared.

"About two days ago I bought a paper for 5 cents and saw that the President-elect was coming to Miami," he related.

"So yesterday I went to a place

Continued on Page Two.

MRS. ROOSEVELT TAKES NEWS CALMLY

She Telephones Immediately to Husband and Is Relieved to Find Him Unhurt.

KEEPS SPEAKING PROGRAM

Assured That "He Is Not Even Excited," She Takes Train Later for Ithaca.

Mrs. Franklin D. Roosevelt returned to her home at 49 East Sixty-fifth Street about 10:30 o'clock last night and found the household upset. The Negro butler's face betrayed his agitation as he admitted her.

"What's it all about?" she demanded.

Stammering, the butler told her that her husband, the President-elect, had been fired upon in Miami. He had only the meager information gleaned from newspapers, which called the house when the first brief reports were received.

Mrs. Roosevelt was met at her home by her daughter, Mrs. Anna Roosevelt Dall, and received the news calmly and without apparent emotion.

"Those things are to be expected," she remarked.

With a calm and steady voice she placed a long distance telephone call which reached the President-elect at the bedside of Mayor Cermak. There followed a few minutes of conversation and then Mrs. Roosevelt turned to the group in the room and said:

"He's all right. He's not the least bit excited."

Leaves for Ithaca.

A few minutes later Mrs. Roosevelt, accompanied only by her maid, was on a railroad train bound for Ithaca, N. Y., to fill a speaking engagement on the program of Cornell University's Home and Farm Week. The train left at 11:35.

Mrs. Roosevelt was at the Warner Club at 321 West Forty-fourth Street when the first of the dramatic incident in Miami was received in New York newspaper offices. She left there without knowledge of what had happened.

In her telephone conversation with Mrs. Roosevelt, members of the household said, the President-elect informed her that it was his belief that the would-be assassin's bullets were aimed at Mayor Cermak, and not at him.

They quoted him as saying that five persons were in the hospital as a result of the shooting, and that starting back for New York last night, as he had planned, however,

Continued on Page Two.

ASSASSIN SHOOTS 5 TIMES

Police and Bystanders Leap for Him and Take Him Prisoner.

ACCOMPLICE TAKEN LATER

Cermak and New York Officer Rushed to Hospital—Now in Serious Condition.

ROOSEVELT DELAYS TRIP

Had Been Warmly Welcomed and Intended to Start for North at Once.

By JAMES A. HAGERTY.
Special to THE NEW YORK TIMES.

MIAMI, Feb. 15.—An unsuccessful attempt was made to assassinate President-elect Franklin D. Roosevelt just after he ended a nine-day fishing cruise on Vincent Astor's yacht Nourmahal.

Although the gunman missed the target at which he was aiming, he probably fatally wounded Mayor Anton Cermak of Chicago and four other persons were hit by five shots from his pistol before a woman destroyed his aim on the last shot by seizing his wrist and a Miami policeman felled him to the ground with a blow of his night stick.

List of the Wounded.

The wounded are:

Mayor Anton Cermak of Chicago, shot through the chest; condition critical.

Miss Margaret Kruis of the Henry Clay Hotel, Miami Beach, a visitor from Newark, N. J., shot through the hand.

Mrs. Joe H. Gill, wife of the president of the Florida Power and Light Company, shot in the abdomen; condition critical.

William Sinnott, a New York policeman, living at 612 West 178th Street, shot in the head; condition critical.

Russell Caldwell, 22, of Miami, shot in the head.

Roosevelt Was Target.

The would-be assassin, who was arrested immediately and lodged in the city prison on the nineteenth floor of Miami's skyscraper City Hall, is Giuseppe Zingara of Hackensack, N. J.

Although early reports made clear that the target was the President-elect, due to his remark, "Well, I got Cermak," it appeared later that Mr. Roosevelt was his target.

"I'd kill every President," he was reported by the police to have said after his arrest.

"I'd kill them all; I'd kill all the officers," he is also reported to have said, indicating that he may be an Anarchist.

Evidence that the attempted assassination of Roosevelt was premeditated was obtained by the police late tonight and Andrea Valemti, who lived with Zingara, was arrested on suspicion of being an accomplice.

A search of Zingara's clothing disclosed several newspaper clippings, mostly from local newspapers announcing Mr. Roosevelt's intended visit to this city.

Clipping on McKinley.

One clipping, however, contained an account of the assassination of President McKinley by the anarchist Czolgosz. This strengthened the police belief that Zingara might belong to some anarchist group, although no direct evidence has been obtained showing such a connection.

Detectives, deputy sheriffs and policemen were working on several clues, obtained by the questioning of Zingara and Valemti.

Zingara is charged with assault, with intent to kill, pending the preferring of the more serious

"All the News That's Fit to Print."

The New York Times.

LATE CITY EDITION
WEATHER—Fair today; tomorrow cloudy, warmer, rain following
Temperatures Yesterday—Max.: 40; min., 26.

Copyright, 1933, by The New York Times Company.

VOL. LXXXII....No. 27,435.

Entered as Second-Class Matter,
Postoffice, New York, N. Y.

NEW YORK, MONDAY, MARCH 6, 1933.

P

TWO CENTS in New York City. | THREE CENTS Within 200 Miles | FOUR CENTS Elsewhere Except in 7th and 8th Postal Zones

ROOSEVELT ORDERS 4-DAY BANK HOLIDAY, PUTS EMBARGO ON GOLD, CALLS CONGRESS

HITLER BLOC WINS A REICH MAJORITY; RULES IN PRUSSIA

Stay-at-Homes Turn Out and Give Government 52% of 39,000,000 Record Vote.

NAZIS ROLL UP 17,300,000

Get 44% of Total Poll and Even Wrest the Control of Bavaria From Catholics.

ELECTION IS PEACEFUL

Berlin Is Closely Guarded—The Stahlhelm Holds Parade Under Sunny Skies.

By FREDERICK T. BIRCHALL.
Special Cable to THE NEW YORK TIMES.

BERLIN, Monday, March 6.—With almost mathematical precision the results in yesterday's German elections for the Reichstag and the Prussian Diet bear out the predictions based on the pre-election campaign. Just as two and two make four, so suppression and intimidation have produced a Nazi-Nationalist triumph. The rest of the world may now accept the fact of ultra-Nationalist domination of the Reich and Prussia for a prolonged period with whatever results this may entail.

At 2 o'clock this morning, when 39,000,000 out of the Reich's eligible vote of 44,000,000 counted and with every indication of a probable total vote of 90 per cent, exceeding all precedents this November vote.The Nazis will have at least 288 seats and the Nationalists 53 more, giving them together 341 seats, or a clear 52 per cent in a total of 648.

The tabulated vote follows:

	Vote.	Seats.
National Socialists	17,300,000	288
Nationalists	3,100,000	53
Socialists	7,000,000	118
Communists	4,800,000	81
Centrists and Bavarian People's Party	5,500,000	91
People's Party and Allied Groups	1,014,000	12
State (Democratic)	333,000	5
Total	39,047,000	648

The Nazis have increased their vote to 44 per cent of the adult population, or 11 per cent over that of last November and 6¼ per cent over their previous high-water total of last July. The Nationalist increase is barely 1 per cent over their vote of last November. This, therefore, is a Nazi rather than a Nationalist triumph.

Nazis Control Bavaria.

Apart from the size of the vote—the 90 per cent of the eligible voters being as nearly unanimous as any election in any large country has ever shown—the sensation of the election is that the Nazis have wrested control of Bavaria from the Catholics. They have wiped out the deficit in their November vote compared with that of July and have beaten the Bavarian People's party by approximately 600,000. This is likely to dispose of any dream of restoring the Wittelsbach monarchy in Bavaria, as it will of the idea of a possible secession of Bavaria from the Reich.

More than this, in the city of Cologne, the Catholic capital of Germany, under the influence of terror a weakening of the Centrists has almost held their own. The so-called stay-at-home vote came out with a vengeance and almost the whole of it went to the Nazis; while, in addition, the Hitlerites gained a full 10 per cent from the other parties.

Gain 4,000,000 Votes.

The Nazis have increased their own vote by more than 4,000,000, or almost 30 per cent over the November total. The Centrists and Socialists throughout the country have almost held their own. The Communists lost more than 20 per cent, but their lost votes did not go to the Socialists, as had been expected. While a few may have expected

Continued on Page Eight.

Pinehurst, N. C.—Complete change of climate, scenery, flawless service and modern days, all expenses, $110 (golf). Carolina Hotel and r.r. fare; 507 at Holly Inn.—Advt.

Mob Attacked Stalin's Home In Wide Revolt, Tokyo Hears

Wireless to THE NEW YORK TIMES.

TOKYO, Monday, March 6.—Private information reaching Tokyo states that discontent due to famine conditions is so acute in Soviet Russia that a mob attacked Joseph Stalin's house in Moscow on Jan. 20 and was driven off by troops after 400 persons had been killed. Other reports from Siberia, partly corroborated by information reaching military circles here, indicate the farmers are in widespread revolt. Serious disturbances occurred at Irkutsk, and 80,000 men are said to have joined the revolt, including Communists and Red soldiers.

The Japanese discount a good part of these rumors, but they come from too many sources to be entirely ignored. It is believed these disturbances are much more serious than the Soviet Government has admitted.

CERMAK NEAR END; LAPSES INTO COMA

Death Is Imminent From Shot Aimed by Zangara at Roosevelt.

FAMILY AT HIS BEDSIDE

Third Transfusion Futile in 19-Day Fight to Save Chicago Mayor in Miami Hospital.

By The Associated Press.

MIAMI, Fla., Monday, March 6.—Physicians of Mayor Anton Cermak early this morning relinquished hope for his life.

In a bulletin issued at 12:30 A. M. the physicians said that Mayor Cermak was in a condition of coma and that he probably would live only a few hours. The bulletin said Mr. Cermak was "failing rapidly."

It was issued after a third blood transfusion had been administered yesterday in an attempt to save his life.

The Mayor's right kidney, punctured on the night of Feb. 15 by a bullet from the pistol of the assassin, Joseph Zangara, in an attempt to kill Franklin D. Roosevelt, was aspirated yesterday and physicians found a gangrenous condition.

Father Morrison of St. Bartholomew's Church in Chicago entered the sun porch room at 1:15 A. M. Mayor Cermak's wife was a Roman Catholic and his children are of that faith.

Dr. Frederick Tice of Chicago told newspaper men at 1:25 A. M. that the Mayor probably would live an hour. He said Cermak's breathing was very labored. He called members of the family and said Mr. Cermak's life was "a matter of another hour."

Members of Family Weep.

Members of the family, summoned to the bedside, emerged weeping.

Joseph Cermak, a brother, his wife and Mr. John Kallal, a sister, came from the sun porch at 12:35 A. M. Mrs. Cermak and Mrs. Kallal took their seats on the lawn before the sun porch door and wept. Vivian Graham, a granddaughter, emerged soon and joined the group. Daughters of the Mayor had been at his side a short time before.

At midnight newspapermen were allowed to go into the sun porch where the Mayor lies in an oxygen room and see the patient through the glass window of the oxygen apparatus.

The Mayor lay back on his pillow, hands folded over his chest, breathing heavily. Dr. Frank Jirka and Dr. E. S. Nichol were attending him.

Dr. Jirka, who is Mr. Cermak's son-in-law, said the Mayor recognized members of the family. "My wife asked him if he knew her. He told her, 'Yes, kiss me.'"

The greatest air of concern prevailed in the little sun porch, where a heavy guard of police and detectives was maintained.

"Reaction" After Transfusion.

After the blood transfusion yesterday afternoon Mr. Cermak suffered a "slight reaction," causing a weakening of the pulse and an irregular respiration, the doctors said.

Reports immediately upon conclusion of the transfusion were that the operation apparently was successful. One pint of blood given by Thomas Pendray Jr. of Miami was

Continued on Page Fourteen.

JAPANESE PUSH ON IN FIERCE FIGHTING; CHINA CLOSES WALL

Jehol Forces Offer Stoutest Resistance of Campaign as They Are Cornered

BUT LOSE ANOTHER PASS

Chang's Troops at Kupei Bar Retreat Southward to the Peiping Area.

NANKING ADMITS DEFEAT

Asserts 'What Will Happen Next Depends on Military'—Tientsin Fears Clashes.

By The Associated Press.

TOKYO, March 5.—Rengo (Japanese) news agency dispatches from Chengteh (Jehol City) today said the final phase of the Japanese campaign in Jehol Province, a move to seize passes in the Great Wall north and northeast of Peiping, was producing some of the most bitter fighting of the whole drive. Cornered Chinese units were resisting desperately.

The Sixteenth Infantry Brigade of Major Gen. Tadashi Kawahara, en route to Koupei Pass through the wall, fought fiercely with remnants of the troops of Tang Yu-lin, Governor of Jehol Province, ten miles west of the provincial capital, Chengteh. Thereafter the detachment advanced to Changshanku, which is sixteen miles northeast of the pass.

Marshal Chang Hsiao-liang, military commander of North China, was reported to have sealed the pass against Governor Tang and his followers. Governor Tang himself was reported to have fled to Fengning, which is about forty miles northwest of Chengteh.

Pass in Wall Taken.

Fighting in the shadow of the Great Wall preceded the occupation by the Fourteenth Infantry Brigade of Major Gen. Heijiro Hattori of Fanchia Pass, which is one of three important Great Wall passes south of Chengteh. General Hattori faced a large Chinese force south of the wall.

Major Gen. Kaoru Nakamura, commanding the Thirty-third Infantry Brigade, en route from Lingyua to Cuiehling Pass, summoned an air squadron to aid him before he succeeded in routing remnants of Marshal Chang's Sixteenth Brigade.

The Fourth Cavalry Brigade of Major Gen. Kennosuke Mogi, pushing on from Chifeng, 100 miles northeast of Chengteh, captured Weichang, fifty-five miles to the southwest, the centre of the Jehol opium-producing region, after stiff fighting.

Thousands of Chinese Dead.

Special Cable to THE NEW YORK TIMES.

SHANGHAI, Monday, March 6.—While members of the Nanking Government are expected to discuss a unified policy at Peiping this week, Jehol reports today tell of indescribable confusion among the Chinese forces there, with thousands killed, wounded and missing among the troops in Marshal Chang Hsiao-liang's best brigades, which originally totaled 20,000.

War Minister Ho Yin-ching arrived by airplane at Peiping at noon, and Acting Premier T. V. Soong and others are expected to follow him there for a belated stocktaking of the present situation. The Chinese troops in Jehol appear to be scrambling for the passes out through the Great Wall, with the Japanese bombing Chinese concentrations near Kupei and Haifeng passes and at Dolonnor, in Northern Jehol.

The Japanese artillery is in action at Sanshihchiatze, between Pingchuan and Lingyuan.

The Japanese brigade led by General Hattori is expected to attack the main Chinese forces tomorrow at Paishihlatsushan Hill, twenty miles south of Pingchuan and thirty-three miles from Haifeng Pass.

The Charhar Provincial Government is reported to be negotiating the occupation for inclusion of that province in Manchukuo, but the Chinese military deny this.

The Nanking Foreign Office yesterday made this terse and inclusive statement:

"Jehol is lost. What will happen

Continued on Page Eight.

Relief Wages Will Be Paid Despite Holiday, Gibson Says

Harvey D. Gibson, chairman of the Emergency Unemployment Relief Committee, declared yesterday that the bank holiday would not interfere with the payment of wages to unemployed men and women holding emergency jobs through the committee's work and relief bureau.

"Emergency wages must be paid and some way must be found to pay them," Mr. Gibson said. "I have no doubt that we will find a way to do it. We are not worried about it at all." Arrangements can certainly be made to meet the emergency relief payroll."

The weekly payroll of the committee exceeds $1,000,000.

BEWILDERED CITY STILL PAYS IN CASH

Faces Use of Scrip Calmly and Continues to Patronize the Theatres and Stores.

HOPEFUL MOOD PREVAILS

Merchants and Travel Lines Uncertain on Use of Tender—Many Extending Credit.

Bewildered but still cheerful, the city followed its usual routine yesterday, talked of the possibility of using scrip instead of cash, but still patronized the movie theatres, restaurants and concert halls.

Railroads reported, generally, that there had been no appreciable decrease in week-end travel, that there had been "no embarrassment" and that they were carrying on as usual, on an all-cash basis.

A spokesman for the Pennsylvania Railroad reported that the outward movement yesterday was good and some way might arise from the banking situation, but no decision was reached so far as could be learned.

Airplane lines and steamship lines, on the other hand, were accepting checks from old clients and were following a policy of being "reasonable" about accepting checks from other customers.

"We will maintain a sensible and reasonable attitude during this crisis," said John Gammie, assistant manager of the Cunard Line. "We will try to carry on as much as we did in ordinary times. We haven't taken up the matter of scrip, but it is likely that a meeting of steamship line officials may be called to decide on a policy with regard to it."

Rise in Grocery Store Sales.

Increased sales were reported in most of the chain grocery stores in the poorer districts on Saturday, owners reported yesterday. They believed it might have been caused by a desire to stock up before an inflation policy might be decided upon by the government.

The Grand Union Grocery Stores, on official said last night, are planning to issue coupon books redeemable for food at their stores. The books would be sold to industrial and commercial concerns that would use them as part payment to employees. The same official considered it likely that guaranteed Clearing House scrip might be acceptable at the Grand Union stores.

A spokesman for the Great Atlantic and Pacific Tea Company, which maintains chains of grocery stores in several States, said his concern had not yet formulated any

Continued on Page Three.

BANKS HERE ACT AT ONCE

City Scrip to Be Ready Today or Tomorrow to Replace Currency.

EMERGENCY STEP PRAISED

Financiers Look for Little Interruption in Business Under Federal Program.

'TRUST DEPOSITS' TO AID

Cash Now Can Be Placed in New Accounts and Drawn Upon Without Limitation.

Clearing House certificates will be issued in New York, if needed, just as soon as they can be printed, possibly today and probably not later than tomorrow, as a result of last night.

The President's emergency decree not only made the banking holiday national and extended it through Thursday when Congress meets in special session, but it also gave the banks permission to issue scrip in the form of Clearing House certificates to take the place of regular currency.

Thus there will be little or no interruption in the ordinary routine of New York's business affairs, which can be carried on with scrip as a substitute medium of exchange just as well as with other currency. Paychecks, for instance, would be converted into scrip by the banks, which would be open for that purpose and for receiving new deposits.

Leading bankers indicated their approval of the President's proclamation last night and signified their belief that the use of scrip would be just as successful in New York as it was in the 1907 panic.

May Pay in Currency.

There is a possibility, some bankers said, that the New York banks might pay out currency when they reopen in place of, or in addition to, clearing house certificates. Such action would be possible only with the express permission of the Secretary of the Treasury under the President's order. These bankers said that the local banks have large amounts of till money on hand and that they could, if permitted, meet substantial demands from their depositors out of these cash holdings. From the standpoint of the central banking system the paying out of till money to the public would have no effect upon the position of the national currency, since it is already a part of total money in circulation.

Subject always to the sanction of the Secretary of the Treasury, the banks will be able, under the President's proclamation, to operate along nearly normal lines. The provision for creation of special trust accounts, business men, merchants and wage depositors for any cash they receive instead of having to face the dangers of carrying large amounts of currency. Those who withdrew money from the banks just before the shutdown and who have since been worrying about its safety will be able to redeposit the funds in special trust accounts and be assured of getting it back again without limitation.

Lehman Defers State Action.

When informed of the President's proclamation late last night, Governor Lehman withheld comment for the present as to whether he would issue a new decree extending the New York State holiday. Although such an action probably would be regarded as a mere formality, it was thought likely that the Governor would take it. Before President Roosevelt's proclamation was made public, Governor A. Harry Moore of New Jersey issued a decree last night extending the banking holiday in New Jersey indefinitely.

In both New York and New Jersey the banking holiday was proclaimed first for two days—Saturday and today—and was to have ended with the close of business this afternoon. Under the original proclamations by Governors Lehman and Moore the New York and New Jersey banks were to have been reopened tomorrow morning.

All security and commodity exchanges remain closed, barring unexpected changes in present

Continued on Page Two.

The President's Bank Proclamation

Special to THE NEW YORK TIMES.

WASHINGTON, March 5.—The text of President Roosevelt's proclamation on the banking situation, issued at the White House at 11 o'clock tonight, was as follows:

BY THE PRESIDENT OF THE UNITED STATES OF AMERICA.

A Proclamation

WHEREAS there have been heavy and unwarranted withdrawals of gold and currency from our banking institutions for the purpose of hoarding; and

WHEREAS continuous and increasingly extensive speculative activity abroad in foreign exchange has resulted in severe drains on the nation's stocks of gold; and

WHEREAS these conditions have created a national emergency; and

WHEREAS it is in the best interests of all bank depositors that a period of respite be provided with a view to preventing further hoarding of coin, bullion or currency or speculation in foreign exchange and permitting the application of appropriate measures to protect the interests of our people; and

WHEREAS it is provided in Section 5 (b) of the act of October 6, 1917 (40 stat. L. 411) as amended, "that the President may investigate, regulate or prohibit, under such rules and regulations as he may prescribe, by means of licenses or otherwise, any transactions in foreign exchange and the export, hoarding, melting or earmarkings of gold or silver coin or bullion or currency * * *";

WHEREAS it is provided in Section 16 of the said act "that whoever shall wilfully violate any of the provisions of this act or of any license, rule or regulation issued thereunder, and whoever shall wilfully violate, neglect or refuse to comply with any order of the President issued in compliance with the provisions of this act, shall, upon conviction, be fined not more than $10,000 or, if a natural person, imprisoned for not more than ten years or both * * *";

NOW, THEREFORE, I, FRANKLIN D. ROOSEVELT, PRESIDENT OF THE UNITED STATES OF AMERICA, IN VIEW OF SUCH NATIONAL EMERGENCY AND BY VIRTUE of the authority vested in me by said act and in order to prevent the export, hoarding or earmarking of gold or silver coin or bullion or currency, do hereby proclaim, order, direct and declare that from Monday, the sixth day of March, to Thursday, the ninth day of March, nineteen hundred and thirty-three, both dates inclusive, there shall be maintained and observed by all banking institutions and all branches thereof located in the United States of America, including the Territories and Insular Possessions, a bank holiday, and that during said period all banking transactions shall be suspended.

During such holiday, excepting as hereinafter provided, no such banking institution or branch shall pay out, export, earmark or permit the withdrawal or transfer in any manner or by any device whatsoever of any gold or silver coin or bullion or currency or take any other action which might facilitate the hoarding thereof; nor shall any such banking institution or branch pay out deposits, make loans or discounts, deal in foreign exchange, transfer credits from the United States to any place abroad, or transact any other banking business whatsoever.

During such holiday, the Secretary of the Treasury, with the approval of the President and under such regulations as he may prescribe, is authorized and empowered (a) to permit any or all of such banking institutions to perform any or all of the usual banking functions, (b) to direct, require or permit the issuance of clearing house certificates, or other evidences of claims of assets of banking institutions, and (c) to authorize and direct the creation in such banking institutions of special trust accounts for the receipt of new deposits which shall be subject to withdrawal on demand without any restriction or limitation and shall be kept separately in cash or on deposit in Federal Reserve Banks or invested in obligations of the United States.

As used in this order the term "banking institutions" shall include all Federal Reserve Banks, national banking associations, banks, trust companies, savings banks, building and loan associations, credit unions, or other corporations, partnerships, associations or persons, engaged in the business of receiving deposits, making loans, discounting business paper, or transacting any other form of banking business.

IN WITNESS WHEREOF I have hereunto set my hand and caused the seal of the United States to be affixed.

Done in the City of Washington this 6th day of March, 1 A. M., in the year of Our Lord One Thousand Nine Hundred and Thirty-three, and of the Independence of the United States the one hundred and fifty-seventh.

(SEAL)   FRANKLIN D. ROOSEVELT.

By the President:
      CORDELL HULL,
          Secretary of State.

ROOSEVELT MEETS GOVERNORS TODAY

Conference Will Centre on Bank Problem—Confidence in President Apparent.

Special to THE NEW YORK TIMES.

WASHINGTON, March 5.—The Governors conference which President Roosevelt called nearly a month ago to discuss with him interlocking governmental problems will meet with him tomorrow morning in the White House at 11 o'clock. But its discussion will be largely directed toward the more immediate issue of banking moratoriums, with the possibility that what is done may indicate the eventual Federal action to be suggested by President Roosevelt.

The present situation so far overshadows the issues which Mr. Roosevelt stressed in originally calling the conference that they have become entirely secondary. It was his first intention to confine the discussion to a limitation on overlapping Federal and State

Continued on Page Six.

USE OF SCRIP AUTHORIZED

President Takes Steps Under Sweeping Law of War Time.

PRISON FOR GOLD HOARDER

The Proclamation Provides for Withdrawals From Banks Against New Deposits.

CONGRESS SITS THURSDAY

Day of Conference With the Cabinet and Financial Men Precedes the Decree.

Special to THE NEW YORK TIMES.

WASHINGTON, March 5.—To prevent the export, hoarding or earmarking of gold or silver, coin or bullion or currency, President Roosevelt issued a proclamation at 11 o'clock tonight, in which he ordered a bank holiday from tomorrow through Thursday, March 9. Earlier in the day he had summoned a special session of Congress to meet on Thursday.

This sweeping action was taken after a day of conferences, among officials and bankers, the President taking recourse to war powers granted under the trading-with-the-enemy act.

As a result of the proclamation all banking activities will be suspended during the holiday, except as permitted by regulations of the Secretary of the Treasury, thus taking this country technically off the gold standard until the four-day period expires.

In order that there may not be a complete suspension of all banking and exchange operations, the proclamation authorizes the issuance of Clearing House certificates, which may be used as currency until the banks return to more normal functioning.

Points of the Proclamation.

The main points in the proclamation are:

1. A national banking holiday from March 6 to March 9 inclusive.

An embargo on the withdrawal of gold and silver for export or domestic use during that period, except with permission of the Secretary of the Treasury.

2. The issuance of Clearing House certificates or other evidence of claims against the assets of banking institutions to permit banks to carry on.

4. Authorization to banking institutions under regulations of the Secretary of the Treasury to receive new deposits and make them subject to withdrawal on demand without any restrictions or limitations.

Friends of the President had had a definite three-point program for the solution of the banking problem and that tonight's action included two of them. The first, they said, was a protection of the currency against unreasonable withdrawal. The second was to furnish a temporary currency. The third is permanent reorganization of the whole banking system, which, they predicted would be proposed to the special session of Congress meeting here Thursday.

Officials Act Quickly.

The Federal Reserve Board and Secretary Woodin, with the advice of former Secretary Ogden L. Mills, acted immediately after the issuance of the proclamation to make it effective.

The proclamation was issued at 11 o'clock, bringing to an end a series of conferences held by Treasury officials and the new Cabinet throughout the day.

The proclamation affects all Federal Reserve Banks and national banks, trust companies, savings banks, building and loan associations, credit unions or other institutions engaged in any form of banking business.

The proclamation provides for a fine of $10,000 or imprisonment of not more than ten years for any violation of its provisions by gold hoarding or otherwise.

The President acted under Section 5 (b) and Section 16 of the trading-with-the-enemy act to place these extraordinary restrictions on the nation's banking structure. The courts have interpreted the act as giving the President authority to bring about a complete suspension of gold and silver payments as well as an embargo on their export.

Section 5 (b) of the trading-with-

ON GOLD STANDARD, WOODIN DECLARES

Other High Officials Concur in His View of Suspending Payments for Period.

Special to THE NEW YORK TIMES.

WASHINGTON, March 5.—Secretary of the Treasury William H. Woodin declared tonight emphatically that the United States had not gone off the gold standard on account of the proclamation of the President. He was supported in this view by other high officials of the administration, both in the executive and legislative branches, among them Senator Key Pittman, chairman of the Committee on Foreign Relations.

Secretary Woodin said:

"It is ridiculous and misleading to say that we have gone off the gold standard, any more than we have gone off the currency standard.

"We are definitely on the gold standard. Gold merely cannot be obtained for several days. In other

"All the News That's Fit to Print."

The New York Times.

LATE CITY EDITION

WEATHER—Rain and warmer today; tomorrow fair and colder.
Temperature Yesterday—Max., 57; Min., 45

Copyright, 1933, by The New York Times Company.

VOL. LXXXIII....No. 27,692.

Entered as Second-Class Matter,
Postoffice, New York, N. Y.

NEW YORK, SATURDAY, NOVEMBER 18, 1933.

TWO CENTS In New York City. | THREE CENTS Within 200 Miles | FOUR CENTS Elsewhere Except In 7th and 8th Postal Zones

---

WRIT BARS TAX AID FOR CITY SUBWAY; 5-CENT FARE HIT

Appellate Division Finds That 3 Years of Trial Operation Began Sept. 10, 1932.

$12,000,000 SAVING SEEN

Huge Service Charge Must Be Taken From Budget if Decision Is Upheld.

LAGUARDIA TO ACT AT ONCE

Will Speed Negotiations as Unity Is Seen as Sole Hope of Averting Fare Rise.

The Appellate Division ruled yesterday, in a 4 to 1 decision, that the city no longer has any right to use tax funds to pay interest and amortization on bonds issued to finance construction of the Eighth Avenue subway. Reversing a ruling made in June by Supreme Court Justice John J. Walsh, the court granted a taxpayer's application for a temporary injunction against such payments.

If the decision is upheld, it will mean that approximately $12,000,000 must be stricken from the debt service appropriation in the 1934 budget, which is $26,000,000 out of balance. City officials, including George McAneny, Controller, and John H. Delaney, chairman of the Board of Transportation, indicated that an immediate appeal would be taken, which would automatically stay the temporary injunction.

Five-Cent Fare Imperiled.

In transit and financial circles the decision was regarded as of vital importance to the future of the five-cent fare. Responsible city officials, although declining to be quoted, indicated their belief that affirmation of the ruling by the Court of Appeals would mean that the nickel fare could be preserved, if at all, only by speedy unification of all rapid transit lines under city ownership and control.

In effect the decision fixed Sept. 10, 1932, the date of the opening of the Eighth Avenue line, as the beginning of the three-year trial period allowed the city if it elected to operate its own subways on a 5-cent fare. At the end of that period, under the State laws, the fare must be sufficient to pay all expenses, including fixed charges of every nature. It has always been the city's contention that the three-year period would not begin to run until after the entire system, including the Sixth Avenue line, for which no contracts have yet been let, was completed and in operation.

City Faces Dilemma.

Affirmation of the decision by the Court of Appeals, it was said in financial circles, would leave the city in a serious dilemma, so far as the fare question was concerned.

The consensus was that while it would mean speedy unification highly desirable from the city's point of view, the prevailing economic conditions, together with the strictures placed upon the city's fiscal freedom by the four-year financing compact with its bankers, might well force a general upward revision of all traction fares, without unification.

In any event, it was said, consummation of a unity plan which would preserve the five-cent fare and still be workable would be quite difficult under existing conditions. City officials made light of this viewpoint, declaring that the pressure of economic conditions was such that the traction companies would be glad to "get out from under" at prices which would permit the city to engage in unified ownership and control of rapid transit lines and still continue the five-cent fare. None of these officials, however, would be quoted, preferring to leave the problem to the incoming Fusion administration.

LaGuardia to Act at Once.

Coincident with the handing down of the Appellate Division's ruling was the receipt of word from the Canal Zone that Mayor-elect F. H. LaGuardia planned to begin unification negotiations immediately upon his return to the city next week, instead of waiting until he assumed office on Jan. 1. Mr. LaGuardia and his advisers, it was understood, reached the conclusion some time ago that the unification problem must be settled speedily if the five-cent fare was to be preserved.

The issue upon which the Appellate Division ruled was raised last February in a taxpayer's action brought by William Church Osborn and the Anahma Realty Corporation, under the sponsorship of the Citizens Budget Commission. The decision upheld their contention that the beginning of operation of the Eighth Avenue subway on the

Continued on Page Nine.

Bolan and Aide Quell Fire in Car on 5th Av.

Police Commissioner Bolan usurped the duties of fire chief yesterday and directed a one-man fire company in the extinguishing of a blaze.

As the commissioner was being driven up Fifth Avenue, he noticed smoke coming from beneath an expensive limousine. Signaling his chauffeur to stop at Fifty-eighth Street, the commissioner and the driver, Detective Bernard Shanley, went into action with a hand extinguisher. Shanley did the pumping and the commissioner "kibitzed."

Meanwhile a pedestrian had turned in an alarm, but when a fire truck rolled up its work had been done. The limousine was owned by former Governor R. L. Beeckman of Rhode Island, whose home is at Newport. The fire was under its floorboards, and was caused by a short circuit.

BREWERS WIN FIGHT ON ALCOHOL LABEL

State Board Rules They Need Not Show Strength of Beer After Repeal.

RUSH FOR LIQUOR PERMITS

10,000 Seek Applications for Licenses for Restaurants, Hotels and Clubs.

Edward P. Mulrooney, chairman of the State Alcoholic Control Board, announced yesterday that after Dec. 5, the day repeal goes into effect, brewers would not be required to state the alcoholic content of their brew on beer bottle labels.

He explained that this was ordered by the board at the request of the brewers to eliminate unfair competition. Mr. Mulrooney said the board would test the beer for sale in this State from time to time to see that it was palatable and had at least the present alcoholic content.

Representatives of about 10,000 restaurants, hotels and clubs appeared during the day at the temporary offices of the City Alcoholic Beverage Control Board for applications for licenses to sell liquor and wine for consumption on the premises.

Wait Nine Hours in Cold.

Many of the applicants waited for more than nine hours in the cold. Hundreds were turned away because the supply of blanks had been depleted. Applications for club licenses had not arrived and will not be available until this morning.

When the offices of the board were closed for the day, more than 6,000 application blanks for permission to sell liquor in restaurants and hotels had been distributed. At closing time fifty-six restaurant liquor license applications and one hotel liquor application, one drug store application and one restaurant wine application had been filed.

The restaurant applications were the first to be distributed. The hotel license applications were not received from the printer until 11 o'clock in the morning. The supply ran out about 4 in the afternoon and did the restaurant application forms.

There was no disorder attendant on the passing out of the applications. The blanks were handed out rapidly as soon as they were received at the Reade Street premises. Applicants as well as officials of the State and city boards were disappointed that there were not enough to take care of all applicants during the entire day.

State Regulations Clarified.

Mr. Mulrooney clarified some of the regulations of the State board governing the sale of wine and liquor for off-premises consumption. He ruled that the 1,500-foot distance could not apply to stores that sell only wine at retail. The board will waive the 1,500-foot rule in these cases whenever it deems such action necessary and every case will be passed on by the board.

The 1,500 foot rule was explained in more detail by Mr. Mulrooney. He said the measurement to separate liquor retail stores is not to be made by the board "as the crow flies," but such distances will be measured as the street and block runs. "The measurement guide will be as one walks or rides on a bicycle," Mr. Mulrooney said.

Long after those in line had been told to return today or Monday for restaurant and other licenses, word was received from the State Board that additional restaurant licenses were available and would be sent over immediately to the City Board. Those who wanted this form of application received the blanks until the board offices closed. Applicants for hotel and club licenses were told to return today or Monday.

The regulation requiring restau-

Continued on Page Nine.

FLIGHT OF DOLLAR SET AT ONE BILLION BY LONDON EXPERTS

Americans' Investments in Britain in Past 3 Months Put at $375,000,000.

BAN IS DISPUTED HERE

Washington Opinion on Volume Is Divided—Dollar Rises Again in World Markets.

By CHARLES A. SELDEN.
Special Cable to THE NEW YORK TIMES.

LONDON, Nov. 17.—A tangible estimate in a reliable quarter of American capital which has "flown" to Great Britain in the last three months is only $75,000,000, roughly $375,000,000.

That figure was obtained today from a source whose periodical estimates of foreign investments in this country and British investments abroad are accepted as authentic by the British Board of Trade. Its figures are often used in compiling Board of Trade documents and statements to Parliament.

The financial expert and his advisers who reach the conclusion that $75,000,000 will amply cover the American flight of capital to England also venture the suggestion that such flight from the United States to all countries in the last three months would not exceed $200,000,000, or roughly $1,000,000,000. But they feel much surer of their estimate for this country than of the aggregate figure, although they regard the latter as reasonable for all countries to which the dollar has been going.

"Loose Talk" of Billion Loss.

There has been much loose talk in London about the flight of $1,000,000,000 to Great Britain alone. That is regarded as absurd, but there is a simple explanation for such an exaggeration. It is that $1,000,000,000 is a rough estimate of the total American capital invested in this country, chiefly in industrial and mercantile concerns which have their parent houses in the United States and branch or subsidiary concerns in England, like Ford, General Motors, Woolworth, &c. These investments, of course, are permanent and long antedated the Roosevelt administration. When the flight of American capital did begin and attempts were made to measure it by the amount of American capital in this country, it was sensational but easy to garble the figures on permanent investments as a part of the money which had left the United States.

The wonder in financial circles in London is not that the flight is not larger because of President Roosevelt's policy, but that it has been even $75,000,000, despite the reluctance to buy dollars. There is a simple reason to purchase American currency today if there is a virtual assurance that it is going to be cheaper tomorrow, and there is no assurance whatever when President Roosevelt is going to end the depreciation.

So, under existing circumstances, the British market for the dollar is confined to those who need American currency to pay bills or buy goods in the United States. Even they are inclined to postpone purchases of dollars on the chance that they are going to go even lower.

American currency bought here for discharging obligations or buy-

Continued on Page Two.

Australia Plans to Cut Curbs on Immigration

Wireless to THE NEW YORK TIMES.

CANBERRA, Australia, Nov. 17.—Suggestions for relaxing the restrictions on immigration will be placed before the Commonwealth Cabinet by J. A. Perkins, Minister of the Interior.

Mr. Perkins told the House of Representatives today there was a growing feeling that it was time to modify the restrictions.

"No sweeping change is contemplated," he said, "but the Ministry is well aware of Australia's need for population. However, the economic position, although it is improving, is still sufficiently acute to justify the continuance of some restrictions on the entry of immigrants."

SEEK A WOMAN AIDE IN HART ABDUCTION

Police on Coast Think She Helped in Ransom Notes to Dead Boy's Father.

NEW WITNESSES FOUND

Seller of 22-Pound Bricks for Murder Identifies Thurmond—Victim's Body Still in Sea.

Special to THE NEW YORK TIMES.

SAN JOSE, Calif., Nov. 17.—Waters of San Francisco's lower bay still held the body tonight of Brooke L. Hart, but authorities moved swiftly in perfecting a case against his confessed kidnappers and slayers, John Holmes and Thomas H. Thurmond.

Bit by bit they put together the many clues which, by their very unpremeditated simplicity, had for almost a week served to confuse investigators and aid in the kidnappers in escaping detection.

Motive for the crime has apparently been established. Ransom of $40,000 was demanded, according to the confession of Thurmond, to enable Holmes to satisfy the insatiable demand of "a woman for finery and a 'good time.'"

In this connection, authorities disclosed information indicating that a woman helped prepare one of the ransom notes sent to Alexander J. Hart, wealthy San Jose merchant and father of the slain 22-year-old youth.

The woman's name is known, Sheriff Emig announced, and she is sought for questioning.

Sheriff Emig said that Wesley Shaves of Campbell, home town of Holmes, reported seeing a woman and a man helping another man write a note last Monday. This preceded by some hours the mailing of the first ransom letter in the case. Shaves will be asked to view the prisoners.

Friend Chosen for Go-Between.

One more vital point in identification was established during the day, coincidentally with disclosure that Charles O'Brien Jr., friend of the slain youth and proprietor of a confectionery, had been selected by the kidnappers as the intermediary in the ransom negotiations.

O'Brien identified Thurmond, it was announced, as the man who leaped on the running board of his automobile at dusk last Tuesday, put his hand on the door handle, looked inquiringly at O'Brien and then dropped off and disappeared. Less than an hour later O'Brien received a telephone call, supposedly from Thurmond. The person instructed him to have Mr. Hart drive south on the coast highway "toward Los Angeles" the fol-

Continued on Page Seven.

UNITED STATES RECOGNIZES SOVIET, EXACTING PLEDGE ON PROPAGANDA; BULLITT NAMED FIRST AMBASSADOR

TRADE AWAITS CREDITS

Russians Ready to Buy $520,000,000 Goods, Says Brookhart.

ARRANGEMENT EXPECTED

Deal for $50,000,000 Cotton Likely at Start—Soviet Declared 'Good Risk.'

EXPORT GUARANTEE SEEN

Government Will Underwrite Sales, Iowan Holds—Predicts Work for 300,000.

Special to THE NEW YORK TIMES.

WASHINGTON, Nov. 17.—Russian orders for American goods worth $520,000,000 are immediately available to the United States if the government will extend the credit necessary for financing such exports, it was stated today by Smith W. Brookhart, special adviser to the Agricultural Adjustment Administration. He thought the needed credit would be provided.

On the same condition, he said, a continuing annual market would exist in Russia for a similar amount of American products for many years to come. The former Iowa Senator said he had discussed trade possibilities with M. Litvinoff since the latter's arrival in the United States and added:

"We will be able to sell them two or three times as much as they expect to sell us, if the proper credits are extended."

A long-time advocate of Russian recognition, Mr. Brookhart has been negotiating with the Amtorg Trading Corporation on behalf of the Adjustment Administration for the sale of surplus farm products to Russia. He said today that the first deals with the Russian Government would be in shipments of cotton and cotton textiles, live stock and heavy machinery.

Demand for $50,000,000 Cotton.

He thought the cotton deals would come first with government-financed exports of raw cotton worth from $50,000,000 to $60,000,000. An additional $30,000,000 is expected by Mr. Brookhart in orders for cotton textiles, and to this he added another $30,000,000 in live stock. Other items included in the $520,000,000 of orders which Mr. Brookhart said awaited only the extension of credits were about $400,000,000 of so-called heavy equipment, such as rolling mill apparatus and machine tools. In this total $400,000,000 of heavy equipment would be about $100,000,000 of railroad equipment, including rolling stock and other materials.

Such orders as were described by Mr. Brookhart as being immediately available would, he said, provide direct employment for 300,000 to 400,000 presently idle workers, and additional work indirectly for several thousands more.

These orders are definitely provided for in the present Five-Year Plan, according to Mr. Brookhart. He said that large orders outside the plan were being contemplated, and recalled that M. Litvinoff at the recent London Economic Conference expressed the intention of his government to buy $1,000,000,000 of products, apart from such plans.

Calls Russians "Good Risk."

"There's no reason why we shouldn't be able to get more than half of those orders if we go after them," he said.

Mr. Brookhart placed much weight in the utmost scrupulousness of the Russian Government about paying its debts.

"It's far better credit risk than Wall Street," he said, "and the best credit risk in the world, other than the United States Government itself."

Characterizing the Soviet Government as "the most stable one in Europe," Mr. Brookhart continued:

"They conduct all their operations on a five-year plan and the second one started last January. They won't buy any more than they see themselves able to pay for, and in that way they never get in over their head.

"They will buy beyond those periods only if credit is extended enabling them to buy abroad, and it is a fact worth noting that they

Continued on Page Four.

Points Conceded by Russia

Special to THE NEW YORK TIMES.

WASHINGTON, Nov. 17.—The exchange of agreements and concessions made public at the White House today in connection with the resumption of diplomatic relations with Russia was said in informed quarters to include virtually every concession the Soviet Government has ever made to any country. These points, the basis of recognition, are:

1. The Soviet Government promises "to respect scrupulously the indisputable right of the United States to order its own life within its own jurisdiction in its own way," pledging itself not to disseminate Communist propaganda in this country nor to attempt in any way to overthrow American institutions.

2. The Soviet Government expressly agrees to permit complete freedom of worship to Americans resident in Russia, including rites in the English or any other language, and leasing, erecting or maintaining buildings for the purpose.

3. A consular convention will be negotiated immediately, in which United States citizens will have rights of legal protection "not less favorable" than those enjoyed by "nationals of the nation most favored in this respect."

4. Preparatory to a final settlement of claims and counter-claims, the Soviet will not prosecute any claims against Americans as the successor of prior governments of Russia, or otherwise.

5. The Soviet Government waives all claim to damages arising from the American military expedition to Siberia in 1918.

In addition to the agreements signed, there took place an exchange of views regarding methods of settling all outstanding questions of indebtedness and claims.

TRIUMPH HAILED BY SOVIET PEOPLE

Recognition Is Likened to the Tale of the Ugly Duckling Which Became Swan.

NEWS TOO LATE FOR FETES

Mezhlauk and Sokolnikoff Are Regarded as Candidates for Envoy to Washington.

Special Cable to THE NEW YORK TIMES.

MOSCOW, Saturday, Nov. 18.—Word of the recognition of the Soviet by the United States came to Moscow in the dead of night because of the difference in time, but not too late for a communique to appear in every morning newspaper. Trusts, restaurants and trams will be buzzing with the news later in the morning.

Official comment is not available at this hour, but to the Soviet leaders recognition by the greatest of capitalistic powers brings the same degree of elation felt by the "ugly duckling" of Hans Christian Andersen when it was recognized as a beautiful swan.

"It hid its head under its wing," said the old fairy tale, "and felt too happy—but had no thought of pride. It remembered how it had been mocked and persecuted, and now every one said it was lovelier than all."

Soviet leaders have been living all their lives as "ugly ducklings." They are almost afraid to believe the fairy tale has reached its traditional ending.

Youth Hails Event.

But to the komsomols (young revolutionaries and future Soviet leaders) of recognition comes as part of their birthright, somewhat unexpectedly delayed. It is almost impossible to explain to them why the United States has not recognized the U. S. S. R. before. From their point of view, purely Marxian, the economic and political situation has been demanding such action for three years.

To Soviet economists, engineers and scientists it brings a hope of easier budgeting, with new equipment to realize their plans for products which are necessary to develop Russia's natural resources.

To artists, writers and actors come greater possibilities of travel to that strange land where movie stars receive unbelievable salaries, and where no party line shapes the theme of plays or poems or guides the painter's brush.

To the Red Army it probably is interpreted as meaning one less enemy in the next war.

Peasants Are Pleased.

To the peasant in the fields it shows that "Uncle Kalinin" was right, right again. Now perhaps he will manage to get some more of those American chickens for me."

To the workers it is one more triumph for the policies of Joseph Stalin and Maxim Litvinoff.

Continued on Page Six.

LITVINOFF PLEDGES SOVIET FRIENDSHIP

Looks to Cooperation With America for Peace Under Economic and Cultural Ties.

ASSURANCE ON NATIONALS

Roosevelt Got This First, He Says in Speech—Disavows Moscow Link to Reds Here.

Special to THE NEW YORK TIMES.

WASHINGTON, Nov. 17.—Foreign Commissar Litvinoff disclosed in a statement before the National Press Club tonight that the first commitment sought by President Roosevelt as a requisite to recognition of Russia was an assurance of the Soviet policy toward nationals of other countries.

M. Litvinoff, in answer to a question, also took occasion to disavow the Communist party of America so far as it claims to represent the governing group in Russia.

"The Communist party of America is not concerned with the Communist party of Russia and the Communist party of Russia is not concerned with the Communist party of America," he said.

Creation of Understanding.

M. Litvinoff said that he gladly supplied President Roosevelt with all the information he desired concerning the Soviet policy toward nationals of other governments. He put his answers as convincingly as he could, to cut away a sixteen-year accumulation of false ideas concerning Russia which had sprung up here in the absence of normal diplomatic relations.

The obviously happy diplomat traced the history of recognition as it came to a full realization today. He added that his government would seek to make the new relations with the United States not merely a conventional or technical diplomatic intercourse, but such an understanding between two countries which have never had a common ground for cooperation in economics, culture and international peace.

Address by M. Litvinoff.

M. Litvinoff's speech was as follows:

"I am happy today because the hopes which I have cherished for sixteen years have been realized. Ever since the beginning of my diplomatic activities I have been striving to obtain a good understanding between the Soviet Union and the United States.

"Toward that end I proposed to my government in 1918, during the war, that it send me to Washington. My request was happily granted. Many historical events might have taken different shape, if we could then have entered into relations with the United States.

"At the end of 1918 I made another attempt in the same direction by sending a long telegram and making certain proposals to President Wilson through his arrival in Europe. I failed again, but I con-

Continued on Page Five.

PRESIDENT REVEALS PACT

Reads to Press Letters in Which He and Litvinoff Bind Nations.

FREE WORSHIP CONCEDED

Russia Also Agrees to Allow Americans Own Counsel if Brought to Trial.

WORLD PEACE IS STRESSED

Russo-American Claims Will Be Adjusted Through Regular Diplomatic Channels.

The notes of the President and
Maxim Litvinoff, Page 2.

By WALTER DURANTY.
Special to THE NEW YORK TIMES.

WASHINGTON, Nov. 17.—Official relations between the United States and the Soviet were established at ten minutes before midnight yesterday. Or, to express it more simply, the United States recognized the U. S. S. R. at that hour after sixteen years and nine days of the Soviet Government's existence. The fact of the establishment of relations was announced this afternoon by President Roosevelt, but historically speaking the date was 11:50 P. M., Nov. 16.

The undertakings of the two governments were set forth in eleven letters and a memorandum exchanged between the President and Maxim Litvinoff, Soviet Commissar for Foreign Affairs, covering agreements and concessions completed in ten days of negotiation.

Subject to the approval of the Soviet Government, William C. Bullitt of Philadelphia, special assistant to the Secretary of State, was designated to be the first American Ambassador to the U. S. S. R.

The pact, read to the press by Mr. Roosevelt at his press conference this afternoon, covers propaganda, freedom of worship, protection of nationals and debts and claims.

Anti-Propaganda Pledge.

The most complete pledge against Bolshevist propaganda that has ever been made by the Soviet Government, and includes "organizations in receipt of any financial assistance from it" as well as persons or organizations under the jurisdiction or control of the government. Complete freedom of worship is assured Americans, as well as assurance against discrimination because of "ecclesiastical status."

To Americans is accorded "the right to be represented by counsel of their choice" if brought to trial in the U. S. S. R., which represents perhaps the most definite concession that M. Litvinoff made. The President made reciprocal pledges except regarding religion, which the Soviet did not desire.

Debts and claims were left to be threshed out later for "a final settlement of the claims and counter-claims" between the governments "and the claims of their nationals." Claims arising out of the military occupation of Siberia by American forces, or assistance to military forces in Siberia after 1917, were waived, but the Murmansk occupation was not mentioned.

One may surmise that the article relating to propaganda was drawn up after the most careful consideration by the Americans of the propaganda clause or clauses between the Soviet and Afghanistan, or both, but it goes further than either of these two, and might almost be termed a diplomatic victory of high order.

The question of religious freedom has great political importance and is treated with corresponding detail. Americans are allowed every thing they can want in this respect, but it is worth noting that M. Litvinoff takes the opportunity of "slipping something over" in a quiet way by quoting the laws of the Soviet Union to show that many of the reports upon the restriction of religious liberty in that country have been exaggerated. The American side, however, scores a tactical success in M. Litvinoff's admission that "no persons having ecclesiastical status"

Continued on Page Two.

Roosevelt Leaves for Warm Springs; Will Speak at Savannah This Morning

Special to THE NEW YORK TIMES.

WASHINGTON, Nov. 17.—President Roosevelt left Washington late this afternoon for Warm Springs, Ga., where he plans to spend the Thanksgiving holidays.

He is going on a special train by a circuitous route in order to visit Savannah and make a speech tomorrow morning as part of the ceremonies celebrating the bicentennial of that city.

The stop there will be brief, however, and the President will take all his meals aboard the train except special train, which is due at Warm Springs late tomorrow evening.

At Warm Springs the President will divide his time between official duties and the children at Warm Springs Foundation, which he helped to establish as a place for special treatment for victims of infantile paralysis.

He is expected to have an active schedule, beginning on Monday, when, as will receive Sumner Welles, Ambassador to Cuba. Events in the island republic reached a stage a few days ago where Ambassador Welles believed

they required a personal conversation between himself and the President, so the President invited Mr. Welles to come from Havana for a conference.

Mr. Roosevelt was accompanied on the train by only one member of his family, Mrs. James Roosevelt, his mother. Other arrangements detained his wife here, but she will join the President in time to spend Thanksgiving Day with him.

His party included a large staff from the White House offices which will handle the business of the Chief Executive, with the assistance of telephone and telegraph, much the same as if he were in Washington. This staff is under the direction of Stephen T. Early, assistant White House secretary, and Miss Marguerite A. Le Hand, the President's personal secretary. It includes six others, stenographers and telephone operators, in addition to the White House Secret Service with him.

Fifteen newspaper correspondents and twelve news picture men completed the party.

NRA

"All the News That's
Fit to Print."

The New York Times.

LATE CITY EDITION
WEATHER—Cloudy, warmer and
rain today; tomorrow colder.
Temperatures Yesterday—Max., 48; min., 38.

Copyright, 1933, by The New York Times Company.

VOL. LXXXIII....No. 27,709.   Entered as Second-Class Matter,
Postoffice, New York, N. Y.   NEW YORK, TUESDAY, DECEMBER 5, 1933.   M P P   TWO CENTS In New York | THREE CENTS | FOUR CENTS Elsewhere Except
City.   Within 200 Miles | in 7th and 8th Postal Zones

ALDERMEN REDUCE CITY'S 1934 BUDGET BY ONLY $3,604,264

Tammany Men Ignore Pleas for Economy and Adopt Total of $551,004,248.

$20,934,248 FUNDS NEEDED

McAneny Committee Offers Program of New Revenue to Meet This Deficit.

$40,547,000 SAVING ASKED

Baldwin's Minority Report Urging Job and Pay Cuts Is Rejected.

Ignoring all last-minute pleas for drastic economies to fit the city's impaired financial position the Board of Aldermen adopted, at 1 o'clock this morning, a 1934 budget aggregating $551,004,248, after cutting a scant $3,604,264.74 from the tentative figure of $554,605,512 set by the Board of Estimate on Oct. 31.

By its action, which followed faithfully the recommendations of a joint Board of Estimate and Board of Aldermen budget committee headed by Controller George McAneny, the Tammany board bequeathed to the incoming finance administration of Mayor-elect F. H. LaGuardia the problem of overcoming a minimum deficit of $20,934,248 in order to put the city's financial house in order.

The only departure by the board from the path laid down for it by the joint report was to abolish the post of Deputy Clerk of the City Court in Kings County, held by a supporter of Joseph V. McKee at the recent election. The spirited debate over this additional saving of $4,640 caused a split in the ranks of the board, so that the final vote on adoption of the budget was 91 to 3, with Alderman Joseph Tinsley of the Bronx and Walter Hart of Brooklyn supporting the negative ballot cast by Alderman Joseph Clark Baldwin 3d, the sole Republican member.

Act to Wipe Out Deficit

To close the gap between the deficit of $24,608,512 handed to it by the Board of Estimate, the lower board adopted resolutions which approved a program estimated by the McAneny committee to increase the 1934 annual fund by $8,930,000 in new revenues from various licenses, inspections and service fees; by $1,500,000 from tax arrears funds due to the 10 per cent penalty effective on Jan. 1, and by some $10,-500,000 by way of restoration of money spent by the city out of tax revenues to meet interest and amortization of the city subway bonds.

The last-mentioned item was included on the assumption that the Court of Appeals would affirm the recent decision of the Appellate Division holding that the city had no right to make such expenditures. Before the money thus spent can be restored, however, the Board of Transportation will have to market a new form of city security in the shape of certificates of indebtedness.

The McAneny report summarized the various means by which the deficit gap was to be closed:

Further reductions in the budget $3,604,264
Increased revenue from tax penalties 1,500,000
Restoration to general fund of transit carrying charges paid from the budget during the current year 10,512,500
New sources of revenue 8,930,000

Total $24,643,124

Final Approval Likely.

The Board of Estimate has until Dec. 31 to put the seal of its approval upon the lower board's action, but there is little doubt that it will do so. It received the joint committee's report in executive session before the Board of Aldermen met and later approved it in open meeting and sent it along with the recommendation that it be approved by the other branch of the Tammany Legislature.

Before the Board of Aldermen put through the program of the McAneny committee it rode down without ceremony a minority report of the finance committee, submitted by Alderman Baldwin. He urged drastic reductions in the number of jobs in virtually every city department, as well as substantial pay cuts in the higher brackets, declaring that his program would bring a total saving of $40,547,200, which would to augments by new revenues to bring the total saving to $48,475,998.

An outstanding feature of his program was the suggestion that $16,000,000 be saved in 1934 by giving all city and county employees with salaries of more than $2,000 a month's leave without pay.

Not a single elimination of pay——

Continued on Page Four.

"When You Think of Writing
Think of Whiting."—Advt.

Republicans Assert Nation Rebels At Roosevelt 'Top Sergeant' Rule

'We Are Not in War,' Declares Statement by National Committee, Which Charges 'Dictatorship' Tactics—Excerpts From Smith's Editorials and Speech Are Quoted.

Special to The New York Times.

WASHINGTON, Dec. 4.—Under the caption "Tories, Chiselers, Dead Cats, Witch Doctors, Bank Wreckers, Traitors" the Republican National Committee resumed its campaign against the Roosevelt recovery program tonight.

The second major onslaught by the committee was issued from headquarters of the committee in the form of a printed document of thirty-five pages in which it is proclaimed that "The Forgotten Man of 1932" is still forgotten, that the radio is being censored and that private initiative is in the "guardhouse." The statement asserts that "the American people object to the attempt upon the part of this administration to conduct itself along the lines of a dictatorship."

Whether or not the attack did not originate with the partisan opponents of President Roosevelt, but came "from outstanding members of the Democratic party," found "virile expression" in the editorial columns of staunch Democratic

Continued on Page Two.

been more protected from partisan criticism than has that of President Roosevelt. No other administration in history, it is declared, has had its requests for legislation granted 100 per cent; granted, it says, with little or no partisan opposition. Congress, it continued, gave President Roosevelt more power than it gave Lincoln to save the Union or Wilson to wage the World War.

"A month or six weeks ago," the committee statement continued, "there began to be criticism of the policies of the administration. It was pointed out in the columns of the public press that the President's recovery program was not working, because it was not workable, that many of the policies ran contrary to fundamental economic laws, sound business practice, plain common sense and particularly to the spirit of American institutions and the convictions and traditions of the American people."

This criticism, it is asserted, did not originate with the partisan opponents of President Roosevelt, but came "from outstanding members of the Democratic party," found "virile expression" in the editorial columns of staunch Democratic

DAWES BANK LOAN DUE RFC ON DEMAND

Status Shifted When $62,157,596 Balance of $90,000,000 Was Unpaid a Year Ago.

$2,283,958 INTEREST PAID

More Time Asked of Senators to Itemize $91,633,679 Face Value Collateral.

Special to The New York Times.

WASHINGTON, Dec. 4.—The remainder of the $90,000,000 loan from the Reconstruction Finance Corporation to the Central Republic Bank and Trust Company of Chicago, of which former Vice President Dawes became chairman of the board several weeks before the advance was made, has been overdue almost a year and never renewed, Chairman Jones of the RFC has reported to the Senate Banking Committee.

Of the principal there was still due $62,157,596.83 on Nov. 5. Mr. Jones informed Chairman Fletcher. On that date the repayments on the loan amounted to $27,842,403.15.

The bank also has paid $2,283,958.95 in interest to the RFC, bringing total payments to $30,126,362.10. The bank owed the RFC $1,839,192.14 in accrued, overdue and unpaid interest.

The $90,000,000 loan was made several weeks after General Dawes resigned as chairman of the RFC to become chairman of the board of the Central Republic Bank and Trust Company. He said at the time that the bank negotiated the loan to put itself in an "impregnable position" and that it was "for current requirements and not for the purpose of liquidation."

Three Disbursements on Loan.

The report of Chairman Jones to Senate committee, submitted at the request of Chairman Fletcher, disclosed that the loan was granted in two authorizations, one of $16,-000,000 on June 25, 1932, and another of $74,000,000 two days later. The RFC disbursed the loan to the bank in three instalments, one of $10,000,000 on June 27, 1932; another of $30,000,000 on June 29, 1932, and a third of $50,000,000 on Oct. 4, 1932.

The loan became due on Dec. 23, 1932. The committee was informed that the loan has never been renewed, and is now regarded by RFC officials as having the status of a demand note. It is not being considered by them as in default, although long overdue.

Under its statute of a demand note the loan may be called at any time. Officials pointed out, however, that the RFC has not yet called any overdue loans.

Chairman Fletcher, acting for the banking committee, requested Mr. Jones, in reporting on the status of the loan to submit an itemized report of the collateral and its present market value. As the collateral consists of some 7,000 items, it was explained that the RFC was not able to complete the itemized list in time to be submitted with the report.

The collateral is on deposit at the Federal Reserve Bank of Chicago. The Senate committee was informed that it has a face value of

Continued on Page Two.

BRITAIN WILL AVOID HARDSHIP TO IRISH

Thomas, Dominions Secretary, Is Conciliatory on Eve of Reply to de Valera.

LOSS ON ANNUITIES CITED

Plebiscite Is Considered on Plan for Declaration of an Irish Republic.

Wireless to The New York Times.

LONDON, Dec. 4.—On the eve of making his anxiously awaited pronouncement on Anglo-Irish relations tomorrow, J. H. Thomas, Dominions Secretary, told the House of Commons today that Britain had "no intention of imposing any hardship on the Free State."

Taxes on Irish goods entering Britain, he said, had yielded about £2,900,000 ($10,240,000) less to date than the amount of the Free State's default on annuity payments. The default so far had totaled £7,333,000.

Rejecting the suggestion by a Conservative member that the duties be increased, Mr. Thomas explained:

"We are more concerned at getting the money due to this country than over imposing new duties."

The Cabinet met two hours today to discuss the government's reply to President de Valera of the Free State, which Mr. Thomas will read in Parliament tomorrow. Mr. de Valera is said to have asked what Britain's attitude would be toward a declaration of an Irish republic.

No hint as to its contents has been given but it is felt it may prove more conciliatory than was once expected.

It is understood the Admiralty is taking steps to repurchase certain wharves and docks at Milford Haven, Wales, which about a year ago were handed over to the government disposals board.

These docking facilities were constructed during the World War as a submarine base and a depot for units engaged in fighting German submarines. One of the reasons suggested for this new activity on the part of the Admiralty is that the government is preparing to surrender its right to dock naval vessels in certain ports in Southern Ireland under the terms of the Free State treaty.

Plebiscite Proposed.

Special to The Associated Press.

DUBLIN, Dec. 4.—A clear-cut plebiscite on the establishment of an Irish republic, similar to the national balloting invoked by Chancellor Hitler in Germany last month, was the plan advanced today to decide whether President de Valera has the support of the Irish people.

The Irish Cabinet meets tomorrow to consider Britain's answer to President de Valera's inquiry regarding Britain's attitude toward Irish secession.

McEntee Concil story.

Special Cable to The New York Times.

DUBLIN, Dec. 4.—President de Valera's government is simply "sitting tight" until J. H. Thomas makes his statement in the Commons tomorrow.

A significant reference to the developing crisis was made by a member

Continued on Page Ten.

MONTEVIDEO PLANS AMERICAN PARLEY TO REVIVE TRADE

Steering Committee Adopts Argentina's Suggestion to Speed Recovery.

EUROPE TO GET BID LATER

Revival of London Conference Will Be Urged to Formulate World Economic Program.

By JOHN W. WHITE
Special Cable to The New York Times.

MONTEVIDEO, Dec. 4.—The steering committee of the Pan American Conference today unanimously approved a resolution presented by Foreign Minister Carlos Saavedra Lamas of Argentina, proposing the creation of a preparatory committee for a Pan American economic and commercial conference.

Señor Saavedra Lamas, in a long speech supporting his suggestion, proposed that the United States Secretary of State, Cordell Hull, in the name of all Pan American republics, undertake to persuade the European nations to reconvene the London Economic Conference with a prearranged program designed to coordinate the recovery plans of European and American States.

Broader Outlook Is Taken.

Two developments at the Pan American conference today marked a trend toward broader international cooperation. First, the steering committee voted to admit observers of Spain and Portugal to the conference, and second, the Secretary-General of the conference published a memorandum from the League of Nations which sought to concentrate in the League peace efforts in this hemisphere, as well as elsewhere.

Members of the United States delegation here denied tonight that Secretary Hull had committed himself to preparations for a Pan-American economic conference or to the reconvening of the London conference, as was first reported.

Señor Saavedra Lamas, it was stated, had suggested to Mr. Hull the appointment of an economic committee within the present conference to study several subjects which the Argentine Foreign Minister proposed to submit. The chief of the American delegation, it was stated, agreed this would be a good idea and expressed special interest in facilitating the economic work of the present conference.

Mr. Hull, according to the American spokesman, had no knowledge of the nature of the subject Señor Saavedra Lamas proposed to introduce. Therefore, it is argued, his attitude could scarcely be interpreted as approval of a list of topics not yet given out.

"Economic Justice" Is Urged.

"After a half-century of existence we must suppose that Pan American organizations have acquired sufficient experience to enable it to assume a definite rôle," said Señor Saavedra Lamas. "That rôle must not be reduced to a mere expression of sentiments or to mere spiritual communion. It must have content, and this content, under the force of present circumstances, cannot be purely moral or entirely juridical. In the historical hour in which we are living, Pan Americanism must have an economic content. The Treaty of Versailles said:

Continued on Page Three.

Rare Stone Stolen From Barnard Arch; Theft May Delay Sculptor's Work a Year

A sample specimen of labradorite, which is to be the base of George Grey Barnard's peace war memorial, was taken by vandals from the front of the full-sized model of the arch, now on public exhibition in the former power house at 216th Street and the Harlem River.

The theft was disclosed yesterday through a public notice written by the noted sculptor, in which he appealed to the person or persons who removed the mineral to bring it back. He began work on the war memorial on Armistice Day fifteen years ago, and the loss of the labradorite sample, he said, would delay his work another year.

In his appeal, posted in the exhibition hall, Mr. Barnard pleaded for the return of the sample specimen, which he said was the particular piece he required to continue his work on the arch. It was mailed to him at his studio and home, 700 Fort Washington Avenue, promising that no questions would be asked.

"To me it adds endless search and delay in the matching of my materials," he wrote. "I trusted those to whom I dedicated the rainbow arch, so I left it unsecured, valuable to me as it is. Please respect my faith in you."

The sculptor and his friends

search every day at the foot of the massive war memorial in the hope that whoever removed the mineral may have brought it back.

More than ten days have elapsed since the sample disappeared, but so far there has not been the slightest clue as to the manner in which it disappeared or its probable whereabouts. The belief has been voiced that a visitor may have taken it as a souvenir, never realizing the intrinsic value to the sculptor and his life work, which symbolizes the hope for peace.

The sample measures 9 by 5 inches and is described as a very rare kind of labradorite. It was brought to New York from Dr. Grenfell's island in Labrador. Dr. Grenfell's island in Labrador. In it come the finest specimens. Beautifully iridescent, it attracted much attention during the short period it was on display. Labradorite is a triclinic feldspar, showing a gorgeous play of blue, green and other colors. Against it, when the memorial is completed, the heroic figures of marble will stand out in bold relief.

The arch, the full-sized model of which was placed on view on Nov. 16, is to be Mr. Barnard's tribute to the American young men who lost their lives in the World War. He plans to build it at his own expense. Eight years will be required for construction.

CARDINAL ATTACKS NAZI CHURCH PLAN

Faulhaber Asks Protestants to Join Catholics in Defense Against Paganism.

REICH BISHOP RETREATS

Mueller Quits Hitlerite Group and Bars Political Links by His Cabinet Members.

By GUIDO ENDERIS.
Wireless to The New York Times.

BERLIN, Dec. 4.—A call to German Protestants to make common cause with Catholics in defense of Christianity against pagan and racial teachings by Nazis was issued from the pulpit of St. Michael's Church in Munich by Cardinal Faulhaber yesterday. He warned that efforts were being made to repudiate the Old Testament and even Christ for the sake of racial ideology.

"In such a situation," he continued, "a bishop cannot keep silence. Not blood but faith is the foundation of religion.

"There is a big difference between the children of Israel before and after the death of Christ. After Christ's death Israel was relieved of being the medium of revelations."

Demands Old Testament.

Therefore, he explained, it is necessary to distinguish between the Holy Writ of the Old Testament and the Talmud writings of a later period. The latter, in his view, were not inspired by the Holy Ghost, while from the Old Testament "comes the message of the only and almighty God."

"The Holy Writ of the Old Testament must, therefore, be kept in high honor," the Cardinal said, "and must not be eliminated from schools or textbooks. German chemists obtained inspiration from the Bible through the centuries and many expressions would have to be rooted out of the German language if the Old Testament is to be banned."

In appealing to Protestants for concerted defense against all attacks on the Old Testament the Cardinal said that for Protestantism the Old Testament was more important as the basis of faith than for Catholicism.

Mueller Quits Nazi Group.

The conflict in German Protestantism took a sensational turn today when the Rev. Dr. Ludwig Mueller, Reich Bishop of the Evangelical Church, resigned his protectorate of the Nazi German Christians' Society, the political organization which elevated him to office. Simultaneously, in a personal letter to members of his ecclesiastical cabinet and all officials in the administration of the Reich Church he forbade membership in

Continued on Page Twelve.

SUPPLIES TIED UP HERE

Toasts to End of Dry Era May Have to Be Drunk in Contraband.

AMPLE STOCKS IN STORAGE

But Dealers Will Be Unable to Sell Today—Applicants Besiege State Board.

1,000 CAFES ARE LICENSED

Extra Police to Curb Revelry in Midtown Area—Liquor Ships Race for Port.

Although the sale of alcoholic beverages becomes legal tonight, wines and whiskies will be available only in the 1,000 restaurants, clubs and hotels that have licenses.

Dinners, dances and other formal fêtes that are to be held tonight at licensed places to mark the end of prohibition, will go on as scheduled, but there will be no legal liquor for parties at home.

In deciding to wait until 9 P. M. to ratify the repeal amendment, Utah made it impossible for New Yorkers to obtain legal bottled goods for consumption off the premises. Retail liquor stores must close here by 8 P. M. Restaurants and cabarets that expected an influx of individual celebrants will reap the benefit.

Hotel Guests Excepted.

In hotels, bottled goods may be sold to guests, if they have rooms. The action also limits celebrations to six hours, unless the police confer at 3 A. M. is extended today. Previously it had been announced the curfew might be deferred until 4 A. M. if that was desired by the public, but no requests had been received.

Up to late yesterday only about a dozen licenses had been issued for retail liquor stores. Clerks in the offices of the New York State and City Alcoholic Beverage Control Boards worked late last night to get more out in time.

In appealing to Protestants for concerted defense against all attacks on the Old Testament the beards had devoted their activities earlier in an effort to get out the store licenses. Then they changed their plans and issued permits for restaurants and clubs with a whole day in which to do so, they may be able to issue more neighborhood restaurant licenses.

Whether enough legal wines and whisky would be available in view of the confusion and delay attending issuance of licenses, and the inability of the liquor stores to open was regarded as highly doubtful last night. Thus New York faced the anomalous situation of heralding the return of legal drinking with bootleg drinks.

Jersey May Be Officially Dry.

In New Jersey there was confusion also because of the failure of Governor A. Harry Moore to act on a State control bill passed by the Legislature last week and which the New Jersey Attorney General contends is unconstitutional. If Governor Moore vetoes the bill, and if the Legislature fails to repass it the State would be bone-dry even to 3.2 beer because of a law passed in 1898, which prohibits the sale of any alcoholic beverage without a license. The 3.2 beer law is operative only until the expiration of national prohibition. Meanwhile, authorities in various communities were going ahead with plans for local licensing and other control. Whether the 300 or more trucks set for the dash from licensed warehouses to restaurants, hotels and clubs that have licenses will be able to fill orders in a ratio to their receipt could not be ascertained.

Edward P. Mulrooney, chairman of the State control board, predicted that "the rush for liquor will be somewhat dampened because the public is short of money, and there will be a shortage of liquor for some time."

Informed last night that Utah had decided to delay ratification, Mr. Mulrooney made the following comment:

"That will not alter our plans in any way. It will merely mean that the liquor licenses will not be effective until several hours later than was expected."

In all discussion of prices for consumption in public the reservation was made yesterday that the schedules proclaimed in effect today would be temporary, pending a determination of the public taste for some time.

Preparations by those who intend to engage in the industry gave little indication that there was a fear of lack of demand. And the liquor shortage was said by other officials

Continued on Page Sixteen.

Utah Decides to Vote After 9 P. M. Our Time

By the Associated Press

SALT LAKE CITY, Utah, Dec. 4.—Delegates to Utah's convention to ratify prohibition repeal, which will meet here tomorrow amid much ceremony to cast for their State the deciding vote in the nation, agreed tonight to recess after the appointment of credentials and resolutions committees tomorrow afternoon and to reassemble at 7 P. M. (9 P. M. Eastern Standard Time) for final action.

"We are determined no other State shall take this glory away from Utah," said Franklin Ritter, president of the Utah League for Prohibition Repeal and a delegate to the convention, in commenting upon Utah's apparent determination to await ratification by Pennsylvania and Ohio before acting, in order to be the thirty-sixth State to ratify.

REPEAL CUTS PRICE OF DRINKS IN HALF

Cocktails Will Be 25 Cents in Some Places Celebrating End of Prohibition.

WHISKY AT $3 A QUART

Imported Champagne Offered at $5 to Take Home, or $8 at Hotel Table.

The price of drinks will be brought down today by repeal to almost half the recent bootleg and speakeasy level.

Although there were differences of five or ten cents among the lists tentatively issued by the various licensed establishments yesterday, the cost of a cocktail seemed generally about thirty cents and a highball about forty-five, while a bottle of imported still wine would be served for about $2.50 and champagne $8.

Retailers said blended whisky would be about $3 a quart.

Cover charges seemed generally to have been repealed with prohibition. While many establishments raised their dinner prices and supper dance prices about a dollar for repeal night celebrations, the public may dance and eat thereafter in first-class hotels and restaurants where wine and liquor is served for about $2 a person.

A survey of representative speakeasies that have ministered to the dry years revealed yesterday that they would reduce their prices to the repeal level.

A controlling influence seems to have been exercised on the cost of repeal drinking by the schedule of prices published by the Society of Restaurateurs. It has been adopted in licensed Childs Restaurants and has been raised five or ten cents in hotels, restaurants and speakeasies where the maintenance of a more expensive establishment seems to warrant it.

Restaurateurs' List.

As republished today by the Society of Restaurateurs for the guidance of repeal drinkers, the prices of liquors for consumption on the premises should be:

Cents.
Gin and whiskey cocktails 30
Rum cocktails 30
Old fashioned 30
"Rye whisky 30
*Scotch whisky 45-60
Dubonnet 30
Gin fizz 30
Sherry flip 30
Cordials 30
Pousse café 35
Cuban daisy 30
Sidecar 30
Silver fizz 30
Sherry 30
*Singer ale and seltzer for highballs charged extra at 5 to 10 cents.

A few places offer cocktails even below the society's schedule. For instance, a cocktail is promised for 25 cents; as also in the Childs restaurants, whose president, G. D. Strohmeyer, said yesterday that the proposed "Childs Special" was unlike anything he had ever seen, but that he found it very palatable. He said it was a clear drink, midway between green and yellow. He believed it was made with a gin base.

Continued on Page Sixteen.

DELLA ROBBIA ROOM Opens Tonight.
Dinner $1.50. Cocktails .25. Dancing.
Vanderbilt Hotel. AB. 4-4000.—Advt.

FINAL ACTION BY UTAH

Pennsylvania, Ohio Will Precede Western State in Ending Dry Law.

WASHINGTON IS PREPARED

Proclamations on Ratification and Taxes Await Last State's Action.

DRYS MAKE A LAST STAND

Capital Holds Fight for Writ Futile—Doran Resigns to Head Distillers.

Special to The New York Times.

WASHINGTON, Dec. 4.—National prohibition will pass into history as an unsuccessful experiment late tomorrow afternoon or evening—thirteen years, ten months, eighteen days and a few hours after it was declared in effect.

By that time the States of Pennsylvania, Ohio and Utah, by duly authorized conventions, will have ratified the Twenty-first Amendment to the Constitution, which also will establish in history the first repeal of an amendment—the Eighteenth.

Actual repeal of the Eighteenth Amendment, which will carry with it a collapse of the Volstead Act except as it applies to strictly Federal territory, will come when the last of the three State conventions has voted. However, an official proclamation is to be issued by Acting Secretary of State Phillips the minute that telephonic or telegraphic advice reaches Washington that ratification is an accomplished fact.

Four Tax Levies Will Pass.

A similar proclamation is also expected to be made by President Roosevelt. By that proclamation, provided in the National Industrial Recovery Act, four "recovery" taxes, levied to supply $220,000,000 a year to finance the huge public works program, will be automatically repealed—three as of Jan. 1 and one as of July 1—to be supplanted by the pre-prohibition levies on alcoholic beverages.

While preparations were going forward today for the formalities of repeal, the Federal Government also was perfecting its plans for assuming control of the liquor traffic until Congress meets and determines a policy of its own.

The new Federal Alcohol Control Administration, provided for in fair competition codes for various branches of the liquor trade, was officially set up in Washington today.

Headed by Joseph H. Choate Jr. of New York, the new administration took office in the Transportation Building and settled quietly to its immediate two-fold task—to regulate the industry to the best social and commercial advantage possible, and to supply at the same time every legitimate demand for alcoholic beverages that might be made by a people so long athirst.

Dr. Doran Resigns His Post.

The last passage of prohibition witnessed the passing from government service of the individual who has been closest to enforcement from the time of the birth of the "noble experiment" at midnight Jan. 16, 1920, until the day it finally passed away.

Dr. James H. Doran, lately Commissioner of Industrial Alcohol but at one time Commissioner of Prohibition, resigned the former position to become head of the new code authority of the distilling industry.

In his new capacity Dr. Doran will be the chief contact between the liquor-making industry and whatever Federal body may now or hereafter regulate the traffic. Dr. Doran entered the government service as a chemist twenty-six years ago and he is generally acknowledged as probably the leading authority in the United States on all phases of the liquor problem.

Commenting on Dr. Doran's resignation, Mr. Choate said:

"The FACA is very much pleased with the spirit of cooperation shown by the distilled spirits industry and feels that Dr. Doran's connection with the industry will insure an effective operation of the newly constituted association. Throughout his twenty-six years of government service he has earned

Continued on Page Sixteen.

NRA

"All the News That's Fit to Print."

The New York Times.

Copyright, 1933, by The New York Times Company.

LATE CITY EDITION

WEATHER—Rain and warmer to-day; tomorrow fair and colder.
Temperature Yesterday—Max., 44; Min., 34.

VOL. LXXXIII....No. 27,710.

Entered as Second-Class Matter,
Postoffice, New York, N. Y.

NEW YORK, WEDNESDAY, DECEMBER 6, 1933.

MP

TWO CENTS In New York City. | THREE Cts. Within 200 Miles | FOUR CENTS Elsewhere Except in 7th and 8th Postal Zones

LINDBERGHS AT SEA ON BRAZIL FLIGHT; 'O. K.' SHE REPORTS

630 MILES FROM AFRICA

Breeze Starts Fliers After Twenty Attempts in Dead Calm.

MOON LIGHTS THEIR WAY

10,000 Natives See Take-Off as Motor's Roar Stirs Them From Slumber.

RIDE THROUGH SQUALLS

Wife Radios Every Fifteen Minutes of Progress on 1,800-Mile Flight.

Colonel and Mrs. Charles A. Lindbergh were flying across the South Atlantic from Africa to Brazil this morning, reporting their progress by radio every fifteen minutes and their location every half hour.

At 2:20 A. M., New York time, five hours and twenty minutes after taking off from Bathurst, Gambia, in bright moonlight, they were 630 miles on their way across the Southern Ocean.

The first message from the plane was picked up by the Miami, Fla., station of Pan American Airways soon after 9:02 P. M. last night, New York time. It reported that the plane had taken off from Bathurst at that time. At 10 P. M., New York time, another message picked up by the Bahia, Brazil, station of Pan American Airways advised that the plane was flying Course 224 true, and gave its position, which Pan American officials estimated to be about 115 miles southwest of Bathurst. At 10:40 P. M. another message, also picked up by the Bahia station, reported "everything O. K.," and said the plane's position would be given every half hour and a progress O. K. sent out every fifteen minutes. The first progress O. K. was received by the Pan American station at Miami at 11 P. M., New York time.

Made 240 Miles in Two Hours.

At 11 P. M., the Bahia station also picked up a message. It gave for the plane a position approximately 240 miles southwest of Bathurst and right on her course. The operators at Bahia said that in her first message, Mrs. Lindbergh reported considerable static. But her messages, they said, were coming into Bahia strong, fast and clear, as if they were being sent by an experienced wireless operator.

The next message was received by the Pan-American station at Para, Brazil, at 11:50 P. M., New York time. It reported that the plane was flying at an altitude of 2,000 feet and making about 100 knots. There was unlimited visibility, the message said, with the sky about one-tenth overcast, and a quartering ten-knot tail wind.

At 12:30 this morning, the Pan American radio station at Miami and the Chatham, Mass., station of the Radiomarine Corporation each picked up a message from the plane giving a position approximately 446 miles southeast of Bathurst. The message said the plane was flying at an altitude of 1,200 feet, that there was visibility of about ten miles, that the sky was nine-tenths overcast, and that there was a quartering tail wind of 10 knots.

Squalls Met at Daybreak.

A message was received at 1:27 this morning at Pará, Brazil, reporting "skies eight-tenths overcast, scattered squalls, visibility three miles, daybreak; all's well."

At 1:50 A. M. the Bahia station picked up a message, "All's well."

At 2:20 A. M. a message was received at the Pará station reporting the plane's position as 630 miles southwest of Bathurst, flying at 1,200 feet, the skies nine-tenths overcast, frequent squalls, calm seas and no wind. That position indicated the Lindberghs had covered about one-third of the distance to Natal.

Natives Awaken for Start.

Special Cable to THE NEW YORK TIMES.

BATHURST, Gambia, Wednesday, Dec. 6.—With bright moonlight turning the waters around the little island of St. Mary, on which

Continued on Page Twenty-six.

Lindbergh Flight to Fame Twice as Long as New Hop

On the morning of May 20, 1927, six years and six months ago, Captain Charles A. Lindbergh, a mail pilot, left Roosevelt Field for Paris.

He flew alone, and veteran pilots shook their heads when they saw him take off. His silver plane, dripping with rain, lumbered slowly—too slowly—down the muddy runway. It gathered speed, bounced from the ground and settled back again. It barely cleared a tractor at the end of the runway and just climbed over low telephone wires at the end of the field.

Thirty-three and a half hours later the young mail pilot brought his gray plane down at Le Bourget. That famous flight covered 3,610 miles. The present flight, also in a single-engined plane, is about 1,875 miles.

PWA READY TO BAR CITY SUBWAY LOAN

Security for $25,000,000 Advance to Finish System Is Held Inadequate.

BANKERS' PACTS A FACTOR

Officials Here Say Attitude of Washington Is Based on a Misunderstanding.

Special to THE NEW YORK TIMES.

WASHINGTON, Dec. 5.—Inability of New York City to furnish security satisfactory to the Public Works Administration has caused the latter to abandon the allotment of $25,000,000 for completion of the Eighth Avenue subway.

New York officials were not here notified, but it was learned from reliable sources that the application for the loan would be refused.

At his press conference today Secretary Ickes said there was "nothing new" to report on the loan. He added, however, that the matter was held up by the question of security.

Senator Wagner announced virtual assurance of the loan more than two weeks ago. Since then the matter has been before the Special Board of Public Works, while PWA engineers and lawyers were investigating.

Application Signed by Mayor.

The application, for $25,000,000, signed by Mayor O'Brien, was on a loan and grant basis, 30 per cent of the cost of materials and structure to be an outright grant and the rest a loan on security furnished by the city.

The amount of money which completion of the subway would require is indefinite. Public Works Administration officials have scaled the sum down to some $22,500,000 under one estimate.

The money would be applied to equipping, tracking and finishing some eighteen miles of subway already dug, mainly in Brooklyn and Queens, and to the building of stations. Seven thousand men would obtain work through the Winter, it was estimated, and large supplies of capital goods would be purchased.

The allotment was discussed at the recent conference between Secretary Ickes and Mayor-elect La-Guardia, but it was not gone into in any detail.

The attitude of the PWA, it was learned, is that the city has tied up the revenues of the subway by its financing agreements with the banks, and would be operating on a margin too slender to enable it to guarantee any return on the investment, even if the PWA funds allowed the subway to open its lines of route and thus tap new sources of revenue.

Unification Another Problem.

The PWA feels that the situation is further complicated by the New subway lines. If the other lines were taken over by the city under the unification plan, a campaign promise of the Mayor-elect, the PWA feels that there would be a general scaling down of the demands of existing creditors and a consequent loss to the government on its investment. The question of the 5-cent fare is not worrying the administration. Secretary Ickes has already ex-

Continued on Page Twenty-seven.

TAX PLAN OFFERED TO CURB EVASIONS, RAISE $237,000,000

House Subcommittee Urges a Check on Personal Holding Concerns by 35% Levy.

WOULD INCREASE SURTAX

Normal Income Tax of 4% and Revision of Capital Gains Are Also Proposed.

Special to THE NEW YORK TIMES.

WASHINGTON, Dec. 5.—Broad tax reforms designed to increase the Federal revenue $237,000,000 a year and prevent "the avoidance and evasion of the internal revenue laws" were recommended today in a report submitted to the House Ways and Means Committee by a subcommittee.

The full committee immediately began study of the suggestions, and Representative Doughton, the chairman, said a completed bill would probably be ready for presentation soon after Congress meets next month.

Changes sought are aimed principally at persons whose incomes are in the higher brackets, as well as corporations now legally permitted to take advantage of what committee members said were "unfair but legal" provisions of the revenue laws.

Some discord was apparent within the committee, but no member would publicly express his feelings. "It isn't law yet, and it is not even past the committee," said one member. "It must go to the House and Senate."

Nine Changes are Urged.

Nine phases of the present law were recommended for modification as follows:

1. Establishment of a normal income tax rate of 4 per cent, instead of the present 4 per cent on the first $4,000 and 8 per cent on the remainder of net income, and revision of the surtax rate on a graduated scale, with the brackets reduced from 55 to 27; estimated to increase revenue $36,000,000 annually.

2. Change for three years in the depreciation and depletion section of the 1932 Revenue Act by reducing allowances by 25 per cent; estimated to add $85,000,000 for each of the three years.

3. Revision of the capital gains and losses section by revising the method of adjustment and prescribing a scale-length of ownership; estimated to add $30,000,000.

4. Amendment of the personal holding companies' section to prevent persons with large incomes from forming companies to evade taxes; estimated to add $25,000,000.

5. Abolition of certain sections of the "exchanges and reorganization" provisions to "close the door to one of the most prevalent methods of tax avoidance"; estimated to add $18,000,000.

6. Imposition of a tax on dividends paid out of corporation earnings accumulated before March 1, 1913; estimated to add $6,000,000.

7. Amendment of the foreign tax credit sections of the 1932 act; estimated to add $10,000,000.

8. Withdrawal of permission for corporations which are affiliated through 95 per cent stock ownership to file consolidated returns; estimated to add $20,000,000.

9. Revision of the partnership losses section of the 1932 Revenue Act; estimated to add $7,000,000.

Eager to expedite the "major problems," the subcommittee passed over a group of minor matters, according to the chairman, Representative Sam B. Hill of Washington. He said the subcommittee would continue study of these problems,

Continued on Page Fourteen.

Italy to Quit League Unless It Is Reformed; Demands Altered Aims and Set-Up at Once

By ARNALDO CORTESI
Wireless to THE NEW YORK TIMES.

ROME, Wednesday, Dec. 6.—At the end of a long sitting lasting far into the night, the Fascist Grand Council, which had been convoked to decide on Italy's relations with the League of Nations, passed a suspended sentence on Geneva.

After having discussed every aspect of the probable effect of Italy's withdrawal, the Grand Council decided "to render Italy's further participation in the League dependent on radical changes in that organization to be brought about within the shortest possible time, which changes must affect the League in its constitution, in its methods and in its objectives."

While Mr. Ickes has already ex-Continued on Page Fifteen.

debt instalment due on Dec. 15. In view of the impossibility of concluding negotiations on the debt problem, the Grand Council decided "to effect on Dec. 15 a token payment of $1,000,000 as renewed proof of Italy's good-will, while awaiting a final settlement of this whole question."

Since the breakdown in the disarmament negotiations Premier Mussolini has been advocating efforts outside Geneva and the League of Nations. He has favored action under the Four-Power Pact initiated by Great Britain, France, Italy and Germany, or at any rate negotiations by the leading powers including the United States.

As to reforms in the League, the press has suggested that the League be divorced from the Versailles Treaty, and that its constitution be revised to give the larger powers a freer hand in directing its affairs.

State House Bootlegger Is Barred in Maryland.

Special to THE NEW YORK TIMES.

ANNAPOLIS, Md., Dec. 5.—Wet legislators here will patriotically support legal liquor. The State House bootlegger received formal notice today to discontinue his trade. The notice was served by a policeman on duty at the Capitol.

Throughout this session, the bootlegger has conducted a thriving business; a business which, he says, has been especially arduous because of the sudden demands made on him by legislators and their desire for prompt service.

While his services were cut off eight hours before post-prohibition stuff could be brought, the bootlegger thought the legislators had obtained a sufficient reserve to carry them through until evening and legal liquor.

RATIFYING BY UTAH ENDS PROHIBITION

With Impressive Ceremony, the 36th State Follows Ohio and Pennsylvania in Day.

CONVENTIONS ALL SOLEMN

Moderation Pleas Are Made at Columbus—Hush Greets Vote at Harrisburg.

Special to THE NEW YORK TIMES.

SALT LAKE CITY, Dec. 5.—The Eighteenth Amendment to the Constitution of the United States passed out of existence officially at 3:32¼ o'clock this afternoon, Mountain standard time (5:32¼ New York time) with the ratification of repeal by the convention of Utah, the thirty-sixth required State.

The passing of national prohibition was marked by impressive ceremony in the hall of the House of Representatives in the State Capitol here.

To Delegate S. R. Thurman, a repeal leader of Salt Lake City, whose father was a member of the State's constitutional convention in 1895 before Utah was admitted to the Union, fell the honor of being the last to record his vote, the roll being called in alphabetical order.

His "Yea," placing the Twenty-first Amendment to the Constitution in effect, was greeted by enthusiastic applause from the audience of a few hundred persons.

About ninety seconds later Ray L. Olson of Ogden, president of the convention, who had been manager of the repealists' campaign, brought down his gavel and announced that the repeal amendment had been ratified. Notification was transmitted immediately to the White House by a special wire from the Capitol.

At the same time Delegate A. S. Brown, former president of the Salt Lake Chamber of Commerce, sent out word to President Roosevelt over the Columbia Broadcasting System. He congratulated the President on the successful culmination of the repeal movement.

The whole proceedings were in keeping with the historic aspect of the occasion. Besides high officials

Continued on Page Five.

CITY TOASTS NEW ERA

Crowds Swamp Licensed Resorts, but the Legal Liquor Is Scarce.

CELEBRATION IN STREETS

Marked by Absence of Undue Hilarity and Only Normal Number of Arrests.

MANY SPEAKEASIES CLOSE

Machine Guns Guard Some Liquor Trucks—Supplies to Be Rushed Out Today.

Slowly gathering momentum from the time when the news began to spread just at nightfall that national prohibition was no more, the public rejoicing at the end of the long dry reign was carried on last night with restraint and absence of undue hilarity.

Throngs of New Yorkers ventured into Times Square and other centres of the metropolis and many of the thousand restaurants, hotels and clubs fortunate enough to have received their licenses for the sale of alcoholic beverages were swamped.

But gay as were their spirits, they were well-behaved. With the city's entire police force of 19,000 men mobilized to guard against overexuberant celebrants, arrests did not exceed the normal number for any day of the last five years. Incidentally, official word that repeal was a fact did not go out to the police until 9:20 P. M., just four hours after Utah acted.

Stores Fail to Get Stocks.

The thronging to places of public entertainment was enhanced by the fact that only a handful of New Yorkers was able to drink a toast to the occasion with lawful liquor in their own homes. Because Utah did not make repeal effective until 5:32¼ P. M., retail liquor stores with only two exceptions were unable to obtain wines and whiskies from the warehouses in the brief time left.

Indeed, the supply of lawful liquor even in the licensed places was woefully scant. Only fifty-four truckloads of bonded liquor were released from the warehouses before they closed last night, and the two largest warehouses shut their doors before the Twenty-first Amendment displaced the Eighteenth.

With 3,000 places licensed to dispense the newly legalized beverages in the metropolitan area and 2,000 more up-State, hardly one in a hundred was able to move in a stock for the few hours available. Some of the others, of course, had had the foresight to lay in supplies under medicinal permits during the dying days of prohibition.

Bootleggers and speakeasies came to the rescue, however, despite a stern warning from Police Commissioner Bolan that his men would not tolerate any such activity. They operated with a little more caution than usual, but nevertheless they took advantage of the occasion to dispose of a large part of their unlawful stocks. The raids threatened by Mr. Bolan proved few and on little known places.

Many Cordial Shops Close.

Cordial shops and other neighborhood dispensaries during the long drought showed fear of police activity last night for the first time in years. Hundreds of them closed their doors, others dealt only with long-known and trusted customers, and only a scattering number, principally in downtown Manhattan, carried on business as usual. Some of them carried signs promising to open as licensed liquor stores in a few days.

There was even hope, however, that New York's long reliance on contraband cheer was near its end. The warehousemen promised deliveries on a large scale would begin today, with 600 trucks licensed to speed legal liquors throughout the city and its suburbs.

A cargo of 6,200 cases of assorted wines and spirits worth about $170,000 arrived on the White Star liner Majestic from France and England late in the afternoon, but the ship was delayed five hours by

Continued on Page Four.

The Repeal Proclamation

Special to THE NEW YORK TIMES.

WASHINGTON, Dec. 5.—The text of the proclamation by William Phillips, Acting Secretary of State, certifying to the adoption of the Twenty-first Amendment repealing prohibition, follows:

WILLIAM PHILLIPS,
Acting Secretary of State of the United States of America.

To all whom these presents shall come, greeting:

KNOW YE, That the Congress of the United States, at the second session, Seventy-second Congress, begun and held at the city of Washington on Monday, the fifth day of December, in the year one thousand nine hundred and thirty-two, passed a joint Resolution in the words and figures as follows:

JOINT RESOLUTION.

Proposing an amendment to the Constitution of the United States.

Resolved by the Senate and House of Representatives of the United States of America in Congress assembled (two-thirds of each House concurring therein), That the following article is hereby proposed as an amendment to the Constitution of the United States, which shall be valid to all intents and purposes as part of the Constitution when ratified by conventions in three-fourths of the several States:

ARTICLE.

Section 1. The Eighteenth Article of Amendment to the Constitution of the United States is hereby repealed.

Section 2. The transportation or importation into any State, Territory, or Possession of the United States for delivery or use therein of intoxicating liquors, in violation of the laws thereof, is hereby prohibited.

Section 3. This article shall be inoperative unless it shall have been ratified as an amendment to the Constitution by conventions in the several States, as provided in the Constitution, within seven years from the date of the submission hereof to the States by the Congress.

And, further, that it appears from official notices received at the Department of State that the amendment to the Constitution of the United States proposed as aforesaid has been ratified by conventions in the States of Arizona, Alabama, Arkansas, California, Colorado, Connecticut, Delaware, Florida, Idaho, Illinois, Indiana, Iowa, Kentucky, Maryland, Massachusetts, Michigan, Minnesota, Missouri, Nevada, New Hampshire, New Jersey, New Mexico, New York, Ohio, Oregon, Pennsylvania, Rhode Island, Tennessee, Texas, Utah, Vermont, Virginia, Washington, West Virginia, Wisconsin and Wyoming.

And, further, that the States wherein conventions have so ratified the said proposed amendment constitute the requisite three-fourths of the whole number of States in the United States.

NOW, therefore, be it known that I, William Phillips, Acting Secretary of State of the United States, by virtue and in pursuance of Section 160, Title 5, of the United States Code, do hereby certify that the amendment aforesaid has become valid to all intents and purposes as a part of the Constitution of the United States.

In testimony whereof, I have hereunto set my hand and caused the seal of the Department of State to be affixed.

Done at the city of Washington this fifth day of December in the year of our Lord one thousand nine hundred and thirty-three.

WILLIAM PHILLIPS.

Roosevelt Proclaims Repeal; Urges Temperance in Nation

President's Announcement Is in Accordance With the Instruction of Congress Contained in the Recovery Act—Declares Social Evils of Liquor Shall Not Be Revived.

Special to THE NEW YORK TIMES.

WASHINGTON, Dec. 5.—President Roosevelt's proclamation of the repeal of the Eighteenth Amendment is as follows:

By the President of the United States of America.

A Proclamation.

Whereas the Congress of the United States in the second session of the Seventy-second Congress, begun at Washington on the fifth day of December in the year one thousand nine hundred and thirty-two adopted a resolution in the words and figures following: to-wit—

JOINT RESOLUTION.

Proposing an amendment to the Constitution of the United States.

Resolved by the Senate and House of Representatives of the United States of America in Congress assembled (two-thirds of each House concurring therein), That the following article is hereby proposed as an amendment to the Constitution of the United States, which shall be valid to all intents and purposes as part of the Constitution when ratified by conventions in three-fourths of the several States:

ARTICLE.

Section 1. The Eighteenth Article of amendment to the Constitution of the United States is hereby repealed.

Section 2. The transportation or importation into any State, Territory or possession of the United States for delivery or use therein of intoxicating liquors, in violation of the laws thereof, is hereby prohibited.

Section 3. This article shall be inoperative unless it shall have been ratified as an amendment to the Constitution by conventions in the several States, as provided in the Constitution, within seven years from the date of the submission hereof to the States by the Congress.

Declares Amendment Repealed.

Whereas, Section 217 (a) of the Act of Congress entitled "An act to encourage national industrial recovery, to foster competition and to provide for the construction of useful public works, and for other purposes," approved June 16, 1933, provides as follows:

Section 217 (a) The President shall proclaim the date of—

(1) the close of the first fiscal year ending June 30 of any year after the year 1933, during which the total receipts of

Continued on Page Two.

FINAL ACTION AT CAPITAL

President Proclaims the Nation's New Policy as Utah Ratifies.

PHILLIPS SIGNS DECREE

Orders 21st Amendment in Effect on Receiving Votes of Three Final States.

RECOVERY TAXES TO END

$227,000,000 a Year Automatically Dropped—Canadian Whisky Quota Is Raised.

Special to THE NEW YORK TIMES.

WASHINGTON, Dec. 5.—Legal liquor today was returned to the United States, with President Roosevelt calling on the people to see that "this return of individual freedom shall not be accompanied by the repugnant conditions that obtained prior to the adoption of the Eighteenth Amendment and those that have existed since its adoption."

Prohibition of alcoholic beverages as a national policy ended at 5:32¼ P. M. Eastern Standard Time, when Utah, the last of the thirty-six States, furnished by vote of its convention the constitutional majority for ratification of the Twenty-first Amendment. The new amendment repealed the Eighteenth, and with the demise of the latter went the Volstead Act which for more than a decade held legal drinks in America to less than one-half of 1 per cent of alcohol and the enforcement of which cost more than 150 lives and billions in money.

Earlier in the day Pennsylvania had ratified as the thirty-fourth State and Ohio as the thirty-fifth.

Proclamation by President.

President Roosevelt at 6:55 P. M. signed an official proclamation in keeping with terms of the National Industrial Recovery Act, under which prohibition ended and four taxes levied to raise $227,000,000 annually for amortization of the $3,300,000,000 public works fund were repealed.

But the President went further. Accepting certification from Acting Secretary of State Phillips that thirty-six States had ratified the repealing amendment, he improved the occasion to address a plea to the American people to employ their regained liberty first of all for national manliness.

Mr. Roosevelt asked personally for what he and his party had declined to make the subject of Federal mandate—that saloons be barred from the country.

"I ask especially," he said, "that no State shall, by law or otherwise, authorize the return of the saloon, either in its old form or in some modern guise."

Makes Personal Plea.

He enjoined all citizens to cooperate with the government in its endeavor to restore a greater respect for law and order, especially by confining their purchase of liquor to duly licensed agencies. This practice, which he personally requested every individual and every family in the nation to follow, would result, he said, in a better product for consumption, in addition to the "break-up and eventual destruction of the notoriously evil illicit liquor traffic" and in tax benefits to the government.

The President then announced that it was his administration's aim to see that the social and political evils of the preprohibition era shall not be revived or permitted again to exist. Failure of citizens to use their new freedom in helping to advance this policy, he said, would be "a living reproach to us all."

He expressed faith, too, in the "good sense of the American people" in preventing excessive personal use of relegalized liquor. "The objective we seek through a national policy," he said, "is the education of every citizen toward a greater temperance throughout the nation."

As a means of enforcing his policy, the President has the Federal Alcohol Control Administration ready to regulate the liquor traffic and regulate it at the source of supply.

In its first major step today, the

Continued on Page Two.

NRA
"All the News That's Fit to Print."

The New York Times.

LATE CITY EDITION
WEATHER—Showers today; tomorrow fair, somewhat cooler. Temperatures Yesterday—Max., 91, Min., 75

Section 1

Copyright, 1934, by The New York Times Company.

VOL. LXXXIII....No. 27,917.

Entered as Second-Class Matter, Postoffice, New York, N. Y.

NEW YORK, SUNDAY, JULY 1, 1934.

Including Rotogravure Picture, Magazine and Book Sections.

F

TEN CENTS | TWELVE CENTS Beyond 200 Miles. Except in 7th and 8th Postal Zones.

EXCHANGE, LABOR BOARDS NAMED; FARM BILL SIGNED

KENNEDY IN 'CHANGE POST

The Others Are Mathews, Landis, Healy, Pecora for Varying Terms.

WIRE BOARD IS CHOSEN

Members Are Sykes, Brown, Case, Stuart, Payne, Gary and Walker.

RAIL PENSIONS APPROVED

Clark Howell Heads Air Study—Moffett Made Administrator of the Housing Act.

President Clears His Desk

On the eve of his departure this evening on the cruiser Houston for a month's cruise, President Roosevelt cleared his desk last night.

He named the two commissions to regulate the Stock Exchanges and the operations of telegraph, telephone and radio companies.

He signed the Frazier-Lemke bill setting up new methods for the compromising of agricultural indebtedness.

He signed the railroad employes' pension bill.

He appointed James A. Moffett of New York, prominent oil executive, Administrator of the Housing Act.

He appointed an Aviation Commission, with Clark Howell as chairman.

He created an impartial Labor Relations Board, abolishing the old one and eliminating the NRA from a rôle in settling labor disputes.

Picks Exchange Board

Special to The New York Times.

WASHINGTON, June 30.—As his last act tonight in cleaning up essential business before sailing from Annapolis for a month's holiday today, President Roosevelt named the personnel of the Securities and Exchange Commission.

He did not designate a chairman, there being some doubt as to his authority to do so, but it was understood in well-informed quarters that responsibility for the commission's work under the sweeping Stock Exchange Control Act would fall upon Joseph P. Kennedy, New York financier, who was designated to serve for five years. Four other commissioners were named for periods varying from one to four years.

The personnel of the commission follows:

JOSEPH P. KENNEDY of New York, five-year term.

GEORGE C. MATHEWS of Wisconsin, four-year term.

JAMES M. LANDIS of Massachusetts, three-year term.

ROBERT E. HEALY of Vermont, two-year term.

FERDINAND PECORA of New York, one-year term.

Messrs. Mathews and Landis are members of the Federal Trade Commission. Mr. Pecora was counsel for the Senate Banking and Currency Committee during the period in which it acted publicly for the first time in twenty years the manifold operations of securities exchanges and investment banking houses. As committee counsel he played a large part in shaping the law under which the commission will operate.

The naming of the Securities and Exchange Commission came after President Roosevelt, in a day of intensive work, had also named the Communications Commission and a commission to plan coordination of aircraft development, and had signed statements announcing the signing of the Frazier-Lemke Farm Mortgage Bill and the Railroad Pensions Bill.

Kennedy Close to Farley.

The membership of the Securities and Exchange Commission had been pretty generally forecast, but even so its composition was full of surprises, particularly the obvious placing in line for the chairmanship of Mr. Kennedy.

This is the first emergence of the New Yorker from what seemed to be political eclipse since the campaign of 1932, when he was distinguished with as a heavy contributor and important raiser of campaign funds, and because of his

Continued on Page Twenty-one.

Major Sports Results

Track—Bill Bonthron of Princeton broke the world's record for the 1,500-meter run in the national A. A. U. championship meet at Milwaukee. Timed in 3:48.8, he beat Glenn Cunningham by two feet. It was the fifth meeting between the stars and the triumph gave Bonthron the edge with three victories.

Tennis—Four Americans advanced at Wimbledon. Frank Shields defeated Christian Boussus of France and George M. Lott Jr. halted Harry Hopman of Australia. Miss Helen Jacobs conquered Mlle. Jacqueline Goldschmidt of France and Miss Sarah Palfrey beat Miss J. Jedrzejowska of Poland.

Baseball—Routing Carl Hubbell, the Dodgers stopped the Giants, 8–4, before 12,000 at the Polo Grounds. At Washington the Yankees won over the Senators, 4—1, when rain caused the game to be called off in the fifth inning.

(Full details in Sports Section.)

JOHN JACOB ASTOR WEDS ELLEN FRENCH

Notables Fill Newport Church for Ceremony Climaxing Weeks of Social Activity.

ONLOOKERS PACK STREETS

Crowd Delays Both Bride and Bridegroom—Astor's Mother Sits in a Front Pew.

By RUSSELL B. PORTER.

Special to The New York Times.

NEWPORT, R. I., June 30.—Two of America's oldest families, prominent in both landed wealth and in social position, were united in marriage here today at the wedding of John Jacob Astor 3d and Miss Ellen Tuck French.

The bridegroom is the third of his name in American life. The first John Jacob Astor, fur trader, founded the family in early American days. The second lost his life in the sinking of the Titanic, and the third John Jacob Astor, today's bridegroom, was born ... few months later. He is a half-brother of Vincent Astor, and inherited with the latter the great Astor fortune.

The bride is a granddaughter of Amos Tuck French and is related to the Vanderbilt family.

These young members of old families, the bridegroom only 21 years old and the bride 18, were joined together in a setting replete with symbols of early American tradition.

They were married according to the ancient simple ritual of the Protestant Episcopal Church, whose worshipers came to New England with the first settlers, in old Trinity Church, a long, narrow, weather-beaten granite headstones bearing the names of men and women who played leading parts in shaping the history of the colonies and of the first days of the Republic.

All around the church, which is right in the centre of this fine old city, old frame buildings of Colonial architecture, with Grecian columns, steeply slanting roofs and gables, crowding close to the building line of the street in the heart of the city.

The time joined with the place in celebrating the event with appropriate ceremony, for not only was it in the midst of the Summer season, when Newport's social colony is always in full swing, but it was coincident with a visit of a large part of the United States fleet. From time immemorial the navy has been associated with Newport, and

Continued on Page Eighteen.

FORD WILL ACCEPT NRA AND ITS CODE, JOHNSON IS TOLD

General Announces He Awaits Signed Certificate From Auto Maker.

SAYS HE ASKED CHANGES

Recovery Head Asserts His Suggestions Have Been Approved in Detroit.

Special to The New York Times.

WASHINGTON, June 30.—General Johnson believed tonight that he was nearing such a settlement of his ten months' feud with Henry Ford as would let the NRA put another feather in its cap and at the same time allow the automobile maker to re-enter the fertile field of government business.

General Johnson today read a copy of an unsigned letter purporting to be from the Ford Motor Company to a local dealer, setting forth the claims that that firm had been complying and would continue to comply with "pertinent" provisions of the Automobile Code.

The Recovery Administrator stated that if the letter, with certain revisions which he suggested, were returned to him signed by Henry Ford or any other authorized executive of the Ford Company despite a "crack-down" campaign against the company and recommend that President Roosevelt that it be allowed to resume bidding on government contracts.

A large order of motor trucks for the army, which War Department officials prefer should be Ford products, is said to be the immediate stake in negotiations between the NRA and Mr. Ford. Harry H. Woodring, Assistant Secretary of War, has made overtures to General Johnson within the last thirty-six hours to learn what the Ford company would have to do to qualify to bid.

Representative Kvale of Minnesota, active in the House Military Affairs Committee investigating War Department purchases, accompanied the Ford dealer when he called to show the unsigned letter to General Johnson this afternoon.

Talks To Ford Adviser.

General Johnson believed the letter to be entirely authentic and to have originated at the Detroit offices of the Ford Company despite the circumstances under which it was shown to him. This belief was intensified by a telephone conversation which he had with William J. Cameron, editorial adviser to Mr. Ford, regarding the suggested revisions.

The letter, according to General Johnson, was addressed to the Northwest Motor Company of Bethesda, Md., the local dealer that has tried so consistently to keep in contractual relations with the government and departmental requirements regardless of Mr. Ford's refusal to sign a compliance certificate for his code.

"Its original form the letter said that although the company had complied and would continue to comply with the provisions of the automobile compact, it reserved its 'constitutional rights' as guaranteed by the fundamental law."

This was the section to which General Johnson objected. He told R. P. Sabine, president of the Northwest Motor Company, and Representative Kvale that President Roosevelt would not stand for

Continued on Page Three.

POLICE FILL THE STREETS

Goering's Forces Keep Curious Throngs on Constant Move.

MACHINE GUNS MOUNTED

Public Buildings on Unter den Linden and Wilhelmstrasse Are Heavily Guarded.

NEWS IS AT A PREMIUM

Rumors Are Rampant as Only a One-Sheet Paper Provides Authentic Information.

Copyright, 1934, by The Associated Press.

BERLIN, June 30.—With the peaceful cool of a Summer evening made strangely tense by squads of armed police and the presence of machine guns, this capital city was facing tonight the possibility of a new unnamed, undefined political event.

Crowds of curious spectators, only partly informed as to events through limited press dispatches, surged up and down Wilhelmstrasse, where public buildings were massed with police ever ready to keep them on the move.

In front of the home of Captain Ernst Roehm, suicide deposed leader of the storm troops, was bristling truckloads of Prussian Premier Hermann Goering's special police. They formed an impressive barricade separate from the thousands who dragged their feet in slow response to demands that streets and sidewalks be kept clear.

Show of Force Excites Crowds.

The presence of police everywhere one turned was a direct stimulant to the excitement of the street and thoroughfare. Never in the history of Berlin, it was pointed out, had so many police appeared in the streets at one time with such obvious readiness for action. In addition to the regular police forces, augmented by armed reserves, there was the steel-helmeted, green-clad police of Premier Goering.

The sudden appearance of a police machine gun detachment, with ammunition ready, in historic Potsdammer Platz brought a final touch to the grimness of the situation. The sight of another similar detachment riding up and down Unter den Linden left no doubt in the public mind as to the nature of the emergency.

Men and women rushed like hounds on the scent wherever carriers appeared with copies of one newspaper which had printed one page only for free distribution. This carried a brief account of Captain Roehm's discharge by Chancellor Hitler.

Reactions to the news were various and could be read at will on the faces of newspaper readers. Persons obviously of a conservative mind wreathed their faces in smiles as they read what had happened.

Continued on Page Two.

HITLER CRUSHES REVOLT BY NAZI RADICALS; VON SCHLEICHER IS SLAIN, ROEHM A SUICIDE; LOYAL FORCES HOLD BERLIN IN AN IRON GRIP

THREE OF THE LEADERS WHO DIED IN THE REICH MUTINY.

Times Wide World Photo. Captain Ernst Roehm, ousted Storm Troop head, who committed suicide.

Associated Press Photo. Karl Ernst, Berlin Storm Troop leader, arrested and later shot.

Times Wide World Photo. General Kurt von Schleicher, slain by arresting officers.

HITLER COMMANDS NAZI ABSTINENCES

Forbids the Troopers to Spend Money on Banquets and Bans Moral 'Debauches.'

WANTS 'MEN, NOT APES'

Chancellor Asserts All Must Be on Best Behavior or Be Expelled From Ranks.

Wireless to The New York Times.

BERLIN, June 30.—Chancellor Adolf Hitler issued these eleven commands today to Viktor Lutze, new Chief of Staff of the Storm Troops:

In naming you Chief of Staff of the Storm Troops I expect that you will accept the series of duties that I herewith inform you of:

1—I demand of a Storm Troop leader, just as from a Storm Trooper, blind obedience and unquestioning discipline.

2—I demand that every Storm Troop leader recognize, like every other political leader, that his behavior and reputation must be an example for his organization and for our whole body of followers.

3—I demand that Storm Troop leaders, exactly as in the case of political leaders, be expelled from the Storm Troops without hesitation as soon as their behavior disgraces them in the eyes of the public.

Demands Simplicity.

4—I demand specially from the Storm Troop leader that he be an example of simplicity, not of display. I do not desire Storm Troop leaders to give costly dinners or that they attend such dinners. There was a time when we were not invited to such affairs, and we have nothing to seek there now. Millions of our fellow citizens have not even the necessaries of life. They are not oblivious of those whom fortune has favored, but it is unworthy of a National Socialist to increase the gulf between fortune and misery, which is already great enough.

I prohibit the use of Storm Troop or party funds for festivals and the like. It is shameless to stage debauches with the pennies of our poorest citizens. The luxurious headquarters in Berlin, in which it has now been discovered that some 30,000 marks monthly were spent for banquets, is to be done away with immediately.

State Dinners Excepted.

I prohibit for all party groups banquets and dinners paid for out of any variety of public funds. I forbid all party and Storm Troop leaders to partake of such banquets. The only exceptions are functions necessary for reasons of State, notably those for which the Reichswehr and the Reich Foreign Minister are concerned. I forbid all party leaders and Storm Troop leaders to give so-called diplomatic dinners. A Storm Troop leader does not need to engage in representation, but simply to do his duty.

5—I do not desire Storm Troop leaders to undertake business trips in expensive limousines or cabriolets, or to employ public funds for such trips. The same

Continued on Page Eight.

Hitler Alone Had Power To Order Shooting of 7

Special Cable to The New York Times.

BERLIN, June 30.—Over its report of the deaths of seven storm troop leaders who yesterday were in power in Germany, the Völkischer Beobachter, Chancellor Hitler's own newspaper, carried the headline, "Seven Storm Troop Leaders Shot. End of Convicted Traitors."

The German words used for the verb and adjective taken together in this connection carry a wider meaning than the English equivalent, as is the case with so many German words. They imply that the men were proved guilty and executed.

These men were shot on the spot without trial on the mere allegation of their guilt by order of a higher authority. The only authority which could give an order for their execution unchallenged was Adolf Hitler, who, according to the same article in this newspaper, "is the supreme conscience of the German people."

GOERING POLICE NET CATCHES LEADERS

Suicides and Killings Follow Raids on Homes of Notables in Berlin and Vicinity.

By OTTO D. TOLISCHUS.

Wireless to The New York Times.

BERLIN, June 30.—General Kurt von Schleicher, former Premier, was killed with his wife while "resisting arrest with a weapon in his hand," according to an official communiqué.

The communiqué was one of a long series issued throughout the day as the criminal police of Premier Hermann Goering of Prussia rushed about Berlin and its vicinity, leaving a heavy wake of arrests, suicides and killings among prominent persons.

General von Schleicher met death at his villa in Neubabelsberg, between Berlin and Potsdam. His wife, Frau Elizabeth von Schleicher, it is stated, fell while trying to shield him with her body during an exchange of shots.

From that point tragedy quickly spread. One squad of General Goering's police rushed to the office of Vice Chancellor Franz von Papen in Voss Strasse, next to the Chancellery, and asked the Vice Chancellor to accompany them to his home. There they kept Colonel von Papen under house arrest, and questioned him regarding his relations with General von Schleicher. The amenities were preserved, and later it was stated Colonel von Papen was "at liberty."

Von Papen Visitors Barred.

Visitors to Colonel von Papen's house, however, were not allowed to see him. His secretary and a Reichswehr officer assured every one that Colonel von Papen was in good spirits, had just finished tea and was smoking his afternoon cigar.

His office meanwhile had been occupied by black uniformed special guards, men with field equipment, rifles and hand grenades. To inquirers they insisted they were merely Colonel von Papen's regular guard, placed there to protect him. Visitors noted, however, that all doors of the building stood open, as if a whirlwind had swept through.

In the face of this action, Colonel

Continued on Page Two.

NAZI CHIEFS TELL OF ENDING REVOLT

Hitler and Lutze Appeal to the Storm Troops to Be Faithful to Their Movement.

RAID DESCRIBED BY PARTY

Leader of War Veterans Urges Them to Be Calm and to Be Loyal to Government.

Wireless to The New York Times.

BERLIN, June 30.—A series of statements was issued today by German leaders on their success in crushing the radical Nazi revolt.

NAZI PARTY STATEMENT.

A communiqué from the National Socialist party read:

Munich, June 30.

For many months individual elements have been trying to drive a wedge and produce conflicts between the Storm Troops and the party, as well as between the Storm Troops and the State. Suspicions of this became more and more confirmed, but it was also plain that these endeavors were to be charged to a limited clique of certain leanings.

Chief of Staff Roehm, in whom the leader placed an exceptional amount of confidence, not only did not oppose these endeavors but undoubtedly sponsored them. His well-known unfortunate characteristic gradually led to intolerable burdens which drove the leader of the movement and the Highest Leader of the Storm Troops (Hitler) into most serious conflicts of conscience.

Chief of Staff Roehm established contacts with General von Schleicher without the knowledge of Der Fuehrer (the leader). His go-betweens were another Storm Troop leader and an obscure person well known in Berlin, to whom Der Fuehrer had always strongly objected.

Since these negotiations also led—of course without the knowledge of Der Fuehrer—finally to contacts with a foreign power, or rather to its representative, it was not possible to avoid intervention both from the standpoint of the party and the State.

Provocative incidents brought about according to the plan caused Der Fuehrer to fly from Bonn to Munich at 2 o'clock this morning, after visiting labor camps in Westphalia, in order to remove and arrest the most seriously compromised group of leaders. Der Fuehrer himself went with only a few companions to Wiessee in order to still any attempts at resistance.

The execution of the arrests revealed such immorality that any trace of pity was impossible. Some of the Storm Troop leaders had taken male prostitutes along with them. One of them was even disturbed in a most ugly situation and was arrested.

Der Fuehrer gave orders for this plague to be done away with ruthlessly. In the future he will not permit millions of decent people to be compromised by a few of this sort of men. Der Fuehrer instructed Premier Goering to take similar action in Berlin and especially to arrest the reactionary accomplices of this political plot.

At noon today Der Fuehrer

Continued on Page Four.

STORM TROOP CHIEFS DIE

Killed or Take Own Lives as Chancellor and Goering Strike.

REACTIONARIES ALSO HIT

Wife Shot With Schleicher as He Resists Police—Head of Catholic Action Slain.

HITLER FLIES TO MUNICH

Tears Off Rebels' Insignia and Arrests and Ousts Roehm—Papen Held but Freed.

By FREDERICK T. BIRCHALL.

Wireless to The New York Times.

BERLIN, June 30.—On the eve of a self-proclaimed month of peace Germany has passed today through the throes of a violent purging that must profoundly affect her future. It is neither a revolution nor a coup d'état nor a counter-revolution but authoritative action intended to head off any of the three.

Chancellor Hitler in Munich, backed by General Hermann Wilhelm Goering, Premier of Prussia, in Berlin, has struck simultaneously at the rebel elements in his own Storm Troops and at certain reactionary elements supposedly allied with them on suspected of being an allied for their own ends in an attempt to upset the present régime in Germany.

When the day was over many Storm Troop leaders had been shot to death or had committed suicide. In addition, General Kurt von Schleicher, Herr Hitler's predecessor as Chancellor, had been slain while resisting police who attempted to seize him as one of the plotters.

[Captain Ernst Roehm, chief of staff of the Storm Troops, committed suicide after having been ousted by Chancellor Hitler, according to The Associated Press, while Heinrich Klausener, chief of the Catholic Action, was shot to death by a Nazi special guard.]

The Official Version.

The official version is that the attempt was a joint effort "to bring pressure" on the government with a threat of violent action behind it. There is mention of a "foreign power" as being involved. The discerning interpret this reference as being to Russia and the ultimate aim of the rebels as a new national bolshevism.

Whatever the cause, Chancellor Hitler has acted swiftly and decisively. Flying to Munich in the early hours of this morning from Bonn, where he had been ostensibly inspecting work camps, he assembled his trusted special guards in that city and proceeded to gather in the suspected leaders, who had already proceeded to preliminary action.

Captain Roehm, the leader of the conspiracy, was arrested in his bedroom in his country house outside Munich by Herr Hitler himself and then and there deposed from all his offices. His fellow-conspirators were gathered in by the dozen in Munich and around it.

The official story told to foreign correspondents by General Goering this afternoon says that some of them, both in Munich and in Berlin, committed suicide and others were shot while resisting.

Goering Acts Swiftly.

Almost simultaneously in Berlin General Goering, by arrangement with Chancellor Hitler, was taking similar action. It came swiftly and unexpectedly just before noon. But here the members of the reactionary group believed to be acting with the rebel Storm Troop leaders were equally the objects of the assault.

Karl Ernst, leader of the Berlin Storm Troops, was traced to a house near Bremen and surrounded there. He is dead and the official version is that he was shot while resisting arrest. The unofficial version is that he was brought by airplane to Berlin and executed on his arrival.

Police and special guards at the very outset sought to seize General von Schleicher at his villa outside Potsdam. It is said that he attempted to draw a pistol. A volley of shots brought him down and his wife and was arrested.

Vice Chancellor Franz von Papen, who seems to have been sus-

Continued on Page Two.

Dillinger Raids Bank in South Bend, Ind., Reported Shot; Officer Slain, Loot $28,000

By The Associated Press.

SOUTH BEND, Ind., June 30.—A bandit quintet with John Dillinger reported to be in command, stormed the Merchants' National Bank today, scooped up $28,439 and fled in a wild barrage of bullets, leaving a slain policeman and four wounded men in their wake.

The ruthless raiders engaged in gun battles with a detective, two officers and a jeweler as they fled from the bank and made their way to the escape car a half block away. More than fifty shots raked the street in the heart of the city.

Detective Harry Henderson, who identified the bandits' leader as Dillinger, said he believed that he had shot the long-sought gunman as the quintet's car sped away.

Patrolman Harold Wagner encountered the three gangsters who carried out the actual robbery as they were hurrying from the bank. He was fatally wounded before he could reach his pistol.

Those wounded were P. G. Stahley, manager of the Birdsell Manufacturing Company; Jake Soloman, Delos N. Coen, a cashier, and Samuel Toth. At Epworth Hospital it was found that a bullet had struck Soloman in the hip and

---

coursed upward. His condition was described as critical. Toth was wounded in the eye as a bullet smashed the windshield of his automobile.

Leaving an outpost, believed to be John Hamilton, on guard at their automobile, and another bandit closer to the bank, the man identified by a police detective as Dillinger, with two henchmen, one of them believed to be "Baby Face" Nelson, rushed into the bank about noon. Cowing the twenty-five customers with a machine gun, the man identified as Dillinger took up a strategic post and sent a score of slugs into the ceiling while his confederates snatched up $28,439. C. W. Coen, vice president of the institution, who took cover under a desk three feet from the gunner, declared he was positive the leader was the desperado Dillinger.

Bundling their loot, the three commandeered Stahley, Coen and several other patrons and used them as human shields as they marched out the door. Wagner, the man toward them from across the crowded street. The machine gun-ner shot him down, three bullets entering the policeman's body.

NRA — "All the News That's Fit to Print."

The New York Times.

LATE CITY EDITION
POSTSCRIPT
Fair, slightly cooler today;
tomorrow fair.
Temperature Yesterday—Max., 89; min., 73.

Copyright, 1934, by The New York Times Company.

VOL. LXXXIII....No. 27,939.

Entered as Second-Class Matter,
Postoffice, New York, N. Y.

NEW YORK, MONDAY, JULY 23, 1934.

TWO CENTS In New York City. | THREE CENTS Within 200 Miles | FOUR CENTS Elsewhere Except in 7th and 8th Postal Zones

15 KILLED, 18 HURT AS BUS FALLS 35 FEET AND BURNS ON AN OUTING AT OSSINING

MANY TRAPPED IN FLAMES

Machine Out of Control Plunges Off Ramp Into Lumber Yard.

GASOLINE TANK EXPLODES

Injured Struggle in Vain to Open Jammed Doors of Old-Fashioned Coach.

4, AFIRE, LEAP INTO RIVER

Members of Young Democrats' Club of Brooklyn Bound for Sing Sing Ball Game.

Fifteen persons were killed and eighteen injured, yesterday, when a bus containing about forty men, women and children plunged thirty-five feet from a ramp near the Ossining railroad station and burst into flames.

The bus was one of seven that had been chartered by the Young Men's Democratic League of the Twentieth Assembly District in Brooklyn to take their friends to a ball game in Sing Sing.

Speeding, out of control, down the tortuous Secor Road hill, it mounted the ramp that crosses the New York Central tracks near the Ossining station, crashed through the fragile iron railing on one side of the ramp and landed on its four wheels in a lumber yard.

Gasoline Tank Explodes.

The driver, apparently, failed to turn off the ignition; and as the bus struck the ground the gasoline tank exploded with a deafening roar. Sheets of flame shot out in all directions, and while passengers inside scrambled for the exits, fire enveloped the vehicle and the adjacent lumber piles.

The bus, one of the old-fashioned type with no centre aisle, had eight seats running crosswise and doors on either side of each seat. A few of the doors were opened without difficulty, enabling those inside to escape. But many of the doors, thrown out of alignment by the crash, refused to open.

The occupants of these seats were penned up, and with the flames mounting around them began screaming for help. Those who had escaped tugged vainly at the closed doors. With the aid of witnesses to the crash they succeeded in opening several doors and releasing some of those inside.

Four Leap Into the Hudson.

Four men, who had escaped from the bus with their clothing in flames, rushed to the near-by Hudson River and threw themselves in. Two others raced down along the New York Central Railroad tracks. In the river were rescued by Frank McLaughlin, former Fire Chief of Ossining. What became of the two who ran along the tracks could not be definitely ascertained last night, but it is believed that they were taken in charge by near-by residents and rushed to a hospital.

Thomas McGuire Jr. of 828 Halsey Street, Brooklyn, who had escaped from the bus with a broken arm and secondary burns, rushed back to rescue his father, who had been critically burned. Others who had escaped from the bus made every effort to save those still inside. So did witnesses to the accident. George Adcock, an Ossining fireman, got credit for seven rescues. But the old wooden framework of the bus and the sun-dried lumber piled near by burned like tinder and the rescue work had to be abandoned.

All ambulances in Ossining were brought to the scene of the crash and secondary burns, rushed back to rescue his father, who had been critically burned. Others who had escaped from the bus made every effort to save those still inside. So did the witnesses to the accident. George Adcock, an Ossining fireman, got credit for seven rescues. But the old wooden framework of the bus and the sun-dried lumber piled near by burned like tinder and the rescue work had to be abandoned.

All ambulances in Ossining were brought to the scene of the crash and the injured removed to the Ossining, Grasslands and Tarrytown Hospitals. Father John Kelly of Briarcliff, who chanced to be passing in an automobile, had arrived in time to assist in the rescue work. He also administered the last rites of the church to some of the more seriously injured. Afterward, he went to the Ossining Hospital, where he administered the last rites to others.

The regular staff at the Ossining hospital was swamped with work and was reinforced by numerous volunteers. These included Drs. Robert Bloom, James Kearney, John Schofmeister, Edward Huntington of Ossining, Edward Hunt-Miller of Croton.

Many prominent women in the vi-

Continued on Page Three.

Victims of Bus Accident

A partial list of the dead and injured in the bus accident at Ossining, as compiled last night, follows:

THE DEAD.

GALLER, ABRAHAM, 666 Hancock Street, Brooklyn.
HAYES, Mrs. WILLIAM, 27 Cornelia St., Brooklyn.
INCARNATO, FRANK, 29 years old, driver of the bus, 662 Ninety-second St., Brooklyn.
McNICHOLAS, JOHN, Jr., 36, 412 Irving Av., Brooklyn.
An unidentified person.

MISSING (BELIEVED DEAD).

GALLER, Mrs. ABRAHAM, 666 Hancock Street, Brooklyn.
LUFF, ARTHUR, 9 Woodbine St., Brooklyn.
His sister, whose name was not determined.
MEHEY, JOSEPH, 27 Cornelia St., Brooklyn.
McDONALD, Mr. and Mrs. JOSEPH, 100 Gates Av., Brooklyn.
McDONALD, BERNADETTE, 13 years old, their daughter.
MURRAY, Mr. and Mrs. JAMES, 15 Cornelia St., Brooklyn.
THOMPSON, Mrs. ROSE, 9 Woodbine St., Brooklyn.

THE INJURED.

Ossining Hospital.
CONNORS, FRANK, 542 Bainbridge Av., Brooklyn, critical.
CORCORAN, JOSEPH, 666 Putnam Avenue, Brooklyn, not serious.

ELLERY, JAMES, 712 Knickerbocker Av., Brooklyn, left hospital after treatment.
MAYER, WILLIAM, 27 Cornelia St., Brooklyn, not serious.
HAYES, JAMES, 12, his son, critical.
NUFF, FRANK, 521 Monroe St., Brooklyn, not serious.
McCANN, DANIEL, 275 Central Av., Brooklyn, critical.
McGUIRE, THOMAS, 826 Halsey St., Brooklyn, critical.
MERKEL, Mrs. TERESA, 290 Highland Blvd., Brooklyn, left hospital after treatment.
REITMEYER, JOHN, 1,318 Gates Av., Brooklyn, critical.
SCHWARTZ, Mrs. ARCHIBALD, 116 Liberty St., Brooklyn, not serious.

Grasslands Hospital.
KNAUER, FRANK, of 75-97 Sixty-fourth St., Glendale, Queens.
LALOF, MARY, 9 Woodbine Street, Brooklyn; not serious.
McGUIRE, THOMAS, Jr., 826 Halsey Street, Brooklyn; not serious.
SCHNEIDER, EDWIN, 105-11 195th Street, Hollis, Queens; not serious.
SCHWARTZ, ARCHIBALD, 116 Liberty Street, Brooklyn, not serious.

Tarrytown Hospital.
MICKEY, GEORGE, 17 Woodbine Street, Brooklyn; not serious.
MURRAY, WILLIAM, 15 Cornelia Street, Brooklyn; not serious.

BUS BRAKES WEAK, SURVIVORS ASSERT

'We'll Take a Chance,' Driver Said—Stopped Twice for Makeshift Repairs.

MAN SAW WIFE PERISH

Tried to Pull Her From Wreck, but Flames Drove Him Back, He Testifies at Inquest.

Special to The New York Times.

OSSINING, N. Y., July 22.—Walter Thompson of 9 Woodbine Street, Brooklyn, a survivor of the bus accident that cost fifteen lives here today, testified tonight at the official inquest that the bus driver knew his brakes were bad.

Thompson was the first witness called by Dr. Amos O. Squire, Medical Examiner for Westchester County. His story of the bad brakes and the driver's makeshift repairs was corroborated by other witnesses and in unofficial accounts obtained by newspaper men from other survivors here and in Brooklyn.

"Several times on the way up," Thompson told Dr. Squire, "the driver had trouble with his brakes. I noticed that finally he got up and turned the foot brake around as if he were screwing it on the shaft. After each time the brake held better, and then it seemed to loosen up. At one point the emergency brake held all right, but on the hill in Ossining it was no good.

"We'll Take a Chance."

"I said to him, 'Your brakes are bad.' I told him he'd better be careful and that he ought to stop and fix them.

"The driver said: 'The bell with it. We'll take a chance. I guess we'll get through.' He was completely sober. I thought that he was a good chauffeur—that's what I told the man in the seat with me.

"When we got on the hill on Main Street here and were coming down from the top at a pretty good pace, we got to where he should have taken a turn at Hunter Street [a right-angle turn off Main Street which would have led to the prison] and there were two automobiles parked on the street which partly blocked the turn.

"The driver turned out, swung away over and cleared the automobiles and went on down the hill, swinging from curb to curb almost all the way down the hill. He couldn't get control again.

"Yelled to All to Jump.

"Just before the bus crashed through the railing the driver yelled, 'Everybody jump!' We went right through the railing, and the bus fell front first when the hind wheel hit the foundation for the railing, raising up the rear of the bus. The bus struck on the front.

"The motor backed up and down the steering wheel drove the chauf-

Continued on Page Three.

TREASURY OFFERS MORTGAGE BONDS

$100,000,000 in 3% 14-Year Farm Corporation Securities to Go to Highest Bidders.

SALE USHERS NEW POLICY

Marks First Time Treasury Has Acted as Fiscal Agent— Ready Market Expected.

Special to The New York Times.

WASHINGTON, July 22.—The Treasury Department today announced an offering to the public of $100,000,000 of Federal Farm Mortgage Corporation 3 per cent bonds, thus inaugurating a new policy under which the department acted as the agent of one of the emergency recovery set-ups in floating securities which the corporation was authorized by law to sell to obtain funds.

In the past the Treasury, except in the case of short-term Treasury bills which are sold on a discount basis, has judged the market, determined upon the interest at which a security should be offered and then has sought subscriptions at par or at a small stipulated premium. Such offerings have been for the purpose of covering the Treasury's own requirements.

In the present offering, however, which the Treasury is making on behalf of the emergency corporations, the department did not have discretion in fixing the interest rate the securities shall carry. It has, therefore, offered the mortgage corporation's bonds to the highest bidders, but in no case at less than par and accrued interest. The bonds will be dated May 15, 1934, mature on May 15, 1948, and may be redeemed at any May 15, 1944, or on any subsequent interest payment date which comes semi-annually on May 15 and Nov. 15 of each year.

At present Treasury 3s are selling in the market at slightly over 102, and outstanding bonds of the mortgage corporation are quoted at just over 101. The latter are guaranteed as to principal and interest by law.

Substantial Premium Expected.

In connection with the present offering the Treasury Department expects to market the $100,000,000 issue readily and at a substantial premium. The bonds are exempt both as to principal and interest from Federal, State, municipal and local taxation, except surtaxes, estate, inheritance and gift taxes. They will be issued in denominations of from $100 to $10,000.

The decision to have the Treasury market the bonds and thus further centralize the handling of government-backed security offerings in the public market was reached after conferences between Treasury officials and officials of the Farm Credit Corporation, under the supervision of which the Federal Farm Mortgage Corporation activities are arranged.

To a certain extent it is in line with the policy adopted some time ago to suspend the direct sale of debentures by the RFC to banks

Continued on Page Three.

2,320 Planes for Army Asked in Baker Report

Board Declares Congress Should Provide Funds—Separate Unit Plan Rejected —Mail Flying Praised.

Special to The New York Times.

WASHINGTON, July 22.—Holding that the strengthening of the air forces was essential to adequate national defense, the War Department's special aviation committee recommended today an increase in the aviation strength of the army to 2,320 planes and a corresponding increase in the flying personnel. The present authorized strength of the army air corps is 1,800 planes, which the committee reported to be more than 300 short.

The committee, headed by Newton D. Baker, former Secretary of War, and composed of eleven civilian and military generals, declared against consolidation of the army and navy aviation services into a single unit. Its report praised the spirit and manner in which the army carried the mail under difficulties during the period of the cancellation of the air mail contracts. With this was mingled criticism of the actual performance, coupled as it was with fatalities, and whatever there was of failure was attributed to lack of proper equipment and to insufficient training.

While expressing the opinion that the United States was comparatively free from the threat of serious overseas air invasion because of the failure so far to develop an airplane capable of crossing the Atlantic or Pacific with an effective military load, attacking vital air bases, the committee held that the army's air corps must be ready at all times for war service.

"The next great war is likely to begin with engagements between opposing aircraft, either sea-based or land-based," the report read, "and early aerial supremacy is quite likely to be an important factor.

Continued on Page Six.

The recommendations of the Baker committee are on page 6.

FALL BUSINESS RISE PREDICTED BY NRA; SUMMER DROP CUT

Upward Trend Held Definite by Leon Henderson, Citing Homely Indicators.

LESS FAMILY DOUBLING-UP

This Despite Increase in Marriages—Small Loans Are Being Rapidly Repaid.

Copyright, 1934, by The Associated Press.

WASHINGTON, July 22.—The NRA has been informed by its experts to "gamble" on a substantial Fall rise in business and a less than usual slump during the remainder of the Summer.

Leon Henderson, chief of the Blue Eagle's research and planning division, held this conclusion today as he based his conclusion on the basis of a mass of statistical and other data. His advice to NRA is based upon an expectation of an upswing.

Mr. Henderson's searchers have reported to him that the decline thus far this Summer has been less than normal, and that there are new numerous signs of an upward trend in business generally.

There is no expectation, however, of a boom development. Mr. Henderson employs most careful language in his estimate of the future. He himself referred today to his attitude as a "gamble" on the basis of the best facts available.

The research chief is paying especial attention to what he describes as his "homely indicators." For instance, there has been a gain in the sale of living room rugs, one of the first things which housewives like to replace when funds are available.

There also has been a decline in the number of bachelors, he points out. In one city the number of bachelors before the depression was 10,000. This increased to 20,000 at the height of the depression and is now about 22,000, the expert conclusion being that men with funds are less fearful of marriage.

Families Again Spring Out.

For another thing, Mr. Henderson's "doubling-up" indicator in reference to housing shows that families which have been crowded now are spreading out and filling vacant apartments and houses.

Small personal loans, his figures show, are being paid up in full at an increasing rate. The index shows the rate of repaying at a record high for the depression, and higher even than in the month when soldiers' cash bonus payments were largest. Similarly, the rate of repayment of building and loan obligations is up and the amount of unrented property held by building and loan associations is down. Repayments to the Home Owners Loan Corporation and Farm Credit Administration are also holding up well.

Mr. Henderson said he was paying increasing attention to this type of statistical indicator because, first, it shows the status of the ordinary person better than the customary type of business statistics, and second, because it tends to get at the beginning of the buying process rather than at the end. Of particular significance, he said, are the indicators showing a reduction in personal debt. He holds this to be one of

Continued on Page Two.

FRENCH FACTIONS WARNED BY LEBRUN TO RESTORE TRUCE

President Says Public Will Be Severe With Those Blocking Doumergue's Work.

PREMIER TO SEEK ACCORD

Tardieu Is Said to Be Ready to Make Peace With Herriot to Prevent Cabinet Shifts.

By The Associated Press.

AURILLAC, France, July 22.—President Lebrun took a hand in the bitter Cabinet clash today by warning that there must be no interference with the government of Premier Doumergue.

France will not tolerate anything which blocks M. Doumergue's work, M. Lebrun said as he unveiled a monument at the birthplace of the assassinated President, Paul Doumer.

M. Lebrun made no direct reference to the Cabinet dissension in which Edouard Herriot and André Tardieu, both Ministers without portfolio and both former Premiers, are the chief figures. But he said pointedly that party fights must be forgotten.

The President expressed pride in M. Doumergue's "wisdom and prudence" and asserted his work must go on.

"Public opinion will not accept a situation that stops its beneficial work," M. Lebrun said. "It will be severe toward those who do not do everything to assure for the future what the wisdom of the efforts of today already is permitting us to hope is being achieved."

Critical Week for France.

Wireless to The New York Times.

PARIS, July 22.—This coming week seems likely to be as critical for France as was that following the rioting of Feb. 6. There is only this difference in the situation, that this time there is a common core of confusion.

It is believed the country as a whole at this vacation time wants a real truce to politics. It has put its trust in Premier Doumergue, and among persons of all classes of opinion one hears expressions of resentment because his Ministers could not keep the truce while his back was turned. Whatever he does will have the approval of most persons, but it also is true that whatever he does is almost certain to arouse resentment in one camp or the other.

In the two camps feeling is running high. André Tardieu's friends on newspapers are reiterating that the Radical Socialists are responsible for breaking the truce and are seeking to thrust them out of the Cabinet because they spoke the truth about Camille Chautemps.

To that the reply of the Radical Socialist press is to describe M. Tardieu as "the man who brought down French bonds."

Newspapers like the Petit Parisien, which more nearly represent average opinion, are afraid of the whole situation. They are careful to remain outside the quarrel. They are too well aware of its dangers to get at the beginning of the Dreyfus affair. There is no concealment of the fact that below the wave covering most of the country, which is possible only in the person and authority of Premier Doumergue, there is an atmosphere

Continued on Page Four.

HOT WAVE ABATES; SEVEN DROWN HERE

Highest Temperature Is 89 at 4:30 P. M. After Cool Morning—One Heat Death.

DROUGHT SPREADS IN WEST

Total Dead in Nation From Weather 272—Cattle and Crops Loss Mounts.

After three days of oppressive heat and high humidity, the weather here moderated somewhat yesterday.

The day's maximum temperature was 89 degrees at 4:30 P. M.; but the humidity remained comparatively low throughout the day, and a brisk northerly breeze tempered the heat of the sun.

The combination here of the warm sun and cool breeze made perfect weather for the seashore, and all the near-by beaches again were thronged with large Sunday crowds. For the fourth time this season the crowd at Coney Island was estimated at more than 1,000,000. At the Rockaways, it was estimated, there were more than 500,000; at Long Beach, more than 300,000, and at Jones Beach, more than 150,000.

The crowd at Jones Beach was one of the largest of the year. The causeway there was lined through out the day with automobiles, and both bathhouses did a near-capacity business.

One heat death and one prostration were reported during the day. An unidentified man about 55 years old was stricken with a heart attack induced by the heat at Sheriff and Delancey Streets and died.

Seven Persons Drowned.

Seven drownings were reported:

JOSEPH CERILLA, 16 years old, of 105 Bergen Street, Brooklyn, drowned while bathing off West Twenty-fifth Street, Coney Island.

JAMES CUNNINGHAM, 36, employed at the Broeklin Hospital in Summit, N. J.; drowned off Beach 100th Street, Rockaway Beach.

ALLAN SNYDER, 23, of 323 Winget Street, West Philadelphia, drowned in Mirror Lake at Browns Mills, N. J.

FRANK BELTTERNICK, 25, of 300 Seventh Street, Jersey City; drowned in New York Bay off Linden Avenue, Jersey City.

CATHERINE LeCONTE, 3, of 343 East Third Street, Brooklyn; drowned in Lake Ronkonkoma, L. I.

WILLIAM MAGNER, 72; drowned in Bairns Creek at Salem, N. J.

MILTON WEYLANDT, 18, of 323 Washington Road, Port Richmond, S. I.; mixed with heart attack and drowned in Lake Hopatcong, N. J.

It was said last night at the Weather Bureau that today probably would be fair and slightly cooler.

272 Dead in Nation.

Deaths in the protracted heat wave covering most of the country passed 256 reported. The Associated Press reported.

Hundreds of prostrations were recorded.

The Southwest and Midwest were hardest hit. Only slight relief for scattered areas was in immediate prospect.

In the grain belt crops wilted and

Continued on Page Eleven.

DILLINGER SLAIN IN CHICAGO; SHOT DEAD BY FEDERAL MEN IN FRONT OF MOVIE THEATRE

Cummings Says Slaying of Dillinger Is 'Gratifying as Well as Reassuring'

By The Associated Press.

WASHINGTON, July 22.—Smiling in elation, Attorney General Cummings tonight termed the slaying of John Dillinger by Federal agents "gratifying as well as reassuring."

The Attorney General was notified just before he boarded the train for the West, the first leg of a journey to Hawaii. At Union Station he dictated the following statement:

"The search for Dillinger has never been relaxed for a moment.

"He has escaped capture on several occasions by the narrowest of margins.

"The news of tonight is exceedingly gratifying as well as reassuring."

Mr. Cummings said the end of the Indiana bandit reflected great credit on the Chicago office of the division of investigation.

J. Edgar Hoover, chief of the Bureau of Investigation, rushed to his office at word that the desperado had been shot down. He told news men:

"This does not mean the end of the Dillinger case.

"Any one who ever gave any of the Dillinger mob any aid, comfort or assistance will be vigorously prosecuted."

He referred directly to George (Baby Face) Nelson, Homer Van Meter and another gangster. Nelson, named by the department as the killer of Special Agent W. Carter Baum in the Dillinger outbreak in the Wisconsin woods last April, was described by Mr. Hoover as a "rat."

REACHED FOR HIS GUN

Outlaw's Move Met by Four Shots, All Finding Their Mark.

HAD LIFTED HIS FACE

Desperado Had Also Treated Finger Tips With Acid to Defeat Prints.

TWO WOMEN WOUNDED

Agents, Tipped Fugitive Was Going to Theatre, Waited While He Saw Show.

Special to The New York Times.

CHICAGO, July 22.—John Dillinger, Public Enemy No. 1, and the most notorious criminal of recent times, was shot and killed at 10:40 o'clock tonight by Federal agents a few seconds after he had left the Biograph Theatre at 2,423 Lincoln Avenue, on Chicago's North Side.

One bullet penetrated the head and another the chest of the desperate outlaw. He died as he was being taken to the Alexian Brothers Hospital. The body was later removed to the county morgue, where the identification of Dillinger was made positive.

According to Melvin H. Purvis, chief of the investigating forces of the Department of Justice in Chicago, and leader of the band of sixteen men who had waited for more than two hours while the desperado viewed his last picture show, Dillinger attempted to put up a fight.

"He saw me give a signal to my men to close in," Chief Purvis said. "He became alarmed and reached into a belt and was drawing the .38-calibre pistol he carried concealed when two of the agents let him have it. Dillinger was lying prone before he was able to get the gun out and I took it from him."

Surgical Disguise Fails.

Dillinger had taken great precautions to prevent his being recognized. His face had been lifted by a surgical process since his last picture was taken and he had dyed his hair a darker shade than its natural reddish brown.

"It was a good job the surgeons did," Chief Purvis said, "but I knew him the minute I saw him. You couldn't miss if you had studied that face as much as I have."

Two women, passers-by who had no connection with the outlaw, were wounded by stray bullets fired by the Federal agents. They are Mrs. Etta Natalsky, 45 years old, of 2,452 Lincoln Avenue, and Miss Theresa Paulus. Each was struck in the left leg. Their injuries, it was said, were not serious.

Patrons of Gangster Film.

Chief Purvis and twelve of his own men, accompanied by Captain Timothy O'Neil and three members of the East Chicago police force, went to the vicinity of the small theatre at about 8:30 P. M. They had received information during the afternoon that Dillinger would attend the performance of "Manhattan Melodrama," a gun and gun movie featuring Clark Gable and William Powell, in the evening.

The sixteen men were posted strategically, some at all possible exits of the theatre, with groups to the north and south, and one detail on the opposite side of busy Lincoln Avenue. Chief Purvis, seating himself in his automobile a few feet south of the show house, watched.

It was about 8:30 P. M. when Dillinger walked up to the entrance and bought a ticket, or tickets. A Chicago policeman who happened to be at the scene said he was accompanied by two women, one dressed in red, but Chief Purvis said he saw none. Passing into the theatre, Dillinger took a seat.

While he was inside, the agents completed their preparations for his emergence. There were so many of them, and their actions seemed, to the theatre manager and to observers in the neighborhood, so suspicious that the police were notified.

Policemen Frank Slattery, Edward Meisterheimer and Michael Garrity, who investigated, were told by Federal badges by the watchers and interfered not at all, al-

Continued on Page Nine.

THREE DOOMED MEN FLEE TEXAS PRISON

Another Convict Killed Climbing Wall, Two Others Shot in Death House Break.

GUARD ALSO IS WOUNDED

Trio of Killers, One of Them an Aide of Clyde Barrow, Escape in Waiting Car.

By The Associated Press.

HUNTSVILLE, Texas, July 22.—Three of the most desperate killers in the Southwest—Raymond Hamilton, Blackie Thompson and Joe Palmer—escaped from the death house of the State penitentiary here today in a daring break in which one convict was killed, two others wounded and a guard shot.

The three convicts who were shot, all knife-bandits and life-termers, were mowed down by the gunfire of guards as Hamilton, Thompson and Palmer scampered over the wall to two waiting automobiles.

Whitey Walker was killed by the shots of guards whom the convicts engaged in battle. Charlie Frazier, the other man who engineered the break, was shot from the ladder with which he was scaling the wall and was believed to be fatally wounded. Roy Johnson, the third bank robber, was shot and less seriously hurt.

H. E. George, the guard, was momentarily stunned by a bullet creased his scalp. He was not seriously hurt.

The break occurred while the prison yard was almost deserted. All officials and guards not actually on duty were practically all convicts were attending a ball game between the prison team and a Conroe team at the athletic field beside the walls.

The escape was the first ever made from the death house, which is located in the centre of the prison. In daring and cool execution, the break has no parallel in the annals of the penitentiary.

Guard Forced to Unlock Cells.

At 4:30 P. M. inside Guard Lee Braswell approached the death house to feed the five inmates. Inside guards are not permitted to carry weapons, as they come closely into contact with the convicts, and it would be possible for the latter on occasions to overpower and disarm them.

As Braswell approached the door, Frazier, crouched against the wall, stepped forward and thrust the muzzle of a .45-calibre revolver against his ribs. In his other hand the convict held another .45.

Frazier marched Braswell into the death house, and compelled him to unlock the cells in which Hamilton, Palmer and Thompson were incarcerated. These convicted murderers came out, and Frazier handed Hamilton his extra gun. Braswell was locked in Hamilton's cell.

The quartet of desperadoes sped from the death house and were joined at the door by Walker and Johnson. A few feet from the death house they encountered W. T. Mc-

Continued on Page Eleven.

"All the News That's Fit to Print."

The New York Times.

LATE CITY EDITION

WEATHER—Showers, cooler to-day; fair, cooler tomorrow.
Temperatures Yesterday—Max., 93; min., 66.

Copyright, 1934, by The New York Times Company.

VOL. LXXXIII....No. 27,942.

Entered as Second-Class Matter,
Postoffice, New York, N. Y.

NEW YORK, THURSDAY, JULY 26, 1934.

P

TWO CENTS In New York City. | THREE CENTS Within 200 Miles | FOUR CENTS Elsewhere Except in 7th and 8th Postal Zones

DEATHS FROM HEAT INCREASE TO 1,213 IN THE COUNTRY

Temperatures Continue to Stay Above 100 Degrees in Western Cities.

MISSOURI SUFFERS MOST

Records Show 312 Deaths in State—Intense Drought Suffering in Huge Area.

WALLACE IS PESSIMISTIC

He Says Situation Will Be Very Serious Unless Relief Comes in Two Weeks.

The Daily Heat Record

Following are the maximum heat records set yesterday in Western cities, with deaths for the day and the forecast:

City.	High	Deaths	Forecast.
Chicago	92	76	Cooler.
Cincinnati	106	37	Slightly cooler.
Des Moines	104	5	Showers, cooler.
Omaha	100	8	Possible showers.
St. Louis	108	76	Showers, cooler.
Kansas City	108	13	Showers, cooler.

By The Associated Press.

Wind and rain combined forces to afford some slight relief to people on the Atlantic, Pacific and Gulf coasts yesterday, but there was no relief for the parched fields, panting beasts and the perspiring populace of the Middle West where the toll of death and damage continued to mount.

Fatalities listed as "heat deaths" reached 1,213 persons. Thousands of head of livestock have been destroyed and the market value of many additional thousands seriously reduced during the past sixteen days, when most of the nation has suffered under temperatures around the century mark. Irreparable damage has resulted to crops in all great producing areas.

On forecasts from the Weather Bureau of continued drought, Dr. Elwood Mead, Reclamation Commissioner, said that tens of thousands of persons in the Dakotas and eastern slopes of the Rockies "must be evacuated."

The Atlantic Coast was favored with lower temperatures and showers in many places. Several baseball games were postponed. The Pacific Coast also continued to enjoy comfortable weather.

Water shortage is serious in many communities. Two down-State Illinois counties reported the situation "was becoming desperate." Some Iowa cities have been hauling water in tank cars. Hundreds of new wells have been sunk throughout the Middle West.

Grasshoppers, chinch bugs and other insect pests daily add their ravages to the farmers' worries.

Missouri Sweep States.

Missouri with 312 victims continued to lead the list of States. Illinois was second with 300 and Ohio had 127. Among the others were Indiana 84, Nebraska 61, Iowa 62, Minnesota 32, Kansas 29, Kentucky 42, Texas 28, Michigan 19, Pennsylvania 18, Wisconsin 15, Oklahoma 10, South Dakota 7, West Virginia 12, Tennessee 5, New York 4, Massachusetts 3, Maryland 3, Connecticut 4, District of Columbia 2, Arkansas 2, Alabama 1.

Chicago, where a new all-time high record of 104.8 degrees, officially 105, was recorded Tuesday, dropped to a maximum of 93 yesterday, although the humidity continued excessive. St. Louis and Kansas City, with highs of 110 for the previous day, turned in marks of 108 and 106 respectively.

Cincinnati equaled its 106-degree mark for the second successive day, but some hope of relief was held out for Thursday, after a slight drop came in the early afternoon. Cleveland, swept by a lake breeze, enjoyed a 78 at 2 P. M. (Eastern standard time).

The Pacific Coast had little change in temperature and no heat fatalities. Seattle and Los Angeles had 80, Portland 84 and San Francisco 68 degrees.

Oklahoma City dropped from 104 Tuesday to 96 at noon Wednesday. Michigan cities in the midnineties showed a 10 degree drop. Baltimore had a 98, Indianapolis 105, Lincoln 97, Huntington (W. Va.) 100, Pittsburgh 96, Philadelphia 86, St. Paul 76, Milwaukee 84, Cumberland (Md.) 105, Ottumwa (Iowa) 104, Duluth 74, Omaha 161, Springfield (Ill.) 101, Carbondale (Ill.) 112, Louisville 100, Lawrence (Kan.) 111, Columbia (Mo.) 111, Newkirk (Okla.) 105, Topeka (Kan.) 109, Emporia 115.

Oklahoma's parched surface faced a new menace—forest fires, eighteen of which were reported licking up the valuable pasturage—and the State relief administration asked $500,000 immediately to fight conditions, "the worst on record."

Although its cattle purchase ma-

Continued on Page Eleven.

Will Not Tell of 'Hanging,' Reporters Go Back to Jail

By The Associated Press.

DANVILLE, Ky., July 25.—Jack Durham and Wesley Carty, newspaper men who refused to tell the police court about their advance information on a hanging in effigy, went back to jail today to serve another six hours. Judge J. W. Harlan ordered them to appear in court again tomorrow.

At the close of today's hearing, after Durham and Carty repeated their refusal to disclose their information on the ground that it was given them in confidence, Judge Harlan said:

"Well, boys, if this is going to be an endurance contest, I can stand it. You understand that this is a challenge to the court."

Yesterday Durham and Carty served a jail sentence of three hours. Monday they were fined $10.

BUS CRASH WITNESS RECEIVES A THREAT

Another Tells Court 'the Boss' Ordered Him to Say Falsely He Overhauled Coach.

3 ARE HELD AS WITNESSES

De Marco, of Rialto Company, Before Grand Jury—New Jersey Pushes New Laws.

Three men were held as material witnesses and Westchester County authorities were told of a threat to one witness and an order to another to commit perjury as the grand jury opened at White Plains yesterday its investigation of the Ossining bus disaster.

Indictments for manslaughter, predicted by the District Attorney's office the day before, did not materialize, and the grand jury heard only one witness before adjourning until next Wednesday. But District Attorney Frank H. Coyne and his aides received evidence, they said, that caused them to characterize many of the companies identified with the Rialto Bus Corporation as "phony, paper corporations with dummy directors."

Jersey Prepares Laws.

Before the end of the day the effects of the investigation had spread far beyond the county to which the accident that cost the lives of nineteen persons occurred.

Aroused by the tragedy and the resultant indications of faulty brakes, inadequate equipment, and lack of legislation to authorize inspection and supervision of sightseeing and chartered buses, New Jersey authorities followed the lead of New York State and prepared to provide remedial laws.

At Albany a resolution authorizing legislative investigation of the bus accident was introduced, and in New York and neighboring States local authorities of various towns and cities were taking the responsibility for inspection and supervision into their own hands.

There were suggestions that bus transportation systems be investigated with a view to more adequate control, and that the Federal Government investigate the tax returns of some companies.

Bus Official Testifies.

The single witness before the White Plains grand jury yesterday was Nicola De Marco, assistant manager of the Rialto garage at 434 East 105th Street, where the buses that took the Young Men's Democratic League of the Twentieth Assembly District, Brooklyn, on the fatal trip to Ossining were stored. De Marco, who appeared jaunty, had been described by Max E. Greenberg, attorney for the Rialto concerns, as one of those

Continued on Page Twelve.

KENNEDY PLEDGES SECURITIES ACT AID TO BUILD BUSINESS

Chairman Says Commission Will Encourage Legitimate Stock Market Operations.

PROMISES NEW STANDARDS

Speaking at Luncheon, He Assures Capital and Investors Alike of Proper Profit.

The text of Chairman Kennedy's speech is on Page 13.

Special to The New York Times.

WASHINGTON, July 25.—Joseph P. Kennedy spoke words of reassurance today to both capital and investors in connection with the new Securities Act. As chairman of the Securities and Exchange Commission he delivered his first speech since assuming office when he appeared at a luncheon of the National Press Club.

He told business generally that there would be no vindictiveness in the enforcement of the stock market law, but rather an effort to develop the financial market.

If business does the "right thing" it will be protected and have a chance to live and prosper, Mr. Kennedy said in assuring governmental protection of all business.

The commission's job, although essentially a technical one, would be done, said Mr. Kennedy, "in a businesslike way without political publicity of any sort." Public scrutiny of the commission's activities would never be discouraged or avoided, he declared.

"In our hands has been placed the responsibility of giving all the aid of which government is capable to the better organization of the mechanism through which the savings of the people find their way into securities," Mr. Kennedy said.

Some Old Practices Past.

"Everybody says that what business needs is confidence. I agree. Confidence that if business does the right thing it will be protected and given a chance to live, make profits and grow, helping itself and helping the country. But the old things business did, the old practices it followed, are, some of them, no longer the right ones."

The commission did not view business with suspicion, nor was there any intention by any member of it that business must be "harassed and annoyed and pushed around," he said.

"Domestic tranquillity is as essential to business as it is to our political system, and it was stated as one of the primary objects to be achieved through the Constitution," Mr. Kennedy went on. "We of the Securities and Exchange Commission do not regard ourselves as coroners sitting on the corpse of financial enterprise. On the contrary, we think of ourselves as the means of bringing new life into the body of the security business.

"We are not working on the theory that all the men and all the women connected with finance, either as workers or investors, are to be regarded as guilty of some undefined crime. On the contrary, we hold that business based on good-will should be encouraged so that it may be helpful."

It would be an "idle thing" to deny that business confidence was lacking in the United States, Mr. Kennedy said, and this was especially true in the case of securities. In times of change capital was notoriously timid, but there was nothing unusual in this; it was caution born of experience.

Mr. Kennedy made plain that the commission was not proceeding as a prosecutor hopeful of bringing

Continued on Page Thirteen.

French Forest Fires Menace Thousands; Whole Mediterranean Fleet Standing By

By The Associated Press.

TOULON, France, July 25.—The entire French fleet in the Mediterranean was ordered to be prepared to speed to Toulon today to evacuate thousands of persons menaced by forest fires in the region of Bormes and Lavadou.

Several thousand persons were reported to have been trapped by a serious fire, and high winds were whipping up the flames.

Orders for the fleet to stand by were radioed by Admiral DuBois after the commandant of the marines fighting the flames had reported that roads were blocked and that the fire was surrounding the villages, cutting off escape.

The village of Bormes, whose inhabitants returned home after having left it last night, was again evacuated.

Officials said that about 25,000

acres of pine trees have been destroyed.

ATHENS, July 25 (AP)—Six persons died of heat here today as the temperature rose as high as 115 degrees. Many forest fires were burning throughout Greece.

WARSAW, July 25 (AP)—The area around Sandomierz, where the surging Vistula River has spread itself into an enormous lake, was the outstanding danger spot today in Poland's flood-devastated scene.

Ten thousand persons already have been evacuated from the section, and many more are expected to be ordered to move by military patrols. The evacuation everywhere was under way.

Although it rained persistently last night, there were reassuring reports from the central section of the Vistula today.

Germany Recalls Envoy For Actions in Vienna

Special Cable to The New York Times.

BERLIN, Thursday, July 26.—The German Government at 2 o'clock this morning announced the recall of Dr. Kurt Rieth, German Minister to Austria, and Germany's intention of arresting the assassins of Chancellor Dollfuss, on behalf of whom Dr. Rieth intervened, should they reach German territory. The announcement reads:

"At the request of Austrian governmental authorities and Austrian rebels, respectively, German Minister to Vienna Rieth consented, without asking the German Government itself, to an agreement concluded between the two relative to the safe passage of the rebels to Germany. He was thereupon immediately recalled from his post."

The second official announcement said that the agreement reached between the Austrian rebels and the Austrian Government for safe passage of the rebels did not concern the German Reich and implied no legal obligations for the German Government.

BERLIN DECLARES HANDS-OFF POLICY

Asserts Austrian Revolt Is a Purely Internal Affair and No Concern of Reich.

PARIS AND LONDON GRAVE

Insist Vienna's Independence Must Be Preserved—British Fear Crisis Like 1914.

By FREDERICK T. BIRCHALL

BERLIN, July 25.—Throughout the day there has been the keenest interest as to what was happening in Vienna. And information to the public has been correspondingly meager and inaccurate and colored by the National Socialist interest.

Telephone communications during this afternoon were fragmentary and liable to interruption, both from the Austrian and from the German end. Tonight, when this was being written, it is cut off altogether. Since Paris, Rome and London report a similar condition, the interruption probably is from the Austrian end.

The last reliable communication between Berlin and Vienna was between two Americans at about 5 o'clock. The Vienna informant was then able to assure his Berlin questioner that the Dollfuss party had regained full control and that the Chancellor "had withdrawn several promises extorted from him under duress."

Version Reaching Berlin.

At the Austrian Legation it was stated that some 300 Nazis had seized the official radio station earlier in the day, had announced that the Chancellor had resigned and had issued other falsehoods; that the police had since captured them and that the Austrian Minister of Justice had issued an explanation.

At 6 o'clock communication had ceased, and the legation professed not to know whether any Nazis had entered the Chancellery. It was stated, however, that a military cordon had been established around it and that the revolt had failed.

However, every time the press attaché at the legation told an inquirer over the telephone that it was Austrian Nazis that had invaded the radio station, the connection with the legation was immediately broken. Eventually the abandoned all attempt at plain speech and simply said that the disturbers "belonged to the party that one would expect."

Safe Conduct Demanded.

It was understood here tonight that the assassins of Chancellor Dollfuss, wherever they came from, demanded safe conduct to Germany after their crime and further demanded and obtained intervention by the German Ambassador to insure it.

The official German reaction is that this is purely an Austrian internal situation with which Germany has nothing to do and off which she is keeping her hands. It is said that she has kept the Austrian émigrés scattered; that she has moved or called the Aus-

Continued on Page Three.

INTERVENTION IS HINTED

Rome Reports Appeal to Powers by Austria to Guard Independence.

75,000 TROOPS AT BORDER

Italian Forces Whip Equipment Into Order and War Fleet Is Steaming Northward.

VIENNA CONFERENCE TODAY

Representative of Italy, France, Britain and the Little Entente Expected to Act.

By The Associated Press.

ROME, July 25.—A statement emanating from official sources tonight said the Austrian Government had requested intervention by European powers to guarantee Austria's integrity.

The statement, which was given to the government-controlled press, was published soon after it was announced that Premier Mussolini had issued wartime military orders to army, navy and air forces to the north of Padua.

The inspired press reported that the diplomatic representatives of Italy, France, Britain and the Little Entente would hold an urgent conference at Vienna tomorrow to determine what action should be taken. The conference also will decide which of the powers should intervene in case armed assistance is determined upon.

Italian troops are prepared to march into Austria on short notice. Fulvio Suvich, Under-Secretary of Foreign Affairs, was remaining at the Foreign Office throughout the night to keep in touch with the Austrian situation and to confer with Premier Mussolini by telephone. The Premier at the same time was keeping a vigil at Riccione.

No effort was made to disguise the fact that the Austrian question is viewed here in a very grave light.

Responsibility of Italy.

"Italy is in the first line of defense for the peace of Europe," said an authoritative editorial in the newspaper Il Popolo di Roma. "It is difficult, if not impossible, to deny that Germany has had grave responsibility in that which has occurred in Austria.

"For months the radio at Munich has issued insult and calumny against Dollfuss and his government. All the efforts of the powers to obtain an end to this campaign, which is against all the principles of international politics, were wrecked by the ill will of German leaders."

The army and air force at Padua was commanded by the Premier to be in instant readiness to move across the Austrian frontier. Leaves were canceled, and each unit was held to keep itself in full strength with all of its mechanical war devices in order. The order applied to 75,000 men from Padua north.

At the same time, an official communiqué was issued stating that the First Naval Squadron had left Fort Ancona.

The communiqué did not give the destination of the squadron, but naval circles said that it is moving into the Northern Adriatic, particularly Port Trieste, to keep in touch with Austrian developments.

Situation Is Held Grave.

By ARNALDO CORTESI.

Wireless to The New York Times.

ROME, July 25.—The Austrian Nazi outburst caused profound consternation in Italy today, but no particular surprise, as it had been felt for several days that things were rapidly approaching a crisis there as a result of the government's energetic repressive measures.

"It was held prisoner all day," he said, "and, like the others, know nothing. Chancellor Dollfuss is dead. I saw wounds on his neck and on his head. He died at 5 P. M. We believe that he was shot shortly after 12 o'clock when the Nazis broke into his office. It was a terrible blow."

At 9 P. M. the Chancellor's office was finally evacuated by the rebels under a guarantee of safe conduct to the German frontier. The telephone service began to function normally again.

I learned that two men in military uniforms confronted the Chancellor at 12:30, and when he drew a revolver they shot him down.

The first intimation I had that there was anything unusual in

Continued on Page Two.

AUSTRIAN NAZIS KILL DOLLFUSS, REVOLT FAILS; 147 PLOTTERS HELD; MARTIAL LAW IN EFFECT; ITALIAN ARMY, NAVY, PLANES READY TO ACT

KILLED IN VIENNA REVOLT.

Times Wide World Photo.

Chancellor Engelbert Dollfuss.

Eight Nazis Hold Off 1,000 Men For Hours at Vienna Radio Plant

Correspondent of The New York Times Witnesses Battle From Restaurant Table—Machine Guns and Bombs of Police and Heimwehr Force Their Surrender.

By G. E. R. GEDYE

Wireless to The New York Times.

BRATISLAVA, Czechoslovakia, July 25.—I had to cross the Austrian frontier, because the Austrian authorities severed all telegraph and telephonic communication and are severely censoring telegrams. I can tell the astounding story of how fewer than 200 Nazis held the Austrian Cabinet prisoners all day long in the Chancellor's office.

Chancellor Dollfuss was shot dead by the Nazi revolutionaries because he drew a revolver on being arrested by the Nazis.

Life in Vienna went on normally all day, except for the desperate battle, at which I was present.

The battle raged at the offices of Ravag, the Austrian radio broadcasting company. I left this battle in its earlier stages at 1:30 P. M. to follow an armored car which drove to the Chancellor's offices, where trucks were lining up with machine guns.

No more than any one else could I suspect that what seemed to be merely a precautionary measure was in reality an attempt to rescue members of the Austrian Government who were being held prisoners, facing the rifle and pistol muzzles of the desperadoes within the Chancellery.

Until late in the afternoon no one had an inkling that the Chancellor and nearly all his Cabinet, together with the huge staff of civil servants, were being held prisoners. Most of the civil servants were driven into the courtyard and kept there under guard.

Dollfuss Shot in Head.

After their release I spoke tonight with Dr. Schmitt, one of the officials of the Chancellor's Department. He seemed on the point of collapse.

Vienna was when I was passing through Johannesgasse shortly before 1 o'clock, when four or five revolver shots were fired. Several policemen took cover at the side of a house and occasionally fired shots at the Ravag building. They did not seem to know what was really afoot. Within a few minutes motor trucks filled with policemen with rifles, with fixed bayonets and with steel helmets began to pour into one end of Johannesgasse. In a few minutes the cracking of rifle fire was added to the popping of revolvers. The astounded passersby had no idea of what was in progress.

Woman Tells of Raid.

A woman, white and trembling, was allowed to come through the police cordon into the street where the firing was now general.

"I saw everything that happened from our house opposite Ravag," she told me. "A group of eight young men tried to enter Ravag about half an hour ago. When the policeman at the door challenged them they shot him dead.

"Inside the building they were resisted by one of the directors, a man named Holt. They shot him dead, also, and on entering the studio they placed their revolvers at the head of the announcer and forced him to broadcast a statement that the Dollfuss Cabinet had fallen. Dr. Rintelen, they stated, had become Chancellor and was forming a new Cabinet.

"Then a police alarm was given ...d the shooting started."

I was informed by the police that it was correct that only eight Nazi youths had carried out this coup and subsequently had repelled for nearly three hours the biggest force the Vienna police could bring to bear on them in the narrow street. With their revolvers they defended themselves against a heavy attack with machine guns.

As I watched the fighting, truck after truck loaded with police and Heimwehr men rolled up until there must have been 1,000 men taking part in the attack, which was pressed with tremendous vigor. The police were in an ugly temper. One of them marched up to the Terrace Restaurant, where I had ordered a meal as an excuse to remain on the scene after the street had been cleared, and drove me with his clubbed rifle into the restaurant.

Machine guns were now taken

Continued on Page Two.

ALL OF REBELS PRISONERS

Passage to Germany, Arranged by German Minister, Revoked.

MOB TRIES TO LYNCH THEM

Their 'Chancellor' Is Also Held, While Kurt Schuschnigg Succeeds Dollfuss.

VIENNA IS QUIET AGAIN

But Armed Guards Patrol the Streets—Reports of Fighting in Styria, Nazi Stronghold.

Wireless to The New York Times.

VIENNA, Thursday, July 26.—Calm and quiet settled over Vienna this morning. There was no external evidence of the sensational attack on the Federal Chancellery yesterday by 147 Austrian Nazis who killed Chancellor Engelbert Dollfuss and seized members of the Austrian Cabinet as hostages.

The fate of the rebels seemed to be decided. Though they obtained a pledge of safe conduct into Germany before they released the Cabinet members the Austrian Government early this morning issued a communique saying that this had been revoked.

The safe conduct, it was pointed out, had been granted with the consent of President Miklas, after a consultation with representatives of great powers in Vienna, on condition that nobody was killed in the building, but as Chancellor Dollfuss had died following the rebel attack the Nazis will be tried according to Austrian law.

Rebels Under Strong Guard.

The rebels are prisoners in Marokkaner Barracks in Vienna, strongly guarded. Their leader is a man named Holsweber, a former army sergeant. In addition to the barracks guard, policemen, armed with rifles, still patroled the streets and trucks rumbled along the boulevards bringing in more troops.

[A dispatch from Vienna in a late edition of The London Mail said that Heimwehr troops and civilians had sought during the night to lynch the assassins of Chancellor Dollfuss, The Associated Press reported. The dispatch said police, heavily armed, had repulsed all attempts to get at the prisoners by threatening to fire into the approaching crowd.]

Dr. Anton Rintelen, the rebels' candidate for the Chancellorship, has been arrested and is now in military custody in the Building of the Ministry of War.

Reports of alleged Italian military movements along the Austrian border are believed here to be greatly exaggerated. Only those measures were taken which had been prepared automatically in the event of Austrian internal disorder. It is understood that Italian Army airplanes are held ready for flight over Austria in case of need.

It was believed in political circles here today that Ministers of the Great Powers will call on Acting Chancellor Kurt Schuschnigg to ask his plans and that he will accept the office of Chancellor.

Cabinet Holds Rebels.

Copyright, 1934, by The New York Times Company.

VIENNA, July 25.—A group of Austrian Nazis today seized the federal Chancellery, killed their bitter enemy, Chancellor Engelbert Dollfuss, and held the government building until they received a guarantee of safe conduct to Germany, a guarantee which was revoked when it was discovered that Dr. Dollfuss was dead.

The police were placed in Marokkaner Barracks, stripped of their uniforms and were ordered held after a Cabinet meeting under the leadership of the new Chancellor, Dr. Kurt Schuschnigg, Minister of Education.

An official communiqué stated that the fact that Dr. Dollfuss was killed canceled the promise of safe conduct, in return for which

Continued on Page Two.

NRA

"All the News That's Fit to Print."

The New York Times.

5:30 A. M. EXTRA

WEATHER—Cloudy, warmer to-day; local showers tomorrow.
Temperature Yesterday—Max., 81; Min., 67

Copyright, 1934, by The New York Times Company.

VOL. LXXXIII....No. 27,949.

Entered as Second-Class Matter, Postoffice, New York, N. Y.

NEW YORK, THURSDAY, AUGUST 2, 1934.

P

TWO CENTS In New York City. | THREE CENTS Within 200 Miles | FOUR CENTS Elsewhere Except in 7th and 8th Postal Zones

TWO REFORM BILLS ARE SIDETRACKED; LEHMAN FIGHTS ON

Quorum Lacking for Report on County Plans as Republicans Walk Out of Committee.

BATTLE ON FLOOR IS DUE

Governor, Assailing 'Despicable' Action, Is Expected to Spur Democrats in Assembly.

SMITH TARGET IN SESSION

Republicans Deny Entering Agreement—Say He Is Trying to 'Bedevil' Situation.

By W. A. WARN.
Special to The New York Times.

ALBANY, Aug. 1.—The Assembly Judiciary Committee met this afternoon and voted to report eleven minor bills, but failed to take any action on the proposed constitutional amendments, sponsored by Senator Dunnigan and Senator Mastick, to prepare the way for county government reform.

The Republican majority in the Assembly contrived to block these yesterday after their adoption in the Senate, sending them back to committee.

Governor Lehman pronounced as "despicable" the failure of the committee to act on the measures, the adoption of which he and ex-Governor Smith, as head of the New York City Charter Revision Commission, have so much at heart.

The Governor said he was firmly backing the position taken by Mr. Smith in a telegram transmitted on behalf of the entire Charter Commission to Speaker McGinnies yesterday protesting against the action of the Republican majority in "repudiating" its agreement to pass the County Reform Bills.

Governor Is Silent on Plans.

Governor Lehman has not indicated what further steps he may be contemplating to force favorable action on the two sidetracked measures.

They have both been adopted by the Senate, together with another proposed amendment to the Constitution, in which both the Mastick and Dunnigan proposals are joined and which the Assembly yesterday concurred in by unanimous vote.

While the Judiciary Committee, like the Assembly itself, has a Republican majority, it has become apparent through developments of the last few days that the Democrats in the Legislature are no more eager to pass these constitutional amendments than are a majority of the Republicans.

While engaging on the floor of the Assembly today in an apparent effort to make political capital out of the Republican blockade established yesterday against the Dunnigan and Mastick measures, the Democrats do not bestir themselves to rescue the amendments.

Chance for Steingut to Act.

Assemblyman Steingut, minority leader, has not filed the necessary three days' notice of a motion to take the two resolutions from the Judiciary Committee, possibly on the assumption that the committee had not had an opportunity to act when the Assembly met today.

Now that the committee has met and failed to act the way is open for Mr. Steingut to proceed, but unless action is taken by the Assembly before the end of the week the adoption of the two resolutions would be to no purpose.

Under the Election Law, Monday is the deadline for publication of notice that the amendments are to be submitted to the 1935 Legislature for concurrent action.

Governor Lehman was aroused when he learned of developments at the committee meeting.

"The action in refusing to report or act on the bills is despicable," he said. "I am back of the position taken by Governor Smith 100 per cent.

"Until I learned of the action of the Judiciary Committee in refusing to report the bills, I was convinced that in accordance with the agreement reported by former Governor Smith, the bills would be reported out and passed.

"There is still time to pass these bills, and they should be passed. I am amazed that any condition like this could exist."

Lehman Action Is Expected.

Hence, with the Governor so stirred by the situation, observers at the capital believe he will move to compel more vigorous intervention by the Assembly Democrats to save the measures.

Most of the Democrats, and Republicans also, have already paid their legislative labors for the week and returned to their homes or gone to the Saratoga races or elsewhere. In order to get anything

Continued on Page Four.

Giant Seaplane Tops All Records; Lindbergh Hails Test of Clipper

Sikorsky Machine, Under Transport Conditions With a Full Load, Averages 157.5 Miles an Hour Over a 1,242-Mile Course —Range Would Cover Ocean Trade Routes.

By REGINALD M. CLEVELAND.

BRIDGEPORT, Conn., Aug. 1.—All existing world's records for transport seaplane flight (previously held abroad) were toppled like ninepins here today as the giant Sikorsky S-42, the Brazilian Clipper, carrying a full transport load and with Colonel Lindbergh in charge for Pan American Airways, flew 1,242.5 miles at an average speed of 157.5 miles an hour. Eight long-standing and recent world marks were shattered by impressive margins. The two other official ones had already been won by the plane in previous test flights.

As Edwin C. Musick, chief pilot of the airlines, and the four-engined flying boat four times over a course of 311 miles which included Manhattan's river front, Long Island Sound and the Atlantic Ocean, it was evident that history was being written for American aviation.

Starting at the Stratford, Lighthouse, the course ran through five control points, George Washington Bridge, Staten Island Lighthouse, Fire Island Lighthouse, Block Island, Point Judith Lighthouse and back to the place of beginning. The elapsed time for the flight

was 7 hours, 53 minutes, 58 seconds, for a distance equal to that from Newfoundland to the Azores. Yet Pilot Musick used only 69 per cent of the 3,000 horsepower of the four Pratt & Whitney Hornet engines streamlined into the wide silver wing. He had fuel enough for another lap when he landed. The margin of range, with a full load, for any of the ocean trade routes, Atlantic or Pacific, by way of the islands, had been amply proved.

Cruising speed only was used and less than full horsepower because the flight was an acceptance test for the airline of this craft, which will cut two days' time from the run between Miami and Buenos Aires and put that South American capital within five and one-half days of New York.

Strictly transport conditions prevailed during the flight.

When the plane crossed the starting line against the blue of a morning sky at 9:24:38, Eastern daylight time, she had only six persons aboard. They were Colonel Lindbergh, as official representative of Pan American Airways' technical

Continued on Page Seven.

NEW ORLEANS TENSE AS POLICE AWAIT A MOVE BY TROOPS

300 More Patrolmen Sworn In as the Militia Removes Machine Guns From View.

GUARD FORCE IS REDUCED

Gov. Allen Orders Guardsmen to Investigate Alleged Gambling and Vice Graft.

Special to The New York Times.

NEW ORLEANS, Aug. 1.—New Orleans anxiously watched the growing tension tonight as armed State and city forces faced each other in a political crisis precipitated by the tactics of Senator Huey Long.

George Reyer, Superintendent of Police, completed tonight the swearing in of 500 supernumerary policemen for emergency use. The machine guns manned by National Guardsmen, which have been protruding from the windows of the registration office, were removed.

The 500 emergency policemen, called for service by order of Mayor Walmsley, were armed with automatic shotguns and pistols. They were divided into two platoons, 300 on the day shift and 200 on night duty.

Of the former, 200 will be held at police headquarters, and 100 stationed at the City Hall and the First Precinct station. All of the men on night duty are stationed at police headquarters, with police automobiles and patrol wagons held in readiness to transport them wherever they might be needed.

Policemen now ready for duty number 1,300. All regular members of the department have been instructed to be ready for duty at all times, day or night.

Explains Machine Guns.

The appearance of machine guns in the registration office was explained by Adjt. Gen. Fleming at a conference with Mayor Walmsley this afternoon.

"The members of the artillery unit guarding the registration office," Adjutant General Fleming said, "were relieved Tuesday night by members of the machine gun unit. The machine gun unit always carries its machine guns along wherever it is sent."

He denied the machine guns were intended for intimidation.

Mayor Walmsley and the Finance Commissioner, A. Miles Pratt, in statements issued today, denied there was any intention on the part of the city government to seize any records in the registration office.

The presidents of the chief organizations of business men met today and debated the situation. They adopted a resolution which censured no one and asked the world to understand that "the business of this city is being conducted along the usual, efficient lines with no interruptions whatsoever."

Three members of the new police commission created by the Long-controlled Legislature to take supervision of the police force out of the hands of the Mayor and Council filed their credentials. No attempt was made to call a meeting of the board.

Prosecution of the 500 odd men charged with miscounting ballots at an impossible under a law taking effect today, District Attorney Stanley nolle prossed the cases. The charges were brought after a

Continued on Page Fourteen.

Wagner and Prall Hurt in Auto Plunge; Senator Drives Into Brook to Avoid Crash

Special to The New York Times.

WESTPORT, N. Y., Aug. 1.—Trapped on a curve of a narrow Adirondack highway, Senator Robert F. Wagner drove his automobile over a twenty-foot embankment into a mountain brook rather than have a collision with an oncoming car near here this morning. Senator Wagner and Representative Anning S. Prall, his only companion, were both seriously but not critically injured.

Senator Wagner suffered two fractured ribs on the right side, several lacerations of the face and knees and numerous body bruises. He may also have concussion of the brain. Representative Prall suffered a compound fracture of both bones of his lower right leg and lacerations of the hands and forehead.

Witnesses of the crash carried the injured men three miles to the offices of Dr. Harold J. Harris here, who turned his machine off the road. It tumbled down the embankment into the brook but did not overturn. Both occupants were thrown against the windshield and dashboard, but were conscious when they were extricated from the wreckage, and remained so while they were being brought to the offices of Dr. Harris here.

Dr. Harris said that he thought it would be best for Senator Wagner to remain in the recovery room in his offices for several days, but

that Mr. Prall might be taken to a New York City hospital tomorrow. He said there was "no evidence of skull fractures or concussions, but we never are sure until after twenty-four hours."

The legislators were on their way north on a fishing expedition when the accident occurred. They were bound for the Seigneur Club at Lucerne, Que. Senator Wagner had only recently returned from Portland, Ore., where he attempted to adjust the marine workers' strike and was fired on by mistake.

The highway through the mountains between Wadhams and this village, which is on Lake Champlain, is narrow and winding. Senator Wagner attempted to pass a truck on a curve, only to find another truck approaching from the opposite direction.

Rather than hit either truck he turned his machine off the road. It tumbled down the embankment into the brook but did not overturn.

Overnight Air Service To West Coast Starts

Starting overnight service between the nation's coasts on the "Lindbergh Line," a fourteen-passenger Douglas plane of the Transcontinental & Western Air Line took off from Newark Airport yesterday afternoon at 5:25 Eastern daylight time. It is due in Los Angeles at 7 this morning.

Elliott Roosevelt, second son of the President; Lieut. Commander Frank M. Hawks, noted speed pilot; two paying passengers, newspapermen and airline officials were aboard as passengers.

The plane also carried two copies of The New York Times addressed respectively to Frank L. Shaw, Mayor of Los Angeles, and Harry Chandler, publisher of The Los Angeles Times.

20% CUT IN NAVIES URGED BY SWANSON

But Secretary, in Rejoinder to Tokyo Premier, Says 5-5-3 Ratio Should Continue.

OUR PLANE PROGRAM CUT

Navy Now Thinks Equipping of All Ships Will Require 274 Fewer Than 1st Estimate.

Special to The New York Times.

WASHINGTON, Aug. 1.—A general reduction of 20 per cent in naval armaments by all the powers signatory to the London Naval Treaty was advocated today by Secretary Claude A. Swanson, but he insisted that the 5-5-3 ratio of naval strength fixed by the Washington treaty of 1922 should stand intact. If agreed to by the powers, the 20 per cent reduction should be a real and not a "blue print" one, he declared.

Meanwhile, Admiral William H. Standley, chief of naval operations, made known that the navy had revised its estimates, but had reached no final decision on the number of planes necessary under the Vinson Naval Building Bill to outfit old and new ships in the next five years. High navy officials now figure that only 910 new planes would be needed, or 274 fewer than previously had been estimated. The navy now has 1,000 planes.

No comprehensive reason was given by naval officials for this reduced estimate, but it was partly explained by the fact that when the earlier estimates were made no decision had been reached to abandon the building of flying-deck cruisers.

Secretary Swanson's statement came as a rejoinder to yesterday's declaration by Premier Keisuke Okada that, while Japan did not expect to attain parity with the United States and Britain at the 1935 naval conference, she could not favor continuation of the present ratio system, which "hurts the self-respect of nations."

Asked to comment on the Japanese Premier's speech, Mr. Swanson said:

"I adhere to the same position I always have. The naval powers are in London and distributed to the naval powers the naval strength they thought was just and right. Naval strength is relative. Both naval and military armaments are relative.

"I represented the navy at the Geneva conference and we offered there the proposition to have any reductions up to 33 1-3 per cent in the different categories of ships.

Continued on Page Three.

VON HINDENBURG DIES AT 86 AFTER A DAY UNCONSCIOUS; HITLER TAKES PRESIDENCY

Times Wide World Photos.

PRESIDENT PAUL von HINDENBURG

END COMES AT 9 A. M.

Reich President Dies at His Home in East Prussia.

MADE A VALIANT FIGHT.

Disappearance of House Flag at Neudeck Announces News to World.

THERE HAD BEEN NO HOPE

He Lapsed Into Coma After Hitler Reached Bedside for Last Meeting.

By The Associated Press.

NEUDECK, Germany, Thursday, Aug. 2.—President von Hindenburg died at 9 A. M. today.

The President's death was indicated to correspondents by the disappearance of the house flag from the flagstaff.

Death came to the 86-year-old leader of the German people and former war marshal after a valiant fight against a complication of ailments.

Chancellor Hitler has assumed the Presidency.

Unconscious For Hours.

By GUIDO ENDERIS.

BERLIN, Thursday, Aug. 2.—A physician's bulletin at 6 o'clock this morning stated that President Paul von Hindenburg remained in the state of unconsciousness into which he lapsed last evening. His death was believed to be a matter only of hours.

The President had consistently lost strength since early morning. All hope that his once rugged constitution would carry him along for a time was definitely dispelled by bedside bulletins that reached Berlin from Neudeck during the day.

At midnight the Propaganda Ministry announced that no further bulletin would be forthcoming during the night. This secretiveness served only to heighten the mystery surrounding Chancellor Hitler's convocation of his Cabinet. Neither foreign correspondents in Berlin nor those besieging the President's estate at Neudeck had been able to break the news embargo which hedged the Field Marshal's deathbed. Only what seeped through official quarters was placed at the disposal of the German and foreign press.

Hitler Advances Time of Visit.

Chancellor Hitler advanced the hour of his flight to Neudeck by more than an hour yesterday morning because of an urgent summons from Professor Ferdinand Sauerbruck, the President's chief physician. It was reported Dr. Sauerbruck notified Herr Hitler that the patient was rapidly sinking.

The last meeting between the President and the man whom he elevated to the Chancellorship after rebuffs which have now become historic, received only brief mention in the day's official bulletins. Herr Hitler found the President momentarily conscious and assured him of the prayerful thoughts of the saddened nation. The President shook the Chancellor's hand and thanked him cordially for his visit; then he dropped into a fresh sleep.

Herr Hitler flew back to Berlin late in the afternoon. Among those who accompanied him to Neudeck was Ernst F. S. Hanfstaengl, chief of his Anglo-American publicity department, but only Herr Hitler was admitted to the sick chamber.

Hope that the President would linger on vanished early last evening when Dr. Sauerbruck, on behalf of the attending physicians, announced that the patient was lapsing into unconsciousness and that his heart action was fast failing. A bulletin issued at 2:30 P. M. stated that the President was then steadily losing ground, despite a restful night. He was conscious most of the forenoon and was able to converse with those around him during part of the afternoon.

Up to two months ago President von Hindenburg's rugged frame and his soldierly bearing gave no evidence of physical decline. The collapse began to set in a month ago when it was discovered that atrophied prostate gland precluded recourse to a major operation so

Continued on Page 13. [Preceding Page 4.]

SOCIALIST SUPPORT SOUGHT BY AUSTRIA

Neutrality of the Party in Fight With Nazis to Be Rewarded by Release of Leaders.

FOE HANGED IN INNSBRUCK

Minor Rebels to Be Held and Put at Hard Labor—Officials Linked to Putsch.

By G. E. R. GEDYE.
Wireless to The New York Times.

VIENNA, Aug. 1.—There are signs that the Austrian Government is preparing for radical changes in policy and is contemplating steps calculated to obtain from the Social Democrats the assurance of at least neutrality toward the government's fight to the finish with the Nazis.

For eighteen months the Nazis have carried on terroristic activities in Austria, involving a considerable loss of life and enormous property damage. But until yesterday the death penalty had been reserved exclusively for Socialists.

Even the stern ordinance directed against Nazi terrorists, which Chancellor Dollfuss introduced fourteen days before he was slain, proclaiming death as the only admissible penalty for those possessing explosives, had a Socialist for its first victim. He was hanged the night before Dr. Dollfuss was assassinated.

Three Nazis Now Hanged.

Yesterday, however, two Nazis at last were hanged. Today another Nazi was hanged in Innsbruck, Friedrich Wurnig who shot and killed Police Commandant Franz Hickel of Innsbruck on the day of the Dollfuss slaying.

The legislators were on their way north on a fishing expedition when the accident occurred. They were bound for the Seigneur Club at Lucerne, Que. Senator Wagner had only recently returned from Portland, Ore., where he attempted to adjust the marine workers' strike and was fired on by mistake.

The first move to conciliate the Socialists was the release of prominent leaders who have been imprisoned without trial since February. It is likely they will be freed in a day or so. The leaders to be released are Burgomaster Karl Seitz, head of the party, and Herr Danneberg, Herr Helmer, Frau Proft and Frau Postranetzny, members of the central executive committee of the party, and more officers of the Republican Defense Corps, General Koerner, Major Eiffler and Captain Loew.

Whether such release will have

Continued on Page Three.

HITLER CONSULTS CABINET IN SECRET

Ministry Meets Two Hours in Emergency Session—Von Papen in Attendance.

NEW ELECTION POSSIBLE

Friend Says Chancellor Intends to Occupy the Presidency— Army an Unknown Factor.

Wireless to The New York Times.

BERLIN, Aug. 1.—Chancellor Hitler convoked the German Cabinet for an emergency session at 9:30 o'clock tonight.

The Ministers, among them Vice Chancellor Franz von Papen, had been hastily summoned. They remained with the Chancellor about two hours.

Beyond a more-than-laconic bulletin announcing that the Cabinet had been called, nothing was divulged. There was no indication as to the purpose of the session, and this quickly gave rise to rumors that President von Hindenburg had already died, but that the announcement was being withheld until tomorrow.

The reading public has received only official communiqués concerning the Reich President. The controlled press appears to have been instructed to abstain from any speculative comment on the implications involved in a vacancy in the Presidency.

Hitler Is Seen Taking Power.

Copyright, 1934, by The Associated Press.

BERLIN, Aug. 1.—Adolf Hitler intends to be both President and Chancellor of Germany, one of his close friends told The Associated Press today.

This would give to Herr Hitler a dictatorship as absolute as any in the world.

Despite gripped many Conservatives who had looked upon President von Hindenburg as an anchor against extreme Nazism.

Herr Hitler's plan, The Associated Press informant said, is to call the Cabinet together to read a brief law assigning the dual power to himself.

"The whole thing will take but a few minutes," he said, "for the Cabinet will, of course, endorse the proposal. It will simplify the Führer's [Hitler's] will work immensely if he need not first ask somebody whether he may do this or that."

An indication of the reliability of this source is that Sunday he revealed the President's turn for the worse and was the first to tip off the fact that Herr Hitler was going to Venice to meet Premier Mussolini.

Under the German Constitution, Dr. Erwin Bumke, President of the Supreme Court, would become Act-

Continued on Page Two.

SMITH ACTS TO QUIT IN CHARTER DISPUTE

Reported Ready to Resign if Board Does Not Agree to Reconsider City Rule Vote.

LETTER ALREADY DRAFTED

Seabury Said to Be Weighing Similar Action—Crucial Meeting Tonight.

Alfred E. Smith will resign from the New York City Charter Revision Commission unless the commission at tonight's meeting changes its decision to retain the city legislature in substantially its present form, according to reports last night in Albany from a source close to the former Governor.

Mr. Smith was said to have long been disgusted with the slowness to thoroughgoing reform of the city charter among members of the commission. According to the report from Albany, Mr. Smith was quoted as saying in private conversation that he was "sick and tired of the bickering and opposition in the commission" and that he "would like a vacation."

The fact that the former Governor has for some time been considering resignation or taking some other drastic action to bring sharply to public attention the failure of the commission to make real progress was confirmed by persons in the city close to Mr. Smith.

Letter Already Drafted.

It was felt that Mr. Smith might be led to resign at tonight's meeting if the commission voted to restore to the Borough Presidents their administrative and patronage powers, as some members of the commission fear will be done. According to a report by The Associated Press, Mr. Smith has already drafted his letter of resignation.

Samuel Seabury, vice chairman of the commission, declined last night to deny or to comment on a report that he also intended to resign. Earlier in the day Mr. Seabury had stated that he would make no comment until after the outcome of tonight's meeting on what he plans to do in case the opposition on the commission succeeds in restoring borough government.

These reports came as fear was expressed by members of the commission and civic organizations favoring drastic charter revision that a successful drive would be made tonight's meeting to restore to the Borough Presidents their present administrative and patronage powers. Such a result, it was said, would largely nullify all the progress made by the commission toward stripping Borough Presidents of their powers and for a single chamber legislature.

Confusion existed yesterday among members of the commission, as well as among civic organizations, over the effect of the action taken Tuesday night by the commission to revamp the Board of Estimate and to revamp the Board of Aldermen into a smaller but much stronger Council.

Many condemned it as merely retaining the present form of city legislature, while others saw in it

Continued on Page Four.

BUSINESS TAX YIELD IS UNDER $3,000,000

$2,092,681 Total, With Mail Returns Still Due, Far Short of $8,000,000 Expected.

BUDGET NOW UNBALANCED

Mayor Denies City Plans to Restore Half of Pay Cut— Chides Levy on Figures.

The city's hope of realizing $8,000,000 from its new business tax received a severe blow last night when Controller Joseph D. McGoldrick announced that the total collected up to 6 P. M. on the final day for payment was only $2,092,-681.47.

It was pointed out, however, that a last-minute ruling permitting payment of taxes by mail without penalty, provided the letters containing tax checks or money orders were postmarked before midnight, would probably bring in additional payments today.

Nevertheless it was predicted that the total return, even with the last-minute checks, could not possibly come to much more than $3,000,—only three-eighths of the sum the city had hoped to garner from the new tax.

McGoldrick Withholds Comment.

Mr. McGoldrick withheld comment on the tax payments pending the final compilation today. It was indicated, however, that he was convinced that the total returns would be materially less than the sum expected when the tax was imposed.

Failure of the revenues from the business tax to come up to expectations will have the effect of unbalancing the city budget, it was said. The budget was balanced after the passage of the City Economy Bill by salary reductions and furloughs and by imposition of new taxes, of which the business tax was one.

A total of $1,094,800.27 was received yesterday in payment of the tax in the City Collector's office in the five boroughs. During the day 16,748 returns were filed.

Several times recently administration spokesmen have expressed the fear that the business tax revenue would be materially below the original estimates. None, however, believed that the revenue would be as small as last night's figures indicated it would be.

In view of the fact that failure to pay the tax on time brings with it a 10 per cent penalty plus payment of 5 per cent interest a month on the whole tax sum due, it was felt in the Finance Department that few concerns would withhold their payments. It was not disclosed how many payments were made under protest and threat of court action to test the constitutionality of the tax measure.

Cut in Reserve Is Hailed.

The revision of the "bankers'" agreement to provide reduction in the tax delinquency reserve fund in the budgets of 1935, 1936 and 1937 from the original $50,000,000 to $25,000,000 was praised yesterday by Peter Grimm, chairman of the Citizens Budget Commission. Mr. Grimm telegraphed Controller McGoldrick and Governor Lehman who are mainly responsible for

Continued on Page Nine.

NRA
WE DO OUR PART

"All the News That's Fit to Print."

The New York Times.

LATE CITY EDITION
WEATHER—Clearing today; tomorrow generally fair.
Temperature yesterday—Max. 72; Min. 61.
Detailed Weather Report, Page 19, Sec. 2.

Section 1

Copyright, 1934, by The New York Times Company.

VOL. LXXXIII....No. 27,987.

Entered as Second-Class Matter,
Postoffice, New York, N. Y.

NEW YORK, SUNDAY, SEPTEMBER 9, 1934.

Magazine and Book Sections.
Including Rotogravure Picture.

F +

TEN CENTS | TWELVE CENTS Beyond 200 Miles.
Except in 7th and 8th Postal Zones.

MORRO CASTLE BURNS OFF ASBURY PARK; 200 TO 250 ARE LISTED AS DEAD OR MISSING

GORMAN PROPOSES STRIKE ARBITRATION IF ALL MILLS CLOSE

Union Leader Would 'Avoid Murders' While President's Board Settles Issue.

BUT WIDENS WALKOUT

Calls Out 50,000 More Workers as Employers Plan Mill Openings Tomorrow.

HOSIERY STRIKE ORDERED

Labor Chiefs Direct 85,000 to Quit Wednesday—Green Confers on Textile Peace Plan.

By LOUIS STARK
Special to The New York Times.

WASHINGTON, Sept. 8.—Francis J. Gorman, chairman of the textile strike committee, proposed tonight that President Roosevelt's textile board arbitrate the issue in the textile strike which began Sept. 1.

In a radio broadcast over the Columbia System, Mr. Gorman suggested that arbitration begin on Monday; that both sides agree to accept the findings of the textile board and that pending arbitration the mills be closed "so that further murder of our fellow workers may be avoided."

An additional 50,000 textile workers in miscellaneous lines will be called out on Monday, said Mr. Gorman. These operatives are in the plants making upholstery and drapery, carpets and rugs, pile fabric, plush and velvets. The strike extension is made in face of the reported plan of employers to open next week mills closed by the general textile walkout.

While Mr. Gorman was still speaking over the radio, the National Executive Board of the American Federation of Hosiery Workers at an emergency session issued an order calling a strike of select an agency for hosiery mills where no contractual relations exist between employers and employes. The order covered both seamless and full-fashioned sections of the industry and applied to about 85,000 workers in twelve States, union spokesmen said.

Strike Threat in Dye Industry.

Mr. Gorman announced that unless employers in the dye industry met demands of the union employes in that industry would be called out some time next week.

Governor J. G. Winant, chairman of the textile board, declined tonight to comment on Mr. Gorman's arbitration proposal. He would not say whether the board would take the initiative and seek the view of the employers on the arbitration request or wait instead the unsolicited action of the manufacturers.

Under the President's executive order the Winant Board is authorized "upon the request of the parties to a labor dispute, [to] act as a board of voluntary arbitration or select a person or agency for voluntary arbitration."

The textile board's next appointment with George A. Sloan, president of the Cotton Textile Institute, is scheduled for Tuesday.

Green Discusses Arbitration.

Arbitration as a way out was also discussed before the board this afternoon by William Green, president of the American Federation of Labor. On leaving the board's offices Mr. Green said that he had brought up the subject of arbitration as a possible way to end the controversy peaceably, but that no concrete or definite line of procedure had been outlined.

No comment was obtainable here as to the view of the manufacturers or the union arbitration proposal.

In making his announcement Mr. Gorman stressed the need for a peaceful atmosphere before the controversial issues could be settled. He declared that the employers have stated that they would open the mills on Monday, asserted that "they have hired guards, and in some places misled members of the American Legion and Mr. Sloan has brought an American Legion regiment to be working with these private armies of so-called guards."

In a telegram to Edward A. Hayes, commander of the American Legion, Indianapolis, Mr. Gorman asked that Mr. Sloan be announced the closed mills would resume operation on Monday. He declared that "great bands of strike-breakers have been deputized and armed and American Le-

Continued on Page Two.

Sailor Missing 12 Years 'Found' on Morro Castle

By The Associated Press.

ST. LOUIS, Sept. 8.—A St. Louisan, given up for dead by his family more than a decade ago, came back into the world for them today as a result of the Morro Castle disaster.

A crew member of the stricken vessel, carried on the roster as Roger Klinger, was identified by his brother today as Gustav Lehmann, who left his home here twelve years ago.

The brother, Edward H. Lehmann, said his missing relative had assumed "Klinger," the name of another branch of the family, to avoid rejection by navigation companies. He was turned down as Gustav Lehmann for failure to pass a physical examination the brother said.

"The last time we saw Gustav," Edward said, "was twelve years ago. He went to Detroit after that and that was the last city from which we ever received a letter from him."

5 LOST IN STORM WHEN BOATS UPSET

3 Missing, 5 Washed Ashore Off Jersey—Two on Tug Drowned in Bay.

4.8 INCHES OF RAIN HERE

Floods Disrupt Land Travel—Ships Torn From Moorings by Wind in Hudson.

A wind and rainstorm lashed the New Jersey and Long Island coasts last night, disrupting land and water transportation and capsizing two boats, causing a loss of five lives.

Two seamen were drowned and three others rescued after they had been in the water two hours when a tugboat of the Tracy Towing Company overturned in New York Bay off the foot of Sixty-fifth Street, Brooklyn. The tug, the William Tracy, was steaming from Brooklyn to New Jersey when she overturned without warning in a sudden gust of wind and plunged the five men into the water.

The drowned were Robert Whitaker, fireman, and Benjamin Elder, deckhand, both of Brooklyn. Those rescued, all of Brooklyn, were Captain William McNally, John Duffy and David Donaldson. They were landed in Jersey City and taken to the Jersey City Medical Centre, where they were reported to be in serious condition.

The thirty-five-foot schooner Neshaminy, with a party of eight men aboard, was capsized two and one-half miles off Brigantine Beach, N. J. Five of the men succeeded, with the aid of life-preservers, in reaching shore. Coast Guardsmen searched for the three others without success.

Boat Is Washed Ashore.

The missing men are Captain Robert McCleary, 35, Harry Clayton, 45, and Edward Clayton, 30, his brother, all of Philadelphia. Coast Guard boats put out to search for them after the five survivors had been washed ashore. At 8:30 P. M. the Neshaminy, the boat in which the party of eight had been fishing, was washed up at Brigantine.

Those rescued are George Sharp, 35, of Langhorne, Pa.; George Oldham, 30, of Newportville, Pa., and Earl Widdop 35, Claude Pieminck, 32, and Charles Wensel, 28, of Philadelphia. Wensel and Oldham were in a serious condition at Atlantic City Hospital.

They said that, although their boat was seaworthy and in good condition, "was no match for the gale that blew off the northeast. Sharp, Harry Clayton and Oldham were in the pilot house when a big wave came along and turned the craft over. They had to be through glass windows to get free.

Craft Break Loose in Hudson.

Shipping in the Hudson River had a bad time at the height of the storm. The U. S. S. Oklahoma, anchored in midstream off Seventy-ninth Street, was forced to pull her hook and manoeuvre about to escape being hit by a lighter with a derrick aboard which had broken moorings on the Jersey side.

From the Oklahoma signals telling what was going on were flashed to the shore patrol, in command of Ensign Albert G. Pelling. He notified the Police Department, and marine division headquarters, as well as

Continued on Page Thirty-five.

AN AIR VIEW OF THE BURNING LINER MORRO CASTLE OFF THE JERSEY COAST.

Rescue Liners Pick Up 157; Craft Near By Speed to SOS

Four Large Vessels Put Out Lifeboats to Circle Water With Coast Guard—Many of the Saved Are Injured.

From north, east and south passenger and freight ships altered their courses yesterday at full speed to the fire-illumined point off Shark River Inlet, above Sea Girt, N. J., where the Ward liner Morro Castle with 318 passengers and a crew of 244 was burning.

Off Ambrose Light the Monarch of Bermuda and the City of Savannah turned around and sped southward through the dark about twenty miles to the distressed ship. From the east, seven miles, came the freighter Andrea S. Luckenbach. From the south, further away than the others, the President Cleveland sped through the night.

The S O S from the Morro Castle was received by the Monarch and the Savannah at about the same time, 4:30 A. M. daylight time. The Luckenbach ship had been attracted by the sight of the flames and radio confirmation that the Morro Castle needed help came from a land station.

Rescues Began in the Dark.

The sea was turning the color of gun metal in a murky dawn when the Monarch and the Savannah arrived to find that the Luckenbach was already on the scene, as well as several Coast Guard craft.

They came upon a scene of confusion and horror. The liner was blazing from B deck upward. On the surface of the water were passengers and members of the crew who had jumped.

"I messaged the Luckenbach," Captain Francis said, "and the message came back that she could be there in a half-hour. I needed an hour. I messaged again—'Do you want assistance?' and the word came back, 'Yes.'

"We reached the Morro Castle about 7:30 A. M. It was turning daylight. From four or five miles away we could see the great red glare of light on the gray sea. We came within 100 yards of the Morro Castle and lowered four boats. One, under the command of Staff Captain Leslie Banyard, picked up thirty-one persons. We took them mainly out of the water and off the poop deck."

Acts of Heroism Related.

Passengers on the Monarch of Bermuda, disturbed by the bustle, were awake and about. They could feel the heat of the burning ship, see the flames climbing from A and B decks upward, shooting fifty to sixty feet in the air.

Passengers and members of the crew dotted the water or hung over the sides on ropes afraid to let go. Some still were jumping from B and C decks. One passenger saw a stewardess with a child on her back jump into the water and swim toward one of the rescue boats. Captain Francis, who stayed on his bridge, saw a woman, with a 4-year-old Robert Lione of Long Island City, enact a similar scene of heroism. The boy was lifted into one of the Monarch's boats.

On the waters around the flaming ship by that time were boats from the Luckenbach, the City of Savannah, Coast Guard boats, from the Jersey shore and from Staten Island. Two boats put out from the President Cleveland three and a half miles away.

Aboard the Monarch two primary concerns were manifest. One was to get as adequate as possible medical attention for the injured, most of whom were suffering from surgical shock, smoke-injured eyes, and exhaustion, and the other was to

Continued on Page Twenty-eight.

of them, on the fire-free forecastle determined not to leave their ship.

Captain Francis said this way out of Ambrose Light when, at 5:30 A. M., daylight saving time, he received an S.O.S. from the Morro Castle. He turned his ship about and made all speed (20 knots) toward the spot off Sea Girt, N. J., about twenty miles away, where the Morro Castle reported she had anchored.

It was not yet daylight, the weather was squally with a heavy sea, as the Monarch headed south. The Andrea S. Luckenbach, freighter, of the Luckenbach line, at least a half-hour nearer the Morro Castle than was the Monarch.

The water was being combed by the Coast Guard craft and two lifeboats from the Luckenbach. Four of the lifeboats from the Morro Castle had been successfully lowered, six on the port side having been made inaccessible by the flames.

The rescuing ships stood by until they could no longer be of service, and then steamed for New York, carrying in all 157 survivors including at least forty members of the Morro Castle's crew, and one woman. She already was dead when taken from the water.

The work of rescue began at about 6 A. M., daylight saving time, when the Morro Castle had been burning at least two hours. By 10 o'clock there were apparently no more living persons to be taken from the water.

The Monarch of Bermuda had gathered seventy-one survivors and the body. The City of Savannah—both of these ships pushed to within 100 feet of the flaming liner—had sixty-five and the Luckenbach twenty-one. The President Cleveland from a point about half a mile away, lowered two boats, but these returned without having lifted any person from the water.

Captain A. R. Francis of the Monarch stood by for two and half hours in a choppy, wind-beaten sea while four power-driven lifeboats lowered circled the immediate water. In this way those aboard listened to the safety persons, cold and young, exhausted, hysterical and unconscious.

At times his ship swept within sixty feet of the burning ship, and then, learning that he had nineteen persons aboard with injuries, twelve of them in a critical condition, Captain Francis headed for New York to provide adequate hospital attention as quickly as possible.

Leaves Burning Ship at Anchor.

He left the Morro Castle anchored with her bow to the wind, the flames being thus swept to stern. A few valiant seamen, 14 to 20

List of Victims in Sea Disaster and Survivors

Passengers and members of the crew reported accounted for, insured or missing, together with a list of the identified dead in the burning of the Ward liner Morro Castle, on the basis of the latest available information, were as follows:

SURVIVORS.

Passengers.

ADAMS, JANE, Point Pleasant, N. J.; injured, shock and submersion.
AGUIAR, VAL, Las Vegas, Venezuela.
ARNETH, PAUL, Brooklyn.
ASCHOFF, THORP H., 150-15 Stoneford Avenue, Flushing, Queens.
ATICELLO, MARCO, Brooklyn.
ASCHOFF, Mrs. T. H., same address.
BARSTEAD, LLOYD C., 1,891 Harrison Avenue, Bronx.
BARSTEAD, Mrs., same address.
BECK, Miss EMILY C., Philadelphia.
BEACH, AGNES, 205 East Seventy-eighth Street.
BEHR, Miss C.
BEHR, Mrs E.
BERGENSTEIN, Miss DOROTHY.
BIREN, ROSE, Philadelphia.
BLANCO, BOB, Havana.
BLONDEAU, Mr. JULES, Philadelphia; shock and submersion.
BLONDEAU, Mrs. JULES, Philadelphia; shock and submersion.
BODNER, S., 85 Summit Road, Elizabeth, N. J.
BODNER, Mrs. S., same address.
BORMAN, H., 362 Roosevelt Avenue, Freeport, L. I.
BRADY, Mrs. E. J., Overbrook, Pa.
BRADBURY, Miss MARTHA, Pennsylvania.
BREGSTEIN, Dr. J. JOSEPH, 7,825 Fourth Avenue, Brooklyn.
BREGSTEIN, MERVIN G., same address.
BRINKMAN, HARRY, Brooklyn.
BRINKMAN, Mrs.
BRODIE, Miss H.
BROWN, Miss FLORENCE.
BROWN, Miss IDA, Philadelphia; shock and submersion.
BUDLONG, Miss MARJORIE, Hillside, N. J.
BUQUETS, OFELIA
BUQUETS, Mrs.
BUQUETS, FRANCOIS
BURRELL, Dr. J. H., Buffalo.
BURRELL, Mrs J. H.
BUTE, JAMES, Brooklyn.
BYRNE, W. E., 330 West Ninety-fifth Street; burns.
CALETA, JUAN, Cuba.
CANNAVAN, Miss K., 20 Butler Place, Brooklyn.
CANNON, THOMAS
CARPENTER, Mrs MADGE, 41-08 171st Street, Flushing, Queens.
CASEY, CAROLINE, Philadelphia.
CHRESLER, Miss L., Brooklyn.
CLARKE, WILLIAM F., 156-14 Channel Street, Howard Beach, L. I.; injured.
COCHRANE, Dr. CHARLES, Brooklyn.
COCHRANE, Miss C. M.
COHEN, Mrs. A., Hartford, Conn.
COHEN, Mrs. A., Hartford, Conn.
COHN, Miss GERTRUDE.
COLL, Mrs J. P.
CONROY, Miss ANNE.
CONWAY, Miss ANNE, Brooklyn.
COTTER, Miss M. V.
CULLEN, Miss UNA
DAVIS, Mrs. MINNIE, 200 Pine Street, Brooklyn, burns on both legs.
DAVIDSON, Miss LILLIAN, 33 Athens Street, Clifton. N. J.
DAVIDSON, SIDNEY.
DAVIDSON, Mrs. SIDNEY.
DESERVINE, MADELINE.

Continued on Page Twenty-six.

Survivors Tell of Leaping Into Sea to Escape Flames

Many Sang and Prayed on Decks—Reluctant Women Pushed Overboard or Into Boats —Ship's Plates Red Hot.

Survivors of the Morro Castle, telling of their experiences on the fire-swept liner yesterday, painted in broad strokes a story of heroism and panic.

Some of them told of jumping from the flame-swept decks of the Morro Castle and swimming for six or seven hours before coming ashore or being picked up off the Jersey coast. Others, brought to New York on the rescue vessels, told of being picked up from the water.

Many told of being forced to jump into the sea many feet below from the crowded decks when the approaching flames left them no other course. Members of the crew described a gallant attempt to subdue the fire—a fight doomed from the start because of low water pressure.

Others told of how frightened passengers crowded aft in the vessel and were cut off from the bulk of the crew by the flames which were sweeping the midsection. They told of women banding together and singing such songs as "Hail, Hail, the Gang's All Here" in an attempt to bolster the courage of the rest.

Chief Officer Takes Charge.

The outstanding hero to the crew was W. F. Warms, the chief officer who became the acting captain of the Morro Castle. They told of his standing on the liner's bridge as it was aflame, shouting orders to his men, thinking only of saving his passengers and crew. All the passengers and all the few members of the crew who appeared among them. The crew members explained that this was due to the fact that they were cut off from the aft section of the vessel by the flames amidship.

A small group of seamen and stewards, however, aided greatly in adjusting life belts for passengers and forcing them to jump into the sea, where they stood at least some chance for their lives.

Rescued stewards laid part of the death toll to the modesty of women passengers who waited in their cabins to dress—waited too long—and found themselves cut off by the flames.

The rough weather, too, was blamed by some of the crew for the heavy loss of life. At least a third of the passengers were seasick at the time the fire began, they said. Many of these, survivors believed, were likewise trapped in their cabins.

The virtual cutting in two of the ship by the flames made it impossible to lower many of the lifeboats. All those on the port side were burned. There were ample life belts, however.

The survivors told their stories in hospitals and impromptu shelters along the Jersey coast, where they were housed after they were brought ashore. Others described their experiences when they arrived in New York on the rescue ships.

At least five couples jumped from the rails together to swim to shore and safety. Two of them made their way to the Jersey coast. Another couple were picked up by rescue boats. In two other instances, however, the wives were saved and their husbands drowned.

At least a score of these safe in New Jersey told of swimming ashore, or nearly ashore, from the burning liner. Some, including sev-

Continued on Page Twenty-seven.

MANY BURNED IN CABINS

Flames Cut Off Escape of Tourists Returning From Cruise to Cuba.

STORM HAMPERS RESCUERS

Darkness and Pounding Seas Add to Death Toll—Captain Had Died Shortly Before.

SWEEPING INQUIRIES SET

Speed of Conflagration and Cause a Mystery—Crew Is Praised and Scored.

A page of photographs of the Morro Castle disaster, Page 24.

By RUSSELL B. PORTER.

In one of the worst marine disasters on record, the liner Morro Castle was swept by fire of unknown origin early yesterday morning off the New Jersey coast, with heavy loss of life.

The scene of the tragedy was not far from where the dirigible Akron was wrecked during a storm off Barnegat Lighthouse last year.

By a strange coincidence, Captain Robert Willmott, master of the Morro Castle, died of a heart attack following acute indigestion about 8:45 o'clock Friday night, nearly eight hours before the SOS went out at 4:23 A. M., New York daylight time. When the fire started, the liner was under the command of Chief Officer William F. Warms, who remained aboard the burning ship until taken off by a Coast Guard cutter late yesterday afternoon.

The exact number of dead and missing was not finally determined last night, but it was believed to be between 200 and 250.

Reports to the offices of the Ward Line, operators of the Morro Castle, were that 161 passengers and 147 of the crew, or a total of 308 persons, were known to have been saved. According to the line, the ship had carried a total of 562 persons, including 318 passengers and a crew of 244. This would indicate a death toll of 254, but it was emphasized that other survivors had not yet been reported.

Later information indicated that the survivors numbered at least 237, for, in addition to the 268 survivors here or bound here, there were thirty-six in the Fitkins Memorial Hospital at Asbury Park and twenty-one in the Point Pleasant (N. J.) Hospital here last night. This would cut the possible death toll to 237.

171 Bodies Are Recovered.

The New Jersey National Guard, which was assembling at Camp Moore, Sea Girt, all the bodies washed ashore at fifteen or more coast communities, estimated that reports from these places indicated that a total of 171 bodies had been recovered.

At midnight last night fifty-eight bodies of unidentified dead had been taken to Camp Moore from various New Jersey communities. Thirty-three were men, twenty-two women and three children. Other bodies were to be taken there during the night.

Confusion existed over the number of survivors and dead partly because of the many places to which survivors and bodies were taken at first and partly because the steamship line did not have an accurate list of the crew. The figure finally announced for the crew may be revised.

Two hundred and fifty-four survivors were brought to New York and New Jersey during the afternoon and night. These included seventy-one persons rescued by the City of Savannah, sixty-five by the Andrea S. Luckenbach and ninety-seven brought here by train from various New Jersey coast points where they had gone ashore. Fourteen more were on their way here aboard a Coast Guard vessel.

Of the 268 here or on their way here last night, 140 were members of the crew and 128 were passengers.

Nine bodies were brought to New York, and were taken to the Morgue at Bellevue Hospital. Five were men and four were women.

Continued on Page Twenty-six.

NRA
WE DO OUR PART

"All the News That's
Fit to Print."

The New York Times.

LATE CITY EDITION
WEATHER—Cloudy, rain or snow today; tomorrow rain.
Temperature Yesterday—Max.: 46; Min.: 36
Detailed Weather Report Page 42.

VOL. LXXXIV....No. 28,145.

Entered as Second-Class Matter,
Postoffice, New York, N. Y.

NEW YORK, THURSDAY, FEBRUARY 14, 1935.

Copyright, 1935, by The New York Times Company.

P   TWO CENTS | In New York City. | THREE CENTS | FOUR CENTS Elsewhere Except Within 200 Miles in 7th and 8th Postal Zones.

HAUPTMANN GUILTY, SENTENCED TO DEATH FOR THE MURDER OF THE LINDBERGH BABY

MACON'S MEN LAND, SAVED FROM DEATH IN SKY AND ON SEA

Calm Heroism and Unbroken Navy Discipline Revealed as Survivors Reach Port.

ADMIRAL TELLS OF HORROR

Saw Gasoline Flames Spread Over Water to Airship's Crew as the Cruisers Came Up.

WILEY DESCRIBES PLUNGE

Naval Court Is Ordered for Today as Field Inquiry Into the Cause Is Started.

Special to The New York Times.

SAN FRANCISCO, Feb. 13.—Eighty-one officers and men of the eighty-three who set out on the dirigible Macon to join the fleet off the California Coast came home today to tell how the giant airship was destroyed yesterday evening and death which snatched at them from sky and sea was beaten back.

They stood huddled on three rescue cruisers in San Francisco Bay, laughing, asking for cigarettes, and between puffs relating this latest epic of man's defeat amid his conquests of space.

But though they could describe the first alarm and the fall, of flying minutes after the Macon struck, and dragging anxiety as the navy swept the misty seas in search of them, they were mute on the cause of the disaster.

Some fabric tore away on her fins and along her backbone; gas cells burst, the great structure shuddered and soared and descended and hit, and suddenly they were tumbled out pell mell into the water, fighting for their lives. Flaming gasoline was ignited around them by calcium flares of mercy.

This was the story in brief, different for every man, yet somehow merging into one clear picture of the whole.

Three Warships Reach Port.

The warships Richmond, Cincinnati and Concord brought in the survivors. Lieut. Commander Herbert V. Wiley, the Macon's skipper, was aboard the Concord. When he described what happened it was in terms of telephone calls, buoyancy and lack of it, jettisoned gasoline and crumbling gas cells and frames. He was in the control car, a city block from the source of trouble.

The story of men is another narrative. The Macon was humming along, not far at sea south of Monterey Bay. The weather was dark gray and filled with drizzle, but the world's greatest dirigible had seen many such days. She had met the fleet plowing northward toward San Francisco; she was accompanying it, and soon she would go to her home in Sunnyvale.

The time was a little later than 5 o'clock in the afternoon, and daylight was already failing. There was a slight jar. It jerked at the wheel in the helmsman's hands. Some said they did not feel the jar, but immediately noticed the inclination of the ship, nose upward.

However, there were subsequent "jars." Lieutenant C. S. Rounds described them as a "shudder."

"But it was equally outside," he said. "I doubt if many of us in the first sixty seconds anticipated serious trouble. Even when the 'stand by' orders came, I thought it was a minor crisis of navigation."

Gas Cells Begin to Go.

But those jars were the rupturing of gas units; then No. 1, then No. 2, away aft. Lieutenant Rounds was forward and began to fall. It was no excitement for the first four or five minutes, except ing among those aft who were whipping telephone calls into the control car. The airship was riding rapidly.

Then No. 9 cell burst. About that time it dawned on all that this was no minor crisis.

They stuck by their posts. They slipped gasoline tanks aft and devalved the forward cells to level her out, but it was no good.

Having soared into the mist in a last living effort, the Macon lost buoyancy and began to fall. It was then that Commander Wiley sent out the message that they were falling and first mentioned abandoning ship.

The man who sent the electric

Continued on Page Two.

CAVALIER HOTEL, Virginia Beach, Va. Opens Feb. 20. Golf and all sports.—Advt.

Opera Threatened Again As Board Balks at Deficit

Metropolitan Directors Cast Doubt on Next Season Unless Production Costs Are Cut and Popular Subscription Enlarged.

There may be no opera at the Metropolitan next season. The board of directors of the Metropolitan Opera Association has decided that opera cannot be continued on the basis of the enormous losses incurred in the last five seasons.

After a meeting of the executive committee yesterday in the office of Paul D. Cravath, chairman of the board, Mr. Cravath issued the following statement:

"The directors of the Metropolitan Opera Association have decided that it is not feasible to give opera at the Metropolitan Opera House next season on the basis of continuing to incur the large deficits of the last five seasons.

"They have requested the preparation of a plan for reducing the cost of producing opera, and increasing the support of the public through subscriptions for seats, that will render the continuation of opera financially possible."

The members of the committee would not elaborate on this statement last night. One member intimated that the announcement had a twofold purpose; to quiet the rumors that have been at large in the last few weeks and to gauge the public reaction as to its willingness to participate in assuring the Metropolitan's future.

It was emphasized that neither the full board nor the executive committee had abandoned the Metropolitan to whatever fate might befall it, and that, despite the immediate doubts, there was every intention to continue consideration of the opera's future.

Besides Mr. Cravath, the members of the executive committee who attended the meeting were Mrs. August Belmont, Cornelius N. Bliss, Frederic Potts Moore, David Sarnoff and Allen Wardwell, Robert S. Brewster, the new president of the Metropolitan Opera and Real Estate Company, and Myron C. Taylor were the only members absent.

The executive committee has been holding frequent meetings since Fall to determine ways and means of continuing opera at the Metropolitan. The first question before it was the establishment of a policy and financial program. The second, depending on the first, was the naming of a general manager to succeed Giulio Gatti-Casazza, whose resignation takes effect next April.

Many plans for the continuation of Metropolitan Opera were proposed and discussed at these meetings.

Continued on Page Twenty-five.

HOPE GAINS IN ROME FOR PEACE IN AFRICA

But Italy Is Reported Ready to Spend $850,000,000 in the Event of War.

REPLY TO DEMANDS ASKED

Plan for Solution Reported in Addis Ababa—Fascist Grand Council to Meet.

By ARNALDO CORTESI
Wireless to The New York Times.

ROME, Feb. 13.—The optimistic forecasts made yesterday as to a peaceful solution of the Italo-Abyssinian crisis became more positive today following a meeting between Negradas Yesus, Abyssinian Chargé d'Affaires, and Fulvio Suvich, Italian Foreign Under-Secretary. Although it is stated semi-officially that no actual solution has been reached, the impression is that good progress has been made. Special emphasis is laid on the fact that Signor Suvich began by assuring the Abyssinian envoy that Italy was animated by the most peaceful intentions, to which the envoy replied that his Emperor also wished to avoid war. Signor Suvich then complained that the demands submitted to Emperor Haile Selassie by the Italian Minister at Addis Ababa remained unanswered.

Then the Italian Under-Secretary went on to discuss possible solutions of the crisis. These include the establishment of a neutral zone on the Abyssinian side of the frontier, but it is positively stated that no indication that this condition will be accepted by the Emperor has yet been received by Italy.

The Abyssinian envoy sent a long report of his conversations with Signor Suvich to Addis Ababa, and it is hoped by Italian officials that a reply will be forthcoming in the next few days.

There has been no let-up in the feverish activities to prepare a strong Italian expeditionary force for dispatch to Africa. In view, however, of today's favorable development hope is beginning to be entertained that it may never be necessary for the force to leave Italy.

Mussolini Studies Note.

ROME, Feb. 13.—Premier Mussolini gave deep study tonight to an Abyssinian note calling Italians to provocations in recent border conflicts. This note, Italian officials said earlier today, made the situation "very serious."

Nevertheless, there appeared this evening to be less concern in government circles over the prospect of hostilities in Africa, although an authoritative source said Italy was prepared to spend about $850,000,000.

Continued on Page Sixteen.

LEHMAN TAX BILLS VOTED BY SENATE

Four-Cent Gasoline Levy and Budget Are Among the 11 Measures Approved.

FEARON ATTACKS FIGURES

He Predicts a $100,000,000 Deficit at Fiscal Year End— Five Proposals Held Up.

By W. A. WARN.
Special to The New York Times.

ALBANY, Feb. 13.—Eleven of the measures included in Governor Lehman's fiscal program were passed in the Senate today. Action on five was deferred, not because the Democrats did not have the votes to pass them, but because legislative leaders doubted whether passage of them would be within the requirements of the Constitution, until after the main budget bills, already passed in the Senate, had been passed in the Assembly also.

Every Democrat in the Senate voted for the Governor's bills. The Republican vote was split in many instances. Senator Fearon, leader of the Republican minority, voted for the main budget bill, but not until he had first denounced it as a measure which did not comply with the Constitutional provision for a balanced budget and had accused Governor Lehman of financial juggling in drafting his measures.

The Senator cited figures intended to show that Mr. Lehman had constantly blundered in estimating revenues. He declared that these futile processes had been repeated by the Chief Executive in making up his new budget, with the probable result that the Governor would be confronted with a $100,000,000 deficit when the next fiscal year ends instead of the $3,000,000 surplus of the Governor's own estimate, cited in his budget message to the Legislature.

Sees 700 New Jobs.

Senator Fearon accused the Democrats of putting more than 700 new jobs into the budget bill without telling anybody anything about it. He said they had refused the taxpayers a public hearing on the budget bill at a time when the Governor himself was demanding public hearings in towns and counties on local budgets.

Senator Dunnigan, Democratic leader, came to the defense of the Governor and the debate was shot through and through with partisan charges. At times it became quite heated, with Senators Fearon and Dunnigan striding up and down the centre aisle.

Senator Fearon gave Senator Twomey, Republican floor leader of the Senate, some moments of embarras

Continued on Page Six.

BON AIR VANDERBILT, AUGUSTA, GA. 18 hrs. to sunshine. Round trip $33.50.—Advt.

SENATE COMMITTEE ADOPTS WORK BILL; TRUCE OVER WAGES

Drive for Pay Under 'Prevailing' Rates Is Beaten and the 'Dole' Also Is Rejected.

ROOSEVELT RETAINS POWER

But His Scale Must Not Cut Private Wages—Floor Fight Due as Labor Protests.

Special to The New York Times.

WASHINGTON, Feb. 13.—After hours of struggle today, the administration leadership, supported by Senator Glass, regained control of the Senate Appropriations Committee and finished a redraft of the $4,880,000,000 relief bill deemed acceptable to President Roosevelt.

Mr. Glass prepared to report the revised measure formally to the Senate tomorrow or next day. Leaders hope it may be acted upon finally before the unemployment funds in the present relief coffers are depleted entirely.

Today's action in the Appropriations Committee was considered both by the administration and organized labor as a victory for the Roosevelt supporters. Instead of yielding to the demand of the American Federation of Labor for an irrevocable "prevailing wage" provision, the committee adopted an amendment giving the President control over pay rates, but with the added prescription that he must pay the "prevailing" scale if he finds the new works program is depressing, or is likely to depress, private wage structures in any locality.

"Ill Advised," Says Mayor.

William Green, president of the A. F. of L., said tonight that the substitute was "unacceptable and unsatisfactory to labor," adding that the federation would make its appeal directly to the Senate membership.

"Dole" Amendment Is Beaten.

The committee also withstood a drive from another group and again voted down, by 12 to 11, the so-called "dole" amendment which would have provided a cut in the appropriation to $2,880,000,000 and thereby, according to its supporters, force the President to rely more on direct relief than upon the more expensive new public works.

Thus, after three weeks of varying degrees of fright, administration leaders apparently had taken hold again. They proposed to move at once to break the log-jam of legislation which has backed up behind the relief program, and expressed confidence in predicting that this measure would be well on its way through the Senate before another week had gone.

Through all of its vicissitudes in the committee, the bill emerged today without any change which leaders regarded as a serious violation of the principles laid down by the President in his annual message. He called then for a lump-sum appropriation and for adequate discretionary authority to spend it in a self-diminishing, largely self-liquidating works program, designed to return 3,500,000 able-bodied persons now on relief to employment at lower than prevailing wages.

All of the trouble on the measure,

Continued on Page Eight.

Girl Dies in Leap Off Empire State Tower; Impact Smashes Heavy Marquee in 33d St.

Disconsolate because of a quarrel with her fiancé, a 20-year-old girl jumped from the observation landing just before 8:30 o'clock last night, her body crashing into a glass and metal marquee nearly a quarter of a mile below.

The impact of the fall, which shattered frosted glass, light bulbs and the sheet-iron covering of the canopy, was at first mistaken for an explosion by passers-by and shop employees in the vicinity. Witnesses in buildings on the opposite side of Thirty-third Street said the young woman's body had struck a sixth-floor set-back of the building before hurtling onto the marquee.

From the contents of her handbag, which was clutched tightly in her fingers, the girl was identified as Irma P. Eberhardt of the Laura Spelman Hall Branch of the Y. W. C. A., 607 Hudson Street. Except for a Y. W. C. A. membership card the black bag contained only 83 cents in change and a compact of lipstick and rouge.

At the moment Miss Eberhardt jumped from the Empire State Tower race, according to the police, Raymond Rebecchi of 5,716 136th Street, Flushing, was at the Charles Street station reporting her disappearance to Detective Frank Campbell. Before he had finished, word of her death was received from the police of the West Thirtieth Street precinct.

Rebecchi said he had told Detective Campbell that he and Miss Eberhardt had quarreled on Tuesday, but that he had called at the Y. W. C. A. last night in the hope of effecting a reconciliation. He asked her to go to dinner, he said, and while he went to a lavatory to wash his hands the young woman vanished.

Rebecchi said he had told the police he waited about half an hour in the foyer when he received a telephone call from Miss Eberhardt. "I'm going to kill myself," she said and hung up the receiver. Alarmed, the young man hurried to the police station.

ELEVATORS TIED UP IN 200 BUILDINGS IN STRIKE FLARE-UP

Union Disclaims Action After New Delay in Decision, but Admits Patience Is Gone.

UPTOWN APARTMENTS HIT

Madison Square Offices Also Are Affected—Spread of the Walkout a Possibility.

A general strike of building service employes in office and apartment house buildings loomed last night after sporadic walkouts affecting more than 200 buildings and 3,500 employes were staged in various parts of the city yesterday.

The strikes were called by a so-called "rank and file committee" of members of the Building Service Employes Union, claiming a membership of 140,000, as the arbitration committee headed by Major Henry H. Curran, appointed last December by Mayor La Guardia to settle the differences between the union and realty interests, was struggling to complete its labors and present an award.

The committee was to have made known its award yesterday. It failed to do so, however, and last night Major Curran announced that the award would not be made public until today. The committee remained in session all evening at Major Curran's office, 280 Madison Avenue.

Mayor La Guardia, on being informed of the walkouts, which occurred in the Harlem, Washington Heights and Madison Square sections, termed the strikes as "ill advised."

At the office of the union, 1,450 Broadway, responsibility for the strikes was disclaimed. The walkouts were characterized as "unauthorized," but the statement was added, "We cannot hold them back any longer—our men have lost patience waiting for the award."

Detectives of the West 123d Street Precinct, cruising in a radio car, arrested sixteen men shortly before 1 o'clock this morning, charging them with disorderly conduct for alleged intimidation of building-service employes in three Harlem apartment houses. According to the officers, the sixteen men, nine of whom were Negroes, had entered the apartment houses and compelled attendants on duty to quit their jobs.

Six of the prisoners were picked up at 50 West 112th Street, three at 56 West 112th Street, and seven at 1,980 Seventh Avenue. All will be arraigned in the Fifth District Court today.

Promised to Work for Peace.

A fortnight ago James J. Bambrick, after a meeting of the union's executive committee and the presidents of its fifteen locals in the city, had promised Major Curran that every effort would be used to prevent any strikes, pending the outcome of the arbitration proceedings.

This was in response to a plea from Major Curran to keep the men from striking lest such action jeopardize the arbitration award.

Continued on Page Eight.

BRUNO RICHARD HAUPTMANN
Being taken to his cell after hearing death sentence last night.

Times Wide World Photo.

HAUPTMANN IN CELL FALLS IN COLLAPSE

After Hearing Verdict Without a Sign, He Breaks Down in Fit of Weeping.

WIFE SOBS AFTER HE GOES

Both Prepared for Worst by Warning of Fisher Against Outburst in Court.

By CRAIG THOMPSON.
Special to The New York Times.

FLEMINGTON, N. J., Feb. 13.—For the first time since his arrest Bruno Richard Hauptmann was reported tonight to be in a state of collapse.

When he was marched out of the court room, manacled to Constable Hovey Low on his left and State Trooper Hugh Stockberger on his right, he was pale but erect as this step seemed firm.

He went through the back rooms to his cell tier, which was occupied by him alone. The minute the door was slammed shut behind him, according to the reports, he slumped, his face striking the floor.

There was a hush in the court room when Hauptmann came in at 10:30 o'clock tonight. For the first time since the trial started he was in irons, manacled to two of his nine guards. The bell in the belfry had already announced that the jury had reached a verdict, and the shouting of the throng outside was an overtone to the inside hush.

Wife Comes to His Side.

Hauptmann walked across the room from the rear door and took his seat. He sat down stiffly, a little awkwardly, as if the manacles impeded his motions.

At almost the same moment his wife, her normally red face growing pale, edged up the outside aisle and around the seats inside the rail to a place close to her husband. She twisted her fingers into a smile, but her husband, after one glance, looked away.

In the two minutes that passed before the jurors began to file in there was a vivid little picture. C. Lloyd Fisher, the one member of Hauptmann's counsel who has been closest to him, visiting him daily in the jail and taking his life story before the trial, leaned over and put his arm around the prisoner's shoulder.

He whispered: "This is only the beginning. Don't show a sign, because, if you do, it will count against you."

Then the attorney leaned over and placed his arm around Mrs.

Continued on Page Eleven.

ACCUSTOMED TO ENTERTAIN THE Famous—Try the Willard Hotel, Washington, D. C.—Advt.

JURY COURAGEOUS, WILENTZ DECLARES

Nation Indebted to Them, He Says—Thanks Aides, Foley and New York Police.

'ENDS OF JUSTICE SERVED'

Peacock Says Verdict Is Reply to 'Mothers' Prayer'—Law Points Raised by Defense.

From a Staff Correspondent.

FLEMINGTON, N. J., Feb. 13.—Attorney General David T. Wilentz, commenting tonight upon the Hauptmann verdict, thanked all those associated with the prosecution, and paid special tribute to the jury.

"The tremendous responsibility imposed upon the Hunterdon County jury was shouldered without flinching," he said. "The nation is indebted to these courageous men and women.

"The proper presentation of the case was due in the main to the work of the New Jersey State police. District Attorney Samuel J. Foley of the Bronx and his assistants labored unceasingly and to them I extend my deep thanks, as well as to Inspectors Henry Bruckman, John J. Lyons, the members of the New York police and the agents of the Federal Government."

Mr. Wilentz added that it had been his unwelcome duty to prosecute the case and added that he hoped society would be served by his efforts and those of his associates.

Former Judge George K. Large of Flemington, special counsel to the State, said, "The verdict was fully justified by the evidence."

"Truth Will Prevail."

Assistant Attorney General Robert Peacock said:

"The verdict proves again that truth will prevail. All during the time I was preparing the case at the request of the Attorney General I felt that the simple truth presented in terms the jury could understand would adequately serve the ends of justice.

"The verdict is the answer to the prayers of the mothers of this nation that those who harm their children shall be punished and that men of the accomplishments of Colonel Lindbergh will be able to maintain homes in the quiet assurance that their families in the hour of their absence shall be protected by the arm of the law."

Colonel H. Norman Schwarzkopf said:

"I feel that the verdict is in accordance with the evidence and that the ends of justice have been served.

Continued on Page Eleven.

When You Think of Writing Think of Whiting.—Advt.

JURY OUT FOR 11 HOURS

One of 2 Women Who Held Out for Mercy Near Tears at End.

DEFENDANT PALE, SILENT

Fails to Glance at Wife as He Is Led Back to Cell— She Is Calm.

DEFENSE PLANS TO APPEAL

Execution Set for the Week of March 18—Court's Charge Attacked as Biased.

Judge's charge to the jury and exceptions granted, Pages 10, 11.

By RUSSELL B. PORTER.
Special to The New York Times.

FLEMINGTON, N. J., Feb. 13.—Bruno Richard Hauptmann was convicted of murder in the first degree at 10:45 o'clock tonight for the killing of Charles A. Lindbergh Jr. at Hopewell on the night of March 1, 1932.

He was sentenced to die in the electric chair at the State prison in Trenton some time during the week of March 18.

The jury of eight men and four women returned its verdict after having been out for eleven hours and twenty-four minutes since it retired from the court room at 11:21 o'clock this morning to deliberate on the jury room.

Handcuffed to two guards, Hauptmann stood between them silent and motionless, his face ashen white and terror in his deep-set eyes, while he heard the jury state its verdict and the judge pronounce sentence.

A few minutes later he was led away to his cell in the county jail. He did not even cast a glance of recognition toward his wife, who sat a few feet away. She looked at him with red-rimmed eyes, but did not weep.

Colonel Charles A. Lindbergh, who attended every session of the thirty-two court days of the trial from its beginning on Jan. 2, six weeks ago, and who heard Supreme Court Justice Thomas W. Trenchard deliver his charge to the jury this morning, was not in court when the verdict was returned. He had returned to his home in Englewood in the afternoon.

Woman Juror Near Tears.

Mrs. Verna Snyder, juror No. 3, was biting her lips to keep from crying and her eyes were wet with tears as she left the jury box. According to well founded report, she and Mrs. Rosie Pill, juror No. 2, had held out to the last ballot for a verdict of guilty with a recommendation providing imprisonment at hard labor for life.

All the rest of the jurors were grave but appeared serene, as if they were satisfied that they had done their duty.

At 10:28 Sheriff Curtiss came out of the judge's chambers and gave an order to a deputy sheriff. The latter left the room and mounted the stairs to the cupola on the roof of the white court house. In a moment the 125-year-old bell, older than the court house itself, began to toll. By an old custom, revived a few years ago, the bell is rung to notify the town that a jury has reached a verdict and is about to return to the court room. "There's the bell!" the whisper spread through the court room.

"Quiet! Quiet!" cried the guards as the reporters murmured among themselves, but both the murmurs and the shouts were drowned out by the noise of the crowd in the street, which at this moment rose to a roar.

Prisoner Is Brought In.

Mr. Fisher of defense counsel came in and indicated that Hauptmann was already on the way from his cell. At 10:31 the prisoner was brought in. The Sheriff and five State troopers led the way.

Hauptmann's gait was unusual as he appeared in the doorway. For the first time since the trial began, he was brought into court manacled.

Continued on Page Twelve.

"All the News That's Fit to Print."

The New York Times.

LATE CITY EDITION

WEATHER—Fair, continued warm today; tomorrow cloudy, showers.
Temperature Yesterday—Max., 85; Min., 73

Copyright, 1935, by The New York Times Company

VOL. LXXXIV....No. 28,329.   Entered as Second-Class Matter, Postoffice, New York, N. Y.   NEW YORK, SATURDAY, AUGUST 17, 1935.   P   TWO CENTS In New York City. | THREE CENTS Within 200 Miles | FOUR CENTS Elsewhere Except In 7th and 8th Postal Zones.

ROOSEVELT CALLS CHIEFS TO ARRANGE CONGRESS WIND-UP

Conference Tomorrow Is Expected to Set Program for Adjournment Thursday.

FIVE MAJOR BILLS FAVORED

Wealth Tax, Banking, Coal, Alcohol Control and Gold Ban Measures Slated to Pass.

UTILITY DEADLOCK HOLDS

Holding Company Curb and Other Major Bills Likely to Wait Till Next Session.

By The Associated Press.
WASHINGTON, Aug. 16.—A semi-final conference of Democratic leaders to make arrangements for a prompt adjournment of Congress was called tonight by President Roosevelt for Sunday night.

The expectation of some of the party chiefs was that at that meeting the President would disclose which measures he was willing for Congress to drop and which he wanted enacted before adjournment.

Among those invited to the conference, beginning at 8:30, were: Vice President Garner, Speaker Byrns, Senator Robinson of Arkansas, the Democratic leader; Chairman O'Connor of the House Rules Committee, Chairman Harrison of the Senate Finance Committee and Chairman Doughton of the House Ways and Means Committee.

It was indicated by one of the conferees that any agreement reached Sunday night, however, would be subject to possible modification if particular pressure developed for the enactment of any measure.

Conjecture on Program.

From what they already had heard directly and indirectly from the President, some of the conferees, talking privately, said the meeting made more clear the possibilities of an end to the present session by the end of next week at the latest.

Some were talking about an adjournment Tuesday, or Thursday. Most agreed that it probably would be the latter part of next week before everything could be wound up to the satisfaction of the President.

The expectation of some of the conferees was that the President would renew his insistence upon enactment of:
1. The Guffey Coal Stabilization Bill, which proponents and some opponents say will pass the House Monday and be approved by the Senate early next week.
2. The Federal alcohol control plan.
3. The $250,000,000 Tax Bill.
4. The Omnibus Banking Bill, on which conferees reached an agreement late today.
5. The measure forbidding suits for gold payments on government contracts.

Six Bills May Be Shelved.

Their belief was that unless action was hastened the following would be left behind when this session ended, with their present status remaining the same until the next session:
1. The Utilities Bill;
2. The rivers and harbors legislation;
3. The measure expanding Federal control over food and drugs;
4. Railroad reorganization;
5. General oil regulation;
6. The Ship Subsidy Bill.

Leaders said the Utilities Bill probably would be left behind, not because the President did not want the legislation, but because the conference deadlock could not be broken.

A possibility was seen by some that the Rivers and Harbors Bill might be insisted upon because it would legalize the millions already spent by the Federal Government on a number of projects, such as the Parker Dam. And they added that they had but scant doubt that before Congress had adjourned it would ratify the oil compacts entered into in Dallas last February.

House Tax Conferees Named.

Special to The New York Times.
WASHINGTON, Aug. 16.—A determined drive to adjourn Congress by Tuesday night, with Thursday as the latest alternate date, was started today following formal commitment of the Wealth-Tax Bill to conference and a conference agreement on the Eccles Banking Bill.

The promise of Tuesday adjournment was held out by Senator Robinson as the Senate voted to take a recess until Monday. Early in the day he had informed the Senate of his desire to quit at that time and in so doing issued a warning

Continued on Page Fourteen.

Davey Sets Ohio Vote for 1936, Defying Opponents of New Deal

Governor, Here, Denies Delaying Test on Advice of Roosevelt Forces, Gives Economy as Reason—He and President Are Accused of 'Conspiracy' by Republican Leader.

Governor Martin L. Davey of Ohio moved formally yesterday to defy Republican demands for a special State-wide election this year for Representative at Large to test New Deal sentiment in the State.

The Governor was visiting New York City during the day and telephoned his office in Columbus to frame an order in legal form setting the election for next year. All that remains to put the order into effect is the signature of the Governor, which he said he would affix when he reached Ohio tonight.

With the Republican national leaders, heartened by a victory in the Rhode Island Congressional elections, demanding that Ohio vote this November to fill the vacancy caused by the death of Representative Charles V. Truax, the Governor insisted that the election should be held next year to avoid imposing the expense of a special election.

He ridiculed the charge made by his political adversaries that the election was being postponed until next year, apparently under advice from the Roosevelt forces at Washington, to prevent an early test of the New Deal in such a key State as Ohio.

"There is no moral justification of loading that extra cost for a special election on the units of the State," Governor Davey said at the Hotel Biltmore. "The good and ample reason for this order is that a recent referendum reducing the tax limit from 15 mills to 10 mills on the dollar has, with the aid of the depression, depleted the treasuries of the counties and the cities so badly that they could not well stand the expense of a special election.

"Now I want to point out that no district in Ohio will be without representation meanwhile, since this post is that of a Representative at Large. I have an excellent precedent for this action, since the same course was followed in my

Continued on Page Seven.

ROOSEVELT RESTS AT HYDE PARK HOME

Joins Family on Two-Day Visit to Celebrate 21st Birthday of Franklin Jr.

AVOIDS ISSUE ON HOOVER

President Intercedes for Man Caught in Act While Stealing Ride on His Train.

From a Staff Correspondent.
HYDE PARK, N. Y., Aug. 16.—President Roosevelt returned to Hyde Park House today for a brief period of quiet contemplation before undertaking the direction of strategy designed to bring the current session of Congress to a satisfactory conclusion from the administration standpoint.

He came here overnight aboard a special train which arrived at 8:30 o'clock this morning for the announced purpose of attending a family party tomorrow in celebration of the twenty-first birthday anniversary of Franklin D. Roosevelt Jr., his third son.

However, an impromptu "press conference" held by Mr. Roosevelt while he sat in an automobile for the ride from the train to his mother's estate overlooking the Hudson River gave ample indication of the many problems awaiting a directing hand, if not a definite solution, by the President.

These problems he plans to tackle actively on Sunday, when he will return to the White House for a long series of conferences with the individuals and groups representing the administration leadership on Capitol Hill.

A cheery confidence was radiated by Mr. Roosevelt today as he was subjected to a barrage of questions by reporters who clustered around his automobile in the bright morning sunlight.

Questioned on Utility Bill.

The questions dealt principally with the Utility Holding Company Bill, which has been deadlocked in conference between the House and Senate for some time, and the Tax Bill which was sent to conference yesterday after the Senate had approved a measure considerably different than the House bill.

Asked if he expected enactment of the Utility Bill this session, Mr. Roosevelt replied smilingly that he hoped so, with an inflection in his voice which some reporters interpreted as indicating that he intended to have this done.

Would he be willing, he then was asked, to accept the House bill, which differs from the Senate bill and administration recommendations in its omission of the celebrated "death sentence" section? At this question, Mr. Roosevelt smiled and closed the topic with the assertion that he could not comment on details.

A request for comment on the action of the Senate in passing the Tax Bill in changed form brought the rejoinder from the President that the Tax Bill had not been finally passed by Congress yet; that it was still an open question.

Renewed efforts by correspondents to get specific comment from the President on the recent statement by former President Hoover were unavailing. Mr. Roosevelt to set forth definitely his plans regarding possible changes in the Constitution, elicited from the President only the reply that he had read Mr. Hoover's statement very hurriedly and therefore was in no position to comment.

Aside from the conferences Mr.

Continued on Page Fourteen.

CONFEREES AGREE ON BANK MEASURE

Glass and His Senators Win on Nearly All Points, Ending Long Battle on Bill.

ONE VICTORY FOR HOUSE

Effort to Force State Banks Into Reserve Is Put Off— Swift Finish Planned.

Special to The New York Times.
WASHINGTON, Aug. 16.—Unanimous agreement on every feature of the hotly contested bill to change the nation's banking laws was reached by Senate and House conferees late today and arrangements were made to hurry this highly important measure through both branches of Congress early next week.

Senator Glass and his conservative colleagues of the Senate conferees won a smashing victory over Representatives Steagall and Goldsborough of the House conferees in almost every particular, but the two House liberals succeeded in postponing efforts to force State banks into the Federal Reserve System.

Senator Glass was delighted by the outcome. He and the other members of the conference asserted that the bill would go through both branches with ease.

Action will be taken on the conference report in the House Monday. The conferees arranged to file formal reports to both branches tomorrow.

The end of the conference marks a long and bitter fight over the policies of Marriner S. Eccles, governor of the Federal Reserve Board, as expressed in the bill passed by the House, and the views of the Glass group as set forth in the Senate bill.

Opinion tonight was that Mr. Glass, veteran banking legislator, had once more come out the victor.

Reserve Board Is Increased.

He and the other Senate conferees succeeded in carrying out their views on the open market committee, particularly in the aspect that government securities must be purchased on the open market and not direct from the Treasury.

Likewise, Senate conferees prevailed in their insistence that the Federal Reserve Board must be increased from the present six to seven members, with the Secretary of the Treasury and the Controller of the Currency eliminated as members ex officio.

The suggested permission of the Senate bill for banks of deposit to underwrite securities was stricken out at the request of President Roosevelt, Senator Glass stated.

The provision of the Senate bill that bankers may serve on not more than two bank boards simultaneously was retained but made subject to the discretion of the Reserve Board, however.

A big feature of the bill is the arrangement for the open market committee, which would be composed of seven Reserve Board members and five representatives of the twelve regional Reserve Banks. This committee would have power to influence the flow of credit by purchase and sale of government bonds by the Reserve Banks.

Policy Is Mandatory

The policy laid down by the committee would be mandatory upon the Reserve Banks.

Following the view of Mr. Eccles, the House gave complete voting control of open market operations entirely to the Reserve Board.

Continued on Page Fourteen.

HOPSON ADMITS TRYING TO CONTROL PRESS WITH ADS

He Also Tells Senators He Urged Move to Kill Utility Bill in Conference.

ATTACK ON TIMES RENEWED

House Committee Told That His 1934 Income Was Between $300,000 and $500,000.

Special to The New York Times.
WASHINGTON, Aug. 16.—Howard C. Hopson, who now admits that he was the guiding influence of the $900,000 lobby that the Associated Gas and Electric Company waged against the Wheeler-Rayburn bill, was forced to state before the Senate lobby inquiry committee today that the company had not hesitated to use the advertising columns of newspapers as a club to minimize unfavorable publicity.

He also said he had suggested to another high utility holding company official that a campaign be waged to kill the administration's utility program in conferences of the two branches of Congress. As matters stand tonight every indication is that the Wheeler-Rayburn bill will die in conference, where for more than a month the conferees of the Senate and House have been deadlocked. All hope had not been given up by the measure's advocates, however.

Earlier in the day, before the House investigating committee, Mr. Hopson for the first time gave figures on his income last year. He said he had received "some three or four or five hundred thousand dollars" from his private companies.

Admits Borrowing Millions.

He also said that the A. G. E. had borrowed several million dollars since the first of the year, and that he had it not been for the Wheeler-Rayburn bill the borrowings might have been a million dollars less.

He was directed to supply the names of the banks from which the money was borrowed, and said he would do so.

Before the Senate committee Mr. Hopson again made charges involving The New York Times, declaring in the "strong influence" of the Morgan and Carlisle interests, and that because of this alleged influence the A. G. E. should expect at "more or less frequent intervals" "unpleasant attacks from that quarter."

The charges were made in a telegram to the H. C. Hopson Company, New York, which was signed by Duncan Robertson, Mr. Hopson's private secretary.

The telegram was in fact his own, said Mr. Hopson, explaining that it was his custom to have Mr. Robertson sign practically all of his messages to his New York office.

Messages to Hearst Admitted.

William Randolph Hearst was pictured before the committee as the writer of an editorial printed in the Hearst newspapers Sunday, June 2, which Senator Black asserted was strikingly along lines suggested by Mr. Hopson in a telegram to Mr. Hearst dated May 31.

Mr. Hopson admitted sending frequent messages to Mr. Hearst, was pilloried, however, and documents placed in evidence showed

Continued on Page Twenty-six.

Lawyer Charges Judge Downs Beat Him; Sues for $50,000 in Contempt Case Row

County Judge Thomas Downs of Queens was sued in the New York Supreme Court yesterday by Lorenzo C. Carlino, a lawyer, for $50,000 damages. The lawyer charged that Judge Downs, after finding him guilty of contempt of court in a trial, and fining him $250, had knocked him down and kicked him at the St. Albans Golf Club in Queens.

Mr. Carlino alleges that his appeal from the contempt order was based on the ground that it was a violation of the Judiciary Act which requires that a contempt order cite the specific facts upon which it is based. The lawyer further asserts that he got the order from the Appellate Division restraining Judge Downs from making any change in the order pending the appeal.

Mr. Carlino served the order on Judge Downs at the golf club on May 7 last, he alleges, when the jurist was about to step into his car. He says that as soon as he showed a signature of Presiding Justice Lazansky on an injunction order, "the defendant, Thom-

as Downs, struck the plaintiff, knocked him down, then kicked him while on the ground and trampled upon the order while it was served upon him. Defendant called plaintiff vile, filthy names and otherwise used vile and filthy language."

In addition to the suit against Judge Downs the lawyer asks $25,000 damages from Sheriff Peter J. McGarry of Queens for brutal treatment when he was arrested on the contempt order, which was later set aside by the Appellate Division.

Judge Downs denied last night he had assaulted Mr. Carlino.

"I was getting into my automobile parked in front of the club house about 10 o'clock one night more than three months ago," the judge explained, "when a man I did not recognize in the darkness rushed out at me from some shrubbery. I was all alone and had received only a few slaps before as I hit the man at once. He fell down and a paper dropped to the ground. The man picked up the paper and ran away."

COAL BILL SPLITS HOUSE DEMOCRATS; PASSAGE HELD SURE

Widest Party Schism Since 'Death Sentence' Marks 'Must' Measure Debate.

VICTORY BY 30 CLAIMED

Administration Leaders Are Confident Despite Attacks as Unconstitutional.

Special to The New York Times.
WASHINGTON, Aug. 16.—In the face of the most serious party schism which has yet confronted any of President Roosevelt's projected reform, the Guffey-Snyder Coal Bill was maneuvered by House leaders tonight into a position for final action on Monday.

With general debate on the measure concluded, they planned to carry it through the amending stage tomorrow and adjourn before the vote on passage.

Not since the vote on the President's demand for the "death sentence" for utility holding companies has the rank and file of the Democratic majority been so thoroughly split as on the merits of the Guffey-Snyder measure, and leaders were working overtime to make good their prediction that the bill would pass by about thirty votes.

Although they conceded that the final count would be close, all said enough votes had been obtained to assure passage of the administration "must" measure. Their estimate of thirty votes was verified by Republican leaders.

'Stalwarts' Oppose Measure.

Shouts of "unconstitutional," "communism," and "regimentation" from some of those who have been among the staunchest supporters of the administration on some other reform programs marked consideration of the bill on the floor today.

The opposition among Democrats was so strong that Republicans either sat back to watch them denounce the measure or left the floor entirely.

Emphasizing the broad difference of opinion on the constitutionality of the measure was the performance of each Ways and Means Committee "stalwart" as Representatives McCormack of Massachusetts, Cooper of Tennessee and Fuller of Arkansas, all of whom took the floor to oppose it, and sometimes on Republican time. The bill had been reported favorably by the committee by a vote of 12 to 11.

The special rule for consideration of the bill was adopted 241 to 94, after a perfunctory debate. Representative McCormack, one of the two Democrats on the Ways and Means Committee who abstained from voting on reporting out the measure, said that he would vote for the rule but against the bill.

He told other members that there would be no inconsistency in such a position, and that he thought the bill should have a chance for consideration on the floor.

Representative Fuller of Arkansas asked Speaker Byrns's attention to the distribution by pages in the hall of copies of the bill bearing typewritten slips which said:

"Bituminous Coal Bill as amended and reprinted. Controversial propaganda largely eliminated. Ten per cent of tonnage output operators favored bill and more than 95 per cent of labor."

Representative Snyder of Pennsylvania, co-author of the bill, said that he had pasted the slips on the measure and had instructed the

Continued on Page Seven.

WILL ROGERS, WILEY POST DIE IN AIRPLANE CRASH IN ALASKA; NATION SHOCKED BY TRAGEDY

Sergeant Morgan's Report of the Death Of Rogers and Post as Seen by Natives

Special to The New York Times.
SEATTLE, Wash., Aug. 16.—The radio message sent by relays from Point Barrow, in which Staff Sergeant Stanley R. Morgan informed the world of the tragic death of Will Rogers and Wiley Post, read as follows:

"Ten P. M. native runner reported plane crashed fifteen miles south of Barrow.

"Immediately hired fast launch, proceeded to scene.

"Found plane complete wreck, partly submerged, two feet water.

"Recovered body Rogers, then necessary tear plane apart extract body of Post from water.

"Brought bodies Barrow. Turned over Dr. Greist.

"Also salvaged personal effects, which am holding. Advise relatives and instruct this station fully as to procedure.

"Natives camping small river fifteen miles south here claim Post, Rogers landed and asked way to Barrow.

"Taking off, plane misfired on right bank while only fifty feet off water.

"Plane, out of control, crashed nose on, tearing right wing off and nosing over, forcing engine back through body of plane.

"Both apparently killed instantly.

"Both bodies bruised.

"Post's wrist watch broken, stopped 8:18 P. M."

The message was received by Colonel George E. Kumpe, in charge of the army signal corps headquarters here. It had been relayed through two radio stations and took about two hours to reach Seattle.

Sergeant Morgan won fame last Spring when he stayed at his post through a severe influenza epidemic while others, including his wife and 2-year-old son, Barrow, lay seriously ill. Sergeant Morgan and Dr. Henry W. Greist, the Presbyterian medical missionary, waged a bitter fight against the epidemic. While Dr. Greist ministered to the sick, Sergeant Morgan radioed for the aid which finally defeated the epidemic.

ETHIOPIANS OFFER ITALY GUARANTEES

Bar Military Occupation, but Propose Mine, Rail, Trade and Settlement Rights.

ASK ROME TO STATE CASE

Britain and France Hold That Frank Presentation of Demands Is Essential.

By FREDERICK T. BIRCHALL.
Wireless to The New York Times.
PARIS, Aug. 16.—Throughout the day and until late this evening, with only an interval for luncheon, Premier Pierre Laval, Anthony Eden of Great Britain and Baron Pompeo Aloisi of Italy have been in conference at the Quai d'Orsay over the Italo-Ethiopian problem in an effort to avert a war, with its resultant repercussions in Europe.

The first day's deliberations closed with one definite, positive step taken toward results. The British and French have made a joint informal request to the Italians to state fully and frankly their complaints against Ethiopia and their consequent claims upon her.

From a British source it is learned that the Ethiopian Government, which is not represented at this conference, has shown a disposition to concede several points that may go far toward satisfying the Italian claims where these are made.

Offers Security Guarantees.

The Addis Ababa government, for instance, has expressed willingness to provide the most complete guarantees of security from Ethiopian aggression for the present Italian colonies and such economic concessions as may be agreed upon, provided the guarantee expected fall short of military occupation.

Emperor Haile Selassie is willing to grant reasonable rights for developing mineral and commercial possibilities within the Ethiopian territory, specific concessions to Italy being made in both fields.

He is further willing to consider granting some rights to Europeans to settle in Ethiopian territory and develop it while maintaining their original nationality. This last point would go a long way toward compliance with the Italian wishes.

Finally, he is willing to renew and even extend by making further concessions the old understanding with Italy, giving her permission to undertake a certain amount of commercial road and railroad construction in this country. This again anticipates an obvious Italian demand.

No answer to the Franco-British query was forthcoming from Rome tonight. Indeed, an immediate response was not expected. Baron Aloisi agreed to submit the request to Rome and to report the result as soon as possible. He received assurance from the others that if Italy would comply with this re-

Continued on Page Three.

CAPITAL SADDENED BY ROGERS DEATH

Both House and Senate Halt Business for Tribute to the Humorist and to Post.

GARNER DEEPLY AFFECTED

Robinson Hails 'Best Loved Citizen'—Deaths 'Real Loss,' Speaker Byrns Says.

Special to The New York Times.
WASHINGTON, Aug. 16.—The death of Will Rogers and Wiley Post shocked and saddened the capital, which knew Rogers as a frequent visitor and liked him as an amiable "josher" of politicians.

Legislative machinery stopped briefly in tribute. The Senate dropped other business to honor the humorist, a friend of Presidents, diplomats and political leaders. The House also listened to a speech of eulogy, while from all quarters came expressions of sorrow over his death.

As soon as the Senate convened, Senator Robinson, the Democratic leader, took the floor and said:

"Probably the most widely known private citizen in the United States and certainly the best beloved met his death some hours ago in a lonely, far-away place.

"I do not think of Will Rogers as dead. I shall remember him always as a sensible, courageous, loyal friend, possessed of unusual and notable talents.

"He made fun for all mankind. In nothing that he ever said was there an intentional sting. He was kind, generous, patriotic.

"His companion was a courageous representative of a gallant group who, on wings of adventure, sought remote places and conquered long distances."

News Saddens McNary.

Senator McNary, the Republican leader, said:

"Mr. Rogers has brought happiness, joy and good feeling to the hearts of millions of Americans. In common with all his fellow-citizens, I regret his tragic end and that of his doughty and valiant companion."

Vice President Garner, a friend of long standing, who shared the humorist's dislike of ceremonial attire, could only say, when informed of his death:

"Awful bad! Awful bad!"

Mr. Rogers had boomed Mr. Garner for the Presidency three years ago. He had found the monoplane a complete wreck, partly submerged. The right wing was broken off.

Speaker Byrns, addressing the House, mentioned Mr. Rogers's in-

Continued on Page Four.

10-MINUTE HOP THEIR LAST

Engine Fails on a Take-Off for Final 15 Miles to Point Barrow.

LANDED TO GET BEARINGS

Startled Eskimos See Huge Bird Plunge to River Bank From 50 Feet Above Water.

ONE RUNS 3 HOURS TO TELL

Humorist Revealed as Financing a Trip Around the World With Famous Pilot.

(Copyright, 1935, by The Associated Press.)
POINT BARROW, Alaska, Aug. 16.—Will Rogers, beloved humorist, and Wiley Post, master aviator, were crushed to death last night when a shiny, new airplane motor faltered and became an engine of tragedy near this outpost of civilization.

Both were killed when their red Arctic sky cruiser slipped and fell fifty feet head-on into a river bank. The 550-horse-power motor, driven back into the fuselage, snuffed out the lives of the two men instantly.

A native runner raced to Point Barrow with word of a plane crash. Sergeant Stanley R. Morgan of the Army Signal Corps dashed to the scene to learn the full significance of the tragedy.

First he took the body of Rogers from the cabin. Then he was forced to tear the plane apart to recover that of the flier who had flown around the globe—once alone.

Bodies Are Taken to Barrow.

The bodies were brought here and given to the care of Dr. Henry W. Greist, a Presbyterian medical missionary.

It was a trifling ten-minute flight that ended the careers of two famous figures long accustomed to flying. Although Rogers—gentle master of the "wise crack"—never became a pilot, he was perhaps the world's foremost airplane passenger.

Resuming a happy-go-lucky aerial tour of Alaska, a prelude to a flight to Siberia and on to Moscow, the noted travelers left Fairbanks late yesterday for a 500-mile hop to Point Barrow, northernmost white settlement in America.

Post "sat down" on Harding Lake for a while, but resumed the journey soon.

Apparently uncertain of his bearings, he brought his pontooned plane to the surface of a shallow river fifteen miles southwest of here to ask natives the way to Point Barrow.

Rogers chatted with the Eskimos. Post tinkered with the plane during the brief stop. Soon after 5 P. M. (11 P. M. Eastern daylight time) they took off for the last little hop.

Motor Misfires on Take-Off.

The natives told the story to Sergeant Morgan. They said the motor of Post's new specially built plane misfired soon after it rose. The pilot quickly banked to the right; then the ship plummeted nose first, out of control. It dived into the edge of the stream, where the water was only two feet deep.

When Sergeant Morgan arrived at the scene by launch, he said today, he found the monoplane a complete wreck, partly submerged. The right wing was broken off.

The soldier said Post's watch had stopped at 8:18 P. M., apparently the time of the accident. [The difference in time indicated by the aviator's watch and that reported by the natives probably is accounted for by the time zones through which he had flown.]

The runner arrived here at 10 P. M. with word of the tragedy. Recovering the flier's personal effects, Sergeant Morgan turned to the grim task of identifying the aviators. He made out the bodies as those of Rogers and Post and from Morgan's superior, Colonel George E. Kumpe, at Seattle.

The unrelenting Arctic, grave of other such noted fliers as Carl Ben Eielson and Frank Dorbandt, played a leading part in this new tragedy.

Rogers and Post had made Fairbanks in the face of poor flying conditions. The stop at Harding Lake enabled them to await the

Continued on Page Four.

"All the News That's Fit to Print."

The New York Times.

LATE CITY EDITION
Cloudy, slowly rising temperature today. Tomorrow cloudy, probably followed by rain or snow.
Temperature Yesterday—Max., 31; min., 13.

VOL. LXXXV.....No. 28,486.

Entered as Second-Class Matter,
Postoffice, New York, N. Y.

NEW YORK, TUESDAY, JANUARY 21, 1936.

P

TWO CENTS In New York City. | THREE CENTS Within 200 Miles | FOUR CENTS Elsewhere Except in 7th and 8th Postal Zones.

Copyright, 1936, by The New York Times Company.

KING GEORGE V DIES PEACEFULLY IN SLEEP; PRINCE OF WALES BECOMES EDWARD VIII

BONUS BILL PASSES IN SENATE, 74 TO 16; HOUSE TO CONCUR

BOND PLAN IS TRIUMPHANT

All but 2 Minor Changes Are Beaten in 3-Hour Final Session.

INFLATIONISTS FIGHT HARD

But Neely Move to Pay With Currency and 'Protect' the Taxpayer Loses, 65-23.

14 'ANTIS' SWING OVER

Cost Put at $2,491,000,000 to $2,664,000,000 or More— House Acts Tomorrow.

Special to THE NEW YORK TIMES.

WASHINGTON, Jan. 20.—By a vote of 74 to 16 the Senate today passed after about three hours' further consideration the "baby bond Soldiers' Bonus Bill, whose total cost in outlays soon and eventually is estimated at from $2,491,000,000 to $2,664,000,000.

The measure now goes to the House, where concurrence, in a vote set for Wednesday, is regarded as certain. The vote there is being deferred, Speaker Byrns said, to allow absent members to return in time to go on record on final passage.

The overwhelming Senate support of nearly 5 to 1 for prepayment of the adjusted compensation certificates, due in 1945, was furnished by fifty-six Democrats, fifteen Republicans, one Farmer-Laborites and one Progressive.

Only nine Democrats and seven Republicans were recorded against. Thirteen names had been called without a dissenting vote before Senator Brown answered "no."

Twelve more names were called before the next opposing vote, that of Senator Couzens, the first Republican to say "no."

The following, who voted for the baby bond bill today, had stood against the Patman currency bonus bill May 7:

Ashurst, Bailey, Barkley, Dieterich, Guffey, Harrison, Lonergan, Radcliffe, Robinson and Walsh, Democrats; Austin, Barbour, McNary and White, Republicans.

The following Senators who did not vote on passage of the Patman bill last May voted affirmatively today: Gore, O'Mahoney and Reynolds, Democrats, and Norbeck and Nye, Republicans.

Many Veterans in Gallery.

Veterans packed the galleries today and even the diplomatic section was well filled. Some of the veterans wore overcoats saved in salvage stores since. Some had apparently not shaved for several days. They had but one concern: this vote. They listened intently to the debate, to the voting—and departed jubilant.

High up in one of the public galleries Ray Murphy, National Commander of the American Legion, and James E. Van Zandt, National Commander of the Veterans of Foreign Wars, took their seats soon after the session began.

On the final roll-call they kept pace with the vote on their own tally sheets.

"I am pleased. That is all, and I have nothing more to say," Mr. Murphy said afterward as he was being congratulated on all sides.

The Senate had met at noon and at 3:14 P. M. the vote was over and adjournment was quickly taken. Most observers agreed that practically every member who voted for the bill today would vote to override a veto, should President Roosevelt return the bill after the expected concurrence of the House. That would more than suffice to override.

Instead of paying the cost of the certificates in cash, as provided in

Continued on Page Fourteen.

Not a snowflake in Atlantic City. Bask in the sun at Hotel Traymore.—Advt.

House Votes Bill to Bar Foreign Mail Divorces

Special to THE NEW YORK TIMES.

WASHINGTON, Jan. 20.—A bill designed to restrict "mail order" divorces from Mexico, by closing the mails to all correspondence about them, passed the House and went to the Senate today.

Introduced by Representative Healey, of Massachusetts, the bill provides that every sort of communication designed to give information or to solicit divorce business in a foreign country is not mailable. The bill provides a fine of $5,000 and a maximum prison sentence of five years or both.

There has been much agitation for such a bill owing to the issuance of many fraudulent Mexican divorces.

DR. ROBINSON UNFIT, ALUMNI UNIT FINDS

City College Committee Holds President Lacks Qualities Vital to Leadership.

MINORITY DEFENDS RULE

12-to-4 Report on Long Study of Campus Disorders Is Sent to Graduates.

Dr. Frederick B. Robinson, president of City College, lacks "the human qualities necessary to achieve the widespread confidence of his faculty and his student body and to provide genuinely inspired, resourceful and socially imaginative leadership," in the opinion of a special committee of the Associate Alumni of the college. The committee for more than a year has been studying the factors responsible for the frequency of undergraduate demonstrations at the institution.

Twelve members of the committee signed the report, which was mailed last night to 1,500 members of the association. Four others signed a minority draft, warmly defending the record of the Robinson administration. One committeeman did not vote because of his inability to attend meetings.

The committee was appointed on Dec. 17, 1934, by Dr. Stephen P. Duggan, director of the Institute of International Education and then president of the alumni organization. His action followed adoption at the association's annual meeting of a resolution directing him to appoint a committee to "seek all significant facts concerning present conditions in the City College and the nature of the present relations between the administration and the student body and the staff."

The group was to have reported its findings at a special meeting of the alumni a month later, but the mass of testimony gathered by it in "tapping every disclosed source of authentic information" soon made it apparent that the committee's deliberations must be extended.

Alumni Meeting Called.

A special meeting of the Associate Alumni has been called for next Monday night at the college's Twenty-third Street building by Federal Judge Clarence G. Galston, president of the association. Both the majority and the minority reports will be discussed.

Signers of the majority draft were Dr. Henry Moskowitz, '99, chairman of the committee and executive adviser of the League of New York Theatres; Dr. Paul Abelson, impartial chairman in the arbitration of labor disputes; Dr. Louis I. Dublin, '01, third vice president of the Metropolitan Life Insurance Company; Waldemar Kaempffert, '97, science editor of THE NEW YORK TIMES; Professor Charles V. Morrill, '03, of the medical faculty of Cornell University; Dr. Henry Neumann, '00, leader of the Brooklyn Society for Ethical Culture; Louis Salant, '98, attorney; Jonar J. Shapiro, '18, attorney; Professor Herbert Wechsler, '28, of Columbia

Continued on Page Two.

QUICK AAA REFUND SHARPLY ORDERED BY SUPREME COURT

Mandate Is Swiftly Issued as Government Fights for 200 Millions Held in Escrow.

CONTRARY RULING CITED

President Calls Conference of Congress Leaders and Aides to Seek Way Out.

Special to THE NEW YORK TIMES.

WASHINGTON, Jan. 20.—With sudden swiftness breaking a precedent of years, the Supreme Court today issued mandates making immediately effective its recent decisions declaring the Agricultural Adjustment Act unconstitutional and ordering $200,000,000 of impounded AAA taxes returned to processors.

The impact of the action was immediately felt in administration circles. President Roosevelt summoned a group of Congressional and farm leaders to meet at the White House tomorrow to discuss the situation created by the release of the $200,000,000, and the farm situation in general.

Announcement of the court's mandates came two and a half hours after the justices had left the bench and entered upon a two-week recess to catch up with their work. Court attachés said they could not remember when the justices had acted so quickly except in urgent matters such as murder cases. Usually all orders are handed down from the bench while the court is in session, and it was assumed that this would be the procedure today.

One of the orders tersely refused a government request made earlier in the day for reopening of the Louisiana rice millers' case through which the $200,000,000 was ordered turned back to the processors. It also granted the mandate sought by the rice millers and directed that their own impounded $200,000 taxes be released. The other order directed immediate issuance of a mandate releasing $80,000 in the receivership proceedings of the Hoosac Mills, victors in the AAA case decided on Jan. 6.

President Is Urged to Act.

Court action came even while government officials were studying plans to prevent the sequestered $200,000,000 from being recovered by processors without stern legal fights. In the face of the justices' swift moves, the President's advisers urged him to call tomorrow's conference as the present tentative strategy might have to be materially altered.

At the White House, it is understood, will be Senators Bankhead and Smith, and Representative Jones of Texas, Congressional farm leaders and possibly Senator Robinson, Democratic floor leader and Speaker Byrns. Secretary Wallace and Chester C. Davis of the AAA, M. G. White, solicitor for the Agricultural Department and representatives of the Treasury and Department of Justice are also expected to participate.

Government legal officers said it would be necessary for all processors with taxes impounded as part of the $200,000,000 to make applications in the Federal courts before their money could be released. The money, it was stated, would not be automatically given back without

Continued on Page Nine.

Lieut. Giovannoli Named for Cheney Award; Faced Death in Rescues From Burning Plane

Special to THE NEW YORK TIMES.

WASHINGTON, Jan. 20.—Lieutenant Robert K. Giovannoli of Lexington, Ky., on duty with the Army Air Corps at Dayton, was selected today to receive the Cheney Award for 1935, in recognition of his "extreme bravery" in the rescue of two men from a burning plane at Dayton on Oct. 30.

Lieutenant Giovannoli was born in 1904 in the District of Columbia, is a graduate of the University of Kentucky, and was commissioned in 1930.

"Probably not in the entire history of the Air Corps has a more heroic action been recorded," the War Department said of Lieutenant Giovannoli's act. An experimental bombing airplane crashed at Wright Field, the citation said in part, the wreckage catching fire. Three of the crew were rescued, but Major Ployer P. Hill, pilot, and Leslie Tower, civilian test pilot, were trapped in the all-metal cockpit.

Lieutenant Giovannoli extricated Tower through a window of the compartment through the window. He worked with "seemingly superhuman energy" four or five minutes and cut loose with a pocket knife the pilot's shoe which had become wedged in the wreckage. He then raised the pilot and passed him through the window to waiting hands.

"His own escape from a perilous position in which he suffered serious and painful burns was considered miraculous," the citation said.

Major Hill died several hours later and Mr. Tower several days later.

GREAT BEAR Ginger Ale, Lime Dry and Sparkling Water made with Great Bear Spring Water. Wholesome. BA. 4-0045.—Advt.

NEW KING 41 YEARS OLD

Adopts Name Edward in Signing Notice to London's Mayor.

FACES AN ARDUOUS LIFE

An Ardent Rider and Flier, He Must Settle Down to More Prosaic Tasks.

CORONATION A YEAR AWAY

Period of Court Mourning Will Precede It—Heir to Throne Flew to Sandringham.

By FREDERICK T. BIRCHALL.
Special Cable to THE NEW YORK TIMES.

LONDON, Tuesday, Jan. 21.—Edward VIII, who at the age of 41 became King at the moment of his father's death just before midnight, will be publicly proclaimed as sovereign today.

According to ancient custom, a crier will call out from the steps of the Royal Exchange, "The King is dead, long live the King!" Ceremonial announcements of the same description will be made in every city, town and village in the country.

The new King himself, who is still at Sandringham, may be expected to remain there in such seclusion as can be permitted to him. His great loss came to him last night after a day more strenuous than most of those he has experienced in a life already inured to ceremonial hardships and quick movement.

Visited London Sunday.

King Edward, then the Prince of Wales, was in London Sunday night, having come here in the afternoon to see Prime Minister Stanley Baldwin and to arrange for a special meeting of the Privy Council at Sandringham which, in King George's presence, would appoint a Council of State, now useless and obsolete, to act should the late monarch's illness have continued over a long period.

Edward, with his brother, the Duke of York, flew back to Sandringham yesterday morning and was present when the Privy Council appointed this intended Council of Regency. Thereafter he was close by his father's death chamber until the end came.

His first task was to console his weeping mother, to whom he is deeply attached and whose favorite son he is. But his duties as King brooked no delay. Already they pressed upon him, and within less than an hour of his father's death and his own accession to the throne he had undertaken his first official act as King by sending the following telegram:

Sandringham, 12:28 A. M.
Lord Mayor, London.

I am deeply grieved to inform you that my beloved father, the King, passed away peacefully at 11:55 P. M. tonight.

EDWARD.

In the next few days, until the funeral is over, he will have to take care of the strenuous life of duty awaiting him. He will be consulted upon a thousand matters of procedure. He must preside over

Continued on Page Five.

THE DEAD KING.

THE NEW KING.

MONARCH'S DEATH STIRS WASHINGTON

Roosevelt Cables Condolences —He Is Expected to Appoint Special Envoy for Funeral.

GRIEF IN WORLD CAPITALS

Bitterness Abates in Rome— New Ruler Wins Praise in Berlin—Paris Is Moved.

Special to THE NEW YORK TIMES.

WASHINGTON, Jan. 20.—The death of King George caused deep sorrow and brought many expressions of grief here tonight. Official messages of condolence were sent to London by President Roosevelt and Secretary of State Cordell Hull.

Sir Ronald Lindsay, the British Ambassador, and the Ministers of Legations maintained here by British Dominions were deeply grieved. They refrained, however, from making any statements until they had been officially notified of the death by their governments. Official periods of mourning will be declared by these missions by authority of royal decree. In addition to the British Embassy, these are maintained here by legations of Canada, the Irish Free State and the Union of South Africa.

It is likely that President Roosevelt will designate a Special Ambassador to represent him at the funeral. A decision on this question, however, is being delayed until official information on the funeral arrangements has been received from the United States Embassy in London.

Messages by the President.

The following message was sent by the President to the new King:

It is with deep sorrow that I learn of the death of His Majesty your father. I send to you my profound sympathy and that of the people of the United States, in whose respect and affection he had the privilege of knowing to a high and unique place.

Mr. Roosevelt also sent condolences to the governmental heads of the British Dominions—Australia, Canada, the Irish Free State, New Zealand and the Union of South Africa. The message to Lord Tweedsmuir, Governor General of Canada, was typical. It follows:

Upon the occasion of the death of His Majesty King George, I offer to Your Excel-

Continued on Page Five.

Death Bulletin Posted At Sandringham House

By The Associated Press.

SANDRINGHAM, England, Tuesday, Jan. 21.—The last bulletin posted at "Jubilee Gate" of Sandringham House was done with rural simplicity.

Down the darkened drive a bareheaded youth rode a bicycle with a dim oil lamp flickering in front of him.

In an old brown leather case, which he carried in one hand while the other gripped a handlebar, he brought the announcement of the death of the Sovereign of the world's largest empire.

The chimes of the Sandringham church clock, striking half an hour after midnight, had just died away. Only the moaning of the wind through the elms bordering the drive broke the silence.

The youth, without dismount ing, delivered the case at the lodge gate to one of the King's servants. The bulletin was taken out of the case and slowly, in the light of two great lanterns of the lodge, the gatekeeper walked across the drive and posted it.

LONDON SADDENED BY NEWS OF DEATH

Hushed Crowd at Buckingham Palace Receives Word From Mourning Servant.

END SEEMED ANTICIPATED

Quietness in Piccadilly Circus Long Before Midnight Showed Stress of Nation.

By FERDINAND KUHN Jr.
Special Cable to THE NEW YORK TIMES.

LONDON, Tuesday, Jan. 21.—The hand of death lay upon London last night. It was a stunned and silent crowd of several hundreds that stood outside Buckingham Palace just after midnight when the notice announcing that the King had died was posted on the railing.

Few in the crowd could read what it said, but all knew what it meant. Heads were bared as if by a common signal, and all conversation was hushed to whispers.

One light glowed in a window high up in a corner of the palace. A sentry in gray tramped back and forth along the sidewalk as though nothing had happened.

The crowd stayed long after midnight, apparently unwilling to believe or unable to realize the King had died. Some attraction had drawn those hundreds to the palace, although the King was lying at Sandringham far away. After all, it was his home in his capital and it was to this building that thousands had come to acclaim him on Armistice Day and hundreds of thousands on the sunlit morning of his Jubilee.

Slowly the crowd melted away. By this time newsboys were shouting through the empty streets near by and their black-bordered placards announced that a great reign had ended.

But the palace sentry still marched up and down as he had done all night, apparently unwilling to believe what had happened. One King had died but another was on the throne and Great Britain had not changed at all.

Even before the sad news came the King's capital seemed to anticipate it. The electric signs of Piccadilly Circus flashed their messages as brightly as ever, but all the gayety had gone out of the life of the great city.

Parliament will convene today as by law it must without summons whenever a sovereign dies. Mr. Baldwin has fixed the hour for the session at 6 o'clock in the evening.

The theatres were half empty and the streets were strangely deserted as millions sat at their radios listening for news from Sandringham.

Early in the evening a vaudeville program from a broadcasting studio

Continued on Page Ten.

DEATH IS MOURNED BY WHOLE EMPIRE

Aga Khan Honors the King's Memory in Bombay—Salute Is Fired in Singapore.

Special Cable to THE NEW YORK TIMES.

LONDON, Tuesday, Jan. 21.—Within a few minutes of the King's death almost every corner of the earth had heard the news.

In Bombay, India, the Aga Khan declared that the "King Emperor was not only a great ruler but also a great man." He added:

"I am sure that the new King Emperor will, with his knowledge of the world and the whole empire, be a worthy successor."

Mahatma Gandhi announced from his Bombay sick bed that he had sent "respectful condolences" to the royal family through the Viceroy, the Earl of Willingdon.

In Cape Town most persons were asleep when the news of the King's death was received, but at the Government House high officials waited near telephones.

When Melbourne, Australia, received the news in the middle of the morning public offices were closed. All sports were canceled. Sir Isaacs, performing his last duty as Governor General of the Commonwealth, sent a message of sympathy to the royal family.

Hushed crowds in Wellington,

Continued on Page Five.

FAMILY WITH KING AT END

Queen Breaks Down as Long Vigil Closes at Sandringham.

HOPE HAD RISEN A LITTLE

Ruler, 70, Had Signed Paper Naming Council of State to Act in Illness.

PARLIAMENT MEETS TODAY

Theatres and Stock Exchange to Be Closed and Ships at Sea Will Lower Flags.

Outline of the life and reign of King George V, Pages 5 to 10.

By CHARLES A. SELDEN.
Special Cable to THE NEW YORK TIMES.

LONDON, Tuesday, Jan. 21.—George V, King and Emperor, passed peacefully last night in the twenty-sixth year of his reign and the seventy-first year of his life out of a world in which he had faced manifold much tribulation. His eldest son, as Edward VIII, now reigns in his stead over Great Britain, Ireland and the great British Empire overseas.

The King died five minutes before midnight in his own house of Sandringham in Norfolkshire, where he had spent the happiest hours of his life. His Queen and his children, all except one—Henry, Duke of Gloucester, who a himself ill in London—were at the bedside as the King's life ebbed away.

He suffered no pain, the doctors say. Throughout the last twelve hours his strength slowly failed until he fell asleep.

Canterbury Blesses Him.

Just before the end came the Archbishop of Canterbury, the King's lifelong friend, who had shared this last vigil with the royal family, bent over the dying monarch and gave him a last blessing.

A few moments later life was extinct and the news was being telephoned to Prime Minister Stanley Baldwin by Sir John Simon, Secretary of State for Home Affairs, who in virtue of his office had also remained at Sandringham near the King's chamber, and the news was being flashed also to the whole world.

The official bulletin of the death was as follows:

Death came peacefully to the King at 11:55 o'clock tonight in the presence of Her Majesty the Queen, the Prince of Wales, the Duke of York, the Princess Royal and the Duke and Duchess of Kent.

FREDERIC WILLANS,
STANLEY HEWETT,
DAWSON OF PENN.

From the death chamber there are already coming affecting stories of the last solemn scene. The Queen, who had maintained a constant watch both day and night from the room adjoining the King's bedroom, had at last been persuaded to take some food. Then she joined the others at the bedside. When the end came the iron self-control she had kept through the long, anxious days broke down at last. She turned to her son, the new King, and they exchanged an affectionate embrace. Each looked lovingly at the dead monarch, then with slow steps they turned away and went to another room, where they did their best to console each other.

Ships to Lower Flags.

Immediately on hearing the news from Sandringham the Admiralty Office in London flashed it to all British warships on the seven seas. Today all their flags will fly at halfmast.

Parliament will convene today as by law it must without summons whenever a sovereign dies. Mr. Baldwin has fixed the hour for the session at 6 o'clock in the evening.

In the House of Commons the Speaker will take the chair wearing his black gown and black shoe-

Continued on Page Five.

"All the News That's Fit to Print."

The New York Times.

LATE CITY EDITION
Fair and somewhat warmer today.
Tomorrow rain and warmer.
Temperatures Yesterday—Max. 39; min. 17.

Section 1

Copyright, 1936, by The New York Times Company.

VOL. LXXXV....No. 28,533.

Entered as Second-Class Matter,
Postoffice, New York, N. Y.

NEW YORK, SUNDAY, MARCH 8, 1936.

P

Including Rotogravure Picture,
Magazine and Book Review.

TEN CENTS | TWELVE CENTS Beyond 200 Miles
Except in 7th and 8th Postal Zones.

STRIKE PEACE HOPE REVIVED AS MAYOR OFFERS A NEW PLAN

OWNERS ARE RECEPTIVE

Realty Board Acts Today on Move to Submit to Arbitration.

UNION ASSENT IS HINTED

Resumption of Negotiations Is Held Likely After La Guardia and Strikers Confer.

300 AT TUDOR CITY QUIT

More Park Av. Buildings Also Affected—Closed-Shop Issue No Longer a Factor.

Hope for settlement of the strike of elevator operators and other building service employees was revived last night after another appeal to both sides made by Mayor La Guardia to submit the dispute to arbitration.

The Mayor made his proposal in identical telegrams addressed to the Building Service Employees Union, the strike organization, and the Realty Advisory Board, which has played the rôle of spokesman for large realty interests in the strike. Accompanying the Mayor's proposal was a detailed plan of settlement minus the closed shop.

The fact that the Mayor dispatched his peace plan after he had conferred at City Hall with strike leaders was taken as a clear indication that it was acceptable to the union, which had previously indicated its readiness to abandon the closed-shop demand.

William D. Rawlins, executive secretary of the Realty Advisory Board, declared after receipt of the Mayor's telegram that the peace plan might be looked upon with favor in the form in which it was submitted.

He announced that the directors of the Realty Advisory Board would consider the Mayor's proposal at a meeting this afternoon at the board's offices, 12 East Forty-first Street. The proposal will be analyzed by Walter Gordon Merritt, counsel for the board, after which a reply to the Mayor will be drafted.

New Negotiations Hoped For.

It was hoped last night that today's meeting of the Realty Advisory Board's directors would lead to a resumption of negotiations at City Hall tomorrow morning and to a settlement of the strike.

The Mayor's appeal for peace came after another day in which there were no important strike developments.

Although the union called out some 300 employees in Tudor City, preliminary to extending the walkout in the Grand Central area tomorrow, and appeared to be holding its lines in other parts of the city, there was no marked extension of the strike during the day.

Upon the intervention of the Mayor the union called off the strike in some 170 buildings controlled by the New York State Mortgage Commission after the commission had agreed to abide by any settlement ultimately reached with the realty interests of the city. The commission controls about 140 buildings in Manhattan and thirty in the Bronx.

In making known the dispatch of telegrams to the contending groups, pleading with them to bring the strike to a termination, Mayor La Guardia said:

"I am convinced that the strike can be settled if both sides are willing to do so. Resistance on one side and provocation on the other will get nowhere. Misrepresentations from either side are not helpful. The real issue now is wages and working conditions, and surely arbitration should be accepted by both sides.

"The Mayor will maintain law and order, protect life and property, and that goes for both sides. He will continue his efforts to end this controversy regardless of abuse from either side."

Closed-Shop Demand Eased.

The Mayor's plea was made public after he had conferred again with James J. Bambrick, strike leader, and other union spokesmen. His statement that "the real issue now is wages and working conditions" was taken as another indication that the union was willing

Continued on Page Thirty-seven.

Butler and Shaw Swap Retorts Not 'Courteous'

By The Associated Press.

SAN PEDRO, Calif., March 7.—Nicholas Murray Butler and George Bernard Shaw let go with both barrels of caustic sarcasm today at each other through the medium of interviews.

Said Dr. Butler, president of Columbia University, with regard to the gibes of G. B. S. at the American Constitution and the President:

"Anything George Bernard Shaw may say about politics is too ludicrous to comment upon. This won't surprise Mr. Shaw because it represents an opinion I have had about him for a long time. And he knows it."

Said G. B. S.:

"I suppose if Dr. Butler had an automobile that had been running for thirty years and was still running he would insist that it shouldn't be exchanged for a new motor car. That is the way with your Constitution. Dr. Butler's antiquated automobile wouldn't bring much of a 'trade-in.'

"Anyway I'm 'G. B. S.' and Dr. Butler isn't 'N. M. B.'"

LEHMAN CRIME PLEA POLITICS, SAYS IVES

Speaker Ascribes Attack on Assembly Members to Quest for Re-election Issue.

DEFENDS ALL COLLEAGUES

He Calls on the Governor for 'Appropriate Action' on Dodge and Geoghan.

The text of Mr. Ives's address is printed on Page 38.

Special to The New York Times.

ALBANY, March 7.—Governor Lehman is making a "political football" of his crime program and picking a fight with the Legislature merely to develop an issue on which to run for re-election, Speaker Irving M. Ives of the Assembly asserted tonight in a State-wide radio broadcast.

The Speaker went on the air over WOKO and a chain of stations to reply to the radio attack of two weeks ago in which the Governor charged that "powerful groups of lawyer legislators" were banding together to hamstring his program in the Assembly.

Mr. Ives offered a detailed statement of his position on the crime bills, saying that his attitude was that of many Democrats and Republicans, and demanded that Governor Lehman "take appropriate action" in the cases of District Attorney William C. Dodge of New York and District Attorney William F. X. Geoghan of Kings. He said:

"Two glaring examples of the failure of law enforcement are to be found in New York City. The first is the case of District Attorney William F. X. Geoghan of Brooklyn, who, unable to secure conviction in the notorious Drukman case, was superseded by Special Prosecutor Hiram C. Todd, who obtained these convictions with admirable promptness.

Demands Governor Act.

"The second example is that pertaining to District Attorney William C. Dodge of New York County, who, after having shown himself unable to break up racketeering gangs which for years have been preying upon the public of New York, was finally superseded in this assignment by Attorney Thomas Dewey as special prosecutor. Where Mr. Dodge failed, Mr. Dewey has not failed and instead has obtained a number of convictions.

"Obviously, there must be some laxity of law enforcement somewhere in these cases, and I recommend that the Governor, in view of the facts, take appropriate action."

The Speaker enumerated "certain basic truths that have emerged from the confusion and misunderstanding which this anti-crime controversy has provoked."

He declared that "the intemperate charges directed at the Assembly by the Governor are utterly false and ridiculous."

He asserted that "the Governor sought to claim credit for inaugurating all anti-crime programs offered in this State in the 1935 session of the Legislature, as he

Continued on Page Thirty-eight.

HOOVER DECLARES FREEDOM IN PERIL, LIFE 'MORTGAGED'

He Tells Colorado Republicans We Face Enslaving Taxes, Repudiation or Inflation.

'COMMON MAN' MUST PAY

Future 'Fireside Talks' Will Be With Collector, He Says— Hits 'Planned Economy.'

The text of Mr. Hoover's speech is printed on Page 36.

Special to The New York Times.

COLORADO SPRINGS, March 7.—Crushing taxes, repudiation of debts or inflation are certain sequels to the New Deal, Herbert Hoover declared tonight before the Young Republican League of Colorado in a speech which was broadcast nationally.

The administration's spending and what he regarded as its steps toward dictatorship have failed to solve the problems of the depression or end unemployment, he said. The former President asserted that the youth of the nation faced a choice between the old American system, with its political liberty and equality of economic opportunity, and a "planned economy" involving regimentation and bureaucracy.

The freedom and opportunities of youth "are being mortgaged," Mr. Hoover asserted, adding that "taxation enslaves as well as dictatorship."

More Taxes "Inevitable."

He warned that the nation's "future fireside talks" would be with the tax collector, and some believed that present taxes on wealth, designed to complete the cycle of "shirtsleeves to shirtsleeves in three generations," take the shirt also.

"Do not mistake," he went on. "The new taxes of today are but part of them. More of them are as inevitable as the first of the month. The only alternatives are repudiation or inflation. No matter what nonsense you are told about corporations and the rich paying the bill, there will be two-thirds of it for the common man to pay after the corporations and the rich are sucked dry."

He said, further:

"And where do we get to after all this attempt to supplant the American system? At the time of the election in 1932 the American Federation of Labor reported 11,600,000 unemployed. Today, after three years of the New Deal, they report 11,600,000 unemployed.

"To get these people back to their jobs was the outstanding job of our government. It was because we cure give for all these doings. But the grim fact remains that it has failed in its primary purpose. And $15,000,000,000 will be added to the national debt before the New Deal is over."

The Record on Platform Pledges.

Mr. Hoover contrasted the administration's actions and party platform promises of 1932, and said that when he was President all but two of the thirty-seven Republican platform promises were carried out, despite depression difficulties. Two secondary promises, he said, "broke against the obstinacy of a Democratic Congress."

The trend of events in this country since 1932, he said, followed the pattern of European nations that succumbed to dictatorship, and he added that the New Deal had "imitated the intellectual and vocal technique of typical European revolution."

The great contributions to civili-

Continued on Page Thirty-six.

Rumania's War Council Called to Special Session

By The Associated Press.

BUCHAREST, March 7.—The Rumanian Defense Council tonight was called to a special session Monday, to devise means for improving and rapidly increasing the nation's armaments. The council consists of King Carol, former Premiers and the general staff of the army.

The semi-official newspaper, Dimineata, predicted that the League of Nations would apply economic sanctions against Germany as a result of remilitarizing the Rhineland.

Commenting on Chancellor Adolf Hitler's speech before the Reichstag, the newspaper said, "Germany is laughing today, but France and England will be laughing tomorrow."

PARIS APPEALS TO LEAGUE

Rejects Reich Proposal of a Substitute for Locarno Treaty.

ALLIES SUPPORT PROGRAM

Russia and Czechoslovakia to Aid to 'Limit' in Effort to Clear Rhineland.

BELGIUM ACTS AT BORDER

French Officials Say Military Moves to Drive Back Germans Await Geneva Decisions.

By P. J. PHILIP.
Wireless to The New York Times.

PARIS, March 7.—France has laid Germany's latest treaty violation before the Council of the League of Nations. That is the procedure called for in the situation.

At the same time the French Government today made it quite clear that there could be no negotiation with Germany of any substitute for the Treaty of Locarno or anything else as long as a single German soldier remained in the Rhineland in contravention of Germany's signed undertakings.

While no public mention of French troop movements is being made here, it is obvious that the necessary precautions will be taken, probably on the same scale as last March, when the Reich government denounced the military clauses of the Treaty of Versailles and reorganized her army.

[France ordered all northeastern border fortifications garrisoned at full strength, The Associated Press reports, and Belgium cancelled leaves for troops garrisoning her eastern frontier.]

Withdrawal Held Essential.

What is essential, in the French view, is that the German Government must be compelled, by diplomatic pressure first and by stronger pressure if need be, to withdraw from the Rhineland. For what is found most intolerable in all today's happenings is this new, renewed appearance of the mailed fist in diplomacy—of, in French opinion, in the service of common peace and order, but as a menace and provocation.

Everything that can be done to avoid war will be done. But there should be no mistaking this fact in Germany or elsewhere: that rather than submit to this last crashing piece of Teutonism, France will fight.

Meanwhile, as always, the French have presented their case. The Cabinet met twice today, once in reduced numbers at the Elysee Palace with President Albert Lebrun and later at the Quai d'Orsay. Between the two meetings Foreign Minister Pierre-Etienne Flandin called in the Ambassadors of all signatory powers of the Locarno agreements for consultation and to acquaint them with his Government's views.

General Marie Gustave Gamelin, chief of the General Staff, took part in the Elysée Palace meeting.

The Cabinet will be summoned for tomorrow morning to be kept fully apprised of the situation and to learn the attitude of other governments whose opinions have been sought by French diplomatic representatives.

After the second Cabinet meeting, Mr. Flandin, in the famous clock room at the Quai d'Orsay, read to the biggest assembly of newspaper men there had been there since the days of the Versailles treaty a long declaration setting forth his government's views and decisions. It was a direct indictment of German veracity and an exposure of all treaty infractions involved in today's action.

Invokes Mediation Clause.

One of his most damning declarations was the invocation of that section of the Locarno Pact by which France and Germany agreed that if any difference should arise between them which could not be dealt with by ordinary diplomatic means, they would submit it to conciliation and arbitration. That procedure, it is argued here,

Continued on Page Thirty.

MUSSOLINI ACCEPTS PEACE PARLEY BID

League Invitation Satisfactory in Principle as Basis for Talks, He Tells Cabinet.

ITALY WILL NOT AID PARIS

Imposition of Sanctions Said to Have Freed Nation of Locarno Obligations.

By ARNALDO CORTESI.
Wireless to The New York Times.

ROME, March 7.—At almost the minute when Chancellor Adolf Hitler, in Berlin, was announcing the reoccupation of the Rhineland, Premier Benito Mussolini, in Rome, was informing the Italian Cabinet Council that he had decided to accept "in principle" the invitation of the League of Nations to negotiate peace with Ethiopia.

These two facts, though seemingly unrelated, are likely to have some important repercussions on each other. The turmoil created in Europe by Hitler's move, which has directed attention from East Africa and pushed sanctions into the background, is expected to help Mussolini to drive a hard bargain with the Negus and to settle the Italo-Ethiopian conflict with all possible speed.

Italy, as soon as her best energies are no longer fettered in Africa, will be able to make her weight felt in the European balance of power and participate in the process of readjustment in the next few years.

The text of Mussolini's reply to the League's peace appeal is not yet known and will not be made public until it has arrived at Geneva. Therefore, it is still uncertain whether he has agreed to negotiate or whether he has pledged his acceptance with important reservations.

Newspapers, usually regarded as the government's mouthpieces, are at variance on this point. The Giornale d'Italia thinks, as the invitation of the League contained no limitations, there can be no conditions in Mussolini's reply. The Tribuna on the contrary says that Mussolini's acceptance does not tie him down to anything and implies the widest reservations. It also

Continued on Page Thirty-nine.

Brief Attack of Cold Is Repelled by Sun; Rising Temperatures Forecast for Today

Winter tried to take possession of the city again yesterday, just two weeks before the official arrival of spring. But a bright sun in a clear sky turned Winter back with a jump of 7 degrees in temperature within little more than an hour in the afternoon.

The average temperature for the day was 26, which is seven degrees below the normal. The coldest March 7 in the records of the Weather Bureau was in 1890, when the mercury dropped to 6, and the warmest was in 1921, when it rose to 69.

Since Jan. 1, when the day was 9 hours and 17 minutes long, the length of the day has increased gradually and will be 11 hours and 32 minutes today. On March 18 the vernal equinox will begin with the day and night each 12 hours long. Two days later, on March 20, at 1:58 P. M., Spring will begin.

at noon. At 3 P. M., when the mercury stood at 32, a shift in light winds from the north to the southwest sent it up quickly to a high of 39 at 4:15, after which it fell slightly.

A forecast for continuing rising temperatures and fair skies is expected to bring a moderate day of above-freezing weather today and warmer weather and rain tomorrow.

From midnight Friday until 3 o'clock yesterday afternoon the mercury remained below freezing and brought a renewed touch of Winter to the city. At 8 A. M. the temperature dropped to a low of 17—the coldest since the days of snow and ice on Fifth Avenue and Broadway.

Within the next hour the mercury rose ten degrees and then dropped back for several hours before renewing an upward course.

HITLER SENDS GERMAN TROOPS INTO RHINELAND; OFFERS PARIS 25-YEAR NON-AGGRESSION PACT; FRANCE MANS HER FORTS, BRITAIN STUDIES MOVE

GERMAN ARMY AGAIN ON THE RHINE.
The shaded portion of the map shows the district demilitarized under the Treaty of Versailles. It included all German territory to the west of the Rhine and a zone fifty kilometers wide along the east bank. The stars show where the principal garrisons were established.

GERMANY'S ACTION ASSAILED BY EDEN

He Uses Severe Tone Toward Reich Envoy, but Attitude of Cabinet Is Deemed Milder.

By AUGUR.
Special Cable to The New York Times.

LONDON, March 7.—Foreign Secretary Anthony Eden used strong words to condemn the German Government's action when Ambassador Leopold von Hoesch of Germany presented to him this morning Chancellor Adolf Hitler's memorandum concerning the Rhineland.

Mr. Eden said the British Government must consider the entry of German regular troops into the forbidden zone to be in defiance of treaty obligations and a flagrant breach of a territorial frontier. But to Charles Corbin, the French Ambassador, Mr. Eden said that the government, while determined to comply with treaty obligations, was equally desirous of avoiding hasty action and it advised the French Government to study the points of the German offer, for they appear to be not without value.

Action Had Been Expected.

The fact is that at the bottom of their hearts Cabinet Ministers here are not so displeased with Hitler's proposals as it officially must be said they are. For sometime past the demilitarized zone has been written off as lost. A chance to obtain a solid counter-value for a hopeless item on the balance sheet appears attractive for practical politicians in London.

The real question awaiting reply is whether Hitler offers advantages that upon closer inspection may be found ephemeral once the fact of the illegal military occupation of the Rhineland is accepted without demur.

Officials in Berlin, it is known here, were alarmed when Foreign Minister Pierre-Etienne Flandin of France put a direct question to Mr. Eden concerning British aid in case of an infraction by Ger-

Continued on Page Thirty-three.

ARMY MARCHES IN AS HITLER SPEAKS

In Full War Equipment It Goes to Rhineland, Ending Its Advance Near Frontier.

By OTTO D. TOLISCHUS.
Wireless to The New York Times.

BERLIN, March 7.—Germany today resumed her "watch on the Rhine" when, with an astonishing bravado that dared challenge Europe to war or to peace and left the world breathless for the moment, the new German Army crossed the military frontier, which hitherto had separated it from France, and occupied the demilitarized Rhineland zone created by the Versailles treaty and reaffirmed at Locarno.

The move was carried through with that German efficiency that drew from foreign military experts tribute to the German Army command and amid manifestations of both popular enthusiasm and grave concern among the population.

It brought back echoes of the last German westward march nearly twenty-two years ago, but also it was made to look like a dress rehearsal for more serious business.

Even while Chancellor Adolf Hitler was serving notice of the contemplated move to diplomats of the Locarno powers assembled in the chancellery at 11 A. M. field-gray masses of the troops of occupation were already on the march.

Planes Circle Cologne.

A few minutes before Hitler began to announce this move to the world in his speech before the Reichstag the first military flying squadrons already were circling Cologne's cathedral spires. As he began to talk infantry, artillery, motorized cavalry, tanks, machine-gun units, anti-aircraft artillery and all other paraphernalia of modern warfare already were closing the Rhine bridges, and two hours after he had finished, his advance guards already had reached Saarbruecken, their westernmost point for the present, only three kilometers from the French frontier.

According to an official announcement, troop movements also continue all day tomorrow. Occupation of the zone, which comprises

Continued on Page Thirty-one.

VERSAILLES CURB BROKEN

Hitler Smashes Locarno Citing Franco-Soviet Treaty as Reason.

READY TO REJOIN LEAGUE

Battle for Equality Ended, He Tells Joyous Reichstag— Sets Vote for March 29.

URGES AIR PACT IN WEST

Bilateral Neutralization of Rhine Proposed—Hand Is Extended to Lithuania.

Hitler's Reichstag speech and other texts on Pages 31, 32, 33.

By GUIDO ENDERIS.
Wireless to The New York Times.

BERLIN, March 7.—Germany today cast off the last shackles fastened upon her by the Treaty of Versailles when Adolf Hitler, as commander-in-chief of the Reich defense forces, sent his new battalions into the Rhineland demilitarized zone.

The Chancellor's marching orders were timed to synchronize with Germany's notification to the powers concerned and to a listening Reich that she no longer considered herself bound by the Locarno terms because the fundamental basis and inherent purpose of that pact had been destroyed through the conclusion of the mutual assistance treaty between France and the Soviet Union.

Hitler related to the Reichstag all he had done. After he had proposed a daring peace program he was greeted with a burst of enthusiasm when he announced that with complete sovereignty over all German territory restored, the Reich was prepared not only to return to the League of Nations, but also to cooperate in any system of collective security that gave promise of success.

Sees Struggle Closed.

"After three years of ceaseless battle," Hitler concluded, "I look upon this day as marking the close of the struggle for German equality which was voluntarily negotiated with France and Belgium in 1928 and for which Great Britain and Italy stood sponsors, provoked less jubilation in the Reichstag than did the news that German troops at that very hour were again marching to their peace garrisons in the Rhineland. That news unloosed a cyclone of rejoicing as the 660 Deputies rose to greet it.

But the Chancellor's speech as a whole must be counted an outstanding political pronouncement and oratorical achievement with respect to both its contents and forceful delivery and also the intense sincerity that marked the recital of the reasons that had determined him to abrogate Locarno.

Offers Non-Aggression Pacts.

The speech was easily Hitler's most effective utterance on German foreign policy. While it was not free from recriminations and indictment of France's refusal to grasp Germany's outstretched hand, that hand was once more revealed as offering France and Belgium a twenty-five-year non-aggression pact at the very moment when the roll of German regimental drums was being heard along the Rhine for the first time since 1919.

The proposed non-aggression pact, which Hitler said was open also to the Netherlands, constituted the only part of his seven-point peace scheme that he offered as a substitute for the Locarno accord.

Germany is also prepared, he continued, to negotiate immediately for the creation of a demilitarized

Continued on Page Thirty.

The New York Times.

LATE CITY EDITION
Generally fair and slightly cooler
today. Tomorrow fair and warmer.
Temperatures Yesterday—Max., 77; Min., 62

Copyright, 1936, by The New York Times Company.

VOL. LXXXV.....No. 28,629.   Entered as Second-Class Matter,
Postoffice, New York, N. Y.   NEW YORK, FRIDAY, JUNE 12, 1936.   PP   TWO CENTS   In New York City. | THREE CENTS Within 200 Miles. | FOUR CENTS Elsewhere Except In 7th and 8th Postal Zones.

REPUBLICANS NAME LANDON UNANIMOUSLY; HE ACCEPTS PLATFORM, ADDING OWN IDEAS

SOVIET TO SET UP NEW PARLIAMENT WITH TWO HOUSES

One Chamber to Be Composed of Deputies Elected by Secret Vote of the People.

'SENATE' WILL BE PICKED

It Will Contain Delegates of the Republics—Freedom of Speech Due for All.

PRESS ALSO IS AFFECTED

Liberty of Worship and Equal Rights for Women Among Features of Charter.

By WALTER DURANTY

Wireless to The New York Times.

MOSCOW, June 11.—The proposed new Soviet Constitution, which will be published tomorrow, is strikingly different from the earlier Constitution, which became law July 6, 1923.

The first section in the initial section there is no reference as before to the severance of the world into the camps of socialism and capitalism—no mention of imperialist hostility or of a union of international workers or that "the bourgeoisie of the world have been unable to organize the collaboration of peoples."

Allows Private Farming

Instead, the new first section stresses the success of socialism in the Union of Soviet Socialist Republics, declares the means of production, commerce, finance, the railroads, &c., now belong to the State and outlines the position of collective farms, with the note that their property belongs to them "eternally," but the Constitution allows private farming and private sale of produce on the condition that it be direct and not involve any profit from or exploitation of a third party.

That, in short, is the basic principle of the Soviet State today as expressed by the new Constitution—that no individual or group can profit by the labor of others and that everything that matters is the property of the community, worked for the community's benefit.

The first section concludes with these significant sentences: "The economic life of the U. S. S. R. is directed by the State's economic plan toward increasing the general wealth.

"In the U. S. S. R. there is established the principle of socialism. 'From each according to his capacity, to each according to his work.'"

Here you get the basic principle of Stalinism, or Soviet socialism, at its present stage as compared with the ultimate goal of Marxian communism, the motto of which is, "From each according to his capacity, to each according to his needs." In other words, the Socialist principle of greater rewards for greater service still prevails over the ultimate ideal of Communist equality.

The second change is that instead of seven federated republics in the U. S. S. R. there will henceforth be eleven, the Caucasian Federation being split into three—Georgia, Azerbaijan and Armenia—and Kirghizia and Kazakstan are added. This is only a formal difference for administrative purposes, and the federated republics as before, retain the right to secede from the union at will.

New Parliament Provided

The third change, however, is more important, affecting the whole electoral system. Instead of provincial Soviets being elected by lists on open ballot and then their choosing delegates to the All-Union Soviet Congress, there are now to be secret ballots for individual Deputies on the basis of one Deputy to each 300,000 members of the population.

These Deputies will be elected to what will be equivalent to the House of Representatives in the United States. And instead of these Deputies sitting jointly with the Congress of Nationalities, there will henceforth be two houses with equal powers of action and initiative, in which the House of Nationalities will be chosen by provincial councils in the ratio of ten Deputies from each federated republic, five from each autonomous

Continued on Page Five

Hoover Calls Platform 'Fighting, Progressive'

Former President Herbert Hoover last night called the Republican platform and Governor Landon's specific statements upon it, as read at the Cleveland convention, "fighting and progressive."

Through his secretary Mr. Hoover made public this statement:

"The platform admirably covers the principles and methods I have so repeatedly advocated. The platform is the fighting, definite and progressive statement the country needs.

"When put into force by the American people, these principles will regenerate the country. Governor Landon's statement amply covers any other points that may be in question."

BORAH IS 'STUNNED' BY LANDON'S PLEA

Nominee Should Have Acted 'Sooner,' He Says When Told of Gold, Wage Demands.

SILENT AS TO HIS SUPPORT

Senator Leaves for Washington After Winning Victory on His Platform Goals.

By The Associated Press.

CLEVELAND, June 11.—The Plain-Dealer says Senator Borah appeared "stunned" when informed at Akron tonight that Governor Landon had declared for a gold-backed currency and a constitutional amendment, if necessary, to permit State regulation of wages and hours.

Informed of the nominee's telegram to the Republican convention, Mr. Borah said:

"Well, that's his business. Why didn't he send it sooner?"

The Plain-Dealer says Mr. Borah ran his hands over his face four or five times. Asked if he had any more comment, he said:

"I shall wait until morning and see what they do."

Mr. Borah was on a train en route to Washington, having left Cleveland just a few minutes before the delegates adopted the platform. He had fought to have any mention of the gold standard eliminated from the platform.

Platform Pleases Him

Special to The New York Times.

CLEVELAND, June 11.—Senator Borah expressed himself thus afternoon as well pleased with the platform sent to the national convention by the committee on resolutions.

But the question whether he would support the man whom the convention was to select as party standard bearer remained unanswered when the Idaho Republican left for Washington.

At the final draft of the platform had been completed and become available for examination, it was reported that Senator Borah had examined it and was satisfied with the language of the planks as

Continued on Page Fourteen

'VICTORY' LANDON PLEDGE

He Promises to Wage One of Party's Most Forceful Campaigns.

THANKS HIS TOWNSMEN

With Wife at His Side on the Front Porch He Hails Their Loyalty.

TOPEKA HAILS THE CHOICE

Citizens Decorate City and Parade to Governor's Home When Nomination Is Flashed.

By WARREN MOSCOW

Special to The New York Times.

TOPEKA, Kan., June 11.—With thousands of his neighbors and other citizens of Topeka gathered around the yellow brick Executive Mansion at Eighth and Buchanan Streets, Governor Alfred M. Landon delivered to them tonight a simple message of his appreciation of their loyalty and affection as they gathered to celebrate his nomination as the Republican candidate for President.

Earlier, in a statement issued to the press, he had pledged himself to lead a harmonious party to victory next November.

It was exactly 11:14 o'clock, Central standard time, when the Governor and Mrs. Landon stepped out to meet a deafening roar of applause from the crowd.

The air rang with cheers, torches and flares blazed and band after band blared "Oh, Susanna" as the Governor and Mrs. Landon left the study in which they had spent most of the evening to appear on the front porch.

Thanks His Townsmen

The Landons' neighbors and all Topeka had been preparing to celebrate his actual nomination and had been awaiting only a radio flash from the convention hall in Cleveland apprising them of the fact. The city was decorated with flags and bunting, and paraders formed in line, with all the city's bands and bugle and fife and drum corps ready to blow their heartiest. Finally word of the nomination came and the paraders marched to the Executive Mansion.

Governor Landon, when he stepped forward into the glare of the floodlights arranged around the house, was at ease, though toward the end of his talk he was plainly affected. He wore a gray business suit, with a white shirt and attached soft collar.

Mrs. Landon's mother, and Joe Cross, a cousin of Mrs. Landon, were on the porch swing, while the Governor and Mrs. Landon faced the cheers of the more than 15,000 paraders.

Governor Landon in his greeting said:

"Mrs. Landon and I are deeply touched by this expression of your good will and good wishes. We are proud, too, that so many of our friends from surrounding towns

Continued on Page Thirteen

Roll-Call of the States On Landon's Nomination

Special to The New York Times.

CLEVELAND, June 11.—Following is the vote by States for Governor Landon when roll was called on the nomination for President:

State or Territory.	No. of Deleg.	State or Territory	No. of Deleg.
Alabama	13	New Jersey	32
Arizona	6	New Mexico	6
Arkansas	11	New York	90
California	44	North Carolina	23
Colorado	12	North Dakota	8
Connecticut	19	Ohio	52
Delaware	9	Oklahoma	21
Florida	12	Oregon	10
Georgia	14	Pennsylvania	75
Idaho	8	Rhode Island	8
Illinois	57	South Carolina	10
Indiana	28	South Dakota	11
Iowa	22	Tennessee	17
Kansas	18	Texas	25
Kentucky	22	Utah	8
Louisiana	12	Vermont	9
Maine	11	Virginia	17
Maryland	16	Washington	16
Massachusetts	33	West Virginia	15
Michigan	38	Wisconsin	6
Minnesota	22	Wyoming	6
Mississippi	11	Alaska	3
Missouri	30	Dist. of Columbia	3
Montana	8	Hawaii	3
Nebraska	14	Philippine Islands	2
Nevada	6	Puerto Rico	2
New Hampshire	11	Total	984

West Virginia gave one vote for Borah. Wisconsin gave 18 votes to Borah.

VANDENBERG LOOMS AS RUNNING MATE

Senator Agrees to Reconsider Refusal and Landon Men Believe He Will Accept.

STEIWER SECOND CHOICE

Kansans May Pick Him if Other Plan Fails—Borah Backs Gannett—Knox Boomed.

By CHARLES R. MICHAEL

CLEVELAND, June 11.—The Landon forces have not yet abandoned the hope of persuading Senator Vandenberg to accept the nomination for Vice President, despite reiteration of his announcement of last week that his decision to remain in the Senate was "final."

Although he continued his refusal earlier in the day, the Michigan Senator agreed this evening to confer again with the Landon forces after adjournment tonight. At this time he was expected to determine whether he would bow to the request of Governor Landon.

Confidence was expressed at the Kansan's headquarters that Mr. Vandenberg would be nominated tomorrow.

There is a strong movement in favor of Colonel Knox. His selection, however, is opposed by Colonel Robert R. McCormick, publisher of The Chicago Tribune.

Frank E. Gannett of Rochester, N. Y., a Borah supporter, came into the situation as a compromise candidate. Members of the New York delegation were told that Senator Borah desired his nomination and "would vigorously support

Continued on Page Twelve

THE PLATFORM IS VOTED

Containing 14 Planks, It Is Declared Largely a Liberal Victory.

WORLD COURT IS BARRED

States' Rights Are Stressed— Social Security Would Be on Pay-as-You-Go Basis.

BANS 'SCARCITY' POLICY

Farm Statement Sets Broad Aims on Crops and Credit Help —Trading Act Repeal Urged.

By FELIX BELAIR Jr.

CLEVELAND, June 11.—After laboring for three days and nights to draft a declaration of political principles that would come near to satisfying the expected Presidential candidate and placate potential party bolters, the resolutions committee of the Republican National Convention brought forth tonight a platform on which it hopes the party can carry the national elections in November.

It was a composite of compromises in which the demands of Governor Landon, the assured nominee, were subordinated in several important instances to those of the more conservative Eastern delegations on matters of social and economic progress.

Throughout its preamble and fourteen planks the document used condemned abuses it connected with the present administration.

While it urged continuance of several reforms inaugurated by the Roosevelt administration, such as regulation of security markets for the protection of investors, social security and unemployment relief—with the latter two administered by the States—these were far outnumbered by the departures from present national policy that it proposed.

Main Points of Platform

The outstanding declarations of the platform were:

1. Constitutional and local self-government must be preserved as well as the authority of the Supreme Court as final protector of citizens' rights, and maintenance of our system of free enterprise, private competition and equality of opportunity.

2. Absorption of the unemployment by private industry and agriculture holds the only answer to that problem, and to that end restriction of production should be abolished, and all policies that raise production costs and cost of living discontinued. Legitimate business should be encouraged and the government withdrawn from competition with industry.

3. Responsibility for relief of the needy must be returned to the States, which should receive Federal grants in proportion as the States contribute. This should be combined with a system of public works, such projects to be undertaken only on their merits.

4. The States should enact Old-Age Pension Laws for persons over 65 and the government make contributions to support such systems according as States contribute, but all such programs should be financed on a pay-as-you-go policy, by widely distributed taxation.

5. Labor's right to organize and bargain collectively through representatives of its own choosing without interference must be protected. State laws and interstate compacts should be undertaken to abolish sweatshops and child labor.

6. Scarcity economics should be abolished in agriculture; a national land use program should be pursued for the protection and restoration of land resources; experimental aid to farmers should be developed for production of new crops and promotions of new agricultural uses of non-food crops; farmers protected from foreign importations. Farm credits at rates comparable with those in industry should be fostered together with decentralized nonpartisan control of the farm credit administration. A form of subsidy should be instituted to take care of exportable surpluses

Continued on Page Fourteen

NOMINATED FOR PRESIDENT
Alfred Mossman Landon

© New York Times Studio Photo.

The Text of the Platform

Special to The New York Times.

CLEVELAND, June 11.—Following is the text of the party platform as adopted by the Republican National Convention tonight:

America is in peril. The welfare of American men and women and the future of our youth are at stake. We dedicate ourselves to the preservation of their political liberty, their individual opportunity and their character as free citizens, which today for the first time are threatened by government itself.

For three long years the New Deal administration has dishonored American traditions and flagrantly betrayed the pledges upon which the Democratic party sought and received public support.

The powers of Congress have been usurped by the President.

The integrity and authority of the Supreme Court have been flaunted.

The rights and liberties of American citizens have been violated.

Regulated monopoly has displaced free enterprise.

The New Deal administration constantly seeks to usurp the rights reserved to the State and to the people.

It has insisted on passage of laws contrary to the Constitution.

It has intimidated witnesses and interfered with the right of petition.

It has dishonored our country by repudiating its most sacred obligations.

It has been guilty of frightful waste and extravagance, using public funds for partisan political purposes.

It has promoted investigations to harass and intimidate American citizens, at the same time denying investigations into its own improper expenditures.

It has created a vast multitude of new offices, filled them with its favorites, set up a centralized bureaucracy and sent out swarms of inspectors to harass our people.

It has bred fear and hesitation in commerce and industry, thus discouraging new enterprises, preventing employment and prolonging the depression.

It secretly has made tariff agreements with our foreign competitors, flooding our markets with foreign commodities.

It has coerced and intimidated voters by withholding relief to those opposing its tyrannical policies.

It has destroyed the morale of many of our people and made them dependent upon government.

Appeals to passion and class prejudice have replaced reason and tolerance.

To a free people, these actions are insufferable. This campaign cannot be waged on the traditional differences between the Republican and Democratic parties.

The responsibility of this election transcends all previous political divisions. We invite all Americans, irrespective of party, to join us in defense of American institutions.

CONSTITUTIONAL GOVERNMENT AND FREE ENTERPRISE

We pledge ourselves:

1. To maintain the American system of constitutional and local self-government, and to resist all attempts to impair the authority of the Supreme Court of the United States, the final protector of rights of our citizens against the arbitrary encroachments of the legislative and executive branches of government. There can be no individual liberty without an independent judiciary.

2. To preserve the American system of free enterprise, pri

Continued on Page Fourteen

LANDON SENDS TELEGRAM

To Back Constitutional Amendment if States' Wage Laws Fail.

FOR GOLD AT PROPER TIME

In His Message to Convention He Specifies Exceptions in Accepting the Platform.

BORAH WINS HIS PLANKS

Vandenberg Is Expected to Be Vice Presidential Choice at Final Session Today.

By ARTHUR KROCK

Special to The New York Times.

CLEVELAND, Ohio, June 11.—An unbossed Republican National Convention, yet working like a machine, at 11:41 o'clock tonight unanimously nominated Alfred M. Landon of Kansas for President, adopted unanimously a platform embracing certain social welfare ideas of the New Deal (which otherwise is excoriated) and seated party control in a group of young Kansas politicians and editors who entered the national political field less than two years ago.

At a final session tomorrow Arthur H. Vandenberg of Michigan is expected to accept the Vice Presidential nomination.

Eighteen Borah delegates from Wisconsin and the Senator's campaign manager (Delegate Carl G. Bachmann of West Virginia) voted for Mr. Borah on the first ballot, which prevented a nomination by acclamation under the rules. But Wisconsin then moved to make the nomination unanimous, and it was done.

Hamilton Reads Message

Two dramatic events colored the night session. Before John D. M. Hamilton, the chief of staff of the nominee, presented his name to the convention, he read at Mr. Landon's request a telegram from the Governor "interpreting" three planks of the platform and stating reservations. These planks, relating to currency, civil service and State control of wages and hours, had been revised by the resolutions committee from the text submitted by the Governor as a part of the week-long effort to placate Senator Borah and win his support in the campaign.

Governor Landon "interpreted" a "sound currency" to mean a currency eventually convertible into gold, insisted that the civil service should extend as far as the government's under-secretariat and pledged himself to support a constitutional amendment to permit regulation of wages and hours if the statutory method were not effective. He said "in good conscience" he must make these intentions known in advance.

The other element of drama was when all the other Presidential candidates but Senator Borah, who had already left for Washington, took the platform and seconded the nomination of Mr. Landon. Mr. Borah is only fairly well-pleased with the platform, and he expects to survey Mr. Landon's speeches and the personnel of his campaign cabinet for a couple of months before deciding whether to support the candidacy. Herbert Hoover, the other eminent Republican whose opposition was feared by the Landon group, phoned here today that he was satisfied with the platform.

Senator Vandenberg was among those seconding the nomination. Colonel Knox, L. J. Dickinson, Robert A. Taft and Harry Nice, the other aspirants, followed.

Harmony the Landon Goal

Harmony among all Republicans and the support of anti-New Deal Democrats have all along been stated as the twin goals of the Landon managers, and, except for Mr. Borah, the harmony seems to have been effected.

The end of the session, amid a series of ecstatic demonstrations for Mr. Landon and Mr. Vandenberg, came after a day of anxious concern to the Kansas syndicate which, at midnight last night believed that all its worries were over. Mr. Landon's differences with the resolutions subcommittee, and with Mr. Borah, and the latter's objections to revision of planks he had been asked to swallow, caused the snarl.

But by 7 o'clock tonight, except

Continued on Page Twelve

Gov. Landon's Statement on Platform

Special to The New York Times.

CLEVELAND, June 11.—Governor Landon, while approving most sections of the platform, sent the following message which was read to the convention before he was placed in nomination by John M. Hamilton.

To the delegates of the Republican National Convention:

My name is to be presented for your consideration as a candidate for the nomination for President of the United States. The platform recommended by your committee on resolutions and adopted by the convention has been communicated to me.

I note that according to the terms of the platform, the nomination tendered by this convention carries with it, as a matter of private honor and public good faith, an undertaking by each candidate to be true to the principles and program herein set forth.

If nominated, I unqualifiedly accept the word and spirit of that undertaking.

However, with that candor with you and the country are entitled to expect of me, I feel compelled before you proceed with the consideration of my name to submit my interpretation of certain planks in the platform so that you may be advised as to my views. I could not in conscience do otherwise.

Under the title of Labor the platform commits the Republican party as follows:

"Support the adoption of State laws and interstate compacts to abolish sweatshops and child labor, and to protect women and children with respect to maximum hours, minimum wages, and working conditions. We believe that this can be done within the Constitution as it now stands."

I hope the opinion of the convention is correct that the aims which you have in mind may be attained within the Constitution as it now stands. But, if that opinion should prove to be erroneous, I want you to know that, if nominated and elected, I shall favor a constitutional amendment permitting States to adopt such legislation as may be necessary adequately to protect women and children in the matter of maximum hours, minimum wages and working conditions. This obligation we cannot escape.

The convention advocates "a sound currency to be preserved at all hazards." I agree that "the first requisite to a sound and stable currency is a balanced budget."

The second requisite, as I view it, is a currency expressed in terms of gold and convertible into gold. I recognize, however, that the second requisite must not be made until and unless it can be done without penalizing our democratic economy and without injury to our producers of agricultural products and other raw materials.

The convention pledges the party to the merit system and to its restoration, improvement and extension.

In carrying out this pledge I believe that there should be included within the merit system every position in the administrative service below the rank of assistant secretaries of major departments and agencies, and that this inclusion should cover the entire Postoffice Department.

ALF M. LANDON.

"All the News That's Fit to Print."

The New York Times.

LATE CITY EDITION

Cloudy, possibly showers today, somewhat cooler. Tomorrow cloudy, possibly showers and cooler.

Temperatures Yesterday—Max.: 86; Min.: 63

Copyright, 1936, by The New York Times Company.

VOL. LXXXV.....No. 28,644.

Entered as Second-Class Matter, Postoffice, New York, N. Y.

NEW YORK, SATURDAY, JUNE 27, 1936.

PP

TWO CENTS In New York City.
THREE CENTS Within 200 Miles.
FOUR CENTS Elsewhere Except in 7th and 8th Postal Zones.

ROOSEVELT NOMINATED BY ACCLAMATION; DEMONSTRATIONS FOR HIM AND LEHMAN

RAIL PENSION LAW VOIDED BY COURT; WRIT HALTS TAXES

District of Columbia Court Rules 1935 Act and Its Tax Legislation Unconstitutional.

CITES FINDING ON 1934 LAW

Bailey Holds Supreme Court Decision on This Also Invalidates Substitute Measures.

CARRIERS WIN INJUNCTIONS

Federal Board Plans a Quick Appeal as 1,000,000 Workers Face Loss of the Benefits.

Text of Justice Bailey's decision on rail pensions is on Page 28.

By LOUIS STARK
Special to The New York Times.

WASHINGTON, June 26.—On grounds similar in part to those expounded by the United States Supreme Court majority on May 6, 1935, in invalidating the 1934 Railroad Retirement Act, Justice Jennings Bailey in the District of Columbia Supreme Court today declared unconstitutional the 1935 Railroad Pension Law and its companion tax measure, providing the levying and collection of taxes to finance railway men's pensions.

The Tax Act and the Pension Act itself were "inseparable," the two dovetailing "into one another so as to create a complete system," the court declared in the ruling.

The decision was the second blow delivered to the pension aspirations of a million railway workers in the last fourteen months, the Supreme Court having previously held the first Pension Law invalid as a violation of the due process clause of the Constitution.

The first decision was announced while the Social Security Act was pending, and gave rise to the question whether the taxation feature of the Social Security Act would stand up when attacked in the Supreme Court. Today's decision revived the doubts as to the constitutionality of the Social Security Act.

In today's decision, Justice Bailey stated that on Aug. 29, 1935, Congress had approved two acts, one creating a pension system for railway employees and the other levying an excise tax of 3½ per cent of the payroll, to be paid by the carriers, and a similar tax to be deducted from the employee earning up to $300 a month.

Laws Held Interdependent

"The provisions of the two acts in question are so interrelated and interdependent that each is a necessary part of one entire scheme," the opinion stated. "This is not only apparent from the terms of the acts themselves but is shown by their legislative history. It was clearly the intention of Congress that the pension system created by the Retirement Act should be supported by the taxes levied upon the carriers and their employees."

Holding that the Taxing Act was unconstitutional, Justice Bailey said that it sought to collect revenue, not to provide for the expenses of government, "but solely for a purpose which the United States Supreme Court has held not to be within the domain of the Federal Government."

Whether the twenty-one standard railway unions would attempt to open direct negotiations with the Class I roads, which won a victory by the decision today, in an effort for an agreement on a voluntary pension arrangement, could not be ascertained in advance of early conferences among the unions.

Counsel Will Meet Judge

It was assumed that the decision would be appealed to the Supreme Court, but in the absence of Attorney General Cummings no statement was forthcoming from the Department of Justice.

Counsel for the Railroad Retirement Board and the Federal law officers will meet in Justice Bailey's chambers on Tuesday to draw up the formal court order.

The decision enjoined the Railroad Retirement Board from compelling the railroads to "assemble, compile or furnish any of the information and records required, or which may be required to be furnished under said Retirement Act."

It also enjoined Commissioner of Internal Revenue Guy T. Helvering

Continued on Page Twenty-eight

Warships of Five Nations To Meet in Chilean Fete

Special Cable to The New York Times.

SANTIAGO, Chile, June 26.—Warships of five Latin American nations—Argentina, Brazil, Peru, Ecuador and Chile—will meet in Valparaiso Bay early in September, it was announced today.

They will be present to participate in celebrations marking the 400th anniversary of the founding of the city of Valparaiso.

The meeting is considered an excellent occasion to reawaken cordiality among Latin Americans.

A great display of Chile's air forces is contemplated.

DRUKMAN JURORS DEBATE FOR HOURS

Get Case Accusing Five of Plot in Brooklyn Murder at 2 P. M. and Sit Into the Morning.

POLICE GUARD JURY ROOM

Judge Holds Charges 'of Great Importance' and Menace to the Jury System.

The Brooklyn blue ribbon jury which listened for four weeks to testimony in the Drukman conspiracy trial had not yet agreed, at 3:30 A. M. today, on verdicts for the five defendants charged with plotting to obstruct justice in the Samuel Drukman murder case.

Shortly before midnight the police cleared hundreds of persons out of the building and an army of scrubwomen took possession of the marble floors and corridors. The sodden crowds milled about in the street that were ordinarily the sidewalks are deserted at that hour of the night. Scores of persons coming from the theatres swarmed in taxicabs to get news.

At that time there had been no word from the jury room since the jurors returned from dinner. No persons were allowed above the ground floor of the building, except the uniformed court officers guarding the vicinity of the jury room. Justice Rogers had given no indication whether he would lock up the jury for the night.

Get Case at 2 P. M.

The jury had been deliberating, with time out for dinner, since 2 P. M. yesterday. Supreme Court Justice Erskine C. Rogers, presiding at the extraordinary term of the court, charged the jury for an hour and forty-five minutes in the morning. Then the jurors went out to lunch, and at 2 o'clock began their deliberations.

Shortly before 5 o'clock they sent two communications to the judge, one asking for testimony dealing with certain tapped-wire conversations and for the testimony of witnesses whose stories, partly contradicting each other, dealt with the State's charge that the defendant, William W. Kleinman, had been sent in an automo-

Continued on Page Four

LEHMAN FOR SOCIAL ISSUE

He Denounces 'Callous' Republican Fight on Security Plan.

'GHASTLY' PHILOSOPHY HIT

President's Program Is Held 'Most Humane Measure of Our Lifetime.'

'MIRACLE' UPTURN HAILED

Governor Also Predicts Fresh Business Expansion—He Will Confer With Roosevelt.

Text of Governor Lehman's seconding speech is on Page 7.

By W. A. WARN
Special to The New York Times.

THE MUNICIPAL AUDITORIUM, PHILADELPHIA, June 26.—In one of the most impressive addresses of his public career, Governor Lehman of New York appeared before the Democratic National Convention tonight amid a great ovation to second the nomination of President Roosevelt on behalf of the President's and his own home State. He painted a picture of the reaction which would follow in the event of a Republican election victory this Autumn.

Governor Lehman said that in New York the Republicans in the Legislature had bitterly fought progressive measures, especially the social welfare legislation that had been recommended by himself and his immediate predecessor in the Governorship, now the President.

At no time did Governor Lehman mention former Governor Smith, with whom he has been on terms of warm friendship since he entered public life.

'Callous' Policies Scored

In his arraignment of Republican leaders in New York Governor Lehman described their policies as "cruel," "callous" and "reactionary," and declared that the social philosophy which inspired their action was undoubtedly the guiding star of Republican leaders in the nation.

Mr. Lehman declared that President Roosevelt had supplied leadership which was needed as never before when he took office and had lifted the country out of an abyss of despair and panic as by "a miracle." The Governor predicted that upon the foundation laid by the President there would be witnessed an expanding improvement in business during the present year.

"For the real progress that has been made, for the great economic reconstruction of this country, for the hope and confidence that again lie in the breasts of millions of our people—one man above all others deserves our gratitude—Franklin D. Roosevelt," Governor Lehman said.

Governor Lehman met a charge

Continued on Page Seven

3 Guilty of Fraud, Fourth's Fate in Doubt In Failure of $81,000,000 Title Company

J. Crawford Stevens, president, and Reginald P. Ray, vice president, of the defunct Westchester Title and Trust Company, were found guilty at 12:20 A. M. today on all counts of a twenty-count mail fraud indictment by a Federal jury which had deliberated for more than eight hours.

Philip H. Kuss, also a vice president, was found guilty on twelve of the twenty counts, and the jury failed to reach an agreement on the guilt or innocence of Frederick P. Condit, chairman of the executive committee, who is also a vice president and trustee of the Title Guarantee and Trust Company.

Judge Robert P. Patterson ordered the jury locked up for the night. It will continue its deliberation this morning on Condit.

Stevens and Ray face prison terms up to ninety-seven years and fines totaling $29,000 each, while Kuss is subject to imprisonment for up to fifty-seven years and fine totaling $22,000.

Shortly before midnight Judge Patterson called the jury into the court room and asked whether they had been able to approach a verdict. Foreman Swain, foreman, said that agreement had been reached regarding three of the defendants but that the jury was deadlocked as to the fourth. Judge Patterson then said that he would accept a

partial verdict and the jury retired, to return about twenty minutes later.

Former Mayor John J. Fogarty, of Yonkers, representing Stevens and Kuss, and Monroe Cahn, attorney for Ray, objected strenuously to the court's procedure in accepting an incomplete verdict.

Of the twenty counts in the indictments, nineteen concerned the mailing of sales-promotion literature containing statements which the government charges were misleading. The twentieth charged that mortgage certificates issued by the company were absolutely safe, depression proof and secured by Westchester County homes or improved property and politics.

Judge Patterson pointed out that Mr. Condit was not a salaried officer of the company and was not active in its affairs. The jury's duty, he explained, was to determine only whether he participated in arranging for year-end loans in 19- and 1932 and whether, if he did so, he knew this was done to produce financial statements which might mislead the public.

President Thanks Lehman, Hails Tribute to Him

Special to The New York Times.

MUNICIPAL AUDITORIUM, PHILADELPHIA, June 26.—President Roosevelt tonight sent the following telegram to Governor Lehman:

"I thank you, my old friend, from the bottom of my heart for all you said tonight.

"That wonderful tribute to you came from the hearts of every State, and you rightly deserved it. My love to you both.

"FRANKLIN D. ROOSEVELT."

The both includes Mrs. Lehman.

ROOSEVELT HINTS OF FARLEY DECISION

His Deferring of Reply Till End of Convention Is Construed as Forecasting Cabinet Change.

CLOSER TO PHILADELPHIA

President Keeps Telephone Busy—Acceptance Speech Will Dwell on Platform.

By CHARLES W. HURD
Special to The New York Times.

WASHINGTON, June 26.—President Roosevelt hinted today of early settlement of the question as to how long Postmaster General Farley would remain in the dual position of Cabinet member and chairman of the Democratic National Committee.

In response to a question at a White House press conference whether he was prepared to discuss Mr. Farley's expected resignation, President Roosevelt replied that he could not say anything until after the convention. His remark was construed as at least partial confirmation of reports that Mr. Farley would resign from the Cabinet in the near future.

Mr. Farley has remained in the Cabinet for more than two years since the President issued a dictum last week that Cabinet officers must hold government office, a rule which he enforced with severity except in the case of the party chairmen.

Keen Over Convention

The press conference, the President's last before he will go to Philadelphia tomorrow night to accept renomination, came in the midst of a day divided almost equally between routine work on bills left by Congress and political work, including the polishing of his speech of acceptance.

The President was cheerful over the smooth running of the Philadelphia convention, but marks of fatigue on his face reflected the late and irregular hours he has kept during the week.

For the first time he admitted an active interest in the convention, saying that he had used the telephone at 1:30 this morning. Denying reports that memoranda on the final draft of the platform had been sent to him by airplane for approval, he laughingly asked newspaper correspondents if they did not agree that the telephone was a simpler means of communication.

His early morning call to Philadelphia was made to congratulate Senator Wagner, chairman of the resolutions committee, on his delivery of the platform before the convention. The radio brought it to the White House.

Mr. Roosevelt said that he also tried to reach Marvin H. McIntyre, one of his secretaries sent to Philadelphia as an observer, but was unable to do so at that hour.

Rough Draft Still 'Too Rough'

As for the platform, much of which obviously was substantially written in advance of the convention by, if not by, Mr. Roosevelt, he said that he had only read part of the final text.

What the President wishes to say publicly about the platform will constitute the main portion of his speech tomorrow night.

This speech, a comparatively brief document of about 2,000 words, was almost completed, having been dictated last night by the President, but he said that he probably would make several changes in it because the rough draft, in second reading this morning, appeared to be literally "too rough" in spots.

In further conversation the President said that he intended to stay within the borders of the United States until after election and that there would be no cruises to Hawaii.

Continued on Page Nine

DRAMA IN NIGHT SESSION

One Big Moment Is Held Back When Lehman Speech Is Delayed.

HE GETS TWO OVATIONS

Acclaim in Drafting Movement Rivals That for President as Name Is Ratified.

DOOLING LEADS PARADE

'It Was Swell,' Says Governor, but Gives No Intimation of What Answer Will Be.

By TURNER CATLEDGE
Special to The New York Times.

THE MUNICIPAL AUDITORIUM, PHILADELPHIA, Saturday, June 27.—With two prolonged demonstrations for Governor Herbert H. Lehman and another for President Roosevelt, the Democratic National Convention, at its session which ended nearly an hour after midnight this morning, attempted by a frank show of its enthusiasm to tie together the personalities of these two leaders for the campaign.

When the convention adjourned at 12:55 this morning until 10 A. M. today, it was in the midst of an ovation to President Roosevelt. It was the second given him during the day's two sessions, the other, lasting an hour and four minutes, being when he was placed in nomination in the afternoon.

The first outburst for Governor Lehman rivaled anything seen at this convention. It came when Chairman Robinson announced at about 10 P. M. that the New York Governor would take the rostrum to second the nomination of President Roosevelt.

Culmination of 'Draft' Move

It was the culmination of the "draft Lehman" movement which started even before the convention began and which last night saw every State, Territory and District represented here join in a concerted movement to add what they all considered a "dynamo of strength" to the Democratic ticket next Fall.

The demonstration was started by the New York delegation, led by James J. Dooling, leader of Tammany; Frank V. Kelly, Brooklyn leader; Senator Robert F. Wagner, and Borough President James J. Lyons of the Bronx. Just behind came George Gordon Battle. The New Yorkers were smiling and shouting as they were joined by delegates from other States.

The instant Governor Lehman's name was mentioned by Senator Robinson, permanent chairman of the convention, the delegates, alternates and spectators literally exploded with enthusiasm. They had been waiting impatiently for nearly an hour while the convention was doing the routine work of polling the delegations on the final draft of the platform and then put to him by airplane for approval.

Lehman Stops the Outburst

As Mr. Lehman raised his voice, however, the demonstration quickly subsided. The demonstration lasted eleven minutes and might have gone on for an hour had it not been halted.

What the President wishes to say publicly about the platform will constitute the main portion of his speech tomorrow night.

Mr. Lehman, as he stood before the late demonstration, started to proceed with the seconding speeches and was ready to present Mrs. Emma Guffey Miller to speak for Pennsylvania, but the New Yorkers kept parading, and she stood politely and to all outward appearances behaving like perfectly normal average citizens.

A second later the entire scene had changed from a relatively dignified assemblage of patriots to one resembling what might take place in the psychopathic ward of a great

Continued on Page Nine

RENOMINATED FOR PRESIDENT
Franklin Delano Roosevelt,
from a photograph for which he posed at the White House last Saturday.

© Photo by New York Times Studio.

OUTBURSTS ALARM PROF. CEREBELLUM

Psychiatrist Diagnoses Campaignomania Which Affects Delegates at Times.

By F. RAYMOND DANIELL
Special to The New York Times.

THE MUNICIPAL AUDITORIUM, PHILADELPHIA, June 26.—Campaignomania, an occupational disease common to politicians at recurrent intervals, notably in Presidential years, broke out on the floor of the Democratic convention today and spread rapidly until a large proportion of the visitors in the balconies was infected.

Isolated cases of the malady have been noted among the delegates since they began assembling here early this week. But the outbreak did not reach epidemic proportions until this afternoon, when the magic name of Franklin Delano Roosevelt fell from the lips of John E. Mack from the cluster of microphones before him.

The symptoms were recognized and the diagnosis made by Professor Cerebrus Cerebellum, a noted psychiatrist from Brownsville, Brown County, Ind., close friend of those other Brown countians, Godfrey Gloom and Abe Martin, who once remarked that a "lot of people believe in Providence who never heard of Rhode Island."

As the professor explained it, campaignomania is a disease characterized by more or less violent manifestations of short duration. There is no immunization against it, he said, and the more dignified statesmen are especially susceptible to its ravages at convention time.

Case History Is Revealing

In the interest of science, the professor suggested that a detailed and objective study of the apparent aberrations of reflexes of the patients be made and published for the benefit of students of psychiatry and politics. Therefore the following:

1:23 P. M. when Mr. Mack mentioned the name of Mr. Roosevelt, the delegates and guests were slumped in their seats, listening politely and to all outward appearances behaving like perfectly normal average citizens.

A second later the entire scene had changed from a relatively dignified assemblage of patriots to one resembling what might take place in the psychopathic ward of a great

Continued on Page Eight

GARNER ON SCENE, MET WITH ACCLAIM

Vice President Passes Through Cheering Crowds From Station to His Hotel.

By CHARLES R. MICHAEL
Special to The New York Times.

PHILADELPHIA, June 26.—Jovial Jack Garner, Vice President, arrived here at 7 o'clock tonight to participate with President Roosevelt in the notification ceremonies tomorrow night. Escorted by 175 mounted policemen from the Thirtieth Street station, he was cheered by the crowds, whose attention was attracted by shrieking sirens as he and the reception committee proceeded to his hotel. He acknowledged the acclaim from the sidewalks by standing up in his car.

At the hotel the Texas delegates, massed in the street under their Lone Star banner, gave him a rousing welcome.

Mr. Garner was met at the station by a committee composed of Attorney General Cummings, Postmaster General Farley, Senators Robinson and Connally and Governor and Mrs. Earle. As he left his car he turned to the captain commanding the police escort and said:

"I have never seen a better lot of officers than you have here. You remind me of the Texas Rangers and your presence makes it home-like."

Is Guest at Reception

The Vice President attended a reception given in his honor by the Texas delegation and later participated briefly in the dinner of the Young Democrats. He did not make a speech and tarried only long enough to greet them. He told them as he left that the future of the country and the Democratic party depended upon their efforts.

Mr. Garner spent the evening in his hotel chatting with old friends. Many came to visit him. He will not make any public appearance until tomorrow, when he is scheduled to accept renomination for the Vice Presidency before President Roosevelt makes his acceptance speech.

Since becoming Vice President, Mr. Garner has refrained from discussing public questions. He remained true to that policy tonight and declined to comment upon the political outlook.

ENTHUSIASM RUNS HIGH

Eight Hours of Oratory Precede Acclamation in Early Morning.

CHEER PRESIDENT AN HOUR

Delegates in Ecstatic Climax When Name Is Presented to Convention by Mack.

LEHMAN TOPS SECONDERS

Received So Enthusiastically as to Leave No Doubt of Desire That He Run Again.

Text of former Justice Mack's nominating speech is on Page 6.

By ARTHUR KROCK
Special to The New York Times.

THE MUNICIPAL AUDITORIUM, PHILADELPHIA, Saturday, June 27.—After more than eight hours of eulogistic oratory and demonstrations, which kept the Democratic National Convention in session from 1 P. M. yesterday until 12:55 o'clock this morning, Franklin Delano Roosevelt was nominated for re-election by acclamation. Vice President Garner will be similarly honored this afternoon.

Fifty-seven speeches were made by the orators in the seconding talkathon, representing every State, territory, possession and the District of Columbia. They included twelve Governors, eight Senators, one Senator-elect, eight women, a Cabinet officer and the Governor General of the Philippine Islands. Senator McAdoo, when called to the chair, also spoke in favor of the nomination but was not strictly a seconding speaker.

On motion of Governor Berry of South Dakota the rules were suspended and the roll-call was dispensed with, the nomination coming at 12:42 A. M.

Final, Noisy Celebration

Senator Robinson's announcement from the platform that the President had been chosen by acclamation—thus "beating Cleveland"—loosed another and the final demonstration of the all-day, all-night session. It was just like the rest and was still in progress when the chairman heard, put and declared passed a motion to recess until 10 o'clock this morning—an action unknown to nearly all the shouting, parading, horn-tooting demonstrators.

Rarely has the flow of harmonious oratory been equaled in a national political gathering as a few conservatives joined a long parade of New Dealers in extolling the President. Going a step beyond the Republican convention at Cleveland two weeks ago, the Philadelphia delegates cast not a single vote against Mr. Roosevelt. A score of Wisconsin and West Virginia kept Governor Alf M. Landon from enjoying the same distinction.

Much more exciting than the actual nomination was a series of tumultuous uprisings to honor Governor Herbert H. Lehman of New York, who made the chief seconding speech at 10 o'clock last night. The effort was in part arranged to convince Mr. Lehman that he must stand for re-election. At the same time a great deal of it was spontaneous and sincere. When Mr. Lehman was finally permitted to leave the platform he received a telegram from the President at Washington. Though beset with importunities, he declined to admit any change in his intention to retire.

Stresses Roosevelt's Record

The Governor stressed the President's bent and record in behalf of social welfare, and, by his scathing attack upon the Republican leadership at Albany, intimated what the chief campaign issue in that State will be if the Democrats can make it so.

When the President's name was formally proposed by John E. Mack of Poughkeepsie, a demonstration of more than an hour's duration interrupted the proceedings. Whatever the feelings of many Democrats who will go along this year for a number of reasons, and some of whom excused themselves on grounds frowned upon from prominent participation in the oratory of the day, there is no doubt that these expressed the feeling of the overwhelming majority of the delegates.

Although a fair percentage of the

Continued on Page Eight

"All the News That's Fit to Print."

The New York Times.

FINAL EXTRA
Rain and much colder today. To-morrow fair, with little change in temperature.
Temperature Yesterday—Max., 73; Min., 65

Copyright, 1936, by The New York Times Company.

VOL. LXXXVI.....No. 28,774.

Entered as Second-Class Matter, Postoffice, New York, N. Y.

NEW YORK, WEDNESDAY, NOVEMBER 4, 1936.

TWO CENTS In New York City. | THREE CENTS Within 200 Miles. | FOUR CENTS Elsewhere Except In 7th and 8th Postal Zones.

ROOSEVELT SWEEPS THE NATION; HIS ELECTORAL VOTE EXCEEDS 500; LEHMAN WINS; CHARTER ADOPTED

FEW HOUSE SHIFTS

Democrats May Add to Vast Majorities in Both Chambers

THREE SENATORS TRAIL

Barbour, Hastings and Metcalf Appear to Have Lost Seats.

90 HOUSE RACES IN DOUBT

Democrats Elect 254, While Republicans Obtain 84, and Progressives 6.

By TURNER CATLEDGE

Republican hopes of making heavy inroads upon the huge Democratic majorities in Congress were apparently smothered under the pro-Roosevelt landslide in yesterday's election.

As the size of the New Deal avalanche continued to grow into the early morning hours the Democrats gave promise of actually increasing their lop-sided majority in the Senate and more than offsetting Republican gains of new House seats by capturing places now held by anti-New Dealers. If the trend of the count persists in the tardy tabulations today the Democrats may hold their own or actually add to their majorities in both branches of Congress.

In the wreckage left by the Democratic sweep also appeared the Senatorial careers of three outstanding Republican Senators—Barbour of New Jersey, Hastings of Delaware and Metcalf of Rhode Island. As the count from their respective States stood early today, these three incumbents appeared defeated.

Moreover, the Democrats threatened to pick up still another Republican Senate seat, that formerly occupied by the late Senator Cousens, and they were pressing hard upon Senator Lester J. Dickinson of Iowa, whose opposition to the administration's farm relief program won for him the enmity of many farmers in his State.

Lodge Leading Curley

The only present Democratic Senate seat which appeared definitely lost to the Democrats was that held by Senator Marcus Coolidge of Massachusetts. Henry Cabot Lodge 2d, Republican, was well ahead of Governor James M. Curley for this post, despite the State's substantial majority for the remainder of the Democratic national and State ticket.

Still another Democratic berth was threatened. Senator W. J. Bulow, Democrat, was trailing Chandler Gurney, Republican, by a slight margin in South Dakota.

The veteran Senator Norris, who left the Republican fold to stand for re-election as an Independent in Nebraska, was leading over former Representative Robert G. Simmons, Republican, and Terry Carpenter, "regular" Democrat.

Representative Ernest Lundeen, Farmer-Laborite candidate, was piling up a commanding lead over former Governor Theodore Christianson, Republican, in Minnesota.

Senator Borah, Republican dean of the Senate, was doing the same to his opponent, Governor C. Ben Ross, Democrat.

As the Senate count stood early today, the Democrats appeared to have elected twenty of the thirty-six Senators who were up for election this year and the Republicans six, while ten were still in doubt. On this showing the Democrats would have a membership of at least sixty-seven Democrats in the new Congress, the Republicans seventeen, Farmer-Laborites one, and Progressives one. The Democrats stood a good chance to pick up still others out of the ten in

Continued on Page Three

Landon Congratulates President, Who Replies

Special to THE NEW YORK TIMES.

TOPEKA, Wednesday, Nov. 4.—Governor Landon conceded his defeat in a message of congratulation to President Roosevelt at 1:30 o'clock this morning, Eastern standard time.

His message read as follows:

"The nation has spoken. Every American will accept the verdict and work for the common cause of the good of our country. That is the spirit of democracy. You have my sincere congratulations."

"ALF M. LANDON."

Governor Landon decided to send the message after he had retired for the night at the Executive Mansion, with the word that no statement would be issued during the night.

Special to THE NEW YORK TIMES.

HYDE PARK, N. Y., Wednesday, Nov. 4.—Half an hour after receiving Governor Landon's message President Roosevelt sent the following reply:

"I am grateful to you for your generous telegram and I am confident that all of us Americans will now pull together for the common good. I send you every good wish."

UNION PARTY VOTE FAR BELOW BOASTS

Coughlin Group Appears to Have Exercised Little Influence on the Electorate.

SUPPORT OF LEMKE WEAK

Even in Ohio and South Dakota His Showing in the Early Returns Is Poor.

By F. RAYMOND DANIELL

Representative William Lemke, the Presidential candidate of the so-called "lunatic fringe," made scarcely a dent in the great totals the nation piled up for President Roosevelt and Alfred M. Landon in yesterday's voting.

Showing his greatest strength in Illinois, Pennsylvania and Massachusetts, the North Dakota Representative, who had the backing of the Rev. Charles E. Coughlin, Dr. Francis E. Townsend and the Rev. Gerald L. K. Smith, still remained a negligible factor in the outcome of the election.

Despite confident predictions by the Union party's backers last August that Mr. Lemke would take enough votes from Mr. Roosevelt to deprive him of a majority in the Electoral College, thus throwing the election into the House of Representatives, nowhere did he poll a substantial enough vote to hurt either major party candidate.

In his home State of North Dakota the co-author of the Frazier-Lemke bill was trailing far behind the President and his Republican opponent. The first seventy-eight precincts reporting gave Mr. Lemke only 1,280 to Mr. Roosevelt's 11,644 and Mr. Landon's 5,332.

Here in New York, Father Coughlin's candidate for the House of Representatives in the Sixteenth Assembly District was running against former State Senator John A. Hastings, an intimate friend of former Mayor James J. Walker. His opponent was Representative John J. O'Connor, who incurred Father Coughlin's wrath by threatening to kick the priest out of Royal Oak from the Capitol to the White House. Mr. O'Connor seemed an easy winner in the Sixteenth.

Two reasons were advanced to explain the failure of Mr. Lemke to make a better showing. The first was that Father Coughlin, the Rev. Mr. Smith and Dr. Townsend were inflationists when it came to estimating the size of their following, which each placed in the neighborhood of 6,000,000 voters. The second was that the men and women who cheered so loudly at the Cleveland convention of the National Union for Social Justice and the Old Age Revolving Pensions Ltd., became Republicans and Democrats again after returning home.

The early vote for Representative William Lemke, even in States where Father Coughlin's National Union for Social Justice boasts a

Continued on Page Five

BIG CHARTER VOTE

8-Hour System for Firemen Also Wins Easily

VOTING CHANGE APPROVED

Brunner Is Victor Over Morris by Large Plurality.

ROOSEVELT SWEEP HERE

President's Vote and Margin, Which Reached 1,356,458, Set Highest City Record.

By RUSSELL B. PORTER

President Roosevelt piled up the largest vote and plurality ever accorded to a candidate for any office in the history of New York City at yesterday's election.

With all the city's 3,799 election districts in, the President had the extraordinary plurality of 1,356,458, which was considerably larger even than his campaign managers had estimated.

This was about 50 per cent larger than his 1932 plurality and about three times former Governor Alfred E. Smith's city plurality when he ran against Herbert Hoover in 1928.

The total Presidential vote was 2,747,240, or over 500,000 more than the total vote cast in the 1932 Presidential election and the 1933 Mayoralty election, the previous records.

Governor Lehman ran behind the President, but had a plurality of 921,938 with no election districts missing. He ran about 2 to 1 ahead of William F. Bleakley, his Republican opponent, while President Roosevelt's ratio was 3 to 1 over Governor Landon. Governor Lehman's plurality was not as large as in 1932, when it was 989,844, but was larger than two years ago, when it was 803,956.

Brunner an Easy Winner

In the day's only election for city office, William F. Brunner, Democrat, had a final plurality of 881,880 over Newbold Morris, Republican, in the contest for President of the Board of Aldermen, with no election districts missing.

The voters approved all three local questions on which referenda were taken. They accepted the new city charter by 927,396 to 583,044, an affirmative majority of 344,354, with 689 election districts missing.

With 78 election districts missing, they voted 898,389 for and 551,914

Continued on Page Four

Smith Plans Comment On the Election Today

Alfred E. Smith, former Democratic candidate for President who espoused the cause of Alfred M. Landon in this campaign said last night that he probably would issue a statement today setting forth his views on President Roosevelt's sweeping victory.

Earlier in the evening he had called THE NEW YORK TIMES to ask how the election was going. He was informed that President Roosevelt was leading in all but a handful of States. He made no comment but when he was asked if he were going to a party of Jeffersonian Democrats in the apartment of Raoul Desvernine, Liberty League lawyer, to which he had been invited, he replied:

"No, I'm going to bed."

P. S.—The former Governor did not retire at once. He called up an hour later to get the latest returns.

DEMOCRATS RETAIN STATE SENATE LEAD

They Are Assured of 30 Seats of the 51, One More Than Their Previous Number.

FAIL TO WIN ASSEMBLY

Republicans Are Beaten for Five Places, but Still Hold a Bare Working Majority.

By W. A. WARN

The Democrats will control the State Senate by a substantial majority and the Republicans will have a bare working majority in the Assembly, according to complete returns from the legislative elections.

The latest returns give the Democrats thirty seats out of fifty-one in the Senate, a net gain of one over their present quota. The Republicans suffered a loss of five seats in the Assembly, but still retain seventy-six seats, which gives them the constitutional majority necessary to pass bills and prevail on important parliamentary motions.

The result in not a few of the districts, however, on the face of the latest returns was so close that in some instances a demand may be made by the losers for recount proceedings.

This city will lose its only Republican Senator in the defeat of Senator Joseph C. Baldwin 3d in the Seventeenth Senatorial District, situated in Manhattan. Leon A. Fischel, Democrat, carried the district by a plurality somewhat below 5,000.

The Democratic solidarity of Albany County in its legislative representation surprisingly was broken. A Republican candidate for Assembly, John McBain, nominated in

Continued on Page Five

LEHMAN VOTE CUT

Bleakley Gets a Surprising Total in the City

SWEEP HELPS GOVERNOR

Roosevelt Strong in Industrial Cities—Gets Big Up-State Poll.

OTHER DEMOCRATS SAFE

Bray, Tremaine, Bennett and Others of State Ticket Regarded Certain of Victory.

By JAMES A. HAGERTY

Governor Herbert H. Lehman was re-elected Governor of New York yesterday for a third term. The indicated plurality for the Governor over former Supreme Court Justice William F. Bleakley, his Republican opponent, was about 600,000.

Governor Lehman, who was urged to become a candidate for re-election to help President Roosevelt, ran far behind the President in New York City. With all the election districts reported, his plurality in New York City over 921,938 as compared with the city plurality of 1,356,458, or more than the million and a quarter predicted by Postmaster General Farley, for President Roosevelt. President Roosevelt's plurality in the State was indicated at about 1,150,000.

The tremendous vote for President Roosevelt in New York City and the failure of Governor Landon to carry up-State by much more than 200,000 indicated that the defection of former Governor Alfred E. Smith and other Jeffersonian Democrats had little effect on the Presidential vote, although there apparently were influences within the Democratic party working against Governor Lehman in New York City.

The tremendous vote for President Roosevelt swept to victory the other State-wide Democratic candidates for re-election, Lieut. Gov. M. William Bray, Controller Morris S. Tremaine, Attorney General John J. Bennett Jr., and Mrs. Caroline O'Day and Matthew J. Merritt, Representatives at Large.

Incomplete returns also indicated the election of Harlan W. Rippey, Democratic candidate for Associate Judge of the Court of Appeals over Supreme Court Justice James P. Hill, Republican candidate.

City Margin Is Unprecedented

President Roosevelt carried New York City by the unprecedented plurality of 1,356,458, the total vote being 2,016,204 for the President and 659,746 for Governor Landon. This was more than 50,000 in excess of the results forecast in the surveys made by the five Democratic county leaders, which they believed should be scaled down 10 per cent to give the probable results. Governor Lehman's New York City plurality increased with the late returns, and he did not run as far behind the President as the early returns had indicated he would do.

With all election districts reported, the vote for Governor in New

Continued on Page Five

©New York Times Studio Photo.

FRANKLIN D. ROOSEVELT

DEMOCRATS SWEEP ALL PENNSYLVANIA

President Wins by More Than 550,000 in First National Party Victory in 70 Years.

PHILADELPHIA IS CARRIED

Whole State Government and the Legislature Go to Democratic Control.

Special to THE NEW YORK TIMES.

PHILADELPHIA, Wednesday, Nov. 4—Pennsylvania, the Keystone State of Republicanism, has swept yesterday by the Democrats for the first time in a Presidential election since the Civil War era.

With unprecedented Democratic pluralities in Philadelphia and Allegheny Counties, with greatly diminished Republican pluralities in the commuting counties about Philadelphia, and with even the rural districts only half heartedly Republican, President Roosevelt carried the State by a margin which exceeded 550,000 votes.

Returns from 6,733 of the State's 8,010 divisions gave:
Roosevelt, 2,010,343.
Landon, 1,469,679.
Lemke, 44,253.

Complete returns from the 1,291 divisions in this city gave:
Roosevelt 521,941.
Landon, 322,229.

This city plurality of 199,712 exceeds that for Herbert Hoover in 1932 for the whole State by 40,000.

Democrats Get Legislature

George H. Earle in 1934 seized the Governorship for the Democrats for the first time in forty-four years. Since assuming office he has been at odds constantly with a Republican-controlled State Senate, which has succeeded in balking many of his plans for putting a "little New Deal" in effect in Pennsylvania.

As a result of yesterday's election

Continued on Page Three

JERSEY'S 16 VOTES SAFE FOR NEW DEAL

Upsets in Republican Areas Add to Huge Pluralities in Democratic Counties.

SMATHERS SEEMS WINNER

Senate Aspirant Runs Behind Roosevelt but Has Lead Over Barbour, Incumbent.

New Jersey's sixteen electoral votes seemed at 5 o'clock this morning in possession of President Roosevelt. Reports from 1,719 of the State's 3,581 election districts gave him 493,071 votes to 295,794 for Governor Landon.

Hudson County, the great Democratic stronghold run by the State leader, Mayor Frank Hague of Jersey City, was responsible for this tremendous lead in what had been a doubtful State until the count began. It seemed quite likely that, although Mr. Landon made gains in other areas, he never could overcome the Hudson County handicap, particularly since several normally powerful Republican communities deserted Landon for Roosevelt.

Keeping pace with the Democratic territories, but dropping behind him in many Republican sections which the President dominated, was Senator William H. Smathers, Democrat, had in 1,656 districts a total of 404,546 for United States Senator.

His Republican opponent, W. Warren Barbour, the incumbent, was gathering many hundreds here and there, outside Hudson County, having a total in the same districts of 297,000. Though this seemed a difficult lead to overcome, Mr. Barbour was quite confident that the great number of unreported districts would offset the Democratic advantage and pull him through for another stay in Washington.

Even Mayor Hague's prediction of 125,000 plurality in Hudson County for Roosevelt was so far surpassed as to give him a happy surprise. In 840 districts out of 924 in that county, the President received 264,—

Continued on Page Eleven

POLL SETS RECORD

Roosevelt Electoral Vote of 519 Seen as a Minimum

NO SWING TO THE BOLTERS

'Jeffersonian Democrats' Fail to Cause Rift as Expected.

NEIGHBORS HAIL PRESIDENT

Landon Concedes Defeat and Sends His Congratulations to Victorious Rival.

By ARTHUR KROCK

Accepting the President as the issue, nearly eight million more voters than ever before had gone to the polls in the United States—about 45,000,000 persons—yesterday gave to Franklin Delano Roosevelt the most overwhelming testimonial of approval ever received by a national candidate in the history of the nation.

Except for the small corner of New England occupied by Maine, Vermont and New Hampshire—which was oscillating between Republican and Democratic in the early morning hours of Wednesday—the President was the choice of a vast preponderance of the voters in all parts of the country, and with him were re-elected as Vice President John N. Garner of Texas and an almost untouched Democratic majority in the House of Representatives. The Democratic national ticket will have a minimum of 519 electoral votes and a possible popular majority of ten millions.

The Democratic candidates for President and Vice President, Governor Alfred M. Landon of Kansas and Colonel Frank Knox of Illinois, are the worst-beaten aspirants for these offices in the political annals of the United States, with the exception of William H. Taft in 1912, when Colonel Theodore Roosevelt led a formidable revolt in the Republican party and Mr. Taft carried only Vermont and Utah. Yesterday Utah was also in the President's campaign bag. He had carried forty-five States as contrasted with the forty-two he won from Herbert Hoover in 1932. And to assure his reputation as the greatest vote-getter in the annals of the United States he—a Democrat—had overwhelmingly swept Pennsylvania, unfailingly Republican for generations in national elections.

The following table contains a list of the States carried by the President, with a total of 519 electoral votes, to which the vote of New Hampshire may yet be added:

Landon Sends Congratulations

After hours of hopeful waiting on the Northeast States, Mr. Landon and the Republican national chairman, John D. M. Hamilton, announced their intentions of letting the night pass before agreeing to the fact of the stupendous party defeat. Even Mayor Hague's prediction of 125,000 plurality in Hudson County for Roosevelt was so far surpassed. All the important newspapers supporting the Republican ticket (about 90 per cent of the metropolitan and country

Continued on Page Three

Roosevelt, Speaking to Victory Procession At Hyde Park, Predicted Record Sweep

By CHARLES W. HURD

Special to THE NEW YORK TIMES.

HYDE PARK, Nov. 3—With wire returns indicating a landslide for President Roosevelt far in excess of the majority necessary to re-elect him, President Roosevelt said tonight that he thought the "sweep" might carry every section of the United States.

Speaking to several hundred loyal followers who made a victory procession through rain from Hyde Park to Mr. Roosevelt's home, Hyde Park House, at 10:30 P. M., he said:

"The returns are not all in yet, so I can't say anything official or final, but it looks as though we are going to have one of the largest sweeps ever heard of in the United States."

"As a matter of fact, from the returns now, it looks as though this sweep has carried every single section of the country," he exclaimed.

The President, laughing and happy, spoke while standing on the open porch of his house, looking out over a crowd whose faces were illuminated by red-fire torches and the calcium flares used for light for motion pictures.

He waved aside sound microphones, saying: "This is just a home party."

The crowd cheered the President, Mrs. Roosevelt, and his mother, Mrs. Sara Delano Roosevelt.

The assemblage cheered loudly when Mr. Roosevelt said one of his happiest moments came with the word that he had carried the village of Hyde Park, although he lost the township.

The crowd remained for half an hour, with some enthusiastic persons shouting "How about 1940?"

Mr. Roosevelt leaned on the arm of his son, Franklin Jr. Beside him were his wife and mother. Grouped behind him was a small party including his daughter, Mrs. Anna Boettiger, and Mr. Boettiger, her son-in-law, and other relatives.

Others in the party included Secretary and Mrs. Morgenthau, Frederick A. Delano and members of the White House staff and newspaper correspondents.

"All the News That's Fit to Print."

The New York Times.

LATE CITY EDITION
Cloudy, mild, with occasional rain today; clearing, colder tonight. Tomorrow colder.
Temperatures Yesterday—Max., 53; Min., 38

Copyright, 1936, by The New York Times Company.

VOL. LXXXVI....No. 28,811.   Entered as Second-Class Matter, Postoffice, New York, N. Y.   NEW YORK, FRIDAY, DECEMBER 11, 1936.   P   TWO CENTS In New York City. | THREE CENTS Within 200 Miles. | FOUR CENTS Elsewhere Except in 7th and 8th Postal Zones.

EDWARD VIII RENOUNCES BRITISH CROWN; YORK WILL SUCCEED HIM AS GEORGE VI; PARLIAMENT IS SPEEDING ABDICATION ACT

CODE FOR INDUSTRY VOTED HERE TO BACK AIMS OF NEW DEAL

Association of Manufacturers Pledges Cooperation for 'Era of Good Feeling.'

ASKS FOR CENSUS OF IDLE

Moley Urges Business Join in Federal Planning—McCarl for Industrial Board.

LABOR GIVES 30-HOUR PLAN

Industrial Progress Council in Washington Hears Program for a Shorter Week.

Industry and New Deal

The National Manufacturers Association meeting here adopted a code for industry pledging "era of good feeling" and cooperation with social aims of New Deal. The text of the code is on Page 30.

The Council for Industrial Progress in Washington heard labor's plan to promote employment by a thirty-hour week and Federal regulation of working conditions. Employers did not oppose new labor laws, but spokesmen insisted that they should conform to the Constitution. Page 33.

Code Is Adopted Here

A declaration of principles for American industry, calling for an era of good feeling both at home and abroad, pledging cooperation with the government in the national interest and embracing, at least in principle, some of the most important social reforms of the New Deal, was adopted yesterday afternoon at the final session of the forty-first annual convention of the National Association of Manufacturers, held in the Waldorf-Astoria Hotel.

The declaration was in harmony with the keynote speech delivered at Wednesday's session by Colby M. Chester, chairman of the General Foods Corporation and president of the association, and in striking contrast to the bitter criticisms of the New Deal uttered by industrialists at previous meetings.

In closing the convention Mr. Chester asserted his belief that it had "written a new, sound and progressive note in the industrial life of this nation in the declaration of principles," and predicted that it would have the support of "a united industry" within the year.

Census of Idle Is Urged

Resolutions were adopted urging a government census of unemployed and opposing governmental ownership of the railroads or any transportation systems.

Addresses were made by Raymond Moley, editor of the magazine Today; John R. McCarl, former Controller General; George H. Mead, president of the Mead Corporation and chairman of the business advisory council to the Department of Commerce, and James A. Emery, general counsel of the association.

Mr. Moley urged joint economic planning by the government and business. He warned industry that it must recognize the meaning of the election returns—that the people voted for security of wages and living standards—and offer them a rational plan to attain these ends if it does not wish to be compelled to submit to impractical and drastic legislation.

A balanced budget through the reduction of relief expenditures and other government spending was advocated by Mr. McCarl. He urged industry to accept the responsibility for reducing the need for relief by giving more jobs. He also suggested that business organize a National Industrial Board to cooperate with the government in the "collective" solution of social and economic problems.

According to Mr. Mead, business wants "constructive regulation," contrary to a general public impression, although it is opposed to "government ownership or control." Business also believes in economic security, he said, adding that a "practical" economic security and a

Continued on Page Thirty-one

4,336,000,000 Francs Set As French Budget Deficit

Wireless to THE NEW YORK TIMES.

PARIS, Dec. 10.—There will be a deficit of 4,336,000,000 francs in the French budget during the coming year, according to figures put before the Chamber of Deputies this morning by the finance commission.

The ordinary expenditure under the budget is estimated at slightly more than 48,000,000,000 francs and the income at 43,685,000,000 francs. With these figures before them, the Deputies began to vote in rapid succession for most of the 140 articles in the law having to do with the collection of revenue despite the protest of one Right Deputy who argued that to vote revenues before expenditures was contrary to all good sense and logic.

JAPAN WITHDRAWS DEMANDS ON CHINA

Indicates Dropping of Moves for Anti-Red Cooperation and Autonomy of North China.

ARMY IS UNDER CRITICISM

Foreign Office Wants Public to Know the Military Interfere With Major Policies.

By HUGH BYAS
Wireless to THE NEW YORK TIMES.

TOKYO, Dec. 10.—Withdrawal of all the Japanese demands regarding North China autonomy and of that for cooperation against communism was implied in a statement issued to the press today by Eiji Amau, Foreign Office spokesman.

Japan asks Nanking to fulfill the agreements already reached on lesser points, but the request is not accompanied by a threat or warning except that if Japanese lives or property are endangered or Japanese rights violated the government will take "adequate measures."

Ambassador Shigeru Kawagoe's failure to obtain satisfaction from China, even in minor matters, is explained as due to Chinese indignation over the invasion of Suiyuan Province by Mongols and Manchukuoans.

Mr. Amau said nothing to connect the Japanese Kwantung Army with these events, but the public was already aware that Manchukuo's Premier had proclaimed sympathy with the Mongolian rising and knew he would not have taken such a step without being prompted.

Mr. Amau's statement, read in conjunction with Foreign Minister Hachiro Arita's answer to the Privy Council yesterday, suggested that the Foreign Office wants the public to know how the Kwantung army interferes with major policies on which all branches of the Tokyo government have agreed.

The statement claims that a definite agreement was reached with China regarding suppression of anti-Japanese movements—including revision of the control of the press and of Kuomintang (Nationalist party) branches—engagement of Japanese advisers, control of Korean exiles and reduction of tariffs.

Consulate Involved

China further agreed to reopening of the Chengtu Japanese Consulate and accepted most of Japan's demands for settlement of recent incidents.

A hitch occurred over air services. No agreement was reached regarding joint defense against communism though both sides concurred on several items.

Economic cooperation in North China was agreed on in principle. This stage having been reached, the Chinese, "taking advantage of the Suiyuan affair," broke off negotiations, threatened to repudiate all the concessions already made and evaded Ambassador Kawagoe's repeated requests for a further interview with Foreign Minister Chang Chun. Mr. Kawagoe was said to have handed Mr. Chang a note embodying the agreed points, requesting that they be put into effect.

"Japan is now watchfully waiting for China's response and is prepared to take adequate measures if China fails to control anti-Japanese movements or if Japanese life and property interests are jeopardized," said the statement.

It is pertinent to note that Mr.

Continued on Page Twelve

CROWDS IN LONDON CALM

News Is Received With British Reserve as Thousands Gather.

QUEEN MARY IS CHEERED

Many Break Through Police Lines When She Calls at Home of Duke of York.

TENSION OF WEEK ENDED

People Sad at Losing Edward but Relieved the Suspense at Last Is Over.

Wireless to THE NEW YORK TIMES.

LONDON, Dec. 10.—As the news of King Edward's abdication sped to the far corners of the empire this afternoon Britain received confirmation of her worst fear with mixed emotions, sadness at losing so popular and beloved a sovereign and relief that the gnawing suspense of the last week at last had drawn to an end.

Massed thousands stood silently outside the towering iron gates of Parliament while the terse, restrained statement of the first monarch in England's history ever to renounce the throne voluntarily was read to the House of Commons. Presently, as the twilight shadows of Westminster Abbey lengthened over Parliament Square, word sped from mouth to mouth that the reign of Edward was coming to an end.

Although the atmosphere a few minutes before had been highly charged with tension and anxiety the news was received calmly and with typical British reserve. There was no demonstration and no show of feeling save for the serious, strained faces in the crowd and the flutter of women's handkerchiefs here and there.

Crowds Gather Throughout Day

Throughout the day, from dawn until after midnight, crowds of varying proportions gathered outside all the historic buildings associated with the historic happenings of the day. People clustered about No. 10 Downing Street, the Houses of Parliament and all the royal residences, standing stolidly and silently when allowed or moving along without protest if required. If any emotion was perceptible that could be described as a corporate reaction, it was one of bewilderment and incredulity that such a thing ever could actually happen.

A throng composed mostly of women, which at times reached 10,000 or more, stood on the pavement before Buckingham Palace forming

Continued on Page Twenty

Edward Plans Radio Talk To British Empire Tonight

Special Cable to THE NEW YORK TIMES.

LONDON, Dec. 10.—King Edward will broadcast to the empire tomorrow night at 10 o'clock, immediately after he has signed the Abdication Act and ceased to be King, in the character of a private person. It is expected Parliament will have disposed of its business by then.

[American networks will broadcast the message at 5 P. M., Eastern Standard Time.]

The British Broadcasting Corporation has arranged for a worldwide hook-up.

Many persons feel the King's decision to broadcast is not wise. He has already sent a message to Parliament with a penciled note to the Prime Minister, commending the Duke of York to the support of the whole empire. These will be broadcast four times tonight and printed in every British newspaper.

MRS. SIMPSON CRIES LISTENING AT RADIO

Shaken and Exhausted by the Climax in Career of King Who Forsook Throne for Her.

WILL REMAIN AT CANNES

Edward Will Not Visit Her Now —Britons in France Question Her Course.

Wireless to THE NEW YORK TIMES.

CANNES, France, Dec. 10.—With tears streaming down her face, Mrs. Wallis Warfield Simpson, for whose sake Edward VIII has abdicated as King and Emperor of the greatest empire the world has ever known, listened today as did all the rest of the world to the news over the radio from the scene in the British Parliament.

She heard the words announcing that the King Emperor of whom so much had been expected had laid down his scepter and crown so as to be free to marry her some months hence and live the life of an ordinary mortal.

Says King Won't Go to Riviera

At 1 o'clock this afternoon the following statement was made by Herman L. Rogers, at whose villa Mrs. Simpson is staying:

"There is definitely no change so far as Mrs. Simpson's plans are concerned. She will stay here until after Christmas. She is now at the villa and is in the best of health. There has been no change in the household.

"It cannot be stated if she has

Continued on Page Twenty

BALDWIN TELLS OF EVENTS

Relates to the Commons How He Warned King Against Marriage.

DENIES ANY BITTERNESS

Says Ruler, Far From Feeling Resentment, Had Become a Firmer Friend to Him.

LEGAL ISSUE IS REFUTED

Churchill Declares It Is Now Clear That There Was Never a Constitutional Crisis.

By CHARLES A. SELDEN
Special Cable to THE NEW YORK TIMES.

LONDON, Dec. 10.—The momentous session of Parliament that received today King Edward's message of abdication was best described by Prime Minister Stanley Baldwin himself when he said near the close of his narrative of the crisis:

"This House of Commons today is a theatre which is being watched by the whole world."

Never since the first British Parliament was called by Simon de Montfort 672 years ago had it been the theatre for such an impressive tragedy as that enacted today.

There have been greater political issues, perhaps, and more fateful struggles between Crown and Commons. There have been long Parliaments, short Parliaments and rump Parliaments. But there has been no precedent for today's enactment of the tragedy in which a monarch signed away his sovereignty over an empire of 500,000,000 people for the love of a woman.

And while the play was on, the wars of one hemisphere and the efforts in the other hemisphere to end wars were merely side shows.

Extra Police on Hand

Standing room only was the situation in the legislative chamber on which there was not even standing room left in the acres of lobbies and for many blocks outside on the streets that lead to the Houses of Parliament.

So many extra companies of police were assigned to duty around the buildings that it was feared serious disorder was anticipated by the authorities, but nothing could have been further from the fact. There was as much decorum in witnessing the self-effacement of Edward VIII as there was last January when the multitudes gathered to mourn for his father and to proclaim him.

Needless to say, the House itself was filled as it had not been since the session at which war was declared in 1914. In the diplomatic gallery, every seat was taken by Ambassadors and Ministers from nearly all nations.

What little daylight sometimes seeps into the Commons chamber on a Winter afternoon was completely shut out by a dense fog, so there was nothing but mellow illumination from the lights above the stained glass ceiling.

House Is Ill at Ease

The House was ill at ease during the hour's interval prior to the great moment when Prime Minister Baldwin entered with the King's message of abdication. The familiar cry, "Prayers are over," after the customary, brief devotional exercise with which every session opens, was followed by many involuntary, at least unusual, "Amens," suggestive of a devout wish that for this once they might be answered quickly.

There was no "King's men" in this House. But it was equally true there were no anti-King men.

Popular Reign Indicated

The King's own message was received with sorrow and sympathy. When Mr. Baldwin made his long statement of the events that preceded the decision to abandon the throne, there vanished the last trace of the bitterness that had developed in the last week from fear that the Crown might try to override the Commons.

"We are not judges," said Mr. Baldwin, and it was one of his utterances to which members gave their warmest assent.

"While there is not a soul among us who will not regret this from the bottom of his heart," said the

Continued on Page Eighteen

SUCCESSOR TO THE BRITISH THRONE
The Duke of York

Associated Press Photo.

YORK GETS OVATION AT HOME IN LONDON

Cheering and Singing Theatre Crowds Surge About His Car While Auto Horns Salute.

HE DOFFS HAT TO THRONG

New Monarch Expected to Use Name 'George' as Symbol of Strength and Steadiness.

Special Cable to THE NEW YORK TIMES.

LONDON, Dec. 10.—Thousands of Londoners shouted a welcome tonight to a shy and awkward young man who was ready to step into the dazzling light of the greatest throne on earth.

With the abdication of King Edward VIII, the 41-year-old Duke of York was about to take his place as the latest in the long line of English sovereigns. And tonight, in front of his town house at 145 Piccadilly, the crowds had their first chance to show him that they were glad.

A surging throng of theatre-goers on the way home surrounded his car as he returned after having dinner with Edward at Fort Belvedere. Cheering and waving hats, they filled the wide roadway in front of the house and blocked traffic so completely police were powerless to keep it moving.

Before the Duke entered the house he turned to the crowd and raised his hat several times. That was the signal for a great demonstration. Hundreds of motorists set up a deafening salute with their horns, while the crowd began singing the national anthem and "For He's a Jolly Good Fellow."

Popular Reign Indicated

It was a demonstration of some importance in the story of the British throne, for it showed that the Duke may be a popular King even without any of the brilliant qualities of his elder brother.

Tomorrow night he will become King, and Saturday morning his accession will be proclaimed with the stately pageantry that has come down unchanged from medieval times. For individual kings may come and go, but the British monarchy that has survived many shocks before this will keep its place as the keystone of the vast and loosely jointed empire.

Heralds in uniforms of gold will

Continued on Page Sixteen

EDWARD CHEERFUL AFTER TAKING STEP

Reported Like Man Who Has Had Crushing Load of Worry Lifted From Shoulders.

PACKS FOR HIS DEPARTURE

Knowledge That He Will Not Be Barred From Returning to England Relieves Him.

By FERDINAND KUHN Jr.
Wireless to THE NEW YORK TIMES.

LONDON, Dec. 10.—The blue and white flag of the Duchy of Cornwall fluttered slowly to the foot of its mast at 10 o'clock this morning on the high turret over Fort Belvedere.

It was a signal that made history, for at that moment King Edward was renouncing the greatest throne on earth so that he could marry the woman he loved. With the three brothers as his only witnesses, he signed the instrument of abdication as his "final and irrevocable decision" to retire into private life.

He will remain King until tomorrow afternoon, when the Abdication Bill is expected to reach him from Parliament. As soon as he signs it, however, his unhappy days as King will come to an end after the short reign in 453 years. The Duke of York will come to the throne as George VI and Edward will leave England as the first man in all the 1,000 years of the British monarchy to have left the throne of his own accord.

Edward Again Cheerful

Although he has not shown himself to the public for almost a week, it was reported on good authority tonight that he was like a man who had had a crushing load of worry lifted from his shoulders. The depression and jumpiness of the last few days had vanished and the King was said to be cheerful and purposeful, superintending the packing of his belongings, dealing with State papers, which arrived incessantly from London, and looking forward to more happiness than he has known in a long time.

Workmen and tractors were busy all day on Edward's private flying field at Smith's Lawn in Windsor Great Park, apparently preparing it for the take-off of an airplane. Four police cars were on duty and a cordon of police were

Continued on Page Sixteen

KING MAKES HIS DECISION

Chooses Woman Over Throne After 'Long and Anxious' Thought.

FINALE LIKELY TOMORROW

New Reign, Expected to Bring Back Calm of George V's, Is to Be Proclaimed Then.

CROWNING PLAN MAY HOLD

Edward Can Use Either of Two Titles, Earl of Rothesay or Baron of Renfrew.

Edward's letter, the Abdication Bill, Baldwin's speech, Page 17.

By FREDERICK T. BIRCHALL
Special Cable to THE NEW YORK TIMES.

LONDON, Dec. 10.—Some time Saturday morning, perhaps as soon as tomorrow night, Edward VIII will cease to be a King and Emperor. He has made his choice between a woman and a throne and the woman has won.

Today at Fort Belvedere, his country home near Windsor Castle, and in the presence of his three brothers, the Dukes of York, Gloucester and Kent, the King signed a message to his Ministers announcing his determination "after long and anxious consideration" to renounce the throne to which he had succeeded on the death of his father. The message, is "my final and irrevocable decision."

The message was carried by Prime Minister Stanley Baldwin this afternoon to a crowded session of the House of Commons and there read, not without emotion, by the Speaker.

Bill Introduced in House

There is no question of whether the House should accept it. Under the British Constitution there can be none, for it was an expression of the King's will and the King rules, though he does not govern, Britain and the empire. So immediately afterward, as soon as the Prime Minister in a speech that will be memorable for the restrained feeling it expressed and the leaders of the Opposition each after his fashion had voiced their regret, a bill was introduced that will implement the monarch's decision.

Tomorrow this formal bill of abdication will be pushed through all its stages in both houses, Commons and Lords. It will then be carried to the King for his royal assent. The moment he signs it, he ceases to be King and his brother, the Duke of York, who is nearest to him, will reign in his stead.

The new King will take the throne, according to the best information available tonight, as George VI and for that choice there is a reason. It is desired, now that this storm is over and the skies are clearing, to get back to the ordered peace and quiet stability of the monarchy under the last King George, to leave behind that brief era of conflict between will and duty and to concentrate anew on the empire and its common destiny.

Proclamation Likely Tomorrow

Another era will begin probably at noon on Saturday when the accession of the new King is proclaimed from the balcony of St. James's Palace, again at old gray Charing Cross and finally from the steps of the Royal Exchange in the City of London, each time with all the pomp and ceremony that the monarchy has upheld here throughout a thousand years. Kings may change but the old order remaineth; that is to be Britain's watchword still.

And thus, in circumstances that will arouse wonder and pity as long as history continues to be written, ends the brief reign of King Edward VIII. That has lasted ten months and twenty-two days before this strange storm that love of woman created has burst to a close, and the empire still endures. Even a monarchal

Continued on Page Sixteen

Soviet Orders Militia Punished for Arrests Without Warrants in Spite of New Charter

Special Cable to THE NEW YORK TIMES.

MOSCOW, Dec. 10.—The first charges of violating the new Constitution were brought at Kazan today in connection with the arrests of eleven persons there by the militia on its own initiative.

According to the new Constitution, "no one may be subjected to arrest except upon the decision of a court or with the sanction of the prosecutor." Apparently no such authorization was obtained, and Moscow authorities have called the Kazan militia's action an "outrageous violation" of the Constitution and ordered that the guilty be suitably punished.

According to an investigation in Kazan, a doorman at a restaurant was arrested this week purely on suspicion. When he failed to arrive home his father made inquiries, and on finding his son in jail complained to the public prosecutor. The latter showed little interest. A correspondent of the Moscow newspaper Izvestia then took up the matter and spurred the prosecutor to visit the jail, where he found eleven persons arrested without warrants.

Today also the first Soviet death sentence for the infringement of private ownership and personal property and the murder of a private individual was imposed in a Moscow court.

Because of the new legal guarantees many more lawyers than hitherto will be needed. Accordingly steps are being taken to enroll thousands more students in the law schools already established, and plans are being formed for the creation of many more schools in the various republics.

shop had been selling valuable old books to two highly paid ballet dancers. Thus the employes had learned their clients had money and valuables. They invaded the young dancers' home in their absence, killed their mother and cook with a brass pestle and looted the apartment. The criminals were traced, arrested, convicted and tonight they will be shot.

Hitherto the death penalty has been imposed in murder cases only where the safety or welfare of the State was involved, the normal penalty for an ordinary murder being not more than ten years.

Nikolai V. Krylenko has assumed his duties as head of the All-Union Commissariat for Justice, newly created under the Constitution. Today he began reorganizing the whole legal profession of the country into voluntary associations, which will give legal aid to any accused persons demanding their services. Any accused person is entitled to free legal counsel if he desires. Legal aid offices are also being established by trade unions.

Continued on Page Twelve

"All the News That's Fit to Print."

The New York Times.

LATE CITY EDITION
Fair today, little change in temperature. Tomorrow cloudy and warmer, followed by rain.
Temperature Yesterday—Max., 37; Min., 27

Copyright, 1937, by The New York Times Company.

VOL. LXXXVI.....No. 28,868.

Entered as Second-Class Matter, Postoffice, New York, N. Y.

NEW YORK, SATURDAY, FEBRUARY 6, 1937.

TWO CENTS In New York City. | THREE CENTS Within 200 Miles. | FOUR CENTS Elsewhere Except in 7th and 8th Postal Zones.

PROGRESS IS MADE IN MOTORS PARLEY; EVICTION DEFERRED

WORKING ON TERMS

Subcommittee Begins Study of Specific Issues in Strike

WILL REPORT THIS MORNING

Pressure From Roosevelt Is Credited With Averting Complete Collapse

MURPHY BLOCKS OUSTERS

Halts Arrest of Union Men After Court Issues Eviction Writs at Flint

Developments in Auto Strike

DETROIT — President Roosevelt's pleas avert a new deadlock in the auto crisis conferences. After all-day sessions a subcommittee is named and begins a study of specific issues pending a new joint meeting today.—Page 1.

FLINT—Judge Gadola signs writs for arrest of union leaders and sit-down strikers, but Sheriff, after asking aid of troops, delays action.—Page 2.

NEW YORK—Federal Council of Churches of Christ in America condemns sit-down strikers as a "dangerous weapon." It also assails General Motors for its speed-up program.—Page 2.

Negotiations Go On
By LOUIS STARK

Special to THE NEW YORK TIMES.

DETROIT, Feb. 5.—John L. Lewis, chairman of the Committee for Industrial Organization, and William S. Knudsen, vice president of General Motors Corporation, comprising a subcommittee designated at today's joint conference of spokesmen for both sides in the automobile strike dispute, sat down tonight with Governor Frank Murphy to formulate a report to go before the full committee to-morrow.

The subcommittee was named today after President Roosevelt's repeated telephonic intervention had saved the deadlocked automobile conference from collapsing. When the second session of the conference closed at 8 o'clock this evening Governor Murphy announced that progress had been made.

While the Governor divulged no details of the conference session today, it was learned that Mr. Lewis had made an important concession toward meeting General Motors spokesmen part way. He agreed to drop his demand that the union be the sole bargaining agency in all the sixty-nine plants of the corporation and to limit this demand to twenty plants where union men are on strike.

Company Reported Wavering

The corporation committee, it was reported, appeared tentatively to be willing to grant sole bargaining rights to the union in six plants on certain conditions, but made no definite commitment that could be regarded by the union as unqualified acceptance of its position in these six plants. Actual and positive agreement on this point awaited further clarification at the hands of the subcommittee tonight.

In announcing progress tonight Governor Murphy, flushed and beaming, warned against over optimism. He indicated that as yet there was no absolute assurance that whatever progress has been made would broaden out until a complete settlement had been written.

Nevertheless, Mr. Murphy's announcement that a sub-committee had been appointed to meet tonight to explore the various subjects in dispute, presumably collective bargaining, wages, hours and creation of machinery for the settlement of disputes, gave rise to hope in many quarters that a settlement might be in sight.

The full joint conference of three on each side will convene again at 10 o'clock tomorrow morning to hear the reports being prepared tonight by the sub-committees.

Frances Murphy Plea

Governor Murphy pressed home to both sides today the admonition of President Roosevelt that the nation looked to them to settle their dispute in a manner betokening public-spirited citizens in a civilized community, and without the indus-

Continued on Page Two

Great-Grandmother, 72, Joins Picket Line in Flint

By The Associated Press.

FLINT, Mich., Feb. 5.—A 72-year-old great-grandmother joined union pickets today in front of Fisher Body Plant No. 1, held by sit-down strikers.

She was Mrs. Rebecca Goddard of Clio, Mich., who said she had nine or ten relatives, including a son, inside the plant.

"I just came down from Clio to show some of my neighbors," she said. "There are a lot of sit-down grouches up there. You don't know what sit - down grouches are? Why, they're people who don't believe in the union."

She was asked if it was true she was a great-grandmother.

"Certainly," she replied. "I have six children, twenty grandchildren and about ten great-grandchildren. My youngest son, Robert, is in that plant right now."

She said she also had some grandchildren and nephews in the plant.

FRIARS FACE TRIAL AS SPANISH REBELS

'People's Court' Will Assemble Monday for Case Against 60 Escorial Guardians

1,500 OTHERS ARE INDICTED

Speedy Hearings Are Planned for Prisoners Who Fill the Jails in Madrid

By The Associated Press.

MADRID, Feb. 5.—A special "people's court" will sit in judgment on the Augustinian friars who dwelt in the Escorial monastery built by King Philip II nearly 400 years ago, the government announced today.

The monks are charged with holding "anti-government tendencies" in the civil war. So far the government has kept possession of Escorial, northwest of Madrid, despite encirclement and siege by insurgent armies.

There are perhaps 60 of the friars, and there are nearly 1,500 more persons who are similarly indicted by the Leftist régime in Spain.

Trials Begin Monday

The friars will be tried by a court made up of a judge and two "representatives of the people." The court's session will begin Monday, and it has been instructed to conclude the trial within twenty days.

Simultaneously, Wenceslao Carrillo, Director General of Public Safety, announced he would immediately begin to examine the cases of all prisoners in Madrid's teeming jails with a view to liberating those against whom there is insufficient evidence of Rebel activity. The others will be rushed to trial.

The Augustinian friars were custodians of the edifice which housed the tombs of the Spanish Kings since Philip II had it built to commemorate a victory over the French in 1557. He intended it as a retreat from Madrid's court gayety.

When the military uprising plunged Spain into civil war the large Escorial monastery was converted into a temporary prison for 500 Summer residents of the town. On their release a wing of the vast, rectangular structure was converted into barracks. The treasures the monks had guarded were stored in other parts of the building.

Constant improvements on the building, even in modern times, gave Spaniards a figure of speech. They have come to say "This is work on Escorial" when they wish to describe some task never finished.

State Monument Planned

Since the advent of the Spanish Republic it had been planned to remove the friars to allow conversion of the monastery into a national monument along with royal palaces and other properties. But the war gave a different aspect to their evacuation.

The mausoleum has but one vacant sepulcher, that reserved for former King Alfonso XIII, now an exile with slight chance of lying with his predecessors.

One of the friars' most-prized possessions was a rich library of Arabic, Hebrew and Spanish manuscripts. They had a school of higher education bearing the name of Alfonso's father, Alfonso XII, and a university, similarly named, devoted to the education of the sons of the Spanish nobility.

$100,000 CAFE SHUT BY RACKET BOMBS, OWNER TESTIFIES

Stench Missiles Used for Ten Months After He Refused to Pay $3,000, He Says

FOUR OTHERS TELL ILLS

Restaurant Manager Describes Threats to His Children and $2,000 Demand

A $100,000 example was given to the Supreme Court jury showing evidence in the restaurant racket trial yesterday by Hyman Gross, who had been one of the owners of the Gerard Cafeteria, on Broadway at Times Square, which was closed by a stench bombardment ten months after it opened.

The experience of Mr. Gross, who had refused to pay Louis Beitcher, the racket's collector, $3,000, was one of five cases, three of attempted extortion and two of extortion placed in the record before Justice Philip J. McCook during the day.

In another, John A. Miller, manager of the Anne Miller restaurant, then at 43 West Eighth Street and a place patronized by Juror No. 5, Franklin H. Middleton, told of kidnap threats against his children and a demand for $2,000. Harry A. Vogelstein, one of the defendants, Miller said, told that "only saps" picketed.

Tells of $1,750 Payment

Isidoris Coviris, one of three owners of the Broadway Cafeteria at 2,230 Broadway, testified that he paid Beitcher $1,750 to purchase protection from the "rights of the union," and Richard M. Decker, owner of a night club called the Congress Restaurant at 1,657 Broadway, told of a sudden strike called by Local 16 of the Waiters Union to force him to join the Metropolitan Restaurant and Cafeteria Association, which he did at a cost of $285.

Two of Mr. Decker's waiters had worked for Jules Martin, the man who organized the racket for Arthur (Dutch Schultz) Flegenheimer, when he operated a restaurant in West Forty-eighth Street.

The flow of witnesses was speeded up by the fact that attorneys for the eight defendants, including three officials of Local 16 of the Waiters Union, two of Local 302 of the Cafeteria Workers Union, and three others, two of them lawyers, connected with the Metropolitan Association, shortened their cross-examination.

Run Short of Witnesses

Toward the end of the day the prosecution, conducted by William B. Herlands and Milton C. Schilback, two of Special Prosecutor Thomas E. Dewey's chief assistants, ran short of witnesses and a half-hour wait followed while more were produced after telephone calls.

Mr. Gross was examined by Mr. Schilback. He said his regular business was real estate, but in July, 1933, after he and associates "had spent $100,000 to build the place," the Gerard was opened at 1,508 Broadway. He had personally put up $40,000, he said.

Before they opened, Max Pincus, then in Local 302 but now dead,

Continued on Page Thirty-six

SIX ON HIGH BENCH ELIGIBLE TO RETIRE

They and Six Justices of the Circuit Courts Could Come Under Roosevelt Plan

13 OTHER JURISTS LISTED

These Members of the Lower Courts Also Have Reached 70, With 10 Years of Service

Special to THE NEW YORK TIMES.

WASHINGTON, Feb. 5.—Not only six of the nine justices of the Supreme Court but half a dozen of the judges of the Federal Circuit Courts and an undisclosed number of the judges of the District Courts would be eligible for retirement as having reached the age of 70 after ten years of service on the bench, as urged by President Roosevelt.

There are forty-three judgeships in the Circuit Courts and 163 in the District tribunals, but in some instances there are still vacancies in appointments.

Preferring not to single out individuals, the Department of Justice refused to reveal the details today, but it was established from other sources that about six of the Circuit justices could retire on these qualifications.

As President Roosevelt stated that twenty-five out of a total judiciary of 237 could thus leave the bench, and as it is known that six Supreme Court and six Circuit justices were so classed, the thirteen others must be members of the district benches and special Federal courts.

Chief Justice Hughes is, of course, among those who will be in the 70-year-old, ten-year service class this year. In fact, he will be 75 years old April 11 and Justice Van Devanter will be 78 just six days later.

Justice McReynolds's seventy-fifth birthday fell on last Wednesday. Justice Brandeis, oldest member of the court, reached the age of 80 Nov. 13 last. Justice Sutherland will be 75 on March 25 and Justice Butler 71 on March 17. Justice Stone will be 65 Oct. 11.

Continued on Page Ten

BILL IS INTRODUCED

Robinson and Bankhead Act for Passage by Senate and House

MAJORITY FOR PROPOSAL

But Most Conservative Democrats Are Silent and Republicans Are Hostile

SPECULATION ON JUSTICES

Those Mentioned for New Places Include J. M. Landis, Richberg and Frankfurter

By TURNER CATLEDGE

Special to THE NEW YORK TIMES.

WASHINGTON, Feb. 5.—President Roosevelt's proposals for a comprehensive reform of the Federal judiciary fell today like a bombshell upon a Congress which thought it already had experienced the ultimate in surprises when it heard his recent messages on the reorganization of the executive branch.

Not even the closest of the President's Congressional advisers knew of the plan until they were called to the White House this morning and told to prepare for the shock at noon.

Regardless of the far-reaching nature of the proposals, the balance of Congressional reaction was decidedly in their favor. Judging from the content of the comment, this was due to three main factors—the resentment in Congress at recent decisions of the Supreme Court holding its acts invalid, the continuing faith of the so-called "liberal" element in Mr. Roosevelt and his works, and the unquestioning loyalty of the leadership in both houses to him and his program.

Republican Protest Vehement

On the other side of the scales were the spontaneous objections of the Republicans, characterized by a vehemence akin to that of the last Presidential campaign, and the disapproving attitude of a number of conservative Democrats.

Most of the conservative Democrats declined to comment.

Although the President's plan for a non-amendment approach to the issues raised by the court's interpretations ran counter to the plans of several outstanding legislators, notably Senator Robinson and Senator Ashurst, the leadership started laying general plans for its enactment. Senator Robinson predicted that the recommendations would receive "favorable consideration" in the Senate, and Speaker Bankhead promised quick action in the House on what he considered a "sound principle" of judicial reform.

The details of the plan, particularly the effective proposal for appointment of six new justices to the Supreme Court, brought forth limitless speculation as to the possible appointees. High on practically every list of possibilities were Senator Robinson, James M. Landis, who will shortly resign as chairman of the Securities and Exchange Commission to become dean of the Harvard Law School; Felix Frankfurter, Professor of Law at Harvard; Donald R. Richberg, former general counsel of the National Recovery Administration; Senators Wagner and Ashurst and Chairman Sumners of the House Judiciary Committee.

The reform proposals were submitted in accordance with the best approved New Deal practices. They were worked out in every essential detail by the President with his administrative advisers, then the Congressional leaders were called in and informed of the scheme. Later a message, with supporting data and the draft of a bill, were sent to Congress.

The only difference today from the practice followed with most of the other measures of major importance was that the documents-message, supporting data and bill draft—were channeled together in a single sheaf of papers, and representatives of the press were called in to be informed in advance of their specifications. The latter was not exactly an innovation, as the President follows this practice regularly on involved budget matters and recently used it in presenting and explaining his plan on executive reorganization.

The President's attitude in explaining the proposal today was in

Continued on Page Nine

ROOSEVELT ASKS POWER TO REFORM COURTS, INCREASING THE SUPREME BENCH TO 15 JUSTICES; CONGRESS STARTLED, BUT EXPECTED TO APPROVE

Supreme Court Keeps Up With Its Work, Say Aides

By The Associated Press.

WASHINGTON, Feb. 5.—Supreme Court attaches said today that the tribunal was up to date in handling its business.

They explained it had been so since soon after William Howard Taft became Chief Justice in 1921. When he went on the bench, fulfilling a lifelong ambition, the tribunal was from two to three years behind in its work. He speeded up disposition of the litigation so that soon afterward it was abreast of the docket.

President's Message

Special to THE NEW YORK TIMES.

WASHINGTON, Feb. 5.—Following are the text of the President's message to Congress on the judiciary, the draft of his proposed bill and the text of the letter of Attorney General Cummings to the President:

I have recently called the attention of the Congress to the clear need for a comprehensive program to reorganize the administrative machinery of the executive branch of our government. I now make a similar recommendation to the Congress in regard to the judicial branch of the government, in order that it also may function in accord with modern necessities.

The Constitution provides that the President "shall from time to time give to the Congress information of the state of the Union, and recommend to their consideration such measures as he shall judge necessary and expedient." No one else is given a similar mandate. It is therefore the duty of the President to advise the Congress in regard to the judiciary whenever he deems such information or recommendation necessary.

I address you for the further reason that the Constitution vests in the Congress direct responsibility in the creation of courts and judicial offices and in the formulation of rules of practice and procedure. It is, therefore, one of the definite duties of the Congress constantly to maintain the effective functioning of the Federal judiciary.

The judiciary has often found itself handicapped by insufficient personnel with which to meet a growing and more complex business. It is true that the physical facilities of conducting the business of the courts have been greatly improved, in recent years, through the erection of suitable quarters, the provision of adequate libraries and the addition of subordinate court officers. But in many ways these are merely the trappings of judicial office. They play a minor part in the processes of justice.

Since the earliest days of the republic, the problem of the personnel of the courts has needed the attention of the Congress. For example, from the beginning, over repeated protests to President Washington, the justices of the Supreme Court were required to "ride circuit" and, as circuit justices, to hold trials throughout the length and breadth of the land—a practice which endured over a century.

In almost every decade since 1789, changes have been made by the Congress whereby the numbers of judges and the duties of judges in Federal Courts have been altered in one way or another.

Continued on Page Eight

STOCKS DROP FAST ON COURT MESSAGE

Sweeping Declines Stop a Rise, Making Market the Year's Second Largest

BRIEF RALLIES ARE FUTILE

List Closes Only Slightly Above Day's Lows—Some Bankers Say Effect Will Be Mitigated

President Roosevelt's proposals for changes in the Federal judiciary came as a stunning surprise to the financial community yesterday. They evoked uncertainty and alarm among bankers and business men which found expression in a sweeping decline of stock prices.

Prices of representative issues on the New York Stock Exchange, which had been advancing during the morning, broke swiftly as the President's message was being read. The volume of dealings increased, the stock ticker fell five minutes behind the pace of trading and earlier gains were quickly turned to losses of one to three or four points.

Brief rallies in the afternoon gave way to renewed selling and closing prices were only slightly above the lowest levels of the day.

From the standpoint of number of shares dealt in, the market was the second largest of the year, the total of transactions being 3,321,000. On the basis of number of issues to appear on the tape, 975, it was the broadest market since Nov. 12.

Course Unexpected by Many

A sample of the net declines among important issues showed: United States Steel down 2% points at 96%; Bethlehem Steel, off 2% at 81%; Allied Chemical, 5 points lower at 235; Allis Chalmers, off 2¾ at 75¼; Anaconda Copper, down 1¼ at 54%; Chrysler, off 2 at 126%, and Standard Oil of New Jersey, off 1% at 70%.

Domestic corporation bonds were irregularly weaker, while the market for government securities showed declines fairly evenly matched by advances.

The response of financiers to the news was based upon concern and uncertainty over its implications rather than upon disagreement with the President's objectives. In spite of rumors which have been heard from time to time that Mr. Roosevelt might seek to enlarge the Supreme Court, it had been felt by most bankers that such a course was unlikely.

Consequently, as the chief executive of one big bank expressed it, the financial community was "flabbergasted" at the suddenness of the announcement, the drastic character of the changes proposed and the implications of criticism of

Continued on Page Ten

AIM TO PACK COURT, DECLARES HOOVER

Roosevelt Move Transcends Any Partisanship Question, Ex-President Holds

WIDELY CRITICIZED HERE

'Shameful Day' in Our History, Colby Asserts—Justice Black Hails 'Greatest Advance'

President Roosevelt's message to Congress asking for authority to appoint Federal judges in addition to those more than 70 years old was characterized last night by Herbert Hoover, his predecessor in the White House, as a proposal for "packing" the Supreme Court to get through New Deal measures.

Mr. Hoover declared that the President's proposal went far beyond any question of partisanship, and advised that Congress delay action on it until the people had time to formulate their views. His comment, made public at his suite in the Waldorf-Astoria, was as follows:

"Stripped of subsidiary matters, some of which are admirable, the President's action amounts to this:

"The Supreme Court has proved many of the New Deal proposals as unconstitutional. Instead of the ample alternatives of the Constitution by which these proposals could be submitted to the people through constitutional amendment, it is now proposed to make changes by 'packing' the Supreme Court. It has the implication of subordination of the court to the personal power of the Executive. Because all this reaches to the very depth of our form of government, it far transcends any question of partisanship.

"The Congress should delay action until the people have had ample time to formulate their views on it. In the long sweep of the Republic a few months are not too much to consider a vital change in the repeated judgment of the American people over 150 years. That judgment has always been that their liberties have depended greatly on the independence of the court and that they themselves should determine changes in the Constitution."

Reaction to the President's proposal among New York City lawyers was generally strongly unfavorable. Former Justice Clarence J. Shearn, president of the Bar Association, asserted that it was an attempt to pack the Supreme Court for cases in which the Federal administration would have a political interest and called on all opposed to "mobocracy" or dictatorship to fight it.

Bainbridge Colby, Secretary of State during the Wilson administration, declared it was an attempt to

Continued on Page Nine

SURPRISE MESSAGE

Asks Authority to Name New Justices if Old Do Not Quit at 70

SEES NEED OF 'NEW BLOOD'

Constitutional Amendment and Statutory Judiciary Curb Would Be Side-Stepped

LOWER COURTS AFFECTED

Bench Would Be Expanded, Appeals Speeded and Defense Assured in Injunctions

By ARTHUR KROCK

Special to THE NEW YORK TIMES.

WASHINGTON, Feb. 5.—The President suddenly, at noon today, cut through the tangle of proposals made by his Congressional leaders to "bring legislative and judicial action into closer harmony" with a broadaxe message to Congress recommending the passage of legislation to effect drastic Federal court reforms.

The message—prepared in a small group and with deepest secrecy—was accompanied by a letter from the Attorney General and by a bill, drawn at the Department of Justice, which would permit an increase in the membership of the Supreme Court from nine to a maximum of fifteen if judges reaching the age of 70 declined to retire; add a total of not more than fifty judges to all classes of the Federal courts; send appeals from lower-court decisions on constitutional questions direct to the Supreme Court, and require that government attorneys be heard before any lower-court injunction issue against the enforcement of any act of Congress.

Avoiding both the devices of constitutional amendment and statutory limitation of Supreme Court powers, which were favored by his usual spokesmen in Congress, the President endorsed an ingenious plan which will so empower him as to give him the power to name six new justices of the Supreme Court.

Power Left to the President

Under the provisions of the bill drawn by the Department of Justice for Congress, if the six now sitting justices who are more than 70 years of age do not resign, the President is empowered to name a new member for each justice in that category. These are the Chief Justice and Justices Brandeis, Van Devanter, Butler, McReynolds and Sutherland. Thus, after the passage of the bill, which is generally expected, the court will number anywhere from nine to fifteen justices.

Although the message—an unusually long one for the President—was a general criticism of the effects upon government and private litigants of overburdened courts and superannuated judges, and stressed a general plea to Congress to make provision for "a constant and systematic addition of younger blood" to "vitalize the courts," Congress instantly recognized its outstanding feature and purpose. Although the message outlined basic defects in the administration of justice in the United States, and contained many reforms to which no exception will be taken, Congress quickly sensed that the President had hurdled the present majority of the Supreme Court on his way to the goal he outlined in his opening message of the session. This, as he stated it, is to find "means to adapt our legal forms and our judicial interpretation to the actual present needs of the largest progressive democracy in the modern world."

Variety of Emotions Aroused

That passage was the one which brought out most cheers from the floors of Congress when the President uttered it. To achieve this aim was the object of all the proposed amendments and statutes which have heaped high in the Congressional hoppers since the opening of the session. When members of the Senate and the House became aware of the ingenious but effective manner in which the President planned to attain his objective without touching the Constitution or the powers of the court, they were torn by a variety of emotions.

Senator Robinson, the majority leader in his branch, said the case

Continued on Page Eight

West Virginian Saved After 8 Days in Mine; Had No Food, Forced to Drink Sulphur Water

By The Associated Press.

FLEMINGTON, W. Va., Feb. 5.—Eight foodless days of utter darkness while lost in the débris-choked passageways of an abandoned mine ended today for Robert Johnson, 36-year-old rural mail carrier.

"I sure thought I was a goner," he said.

Johnson told from his cot in a hospital of praying through the long hours in the damp mine, of giving up all hope, then of seeing a dim glow of lamps carried by rescue workers.

"Thank God, my prayers were answered," he sobbed fervently before a sleeping potion administered by physicians put him to sleep.

Doctors had broken his long fast—he had only sulphur water to drink in the mine—with plenty of black coffee, then with bowls of strained soup.

Rescue crews found Johnson nearly two miles from the mine entrance early today. He was huddled behind a heap of jagged chunks of slate in the mine in which he operated to dig coal in his spare time for sale to neighbors.

The crews had expected difficulty in removing the slate, but had little actual trouble in reaching the imprisoned man.

Three of the scores of volunteers who had searched the mine day and night since Johnson disappeared on Jan. 27 heard his feeble cries for help while exploring a narrow tunnel.

His first words were to assure himself he hadn't merely imagined a light had cut through the dark.

C. F. Pride, assistant safety director for the State Department of Mines quoted him:

"I told myself, 'Bob, please don't lose that light.'" He didn't.

As the rescue party came closer he called to Mike Stanko Jr., Edward Whitehair and William Westfall, all his friends and neighbors:

"Take your time, I'll guide you by your light."

They cautiously approached the heap of slate, reached through a hole and gripped Johnson's hand—assurance he was safe.

Then word went to the surface, sped through this little community of about 400 population in Northeastern West Virginia. Pride and eight others gathered stretchers and blankets. They hurried into the mine, waded and swam through a deep pool of water covering nearly an acre where originally, many believed, Johnson had drowned while trying to open clogged drains.

After Johnson was taken out on the mountainside, he was carried a quarter of a mile down a snow-covered path to a waiting ambulance. There he was joined by his wife—among his first questions was "How's my wife?"—and hurried to a hospital fifteen miles away in Clarksburg, the nearest large city.

"All the News That's Fit to Print."

The New York Times.

LATE CITY EDITION
Fair today, temperature unchanged. Tomorrow fair, little change in temperature.
Temperatures Yesterday—Max. 71; Min. 56

VOL. LXXXVI....No. 28,958.   Entered as Second-Class Matter, Postoffice, New York, N. Y.   NEW YORK, FRIDAY, MAY 7, 1937.   P   TWO CENTS In New York City.   THREE CENTS Within 200 Miles.   FOUR CENTS Elsewhere Except in 7th and 8th Postal Zones.

Copyright, 1937, by The New York Times Company

HINDENBURG BURNS IN LAKEHURST CRASH; 21 KNOWN DEAD, 12 MISSING; 64 ESCAPE

ANARCHISTS RENEW BARCELONA STRIFE; 5,000 LEAVE BILBAO

Revolters, Regaining Part of Catalan Capital, Demand Shock Troop Dissolution

SOCIALIST MINISTER SLAIN

Insurgents Reported Gaining Unresisted in Aragon as Foes Withdraw 12,000

EVACUATION IN NORTH SPED

British Warships Protect Craft Taking Women and Children From Bilbao to France

The Spanish Situation

PERPIGNAN—Anarchists were reported to have regained positions in Barcelona and to have demanded the dissolution of the government's shock troops. Withdrawal of 12,000 men from the Aragon front, to deal with the situation, was also reported, leading to an advance by the Rebel armies. Page 1.

ROME—A heavy concentration of Rebels, including Italians, to rescue the Italians cut off at Bermeo, was under way on the Bilbao front. Page 10.

BILBAO—Five thousand women and children were taken from the city, and vessels carrying them to France were guarded by British warships. More refugees were preparing to leave. (Follows the above.) Page 10.

LONDON—Foreign Secretary Eden revealed that the British Government had evidence that Guernica was destroyed by airplanes. He favored a neutral inquiry. Page 10.

Anarchists Give Ultimatum

Special Cable to The New York Times.

PERPIGNAN, France, May 6.—The Anarchists are reported to have regained control in parts of Barcelona this afternoon after the Catalan Generalidad believed it had dominated the situation.

The Anarchists issued an ultimatum to the government demanding the dissolution of the shock troops patroling the city, the government's chief support, within twenty-four hours and declaring that otherwise they would take matters into their own hands and use every means in their power to suppress the shock troops.

The Anarchists also have obtained the upper hand at Junquera in addition to Figueras, according to news received here, and threaten, it is alleged, to use asphyxiating gas unless their ultimatum is obeyed.

Anarchist broadcasts have been picked up here stating that the casualties in the disorders in Barcelona since the Anarchist rebellion Tuesday amounted to 400 dead and 2,000 wounded. Declaring that "enough blood has flowed," the broadcasts continue to appeal for calm every ten minutes, and it is therefore believed that trouble still persists in Barcelona.

French Consulate Menaced

The French Consulate was threatened by Anarchists, who asserted that Egatist sympathizers had taken refuge there. The consul appealed to French warships in the harbor and 200 armed sailors reinforced the consulate guard.

Telephonic communication with Barcelona is still cut off tonight, and telegraphic and telephonic communication with the interior of Catalonia, which was re-established yesterday, was again interrupted this morning.

The Spanish Consul at Perpignan has recommended that Frenchmen and others should not go further than Figueras, and trains do not proceed beyond Gerona.

Francisco Ascaso, leader of the Anarchists in the Aragon Government, is reported to have been murdered.

Rebels Gain on Aragon Front
By The Associated Press.

PERPIGNAN, France, May 6.—Reports of an unresisted Insurgent advance along the whole Aragon front of Northeastern Spain and of the withdrawal of 12,000 government troops from it to keep the peace in troubled Barcelona, put a new and serious face on the Catalan Anarchist insurrection tonight. The reports emanated from Insurgent

Continued on Page Ten

Judge Sentences Himself By Signing Papers Unread

Wireless to The New York Times.

MOSCOW, May 6.—A judge on one of the most important benches of the Moscow District Court who has the bad habit of signing without reading any document placed before him has just sentenced himself to jail.

The court clerks, deciding he needed a lesson in "Bolshevik vigilance," presented to him a sheaf of papers including one reading "To the chief of Butyrky prison: Under Magistrate Abramson is sent to you for further detention." Judge Abramson signed all the papers and picked up his newspaper again.

The clerks, of course, extracted the sentence and were passing it around laughingly when the judge found out about it. He destroyed it in a rage, declaring such jokes tended to undermine Soviet justice.

The government learned about it, however, and today Investia delivered to Judge Abramson a stinging rebuke for perfunctoriness, reminding him that he dealt not in inanimate goods but in human fate.

HUGHES SEES CHOICE IN LAW OR TYRANNY

Courts Must Be Maintained, He Tells Law Institute, or We Replace Reason by Force

TEST OF BAR TO ROOSEVELT

Stewardship Is Questioned by Laymen, He Writes in Warning of 'Critical Audience'

Text of Chief Justice Hughes's address is on Page 17.

Special to The New York Times.

WASHINGTON, May 6.—Chief Justice Hughes made what his hearers construed as a reference to the Supreme Court when he told the American Law Institute today that if society is to choose the processes of reason as opposed to the tyranny of force, "it must maintain the institutions which embody those processes." It was the second time that the Chief Justice of the United States has broken his silence since the controversy over reorganization of the Supreme Court started three months ago.

Vigorous applause, lasting more than a minute, followed the Chief Justice's words, with which he concluded a speech in which he avoided any direct reference to the court issue.

President Roosevelt in a message to the institute likewise refrained from any positive statement about the Supreme Court, but remarked that "law interpreters," among other legal experts, are facing a sometimes critical audience.

President on Lawyers' Position

"I am happy to greet you members of the bench, the bar and the law school faculties who have assembled for the fifteenth annual meeting of the American Law Institute," the President stated.

"I have followed with interest your accomplishments within recent years in the restatement of the law and your proposals for the improvement in the administration of criminal justice.

"Today our stewardship as lawyers is being questioned. The laymen of America are not, perhaps, quite so disposed to make a complete delegation of law matters to law men. At least the layman asserts his right to evaluate us.

"Law scholars, law practitioners, lawmakers, law administrators, and law interpreters have the stage today. But more significant, they must play their rôles before an intense and sometimes critical audience.

"But this is well. The virtue of the common law was its adaptability to growth and improvement, in generations present and future the lawyer likewise will be measured by the same test.

"It is encouraging today that so many outstanding leaders of the profession assemble to give service in the important and worth-while task to which the American Law Institute is dedicated. I extend again my warm and cordial greetings to your membership and my best wishes for continued success."

Only at one other time since President Roosevelt made his recommendations to Congress on Feb. 5 has the Chief Justice made any

Continued on Page Seventeen

NOTABLES ABOARD

Merchants, Students and Professional Men on the Dirigible

LEHMANN IS A SURVIVOR

Veteran Zeppelin Commander, Acting as Adviser on Trip, Is Seriously Burned

CAPT. PRUSS IS ALSO SAFE

C. L. Osbun, Sales Manager, Who Survived a Plane Crash, Escapes Second Time

Notables from many walks of life were among the passengers on the ill-fated Hindenburg. They included merchants, students and business and professional men and women. Many of the survivors owed their lives to the fact that they were apparently near windows in the dirigible when the accident happened and were able to leap through them to the ground in safety.

Among the survivors listed were Captain Ernst Lehmann, veteran Zeppelin commander; Captain Max Pruss, the new Hindenburg commander; Herbert O'Laughlin of Chicago, employed by the Consumers Company of Elgin, Ill.; Clifford L. Osbun, export sales manager of the Oliver Farm Equipment Company of Chicago, and Ferdinand Lammot Belin Jr. of Washington, D. C.

Lehmann's Condition Grave

Early this morning Dr. E. G. Herbener, staff surgeon at the Paul Kimball Hospital in Lakewood, said that Captain Lehmann was on the doubtful list. Captain Lehmann is suffering from shock and second and third degree burns of the face and body. Captain Pruss is suffering from second and third degree burns of the face, forehead and arms and will probably recover, Dr. Herbener said.

Among the passengers who were still unaccounted for were John Pannes, passenger traffic manager of the Hamburg-American Line and North German Lloyd at New York, and his wife; Ernst Rudolf Anders, partner of the firm of Seelig & Hille, tea merchants of Dresden, Germany, and his son, R. Herbert Anders, and Hermann Doehner of Mexico, D. F.

Captain Lehmann and Captain Pruss were in the control gondola when the crash occurred. Both officers, together with several other members of the crew, leaped through the gondola windows to safety.

Lehmann an Adviser

Captain Lehmann, who was serving as adviser aboard the Hindenburg, had been commander of the ship until this year. He has had long experience with the lighter-than-air craft, and has been associated with Hugo Eckener, world-famous authority on Zeppelins, since 1921.

He was born March 12, 1886, at Ludwigshafen, on the Rhine, the son of a chemist. He became a naval cadet in 1905 and later entered the Polytechnic Institute at Charlottenburg, where he studied. During the World War Captain Lehmann received the German Iron Cross award. After the war, as second in command of the dirigible, he brought the dirigible Los Angeles to Lakehurst in 1924. When the Hindenburg was completed in 1936 Captain Lehmann was placed in command, a position he held until recently, when Captain Pruss was elevated as commander of the ship. Mr. Osbun's escape from the disaster marked the second time that he had narrowly missed death as the result of a flying accident. Last year he was aboard a transport plane when it was forced down on route from Puerto Rico to Buenos Aires. Soon after he was transferred to a motorboat with other passengers and the motorboat blew up. Mr. Osbun escaped injury, but two other passengers were seriously burned.

Mr. Osbun declared that he was talking to fellow passengers in the dining salon, looking down through the observation window watching the ship being moored, when the disaster occurred. He was apparently blown through the window and thrown to the ground, suffering injuries. He was taken to the Paul Kimball Hospital in Lakewood.

Mr. Osbun is 37 years old, the fa-

Continued on Page Nineteen

THE HINDENBURG IN FLAMES ON THE FIELD AT LAKEHURST
The giant airliner as she settled to the ground near her mooring mast at 7:23 o'clock last night.
Associated Press Photo.

DISASTER ASCRIBED TO GAS BY EXPERTS

Washington Sees Dangerous Combination of Hydrogen and Blue Gas as Cause

Special to The New York Times.

WASHINGTON, May 6.—Washington airship experts and Congressional leaders received the news of the Hindenburg disaster with amazement and expressions of sorrow. But in every instance those who commented pointed out that the three disasters of the United States Navy were structural, while that of the German craft was due to the use of a combination of hydrogen and blue gas, the most dangerous of all gases for inflation of airships.

Dr. Hans Luther, the German Ambassador, said the disaster must not cause the world to lose faith in dirigibles and that it could not have been caused by technical defects.

"It is terrible," the Ambassador said. "I was horrified by the news, but it could not have been a technical matter. It must not cause us to lose faith in dirigibles because the Graf Zeppelin has operated safely and efficiently for eight years on the run from Europe to South America and elsewhere.

Secretary Hull sent the following message tonight to Konstantin von Neurath, the German Minister of Foreign Affairs:

"I extend to you on behalf of the Government of the United States my profound sympathy at the tragic accident to the dirigible Hindenburg and the resultant loss of life to passengers and crew."

"It is too terrible to believe," Admiral A. B. Cook, Chief of Naval Aeronautics, said. "From what I

Continued on Page Twenty-one

Airship Like a Giant Torch On Darkening Jersey Field

Routine Landing Converted Into Hysterical Scene in Moment's Time—Witnesses Tell of 'Blinding Flash' From Zeppelin

By CRAIG THOMPSON
Special to The New York Times.

LAKEHURST, N. J., May 6.—The Hindenburg, giant silver liner of the air, suddenly became a torch above the naval air station here tonight. What began as a routine landing of the transatlantic airship ended in a holocaust.

The ground crew, officials of the naval air base, spectators, reporters and press photographers were going about their customary business of aiding or watching the ship nose into the mooring mast.

Two ground lines had been dropped from the nose. These, attached to the cars running on a circular track around the mast, were holding the ship nose down at a thirty-degree angle, and helping it jockey into a position favorable with the wind for a mooring.

A thunderstorm had passed over the field a short time before and a drizzly rain was still falling. Twilight was beginning, although the visibility was still good.

So suddenly that it left spectators on the verge of hysteria for some time afterward, the ship burst into flame. Some one in the ground crew yelled "Run for your lives!" and the crew did. The stern of the ship settled and the photographers, squinting through the view finders of their cameras, ran toward the ship.

The occurrence sounded, witnesses said, like two explosions, one following the other about thirty seconds apart. Some said they saw one burst of flame, others two, but those who described it as explosions gave way to the sounds of human screams.

In the "heavier-than-air" hangar, the pilot of an American Air Lines plane, waiting to ferry passengers from the airship into Newark, watched from a window.

"It seemed to happen so fast that I didn't think anybody could escape," he said afterward.

He was wrong, for about at that moment a man ran into the hangar. "His face was black, but he seemed to be all right otherwise. He wanted to telephone his mother in Chicago."

The passenger was Herbert James O'Laughlin of Chicago. On the field was an army detachment from Philadelphia, detailed there for just an emergency. This detail promptly went to work, trucks scurrying over the field seeking the injured, while in the hangar telephone calls were being put through to all points in New Jersey and New York City calling for ambulances, doctors, nurses, medicine.

All this occurred while the flames spread toward the uptilted nose of the ship, while the stern was going to the ground to be followed shortly by the entire length, girder and strut, the bared ribs of the ship from which the skin had disappeared.

Robert Seelig, Murray Becker and Larry Kennedy, all newspaper camera men, related what they had seen.

"There was a noise that sounded like bullets coming out of the gondolas," Seelig said. "I saw nobody

Continued on Page Twenty-one

GERMANY SHOCKED BY THE TRAGEDY

At First Disbelieving, Line's Officials Tell of Receiving Message of Landing

Special Cable to The New York Times.

BERLIN, Friday, May 7.—It was a few minutes after 1 o'clock this morning when the first news of the disaster to the Hindenburg reached Berlin by telephone from The New York Times Bureau in London. The bureau forwarded the brief bulletin to the effect that the airship had been destroyed while making its landing. No details were given.

At that hour the German newspapers were without news. Several first editions, in fact, had reported the Hindenburg's supposedly safe arrival on the strength of an erroneous telegram received by the company in Frankfort on the Main. It was almost two hours later before the news of the disaster with some few details reached the newspapers through the medium of the German official news agency.

Facts Difficult to Get

In the meantime such facts about the airship and its passengers proved difficult to obtain. The Frankfort and Berlin offices of the Zeppelin company were closed and no complete list of the passengers or crew was available. A list of twenty-one names comprising foreign passengers out of a total of thirty-nine was obtained by telephone from Frankfort, where this correspondent had retained it since the sailing day.

Dr. Hugo Eckener, veteran of the Zeppelin service, was in Austria, when he had lectured last night in Vienna. The Vienna bureau of The New York Times traced him to Graz and obtained his ad-

Continued on Page Nineteen

SHIP FALLS ABLAZE

Great Dirigible Bursts Into Flames as It Is About to Land

VICTIMS BURN TO DEATH

Some Passengers Are Thrown From the Blazing Wreckage, Others Crawl to Safety

GROUND CREW AIDS RESCUE

Sparks From Engines or Static Believed to Have Ignited Hydrogen Gas

A page of photographs of the disaster and survivors Page 20.

By RUSSELL B. PORTER
Special to The New York Times.

NAVAL AIR STATION, LAKEHURST, N. J., May 6.—The zeppelin Hindenburg was destroyed by fire and explosions here at 7:23 o'clock tonight with a loss of thirty-three known dead and unaccounted for out of its ninety-seven passengers and crew.

Three hours after the disaster twenty-one bodies had been recovered, and twelve were still missing. The sixty-four known to be alive included twenty passengers and forty-four of the crew. Many of the survivors were burned or injured, and were taken to hospitals here and in near-by towns.

The accident happened just as the great German dirigible was about to tie up to its mooring mast four hours after flying over New York City on the last leg of its first transatlantic voyage of the year. Until today the Hindenburg had never lost a passenger throughout the ten round trips it made across the Atlantic with 1,002 passengers in 1936.

Two Theories of Cause

F. W. von Meister, vice president of the American Zeppelin Company, gave two possible theories to explain the crash. One was that a fire was caused by an electrical circuit "induced by static conditions" as the ship valved hydrogen gas preparatory to landing. Another was that sparks set off when the engines were throttled down while the gas was being valved caused a fire or explosion.

Captain Ernst Lehmann, who commanded the Hindenburg on most of its flights last year and was one of tonight's survivors, gasped, "I couldn't understand it," as he staggered out of the burning control car. Captain Max Pruss, commanding officer of the airship, and Captain Albert Stampf were also among the survivors.

Captain Lehmann was critically burned and injured; the other officers were also burned, but less seriously.

Experts in lighter-than-air operations who saw the accident said tonight that when the two landing lines were dropped by the dirigible at 7:20, they were immediately made fast to the mooring cars on the circular track about the mooring mast. The crew began to make the lines taut, but the ship had become too much momentum, according to these observers, and drifted several hundred yards past the mast. The starboard line pulled as the nose of the ship passed over the mooring mast at the top.

Order Not Heard

Captain Pruss, making his first trip in command of the dirigible, signaled and shouted, "Pay out!"

This order was heard by the operator on one mooring car, but not by the other, as the shout went against the wind and could not be heard. Consequently, one mooring car paid out and the other did not. The result was that the ship was thrown off its balance and lost the perfect equilibrium it had previously had.

Its nose dipped, forward ballast was dropped and the elevators were set to raise the ship. Instead the ship was held tight by the yaw line. The nose was pulled down opposite to that which they were intended to raise it. The tail dropped sharply and the bottom rudder hit the

Continued on Page Nineteen

"All the News That's
Fit to Print."

The New York Times.

LATE CITY EDITION
Showers and cooler today. Tomorrow generally fair and continued cool.
Temperatures Yesterday—Max., 73; Min., 56

Copyright, 1937, by The New York Times Company.

VOL. LXXXVI.....No. 28,964.
Entered as Second-Class Matter,
Postoffice, New York, N. Y.

NEW YORK, THURSDAY, MAY 13, 1937.

P P

TWO CENTS in New York City. | THREE CENTS Within 200 Miles. | FOUR CENTS Elsewhere Except in 7th and 8th Postal Zones.

C. I. O. STEEL STRIKE SHUTS TWO PLANTS OF JONES-LAUGHLIN

27,000 MEN ARE IDLE

Corporation Puts Blame on Murray, Says It Will Sign Pact

DRIVE AT INDEPENDENTS

Picketing Begins at Pittsburgh and Aliquippa Mills, Backing Recognition for Union

REPUBLIC BARS CONTRACT

Cleveland Letter Tells 55,000 Workers Company Will Not Agree to a Closed Shop

By The Associated Press.

PITTSBURGH, May 12.—Thousands of union steel workers picketed the giant plants of the Jones & Laughlin Steel Corporation tonight in the first major steel strike since John L. Lewis began his drive to organize the nation's millmen into one big union.

The strike began at 11 P. M. as the first move in the campaign of the Steel Workers Organizing Committee to obtain written collective bargaining contracts with the independent steel producers of the country, employing about 202,000 men.

Cheers from the picket lines greeted union members on the early night shifts who walked from the mills in Pittsburgh and Aliquippa, in answer to the strike order of Philip Murray, chairman of the S. W. O. C.

Walkout on Murray's Order

Mr. Murray ordered the walkout after a two-hour conference with H. E. Lewis, chairman of the board of Jones & Laughlin had failed to effect an agreement on the union's demand.

The corporation, in a formal announcement, stated that it had offered to sign a contract provided an identical contract could be granted to non-union workers as its 27,000 employees.

The company also announced that it had offered to grant a sole collective bargaining contract to the group obtaining a majority vote at an employees' election, supervised by the National Labor Relations Board.

A company representative said no attempt would be made to operate the plants "for the time being."

Mr. Murray declined to state what effect the Jones & Laughlin strike would have on union activities at other independent companies, and he would not comment on the company's statement.

The Steel Workers Organizing Committee, as an affiliate of the Committee for Industrial Organization, received a rebuff from Republic Steel Corporation at Cleveland during the day.

The Republic corporation, with 55,000 employes, made public a letter to its workers, refusing to sign a C. I. O. contract. It said, "Republic does not believe in the closed-shop principle."

Biggest Steel Strike Since 1919

The Jones & Laughlin walkout is the biggest strike aimed at the steel industry since 1919. The 1919 strike cut production 40 per cent.

Mr. Murray said the Jones & Laughlin mills would be shut "tight," except for maintenance crews, which were ordered to keep up the blast furnaces.

A further conference would be held with the company tomorrow, Mr. Murray said.

Flames from the blast furnaces shot high into the air, intermittently lighting up the faces of the crowds of men, women and children who packed the streets in front of mill gates more than an hour before the strike call went into effect.

Two score municipal police mingled with the crowd, but made no attempt to break the picket lines.

Without disorder, the union men prevented non-union workers from entering the mill gates.

They held two American flags across the main entrance at the Aliquippa works.

Night Shift Men Parade

The throng was increased by the night shift members for they fell into line, clasped arms with one another, and paraded in front of the gates.

A light rain before midnight sent many of the women and children of the strikers' families to their

Continued on Page Four

---

142 PLAYGROUNDS, CLOSED BY MOSES, SEIZED BY POLICE

Patrolmen Force Locks to Reopen Them as Park Head Defies Mayor on Control

STAFF FURNISHED BY WPA

Somervell, in Control Again, Provides Labor That Moses Lost in Personnel Cuts

One hundred and forty-two playgrounds in the city became the battlefield yesterday for confused conflict between Mayor La Guardia, Lieut. Col. Brehon B. Somervell, WPA Administrator, and Police Commissioner Lewis J. Valentine on the one side, and Park Commissioner Robert Moses on the other. By nightfall, however, "New York's finest" were in full control.

With the Mayor heading by train for California but keeping in touch with the situation by long-distance telephone, the police late in the afternoon picked or broke the padlocks on the playgrounds which had been closed by Mr. Moses because WPA play directors had been withdrawn, and replaced them with police padlocks.

Facilities Normal Today

Today the playgrounds will be reopened to the children, with WPA directors working for the Police Department under direct WPA jurisdiction, aided by 135 men and women from the police juvenile aid bureau. The children can play in safety, the police promised.

The police advanced on the locked gates of the playgrounds only after Mr. Moses had announced to the press there would be "no armed conflict between his park guardsmen and the police" and after he had refused the request of Commissioner Valentine for keys to the padlocks.

The Park Commissioner, asserting that no one was more interested in keeping the playgrounds open for the children than he, stood off the Police Commissioner on legal grounds. The Mayor's order to have the police take over any closed playgrounds, in effect transferring jurisdiction to the police, was a "clear violation of the charter and absolutely illegal," he declared.

Keep Up Other Play Areas

Playgrounds that had been locked "because of the outrageous way in which the WPA has done this" will stay locked, Mr. Moses said, but he added that "if the police want to take the locks off, it will be all right." The 215 playgrounds which were manned by Park Department employes will continue to be run by the department, he said.

The Mayor, anticipating a playground crisis because of the long feud between Mr. Moses and the WPA administrator, had issued his order to the police Tuesday night when he left for California. The order was made public at City Hall by his secretary, Lester Stone, after Mr. Moses had announced the closing of the playgrounds.

With the playgrounds still locked at 3 o'clock, Mr. Stone put in a telephone call for the Mayor at Toledo, and when the Mayor's train arrived informed him of the general situation. He then announced that the Mayor issued the following statement:

"I confirm my order to keep all the playgrounds open. The children of the city, for whom the playgrounds were built, cannot be made to suffer, and I expect the Police Department to reopen the play-

Continued on Page Two

Home Relief Families Get $1,200,000 WPA Clothes

Distribution to home relief families of 2,056,989 articles of clothing made by seamstresses on WPA sewing projects was reported yesterday by Miss Charlotte E. Carr, executive director of the Emergency Relief Bureau. The clothing, which had an estimated retail value of $1,200,000, was distributed between April 13, 1936, and April 23, 1937.

In addition to these WPA products, home relief families received $2,562,410 in cash for the purchase of apparel.

The cash sum to be distributed by the ERB as a clothing allowance for the quarter ending June 30 has been raised to $1,500,000, Miss Carr announced. Of this amount $750,000 was disbursed last month.

REBELS BEAT BACK ATTACK ON TOLEDO

Report Loyalists Have Lost 3,000 There—Government Claims 7-Mile Gain

BILBAO SUBURBS BOMBED

More Than 100 Missiles Were Dropped—Madrid Shelled, Toll Rising to 217

By The Associated Press.

TOLEDO, Spain, May 12.—Heavy government attacks against Insurgent Toledo developed today into a mass offensive in which Insurgents said, the attackers suffered "unprecedented slaughter."

Government prisoners estimated the dead in the campaign at more than 3,000, with total casualties not calculated. Insurgent reports said.

Waves of government infantry charged Insurgent positions south of the Tagus River as a climax to four days of fighting.

Insurgents braced their lines tonight along a six-mile front south of the Tagus. Estimates of government troops in the offensive ranged from 18,000 to 22,000 men.

No-man's land was covered with dead and wounded after a terrific battle yesterday. Squads from both armies roamed the area in the night looking for wounded.

The brilliant defense of Insurgent militiamen in one sector, it is stated, won for them the collective award of the Laureada, the highest honor for bravery in the Spanish Army.

Insurgent reports said Insurgent employes taken by the Insurgents were quoted as saying the government army in the Toledo sector included two brigades of the Lister Division and two other international outfits, the Campesina Battalion and the Dimitroff Battalion, in addition to the units already on the front. Apparently they were sent to reinforce government troops trying to recapture the city won by Insurgents last October, when they freed comrades besieged in the Alcazar.

[The government asserted its troops had advanced about seven miles on the Toledo front.]

100 Bombs Dropped Near Bilbao

BILBAO, Spain, May 12 (P).—Insurgent airplanes dumped more than 100 bombs into the suburbs of Bilbao today but did not fulfill General Emilio Mola's threat to blast the Basque capital to bits.

Terror-stricken inhabitants, mindful of the Insurgent Northern commander's warning he would bombard the city "without mercy" if it did not surrender by today, ducked for cover three times as nine bombing planes and seven pursuit planes roared over Bilbao. Several gasoline tanks were set afire and nearby buildings were destroyed. Clouds of dark smoke billowed over the city.

Basque officials asserted they were informed General Mola had chosen today for the expiration of his ultimatum because the eyes of the world would be turned away from the Spanish civil war toward the London coronation. They said, the indignation that would follow a violent attack on the civilians in the city thus would be lessened, they said.

One person was killed and several wounded in the air bombing of the town of Sorroza. Planes also bombed Larrauri and Manguia, north of Bilbao.

Bilbao's food situation was grave again. Bread supplies were almost exhausted. Only enough for

Continued on Page Thirteen

GEORGE VI AND ELIZABETH CROWNED IN ABBEY; MILLIONS OF THEIR SUBJECTS ACCLAIM THEM; KING, ON AIR, PLEDGES SERVICE TO THE EMPIRE

Times Wide World Radiophoto.

THE ROYAL FAMILY ACKNOWLEDGES GREETINGS OF CORONATION CROWDS

King George VI, Queen Elizabeth and the Princesses Elizabeth and Margaret Rose on the balcony of Buckingham Palace after the ceremony at Westminster Abbey. Behind the Queen, on the left, is Lady Ursula Manners, daughter of the Duke of Rutland, and on the right Lady Diana Legge, daughter of the Earl of Dartmouth, both train bearers for the Queen. Behind King George are two members of the Palace staff.

YOUNGER PRINCESS IS BORED BY AFFAIR

Margaret Rose, 6, Even Goes to the Extent of Yawning at Archbishop of Canterbury

OLDER SISTER NUDGES HER

Elizabeth, for the First Time, Takes Precedence Over Other Ladies of Royal Family

By The Associated Press.

LONDON, May 12.—Two little Princesses saw their father crowned King today, but their reactions were very different.

Eleven-year-old Princess Elizabeth sat primly in her seat in the royal box, her attention fastened on the dramatic spectacle before her. One day she may play the leading rôle in such a ceremony, for she is heir presumptive to the throne.

Beside her, Princess Margaret Rose, 6½, tried her best to act as a princess should at a coronation. But she couldn't keep from squirming and lounging in her seat as the proceedings went on, and once she yawned right at the venerable Archbishop of Canterbury, head of the Anglican Church.

The little girls had risen at 7:30 for the great day. They peeped out of the nursery windows of Buckingham Palace to see whether

Continued on Page Sixteen

Vast Throngs Cheer Royalty In Procession and at Palace

Rain Fails to Lessen Enthusiasm of More Than 1,000,000 on London Route—Queen, Queen Mother, Baldwin Get Ovations

By CHARLES W. HURD
Wireless to THE NEW YORK TIMES.

LONDON, May 12.—The most representative military spectacle the British Empire could muster escorted King George today through six miles of London streets to signalize his coronation, while more than 1,000,000 Londoners and visitors from all countries looked on and cheered even in the last hour, when a cloudburst fell from the skies.

The procession was at once a display of most impressive pageantry and a graphic demonstration of British feeling that the monarchy is an integral part of the empire's soul.

There were plenty of cheers for the troops and the famous personages in line, but most were reserved for four persons—the King and Queen, who got the greatest ovation; Queen Mary, whose popularity is undimmed, and Prime Minister Stanley Baldwin, who steered the throne through its greatest modern crisis last December.

Following their triumphal ride the royal family had another great ovation from the crowds at Buckingham Palace when, in response to cheers, the King appeared on the balcony wearing his robe and crown. The crowd roared, "God save the King!" and then sang "For He's a Jolly Good Fellow."

More prolonged cheers were given Princess Elizabeth and Princess Margaret Rose when they joined their parents. There was an ovation for Queen Mary when she appeared to stand between the King and Queen.

The King and Queen, although tired by the day's responsibilities, made four more appearances later in the evening. Responding to the cheers of the crowds, they walked out on the balcony at 9 o'clock. Immediately after the loud-speakers were employed to announce that they would appear no more tonight. However, they made bows from the balcony three more times, the last at 11:50.

Heavy Rain in Afternoon

By seven o'clock this morning most of the stands along the parade route were filled with ticketholders who had tucked their lunches and mackintoshes under their chairs and hoped they would not have to use the coats despite the lowering skies. Hope for good weather became large when, almost coincident with the King's departure from Buckingham Palace, the sun peeked momentarily through the clouds, but it was its first and last appearance. Thenceforward the clouds yielded intermittent showers, followed by a heavy downpour starting at 3 o'clock.

Continued on Page Eighteen

RITE IS MEDIEVAL

WestminsterRelivesPast Age as Ruler Comes Into His Kingdom

KING A FRAIL, GRAVE FIGURE

Anointed and Robed in Regal Garb, He Receives Crown and Is Cheered by Peers

GIVES VOW WITH EMOTION

Queen, Serious and Nervous, Takes Place on Throne—Historic Service Drags

By FREDERICK T. BIRCHALL
Wireless to THE NEW YORK TIMES.

LONDON, May 12.—In a setting of medieval splendor such as seemed scarcely to belong to this day and age George VI was crowned King and Emperor in Westminster Abbey today.

He rode there with his Queen in their golden coach drawn by eight gray horses through streets lined with troops brought from all parts of the empire, and millions of his subjects acclaimed him as he passed.

In the Abbey he went through the ceremony of being accepted by his people. He took a vow to serve his people, to maintain and obey the laws passed by their Parliament, to be just and to temper justice with mercy.

Anointed With Holy Oil

He was disrobed of the outer garments he had worn on entering and anointed on his hands, breast and forehead with holy oil and thus dedicated to the kingship. Then he was freshly robed in cloth of gold and royal purple. The Sword of State was girt to his side and his heels were touched with the Spurs of Power.

They put the Ring on his finger. Two scepters—emblems of power and justice, equity and mercy—were placed in his hands. Then St. Edward's ancient crown of pure gold and costly jewels was pressed upon his bowed head with a prayer to God to crown him with all principal virtues.

Trumpets sounded, drums rolled and the Abbey sprang into full illumination at his crowning, while outside the church bells rang for joy and guns thundered a royal salute. The peers of this realm surrounding him put on their own coronets and the great edifice rang with the shout, "God save the King!" Archbishops, Bishops, the King's royal brothers and the nobles of his realm knelt in turn before him and swore fealty.

Then Queen Is Crowned

Then the Queen was anointed and crowned in like manner and took her place on her lower throne beside him. They went together to the high altar, knelt in prayer and partook of the communion. Finally, in a new splendid procession, they passed down the great nave and out among the plain people who are the mainstay of their kingdom, yet had had little share in all this ceremony. And throughout the long drive they were again acclaimed in a thunder of cheers echoing through all London—"God save the King!"

The pageant within the Abbey followed the lines that already have been so fully described in advance. The King and Queen entered the Abbey at 11:20 A. M. from the temporary annex, to which the street procession had carried them. They left it at 2:40 P. M. The historic service had dragged a little.

Most of those within the edifice had arrived before 7 o'clock. Few were able to depart before 3:30. The last did not get away before 8. That was due to bad management and it made a long day for many persons no longer young.

So the sixth George and the second Elizabeth, his consort, came at last into their kingdom. Into one kindred and equal great States that overspreads the world. To keep these firmly linked and insure justice to their countless millions is the highest of distinctions is service the highest of distinctions to others.

Continued on Page Sixteen

GEORGE VI THANKS PEOPLE OF EMPIRE

His Broadcast Is Received as Promise of a Reign Like That of His Father

HE GREETS THE DOMINIONS

Recalls That Kingship Arises From 'Will of Free Peoples' Associated in Amity

By FERDINAND KUHN Jr.
Wireless to THE NEW YORK TIMES.

LONDON, May 12.—With the cheers of London crowds still ringing in his ears, King George gave his personal thanks tonight to his peoples throughout the empire and promised to serve them faithfully in the years ahead.

He chose the evening of his coronation day to speak into the microphone from his study in Buckingham Palace as his father had after his silver jubilee two years ago. He talked not only as a king who had just had a crown placed on his head but as a simple young man without great brilliance who had been called to great responsibilities and was determined to live up to them.

Voices Thanks for Loyalty

It was an unassuming little speech, and there was more than a hint of George V in the new King's voice when he said:

"I cannot find words with which to thank you for your love and loyalty to the Queen and myself. Your good will in the streets today and your countless messages from overseas and from every quarter of these islands have filled our hearts to overflowing. I will only say this: that if in the coming years I can show my gratitude in service to you that is in the way above all others that I should choose."

All this, so sincerely meant and so modestly spoken, might have come from the lips of George V if there had been a broadcast on the day of his coronation. It was evident in every sentence that in his coronation George V had set the pattern for this reign of the son who resembles him so closely in his temperament and in his attitude toward his royal job.

Later in his speech King George recalled that he had assumed his crown not only by the grace of God, but "by the will of the free peoples of the British Commonwealth," a reminder that he, like his father, realizes the source whence his kingship comes.

He talked, too, of today's ceremonial as a solemn "dedication" of himself and his Queen, and in one moving passage he reminded uncounted millions of listeners that

Continued on Page Seventeen

Housewives Entitled to Fixed Salaries, Like Any Worker, Mrs. Roosevelt Holds

The suggestion that wives who stay at home to look after the household should receive a definite salary for their work was advanced last night by Mrs. Franklin D. Roosevelt, wife of the President.

Remarking that a housewife earns the right to a salary, "without any question," Mrs. Roosevelt added that "any girl who is needed at home has a job just as surely as the girl who operates a machine in a factory; if she is not needed at home, she loses out by not working."

Mrs. Roosevelt expressed her views in a discussion of "The Home Work for Women," with Miss Rose Schneiderman, president of the Women's Trade Union League and secretary of the New York State Department of Labor. The discussion was broadcast over a radio network.

Asked for her opinion of the most vital question facing working women, Miss Schneiderman said that the working conditions of women were bettered "those of men automatically rise too."

"When women work long hours and for next to nothing," she continued, "they are not only competing against each other, but are pulling down the wages of their men folks."

Asked by Mrs. Roosevelt if she thought men resented women in industry, Miss Schneiderman replied that emotionally they did, "sometimes."

"But can you imagine," she continued, "what would happen if the 11,000,000 working women in the United States suddenly quit their jobs and just waited for the men to support them?"

business and industry and are willing to work for much less pay, she said.

Mrs. Roosevelt remarked that there was no question that "a woman who works to give her children the necessities and some of the advantages of life should have her work day limited to eight hours."

Miss Schneiderman said that when the working conditions of women were bettered "those of men automatically rise too."

"When women work long hours and for next to nothing," she continued, "they are not only competing against each other, but are pulling down the wages of their men folks."

Asked by Mrs. Roosevelt if she thought men resented women in industry, Miss Schneiderman replied that emotionally they did, "sometimes."

"But can you imagine," she continued, "what would happen if the 11,000,000 working women in the United States suddenly quit their jobs and just waited for the men to support them?" Women often carry a feeling of inferiority into

"All the News That's Fit to Print."

The New York Times.

LATE CITY EDITION
Partly cloudy and cooler today.
Tomorrow fair with little change in temperature.
Temperatures Yesterday—Max.: 75; Min.: 64

Copyright, 1937, by The New York Times Company.

VOL. LXXXVII....No. 29,111.

Entered as Second-Class Matter,
Postoffice, New York, N. Y.

NEW YORK, THURSDAY, OCTOBER 7, 1937.

PPP

TWO CENTS In New York City.
THREE CENTS Within 300 Miles.
FOUR CENTS Elsewhere Except in 7th and 8th Postal Zones.

61,000 SEE YANKS CRUSH GIANTS, 8-1, IN SERIES OPENER

Hubbell Routed in Sixth as Victors Stage Seven-Run Uprising at Stadium

GOMEZ PITCHES SUPERBLY

Holds Rivals to Six Hits and Yields Only Tally in Fifth—Lazzeri Gets Homer

DIMAGGIO STAR IN RALLY

Singles With Bases Full to Start the Onslaught—Gate Receipts Are $234,256

By JOHN DREBINGER

Bursting out of the misty haze like an enveloping flame such as a man might encounter on locating that leak in a gas pipe with the aid of a match, the Yankee juggernaut exploded only once at the Stadium yesterday, but that once sufficed to blow the opening clash of the 1937 world series virtually into atoms.

It came with cyclonic effect in the sixth inning, toppled Carl Hubbell like a reed in a high gale, tossed Colonel Bill Terry and his Giants into such confusion that they even nominated a relief pitcher who was sitting awed and spellbound in the dugout, and went on to hurtle seven runs across the plate.

Two rounds later the venerable Anthony Lazzeri wafted a towering home run into the stands and the sum total of all this was a smashing victory for Marse Joe McCarthy's amazing American League champions behind their own left-hander, Vernon Gomez. The final score, 8 to 1, left a crowd of 61,000 almost as stunned and bewildered by it all as were the crestfallen National Leaguers.

Clings Tenaciously to Lead

For five innings, Hubbell, ace pitcher of his circuit, strove heroically to repeat his notable triumph in the series opener of 1936. In four of these rounds, in fact, the work of the famous screwball maestro was absolutely flawless as he clung tenaciously to a one-run margin he had gained over his left-handed adversary.

But in this, perhaps, he made a mistake, for it is a matter of scientific knowledge that at times it is extremely dangerous to keep a highly volatile explosive too tightly bottled up. Something simply had to give and in the sixth it was ol' Hub himself.

Confronted by the inviting set-up of the bases full and nobody out but a few less hardy Giant rooters who doubtless already felt what was coming, Joe DiMaggio, he whom they call the wonder player of his time, crashed a single to center field to start the avalanche of Yankee runs pouring across the plate.

More Shells Are Fired

Presently the bases again filled. In fact, those Yankees seemed to keep the bases filled for an almost interminable period while Bill Dickey and George Selkirk fired more shells into the gaunt frame of ol' Hub, who was unmistakably going down with all his comrades on board.

Finally, with the seven big tallies tucked away, the Yankee storm subsided, leaving only Gomez to move serenely on to his fourth victory in world series warfare.

The singular Castillian, who once made the classic remark that he would rather be lucky than good, now reveled in the picture of combining both of these rare qualities so vital to success in any venture.

For not only had fortune smiled on him to the extent of having runs poured in for him in a carload lot, but he was undeniably superb as well. He pitched smoothly and easily, held the straining National League standard bearers to all blows, only two of which did any damage at all, and all in all was a far cry from the Gomez who stumbled badly to two victories last Fall behind a similar withering barrage.

Open Gaps in Stands

As had been half feared, the capacity crowd which was expected to total 70,000 did not materialize. There were a few open gaps in the lower end of the reserved sections and, what was even more surprising, the unreserved upper tier revealed vacant spaces as well.

The paid attendance totaled 60,573, more than 6,000 short of the all-time record set last year, and the receipts were $234,256.

Following a night of heavy rains which for a time threatened to postpone the whole program a day, a clear but intensely humid morning greeted the early arrivals. It assured a ball game, even if the sun remained behind a haze that hung over the arena like a smoke screen throughout the sultry afternoon.

The bulk of the crowd, in fact,

Continued on Page Thirty-two

Only Three Days Remain For Registration Here

Registration throughout the city continued yesterday to lag behind both last year's figures and those of 1933, the year of the last Mayoralty campaign. The total registration for the first three days of this year was 960,403, which compared with 962,072 in 1933, and 1,152,272 last year, when the all-time record was set.

Yesterday's registration did, however, show an upturn in most boroughs, and in Manhattan and the Bronx exceeded the 1933 total for the same period, although it lagged far behind the 1936 figures.

Residents of New York who desire to cast a vote in the municipal election on Nov. 2 must qualify by registering this week. There are only three days left. Registration places will be open from 5 P. M. to 10:30 P. M. today and tomorrow, and from 7 A. M. to 10:30 P. M. on Saturday.

MAYOR AND TAYLOR BREAK OVER BUDGET

La Guardia Quits Meeting in Rage, Charging Political Plot by Colleagues

WON'T CUT PAY, HE SAYS

Insists Controller Must Make Up Shortage Due to Cut in Water Rates

Enraged to the point of tears by the attempts of Democratic members of the Board of Estimate to make him responsible for finding the additional $12,000,000 for next year's budget, Mayor La Guardia slammed out of an executive session of the board yesterday after the bitterest battle he has ever had with Controller Frank J. Taylor.

Controller Taylor suggested in the course of the executive session that the Mayor order the Budget Director to reduce salaries next year to make up the $12,000,000 taken off the city's revenues when the Aldermen cut city water rates last Monday. Through the closed doors of the Mayor's sledge-hammer blows on the table were plainly heard.

"Damn it," he shouted, "you're not going to put me on the spot. I'm a candidate too. Your Democratic Aldermen overrode my veto on the water rates, and now you want me to take the rap. I'll be damned if I will."

Tells Colleagues to Do Cutting

"Mahoney and the rest of you are going around town taking credit for getting the water rate cut through, and now you want me and my Budget Director to take the rap by trying to make us cut salaries in the budget next year.

"You cut the revenue," the Mayor stormed at his colleagues. "Now go ahead and cut the budget. I warned you that your colleagues would have to cut relief or cut salaries, if you cut the water rate. Now, damn it, you go ahead and do it. I won't."

With a mighty tug, the door of the chamber flew open and the Mayor charged out, his face a choleric red and tears of rage starting from his eyes. He tore by every one in the hall, clattered down the stairs and dashed into his office, and every door in his path got a resounding slam as he went.

The board formally adopted the Mayor's executive budget of $589,222,376 yesterday, and it became the tentative budget through that action. The open meeting at which the vote was taken was marked by sharp exchanges among the Mayor, Mr. Taylor and Borough President James J. Lyons of the Bronx.

"The Controller is the financial officer of the city—let him find the $12,000,000 to make up the water rate cut," the Mayor remarked.

"I won't take that responsibility," said Mr. Taylor. "It's your budget."

"Well, I can't print the money," the Mayor shot back.

Lyons in Clash

Mr. Lyons tried to introduce a motion stating that the Mayor was equally responsible with other members of the Board of Estimate for local legislation which increases the budget by $22,905,038. In his budget message last Saturday the Mayor said these were items over which he had neither power nor control.

"The Borough President of the Bronx doesn't know what he's talking about and apparently can't read English," the Mayor lashed out. "He is one of those who is trying to force the rate up, or salaries down, through the cut in water rates."

"We're not going to tamper with the

Continued on Page Eleven

MAN ABOUT TOWN, 15 W. 51 St. Continuous. Dinner. Supper. Music. Entertainment.—Advt.

LONDON AND PARIS SAID TO GIVE ITALY 24 HOURS TO REPLY

Patience Is Exhausted in Issue of Withdrawal of Italians From War in Spain

SHOW OF FORCE EXPECTED

Opening of French Frontier to Arm Madrid Is Held to Be Sufficient

Twenty-four hours in which to reply to the invitation to a three-power meeting on withdrawal of "volunteers" from Spain was understood to have been given to Italy yesterday by Great Britain and France. An Anglo-French display of force was indicated if a prompt reply from Italy was not forthcoming. In Rome it was said the answer was not yet ready. [Page 1.]

Rain and fog continued to hold up the Insurgent drive near Gijon on the north coast of Spain. In the southwest around Huelva the Rebels were harassed by guerrilla warfare. [Page 20.]

In London, a group of British Protestants, having issued an appeal for a united Christian front to combat anti-church activities in connection with the civil war, was collecting funds to help this work. [Page 20.]

Firm Stand Toward Italy

By The Associated Press.

LONDON, Oct. 6.—France and Great Britain tonight gave Premier Benito Mussolini twenty-four hours' grace to respond to their joint bid for a three-power discussion of the withdrawal of "volunteers" from Spain.

The two governments, alarmed by the new Italian aid to the Spanish Insurgents, strongly indicated their patience with Mussolini was not unlimited after Foreign Secretary Anthony Eden conferred lengthily with Prime Minister Neville Chamberlain and Ambassador Charles Corbin of France.

"The two governments have agreed on the desirability of receiving an early reply from Italy," said a statement issued following the conferences.

Show of Force Suggested

The feeling grew in authoritative quarters that a stern show of Anglo-French force might be the only way to get Italian Black Shirt legions out of Spain, a problem that worries Britain as much as the Far Eastern crisis does.

"We may have to take quick, very decisive action to strangle at its source the prolonged Italian intervention in behalf of the Insurgents," said one informed source, though just what direct action the British Cabinet might take remained a secret.

The opinion was expressed that Italy's obvious attempts to impress Britain and France of her strength —by sending new, powerful planes and troops to Spain—actually were

Continued on Page Thirteen

Rome Held Ready to Aid Any U. S. Peace Parley

By The Associated Press.

ROME, Oct. 6.—Diplomatic circles here were stirred by the potentialities of President Roosevelt's comments on world affairs.

There was considerable speculation in Fascist circles over whether the President, in announcing more active American cooperation in the cause of world peace, was planning an international conference to halt "international anarchy and instability" and if his strength was great enough to obtain a positive peace agreement.

Informed sources said Italy would be willing to take part in such a parley if sufficient preliminary work preceded the actual conference.

American condemnation of Japan as a treaty violator in China fell sharply athwart an Italian tendency to justify Japanese activity. For example, the Popolo d'Italia of Milan said yesterday, "We fully understand and justify" Japanese efforts at expansion.

Reliable sources reported that weeks ago the Fascist press was instructed to play up the Japanese side of the Sino-Japanese conflict.

JAPANESE CONFER ON CENSURE BY U. S.

Emergency Conference Called by Foreign Office as Extras Appear With Condemnation

ROOSEVELT IS CRITICIZED

But Press Is Convinced That We Will Shun Entanglement in Other People's Quarrels

By The Associated Press.

TOKYO, Thursday, Oct. 7.—The Japanese Foreign Office called an emergency conference today following the United States action condemning Japan as a treaty violator.

Simultaneously, newspaper extras began appearing with the bare text of the pronouncement issued by the State Department in Washington. No comment was published immediately. Excitement spread through the streets as crowds clustered around the newsboys.

Government officials earlier had reserved comment on the action by the United States and by the League of Nations Assembly also condemning Japan for her role in the undeclared war with China.

They said they were awaiting

Continued on Page Twelve

Hepburn Government Wins in Ontario; He Hails Victory as Endorsing Fight on CIO

Special to THE NEW YORK TIMES.

TORONTO, Oct. 6.—After three stormy years in office, Premier Mitchell Hepburn of Ontario was re-elected tonight by a majority almost as sweeping as that which first swept him into power in 1934.

The Conservatives lost their leader, Earl Rowe, who was defeated by Mr. Hepburn's Minister of Education, Dr. L. J. Simpson. All the other Liberal Ministers were re-elected, with the exception of Duncan Marshall, who held the portfolio of agriculture.

Mr. Hepburn's Liberal party won 63 and the Conservatives 23 out of the Legislature's ninety seats. Two Liberal Progressives, one Independent Liberal and one United Farmer were returned. Labor, Social Credit and Communist candidates were left at the post. The Cooperative Commonwealth party (Fabian Socialist) won the one seat it held in the last Legislature.

The result was interpreted by Mr. Hepburn chiefly as an endorsement of his determined stand last Spring against the incursion of C. I. O. organizers from the United States. "The people of Ontario," he declared, "may rest assured they will have another five years of industrial peace. Ontario has given endorsement to the first jurisdiction that had enough courage openly to defy and resist the threatened C. I. O. invasion."

Ontario farmers, to whom Mr. Hepburn made his chief appeal, gave him solid support. In Oshawa,

where the General Motors strike last Spring provoked his intervention and caused the resignation of two Ministers from his Cabinet, a Liberal candidate, Gordon Conant, was returned. Northern Ontario, whose miners were said to have been recruited by the C. I. O., gave the Government almost as large a vote as in 1934.

Against this, however, was the fact that in Windsor and Toronto, David A. Croll and Arthur W. Roebuck, two former Hepburn Ministers, who lost their Cabinet portfolios as the result of an open break with the Premier over the C. I. O. issue, were re-elected with handsome majorities.

Credit for his victory is given both by the government's friends and foes to Mr. Hepburn himself. For eight weeks he waged what was virtually a one-man campaign, principally on his opposition to the C. I. O. and communism which, he contended, was following hot on its heels.

TORONTO, Oct. 6 (Canadian Press).—The Conservatives gained nine seats from the Liberals in the Ontario election: Dufferin-Simcoe, Fort William, Hastings West, Leeds, Peel, Prince Edward-Lennox, Simcoe East, Toronto Riverdale, Victoria. The Liberals gained three from the Conservatives: Peterborough, Toronto Bracondale, Toronto St. David, and one from the Cooperative Commonwealth party, Hamilton East.

U. S. CONDEMNS JAPAN AS INVADER OF CHINA; DROPS NEUTRALITY POLICY TO BACK LEAGUE; GENEVA CALLS MEETING OF 9-POWER NATIONS

LEAGUE UNANIMOUS

Fifty Countries Endorse Move for a Parley to Seek Settlement

19 NATIONS ARE INVITED

Germany and Russia Also Are Expected to Be Asked— Roosevelt Speech Hailed

Wireless to THE NEW YORK TIMES.

GENEVA, Oct. 6.—With the tacit approval of fifty other countries and the remaining two, Poland and Siam, abstaining, the League of Nations Assembly adopted tonight the resolution of its Far Eastern Advisory Committee. This resolution authorizes League members who are parties to the Nine-Power treaty to invite the United States and other interested powers to initiate the consultation provided for in this treaty with a view to ending the Sino-Japanese conflict by agreement.

Then, instead of closing the session, the Assembly followed the precedents set during the Manchurian and Ethiopian crises and recessed. By this action Aga Khan, as President, was left free to call another session whenever he considers it necessary.

Tonight's meeting was brief, lasting slightly more than a half hour. There were only two speakers, Carl J. Hambro of Norway and Stefanus F. Qie of South Africa. Both supported the resolution.

Declares Move Adopted

When they had finished and no further speakers expressed a wish to be heard the President announced that unless a vote were requested he would take it that the Assembly did not want one. There being no objection he declared the resolution adopted.

Immediately thereafter, in accordance with the Assembly's decision, he signed letters to seventeen League members who are signatories of the Nine-Power treaty, inviting them to initiate the consultation provided for under the pact's Article VII at the earliest possible moment. The seventeen League signatories are Australia, Belgium, Bolivia, Canada, China, Denmark, France, India, Italy, Mexico, the Netherlands, New Zealand, Norway, Portugal, Sweden, the United Kingdom and the Union of South Africa.

[Article VII of the Nine-Power treaty, signed at Washington Feb. 6, 1922, reads: "The Contracting Powers agree that whenever a situation arises which in the opinion of any one of them involves the application of the stipulations of the present treaty and renders desirable discussion of such application, there shall be full and frank communication between the Contracting Powers concerned.]

League circles hinted that an invitation from Washington to hold the consultation in the capital of the United States would be particularly acceptable, as under those circumstances the Japanese might be disposed to accept. The British are especially known to hold this view.

Besides Japan, the United States and the seventeen other countries mentioned above, Germany and Soviet Russia are almost certain to be invited, though it is regarded as unlikely that Germany will accept.

Since the Advisory Committee meets again within a month it is hoped here that consultation will be called within a fortnight. The results could then be transmitted to the Advisory Committee when it meets and, if the circumstances require it, the Assembly might be reconvened.

Other Measures Threatened

GENEVA, Oct. 6 (AP).—The League put pressure on Japan tonight to end her undeclared war on China. The League Assembly threw its "moral support" to China, called on the Nine-Power treaty group to act and told Japan there might be other measures if she did not quit her war.

"China's principal need is that something should be done by outside nations to help her, but that outside nations should cease helping her enemy," Mr. Stimson declared after an exhaustive analysis of the situation, in which he branded Japan as a militarist aggressor acting in violation of international obligations under the Nine Power treaty.

While rejecting the idea of armed intervention in the Sino-Japanese conflict, Mr. Stimson emphasized that "that is very far from saying that the only alternative is a passive and shameful

Continued on Page Twelve

U. S. Statement on Japan

Special to THE NEW YORK TIMES.

WASHINGTON, Oct. 6.—Following is the text of the State Department statement issued today condemning Japan's action in China:

The Department of State has been informed by the American Minister to Switzerland of the text of the report adopted by the advisory committee of the League of Nations setting forth the advisory committee's examination of the facts of the present situation as between China and Japan. Among the principles which in the opinion of the Government of the United States should govern international relationships, if peace is to be maintained, are abstinence by all nations from use of force in the pursuit of policy and from interference in the internal affairs of other nations; adjustment of problems in international relations by process of peaceful negotiation and agreement; respect by all nations for the rights of others and observance by all nations of established obligations; and the upholding of the principle of the sanctity of treaties.

Since the beginning of the present controversy in the Far East the Government of the United States has urged upon both the Chinese and the Japanese Governments that they refrain from hostilities and has offered to be of assistance in an effort to find some means, acceptable to both parties to the conflict, of composing by pacific methods the situation in the Far East.

The Secretary of State in statements made public on July 16 and Aug. 23 made clear the position of the Government of the United States in regard to international problems and international relationships throughout the world and as applied specifically to the hostilities which are at present unfortunately going on between China and Japan. Among the principles which in the opinion of the United States should govern international relationships, if peace is to be maintained, are abstinence by all nations from use of force in the pursuit of policy and from interference in the internal affairs of other nations; adjustment of problems in international relations by process of peaceful negotiation and agreement; respect by all nations for the rights of others and observance by all nations of established obligations; and the upholding of the principle of the sanctity of treaties; that international anarchy de-

Continued on Page Twelve

STIMSON FAVORS ACTION ON JAPAN

Urges Joint Move by U. S. and Britain to Stop Supplying War Goods to Tokyo

HE PRAISES ROOSEVELT

Terms Chicago Speech 'an Act of Leadership'—Supports Our Backing of League

The text of Mr. Stimson's letter is on page 12.

An appeal that the United States lend support to the League of Nations "by a statement of its concurrence" in efforts to stop Japan's war upon China was made yesterday by former Secretary of State Henry L. Stimson in a letter to THE NEW YORK TIMES discussing the Sino-Japanese situation.

Mr. Stimson, whose letter had been completed before President Roosevelt made his Chicago address, added a paragraph in which he hailed the talk, which called for "concerted action" for peace and assailed war makers. He referred to it as "an act of leadership" which, he hoped, "will result in a new birth of American courage in facing and carrying through our responsibilities in this crisis."

"In this grave crisis in the Far East we not only must not fear to face issues of right and wrong but we must not fear to cooperate with other nations who are attempting to face those issues," Mr. Stimson declared.

Failure to act, he warned, will not keep this country out of war, but will endanger our own peace.

Assails Neutrality Laws

Assailing the recent neutrality legislation of the United States as a "policy of amoral drift" which, if continued, will make our entanglement in war more certain, Mr. Stimson suggested as one measure of practical action that the United States and Great Britain stop supplying Japan with munitions essential to the pursuit of her military and naval operations. The United States and the British Empire, he pointed out, now furnish Japan with the bulk of these commodities.

OSTRACIZE JAPAN, PITTMAN DEMANDS

Senator Asserts an 'Economic Quarantine' Would End Conflict in 30 Days

HOLDS WORLD SHOULD ACT

Calls on 'Civilized' Nations, Especially Britain, to Join U. S. in Strong Move

Special to THE NEW YORK TIMES.

RENO, Nev., Oct. 6.—Senator Key Pittman, chairman of the Senate Foreign Relations Committee, recommended an economic quarantine of Japan in a statement issued here tonight.

He declared that President Roosevelt has been very "patient and has made every effort to persuade the military government of Japan to abandon its unlawful, immoral and brutal conduct in China," and that "the continued conduct of the Japanese Government in China has conclusively proved to the world that Japan's 'excuse' that she has been only protecting her subjects in China is false.

"Great Britain is more directly affected by Japan's aggression in the United States or any other country. Great Britain backed out in 1932 and left our Government out of the League. Japan has offered the excuse of a hold-up—that is, the hold-up man needs money and the victim has it.

"Great Britain has suggested the method of compelling Japan to desist from its barbarous warfare of destruction. He holds that Japan is disseminating war disease which may involve the world and thus Japan should be quarantined as every civilized community quarantines against contagious disease.

"The Neutrality Act was not intended to meet such contagion. It was intended solely to eliminate certain causes that might lead us into foreign war. What is required now is a quarantine to prevent spread of the war disease and to stamp it out.

Continued on Page Twelve

TWO PACTS CITED

State Department Says Tokyo Breaks 9-Power and Kellogg Treaties

EMBARKS ON NEW COURSE

Acceptance by Washington of Bid to Conference Asked by League Is Foreseen

By BERTRAM D. HULEN

Special to THE NEW YORK TIMES.

WASHINGTON, Oct. 6.—Japan was condemned by the United States for her action in China and accused of having violated the Nine-Power treaty for safeguarding China and the Kellogg-Briand anti-war pact in a formal statement issued late today by the State Department.

The declaration aligned this country with the League of Nations in the condemnation of Japan as an aggressor. It is to be followed, from all indications, by American acceptance of an invitation, which has not yet been received, to participate in a conference called under the Nine-Power treaty to consider what the interested nations should do to meet the emergency.

The statement, which was issued in response to official notification of the analysis and the conclusions on the Sino-Japanese controversy by the League of Nations, marked a radical shift in American policy and represented the first step in implementing the views President Roosevelt enunciated in his Chicago speech yesterday.

New Course for U. S. Seen

Together the two moves mean, in diplomatic and political opinion, that President Roosevelt has made a direct letter of American neutrality policy and is embarked on a new course of dealing actively with aggressor nations.

The State Department statement reviewed the efforts Secretary Hull has made heretofore to encourage peace between Japan and China, recalled the pertinent points of President Roosevelt's Chicago speech, and concluded by saying: "In the light of the unfolding developments in the Far East the Government of the United States has been forced to the conclusion that the action of Japan in China is inconsistent with the principles which should govern the relationships between nations and is contrary to the provisions of the Nine-Power treaty of Feb. 6, 1922, regarding principles and policies to be followed in matters concerning China, and to those of the Kellogg-Briand pact of Aug. 27, 1928. Thus the conclusions of this Government with respect to the foregoing are in general accord with those of the Assembly of the League of Nations."

The condemnation of Japan marks the first time that the United States has declared a nation as aggressor or a violator of treaties.

First Move of the Kind

Similarly, the call for a conference under the Nine-Power treaty constitutes the first time that that pact has been invoked. Secretary of State Henry L. Stimson planned to invoke it in 1932 at the time of Japan's invasion of Manchuria, but was dissuaded when Great Britain displayed no enthusiasm for the plan. Instead, Mr. Stimson invoked American rights under the newly implemented the Kellogg-Briand pact by announcing the United States would not recognize gains won contrary to its terms.

[This is the second instance within eight days in which the United States has supported action taken by the League of Nations. Secretary Hull issued a statement on Sept. 28 condemning Japanese bombings of open cities in China when the League had adopted a resolution taking a similar stand.]

Officials in issuing the statement were thoroughly aware of the significance of the step and of its implications in relation to association of the United States with the League of Nations and in the respect that it gives the Kellogg-Briand pact.

They appreciated, although perhaps only in broad outline, that it might well lead to similar steps in future emergencies and that it might also produce adverse reactions from isolationist elements in this country. Even today peace organizations attacked President

Continued on Page Twelve

"All the News That's Fit to Print."

The New York Times.

LATE CITY EDITION
Partly cloudy, continued cold today. Tomorrow cloudy, probably snow, temperature unchanged.
Temperatures Yesterday—Max., 32; Min., 19

Copyright, 1937, by The New York Times Company

VOL. LXXXVII....No. 29,178.   Entered as Second-Class Matter, Postoffice, New York, N. Y.   NEW YORK, MONDAY, DECEMBER 13, 1937.   PPP   TWO CENTS in New York City.   THREE CENTS Within 200 Miles.   FOUR CENTS Elsewhere Except in 7th and 8th Postal Zones

DIES CLAIMS VOTES TO BEAT WAGE BILL BY RECOMMITTAL

But Despite His Poll House Leaders Hope to Pass Measure This Week

HARD FIGHT IN PROSPECT

Some Expect Norton Change in Administration to Be Turned Down

CROP PLAN TEST IS NEAR

Senate Action This Week Seen —Harrison Predicts Tax Revision by Feb. 1

Special to THE NEW YORK TIMES.

WASHINGTON, Dec. 12.—Congressional leaders plan to make a determined effort to send to conference this week two of the four measures for which the special session was called, the Farm Bill voted by the House last week and the Wages and Hours measure, which has long been tied up in the House Rules Committee.

The latter bill faces perhaps the bitterest fight of the session. When the House convenes tomorrow noon Representative Mary Norton, chairman of the Labor Committee, will call up the measure, changed in many respects from the Black-Connery bill passed by the Senate at the last regular session.

By means of a discharge petition to which 218 signatures were obtained ten days ago to force it out of the Rules Committee, the bill comes before the House, where its enemies threaten the strongest vote of opposition.

Representative Dies of Texas, a member of the Rules Committee, disclosed tonight that with other opponents he had been quietly talking a poll of the House and felt that they had enough backing to force recommittal of the bill.

Count 202 for Recommittal

"Our poll shows that 202 House members will vote for recommittal," he said. "It indicated that two-thirds of the Republicans in the House favor recommittal."

He added that at least thirty-five of the members who signed the discharge petition would vote for the motion to recommit, and that Southern foes of the measure could count on enough additional votes from the Middle West and rural towns in the East to give them a majority when the test came.

"If the bill passed, taking the most optimistic figures, it would affect not more than 500,000 workers after you deduct those who are exempt and those who are engaged in interstate employment," said Mr. Dies.

"This bill can only help a handful but at the same time its passage would increase the cost of living and thus affect the whole nation. Its real effect would be to lower wage scales and lengthen hours."

Representative Cox of Georgia, likewise a member of the Rules Committee, also expressed hostility to the measure.

"The passage of this measure is the worst thing that could take place at this time," he said. "It would throw a million out of work."

The House leadership expresses equal confidence that a wages and hours measure in some form will be passed by the end of Wednesday's session.

Boland Predicts Passage

Representative Boland, the Democratic whip, canvassed the situation over the week-end, and predicted that a bill resembling in essentials the Senate measure, which provides for a five-man administrative board with differentials as to minimum wages and maximum hours for various parts of the country, would be approved.

The leaders will fight the motion to recommit and say they regard a victory in that fight as virtually certain. Mr. Boland said a handful of those who signed the discharge petition might vote to recommit, but that there were enough votes to compensate for such a defection.

Besides having to thwart efforts of Southern members to have it recommittal, the leadership faces what may develop into a major struggle over the content of the legislation to be passed. Representative Dockweiler of California seeks to substitute for the bill a measure, strongly backed by the American Federation of Labor, which provides for a flat forty-hour maximum work week and a forty-cent minimum wage, with Federal courts and the administration by existing agencies, with Federal courts and the ag-

Continued on Page Twelve

Convicts Kill Captive Guard As Governor Begs Mercy

South Carolina Executive Pleads 2 Hours for Hostage Held in Prison Office, Then Troops Rout 6 Men With Gas

By The Associated Press.

COLUMBIA, S. C., Dec. 12.—A machine-gun company of National Guardsmen fired tear-gas shells today to subdue six convicts who stabbed a prison guard captive to death and barricaded themselves in the captain's office in a desperate attempt to escape from the State penitentiary.

The victim, Captain Olin Sanders, was stabbed five times after the felons had defied a dramatic two-hour plea by Governor Olin Johnston to give themselves up.

The youthful Governor shouted to them through the door of their barricaded refuge, urging them to submit to avoid bloodshed and obviate the necessity of calling out the National Guard.

"Get us a car. Open the gates. Otherwise it'll be too bad for Sanders," one of the felons retorted.

In vain the Governor begged them to release their captive. Two hours later the khaki-clad troopers arrived. Another plea was made by Adjt. Gen. James C. Dozier, commanding the guardsmen. Again the convicts bluntly refused, announcing they would stay there "until hell freezes over."

Governor Johnston made one final effort to persuade them.

"If you fellows will walk out there and let Captain Sanders walk out first, I'll see that nothing goes against your record," he promised.

A hoarse rumble of defiance replied, and Governor Johnston signaled the guardsmen.

"Go ahead, boys—let them have it."

A barrage of tear gas brought quick surrender. Gasping and choking, with tears streaming down their cheeks, the desperadoes emerged, one by one, with their hands up.

On the floor, bleeding profusely from stab wounds, lay Sanders. He died in a hospital a few minutes later.

The victim apparently was stabbed immediately after the guardsmen opened their tear-gas attack.

Prison officials said that Sanders was unarmed at the time of the attack because strict prison rules forbade carrying a gun into the prison yard.

Guards said he had "checked"

Continued on Page Four

SLOAN BACKS FUND BY $10,000,000 GIFT

General Motors Head Endows Foundation He Established for Economic Research

ASKS THAT STOCK BE HELD

Transfer of Holdings in His Own Concern Explained— Gains in Education Sought

Alfred P. Sloan Jr. announced plans yesterday for endowing the Alfred P. Sloan Foundation for economic research with securities worth about $10,000,000. A little more than one-third of the proposed endowment, his statement said, consists of common stock of General Motors Corporation, of which Mr. Sloan is chairman.

Lest the public misapprehend the situation, Mr. Sloan included in his statement announcing the gift a promise to recommend to the trustees of the fund that they retain the General Motors stock in their portfolio. Under SEC rules the transfer of ownership of the stock is a matter of public record.

The trust Mr. Sloan purposes to endow was established by him on July 6, 1936, as a non-profit corporation under the laws of Delaware. Harold S. Sloan, his brother, a former Associate Professor of Economics at State Teachers College, Montclair, N. J., was named executive director of the fund.

The organization of the trust was not announced until Feb. 27, 1937. At the time it was explained that the founder had been too busy with labor troubles to determine details of the fund's operation or the size of the endowment needed for its work. In the meantime, Harold Sloan established an office at 30 Rockefeller Plaza.

Sloan Explains His Gift

Mr. Sloan's statement, announcing his intention of transferring $10,000,000 of securities to the fund, follows:

"I take this means of announcing that I am in the process of donating as an endowment to the Alfred P. Sloan Foundation, which I have been developing for some years past, securities of an estimated worth of approximately $10,000,000. The specific purpose of this statement is twofold: first, to avoid any misconception as to the aims involved, and, second, to establish the objectives that I have in mind.

"I particularly wish to emphasize the fact, even if it appears self-evident, that this transaction has nothing whatsoever to do with General Motors Corporation or my official relationship with same. It is entirely a personal matter. However, among the securities involved are over 100,000 shares of common stock of General Motors.

"Due to government regulations, changes in my General Motors holdings are a matter of public record on account of my official relationship with that organization; hence it is important, especially in the period of uncertainty now existing, that no prejudice should develop as to the reasons for the action that I am taking. I shall recommend to the trustees of the foundation that they continue to hold these securities as part of its portfolio.

"As to the objectives: The Alfred P. Sloan Foundation has as its general purpose, in common with all

Continued on Page Ten

PRINCETON SENIOR IS KILLED IN FIRE

Lawrence H. Clark, 21, Found Slumped in Dormitory After Flames Sweep His Room

VICTIM OF DENSE SMOKE

Fellow-Student Arouses Seven Other Sleepers, but Fails to Locate His Friend

Special to THE NEW YORK TIMES.

PRINCETON, N. J., Dec. 12.—Lawrence H. Clark, a 21-year-old senior at the university here, was killed this morning by smoke from a fire which apparently originated in an upholstered chair in his dormitory room at 43 Mitchell Hall. He died in the room of another student across the hall from his own, his body partly draped in bedclothing which he had sought before running out into the cold.

At about 3:45 o'clock Richard B. Duane Jr., a sophomore, of Locust, N. J., and the occupant of the room in which Clark's body was found, was awakened by the noisy entrance of Clark from the hall. He saw Clark drop on one knee, seemingly having tripped over the door sill. Duane's room was instantly filled with smoke, and, clad only in pajamas and a pair of hastily snatched shoes, he ran out of the building and to the university police office on the campus, where he turned in a fire alarm. He said he believed Clark had followed him out.

Awakens Other Students

After turning in the alarm, Duane ran back to the dormitory and awakened the other students by shouting through the building. Five students were asleep in two double rooms on the ground floor and four more in single rooms on the second floor. Only when they were all out, shivering in heavy coats over pajamas, did Duane realize that Clark was not among them.

He went back into the building, climbing the stairs to the second floor, and finding that the flames, mounting through the ceiling in Clark's room, had cut off the electric current, he struck a match. By the imperfect light he looked over his own room, but could not enter Clark's because of the smoke, and concluded that Clark had somehow got out.

Back downstairs again, he once became alarmed at the absence of Clark and once again went into the building. This time the smoke was so thick he could not even reach the second floor.

All the fire apparatus of Princeton had arrived meanwhile. The clangor had resulted in the assembly of a large number of students, police and others. The firemen, on ladders, attacked the fire through the windows of Clark's room.

In a few moments it had been subdued sufficiently to permit a more thorough search. In Duane's room Clark's body was found, wedged between a chest of drawers and the wall, at the foot of Duane's bed. Apparently he had sought to find clothing in Duane's room, became blinded by the smoke and dropped unconscious. The bedclothing from Duane's bed was partly draped around his body.

Clark was taken to the university hospital immediately and, although apparently dead, Dr. C. Douglas

Continued on Page Eight

RUSSIA'S MILLIONS VOTE STALIN TICKET AMID HOLIDAY AIR

Bands Play as Most of Nation's 90,000,000 Electors Join in First Secret, Direct Poll

SUPREME SOVIET CHOSEN

Heads of Air and Tank Corps, Removed From Ballot, Are Believed in Trouble

By HAROLD DENNY
Wireless to THE NEW YORK TIMES.

MOSCOW, Dec. 12.—The Soviet Union elected its first Supreme Soviet under its new constitution today in a beautifully conducted vote that was carried out with all the precision, order and colorful decor of a May Day parade or a Bolshoi Theatre spectacle.

The authorities succeeded fully as well as they could have expected in bringing out the total electorate numbering probably 90,000,000 to vote for the only ticket in the field—the ticket headed by Joseph Stalin himself and including virtually every high government and Communist party official.

Thus the present Soviet regime can now show the world the most complete endorsement in terms of number of votes cast ever given to any government in the world's history.

Huge Turn-Out at Polls

As there was no semblance of opposition in today's election the only question was how many votes would be cast. It seemed tonight on the basis of this correspondent's visits to typical polling places in Moscow and several surrounding villages and of radio reports from all parts of the Soviet Union that virtually every one, male and female, above the age of 18 who was able to get to the polls afoot, on skis or in automobiles, trucks or sleighs had voted, and naturally for the one ticket.

Agitators went through dwellings hunting for non-voters. Where they found sick persons who were able to leave their beds cars were summoned to transport them to the polls. In one election district in Moscow a number of ill persons reported they were unable to leave their beds and requested that ballots be sent them so they could vote.

It could not be determined what was done in most such cases, but in one at least an absentee vote by a bedridden elector was allowed. This case was that of Constantin Stanislavsky, famous director of the Moscow Art Theatre, who is now 75 years old and ill of pneumonia. A ballot was sent to him and he sealed it himself and dispatched it by a member of his family, who deposited it in a box in Mr. Stanislavsky's election district here.

Results Are Broadcast

All afternoon and evening election results were broadcast as in the United States. As there was no contest, however, the bulletins were devoted to what percentage of the eligible vote had been cast.

So expeditiously were the polls handled that most polling places had little to do after midday. Bulletins late tonight showed that very nearly 100 per cent of the total possible vote had been cast in Moscow and other big centers.

As far as Moscow was concerned

Continued on Page Sixteen

Doctor Arrested in Park Ave. Hit-Run Death; Traced by Car Part Found Near the Victim

Dr. John E. Toole, 41 years old, Yale graduate and urologist, was awakened by detectives at his home, 120 East Eighty-fifth Street, shortly after 7 o'clock yesterday morning and arrested on a technical charge of homicide. The arrest followed an all-night investigation of the death of Miss Mary McCormack, 60, of 22 East 119th Street, who was hit and dragged more than 100 feet by an automobile at 10 o'clock Saturday night as she was crossing Fifty-eighth Street at Park Avenue. The motorist failed to stop.

Detectives Charles L. McGowan and Hugh Fox took Dr. Toole to the East Fifty-first Street station, where he denied responsibility for the death of the woman, whose body was not identified at the morgue until yesterday afternoon. The identification was made by her sister, Anna McCormick, a housekeeper in the home of Dr. Nicholas Murray Butler, president of Columbia University.

Dr. Toole insisted his automobile did not hit any pedestrian, the detectives quoted him as saying he felt a jar when the car was passing Fifty-eighth Street on Park Avenue. The doctor explained he thought he had passed over a depression in the street and kept on toward his home.

When the body of Miss McCormack was picked up, near by was

found part of a broken automobile radiator grill and the emblem of a Dodge car. A search of all garages in the city was started for an automobile with broken grill-work and a missing emblem. The search was not until early yesterday morning that such a car, with the front blood spattered, was found in a garage at 150 East Eighty-fourth Street. The detectives said the piece of broken radiator fitted perfectly into the frame. The automobile was listed as the property of Dr. Toole. When the detectives called at his home, Dr. Toole was asleep. He was said to have admitted he drove the automobile Saturday night, but insisted that beyond the slight jar at the scene of the accident he did not notice anything out of the ordinary. Miss McCormack was crossing Park Avenue from west to east when she was struck by a northbound automobile traveling at considerable speed.

Dr. Toole was taken from the East Fifty-first Street police station to police headquarters, where he was booked and remained pending arraignment this morning in Homicide Court.

Dr. Toole, who is single, is a graduate of the Yale class of 1920. He practices here and in Hempstead, L. I., specializing in urology and radiology.

U. S. GUNBOAT SUNK BY JAPANESE BOMBS; 1 DEAD AND 15 HURT; 54 SAVED, 18 MISSING; BRITISH WARSHIP HIT, SEAMAN DEAD

NANKING INVESTED

Japanese Expect Its Fall Soon Because Troops Are Rushing In

VITAL GATE IS CAPTURED

Naval Force Is Expected to Arrive Today to Join Land and Air Assault

By HALLETT ABEND
Special Cable to THE NEW YORK TIMES.

SHANGHAI, Monday, Dec. 13.—Japanese troops, preceded by tanks, have been pouring into Nanking since 4 A. M., when they captured Chungshan gate. The city's capitulation is imminent, according to Japanese army headquarters.

The Nanking fighting continued unabated throughout last night under clear skies and a half moon. The Japanese took yesterday the shores of Lotus Lake, which borders Nanking's north wall. Colonel and Mrs. Charles A. Lindbergh landed on this lake after their flight to China in September, 1931.

Japanese flags flew along all of the south wall before sunset yesterday. The Japanese first held Kwanghwa gate and the corner west of the gate and Chunghwa gate and another corner near it.

The Japanese Army contingent that crossed to the north bank of the Yangtze to Wukiang Sunday has captured Pukow, the southern terminus of the Tientsin-Pukow railway, directly opposite Nanking. They thus cut off the last chance of escape for the Chinese forces in the Nanking and near-by areas.

Chinese Show Bravery

Once more the rank and file of Chinese soldiery demonstrated at Nanking their extraordinary ability to take terrible punishment and hold fast under conditions which ordinarily would disheartn any fighting men.

Mostly unpaid and underfed, without any provisions for their wounded, the Chinese forced the Japanese to pay a terrific price for every foot gained around the gates. As in 1900, when Chinese forces held Tientsin's walls until a hill of corpses exceeded 7,000 and conspicuously again at Tsinan in Shantung in 1928, when they fought with similar valor, the Chinese contested every foot of the Japanese advance.

From many vantage points on the wall at Kwanghwa gate, from Purple Mountain and from other dominant heights surrounding the city the Japanese for nearly fifty hours poured shells of all sizes and machine-gun fire into the area inside Nanking's wall. There were almost hourly aerial bombings, but the Chinese continued their suicidal battle.

With the city surrounded on all land fronts the Japanese crossed the Yangtze River yesterday at Taiping, between Nanking and

Continued on Page Fifteen

Old Treaty Permits U. S. Patrol; Ships Not on Aggressive Mission

Nationals Are Protected on Yangtze Through Agreement—Silver Island Blockade by Chinese Not Responsible for Difficulties

Special to THE NEW YORK TIMES.

WASHINGTON, Dec. 12.—The United States gunboat Panay, sunk today by bombs in the Nanking battle area, was one of six or seven such patrol boats maintained in the Yangtze River by the United States under the Sino-American treaty of 1858. Other nations also maintain patrols in the river.

This treaty was conceded by China following the joint attack on that country by Britain and France in 1857-58, when they captured Canton and reduced the Taku forts guarding Tientsin. The United States and Russia did not join in the war but they insisted on sharing the rights gained by the others.

Among these was permission for foreigners to travel in the interior of China and the entrance of Christian missionaries into this field. Four ports were opened on the Yangtze and extraterritorial rights were granted to the nations concerned so they could protect their nationals. In order to protect these

foreigners and their trade and religious activities the patrol of the river was established.

Commander L. P. Lovette, naval press relations officer, who formerly commanded such craft said tonight that these vessels comprised a sort of civil "police force" for the United States and China.

Naval orders say that these boats are on duty for the special purposes of protecting United States nationals from violence, to protect them in times of emergency, to maintain uninterrupted communications, and to protect United States diplomatic and consular establishments.

He said the ships acted as police not only for the United States but for China, offering protection to China's citizens as well as to our own in times of violence or emergency. Sometimes, he said, it became necessary for the ships

Continued on Page Fourteen

JAPAN TAKES ONUS

Officers Admit Attack on Panay With Regrets— Craft Sought Safety

BRITISH VESSELS TARGETS

Two Fire at Planes as Bombs Are Aimed at Them—Two Standard Oil Ships Sunk

By The Associated Press.

SHANGHAI, Monday, Dec. 13.—Japanese bombs sank the United States gunboat Panay in the Yangtze River twenty-three miles above Nanking yesterday.

One American sailor died of his wounds. His name was not given. Eighteen other persons were unaccounted for.

There were fifty-four known survivors, some of them wounded. Among the wounded were Lieut. Comdr. James J. Hughes, commander of the Panay, and Lieutenant Arthur F. Anders, executive officer.

[Ambassador Nelson T. Johnson reported to the State Department at Washington that fifteen of the survivors had been wounded, some of them seriously, according to The Associated Press. One of the injured was an Italian seaman, he said.]

The gunboat's normal complement was fifty-five officers and men. In addition, the "mercy ship" carried at least nine American refugees, including four embassy officials.

Two Standard Oil Company ships were also sunk at the same time. No word was received of the fate of those aboard these vessels.

The Japanese Navy quickly accepted responsibility for the grave incident. A Japanese communiqué pledged immediate steps to place the blame on the military units responsible, and it regretted the bombing "most deeply."

British Gunboat Shelled

Earlier British naval reports said that Colonel Hashimoto, senior Japanese naval officer, had declared he had ordered a "fire on every ship on the river." This statement was made in reply to a British protest against shelling of the British gunboat Ladybird at Wuhu. A British seaman was killed and two other Britons were wounded there.

An Insurgent communiqué announced the government lines had collapsed under the offensive, which hit "like a bolt of lightning."

"The Reds [Government] were unable to resist the attacks," the Insurgents declared.

Rear Admiral Harry E. Yarnell, commander of the United States Asiatic Fleet, canceled his departure for Manila, scheduled for tomorrow, in face of the serious incident.

Other Ships Rush to Aid

The U. S. gunboat Oahu and the British gunboat Bee steamed under forced draught for the scene of the sinking.

The Bee was expected to reach the scene of the sinking tonight but, because of the distance down the Oahu was not expected until Tuesday.

The 450-ton Panay, especially made for river service in China, had stood by to save Americans during the Japanese siege of Nanking. Anchored in the Yangtze, the Panay was a haven for Embassy officials and other refugees when the Japanese shells crashing dangerously near caused her to seek safety up the river.

It was while steaming away from the battle zone that the vessel was sent to the bottom by Japanese bombs.

Among those aboard the Panay were George Atcheson Jr., second secretary in charge of the United States Embassy at Nanking; J. Hall Paxton, assistant military attaché, and Emile Gassie, embassy clerk.

The United States Consulate here said that other civilians believed to have been aboard were: Norman Alley, Fox Movietone cameraman; Weldon James, United Press correspondent; Norman Soong, a correspondent; Norman Bong, a Chinese-American born in China; James Marshall, Collier's correspondent of The New York Times; Roy Squires, American born in China; and Standard Oil Company representa-

Continued on Page Fourteen

TROTSKY CLEARED BY DEWEY BOARD

International Group Finds He and Son Were 'Not Guilty' of Plot Against Soviet

A 'FRAME-UP' IS CHARGED

New Evidence Contradicts the Moscow Verdicts on 21 Counts, Report Says

An international commission of inquiry headed by Dr. John Dewey declared last night that Leon Trotsky was "not guilty" of the charges against him in the Moscow trials of August, 1936, and January, 1937, and that the trials were a "frame-up."

The commission's verdict of "not guilty" applied also to Leon Sedov, Mr. Trotsky's son now residing in Paris and condemned in absentia with his father in the two trials.

Dr. Dewey announced the commission's findings at a mass meeting in the Hotel Center, 108 West Forty-third Street, attended by more than 2,000 persons, including many prominent liberals and representatives of various schools of political thought specially invited to hear a summary of the commission's report.

The report, a document of 80,000 words, will be published in book form, continuing the series of publications begun with the record of the preliminary hearings held by the commission last April in Mexico City and at which Mr. Trotsky testified at great length and was subjected to exhaustive interrogation.

Contradicts the Verdicts

The commission's conclusions, as reported by Dr. Dewey at last night's meeting, flatly contradicted the verdicts of the Moscow court on twenty-one separate counts. On the basis of "much new documentary evidence" assembled over a period of nine months in Mexico, the United States, Canada and European countries, and study of the official Soviet trial records, the commission reached the conclusion that the charges were untrue.

"The accusation of collusion with foreign powers to discredit them, and that: 'independent of extrinsic evidence the conduct of the Moscow trials was such as to convince any no prejudiced person that no effort was made to ascertain the truth.'

At the same time, the commission expressed the belief that the confessions were obtained by duress.

The Chief Findings

Supporting itself upon a "mass of new documentary evidence and affidavits," the commission offered

Continued on Page Thirteen

3 DRIVES STARTED BY SPANISH REBELS

Collapse of Loyalists Is Said to Have Resulted at Toledo, Brunete and Teruel

MADRID IS AGAIN SHELLED

Insurgents Claim 270 Planes Took Part in Friday Battle, With Victory for Them

By The Associated Press.

HENDAYE, France, at the Franco-Spanish Frontier, Dec. 12.—The Spanish Insurgent armies launched today their long-awaited general offensive. Insurgent authorities announced at Irun they struck simultaneously on the Toledo, Brunete and Teruel fronts.

An Insurgent communiqué announced the government lines had collapsed under the offensive, which hit "like a bolt of lightning."

"The Reds [Government] were unable to resist the attacks," the Insurgents declared.

The offensives at Brunete and Toledo were directed at Madrid, Spain's long besieged capital, while the drive on the Teruel front is faced toward Valencia.

270 Planes in Battle

Insurgent dispatches today gave further details of Friday's aerial battle near Saragossa. They said massed air fleets totaling 270 warplanes had clashed. Twenty-five Government planes were shot down and only one Insurgent plane was lost, it was said.

When 100 Government planes encircled the supposed raiders, 150 Insurgent warplanes suddenly swooped, putting the Government fleet to flight with a quarter of its strength lost in a few minutes.

Insurgent planes made a number of fresh incursions in Government zones Saturday, meeting renewed resistance. One Insurgent squadron invaded the Aragon front, east of Saragossa, bombing the outskirts of Castejon del Puente. A Government communiqué said that the raid was checked with a minimum of damage.

Madrid Heavily Shelled

By HERBERT L. MATTHEWS
Wireless to THE NEW YORK TIMES.

MADRID, Dec. 12.—Many dinners were spoiled in Madrid tonight when the Rebels chose from 7:40 to 8:30 to bombard the center of the city with considerable intensity. They may not have been good dinners, for the Madrileños are not suffering from any great surplus of food this Winter.

We had a perfectly good dish of succotash partly ruined in our flat by one of three shells which hit

Continued on Page Fourteen

"All the News That's Fit to Print."

The New York Times.

LATE CITY EDITION
Fair and moderately cold today.
Tomorrow fair, with slowly rising temperature.
Temperatures Yesterday—Max., 38; Min., 29

Copyright, 1938, by The New York Times Company.

VOL. LXXXVII....No. 29,248.

Entered as Second-Class Matter,
Postoffice, New York, N. Y.

NEW YORK, MONDAY, FEBRUARY 21, 1938.

PP

TWO CENTS in New York City. | THREE CENTS Within 200 Miles. | FOUR CENTS Elsewhere Except in 7th and 8th Postal Zones.

FEDERAL AGENCIES CONSIDER FORCING RAILROAD MERGERS

Groups Shaping Rehabilitation Plans Believe Plight Inclines Congress to Idea

FAVOR THREE YEARS' GRACE

Would Allow Time for Voluntary Consolidations, With Federal Action Afterward

FOR TEMPORARY POOLING

Some Officials Hold This a Need Until a Long-Range Plan Becomes Effective

By JOHN H. CRIDER
Special to The New York Times.

WASHINGTON, Feb. 20.—Legislation for forced consolidations of railroads is being considered seriously in at least three of the government offices now preparing plans to be laid before President Roosevelt at his rail conference scheduled for the coming week.

It was learned that some officials are advancing a plan which would apply the "death sentence" technique of the Holding Company Act to railroad consolidations. Under this procedure the railroads would have a certain period of years in which to submit voluntary unification plans, after which a government agency would prepare a plan for them.

"Like most remedies for the nation's rail problems, the idea of forced or compulsory consolidation has been considered for years, with little favorable response from Congress, even for milder remedies than the one now gaining ground. Rail reformers are hopeful that this time Congress will relent in view of the unusually weak plight of the railroads.

"Wasteful" Competition a Factor

President Roosevelt, Senator Burton K. Wheeler, in charge of the Senate investigation of railroad finances, and the Interstate Commerce Commission in its annual report have stated that "wasteful" competition is one of the fundamental railroad ills.

The I. C. C. went so far in its annual report as to state that "no competitive industry can work out its salvation through a price-increasing policy alone." The best expert opinion in official Washington seems to be that a rate increase, such as the $517,000,000 rate rise which the I. C. C. is expected to grant to the railroads can be at most only a temporary remedy.

It is felt that compulsory consolidations cannot solve the immediate economic emergency faced by the railroads and that rate increases and perhaps some form of pooling may have to be employed until a long-range plan can be effected. Pooling is condemned by some as an incentive to inefficiency since the weak railroads are carried along by the strong.

Senator Wheeler's investigating committee, the I. C. C., the Securities and Exchange Commission, and the Reconstruction Finance Corporation are among the government agencies now formulating plans to be considered at the White House conference.

Financial Position Weak

The current efforts in official circles to work out a permanent solution to the railroad problem arises from the unusually weak financial position of the country's railroads, due partly to increased operating costs, the decline in general business activity, and competition from other forms of transportation, but the real work was started when the President discussed the problem at a press conference on Dec. 10. He questioned the necessity for maintaining parallel lines of railroad with inadequate traffic.

He also referred to the reports of Commissioner Joseph B. Eastman of the Interstate Commerce Commission as Federal Coordinator of Transportation in 1933 and 1934 which discussed the problems of consolidation at some length. As a consequence there has been a considerable demand for these reports, particularly for the first one, which contained in the appendix a report by Leslie Craven, counsel to the coordinator, upholding the constitutionality of compulsory consolidations and recommending a modification of the method employed in England.

Some of those now preparing plans to lay before the President feel with Mr. Craven that under "any consolidation program which is non-compulsory and not fully comprehensive, it is almost certain that uneconomic and inefficient groupings will result due to the inevitable inclination of the carriers which initiate consolidations to grab favorable lines in the effort

Continued on Page Eight

Swiss Make Romansh Fourth Official Tongue

By The Associated Press.

BERNE, Switzerland, Feb. 20.—Swiss voted by an overwhelming majority today to establish Romansh as the fourth official language of Switzerland.

The vote was considered by some observers as a slap at Italy, where Fascisti say Romansh, an obscure language that is spoken only in part of Grisons canton, is an Italian dialect.

German is spoken by about 71 per cent of the Swiss, French by 22 per cent, Italian by 6 per cent and Romansh by 1 per cent.

A resolution giving the Federal Council power to prevent arms shipments to warring nations and providing for partial control of armament industries also was approved.

TENEMENT BLAZE KILLS 3, INJURES 9

Families Routed in 165th St. Fire, Third in Building Unit in Less Than Two Years

DARING RESCUES CUT TOLL

Cripple Is Carried to Safety— Man Leaps to Death, Wife Is Killed Shielding Baby

The third fire since June, 1936, in adjoining three-story buildings at 761-63 East 165th Street, between Forest and Tinton Avenues, the Bronx, killed three persons early yesterday morning and caused injuries to nine others, including an infant orphaned by the blaze.

Hampered by the collapse of a stairway under which the flames were believed to have started, firemen of seven engine companies and two hook-and-ladder units made a series of dangerous rescues from the second and third floors of No. 763, virtually all of which was destroyed except its yellow-brick front.

At first it was believed that the fire was incendiary, but after an all-day investigation Assistant District Attorney George Pilzer and Assistant Fire Marshal Martin Scott announced at 9:30 o'clock last night that the fire was not of suspicious origin. They had spent Hours questioning tenants of the building and others living near by.

One of those hurt was a passer-by who aided in the rescue work. Another volunteer, boosted on the shoulders of friends before the apparatus arrived, cut his hand in smashing a second-floor window to free tenants. The two were Thomas Smith, 35, of 1,009 Union Avenue, who suffered a sprained knee and cut thumb, and Joseph Barrett, 27, of 486 East 165th Street, whose left hand was injured.

Francis Dunn, 38, of 857 Fox Street, who was later cut on the head by falling glass, turned in the alarm at 3:04. He was on his way home when he noticed curling flames in the building. By the time the first fire apparatus arrived, Smith, Dunn and others had awakened all the tenants in No. 761 and the building had been cleared.

Flames Burst Through Roof

The blaze centered, however, beneath the stairway of No. 763 and spread rapidly to the top, where it divided and ate its way into the top floor of both units of the building. One witness said it suddenly burst through the roof like a greased chute.

Smoke in the hallway thickened, but members of Engine Company 50 tried to get up the stairs anyway. Fireman Terence A. Nugent, who subsequently needed medical aid, was one of those nearly trapped when the stairs crumbled.

While his colleagues swung their ladders toward the building, a man appeared at the third floor window over the entrance, clambered to the sill and stared down, terrified.

A confusion of shouts rose from the street. Some cried "Jump!" Others yelled "Back! Back!" The man jumped. But while would-be rescuers extended their arms, his body struck the broad, jutting cornice between the second and ground floors. The deflection catapulted him beyond them to the street, and he was fatally injured. He was William Theofanus, 62, whose wife, Armione, 41, was burned in the bedroom while shielding their baby, 5-month-old Betsy. The fire-fighting crew of a second alarm, rescues by ladder were accomplished with comparatively little difficulty. But in the case of William Sculla, 45-year-old paralytic, Firemen John Mullen and Vincent Howard risked their lives to fight their way to his bed.

Continued on Page Twenty

ORTIZ INAUGURATED AMID WIDE ACCLAIM BY THE ARGENTINES

Nation Greets Six American Airplanes as a Major Part of Colorful Ceremony

PRESIDENT IS A CIVILIAN

Public Reaffirms Its Faith in Free Rule, Regarding U. S. as Example and Friend

By JOHN W. WHITE
Special Cable to The New York Times.

BUENOS AIRES, Argentina, Feb. 20.—Dr. Roberto M. Ortiz was inaugurated the twenty-first constitutional President of the Argentine Republic this afternoon in a colorful ceremony amid widespread popular acclaim. In Argentina lawyers have the title of Doctor and this puts the Presidency again under a civilian title; the last two Presidents were generals.

The presence of six giant U. S. Army bombers of the type known as "flying fortresses" associated the United States with Argentina on this occasion in a manner in which no foreign country has participated at any inauguration in recent years. The planes arrived on Friday after a nonstop-smashing flight from Miami, bearing a letter from President Roosevelt to President Ortiz, expressing the best wishes of the American Government and the American people for his forthcoming government.

Nothing that the United States has done in Latin America, with the possible exception of President Roosevelt's visit a year ago, has ever aroused such an enthusiastic response on the part of the Argentine people. The newspapers have published the most laudatory editorials extending a hearty welcome to the American fliers and expressing their appreciation of the good-will of the government that sent them.

Faith in Democracy

People here have seized upon the visit of the United States fliers as an opportunity to reaffirm their faith in democracy and express their disapproval of totalitarian regimes. South America, including Argentina, has been subjected to such intense propaganda from European totalitarian countries, especially Italy, during the last year that this propaganda has now reached the state expressed in the Spanish words "contra producente" —working to defeat its own aims.

The people have become resentful of this high-pressure propaganda. They have enthusiastically greeted the big American fighting planes as messengers of peace and good-will from the country to which the South Americans have always looked as their model democracy.

Public opinion in Argentina was very cold to the intimation that the Italian planes that recently visited Brazil might come to Buenos Aires for the inauguration. The Italians changed their minds and did not come. No foreign mission has ever been more enthusiastically received than the American aviators whose flight was not announced until two days before they started.

Italian newspapers both here and in Italy have not mentioned the American flight. German papers here gave it a paragraph hidden away on an inside page. Both devoted pages to two recent Italian flights.

This was an ideally beautiful Summer day with the bright blue sky and blazing sun that are featured in the Argentine flag. The Argentine Army and Navy Flying

Continued on Page Seven

King Issues Fascist Charter for Rumania; Constitution Sets Up a Corporative State

Wireless to The New York Times.

VIENNA, Feb. 20.—A dictatorial Constitution was given to Rumania tonight by a proclamation signed by King Carol. It was not countersigned by any of his Ministers.

The democratic parliamentary system is abolished and replaced by a Fascist corporative Chamber and Senate, where various trades and occupations will be represented. The distribution of land under the land reform scheme stands, but increased compensation will be given for mineral rights taken over by the State. Special measures will be taken against corruption. Trial by jury is abolished.

In the proclamation Carol says: "I have been moved by one idea only—the love of my people and the need to rescue the fatherland."

The Constitution promises to peoples that have lived for centuries on the soil of present-day Rumania that would lay down general principles of policy, and a Cabinet to frame legislation that would be submitted to the King and the Crown Council.

A corporative State, such a dual system would resemble that of Italy, with her Fascist Grand Council and Cabinet.

form of taking a plebiscite of the people's views on this dictated Constitution.

King Carol assumed direct control of the Rumanian Government early this month, when he forced the pro-Fascist Premier Octavian Goga out of office to make way for a national Cabinet headed by Dr. Miron Cristea, Patriarch of the Rumanian Orthodox Church.

The King suspended the Constitution, promising to replace it as soon as the situation created by M. Goga's leanings toward Germany and Italy and his anti-Semitism had calmed.

The new Constitution had been generally expected to provide for a dual administration: a Crown Council, composed of distinguished Rumanians, that would lay down general principles of policy, and a Cabinet to frame legislation.

There are rumors that on Thursday Rumania will go through the

Roosevelt Silent on Hitler, But May Give Views Soon

Special to The New York Times.

HYDE PARK, N. Y., Feb. 20.—The temporary White House was completely silent tonight on President Roosevelt's reaction to the address of Chancellor Hitler to the German Reichstag. But there were suggestions that he might soon make known in an informal way the views of his Administration toward the political situation abroad.

Marvin H. McIntyre, the President's secretary, insisted that Mr. Roosevelt passed the day resting from the cares of his office, and that he had talked only with members of his immediate family and the vestryman of St. James Episcopal Church here.

Despite the official reticence, however, there was no doubt that the President was in close touch with the State Department.

EDEN'S RESIGNATION DISTRESSES FRANCE

Belief Prevails That British 'Capitulation' Must Reduce Leadership of Paris

SMALL ALLIES FEARED FOR

Chautemps and Delbos Confer With Ambassador Phipps, Calling Him Urgently

By P. J. PHILIP
Wireless to The New York Times.

PARIS, Feb. 20.—The resignation of British Foreign Secretary Anthony Eden has caused much more concern in France than anything that Chancellor Adolf Hitler said today. Immediately after the announcement was made, Ambassador Sir Eric Phipps hurried over to see Premier Camille Chautemps and Foreign Minister Yvon Delbos, presumably to assure them that British friendship for France and Anglo-French cooperation would not come as close as ever.

But such assurances are not likely to alter the conclusion that what is called here the Germanophile clique in Great Britain has won, and that henceforth France will be reduced to a very different role in European affairs from that which she has been accustomed to play.

It is a poor consolation to be told by Hitler that she has nothing to fear from Germany "if she minds her own business." And it will be meat for much criticism of M. Delbos and his aides that this abandonment should be the reward of their steady support of British policy during the past two years, or rather, as it will be called, their constant subservient agreement.

Bitter Clash Forthcoming

It is too early to forecast what the effects will be here. What is clear, however, is that there will be a bitter fight between those who clamor for complete abandonment of the non-intervention policy in Spain and a frank espousal of the republican cause, and those who will counsel prudence and that France

Continued on Page Three

BRITAIN IS SHOCKED

Foreign Secretary Quits Over Issue of Seeking Deals With Dictators

CRANBORNE GOES OUT, TOO

Two Other Ministers Waver— Outburst Is Expected in Commons Today

By FERDINAND KUHN Jr.
Special Cable to The New York Times.

LONDON, Feb. 20.—Foreign Secretary Anthony Eden resigned from the British Cabinet tonight, no longer willing to approve or support the methods of Prime Minister Neville Chamberlain and the majority of his colleagues in seeking settlements with Italy and Germany.

He took with him into retirement Viscount Cranborne, Under-Secretary for Foreign Affairs. At least two other Ministers—Walter E. Elliot, Secretary of State for Scotland, and William S. Morrison, Minister of Agriculture—had contemplated resigning with Mr. Eden, but late tonight they had not carried their intentions to the point of action.

Viscount Halifax, Lord President of the Council, will direct the Foreign Office temporarily, with Mr. Chamberlain himself probably taking charge of foreign affairs for a time in the House of Commons.

Eden Is Determined

The Cabinet had tried for more than three hours in the afternoon to persuade Mr. Eden to change his mind, but this time nothing could shake his determination.

As a last resort the Ministers begged Mr. Eden to accept some other office or to say he was resigning on grounds of ill health. But he refused all such suggestions. A break had come on a question of policy and he saw no reason why he should conceal it.

Tonight, pale and haggard, Mr. Eden walked abruptly across Downing Street, where a crowd was waiting to cheer him, and called at No. 10. Inside the historic Prime Minister's house Mr. Chamberlain was in anxious consultation with his Ministers.

But Mr. Eden stayed only long enough to hand in a formal letter of resignation. After four minutes he strode back to the Foreign Office in the adjoining street. In his two years and two months of incessant responsibilities it was at an end.

Refers to 'Difference'

"The events of the last few days," wrote Mr. Eden, "have made plain a difference between us on a decision of great importance in itself and far-reaching in its consequences. I cannot recommend to Parliament a policy with which I am not in agreement."

Mr. Eden went on to admit a "difference of outlook between us in respect to international problems of the day and also as to the methods whereby we should seek to resolve them." He reminded Mr. Chamberlain that it was not in the interests of the nation that Ministers should work "in uneasy partnership," especially the Foreign Secretary and the Prime Minister.

The letter ended with a note of thanks for "help and counsel" and a polite and doubtless sincere assurance that "our differences, whatever they may be, cannot efface that memory nor influence our friendship."

The stilted wording of Mr. Chamberlain's reply showed what a shock to him and his Cabinet this resignation had been. The Prime Minister wrote of his "most profound regret" and of the "distinction" with which Mr. Eden had administered the Foreign Office. His regret was all the greater, said Mr. Chamberlain, "because such differences as he feels, in other words, that Mr. Eden's fall has caused a personal enemy to disappear as head of the British Foreign Office.

It cannot be doubted that his resignation will take advantage of the new situation.

Continued on Page Two

Eden=Chamberlain Letters

By The Associated Press.

LONDON, Feb. 20.—The texts of Foreign Secretary Anthony Eden's letter of resignation to Prime Minister Neville Chamberlain and the Prime Minister's reply follow:

My Dear Prime Minister:

The events of the last few days have made plain a difference between us on a decision of great importance in itself and far-reaching in its consequences.

I cannot recommend to Parliament a policy with which I am not in agreement.

Apart from this, I have become increasingly conscious, as I know you have also, of the difference in outlook between us in respect to the international problems of the day and also as to the methods whereby we should seek to resolve them.

It cannot be in the country's interest that those who are called upon to direct its affairs should work in uneasy partnership, fully conscious of differences in outlook yet hoping they will not recur.

This applies with special force to the relationship between the Prime Minister and the Foreign Secretary.

It is for these reasons that with very deep regret I have decided that I must leave you and your colleagues with whom I have been associated during years of great difficulty and stress.

May I end on a personal note?

I can never forget the help and counsel you have always so readily given me, both before and since you became Prime Minister.

Our differences, whatever they may be, cannot efface that memory nor influence our friendship.

Yours ever,
ANTHONY EDEN.

Mr. Chamberlain's Reply

My Dear Anthony:

It is with the most profound regret, shared by all our colleagues, that I have received your intimation of your decision

Continued on Page Three

ITALY IS JUBILANT AS EDEN QUITS POST

Sees Relations With Britain Improved With Change in the Foreign Office

HITLER SPEECH IS HAILED

But Strain on Friendship Is Seen if Reich Interferes Actively in Austria

By ARNALDO CORTESI
Wireless to The New York Times.

ROME, Feb. 20.—The news of the resignation of Anthony Eden, British Foreign Secretary, reached Rome late this evening and quickly spread through the city, causing great satisfaction everywhere, as was to be expected. In the Foreign Office Mr. Eden's resignation is believed to remove one of the great obstacles to the conclusion of an Italian-British understanding and, as this is still one of the main objectives of the present foreign policy, it is thought that official negotiations soon will be opened with better chances of success than in the past.

Italians have, whether rightly or wrongly, been convinced that for a long time there has been a conflict of opinion in the British Cabinet between one school of thought, headed by Prime Minister Neville Chamberlain, that was in favor of an agreement with Italy, and another, headed by Mr. Eden, that made an agreement dependent on conditions, such as the withdrawal of Italians from Spain, that Italy could not accept or was not willing to accept.

Mr. Eden's resignation is regarded as a victory for Mr. Chamberlain's faction and, therefore, likely to bring an Italian-British understanding nearer by insuring that Italy's desire to make friends with Britain is met by an equal desire on Britain's part to make friends with Italy.

Claim Personal Defeat

It is thought in Italy that Mr. Eden is more or less smarting under the failure of his scheme to upset Premier Benito Mussolini's plans in Ethiopia by means of sanctions and that it is believed were actuated by personal animosity against Italy.

Mr. Eden has, therefore, always been the target of strong attacks by the Italian press, which, sometimes openly and sometimes by innuendo, accused him of allowing his private grudges to play too large a part in his handling of his country's foreign affairs. Italians feel, in other words, that Mr. Eden's fall has caused a personal enemy to disappear as head of the British Foreign Office.

It cannot be doubted that his resignation will take advantage of the new situation.

Continued on Page Five

NAZIS CELEBRATE IN AUSTRIAN FETES

Great Strength Is Shown in the Provinces, but Numbers Are Small in Vienna

HITLER THREAT IS FEARED

Patriots Are Bitter, Hearing No Pledge of Independence in Chancellor's Talk

By G. E. R. GEDYE
Wireless to The New York Times.

VIENNA, Feb. 20.—Throughout Chancellor Adolf Hitler's speech Vienna's streets were like those of a dead city. Patriots and Nazis alike were indoors, patiently listening, the former hoping to hear the promises made at the Berchtesgaden meeting with the Austrian Chancellor fulfilled, the latter to learn whether there would be flaming words with which to light the torch of a Nazi uprising.

Instructions had come from Munich for small but peaceful Nazi demonstrations today. A Nazi journalist told me today, however, that three or four days hence there would be large-scale demonstrations. He produced the date. Presumably it is Thursday, when Chancellor Kurt Schuschnigg speaks.

It has become fairly common knowledge here that Hitler solemnly promised Dr. Schuschnigg that if he accepted the terms dictated under the threat of invasion Germany would today recognize Austria's independence, the political monopoly of the Fatherland Front and guarantee suspension of the support of the Austrian Nazis with money and propaganda material from Germany.

Threat to Austria Seen

When the speech ended without the least effort by Hitler to fulfill his part of the bargain, there was great indignation. But more serious than this was the bitterness caused by Hitler's silence on the question of Austrian independence, which was taken as equivalent to a threat that soon would be put into execution.

During the broadcast Vienna Nazis listened quietly in their favorite cafes. Immediately after ward street demonstrations began, but not on any serious scale. Three hundred Nazis marched past the German Legation singing the "Horst Wessel Song" and shouting "Heil Hitler." The police allowed the demonstrators to march but did not allow them to stand outside the legation. Soon afterward similar small

Continued on Page Three

HITLER DEMANDS RIGHT OF SELF-DETERMINATION FOR GERMANS IN AUSTRIA AND CZECHOSLOVAKIA; EDEN RESIGNS IN CRISIS OVER BRITAIN'S POLICY

NAZI POWER CITED

Status Quo Repudiated by Fuehrer—Restates Colonial Demands

TONE OF TALK ANTI-BRITISH

Resignation of Eden Is Hailed as Greatest Victory of German Diplomacy

Chancellor Hitler in a militant speech to the Reichstag yesterday made a strong point of the right for "self-determination" for the 10,000,000 Germans in Austria and Czechoslovakia. He indicated force must be used in the end to break the status quo. He promised to go ahead with plans to enlarge the army. He assailed British policy, making a direct attack on Mr. Eden, and demanded colonies.

Disputes in the British Cabinet over proposed negotiations for a settlement with Italy and Germany led to the resignation of Foreign Secretary Eden. Viscount Halifax took temporary control of the Foreign Office, but Prime Minister Chamberlain will direct his policies.

France was fearful of losing her position as leader on the European Continent as a result of Mr. Eden's retirement. Italians, on the other hand, were jubilant over the passing of the Secretary, long regarded as a foe of their country.

Nazis held large demonstrations in Austrian provinces, but made a poor showing in Vienna.
[All stories on Page 1.]

Main Points of Hitler's Speech to the Reichstag on Page 4.

Hitler Shows Militancy

By OTTO D. TOLISCHUS
Wireless to The New York Times.

BERLIN, Feb. 20.—In the most militant speech of his career, which is already hailed here as the final cause for the overthrow of British Foreign Secretary Anthony Eden, Chancellor Hitler outlined today for the Reichstag those principles and conditions through which National Socialist Germany proposes to retain her place in the sun and which, in her view, is alone able to preserve peace.

In some respects this most anxiously awaited speech was sufficiently vague to allay some of the worst fears in certain capitals, already primed for sensational extras. In respect to the two events which have most alarmed the world recently, namely the reorganization of the government and the army command and Austria's "cold Anschluss" with the Third Reich, it was even disappointing in its paucity of new revelations.

In both of these cases Hitler has stuck entirely to the understatements of the official communiqués previously published.

Right of Self-Determination

The speech's real keynote was the proposition that by virtue of their efficiency and accomplishments the German people, organized in and represented by the National Socialist Third Reich, constituted a great power therefore entitled to equal rights with all other great powers, including the right of self-determination. This right of self-determination, according to Wilson's fourteen points, was specifically proclaimed by Hitler for the "10,000,000 Germans" living in the two states adjacent to German borders.

These States are Austria, with nearly 7,000,000 inhabitants, and Czechoslovakia, with a German minority of more than 3,000,000.

Despite the occasional vagueness there was no possibility of mistaking the final implications of this speech, with which the world will have to reckon henceforth. It was a frank repudiation of the status quo conception of world politics and an equally frank avowal of power politics based on the vital, if egotistic, interests of nations—a dedication to the proposition that might commands a new right.

League Policies Repudiated

It is in this sense that the whole speech was also an outspoken repudiation of the legalistic conception of peace as represented by the League of Nations policy of Mr. Eden. Further underlined by the open if ironic attacks upon Mr. Eden per-

Continued on Page Three

"All the News That's Fit to Print."

The New York Times.

LATE CITY EDITION
Generally fair and warmer today.
Tomorrow mostly cloudy, mild temperatures, colder at night.
Temperature Yesterday—Max. 46; Min. 26

Copyright, 1938, by The New York Times Company.

VOL. LXXXVII..No. 29,267.

Entered as Second-Class Matter,
Postoffice, New York, N. Y.

NEW YORK, SATURDAY, MARCH 12, 1938.

PP

TWO CENTS In New York City. | THREE CENTS Within 300 Miles. | FOUR CENTS Elsewhere Except in 7th and 8th Postal Zones.

A. E. MORGAN DEFIES PRESIDENT'S AIRING OF TVA BOARD ROW

Again and Again He Declines at Hearing in Roosevelt's Office to Give 'Facts'

SAYS IT IS UP TO CONGRESS

He Is Told He Should Resign if Not Willing to Support Accusations He Made

TWO COLLEAGUES HEARD

Lilienthal and H. A. Morgan Put Before Chief Executive Data Defending Their Course

A summary of Mr. Roosevelt's inquiry in TVA on Page 8.

By TURNER CATLEDGE
Special to The New York Times.

WASHINGTON, March 11.—President Roosevelt met open defiance today in his efforts to investigate dissension in the Tennessee Valley Authority when Arthur E. Morgan, chairman of the board, refused to submit evidence in support of his charges against his fellow-directors and reiterated, instead, his demand for a Congressional investigation.

Chairman Morgan sat with the other board members, Dr. Harcourt A. Morgan and David E. Lilienthal, for six hours in the President's office, the most unusual meeting of its kind ever held in Washington.

Time and time again the President heard the chairman ask him to bring forth evidence to back his charges. He heard the other directors spread before the President the grounds on which they had counter-charged that the chairman was undermining the TVA and that they could work with him no longer.

Dr. Morgan even heard the suggestion from the President's lips that he should resign if he were unwilling to support with facts his accusations that "fairness" and "decency" were impossible in the TVA administration with the other two members on the board.

Says He Is an "Observer"

Except for rare intervals when he defended himself with a sentence or two against the charges of his associate directors, Chairman Morgan remained openly defiant of the proceedings. Throughout, he maintained the position he had stated shortly after 11 A. M. when he marched into the President's office behind the others:

"I am an observer and not a participant in this alleged process of fact finding."

As the conference temporarily ended early tonight, President Roosevelt told the three TVA board members that it was their duty to the country not to continue their "personal" row any longer. He told them that if they could not reach a settlement among themselves, it was the duty of those who could not see their way to do so, to resign. He gave them until 11 A. M. next Friday to submit any other statements or evidence to prove their charges and, furthermore, to determine whether they would be able to compose their differences without a resignation.

This statement from the President was widely interpreted in Washington as an ultimatum to Chairman Morgan either to drop or substantiate his statement by next Friday or quit.

Expect Morgan to Resist

Simultaneously the Presidential statements aroused wide speculation as to whether Mr. Roosevelt had the power to remove Chairman Morgan or any of the other TVA directors. From Dr. Morgan's attitude, observers concluded that he would resist any effort at ouster until his case was heard before a Congressional committee.

Various data concerning the dispute were brought into the open at the Presidential hearing and the two groups made it plainer than ever that they are separated by a chasm of professional and personal feeling which will require little short of a political miracle if it is to be patched up.

Opening the meeting with a statement of the necessity, in the public interest, of disclosing the facts upon which Chairman Morgan had based his charges against the other directors, the President turned to Dr. Morgan for a reply, but he received, instead, a refusal to answer.

The President read the accusations made in recent statements by Chairman Morgan and at the end of each asked for specifications. As often as Mr. Roosevelt demanded "facts," Dr. Morgan stood on his previous statement, in which he said in effect that he would have nothing to do with the President's personal inquiry.

The questioning revealed that Dr.

Continued on Page Nine

Flower Peddler Freed By Defiant Magistrate

In defiance of a letter from Chief Magistrate Jacob Gould Schurman urging city magistrates to impose heavier fines on flower vendors, Magistrate Sabbatino suspended sentence yesterday on a peddler in Coney Island Court, declaring that "nobody can tell me what to do except my Creator, through my conscience."

After releasing Thomas Hyden, 23-year-old peddler, of 357 Eighty-seventh Street, Brooklyn, Judge Sabbatino made public the letter from his chief. Terming the instructions "insulting," he said:

"In the letter I received, I was told that I should sentence floral peddlers to pay fines of $5 or to serve two-day jail terms, and should be even stricter with second offenders. The people of this city should heed the many robberies that are committed instead of worrying about floral peddlers."

WHITNEY ARRESTED ON SECOND CHARGE

Accused by the State of Using $109,384 Yacht Club Fund to Get a Loan

BAIL PLACED AT $25,000

Prompt Indictment Will Be Sought—Bennett-Dewey Feud Is Revealed

For the second time in two days Richard Whitney, senior partner of the brokerage firm which bears his name and former president of the New York Stock Exchange, was arrested, fingerprinted, photographed, haled into court and held in bail yesterday on a charge of grand larceny in the first degree.

This time he was accused of the theft of bonds with a face value of $153,200 and present market value of $109,384 belonging to the New York Yacht Club, of which he had custody as treasurer of the club, and their use as collateral for a personal loan of $100,000 from the Public National Bank and Trust Company of New York without the permission or knowledge of the club. His charge after arraignment in the Felony Court before City Magistrate Thomas A. Aurelio, who held him for the grand jury.

The penalty fixed by law for conviction on the charge of grand larceny in the first degree is from five to ten years in State's prison for each offense.

Total Bail $35,000

Mr. Whitney now has his liberty on $35,000 bail, as he was freed in $10,000 on Thursday by Judge William Allen in the Court of General Sessions on the charge of stealing $105,000 in securities from the estate of his father-in-law, George H. Sheldon, of which he was an executor and trustee, and of which his wife, his sister-in-law, the widow of Judge Daniel F. Murphy of the Court of Special Sessions; Harvard University and St. Paul's School at Concord, N. H., were the beneficiaries.

Ambrose V. McCall, Assistant State Attorney General, has been conducting daily hearings on behalf of Attorney General John J. Bennett Jr. since the Whitney firm was suspended by the Stock Exchange on Tuesday, informed Magistrate Aurelio that his investigation had already shown shortages of nearly $1,000,000 in the Whitney accounts. He said that in view of this and other circumstances Attorney General Bennett regarded the $10,000 bail asked by District Attorney Thomas E. Dewey of New York County in the Sheldon estate case as entirely insufficient.

Feud Is Revealed

Mr. McCall's statements brought into the open a feud that has been developing behind the scenes since District Attorney Dewey called a witness from the Attorney General's inquiry before the grand jury and obtained the indictment in the Sheldon case by a surprise move.

Hurrying here from Albany yesterday morning, Attorney General Bennett made no secret of his resentment at Mr. Dewey's action. He said that a district attorney had never before stepped into a case while it was under investigation by the Attorney General, and that he saw no necessity of Mr. Dewey acting as he had done. In the ordinary course of events, Mr. Bennett explained, his office would have presented the Sheldon case to the grand jury and prosecuted it just as it intends to do with the grand jury charge that ever that he was concurrent jurisdiction with the State prosecutor.

In view of the indictment obtained by Mr. Dewey, the Attorney General said he did not intend to accept Mr. Whitney's offer to testify on the State investigation. If it had not been for Thursday's indictment, he added, the broker would have

Continued on Page Eighteen

TAX BILL IS PASSED BY HOUSE, 294 TO 97; SENATE TO SPEED IT

Three Hours of Continuous Voting on Amendments Precede House Action

'THIRD BASKET' IS OUT

Liquor, Pork Import Levies Replace It—Profits, Gains Imposts Are Retained

By CHARLES W. HURD
Special to The New York Times.

WASHINGTON, March 11.—The House passed the new Tax Bill today after three hours of continuous voting, in which a roll-call confirmed its former informal action eliminating a special levy of 20 per cent on the income of large closely held corporations. Adopted in place of the "third basket" surtax were new taxes on liquor and imported pork products. Final passage was voted 294 to 97.

The bill, which is expected to yield between $5,000,000,000 and $5,300,000,000 annually was ordered sent to the Senate immediately. There the Finance Committee will begin studies of it on Monday in expectation of a quick report.

Final House action on the bill occurred in the presence of almost all members on the floor, that being in itself a rare occurrence.

These members, permitted by the leadership only to vote and not to debate, carried on loud conversation among themselves, laughed and occasionally applauded as some member shouted "Aye" or "Nay" in response to his name through the dreary succession of roll-calls, one teller count and one standing division.

New Corporation Clause Voted

The most important change in the bill, as compared with current tax laws, consists of readjusted rates and schedules for corporation taxes, reported in detail previously, which are expected to make their burden more equitable.

However, the House refused again today, by an overwhelming vote on a roll-call, to reconsider its action in completing in effect the much criticized undistributed profits tax and the capital gains tax.

The results of the roll-calls, in the order in which they were taken, follow:

The House adopted, 233 to 153, the McCormack Amendment which eliminated the "third basket" contained in Section 1B.

It adopted, 201 to 182, an amendment by Representative Thompson of Illinois placing a new excise of six cents a pound on imported pork and three cents a pound on imported pork.

If approved, 290 to 96, an additional tax of 25 cents a gallon on spirits, proposed by Representative Robertson, to be added to the $2 rate now in effect.

It defeated, 292 to 94, a motion by Representative Treadway of Massachusetts, to recommit the bill to the Ways and Means Committee with instructions to eliminate the undistributed profits tax and to modify the corporate gains.

The final roll-call was on adoption of the bill.

A teller vote resulted in approval, by 125 to 96, of an amendment by Representative Boileau to include Engleman spruce among woods ex-

Continued on Page Nine

Netherlands Likens Crisis To Invasion of Belgium

Wireless to The New York Times.

THE HAGUE, The Netherlands, March 11.—The news of the dramatic events in Austria has seriously impressed The Netherlands, where it is considered the most alarming intelligence for smaller European countries since August, 1914, when German troops invaded Belgium.

Although German relations with The Netherlands are quite different from those with Austria, it is felt that some pretext or other might serve the Reich some day to intervene in The Netherlands' internal affairs as well.

The attitude of the British Government in the face of the new situation is impatiently awaited. In any case the lesson of Austria will not be lost on The Netherlands.

ITALY GETS SHOCK

Visit of Hitler Probably Will Be Canceled as Result of the Coup

ROME-BERLIN AXIS SHAKEN

Parleys With Britain Likely to Be Speeded and Accord Is Now Thought Probable

By ARNALDO CORTESI
Wireless to The New York Times.

ROME, March 11.—The news from Austria struck Italy with the impact of a exploding bomb and left an official world here aghast.

An official spokesman told an unusually large audience of newspaper men this evening that the Italian Government considered the situation so grave that it did not feel it could make any statement at present.

The general impression is, however, that whatever Italy may decide to do she will not make any attempt to intervene in Austria militarily and will not concentrate divisions as those before the Brenner Pass as in July, 1934, after the assassination of Chancellor Engelbert Dollfuss. Certainly no troop movements have been reported.

The greatest uncertainty and confusion reigned in Italian quarters, where the day's developments apparently were entirely unexpected. But it seems clear that Chancellor Hitler's action in forcing Chancellor Kurt Schuschnigg to resign has shaken the Rome-Berlin axis to its very foundations. Whether the axis will be able to survive depends on the turn of events in the next few days and the explanations Berlin furnishes in reply to Rome's inquiries. Worth recording in any case are the widespread rumors that Hitler's visit to Italy in May will be canceled. Such a cancellation would be an unmistakable symptom that the axis was doomed.

No Hint to Rome

The very surprise and shock caused by Dr. Schuschnigg's resignation prove that Hitler did without giving the Rome end of the axis the slightest inkling of his intentions. As late as last night Italian circles close to the government were still saying that the Austrian plebiscite would lead to a clarification, which Rome heartily favored. Now the latest developments have brought the Italo-German situation to a climax.

It is declared here that Hitler could not have chosen a better moment for a coup in Austria. The Anglo-Italian negotiations are not yet properly under way and therefore Italy cannot definitely count on British support in any action she might meditate in Central Europe. France is in the throes of a Cabinet crisis, while Russia is going through a far from happy period internally.

The events in Austria are also likely to have deep repercussions on the Anglo-Italian negotiations. Italy obviously will now enter them in a much weaker position, since her principal strength in relation to Britain hitherto was that in the field of foreign politics she and Germany acted as a unit. The wabbling of the axis cannot but increase for Italy the "necessity of reaching an understanding with Britain and thus deprive her of a considerable part of her bargaining points.

Agreement Facilitated

On the other hand, the events in Austria cannot but make both Italy and Britain more determined to reach an agreement as soon as possible.

Even if the Rome-Berlin axis survives this blow, it is doubtful whether it will ever again regain the strength it had hitherto. Public opinion is convinced Germany has betrayed Italy; therefore it is difficult to imagine that the atmosphere of perfect cordiality and mutual confidence existing hitherto can ever be restored. Perhaps an open break will be avoided so as to gloss over the fact that a pillar that has upheld the whole of Italian foreign policy in the last two years has fallen to the ground, but it seems that the process of a breaking up of the axis has begun.

No course appears open to Italy but to save what she can of her position in Central Europe by diplomacy. Germany today is very conscious of her military sense from the German viewpoint, so the use of force can in all probability be relied out.

Perhaps Germany still counts

Continued on Page Two

NAZIS SEIZE AUSTRIA AFTER HITLER ULTIMATUM; GERMAN TROOPS INVITED TO MAINTAIN ORDER; SEYSS-INQUART CHANCELLOR; POWERS PROTEST

The Austrian Situation

Following an ultimatum from Berlin, the Schuschnigg government in Austria retired yesterday evening and was succeeded by one headed by the Nazi leader, Arthur Seyss-Inquart, as Chancellor. He immediately asked Germany to send troops to help in preserving order. Some 50,000 highly armed and mechanized forces marched to the border. Both Munich and Vienna report some crossed into Austria. Berlin denies this. Nazi mobs took possession of Vienna and raided the Jewish quarter. The swastika was flown over public buildings, and Fatherland Front forces were disarmed. There were similar demonstrations in other cities.

Europe was aghast at the coup of Hitler. His action struck Italy with the force of an exploding bomb. The impression was that Italy would not retort with force, but it was believed the Rome-Berlin axis had been shaken and that Hitler's visit to Rome might be canceled. No advance notice of Germany's intention is believed to have been given to Mussolini.

Britain delivered a sharp protest to Berlin, saying Germany's action was bound to produce "the gravest reactions, of which it is impossible to foretell the issue." Other warnings were delivered earlier, but Foreign Minister von Ribbentrop retorted that Germany saw no reason to confer with Britain until her purposes had been achieved elsewhere.

In Paris it was understood Italy had been asked if she would join in a united effort to save Austria, but had refused. France, however, took action similar to that of Britain in protesting the Reich's action. The parties tried to get together to form a new Cabinet to deal with the situation, but they were still too deeply divided to make that accomplishment possible. It was believed Léon Blum would not be able to gain sufficient support to head a government. [All the above dispatches on Page 1.]

Premier Negrin of Spain announced that Italy and Germany had made unofficial proposals for some agreement with the Loyalists, but they were determined not to enter on negotiations. [Page 2.]

ROME CHECKS PARIS ON AID FOR VIENNA

Refuses to Cooperate With France and Britain for the Support of Austria

FAILURE FOR BLUM IS SEEN

Premier Designate Is Unable to Form Union Government From All the Parties

By P. J. PHILIP
Wireless to The New York Times.

PARIS, March 11.—It was learned here tonight that yesterday the French and British Governments jointly sounded out Italy as to whether cooperation could be expected in maintaining Austrian independence and that they received a firm negative reply.

However, Nazi Germany's annexation of Austria this evening has profoundly affected the French political situation and, in the opinion of every political party, made the immediate constitution of a government essential. That being so, Premier-designate Léon Blum tonight, after a day of continuous negotiation and argument with the party and another, informed the press that toward noon tomorrow he will announce his decision and intentions.

It is believed that he hopes to be able to announce the formation of a national government including most, if not all, of the parties. Before then, however, he will meet the National Council of the Socialist party, which last January ran counter to his wishes and by a small majority opposed every Socialist Minister in the Chautemps Cabinet.

What course events will take depends on M. Blum's ability to persuade his own party that the time has come for them to take the lead in the formation of a government which will represent France and not

Continued on Page Two

Mechanic on New Army Planes Held as Spy; Trapped by Counter-Espionage in Plant

Following several days of intensified counter-espionage activities around Long Island air fields, Federal authorities yesterday arraigned Otto Hermann Voss, a naturalized German mechanic employed in the Seversky aircraft plant, for espionage. Waiving examination, Voss was held in $10,000 bail.

The government invoked the last severe World War statute under which two renegade soldiers and a German woman were held as German spies on Feb. 26. Voss was charged with engaging and inducting others to deliver "to agents of a foreign power certain documents, writings, code books, signal books, photographs, instruments and information relating to the defense of the United States." The maximum punishment for conviction is imprisonment for twenty years.

The background of the case was not revealed beyond what appeared in the complaint and the few words spoken by Lester C. Dunigan, assistant United States attorney, at the arraignment before United States Commissioner Isaac Platt. Mr.

Dunigan said that after a conference with John F. Dailey, Acting United States Attorney, it had been decided that any statement at this time "would be out of order."

It was reported, however, that four men who were plant mechanics worked away from the plant three weeks until two Department of Justice agents arrested him Wednesday. Then they disappeared. Voss worked in the "day-dreaming" or experimental section of the plant's assembly division, where Major de Seversky tests new ideas and materials.

Voss, it was learned, visited Germany for about a month last Summer. His wife at their home at 225 Jericho Turnpike, Floral Park, was on the verge of collapse after two long sessions of questioning by Federal agents. They were at her home on Wednesday and Thursday. Mrs. Voss asserted her husband was innocent and believed he came under suspicion when his name was found in a paper on the person of a friend arrested as a spy suspect recently.

The defendant, 39 years old, was silent at his arraignment. He is 6 feet tall with old scars on both cheeks. Mr. Dunigan said Voss worked at the plant at intervals for several years. His alleged illegal activities were dated from Jan. 2, 1936. Mr.

BRITISH APPALLED BY REICH METHODS

Government Sends to Berlin a Sharp Rebuke Assailing the Tactics Employed

LONDON NOT TO INTERVENE

German Troops Start Across Border While Ribbentrop Is Guest of Chamberlain

By FERDINAND KUHN Jr.
Special Cable to The New York Times.

LONDON, March 11.—At the very moment when German troops were crossing the Austrian frontier the British Government tonight delivered to Berlin one of the sharpest protests it has yet made in its post-war relations with Germany. [France also protested to Germany along the same lines as the British rebuke, it was reported in Paris.]

The strength of the protest showed how strongly the British Government felt over the day's events and particularly over the methods by which Germany had finally attained her ends in Austria.

Referring especially to the second German ultimatum that preceded the actual invasion, the British described it as "the coercion, backed by force, of an independent State in order to create a situation incompatible with its national independence."

Such action, it was pointed out, was bound to produce the "gravest reactions of which it is impossible to foretell the issue."

The protest was delivered at the Wilhelmstrasse by Sir Nevile Henderson, the British Ambassador.

British Warning Disregarded

Britain's warning was tonight obviously disregarded the warnings of the British Government earlier in the day that threat or use of force would damage the prospects of the Anglo-German talks and threaten future chances for reconciliation in Europe.

The warning was delivered personally to Joachim von Ribbentrop, German Foreign Minister, by Prime Minister Neville Chamberlain and Foreign Minister Viscount Halifax after luncheon at 10 Downing Street.

But the British Minister's words produced no effect upon Herr von Ribbentrop or upon his master in Berlin. Herr von Ribbentrop is said to have told Mr. Chamberlain, indeed, that the Fuehrer saw no reason for starting negotiations for reconciliation with Britain until German purposes "elsewhere" had been achieved.

While these words were being spoken the German Army was rolling along the express highways leading to the Austrian border and Berlin was preparing the ultimatums that forced the Austrian Government from power.

Britain will, of course, do nothing in the way of intervention. At this late stage in the absorption of Austria there is little left for Britain

Continued on Page Three

REICH ARMY MOVES; 50,000 AT FRONTIER

Force of Infantry, Artillery and Engineers Said to Have Entered Austria With Planes

BUT BERLIN MAKES DENIAL

Bavarian Roads Choked, Cars Taken Over—Border Towns Fired by Excitement

Wireless to The New York Times.

MUNICH, Germany, Saturday, March 12.—With a dramatic suddenness that stunned the world the German Army embarked yesterday on its first campaign beyond the Reich's borders and without firing a shot achieved a victory that laid Austria prostrate at its feet, transformed the European equilibrium and set the borders fixed by the peace treaties into motion for a readjustment, of which the end is not yet in sight.

All day yesterday German forces, some 50,000 strong, made up of infantry, cavalry, artillery, motorized divisions, air force units and engineers with bridge building materials were moving to the Austrian frontier. Their mission was to avenge what is termed in Germany "the betrayal of Berchtesgaden"—Chancellor Kurt Schuschnigg's recent proclamation of a plebiscite on Austrian independence.

Last night, following Dr. Schuschnigg's overthrow and a telegram from the new Chancellor, Dr. Arthur Seyss-Inquart, to Chancellor Hitler requesting German military aid in preventing bloodshed, German troops were reported to have marched into Austria in close formation at three points—Salzburg, Kufstein and Mittenwalde.

[According to an Associated Press dispatch from Vienna, German troops crossed also at Passau, on the way to Linz, Austria, and a contingent of Reich troops, numbering about 1,000 men in trucks, was expected to reach Vienna at 6 A. M., New York time.]

Orders No Resistance

Information given out at the Munich army headquarters said the troops had begun to cross the border shortly after 10 o'clock, although their coming had been heralded by Dr. Seyss-Inquart in semi-hourly broadcasts beginning soon after 7 o'clock. The broadcasts included instructions to the Austrian military and civil authorities and the population not to resist the troops.

Whether the statements of the Munich army headquarters are correct or whether insistent denials in Berlin of a German march into Austria are the real truth does not much matter, for, even if the troops did halt at the border without crossing it, theirs is still the victory. It was their march that turned the tide in Austria and, after a bloodless Sebastos, enabled the Austrian

---

SCHUSCHNIGG GOES

Resigns After Threat of Invasion as Powers Fail to Back Him

PLEBISCITE IS CALLED OFF

Goering and Hess Expected in Vienna Today—Nazis Rule Streets, Rout Foes

Censorship Imposed
By The Associated Press.

VIENNA, March 11.—Censorship has started.

An order posted in the correspondents' room in the Central Telegraph Office tonight said all telephone conversations from the room must be in German.

Correspondents for the International News Service, an American organization, were detained against their will, without charges, at the office.

By G. E. R. GEDYE
Wireless to The New York Times.

VIENNA, Saturday, March 12.—Under threats of force from Berlin, Chancellor Kurt Schuschnigg of Austria yielded last evening and resigned in dramatic circumstances. The Nazis, with Dr. Arthur Seyss-Inquart, Interior Minister in the Schuschnigg Cabinet, as Chancellor, are in power.

To an unprepared public listening over the radio to a typical program of pleasant Viennese melodies the voice of the man who may have been the last Chancellor of an independent Austria announced at 7:45 P. M. that, in his own words, he had "yielded only to force" to avoid bloodshed and that under the threat of a German invasion that was to start at the very moment he spoke, he had resigned his office.

Plebiscite Is Postponed

Apart from the statement in a broadcast at 6 o'clock that "the Chancellor and Fatherland Front Leader, in consultation with President Miklas, has decided to postpone the plebiscite," there was no warning for the public when the program was interrupted for the announcer to say, "An important declaration is just coming." Then, without even mention of Dr. Schuschnigg's name, his voice was heard at the microphone.

When Dr. Schuschnigg had finished, thousands of Nazis began swarming into Vienna's streets to take over control unopposed. An hour afterward Dr. Seyss-Inquart also addressed the nation over the radio, calling on every one to maintain order and declaring that there was no question of resistance if the German Army should march in.

Dr. Seyss-Inquart's first official act as Chancellor appears to have been a message to Chancellor Hitler requesting the speedy dispatch of German troops to his support. The message read:

"Following the retirement of the Schuschnigg government, the Provisional Government of Austria regards the restoration and maintenance of law and order in Austria as its first duty.

"To this end it urgently requests the German Government to support it in this undertaking and assist it in the prevention of bloodshed. I therefore appeal to the German Government for the earliest possible dispatch of troops."

Up to noon Dr. Schuschnigg had remained firm in the face of all threats. Then came the first ultimatum from Germany, conveyed by Dr. Edmund Glaise-Horstenau, Minister Without Portfolio in the Schuschnigg Cabinet, on his return from Berlin. Austria was to postpone the plebiscite or she would be invaded.

Final Ultimatum Delivered

At 4 P. M. an airplane landed in Vienna. It brought Dr. Schuschnigg a final and, this time, an official ultimatum. The man who delivered it was believed to have been Josef Buerckl, Nazi leader in the Saar.

At first it was rumored that Field Marshal Hermann Goering and Rudolf Hess, deputy leader of the German Nazi party, had arrived with the ultimatum and were going to speak to the crowds in the Karlsplatz at 10 P. M., but this belief later proved unfounded. It was stated later, however, that Marshal Goering and Herr Hess would arrive today.

In any event, this ultimatum was quite different from that Dr. Glaise-Horstenau had delivered. It was as

Continued on Page Three

"All the News That's Fit to Print."

The New York Times.

LATE CITY EDITION
POSTSCRIPT
Showers today, cooler tonight.
Tomorrow fair.
Temperature Yesterday—Max., 75; Min., 63

Copyright, 1938, by The New York Times Company.

VOL. LXXXVII....No. 29,454.   Entered as Second-Class Matter, Postoffice, New York, N. Y.   NEW YORK, THURSDAY, SEPTEMBER 15, 1938.   P   THREE CENTS NEW YORK CITY and Vicinity | FOUR CENTS Elsewhere Except in 7th and 8th Postal Zones.

GEORGE IS WINNING IN GEORGIA POLL; CAMP RUNS THIRD

TALMADGE SECOND

Choice of President in 'Purge' Primary Admits His Defeat

TALMADGE CLAIMS VICTORY

Former Governor Lost Lead Won in the Early Returns in Rural District Counts

Senator George went into the lead on the late count from the Georgia Senatorial primary after a nip-and-tuck race in the return with Former Governor Eugene Talmadge, an even more direct critic of the New Deal than the Senator whom President Roosevelt marked for elimination in the party "purge." Lawrence Camp, the choice of the President, trailed throughout the count and conceded defeat. [Page 1.]

Democrats of Connecticut, in State convention, renominated Senator Lonergan and Governor Cross. Attorney General Cummings advocated letting "the dead past bury its dead." [Page 14.]

Former Governor Frank D. Fitzgerald of Michigan won over two opponents and will oppose Frank Murphy for the Governorship. [Page 16.]

Senator Tydings's lead in Maryland's popular vote rose to 56,000 on late returns. [Page 15.]

'Purge' Again Defeated

By TURNER CATLEDGE
Special to THE NEW YORK TIMES.

ATLANTA, Thursday, Sept. 15.—President Roosevelt's drive to "purge" less than 100 per cent followers from the Senate was rounded out here early today in the apparently disastrous finish.

Senator Walter F. George, whom the President personally requested Georgia voters to oust from the seat which he has held in the Senate for 16 years, forged ahead in the returns from yesterday's Democratic Senatorial primary. The Senator was leading both in popular and county unit votes at midnight.

The runner-up was former Governor Eugene Talmadge, a more consistent and certainly more bitter critic of the President and the New Deal than Senator George. After running ahead in the early returns, Mr. Talmadge dropped behind the Senator, but at the same time went on the radio and claimed the nomination, saying that if he lost, it would be stolen from him.

Federal District Attorney Lawrence Camp, over whom the President waved the once-magic New Deal wand in his celebrated speech at Barnesville five weeks ago today, ran a poor third and formally conceded defeat at 11:20 P. M.

79 of 159 Counties Complete

At midnight 70 of the State's 159 counties had reported complete returns, accounting for 170 of the total 410 county unit votes, a majority of which a candidate must receive to be nominated. Out of the number Senator George had collected a total of 113 county unit votes in forty-two counties; Mr. Talmadge 54 unit votes in twenty-six counties, and Mr. Camp six in two counties.

Senator George had amassed 100,-082 popular votes; Mr. Talmadge 75,951 and Mr. Camp 55,265. Senator George was leading in counties having a total of 192 unit votes; Mr. Talmadge in counties having a total of 194 and Mr. Camp in counties with a total of 7. However, a trend toward Mr. George had set in late in the evening and was still running.

In a radio broadcast at 11:20 P. M., Mr. Camp said:

"I am deeply grateful to all the people who have supported me in this fight. I regret the fight was not successful at this time, but I believe that the fight for liberalism will be successful in the end and that the people will demand liberal representation. I bow to the will of the electorate and offer my congratulations to the successful candidate."

On many of the first returns Mr. Talmadge would be leading in one county after another, with only one to three boxes in each to be heard from. But in most of these, when the county tabulation was complete

Continued on Page Eighteen

When New Think of Visiting Times of Willard.—Advt.

Corcoran 'Deaf and Dumb' When Queried on Tydings

Thomas G. Corcoran, one of President Roosevelt's closest advisers in the current "purge" campaign, visited the office of Lieut. Col. Brehon B. Somervell, Works Progress Administrator. He smilingly denied that there was any political significance to his visit.

Asked whether he had anything to say about Senator Millard Tydings, Mr. Corcoran replied:

"I never have anything to say. Professionally I am deaf, dumb and blind."

RED HOOK HOUSING TO COST $12,000,000, A $4,600,000 SAVING

Total Per Room of $1,125 Is About Half That for Harlem and Williamsburg Projects

BIDS FAR BELOW BUDGET

Rheinstein Wires Mayor That Queensbridge Should Now Provide for 9,000 More

The total cost of the Red Hook low-rental housing development, including land, will be about $12,000,-000, or approximately $4,600,000 less than the $16,592,766 provided in the budget allowed by the United States Housing Authority, it was announced yesterday by Alfred Rheinstein, chairman of the New York City Housing Authority.

Mr. Rheinstein, who is also Commissioner of Housing and Buildings, telegraphed Mayor La Guardia at Prescott, Ariz., that the bids for the Red Hook superstructures, which were opened Tuesday, showed that the project could be completed at a cost per room, including land, carrying charges and overhead, of $1,125.

Cost of Other Projects

The cost per room of Williamsburg Houses, built by the housing division of the Public Works Administration, was $2,284, while Harlem River Houses cost $2,150 a room, Mr. Rheinstein said, adding that the lower cost for Red Hook was due to "an accurate definition of the problem, careful planning, unusual cooperation of the building industry and a favorable market."

Mr. Rheinstein expressed confidence that similar economies would be revealed when bids for the $16,-500,000 Queensbridge development were opened some time next month. He advised Mayor La Guardia that as a result it would be possible to provide housing in the Queensbridge development for 31,000 persons, or 9,000 more than the plans approved by the Federal authorities contemplated.

"This saving undoubtedly will permit slum clearance which, in the past, was a doubtful prospect because of the high cost of land in New York City," Mr. Rheinstein said in discussing the reduction in cost.

"This is the first fruit of intensive effort by an organization which has labored with great skill and faithfulness. Credit is due Alfred Easton Poor, the chief architect, and his associates; to the engineers and to our own technical staff, which is headed by Allan S. Harrison."

Rheinstein Praises Builders

Mr. Rheinstein paid tribute to the cooperative attitude of the building industry, which he said had been a factor in the saving. He said the building industry and the Housing Authority had worked in close harmony and "on a practical basis" for many months.

The text of Mr. Rheinstein's telegram to the Mayor follows:

"Bids on the superstructures for Red Hook opened last night. Total cost, including land, carrying

Continued on Page Thirteen

TRANSIT EXPANSION TO COST $827,102,344

Delaney Submits Long-Range Program to Planning Board —Many Items Must Wait

A long-range program for expansion of the city's rapid transit facilities, at an estimated total cost of $827,102,344, was submitted to the City Planning Commission yesterday by the Board of Transportation.

In submitting the program, John H. Delaney, chairman of the board, explained that it was not to be regarded as inflexible, but as subject to changes in the city's financial condition, the volume of rapid transit traffic, the fate of pending transit unification proposals and other factors.

"This board," Mr. Delaney wrote, "is aware that the financial resources of the city are not sufficient to permit the adoption at this time of any considerable part of this future program, but is of the opinion that the City Planning Commission should have before it a comprehensive outline of what this board deems to be the most useful development of transit facilities during the coming years."

Early Unification Assumed

Explaining that the list of projects was arranged generally in the order of priority desired, Mr. Delaney declared that it was drawn on the assumption that "rapid transit unification will be effected in the near future."

The list is a comprehensive summary of the many rapid transit projects put forward by the Board of Transportation since it began to function in 1924. It includes the proposed additional system based upon a trunk line subway under Second Avenue, the proposed acquisition of parts of the Long Island Railroad right of way in Queens, the recapture of the Hudson & Manhattan Railway tubes in Manhattan and the building of a rapid transit tunnel between Brooklyn and Staten Island.

The list, which will come before the City Planning Commission for consideration this afternoon, includes the proposed demolition of the Sixth Avenue elevated line at an estimated cost of $225,000, less possible salvage. Proceedings are now pending under which the city hopes to acquire the line itself at a cost of $12,500,000.

Projects as Submitted

Following is the complete list of projects submitted by the Board of Transportation:

Transportation building..$2,000,000
Rockaway Line, Acquisition and Reconstruction, Queens—Four and two tracks; subway, embankment and elevated....$40,568,364
Fulton Street Line Extension:
Via Pitkin Avenue and Linden Boulevard, Grant Avenue to 105th Street, with provision for a connection to the Rockaway line, Brooklyn and Queens; four tracks, subway $21,200,000
Connection from Rockaway line to Fulton Street extension, Queens; two tracks, subway and open cut.................$2,220,000
Hillside Avenue Extension—178th Street to 213th Street, Queens; four tracks, subway.......$22,750,000
Flushing Line—I. R. T. Extension:
Via Roosevelt Avenue, public streets and property formerly parallel and adjacent to L. I. R. R.; Main Street, Flushing, to Bell Boulevard, Bayside, Queens; four tracks to 164th Street, thence two tracks to Bell Boulevard; subway, embankment and open cut....$5,500,000
Via 149th Street and 11th Avenue, from Roosevelt Avenue to 192d Street, College Point, Queens; two tracks, elevated throughout........$7,900,000

Continued on Page Fourteen

Ultimatum of Henlein Disavowed in Germany

Wireless to THE NEW YORK TIMES.

BERLIN, Sept. 14.—The ultimatum sent to the Czech Government by the Sudeten party yesterday is declared here to have been drawn up without Chancellor Adolf Hitler's approval.

It was stated here today that Konrad Henlein did not communicate with Berchtesgaden yesterday because of alleged telephone communication with Germany. Herr Henlein is thereupon said to have dispatched his belligerent statement to the Czech Government on his own responsibility.

Apparently he was not sharply reproved for doing so, and his subsequent decision to break off negotiations with Prague had Hitler's complete approval.

The German Foreign Office stated today that it was unable to get in touch with the German Legation in Prague between 8 P. M. and midnight.

PRESIDENT SPEEDS BACK TO CAPITAL

Tells Rochester, Minn., Crowd That the European Crisis Changed His Plans

By HENRY N. DORRIS
Special to THE NEW YORK TIMES.

ON BOARD THE PRESIDENTIAL TRAIN EN ROUTE TO WASHINGTON, Sept. 14.—President Roosevelt sped toward Washington tonight to be at the seat of government during the present crisis in Europe.

Concerned over what he described in extemporaneous remarks at Rochester, Minn., as the "extremely serious" situation in Europe, Mr. Roosevelt cut short his visit to his special train after he had paid his son a morning visit, the President said to several hundred Rochester citizens gathered to bid him farewell:

"I am going back now, not to my house on the Hudson River, but straight through to Washington, because, as you know, having read the newspapers, the condition of affairs in other parts of the world is extremely serious. That is why, as President, I have to go back to the national capital."

Until this morning the President was undecided as to going to Hyde Park or Washington, but after a long conversation with Secretary Hull, Mr. Roosevelt ordered that the train go direct to the capital. After he reaches Washington tomorrow night he is expected to go

Continued on Page Twelve

Americans Informally Told to Return Home; Many Ship Bookings to Europe Canceled

By The Associated Press.

BERLIN, Sept. 14.—American travelers have been advised "unofficially and informally" by the United States Consulate here to return home "if they could conveniently alter their European travel plans," officials said today.

Members of the consulate staff disclosed that "numerous United States citizens had inquired what they ought to do in view of the critical situation in Central Europe."

The officials said, however, that American residents in Berlin have not been advised to leave Germany. Consulates of other countries have given their nationals similar advice.

Special to THE NEW YORK TIMES.

WASHINGTON, Sept. 14.—Asked about a press report that the American consulates in London were advising Americans to book early passages for home, Secretary of State Cordell Hull said he had received nothing officially on the subject.

He pointed out that some years ago a survey was taken of possible eventualities in various parts of the world and general instructions were then issued to consulates for their guidance "in such matters as a threatening war situation. Those instructions, he said, had not been supplemented by special instructions in the present crisis.

Special to THE NEW YORK TIMES.

LONDON, Sept. 14.—The United States cruiser Nashville anchored in the Thames off Gravesend today after a hurried trip down from Portland—a move made ostensibly to "let the

men see another port" but in reality, London suspected, to care for American residents in case of danger.

WASHINGTON, Sept. 14 (P).—It was announced today that a bombproof cement and steel shelter was being built under a wing of the American Legation in Prague, Czechoslovakia.

It was authorized by the State Department after the Czech Government had given its approval.

The American Embassy in Berlin is also about to undergo extensive repairs, and it is reported another bombproof shelter may be built there.

Shipping executives said last night that European developments of the last few days had affected shippings in both passenger and freight fields. Tramp ships of foreign registry, which are generally available for service to any part of the world depending upon the nature of the freight, were said yesterday to have been withdrawn from the market.

In the passenger field cancellations of bookings have already been reported. Nine cancellations were reported last night on a ship scheduled to sail during the next few days.

The ship lines also have notified their booking clerks to restrict their promises of accommodations on ships in westbound sailings during the next few weeks.

There have been no cancellations of sailings from Europe as yet. The Europa will dock here today and the New York of the Hamburg Line tomorrow.

FIGHTING IS BITTER

Dead Mount to 23 as Six Are Killed in a Struggle in Eger

GERMAN ARMS ARE SEIZED

Troops Victorious After Long Struggle in Schwaderbach —Martial Law Extended

By G. E. R. GEDYE
Wireless to THE NEW YORK TIMES.

PRAGUE, Czechoslovakia, Thursday, Sept. 15.—After perfect order had apparently been restored in most of the Sudeten German areas yesterday, further serious firing on the police occurred in Eger last night that developed into a pitched battle, with six killed.

A government communiqué last night said that investigations into events in various parts of the frontier areas had established that the shooting of individual police and attacks on various gendarmerie stations and State buildings that set in immediately after Chancellor Adolf Hitler's speech at Nuremberg were part of an attempted revolt.

Despite the restoration of order, it asserted, danger still remained that irresponsible elements would continue their "cruel and ruthless attempts at violence against fellow citizens of a different race and different political opinions."

"Altogether," the communiqué declared, "there have been twenty-three deaths—thirteen Czechs, of whom ten belonged to the forces of public order. Of the German assailants ten were killed. Of the seventy-five wounded fourteen are Germans; thirty-seven of the others are police and gendarmes."

Moderate Measures Stressed

"These figures clearly show with what reserve and moderation the necessary measures have been taken. Firearms have been employed only on absolutely unavoidable occasions; the attackers have had machine guns and even hand grenades among their arms.

"The government has had every right to suppress this revolt and to do it energetically in the interests of the State and for the sake of European peace."

The fighting that left Eger absolutely normal in the afternoon, save for many drawn shutters concealing the wreckage of Monday night's wave of violence following Hitler's speech. An occasional double police patrol with rifles and bayonets indicated that martial law was in force.

Late in the evening it was reported that a police patrol had been fired on from the headquarters of the Henlein party in the Hotel Victoria in the town.

The fighting began, according to the official account, when, acting on information that there was a secret munitions depot in the party headquarters, two police detachments in armored cars were sent to carry out a search. They found the doors of the hotel closed and were received with fire from the windows.

Armored Cars Return Fire

The armored cars returned the fire and with the help of hand grenades the doors were finally burst open. Inside a considerable armory of German revolvers and automatic pistols and a radio transmitting station were found. Those inside who had not already escaped were arrested.

During these operations the police were constantly fired on from the cellars of the neighboring Hotel Wenzel. The shooting continued until late in the evening, when that hotel was taken by storm and every one found inside was placed under arrest.

The six persons killed included one policeman, one Czech railwayman and one Henleinist. Three bodies of persons apparently killed by stray bullets were lying in the market square. One was a woman. Their identity has not been established.

By 9:30 P. M. order was not yet restored in Eger. The ringleaders were arrested and will be tried summarily by a military court.

The only other place in the republic where the Henleinist revolutionaries were still causing trouble last night was the village of Schwaderbach, near Graslitz. Schwaderbach is really a suburb of the German town of Sechsenberg. There the Henleinists had been armed, allegedly by Germany, not

Continued on Page Four

CHAMBERLAIN OFF BY PLANE TO SEE HITLER; WILL MAKE A PERSONAL PLEA TO AVERT WAR; PRAGUE FIRM AS SUDETENS BATTLE THE POLICE

Chamberlain Visit Stuns Reich; Hitler Looks to British Fair Play

Czech-Sudeten Crisis Seen as Drawing Further Away From Brink of War as Result—Berlin to Delay Action

By GUIDO ENDERIS
Wireless to THE NEW YORK TIMES.

BERLIN, Sept. 14.—The Czech-Sudeten German crisis drew further away from the brink of war tonight with the announcement that Prime Minister Neville Chamberlain and Chancellor Adolf Hitler would meet in Berchtesgaden tomorrow afternoon for a man-to-man talk.

Following a day of nervous apprehensions over the intensification of the situation in Sudetenland and the breakdown of negotiations between the Czech Government and Konrad Henlein the news that the British Prime Minister had sought an appointment with Hitler stunned the unsuspecting radio public tonight. Mr. Chamberlain's visit was announced in a communiqué containing the Prime Minister's message and Hitler's reply, which was remarkable alike for its informally personal formulation and its dramatic contents.

Mr. Chamberlain, it is expected, will reach Hitler's mountain chalet early tomorrow afternoon. He will land at Munich and will immediately motor to Berchtesgaden, which once again is to become a cynosure of world-wide curiosity. The an-

Continued on Page Two

TOKYO CZECH STAND ALARMS SHANGHAI

Pledge to Back Reich and Italy by Arms, if Necessary, Seen as Threat to Foreigners

By HALLETT ABEND
Special Cable to THE NEW YORK TIMES.

SHANGHAI, Sept. 14.—Consternation over the European crisis spread and deepened here and in other centers of foreign residence in China upon receipt from Tokyo of a declaration by a Foreign Office spokesman to the effect that Japan is prepared to join forces with Germany and Italy in accordance with the anti-Comintern agreement.

This statement apparently implies an immediate spread of a European conflict to the Far East and places enormous interests in jeopardy.

An immediate question arises concerning the British and French concessions in Tientsin, where there are stationed only a handful of troops of each nation. There, presumably, Japan and Italy would act in unison since Italy has her own Tientsin concession, a considerable Tientsin garrison and a river gunboat.

Limited Forces

At Shanghai there are only two regiments of British troops, about 4,500 French forces and Annamites and 1,200 United States Marines. Anchored in the Whangpoo River are three French warships, one British cruiser, two Italian light cruisers, the U. S. S. Asheville, ocean-going gunboat, and the U. S. S. Oahu, river gunboat, while numbers down stream are many Japanese men-of-war of all sizes. Other fighting craft, however, are within striking distance. The British have a force at Hong Kong while the United States Asiatic Fleet bases at Manila and spends its Summers on the China coast.

British interests in the International Settlement and also the French Concession at Shanghai are utterly indefensible and the entire surrounding countryside is in the hands of the Japanese Army.

At Canton there are only two foreign concessions, the British and French, both on the Island of Shameen. There is nothing larger than the river gunboats, but the navy craft would be dispatched from Hong Kong, which is well-garrisoned and stoutly defensible from land and sea.

Inexplicable to Americans

Special Cable to THE NEW YORK TIMES.

TOKYO, Sept. 14.—A statement by a Foreign Office spokesman early today that the Comintern is primarily responsible for the Sudeten trouble is considered inexplicable to American and other foreign circles in Tokyo.

The only other place in the republic where the Henleinist revolutionaries were still causing trouble last night was the village of Schwaderbach, near Graslitz. Schwaderbach is really a suburb of the German town of Sechsenberg. There the Henleinists had been armed, allegedly by Germany, not

The afternoon edition of the newspaper Miyako editorially supports this statement but other papers are silent.

The Miyako praises Chancellor Adolf Hitler's Nuremberg speech, saying that it will have

Continued on Page Seven

FRENCH HOPES RISE ON BRITAIN'S MOVE

Daladier Not Only Endorses the Chamberlain Plan, but Claims Initiative in It

By P. J. PHILIP
Wireless to THE NEW YORK TIMES.

PARIS, Sept. 14.—With special trains ready outside Paris to take the civilian population away and with the president of the American Chamber of Commerce here asking that provision for gas masks be made for American citizens, all seemed set tonight for a tragic finale to the tension of past days and weeks, when the news of Prime Minister Neville Chamberlain's proposal to visit Chancellor Adolf Hitler caused such surprise and relief as had not been experienced since the news broke in November, 1918, that the Germans were seeking an armistice.

Of course, there are all kinds of different opinions about the British Prime Minister's action. There is, first, the official one. In a communiqué issued late this evening Premier Edouard Daladier in some ways claims credit for the suggestion, for he always has been a partisan of a get-together policy with Germany, and late last evening, he says, he suggested by telephone to Mr. Chamberlain that something should be done for having something like a three-power conversation to consider the situation.

Tells of Taking Initiative

In his statement this evening M. Daladier said:

"At the end of yesterday afternoon, in the presence of a rapid sequence of events in Czechoslovakia, which made local negotiations difficult, I took the initiative in establishing direct personal contact with the British Prime Minister with a view to examining the possibility of attempting exceptional procedure that would permit an examination with Germany of the most effective means of assuring a friendly solution of the differences that separate the Sudetens and the Prague government and, in consequence, of maintaining peace in Europe.

"I am, therefore, extremely happy at the agreement in the ideas of the two governments."

The British Prime Minister's action has, therefore, official French sanction and approval. At the same time the French, because of the fact that the British are acting alone, are relieved of certain grave embarrassments. They are bound by their treaties with Czechoslovakia to go to that country's aid if her territorial integrity is threatened.

But the French are on record as defenders of minorities, and the behavior of the Sudeten Nazis during these last few weeks has left no doubt in any French mind that, whatever they may want, they do not want to continue under the old regime or anything like it. From a purely French viewpoint, therefore, the whole basis on which war might

Continued on Page Ten

LONDON HAILS PLAN

Prime Minister Hopeful of a Temporary Accord at Berchtesgaden

KING HASTENS TO CAPITAL

In Case of a Rebuff Britain Will Have Stressed to World Her Efforts for Peace

Prime Minister Chamberlain, in a dramatic move to avert Europe's threatened war, is flying to Germany to meet Chancellor Hitler face to face. The step, which was approved by the full British Cabinet yesterday, was understood to have been suggested by Premier Daladier of France. [Page 1.] It electrified Germany, where Hitler conferred all day with his diplomatic advisers. [Page 1.]

This development came after a day of continued violence in the Sudeten areas of Czechoslovakia. In the border town of Schwaderbach Henleinists seized the police station and for hours held the Czech forces at bay. Prague charged that they were helped by arms from abroad. In Eger six were killed in a police attack on Henleinist headquarters. [Page 1.]

Meanwhile Konrad Henlein said events had left his original demands far behind and he balked at further negotiations. [Page 10.]

As a solution to the Sudeten German problem a letter published in Italy, attributed to Premier Mussolini, called on Viscount Runciman, British mediator, to sponsor a plebiscite. [Page 5.]

At Geneva preparations were made to convene the League Council immediately after any German invasion of Czechoslovakia. [Page 6.]

A Tokyo statement that Japan would support her anti-Communist allies, Germany and Italy, with arms if necessary caused alarm in foreign circles in China because of the peril to huge foreign interests there. [Page 1.]

While Washington took hope from the Chamberlain development [Page 2], American tourists in Germany were advised as a precautionary measure to leave the country. [Page 1.]

Locally, the stock market again was hit by a wave of selling [Page 2], and underwriters suspended rates on marine insurance, with higher ones likely to be fixed today. [Page 3].

Chamberlain Flying to Reich

By FERDINAND KUHN Jr.
Special Cable to THE NEW YORK TIMES.

LONDON, Thursday, Sept. 15.—Prime Minister Neville Chamberlain flew today from the Heston Airdrome for Berchtesgaden, Germany, to keep an appointment with Chancellor Adolf Hitler in a last attempt to save Europe from war.

At 8:36 A. M. the wheels of the big silver Lockheed monoplane lifted from the runway into a cloudless sky. Its first stop will be Munich, 600 miles away, whence Mr. Chamberlain will go to Hitler's mountain chalet by automobile.

He made a statement for the newsreels as follows:

"I am going to meet the German Chancellor because the situation seems to me to be one in which discussions between me and him would be fruitful. My policy has always been to seek peace. The Fuehrer's ready acceptance of my invitation leads me to hope my visit will not be without result."

Only about 100 newspapermen, photographers and officials who allowed near the airplane. They cheered and shouted, "Good luck! God speed you!"

A moment later Mr. Chamberlain turned and bowed his head to enter the plane. But photographers called him back and then the Prime Minister found time to joke. He struck a stiff attitude, his hands on his hips, like an old-fashioned daguerreotype.

The crowd gasped and then gave three cheers, waving hats. The individual cries redoubled and Mr. Chamberlain's face broke into a surprised smile and he waved his own hat. Within five minutes after the engines had been warmed up

"All the News That's Fit to Print."

The New York Times.

LATE CITY EDITION
Generally fair and cooler today; continued cool tonight. Tomorrow fair, slowly rising temperature.
Temperatures Yesterday—Max., 82; Min., 67

Copyright, 1938, by The New York Times Company.

VOL. LXXXVII....No. 29,455.

Entered as Second-Class Matter, Postoffice, New York, N. Y.

NEW YORK, FRIDAY, SEPTEMBER 16, 1938.

PP

THREE CENTS NEW YORK CITY and Vicinity | FOUR CENTS Elsewhere Except in 7th and 8th Postal Zones.

ANTI-RED WRITERS BARRED FROM WPA, WITNESS DECLARES

Former Newspaper Man Tells of Communist Grip on 40% of Project Workers

TIES PARTY TO HAGUE ROW

Says Agents Provocateurs Were Used—Calls Alliance Job Clearing House

An elderly man of Colonial ancestry, who was a Communist until fifteen days ago, told a Dies Congressional subcommittee investigating un-American activities yesterday that the Communist party had a grip on 40 per cent of the workers on the WPA Federal Writers Project and that the Workers Alliance was a sort of clearing house for project job applicants through which few non-Communists could now pass.

Before the first open session of the subcommittee was completed in Room 1604 of the Federal Court House in Foley Square, witnesses had sketched out a program of Communist party undercover activities in various fields. Some of the workers in the writers' project, active and detached, it was said, had been used as agents provocateurs in the recent civil liberties quarrel in Jersey City, among Long Island utilities workers, in Pennsylvania steel centers and in Florida.

Recruiting for the Spanish Loyalist army was linked by one witness with the Robinson-Rubens false passport ring that operated through the office of former County Clerk Albert Marinelli.

Returned veterans of the Loyalist Army, it was testified, were to be grouped into cadres on which to build a "Red army" in the United States.

Three of the four witnesses said they were members of the Communist party until recently, and one admitted that more recently he had switched over to the German American Bund.

Starnes Is Chairman

The hearing was held under the chairmanship of Representative Joe Starnes of Alabama, a Democrat. With him were J. Parnell Thomas, Republican Representative from New Jersey, and S. W. Birmingham, chief investigator of the committee. Arthur D. Healey, a Massachusetts Representative and the only other member of the subcommittee, was absent.

The committee's first witness, who told about affairs in the writers' project, spoke from first-hand knowledge. He was Edwin P. Banta, a librarian for the project, of 215 East Seventeenth Street. Born in Newark in 1872, he is a sturdy man with a strong voice.

"How long have your forebears lived in this country," asked Mr. Starnes.

"Since Feb. 12, 1659," responded the witness.

Mr. Banta testified he had worked as a reporter on the old New York World for twelve years, had spent some time on The New York American and was employed by The New York Times from 1930 to 1932 as a clerk in the classified advertising department.

Obtaining employment in the reporters' unit of the Civil Works Administration on Jan. 23, 1934, which later became the WPA writers' group, Mr. Banta said he soon became aware that many of the workers were Communists. His membership began, he explained, with an invitation to a "lecture" in Irving Plaza, received from Ralph De Sola, who was a witness too.

Tells of "Lecture"

The "lecture," it turned out, was a Communist party meeting and Mr. Banta said he was "surprised to find that at least 40 per cent of those at the meeting" were his colleagues on the project. That night Banta was enrolled as a member of Branch 2, Section 24, Unit 36-B, of the Communist party. He had paid 50 cents for admission and added 50 cents more for dues.

Mr. Banta declared he "stayed in until Sept. 1, 1938," and later revealed he had been denounced by party members as a "stool pigeon" after he received a subpoena from the Dies committee. His reason for joining or quitting the radical organization, but in references to certain few members of the project he testified that they enrolled to protect their jobs.

Once a member of the party Banta attended its meetings, solicited advertisements for "Red Pen," a Communist paper, and generally became known as a good Communist. To the Workers Alliance, which he had joined about the same time, he became a dues collector.

Continued on Page Sixteen

New Anti-Parking Drive Against Trucks Starts

In an attempt to alleviate the heavy traffic problem in the midtown area, the Police Department initiated a new "no parking" drive at 7 o'clock yesterday morning. According to the new regulations, trucks will be prohibited from parking, other than to make deliveries, in the area bounded by Fourteenth to Fifty-ninth Street and from Third to Ninth Avenue from 7 A. M. to 6 P. M.

In all instances trucks making deliveries must move as soon as those deliveries have been made. Coal trucks will get a longer time than delivery trucks, but all must "move on as soon as possible." Warnings will be given to violators this week and summonses next week.

TRUCKING IS TIED UP BY 'OUTLAW' STRIKE

Insurgent Members of A. F. L. Union Halt Most Interstate Shipments in City

An "outlaw" strike supported by insurgent members of Local 807 of the International Brotherhood of Teamsters, an A. F. of L. affiliate, halted most interstate trucking in and out of this city yesterday. Local trucks were tied up to a lesser degree, despite efforts by roving bands of strikers in the downtown waterfront district to force trucks back to their garages.

Officers of the union, disavowing any responsibility for the walkout, sent "missionary squads" into the downtown area to instruct drivers to continue at their duties and to seek to dissuade the insurgents from interference with truck movements. Thomas Hickey, secretary of the union, said he hoped all the men would be back at work this morning, but the rebels showed little sign of responding.

A flat order to participants in the unauthorized strike to return to work today and to iron out their differences with the union leadership later was issued last night by the executive committee of Local 807. It was impossible to determine at once whether this order would prove more effective in returning the dissident teamsters to their posts than had the union's earlier efforts at "persuasion."

Food Shipments Affected

The transportation of general merchandise from Boston, Baltimore, Philadelphia and other distant centers was cut off almost completely by the intra-union disagreement. Shipments of perishable foodstuffs were affected also, but the Department of Markets said it had no reports that the city's food supply was in jeopardy.

The revolt in the ranks of Local 807 grew out of a meeting Wednesday night at the Manhattan Opera House, at which members of the executive committee reported on negotiations with the Merchant Truckmen's Bureau for a contract to replace the one that expired on Sept. 1.

An offer by the employers to renew the agreement on the terms which prevailed last year was rejected by the meeting, Mr. Hickey said, but no strike vote was taken and the understanding was that negotiations were to be resumed.

The union demanded that hours be cut from forty-seven to forty a week without any reduction in the men's weekly pay. The employers, contending that hourly rates were 42 per cent above those prevailing in other large cities, asked that last year's standard be cut. This was the position of the two groups when conferences for a new contract began six weeks ago, and still represents their official position, according to spokesmen on both sides, although no compromise offers have been made in the negotiations.

Limited to One Local

Although a joint committee representing three affiliates of the International Brotherhood of Teamsters, Locals 807, 816 and 282, is involved in the wage conferences, yesterday's developments indicated that the strike movement was limited to members of Local 807. This union and seventy of its officers and members were indicted by a Federal grand jury last May on charges of violating the Anti-Racketeering and Anti-Trust Laws. The charges have not come to trial. Arthur G. McKeever, managing director of the Merchant Truckmen's Bureau, laid the strike move to "malcontents" in the ranks of Local 807. One employer spokesman asserted the strikers as "radicals" and said their strategy was greatest among the "malcontents" in New York of out-of-town trucks, as this branch of service was the one most recently organized by the union.

When interstate trucking began to reduce railroad freight traffic in the metropolitan district, the New York local insisted that all trucks coming into this city from other communities employ a member of Local 807, at the full day's pay of $9.42, to drive inside the city limits

Continued on Page Eight

MAJORITY PILED UP FOR GEORGE DOOMS 'PURGE' IN GEORGIA

Talmadge, Foe of New Deal Who Ran Second, Ponders Steps for Contest in Senate

COX, HOUSE CRITIC, AHEAD

R. E. Baldwin for Governor and J. A. Danaher for Senator on Connecticut G. O. P. Slate

Senator George won a majority of the county unit vote in Georgia's primary, assuring him the Democratic renomination for the Senate, despite President Roosevelt's opposition. Former Governor Talmadge, New Deal foe who ran far ahead of Lawrence Camp, Mr. Roosevelt's choice, hinted that a contest of Senator George's victory will be filed with the Senate. [Page 1.]

All eight of the Democratic Senators seeking renomination after opposing President Roosevelt's Court Bill, have been successful in primaries or conventions, three despite his direct intervention against them at the polls. [Page 6.]

Leaders in "unbossed" Connecticut Republican convention agreed on R. E. Baldwin for Governorship and J. A. Danaher for Senate choice in nominations to be made today. [Page 6.]

George Is the Winner

By TURNER CATLEDGE
Special to THE NEW YORK TIMES.

ATLANTA, Sept. 15.—Senator George's victory in the face of President Roosevelt's attempt to "purge" him from the Senate was confirmed today on late returns from yesterday's Democratic primary. This was the culmination result of a contest so hotly fought that it may go before the Senate privileges and elections committee of which Senator George is chairman.

Hot on the Senator's heels was former Governor Eugene Talmadge, the man with the red galluses and the Napoleon haircut, and one of the bitterest political enemies of the President and the New Deal to be found in the party.

Federal District Attorney Lawrence Camp, picked by Mr. Roosevelt to drive Mr. George from his Senate seat, was never able to go above third place from the time the count started.

Mr. George passed the finish line early this afternoon when complete returns from seventy-one of the State's 159 counties gave him a majority of the county unit vote, on which a nominee is selected. At that time he was leading with 208, or two more than an actual majority of the total of 410 unit ballots and was still going strong. He was also far ahead in the total popular vote.

Says Democracy Triumphed

In a broadcast from his home at Vienna Senator George declared that "the principle of Democracy has triumphed." Throughout his campaign the Senator had denounced the intervention of the President in the primary, characterizing it at one time as the "second march through Georgia."

After the broadcast the Senator left his home for Atlanta to par-

Continued on Page Five

Lynch, Princeton Football Star, Falls Dead; Heart Attack Fatal as He Ends Practice

Special to THE NEW YORK TIMES.

PRINCETON, N. J., Sept. 15.—William E. (Bill) Lynch, a senior at Princeton University and varsity fullback for the last two years, fell over backward and died of acute heart disease at 6 o'clock tonight as he was completing a jog around the field with his teammates at the end of a two-and-a-half hour practice session.

Lynch collapsed just outside the fieldhouse, where the players were going to take a shower at the end of their run around the field. Artificial respiration was begun at once by Charles Ceppi, line coach, a physician, and George M. Bohler, head trainer. Dr. Harry R. McPhee, chief physician to the team and associate professor of health and physical education at the university, was rushed to the scene. Artificial respiration, under Dr. McPhee's direction, was continued while Lynch was being carried to Princeton Hospital and for three hours after he was stricken. Dr. McPhee said there had been no indication of heart disease before.

"Last Friday, before he began football practice, I gave Lynch a thorough physical examination,"

Dr. McPhee said. "In my opinion he was in the best condition in which he had reported since he had been in college. I attributed his good condition to the fact that he had been in training all Summer; he was on the United States track team in Europe."

Lynch was 22 years old. He was the son of Mr. and Mrs. Leigh B. Lynch of 1,095 Fairfax Drive, Birmingham, Mich. His father, an executive at the Hudson auto plant in Birmingham, was an all-American halfback when he was at Brown. His brother, Leigh B. Lynch Jr., was the all-Eastern tackle at Brown in 1935.

Lynch prepared for Princeton at Westminster School, where he was active on the student council, on publications and in the W Club. At Princeton, besides his football activities, he was manager of the Elm Club, an eating club, held a scholarship and was majoring in English.

This year he was to have been shifted to quarterback. He was noted for his drop-kicking ability, and on Oct. 10, 1936, in the game with Rutgers, drop-kicked the first such goal in six years in Palmer Stadium, a distance of 46 yards.

Hungarians on Czech Soil Ask 'Self-Determination'

By The Associated Press.

BUDAPEST, Hungary, Sept. 15.—The Hungarian Revisionist League sent a message to Prime Minister Neville Chamberlain at Berchtesgaden today, asking him to "urge the right of self-determination" for the Hungarian minority in Czechoslovakia.

At the same time the league issued a proclamation "to all the peoples of the world," asking sympathy and support for "the right of self-determination of 1,000,000 Hungarians," the number estimated by the league to be in Czechoslovakia.

The league was formed to seek restoration to Hungary of territory lost in treaties at the end of the World War, including part of Czechoslovakia.

EXPECT WIDE PLAN

French Look for Series of Meetings and Then European Parley

CHAMBERLAIN IS PRAISED

Calling of Parliament Likely to Win Over World Opinion

By P. J. PHILIP
Wireless to THE NEW YORK TIMES.

PARIS, Sept. 15.—Today's meeting between Prime Minister Neville Chamberlain and Chancellor Adolf Hitler at Berchtesgaden, Germany, was only a preliminary contact, according to all information and opinion here, in a series of meetings that may develop into another peace conference. This conference, if it ever takes place, will be between equals and will not be an imposed peace of victors on the vanquished.

Toward it the first step will be most probably an almost immediate interview between Mr. Chamberlain and Premier Edouard Daladier of France. London on Saturday is to be mentioned as the probable place and time of the meeting. That would be a logical outcome of today's meeting. Its alternative is war.

Of what actually happened at Berchtesgaden little, almost nothing, has been allowed to leak out. For those who know what has been in both the German Chancellor's and the British Prime Minister's minds to reconstruct their conversation in broad outline. As a basis they set the ideas that follow.

War Views of the Two Men

Mr. Chamberlain does not want his country or any country involved in a major war. Hitler does not want to engage in a war into which Great Britain might be drawn. Both men are forthright in speaking their minds, and there is no doubt Hitler was flattered by the British Prime Minister's visit.

It removes the German Chancellor from any possibility of being regarded as a political outcast from the European concert. Mr. Chamberlain went to him as an equal, and that has been in these past twenty years what Germany has wanted more than anything else.

There is no doubt also that both men were concerned with the wide problem of peace more than with what is in reality the detail of the Sudetens' quarrel with the Czechoslovaks and the inclusion of the former in Czechoslovakia under the Treaty of Versailles.

Even if it came to war and Germany were beaten, the problem would remain. So, Hitler argues, what is the use of fighting? The Chancellor did not insist on the Sudetens' attachment to Germany.

In the last few years, under similar conditions, and what happened even to foreign exchange, or to American dollars, you will just see that I think we are proving to the world that the United States is the financial center of the world, and we can resist the kind of nervousness which people who have money are feeling at this time."

Continued on Page Twelve

Sudeten Leader Flees Country After Urging Union With Reich

Says Germans and Czechs Can No Longer Live in Same State—Martial Law Extended—Runciman Goes to London

By The Associated Press.

PRAGUE, Czechoslovakia, Sept. 15.—The inner council of the Czechoslovak Cabinet tonight ordered the arrest of Konrad Henlein, the Sudeten German leader, as a traitor.

Announcement of the action came suddenly after Herr Henlein earlier had issued a proclamation declaring the Sudeten Germans wanted union with Germany.

The proclamation and the government's drastic countermove apparently brought to an end all present possibility of an understanding between the Sudeten German party and the Czechoslovak regime.

Earlier the government had extended martial law in the Sudeten areas, bringing about two-thirds of the population of 3,500,000 under military rule.

The government clamped martial law tighter upon the German cities, adding the communities of Reichenberg, Rumburg and Schluckenau—all near the German frontier in Northwestern Czechoslovakia—to the number under control of troops. It also placed the city of Warnsdorf, on the German frontier, under martial law after reports circulated that Sudeten Germans were gather-

ing at near-by Komotau for a march on Warnsdorf. The march failed to materialize.

Henlein Issues Proclamation

By G. E. R. GEDYE
Wireless to THE NEW YORK TIMES.

PRAGUE, Czechoslovakia, Sept. 15.—Konrad Henlein has finally dropped altogether the pretense maintained for years that despite differences with Prague he was a loyal citizen and has openly raised the standard of revolt. Characteristically, it was raised not via Czechoslovakia but via the German radio.

At noon Germany broadcast what was allegedly Herr Henlein's proclamation "to the Sudeten Germans, German peoples and the whole world," in which he openly declared himself a rebel against the State, adding that the Sudeten Germans and Czechs could no longer live together in the same country and that he and his followers desired an schluss with Germany. The government immediately announced that necessary measures would be taken against whoever was responsible for the proclama-

Continued on Page Thirteen

EXCHANGE IS FRANK

Briton to Fly to London Today but Will Return for New Meeting

NEXT ONE IN A FEW DAYS

Fuehrer Insists the Sudetens Can No Longer Remain in Czechoslovakia

Prime Minister Chamberlain and Chancellor Hitler conferred three hours at Berchtesgaden yesterday and the former returned to a hotel. He will fly to London today to consult his Cabinet, and it was announced he would again visit Hitler in a few days. The official communiqué told only of a "comprehensive and frank exchange of opinion."

Paris believed the Berchtesgaden meeting would be only preliminary to a series of further ones leading to a peace conference, in which Germany would be treated as an equal. Premier Daladier was expected to confer immediately with Mr. Chamberlain.

The Prague Government ordered the arrest as a traitor of Konrad Henlein, Sudeten leader, following a proclamation demanding union of the Sudeten districts with the Reich. He took refuge in Germany. More districts were placed under martial law. Viscount Runciman was recalled to London.

Preparations were made in London to summon Parliament to hear Mr. Chamberlain's report. A special Cabinet meeting was called for this afternoon. There was renewed nervousness over the sudden return of the Prime Minister.

Secretary of the Treasury Morgenthau said foreign money was coming into the United States in unprecedented volume. He saw no reason for alarm in this situation. [All the above dispatches on Page 1.]

Marine insurance companies here and in London put all war risks on a ship to ship basis and increased them sharply on business taken. [Page 15.]

Three-Hour Conference Held

Wireless to THE NEW YORK TIMES.

BERCHTESGADEN, Germany, Sept. 15.—The German-Sudeten man question was discussed for three hours by Prime Minister Neville Chamberlain and Chancellor Adolf Hitler at the latter's highland chalet near Berchtesgaden this evening.

The conversation was then adjourned to permit Mr. Chamberlain to return to London tomorrow morning and inform the British Cabinet of the German demands, and presumably also to communicate with the French Government. He will again visit Hitler in a few days for further consultations, it was officially announced.

It was suggested that a more convenient place than Hitler's Alpine home would be selected for the next conversation, according to The Associated Press.]

The only authoritative information as to the course and contents of today's conversation is contained in a meager communiqué that affords no clue to the motives that may have prompted the Prime Minister to decide to return to London tomorrow. The communiqué reads:

Berchtesgaden, Sept. 15, 1938. The Fuehrer and Reich Chancellor had a discussion today at Obersalzberg with the British Prime Minister, in the course of which a comprehensive and frank exchange of opinion on the present situation took place.

The British Prime Minister will return to England tomorrow to confer with the British Cabinet. New discussions will take place in a few days.

Inquiries for something more illuminating than the slender information revealed in the official statement produced a warning against conjectures on today's initial conversation. Both the German and the British affected a show of restricted optimism over the outcome of the day's contacts, but neither would divulge the nature of the information Mr. Cham-

Continued on Page Fifteen

ROOSEVELT ALERT, SILENT ON CRISIS

Confers With Hull on Reaching Capital—Cancels Today's Press Conference

Special to THE NEW YORK TIMES.

WASHINGTON, Sept. 15.—President Roosevelt returned to the capital tonight and immediately went into conference with Secretary Hull to learn details of the European crisis.

Arriving at 7 o'clock from Rochester, Minn., where he went to be at the bedside of his son, James, Mr. Roosevelt received Secretary Hull in his private car and they conversed for ten minutes. Secretary of War Woodring also boarded the train.

So grave did the President consider the situation that he canceled tomorrow's press conference, for fear that any comment he might make there might be misinterpreted. Stephen T. Early, the President's secretary, insisted that there was no special significance in this other than that the President felt he was not in a position to discuss European affairs.

Cabinet Session Is Called

The President called a Cabinet meeting for tomorrow to lay before his advisers all the information he has received. He is expected then to state whether he will go to Poughkeepsie Saturday to make an address in connection with the 150th anniversary of New York's ratification of the Constitution.

Attachés of the White House said the engagement would be kept, but a final decision would wait on what probably took place in Czechoslovakia within twenty-four hours.

Mr. Roosevelt caught up with official business during the afternoon as his special train moved through Western Maryland. Twice during the day he received reports from Rochester, where his son is convalescing from his operation. The reports were good.

Although crowds met the train at every stop, Mr. Roosevelt remained in his car, keeping to his intention

Continued on Page Eleven

RECORD RUSH HERE BY FOREIGN CAPITAL

Dollar Buying Abroad Reaches New High—Morgenthau Says U. S. Will Be Haven for Money

Special to THE NEW YORK TIMES.

WASHINGTON, Sept. 15.—As a result of the tense situation in Europe foreign money is coming into the United States in unprecedented volume, Henry Morgenthau Jr., Secretary of the Treasury, said today. He declared that there was no reason to be alarmed because of this and added that "if people want to send their money here as a haven of refuge we will take good care of it for them."

"When you consider the nervousness all over the world due to the European situation," Mr. Morgenthau said, "it has been extremely remarkable that there has been as little fluctuation in foreign exchange as there has been, and the reason that there is as little as there is, is due to the fact that Congress has given the United States Treasury the necessary legislation and the means by which to see that no groups should manipulate the dollar to the disadvantage of the American business men. I think the record speaks for itself."

The Secretary explained that he referred to the stabilization fund as well as operations under the tripartite agreement of 1936.

U. S. Financial Center

Asked if he still felt that the tri-partite agreement was working smoothly, Mr. Morgenthau said:

"Conditions are what they are, and if you compare this with any other time during the last few

One significant detail that might be added to the official communication that another meeting will take place shortly is that it was reported at Berchtesgaden this evening that Hitler declared he would not wish the British Prime Minister to make a second long voyage to such a remote corner as Berchtesgaden and that he would gladly meet Mr. Chamberlain in some more convenient town in Germany.

Mr. Chamberlain's reported intention to summon the British Parliament for the purpose of making a full statement of his hopes and intentions is regarded here as a master stroke. In that way, it is believed, he will be able to mobilize the British Empire and probably get a great part of world opinion behind him in his efforts to deal with the problem of armed Europe as a whole and not merely with the incidental issue of Czechoslovakia.

Over his colleague, Premier Daladier, the British Prime Minister will have this advantage, that he will do most of the talking to his own country.

"Let me go through this again,"

Continued on Page Fourteen

BRITAIN WILL ISSUE PARLIAMENT CALL

Special Session Next Week to Hear Chamberlain—London, Nervous, Speculates on Trip

By ROBERT P. POST
Special Cable to THE NEW YORK TIMES.

LONDON, Sept. 15.—The British Parliament will be called into special session some time next week to hear Prime Minister Neville Chamberlain's report on his Berchtesgaden conference. This was decided today at a meeting in the Downing Street of Sir John Simon, Chancellor of the Exchequer; David Margesson, government Chief Whip, and Edward Algernon Fitzroy, Speaker of the House of Commons.

But this meeting was held before astonished Britain learned that Mr. Chamberlain had cut short his projected stay at Berchtesgaden and was flying back tomorrow to preside over another special Cabinet meeting, hastily summoned tonight to meet tomorrow afternoon.

It is still in doubt what effect the news Mr. Chamberlain brings from Chancellor Hitler's mountain retreat will have on the plans for convoking Parliament—a convocation easily made at short notice through use of the British Broadcasting Company facilities and requiring no formalities as Parliament is only in recess.

Nervousness Returns

Naturally, under the circumstances, London is full of speculation and rumor. The distinct slackening of tension that had been felt here today as Mr. Chamberlain's plane left Heston Airport in the morning, was succeeded at night by renewed nervousness. It is true that no time limit had been placed on Mr. Chamberlain's visit, but it was distinctly understood he expected to stay several days at least. That being the case, it is easy to understand the wave of disillusionment that swept over Britain on the news that he had ordered his plane ready for the return journey almost before its engines had had time to cool.

In the view of many here, however, there is a much brighter side to the picture. The negotiations clearly are not broken off and the fact that it was declared definitely that the face-to-face negotiations of the heads of the two States would continue is bound to be taken as an indication that Mr. Chamberlain's new technique still has profound possibilities. As one qualified observer put it, "As long as he is going back it's all right."

The general attitude of the government is that since the entire future hung on what went on at Berchtesgaden it was useless to speculate or even discuss the future until the conference was over and its results were ready to be assayed. The fact that Mr. Chamberlain is bringing home some of these results more speedily than was expected

Continued on Page Twelve

"All the News That's Fit to Print."

The New York Times.

LATE CITY EDITION
Cloudy, little change in temperatures today; showers tonight.
Tomorrow fair, cooler.
Temperatures Yesterday—Max., 71; Min., 56

Copyright, 1938, by The New York Times Company.

VOL. LXXXVIII...No. 29,466.   Entered as Second-Class Matter, Postoffice, New York, N. Y.   NEW YORK, TUESDAY, SEPTEMBER 27, 1938.   PPPP   THREE CENTS NEW YORK CITY and Vicinity | FOUR CENTS Elsewhere Except in 7th and 8th Postal Zones

TRUCK FIRMS HALT THE MAYOR'S PLAN; DRIVERS ACCEPT IT

Operators Reject Peace Terms as 'Unfair' After All-Day Conference Fails

CITY HAS A FLEET READY

1,000 Sanitation Vehicles Are Mobilized for Emergency— 15,000 Quit in Jersey

Convinced that further negotiations between union and operator representatives would produce no settlement of the truck drivers' strike that has paralyzed shipping in New York City for more than a week, Mayor La Guardia submitted a compromise proposal to the negotiators whom he locked in City Hall last night and demanded an end of the strike by noon today.

Michael J. Cashal, vice president of the International Brotherhood of Teamsters, submitted the Mayor's proposal to the strikers' committee and within a few minutes announced their acceptance.

The Mayor's proposal was unanimously rejected by the truck operators early this morning at a meeting at the Capitol Hotel, Eighth Avenue and Fifty-first Street, attended by more than 300 members of the Merchant Truckmen's Bureau and the Highway Transport Association.

The vote was taken at about 1:40 A. M. at the end of a two-hour meeting at which members of the operators' negotiating committee reported on the Mayor's plan and asked for instructions.

The operators also voted to set up a committee to enlist support among shippers and to seek to persuade operators not to sign separate agreements.

Although the committee made no formal recommendation for acceptance or rejection of the Mayor's proposal, members of the committee assailed it as "unfair" and requiring the operators to concede everything while the union gave nothing in return.

Rise in Costs Seen

D. L. Sutherland, president of the Highway Transport Association, estimated that the proposal, if accepted, would raise costs between 7 and 9 per cent. He termed the proposal "not a compromise but a piece of political skulduggery." Operators at the meeting applauded declarations from the floor that it was time to make a stand and fight it out.

The operators met late in the afternoon, and recessed until evening to hear reports on the City Hall negotiations. The committee arrived from City Hall at about 11:30 P. M. and discussion of the Mayor's plan began a few minutes later. The operators will meet again at the Capitol Hotel at 3 P. M. today.

The operators' committee is to report its answer at City Hall at 9 o'clock this morning, in accordance with the Mayor's request. Arthur G. McKeever, managing director of the Merchant Truckmen's Bureau, told the Mayor at the conclusion of the City Hall conference last night that some points would require clearing up and would have to be submitted to the operators' organizations.

In the meantime, the Mayor ordered mobilization of the Department of Sanitation's emergency fleet of 1,000 trucks, which began arriving at City Hall Plaza shortly after 12 o'clock. The fleet was being mobilized to handle any essential food stuffs or other material held up by the strike.

2-Year Contract Urged

Mayor La Guardia's proposal was for an agreement to run for two years. Where the union had demanded a forty-four week at the forty-four-hour rate of pay, the Mayor proposed a forty-four-hour week at forty-seven hours' pay, an eight-hour day, beginning at 8 A. M., with no man to be permitted to work more than forty-four hours weekly.

The Mayor submitted his compromise plan at a joint meeting of driver and operator committees of eleven members each at City Hall. He expressed a determination to end today the strike which he pointed out had caused not only losses to the business community but hardship to citizens, particularly those in the storm-stricken areas.

The plight of the hurricane-swept communities of New England, which need building supplies and materials, was described by Governors Robert E. Quinn of Rhode Island and Wilbur L. Cross of Connecticut in telegrams to the Mayor to send storm relief supplies moving again.

Meanwhile, the strike of 15,000 drivers in New York City had spread to 15,000 drivers in North New Jersey, while a strike of bus drivers, not involved in the dispute, had halted the transportation of

Continued on Page Six

Southampton Declines WPA Storm Clean-Up Aid

Special to THE NEW YORK TIMES.

SOUTHAMPTON, L. I., Sept. 26.—The Village Board of Southampton voted today to decline an offer of WPA aid in cleaning up after Wednesday's hurricane. Many trees were blown over and considerable damage was done to the waterfront of this exclusive Summer resort.

After the Village Board meeting Mayor Albert P. Loening said:

"The Village Board has declined WPA aid in cleaning up the highways and for other rehabilitation work in the village. In Southampton we have always been able to handle our own affairs in the 300 years of our existence. The Village Board appreciates WPA offers of help, but the members feel that the sister communities of Southampton, which sustained greater damage, should receive whatsoever assistance was gone to us."

LABOR LAW CHANGE DEMANDED BY FREY

Its Administration 'Disrupting' Factor in Industry, He Tells Metal Trades Group

By The Associated Press.

HOUSTON, Texas, Sept. 26.—John P. Frey, chief of the A. F. of L. Metal Trades Department, attacked Federal regulation of wages and industrial relations today in his annual report to the metal trades conference, and called for greater cooperation between labor and industry.

Mr. Frey said that the trade union movement was founded on "self-government in industry instead of government by bureaus and administrators."

Congress, he declared, would do much to prevent recurring depressions by establishing "the proper and adequate rules under which business is to be conducted."

"Business and organized labor, through the conference room and collective bargaining, must then work out the problem of stable production and the economically sound division of the wealth being created," he said.

Mr. Frey's report criticized both the Wage-Hour Law and the National Labor Relations Act. The administration of the latter, he said, was a "disrupting" factor in American industry.

"Both the law and the personnel must be changed before the board under the Wagner act can constructively and sanely apply its authority to protect the right of wage-earners to be represented by organizations of their own choosing," he said.

The Wage-Hour Law, he continued, conferred "extraordinary authority" on the administrator amounting to "bureaucratic or commissar control."

Communist Activity Assailed

The metal trades chief also criticized the activity of Communists in the labor movement, the political ventures of the rival C. I. O. and its contributions to political campaigns.

In less specific terms, he struck at centralization of government authority, "college professors and theorists in administrative posts," and at a "super-intelligent, highly educated minority" he said was preaching that workers should trade their independence for security.

"Should the day come," he continued, "when American workmen, instead of depending upon themselves, depend upon controllers for leadership and guidance, then American wage-earners will have lost their independence and their capacity for self-government."

Recalling some of the political activities of the C. I. O., Frey said:

"The definite entry of the C. I. O. into the political fields creates an issue which we cannot escape. The political activities of the C. I. O. have led many representatives in State Legislatures and in Congress to give more consideration to the probabilities of C. I. G. strength than the merits of the legislative measures coming to their attention.

"The nonpartisan political policy of the American Federation of Labor serves to indicate the most effective method of meeting this problem." (The federation's policy has been to reward its friends and punish its enemies regardless of party.)

The political representatives of the C. I. O.'s United Mine Workers in the 1936 Democratic Presidential campaign and later in the 1938 Pennsylvania Democratic primary, Mr. Frey declared, "eclipsed all political records."

"These enormous campaign expenditures," he added, "are an evidence of what labor may expect if it is to indulge in partisan politics, a larger expenditure for political purposes than for all other trade union activities combined."

Reiterating some of his anti-communism testimony before the Dies House committee investigating un-American activities, Mr. Frey

Continued on Page Five

PREPARE TO FIGHT 'OLD GUARD' SLATE ON DEWEY TICKET

Republican Liberals Fear Move to Give All Other Places to Conservatives

SPRAGUE BOOM IS HINTED

Young Element in Party Hears He Is Talked for Long-Term Senate Nomination

By JAMES A. HAGERTY
Special to THE NEW YORK TIMES.

SARATOGA SPRINGS, Sept. 26.—Reports of a possible clash between the liberal and Old Guard elements in the Republican party over the nomination of candidates other than for Governor reached here tonight as the first of the delegates arrived for the opening of the State convention Wednesday.

There was no difference of opinion over the desirability of nominating District Attorney Thomas E. Dewey of New York County for Governor, but fear was expressed by some of the liberal faction than the conservative party leaders might try to name conservatives for the rest of this ticket.

This feeling is likely to be reflected at meetings of the board of governors of the State Association of Young Republican Clubs tomorrow afternoon and of the executive committee of the association tomorrow evening. The board of governors will confine itself to making suggestions for the platform while the executive committee will make recommendations concerning candidates.

The Young Republicans favor the nomination of Edward Corsi of Manhattan for the short Senatorial term. They are not wholly satisfied with all of those suggested for nomination for the full Senatorial term of six years.

Mentioned for Long Term

The word here is that J. Russell Sprague of Nassau County and Representative Bruce Barton of Manhattan are under consideration for either nomination in addition to Edward H. Butler, publisher of The Buffalo Evening News, and Jerome D. Barnum, publisher of The Syracuse Post-Standard.

District Attorney Alfred L. Simon of Saratoga County, president of the Association of Young Republican Clubs, has the support of this section for nomination for Attorney General. State Senator Benjamin F. Feinberg of Clinton County has strong support for this nomination.

The boom for Assemblyman Jeremiah J. Wadsworth of Livingston County arrived tonight in the custody of Mark Welch, his campaign manager. State Senator Frederic H. Bontecou of Dutchess County also is a candidate for this nomination. Delegates from Western New York brought a boom for E. E. Holmquist, Jamestown furniture manufacturer, for the nomination for Controller.

Miss Katherine Kennedy, acting secretary of the Republican State Committee, was overwhelmed with requests for tickets of admission to the convention on her arrival. There will be 1,936 delegates and the same number of alternates, in excess of 1,800 more than at any previous convention of the party, and the convention hall seats only

Continued on Page Four

Geoghan, Angered by Rumors, Subpoenas Officials to Inquiry Into 'Corruption'

For the second time within two months, District Attorney William F. X. Geoghan of Brooklyn proceeded yesterday to conduct a personal investigation into rumors of "official corruption" involving a member of his office and this time centering about a fur swindle in which five policemen and four other persons have been indicted.

Making one of his rare appearances before a grand jury, Mr. Geoghan spent several hours in the afternoon interrogating two witnesses, including Police Inspector Michael F. McDermott. Afterward, he announced that he had issued grand jury subpoenas for the appearance today and tomorrow of William B. Herlands, Commissioner of Investigation, Chief City Magistrate Jacob Gould Schurman Jr., Magistrate Matthew J. Troy, S. Harvey Posner of the Citizens Committee for Crime Control, and "others reported to know something about this matter."

"Aspersions have been cast upon my office and I now propose to have a show-down," Mr. Geoghan, angered, declared. "With the aid of this grand jury, I am going to probe these charges of reported, or rumored, official corruption in connection with this case.

"I will subpoena any single person connected in any way with this matter. If anyone has anything to say, let him say it before this grand jury. I want it all on the record in black and white. I'm the prosecutor of this county and if there is anything to this I'll prosecute it to the limit."

Later in the day Mr. Geoghan announced that the investigation concerned Isidore Jaffe, 48 years old, of 332 East Fourteenth Street, Brooklyn, a suspect in the fur swindle, against whom grand larceny charges twice have been dismissed because of insufficient evidence, and who is alleged to have said that he was freed "because I paid plenty." Mr. Geoghan said that Jaffe had been an informer in the case and that he had made a statement recently denying the payment of money and explaining that he "was only trying to throw the others off the trail."

It was just two months ago that Mr. Geoghan, acting on the basis of rumors and unofficial charges, initiated a personal investigation into reports that one of his staff assistants had accepted a bribe of $100 to "fix" a perjury case. As a result William F. McGuinness, suspended assistant district attorney of Brooklyn, and George F. Murphy, city-employed elevator operator, recently were indicted for conspiracy to obstruct justice and are awaiting trial.

BRITAIN PLEDGES AID IF CZECHS ARE ATTACKED; ALSO GUARANTEES SURRENDER OF SUDETEN AREA AS HITLER IN SPEECH KEEPS PEACE DOOR OPEN

Reich Is Accelerating Inflation of Currency

Wireless to THE NEW YORK TIMES.

BERLIN, Sept. 26.—Inflation of German currency is being accelerated alarmingly by military preparations. Contrary to the general rule for the third week in September the Reichsbank return for Sept. 23 shows a large increase in loans and a substantial rise in banknote and total circulation.

In consequence the Sept. 30 return will show a very serious inflation in the total.

On Sept. 23 the bills portfolio was 1,785,000,000 marks higher than in the same period in 1937. The note circulation was 2,078,-000,000 marks higher, which means a 40 per cent rise in one year.

The total note circulation is 8,786,000,000 marks, against 6,565,-000,000 marks for the same period in 1937. Reichsbank gold and exchange reserves show virtually no change.

BENES IS ASSAILED

Hitler Says Czech State Was Conceived as Lie by 'Mad' Statesmen

SUDETENLAND ONLY CLAIM

Address Seen as Facade Behind Which Anything Can Happen —Oct. 1 Still Deadline

Text of Chancellor Hitler's speech is on Page 17.

By FREDERICK T. BIRCHALL
Wireless to THE NEW YORK TIMES.

BERLIN, Sept. 26.—For an hour tonight, facing directly an audience of 15,000 in the Sportpalast, Chancellor Hitler addressed the German people listening in by order at loud-speakers over all the land and his speech was far from being the expected defiance of British and French public opinion steadily rising against his Czechoslovak ultimatum.

Uncompromising in the matter of his demands for the evacuation of Sudeten German areas, he stressed equally his having agreed to a plebiscite in the disputed territories after German forces came into possession of them.

It was notable that Herr Hitler had really harsh words only for President Eduard Benes and the present Czechoslovak State, which he characterized as "conceived as a lie and conducted as a swindle for twenty years." The Czech people escaped vituperation and Herr Hitler addressed soothing phrases to the Poles, Ukrainians, Slovaks, French, British and even Hungarians, all of whom he reminded of his manifested desire to seek no quarrel with them.

While utterly uncompromising in his insistence that the Sudeten areas should be surrendered by Saturday he stressed the sweet reasonableness of this demand rather than the desire to acquire them forcibly. The Czech Government, he argued, had already consented to surrender the territories; he only wanted it to keep its word. The British and French had agreed to it and they should stand by their agreement.

The fact that his memorandum handed to Prime Minister Neville Chamberlain had extended beyond the original limits of the areas to be surrendered and that the conditions for evacuation were harsh and humiliating beyond any expectation, Herr Hitler ignored. He dwelt over the demand for German military occupation of the disputed areas also pending and during the plebiscite stressing instead that he had granted Mr. Chamberlain's request to have an international commission manage the plebiscite.

Way Left Open for Hitler

The speech, in fact, while firm and impassioned in the Hitler manner, left the impression clearly to the very reticence that it was a facade behind which anything can happen without in the least controverting its contents. Herr Hitler can negotiate—through France and Britain for a peaceful surrender or he can wait the prescribed period and then march in dealing as harshly as he chooses with the Czech resistance. Either way he will be consistent and he can claim and will probably receive the initial applause of his people.

It is common knowledge that Sir Horace Wilson of the British Foreign Office arrived by air from London bringing a message from Mr. Chamberlain that had the endorsement of the French ministers who had gone to London as well as the French Cabinet, and that Sir Horace was closeted with Herr Hitler for more than a half hour before his speech. The message, it is understood, was a final appeal not to close the door to negotiation.

Continued on Page Twelve

Two British Declarations

By The Associated Press.

LONDON, Tuesday, Sept. 27.—Following are the texts of the authoritative statement issued yesterday on Britain's decision to join in defending Czechoslovakia in case of attack and of Prime Minister Chamberlain's statement early this morning replying to Chancellor Hitler's speech:

Statement of Policy

It is stated in official quarters that during the last week Prime Minister Chamberlain has tried with the German Chancellor to find a way of settling peacefully the Czechoslovak question.

It is still possible to do so by negotiation.

Germany's claim to transfer of the Sudeten areas has already been conceded by the French, British and Czechoslovak Governments.

But if, in spite of all efforts made by the British Prime Minister, a German attack is made upon Czechoslovakia, the immediate result must be that France will be bound to come to her assistance and Great Britain and Russia will stand by France.

It is still not too late to stop this great tragedy and for the peoples of all nations to insist on settlement by free negotiation.

Chamberlain Declaration

I have read the speech of Chancellor Hitler and I appreciate his reference to the efforts I have made to save peace.

I cannot abandon those efforts since it seems to me incredible that the peoples of Europe who do not want war with one another should be plunged into a bloody struggle over a question on which agreement has already been largely obtained.

It is evident that the Chancellor has no faith that the promises made will be carried out. These promises were made not to the German Government direct but to the British and French Governments in the first instance.

Speaking for the British Government, we regard ourselves as morally responsible for seeing that the promises are carried out fairly and fully and we are prepared to undertake that they shall be so carried out with all reasonable promptitude, provided that the German Government will agree to settlement of terms and conditions to the transfer by discussions and not by force.

I trust that the Chancellor will not reject this proposal, which is made in the same spirit of friendliness as that in which I was received in Germany and which if it is accepted will satisfy the German desire for union of the Sudeten Germans with the Reich without the shedding of blood in any part of Europe.

CZECHS RESIGNED AFTER HITLER TALK

No Hope Taken by the People From Speech—Officials Are Urged to Stand Fast

By G. E. R. GEDYE
Wireless to THE NEW YORK TIMES.

PRAGUE, Czechoslovakia, Sept. 26.—Knowledge that Chancellor Adolf Hitler would speak tonight hung like a thundercloud over the political atmosphere of this capital all day. Czechoslovakia had already rejected the Godesberg memorandum as furnishing no basis whatever for discussion, and it was felt quite possible that Herr Hitler's speech would contain an announcement that German troops would be ordered to attack Czechoslovakia.

People learned from shops and offices with unusual speed fcr the comparative safety and security of their homes and far more than the usual number of gas masks were carried by civilians in the streets during the afternoon and evening.

The fact that Dr. Joseph Goebbels, German Propaganda Minister, with his well-known desire for war, introduced Herr Hitler tonight seemed at once an ominous sign. When the speech of the German Chancellor closed without a declaration of hostilities there was a slight relaxation of tension here. The relaxation, however, did not go very far because it is universally felt that the speech of Herr Hitler now makes war inevitable by Saturday.

Czechoslovakia Is Silent

It is not likely that there will be any official Czechoslovak reply to the speech, which, it is felt here, did nothing but repeat the Godesberg memorandum, with no important variations. That memorandum had already been rejected, and Czechoslovakia has nothing more to say.

There is full confidence that when the blow falls both of Czechoslovakia's allies, France and Russia, will fulfill their treaty obligations to the letter, as well her allies of the Little Entente, Rumania and Yugoslavia, should their intervention be necessary by reason of Hungary's participation in an attempt to wreck this country.

As for Britain, the news received here concerning last night's Cabinet sitting awakened a strong hope that she also would join her friends.

Meantime, until dusk falls with its unnaturally darkened streets and pitch black windows, daily life continues almost normal in Prague. The virtually complete absence of taxicabs—perhaps six are plying in the entire city, for nobody uses them—makes it necessary to fight for a place in street cars, where Russian conditions prevail. The cars are packed from morning to night with passengers clinging to every inch of space, even on the steps.

For those who have no automobiles of their own, the street cars are now the only means of transport.

Continued on Page Fourteen

FRANCE SEES ISSUE DRAWN FOR HITLER

Ministers Say Chancellor Must Choose Now Between War and Peace

By P. J. PHILIP
Wireless to THE NEW YORK TIMES.

PARIS, Sept. 26.—From their London conference Premier Edouard Daladier and Foreign Minister Georges Bonnet returned this afternoon by air to find there was no necessity even for calling a Cabinet meeting before tomorrow morning. Events had spoken for themselves. There was no need to speak.

M. Daladier's reply to President Roosevelt, Prime Minister Neville Chamberlain's final appeal to Chancellor Adolf Hitler, the decision of Foreign Minister Georges Bonnet to summon at once the Council of the League of Nations if Czechoslovakia should be attacked, interviews that General Marie Gustave Gamelin, Chief of Staff of the French Army, had had, London warnings, preparations against air attack that are being made here, and finally Chancellor Hitler's speech all contributed to make the situation clear to every one. If Herr Hitler insists on having his way, he will have war. There is no other issue.

Opens Way for Russia

By deciding to summon at once the League Council, M. Bonnet is opening the way for Russian intervention with the consent of Rumania. The only uncertain element in today's doings, as far as the French public was concerned, was exactly what was contained in Mr. Chamberlain's appeal to Herr Hitler, which had been sent with M. Daladier's full approval. Everything else that had been done and said seemed to point to war.

London reports take today of a proposal to Herr Hitler to negotiate with the Czechoslovaks and a warning that if he does not reach a satisfactory settlement and tries force, Great Britain and Russia will automatically join France in protection of Czechoslovak independence, swiftly changed the outlook. Even Chancellor Hitler's speech was found, in the light of these reports, to read somewhat differently than it had sounded. There were significant omissions. It will not be until his reply, which Sir Horace Wilson is taking to London tomorrow, is made public that any one can be quite sure, if even then.

Fears of the general public who heard or read Herr Hitler's speech concurred that it looked like war. In inner circles of those engaged in the immense diplomatic game it is still hoped, even believed, that inch by inch the German leader can be forced from his position.

No one here has any quarrel with the German people. It is the Nazi system, personified in Hitler, that they fear, and Goebbels that at the speech reminded them of what France believes in. If some check can be interposed to that system without war, then so much the

Continued on Page Fourteen

ENTENTE REVIVING

London Warns It Will Share Defense With Paris and Moscow

APPEALS TO HITLER ANEW

Offers to Enforce the Cession Pledge of Czechs—Meeting of Parliament Tomorrow

Britain announced last night that she and Russia "will certainly stand by France" if that nation should go to the defense of Czechoslovakia. This information was not delivered to Herr Hitler before his speech but a personal note from Prime Minister Chamberlain was given to him urging further negotiations. Mr. Chamberlain announced he would see that Sudeten territory was transferred to Germany fairly if she did not go to war.

Herr Hitler refrained from defiance in his speech to the German people. He was uncompromising in his demands for annexation of Sudeten territory and threatened to take it if surrender was denied but was believed to have left the door open to negotiations.

Czechoslovakia gave no indication that she would make a reply to Herr Hitler's speech, and the people resigned themselves to the worst. It was felt in Prague that the speech made war inevitable by Saturday.

The French Premier and Foreign Minister, on their return from London, declared the issue had boiled down simply to whether Hitler wanted war. If Germany should attack, the League Council is to be convened to give Russia a chance to intervene with Rumania's consent.

President Roosevelt called a special session of the Cabinet for today "because of the existing situation" and the State Department rushed activities in getting Americans out of Europe. [All the above dispatches on Page 1.]

Premier Mussolini appealed to Britain and France to abandon Czechoslovakia before it was too late. [Page 10.]

Germans and French strung barbed wire along the Rhine and challenging signs were erected on both sides. [Page 14.]

Britain Is Pledged to Fight

By FERDINAND KUHN Jr.
Special Cable to THE NEW YORK TIMES.

LONDON, Tuesday, Sept. 27.—The British Government took its most momentous decision in twenty years yesterday by accepting a clear-cut military commitment in case of German aggression against the Czechoslovak Republic.

An authoritative statement came from Downing Street last night that if a German attack was made against Czechoslovakia "the immediate result must be that France will be bound to come to her assistance and Great Britain and Russia will certainly stand by France."

So at the eleventh hour and as a last resort the hesitations of the past week have been wiped away. Prime Minister Neville Chamberlain's carefully qualified warning to Germany on March 24 and that of Sir John Simon, Chancellor of the Exchequer, last month have been swept into the forgotten past by the rush of tremendous events.

Triple Entente Revived?

From now on France knows she can count definitely, without quibbles and evasions, upon British help if she springs to the defense of Czechoslovakia. Britain has had to swallow her dislike of Continental commitments and by an odd twist of history Conservative Britain and Bolshevist Russia will find themselves, if war now begins, allied once more in spite of all their mutual antipathies of the past twenty years.

In other words, if Chancellor Hitler fulfills last night's threat to "go and liberate our Germans" in Czechoslovakia, Britain has had to swallow her dislike of Continental commitments and by a twist of history Conservative Britain and Bolshevist Russia will find themselves allied once more in spite of all their mutual antipathies of the past twenty years.

There is one big "if" in the decision taken by the united British Cabinet early yesterday morning and approved by the heads of the British and French Governments later in the day. The new alignment of Britain, France and Rus-

Continued on Page Sixteen

3 NATIONS IN REPLY PRAISE ROOSEVELT

Germany Is Silent, but Czechs, British and French Send Notes—U. S. Cabinet Called

Replies by Benes, Chamberlain and Daladier are on Page 10.

Special to THE NEW YORK TIMES.

WASHINGTON, Sept. 26.—A Presidential call for a special meeting of the Cabinet tomorrow afternoon, "because of the existing situation," coupled with feverish activity at the State Department on behalf of Americans caught in European danger zones, combined today to make official Washington keenly aware of the fast-developing war crisis in the wake of Chancellor Adolf Hitler's Berlin address.

At the White House and the State Department, particularly, there was an obvious effort to present an appearance of calm in the face of an admittedly serious situation in Europe. President Roosevelt remained in his blue-paneled study in the White House, from which in the early hours this morning he authorized his appeal for peace to the European powers directly concerned.

Replies were received from the British, French and Czechoslovak representatives at President Roosevelt's eleventh-hour peace plea and they were relayed to the White House as quickly as they were received at the State Department. At the close of business for the day no reply had been received from the German Government, and officials did not know when to expect one.

[Advices from Berlin showed that no mention was made of Mr. Roosevelt's message in the German press and Herr Hitler did not mention it in his speech.] Mr. Roosevelt conferred with

Continued on Page Ten

"All the News That's Fit to Print."

The New York Times.

LATE CITY EDITION
Generally fair, cooler today. Tomorrow cloudy, probably followed by rain; temperature unchanged.
Temperatures Yesterday—Max., 72; Min., 54

Copyright, 1938, by The New York Times Company.

VOL. LXXXVIII...No. 29,468.   Entered as Second-Class Matter, Postoffice, New York, N. Y.   NEW YORK, THURSDAY, SEPTEMBER 29, 1938.   PPP   THREE CENTS NEW YORK CITY and Vicinity | FOUR CENTS Elsewhere Except in 7th and 8th Postal Zones

DEWEY SLATE HITS CONVENTION SNAG; KEY POSTS IN DOUBT

Barton and Heck, at Opening Session, Score New Deal on 'Vote Buying' and 'Waste'

LEHMAN UNDER PRESSURE

Farley Says He Will Be Drafted —Hoover in West Backs Roosevelt Peace Plan

The Republican State Convention opened with a snag developing over completing the Dewey slate. Bruce Barton and Oswald D. Heck condemned the New Deal on "vote buying" and as failing to solve the unemployment problem. [Page 1.]

At Rochester, on the eve of the Democratic State convention, the leaders were exerting all their pressure to induce Governor Lehman to run again and Chairman Farley expressed the opinion that the convention would draft him. [Page 21.]

Herbert Hoover in a speech in Kansas City backed President Roosevelt's peace efforts, but attacked his home policies. [Page 22.]

Senator Vandenberg told the Michigan League of Women voters that the "yes-but-man" was the essential factor in a system of "nonpartisan politics" that he asserted would be a strengthening element in the development of the two major parties. [Page 23.]

Speeches at the Republican Convention, Pages 18, 19; Hoover's Kansas City speech, Page 22.

State Republicans Meet

By JAMES A. HAGERTY
Special to THE NEW YORK TIMES.

SARATOGA SPRINGS, Sept. 28.—With complete agreement on District Attorney Dewey as the candidate for Governor, the slate makers at the Republican State Convention struck a snag today when Mayor Rolland B. Marvin of Syracuse refused to be drafted for the nomination for the long Senatorial term.

Concurrently, a difference of opinion developed between Kenneth F. Simpson, New York County chairman and national committeeman, and Edwin F. Jaeckle, Erie County leader, and there was a revolt of a minority of the Brooklyn delegation, who expressed opposition to the candidates for the nomination for Controller suggested by John R. Crews, Brooklyn leader.

Agreement seemed to have been reached on the nomination of Edward Corsi of Manhattan for the short Senatorial term, to fill the vacancy caused by the death of Senator Royal S. Copeland, and on the nomination of Richard B. Scandrett Jr. of Orange County and Mrs. Helen Rogers of Buffalo for Representatives at Large. The selection of candidates for the long Senatorial term, Lieutenant Governor, Attorney General and Controller awaited the results of further conferences to be held after the night session of the convention.

The name of Jerome D. Barnum, publisher of The Syracuse Post-Standard, was the only one mentioned for the long Senatorial term nomination after it became known that Mayor Marvin had repeatedly refused efforts to draft him.

Marvin Favors Present Posts

Mr. Marvin is under commitment to serve the three remaining years of his Mayoralty term. He also is the head of the Onondaga Republican organization, and is reported to be reluctant to leave these two positions.

The nomination of Mr. Barnum, understood to be opposed to any possible alliance with the American Labor party, would not be satisfactory to sponsors of Mr. Dewey's candidacy, it was said.

Mayor Marvin called members of the Onondaga County delegation together for a conference. He said at midnight that his position was unchanged and that he would not take the nomination for Senator. Reluctant to lose him, those back of Mr. Dewey's candidacy will make a further effort tomorrow to get him to run. In case of failure, the indications tonight were that the nomination would go to Mr. Barnum.

No meeting of the executive committee of the State committee was held tonight and the conferences which went on were confined to a small number of the party leaders. Resentment among the delegates and leaders of the less populous counties increased as no apparent progress was made in agreeing on a ticket, and a meeting of the county chairmen of rural counties was called for tomorrow morning in the Grand Union Hotel at which it is expected that protests will be

Continued on Page Eighteen

When You Think of Writing Think of Whiting—Advt.

Gain of 369,000 Jobs Shown in August Survey

The National Industrial Conference Board reported yesterday that 10,590,000 were unemployed in August, a drop of 369,000 from the July total. This estimate included as unemployed 3,475,000 workers in the WPA, Civilian Conservation Corps and other government works agencies.

The hiring of 338,000 additional workers in manufacturing helped increase total national employment to 43,453,000, or 422,000 above the July figure. Construction employment rose by 126,000, transportation 12,000, forestry and fishing 5,000 and agriculture 3,000, according to the report.

Declines of 41,000 in employment in the service industries and of 32,000 in trade, distribution and finance were recorded.

TRUCK PEACE NEAR; MANY OWNERS SIGN

Only the Out-of-Town Haulers Still Oppose Mayor's Plan— Shipments Move Again

An end of the two weeks' strike of 15,000 truck drivers today was expected last night when the Merchant Truckmen's Bureau, representing local operators, voted to accept the compromise terms of Mayor La Guardia. The Highway Transport Association, representing long-distance haulers, voted to reject the terms, but decided later to defer action until today.

The Highway Transport Association adopted a five-point resolution and voted to continue to see Mayor La Guardia this morning, to defer action meanwhile on the Mayor's compromise, to register a vote of confidence in its wage scale committee, to draw up as soon as possible a new contract to be submitted to the Mayor and to meet again this evening at 8 o'clock. At the second meeting the long-distance haulers rescinded their rejection of the Mayor's plan.

Offers to Name Committee

The Mayor appealed to the operators to end the dispute, told them that disaffections in their ranks had resulted in separate agreements releasing 2,500 trucks during the day and, incidentally, admitted that he had no desire to continue "in the trucking business," referring to his emergency mobilization of 800 obsolete trucks of the Department of Sanitation.

The Mayor's appearance before the operators apparently turned the tide in favor of a settlement. He offered to appoint a fact-finding committee to study economic and other factors in the trucking industry and to make recommendations on wages and working conditions. Furthermore, the Mayor was able to cite the widespread response of truck operators to sign separate agreements following the appeal he made to the operators when their organizations rejected his compromise offer.

As a result of these disaffections the movement of commerce had resumed to such an extent that merchants reported increasing shipments and Port Authority executives noted a rise in truck traffic through the Holland Tunnel.

The compromise plan which the Mayor submitted late Monday night provides among other things for a forty-four-hour week at the rate of forty-seven hours' pay. The strikers originally demanded a forty-hour week at forty-seven hours' pay.

Decide to Vote Separately

The Merchant Truckmen's Bureau and the Highway Transport Association, which had met jointly 500 strong to consider every proposal up to last night, finally decided to vote separately on the Mayor's compromise terms. At the time of the division their number had dwindled to about 300 and of that number only half cast ballots. The ballot of the Merchant Truckmen's Bureau totaled about eighty.

The bureau's members accepted the Mayor's terms, it was learned, after the joint wage scale committee of nineteen had been reduced to four members by disaffections. The four members of the "old guard" who stood pat were P. J. Murphy, president; Arthur G. McKeever, managing director; Ted Ficke, past president, and Hugh B. Sheridan, chairman of the joint wage scale committee.

The end of the strike was assured when the United States Trucking Corporation and other important operators announced soon after Mayor La Guardia's address that they would follow the lead of Daniels & Kennedy and hundreds of other operators who already had signed separate agreements with the International Brotherhood of

Continued on Page Twenty-six

HITLER HALTS WAR MOVES, CALLS 4-POWER CONFERENCE; MEETS MUSSOLINI, CHAMBERLAIN AND DALADIER TODAY; MUNICH TALK MAY COVER WHOLE EUROPEAN SITUATION

BERLIN IS RELIEVED

Hopes Talks on Czechs May Lead to Wider European Accord

ROOSEVELT PLEA A FACTOR

Hitler Described as Desirous of Removing Parley From 'Benes Atmosphere'

By GUIDO ENDERIS
Wireless to THE NEW YORK TIMES.

BERLIN, Sept. 28.—Announcement today of the four-power conference in Munich tomorrow followed a day of high-pressure diplomatic exchanges and long-distance telephone calls between Berlin, London, Paris and Rome. It burst in upon the stagnant political atmosphere like a freshening breeze.

The circumstances under which the four Premiers will meet is not unlike that existing when Neville Chamberlain, the British Prime Minister, undertook his dramatic flight to Berchtesgaden.

With the German ultimatum nearing its deadline it was recognized that the statesmen concerned with the Czech crisis were largely talking past each other and that only a frank, intimate exchange across a conference table gave promise of breaking the deadlock.

Chancellor Adolf Hitler, accordingly, determined not only to react to Mr. Chamberlain's appeal but to expand the British Prime Minister's suggestion by making further conversations a four-power affair.

Roosevelt's Plea a Factor

There were other factors, too, that pressed for early inter-governmental action. One of decisive weight, it was admitted here, was President Roosevelt's second appeal to Chancellor Hitler, which reached Berlin early this morning.

In view of the atmosphere of recrimination engendered by foreign and German press controversies over the German memorandum, the proposal that the four statesmen meet provoked no surprise in Berlin diplomatic quarters. It was realized that important time had been lost through the fruitless Hitler-Chamberlain negotiations at Berchtesgaden and Godesberg. The outcome of those negotiations, it now seems, contributed to making the Czech crisis even more complicated and acrimonious. Charges that Czech mobilization was undertaken at British instigation also provoked irritation here. Meanwhile Herr Hitler watched developments with a calm born of unconcern, convinced that the German case was securely grounded and that Great Britain would not abandon her peace initiative merely because of conflicting interpretations of the German memorandum.

Continued on Page Six

Chamberlain Off to Reich; Cites 'Try, Try, Try Again'

By The Associated Press.

HESTON AIRPORT, London, Thursday, Sept. 29.—Prime Minister Neville Chamberlain took off for the four-power conference at 8:35 o'clock this morning (2:35 A. M. in New York).

Most of the Cabinet and a large crowd cheered him. Like admiring schoolboys, the Ministers had brought a gift of fruit for him to eat en route on this third journey to Chancellor Adolf Hitler in the cause of peace.

Standing outside his plane, the Prime Minister said:

"When I was a little boy, I used to repeat: 'If at first you don't succeed, try, try, try again.' That's what I'm doing."

BRENNER PASS, Thursday, Sept. 29 (AP).—Premier Benito Mussolini and his Foreign Minister, Count Galeazzo Ciano, arrived here today by special train at 6:08 A. M. (12:08 A. M. in New York) on their way to Munich. They were greeted by Rudolf Hess, Chancellor Hitler's deputy in party affairs. An hour later the train continued toward Munich.

PARIS, Thursday, Sept. 29 (AP).—Premier Edouard Daladier, accompanied by his staff, left Le Bourget Field by airplane today at 8:45 A. M. (2:45 A. M. in New York) for Munich.

CZECHS SUSPICIOUS OF MUNICH PARLEY

Fear Four-Power Accord at Their Expense—Hope Hitler Simply Aims to Save Face

By G. E. R. GEDYE
Wireless to THE NEW YORK TIMES.

PRAGUE, Czechoslovakia, Sept. 28.—Prime Minister Neville Chamberlain's speech tonight and the forthcoming conference in Munich had a mixed reception here. In official circles a reserved attitude was maintained.

For years what Europe's small nations that have remained outside the German orbit have most dreaded is a four-power pact in which the so-called Western democracies would in the end find themselves led by the nose by the two Fascist powers. This four-power conference looks to Czechoslovak eyes alarmingly like that.

An early release of the Czechoslovak News Agency tonight labeled it the "Fuehrer Conference," an innocent misprint, which was corrected subsequently to the "Vierer Conference," or Conference of Four.

There is another interpretation that seems not without foundation—that Chancellor Adolf Hitler, accompanied by Premier Mussolini and the Nazi party find themselves losing the war within their own

Continued on Page Seventeen

DUCE SWAYS HITLER

Persuades Him by Phone to Delay Mobilizing and Join Parley

HEEDS CHAMBERLAIN PLEA

Appeal by Roosevelt Is Also Delivered to Mussolini— Italian Hopes Soar

By ARNALDO CORTESI
Wireless to THE NEW YORK TIMES.

ROME, Sept. 28.—The war clouds hanging over Europe were torn asunder in dramatic fashion this morning and admitted a pair ray of sunshine when Premier Benito Mussolini had a long personal telephone conversation with Chancellor Adolf Hitler of Germany and prevailed upon him to postpone German mobilization and give his adherence to a conference in Munich at noon tomorrow among Prime Minister Neville Chamberlain of Britain, Premier Edouard Daladier of France, Herr Hitler and Signor Mussolini himself.

Premier Mussolini telephoned the German Chancellor after the first of two calls by the Earl of Perth, the British Ambassador to Rome, on Count Galeazzo Ciano, the Italian Foreign Minister. On his first visit Lord Perth delivered the following message to Signor Mussolini from Mr. Chamberlain:

I have today addressed an appeal to Chancellor Hitler to abstain from the use of force to solve the Sudeten problem, which I feel sure could be solved by means of a brief discussion while giving him essential territory, population and the protection of both Sudetens and Czechs during the transference.

I offered to go myself to Berlin to discuss a compromise with the German and Czech representatives and, if the Chancellor so desires, also with the representatives of Italy and France.

I trust that Your Excellency will inform the German Chancellor that you are willing to be represented and will exhort him to adhere to my suggestions. I have guaranteed that the Czech promises will be carried out and I am confident that complete agreement could be reached within a week.

Roosevelt Appeal Received

William Phillips, the United States Ambassador, was received by Signor Ciano at 4 o'clock this afternoon and delivered a personal message from President Roosevelt. It is understood that Signor Mussolini expressed his appreciation of the President's efforts on behalf of peace and declared himself happy to be able to announce that acceptance in accordance with Mr. Roosevelt's suggestion had already been adopted with the decision to hold the Anglo-French-Italian-German conference in Munich tomorrow.

A summary issued by Stefani, official Italian news agency, said, according to The Associated Press, that the President in his message, "after having recalled efforts exerted by him to assure a peaceful solution of the German-Czechoslovak conflict and after having emphasized the tragic consequences that a European war would have for every one, asked Il Duce to lend his aid to settle the controversy by negotiation or other peaceful means and without recourse to force."

Lord Perth first called on Count Ciano at 10 A. M. and then at noon. As Signor Mussolini's telephone call to Herr Hitler occurred between the two visits, Count Ciano was able to inform the British Ambassador on the second that Signor Mussolini had induced Herr Hitler to agree to a conference.

Signor Mussolini assured Herr Hitler personally, as well as through an official step through the Italian Ambassador to Berlin, that Italy was ready to stand by her pledges to Germany but begged him not to disregard the opportunity Mr. Chamberlain offered for getting what he wanted without using violence.

The Italian Premier left for Munich by special train at 6 o'clock this evening accompanied by Count Ciano.

The wave of hopefulness that swept over Italy when this news became known is heightened by reports that Signor Mussolini succeeded in inducing Herr Hitler not only to meet Mr. Chamberlain but

Continued on Page Nine

German Liners Are Called Home; Thousands of Tourists Stranded

Other Lines Take as Many as Possible— 2,000 on the Washington—Freighter Slips From Puerto Rico and Eludes a Cutter

Germany withdrew the far-flung tentacles of her mercantile marine yesterday in a drastic move that threw shipping on the Atlantic into unprecedented confusion, turned liners around at sea and sent two vessels out from New York Harbor empty, before all their prospective passengers could be warned.

With other steamship companies altering schedules on a moment's notice in efforts to accommodate stranded passengers and shipping on extra cots, lifebelts and other equipment required by international safety laws, the entire industry was in a state of disruption unknown here since the World War.

There was no explanation for the recall other than the war scare. Local shipping officials, long accustomed to soldierly discharge of orders from the Reich Government, said they knew only that the order had been issued and had been complied with as quickly as circumstances permitted. It was construed here as an attempt to get the fleet into safe German harbors to avoid possible repetition of the elimination of the German merchant marine in the World War.

All the way across the Atlantic, from the North Sea to America, German ships are either plowing along on their usual courses devoid of passengers and carrying only such cargo as could be shipped at the last moment or are retracing their courses and omitting ports that in more peaceful times are regularly on their schedules.

The first ship affected was the 50,000-ton express liner Europa, which turned around in the English Channel before reaching Cherbourg and Southampton and hurried back toward Bremerhaven, leaving hundreds of passengers waiting on piers in the French and English ports.

Her sister ship, the Bremen, had sailed from New York at 12:25 A. M. yesterday, on schedule. At the end of the day, however, the recall order had been extended to the entire fleet of the German lines with a few exceptions in which execution of the order was impossible. Early yesterday morning, after a few hours of hurried preparation, the Hamburg-American liner Hansa steamed out of New York, leaving

Continued on Page Twelve

WASHINGTON'S HOPE FOR PEACE MOUNTS

Roosevelt Made Final Plea to Hitler on Hearing Reich Might March Yesterday

Special to THE NEW YORK TIMES.

WASHINGTON, Sept. 28.—Upon receiving official confirmation through diplomatic channels of the summoning of the four-power conference at Munich tomorrow, the White House, through Stephen T. Early, secretary to the President, said today that the meeting "offers great hope and encouragement."

This was the one definite Administration comment on the development, but the relief here was evidenced in a relaxation of the tension that had gripped the government. For the first time in several days it was really believed that the grave danger of war could be averted.

Mr. Early revealed that President Roosevelt had decided to send his plea early last night during a two-hour conference on the day's developments with Secretary of State Cordell Hull and Sumner Welles, Undersecretary of State.

Previously, at his late afternoon press conference, the President had rather indicated that there would be no developments during the night, but the unofficial reports of possible German military movements this morning decided his course. When he reached his decision he dictated the telegram instead of writing it in longhand, as he did his earlier peace appeal that was dispatched early Monday morning.

This illustrates, Mr. Early said, how closely the President has watched the situation by reading press dispatches and listening to the radio when he was confined to the Executive Mansion by a head cold.

"It is a great advantage," Mr. Early said, "to have the President sitting in the White House knows that anything more than the first Anglo-French settlement proposal will mean the dooming of Czechoslovakia."

Stresses No Involvements

It was also disclosed by Mr. Early that the President's suggestion for a conference to decide the detailed questions at issue would enlarge the negotiations to include Poland, Russia and Hungary. At the same time Mr. Early stressed that the United States has no involvements in Europe.

According to Mr. Early the President decided to send his plea early last night during a two-hour conference on the day's developments with Secretary of State Cordell Hull and Sumner Welles, Undersecretary of State.

There was no official confirmation, but Mr. Roosevelt felt that he should make his last effort then or never. If the troops marched today it would be too late.

Continued on Page Eight

FRENCH NOW WANT SOLID PEACE BASIS

Nation Firmer Toward Hitler —Mussolini Moves Watched —Many Abandon Paris

By P. J. PHILIP
Wireless to THE NEW YORK TIMES.

PARIS, Thursday, Sept. 29.—How much can one buy for two or three and one? Is Premier Edouard Daladier of France strong enough to carry this immense argument? In which camp will Premier Benito Mussolini of Italy be? Will Chancellor Adolf Hitler scream, as he did at Berchtesgaden? Will it bring real peace?

All these and a thousand other questions poured out in an unceasing stream yesterday as bit by bit the news leaked out in France that this ever-towering crisis, which has seemed each day certain to crash in a great welter of blood and ruin, had shot up to a new pinnacle with hope perched higher than ever.

And now what? After these successive days crowded with events, with their alternating hopes and fears, even peace will seem an anti-climax. To satisfy French sentiment in the present grim mood it must at least be a real peace, such a peace of confidence as there is between Britain and France or between France and the United States. Is that possible with Adolf Hitler and Benito Mussolini in power in their respective countries with Nazi and Fascist systems?

Daladier Must Be Wary

M. Daladier is going to go warily. His people are not trustful by nature—and, perhaps, with cause. And yet it is realized that the French Premier cannot go to this conference with nothing to offer. There must be something for Signor Mussolini, whose ways have seemed devious, but to whom in the end and for whatever cause a debt of gratitude seems due for yesterday's action.

There must be something for Herr Hitler, if only a Roman triumph in a Mercedes car through the winding streets of Karlsbad, Czechoslovakia. M. Daladier is big enough to do it, but is well aware that such a war might be localized are very small. He has other reasons, some of which go back to the annexation of Austria and others that look forward to the future and see the necessity of doing a service for peace.

Can Herr Hitler, who has never gone back from what he said he would, do so now? That is the great question of tomorrow. If Signor

Continued on Page Thirteen

COMMONS JUBILANT

Chamberlain's News of a Delay by Hitler on Czechs Stirs Bedlam

FINAL PLEAS SUCCESSFUL

Mussolini and Roosevelt Are Credited—Germany Warned She Would Attack Today

As Prime Minister Chamberlain was delivering a grave speech to the House of Commons yesterday two slips of paper were handed to him that bore tidings which instantly dispelled the war clouds hanging over Europe. The slips related that Chancellor Hitler had agreed to meet Mr. Chamberlain, Premier Daladier and Premier Mussolini at Munich today for a peace conference, and meanwhile had deferred his war measures.

This development resulted from a Chamberlain appeal to Herr Hitler, a second Roosevelt appeal from an appeal by Mr. Chamberlain to Signor Mussolini. The Italian Premier promptly got in touch with the Chancellor and begged him not to disregard the opportunity for peace.

There was talk in Rome that 'he Munich conference would range over the whole European situation, including Spain, and also that Signor Mussolini might forsake the cause of the Spanish Insurgents.

Washington was hopeful. It was revealed in the capital that President Roosevelt had sent a personal message to Premier Mussolini asking his intervention.

Berlin was relieved by the new turn, as was Paris, but the French are insistent that a real settlement must develop out of the four-power talks. Prague was suspicious, fearing that a settlement would be at its expense.

Meanwhile, as a result of German action in recalling merchant ships, many of which sailed without passengers, the Atlantic tourist trade was thrown into confusion.

[All the above dispatches on Page 1.]

The stock market reacted favorably to the good news in Europe with gains of 1 to 4 points. [Page 7.]

Mr. Chamberlain's speech is printed on Page 14; British White Paper, Pages 16-17.

Hitler Agrees to Parley

By FERDINAND KUHN Jr.
Special Cable to THE NEW YORK TIMES.

LONDON, Thursday, Sept. 29.—Prime Minister Neville Chamberlain won the greatest and sweetest triumph of his life yesterday when he suddenly announced to a wildly cheering House of Commons that Chancellor Adolf Hitler had summoned a four-power meeting for tomorrow at Munich, Germany, to find a peaceful way out of the Czech crisis. A "last last" appeal from Mr. Chamberlain to Herr Hitler and another to Premier Benito Mussolini, together with the second message from President Roosevelt, had produced the desired result in Berlin in what was only twenty-four hours after Herr Hitler had sent word to London that Germany would mobilize yesterday and march across the Czech frontier today unless his demands upon Czechoslovakia were fulfilled.

Instead, Mr. Chamberlain is flying to Munich this morning and hopes to meet Herr Hitler, Signor Mussolini and Premier Edouard Daladier of France about midday. The same advisers who went to Godesberg are accompanying Mr. Chamberlain, with the addition of Frank Ashton-Gwatkin, the expert who served with Viscount Runciman's mediatory mission in Prague.

Whether the meeting at Munich succeeds or not, there was a strong belief throughout Britain today that Europe might soon awaken from its nightmare. Relief and thankfulness, without parallel since the Armistice, swept the country at the

Continued on Page Fifteen

WALTER WINCHELL SAYS: "FRED'S another American triumph in 'Liquitint' at the John Golden Theatre."—Advt.

Italy Reported Forsaking General Franco; Angry at His Neutrality in Czech Quarrel

Wireless to THE NEW YORK TIMES.

ROME, Sept. 28.—In connection with the other problems now confronting Europe, a report circulated in Rome today that, although still lacking confirmation and indeed officially denied, nevertheless is worth noticing.

It was stated that the Italian Government, increased at Generalissimo Francisco Franco's declaration of absolute neutrality in the present European crisis, had decided to withdraw all Italian troops from Spain immediately. Some reports even went as far as to say that the first contingents were already on their way back.

It is obviously useless, say many indignant Italians, to continue spending Italian money and shedding Italian blood in Spain if Italy cannot count on General Franco in an hour of need.

All such reports must be accepted with the greatest prudence, since Italy is heavily committed in Spain and can scarcely afford to see General Franco lose. Nevertheless, Italian enthusiasm for the Spanish venture has waned noticeably of late. Hence it is not to be excluded that some compromise solution would be broached at the conference in Munich, Germany, tomorrow.

The offer of the Spanish Premier, Dr. Juan Negrin, to withdraw all foreign volunteers on the Loyalist side seems to offer a possible starting point for negotiations aiming at the institution of a constitutional monarchy in Spain with definite safeguards for the two warring parties.

Elimination of the Spanish question would have the immediate advantage for Italy of permitting application of the Anglo-Italian agreement and facilitating the resumption of Italo-French negotiations. It is deemed significant, in any case, that the Italian Foreign Minister, Count Galeazzo Ciano, before his departure for Munich, had a long conversation with the Spanish Ambassador here.

Wireless to THE NEW YORK TIMES.

GENEVA, Sept. 28.—In the League of Nations Assembly's political committee tonight the request of the Spanish Premier, Dr. Juan Negrin, for a League Commission to verify the withdrawal of non-Spanish combatants from the Loyalist army hit a snag.

The British and French agreed to it on the condition, which Spain accepted, that this should not prevent the London Non-Intervention Committee later from sending its commissions to both sides for the same purpose if Generalissimo Francisco Franco later accepted the plan. Negrin, however, opposed this and insisted that only the Non-Intervention Committee should act in this respect.

Continued on Page Nine

The New York Times.

"All the News That's Fit to Print."

LATE CITY EDITION

Mostly cloudy, not quite so cool today. Tomorrow probably fair with moderate temperatures.

Temperatures Yesterday—Max., 48; Min., 44

Copyright, 1939, by The New York Times Company.

VOL. LXXXVIII...No. 29,680.

Entered as Second-Class Matter, Postoffice, New York, N. Y.

NEW YORK, SATURDAY, APRIL 29, 1939.

P

THREE CENTS NEW YORK CITY and Vicinity | FOUR CENTS Elsewhere Except in 7th and 8th Postal Zones

MOSCOW AVIATORS DOWN IN CANADA; RELIEF IS RUSHED

One Flier Hurt and Plane Is Badly Damaged in Landing on New Brunswick Marsh

ON DASH TO NEW YORK

Mishap in Northern Wilds Comes After 23 Hours and 40 Minutes in the Air

By Telephone to THE NEW YORK TIMES.

MISCOU PLAIN, N. B., April 28.—Forced down on their flight over the Arctic Circle route from Moscow to New York, Colonel Vladimir Kokkinaki and his co-pilot, Major Mikhail Gordienko, Soviet airmen, wrecked their twin-motored monoplane in landing in a marsh five miles from this village on Miscou Island, northeasternmost point of the Province of New Brunswick.

Clearing the ice covering Chaleur Bay on the west and the Gulf of St. Lawrence on the east, the airmen found a landing spot on the snow-covered marsh to bring their flight to a halt, but in making the landing both right and left wings were smashed, the two propellers shattered and one of the two engines was torn from the fuselage.

One of the fliers was injured in landing, but it was believed that he was not badly hurt. He made light of his injury, indicating that it was only a broken rib and, with the aid of his comrade, made himself comfortable in an improvised bed beside the wrecked plane, sheltered from the frozen marshland by a single blanket. It was cold, but not severely so.

The fliers had made their presence known to the residents of this hamlet and others of the 1,200 on Miscou Island by circling before landing. Their motors sputtered as if they were having engine trouble or were running short of fuel. It was thought at first, because they were flying so low, that they might land here, but they continued on.

Inhabitant Finds Plane

When the big red plane swung down toward the marsh and it was apparent the fliers were going to land, Lawrence Vibert of this village set out to find them. He discovered them on the marsh, five miles from the village, resting beside their plane. Vibert was unable to speak to them, however, for the fliers spoke only Russian.

For several minutes Vibert tried to make himself understood in English and French and the Russians attempted to talk with him in their native tongue. Gesticulating, the uninjured airman at last hauled out a map and showed Vibert that the plane had flown from Moscow along a course set out on the paper and that it was due in New York at 4 P. M. The plane had been 23 hours 40 minutes in the air.

Vibert, by gestures, attempted to get the fliers to leave their wrecked plane in the desolate marsh and come to his house for shelter. Both pilots gestured that they would remain on guard beside their plane, and the injured man, lying on the frozen ground in his improvised bed, indicated that he was comfortable so long as he did not attempt to move.

Returning to the village, Vibert telephoned to Miss Jeannette Newton, telephone operator at Shippigan, a railroad trunk station on the mainland twenty-five miles from here, and reported his discovery. Loading up with food and fuel and blankets at his house, he started trudging back to the plane, intending to stay through the night with the airmen.

Vibert said as far as he could discover the men had a single blanket and no tent or other material to afford shelter from the cold.

Stay to Guard Plane

It was believed the men were remaining by their plane to guard it, as the injured flier did not indicate that he felt he was hurt too badly to be moved by villagers, who were ready to send out a stretcher for him. However, no medical aid could be sent to the men as Dr. A. Robichaud of Shippigan (the nearest physician) would have to cross two dangerous ice-covered strips of water and two islands to reach them.

A rescue party headed by Constable Marcel Therriault of the Royal Canadian Mounted Police, stationed at Shippigan, will escort Dr. Robichaud to the scene at dawn. Once the party takes the men off the island, they will be able to go from Shippigan to the railroad terminal at Bathurst and thence down to Moncton and St. Johns.

The end of the flight in this section of the Canadian wilds was caused by lack of knowledge of the terrain, the same cause which prevented several Moscow-New York airmen, flying the Pacific route, from reaching their destination non-stop. Colonel Kokkinaki and

Continued on Page Two

Daylight-Saving Time Starts At 2 Tomorrow Morning

Daylight-saving time will go into effect at 2 A. M., Eastern standard time, tomorrow. Before retiring many New Yorkers will turn their clocks and watches forward one hour.

More than 30,000,000 persons in the United States are affected by the time change, of whom about 10,000,000 are in New York. Daylight saving will continue in effect until the last Sunday in September, when the lost hour of sleep will be regained.

As has been the custom in past years, most railroad time-tables will continue to show Eastern standard time, while nearly all the trains will be changed an hour to conform to the new daylight time. The Long Island Railroad, however, will operate all its trains on the new time.

THRONGS ARRIVING FOR START OF FAIR

Incoming Travel Rises, Hotels Filling Up With Visitors for Opening Fete

The advance guard of World's Fair visitors began to trickle through New York's celebrated air terminals, bridges and tunnels yesterday, with indications that many thousands would arrive today, tonight and tomorrow morning for Sunday's official opening.

With the Weather Bureau predicting "probably fair" for tomorrow, with more than thirty vessels of the Atlantic fleet massing here, and, with the Bronx-Whitestone Bridge to be dedicated today. Fair officials were confident that their estimate of an attendance of 1,000,000 for the opening day would be realized.

Although the Fair will not be 100 per cent ready, by any means, when the gates open, the management was satisfied that it would be as nearly ready as any other World's Fair has been, or even so. They felt that this one will be so much bigger than previous fairs that even in its incompleted stage it will have so much more to see than any one can possibly cover in a day that no one will be disappointed at the failure of some of the exhibits to be ready.

Most of Features Ready

Bad weather in the last few weeks, labor troubles and the foreign situation were given as factors that have delayed construction and the receipt of exhibits in some cases. It was emphasized, however, that the buildings that will not open, or will open in a seriously incomplete condition, will be in a distinct minority.

Even in the amusement zone, which is the most retarded part of the Fair from a construction standpoint, it was said that fifty-five or more attractions would be ready for business when the first-day crowds arrive. The management promised that the streets in the amusement zone would be satisfactorily paved by tomorrow.

Both at the Fair Grounds and throughout the rest of the city New York was getting ready to entertain the throngs of visitors expected. All over the city the Fair's orange and blue colors and its tryIon and perisphere symbols were displayed on public and private buildings, including City Hall.

40,000 Work at High Speed

Despite the damp, misty rain that prevailed most of the day, about 40,000 men were working at high speed inside the Fair Grounds, putting up many-colored flags, pennants and banners, taking down scaffolding and doing other last-minute jobs. Trucks and automobiles, which will be barred from the Fair after today, continued to dash about, and the wheel-chairs and buses in which visitors will be able to go from place to place throughout the 1,216-acre tract began to appear in large numbers.

Hotels, restaurants and bars, as well as railroad stations, throughout the city also were filling up with people from out-of-town who exhibited an eager friendliness and talkativeness unusual to New Yorkers, and told utter strangers their personal histories and their views on the foreign situation, as well as their plans for visiting the Fair.

The police, especially the traffic policemen, began to shift their hands full with visitors unaccustomed to the ways and regulations of the metropolis. Just outside Pennsylvania Station yesterday afternoon an elderly woman, evidently from out-of-town, and a traffic policeman to the test, and he came through with flying colors under

Continued on Page Three

LEGISLATURE VOTES REPUBLICAN BUDGET, SLASHING LEHMAN'S

Both Houses, on Party Lines, Pass $388,000,000 Bill, a $31,000,000 Reduction

GOVERNOR PLEADS IN VAIN

Warns of Harm to Public Service—Majority Holds Cut Vital—Court Test Ahead

By WARREN MOSCOW
Special to THE NEW YORK TIMES.

ALBANY, April 28.—Both houses of the Legislature, by practically a straight party vote, adopted the Republican budget late today. The Assembly balloted 82 to 64 for the measure and the Senate approved it, 27 to 24.

The total of the budget, as revised by the Republican majority, is $388,000,000, as contrasted with the $419,000,000 budget submitted by Governor Lehman, a reduction on paper of $31,000,000. The Governor submitted a budget of $415,000,000, but by transferring special fund revenues and appropriations to the general fund the totals of the Governor's budget and that of the Republican majority were raised by about $4,000,000 of bookkeeping transactions.

The vote in the Assembly came late in the afternoon after an all-day debate wherein the Democrats charged the Republicans with crippling State services, and the repudiation of platform pledges, and the Republicans retorted that a check in spending was necessary.

Senate Session Is Short

The Senate, worn out by the Assembly debate, to which most of the Senators listened as visitors, cut its discussion to less than an hour. The only deviation from party affiliation in either house came in the Assembly, where Joseph Boccia, Republican of New York City, elected with the support of the American Labor Party, voted with the Democrats against the revised budget.

Both houses acted after they had received another special message from Governor Lehman, in which the Governor accused the Republicans of hampering State services, and pursuing an unconstitutional course of action.

The budget will now go to the Governor, who has the power to veto any addition to estimates and also any of the special acts necessary to carry out the Republican program. These special acts have not yet been passed. He has no power to veto cuts in the budget. Both sides have served notice that the question of the constitutionality of the "lump sum" budget prepared by the Republicans will be carried to the Court of Appeals, but it is not now known whether the Governor will attempt to veto the budget on the grounds that it is unconstitutional or sign it for the purpose of expediting a test case.

Nor is it certain how the test case will be brought. The most probable sponsor is the State Association of Civil Service Employes, which has announced that it would bring an action if the Republicans carried out their announced plans. This they did today.

On the floor of the Assembly the

Continued on Page Four

$325 Car Set to Go 50 Miles Per Fuel Gallon; Crosley Puts Its Speed at 50 Miles an Hour

Special to THE NEW YORK TIMES.

INDIANAPOLIS, April 28.—A new low-cost, two-cylinder automobile, designed for a top speed of fifty miles an hour and a gasoline mileage of fifty to the gallon, was introduced to distributors and newspaper men today at the Indianapolis Motor Speedway here by Powel Crosley Jr., Cincinnati manufacturer and owner of the Cincinnati Baseball Club.

Radical in design, the car will sell f. o. b. for $325 for the two-passenger convertible coupe and $350 for the four-passenger convertible sedan, the only models in which it is to be manufactured, at Richmond, Ind. The car will be manufactured in Cincinnati as well, but Richmond will be the final shipping point.

It is said that the car will accommodate persons taller than six feet, although the automobile itself is only ten feet long from bumper to bumper, mounted on a wheelbase of eighty inches. It has three speeds forward and reverse, four-wheel mechanical brakes and is equipped with safety glass.

The two-cylinder engine is of a light aviation four-cycle type. An aviation-type suction blower, an integral part of the flywheel, provides air cooling. The drive shaft runs straight to the rear axle without

going through universal joints as in the conventional car.

The Crosley automobile weighs only 925 pounds and has a gasoline tank of four-gallon capacity which is estimated to be at least a 200-mile fuel supply. The crankcase holds only two quarts of oil.

The gear shift and steering arrangements are not essentially different from those of other makes. The cars shown at the introductory display today were in the standard colors of gray, yellow and blue. They had red wheels with chrome hub caps and black tops. The car can be used as a light commercial vehicle by the removal of one of the seats in the convertible coupe for added transportation space, offering a quarter-ton carrying capacity, Mr. Crosley said.

"I always wanted to build a practical car that would not only operate at a low cost, but also would sell at a low price," Mr. Crosley stated. "I have been dreaming of this car for twenty-eight years."

The car was christened by Lewis L'Hommedieu Crosley, grandson of the manufacturer, who broke a bottle containing a sample of all standard brands of gasoline.

Crosley officials announced that the new cars would be manufactured at the rate of about 200 a day.

Riot in Saar Reported Over New 60-Hour Week

Special Cable to THE NEW YORK TIMES.

PARIS, April 28.—A French news agency reports that twenty Saar workers have been jailed for rioting against the new sixty-hour week.

At Forbach on the French frontier gendarmes reported that all was quiet on the eastern front. Metz and Strasbourg also reported apparent quiet across the frontier.

Wireless to THE NEW YORK TIMES.

VIENNA, April 28.—Twelve men, most of them former officers of the Austrian Army, were arrested today in a wine cellar in the center of Vienna. They are suspected of a monarchist conspiracy. All are known to have monarchist sympathies.

ROME-LONDON PACT MAY BE NEXT TO GO

Following of Hitler's Lead Is Rumored in Italy — Public Fears Step Toward War

By HERBERT L. MATTHEWS
Wireless to THE NEW YORK TIMES.

ROME, April 28.—Amid a general fear of an approaching war, which Chancellor Adolf Hitler's address intensified here today, came rumors that Italy might in her turn denounce the Anglo-Italian Pact of April 16, 1938. These reports, however must be taken cautiously and they cannot be confirmed in official quarters.

These reports are, perhaps, more symptomatic of the rising tension in Italy since the announcement of British conscription than a true foreshadowing of events to come. But something is expected.

Herr Hitler's reply to President Roosevelt was very different from Premier Benito Mussolini's mild protestation of peace, and there well may be some return from this end of the Axis to bring Italy's policies into line with Germany's.

Alarm Felt by Public

Herr Hitler's speech has been interpreted by the ordinary Italian as another step toward war and, from that viewpoint it has brought regret and disappointment. Such feelings, of course, are not expressed in official circles or to be found in the press.

Herr Hitler's reaffirmation of the strength of the Axis echoes what is constantly being said here and because of that the official attitude is praise as a matter of policy. The newspapers reflect the same attitude and outwardly one gets the impression of complete harmony.

Yet, when there is a controlled press, the commentator has to distinguish between spontaneous natural feelings, as far as they are

Continued on Page Five

POLAND PREPARED

Return of Danzig to the Reich Opposed as Well as a Corridor Road

ARMS PLAN TO BE RUSHED

Attempts to Exert Pressure Will Be Met by Poles—End of Pact Seen as Warning

By JERZY SZAPIRO
Wireless to THE NEW YORK TIMES.

WARSAW, April 28.—The memorandum from the Reich government outlining its views in the present state of Polish-German relations was delivered to the Foreign Office here today by the German Chargé d'Affaires at the very moment Chancellor Hitler began his speech.

No information is obtainable here as to the contents of the memorandum but official circles declare that it will be examined carefully and attentively. There is a tendency to regard the document as a preliminary step to the opening of new negotiations between Poland and Germany with a view to concluding a new agreement replacing the 1934 non-aggression pact that Herr Hitler denounced today.

The Poles, it is understood, are prepared to negotiate a new understanding and to discuss the Danzig problem but under normal conditions without pressure or intimation.

[Poland intensified her military precautions at the Polish-German frontier where many of Poland's 1,300,000 men were under arms and military activity especially was noticeable near Danzig, The Associated Press reported.]

The memorandum, it is believed, repeats in more diplomatic form the views Herr Hitler expressed in his speech and declares that the non-aggression pact must be considered non-existent because it was violated by the Poles when they entered an agreement with Britain.

Official circles explained that so far as Danzig is concerned the Germans, during the last five years, have always maintained that the fate of this provincial city was of minor importance to them but that the Danzig problem should not adversely affect Polish-German relations and undermine the non-aggression agreement.

As far as German communications through the so-called Corridor, they have always been treated favorably by the Polish Government although Germany violated certain conventions in connection with traffic such as, for instance, the prompt payment for railroad transit.

Road Held Out of Question

The extra-territorial road through the Corridor is out of the question, it was added. Such a demand, it was said, had already served the Germans as a pretext to disrupt a neighboring country; what methods could not be applied to Poland.

The Polish-German non-aggression pact, it was further said, was a bilateral arrangement and a unilateral denunciation of the agreement was sure to provoke a strong reaction. Germany never received the right to decide what was best for Poland's interests, it was added, and the 1934 pact could never be interpreted as preventing Poland's cooperation with the western powers.

The question of whether the Polish-British agreement was contrary to the non-aggression pact should be left for diplomatic exchanges, it was said. In this case such exchanges were impossible by the fact that since April 6—the date of Prime Minister Neville Chamberlain's pronouncement of the Polish-British guarantee—diplomatic contacts with the Reich government have been cut off because Foreign Minister Joachim von Ribbentrop would not see the Polish Ambassador, Josef Lipski, and the German Ambassador here, Hans Adolf von Moltke, never returned from his Easter vacation.

Statement Surprises Warsaw

Warsaw was surprised by Herr Hitler's revelation that he had offered the extension of the Polish-German non-aggression pact for twenty-five years and a common Polish-Hungarian-German guarantee of Slovakia's independence in return for Danzig's incorporation in the Reich and a motor road through the Corridor. It was insisted in official circles that up to now in rejecting the Chancellor's proposal Warsaw was not, therefore,

Continued on Page Seven

HITLER SAYS NO TO ROOSEVELT, INSISTS ON DANZIG; SCRAPS POLISH, BRITISH NAVAL AND MUNICH PACTS; WARSAW DEFIANT; ITALY MAY END LONDON TREATY

President Tells Norwegian Guest Hitler Leaves Door Open 'an Inch'

Remark to Crown Princess at Poughkeepsie Roosevelt's Only Comment on Speech— He Slept Through the Broadcast

By FELIX BELAIR Jr.
Special to THE NEW YORK TIMES.

POUGHKEEPSIE, N. Y., April 28.—"It left the door about an inch open," President Roosevelt commented on Chancellor Adolf Hitler's reply to his address before the Rome-Berlin Axis pledge a ten to twenty year guarantee of the territorial integrity of thirty-one European States, in which the Nazi chief called for specific proposals on the basis of absolute reciprocity.

The Chief Executive's off-hand judgment, presumably directed at the opportunities for an amicably negotiated settlement of Germany's demands within the limits of Chancellor Hitler's statement of his attitude, was offered in response to a direct question from Crown Princess Martha of Norway as to what he thought of the speech.

Fewer than fifty persons were within earshot of the exchange that followed, and some of it was missed entirely amid the hub-bub that followed the handshaking and picture taking of the President and Mrs. Roosevelt with the Princess Martha and Crown Prince Olav and their entourage as they debarked at a lumber yard dock at Poughkeepsie.

Without waiting for a formal introduction to the royal couple by George Summerlin, chief of protocol

Continued on Page Eight

FRENCH SEE PERIL IN BOND TO POLES

Fear Call to War for Danzig Which They Do Not Regard as a Good Issue

By P. J. PHILIP
Wireless to THE NEW YORK TIMES.

PARIS, April 28.—Both in official circles and among the general public Chancellor Hitler's speech today has been judged as unlikely to increase, although it does not diminish, the present state of tension.

In manner it sounded aggressive. In matter it is described as being a very astute lawyer's presentation of the German case, carefully compiled, well argued and marked by a tendency toward caution.

This tendency is shown in the inclination to appeal to juries—the British, French and American peoples—by insinuating that their governments are hostile judges. It is shown also, it is considered here, in the manner in which, while the Chancellor denounces the Anglo-German naval agreement and the German-Polish accord he still seems to leave the doors open for future arrangements.

Where he was least at ease was in defense of his action regarding Bohemia. He devoted twenty typewritten pages, nearly a fifth of the whole speech, to that question as if it needed all that space to convince himself as well as his listeners that he had not departed from his doctrine and policy. He seemed, French experts judged, uncomfortable, as if he knew instinctively that he had acted in contradiction to himself.

Uneasiness Over Danzig

By far the greatest importance is attached to his denunciation of the pact with Poland and his account of the rejection by Warsaw of the offer he had made concerning Danzig and the Corridor through the Polish Corridor. While the Chancellor-based denunciation of the pact with Poland on the fact that that country had joined the ranks of the western nations in an agreement that he considers hostile to Germany there seems little doubt that his major reason was the rejection of the Danzig agreement by Warsaw, for the Franco-Polish treaty existed when the Germano-Polish pact was made.

There is uneasiness here because Warsaw was solely responsible for rejection of the German proposal. Paris was not informed until afterward and even then not fully of all its terms. That Germany had proposed that Poland and Hungary should participate in a guarantee of the independence of the Slovak State was news to the French Foreign Office.

Continued on Page Six

BRITAIN UNSOLACED BY HITLER'S SPEECH

Finds Situation Full of Danger —Home Fleet Concentrates —Russian Plan Speeded

By FERDINAND KUHN Jr.
Wireless to THE NEW YORK TIMES.

LONDON, April 28.—The British Government pushed ahead today with its conscription plans and its defensive alliances in spite of the comparatively mild and almost apologetic tone of certain passages in Chancellor Adolf Hitler's speech.

Prime Minister Neville Chamberlain met his leading Cabinet colleagues to discuss the draft of the conscription bill that will be published Monday night and debated in the House of Commons Thursday. At the same time British diplomacy showed no signs of slackening in its efforts to bring Russia and Turkey into the anti-aggression front of Europe.

Soviet Ambassador Ivan M. Maisky returned here today from his consultations in Moscow and after a message saying that Viscount Halifax, Foreign Secretary, would be delighted to see him at the Foreign Office at his earliest opportunity. So the two men arranged to compare notes tomorrow morning on the progress of the Anglo-Russian talks, which aim to create an Eastern front against Germany in case of war.

British Fleet Assembles

By coincidence or design, warships of the British Home Fleet, led by the giant battleship, Nelson, assembled at Portland today after their Easter leave. The ships concentrated while Herr Hitler was speaking, just as last September they arrived at their battle stations in Scotland on the day of the Nuremberg speech that helped to precipitate the Czech crisis.

Such friendly references as Herr Hitler made to Britain today may, no doubt, be reciprocated publicly by Mr. Chamberlain in the House of Commons next week. Taking a leaf from Herr Hitler's book, the Prime Minister can say with perfect sincerity that he admired Germany's past achievements and would regard war between Britain and Germany as a needless tragedy for mankind, but the British found nothing in the speech to justify even the slightest abandonment of their new policy, which has led them in six short weeks to assume military responsibilities to three countries in Eastern Europe and to impose compulsory military training at home.

In fact, the more Herr Hitler's speech was studied here today the less reason was found for the optimism that short prices upward on the Stock Exchange this afternoon. The speech, as viewed in high quarters

Continued on Page Six

BID TO POLES BARED

Chancellor Reports 25-Year Pact Offer for Free City's Return

SPEECH A BLISTERING ONE

Nazi Leader Willing to Give Non-Aggression Pledges to Nations Asking for Them

Chancellor Hitler, in a scornful speech before the Reichstag yesterday, denounced three treaties, replied in critical tones to President Roosevelt's truce proposal and defended his actions in Europe. One pact he abrogated was the non-aggression treaty with Poland [text of note to Warsaw, Page 7], and at the same time he emphasized he wished the return of Danzig and session of a right-of-way across Pomorze. Another accord he canceled was the Anglo-German naval treaty [text of note to London, Page 6], and the third was the Munich consultative agreement with Britain. To Mr. Roosevelt, the Chancellor declared he was ready to pledge non-aggression to the thirty-one nations named by the President provided such pledges were reciprocal and the other nations took the initiative. [Page 1; text of the speech, Pages 9, 10 and 11.]

Poland's reaction was one of firm refusal to cede any territory and of renewed military precautions. [Page 1.]

Rumors circulated in Rome that Premier Mussolini might follow his partner's lead by denouncing the Anglo-Italian agreement. [Page 1.]

In the opinion of President Roosevelt the Chancellor "left the door about an inch open" [Page 1], and the State Department seemed to agree. [Page 8.]

London found the speech had done nothing to relieve the tension [Page 1], Paris was somewhat encouraged over the danger spot at Danzig [Page 1], while Moscow took solace in the thought that the Chancellor had divided Europe into two camps and thus removed the long-standing Bolshevist bogey. [Page 5.]

Chancellor Hitler Speaks
By GUIDO ENDERIS
Wireless to THE NEW YORK TIMES.

BERLIN, April 28.—An American President's political philosophy underwent searching scrutiny by Chancellor Adolf Hitler before the National Socialist Reichstag today and he found it wanting.

But President Roosevelt's peace appeal of April 15 to Herr Hitler was not the only document to crumble in the white heat created by one of the most blistering speeches that the Chancellor has delivered before the Reichstag.

Today that body literally worked itself into a frenzy of approval as Herr Hitler announced the abrogation of the German-Polish non-aggression pact of 1934, the Anglo-German naval agreement of 1935 and the Anglo-German consultative pact concluded between Herr Hitler and Prime Minister Neville Chamberlain in Munich last September.

If the political equilibrium is in an already restless Europe is not placed further in jeopardy by the German Government's decisions announced today it will be because of calmer judgments in Chancelleries elsewhere, which probably can discount today's speech on the ground that it was motivated by internal considerations.

Diplomats Gasp at Decisions

The tension in the chamber of the Kroll Opera House mounted as Herr Hitler announced the decisions, which made neutral spectators and the occupants of the diplomatic gallery gasp at the manner in which he defied Britain and fretted the nerves of Polish statesmen. His caustic rejection of President Roosevelt's message concluded a two-hour speech already packed with thrills. The climactic effect was attributable to the shriveling sarcasm bestowed upon the President's proposals.

Herr Hitler left with them as twenty-one points, each of which gave him a succulent opportunity

Continued on Page Eight

"All the News That's Fit to Print."

The New York Times.

LATE CITY EDITION
Generally fair and continued cool today. Tomorrow fair, slowly rising temperatures.
Temperature Yesterday—Max., 60; Min., 45

Copyright, 1939, by The New York Times Company.

VOL. LXXXVIII...No. 29,682.

Entered as Second-Class Matter,
Postoffice, New York, N. Y.

NEW YORK, MONDAY, MAY 1, 1939.

PP   THREE CENTS NEW YORK CITY and Vicinity | FOUR CENTS Elsewhere Except in 7th and 8th Postal Zones.

POLES CONSIDERING COUNTER DEMANDS IN REPLY TO HITLER

Military Circles Say Claim on Danzig Should Be Dropped Before Further Parleys

BALTIC OUTLET STRESSED

Reich Specification of Width of Right of Way in Corridor Said to Be 15.5 Miles

In Warsaw there were indications yesterday that the Polish reply to Germany might call for a dropping of the Nazi demands regarding Danzig and the replacing of the League of Nations link to the Free City by a new Polish one. It was also reported that Chancellor Hitler in a detailed demand had asked a fifteen-and-a-half-mile motor road right-of-way across Pomorze. [Page 1.]

Both Paris and London seemed to be hopeful that a Polish-German compromise on Danzig could be reached. Reports from the two capitals indicated a disinclination to be forced to fight on this issue. [Page 2.]

The question of peace or war, however, was considered by Nazi spokesmen to have been put up to the democracies and their partners. [Page 13.]

With the arrival of the German Army commander in Rome it was believed new pressure was being put on Italy by Germany for a full-fledged military alliance. But it was significant that according to all reports the Brenner Pass between the two countries was being fortified on both sides. [Page 11.]

Poles to Use Hitler Tactics

By JERZY SZAPIRO
Wireless to THE NEW YORK TIMES.

WARSAW, Poland, April 30.—The German memorandum delivered to the Polish Foreign Office on Friday while Chancellor Adolf Hitler was attacking Poland will be answered in the same manner. A Polish memorandum, repudiating the German accusation and rejecting Danzig's incorporation into Germany and a highway across Pomorze [the Polish Corridor], but leaving the door open for further negotiations, will be delivered at the Berlin Foreign Office while Foreign Minister Josef Beck and Premier Felicjan Slawoj-Skladkowski are addressing the Sejm [Parliament], probably on Friday.

[It was reported in Poland that Chancellor Hitler had demanded a German motor road right of way across Pomorze 15.5 miles wide, The Associated Press stated.]

Certain influential military circles hold that Warsaw should not enter into new negotiations with the Nazis unless the Germans withdraw their demands regarding Danzig. This view is expressed in the military journal, Polska Zbrojna, which published one of the strongest criticisms of Herr Hitler's speech and of German policy generally.

"Danzig is at the mouth of a great Polish river," it says, "and we cannot give it up. The Polonization of Danzig is notable; wherefore, why should the Germans show so much interest in what to them is but one of their provincial towns?"

Poland to Make Demands

The Gazeta Polska, official organ of the Polish Government, tomorrow will publish a noteworthy statement concerning the position of Danzig.

"Germany," it will say, "has shown her regard for international engagements by her recent occupation of Memel, by her denunciation of solemn treaties. She has demonstrated quite clearly that German policy aims at separating Poland from her outlet on the Baltic Sea, the importance of which to Poland needs no emphasis.

"The policy of Berlin thus creates a situation that forces Poland to go further in her demands concerning the status of Danzig than she did formerly when concluding with Germany the pact of 1934."

Although it is not explicitly stated, there is reason to believe that Poland's demands will include the transference of the functions of the League Commissioner to the Polish Government.

Will Close Exchanges

The Polish official answer to the German memorandum, it is believed, will close German-Polish exchanges for the time being. The Poles expect to delay the negotiations until there is a clear clarification of the European situation. No chances are being taken, however. All the military precautions ordered last month are still in force and the army is strengthened by

Continued on Page Twelve

Rider Will Ask Pensions For Congress Members

By The Associated Press.
WASHINGTON, April 30.—A quiet campaign to give pensions to members of Congress has materialized into a legislative proposal.

Chairman Ramspeck of the House Civil Service Committee said today that he intended to add provisions for the pensions to a bill making amendments to the Civil Service Law which has just been passed by the Senate.

Under the proposal, the government and the members would bear about equal shares of the cost. Five per cent of the salary of each member would be deducted monthly and would go toward the purchase of an annuity to be added to the amount to be paid by the government.

Civil service workers receive pensions which increase with length of service. They contribute 3½ per cent of their salaries.

Mr. Ramspeck reported that almost every member he had talked to favored the pension idea.

"They're getting security-minded," he added, laughing.

PARI-MUTUEL VOTE AGAIN UP IN STATE

Republicans Plan Assembly Test on Betting System— Democratic Split Reported

Special to THE NEW YORK TIMES.

ALBANY, April 30.—The question of pari-mutuel betting on horseracing is returning to plague the 1939 session of the Legislature.

Pressure from pari-mutuel advocates has resulted in a decision on the part of Republican leaders to put the matter to a vote on the Assembly floor. If the proposed constitutional amendment should be passed by both Houses this year, it would be submitted to the people for approval in the Fall, as the 1938 Legislature approved the system.

Despite considerable support on the Republican side, there is no guarantee that the pari-mutuel proposal will pass in either House. The Democrats, who have blown hot and cold on the measure for years, are again reported to be divided on the subject.

In one recent year the proposed amendment was passed by the Senate, and when it came up a second time, as is required by the Constitution, its original sponsor voted against it. Last year John J. Dunnigan, the Democratic leader of the Senate, pushed the proposal through the Upper House, and it gained approval in the Republican controlled Assembly as well.

Senate Sponsor Now Lacking

With the intervening elections, the Republicans gained control of the Senate as well and Senator Dunnigan has made no move to introduce the proposal in this session. In fact, it has yet to have an official sponsor there. However, John D. Bennett and Norman F. Penny, Nassau County Republican Assemblymen, have introduced in the Assembly resolutions identical with the Dunnigan resolution of the year before, and passage this year by both Houses would constitute the required second action by the Legislature, even if the sponsors are not the same.

In the Assembly the practice of the Republican leadership, under Speaker Heck, is to refuse to throttle in committee any bill of the type of the pari-mutuel proposal, because of rumors always circulated about bookmakers' lobbies. Putting the bill out for a vote leaves it up to the individual membership. The Republicans will seek passage of the measure in the Assembly, but its final fate would appear to rest on the number of Democratic votes it can command.

Whether the matter will be brought to a vote this week, or the following week, was not disclosed today.

Sales Tax Vote Awaited

Tomorrow night the Legislature is expected to adopt the rest of the budget bills, and either then, or the next day, adopt the tax program which will be used to finance the Republican budget. The new taxes on this program are the increase in the liquor tax, effective May 1, and the two-cent-per-package cigarette tax, effective July 1.

Later in the week the sales tax probably will come up for a vote, with its eventual fate still depending on the support the Republicans can muster for it in the Senate, where they control by a margin of only two votes. The political aspects of the battle over the budget itself appear to make it unlikely that the Republican sales tax idea can gain any Democratic votes on the Senate side.

Local bills have been cleaned up to a large extent in both houses, and after the enactment of the tax bills, the settling of the sales tax problem, the revision of the unemployment insurance law, and the enactment of a housing measure, the Legislature will be in a position to quit and go home, to await a possible special-session call.

CONGRESS FACING SEVEN BIG ISSUES AS TIME SHORTENS

None Is on Week's Calendars, But All Except Taxes Are in Legislative Process

WAY CLEARED FOR ACTION

Routine Money Bills Passed, Reporting of Vital Measures to Floor Is Expected

By LUTHER A. HUSTON
Special to THE NEW YORK TIMES.

WASHINGTON, April 30.—Congress has been in session nearly four months and has disposed of only two of the major controversial items on its calendar. At least seven important issues remain to be settled in the two months that remain of the session if present plans are followed and a late Summer sitting is avoided by adjournment around July 1.

None of the major measures is on the calendar of either chamber for this week. The most progress that can be expected is that one or more of these measures may come from committees to the floor of the House or Senate.

The two issues that have been settled are the limited authorization for the President to reorganize executive agencies and the passage of national defense, for which necessary appropriation bills have been passed. The decks also have been cleared of considerable of the routine, most of the important departmental appropriation bills having been disposed of.

Major Questions Outstanding

The following matters remain to be dealt with:

Amendments to the Social Security Act, the National Labor Relations Act and the Wages and Hours Act.

Revision or extension of existing neutrality laws.

The amount of the appropriation and the method of disbursement for relief during the 1940 fiscal year.

A farm program including the highly controversial question of export and domestic subsidies on farm products.

Legislation to repeal, modify or continue in effect certain provisions of the tax laws that are estimated to yield an annual revenue of around $2,000,000,000 even if general tax revision is not attempted.

Except for tax proposals, all of these measures are in the legislative mill. On some of them committee hearings are in progress; on others committee action has ended. There is a possibility that proposed amendments to the Wages and Hours Law may come up in the House tomorrow. Representative Mary Norton, chairman of the Labor Committee, has indicated that she will try to bring up under suspension of the rules the proposals which her committee has approved. If this is not done, the proposals must lie over at least a week.

To Hear Green on C. I. O. Charges

On Capitol Hill tomorrow, however, interest probably will center on the hearing by the Senate Education and Labor Committee on proposed amendments to the National Labor Relations Act, where William Green, president of the American Federation of Labor, will be the witness.

Mr. Green is expected to reply to

Continued on Page Twenty-four

Hague Ignores Own Plea for Patriotic Rally; Skips Americanization Fete for Ball Game

Special to THE NEW YORK TIMES.

JERSEY CITY, N. J., April 30.—Mayor Frank Hague, who issued a proclamation yesterday calling on people of Jersey City to "show your Americanism" by attending the city's tenth annual celebration today of Americanization Day, did not appear at that event this afternoon. Instead he attended the double-header baseball game between the Jersey City and Toronto teams of the International League at Roosevelt Stadium.

"As Mayor of Jersey City, I earnestly and respectfully invite all the people of our city to participate actively in the Americanization Day exercises, Sunday, April 30, 2 P. M., at Pershing Field," declared the Mayor's signed proclamation, published yesterday in newspaper advertisements.

"Show your Americanism by parading or being present Sunday afternoon. It is my request that the American flag be displayed on all buildings and buildings Sunday. Every citizen should remove his hat as the colors pass by."

Representative Edward J. Hart, Democrat, and another speaker. Governor A. Harry Moore, was present, but did not speak.

The Americanization Day celebration is sponsored by Captain Clinton Fisk Post, Veterans of Foreign Wars.

... sey City Mayor, was whisked away by police several months ago when he attempted to speak there.

A crowd estimated at 4,000 persons assembled in the field today and 10,000 others marched there. During the parade and speechmaking, however, the Mayor was driven away—some of them after several hours in line—when ships' officers and the beach guard said the men-of-war were unable to accommodate any more visitors.

"As Mayor of Jersey City," he occupied a box at the baseball stadium with his nephew and private secretary, former Judge Frank Hague Eggers. The Jersey City team won both games.

Commissioner Arthur Potterton, who spoke at Pershing Field, declared that "Jersey City takes the lead to show the world that nothing un-American will creep into our lives in this part of the State." Referring to other parts of the State and the nation, he said that "we have given them the courage they did not possess."

The proclamation listed Mayor Frank Hague among the speakers at Pershing Field, from which representative Jerry O'Connell, Montana Democrat and foe of the Jer-

PRESIDENT OPENS FAIR AS A SYMBOL OF PEACE; VAST SPECTACLE OF COLOR AND WORLD PROGRESS THRILLS ENTHUSIASTIC CROWDS ON THE FIRST DAY

Times Sq. May Be Closed To Autos During Fair

Times Square may be turned over as a playground for World's Fair visitors if their numbers become great enough to warrant special police arrangements in the theatrical area.

Police Commissioner Valentine said yesterday that the Fair crowds may approximate the number of American Legion members who came to New York for their national convention in September, 1937. If that should develop, Mr. Valentine said, it would be advisable to turn over Times Square to the city's guests. Automobile traffic would be routed north and south on either side of the Square, as it was during the Legion convention. For the last two weeks heavy police details have handled the crowds in Times Square, directing pedestrians to the right to obtain the maximum amount of order.

ROOSEVELT SPEAKS

He Sees Nations of This Hemisphere United in Desire for Peace

U. S. DEMOCRACY STRONG

Exposition Here and in West Born of Singleness of the American Ideal, He Says

By FELIX BELAIR Jr.

In his first public utterance since Chancellor Hitler's virtual rejection of his plan to assure the peace of Europe for another ten years, President Roosevelt served notice on the world yesterday that the nations of the Western Hemisphere were "united in a desire to encourage peace and good-will among all nations" and voiced their hope that time would break down the barriers to tranquillity on the Continent.

In a brief address dedicating the New York World's Fair to the cause of international amity and declaring it "open to all mankind," the President said that the American wagon was hitched to the star of peace, and asked that the months ahead "may carry us forward in the rays of that hope."

Avoids Any Direct Reference

For those who had expected a more direct reference to the state of affairs in Europe or something that might be interpreted as a reply to the German Chancellor's all but complete throwdown of his peace guarantee proposal there was disappointment, for his attitude regarding that had to be inferred from what he said of the traditional aspirations of the American republics.

Of recent years American historians would write that "sectionalism and regional jealousies diminished and that the people of every part of your land acquired a national solidarity of economic and social thought such as had never been before," the President said.

He added that "wise tolerance" almost as much as the American form of government had made possible this unity of sentiment in a nation made up of so many different creeds and national derivations. The President recalled that democratic government had endured unchanged in this country longer than in any other country on the globe at any period of history, a circumstance he attributed to the wisdom of the framers of the Constitution.

He Sees Aim Accomplished

"That this has been accomplished," the President added a little later, "has been due in fact to our own form of government itself and, secondly, to a spirit of wise tolerance which, with few exceptions, has been the rule.

"We in the United States, and, indeed, in all the Americas, remember that our population stems from many races and kindreds and tongues. Often, I think, we Americans offer up the silent prayer that the continent of Europe, from which the American hemisphere was principally colonized, the years to come will break down many barriers to intercourse between nations —barriers which may be historic, but which so greatly, through the centuries, have led to strife and hindered friendship and normal intercourse."

From the distant reaches of the Court of Peace, at the head of which he spoke in front of the Federal Building, the President's voice came echoing back. The spectators sat motionless on folding chairs down the long concourse ending with the Trylon and Perisphere as Mr. Roosevelt slowly spoke the principal address of the day.

Not until the completion of his remarks, which carried for at least half a mile through the amplifiers arranged for the occasion, was there a suggestion of applause. The President deliberately had phrased his speech so as not to play upon the emotions and he received none of the clapping that punctuated a preceding address by Mayor La Guardia until he finished what he had to say.

The throng that came to hear him was apparently too much absorbed in his remarks to give any outward demonstration of approval until his concluding pronunciation:

"I hereby dedicate the New York

Continued on Page Four

RUSSIAN AVIATORS, RESCUED, ARRIVE

Two Who Crashed in Canada Here in American Plane— One Fainted During Flight

Brig. Gen. Vladimir Kokkinaki and Major Mikhail Gordienko, the two Soviet airmen who crashed Friday night in a swamp off the coast of New Brunswick were landed in a rescue plane last night at Floyd Bennett Field at 10:31 o'clock.

The two men were brought to New York in the plane of Commodore Harold Vanderbilt, which was chartered by Soviet and American officials for the rescue work, which took more than thirty hours.

They and the rescue party, which left here Friday night after word of the crash of the Moscow-New York non-stop flight came through from Miscou Point, N. B., were "ferried" to the end of the scheduled flight in an American airplane.

Their own craft, in which they sped toward New York from Moscow in 23 hours and 40 minutes, still lay in the frozen morass where Major Gordienko squashed it in an emergency landing. He landed it because General Kokkinaki had fainted at an altitude of more than 27,000 feet. He was learned yesterday when the party first brought the two men as far south as Moncton, N. B.

In recounting last night the events which led up to the forced landing at the field General Kokkinaki said the main difficulty of flying in the substratosphere was at 27,000 feet, where his compass liquids froze and his radio reception was so poor that he could not tune in the directional beams. He offered this explanation as a reason why the ship apparently lost its course, having been reported in the same area for nearly four and a half hours prior to its final landing. In the plane were the two Russian aces; Russell Thaw, pilot, and his co-pilot, John Revely; V. P. Butosov; Dr. Louis S. Spector and Peter Baranov, all of the Am-

Continued on Page Twenty-four

Crowds Awed by Fair's Vastness And Medley of Sound and Color

Opening Day Has Everything, Including All Kinds of Weather—Spirit of Gayety Wanes When Pelting Rain Menaces Finery

The Fair had everything for its opening yesterday, including all kinds of weather. Early trains rolled to the Flushing Meadows under skies clear and blue, flooded with rich sunlight, carrying thousands come to look upon the miracle wrought by Grover Whalen's armies in the last three years.

Silk-hatted dignitaries, sailors on shore leave, men and women of all ages, dressed for fair weather and a great holiday. They came in hordes down the railroad and subway ramps, forty and fifty abreast, to gaze upon the wonders, to buy guide books from the shouting peddlers and to scramble for the observation cars.

Wealthier fairgoers climbed into motor-driven and man-powered chairs for their first tour of the grounds. Hundreds of thousands preferred to make it on foot, all a little bewildered and puzzled by the tremendous sweep of grounds, by the dazzling color, almost blinding in the bright sun. Guides, ushers, policemen and policewomen were breathless the first hour trying to keep up with the flood of questions. Men and women, rank amateurs at reading maps, assembled in the walks or took over the benches, to puzzle out the direction of the various exhibits. Thousands were

Continued on Page Two

CITY AND THE FLEET TAKE TURN AS HOST

1,000 Officers and Men Under Admiral Johnson Help Open Fair—Ships Draw Crowds

By HANSON W. BALDWIN

The city played host to the navy yesterday and the navy played host to the city.

It was—all things considered—an even exchange. Some 1,000 officers and men of the thirty-five visiting men-of-war, led by Rear Admiral Alfred W. Johnson, commanding the Atlantic Squadron, took part in the opening ceremonies for the World's Fair, and thousands of others rolled along Broadway and throughout the five boroughs with that peculiar to sailors home from the sea.

But the boats that brought the parties ashore took crowds of visitors back to the ships, while other thousands climbed the gangways of ships berthed at piers and stared with absorbing interest at turrets, the burnished muzzles of guns, the ranks of planes aboard the aircraft carrier Ranger, the ominous black hulls of the submarines and the torpedo tubes of the destroyers.

It was the visiting squadron's second day—and first Sunday—in port, and the public took full advantage of it. The men-of-war were a rival attraction, and a stellar one, to the World's Fair, and the crush of visitors was more than the navy could handle.

Estimates of Throng Vary

The crowd estimates varied widely. The police said 23,000 got aboard, while the navy thought 56,-000 had crowded onto the battleships, cruisers, destroyers, submarines and auxiliaries in the few hours of the afternoon that the ships received the public. Perhaps 10,000 to 15,000 others were turned away—some of them after several hours in line—when ships' officers and the beach guard said the men-of-war were unable to accommodate any more visitors.

The visiting hours were supposed to have been from 1 to 5 P. M., but at the Ninety-sixth Street landing no more visitors were permitted to leave shore after 3:25 P. M. Naval officials explained that it took some time to clear the ships of visitors, especially when the vessels were lying out in the stream and all visitors had to be transported by small ships.

They explained that it was necessary at times to allow no visitors to leave the shore landing places later than 4 P. M. There was, however, despite the navy's announcement that all ships would be open daily from 1 to 5 P. M., considerable variation on individual ships.

The Ranger, aircraft carrier berthed alongside a pier at Canal

Continued on Page Ten

LIGHT AUTO TRAFFIC SURPRISE TO POLICE

Elaborate System to Cope With Expected Snarls on Roads Goes Unused

Although Police Department traffic experts were ready for the worst, streams of automobiles flowed evenly along principal Queens highways yesterday and not a single accident involving a serious injury was reported.

An elaborate system for emergency communications, worked out to cope with expected road snarls, went unused as 3,300 patrolmen, 523 of the traffic division, and 300 detectives—a total of 4,123—worked overtime to assure a safe and orderly opening to the World's Fair.

By 11 P. M. most of the motorists had either gone home or were on their way there and reports to police centers indicated there was no more congestion than there had been on the way out.

The only mishap on the record-spoiling what otherwise would have been a virtually incredible perfect mark—occurred at 1:10 P. M. just outside the Fair Grounds, at Lawrence and Sanford Avenues.

Louis Hoffman, 70 years old, of 1,296 Spofford Avenue, the Bronx, suffered lacerations of the left leg when struck by a car that the police said was driven by Louis Azzolone of 37-41 108th Street, Corona, Mr. Hoffman went home after treatment by an interne from Flushing Hospital. The driver was not held.

Policeman Is Injured

A patrolman was hurt inside the grounds a little later, when a crush developed outside the French Building. There were seven children lost, a man had an epileptic fit, and fifty peddlers were arrested for operating on the ramp leading from the combined I. R. T.-B. M. T. subway terminal, but otherwise, the first day was as safe as a lamb was.

A false fire alarm was turned in at the box in the R. C. A. building shortly before the opening parade, while the walks near the theme center were cluttered with people. Fire Chief Thomas F. Dougherty said it was "malicious." Patrolman Bartholomew Nicastro, 35 years old, of 113-02 175th Street, St. Albans, was the man injured. The accident occurred at about 2 P. M. when the resurgent crowd he was trying to keep back threw him against a wooden "horse," which had been used in construction work. He was treated for a cut right leg by one of the Fair surgeons under Dr. Joseph Peters and remained on duty. In general, the Fair's day first aid stations had a dull day.

A checkup by the Fair police and at 10 P. M. indicated that the stations

Continued on Page Four

NATIONS IN PARADE

Mayor and the Governor Voice Welcome to the 'World of Tomorrow'

WEATHER REDUCES THRONG

Attendance Reported Above 600,000—Centers of Religion and Freedom Dedicated

By RUSSELL B. PORTER

The biggest international exposition in history was officially opened at 3:12 o'clock yesterday afternoon when President Roosevelt formally dedicated the New York World's Fair of 1939 in an address before a gathering of 60,000 persons at the open-air Court of Peace.

Governor Lehman, Mayor La Guardia, Sir Louis Beale, British Commissioner General to the Fair and spokesman for the nearly sixty foreign nations that have exhibits, and Grover A. Whalen, president of the Fair Corporation, also made speeches at the opening ceremonies. They joined the President in emphasizing the message of peaceful progress that the Fair brings to mankind in an era when the whole world is troubled by war and threats of war.

When the President declared the Fair open he brought to a climax ceremonies that included a parade of 20,000 uniformed soldiers, sailors and marines, foreign groups in picturesque native costumes from nearly all the countries of Europe, Asia and the Americas, and the workmen who built the Fair in their overalls and white caps.

Starting at the Trylon and Perisphere, the Theme Center of the Fair, the parade passed down Constitution Mall to the Court of Peace with flags waving, bands playing and spectators applauding until it ended with a colorful pageant in the Court of Peace.

Spectacle Impresses Visitors

Although the official exercises were the important part of the day from a formal viewpoint, actually the Fair itself made the greatest impression upon the visitors, judging from their comments as they strolled through the 1,216-acre Fair Grounds and as they journeyed homeward last night.

What they saw was a spectacle of surprising beauty and magnificence, especially last night when the whole Fair, bathed in soft, glowing colors with the most modern lighting effects, and when fireworks combined with flame, water and color displays on the Lagoon of Nations, the pools in Constitution Mall and the surface of Fountain Lake.

In the daytime also the Fair is a beautiful sight, with the whole scene dominated by the 700-foot Trylon and the 200-foot Perisphere, from which radiate a rainbow of many-colored buildings of modernistic, functional architecture, some bizarre in shape and hue, others strikingly handsome and impressive in their suggestion of strength and use.

Green trees, shrubbery and lawns, playing fountains, shady benches and restful spots on all sides make a garden spot of this artificial city within a city which has been constructed within the past three and one-half years on what was formerly the ash dumps of the Flushing Meadows, and will be a real city park after the Fair is over.

See "World of Tomorrow"

In the nine crystal ball of the Perisphere, visitors peered to see what "the World of Tomorrow" would be like, finding it to be a conception of more and more progress in democracy and in the advance of science, industry, commerce, transportation, communication, the arts and the professions to bring peace and happiness to mankind. They found the same ideas expressed in the streamlined, futuristic dimensions of the buildings, statues, murals, dioramas, and exhibits of the Fair as a whole.

Like the worlds of yesterday and today, and also like the City of New York, which has the reputation of never being finished but of always changing, the "World of Tomorrow" has a great deal of unfinished business before it. The heart of the Fair, the half-mile stretch between the Theme Center and the Court of Peace where the official ceremonies were held, was virtually complete yesterday, but many other sections

Continued on Page Three

93

"All the News That's Fit to Print."

The New York Times.

LATE CITY EDITION
Partly cloudy and warm with scattered showers today and tomorrow.
Temperature Yesterday—Max., 86; Min., 70

Copyright, 1939, by The New York Times Company.

VOL. LXXXVIII...No. 29,797.

Entered as Second-Class Matter.
Postoffice, New York, N. Y.

NEW YORK, THURSDAY, AUGUST 24, 1939.

PP

THREE CENTS NEW YORK CITY and Vicinity | FOUR CENTS Elsewhere Except in 7th and 8th Postal Zones.

GERMANY AND RUSSIA SIGN 10-YEAR NON-AGGRESSION PACT; BIND EACH OTHER NOT TO AID OPPONENTS IN WAR ACTS; HITLER REBUFFS LONDON; BRITAIN AND FRANCE MOBILIZE

U.S. AND ARGENTINA PLAN TRADE PACT, WELLES DISCLOSES

Our Commerce Will Get Full Equality With That of All Foreigners, He Asserts

BEEF NOT TO BE INCLUDED

Long Preliminary Talks Ease Difficulties, With Offset Seen to Our Recent Losses

Special to THE NEW YORK TIMES.

WASHINGTON, Aug. 23.—The United States intends to negotiate a reciprocal trade treaty with Argentina as a move to put American commerce with that republic on a footing of equality with that of European competitors, Sumner Welles, Acting Secretary of State, said today. There have been more than four years of preliminary discussion.

The State Department, making public a list of products upon which this country would make tariff concessions, set Oct. 4 as the closing date for submission of briefs by interested Americans and Oct. 16 for the opening of public hearings.

It was emphasized that fresh, chilled or frozen Argentine meat, the entry of which into this country is banned by the Tariff Act of 1930, and fine wools would not be a subject of discussion in the negotiations. This was expected to remove the most serious objections which might have been advanced to conclusion of a reciprocal agreement. Barring of the entry of Argentine fresh beef here has long been a subject of some friction between the two countries in their commercial relations.

"It may be noted that during the fifteen-year period 1924-38 our exports to Argentina have exceeded our imports from that country by $486,900,000," Mr. Welles said in a statement.

Trade Cut by Foreign Facts

"Our trade with Argentina has suffered in recent years for lack of a trade agreement. The trade of certain European countries with Argentina has been developing at our expense under the influence of their commercial agreements with Argentina. The placing of American commerce in Argentina on a footing of full equality with that of our European competitors is a subject which was gone into fully in preliminary discussions leading up to the present announcement.

"The agreement will enable us to maintain our competitive position in a market of great present and prospective importance.

"On our side we must, of course, offer reciprocal benefits. The products of interest to Argentina with respect to which consideration will be given in the course of the negotiations, with a view to seeing what concessions could be granted, are listed in connection with the announcement of the proposed negotiations. The concessions, which will in due course be formulated, should, of course, permit an increase in Argentina's exports to this country, but will not have injurious effect upon American production.

"The types of wool included in the list are the coarser types, of which there is only a very small production in this country."

Barter Agreement With Germany

It was presumed that in referring to European competitors Mr. Welles was speaking principally of Germany, which concluded a barter agreement with Argentina after the Pan-American Conference in Lima last December. England has long been a large trader with Argentina, however, and is a heavy buyer of Argentine beef.

Among the products upon which the United States will consider lowering duties in favor of Argentina are:

Tallow, oleo oil and oleo stearin, extract of meat, including fluid, pickled or cured beef packed or not packed in air-tight containers; dead turkeys, dead birds, chicken eggs, corn or maize, including cracked corn; asparagus in its natural state, and rabe wools.

With the possible exception of that made with Brazil, a reciprocal trade treaty with the Argentine would be the most important type to be consummated with a Latin-American country, officials indicated. Be-

Continued on Page Thirty-five

BRITAIN ACTS FAST

Air Force Is Ready for Hostilities—Warships Mass in Skagerrak

EXPORT EMBARGO IS FIXED

Parliament Meets Today in an Emergency Session—King to Convene Privy Council

By FERDINAND KUHN Jr.
Special Cable to THE NEW YORK TIMES.

LONDON, Aug. 23.—The British Government prepared for action today with every indication that it was ready to go to war with Germany whenever a call for help from Poland should come.

Warning notices went out to reservists in all departments of the armed and civilian services; the King was returning to London to hold a meeting of the Privy Council tomorrow; Londoners were ordered to darken their windows until further notice; the air force was poised for instant action, and a concentration of an undisclosed number of British warships was reported in the Skagerrak, between the Norwegian and Danish coasts, as if to remind Germany of the blockade that she had to endure during the World War.

In the face of Herr Hitler's rebuff Britain went ahead with war preparations, including the sending of notices to reservists, poising of the air force and concentration of warships in the Skagerrak, south of Denmark. Parliament prepared to meet today to grant the government sweeping emergency powers. [Page 1.] Reinforcements were reported being sent to the Mediterranean, where the bases at Gibraltar and Malta were on the alert. [Page 3.] The dominions, led by Canada and Australia, were beginning to swing into line behind Britain. [Page 6.]

France, convinced that Germany intends to invade Poland within a few days, called up further reservists after a meeting

Parliament Session Today

Tomorrow both houses of Parliament will meet in emergency session to give the government sweeping powers of a sort unknown in democratic England since World War days. The new law will be something like the old Defense of the Realm Act, enabling the government to issue Orders in Council, without prior or subsequent Parliamentary sanction, for any purpose that the national interest may require.

The real business of the Parliamentary session, however, will be to hear a complete review of the international situation by Prime Minister Chamberlain in the House of Commons and by Viscount Halifax, the Foreign Secretary, in the House of Lords. All indications are that the Prime Minister's words and the subsequent debate will be more somber in tone than anything heard in the Commons chamber since Aug. 3, 1914, when Sir Edward Grey made his famous speech on the eve of the World War.

Everywhere it was agreed that a crisis of the utmost gravity now confronts Britain, a crisis far more serious than that of last Autumn, when this country was not committed as it is now. The British determination to carry out all the pledges to Poland was reaffirmed in the government message handed to Chancellor Hitler today by Sir

Continued on Page Two

The Developments in Europe

The signing of the Russo-German non-aggression pact, which many world capitals feared might be Chancellor Hitler's "go-ahead signal," took place in Moscow early this morning, half a day after German Foreign Minister von Ribbentrop had arrived in the Russian capital. The pact, which runs for ten years, in addition to prohibiting attack by either party against the other, forbids either to join any association of powers aimed at the other. Moreover, it provides that if one party is an "object of warlike acts" the other will not support such acts. [Page 1; text of the treaty, also Page 1.]

Signature of the pact followed a day that seemed to bring Europe closer to the brink. When the British Ambassador to Germany conveyed to Chancellor Hitler a warning that Britain would fight for Poland he was bluntly rebuffed. In Berlin word was circulated that the German Army would march at 6 P. M. today (noon in New York). [Page 1.]

In the face of Herr Hitler's rebuff Britain went ahead with war preparations, including the sending of notices to reservists, poising of the air force and concentration of warships in the Skagerrak, south of Denmark. Parliament prepared to meet today to grant the government sweeping emergency powers. [Page 1.] Reinforcements were reported being sent to the Mediterranean, where the bases at Gibraltar and Malta were on the alert. [Page 3.] The dominions, led by Canada and Australia, were beginning to swing into line behind Britain. [Page 6.]

France, convinced that Germany intends to invade Poland within a few days, called up further reservists after a meeting of the Permanent Committee on National Defense. [Page 1.]

Poland remained outwardly calm, still doubting that Herr Hitler would risk precipitating a general war. [Page 2.]

In Turkey allegiance to the coalition powers was affirmed, although German Ambassador von Papen was flying to Angora from Germany, presumably to try to break that allegiance. [Page 1.] But in Rumania, another State guaranteed by France and Britain, informed circles said that country would strive to remain neutral [Page 7.]

Only in Rome were signs of war lacking. Although the press continued to attack Poland, no unusual defense preparations were evident. [Page 1.]

In an attempt to head off disaster King Leopold of the Belgians, speaking for the seven Oslo powers, appealed for peace. [With the text of the appeal, Page 5.]

President Roosevelt, disturbed by the outlook, was speeding back to Washington [Page 1], where officials were clearing the decks for action if it became necessary to safeguard United States neutrality and help Americans to escape from danger zones. [Page 3.] The State Department advised citizens not to go to Europe [Page 3] and those who were trying to return home found ships still running normally from foreign ports. [Page 3.]

In the Far East the army and navy leaders in Japan were understood to have shaped a policy to be followed in view of the new situation arising from the Russo-German treaty. [Page 4.] In China some observers believed the treaty would mean increased Soviet aid in resisting Japan. [Page 4.]

FRANCE MOBILIZES; NOW EXPECTS WAR

People Confident of Strength to Meet Aggressor as Hopes of Peace Diminish

By P. J. PHILIP
Wireless to THE NEW YORK TIMES.

PARIS, Thursday, Aug. 24.—Convinced by a report from French Ambassador Robert Coulondre at Berlin and by a reply that Chancellor Adolf Hitler gave in answer to Prime Minister Neville Chamberlain's message through British Ambassador Sir Nevile Henderson at Berchtesgaden that an invasion of Poland is intended by the German Government within the next few days, the French Government last night decided to call up a further contingent of reservists today.

This decision was communicated to the press in an official statement from Premier Edouard Daladier's office as follows:

"On account of the international situation the French Government has decided to complete military measures already taken by calling up an additional contingent of reserve soldiers."

During last night notices were

Continued on Page Five

Sidney Howard Killed by Tractor on Estate; Playwright Is Crushed in Berkshire Garage

Special to THE NEW YORK TIMES.

TYRINGHAM, Mass., Aug. 23.—Sidney Coe Howard, playwright, was crushed to death today by a two and a half ton tractor in his garage on his 700-acre estate here.

Mr. Howard had put up a house of hard work on a new play based on Carl Van Doren's "Benjamin Franklin" and, as was his custom, was going to seek relaxation in physical work on his estate, which included one of the most modern dairy farms in this part of the State. The chore he had set for himself was harrowing a twenty-eight-acre field which he had recently bought to extend his property.

Driving alone to the garage a quarter of a mile from his studio in the fields, Mr. Howard entered, turned on the ignition switch of the machine and cranked it. The machine lurched forward, pinning the playwright against the wall of the structure. The tractor, put in the garage the night before by an employe, was believed to have been left in high gear.

Fred L. Fairbanks, superintendent of the estate, discovered Mr. Howard while on an inspection trip. The garage, a former Shaker schoolroom, is set off by itself on the estate and is seldom visited by any one except by those on business.

Mr. Fairbanks found his employer in, an upright position, his head bent over his chest. He was pinned at the chest by the hood of the tractor, which had stalled after crushing him against the wall.

After starting the tractor and moving Mr. Howard's body, Mr. Fairbanks ran to the nearest telephone on the estate to notify Mr. Howard and summon aid. Mr. Howard was shopping in Lee, five miles away. When she returned

Continued on Page Nineteen

TURKEY REAFFIRMS PLEDGES TO ALLIES

Will Honor Pact With France and Britain—German Envoy Flies to Woo Her

Special Cable to THE NEW YORK TIMES.

ISTANBUL, Turkey, Aug. 23.—No official pronouncement has yet been made about the Russo-German non-aggression pact. In official quarters the position of Turkey is said to be unchanged; she has made agreements for mutual assistance against aggression with France and Britain and stands by them.

The Turkish people are still bewildered over yesterday's news, but less alarm about its possibilities is noticeable since last night's official British communique was published.

Until the Turkish Government has authentic information about the terms of the pact Turkish newspapers will be reticent. Cumhuriet, only Turkish newspaper with an editorial on the subject, assumed the Soviet Union would stipulate that if Germany was guilty of aggression against any of her Western neighbors, the pact would become null and void.

Cumhuriet added that although a pact of non-aggression was not an alliance, it implied friendly feeling and, it believed, therefore, that the anti-Comintern pact was political, not ideological, and that the Russo-German pact may be regarded as a truce.

Von Papen Flies to Turkey

BUDAPEST, Hungary, Aug. 23 (AP).—Franz von Papen, Germany's Ambassador to Turkey, passed by plane through Budapest today, en route from Salzburg to Angora.

Diplomatic circles conjectured his mission now was to renew attempts to draw Turkey out of the British-French bloc. They recalled German and Italian claims that Turkey's alliance with Britain and France was dependent upon Russia's not joining the opposition camp.

Wireless to THE NEW YORK TIMES.

BUDAPEST, Hungary, Aug. 23.—The international situation was dis-

Continued on Page Five

QUICK ACTION SEEN

Berlin Talks of 6 P. M. Deadline for Move Against Poland

DICTATOR WARNS BRITISH

Henderson So Wrought Up on Leaving Parley With Hitler That He Is Speechless

By OTTO D. TOLISCHUS
Wireless to THE NEW YORK TIMES.

BERLIN, Thursday, Aug. 24.—While Foreign Minister Joachim von Ribbentrop was in Moscow discussing, in the view of some German quarters, not so much a new non-aggression pact as "Poland's fourth and final partition," Chancellor Hitler yesterday received Sir Nevile Henderson, the British Ambassador, for a fifteen-minute conference.

According to reliable information, the conference ended on a rather blunt note that is interpreted in diplomatic quarters as possibly Herr Hitler's last word. The communique, issued last night, reads:

"Complying with the wish of the British Government, the Fuehrer received Sir Nevile Henderson at the Berghof today. The Ambassador delivered a letter from the British Prime Minister addressed to the Fuehrer, which was drawn up in the same sense as yesterday's British communication regarding the Cabinet session.

"The Fuehrer left no doubt in the mind of the British Ambassador that the obligations assumed by the British Government could not induce Germany to renounce the defense of her vital national interest."

Hitler's Tone Reported Blunt

Actually Herr Hitler's tone to Sir Nevile was reported to have been even more blunt than the communique indicates. In effect, Herr Hitler told the Ambassador that Britain had no business in Eastern Europe and that her guarantee of Poland merely encouraged Polish resistance to German demands, therefore it was up to Britain to persuade the Poles to yield or face the consequences.

Sir Nevile left the conference so wrought up he was speechless. Not trusting his memory to repeat the exact shadings of Herr Hitler's answer, he asked that it be put in writing and he received it in a half hour later. So it is couched in the same strong terms that Herr Hitler used to him before.

At the same time there are also well-authenticated reports that, in addition to Prime Minister Chamberlain's letter, Sir Nevile also delivered to Herr Hitler an oral message that if Herr Hitler would give the Poles time Britain would try to induce Poland to come forth with new proposals. In that connection some circles launched—perhaps not unintentionally—the suggestion that Foreign Minister Josef Beck of Poland might after all ask to see Herr von Ribbentrop and even Herr Hitler. A preliminary meeting with the former might be arranged at Riga, Latvia, on Herr von Ribbentrop's return from Moscow. But Polish circles declare the suggestion was "extremely unlikely" because it spelled surrender.

As during the last few days the word in Berlin is that the zero hour, which will set the German Army on the march, will come today, and these rumors are supplemented with the additional detail that the exact hour is 6 P. M. (noon, New York time), which might mean "contact with the enemy" some time tomorrow. Furthermore, orders to postpone action, issued after Herr von Ribbentrop's departure for Moscow, have been canceled again.

Germans Elated by News

How much all that is merely a part of the "war of nerves" and how much is bitter reality remains to be seen. In fact the tension developing in Germany, at least in an atmosphere of fantastic unreality, is made no more real by the delayed Summer heat that lures the populace to the woods and beaches, and, together with the elation over the Russian pact and renewed confidence in Herr Hitler's diplomatic superiority over the democratic statesmen, helps to hide the war clouds.

However, the rebuff to Britain yesterday, which in some quarters is compared with the rebuff administered to the French Ambassador by King William of Prussia just preceding the Franco-Prussian War

Continued on Page Two

Text of the Berlin-Moscow Treaty

By The Associated Press.

MOSCOW, Thursday, Aug. 24.—The text of the German-Russian non-aggression pact announced here today follows:

The German Reich Government and the Union of Soviet Socialist Republics, moved by a desire to strengthen the state of peace between Germany and the U.S.S.R. and in the spirit of the provisions of the neutrality treaty of April, 1926, between Germany and the U.S.S.R., decided the following:

Article I

The two contracting parties obligate themselves to refrain from every act of force, every aggressive action and every attack against one another, including any single action or that taken in conjunction with other powers.

Article II

In case one of the parties of this treaty should become the object of warlike acts by a third power, the other party will in no way support this third power.

Article III

The governments of the two contracting parties in the future will constantly remain in consultation with one another in order to inform each other regarding questions of common interest.

Article IV

Neither of the high contracting parties will associate itself with any other grouping of powers which directly or indirectly is aimed at the other party.

Article V

In the event of a conflict between the contracting parties concerning any question, the two parties will adjust this difference or conflict exclusively by friendly exchange of opinions or, if necessary, by an arbitration commission.

Article VI

The present treaty will extend for a period of ten years with the condition that if neither of the contracting parties announces its abrogation within one year of expiration of this period, it will continue in force automatically for another period of five years.

Article VII

The present treaty shall be ratified within the shortest possible time. The exchange of ratification documents shall take place in Berlin. The treaty becomes effective immediately upon signature.

Drawn up in two languages, German and Russian.

MOSCOW, 23d of August, 1939.

For the German Government:
RIBBENTROP.

In the name of the Government of the U.S.S.R.:
MOLOTOFF.

NO MILITARY MOVES APPARENT IN ITALY

Country Remains Tranquil as Regime Fails to Whip Up Any War Fervor Among People

By HERBERT L. MATTHEWS
Wireless to THE NEW YORK TIMES.

ROME, Aug. 23.—The Italian ship of state sailed tranquilly on the edge of the European tornado today. There have been no conferences, communiques, evacuation or orders, special mobilization or troop movements.

There have been only some diplomatic visits to Count Ciano, the Foreign Minister, including those of the British and French Ambassadors. This is the fourth time this past Thursday that Sir Percy Loraine saw Count Ciano, which shows the degree of pressure the British are bringing to bear as well as their anxiety to make the Italian leaders realize Britain's determination to support Poland. Presumably, Sir Percy delivered a copy of the same note that was presented to Chancellor Hitler, although that has not been admitted.

André François-Poncet's visit was his first since returning to Rome last Friday. He has tried steadily to see the Foreign Minister but hitherto without success. It is believed he also impressed on Count Ciano France's intention to abide by her pledges.

To Get War Supplies Report

Back at the White House in the early afternoon the President will have before him a report of the War Industries Committee on the status of the nation's munitions and other heavy industries. The committee has been canvassing the aviation and other industries in the past few days with a view to American preparedness.

The Hungarian Minister, Baron Frederick Villani, also saw Count Ciano today, receiving reports about Germany's demands on Budapest.

Italian People Are Calm

The Italian people are not being whipped up to the fervor that would be required to enter a war in the next few days. Nowhere do you see air shelters being hastily dug or gas masks being distributed.

Only in the newspapers do the commentators warn their readers that a conflict seems near, while relatively full accounts of the developments in various capitals are given. The British Cabinet's statement last night is published fully in all newspapers here, whereas the German press ignored it. If readers trusted their Italian newspapers this evening they would have a biased but reasonably correct appreciation of the dangers of the present situation.

They know their country is making no last-minute efforts to meet the

Continued on Page Four

PRESIDENT SPEEDS TO ACT ON CRISIS

Disturbed by War Threat, He Will End Cruise Today and Board Train at Red Bank

By FELIX BELAIR Jr.
Special to THE NEW YORK TIMES.

RED BANK, N. J., Aug. 23.—Admittedly disturbed by the European war crisis, President Roosevelt is hurrying here aboard the cruiser Tuscaloosa after scrapping plans for a more ceremonious landing at Annapolis in order to be back at the White House in the event of an outbreak of hostilities.

A small White House secretarial staff is awaiting the arrival of the President off Sandy Hook early tomorrow to give him a bundle of official diplomatic reports on latest developments abroad. Mr. Roosevelt plans to study the reports aboard his special train en route to Washington.

After debarking from the Tuscaloosa about 3 A. M. tomorrow the President will motor here with Brig. Gen. Edwin M. Watson, his first since returning to Rome, T. McIntire, White House physician. He is expected to stop long enough before entraining for the capital to telephone Secretary of State Cordell Hull, as well as to the embassies in London and Paris about overnight developments.

To Get War Supplies Report

Back at the White House in the early afternoon the President will have before him a report of the War Industries Committee on the status of the nation's munitions and other heavy industries. The committee has been canvassing the aviation and other industries in the past few days with a view to American preparedness.

Prior to the departure of the White House staff late today it was understood the War Industries Committee had drafted a report informing the President that the aviation and several other industries were prepared for any emergency that might arise and that aircraft manufacturers were ahead of schedule on orders of military planes from France and Great Britain.

Among Presidential intimates as well as the capital's political observers interest centered during the day on the question of whether Mr. Roosevelt considered the situation abroad sufficiently grave to call a

Continued on Page Three

BARS HOSTILE UNION

Treaty Forbids Either to Join Any Group Aimed at Other

ESCAPE CLAUSE OMITTED

Von Ribbentrop's Car, Flying Swastika, Passes Beneath Red Flag at Kremlin

By The Associated Press.

MOSCOW, Thursday, Aug. 24.—Germany and Soviet Russia early today signed a non-aggression pact binding each of them for ten years not to "associate itself with any other grouping of powers which directly or indirectly is aimed at the other party."

By the pact they also agreed to "constantly remain in consultation with one another" on their common interests and to adjust differences by arbitration.

The non-aggression clauses bound each power to refrain from any act of force against the other and if either party is "the object of warlike acts by a third power" to refrain from supporting that third power.

The pact did not include the usual escape clause providing for its denunciation in case one of the contracting parties attacked a third power. This provision has been written into most non-aggression agreements signed in the past by Moscow.

Arrives by Plane

By G. E. R. GEDYE
Special Cable to THE NEW YORK TIMES.

MOSCOW, Thursday, Aug. 24.—With the meticulous punctuality of a perfectly staged arrival, two huge Focke-Wulf Condor planes conveying Joachim von Ribbentrop, the German Foreign Minister, and his thirty-two assistants, landed at the Moscow airdrome on the stroke of 1 P. M. yesterday.

Adequate but not excessive police precautions were taken at the airdrome. For the first time the Soviet authorities displayed the swastika banner, five of which flew from the front of the airdrome building, but were placed so as not to be visible from the outside.

Vyacheslaff M. Molotoff was not present to welcome Herr von Ribbentrop, probably because he is of higher rank than Herr von Ribbentrop. Instead the visitor was received by Vladimir P. Potemkin, Vice Commissar of Foreign Affairs; Mr. Barkoff, protocol chief; Mr. Merkuloff, Vice Commissar of Internal Affairs, under whom falls the NKVD, formerly the GPU; Mr. Alexandroff, chief of the Central European Department of the Foreign Office, and General Suvoroff, commander of the Moscow garrison.

Almost the entire staff of the huge German Embassy, headed by the Ambassador, Count Friedrich Werner von der Schulenburg, with the military, naval and air attachés in uniform, was present. The German civilians mostly wore top hats and cutaway coats.

The Italian Ambassador, Augusto Russo, with his military attaché in uniform, also was present. The feature of the reception that commented upon was the absence of any Japanese representative.

The German Embassy staff stood lined up like troops on parade. As each was presented to Herr von Ribbentrop he sprang to attention, clicked his heels, gave the Hitler salute and shook hands, again saluting and heel-clicking.

In Old Austrian Embassy

From the airdrome the party drove to the city through streets where police in their white Summer jackets stood every ten paces. For Herr von Ribbentrop the Soviet Government provided a large American car from the Kremlin car park, flying the swastika flag.

The party drove directly to the former Austrian Embassy, where they are being housed. Subsequently Herr von Ribbentrop and leading members of his mission had luncheon at the embassy with Count von der Schulenburg.

At about 3:30 P. M. Herr von Ribbentrop, accompanied by Count von der Schulenburg and an expert translator when, the Germans brought from Berlin, drove through the gates of the Kremlin with its

Continued on Page Six

"All the News That's Fit to Print."

The New York Times.

Copyright, 1939, by The New York Times Company.

EXTRA
Partly cloudy and somewhat warmer today. Tomorrow generally fair with moderate temperatures.
Temperatures Yesterday—Max., 67; Min., 61

VOL. LXXXVIII...No. 29,805.   Entered as Second-Class Matter, Postoffice, New York, N. Y.   NEW YORK, FRIDAY, SEPTEMBER 1, 1939.   THREE CENTS NEW YORK CITY and Vicinity | FOUR CENTS Elsewhere Except in 7th and 8th Postal Zones.

GERMAN ARMY ATTACKS POLAND; CITIES BOMBED, PORT BLOCKADED; DANZIG IS ACCEPTED INTO REICH

BRITISH MOBILIZING

Navy Raised to Its Full Strength, Army and Air Reserves Called Up

PARLIAMENT IS CONVOKED

Midnight Meeting Is Held by Ministers—Negotiations Admitted Failure

By The Associated Press.

LONDON, Friday, Sept. 1.—The British Parliament was summoned to meet today at 5 P. M. [12 noon in New York].

British Call Up Forces

By FERDINAND KUHN Jr.
Special Cable to THE NEW YORK TIMES.

LONDON, Friday, Sept. 1.—All attempts to bring about direct negotiations between Germany and Poland appeared to have broken down tonight as Great Britain mobilized her fleet to its full strength, stretched her other defensive preparations close to the limit and began moving 3,000,000 school children and invalids from the crowded cities into the safety of the countryside.

Censorship was established over cables after London had been cut off for hours from communication with the Continent.

It was the peak of the crisis, but a day of rumors had not shifted the fundamental issue nor given a conclusive answer to the question of peace or war.

At midnight the British Government was not yet convinced that Germany really intended to attack Poland and provoke a world war.

Terms Called Smoke Screen

All that had happened during yesterday, including the sudden broadcasting of Chancellor Hitler's sixteen-point demands, was interpreted here as a smoke screen rather than as the flash of guns.

After hearing Herr Hitler's "terms" officials here quietly announced tonight that "the government primarily interested in the proposals is, of course, the Polish Government."

Until the Polish Government has had time to consider them, it was said in Whitehall that "it would be highly undesirable for any comment to be made."

It was fully expected that Poland would reject them later today; indeed, Polish circles here were describing them tonight as "utterly unacceptable," for they would involve dismemberment of Poland and loss of Poland's capacity to defend her independence. In any event, there was no sign of any intention here to put pressure on Warsaw to accept.

Much might have been said about the German "proposals" here tonight if the government had not been so anxious to leave the first decision to Warsaw without any prompting. That the British regarded them as artful went without saying, since they conveyed a firm impression of reasonableness that was not borne out by the terms themselves.

Until the announcement on the German wireless tonight, the British Government had not been told about them officially, and the Polish Government was not informed until Josef Lipski, Polish Ambassador to Berlin, visited Foreign Minister Joachim von Ribbentrop a few minutes before the broadcast took place.

Shortly after midnight last night, Sir Nevile Henderson, the British Ambassador in Berlin, had heard the "points" read to him by Herr von Ribbentrop, but the reading could not even take notes of them in detail. In any event, he was told Herr Hitler's "points" were not being given to him or his government officially, on the ground that it was already too late.

Time Limit Expired

On Tuesday Herr Hitler had asked that a Polish negotiator should arrive in Berlin within twenty-four hours; and as nobody had arrived from Warsaw when the time limit expired, Sir Nevile was told that the "points" could not be communicated officially to his German time table was in

Continued on Page Four

Bulletins on Europe's Conflict

London Hears of Warsaw Bombing

LONDON, Friday, Sept. 1 (AP).—Reuters British news agency said it had learned from Polish sources in Paris that Warsaw was bombed today.

French Confirm Beginning of War

PARIS, Friday, Sept. 1 (AP).—The Havas news agency said today that official French dispatches from Germany indicated that "the Reich began hostilities on Poland this morning."

The agency also reported that the Polish Embassy here had announced that "Germany violated the Polish frontier at four points."

"German reports of pretended violation of German territory by Poland are pure invention, as is the fable of 'attack' by Polish insurgents on Gleiwitz," the embassy announcement said.

Attack on Entire Front Reported

LONDON, Friday, Sept. 1 (AP).—A Reuters dispatch from Paris said:

"The following is given with all reserve: According to unconfirmed reports received here, the Germans have begun an offensive with extreme violence on the whole Polish front."

First Wounded Brought Into Gleiwitz

GLEIWITZ, Germany, Friday, Sept. 1 (AP).—An army ambulance carrying wounded soldiers arrived at the emergency hospital here today at 9:10 A. M.

The men, carried in a wagon, were on stretchers. One had on a first-aid field bandage. It could not be ascertained where the ambulance came from.

At about 9:30 a half-mile long truck train manned by the engineering corps drove through the heart of the city with pontoon bridge building material. In the train were caterpillar tread, twenty-passenger motor vans.

Obviously the train had been on the road for a considerable time. All equipment was thickly covered with gray mud.

A scouting plane of the air force was patrolling an area over Gleiwitz.

Early today Gleiwitz residents reported that artillery fire

Continued on Page Four

DALADIER SUMMONS CABINET TO CONFER

News of Attack on Poland Spurs Prompt Action— Military Move Thought Likely

By The Associated Press.

PARIS, Friday, Sept. 1.—Edouard Daladier, Premier and War Minister of France, informed that German troops crossed the Polish frontier today, summoned an urgent meeting of his Cabinet for 10:30 A. M.

It was probable that Parliament would be called tomorrow.

Reports of the German invasion came from Berlin and from the Polish Embassy here. The Ministers were called to the Elysée Palace to meet with President Albert Lebrun.

Upon receipt of word of the German operations M. Daladier rushed to the War Ministry and called General Marie Gustave Gamelin, supreme commander of land, sea and air forces, into consultation.

A little later Daladier summoned Foreign Minister Georges Bonnet.

The Polish Embassy said that Germans violated the Polish frontier at four points and at the same time it characterized German charges that Poles had crossed into Germany as "pure invention."

Havas, French news agency, announced that "a German declaration of war against Poland probably will lead France and Great Britain to take new military measures."

Britain and France are committed to aid Poland in any fight to save her independence.

Ministers Stand Firm

By P. J. PHILIP

PARIS, Aug. 31.—The Cabinet met with President Albert Lebrun for more than two hours this evening at the Elysée Palace. At the close of the meeting Minister of the Interior Albert Sarraut handed the press the following communiqué:

"MM. Edouard Daladier, President of the Council, and Georges Bonnet, Minister of Foreign Affairs, laid before the Cabinet the detailed account of the international situation as a whole.

"The Cabinet was unanimous in formally maintaining the engagements taken by France."

Later M. Daladier had further conversations with M. Bonnet, Fi-

Continued on Page Four

BRITISH CHILDREN TAKEN FROM CITIES

3,000,000 Persons Are in First Evacuation Group, Which Is to Be Moved Today

By FREDERICK T. BIRCHALL
Special Cable to THE NEW YORK TIMES.

LONDON, Friday, Sept. 1.—The greatest mass movement of population at short notice in the history of Great Britain is under way. It is an evacuation, under government order, of little children, invalids, women and old men from congested areas.

From London, Birmingham, Manchester, Liverpool, Edinburgh, Glasgow and twenty-three other cities the great exodus is going on as this dispatch is being written. The numbers are stupendous. Some 3,000,000 of these helpless human beings are being taken out of danger of German bombs.

Nothing like it has ever been attempted anywhere; yet it is going on without mishap—so far, indeed, without serious confusion.

Scenes everywhere were much the same whether in the aristocratic West End or the proletarian East Side, but one that this correspon-

Continued on Page Three

Soviet Ratifies Reich Non-Aggression Pact; Gibes at British and French Amuse Deputies

By G. E. R. GEDYE
Special Cable to THE NEW YORK TIMES.

MOSCOW, Aug. 31.—With Premier and Foreign Commissar Vyacheslaff M. Molotoff, working under high pressure—so suddenly applied without any previous indication and contrasting so sharply with earlier delaying tactics that it was to suggest German insistence that the matter be finally settled—the Supreme Soviet [Parliament] tonight unanimously ratified the Russo-German non-aggression pact.

Ratification, which was first foreshadowed at midday, was preceded by a speech by Mr. Molotoff so precise in its definition of Soviet obligations to refrain from participating on the side of Great Britain and France in any war against Germany, so voluble in its defense against charges of inconsistency and suspicious of the existence of a secret German-Soviet pact entitling the latter to participate in a partition of Poland.

Mr. Molotoff's speech contained nothing to justify constantly repeated suspicions of the existence of a secret German-Soviet pact entitling the latter to participate in a partition of Poland.

The Premier's speech contained much trenchant and seemingly irrefutable evidence of blunders in the British and French Governments in handling the question of Soviet cooperation. It was not dif-

Continued on Page Eight

HOSTILITIES BEGUN

Warsaw Reports German Offensive Moving on Three Objectives

ROOSEVELT WARNS NAVY

Also Notifies Army Leaders of Warfare—Envoys Tell of Bombing of 4 Cities

By JERZY SZAPIRO
Wireless to THE NEW YORK TIMES.

WARSAW, Poland, Friday, Sept. 1.—War began at 5 o'clock this morning with German planes attacking Gdynia, Cracow and Katowice.

At Gdynia three bombs exploded in the sea.

The regular German Army started an offensive in the direction of Dzialdowka—in Upper Silesia and Czestochowa. The German plan apparently is to cut off Western Poland along the line of Dzialdowka-Lodz-Czestochowa.

The offensive is developing, from East Prussia, toward Silesia and northwards from Slovakia.

At 9 o'clock an attempt was made to bombard Warsaw. The planes, however, did not reach over the suburbs.

A military attack on the garrison at Westerplatte in the Danzig area was repulsed.

The Foreign Office at 8:45 A. M. issued a communiqué saying that military action had begun in Westerplatte in the Danzig area as well as in Buschkowa near Gdynia, and in Dzialowka, Chojnice and Lowa.

Hostilities have begun and Poland has been attacked, said the communiqué.

Three cities in Upper Silesia suffered artillery bombardment, particulars of which are lacking, it was said.

While this dispatch was being telephoned, the air-raid sirens sounded in Warsaw.

Danzig Fighting Reported

WARSAW, Poland, Friday, Sept. 1 (AP).—It was reported today that Tczew and Czestochowa was bombed by German airplanes early this morning.

There was no official confirmation of the bombing.

Fighting was reported at Danzig. It was reported that German troops had attacked Polish defenses near Mlawa, bordering the southern part of East Prussia.

There was no announcement of the damage resulting from the bombing.

Mist and clouds were overhanging the city. A light drizzle afforded momentary protection against air raids. Warsaw went to work as usual.

Roosevelt Warns Navy

WASHINGTON, Friday, Sept. 1 (AP).—President Roosevelt directed today that all naval ships and army commands be notified at once by radio of German-Polish hostilities.

The White House issued the following announcement:

"The President received word at 2:50 A. M. Eastern standard time

Continued on Page Five

FREE CITY IS SEIZED

Forster Notifies Hitler of Order Putting Danzig Into the Reich

ACCEPTED BY CHANCELLOR

Poles Ready, Made Their Preparations After Hostilities Appeared Inevitable

Special Cable to THE NEW YORK TIMES.

DANZIG, Friday, Sept. 1.—By a decree issued early this morning Albert Forster, Nazi Chief of State, proclaimed the annexation of the Free City to the Reich, thus settling by a fell stroke the original point of contention in the international crisis.

In a telegram to Chancellor Hitler Herr Forster explained his action as necessary to remove "the pressing necessity of our people and State." Herr Forster also issued a proclamation to the people of Danzig saying the hour awaited for twenty years had arrived because "our Fuehrer, Adolf Hitler, has freed us."

[A NEW YORK TIMES dispatch from Berlin this morning said Herr Hitler telegraphed Herr Forster today thanking him and all Danzigers and stating:

"The law for reannexation is in effect immediately."

The Chancellor stated, furthermore, that Herr Forster was appointed head of the civil administration of the Danzig area.]

In a four-article decree Herr Forster declared the Constitution of Danzig no longer valid. He declared himself sole administrator of the Danzig part of the German Reich, and he declared that until the Reich's legal system had been introduced by command of Herr Hitler all laws except the Constitution remained in effect. Then Herr Forster immediately wired Herr Hitler of his action, begged the Chancellor to give his approval of the move and through Reich law complete the annexation.

The German flag is now flying everywhere over Danzig, Herr Forster said, and all church bells resound to the event. "We thank God," he declared, "that He gave the Fuehrer the strength and the possibility to free also us from the evil Versailles treaty."

Hitler Accepts Danzig

BERLIN, Friday, Sept. 1.—The German official news agency, D. N. B., announced today that Albert Forster, Nazi Chief of State in Danzig, had proclaimed the reunion of the Free City with the Reich.

Herr Hitler today accepted the Free City of Danzig into the Reich.

"I acknowledge your proclamation of the return of the Free City of Danzig to the Reich," Herr Hitler's telegram said. "I thank you, Gauleiter Forster, and all Danzig men and women, for your loyalty which you have displayed for so many years.

"Greater Germany welcomes you with joy in her heart.

"The law of reunion will be enacted forthwith. I appoint you, Herr Forster, chief of the civil administration in the Danzig territory."

Forster's telegram to Herr Hitler read:

My Fuehrer,

I have just signed and then put into effect the following basic law:

The basic State law of the Free State of Danzig and the German Reich is effective Sept. 1, 1939.

To lift the immediate distress of the people and State of the Free City of Danzig, I decree the following basic State law:

ARTICLE I

The Constitution of the Free City of Danzig has been suspended and effective immediately.

ARTICLE II

All legal and administrative power will be executed exclusively by the head of State.

ARTICLE III

The Free City of Danzig with its territory and its peoples form

Continued on Page Five

Hitler Acts Against Poland

The port of Gdynia, north of Danzig (toward top of map), was blockaded this morning. At Gleiwitz (shown by cross) artillery fire was heard after a Polish-German skirmish had been reported there. Cracow, to the east, was among Polish cities said to have been bombed.

Hitler Tells the Reichstag 'Bomb Will Be Met by Bomb'

Chancellor Vows 'Fight Until Resolution' Against Poland—Gives Order of Succession As Goering, Hess, Then Senate to Choose

Chancellor Adolf Hitler of Germany, in a world broadcast this morning, opened "a fight until the resolution of the situation" against Poland, announcing that "from now on bomb will be met by bomb."

At the same time he announced, to face any eventuality, that if anything "happened" to him, Field Marshal Hermann Goering was to be in charge; if to Marshal Goering, Rudolph Hess; if to Herr Hess, the Senate, which he proposes to appoint, will select a successor.

The Chancellor, after attempting to narrow the conflict with Poland by assuring the Western powers that he had no designs on their frontiers, by assuring the neutrality of the sideline powers and by acknowledging the friendliness of Italy and the new relations with Russia, issued a defy to Poland's allies.

Says He Will Carry on

"I shall carry on this fight regardless of against whom I may come," he declared.

At the same time he held the door open for Poland to capitulate to his demands, declaring that he did not intend to make war against women and children. He said that if a solution did not come from the present Polish Government, it would come from a future Polish Government.

The Chancellor expressed confidence, toward the close of his address, that his decision, which was being broadcast over amplifiers hastily erected by electricians at the last moment in the streets of Berlin and the provincial capitals, would be accepted by the German people.

The scene enacted in the Kroll Opera House in Berlin was carried over sound waves to most of the nations of the world. From Berlin hook-up has been arranged with the three major networks of the United States, and, according to the announcer for the combined broadcasting system, over the Italian, Hungarian, Spanish, Norwegian, Swedish, Danish, Yugoslav, British and French national networks.

The summons to the Reichstag, ordered by Herr Hitler himself, had been sent out only a few hours before the meeting. Most of the members had been awaiting the signal, and when the opera house opened shortly before 10 o'clock [5 o'clock, New York time] this morning, they were dressed in the uniforms of their military formations.

After Herr Hitler finished speaking the deputies enacted a law incorporating Danzig into the Reich, declaring Danzig citizens were now Germans, voiding the Constitution of the Free City and extending its territory the jurisdiction of German law.

At 5:10 A. M., Marshal Goering opened the meeting and turned the floor over to the Chancellor.

In the early part of his address, Herr Hitler electrified his audience by assuring the Western powers that he had no designs on them under the tortures that the Versailles treaty has been inflicting upon us.

Then, speaking with measured deliberateness of Germany's claims to the pre-war German areas, he announced, as he had on a previous occasion:

"The Treaty of Versailles is, for us Germans, and has been, for us Germans, not a law."

Anticipating what the announcement's reiteration would lead to, the Deputies roared applause. Then Herr Hitler, his indignation rising as he proceeded, set about building up the German case, asserting that his proposals for a peaceful solution of the problem of Danzig and the Polish Corridor had been rejected, and charging that the Poles had visited atrocities on Germans, especially women and children, "killing many of them."

SUMMARY OF SPEECH

A summary of Herr Hitler's speech was translated as follows:

"For months we have been suffering under the burdens of the Treaty of Versailles. Danzig was and is a German city. All these regions owe only to Germany their cultural development.

"Minorities in the Polish Corridor have been shamefully mistreated. Here, as in other respects, I have tried to solve the problems by peaceful means. In the fifteen years of National Socialism we have been

Continued on Page Three

HITLER GIVES WORD

In a Proclamation He Accuses Warsaw of Appeal to Arms

FOREIGNERS ARE WARNED

They Remain in Poland at Own Risk—Nazis to Shoot at Any Planes Flying Over Reich

By OTTO D. TOLISCHUS
Special Cable to THE NEW YORK TIMES.

BERLIN, Friday, Sept. 1.—Charging that Germany had been attacked, Chancellor Hitler at 5:11 o'clock this morning issued a proclamation to the army declaring that from now on force will be met with force and calling on the armed forces "to fulfill their duty to the end."

The text of the proclamation reads:

To the defense forces:

The Polish nation refused my efforts for a peaceful regulation of neighborly relations; instead it has appealed to weapons.

Germans in Poland are persecuted with a bloody terror and are driven from their homes. The series of border violations, which are unbearable to a great power, prove that the Poles are no longer are willing to respect the German frontier. In order to put an end to this frantic activity no other means is left to me now than to meet force with force.

"Battle for Honor"

German defense forces will carry on the battle for the honor of the living rights of the reawakened German people with firm determination.

I expect every German soldier, in view of the great tradition of eternal German soldiery, to do his duty until the end.

Remember always in all situations you are the representatives of National Socialist Greater Germany!

Long live our people and our Reich!

Berlin, Sept. 1, 1939.

ADOLF HITLER.

The commander-in-chief of the air force issued a decree effective immediately prohibiting the passage of any airplanes over German territory excepting those of the Reich air force or of the government.

This morning the naval authorities ordered all German mercantile ships in the Baltic Sea not to run to Danzig or Polish ports.

Anti-air raid defenses were mobilized throughout the country early this morning.

A formal declaration of war against Poland had not yet been declared up to 8 o'clock [3 A. M. New York time] this morning and the question of whether the two countries are in a state of active belligerency is still open.

Reichstag Will Meet Today

Foreign correspondents at an official conference at the Reich Press Ministry at 8:30 o'clock [3:30 A. M. New York time] were told that they would receive every opportunity to facilitate the transmission of dispatches. Wireless stations have been instructed to speed up communications and the Ministry is installing additional batteries of telephones.

The Reichstag has been summoned to meet at 10 o'clock [5 A. M. New York time] to receive a more formal declaration from Herr Hitler.

The Hitler army order is interpreted as providing, for the time being, armed defense of the German frontiers against aggression. This action is also suspected of forcing international diplomatic action.

The Germans announced that foreigners remain in Polish territory at their own risk.

Flying over Polish territory as well as the maritime areas is forbidden by the German authorities and any violators will be shot down.

When Herr Hitler made his

Continued on Page Three

CHAMBERLAIN ANNOUNCES BRITAIN IS AT WAR WITH GERMANY

"All the News That's Fit to Print."	The New York Times.	EXTRA Generally fair, little change in temperature today. Tomorrow cloudy, showers in afternoon or night. Temperatures Yesterday—Max., 80; Min., 64	Section 1

NEWS INDEX, PAGE 21, THIS SECTION

Copyright, 1939, by The New York Times Company.

VOL. LXXXVIII....No. 29,807 — Entered as Second-Class Matter, Postoffice, New York, N. Y. — NEW YORK, SUNDAY, SEPTEMBER 3, 1939. — P — Including Rotogravure Picture, Magazine and Book Review. — TEN CENTS | TWELVE CENTS Beyond 200 Miles Except in 7th and 8th Postal Zones.

BRITAIN AND FRANCE IN WAR AT 6 A. M.; HITLER WON'T HALT ATTACK ON POLES; CHAMBERLAIN CALLS EMPIRE TO FIGHT

SOVIET IN WARNING

British-French Action to Bring Western Border Revision, Berlin Hears

NAZIS GREET MISSION

Hitler to Receive New Russian Ambassador and General Today

By OTTO D. TOLISCHUS
Wireless to THE NEW YORK TIMES.

BERLIN, Sunday, Sept. 3.—According to well-informed quarters here Moscow is already supposed to have notified Paris and London that if France and Britain join in the present Reich-Polish conflict Russia will find herself compelled to revise her Western borders.

This is tantamount to the threat that any British and French help to Poland will merely hasten the partition of Poland between Germany and Russia. There are hints that Russia might also seek other "compensation" in regions even less convenient to Britain.

As an impressive demonstration of this new cooperation there arrived today by air from Stockholm a new Russian Ambassador and a new embassy secretary, both of whom were said to be very close to Premier Vyacheslaff Molotoff, and a Russian military mission headed by a commanding general.

Officials Greet the Mission

The new Ambassador is Alexander Shkhvartzeff, who, it is pointed out here, collaborated with Mr. Molotoff in the Commissariat of Foreign Affairs in Moscow. The new embassy secretary is Vladimir Perloff, up to now Mr. Molotoff's secretary and interpreter.

The military mission consists of General Maxim Purjakoff, designated as the Military Plenipotentiary of the U. S. S. R., and his staff; Brig. Gen. Michae' Beljakoff, Colonel Nikolai Skornjakoff, Major Basanoff and Captain Alexander Seditch.

To show the importance of the occasion the members were met at Tempelhof Airfield by Dr. Ernst Woermann, Under-Secretary of State in the Foreign Office; Baron Alexander von Doernberg, Chief of Protocol, and other Foreign Office officials. Lieut. Gen. Seifert, commander of Berlin, headed the list of army officers greeting the Russians. A guard of honor presented arms.

The Russians received an ovation as their automobiles, flying the hammer-and-sickle flag of the Soviet Union, passed the Reich Chancellery. Those assembled along the street gave the Nazi salute.

Hitler to Receive Envoy

Adding importance to all this is the fact that it was announced at midnight that Herr Hitler would receive the new Ambassador, together with the Military Plenipotentiary, for the submission of credentials later today, which sets a precedent for diplomatic speed.

That such a formidable military mission was sent here to work out close collaboration with the German Army is taken for granted now. But German quarters still hold that the consultative clauses of the German-Russian pact are sufficient to cover all the collaboration necessary and a formal military alliance may be signed only as the last trump card to impress London and Paris.

Ambassador Joseph Lipski and his whole embassy staff left Berlin this morning under safe conduct en route to Sweden, which has also taken over the representation of Polish interests. The German Embassy staff was supposed to have left Warsaw at the same time. German interests in Poland are being represented by the Netherlands. Official quarters hold, however, that this merely represents a "cessation of direct diplomatic relations," not a formal break of relations, just as there is no declared state of war.

Meanwhile, since the German-Polish conflict is now being arbitrated by the roar of cannon the re-

Continued on Page Sixteen

Announcement of Final Ultimatum

By The Associated Press.

LONDON, Sunday, Sept. 3.—*Following is the text of today's communique revealing the final ultimatum to Germany:*

On Sept. 2 His Majesty's Ambassador in Berlin was instructed to inform the German Government that unless they were prepared to give His Majesty's Government in the United Kingdom satisfactory assurances that the German Government had suspended all aggressive action against Poland and were prepared promptly to withdraw their forces from Polish territory, His Majesty's Government in the United Kingdom would without hesitation fulfill their obligations to Poland.

At 9 A. M. this morning His Majesty's Ambassador in Berlin informed the German Government that unless not later than 11 A. M., British Summer time, today, Sept. 3, satisfactory assurances to the above effect had been given by the German Government and had reached His Majesty's Government in London a state of war would exist between the two countries as from that hour.

His Majesty's Government are now awaiting the receipt of any reply that may be made by the German Government.

The Prime Minister will broadcast to the nation at 11:15 A. M.

21 CIVILIANS KILLED IN RAID ON WARSAW

Women, Children Die as Bomb Hits Workers' Apartment— State of War Decreed

By The Associated Press.

WARSAW, Poland, Sept. 2.—Twenty-one dead and more than thirty wounded were counted tonight after German bombs had struck an apartment house in a Warsaw workingmen's quarter.

The bombs tore off the side of the apartment house as if it had been made of paper. Rescue workers still were clearing away the resultant pile of debris in a search for further casualties when this correspondent inspected it.

One of the bombs had dug a crater fully twenty feet in diameter, and the open ground was piled high with furniture and belongings.

In the center of a large park in the southern section of Warsaw, this writer also saw where a bomb had struck a simple wooden dwelling, killing two persons and wounding one. In an open field near the Vistula River, where ten light bombs apparently had been released simultaneously, they had dug craters in a 100-yard circle.

With the writer on this tour of inspection of the damage done by the German air bombings were C. Burke Elbrick, secretary of the American Embassy; Clifford Norton, charge d'affaires of the British Embassy, and officials of the Polish Foreign Office.

During the tour the party twice was forced to take refuge because of air-raid alarms, five of which in all sounded through the city today. Once the party took cover in a shallow dugout filled with working men, their wives and their crying children.

The worst scene of damage was at Kolo, the workingmen's quarter, where, in addition to wrecking one apartment building, the bombs had smashed windows in several others.

An old man gulped back tears as he said his wife and two children were dead. A woman, still staring blankly into space, said:

"My husband is gone."

An official news service communiqué stated that yesterday German raiders dropped 120 bombs on No. 3, a transcontinental crossing in the suburbs still undetermined.

President Ignaz Moscicki declared that Poland was under a "state of war" today as official reports said that Polish forces were resisting German invasion on three fronts.

The "state of war" was proclaimed

Continued on Page Fourteen

News dispatches from Europe are now virtually all subject to censorship

PARIS AUTHORIZED WAR DECLARATION

Chamber Voted Credits After Hearing Daladier— New Ultimatum Being Drawn

By The Associated Press.

PARIS, Sept. 2.—Premier Edouard Daladier today received implied authority from the Chamber of Deputies to declare war on Germany.

With that to support them, he and his Cabinet met at the War Ministry at 7:30 tonight to frame a demand that Chancellor Hitler reply to the British-French "last warning" of yesterday.

The power to declare war was vested in a war budget bill of 69,-000,000,000 francs, which the sober Deputies, many wearing army uniforms, adopted unanimously by a show of hands after hearing M. Daladier say the government was still willing to negotiate if Germany would cease hostilities in Poland.

Whether the Premier uses the authority vested in him by adoption of the budget depends upon the possibility—frankly viewed as slight—that Herr Hitler would avail himself of a last-minute loophole for peace.

The Premier told the finance committee after the Chamber session that he planned to call the Chamber to approve an actual declaration of war if that became necessary, but he may simply ask for approval after, rather than before, the action itself.

"The government will take the same chance as Parisians," M. Daladier told a Deputy who asked whether the government planned to leave Paris immediately.

The session was held in a tense atmosphere from 3 to 3:55 P. M.

Continued on Page Fifteen

ROME ASKED PEACE

Pressed Its Proposal for a 5-Power Parley on Britain and France

WAR MEASURES CUT

Press Expressed the Hope Germany Would Win in Poland

By The Associated Press.

ROME, Sept. 2.—Premier Mussolini tonight sought to prevent Polish-German hostilities from spreading into a general European war by arranging a negotiated settlement.

Conferences that the British and French Ambassadors had with Foreign Minister Count Ciano were believed to be connected directly with an Italian proposal of a five-power conference disclosed in London by Prime Minister Neville Chamberlain and Foreign Secretary Viscount Halifax.

The possibility of halting the German-Polish conflict and arranging a peaceable settlement had been asked to use his influence on Adolf Hitler to halt fighting in Poland, call his army back and negotiate a settlement of his demands on the Poles.

For Wide Settlement

Here it was regarded as certain that any five-power conference proposed by Premier Mussolini would be not merely for settling the German-Polish conflict but would be aimed at complete revision of the Treaty of Versailles.

Under such a revision Italy and Germany would seek the political and economic concessions that they consider necessary to end European tension once and for all. This has long been Signor Mussolini's idea and Italian newspapers recently have been stressing it as the only real solution. [Italy has been demanding from France concessions concerning Tunisia, the Suez Canal and Jibuti, French Somaliland port.]

While the Ambassadors of France and Britain conferred with Foreign Minister Ciano Italy continued her policy of watchful waiting and avoidance of any military "initiative".

The important commentator, Virginio Gayda, in the Giornale d'Italia noted uneasily that French and British war preparations made it seem that only a miracle could prevent a "more general explosion." Italy, he said, rested on her arms, confident she had done everything possible to avoid war. He said she was following events

Continued on Page Three

NAZIS REPORT GAINS

Hitler's Aims in Corridor Already Won, They Say, Telling of Big 'Trap'

RESISTANCE IS NOTED

But Armies Drive On and Navy Is in Command of Baltic, Germans Hold

Special Cable to THE NEW YORK TIMES.

BERLIN, Sunday, Sept. 3.—Despite the British and French ultimatums, the German armies reported continued advances into Poland yesterday.

By nightfall, it was asserted, not only had they attained the German war aims in the Polish Corridor as outlined in Chancellor Hitler's "sixteen points" but they were pushing forward in a concentric drive toward Warsaw. According to one report, the German forces stood less than fifty miles north of the Polish capital, and a big battle was believed developing along the Narew River.

According to the latest communiqués of the army command, which apparently have already been overtaken by developments, the German armies operating out of East Prussia and Pomerania had virtually cut the Corridor along the Netze and Vistula Rivers, so that all Polish troops remaining in the bottleneck north of it were hopelessly trapped.

Claim Capture of Teschen

In the South the Germans were reported to have taken the heavily fortified Jablunka Pass, the main strategic highway from Slovakia into Poland; to have captured Teschen and Pless [Pszcznya] and to be breaking through the Polish bunker line approaching Biala. This army group apparently has the task of capturing the Upper Silesian industrial section and the Teschen coal mines, taken by Poland from Czecho-Slovakia, and then of advancing along the Vistula toward Sandomierz, the new Polish armament and industrial center.

At the same time two other German Army groups, operating from the north out of East Prussia and from the southwest out of Silesia, apparently were conducting a pincers movement on Warsaw. The southwestern group was declared to have taken Wielun and to be advancing toward Radomsk and Sierads.

The Northern army group, according to a communiqué, was advancing on Przasnysz, but, according to private reports, is already beyond that town and approaching a larger Polish army that is supposed to have taken a stand on the Narew, where the first real battle of the undeclared war may take place.

Reich Claims 'Air' Domination

The communiqué asserted also that the German air force, after many bombing expeditions against air fields, railroads, military transports, retreating marching columns and other military objectives, in which many planes and the munition factory at Skarzysko-Kamien was destroyed, now has "unchallenged air domination over the entire Polish territory and so is now free for other tasks in protection of the Reich."

In addition, the Germany Navy, which said it had bombed the fortifications and port of Hela and also Gdynia, reported the sinking of a Polish torpedo boat near Hela. It was said to command the Baltic so completely that the fishing embargo was lifted last night.

A communiqué announced by the high command early today, according to the official German News Bureau, declared:

"The German air force yesterday again proved its absolute superiority. The whole air area over the battle zone and the hinterland is completely controlled by the German air force. Attacks were confined exclusively to military objec-

Continued on Page Twelve

Text of Chamberlain Address

The following is the text of the address by Prime Minister Chamberlain from 10 Downing Street this morning:

I am speaking to you from the Cabinet Room from 10 Downing Street. This morning the British Ambassador in Berlin handed the German Government the final note stating unless we heard from them by 11 o'clock [6 o'clock New York time] that they were prepared at once to withdraw their troops from Poland a state of war would exist between us. I have to tell you now that no such undertaking has been received and consequently this country is at war with Germany.

You can imagine what a bitter blow it is to me that all my long struggle to win peace has failed. Up to the very last it should have been quite possible to arrange a peaceful settlement between Germany and Poland.

Hitler has evidently made up his mind to attack Poland whatever may happen. Hitler claims that his proposals were shown to Poland and to us. That is not a true statement. The proposals never were shown to the Poles or to us. The German Government prepared the proposals in German and the same night the

German troops crossed the Polish frontier. Germany will never give up force and can only be stopped by force.

We are prepared to uphold our treaty with Poland and to protect them from the wicked and unprovoked attacks on the Polish people. France is joining Britain in fulfillment of her pledges. We have a clear conscience and the situation has become intolerable. Now that we have determined to finish it I know that you will all play your part.

When I have finished speaking several detailed announcements will be made on behalf of the government giving you plans under which it will be possible to carry on the work of the nation in these days of stress which may be ahead, but these plans need your help. You may be taking part in one of the fighting services or one of the other branches.

It is of vital importance that you carry on with your jobs. May God bless you all and may He defend the right for it is the evil things we shall be fighting against—brute force, broken promises, bad faith. But I am certain that right shall prevail.

Bulletins on European Conflict

Air Raid Warning in London

LONDON, Sept. 3 (Sunday).—Air raid sirens sounded an alarm in London today at 11:32 A.M. (5:32 A.M., E.S.T.). The whole city was sent to shelters by the wail of the alarm but all clear signals were sounded seventeen minutes later.

Ribbentrop Gives Reply to British Envoy

BERLIN, Sunday, Sept. 3 (AP).—German Foreign Minister Joachim von Ribbentrop received British Ambassador Sir Nevile Henderson at 9 A. M. [4 A. M. in New York] today to hand him Germany's answer to the "final warning" of Britain and France. Herr von Ribbentrop was expected to see the French Ambassador, Robert Coulondre, shortly before noon.

American Diplomats' Families Leave Reich

BERLIN, Sunday, Sept. 3 (AP).—About fifty women and children of the United States Embassy and consular staffs, as well as several other American families, left Berlin today at 8:50 A. M. [3:50 A. M. in New York] for Copenhagen in compartments reserved for them in a regular train. They were due in Copenhagen at 5:35 P. M. [12:35 A. M. in New York].

War Announced in France

PARIS, Sunday, Sept. 3 (AP).—The radio announced to the French nation today that British Prime Minister Chamberlain had proclaimed Great Britain at war with Germany.

"No News" at the German Embassy

LONDON, Sunday, Sept. 3 (AP).—At the German Embassy in London at 9:30 A. M. today [5:30 A. M., New York], a half hour before the expiration of the British ultimatum, it was said, "There is no news." A spokesman said, "We are in constant communication with Berlin."

Denies Poles Got Five-Power Parley Offer

LONDON, Sunday, Sept. 3 (AP).—Exchange Telegraph Agency, British news agency, said today that Count Edward Raczynski, Polish Ambassador in London, informed it that "the Italian Government did not approach Poland" concerning a reported five-power conference to settle German-Polish issues.

"Apart from the declarations made yesterday in the British Parliament and apart from contradictory reports in the press," the agency quoted him, "the Polish Government has not knowledge of such a scheme."

Exchange Telegraph said the Ambassador declared that "any talk of such a conference" would be "ludicrous and fantastic" as long as "a single enemy soldier stands on Polish soil."

1,000 Americans Sail on French Liner

PARIS, Sunday, Sept. 3 (AP).—The French Line said today that the Ile de France had sailed from Havre with more than 1,000 Americans on board, bound for home.

Heavy Fighting Is Reported in Silesia

WARSAW, Sept. 2 (AP).—Although official information was lacking, it was reported tonight that severe fighting be-

Continued on Page Twelve

TO END OPPRESSION

Premier Calls It 'Bitter Blow' That Efforts for Peace Have Failed

WARNING UNHEEDED

Demand on Reich to Withdraw Army From Poland Ignored

Prime Minister Neville Chamberlain announced to the world at 6:10 o'clock this morning that Great Britain and France were at war with Germany. He made the announcement over the radio, with short waves carrying the measured tones of his voice throughout all continents, from 10 Downing Street in London.

Mr. Chamberlain disclosed that Great Britain and France had taken concurrent action, announcing that "we and France are, today, in fulfillment of our obligations, going to the aid of Poland."

France, however, had not made any announcement beyond stating that the French Ambassador to Berlin would make a final call upon Foreign Minister Joachim von Ribbentrop at 6 o'clock this morning, and it was assumed the French had proclaimed the existence of the state of war.

Speaks With Solemnity

With the greatest solemnity Mr. Chamberlain began his declaration by reporting that the British Ambassador to Berlin had handed in Great Britain's final ultimatum and that it had not been accepted. Without hesitation he announced Britain's decision and, after touching briefly on the background of the crisis, he expressed the highest confidence that "injustice, oppression and persecution" would be vanquished and that his cause would triumph.

Mr. Chamberlain appealed to his people, schooled during the last year as the crisis deepened in measures of defense and defense, to carry on with their jobs and begged a blessing upon them, warning that "we shall be fighting against brute force."

The declaration came after Great Britain had given Chancellor Adolf Hitler of Germany extended time in which to answer the British Government's final ultimatum of Friday. In the final ultimatum Herr Hitler had been told that unless German aggression in Poland ceased, Britain was prepared to fulfill her obligations to Poland.

Warning Was Sharp

Britain's last warning at 4 o'clock this morning, New York time, left no doubt as to her stand, for the phrase, "fulfillment of Britain's obligations to Poland," was replaced by a flat statement that a state of war would exist between the two countries as of the hour of the deadline.

After Mr. Chamberlain had finished his statement, which had been introduced as "an announcement of national importance," the announcer warned the British people not to gather together, broadcast an order that all meeting places for entertainment be closed, and gave precautions to prepare the people against air bombings and poison gas attacks.

Mr. Chamberlain began his

Continued on Page Fifteen

Fuller Breaks Own Bendix Race Records; Crosses Continent in 8 Hours 58 Minutes

Frank Fuller, San Francisco sportsman pilot, broke his own record in the Bendix Trophy Race from Burbank, Calif., to Cleveland yesterday and then kept on to Bendix, N. J., to break his own record for a transcontinental crossing in the event, opening feature of the National Air Races and the country's outstanding air derby.

Flying a stripped-down Seversky military plane equipped with the same twin Wasp engine he had in the 1937 race, with his earlier records were set, Fuller flew the 2,450 miles from Burbank to Bendix in an elapsed time of 8 hours 58 minutes 8.45 seconds. His average speed was 273.14 miles an hour. His elapsed time in 1937 was 9 hours 25 minutes.

The record for a transcontinental flight is 7 hours 28 minutes, established by Howard Hughes in a specially built plane about two years ago.

In crossing the finishing line of the Bendix, Fuller, a wealthy paint manufacturer, won first place. As the first to fly over the line in Bendix he won another $1,000, and for breaking his 1937 record he won $2,500.

Fuller reached Bendix at 4:24:53 P. M., Eastern daylight time, and proceeded, without landing, to Floyd Bennett Field, where he brought his plane to earth at 4:35 P. M.

Max Constant of Burbank was the second racer to fly over Bendix, reaching there at 6:13:39 P. M. Arthur C. Bussy of Royersford, Pa., appeared at 7:06:15 P. M.

Although Constant arrived at Bendix ahead of Bussy, he took off from Burbank before him and Bussy was declared the second prize winner of an elapsed time of 8 hours 56 minutes 48 seconds. His average speed was 273.14 miles an hour. He won the $2,500 first prize for the flight to Cleveland and an additional $500 for continuing to Bendix and Floyd Bennett Field.

Mrs. Arline Davis of Cleveland landed at Newark Airport at 5 P. M., believing that she had cracked the official marker at Bendix and thereby won the $2,500 prize for the first woman to finish

Continued on Page Three

HOTEL ESSEX—Boston's popular hotel opposite Terminal Station. Famous bar. Booklet.—Advt.

ADELPHIA HOTEL, Philadelphia, Pa. Chestnut at 13th. Nearest Everything. Rooms now $3.50 up. Edward F. Kehl, Mgr.—Advt.

96

"All the News That's Fit to Print."

The New York Times.

LATE CITY EDITION
POSTSCRIPT
Generally fair with showers tonight, continued warm.
Temperatures Yesterday—Max.,79; Min.,64

Copyright, 1939, by The New York Times Company.

VOL. LXXXVIII...No. 29,808.

Entered as Second-Class Matter,
Postoffice, New York, N. Y.

NEW YORK, MONDAY, SEPTEMBER 4, 1939.

P

THREE CENTS NEW YORK CITY and Vicinity | FOUR CENTS Elsewhere Except in 7th and 8th Postal Zones.

BRITISH LINER ATHENIA TORPEDOED, SUNK; 1,400 PASSENGERS ABOARD, 292 AMERICANS; ALL EXCEPT A FEW ARE REPORTED SAVED

ROOSEVELT IN PLEA

President, on Air, Asks the Nation to Observe True Neutrality

CALLS ALL TO UNITY

Draws Ring Around Americas—'Even a Neutral' May Judge, He Says

By TURNER CATLEDGE
Special to The New York Times.

WASHINGTON, Sept. 3.—In an extraordinary message broadcast by radio to "the whole of America," President Roosevelt tonight called for an adjournment of all partisanship and selfishness and substitution of complete national unity in the United States to the end that the newest world war may be kept from the Western Hemisphere.

He declared that, as long as it remained within his power to prevent, "there will be no blackout of peace in the United States."

Linking the present European conflagration to the "invasion of Poland by Germany," the President announced that a proclamation of American neutrality was being prepared for issuance under the present Neutrality Act.

"I trust that in the days to come our neutrality can be made a true neutrality," he added.

Would Seek a "Final Peace"

But it seemed clear to him, he said, "even at the outbreak of this great war," that the influence of America should be consistent "in seeking for humanity a final peace which will eliminate, as far as it is possible to do so, the continued use of force between nations."

In his flat declaration that "this nation will remain a neutral nation," the President said he could not ask that every American remain neutral in thought as well. "Even a neutral has a right to take account of facts," he said. "Even a neutral cannot be asked to close his mind or his conscience."

The President gave no inkling of his intentions about calling Congress into special session to revise the stringent Neutrality Law which places certain mandatory obligations upon him. The universal opinion among observers at the capital was that he would issue a call soon, and that it might come upon the heels of the obligatory neutrality proclamation, placing an embargo on arms and munitions of war to Germany, Poland, France and England. White House sources said the neutrality proclamation could be expected within the next forty-eight hours.

Gives Ideas of Safety

Under the law, the neutrality proclamation, which carries with it the proclamation of an arms embargo, is required as soon as the President makes a finding that a state of war exists between two or more countries. Officials were standing today on the technicality that this government had not been officially notified of Britain's and France's declarations. They conceded, however, that this was a mere technicality.

In the course of his message, the President drew a ring around the Western Hemisphere, saying in substance that this was the area which the United States must and would seek to protect and keep neutral.

This country, he said, had certain ideas and ideals of national safety "and we must act to preserve that safety today and to preserve the safety of our children in future years."

That safety, he continued, is and will be bound up with the safety of the Western Hemisphere "and the seas adjacent thereto."

"We seek to keep war from our firesides by keeping war from coming to the Americas," he said.

Recalls Efforts for Peace

He claimed historic precedent, going back to the days of George Washington, for this country's assuming the responsibility of protecting the whole of the Americas. It is serious enough and tragic enough to every American family in every State in the Union to live in a world torn by wars on other continents, he said. Therefore he considered it our national duty to use

Continued on Page Six

Poles Charge Aerial Gas Attacks on Cities As Germany Agrees to 'Humanize' the War

LONDON, Sept. 3 (AP).—The Polish Ambassador to London, Count Edward Raczynski, tonight declared that new German air attacks in all parts of Poland had disclosed that the civilian population was suffering with the Germans using gas in their raids.

WARSAW, Sept. 3 (Polish Telegraphic Agency).—German bombers threw gas bombs on the unfortified village of Grudisk in the county of Ciechanow.

Wireless to The New York Times.

BERLIN, Sept. 3.—It was announced today that Germany and the Western Powers had agreed to "humanize" the war by not employing poison gas, not bombing open cities from the air, even when in the zone of war operations, and not taking military measures against civilians as long as both sides observed the agreement.

The reported dropping of gas bombs on Polish towns represents the first use of gas from planes in European warfare.

The inauguration of this form of attack recalls that in 1915 the Germans began the use of poison gas on the battlefields and the Allies followed suit.

In 1917 the German General Staff gave consideration to the use of gas from planes in attacking cities, but after a long debate it was decided not to do so. The reason was that the British and French air forces combined were superior to the air force of the Germans, and the fear of what might happen to German cities deterred the Germans from using gas in air attacks at that time.

ITALY FAILS TO ACT AS HER ALLY FIGHTS

Rome Plans to Stay Neutral Unless Attacked—Fascist Moves Kept Secret

By HERBERT L. MATTHEWS
Special to The New York Times.

ROME, Monday, Sept. 4.—Although Great Britain and France are at war with Germany, Italy has taken no step to join her Axis partner. She remains friendly to Germany but neutral, and she will make no move against the French and British unless attacked. This was made clear in Premier Mussolini's newspaper, the Popolo d'Italia, this morning, which reaffirmed the declaration of neutrality contained in the Council of Ministers' communiqué Friday.

Whether there is any possibility of Italy going beyond that attitude toward one side or the other cannot be stated yet, for the Italians continue to be completely secret. Since history always repeats itself, one may well suppose that the French and British are doing everything they can to win Italian benevolence, if not aid. That is the normal and natural thing for them to do whether they have hopes for success or not. After all, diplomatic relations between Rome and Paris and London continue on a friendly basis, and none need be surprised if André François-Poncet and Sir Percy Loraine, the French and British Ambassadors, who see Count Ciano, the Foreign Minister, so often these days, should be exerting their greatest efforts to win Italy away from Germany. It is their business to do so.

Attitude Is Not Changing

None can say yet what success, if any, they are having. So far as today is concerned there is that Popolo d'Italia article to go upon, which indicates clearly enough that Italy is not changing her attitude because Britain and France have entered the conflict. Although it was printed before those countries acted it was written at a time when there could be no doubt of what was going to happen.

The editorial begins by saying that the Council of Ministers' communiqué should be "re-read and meditated." Its words were "sculptured in stone," says the editorial, meaning that it was meant to last.

From Premier Mussolini's efforts for "peace with justice," two things are to be deduced it continues:

First, that notwithstanding certain foreign interpretations which are too hasty or ingenuous nothing is changed on the plane of Italo-German friendship.

Second, that Signor Mussolini has worked not only for the solution of the German-Polish problem but for all other problems which like this one now being solved by arms, have their origin in the Versailles Treaty.

"It is therefore natural," the article goes on, "that whatever happens, whether the German-Polish conflict remains localized or spreads to a catastrophe, the Duce's work—that is to say the work that

Continued on Page Seven

HITLER WITH ARMY ON EASTERN FRONT

Leaves Berlin After Placing Blame for War on Britain—Allied Envoys Depart

By OTTO D. TOLISCHUS
Wireless to The New York Times.

BERLIN, Sept. 3.—At 9 o'clock tonight Chancellor Hitler left Berlin, presumably for the Eastern Front. He had previously sent a message to the Eastern Army stating that he was joining them.

He left the city in a heavily guarded special train that mounted anti-aircraft artillery. He was accompanied by his Foreign Minister, Joachim von Ribbentrop, and by Field Marshal Hermann Goering. It was supposed that their destination was Stolp, Pomerania, where the headquarters of the Eastern Army is believed to be located.

The departure of the Chancellor ended a day of proclamations from the chancellery. There was an appeal to the German people, a proclamation to the Nazi party, a message to the soldiers of "the East Army and another to the troops manning the Westwall. There was also given out the text of a German memorandum answering the British ultimatum.

Perhaps the most significant feature of all these proclamations and of the memorandum is that they do not mention France, sidetrack

Continued on Page Nine

The Developments in Europe

Britain and France plunged into war yesterday morning and soon events began to gather momentum.

The most sensational was the torpedoing and sinking of the British liner Athenia off the Hebrides this morning. She was carrying 1,400 passengers, including 292 Americans, from Liverpool to Montreal. The news shocked the White House. [Page 1.]

On top of this came charges by Poles that the Germans had dropped gas bombs on towns. [Page 1.]

Britain, following her tactics of the last war, quickly blockaded Germany and closed the entrances to the Mediterranean as well. The British public was calm and grimly determined after it had heard Prime Minister Chamberlain gravely announce on the radio that "this country is at war with Germany." [Page 1.] He m. de the same announcement in the House of Commons, where he immediately received the support of such former opponents as Winston Churchill and David Lloyd George. In a new War Cabinet Mr. Churchill resumed the post of First Lord of the Admiralty, which he had held in the last war; Lord Hankey, another veteran statesman of that conflict, became Minister Without Portfolio, and Anthony Eden

became Secretary for the Dominions. [Page 8; texts of Mr. Chamberlain's addresses and of addresses in the Commons, Page 8.]

In France Premier Daladier, declaring that the responsibility for bloodshed was Chancellor Hitler's, said that France's cause was the cause of justice. [Page 1; text of Daladier's radio speech, Page 8.]

Herr Hitler in a series of statements during the day put the blame for the strife on the British whom he accused of seeking to encircle Germany. He left for the Polish front. [Page 1; texts of these statements, Page 2.]

On that front the Poles were reported to have carried the fighting to German soil in one sector, but were declared to be giving ground in Silesia and at points in Pomorze [Page 1.]

Russia likewise kept a middle-of-the-road position [Page 6.]

President Roosevelt, in an extraordinary message radioed to "the whole of America," called for national unity as a measure for keeping the Western Hemisphere from becoming embroiled. [Page 1; text of the message, Page 6.]

POLES REPORT GAIN

Tell of Fighting on Foe's Soil After Horsemen Retake 2 Towns

SHELL GERMAN AREA

But Invaders Announce Wide Advances—They Capture Rail Center

By The Associated Press.

LONDON, Monday, Sept. 4.—An Exchange Telegraph dispatch from Warsaw reported early today that Polish troops had crossed the German frontier north of Breslau and were fighting on German soil.

Quoting a Polish short-wave radio broadcast, the news agency said the troops had crossed between Rawicz and Leszno. These towns are on the border about twenty-five miles apart and approximately forty-five miles north of Breslau. The report said Polish cavalry was in the action.

[The Polish Telegraphic Agency reported earlier that Polish cavalry had driven German forces from Rawics and Leszno, which they had captured in a surprise attack on Friday.]

The agency quoted the following communiqué issued last night by the Polish supreme command:

"During the day the German air force carried out raids on numerous unfortified towns, including Warsaw, Deblin, Radom and Cracow. Near Radom and Cracow twenty-six enemy aircraft were brought down. The total number brought down today was sixty-four. The Polish losses amounted to eleven machines. German raiders did not spare the peasant population working in the fields near their villages.

"Considerable enemy forces launched a strong attack in the direction of Silesia and in the direction of Podhale. Under the pressure of the enemy, Polish forces were compelled to abandon Czestochowa on the Silesian frontier.

"Our lines were slightly pressed in the Silesia sector. In the north Polish troops recaptured Puck and Orlowo,"

In an air encounter over Poznan late yesterday, Exchange Telegraph said, six German bombers were shot down near Wolbrom after they had dropped a number of gas bombs.

The agency said that the German radio had announced that a German Army had crossed the Warta (Warthe) River yesterday east of Wielun in Western Poland.

An attempt by Polish troops to

Continued on Page Four

BRITISH NAVY ACTS

It Cuts Off Entrances to the Baltic, North and Mediterranean Seas

LONDON IS UNSHAKEN

Declaration of War Is Met With Resolve—Air Alarm Orderly

Special to The New York Times.

WASHINGTON, Monday, Sept. 4.—The British Government has ordered a naval blockade of Germany, according to information reaching officials here tonight. This government has not been informed officially by the British Government of this fact, however.

It was understood here that the naval blockade went into effect immediately upon the declaration of war and that British naval vessels were blocking the entrance to the Baltic Sea near Skagerrak and were stretched across the North Sea near the Scandinavian peninsula. It was also understood here that the entrances to the Mediterranean at Gibraltar and Suez were being carefully controlled.

Both Britain and France were cloaking their naval and military moves with greatest secrecy and neither the Navy nor the War Department had specific information about them up to 8 o'clock, Eastern standard time, tonight.

Britain Is Determined

By FREDERICK T. BIRCHALL
Special Cable to The New York Times.

LONDON, Monday, Sept. 4.—At last midnight Great Britain had been at war with Germany for thirteen hours. France had been at war for seven hours—since 5 o'clock.

A darkened London, in which only hooded red and green crosses at the traffic halts, invisible from above, indicate that there are streets, houses and human life below a clear starry sky, awaits calmly the air attacks that it confidently expects despite Chancellor Hitler's professed desire to avoid bombing open cities. Even these tiny indications will be extinguished the moment that sirens hoot their warnings of approaching raiders.

There are few people in the streets because the authorities have broadcast warnings to every one to stay at home and to go out no more than is necessary. Cinemas, theatres and every other form of entertainment likely to draw a crowd have been shut down by order for the time being, at least. Only the churches have held their customary services.

People Grimly Determined

Thus war has come to Britain, to a people grimly determined to meet it and to see it through. The predominating sentiment, if any, is one of relief that the long period of suspense is over. Throughout the land the watchword now is "Let's get on with it."

War became a reality yesterday morning just after the church bells had ceased ringing. It came in the shape of a sudden interruption of the regular radio program by an announcer:

"The Prime Minister will broadcast an important announcement to the nation."

Then came Mr. Chamberlain's well-known voice, quiet and sad but clear and firm:

"I am speaking to you from the Cabinet room at 10 Downing Street."

Then followed his terse narration of the course of events. That morning (it was actually at 9 o'clock, two hours earlier) the British Ambassador at Berlin had handed Foreign Minister Joachim von Ribbentrop a final note stating that unless the Germans had agreed by 11 o'clock to withdraw their troops from Poland, a "state of war would exist between us."

"I have to tell you now," continued Mr. Chamberlain in the same level tones, "that no such

Continued on Page Four

FIRST SHIP SUNK IN THE WAR
The Athenia, with 1,400 aboard, torpedoed off the Hebrides.
Wired Photo—Times Wide World

List of the American Passengers Aboard the Torpedoed Athenia

Special to The New York Times.

WASHINGTON, Monday, Sept. 4.—The list of American citizens who embarked on the liner Athenia in Liverpool follows; no addresses were given in the cable received at the State Department from Ambassador Joseph P. Kennedy:

Ralph Ruffieau	Sarah Warenreich	Ernest Ratcliffe	Ethel Russell
Katheryn McGuire	John Hughes	Faith Ratcliffe	William Bohn
Hasel Casserly	Gertrude Reed	Irene de Munn	Ada Bohn
Charles Grant	George Cattle	Edward O'Connell	Montgomery Evans
Florence Malik	Rhoda Thomas	Aileen Philipsen	Franklin Dexter
Edith Bridge	William Hinds	Mary Steinberg	Cathleen Schurr
Harry Bridge	J. Davis	Ralph Child	Agnes Stappel
Robert Harris	William Peers	Peter Birchall	Lillian Eilstrap
Gustaf Petersen	Lillian Peers	Duncan Wood	Rose Churchill
Margaret Buchan	Charles Prince	Ellin Ratcliffe	Ellen Howland
Laura Cattle	Harold	Donald Gifford	Mirarine Dexter
Mrs. Thomas	Etherington	Jozef Karnowski	Maud Shearer
Kerr	Ellen Harrington	Doris O'Connel	Alexander
Kate Hinds	Jessie Forle	John Youngquist	Sheshunoff
Herbert	Francis Cooley	Donald Edwards	Cosby Eilstrap
Spierelberg	Charles Prince (two Charles Princes)	John Lawrence	Sarah Burdett
Mrs. Davis		Tryphene Humphrey	Yvette Pepin
Margaret	Geoffrey Etherington	Louise Horte	Ena Logan
McGuire	R. Casey	Mary, Dick and Edward Belton	Herbert Bonn
Elizabeth Wiss	George Kelliher	Elsa Philipsen	Thomas Quine
William	Harry Treheance	Adolph Sadowski	Lulu Swiegard
Buchanan	Ella Trehearne	John Harju	Romona Allen
Master Charles	Annie Word	Charles Stork	Gus Anderson
Grant	Duncan Wood (Two Duncan Woods)	Harold Ruggs	Eleanor Crowley
Bernice Jansen		Adolph Leocha	Harriet Tolley
Constance Bridge		Florence Dery	Janet Elsen
		Wiktor Ponjola	Annie Quine
			Carol Allen
			Susan Allen

The following Americans boarded the Athenia at Glasgow, the American Consulate there reports:

James Boyle	Margaret Wilkes	Joseph MacDonald
Cathryn Brennan	Donald Wilkes	Elmetta MacDonald
Margaret Campbell	William Wilkes	
Elva Campbell	Myrtle Barber	Gus Anderson
Agnes Craig	Barbara Bradfield	Caroline Rice
William Diller	Joan Outhwaite	William Bown
Margaret Diller	Alberta Wood	Ada Bown
Louis Diven	Lucile Lucas	Elizabeth Lewis
Mary Diven	Elizabeth Martin	May Lewis
Ma, y Dowie	Gertrude Martin	Donald Lewis
Thomas Fielder	Ila Vincent	William Aitken
John Bernard	Michael Flynn	Anne Baker
Margaret Ford	Alice Robinson	Alma Bloom
Cora Gilroy	Robert Townsend	Dorothy Feder
Don Gilroy	Bainbridge Hayden	Martha Bonnet
Helen Hannah	Dirus Ekaube	William Brown
Jar Hannah	Doris Elaine Kent	George Calder
Harriet	William Ralph Singleton	Alice Chalmers
L'Fadzean	Sarah Bloom	William Chalmers
Mary McKellar	Olive Bloom	Margaret Doggett
Alexander Nichol	Fred Tinney	Eileen Duncombe
Edith Nichol	Madeline Tinney	
Marion Nichol	Charles Cotterman	
Alice Tocklington	Simeon Price	
John Pringle	Elizabeth Alton (two listed)	
Lottie Tringle	Louis Burns	
Katherine Scott	Mary Burns	
Essie Mallery	Harrietta Jones	
William Mallery	Joan Moffett	
Helen Stewart	Elsie Moffett	
Edgar Wilkes		

The names of the Americans who boarded the Athenia at Belfast could not be obtained up to 5 o'clock this morning.

News dispatches from Europe and the Far East are now virtually all subject to censorship.

HIT OFF HEBRIDES

Ship Bound for Canada Carried Some Children Among Americans

CAPITAL IS SHOCKED

President's Aide Notes Liner Had Refugees, Not Munitions

By The Associated Press.

BELFAST, Northern Ireland, Monday, Sept. 4.—All persons aboard the sunken British liner Athenia, except some killed by a German torpedo, were reported saved today.

An agent of the ship's owners here issued the report. He said all survivors had been picked up by other vessels.

By The Associated Press.

LONDON, Monday, Sept. 4.—The British liner Athenia, with 246 United States citizens among her 1,400 passengers, was torpedoed and sunk 200 miles off the Hebrides, the British Ministry of Information announced early today. [Washington reports 292 Americans were aboard the Athenia.]

The United States Embassy, checking on the departures of Americans hurrying home in flight from the European war, said 101 boarded the ship at Liverpool and 145 at Glasgow. [Forty-six more Americans boarded the vessel at Belfast, Washington was informed.]

The Athenia sailed Saturday from Liverpool.

The British Ministry of Information said the 13,581-ton ship reported to the Admiralty she had been torpedoed 200 miles off the Hebrides, west of Northern Scotland.

The Ministry of Information said the last official information received by the Admiralty from the ship was that she was sinking "rapidly." Since there were no further advices, it was then assumed she had gone down.

Stephen Early, secretary to President Roosevelt, said in Washington that official reports indicated the Athenia was carrying "mostly Canadians and some Americans."

"I'd like to point out," he said, according to The Associated Press, "that, according to official information, the ship had gone from Glasgow to Liverpool and was bound for Canada, bringing refugees."

["I point this out to show that there was no possibility, according to official information, that the ship was carrying any munitions or anything of that kind."]

292 Americans Were Aboard

WASHINGTON, Monday, Sept. 4 (AP).—Dispatches to the State Department indicated today that at least 246 [later news brought the figure to 292] Americans were aboard the liner Athenia, torpedoed in the North Atlantic.

White House Is Informed

Special to The New York Times.

WASHINGTON, Monday, Sept. 4.—Information received here last night that the Cunard White Star liner Athenia had been torpedoed off the coast of Ireland while en route to the United States brought a prompt acknowledgment from the White House acknowledging receipt of the news and information from the State Department that it had received eighteen long-distance calls within a few minutes of a radio broadcast of the news. The calls appealed for information about relatives aboard.

The White House said that the vessel was bound from Glasgow and Liverpool to Montreal with a large group of Canadian passengers and with an undetermined number of Americans aboard.

At 6 A. M., British Summer Time [1 A. M. in New York] Ambassador Joseph P. Kennedy cabled State Department as follows:

"Admiralty unable as yet to indicate whether Athenia had rescue arrangements; 101 American citizens embarked on her at

Continued on Page Five

The New York Times.

LATE CITY EDITION
Generally fair and cooler today and tonight. Tomorrow fair with moderate temperature.
Temperature Yesterday—Max., 84; Min., 64

Section 1

VOL. LXXXVIII....No. 29,821   Entered as Second-Class Matter, Postoffice, New York, N. Y.   NEW YORK, SUNDAY, SEPTEMBER 17, 1939.   PPP   Including Rotogravure Picture, Magazine and Book Review.   TEN CENTS   TWELVE CENTS Beyond 200 Miles Except in 7th and 8th Postal Zones.

Copyright, 1939, by The New York Times Company.

SOVIET TROOPS MARCHED INTO POLAND AT 11 P. M.; NAZIS DEMAND WARSAW GIVE UP OR BE SHELLED; FIERCE BATTLE IS RAGING ON WESTERN FRONT

2 SENATORS BLAST EMBARGO REPEAL AS LEADING TO WAR

Clark, Disavowing Filibuster, Asks Prolonging of Session to Curb Rule by Decree

DEFENDS 'INSULATIONISTS'

Vandenberg Calls Favoring Any Belligerent 'Unneutral' and Urges 'Middle Ground'

By TURNER CATLEDGE
Special to The New York Times.

WASHINGTON, Sept. 16—The fight over lifting the embargo against export of arms was intensified further today as Senators Clark of Missouri and Vandenberg of Michigan aimed new blasts at the Administration's program to alter the Neutrality Act at the special session of Congress.

Following upon the radio address last night of Colonel Lindbergh, the Senators, a Democrat and a Republican, took up Senator Borah's thesis—that the issue was more of intervention or non-intervention in the affairs of Europe than of mere methods of neutrality.

Senator Clark's remarks were contained in a statement telegraphed from his home in St. Louis for release at the capital.

Senator Vandenberg made his plea to his own constituents at a Republican rally at Grand Rapids, telling them not to allow their minds to be taken off domestic problems by the agitation over the conflict abroad.

In his address, Senator Vandenberg declared that the arms embargo should not be repealed by a revision of the present neutrality laws.

"In my view," he said, "it is not 'neutrality' for us to change that code today to make it fit some favored belligerent, no matter what our sympathies. In my view, that is unneutrality. It is trying to be half in this war and yet to safely stay out. I do not believe there can be any such middle ground."

Clark for Check on Executive

"I welcome the President's call for an extraordinary session of the Congress," Senator Clark said in his statement.

"Since the President has by proclamation declared the existence of a national emergency, it is the duty of the Congress to remain in session and share fully in the responsibilities of government during the duration of the national emergency. This is and should remain a government by law and not by decree.

"So far as the Neutrality Act is concerned there has been no suggestion of a 'filibuster' on the part of any of the Senators who oppose the emasculation and perversion of the whole neutrality policy heretofore adopted by the Congress and approved by the President by the repeal of the provision for a mandatory arms embargo.

"The suggestions of a 'filibuster' have been put out in inspired articles from Washington and Hyde Park designed to promote a gag rule and stifle free and fair discussion of perhaps the most important question of public policy which has confronted the Congress of the United States since that tragic day in 1917 when the decision was made to throw the United States into the World War.

Sees Decision on "Taking Sides"

"We are now to determine whether or not we have learned anything from that awful experience by deciding whether by repealing the arms embargo we shall again deliberately set our feet on the path which inevitably leads to war.

"Those of us who oppose the abandonment of a bona fide neutrality policy stand precisely where President Roosevelt stood in his eloquent Chautauqua speech in 1936 when he was a candidate for re-election when he said in defending the law containing a mandatory arms embargo:

"'We are not isolationists except in so far as we seek to isolate ourselves completely from war.'

"My friend, Senator Elbert Thomas of Utah, one of the leading revisionists, let the cat out of the bag the other night as to the real position.

Continued on Page Thirty-seven

HOTEL ESSEX—Doctor's popular hotel—opposite Pennsylvania Station. Famous for food.—Advt.

White House Gate Closed To Keep Out Trysting Cars

Special to The New York Times.

WASHINGTON, Sept. 16—Neither war rumors of wars, but the popularity among motorists of the White House grounds on Summer nights is the reason one of the iron gates on Pennsylvania Avenue is now closed after dark and a guard stands at the other, day and night, to tell all comers that only those having appointments may park their cars inside.

People have been driving in, especially at night, and parking there, Mrs. Roosevelt revealed at a press conference today. And though it is a pleasant place to sit, under the trees, the White House driveway is really not a good trysting place, she said. Too many motorists were attracted by it.

As the number of parking parties increased, so did the problem of keeping the driveway open and free of obstruction. Now an extra all-night guard is on duty, from dark to dawn, to keep it so.

LATIN TRIP FOR FAIR PLEDGED BY MAYOR

'If They Want Me to Go, I Am Going,' He Says—Crowds Set New Record for Saturday

By SIDNEY M. SHALETT

• Clarifying his position as the possible World's Fair ambassador of good-will to South America, Mayor La Guardia, in two statements yesterday, agreed that he would go "if necessary," but hinted that the trip might not take place for at least several months.

There was even a third statement issued by Stanley Howe, the Mayor's executive secretary, to settle the "incident" created Friday night when Grover A. Whalen, Fair president, announced in the Mayor's absence that La Guardia would fly "at an early date" to sell the United States' neighbors to the South on the idea of participating in the 1940 exposition.

As Mr. Howe viewed it, the Mayor would like, with permission of the State Department, to make a trip both to sell South American nations on the 1940 Fair and to "unsell" them on any totalitarian ideas that may have crept in.

These matters yesterday were exceedingly important to the administrators who run the Fair, but despite all the flurry about South American envoys and European participation the Fair itself was entertaining the biggest Saturday crowd in its history. From early morning on thousands of visitors streamed past the turnstiles, and early in the evening it became evident that a new record for a Saturday would be set.

The Mayor issued his first statement shortly after noon, after a hurried dash from the World's Fair City Hall to Hoboken to see Mr. Whalen off on the Statendam. The Fair president, who had made the announcement Friday in which the Mayor did not fully concur, was sailing for Europe as salesman for the 1940 Fair.

Boat Held Up for Mayor

Arriving at the dock only four minutes before sailing time, Mayor La Guardia induced the captain to hold up the boat until he could hurry aboard, have a word with Mr. Whalen and pose with him for a farewell picture. It was such an eleventh-hour affair that the last gangplank was partly dismantled and had to be made secure again before the Mayor and his retinue could leave the ship.

Then, on the pier, the Mayor gave out the following statement concerning the South American plans:

"There are a great many preliminaries. If it can do the Fair any good, and if these necessary preliminaries can be made, and if there is a real need, I'll go. But there is nothing definite yet."

Then he whisked off in his car. His next appearance, late in the afternoon, was at a ceremony at the United Spanish War Veterans at the Court of Peace at the Fair. There he was asked again if he would fly south, and this time he made it a little stronger.

"I'll do anything that is helpful and necessary for the World's Fair," the Mayor said. "If they want me to go, I am going. Of course, that requires a good deal of preliminary preparation and is already—

Continued on Page Forty-eight

6 U. S. SHIPS KEPT IN PORT AS SEAMEN HOLD OUT FOR PAY

Stalemate Results Over War Risk Insurance Demands— No Solution Seen Near

FRIED CALLS 12 SAILORS

Plans Inquiry on Tie-Up of American Trader—Owners Say Capital Must Act

American merchant shipping was badly hampered in New York harbor yesterday when the crews of six vessels refused to sail their ships, insisting on concrete concessions to their demands for extra compensation for entering European waters affected by the war.

With Federal agencies already overburdened by the unusual duties laid on them as a result of the war, confusion reigned on the waterfront, and at a late hour there appeared to be little chance of solution or compromise.

Two of the ships, one with passengers, were to have sailed Friday afternoon but their crews staged a sit-down strike after signing the ship's articles. In other cases, the men declined to sign the articles, leaving vessels with no manning force.

Fried Sends Out Summonses

On the United States liner American Trader, which was at the Chelsea piers of the company with passengers and cargo, twelve union men received summonses from the office of Captain George Fried, supervising inspector of the Bureau of Marine Inspection and Navigation.

The summons in each case was returnable immediately at 45 Broadway, but a representative of the National Maritime Union appeared in the men's stead and received an adjournment until 10 A. M. tomorrow, allowing the union time to obtain counsel for them.

Captain Fried had boarded the American Trader on Friday night and had been at the piers yesterday, but he declined to reveal the nature of the charges to be filed against the men, saying that the public would be admitted to the hearing.

He also declined to explain why only twelve of the seventy seamen had been called, or to say how they had been selected.

Will Set Up Special Board

He planned to constitute a "C" board to preside at the inquiry, headed by himself and including Captain Karl Nielsen and Howard C. Bridges, inspectors of the district. The "C" board would sit in the same manner as a grand jury, to determine if charges should be filed against the men.

The National Maritime Union, which has disclaimed responsibility for the strike on Friday, issued a

Continued on Page Forty-six

Blast Shakes Offices Of Reich Air Ministry

By The Associated Press.

BERLIN, Sunday, Sept. 17—An explosion occurred in the Air Ministry headquarters on the Leipzigerstrasse early today. Firemen and police closed off an extensive area around the building.

The Propaganda Ministry acknowledged that there had been an explosion, but no immediate explanation was forthcoming. It was reported that no one had been injured. There was shattered glass in the street, but the extent of the damage was not immediately apparent.

The Propaganda Ministry refused to speculate whether the blast might have been caused by a bomb. It said merely that an investigation was under way.

"The persons responsible are being sought energetically," a Propaganda Ministry spokesman declared.

The blast came during the regular nightly blackout and the streets were deserted.

TOKYO MINIMIZES SOVIET AGREEMENT

Denies Non-Aggression Pact Is to Follow Truce—Policy on Russia Is Held Unchanged

By HUGH BYAS

Wireless to The New York Times.

TOKYO, Sept. 16—Japanese officials emphatically deny and characterize as "absolute nonsense" reports that a non-aggression pact with Russia is under negotiation or is contemplated. They also deny that Germany had a hand in arranging the armistice on the Manchukuoan-Mongolian border or that German influence could induce Japan to change her policy toward the Soviet.

The Japanese Government regards the armistice as a means of terminating the border fighting. It is part of the new Cabinet's policy for a speedy settlement of the China "incident." Not only does it assure peace on the Mongolian frontier, it is asserted, but it shows Generalissimo Chiang Kai-shek that he cannot expect further diversions in the north, and it helps demonstrate that the Soviet has lost faith in the possibility of a Chinese victory.

According to Domei, the Japanese news agency, the armistice is a definite help toward a settlement in China by enabling Japan to devote her entire energy to the impending peace moves. When asked what Russia receives, the Japanese answer is that she wins a cessation of potentially serious disputes with Japan and possibly certain territorial concessions during the frontier adjustment.

On the broader question whether the armistice is a first step toward a revolutionary realignment of world forces, officials suggest that the move is adequately explained

Continued on Page Thirty-two

Major Sports Yesterday

BASEBALL

The Yankees clinched their fourth consecutive American League pennant under Manager Joe McCarthy and equaled the record set by John McGraw's Giants of 1921 to 1924. It was the eleventh flag victory for the New Yorkers, who beat the Tigers at the Stadium, 8–5. The second-place Red Sox lost. In Cincinnati the Reds halted the Giants, 6–1, and maintained their lead of three and a half games over the victorious Cards.

GOLF

Marvin (Bud) Ward of Spokane defeated Ray Billows of Poughkeepsie, N. Y., 7 and 5, to win the national amateur championship on the North Shore Country Club links, Glenview, Ill. Ward is the first Pacific Coast golfer to take the title.

TENNIS

Welby Van Horn upset John Bromwich, 2–6, 4–6, 6–2, 6–4, 6–5, to gain the final of the national singles championship with Robert L. Riggs, who eliminated Joe Hunt, 6–1, 6–2, 4–6, 6–1. Miss Alice Marble and Miss Helen Jacobs entered the women's final.

HORSE RACING

Hash won the Edgemere Handicap at Aqueduct, where Merry Knight annexed the Junior Champion Stakes. At Chicago, Challedon captured the Hawthorne Gold Cup. Farndale took the Foxcatcher National Cup Steeplechase at Fair Hill, Md.

POLO

The Bostwick Field four beat Westbury, 9–6, in the first match of the national open tournament.

[Complete Details of These and Other Sports Events in Section 5.]

GERMANS SET BACK

Heavy Counter-Attacks Repulsed by the French Drive

NAZIS BLAST TOWNS

Gamelin Hits at Three Points in Saar Area, Hardest on Moselle

By G. H. ARCHAMBAULT

Wireless to The New York Times.

PARIS, Sept. 16—The French are bringing up more and more troops on the western front, where the fighting grows fiercer daily. That is the salient point in the French headquarters communiqués today. This morning's bulletin, Communiqué 25, said:

"There was a restless night on numerous parts of the front. Enemy artillery was very active in the region south of Saarbruecken.

"Our troops made some progress east of the Moselle.

"A strong enemy counter-attack, following artillery preparation, was driven back in the region near the lower valley of the Nied River."

This evening Communiqué 26 announced:

"There was great activity on both sides on the part of artillery and of first-line troops on the entire front.

"The enemy is constantly reinforcing before us.

"At several points the enemy abandoned and destroyed several of his villages from which he retreated."

Battle West of Saarbruecken

The heaviest fighting at present is on that portion of the front running some twenty miles west of Saarbruecken. The object is the possession of observation points dominating not only the Saar Valley but also certain parts of the Westwall.

The specific purpose of the German attack near the River Nied, which is a tributary of the Saar, is to regain a number of observation points along the plateau from which the town of Saarlautern can be brought under the fire of French guns.

After artillery preparation the German infantry left its cover for a swift attack. The duration of this preparation, however, had sufficiently indicated its purpose. The French guns came into action as soon as the infantry got on the move and the attack was soon stopped. It is reported that the Germans employed a relatively large force for this attempt.

There is also heavy fighting for the Saar bridgeheads. The possession of the banks of the river at divers points is important for the bringing up of heavy tanks.

That the Germans should be bringing up reinforcements continuously, as reported in the evening communiqué, may imply the intention of attempting stronger counter-attacks than any hitherto. It may even suggest an endeavor to wrest the initiative from the French. It is manifest that important developments may be expected soon.

Three Main Sectors

As the second week of the war ends, the operations on the west front are clearly divided into three main sectors. These are, reading the map from the east to the west:

1. From the Rhine, in the vicinity of Lauterbourg to the highway from Zweibrucken to Bitche.

2. From this highway to a point on the Saar north of Forbach, taking in Saarbruecken, the industrial heart of the Saarland.

3. From this point west of Saarbruecken to the Moselle River in the vicinity of the village of Peri.

In each of these three sectors French troops are operating on German soil.

At the beginning of the hostilities the eastern sector was the most active, with the French occupation of the forest called Bienwald, in order to gain ground at the point where the Maginot Line and the Westwall describe a right angle before following the Rhine southward. In that valley itself scarcely a shot has been fired as yet; the garrisons of the respective fortified lines are merely sentries.

Continued on Page Forty-two

The International Situation

A Poland already tottering under the blows of the German military machine was subjected to another invasion last night, this time by Soviet forces, according to an official announcement in Berlin.

It was declared that the Russian Government had informed the Polish Ambassador that it was marching in "to protect its own interests and to protect the White Russian and Ukrainian minorities."

Nevertheless, Moscow said, Soviet neutrality is being maintained. Berlin said the action had German sanction. [Page 1.]

The German sweep in Poland was unabated. Kutno, Bialystok and Przemysl fell. But at Warsaw the invaders were still encountering furious resistance. As a result they issued an ultimatum to the Poles to quit Warsaw within twelve hours on pain of bombardment of the entire city. [Page 1.] The effects of previous bombardments and air raids on the Polish countryside were described by a correspondent, who found towns in flames, inhabitants wailing over ruins of homes and chaos everywhere. [Page 28.] In general, military experts found that Poland's despair was undermining her resistance. [Page 40.]

Meanwhile, the "Battle of the Saar," snowballing daily into a major engagement, was being fiercely fought. The French reported that after a heavy artillery exchange the Germans had destroyed and abandoned several villages and had retreated. [Page 1.]

In the face of continued harrying of commerce by German submarines, which yesterday sank two more British ships, the Admiralty set up convoy service for merchant vessels. [Page 1.] Three South American countries, Argentina, Brazil and Uruguay, fearing violations of their neutrality by belligerent warships, were negotiating to pool their naval strength for protection of the entire coast of South America. [Page 31.]

The full significance of the Russo-Japanese truce on the Mongolian border was still unclear, as was Germany's role, if any, in its conclusion. Japanese officials emphatically denied reports that a non-aggression pact with Russia would follow, insisting that Japan remained an anti-Comintern power. [Page 1.] But one result of the new truce emerged in the form of reports that the Japanese, freed of fears for the Manchukuoan border, had launched a general offensive in Central China. [Page 30.] In London news of the truce was received with equanimity; statesmen there had become accustomed to surprises from Moscow. [Page 34.]

In this country Senators Clark and Vandenberg rallied to Senator Borah's fight against alteration of the Neutrality Act. [Page 1.]

MERCHANT CONVOYS SET UP BY BRITAIN

Guard Pressed After Her Loss of 21 Ships—Three More Vessels Are Victims

By The Associated Press.

LONDON, Sept. 16—The British Admiralty pressed into service tonight convoys for merchant ships after it was disclosed authoritatively that enemy craft had sunk twenty-one British ships, involving a tonnage of 122,843, during the first two weeks of the war.

The use of convoys was not instituted by the British in the last war until 1917.

While slim cruisers and racing destroyers roved and struck on the shipping lanes, planes of the Royal Aircraft patrolled the skies around the United Kingdom in redoubled efforts to halt the persistent shipping losses to U-boats or mines. Despite the casualties, naval quarters expressed optimism about the situation at sea.

Understatement in Reports

Increasing patrol activity and the Admiralty's cautious announcement that "a number of U-boats have been destroyed," was taken by naval authorities to tell a story of far greater successes than the guarded statement indicated.

Britain placed responsibility on Germany for the sinking last night of the 8,000-ton Belgian motorship Alex Van Opstal in the Channel off Weymouth, asserting she was sunk by mine or torpedo in violation of international law.

[In Brussels, Belgian authorities refrained from lodging a protest, pending a report from the master of the vessel as to whether she was sunk by torpedo or mine.]

A British communiqué said there were no British mines in the neighborhood, that Germany had sent no notification of German mines there and that attack without warning was in violation of the submarine protocol to which Germany subscribed.

[The Alex Van Opstal left New York on Sept. 6 for Antwerp with eight passengers and 3,400 tons of grain.]

The latest ship to be added to the list of British losses was the tanker Cheyenne of the Anglo-American Oil Company, any, which was announced officially to have been attacked and sunk by a submarine off the southwest coast of Ireland.

The Anglo-American Oil Company, according to Poor's Manual—

Continued on Page Forty-six

ORDER GIVES POLES 12 HOURS TO LEAVE

Nazis Say Citizens Will Have to Take 'Consequences' Today Since Army Is Defiant

Wireless to The New York Times.

BERLIN, Sept. 16—The German Army High Command has given Warsaw until 3:10 o'clock tomorrow morning to decide whether or not to surrender. In the event the Polish capital does not give in to the German troops now surrounding it on all sides, the city will "take the full consequences of being regarded as a military factor."

[The German High Command reported at 4:30 o'clock this morning, an hour and twenty minutes after expiration of the ultimatum, that its army in the field had had no word from the Polish authorities. The Associated Press reported.]

The notice was served in the form of a double ultimatum: First, a military ultimatum expiring at 3:10 o'clock tomorrow morning, and the second ultimatum to the civilian population to leave the city by 3:10 o'clock in the afternoon [10:10 A. M. New York time.]

A German officer entered Warsaw with a white flag at 8 o'clock this morning to demand the surrender of the city. According to the report of the official German News Agency the commandant of the city refused to see him or accept a written demand for the surrender of the city.

The officer, it is stated, thereupon returned to the German lines and this afternoon a squadron of the German air force dropped the pamphlets.

Nazis Cite Law Violation

Warsaw already has been subjected to a partial bombardment by the German air force and artillery but, according to German report, only objects of a military nature have been fired upon. Preparations for defense by the civilian population, however, are regarded by the German High Command as being a "violation of international law depriving the city of its character as an open city." German shells and German bombs will crash into the city tomorrow afternoon unless it is "surrendered without resistance" by dawn tomorrow.

"The patience of the German Army is now exhausted," states the official news agency. "The German Army is no longer willing to observe inactively the conditions which are a slap in the face of all international law, but is determined to put an end to these activities of the Warsaw power holders which, though of no importance whatever in a military sense, constitute a

Continued on Page Forty

FRONTIER CROSSED

Reich Ministry States That Invasion Has German Sanction

ENVOY IS NOTIFIED

Soviet Pleads Need to Aid Minorities, but Claims Neutrality

By The United Press.

BERLIN, Sunday, Sept. 17—A spokesman for the Propaganda Ministry announced that Russian troops had marched into Poland today at 4 A. M. Moscow time [11 P. M. Saturday in New York].

The Soviet troops entered Poland with the full knowledge and approval of the German Government, he said.

The spokesman made his statement after D. N. B., the official German news agency, had reported from Moscow that the Soviet Government had informed the Polish Ambassador, Dr. Waclaw Grzybowski, Saturday night that Soviet troops were about to cross the frontier.

The agency said that the note handed to the Ambassador said the troops would cross the frontier along its entire length from Polozk in the north to Kamenets-Podolsk in the south "in order to protect our own interests and to protect the White Russian and Ukrainian minorities."

The Soviet Government, the agency said, told the Poles that it maintained its neutrality despite its military action, but added that its treaties with the Polish State could be regarded as canceled because the Polish State could no longer be regarded as existing.

To Occupy Two Districts

MOSCOW, Sunday, Sept. 17 (P)—Soviet Russia has decided to send her army across the Polish frontier today and to occupy the Polish Ukraine and White Russia.

The government was understood unofficially to have sent a note last night to the Polish Ambassador here saying that the Red Army would enter the Polish Ukraine and White Russia today from Polozk to Kamenets-Podolski.

Copies of this note was said also to have been sent simultaneously to all diplomatic representatives here saying the action was taken because Poland no longer exists. It was said to have declared there no longer is a Polish Government because its whereabouts are unknown.

The note was said to have declared that "the Soviet Union will retain neutrality, but feels it necessary to protect White Russian and Ukrainian minorities in Poland and will do everything to keep peace and order."

[Poland not only has a non-aggression pact with Russia but in mutual assistance treaties by which the British and French are pledged to aid Poland in defense of her independence against any aggression. Polish invocation of this treaty brought Great Britain and France into war against Germany on Sept. 3, two days after a German army invaded Western Poland.]

Covers Entire Frontier

The scene of the Russian action would extend across the whole of Russia's Polish frontier.

It would include neighboring Russia's frontier with Rumania. Rumania holds Bessarabia, severed from Russia after the World War, and the Soviet Government never has relinquished its claims on this territory.

Russia's decision to act came after she had sent a vast number of men to her western frontier in semi-mobilization, and had followed with her "peace" with Japan.

It was believed here that the Polish Embassy in Moscow would leave and that, possibly, the British also would leave, since they are allies of Poland.

Man Power Is Threat

If necessary, Soviet Russia could throw nearly 2,000,000 trained soldiers against the struggling Poles. The official Communist party newspaper Pravda this Spring estimated Russia's peacetime army at 1,800,000. This estimate did not include the millions of semi-trained

Continued on Page Thirty-five

Dispatches from Europe and the Far East are now subject to censorship.

"All the News That's
Fit to Print."

The New York Times.

LATE CITY EDITION
POSTSCRIPT
Mostly cloudy, mild temperatures
today, followed by light rain.
Temperatures Yesterday—Max., 51; Min., 30

Copyright, 1939, by The New York Times Company.

VOL. LXXXIX...No. 29,895.   Entered as Second-Class Matter,
Postoffice, New York, N. Y.   NEW YORK, THURSDAY, NOVEMBER 30, 1939.   P   THREE CENTS NEW YORK CITY
and Vicinity | FOUR CENTS Elsewhere Except
In 7th and 8th Postal Zones.

RUSSIANS START THEIR INVASION OF FINLAND; PLANES DROP BOMBS ON AIRFIELD AT HELSINKI; WAR STARTS AS U. S. MOVE FOR PEACE IS MADE

KUHN FOUND GUILTY ON ALL FIVE COUNTS; HE FACES 30 YEARS

Leader of the Bund Here Will Be Sentenced Tuesday as Thief and Forger

JURY OUT FOR 8½ HOURS

Defense Counsel Rebuked by the Court as Clashes Mark Final Day of Trial

Fritz Kuhn, the leader of the German-American Bund, was convicted shortly after 10 o'clock last night of grand larceny and forgery in General Sessions Court.

He stood up, with only his forefinger on his left hand waving along the side seam of his trousers, and heard without a blink the verdict of a jury that had deliberated eight and a half hours. The maximum sentence he can receive is thirty years, and the day on which he will hear his plea was set by Judge James G. Wallace as Tuesday.

Pending the sentence Judge Wallace told Peter L. F. Sabbatino, the counsel who had defended Kuhn during his trial in General Sessions Court, that action on a promised contempt of court would be suspended until then. He gave Mr. Sabbatino leave to make any motions he desired in the intervening time.

Kuhn marched off to the Tombs with the stoical attitude of a good German soldier, which he says he once was. There was no tremor on his face, and the three courtroom bailiffs who surrounded him when Morris C. Bullock, the foreman of the jury, pronounced him guilty, had only to tug at his sleeve to lead him away to prison. There was not even an interchange of glances between him and Mr. Sabbatino or Wilbur V. Keegan, associate counsel.

What the Verdict Meant

The verdict was that he was guilty of grand larceny in the first and second degree in the theft of $717 from the bund to pay for the transportation of the furniture of Mrs. Florence Camp across the country, and of second degree larceny and two counts of forgery in the "Murray transaction."

The Murray transaction was a $500 item which Kuhn listed on the bund books of record and told the bund members that he had paid to James D. C. Murray for legal services. These two items, totaling $1,217, were all that the jury had to pass on of an indictment which originally charged thefts amounting to more than $14,000.

One pair of counts, dealing with more than $8,000 charged against Kuhn as a theft had been eliminated before the trial began and Judge Wallace knocked out another pair charging that he had stolen $4,424 of the bund funds because, the judge ruled, the prosecution had not proved this beyond a reasonable doubt.

During a long afternoon and early evening while the jury was out, Kuhn sat in the court room talking to his counsel. He had sandwiches brought in to him and munched on them while Assistant District Attorney Herman J. McCarthy, who prosecuted him, walked the corridors of the Criminal Courts Building.

Part of Charge Is Re-read

After seven and a half hours the jury came in shortly before 9 P. M. to ask Judge Wallace for a re-reading of a part of his charge dealing with the Camp transactions.

When the verdict finally did come in a half-hour later he stood up again. But this time the bailiff who was behind him asked him to step outside the rail enclosing the space for the attorneys, and as he stood there two other bailiffs came up behind him.

The precaution of three men surrounding the man who says his war record covered service as a machine gunner in Alpine service during the World War was not necessary. He made no move and there was no sign of emotion on his face. The index finger of his left hand wiggled spasmodically. But he did not even move his head.

Then, in a voice that was not even audible a few feet away, he gave his "pedigree" to a bailiff. He said he was born in Germany forty-two years ago and revealed

Continued on Page Twelve

Must Stay Day in Mexico Or Pay San Diego Duties

Special to THE NEW YORK TIMES.

WASHINGTON, Nov. 29 — The twenty-four hour limit goes into effect Friday on the Mexican border in the San Diego Customs District and persons wishing to avail themselves of the $100 customs exemption on goods brought into this country must stay in Mexico at least twenty-four hours.

Collectors have been instructed that in their discretion they may permit tourists staying a shorter time to bring in products with an aggregate value of not more than $5 without paying duty.

The unusual situation in the San Diego district is created by the proximity of the Free Port of Tijuana, into which European merchandise may enter duty-free. Large retail establishments there maintain billboards along the roads to Tijuana advertising bargains on selected European imports.

CITY WILL SET UP A 'BOOSTER' BUREAU

Mayor Reveals Plans for New Department to Attract More Business Here

Reviewing the accomplishments of his administration before a gathering of merchants and property owners yesterday, Mayor La Guardia disclosed plans for still another project for the betterment of the city—a Department of Commerce—to bring more business and industry here.

He told the Central Mercantile Association at its Fall luncheon in the Hotel Pennsylvania that he had often boosted New York on his frequent flights out of town and that now he would have a municipal organization for this purpose, "and I am going to out-small-town the smallest town in the country."

The Mayor had reviewed the difficulties of city finance, education costs, the new pension plan for policemen and firemen, the Sixth Avenue improvement, transit unification, plans for North and South Avenues, the North Beach Airport and the new information bureau under the Park Avenue ramp in Pershing Square, not mentioning other accomplishments.

Will Combat Adverse Reports

"We have been confronted with a lot of small-town stuff about business in New York being more costly than elsewhere," he then went on. "I am going to out-small-town the smallest town in the country. I am going to establish a 'Department of Commerce which will have the function of providing information and advice to business men interested in coming to New York."

The Mayor's bureau will add no cost to the city government, he said, because he will "pick up employees from various city departments to do the work." He also will invite business and labor here to cooperate, he said, adding that "labor will have to assume its responsibility and I expect it to do its part."

The first step in the functioning of such a new program, the Mayor said, has already been taken in his invitation to the film industry to return to New York. He said there was no reason why this industry should be centered in one city "but we should have our share." He reported that, "notwithstanding ridicule and opposition, we are making progress."

Ryan Seen as Likely Head

A report that a municipal department of commerce would be established was published last Sunday but had not been publicly acknowledged by the Mayor until yesterday. The report said that Clendenin J. Ryan, Deputy Commissioner of Sanitation, would head the new department and would be sworn in as its first Commissioner this week.

In his address, which lasted for more than an hour, the Mayor dwelt particularly on his new pension plan for policemen and firemen. The establishment of the plan was prompted by the fact that any pension plan in existence July 1, 1940, will, under constitutional amendment, become a contractual obligation of the city.

The Mayor noted that the Legislature had failed to provide the policemen and firemen pension system

Continued on Page Twelve

DIES AT RALLY HERE WARNS U.S. TO STOP ITS 'APING' OF EUROPE

10,000 Cheer His Plea for National Unity and a Fight on All Alien Forces

HE PLEADS FOR TOLERANCE

Calls on Administration to Provide Funds to Continue Work of His Committee

Speaking last night in Madison Square Garden before an enthusiastic throng estimated at 10,000 to 12,000 persons, representing many patriotic and religious organizations, Representative Martin Dies of Texas denounced communism, fascism and nazism as alien forces tearing at American unity. He made a strong plea also for racial and religious tolerance.

Asserting that there was an organized campaign to discredit the work of the Congressional Committee Investigating un-American Activities which he heads, Mr. Dies made a demand for public funds with which to continue hearings on subversive groups next year. He also called on the Administration, which he implied was opposed to the drive against foreign "isms."

On this question Mr. Dies got strong support from the audience and from the other speakers, who urged those present to demand from Congress an appropriation that would preserve the committee as it is.

The husky, 6-foot Representative who has achieved national prominence since he was named chairman of the committee in 1938 was escorted to the platform by a guard of American Legionnaires as the drums of the Seventh Regiment band announced him with a fanfare.

Mr. Dies's-speakers were Colonel George U. Harvey, Borough President of Queens; Joseph P. Ryan, president of the International Longshoremen's Association; Jeremiah Cross, past State commander of the American Legion; Laurens Hamilton, president of the New York State chapter, Sons of the American Revolution, and Jean Mathias, New York State commander, Jewish War Veterans of the United States.

As chairman of the meeting, Merwin K. Hart, president of the New York State Economic Council, opened the meeting at 8:30 P. M. Frederick Jagel of the Metropolitan Opera sang the "Star-Spangled Banner," although he advocates the adoption of a new anthem for the United States.

Among those who attended, it was reported but not confirmed, were

Continued on Page Thirteen

Intelligence Chief Quits; Dutch Blame Venloo Case

Wireless to THE NEW YORK TIMES.

AMSTERDAM, the Netherlands, Nov. 29—Major Gen. J. W. van Oorschot, 64-year-old head of the Netherlands intelligence service, resigned today. He had headed the department since 1919.

Observers are inclined to link his resignation with the Venloo frontier incident.

THE HAGUE, the Netherlands, Nov. 29 (UP)—The Venloo incident involved the shooting of a Netherlands intelligence officer, Lieutenant Klop, and the kidnapping of two British intelligence agents and a chauffeur by German Gestapo (secret police) agents. General J. W. van Oorschot, who resigned today, was responsible for sending Lieutenant Klop to Venloo.

The British version of the incident was that two British intelligence officers, Sigismund Payne Best and Captain Richard Henry Stevens, went to Venloo to investigate presumably legitimate German peace talk on Nov. 9.

REICH OIL SITUATION VIEWED AS CRITICAL

Germany Isolated From Great Sources of Supply—Imports From U. S. Virtually Ended

Special to THE NEW YORK TIMES.

WASHINGTON, Nov. 29.—The oil situation in Germany, especially the Reich's reserve of fuel oils, is the most serious problem facing the Hitler government today, in the opinion of American naval and military experts. Export data in the Department of Commerce appear to substantiate this opinion.

Germany is one of the few great nations without oil resources and since the war started she has received virtually no crude, lubricating or gasoline supplies from the United States. One market that under normal conditions would be in a position to make up at least part of the deficit.

Official statistics, plus reports considered reliable, all indicate that Germany is completely isolated from the great oil markets of the world. So grave is the situation that Germany is making frantic efforts to develop synthetic gasoline plants, which, it is hoped, may be in partial operation by the middle of 1940. Even the Germans do not expect the plants to be operating to capacity before the end of 1941.

Any hopes the Germans might have of getting appreciable quantities of oil from the Russian fields are dispelled, according to official information, by the fact that Russia is having a hard time producing enough for her own needs. This

Continued on Page Seven

HULL ACTS QUICKLY

Offer of Good Offices in Ending Dispute Sent to Finland and Russia

HELSINKI LIKELY TO AGREE

But Moscow's Reaction Is Held to Be Highly Problematical —Pittman Assails Soviet

U. S. Offer Received

By The United Press.

MOSCOW, Thursday, Nov. 30—The United States' offer to mediate in the Soviet-Finnish dispute was received at the American Embassy here at 10:30 A. M. (3:30 A. M. Eastern Standard Time).

The offer will be presented or delivered to the Soviet Foreign Office some time this morning by Walter Thurston, Chargé d'Affaires.

By BERTRAM D. HULEN
Special to THE NEW YORK TIMES.

WASHINGTON, Nov. 29.—The increasingly serious developments in relations between Russia and Finland led the United States today to proclaim her readiness to extend good offices for a pacific adjustment of the points at issue, if that should be agreeable to both parties.

The move was made in an effort to leave no stone unturned that would prevent a spread of European hostilities. It was in the form of a statement issued by Secretary of State Cordell Hull after several telephone conversations with President Roosevelt. In particular, it represented their views of a way in which the American Government could throw its weight into the solution of the dispute by peaceful processes only, this government would, if agreeable to both parties, gladly extend its good offices.

Text Is Cabled to Envoys

The force of a diplomatic appeal was given the statement when Secretary Hull late today cabled the text to the United States Legation in Finland and the United States Embassy in Russia with instructions that it be delivered to the Foreign Offices.

The statement was issued at 3:05 P. M., one hour before word was received of Russia's severance of diplomatic relations with Finland, and an hour and a half before its press carried reports of the speech of Vyacheslaff M. Molotoff, Soviet Premier and Foreign Commissar.

In comment on the statement the State Department said it did not constitute intervention, nor did it necessarily mean mediation. It simply meant, it was stated, that this government is using what efforts it can to help Russia and Finland settle the dispute themselves.

Although Secretary Hull merely expressed a readiness to extend good offices if Russia and Finland are agreeable, his action threw open the possibility of an adjustment that might be worked out along any one of several lines. An offer of good offices, mediation and arbitration are the three recognized methods for pacific adjustment of disputes under The Hague conventions of 1907 and have been utilized by the United States on many occasions, particularly in Latin America.

In the case of an offer of good offices the country making the tender sets no limitations upon the forms that will be used in seeking to facilitate an adjustment. It could be by diplomatic conversations, mediation, arbitration, reference to a commission of inquiry or any other method. The country making the tender, moreover, usually does not figure in the ad-

Continued on Page Six

The International Situation

Soviet Russia severed diplomatic relations with Finland last night and this morning the Red Army crossed the border while Soviet planes bombed the airfield at Helsinki. Explaining the break over the radio, Premier Molotoff said that Finnish hostility had become "unbearable," and virtually demanded that a different government be set up in Helsinki. He also indicated rejection to a tender of good offices by the United States. [Page 1.] This offer had been made by Secretary Hull after he had been in touch with President Roosevelt. [Page 1.]

Finland, meanwhile, revealed that the Russian action had been taken before she had delivered a note to the Kremlin offering to withdraw troops from the border and suggesting conciliation. [Page 1.]

London evinced friendliness for the Finns and welcomed the news of the American offer. [Page 6.] Likewise Italy, fearing that near-by Rumania might next claim Russia's attention, expressed through her press sympathy for the Finns. [Page 7.] Germany, on the other hand, supported Russia, although she indicated that her attitude if a conflict began would be one of "benevolent neutrality." [Page 4.]

Japan, a possible sufferer from the hostilities at sea, studied measures of reprisal against the Anglo-French blockade of German exports. It was reported that such measures might include seizure of Allied cargoes in the Orient. [Page 1.]

In the Balkans the Rumanian Foreign Minister turned down Hungary's revisionist demands, but at the same time invited her to help improve relations between the two countries. [Page 10.]

Today Premier Daladier will go before the French Parliament and ask, with every expectation of success, that his emergency powers be continued. [Page 9.]

The Reich's most serious problem of the moment, according to Washington experts, is its critical oil situation. Germany was revealed as completely isolated from the world's oil markets. [Page 1.]

There was little actual war activity during the day. The British reported having driven off two German air raid attempts. [Page 2.] The French said one of their patrols had penetrated deep into German territory in the Vosges sector and had brought back valuable information. [Page 8.] And at sea two more British ships were sunk. [Page 3.]

JAPAN MAY SEIZE CARGOES OF ALLIES

Studies Plan for Reprisals if Anglo-French Ban on Reich Exports Continues

By HUGH BYAS
Wireless to THE NEW YORK TIMES.

TOKYO, Thursday, Nov. 30—The Japanese Government is considering retaliatory measures against Great Britain's two-way blockade of Germany. These may include seizure of Anglo-French ship cargoes in Far Eastern waters.

This threat appears in the newspaper Nichi Nichi this morning as part of the report of a conference held at the Foreign Office yesterday to discuss the British reply to Ambassador Mamoru Shigemitsu's protest against the Order in Council for seizure of German exports on neutral ships.

Reports from other sources indicate that interference with Anglo-French shipping in the Far East still is a somewhat distant possibility, depending on the British response to Japan's demand for special consideration under the German imports. Asahi says that Mr. Shigemitsu has been instructed to press the British Government to give assurances that Japanese trade will receive special consideration in enforcement of the blockade.

The Foreign Office conference in which Foreign Minister Kichisaburo Nomura, Vice Foreign Minister Masayuki Tani and several bureau chiefs participated, found the British order had been formulated in flexible terms so that its effect could not be ascertained until it had been enforced. It was decided to await the text and to continue the policy of pressing Britain to give consideration to Japan's "important" imports from Germany.

If the Japanese representations to Britain are disregarded, a further measure will be considered in the terms of Japan's original protest, which threatened appropriate counter-measures.

Continued on Page Three

BORDER IS CROSSED

Soviet Artillery Opens Fire as Troops March in Karelian Sector

AIR RAID WARNING SOUNDED

People Run to Shelters as the Capital Sees Russian Planes —Five Bombs Are Dropped

Special Cable to THE NEW YORK TIMES.

COPENHAGEN, Denmark, Thursday, Nov. 30—At 9:15 A. M. today the first Russian troops crossed the Karelian frontier into Finland. At 9:20 o'clock an air raid warning was sounded in Helsinki, causing panic in the streets.

At 9:25 o'clock Russian bombers flew over the Finnish capital.

Five Bombs Dropped

HELSINKI, Finland, Nov. 30 (UP)—Five bombs were dropped on the city's airfield today. A report from the border station at Terijoki said Russian troops had opened artillery fire against the Finns early this morning.

The bombing of Helsinki occurred a few minutes after a Russian two-motored airplane flew over the city, driving people to shelter.

Earlier, a squadron of six Russian airplanes had been sighted over the Gulf of Finland, approaching the city.

Finnish anti-aircraft guns fired on the squadron as well as on the single plane over the capital. Finnish anti-aircraft batteries fired on the plane here and coastal batteries attacked the Russian squadron in the gulf.

FINLAND IS BLOCKED IN MEDIATION PLEA

Note Delivered After Rupture Offers to Recall Troops— Soviet Move Awaited

The text of the last Finnish note appears on Page 5.

By The Associated Press.

HELSINKI, Finland, Thursday, Nov. 30—Profoundly disturbed by Moscow's action rupturing diplomatic relations, but still determined to stand fast, Finns uneasily awaited developments today, fearing the beginning of hostilities at any time. But early this morning officials said there had been no troop movements across the borders so far as they could learn.

It was all the more shocking to the Finns because the Moscow action came before they could deliver a note to the Kremlin offering to withdraw Finnish defense forces from the frontier as a gesture toward settling their quarrel.

The offer was made by Foreign Minister Eljas Erkko in his reply to Russia's denunciation of the 1932 Finnish-Soviet non-aggression treaty.

"My government is ready to settle with the Soviet Government the question of the removal of Finnish defense forces on the Karelian Isthmus, with the exception of frontier customs guard forces, to such a distance from Leningrad that it could not even be alleged that they threaten its security," Mr. Erkko's note said.

Making a Sincere Effort

He prefaced this statement with the explanation that Finland was motivated by a desire "to prove emphatically that there is a sincere effort to reach an accord with the Soviet Government and refute the Soviet Government's allegations that Finland has adopted a hostile attitude toward the U.S.S.R. and is desirous of threatening the security of Leningrad."

Despite the breaking off of diplomatic relations, and despite the midnight broadcast of Soviet Premier Vyacheslaff M. Molotoff, who announced the action, Finland's note answering Moscow's denunciation of their non-aggression pact was delivered to the Kremlin at 1:10 A. M., Moscow time.

It was almost three hours after Mr. Molotoff had notified the Vice Commissar of Foreign Affairs, Vladimir Potemkin, had notified the Finnish Minister that relations were broken.

The Finnish answer said the Russia unjustified in denouncing the non-aggression pact and suggested that a conciliation commission be named to examine the controversy.

The news from Moscow spread rapidly through Helsinki. Grim Finns gathered in clusters to discuss the situation. Government of-

Continued on Page Five

Molotoff Proclaims Split

By G. E. R. GEDYE
Wireless to THE NEW YORK TIMES.

MOSCOW, Thursday, Nov. 30—Premier Vyacheslaff M. Molotoff announced in a thirteen-minute radio speech last midnight the breaking off of diplomatic relations with Finland by the Soviet Union through the recall of all Soviet diplomatic, consular and economic representatives in Finland. At the same time he warned all units of the Red Army and Red Navy to stand ready for every emergency.

In contrast to the last Soviet note to Finland and in glaring contrast to the abusive violence of the inspired press and radio campaign, Mr. Molotoff's speech, except for one important particular, refrained entirely from international usage.

Although it accepted, of course, without any effort to substantiate their accuracy, all the Soviet charges concerning the alleged extraordinary violations of the frontier by the Finns in the last few days, the language was restrained and contained indications that the Soviet was prepared to grant concessions to reach a settlement—with the "Finnish people." In that, however, lay the important exception to conformity with international usage.

Appeals to 'Finnish People'

Despite the sentences asserting no desire to interfere in internal Finnish affairs and that the Finnish regime's relations with other States was exclusively the affair of Finland, the speech directly appealed over the heads of the present Finnish Government "to the Finnish people." Thus it confirmed the belief expressed more than once that the Soviet Union intended to try to force the surrender of the bases demanded from Finland through a change in the Finnish Government rather than through involving the Soviet Union in an invasion of Finnish territory.

By these passages of his speech Mr. Molotoff would seem to have confronted the Finnish Government with the alternatives of immediately recalling its diplomatic mission from Moscow at the peril of a still further increase in Soviet military pressure, if not of invasion, or of resignation. If the latter alternative were chosen, it would open the

Continued on Page Four

Unofficial Thanks to Be Given Here Today By Irreconcilables Clinging to 'Old Style'

It will be just another day on New York's official calendar today, but half the nation, led by New England, will observe Thanksgiving with a determination to make the celebration of the traditional day outshine the "new Thanksgiving" fixed by President Roosevelt and marked by the other half of the country a week ago.

They will 'be 'oin'-d here in unofficial joy by those New York irreconcilables who refuse to eat turkey on any but the last Thursday of November, by those who have children coming home from school or college in "old-style" States, and by those who feel that any holiday is worth celebrating again even if it did occur only seven days before. These double celebrators will be following the example of Colorado, Mississippi and Texas, which are observing a second holiday in addition to the one last week.

Including these three, twenty-six States have proclaimed today as Thanksgiving Day. Americans in Sao Paulo, Brazil, dissenting from their fellows in Rio de Janeiro, and most other Americans abroad will observe the day—which has been termed the "Republican Thanksgiving" in contrast to the "New Deal Thanksgiving" of Nov. 23.

In New York many theatres are giving special matinees, and numerous restaurants will have turkey dinners for those who wish to partake. Private clubs are in some cases holding special events which were scheduled for today before the President changed the date. The Volunteer Rescue Army, which fed turkey to 2,018 unemployed last week, will give the same menu today for 3,000 at its chapel at 379 First Avenue.

Magistrate Henry H. Curran, sitting in Felony Court yesterday, declared he would observe the holiday today to "give thanks for the twenty-three States that didn't fall for this tyrannical novelty which came out of Washington." But he will eat chicken because "it's not fair to make the turkeys suffer on two days."

In Highland Park, N. J., a suburb of New Brunswick, school pupils will be dismissed at 1 P. M. as a "gesture toward those who believe the day is still the old-time Thanksgiving."

Rutgers University, in New Brunswick, will observe its second Thanksgiving today to permit students to go to Providence, R. I., to the Brown-Rutgers football game. Mayor C. D. White of Atlantic City has also proclaimed today as a second Thanksgiving.

The nation's principal observance

Continued on Page Five

Norway Adds Her Protest

OSLO, Norway, Nov. 29 (UP)—Foreign Minister Halvdan Koht announced today that the Norwegian Government has made representations to the Allied Governments regarding their decision to seize German exports.

The Norwegian Government, Mr. Koht said, "fails to see how such a move can be in accord with international law." He added that Norway claimed the right to demand compensation for any losses involved, and urged Great Britain to reconsider her decision. Norway is

Continued on Page Three

Dispatches from Europe and the Far East are subject to censorship.

"All the News That's Fit to Print."

The New York Times.

LATE CITY EDITION
Cloudy and colder today. Tomorrow partly cloudy with slowly rising temperatures.
Temperature Yesterday—Max., 43; Min., 31

VOL. LXXXIX...No. 29,909.

Entered as Second-Class Matter, Postoffice, New York, N. Y.

NEW YORK, THURSDAY, DECEMBER 14, 1939.

Copyright, 1939, by The New York Times Company.

PP

THREE CENTS NEW YORK CITY and Vicinity | FOUR CENTS Elsewhere Except in 7th and 8th Postal Zones

BRITISH DEFEAT NAZI RAIDER IN ALL-DAY FIGHT; SHE RUNS TO MONTEVIDEO WITH 36 DEAD, 60 HURT; U-BOAT SUNK, REICH CRUISER HIT IN NORTH SEA

A.F.L. LEADER SAYS NLRB 'PLAN' SAVED LEWIS' COAL UNION

Area Jurisdiction Ruling Led Thousands to Quit the Rival P.M.W., Ozanic Tells Inquiry

'SHOOTING' ORDER CHARGED

NLRB Report Said U. M. W. Officer Urged This Treatment for Progressive Miners

By The Associated Press.

WASHINGTON, Dec. 13—Joe Ozanic, young leader of the Progressive Mine Workers (A. F. L.), charged before a House investigating committee today that the National Labor Relations Board had followed a "plan" to give the United Mine Workers (C. I. O.) "a way out" in the desperate rivalry between the two unions.

The "plan," as he described it, was embodied in a controlling decision, which certified the C. I. O. union as the bargaining agent for all the coal mines in a specified geographic area. This was done, he said, despite provable majorities for the Progressives in individual mines affected.

As a result, he asserted, the United Mine Workers and employers in the field had forced thousands of Progressive members to switch to the C. I. O. union, and pay its dues, regardless of their own desires in the matter.

In one instance which he cited, that of the Acme Semi-Anthracite Coal Company of Williams, Okla., members of the Progressive union were unemployed, he said, because their jobs had been taken by miners imported by the United Mine Workers.

Bitterness of Feud Evidenced

All the accumulated bitterness of the fierce battle between the C. I. O. and the American Federation of Labor was epitomized for the committee in the day's testimony. Mr. Ozanic spoke repeatedly of "Dictator John L. Lewis," and of alleged "coercion" by C. I. O. members against his own followers.

At one point Edmund M. Toland, the committee's counsel, introduced a memorandum from Philip G. Phillips, the West Virginia regional director of the Labor Board, which quoted "Van Bitner" as having advised United Mine Workers' organizers to shoot Progressive organizers "faster than they would shoot a rabbit."

"Who is Van Bitner?" Chairman Smith, Democrat of Virginia, inquired.

"Van Bitner," Mr. Ozanic replied, "why, he's the provisional district president for District 17 of the United Mine Workers. He was appointed by Dictator John L. Lewis and never in his life elected by the United Mine Workers. That, gentlemen, is Mr. Bitner."

Later when Van A. Bitner, who spells his name with two "t's" and is president of District No. 17, and also a member of the U. M. W. International Board, denied that he had ever made the shooting statement.

Denial by U. M. W. Official

"That statement of Phillips is absolutely untrue and made out of whole cloth," he told reporters. The memorandum mentioned that "Bitner" spoke at a Labor Day meeting in Charleston, W. Va., but the U. M. W. official said that union held no Labor Day meeting in Charleston in 1938.

When Mr. Ozanic took the stand he told the committee that he started work as a coal miner at the age of 15 and was a member of the United Mine Workers of America.

After twenty-two years in that union, he said that he had fellow-miners in the Illinois fields "seceded" because of the U. M. W.'s dictatorial policies" and formed the Progressive Mine Workers of Illinois in 1932.

The new union soon recruited 28,000 of the State's 42,000 miners, he said, and, he cited, still had them. After the Progressives received an international charter from the A. F. L. in 1938, Mr. Ozanic said, it recruited an additional 80,000 workers in coal fields outside Illinois. To the bitter, however, recovered.

Continued on Page Eighteen

When you think of Writing Think of Whiting—Advt.

Revolutionary Landmark In Queens Being Razed

The old frame building in Elmhurst, Queens, used during the Battle of Long Island as the headquarters of the British Army, was being razed by its present owner yesterday despite efforts of Borough President George U. Harvey to have the property purchased by the city and restored as a historic landmark.

The building, which stands at Fifty-seventh Avenue and Queens Boulevard, was erected in 1762. On Sept. 3, 1776, General William Howe, commanding the British forces, wrote his official report to the King on what happened during the Battle of Long Island six days before, while using the house as his headquarters.

The present owner, Dr. Hevia, Cuban tobacco planter, who has a home in Richmond Hill, decided to raze the building when it became in need of repair. He has no plans for future use of the land.

RALLY HERE SCORES REICH AND SOVIET

Hoover, Landon, La Guardia and Green Are Heard by 20,000 in Garden

Before a mass meeting of more than 20,000 persons who filled every seat in Madison Square Garden last night, former President Herbert Hoover, former Governor Alf M. Landon of Kansas, Mayor La Guardia and William Green, president of the American Federation of Labor, headed prominent Christian and Jewish speakers who joined in protest against the persecution of Jews by Nazi Germany and in an appeal for the mobilization of the moral forces of the world against Hitlerism and Stalinism.

The meeting, held under the auspices of the American Jewish Congress and the Jewish Labor Committee, unanimously adopted by rising vote a resolution asking President Roosevelt to convey American condemnation of the persecution of the Jews in Nazi Poland to the German Government and to use every possible means to succor the victims of the oppression. It was decided to appoint a committee representing the two organizations to take the resolution to Washington.

Hitler and Stalin Booed

Cheering every reference to President Roosevelt's neutrality program, the audience booed equally every mention of Hitler and Stalin. They laughed loudly when speakers ridiculed Nazi and Communist propaganda that Hitler and Stalin are working for peace against the imperialist war aims of England and France.

They also applauded statements that the real issue was the defense of democracy against totalitarianism, whether its label was Nazi, Fascist or Communist, and that Anti-Semitism was only the first step toward the destruction of all religions, labor unions and civil liberties. Many in the audience came to the Garden because of their Jewish faith, but the meeting was not a demonstration in which Jewish membership predominates.

The speakers and the audience made it clear that their protests were aimed at the Russian invasion of Finland as well as German aggression in Poland, and that their appeals for help were directed in behalf of the Finns as well as the Jews in Poland, Austria, Czechoslovakia and Germany.

It was announced that part of a collection taken up at the meeting to defray its expenses and to help Jewish victims of Hitlerism would be turned over to former President Hoover's Finnish relief fund if the collection was large enough. The total was not announced, as the contributions were not to be counted until today.

About seventy policemen were stationed outside the Garden in case of disturbances, but there was no trouble.

Several hundred persons were turned away when the gates of the Garden were closed by Fire Department order at 8:35 P. M., half an hour after the meeting opened. About 200 clustered outside the police lines despite the rain.

Mayor La Guardia received the biggest ovation of all the speakers when he arrived on the platform after flying in from Chicago on a night plane. He expressed his "horror" at what is taking place in Europe and said he hoped that what

Continued on Page Eight

RUSSIA CONDEMNED

League Certain to Expel Her as Committee of 13 Calls Her Aggressor

PLANS AID TO FINNS

U. S. Will Be Invited to Help—Victim One of Invader's Judges

Text of League report on Russia is on Page 6.

By F. J. PHILIP
Wireless to The New York Times.

GENEVA, Dec. 13—Soviet Russia, it is now considered certain, will be thrust forth from the company of the League of Nations, having, in the opinion of her fellow-members, by her own acts placed herself outside the Covenant.

A report by thirteen of them—the committee appointed by the Assembly to consider Finland's appeal—held today that Russia has been the aggressor and called on member States to lend all possible aid to the victim. It also offered the facilities of the League to coordinate such help and suggested that non-members be invited to cooperate.

The report was drafted by a representative composed of the representatives of Great Britain, France, Sweden, Bolivia and Portugal.

In the public meeting of the Assembly during the morning Argentina demanded the expulsion, declaring that she would no longer remain a member of the League if the Soviet Union continued to enjoy that title.

Russia Not Represented

The Russian Government was not there to defend itself and no one cared to assume its defense. Jacob Suritz, Soviet Ambassador to France, anticipating events, had left Geneva on the morning train.

Alternative suggestions to that of expulsion proposed by Argentina were invited. It was stipulated that they should be heard in private committee so as to avoid embarrassment to those who feel that their geographic position as Russia's neighbors affects their judgment of both the legal and moral aspects of the question.

Cuba wanted to speak after Argentina in the Assembly, but was overruled as Mexico and India already had agreed to submit their proposals in private.

The Assembly then prepared one more step on the way to expulsion by electing the Union of South Africa and Finland to the council in the place of New Zealand and Sweden, re-electing Bolivia and shelving until after the council shall have taken its decision on the Russian issue the re-election of

Continued on Page Six

Liner Columbus Cleared For Transatlantic Dash

By The Associated Press.

VERACRUZ, Mexico, Dec. 13—Port authorities disclosed tonight that the 32,581-ton German liner Columbus had obtained clearance papers for a transatlantic voyage and was prepared to sail without further notice.

All crew members on shore leave have been ordered to report aboard to prepare for a "long voyage."

The ship's representatives said her destination was Oslo, Norway.

It was believed that the Columbus would slip from port shortly, but in view of persistent rumors of British warships in the Gulf of Mexico and Caribbean she was expected to sail as secretly as possible, probably at night without lights.

The same agency also arranged for the departure of the German freighter Arauca, also here since the start of the war. The crew was busy this afternoon painting the vessel black.

FINNS REPORT GAIN IN COUNTER-THRUST

Say Russians Are Hurled Back as Major Battle Impends— Soviet Is 'Invaded'

By The United Press.

COPENHAGEN, Denmark, Thursday, Dec. 14—Heavily reinforced Finnish troops early today were reported to be laying siege to the strategic town of Salla, just above the Arctic Circle, where the Russians were said to have lost 7,000 men.

The Finns, concentrating large forces in an effort to prevent the Red Army from reaching the Gulf of Bothnia and cutting Finland in two, hoped to recapture Salla today, frontier dispatches said.

Salla is about 125 miles northeast of the top of the Gulf of Bothnia at the Swedish-Finnish border and slightly northeast of the town of Kemijaervi, where fierce fighting was reported.

Thrust Into Russia Reported

[Finnish forces had carried the war to Russian soil in a strong drive north of Lake Ladoga, according to unofficial reports in Helsinki. This followed closely the reported bombing of the Soviet's Leningrad-Murmansk railway, which was said to have halted an attempt to transport submarines to the Arctic.]

Against the Russians' reported losses of 7,000 men in the new Finnish counter-offensive, the Finns claim to have lost only 250 men.

Continued on Page Nine

NORTH SEA SUCCESS

British Submarine That Spared Bremen Said to Have Scored Twice

NEW TACTICS IN AIR

Planes Patrol Nazi Base to Prevent Laying of Mines at Night

Special Cable to The New York Times.

LONDON, Dec. 13—The British Admiralty announced tonight that the British submarine that sighted and spared the German liner Bremen a few days ago had sunk a German U-boat and torpedoed a German cruiser in the North Sea.

The announcement marked the first time that any British submarine had been in action against enemy seacraft. Details of the British submarine's exploit were not given and officials would not make any comment on the identity of the German cruiser involved.

When asked whether the cruiser had sunk after the torpedoing the officials pointed out that the communiqué specified sinking in the case of the U-boat but used the word "torpedoed" in the case of the cruiser. This was taken to mean the cruiser had been damaged. When the action took place was not revealed.

New Air Patrol Fixed

The Air Ministry issued today a statement hinting at new tactics in the evolving strategy of war in the air and on the sea. British planes, it was said, had maintained an all-night watch over the German seaplane bases at Sylt, Borkum and Norderney in Helgoland bight.

The official announcement indicated that a new arm of defense against air attack had been formed and that it was its duty to squelch attacks from the air on enemy territory instead of awaiting the arrival of Nazi air armadas.

Hindsight is sometimes helpful in interpreting the mysterious diplomatic manoeuvring in these uncertain times, but yesterday's announcement that a British submarine failed to sink the Bremen and the latest announcement that British planes roamed harmlessly over German naval bases last night do not help much in understanding the way this strange war is developing. Presumably, the British Admiralty thinks more was gained diplomatically by the strict observance of international law than could have been gained by the sinking of the queen of Germany's merchant navy. Likewise, it may be presumed the British feel there is more to be gained by sending planes to hover over the nests of Germany's mine-laying fleet than by bombing their bases and that it is better to hold the threat of attack above the Nazi fliers' heads than to try to drive them from British coasts with all the advantage that falls to the fighter who comes fresh to the fray.

Nazis Scoff at Statement

The Germans, of course, scoff at the British statement that they could have sunk the Bremen but did not think it sporting or legal. The truth is, the Germans say, that the British are just trying to put the best face possible on their naval impotence.

The official announcement of the new patrols over the German bases in Helgoland Bight said they were "continuously maintained." That purpose, it was said, was "to interrupt the activities of mine-laying aircraft operating from these bases." Despite anti-aircraft opposition "the operations were successfully carried out."

Today's Air Ministry statement indicated that Britain's method of meeting the new magnetic mine menace included not only some method of sweeping up the destructive eggs laid by planes and submarines in coastal shipping channels but also contemplated measures to prevent their being laid at all. Aviation experts said there was much about the establishment of what already have been dubbed "security patrols" that is mysterious.

It was pointed out, for instance, that the official statement rather indicated that bombing planes were used, that they circled more or less

Continued on Page Four

The International Situation

Britain's far-flung sea power caught up with a raiding German pocket battleship yesterday in the Western Hemisphere.

A running battle was fought during the day and last night off the Uruguayan coast between the Nazi craft, identified as the Admiral Graf Spee, and two small British cruisers, the Ajax and the Achilles. The cruiser Exeter had also been in the battle, but was damaged and forced to drop out. The pursuit continued with hits scored on both sides until the pocket battleship raced into neutral Montevideo harbor badly damaged and with thirty dead aboard. The Ajax and the Achilles followed and lay outside the harbor. [Page 1.]

Under international law Uruguay must now determine the minimum repairs needed to make the German ship seaworthy, and when these repairs have been made the vessel must either put to sea or be interned for the duration of the war. [Page 4.]

London claimed another naval success, reporting that the British submarine that had sighted the liner Bremen on her dash to Germany had sunk a U-boat and torpedoed a German cruiser. At the same time the Air Ministry indicated a new policy of an all-night air patrol over German seaplane bases to frustrate aerial mine-laying. [Page 1.]

Following his adventurous voyage homeward, the Bremen's commander declared at a reception that he believed the fleet had been held up in New York last August to help the British. [Page 3.]

While the Finns reported having thrown the Russians back in counter-offensives and were unofficially said to have carried the war to Russian soil [Page 1], a League of Nations committee condemned Russia as an aggressor, called for all possible aid to the Finns by members and non-members alike and suggested expulsion of the Soviet, a development that now seems certain. [Page 1.]

What the League was doing was still kept from the Soviet people. [Page 8.] But a hint that Moscow was not insensitive to criticism was seen in the hasty summoning home of the new Russian Ambassador to Rome, who had not yet had time to present his credentials. [Page 1.]

While the British House of Commons in its first secret session since the World War debated Opposition charges of government bungling on supplies [Page 11], peace talk in Britain, though confined to non-official sources, was emphasized by a policy of an all-night air patrol by Foreign Secretary Halifax to characterize the debate as "unfortunate." [Page 1.]

SOVIET CALLS HOME NEW ROME ENVOY

Italians Believe He Will Be Asked How Seriously They Mean Balkan Warning

By HERBERT L. MATTHEWS
By Telephone to The New York Times.

ROME, Dec. 13—Nikolai Gorelchin, the new Russian Ambassador, who has not yet had time to present his credentials, was hastily summoned back to Moscow by telegram and left Rome on Monday, it was learned today. The Russian Embassy claims it is a mere informative visit without particular significance and that Mr. Gorelchin, on the new Count Ciano, the Foreign Minister, last week, will return to Rome shortly.

However, it is at least a coincidence that his sudden recall should come at a time when there are almost daily hostile demonstrations against Russia and when the Fascist Grand Council, to say nothing of the entire Italian press, has been issuing warnings to Moscow to keep out of the Balkans. One is entitled to suppose that Joseph Stalin wants to know just what the Italians mean and how serious they are with their threats.

Italy's Earnestness Clear

If that is what his visit is about, Mr. Gorelchin will doubtless inform his government that Italy means business, for genuinely strong measures are being taken to parry the expected Russian thrust, should it try to go beyond Bessarabia. On the other hand, the Soviet Government may have become sensitive about criticism and hostility and may not intend to send Mr. Gorelchin back here.

In connection with the press criticism, Roberto Farinacci's newspaper, the Regime Fascista, offers a novel explanation for the Russo-German alliance. After saying that Finnish resistance has proved Russian weakness, the writer concludes:

"So when England, France and the Osservatore Romano [the Vatican City newspaper] speak of the Russian peril, it is in bad faith. Russia preferred the German alliance because she thought that if she had to fight Germany she would be beaten."

Premier Georges Kiosseivanoff of Bulgaria, in an interview with the Giornale d'Italia's correspondent today, says that while Bulgaria has not renounced "the realization of

Continued on Page Seven

BRITISH PEERS URGE NEW PEACE MOVES

Mediation Call Hurts Nation, Halifax Replies—Commons Holds Secret Session

Special Cable to The New York Times.

LONDON, Dec. 13—The question of making peace now and without military victory arose in the House of Lords today in a debate described by Foreign Secretary Viscount Halifax as "unfortunate because it would create a wrong impression abroad that Britain was not united in her determination to fulfill her war aims."

The debate centered around the problem of whether a lasting peace could be obtained at this time and whether a long war would not mean that the country paid a terrible price in vain.

[Meanwhile the House of Commons in its first secret session since the last war debated for seven hours and a half Opposition charges that the government is bungling the production of vital war supplies.]

The debate was precipitated by a suggestion from the Earl of Darnley that Britain take u, the Belgian and Netherland proposal for mediation, which, he said, is still open. Supported by Lord Arnold and the Bishop of Chichester, he said Britain had not done enough after the Versailles treaty to conciliate Germany and warned against a "revenge-producing victory."

Three Peers Reply

Lord Balfour, Viscount Samuel and Lord Snell opposed the Earl amid cheers. Lord Balfour declared there was a reign of violence and terror in Germany, "and as long as that persisted any idea that there was a change of heart or that a freely negotiated peace was possible was illusory."

Lord Darnley maintained that Chancellor Hitler's actions were aimed partly to make Germany free and prosperous but chiefly to make her free from any danger in the future, and every threat made against him made him think aggression more necessary.

Lord Arnold said it was unfortunate the Earl's proposal could not be discussed at a secret session. He contended that laying down peace conditions in advance did not help negotiations, and hindered them. He added:

"If a satisfactory peace could be secured in other respects, this country would not wish to continue the war on account of Austria."

Lord Arnold believed that if the war continued until Herr Hitler was overthrown by revolution, Germany would become Communist and enter into an alliance with Russia. He feared that communism might spread over Eastern Europe and "not only would any peace at the end of a long war be

Continued on Page Twelve

Davies Will Resign as Envoy to Belgium To Become an Adviser on Europe to Hull

By FELIX BELAIR Jr.
Special to The New York Times.

WASHINGTON, Dec. 13—Joseph E. Davies is soon to give up his post as Ambassador to Belgium and take a place in the special division of the State Department dealing with war emergencies.

The Ambassador's resignation is lying on the President's desk. Whether it was offered when Mr. Davies called on the President today or was sent ahead of his return to the United States was not ascertained. The resignation was technical, in any event. Arrangements for the transfer were completed several weeks ago.

The duties to be assigned to Mr. Davies will be similar to those now being performed by Hugh R. Wilson, who recently resigned as Ambassador to Germany, and Breckinridge Long, former Ambassador to Italy. President Roosevelt is said to be desirous of putting the details of the emergency situations abroad in the hands of diplomats who have had experience in the field.

Mr. Davies entered the diplomatic service as Ambassador to Russia and later was transferred to Brussels. He has been credited at various times with an ambition to represent this country in London. He returned to this country yesterday.

ostensibly to participate in negotiations over revision of the reciprocal trade agreement with Belgium.

It was at the Executive Office today after conferring with the President, Mr. Davies said that he wanted to be on record as having stated that he was not a candidate for the Secretaryship of the Navy, a post with which the issue has had been connected in recent rumors. Mr. Davies will probably go back to Brussels to wind up the affairs of his ambassadorship and also to participate in official activities incident to the start of operation of the trade agreement.

After it became known that information regarding Mr. Davies's resignation had been obtained by The New York Times, a spokesman of the State Department said that Mr. Davies had been instructed to return here and that he reported today to the President, Secretary Hull and Under-Secretary Welles. The spokesman issued this statement:

"No decision has been reached as to what his future duties will be either in Washington or in the event that he returns to Belgium.

PREY OF 3 CRUISERS

Pocket Battleship Puts In South America Port After 18-Hour Fight

EXETER FORCED OUT

Foe Badly Damaged 1 Ship, but Two Others Continue Chase

By JOHN W. WHITE
Special Cable to The New York Times.

BUENOS AIRES, Argentina, Thursday, Dec. 14—The German pocket battleship Admiral Graf Spee struggled into Montevideo harbor shortly before midnight with thirty-six of her crew dead, sixty wounded and the ship badly damaged as the result of an eighteen-hour running battle with the British cruisers Exeter, Ajax and Achilles.

Shortly after the Graf Spee's arrival two British cruisers, the Ajax and the Achilles, arrived in the outer roads off Montevideo, but at an early hour this morning had not reported to the authorities ashore regarding their casualties.

[Returning from a visit aboard the Admiral Graf Spee, the German Minister to Uruguay, Otto Langman, said that the dead included a lieutenant and the wounded the commander of the ship, The Associated Press reported. His statement that the ship was the Spee and not the Admiral Scheer is reported at first was the first indication that the Graf Spee had been operating in the Atlantic.

[The spokesman for the German Legation at Montevideo said that "there are thirty-six dead and sixty wounded aboard the Graf Spee, mostly because the British used mustard gas shells," The United Press reported. The spokesman said that the damage to the battleship was insignificant.

[Captains of six British ships captured by the Graf Spee off the South American and South African coasts will be landed at Montevideo, the spokesman added.]

Open Fire on the Spee

The British squadron was under the command of Commodore H. H. Harwood.

Contact with the Graf Spee was established six times during the morning when the pocket battleship attacked the Ajax while the latter was convoying the French passenger liner Formosa from Rio de Janeiro to Montevideo. The Ajax called for help and the Exeter and Achilles arrived at full speed and opened fire on the battleship.

The four warships fought an intense artillery duel from 6 o'clock until 10. Despite the Admiral Spee's speed and heavier armament she was repeatedly hit by shells from the British cruisers, especially the Exeter. The Spee, accordingly, directed her main efforts to putting the Exeter out of commission. By this time all four warships were running southward, the Formosa having dropped back for safety.

The Exeter, finally disabled, was forced to drop out of the battle but by this time the Spee was so badly damaged that the commander began running at full speed for the River Plate, closely followed by the Ajax and Achilles.

The battle apparently lasted on and off all day, as the firing was renewed twice after the warships were within sight of the Uruguayan shore. Just after the warships passed Punta del Este, which projects far out to sea, the two British cruisers turned westward toward the shore to take advantage of the setting sun by getting the Graf Spee silhouetted against the reflected light in the eastern sky while they were protected by the shadow of the land.

Spee Changes Her Course

This forced the Spee to change her course and dash disadvantageously to the southeast. Then the British warships renewed their heavy firing, which continued until well after dark. Under cover of night the Graf Spee changed her course and finally reached the refuge of Montevideo.

Continued on Page Four

1940 - 1949

"All the News That's Fit to Print."

The New York Times.

LATE CITY EDITION
POSTSCRIPT
Cloudy, preceded by rain today.
slightly colder tonight.
Temperature Yesterday—Max., 51 | Min., 44

Copyright, 1940, by The New York Times Company.

VOL. LXXXIX...No. 30,026.

Entered as Second-Class Matter,
Postoffice, New York, N. Y.

NEW YORK, TUESDAY, APRIL 9, 1940.

P

THREE CENTS NEW YORK CITY and Vicinity | FOUR CENTS Elsewhere Except in 7th and 8th Postal Zones.

GERMANS OCCUPY DENMARK, ATTACK OSLO; NORWAY THEN JOINS WAR AGAINST HITLER; CAPITAL IS REPORTED BOMBED FROM AIR

HOUSE TO CONSIDER WAGE ACT CHANGES EARLY NEXT WEEK

Leaders in Surprise Moves Also Slate Bill for Court Review of Agency Rulings

LABOR LAW ACTION LIKELY

Proponents of Amendments Expect Drive to Dispose of All Labor Legislation

House consideration next week was slated for the bill to amend the Wages and Hours Act and for the Logan-Walter bill to provide for a court review of decisions by governmental agencies. [Page 1.]

A refusal by the Supreme Court to review the Labor Board's order in the Republic Steel case sustained the reinstatement of 5,000 C. I. O. strikers with $5,000,000 back pay. [Page 20.]

The Socialist party convention, at Washington, stated in a resolution that "the interests of American working men and women will best be served by the making of an immediate peace between the C. I. O. and the A. F. L." [Page 1.]

Colonel Harrington, WPA Administrator, will be questioned Thursday by the House Appropriations Subcommittee on evidence gathered by its investigators bearing on the 1941 relief outlay. [Page 20.]

The NLRB refused to relieve Mrs. Elinore M. Herrick of further responsibility in connection with the election of employes of the Consolidated Edison Company of New York after a charge of collusion with the company. [Page 20.]

Two Revision Bills Slated

By HENRY N. DORRIS
Special to The New York Times.

WASHINGTON, April 8—House leaders decided today on consideration early next week of the Barden bill to amend the Wages and Hours Act, a decision which occasioned surprise in labor quarters since it had been assumed this measure would follow the Smith or Norton amendments to the National Labor Relations Act.

But this was not the only surprise, because the tentative calendar for next week also contained a place for the Logan-Walter bill providing court review of any decision of a governmental agency which has the force of law.

When these two measures are out of the way, proponents of amendments to the Wagner Act expect to win consideration of their measures. Just how they will manage this was not revealed, but it was said by one member that the procedure was for a "Bang! Bang! Bang!" program that would wipe the House calendar clean of labor legislation that has "plagued" it for more than a year.

The Barden bill has been pending since last August, when a rule was granted for its consideration. It was never considered, however, because of the "compromise" by which the lending-spending and United States Housing Authority bills—desired by the Administration—were cleaned up. Both of these failed to obtain consideration, but they served to crowd out the Barden bill, which primarily aims at a redefinition of the "area of production" provision of the Wages and Hours Act.

Would Remove "Ambiguities"

The amendment proposed by Representative Barden of North Carolina, a member of the House Labor Committee, proposes to remove the "ambiguities" of the "area of production" clause and the ruling subsequently made on it by the former Wages and Hours Administrator, Elmer F. Andrews.

Under that ruling processing plants located within ten miles of the area where agricultural products are grown or harvested are exempt from the provisions which require them to pay a minimum wage of thirty cents an hour or work their employes not to exceed forty-two hours per week without overtime pay of time and a half. The Barden amendment proposes

Continued on Page Twenty

The International Situation

War caught up two more countries in its clutches today as the Germans invaded Denmark and attacked Norway.

In the early morning Nazi troops crossed the southern border of Denmark, landed on Danish soil from warships and occupied the Danish capital, Copenhagen—all apparently without resistance. [Page 1.]

Almost at the same time a diplomatic dispatch to Washington announced that Norway was at war with Germany. [Page 1.] This development followed an attempt by German warships—more than 100 of which were sighted last night moving northward in the Kattegat—to force an entry, with aerial support, into Oslo Fjord. At latest reports German troops were debarking on the Norwegian coast and had entered Narvik, Bergen and Trondheim, while the Norwegians were said to have moved their capital, which was reported bombed.

Berlin explained it was taking Denmark and Norway under its "protection" to prevent any hostile attack upon them. [Page 4.]

There had been at least one suggestion yesterday of German troop movements in Scandinavia. A Nazi transport had been torpedoed off Southern Norway with a loss of 150 out of some 300 uniformed men aboard. In the same neighborhood a large German tanker was sent to the bottom. [Page 1.]

The mining of Norwegian waters had taken Norway completely by surprise and eight German freighters were apparently in the same predicament, as they were trapped in those waters and unable to get home. With British warships patrolling the mine fields the ore traffic at Narvik was halted and it seemed likely that Swedish iron shipments would be halved. [Page 3.] Norway protested to both Britain and France against the mining, terming it "an open breach of international law" and demanding that the mines be removed. [Page 1.] London had expected the protest and discounted it. But the British were believed to be ready to go to Norway's aid against the Germans. [Page 2.]

With a loophole in the block-ade apparently plugged in Scandinavia the British gave some of their attention to the Balkans; their envoys to the countries of that region began their conferences. [Page 9.] At the same time Southeastern Europe was startled by Rumania's detention of a fleet of British barges carrying dynamite, which, according to the Germans, was to have been used for blocking the Danube. British quarters insisted the explosives were to have been used only for destroying river craft in the event of a German invasion of Rumania. [Page 1.]

REICH SHIP IS SUNK

150 Lost Off Transport Torpedoed by British Off South Norway

ALL MEN IN UNIFORM

Large Nazi Tanker Also Sunk by Allies, but Crew Is Rescued

Special Cable to The New York Times.

OSLO, Norway, April 8—A British submarine torpedoed and sank the German troop ship Rio de Janeiro today off Lillesand, on the south coast of Norway. At least 150 German soldiers are believed to have perished.

It is reported here that the German transport, formerly a freighter on the South American run, had at least 300 men aboard and that fewer than 150 are accounted for. The ship, of 5,261 tons, was out of Hamburg and was classified here as a transport because all the men aboard were in uniform.

Another large German vessel, the tanker Posidonia, was also reported torpedoed today off the Norwegian coast, but without loss of life.

[Lloyd's Register of shipping does not list a German tanker Posidonia. The Associated Press, in recording the report of still a third sinking, that of the German tanker Kreta, indicated that there might be some confusion over the Posidonia's case, since the Kreta, apparently to conceal her identity, had sent out the call letters of the Posidonia. Other reports said that the Posidonia used the Kreta's signals.]

The report of the torpedoing of the Rio de Janeiro, received here states that the British submarine intercepted the transport off the Norwegian coast, hailed her and fired a warning shot across her bows. This was disregarded and the troopship altered her course, speeding toward land or territorial waters. The submarine then fired a torpedo.

Some Jump Overboard

With the explosion some of the Germans immediately jumped overboard. A Norwegian fishing vessel was near by and went to the rescue, taking these men out of the water.

As the transport appeared to be settling, the submarine fired a second torpedo, with terrific result. An iron bar from the ship was hurled 150 feet and struck the rescuing fishing vessel, killing three of the Germans who had been taken aboard.

The fishing vessel continued its work of rescue and was aided by other fishing craft that hurried out when an alarm was sounded along the coast. These ships took a total

Continued on Page Five

NAZIS IN NORWAY

Troops Debark at Ports —Government Leaves Oslo for Hamar

NARVIK IS OCCUPIED

Air Attacks on Capital Reported—Civilians Are to Be Evacuated

Sweden Is Mobilizing

By The United Press.

STOCKHOLM, Sweden, April 9—The Swedish radio announced today that the government had ordered general mobilization.

Wireless to The New York Times.

LONDON, Tuesday, April 9—The Paris correspondent of Reuters, British news agency, reported this morning that the Oslo radio had announced that German troops had debarked in Norwegian ports at 3 A. M.

[Mrs. J. Borden Harriman, United States Minister to Norway, notified the State Department early this morning that she had been informed by the Foreign Minister that Norway considered herself at war with Germany.

[Mrs. Harriman also reported that at 5:30 A. M. Norwegian shore batteries were still engaged in battle with four invading German warships that were trying to force entry into Oslo Fjord.]

It was also announced that the Norwegian Government had left Oslo for Hamar, in Central Norway.

Reuters further reported that the Germans had occupied the cities of Bergen and Trondheim.

[The Oslo radio announced this morning that the Norwegian Government had ordered general mobilization after an all night session of the Cabinet, The Associated Press reported.]

Reuters also reported from Paris that the Oslo radio announced this morning that the Germans had occupied Narvik.

The Norwegian legation here issued the following communiqué this morning:

"The German Minister in Oslo saw the Norwegian Foreign Secretary at 4:30 o'clock this morning and demanded that Norway should be handed over to the German administration. If this was not done all resistance would be defeated. This demand was refused and hostilities have started."

LONDON, Tuesday, April 9 (AP) —A Reuters, British news agency,

Continued on Page Two

NEW THEATRE OF WAR IS OPENED

German troops invaded Denmark at 5 A. M. today. A few hours previously German warships attempted to force an entry into Oslo Fjord (cross). This action, which brought Norway into the war against the Reich, followed the sighting last night of a German armada steaming northward off Lessoe (3). Near Lillesand (1) a German troop transport was torpedoed by a British submarine and a U-boat was rumored to have been sunk. Off Faerder Light (2) one and perhaps two German tankers were sent down. The Allied mine fields off Norway are indicated by arrows.

NORWAY DECLARES WAR ON GERMANY

Washington Notified of Action by U. S. Minister at Oslo— Warships Sent There

Special to The New York Times.

WASHINGTON, Tuesday, April 9—Norway was at war with Germany. This was the word received soon after 1 o'clock this morning tested to Paris and London against the mining of her waters at dawn by a sudden move by which the Allies hope to cut off Germany's Swedish ore shipments through Norway's western coastal waters.

In a public statement Mr. Koht charged the Allies with an "open breach of international law" and demanded that the mines "be removed at once and that the guard by foreign warships cease." Britain was appticating Norway's waters near the new mine fields, stating such action would be for forty-eight hours to warn away neutral vessels.

In all Scandinavian statesmen, in realization that the dreaded day had arrived bringing the European war to the north, gathered to discuss the cloudy future and await a feared retaliation from Germany.

Leaders of the Norwegian Parliament, which was called into special session, said they were behind the government's action in the crisis. A Cabinet meeting was held in Oslo, which military and naval leaders attended.

Political Leaders Meet

Leaders of all of Denmark's political parties met in Copenhagen, and in Stockholm Swedish leaders watched gravely. The Swedish Foreign Office announced there had been no violation of Swedish waters, but officials admittedly were worried.

The Oslo newspaper Arbejderbladet, a government organ, said that "the situation is particularly grave for our country, but in such times we must keep our heads cool."

"Any tendency toward nervousness or panic would only make it worse," the paper said. "Norway naturally will protest in a most emphatic way against any closing of her waters and demand respect for international laws. But it is a question

Continued on Page Four

ALLIED MINES BRING A PROTEST BY OSLO

Breach of International Law Charged by Koht—Sweden Takes Defense Measures

By The Associated Press.

OSLO, Norway, April 8—Foreign Minister Halvdan Koht told Parliament today that Norway had protested to Paris and London against the mining of her waters at dawn by a sudden move by which the Allies hope to cut off Germany's Swedish ore shipments through Norway's western coastal waters.

In a public statement Mr. Koht charged the Allies with an "open breach of international law" and demanded that the mines "be removed at once and that the guard by foreign warships cease." Britain was applicating Norway's waters near the new mine fields, stating such action would be for forty-eight hours to warn away neutral vessels.

In all Scandinavian statesmen, in realization that the dreaded day had arrived bringing the European war to the north, gathered to discuss the cloudy future and await a feared retaliation from Germany.

Leaders of the Norwegian Parliament, which was called into special session, said they were behind the government's action in the crisis. A Cabinet meeting was held in Oslo, which military and naval leaders attended.

COPENHAGEN TAKEN

Troops Cross Border as Ships Debark Others in Sudden Nazi Blow

DANES FALLING BACK

Germans Say They Act to Forestall Foe and Protect Neighbor

By SVEND CARSTENSEN
Wireless to The New York Times.

COPENHAGEN, Denmark, Tuesday, April 9—German troops crossed the Danish frontier at 5 o'clock this morning.

Three German cruisers arrived at that same hour at Middelfart and troops immediately occupied streets of the town.

Copenhagen was also occupied by German troops this morning.

The invasion came without warning. For some hours before the crossing of the border reports had circulated here that the Germans of South Jutland were expecting German troop trains carrying 45,000 men to arrive at the town of Flensburg during the night. That German town on the border was characterized as a convenient port for shipping troops northward, and although Danish border guards had been put in the highest state of preparedness it was not thought that there would be any threat to Denmark.

This belief had been bolstered by the fact that the fleet of more than a hundred German warships that passed through the Great Belt into the Kattegat and Skagerrak yesterday and early today included troopships—and it was presumed that this fleet was on the way to Norway to retaliate against the British Navy.

More Centers Seized

Mr. Carstensen left Copenhagen after the entry of German forces and went to Kolding, where he filed the following dispatch:

Special Cable to The New York Times.

KOLDING, Denmark, Tuesday, April 9—The German occupation continues here. It is reported that two ferry points on the Great Belt —Nyborg and Korsoer—have been occupied.

Troops have landed at Middelfart on a large scale. A Little Belt bridge has been reported seized and the city of Aalborg in North Jutland has been occupied.

Although there were no reports of clashes between Danish troops and the invaders today, military resistance was expected at Haderslev, about thirty miles north of the German border. The placing of guns and erection of barricades were reported from that town.

After leaving Copenhagen I observed from my automobile swarms of fast German planes flying over towns dropping badly printed leaflets that laid responsibility for Germany's invading Denmark and Norway to what was termed a British intention to make Scandinavia a theatre of war.

The leaflets used Winston Churchill, Britain's First Lord of the Admiralty, "the century's greatest warmonger," who planned to police Norwegian and Danish waters against the wills of the two countries.

The statement said that, since Norway and Denmark were unable to resist effectively, Germany had resolved to act in advance of a British attack and by force took "protection" of Danish and Norwegian neutrality and "guard" the countries during the war. It was asserted that Germany did not intend to obtain bases for her fight against Britain but solely aimed at preventing Scandinavia from being a battlefield for "British expansion of the war."

According to the statement, negotiations were going on between the German and Danish Governments to make Denmark "secure" and assure that her army and navy were maintained and the Danish people's freedom respected. The country's independence, it was said, is fully secured. The ...

Continued on Page Two

ROOSEVELT EFFIGY 'FRONT' GUN TARGET

Healy Also Swears Cassidy Wanted 12 in Congress Shot in Capital as Gesture

Denis A. Healy, star prosecution witness in the trial of seventeen men indicted for conspiring to overthrow the United States Government, testified yesterday in the Brooklyn Federal Court that some of the defendants had used a likeness of President Roosevelt's head as a target during rifle practice.

He swore that John F. Cassidy, a defendant who was prominent in the Christian Front, had favored "going to Washington and shooting twelve Congressmen to show that the Christian Front means business," and he testified that William Gerald Bishop, another defendant, wanted to place Major General Van Horn Mosely, U. S. A. retired, at the head of a dictatorship after overthrowing the present government.

Telling of how members of the group practiced making crude bombs out of empty beer cans, Healy said that they had discussed committing acts of sabotage here if the United States entered the war. He described that Bishop had boasted to him of knowing who was responsible for an explosion he said had occurred on an oil tanker in the lower bay a few days earlier.

Cross-Examination Begun

Healy finished his direct testimony at 2:30 P. M. yesterday after having been on the witness stand for five hours, beginning Friday afternoon. He began at once a hammering cross-examination at the hands of defense counsel, which they estimated would last for at least two full court days in their effort to discredit his story of having been a once been convicted of street fighting, for which he received a suspended sentence.

Conceding that he had testified for the government in a previous case, Healy insisted that he was a "professional witness," as was charged by former Magistrate Leo J. Healy, counsel for eleven of the defendants. He said the government had arranged a leave of absence for him from the New York Central Railroad, and was paying him the same salary while he was

Continued on Page Sixteen

BRITISH EXPLOSIVES HELD BY RUMANIANS

Fleet of Barges Detained at Danube Port—Nazis Charge Plot to Block River

By The Associated Press.

BUCHAREST, Rumania, April 8—Detention of a fleet of dynamite-laden British barges, said by Germans to be designed to blow up a narrow Danube gateway and block a German supply line, today electrified Southeastern Europe with the fear war soon might spread to this quarter of the world.

Rumanian police, acting on a tip said to have been supplied by the pro-Nazi Iron Guard, halted the fleet near Giurgiu, Danube River port whence Germany ships much-needed Rumanian oil supplies. Aboard were tons of dynamite.

Germans alleged the British planned to blockade the spot in the Danube known as the Iron Gate by sinking the barges and wrecking the narrow channel where the river cuts through the Carpathian barrier between high cliffs. The Iron Gate is 280 miles up river from Giurgiu.

Official British quarters, acknowledging the barges were loaded with explosives, insisted they were to be used only for destroying Allied river craft in case of a German invasion of Rumania.

The only official British statement on the matter was a communiqué saying merely that Rumanian authorities had seized two cases of firearms which a British barge captain had neglected to declare in passing customs.

Troops Guard Gateway

The British aim was reported in Germany to be the blocking of the Iron Gate with sunken barges and blasting of the narrow artificial channel through which all river shipping must pass.

Two hundred Rumanian and Yugoslav soldiers armed with machine guns tonight were guarding the gateway where the Danube forms the boundary between Rumania and Yugoslavia. Giurgiu was turned into a military zone by the Rumanian Army, which banned all entries without special permits.

The German version of the seizure, said to have taken place Saturday, reported more than 100 British Army, Navy and Air Force men, who were to have participated in the coup, had been arrested.

Both the Rumanian Foreign Office and British quarters, however, insisted there was no basis for the German reports that Britons had been seized aboard the barges, and official London sources declined to

Continued on Page Eight

Canadian Premier to See Roosevelt Soon, Stopping Off En Route South for a Vacation

By FREDERICK T. BIRCHALL
By Telephone to The New York Times.

OTTAWA, April 8—Prime Minister W. L. Mackenzie King will leave Ottawa in a few days for a short holiday in the South of the United States. On his way through Washington he will pay a visit to President Roosevelt at the White House.

This will be Mr. Mackenzie King's first visit to Washington since war was declared. There are several questions he would like to take up with Mr. Roosevelt. There are doubtless also matters the President will be glad to discuss with the Canadian Prime Minister.

While there is no information here as to the precise subjects that may figure in the conversation, some of those ripe for discussion are well known. Among these are the progress of the St. Lawrence Waterway project, continuance of the trade agreements renewed last year and the extent to which the United States and Canada's war effort.

As to the St. Lawrence project, it is known that all administrations are anxious to have the treaty signed with as little delay as possible so that it may be submitted to Congress in time for consideration before adjournment. Since the

project again came up opposition to it has developed in both countries. It will not have easy sailing.

Among matters even more pressing are the exemption of Americans resident in Canada from the conditions affecting the ownership of foreign currency and securities and the status of American fliers who desire to come here and enlist under for Air Training Plan and for overseas service.

It has been strongly urged that Canada modify for these the oath of allegiance now required from all who join her forces, which does not automatically give them Canadian citizenship, while causing them to lose their own.

Another point of interest is Canada's desire to obtain more airplanes for use in the initial stages of the commonwealth air training plan. The present prospect is that there will be a shortage of planes until Canadian plants, now in receipt of about $40,000,000 worth of orders, can reach the stage of advanced production.

Any or all of these topics may be profitably discussed between the

Continued on Page Five

"All the News That's Fit to Print."

The New York Times.

LATE CITY EDITION
POSTSCRIPT
Fair, not much change in temperature today. Tomorrow cloudy.
Temperature Yesterday—Max 65, Min 47

Copyright, 1940, by The New York Times Company

VOL. LXXXIX...No. 30,057.   Entered as Second-Class Matter, Postoffice, New York, N. Y.   NEW YORK, FRIDAY, MAY 10, 1940.   THREE CENTS NEW YORK CITY and Vicinity | FOUR CENTS Elsewhere Except In 7th and 8th Postal Zones

NAZIS INVADE HOLLAND, BELGIUM, LUXEMBOURG BY LAND AND AIR; DIKES OPENED; ALLIES RUSH AID

U.S. FREEZES CREDIT

President Acts to Guard Funds Here of Three Invaded Nations

SHIP RULING TODAY

Envoy Reports to Hull on Germany's Attacks by Air and Land

Special to THE NEW YORK TIMES.

WASHINGTON, Friday, May 10—President Roosevelt early today ordered the freezing of all credits held by Belgium, the Netherlands and Luxembourg in this country.

He called a conference for 10:30 A. M. of heads of the State, War and Navy Departments to consider pressing problems of neutrality.

The President acted swiftly when news of Germany's invasion of the three European neutral countries reached Washington and galvanized high officials into action. His order with regard to the freezing of all the invaded countries' credits and cash balances here was a counterpart of the action taken after Germany invaded Norway and Denmark.

Congress this week completed action on legislation that specifically authorizes the President to freeze to freeze all such cash and credits of any belligerent. The object is to prevent these resources from falling into the hands of the invading power.

Ships to Be Considered

The President's order directed Secretary of the Treasury Henry Morgenthau Jr. to freeze all Belgian, French and Luxembourg credits before the markets open this morning.

It was announced also that the conference to be held at 10:30 will consider the question of Belgian and Netherland ships that may be in United States ports. Attorney General Robert H. Jackson also will attend this conference.

The White House, meanwhile, indicated some skepticism of the official explanation of the invasion given by German Propaganda Minister Joseph Goebbels, who was reported to have said that the Germans moved because of information that Great Britain and France intended to invade the Low Countries involved.

"Nevertheless," said Stephen T. Early, Presidential secretary, after he had quoted the Goebbels statement, "it remains to be seen who invaded who."

It was announced that the President would remain awake throughout the night, if necessary, to receive reports and consult with officials. Sumner Welles, Under-Secretary of State, at 1:45 A. M. joined the group of State Department officials who remained on duty at the department.

Report From Ambassador

A general invasion of the three neutrals by heavy German land and air forces was reported to the State Department and Mr. Roosevelt early today by Ambassador John C. Cudahy at Brussels.

After trying vainly to re-establish telephone connection with Secretary of State Cordell Hull, over which he had relayed a "blow-by-blow" description of developments several hours earlier, the Ambassador got through the following terse message:

"German planes continue to cross the border and are bombing the airport near Brussels. It seems to be a general attack on all three countries."

A State Department press liaison officer who was relaying latest diplomatic bulletins to reporters as they came in by transatlantic telephone, dropped the cryptic remark:

"As the American Ambassador spoke from Brussels, an enemy military attaché stood at his elbow."

After relaying the information to the President that the Belgian Government had ordered all hands to stand by, Ambassador Cudahy again called Secretary Hull between 10 and 11 o'clock and said he had been informed by officials in Brussels that one German and

Continued on Page Two

The International Situation

In the midst of Britain's Cabinet crisis Germany struck another powerful blow early this morning by invading the Netherlands, Belgium and Luxembourg.

After swarms of planes had engaged in air fights over Amsterdam, parachute troops, some of them clad in Netherland uniforms, descended at strategic points while planes bombed air fields. The Netherlands resisted the incursion and promptly opened the dikes that are part of her water defense system. [Page 1.]

Parachute troops likewise made surprise landings in Belgium and bombs from 100 planes blasted the Brussels airport. [Page 1.]

Appeals for help were dispatched to the Allies by the invaded countries and it was understood that machinery of assistance was being set in motion. Queen Wilhelmina in a proclamation issued at The Hague declared, "I and my government will do our duty." [Page 1.]

As in the case of Norway, Berlin explained that the German action had been taken to forestall the Allies; an announcement said that an attack on Germany had been planned through the territory of the Low Countries. What the Reich was doing, it was declared, was safeguarding the neutrality of those countries. [Page 1.]

President Roosevelt lost no time in acting on the new situation. After night conferences he ordered the freezing of credits of the three invaded countries. Further measures are to be taken today. [Page 1.]

London, meanwhile, announced that British troops had occupied Iceland to prevent a possible German seizure of that former Danish possession. [Page 1.]

Before all these happenings Neville Chamberlain had appeared to be on his way out as Prime Minister, but today it was expected the new developments might save him.

Following upon his relatively narrow escape in the House of Commons vote on Wednesday night, Mr. Chamberlain set about yesterday to see what could be done to satisfy his critics. He offered Cabinet posts to two leaders of the Labor Opposition, but they refused to serve under him. As to whether they would serve under another Conservative, they delayed their reply. If Mr. Chamberlain steps out of office, it is thought probable his

Bombs Drop on Swiss Soil

By The United Press.

BERNE, Switzerland, Friday, May 10—The army staff announced today that foreign airplanes had dropped bombs in the Berne Jura Alpine district between Delemont, near the frontier, and Mount Terr, damaging a railroad.

Traffic continued over the road, the army staff said. It added that other foreign planes were flying over Swiss territory near Basle but that no details had been received.

Italians Reported Massing

By The United Press.

BUENOS AIRES, Argentina, Friday, May 10—The Madrid radio was heard broadcasting today that the British had closed the Strait of Gibraltar and that Italy was massing troops on the French frontier.

Special Cable to THE NEW YORK TIMES.

LONDON, Friday, May 10—The British Government received appeals for help early today from both the Netherlands and Belgium.

The British and French reply to the Netherland-Belgian appeals was prompt. Representatives of the respective governments here (early New York time) they could expect all the help Britain could give them.

The Netherland Legation here received assurance that its country and Belgium were now regarded as Allies of Britain and France.

Within a few minutes after receipt of official news of the invasion of the Low Countries, the British Cabinet was called to 10 Downing Street and was in session with Prime Minister Neville Chamberlain.

According to information here, the Belgian Cabinet was in Brussels and Premier Hubert Pierlot conferred with King Leopold.

The German invasion of the Low Countries had been expected in London, and it must be presumed the Allies were ready for it to some extent.

Allies Visible to Planes

The biggest handicap to the British and French was in the timing of the German thrust at dawn. This prevented the Allies moving troops under cover of darkness, and since hundreds of German planes already had flown over practically all of Netherland and Belgian territory for some hours, the disposition of Allied troops and their every movement must have been known to the German High Command.

While the Netherlanders and Belgians had taken every precaution

Continued on Page Four

ALLIED HELP SPED

Netherland and Belgian Appeals Answered by British and French

TACTICS ARE WATCHED

London Thinks Move an Effort to Get Bases to Attack Britain

place will be taken by the present Foreign Secretary, Viscount Halifax, with Winston Churchill acting as government spokesman in the Commons, from the floor of which the peer would by tradition be barred. [Page 1.]

A new offset to the Norwegian reverses was a London announcement that British submarines had attacked three German convoys and scored eleven torpedo hits, in addition to destroying two ships sailing home. [Page 6.]

Moreover, the Allies' Narvik campaign seemed to be making progress. From that far northern area it was reported that two Allied columns closing in on the railway to the port were within ten miles of each other near the Swedish border. Their intention apparently was to join and drive westward along the railroad to Narvik itself, which is held by the Nazis. The Germans, in their effort to thwart the besiegers, were said to be landing parachute troops and supplying them by air. [Page 4.]

In the aftermath of the campaign in the south of the country Foreign Minister Koht disclosed that four of Norway's six divisions had been lost—killed, wounded or captured by the Nazis or interned by Sweden. [Page 6.]

BRUSSELS IS RAIDED

400 Reported Killed—Troops Cross Border at Four Points

PARACHUTE INVASION

Mobilization Is Ordered and Allied Aid Asked—Luxembourg Attacked

Wireless to THE NEW YORK TIMES.

BRUSSELS, Belgium, Friday, May 10—The invasion Belgium had feared since the outbreak of the European war came before dawn this morning. About a hundred German planes flew over this city and bombed the airport.

The airfield at Antwerp also was bombed. Parachute troops were landed at Hasselt in Eastern Belgium. Artillery fire was reported heard along the German and Luxembourg frontiers.

Anti-aircraft guns at the airport opened fire at the first invaders and kept up a steady barrage. Those in the center of the city went into action at 5:30 A. M.

Above the drone of airplane engines could be heard the staccato of machine guns. Bombs wrecked many houses in the vicinity of the airport and caused some loss of life. [Exchange Telegraph (British news agency) said 400 persons had been killed in the first raid.]

Reports from Antwerp and other parts of the country said German planes had flown constantly over since 4:30 A. M., keeping anti-aircraft batteries steadily in action.

Premier Hubert Pierlot and Foreign Minister Paul-Henri Spaak conferred with King Leopold and then called an emergency meeting of the Cabinet. The betting had been broadcast repeated summonses to all soldiers to join their units at once. A "state of alarm" was decreed throughout the country with the appearance of the first planes.

The Belgian radio also stated German parachute troops had fluttered down at Nivelles, less than twenty miles south of Brussels, and at Saint Trond, about thirty-five miles east of the capital. The broadcast stated that Germany had made no demarche in Brussels before the invasion.

Wireless to THE NEW YORK TIMES.

LONDON, Friday, May 10—The Germans crossed the Belgian frontier at four points this morning, according to an announcement made

Continued on Page Two

NAZIS SWOOP ON THE LOW COUNTRIES

By land and air German troops descended this morning upon the Netherlands, Belgium and Luxembourg. The principal land incursion into the Netherlands was at Roermond.

Ribbentrop Charges Allies Plotted With the Lowlands

By GEORGE AXELSSON
Wireless to THE NEW YORK TIMES.

BERLIN, Friday, May 10—Foreign Minister Joachim von Ribbentrop at 9 o'clock this morning announced that Reich forces had launched military operations against Holland, Belgium and Luxembourg to "protect their neutrality."

It was reported that German troops had occupied Maastricht, the Netherlands, and had "landed" contingents in Brussels, probably meaning parachute troops.

Herr von Ribbentrop said that Germany had received unimpeachable proof that the Allies were engineering an imminent attack through the Lowlands into the German Ruhr district wherefore the Germans felt compelled to take corresponding measures. He said the time had come for settling the final account with the "Franco-British leaders."

And thus the war to a decisive finish has at last started in the West. This was the assumption when Herr von Ribbentrop informed the world through news-paper men that the German action meant that she had decided to settle all accounts with the Allies.

"France and Britain dropped their masks," said Herr von Ribbentrop. "The alarm in the Mediterranean was a feint behind which the Allies were preparing an onslaught on German territory which the Reich could not tolerate."

The notes—handed to The Hague and Brussels simultaneously, and a shorter note to the Grand Duchy of Luxembourg just prior to their invasion by Germany—accused the Lowlands with having been overwhelmingly partial toward the Allies, adding that the attitude of the press was objectionable to the Reich.

A memorandum similar in tone to that handed to Denmark and Norway last month added:

"In the life-and-death struggle thrust upon the German people, the government does not intend to await an attack by Britain and France inactively allowing the war to be carried through Belgium and Holland onto German soil. The government, therefore, has issued orders to safeguard the neutrality of the two countries with all the military means of the Reich."

Ribbentrop Reads Statement

In eight points the memorandum outlines the German argument that Belgium and Holland had not observed the strictest neutrality upon which German respect for their territories was founded. The document accuses them with having even supported Germany's enemies in their hostile intentions. Belgium fortified exclusively her Eastern frontier against Germany, leaving the French frontier unfortified, one argument reads.

Berlin slept peacefully unaware

AIR FIELDS BOMBED

Nazi Parachute Troops Land at Key Centers as Flooding Starts

RIVER MAAS CROSSED

Defenders Battle Foe in Sky, Claim 6 Planes as War Is Proclaimed

First Bombing in France

Special to THE NEW YORK TIMES.

PARIS, Friday, May 10—The Bron airdrome, a big airport near Lyon, was bombed by German planes today. One German aircraft was shot down. The alarm was first given at 4:25 A. M. The all-clear signal was given at 6:45 A. M.

WASHINGTON, Friday, May 10 (UP)—United States Ambassador William C. Bullitt telephoned the State Department from Paris at 4 A. M. today that the Germans had bombed a number of fortified towns in France, "such as Dunkerque and Calais."

By The United Press.

AMSTERDAM, The Netherlands, Friday, May 10—Germany invaded the Netherlands early today, land troops being preceded by widespread air attacks on airdromes and by the landing of parachute troops.

The Netherlands resisted and announced she was at war with Germany. Anti-aircraft batteries engaged swarms of German aircraft when they appeared simultaneously over a score of Netherland cities.

An official proclamation said:

"Since 3 A. M. German troops have crossed the Netherland frontier and German planes have tried to attack airports. Inundations are effective according to plans. The army anti-aircraft batteries were found prepared. So far as is known six German planes have been shot down."

[French, Belgian and British planes were sighted over the Netherlands this morning, a Reuter (British news agency) dispatch said in quoting the Netherland radio station at Hilversum, near Amsterdam.]

German troops were first reported crossing the Netherland frontier near Roermond, eight miles south of the Belgian frontier. German planes landed troops by parachute at strategic points near Rotterdam, The Hague, Amsterdam and other large cities.

A large number of the German troops landed by parachute were said to be dressed in Netherland military uniforms.

Other Germans crossed the Maas River in rubber boats to Netherland territory. They were said to be reaching the Netherland side in "considerable numbers."

A fierce air battle raged over Amsterdam as Netherland fighter planes dived repeatedly on German bombers and troop transport planes with chattering machine guns.

Schiphol Airdrome outside Amsterdam, the nation's largest, was heavily bombed. Military authorities immediately threw a heavy guard around the airdrome in an effort to defend it against German parachute troops.

Planes identified as German Heinkels bombed Schiphol Airdrome repeatedly, loosing some thirty heavy caliber bombs on the landing field between 5:15 and 5:30 A. M.

Reports poured in of planes in great numbers over a score of Netherland cities. Netherland authorities, hurriedly organizing defense, flashed orders to the whole country to be on the alert against parachute troops.

Fifty planes were over Nijmegen, sixty miles southeast of Amsterdam on the German border.

A number of parachute troops reportedly landed at Sliedrecht, Delft and several other points. Delft is twelve and a half miles from The Hague. About 100 parachute troops

Continued on Page Three

MUSSOLINI TO LET 'ONLY FACTS' SPEAK

Press Assures Yugoslavia, but Reminds Her of Fate of Poland and Norway

By HERBERT L. MATTHEWS
By Telephone to THE NEW YORK TIMES.

ROME, May 9—The fourth anniversary of the founding of the new Italian Empire was celebrated today in an atmosphere of warlike preparation. The army was honored, Italian armed strength was glorified and the country was told by its leading commentators that the empire would soon earn that "freedom of the seas" which to Italians means domination of the Mediterranean.

Rome, like every other city in the empire, resounded today to martial music while thousands of soldiers paraded through streets from whose buildings hung innumerable flags. The great ceremony was at the Piazza Venezia this morning. Premier Mussolini awarded gold and silver medals to the kin of soldiers fallen in Fascismo's three wars in Ethiopia, Spain and Albania. Later, responding to the insistent appeal of the thousands of men massed below his balcony, he spoke very briefly, only to say that he was resuming this cloak of silence.

"May 9, 1936, was a great day in the history of the country, a day of solar victory," he said. "After my speeches, you must accustom yourself to my silence. Only facts will break it."

Small groups in the crowd thereupon began yelling "Tunisia!" and "Malta!" but the cries were not general.

At the same time this morning

Continued on Page Seven

ICELAND OCCUPIED BY BRITISH FORCE

Secret Expedition Is Justified as Thwarting Action There by Germany

By JAMES MacDONALD
Special Cable to THE NEW YORK TIMES.

LONDON, Friday, May 10—Forestalling a possible German swoop on the strategically valuable former Danish dominion of Iceland, the British have landed an expeditionary force there, it was announced this morning by the Foreign Office.

Neither the size of the British contingent, which was sent out in the deepest secrecy, nor its place of landing was revealed in the official communiqué.

The landing of the expeditionary force was still going on at an early hour this morning. Observers guessed that the landing place must be Reykjavik.

TEXT OF COMMUNIQUE

The official announcement read as follows:

Since the German seizure of Denmark it has become necessary to reckon with the possibility of a sudden German descent on Iceland.

It is clear that in the face of an attack on Iceland, even on a very small scale, the Icelandic Government would be unable to prevent their country being fully completely into German hands.

His Majesty's Government have accordingly decided to preclude this possibility which would

Continued on Page Three

Chamberlain Saved by Nazi Blow In Low Countries, London Thinks

By RAYMOND DANIELL
Special Cable to THE NEW YORK TIMES.

LONDON, Friday, May 10—The first effect of the German attack on the Low Countries is expected to be that Prime Minister Chamberlain will be saved just when it looked as if he was sure to fall.

It was believed that the Labor party, which so far has refused to serve under him in a truly national government, and only yesterday rejected a formal offer to do so, will now close ranks, forget political difficulties and take any Cabinet job offered to its leaders. Furthermore, the Labor party conference, which was supposed to start at Bournemouth on Monday, now will probably be called off.

There is just a possibility that Mr. Chamberlain may quit immediately and turn his seals of office over to First Lord of the Admiralty Winston Churchill. This was a strong but unconfirmed rumor as the House, despite the gravity of the internal crisis and perils abroad, decided to take its usual twelve-day Whitsuntide holiday, subject to recall in the event of major developments, which followed promptly.

Mr. Chamberlain's efforts to broaden the base of his Cabinet by

Until the invasion of the Low Countries was known, the con-

sensus of political observers here had been that the end of the Chamberlain Government could not be long delayed.

The two questions uppermost were how soon it would take place and who would succeed him at No. 10 Downing Street. The betting had been that it would be sooner rather than later and that Foreign Secretary Viscount Halifax would be the next Prime Minister, with Mr. Churchill serving as his spokesman in the House of Commons, from whose floor the present Foreign Secretary, as a peer, is barred by tradition.

The troubles of the 71-year-old Prime Minister, who struggled vainly to maintain Europe's peace by appeasement and who was accused in the House of Commons of bungling the business of war-making, increased rather than diminished during the day. However, despite the gravity of the internal crisis and perils abroad, decided to take its usual twelve-day Whitsuntide holiday, subject to recall in the event of major developments, which followed promptly.

Mr. Chamberlain's efforts to broaden the base of his Cabinet by

Continued on Page Five

Dispatches from Europe and the Far East are subject to censorship at the source.

HOLLAND'S QUEEN PROTESTS INVASION

Wilhelmina Vows She and the Government Will Do Duty—Bars Negotiation With Foe

By The United Press.

THE HAGUE, the Netherlands, Friday, May 10—Queen Wilhelmina said today in a statement on the German invasion of the country that "I and my government will do our duty."

The Queen, in a proclamation addressed to "my people," said:

"After our country, which observed strict neutrality during all these months, and while Holland had no other plan than to maintain strictly this attitude, Germany last night made a sudden attack on our territory without any warning.

"This was done notwithstanding a solemn promise that the neutrality of our country would be respected so long as we ourselves maintained that neutrality.

"I herewith direct a flaming protest against this unprecedented violation of good faith and violation of all that is decent in relations between cultured States.

"I and my government now will do our duty.

"Do your duty everywhere and under all circumstances. And let every one go to the post to which he has been appointed and, with the utmost vigilance and with that inner calm and serenity which comes from a clear conscience, do his work."

The Netherland general military headquarters in a communiqué said:

"Never will the High Command or government enter into negotiations with the enemy."

"All the News That's
Fit to Print."

The New York Times.

LATE CITY EDITION
Fair, continued cool today. Tomorrow increasing cloudiness,
slightly warmer.
Temperature Yesterday—Max., 64; Min., 53

VOL. LXXXIX...No. 30,065.

Entered as Second-Class Matter,
Postoffice, New York, N. Y.

NEW YORK, SATURDAY, MAY 18, 1940.

Copyright, 1940, by The New York Times Company.

PPPP   THREE CENTS   NEW YORK CITY   FOUR CENTS Elsewhere Except
and Vicinity   in 7th and 8th Postal Zones

NAZIS PIERCE FRENCH LINES ON 62-MILE FRONT; TAKE BRUSSELS, LOUVAIN, MALINES AND NAMUR; WASHINGTON SPEEDS ITS BIG DEFENSE PROGRAM

ROOSEVELT IS BUSY

Calls Parley on Great Air Force, Considers Bigger Sea Patrol

UNITY IN CONGRESS

Partisanship Shelved in Drive—Midwest May Get Arms Plants

By FELIX BELAIR Jr.
Special to THE NEW YORK TIMES.

WASHINGTON, May 17—National defense preparations were begun by government agencies today on a scale unapproached since the World War.

In response to President Roosevelt's preparedness message calling for an impregnable America, first steps were taken toward proposed far-reaching undertakings, such as construction of airplane and munitions factories in the Middle West, out of reach of possible quick bombing raids.

The President followed his request to Congress for a goal of 50,000 first-line fighting planes by calling a conference of aviation industry leaders with army, navy and Treasury officials in the office of Secretary Morgenthau Monday morning. Earlier in the day he disclosed plans to recommission thirty-five more World War destroyers for emergency patrol duty at a cost of $6,000,000.

Developments of the Day

As the executive and legislative branches gave evidence of the "partnership" for which the President appealed in his $1,182,000,000 national defense message yesterday, the preparedness campaign brought the following developments:

1. The House Military Affairs Committee began hearings on the President's defense program envisaging an army nucleus of 750,000 regulars and 250,000 reserves, fully equipped for active service by June 30, 1941.

2. Military authorities shaped plans calling for a $300,000,000 outlay to bring actual aircraft production up to 30,000 planes a year as quickly as possible under a program specifying a number of factories between the Allegheny and Rocky Mountains capable of producing a hundred planes a month, the government to build the plants and rent them on a "fixed-fee basis."

3. House leaders organized a drive for modification of the Walsh-Healey Act to permit the President to waive forty-hour week limitations governing shipbuilding to speed up the present expansion program.

4. Mr. Roosevelt made known plans to call to Washington soon several recognized industrialists to speed industrial mobilization required to carry out his unprecedented peacetime defense program.

5. The White House placed its stamp of approval on plans of Colonel Frank Knox, Chicago publisher, to sponsor the creation of a chain of aviation training camps throughout the country to supplement the military and naval training facilities.

6. The Navy Department considered proclaiming all industrial navy yards, air bases and fields as restricted areas and sought ways and means of increasing the number of its skilled mechanics from 75,000 to 150,000 or 200,000 men. The President's defense plan included the placing of the navy's expansion program on a twenty-four-hour basis instead of eight hours as at present.

Leaders Discard Partisanship

Political leaders, meanwhile, declared a moratorium on partisanship to expedite early enactment of legislation carrying out the President's plan to make our defenses invulnerable. The statement of former President Hoover endorsing Mr. Roosevelt's message to Congress was received by the White House as "an indication of national unity which we welcome and that political differences are being cast aside in the emergency."

The President, apparently convinced of Republican good will for his program, invited Alfred M. Landon to a White House luncheon conference next Wednesday.

In announcing the President's endorsement of the aviation training plan suggested by Colonel Knox, Stephen T. Early, White House

Continued on Page Six

The International Situation

The War in the West

German arms struck yesterday along the whole Western Front from the Netherland border to the northern anchor of the Maginot Line at the Luxembourg corner. As night fell the situation was as follows:

The Nazis claimed that on the northern wing against the British and Belgians they had penetrated to the outlying forts of Antwerp and occupied Malines and Louvain and that advance units were in Brussels, the Belgian capital. On the southern wing, against the French, the German High Command said it had broken through the fortifications along the Belgian-French border for a distance of 100 kilometers (62 miles) from just south of Maubeuge to Carignan, south of Sedan, and had penetrated into France as far as to Le Cateau, La Capelle and to a point north of Rethel. The communiqué admitted, however, that the lines were changing hourly. The Germans claimed 12,000 French prisoners, including two generals. On the central Belgian front advances were reported at Namur and Wavre. [Page 1.]

The Allies did not deny that the situation was critical. General Gamelin, supreme commander of the Allied forces, issued a general order to all troops stating that the "fate of our country, of our Allies, the destiny of the world depend on the battle now being fought." The command was, "Conquer or die." The order recalled Marshal Joffre's famous message to the French Armies before the 1914 First Battle of the Marne, where the "taxicab army" from Paris stopped the Kaiser's legions, and saved Paris. A communiqué said that the Germans had penetrated as far as Avesnes and Vervins, about fifteen miles into France along the Belgian border. It estimated the Germans had engaged the "greatest part" of their heavy tank divisions in the attack. Attacks south of Sedan in the vicinity of Montmedy and Sedan were said to have been repulsed. Allied bomber and fighter squadrons were reported carrying out their missions of harassing enemy troop concentrations and rear lines of communication. [Page 1.]

While London admitted a withdrawal of its forces to a new defense line behind Brussels, advices from field headquarters in Belgium indicated the retreat had been orderly and that British air forces were more than holding their own in harassing the enemy and protecting their own rear from German bombing and machine-gunning attacks on communication lines. [Page 1.]

The Air Ministry at London said the German advance was not being made without cost. It estimated German plane losses in the last seven days at 1,000. However, it said, large reserves (estimated at 23,000 planes) made it probable the German air effort could be sustained for some time. [Page 4.]

Tragic victims of the horror were innumerable numbers of refugees who choked all roads in Belgium not already filled with troops and guns moving up to the fighting lines, homeless, unfed, many wounded, seeking a sanctuary which appeared not to exist. [Included in the above.]

Repercussions Elsewhere

Scenes in government departments reminiscent of World War days were seen in Washington as the Federal agencies involved moved to put into effect the needed defense measures outlined by President Roosevelt in his speech to Congress Thursday. The President called a conference of Army, Navy and Treasury officials and aviation leaders to discuss his program to build up the United States air force to 50,000 planes. [Page 1.]

War fever mounted in Rome. Premier Mussolini's newspaper, Popolo d'Italia, thundered: "The Italian people must now or never achieve their Mediterranean destiny." The Senate, in an atmosphere of war hysteria, heard a budget report with a record deficit and warning of more taxes; the stock market suffered another "Black Friday" recession. [Page 1.]

On the Balkan diplomatic front Russia was reported bringing pressure on all interested countries to retain the status quo there under threat of forming an alliance with Yugoslavia and Bulgaria and reviving the idea of a union of all the Slavs in Europe. [Page 5.]

GAMELIN IN APPEAL

Says Fate of Nation and World's Destiny Hang on Present Conflict

FIGHTING IS AT PEAK

Full Air Forces Battle— Attacks at Sedan and Montmedy Repulsed

By G. H. ARCHAMBAULT
Wireless to THE NEW YORK TIMES.

PARIS, May 17—"The fate of our country and that of our allies and the destiny of the world depend on the battle now being fought."

Thus begins a general order to all troops issued this evening by General Maurice Gustave Gamelin, supreme Allied commander.

Taken in conjunction with the communiqué issued from General Headquarters tonight, it reveals the situation as tragic.

"Today the German attack developed on a massive scale," the communiqué stated, "not only in Belgium but in the region of Avesnes and Vervins. On those fronts the enemy engaged the greater part of his heavy tank divisions. The battle took the form of a veritable melee."

Avesnes and Vervins are in the North of France, the latter some fifteen miles from the Belgian border.

[Cannonading was heard today on the outskirts of Paris, according to The Associated Press. It was not learned whether this was anti-aircraft or other fire.]

All United in Battle

General Gamelin's order adds that British, Belgian and Polish soldiers are fighting by the side of the French, together with foreign volunteers. The British Air Force, he added, like the French, is fighting to the last man.

Every troop that cannot advance, the general asserted, must die where it stands rather than abandon the portion of national soil entrusted to it. Concluding, he said: "As always in the critical hours of our history, the watchword today is 'Conquer or die.' We must conquer."

This general order so reminiscent of that issued by Marshal Joffre in 1914 on the first day of the Battle of the Marne tells the story. There are no details. A terrific struggle is being fought for the future of mankind. All else is of no moment. That the Allied General Headquarters has not departed from its calm is indicated in the remainder of the communiqué, which proceeds to refer to minor incidents as follows:

"Further to the east the enemy attacked in the region of Sedan and Montmedy without success.

Aviation Continues Activity

"In close collaboration with the Royal Air Force our aviation continued its energetic and efficacious action against ground troops, crossroads and railways. While assuring the protection of our troops our fighters engaged in numerous encounters. Many enemy planes were brought down. In the present conditions of open warfare it is not possible to know the exact number."

Nor is it of moment to refer to any relating to the actions on the Meuse. They all pale into insignificance with the day's developments. Since the outline of the pocket formed by the German drive was indicated by a spokesman for the general staff last night, the Stock Exchanges had a singularly black day; the great successes claimed by Germany on the French front provided a temptation of the first magnitude for the Fascist leaders.

The temperature in the Senate session was feverish. Every time the name of King Victor Emmanuel or of Premier Mussolini was mentioned there was a remarkably emotional reaction. Count Suardo, the President of the Senate, spoke words like these:

"The Italian people press around you, Duce, to form an iron block of energy and will, ready for your orders wherever you wish to guide them, because they know that the road you will take at short notice to preserve our vital rights has just one goal—the grandeur and power of Italy."

The German thrust through Bel-

Continued on Page Three

COL. KNOX TO FORM AIR 'PLATTSBURGS'

Roosevelt Authorizes Civilian Groups to Promote Training of Students as Pilots

Special to THE NEW YORK TIMES.

CHICAGO, May 17—With the authorization of President Roosevelt, Colonel Frank Knox, publisher of The Chicago Daily News and Republican Vice Presidential nominee in 1936, stated here today that a civilian group would be formed to cooperate with the government in training 10,000 pilots at volunteer camps this Summer in the same army corps area. Colonel Knox discussed the project in a White House conference yesterday with the President.

The training camps will be opened about July 1, Colonel Knox said, and will be designed primarily to accommodate 10,000 college students who have been receiving preliminary training through the Civil Aeronautics Authority.

"What we are undertaking," Colonel Knox said, "is not to replace any of the present activities, but to extend and increase them. We can turn out airplanes rapidly, but not top pilots, and we need at least two pilots for each plane."

World War Comparison

Colonel Knox described the new organization as a parallel to the training camps of the last World War, such as Plattsburg, N. Y.

The cost of promoting the volunteer enlistments in the camps will be financed privately, he continued. The army has agreed for its part to provide tents, reserve officers for training, cooks and camp sites.

"Most of all," Colonel Knox said,

Continued on Page Seven

WAR BASIS EVIDENT IN ITALIAN BUDGET

With Record Deficit Figures, Senators Cheer Belligerent Speeches of Leaders

By HERBERT L. MATTHEWS
Wireless to THE NEW YORK TIMES.

ROME, May 17—While nothing startling happened in Italy today, there have been a number of minor developments to drive home further the feeling that Italian intervention in the European war is not very far off.

The Senate held a session in the morning full of genuine war fervor. The Minister of Finance, Count Paolo Thaon di Revel, presented what amounts to a war budget and admitted a deficit for this year of more than 26,000,000,000 lire. Premier Mussolini's own newspaper, in a highly significant editorial, as good as told the nation that it was about to enter the conflict. The Stock Exchanges had a singularly black day; the great successes claimed by Germany on the French front provided a temptation of the first magnitude for the Fascist leaders.

The temperature in the Senate session was feverish. Every time the name of King Victor Emmanuel or of Premier Mussolini was mentioned there was a remarkably emotional reaction. Count Suardo, the President of the Senate, spoke words like these:

"The Italian people press around you, Duce, to form an iron block of energy and will, ready for your orders wherever you wish to guide them, because they know that the road you will take at short notice to preserve our vital rights has just one goal—the grandeur and power of Italy."

At the end of Count Suardo's

Continued on Page Five

GERMANY'S SWIFT COLUMNS SWEEP TO NEW SUCCESSES

Nazi forces, breaking through the extension of the Maginot Line in Northern France across the Belgian border, have reached the vicinity of Avesnes (4) and Vervins (5) and are reported north of Rethel (6) in a thrust toward Laon. The Allies claim to have halted a further attempt to widen the gap south of Sedan (7). In Belgium the Germans occupied Louvain and Malines (1) and claim to have reached the outer fortifications of Antwerp; they also crashed through the Dyle River defenses and marched into Brussels (2) as British forces withdrew to the west, and reported the capture of Namur (3). The dotted line indicates approximate Allied fixed positions.

Gamelin, 1940; Joffre, 1914

Gamelin Order
By The United Press.

PARIS, May 17—Following is the text of General Maurice Gustave Gamelin's order of the day to the French armies:

"The fate of our country and that of our Allies and the destiny of the world depend on the battle now being fought.

"English, Belgian and Polish soldiers and foreign volunteers fight at our side.

"The British Air Force is engaged up to the hilt like ours.

"Every unit that is unable to advance must accept death rather than abandon that part of the national territory entrusted to it.

"As always in the critical hours of our history the watchword today is 'Conquer or die.' We must conquer."

Joffre Order

Following is the text of the order addressed by Marshal Joffre to all army headquarters and to troops on Sept. 6, 1914:

"We are about to engage a battle on which the fate of our country depends and it is important to remind all ranks that the moment has passed for looking to the rear; all our efforts must be directed to attacking and driving back the enemy.

"Troops that can advance no further must, at any price, hold on to the ground they have conquered and die on the spot rather than give way. Under the circumstances which face us, no act of weakness can be tolerated."

BELGIANS REMOVE CAPITAL TO OSTEND

Vacating of Brussels Laid to 'Obvious Necessity'—U. S. Envoy Remains at Post

Wireless to THE NEW YORK TIMES.

PARIS, May 17—The removal of the Belgian capital from Brussels to another point in Belgian territory was announced today in a broadcast from Brussels by M. Vanderpoorten, Minister of the Interior, speaking for Premier Hubert Pierlot.

[The Belgian Government is now established at Ostend, on Belgium's North Sea coast, The Associated Press reported in a dispatch from Ostend.]

"This painful decision," he said, "has been forced upon us by obvious necessity. The Allied troops are defending themselves step by step, but the rapidity of movement that armies have today causes events to transpire with greater rapidity than ever. After a few days of war we find ourselves in a situation which, without being so grave, recalls in certain respects what it was after the first weeks of war in 1914. We shall soon witness, we firmly believe, the same recovery which took place then."

The Minister praised the courage of the Belgian Armies and people, and added:

"The Premier yesterday after-

Continued on Page Four

FRANCE PAYS PRICE FOR SHIFTING UNITS

Penetration by Nazi Armored Forces Laid to Fact Aid Had to Be Rushed to Neutrals

Wireless to THE NEW YORK TIMES.

PARIS, May 17—Outside military circles, the public mind not only here but seemingly all over the world is much exercised over the swift advance of German armored columns into French territory.

The briefest explanation is that the Allies had paid that price for moving immediately to the aid of Belgium and the Netherlands despite the fact that both countries steadfastly refused to consider any joint plan of campaign in the event of invasion.

Apparently what seems most inexplicable to the layman is that the line of defenses along the French frontier should have been penetrated. The answer is twofold:

First, these defenses were not the Maginot Line of solid permanent concrete works that extends only from Montmedy eastward to the Rhine, but field fortifications—trenches, ditches, pits and the like—reinforced since the war by pill boxes and blockhouses.

Second, that the value of field works is determined by the forces behind them.

Since the Allied High Command decided early in the campaign to

Continued on Page Four

NAZIS REPORT ROUT

Allies 'in Full Retreat' Westward Into France, Germans Declare

AIR VICTORIES NOTED

Sedan Prisoners Said to Total 12,000, Among Them 2 Generals

By GEORGE AXELSSON
Wireless to THE NEW YORK TIMES.

BERLIN, May 17—Brussels, Malines and Louvain have fallen to the relentlessly advancing Germans, who also claim to have broken into France across the defenses of the Maginot Line extension on a wide front, standing not more than ninety miles from Paris at the nearest point.

The German High Command today broke a three days' silence on its Western Front operations to announce two major successes. First was the driving of a sixty-two-mile wedge into the French lines from south of Maubeuge to Carignan, southeast of Sedan. Second was a break through the Belgian Dyle line positions south of Wavre, along with the capture of Namur.

The spearhead of the German advance into France—where, a General Headquarters communiqué significantly says, "our infantry units and air force are pursuing the enemy in full retreat westward"—is tonight said to be in the vicinity of La Capelle and Le Cateau, halfway between Maubeuge and St. Quentin.

In the sector southeast of Sedan the Germans, according to their communiqué, have taken 12,000 prisoners, including two generals, and also captured abundant war material.

British Thrown in Tank Units

In Belgium, the Germans early this morning already had advanced their lines to Malines, the vicinity of Louvain and south of Brussels in the Waterloo area, making the military situation of the capital seem hopeless for the defenders.

Here, it is admitted, the British had thrown in particularly powerful tank units in a desperate attempt to stem the German advance to the coast. The time were swaying back and forth along this entire sector, with tank meeting tank and infantry against infantry in vicious hand-to-hand encounters of a ceaseless attack and counterattack.

The Germans evidently were following the Polish campaign method of launching giant tanks in wild forward lunges fanwise, as though along the fingers of an outspread hand, and trusting to skill and chance to hold the spearheads and eventually close the gaps between.

With Paris and the English Channel coast directly threatened, the military plight of the Allies appears most grave, as seen from Berlin. The British, it is said, must now devote every ounce of their resources to saving the coast, while the French must be equally concerned with the defense of their capital, rendering mutual aid difficult if not impossible.

French Attacks Said to Fail

The Germans admit violent French attacks on their south flank, presumably in the Longwy sector, but say these attempts to relieve the main fronts met with no success. Instead, it is claimed, the Germans gained further ground in their counter-attacks.

That the struggles in Belgium and France have changed their aspect in the last forty-eight hours is observed by military observers here. Only Wednesday the two battle zones, that in front of Brussels and that to the south in France, formed one connected front from Antwerp by Charleville to Sedan.

The German break through between Namur and Givet and the thrust at the point where the Maginot Line crosses the Meuse was thrust at the point where the south flank of the Belgian battle zone joined the northern flank of the French. Widening of the breach between Namur and Givet and the rapid German push westward in the Maubeuge sector are said to have separated the two battle lines and doubled over the flanks.

The Belgian break is now reported turned back, with the Sambre River westward where, according to the Germans, the Allies are now threatened with a flanking move-

Continued on Page Two

BRITISH FALL BACK BEHIND BRUSSELS

'Adjustment' West of City Is Announced—Troops Steady Against Nazi Blows

Special Cable to THE NEW YORK TIMES.

LONDON, May 17—The War Office announced tonight that the British Army in Belgium had retired the night before to positions west of Brussels, "certain adjustments at the front having become necessary."

"This readjustment," the communiqué said, "was carried out without interferences. There is no question of any collapse or break through in this sector as suggested by the German communiqué."

By HAROLD DENNY
Wireless to THE NEW YORK TIMES.

WITH THE BRITISH ARMY IN BELGIUM, May 17—The Germans renewed today their assaults on the British positions, hurling tanks supported by airplanes with especial severity on the right side of the British line.

The British are withstanding these terrific mechanized assaults with great steadiness and can be counted upon to continue doing so. The British Expeditionary Force is fighting under the French High Command, and its employment is governed by the working out of the grand battle plan. The British are playing the role assigned to them no matter what their local situation. Should the French be hard pressed in the Sedan area—enough, that is, to threaten the splitting of the Allied general line—a realignment of the British forces might be necessary.

British Staff Pleased

British staff officers are pleased with the fine qualities their troops are exhibiting against attacks such as soldiers never had encountered before this war. They are equally confident of the ability of the French High Command to meet any situation presented by the German drive. The French seem to have the gift of choosing the exact moment to strike most effectively.

The British now are fighting side by side with the Belgians, who made contact with them in the vicinity of Malines.

British resistance to the German

Continued on Page Three

Dispatches from Europe and the Far East are subject to censorship at the source.

The New York Times.

LATE CITY EDITION
Cloudy, little change in temperature today. Tomorrow rain, not
much change in temperature.
Temperature Yesterday—Max.,78; Min.,58

Copyright, 1940, by The New York Times Company.

VOL. LXXXIX No. 30,069.　　NEW YORK, WEDNESDAY, MAY 22, 1940.　　THREE CENTS NEW YORK CITY | FOUR CENTS Elsewhere Except in 7th and 8th Postal Zones.

NAZIS AT CHANNEL, TRAP ALLIES IN BELGIUM; CROSS AISNE RIVER 60 MILES FROM PARIS; FRANCE CAN'T DIE, REYNAUD TELLS PEOPLE

PRESIDENT SPEEDS DEFENSE PROGRAM; APPEALS FOR UNITY

At Press Talk He Condemns Nazis as Machine-Gunning Fleeing French Civilians

MOVES ON 'FIFTH COLUMN'

New Reorganization Order Will Put Immigration Bureau in Justice Department

As President Roosevelt outlined yesterday at his press conference further details of plans for the nation's defense [Page 1] various departments of the government took action to speed up preparedness. The navy submitted to Congress a program calling for 10,000 planes and 16,000 pilots. It also ordered a forty-eight-hour work week in navy yards and the hiring of 15,000 more civilian employees. [Page 13.]

Senator Pepper offered a resolution authorizing the President to sell to any invaded country any of the army's or navy's airplanes. The Senate sped action on the War Department Appropriation Bill, now increased to almost $1,500,000,000 in cash grants and close to $325,900,000 in contract authorizations. [Page 10.]

The President asked the House to lift its $50,000 limit on WPA grants, because such a restriction would hamper projects for defense. [Page 8.] He also vetoed a $109,985,450 Rivers and Harbors bill in order to give preference to military projects. [Page 11.]

States 3-Point Plan

By FELIX BELAIR Jr.
Special to The New York Times.

WASHINGTON, May 21—President Roosevelt today coupled an appeal for national unity behind his preparedness drive with the grimmest picture of German military tactics yet painted in any official American quarter—a picture of the deliberate machine-gunning of millions of fleeing French women, children and old men by Nazi war planes. He said Americans well understood the implications of such ruthless methods and would be guided accordingly.

Then the President, employing the gravest tone he has used in referring to the war in Europe, outlined the following three-point policy which he said would govern the nation's defense preparations:

Not a single war millionaire will be created in this country as a result of the war disaster.

Labor will not attempt to take advantage of its collective power to foment strikes and interfere with the national defense program to squeeze higher wages from employers in the so-called war industries.

Under no circumstances will the Administration sanction a weakening of the social legislative gains attained during the last seven years. Labor standards prescribed in the Walsh-Healey act and the Wage Hour Law must not be relaxed in the name of the national defense.

Plans Attack on "Fifth Column"

As the President gave further impetus to the preparedness drive there were the following developments in his national defense program:

1. Mr. Roosevelt sought to strengthen the country against "fifth column" activities by providing for an early transfer of the Bureau of Immigration and Naturalization from the Department of Labor to the Department of Justice. He said he would send to Congress tomorrow another reorganization plan giving effect to the transfer proposal.

2. With full Administration backing, chairmen of the Senate and House Naval Affairs Committee introduced companion bills to spend an additional $124,000,000 for a naval air armada of 10,000 planes and 16,000 pilots. Introduced by Senator Walsh and Representative Vinson after a White House conference, the proposed legislation would increase the navy's authorized aerial fleet by 7,000 units, of

Continued on Page Ten

The International Situation

On the Battle Fronts

Eleven days after the start of their offensive on the Western Front, the Germans yesterday drove a spearhead to the English Channel, cutting off the Allied troops in Belgium and the northwest tip of France from the main body of the French Army. The German command estimated that half a million to a million men had thus been trapped between a steadily pressing mass of German attackers and the North Sea. [Page 1.]

The German thrust, described by Berlin as "the greatest attack of all time," swept sixty miles along the Valley of the Somme, reaching Abbeville, on the estuary of that river. Amiens and Arras fell. The Germans claimed that their air force, aided by submarines and torpedo-carrying mosquito boats, was in command of the Channel. However that may be, French and Belgian ports, from which the British must embark if all effort to hold the northern line is abandoned, were being unmercifully bombed last night. Despite all this activity in the west, the Germans did not let up in the southern part of their huge salient. The push toward Paris continued, with semi-official sources in Berlin saying the invaders had crossed the Aisne at Soissons, sixty miles from the capital. [Included in foregoing.]

Paris contended that only motorcycle troops had reached Abbeville. Despite the breakthrough, French authorities said there still was furious fighting in the neighborhood of Cambrai, far to the German rear, where the invaders had not yet succeeded in consolidating their positions. But there was as yet no sign of large-scale counterattack. [Page 1.]

The French admitted that the Somme Valley above St. Quentin was in chaos. Parachutists set hundreds of fires around Arras and Amiens; in the triangle between the Belgian border, Amiens and the Channel, not one railway station stood intact. [Page 1.]

The Germans apparently had succeeded in capturing the commander of the French Ninth Army, General Henri Honoré Giraud. A Berlin dispatch said the capture had been "half-tragic, half-comic"—that the general had walked into his headquarters and found German officers there. Paris admitted there had been no communication with the general for forty-eight hours. [Page 1.]

Early this morning waves of Allied fliers bombed Aachen (Aix-la-Chapelle), on the west border of Germany. Bombs showered on the city and on Westwall fortifications. This raid was outstanding among many aimed at the German rear. The British Air Ministry announced that during the night German planes had dropped bombs on two districts in Southeastern England; no damage or casualties were reported. [Page 1.]

Alfred Duff Cooper, British Minister of Information, warned his countrymen by radio that they might expect invasion at any time. Volunteer "parashoots" were rushed to positions guarding points vulnerable to attack by German soldiers floating down from the skies. [Page 3.]

Premier Reynaud, addressing the French Senate, said the inefficient training and handling of General André Georges Corap's army was responsible for France's plight. "Unbelievable faults" would be punished, he declared. The Premier said the classic French conception of war had been demolished by armored divisions, fighting planes and disorganization of the rear by parachutists. He emphasized his faith in France to surmount her period of trial, and asserted: "Abroad they are beginning to understand * * * that what is happening affects them and their children. Let them not come to this understanding too late." [Page 1.]

Repercussions Elsewhere

Italy, which is expected shortly to join the German side, closed the border between Italian-owned Albania and Yugoslavia, where Allied sentiment has been strong. There were reports in Yugoslavia that munitions were being rushed in below the border and that barrack and other military construction work was being pressed in twenty-four-hour shifts. [Page 5.]

President Roosevelt, at a press conference in Washington, appealed for national unity in preparedness. He set forth three points to govern policy in building up our defenses: (1) No war millionaires will be created; (2) labor must not take advantage of its collective power to foment strikes interfering with the defense program; (3) there must be no weakening of social legislation of the last seven years, notably laws affecting labor standards. [Page 1.]

HENDRICKSON LEADS IN JERSEY PRIMARY

Willkie Gets Surprise Write-In Vote Against Dewey in Presidential Contest

A write-in vote for Wendell L. Willkie in the New Jersey primaries yesterday disclosed surprising strength for the utilities executive as a candidate for President. State Senator Robert C. Hendrickson of Gloucester County was leading former Governor Harold G. Hoffman for the Republican nomination for Governor.

A total of 2,296 election districts out of 2,681 in the State gave 166,650 votes to Mr. Hendrickson and 144,290 to Mr. Hoffman, a commanding lead of 21,360 for Mr. Hendrickson.

Contrary to pre-election predictions, Hendrickson carried Bergen and Union Counties on the basis of incomplete returns. His margin in both counties was small, however. His plurality in Essex County was larger than had been expected.

State Senator Winant Van Winkle, a Hendrickson supporter, was slated for renomination in Bergen County by a Hoffman candidate, Lloyd L. Schroeder. Complete returns gave Schroeder 27,306 votes to 26,251 for Van Winkle.

District Attorney Thomas E. Dewey entered the Republican primary as a preferential candidate

Continued on Page Sixteen

ALLIES FIGHT BACK AT FURIOUS DRIVES

Admit Penetration of Nazis to Abbeville, but Look for Re-forming of Lines

By The Associated Press.

PARIS, May 21—The Allies, with their backs to the English Channel, tonight fought against a new German advance that spread a path of fire across Northern France and threatened to isolate England.

The French High Command's night communiqué admitted the Germans had driven their advance guard to Amiens and Arras, on the edge of the coastal plain leading to the English Channel.

A War Ministry spokesman said that German motorcycle troops had pushed on to the outskirts of the Abbeville region. The city of Abbeville is on the Somme estuary, twelve miles from the Channel's open waters, and about twenty-five miles west of Arras and Amiens. The War Ministry spokesman said he believed the French still held Abbeville itself, but that he could "give no official confirmation."

German motorcycle units thrust along roads to the west of Arras and Amiens behind advance bombardments and machine gunning from Nazi planes. Other roads leading from the French towns, filled with refugees, were reported strafed by the Germans from the

Continued on Page Four

PREMIER IS CANDID

'Unbelievable Faults' in Allied Defense to Be Punished, He Says

'DISASTER' ADMITTED

But France Is Told Hope and Savage Energy Can Still Bring Victory

The text of Premier Reynaud's address is on Page 6.

By P. J. PHILIP
Wireless to The New York Times.

PARIS, May 21—Announcing quietly, and a chilly silence, that since 8 o'clock this morning the advancing German forces had occupied Amiens and Arras, Premier Paul Reynaud in the Senate this afternoon called on the people of France, soldiers and civilians alike, to be worthy of the "grandeur of the hour in which we are living" and to "rise to the height of the misfortunes of our country."

Succinctly, sparing no one, he told the tragic story of the mistakes that had been made in the Belgian campaign, of the lack of preparation, of the terrible exactness of the German calculations and their consequences.

The Germans had broken the hinge on which the whole left wing of the Allied armies swung, the Premier explained. They had pounded through the breach and driven forward with their armored divisions and airplanes far behind the French northern defense line. The French classic conception of war had been utterly routed by this new conception which disorganized the country behind the lines while it piled hammer blow on hammer blow at strategic points.

Cites "Unbelievable Faults"

There had been, he went on, "unbelievable faults which will be punished." Bridges over the Meuse that should have been destroyed had not been destroyed. Describing what happened to General André Corap's army, he called it a "disaster" and "total disorganization." M. Reynaud seems not to have given up hope. He demanded that that hope should be backed by confidence and savage energy on the part of all who are fighting and working for the salvation of the country.

This new method of war must be met by new methods of defense, he held. France had in the past not repeatedly overcome such initial mistakes and miscalculations; she had risen from the pit of defeat to victory under Marshal Henri Philippe Pétain and Marshal Foch's lieutenant, General Maxime Weygand, in the past and could do so again.

There was an indirect word directed toward American and all the peoples far removed from the struggle. They were beginning to understand and to see that their future also was involved, M. Reynaud declared.

Continued on Page Six

NAZIS SPRINT TO COAST AND PUSH NEARER TO PARIS

Allied forces have been put in peril by a German spearhead driven between French and Belgian troops at Valenciennes (2) and by the westward push of the German right wing in Belgium, where the Belgians were engaged east of Ghent (1). Even more serious, however, was the advance to Abbeville (4) near the shore of the English Channel. As fighting raged north of Cambrai (3) motorised units swept south of that town and then, while some of them moved northward to Arras, the rest raced along the Somme valley, took Amiens and continued on to the coast. Nor was the threat to Paris lessened. At Amiens the Nazis claimed to have a bridgehead across the Somme, while to the east the German advance beyond Laon (5) was semi-officially declared to have resulted in the capture of Soissons, within sixty miles of Paris, and threats to both Noyon and Compiegne. At Rethel (6), however, the French said they were clinging to the south bank of the Aisne. The approximate limit of the German advance is shown by the broken line, which is based on dispatches received from both Berlin and Paris.

'Chutists and Cyclists Set Fires Behind Allied Lines

By The United Press.

PARIS, May 21—Germany unleashed the full fury of "total war" on Northern France today, dropping parachutists with torches to set fire to wide areas around Arras, Amiens and other cities in the Nazi drive to the English Channel.

Hundreds of German planes rained incendiary bombs on every city, village and community in the Picardy and Flanders lowlands, military dispatches said.

At the same time giant air transports unloaded aerial incendiaries who were instructed to race through the countryside and set fire to munitions factories, railway stations, munitions and fuel dumps and other such objectives in scores of cities between Cambrai and the sea.

In the triangle between the Belgian frontier, the Channel and Amiens, not one railway station stood intact tonight, military spokesmen said.

Property losses were tremendous along a corridor of destruction thirty-five miles wide in which not a building stood undamaged and

Continued on Page Two

Women, Children Begin Evacuation of Gibraltar

Wireless to The New York Times.

GIBRALTAR, May 21—Women and children are being evacuated from Gibraltar. The first batches left today for French Morocco. Others will follow tomorrow and subsequent days.

The action follows an official announcement today that the Governor of Gibraltar, Lieut. Gen. Sir Clive Liddell, had received instructions from the War Cabinet that owing to the international situation the evacuation of women and children from Gibraltar would be compulsory immediately.

Nazis Report Capture of Giraud; Say General Walked Into a Trap

Wireless to The New York Times.

BERLIN, May 21—The Germans told an astounding story today of how General Henri Giraud, commander of the French Ninth Army, was captured. In a lightning advance in the Cambrai sector, Nazi forces occupied the château headquarters of the French Ninth Army. Here they learned that the commanding general had left, having been relieved by order of the new Commander in Chief, General Maxime Weygand, by General Giraud, who had been head of the Seventh Army.

According to accounts here, the Germans on their high-speed "mystically and taking General Giraud and his staff into custody as they arrived to take charge, ignorant of the situation. The story of the capture leaked out in Berlin yesterday, but the High Command did not treat it spread, hoping that dispatch riders and others attached to the Ninth Army headquarters,

Continued on Page Five

500,000 'ISOLATED'

Swift Thrust to Coast Cuts Off Huge Force, Berlin Claims

SOISSONS 'TAKEN,' TOO

Invaders Stab at Paris as Threat to Britain Progresses

By GEORGE AXELSSON
Wireless to The New York Times.

BERLIN, May 21—In a crowning series of staggering blows dealt to the Allies in the last few days, the Germans claim tonight to have reached Abbeville on the Picardy coast, fifteen miles from Le Tréport on the English Channel. Thus they have now virtually achieved their aim to isolate the combined Allied armies in the western corner of Belgium and the northwestern tip of France. Unless they can fight their way out, this should seal the fate of the Belgian Army and numerous divisions of the French totaling perhaps between 500,000 and 1,000,000 men, including whatever British forces are left in this area.

[The German thrust toward Paris has reached the region of Reims, it was said in official German circles early today, according to an Associated Press dispatch from Berlin.]

In an apparently masterful enveloping movement rapidly closing in, the Germans claim to have definitely broken up the entire French Ninth Army, taking prisoner its commander, General Henri Giraud, with his complete staff. The mission of the Ninth Army was to insure liaison between the strong Allied units in Belgium and the Maginot Line south of Sedan.

En route to Abbeville, the Germans say, they occupied Amiens and Arras. The River Somme up to the estuary that the German tried until to reach in the "risk it all" drive in March, 1918, should thus be in their hands after brisk fighting that apparently lasted fewer hours than it did months during the World War.

Soissons Reported Taken

At the same time they are pushing toward Paris, and it is semi-officially said here tonight that they have separated the main French and British armies and trapped the entire British expeditionary force in an untenable position, the Allied High Command recognized tonight. The writer left one of the Channel ports today when the German drive was reaching its peak. It was directly menaced by advancing German mechanized units.

With perhaps 1,000,000 Allied troops hopelessly cut off and squeezed by powerful German armies between the mouths of the Rivers Scheldt and Somme, the question arises here in the minds of neutral military observers: How could the Allied Army leaders have permitted a situation threatening such a major disaster?

One explanation is that it is perhaps the outcome of a desperate French attempt at a counter-offensive aimed at the flank of the German right wing without having sufficiently insured the rear lines of communication. It is suggested that German tanks of the mastodon type may have charged the French laterally, cutting off their supply lines and forcing the bulk of the attackers clear through the fronts into the jaws of German tongs as flocks of Nazi dive-bombers efficiently supported the deadly ground work of the tank divisions.

French Effort Criticized

In this connection, it is asked here: What has happened to the French artillery? Is it a matter of record that the French have the most efficient artillery, from light field pieces including the famous 75's up to railway and other heavy long-range guns.

None of these, or more than French supertanks reputedly weighing in the neighborhood of fifty tons, have figured in reports of the fighting available here. The superiority of the German tank and of the German plane seems definitely established, in the eyes of observers here.

With the Channel ports from Ostend to Boulogne strongly compromised, a powerful German bid for final victory seems at a decisive stage. As seen from here, the Allied position is not altogether

Continued on Page Two

BRITISH FIGHT HARD TO AVOID DISASTER

Their Whole Force in Belgium Is Trapped in Untenable Position, Allies Admit

By The United Press.

LONDON, May 21—The lightning German thrust to the English Channel has separated the main French and British armies and trapped the entire British expeditionary force in an untenable position, the Allied High Command recognized tonight.

The British have their choice of attempting evacuation under a rain of German bombs over the entire Channel area or facing the enemy in a last-ditch effort to hold the only avenue of escape left to them—the Channel ports of Calais, Boulogne, Ostend and Blankenberge. In either event, the B. E. F. is fighting desperately to escape annihilation.

[In Berlin it was said that the British had received orders to embark for England and that "our planes are bombing embarkation centers."]

Le Touquet Threatened

The Germans are completing encircling tactics in their drive on the coast between Abbeville and Le Touquet, where they are due to reach at any hour.

[Le Touquet is about twenty miles north of Abbeville, from which a double-trunk railroad line runs to the French resort.]

German mechanized divisions were rumbling along roads leading to the principal ports. British forces were rushing to oppose them, but the Nazis were flushed with victory and no obstacle seemed capable of checking them.

The roads were crowded with refugees from Northern France, Belgium and the Netherlands. They blocked the roads and made Allied military manoeuvres more difficult.

The B. E. F. at present is awaiting the order of the Commander in Chief to make a terrific last stand in which it would throw all it possesses of gun power, tanks, infantry divisions and aircraft.

The French, on the other (southwestern) flank of the German columns, have been counterattacking

Continued on Page Two

AACHEN IS BOMBED HEAVILY BY ALLIES

Troop Concentrations There —German Bombs Dropped in Southeast England

By The United Press.

AACHEN, Germany, Wednesday, May 22—Waves of Allied bombing planes early today attacked this German city along the German Westwall fortifications, bombing and battling Nazi Messerschmitt fighters.

The first air raid alarm was sounded at 12:45 A. M., when the first enemy bombers appeared over the city and began dropping bombs. The city was met by anti-aircraft fire for fifteen minutes and Messerschmitt fighters went into the sky to battle the raiders. From then on the Allied planes came in waves and were still sweeping upon the city at 1:05 A. M.

[Aachen, also known as Aix-la-Chapelle, lies at the point of the German, Netherland and Belgian borders and was the "jumping off" place for the German invasion of Belgium on May 10.]

Continued on Page Four

Dispatches from Europe and the Far East are subject to censorship at the source.

"All the News That's Fit to Print."

The New York Times.

LATE CITY EDITION
Partly cloudy today, showers tonight, little change in temperature. Tomorrow showers.
Temperatures Yesterday—Max., 64; Min., 53

Copyright, 1940, by The New York Times Company

VOL. LXXXIX...No. 30,077.

Entered as Second-Class Matter, Postoffice, New York, N. Y.

NEW YORK, THURSDAY, MAY 30, 1940.

THREE CENTS NEW YORK CITY and Vicinity | FOUR CENTS Elsewhere Except in 7th and 8th Postal Zones

ALLIES ABANDONING FLANDERS, FLOOD YSER AREA; A RESCUE FLEET AT DUNKERQUE; FOE POUNDS PORT; ONE FORCE CUT OFF FROM THE SEA AS LILLE FALLS

PRESIDENT TO ASK $750,000,000 MORE FOR ARMY PROGRAM

Nazi Blitzkrieg Held to Show the $3,300,000,000 Allotted Fails to Meet Needs

FOR TANKS, GUNS, PLANES

Tax Bill to Be Offered in House Today—D. M. Nelson Named Procurement Director

By FELIX BELAIR Jr.
Special to THE NEW YORK TIMES.

WASHINGTON, May 29—On the eve of his first meeting with the reconstituted Council of National Defense, President Roosevelt was putting finishing touches today on a new request for $750,000,000 as a supplemental appropriation for further expansion and mechanization of the military establishment to take account of European war developments since he sent his preparedness message to Congress two weeks ago.

The projected increase in funds for the Army, over and above the omnibus $3,300,000,000 defense program already pending, was mapped by the President in a White House conference with Treasury and War Department officials.

It was the President's plan to send up the supplemental request in a few days. Subject to additions, the new program contemplates placing orders immediately for the following:

About 3,000 new pursuit and bombing planes.

Between 1,500 and 2,000 tanks.

About 500 heavy howitzers.

A supply of aerial bombs of various sizes, to cost between $20,000,000 and $30,000,000.

Other modern weapons of war which have been developed in Army laboratories, but not yet put into actual production.

German Drive Appraised

There was no official announcement on the results of the meeting, and Secretary Woodring, who acted as spokesman for the group, said only that they had reviewed "the whole military situation."

From others present, however, it was learned that the nation's military establishment had been reappraised in the light of Germany's advances in Western Europe since the President's preparedness message was first submitted to Congress.

Other developments in the national defense program were:

1. The Senate Naval Affairs Committee brought out a measure increasing the air force limit of the Navy to 10,000 planes and 16,000 pilots, with a report warning that "the country at this time is facing the possibility that the Allies may be defeated and that we may have to defend ourselves in both oceans at the same time."

2. Senate leaders were planning to take up tomorrow the $1,500,000,000 bill providing an 11 per cent increase in under-age surface tonnage, with indications that the measure would be disposed of without delay.

Procurement Officer Named

3. Secretary Morgenthau named Donald M. Nelson, executive vice president of Sears, Roebuck & Co., as director of the Treasury's Procurement Division, thereby adding another business executive to the list of those on whom the administration is relying for the success of the defense program.

4. Administration - Congressional plans for placing emergency rearmament financing on a "pay-as-you-go" basis gathered momentum, with an announcement by Representative Doughton, chairman of the House Ways and Means Committee, that he would introduce emphatically a measure raising the statutory debt limit by $3,000,000,000 and imposing upward of $656,000,000 in new defense taxes.

5. Secretary Hull modified aviation restrictions under the Neutrality Act to permit the delivery of American planes by American pilots to Halifax, N. S., thereby removing the ban on through deliveries over the Maritime Provinces.

6. White House sources explained that there would be the closest possible relations between the

Continued on Page Eight

When You Think of Writing Think of Whiting.—Advt.

ALLIES STRIKE FOR COAST IN EVER-TIGHTENING POCKET

To keep the exit at Dunkerque (1) open French and British sea, land and air forces were waging a furious struggle yesterday; to retard the German advance the Allies were understood to have opened sluice gates on the Yser to flood the region below Nieuport (2). In the sector that had been held by the Belgians the Nazis pushed to Ostend and Dixmude (3). Farther south they were reported to have taken Ypres (4). Their most important operation of the day, however, was the bisecting of the pocket by the capture of Lille and Armentieres (5), thus cutting off from the sea the Allied forces in the lower section. Along the Somme the French eliminated a German bridgehead west of Amiens (6). The broken lines show the approximate battlefronts.

HULL ORDER SPEEDS PLANES TO ALLIES

Allows Our Pilots to Fly Craft Over Three Canadian Maritime Provinces

Special to THE NEW YORK TIMES.

WASHINGTON, May 29—The way was opened today for expediting deliveries of American airplanes to the Allied fighting lines when Secretary Hull modified regulations of the Neutrality Act to permit the delivery of such aircraft by American pilots to ports in the three eastern Canadian provinces.

The step was designed to facilitate deliveries to the Allies because of the urgency of their military situation. It was taken at the request of the French Government.

Mr. Hull ruled that "American nationals may travel in belligerent aircraft over the Canadian Provinces of New Brunswick, Nova Scotia and Prince Edward Island."

This means that pilots from the United States may fly new planes to Halifax, whence they will be flown across the Atlantic by pilots of the Allies or sent across by ship.

American pilots have been delivering planes in Ottawa and other Canadian cities. As before, they must still conform under the new order to regulations by pushing planes over the Canadian border from the United States.

Previously, while American pilots could fly planes over Canadian territory, once they were pushed over the border the fliers could not enter the three eastern maritime Provinces because American ships are barred from them and aircraft regulations conform to shipping rules. Newfoundland was excluded from the modification today because there was no actual need for including it.

Berlin Exchange Slumps As Optimism Is Decried

Wireless to THE NEW YORK TIMES.

BERLIN, May 29—In what was apparently a strong reaction to warnings against over-optimism, which have been circulated generally among the population following the German victories in the West, the Berlin Boerse today took a sudden nose dive.

Most values dropped between 1 and 4 per cent. In shipping, Hapag dropped 5 per cent and North German Lloyd dropped 2 per cent. Fixed interest securities were quiet and generally unchanged. The close was irregular, with call money at 1⅛-2%.

Utilities, motor works and other heavy industries led the recession, while metal works in the Rhineland were among those that showed the maximum decline.

URUGUAY ON GUARD FOR FIFTH COLUMN

Check on Assembly, Increase in Army Urged—Nazis Take Bold Tone in Ecuador

Special Cable to THE NEW YORK TIMES.

MONTEVIDEO, Uruguay, May 29—The Uruguayan Government is frankly alarmed over Nazi fifth column activities.

After several Cabinet meetings at which the problem was closely studied, President Alfredo Baldomir has sent to Congress, with a request for urgent action, two bills. One provides for general rearmament and the other modifies Article 38 of the Constitution, which guarantees the right of assembly.

It has been rumored in well-informed diplomatic circles in more than one South American capital yesterday and today that Uruguay fears an invasion of Nazi fifth columnists from Southern Brazil. Official circles tonight emphatically denied any such fear and also denied that Uruguay had requested assistance from any other government.

The President's office earlier in the day, however, had published the details of the plans for rearmament and for modifying the constitutional guarantees.

Article 38 of the Constitution says that "all persons have a right to form themselves into associations," whatever may be the object sought, except that they do not constitute an association declared by law to be illicit.

Since the law doesn't define what constitutes an illicit association, the bill that President Baldomir sent to Congress yesterday defines such il-

Continued on Page Six

ITALY BARS IMPORTS EXCEPT BY BARTER

Cancels Permits to Bring In Goods or to Buy Exchange for Payments Abroad

By HERBERT L. MATTHEWS
By Telephone to THE NEW YORK TIMES.

ROME, May 29—The Ministry of Foreign Exchange issued an order today to all banks and industrial firms canceling permits for importation and permission to acquire foreign currency to pay for imports. Thus Italy cuts herself off commercially from the world, except for barter agreements, and even there Italian ships coming in are not departing to bring back further imports.

This is the most serious indication yet given of the expectation of war, certainly as serious as the postponement of the sailing of those ships announced last Friday.

The Conte di Savoia is due back from New York Sunday. No one expects her to depart, even on June 23, when she is scheduled to go. She will leave only the Conte Grande out of the Mediterranean among the large Italian ships. She sailed for South America a week ago.

[The steamship Roma arrived yesterday at Naples, according to The Associated Press, and is now expected to remain there instead of proceeding to Genoa, as scheduled. The Roma was to have left Genoa for New York June 21.]

Trade with the United States will suffer most heavily by the decision taken today. It has been possible for importers to acquire dollars at

Continued on Page Four

11,000 Times Speedier Way Found To Obtain Atomic Power Element

By WILLIAM L. LAURENCE

Development of a process that speeds up by 11,000 times the extraction of U-235, the element recently discovered to possess 5,000,000 times the power output of coal, promising to make it possible to utilize atomic energy as a new source of enormous power for all purposes, and to place in the hands of the nations at war, especially Germany, the most powerful fuel ever to be discovered, is to be announced in the forthcoming issue of Nature, leading British scientific weekly, advance proofs of which have reached THE NEW YORK TIMES.

Germany, more than any other European nation, has been concentrating on developing this power. If the tests succeed the Allied blockade could be materially offset.

The new process for extracting U-235 that promises to revolutionize methods of power production and to usher in a new civilization based on the utilization of atomic power, was developed by Professor Wilhelm Krasny-Ergen of the Wenner-Grens Institute, Stockholm, Sweden, one of the leading scientific research institutions in Europe.

On May 6 it was announced that a tiny amount of U-235, a relative of uranium, had been isolated at the University of Minnesota and at the General Electric Company, and that pioneer experiments at the physics laboratories at Columbia University, under the direction of Professor

NAZIS TIGHTEN TRAP

They Drive a Line Across Pocket, Encircling Foes in South

SAY YPRES IS TAKEN

Zeebrugge and Ostend Fall—Large Stores Are Reported Seized

By GEORGE AXELSSON
Wireless to THE NEW YORK TIMES.

BERLIN, May 29—Remnants of the Allied Armies cut off in Flanders came a step nearer to being wiped out today when the Germans, simultaneously pressing from east and west toward the middle, managed to drive a wedge right across the pocket, thus separating the French and British divisions north of Lille from those in the south, who now are surrounded on all sides, no longer having access to the sea.

The Germans tonight claim to be in the city of Lille, Ypres and Armentières and to have burned Dunkerque under heavy artillery bombardment. The Belgian capitulation permitted the Germans to take Bruges, Zeebrugge, Ostend and Thourout without a struggle.

Piercing the Allied lines at Lille, Ypres, however, fortifications still seem to hold out, permitted the Germans to make two pockets out of the big one. The smaller of these, south of Lille, is square with the sides between nine and twelve miles long, and inside this narrow space are compressed the French divisions that only a few days ago tried to break the strong German hold at Valenciennes, as well as British contingents that figured in desperate resistance in the sector between Arras and Cambrai.

Hemmed in with these troops is an incalculable number of refugees and other civilians, who are exposed to bombs and shell fire on the same terms as the soldiers fighting one another in this area.

The larger northern pocket reaches from Lille to the sea, and although it is some thirty miles wide the situation of the troops enclosed in it appears to be hardly more enviable than that of their comrades surrounded to the south. They are being hard pressed on three sides by withering German fire as well as from the air.

Their only chance of retreat, should they choose this way out, seems to be the narrow strip of coast between Dunkerque and Nieuport, but the Germans are said to be continuously shelling and bombing this district, making an exit, even if protected by Allied warships, seem most difficult.

Crowded together in an area bounded by Dixmude, Ypres—which the Germans claim to have taken by storm tonight—Armentières, Bailleul and Bergues, remnants of the British Expeditionary Forces and whatever French and Belgians remain thereabout appear to have a choice only between death or surrender.

The situation up there, according to latest reports received in Berlin, indicates that the Allies have chosen to fight to the last. The Germans stand before Dixmude, where the British are holding them, and a similarly bitter struggle is raging at

Continued on Page Four

The International Situation

On the Battle Fronts

The Battle of Flanders became yesterday a wholly rear-guard action, with the Allies trying to evacuate as many as possible of the troops caught in the German pocket. The trapped men fought on "desperately but not despairingly," Paris reported. [Page 1.]

The desperate situation of the Allied army of the north was made evident by Berlin dispatches telling of the success of the German effort to cut the opposing forces in two. The invaders drove a wedge between the two Allied wings to the north of Lille. Thus there are now two pockets; the forces south of Lille are completely surrounded, in a square-shaped area whose sides measure only nine to twelve miles. The pocket above Lille was greatly reduced by German advances pressing down from the north and up from the south. [Page 1.]

Early this morning shattered remnants of the British Expeditionary Force began arriving at British ports. Most of the men were wounded. To the survivors still in Flanders King George sent a message saying they had displayed "gallantry that has never been surpassed in the annals of the British Army." [Page 1.]

The Allies recorded a victory in Norway. They took Narvik, and the Germans admitted its loss. The British said their warships had sunk seven German troop transports in the Narvik area in the last three days. [Page 1.]

The French asserted that they had eliminated a German bridgehead on the Somme west of Amiens, and had repulsed a German thrust near Rethel, on the left flank of the invaders. [Included in the foregoing.]

Repercussions Elsewhere

Britain took drastic measures to guard against possible fifth column activities on the part of aliens. Beginning June 3, all aliens must be in their "ordinary place of residence" from 10:30 P. M. to 6 A. M.; they are forbidden to own bicycles, boats or aircraft without special permission. [Page 3.]

Italy, by decreeing an end to import and foreign currency permits, cut herself off from the world commercially, except for her barter arrangements. And even they have ceased to mean anything, as Italian vessels no longer are being sent abroad for cargoes. The new regulations gave the strongest indication yet of Italy's intention to join Germany in the field soon. [Page 1.]

Because Russia had refused to accept Sir Stafford Cripps, Left-Wing Labor member of the British Parliament, as a "special trade envoy," London conferred Ambassadorial status on him. Sir Stafford is in Athens, en route to Moscow. With offers of improved trade with Britain, he will seek to woo Russia away from Germany. [Page 4.]

The Nazi fifth-column technique stirred fears in South America. Uruguay's Congress received from President Baldomir two bills, one of which would provide for rearmament, the other modifying the Constitution to deny the right of assembly to anti-democratic organizations with foreign connections. [Page 1.]

What has happened in Flanders impelled a reappraisal in Washington of American defense plans, with the result that President Roosevelt decided to ask Congress for $750,000,000 (in addition to the $3,300,000,000 already projected) to be used to buy 3,000 pursuit and bombing planes, 1,500 tanks, 500 heavy howitzers and at least $20,000,000 in aerial bombs. [Page 1.] The Senate Naval Affairs Committee, recommending House-adopted bills to speed air and naval preparedness, said the country's defense plans must be based on the possibility of defeat for the Allies. [Page 9.]

COAST FIGHT RAGES

Communications Lines and Bases Bombarded Constantly by Nazis

DUNKERQUE SHELLED

Allies Inflicting Heavy Losses as They Battle in Rear-Guard Actions

By G. H. ARCHAMBAULT
Wireless to THE NEW YORK TIMES.

PARIS, May 29—The full import of the Belgian defection during the course of the battle in Flanders may be gathered from the indication given tonight by a spokesman for the General Staff that King Leopold's army represented about half the Allied forces engaged on that front.

French and British in that area continue to fight desperately, though not despairingly yet, with the knowledge that at present at least little help can be given them. Their valor is described as very comforting in the circumstances, and it is added that whatever happens their honor will be safe.

Breaking the anonymity rule that has prevailed hitherto, it was announced this evening that, under General Georges Maurice Jean Blanchard's direction, General René-Jacques-Adolf Prioux is striving to fight his way to the coast in the general direction of Dunkerque, where Vice Admiral Jean Marie Abrial of the French Navy is co-operating and is holding that base, where he has organized a service of supplies with vessels of all kinds of tonnage.

Prioux a Cavalry Man

General Prioux was a corps commander at the beginning of the war; he is sixty-one years of age and comes from the cavalry arm.

No one has yet come from that inferno in Flanders to describe the scene; doubtless it baffles the imagination. For the battle is being waged on land, in the air, on the sea and under the sea. Every engine of death yet devised by man is in action, and the fight never ceases day or night. Nor is it confined to the actual battlefield. All bases, all lines of communication are bombed continually on both sides, with the Germans concentrating a great effort on Dunkerque.

The communiqué issued from French General Headquarters this morning said that "information from accurate sources warrants the affirmation that the losses suffered by the Germans in the engagements yesterday and last night were particularly high."

The French and British are fighting mostly rear-guard actions, but whenever any unit finds itself in approximately equal strength it counter-attacks "to progress over the enemy dead."

Position Very Critical

Nevertheless despite heroic deeds it cannot be gainsaid that the position of the Allied division is very critical.

The exact position of General Blanchard's forces is not known; his front in any case must be very fluid. Doubtless he has shortened his lines in order to constitute a sort of mobile fortress moving toward the sea and fighting every inch of the way. The tragic aspect of its situation lies in the fact that the prime task of Leopold's army was to cover the coast.

It is revealed today in this connection that it was at the Belgian King's repeated insistence that the Allies took up positions on the Schelde to protect Antwerp and also that the order to retreat was deferred until May 15, although the Allied High Command had urged withdrawal on the eleventh or twelfth.

There is confirmation today of the indication given yesterday in these dispatches that before the capitulation news came French detachments between the Belgians and the sea. It is hoped that though relatively small they may have acted effectively along the coast. It is believed, moreover, that it has been possible to flood that part of the country west of the Yser River. While lines of this last war in this very region.

On the coast the Allies have lost Ostend. They hold Nieuport and

Continued on Page Two

ALLIES GET NARVIK IN LAND-SEA FIGHT

Warships Support Troops in Final Thrust From Beis and Rombaks Fjords

By JAMES MacDONALD
Special Cable to THE NEW YORK TIMES.

LONDON, May 29—Narvik, Norway's important iron ore port, the prize of an unrelenting struggle ever since Germany invaded Norway on April 9, has been captured by Allied forces, the War Office and Admiralty announced in a joint communiqué today. The communiqué also announced the capture of Fagerness, on the shore of Narvik Harbor, and Forsneset, five miles east of Narvik on the railway line over which Swedish iron ore reaches Narvik for shipment to Germany.

Fierce fighting by Norwegian, French, British and Polish forces continues in the district. An unofficial report received here today said British naval forces had sunk seven German troop transports in Narvik waters since Sunday.

British warships are reported high up in Rombaks Fjord, shelling German positions on the Ofoten railway. In a narrow part of the fjord the Germans have sunk four ships in an attempt to block off the British naval vessels.

Other reports reaching London today said German planes had raided Bodoe, at the entrance to Vaest Fjord, about ninety miles south of Narvik, last evening, dropping 200 bombs and machine-gunning the town. Of the population of 6,000, it is said at least 5,000 are now

Continued on Page Five

HARRIED B. E. F. MEN ARRIVING IN BRITAIN

Many of Wounded Had to Wade Out to Boats Under Constant Fire of German Forces

By The United Press.

LONDON, Thursday, May 30—Shattered remnants of the British Expeditionary Force—blood-stained, muddy and walking like men asleep—began arriving in British ports today.

Most of the first arrivals were wounded. They described a constant, pitiless German bombing and strafing bombardment of the French ports from which Viscount Gort is attempting to save his trapped divisions.

They said the shattered British forces were "dying off a stretch of coast thirty miles long."

German bombs rained down continually, even on hospital ships, they said. Quays and harbor works of the French ports were under terrific German air attack, which went on all through last night.

Allied warships and the Royal Air Force worked and fought like beavers to aid the rescue of the battered armies of Flanders whose fate was teetered on the Channel's brink. Under a screen of intense curtain fire from long-range naval guns, the B. E. F. was backing out through the Dunkerque zone.

Continued on Page Five

Dispatches from Europe and the Far East are subject to censorship at the source.

105

"All the News That's Fit to Print."

The New York Times.

LATE CITY EDITION
Cloudy with showers and little change in temperature today and tomorrow.
Temperature Yesterday—Max., 85; Min., 57

Copyright, 1940, by The New York Times Company.

VOL. LXXXIX..No. 30,089.

Entered as Second-Class Matter,
Postoffice, New York, N. Y.

NEW YORK, TUESDAY, JUNE 11, 1940.

THREE CENTS NEW YORK CITY and Vicinity | FOUR CENTS Elsewhere Except in 7th and 8th Postal Zones.

ITALY AT WAR, READY TO ATTACK; STAB IN BACK, SAYS ROOSEVELT; GOVERNMENT HAS LEFT PARIS

NAZIS NEAR PARIS

Units Reported to Have Broken Through Lines to West of Capital

SEINE RIVER CROSSED

3 Columns Branch Out From Soissons—Enemy Held, French State

By The Associated Press.

PARIS, June 10—Marauding German tanks were reported tonight to have reached the Paris region itself as the government left the capital.

While some German armored advance guards were said to have penetrated to the environs of Paris in isolated raids through the French lines, the main front was about thirty-five miles west and northeast of the capital. Although steadily approaching, the battle's roar still could not be heard there.

[The German High Command has no knowledge that Nazi tank units have reached the Paris region, The United Press reported.]

The battle, which had been waged heretofore on familiar World War territory for the most part, swung all along the Seine in an effort to prevent the Germans from effecting further passages and taking the capital from the rear.

The French took their main stand west of Paris all along the Seine in an effort to prevent the Germans from effecting further passages and taking the capital from the rear.

In the central sector of the Oise Valley, directly north of Paris where the Germans had suffered tremendous losses, they held back their infantry and sent out dive bombers in an effort to break down French resistance.

They broadened their salient, however, farther east, where they had crossed the Aisne. Three columns fanned out from Soissons through La Ferte Milon and Fere en Tardenois and toward Flames.

Hold Firm on East Flank

These were just north of Chateau Thierry and the Marne, where they were stopped in their 1918 thrust by Americans fighting with the French.

On the east flank, where the French have been holding firm, fresh German infantry, tanks and planes battered the French lines, but with small gains.

But France, besieged on two sides by Germans driving on Paris from the north and the Italians entering the war on the south, proclaimed her grim determination to carry on the fight.

The main combats were centered in the Seine Valley to the west of Paris, with the high German commander declaring that some German elements had crossed the Seine at certain points, and in the Ourcq River Valley to the northeast of the capital.

The communiqué, however, said the "enemy is held everywhere by vigorous counter-attacks."

The French communiqué was filed from Paris, but was issued "Somewhere in France." The regular press conference of the War Office was not held this morning, as only a few attachés were in the office.

The High Command reported that the German break-through to the Paris region resulted from increased pressure applied by the Nazis between the route from Amiens to Rouen and from Amiens to Vernon as far as the lower Seine.

In the other principal area of combat, east of the Oise River, German columns coming down from the region of Soissons have resumed their attack toward the Ourcq River.

The German offensive in the

Continued on Page Two

FRESHEN UP for a tough job! Be cool when there's work to be done . . . Smoke a soothing pipe of tobacco to keep your head clear as a bell.—Advt.

The International Situation

On the Battle Fronts

Italian guns will speak today in Europe. Italy's declaration of war against France and Britain became effective at 12:01 A. M., Rome time. Before 100,000 men and women, packed in the Piazza Venezia and near-by streets, Premier Mussolini yesterday announced his decision. It was war against "the plutocratic and reactionary democracies of the West." For the present that does not include the United States, but Rome reports that few Italians, from Signor Mussolini down, believe they will see the end of this war without having America against them.

The Italian Premier specifically excluded Turkey, Switzerland, Yugoslavia, Greece and Egypt from his military designs. Rome hoped Turkey would fail to keep her agreement to support the Allies in a Mediterranean war. Demonstrators in Rome carried placards naming Italian objectives in the war—Tunisia, Jibuti, Corsica, Suez, Malta, Cyprus. There were reports that action against some of these places already had started. But Rome was convinced that nothing big would get under way until today. [All the foregoing. Page 1, Column 8.]

The sixth day of the Battle of France brought the German invaders still closer to Paris; at one point—south of Beauvais—they were said to be within twenty-five or thirty miles of their goal. On the French left wing the Germans crossed the Seine at several points in a dangerous advance that threatened to en-

velop the capital. In the center, they pushed through to the Ourcq Valley, a movement that similarly threatened to flank Reims. On the French right wing the German pressure was furiously increased; but the French said no great gains had resulted. Information from the French side was less complete than usual because the government press bureau was evacuated from Paris and had not yet established a stable headquarters. [Page 1, Column 1.]

The French Government moved, apparently to the neighborhood of Tours. An exodus of civilians from Paris got under way. [Page 1, Column 2.]

Berlin analyzed the front thus: A semicircle had been thrown around Paris, from which three wedges were being driven into the defense lines. The first, in the lower Seine Valley, succeeded in cutting off the extreme left of the French Army, which can now be pushed to the coast. The second was progressing toward the Marne from the Aisne below Soissons. The third, on the French right, had pierced the Aisne and was headed toward Reims. [Page 1, Column 5.]

London admitted the loss of the airplane carrier Glorious, two destroyers, a transport and an oil tanker—totaling 50,706 tons—in an engagement in the North Sea. King Haakon of Norway arrived in Britain with his government. Some Norwegian troops also were carried off and will continue the war on the Western Front. [Page 16, Column 3.]

Repercussions Elsewhere

President Roosevelt, in a broadcast speech, termed Italy's entry into the war a threat to the American way of life. "The hand that held the dagger has struck it into the back of its neighbor," he said. Declaring it an "obvious delusion that we of the United States can safely permit the United States to become a lone island in a world dominated by the philosophy of force," he advocated all possible material aid to the Allies. [Page 1, Column 4.]

Switzerland reported much military activity, but no rumble of guns, in mountain passes between France and Italy. The Swiss were concerned about rumors that there were new German troop concentrations on the country's northern frontier. [Page 5, Column 5.]

Turkey stood ready to fulfill her engagements to the Allies under the mutual-assistance pact of last October. It was believed that the first step, once Italy made that pact operative by an aggressive move in the Mediterranean, would be the placing of Turkish ports and air fields at the disposal of the Allies. [Page 1, Column 7.]

Belgrade heard reports that the Italians had landed troops and much mechanized equipment at the Italian-owned port of Zara, which is on the Yugoslav coast, and has evidenced its unwillingness to find the means through pacific negotiation, for the satisfaction of what it believes are its legitimate aspirations. [Page 1, Column 6.]

Berlin, jubilant over the entry of the Italians, expressed the belief that Premier Mussolini's mil-

OUR HELP PLEDGED

President Offers Our Full Material Aid to Allies' Cause

AMERICA IN DANGER

Fate Hangs on Training and Arms, He Says at Charlottesville

The text of the President's speech will be found on Page 6.

By FELIX BELAIR Jr.
Special to THE NEW YORK TIMES.

CHARLOTTESVILLE, Va., June 10—"On this 10th day of June, 1940, the hand that held the dagger has struck it into the back of its neighbor." In these words tonight President Roosevelt condemned the decision of Premier Mussolini which took Italy into the war on the side of Germany.

The remark was interpolated by the President in an address at the graduation exercises of the University of Virginia here. There could be no missing the depth of his feeling, since he put into the words all the emphasis at his command.

Italy's intervention was denounced furthermore as a definite threat to the way of life and the trade and commerce of the Americas. This government, he said, would give all material aid to France and Great Britain as "opponents of force."

The Chief Executive of the United States spoke to the nation and to the world only a few hours after Premier Mussolini announced his decision to join hands with Chancellor Hitler and unleashed his fascist legions against France and Great Britain. More details were revealed by Mr. Roosevelt of his correspondence with the Italian dictator in an effort to keep Italy at peace and to prevent the spread of war to the Mediterranean basin.

"To the Regret of Humanity"

"Unfortunately—unfortunately, to the regret of all of us and to the regret of humanity—the chief of the Italian Government was unwilling to accept the procedure suggested, and he has made no counter proposal," the President said.

And a moment later:

"The Government of Italy has now chosen to preserve what it terms its freedom of action and to fulfill what it states are its promises to Germany. In so doing it has manifested disregard for the rights and security of other nations, disregard for the lives of the peoples of those nations which are directly threatened by the spread of this war, and has evidenced its unwillingness to find the means through pacific negotiation, for the satisfaction of what it believes are its legitimate aspirations."

The President bespoke the prayers and hopes of this nation for those peoples beyond the seas who were battling for their freedom.

"In our American unity," he

Continued on Page Six

Nazi Tide Laps at Paris as Italy Joins War

On the western end of the line the Germans pushed a wedge to the Seine southeast of Rouen (1) and struck mighty blows in the region of Beauvais (2). In the center they reached the Ourcq River below Soissons (3). To the east they crossed the Aisne at two points near Vouziers (4).

Italy's announcement of her entry into the war was accompanied by no attack anywhere. One report had Italian troops invading the French Riviera (1), but this was unsupported. Rome's troops landed on two Italian-owned points on the Yugoslav coast: Zara (2) and Lagosta (3). In Albania (4) Italian military preparations were accelerated.

NAZIS CLAIM BREAK IN SUPPLY ARTERY

Paris Cut Off From Havre by Thrust to Seine East of Rouen, Berlin Says

By C. BROOKS PETERS
Wireless to THE NEW YORK TIMES.

BERLIN, June 10—German forces in Northern France are fighting tonight to shorten the radius of action before Paris by drawing about Paris, according to reports received here. Apparently they are attempting to drive three wedges into the remaining French territory north of the capital.

The first is on the Germans' extreme right wing, which is reported to have reached the lower Seine east of Rouen and therewith cuts off Paris from Havre. Mass tank formations, assisted by light motorized forces, are claimed here to have made more than a sixty-mile ad-

Continued on Page Eleven

Three Italian Freighters Are Scuttled by Crews

LA LINEA, Spain, Tuesday, June 11—Two Italian merchant ships, the 10,000-ton Chelina and the 2,000-ton Numbolla, were scuttled by their crews in Gibraltar waters late yesterday [Monday] when their crews heard the radio news that Italy had gone to war.

RIMOUSKI, Que., June 10 (UP)—The 3,921-ton Italian freighter Capo Noli was set afire by her crew tonight as she proceeded down the St. Lawrence. The scuttling attempt failed.

The Marine Department said the Canadian pilot grounded the freighter near the Father Point pilot station. A naval control boat extinguished the flames.

The government salvage boat Lord Strathcona left Quebec tonight for the site with a large derrick in tow. The Capo Noli will be taken over by the Canadian Government and her crew probably will be interned.

TURKEY PREPARES UNDER ALLIED PACT

Partial Mobilization Expected Today—Troops Are on Move —Precautions in Balkans

By J. W. KERNICK
Special Cable to THE NEW YORK TIMES.

ISTANBUL, Turkey, June 10—Turkey, speeding her military preparations as a result of Italy's entry into the war, stood ready tonight to fulfill her obligations under her mutual-assistance agreement with Britain and France.

That accord, concluded last October, stipulates that Turkey will aid the Allies every assistance in her power in the event of hostilities in the Mediterranean as a result of aggressive action by a European power. Hence Turkish aid can be invoked as soon as the first shot is fired.

The Italian action has already resulted in the calling of several classes to the colors by the Turkish Government. It is believed that the next move will be to place ports and airfields at the disposal of the Allies.

[The Turkish Cabinet met last night to consider the question of war or peace, The Associated Press reported, but it was believed that Turkey's entrance into the war would be by gradual steps, not immediately.]

Italy's declaration of war caused neither surprise nor excitement in Turkey. The Turks had suspected for some time and lately became certain that Premier Mussolini could not forever remain an onlooker while Chancellor Hitler marched.

Premier Mussolini's assurances that he did not intend to attack Yugoslavia, Turkey, Greece, Switz-

Continued on Page Four

Soviet Action Discounted

Russia has washed her hands of the struggle. The Italians know that any disturbance in the Balkans will immediately bring her in; but as long as the struggle is confined to the west and south the Soviet will do nothing either to hinder or help. This was told to your correspondent a few hours ago by a very authoritative source.

It was emphasized there were no elements about furnishing material or anything else, nor any threats or promises.

The Italian Ambassador, Augusto Rosso, left in the morning for Moscow and Ivan Gorelkin, Soviet Ambassador, is coming back to Rome, thus ending a long period without such representation. The Italians were anxious to restore full diplomatic relations in this critical period, according to the view taken by the informant, and the Russians agreed, but without compromising themselves.

It is thus appears that Premier Mussolini has embarked on this dangerous venture without really knowing what Soviet Russia will do in the long run.

President Roosevelt's speech clearly has come too late. There was nothing that the United States could do to halt this conflict, the Italians say. Whatever broke Mr. Roosevelt may have exercised was overcome by the momentum of Italian Fascist policy. Once it was set in motion, nothing could stop it. The Italians do not believe that the United States can affect the issue, whatever it does. They are

Continued on Page Four

DUCE GIVES SIGNAL

Announces War on the 'Plutocratic' Nations of the West

ASSURES 5 NEUTRALS

Bid Is Made to Russia, But Rome Has No Pledge of Aid

'Hostilities' Are Reported

"Hostilities were started four hours ago, Central European time," Radio Roma, the official Italian short-wave radio, said last night at 11 o'clock Eastern daylight time in a broadcast recorded by Columbia Broadcasting System's short-wave listening station.

"The first Italian war bulletin is expected to be issued within a few hours."

At 11 A. M. today, however, the official British wireless said that "there have been no reports as yet of any engagements growing out of Italy's entrance into the war," Columbia's listening station reported.

By HERBERT L. MATTHEWS
By Telephone to THE NEW YORK TIMES.

ROME, Tuesday, June 11—Italy declared war on Great Britain and France yesterday afternoon, to take effect at one minute past midnight. The land, air and sea forces of the Italian Empire were already in motion.

It is a war, as Premier Benito Mussolini announced to the people from his balcony at the Palazzo Venezia at 6 in the evening, against "the plutocratic and reactionary democracies of the West." For the moment that does not include the United States, but few Italians believe that they will see the war to a finish without having the Americans against them.

Signor Mussolini expressly excluded Turkey, Switzerland, Yugoslavia, Greece and Egypt as enemies unless they attacked Italy or the Italian possessions.

Turkey provides the burning question of the day. Italians are absolutely convinced that the Turks will not move against them and will not honor their agreement with the Allies. It is hoped to confine Italian activity to France, Great Britain and the Mediterranean and to keep the Balkans tranquil. If that can be done, Italians think, the Turks will remain quiet.

FRENCH MINISTRIES MOVED SOUTHWARD

Tours Is Believed New Capital, but Reynaud Goes to Army —No Civilian Panic

By The Associated Press.

PARIS, June 10—The French Government left Paris tonight.

"Paul Reynaud, Premier, has gone with the armies," said a communiqué, which also declared:

"The High Command asked the Ministers to effect their withdrawal to the provinces in conformity with established dispositions. This withdrawal has been effected."

The announcement of the departure of the Ministers was made only after they were safely installed "somewhere in France" in the southern provinces.

The government transfer at General Maxime Weygand's request was approved last night at a Cabinet meeting.

Under cover of darkness the Ministers drove to their new offices

Continued on Page Ten

ADELPHIA HOTEL, Chestnut at 13th. Rooms now $2.50 up.—Advt.

BRITISH NAVY GUNS HAMMER AT NAZIS

Shelling From Sea, Rushing of Troops and Planes Mark London's Share in Battle

By HAROLD DENNY
Special Cable to THE NEW YORK TIMES.

LONDON, June 10—Britain was rushing all available forces today into the battle in France, which was officially called here the "Battle of Paris and London" because of the Nazi threat to England. This reinforcement across the English Channel will continue, it was stated, "despite the imminent danger of German invasion of the United Kingdom."

The guns of British warships pounded the Germans to support Allied troops near the coast.

"Important contingents" of new troops have already gone to France, it was announced.

Even closer cooperation of the

Continued on Page Twelve

La Guardia Warns of Strict Neutrality Here; Consuls Told to 'Adhere to Consular Duties'

Mayor La Guardia went on the air over WNYC, the city broadcasting station, yesterday afternoon with a strong plea to the million persons of Italian blood in this city to preserve strict neutrality in the face of Italy's declaration of war.

Moving with characteristic rapidity, the Mayor telephoned the city broadcasting studio in the New York City Building at the World's Fair and said he would be on the air ten minutes later. He thought over the message he wanted to deliver while driving over from the World's Fair and, while en route, prepared to speak immediately upon his arrival. Meantime, Morris B. Novik, director of the station, had made arrangements to rebroadcast the Mayor's talk over five commercial stations at intervals later in the day.

Speaking slowly and impressively,

the mayor stated his policy that the European war must be fought on the battlefields of Europe and not on the sidewalks of New York.

Recalling his war service as an ally of the Italian forces in Italy, the Mayor said he fully realized that the Italian entry into the war on the opposite side must be as painful to others of Italian blood as it was to him. Nevertheless, he insisted that the national policy of neutrality must be observed in the city. While he begged full protection to consular officers of various European governments in the city, the Mayor made clear that those officials must stay within the bounds of their consular duties.

The Mayor's speech follows:

This is F. H. La Guardia, Mayor of the City of New York, talking. On Sept. 1, 1939, when the Nazi

Continued on Page Eight

ITALIANS REPORTED ON YUGOSLAV COAST

Said to Have Landed at Two Places Controlled by Rome— Mass on Greek Border

By The United Press.

BELGRADE, Yugoslavia, Tuesday, June 11—Large numbers of Italian troops were reported early today to have been landed along the Yugoslav coast at two Italian points as the Yugoslav Government prepared to fight in defense of its territory if necessary.

[It was reported from Berlin yesterday that Italian forces had invaded France through the Riviera, but this was denied in Rome, and German military quarters said later that they had no knowledge of any such movement.]

Reports from Split on the Adriatic coast said that large forces of Italian troops had been landed at

Continued on Page Four

Dispatches from Europe and the Far East are subject to censorship at the source.

"All the News That's Fit to Print."

The New York Times.

LATE CITY EDITION
Partly cloudy, warmer today, followed by showers tonight. Tomorrow fair, temperature unchanged.
Temperature Yesterday—Max., 78; Min., 65

VOL. LXXXIX...No. 30,093.

Entered as Second-Class Matter,
Postoffice, New York, N. Y.

NEW YORK, SATURDAY, JUNE, 15, 1940.

THREE CENTS NEW YORK CITY and Vicinity | FOUR CENTS Elsewhere Except in 7th and 8th Postal Zones.

Copyright, 1940, by The New York Times Company.

GERMANS OCCUPY PARIS, PRESS ON SOUTH; CAPTURE HAVRE, ASSAULT MAGINOT LINE; FRENCH ARMY INTACT; SPAIN SEIZES TANGIER

HITLER IS DOUBTED

Roosevelt Skeptical of Pledge He Will Not Cross Atlantic

HAS RECOLLECTIONS

U. S. Doing All It Can for Allies, He Asserts of French Appeal

By FELIX BELAIR Jr.
Special to THE NEW YORK TIMES.

WASHINGTON, June 14—President Roosevelt replied today to Adolf Hitler's reported denial of territorial aspirations in the Western Hemisphere with a reference to the German Chancellor's regard of broken pledges to respect the integrity of European nations over a considerable period of time.

As a part of the same answer the President said the United States was doing and would continue to do everything in its power to give aid to the Allies. He said, in effect, that Chancellor Hitler's statement in an interview that he would confine his activities to Europe was to be taken with considerable quantities of salt.

The President followed up this with an announcement of plans to mobilize American scientific genius in the interest of national defense.

"That brings recollections," the President said when asked at his press conference for his reaction to statements credited to the German Chancellor in an interview published in Hearst newspapers today. Reporters were not permitted to quote directly the rest of the President's statement, in which he said his observation might be enlarged upon with dates and nations going back over quite a period of years.

Many Rumors in Washington

Mr. Roosevelt's press conference remark was the high point of a day in which Washington was thick with rumors of the formation of a new French Cabinet without Premier Reynaud, that France would soon seek a separate peace with the Germans and that the President had been asked by France or Great Britain to propose a declaration of war against the Nazi government.

Both the White House and State Department denied that any proposal had been received from the Allied governments that the United States declare war.

Secretary Hull was asked in connection with the French situation whether the question of a declaration of war by the United States had been projected or raised in any way. He replied that so far as he knew nothing was involved beyond the sale of supplies, under terms and conditions that every one knew.

The question was asked of the Secretary of State at his press conference, which was held at 1 o'clock. Mr. Hull said the appeal Premier Reynaud was then being decoded, that he had not seen it, but he understood it was the same that the French Premier gave by radio last night. Later the French Ambassador, Count de Saint-Quentin, said he assumed it was that or its equivalent.

Day's Other Developments

These other developments in the legislative and executive branches during the day stood out:

1. The President let it be known, by inference, that no accumulation of circumstances in the European war would alter this country's determination to arm to the teeth.

2. The House passed and sent to the Senate a bill authorizing the Reconstruction Finance Corporation to organize and lend money to corporations for plant expansion and acquisition of strategic materials for national defense.

3. State Department officials made no secret of their belief that France would undertake negotiations with Germany looking to a separate peace and that reorganization of the French Government probably would be attempted with this in mind.

4. Administration sources said legislation would be introduced next week to embargo exports of scrap iron as a measure of national defense.

5. Attorney General Jackson

Continued on Page Ten

The International Situation

On the Battle Fronts

Paris was taken over yesterday by the German war machine. Led by dust-stained tanks, followed by motorized divisions and then by infantry, the German Army marched down the Champs Elysées. Tense, grim-faced Parisians—the few who had remained behind—stood silently on the curbs as a hostile force marched through the famous boulevards of the "City of Light" for the first time since 1871. Shops were closed and shuttered. [Page 1, Column 7.]

In Berlin there were scenes of wild rejoicing. On Chancellor Hitler's orders church bells were rung for a quarter of an hour and the Nazi flag was ordered displayed for three days. [Page 2, Column 2.]

Berlin said that the fall of Paris—described as "catastrophic" morally and economically for the French—had completed the second phase of the war. The first was the Battle of Flanders. The third, the High Command communiqué said, was pursuit and "final destruction" of all the French forces. The chief drive of this "final" phase appeared to be directed against the flank of the Maginot Line through Champagne and the Argonne Forest—famous World War battlefield of American troops. Montmédy, western anchor of the line, was reported conquered. Spearheads had driven as far east as Vitry-le François, between Paris and Nancy. Verdun was said to be threatened. On the coast Havre's fall was claimed. [Page 1, Column 8.]

The war appeared to be developing for Italy. First reports of action on her Alpine frontier were reported in a communiqué. It was divulged for the first time, too, that the Italian fleet was at sea in force. [Page 1, Column 3.] Attacks in Africa were reported, both by the Italian air arm and by Allied troops against Libya, Eritrea and Ethiopia. Successes were claimed by the Italians in all actions. [Page 4, Column 1.]

The French Government abandoned Tours as its provisional capital and started southward, apparently for the port of Bordeaux. It was the seat of the French Government for a short time in 1914. [Page 1, Column 6.]

Repercussions Elsewhere

Spanish troops yesterday took over control of Tangier, the small internationally-policed territory in Northern Africa fronting on the Straits of Gibraltar. Madrid said the action had been taken to "guarantee its neutrality" and had been done with the full consent of the other three guarantors—Britain, France and Italy. Berlin said the consent of the Allies was given after the act. Return of Tangier has been one of the most frequently expressed territorial demands of Franco-Spain. That of British-held Gibraltar is the other. [Page 1, Column 4.] In Washington Secretary Hull said the United States would insist on its extraterritorial rights in Tangier under the treaty of 1906. [Follows the foregoing.]

"That brings up recollections," President Roosevelt said at his press conference when a purported interview with Chancellor Hitler was shown to him quoting the German leader as saying he had no aspirations in this hemisphere. The President's reference was to similar statements made about European countries. Driving ahead with the American defense program, the President announced the appointment of a scientific research commission to work with the defense advisory commission. [Page 1, Column 1.]

MOROCCANS MOVE IN

Spanish Troops Take Over Zone in Which U. S. Has Rights

'GIBRALTAR' NOW CRY

Madrid Students Parade and Shout for Return of the Famous Rock

By T. J. HAMILTON
Special Cable to THE NEW YORK TIMES.

MADRID, June 14—The Spanish Government announced early this afternoon that with the object of guaranteeing "the neutrality of the international zone" in Morocco, Moroccan troops entered Tangier this morning.

It was stated officially that the action had been taken in agreement with Great Britain, France and Italy, who are other guarantors of the zone under a convention of 1903. The United States, which is also a signatory to the convention, received a copy of the announcement in a note delivered to the United States Embassy here at 11 A. M.

The text of the communiqué follows:

"With the object of guaranteeing the neutrality of the international zone and the city of Tangier, the Spanish Government has decided to take charge provisionally of the surveillance, police and public safety services of the international zone; forces of Moroccan troops entered this morning with this object.

"All existing services are assured and they continue functioning normally."

Coveted by the Spanish

Next to Gibraltar, Tangier occupies the front rank in Spanish territorial aims. In the last few days newspapers have devoted special attention to it among African territories that the French, assertedly with the connivance of the British, took away from Spain.

Although the first extra newspapers did not appear on the streets until 4 P. M., word that Tangier had been occupied spread quickly. By noon flags were appearing on houses throughout Madrid and members of the Falange youth movement were marching in uniform through the streets.

The news helped to bring an extra welcome for General Franco when he arrived late in the afternoon to open an exposition showing accomplishments of the government in rebuilding devastated regions. The press confined itself to printing the text of the government communiqué and relating the history of the international zone.

However, there were four demonstrations during the day, in which university student Falangistas predominated, all shouting, "Tangier is ours!" Some of these demonstrations passed the French and British Embassies.

British circles emphasized tonight that the occupation of Tangier had taken place with the complete agreement of Britain and France, who along with Italy and Spain were guarantors of the interna-

Continued on Page Six

FRENCH NOTE LULL

Battle Continues Along Front—At Some Points Its Violence Abates

ATTACK IS REPULSED

Nazi Losses Are Heavy in Maginot Assault— Loire Next Barrier

By G. H. ARCHAMBAULT
Wireless to THE NEW YORK TIMES.

TOURS, France, June 14—Is there any significance in the fact that although the battle continued to be waged today all along the front from the coast to the Argonne, it was notable that at certain points its violence was abating?

That question is in every mind tonight, for it may contain confirmation of the belief that the Germans have now engaged the maximum of their available forces.

The communiqué issued tonight gives little information on the day's operations, but it implies that all the retreating French forces continue to fight rear-guard actions and that at several parts of the front they have, in addition, counter-attacked the advancing Germans.

The only reference to Paris is as follows: "The prescribed withdrawal has been effected in conformity with our plans."

But if there has been a relative lull on the main line of battle the Germans were very active in front of the Maginot Line, especially west of the Saar River. Early in the morning they launched a violent attack with the now customary accompaniment of tanks and dive-bombing planes. The French claim to have thrown back the attacking force, on which they inflicted heavy losses.

Present Front Uncertain

Manifestly this attack must be considered in correlation with the fighting in the Argonne, farther to the west.

It is impossible tonight to indicate the present front even approximately. It is really one long line of pockets and salients, a situation calling for great qualities of generalship in order to preserve cohesion of the French forces.

Meanwhile, with the withdrawal of the French troops charged with the defense of Paris the first phase of the Battle of France was ended in defeat. It may be called the Battle of the Seine. The next phase may be the Battle of the Loire.

The issue was clear from the moment it was decided to declare Paris an open city and the news of withdrawal cannot have surprised many. A communiqué issued this morning from French General Headquarters explained that there were insufficient strategic reasons for defending the capital to justify risking destruction of France's very heart.

From the military point of view it is clear now that a battle for Paris would merely have immobilized troops, added to the loss of life and brought about no com-

Continued on Page Three

Will Fight On, British Insist, Even if the French Capitulate

London Letting Ally Make Decision on the Immediate Course as Help Is Speeded— New Nazi Peace Offensive Expected

By The United Press.

LONDON, June 14—Britain has agreed to accept any decision France may make regarding military and political policy, but if France is lost as an ally the British will fight on alone against Chancellor Hitler's war machine, it was understood tonight.

The British Government has agreed this week to any choice the French Government might make in regard to these military and political matters, which weigh more heavily with each hour of Germany's increased drive, provided the choice had the approval of Generalissimo Maxime Weygand.

Foreign observers in London said against the Maginot Line, particularly the strong flanking attack south of Montmédy and from Vitry-le-François, as of far greater strategic importance than yesterday's German occupation of undefended Paris. Nevertheless, the psychological importance of the fall of Paris and the effect on French morale are not underestimated.

The impression prevails in foreign embassies in London that Herr Hitler would respond affirmatively to any possible French peace overture, but would impose harsh con-

ditions as his price for ending the war in France. These conditions, it was felt, might range from dismantling the $500,000,000 Maginot Line to the return to Germany of Alsace-Lorraine and other territorial and economic and financial concessions.

There are strong indications, however, that Herr Hitler would refuse to negotiate with Britain, since he is intent on smashing Britain's financial and industrial power.

How far Germany would be prepared to bid for a completely Nazi-dictated peace presumably would depend upon the extent of the German losses suffered in the war.

If Britain should be compelled to fight on alone without France as an ally she would be able, it is felt in British quarters, to carry on until Autumn with United States aid.

The British Navy is relatively intact despite Germany's claims to the contrary. Then, it is asserted, starvation might seriously menace Germany and Italy during the Winter, impairing their military strength and the security of their home fronts.

British morale appears to be firm.

Continued on Page Five

2 FORCES TAKE CITY

Berlin Says Industrial Losses May Be Worst Feature for French

MONTMÉDY CAPTURED

Anchor of Maginot Line Lost—Nazis Report Foe Is Routed

By C. BROOKS PETERS

BERLIN, June 14—Today, for the third time within the last century and a quarter, victorious German troops marched into Paris. This time, however, the legions, the clatter of whose hobnailed boots resounds throughout Paris and the entire world, are more than just German soldiers. They are the bearers of a proposed new order for Europe and perhaps the world, a major tenet of which is to destroy the old one.

With the capitulation of Paris, the Germans claim that the destruction of the remaining French forces is but a matter of "the shortest time." Well-informed quarters in Berlin put that time at two weeks at most.

For the German High Command announced today that the second phase of the western campaign had been completed successfully, the resistance of the French northern fronts has been broken and the enemy is "in full retreat along the entire front from Paris to the Maginot Line near Sedan."

Retreat Called Rout

If the statements of German military officials in Berlin are correct, this "full retreat" is really a rout. For the French, forced from their positions, have had no time to construct new ones but are being constantly harassed by German tanks, other motorized units and planes as they move southward, it is declared.

Early this morning, the Germans declare, they unleashed a frontal attack on the Maginot Line along the entire Saar front. Farther east, the fall of Montmédy, "anchor" of the Maginot Line, was claimed as well.

The extreme right wing of the German forces was not idle either. For yesterday it captured Havre, Berlin heard, and thus added approximately another hundred miles to the stretch of French coast that already is in German hands.

Advance on Cherbourg

The lower Seine, however, according to the High Command, was the scene of a wide front. The extreme right wing, it is believed, now is advancing on Cherbourg further to cut France off from Great Britain and provide the Germans with still another base for a future raid on the British Isles.

The front is now about 300 miles long as the crow flies, Germans declare, from Havre to the Rhine.

Although no information has been officially released here relative to the progress of the attack on the Maginot Line, it was said in usually informed quarters tonight that the force of the German drive in this sector already has broken through in several places.

Escape Held Impossible

Forces of the German left wing are reported pushing forward in a southeasterly direction in what now appears to be a plan to storm the triangle of the Maginot fortifications from several sides, while an advance west of the fortifications to Belfort—southern tip of the Maginot Line—would cut off the avenue of escape for the French troops manning the line.

This German left wing yesterday was said to have captured Vitry-le-François and crossed the Marne-Rhine Canal, which connects that town with Strasbourg. Still farther west another tentacle of the German left wing last evening was reported to have reached the famous Hill 304 (Dead Man's Hill), northwest of Verdun, in which sector in 1916, Germans say, they lost 80,000 men.

In that hub from which radiate eleven streets stands the Arc de Triomphe and the tomb of the Unknown World War Soldier, where flickers the Eternal Flame.

German reports indicated that the parade through Paris swung around

Continued on Page Two

COLONNA PROTESTS ON ITALIAN CHARGES

Envoy Sees Hull—Inquiry Here Widened—German Agent to U. S. Warns of Reprisals

Special to THE NEW YORK TIMES.

WASHINGTON, June 14—The Italian Ambassador, Don Ascanio dei Principi Colonna, protested to Secretary of State Cordell Hull today what he considered to be an unjustified effort to foment anti-Italian feeling in the United States.

The protest was directed specifically to the charges made in New York yesterday that the Italian Consulate General there, under orders of Premier Benito Mussolini, was seeking to promote fascism in this country by ideological propaganda. He also implied there were similar activities against Italy in other American cities.

His concern was especially manifested over publication of these charges by newspapers. The fact that the New York charges were issued through Police Commissioner Valentine apparently was not mentioned. No reference was made directly to President Roosevelt's Charlottesville address denouncing Italy.

In making the protest, Prince Colonna declared that Italian consuls in this country restrict their activities to their legal functions and that Italian nationals in the United States are careful to avoid

Continued on Page Nine

ITALIANS IN CLASH ON FRENCH BORDER

Report Attack Repulsed— Fleet Action Revealed— Coast Is Shelled

By HERBERT L. MATTHEWS
By Telephone to THE NEW YORK TIMES.

ROME, June 14—The war began to develop for Italy on land, sea and air, according to this morning's communiqué, with the first activity on the Italo-French frontier and an indication that the Italian Fleet was on its way on some great mission.

The taking of Tangier by the Spaniards is considered a first-rate victory for the Axis, but, of course, the fall of Paris dominates everything else.

Among Fascisti here there is rejoicing over the fate of Paris. The newspaper Lavoro Fascista cheers in an eight-column box whose sentiments are typical.

"C'est Paris," it says. "Capitalists, Jews, Masons and snobs all over the world are in mourning. The spiritual capital of all the old civilization has fallen. Paris itself 'la ville lumière'—Paris tout entier.'"

As the war shapes up, even this early, the Mediterranean seems more than ever certain to become Italy's main theatre of operations. To be sure, there was some activity on the French frontier yesterday—the first time in that direction. There were clashes by patrols and "enemy" at-

Continued on Page Four

British Call on U. S. for Munitions at Once; French Order 120 Bombers Here for 1941

By RAYMOND DANIELL
Special Cable to THE NEW YORK TIMES.

LONDON, June 14—In circles close to the government it was said today that every gun, every ounce of war materials that the United States can spare was needed urgently and needed quickly if the cause for which the Allies were fighting was not to be lost on the battlefields of France. It is not a matter of months but of weeks, even days, it was added by those in a position to know the facts, of which the ordinary people in this country only now are becoming fully aware.

Withdrawal of the battered French armies behind their abandoned capital and contemplation of the possibility that the Government of France may be forced to withdraw from Europe to Africa, led to expressions that made increasingly apparent the extent to which the

After the Anglo-French Purchasing Commission yesterday had announced that French purchases of war material in the United States were being stepped up, the French signed a contract at 7 P. M. for 120 "flying fortresses" to be delivered in the second and third quarters of 1941. The planes are to be built by the Consolidated Aircraft Corporation.

In an interview earlier in the day a spokesman for the Anglo-French commission said that contracts for "many millions of dollars" had been placed during the day.

Instead of curtailing purchases following the capture of Paris by the Germans, France is sending more purchasing experts, this spokesman said. In response to a question relative to the ability to pay cash for purchases, he added:

"There is no immediate end of our

Continued on Page Four

"All the News That's Fit to Print."

NEWS INDEX, PAGE 33, THIS SECTION

The New York Times.

LATE CITY EDITION
Cloudy today with little change in temperature. Tomorrow cloudy and slightly warmer.
Temperatures Yesterday—Max., 72; Min., 52

Section 1

Copyright, 1940, by The New York Times Company.

VOL. LXXXIX. No. 30,101.

Entered as Second-Class Matter,
Postoffice, New York, N. Y.

NEW YORK, SUNDAY, JUNE 23, 1940.

Including Rotogravure Picture, Magazine and Book Review.

TEN CENTS

TWELVE CENTS Beyond 200 Miles, Except West of Pa.—South of Md.—North of Mass.

FRENCH SIGN REICH TRUCE, ROME PACT NEXT; BRITISH BOMB KRUPP WORKS AND BREMEN; HOUSE QUICKLY PASSES 2-OCEAN NAVY BILL

REPUBLICAN FIGHT LOOMS ON WAR ISSUE AT THE CONVENTION

Dewey, Taft and Willkie Reach Philadelphia to Appeal to the Delegates

NO GROUP HAS CONTROL

Rival Candidates Make Ballot Claims—Willkie Stronger—Hoover Possibility Seen

A battle between divergent views on the war and peace issue loomed yesterday among delegates to the Republican National Convention, opening tomorrow. Messrs. Dewey, Taft and Willkie, rival candidates for the Presidential nomination, reached Philadelphia to press their campaigns. No leader or group of leaders was in a position to dominate the proceedings or the committee on resolutions. The effect of a speech by Mr. Hoover to the convention Tuesday is expected to decide what, if any part, he will play as a Presidential nominee. [All the foregoing Page 1, Column 1.]

In press conferences Mr. Dewey declared for aid to the Allies without violating international or domestic law or entering the war; Mr. Willkie for aid to the Allies without going to war, and for reciprocal trade treaties. [Page 2, Column 1.]

The national committee approved a change in the rules under which districts which fail to show a poll of 1,000 Republicans would be deprived of representation at future conventions. Other rules changes approved would ease penalties on States which do not give a majority for the national ticket. [Page 2, Column 4.]

Drafters of the platform, split over aid to the Allies, hinted that a stand on the foreign policy plank might be left largely to the decision of the Presidential nominee. [Page 3, Column 1.]

Convention Unbossed

By JAMES A. HAGERTY
Special to The New York Times.

PHILADELPHIA, June 22—The Republican National Convention, which will convene here Monday in the Municipal Auditorium, will open without a boss or even under the control of any particular group of minor bosses.

This was the indication, today, when District Attorney Thomas E. Dewey of New York, Senator Robert A. Taft of Ohio and Wendell L. Willkie, president of the Commonwealth and Southern Corporation, just now regarded as the three leading candidates for the Presidential nomination, arrived in the convention city to make direct appeals to the delegates.

With no leader or group of leaders in a position to dominate either the convention or the committee on resolutions, the delegates face the prospect of a hotly contested fight for the nomination for President, and an equally bitter floor contest on the resolution on foreign relations.

Little difficulty is expected in putting through the rest of the platform which is expected to follow the recommendations of the program committee headed by Dr. Glenn Frank.

Alfred M. Landon, nominee for President in 1936, who is chairman of the subcommittee on foreign relations of the committee on resolutions, continued his efforts to get a plank that would be satisfactory both to the isolationists and those favoring a declaration of aid to the Allies, but the formula, so far as could be learned, had not been found tonight.

Candidates Give Views

Mr. Dewey, Mr. Willkie and Senator Taft each had a press conference. Mr. Dewey declared for aid for the Allies without violating international or domestic law or getting into the war. Mr. Willkie, who was nearly mobbed by supporters in the Bellevue-Stratford Hotel, also declared for aid to the Allies without going to war and

Continued on Page Two

Major Sports Results

BASEBALL

New York's major league teams all met defeat yesterday. The Reds downed the Giants, 3–1, on Ernie Lombardi's home run with one man on base, the Pirates beat the Dodgers, 7–2, and the Tigers won from the Yankees, 3–2. Despite the setback, the Dodgers stayed in first place in the National League.

RACING

Your Chance won the $13,350 Dwyer Stakes at Aqueduct after Snow Ridge, first past the finish line, was disqualified for bumping in the stretch. Gen'l Manager was placed second and Andy K. third. The crowd of 20,520 bet $1,076,417 on the seven races, this being Aqueduct's first million-dollar day.

TRACK AND FIELD

The University of Southern California won its sixth successive National Collegiate A. A. championship in the meet at Minneapolis. The New York A. C. easily retained the metropolitan A. A. U. senior title.

[Complete Details in Section 5.]

CITY WPA TO PURGE 1,000 NAZIS, REDS

Signing of Affidavits to Be Started Tomorrow—FBI to Aid in Investigations

Without waiting for President Roosevelt to sign the new Relief Appropriations Act, Colonel F. C. Harrington, National Work Projects Commissioner, set in motion yesterday the machinery for purging the WPA rolls of Communists and Nazis by July 1.

The purge in this city will begin tomorrow, and the local administrator, Lieut. Col. Brehon B. Somervell, estimated that at least 1,000 WPA workers would lose their jobs before it was completed. All of the 101,000 persons on the rolls here, and 1,700,000 in other parts of the country, will be required to sign affidavits disavowing Communist or Nazi affiliations. The maximum penalty for false statement will be $2,000 fine and two years' imprisonment.

Colonel Somervell made clear that his office would not rely on affidavits alone in carrying out the mandate of the new law. The registration lists of the Board of Elections will be compared with the WPA payroll to turn up the names of Communists. The full facilities of the Federal Bureau of Investigation, the Police Department and the WPA's own Bureau of Investigation will be invoked as a further means of identification.

Dies Records to Be Used

Still another source of data, Colonel Somervell revealed, will be the reports and testimony gathered by the Dies committee and the record compiled in the recent trial of Fritz Kuhn, leader of the German-American Bund.

Because of the "well-known practice of Communists to deny membership in the party and to use false names in enrollment with the WPA," the administrator called upon all "responsible citizens" to make available any information they had on subversive activities among Federal relief employees. He said he expected at least 50,000 letters, and he promised that "grudge letters would be carefully sifted out from those submitting authentic information."

Although Congress did not complete action on the new Relief Act until yesterday morning, WPA officials in this city have been collecting material on Communists and Nazis on their rolls for several weeks. More than 1,000 names of persons tentatively identified as members of un-American groups are now under scrutiny, it was learned.

Under the wording of the law, Colonel Somervell said, a person does not have to be a member of the Communist party to be ineligible for WPA employment. He said he regarded Trotskyites within the meaning of the law, and indicated that other "splinter groups" would be subject to a similar interpretation. The administrator said he would function as the court of last resort in determining whether a person entertained subversive views.

The WPA purge creates a problem for municipal relief authorities.

Continued on Page Thirteen

FOR 200 NEW SHIPS

70% Increase in Fleet Authorized as Congress Recesses Till July 1

TO COST 4 BILLIONS

Chambers Enact Tax, Defense and Relief Fund Measures

Special to The New York Times.

WASHINGTON, June 22—Congress took a recess at 9:10 o'clock tonight, adopting a resolution to reassemble on July 1 after the Republican National Convention at Philadelphia, and to take a similar week's recess during the Democratic National Convention at Chicago.

As a night session began to clear the decks for the recess, the House gave a dramatic flourish to a day devoted to pressing legislation by passing and sending to the Senate the "two-ocean" navy bill. No dissent was heard in the voice vote.

Within less than two hours, the House then gave its approval to the construction of the world's mightiest navy, designed for defense of the Western Hemisphere. The Senate did not have time to act.

The "two-ocean" navy bill would authorize about 200 warships, a 70 per cent increase in the nation's fleet, or an expansion of 1,325,000 tons of combatant and auxiliary vessels to be built in the next six years at an estimated cost of $4,000,-000,000.

Naval Air Force Augmented

Besides the increase in tonnage, the two-ocean navy measure would increase the naval air force authorized strength from 10,-000 to 15,000 planes.

It provides for $25,000,000 for "mosquito" torpedo boats, and authorizes an appropriation of $150,-000,000 to expand shipbuilding facilities at government and private yards.

It provides also for the expenditure of $20,000,000 for expansion of facilities for armor plate manufacture and $50,000,000 for added facilities for construction of guns.

In calling for enactment of the bill, as recommended by Admiral Harold R. Stark, Chief of Naval Operations, Chairman Vinson of the House Naval Affairs Committee said that when the bill became law the Administration would ask for $175,000,000 for an immediate start on the program.

Mr. Vinson and Representative Maas of Minnesota, ranking minority member on the committee, led the brief debate by asserting that the United States should not depend upon the Navy of any other power for its defense.

"The time has come to realize that if the United States is to remain free and independent it must depend upon itself," Mr. Maas said. "It is foolish to risk our defense on the thin thread of a (the Panama) canal."

The Navy now has 307 ships in

Continued on Page Fourteen

British Torpedo and Bomb the Scharnhorst; Submarine, Planes Waylay Nazi Battleship

By HAROLD DENNY
Special Cable to The New York Times.

LONDON, June 22—The Germans' 26,000-ton battle cruiser Scharnhorst has been seriously damaged by a British submarine and airplanes off the Norwegian coast, according to reports given out tonight by the Admiralty and the Air Ministry.

The Scharnhorst was believed to be lying at bay with German destroyers and war planes clustering about her protectively, awaiting further attack by British naval units summoned by the Royal Air Force bombers.

The battle with the Scharnhorst and her escorting forces was the most important of three attacks on German and Italian naval craft reported in London.

The other incidents were the almost unbelievably exploit of the capture of a Italian submarine by a British trawler in the Gulf of Aden opposite British Somaliland and the sinking by an airplane of a German supply ship in the North Sea.

The Scharnhorst and her sister ship the Gneisenau, the most powerful of German war vessels, had previously taken severe punishment. She was heavily pummeled in April by the British battleship Renown off Narvik, Prime Minister Winston Churchill then reported.

On June 13 she was reported here to have been badly bombed, with one—perhaps two—British bombs making direct hits on the center of the ship when she was in Trondheim Fjord.

"One of our submarines sighted the Scharnhorst soon after she left Trondheim Fjord," the day's reports said. "The battle cruiser was clearly on passage to a safe port where she could repair damage sustained when hit by at least one heavy bomb during an attack by the aircraft of the fleet arm on June 13."

This latest encounter with the Scharnhorst touched off an exceptional

Continued on Page Twenty-one

$5,377,552,058 Voted For Defense This Year

By The Associated Press.

WASHINGTON, June 22—Here are the defense appropriation totals, including contract authorizations, which Congress has approved thus far this session:

Regular Army......	*$1 $23,254,624*
Regular Navy bill...	*1,492,542,750*
Supplemental defense	1,768,913,908
Urgent deficiency.....	28,000,000
Emergency deficiency	252,340,776
Strategic materials (in Treasury appropriation)	12,500,000
Total	**$5,377,552,058**

*To which supplemental sums were added by the Senate.

There are also items intended for defense in the Civil Aeronautics Authority, Civilian Conservation Corps, WPA and the Army Civil Functions Supply Bills.

COMMITTEE LEANS TO KNOX REJECTION

But Senate Naval Group Votes to Hear Him July 1—Stimson Will Testify Next Day

By HAROLD B. HINTON
Special to The New York Times.

WASHINGTON, June 22—Confirmation of Colonel Frank Knox as Secretary of the Navy probably will be opposed by the Senate Naval Affairs Committee, according to some members questioned after a stormy executive session today. If members maintain the opposition shown today, an adverse report will be made to the Senate, it was said.

The Naval and the Military Affairs committees, to which the nominations of Colonel Knox and Henry L. Stimson as Secretary of War have been referred, will hear the nominees in person during the week of July 1, when Congress reassembles after its recess for the Republican National Convention.

There is no indication that the Military Affairs Committee will recommend rejection of Colonel Stimson, although he will probably be closely questioned by such isolationist members as Senators Reynolds and Lundeen.

The Naval Affairs Committee will give Colonel Knox a more searching examination, it was believed. Some members, it was reported, favored rejecting the nomination today, but counsel prevailed that no nominee should be disapproved without having a chance to be heard.

Senator Walsh, the chairman, announced after the meeting that Colonel Knox would be required to appear on July 1. In other quarters it was said that eleven members attended today's meeting and that most of those who spoke were opposed to the nomination. Only Senators Hale and Barbour took no part in the discussions.

The most outspoken opponents, according to these reports, included Senators Walsh, Tydings, Smith of South Carolina, Byrd, Holt and Gillette, all Democrats. Senator Johnson of California, a Republican, also indicated his opposition. Others attending the meeting were

Continued on Page Fifteen

ARMS PLANT IS HIT

R.A.F. Raiders Continue Assault Upon Nazis' Bases of Supply

SCORE NEAR BERLIN

Plane Factory Is Target—Germans Retaliate Along English Coast

By JAMES MacDONALD
Special Cable to The New York Times.

LONDON, June 22—Royal Air Force bombers pounded the big Krupp arms works at Essen and important aircraft factories and military stores at Bremen, Kassel, Rothenburg and Goettingen and a big naval depot at Willemsoord in German-occupied Netherlands in a heavy series of air raids last night, according to the Air Ministry's communiqué today.

As against their boast of heavy damage done to the Nazis, British officials insisted that Nazi airmen had accomplished little in their retaliatory raids in this country this morning and last night.

Three persons were killed in a Suffolk town and three wounded elsewhere, it was announced. It was declared that bombs burst sporadically in "several counties on the east coast," but that most of them fell in open country, causing small damage. The German raids, it was said, were less intense than those of Tuesday and Wednesday nights. The Ministry did not state whether or not any Nazi planes were shot down, or if any defending fighter machines were lost.

All Appears Quiet

Meanwhile all appeared quiet on the British home air front tonight. There were no unwelcome noises of purring enemy motors that were picked up by the sensitive sound-detecting devices on the ground.

[Alexandria, Egypt, fought off three Italian air raids yesterday, the first of the war. British fliers attacked Tobruk, Libya, and reported hitting a large warship. Rome said bombers had destroyed a British naval base in Egypt and raided Marseille and Bizerte, Tunisia.]

Many sections of British planes are reported to have taken part in widespread raids on German objectives last night, but only one was shot down and only two are reported missing.

Two Planes Missing

Many planes were engaged in the big raids over Germany. They returned with only two missing.

British raiders over Bremen directed their attack against the main building of the Focke-Wulf airplane factory. They made direct hits with incendiary and explosive bombs in the middle of the factory buildings. Two violent explosions were seen by the British fliers after their bombs burst.

The airfield adjoining the factory was also bombed and one hangar was badly damaged, according to assertions made here.

Another section of the raiders reported that they had hit several buildings of the Krupp plant at Essen as well as railroad sidings near by. The exact extent of the damage done there, however, was not disclosed in London.

The objective at Kassel was the Fieseler aircraft factory and it was said that several bombs were seen exploding directly on the target. Airplane hangars were damaged at Rothenburg, where also military buildings and the air field were hit. Another attacking force dropped bombs on the aircraft storage depot

Continued on Page Twenty-one

The International Situation

In Europe and Africa

An armistice between Germany and France was signed in the Forest of Compiègne yesterday at 6:50 P. M. German time (12:50 P. M. New York time). Immediately after the signing the French representatives left by a German plane, German-piloted, for Rome, where they will sign a companion document with Italy. Six hours after the signatures have been appended to the Italian armistice the order to cease fire will become effective. The terms of the armistice are still withheld; in Bordeaux they were described as "hard but honorable." London reported, without confirmation, that these were the principal provisions: (1) Occupation of France by Germany and Italy for the duration of the war with Britain; (2) surrender of all war stores; (3) surrender of all gold and foreign currency reserves; (4) delivery of coal and other raw material supplies to Germany for a fixed period. [Page 1, Column 8.]

Prime Minister Churchill said he had heard "with grief and amazement" of the French acceptance of terms that, to his mind, would mean that France and her empire would be entirely at the mercy of the dictators. He called on the French people to continue resistance. This call was reiterated by General Charles de Gaulle, former French Under-Secretary of War, who broadcast from London, calling on all French people not under Axis guns to mobilize to carry on the war. [Page 1, Column 6.]

The French negotiators arrived in Rome by plane from Compiègne. [Page 27, Column 1.]

Berlin announced that 500,000 French soldiers, encircled in Alsace-Lorraine, had surrendered, among them three army commanders. Only isolated resistance was left in that part of France. The Germans took the port of Lorient, on the southern coast of Brittany. According to Swiss reports, the French repulsed a German attack on L'Ecluse Fort, which dominates the Rhone at the Swiss border. [Page 22, Column 1.]

British bombers struck at the famous Krupp armaments works at Essen and at aircraft factories at several other points in Germany. In a raid on Willemsoord, German-held base in the Netherlands, the British said they had sunk two ships, set one afire and destroyed naval storehouses. Berlin reported that nearly 100 planes took part in Friday night's bombing of Britain, the Germans admitted, injuring seven persons and damaging buildings. [Page 1, Column 5.]

The British reported that the German battleship Scharnhorst, 26,000 tons, had been both torpedoed and bombed, with "considerable damage" resulting. The action took place off the Norwegian coast. A destroyer was torpedoed in the same fight, London said. The British trawler Moonstone informed the Admiralty that it had captured a large Italian submarine in the Gulf of Aden. Depth charges forced the submarine to the surface, where guns were brought into play. The Italian commander and several officers were reported killed; three officers and thirty-seven men were captured. [Page 1, Column 3.]

Three groups of Italian bombers attacked the Allied naval base at Alexandria, Egypt, early yesterday. They were driven off, the British reported, by the combined fire of both French and British naval units, and no warships were hit. Rome claimed to have sunk three enemy ships in the Mediterranean. [Page 1, Column 7.]

By the emphatic denial of an official government statement, Russia denied that troops were being concentrated on the German frontier. [Page 22, Column 7.]

Developments Elsewhere

Within less than two hours, the House of Representatives adopted the "two-ocean" navy bill, which will give the United States the most powerful navy in the world—a navy 70 per cent greater than the present one. [Page 1, Column 3.]

After a stormy session of the Senate Naval Affairs Committee, it appeared in Washington that Colonel Frank Knox, Republican, would not be approved by the committee for Secretary of the Navy, Colonel Henry L. Stimson, Republican, nominated for Secretary of War, also faces hard going before the Military Affairs Committee. But confirmation of both appointments is expected when the issue gets to the floor. [Page 1, Column 4.]

In Hyde Park, where he was spending the week-end, President Roosevelt contemplated the possibility that the United States might have to shift the fleet to the Atlantic to face a superior sea power of the totalitarian nations. [Page 16, Column 1.]

NAZI TERMS SIGNED

But Hostilities Persist as French Fly to Get Italy's Demands

SEVERITY PROTESTED

Huntziger Voices View at Close of 27-Hour Compiègne Parley

By GUIDO ENDERIS
Wireless to The New York Times.

BERLIN, June 22—The armistice treaty between Germany and France was signed today in the forest of Compiègne at 6:50 P. M. German Summer time [12:50 P. M. New York time]. Col. Gen. Wilhelm Keitel, Chancellor Hitler's plenipotentiary, signed for Germany and General Charles Huntziger for France.

Its contents will not be made public for the present, but it is announced that the agreement does not provide for immediate cessation of hostilities. The fighting is to end six hours after the Italian Government has notified the German High Command of the signing of an armistice treaty between Italy and France.

As the latter is now believed to be a mere formality, already agreed upon by the leaders of the Axis Powers in their discussion in Munich last Tuesday, its conclusion is expected within the next forty-eight hours. The French delegation that conferred at Compiègne also will negotiate with Italy. Such procedure, it is predicted, will end the war on the Continent early in the coming week.

Scene in Car Dramatic

The French delegation returned to Compiègne from Paris at 10 A. M. and continued its deliberations throughout the day, during which it was in constant communication with the Bordeaux government. To expedite contacts, German military authorities installed a direct telephone wire at Compiègne between its seat and Bordeaux. The German radio broadcast announcing the signing of the treaty closed with the words, "We thank our Fuehrer." There was a dramatic scene in the armistice car at Compiègne before the formalities were completed. General Huntziger, in a choked voice, announced that his government had ordered him to sign.

"Before carrying out my government's order," he said, "the French delegation deems it necessary to declare that in a moment when France is compelled by fate of arms to give up the fight, she has a right to expect that the coming negotiations will be dominated by a spirit that will give two great neighboring nations a chance to live and work once more. As a soldier you will understand the onerous moment that has now come for me to sign."

After the signatures were affixed, General Keitel requested all members to rise from their seats, and then said:

"It is honorable for the victor to do honor to the vanquished. We have risen in commemoration of those who gave their blood for their countries."

Talks With Italy Speeded

The French delegation left Compiègne for Paris tonight and is expected to take up negotiations with Italy without further delay to bring the hostilities to a quick close.

With an Italian-French armistice in imminent prospect, military activities are now expected to give way to diplomatic negotiations and its not improbable that Germany, Italy, France and possibly also Belgium will meet in conference in some German city to discuss steps for an approach to honorable peace.

Meanwhile there is no indication in German official or press utterances to suggest that Germany is not grimly determined to prosecute her war on Britain with all possible speed, and this determination has received fresh impetus through uninterrupted attacks by British bombers on German objectives.

With French Channel ports now available as Germany air bases, raids on English coastal points also have increased in recent days and the final liquidation of the war in

Continued on Page Twenty-eight

GENERAL SUMMONS FRENCH TO RESIST

De Gaulle Offers to Organize Fight Abroad—Churchill Supports His Stand

By RAYMOND DANIELL
Special Cable to The New York Times.

LONDON, Sunday, June 23—A broadcast to the French people by one of their own military leaders calling on them to continue the fight against Germany by every means in their power was made from here last night.

General Charles de Gaulle, assistant and adviser to Paul Reynaud when the former Premier was also War Minister, told his countrymen the proposed armistice would be not only capitulation but "submission and slavery."

[The general undertook to organize such French resistance as was possible himself and urged French fighting men and technicians everywhere to join him in the task, according to The United Press.]

General de Gaulle's arguments were reinforced early this morning by Prime Minister Winston Churchill in a statement expressing "grief and amazement" at the terms. He indicated they would transform France into an active enemy, and he too urged French-

Continued on Page Twenty-seven

ALEXANDRIA FIGHTS FIRST ITALIAN RAIDS

20 Bombs Fall in 3 Attacks—Warship Reported Fired by R. A. F. at Tobruk

By JOSEPH M. LEVY
Wireless to The New York Times.

CAIRO, Egypt, June 22—Alexandria experienced its first bombing this morning when twenty bombs were dropped in three Italian air raids. Two persons were killed; twenty-three were injured.

During the first raid a native woman, who was killed when bombs hit among palm trees growing in a village close to the city, and a man who was killed by a bomb that demolished four Alexandria houses. Here nineteen persons were injured.

[Another air raid warning sounded in Alexandria early today, but no planes appeared, The Associated Press reported, and the all-clear signal was given in fifteen minutes.]

Bombs were reported dropped indiscriminately on the city, harbor and native villages, on planes flying high and dodging in their attempt to avoid anti-aircraft fire. Two Italian planes were reported badly damaged. It is not certain whether either was shot down. Only a few bombs fell in the city.

Continued on Page Twenty-three

"All the News That's
Fit to Print."

The New York Times.

LATE CITY EDITION
Fair, with little change in temperature today and tomorrow.
Temperature Yesterday—Max., 80; Min., 63

Copyright, 1940, by The New York Times Company

VOL. LXXXIX..No. 30,174.

Entered as Second-Class Matter,
Postoffice, New York, N. Y.

NEW YORK, WEDNESDAY, SEPTEMBER 4, 1940.

THREE CENTS NEW YORK CITY and Vicinity | FOUR CENTS Elsewhere Except In 7th and 8th Postal Zones.

ROOSEVELT TRADES DESTROYERS FOR SEA BASES; TELLS CONGRESS HE ACTED ON OWN AUTHORITY; BRITAIN PLEDGES NEVER TO YIELD OR SINK FLEET

R. A. F. REPELS RAIDS

Fliers Turn Back Three Drives on London—Reich Perfecting Technique

PLANES REACH BERLIN

2½-Hour Alarm in City —British Hit Hard at French Coast

By JAMES B. RESTON
Special Cable to THE NEW YORK TIMES.

LONDON, Wednesday, Sept. 4.—German bombers started ringing that big London doorbell early yesterday morning. They rang it again in the afternoon while Prime Minister Winston Churchill and his Ministers were commemorating the first anniversary of the war, and they kept ringing it right up till last midnight, when the third "all clear" of the day was sounded over the capital.

It was a day of fierce air battles, fought at great height in blue and silver sky all over Southeast England, and at the end, though Reich Marshal Hermann Goering's night shift was still operating all over the island, the British Air Ministry announced that twenty-five Nazi planes had been shot down to fifteen of Britain's planes. Eight British pilots were said to be safe, though it is not known whether they are in condition to fly.

[British bombing planes flew high over Berlin shortly after last midnight. Berlin spokesmen were quoted as saying that most of the Royal Air Force planes were turned back by severe anti-aircraft fire between Wittenberg and Magdeburg, but several planes escaped through the anti-aircraft barrage and reached Berlin, where they were again met with anti-aircraft fire.]

These German bombers, which have already overwhelmed five countries in the past twelve months, have now perfected a technique in attacking this vast, sprawling city, and they tried to work it again yesterday morning in the first raid.

Two Formations Meet

Just at 10 o'clock, timed to perfection, one wave of bombers approached the Thames Estuary from their bases in Belgium. Simultaneously, another formation, flying high through a light haze, came up from bases in France and met them over the Kentish coast. Altogether they were about 250 of them, and defying anti-aircraft batteries at first they started along the banks of the Thames toward London.

As they came inland, however, they met first one, then a second squadron of British fighters, who dived through Nazi fighter patrols into the bombers, broke up the formation and then attacked them singly and drove them back over the coast.

Some German bombers dropped their dynamite in Kent and Essex, but all that is said about the effect of these bombs is that they caused few casualties and little damage.

What can be said is that, if these bombers were trying to get into the heart of London to attack objectives here, they certainly failed, for while sirens were sounded everywhere in Greater London nobody in the heart of the city saw any fighting.

There was an interesting sidelight to the second mass raid of the day. At 2:45 P. M. Mr. Churchill, who somehow contrives to look more confident every day, walked into Westminster Abbey to attend the special service in commemoration of the day a year ago when Britain declared war on Germany. Alongside him walked tall, gaunt Viscount Halifax, Foreign Secretary; dapper Arthur Greenwood, Minister without portfolio; Sir Kingsley Wood, Chancellor of the Exchequer; Anthony Eden, War Secretary, and Joseph P. Kennedy, United States Ambassador to Great Britain.

They took their places in the cool church beside a great audience. At 2:50 P. M., as they were sitting there waiting for the service to start, air-raid sirens started echoing through the great cathedral.

Mr. Churchill got up, walked over to the cloisters and had a long talk with the Dean. In a few minutes he returned and took his place beside his Ministers in the cathedral. It was announced that the service would proceed.

Around the city the British fight-

Continued on Page Three

The International Situation

Destroyer-War Base Deal

Completion of a deal by which the United States will transfer to Britain fifty over-age destroyers and obtain ninety-nine-year leases on eight shore and island bases stretching from Newfoundland to British Guiana was announced by President Roosevelt yesterday in a message to Congress. Coincidentally, the British Government pledged not to scuttle or surrender its fleet under any conditions. [Page 1, Column 8.]

The objective of the arrangement with Britain is to build a 4,500-mile iron fence in the Atlantic to assure this country's safety for a century, an authoritative State Department source said. To attain this, any interpretations of international law and parts of treaties in conflict must be subordinated, he said. Since this country's purpose is its defense, no well-intentioned nation can call the move a hostile act, he declared. [Page 1, Column 7.]

President Roosevelt, en route to Washington, disclosed that he looked upon the agreement as a means of keeping an enemy from the country's front door. Listing it as in some ways more important for defense than Jefferson's Louisiana purchase, he hinted there might be other similar arrangements. [Page 1, Column 6.]

The President had acted on an opinion from Attorney General Jackson, who held that the Executive had the right to negotiate the transfer without Senate consent and the constitutional power to dispose of the vessels. [Page 1, Column 5.]

Wendell L. Willkie, Republican Presidential nominee, said the country would undoubtedly approve the arrangement, but criticized Mr. Roosevelt's failure to obtain Congress's approval. [Page 1, Column 3.]

London rejoiced. A Foreign Office spokesman described the agreement as a practical method for each nation to contribute to the other's defense requirements. [Page 1, Column 4.]

Axis spokesmen did not challenge the deal's legality under neutrality laws. In Berlin it was belittled as unlikely to affect the war's outcome. It was said to be a bargain for the United States and evidence that Britain was "cracking up." In Rome it was expected the Italians would be embittered. [Page 15, Column 1.]

Developments in Congress

The House opened debate on the Selective Service Training Bill, the discussion following the lines of the Senate's deliberation. Indications were that the bill would pass by a good margin, the principal controversy centering on the question of industrial conscription. Leaders planned for final action Friday. [Page 17, Column 1.]

The Senate Finance Committee opened hearings on the excess profits tax and defense expansion amortization bill. The probability of changes in the measure increased as witnesses hit at its effects on business. [Page 10, Column 1.]

The War in Europe, Asia and Africa

German bombers hammered at Britain's airfields, harbors and naval bases, engaging the Royal Air Force in battles all over Southern England. Three raids on London were repelled. [Page 1, Column 1.]

Several R. A. F. bombers reached Berlin early today to provoke violent anti-aircraft fire after the British had loosed a powerful aerial counter-offensive in which their planes had bombed German industrial centers, the French coast and Italian power stations. [Page 3, Column 1.]

In the central Mediterranean, new type Italian bombers scored a victory, damaging a British battleship, an aircraft carrier, a cruiser and a destroyer, the Rome High Command announced. The R. A. F. again pounded Assab, port in Italian Eritrea. [Page 4, Column 6.]

Led by Tahiti, France's most important colony in Oceania, the French-protected Society Islands have voted to throw in their lot with Britain, repudiating Vichy, it was reported. [Page 6, Column 1.]

A virtual Japanese ultimatum demanding a military base and passage for troops was reported to have been rejected by French Indo-China and conflict there was believed inevitable. [Page 6, Column 2.]

In an attempted Iron Guard coup three gunmen broke through King Carol's palace guard and fired several shots into the air. Others equally vainly besieged a radio station, fought with troops. [Page 1, Column 2.]

A clash between Hungarian and Rumanian troops over the occupation of Transylvania was reported at Bucharest. [Page 4, Column 1.]

BUCHAREST CHECKS IRON GUARDS' COUP

Shots Fired in Front of Royal Palace — Handbills Call On Carol to Abdicate

By EUGEN KOVACS
Wireless to THE NEW YORK TIMES.

BUCHAREST, Rumania, Sept. 3.—A group of the Iron Guards, dissatisfied with the conduct and policy of other Iron Guards who are Ministers and who participated in the Crown Council, gathered and carried out several attempts tonight against different public buildings in Bucharest. All these attacks failed.

A small group consisting of three persons appeared in an automobile this evening at 8:30 before the Royal Palace and one of them fired two shots in the air. A policeman on duty in front of the gates of the palace fired at the car but failed. The man who fired the shots tried to escape, however, but was arrested, while the car disappeared.

The regular news bulletin broadcast at 10 o'clock was cancelled.

A second group, consisting of young men wearing civilian uniforms and disguised as Iron Guards, attacked the Bucharest radio station. The guard fired and succeeded in repelling the attacking group.

At the cable of transmission the Central Telephone Exchange a man was found who cut off some lines so that the telephone connection with abroad was cut off for a while. At the State Railway quarters works in the suburb of Grivitza announced

Continued on Page Four

WILLKIE FOR PACT, BUT HITS SECRECY

Regrets President Did Not Put Deal With Britain Before Congress and People

By JAMES A. HAGERTY
Special to THE NEW YORK TIMES.

RUSHVILLE, Ind., Sept. 3.—Asked today to comment on President Roosevelt's announcement of the agreement to turn over to Great Britain fifty over-age destroyers in return for air and naval bases in British Western Hemisphere areas, Wendell L. Willkie, Republican nominee for President, declared that the country undoubtedly would approve the program, but criticized the President's failure to obtain prior approval of Congress as smacking of totalitarianism.

In a statement prepared with care and with realization that it might have important foreign repercussions, Mr. Willkie said:

"The country will undoubtedly approve of the program to add to our naval and air bases and assistance given to Great Britain. It is regrettable, however, that the President did not deem it necessary to secure the approval of Congress or permit public discussion before its adoption.

"The people have a right to know of such important commitments prior to and not after being made. We must be extremely careful in these times when the struggle in the world is between democracy and to-

Continued on Page Fourteen

BRITISH JUBILANT

Destroyers Strengthen Their Fleet at Point of Greatest Strain

MORAL EFFECT GREAT

But Press Warns People Gesture Does Not Mean U. S. Will Enter War

By RAYMOND DANIELL
Special Cable to THE NEW YORK TIMES.

LONDON, Sept. 3.—It would be impossible to overstate the jubilation in official and unofficial circles caused today by President Roosevelt's announcement that fifty United States destroyers were coming to help Great Britain in her hour of peril. They will be manned by British crews and will fly the white ensign of the Royal Navy, it is true, but they are coming, nevertheless.

It was tangible proof that American talk of giving "all aid short of war" was more than idle chatter and that this country's friends across the Atlantic, despite German propaganda and the heavy bombardment of British cities and towns, had decided there was still lots of fight left in the British lion and that it was not too late to help turn the tide against totalitarian domination of Europe.

Destroyer Losses Offset

Under the arrangement, the United States gained security against future aggression, while the British fleet at one stroke acquired fifty 1,200-ton destroyers as an offset to the thirty lost since the beginning of hostilities.

These destroyers are badly needed at this stage of the war with British seapower engaged in a death grapple with the German Empire. Since the French were knocked out as an ally, the whole job of protecting convoys and maintaining the lifelines of the Empire against the new enemy in the Mediterranean has fallen upon the British fleet, while the air force has concentrated chiefly on destroying the enemy's supplies and defending the homes of the people of this island, which is under repeated bombardment from the air throughout its length and breadth.

Added to this multiplication of the navy's duties has been the necessity of blockading the whole Continent of Europe while standing by to resist the very real threat of a German invasion which, as War Secretary Anthony Eden warned today, still hangs over this country.

As great as was Britain's need the material gain by today's transaction was matched in British minds by the intangible implications of most open indication yet of Anglo-American cooperation for defense against the Nazi threats. The Times, London, will point out editorially tomorrow that such cooperation between a belligerent and a neutral is "a new departure" but one that is dictated by the necessities of modern war. The editorial goes on to say:

"The tragic fate of some of the smaller peoples of Europe might have been averted if they had not been restrained from planning for

Continued on Page Fifteen

RULING BY JACKSON

Opinion Holds Transfer by President Needs No Senate Action

AN 'EXECUTIVE' DEAL

Opponents in Congress Seek to Find Means of Obstructing It

Attorney General Jackson's opinion is printed on Page 16.

By LEWIS WOOD
Special to THE NEW YORK TIMES.

WASHINGTON, Sept. 3.—President Roosevelt has unqualified power to exchange fifty over-age destroyers for British naval and air bases in the Western Hemisphere without Senate consent, in the opinion of Attorney General Jackson, made public today, but, while Mr. Jackson asserted the Executive's right to dispose of naval vessels, he again refused to sanction the legality of delivery of "mosquito boats" now under construction.

Under a World War law the Attorney General ruled that it would be entirely proper to transfer the destroyers, since these were not built "with the intent that they should enter the service of a belligerent," but turning over the uncompleted mosquito boats, he argued, would be impossible, as this would legally mean that they were intended for a belligerent.

Opponents of the British-American deal sought tonight to find means of obstruction and delay, but this seemed to hinge upon the extent to which the direct interest of a taxpayer could be proved and the general opinion here was that the adversaries were blocked from court action and could depend only upon sufficient massing of public opinion. Apparently the Administration felt legally secure.

Writing his opinion to President Roosevelt last Tuesday, Mr. Jackson went into detail as to constitutional power and especially stressed the responsibility of the Executive to use every authority for national defense at a time when "present world conditions forbid him to risk" any constitutionally avoidable delay.

"No Future Commitments"

The Attorney General conceded that the wide Presidential power over foreign relations was not unlimited, but in this case, Mr. Jackson contended, there were no promises or future commitments by the United States which would require Senate consent or, indeed, any Congressional action. The agreement provided an opportunity to establish naval and air bases for coastline defense, he maintained, but needed no appropriation of money. Thus it was unnecessary for the Senate to ratify "an opportunity that entails no obligation," he declared.

Alluding to precedents, Mr. Jackson remarked that the "proposition falls far short" of the acquisition of the Louisiana Territory by President Jefferson from a belligerent during a European war. Outside of constitutional power, he went on,

Continued on Page Sixteen

Writer on British Destroyer Sees U-Boats in Raids and One Sunk

By BRYDON TAVES

ABOARD A BRITISH DESTROYER, in the North Atlantic, Sept. 3 (UP)—Germany is shooting the works to make good the threat of total blockade of the British Isles, but after eight days aboard a little British flotilla here I can say that hundreds of ships are entering and leaving British ports each week.

German submarine and air attacks marked day voyage. Not one day passed without action. The British crew was either manning gun and depth-charge stations to fight off a U-boat or manning anti-aircraft stations to fight attacking planes.

I saw one British merchantman take a long-range torpedo squarely amidships and sink within a half hour. The next day our destroyer owned the score.

A "tin-fish," meant for us, [missing] by a scant thirty feet as we [missing]

whipped around. Then we rocked from the concussion of our own depth charges and I saw an oil patch spread slowly over the surface, marking that U-boat's end.

The destroyer was engaged in a typical convoy job, and its duties were something between those of a conscientious sheep dog and a sister of charity lending a bunch of orphans across Times Square.

We were one destroyer and one smaller warship escorting a thirty-ship convoy spread over fifteen square miles of ocean. Watching the line of hulls stretching out behind us, I remembered what a naval officer in a convoy control room in a West coast port told me just before I sailed.

"Give me fifty more American destroyers," he said, "and I will

Continued on Page Four

UNITED STATES ACQUIRES DEFENSE BASTIONS

Bases at the places indicated by circled dots are being leased by Great Britain to this country for ninety-nine years. The leases for those in Newfoundland and Bermuda are in effect outright gifts; the leases for the others are in exchange for fifty over-age United States destroyers. The bases in the Caribbean area will supplement present American defense centers (black diamonds) in guarding approaches to the Panama Canal.

LINE OF 4,500 MILES

Two Defense Outposts Are Gifts, Congress Is Told—No Rent on Rest

FOR 50 OLD VESSELS

President Holds Move Solely Protective, 'No Threat to Any Nation'

Texts of messages on leasing of naval bases is printed on Page 10.

By FRANK L. KLUCKHOHN
Special to THE NEW YORK TIMES.

WASHINGTON, Sept. 3.—President Roosevelt informed Congress today that he had completed an arrangement by which the United States will transfer to Great Britain fifty over-age destroyers and obtain from Britain ninety-nine-year leases for sea and air bases at eight strategic continental and island points in the Western Hemisphere.

The new American defense line thus established will stretch 4,500 miles from Newfoundland to British Guiana and include other bases on the islands of Bermuda, the Bahamas, Jamaica, St. Lucia, Trinidad and Antigua.

It is intended to make difficult, if not impossible, naval and air attacks upon the United States and much of the New World. The exact sites of the bases will be determined later by the two governments.

A solemn pledge by the British Government to the United States not to scuttle or surrender the British fleet under any conditions was revealed coincidentally by the State Department's publication of correspondence between Secretary Hull and the British Ambassador, the Marquess of Lothian.

Secretary Hull was informed that it represented the "settled policy" of His Majesty's Government not to "surrender or sink" the British fleet.

Reshaping of Naval Defense

The deal, carrying with it far-flung international as well as domestic implications, was hailed by President Roosevelt as the most important since the Jefferson Administration completed the Louisiana Purchase in 1803.

Informed official circles contended that it assured the British Fleet an an Atlantic ocean for the United States and made it possible for the American Fleet to remain in the Pacific.

Some thought it might lead to an informal defensive alliance between this country and Australia similar to the arrangement recently completed administratively with Canada, although others disagreed on this point.

President Roosevelt informed Congress that the British Government had given the right to bases in Newfoundland and Bermuda as an outright gift, "generously given and gladly received," but that "the other bases mentioned have been acquired in exchange for fifty of our over-age destroyers."

Previously, the President had insisted that the destroyer and base deals were separate.

Legal Basis for Procedure

Mr. Roosevelt explained in his message that he had acted upon a legal opinion by Attorney General Jackson which held that the Chief Executive had the right to dispose of the destroyers and complete the deal without consultation with the Senate and without its approval.

The President made clear that he would not seek the Senate's endorsement by remarking that he sent his statement merely "for the information of Congress."

Chairman Walsh of the Senate Naval Affairs Committee and several other Senators publicly condemned the proposed deal as illegal under domestic and international law when it was reported in the press some weeks ago that President Roosevelt had agreed to give Britain fifty destroyers after plans from Prime Minister Winston Churchill.

In view of Senator Walsh's stand, some Senators privately expressed the opinion that there might be an attempt to have the Naval Affairs Committee open an investigation of the whole transaction.

After the President's message was

Continued on Page Twelve

ROOSEVELT HAILS GAIN OF NEW BASES

Exchange of Over-Age Ships for British Leases Offers Outer Defense Line, He Says

By CHARLES HURD
Special to THE NEW YORK TIMES.

ON BOARD ROOSEVELT TRAIN, Sept. 3.—President Roosevelt indicated that the chief value of the trade with Great Britain of fifty over-age destroyers for naval and air base sites in British crown colonies in the Western Hemisphere lies in the fact that this outer line of defenses would keep any enemy away from this country's front door.

For that reason, he said, his agreement with the British Government was more important for the defense of this country than anything since the Louisiana Purchase in 1803, which assured United States military control over the Mississippi River.

There may be other similar negotiations, he added, but he cautioned newspaper reporters not to try to guess where they would be, listing the odds at 10 to 1 that such guesses would be wrong.

The President did not deny a suggestion made by a reporter that perhaps Greenland might be the site for another base. He merely renewed his caution against speculation.

The President's view of the agreement, which has been known to be in progress for several weeks, was given at a special press conference on his private train at the same hour that his offices in Washington sent to Congress a message that the exchange was accomplished.

A dozen newspaper reporters heard Mr. Roosevelt read the text of the message to Congress, which he completed during a trip from Hyde Park, N. Y., to Tennessee, North Carolina and West Virginia. He read the message, after laughingly telling them that there was no story. While the document, with supporting papers, was being made public in Washington at noon, he began his press conference at 11:30 A. M.

Mr. Roosevelt called the press conference to meet in the tiny vestibule of his private car forty-five minutes after he departed from South Charleston, W. Va., where he inspected the work being done to high productivity a long abandoned Navy ordnance plant built in 1917-18 to construct armor plate and shells.

Among the statements he made,

Continued on Page Ten

SHIP TRADE IS HELD NOT HOSTILE ACTION

State Department Stresses Defense Phase of Exchange of Vessels for Bases

Special to THE NEW YORK TIMES.

WASHINGTON, Sept. 3.—No country could consider the transfer of fifty United States destroyers to Great Britain and the obtaining by this country of naval and air base sites in British New World territory as a hostile act, an informed State Department source said today.

Only a nation seeking world conquest could use this as a pretext for belligerent action, the source asserted.

The intention of this government in completing the agreement was merely to strengthen its own defenses and no other considerations were entertained, State Department officials said, in insisting that the United States had the opportunity of obtaining a 4,000 or 5,000 mile ring of steel around the eastern part of the hemisphere on terms unequaled since the Louisiana Purchase. They added that the protection would last for 100 years.

It was made clear that it was no time to consider any technical provisions which might be sought in international law by opponents of the agreement but that in these dangerous days, when the world is almost literally on fire, defense considerations must come first.

This view was expressed in answer to questions and comments about the Second Hague Convention of 1907, of which the United States and Germany are signatories, but Great Britain is not.

Hague 1907 Convention Is Quoted

Article VI of this convention asserts:

"The support in any manner, directly or indirectly, by a neutral power of a belligerent power, by warships, ammunition or war materials of any kind whatever, is forbidden."

Article VIII says:

"A neutral government is also bound to display the same vigilance to prevent the departure from its jurisdiction of any vessel intended to cruise, or menace in hostile operations, which had been adapted entirely or partly within the said jurisdiction for use in war."

Article XXVIII, however, states:

"The provisions of this present convention do not apply except to the contracting powers and then only if all the belligerents are parties to the convention."

One could accurately visualize a situa-

Continued on Page Sixteen

"All the News That's Fit to Print."

The New York Times.

LATE CITY EDITION
Fair and cooler today. Tomorrow fair and continued cool.
Temperatures Yesterday—Max., 72; Min., 64

Copyright, 1940, by The New York Times Company.

VOL. LXXXIX..No. 30,181.

Entered as Second-Class Matter, Postoffice, New York, N. Y.

NEW YORK, WEDNESDAY, SEPTEMBER 11, 1940

THREE CENTS NEW YORK CITY and Vicinity | FOUR CENTS Elsewhere Except in 7th and 8th Postal Zones

BRITISH BOMB BERLIN, HIT REICHSTAG BUILDING AND OTHER LANDMARKS IN CENTER OF THE CITY; GERMANS POUND AT LONDON IN 8-HOUR ATTACK

ROOSEVELT TO TALK 'POLITICS' TONIGHT BEFORE TEAMSTERS

First Avowed Campaign Talk Will Be a Paid Broadcast Over Two Networks

'HISTORY' WILL BE A TOPIC

President Professes Not to Know if 8-Year Survey Would Be Political or Historical

By CHARLES HURD
Special to The New York Times.

HYDE PARK, N. Y., Sept. 10—President Roosevelt dropped tonight the nonpolitical attitude which he has heretofore adopted. He will deliver tomorrow night a major speech in Washington before the annual convention of the Brotherhood of Teamsters, Chauffeurs, Stablemen and Helpers, A. F. of L.

He will speak over two nationwide radio networks on broadcast time to be paid for by the Democratic National Committee, instead of getting facilities free from all four networks available.

The decision was announced by Stephen T. Early, White House secretary, who told news correspondents:

"I expect that President Roosevelt in all probability will deliver the labor speech of the campaign."

The decision that this speech would be Mr. Roosevelt's first bid for re-election apparently was made at the last minute. The President at a press conference earlier indicated that he did not consider the speech to be political.

Mr. Early, who acted as Presidential spokesman later, said that the decision was dictated ... was content by a desire not to burden the radio circuits by carrying the talk as an unpaid news service by all the radio companies and thereby making them liable for granting equal facilities and time to Wendell L. Willkie.

New Phase of the Campaign

The White House announcement, made only a few hours before the President left on his train for the capital, opened a new phase of his activities as they concern this election year. Heretofore he has insisted that his inspection trips and his talks were made as duties of the President.

He will speak nonpolitically in Philadelphia on Sept. 20, when he receives a degree from the University of Pennsylvania, and here on Oct. 5, when he dedicates in one ceremony a new high school and two grade schools.

This attitude also will characterize other similar trips and talks in the future, but White House sources recalled that Mr. Roosevelt made for himself a loophole in the noncampaign rule in his radio address to the Democratic National Convention at Chicago, on July 19.

In that speech he said:

"Since last Summer I have been compelled to abandon proposed journeys to inspect many of our great national projects from the Alleghanies to the Pacific Coast. Events move so fast in other parts of the world that it has become my duty to remain either in the White House itself or at some near-by point where I can reach Washington and even Europe and Asia by direct telephone.

"I do expect, of course, during the coming months, to make my usual periodic reports to the country through the medium of press conferences and radio talks. I shall not have the time or the inclination to engage in purely political debate, but I shall never be too busy to call the attention of the nation to deliberate or unwitting falsifications of fact which are sometimes made by political candidates."

Early Asails President's Stand

On returning from a work session with the President at the Hyde Park home in late afternoon, Mr. Early gathered reporters in his office and recalled that statement by Mr. Roosevelt, laying emphasis on the President's earlier stipulation that he would use the press conferences and radio speeches to reply to political attacks.

"The address tomorrow night will be at radio time to be paid for by the Democratic National Committee, too," Mr. Early said, and he added, "That is all."

The announcement served to fix the proposed speech, which Mr. [continued]

Continued on Page Fifteen

La Guardia to Reveal Choice for President

Special to The New York Times.

WASHINGTON, Sept. 10—Mayor La Guardia will announce his choice for President in a nationwide radio broadcast Thursday evening over the NBC Red Network, he announced here today.

The Mayor, here as chairman of the United States section of the United States-Canadian Joint Defense Commission, issued a typewritten announcement to this effect. It has been reported that the Mayor would work for President Roosevelt's re-election, but he refused to go beyond his formal announcement.

The Democratic National Committee will pay the bill for Mayor La Guardia's broadcast tomorrow evening, Edward J. Flynn, chairman of the committee, said yesterday. The speech will be delivered from 7:15 to 7:30 P. M. and be repeated later from 11:15 to 11:30 P. M. for Pacific Coast listeners.

Mr. Flynn said that the Mayor had requested the broadcast to him several days ago.

LEHMAN DEPLORES STATE TAX CURBS

Asserts Attempts at 'Economic Isolation' Are a Threat to Democratic Way of Life

Charging that several States have deliberately attempted a policy of "economic isolation" in recent years, Governor Lehman warned last night that their efforts to "stifle the flow of trade across State lines" might eventually threaten our democratic way of life.

Governor Lehman, Governor A. Harry Moore of New Jersey and Governor Raymond E. Baldwin of Connecticut spoke at the annual dinner of the National Tax Association, which is holding its thirty-third annual conference at the Hotel Pennsylvania. Their addresses followed a day of discussion of current tax problems by many governmental and university specialists in the field.

Governor Moore pointed out that at present three-quarters of the cost of government in New Jersey is defrayed by taxes on real property, and he contended that this is too narrow a tax base. In working out replacement taxes, however, he said, care must be taken not to impose taxes that would harm the State's industries in their competitive position with other States.

Governor Baldwin, pointing out that Connecticut has a balanced budget without a sales tax or a State income tax, said that in his State an indicated deficit of $1,500,000 when he took office in January, 1939, has been changed to a surplus of $1,000,000 by a policy of government "friendly" to business, labor and agriculture, with resultant increased production.

Sees Struggle by States for Gain

In his assault on State tax policies that are creating interstate trade barriers, Governor Lehman said that over a period of years there has arisen "a shameless struggle for gain at the expense of sister States." He said that these policies were of "questionable material benefit" to the States that employ them.

"Laws have employed the power of government not for purposes of revenue but rather to stifle the flow of trade across State lines in behalf of domestic interests and enterprises," Governor Lehman said. "The net result has been to limit open competition, raise prices, lower standards of quality and, finally, to affect adversely the national income."

Turning to the "political and economic implications" of this trend, Governor Lehman said that "while our democratic way of life is being challenged more fiercely than at any recent stage of our national history, we quibble among ourselves over questionable material benefits."

"If the time over arrives when boundary lines of the forty-eight States assume greater significance than as mere geographic borders and our democracy is doomed," Governor Lehman continued. "National strength and stability in times of crisis are strongly dependent upon singleness of purpose.

Continued on Page Twenty-nine

WILLKIE OPPOSES DELAYING OF DRAFT DESPITE PRESSURE

Hopes the Senate and House Conferees Will Eliminate the Fish Amendment

HE REBUFFS ISOLATIONISTS

Takes Stand in Face of 140 House Republicans Who Voted to Wait

By JAMES A. HAGERTY
Special to The New York Times.

RUSHVILLE, Ind., Sept. 10—Disregarding strong pressure from members of the Republican organization, Wendell L. Willkie came out today against the House amendment to the Burke-Wadsworth selective service bill, which, if accepted by the Senate, would delay the draft until after the November election.

"I hope that, as a result of the conference between House and Senate conferees on the selective service bill, the Fish amendment is eliminated," Mr. Willkie said in a formal statement.

In opposing any delay in the draft, or selective service for national defense as Mr. Willkie prefers to phrase it, the Presidential nominee ran counter to 140 Republicans in the House who voted for the amendment, including Representative Joseph W. Martin Jr., chairman of the national committee. Only twenty-two Republicans voted against the amendment.

Resists Isolationist Pressure

Mr. Willkie's declaration confirmed the assertion he made in his speech Saturday night that never during his campaign would he take any position in which he did not believe. He is known to regard the international situation as so serious that there should be no avoidable delay in any of the preparations for national defense. He declared for "selective service" in his acceptance speech and explained afterward that he meant selective service now, not later.

Since that time he has resisted pressure from leading members of his party to modify his position and take more of an isolationist stand. He has been frank at all times regarding his views on foreign policy. He has said frequently that he favored aid to Great Britain, short of war, adding that when he said "short of war" he meant "short of war." In criticizing President Roosevelt's exchange of over-age destroyers for defense bases in British possessions, he favored the trade but attacked the method used by the President as dictatorial.

Research Aides Arrive

Members of the research staff which will accompany Mr. Willkie on his trip to the Pacific Coast arrived here today. Among them were Russell W. Davenport, who resigned as managing editor of Fortune to join the movement to nominate Mr. Willkie; Raymond Leslie Buell, former director of The Foreign Policy Association, and Elliott

Continued on Page Fourteen

Italians Jail Prince Doria as Anti-Fascist; Prince Torlonia Also Reported Arrested

By CAMILLE CIANFARRA
Wireless to The New York Times.

ROME, Sept. 10—Prince Filippo Andrea Doria-Pamaghili-Landi, 54-year-old head of an Italian princely family, has been put in a concentration camp, it is learned.

It is also reported, but without confirmation, that 25-year-old Prince Alessandro Torlonia, whose mother was Elsie Moore of New York and who married a daughter of the King of Spain, also has been arrested.

Circles close to the government emphatically denied this evening that the "alleged" arrests of two Roman princes were part of a round-up of anti-Fascists.

"No such round-up has taken place," they stated, "and all reports to the contrary are completely unfounded."

Prince Doria's arrest is stated to have been caused by remarks unfriendly to the Fascist regime, which he made publicly last June in a concentration camp for remarks ... going to friends of the family, he is [continued] ... doing manual labor. Since it is feared he is affected by heart trouble and rheumatism, there is considerable apprehension for his life among his friends.

Prince Doria, after the death of his first wife, married Mary Dykes, who is generally credited with having kept him alive with her constant care.

His anti-Fascist feelings are well known in Rome. He heartily disapproved the Ethiopian campaign.

On Dec. 14, 1935, the "day of the oath," when, following the adoption of sanctions against Italy by the League of Nations, Italian women were asked to donate their wedding rings to increase Italy's gold reserve, Prince Doria refused to display the Fascist ... quietly to the family ... [continued]

This gesture did not escape

Continued on Page Six

Ford's Party Leaves $46 As Tip After Luncheon

By The Associated Press.

DETROIT, Sept. 10—Ethel Gaff, 19-year-old Fort Wayne (Ind.) hotel waitress, need not worry about the $46 left on the table after Henry Ford and his party ate a $4 luncheon. It was the change from a $50 bill which paid for the luncheon.

Miss Gaff was reported in doubt as to whether the money was a tip or whether the automobile manufacturer had forgotten it in his hurry to resume his motor trip.

"I paid the check, and I left the money purposely as a tip for the young lady," Harry Bennett, personnel director of the Ford Motor Company, said today. "She did a very good job in taking care of us, and particularly in keeping curiosity seekers away from Mr. Ford."

PLANE PRODUCTION HAILED BY KNUDSEN

He Says in Buffalo Interview We Will Have 11,000 Combat Craft by April, 1942

By The Associated Press.

BUFFALO, Sept. 10—In nineteen months the Army and Navy will have about 11,000 combat airplanes, fighters and bombers, William S. Knudsen of the National Defense Commission said today as he approached the end of a nation-wide tour of aircraft plants with Major Gen. H. H. Arnold, chief of the Army Air Corps.

"We know the United States is making the best airplanes," he said, and added:

"I believe that presently we can say we are making the most airplanes."

The figure of 11,000 was based on a total production by April 1, 1942, of 33,000 planes, 14,000 destined for Great Britain and 19,000 for the armed services of the United States. General Arnold said that of those to be delivered to the Army and Navy, about 60 per cent would be so-called combat types.

Mr. Knudsen said the current American airplane production of 900 a month, including both military and large commercial types, would be doubled in twelve months. Seated in the office of Burdette S. Wright, president of the Curtiss Aeroplane Division of the Curtiss-Wright Corporation, he fixed at three a day the delivery of new Curtiss P-40 fighter planes to the Air Corps.

General Arnold added that 524 P-40's, one of the newest types of American fighters, were on order for the Air Corps, and that 140 had been delivered.

The visitors saw two of these fighter planes, the American counterpart of British and German pursuit craft, streak at 320 miles an hour across Buffalo's Municipal Airport in a rare public demonstration of the country's military air rearmament drive.

Delivery of P-40's to both the Air Corps and to Great Britain's Royal Air Force has been slowed down by the limited manufacture of engines by the Allison Engineering Corporation, a General Motors subsidiary at Indianapolis, but Mr. [continued]

Continued on Page Fourteen

LONDON IS HARRIED

Night Invaders Resume Bombing After 4 Raids by Day Are Repelled

BRITONS CARRYING ON

People Now Sleep in the Shelters—Water and Gas Impaired

By RAYMOND DANIELL
Special Cable to The New York Times.

LONDON, Wednesday, Sept. 11—As darkness fell last night a waxing moon rose above the smoldering embers of the previous night's great fires, which threatened for a time to destroy the beautiful St. Paul's Cathedral and St. Mary-le-Bow Church, whose sweet-toned chimes for generations have lulled the Cockney children to sleep. The German Air Force then returned in force to London to continue the attack that has made life in this capital a nightmare since Saturday.

The all clear was sounded at 4:39 this morning, after the raid had been in progress for eight hours and twenty-four minutes.

[Nazi bombers smashed at London with increasing violence early today, The Associated Press reported. Until early this morning, it was stated, the attack was much less ferocious than the previous three. Then the pace stepped up until four separate squadrons were wheeling about the capital at the same time at opposite points of the compass.]

The screams of their bombs, the earth-shaking crashes, the blaze that lit the sky, the clangor of fire engines and ambulances, the bark of anti-aircraft guns and nerve-racking hum of engines droning like a mosquito that does not bite, brought another sleepless and hideous night to 7,000,000 harried persons who are trying to carry on in the face of an attack that spares neither humble workmen's homes nor the homes of the nobility.

Bombing Is at Random

For nine hours last night explosive-laden planes roared overhead, dropping high explosive and incendiary bombs apparently wherever the spirit moved the man in charge of the bomb racks to press the button. They released death and destruction upon helpless civilians who shuddered each time the ground shook beneath them.

Two hospitals, one filled with ailing children and the other a maternity hospital, suffered heavy damage. It is not accurately known at present, while the raid is still going on, how many homes were wrecked or persons killed, for the rescue workers are still digging among the ruins.

It was estimated, however, that Sunday night's raid caused at least 286 deaths and injured 1,400 persons, including the lame, halt and blind, into hospitals, seriously injured.

Question of Morale

But it is not the dead or the injured, or even the extensive property damage that really counts in this battle for London, which is a mere prelude to the Battle for Britain. It is what is happening to the city's life and the nerves of its people that matters the most.

They are standing up to the punishment that is being rained on them from the skies with a courage that makes the eyes of a seasoned observer smart at times. There is no doubt about their bravery, but one cannot help but wonder how long any people's nerves can stand up under this kind of bombardment, in which every one knows that each breath may be the last one, and in which the suspense is awful.

That does not mean that a defeatist attitude is growing. Far from it. These people are getting madder by the minute.

Many homes are without gas and ... Citizens are forced to undergo tremendous inconveniences in getting to and from the places where they earn their livelihood, and their ingrained politeness to one another in the housing a strain.

There is hardly any one who has not a friend who has lost his home or has had a narrow escape from death or injury. Monday night bombs dropped on every section of London. Slum hovels, wealthy homes, office and luxury apartments, all felt the [continued]

Continued on Page Two

The International Situation

The War in Europe and Africa

Berlin last night suffered the most intense raid yet inflicted by Royal Air Force planes. Earlier British craft had ranged over Northwestern Germany, Belgium, the Netherlands, France and the Norwegian coast, raiding twenty-five places. Relays of planes blasted Hamburg wharves, a Berlin power plant, docks, factories, barges and supplies at Continental ports. Four bombers failed to return, the Air Ministry reported. [Page 1, Column 8.]

With fires from Monday's attack still smoldering, Nazi bombers swooped down upon London again last night to plague the harassed city its fourth sleepless night. The crash of descending bombs started at dusk, when the air-raid sirens sounded the fifth warning of the day. Previous raids had been limited apparently to reconnaissance flights and the planes had been driven off by British fighters. The early alarms were so timed that they drove workers to air-raid shelters at lunch time, at tea time, and again at the height of the evening rush hour with people jammed around crippled transit facilities. Though harassed at their daily tasks after a sleepless and strained night Londoners' morale was unbroken and they were getting "madder by the minute." [Page 1, Column 5.]

Women and children, many dazed from shell shock, jammed the railroads, begged rides from motorists and pleaded with the authorities to have homes for them in an exodus from battered London. The menfolk were carrying on. The Minister of Transport asked that every one refrain from unnecessary travel; the Minister of Health broadcast a plea for aid to the homeless. [Page 6, Column 5.]

Prince Filippo Andrea Doria-Pamphili-Landi, 54-year-old head of an Italian princely family, is now doing manual labor in a concentration camp for remarks unfriendly to the Fascist regime, it was learned in Rome. Reports that Prince Alessandro Torlonia, whose mother was Elsie Moore of New York and who married a daughter of the King of Spain, had also been arrested were unconfirmed. The government denied that there had been a round-up of anti-Fascists. [Page 1, Column 3.]

American Developments

The American Red Cross sped plans to provide relief for victims of German air raids in London and other British cities. The Washington office of the Red Cross ordered 500,000 garments shipped from its New York warehouses, made preparations to send additional medical supplies, and cabled funds for purchase in London of twelve mobile canteen units of eight vehicles each for feeding homeless civilians. [Page 14, Column 4.]

House and Senate conferees on the conscription bill spent the day tabulating the differences between the two adopted versions of the measure without conclusive results. Washington opinion is that the final version will accept the House age limits of 21 to 45 and that the Fish amendment to delay the draft sixty days will be dropped. [Page 12, Column 3.]

The Senate agreed to limit debate on the Export-Import Bank Bill to ten minutes today after spending yesterday in fruitless debate. Senator Taft has offered the only amendment, restriction of loans to help Latin-American production of strategic, critical or non - competitive products. [Page 11, Column 1.]

RAID NAZI CAPITAL

Miss U. S. Embassy, Hit Brandenburg Gate, Germans Say

AIM HELD DELIBERATE

R. A. F. Hammers 25 Vital Points to Weaken Foe's Offensive

By PERCIVAL KNAUTH
Wireless to The New York Times.

BERLIN, Wednesday, Sept. 11—The Royal Air Force this morning attacked the heart of Berlin's governmental center, dropping explosive and incendiary bombs in the immediate vicinity of the Wilhelmstrasse and the Reich's Chancellory. Appearing over the capital a few minutes after midnight when the moon nearly at full to guide them, the British fliers steered their course straight down "Via Triumphalis" bisecting Berlin from east to west and dropped a veritable hail of incendiary bombs on the famous Unter den Linden and Brandenburg Gate.

Two houses away from the American Embassy incendiary bombs set a small fire. Three hundred yards up the "East-West Axis"—a bomb estimated at between 500 and 1,000 pounds in weight smashed into the broad asphalt speedway, rocking buildings in a half-mile radius. Incendiary bombs splattered on the rooftops, on the Brandenburg Gate, the Academy of German Art, the House of German Engineers and the old Reichstag building, setting small fires, which, however, were said to have been quickly extinguished.

In The New York Times office near the Wilhelmplatz detonations of half a dozen explosive bombs in the vicinity of the cellar were heard in the underground air-raid shelter. Incendiary bombs were said to have set small fires in a Jewish hospital, close to the university buildings, and the Charité Hospital.

The Catholic Saint Hedwig's Hospital, second largest in Berlin, likewise was said to have been struck by incendiary bombs which started several fires.

Two Injured by Bombs

In the Invalidenstrasse, close to the central business section, explosive bombs injured two persons and blasted the front of an apartment house as well as part of another house. In Dorotheenstrasse, which runs parallel to Under den Linden, a dud bomb buried itself many feet deep in the street, while another ripped a wide hole in the office building.

An American news agency, with offices on the top floor of a building on this street, had a narrow escape when a bomb struck a house next door.

The British apparently attacked in four waves coming from the west. German military observers estimated the altitude of the first wave at about 18,000 feet, with each successive wave flying at a lower height, the last dropping its bombs from an altitude of about 6,000 feet. They flew straight into the city and when over the governmental district dropped numerous flares, which were followed by both explosive and incendiary bombs. Some planes were reported to have flown low and machine-gunned anti-aircraft, artillery and searchlight batteries. The ground defenses followed the planes with a steady barrage, which was louder over the center of the capital than ever heard before.

Official German quarters asserted the attack on the governmental district were obviously premeditated and designed to destroy government buildings. R. A. F. fliers, it is asserted, had every opportunity of sighting their objectives both in the light of the great moon of flares and the bright moon. It is concluded here, therefore, that the order had been given to attack the governmental district, for it is claimed that "all military objectives whatever were strictly avoided."

What form the German retaliation for this attack will take cannot as yet be said. However, German quarters always have been very clear in stating that retaliation will follow a hundredfold in the same manner as the British attack. Never before has governmental districts in Berlin [continued]

Continued on Page Four

INCENDIARY 'CARDS' A BRITISH WEAPON

Damp Discs, Dropped by R.A.F. by Thousands, Dry and Ignite—Nazis Incensed

By The Associated Press.

LONDON, Sept. 10—Britain disclosed tonight a new "secret weapon" in the form of innocent-looking bits of chemically treated cardboard dropped by the millions on Germany as delayed fire-bombs that burst into flame in unexpected quarters.

Germany, in first making public the new British tactics, acknowledged that the fire-secreting "calling cards" carried something more than a mere nuisance threat.

British authorities, in subsequently admitting use of the new weapon, described it only as a "self-igniting leaf," and declined to furnish details.

But the authentic German description, given after chemical analysis, sounded like a sequence from some fertile adventure fiction or a passage from a detective thriller.

The cards, composed of guncotton and phosphorus, are carried in a moist state, the Germans said. Scattered over the countryside in lots of a quarter-million from a single plane, they dry out naturally and spring suddenly into flame about eight inches high when warmed by natural processes to a moderate temperature.

Implying that the cards also bear a printed message, the Germans said they were particularly dangerous because people had been picking [continued]

NAZIS SEE BATTLE AS FIGHT TO FINISH

Air Attacks on London Will Be Pressed Till British Yield, It Is Said in Berlin

By The United Press.

BERLIN, Sept. 10—Nazis, angered by British bombing of Berlin and other cities, reported tonight that the German Air Fleet was roaring against London again in an offensive that would be pressed relentlessly until the British capitulate.

A new wave of German bombers flying against London with guns cut remorseless and incessant warfare, Nazis said, until "the smoking ruins of industrial and military objectives, decimation of the British Air Force and shattered morale of the British people bring into power a government that will accept German terms."

The German terms were regarded here as unconditional capitulation. Official German quarters were silent regarding any peace terms, but there were many unofficial suggestions that the collapse of Britain is "only a matter of weeks."

The Nazi press said that "now it is an eye-for-an-eye and a tooth-for-a-tooth" battle and that "the sword of the German air force strikes pitilessly."

"What effects the heavy caliber bombs have were clearly revealed by Warsaw and Rotterdam," one newspaper said. "If London wishes to taste a similar fate to the full extent, then let Churchill and his criminal clique continue to send pirates at will to Germany."

The Propaganda Ministry said [continued]

Continued on Page Four

"All the News That's Fit to Print."

The New York Times.

LATE CITY EDITION
Cloudy, much colder today. Tomorrow partly cloudy and rather cold
Temperatures Yesterday—Max., 68; Min., 52

Copyright, 1940, by The New York Times Company.

VOL. XC. No. 30,237.

Entered as Second-Class Matter,
Postoffice, New York, N. Y.

NEW YORK, WEDNESDAY, NOVEMBER 6, 1940.

THREE CENTS NEW YORK CITY and Vicinity | FOUR CENTS Elsewhere Except in 7th and 8th Postal Zones.

ROOSEVELT ELECTED PRESIDENT; CERTAIN OF 429 ELECTORAL VOTES; DEMOCRATS KEEP HOUSE CONTROL

RETAIN HOUSE GRIP

Democrats, Holding 225 Seats, Gain at Least Ten From Rivals

65 ARE NOW IN DOUBT

Latest Figures Indicate Republican Gain of 1 to 3 Senators

By TURNER CATLEDGE

Unless further complete returns today show more Republican winners in yesterday's election, the Democrats not only will have met successfully the challenge of their opponents to control the house but may actually repair some of the damage to their huge majority in the 1938 Congressional election.

The Republicans, on the other hand, may have added from one to three to their roster in the Senate, but this remains to be determined by complete reports.

Returns received up to 4 o'clock this morning indicated that the President's party had dropped only four seats to the opposition, while they had picked up at least ten now held by Republicans. This made the count 225 Democrats, 143 Republicans, one Independent Democrat and one American Labor ,with sixty-five seats still in doubt.

The present House is composed of 259 Democrats, 167 Republicans, one Farmer-Laborite, two Progressives and one American Labor member, with five vacancies due to deaths and resignations.

The status of the Senatorial tabulation at that hour, with thirty-six States in contest—thirty-three for full and three for unexpired terms—showed Democrats, 18; Republicans, 7, and 11 still in doubt. This made sure that the new Senate would have at least 62 Democrats, 22 Republicans, 1 Independent, leaving the 11 in doubt. The present ratio of the Senate is 69 Democrats, 24 Republicans, 1 Progressive, 1 Independent and 1 Farmer-Laborite (Senator Shipstead of Minnesota, who ran this year as a Republican).

The Senate's lone Progressive, Senator Robert M. La Follette, trailed Fred H. Clausen, his Republican opponent, in the earlier returns from Wisconsin, but along in the morning hours he forged ahead and won from the Badger State indicated that he might pull through in the toughest fight of his career.

The four seats dropped by Democrats to Republicans were in the Eighth Massachusetts, Sixteenth New York, Fourth California and the Sixth Missouri districts. More than offsetting these were the ten picked up by the Democrats, including the First, Second and Fourth Connecticut districts and the Congressman at Large of that State; the First and Second Rhode Island districts, the Fifth and Twenty-second Pennsylvania districts and the Forty-first New York and the Sixteenth Ohio districts. The Democrats made a clean sweep of the delegations in Connecticut and Rhode Island, annexing six seats held in these two States. Perhaps the greatest upsets in the House were the defeats of Representative Phil Ferguson, Democrat, of Oklahoma by Ross Rizley, Republican, and of the Democratic Representative James Fay of the Sixteenth New York by William E. Pfeiffer, Republican.

Incumbent Democrats Sticking

Incumbent Democrats were holding tenaciously to leads in most of the other contests in which they were involved and New Deal nominees were threatening sitting Republican Congressman in a number of districts, particularly in States where the Roosevelt victory was assuming landslide proportions in the popular vote.

The Republicans had entertained no hope from the start of capturing the leadership of the House, but they claimed chances of picking up from five to ten new seats to add to the twenty-four they now hold.

Continued on Page Two

THE VOTE FOR PRESIDENT

State	Districts Total	Reported	Roosevelt, Democrat.	Willkie, Republican.	Thomas, Socialist.	Electoral Vote—Roosevelt.	Willkie.
Alabama	2,300	1,107	140,984	21,224	......	11	
Arizona	430	270	40,287	21,603	......	3	
Arkansas	2,169	642	37,258	8,586	......	9	
California	13,692	9,394	1,043,200	743,522	......	22	
Colorado	1,610	387	43,150	54,301	......		
Connecticut	169	166	412,648	358,159	......	8	
Delaware	249	200	50,890	40,312	......	3	
Florida	1,451	895	246,183	52,531	......	7	
Georgia	1,720	896	196,657	29,046	......	12	
Idaho	792	300	36,113	30,155	......		
Illinois	8,378	6,017	1,314,763	1,375,692	......	29	
Indiana	3,968	2,185	576,754	576,872	......		
Iowa	2,453	1,505	356,657	376,859	......		
Kansas	7,734	1,377	147,821	216,802	......		
Kentucky	4,341	2,240	297,123	193,622	......	11	
Louisiana	1,712	481	137,518	22,987	......	10	
Maine	629	653	154,732	163,782	......		5
Maryland	1,331	1,194	351,234	241,447	......	8	
Massachusetts	1,810	1,151	636,856	575,950	......	17	4
Michigan	3,630	1,349	387,245	387,758	......		19
Minnesota	3,696	919	258,715	216,433	......	11	
Mississippi	1,668	635	87,190	4,179	......	9	
Missouri	4,479	2,914	526,667	480,110	......	......	
Montana	1,196	262	43,057	26,829	......	4	
Nebraska	2,043	1,227	124,825	169,063	......		
Nevada	260	177	15,545	11,213	......	3	
New Hampshire	294	287	115,932	103,671	......	4	
New Jersey	3,630	2,038	529,922	564,294*	......	16	
New Mexico	914	413	80,999	39,300	......	3	
New York	9,319	9,297	3,231,032	3,021,536	......	47	
North Carolina	1,926	-686	560,558	175,507	......	13	
North Dakota	2,262	631	73,669	73,330	......	......	
Ohio	8,675	7,722	1,465,514	1,385,759	......	26	
Oklahoma	3,613	2,805	355,766	249,117	......	11	
Oregon	1,663	923	89,971	89,539	......		5
Pennsylvania	8,113	7,132	1,912,401	1,670,032	......	36	
Rhode Island	259	259	181,881	138,432	......	4	
South Carolina	1,277	953	81,867	4,144	......	8	
South Dakota	1,936	1,054	61,211	83,369	......		4
Tennessee	2,300	1,891	257,724	119,636	......	11	
Texas	254	244	504,433	118,196	......	23	
Utah	831	345	63,396	39,941	......	4	
Vermont	246	246	64,244	78,355	......		3
Virginia	1,714	1,522	223,388	103,030	......	11	
Washington	3,018	1,063	154,500	102,022	......	8	
West Virginia	2,300	1,018	217,064	155,680	......	8	
Wisconsin	3,038	1,782	408,666	377,717	......	12	
Wyoming	696	490	32,889	31,785	......	3	
						429	51

*Hudson County returns incomplete.

ROOSEVELT WINNER IN MASSACHUSETTS

Indicated Margin Is Below That of 1936—Saltonstall Ahead in a Close Race

Special to THE NEW YORK TIMES.

BOSTON, Nov. 5—President Roosevelt carried Massachusetts over Wendell Willkie in today's election. Indications tonight were that his margin would be smaller than the 174,000 by which he captured the State's 17 electoral votes four years ago.

The Democratic surge was great enough to re-elect Senator Walsh over Henry Parkman Jr. by a substantial margin and to endanger Governor Leverett Saltonstall's re-election in his contest with Attorney General Paul A. Dever.

Lieut. Gov. Cahill, State Secretary Cook, State Treasurer Hurley and State Auditor Cook apparently were re-elected, while Robert T. Bushnell seemed to have won his contest for Attorney General on the basis of returns which had been counted late tonight.

President Roosevelt was strongest in the industrial cities outside Boston. He carried Lynn by almost 6,000 votes and New Bedford by a ratio of nearly 2 to 1. It was estimated that Roosevelt's margin in Boston would approach 100,000. He carried Somerville by 4,100 votes.

Governor Saltonstall fared much

Continued on Page Four

The War

Leading developments yesterday in the war, accounts of which appear on Page 25—the first page of the second section, —were as follows:

1. A German pocket battleship appeared in mid-Atlantic and shelled a British convoy.

2. Prime Minister Churchill emphasized before the Commons the growing U-boat threat and said bases in Ireland were needed by Britain.

3. In the Greek-Italian hostilities Rome reported an advance in the Yanina sector, the Greeks were said to be closing in on Koritza and a Yugoslav town was bombed by Italian-type planes.

The summary headed "International Situation" also appears on Page 25.

FLASH — a Want Ad Just telephone The New York Times—LAckawanna 4-1000.

NEW JERSEY VOTE GOES TO PRESIDENT

Willkie Margin Cut in Normal Republican Areas—Edison and Barbour Win

By RUSSELL B. PORTER

On the basis of incomplete returns at 4 o'clock this morning, President Roosevelt appeared to have carried New Jersey and its sixteen electoral votes by a safe plurality—over Wendell Willkie—drastically reduced from 364,000 margin in 1936 and closer to his 31,000 edge in 1932.

The same returns indicated the election of Charles Edison, former Secretary of the Navy and son of the late Thomas A. Edison, the inventor, over his Republican opponent, State Senator Robert C. Hendrickson. Mr. Edison appeared to have polled more votes than the President.

United States Senator W. Warren Barbour, Republican candidate for re-election, ran far ahead of his ticket, and decisively defeated James H. R. Cromwell, former Minister to Canada and husband of Doris Duke, the tobacco heiress.

Eight hours after the polls closed at 8 P. M. there was still considerable uncertainty over State-wide totals. Only one-half of the State's 3,631 election districts had reported their results by that time, and only a few comparatively of these were from the strong Democratic counties—Hudson, where Mayor Frank Hague of Jersey City, vice chairman of the Democratic National Committee, piled up a big Roosevelt vote, and Camden and Middlesex, where big industries with strong Roosevelt labor strength are located.

Big Vote Adds to Delay

The delay in recording the vote from these counties was caused partly by the record-breaking vote, brought out by perfect weather and unprecedented heavy registration, partly by the fact that voting machines are not used in these counties, and partly by the traditional withholding of the Hudson County vote until after the Republican counties have reported.

Surrogate John H. Gavin of Hudson County, spokesman for Mayor Hague, estimated early this morning, with the vote still incomplete, that Hudson would give the President and Mr. Edison a plurality of 110,000, including 60,000 in Jersey City. Mr. Cromwell was running far behind.

Four years ago Mr. Roosevelt re-

Continued on Page Twelve

CITY MARGIN WIDE

Lead Totals 727,254— Queens, Richmond Won by Willkie

P. R. SYSTEM UPHELD

Abolition Move Defeated by About 206,550— Simpson Is Elected

By LEO EGAN

Franklin D. Roosevelt piled up a plurality of 727,254 in New York City yesterday as voters in record-breaking numbers went to the polls under clear skies to record their choice for President. This was far short of the 1,375,396 plurality given to him in 1936, when he was a candidate for a second term.

The President carried the three most populous counties in the city, but lost Queens and Richmond. Queens gave Wendell Willkie a plurality of 36,875.

Senator James M. Mead, seeking re-election on the Democratic ticket, ran slightly ahead of the President. He carried the city by 845,063, carrying all five counties.

The President's pluralities of 350,-610 in Kings, 219,066 in the Bronx and 195,017 in Manhattan were much less than his supporters had counted on except in Manhattan, but they were enough to please them. The Manhattan plurality was larger than expected.

Results in Other Contests

Other features of yesterday's voting in the city were the defeat by an indicated plurality of 206,550 of the proposal to repeal the proportional representation method of selecting members of the City Council, the apparent defeat of Representative James H. Fay in the Sixteenth District, the election of Kenneth F. Simpson, New York County Republican leader, for the Congressional seat now held by Representative Bruce Barton; the election of John Cashmore and Samuel S. Leibowitz, the Democratic candidates for Borough President and County Judge, respectively, in Brooklyn, and the re-election of Representative Vito Marcantonio, outstanding Congressional foe of conscription and the Roosevelt defense program, in the Twentieth Congressional District on Manhattan's upper East Side.

The President carried all but two Assembly districts in Manhattan, losing the Fifteenth and Tenth, and all but three in King's losing the Ninth, Tenth and Twentieth. He swept all eight districts in the Bronx and lost three out of six in Queens.

In all but one borough the friends of proportional representation were able to beat back the proposal to repeal it. If the proposal had been carried the voters would have elected Councilmen next year on the basis of State Senate districts with

Continued on Page Four

WINNERS OF PRESIDENCY AND VICE PRESIDENCY
Franklin Delano Roosevelt — Henry Agard Wallace

DEMOCRATS CARRY STATE BY 230,000

Mead, O'Day, Merritt and Desmond Join President in New York Victory Column

By JAMES A. HAGERTY

For the third time President Franklin D. Roosevelt car.ied his home State of New York with its forty-seven electoral votes in yesterday's election, this time by a plurality of about 230,000, over Wendell L. Willkie, his Republican opponent.

The vote in New York City with 40 election districts missing out of 4,051 gave Willkie 1,241,501 and Roosevelt 1,937,017, an actual plurality for Roosevelt of 695,516 and an indicated plurality of 700,823.

Outside New York City in 5,004 out of 5,268 election districts, President Roosevelt had a total vote of Willkie 1,685,043, Roosevelt 1,219,817, an actual plurality of 465,276 for Willkie and an indicated plurality of 489,924. This gave the President an actual plurality of 230,240 one these returns and an indicated plurality of 215,000, which may be slightly higher because of the small number of votes in the unreported districts.

Continued on Page Ten

Bonfires of All Buttons Urged to Heal Bitterness

Public bonfires of all the Democratic and Republican campaign literature and buttons were suggested yesterday by William Allen White, national chairman of the Committee to Defend America by Aiding the Allies, as a means of "healing partisan bitterness and for launching a nation-wide campaign to safeguard American democracy."

Mr. White, in a statement issued last night, urged "unity mass meetings" as soon as possible after election, in a message to the representatives of the group's 717 local chapters in the forty-eight States.

The meetings should be held, he said, "not in the spirit of exultation on the part of the victorious party but with the idea that we destroy the symbols of partisan bitterness and unite now on a national program of safeguarding American democracy."

PRESIDENT TAKES KEYSTONE STATE

Republican Chairman Concedes Pennsylvania—Guffey Ahead in Senate Race

Special to THE NEW YORK TIMES.

PHILADELPHIA, Wednesday, Nov. 6—Aided by impressive strength in the industrial areas, President Roosevelt apparently duplicated his feat of 1936 and won the thirty-six electoral votes of traditionally Republican Pennsylvania in yesterday's election.

The trend in the senatorial contest between Senator Joseph F. Guffey, Democrat, and Jay Cooke, chairman of the Philadelphia Republican Committee, was in the direction of the re-election of Mr. Guffey, who campaigned on his record of "100 per cent Roosevelt support."

The Democrats, it seemed likely, would gain an undetermined number of seats in the State's Congressional delegation, which had been Republican by nineteen to fifteen, and they appeared to have an even chance of wresting control of the State House of Representatives from the Republicans, which took it over two years ago. The Republicans were hopeful of salvaging their majority in the State Senate.

James F. Torrance, Republican State Chairman, conceded Pennsyl-

Continued on Page Four

BIG ELECTORAL VOTE

Large Pivotal States Swing to Democrats in East and West

POPULAR VOTE CUT

First Time in History That Third Term Is Granted President

By ARTHUR KROCK

Over an apparently huge popular minority, which under the electoral college system was not able to register its proportion of the total vote in terms of electors, President Roosevelt was chosen yesterday for a third term, the first American in history to break the tradition which began with the Republic. He carried to victory with him Henry A. Wallace to be Vice President, and continued control of the House of Representatives by the Democrats was also indicated in the returns.

But in many of the larger States so many precincts were still missing early this morning, and the contest in these States was so close, that Wendell L. Willkie, the Republican opponent, whose name Mr. Roosevelt never mentioned throughout the campaign, refused to concede defeat. He said it was a "horse race," and that the result would not be known until today. He went to bed in that frame of mind.

As the returns mounted there seemed little, however, to sustain Mr. Willkie's hope. New York, Massachusetts, Connecticut, Rhode Island, Pennsylvania, Ohio and Illinois, of the greater States, all appeared to have been carried safely by the President. The Solid South had resisted all appeals to revolt against Mr. Roosevelt's quest for a third term. The Pacific and Mountain State were following the national trend.

States for Mr. Roosevelt

States sure or probable for the President are:

Alabama, Arizona, Arkansas, California, Connecticut, Delaware, Florida, Georgia, Illinois, Kentucky, Louisiana, Maryland, Massachusetts, Missouri, Minnesota, Mississippi, Montana, Nevada, New Hampshire, New Jersey, New Mexico, New York, North Carolina, Ohio, Oklahoma, Pennsylvania, Rhode Island, South Carolina, Tennessee, Texas, Utah, Virginia, West Virginia and Wisconsin—electoral votes, 429.

States sure or probable for Mr. Willkie:

Kansas, Maine, Michigan, Nebraska, North Dakota, South Dakota, Vermont—electoral votes 51.

States doubtful or insufficiently reported:

Colorado, Idaho, Indiana, Iowa, Oregon, Washington and Wyoming—electoral votes, 51.

The Doubtful Vote

Listing as doubtful nine States, including several like California, Ohio and Indiana, which seem certain to join the Democratic column, there were at 3 A. M. only 51 electoral votes in possible dispute. The President had an apparently certain total of 429, while with more or less security in Mr. Willkie's column were only 51 votes.

No shift or series of shifts could affect the electoral result and the indications were that the President's total would reach from 420 to 470.

Either figure would be much less than the nearly clean sweep he had in 1932, when he carried forty-two States, and in 1936, when only Maine and Vermont went Republican. And unless the Far West and the Mountain States shall be shown to have given incredible majorities and less than his indicated lead in the Eastern States pile up the President's states higher than indications seem to make possible, Mr. Roosevelt's popular majority will be far less than he had against Herbert Hoover and Alf M. Landon.

ROOSEVELT LOOKS TO 'DIFFICULT DAYS'

But Tells Celebrators That He Will Carry On for the Country 'Just the Same'

By CHARLES HURD

Special to THE NEW YORK TIMES.

HYDE PARK, Wednesday, Nov. 6—Standing on the portico of his mother's home here, Franklin D. Roosevelt early today acknowledged his re-election with a promise to continue to be "the same Franklin Roosevelt you have known."

He made this statement to several hundred residents of Hyde Park and vicinity who formed a torchlight procession that carried out a tradition marking Democratic political victories with rallies at the old house, a parade formed by Democrats as soon as returns indicated the victory.

"We are facing difficult days in this country," Mr. Roosevelt told the throng, "but I think you will find me in the future just the same Franklin Roosevelt you have known many past years."

The President leaned on the crowd as he leaned on the arm of his third son, Franklin Jr., in the bright light of flares set in place by motion-picture camera men.

He smiled and waved while hundreds of people trooped through the grounds from cars parked first in the driveways and afterward on the Albany Post Road, some of them a quarter of a mile away.

President Faces His Neighbors

Behind the President were grouped about forty guests who had been entertained by Mrs. Roosevelt at supper at her cottage at Val-Kill. But the President faced a crowd in which there were no prominent politicians, no industrial leaders. These were exclusively his neighbors, who bear to him the same relationship as the villagers bore to his father when he was a young Democratic leader and a friend of President Cleveland.

President Roosevelt walked on to the front porch of the Hyde Park house just before midnight, when he finally drove a vigil over table on which he marked election returns behind locked doors in the dining room of his home.

The first glare of red flares was seen far off down the driveway. Ten minutes later, exactly at midnight, a town band marched into the car park in front of the house.

The President, with Franklin Jr., stood at the right side of the porch.

Continued on Page Two

Willkie Retires Refusing to Give Up; He Declines Any Statement Before Today

Grimly clinging to his avowed determination not to give up the fight, Wendell L. Willkie said at 1:30 this morning that he intended to go to bed in his suite at the Hotel Commodore, and that he would have no statement to make concerning the election until some time after he wakes up this morning.

This information, relayed from his fourteenth-floor suite to the waiting crowd of reporters in the press headquarters downstairs, was the only word that came from Mr. Willkie after he had briefly appeared before a crowd of cheering campaign workers at 12:20 A. M., to say that he was neither afraid nor disheartened, and repudiate indignantly suggestions that he should concede his defeat.

When he appeared at that time before about 1,500 faithful supporters in the Grand Ball Room of the Commodore Hotel, Mr. Willkie pleaded with them not to quit and expressed his confidence that the fight they had jointly waged would eventually be won.

His appearance before his campaign workers came after hours of seclusion in his private suite, where he repeatedly characterized the election as a "horse race" and predicted that the result would not be known definitely until some time today. Mr. Willkie appeared before the crowd of campaign workers at 12:19 A. M.

Holding up both hands to ask for silence while they gave him an earsplitting ovation, Mr. Willkie said:

"Fellow workers: I first want to say to you that I never felt better in my life. I congratulate you in being a part of the greatest crusade of this century. And that the principles for which we have fought will prevail in as sure end that the truth will always prevail.

"And I hope that none of you are either afraid or disheartened because I am not in the slightest.

"I just wanted to come down and thank you so much for being my fellow fighters in this struggle—to

Continued on Page Five

The New York Times.

LATE CITY EDITION
Occasional rain, little change in temperature today. Tomorrow partly cloudy, continued cool.
Temperature Yesterday—Max. 47 ; Min. 40

Section 1

VOL. XC No. 30,388. Entered as Second-Class Matter, Postoffice, New York, N. Y. NEW YORK, SUNDAY, APRIL 6, 1941. Copyright, 1941, by The New York Times Company Including Rotogravure Picture, Magazine and Book Review New York City and Vicinity TEN CENTS

GERMANS INVADE YUGOSLAVIA AND GREECE; HITLER ORDERS WAR, BLAMING THE BRITISH; MOSCOW SIGNS AMITY PACT WITH BELGRADE

U. S. STEEL STRIKE IS CALLED BY C. I. O., EFFECTIVE TUESDAY

Murray Says Wage Talks Failed and Plans Picketing in Tie-Up Involving 261,000 Men

ROOSEVELT MAY STEP IN

President Is Reported to Have Summoned C. I. O. Chief in Move to Bar Walkout

By The Associated Press.

PITTSBURGH, April 5 — The C. I. O. Steel Workers Organizing Committee tonight ordered its members in all steel mills of the giant United States Steel Corporation, employing about 261,000 wage-earners, to stop work at midnight next Tuesday.

The union said that negotiations for a wage increase and other benefits had collapsed.

Philip Murray, C. I. O. president and chairman of the Steel Workers Organizing Committee, telegraphed instructions to local union units of the corporation to establish continuous picket lines at all plant gates.

[The United Press reported from Pittsburgh last night it had learned authoritatively that President Roosevelt, concerned over the threatened stoppage, had invited Mr. Murray to a White House conference tomorrow or Tuesday.]

The company produces more than one-third of America's steel, an amount exceeding all of that made in England. It hold millions of dollars in defense contracts.

Mr. Murray termed the cessation of work a "lockout" rather than a strike, asserting that the company had rejected his suggestion to continue negotiations, which had begun March 20, another week, with any agreement to be retroactive to April 1. The company was said to be willing to make the agreement retroactive only to April 8.

The sudden development, threatening to spread the nation's strike area to the vital steel industry, came during an interim of wage negotiations, which still are scheduled to be resumed Monday at 10 A. M.

Mr. Murray called in 100 local union leaders today for conference. It was the third such meeting since the union made known its nine-point demands, which included a wage increase of 10 cents an hour, a closed shop, check-off union dues by the company, liberalized vacations and establishment of seniority rights.

The company's minimum pay, established in 1937, is 62½ cents an hour, with the average pay of wage earners about 87 cents an hour. This contract expired April 1 and was extended to April 8.

The company's original counter-offer of a 2½ cents an hour wage rise was rejected by Mr. Murray. Tonight it was learned this offer had been raised to five cents an hour but again was refused by the union. The company contended it made but $60,000,000 of its $102,000,000 profit last year in its steel plants. The other profits came from coal, cement shipping and other subsidiaries. The company has insisted it cannot increase wages without increasing the price of steel. The Government has firmly refused to sanction any such price advance.

In his instructions to local unions, Mr. Murray said:

"The Carnegie-Illinois Steel Company has either rejected entirely or submitted unsatisfactory counter proposals with respect to each of the points offered by the S. W. O. C. in its program.

"The S. W. O. C. will attempt to arrive at an agreement with the companies involved to provide for the continuance at work of the necessary maintenance men during the suspension of operations. Further instructions regarding this situation will be forwarded to you by wire.

"Peaceful picket lines shall be established at all plant gates and maintained at all times during the cessation of work. There should be no violence or other unlawful acts on the part of members or representatives of the S. W. O. C."

No comment was forthcoming from the company on the development.

Continued on Page Forty-nine

The International Situation

SUNDAY, APRIL 6, 1941

Germany's armies this morning launched a vast attack upon Yugoslavia and Greece. The move was announced over the Berlin radio in an order of the day from Reichsfuehrer Hitler, read by Propaganda Minister Goebbels; it denounced "the Belgrade government of intrigue" and said German troops would not lay down their arms until "this band of ruffians" and every last Briton had been eliminated from Southeastern Europe. [Page 1, Column 8.]

As Belgrade's first air raid was reported, it was believed the principal Nazi attacks had been launched from Bulgaria, one across Southern Yugoslavia and another southward toward Salonika. Bulgaria's army was said to have an active role, though Hungary's was believed inactive for the present. The Yugoslavs were expected to fight a rear-guard delaying action until they reached their strong natural defense positions. The Belgrade Government had planned to evacuate the capital, going to some southern point. The United States Minister was reported remaining in Belgrade. [Page 1, Column 5.]

With dramatic suddenness Yugoslavia and Soviet Russia signed a five-year non-aggression and friendship pact providing that if either signatory became the victim of aggression by a third State the other would maintain a policy of "strictest friendship." The pact will take effect immediately and the articles of ratification will be exchanged in Belgrade "at the earliest possible moment." [Page 1, Column 4.]

On the African front, British Headquarters in Cairo reported that an Axis advance east of Bengazi, Libya, "has been successfully held and the situation is well in hand." Empire forces in Ethiopia were driving on the Awash River, to a point only eighty miles from Addis Ababa, while other units driving down on the capital from Eritrea captured Adowa and Adigrat. [Page 1, Column 6; Map, Page 7.]

The British Air Ministry augmented early brief accounts of the R. A. F. attack on Brest Friday night and early Saturday by stating that the 26,000-ton German battleships Gneisenau and Scharnhorst had been "very, very lucky" if they had escaped serious damage from new and powerful British bombs. R. A. F. aircraft, it was said, had dived to 1,000 feet to unleash their missiles on the Nazi raiders and had fired oil stores and warehouses near by, while other British planes dropped bombs on Rotterdam and the Ruhr. [Page 9, Column 1.]

The sharp British blow at the two German raiders coincided with a Berlin claim that 718,000 tons of British and Allied shipping had been sunk during March by German surface craft, U-boats, mines and airplanes. A German auxiliary cruiser operating "overseas" was said to have sunk the British auxiliary cruiser Voltaire of 13,255 tons. Moreover, Berlin said, U-boats in two days had sunk eighteen ships, totaling 106,000 tons, in a British convoy. [Page 13, Column 1.]

President Roosevelt's hint that he might soon lift combat-zone restrictions on the Red Sea to permit passage of American ships with war supplies for Britain aroused considerable interest in Washington. Senator George, chairman of the Senate Foreign Relations Committee, was said to feel that such action would necessitate Congressional amendment of the Neutrality Act; other members of Congress were believed to hold the President already had power to do this through provisions of the Lease-Lend Law. [Page 1, Column 1.]

Uruguay formally seized two Italian and two Danish ships in her harbors and placed the crews, comprising 119 men, under the direction of the Italian and Danish consuls, respectively. Many of the Danish seamen were reported to have expressed pleasure over the seizures and to have exhibited pro-British emblems. [Page 19, Column 1.]

COAL TIE-UP ENDED IN 65% OF THE MINES

Southern Operators Hold Out but Contract for Rest Will Be Signed Tomorrow

Yielding to pressure from the Federal Government, representatives of 65 per cent of the nation's soft-coal producers agreed yesterday to sign a new contract with the United Mine Workers Tomorrow. At least 300,000 miners are expected to return to work Tuesday or Wednesday, ending a week's stoppage that threatened to cut off vital fuel supplies for defense industries.

Dr. John R. Steelman, director of the United States Conciliation Service, who succeeded in breaking the four-week deadlock between the C. I. O. union and the operators, predicted that virtually all the mines would be open within a week. Other government officials said they believed the settlement in the soft-coal fields would provide a key to peaceful adjustment of employer-union differences in steel and anthracite, thus removing the threat of delay in the defense program and insuring uninterrupted work for 1,000,000 men.

Thirteen associations of Southern bituminous operators were the sole holdouts against the tentative accord effected by Dr. Steelman, and there were indications that their ranks were crumbling. Union officials said scattered companies in the Southern States had indicated their intention of signing with the John L. Lewis organization, whether or not their associations went along. The union relied on the pressure of competition to bring the others into line in a few days.

Under the terms of the proposed contract the United Mine Workers will win its full demand for a basic wage of $7 a day. This represents an increase of $1 over the rate previously in effect in the North and $1.40 over the Southern rate. The union's insistence on abolition of the

Continued on Page Thirty-three

KNUDSEN ASSAILS RADICALS IN LABOR

Charges They Hamper Output for Defense—Cooperation by All Vital, He Warns

Text of Mr. Knudsen's address appears on Page 40.

Asserting that the most serious aspect of the strike in the Allis-Chalmers plant in Milwaukee was not the time lost in the production of defense materials but the fact that it showed that "radical" labor leaders could tell the State and Federal Governments "where to get off," William S. Knudsen last night proposed a program for dealing with labor difficulties that he said would eliminate 90 per cent of the strikes.

The director-general of the Office of Production Management, who spoke at the Army Day dinner of the Military Order of the World War at the Hotel Waldorf-Astoria, said that the labor situation during the last month had grown worse and warned that the epidemic of strikes must be stopped or the effort for defense and aid to Great Britain, Greece and Yugoslavia would fail.

Interrupted by applause when he started to discuss the labor situation, Mr. Knudsen declared that time was the all-important element in America's defense program and declared that if the nation could put on a "little steam" in production during the eighty-nine days remaining before the Fourth of July "we might save a lot of blood later on."

"I do not believe that legislation against strikes is necessary or enforceable," Mr. Knudsen said, "but I do believe that during the emergency period a definite procedure should be followed in order that strikes may be held to a minimum.

"For instance, I believe that strike votes should be taken under the supervision of the Labor Department. I believe a certain mini-

Continued on Page Forty

TREATY NOW VALID

Moscow Discloses That Pledge of Friendship Was Made Yesterday

PEACE IS TERMED AIM

Strictest Neutrality Is Provided—Accord Is Hailed in London

By The Associated Press.

MOSCOW, Sunday, April 6—Soviet Russia and Yugoslavia have signed a treaty of friendship and non-aggression after several days of negotiation, Tass, Soviet official news agency, announced early today.

The agency said the pact had been signed yesterday by the Russian Premier and Foreign Commissar, Vyacheslaff M. Molotoff, and Milan Gavrilovitch, former Yugoslav Cabinet Minister and Yugoslavia's representative in Moscow.

The treaty declared that Russia and Yugoslavia were "inspired by the friendship existing between the countries and convinced that the preservation of peace forms their common interest" and hence had decided to conclude the pact.

The treaty was for five years.

Its first article provided neither country would attack the other and that each would respect the sovereign rights and territorial integrity of the other.

It provided that, in case of aggression against one of the countries by a third power, the other would observe a policy of friendly relations with the country attacked.

TEXT OF THE TREATY

MOSCOW, Sunday, April 6 (UP) —Tass News Agency gave out today the text of the treaty between the Soviets and Yugoslavia, as follows:

A treaty on friendship and non-aggression between the Union of Soviet Socialist Republics and the Kingdom of Yugoslavia.

The Presidium of the Supreme Soviet U. S. S. R. and His Majesty the King of Yugoslavia, inspired by friendship existing between the two countries and convinced that preservation of peace forms their common interest, decided to conclude a treaty on friendship and non-aggression and appointed for this purpose their representatives:

Presidium of the Supreme Soviet U. S. S. R.—Vyacheslaff M. Molotoff, chairman of the Council of Peoples Commissars and Peoples Commissar of Foreign Affairs; His Majesty the King of Yugoslavia—Milan Gavrilovitch, Envoy Extraordinary and Minister Plenipotentiary of Yugoslavia, Bozhin Simich and Colonel Dragutin Savich, which representatives, after exchanging their credentials found in proper form and due order, agreed on the following:

ARTICLE I

The two contracting parties mutually undertake to desist from

Continued on Page Twenty-five

New Army Marches in Rain Here; Nation Joins in Military Tribute

By HANSON W. BALDWIN

The new Army of the United States paraded down the Fifth Avenue of many cities yesterday as the nation opened an unprecedented week-end celebration of Army Day.

Veterans of past wars marched with youngsters who may become veterans of a future war, as the muffled beats of drumheads dampened by the rain epitomized the somber attitude with which thousands of spectators in many cities viewed their marching men. Not since 1917 and another war has the nation so taken the Army—now truly a national army—to itself with quiet, restrained pride.

For the music of the bands was but a faint echo in people's minds of the growing thunder of Europe's guns, and the serious attitude of the onlookers was matched in New York, Washington and other American cities by the weather. The skies were a sullen gray and the peaks of New York's skyscrapers were

veiled in the rain as the Army marched and drumheads burst and slickers poured off torrents of the rain.

The New York parade along upper Fifth Avenue, which had been expected to be the greatest Army Day event in the city's history, lost considerably in volume but gained in solemnity because of the weather. Not many more than half of the expected 50,000 marchers participated, and the sparse, umbrellaed crowd that watched could not have numbered at its peak more than 30,000 to 40,000. The crowd dwindled at times during the two-hour parade to less than half that number. The march past into a real test of soldiering, particularly for 4,500 men of the Forty-fourth Division from Fort Dix, N. J., who had negotiated seventy-eight miles of roads slick with rain in motor convoys to participate in the parade.

Mayor La Guardia, huddled in

Continued on Page Forty-two

YUGOSLAVIA FIGHTS

Belgrade Has Air Raid as Armies Resist, Berne Hears

DRIVE FROM BULGARIA

Greeks Announce Nazi Attack—Stukas Clear Path, Germans Say

By RAY BROCK
Wireless to THE NEW YORK TIMES.

BELGRADE, Yugoslavia, Sunday, April 6—At 3:25 o'clock this morning the air-raid sirens in Belgrade sounded an alarm. For the Yugoslavs it was the first indication that the nation was at war.

An hour later, at 4:32, two Yugoslav fighter planes appeared over the city, flying in an easterly direction. They came from the Zemun airdrome. Two more fighter planes appeared a short time later.

[At this point wireless connections with Belgrade were cut.]

Greeks Announce Attack

The Greek High Command announced in a communiqué broadcast from Athens that since 5:15 A. M., Athens time, the German troops had been attacking Greek troops on the Bulgarian border, the Columbia Broadcasting System announced this morning. No further details were in the communiqué as it was received here.

The German Propaganda Ministry announced in a broadcast from Berlin, according to CBS, that swarms of German planes, including Stuka dive-bombers, were "pouncing like hornets" on Greek and Yugoslav airdromes and railways in an effort to cripple the resistance to the invading German armies. The Nazi Propaganda Ministry also asserted that the planes were clearing a path for tanks and infantry, and that parachute troops were landing at strategic points within the Greek-Yugoslav defenses. There was no confirmation of these claims.

Belgrade Has Second Alarm
By Telephone to THE NEW YORK TIMES.

BERNE, Switzerland, Sunday, April 6—The Belgrade correspondent of THE NEW YORK TIMES reported at 5:30 o'clock this morning that naturally he had heard of the situation, but that "you wouldn't know the difference." Aside from two air-raid alarms in the capital early this morning, no incident had yet occurred. Reports as to the exact location of the fighting were very scant.

On the Greek frontier the invasion doubtlessly came from Bulgaria through the Struma Valley with a secondary attack down the Vardar Valley. This latter attack, however, would entail driving across the southeastern border of Yugoslavia—the Third Army region based on Skopje under General Ilija Brasitch.

For some time before the Yugoslav crisis began to take on even fainfly menacing tones, the Yugoslav High Command had been re-

Continued on Page Twenty-four

Hitler's Order of the Day

Adolf Hitler's declaration that Germany was at war with Yugoslavia was read over the Berlin radio early today by Propaganda Minister Joseph Goebbels. As heard by the National Broadcasting Company's station in New York and translated from the German, it read:

In the name of the Fuehrer, Adolf Hitler, I am reading the following order of the day to the German Army of the East:

Berlin, April 6, 1941.

Soldiers of the Southeast Front:

Since early this morning the German people are at war with the Belgrade government of intrigue. We shall only lay down arms when this band of ruffians has been definitely and most emphatically eliminated, and the last Briton has left this part of the European Continent, and that these misled people realise that they must thank Britain for this situation, they must thank England, the greatest warmonger of all time.

The German people can enter into this new struggle with the inner satisfaction that its leaders have done everything to bring about a peaceful settlement.

We pray to God that He may lead our soldiers on the path and bless them as hitherto.

In accordance with the policy of letting others fight for her, as she did in the case of Poland, Britain again tried to involve Germany in the struggle in which Britain hoped that she would finish off the German people once and for all, to win the war, and if possible to destroy the entire German Army.

In a few weeks long ago the German soldiers on the Eastern Front, Poland, swept aside this instrument of British policy. On April 9, 1940, Britain again attempted to reach its goal by a thrust on the German north flank, the thrust at Norway.

In an unforgettable struggle the German soldiers in Norway eliminated the British within a period of a few weeks.

What the world did not deem possible the German people achieved. Again, only a few weeks later, Churchill thought the moment right to make a renewed thrust through the British Allies, France and Belgium, into the German region of the Ruhr. The victorious hour of our soldiers on the West Front began.

It is already war history how the German Armies defeated the legions of capitalism and plutocracy. After forty-five days this campaign in the West was equally and emphatically terminated. Then Churchill concentrated the strength of his Empire

Continued on Page Twenty-six

BRITISH HALT DRIVE IN LIBYA, GET ADOWA

Axis Checked East of Bengazi —South Africans Within 80 Miles of Addis Ababa

Wireless to THE NEW YORK TIMES.

CAIRO, Egypt, April 5—The British announced today that their forces in Libya had halted the advance of German and Italian armored units somewhere east of Bengazi. The situation here after the recapture of that port by the Axis was said to be "well in hand."

At the same time the swift progress of the British Imperial forces in East Africa resulted in the capture of Adowa (and of near-by Adigrat, according to The Associated Press) with South African troops in Ethiopia crossed the Awash River and struck to within eighty miles of Addis Ababa.

[Massawa, the Red Sea port toward which the British armies of East Africa are racing, was reported to have defied a British demand for surrender, according to an Associated Press dispatch from Khartum.]

South African Advance

After the British in the last two days took the two most easily defendable areas in East Africa, Italian resistance appeared to be crumbling fast. The South African troops, who have marched all the way from Italian Somaliland now are moving westward along the Jibuti railway. After a brisk but brief battle at the crossing of the Awash, this column is pushing through the African hill country toward the higher rolling grassland plateau around Addis Ababa.

It is said the South Africans averaged a twenty-five-mile advance every day in the last two months. North of the capital, combined British and Indian forces are pursuing the fleeing Italians toward Dessye through difficult mountainous terrain. Between Asmara and Adowa they advanced with only slight skirmishing at many points that might have become other Cherens had Italian morale been good.

The occupation of Adowa frees the battle site where in 1896 Ethiopia's Emperor Menelik routed the Italians, killing 5,000 and capturing 4,000, thus preserving his nation's independence until 1936. The town itself has a population of 6,000.

Despite the lightness of the fighting in this area, advancing British forces surprised and captured a battalion of Italian infantry. Italians are running southward, apparently almost wholly disorganized, throwing away their rifles and surrendering on the slightest excuse.

Continued on Page Seven

NAZI TROOPS MARCH

Goebbels Reads Order to Germans to Rid Europe of All Britons

QUICK BLOW PLEDGED

Greece Told She Invited It—U. S. Is Said to Share Blame

By DANIEL T. BRIGHAM

BERNE, Switzerland, Sunday, April 6—At 5 o'clock this morning German forces attacked Yugoslavia and Greece in the long-awaited culmination of the Balkan war of nerves.

The news broke on the world with startling suddenness when a German radio station announcer with a triumphant blast this morning introduced Dr. Joseph Goebbels, Minister of Propaganda, who then read Reichsfuehrer Hitler's order of the day to "my forces in the Southeast Europe."

"Since dawn this morning," said Dr. Goebbels, "the German Reich has been at war with Yugoslavia and Greece."

It was indicated that the friendship pact signed between Yugoslavia and Russia yesterday was one of the factors of which Germany complained. This was another version of the Nazi charges of "aggressive encirclement of Germany," which have been used since Herr Hitler's advent to power.

Yugoslav Arming Held Cause

Another source of grievance, it would seem, was Belgrade's mobilization, a point that Herr Hitler mentioned in his order of the day as one of the chief reasons for the attack.

Immediately after Dr. Goebbels's broadcast, telephone communications to the eastward from this city —and south to Rome—were cut off.

[United States and British encouragement to the Yugoslavs in their resistance to German demands was also cited as grounds for Germany's attack, according to The Associated Press. Alleged American offers of material aid were also quoted.]

The German Army was told it would not lay down its arms until the "ruffians" and "plotters" in Belgrade had been deposed and the last Briton driven out of this territory.

Friendship for Greeks

German soldiers have been fighting in Greece since dawn today, the proclamation stated. It was indicated that the battle in Greece was not directed against the population but only against the "world enemy," Great Britain, who had dispatched troops there for an attack against the interests of the Reich.

Germany, Herr Hitler was quoted as saying, does not consider herself at war with Greece and will not molest any Greek who does not take up arms against the German Army, but any who lends his support to the British will be crushed.

"Soldiers of the Southeast Front," the Reichsfuehrer proclaimed, "your hour has now come."

He then told these troops that they must emulate their comrades at war with Greece and will not molest any Greek who does not take up arms against the German Army, but any who lends his support to the British will be crushed. The general mobilization in Yugoslavia was considered by the Reich as final proof that Britain had mixed into the internal affairs of Yugoslavia and would lead that country into hostile acts against Germany.

Yugoslav Provocation Charged

BERLIN, Sunday, April 6 (P)— The German radio, in broadcasting Reichsfuehrer Hitler's order to the German Army, quoted him as saying Germany was unable longer to endure the Yugoslav attitude. The Reich was said to be reacting to alleged "attacks and murdering" of Germans in the Yugoslav Kingdom.

The order said the greatest patience had been exercised by Germany respecting Yugoslavia and Greece, but that now the moment for action had arrived.

It was said that Herr Hitler had frequently called attention to the dangers in the Southeast.

Now, it was said, Germany

Continued on Page Twenty-six

NAZI UNITS CROWD YUGOSLAV BORDERS

Some Are Reported in Albania, Many in Southern Hungary— German Plane Downed

By C. L. SULZBERGER
By Telephone to THE NEW YORK TIMES.

BELGRADE, Yugoslavia, April 5 —The German military encirclement of Yugoslavia was made complete last night.

The German military encirclement of Yugoslavia was made complete last night with the reported jamming of eight new divisions reportedly jammed the Hungarian roads, a powerful armored unit concentrated at Bela Crkva, on the Rumanian frontier one and a half hours' drive from Belgrade, and the first Nazi troops entered Albania.

British information sources reported from Bucharest and Budapest that the invasion of Southeastern Yugoslavia by the German Army of the Struma was ready to begin at any moment.

It is only worth noting that most of the more pessimistic predictions emanate from German-controlled countries, such as Hungary, Rumania and Bulgaria, or from the Croat capital of Zagreb, which is the center of the small but active German-inspired Fascist movement.

The facts of the situation are clear. Once more the normal peasant life of Hungary has been thrown into turmoil by the huge disruption caused by the passage of German Armies, and eight separate divisions are said to have been sighted. The motorized units on three points of the Hungarian southern frontier— Mohacs, Szeged and Nagy Kanizsa —were increased, as were the concentration in the Rumanian Banat.

An absolutely reliable source said German soldiers were known to have arrived in Albania, the debarkation point coming as somewhat of a surprise and indicating the probability that airplane transport was employed. Four Tyrolean mountain divisions have entered Italy in the last four days.

The government ordered the closing of all frontiers this morning. Outerbridge Horsey, secretary of the United States Legation in Budapest, who is coming here by train for emergency work, was stopped at the Hungarian frontier and the legation here is trying to facilitate his transport now by automobile.

All Danube traffic on the Yugoslav stretch of the river has been halted. A German Messerschmitt plane was shot down yesterday while cruising over Maribor and it crashed at Ptuj.

Circulation through the country save with special military permit has been halted. All cars are being requisitioned by the police and are being requisitioned unless they have special passes. A new War Press Bureau has been established. At the same time Yugoslav technical con-

Continued on Page Twenty-six

"All the News That's Fit to Print."

The New York Times.

LATE CITY EDITION
Fair and continued cool today and tomorrow.
Temperatures Yesterday—Max., 67; Min., 40

Copyright, 1941, by The New York Times Company.

VOL. XC..No. 30,425.

Entered as Second-Class matter.
Postoffice, New York, N. Y.

NEW YORK, TUESDAY, MAY 13, 1941.

THREE CENTS NEW YORK CITY and Vicinity

HESS, DESERTING HITLER, FLIES TO SCOTLAND; BERLIN REPORTED HIM MISSING AND INSANE; DARLAN MEETS HITLER; R. A. F. POUNDS PORTS

COAST SHIPYARDS SHUT BY PICKETS; RETURN REJECTED

Navy and Maritime Work Stops as Other Crafts Refuse to Pass Heavy Lines

POLICE STAY IN RESERVE

Union Leaders Declare Fight to Finish as Meeting Votes Against Lapsing Strike

By FOSTER HAILEY
Special to The New York Times.

SAN FRANCISCO, May 12—A request from the Office of Production Management that striking machinists in eleven shipbuilding yards in the San Francisco Bay area return to work pending an attempt to settle their wage and hour demands in conference was unanimously rejected today by a mass meeting of those of the strikers affiliated with the American Federation of Labor.

Picket lines around the eleven plants, established by the 1,200 A. F. of L. machinists and the 700 who belong to the Congress of Industrial Organizations, brought a complete halt to operations as 15,000 to 18,000 other workers who are not on strike refused to pass through the machinists' picket lines.

The strike was called Friday midnight by Local 68 of the A. F. of L. and Lodge 1304 of the C. I. O. The latter is affiliated with the Steel Workers Organizing Committee, headed by Philip Murray, president of the C. I. O. The walkout is in protest against hourly wage and overtime provisions of a master contract for the whole coast signed April 23 in Seattle by representatives of labor, the OPM and the shipbuilders.

Reason for Refusal to Return

The request to go back to work pending a conference came from Joseph Keenan, A. F. of L. representative of the OPM. It was presented to a mass meeting of about 1,000 members of Local 68 by its business agents, E. F. Dillon and Harry Hook, who later said:

"Our members took the position, and passed a resolution to the effect, that inasmuch as we've never been able to get an agreement out of Bethlehem in the past twenty-two years, we don't feel any good purpose would be served by sending the men back to work before an agreement is reached now.

"We feel it would only prolong the controversy and probably result in a repetition of what we are going through now."

Although Bethlehem Shipbuilding, a division of Bethlehem Steel, is only one of the eleven plants involved in the strike, it is by far the largest, employing about 900 of the 1,200 A. F. of L. machinists who are on strike, and it is considered the bellwether of the group.

Out to Compel Settlement

"We intend to tell Mr. Keenan, if he telephones us from Chicago, the attitude of the strikers," Mr. Dillon said. "When he made the request yesterday he said he would call back today. (He had not called up to late tonight.)

"We would be glad to have a representative of the OPM on the ground here to go into a thorough analysis of the situation.

"As things stand now, the strike will continue in effect until we are able to make some agreement with the C. I. O. machinists, since the request was not directed to them, but pickets handed out leaflets signed by J. P. Smith, business agent of Lodge 1304, asserting that "hard-won conditions must be preserved and employers, under a smoke screen of national defense, are not going to destroy them." The C. I. O. was not represented in the negotiations for the master contract.

In a joint statement, Mr. Dillon and Mr. Hook said that the machinists, because of the "friendly attitude and fine spirit of the other metal trades organizations," intend to see to it that all such metal trades men that respected our picket lines will be returned to their jobs without discrimination," and "on a basis satisfactory to them."

Appraised of the strikers' position, Frank M. Fox, chairman of the Bay Area Shipbuilders Negotiating Committee and authorized spokesman

Continued on Page Sixteen

'Peace' Pickets Routed At White House Gates

Special to The New York Times.

WASHINGTON, May 12—One soldier and one Marine tonight broke up a line of eight pickets marching in front of the White House who represented the American Peace Mobilization. This organization has been charged with being a Communist Front group.

At the hour all Washington theatres were letting out, police emergency cars and motorcyclists roared through downtown Washington to the White House. The two assaulters were arrested and one picketeer was removed to Emergency Hospital where he was reported slightly injured. The picketing continued.

Tonight's fracas followed one at 3 A. M. when a larger group of soldiers and Marines attacked the pickets, tore up their placards and warned them they would be back if the picketing continued. In an earlier assault the policemen did not interfere. Tonight the assailants were seized and one was charged with simple assault. The police then closed and manned the White House gates for the night.

ROOSEVELT TO TALK TO NATION MAY 27

'Fireside Chat' Two Weeks From Today Is Substituted for Address Tomorrow

By FRANK L. KLUCKHOHN
Special to The New York Times.

WASHINGTON, May 12—President Roosevelt will make a "fireside chat" to the nation May 27, but will not make his scheduled speech before the Pan American Union Wednesday night, it was announced at the White House today.

This change in plans was interpreted generally to mean that the President has in mind no important announcement on American foreign policy for two weeks and that, at least for this period, he does not contemplate any new type of aid for Britain.

The Executive seldom makes fireside chats except upon important matters, however, and his talk on the 27th is generally expected to present an outline of the current position of the United States as he sees it and the future steps that should be taken.

Mr. Roosevelt completed his seventh day in bed because of illness today, and his widely publicized speech was canceled to give him time to recover fully, according to official statements.

Stephen T. Early, White House Secretary, emphasized, however, that the President had never intended his talk before the Pan American Union to be of "world-shaking" importance.

Pressure on President

In informed circles it was understood that the Executive did not intend to be pushed into any important steps and that he considered the present time poor for any announcement of vital importance.

Speaking of the canceled Wednesday address, Mr. Early said:

"So, despite reports from abroad, there will be no world-shaking pronouncement from President Roosevelt Wednesday night, as this office has stated right along."

Three Cabinet officers, Secretaries Henry L. Stimson, Frank Knox and Claude Wickard, have urged use of the American Navy to protect shipment of war supplies to Great Britain, their speeches generally being interpreted as an appeal for escort of convoys by the American Navy. Other individuals or groups publicly have urged the Executive to go so far as to ask for a declaration of war. Pressure has come from all sides on these controversial questions and others.

The decision to cancel Wednesday night's speech was revealed through White House announcement of a resolution adopted by the Board of Governors of the Pan American Union.

Diplomats Ask Postponement

"The Ambassadors, Ministers and chargés d'affaires of the republics of Latin America," the resolution said, "realizing that President Roosevelt has recently been indisposed and in view of the fact that the reception to be tendered him would involve a strain upon him, take the liberty of suggesting that the reception be postponed until such time as President Roosevelt may

Continued on Page Eight

HAMBURG HIT HARD

Miles of Docks Fired in British Bombing a Second Night

BREMEN LIKE TARGET

U-Boat Yards and War Plants of Reich Bases Kept Under Attack

By DAVID ANDERSON
Special Cable to The New York Times.

LONDON, Tuesday, May 13—Nine miles of docks along the River Elbe at Hamburg were laced with heavy British bombs and thousands of incendiaries over Sunday night when the Royal Air Force followed up its attack of the previous night with another vigorous raid on German war ports.

The Hamburg docks were "threaded and crossed with fire, continuing the destruction and disorganization of vital parts of this great seaport," the British Air Ministry reported.

Bremen, the Reich's second port in the size of its war activities, was attacked also with what R. A. F. officials moderately termed a "heavyweight of high-explosive and incendiary bombs."

Shipbuilding yards and especially the plants of the two ports where Germany has built most of her U-boat fleet were the target.

Previous Havoc Extended

Explosives hammered down on industrial works in both cities, the Air Ministry stated, and vast fires were started to continue the havoc of previous attacks.

Last night "objectives" at the German industrial center of Mannheim, also a frequent target for the British, were attacked by R. A. F. bombers, a brief official report early today said.

Sunday night attacks were made by the R. A. F. on a number of other targets in the Reich, including Emden again, and the docks of Rotterdam were also bombed.

Four aircraft of the Bomber Command were missing from all these operations, British officials said. The Coastal Command carried out Sunday night attacks on docks at the Netherland port of Ijmuiden, and on the Nazi seaplane base on the island of Texel without loss.

The attacks seemed to mark a definite stepping-up of the R. A. F. offensive, as officials of the Bomber Command, in giving some detail of the operations, said the objective was to strike Hamburg again before that city could "recover from the impact of the attacks made Saturday night."

Weather Right for Bomb-Aimers

Fine weather and the brilliant moonlight enabled the British pilots to pick their spot with relative ease over "the vast expanse of docks which was the particular focus" of this raid, it was stated.

An R. A. F. flier's account of the Bremen attack said:

"It was not so cold as when we visited Bremen three nights before, but there was the same bright sky. All the way over there were patches of cloud which looked like stepping

Continued on Page Two

Russians See Advantage In R.A.F. Planes' Big Load

By The Canadian Press.

LONDON, May 12—Increased bomb loads carried by Royal Air Force bombers "partly offset" the German advantage of having air bases close to Britain, Red Star, organ of the Soviet Army, said in an article quoted today by the British Broadcasting Corporation.

The article commented on "the tremendous load of bombs that now can be carried by a single British machine."

In a review of war developments, the newspaper observed that "the hardest blows delivered by the German Air Force in recent weeks have been aimed at British ports and centers of shipbuilding" and also that "the experience of the last war proved that British and United States industry made up for sinkings by U-boats."

PAPEN SEES HITLER, RETURNS TO TURKEY

Envoy Is Expected to Reveal Nazi Plans for Near East—Soviet Move Studied

The following dispatch was received by direct voice broadcast through the Ankara wireless station last night. C. L. Sulzberger prefaced the broadcast in this way:

"The following direct broadcast from Ankara to The New York Times, New York City, contains news dispatches for The Times. These are exclusive property of the New York Times Company. Dispatches follow."

By C. L. SULZBERGER
Special Broadcast to The New York Times.

ANKARA, Turkey, May 12—Franz von Papen, the German Ambassador to Ankara, came back to his post today aboard a large camouflaged Junkers troop transport plane, following a series of last-minute conferences with Reichsfuehrer Hitler at the latter's Obersalzburg retreat.

The Ambassador, who was accompanied by his wife and daughter, was met at the Ankara Airport by the diplomatic representatives of the countries that have signed the tripartite accord. He appeared in excellent spirits and conferred for several minutes with the Italian Ambassador.

Herr von Papen has been expected back almost daily for the better part of the last fortnight and the fact that he continually delayed his return and then at the last minute had a long personal conversation with Herr Hitler is regarded as significant.

Events are shaping up rapidly in the Middle East, and the only hand that now remains to be disclosed fully is that of Germany. Russia has abandoned her disinterest in this area by according full diplomatic recognition to the bellicose Rashid Ali Beg Gailani government of Iraq.

Britain, already engaged in extensive military operations in Iraq, has

Continued on Page Five

ADMIRAL HAS TALK

Berlin Says Ribbentrop Was Present—Place Is Not Disclosed

VICHY PRESS TENSE

U. S. Attitude Is Cause of Worry—Leahy May Protest Attacks

By The Associated Press.

BERLIN, Tuesday, May 13—Reichsfuehrer Hitler has received the French Vice Premier, Admiral François Darlan, in the presence of German Foreign Minister Joachim von Ribbentrop, it was officially announced early today.

The communiqué announcing the meeting did not say where or when it took place.

The announcement said:

"The Fuehrer, in the presence of the Reichsminister of Foreign Affairs, received the vice president of the French Ministerial Council, Admiral Darlan."

Hitler-Stalin Talk Forecast

BERLIN, Tuesday, May 12 (P)—Separate meetings of Reichsfuehrer Hitler with Premier Joseph Stalin and Premier Benito Mussolini were considered in diplomatic circles here tonight as likely to result from the current political moves over Europe.

These circles said, probably would be complete economic if not military organization of the Axis-dominated Continent.

Observers listed the current shakeup of Spain's civil and military organization and Vice Premier Admiral François Darlan's negotiations with the Germans as indications of forthcoming conferences of Herr Hitler and Mr. Stalin and Signor Mussolini.

U. S. Gives Press Concern

By G. H. ARCHAMBAULT
Wireless to The New York Times.

VICHY, France, May 12—For the time being it is not possible to separate the two hemispheres in any discussion here of the world situation. That the situation is tense and is likely to remain so, at least until President Roosevelt has spoken, is admitted.

In every newspaper as well as in every conversation the United States and what it may or may not do is a recurrent topic.

There are some here who surmise that it may have been mentioned in Paris during the visit there of Vice Premier Admiral François Darlan, who is expected back in Vichy tomorrow to report to Marshal Henri Philippe Pétain, who himself returned this morning after a few days' rest in his Riviera estate.

A semi-official commentary declared today that the Marshal has expressed his satisfaction to the Admiral with the progress of his negotiations hitherto.

It is understood that another Admiral—William D. Leahy, the United States Ambassador—will see Marshal Pétain in the near future for one of their periodical conversations on food supplies and cognate subjects.

To Stick to Collaboration

While there is complete official silence regarding the negotiations with Germany, as also regarding the United States, the Inter-France News Service, which circulates editorials "for free reproduction by any newspaper," advanced the following arguments:

"Should war occur between the United States and Germany and should it be prolonged, the political reasons which led France to follow the road of collaboration would be reinforced by even more decisive practical reasons. For war between the United States and the Axis would immediately create a European solidarity that would be stronger than any sentimental factor.

"An American blockade, which would necessarily extend to all our coasts, will develop the notion of a common interest among the peoples of all Europe, since from Brest to Koenigsberg and from Narvik (Norway) to Cadiz (Spain) we should be compelled to do without everything. Europe will be in a common front from Portugal to Brazil, to dispense with cotton from the United States and oil from Mexico. The French

Continued on Page Five

Nazis Allege 'Hallucinations'; Silent on Glasgow Arrival

Arrest of Hess's Aides Ordered Since Hitler Forbade Him to Fly—Letter He Left Said to Show Disordered Mind

By Telephone to The New York Times.

BERLIN, May 12—Authoritative quarters in Berlin refused to comment late tonight on a British statement that Rudolf Hess, 47-year-old deputy leader of the National Socialist party and Reichsfuehrer Hitler's personal representative, had bailed out of a Messerschmitt plane near Glasgow, Scotland, and was in the hands of the British authorities. Earlier in the evening the Germans had officially reported Herr Hess to be missing.

The man who, on Sept. 1, 1939, was designated by Herr Hitler as his second choice, next to Reich Marshal Hermann Goering, in the line of succession for leadership of the German State, was last heard of in Augsburg, in Bavaria, on Saturday. He was reported to have taken an airplane there for an unknown destination in violation of Herr Hitler's orders prohibiting him from flying because of physical disability.

The announcement said:

"The news of the mysterious disappearance of Herr Hess has been released, forty-eight hours after he had been reported missing, in the following communiqué:

"Rudolf Hess has met with an accident.

"Party Comrade Hess, who, because of a disease that for a year has progressively worsened has been categorically forbidden by the Fuehrer to continue his flying activities, recently found means to come into possession of an airplane.

Continued on Page Four

The International Situation

TUESDAY, MAY 13, 1941.

A laconic announcement from 10 Downing Street gave to the astounded world last night the news that Rudolf Hess, deputy leader of the Nazi party in Germany and the third most powerful figure in the Reich, had landed by parachute in Scotland and is in safe custody in a Glasgow hospital suffering from a broken ankle. The official statement gave no direct explanation for the dramatic development, but it was presumed that the man who was named at the outset of the war by Adolf Hitler as his second in succession had deliberately fled Germany.

Herr Hess flew to Scotland in a Messerschmitt 110, a plane incapable of carrying sufficient fuel for his return to Germany. The plane crashed Saturday night on the Duke of Hamilton's estate. The flier established his identity in the hospital, and the Foreign Office dispatched an attaché to interview him there. [All the foregoing, Page 1, Column 8.]

Berlin issued a communiqué earlier in the day stating that Herr Hess, apparently suffering from "hallucinations" induced by a long-standing ailment, had taken off by plane from Augsburg Saturday evening against the express orders of Herr Hitler and was "missing" and presumably had "met with an accident." It was announced that Herr Hess's adjutants had been ordered arrested. [Page 1, Column 6.]

Hundreds of German bombers flew over South England and the Midlands Sunday night, attacking airdromes and other objectives, and causing destruction over widespread areas. Nine Nazi planes were shot down. A Berlin statement that forty-five British airfields were attacked was contradicted by the British, who said the military damage was "not considerable." Few raiders were reported over Britain last night. [Page 6, Column 1.]

Over Sunday night the R. A. F. was sending wave after wave of bombers against German ports, particularly Hamburg and Bremen. Nine miles of docks and shipyards on the River Elbe were laced with fires from British incendiaries, and attacks were made on Emden, Rotterdam and Ijmuiden. Last night British planes again bombed Mannheim. [Page 1, Column 3.]

The return to Ankara of German Ambassador von Papen

from an extended visit to Berlin gave rise to a belief that Germany would propose a far-reaching economic treaty to all but isolated Turkey. Ankara also looked for an early meeting between the Ambassador and the Iraqi Defense Minister, who has been visiting Ankara. [Page 1, Column 4.]

The situation in Iraq was described by the British as now "stabilized." R. A. F. planes harried remnants of Iraqi forces, and British mechanized forces completed the occupation of Rutbah, a vital point on the oil pipe line and site of an airplane base. [Page 2, Column 6.]

The British forces in Ethiopia tightened their pincer around Alagi, the last Italian stronghold on the Asmara-Dessye road. The Italian garrison at Gondar was said to be virtually isolated. In North Africa, the Admiralty announced, British warships bombarded Bengazi Saturday night, but Rome advised the British vessels had been routed after having suffered direct hits. [Page 3, Column 4.]

Identified by Official

Ivone A. Kirkpatrick, who used to be first secretary in the British Embassy in Berlin, was the official sent to Scotland, and the Ministry of Information announced early this morning that Herr Hess's identification had been definitely established.

Earlier the Germans had announced that Herr Hess, who was outranked only by Reichsfuehrer Hitler and Reich Marshal Hermann Goering in the Nazi hierarchy, had been suffering from hallucinations and had violated Herr Hitler's orders in taking the plane.

It was just before nightfall Saturday that Herr Hess was found by a Scottish farm worker; he was groaning in agony, with his parachute wrapped around him. He was taken first to a little two-roomed cottage and then was turned over to the military authorities. This morning he was in a military hospital somewhere near Glasgow.

That is the bare outline of the facts as they are known so far. What do they mean? The Germans have already announced that Herr Hess's 'adjutants' have been arrested. The British are inclined to believe that there may be another purge in Germany—a purge similar to the one following the arrest of Captain Ernst Roehm, who was also one of Herr Hitler's closest collaborators, on June 30, 1934.

But from this distance it is almost impossible to say what this development means as far as Germany is concerned. One can record only what the British believe it means. One Briton told the writer that "this is the first 'break' we have had since the war started." Alfred Duff Cooper, the Minister of Information, himself acted as messenger boy to take the British

Continued on Page Four

BRITISH ASTOUNDED

Hitler's Deputy Is in Hospital After Bailing Out of War Plane

HAS A BROKEN ANKLE

London Believes Hess's Flight May Portend a New Purge in Reich

By ROBERT P. POST
Special Cable to The New York Times.

LONDON, Tuesday, May 13—Rudolf Hess, deputy leader of the German Nazi party and the third-ranking personage in the German State, parachuted to earth in Scotland on Saturday night and is now a prisoner of war.

That may sound like something from a mystery thriller by Oppenheim. But in sober truth, 10 Downing Street issued last night the strangest and most dramatic document ever to come from the official home of a British Prime Minister.

THE BRITISH STATEMENT

This statement said:

Rudolf Hess, the Deputy Fuehrer of Germany and party leader of the National Socialist party, has landed in Scotland in the following circumstances:

On the night of Saturday, the tenth, a Messerschmitt 110 was reported by our patrols to have crossed the coast of Scotland and to be flying in the direction of Glasgow. Since a Messerschmitt 110 would not have fuel to return to Germany, this report was at first disbelieved.

Later on a Messerschmitt 110 crashed near Glasgow with its guns unloaded. Shortly afterward a German officer who had bailed out was found with his parachute in the neighborhood, suffering from a broken ankle.

He was taken to a hospital in Glasgow, where he at first gave his name as Horn, but later on he declared that he was Rudolf Hess.

He brought with him various photographs of himself at different ages, apparently in order to establish his identity.

These photographs were deemed to be photographs of Hess by several people who knew him personally. Accordingly, an officer of the Foreign Office closely acquainted with Hess before the war has been sent up by airplane to see him in the hospital.

Continued on Page Four

Bodies of Brewster and Wife Found In Plane Wreckage in Alleghenies

The bodies of Benjamin Brewster, New York investment broker, and his wife, the former Leonie de Bary Lyon, who disappeared Friday on a projected flight from Roosevelt Field to Warren, Ohio, were found last night in the charred wreckage of their plane on a rugged mountain top forty miles north of Harrisburg.

The discovery was made after several pilots reported they had seen the badly damaged wreck nestled in tree branches on Shade Mountain near Beavertown.

The report that the bodies had been found was telephoned to Private Charles Hicklin of the Pennsylvania Motor Police by Private John Zeigler, one of a party sent out from the barracks at Selinsgrove.

The bodies were taken in charge by Dr. Charles W. Strand, coroner of Snyder County, who will remove to Middleburg as soon as permission is received from members of the Brewster family.

Late last night positive identification was made by Whitney Stone,

vice president of the Stone & Webster Company, a brother-in-law of Mr. Brewster. In a telephone conversation with his sister, Mrs. Edward C. Brewster, Mr. Stone said the plane crashed against the side of a 1,500-foot mountain and then exploded. A reward of $1,000 had been offered by Mr. Stone to the person locating the plane.

The Brewsters' plane was a radio-equipped black and green Beechcraft with a Wright motor. Mr. Brewster was a prominent sportsman pilot and had more than 1,000 flying hours to his credit.

The tangled, charred wreckage was sighted at about 5 P. M. (daylight saving time) by two private pilots from Philadelphia, who were searching the mountain by air. They reported having circled the scene and sighted a twisted wing lying near by. The wings, red and apparently had escaped the flames, and its black and green striping could be seen clearly. These fliers,

Continued on Page Nineteen

113

The New York Times.

VOL. XC. No. 30,465.   Entered as Second-Class Matter, Postoffice, New York, N. Y.   NEW YORK, SUNDAY, JUNE 22, 1941.   Copyright, 1941, by The New York Times Company.

LATE CITY EDITION
Partly cloudy and continued
warm today and tomorrow.
Temperatures Yesterday—Max., 91; Min., 75

Section
1

Including Rotogravure Picture,
Magazine and Book Sections   TEN CENTS
New York City and Vicinity

HITLER BEGINS WAR ON RUSSIA, WITH ARMIES ON MARCH FROM ARCTIC TO THE BLACK SEA; DAMASCUS FALLS; U.S. OUSTS ROME CONSULS

MUST GO BY JULY 15

Ban on Italians Like Order to German Representatives

U. S. DENIES SPYING

Envoys Told to Protest Axis Charges—Nazis Get 'Moor' Text

By BERTRAM D. HULEN
Special to The New York Times.

WASHINGTON, June 21—The Italian Embassy was directed by the State Department in a note published today to close all its consular offices and other agencies in this country having connections with the Italian Government by July 15. This was the reply to the Italian demand for the closing of all American Consulates in Italy.

At the same time Sumner Welles, Under-Secretary of State, announced that he had sent to Dr. Hans Thomsen, the German Chargé d'Affaires, the text of President Roosevelt's message to Congress yesterday denouncing the sinking of the American freighter Robin Moor in the South Atlantic on May 21.

This message, which accused Germany of being an international outlaw, engaging in piracy and attempting to intimidate the United States by the sinking and to drive American commerce from the seas, contained notice that this country would not yield before such measures and stated that compensation would be sought for the sinking.

It was transmitted "for the information" of the German Government, but constituted in effect a note of protest. A further communication will be sent asking damages when a final determination has been reached of the extent of damages that should be sought.

Will Deny Improper Acts

In addition, the State Department instructed the American Embassies in Berlin and Rome to inform the respective governments that the United States proposes to end all allegations of improper acts by American consular officials in those countries and to complete arrangements for the withdrawal of the consular officials and their staffs by July 15, the limit set by the German and Italian Governments.

The Axis governments had charged that the American Consuls had spied for the British. No reply has been made by the State Department to the German protests against the order closing Nazi consulates in this country, but the protest will be rejected. The United States alleged subversive activities as the reason for the demand for them to be closed by July 10.

The note to the German and Italian Embassies were sent by messenger last night. However, no direct charge of improper activities was made against the Italian consuls in the note. Mr. Welles sent to Don Ascanio dei principi Colonna, the Italian Ambassador. He merely stated that the continued functioning of Italian consular establishments within United States territory "would serve no desirable purpose."

In addition, the closing of Italian agencies having connections with the Rome government was requested. The Italian Embassy, as in the earlier case of the German Embassy, was exempted, but the closing of the office of the Italian Commercial Counselor in New York was demanded, along with the consulates.

Welles Note to Colonna

The note from Mr. Welles to Prince Colonna follows:

June 20, 1941

His Excellency
Don Ascanio dei principi Colonna
Royal Italian Ambassador
Excellency:

I have the honor to inform Your Excellency that the President has directed me to request that the Italian Government promptly close all Italian consular establishments in United States territory and remove therefrom all Italian consular officers.

Continued on Page Two

FOR WANT AD RESULTS try The
New York Times. It's easy to order your ad.
Just telephone LAckawanna 4-1000.—Advt.

Hope Dims for Submarine; Diver Balked at 370 Feet

Knox Believes All 33 Are Dead on the O-9 and Expects Rites at Scene for Navy 'Heroes'—Pressure Halts Descent

By RUSSELL PORTER
Special to The New York Times.

PORTSMOUTH, N. H., June 21—As hope faded rapidly for the crew of the Submarine O-9, which failed to rise after submerging yesterday morning twenty-four miles east of this city, it became known tonight that the Navy might be unable to complete its salvage operations, and might be compelled to leave the bodies entombed where they lie—440 feet below the surface of the Atlantic.

This theory was based upon the assumption that the two officers and thirty-one men must already be given up as lost, but that assumption has become stronger with every new development since the submarine was reported missing.

Last night cork insulation from the interior of the hull was picked up, showing that at least part of the submarine had collapsed, and early today, after fourteen hours of dragging, grapnels located an object believed to be the sunken craft. Since then no signals from the O-9 have been received on the sensitive sound-detection devices on the salvage ships in response to their repeated messages.

The view that the O-9's fate was sealed was strengthened this afternoon when reporters and photographers, visiting the scene in a

Navy press boat, saw one of the Navy's most experienced divers fail in an attempt to reach the O-9 after descending 370 feet, or within seventy feet of where the Navy believes it has located the submarine with grapnel lines.

The diver, George Crocker, 30 years old, of Seattle, asked to be hauled up when he became convinced that he was not getting enough air pressure from his life lines of helium-oxygen mixture to overcome the increasing sea pressure as he went lower and lower.

A message from the Falcon said:
"Diver descended 370 feet. Had difficulty in breathing. Brought to surface. Will continue attempts by varying diving techniques."

On the salvage ship the dive was called "the most dangerous in submarine history." It was pointed out that no one had ever made a successful "working" dive at 440 feet and that any diver who went down so far, where he would have to grope his way in complete darkness under terrific sea pressure, 195.8 pounds to the square inch, could do so only at extreme risk to his life.

Colonel Frank Knox, Secretary of the Navy, returning tonight to

Continued on Page Thirty

ARMY ASKS GUARD BE KEPT IN SERVICE

Recommends Congress Act to Hold State Troops, Reserve Officers Indefinitely

By HALLETT ABEND
Special to The New York Times.

WASHINGTON, June 21—Members of the National Guard and Reserve Officers Corps will be kept in active service beyond the single year planned when they were called, if a recommendation made today by the War Department is approved by President Roosevelt and Congress.

Instead of a return to civilian life, starting Sept. 15, their terms of service in uniform may be extended indefinitely, or at least until the Army selectees have been sufficiently trained in numbers to permit the Guardsmen to be demobilized. The recommendation to the President does not specify any limit to the proposed extension of service.

At present there are 289,800 National Guardsmen, including their 21,800 officers, on active duty with the Federal Army. They were inducted into service in increments beginning Sept. 15 of last year. Some went into uniform as late as March of this year. Their terms of service, at time of induction, were limited to twelve months, which may not be extended except by act of Congress.

341,300 Would Be Affected

In addition to the National Guardsmen, who comprise eighteen divisions and one cavalry brigade now on active service, the government has called up 51,500 Reserve officers under the same terms, making collectively 341,300 officers and men who would be affected.

Today's War Department recommendation to the President that steps be taken to retain in the service these Guardsmen and Reserve officers was taken, according to the official announcement, because "the War Department has been flooded with queries from the field" as to whether or not the specified one-year limit of service would hold good or be changed.

"These queries are to be expected," continues the announcement, "because whatever the decision, there are many adjustments which the citizen-soldier must make in his affairs."

As yet no decision has been reached in the War Department whether or not to seek authority to retain selectees in the Army beyond the one-year training period specified in the Selective Service Act, but presumably such a step

Continued on Page Nineteen

NAVY MAY REPLACE SHIPYARD STRIKERS

Weighs Putting Own Machinists to Work to End Long Tie-Up in San Francisco

By the Associated Press.

SAN FRANCISCO, June 21—Striking A. F. L. machinists in a $300,000,000 defense program have come to a showdown with the United States Navy and their own international officers.

Reliable reports, not officially denied, indicated that the Navy might install its own machinists in the huge Bethlehem shipyards Monday if the local union did not heed the order of its international president to call off the strike by that time.

The same reports indicated that the Army also might be on hand

Continued on Page Twenty-eight

The International Situation

SUNDAY, JUNE 22, 1941

At 5:30 o'clock this morning, Berlin time, two statements were read over the German radio that constituted a declaration of war upon the Soviet Union by Germany. A proclamation of Adolf Hitler, read by Propaganda Minister Goebbels, said that Russia, with Britain and the United States, had sought to "throttle" Germany and that he had therefore decided to put the fate of the German people into the hands of the army. A statement by Foreign Minister von Ribbentrop contained the actual declaration of war. The Finns and the Rumanians were mentioned as allies. Berlin reported subsequently that troops were on the move in the Syrian campaign. [Page 1, Column 8; with map.]

Today's War Department recommendation to the President that steps be taken to retain in the service these Guardsmen and Reserve officers was handed particularly for airdromes, and engaged German air defenses. The British reported downing twenty-six Nazi planes in these attacks for a loss of five of their own. Late last night the British were continuing their attacks across the Channel. [Page 1, Column 4; Map, Page 18.]

The Libyan theatre was quiet, but British pressure in East Africa was indicated by a protest from Vichy against what was declared to be a virtual ultimatum from General Wavell to the Free French or suffer an intensified blockade. London confirmed the representations of General Wavell. [Page 14, Column 1.]

Washington announced the accelerated pace of its anti-Axis diplomatic offensive. The Italian Embassy was instructed to close the forty-nine Italian consulates and seven agencies in this country before July 15. President Roosevelt's message to Congress on the Robin Moor was handed to the German Embassy while the State Department instructed the United States embassies in Berlin and Rome to inform those governments that the United States objected categorically to any allegations of improper acts by United States consuls. [Page 1, Column 1.]

Italian consular circles were silent concerning the Washington order, but Italian anti-Fascist quarters expressed jubilation. [Page 3, Column 1.]

R. A. F. BLASTS FOE

Bags 26 Nazi Planes in Record Day Raids on Invasion Coast

GERMANY IS BOMBED

British on 11th Straight Night Offensive Into Western Reich

Special Cable to The New York Times.

LONDON, Sunday, June 22—Twenty-six Nazi fighter planes were destroyed in daylight yesterday by Royal Air Force fliers on their fifth straight day of raiding the Germans' invasion coast and air bases in Northern France.

Twice before dark, waves of R. A. F. warcraft—reportedly numbering at least 150 planes each—swept over the Channel in offensive operations.

Bombers attacked the Nazi's airdromes on each occasion while strong forces of fighters blasted the way for the big planes through formations of German defense fighters. While the major raids were going on, other strong R. A. F. units patrolled over the French coast and battled Messerschmitts.

Attack Goes On; Big Bombs Used

Last night and early this morning the R. A. F. was still attacking the invasion coast, using some of the latest type of high-powered bombs.

Explosions rolled across the Channel like peals of thunder, shaking the ground and rocking buildings for miles along the Kentish coast, observers there reported.

A night curtain of fog hung over the Strait of Dover and little could be seen of the raids. The latest British attacks were apparently being made in the Boulogne area, where some of the heaviest daylight bombing was carried out.

Meanwhile R. A. F. bomber forces again attacking Western Germany, officials here said briefly early today. The attacks marked the eleventh consecutive night in which the British have bombed industrial centers and war bases in the Reich.

Two Nazi bombers were shot down during the night in small scattered enemy raids on the east and southeast coasts of England. A few German bombs were reported dropped there; there were no accounts of casualties or damage.

The R. A. F. coastal patrol squadrons reported destroying at least two enemy planes and one Nazi

Continued on Page Eighteen

SYRIAN CITY TAKEN

French Withdraw After a Hard Fight—British Closer to Beirut

TADMUR PUSH IS ON

Allied Planes Harassing Vichy Troops, Whose Defense Falters

By C. L. SULZBERGER
By Telephone to The New York Times.

ANKARA, Turkey, June 21—French troops evacuated the city of Damascus today after a persistent bombardment by British artillery and withdrew to new positions outside the Syrian capital, according to official advices from Beirut. Early in the afternoon it was learned that the Allied vanguard was already beginning to enter the city proper. This evening the British reported complete occupation.

The Damascus airport at Mezze has been taken by Indian detachments of the Allied forces and one of the key points east of Damascus has been surrounded by Druz tribesmen fighting on the side of the British.

The Beirut radio announced that a British motorized column pushing westward from Iraq was now heading toward Tadmur. The British column, it was said, had been constantly by the French Air Force, which has just been reorganized and reinforced by French squadrons coming from North Africa. Some German planes also were said to have arrived in Syria.

Advance in High Gear

It is clear that the Allied advance is beginning to move into high gear. Unconfirmed reports that the British forces have reached Beirut indicate that it may also fall soon. Beirut's fate depends largely on whether the British will call in their superior naval forces to shell the city proper. So far this has been avoided in order to keep damage and casualties at a minimum.

[A dispatch from Cairo said that Australian forces had been progressing toward Beirut for two days and had passed Ras Damour.]

The Allies, convinced of the seriousness of the French resistance, evidently have begun to fight this undeclared war in earnest and intend to get it over with at fast at any cost. The main center of French resistance in the east has been Damascus, and the capture of the city is of great importance.

The Allied counter-move to the French attack in the south, which developed earlier in the week, is now proceeding with dispatch in the Merdjayoun district. The fortress of Merdjayoun is in Allied hands and it is obvious that the region is being rapidly cleared, since the coastal advance is dependent to a large degree on a corrollary advance in the center.

Considerable concentrations of French artillery had been brought up around Damascus. The French dug in and placed batteries in many of the villas and gardens in the outer sections of the city. These batteries were slowly picked off by British gunners with Royal Air Force support, but the principal British effort was artillery shelling. The British sought to avoid excess damage by aerial bombardment, which is less accurate than artillery fire.

Tadmur Believed in Peril

The French admission that a British column is pressing toward Tadmur would seem to indicate that perhaps the town is endangered. Several days ago reliable sources here reported the existence of a British column, but this was disbelieved by Beirut.

While there have been new reports that the trouble for the British in Iraq is far from over, the fact that they are able to spare considerable forces from there would indicate that everything is under control. It is known that British forces also are working westward along the North Syrian frontier toward Aleppo, but the exact strength of these units is not known here.

British military circles admit that the Syrian adventure can no

Continued on Page Twelve

WHERE GERMAN ARMIES MARCH ON RUSSIA

Shown on the map is the western frontier of the Soviet Union, a battle line of more than 2,000 miles. Berlin indicated an attack from Norway to Rumania.

The Hitler Proclamation

The text of Adolf Hitler's proclamation, as recorded here by Columbia Broadcasting System, follows:

It was a difficult step for me to send my Minister to Moscow in order to attend to work against the policy of encirclement of Britain.

I hoped that at last it would be possible to put away tension.

Germany never intended to occupy Lithuania. The defeat of Poland induced me to again address a peace offer to the Allies. This was declined because Britain was still hoping to bring about European coalition.

That is why Cripps [Sir Stafford Cripps, British Ambassador] was sent to Moscow. He was commissioned under all circumstances to come to an agreement with Moscow. Russia always put out the lying statement that she was protecting these countries [evidently Lithuania, Estonia and Latvia, the Baltic States].

The penetration of Russia into Rumania and the Greek liaison with England threatened to place new, large areas into the war. Rumania, however, believed she was able to accede to Russia only if she received guarantees from Germany and Italy for the remainder of the country. With a heavy heart, I did this, for if Germany gives guarantees, she will fulfill them. We are neither Englishmen nor Jews.

I asked Molotoff [Soviet Foreign Commissar V. M. Molotoff] to come to Berlin, and he asked for a clarification of the situation. He asked, "Is the guarantee for Rumania directed also against Russia?"

I replied, "Against every one."

And Russia never informed us that she had even more far-reaching intentions against Rumania.

Molotoff asked further, "Is Germany prepared not to assist Finland, who was again threatening Russia?"

My reply was that Germany has no political interests in Finland, but that another attack on Finland could not be tolerated, especially as we do not believe that Finland is threatening Russia.

Molotoff's third question was, "Is Germany agreeable that Russia give guarantees to Bulgaria?"

My reply was that Bulgaria is a sovereign State and I did not know that Bulgaria needed guarantees. Molotoff said Russia needed a passage through the Dardanelles and demanded bases in the Bosporus.

A few days later [Russia] concluded the well known friendship agreement which was to incite the Serbs against Germany. Moscow demanded the mobilization of the Serbian Army.

When I still was silent, the men in the Kremlin went one step further. Russia offered to deliver war material against Germany. This was at the same time that I advised Matsuoka [Japanese Foreign Minister Yosuke Matsuoka] to bring about a lessening of the tension with Russia.

Serbian officers flew to Russia, where they were received as allies. Victory of the Axis in the Balkans at first foiled the plan to involve Germany in a long war and then, together with England and with the hope of American supplies, to throttle Germany.

Now the moment has come when I can no longer look at this development. Waiting would be a crime against Germany.

For weeks the Russians have been committing frontier violations. Russian planes have been crossing the frontier again and again to prove that they are the masters. On the night of June 17 and again on June 18 there was large patrol activity.

The march of the German Armies has no precedent. Together with the Finns we stand from Narvik to the Carpathians. At the Danube and on the shores of the Black Sea under Antonescu [Rumanian Dictator Ion Antonescu], German and Rumanian soldiers are united.

The task is to safeguard Europe and thus save all.

I have therefore today decided to give the fate of the German people and the Reich and of Europe again into the hands of our soldiers.

BAD FAITH CHARGED

Goebbels Reads Attack on Soviet—Ribbentrop Announces War

BALTIC MADE ISSUE

Finns and Rumanians Are Called Allies in Plan of Assault

Statement by von Ribbentrop is printed on Page 6.

By C. BROOKS PETERS
By Telephone to The New York Times.

BERLIN, Sunday, June 22—As dawn broke over Europe today the legions of National Socialist Germany began their long-rumored invasion of Communist Soviet Russia. The non-aggression and amity pact between the two countries, signed in August, 1939, forgotten, the German attack began along a tremendous front, extending from the Arctic regions to the Black Sea. Marching with the forces of Germany are also the troops of Finland and Rumania.

Adolf Hitler, in a proclamation to the German people read over a national hook-up by Propaganda Minister Dr. Joseph Goebbels at 5:30 this morning, termed the military action begun this morning the largest in the history of the world. It was necessary, he added, because in spite of his unceasing efforts to preserve peace in this area it had definitely been proved that Russia was in a coalition with England to ruin Germany by prolonging the war.

Herr Hitler, in his proclamation as reported here, made one vitally interesting statement, namely, that the supreme German military command did not feel itself able to force a decisive victory in the West—apparently on the British Isles—when large Russian troop concentrations were on the Reich's borders in the East.

The Russian troop concentrations since began in August, 1940, Herr Hitler asserted. "Thus, there occurred the effect intended by the Soviet-British cooperation," he added, "namely, the binding of such powerful German forces in the East that a radical conclusion of the war in the West, particularly as regards aircraft, could no longer be vouched for by the German High Command.

[The German radio announced early today that documentary proof would shortly be given of a secret British-Russian alliance, made behind Germany's back.]

Designed "to Save Reich"

The German action, Herr Hitler explained to his fellow-National Socialists, is designed to save the Reich and with it all Europe from the machinations of the Jewish Anglo-Saxon warmongers.

The German Foreign Minister, Joachim von Ribbentrop, with Dr. Goebbels on the air with a declaration of the Reich Government read before the foreign correspondents in the Foreign Office. Herr von Ribbentrop said he received V. G. Dekanosoff, the Russian Ambassador, this morning and informed him that in spite of the Russian-German non-aggression pact of Aug. 23, 1939, and an amity pact of Sept. 28, 1939, Russia had betrayed the trust that the Reich had placed in her.

"Contrary to all engagements which they had undertaken and in absolute contradiction to their solemn declarations, the Soviet Union had turned against Germany," the Reich note asserted. "They have first not only continued, but even since the outbreak of war intensified their subversive activities against Germany in Europe. They have second, in a continually increasing measure, developed their foreign policy in a tendency hostile to Germany, and they have third massed their entire forces on the German frontier ready for action."

The Soviet Government, it was charged, had violated its treaties

Continued on Page Seven

"All the News That's Fit to Print."

The New York Times.

LATE CITY EDITION
Increasing cloudiness with rising temperature today. Tomorrow cloudy, somewhat colder.
Temperatures Yesterday—Max ,34; Min.,25

VOL. XCI No. 30,634.

Entered as Second-Class Matter, Postoffice, New York, N. Y.

NEW YORK, MONDAY, DECEMBER 8, 1941.

THREE CENTS NEW YORK CITY and Vicinity

JAPAN WARS ON U. S. AND BRITAIN; MAKES SUDDEN ATTACK ON HAWAII; HEAVY FIGHTING AT SEA REPORTED

CONGRESS DECIDED

Roosevelt Will Address It Today and Find It Ready to Vote War

CONFERENCE IS HELD

Legislative Leaders and Cabinet in Sober White House Talk

By C. P. TRUSSELL
Special to THE NEW YORK TIMES.

WASHINGTON, Dec. 7—President Roosevelt will address a joint session of Congress tomorrow and will find the membership in a mood to vote any steps he asks in connection with the developments in the Pacific.

The President will appear personally at 12:30 P. M. Whether he would call for a flat declaration of war again Japan was left unannounced tonight. But leaders of Congress, shocked and angered by the Japanese attacks, were talking of a declaration of war on not only Japan but on the entire Axis.

The plans for action tomorrow were made tonight in a White House conference at which the President, surrounded by his Cabinet and by Congressional leaders of both parties, went through reports, some official, some unconfirmed, of the continued assaults of the Japanese upon American Pacific outposts.

Meet Far Into Night

The conference lasted until after 11 o'clock and at its close an official statement was issued. This said that the President had reviewed for his conferees the latest advices from the Pacific and declared:

"It should be emphasized that the message to Congress has not yet been written and its tenor will, of course, depend on further information received between 11 o'clock tonight and noon tomorrow. Further news is coming in all the time."

Congressional leaders asserted as they left the White House that they did not know what the President would say tomorrow.

"Will the President ask for a declaration of war?" Speaker Rayburn was asked.

"He didn't say," answered the Speaker.

Asked whether Congress would support a declaration of war, Mr. Rayburn observed:

"I think that is one thing on which there would be unity."

Politics Declared Dropped

"There is no politics here," said Representative Joseph W. Martin Jr., Minority House Leader. "There is only one party when it comes to the integrity and honor of the country."

"The Republicans," said Senator Charles L. McNary of Oregon, the Senate minority leader, "will all go along, in my opinion, with whatever is done."

Unless international developments and plans changed overnight, it was indicated, the Presidential recommendations would be directed for the present, at least, at Japan only. This was asserted authoritatively in the face of widespread expectation that an

Continued on Page Six

NEWS BULLETINS

are broadcast by The New York Times every hour on the hour over Station WMCA— 570 on the dial.

WEEKDAYS
8 a. m. through 11 p. m.
SUNDAYS
9 a.m., 1 p.m., 5 p.m., 11 p.m.

TOKYO ACTS FIRST

Declaration Follows Air and Sea Attacks on U. S. and Britain

TOGO CALLS ENVOYS

After Fighting Is On, Grew Gets Japan's Reply to Hull Note of Nov. 26

By The Associated Press.

TOKYO, Monday, Dec. 8—Japan went to war against the United States and Britain today with air and sea attacks against Hawaii, followed by a formal declaration of hostilities.

Japanese Imperial headquarters announced at 6 A. M. [4 P. M. Sunday, Eastern standard time] that a state of war existed among these nations in the Western Pacific, as of dawn.

Soon afterward, Domei, the Japanese official news agency, announced that "naval operations are progressing off Hawaii, with at least one Japanese aircraft carrier in action against Pearl Harbor," the American naval base in the islands.

Japanese bombers were declared to have raided Honolulu at 7:35 A. M., Hawaii time [1:05 Sunday, Eastern standard time].

Premier-War Minister General Hideki Tojo held a twenty-minute Cabinet session at his official residence at 7 A. M.

Soon afterward it was announced that both the United States Ambassador, Joseph C. Grew, and the British Ambassador, Sir Robert Leslie Craigie, had been summoned by Foreign Minister Shigenori Togo.

The Foreign Minister, Domei said, handed to Mr. Grew the Japanese Government's formal reply to the note sent to Japan by United States Secretary of State Cordell Hull on Nov. 26.

[In the course of the diplomatic negotiations leading up to yesterday's events, the Domei agency had stated that Japan could not accept the premises of Mr. Hull's note.]

Sir Robert was summoned by

Continued on Page Five

The International Situation

MONDAY, DEC. 8, 1941

Yesterday morning Japan attacked the United States at several points in the Pacific. President Roosevelt ordered United States forces into action and a declaration of war is expected this morning. [Page 1, Columns 7 and 8.] Tokyo made its declaration as of this morning against both the United States and Britain. [Page 1, Column 2.] The first Japanese assault was directed at Pearl Harbor Naval base in Hawaii. Many casualties and severe damage resulted. [Page 1, Columns 4 and 5; Map, Page 13.] United States Army aircraft took off from the Philippines this morning and some points in the Archipelago were bombed. [Page 8, Column 2.] Singapore and Hong Kong were bombed and a Japanese landing in Northern Malaya and a move on Thailand were reported. [Page 1, Column 3.] In Shanghai, Japanese marines occupied the waterfront; a British gunboat was sunk, a United States gunboat seized. [Page 9, Column 2.]

Factional lines dissolved as an angered Congress prepared to meet this morning. [Page 1, Column 1.] Secretary of State Hull accused Japan of having made a "treacherous and utterly unprovoked attack" after having been "infamously false and fraudulent." [Page 1, Column 6.] He released the text of diplomatic exchanges with Japan [Page 10],

while the President gave out the text of his fruitless appeal to the Japanese Emperor. [Page 12.] The White House was the hub of Washington activity and news bulletins were released there. [Page 12, Column 3.]

The Federal Bureau of Investigation was ordered to begin a round-up of some Japanese in this country. [Page 6, Column 3.] As New York City went on a war footing and public precautions were taken, the FBI began the detention of Japanese nationals. [Page 1, Column 4.]

Prime Minister Churchill notified Tokyo that a state of war existed. [Page 4, Column 1.] Declarations were made last night or early today by Australia, Canada [Page 14 Column 1], the Netherlands Indies [Page 7, Column 2] and Costa Rica. [Page 15, Column 1.]

Libya was the scene of a renewed tank battle and the Tobruk corridor was reported again clear of Axis forces. [Page 20, Column 2, with map.] On the Moscow front the German line was broken at two places, said Soviet sources. [Page 37, Column 2.]

FOR WANT AD RESULTS use The New York Times. It's easy to order your ad. Just telephone LAckawanna 4-1000.—Advt.

Continued on Page Two

Continued on Page Three

PACIFIC OCEAN: THEATRE OF WAR INVOLVING UNITED STATES AND ITS ALLIES

Shortly after the outbreak of hostilities an American ship sent a distress call from (1) and a United States Army transport carrying lumber was torpedoed at (2). The most important action was at Hawaii (3), where Japanese planes bombed the great Pearl Harbor base. Also attacked was Guam (4). From Manila (6) United States bombers roared northward, while some parts of

the Philippines were raided, as was Hong Kong, to the northwest. At Shanghai (5) a British gunboat was sunk and an American gunboat seized. To the south, in the Malaya area (7), the British bombed Japanese ships, Tokyo forces attempted landings on British territory and Singapore underwent an air raid. Distances between key Pacific points are shown on the map in statute miles.

JAPANESE FORCE LANDS IN MALAYA

First Attempt Is Repulsed— Singapore Is Bombed and Thailand Invaded

By The Associated Press.

SINGAPORE, Monday, Dec. 8—The Japanese landed in Northern Malaya, 300 miles north of Singapore, today and bombed this great British naval stronghold, causing small loss of life among civilians and property damage.

About 300 Japanese troops landed on the east coast of Malaya and began filtering through jungle-fringed swamps and rice fields toward Kota Bahru airdrome, which is ten miles from the northern terminus of a railroad leading to Singapore.

An official report from the

Continued on Page Two

Tokyo Bombers Strike Hard At Our Main Bases on Oahu

By The United Press.

HONOLULU, Dec. 7—War broke with lightning suddenness in the Pacific today when waves of Japanese bombers attacked Hawaii this morning and the United States Fleet struck back with a thunder of big naval rifles. Japanese bombers, including four-engined dive bombers and torpedo-carrying planes, blasted at Pearl Harbor, the great United States naval base, the city of Honolulu and several outlying American military bases on the Island of Oahu. There were casualties of unstated number.

[The United States battleship Oklahoma was set afire by the Japanese attackers, according to a National Broadcasting Company observer, who also reported in a broadcast yesterday that two other ships in Pearl Harbor were attacked.

[The Japanese news agency, Domei, reported that the battleship Oklahoma had been sunk at Pearl Harbor, according to a United Press dispatch from Shanghai.

[Governor Joseph B. Poindexter of Hawaii talked with President Roosevelt late yesterday afternoon, saying that a second wave of Japanese bombers was just coming over, and the Gov-

Continued on Page Thirteen

ENTIRE CITY PUT ON WAR FOOTING

Japanese Rounded Up by FBI, Sent to Ellis Island—Vital Services Are Guarded

The metropolitan district reacted swiftly yesterday to the Japanese attack in the Pacific. All large communities in the area, including New York City, Newark, Jersey City, Bayonne and Paterson, went on immediate war footing.

One of the first steps taken here last night was a round-up of Japanese nationals by special agents of the Federal Bureau of Investigation, reinforced by squads of city detectives acting under FBI supervision. More than 100 FBI men, fully armed, were sent to the detail.

The prisoners were sent to Ellis Island, where they will be held pending action at Washington. It was indicated hundreds would be detained.

Earlier Mayor La Guardia had convened his Emergency Board and directed that Japanese nationals be confined to their homes pending decision as to their status and had their clubs and other meeting places closed and put under police guard.

A police sergeant and five policemen went to the Japanese Consulate at 630 Fifth Avenue in Rockefeller Center where the Consul General, Morito Morishima, and his staff were preparing to leave, and posted a guard there. The Consul General and his staff were escorted to their homes when they left. They were not to move about the city without police attendance.

Rear Admiral Adolphus Andrews, commander of the North Atlantic Squadron, told reporters at a conference in the Federal

Continued on Page Three

Lewis Wins Captive Mine Fight; Arbitrators Grant Union Shop

The three-man arbitration board appointed by President Roosevelt to arbitrate the union shop dispute in the captive coal mines last night reversed the decision of the National Defense Mediation Board and ruled that all workers in the captive mines should be required to join John L. Lewis's United Mine Workers as a condition of employment.

The decision was made by a two-to-one vote, with Benjamin F. Fairless, president of the United States Steel Corporation, dissenting. Dr. John R. Steelman, who took a leave of absence from his post as director of the United States Conciliation Service to serve as chairman of the arbitration panel, and Mr. Lewis voted in favor of extension to the captive mines of the union shop provision of the standard Appalachian agreement.

Despite his dissent, Mr. Fairless promised that the coal mining subsidiaries of United States Steel would put the ruling into effect. All eight steel companies operating captive mines had given formal as-

surances before the decision was reached that they would accept it as binding.

The arbitration award ended a dispute in which Mr. Lewis had repeatedly defied the President by calling strikes that menaced the production of steel and that had had its repercussions in the enactment by the House of the Smith anti-strike bill.

In explaining his vote for the union shop, Dr. Steelman pointed out that 95 per cent of the 53,000 captive miners had voluntarily assumed membership in Mr. Lewis's C. I. O. union and that 99.5 per cent of all the miners in the nation were now members of the union.

Since the bulk of the industry, including many owners of captive mines, was already operating under the union shop, it could not be argued that the United Mine Workers was endeavoring to take

Continued on Page Forty-three

HULL DENOUNCES TOKYO 'INFAMY'

Brands Japan 'Fraudulent' in Preparing Attack While Carrying On Parleys

Texts of Secretary Hull's note and Japan's reply, Page 10.

By BERTRAM D. HULEN
Special to THE NEW YORK TIMES.

WASHINGTON, Dec. 7—Japan was accused by Secretary of State Cordell Hull today of making a "treacherous and utterly unprovoked attack" upon the United States and of having been "infamously false and fraudulent" by preparing for the attack while conducting diplomatic negotiations with the professed desire of maintaining peace.

But even before he knew of the attack, Mr. Hull had vehemently brought the diplomatic negotiations to a virtual end with an outburst against Admiral Kichisaburo Nomura, the Japanese Ambassador, and Saburo Kurusu, special envoy, because of the insulting character of the reply they delivered.

Continued on Page Eleven

GUAM BOMBED; ARMY SHIP IS SUNK

U. S. Fliers Head North From Manila— Battleship Oklahoma Set Afire by Torpedo Planes at Honolulu

104 SOLDIERS KILLED AT FIELD IN HAWAII

President Fears 'Very Heavy Losses' on Oahu— Churchill Notifies Japan That a State of War Exists

By FRANK L. KLUCKHOHN
Special to THE NEW YORK TIMES.

WASHINGTON, Monday, Dec. 8—Sudden and unexpected attacks on Pearl Harbor, Honolulu, and other United States possessions in the Pacific early yesterday by the Japanese air force and navy plunged the United States and Japan into active war.

The initial attack in Hawaii, apparently launched by torpedo-carrying bombers and submarines, caused widespread damage and death. It was quickly followed by others. There were unconfirmed reports that German raiders participated in the attacks.

Guam also was assaulted from the air, as were Davao, on the island of Mindanao, and Camp John Hay, in Northern Luzon, both in the Philippines. Lieut. Gen. Douglas MacArthur, commanding the United States Army of the Far East, reported there was little damage, however.

[Japanese parachute troops had been landed in the Philippines and native Japanese had seized some communities, Royal Arch Gunnison said in a broadcast from Manila today to WOR-Mutual. He reported without detail that "in the naval war the ABCD fleets under American command appeared to be successful" against Japanese invasions.]

Japanese submarines, ranging out over the Pacific, sank an American transport carrying lumber 1,300 miles from San Francisco, and distress signals were heard from a freighter 700 miles from that city.

The War Department reported that 104 soldiers died and 300 were wounded as a result of the attack on Hickam Field, Hawaii. The National Broadcasting Company reported from Honolulu that the battleship Oklahoma was afire. [Domei, Japanese news agency, reported the Oklahoma sunk.]

Nation Placed on Full War Basis

The news of these surprise attacks fell like a bombshell on Washington. President Roosevelt immediately ordered the country and the Army and Navy onto a full war footing. He arranged at a White House conference last night to address a joint session of Congress at noon today, presumably to ask for declaration of a formal state of war.

This was disclosed after a long special Cabinet meeting, which was joined later by Congressional leaders. These leaders predicted "action" within a day.

After leaving the White House conference Attorney General Francis Biddle said that "a resolution" would be introduced in Congress tomorrow. He would not amplify or affirm that it would be for a declaration of war.

Congress probably will "act" within the day, and he will call the Senate Foreign Relations Committee for this purpose, Chairman Tom Connally announced.

[A United Press dispatch from London this morning said that Prime Minister Churchill had notified Japan that a state of war existed.]

As the reports of heavy fighting flashed into the White House, London reported semi-officially that the British Empire would carry out Prime Minister Winston Churchill's pledge to give the United States full support in case of hostilities with Japan. The President and Mr. Churchill talked by transatlantic telephone.

This was followed by a statement in London from the Netherland Government in Exile that it considered a state of war to exist between the Netherlands and Japan. Canada, Australia and Costa Rica took similar action.

Landing Made in Malaya

A Singapore communiqué disclosed that Japanese troops had landed in Northern Malaya and that Singapore had been bombed.

The President told those at last night's White House meeting that "doubtless very heavy losses" were sustained by the Navy and also by the Army on the island of Oahu [Honolulu]. It was impossible to obtain confirmation or denial of reports that the battleships Oklahoma and West Virginia had been damaged or sunk at Pearl Harbor, together with six or seven destroyers, and that 350 United States airplanes had been caught on the ground.

The White House took over control of the bulletins, and the Navy Department, therefore, said it could not discuss the matter or answer any questions how the Japanese were able to penetrate the Hawaiian defenses or appear without previous knowledge of their presence in those waters.

Administration circles forecast that the United States soon might be involved in a world-wide war, with Germany supporting Japan, an Axis partner. The German official radio tonight attacked the United States and supported Japan.

Axis diplomats here expressed complete surprise that the Japanese had attacked. But the impression gained from their attitude was that they believed it represented a victory for the Nazi attempt to divert lease-lend aid from Britain, which was the

Continued on Page Four

The New York Times.

LATE CITY EDITION
Cloudy followed by clearing and colder today. Tomorrow fair and moderately cold.
Temperatures Yesterday—Max., 44; Min., 25

VOL. XCI. No. 30,635.

Entered as Second-Class Matter, Postoffice, New York, N. Y.

NEW YORK, TUESDAY, DECEMBER 9, 1941.

THREE CENTS NEW YORK CITY and Vicinity

Copyright, 1941, by The New York Times Company.

U. S. DECLARES WAR, PACIFIC BATTLE WIDENS; MANILA AREA BOMBED; 1,500 DEAD IN HAWAII; HOSTILE PLANES SIGHTED AT SAN FRANCISCO

TURN BACK TO SEA

Two Formations Neared City on Radio Beams, Then Went Astray

ALARM IS WIDESPREAD

Whole Coast Has a Nervous Night—Many Cities Blacked Out

By LAWRENCE E. DAVIES
Special to THE NEW YORK TIMES.

SAN FRANCISCO, Dec. 8—Two formations of "many planes," described as undoubtedly enemy aircraft, flew over the San Francisco Bay area tonight, it was announced officially by Brig. Gen. William O. Ryan, commander of the Fourth Interceptor Command. After a progressive blackout had blotted out naval and military establishments and whole cities along the Pacific Coast.

Conflicting reports spread, contributing to the "war of nerves," as the sirens wailed and broadcasting were silenced.

After another spokesman, through an error, had declared the blackout to be an air raid test, General Ryan said at the Presidio that it was no test but "the real thing."

The ships were detected first about 100 miles at sea, he said. In two formations they headed for the Monterey Peninsula, about eighty miles south of this city, and for San Francisco Bay itself.

Radio detectors plotted their course, bringing one formation in just north of the Golden Gate and the other to a point near Fort Barry, at the south end of the Golden Gate Bridge.

Planes Turn Back to Sea

After flying northward for some distance the planes turned south to a point thirty-five or forty miles down the peninsula section below San Francisco. Apparently trying to orient themselves, they flew about a while longer and then headed southwest to sea, General Ryan said.

The commanding officer, whose station is at Riverside and who said he just "happened" to be at the Presidio tonight, declared that the planes believed from radio beams to these shores. When radio stations on the West Coast were silenced as part of the blackout the enemy craft apparently were not sure of their position.

No American planes were sent to the attack, he said, because "you don't send planes up unless you know what the enemy is doing and where he is going and you don't send planes up in the dark unless you know what you are doing."

Although there was no official explanation for the absence of anti-aircraft fire, it was indicated that the planes were hardly close enough for effective use of the guns.

Plane Carriers Rumored

Although General Ryan had no information, he said, as to the presence of enemy aircraft carriers hovering off the Pacific Coast, rumors of their presence back broadcast during the day and this, it was acknowledged, would be the logical explanation for the appearance of the planes.

Lieut. Gen. John L. Dewitt,

Continued on Page Twenty-eight

NEWS BULLETINS

Please do not telephone The New York Times for war news. Every hour on the hour news bulletins are broadcast over Station WMCA—570 on the dial.

WEEKDAYS
8 a. m. through 11 p. m.
SUNDAYS
9 a.m., 1 p.m., 5 p.m., 11 p.m.

Philippines Pounded All Day As Raiders Strike at Troops

Air Base Near Capital Among Targets Hit by Japanese—Landing on Lubang With Aid of Fifth Columnists Reported

By H. FORD WILKINS
Wireless to THE NEW YORK TIMES.

MANILA, Tuesday, Dec. 9—After a day of widespread aerial attacks throughout the Philippines, Japanese bombers swept in over Manila Bay early this morning and attacked Nichols Field, the United States Army air base on the outskirts of this capital, and for Mindoro.

This morning's attack, which began shortly after 3 o'clock, was the first in the Manila area. The damage was believed to have been slight, but some casualties were reported. [A National Broadcasting Company correspondent reported that an official statement issued in Manila after the raid said: "In the raid on Nichols Field, which was conducted by approximately ten Japanese bombers, one hangar was damaged and one officers' quarters was burned. The casualty list consists of one soldier killed and twelve slightly wounded—all Americans."]

The reported landing on Lubang, sixty miles southwest of Manila, was not officially confirmed, but the reports received credence here. [Other unconfirmed reports, relayed by the Columbia Broadcasting System, told of landings in the Davao region, on the southern island of Mindanao.]

The Manila area's first experience with bombs was a climax to a day and night of tension and activity. The explosions could be

Continued on Page Nine

PLANES GUARD CITY FROM AIR ATTACKS

Army Interceptors Join the Navy Patrols—Anti-Aircraft Apparatus Set Up Here

While long lines of men of fighting age waited impatiently outside of every Army, Navy and Marine Corps recruiting office in the city yesterday, representatives of the city, State and Federal Governments went ahead with the grim business of making New York City ready for war.

Beginning at dawn yesterday Army fighting planes took off at regular intervals from Mitchel Field to maintain, in conjunction with a Navy patrol, a constant fighting force in the air, so there could be no repetition here of the surprise in Hawaii. At the same time the First Interceptor Command called to active duty 40,000 volunteer civilian aircraft spotters at 1,300 posts scattered through thirteen eastern coastal States and the District of Columbia.

Anti-Aircraft Guns Set Up

The Sixty-second Coast Artillery of Fort Totten, Bayside, Queens, set up anti-aircraft apparatus at vantage points around the city. One base was in Prospect Park, Brooklyn.

Air raid wardens went on duty at midnight in every part of the city, as a result of a series of conferences among Police and Fire Department officers and representatives of the Board of Education and the Department of Housing, at which it was agreed that air raid warnings would be broadcast by the blowing of the sirens of all police radio cars and emergency trucks and all Fire Department apparatus.

Alternating long and short blasts of the sirens will be sounded from the moment the Army notifies the Police and Fire Departments of the approach of an enemy and will be continued throughout the duration of the raid. The all-clear signal will be given by a series of short blasts from the sirens, it was agreed.

Teachers to Be Warned

The Police and Fire Departments, with their network of communications reaching into every neighborhood in the city, also undertook to advise the 800 public schools of an impending raid when the alarm is sounded, so the teachers can shepherd their pupils to their homes in accordance with plans already made.

Precautions against sabotage of bridges, tunnels, railroads, reservoirs, dams, power plants and other points of key importance throughout the city also were discussed at conferences of high police officials with Commissioner

Continued on Page Twenty-six

MALAYA THWARTS PUSH BY JAPANESE

Thailand Capitulates and Is Seen Virtually in Axis—Two Raids on Singapore

By F. TILLMAN DURDIN
Wireless to THE NEW YORK TIMES.

SINGAPORE, Dec. 8—The Japanese in the first eighteen hours of their attack on the Malaya peninsula have forced Thailand to capitulate, but do not now appear to have achieved any appreciable success in an invasion of British Malaya.

There was an air raid on Singapore this morning. Prai, on the mainland opposite Georgetown, more commonly known as Penang from the name of the island on which it is located, was also bombed, but damage was said to be slight.

[Bombs again started dropping on Singapore at 4 A. M. today, The Associated Press re-

Continued on Page Ten

The International Situation

TUESDAY, DECEMBER 9, 1941

The United States yesterday made a formal declaration of war on Japan after President Roosevelt had addressed a joint session of Congress. [Page 1, Column 8.] The Senate approved it by unanimous vote [Page 6, Column 1] while one woman in the House of Representatives dissented. [Page 6, Column 4.]

In the national effort the Supply, Priorities and Allocations Board mapped expanding production [Page 36, Column 1], leaders of organized labor pledged support [Page 36, Column 4], and Mayor La Guardia issued a proclamation giving air raid defense instructions [Page 34, Column 1.]

In San Francisco two formations of enemy aircraft were sighted over the city, which was blacked out. [Page 1, Column 1.] White House announcements indicated that the battle of the Pacific was raging with the United States still on the defensive. [Page 1, Column 4; Map, Page 4.] There were extensive air attacks in the Philippines [Page 1, Columns 2 and 3; Map, Page 9], raids on Hong Kong [Page 11, Column 1] and a Tokyo report that both Guam and Wake had been put under the Japanese flag. [Page 12, Column 1; with map.] The British were mopping up on a Japanese landing party in Malaya, but Thailand had yielded. [Page 1, Column 3; Map, Page 10.]

The small detachment of United States Marines at Tientsin and Peiping were disarmed and detained by the Japanese and they closed the United States Consulate in Shanghai [Page 3, Column 1.] Imperial Headquarters in Tokyo made sweeping claims of victory in the battle of the Pacific, listing great damage to the United States forces. [Page 1, Column 5.]

In London, Prime Minister Churchill announced Britain's declaration of war to Parliament and made a stirring address to the world. [Page 14, Column 1.]

The American nations began to line up behind the United States. A conference will be held, but seven countries have already declared war on Japan, two have broken diplomatic relations and act. [Page 22, Column 3.] China decided to declare war not merely on Japan but on Germany and Italy as well. [Page 9, Column 4.] The various European governments in exile also supported the United States. [Page 18, Column 1.] Russia's position is obscure. [Page 2, Column 2.]

The United States accused Germany of having egged Japan on; said lease-lend would continue. [Page 1, Column 6.] Berlin gave out word that Winter had stopped the Germans short of Moscow and that the capture of the Russian capital had been put off until Spring. [Page 1, Column 1.]

In Libya, the Axis armored forces were attacked from three directions by the British and what was expected to be a major engagement was eventually merely a rearguard action. [Page 24, Column 3.]

BATTLESHIP LOST

Capsized in Pearl Harbor, Destroyer Is Blown Up, Other Ships Hurt

FLEET NOW IS FIGHTING

Aid Rushed to Hawaii— Some Congressmen Sharply Critical

By CHARLES HURD
Special to THE NEW YORK TIMES.

WASHINGTON, Dec. 8—The Battle of the Pacific spread tonight over a 5,000-mile "front" from Hawaii to the Philippines while a badly battered United States Fleet fought back at Japanese sea and air forces that launched severe attacks yesterday afternoon.

Tonight the Japanese were reported to be launching their main attack at the Philippines, particularly at Cavite, site of Honolulu and the Pearl Harbor naval base, probably has cost about 1,500 lives and resulted in an equal number of wounded persons.

To the toll of lives announced for this region, and undisclosed casualties in the Philippines and at other points, was added official word that one "old battleship" had capsized in Pearl Harbor, a destroyer had exploded and that several other

Continued on Page Four

LARGE U. S. LOSSES CLAIMED BY JAPAN

Tokyo Lists 2 Battleships, 1 Mine-Sweeper Sunk, 4 Capital Ships, 4 Cruisers Damaged

3,000 Casualties on Oahu

TOKYO, Tuesday, Dec. 9 (From Official Broadcasts, Distributed by The Associated Press.)—Japanese Imperial Headquarters announced last night the sinking of two United States battleships and a mine-sweeper, severe damage to four other American capital ships and the two cruisers and the destruction of about 100 American planes in Japan's surprise blows at Hawaii, the Philippines and Guam.

The official news agency, Domei, quickly interpreted "these magnificent early gains" as giving Japan naval mastery over the United States in the Pacific, and said that any force that the United States could muster now "would be regarded as utterly inadequate to accomplish any successful outcome in an encounter with the thus-far-intact Japanese fleet."

In addition, "many enemy merchant ships were captured" in the Pacific, it was announced, and the communiqué listed an unconfirmed report that a Japanese submarine had sunk an American aircraft carrier off Honolulu.

"No Japanese ships were lost during the fighting," it added.

Domei said today it was "understood that Japanese forces had destroyed more than 300 American planes, including 200 in dogfights and on the ground in Hawaii. The others, it said, were "believed" destroyed in the Philippines. Of the total, the news agency said, thirty were Fortress planes and thirty long-range bombers.

Japanese newspapers identified the two American battleships declared sunk Sunday at Pearl Harbor, Hawaii, as the 31,800-ton West Virginia, and the 29,000-ton Oklahoma. [An Italian broadcast, however, quoted Domei as listing the Oklahoma and the 33,100-ton Pennsylvania as lost. In Berlin, D. N. B. said in a Tokyo dispatch that an American transport ship carrying 350 men had been sunk off Manila.]

Japanese planes were reported to have again attacked the Philippines and British Hong Kong yesterday, inflicting "heavy damage" in a follow-up of the raids launched Sunday. "Twelve out of fourteen enemy planes on the ground were

Continued on Page Thirteen

The President's Message

Following is the text of President Roosevelt's war message to Congress, as recorded by THE NEW YORK TIMES from a broadcast:

Mr. Vice President, Mr. Speaker, members of the Senate and the House of Representatives:

Yesterday, Dec. 7, 1941—a date which will live in infamy—the United States of America was suddenly and deliberately attacked by naval and air forces of the empire of Japan.

The United States was at peace with that nation, and, at the solicitation of Japan, was still in conversation with its government and its Emperor looking toward the maintenance of peace in the Pacific.

Indeed, one hour after Japanese air squadrons had commenced bombing in the American island of Oahu, the Japanese Ambassador to the United States and his colleague delivered to our Secretary of State a formal reply to a recent American message. And, while this reply stated that it seemed useless to continue the existing diplomatic negotiations, it contained no threat or hint of war or of armed attack.

Attack Deliberately Planned

It will be recorded that the distance of Hawaii from Japan makes it obvious that the attack was deliberately planned many days or even weeks ago. During the intervening time the Japanese Government has deliberately sought to deceive the United States by false statements and expressions of hope for continued peace.

The attack yesterday on the Hawaiian Islands has caused severe damage to American naval and military forces. I regret to tell you that very many American lives have been lost. In

Continued on Page Six

The President signs the declaration of war —Associated Press Wirephotos

U. S. TO CONTINUE AID TO BRITAIN

White House Charges Nazis Sought Pacific War, but Will Fail to Gain Ends

Special to THE NEW YORK TIMES.

WASHINGTON, Dec. 8—A statement accusing Germany of having done everything in her power "to put Japan into the war" was issued this evening at the White House.

The statement declared that Germany's objective was "to put an end to the lease-lend program," which has aided the European enemies of Germany, including Britain and Russia and Turkey. It added that this program would continue "in full operation" and that the German attempt to end lease-lend shipments was "100 per cent" mistaken.

This statement took full cognizance of the belief in diplomatic circles here that Germany would carry out its pledges to Japan, its Axis ally, by declaring war on the United States and that Italy would

Continued on Page Seventeen

NAZIS GIVE UP IDEA OF MOSCOW IN 1941

Winter Forces Abandonment of Big Drives in North Till Spring, Berlin Says

By The Associated Press.

BERLIN, Dec. 8—Winter has stopped the Germans short of Moscow and the capture of the Soviet capital is not expected this year, a military spokesman declared tonight.

[A surprise Russian attack on Eastern Crimea from the Caucasus was revealed in a Moscow broadcast. A counter-attack from Sevastopol also was reported. The Soviet claimed important progress around Taganrog and on Moscow's defense lines.]

It seemed likely from the spokesman's statement that until Spring there could be no further major German offensive except that along the extreme southern front. This word reduced the Russian campaign to secondary interest for the Germans for the first time, and attention focused instead on Ja-

Continued on Page Twenty-five

UNITY IN CONGRESS

Only One Negative Vote as President Calls to War and Victory

ROUNDS OF CHEERS

Miss Rankin's Is Sole 'No' as Both Houses Act in Quick Time

By FRANK L. KLUCKHOHN
Special to THE NEW YORK TIMES.

WASHINGTON, Dec. 8—The United States today formally declared war on Japan. Congress, with only one dissenting vote, approved the resolution in the record time of 33 minutes after President Roosevelt denounced Japanese aggression in ringing tones. He personally delivered his message to a joint session of the Senate and House. At 4:10 P. M. he affixed his signature to the resolution.

There was no debate like that between April 2, 1917, when President Wilson requested war against Germany, and April 6, when a declaration of war was approved by Congress.

President Roosevelt spoke only 6 minutes and 30 seconds today compared with Woodrow Wilson's 29 minutes and 34 seconds.

The vote today against Japan was 82 to 0 in the Senate and 388 to 1 in the House. The lone vote against the resolution in the House was that of Miss Jeannette Rankin, Republican, of Montana. Her "No" was greeted with boos and hisses. In 1917 she voted against the resolution for war against Germany.

The President did not mention either Germany or Italy in his request. Early this evening a statement was issued at the White House, however, accusing Germany of doing everything possible to push Japan into the war. The objective, the official statement proclaimed, was to cut off America's lend-lease aid to Germany's European enemies, and a pledge was made that this aid would continue "100 per cent."

A Sudden and Deliberate Attack

President Roosevelt's brief and decisive words were addressed to the assembled representatives of the basic organizations of American democracy—the Senate, the House, the Cabinet and the Supreme Court.

"America was suddenly and deliberately attacked by naval and air forces of the Empire of Japan," he said. "We will gain the inevitable triumph, so help us God."

Thunderous cheers greeted the Chief Executive and Commander in Chief throughout the address. This was particularly pronounced when he declared that Americans "will remember the character of the onslaught against us," a day, he remarked, which will live in infamy.

"This form of treachery shall never endanger us again," he declared amid cheers. "The American people in their righteous might will win through to absolute victory."

Then, to the accompaniment of a

Continued on Page Five

President to Talk On Radio Tonight

By The Associated Press.

WASHINGTON, Dec. 8—President Roosevelt will make a radio address to the nation tomorrow night at 10 P. M., Eastern standard time, at which time the White House said he would make "a more complete documentation" of the Japanese attack than has yet been possible.

Stephen Early, Presidential secretary, announced that the Chief Executive would speak for half an hour and that the address would be carried by all networks.

Mr. Roosevelt began dictating the speech tonight in his White House study.

"All the News That's Fit to Print."

The New York Times.

LATE CITY EDITION
Partly cloudy, slightly warmer today. Tomorrow mostly cloudy, moderate temperature.

Copyright, 1941, by The New York Times Company.

VOL. XCI..No. 30,642.

Entered as Second-Class Matter, Postoffice, New York, N. Y.

NEW YORK, TUESDAY, DECEMBER 16, 1941.

THREE CENTS NEW YORK CITY and Vicinity

KNOX REPORTS ONE BATTLESHIP SUNK AT HAWAII, 5 OTHER CRAFT LOST, BUT MAIN FLEET IS AT SEA; PRESIDENT LAYS PERFIDY TO JAPAN'S EMPEROR

AIR WARDEN ORDERS WILL BE BACKED UP BY $500 PENALTIES

Alternate Jail Sentences Are Provided in Bill Council Will Act Upon Today

5 NEW SIRENS DELIVERED

Devices May Be Heard One to Two Miles—Tests Tomorrow —School Rules Unchanged

Failure to obey civil defense regulations or refusal to comply with the orders of air raid wardens would be made punishable by a jail term of not more than six months or a fine of not more than $500 by a local law to be introduced at this afternoon's meeting of the City Council by majority leader Joseph T. Sharkey of Brooklyn.

The measure, which was requested yesterday by Mayor La Guardia, also provides that during an air raid all except duty authorized persons must immediately leave streets, parks and open spaces and proceed to the nearest cover, and that vehicles must be parked immediately and their passengers take to the nearest shelter.

After the air-raid alarm last Tuesday and Wednesday many air raid wardens complained that crowds thronged into the streets to see what was going on and ignored their directions to seek shelter. The legislation sought by the Mayor is intended to correct this condition and to give the wardens legal authority to disperse crowds which might be subject to heavy casualties in an actual raid.

Warden Cards Printed

The Police Department has completed the printing of 200,000 identification cards for air-raid wardens, it was learned last night at the office of the Coordinator of Civilian Defense at Police Headquarters, and is about to begin issuing them to qualified wardens. Zone wardens will receive white cards, sector wardens yellow cards and post wardens salmon-colored cards.

Each warden must affix a photograph of himself, chauffeur size, to his card and return it to the police through his local precinct. A Police Department seal will then be placed over his picture and signature to guarantee the validity of the card to the holder. The cards will be two by three inches in size.

Five big "siro-drones," the first of seventy to be delivered this week, arrived yesterday at the office of the Thomas W. Rochester, chief engineer of the Police Department. The five included two different types, one of which is supposed to be audible within a radius of two miles and the other with a range of one mile.

Can Be Heard Mile

Both sirens are about three feet high, with horns twenty inches in diameter, and are electrically operated. The type with a radius of one mile is operated by a one-horsepower motor and the louder horn by a five-horsepower motor. They are ordinarily used as factory whistles and fire alarms in small towns and are manufactured by the H-O-B Company, Inc., of Stapleton, S. I.

Mayor La Guardia, Police Commissioner Valentine, and other local officials and civilian defense leaders will attend tests of both types of the new "siro-drones" tomorrow afternoon. The Mayor's party is to arrive at Spring and Lafayette Street, near Police Headquarters, at 4:30 P. M. to try out the sirens after they have been placed on a Police Department tower truck.

Earlier tomorrow afternoon, at 4 o'clock the Mayor and his entourage will visit the building of the New York Edison Company at Fortieth Street and East River for a trial of the big whistle, operated by steam and electricity, that is mounted on the structure.

Continued on Page Twenty-four

'Keep Flag Flying,' MacArthur's Order

Wireless to THE NEW YORK TIMES.
MANILA, Dec. 15—Morale at headquarters of the United States Army's Far Eastern Forces is above par.

An officer on the staff of General Douglas MacArthur, Commander in Chief, suggested to him that the American flag atop the bastion that marks the headquarters might serve as a target for Japanese planes. General MacArthur laughed and said:

"Take every other normal precaution for the protection of the headquarters, but let's keep the flag flying."

18-64 AGE LISTING FOR DRAFT RUSHED

House Committee for Military Service at 21, Senate Group for Minimum of 19

By HENRY N. DORRIS
Special to THE NEW YORK TIMES.

WASHINGTON, Dec. 15—Congressional committees speeded legislation today to give full wartime powers to the President and extend the registration requirements of the Selective Service Act to all men from 18 to 64, inclusive.

The House Military Affairs Committee gave final approval to a bill carrying the Selective Service changes. The Senate Military Affairs Committee gave tentative approval to a bill, withholding full approval pending testimony in executive session tomorrow by Brig. Gen. Lewis B. Hershey, Selective Service Administrator.

The bills as they stood tonight differed on the ages subject to military service. The Senate bill contains tentatively the War Department recommendation for the age brackets 19 to 44, inclusive. The House committee approved the bracket 21 to 44, inclusive.

About 41,000,000 men would be affected by the overall registration requirement, which is planned not only to provide an army of 2,800,000 to 7,500,000 but to ascertain

Continued on Page Thirty-one

The International Situation

TUESDAY, DECEMBER 16, 1941

Secretary of the Navy Knox yesterday reported losses to the United States Fleet in the Pearl Harbor attack as one battleship, a target ship, a minelayer and three destroyers. Casualties, as he gave them out, were heavier than had been previously reported. He said that defense forces were "not on the alert" and that the Japanese had been aided by a great "fifth column." An investigation is going forward. [Page 1, Column 8.]

The situation in the Philippines appeared to be stabilized, with an air raid on the naval station at Olongapo the only major operation. Midway, as well as Wake, was said in reports from Washington to be still holding out. [Page 1, Column 5; Map, Page 2.] British troops, resisting a Japanese attack in force on the Malay Peninsula, were declared to have dug in on a stronger defense line in southern Kedah and to have abandoned the southern tip of Burma. [Page 14, Column 3.] British and Netherland air units fought off strong Japanese forces. [Page 1, Column 5 and 6.] At Hong Kong the British had retired from the mainland and were strongly defending the island. The thrust in relief was gaining momentum. [Page 10, Column 2.] Tokyo's Premier claimed his foes in collapse, but warned of a long war. [Page 1, Columns 6 and 7.]

President Roosevelt, in a message to Congress outlining the events leading up to the war, laid stress on the Japanese bad faith, in which, he implied, the Emperor himself was involved. [Page 1, Column 4.] In a broadcast to the nation on the anniversary of the ratification of the Bill of Rights, he made Adolf Hitler the chief object of his attack and pledged

our victory for the sake of liberty. [Page 30, Column 2.]

The President also made his quarterly report to Congress on lease-lend aid and emphasized that our entrance into the war increased its necessity. [Page 4, Column 1.] Military Affairs Committees of the Senate and House approved bills to register all males between 18 and 65 years, but differed slightly on the age for military service. [Page 1, Column 8.]

Moscow reported the recapture of Klin and said the drive around Tula was successful; indeed, there were continued victories of the Russian offensive on all fronts. [Page 1, Column 3; Map, Page 15.]

The Axis also continued to give ground in Libya and the Nazis were reported to be throwing their last tank and infantry strength into a desperate delaying action. [Page 16, Column 1.] Their supply lines were said to have been further impaired with the sinking in the Mediterranean of a large supply ship and the sinking or damaging of half a dozen smaller vessels. [Page 17, Column 1.]

Vichy heard of fresh attacks on Nazis in Paris, including the bombing of a restaurant. There were reports that Marshal Pétain had refused the Germans the use of the French fleet and bases in Tunisia. [Page 18, Column 3.] Secretary of State Hull expressed friendly and encouraging sentiments toward the French people at his press conference. [Page 19, Column 1.]

As the American republics took further actions in support of the United States, Argentina contemplated instituting a state of siege to curb Axis activities. [Page 9, Column 1.]

RUSSIANS TAKE KLIN

Vital Rail Point in Center Seized as Push Gains on Every Front

NAZIS FLEE IN NORTH

Lose 3 Towns in Tula Area—Soviet Claims Crimean Advance

By DANIEL T. BRIGHAM
By Telephone to THE NEW YORK TIMES.

BERNE, Switzerland, Tuesday, Dec. 16—Smashing through ever-weakening German lines of defense, Soviet troops continued their brilliant operations in the fighting yesterday, recapturing Klin, important rail point on the Moscow-Leningrad line, and three communications centers south of Moscow.

The Red Army also advanced in the Volkhov area, southeast of Leningrad, and in Crimea the Germans were pushed back to the outskirts of Balaclava by Russian troops from Sevastopol, a Russian military spokesman announced on the Moscow radio this morning.

In operations intended to disengage the entire Leningrad-Moscow rail line, the Russians carried out encircling movements north of the Valdai Heights that enabled them to smash the German Thirty-ninth Army Corps. According to the spokesman, 20,000 Germans were killed or wounded in this action.

The remainder of the German force was reported to be fleeing in a southwesterly direction in an attempt to rejoin a "fairly large German force" with its back to Lake Ilmen. However, a Russian column threatens the Germans' southern wing on that sector.

On the Leningrad end of the front Red Army troops began a wide-scale operation southwestward from Tosna. It is understood that the main objective is to straighten out a deep salient that the Germans have held for more

Continued on Page Fifteen

U. S. 'WHITE PAPER'

President in Message Reveals How Tokyo Hid Treacherous Aims

AS HITLER DID LATER

Tyrants Will Fall in End to the Free Peoples, He Says on Radio

The President's message to Congress is on Page 6.

Special to THE NEW YORK TIMES.

WASHINGTON, Dec. 15—Emperor Hirohito was accused today by President Roosevelt, in effect, of personal complicity in Japan's course of carrying on peace negotiations with the United States while putting into operation the plan for a treacherous attack upon this country.

The Emperor is regarded by most Japanese as a divinity whose personal honor must be above reproach, and diplomatic circles here expressed the opinion today that the revelation of perfidy might have serious repercussions within Japan later.

The President revealed in a message transmitted to Congress the details of the reply from the Emperor to his personal appeal for peace on Dec. 6. The message, which was looked upon as the equivalent of an American White Paper, outlined the whole course of American-Japanese relations and of step-by-step execution of the joint German-Japanese-Italian plan for world conquest.

[The issue of the war is whether a revival of barbarism is to be forced on the self-respecting peoples of the world by tyrants, President Roosevelt declared last night in his radio address on the 150th anniversary of the ratification of the Bill of Rights. Whereas Hitler's idea is that the individual has no rights whatsoever under an absolute master, the state, the President pledged that this nation will not lay down arms until "liberty is once again secure in the world we live in."]

Talked Peace After War Started

The President emphasized that Hirohito's reply to his peace appeal was delivered orally to Ambassador Joseph C. Grew in Tokyo three hours and forty minutes after Japanese planes and submarines had started the war by a surprise attack on Pearl Harbor.

The full text of the Emperor's reply was not made public, but he was quoted as saying, in part, after Japan had begun the war:

"Establishment of peace in the Pacific, and consequently of the world, has been the cherished desire of His Majesty, for the realization of which he has hitherto made his government to continue its earnest endeavors."

Japan's real reply, the President stressed, had been given earlier by the long-prepared attack without warning on American bases in the Pacific. "There," he said, "is the record, for all history to read in amazement, in sorrow, in horror and disgust."

After outlining the attempt that Hirohito's reply was made while friendly relations with the Japanese from the time Commodore Perry opened Japan to the outside world in 1853, and telling of continued American efforts to maintain a peace based on justice and fair-dealing in the Orient, the President stated that Japan openly entered a league of fascism against the free world under the pretext of signing the anti-Comintern Pact in 1936.

Tells of Axis Accord Against Us

He offered evidence to show that Japan, Germany and Italy arranged together to time their blows against free nations in the best manner to effect joint plans for world dominance, and mentioned how the three finally and openly concluded last year "a treaty of

Continued on Page Six

ENEMY MAKES SOME GAINS IN MALAYA AND SOUTH BURMA

British defenders of Victoria Point (1) were reported to have withdrawn as a Japanese force pushed westward across the Kra Isthmus. An announcement of fighting in Southern Kedah (2) indicated that the Japanese had made progress in that area. "Some activities" were reported in Kelantan (3). Ipoh (4) had an air raid alarm. Frame on inset shows the area covered by large map.

Allied Fliers Match Japan's In North Malaya Fighting

By F. TILLMAN DURDIN
Special Cable to THE NEW YORK TIMES.

SUNGEI PATANI, North Malaya, Dec. 14 (Delayed)—Against Japanese based on airdromes in Thailand that apparently had been prepared for them long before the attack on Malaya began, British, Australian and Netherland air units in this region are putting up a courageous and effective opposition. One Royal Air Force source told me that the Japanese were operating from five different airfields in Southern Thailand within forty-eight hours after the war broke out.

[Japanese forces pushed into the southern part of the State of Kedah, Northern Malaya, and took Victoria Point, the tip of Southern Burma, the British announced. The Japanese, however, moved at a heavy cost in lives, it was said. The Japanese were entrenched on the eastern side of the peninsula south of Kota Bharu. Penang was not raided yesterday, but Japanese bombers attacked Ipoh, tin mining center.]

The Navy sustained damage to some of their vessels. This damage varies from ships which have been already repaired and are ready for sea, or which have gone to sea, to a few ships which will take from a week to several months to

Continued on Page Fourteen

FILIPINOS BEAT OFF 154 ENEMY BOATS

Lingayen Guns Blast Japanese for 3 Days—Invading Planes Bomb Olongapo Naval Base

By The United Press.

MANILA, Tuesday, Dec. 16—First details reached here today of an engagement at Lingayen Beach, 110 miles northwest of Manila, where a Filipino Army division, lining the shore with artillery, blasted 154 motorboat loads of invading Japanese soldiers without letting one of them reach land alive.

The fighting lasted three days. It began last Wednesday night and at last report the Filipinos were holding the beach. The colonel in command sent word to Manila that his force would stand their ground "to the last man."

Details were brought here by a correspondent of The Philippines Herald, who quoted the colonel, whom he did not identify, as having said:

"We eagerly awaited the Japanese attempt to land. They showed up Wednesday night. I counted 154 motorboats in all. We held our fire until they were near.

"Then our artillery roared into action. Most of the boats were destroyed. A few managed to escape to warships which must have been anchored far beyond the horizon. Since then the enemy has attempted to land, but each time he has been frustrated."

The correspondent reported that the colonel promised to fight to the last man "to a man voicing the sentiments of men of all ranks whom I interviewed. The colonel was said to be con-

Continued on Page Six

Knox Statement on Hawaii

By The Associated Press.

WASHINGTON, Dec. 15—The text of Secretary Knox's statement detailing losses in the Japanese attack on Pearl Harbor follows:

My inspection trip to the island enables me to present the general facts covering the attack which hitherto have been unavailable.

1. The essential fact is that the Japanese purpose was to knock out the United States before the war began. This was made apparent by the deception practiced, by the preparations which had gone on for many weeks before the attack, and the attacks themselves, which were made simultaneously throughout the Pacific. In this purpose the Japanese failed.

2. The United States services were not on the alert against the surprise air attack on Hawaii. This fact calls for a formal investigation, which will be instituted immediately by the President. Further action is, of course, dependent on the facts and recommendations made by this investigating board. We are all entitled to know it if (a) there was any error of judgment which contributed to the surprise, (b) if there was any dereliction of duty prior to the attack.

3. My investigation made clear that after the attack the defense by both services was conducted skillfully and bravely. The Navy lost:

(a) The battleship Arizona, which was destroyed by the explosion of, first, its boiler and then its forward magazine due to a bomb which was said to have literally passed down through the smokestack;

(b) The old target ship Utah, which has not been used as a combatant ship for many years, and which was in service as a training ship for anti-aircraft gunnery and experimental purposes;

(c) Three destroyers, the Cassin, the Downes and the Shaw;

(d) Minelayer Oglala. This was a converted merchantman, formerly a passenger ship on the Fall River Line and converted into a minelayer during the World War.

Continued on Page Seven

Tokyo Premier Claims Triumph, Then Warns of War to Be Fought

By The Associated Press.

TOKYO, Tuesday, Dec. 16 (From Japanese Broadcast) — Premier Hideki Tojo, addressing an extraordinary session of the Japanese Diet, today reiterated his assertions that Japan had declared war on the United States only after trying all means of peaceful settlement. He declared:

"Our fighting services have speedily broken through the enemy key positions within less than ten days. The bulk of the American Fleet which had been at Hawaii is destroyed, and the main body of the British Far Eastern Fleet is crushed; the encircling front against Japan, the strength of which the enemy has exaggerated and given wide publicity in an attempt to intimidate Japan, is shattered at various places.

"The anti-Japanese encircling front already is on a fair way to collapse."

He nevertheless cautioned the Japanese that "a war remains waiting to be fought."

Japanese Imperial Headquarters reported that Japanese expeditionary forces had landed on British Borneo at dawn today despite a heavy gale.

The headquarters also reported that Japanese Army and Navy forces completed occupation of the island of Guam last Friday.

A joint communiqué of the army and navy sections of Imperial Headquarters warned Japanese yesterday "against the lurking danger of enemy submarines off Japan's island coasts and urged them to

Continued on Page Thirteen

HEROIC ACTS CITED

2,897 Defenders Killed in Gallant Battle— Base Not 'on Alert'

FIFTH COLUMN ACTIVE

2-Man Submarine Used —Roosevelt to Name Inquiry Board

By CHARLES HURD
Special to THE NEW YORK TIMES.

WASHINGTON, Dec. 15—Japan did not administer a knockout blow or destroy the effectiveness of American naval forces in the Pacific when she attacked at Pearl Harbor, Hawaii, at dawn on Dec. 7, and thus failed to achieve her objective, Secretary of the Navy Frank Knox reported today on his return from a flight to Hawaii to investigate the attack.

High Japanese officials had asserted that the blow struck at Pearl Harbor destroyed American naval supremacy in the Pacific. Mr. Knox evidenced a different view when he said:

"The Japanese failed to knock out the United States before the war began."

Fleet Now Hunts Enemy

The Secretary said the United States Army and Navy forces in Hawaii "were not on the alert" against the surprise attack "of the Japanese and in consequence losses had been heavy. After the action started, however, he said, our soldiers and sailors fought bravely, and he added that all remaining effective units of the Pacific Fleet "are at sea seeking contact with the enemy."

He listed the destroyed vessels as the battleship Arizona, the destroyers Cassin, Downes and Shaw, the minelayer Oglala and the target and training ship Utah. In addition, he said that the battleship Oklahoma had capsized and that an unannounced number of vessels had been damaged.

The Navy casualties in this action were given by Mr. Knox as 91 officers and 2,638 men killed and 20 officers and 636 men wounded. Late this evening the Army announced that its losses in this engagement totaled 168 officers and men, bringing the aggregate service losses to 2,897.

Attack's Objective Failed

Mr. Knox gave his report at a special press conference a few hours after his return from Honolulu. He supplemented a prepared statement by replies to questions that emphasized the fact that the Japanese failed in their attack with carrier-borne planes and submarines, eluded the naval patrols at sea, caught the Army Air Force on the ground and destroyed the great majority of planes there, and showed a detailed knowledge of objectives.

Against these adverse reports, Mr. Knox reported that the sailors and soldiers fought bravely and well after the action started, and he told reporters that the Japanese failed in their objective, which was to knock out the Pacific fleet before the war started.

Responsibility for the errors committed, he said, will be investigated immediately by a Presidential commission. He declined to anticipate the results of such an investigation. After calling on President Roosevelt this evening, Mr. Knox said the President would name the inquiry board tomorrow. The Japanese losses for this engagement were listed by the Secretary as three submarines, including one large and one small destroyed and a small one captured, and forty-nine planes.

One reason for the success of the Japanese, he asserted, was cooperation from the Hawaiian Islands themselves.

"The most effective fifth-column work in this war was done in Hawaii, with the exception of Norway," Mr. Knox said.

He declined to elaborate on steps

Continued on Page Seven

The New York Times.

LATE CITY EDITION
Rain today and not much change
in temperatures.
Temperature Yesterday—Max., 53; Min., 35

Copyright, 1942, by The New York Times Company.

VOL. XCI. No. 30,757.

Entered as Second-Class Matter,
Postoffice, New York, N. Y.

NEW YORK, FRIDAY, APRIL 10, 1942.

THREE CENTS NEW YORK CITY
and Vicinity

JAPANESE CAPTURE BATAAN AND 36,000 TROOPS; SINK TWO BRITISH CRUISERS; ITALIANS LOSE ONE; INDIA REPORTED AGREEING ON NATIVE COUNCIL

SENATOR AND JONES CLASH OVER ATTACK ON WAR PLANT DEAL

Bunker Charges DPC Condones 'Unconscionable Profits' for Nevada Magnesium Plant

UNTRUE, SAYS SECRETARY

Fees Paid to 9 Contractors, He Adds, Will Be Less Than 2% of Cost of 70 Millions

Special to The New York Times.

WASHINGTON, April 9—Senator Bunker, Democrat, of Nevada, today attacked the Defense Plant Corporation, an RFC subsidiary, charging that the terms of its contract with Basic Magnesium, Inc., for a plant at Las Vegas, Nev., meant "unconscionable profits." Secretary Jones, as head of the RFC, immediately replied that the charges were misleading and untrue, and, in effect, challenged Senator Bunker to press them without benefit of Senatorial immunity.

The Secretary of Commerce replied to Senator Bunker in a statement.

"Senator Bunker's statements accusing RFC officials of wrongdoing," he said, "are unworthy of a United States Senator and cannot go unchallenged. The Senator must know these statements are untrue.

"The magnesium plant that is being built by the government near Las Vegas, Nev., will cost approximately $70,000,000 and have an estimated annual capacity of 112,000,000 pounds of metallic magnesium.

Says Fees Total Less Than 2%

"Nine separate contractors are participating in the construction. The fees to be paid the nine contracting and engineering firms, together with the fee to Basic Magnesium, Inc., for its engineering plans, supervision and 'know-how,' will aggregate less than 2 per cent of the total cost of the plant.

"The operating or management fee of the plant is to be half cent per pound of magnesium produced, which is approximately 2 per cent of the estimated cost.

"The royalty for the ores will not exceed ¼ cent per pound of magnesium metal produced.

"No irregularities have been discovered in the construction of the plant that would warrant the irresponsible statements made by Senator Bunker. The plant is wholly owned by the government and will be operated for its account. All expenditures in connection with the construction of the plant as well as its operation are carefully audited as the work progresses.

"Defense Plant Corporation contracted with Basic Magnesium, Inc., for the construction of this plant at the request of OPM and the War Department, and the government's interest is fully protected.

Continued on Page Eighteen

Cripps Said to Have Accord On National Regime in India

Plan Is Reported to Envisage Rule by a Council With Briton Directing Army and Native in Defense Ministry

By The United Press.

NEW DELHI, India, April 9—Great Britain and India are in general agreement on a self-government plan that will establish the first all-Indian national government in two centuries and provide for an executive council of fifteen members, all but one of them to come from the various political parties, it was learned tonight.

The plan was reported to be acceptable, with the exception of a few minor adjustments, to the two major political groups—the All-India Congress party and the Moslem League.

Under the plan a native government minister will handle all Indian defense matters except war strategy and tactics, which a British military chief will control.

With only final details to be smoothed out, formal announcement of the settlement was predicted for late tomorrow or Saturday.

It was learned that an executive

Inquiries late tonight revealed that under the agreement reached between the Congress party and Sir Stafford Cripps, British negotiator, the new national government would be directed not by a Cabinet but by the Executive Council of the Viceroy of India, the Marquess of Linlithgow.

The importance of that point in the agreement, it was said, was the fact that a Prime Minister would not be appointed and asked to form a Cabinet—the usual constitutional procedure—but that the Viceroy would appoint members to the council, after receiving the names of nominees by the various Indian parties.

Under the new government, the country would be mobilized to resist the Japanese, who are drawing closer.

Continued on Page Six

2 Police Officials Suspended On Amen's Charges of Graft

In an unexpected move that may present a test case of far-reaching effect in the Police Department, Special Prosecutor John Harlan Amen's two extraordinary grand juries returned supplemental presentments yesterday against two high-ranking police officers who had sought retirement while under investigation in connection with alleged police protection of a $100,000,000 city-wide gambling racket.

The two, Inspector Camille C. Pierne of the Tenth Division in Brooklyn and Lieutenant Terence J. Harvey of the Brooklyn Borough headquarters squad, were named in Wednesday's presentments that bared the existence of police graft estimated at more than $1,000,000 a year, but no specific charges were lodged against them on the theory that a mere application for retirement was sufficient to preclude the prosecution of departmental charges against them.

However, Police Commissioner Valentine, after conferring behind closed doors with his aides and later in the afternoon with Mayor La Guardia, issued a statement Wednesday night asserting that he had notified Mr. Amen that inasmuch as the retirement applications of several police officers had not been acted upon by the Police Pension Fund he regarded them as members of the uniformed force and would like to be advised if the grand jury had made any charges against them so that he could be "guided accordingly."

Mr. Amen's reply yesterday was to send a letter to Commissioner Valentine asserting that it was because of his understanding of Mr. Valentine's earlier advice that he had not filed charges against men

Continued on Page Thirty-eight

GASOLINE SUPPLIES CUT AGAIN BY WPB

Deliveries to East and 2 States in Northwest Will Be Reduced From 80 to 66⅔ Per Cent

Special to The New York Times.

WASHINGTON, April 9—The War Production Board issued today an order further curtailing gasoline deliveries to filling stations and bulk consumers in seventeen Eastern States, the District of Columbia and Oregon and Washington.

Effective April 16, deliveries of gasoline to filling stations and bulk consumers in curtailment areas will be cut to 66⅔ per cent of average deliveries in December, January and February, adjusted for seasonal variations. Deliveries have been reduced 20 per cent since March 19.

Secretary Ickes, Petroleum Coordinator, discussing the WPB order, said at his press conference:

"If this curtailment proves satisfactory, we may go to Leon Henderson and tell him we see no need for rationing."

Mr. Ickes added that the matter

Continued on Page Twenty-six

Jesse Jones Shakes Eugene Meyer; Eye-Glasses Broken in Encounter

Special to The New York Times.

WASHINGTON, April 9—Jesse Jones, Secretary of Commerce, and Eugene Meyer, editor and publisher of The Washington Post, were participants in a fistic encounter at the annual dinner of the Alfalfa Club at the Hotel Willard tonight.

A sharp verbal exchange arising from resentment by the Secretary of an editorial in which his testimony before the Senate's Truman committee investigating the rubber situation was criticized preceded the encounter, club members said.

As told by eyewitnesses, Secretary Jones was approached by Mr. Meyer, a long-time critic of the banker, as Mr. Jones entered the small ballroom of the club. Accounts of witnesses vary as to the words which immediately preceded the encounter, but most members agreed that Secretary Jones

grasped Mr. Meyer by the coat and started to shake him. As Mr. Meyer wrenched himself free his eye-glasses fell to the floor and were smashed.

Mr. Meyer, the accounts continue, swung at the Secretary but friends, including John J. O'Connor, former New York Representative, pushed them apart. Secretary Jones left immediately after the fight, while Mr. Meyer stayed for a time chatting with friends.

The men have been frequent adversaries since the Hoover Administration, when both served with the Reconstruction Finance Corporation, of which Mr. Meyer was then chairman. Mr. Jones is also a publisher, owning The Houston Chronicle.

Today's editorial asserted that Mr. Jones had shielded himself behind the President, the British and the Netherlands in defending his handling of the rubber situation.

PLANES GET SHIPS

Japanese Sink Big Naval Units in Bay of Bengal, Blast Base in Ceylon

BRITISH RAID CARRIER

Score Near-Misses, Get 4 Aircraft—2 Fleets Massing for Battle

By RAYMOND DANIELL
Wireless to The New York Times.

LONDON, April 9—The Japanese have struck a heavy blow against the British Navy in the struggle for mastery of the Bay of Bengal, which is the key to the Indian Ocean, in sinking by air attack the heavy cruisers Dorsetshire and Cornwall. In return, near-misses were scored by bombers in an attack on a Japanese aircraft carrier in the Bay of Bengal.

Full enemy control of the Bay of Bengal, the eastern half of which the Japanese command already, would lay the eastern coast of India open to invasion. Renewed aerial attacks today on Trincomalee, the main British naval base on the island of Ceylon, off the south coast of India, made it more apparent than ever that the Japanese were seeking to extend their domination westward.

1,100 Are Rescued

News of the sinking of the 10,000-ton Cornwall and 9,975-ton Dorsetshire was given in an Admiralty communiqué, which placed the encounter with the Japanese planes in the Indian Ocean. The announcement said 1,100 survivors, —including the commanders, Captain A. W. S. Agar of the Dorsetshire and Captain P. O. W. Manwaring of the Cornwall—had been picked up. The Dorsetshire was the ship whose torpedoes administered the coup de grâce to the German battleship Bismarck in the Atlantic last year.

The attack on the Japanese aircraft carrier was announced in a communiqué received tonight from Colombo, Ceylon. In the action, which followed today's attack on Trincomalee, four Japanese planes were shot down. Some of the attacking planes did not return, but their number was not disclosed. While Trincomalee was being raided a couple of Japanese planes appeared over Colombo, but dropped no bombs.

[The Colombo communiqué also revealed that in the attack on Trincomalee the Japanese damaged harbor and airdrome facilities and caused a few casualties among dockyard personnel, The Associated Press reported. Six of the Japanese planes were shot down, six others were probably destroyed and two were listed as damaged. The Japanese, who attacked with "a large force of bombers and fighters," caused no damage in the town of Trincomalee.]

Allied Cargo Ships Sunk

The loss of the Cornwall and the Dorsetshire, coupled with an official statement from New Delhi, India, that several merchantmen have been sunk in recent enemy air and naval attacks in the Bay of Bengal, represents a serious blow not only at British naval strength in that area but against United Nations lines of communication.

The number of merchant vessels lost was not announced, but the total of survivors from them—between 400 and 500, who have landed on the coast of Orissa in India—indicates a considerable number. Tokyo said today that the number of ships sunk was twenty-one, with twenty-three others so severely damaged that they must be regarded as lost.

The Japanese naval force in the Bay of Bengal area is operating hundreds of miles from its presumed base in the Andaman Islands. The distance from the Andamans to Ceylon is more than 1,000 miles. Before the occupation of

Continued on Page Six

IN THE FOX HOLES OF BATAAN

U. S. Troops in action on the Philippine peninsula, the fall of which was announced yesterday
Associated Press Wirephoto (U. S. Army Signal Corps)

ITALIAN CRUISER SUNK BY BRITISH

10,000-Ton Vessel Destroyed by Submarine—Foes Spar in Libyan Fighting

By ROBERT P. POST
Wireless to The New York Times.

LONDON, April 9—A 10,000-ton eight-inch-gun Italian cruiser has been sunk in the Central Mediterranean by torpedoes from a British submarine, the Admiralty announced today.

The cruiser, which may have been convoying reinforcements for Marshal Erwin Rommel in Libya, was accompanied by destroyers and aircraft when Lieut. Comdr. E. P. Tomkinson, who received the Distinguished Service Order with bar in December for his work on submarine patrol, ordered the attack. Eight minutes after his torpedoes struck home, the commander risked attack by the cruiser's escort to show his periscope. The cruiser was heard to break up and sink while the destroyers picked up survivors.

Lieut. Commander Tomkinson's earlier exploits were carried out with the Urge, one of the smallest British submarines. Last April he sank a heavily laden oil tanker of more than 10,000 tons. For this he

Continued on Page Eight

Sacred Saffron of Priests Aids Foe's Burma Advance

By HARRISON FORMAN
Wireless to The New York Times.

CHUNGKING, China, April 9—Clad in the sacred saffron robes of the Poongee—literally meaning "great glory"—the fifth column in Burma is taking advantage of the historic sanctuary provided by Burmese Buddhism. In the past the Poongees have included, besides the genuinely devout, many thieves, bandits and general malcontents, and they have always been a major problem for British administration.

Unlike most other priesthoods, the Poongees require no special training or lifelong vows. Any man may in practice become a Poongee for any period desired, days or years, by the simple procedure of shaving his head, donning a saffron robe, formally renouncing all things worldly before a temple and thereafter living solely by begging, which is not permitted for more than daily needs. In practical example, a business man may welch on a contract or a debt by simply becoming a Poongee, and he thereby is cleansed of all worldly obligations and responsibilities. The Poongees are arrogant and sacrosanct in so far as the police are concerned. They are publicly regarded as holy men who can do no wrong, and the British military confess they are practically helpless in the face of such fanaticism.

An eyewitness on the Burma front reports that at a certain supposedly secret airport there ap-

Continued on Page Five

War News Summarized

FRIDAY, APRIL 10, 1942

Rocky Bataan Peninsula, the finger of land that still defied the Japanese after they had conquered most of the Southwest Pacific, finally succumbed yesterday. Its 36,853 remaining American and Filipino defenders—drained by hunger, exhaustion and disease—could no longer rally to beat off an enveloping movement that broke their lines on the east flank. For three months they had fought against ever-growing odds. Although Corregidor Island and the other forts in Manila Bay stayed in American hands, it was questionable how long they could hold out. [1-8; map, P. 2]

The United Nations suffered a probably greater strategic setback in the Bay of Bengal. Japanese planes sank two British 10,000-ton cruisers, the Dorsetshire and the Cornwall, and a great naval battle loomed with the coast of India at stake. Allied bombers attacked a Japanese naval squadron and scored near-misses on an aircraft carrier. In the Allied attack and in a raid on the Ceylon naval base of Trincomalee, the Japanese lost at least ten planes. [1:6; map, P. 6]

The Japanese naval force in the Bay of Bengal area is operating

ers and damaged two others without a loss of their own. [1:7.] United Nations bombers blasted planes and military targets in a surprise raid on Rabaul, New Britain. [3:1.]

With the threat to India growing daily, the situation and negotiations in New Delhi appeared nearing a successful compromise—the establishment of an Indian national government in which the defense minister would share responsibility with General Wavell. [1:2-3.]

The naval defeat in the Indian Ocean was offset somewhat by the sinking of a 10,000-ton Italian cruiser by a British submarine in the Mediterranean. [1:5.]

Germany flung large units of tanks and planes into the Russian front to feel out the Red Army's strength in virtually every sector, Moscow reports said, but the reinforced Soviet forces broke up their attacks and clung to the initiative. [11:1, with map.]

In occupied Norway, the embittered Norwegian people observed the second anniversary of the German invasion with a "strike" of silence as Quislings and German troops marched in the streets. [9:1.]

DEFENSE CRUSHED

Stimson Reveals Defeat Followed Failure to Get in More Food

CORREGIDOR IS HELD

Wainwright on the Isle Free to Set Course, Roosevelt Tells Him

What Tokyo Reports

By The Associated Press.

TOKYO, Friday, April 10 (From Japanese broadcasts recorded in New York)—The Domei news agency said today that "60,000 Filipino and American troops resisting the Japanese on Bataan Peninsula have begged for a halt in hostilities after six days of fierce Japanese assault."

"Details of the conditions of surrender are not yet disclosed," said the Domei dispatch, "nor is it known yet whether the Japanese forces have decided to accept the terms."

Corregidor was raided twice yesterday by Japanese bombers and tons of explosives were unleashed on military installations, Domei reported.

By CHARLES HURD
Special to The New York Times.

WASHINGTON, April 9—An overwhelming Japanese Army, aided by the allies of hunger, fatigue and disease, today crushed the small mixed force that had held Bataan Peninsula since December.

Japanese forces, heretofore estimated at 200,000 men, including fresh assault troops, and supported by tanks, artillery, bombers and attack planes in profusion, enveloped an exhausted defending army of 36,853 men, as counted officially yesterday afternoon.

The defeat of the American and Filipino forces was officially announced as a "probability" in a War Department communiqué issued as of 5:15 A. M. today. A few hours later Secretary of War Henry L. Stimson announced the defeat at his regularly scheduled weekly press conference. He already had carried the word to President Roosevelt.

Reveals Supplies Were Sent In

When Secretary Stimson met reporters in his conference room he paid the highest praise to the spirit of the defenders in a fight recognized as hopeless from the beginning but pledged that the Philippines would be reconquered. In the same talk he described the extraordinary efforts made to provision the garrison, saying that "several shiploads of supplies" were sent into the Philippines, "but for every ship that arrived safely we lost nearly two."

Army Records Position

This was the first challenge to Japanese air superiority over Burma battlegrounds since the invaders launched their all-out offensive against cities and airports in that theatre early last week. The strength of the A. V. G. force —American-made and American-flown planes fighting under the Chinese banner—was not disclosed.

Official Chinese dispatches disclosed that German officers were mapping the Japanese drive against Chinese lines north of Toungoo in Central Burma. One German officer was reported captured by the defenders and reconnaissance revealed that the Japanese were massing troops in Thailand to the east for a possible envelopment move against the Chinese on the Nazi model.

Chinese spokesmen said the Japanese concentrations in the Chiengmai area across the Thailand border not only menaced the Chinese positions around Toungoo but enabled the invaders to threaten a diversion drive into China's Kwangsi and Yunnan Provinces.

The Toungoo front—one-third of the way to bombed-out Mandalay from captured Rangoon—has been fairly static for a week. A belated Chinese communiqué reported the Japanese attacked south of Yedashe, eighteen miles north of Toungoo, on Monday and that fighting continued after dark that night. Subsequent communiqués

Continued on Page Five

AMERICANS BAG TEN IN BURMA AIR FIGHT

A. V. G. Routs Twenty of Foe Without One Loss—Lull in Land Fighting Continues

By The United Press.

CHUNGKING, China, April 9—Reinforced American Volunteer Group fliers have roared back into the Battle of Burma, destroying ten planes and damaging two others without a loss of their own in a mass dogfight with twenty Japanese Zero fighters in which one American plane was lost but its pilot saved, an A. V. G. communiqué announced tonight.

The battle was fought over the Burmese town of Loi-Win, the communiqué said. [An Associated Press dispatch from Chungking, based on the same official source, said the encounter took place Wednesday over Leiyun in the south of China's Yunnan Province. Neither Loi-Win nor Leiyun appears on available maps.]

Week of Inaction Ended

This was the heavy one for General Wainwright, now that it is assumed here that he lacks transport to take more than a handful of the Bataan forces across the four miles of water that separates Bataan Peninsula from Corregidor. Even so his food is desperately short, Secretary Stimson said on having said this morning that every man in Bataan had been on short rations since Jan. 11. This was a primary reason for the collapse of the defense after five days of savage hand-to-hand fighting.

The long-expected defeat, which by its deferment wrote an epic in American military history, was officially indicated in War Depart-

Continued on Page Two

TO PLACE a Want Ad just telephone The
New York Times—Lackawanna 4-1000.—Advt.

"All the News That's Fit to Print."

The New York Times.

LATE CITY EDITION
Mild today.
Temperatures Yesterday—Max., 74; Min., 52

Copyright, 1942, by The New York Times Company

VOL. XCI. No. 30,783.

Entered as Second-Class Matter,
Postoffice, New York, N. Y.

NEW YORK, WEDNESDAY, MAY 6, 1942.

THREE CENTS NEW YORK CITY
and Vicinity

CORREGIDOR SURRENDERS UNDER LAND ATTACK AFTER WITHSTANDING 300 RAIDS FROM THE AIR; BRITISH HIT MADAGASCAR BASE; VICHY RESISTS

CHARGE ACCOUNTS ARE DUE IN 40 DAYS AS INFLATION CURB

Reserve Board's Regulation, in Effect Today, Is First Check on Such Retail Customers

Bringing retail charge accounts under control for the first time and ruling that installment purchases must be liquidated in twelve months the Federal Reserve Board promulgated yesterday amendment No. 4 to its consumer credit regulation W, carrying into effect the seventh point in President Roosevelt's anti-inflation program.

Under the amendment, which is effective today, charge account customers of retail stores will be required to speed up their payments to complete them within forty days after the end of the month in which purchase is made. If this is not done the account will be transferred to an installment basis requiring liquidation within six months and no further charge account purchases will be permissible until the items in default are paid for.

The amendment also tightened substantially the earlier restrictions on installment sales and broadened the scope of the merchandise covered to forty-six listed classifications, including almost every item used in the American home, and clothing and jewelry as well. The down payment was generally raised to 33 1/3 per cent and the payment period to twelve months.

Explains Aim of Rules

Allan Sproul, president of the Federal Reserve Bank of New York, in announcing the amendment here, said:

"As amended, the regulation is extended to cover a comprehensive list of durable and semi-durable goods for civilian consumption and contemplates that the volume of outstanding consumer credit, already substantially diminished, will be further contracted in keeping with the government's purpose to prevent the rapid bidding up of prices.

"The purpose of this revision is to help make effective the last point in the seven-point program which the President set forth in his special message to Congress of April 27, 1942, as follows: 'To keep the cost of living from spiraling upward, we must discourage credit and installment buying, and encourage the paying off of debts, mortgages and other obligations; for this promotes savings, retards excessive buying and adds to the amount available to the creditors for the purchase of war bonds.' "

With respect to charge accounts, the regulation, in effect and depending upon the date of the purchase, provides for a forty to a seventy day payment period, similar to that in effect in Canada. The average period for payment of

Continued on Page Fourteen

Nazis' War Industry Spurs Plane Output

By Telephone to THE NEW YORK TIMES.

BERNE, Switzerland, May 5—German war industry has been ordered to devote all its attention henceforth to turning out airplanes, even to the detriment of tanks and other matériel. This news from Berlin tonight confirms indications reaching foreign circles here that mastery of the air is the paramount consideration for the moment.

Figures declared to be trustworthy indicate that the peak of plane production in the Reich was reached in June, 1941, when 3,300 were turned out. Now it has fallen to between 2,700 and 2,800. Italy's contribution does not exceed 700 machines a month.

It is understood the Germans' estimate of their opponents' production is: United States, 3,300 planes a month; Britain, 2,400; Russia, 2,600 to 2,900. But the Nazis can draw upon considerable reserves.

WPB CUTS GASOLINE 50 PER CENT IN EAST

Non-Essential Users May Be Down to 5 Gallons a Week After May 16 Order

By The Associated Press.

WASHINGTON, May 5—Gasoline consumption in the East will be slashed 50 per cent below normal starting May 16, the War Production Board said tonight. This means that many of the area's 10,000,000 motorists probably will have to get along with as little as five or six gallons a week.

The reduction will become effective the day the seaboard area begins using ration cards.

[In New York motorists will register for gasoline rationing next Tuesday, Wednesday and Thursday. Rationing will begin on May 15.]

While the overall curtailment will be one-half, informed sources explained that it would amount to about a 60 per cent cut for non-essential users of automobiles, since necessary vehicles will continue to receive their full requirements of fuel.

Action Recommended by Ickes

The WPB action, taken on recommendation of Harold L. Ickes, petroleum coordinator, came shortly after Joseph B. Eastman, defense transportation director, declared "every owner of a motor vehicle in public or private service should realize that he holds this vehicle in trust for the national war effort and that it should be used only for purposes of necessity."

This statement of Mr. Eastman's applied to the whole country, not merely to the East.

Simultaneously with the gasoline order, WPB directed that use

Continued on Page Thirteen

BRONX GRAND JURY CLEARS EVERYONE IN THE FLYNN CASE

County Is 'Singularly Free of Fraud and Corruption,' Presentment Says

The Bronx County grand jury that has been hearing evidence on the paving with city materials and labor of a courtyard on the Lake Mahopac estate of Edward J. Flynn, chairman of the Democratic National Committee, as well as other irregularities in the Bronx, handed up a seventeen-page presentment yesterday, finding that Bronx County is "singularly free of fraud and corruption," but that many irregularities are prevalent.

The grand jury declared that after hearing all the evidence submitted, it did not find that the facts warranted the indictment of any one.

Work on Flynn Estate Reviewed

In discussing the work done on the Flynn estate on Nov. 14, 15, 17 and 18 of last year, the presentment said city employes had been transported to the estate from the city by city-owned station wagons and that the work had consisted of laying 8,000 second-hand granite blocks.

The city employes, the presentment said, were paid in full for their services; 8,000 blocks were returned to the city and the gasoline and oil issued to the city station wagons for the Mahopac trip were returned in full. The cost of trucking the blocks by private concerns was paid by Mr. Flynn. The courtyard was only part of a general alteration on the estate, while the total job to cost more than $30,000.

The evidence adduced, it continued, showed that Mr. Flynn had never expressed any desire that the work be done under city auspices or by city employes and without expense to him, but that the job would be done by a private contractor and paid for by Mr. Flynn. The work done by city employes was under the supervision of Robert J. Moran, Bronx Commissioner of Public Works.

Paul J. Kern, deposed president of the Civil Service Commission, who conducted an investigation into the paving job while still in office, was severely rebuked by the grand jury for hampering the investigation conducted by William B. Herlands, Commissioner of Investigation.

No Conspiracy Found

"In respect to the second phase of the investigation," the presentment said, "the alleged conspiracy between Mayor La Guardia, Mr. Flynn and Commissioner Herlands to suppress the Kern investigation, the charge was entirely without foundation and we feel that it never would have been made but for the fact that Mr. Kern is greatly influenced by what he terms 'his intuition.' "

Mr. Kern had charged that Mayor La Guardia was trying to suppress his investigation in Mr. Flynn's behalf, and that in return Mr. Flynn was to obtain for the Mayor the Democratic nomination for United States Senator.

The grand jurors found that the records of the Department of Highways and Sewers under Commissioner Moran were in a "deplorable condition." They said they believed Borough President James J. Lyons when he testified that he was ignorant of the Mahopac paving job, and "we strongly condemn tha. ignorance." Commissioner Moran, they said, was Mr. Lyons's appointee and the Borough President could not avoid responsibility for the manner in which any subordinate conducted a department.

The Grand Jury's Presentment

In its presentment the grand jury said:

"The subject matter of our investigation resolved itself, naturally, into three phases; (1) The Mahopac

Continued on Page Twenty-eight

Direct Hit on Tirpitz By British Reported

By Telephone to THE NEW YORK TIMES.

STOCKHOLM, Sweden, May 5—British Royal Air Force bombs scored a direct hit on the battleship Tirpitz when she was in Kiel harbor prior to her transfer to her present anchorage at Trondheim, Norway, according to an eyewitness account by a Swedish seaman published in Ny Dag. The observer also reported a great change of morale among German civilians.

"Although the British attacks on Kiel were usually made from a great height, sometimes from 20,000 feet," he is quoted as saying, "the bombs hit their targets with astonishing precision. Thus in every bombing the biggest wharf in Kiel was regularly set ablaze, and on one occasion a British bomber scored a direct hit on the Tirpitz."

FOE ENTERS CHINA ACROSS BURMA LINE

Advance Units Over Border While Main Columns Wait— Planes Aid British Retreat

By DAVID ANDERSON
Wireless to THE NEW YORK TIMES.

LONDON, May 5—The Japanese have entered Yunnan Province in China via the Burma Road, it was announced today. Their vanguards reached the suburbs of Wanting, which is on a small river dividing Burma and China, and Chungking said the Japanese were being engaged by Chinese troops in the hills. The main enemy column was waiting within Burma at Chukok, near by.

The invading force must have made a detour around the Chinese fighting at Kutkai because the battle there was reported still going on. Other Chinese units were believed holding out north of Mandalay on the banks of the Irrawaddy River. British soldiers were continuing their slow retreat west of Mandalay.

"At times their [the Japanese]

Continued on Page Four

BRITISH ADVANCING

Landing Force Reported Within Four Miles of Madagascar Base

'CHUTISTS ARE USED

Warships and Aircraft Make Frontal Assault to Help Troops

By RAYMOND DANIELL
Wireless to THE NEW YORK TIMES.

LONDON, May 5—Small units of British Commandos and regular troops won a bridgehead at Courier Bay in the action against Madagascar and were reported tonight to be fighting their way across a ten-mile-wide isthmus toward the important naval base of Diego Suarez.

[A London dispatch of The Associated Press quoted Vichy reports that waves of British parachutists had been landed at the outset of a double attack in which warships and squadrons of aircraft made a frontal thrust from the sea timed to coincide with the overland assault on the rear of the base by British light armored units landed at Courier Bay.

[The Associated Press said, according to advices released by Vichy sources, the British occupying forces had reached Andrakaka, four miles from Diego Suarez. The French estimated that the attacking forces numbered 20,000 and the French and native defenders about 7,000.]

There were only sketchy accounts of the battle for the big French island, which lies athwart vital United Nations supply routes. However, a joint Admiralty-War Office communiqué issued this afternoon clearly indicated that opposition had been offered by the Vichy French garrison. The capture of a defending battery was reported.

A communiqué issued late to-

Continued on Page Two

JAPANESE FINALLY TAKE CORREGIDOR

Japanese forces attacking from the Bataan Peninsula have forced the surrender of Corregidor and other United States island fortresses at the entrance to Manila Bay.

Laval Protests 'Aggression' But Won't Seek U. S. Break

By LANSING WARREN

VICHY, France, May 5—Replying to the American note expressing approbation of the British occupation of Madagascar, Pierre Laval as Chief of the French Government and Foreign Minister, tonight protested the move as an aggression. He rejected as inadmissible the "pretension of the Government of the United States to forbid France to defend her territory when attacked," and declared that he leaves "to President Roosevelt the share of responsibility that may fall to him in consequence of this aggression."

[In Washington, Secretary Hull made it clear that there would be no deviation from the approval of the British action at Madagascar. After a White House session, Pacific War Council members praised the move.]

M. Laval, in handing his note to the American Chargé d'Affaires, S. Pinckney Tuck, recalled the long record of friendship between France and the United States and added:

"You were present at my recent interview with your Ambassador, Admiral Leahy, and I wish again to repeat to you what I said to him, that no definitive gesture leading to a break will be initiated by France."

Indicates Grave Situation

M. Laval read his reply to the assembled French and foreign press in a salon of the Hotel du Parc, and completed it with comments that indicated the full seriousness of French-American relations because the United States was directly involved in diplomatic controversy with France.

Following is the text of the note as read to the correspondents by M. Laval:

In replying to the note handed in today by the Chargé d'Affaires of the United States of America, the French Government raises the most energetic protest against the aggression of which Madagascar has just been the object on the part of British forces.

It notes the assurance given that Madagascar will be returned to France some day.

It rejects as inadmissible the pretension of the Government of the United States to forbid France to defend her territory when attacked.

The French Government is the sole judge of the obligations imposed by its honor. In that manner, the defenders of Madagascar, have understood correctly their duties. They have not hesitated, despite their numerical inferiority, to carry out their duties according to the most noble tradition of the French Army.

England so often since the Armistice has manifested hostility to France and the aggression

Continued on Page Two

RED ARMY ATTACKS KEY GERMAN BASES

Timoshenko Smashes at Kursk, Kharkov and Taganrog to Forestall Nazi Drive

By The Associated Press.

MOSCOW, May 5—Stealing the jump on Reichsfuehrer Hitler, hundreds of thousands of Russian soldiers, tanks and planes smashed head-on today at three key German bases from which it was believed the Nazi leader was planning his Spring or Summer drive.

Under command of Marshal Semyon Timoshenko, the first Russian general to turn back the German military machine with the recapture of Rostov last November, the Red Army struck at Kharkov, Kursk and Taganrog in the strongest Nazi-held section of the long battle line.

Action was also stepped-up in the northern sectors, particularly the hard-fought Kalinin area northwest of Moscow. The army newspaper Red Star said the Germans were

Continued on Page Ten

OTHER FORTS FALL

American Soldiers Had Held Out in Spite of Supply Shortage

COURAGE IS PRAISED

Roosevelt Views Their Example as Guarantee of Final Victory

By The Associated Press.

AT UNITED NATIONS HEADQUARTERS, Australia, Wednesday, May 6—The American fortress of Corregidor and the other fortified islands in the entrance to Manila Bay surrendered today, it was officially announced here.

Besides the rock that is Corregidor, the United States forts that had held out were Fort Hughes, Fort Drum and Fort Frank.

The end came in the second day of the final Japanese assault, launched at midnight Tuesday, Manila time, with landings from Bataan Peninsula after Corregidor had been pounded again and again by Japanese big guns and aerial bombs. Corregidor alone had had 300 air raids since Dec. 29, when thirty-five Japanese bombers attacked for three hours.

A spokesman for General Douglas MacArthur, who led the brilliant defense of Bataan and the forts at the mouth of Manila Bay until ordered to Australia, made this announcement:

"General Wainwright has surrendered Corregidor and the other fortified islands in Manila Harbor."

There were believed to be about 7,000 men and women altogether on Corregidor and the other fortified islands. Besides the original garrisons, there was a naval detachment consisting originally of some 3,500 Marines and bluejackets who were removed to Corregidor when fighting ceased April 9 on Bataan Peninsula. A group of Army nurses also reached Corregidor.

Troops Half-Starved

By CHARLES HURD

WASHINGTON, May 5—The fortified island of Corregidor in Manila Bay, last bastion of the American defenders of the Philippine Island, Luzon, was fighting a landing attack by Japanese troops today.

The issue of the fighting was not known in Washington at 5 P. M., when the War Department issued a communiqué, but two factors indicated grave concern over the outcome of a contest in which the defenders were outnumbered.

Continued on Page Five

Mrs. Rosenberg in 2 Federal Jobs While Making $22,500 on the Side

By LOUIS STARK
Special to THE NEW YORK TIMES.

WASHINGTON, May 5—Some members of the House Appropriations Committee asserted today that they were determined to write into all future supply bills a provision prohibiting Federal administrative officials from accepting employment outside the government. This came following the disclosure at a closed meeting of an appropriations subcommittee today that Mrs. Anna M. Rosenberg of New York, regional director of the Social Security Board, receives a large income from private industry and also draws pay from another agency.

Mrs. Rosenberg's Social Security Board post pays $7,500 on a full time basis. Beside this Federal position she revealed to the subcommittee today that she received $20,000 a year for part time work as public and labor relations consultant to the Macy-Bamberger stores in New York and Newark, and $2,500 a year for similar services performed for I. Miller, New York shoe dealer.

In addition, Mrs. Rosenberg is a consultant on the staff of Nelson Rockefeller, coordinator of American Affairs. For this service she receives $6,000 a year. Her total earnings therefore are $36,000 a year, $13,500 paid by two government agencies and $22,500 by industry.

Arthur J. Altmeyer, chairman of the Social Security Board, who accompanied Mrs. Rosenberg to the committee meeting today, revealed that when the regional directorship was offered to her six years ago Mrs. Rosenberg made it a condition that she be permitted to continue her work as labor relations consultant for private concerns. Correspond-

Continued on Page Twenty-eight

War News Summarized

WEDNESDAY, MAY 6, 1942

Corregidor, the island fortress at the entrance to Manila Bay, was surrendered to the Japanese after a furious assault. The British were engaged in breaking French resistance to their landing in Madagascar. Japanese forces reached and crossed the Burma-China frontier. Other war fronts were largely unchanged.

The surrender of Corregidor and other island bases was announced by United Nations Headquarters in Australia, following an earlier Washington communiqué stating that the Japanese had started landing operations. The defenders were reported to be short of both food and ammunition. [1:8.]

British landing forces on Madagascar were reported to be within four miles of the Diego Suarez naval base at the northern extremity of the island. The French garrison was resisting, but Vichy reported that some 20,000 British had landed or were preparing to land. London said the Commandos had encountered little resistance. [1:5; map, P. 2.]

The Vichy regime ordered the garrison at Madagascar to resist. Pierre Laval in a note to the United States Government rejected Washington's warning against French belligerent action, but he insisted his government would not be the first to take measures to break relations with the United States. Admiral Darlan, chief of the Vichy military forces, expressed extreme bitterness toward Britain. [1:6-7.]

Secretary of State Hull indicated clearly in his press conference that the United States would adhere to a policy of full support of British occupation of Madagascar. [3:1.]

Meanwhile, Japanese forces in Burma had reached the Chinese frontier in the Burma Road sector and had penetrated a slight distance into China. A battle was raging on the frontier, and the Japanese had been halted, according to Chungking. United States bombers from India attacked successfully Mingaladon airport north of Rangoon. The Japanese said their planes had set on fire the Chinese city of Yungchang, 120 miles inside China in Yunnan Province. [1:4; map, P. 4.]

Chungking said that Chinese guerrillas in Eastern China had raided fifteen Japanese-occupied cities during the past two weeks and destroyed power plants and communications. [6:3, with map.]

The United Nations Australian Headquarters announced successful air attacks on Lae, New Guinea, and Rabaul, New Britain. A Japanese air attack on Port Moresby was repulsed. [4:4.]

On the other side of the world, London announced Royal Air Force attacks on the Skoda munitions plant in Czechoslovakia and factories at Stuttgart in Southwestern Germany. The Germans raided points on the British south coast. [10:2.]

The story was heard in London that a group of German generals had informed Adolf Hitler that if the campaign in Russia this year should fail, they would seek to abolish the National Socialist system. [8:4-5.]

Moscow reported an offensive in the south against German-held Kharkov, Kursk and Taganrog. [1:7.]

Washington disclosed the sinking of three more merchant vessels off the United States coast. [5:1.]

G. M. Defies WLB on Double Pay; Hearing Will Take Up Issue Today

Special to THE NEW YORK TIMES.

DETROIT, Mich., May 5—On the eve of the start of negotiations before a panel of the National War Labor Board between the General Motors Corporation and the United Automobile Workers, C. I. O., C. E. Wilson, president of the corporation, revealed today that it had defied the board on the issue of double-time pay for Sunday and holiday work.

The disclosure came in the release by Mr. Wilson of the texts of exchanges of correspondence among the corporation, the board and the union. The correspondence dated from April 27. It included a copy of the order by the board to Mr. Wilson May 1 that double-time pay for Sunday work be continued by the company to May 18.

In reply to the order, the releases by Mr. Wilson showed, H. W. Anderson, vice president of General Motors, sent the board on May 2 a telegram which said that "we protest and do not agree to comply with your directive order."

The hearings before the NWLB panel are scheduled to open in Washington tomorrow morning. They aim at a renewal of the union contract which expired April 28. The contract has been continued in effect except for a stipulation signed by General Motors April 27 that "pending a final adjustment," double time "will not be paid for Sunday and holiday work." It has been agreed that when a new agreement is reached all its terms will be retroactive to April 28.

Walter P. Reuther, director of the General Motors division of the union, has made known that the union wished to have the Washington hearing open to the public, including the press. In reply to the order, the releases by Mr. Wilson showed, H. W. Anderson, vice president of General Motors, sent the board on May

Continued on Page Fourteen

"All the News That's Fit to Print."

The New York Times.

LATE CITY EDITION
Little change in temperature today.
Temperatures Yesterday—Max., 85 ; Min., 69

VOL. XCI . No. 30,830.

Entered as Second-Class Matter,
Postoffice, New York, N. Y.

Copyright, 1942, by The New York Times Company.

NEW YORK, MONDAY, JUNE 22, 1942.

THREE CENTS NEW YORK CITY
and Vicinity

TOBRUK FALLS, AXIS CLAIMS 25,000 PRISONERS; GERMANS DRIVE WEDGE INTO SEVASTOPOL LINES; JAPANESE ASHORE ON KISKA IN THE ALEUTIANS

'GAS' DROUGHT CUTS HOLIDAY PLEASURE AS CITY SWELTERS

New Yorkers Stay at Home or Drive Only to Suburbs—Many Avoid Main Roads

CROWDS AT SOME RESORTS

Others Are Hard Hit as Travel Is Spotty—Humidity Soars and Mercury Reaches 84°

New Yorkers, afflicted with the first sweltering Sunday of the season under the gasoline shortage, stayed at home yesterday, sitting on the sidewalks or in penthouse or roof gardens, or went to near-by parks and beaches. Pleasure driving was only half of normal, by and large, and the resorts, particularly the distant ones, bore the brunt of the decline. Relatives and friends in the suburbs apparently had many visitors.

The heat was not record-breaking. Temperatures rose from a low of 69 degrees at 8:45 A. M. to a high of 84 degrees at 5:30 P. M. The humidity, however, remained at 75 per cent, which the Weather Bureau said was extremely high for such high temperatures. In the morning two-tenths of an inch of rain fell and skies were overcast long after, accounting for many of the stay-at-homes in the city.

Brooklyn's first heat prostration of the season was reported last night when John Chambers, 45 years old, of 244 West End Avenue, Coney Island, collapsed as he was walking in Flatbush Avenue near East Twenty-sixth Street, Brooklyn. He was removed to Coney Island Hospital, where his condition was described as fair.

Motoring Is Spotty

The drop in pleasure driving, although marked as far as resorts were concerned, and severe if parkway use was an accurate indication, did not fully reflect the gasoline supply situation.. With many stations dry, traffic on the George Washington Bridge was reported normal for a Sunday, through the Holland Tunnel a third off, and over other bridge and tunnel exits the reduction was not significant.

Yet on the Westchester parkways motor traffic was 30 per cent of normal and on the Long Island parkways about 60 per cent of normal. Police traffic experts believed that this reflected the spotty character of the gasoline shortage, which was acute in Westchester and near-by Long Island and some sections of New Jersey, but not serious in others.

Those who had gasoline in their tanks apparently went pleasure driving in spite of the appeals to save gasoline, but avoided the parkways and resorts, where they would be conspicuous. Many, the traffic experts thought, must have gone to visit friends and relatives

Continued on Page Nine

If in Doubt, Put It Out

Carelessness remains the greatest enemy of the Army's dimout regulations, it was said yesterday by civilian lighting experts who have been working with the Army on ways of cutting down the nightly illumination over the city that is used by enemy submarines in spotting shipping off our coast.

Windows and doors thoughtlessly opened for relief from the heat continue to loose light rays that help build up the sky glow over the metropolitan area, these experts said. They urged that whenever a window or door is opened for this purpose, it should be properly shaded or screened to prevent direct rays of light from emerging. These and other precautions should be placed in effect by one hour after sundown, which is at 8:31 P. M. tonight.

Meanwhile, the Army adjures all citizens: "If in doubt, put it out."

Peter of Yugoslavia Reaches Washington

Special to THE NEW YORK TIMES.

WASHINGTON, June 21—King Peter of Yugoslavia arrived here by airplane today. He was accompanied by M. Nincitch, the Yugoslav Foreign Minister.

They will discuss with President Roosevelt and other officials their country's continued opposition to the Axis. One of their objectives, it is understood, will be to obtain lease-lend aid for the guerrilla forces resisting the Nazis in Yugoslavia.

The King and his entourage will spend tonight at Blair House and will leave tomorrow to spend a few days in the country. He is traveling incognito until Wednesday, when he will return to Washington to begin the official program of his visit to the United States.

DIMOUT 'FAILURE' IS LAID TO MAYOR

Defense Council Members Say He Has Not Ordered Police to Enforce Army Rules

Charges that Mayor La Guardia has failed to give the Police Department orders to enforce the Army's dimout regulations, but has endeavored unsuccessfully to get the Army to modify its specifications, were advanced yesterday by two members of the executive board of the Lower West Side Defense Council, acting as a special committee in behalf of the council.

Howard Mulligan, a lawyer, of 103 Waverly Place, and J. B. C. Woods of 38 Perry Street, made public copies of a letter they had sent to the Mayor charging that conditions in their area were "deplorable." Mr. Mulligan explained that he and Mr. Woods had been authorized to take this action at a meeting of the council's headquarters, 27 Barrow Street, last Tuesday evening.

"Nightly, men are dying and ships are being sunk by the enemy off our coast because you, sir, prefer not to carry out the Army's orders," the letter charged.

In his weekly radio broadcast on June 7 Mayor La Guardia an-

Continued on Page Thirteen

RED ARMY RETIRES

Paris Radio Says Nazi Troops Have Reached Town of Sevastopol

AXIS LOSSES SEVERE

Placed at 7 Divisions—Germans Repelled on Kharkov Front

By RALPH PARKER
Wireless to THE NEW YORK TIMES.

MOSCOW, Monday, June 22—The Russian High Command acknowledges in its communiqué this morning that the Germans have succeeded, at a high cost in lives lost, in driving a wedge into the defenses of Sevastopol. But the bulletin also reports the repulse of numerous severe German assaults on the Sevastopol front.

[The German-controlled Paris radio said today that German troops had reached the town of Sevastopol after breaking through the Russian inner defense lines, The United Press reported from London. German sappers smashed their way through the final defense line outside the town with flame throwers, the Paris broadcast claimed.]

[The Germans reported the Red Army forces on the Kharkov front, where fighting on any considerable scale appears to be confined to one narrow sector, are said to have achieved an important success. After two enemy regiments had crossed a river barrier and advanced on the eastern bank, the Russians struck back, driving the Germans into and across the river. The Russians themselves then crossed the river and captured points on the western bank.

Press reports yesterday indicated that the Germans were continuing to pour troops into the Sevastopol fighting and that the situation there was grave. These reports said that waves of German and Rumanian infantry, attacking Russian lines in the southern sector of the Crimean base's defenses while planes dive-bombed Soviet artillery positions, had

Continued on Page Five

NEW LANDING MADE

Japanese Cruiser Is Hit in Army Air Blow at Kiska's Harbor

TRANSPORT IS SUNK

U. S. Fliers See Enemy's Temporary Buildings on Aleutian Isle

By C. BROOKS PETERS

WASHINGTON, June 21—The Japanese forces that have been operating in the western Aleutian Islands since June 3 have succeeded in occupying Kiska, 650 miles west of Dutch Harbor, strategic American operations base, the Navy Department announced today.

Enemy occupation of Attu, westernmost island of the American chain and some 275 miles northwest of Kiska, was acknowledged on June 12.

Flying conditions in the Aleutian region—in which "foul weather and fog" are the general rule, the Navy reported recently—were sufficiently satisfactory in the last few days to permit "some restricted air operations against Kiska," today's Navy communiqué asserted.

Long-range Army aircraft attacked a small force of Japanese ships in Kiska's harbor and reported hits on a cruiser, the Navy announced. An enemy transport was sunk.

Tents of Japanese Seen

The American planes that finally were able to penetrate to the remote island of Kiska, where enemy forces the United States Navy maintained a weather station, observed that the enemy had set up tents and "minor temporary structures on land."

The communiqué added that operations in that area continued to be restricted "by considerations of weather and great distances."

Last Monday the Navy Department reported that Army and Navy planes were continuing air assaults "against the Japanese forces which recently were reported to have landed on western islands of the Aleutian group." At that time the Navy asserted that at least three Japanese cruisers, one destroyer, one gunboat and one transport had been damaged, "some of them severely," by air attacks.

Since the announcement on June 12 of the occupation of Attu naval circles in Washington have minimized the seriousness of the Japanese landings in the western Aleutians, characterizing them as having been inspired primarily by a desire "to save face" after the defeat administered by American Army and Navy forces in the Coral Sea and off Midway Island.

Supply Problem Difficult

Military experts here have stated that supply would be a major problem for any enemy forces that endeavored to establish themselves in the Aleutians. The distance from bases in Japanese territory to the Aleutian Islands is so great, these circles have contended, that aerial transport is not feasible, particularly in view of the uncertain weather conditions. Therefore, supplies must be transported by surface craft, which are constantly exposed to attack by American submarines.

There is, however, a possibility that in the Rat Island group, of which Kiska is one island, the Japanese could conceal submarine mother ships and perhaps even small aircraft carriers, the experts here said. Submarines from such bases might prove effective should Japan attack Russia, they added.

But for the most part, according to the opinion conveyed to reporters in Washington by military circles, the enemy will have to es-

Continued on Page Four

ROMMEL'S FORCES TAKE IMPORTANT PORT IN LIBYA

Tobruk (1) has been overwhelmed and captured with its garrison by the Axis, which also claimed the capture of Bir el-Gobi (2) and the minor port of Bardia (3). There were indications that the Germans were working their way from Bardia southward to Capuzzo for an assault across the border into Egypt. Here they will find defenses between Solum and Sidi Omar (4).

Vancouver Island Shelled; Northwest Coast Dims Out

By P. J. PHILIP

OTTAWA, June 21—Estevan Point on Vancouver Island was shelled by an enemy submarine at 10:35 o'clock, Pacific time, last night (1:35 A. M., Sunday, Eastern war time), Colonel J. L. Ralston, the Defense Minister, announced here today. The submarine was presumed to be Japanese.

The enemy's objective was the government wireless and telegraph station there. No damage was done, said a report from Lieut. Gen. Kenneth Stuart, Canadian Chief of Staff and acting Commander in Chief of the West Corps defenses.

[Coastal dimouts in the States of Washington and Oregon went into effect last night, following the shelling of Estevan Point, which is about 125 miles north of the United States border.]

There is an airfield near Estevan Point, but no report has come through as to whether action was taken against the attacking submarine.

The attack was the first against Canadian soil in the history of Canada as a Dominion. Last month two ships were torpedoed and sunk in the Gulf of St. Lawrence.

The Defense Minister's announcement said:

"The Commander in Chief, West Coast defenses, reported that the Dominion Government telegraph station at Estevan Point, Vancouver Island, was shelled by a submarine at 10:35 P. M. (Pacific time) on Saturday night. No damage resulted."

Estevan Point lies halfway along the western shore of Vancouver Island, about 150 miles northwest of Victoria. Its only importance seems to be the estab-

Continued on Page Four

R. A. F. PAYS EMDEN 2D VISIT IN 2 NIGHTS

Also Hammers Other Targets in Northwest Reich—Hits Ship Off Dutch Coast

By JAMES MacDONALD
Wireless to THE NEW YORK TIMES.

LONDON, June 21—A large number of British bombers hammered Emden, Germany, last night for the second night in succession and also other objectives in Northwest Germany and air bases in the Netherlands.

At the same time new-built Hudson planes of the Coastal Command, ever on the lookout for enemy shipping, searched waters off the Netherland coast, where a Canadian flying crew dropped two bombs on a medium-sized cargo vessel.

The communiqué announcing these operations did not divulge the number of planes engaged, but said that last night the Royal Air Force six bombers and one Coastal Command plane. The R. A. F. losses were increased today when one fighter plane failed to return home from a daylight attack on Dunkerque.

[The Berlin radio went off the air at 1:50 A. M. today, a possible sign that British bombers were again over Germany, The United Press reported from London.

[German planes dropped bombs early today in a sharp attack on the south coast of England, The Associated Press reported. Two of the raiders were shot down and two more Nazi planes destroyed over Europe.]

As in the case of the R. A. F. raids on Emden late Friday night and early yesterday morning, the Air Ministry did not go into details about the targets for the night or indicate the extent of damage.

While patrolling along the Netherland coast during the night Coastal Command fliers caught up with an enemy convoy of three ships. The rear gunner on a Canadian-manned plane said on his return to his base that he saw two bombs hit one vessel amidship, hurling debris high in the air in the resulting explosions. Whether the vessel sank was not determined. What became of her two companion ships was not learned here. Although the sky was clear, there was less daylight activity to-

Continued on Page Five

NEWS PUTS DAMPER ON CHURCHILL VISIT

But Washington Sees Mid-East Crisis as Incidental in His Planning With Roosevelt

By JAMES B. RESTON
Special to THE NEW YORK TIMES.

WASHINGTON, June 21—Washington was in a sober and realistic mood tonight. The fall of Tobruk and the situation for the Russians at Sevastopol have put a damper on speculation that has surrounded the Roosevelt-Churchill talks. The chief immediate concern was viewed as the holding of the second front the United Nations now have in Egypt, rather than opening up new fronts on the European continent.

The President and Mr. Churchill continued their talks during the day, and the chiefs of staff of the United States and Britain, General George C. Marshall and General Sir Alan Brooke, who came to the United States with Mr. Churchill, continued their exchange of information and their planning for the future.

The plain and simple truth about these important discussions is that only a few persons know what has gone on since Mr. Churchill arrived, and they are not telling what they know.

The purpose of the conversations is much less complicated, dramatic and urgent than one would tend to deduce from the secrecy with which they have been surrounded.

It is undoubtedly true, as Stephen Early, White House secretary, has said, that they are dealing with the future plans of the United Nations. Within a matter of hours the battle was over.

Continued on Page Eight

'Never a Dull Moment' at Midway, Reporter Watching Battle Found

The following account of the Battle of Midway is by a correspondent of THE NEW YORK TIMES who was aboard one of the United States warships.

By FOSTER HAILEY
Special to THE NEW YORK TIMES.

WITH THE PACIFIC FLEET, at Sea, June 4 (Delayed)—Today is the day. Mark it on your calendar in red ink, Thursday, June 4. It may be the one on which the tide definitely turned in the battle of the Pacific.

This morning at dawn the Japanese launched planes from a strong striking force northwest of Midway. We are in a position to strike them on the flank. If our planes can only get to their carriers before the Japanese planes attacking Midway car return, the result may be a naval disaster for the Japanese.

"We should be in launching distance soon."

The dawn was a gloomy one, but now the clouds are breaking up.

Continued on Page Two

NAZIS NEAR EGYPT

British Are on Border as Rommel Presses On After Victory

PORT'S LOSS SERIOUS

Plan for a Second Front Seen Upset by Need to Hold New Line

By DAVID ANDERSON
Special Cable to THE NEW YORK TIMES.

LONDON, June 21—A smashing blow delivered yesterday by waves of German tanks, heavily supported from the air, crushed the defenses of Tobruk in Libya. The loss of the town, already claimed by the enemy, who said 25,000 prisoners, including "several generals" had been captured.

The story of what happened, as given by both German and Italian sources, appears to cover the battle fairly fully, but the accuracy of these reports cannot be checked at present. Briefly, it can be said Field Marshal Erwin Rommel's armored units that had passed Tobruk in pursuit of the British Eighth Army did so to make certain whether the British showed any signs of preparing a counterattack.

When the German Marshal was satisfied this was not the case he reversed his forces, bringing back tanks against Tobruk from the south, driving from the vicinity of Ed Duda, and did this fiercely with every ounce of power at his command. At the same time the Luftwaffe began intensive bombing of Tobruk's defenses. Within a matter of hours the battle was over.

Tobruk Long in Battle

Tobruk must have been softer in its last moments than during the many other attacks it beat off during the last seventeen months since it was captured from the Italians on Jan 22, 1941. It has been on the fringe of the Libyan battlefield for some weeks with inevitable strain as strategy wavered between one of concentration of strength there and one of evacuation.

Despite the presence of a large garrison when Tobruk fell it is believed there was not time to lay minefields on its perimeter or otherwise strengthen the British positions to face an immediate storming.

A Cairo communiqué, released here at noon today, paved the way for the worst. It read:

"Yesterday the enemy attacked the perimeter of Tobruk in great strength. In spite of most determined resistance by our forces the enemy succeeded in penetrating the defenses and in occupying a considerable area inside them."

Twelve strong points in the defenses were taken by the first wave of enemy tanks, according to Berlin. This made a wedge two and a half miles wide, and German sources state the British defenders then realized that further resistance was useless.

Bombers Blast Defenses

But they had other reasons for weighing most seriously the advantage of carrying on the fight. The Germans said today that "numerous bombers" ceaselessly attack wrought great destruction in the fortifications and other military works of the port and town.

It was not long after noon yesterday when large formations of German bombers swooped down on a group of four anti-aircraft batteries, all of which were silenced, it was reported by Berlin. Still more of the Luftwaffe's heavy aircraft, laden with high explosives, cruised over a column of twenty tanks, setting many of them ablaze.

Finally, the German radio said, "About 2 P. M. another great attack was made on Tobruk, which lasted three hours without interruption and caused numerous fires.

Continued on Page Two

War News Summarized

MONDAY, JUNE 22, 1942

Tobruk fell yesterday, and the resultant threat to Egypt and the British position in the Eastern Mediterranean changed the war picture drastically, while the Russians acknowledged a significant German advance at Sevastopol, though at the cost of heavy enemy losses.

Tobruk fell to a smashing blow delivered by waves of German tanks according to London reports. The Germans claimed that 25,000 prisoners had been taken. In London the opinion prevailed that they had not time to lay minefields around Tobruk before the Axis attack. [1:8.]

Military observers in London referred to the fall of Tobruk as an "incontestable disaster." The Germans were believed to have obtained a large quantity of stores. General Rommel was expected to drive on Suez. [2:2.]

British bombers attacked Emden, German submarine base, for the second successive night, airfields in the Netherlands and enemy shipping off the Netherland coast. Heavy air attacks were also made on the French and Belgian coasts. [1:5.]

Moscow granted that the defenders of Sevastopol had been forced to fall back as the enemy forced a wedge in their lines, but declared that the action had crippled five German and two Rumanian divisions. Sharp activity was reported in the Kharkov and Leningrad sectors. [1:2.]

President Kalinin of the Soviet Union, in a review of a year of war, stated that the Germans no longer were capable of a general offensive. [5:5; map, P. 5.]

Lord Beaverbrook, addressing a "Salute to Russia" meeting in Britain, again urged the United Nations to open a second front. He asserted that the British Army was now sufficiently prepared. [3:1.]

Chungking reported that the Japanese had been halted in Kiangsi and had lost 1,300 troops in Honan. The Minister of War asserted that the Japanese soon would be so bogged down in China that they would not be able to attack Russia with full strength. [4:1.]

The United States Navy announced that Japanese forces in the Aleutians had succeeded in occupying the island of Kiska, 650 miles west of Dutch Harbor. Bomb hits were made on a Japanese cruiser and a Japanese transport was sunk. [1:4; map, P. 4.]

Colonel J. L. Ralston, Canadian Defense Minister, disclosed that a government telegraph station at Estevan Point, Vancouver Island, had been shelled by a submarine Saturday night, but no damage was done. [1:3-6.]

As President Roosevelt and Prime Minister Churchill continued their conversations yesterday Washington reported that the fall of Tobruk and Russian withdrawals at Sevastopol had checked "second front speculation." Concern was being shown over the necessity for holding the present front in Egypt. [1:7.]

"All the News That's Fit to Print."

NEWS INDEX, PAGE 55, THIS SECTION

The New York Times.

Copyright, 1942, by The New York Times Company.

LATE CITY EDITION
Continued cool today with light winds.
Temperatures Yesterday—Max.,57; Min.,45
Sunrise, 7:54 A. M.; Sunset, 5:45 P. M.

Section 1

VOL. XCII—No. 30,969.

Entered as Second-Class Matter,
Postoffice, New York, N. Y.

NEW YORK, SUNDAY, NOVEMBER 8, 1942.

Including Magazine and Book Sections.

TEN CENTS
New York City and Vicinity

AMERICAN FORCES LAND IN FRENCH AFRICA; BRITISH NAVAL, AIR UNITS ASSISTING THEM; EFFECTIVE SECOND FRONT, ROOSEVELT SAYS

U.S. DRIVES ON BUNA

American Troops Flown to Area Closing In on Big Japanese Base

PAPUA IS OVERRUN

All Except Beachhead of Buna-Gona Seized in New Guinea Push

By The Associated Press.

AT UNITED NATIONS HEADQUARTERS, Australia, Sunday, Nov. 8.—American combat troops are in action near Buna, vital Japanese base on the north New Guinea coast, General Douglas MacArthur disclosed today.

Simultaneously, General MacArthur disclosed that the Allies have occupied Goodenough Island to the northeast of New Guinea, off Collingwood Bay, in an obvious flanking movement.

[American Army troops on Guadalcanal advanced on Friday (Solomons time) in the area to the west of Henderson airfield, the Navy reported yesterday. They crossed the Matanikau River a few miles south of Koli Point, where the Japanese recently landed reinforcements, but met little opposition.]

It was from Buna, in midsummer, that the Japanese began a drive across tortuous trails of the Owen Stanley Mountains which carried to within thirty-two miles of Port Moresby, Allied base on the south coast, before it was stalled. Late in September the Allies began encircling and infiltration movements which rolled the Japanese back and yesterday's communiqué had mentioned bitter fighting at Oivi, which is fifty-five miles south of Buna.

Japanese Resist at Oisi

"American ground troops in force, transported by air from Australia during the last month, have penetrated Central and Northern Papua to the vicinity of Buna," a communiqué stated.

"The Allied forces now control all of Papua except the beach head in the Buna-Gona area."

The surprising development came as a thrust around the eastern end of New Guinea from Milne Bay where Japanese troops landed in July only to be pinned against the sea and slain or forced to their ships.

"Units from Milne Bay," the communiqué said, "have now completed clearing remnants of hostile forces from the islands to the north and have occupied adjacent strategic points."

While this disclosure was being made, Australian ground forces still were meeting fierce resistance at Oivi where the retreating Japanese are making a stand. Today's communiqué said the Australians maintained constant pressure and were resorting to their hitherto successful tactics of local encircling movements in efforts to dislodge the defenders.

The Allied air force continued to support the overland drive with strafing attacks on the Japanese troops.

[Delayed dispatches from Harold Guard, United Press staff correspondent in New Guinea, revealed that the Americans had

Continued on Page Forty-five

When You Think of Writing Think of Whiting—Advt.

LEADS IN AFRICA

Lieut. Gen. Dwight Eisenhower
Associated Press

R. A. F. ROCKS GENOA; U. S. RAID ON BREST

Bombers From Britain Pound North Italy 2 Nights in Row —Hit Nazis on Coast

Special Cable to THE NEW YORK TIMES.

LONDON, Sunday, Nov. 8.—Bombers from Britain struck a heavy blow at Northern Italy over Friday night, blasting the port of Genoa again in support of the Eighth Army's battling of the Nazis and Italians in the African desert.

Again last night the Royal Air Force sent its big bombers over Northern Italy, British officials reported briefly early today. The announcement meant that the R. A. F. from here was seeing to it that the Axis forces in Africa got no help from home.

American heavy bombers, both Flying Fortresses and Liberators, escorted by Allied fighters, carried out a smashing attack on the docks and U-boat pens at Brest in occupied France yesterday afternoon, United States Army headquarters here announced.

Bombs were seen to strike the targets at Brest. The communiqué stressed that sharp Nazi antiaircraft fire and enemy fighter opposition were encountered over the coast of Brittany.

The Brest raiders shot down four Nazi fighters. All the United States bombers returned, but one Allied fighter was lost.

The R. A. F.'s fighter squadrons

Continued on Page Four

NAZIS NEAR LIBYA

British Drive Out to Bar New Stand by Enemy or Reinforcements

FOE BOMBED ALL NIGHT

Pursuers Reported to Be Within 40 Miles of Halfaya Pass

By The United Press.

CAIRO, Egypt, Nov. 7.—The British Eighth Army under Lieut. Gen. Bernard L. Montgomery hurled armored forces, motorized infantry and swarms of planes tonight at the remnants of German General Field Marshal Erwin Rommel's once-proud Afrika Korps—possibly 25,000 out of an original 140,-000—now trying to brace for a stand at Halfaya (Hellfire) Pass on the Libyan frontier, 240 miles west of the Alamein battleground.

The main body of the British forces was reported to be well west of Matruh, 110 miles west of El Alamein, and advance striking forces were believed to be as far as 200 miles west of El Alamein, or close to the Egyptian-Libyan frontier, 240 miles west of El Alamein.

How many men Marshal Rommel had left in the Halfaya area could not be established. Already 20,000 prisoners have been counted in British hands. Marshal Rommel's desert casualties were estimated at approximately 20,000 more. In addition, 75,000 Italian troops had been left far behind the swirling battleground, ready to surrender when the British could find time and men to round them up.

Marshal Rommel entered the battle with a maximum of 140,000 troops in the forward area. It was doubted whether he had more than one or two divisions left to attempt another stand at Halfaya unless he had been able to rush large reinforcements from the rear.

It appeared possible tonight that the Axis forces might not even attempt to stand at Halfaya, but would, instead, continue their headlong flight as deeply as possible into Libya in an effort to open a gap between themselves and the Eighth Army.

Such a manoeuvre, however, may already be doomed to failure. General Montgomery has ordered a great convoys coming thousands off Marshal Rommel's retreat. It was believed that he might have sent a hard-hitting, fast-moving

Continued on Page Twenty-one

SHOCK TROOPS LEAD

Simultaneous Landings Made Before Dawn at Numerous Points

PLANES GUARD SKIES

An Armada Pours Men on the Beaches—Early Actions Satisfactory

By WES GALLAGHER
Associated Press Correspondent

ALLIED HEADQUARTERS IN NORTH AFRICA, Sunday, Nov. 8.—American soldiers, marines and sailors from one of the greatest armadas ever put into a single military operation swarmed ashore today on the Vichy-controlled North Africa shore before dawn, striking to break Hitler's hold on the Mediterranean.

[Reports reaching Allied headquarters in North Africa today disclosed that successful landings had been made by American assault parties on beaches of North Africa near two main objectives outlined in operational plans, an Associated Press dispatch stated.

[British forces reported attempting a landing at Algiers after a bombardment were said by the Vichy radio to have been "beaten off."]

Tall, decisive Lieut. Gen. Dwight D. (Ike) Eisenhower, supreme commander of the huge forces involved in the operation, worked throughout the night directing the first great American blow at the Axis.

Included in the forces were crack combat troops, Rangers (airborne units) and the cream of America's airmen.

British naval and air force units supported the American landing forces, who were preceded by a snowstorm of leaflets and a radio barrage promising the French that the United States had no intention of seizing French possessions and only sought to prevent Axis infiltration.

It undoubtedly was the longest over-water military operation ever attempted, with hundreds of ships in great convoys coming thousands of miles under the protection of British and American sea and air might.

I came on one of these big convoys.

Fighting-fit American soldiers

Continued on Page Five

WHERE THE UNITED STATES PREPARES FOR NEW FRONT

As the survivors of Marshal Rommel's beaten German legions fled westward toward the Libyan border (1), powerful American land, sea and air forces landed behind them at various places in Vichy France's colonies along the Mediterranean (2) and on the shores of the Atlantic, apparently in Morocco (3). British naval and aerial units are assisting them. There was no indication of military action against Vichy's possessions on the western bulge of the Atlantic (4). A large and comprehensive map of the African and Mediterranean theatre of war will be found on Page 1 of Section 4 of this issue of THE TIMES. However, Section 4 had gone to press before the announcement last night of the landing of American troops.

LANDING PLAN KEPT SECRET BY WRITERS

Americans Selected for Duty, Bureaus Sworn to Silence— Eisenhower Slipt Away

By RAYMOND DANIELL
Special Cable to THE NEW YORK TIMES.

LONDON, Sunday, Nov. 8.—For weeks American newspaper men have been the custodians of one of war's biggest secrets. It was not an easy secret to keep because although all that time they had to improvise excuses for the absence of a large number of the members of their London staffs to conceal the fact that they had gone with the expeditionary forces.

Most London offices of Amer-

Continued on Page Fourteen

President's Statement

Special to THE NEW YORK TIMES.

WASHINGTON, Nov. 7—President Roosevelt's statement announcing the opening of a second front in French North and West Africa follows:

In order to forestall an invasion of Africa by Germany and Italy, which, if successful, would constitute a direct threat to America across the comparatively narrow sea from Western Africa, a powerful American force equipped with adequate weapons of modern warfare and under American command is today landing on the Mediterranean and Atlantic coasts of the French colonies in Africa.

The landing of this American Army is being assisted by the British Navy and air forces, and it will, in the immediate future, be reinforced by a considerable number of divisions of the British Army.

This combined Allied force, under American command, in conjunction with the British campaign in Egypt is designed to prevent an occupation by the Axis armies of any part of Northern or Western Africa and to deny to the aggressor nations a starting point from which to launch an attack against the Atlantic coast of the Americas.

In addition, it provides an effective second-front assistance to our heroic allies in Russia.

The French Government and the French people have been informed of the purpose of this expedition and have been assured that the Allies seek no territory and have no intention of interfering with friendly French authorities in Africa.

The government of France and the people of France and the French possessions have been requested to cooperate with and assist the American expedition in its effort to repel the German and Italian 'international criminals, and by so doing to liberate France and the French Empire from the Axis yoke.

This expedition will develop into a major effort by the Allied Nations and there is every expectation that it will be successful in repelling the planned German and Italian invasion of Africa and prove the first historic step to the liberation and restoration of France.

Blow to Knock Italy Out of the War Called Goal of American Invasion

Special Cable to THE NEW YORK TIMES.

LONDON, Sunday, Nov. 8.—Allied Army, Navy and air forces commanded by Lieut. Gen. Dwight D. Eisenhower, commander of all American forces in the European theatre, have struck a powerful blow to free the Mediterranean from Axis control and knock Italy out of the war. That, in the opinion of military observers here, is the meaning of the movement of United States forces that now become part of the gigantic pincers with which it is expected that the last vestiges of the German and Italian forces in North Africa will be annihilated.

The first stage of the battle just beginning will be a struggle for the control of roads, railways and airfields in Algeria and the neighboring colony of Tunisia. Once the control of these has been won, Allied reinforcements and supplies will be able to dispense with the long journey around the Cape of Good Hope that has been one of

Continued on Page Thirteen

U.S. MEETS 'THREAT'

Big Expeditions Invade North and West Africa to Forestall Axis

EISENHOWER AT HEAD

President Urges French to Help, Calls Move Aid to Russia

Roosevelt's appeal to French people and Eisenhower's message to North Africans, Pg. 8.

By C. P. TRUSSELL
Special to THE NEW YORK TIMES.

WASHINGTON, Nov. 7—Powerful American forces, supported by British naval and air forces, landed simultaneously tonight at numerous points on the Mediterranean and Atlantic coasts of French North Africa, forestalling an anticipated invasion of Africa by Germany and Italy and launching effective second-front assistance to Russia, President Roosevelt announced tonight. Lieut. Gen. Dwight D. Eisenhower is in command.

The President made the announcement even as the American forces, equipped with adequate weapons of modern warfare, he emphasized, were making the landings.

President Speaks to France

Soon he was speaking direct to the French Government and the French people by short-wave radio and, in their own tongue, giving assurances that the Allies seek no territory and have no intention of interfering with friendly French, official or civilian. He called upon them to cooperate in repelling "the German and Italian international criminals."

By doing so, he said, they could help liberate France and the French Empire.

[United States and British planes dropped leaflets in France and French Africa containing messages to the people from President Roosevelt and General Eisenhower, London reported.]

General Eisenhower himself, the White House let it be known, also spoke by radio to the French people, explaining the purposes of the invasions.

His proclamation, issued while the American troops were making their landings, gave specific directions to French land, sea and air forces in North Africa as to how they could avoid misunderstanding and prevent action against them by a system of signals. This is a military operation, General Eisen-

Continued on Page Three

Petain Says Vichy Will 'Defend' Lands

By The Associated Press.

LONDON, Sunday, Nov. 8—The Vichy radio said today that Marshal Henri Philippe Pétain had sent President Roosevelt a message expressing his "astonishment and sadness" at learning of "the aggression of your troops against North Africa."

Marshal Pétain said that the reasons given by the President for the landings failed to justify them and added:

"France and its honor are involved. We are attacked and we will defend ourselves."

The Vichy government issued a communiqué opening with an "appeal to Frenchmen not to allow yourselves to be swayed by foreign broadcasts."

Major Sports Yesterday

FOOTBALL

Making both touchdowns in the second half, Notre Dame defeated Army before 75,142 spectators at the Yankee Stadium. With a scoring pass in the first period and several goal-line stands, Navy thrilled 74,000 fans at Philadelphia by upsetting Penn. Both Fordham and Columbia lost free-scoring contests here and the Big Three—Princeton, Yale and Harvard—all went down to defeat. Iowa toppled hitherto unbeaten Wisconsin. Scores of leading games:

Alabama 29	So. Carolina... 0	Miss. State .. 7	Tulane 0
Amherst 35	Trinity 6	Missouri 26	Nebraska .. 6
Boston Coll...29	Temple 0	Moravian 32	C. C. N. Y... 0
Brown 20	Holy Cross..14	Navy 7	Penn. 0
Colgate 35	Columbia 26	Notre Dame..13	Army 0
Cornell 13	Yale 7	Ohio State..39	Pittsburgh ..19
Dartmouth ..13	Princeton ... 7	Oklahoma ...76	Kan. State.. 0
Duke 42	Maryland ... 6	Oregon 14	U. C. L. A... 7
Duquesne ... 7	St. Mary's.. 7	Penn. State..18	Syracuse ...13
Georgia 75	Florida 0	Rice 40	Arkansas .. 7
Ga. Pre-Fl...41	Auburn 14	So. Calif....21	California .. 7
Ga. Tech.....47	Kentucky ... 7	Stanford 20	Washington . 7
Great Lakes..42	Purdue 6	Texas 20	Baylor 0
Illinois 14	Northwestern. 7	Tex. A. & M.27	S. M. U.....20
Indiana 7	Minnesota .. 0	Texas Tech..13	T. C. U..... 6
Iowa 6	Wisconsin .. 0	Vanderbilt ..19	Mississippi . 0
La. State....20	Fordham 13	Wash. State.18	Mich. State .13
Michigan 35	Harvard 7	Williams 31	Wesleyan .. 0

HORSE RACING

Good Morning won the Florence Nightingale Purse by half a length from Too Timely on the war-relief program before 22,099 racegoers who bet $1,550,089 at Belmont Park. Aonbarr defeated Riverland by a neck in the Grayson Handicap at Pimlico.

HOCKEY

The New York Rangers downed the Montreal Canadiens, 4—3, in the overtime opening game at Madison Square Garden.

(Complete Details of These and Other Sports Events in Section 5.)

War News Summarized

SUNDAY, NOVEMBER 8, 1942

The White House announced last night that powerful American forces were landing on the Atlantic and Mediterranean coasts of French North Africa to forestall a German invasion. The announcement stated that the landing was to prevent the creation of an Axis threat to the Atlantic coast of the Americas across the narrow sea in western Africa. France has been assured that the Allies seek no territory. [1:8.]

American correspondents with the African expeditionary force told of simultaneous landings by the United States troops at many points hundreds of miles apart. [1:4.]

Britain's Eighth Army continued its pursuit in North Africa of Marshal Rommel's shattered army. Twenty thousand prisoners had been taken, according to Cairo. British columns were said to be 200 miles west of El Alamein, close to the Libyan border. [1:3; map, P. 4.]

London announced that British heavy bombers had launched a "concentrated and effective" attack on Genoa Friday night and again raided Northern Italy last night. United States bombers attacked the U-boat base at

Brest, France, and other planes from Britain pounded Nazi targets from the Netherlands to the Bay of Biscay. [1:2; map, P. 21.]

Moscow reported that the Soviet armies held on all fronts and killed some 1,800 of the enemy on the Stalingrad and Caucasus fronts. The German advances in the Nalchik region had apparently been halted. [38:4-5.]

General Douglas MacArthur's headquarters announced that American troops in force had been transported by air to New Guinea and had penetrated to the vicinity of Buna, Japanese base on the north coast. [1:1; map, P. 45.]

The United States Navy announced that Army forces on Guadalcanal Island in the Solomons had attacked Japanese troops to the east of the airfield Nov. 6 and had encountered little opposition. Announcement was also made that at least 5,188 Japanese had been killed in land fighting on Tulagi and Guadalcanal since the United States occupation Aug. 7. [46:1 with map.]

United States bombers attacked successfully the docks at Rangoon, Burma, and returned to their bases in India. [46:8.]

"All the News That's Fit to Print."

The New York Times.

LATE CITY EDITION
Continued cool with moderate winds today.

Temperatures Yesterday—Max., 86; Min., 69
Sunrise, 5:27 A. M.; Sunset, 8:31 P. M.

VOL. XCII—No. 31,204.

Entered as Second-Class Matter,
Postoffice, New York, N. Y.

NEW YORK, THURSDAY, JULY 1, 1943.

Copyright, 1943, by The New York Times Company.

THREE CENTS NEW YORK CITY

M'ARTHUR STARTS ALLIED OFFENSIVE IN PACIFIC; NEW GUINEA ISLES WON, LANDINGS IN SOLOMONS; CHURCHILL PROMISES BLOWS IN EUROPE BY FALL

MAYOR FACES FIGHT WITH OPA ON PLAN FOR HANDLING MEAT

Gives Approval for Sales by Slaughterers to Retailers on Consignment Basis

FEDERAL ACTION LOOMS

Price Agency Director Here Promises Move Should Violation Be Found

A direct conflict between Mayor Fiorello H. La Guardia and the Office of Price Administration appeared inevitable last night, after the Mayor had announced that he had approved, on his own responsibility, a plan for independent slaughterers to sell meat to the public at consumer ceiling prices through consignments to retailers, despite the OPA's objections to the plan.

"If they go ahead with a plan that is in violation of the regulations, OPA will be forced to take action," Frank C. Russell, district OPA director, retorted when informed of the Mayor's decision. "Apparently, the Mayor has given his permission for something which the OPA legal department has turned down."

Former Municipal Court Justice Nathan Sweedler of 225 Broadway, who, as counsel for the Eastern States Independent Meat Packers and Slaughterers, proposed the plan approved by the Mayor after the OPA had turned it down, announced that his organization hoped to have meat on sale in some retail shops today and expected to have a large quantity available by Saturday.

Sees Quick Meat Supply

Mr. Sweedler has estimated that his group could provide 25,000 pounds of beef within twenty-four hours after the Mayor gave his approval to the plan and eventually could gear its output to 1,000,000 pounds a week, but the Mayor was even more optimistic. He said that the plan might provide the city with 1,000,000 pounds a week "and it may be 5,000,000 pounds."

Under the plan the meat would be sold on consignment, the retailer keeping 21 per cent of the selling price. According to Mr. Sweedler, the remaining 79 per cent would pay for the cost of livestock, freight and slaughtering. He contends that under his plan meat could be sold at the consumer ceiling prices, and any butcher violating the ceiling would be deprived of meat through a voluntary policing system.

The Mayor announced his approval of the plan to reporters at City Hall and then released a letter to Commissioner of Markets Daniel P. Woolley in which he argued that the plan did not conflict with any existing regulations and that it should be accepted as a temporary measure.

Holds Plan Feasible

"I have carefully studied the report you submitted to me with plan for direct consignment of food from the original processor to retailer direct, and selling by such retailer to consumer at ceiling prices or lower," the Mayor said in his letter. "I do not see how any such plan could conflict with any existing rules or regulations of any Federal agency, provided the producer, farmer or livestock man is paid the market price and the retailer sells at ceiling prices or lower.

"The whole purpose of food control is to make food available and fix ceiling prices. There is nothing in the rules that prevents anyone from selling below ceiling prices. Surely, in the protection of the consumer, we could not or would not prosecute a retailer for selling below ceiling prices provided his food is wholesome and complies with all health requirements and government inspection.

"In fact, if an original processor or retailer wanted to give food

Continued on Page Seventeen

OWI Closes Twelve Regional Branches

By The Associated Press.

WASHINGTON, June 30 — Twelve regional and thirty-six branch offices of the Office of War Information throughout the country began closing at midnight tonight as the fiscal year ended.

The OWI said an official would remain in each of the twelve regional offices for a few days to liquidate the affairs of both the regional and branch offices. The shutdown was made necessary, the OWI said, because the Senate voted to appropriate only $3,000,000 for the domestic branch of the organization and earmarked the amount, allowing none for maintaining the regional and branch offices. The House had voted to abolish the domestic service entirely.

"It isn't likely that the Congressional conference committee, which has yet to act finally, would go above the Senate's $3,000,000, so we are closing down the offices," an agency spokesman said.

CONGRESS CRUSHES SUBSIDY PROGRAM

Ban on Payments to Cut Prices Stays in CCC Bill Passed by Overwhelming Majorities

By The Associated Press.

WASHINGTON, June 30 — Congress, handing the Roosevelt Administration another legislative setback, today forbade use of subsidies to push down retail food prices and ordered the meat-butter price "roll back" ended by Aug. 1.

The ban was incorporated in legislation extending the life of the Commodity Credit Corporation for two more years from midnight tonight and adding $750,000,000 to its present $2,650,000,000 lending powers. Both Senate and House approved the measure by far more than the two-thirds majority which would be necessary to override a veto. The House vote was 160 to 32, and the Senate vote, 62 to 13.

Less restrictive than the original House measure, the bill permits continued use of subsidies, up to $150,000,000 to meet increased transportation costs such as are now being paid on the movement of oil to the East Coast and on coffee imports, and to promote production of critical metals and war-essential foods. It also allows incentive payments on canning and specialty crops, price support for domestic vegetable oils and fats, and payments for sale of wheat for feeding purposes. However, no subsidies could be paid simply to reduce prices.

Before final passage, a provision prohibiting Government agencies from deducting farm benefit payments in calculating agricultural price ceilings was stricken out.

Just before final Congressional action, Lou R. Maxon, deputy administrator of the Office of Price

Continued on Page Eleven

Cattle Grower Says 'Policymakers' Are to Blame in Meat Shortage

By JAY G. HAYDEN
North American Newspaper Alliance

WASHINGTON, June 30 — Joseph G. Montague, general counsel for the Texas and Southwestern Cattle Raisers Association, put the blame for the meat shortage today on "the unofficial policymakers close to the President," thereby bringing into the open a charge which figured behind the scenes in the Congressional rejection of food subsidies and the retirement of Chester C. Davis as Food Administrator.

Speaking before the Senate Agricultural Committee, Mr. Montague said:

"Surrounding the President are a group of people who have no responsibility, yet determine policy and cause confusion in the meat situation. They are entrenched in the seats of Government behind a veil, not only over broad food policy, but day-to-day actions, is being exercised elsewhere."

Mr. Davis is believed to have had substantially · this same thought in mind when he gave as his first reason for resignation that "I find I have assumed a public responsibility while the authority, not only over broad food policy, but day-to-day actions, is being exercised elsewhere."

Mr. Davis, according to his close friends, became convinced that the real policy-makers were the same old New Deal inner cabinet, including particularly Harry L. Hopkins, Associate Justice Felix Frankfurter and Judge Samuel Rosenman, which has functioned prominently throughout the Roosevelt Administration. Whether he was speaking of his own knowledge or merely

Continued on Page Seventeen

When You Think of Writing
Think of Whiting—Advt.

WALLACE AND JONES RENEW THEIR ROW AFTER 2-HOUR TALK

Conference Called by Byrnes Fails 'to Resolve and Determine' Controversy

SHARP STATEMENTS ISSUED

Secretary Says Charge of Delay by RFC in War Effort Is 'Dastardly' and 'Untrue'

By JOHN H. CRIDER
Special to THE NEW YORK TIMES.

WASHINGTON, June 30 — An attempt by the War Mobilization Director, James F. Byrnes, to harmonize the differences between Vice President Henry A. Wallace and Secretary of Commerce Jesse H. Jones, failed today after he had summoned them to his office for a two-hour discussion this afternoon.

Tonight the Vice President issued a statement which somewhat tempered his bitter accusations against Mr. Jones made yesterday but said the fundamental differences remained.

To this the Secretary replied:

"Mr. Wallace in his statement tonight repeats that delays of the RFC have retarded the war effort. This dastardly charge is as untrue as when he first made it. As for the rest of his statement, Mr. Wallace was not authorized to speak for me. I will continue to speak for myself, and as previously stated, I shall insist upon a Congressional investigation."

The Vice President's statement made it clear that the basic differences between himself and Mr. Jones had been altered only to the extent that "Mr. Jones did not object" to Mr. Wallace's plan to ask Congress after its recess for funds for foreign procurement which would make it independent of the Reconstruction Finance Corporation, headed by the Secretary of Commerce.

There was no mention of Mr. Byrnes in the Vice President's statement, although it was the fruit of the War Mobilization Director's efforts to play the role of peacemaker for the Federal Bureaucracy cast for him by President Roosevelt's Executive Order of May 28 calling upon him to "resolve and determine controversies between such agencies or departments."

Meanwhile, the Senate, showing little inclination at this point of being in a mood to grant the broad authority over foreign procurement expenditures sought by Mr. Wallace, inserted in the War Agencies Appropriation Bill an amendment by Senator Kenneth McKellar, Democrat, of Tennessee, providing that B&W could not use for foreign purchases any of the $36,000,000 appropriated without approval of a majority of the

Continued on Page Twelve

UNITED NATIONS FORCES MOVE FORWARD IN THE SOUTHWEST PACIFIC

American troops landed on Rendova and New Georgia Islands without opposition. In New Guinea they occupied Nassau Bay (4), (1), in the vicinity of the enemy air base at Munda, and engaged just below Salamaua; the landing craft encountered only slight the Japanese. The inset shows this area in detail. To the west the resistance. Apparently these widespread operations have as their Allies occupied Woodlark Island (2) and the Trobriand Islands (3) ultimate goal the reduction of Rabaul (5), which was bombed.

76 BILLIONS SPENT IN U.S. FISCAL YEAR

71 of the Total Were for War —Public Debt Up to 140 Billions, Deficit to 55

Special to THE NEW YORK TIMES.

WASHINGTON, June 30 — The United States ended its fiscal year tonight with a record of expenditures of more than $76,000,000,000, receipts of more than $21,000,000,000, a gross public debt of more that $140,000,000,000 and a deficit of more than $55,000,000,000.

The latest figures available at the Treasury were for June 26, four days before the actual end of the fiscal year. On that date total war expenditures for the year were $71,014,000,000, as against $25,515,000,000 on the same date in 1942.

Spending for civilian purposes was $5,375,000,000, as compared with $5,800,000,000 on the same day a year earlier. The War Department spent $41,690,000,000 and the Navy $20,513,000,000. War expenditures of the Agriculture Department' totaled $2,005,000,000. The Maritime Commission spent $2,733,000,000.

In one year the public debt increased from $76,560,000,000 to $140,028,000,000 and the deficit advanced from $19,152,000,000 to $55,242,000,000.

Receipts of $21,625,000,000 up to

Continued on Page Twelve

Prime Minister Warns Axis Allied Attacks Are Imminent

By RAYMOND DANIELL
By Cable to THE NEW YORK TIMES.

LONDON, June 30 — Prime Minister Churchill warned the Axis today that the Allies were preparing heavier blows on land and sea and by air from east, south and west to bring about the unconditional surrender that he and President Roosevelt declared at Casablanca was the price of peace.

In the Mediterranean and "elsewhere," he said, heavy fighting probably would develop "before the leaves of autumn fall," but he added that large-scale amphibious operations take months to prepare.

Significantly, he dwelt at length and in considerable detail upon the growing scale and intensity of the British - American air offensive against Germany from this island, and indicated that Russian air power, long tied down to the battle lines, would soon be able to join in the attack on Nazi industry from the east.

A Major Victory at Sea

Reviewing the Battle of the Atlantic, he said a victory had been won at sea against the submarines two months ago comparable with the Allied conquest of Africa with the capture of 350,000 German and Italian prisoners and vast quantities of war material. He likened the victory in Tunisia to the Russian triumph at Stalingrad.

The Prime Minister was speaking in the ancient Guildhall, where he received the freedom of the City of London, that square mile of the British capital that still bears the

Continued on Page Four

War News Summarized

THURSDAY, JULY 1, 1943

The Allied Southwest Pacific and South Pacific Commands have started a broad offensive against Japanese positions. The first results of the combined naval, air and land operations are:

Landings on Rendova and New Georgia Islands in the Central Solomons, where fighting is going on.

Occupation, without opposition, of the Trobriand Islands and Woodlark Island off the southeastern tip of New Guinea at the north end of the Coral Sea.

A landing at Nassau Bay, ten miles south of Salamaua in New Guinea.

Heavy aerial bombardment of the big Japanese base at Rabaul, New Britain.

Gen. Douglas MacArthur is in general command of the combined operations, with Admiral William F. Halsey Jr. directing the offensive of the South Pacific forces. The battle area extends 500 miles north of Guadalcanal to Rabaul and 750 miles southeast of Rabaul to Salamaua [All the foregoing, 1:8.]

In London, Prime Minister Churchill pledged that after Hitler's defeat "every man, every ship and every airplane in the King's service that can be moved to the Pacific will be sent and there maintained in action * * * for as many years as are needed to make the Japanese, in their turn, submit or bite the dust."

Mr. Churchill then announced that "very probably there will be heavy fighting in the Mediterranean and elsewhere before the leaves of autumn fall." He characterized Tunisia and the campaign against the U-boat as the two greatest Allied victories of the war, and promised that every corner of Germany would be bombed as thoroughly as the Ruhr had been. [All the foregoing, 1:5-6.]

On the other war fronts, Flying Fortresses raided Le Mans in France and the RAF hit targets in western Europe [5:2-3]. Reggio Calabria and Messina were bombed in the Mediterranean [6:2], and Russian troops captured a strong point on the Velikiye Luki front. [7:1.]

Admiral Robert, Vichy's High Commissioner in Martinique, asked the United States for terms under which the West Indies islands could be transferred to other French authority. [1:7.]

MARTINIQUE YIELDS, ASKS TERMS OF U. S.

Robert, 'to Avoid Bloodshed,' Ready to Accept Change of French Authority

The Martinique radio broadcast a statement last night by Admiral Georges Robert, Vichy's High Commissioner on the island, asserting that he had asked the United States Government to dispatch a "plenipotentiary to fix the terms for a change of French authority."

The broadcast said that Admiral Robert had taken the action "to avoid bloodshed." It was recorded by Federal Communications Commission monitors. The United Press said.

The admiral, head of the French islands in the Caribbean under his own rule, loyal to Marshal Henri-Philippe Pétain, French Chief of State.

The reception of the broadcast was marred by technical difficulties, but those portions of the broadcast that could be heard said:

"Communiqué to the population: 'In order to avoid bloodshed between the French and * * * I have asked the Government of the United States, under the double condition of its renewing the guarantee to maintain French sovereignty in these islands and of the non-intervention of American forces, to send a plenipotentiary to fix the terms for a change of French authority.

'* * * my duty to the people and the Marshal * * *

'"Admiral Robert.'"

Recently there have been unconfirmed reports of clashes between the Admiral's troops and elements favoring the rule of the islands by

Continued on Page Eight

BERLIN EVACUATION REPORTED PLANNED

Swedes Hear Exodus Is to Start in Fall—Wuppertal Held Beyond Rebuilding

By GEORGE AXELSSON

STOCKHOLM, Sweden, June 30 — Berlin will evacuate in the Fall women and children not engaged in the war industries, according to reliable war information received here today through private channels.

Fear of heavier and more frequent Allied air raids with the coming of longer nights has prompted this decision, and authorities have already begun the preliminary arrangements, it is stated.

The extent to which the Ruhr has been hit by the RAF raids is indicated by a statement by Adolf Hitler's chief city planning consultant, Armaments Minister Albert Speer, just back from a tour of inspection of the devastated area.

He said it was not worth while to try to rebuild Wuppertal.

Continued on Page Three

Laundry Workers Held Essential But the WMC Restricts Services

Special to THE NEW YORK TIMES.

WASHINGTON, June 30 — The War Manpower Commission extended to the country's laundries today the same preferential treatment in the allocation of manpower as is given to essential war industries.

Laundries classified as "locally needed" by the WMC will be supplied with workers by the United States Employment Service, will be protected from labor piracy and will have their existing labor force stabilized, except that there will be no occupational deferment under the Selective Service Act. They will receive this aid only if they discontinue luxury services to their patrons.

Laundries are expected to cooperate in inducing hotels, boarding houses and tourist homes to change bed linen only once a week for any one patron; limit each patron to one face towel and one bath towel

Continued on Page Ten

2-PRONGED DRIVE

Americans Battle Enemy on New Georgia and Rendova Islands

SALAMAUA IN PERIL

Allies Seize Trobriand and Woodlark Isles— Rabaul Pounded

By SIDNEY SHALETT
Special to THE NEW YORK TIMES.

WASHINGTON, Thursday, July 1—Combined Army and Navy forces under General Douglas MacArthur have opened the long expected offensive against the Japanese in the south and southwest Pacific.

Fighting was in progress on Rendova and New Georgia islands, which were hit by ground, naval and air forces in "closest synchronization," a communiqué from General MacArthur's headquarters in Australia reported today. Nassau Bay, ten miles south of the big Japanese base of Salamaua in New Guinea, fell to the Allies after a slight skirmish, and the Trobriand and Woodlark island groups, 300 to 400 miles west of the New Georgia group, were occupied without opposition.

The Allied push—aimed, observers here believe, at the major Japanese base of Rabaul, on New Britain Island—got under way yesterday, Solomons time, which was Tuesday here.

Nutcracker Move Seen

It was believed here, on the basis of early reports, that the fighting and occupations reported so far were preliminary to major actions to come. If bases in the New Georgias are consolidated, a two-way push against Rabaul might be developing, with one arm advancing northwestward from the Central Solomons and the other swinging across eastward from new bases in New Guinea.

United States heavy bombers carried out an attack on Rabaul during the night, dropping nearly twenty-three tons of high-explosive, fragmentation and incendiary bombs throughout the dispersal areas at the Vunakanau and Lakunai airdromes, the communiqué from Australian headquarters reported. "Several explosions and "numerous fires" were observed, one of which was visible for 100 miles, the announcement said.

The big bombers, which have punished Rabaul extensively in recent weeks, ran into heavy Japanese anti-aircraft fire and interference from some enemy night fighters. One American bomber was missing after the raid.

The Trobriand and Woodlark islands will be valuable as stepping-stones in a chain of fighter-plane bases from the Allies stronghold of Milne Bay, on the tip of New Guinea. Japanese-held Gasmata and Rabaul may be raided with comparative ease with the aid of these bays.

Navy Gives First News

The first report of landing actions came early yesterday when the Navy announced here in a communiqué that combined United States forces had landed June 30 (Solomons time) on Rendova Island, in the New Georgia group, which is only five miles from the important Japanese air base of Munda, on New Georgia Island. On New Georgia details have been received.

A hint that the fighting had extended came later from Secretary of the Navy Frank Knox in Los Angeles, where he is inspecting Pacific Coast installations. The Secretary declared that the Rendova attack was the beginning of "an offensive against the Japanese base at Munda and surrounding bases." Navy officials in Washington yesterday declined, however, to con-

Continued on Page Three

God bless America—Hollywood Bowl
At all dealers. 20c Jul—Advt.

"All the News That's Fit to Print."

The New York Times.

LATE CITY EDITION
Moderately cool with gentle winds today.
Temperatures Yesterday—Max., 90; Min., 73
Sunrise, 6:22 A. M.; Sunset, 7:21 P. M.

VOL. XCII.—No. 31,268.

Entered as Second-Class Matter,
Postoffice, New York, N. Y.

NEW YORK, FRIDAY, SEPTEMBER 3, 1943.

Copyright, 1943, by The New York Times Company.

THREE CENTS NEW YORK CITY

ALLIES LAND IN ITALY OPPOSITE MESSINA; 8TH ARMY LEADS, WITH AIR-NAVAL COVER; RUSSIANS DRIVE AHEAD, CAPTURING SUMY

HULL TO TAKE REINS OVER ALL AGENCIES IN ECONOMIC FIELD

Coordination of OEW, OFRRO and Lend-Lease Under State Department Is Due Soon

NOT ALL FRICTION ENDED

WFA and OEW at Odds—Capital Speculates on What Course Lehman Will Pursue

By JOHN MacCORMAC
Special to The New York Times.

WASHINGTON, Sept. 2—The coordination of the Office of Economic Warfare, the Office of Lend-Lease Administration and the Office of Foreign Relief and Rehabilitation Operations in a way which will give the department complete control over their activities and leave them as instruments executing its policies has been planned and will shortly be put in effect, it was learned today.

Part of the plan in the formulation of a definite and coordinated policy with regard to the international economic activities of the Government. Hitherto there has been a general understanding in theory, but in practice some of the agencies which were supposed to execute economic policy have worked at cross-purposes.

The conflict between the foreign activities of some of the Reconstruction Finance Corporation subsidiaries and those of the Board of Economic Warfare exploded recently in the row between Vice President Wallace and Secretary Jones, which led to the coordination of these activities by the OEW under Leo T. Crowley as its new head.

Some Friction Still Exists

But there is still uncertainty regarding the representative spheres of OEW, Lend-Lease and OFRRO and, for that matter, friction between OEW and the WFA. OEW administration as regards foreign food purchases. The plan, therefore, is to have the State Department effect a final coordination of their efforts, and there is a possibility that some or all of them might be absorbed in the process.

This is not only believed to be the policy of the President and Secretary Hull, but it is understood to be approved by Mr. Crowley and Edward Stettinius Jr., lend-lease administrator. There is some doubt, however, whether ex-Gov. Herbert H. Lehman is willing to subordinate OFRRO to the State Department to the extent desired.

From a spokesman for Mr. Crowley it was learned that close collaboration with the State Department has from the first been one of his objectives. Mr. Crowley has indicated that as soon as the coordination is made and the administrative facilities have been set up, the time will have arrived for a substantial simplification of the Government's foreign economic set-up.

OEW Changes Held Temporary

It was because of these views that the reorganization of OEW announced Tuesday was regarded as of a transitory rather than permanent character.

For instance, James L. McCamy, who was appointed assistant to the director, will soon leave again to join the Bureau of the Budget. Hugh B. Cox, who will act as general counsel, will work only part time with OEW, and the rest of the time as assistant attorney general of the United States. No executive director was named, and Lauchlin Currie, who will act as executive officer, is on "loan" from the President's office.

Before OEW and lend-lease are placed under the State Department, however, the details of foreign economic policy will have been worked out and men of the requisite business ability will have been added

Continued on Page Seven

TO PLACE a Want Ad just telephone The New York Times—LAckawanna 4-1000.—Advt.

Meat Ration Points Are Cut But Butter Will Need More

Thirty-five Meat Items Are Reduced 1 to 2 Points on Report of Larger Supplies—Changes Take Effect Sunday

Special to The New York Times.

WASHINGTON, Sept. 2—Point values of most meats were lowered today by the Office of Price Administration, effective Sunday through September. An exception to the increased purchasing power of red stamps was creamery butter. It will call for twelve instead of ten points a pound. The buying power of blue stamps was reduced by an increase in the point values of many processed fruits and vegetables.

The changes in red stamp values were based on the belief that more meat would be available to civilians for the rest of this month. The ration costs of most lamb and bacon cuts were reduced one to two points a pound. Lower values were fixed for sirloin steak, roasts of beef and several variety meats.

The increase in the point value of creamery butter is not likely to be noticed in most urban areas, where dealers, because of acute shortages, have been restricting customers to a quarter pound at a time and getting three points for the quarter pound, or twelve points a pound.

Farm or country butter was listed separately for the first time in the new point value schedules. To it a point value of six points a pound was assigned. Previously country butter had the same point value as creamery butter. The reduction was intended to spur the movement of farm-churned butter to urban markets to relieve the shortage of creamery butter.

"The further increase in the point value of creamery butter is necessary because purchases near butter-producing areas have been so large at a ten-point value that shortages developed in other parts of the country," the OPA said. "In addition butter production during

Continued on Page Eight

CONGRESS TAX MOVE IRKS MORGENTHAU

Joint Committee Plans to Subpoena Data Direct From Internal Revenue Body

Special to The New York Times.

WASHINGTON, Sept. 2—A conflict has arisen between the joint committee of Congress on internal revenue taxation and the Treasury over the committee's power to obtain tax data direct from officials of any Government department or agency and this may lead to a test in the courts of the committee's authority.

The 1942 revenue act empowered the committee to obtain such data from officials of the Bureau of Internal Revenue or any other department without sending its requests through departmental heads.

The committee, jointly set up by the Senate Finance and House Ways and Means Committees, has seldom disagreed with the Treasury on tax matters in recent years. Of late it has been paying less and less attention to the Treasury's views and insisting on writing its own tax bills.

It was to give Colin F. Stam, the committee's chief of tax experts, opportunity to make use of the fiscal and economic experience to be found in Government departments and particularly in the Internal Revenue Bureau that Congress was asked to authorize it to go over the head of Secretary Morgenthau to his subordinates and to deal similarly with other divisions.

Although neither the Treasury nor Mr. Stam would comment on

Continued on Page Ten

1,330 JAPANESE SAIL ON EXCHANGE LINER

Gripsholm Leaves on Second Trip—Teia Maru to Bring Americans Back Home

The exchange liner Gripsholm, painted white and carrying in huge letters on her side the word "Diplomat," sailed from her anchorage in New York Harbor early yesterday on her second mission to bring Americans who have been interned in the Orient since December, 1941.

Gaily painted like the cruise ship she was before the United States Government chartered her in the spring of 1942 from the Swedish-American Line, the big vessel carried the gold and blue marks of Sweden, painted flags and brilliant lighting arrangements to identify her through submarine-infested waters.

In her cabins there were, according to announcements of the War and State Departments in Washington, 1,330 Japanese civilians who will be exchanged for Americans and nationals of other Western Hemisphere nations in the Orient for Mormugao, Portuguese India, on or about Oct. 15.

The Americans and their fellow internees—1,500 in those lists, including 1,250 citizens of the United States—are to travel from the Orient on the Japanese-flag liner Teia Maru. The Washington announcements said that the Teia Maru was scheduled to leave Japan on Sept. 15, touching at ports in China, the Philippines and Indo-China to take on additional passengers, and calling at Singapore for fuel and water.

Continued on Page Five

Browder Charges 'Bad Faith' Delays Opening a Second Front

Earl Browder, general secretary of the Communist party of the United States, asserted at a party meeting last night in Manhattan Center, 311 West Thirty-fourth Street, that Anglo-American relations would "deteriorate sharply" unless a second front in Western Europe was opened before the end of the summer.

The meeting was a special one called to hear Mr. Browder discuss the present situation. About 3,000 persons were in the hall.

Mr. Browder argued that we should not wait until next spring in the hope that victory can then be "bought much more cheaply," but should land in full force now in an effort to win a quick victory and take some of the burden of land fighting off the Red Army. He said that military occupation by "fighting armies" was the only way nazism could be ended.

Mr. Browder, who is not a military expert, vigorously expressed the opinion that our troops were overwhelmingly able to open a second front whenever their leaders gave the word. But the British and American general staffs, he charged, have acted in the role of "politicians subject to reactionary influence," and posed themselves as military leaders, in which capacity, he said, they realize the need for a second front. Counting out "weakness" as a reason for not opening a second front, he said the only alternative was "bad faith."

Mr. Browder charged that "dark and sinister forces" in this country were accusing the Soviet Union of

Continued on Page Four

AIR BLOWS PRESSED

French Fields Pounded as Fortresses Join British in Sweeps

POWER PLANT IS HIT

Canal Locks Smashed on Key Dutch Route Serving Antwerp

New, Heavy Air Raids As Allies Land in Italy

By The United Press.

LONDON, Friday, Sept. 3—Powerful forces of Allied bombers ranged over the northern flank of the European continent early today, almost simultaneously with the invasion of Italy.

A long procession of bombers streamed out over the British coast, flying so high they could not be seen from the ground, although the roar of their motors was audible.

By The United Press.

LONDON, Friday, Sept. 3—American Flying Fortresses, culminating an evening of widespread activity that saw Royal Air Force Fighter Command planes in their biggest operation of the year, blasted enemy airfields at Mardyck and Denain in northern France late yesterday, a joint British-American communiqué reported today.

Squadrons of British Spitfires and Typhoons escorted medium B-26 Marauder bombers of the Eighth United States Air Force and RAF Boston, Mitchell and Ventura bombers in attacks on targets in Pas de Calais Department.

Fast and deadly P-49 Thunderbolts covered the Fortresses in their hard-hitting foray against the northern French airfields. "Good bombing results were observed on all targets," the joint communiqué said, adding that four enemy aircraft were destroyed—one by the Fortresses and three by Spitfires. One medium and one light bomber and two fighters were lost in the heavy operation.

The B-26 Marauder medium bombers of the Eighth United States Air Force attacked the power station at Mazingarbe, near Bethune, France, "with good results," the fighter pilots reported.

Continued on Page Six

RED ARMY ROLLING

Storms Ukraine Citadel and Seizes Towns on Kiev Rail Line

DONBAS KEYS TAKEN

Nazis Retreat Toward Dnieper—550 Places Fall in Two Days

By The Associated Press.

LONDON, Friday, Sept. 3—Moscow announced early today that five Red armies plunging westward had cut the Bryansk-Kiev railway 150 miles from Kiev, smashed German reinforcements in a six-mile gain on Smolensk and rolled up Axis lines in a new forty-five-mile-wide spurt in the Donets Basin.

Premier Joseph Stalin, in an order of the day, announced late yesterday that the Ukraine citadel of Sumy, ninety miles northwest of Kharkov, had fallen to Gen. Nikolai Vatutin's army, and a communiqué announced the capture of Krolevets and Yampol, two points on the vital Bryansk-Kiev railway linking the enemy's central and southern fronts.

Lisichansk, Voroshilovsk, Slavyanoserbsk and other cities were seized in the Donets Basin, while Budennovka, twenty miles from Mariupol, was taken in the push along the rim of the Sea of Azov, said the communiqué, recorded by the Soviet monitor.

250 More Places Overrun

The swiftness of the Russian advances and the tone of the communiqué indicated that the Germans were engaged in a large-scale retreat toward the Dnieper River, particularly in the huge Donets Basin. The bulletin, however, emphasized that the Germans were fighting stubbornly all along the 600-mile front.

More than 9,000 Germans were killed yesterday as the Red Armies overran nearly 250 cities and villages, many of them strategic prizes, for a two-day bag of nearly 550 localities.

Germany's 1941 invasion lines now have been cracked by the Russians in a 1943 offensive that has carried the Red Army more than half way along the comeback trail

Continued on Page Four

ACROSS NARROW WATERS TO EUROPE

Sept. 2, 1943

Allied forces spanned the Strait of Messina this morning to land on the toe of Italy. This map, a perspective view looking eastward, gives an idea how the mainland appeared to the invaders.

Other Invasions This Year Anticipated in Washington

By ROBERT F. WHITNEY
Special to The New York Times.

WASHINGTON, Friday, Sept. 3—While Washington slept, its somnolent thousands secure in the knowledge that plans laid at Quebec last week would be efficiently carried out, the word was flashed to the capital that the invasion of the Italian mainland had begun. It was the first penetration by the Allies of Fortress Europe and thus a historic event which defied the pledge of Adolf Hitler that his Reich, by its aggressions, would secure its future for a "thousand years."

Unlike the invasion of North Africa by American troops nearly a year ago and the opening of the Sicilian campaign about two months ago, the invasion was not announced in Washington. The first news to the public came in flashes from North Africa.

The announcement, as received here, told of Allied troops swarming across the Strait of Messina. Only on Tuesday Prime Minister Churchill, in his Canadian speech, had stated that the Germans had augmented their forces in Italy and intended to make a battleground of that country.

The Allied invasion was seen here as an answer both to that challenge by the Germans and to the demands that a second front be opened in Europe this year.

When the news came, it was probable that the President and Mr. Churchill, the pair who are directing the strategy of the two English-speaking nations of the United Nations, were awaiting the news of a successful landing together in the White House study, as it is known that when they meet neither one retires early.

It was hoped here in semi-official quarters that the invasion of Italy would answer the prayers of Russia that her Allies in the west would lift some of the load off her shoulders by an attack on the European Continent.

While it was confidently expected that the invasion of Italy

Continued on Page Three

PLANE OUTPUT 7,700 FOR AUGUST, A JUMP

Production This Month May Reach 8,000, WPB Says—Rise Despite New Designs

Special to The New York Times.

WASHINGTON, Sept. 2—Aircraft production last month totaled 7,700 planes, compared with 7,373 in July, the WPB reported today in tones of elation.

On the basis of the August figure, airplane production in September will top 8,000, it was said.

The rise in output last month as compared with July was in the rate called for in the production schedule. Both July and August production were below the original schedule, WPB officials said. But they maintain that the schedules are "unrealistic" in that they do not take into consideration the shifts in production occasioned by design changes and by many other factors.

Schedules have been adjusted three times so far this year, one official said, and are likely to be changed again. He added that "I'd rather make 6,500 planes of the type we needed than to meet the schedules which include many of the types we don't need and would rather not have."

He contended that "we got the planes we wanted. Those we didn't want we didn't get."

The discrepancy between the

Continued on Page Seven

DAWN IS ZERO HOUR

British and Canadians Storm Over Narrow Strait of Messina

ROME SAYS NOTHING

Allies Invade on Fourth Anniversary of Their War Declaration

By MILTON BRACKER
By Wireless to The New York Times

ALLIED HEADQUARTERS IN NORTH AFRICA, Friday, Sept. 3—The Allies have breached the "Fortress of Europe." On the fourth anniversary of the British and French declaration of war against Germany, Allied troops are striving to establish a bridgehead on the Italian side of the Strait of Messina.

Under the thunderous support of Allied sea and air power, the main strip of water to bring the war at long last to the mainland of the Continent that Germany has enslaved.

Preceded by a pounding artillery barrage across the strait and by a number of reconnaissance landings, the main party set foot on the tip of the Calabrian Peninsula, opposite Messina, at 4:30 A. M., today [10:30 P. M. Thursday, Eastern War Time].

No details were available on either this morning's historic assault or the previous reconnaissance missions. The latter were, plainly, those referred to in German broadcasts as landing attempts beginning on Aug. 29, which the Germans said had been repulsed with heavy losses.

[A Mutual Broadcasting System commentator, speaking from Algiers, quoted an official Allied spokesman today as saying that the Allies were "apparently engaged in heavy fighting," The Associated Press reported from London.]

A special communiqué issued here at 7:20 A. M. said merely: "Allied forces under General Eisenhower continued their advance. British and Canadian troops of the Eighth Army, supported by Allied sea and air power, attacked across the Strait of Messina early today and landed on the mainland of Italy."

Field Guns Pave Way

ALLIED HEAQUARTERS IN NORTH AFRICA, Sept. 3 (AP)—British, Canadian and other troops of the British Eighth Army spearheaded the invasion armies, swarming across the Strait of Messina from Sicily under cover of Allied aircraft and the big guns of British and American warships. The Eighth Army's field guns helped to pave the way for the invasion troops with a thunderous barrage that silenced several of the

Continued on Page Two

War News Summarized

FRIDAY, SEPTEMBER 3, 1943

Allied forces crossed the Strait of Messina from Sicily and landed in southern Italy early this morning to start the long-awaited invasion of Europe, according to an official communiqué issued by the Allied Headquarters in North Africa. The landing was the culmination of a series of devastating air blows. [1:8, maps pages 1, 2 and 3.]

The Russian war machine rolled relentlessly on yesterday. The important Ukrainian town of Sumy was captured, the Bryansk-Kiev railway was severed and a wide advance was made in the Donets Basin, with every indication that a German retreat to the Dnieper was in full swing. [1:5, map P. 4.]

Continuing the softening-up process on the Continent, Allied fighters and bombers hit airfields in Northern France shortly after RAF fighters had returned from the Netherlands, where they struck at some of the most vital water communications controlled by the Germans. The bomb racks were unloaded on the strategic Hansweert Canal, where three locks were hit. RAF reported that 107,520 American tons of bombs had been dropped on Germany in the first eight months of 1943. [1:4, map p. 6.]

The Navy Department in Washington still withheld details of Tuesday's raid on the Marcus Islands, but some of the mystery was dispelled by the Japanese, who acknowledged damage to the strategic air and observation base and estimated the American task force at 160 fighter and bomber planes from two carriers. Military observers at Pearl Harbor believe that the Marcus raid was not a feint and that a major blow against Japan's outer defenses is near. [5:1.]

Allied bombers dropped a record of 206 tons of bombs on the Japanese bases at Madang, New Guinea, General MacArthur reported. Ground troops also were strafed at Salamaua. [5:5, with map.]

The Pacific phase of the war is believed to be one of the principal subjects being discussed by Prime Minister Churchill and President Roosevelt in Washington. They have been holding day and night sessions. The Prime Minister also has conferred with high military and supply mission heads. [4:4.]

Another indication of the stepped-up pace to launch a second or a third front was the report from Washington of an August output of 7,700 planes as against 7,373 for July and indications that the figure might top 8,000 in September. [1:7.]

Portugal Weighs Idea of Fighting; Premier Tells People to Prepare

Neutral diplomatic quarters in London reported yesterday that Portugal was contemplating a declaration of war against Japan and might follow it with declarations against other Axis powers, according to The United Press.

The Portuguese action is said to arise from the fact that the Japanese established military control over Macao, in China near Hong Kong, as well as from Japanese occupation of Timor, in the southwest Pacific north of Australia.

LISBON, Sept. 2 (AP)—Premier Antonio de Oliveira Salazar stated today that Portugal's military preparations were defensive but "in the unfortunate times in which we are living may have to be used against foreign enemies as much as against internal elements of national disintegration."

Clamping a tight censorship on speculation regarding the military preparations, Dr. Salazar cautioned against expecting any change in the country's foreign policy.

[The London Evening Standard interpreted the "mobiliza-

Continued on Page Five

statement "following fantastic rumors" and this statement gave the impression Portugal was on the eve of some important action.

Arnold in Britain To Meet Air Chiefs

LONDON, Sept. 2—Lieut. Gen. Henry H. Arnold, chief of the United States Army Air Forces, and Maj. Gen. William C. Lee, commander of an air-borne division, who is known as the father of American parachute troops, arrived in Britain today from the United States. They plunged immediately into a study of the military set-up and recent operations by the Eighth United States Air Force.

General Arnold is here for conferences with Air Chief Marshal Sir Charles Portal, Lieut. Gen. Jacob T. Devers, commanding all United States forces in the European theatre; Maj. Gen. Ira C. Eaker, commander of the Eighth Air Force, and other British and American officers.

"All the News That's Fit to Print."

The New York Times.

LATE CITY EDITION
Continued moderately cool today; moderate winds.
Temperature Yesterday—Max. 74; Min. 67
Sunrise, 6:29 A. M.; Sunset, 7:17 P. M.

VOL. XCII..No. 31,274.

Entered as Second-Class Matter,
Postoffice, New York, N. Y.

Copyright, 1943, by The New York Times Company.

NEW YORK, THURSDAY, SEPTEMBER 9, 1943.

THREE CENTS IN NEW YORK CITY

ITALY SURRENDERS, WILL RESIST GERMANS; ALLIED FORCES LAND IN THE NAPLES AREA; RUSSIANS IN STALINO, CLEAR DONETS BASIN

SOVIET TIDE RISES

Swift Red Army Blows Capture Key City, Free Rich Region

DRIVE NEARS DNIEPER

More Rail Hubs Fall— Thrust Toward Kiev Also Extended

By The United Press

LONDON, Thursday, Sept. 9—The Red Army recaptured Stalino, Russia's twelfth city, yesterday and freed the Donets Basin, which before the war produced more steel than Japan and Italy combined, in a great surge that took it to Grishino, ninety miles east of Duiepropetrovsk on the lower Dnieper River.

While the armies of Gen. Rodion Y. Malinovsky and Gen. Fedor Tolbukhin drove the enemy from the rich Donets Basin, crowded with coal mines and factories, the army of Gen. Konstantin Rokossovsky drove to a point ninety-six miles northeast of Kiev by capturing Borzna, twenty-three miles west of Bakhmach.

Bakhmach and Romni, forty-two miles to the southeast, were surrounded on three sides, a Moscow radio bulletin reported, and the Bakhmach-Kremenchug railroad was cut. The roads leading from Bakhmach to Kursk and Gomel had been cut previously and only the lines to Kiev and Odessa remained open.

Picked Troops Take Stalino

Red Army shock troops, picked from the sixteen infantry divisions that had driven the Germans through city after city in six days of tireless fighting, took Stalino by storm.

The Russian communiqué said the Red Army troops drove in on Stalino throughout Tuesday night and yesterday morning. They fought through the suburbs and then stormed the city from north and south, routing the enemy in a street-by-street fight and capturing a great store of spoils.

Twenty-five miles northwest of Stalino the Russians took Krasnoarmeiskoye, a big railroad junction controlling four of four rail roads leading west from the basin.

In all the Russians took, in addition to Stalino, a city of 462,000 persons, more than 150 towns in the Donbas alone, twenty of them important, in gains of up to twelve and a half miles. During their Donbas offensive the Russians took twelve towns of more than 50,000 persons each.

The Germans at Krasnoarmeiskoye were so swiftly beaten that the Russians took nineteen planes and several loaded railroad trains.

March on Kiev Gains

On the Kiev front, the Russians took more than sixty towns in advances of up to twelve and a half miles. Their capture of Borzna in that area meant that the battle for the Dnieper River line had started. An advance of twenty-three miles to Nezhin would cut the only remaining German supply line east of the river. The Russians had already advanced 101 miles in nine days from Rylsk, half the distance to Kiev.

More than 1,000 Germans were killed at Borzna, and 1,000 were killed in another sector.

South of Bryansk the Russians advanced up to six miles to take several villages. They were reported only twenty miles south of Bryansk. The Soviet communiqué, recorded from the Moscow radio, reported that the Russians were advancing west of the Navlya railroad junction in this area, driving the Germans through dense forests.

West and southwest of Kharkov nearly four miles were gained in some sectors and about 1,200 Germans were killed.

The Germans are southwest of Novorossisk, the Caucasus naval base, seized by the Russians

Continued on Page Twenty-two

When You Think of Writing
Think of Whiting.—Advt.

New Fascist Regime Set Up, Nazis Report

By Cable to THE NEW YORK TIMES.

LONDON, Thursday, Sept. 9—The German radio announced early today that a "National Fascist government has been set up in Italy and functions in the name of Benito Mussolini."

The announcement, called a "proclamation by the National Fascist Government of Italy," said "this Badoglio betrayal will not be perpetrated. The National Fascist Government will punish traitors pitilessly."

The broadcast, in Italian, said nothing about the whereabouts of Mussolini, who has been reported under arrest. It was preceded by the playing of "Giovinezza," the Fascist anthem.

FOE'S MARCUS LOSS 80% NIMITZ SAYS

U. S. Carrier Planes Alone Hit at Japanese Isle—Hell Cat Fighter Excels in Test

By ROBERT TRUMBULL
By Telephone to THE NEW YORK TIMES.

PEARL HARBOR, Sept. 8—Admiral Chester W. Nimitz, Commander in Chief of the Pacific Fleet, issued today a communiqué that gave the first details of the raid on Marcus Island Sept. 1. Coincidentally three naval air officers who participated in the action gave an interview covering all phases of the raid, which they said destroyed a surprisingly well-fortified Japanese air base.

Action Consisted of Bombing

Admiral Nimitz's communiqué said that a United States Pacific Fleet task force under command of Rear Admiral Charles A. Pownall attacked the little island, 1,185 miles southeast of Tokyo, at dawn Sept. 1. The air officers revealed that the action consisted entirely of bombing and strafing by carrierborne aircraft.

They said that the new Grumman F6F Hellcat fighter was employed in combat for the first time in this action.

Continued on Page Four

IN HEART OF ITALY

American 7th Army Is Reported in Van of Naples Operation

MORE POINTS NAMED

Landings Rumored at Genoa, Pizzo, Gaeta and Leghorn

By Wireless to THE NEW YORK TIMES.

ALLIED HEADQUARTERS IN NORTH AFRICA, Thursday, Sept. 9—The Allies have carried the land campaign against the Germans in Italy to the vicinity of Naples in new operations announced within twelve hours of the disclosure by Gen. Dwight D. Eisenhower that the Italian armed forces had unconditionally surrendered.

The news was announced a few minutes past 6:30 A. M. in the following thirteen words:

"Further operations have started on the Italian mainland in the vicinity of Naples."

In the absence of the slightest expansion of the communiqué, no details are available as to the forces participating. The single fact remained that the attack had been pressed near Italy's southern metropolis and port, second only to Genoa, in what obviously was a major amphibious thrust.

Naples is a city of more than 700,000 population—nearer 1,000,000 if the suburbs are included. The assault was launched eighty-three years and two days after Garibaldi entered the city alone in a dramatic liberation gesture, which culminated in the unification of the country ten years later.

Although there is no indication just how near the city itself the landing or landings were carried out, it is plain that Naples is the objective of the sea-borne invaders.

[This dispatch did not indicate the make-up of the landing parties. A Tunis radio broadcast

Continued on Page Four

U. S. SOLDIERS IN LONDON CHEER THE NEWS

Americans in front of the Red Cross Washington Club in the British capital when the news of Italy's surrender was announced.
Associated Press Radiophoto, passed yesterday by censor

Announcements of the Surrender

By Broadcast to THE NEW YORK TIMES

ALLIED HEADQUARTERS IN NORTH AFRICA, Sept. 8—The texts of the proclamations by Gen. Dwight D. Eisenhower and Premier Pietro Badoglio follow:

By GENERAL EISENHOWER

This is Gen. Dwight D. Eisenhower, Commander in Chief of the Allied Forces.

The Italian Government has surrendered its armed forces unconditionally. As Allied Commander in Chief, I have granted a military armistice, the terms of which have been approved by the Governments of the United Kingdom, the United States and the Union of Soviet Socialist Republics. Thus I am acting in the interest of the United Nations.

The Italian Government has bound itself to abide by these terms without reservation. The armistice was signed by my representative and the representative of Marshal Badoglio and it becomes effective this instant.

Hostilities between the armed forces of the United Nations and those of Italy terminate at once. All Italians who now act to help eject the German aggressor from Italian soil will have the assistance and the support of the United Nations.

By PREMIER BADOGLIO

The Italian Government, recognizing the impossibility of continuing the unequal struggle against the overwhelming power of the enemy, with the object of avoiding further and more grievous harm to the nation, has requested an armistice from General Eisenhower, Commander in Chief of the Anglo-American Allied forces. This request has been granted. The Italian forces will therefore cease all acts of hostility against the Anglo-American forces wherever they may be met. They will, however, oppose attack from any other quarter.

CITY 'JUMPS GUN' IN WAR BOND DRIVE

Rallies, Sales Begin on Vast Scale—State Savings Banks Will Invest $600,000,000

As President Roosevelt and Secretary of the Treasury Henry J. Morgenthau Jr. opened the Third War Bond Drive for $15,000,000,000 last night over the radio, it was announced here that in the campaign to raise the State's quota of $4,709,000,000 the mutual savings banks in the State would buy $600,000,000 in Government bonds. The United States Steel Corporation and its subsidiaries will buy $100,000,000 in Government securities, with parts of the total allocated to districts where the corporation operates.

Restive to get its drive under way, New York City held preliminary rallies yesterday as Navy convoys took into the five boroughs Navy gunners who had been meeting were held in Times Square and on the steps of the Sub-Treasury Building at Wall and Broad Streets.

Burgess Hails Italy's Surrender

The thousands assembled in the streets for these two gatherings cheered wildly as speakers and Ticker tape, confetti and torn paper were thrown from the windows of buildings where workers in the financial community were listening to the rally.

The unconditional surrender of Italy is "bullish news" and will be a great help in the bond drive, W. Randolph Burgess, chairman of the War Finance Committee for New York State, said later in the

Continued on Page Sixteen

President Hails Victory But Warns of Real Foes

By JOHN H. CRIDER
Special to THE NEW YORK TIMES.

WASHINGTON, Sept. 8—President Roosevelt hailed the surrender of Italy today as "a great victory for the United Nations" and also "a great victory for the Italian people" against "their real enemies, the Nazis," but cautioned against over-optimism. Addressing the nation on the opening of the Third War Bond drive, the President said "the time for celebration is not yet" and added that "our ultimate objectives in this war continue to be Berlin and Tokyo."

Toward the end of his speech the President interpolated three words which gave basis to report that Allied armies already were on the move again in the Mediterranean when he spoke of troops in landing barges moving up to enemy coasts "at this moment."

"This war does not and must not stop for one single instant," he declared. "Your fighting men know that. Those of them who are moving forward through jungles against lurking Japs—those who are landing at this moment in barges moving through the dawn up the strange enemy coasts—those who are diving their boats down on the target at roof-top level at this moment—every one of these men knows that this war is a full-time job and that it will

Continued on Page Seventeen

Germans Charge Betrayal by Italy In Plot With Russian Government

By GEORGE AXELSSON
By Wireless to THE NEW YORK TIMES.

STOCKHOLM, Sweden, Sept. 8—Berlin's newspapers branded Italy's capitulation as cowardly treachery last night. The German press abounds in scathing denunciation of Premier Pietro Badoglio and King Victor Emmanuel, as well as

"Mussolini was too great a personality for a nation like that," a German official said. This is the second time that Victor Emmanuel has broken his word, because the King "left Germany in the lurch" in 1915 when he joined the Allies.

Forgetting its praise of the Italians during the heyday of the pact, the German press now condemns the Italians as third-rate individuals. "The cowardly perfidy of Badoglio caps the crime," one paper said.

"by being collusion with the Soviet Government, which is treason not only against Italy and Germany but also against all Europe."

Berlin added that the Germans had no intention of giving up their entrenchments in Italy, where they hoped to offer efficient resistance. Italy, since last night, is German-occupied territory to the extent that the Germans have been able to gain a firm footing there. In the Italian provinces occupied by the Germans, Berlin boasts that fascist lines will be revived even if "we leave it to the Italians in those provinces to organize themselves along fascist lines."

Official circles are reviving accusations of broken words of honor

Continued on Page Nine

War News Summarized

THURSDAY, SEPTEMBER 9, 1943

Italy has surrendered unconditionally, and all hostilities between that country and the United Nations ceased yesterday. An armistice was signed last Friday, the same day that Italy was invaded, but the victors reserved the right to withhold announcement until the most favorable moment for the Allies. [1:8; map, P.3.]

No official comment came from Berlin, but the German radio, after withholding the news for hours, was furious at the "treachery." [1:5-6.]

Germany's Balkan satellites were so shaken by the Italian surrender that Bulgaria, Rumania and Hungary were reported ready to follow Italy out of the war. [10:3.]

President Roosevelt, in a radio address last night, termed the surrender a great victory for the United Nations. But he warned: "The time for celebration is not yet. Our ultimate objectives in this war continue to be Berlin and Tokyo." [1:5-6.]

The actual fighting in Italy was of a minor nature. Land forces advanced on both coasts. [3:6.] Airfield were hit by Allied bombers and the Rome radio reported heavy raids on suburbs of the city. [4:1.]

With one Axis partner out of the war, the two others continued to be hit hard. The Red Army captured Stalino and cleared the Donets Basin. [1:1; map, P.22.] Allied bombers from Britain struck enemy airfields in France and Belgium [23:2], while down in New Guinea Japanese troops were providing weak opposition as the Allies closed in on Lae. [22:1.]

The naval task force that raided Marcus Island Sept. 1 destroyed 80 per cent of the Japanese military installations. We lost three planes. [1:2.]

way to sober realization of continued danger when the Germans occupied Milan and other cities and imposed martial law. [3:1.]

General Eisenhower, announcing the surrender, promised support to all Italians who helped fight the Germans. Marshal Badoglio issued a proclamation ordering all fighting against the "Anglo-American forces" to cease and commanding resistance to "attacks from any other quarter."

Allied radios and planes carried messages urging the Italians to take vengeance on their "German oppressors" and to prevent trains, ships and trucks from carrying German troops or supplies. [All the foregoing, 1:8; map, P.3.]

Landings in the Naples area followed only a few hours after the surrender announcement and it was believed the Allies were attempting to cut off German troops in southern Italy. The American Seventh Army was reported among the invading forces. [1:3; map, P. 4.] Earlier, the Italian Navy and merchant marine had been urged to take their ships to designated points and to scuttle the vessels as a last resort to keep them from the Germans. [7:4.]

Wild demonstrations of joy were reported from all over Italy, but in the north they gave

GEN. EISENHOWER ANNOUNCES ARMISTICE

Capitulation Acceptable to U. S., Britain and Russia Is Confirmed in Speech by Badoglio

TERMS SIGNED ON DAY OF INVASION

Disclosure Withheld by Both Sides Until Moment Most Favorable for the Allies—Italians Exhorted to Aid United Nations

By MILTON BRACKER
By Wireless to THE NEW YORK TIMES.

ALLIED HEADQUARTERS IN NORTH AFRICA, Sept. 8—Italy has surrendered her armed forces unconditionally and all hostilities between the soldiers of the United Nations and those of the weakest of the three Axis partners ceased as of 16:30 Greenwich Mean Time today [12:30 P. M., Eastern War Time].

At that time, Gen. Dwight D. Eisenhower announced over the United Nations radio that a secret military armistice had been signed in Sicily on the afternoon of Friday, Sept. 3, by his representative and one sent by Premier Pietro Badoglio. That was the day when, at 4:50 A. M., British and Canadian troops crossed the Strait of Messina and landed on the Italian mainland to open a campaign in which, up to yesterday, they had occupied about sixty miles of the Calabrian coast from the Petrace River in the north to Bova Marina in the south.

The complete collapse of Italian military resistance in no way suggested that the Germans would not defend Italy with all the strength at their command. But the capitulation, in undisclosed terms that were acceptable to the United States, the United Kingdom and the Union of Soviet Socialist Republics, came exactly forty days after the downfall of Benito Mussolini, the dictator who, by playing jackal to Adolf Hitler, had led his country to the catastrophic mistake of declaring war on France three years and three months ago this Friday.

Negotiations Begun Several Weeks Ago

The negotiations leading to the armistice were opened by the war-weary and bomb-battered nation a few weeks ago, it was revealed today, and a preliminary meeting was arranged and held in an unnamed neutral country.

The Italians who had approached the British and American authorities were bluntly told that the terms remained what they had been: unconditional surrender. They agreed, and the document was signed five days ago. But it was agreed to hold back the announcement and its effective date until the moment most favorable to the Allies.

That moment came today, when the Allied Commander in Chief, in a historic broadcast, announced the armistice. He concluded with the reminder that all Italians who aided in the ejection of the Germans from Italy would have the support and assistance of the United Nations.

One hour and fifteen minutes after the General's voice had gone out over the air, Marshal Badoglio faced a microphone in Rome and confirmed the armistice. He concluded with the promise that the Italian forces would oppose attacks "from any other quarter," although they were laying down the arms that they had taken up against the Anglo-American armies.

Military Aspect Emphasized

Although it was emphasized that the armistice was a strictly military instrument, "signed by soldiers," it was disclosed that it contained a clause binding Italy to comply with political, economic and financial conditions to be imposed at the Allies' discretion.

[It was believed that the armistice conditions were substantially the same as those imposed on France in 1940, which allowed the Germans to use all strategic French ports and military bases to wage war against Britain, The United Press reported.]

Immediately after the announcement of the armistice, the Allies made two appeals—one to the Italian people and one to the Italian Fleet—urging them to rally to a cause that was, in effect, the liberation of their own country. The appeal to the people was disseminated by radio and air-borne leaflet, while that to the Navy was broadcast by Admiral Sir Andrew Browne Cunningham, the Allies' Mediterranean naval commander.

The Italian people, particularly transport, railroad and dock workers, were asked not to give the slightest aid to the Germans. The men who man Italian ships received specific instructions how to bring their vessels into the protection of the United Nations.

Although the fear was proved unjustified by Marshal Badoglio's broadcast, the Allies had taken no chances of a German move to forestall his giving the news to the people. As a safeguard, they had obtained from the Italians an agreement to leave one senior military representative behind when the others returned to Rome. This man is now in Sicily and presumably, had Marshal Badoglio not gone on the air, his representative would have broadcast the decision to the Italian public.

As a further earnest of good faith, Marshal Badoglio had arranged to send the text of the proclamation that he made this evening to Allied Headquarters here. He kept his word.

1,181 Days at War and Losses

Italy quit the war after 1,181 days, during which she steadily lost territory and prestige. Last May 7, with the fall of Tunis and Bizerte, the last Italian soldier in North Africa was doomed. Since then, Sicily, part of Metropolitan Italy, was occupied in thirty-eight days.

The Italians endured two raids on military targets in Rome

Continued on Page Three

"All the News That's Fit to Print."

The New York Times.

LATE CITY EDITION
Cloudy and warmer today; fresh winds.
Temperatures Yesterday—Max., 30; Min., 9
Sunrise, 8:18 A. M.; Sunset, 8:34 P. M.

Copyright, 1943, by The New York Times Company

VOL. XCIII.—No. 31,381.

Entered as Second-Class Matter,
Postoffice, New York, N. Y.

NEW YORK, SATURDAY, DECEMBER 25, 1943.

THREE CENTS NEW YORK CITY

EISENHOWER NAMED COMMANDER FOR INVASION; 3,000 PLANES SMASH FRENCH COAST; BERLIN HIT; ROOSEVELT PROMISES NATION A DURABLE PEACE

STRIKE CALLED OFF BY 230,000 IN TRAIN AND ENGINE UNIONS

But Non-Operating Men Meet Carriers and Reject Offer Made for Overtime Pay

GIVE BYRNES NO ANSWER

He Says Agreement Must Meet Requirements Set Forth in the Stabilization Program

By LOUIS STARK
Special to THE NEW YORK TIMES.

WASHINGTON, Dec. 24—The Brotherhood of Locomotive Engineers and the Brotherhood of Railroad Trainmen today canceled notices for a strike of their 230,000 members on Dec. 30 in view of President Roosevelt's offer and their acceptance of arbitration by the Chief Executive.

The conductors, firemen and switchmen's unions, also members of the "Big Five" operating and transportation brotherhoods, representing more than 120,000 employes, have rejected arbitration by the President and have not called off the strike of their members set for Dec. 30.

The other major development today in the railroad wage situation was a three-hour conference in the office of James F. Byrnes, chief of the Office of War Mobilization, participated in by committees of the railroads and the spokesmen for the fifteen non-operating unions, whose 1,100,000 members are scheduled to strike on Dec. 30.

At this meeting it was reported that the non-operating unions asked for a wage increase of 6 cents an hour as compensation for overtime after forty hours. These employes receive overtime after forty-eight hours of service. The carriers are reported to have offered 4 cents an hour for overtime, but it is understood that this was rejected by the unions.

Insists on Negotiations

B. M. Jewell, chief negotiator for the unions, is said to have been pressed by Mr. Byrnes for a reply to the President's demand that the non-operating employes permit him to act as sole and final arbiter in their dispute with the carriers.

The union leader is said to have replied with some asperity that the President last night gave the unions until Monday to reply to the arbitration proposal, and that in the meantime they had obtained from the President authority to proceed and seek an agreement with the carriers, whose committees were headed by Jacob Aronson, vice president of the New York Central Railroad.

The offer of 4 cents an hour for overtime was understood to be above the 4 to 10 cents an hour sliding scale wage increase recommended in the non-operating unions' case by an emergency board, convened by Frank M. Vinson, the Economic Stabilization Director, that rejected the 8 cents an hour proposal of a previous emergency board.

Byrnes's Statement

The conference in Mr. Byrnes's office, which was attended for a short time by Mr. Vinson, ended at 5:30 P. M. and the following statement was issued on Mr. Byrnes's behalf:

"The representatives of the carriers and the non-operating brotherhoods met in the conference room of the Office of War Mobilization.

"The representatives of the carriers were not present at the conference the President held with the representatives of the brotherhoods yesterday afternoon. Justice Byrnes advised the carriers' representatives that the President desired to know whether they would object to his arbitrating the differences between the carriers and the non-operating brotherhoods.

"The representatives of the carriers stated that they were entirely willing to agree that the President should arbitrate the differences just as they had agreed in

Continued on Page Twenty-six

17 Perish as Fire Sweeps 42d Street Lodging House

Scores Hurt in 'Bowery-Type' Building Disaster, Worst of Its Kind Here in Years—Many Trapped Asleep

Sixteen bodies had been removed last night from a five-story brick structure at 437-439 West Forty-second Street, between Ninth and Tenth Avenues, the four upper floors of which were occupied by a "Bowery-type" lodging house, after one of the city's worst fires in years virtually had consumed the entire interior.

A seventeenth victim died at 7:15 P. M. in Roosevelt Hospital, to which most of the score of injured were removed.

The actual loss of life probably never will be known. With most of the victims burned beyond recognition and in many cases nothing remaining for them, the task of counting the dead and identifying them was proving almost impossible. Authorities, after checking for hours, could not even determine

how many persons were in the building at the time of the fire. They were faced with the fact that the lodging house had beds in three-foot by six cubicles, separated by flimsy plywood partitions, and in hall-like dormitories "accommodating" 248 persons. It was said the beds were well filled with restaurant and other night workers.

The fire, believed to have smoldered for three hours, started at 2 P. M. as if set by a hundred torches. Trapped in their sleep many were burned to death in their "cells," rooms so tiny that a lodger had literally to crawl into bed through a special door on a central vertical hinge that folded to permit entry.

The victims groped through confusion

Continued on Page Twenty-six

WLB PEACE OFFER WIRED STEEL UNION

Davis Tells Murray Retroactivity Can Be Reconsidered Within Wage Formula

Special to THE NEW YORK TIMES.

WASHINGTON, Dec. 24—William H. Davis, chairman of the War Labor Board, telegraphed today to Philip Murray, president of the CIO United Steel Workers, that if labor members of the board desired to reconsider their vote on the retroactive pay issue "the public members will favor such reconsideration."

But, while he indicated that a retroactive basis might be approved within the framework of the present ("Little Steel") wage stabilization formula, Mr. Davis stated in his message that the public members could not now determine "any question of retroactivity that might come up in any future change in the wage stabilization policy."

Presuming that any such future change would be applied to "all wage-earners," he wrote that retroactivity in general or in particular ought to be decided when and if the change is made.

[A production stoppage was reported early this morning by The Associated Press with the expiration of contracts at midnight covering 35,000 employees at the Republic Steel Corporation and Youngstown Sheet and Tube Company. At these plants in Youngstown and in Cleveland picketing began.]

"Misunderstanding" Deplored

Mr. Davis's telegram said:

"You are quoted as saying that the proposal of the public members of the War Labor Board as to retroactivity in the steel negotiations violates principles enunciated by the board in the recent cases affecting hundreds of thousands of workers, that the proposal of the

Continued on Page Twenty-six

CITY AN OPEN HOUSE FOR WARTIME YULE

Heart-Warming Parties for Service Men and Women Are Chief Among Festivities

New York was far from a big, cold, gray city as it ushered in its third wartime Christmas last night with heart-warming church services, gay parties, gifts for the ill and unfortunate, and messages of good-will that brought cheer to its teeming millions and to the men and women visitors in the service.

It will not be a white Christmas, according to the weather man, but it will be cold.

Tens of thousands of visitors, many of them members of the families of service men, were in the city for the week-end. Railroads, doing a peak business, were handicapped by the bitter cold in the surrounding country. Utility services were taxed, every train to and from the city was loaded to capacity, with standees in the aisles. Because of the cold, many trains were late.

Grand Central Terminal and the Pennsylvania Station were packed. Policemen kept the crowds moving. Buses and bus terminals throughout the city did a land-office business, too.

Stores Experience Let-Up

Only in the stores did Christmas Eve bring a let-up. While business was brisk, the real crush had subsided and only last-minute shoppers were on hand.

The churches of all faiths welcomed the Holy Day with midnight services, offering prayers for a victorious peace. There were many men in uniform at masses, carol services and communion.

Virtually every Roman Catholic church celebrated a midnight mass by permission of Archbishop Francis J. Spellman. Episcopal churches celebrated communion, while many churches of other faiths held can-

Continued on Page Nine

Biggest of War Plants Will Make Army Bomber Engines at Chicago

By The United Press.

CHICAGO, Dec. 24—The country's largest war plant, a series of structures sprawling over 500 acres of land, was ready today to turn out an unending stream of engines for Army bombing planes.

The giant inland plant on Chicago's South Side was built by the Dodge division of the Chrysler Corporation. Willow Run could be set down in the main building, with enough room left to lay out twenty baseball diamonds.

There are nineteen buildings in the plant, all ready for production. The main building, the machining assembly plant, covers eighty-two acres.

The plant has fourteen cafeterias and kitchens, butcher shops and bakeries to feed employees.

A parking lot a mile and a quar-

ter long will accommodate 14,000 automobiles. The interplant communication system has 500 miles of telephone lines. Utility services are sufficient for a city of 75,000 population.

Officials revealed that the machine engines will turn out parts for 2,200-horsepower, eighteen-cylinder Wright engines.

The plant, already called "Hitler's headache," will employ more than 25,000 persons when it enters mass production.

Prior to the completion of the Chicago plant, the bomber factory owned by the Government and operated by Henry Ford at Willow Run, twenty-five miles from Detroit, was called the largest war production unit in the world. It covers two square miles.

RECORD AIR BLOW

'Forts,' Liberators and Medium Bombers Rock 'Special' Targets

ALL CRAFT RETURN

RAF Pounds the German Capital With 1,120 Tons Before Dawn

By DAVID ANDERSON
By Cable to THE NEW YORK TIMES.

LONDON, Dec. 24—The greatest number of American heavy bombers ever to take off from Britain attacked "special military installations" of the Germans along the coast of northern France today as part of record operations of probably 3,000 Allied warplanes across the Channel.

Before dawn hundreds of the most powerful bombers of the Royal Air Force struck Berlin again with more than 1,120 tons of high explosives and fire missiles.

Several features of the twin-fisted battering by the Allied air forces on the eve of Christmas made the day a memorable one for the enemy, even taking into account the Anglo-American achievements of recent weeks.

Headquarters of the United States Eighth Air Force announced that 1,300 bombers handled by American crews took part in the daylight missions.

An even greater number of RAF, Dominion and Allied planes were out. Every one of the bombers and fighters of the joint forces returned to its base, according to a communiqué issued by headquarters of the United States Army here and the British Air Ministry.

Included in the American force were the largest formations of Flying Fortresses and Liberators ever sent into the air. Since an estimated 750 United States "heavies" at one time have attacked targets in western Germany within the past month, the day's operations entailed the use of close to, if not exceeding, 800 four-motored bombers.

The most concentrated attacks were carried out in the Pas-de-Ca-

Continued on Page Three

TO KEEP IT BY ARMS

President Says 4 Nations Agree on This for as Long as Necessary

'COST MAY BE HIGH'

German Might Must End, He Says on Air, Warning 'Japs' of Bad News

By JOHN H. CRIDER
Special to THE NEW YORK TIMES.

HYDE PARK, N. Y., Dec. 24—President Roosevelt promised the country and the world this Christmas Eve that they could look for insured peace with "certainty," even though "the cost may be high and the time long," and said that the United States, Great Britain, Soviet Russia and China were agreed to use force to maintain that peace "for as long as it may be necessary."

Speaking from the study in the Franklin D. Roosevelt Library, one of his favorite rendezvous, with his family gathered informally around him, the President gave his first comprehensive report on his recent conferences in the Middle East over the most extensive broadcast facilities ever set up in this country.

For the first time the President tempered his "unconditional surrender" ultimatum of Casablanca by stating that the United Nations did not want to enslave the German people but wanted them to have "a normal chance to develop in peace as useful and respectable members of the European family."

Here appeared to be one of the great achievements of the conference at Teheran—a united view by the Allies in Europe on what kind of a post-war Germany they would look for, which closes the gulf which appeared to exist between the Anglo-American "unconditional surrender" demand, and the more hopeful outlook for the future which the Russians have been

Continued on Page Eight

The text of the President's address appears on Page 8.

NEW INVASION COMMANDER IN CHIEF

Gen. Dwight D. Eisenhower
The New York Times, 1943

Pope Prays for Just Peace Kept by Wise Use of Force

By The Associated Press.

LONDON, Dec. 24—Praying that this may be the last war Christmas and that a truly Christian peace may be celebrated in the coming year, Pope Pius XII today called for the world's responsible leaders to check the instincts of hate and vengeance and give rise to "the resplendent dawn of a new spirit of world union."

Raising his voice to a vibrant ring in outlining "the principles for a peace program," the Pontiff called for a "normal measure of power," sanctions and "the employment of force" to achieve and maintain peace, but warned that true peace "can never be a harsh imposition supported by arms" alone.

"An hour like the present—so full of possibilities for vast beneficent progress no less than for fatal defects and blunders—has perhaps never been seen in the history of mankind," said the Holy Father, who spoke on Christmas Eve from the bayonet-circled Vatican, where he has been isolated except by radio since the Germans occupied Rome in September.

The 35-minute address was delivered on the radio in Italian, but an official English language translation later was made available.

Juridical Basis for Peace

"A true peace is not the mathematical result of a proportion of forces, but in its last and deepest meaning is a moral and juridical process," said the Pope, speaking from what he called the "abysmal ruins of this terrible war."

"It (peace) is not, in fact, achieved without the employment of force, and its very existence

Continued on Page Ten

The text of the Pope's address appears on Page 10.

RED ARMY TAKES KEY TO VITEBSK

Gorodok, 17 Miles From Goal, Falls After Russian Feint Outwits Nazi Defense

By The Associated Press.

LONDON, Saturday, Dec. 25—The Russian Baltic Army cracked a model German defense-in-depth line and captured the heavily fortified lake town of Gorodok, seventeen miles north of Vitebsk yesterday, sweeping on over 2,000 German dead in a continuing offensive to take sixty more towns and hamlets, Moscow announced early today.

Resuming their drive after a two-day slow-down, the Russians swept to within fifteen miles of the Vitebsk-Polotsk rail line, an important east-west supply artery for the Germans, as they advanced southward along the Nevel-Vitebsk railroad.

In another fighting area to the south—southwest of Zhlobin—the

Continued on Page Five

GENERAL IS SHIFTED

Choice of 'Big 3' Parley, He Has Montgomery as British Field Leader

WILSON IS SUCCESSOR

Mid-East Head Honored —Spaatz to Direct U. S. Air Strategy

Special to THE NEW YORK TIMES.

HYDE PARK, N. Y., Dec. 24—President Roosevelt announced today the appointment of Gen. Dwight D. Eisenhower to lead the invasion of Europe from the north and west, and from London came word that Gen. Sir Bernard L. Montgomery of North African fame would head the British troops under General Eisenhower to form a proved and hard-hitting team to lead the assault on Adolf Hitler's "Fortress Europe."

The President's announcement of General Eisenhower's selection at the recent Teheran conference to lead the main attack against Germany also set to rest the old rumors regarding the probable appointment of Gen. George C. Marshall, Army Chief of Staff, to that post.

The President, in his radio report today on the recent conferences at Teheran and Cairo, also named Lieut. Gen. Carl A. Spaatz as commander of "the entire American strategic bombing force operating against Germany."

This was taken to mean that while General Eisenhower will confine his command to the mass attack on Europe from the north and west, General Spaatz' command over all American strategic bombardment of Germany extends to operations against Germany from all neighboring bases.

Quashes Marshall Rumors

The President gave a vivid picture in his radio report of complete agreement between Prime Minister Churchill, Premier Stalin and himself regarding a detailed program for the annihilation of Germany by land and air from all directions.

He also paid high tribute to General Marshall, presumably to set old rumors at rest. Some persons have argued that the position to be occupied by General Eisenhower is of greatest importance, but the official decision now revealed seems to give credence to the opinion that the most important position in the Army is that of Chief of Staff, as Washington is the only place from which the whole global operation can be commanded.

"To the members of our armed forces, to their wives, mothers and fathers, I want to affirm the great faith and confidence that we have in General Marshall and Admiral King (Chief of Naval Operations), who direct all of our armed might throughout the world," the President declared.

Their Military Genius Stressed

"Upon them," he said, "falls the responsibility of planning the strategy; of determining where and when to fight. Both of these men have already gained high places in American history; places which will record in that history many evidences of their military genius that cannot be published today."

The announcement from London told not only of General Montgomery's appointment to head the British invasion forces under General Eisenhower but also of Gen. Sir Henry Maitland Wilson's appointment to replace General Eisenhower as commander of the Mediterranean Theatre and Gen. Sir Harold R. L. G. Alexander's appointment to command all Allied forces in Italy.

The Teheran military decision was as much as anything else that the American handling of the invasion of North Africa and of Italy had deeply impressed the United States allies. Those invasions may now be regarded as the testing phase of the main European invasion, since the American officers identi-

Continued on Page Two

War News Summarized

SATURDAY, DECEMBER 25, 1943

President Roosevelt proudly announced to the world yesterday the appointment of General Dwight D. Eisenhower as supreme commander of the Anglo-American invasion forces—a selection, he said, that was made at the Teheran conference, where every point concerning the impending east-west-south attack on Germany had been decided.

It was announced from London that General Wilson would succeed General Eisenhower as commander of the Allied forces in the Mediterranean Theatre; that General Montgomery would be chief of British Army units under General Eisenhower; that General Alexander would head the Allied forces in Italy, and that General Spaatz would be American Air Force commander against Germany. [All the foregoing, 1.]

Peace is certain, but the cost of bringing it about will be high and the realization may be distant, President Roosevelt declared during the Christmas Eve broadcast from his Hyde Park home. He said the United Nations had no desire to enslave the German people but wanted them to develop as respectable members of the European family. As for Japan, he said that empire is now being enveloped in a band of steel and there is plenty of bad news for the Japanese in the offing. [1:5.]

Speaking from the German-surrounded Vatican, Pope Pius XII made a plea for a just peace and declared that a normal measure of power and the employment of force were needed to achieve it, but he decried any harsh imposition supported by arms alone. [1:6-7.]

and British planes of virtually all types—the greatest concentration in air history—bombed the Pas-de-Calais area of France, where, it is believed, the Germans have implanted rocket guns. In this, the fifth straight assault on these targets, the American Eighth Air Force sent 1,300 planes, a record number for any single operation. All Allied planes returned. The attack followed a Royal Air Force blow at Berlin, reportedly hitting the southeast industrial area near Tempelhof. [1:4, map P. 3.]

The fortified town of Gorodok, seventeen miles from Vitebsk on the Vitebsk-Nevel railroad, was successfully stormed by the Russian Army, which drove ahead to capture sixty other places. Southwest of Zhlobin, in southern White Russia, large German tank and infantry attacks were beaten back. [1:7, map, P. 5.]

The British Eighth Army captured Vezzani, three miles southwest of Ortona, where fighting continued in the streets. There was little activity except for patrol thrusts on the Fifth Army front, because of deep mud. Medium Allied bombers struck at the Riviera coast, hitting bridges, railroads and viaducts. [1:6-7.]

Cape Gloucester, which seems to be shaping up as another possible invasion point on New Britain Island, was hit by 300 more tons of Allied aerial bombs, bringing the total tonnage dropped since Dec. 1 to 2,500. [6:1.]

The Navy announced that the United States submarine Grayling was presumably lost with her complement of sixty-five men. [6:2.]

8th Army Wins Town Near Ortona; Americans Take a Hill, Lose One

By MILTON BRACKER
By Wireless to THE NEW YORK TIMES.

ALGIERS, Dec. 24—The Allied armies in Italy kept up pressure all along the line yesterday despite the imminence of Christmas, but were unable quite to complete the capture of Ortona or accomplish substantial gains on the Tyrrhenian half of the front.

Although Canadian units of Gen. Sir Bernard L. Montgomery's Eighth Army had driven back the last German defenders of Ortona to the northwest corner of the shell-blasted and tank-razed town, and apparently intended to deprive the Allies of the full use of the most important port immediately below Pescara as long as possible. Evidence of the toll the Germans have been paying for their desper-

ate defense of the area was the discovery of a new cemetery at the crossroads just southwest of Ortona with at least 100 German graves.

The Eighth Army did manage to wrest from the enemy another village three miles southwest of Ortona and a mile beyond the Ortona-Orsogna road. It was Vezzani, which is three and a half miles from the coast and, like Ortona, just about twelve from Pescara. Other units of General Montgomery's veteran army have also penetrated to the outskirts of Villa Grande, a mile northeast of Vezzani on a secondary road paralleling the coast.

On the Fifth Army front the

Continued on Page Three

"All the News
That's Fit to Print"

The New York Times.

LATE CITY EDITION
Partly cloudy, slightly warmer
today; gentle to moderate winds.
Temperatures Yesterday—Max., 63; Min., 55
Sunrise, 5:25 A. M.; Sunset, 8:22 P. M.

VOL. XCIII. No. 31,544.

Entered as Second-Class Matter,
Postoffice, New York, N. Y.

Copyright, 1944, by The New York Times Company.

NEW YORK, MONDAY, JUNE 5, 1944.

THREE CENTS NEW YORK CITY

ROME CAPTURED INTACT BY THE 5TH ARMY AFTER FIERCE BATTLE THROUGH SUBURBS; NAZIS MOVE NORTHWEST; AIR WAR RAGES ON

TRANSIT MEN BALK AT MAYOR'S INQUIRY INTO OUTSIDE JOBS

Demand for Sworn Statements Covering Family Earnings Evokes Union Protest

RESENTMENT WIDESPREAD

Many Department Heads Cold Toward Policy and Some Authorize Dual Work

By PAUL CROWELL

Widespread resentment among city employes against Mayor La Guardia's crusade to keep them from holding outside jobs on their own time was intensified yesterday. It became known that Investigation Commissioner Edgar Bromberger, by direction of the Mayor, had asked the 35,000 employes of the unified transit system to make sworn answers to forty questions concerning their own employment and that of all working members of their families.

The Transport Workers Union and other organizations representing city transit workers already have registered informal protests and are considering formal action. It was reported that the TWU was prepared to ask its members receiving such questionnaires from Commissioner Bromberger's office to turn them over to the union.

The questionnaire, of a type said to have been sent to employes of other city agencies, asks the transit worker to give full details about his own job, any job he may have outside, any job his wife may hold, any jobs his children may be filling. Full details concerning pay rates on all such jobs are demanded. The workers are asked also how they obtained outside jobs, whether they paid anyone to get them and whether they are making payments to anyone in connection with outside jobs.

Board Members Dislike Policy

The regulations of the Board of Transportation do not forbid the holding of outside jobs and individual members of the board were known to feel that so long as employes were punctual and efficient in their tasks their outside activities were their own affair. Despite this feeling, however, the board is prepared to carry out the policy laid down by the Mayor. An informal survey of other city agencies conducted last week indicated that most of their heads held about the same attitude, but felt that the Mayor's policy must be carried out if he insisted upon it.

The Mayor's insistence that city employes, regardless of departmental rules forego such activities, led him recently to demand that charges be brought against an electrical engineer employed by the Board of Transportation who was teaching one night a week at City College, receiving $12 for each night's work. An exchange of views between the Mayor and the Board of Transportation resulted in a decision to let the employe continue teaching until the end of the current term, with the understanding that he would not resume teaching in the fall.

The electrical engineer, who is a graduate of one of the country's leading technical schools, was certified by the Board of Transportation, after investigation, to be efficient, painstaking and punctual, and the Mayor was told that his outside work made him a better city servant, while the small additional income was a welcome addition to his modest salary. It was also pointed out to the Mayor that there was nothing in the board's rules or the law to bar the outside work. The Mayor is reported to have replied that the man must keep one job or the other, but could not hold both.

Outside work by employes is a live issue in the Board of Transportation, where it is estimated that at least 10 per cent of the 35,000 transit workers have extra work to increase family income. Resentment against the Mayor's

Continued on Page 11

Laval Tries to Shift Funds to Argentina

Pierre Laval, chief of the Vichy government, recently tried to transfer $50,000 from Spain to Argentina, the Brazzaville radio said yesterday in a broadcast recorded by the Columbia Broadcasting System's short-wave listening station.

"A Madrid bank revealed to the Spanish authorities that a deposit of $50,000 had been made with them for transfer to an Argentinian bank," the French radio said. "An inquiry was opened, and the person behind the depositor was discovered: He is Pierre Laval."

The same broadcast reported: "Germans in France have been buying gold at very high prices. Among the German agents arrested by French police for illegal traffic in gold was one who identified himself in order to be freed. He told the police commissioner that he was the director of a bank in a small German town. Because of his age, he had not been drafted into active military service, but his competence in financial matters made possible his being used in this work, in which he had been engaged since 1940."

JOHNSTON IN RUSSIA SCOFFS AT U. S. REDS

Business Leader Also Praises Soviet 'Capitalism'—Calls Ideologies Bridgeable

By The United Press.

MOSCOW, June 4—With straight-from-the-shoulder frankness, Eric Johnston, president of the United States Chamber of Commerce, told 100 Soviet trade leaders yesterday that a gulf separated the economies of the United States and Russia, but that bridges of practical cooperation could be thrown across that gulf.

Mr. Johnston advocated extensive post-war trade and visits between American business and "Soviet capitalists" as one bridge, but said that "each of our countries should be allowed to pursue its own unique economic experiment unimpeded by the other."

Bluntly, he told the Russians that Americans "were most private-minded and most individual-minded and, make no mistake, we are determined to remain so and even become more so."

Mr. Johnston, who arrived in Russia last week, was luncheon guest of A. I. Mikoyan, Soviet Foreign Trade Commissar, at Spiridonovka House. At the table sat Soviet trade experts, members of the Soviet Foreign Office, United States Ambassador W. Averell Harriman and Soviet military men.

At first the Russians appeared nonplussed by Mr. Johnston's bluntness, but later they burst into gales of mirth at his sallies at American Communists and Marxism.

"I shall try to show you my admiration for your heroic deeds and

Continued on Page 6

Enraged Bull Kills 2 Brothers, Gores Neighbor on Long Island

BABYLON, L. I., June 4 — Two dairy farmers, brothers, were found this morning gored and trampled to death on the Ames Farm in North Babylon, victims of their city servant, while the small guernsey bull, which had run wild and scattered their herd of thirty cows over near-by roads. A neighbor, trying to round up the scattered herd, was gored in the groin by the infuriated animal.

State troopers were forced to shoot and kill the belligerent bull. The victims were George W. Ames, 41 years old, and his brother, James Hawley Ames, 35, who operated the Ames Farm on Phelps Lane, North Babylon. So far as is known no one saw the unequal encounter that cost them their lives. Their bodies were discovered, lying about 100 feet apart, several hundred yards from the cow barn.

The first intimation that anything was amiss came with com-

plaints to the State Police in North Babylon that the Ames cows were wandering off the pasture and on the near-by Phelps Lane and Belmont Road. Two State troopers were sent to the farm and succeeded in getting most of the cows back into the pasture along with the bull. They put in a call for two additional troopers to round up the remainder of the herd.

Their suspicions aroused by the fact that the milk delivery truck, fully loaded, was standing in its place although it usually left on its rural route at 8 A. M., the troopers made their way to the farmhouse. There they found Mrs. Kathleen Ames, mother of the two men, and her daughter, Jane L. Ames, a school teacher.

A search of the farm was begun and Trooper Anthony Cherry came

Continued on Page 20

FOE 'EXPLAINS' STEP

Hitler Ordered Troops Out to Save Rome, Germans Assert

ENEMY PLEA BARED

Kesselring Made Last-Minute Renewal of Open-City Offer

By The Associated Press.

LONDON, June 4—The Germans announced tonight in a special communiqué—broadcast after the Allies had liberated Rome—the withdrawal of German troops to the northwest of the city and said that the Allies had received a plan whereby Rome would have been regarded as an "open city."

The open-city proposals were said to have been advanced at 11 P. M. on Saturday, less than twenty-four hours before Rome changed hands. The first word from Adolf Hitler's headquarters in several days asserted that the fight in Italy would continue and that measures were being taken "to force final victory for Germany and her allies." The communiqué said:

"As the front line, in the course of the present fighting in Italy, was gradually approaching nearer and nearer to the city of Rome, there was danger that Rome, one of the oldest cultural centers of the world, would be directly involved in the present fighting. Hitler has ordered the withdrawal of German troops to the northwest of Rome to prevent the destruction of Rome.

"The struggle in Italy will be continued with unshakable determination to break the enemy attacks and to force final victory for Germany and her allies. The necessary measures for an eventual German victory are being taken in close collaboration with fascist Italy and other allied powers.

"The year of invasion will bring Germany's enemies an annihilating defeat at the most decisive moment."

Kesselring's Proposals Listed

Field Marshal Gen. Albert Kesselring, the German commander in Italy, sent the Allies proposals that Rome be regarded as an open city, a special announcement from Hitler's headquarters said. The statement was broadcast by the German radio and was received only after a dispatch filed from Rome had announced the crushing of the last German resistance units within the city. The broadcast said:

"The German High Command announced that the supreme commander of German troops in Italy, Field Marshal Kesselring, had submitted proposals to the Vatican with the request that they should be conveyed to the Anglo-American High Command. The proposals confirmed the recognition of Rome

Continued on Page 4

THE FIRST OF EUROPE'S WAR CAPITALS TO FALL TO THE ALLIES

The sign tells the troops they have entered Rome.

The New York Times (U. S. Signal Corps Radiotelephoto)

U. S. 'HEAVIES' BOMB IN FRANCE ALL DAY

Attack Boulogne Area Twice, Rip Rail, Air Targets Near Paris—Genoa Blasted

By JAMES MacDONALD

LONDON, Monday, June 5—Continuing to pave the way for the Allied invasion of the Continent hundreds of Allied bombers and fighters from Britain scorched a 200-mile stretch of the French coast yesterday and penetrated inland.

Three separate missions were carried out by the Flying Fortresses and Liberators of the United States Eighth Air Force with fighter escort over northwestern France. They met little Luftwaffe opposition; the enemy flak ranged from moderate to heavy.

In the morning and again in the afternoon strong formations of the

Continued on Page 5

Road to Rome Hard Fought, Yet Crowded With Civilians

By MILTON BRACKER
By Wireless to THE NEW YORK TIMES.

IN THE OUTSKIRTS OF ROME, June 4—The Fifth Army's entry into the suburbs of Rome was made along Highway 6—the Via Casilina, which runs into Rome at Centocelle, a suburb test known for its airport. But the advance did not mean a simple triumphal procession into the heart of Rome. It meant going in in careful infantry columns along the sides of the road. Most of the men had their bayonets fixed and they wore deadly earnest expressions because two wrecked Sherman tanks along the approaches told what had happened to other Americans earlier today.

Just before 4 P. M., a huge column of smoke billowed up from the southwest corner of the city, indicating a demolition. At the same time, a mine went off with a terrible burst beyond the farthest of the two tanks, and it tore an Italian woman to pieces. As the afternoon wore on, the sniping

Continued on Page 4

War News Summarized

MONDAY, JUNE 5, 1944

Rome was liberated from the Nazi-Fascist aggressors last night. The first European capital to be wrested from the enemy came under full Allied control when a force that had fought its way up from the old Anzio beachhead knocked out a German scout car in the center of the city. There was fierce fighting with enemy rear-guard detachments at the outskirts of Rome before the city was liberated. [1:6-7.]

Fifth Army units and the vanguard of the Eighth Army, which entered the Eternal City later, were sent in hot pursuit of the fleeing Germans. Rome was found to be 95 per cent intact, with destruction centered in the railroad yards. [All the foregoing 1:8; maps P. 2.]

German artillery and snipers held off the Allied advance between the airport at Centocello and the city limits. Civilians, obviously happy over the departure of the Nazis, remained calm as United Nations troops moved in. [1:5-6.]

Hitler's headquarters announced after the Fifth Army had entered the city that the Germans had withdrawn to new lines northwest of Rome. Shortly before the city fell they dispatched a proposal that Rome be declared an open city. [1:2.]

Capture of Rome, according to military observers in London, made it much more likely that the main objective of the offensive—destruction of the German Tenth and Fourteenth armies—would be accomplished, with pos-

sible enemy losses reaching up to 100,000. [3:1.]

The AMG, following closely upon the victorious Allied forces, was fully prepared to undertake the gigantic task of feeding some 2,000,000 civilians. Vast stocks of food have been accumulated for distribution. [1:6-7.]

Washington withheld official comment until President Roosevelt's radio address tonight, but the capital was interested in how soon King Victor Emmanuel would fulfill his promise to retire when Rome had fallen to the Allies. [1:7.]

American heavy bombers from Britain smashed three times at enemy installations in France yesterday as the air invasion continued unabated against little enemy opposition. Italian-based aircraft struck rail lines on the French-Italian border. [1:4.]

United States troops resumed the offensive against the three airfields on Biak Island, off New Guinea. Thirty Japanese planes were shot down in widespread fights from Biak to Truk. [8:2.] Continued improvement in Allied positions was reported from Burma [8:3] although in China the Japanese made some gains toward Changsha while losing ground in other sectors. [8:4-5.]

Eric Johnston, president of the United States Chamber of Commerce, told 100 Soviet trade leaders at a Moscow luncheon that he would try to bridge the economic gulf separating American and Russian economies by a closer knowledge and greater mutual respect. [1:2.]

AMERICANS IN FIRST

U. S. Armor Spearheads Thrust Through Last Defenses of Rome

FINAL BATTLE BITTER

Fifth and Eighth Armies Rush On Beyond City in Pursuit of Foe

By The United Press.

NAPLES, June 4—The Fifth Army captured Rome tonight, liberating for the first time a German-enslaved European capital. German rear guards were fleeing in disorganized retreat to the northwest.

Except for the railway yards, smashed by the Allies' bombs, the city was 95 per cent intact, United Press correspondents reported, after their arrival in the city.

Late tonight, the British Eighth Army, rushing into Rome from the southeast along the Via Casilina, was reported to be joining the Fifth Army in close pursuit of the hard-pressed enemy remnants, under orders to destroy them to a man if possible. Only enough troops to maintain order and ferret out any German snipers or suicide nests were to be left in Rome while the Allies' main armies pounded on without pausing to celebrate their greatest triumph, coming 270 days after the start of the Italian campaign.

[The Allies battled German rear guards to the edge of the ancient Forum, The Associated Press reported. A force from the old Anzio beachhead completed the mopping up of German forces at 9:15 P. M. by knocking out an enemy scout car in front of the Bank of Italy, almost within the shadow of Trajan's Column.]

Final Stand at Rome's Gates

At the very gates of Rome, the Germans had made a final stand but Lieut. Gen. Mark W. Clark, after having waited three hours for the enemy troops to withdraw in accordance with their own declaration of Rome as an open city, ordered a violent anti-tank barrage. Then masses of Fifth Army men and weapons crashed into the city and began mopping up enemy snipers and a few tanks and mobile guns trying to cover the retreat.

More of the enemy survivors of the Allies' whirlwind offensive were streaming to the northwest in congested retreat to the northwest at the mercy of the Allies' planes, which, during the day, destroyed or damaged 600 enemy trucks and other vehicles. The Germans' jammed traffic columns stretched fifty-five miles to Lake Bolsena.

Direct radio contact with American correspondents in Rome was established tonight. A United Press reporter said that the main entry into the city had been made along the Via Casilina, which passes through the Porta Maggiore at the southeastern edge of the city. Other Allied troops were reported to have fought their way through the Ostiense freight yards, just south of the St. Paul Gate, the main entrance to the city from due south and only one and one-quarter miles from the Venice Palace.

The entry into Rome came with dramatic suddenness after the Al-

Continued on Page 3

CITY'S FALL FOCUSES POLITICAL CHANGES

Victor Emmanuel's Promise to Retire Recalled — Badoglio Cabinet May Step Down

WASHINGTON, June 4 — Pending receipt of final details of the fall of Rome, most Government leaders tonight refrained from direct comment. It was felt that the first official reaction to the Allied victory would come from President Roosevelt in the radio address that the White House announced he would make tomorrow night.

Interest in the news of the capture of the Italian capital centered not so much in the military victory as in the probable political consequences, particularly those stemming from King Victor Emmanuel's recent statement that he planned to retire as Italy's ruler as soon as Rome fell to the Allies.

The King announced April 12 that he intended to turn Italy's affairs over to Crown Prince Humbert, and said the transfer of power would take place "on the day on which the Allied troops entered Rome."

Even more important than this move are the effects the change may have on the future of the Italian Government now headed by Marshal Pietro Badoglio. Developments, it was said, will be watched closely not only as to other high appointments to be made after Prince Humbert takes over control but also as to any alterations in the structure of the Italian Government.

While the diplomatic and politi-

Continued on Page 4

CONQUERORS' GOAL REACHED BY ALLIES

Fifth and Eighth Armies Drive Up From South on Rome in a Historic Campaign

By HERBERT L. MATTHEWS
By Wireless to THE NEW YORK TIMES.

ROME, June 4—The Allies' troops fought their way into Rome this morning and at nightfall they were still fighting on the outer edges, which the Germans were defending despite all their protestations about considering Rome an open city. Other large German units faced entrapment south of Highway 6 unless they could be pulled back across the Tiber or through Rome.

But Rome has been reached—the goal of conquerors throughout the ages, though now was never before able to make the almost impossible south-north campaign. What Hannibal did not dare to do, the Allies' generals accomplished, but at such a cost in blood, matériel and time that it will probably never again be attempted.

All roads from all over the world led to Rome today as a United

Continued on Page 4

AMG Will Rush Food for Rome, Teeming With 750,000 Refugees

By HAROLD CALLENDER
By Wireless to THE NEW YORK TIMES.

ALGIERS, June 4—The fall of Rome will add about 2,000,000 persons to those whom the Allies have assumed responsibility of feeding, Allied authorities estimated today. But the Allied Military Government, now operating under the Allied Control Commission, has long prepared for the task and is believed to be ready.

The normal population of Rome, capital is estimated to have been swollen by 750,000 refugees from Naples and other places.

Allied authorities have stocks of wheat, canned milk and dehydrated vegetables ready to send to Rome quickly with the cooperation of the Fifth and Eighth Armies regarding transport by trucks. At Anzio landing facilities have

been built since the establishment of the bridgehead, and ships can be unloaded at Gaeta.

In the plans already made Rome has been divided into regions for the distribution of foodstuffs by Italian and Allied personnel under the authority of the commission. An emergency system has been prepared to provide strict control over the black market, which otherwise might absorb the local produce destined to go into the Allied pool for distribution on a ration basis to the masses who cannot afford the black market.

Continued on Page 4

President to Talk On Rome Tonight

By The United Press.

WASHINGTON, June 4—A fifteen-minute radio address will be made by President Roosevelt to the nation tomorrow night on the liberation of Rome, the White House announced tonight. Mr. Roosevelt will speak from 8:30 to 8:45 P. M.

The President's message will be broadcast over all major networks.

The New York Times.

6 A. M. EXTRA
Partly cloudy and warmer today; moderate to fresh winds.
Temperature Yesterday—Max., 67; Min., 51
Sunrise, 4:25 A. M.; Sunset, 8:31 P. M.

Copyright, 1944, by The New York Times Company

VOL. XCIII..No. 31,545.

Entered as Second-Class Matter, Postoffice, New York, N. Y.

NEW YORK, TUESDAY, JUNE 6, 1944.

THREE CENTS NEW YORK CITY

ALLIED ARMIES LAND IN FRANCE IN THE HAVRE-CHERBOURG AREA; GREAT INVASION IS UNDER WAY

ROOSEVELT SPEAKS

Says Rome's Fall Marks 'One Up and Two to Go' Among Axis Capitals

WARNS WAY IS HARD

Asks World to Give the Italians a Chance for Recovery

The text of President Roosevelt's address is on Page 5.

By CHARLES HURD
Special to The New York Times.

WASHINGTON, June 5—President Roosevelt tonight hailed the capture of Rome, first of the three major Axis capitals to fall, as a great achievement on the road to-ward total conquest of the Axis. Rome, he said, marked "one up and two to go."

The President spoke for a quar-ter-hour on the radio, as had been announced yesterday, but his speech was notable for its lack of heroics. It was in no sense a speech of triumph, but rather a tribute to the United Nations forces and leadership that drove the Germans from Rome.

With this tribute he combined a solemn warning that much greater fighting lies ahead before the Axis is defeated, as well as high tributes to the Italian people, whom he again welcomed as a peo-ple into the family of nations op-posed to the Axis.

"Italy should go on," Mr. Roose-velt said, "as a great mother na-tion, contributing to the culture and the progress and the good-will of mankind, developing her special talents in the arts, crafts, the sciences, and preserving her his-toric and cultural heritage for the benefit of all peoples.

"We want and expect the help of the future Italy toward lasting peace. All the other nations op-posed to fascism and nazism ought to help to give Italy a chance."

Shrines Should Live, He Says

President Roosevelt saw consid-erable significance in the fact that Rome should be the first Axis capi-tal to fall. He remarked the shrines, "visible symbols of the faith and determination of the early saints and martyrs that Christianity should live and become 'universal,'" and added that "it will be a source of deep satisfaction that the free-dom of the Pope and of Vatican City is assured by the armies of the United Nations."

There is significance, too, he added, in the fact that Rome was liberated by a composite force of soldiers from many nations.

Reviewing the military picture, the President pointed out that "it would be unwise to-inflate in our own minds the military importance of the capture of Rome." He cau-tioned his auditors that while the Germans have retreated "thou-sands of miles" across Africa and back through Italy "they have suf-fered heavy losses, but not great enough yet to cause collapse.

"Therefore," he added, "the vic-tory still lies some distance ahead. That distance will be covered in due time—have no fear of that. But it will be tough and it will be costly."

Turning to the relief problem in the newly liberated people of Italy, Mr. Roosevelt noted that some persons thought of the finan-cial cost, but he maintained that the work would pay dividends "by eliminating fascism" and any fu-ture desire by Italians to "start another war of aggression." Re-lief has been planned, he added, but transport demands are so great that "improvement must be gradual."

He warned Italy that it "cannot grow in stature by seeking to build up a great militaristic empire."

Continued on Page 5

Conferees Accept Cabaret Tax Cut

By The Associated Press.

WASHINGTON, June 5—A House-Senate conference com-mittee agreed today to cut back the cabaret tax from 30 to 20 per cent, but eliminated a provision exempting service men and wo-men from the levy.

The group decided to put the national debt limit at $260,000,-000,000 as originally requested by the Administration.

The action is subject to House and Senate votes. The conferees met informally today, but mem-bers said that the decisions prob-ably would stand as their final recommendation.

The House, at the insistence of a group of Republicans, passed a bill raising the debt ceiling only from $210,000,000,000 to $240,-000,000,000. The Senate then put the figure at $260,000,000,000 and attached a rider reducing the cabaret tax from 30 to 20 per cent and exempting men and wo-men in uniform from paying the tax on their checks.

Some tax experts argued that this exemption would make ad-ministration of the excise on night clubs impossible.

FEDERAL LAW HELD RULING INSURANCE

Supreme Court, 4-3, Decides Business Is Interstate and Subject to Trust Act

Special to The New York Times.

WASHINGTON, June 5—The Supreme Court, by a four-to-three decision today, held that the insur-ance companies of the country, with assets of $37,000,000,000 and annual premium collections in ex-cess of $6,000,000,000, are in in-terstate commerce and thus subject to the Sherman Anti-Trust Law.

The decision upset precedents which began with a contrary deci-sion by the court more than seven-ty-five years ago and has been reaffirmed repeatedly since the adoption of the anti-trust law in 1890.

The majority decision, writ-ten

Continued on Page 13

PURSUIT ON IN ITALY

Allies Pass Rome, Cross Tiber as Foe Quits Bank Below City

PLANES JOIN IN CHASE

1,200 Vehicles Wrecked —Eighth Army Battles Into More Towns

By The Associated Press.

ROME, June 5—The Allies' ar-mor and motorized infantry roared through Rome today without paus-ing, crossed the Tiber River and proceeded with the grim task of destroying two battered German armies fleeing to the north.

Fighter-bombers spearheaded the pursuit, jamming the escape high-ways with burning enemy trans-port and littering the fields with dead and wounded Germans. The enemy was tired, disorganized and bewildered by the slashing assault, which in twenty-five days had in-flicted a major catastrophe and liberated Rome al-most without damage.

Railway Yards Bombed

Five hundred American heavy bombers blasted railway yards at five points in northern Italy be-tween Venice and Rimini along which the Germans might attempt to move reinforcements and equip-ment to bolster their beaten armies. Hour after hour, the Al-lies' planes swept down on high-ways leading northward and tore the fleeing enemy apart. Twelve hundred combat vehicles were de-stroyed from dawn to dark yes-terday, and hundreds more today. Farther north, medium bombers smashed bridges and rail facilities.

[The Germans have abandoned the entire left bank of the Tiber from Ostia, at its mouth, to Rome, according to a Vichy broadcast quoted by The Asso-ciated Press.

[The Germans are already en-trenched in mountain positions

Continued on Page 2

War News Summarized

TUESDAY, JUNE 6, 1944

The invasion of western Eu-rope began this morning.

General Eisenhower, in his first communiqué from Supreme Headquarters, Allied Expedition-ary Force, issued at 3:30 A. M., said that "Allied naval forces supported by strong air forces began landing Allied armies this morning on the northern coast of France."

The assault was made by Brit-ish, American and Canadian troops who, under command of Gen. Sir Bernard L. Montgom-ery, landed in Normandy. Lon-don gave no further details but earlier Berlin had broadcast that parachute troops had landed on the Normandy Peninsula near Cherbourg and that invasion forces were pouring from land-ing craft under cover of war-ships near Havre. Dunkerque and Calais were being heavily bombed, the Germans said.

Later announcements from Berlin said that there was fight-ing between Caen and Trouville and that shock troops had swung into action to halt the invasion. [All the foregoing, 1:8.]

General Eisenhower, in an order of the day to each member of the "great crusade," told his men the enemy would fight sav-agely and added: "We will ac-cept nothing less than full vic-tory. Good luck." In a broad-cast to the "Peoples of Western Europe," he said the day would come when he would need their full help. A special word to France added that Frenchmen would rule the country. [1:6-7.] Almost simultaneously it was an-nounced that General de Gaulle had arrived in London. [6:2.]

The liberation of Rome in no way slowed the Allied pursuit of the tired and disorganized Ger-man armies in Italy yesterday. Armored and motorized units sped across the Tiber River to press hard upon the retreating enemy's heels. Five hundred heavy bombers joined with lighter aircraft to smash rail and road routes leading to northern Italy and to add to the foe's de-moralization. The Eighth Army, despite heavy opposition, espe-cially northeast of Valmontone, captured a number of strategic towns. [1:3; map P. 2.]

King Victor Emmanuel ful-filled his promise and turned over all authority to his son, Crown Prince Humbert. [1:5-6.] President Roosevelt warned the people of the United States in a radio talk last night not to over-emphasize the military sig-nificance of the liberation of Rome. "Germany has not yet been driven to surrender," he said. "Victory still lies some dis-tance ahead. * * * It will be tough and it will be costly." The President appealed to the world to give Italy a chance to contribute her share to a lasting peace. [1:1.]

In the Pacific theatre Ameri-cans were converging on the Biak airfields. Allied planes sank one and damaged two Jap-anese destroyers and shot down at least eighteen aircraft. [8:1.]

FIRST ALLIED LANDING MADE ON SHORES OF WESTERN EUROPE

June 6, 1944

General Eisenhower's armies invaded northern France this morning. While the landing points were not specified, the Ger-mans said that troops had gone ashore near Havre and that fight-ing raged at Caen (1). The enemy also said that parachutists had descended at the northern tip of the Normandy Peninsula (2) and heavy bombing had been visited on Calais and Dunkerque (3).

POPE GIVES THANKS ROME WAS SPARED

Voices Appreciation to Both Belligerents in Message to Throng at St. Peter's

By Wireless to The New York Times.

VATICAN CITY, June 5—Pope Pius XII appeared on the balcony of St. Peter's at 6 P. M. today to thank God that Rome had been spared from the ravages of war while before him in the densely packed square of St. Peter's and the new broad Via Della Concilia-zione tens of thousands of Romans cheered themselves hoarse.

It was the third time today that the Pontiff had showed himself to cheering crowds, as he had ap-peared twice at a window of his office this morning. But this was a solemn, sacred occasion and no one knowing anything about Pius XII can doubt the fervor of his thankfulness that Rome had been saved.

The Pontiff seemed strong and well and his voice carried far, though it was difficult to hear every word he said because of the crowd.

"We must give thanks to God for the favors we have received," said the Pope. "Rome has been spared. This day will go down in the annals of Rome."

He went on to say he hoped that Italians would be worthy of the grace shown them and put aside hatred and all personal vendettas. He then thanked both belligerents —the Allies and Germany—for hav-ing left Rome intact.

After a prayer of thankfulness to the Blessed Virgin and Saints Peter and Paul, guardians of Rome, the Pontiff gave his blessing, "urbe et orbis," as the immense crowd knelt before him.

[The Associated Press estimated the crowd was between 250,000 and 500,000.]

The world has changed for Rome but the Vatican goes on im-perturbably as it has through so many other conquests in centuries gone by. It is neutral in fact and spirit. The Pope and all high of-ficials went about their daily rou-tine today as in the past. Except for the tanks and armored cars running along the street in front of St. Peter's one could never know what had happened today.

Continued on Page 5

Italy's Monarch Yields Rule To Son, but Retains Throne

By The Associated Press.

NAPLES, June 5—Victor Emmanuel III stepped aside as King of Italy today, as he previously had said he would do upon the liberation of Rome, and handed to his 39-year-old son, Crown Prince Humbert, all "royal prerogatives." Italian political pressure had been brought to bear against the throne since the occupa-tion of Naples.

In a decree signed by himself and countersigned by Premier Pietro Badoglio, head of the Ital-ian Liberation Government, the King named his son Lieutenant General of the Realm. The mon-arch, however, retained his title as head of the House of Savoy and remains as King without power.

[The first act of the Council of Ministers after the transfer of royal powers was a formal denunciation of the 1940 armi-stice treaty inflicted on France, The United Press said.]

Victor Emmanuel, who became King July 29, 1900, had announced last April 12 his "irrevocable" de-cision to withdraw from public life "on the day on which Allied troops enter Rome."

Little more than a figurehead since Benito Mussolini assumed the dictatorship of Italy, Victor Em-manuel had won a reputation in the first years of his reign as a sym-pathetic monarch, interested in his people and their problems.

Prince Humbert, tall and erect, opposed fascism in Italy at the start, but later made a truce with Mussolini. In effect, Humbert be-comes the King's regent.

TEXT OF ROYAL DECREE

The King's withdrawal was presented

I, Victor Emmanuel III, by the grace of God and by the will of the nation King of Italy, in col-laboration with the President of the Council of Ministers and with the agreement of the Council, have ordered and order as fol-lows:

My beloved son, Humbert of Savoy, Prince of Piedmont, is nominated our Lieutenant Gener-al. In collaboration with respon-sible Ministers he will in our name superintend all matters of administration and exercise all royal prerogatives without excep-tion, signing royal decrees which will be countersigned and authen-ticated in the usual way.

We order all concerned to ob-serve this decree and to see that it is observed as the law of the State.

Given at Favello June 5, 1944.
VICTOR EMMANUEL.
(Countersigned) Pietro Badoglio.

The withdrawal was presented

Continued on Page 4

EISENHOWER ACTS

U. S., British, Canadian Troops Backed by Sea, Air Forces

MONTGOMERY LEADS

Nazis Say Their Shock Units Are Battling Our Parachutists

Communique No. 1 On Allied Invasion

By Broadcast to The New York Times.

LONDON, Tuesday, June 6—The Supreme Headquarters of the Allied Expeditionary Force issued this communiqué this morning:

"Under the command of Gen-eral Eisenhower, Allied naval forces, supported by strong air forces, began landing Allied armies this morning on the northern coast of France."

By RAYMOND DANIELL
By Cable to The New York Times.

SUPREME HEADQUARTERS, ALLIED EXPEDITIONARY FORCES, Tuesday, June 6—The invasion of Europe from the west has begun.

In the gray light of a summer dawn Gen. Dwight D. Eisen-hower threw his great Anglo-American force into action today for the liberation of the Conti-nent. The spearhead of attack was an Army group commanded by Gen. Sir Bernard L. Mont-gomery and comprising troops of the United States, Britain and Canada.

General Eisenhower's first communiqué was terse and cal-culated to give little information to the enemy. It said merely that "Allied naval forces supported by strong air forces began landing Allied armies this morning on the northern coast of France."

After the first communiqué was released it was announced that the Allied landing was in Normandy.

Caen Battle Reported

German broadcasts, beginning at 6:30 A. M., London time, [12:30 A. M. Eastern war time] gave first word of the assault. [The Associated Press said Gen-eral Eisenhower, for the sake of surprise, deliberately let the Ger-mans have the "first word."]

The German DNB agency said the Allied invasion operations began with the landing of air-borne troops in the area of the mouth of the Seine River.

[Berlin said the "center of gravity" of the fierce fighting was at Caen, thirty miles southwest of Havre and sixty-five miles southeast of Cher-bourg, The Associated Press reported. Caen is ten miles inland from the sea, at the base of the seventy-five-mile-wide Normandy Peninsula, and fighting there might indi-cate the Allies' seizing of a beachhead.

[DNB said in a broadcast just before 10 A. M. (4 A. M. Eastern war time) that the Anglo-American troops had been reinforced at dawn at the mouth of the Seine River in the Havre area.

[An Allied correspondent broadcasting from Supreme Headquarters, according to the Columbia Broadcasting System, said this morning that "German tanks are moving up

Continued on Page A Following Page 5

PARADE OF PLANES CARRIES INVADERS

Witness Says First 'Chutists Met Only Light Fire When They Landed in France

The first eyewitness account of the Allies' invasion of Europe was given in a pool broadcast from London this morning by Wright Bryan of the National Broadcast-ing Company, who accompanied the airborne troops in their land-ings.

His account said the great spear-head of Allied forces landed by parachute in northern France in the first hour of D-day.

"In the navigator's dome in the flight deck of a C-47, I rode across the English Channel with the first group of planes from the United States Ninth Air Force Troop Car-rier Command to take our fighting men into Europe," Mr. Bryan said.

He added that just before he left French soil for the return trip he saw seventeen American para-troops, led by a lieutenant colonel, jump with their arms, ammunition and equipment into German-occupied France.

He declared that his group at the head of the leading wing was met with "only scattering small

Continued on Page B

ALLIED WARNING FLASHED TO COAST

People Told to Clear Area 22 Miles Inland as Soon as Instructions Are Given

By Cable to The New York Times.

LONDON, Tuesday, June 6—The British Broadcasting Corpora-tion began its 8 A. M. news bulle-tin this morning with quotations from a Supreme Headquarters' "urgent warning" to inhabitants of the enemy-occupied countries giving near the coast.

Gen. Dwight D. Eisenhower has directed that whenever possible in France a warning shall be given to towns in which certain targets will be intensively bombed. This warning, the broadcast said,

Continued on Page B

Eisenhower Instructs Europeans; Gives Battle Order to His Armies

Following are the texts of a statement by Gen. Dwight D. Eisenhower broadcast to the people of western Europe and his Order of the Day to the Allied Expeditionary Force as recorded by The New York Times and the Columbia Broadcasting System:

People of western Europe! A landing was made this morning on the coast of France by troops of the Allied Expeditionary Force. This landing is part of the concerted United Nations plan for the liberation of Eu-rope, made in conjunction with our great Russian Allies. I have this message for all of you. Al-though the initial assault may not have been made in your own country, the hour of your libera-tion is approaching.

All patriots, men and women, young and old, have a part to play in the achievement of final victory. To members of resist-ance movements, whether led by national or outside leaders, I

say: "Follow the instructions you have received." To patriots who are not members of organized re-sistance groups I say, "continue your passive resistance, but do not needlessly endanger your lives until I give you the signal to rise and strike the enemy. The day will come when I shall need your united strength. Un-til that day, I call on you for the hard task of discipline and re-straint."

Citizens of France! I am proud to have again under my command the gallant forces of France. Fighting beside the Allies, you will play a vital part in the liberation of their

Continued on Page A Following Page 5

"All the News That's Fit to Print"

The New York Times.

LATE CITY EDITION
POSTSCRIPT
Partly cloudy and warm today
Temperature Yesterday—Max., 84; Min., 64
Sunrise, 5:26 A. M.; Sunset, 8:31 P. M.

Copyright, 1944, by The New York Times Company.

VOL. XCIII..No. 31,566.

Entered as Second-Class Matter,
Postoffice, New York, N. Y.

NEW YORK, TUESDAY, JUNE 27, 1944.

THREE CENTS IN NEW YORK CITY

CHERBOURG FALLS TO AMERICAN TROOPS; ENEMY LEADERS AMONG 30,000 PRISONERS; RUSSIANS CAPTURE VITEBSK AND ZHLOBIN

REPUBLICANS MAKE QUICK END TO WAR THEIR BATTLE CRY

Warren, Keynoter, Says Party Will Bring Victorious Boys Home With All Speed

DISPUTES OVER PLATFORM

Dewey Avalanche Piles Up, With Californian Unchallenged as His Running Mate

Governor Warren's keynote address is printed on Page 10.

By TURNER CATLEDGE
Special to The New York Times.

CHICAGO, Tuesday, June 27—A triple pledge to bring the boys back home quickly and "victorious," to reopen the doors of opportunity to "all Americans," and to guard the peace in the future, was sounded today as a cheering throng as the Republican battle-cry at the opening of the party's twenty-third national convention.

While it was being uttered by Gov. Earl Warren, temporary chairman, in his keynote address to a thundering throng in the Chicago Stadium, THE NEW YORK TIMES learned of a plank which policy writers had evolved Saturday, pledging the party to a post-war cooperative organization "among sovereign nations," to prevent military aggression and attain permanent peace in the future.

Word had come meanwhile from Wendell L. Willkie, the nominee of 1940, that he considered the foreign policy plank, as he understood it, ambiguous, and therefore was disappointed in it.

Willkie's Backers Upset

This note of controversy came as a distinct shock to a group of former backers of Mr. Willkie who have been attempting these last few days to bring him in line with the platform, and with a ticket of Thomas E. Dewey of New York for President and Governor Warren for Vice President, which is considered certain of nomination by tomorrow night.

Meanwhile, another complication appeared in the hitherto placid convention picture when the seventeen Governors who are delegates demanded opportunity to examine and possibly suggest changes in the platform before it is submitted to the convention, probably tonight, for ratification.

The Governors did not protest any particular item in the platform as it was agreed to in principle last night. They did protest the fact, however, that, as one of them put it, an "oligarchy" of Senators, members of the House and other party leaders, had assumed the prerogative of speaking for the party.

The Governors feel, as Governor Warren reflected in his keynote address, that they have been the spearhead and more than members of Congress, for the resurgence of Republicanism during the last three years. What happened here when the Governors demanded and obtained permission to appear before the resolutions committee was another chapter in a protest which first came to light at the Mackinac Island conference in September.

Led by New Englanders

The action was led, as was the move at Mackinac, largely by a New England group, in which Gov. Raymond E. Baldwin of Connecticut and Gov. Sumner Sewall of Maine were active.

These new possibilities of trouble ahead did not divert the main line of appeal upon which the party was centering—an appeal to the soldier vote, to those Americans who are weary of the New Deal, and, above all, to those wanting to avoid the tragedy of war in the future.

It was the note on which Gov. Dwight Green of Illinois opened the meeting with a welcoming ad-

Continued on Page 9

Convention Events Listed for Today

Special to The New York Times.

CHICAGO, June 26—The official program for tomorrow's sessions of the Republican National Convention is as follows:

Tuesday, June 27, 10:15 A. M. (Central War Time)
Convention called to order by the temporary chairman.
National Anthem: Miss Mildred Maule of East St. Louis, Ill.
Prayer: The Rev. Joseph Simonson, pastor of Christ Lutheran Church, St. Paul.
Report of Committee on Credentials.
Report of Committee on Permanent Organization.
Election of permanent chairman and permanent officers.
Address by permanent chairman.
Report of Committee on Rules and Order of Business.
Election of National Committee.
Report of Resolutions Committee.
Recess until 8:15 P. M.
Tuesday, June 27, 8:15 P. M.
Convention called to order by the permanent chairman, Representative Joseph W. Martin Jr.
National Anthem: Miss Mona Bradford of the Chicago Civic Opera Company.
Prayer: Rabbi Abba Hillel Silver of The Temple, Cleveland.
Music.
Address: Herbert Hoover.
Address: Representative Clare Boothe Luce of Connecticut.
Adjourn until Wednesday.

WILLKIE CONDEMNS PEACE-POLICY PLAN

Republican Draft on Foreign Relations Could Be Used to Balk Cooperation, He Says

A few hours after Wendell Willkie had received the text of the proposed Republican foreign-policy plank, the 1940 Presidential candidate issued a statement denouncing the plan as ambiguous, subject to opposing interpretations and capable of being used to throttle effective collaboration by the United States with other countries to maintain peace.

Mr. Willkie's views on the platform committee's suggestions were presented to reporters who had been invited to visit his offices at 15 Broad Street. He explained that he chose this form of making them public because he was not a delegate to the convention.

"We believe," the language proposed for this year's platform is that employed in 1920, Mr. Willkie recalled that thirty-one leading Republicans had assured the country that the 1920 formula "was the surest road to an effective international organization," but that President Harding, immediately after the election, "announced that the League of Nations was dead."

"A Republican President elected under the proposed platform of

Continued on Page 13

ACCORD OF NATIONS FAVORED IN PLANK ON FOREIGN POLICY

'Participation in Cooperative Organization' Provided 'to Attain Permanent Peace'

TAFT PREDICTS ADOPTION

Declaration Calls for Seeking 'Economic Stability,' Pledges Constitutional Procedure

By JAMES B. RESTON
Special to The New York Times.

CHICAGO, Tuesday, June 27—The Republican party platform will favor "participation by the United States in post-war cooperative organization among sovereign nations to prevent military aggression and to attain permanent peace."

The party's Foreign Affairs Committee, headed by Senator Warren Austin of Vermont, has approved unanimously a plank which calls on the future world peace organization to "develop effective cooperative means to direct peace forces to prevent or repel military aggression."

Pending the formation of this world peace organization, the plank recommends that the United States should "pledge continuing collaboration with the United Nations."

Senator Robert A. Taft, chairman of the party's Resolutions Committee, to which the platform will be submitted later this morning, said he was certain that the foreign affairs plank as recommended by Senator Austin's committee would be adopted.

Objectives of Peace Treaties

After stating that the party favored "prosecution of the war to total victory against all our enemies in full cooperation with the United Nations and the speedy return of our armed forces," the plank emphasized that justice in the writing of the peace was the essence of realism.

"We believe that peace and security do not depend upon the sanction of force alone, but should prevail by virtue of reciprocal interests and spiritual values recognized in these security agreements," the Foreign Affairs Committee said.

"The treaties of peace should be just; the nations which are the victims of Axis aggression should have 'participation' in their own self-government, and the organized cooperation of the nations should concern itself with basic causes of world discord."

Elaborating on "cooperation," the committee continued:

"We shall seek, in our relations with other nations, conditions calculated to promote world-wide economic stability, not only for the sake of the world, but also that our own people may enjoy a high level of employment in an increasingly prosperous world. We

Continued on Page 14

ALLIED WARSHIPS SHELLING GERMAN POSITIONS IN CHERBOURG

The U. S. S. Quincy (left) and H. M. S. Glasgow bombarding the port
The New York Times (British Admiralty via U. S. Signal Corps Radiotelephoto)

U. S. TROOPS SCALE LOFTY SAIPAN PEAK

Tapotchau, Dominating Island, Is Reported Won — Carrier Planes Batter Guam and Rota

By GEORGE F. HORNE
By Telephone to The New York Times.

PACIFIC FLEET HEADQUARTERS, Pearl Harbor, June 26—Mount Tapotchau on Saipan Island has been scaled by United States Marines who are now established in positions near the summit. Marines and Army troops have made substantial gains on both the eastern and western shores of the island.

[A front dispatch said that Tapotchau which dominated the island has been the goal of all our men ever since they landed on Saipan, had been captured by troops who held it against a before-dawn Japanese counter-attack Sunday.]

Admiral Chester W. Nimitz stated that the Kagman Peninsula, forming the upper arm of Magicienne Bay, was now entirely in our hands and that troops had

Continued on Page 7

Russians Begin Encircling Mogilev and Orsha Citadels

By The United Press.

LONDON, Tuesday, June 27—The Red Army, tearing out the northern and southern anchors of the German defense line in White Russia, captured the fortress cities of Vitebsk and Zhlobin yesterday and seized more than 1,700 towns and settlements, while the vanguard of their victorious forces advanced more than twenty-five miles toward Minsk for a great pincer assault on that city.

Striking with unprecedented power and speed, four Soviet armies sprinting along a 285-mile front raced to within eighty-four miles of Minsk, approached to within thirty-five miles of the Polish border, outflanked Orsha and drove to within six miles of Mogilev.

Vitebsk, the most powerful Nazi stronghold on the route to East Prussia, and Zhlobin, 175 miles to the south, fell on the fourth day of the Red Army's summer offensive—four days in which Russian troops advanced as much as fifty-six miles, seized 3,040 towns and settlements and killed more than 31,500 Germans.

More than 6,000 of the German garrison of five infantry divisions

Continued on Page 6

VIENNA WAR PLANTS GET HEAVY BOMBING

Italy-Based Planes Pound Oil, Aircraft Works — Weather Cuts Invasion Support

By The Associated Press.

SUPREME HEADQUARTERS, Allied Expeditionary Force, Tuesday, June 27—United States Flying Fortresses and Liberators 500 to 750 strong roared from Italian bases to the Vienna area yesterday through the heaviest Luftwaffe opposition in recent weeks and attacked oil refineries, rail yards and a Nazi aircraft plant.

Poor weather over western Europe halted for the day the pounding from Allied air bases in Britain and Normandy of German supply and communication lines behind the French front.

Indications of renewed Allied aerial activity came last night as the German radio interrupted programs to say an alert had been sounded in all parts of southwestern Germany. In Hungary, where British bombers of the Mediterranean Allied Air Force attacked oil works Sunday night, the Budapest radio went off the air again at 10 P. M.

The Flying Fortresses and Liberators and their escorting Mustangs, Lightnings and Thunderbolts of the United States Fifteenth Air Force shot down large numbers of enemy planes on the route to the Vienna area, headquarters announced.

They struck oil refineries at Schwechat, ten miles southeast of

Continued on Page 5

---

14 WARSHIPS SHELL CHERBOURG AT ONCE

British Newsman Describes Destruction of Batteries Defending Harbor

By DESMOND TIGHE
Reuter Correspondent

ABOARD H.M.S. GLASGOW, off Cherbourg Harbor, June 25 (Delayed)—American battleships and heavy cruisers, supported by two British cruisers and seven destroyers, are firing broadside after broadside into German shore batteries at vital key points on the fringes of Cherbourg harbor in support of the Army.

The bombardment started at exactly eleven minutes past 12 this morning and has lasted for more than three hours with German long-range 450-mm. shore batteries returning the fire vigorously.

As I watched this bombardment from the bridge of H.M.S. Glasgow, victor of the recent Bay of Biscay battle, we are steaming steadily some 15,000 yards off the breakwater of Cherbourg harbor.

Air Resounds With Crashes

Our six-inch guns are blazing away as shells scream into a German fort. The air resounds with the crash of broadsides from the battleships, cruisers and destroyers. The Channel sea is whipped with wicked looking grey-black splashes as we are straddled time and time again by German shore batteries.

The German gunnery is good and although we are plastering their concrete gun emplacements with tons of high explosives some of them keep on firing.

The United States bombardment task force is commanded by Rear Admiral Morton L. Deyo, United States Navy. Admiral Deyo is flying his flag in the heavy cruiser Tuscaloosa. Among the warships in the battle squadron are the battleships Texas, Nevada, Arkansas; the American cruiser Quincy, and the two British cruisers, Glasgow and Enterprise. We are escorted by a

Continued on Page 4

VICTORY IN FRANCE

Capture of Port Seals First Phase of Allied Liberation of Europe

FIGHT SHARP TO END

British Reported Near Main Enemy Highway at Base of Peninsula

5 A. M. Communique

By The Associated Press

SUPREME HEADQUARTERS, Allied Expeditionary Force, Tuesday, June 27—The capture of Lieut. Gen. Carl Wilhelm von Schlieben, commander of the Cherbourg garrison, and Rear Admiral Hennecke, Nazi sea defense commander of Normandy, was announced today in Allied communiqué No. 43 confirming the fall of Cherbourg.

"Cherbourg's liberation came after a final day of fierce fighting in the northwestern part of the city," the communiqué said.

"In the battle the enemy has lost the greater part of four infantry divisions, numerous naval and marine units and line of communication troops."

Of the British gains on the east side of the beachhead, the communiqué said:

"A strong attack toward the Villers-Bocage-Caen main road has secured Cheux and Fontenay, and has advanced several miles in the face of heavy German armor and infantry. Progress continues."

By DREW MIDDLETON
By Cable to The New York Times.

SUPREME HEADQUARTERS, Allied Expeditionary Force, Tuesday, June 27—Cherbourg, France's third greatest port, has fallen to the American troops in the first outstanding victory of the Allied campaign to liberate France.

The fall of Cherbourg, after a siege that lasted a week from the moment the first shells began to pound its defenses, was officially announced here this morning just after 7 o'clock double British summer time [1 A. M. in New York].

With the taking of the city the first phase of the campaign in which the Allies were forced to build up their armies without the use of a large port came to an end. It was estimated here recently that supplies for two divisions could be moved through Cherbourg within forty-eight hours after its fall.

Captives May Total 30,000

Last night American patrols mopped up the remaining German resistance in the vicinity of the naval base and arsenal and cleaned out snipers from buildings along the waterfront, where individual Germans held out until the last.

Although there has been no official estimate of the number of prisoners yet, it is probable the city fall will bring more than 30,000 German soldiers and sailors into the Allied cages.

Cherbourg was the second French port and naval base to fall to Lieut. Gen. Omar N. Bradley. Bizerte in Tunisia was taken by the United States Second Army Corps under his command on May 7, 1943.

The struggle for Cherbourg drew to its victorious close yesterday when in the rain and chill wind doughboys mopped up the port. By nightfall more than one-third of the port had been occupied and by midnight two-thirds of the city was in Allied hands.

At dawn Monday 3,600 German prisoners had been taken and it is probable that twice that number was captured in the mopping up operations yesterday.

The Germans were driven from five remaining strongholds during the early evening by grenade, bay-

Continued on Page 3

War News Summarized

TUESDAY, JUNE 27, 1944

Cherbourg fell to the Americans this morning after General Bradley's troops had fought the desperate German defenders from dock to dock along the ruined waterfront. The enemy held out in four or five strong points, principally around the naval base, until each fortified nucleus had been overrun. Lieut. Gen. von Schlieben, Cherbourg garrison commander, and Admiral Hennecke, head of the German sea force off Normandy, were captured. The total of prisoners may reach 30,000.

At the eastern end of the Normandy line the British opened a new drive from Tilly-sur-Seulles and gained as much as four miles, threatening to cut the Caen-Avranches highway at the base of the Cotentin Peninsula. Since the initial landings three weeks ago the Allies have liberated more than 1,000 square miles of France, have taken more than 50,000 prisoners and have destroyed four German divisions. [All the foregoing 1:8; map, P. 2.]

Three United States battleships headed a force of fourteen Allied vessels that pounded Cherbourg's main fortifications into rubble shortly after noon Sunday. The massed naval rifles poured shells into the targets for more than three hours, clearing the way for the troops. [1:7.]

A British naval intelligence officer said in this city that the Germans had been so skillfully outmaneuvered that they massed their air defenses to counter a feint invasion aimed at Calais and Boulogne, leaving Normandy without protection. [9:1.]

Marines on Saipan, in the Marianas, have scaled Mount Tapotchau and dug in at the summit. The southern part of Garapan, on the west, was in American hands, and the Japanese have been cleared from Kagman Peninsula on the east. Carrier planes did widespread damage to shipping, installations and grounded enemy aircraft at enemy bases on Guam and Rota. [1:4; map, P. 7.]

Allied forces have captured Mogaung in Burma and gained on all fronts from the Indian border to China, where Hsiangta and forty-five of Florence. The Japanese, after seizing Hengchan and Yuhsien, were unable to push closer to Hengyang in China's Hunan Province. [7:4.]

Another vaunted German line crumbled when the Red Army captured Vitebsk and Zhlobin, anchors of the so-called "Fatherland Line." More than 45,000 enemy troops were trapped at Vitebsk, and at one point the Russians drove thirty-five miles from the old Polish frontier. A record number of 1,700 places was liberated in the general advance. Gains were also reported from the Karelian Isthmus on the Finnish front. [1:5-6; map P. 6]

The Fifth Army in Italy entered the port of Piombino without a fight and, inland, advanced to within fifteen miles of Siena and forty-five of Florence. The Eighth Army crossed the Chienti River northeast of Foligno in hard fighting. [6:1.]

United States bombers from Italy smashed oil refineries, rail yards and an airplane plant in the Vienna area. The Luftwaffe offered the heaviest opposition in weeks. [1:6.]

3-Cornered Baseball Game Yields $56,500,000 in Fifth Bond Drive

A crowd of 50,000 baseball fans, all of whom paid their way into the park by buying war bonds, turned out last night at the Polo Grounds to witness a bizarre contest in which the Yankees, Giants and Dodgers participated in a nine-inning contest. The Brooklyn nine won the game, tallying five runs; the Yankees scored one and the Giants nothing.

The program, as arranged by the Fifth War Loan Sports Committee, helped to swell New York's quota in the current bond drive by $56,500,000. Fifty million dollars of this sum came, according to an announcement by Mayor La Guardia, from the coffers of the City of New York. The remainder was contributed by the crowd as "admission fee," plus a one-million-dollar bond purchase of an autographed score card by the Bond Clothing Stores.

During the day the drive moved into high gear with the announcement of many large subscriptions here totalling around $1,000,000,000 and the disclosure that purchases throughout the nation had reached $4,591,000,000, or 29 per cent of the quota for the campaign.

Devised and conceived by Stanley Oshan of the War Finance Committee, the baseball game was followed closely by the huge throng that was seeing three major league teams tangle with each other on the same field for the first time. While Mr. Oshan was the originator of the idea it required a Columbia University professor of mathematics, Paul A. Smith, to produce a method of scoring.

Professor Smith's assistance proved helpful, indeed, for the

Continued on Page 20

Pockets of Nazis Kept on Sniping As Americans Overran Cherbourg

By HAROLD DENNY
By Wireless to The New York Times.

WITH THE AMERICAN FORCES at Cherbourg, June 26—The Germans fought a last-ditch defense in Cherbourg this morning, though the outcome was inescapable. Substantial elements of the American forces got into the city from the south only after a piece-by-piece conquest of succeeding strong points and the Germans were still firing on them in the city and from two pillboxes near the old Polish frontier at Fort du Roule with 88-mm. field-pieces and machine guns. The city has been considerably damaged but less than one would have thought. As a whole it is intact, though many individual buildings have been smashed.

Dominating all was the arsenal where the last important holdout

Continued on Page 4

"All the News
That's Fit to Print"

The New York Times.

LATE CITY EDITION
Fair today and tomorrow with
mild afternoons and cool nights.
Temperatures Yesterday—Max., 75; Min., 55
Sunrise, 6:16 A. M.; Sunset, 7:32 P. M.

Copyright, 1944, by The New York Times Company

VOL. XCIII..No. 31,626.   Entered as Second-Class Matter,
Postoffice, New York, N. Y.   NEW YORK, SATURDAY, AUGUST 26, 1944.   THREE CENTS NEW YORK CITY

ALLIES SWEEP TO TROYES, NAZI ROUT GROWS; GERMAN COMMANDER SURRENDERS IN PARIS; RUMANIA DECLARES WAR, BULGARIA TO QUIT

NELSON UNDER FIRE OF BRADLEY DEWEY; WPB POST IN DOUBT

Former Head of Rubber Agency Defends Program, Accuses Nelson of 'Sniping'

ISSUE PUT TO PRESIDENT

Question of Production Chief's Future Is 'Iffy,' He Says —Krug Takes Firm Hold

By CHARLES E. EGAN
Special to The New York Times.

WASHINGTON, Aug. 25—The question whether Donald M. Nelson will resume his chairmanship of the War Production Board on his return from a special mission to China for President Roosevelt was raised today when the President told his press conference that he did not know whether Mr. Nelson would resume his duties at that time.

The President's statement came soon after Mr. Nelson departed on the first leg of his China journey and the day after the chairman had apparently won a fight with his executive vice chairman, Charles E. Wilson, who resigned yesterday after charging that his usefulness was being impaired by attacks from Mr. Nelson's staff. It supplied another surprising development in the explosive situation which had developed in the WPB over reconversion.

While official Washington speculated whether the President had a more important job than WPB head in prospect for Mr. Nelson or whether the war agency chairman was to be "let out" along with his first assistant, Mr. Nelson came under fire from another quarter when Col. Bradley Dewey, retiring rubber director, accused him of engaging "in typical Washington sniping" at the rubber director's office.

Dewey Takes Issue on Rubber

Colonel Dewey referred to the testimony given by Mr. Nelson before a closed session of the Senate's committee investigating national defense as the type "that has made many good Americans unwilling to give services that otherwise would be of value to the country and to the conduct of the war."

Mr. Nelson had testified that the rubber program was completed, "all but getting the tires." Questioned about Colonel Dewey's then-recent resignation, Mr. Nelson said that to call the rubber program completed would be "like the Army saying they are completed except for the shooting."

Colonel Dewey told reporters that he had never said the task of providing tires was completed, but rather that the synthetic rubber plants were turning out rubber in surplus.

The problem of providing manpower and tire cords no longer required the special powers which were reposed in the Office of Defense Rubber, Colonel Dewey added.

Krug Demands End of Sniping

"These powers are of no value to the problem of manning the plants and providing the much-needed tires," he concluded. "By Presidential directive these were and are the responsibilities of the WPB and of the War Manpower Commission."

J. A. Krug, who was named yesterday by President Roosevelt as acting chairman of the WPB in the absence of Mr. Nelson, took over the reins today. He called over the vice chairmen of the agency into conference this afternoon, and, according to reports, told them that he received a clear grant of authority to run the WPB and to get it back on the "track."

He warned that fights within WPB should end and that he would "fire" anyone who engaged in the future in internal disputes.

Mr. Krug told reporters later
Continued on Page 24

Must Post Ceilings For Diners Monday

The Regional Office of Price Administration reminded restaurant managements yesterday that they have until Monday to file a list of forty food items and the ceiling prices they are required to post on their premises. The list in triplicate must be filed with local war price and rationing boards.

The new OPA national restaurant regulations require the posting of the forty food items and the ceiling prices. Restaurants violating the provisions of the regulation face enforcement action, OPA attachés pointed out. Each list filed by a restaurant will be compared with menus of May, 1943, and, upon approval, a copy of the list, bearing an official stamp to show approval, will be returned to the restaurant owner.

OWN MEN AT FRONT APPEAL TO LABOR

AFL and CIO Leaders in France Link War Supply Shortages to 'Our Quarrels at Home'

By SIDNEY SHALETT
Special to The New York Times.

WASHINGTON, Aug. 25—"We cannot let the men whose lives depend on this equipment pay the price for our quarrels at home," six American labor leaders who are visiting the French battlefields under War Department sponsorship have declared in a message sent back here to their unions.

The message was transmitted through the War Department by William Green, president of the American Federation of Labor, and Philip Murray, head of the Congress of Industrial Organizations.

"Conscious of the partnership that exists between the fighting fronts and the factory," it read, "the War Department has made it possible for us to travel through the battle areas and see at first hand how our soldiers are using the weapons and equipment made by American labor.

Need of Supplies to Save Lives

"As we travel along roads lined with the wreckage of American and German equipment and pass through shattered French cities and, above all, as we pause at military cemeteries and hospitals that are all too plentiful here, we are struck more forcibly than ever before with the horrible destructiveness of modern war and the importance of superior supplies in cutting down the toll of our dead and wounded.

"We are filled with pride for our Army. Its combat efficiency and morale are high. It is well-staffed and well-manned—an Army representative in the highest sense of our great American democracy.

"Everybody knows his job—from generals to privates—and we are determined to get ourselves to the job of finishing this war with the same single-minded determination as the men at the front.

"We do not know whether the war will last a short time or a long
Continued on Page 24

Army Rules Roosevelt Address Was Political, Then Denies It

Special to The New York Times.

WASHINGTON, Aug. 25—The War Department changed its mind today on whether President Roosevelt's speech at Bremerton, Wash., on Aug. 12 was "political," holding first that it was and several hours later reversing itself to hold that it was "not political."

The issue was raised by the Socialist party, which applied to the War Department for equal radio time to address fighting men overseas on the grounds that the President's Bremerton speech, in which he mainly reviewed his trip to Hawaii and the Aleutians, was "political."

Under Title 5 of the Service Men's Voting Law, the Socialists contended, they were entitled to equal time on the air. Earlier this week the War Department had announced that, under an interpretation of the statute, the Democratic, Republican, Socialist and Prohibition parties would have equal recognition for any political radio time.

Under the first ruling by the War Department today the Socialist party was granted equal time to that of the President to address the men overseas.

"The War Department," said a memorandum issued in reply to press inquiries, "has indicated to the Socialist party that, under the statute, it will accede to this request. The other major political parties have asked for and have been furnished copies of the correspondence between the War De-
Continued on Page 9

RED ARMY RACES ON

Russians Attack Galati Gap and Encircle 12 German Divisions

REACH DANUBE DELTA

205,000 Enemy Troops Killed or Taken in Six Days—Tartu Seized

By The Associated Press.

LONDON, Saturday, Aug. 26— Two Russian armies racing toward the heart of Rumania at a better than a mile-an-hour clip yesterday reached the Galati Gap defenses at Tecuci and also drove a spearhead down to the Danube River delta at Kiliya in a six-day whirlwind offensive that Moscow announced had cost the enemy nearly 205,000 in killed or captured.

In perhaps the greatest defeat yet inflicted on the Axis in a comparable period, the Russians also announced they had encircled twelve German divisions of upward of 60,000 men southwest of fallen Kishinev, provincial capital of Bessarabia. Thirteen thousand Germans already have surrendered in two days, and the remainder are being annihilated, said the Moscow broadcast bulletin.

Thousands of Rumanians were abandoning the struggle against the Russians and turning to fight the Germans, dispatches said, as the Second and Third Ukrainian Armies under General Rodion Y. Malinovsky and Feodor I. Tolbukhin linked up in a quick drive on Bucharest, within 113 miles of Bucharest, when they seized Tecuci on the Barlad River.

Danube Delta Reached

A total of 550 towns and villages were swept up by the two armies, and the capture of Tecuci found the Russians within ninety miles northeast of the Ploesti oil wells. General Malinovsky's troops now were at the Galati Gap, a forty-five-mile stretch of defenses prepared along the Putna, Siret and Barlad Rivers just above where those streams empty into the Danube.

To the southeast, a Soviet communiqué said, the Russians had captured Kiliya on the Danube, fifteen miles west of the Black Sea port of Vilkov at the mouth of the delta, and twenty-two miles east of the port of Ismail. General Tolbukhin's Third Army seized that point. To the northwest his troops reached the Prut River on a seventy-mile front between captured Leusheny and Kagul, the latter being thirty miles northeast of the junction of Galati. The capture of Gasanbatyr put the Russians thirty miles from the port of Ismail on the northeast.

Soviet aircraft added to the slaughter by attacking Axis military trains at Galati, the supplementary communiqué said.

In six days the Russians have captured nearly all of lower Bessa-
Continued on Page 6

ALLY FIGHTS REICH

Nazis' Bombers Attack Bucharest—City Held Cleared of Germans

FIGHTING CONTINUES

Bulgaria Called Willing to Surrender to Allies Unconditionally

By SIDNEY GRUSON
By Cable to The New York Times.

LONDON, Aug. 25—The new Rumanian Government, after having denounced German perfidy tonight, openly declared war on the Reich, thereby fulfilling a Russian prerequisite for acceptance of the Rumanian offer to change to the Allied side.

The United States and Great Britain, moreover, have received word from Bulgaria that she is ready to accept unconditional surrender terms. The western allies, it was learned tonight, are now filling in details of the terms. The Rumanian declaration of war came after the Nazis, according to a proclamation broadcast by the Bucharest radio, had bombed the capital heavily and German units had attacked Rumanian forces and machine-gunned civilians of Bucharest and of other places.

Nazis' Flight Called Hopeless

"By these acts of aggression, which occurred simultaneously in various parts of the country, Germany has placed herself in a state of war with Rumania," the proclamation declared. "The Government therefore orders the Rumanian Army to begin the struggle against all German military forces on Rumanian territory for the liberation of the country from German usurpation."

The Germans themselves have acknowledged their position in Rumania as being hopeless. The Nazi-controlled Scandinavian News Service said that encircled German units were trying to break through the Russian lines toward the Carpathians and Transylvania to fight their way to Hungary.

The German "Danube" radio station announced that the Rumanian Army tonight to "refuse to fight against your former allies." But the appeal was falling on deaf ears, for the Bucharest radio shortly before had declared that the capital had been completely
Continued on Page 3

PARISIANS CELEBRATE ARRIVAL OF ALLIES

Patriots crowding around a jeep after its arrival in the French capital yesterday. This picture, one of the first to be taken inside the city, was sent from the new transmitting station set up in Cherbourg.
The New York Times (U. S. Signal Corps Radiotelephoto)

JAPANESE CRUISER FIRED BY U.S. FLIERS

Mast-Head Strike at Manado Also Smashes 7 Freighters —40 Barges Riddled

By FRANK L. KLUCKHOHN
By Cable to The New York Times.

ALLIED HEADQUARTERS IN AUSTRALIA, Aug. 25—A Japanese cruiser and seven Japanese freighters were sunk or severely damaged and forty barges and luggers were shot up as a force of fewer than twenty-five of Gen. Douglas MacArthur's Liberators made a surprise low-level attack yesterday on Manado, in Netherland Celebes, which is the enemy supply point for Halmahera.

The Mitchells braved heavy ack-
Continued on Page 6

Allied Forces Help French To Rid Capital of Nazis

By The Associated Press.

SUPREME HEADQUARTERS, Allied Expeditionary Force, Aug. 25—The Paris radio announced late tonight that the French capital had been liberated and that the German commander had signed a document ordering his troops to cease fire immediately.

The announcement followed entry of American and French troops into the capital during the day. There was no immediate confirmation here.

The latest word at headquarters was that American and French troops had joined Fighting French troops in the heart of the capital after bitter fighting with Germans and French collaborationist militiamen.

Gen. Charles de Gaulle, President of the French Committee of National Liberation, said in a speech broadcast from Paris:

"France will take her place among the great nations which will organize the peace. We will not rest until we march, as we must, into enemy territory as conquerors."

The commander of the Paris region for the French Forces of the Interior, Colonel Raoul, issued this proclamation to his forces, the radio said:

"FFI of the Ile de France (the Paris region), you have unleashed a rising that has liberated Paris. You have improvised your tactics, animated by the strong desire to win, and you have won."

In another broadcast the Paris radio said that the German com-
Continued on Page 3

AMERICANS SEIZE CANNES, PUSH EAST

Drive to 20 Miles From Italy, Spear Along Rhone—Lyon Is Reported in Patriots' Hands

By The Associated Press.

ROME, Aug. 25—American troops lunging suddenly eastward from their Riviera beachhead, in southern France, have captured the famous resort towns of Cannes and Antibes and tonight were fighting forward less than twenty miles from the Italian frontier.

Nice, within short artillery range of the advancing Americans, was expected to fall at any hour.

Other swift Allied columns drove methodically toward the heart of France and a junction with Gen. Dwight D. Eisenhower's armies in the north. Tonight's communiqué said columns probing into the delta of the Rhône valley were close to
Continued on Page 3

Dulles Indicates Republican Idea Is to Cooperate, Yet Criticize

By JAMES B. RESTON

WASHINGTON, Aug. 25—Apparently the Republican party will try to lift the specific question of American participation in a world security organization out of party politics in the Presidential campaign, but there will be no moratorium on discussion of the Administration's conduct of foreign policy as a whole.

This seemed clear today at the close of the first phase of the discussion between Secretary Hull and John Foster Dulles, Governor Dewey's representative on foreign affairs, who issued a joint statement which indicated that they had not reached complete agreement on the subject of how to discuss foreign policy during the campaign nor complete agreement on the American security plan now before the Dumbarton Oaks Security Conference.

But Mr. Dulles told reporters that he hoped the two major parties could reach an agreement on the American security plan now being discussed at the Dumbarton Oaks conversations and he added that he would see Mr. Hull again to that end, but he indicated that no complete agreement had been reached as yet and emphasized that the Republicans would retain their right to criticize freely the Administration's past conduct of foreign relations.

The joint statement by Secre-
Continued on Page 24

War News Summarized

SATURDAY, AUGUST 26, 1944

American forces in northern France entered Troyes, 130 miles from the German frontier, as Allied armies continued yesterday to move forward along a 200-mile front. Our bridgeheads across the Seine south of Paris were widened. The enemy was driven from Montereau, ten miles east of Fontainebleau and was in hurried retreat from the area northeast of Montargis. Far to the northwest, the remnants of the German Seventh Army, trapped with their backs to the Seine, were being driven into the river. [1:8; map P. 4.]

As the famous spire of the Eiffel Tower pierced an early morning fog, French and American forces smashed through to the heart of Paris amid a tumultuous welcome. The Free Paris radio reported that the German commander of the city had surrendered. [1:6-7; map P.5.]

In southern France, Allied troops captured Cannes and Antibes and stood less than twenty miles from the Italian frontier. Other Allied columns were reported closing in on Lyon, Rhône Valley industrial center 170 miles inland from the Mediterranean, and French patriots were said to be in control of the city. [1:7; map P. 2.]

General de Gaulle—who is in Paris—and his followers will have a greater part in the administration of civil affairs in France by new agreements. [5:1.]

More than 3,000 planes from Britain and Italy ranged over Czechoslovakia and Germany, pounding aircraft plants, airfields and experimental and research centers for Hitler's flying bombs and other new weapons of destruction. [4:6.]

The Red Army has reached the Galati Gap, a forty-five-mile path between the Danube delta and the mountains to the west, and seized Tecuci, a railway junction within that gateway to the Balkan plains. Twelve enemy divisions have been encircled southwest of Kishinev. Moscow also reported the capture of the key city of Tartu in the Riga-Tallinn railroad in Estonia in the Russian drive to wipe out two German Baltic armies. [1:3; map, P. 6.]

Chaos mounted in the Balkans. After German planes had bombed the Rumanian capital, the Bucharest radio went on the air to proclaim that King Michael's new pro-Ally Government was at war with Germany. Rumanians were battling Bulgarians as well as Germans. [1:4.] The Russian sweep led Bulgaria to send word to the Allies that she was ready to sue for unconditional surrender. [1:7.]

Allied planes set a Japanese cruiser ablaze and damaged seven enemy freighters near Celebes, an important Japanese supply center for Halmahera Island. [1:5.]

THIRD NEAR MARNE

Berlin Says Americans Have Driven to Reims, 80 Miles Above Paris

SEINE FOE CRUSHED

River Becomes a Scene of Carnage as Bombs Rain on Germans

By DREW MIDDLETON
By Cable to The New York Times.

SUPREME HEADQUARTERS, Allied Expeditionary Force, Saturday, Aug. 26—Three resounding victories were won along the 200-mile-long front in northern France yesterday.

Armored patrols of the United States Third Army rumbled into Troyes, a great road and railroad center 130 miles from the German frontier as the thrust eastward on the extreme right flank of the Allies' line broke through German offensive positions in front of Troyes, thirty-seven miles from the Marne River.

Bridgeheads across the Seine south of Paris were widened from Montereau, ten miles east of Fontainebleau, and was retreating hurriedly from the area northeast of Montargis, taken by other American forces last Thursday.

Report Reims Reached

An unconfirmed report, published in The London Chronicle, said the Germans declared that American troops had reached Reims, eighty miles northeast of Paris.

French and American troops penetrated into the center of Paris yesterday.

Aside from its tremendous effect on French morale, the Allies' occupation of Paris, the most important communications center in France, is a military triumph of first magnitude.

Finally, far to the west, British, American and Canadian forces were driving the remnants of the German Seventh Army pell-mell into the Seine. The Elbeuf pocket replaced Falaise as a graveyard. Enemy forces are now contained in an area less than 300 miles square, with the Seine to the east and north and the Risle to the west and the steadily advancing Allied line to the south.

Planes Batter Fleeing Foe

While field guns and tanks searched the forests for fleeing Germans, hundreds of medium and light fighter bombers scourged the Germans seeking to escape across the Seine.

The battle has become a race for Seine crossings, with Allied forces confident they will have killed, wounded or captured at least 40,000 of the Germans before they reach the Seine.

On the ground forces drove the Germans to the Seine. American and British light naval craft, attacking German ships leaving Le Havre, blew up an escort vessel, an armed trawler and a German E-boat and damaged at least five other craft. Between 3 and 4 o'clock yester-
Continued on Page 4

Von Kluge Killed, Stockholm Hears

By The Associated Press.

STOCKHOLM, Saturday, Aug. 26—Field Marshal Gen. Guenther von Kluge has been killed, the newspaper Dagens Nyheter said today on the basis of information received from Germany.

Circumstances of his reported death were not known here and the newspaper had no additional details.

[There was no immediate confirmation of this report in either London or Allied official quarters.]

Von Kluge, 61 years old, had held command of the German armies on the western front since July 6, when he succeeded Field Marshal Gen. Karl von Rundstedt.

"All the News
That's Fit to Print"

The New York Times.

LATE CITY EDITION
Sunny, cool and windy; fair and
becoming cooler tonight.
Temperatures Yesterday—Max., 69; Min., 51
Sunrise, 7:10 A. M.; Sunset, 6:01 P. M.

Copyright, 1944, by The New York Times Company

VOL. XCIV..No. 31,687.

Entered as Second-Class Matter,
Postoffice, New York, N. Y.

NEW YORK, THURSDAY, OCTOBER 26, 1944.

THREE CENTS NEW YORK CITY

U. S. DEFEATS JAPANESE NAVY; ALL FOE'S SHIPS IN ONE FLEET HIT; MANY SUNK; BATTLE CONTINUES

SPECIAL PRIVILEGE SOLD BY NEW DEAL, DEWEY CHARGES

Says Roosevelt Backs Plan for 1,000 to Put '$1,000 on the Line' to Aid Campaign

PARTY LETTER IS QUOTED

Governor Declares in Chicago Administration Lacks 'Honesty' to Solve Post-War Problems

The text of Mr. Dewey's speech will be found on Page 13.

By ALEXANDER FEINBERG
Special to The New York Times.

CHICAGO, Oct. 25—Governor Dewey declared tonight that "for $1,000 cash on the line to finance the fourth-term drive, this Administration boldly offers for sale 'special privilege,'" which includes the "assisting in the formulation of Administration policies."

Attacking the "rudimentary honesty" of the New Deal, Mr. Dewey, in a major campaign address preceding the appearance of President Roosevelt here Saturday, charged that the Chief Executive himself was the sponsor of the fund raising idea.

The Chicago Stadium, which accommodates 25,000 persons, was packed to capacity, with several thousand others clamoring to obtain admittance. Gov. Dwight H. Green of Illinois presented Mr. Dewey, who was received with tumultuous acclaim. He kept pointing to the microphone to quiet the demonstration, but it was just short of five minutes before he could begin his speech.

Governor Dewey said that the fund raising plan was disclosed in a letter signed by H. L. McAlister and Sam J. Watkins, State finance chairman, and written on the letterhead of the National Democratic Campaign Headquarters, Little Rock, Ark.

Dewey Quotes Letter

Mr. Dewey quoted the letter as follows:

"This is an invitation to you to join the One Thousand Club.

"The idea of such a club originated at a recent conference at the White House between the President, Robert E. Hannegan, chairman of the Democratic National Committee, and Edwin W. Pauley, treasurer of the committee. At this meeting the President commented:

" 'I think it would be a good idea to have a list of one thousand persons banded together from all over the United States to act as a liaison so that facts relating to the public interest are presented factually to the President and members of Congress.'

"Members of this organization undoubtedly will be granted special privilege by party leaders. These members will be called into conference from time to time to discuss matters of national importance and to assist in the formulation of Administration policies.

"To be eligible for membership in the One Thousand Club will require a contribution of $1,000 to the National Democratic campaign fund."

Mr. Dewey declared that "there in crude, unblushing words is the ultimate expression of New Deal policies," adding:

"And the sponsor of this idea is frankly stated in that letter to be the President himself. The man who holds the highest office within the gift of the American people at a conference in the White House sponsors an idea to sell 'special privilege' and a voice in the formulation of Administration policies' for one thousand dollars on the barrelhead."

The Governor said that New

Continued on Page 12, Column 1

No Extra Gasoline For Trip to Polls

By The Associated Press.

WASHINGTON, Oct. 25—Chester Bowles, OPA head, in a letter to Senator Davis, Republican, of Pennsylvania today stated that the OPA could not allow extra gasoline rations for private automobiles to take voters to the polls if other means of transportation are available.

Pennsylvania has no absentee voting law and Senator Davis contended that many persons from his State working elsewhere would be unable to return to cast their ballots unless they received extra gas rations.

"A special ration may be granted to carry persons to and from the polls for the purpose of voting in public elections (including primary elections), provided reasonably adequate alternative means of transportation are not available," Mr. Bowles wrote.

Where no other form of transportation is available those wishing to use cars for voting may apply to their local ration boards on special forms which the boards have available.

WAGNER ACCLAIMS PARTY FARM POLICY

He Says That Dewey Is Vague on Agriculture—Calls His Platform 'Double Talk'

By CLAYTON P. KNOWLES
Special to The New York Times.

SYRACUSE, N. Y., Oct. 25—The farm plank in the Republican platform offers nothing but "double talk" and Governor Dewey, rather than clarifying the issue, puts forward proposals "as vague and airy as a wisp of smoke," Senator Robert F. Wagner declared tonight in a campaign for re-election into this city in the heart of the farm area.

"Mr. Dewey ridicules the so-called alphabetical agencies," he declared. "But how could low-interest loans have been provided without the Farm Mortgage Corporation? How could the number of farms with central electric service have been multiplied three times without the Rural Electrification Administration?

"These programs are not perfect. They need to be improved, they are solid, they can be seen, they can be felt. When Mr. Dewey talks about the farmer, what he proposes is as vague and airy as a wisp of smoke."

His address, broadcast over a State-wide hook-up by the Columbia Broadcasting System, said that Governor Dewey's Commissioner of Agriculture last spring set minimum milk prices "far above

Continued on Page 3, Column 3

PRESIDENT ELATED

Gives News From Halsey That Foe Is 'Defeated, Damaged, Routed'

TEST IS ON, KING SAYS

Practically All Japanese Fleet in the Battle, Admiral Believes

By LEWIS WOOD
Special to The New York Times.

WASHINGTON, Oct. 25—President Roosevelt exultantly announced late today the receipt of a report from Admiral William F. Halsey saying that the Japanese Navy in the Philippine area had been "defeated, seriously damaged and routed" by our forces.

Two hours earlier Admiral Ernest J. King, Commander in Chief of the United States Fleet and Chief of Naval Operations, had disclosed that virtually all of the long elusive Japanese Fleet had been engaged at last in the furious sea battle of the Philippines.

These two startling revelations, exciting Washington as nothing has done since the European invasions, were taken here to mean that the vaunted Japanese naval power had been seriously crippled and the road to Tokyo made much easier. At last, it was presumed, the principal part of Japanese naval strength had been nettled out of hiding and then decisively beaten.

Announcement Is Dramatic

The circumstances of the President's statement were thrilling. When only a half dozen newsmen remained in the White House press room at 5:20 P. M., Press Secretary Stephen T. Early appeared at the door.

"Come quick," he cried, slapping his palms together for emphasis. Rushing to the President's oval-shaped office, the reporters found him seated at his desk, smiling broadly. Obviously he had been interrupted in his late afternoon dictation. Before him lay scattered papers, but directly in front of him was a single sheet of paper, inscribed apparently with his own handwriting.

He had said the President beamingly, a "real flash," just telephoned to him by Admiral William D. Leahy, Chief of Staff to the President as Commander in Chief of the Army and Navy. Picking up the paper, Mr. Roosevelt slowly and distinctly read:

"The President received today a report from Admiral Halsey that the Japanese Navy in the Philippine area has been defeated, seriously damaged and routed by the United States Navy in that area."

For a moment there was a pause. Then no one said a word. Then

Continued on Page 3, Column 3

SEA POWER OF LAND OF THE RISING SUN SHATTERED IN BATTLE

Oct. 26, 1944

Piecing together the statements of Admiral Nimitz and General MacArthur gives this picture of the battle around the Philippines: One Japanese force, including four battleships, ten cruisers and thirteen destroyers, first sighted south of Mindoro (1) steamed east, across the Sibuyan Sea, through San Bernardino Strait and down the coast of Samar (2), where Admiral Kinkaid's combined force (5) attacked it and forced it to retire northward with perhaps ten ships damaged. It was apparently in this action that the American light carrier Princeton was sunk. A second enemy force, first sighted southwest of Negros (3), included two battleships, one or two cruisers and four destroyers. It moved east across the Sulu Sea and through Surigao Strait (4). Admiral Kinkaid attacked this group and it lost one battleship and several cruisers and destroyers; the rest of the force retreated west through the strait. This whole battle scene is at (A) on the inset. A third Japanese force was engaged southeast of Formosa (B).

ALLIES CUT UP FOE IN WEST HOLLAND

British Hammer Germans in One Area of 's Hertogenbosch —Canadians Tighten Traps

By CLIFTON DANIEL
SUPREME HEADQUARTERS, Allied Expeditionary Force, Oct. 25—The Germans were rapidly losing their grip tonight on their strongholds between the North Sea and the British Second Army's salient in the Netherlands.

British forces converging from three sides drove them out of all

Continued on Page 7, Column 2

'17 Hours of Hell' Raised In Sea Battle Off Leyte

By RALPH TEATSORTH
United Press Correspondent

ABOARD ADMIRAL KINKAID'S FLAGSHIP, off the Philippines, Thursday, Oct. 26—The Tokyo Express rammed into the American Navy Limited today. The pride of Japan was wrecked so badly it may never make another long run. It was the day our Navy had dreamed about for considerably more than a year.

It was seventeen hours of concentrated hell and the most amazing thing about the battle was that our Pacific Fleet Carrier Force—which nobody thought could deliver such a terrific punch—held off the bulk of the Japanese fleet all day and had it on the run all afternoon.

When evening came and most of

Continued on Page 4, Column 7

AMERICANS MAKE BIG LEYTE JUMPS

Troops Push Westward on Isle —Southern Coast of Samar to the North Now Held

By The United Press.

ADVANCED HEADQUARTERS ON LEYTE, Thursday, Oct. 26—American dismounted cavalry troops have invaded Samar, third largest of the Philippines and last island barrier on the road to Luzon and Manila, while forces fighting on Leyte have punched nine miles inland to seize the key road junction of Burauen.

Gen. Douglas MacArthur also announced in a special communiqué that Field Marshal Count Juichi Terauchi's Japanese defenders of the northern Leyte front were "disintegrating" under the American hammer blows.

The three-mile American advance that occupied Burauen, southern terminus of an inland highway, split the Japanese lines in northern Leyte and threw the enemy back toward the hills, where Filipino guerrillas were reported in action.

The new American triumphs pushed our lines nine miles inland and raised to thirty-one the number of towns and villages captured. Six airfields also have been seized. The invasion of Samar, on the

Continued on Page 4, Column 4

AIR PLANT IN JAPAN SMASHED BY B-29'S

Omura Target Is 'Perfectly Patterned,' Pilots Say—Foe Lists 100 Planes in Attack

WASHINGTON, Oct. 25—While the remnants of the demoralized Japanese Fleet were fleeing from Admiral William F. Halsey's forces in Philippine waters, United States Army Superfortresses took the war another step closer to the heart of Japan by carrying out a successful mission against the key aircraft assembly plant at Omura on the island of Kyushu.

Twentieth Air Force Headquarters here announced that a medium-sized task force of the mammoth bombers, operating from Twen-

Continued on Page 4, Column 4

BATTLESHIP IS SUNK

Seventh Fleet Smashes Two Japanese Forces Converging on Leyte

REMNANTS IN FLIGHT

They Are Hotly Pursued —Third Enemy Force Is Hit Off Formosa

The Imperial Japanese Fleet has been brought to battle. It is suffering a crushing defeat. Two of its divisions have been routed. One has been almost destroyed. Contact has been made with the main force southeast of Formosa by Admiral William F. Halsey's Third Fleet. That engagement is continuing, said the last communiqué.

Two strong Japanese naval forces converged on Leyte Gulf through the San Bernardino Strait in the Philippines to the north and the Surigao Strait to the south. Vice Admiral Thomas C. Kinkaid's Seventh Fleet smashed these two forces and put the remnants to flight after sinking or heavily damaging every ship in the southern enemy force.

One big Japanese carrier has been sunk. Two more have been heavily damaged and undoubtedly are out of action. One Japanese battleship of the Yamasiro class has been sunk. At least four others have been heavily damaged. Several enemy cruisers and destroyers have been sunk. Many others have been hit, both by bombs and torpedoes.

Enemy Defeated and Routed

The only announced American loss is the converted light-carrier Princeton sunk. Other escort carriers were damaged by fire from one of the enemy battleship forces. Gen. Douglas MacArthur reported triumphantly that "the Japanese Navy has suffered its most crushing defeat of the war." Admiral Ernest J. King, in Washington, said that "practically all" of the Japanese fleet was engaged and that he was confident of the outcome. President Roosevelt called a special press conference to announce receipt of a message from Admiral William F. Halsey reporting that the enemy has been "defeated, seriously damaged and routed."

Pending official word from Pearl Harbor, it appeared the greatest surface and naval air action in the history of naval warfare was being fought and won by the Pacific Fleet, the greatest naval force that ever went down to the sea.

Fate of Leyte Decided

SEVENTH FLEET HEADQUARTERS, Philippines, Thursday, Oct. 26 (P)—Japan lost the first, and possibly the decisive, round in an all-out battle to halt on the Philippines line the American advance toward her home islands.

This occurred early yesterday morning when Admiral Kinkaid's outnumbered fleet battered and put to rout Japanese battle forces converging on Leyte Gulf.

Complete results are lacking as the action is continuing, with planes from Admiral Kinkaid's hurt but still fighting carrier force hitting the surviving enemy warships as they are retiring. But MacArthur and the Japanese forces that came through Surigao Strait fled back through it to the west and the other was in flight in a northerly direction.

[Gordon Walker in a Mutual broadcast from the Philippines said "a Navy spokesman here claimed that practically every

Continued on Page 3, Column 2

U. S. and Britain Recognize Italy; Action Is First With an Ex-Enemy

By BERTRAM D. HULEN
Special to The New York Times.

WASHINGTON, Oct. 25—Diplomatic relations with Italy were resumed by the Allies tonight.

Recognition is being accorded by the United States, the other American republics in the United Nations and Britain. The Soviet Union had previously extended recognition to the Government of Premier Ivanoe Bonomi.

Our action was announced by Edward R. Stettinius Jr., acting Secretary of State, who said that Alexander C. Kirk, who has been serving as our diplomatic representative in Rome with the personal rank of Ambassador, would now be accredited to the Italian Government with the rank of Ambassador.

The announcement by Mr. Stettinius follows:

"After consultation with the other American republics, as provided for in the Resolutions of Rio de

Continued on Page 10, Column 5

It is expected that Italy will now send an Ambassador here. The appointment of Count Carlos Sforza, long a friend of the United States, to the post, has been forecast since it became evident that recognition would not long be delayed.

Announcement of the recognition has been made at London and is expected at the Latin-American capitals, except for Buenos Aires. Argentina never severed relations with Italy, although she did with Germany and Japan.

'17 Hours of Hell' — War News Summarized

THURSDAY, OCTOBER 26, 1944

The Japanese Navy came out to fight in the waters off the Philippines and was severely mauled. One force of four battleships, ten cruisers and thirteen destroyers moved up south of Mindoro into the Sibuyan Sea. Every battleship and at least one cruiser was hit. This flotilla rounded Samar and fled north. We lost an escort carrier.

A second force of two battleships, two cruisers and four destroyers came into the Sulu Sea from southwest of Negros Island. After all the ships had been hit it turned tail and retreated.

A third force, this one with carriers, came down from home waters and the battle was still going on. Most of the engagements were fought from the air and the enemy suffered heavily in plane losses. Our light carrier Princeton was hit and its magazine subsequently exploded. Most of the crew were saved. The Third Pacific Fleet took on the enemy carrier force and the Seventh turned back the two others. [All the foregoing 1:8.]

President Roosevelt, in an impromptu press conference, said that Admiral Halsey had just reported that the Japanese Navy had been "defeated, seriously damaged and routed." Earlier Admiral King had said that almost the entire enemy naval strength was involved in the Philippines battle. Fighting covered an area 600 miles north and south and 250 miles east and west. Navy officials were elated and felt the whole course of the war might be speeded. [1:3.]

On Leyte American troops had pushed twenty miles north of Tacloban and nine miles inland from Dulag. Additional landings on the northern part of Leyte and the southern part of Samar won control of San Juanico Strait, which separates them. [1:7; map P. 2.]

Superfortresses delivered a smashing assault on Japan's key aircraft plant at Omura on the island of Kyushu. One B-29 was missing. [1:6.]

German positions in the Belgium - Netherland pocket were becoming increasingly untenable as Canadian and British troops drew closer and menaced the enemy retreat line. [1:4; map P. 7.] More than 2,200 American and British bombers lashed rail and oil targets in the Reich. Six bombers and one of a great fighter escort were missing. [9:1.]

Russian forces captured the German port and U-boat base of Kirkenes in Norway and thirty other Norwegian villages. [1:6-7; map P. 11.] To the south the Red Army renewed its drive on East Prussia, gained more ground in East Prussia and liberated all of Transylvania by capturing Satu Mare and Carei. [12:1, with map.]

Mount Belmonte, guarding the southern approaches to Bologna, was captured by Americans of the Fifth Army in Italy. The British Eighth Army gained ground in the Adriatic sector. A German withdrawal was indicated. [10:7.]

The United Nations have resumed diplomatic relations with Italy, the first former enemy state to receive recognition. [1:2-3.]

Russians Invade North Norway; Take Kirkenes in Wide Advance

By W. H. LAWRENCE
By Wireless to The New York Times.

MOSCOW, Oct. 25—Entering their ninth country in less than seven months, Red Army forces smashed across the "Norwegian frontier today and liberated the Barents Sea port of Kirkenes and thirty other Norwegian villages just fifty-four months and twenty-one days after the beginning of Adolf Hitler's treacherous invasion of the Scandinavian country.

This new expedition of Russian troops outside the Soviet Union was announced by Premier Joseph Stalin in a special order of the day and was saluted by Moscow's massed guns and highlighted in tonight's communiqué.

It would be wrong to assume from this dash across the Norwegian frontier at its northernmost point that the liberation of

Continued on Page 11, Column 4

back on the soil of that restless country for the first time since June 15, 1941, when the British had to withdraw their poorly equipped forces in the face of numerically superior German forces.

[On its European front the Red Army reopened the battle for Warsaw by outflanking the Polish capital on the north, drove farther into East Prussia against desperate resistance and completed the liberation of Transylvania.]

The Soviet Union's Norwegian campaign brings Allied armies

131

"All the News
That's Fit to Print"

The New York Times.

Copyright, 1944, by The New York Times Company.

LATE CITY EDITION
POSTSCRIPT
Considerable cloudiness and milder today; moderate winds.
Temperatures—Max., 51 ; Min., 37
Sunrise, 7:15 A. M.; Sunset, 3:45 P. M.

VOL. XCIV No. 31,700.

Entered as Second-Class Matter,
Postoffice, New York, N. Y.

NEW YORK, WEDNESDAY, NOVEMBER 8, 1944.

THREE CENTS IN NEW YORK CITY

ROOSEVELT WINS FOURTH TERM; RECORD POPULAR VOTE IS CLOSE; DEMOCRATS GAIN IN THE HOUSE

2-DAY LUZON BLOWS SMASH 440 PLANES, 30 JAPANESE SHIPS

Halsey's Fliers Destroy 249 Aircraft, Sink Four Vessels in Sunday Sweep

MANILA FIELDS RAVAGED

Ports and Installations Hit Hard—Enemy Lines to Leyte Defenders Are Strained

BY GEORGE HORNE
By Telephone to THE NEW YORK TIMES.

PEARL HARBOR, Nov. 7—Admiral William F. Halsey's Third Fleet carriers spread death and damage over southern Luzon Island in the Philippines for the second successive day on Sunday, sinking another five ships and destroying 249 additional enemy aircraft.

It was a major air strike, apparently an all-out effort to annihilate the Japanese air forces supporting enemy counter-attacks on Leyte, where American military leaders have reported the campaign nearing its final stages.

Over the two days, according to Admiral Chester W. Nimitz's communique today, the enemy has lost 440 aircraft, 327 of which were caught and destroyed on the ground and 113 shot down in the air. The principal plane concentrations were found on seven fields in the Manila network. They were Nichols, Clark, Nielson, Lipa, Tarlac, Bambam and Mabalacat.

[The two-day toll of enemy ships sunk or damaged was about thirty.]

Unable to Rise in Strength

As the widespread attacks continue, the enemy air opposition is becoming steadily weaker, as is evidenced by the fact that on the second day all but a few of the lost enemy aircraft were caught on the ground, unable to get into the air.

Terrific damage is being inflicted on port facilities and ground installations in and around Manila harbor. In addition to ships sunk and planes destroyed, many air and surface craft were listed as damaged. Reports on the action were still of a preliminary nature and there was no count of our own losses.

Admiral Nimitz said that oil storage areas were left blazing at the northern section of Clark Field and at the northeast of the field a tremendous explosion was observed, followed by fire. North of Malvar a railroad engine and five tank cars were blown up.

Five Ships Sunk at Manila

In the harbor of Manila the fighters, torpedo planes and dive-bombers sank three cargo ships and an oil tanker, probably sank a destroyer and damaged two destroyers, two destroyer escorts, a trawler and several cargo ships. Fourteen cargo ships were damaged during the two-day attack, in which wave after wave of American planes swept in from the sea to wipe out available enemy strength that might be used to bolster the hard-pressed Japanese forces on Leyte.

Meanwhile the steady attacks on the Bonins and Kuriles are continuing. On Sunday a detachment of the Eleventh Army Air Force, flying hundreds of miles from our Aleutian bases, hit three small transports off Onnekotan Island in the Kuriles and other Liberators flying with it concentrated on land targets of the island base.

Seven enemy fighters fought the big bombers in a running battle, and guns from three Liberators brought down one and probably destroyed another. Two Liberators were damaged.

Otomari and Tori Island, also in the Kuriles, were attacked.

Seventh Air Force Liberators

Continued on Page 19, Column 2

"WILL ENCHANT MOVIE-GOERS' IS HEARALD Tribune's praise of "Greenwich Village." Starts tomorrow at RKO Brooklyn and Queens theatres. Plus account full-length feature "Dangerous Journey"—packed with a thousand thrills.—Advt.

War News Summarized

WEDNESDAY, NOVEMBER 8, 1944

Japanese Lose 440 Planes

Japanese air power in the Philippines received a staggering blow on Saturday and Sunday when Third Fleet carrier planes destroyed 440 enemy aircraft in the Manila and southern Luzon areas. Nearly thirty ships, including a number of warcraft, were also destroyed or damaged. Our fliers reaped their greatest harvest at seven airfields where they wiped out 327 planes on the ground. Port and ground installations suffered terrific damage. Reports were still incomplete and our own losses were not known. [1:1.]

Luzon fields pounded from air

Battle Joined on Leyte

American troops on Leyte were battling elements of four Japanese divisions in the hills north of Ormoc and repulsed three heavy attacks, inflicting great loss on the enemy. The area of Valencia, north of Ormoc, was under American artillery fire. [19:1, with map.]

Tokyo Sees B-29's

The jittery Japanese reported more Superfortresses on reconnaissance flights over Tokyo and surrounding territory. They also said that the Bonins and Volcanos had been bombed. [19:2.] In China the enemy scored by driving to within twenty miles of Liuchow, but in Burma the British captured Kennedy Peak and threatened Fort White and Paletwa. [21:1.]

Grim Fight Below Aachen

The United States First Army fought its way back into the streets of Vossenack in some of the bitterest fighting of the war.

Three German counter-attacks from Schmidt were repulsed. The Sixth Army Group made important advances in the Vosges Mountains and in the Netherlands Allied troops were mopping up the liberated areas. [19:8, with map.]

Soviet Drive Forecast

Behind the lull on Russia's fighting fronts the Red Army was reported to be preparing for a great new offensive. [19:4.] The Athens radio announced that the Greek Government had ordered dissolution of the guerrilla bands Edes and Elas. [19:5.]

Robot Blows at U.S. 'Possible'

A joint Army-Navy statement said that it was "entirely possible" for flying bombs to reach the United States from Europe, but gave no indication such an attack was expected. [19:6-7.]

FISH IS DEFEATED; CLARE LUCE WINS

Congress Veteran Concedes Bennet's Victory—Close Finish in Connecticut

Special to THE NEW YORK TIMES.

NEWBURGH, N. Y., Wednesday, Nov. 8—Representative Hamilton Fish, for twelve terms a Republican member of the House and a leading isolationist and critic of President Roosevelt's foreign policy, conceded his defeat by Augustus W. Bennet just before 1 o'clock this morning.

"From reports I have received to date, it looks like I have lost the district by a 5,000 vote majority," he said.

"It looks as if the Republicans have lost the House, and if that is so, as much as I regret it, I have no great desire to continue to serve as a minority member, which I have for the last fourteen years in an uphill fight."

Mr. Bennet, in a victory statement, paid tribute to those who had supported him from all parties, "including the much-abused Political Action Committee." He hailed his election as the result of the citizens' determination "to eliminate Ham Fish from Congress."

Factors in the Result

Heavy Republican defections to Mr. Bennet in Orange County and strong support for Mr. Fish's opponent in the parts of the district in Rockland, Sullivan and Delaware counties sent the Republican nominee down to defeat in the bitterest Congressional election in this part of the State in years.

Complete returns from Orange County gave Fish 35,126 votes to 27,371 for Bennet, a majority for Fish of 7,755. This indicated that Mr. Bennet's majority for the whole Twenty-ninth Congressional District would be about 5,600.

Complete returns from Orange County gave Bennet 19,706 votes to 12,323 for Fish, a majority of 7,383.

In Sullivan County, with twenty-four election districts missing, including those where Mr. Bennet was expected to run strongest, the vote was Fish 3,877, Bennet 3,776.

Continued on Page 2, Column 7

LETTERS from SANTA CLAUS are thrilling to children—At Greeting Card Counters.—Advt.

ROOSEVELT VICTORY CLAIMED IN JERSEY

Hague Spokesmen Also Say Wene Will Win—Constitution Revision Is Rejected

Despite greatly reduced pluralities in Hudson County, Democratic stronghold of New Jersey, lieutenants of Mayor Frank Hague of Jersey City, Democratic boss of the State, predicted shortly before 4 A. M. today that the State's sixteen electoral votes would be delivered to President Roosevelt, largely by virtue of an estimated plurality of 75,000 votes in Hudson. In 1940 Mr. Roosevelt carried the county by a plurality of 100,877.

Mayor Hague's spokesman also predicted victory for the party nominee for the United States Senate, Representative Elmer H. Wene, although by a close vote, and rejection of the proposed revised State Constitution by a substantial margin.

Mr. Hague himself left headquarters in Jersey City early today without making any statement.

The Jersey City predictions were made despite the fact that eight of the twelve wards in the city had not reported returns up to that hour, but the estimates on the fate of charter revision appeared to be borne out by State-wide returns. At 4 A. M., with 1,311 of the State's 3,657 election districts missing, the vote for rejection was 480,503 to 381,686 for approval.

At the same hour Mr. Dewey was leading Roosevelt by a vote of 481,677 to 456,275, with 1,819 districts missing, and, H. Alexander Smith, Mr. Wene's Republican opponent, was leading the Democratic nominee by a vote of 562,261 to 503,763, on the basis of returns from 2,226 districts.

Five Hudson Communities Bolt

The apparent failure of the Hague machine to deliver the expected large Democratic plurality in the county had caused some political observers to place the State in the doubtful class.

Continued on Page 9, Column 4

GET 11 TO 20 SEATS

Victories Blast Hopes of Rivals to Control the House

SENATE UNCHANGED

Democrats Have 180 in House, Republicans 155, 98 in Doubt

By TURNER CATLEDGE

Democratic gains of from eleven to twenty seats in the House and a possible new place or two in the already one-sided Senate, appeared on returns received up to 5 A. M. today to have followed in the wake of yesterday's fourth-term landslide for President Roosevelt.

Republican hopes of controlling the House appeared to have been blasted beyond any possibility of realization and what in the earlier count seemed to portend a G. O. P. gain in the Senate began to fade with the later returns.

These same reports showed the defeat of Representative Hamilton Fish, Republican, of New York, one of the most controversial figures in the lower house; the possible defeat of Senator John A. Danaher, Republican, of Connecticut; a victory for Mrs. Clare Luce, Republican, in a close race in the Fourth Connecticut Congresional District; a trend in the early count against Senator Gerald P. Nye, Republican "isolationist" of North Dakota, and a neck-and-neck contest in which Senator James J. Davis, Republican, of Pennsylvania, was trailing his Democratic opponent, Representative Francis J. Myers, by a slight margin.

Leading Senators Re-elected

These returns also revealed the re-election of Senator Alben W. Barkley, Democratic Majority Leader, in Kentucky; of Senator Scott Lucas, Democrat, in Illinois; of Senator Robert A. Taft, Republican, in Ohio; of Senator Millard Tydings, Democrat, in Maryland, and numerous other sitting Senators, both Democratic and Republican.

With 98 House seats still in doubt, the Democrats had clinched 180 seats in the House of Representatives of the Seventy-ninth Congress; the Republicans were certain of at least 155; the American Labor party of 1 and the Progressives of one.

Seventeen Senate places were still awaiting the decision of the final count, but the Democrats were certain of 49, or an actual majority. The Republicans appeared certain of thirty-one and with the latest returns received the Democrats had garnered a net

Continued on Page 2, Column 5

ELECTED TO PRESIDENCY AND VICE PRESIDENCY

Franklin D. Roosevelt   Harry S. Truman

ROOSEVELT STRONG IN WAR VOTE TALLY

Partial Count of Ballots of Armed Forces Increases President's Majority

By CHARLES GRUTZNER Jr.

The majority given to President Roosevelt by civilian voters who went to the polls throughout the nation yesterday was increased by the count of war ballots marked, some of them as long as two months ago, by members of the armed forces in camps here and in far-flung theatres of operations.

The decisiveness of the President's victory over Governor Dewey removed the possibility that the outcome of the election might hinge on the soldier vote in some of the eleven States that delayed counting their war ballots, but partial returns from States that counted their war ballots yesterday made it clear that the support of the men and women in the armed forces would be a strong factor in building up the final majority of their Commander in Chief.

A breakdown of the vote into civilian and war ballots was slow in coming in from nearly all of the thirty-seven States that counted their soldier vote yesterday, because election officials were concerned chiefly with transmitting

Continued on Page 4, Column 2

New York for Roosevelt; Wagner Re-elected Senator

By JAMES A. HAGERTY

For the sixth consecutive time, four times as a candidate for President and twice as a candidate for Governor, President Roosevelt carried his home State of New York in yesterday's election and won its forty-seven electoral votes. With 3,609 of the 3,700 election districts in New York City and with 4,978 of the 5,421 election districts outside New York City reporting, President Roosevelt had an actual lead over Governor Dewey, his Republican opponent, of 300,831 and a plurality of about 283,000 for the President in the State was indicated.

Returns from 3,609 election districts out of 3,700 in New York City gave Dewey 1,240,216, Roosevelt 1,966,539. This is an actual plurality of 726,273 and an indicated plurality of 743,700 for Roosevelt.

Returns from 4,978 election districts out of 5,421 outside New York City gave Dewey 1,585,771, Roosevelt 1,160,329. This is an actual plurality of 425,442 and an indicated plurality of 460,785 for Dewey.

Re-elected in the sweep for the President was United States Senator Robert F. Wagner, who defeated Secretary of State Thomas J. Curran by a plurality probably greater than that for Mr. Roosevelt. Also elected was Associate Judge of the Court of Appeals, Marvin B. Dye, who defeated John Van Voorhis, Republican. The President, Senator Harry S. Truman, candidate for Vice President, Senator Wagner and Mr. Dye, all Democrats, also were nominees of the American Labor and Liberal parties.

Returns from 3,566 election districts of the 3,700 in New York City gave Curran 1,183,020, Wagner 1,957,026. This is an actual plurality of 774,006, and an indicated plurality of 802,900 for Wagner.

Returns from 4,797 of 5,421 election districts outside New York City gave Curran 1,468,985, Wagner 1,086,736. This is an actual plurality of 382,249, and an indicated plurality of 433,680 for Curran.

Both Houses of the State Legislature remain Republican. Among the greatest upsets in the State was the defeat of former Mayor Rolland B. Marvin of Syracuse, Republican candidate for State Senator in the Forty-third Senatorial District, by Richard J. P. Byrne, Democratic and American

Continued on Page 2, Column 2

DEWEY STATEMENT ADMITS HIS DEFEAT

Candidate Concedes Loss of Election at 3:12 A. M. and Congratulates Victor

Gov. Thomas E. Dewey, Republican candidate for President, conceded defeat at 3:12 o'clock this morning.

His statement was made at Republican National Headquarters in the Hotel Roosevelt, where both he and Herbert Brownell Jr., chairman of the National Committee, earlier had refused comment on the growing indication of a lopsided electoral college vote for his Democratic opponent, President Franklin D. Roosevelt.

Mr. Dewey said:

It is clear that Mr. Roosevelt has been re-elected for a fourth term, and every good American will whole-heartedly accept the will of the people.

I extend to President Roosevelt my hearty congratulations and my earnest hope that his next term will see speedy victory in the war, the establishment of lasting peace and the restoration of tranquillity among our peoples.

I am deeply grateful for the confidence expressed by so many million Americans for their labors in the campaign.

The Republican party emerges from the election revitalized and a great force for the good of the country and for the preservation of free government in America.

I am confident that all Americans will join me in a devout hope that in the years ahead Divine Providence will guide and protect the President of the United States.

President Roosevelt, from his Hyde Park home, acknowledged, at 3:28 o'clock this morning Gov-

Continued on Page 3, Column 2

MALE WORKERS; No experience required. Express handlers, garagemen, mechanic helpers, experienced mechanics; post-war policy. Offices, warehouse, bronx, Brooklyn, apply Railway Express Agency, 51 S. Railroad Ave., Flushing Freight Stat. 561 9th Ave. or 53 Hudson St., N. Y. City. Essential workers need statement of availability.—Advt.

Roosevelt Leads as Davis Trails, In Mounting Pennsylvania Count

Special to THE NEW YORK TIMES.

PHILADELPHIA, Wednesday, Nov. 8—On the basis of partial returns from all but three of the sixty-seven counties in Pennsylvania, it appeared early that President Roosevelt for the third successive time had captured the State's electoral votes.

Swept on the Roosevelt wave, it appeared, was Representative Francis J. Myers in his race to unseat James J. Davis, 71-year-old Republican Senator who was elected first in 1932 and re-elected six years ago.

Whether the Roosevelt impetus would be sufficient to sweep into office the Democratic candidates for the five State offices remained in doubt. Reports in these instances lagging far behind the count on the two top contests, were inconclusive.

With 6,012 of 8,202 precincts reporting, President Roosevelt was leading Governor Dewey, 1,282,392 to 1,238,986. Among the returns were all the 1,338 precincts in this city where the President gained a lead of 117,000.

The returns showed that once again the soft coal miners in western Pennsylvania and the anthracite miners in the East repudiated John L. Lewis, president of the United Mine Workers of America, by turning in thumping pluralities for Mr. Roosevelt.

On the other hand, with less than half the precincts reporting, President's lead, Republican leaders were hoping that late returns and a fair share of the soldier vote, to be counted on Nov. 22, would mean victory for the party in the State.

Although the President seemed

Continued on Page 8, Column 4

DEWEY CONCEDES

His Action Comes as Roosevelt Leads in 33 States

BIG ELECTORAL VOTE

Late Returns in Seesaw Battles May Push Total Beyond 400

By ARTHUR KROCK

Franklin Delano Roosevelt, who broke more than a century-old tradition in 1940 when he was elected to a third term as President, made another political record yesterday when he was chosen for a fourth term by a heavy electoral but much narrower popular majority over Thomas E. Dewey, Governor of New York.

At 3:15 A. M. Governor Dewey conceded Mr. Roosevelt's re-election, sending his best wishes by radio, to which the President quickly responded with an appreciative telegram.

Early this morning Mr. Roosevelt was leading in mounting returns in thirty-three States with a total of 391 electoral votes and a half a dozen more a trend was developing that could increase this figure to more than 400. Governor Dewey was ahead in fifteen States with 140 electoral votes, but some were see-sawing away from him and back again. Typical of these were Wisconsin, where he overtook the President's lead about 2 A. M.; Nevada where Mr. Roosevelt passed him at about the same time, and Missouri.

In the contests for seats in Congress, the Democrats had shown gains of 11 to 20 in the House of Representatives, assuring that party's continued control of that branch. In the Senate the net of losses and gains appeared to be an addition of one Republican to the Senate, which would give that party twenty-eight members—far short of the forty-nine necessary to a majority. A surprise was the indicated defeat of the veteran Pennsylvania Republican, Senator James J. Davis.

Mrs. Luce's Opponent Concedes

The Congressional races were featured by a mass Democratic attempt, in which the President and Vice President Henry A. Wallace to unseat Representative Clare Boothe Luce of Connecticut. But shortly after 3 A. M., following a night in which the lead had swung back and forth, her election was conceded by her opponent, Miss Margaret Connors. Some hours before, to his neighbors at Hyde Park, the President had expressed rejoicing over Mrs. Luce's "defeat." Her success is the vitriol in the Democratic honey.

Despite the great general victories by the Democrats, the popular vote will evidently show a huge minority protest against a fourth term for the President. Tabulations by the press associations indicated that the disparity between the ballots cast for the two candidates will be so small that a change of several hundred thousand votes in the key States, distributed in a certain way, would have reversed the electoral majority. At 4:40 A. M. The Associated Press reported 16,387,999 for Mr. Roosevelt and 14,235,051 for Mr. Dewey from more than one-third of the country's election districts. This ratio, if carried through, would leave only about 3,000,000 votes between the candidates.

One of the most interesting struggles for the President was that in Wisconsin, where Mr. Dewey took an early lead, lost it again and again. Wisconsin is the State where the late Wendell L. Willkie was beaten for renomination, posing the issue of

Continued on Page 2, Column 2

WOR's news programs will brilliantly sum up the whole election today!—WOR.—Advt.

"All the News That's Fit to Print"

The New York Times.

LATE CITY EDITION
Fair and cold today. Cloudy and slightly warmer tomorrow.
Temperature Yesterday—Max., 33; Min., 19
Sunrise, 6:17 A. M.; Sunset, 1:20 P. M.

Copyright, 1945, by The New York Times Company.

VOL. XCIV...No. 31,771.   Entered as Second-Class Matter, Postoffice, New York, N. Y.   NEW YORK, THURSDAY, JANUARY 18, 1945.   THREE CENTS NEW YORK CITY

RUSSIANS TAKE WARSAW, REPORTED IN CRACOW; WIN A CITY 14 MILES FROM REICH IN 24-MILE GAIN; BRITISH ADVANCE, AMERICANS CLOSE ON ST. VITH

ROOSEVELT URGES WORK-OR-FIGHT BILL TO BACK OFFENSIVES

Letter to May Calls for Prompt Action on 18-to-45 Measure—King, Marshall Tell of Needs

RECENT LOSSES ARE HEAVY

House Group Abruptly Ends Hearings—Approval of Legislation Expected by Tonight

Appeals by the President, Gen. Marshall, Adm. King, Page 13.

By C. P. TRUSSELL.
Special to The New York Times.
WASHINGTON, Jan. 17—President Roosevelt called on Congress today for prompt action on a work-or-fight bill in the years between 18 and 45, since it was vital that the Allied "total offense should not slacken because of any less than total utilization of our manpower on the home front."

In support of his appeal, which was addressed to Chairman Andrew J. May of the House Military Affairs Committee, the President attached a copy of a joint letter sent to him by General Marshall and Admiral King.

Replacements Needed

As "the agents directly responsible" for the conduct of military operations, they also urged "immediate action" on the home front to meet requirements for young and vigorous replacements in battle zones and to provide the necessary manpower to multiply production of critical munitions, build new ships and repair those damaged in combat.

Mr. Roosevelt said that the need for statutory controls to channel 4-F's into essential war work was more urgent now than it was eleven days ago when he asked for it as a stop gap, pending enactment of a national service law, and urged action "without delay" on the May-Bailey bill providing for "limited national service" and covering all 18 to 45 deferred registrants.

Hearings on the May-Bailey bill were ended abruptly, and Mr. May called an executive session of the committee tomorrow. He predicted that the measure, in some form, would be approved by nightfall.

"Time to Act," May Says

"We've discussed this matter long enough," Mr. May said. "It's now time to act."

Committeemen joined their chairman in expected approval of the bill, but they predicted that changes would be made, warned that much care must be exercised in revising the measure, and looked for a "tough" fight when it reached the House floor.

Earlier, the National Association of Manufacturers had organized labor in opposing the bill, as well as national service generally, before the committee.

Frederick C. Crawford, chairman of the NAM executive committee, testified that if legislation were to be written, it should only put teeth into the controls of existing machinery and programs. He said that intensified cooperation between Government, management and labor could supply the manpower demands for the armed service and war production requirements now and in the next six months, when an estimated 1,600,000 men will be required. Recent employment gains were cited.

The President in his letter to Mr. May said that it was true that there had been a trend toward increased placement of manpower in the last fortnight, but he added that there was danger that this trend, accelerated by belief that Congress was about to act on work-or-fight measures, would be reversed by indications that such action was likely to be delayed.

Although the May-Bailey bill is not a complete national service measure, Mr. Roosevelt said, it would "go far" to effect essential

Continued on Page 13, Column 2

Russian Super-Tank Reported by Nazis

By The Associated Press.
LONDON, Jan. 17—A German reporter, speaking on the Berlin radio from the Kielce sector of Poland tonight, paid high tribute to the power of a new Red Army heavy tank, called the Joseph Stalin.

"The Russians are using their new Joseph Stalin super-tank on an ever-increasing scale," the Nazi reporter, Heinz Megerlein, said. "This most powerfully gunned and armored vehicle in the world is more than a match for our best tank, the Royal Tiger."

The German broadcaster said the Russian super-tank carried a 122-mm. [4.8-inch] gun.

The German Royal Tiger tank has been reported to mount a new version of the famous 88-mm. gun.

U. S. POLICY ON ROWS IS FIRM, GREW SAYS

Position, Stated Vigorously, Is Not to Allow Differences to Mar Unity, He Asserts

Joseph C. Grew, Under Secretary of State, declared last night that our State Department has vigorously stated, and would continue to state to its allies, the American position on issues in dispute, but that it was the policy of this Government not to allow these differences to interfere with the unity of action essential to winning the war, or to disrupt that unity after the war.

He made this reply to recent critics of our foreign policy at a meeting in The New York Times Hall, 240 West Forty-fourth Street, at which Senator Warren R. Austin of Vermont called for the earliest practicable meeting to establish the Dumbarton Oaks Organization, and Senator J. William Fulbright of Arkansas assailed our handling of foreign affairs as hesitant, timid, and lacking in forthrightness.

Nicholas Roosevelt was moderator of the meeting, which was arranged by THE NEW YORK TIMES on the topic, "America's Place in World Affairs." The prepared addresses of the three speakers were broadcast over radio stations WQXR and WQXQ. Senators Austin and Fulbright then took part in a discussion and question-and-answer period that followed, for which Mr. Grew was unable to remain.

Fulbright Assails Delay

Senator Fulbright said that our failure to take part in formulating decisions in such pressing matters as the situations in Greece, Italy and Poland was forcing Great Britain and Russia to make their own decisions. He declared that our failure to assume a share of the responsibility for the decisions in the case of Greece had had the effect of making one of our Allies, Great Britain, "the undeserved goat" and had stirred up feeling

Continued on Page 12, Column 2

FOE STIFF IN WEST

Fog and Tanks Help the Germans Slow British and U. S. at Front

OUR AIR ARM BARRED

Montgomery Push Gains Town—Americans Lift Threat to Strasbourg

By CLIFTON DANIEL.
By Wireless to The New York Times.
SUPREME HEADQUARTERS, Allied Expeditionary Force, Jan. 17—While the drive to beat back the German salient continued despite thick, freezing weather and repeated German counter-attacks, which cost the Germans at least twenty-four tanks today, British forces northeast of Aachen also made painful progress into the flank of the Maaseyck bulge.

Beating their way with a flail of tanks through mine fields, dense fog and stinging sleet, they advanced 2,000-odd yards in the first twenty-four hours. Their progress was marked on the map by two river crossings and a village captured—Dieteren. The attack seemed less ambitious than originally appeared, but it still held symbolic value as representing a resumption of the Allied initiative.

The American threat to St. Vith, the last important road junction on the Germans' retreat route from the Ardennes, grew serious today as the battle-wise Old Hickory Division pressed down on the devastated town through knee-deep snow, thick woods and treacherous hills, reaching within five miles of St. Vith's outskirts. A forest belt of two and a half miles and a maze of knobby hills still stand between the town and the attacking Americans, however.

Americans Gain in Alsace

In Alsace American forces attacking the perimeter of the German bridgehead over the Rhine north of Strasbourg not only redressed the setback inflicted by the Germans last night but pushed their way into the western stronghold of the German pocket at Herrlisheim. This advance, though local and limited, will be regarded with satisfaction, particularly by the French, who have been viewing the bridgehead and its threat to Strasbourg with apprehension for many days.

Militarily, Strasbourg does not seem more important than any other city, but politically it is a far greater prize for either the Germans or the French. As the capital of the lost and regained province of Alsace and the "second city of France," it is a major symbol for France, and its loss might have a painful effect on French morale, already at a low ebb because of the unduly severe winter.

However, French forces holding the city are regarded as sufficient at the moment to counter any

Continued on Page 9, Column 1

RED ARMY TEARS GERMANS' DEFENSES IN POLAND ASUNDER

Jan. 18, 1945

Breaking from their Narew River positions, the Russians punched out a salient between Ciechanow and Pomiechowek (1). In an encircling operation they finally toppled Warsaw and some units sped westward to Leszno (2). South of the Polish capital the Warsaw-Lodz railroad was cut with the capture of Zyrardow (3). The rail junction of Skarzysko-Kamienna was being encircled as Soviet forces moved into Szydlowiec and Konskie (4). The Red Army's closest approach to Germany was at the important Polish city of Czestochowa, fourteen miles from the Silesian border (5). Although the Lublin radio reported the fall of Cracow, Moscow merely said that Sadowie (6), eight miles away, had been taken, but the city's capture was obviously at least imminent.

U. S. MEN USE TNT TO SLIT ICY GROUND

Fight Polar Weather in Hills of Ardennes as Well as Atrocity-Bent Germans

By Wireless to The New York Times.
SUPREME HEADQUARTERS, Allied Expeditionary Force, Jan. 17—Up in the Ardennes hills, where the United States First Army is attacking toward St. Vith, the ground is so hard that the troops have to use dynamite and mortar shells to dig slit trenches.

The ground is so steep and slippery with snow that tanks sometimes slide down them like sleds. When pinned down by enemy fire or while waiting to attack Ameri-

Continued on Page 8, Column 2

MacArthur Protects Flank By 17-Mile Dash Along Gulf

By LINDESAY PARROTT
By Wireless to The New York Times.
ALLIED HEADQUARTERS, on Leyte, Thursday, Jan. 18—The pace of the American advance on Luzon in the Philippines has been fastest in the extreme northwest where Gen. Douglas MacArthur's infantrymen have been feeling their way into Bolinao Peninsula, which forms the western shore of Lingayen Gulf. Here, in a sprint of seventeen miles from captured Alaminos, Sixth Army men reached Bolinao, a town on the extreme point of the peninsula.

Other detachments are moving southwestward toward Dasol Bay and the highway that leads west of the Zambales Mountains toward today.

[The capture of Bolinao sealed

Continued on Page 5, Column 3

OUR CHINA STRIKE IN 4TH DAY, FOE SAYS

Tokyo Cites 300-Plane Blow at Coast Ports—B-29's Join in Attack on Formosa Base

By The Associated Press.
PEARL HARBOR, Jan. 17—Tokyo reported today that more than 300 American carrier planes hit the China coast for the fourth successive day, battering Hong Kong, Canton and Hainan Island.

B-29 Superfortresses joined the mounting two-way offensive with new blows against Formosa.

[A new attack on Formosa Wednesday night was reported by General Douglas MacArthur's headquarters on Luzon. The report stated that long-range patrol planes harassed the Okyama airdrome.]

There was no immediate confirmation that Admiral William F. Halsey's Third Fleet planes had

Continued on Page 5, Column 5

RIPS LINE IN POLAND

Red Army Races West After Storming Into Vistula Citadel

KONEFF NEAR SILESIA

Capture of Czestochowa Threatens Heart of Reich's Industries

By The United Press.
LONDON, Thursday, Jan. 18—Russian and Polish troops yesterday captured devastated Warsaw to free its last survivors of five years of Nazi tyranny as the Red Army's greatest offensive surged twenty-four miles across western Poland, taking Czestochowa and reaching within fourteen miles of the German border.

At the same time the Red Army launched another offensive north of Warsaw that carried within 130 miles of Danzig and twenty-two miles south of the East Prussian border. Cracow, the fourth city of Poland, also was reported to have been liberated, but Moscow said only that Russians were eight miles northeast of the city at Sadowie.

Shoulder to shoulder, three crack Soviet armies were driving westward across Poland along a twisting 450-mile front. They were headed straight for Germany and were 260 to 288 miles from Berlin.

Racing Toward Lodz

With Warsaw, the first European capital to be overrun by Adolf Hitler's victory-flushed troops, behind them, the Russians were racing westward toward Lodz, second city of Poland, and Russian spearheads already were thirty-six miles east of Lodz on the main Warsaw-Berlin highway.

German troops were retreating hastily toward the borders of the Reich and Berlin reports indicated that the Nazis might be pulling out of Poland entirely, writing off their 1939 conquest of the country. German newspapers reaching Stockholm said the German High Command had moved the puppet Government General of Poland from Cracow to Central Germany.

The Russians were striking with blitzkrieg speed that paled Germany's lightning marches through Poland in 1939 and France in 1940, and though Berlin protested that its troops were fighting far behind advance Soviet lines, the German Army appeared to be in full rout.

More than 2,300,000 Soviet soldiers were committed to the huge offensive and Moscow dispatches said savagery unparalleled in four winters of war raged on the Eastern Front as the Russians tore gaps in the German lines and split and resplit enemy groups falling back toward the Oder River—the Rhine of the east.

Silesian Center Outflanked

Thousands of German troops were killed yesterday as Soviet troops, advancing at a mile-an-hour clip, outflanked the rich coal and steel region of upper Silesia and split its defenders from the main German armies in the Lodz area. Capturing Slawnlow, the Russians were twenty-four miles northeast of Dabrowa, easternmost industrial center of Silesia.

Premier Joseph Stalin announced the capture of Warsaw, "the capital of our ally, Poland." Just five years, three months and twenty days after Hitler's troops marched into the bombed city, and the free Warsaw radio broadcast to the world: "The city is razed, but we live on."

Marshal Stalin announced the victory in an order of the day. In Moscow victory guns fired without interruption for three hours to mark it and two subsequent orders of the day from the Red Army's Commander in Chief.

The second told of the new offensive north of Warsaw by the Second White Russian Army under the command of Marshal Konstantin K. Rokossovsky, which had all

Continued on Page 6, Column 3

ACCORD ON POLAND AT ONCE HELD VITAL

Red Armies' Sweep to West Seen Spurring Need for 'Big 3' Agreement

By RAYMOND DANIELL
By Cable to The New York Times.
LONDON, Jan. 17—The fall of Warsaw and the swift advance of the Red Armies across western Poland toward the old frontiers of Germany have made it imperative that President Roosevelt and Prime Minister Churchill reach a final agreement with Premier Stalin on Poland's territorial and political future at their next meeting, it is believed here.

There was no indication that the exiled Polish Government under Premier Tomasz Arciszewski is approaching the problems of its relations with Russia with a new sense of urgency but without much outward evidence to support an optimistic view of the outcome.

Mr. Arciszewski, in a statement on the liberation of Warsaw, cited the words of Lieut. Gen. Tadeusz Komorowski [General Bor], just before he and his underground army defending Warsaw yielded to the Germans after a heroic sixty-three-day struggle: "We are fighting for freedom, we are fighting for the right to be free!" Mr. Arciszewski commented: "At this moment these words embody, as

Continued on Page 6, Column 2

War News Summarized

THURSDAY, JANUARY 18, 1945

Warsaw, the first European capital to fall to Hitler's blitzkrieg five years and four months ago, was liberated by Russian and Polish troops yesterday. The First White Russian Army captured the city after a wide encircling dash that swept up more than 800 other places.

The Red Army steamroller, which at its closest point was 260 miles from Berlin, moved north of the Polish capital when the Second White Russian Army, from its two bridgeheads across the Narew River, advanced twenty-four miles on a sixty-two-mile front, freeing Makow, Pultusk, Ciechanow and 500 other communities.

At the southern end of the long surging line the First Ukrainian Army liberated Czestochowa, Radomsko and 700 more inhabited places, and Lublin reported that Cracow had also fallen. This Russian army was only fourteen miles from the Reich. [All the foregoing 1:3.]

Gloom hung heavy over Germany. The enemy press and radio prepared the people for retreat on the Eastern front as the "final onslaught against Germany planned at Teheran" got under way. [6:1.]

The Warsaw victory brought to a climax the diplomatic impasse over recognition of a single Polish Government by all the Allies. The Polish Government in London indicated it would seek an early return to Warsaw and the Moscow-fostered Lublin regime was expected to enter into the capital immediately. [1:7.]

Reverses in the east did not prevent the Germans from stiffening against the new British Second Army drive north of Aachen. The British advanced 2,000 yards, crossed the Roode River in two places and captured two villages, one of which was Dieteren. To the south, Americans took Vielsam and were five miles from St. Vith. The Third Army trapped a German force in the woods southeast of Tettingen. Inconclusive small battles were fought in the Alsace area. [1:3; map, P. 9.]

Some 700 American heavy bombers and 350 fighters carried the air war to oil and submarine plants in the Hamburg-Harburg area and rail targets in northwest Germany. [8:3-4.]

Americans on Luzon speared seventeen miles from Alaminos on the extreme right of the line to capture Bolinao, at the southwest tip of Lingayen Gulf. They also cut across the peninsula toward Dasol Bay, on the China Sea. At the other end of the line patrols entered Pozorrubio while main forces were half a mile from Rosario. Allied planes, in their best, day, destroyed sixty-two enemy aircraft, all but one of which were caught on the ground. [1:5-6; map P. 2.]

Tokyo said that Pacific Fleet carrier planes had hit China for the fourth day, 300 of the Navy's aircraft striking Hong Kong, Canton and Hainan Island. A sizable force of B-29's—Tokyo said eighty—hit air installations at Shinchiku, on Formosa's northwest coast, with good effect, and General MacArthur's fliers again struck Okayama, on the southwest coast. [1:6.]

Douds Receives Formal Charges Aimed at Removal From NLRB

Formal charges aimed at forcing his resignation as regional director of the National Labor Relations Board were received yesterday by Charles T. Douds. The document was signed by Lester A. Asher, associate administrative examiner of the board in Washington.

Filing of the charges was announced in a statement on Tuesday by Harry A. Millis, chairman of the board, who said that Mr. Douds' removal was being sought "to promote the efficiency of the service" and on grounds of a "lack of fitness and capacity to supervise and direct the work of the staff" of the New York office. In making known that removal proceedings had been instituted against Mr. Douds, Dr. Millis voiced an implied reprimand to Mr. Douds for carrying the controversy

between himself and the board into the press.

Mr. Douds, who had refused to comply with the board's previous request that he resign, demanding that formal charges be filed against him so that he might answer them in accordance with prescribed procedure, confirmed receipt of the charges yesterday but declined to discuss them. He made the following statement:

"This afternoon I received formal charges from the board. I first learned of the transmission of these charges from the papers this morning. I will answer these charges to the board and not through the newspapers.

"Dr. Millis implied in his statement this morning that the information already made public on this matter emanated directly or indi-

Continued on Page 34, Column 2

McGuire, Pacific Air Ace, Killed; He Downed 38 Japanese Planes

By The Associated Press.
SAN ANTONIO, Tex., Jan. 17—Major Thomas B. McGuire Jr. of San Antonio and Ridgewood, N. J., the leading American active ace with thirty-eight Japanese planes to his credit, was shot down and killed in the Philippines Jan. 7, Lieut. Gen. George C. Kenney, commanding the Allied Air Forces in the Pacific, informed Mrs. McGuire in a letter dated Jan. 8.

Mrs. McGuire received General Kenney's letter today. The Allied air chief said that the word Major McGuire had been shot down brought him the worst of a number of bad moments he had had to face since the war began.

"I felt that he would make a name for command as well as for leadership and great personal courage," the letter stated.

"Your husband was one of the men the Air Forces can never forget. We will find it more difficult to carry on without him," General Kenney added.

The letter indicated that Major McGuire's plane was in some way disabled in the air, making him an easy prey to defending enemy fighters. Mrs. McGuire said she had received no official notification of her husband's death from the War Department.

Major McGuire became the leading ace when Maj. Richard I. Bong of Poplar, Wis., returned to the United States on leave. Major

Continued on Page 5, Column 2

The New York Times.

LATE CITY EDITION
Fair and warm today. Cloudy and
warm tomorrow.
Temperatures Yesterday—Max. 50 ; Min. 34
Sunrise today: 6:54 A. M.; Sunset, 7:22 P. M.

VOL. XCIV..No. 31,836.

Entered as Second-Class Matter,
Post-office, New York, N. Y.

Copyright, 1945, by The New York Times Company.

NEW YORK, SATURDAY, MARCH 24, 1945.

THREE CENTS NEW YORK CITY

PATTON CROSSES RHINE IN A DARING DRIVE WITHOUT BARRAGE, EXPANDS BRIDGEHEAD ; NAZIS SAY RUSSIANS ARE MOVING ON BERLIN

SENATE, BY 52 TO 36, REJECTS WILLIAMS AS DIRECTOR OF REA

Nineteen Democrats Join With 33 Republicans to Defeat the Former Chief of NYA

HE DENOUNCES HIS FOES

And Declares With Patton of Farmers Union That Issue Is Whether People Shall Rule

By WILLIAM S. WHITE
Special to The New York Times.

WASHINGTON, March 23—The Senate rejected today, 52 to 36, President Roosevelt's nomination of Aubrey Williams to be Rural Electrification Administrator. The adverse vote came through a coalition of Republicans and Conservative Democrats. Most of the latter came from the South, and some of them had been termed "Tories" by the nominee.

Nineteen Democrats joined thirty-three Republicans in voting to deny confirmation to Mr. Williams, the first such denial of an important executive appointment since 1939. Thirty-one Democrats, four Republicans and the Senate's single member of the Progressive party, LaFollette of Wisconsin, voted for the nomination.

Immediately after the Senate vote, the National Farmers Union, of which Mr. Williams has been national director of organization, vowed political vengeance on his opponents, and said that Mrs. Franklin D. Roosevelt would address a "Victory Dinner" for Mr. Williams Wednesday night that would begin "a total war of issues."

The Southern Democrats who opposed Mr. Williams were principally those whose views on economics are radically opposed to the New Dealism of Mr. Williams.

Barkley Upholds Nominee

A last minute speaker for Mr. Williams was Senator Barkley of Kentucky, the majority leader.

"The record shows," he said, "that Williams was not connected with communism, but that he combated communism."

Mr. Williams asserted that he had been rejected by "those who stand for control by the few, fearing an economy in which everybody would share."

Then, in a joint press conference at the headquarters of the Farmers Union, both he and James G. Patton, president of the National Farmers Union, indicated that the Senate's action would be used as the starting point of an intensive national organizing and political campaign by the union to be concentrated in the Deep South.

"We'll be asking some of those Senators out where the people live," Mr. Patton declared. Remarking that the forthcoming "Victory Dinner" had been so named because the vote in the Senate "showed us how we stand," he added:

"This is the first battle in a total war of issues in this country to decide whether the country is to be conducted by the people or for the vested interests. The Farmers Union people will become much more intense in their feelings because of this action. We are going to take whatever steps are necessary to begin to implement our feelings more drastically."

Denies Competence an Issue

Mr. Patton and Mr. Williams have been associated, as individuals, with the CIO's Political Action Committee, although the Farmers Union as an official entity has not been so connected. What the union's precise mechanism would be in its new campaign had not been determined, Mr. Patton said, although he indicated that no consideration had been given to the question of setting up a separate political organization.

Mr. Williams declared that "such Senators" as Bushfield, South Dakota; Willis, Republican, of Indiana; McKellar, Democrat, of Tennessee; Taft, Republi-

Continued on Page 15, Column 7

Women's Jury Bill Goes to Governor

Special to The New York Times.

ALBANY, March 23—With unanimous adoption by the Senate, Governor Dewey received today Assemblyman Philip Schuyler's bill making jury service for women mandatory instead of optional. The only exceptions permitted under the bill are those where a woman has children under 16 years of age or is caring for a sick or invalid person.

Enactment of the measure after several years of experience under permissive jury service follows a considerable demand from women's groups, notable among which is the League of Women Voters.

A year ago former Assemblywoman Jane H. Todd sponsored a similar bill, which passed the Assembly, but died in committee in the upper house. There has been no indication as to what Governor Dewey's views are with regard to the proposal.

RISE OF $14,000,000 IN SCHOOL AID VOTED

Legislature Moves to Adjourn Today—Assembly Passes Merit Rating Truce

By LEO EGAN
Special to The New York Times.

ALBANY, March 23—By unanimous vote in both houses, the Legislature passed and sent to Governor Dewey today a bill revising the apportionment of State aid for education to increase the total by about $14,000,000 over that provided by existing law and $18,000,000 over that required by the old formula.

The Assembly rejected, 66 to 78, the Young-Demo merit rating bill after a debate lasting almost five hours and then passed almost unanimously the "harmonizing" merit rating proposal, which had the endorsement of Governor Dewey, the Ives Committee on Labor and Industrial Conditions, the AFL and the CIO.

A majority of the Assembly Republicans favored the Young-Demo bill and threatened for a time to revolt against their leaders, who, along with Governor Dewey, opposed it.

Bowing to Labor Charged

In private conversation and, according to some reports, at a closed party conference, the Young-Demo backers accused the leadership of bowing to organized labor. There was a great deal of private bitterness over the action of Irving M. Ives, the majority leader, and Oswald D. Heck, the Speaker, in persuading a number of Republicans favoring the Young-Demo plan to switch to the "harmonizing" bill.

The "harmonizing" bill, which in most essentials is identical with the last of the Falk-Gurgino bills, will be taken up in the Senate tomorrow, with passage, in view of the Assembly action, regarded as certain.

By disposing of the educational and merit rating measures, which rank among the most important

Continued on Page 14, Column 3

HOUSE UNANIMOUS IN VOTE TO EXTEND DRAFT ACT A YEAR

Senate Leaders Seek Rapid Action on Measure Free of Civilian Job Issue

NO BREAK IN DEADLOCK

New Compromise to 'Freeze' Workers Is Considered by Conferees—Vote Set Today

By C. P. TRUSSELL
Special to The New York Times.

WASHINGTON, March 23—The House quickly passed by unanimous vote and sent to the Senate today a bill to extend the Selective Service Act for one year beyond May 15.

On the Senate side leaders assumed that chamber also would act promptly on the bill, without the attachment of riders which would link the drafting of men for the armed services to the mobilization of manpower on the home front.

The question of a "labor draft" remained deadlocked, with Senate and House conferees seeking to find a compromise in the conflicting civilian manpower bills which the two branches have passed.

A new compromise, or trade, was proposed today and was scheduled for a vote tomorrow. It was suggested that if the House would abandon its "limited national service," or draft, provisions, the Senate would agree to impose penalties on workers as well as employers for violations of employment ceilings and other War Manpower Commission controls.

Workers Would Be "Frozen"

Under the proposed compromise there would be a "freezing" of essential war workers into their present jobs as long as they were needed.

An expected move to prohibit the sending of draftees into combat zones within five months after their induction into the Army failed to develop in the House.

The Military Affairs Committee, which reported the extension bill yesterday, was told by Maj. Gen. Idwal Edwards, Assistant Chief of Staff in charge of training, that such a restriction would be "very definitely harmful" to an orderly system of providing men for the fighting fronts.

While the House was acting with unanimity, conferees on the manpower bills spent hours this afternoon studying the compromise offered by Senator Austin, Republican, of Vermont, and the amendments to it which have been presented by Representative May, Democrat, of Kentucky.

As a recess was taken, the conferees had before them a proposal for the newer compromise. Concededly, it was not certain that the Senate conferees would be willing to apply penalties to employes when WMC regulations were violated, even though the House conferees should agree to abandon all "labor draft" concepts.

Among Senate conferees there

Continued on Page 15, Column 2

THE RHINE IS BRIDGED AND OUR MATERIEL ROLLS ACROSS

A strong span is stretched on pontoons, over which heavy trucks are carrying supplies to our forces on the east bank.
The New York Times (U. S. Signal Corps)

ODER BRIDGEHEADS REPORTED MERGED

Foe Puts Red Army 6 Miles Past Kuestrin—Danzig and Gdynia Split—Push in South Gains

By The Associated Press.

LONDON, Saturday, March 24—Berlin said last night that the Red Army had reopened a blazing battle for the imperiled German capital, while Moscow announced that Russian forces had split the defenders of the prize Baltic ports of Danzig and Gdynia.

Waves of Russian infantry and tanks were reported by the enemy to have broken through defenses along Berlin's Oder River line and to have swept six miles beyond captured Kuestrin to within thirty-one miles east of the capital. [German reports cited by The United Press said that two Oder bridgeheads had been linked.

Continued on Page 7, Column 2

New Rhine Bridgehead Won Without Loss of Single Man

By EDWARD D. BALL
Associated Press Correspondent

WITH THE UNITED STATES THIRD ARMY east of the Rhine, March 23—The United States Third Army stormed across the Rhine at 10:25 o'clock last night without loss of a man and without drawing a single shot from the Germans until a good twenty minutes after the crossing was made good.

By dawn today a solid bridgehead had been driven into Hitler's inner fortress against opposition that still was spotty and erratic despite some artillery and mortar fire.

Most of the enemy weapons were soon silenced.

By dawn many infantry units had gone across, and by that time the first waves of doughboys had pushed inland.

There was a minimum of noise and confusion at the bridgehead, where droves of assault boats were speeding back and forth with men and supplies.

Within eight hours Lieut. Gen.

Continued on Page 4, Column 4

War News Summarized

SATURDAY, MARCH 24, 1945

The American Third Army has stormed across the Rhine in large force and established a firm bridgehead, the second one now held by our troops. The new crossing was made at 10:25 P. M. Thursday and the bridgehead has been expanded since then. Its site was not officially disclosed, but the Germans said it was near Frankenthal, four and a half miles north of Ludwigshafen.

The mighty German armies once deployed west of the Rhine have been either destroyed or driven to the east bank almost in their entirety. American tanks crashed into Speyer, one of the last enemy strongholds west of the Rhine, while the enemy bridgehead in the Palatinate was compressed further to an area about fifteen miles from east to west with a base of less than twenty miles along the river. Tremendous aerial blows on German communications west of the Ruhr may be part of preparations for a new offensive by Marshal Montgomery. [All the foregoing 1:8; map, P. 2.]

Thousands of Allied bombers again struck in support of the ground forces, seeking to pulverize enemy installations east of the Rhine and soften the foe's power and will to resist. Countless fires were started in the industrial areas of the Ruhr as our flying artillery pounded marshaling yards. [1:7]

The Red Army has renewed its drive on Berlin after breaking through German defenses along the Oder River line, the enemy reported. The Nazis also said the Russians had smashed six

miles beyond Kuestrin to within thirty-one miles of the capital, reaching Golzow on the main Kuestrin-Berlin railroad. Soviet troops on the Baltic split the enemy forces between Danzig and Gdynia by knifing to the Bay of Danzig midway between the two ports. [1:4; map P. 7.]

An American escort carrier, the Bismarck Sea, was lost to enemy action off Iwo Feb. 21, the Navy announced. Another naval bulletin revealed that our carrier planes had caused extensive damage at seven Japanese ports and bases on Kyushu Island during the attack by Fifth Fleet forces early this week. Further details also put at 731 the number of enemy planes destroyed or damaged. [1:6; map P. 10.] The B-29 attack on Tokyo March 9 knocked out 20 per cent of the city's productive facilities for at least three months and the punishment given the Japanese in the five recent aerial assaults against their industrial cities probably was the most severe suffered by any people in a similar period, it was emphasized by General Norstad. [9:4.]

In the Philippines American forces took Naguilian and its airfield, twelve miles northwest of Baguio, on Luzon. [10:6.]

The Japanese opened a new offensive northwest of Hankow in central China with 60,000 troops. The drive apparently had the twin aims of capturing several Allied airfields in its path and seizing the wheat crop. [9:2; with map.] The British, striking south of Mandalay in Burma, continued to cut up the foe. [9:5.]

Moses Threatens to Resign in Row Over 'Talk Out of Mayor's Office'

Park Commissioner Robert Moses, for years one of Mayor La Guardia's staunchest political and administrative supporters, told the Board of Estimate yesterday that he keenly resented "talk right out of the Mayor's office" insinuating that he favored a tree-removal appropriation of $145,000 because he "had to take care of favored contractors."

Commissioner Moses appeared at an adjourned meeting of the Board of Estimate to speak in support of a recommendation by Borough President James A. Burke of Queens that $145,000 be appropriated to make possible the removal, by a private contractor, of the 5,330 trees blown down by the hurricane last September and still cluttering city streets in Queens

and Brooklyn. The hurricane left 16,730 trees to be removed from the streets. Of these 7,933 have been removed by contract and 3,467 by departmental forces of the Park Department, cooperating with employes of the Department of Sanitation and the offices of the borough presidents.

Discussion of the Burke proposal provoked a heated argument between Commissioner Moses and Deputy Mayor Rufus E. McGahen, who insisted that the proposal be referred to Budget Director Thomas J. Patterson for a report in accordance with routine procedure. Before the argument ended Commissioner Moses, pale with anger, indicated his willingness to

Continued on Page 15, Column 5

3D WINS FIRM HOLD

Spans the River at Night Above Ludwigshafen, Catches Foe Asleep

1ST SPEEDS UP PUSH

Palatinate Escape Gap Cut Again—Thousands More Captured

By DREW MIDDLETON
By Wireless to The New York Times.

PARIS, March 23—Troops of Lieut. Gen. George S. Patton's United States Third Army have established a bridgehead over the Rhine in a bold, skillful assault.

The river was crossed at 10:25 o'clock Thursday night. The bridgehead established at that time has been steadily expanded since. [Press services said the crossing was virtually unopposed.]

The Twelfth Army Group, whose announcement was released here tonight, did not locate the bridgehead, but the German radio said that it was east of Frankenthal, four and a half miles north of the northern outskirts of Ludwigshafen.

[Earlier German broadcasts said that Third Army troops had crossed the Rhine at Oppenheim, ten miles south of Mainz, and that other American troops had attempted crossings at Duesseldorf and six miles south of Cologne, The Associated Press reported. The Associated Press said the crossings at Duesseldorf and in the Cologne area had been repulsed.]

Crossing Is Bold Stroke

At his headquarters, Lieut. Gen. Omar N. Bradley, Twelfth Army Group Commander, said that the Allies were in a position to cross the Rhine virtually "anywhere at any time."

The Third Army's crossing of the Rhine was an operation as bold as the character of its commander. General Patton hurled his troops across the river without preparation by artillery or air force in a surprise move that evidently caught the enemy asleep.

Since that time his troops have been striking out from the bridgehead and expanding it.

[A powerful fleet of British heavy bombers battered German troops and positions on the east bank of the Rhine during the night, London officials announced early Saturday, The Associated Press said. British planes also bombed Berlin for the thirty-second straight night.]

A great east-west highway runs through Frankenthal. There was a bridge under construction there in May, 1944. No recent information concerning the bridge is available here.

Frankenthal, where the Germans said the crossing was made, is six miles northwest of Mannheim on the east bank of the Rhine opposite Ludwigshafen. If the crossing was made in this area, as the enemy claimed, then General Patton has placed his troops in a fine position to attack Mannheim from the north or east. Frankenthal also is twenty-five miles southwest of the industrial city of Darmstadt.

Germans Nearly Wiped Out

Meanwhile Gen. Dwight D. Eisenhower's order to destroy the German Armies west of the Rhine is almost fulfilled.

Tanks of General Patton's Third Army rumbled into Speyer, one of the last enemy strongholds west of the Rhine, today, while a series of savage blows by armored and infantry divisions of the Third Army and Lieut. Gen. Alexander M. Patch's Seventh Army hammered the remaining Germans in the Palatinate to a rough triangle fifteen miles from east to west with a base of less than twenty miles along the west bank of the Rhine.

The tremendous aerial assault on the German Army's defense depots and communications in the area north of the Ruhr and west of the Cologne was maintained from early morning today.

Nothing more than routine pa-

Continued on Page 3, Column 1

AIR FLEETS FLATTEN NAZIS AROUND RUHR

U. S. 'Heavies' Strike at 12 Rail Yards, RAF Hits Bridges and Enemy Troops

By SYDNEY GRUSON
By Wireless to The New York Times.

LONDON, Saturday, March 24—Allied airmen poured more thousands of tons of bombs on the Germans east of the Rhine, especially in the Ruhr area, yesterday, in the third successive day of record operations to flatten everything in the path of the American and British Armies massing for a crossing of the Rhine on the northern sector of the Western Front.

Last night, as the Ruhr's industrial towns and the great plain leading to north Germany blazed from countless fires set by thousands of heavy, medium and light bombers, more blows were struck in the aerial softening-up.

More than 1,250 Flying Fortresses and Liberators of the United States Eighth Air Force, all of them escorted by fighters, flew by daylight through towering clouds of smoke rising from the ashes of dead cities.

In weather so clear the heavy bombers' targets could be picked up by naked eye from five miles up, the American and British crews pounded rail yards and

Continued on Page 5, Column 2

U. S. CARRIER LOST IN BATTLE OFF IWO

Bismarck Sea, Escort Craft, Is Victim of Air Blow — Fleet Strike in Ryukyus Reported

By The Associated Press.

GUAM, Saturday, March 24—Loss of the U. S. S. Bismarck Sea, an escort aircraft carrier, to enemy aerial attack off Iwo Island on Feb. 21 was announced by Admiral Chester W. Nimitz today. Most of the Bismarck Sea's company was rescued, he stated. The normal complement of an escort carrier is about 1,500 officers and men.

[Delayed dispatches from the fleet off Iwo said there were more than 300 casualties among the crew of the Bismarck Sea, including 100 who, struggling in the water, were strafed and killed by Japanese fliers.

[The Tokyo radio said early Saturday that American carrier aircraft, which earlier in the week ravaged Japanese air and naval strength in the home islands, made attacks Friday and Saturday (today) on Okinawa Island, Japanese air and naval base in the Ryukyu group, mid-

Continued on Page 10, Column 2

Germans Speed Arms to Mountains As Allies Map Their Destruction

By Wireless to The New York Times.

PARIS, March 23—The Germans are speeding work on a great national redoubt, a defensive position based on the mountains of the southern Reich, where 88 divisions, some regular soldiers and Nazi party officials hope to continue the war after the German field armies have been destroyed.

A reliable source who recently returned from Switzerland said the work on the redoubt had been rushed since the last Russian offensive and the Anglo-American victories west of the Rhine and that, according to neutrals who lately had been in the Reich, the Germans also were constructing another redoubt on the Kiel Canal in the north.

The Swiss, he said, are extreme-

ly worried, since the preparation of the redoubt in the south foreshadows heavy fighting near their borders by Russian as well as American and British armies.

According to this source a nobleman, who must remain unidentified, recently drove from his domain to Vienna and back. Both trips were exceedingly difficult because the Germans had closed many of the roads leading into the redoubt and he had to detour around the position. He reported that the Germans were pouring many hundreds of tons of supplies of all kinds into the redoubt.

The exact limits of the position where the Germans hope to retire

Continued on Page 3, Column 2

"All the News That's Fit to Print"

The New York Times.

LATE CITY EDITION
Clearing and warm today.
Fair, continued warm tomorrow.
Temperature Yesterday—Max., 74; Min., 54
Sunrise today, 6:21 A. M.; Sunset, 7:18 P. M.

Copyright, 1945, by The New York Times Company.

VOL. XCIV...No. 31,856.

Entered as Second-Class Matter,
Postoffice, New York, N. Y.

NEW YORK, FRIDAY, APRIL 13, 1945.

THREE CENTS IN NEW YORK CITY

PRESIDENT ROOSEVELT IS DEAD; TRUMAN TO CONTINUE POLICIES; 9TH CROSSES ELBE, NEARS BERLIN

U. S. AND RED ARMIES DRIVE TO MEET

Americans Across the Elbe in Strength Race Toward Russians Who Have Opened Offensive From Oder

WEIMAR TAKEN, RUHR POCKET SLASHED

Third Army Reported 19 Miles From Czechoslovak Border—British Drive Deeper in the North, Seizing Celle—Canadians Freeing Holland

By DREW MIDDLETON
By Wireless to THE NEW YORK TIMES.

PARIS, April 12—Thousands of tanks and a half million doughboys of the United States First, Third and Ninth Armies are racing through the heart of the Reich on a front of 150 miles, threatening Berlin, Leipzig and the last citadels of the Nazi power.

The Second Armored Division of the Ninth Army has crossed the Elbe River in force and is striking eastward toward Berlin, whose outskirts lie less than sixty miles to the east, according to reports from the front. [A report quoted by The United Press placed the Americans less than fifty miles from the Elbe.]

Beyond Berlin the First White Russian Army has crossed the Oder on a wide front and a junction between the western and eastern Allies is not far off.

[The Moscow radio reported that heavy battles were raging west of the Oder before Berlin, indicating that Marshal Gregory K. Zhukoff had launched his drive toward the Reich's capital. The Soviet communiqué announced further progress by the Red Army forces in and around Vienna.]

Paris is wild with excitement tonight. A special edition of the newspaper France-Soir carries a report by the radio station "Voice of America" that places American forces fifteen and five-eighths miles from Berlin after an airborne landing that had linked up with Lieut. Gen. William H. Simpson's forces advancing eastward from the Elbe. This would put American forces only seventy-five miles from the Red Army vanguard.

No Confirmation at Headquarters

There was no confirmation of this report at Allied Supreme Headquarters, which by its own admission was thirty-six hours behind developments on some sectors of the front.

Resistance was continuing only on the northern and southern flanks. The center had burst wide open. Weimar fell to Lieut. Gen. George S. Patton's infantry, and reports from the front said Erfurt also had been cleared. Schweinfurt and Heilbronn, two German bastions on the south, had fallen to United States Seventh Army force, who were driving on Bamberg, while farther north Third Army forces were about thirty-five miles from the Czechoslovak frontier in the area east of Coburg.

[The German radio reported American Third Army forces at Lichtenberg, nineteen miles from the Czechoslovak border, The United Press said.]

The offensives to liberate the Netherlands and reduce the Ruhr Continued on Page 12, Column 2

Army Leaders See Reich End at Hand

By The Associated Press.
WASHINGTON, April 12— High Army officials told Senators today that the end of organized fighting in Germany probably would come within a few days.

Describing the pell-mell dash of American Armies across Germany, General Staff officers expressed the opinion to members of the Senate Military Committee that a collapse of German arms was imminent.

Those who attended said the army chiefs declared that they were so sure of the results that orders had been drawn for a drastic reduction in shipments of durable equipment to Europe.

Continued on Page 18, Column 3

OUR OKINAWA GUNS DOWN 118 PLANES

Japanese Fliers Start 'Suicide' Attacks on Fleet, Sink a Destroyer, Hit Other Ships

By W. H. LAWRENCE
By Wireless to THE NEW YORK TIMES.

GUAM, Friday, April 13—Japanese attempting to halt the American march to Tokyo, have started "desperate, suicidal" aerial attacks upon our ships and men in the Okinawa area, losing 118 planes on Thursday alone, Fleet Admiral Chester W. Nimitz announced today.

The Japanese succeeded in sinking a destroyer and damaging several other surface units, the communiqué said. All of the damaged vessels remained in action.

It was the first time that the Navy had revealed the suicidal nature of the Japanese air missions against our ships and men. The Japanese radio has been saying that this type of assault was being carried on by a "special attack corps" known in Japanese as "kamakazi," which, translated literally, means "divine wind."

Attack at Low Levels

The Japanese fliers launched their attacks upon our ships and men at a high speed and from low levels, diving directly into a ship or troop concentration to explode their bombs as they crashed.

There was no official estimate of the total number of enemy aircraft engaged in the Okinawa area attack other than the report of the 118 enemy planes destroyed.

Admiral Nimitz reported that the attacks began early on April 12 (Eastern Longitude time) with seven enemy planes shot down during the morning in the vicinity of the Hagushi beaches.

The tempo of the attack was stepped up in the afternoon as the Japanese bore in on our ships in wave after wave. Admiral Nimitz said that ships' guns, carrier aircraft and shore-based anti-aircraft shot down 111 of the attackers.

The revelation of the suicidal Japanese air attacks was the highlight of Admiral Nimitz' regular morning communiqué, which also disclosed the identity of two Marine and two Army divisions that have gone into action on Okinawa. These included the Twenty-seventh Army Division, formed from New York National Guard units, which are seeing action for the first time since the Saipan campaign and previously had engaged in the Gilbert Islands assault. It is com-
Continued on Page 2

Franklin Delano Roosevelt
1882-1945
© Perskie

SECURITY PARLEY WON'T BE DELAYED

State Department Urges That World Be Shown We Plan No Changes in Policy

By JAMES B. RESTON
Special to THE NEW YORK TIMES.

WASHINGTON, April 12—The United Nations Security Conference will open in San Francisco on April 25, despite the death of President Franklin Roosevelt, Secretary of State Edward R. Stettinius Jr. announced tonight.

Mr. Stettinius said that he had been authorized by President Harry Truman to make this announcement after a meeting of the Cabinet at the White House.

Most of the overseas delegations to the San Francisco conference have either arrived in this country or are now on their way, but while this was said to have been a factor in the decision to proceed with the conference, State Department officials urged that every attempt be made to give immediate evidence to the world that President Roosevelt's foreign policy would be sustained by the new Administration.

President Roosevelt had planned to address the San Francisco conference. His interest in an international organization of nations to maintain peace and security had gone back to his service in the Wilson Administration, when he sat in the gallery of the Senate and listened to the debate that resulted in the rejection of the League of Nations Covenant. He had expressed to friends his desire to participate in the San Francisco conference and to see the United States enter the new league during his term in office.

The sudden elevation of Presi-
Continued on Page 2, Column 1

War News Summarized

FRIDAY, APRIL 13, 1945

President Roosevelt died yesterday afternoon, suddenly and unexpectedly. He was stricken with a massive cerebral hemorrhage at Warm Springs, Ga., on the eve of his greatest military and diplomatic successes—the impending fall of Berlin and the opening of the San Francisco Conference to set up a World Security Organization that would make the world free from martial and economic strife [1:7-8.]

Mr. Roosevelt had been sitting in front of the fireplace of his Little White House, having gone to Warm Springs on March 30 for a three-week rest. About 2:15 Eastern war time he said, "I have a terrific headache," lost consciousness in a few moments and died at 4:35. He was 63 years old. [1:6.]

The tragic word spread quickly around the world. Expressions of sorrow poured in from all sections. [4:5.] American soldiers and sailors refused to believe the reports until there was no longer doubt that their Commander in Chief had gone. [4:2-3.]

Harry S. Truman was sworn in as President at 7:09 o'clock last night, and a few minutes later Mrs. Roosevelt left for Warm Springs. [1:7.] The new President immediately called a Cabinet meeting and declared that Mr. Roosevelt's policies would be continued, that the war would be carried on until Germany and Japan surrendered unconditionally and that the San Francisco Conference would open April 25 as scheduled. [1:3.]

Some 500,000 American soldiers of the Third and Ninth Armies, and thousands of tanks, sped along a 150-mile front toward Berlin and Leipzig. The Ninth, surging across the Elbe, according to delayed reports was less than fifty miles from the German capital and 115 from the Russians along the Oder. The Third Army captured Weimar, home of the late German Republic, and was twenty-three miles below Leipzig, with the First closing a pincers from the north. [1:1-2; map P. 2.]

The Moscow radio reported that the Red Army was waging fierce battles east of Berlin, indicating resumption of the drive on that city. Elsewhere Russian troops scored wide gains and cut the last escape railroad from Vienna. [13:1.]

Open cities were ruled out and every German was ordered by Himmler to fight to the death, although Goebbels said "the war cannot last much longer." [12:6-7.]

The Ninth Air Force destroyed at least 117 more German planes yesterday. [11:8.]

In Italy the Eighth Army advanced along a thirty-mile front toward Bologna and the Po Valley; the Fifth Army also made good gains and was eleven miles from La Spezia. [13:8, with map.]

Japanese planes resumed their suicide attacks on American ships off Okinawa, sinking a destroyer and damaging several other vessels. One hundred and eighteen enemy planes were shot down. [1:2.] The American Division invaded Bohol, last of the enemy-held central Philippines. [18:6.] The B-29 attack on Koriyama, 110 miles north of Tokyo, set a new Superfortress distance record. [18:2.]

Secretary of State Stettinius and Secretary of War Stimson, denouncing Germany's "steadily increasing" mistreatment of American prisoners, said those responsible would be brought to justice. [13:6-7.]

Clashes between Right and Left wing elements in Iran were reported from Moscow. [13:2.]

LAST WORDS: 'I HAVE TERRIFIC HEADACHE'

Roosevelt Was Posing for Artist When Hemorrhage Struck —He Died in Bedroom

By The Associated Press.

WARM SPRINGS, Ga., April 12—President Franklin D. Roosevelt's last words were:

"I have a terrific headache."

He spoke them to Comdr. Howard G. Bruenn, naval physician.

Mr. Roosevelt was sitting in front of a fireplace in the Little White House here atop Pine Mountain when what was described as a massive cerebral hemorrhage struck him.

The President's Negro valet, Arthur Prettyman, and a Filipino messboy carried him to his bedroom. He was unconscious at the end. It came without pain.

Dr. Bruenn said that he saw the President this morning and he was in excellent spirits at 9:30 A. M.

"At 1 o'clock," Dr. Bruenn added, "he was sitting in a chair while sketches were being made of him by an artist. He suddenly complained of a very severe occipital headache (back of the head).

"Within a very few minutes he lost consciousness. He was seen by me at 1:30 P. M., fifteen minutes after the episode had started.

"He did not regain consciousness, and he died at 3:35 P. M. (Georgia time)."

The artist sketching Mr. Roosevelt was N. Robbins of 520 West 139th Street, New York.

Only others present in the cottage were Comdr. George Fox, White House pharmacist and long an attendant on the President; William D. Hassett, Presidential secretary; Miss Grace Tully, con-
Continued on Page 4, Column 2

END COMES SUDDENLY AT WARM SPRINGS

Even His Family Unaware of Condition as Cerebral Stroke Brings Death to Nation's Leader at 63

ALL CABINET MEMBERS TO KEEP POSTS

Funeral to Be at White House Tomorrow, With Burial at Hyde Park Home— Impact of News Tremendous

By ARTHUR KROCK
Special to THE NEW YORK TIMES.

WASHINGTON, April 12—Franklin Delano Roosevelt, War President of the United States and the only Chief Executive in history who was chosen for more than two terms, died suddenly and unexpectedly at 4:35 P. M. today at Warm Springs, Ga., and the White House announced his death at 5:48 o'clock. He was 63.

The President, stricken by a cerebral hemorrhage, passed from unconsciousness to death on the eighty-third day of his fourth term and in an hour of high triumph. The armies and fleets under his direction as Commander in Chief were at the gates of Berlin and the shores of Japan's home islands as Mr. Roosevelt died, and the cause he represented and led was nearing the conclusive phase of success.

Less than two hours after the official announcement, Harry S. Truman of Missouri, the Vice President, took the oath as the thirty-second President. The oath was administered by the Chief Justice of the United States, Harlan F. Stone, in a one-minute ceremony at the White House. Mr. Truman immediately let it be known that Mr. Roosevelt's Cabinet is remaining in office at his request, and that he had authorized Secretary of State Edward R. Stettinius Jr. to proceed with plans for the United Nations Conference on international organization at San Francisco, scheduled to begin April 25. A report was circulated that he leans somewhat to the idea of a coalition Cabinet, but this is unsubstantiated.

Funeral Tomorrow Afternoon

It was disclosed by the White House that funeral services for Mr. Roosevelt would take place at 4 P. M. (E. W. T.) Saturday in the East Room of the Executive Mansion. The Rev. Angus Dun, Episcopal Bishop of Washington; the Rev. Howard S. Wilkinson of St. Thomas's Church in Washington and the Rev. John G. McGee of St. John's in Washington will conduct the services.

The body will be interred at Hyde Park, N. Y., Sunday, with the Rev. George W. Anthony of St. James Church officiating. The time has not yet been fixed.

Jonathan Daniels, White House secretary, said Mr. Roosevelt's body would not lie in state. He added that, in view of the limited size of the East Room, which holds only about 200 persons, the list of those attending the funeral services would be limited to high Government officials, representatives of the membership of both
Continued on Page 3, Column 1

TRUMAN IS SWORN IN THE WHITE HOUSE

Members of Cabinet on Hand as Chief Justice Stone Administers the Oath

By C. P. TRUSSELL
Special to THE NEW YORK TIMES.

WASHINGTON, April 12—Vice President Harry S. Truman of Missouri, standing erect, with his sharp features taut and looking straight ahead through his large, round glasses, became the thirty-second President of the United States in a ceremony lasting not more than a minute in the Cabinet Room of the White House at 7:09 o'clock tonight.

The oath was administered by Chief Justice Harlan F. Stone two hours and thirty-four minutes after the sudden death of President Roosevelt at Warm Springs. Mr. Truman had picked up a Bible from the end of the big Cabinet conference table, held it with his left hand and placed his right hand upon the upper cover. After repeating the oath, he bowed his head, lifted the Bible to his lips and kissed it.

Even before he had taken the oath Mr. Truman had asked President Roosevelt's Cabinet to continue in service. He also authorized Edward R. Stettinius Jr., Secretary of State, to announce that the United Nations Conference for International Organization would go on as scheduled.

To the newsmen at the White House he sent this word, through Stephen Early, press secretary:

"For the time being I prefer not to hold a press conference. It will be my effort to carry on as I believe the President would have done, and to that end I have asked the Cabinet to stay on with me."

Soon after he became President, Mr. Truman left the White House for the five-room Connecticut Avenue apartment where he has resided with Mrs. Truman and their 20-year-old daughter, Mary Margaret, for four years. He said he was "going home, to bed."

It was shortly after he had finished presiding over the Senate debate on the United States-Mexican Water Treaty late this afternoon that Mr. Truman received word from the White House of President Roosevelt's death. This was at about 5.15 P. M., a half hour before the news was made public. Reaching for his hat, he dashed out of the office, calling back to his staff that he was going to the White House.

Arriving at the White House, the
Continued on Page 3, Column 6

Byrnes May Take Post With Truman

Special to THE NEW YORK TIMES.

WASHINGTON, April 12— James F. Byrnes, recently resigned as Director of War Mobilization and Reconversion, known to be one of President Truman's warmest friends in official Washington, is expected to be called to the White House for consultation, and possibly to take an important post in the new Administration.

President Truman's admiration of former Justice Byrnes is well known here. He undoubtedly would be more than Mr. Truman's choice as a successor to Cordell Hull as Secretary of State.

135

The New York Times.

LATE CITY EDITION
Clearing and warmer today. Cloudy with moderate winds tomorrow.

Temperatures Yesterday—Max., 51; Min.,44
Sunrise today, 5:54 A. M.; Sunset, 7:55 P. M.

VOL. XCIV.—No. 31,875.

Entered as Second-Class Matter,
Postoffice, New York, N. Y.

Copyright, 1945, by The New York Times Company.

NEW YORK, WEDNESDAY, MAY 2, 1945.

THREE CENTS IN NEW YORK CITY

HITLER DEAD IN CHANCELLERY, NAZIS SAY; DOENITZ, SUCCESSOR, ORDERS WAR TO GO ON; BERLIN ALMOST WON; U. S. ARMIES ADVANCE

MOLOTOFF EASES PARLEY TENSION; NEW MOVES BEGUN

Russian Says Country Will Cooperate in World Plan Despite Argentine Issue

4 COMMISSIONS SET UP

They Will Deal With Council, Assembly, Court and Some General Problems

By JAMES B. RESTON
Special to The New York Times.

SAN FRANCISCO, May 1—The International Conference on International Organization has survived its first basic crisis and after six days of political maneuvering is moving at rapid tempo today toward its primary task—the creation of a world organization which would stop what Field Marshal Jan Christiaan Smuts called "this pilgrimage of death."

The test came last night. Rebuffed by the conference on his attempts to keep Argentina out of the conference and bring the Warsaw Poles in, Soviet Foreign Commissar Vyacheslav M. Molotoff went late last night to Secretary Stettinius's penthouse at the Fairmont Hotel. He immediately made his position clear.

He still disapproved the conference actions on the Poles and the Argentine, but he wanted the conference to succeed; he would cooperate in its labors, and while he was under urgent pressure by the events in Europe to return to Moscow, he would remain at least for a few days until the major issues on the charter were thrashed out among the four sponsor powers. Then, he said, he would have to leave, probably at the week-end or early next week.

"Friendly Meeting" Is Held

Immediately, in what the Foreign Ministers of the United States, Great Britain and China described to their colleagues as "the most friendly meeting of the conference," the big four approved the formation of the working commissions and committees of the conference, and other committees began discussing, not the personalities or procedures of the conference, but the basic questions of creating an organization which would win the support, with the power, of the great nations without violating the rights and principles of all nations.

The three main developments of the day were as follows:

First, the conference approved four commissions to deal with the security council of the proposed organization, the general assembly, the judicial agency and general problems, and established twelve committees to study specific problems under these four commissions. The heads of the four commissions were: Trygve Lie of Norway, Security Council; Field Marshal Smuts, General Assembly; Carraciolo Parra Rez of Venezuela, judicial organization; and Paul Henri Spaak of Belgium, general provisions.

Second, Field Marshal Smuts called on the four major powers to accept the special responsibilities which flow from the special authority given them under the Dumbarton Oaks proposals and urged all the nations here to pay more attention to the spiritual and economic aspects of the new charter than they had in the past.

Third, the Russians began studying in some detail the sixteen amendments to the Dumbarton Oaks proposals which were submitted by the United States. The other delegations started circulating amendments and exchanging views on proposals already circulated.

The facts on the crisis among the Big Three over Poland, Argentina, White Russia and the Ukraine can now be put down with assur-

Continued on Page 18, Column 6

Allies Invade North Borneo; Fighting Fierce, Tokyo Says

Australia Informed of Landing by Treasury Minister—MacArthur Reports Only Air Attacks and New Gains on Luzon

By The United Press.

MANILA, Wednesday, May 2—An official Australian announcement said yesterday that Allied troops had invaded Borneo, the world's third largest island, but Gen. Douglas MacArthur's communiqué early today reported only that heavy bombers were neutralizing enemy bases and airdromes on the oil-rich island.

Tokyo also reported the landings and said they had been made on the ten-square-mile island of Tarakan on the northeast coast, a region rich in oil wells, which the Netherlanders destroyed before the Japanese captured them in 1942. The enemy broadcast said "fierce fighting" was in progress.

[A later Japanese broadcast, picked up in San Francisco, reported that Allied units had landed on Tarakan Island at 6:30 A. M., Tuesday, Tokyo time. The

broadcast said "the enemy had been bombarding the island since April 27, and on Monday morning began approaching the island in their landing attempts." It reported the landing force consisted of "about 5,000 soldiers" and said Japanese forces on the island "are holding secure their positions, obstructing the enemy's advance."]

General MacArthur announced that heavy bombers in attacks on Borneo had struck Kuching, Macassar and Kendari, while medium units and fighters had attacked Japanese gun positions on Tarakan.

General MacArthur announced that on Mindano Island the Twenty-fourth Division, in another swift drive, had advanced eleven miles

Continued on Page 16, Column 2

REDOUBTS ASSAILED

U.S. 3d, 7th and French 1st Armies Charging Into Alpine Hideout

NEAR BRENNER PASS

British in North Close About Hamburg—Poles Gain in Emden Area

Von Rundstedt Caught

By The Associated Press.

WITH UNITED STATES SEVENTH ARMY, Wednesday, May 2—Field Marshal Karl von Rundstedt has been captured by United States Seventh Army troops.

The Seventh Army caught the former German commander in the west in its drive into the Nazis' southeastern redoubt area.

By DREW MIDDLETON
By Wireless to The New York Times.

PARIS, May 1—The last defenses of the Third Reich were crumbling as Allied tanks and infantry swept almost unopposed into the northern and southern redoubts.

Gen. George S. Patton's United States Third Army has resumed its offensive into Austria, crashing to within twenty miles of Linz, and is only fifty-four miles from Amstetten, where Marshal Fedor I. Tolbukhin's Third Ukrainian Army was last reported. According to reports from the front, radio contact has been established between tanks of the United States Eleventh Armored Division and the vanguard of the Soviet armies. Other armored columns of the

Continued on Page 14, Column 1

NAZI CORE STORMED

Russians Drive Toward Chancellery Fortress, Narrowing Noose

BRANDENBURG TAKEN

Stralsund Port Swept Up in New Baltic Gains— Vah Valley Cleared

By C. L. SULZBERGER
By Wireless to The New York Times.

MOSCOW, Wednesday, May 2—Street battles within smoldering Berlin today entered their twelfth day since the Russians first broke into the city, with Nazi die-hards still holding grimly to the central part of the town, whittled down by yesterday's fighting, in which Marshal Gregory K. Zhukoff's First White Russian Army completely occupied Charlottenburg and Schoeneberg and more than 100 blocks in the capital's central region.

Some 14,000 prisoners were taken within the city on Monday, the Russians announced. At the same time, the remnants of a holdout group south of Berlin, part of which had been annihilated in two and the survivors were split ground to death at Wendisch Buchholtz, was split in two and the survivors were swept to death at Wendisch Buchholtz, Koneff's men.

Curiously enough, the midnight communiqué did not mention Marshal Ivan S. Koneff's First Ukrainian Army, which has been working from the southwestern sector of the city toward the desperately defended Tiergarten.

Marshal Zhukoff's forward spearheads meanwhile struck deep into Brandenburg Province, capturing the city of Brandenburg, halfway to Magdeburg from Berlin.

While Gen. Andrei I. Yeremenko proceeded apace in his lightning

Continued on Page 3, Column 3

ADOLF HITLER   The New York Times, 1938

Clark's Troops Meet Tito's In General Advance in Italy

By VIRGINIA LEE WARREN
By Wireless to The New York Times.

AT ADVANCED ALLIED HEADQUARTERS, in Italy, May 1—After advancing fifty-five miles in less than a day along the coastal road rimming the Gulf of Venice, units of one division of the Fifteenth Army Group made contact this afternoon with Marshal Tito's forces at Monfalcone while other troops under Gen. Mark W. Clark continued to sweep German remnants from the valleys of north Italy and to seal off the few remaining escape routes through the Alps.

No details of the meeting at the small seaport northwest of Trieste between Marshal Tito's men, who had driven fourteen miles from Trieste, and leading elements of the Eighth Army's Second New Zealand Division were given to tonight's communiqué.

On the other side of Italy another historic meeting was imminent as Fifth Army troops, continuing their drive along the Gulf of Genoa, advanced on the Aurelian Way to within sixty miles of the French border, which has already been crossed by French troops headed this way.

General Clark announced yesterday that the military power of Germany had virtually collapsed, but there still are drives for him two armies to make and engagements still to be won. The Germans were deprived of two key road junctions leading to mountain passes west of Brenner when Belluno and Udine were occupied this afternoon by units of the Eighth Army.

New Zealand troops in Italy made contact with Yugoslav Partisans at Monfalcone near Trieste and the British entered Udine. While the Eighth Army was closing a trap along the Swiss border, the Fifth neared France.

Continued on Page 13, Column 5

ADMIRAL IN CHARGE

Proclaims Designation to Rule—Appeals to People and Army

RAISES 'RED MENACE'

Britain to Insist Germans Show Hitler's Body When War Ends

By SYDNEY GRUSON
By Cable to The New York Times.

LONDON, May 1—Adolf Hitler died this afternoon, the Hamburg radio announced tonight, and Grand Admiral Karl Doenitz, proclaiming himself the new Fuehrer by Hitler's appointment, said that the war would continue.

Crowning days of rumors about Hitler's health and whereabouts, the Hamburg radio said that he had fallen in the battle of Berlin at his command post in the Chancellery just three days after Benito Mussolini, the first of the dictators, had been killed by Italian Partisans. Doenitz, a 53-year-old U-boat specialist, broadcast an address to the German people and the surviving armed forces immediately after the announcer had given the news of Hitler's death.

[The British Foreign Office said that it would demand the production of Hitler's body at the end of hostilities, The Associated Press reported.]

First addressing the German people, Doenitz said that they would continue to fight only to save themselves from the Russians but that they should oppose the western Allies as long as they helped the Russians. In an order of the day to the German forces he repeated his thinly veiled attempt to split the Allies.

Radio Prepares Germans

Early this evening the Germans were told that an important announcement would be broadcast tonight. There was no hint of what was coming. The stand-by announcement was repeated at 9:40 P. M., followed by the playing of excerpts from Wagner's "Goetterdaemmerung."

A few minutes later the announcer said: "Achtung! Achtung! In a few moments you will hear

Continued on Page 5, Column 4

NEW CIGARETTES FACE PRICE INQUIRY

OPA Calls on Manufacturers of 21-Cent Brands to Prove Quality Merits Charge

By JAMES E. POWERS

Manufacturers of hitherto unheard of brands of cigarettes that have appeared on the market in recent weeks and are being retailed at four or more cents a package higher than ceiling prices for scarce popular brands will be called upon by the Office of Price Administration to show that the new products are of a quality rating the prices charged, it became known yesterday.

Daniel P. Woolley, regional OPA administrator, said an investigation was in progress as a result of complaints by smokers who said they had paid 21 cents a package for cigarettes "they had previously never heard of."

The United Wholesale Tobacco and Cigarette Distributors Association, a sub-jobbers' group, in a telegram to Senator William Langer of North Dakota, who recently introduced a resolution to set up a committee to look into the "black market" in cigarettes, demanded an immediate investigation of the entire cigarette shortage.

Mr. Woolley declared that as a result of OPA prosecution of violators of price ceilings, the black-market condition largely had been corrected here. He said he was centering on the pricing of the new cigarette brands.

Mr. Woolley added that studies were being made to determine

Continued on Page 40, Column 4

HARD COAL 'HOLIDAY' BRINGS WLB BAN

New Order by Board Asserts Output Is Urgent—Seizure Action Is Postponed

By JOSEPH A. LOFTUS
Special to The New York Times.

WASHINGTON, May 1—The War Labor Board issued a new order tonight to the United Mine Workers and the operators to resume the production of hard coal. To give the UMW leaders an opportunity to act on the order it decided to defer for twenty-four to forty-eight hours a recommendation to President Truman for Government seizure of the mines.

The miners went on a holiday today after expiration of their contract at midnight.

Dr. George W. Taylor, WLB chairman, in a telegram to both parties took cognizance of the miners' traditional "no contract, no work" policy.

"The board's order provides for a continuing contract," he said. "It is urgent that production should be immediately resumed."

As in acting on the soft coal dispute a month ago, the WLB provided in the new order that any legal wage adjustment agreed upon or finally ordered be retroactive to the expiration date of the old contract.

Union spokesmen told the WLB at a brief hearing that the Tri-District Scale Committee had voted to advise the miners to return to work when the operators accepted the settlement proposal made by Secretary of Labor Perkins.

Dr. Taylor, in questioning John Owens of the UMW, noted that

Continued on Page 40, Column 3

Eisenhower Halted Forces at Elbe; Ninth Had Hoped to Storm Berlin

By The Associated Press.

WITH THE UNITED STATES NINTH ARMY, in Germany, April 26 (Delayed by Censorship)—A direct order from Supreme Allied Headquarters halted the United States Ninth Army's drive to Berlin at the Elbe River at a time when the major objectives still were predicting that Lieut. Gen. William H. Simpson's forces could reduce the German capital in ten days, "even if the Germans fought hard."

General Eisenhower's order said Berlin would be halted on the Elbe and await the arrival of Russian forces from the east, thereby leaving the capture of the capital to the Red Army. It also was understood that the American First and Third and British and Canadian armies received similar orders to halt at the Elbe.

It was not clear whether General

Eisenhower's order was dictated by political agreement among the Great Powers or in a belief that it was a military necessity.

It was felt by high staff officers in the field, however, that the Ninth and other American forces could push on to the capital without great difficulty. While the order disappointed some staff officers, it was not altogether unexpected. It was known that the Ninth Army had pushed past the eventual British-American occupation area when it crossed the Weser River.

While the staff officers were disappointed, they appointed the American doughboys and tankmen who had to do the fighting and dying to get to Berlin expressed no regret. Almost to a man, they felt they could withdraw

Continued on Page 4, Column 4

War News Summarized

WEDNESDAY, MAY 2, 1945

Hitler is dead, according to the Hamburg radio, and on Monday, the day before he allegedly fell at his command post in the Chancellery in Berlin, he appointed Admiral Karl Doenitz to be the new Fuehrer. The head of the German Navy, who had made his mark directing the enemy's U-boats campaign, pledged continuance of the war. [1:8.]

Washington received the news, as did London, with some skepticism and a desire to see the body. Selection of Admiral Doenitz was considered logical in view of his strong Nazi feelings. [1:7.]

The new development was interpreted in London as a move to counteract Himmler's reported peace bids, but Prime Minister Churchill broadly intimated in the Commons that he might have "information of exceptional importance" to impart before Saturday. Peace will probably come before all enemy forces have surrendered, he said. [1:6-7.] German troops were reported to have begun evacuation of Denmark and to be ready to leave Norway. Count Bernadotte said in Sweden he had no new Himmler proposals, and the Nazis' Scandinavian withdrawals were related there to a prospective general capitulation. [11:1.]

Meanwhile, general Allied progress on the battlefields against slight resistance continued. The United States Third Army, on the day Hitler was declared to have died, captured Braunau, his birthplace. The drive into Austria was resumed and had reached to within twenty miles of Linz and fifty-four of the last known Russian position. The Seventh Army smashed through the Tyrol on a broad front and cleared Munich. The British Second Army, by-passing Hamburg, raced to within eight-

een miles of the Baltic port of Luebeck. [1:4; map P. 14.]

General Eisenhower, it was revealed, personally ordered the halt of the Allied drive on Berlin from the west to permit the Russians to take the capital. [1:2-3.]

The Russians greatly cut down the German holding in Berlin, capturing the districts of Charlottenburg and Schoeneberg and along the Baltic they seized Stralsund. [1:5; maps Pages 2 and 14.]

New Zealand troops in Italy made contact with Yugoslav Partisans at Monfalcone near Trieste and the British entered Udine. While the Eighth Army was closing a trap along the Swiss border, the Fifth neared France. [1:6-7; map P. 14.]

Mussolini and his mistress were buried in unmarked paupers' graves in Milan. [13:1.] Admiral Horthy, former Regent of Hungary, was captured. [4:3.]

Invasion of Borneo was officially disclosed in Australia, although no word of the break into the Japanese-held Netherlands East Indies had come from General MacArthur. On Mindanao in the Philippines, Americans were within six miles of the city of Davao. [1:2-3; map P. 14.]

Seventh Division troops on Okinawa resumed their southward advance, entering the village of Kuhazu. [15:1.] More than 400 starved, naked Allied prisoners of war were liberated by the British as they drove on Rangoon in Burma. [15:3.]

Good progress was made at the San Francisco Conference. Foreign Commissar Molotoff, after assuring Secretary of State Stettinius of his desire that the conference succeed, announced that pressure of events would compel his return to Moscow within a few days. [1:1.]

DOENITZ' ACCESSION VIEWED AS A BLIND

Capital Lays His Designation to General Ignorance of His Allegiance to Party

By The Associated Press.

WASHINGTON, May 1—If Adolf Hitler really designated Grand Admiral Karl Doenitz his successor, military men here believe, he did so for the following reasons:

1. Doenitz is a Nazi supporter who could be counted on to keep German resistance going if possible.

2. But he is not associated in the Allies' minds with German atrocities and the extreme policies of the Nazi party. Therefore, Hitler probably figured that he might be able to get better treatment from the Allies when the hour of surrender came.

3. He is immensely popular with the German people.

There was a disposition here tonight to look for continued organized resistance whose core would now be centered in the Baltic and North Sea port areas. Those places are the homes of the German Navy and especially of the U-boat fleet that Doenitz commanded from 1936 until he succeeded Grand Admiral Erich

Continued on Page 5, Column 1

Copenhagen Writer Again Phones Story

By Cable to The New York Times.

STOCKHOLM, May 1—For the first time in more than five years THE NEW YORK TIMES correspondent in Copenhagen, Svend Carstensen, tonight telephoned a story from the Danish capital. Mr. Carstensen imposed censorship there has been lifted. Mr. Carstensen said:

"The Danes are overjoyed at their imminent liberation, but it is not noticeable on the Copenhagen streets.

"Anxious to avoid trouble on May Day, Copenhageners have been staying indoors. The blackout is still enforced and it is pitch dark in Copenhagen tonight. All Copenhageners are glued to radios listening to broadcasts on Hitler's death.

"We expect King Christian will resume his functions and name a new Cabinet any day now. In the meantime the strictest discipline is being observed so as not to give the Germans any excuses for starting more trouble."

On April 9, 1940, Mr. Carstensen was the first to give the world the news of the German invasion of Denmark in a wireless dispatch to THE NEW YORK TIMES. His dispatch was cleared less than an hour before the Nazis seized the radio station and was the last to be sent.

Churchill Hints Peace This Week; 2-Day Celebration Is Authorized

By CLIFTON DANIEL
By Wireless to The New York Times.

LONDON, May 1—The general belief that peace with Germany will be announced this week persisted in Britain today, encouraged by Prime Minister Churchill himself and by Grand Admiral Karl Doenitz's announcement of the death of Adolf Hitler.

The War Cabinet again held a session tonight but so far as was known did not have any concrete proposal to consider. The chances that Heinrich Himmler will ultimately make an acceptable peace are now held in some quarters to be only "fifty-fifty."

[Stockholm reported, with the return there of Count Bernadotte, that the "imminent liberation" of Denmark and Norway—already taking effect locally in Denmark —as a phase of a prospective general German capitulation that must be acceptable to the Allies' military commands.]

Nevertheless the buoyant Prime Minister told the House of Commons today that he might have "information of importance" to announce before Saturday.

The public's hopes were raised today by a long Home Office circular giving the Government's views on how Britain should observe V-E Day, which the British, it appears, will be expected to celebrate strictly according to form.

The hurrahing will begin with the announcement of the cessation of hostilities by Mr. Churchill over a nation-wide radio network. The King will speak at 9 o'clock that evening. And throughout that day

Continued on Page 10, Column 4

The New York Times.

LATE CITY EDITION
Cloudy with showers today. Partly
cloudy and cooler tomorrow.
Temperatures Yesterday—Max., 64; Min., 47
Sunrise today, 5:45 A. M.; Sunset, 7:59 P. M.

VOL. XCIV..No. 31,881.

Entered as Second-Class Matter,
Postoffice, New York, N. Y.

Copyright, 1945, by The New York Times Company

NEW YORK, TUESDAY, MAY 8, 1945.

THREE CENTS IN NEW YORK CITY

THE WAR IN EUROPE IS ENDED!
SURRENDER IS UNCONDITIONAL;
V-E WILL BE PROCLAIMED TODAY;
OUR TROOPS ON OKINAWA GAIN

ISLAND-WIDE DRIVE

Marines Reach Village a Mile From Naha and Army Lines Advance

7 MORE SHIPS SUNK

Search Planes Again Hit Japan's Life Line— Kyushu Bombed

By WARREN MOSCOW
By Wireless to THE NEW YORK TIMES

GUAM, Tuesday, May 8—In an island-wide American advance on Okinawa yesterday the First Marine Division drove south to the edge of Dakeshi Village, about a mile from Naha, the capital, straightening out the line on our right flank. In the center the Seventy-seventh Army Division used flame-throwing tanks for considerable advances, while the Seventh Army Division moved forward on the left flank.

[Airfields on Kyushu, southern Japan, were bombed Monday and Tuesday by Superfortresses, two of which were lost in heavy air opposition.

[Allied fliers started operating from the Tarakan airfield although fighting continued on that island off Borneo, and in the Philippines American troops made advances on Mindanao and Luzon.]

Japanese Dead at 36,535

As the United States forces on Okinawa resumed their drive, Fleet Admiral Chester W. Nimitz revealed that Japanese killed on the island had mounted to 36,535 on Monday, showing that the Americans were maintaining their rate of 1,000 a day.

The Americans have not yet taken the main Japanese artillery emplacements on Okinawa, which were the principal targets of the fleet off the island. The fleet's guns continued yesterday, along with carrier aircraft, to support the ground movements.

Meanwhile search bombers of Fleet Air Wing 1 continued to give an impressive demonstration of what the tightening air blockade of Japan will mean. Attacking at mast-head height with bombs and machine guns, these long-range aircraft, based in the Okinawa area, sank four more ships in waters off Korea and damaged five others.

The ships sunk were a large cargo ship, a medium cargo ship, a medium oiler and a large fleet tanker. Two small freighters were

Continued on Page 12, Column 2

Leopold Rescued By 7th Army Troops

By The Associated Press

WITH THE UNITED STATES SEVENTH ARMY, Tuesday, May 8—Léopold III, King of Belgium, and his wife, Princess Rethy, have been liberated by the Seventh Army, it was announced today.

They were found near Strobl, eight miles east of Salzburg. The Americans had been told of their whereabouts by civilians.

With the King and his wife were eighteen members of their staff and four children. All were in good health. Elements of the American 106th Cavalry Group had to overpower German Elite Guards to make the rescue. Seventh Army troops are now closely guarding the royal party.

The Pulitzer Awards For 1944 Announced

The Pulitzer Prize awards announced yesterday by the trustees of Columbia University included: For a distinguished novel, to "A Bell for Adano," by John Hersey; for, an original American play of the current season, to "Harvey," by Mary Chase.

Among the newspaper awards were those to Hal Boyle, Associated Press war reporter, for distinguished correspondence; to James B. Reston of THE NEW YORK TIMES for his reporting of the Dumbarton Oaks Security Conference; to Joe Rosenthal, Associated Press photographer, for his photograph of marines raising the American flag at Iwo and to The Detroit Free Press for "distinguished and meritorious public service" in its investigation of legislative corruption at Lansing, Mich.

Further details of the awards will be found on Page 16.

MOLOTOFF HAILS BASIC 'UNANIMITY'

He Stresses Five Points In World Charter, but His View on One Is Questioned

By JAMES B. RESTON
Special to The New York Times.

SAN FRANCISCO, May 7—The major allies who forced Germany's unconditional surrender have reached "unanimity" on the kind of world security organization which should be created at the United Nations conference to protect their newly won victory, Vyacheslaff M. Molotoff, Russian Foreign Commissar, said today.

While the delegates at the conference celebrated the end of the European war, and three Foreign Ministers, T. V. Soong of China, Paul Henri Spaak of Belgium and Trygve Lie of Norway left the conference to deal with urgent official business elsewhere, Mr. Molotoff told the press that the Soviet Union attached the "greatest importance" to five agreements reached by the heads of the Big Four delegations.

First, he said, these leaders agreed to support the principles of justice, international law, human rights and fundamental freedom for all.

Second, he added, the Big Four agreed not to make provision in the security charter for the revision of treaties.

His statement on this point was ambiguous and led to some speculation as to the unanimity of all the Big Four.

Revision Power Called Danger

A reference in the United Nations charter to the necessity of revising treaties, Mr. Molotoff stated, "would play into the hands of enemy countries, which would certainly like to undermine and emasculate these treaties." Furthermore, he declared, to give the new League of Nations authority to consider revision of treaties would be a violation of national sovereign rights, which are guaranteed in the Dumbarton Oaks Charter.

For these reasons, he concluded, "the idea of revising treaties was rejected as untenable."

Third, Mr. Molotoff said, it was agreed among the Big Four that treaties directed against Germany, such as Russia's twenty-year alliances with Britain, France, Czechoslovakia, Yugoslavia and the Warsaw Poles, "should remain in force until such time as the Government concerned felt that the international security organization was really in a position to undertake the accomplishment of the tasks of

Continued on Page 15, Column 2

GERMANY SURRENDERS: NEW YORKERS MASSED UNDER SYMBOL OF LIBERTY

Thousands filling Times Square in spontaneous celebration yesterday
The New York Times

PRAGUE SAYS FOES ACCEPT SURRENDER

Czechoslovak Radio Reports All Fighting in Bohemia Will Be Ended Today

By The Associated Press.

LONDON, Tuesday, May 8—The Czechoslovak - controlled Prague radio announced today that the Germans in Prague and throughout Bohemia, a last major holdout pocket of German resistance, had accepted unconditional surrender.

The announcement came as the United States Third Army was reported to have advanced to the outskirts of the Czechoslovak capital, and three Russian armies hammered toward the same goal from the east and north.

"The German military plenipotentiary is negotiating with the Czechoslovak National Council on the modalities of unconditional surrender," said the broadcast, detailing what purported to be the

Continued on Page 11, Column 2

Wild Crowds Greet News In City While Others Pray

By FRANK S. ADAMS

New York City's millions reacted in two sharply contrasting ways yesterday to the news of the unconditional surrender of the German armies. A large and noisy minority greeted it with the turbulent enthusiasm of New Year's Eve and Election Night rolled into one. However, the great bulk of the city's population responded with quiet thanksgiving that the war in Europe was won, tempered by the realization that a grim and bitter struggle still was ahead in the Pacific and the fact that the nation is still in mourning for its fallen President and Commander in Chief.

Times Square, the financial section and the garment district were thronged from mid-morning on with wildly jubilant celebrators who tooted horns, staged impromptu parades and filled the canyons between the skyscrapers with fluttering scraps of paper. Elsewhere in the metropolitan area, however, war plants continued to hum, schools and offices and factories carried on their normal activities, and residential areas were calmly joyful.

One factor that helped to dampen the celebration was the bewilderment of large segments of the population at the absence of an official proclamation to back up the news contained in flaring headlines and radio bulletins. With the premature rumor of ten days ago fresh in everyone's mind, and millions still mindful of the false armistice of 1918, there was widespread skepticism over the authenticity of the news.

By mid-afternoon loudspeakers were blaring into the ears of the exciting thousands in the amusement district the news that President Truman's proclamation was being held up by the necessity of coordinating it with the announcements from London and Moscow, and that the formal celebration of the long-awaited V-E Day would be delayed until today.

This sobering note gradually

Continued on Page 7, Column 6

SHAEF BAN ON AP LIFTED IN 6 HOURS

Action Comes After Protests From Newspapers and Public —Writer Still Barred

Suspension of filing facilities of The Associated Press in the European theatre was clamped on by Supreme Headquarters, Allied Expeditionary Forces (SHAEF), yesterday in an unprecedented action and was lifted six hours and twenty minutes later.

The ban was continued, however, on all copy submitted for clearance by Edward Kennedy, chief of the press association's staff on the Western Front, who sent the momentous story announcing Germany's final surrender in a dispatch from Reims, France, which was received in New York over the AP wires at 9:35 A. M. (EWT).

It was not until seven hours and fifty-five minutes had elapsed aft-

Continued on Page 4, Column 2

GERMANS CAPITULATE ON ALL FRONTS

American, Russian and French Generals Accept Surrender in Eisenhower Headquarters, a Reims School

REICH CHIEF OF STAFF ASKS FOR MERCY

Doenitz Orders All Military Forces of Germany To Drop Arms—Troops in Norway Give Up —Churchill and Truman on Radio Today

By EDWARD KENNEDY
Associated Press Correspondent

REIMS, France, May 7—Germany surrendered unconditionally to the Western Allies and the Soviet Union at 2:41 A. M. French time today. [This was at 8:41 P. M., Eastern Wartime Sunday.]

The surrender took place at a little red schoolhouse that is the headquarters of Gen. Dwight D. Eisenhower.

The surrender, which brought the war in Europe to a formal end after five years, eight months and six days of bloodshed and destruction, was signed for Germany by Col. Gen. Gustav Jodl. General Jodl is the new Chief of Staff of the German Army.

The surrender was signed for the Supreme Allied Command by Lieut. Gen. Walter Bedell Smith, Chief of Staff for General Eisenhower.

It was also signed by Gen. Ivan Susloparoff for the Soviet Union and by Gen. Francois Sevez for France.

[The official Allied announcement will be made at 9 o'clock Tuesday morning when President Truman will broadcast a statement and Prime Minister Churchill will issue a V-E Day proclamation. Gen. Charles de Gaulle also will address the French at the same time.]

General Eisenhower was not present at the signing, but immediately afterward General Jodl and his fellow delegate, Gen. Admiral Hans Georg Friedeburg, were received by the Supreme Commander.

Germans Say They Understand Terms

They were asked sternly if they understood the surrender terms imposed upon Germany and if they would be carried out by Germany.

They answered Yes.

Germany, which began the war with a ruthless attack upon Poland, followed by successive aggressions and brutality in internment camps, surrendered with an appeal to the victors for mercy toward the German people and armed forces.

After having signed the full surrender, General Jodl said he wanted to speak and received leave to do so.

"With this signature," he said in soft-spoken German, "the German people and armed forces are for better or worse delivered into the victors' hands.

"In this war, which has lasted more than five years, both have achieved and suffered more than perhaps any other people in the world."

LONDON, May 7 (AP)—Complete victory in

Continued on Page 3, Columns 2 and 3

Summary of News of the War and German Surrender

TUESDAY, MAY 8, 1945

The war ended in Europe yesterday after five years, eight months and six days of the bloodiest conflict in history. Grand Admiral Karl Doenitz surrendered unconditionally to the Allies in a little red schoolhouse at Reims, France. At 8:41 P. M. Sunday, New York time, Col. Gen. Gustav Jodl signed for the enemy and Lieut. Gen. Walter Bedell Smith, General Eisenhower's Chief of Staff, for the Allies.

In the absence of any official announcement there was some confusion as to the compliance with the surrender. Fighting had been going on in Czechoslovakia and nothing had been heard from German pockets along the French coast. [1:7-8.]

President Truman planned a broadcast from the White House at 9 o'clock this morning. Washington, gratified that the war in Europe was over, was confused by lack of confirmation. [2:2.]

Prime Minister Churchill will also broadcast at 9 A. M. from London and Premier Stalin is expected to make a simultaneous announcement in Moscow. King George will talk over the radio six hours later. [2:8.] London will celebrate V-E Day today, but, unable to restrain its joy, staged many impromptu celebrations yesterday. [2:7.]

Most New Yorkers took the news calmly and thankfully, sobered by realization that the war in the Pacific was far from over. There were, however, noisy outbursts in such centers as Times Square and Wall Street. Scrap paper showers fluttered from roofs and windows. [1:4-5.]

German Foreign Minister Lutz Schwerin von Krosigk broke the news to his people. The future will be difficult, he warned, and then added: "We must make right the basis of our nation. In our nation justice shall be the supreme law and the guiding principle. We must also recognize law as the basis of all relations between the nations." This sudden, complete reversal in German policy was received with skepticism by the Allies. [3:1.]

Perhaps one reason for this was the announcement from Moscow that 4,000,000 men, women and children had been done to death by gas, shooting, famine, poisoning and torture in the German extermination camp at Oswiecim, Poland. [12:5.]

The actual situation in Czechoslovakia was obscure. Late last night a Patriot broadcast said the Germans were negotiating with the Czechoslovak National Council details of surrender in Prague and Bohemia. Fighting had continued throughout yesterday and German planes had bombed public buildings and hospitals. [1:3; map P. 11.]

The United States Third Army continued its general advance into Czechoslovakia and the Fifth and Seventh Armies joined again in the Alps. The British Second Army moved to Denmark and Poles entered the shattered port of Wilhelmshaven. [11:1.] Breslau fell to the Red Army after an eighty-four-day siege; 40,000 Germans were captured. [11:5.]

Japan accepted the surrender of her Axis partner with a statement that she never had expected German aid and would go on to victory without the Reich. [13:1.]

Infantry and marines on Okinawa scored another general advance after naval bombardment had pulverized Japanese strong points. Pacific Fleet planes sank or damaged thirteen more ships off Korea and Japan. [1:1; map, P. 12.] B-29's maintained their assault on Kyushu airfields. Two of the big planes were shot down. [14:3-4.] On Tarakan Allied troops were within a mile and a half of the eastern shore. Americans gained on Mindanao and Luzon in the Philippines. [12:3-4.]

Foreign Commissar Molotoff said in San Francisco that unanimity on amendments to Dumbarton Oaks assured success of the conference. He declared that the Big Four consultations had ended. [1:2.]

"All the News That's Fit to Print"

The New York Times.

LATE CITY EDITION
Showers, thunder showers; warm and humid today and tomorrow.
Temperature Yesterday—Max., 70; Min., 67
Sunrise today, 5:49 A. M.; Sunset, 8:11 P. M.

Section 1

NEWS INDEX, PAGE 41, THIS SECTION

Copyright, 1945, by The New York Times Company.

VOL. XCIV..No. 31,963.

Entered as Second-Class Matter,
Postoffice, New York, N. Y.

NEW YORK, SUNDAY, JULY 29, 1945.

Including Magazine and Book Review.

TEN CENTS
New York City and Suburban Areas (15c Elsewhere)

SENATE RATIFIES CHARTER OF UNITED NATIONS 89 TO 2; TRUMAN HAILS AID TO PEACE

FOES ARE CRUSHED

With Hiram Johnson Ill, Only Shipstead and Langer Vote 'No'

WORLD OBLIGATION CITED

Leaders Say Today's Ratification Is 'Master Plan,' With Military Pacts Secondary

By JAMES B. RESTON
Special to The New York Times.

WASHINGTON, July 28—The United States Senate paid a first installment on an old debt today. It ratified, 89 to 2, the United Nations Security Charter, successor to the League of Nations Covenant which it rejected twenty-six years ago, and thereby fulfilled Woodrow Wilson's prophecy that one day the upper chamber would reverse its decision.

The vote came 107 days after the death of Franklin D. Roosevelt, who helped guide the Charter past the pitfalls that defeated Wilson's Covenant, and at a moment when American statesmen were settling the fate of a defeated Germany and American warships were closing in on the heart of Japan.

The two Senators who voted against ratification were William Langer of North Dakota and Henrik Shipstead of Minnesota, both Republicans. Mr. Langer, who worked actively for Hiram Johnson and Robert M. La Follette when those two "irreconcilables" were candidates for President, said he was voting against the Charter because it would mean "perpetual war" and the "enslavement" of millions of poor people from Poland to India.

Hiram Johnson Sends Word

Senator Hiram Johnson, Republican, of California, sent word from the Naval Medical Center outside Washington that if he had been well enough to be present he would have joined Mr. Langer and Mr. Shipstead in opposition, but the four other members of the Senate who were with Mr. Johnson in the upper chamber during the League of Nations debate—Arthur Capper, Republican, of Kansas, and Peter G. Gerry of Rhode Island, Kenneth McKellar of Tennessee, and David I. Walsh of Massachusetts, Democrats, all voted for ratification.

As soon as the results were made known, President Truman and Cordell Hull, former Secretary of State, who started work on the Charter in the State Department in 1942, issued statements praising the Senate's action.

"It is deeply gratifying that the Senate has ratified the United Nations' Charter by a virtually unanimous vote," the President's message from Potsdam said. "The action of the Senate substantially advances the cause of world peace."

It was a grim-appearing Senate that rolled off the "ayes" on the final count this evening. Despite the long parliamentary debate in the chamber on the subject, and despite its overwhelming approval at the end, there was no sense of a job finished but merely of a difficult job just beginning.

Since a league to enforce peace had first been mentioned to members of this chamber by Woodrow Wilson in 1914, some 40,000,000 human beings, armed and unarmed, had been killed in two great wars. In the first German war total military casualties were estimated at 37,000,000 men; in the European phase of the second German war some 14,000,000 men had been killed, and our own casualties in this war, still unfinished, were over the million mark.

Chaplain Tells Senate's Hopes

Throughout the debate, the Senate seemed to realize this and to approach the problem more in hope than anything else.

"Under the old order of strife," the Senate's chaplain said in his prayer opening today's session, "we learned how to destroy ourselves. Under a new charter of mutual aid and tolerance of diversity, may we learn at last how to save ourselves."

Today's vote does not put the

Continued on Page 33, Column 4

Truman Deeply Gratified, He Says in Cable Message

President Promptly Recognizes Senate's Action as Advancing 'the Cause of World Peace'—Grew and Hull Applaud

Special to The New York Times.

WASHINGTON, July 28—President Truman was swift to applaud the passage of the World Security Charter. In a message from Potsdam he said:

"It is deeply gratifying that the Senate has ratified the United Nations Charter by a virtually unanimous vote.

"The action of the Senate substantially advances the cause of world peace."

Joseph C. Grew, Acting Secretary of State, and Cordell Hull, former Secretary of State, commended the Senate for its approval of the Charter.

Mr. Grew said:

"The passage of the United Nations Charter by the Senate today is a memorable event in the history of the United States and the world. By their action, the members of the Senate have taken a most important step toward establishing security and peace throughout the world.

"Millions of men, women and children have died because nations took to the naked sword instead of the conference table to settle their differences.

"The United Nations Charter, approved by such an overwhelming majority, represents the labor of citizens of fifty nations, united in their desire for a peaceful world. The Charter itself is the foundation and cornerstone on which the international organization to keep the peace will be built. This organization can survive only through the faith and labor of the citizens of all these nations.

"I congratulate the members of the Senate for their work today."

Continued on Page 33, Column 1

Poles, at Big 3 Meeting, Ask Stettin, Oder-Neisse Border

By RAYMOND DANIELL
By Wireless to The New York Times.

BERLIN, July 28—A delegation of the Polish Government, including Vice Premier Stanislaw Mikolajczyk and, it is believed, Labor Minister Jan Stanczyk, has been here this last week to ask for a final delimitation of their country's western frontier to include Stettin and run from there southward along the east bank of the Oder-Neisse River line.

It was officially announced that Britain's new Prime Minister, Clement R. Attlee, and his Foreign Minister, Ernest Bevin, after formal calls on President Truman, Secretary of State James F. Byrnes, Premier Stalin and Foreign Commissar Vyacheslaff M. Molotoff, had participated today in a plenary session of the tripartite conference.

It is now believed, although there has been no inkling of their plans from official sources, that neither Winston Churchill nor former Foreign Secretary Anthony Eden will return. The new Prime Minister and his Foreign Secretary, who as Labor Minister in Mr. Churchill's coalition Government had access to all secrets of the War Cabinet, are the only new members of the British delegation. Inasmuch as Mr. Attlee sat in at all sessions of the Big Three before his election and saw all the official documents at the conference, it can hardly be said that he is a newcomer to the council table.

Parley Continuity Maintained

The downfall of the Churchill Government has caused little break in the continuity of the conference. Little more than forty-eight hours elapsed between Mr. Churchill's departure from Berlin and Mr. Attlee's return today.

In the absence of the head of the British delegation experts worked steadily to clear the decks

Continued on Page 5, Column 4

WOOLLEY DISMISSES ROSS IN OPA DISPUTE

Refuses to Grant the Public Hearing Demanded by Aide He Suspended June 22

Paul L. Ross, regional enforcement executive of the Office of Price Administration, who was suspended June 22 on charges of maladministration, was discharged yesterday by Daniel P. Woolley, regional OPA administrator, who refused to grant Mr. Ross the public hearing for which he had pleaded.

The discharge, effective at once, was contained in a registered letter mailed to Mr. Ross at noon, and followed by less than forty-eight hours the filing of Mr. Ross' reply to the administrator's charges.

In a brief statement, Mr. Woolley declared "utterly untrue and unfounded" serious counter-charges against him preferred by Mr. Ross in his answer. The enforcement officer had accused Mr. Woolley of hampering the enforcement of OPA regulations, interfering in behalf of certain alleged violators and obstructing the Federal enforcement policies.

Upon learning of his discharge,

Continued on Page 37, Column 5

Kweilin and Three Airfields Seized; Chinese Also Gain in Other Areas

By The Associated Press.

CHUNGKING, China, July 28—Chinese troops recaptured the airbase city of Kweilin yesterday and seized its three former American airfields from the Japanese, the Chinese High Command said tonight. The victory ended a six-week battle.

Kweilin, walled capital of Kwangsi Province, once was the biggest United States airbase in South-Central China. It had been occupied by the Japanese since last November. Its recapture was the most significant victory in the recent comeback of the Chinese armies.

Generalissimo Chiang Kai-shek's veterans smashed into the rubbled streets of Kweilin, 360 miles southeast of Chungking, at 4 P. M. yesterday after mowing down the defenders of the city's south and west gates. Most of the Japanese garrison had fled and enemy rearguard remnants swiftly were routed from machine-gun nests in cellars and on roofs, a communiqué said.

The Japanese, headquarters added, withdrew to the northwest to escape annihilation. Their escape route northeastward to Hengyang was severed several days ago. The Chinese said: "Our troops are in hot pursuit."

Kweilin, abandoned by the United States Fourteenth Air Force eight months ago, was the third former American airbase recovered in three days by the Chinese, whose current drive is rapidly strengthening American air power on the Asiatic mainland.

Continued on Page 3, Column 5

CRIPPLED WARSHIPS OF JAPANESE NAVY SMASHED BY FLIERS

2 Battleships and 3 Cruisers Set Afire in Saturday Strike by the Third Fleet

HYUGA IS FOUND SUNK

Returning U. S. Pilots Report Waters Off Kure Strewn With Burning Vessels

By Wireless to The New York Times.

GUAM, Sunday, July 29—Two Japanese battleships, the Haruna and Ise, and three cruisers were set afire and a third battleship, the Hyuga, which was heavily damaged on Tuesday, was found to be resting on the bottom at her anchorage as United States Third Fleet carrier planes struck heavily Saturday at crippled remnants of the Japanese Navy in the Inland Sea.

An aircraft carrier also was further damaged.

Fleet Admiral Chester W. Nimitz today announced the results of the strike, which were incomplete. No reports had yet been received from British carrier pilots, who also participated.

Enemy Air Opposition Sporadic

The enemy's air opposition was sporadic, with American fighters shooting down one Japanese plane near Task Force 38, another eighteen near the target areas and destroying seventy-five on the ground. Fifty-six other parked enemy aircraft were damaged.

[Pilots returning from the Saturday strike reported waters off the Kure naval base littered with burning ships, and the dispatches said every major Japanese warship was believed to have been put out of action for the duration of the war, The United Press stated.]

The Third Fleet assault was directed at Japanese shipping between the once great ports of Kobe and Kure.

Pilots reported that the Hyuga, a modernized battleship with carrier type runway aft permitting it to handle aircraft, was on the bottom, water lapping over her main deck amidships.

It was disclosed also that Saturday's aerial assault, resulted in the sinking of three submarines, presumably in dry dock, and damage to four destroyers, two destroyer escorts, two medium-size freighter transports, three small cargo ships and an unidentified vessel.

Five Warships Left Burning

Whether these ships were among those damaged in the Tuesday attack, which battered twenty-three warships, was not revealed. However, it is definite that yesterday's attack further damaged six warships on Tuesday, the battleships Haruna and Ise, the cruisers Tone, Aoba and Oyodo and the escort carrier Kaiyo. All ships except the carrier were left burning in the latest assault.

Thus it seems that Admiral Halsey is well along toward his objective—the neutralization of Japan's remaining naval warships in order to provide a thoroughly clear field for future amphibious

Continued on Page 3, Column 2

BOMBER HITS EMPIRE STATE BUILDING, SETTING IT AFIRE AT THE 79TH FLOOR; 13 DEAD, 26 HURT; WIDE AREA ROCKED

WHERE BOMBER CRASHED INTO EMPIRE STATE BUILDING

Hole torn between seventy-eighth and seventy-ninth floors. The New York Times (by Slato)

B-29'S FIRE 6 CITIES IN PROMISED BLOWS

Oil Refinery Target on Honshu Added to List LeMay Gave Japanese in Advance

By Wireless to The New York Times.

GUAM, Sunday, July 29—The Twentieth Air Force early today bombed six out of eleven Japanese cities that hardly twenty-four hours previously had been told that they were on a list of enemy communities marked for aerial destruction by Superfortresses.

Seven task forces of the B-29 bombers, totaling 550 to 600 planes, dropped more than 3,500 tons of incendiaries on the six industrial centers situated from Shikoku in the south to northern Honshu and demolition bombs on an oil refinery near Osaka.

[Gen. Douglas MacArthur reported Okinawa-based Army planes had sunk enemy shipping in Japan's Inland Sea area. He disclosed that our new B-32 super-bomber has been in action since May against the foe on Formosa and along the China coast.]

One of the B-29 task forces, sent

Continued on Page 4, Column 1

Catholic War Relief Office Is Chief Victim of Tragedy

By LARRY RESNER

An agency that has been in the vanguard of supplying aid and comfort to thousands of homeless and destitute persons in the war zones became yesterday, through one of those curious quirks of fate, the victim of the worst local tragedy of the war. The point of greatest impact of the low-flying bomber that crashed into the Empire State Building was at the seventy-ninth floor, where the principal tenant was the War Relief Services of the National Catholic Welfare Conference.

Throughout the war years, this agency has sent many field representatives into the lands laid waste by war to work with other relief and welfare agencies in helping save victims.

And only yesterday, as the bomber struck and destroyed their office, the reduced Saturday staff of workers was busily engaged in arranging the final details of a trip to Europe on Tuesday of two of their principal functionaries.

Only five of an estimated working staff of fifteen to twenty persons in the office, including men and women, were known to have escaped the flames that swept the skyscraper floor as the gasoline of the crashing plane exploded.

W. Paul Dearing, correspondent here for The Buffalo Courier-Express and publicity director of the War Relief Services for the last year, either jumped or was blown from his seventy-ninth-floor office to his death in a ledge on the sev-

Continued on Page 32, Column 3

SURVIVOR LIKENS CRASH TO A QUAKE

Building Moved Twice, Then Settled, Says Occupant Who Felt Shocks in China

By ALEXANDER FEINBERG

The towering Empire State Building that is a city of 102 stories, reaching 1,250 feet high, "moved" twice yesterday when struck by the bomber and then it "settled." That was a dread moment for one who had felt that double movement and the settling many times before.

Recently returned from China after twenty-seven years, the man who told of his sensations when the B-25 struck said the impact was precisely that of an earthquake, to which he is no stranger. Preferring not to give his name, he said he was in an office on the sixty-eighth floor of the building when he felt the double "move-

Continued on Page 28, Column 1

Red Cross and Hospital Groups Speed to Aid of Victims, Rescuers

The last fireman had barely leaped from his truck to the ragged four-alarm blaze caused by the bomber crash in the Empire State Building when hospital disaster units and two Red Cross Service canteen wagons were on the scene to aid the victims and rescuers of the catastrophe.

While fifteen Red Cross aides set up shop and dispensed hot coffee and doughnuts to the toiling fire fighters and others helping them, two disaster units from Bellevue Hospital, replete with the latest equipment, were making their way into the upper reaches of the building to assist in the rescue work.

Only twelve minutes elapsed between the sounding of the first alarm at 9:49 and the fourth alarm and from the moment the Telegraph Bureau at Police Headquarters received the first report made possible by the Potsdam proclamation. [4:5.]

the city's fire-fighting equipment, a small army of police and squads of Army and Navy units, mostly military police and shore patrols, moved with clock-like precision through the fog-shrouded streets.

The fire sirens screeched constantly as apparatus sped to the scene. The second alarm hit at 9:57 A. M., the third at 10 A. M. and the last at 10:01 A. M. After that there were other calls but only for specialized equipment.

The four alarms brought to the scene forty-one pieces of fire-fighting apparatus, including "walkie-talkie" radio units. All were under the immediate command of Fire Commissioner Patrick Walsh. Almost simultaneously the Police Department's ranking officers dispatched more than 400 policemen

Continued on Page 32, Column 6

B-25 CRASHES IN FOG

Hole 18 by 20 Feet Torn Through North Wall by Terrific Impact

BLAZING 'GAS' SCATTERED

Flames Put Out in 40-Minute Fight—2 Women Survive Fall in Elevator

By FRANK ADAMS

A twin-engined B-25 Army bomber, lost in a blinding fog, crashed into the Empire State Building at a point 915 feet above the street level at 9:49 A. M. yesterday. Thirteen persons, including the three occupants of the plane and ten persons at work within the building, were killed in the catastrophe, and twenty-six were injured.

Although the crash and the fire that followed wrecked most of the seventy-eighth and seventy-ninth floors of the structure, causing damage estimated at $500,000, Lieut. Gen. Hugh A. Drum, president of the Empire State, Inc., Corporation, said last night that an inspection by the city's building department and by its engineers and architects showed that the structural soundness of the building had not been impaired.

Landing Advice Disregarded

The plane, en route from Bedford, Mass., to Newark on a cross-country mission, had flown over La Guardia Field a few minutes before the crash, and its pilot, Lieut. Col. William F. Smith Jr., deputy commander of the 457th Bomber Group and recently decorated for his service overseas, was advised by the control tower to land. Instead he asked for the weather at Newark Airport and headed in that direction.

Horror-stricken occupants of the building, alarmed by the roar of engines, ran to the windows just in time to see the plane loom out of the gray mists that swathed the upper floors of the structure. The plane was banked at an angle of about fifteen degrees as Colonel Smith swung it in a curve out of the northeast.

It crashed with a terrifying impact midway along the north or Thirty-fourth Street wall of the building. Its wings were sheared off by the impact, but the motors and fuselage ripped a hole eighteen feet wide and twenty feet high in the outer wall of the seventy-eighth and seventy-ninth floors of the structure.

Brilliant orange flames shot as high as the observatory on the eighty-sixth floor of the building, 1,050 feet above Fifth Avenue, as the gasoline tanks of the plane exploded. For a moment watchers in the street below saw the interior brilliantly illumined by the flames. Then it disappeared again in gray murk and the smoke of the burning plane.

Motor Hits Another Building

One of the plane's two motors hurtled clear across the seventy-eighth floor, tore a hole in the south wall of the building, and plummeted to the roof of the twelve-story office building at 10 West Thirty-third Street, where it started a fire that demolished the penthouse of Henry Hering, noted sculptor, with resulting damage estimated at $75,000.

A propeller was imbedded in the wall of the Empire State Building; the other motor and part of the landing gear crashed into an elevator shaft, where they fell to the sub-cellar 1,000 feet below, and other sections of the fuselage were blown as high as the eighty-sixth floor observatory. The steel girder at the seventy-ninth floor level was bent inward eighteen inches by the shock.

Cascading torrents of flaming gasoline poured through the seventy-eighth and seventy-ninth floors, setting fire to everything that was combustible. The burning fuel ran down stair wells into hallways as far as the seventy-fifth floor, while choking fumes

Continued on Page 25, Column 1

War News Summarized

SUNDAY, JULY 29, 1945

The United States Senate ratified, 89 to 2, the United Nations Security Charter. The two Senators who voted against ratification were William Langer of North Dakota and Henrik Shipstead of Minnesota, both Republicans. [1:1.]

Two battleships and three cruisers, all previously damaged, were hit again in the latest Third Fleet attack on the Inland Sea area, Admiral Nimitz disclosed, and it was found another battleship had been sunk. Returning pilots reported that the Japanese Navy probably was out of action for the rest of the war. [1:4.]

Between 550 and 600 Superfortresses set fire to six of the eleven Japanese cities warned previously of their coming destruction. [1:5; map P. 2.]

Chinese forces took Kweilin and three former United States airfields. Other Chinese pressed toward Kukong, 120 miles north of Canton, gaining thirty miles in two days. [1:2-3; map P. 3.]

The British in Burma reported that the Japanese Twenty-eighth Army had been annihilated with more than 5,500 killed and the remnant fleeing toward Thailand. [3:1.]

Prime Minister Attlee and six new Ministers took the oath of office in London. [5:1.]

A Polish Government delegation was in Potsdam pleading for a western frontier running along the Oder and Neisse Rivers. Meanwhile, the conference was resumed with Mr. Attlee and Foreign Secretary Bevin in the places of Messrs. Churchill and Anthony Eden. [1:2-3; map P. 5.]

General Minami, chief of Tokyo's would-be totalitarian party, said Japan would be ready to discuss peace when East Asia was free from British-American "colonial exploitation." [9:1.]

Captain Zacharias, United States naval spokesman, broadcast to Japan a declaration that peace with Japan had now been

A Polish Government delegation was in Potsdam pleading for a western frontier running along the Oder and Neisse Rivers. Meanwhile, the conference was resumed with Mr. Attlee and Foreign Secretary Bevin in the places of Messrs. Churchill and Anthony Eden. [1:2-3; map P. 5.]

Michel Clemenceau accused Marshal Pétain at the latter's treason trial of having been indirectly responsible for handing over Georges Mandel, former Minister of Colonies, to the Germans who killed him. [12:1.]

"All the News That's Fit to Print"

The New York Times.

LATE CITY EDITION
Partly cloudy, less humid today.
Cloudy and warm tomorrow.
Temperatures Yesterday—Max., 72; Min., 66
Sunrise today, 5:57 A. M.; Sunset, 8:06 P. M.

Copyright, 1945, by The New York Times Company.

VOL. XCIV..No. 31,972.

Entered as Second-Class Matter,
Postoffice, New York, N. Y.

NEW YORK, TUESDAY, AUGUST 7, 1945.

THREE CENTS IN NEW YORK CITY

FIRST ATOMIC BOMB DROPPED ON JAPAN; MISSILE IS EQUAL TO 20,000 TONS OF TNT; TRUMAN WARNS FOE OF A 'RAIN OF RUIN'

HIRAM W. JOHNSON, REPUBLICAN DEAN IN THE SENATE, DIES

Isolationist Helped Prevent U. S. Entry Into League—Opposed World Charter

CALIFORNIA EX-GOVERNOR

Ran for Vice President With Theodore Roosevelt in '12 —In Washington Since '17

Special to THE NEW YORK TIMES.

WASHINGTON, Aug. 6—Senator Hiram Warren Johnson of California, lifelong isolationist who helped prevent this country's entry into the League of Nations and fought all "foreign entanglements" through a second World War, died in his sleep this morning at Bethesda Naval Hospital, nine days after, ill but consistent, he had paired his vote against ratification of the United Nations Charter. Death was caused by a thrombosis of a cerebral artery. Mrs. Johnson was with him when the end came.

When word reached the Capitol of the passing of the oldest member of the Senate in point of service, save Senator Kenneth McKellar, the President pro tempore, the mourning was deep. With great personal affection colleagues paid humble tribute to his integrity of character, his liberalism and his steadfastness to his ideals and convictions. They joined in declaring that the country had lost a great statesman.

Senator Johnson, who was serving the fourth year of his fifth term in the Senate, would have been 79 years old on Sept. 2. Although his health had been failing during the last two years and though the thundering voice which had conveyed his eloquence through innumerable stirring debates had become little more than a whisper, friends believed he planned to seek a sixth term in 1947.

He went to the hospital July 18. Five days before that he had cast the lone vote in the Foreign Relations Committee, of which he was the ranking minority member, against reporting the new World Charter to the Senate without change. He did not participate in the floor debate on this document, which won Senate approval by a vote of 82—2. However, he clashed spiritedly with colleagues while the hearings were in progress.

Funeral arrangements awaited the arrival of the Senator's son, Lieut. Col. Hiram W. Johnson Jr., who was flying here from California.

Capper Becomes the Dean

The death of Senator Johnson made Senator Arthur Capper of Kansas, who last month marked his eightieth birthday, the Republican dean of the Senate. It also elevated him to the ranking minority membership on the Foreign Relations Committee, with which Senator Johnson had been so conspicuously identified through the many years of his unshaken position on foreign policy. Mr. Capper, too, with Senators McKellar, Carter Glass of Virginia, David I. Walsh of Massachusetts and Peter G. Gerry, was in the League fight of 1919 and 1920. He supported it, with reservations.

The career of Senator Johnson, from his entrance into the Senate from the Governorship of California in March of 1917, was one distinctly lacking in compromise or reservation. In 1912 he had bolted his party with Theodore Roosevelt and had become his running mate on the Bull Moose ticket. In 1932 he again bolted to support Franklin D. Roosevelt for the Presidency but broke bitterly with the President when he ran for his third term.

In 1919 Mr. Johnson joined with Senators Lodge, Knox and others

Continued on Page 23, Column 4

Jet Plane Explosion Kills Major Bong, Top U. S. Ace

Flier Who Downed 40 Japanese Craft, Sent Home to Be 'Safe,' Was Flying New 'Shooting Star' as a Test Pilot

By The United Press.

BURBANK, Calif., Aug. 6—Maj. Richard Bong, America's greatest air ace, died today in the flaming wreckage of a jet propelled fighter plane which crashed while he was testing it.

Only 24 years old, he wore twenty-six decorations including the nation's highest award, the Congressional Medal of Honor. He had survived countless air battles and shot down forty Japanese planes without a scratch.

The knowledge he gained in those battles was too valuable to risk, so he was brought home to "safe" duty. He was on that "safe" duty today when his P-80, the Shooting Star, hurtled over a clump of trees and burst like a bomb in a field.

Witnesses did not agree on the cause of the crash. One Army flier said that Major Bong overshot the Lockheed airport. Another witness, John McKinney of North Hollywood reported that he saw something fall out of the plane's tail.

"The plane started to wobble up and down, then went into a left bank and hit the ground," he stated. "It exploded and burned and scattered wreckage over about a block square."

Major Bong was trying to get out of the ship when it crashed. He had released the escape hatch and was partly clear. He had pulled the ripcord to his parachute, and the silken folds lay about the body as the flames swept over it.

With a roaring sigh, the plane, like a giant blowtorch, shot over the airport just before 3 P. M. and then lurched over the trees and nosed down into the field, a mile away.

Smoke and flame surged up and crowds rushed from the airport. By the time anyone could reach the scene the ship had been almost consumed.

The crash scene was near the intersection of Cahuenga and Oxnard Boulevards and barely out-

Continued on page 15, Column 2

MORRIS IS ACCUSED OF 'TAKING A WALK'

Fusion Official 'Sad to Part Company'—McGoldrick Sees Only Tammany Aided

The No Deal ticket, headed by Council President Newbold Morris, "can only serve the interests of Tammany Hall," Controller Joseph D. McGoldrick, candidate for reelection on the Republican-Liberal-Fusion party slate, declared yesterday in a fresh attack on the third-party ticket injected over the week-end into the city Mayoralty campaign.

A short while later Gabriel A. Wechsler, general secretary of the City Fusion party, which supported Mayor La Guardia and Mr. Morris in previous city campaigns, accused Mr. Morris of "taking a walk away from the good government forces."

To both charges Mr. Morris declared he would stand on his statement of Sunday that he was not interested in "just taking votes" away from Judge Jonah J. Goldstein. Republican-Liberal-Fusion candidate for Mayor, or from William O'Dwyer, his Democratic-American Labor party opponent.

"I have no comment," he said, "since I stand on my statement of Sunday. We are waging an affirmative campaign."

Informed that Hyman Blumberg,

Continued on Page 19, Column 6

CHINESE WIN MORE OF 'INVASION COAST'

Smash Into Port 121 Miles Southwest of Canton—Big Area Open for Landing

By The Associated Press.

CHUNGKING, China, Aug. 6—Chinese troops have broken into the South China port of Yeungkong and cleared a fifty-mile stretch of the Chinese "invasion coast" west of Hong Kong, Generalissimo Chiang Kai-shek's headquarters said today.

Swaying block-by-block street fighting is raging in the strategic coastal highway town, 121 miles southwest of Canton, a communiqué said.

By breaking into Yeungkong Chinese forces won control of a fifty-mile coastal stretch leading west to Tinpak, which lies east of Luichow Peninsula on the South China Sea. The coastal area now is open to a virtually unopposed landing should American forces choose it for a staging point for supplies to the armies of South China.

West of Luichow Peninsula another 145-mile coastal stretch extending to the Indo-China frontier is under Chinese control and observers believe the Chinese soon may launch a concerted drive from the west and east that would seal off the Japanese on the Luichow

Continued on Page 2, Column 7

Turks Talk War if Russia Presses; Prefer Vain Battle to Surrender

By SAM POPE BREWER
By Wireless to THE NEW YORK TIMES.

ANKARA, Turkey, Aug. 6—Russo-Turkish relations weigh heavy on Turkish minds these days. All leading editors commented today on various aspects of the Russian claims against Turkey.

The Potsdam conference leaves the situation virtually unchanged so far as the Turks can see, but they seem to agree that they would go to war, however hopeless such a war might be, rather than yield before the threat of force. Suggestions from London and Washington that the Russians have been asked to moderate their demands give little reassurance here.

The Potsdam communiqué created more confusion than confidence and the Turks are still trying to decide whether the fact that the conference did not deal with certain specific questions means that it was a failure.

Many point out that all the really thorny questions still are unsettled. The Turks probably do not see a relative importance among world problems of Russian demands on Turkey, but point out that the important question of principle is involved. The general and apparently-official argument is that the status of the Straits cannot be modified by a bilateral agreement but must be discussed at a conference of the signatories of the Montreux Convention, with America replacing Japan. The signatories were Great Britain, France, Russia, Japan, Turkey, Greece, Rumania, Yugoslavia and Bulgaria.

The grounds for the Russian claims to Kars and Ardahan are not clear, but throughout the Near and Mideast in recent months

Continued on Page 15, Column 1

KYUSHU CITY RAZED

Kenney's Planes Blast Tarumizu in Record Blow From Okinawa

ROCKET SITE IS SEEN

125 B-29's Hit Japan's Toyokawa Naval Arsenal in Demolition Strike

By FRANK L. KLUCKHOHN
By Wireless to THE NEW YORK TIMES.

MANILA, Tuesday, Aug. 7—More than 400 fighters and bombers, speeding at chimney-top level for two hours Sunday over Tarumizu in southern Kyushu in the largest single attack launched by Gen. George C. Kenney's Far East Air Forces to date, leveled that city's munitions factories and aircraft and munitions storage depots and waterfront installations.

Rockets and demolition bombs were poured by waves of B-26 Invaders, B-25 Mitchells and Mustangs and Thunderbolts of the Fifth and Seventh Air Forces from Okinawa, supported by a few B-24 Liberators carrying big bombs.

[Tarumizu, about 350 miles from Okinawa, appeared to be a site at which the Japanese might be preparing a rocket campaign against the American base, said a United Press dispatch. FEAF pilots reported seeing in the area, which has extensive cave construction, what seemed to be Japanese robot planes and also a huge catapult-like machine, extending over the water, that might be a rocket launcher.

[About 125 B-29's hit the Toyokawa naval arsenal of Japan in a demolition bombing Tuesday noon, Strategic Air Forces headquarters at Guam reported.] The planes over Tarumizu met scant resistance, as our fliers took their time to assure the highest

Continued on Page 11, Column 2

REPORT BY BRITAIN

'By God's Mercy' We Beat Nazis to Bomb, Churchill Says

ROOSEVELT AID CITED

Raiders Wrecked Norse Laboratory in Race for Key to Victory

The text of Mr. Churchill's statement is on Page 8.

By CLIFTON DANIEL

LONDON, Aug. 6—The hitherto secret details of the grisly race between Germany and the Allies to find a weapon so destructive that it would insure absolute victory—a race not only between scientists but also between under-cover agents—were recounted in London tonight after it had been disclosed that the first atomic bomb had been dropped on Japan.

"By God's mercy British and American science outpaced all German efforts," said a statement by former Prime Minister Churchill written before he left office and issued from 10 Downing Street by his successor, Clement R. Attlee.

"The possession of these powers by the Germans at any time might have altered the result of the war," Mr. Churchill said, "and profound anxiety was felt by those who were informed."

The British Isles, which endured the terrors of flying bombs and rockets, did hear repeated rumors that Adolf Hitler's V-2 weapon was to be an atomic bomb,' but they never knew until tonight how close they came to being the first victims of its destructive power. Much less did they suspect what

Continued on Page 9, Column 1

Steel Tower 'Vaporized' In Trial of Mighty Bomb

Scientists Awe-Struck as Blinding Flash Lighted New Mexico Desert and Great Cloud Bore 40,000 Feet Into Sky

By LEWIS WOOD
Special to THE NEW YORK TIMES.

WASHINGTON, Aug. 6—A blinding flash many times as brilliant as the midday sun and a massive, multi-colored cloud boiling up 40,000 feet into the air accompanied the first test firing of an atomic bomb on July 16, three weeks ago today. Set in the remote desert-lands of New Mexico, the experiment was seen against a wild background where rain poured in torrents, and lightning pierced the sky up to the zero hour of the explosion at 5:30 A. M.

A steel tower from which the atomic weapon hung was vaporized. In its place was only a huge, sloping crater. At the moment of the explosion a mountain range three miles distant stood out sharply in brilliant light.

"Then," said the War Department in a description, "came a tremendous, sustained roar and a heavy pressure wave which knocked down two men outside the control tower (10,000 yards, or more than five miles, away.)"

Before the detonation scientists waited in tense expectancy. Minutes lengthened seemingly to hours. Lying face downward, with their feet toward the steel tower, the watchers waited, nearly breathless. They were "reaching into the unknown" and did not know what would happen.

On the instant that all was over these men leaped to their feet. The terrible tension ended, they shook hands, embraced each other and shouted in glee. Behind their triumph was sober consciousness of possessing the means to "insure the speedy conclusion of the war and save thousands of American lives."

The scene of the great drama was the Alamogordo Air Base, 120 miles southeast of Albuquerque. Here the scientists strove to unlock the secret upon which $2,000,000,000 had been spent.

Graphic word pictures of the

Continued on Page 5, Column 1

ATOM BOMBS MADE IN 3 HIDDEN 'CITIES'

Secrecy on Weapon So Great That Not Even Workers Knew of Their Product

By JAY WALZ
Special to THE NEW YORK TIMES.

WASHINGTON, Aug. 6—The War Department revealed today how three "hidden cities" with a total population of 100,000 inhabitants sprang into being as a result of the $2,000,000,000 atomic bomb project, how they did their work without knowing what it was all about, and how they kept the biggest secret of the war.

One of these, Oak Ridge, situated where only oak and pine trees had dotted small farms before, is today the fifth largest city in Tennessee. Its population of 75,000 persons has thirteen supermarkets, nine drug stores and seven theatres.

A second town of 7,000 was built for reasons of isolation and security on a New Mexico mesa. The third, named Richland Village, houses 17,000 men, women and children on remote banks of the Columbia River in the State of Washington.

None of the people, who came to these developments from homes all the way from Maine to California, had the slightest idea of what they were making in the gigantic Gov-

Continued on Page 3, Column 2

TRAINS CANCELED IN STRICKEN AREA

Traffic Around Hiroshima Is Disrupted — Japanese Still Sift Havoc by Split Atoms

By The United Press.

WASHINGTON, Aug. 6—The Osaka radio, without referring to the atomic bomb dropped on Hiroshima, hinted tonight at the terrific damage it must have caused by announcing that train service in the Hiroshima and other areas had been canceled.

First mention of the bomb came in a Japanese Domei agency dispatch announcing that President Truman and Prime Minister Attlee had disclosed that the new missile had been dropped on Hiroshima.

The Office of War Information began telling the Japanese today what hit them. OWI branch transmitters in San Francisco, Hawaii and Saipan beamed President Truman's statement on the atomic bomb to Japan.

Edward Barrett, director of the OWI's overseas branch, said that the President's announcement and related information on the atomic bomb will dominate the OWI's normal Japanese transmissions for the next several days.

LONDON, Tuesday, Aug. 7 (U.P.)—The Japanese Domei news agency, in a dispatch recorded by the British radio, said that the new

Continued on Page 7, Column 3

NEW AGE USHERED

Day of Atomic Energy Hailed by President, Revealing Weapon

HIROSHIMA IS TARGET

'Impenetrable' Cloud of Dust Hides City After Single Bomb Strikes

Truman, Stimson statements on atomic bomb, Page 4.

By SIDNEY SHALETT
Special to THE NEW YORK TIMES.

WASHINGTON, Aug. 6—The White House and War Department announced today that an atomic bomb, possessing more power than 20,000 tons of TNT, a destructive force equal to the load of 2,000 B-29's and more than 2,000 times the blast power of what previously was the world's most devastating bomb, had been dropped on Japan.

The announcement, first given to the world in utmost solemnity by President Truman, made it plain that one of the scientific landmarks of the century had been passed, and that the "age of atomic energy," which can be a tremendous force for the advancement of civilization as well as for destruction, was at hand.

At 10:45 o'clock this morning, a statement by the President was issued at the White House that sixteen hours earlier—about the time that citizens on the Eastern seaboard were sitting down to their Sunday suppers—an American plane had dropped the single atomic bomb on the Japanese city of Hiroshima, an important army center.

Japanese Solemnly Warned

What happened at Hiroshima is not yet known. The War Department said it, "as yet was unable to make an accurate report" because "an impenetrable cloud of dust and smoke" masked the target area from reconnaissance planes. The Secretary of War will release the story "as soon as accurate details of the results of the bombing become available."

But in a statement vividly describing the results of the first test of the atomic bomb in New Mexico, the War Department told how an immense steel tower had been "vaporized" by the tremendous explosion, how a 40,000-foot cloud rushed into the sky, and two observers were knocked down at a point 10,000 yards away. And President Truman solemnly warned:

"It was to spare the Japanese people from utter destruction that the ultimatum of July 26 was issued at Potsdam. Their leaders promptly rejected that ultimatum. If they do not now accept our terms, they may expect a rain of ruin from the air the like of which has never been seen on this earth."

Most Closely Guarded Secret

The President referred to the joint statement issued by the heads of the American, British and Chinese Governments, in which terms of surrender were outlined to the Japanese and warning given that rejection would mean complete destruction of Japan's power to make war.

The principal character in the dramatic story of the long search for a method of releasing atomic energy is Dr. Lise Meitner, a woman physicist whom the Nazis expelled from Germany as a "non-Aryan." With her associates, Dr. Otto Hahn and Dr. F. Strassmann, both chemists, she had been working in the Kaiser Wilhelm Institute in Berlin, bombarding uranium atoms with neutrons and then submitting the results to chemical analysis.

That the new bomb may be far from its maximum devastating potential was indicated by the War Department's statement that said:

"The energy we are now able to utilize in the atomic bombs, at 100 per cent efficiency, constitutes

Continued on Page 2, Column 2

War News Summarized

TUESDAY, AUGUST 7, 1945

One bomb hit Japan on Sunday night, but it struck with the force of 20,000 tons of TNT. Where it landed had been the city of Hiroshima; what is there now has not yet been learned.

The attack, dramatically announced by President Truman sixteen hours after the missile had struck, was with an atomic bomb, a "harnessing of the basic power of the universe," he said. "The force from which the sun draws its power has been loosed against those who brought war to the Far East. And the end is not yet."

Details of the missile are closely guarded, but the 125,000 workers who saw materials pour into their factories knew anything go out. The bomb is the result of pooling British-American scientific knowledge begun in 1940. "We have spent two billion dollars on the greatest scientific gamble in history and won," Mr. Truman said, and warned:

"We are now prepared to obliterate more rapidly and completely every productive enterprise the Japanese have above ground in any city. It was to spare the Japanese public from utter destruction that the ultimatum of July 26 was issued at Potsdam. If they do not now accept our terms they may expect a rain of ruin from the air." Secretary of War Stimson detailed the story of research and production and forecast improvements in the destructiveness of the "atomic bomb" several times. Congress will be asked to establish a committee to control peacetime use.

Hiroshima was a major military target, a city of 318,000 persons thickly settled around a quartermaster's depot, an embarkation point, armament and airplane parts plants. [All the foregoing 1:8.]

All production was in the United States at two plants at Oak Ridge, near Knoxville, Tenn., and one at Richland, Wash. A scientific laboratory was maintained in Sante Fe, N. M. [1:6.]

Former President Churchill told of Britain's part, including costly analysis of German "heavy water" plants and the race to outstrip the Nazis. He praised American scientific achievement and gave full credit to President Roosevelt and his advisers. [1:5.]

Tokyo made no mention of what had happened to Hiroshima but rail service in that area was canceled. [1:7.]

Okinawa sent out 400 planes that left Tarumizu, on Kyushu's Kagoshima Bay, in flaming wreckage. About 125 "Superforts" bombed Toyokawa naval arsenal by daylight. [1:4; map p. 11.]

Chinese troops have broken into the port of Yeungkong and have cleared a large stretch of the south China coast west of Hong Kong and east of the Luichow Peninsula. [1:3; map P. 2.]

Moscow, moving to implement Potsdam decisions, has resumed diplomatic relations with Finland and Rumania. [11:4.]

The Germans received an opportunity to develop democratic talents when the United States and Great Britain authorized local trade unions and political parties in their zones of occupation. [12:2.]

France is expected to ratify the United Nations Charter and then the Bretton Woods monetary plan in the near future. [13:6.] Marshal Pétain was accused of having asked Hitler for help in regaining France's colonies. [13:1.]

Argentina has lifted the state of siege in effect since Pearl Harbor. [14:8.]

Reich Exile Emerges as Heroine In Denial to Nazis of Atom's Secret

Special to THE NEW YORK TIMES.

WASHINGTON, Aug. 6—How Germany twice narrowly missed the secret of harnessing atomic energy by splitting uranium atoms and releasing the most powerful destructive force on earth was recalled today in War Department reports on the atomic bomb.

Development of the bomb after more than ten years of experimentation and research marks the first time that Prof. Albert Einstein's theory of relativity has been put to practical use outside the laboratory; the equation by which he showed the existence of a definite relationship of matter, energy and the velocity of light.

That the new bomb may be far

As the War Department tells the story:

"To their amazement, they found the element barium in the debris of the smashed uranium atoms.

only one-tenth of 1 per cent of the total energy present in the material. But even one-hundredth of 1 per cent is still the most destructive force by far on this earth."

The principal character in the dramatic story of the long search for a method of releasing atomic energy is Dr. Lise Meitner, a woman physicist whom the Nazis expelled from Germany as a "non-Aryan." With her associates, Dr. Otto Hahn and Dr. F. Strassmann, both chemists, she had been working in the Kaiser Wilhelm Institute in Berlin, bombarding uranium atoms with neutrons and then submitting the results to chemical analysis.

What is this terrible new weapon, which the War Department also calls the "Cosmic Bomb"? It is the harnessing of the energy of the atom, which is the basic power of the universe. As President Truman said, "The force from which the sun draws its power has been loosed against those who brought war to the Far East."

"Atomic fission" was involved

Continued on Page 2, Column 2

Continued on Page 7, Column 1

139

"All the News
That's Fit to Print"

The New York Times.

LATE CITY EDITION
Thunderstorms, warm, humid; clear
and cooler tonight. Fair tomorrow.
Temperatures Yesterday—Max., 84; Min., 71
Sunrise today, 6:06 A. M.; Sunset, 7:55 P. M.

Copyright, 1945, by The New York Times Company.

VOL. XCIV..No. 31,980.   Entered as Second-Class Matter,
Postoffice, New York, N. Y.   NEW YORK, WEDNESDAY, AUGUST 15, 1945.   THREE CENTS IN NEW YORK CITY

JAPAN SURRENDERS, END OF WAR!
EMPEROR ACCEPTS ALLIED RULE;
M'ARTHUR SUPREME COMMANDER;
OUR MANPOWER CURBS VOIDED

HIRING MADE LOCAL

Communities, Labor and Management Will Unite Efforts

6,000,000 AFFECTED

Draft Quotas Cut, Services to Drop 5,500,000 in 18 Months

By LEWIS WOOD
Special to The New York Times.

WASHINGTON, Aug. 14—All manpower controls over employers and workers were abolished tonight, the War Manpower Commission announced, enabling employers to hire men where and when they pleased.

The end of the war threw on the Government the difficult task of trying to readjust perhaps 8,000,000 war workers into new employment. Nevertheless, the WMC said, all its facilities would be used to help workers find new places, with preference going to veterans, displaced migratory war workers and other preferentials.

At the same time President Truman announced that monthly inductions into the Army would be immediately slashed from 80,000 to 50,000, and said 5,000,000 to 5,500,000 men probably would be released from the service within the next year or eighteen months.

The induction rate, 50,000 monthly, the President said, would be sufficient to maintain the occupation forces and allow men of long service overseas to return to their homes.

Under the WMC program, the manpower controls are to be lifted at once and voluntary community action to hurry reconversion will be substituted. In every community, the number of displaced workers and returning veterans will be ascertained in cooperation with local management-labor groups. Full facilities of the United States Employment Service offices will be made available to all employers. Service for veterans will be enlarged.

The WMC program embraced these seven points:

1. All manpower controls are to be lifted at once and in their place voluntary community action to

Continued on Page 13, Column 3

Hirohito on Radio; Minister Ends Life

The Japanese Domei agency said at 11 o'clock last night that Emperor Hirohito had been "graciously pleased to personally read an imperial rescript accepting the Potsdam declaration."

The Domei English-language wireless dispatch, directed to the United States and recorded by the Federal Communications Commission, said that the Emperor had read the rescript over a nation-wide broadcast at noon Wednesday, Tokyo time.

Previously Domei had reported that weeping people had gathered before the Imperial Palace and "bowed to the very ground" in shame.

Japanese War Minister Korechika Anami committed suicide, Domei reported this morning. The wireless dispatch, directed to the American public, said Anami had taken his life at his "official residence" to "atone for his failure in accomplishing his duties as His Majesty's Minister."

A complete story appears on Page 3.

LIFE INSURANCE LOANS, $1500 up, low interest. Refinanced directly through HUDSON COUNTY NATIONAL BANK, 40 Journal Square, Jersey City 4, N. J.—Advt.

Third Fleet Fells 5 Planes Since End

By The Associated Press.

GUAM, Wednesday, Aug. 15—Japanese aircraft are approaching the Pacific Fleet off Tokyo and are being shot down, Admiral Chester W. Nimitz announced today.

Five enemy planes have been destroyed since noon today, Japanese time, or 11 P. M. EWT. Gen. Douglas MacArthur has been requested to tell the Japanese that American defense measures require the Third Fleet to destroy any Japanese planes approaching United States warships.

GUAM, Wednesday, Aug. 15 (U.P)—When Admiral Halsey received word of Japan's capitulation today, he sent this message to his fliers:

"It looks like the war is over, but if any enemy planes appear shoot them down in friendly fashion."

SECRETS OF RADAR GIVEN TO WORLD

Its Role in War and Uses for Peacetime Revealed in Washington and London

By WILLIAM S. WHITE
Special to The New York Times.

WASHINGTON, Aug. 14—The great drama of radar, the war's most powerful "secret weapon" until the atomic bomb was devised, was displayed before a world audience today.

The Joint Board on Scientific Information Policy permitted the Office of Scientific Research and Development, the War Department and the Navy Department to tell the story of a device of which millions had known vaguely for two years, a device which at least three times stood between survival or defeat by the Axis powers for the United States and Great Britain.

It was radar, short for "radio detection and range," that helped the small surviving British air squadrons to beat the German blitz of 1940, that not only saving the home islands but preserving them as the essential Anglo-American base from which the continental invasion went forward on June 6, 1944.

It was radar, which "sees through" the heaviest fog and the blackest night," that more than any other factor broke in 1942 the German submarine threat in the Atlantic which was threatening to starve and strangle the British homeland.

And it was radar that permitted the remnants of the blasted United States Pacific Fleet to stay alive

Continued on Page 14, Column 3

ALL CITY 'LETS GO'

Hundreds of Thousands Roar Joy After Victory Flash Is Received

TIMES SQ. IS JAMMED

Police Estimate Crowd in Area at 2,000,000—Din Overwhelming

By ALEXANDER FEINBERG

Five days of waiting, of rumor, intimation, fact, distortion—five agonizing days following the first indication of a Japanese surrender, days of alternately rising hopes and fears—came to an end for New York, for the nation and the world, a moment or two after seven o'clock last night. And the metropolis exploded its emotions, harnessed for the most part during the day, with atomic force.

"Official—Truman announces Japanese surrender."

These were the magic words flashed on the moving electric sign of the Times Tower, at 7:03 P. M. that touched off an unparalleled demonstration in Times Square, packed with half a million persons.

The victory roar that greeted the announcement beat upon the eardrums until it numbed the senses. For twenty minutes wave after wave of that joyous roar surged forth.

Restraint was thrown to the winds. Those in the crowds in the streets tossed hats, boxes and flags into the air. From those leaning perilously out of the windows of office buildings and hotels came a shower of paper, confetti, streamers. Men and women embraced—there were no strangers in New York yesterday. Some were hilarious, others cried softly.

By 7:30 P. M. the crowd in the Square had risen to 750,000 persons; by 8:45 it had swelled to 800,000 and the number continued to rise. People were jammed solidly between Forty-third Street and Forty-fifth Avenue. Individual movement was virtually impossible; one moved not in the crowd but with it.

At 10 P. M. Chief Inspector John J. O'Connell estimated that 2,000,000 persons were in the Times Square area from Fortieth to Fifty-second Street, between Sixth and Eighth Avenues. This constitutes an all-time record, police officials said. At that hour people were still pouring into the Square from subways, buses and on foot. Those at the north end of the

Continued on Page 5, Column 1

Two-Day Holiday Is Proclaimed; Stores, Banks Close Here Today

By The Associated Press.

WASHINGTON, Aug. 14—Tomorrow and Thursday are days off for Government workers and holidays for pay purposes for workers in private industry.

And V-J Day, when it comes, will be a premium pay day, too. President Truman announced both rulings tonight.

He directed agency heads throughout the Government to cut their forces down to a bare skeleton staff Aug. 15 and 16 and not to charge the two days against the employes' annual leave. He said it was in "inadequate" recognition of the four-year efforts on "one of the hardest working groups of war workers."

For other workers under war control, Wednesday and Thursday count like Christmas and the few other accepted holidays for purposes of overtime pay and in figuring the number of days worked

Continued on Page 6, Column 7

in a week. Many employers already have obtained approval for regular time pay to workers who take the day off.

Postal service for the next two days will "approximate holiday service," the Postoffice Department said.

Local postmasters will have wide discretion in carrying out the President's wishes. It was indicated, and that postal employes required to work tomorrow and next day will have compensating time off at a later date.

It was presumed, but not specifically stated, that Government workers generally would be off on V-J Day, too.

The White House said that the next two days will be regarded as legal holidays.

PRESIDENT ANNOUNCING SURRENDER OF JAPAN

Mr. Truman reading the message in the White House. Seated are Admiral William D. Leahy, Secretary of State James F. Byrnes and former Secretary of State Cordell Hull. Standing (left to right) are Maj. Gen. Philip Fleming, head of the Federal Works Administration; William H. Davis, Economic Stabilizer; John W. Snyder, Reconversion Director; James Forrestal, Secretary of the Navy; Fred Vinson, Secretary of the Treasury; Tom Clark, Attorney General, and Lewis Schwellenbach, Secretary of Labor.
Associated Press Wirephoto

PETAIN CONVICTED, SENTENCED TO DIE

Jurors Recommend Clemency Because of His Age—Long Indictment Upheld

By G. H. ARCHAMBAULT
By Wireless to The New York Times.

PARIS, Wednesday, Aug. 15—Marshal Henri-Philippe Pétain was convicted at 4:15 A. M. today of intelligence with the enemy and sentenced to death. Because of his age—the former head of the Vichy regime is 89—the jury expressed the hope that the death sentence might not be carried out.

Guards had to arouse Pétain to

Continued on Page 15, Column 5

Terms Will Reduce Japan To Kingdom Perry Visited

By JAMES B. RESTON
Special to The New York Times.

WASHINGTON, Aug. 14—The Allied terms of surrender will not only demobilize and demilitarize Japan but also deprive her of 80 per cent of the territory and nearly one-third of the population she held when she attacked Pearl Harbor. Thus these terms, already approved by President Truman and our major Allies, will not only destroy the vast empire she conquered in the first eighteen months of this war but also reduce her to little more than the territory she occupied when Commodore Perry introduced her to the western world in 1853.

The main terms of surrender, as

Continued on Page 11, Column 2

World News Summarized

WEDNESDAY, AUGUST 15, 1945

World War II became a page in history last night.

President Truman announced at 7 P. M. that he had received the Japanese reply to the Allied note of last Saturday and that he deemed it full acceptance of the Potsdam declaration of July 26. The Chief Executive said that the Japanese surrender would be made to Gen. Douglas MacArthur in his capacity as Supreme Allied Commander in Chief. Allied military commanders were ordered to stop fighting, but the proclamation of V-J Day will await the signing of the peace treaties. [1:7-8.]

Simultaneously with the President's announcement, Admiral Nimitz flashed "cease fire" orders to all units under his command. [8:3-4.]

The official announcement that the Japanese sneak attack on Pearl Harbor had resulted three years and 250 days later in the inglorious end of the Japanese Empire touched off unrestrained celebrations throughout the Allied world. Here in New York the flash on the moving electric sign on the Times Tower, "Official—Truman announces Japanese surrender," signaled a wild demonstration. [1:3.]

Emperor Hirohito announced the Japanese surrender to his people in his first broadcast to the nation. Weeping Japanese gathered outside the Emperor's palace to bow to the ground in

their shame because their "efforts were not enough." [2:2.]

The fury of Allied military might continued to strike the Japanese up to the very last. Even as the Tokyo radio announced that the Japanese reply to the Allied note of Saturday was on its way, our Superfortresses were winging from the Marianas to the Japanese homeland. More than 1,000 planes struck Honshu with 6,000 tons of bombs in a fourteen-hour assault ending early yesterday. [8:1.]

In the midst of rejoicing it was disclosed that the heavy cruiser Indianapolis had been sunk, presumably by an enemy submarine, shortly after she had delivered an atomic bomb cargo to Guam. All men aboard were casualties. [1:6-7.]

The Red Army unleashed fierce new attacks. Russian armored forces raced ninety-three miles unchecked across western Manchuria toward Harbin and other Soviet columns scored new gains all along the 2,300-mile front. [8:6; Pacific area map P. 8.]

The Soviet Union signed "a treaty of friendship and alliance" with China after an agreement had been reached between the two nations on all questions of common interest. [1:6.]

Chinese Communists informed the Generalissimo that they refused to accept his command to remain at their posts. [6:1.]

A French jury sentenced Marshal Pétain to death. [1:4.]

YIELDING UNQUALIFIED, TRUMAN SAYS

Japan Is Told to Order End of Hostilities, Notify Allied Supreme Commander and Send Emissaries to Him

MAC ARTHUR TO RECEIVE SURRENDER

Formal Proclamation of V-J Day Awaits Signing of Those Articles—Cease-Fire Order Given to the Allied Forces

By ARTHUR KROCK
Special to The New York Times.

WASHINGTON, Aug. 14—Japan today unconditionally surrendered the hemispheric empire taken by force and held almost intact for more than two years against the rising power of the United States and its Allies in the Pacific war.

The bloody dream of the Japanese military caste vanished in the text of a note to the Four Powers accepting the terms of the Potsdam Declaration of July 26, 1945, which amplified the Cairo Declaration of 1943.

Like the previous items in the surrender correspondence, today's Japanese document was forwarded through the Swiss Foreign Office at Berne and the Swiss Legation in Washington. The note of total capitulation was delivered to the State Department by the Legation Charge d'Affaires at 6:10 P. M., after the third and most anxious day of waiting on Tokyo, the anxiety intensified by several premature or false reports of the finale of World War II.

Orders Given to the Japanese

The Department responded with a note to Tokyo through the same channel, ordering the immediate end of hostilities by the Japanese, requiring that the Supreme Allied Commander—who, the President announced, will be Gen. Douglas MacArthur—be notified of the date and hour of the order, and instructing that emissaries of Japan be sent to him at once—at the time and place selected by him—"with full information of the disposition of the Japanese forces and commanders."

President Truman summoned a special press conference in the Executive offices at 7 P. M. He handed to the reporters three texts.

The first—the only one he read aloud—was that he had received the Japanese note and deemed it full acceptance of the Potsdam Declaration, containing no qualification whatsoever; that arrangements for the formal signing of the peace would be made for the "earliest possible moment;" that the Japanese surrender would be made to General MacArthur in his capacity as Supreme Allied Commander in Chief; that Allied military commanders had been instructed to cease hostilities, but that the formal proclamation of V-J Day must await the formal signing.

The text ended with the Japanese note, in which the Four Powers (the United States, Great Britain, China and Russia) were officially informed that the Emperor of Japan had issued an imperial rescript of surrender, was prepared to guarantee the necessary signatures to the terms as prescribed by the Allies, and had instructed all his commanders to cease active operations, to surrender all

Continued on Page 2, Column 2

TREATY WITH CHINA SIGNED IN MOSCOW

Complete Agreement Reached With Chungking on All Points at Issue, Russians Say

By Cable to The New York Times.

LONDON, Aug. 14—The Soviet Union and China have signed a treaty of friendship and alliance, the Moscow radio announced tonight, and have reached "full agreement on all other questions of common interest."

The broadcast said the treaty and "other agreements" would be published shortly after they were signed by the two countries.

These are the first fruits of the talks which have been proceeding in Chungking on all points of

Continued on Page 6, Column 3

Cruiser Sunk, 1,196 Casualties; Took Atom Bomb Cargo to Guam

Special to The New York Times.

WASHINGTON, Aug. 14—The American heavy cruiser Indianapolis was sunk by enemy action in the Philippine Sea with 1,196 casualties, every man aboard, the Navy announced today.

The 9,950-ton ship left San Francisco on July 16 on a special high-speed run to deliver essential atomic bomb materials to Guam. The cargo was delivered. The cruiser was lost after having left Guam.

The sinking, which took one of the Navy's heaviest tolls of lives since Pearl Harbor, was disclosed a few minutes before President Truman announced Japan's surrender.

Casualties included five Navy

dead, including one officer; 845 Navy missing, including sixty-three officers; 307 Navy wounded, including fifteen officers; thirty Marine missing, including two officers, and nine enlisted Marine wounded. Next of kin are being notified.

The skipper, Capt. Charles B. McVay 3d, 47, of Washington, was wounded.

The Navy Department also reported for the first time that in a previous action on March 31 the Indianapolis, flagship of the Fifth Fleet, was damaged by a suicide plane off Okinawa. She had been repaired at the Mare Island, Calif., Navy

Continued on Page 10, Column 6

MacArthur Begins Orders to Hirohito

By Wireless to The New York Times.

MANILA, Wednesday, Aug. 15—Gen. Douglas MacArthur in his first action as Allied Supreme Commander today directed Emperor Hirohito and the Japanese Government to furnish a radio station in the Tokyo area for "continuous use in handling radio communications between his headquarters and your headquarters." The message, sent in the clear, called for the "earliest practicable" arrangements to end hostilities.

AGGRESSIVE COUNTRY CLUB, well-located at [illegible]—Restrictions removed. Beautiful homesites now selling at pre-war prices. [illegible] Aug. 19th.—Advt.

FREDERIC MARCH in "A BELL FOR ADANO." "Best play of season."—Mantle, Daily News. Cort Thea. Regs. 8:40. Mat. Today & Sat.—Advt.

"All the News That's Fit to Print"

NEWS INDEX, PAGE 33, THIS SECTION

The New York Times.

LATE CITY EDITION
Clearing early today; cooler.
Clear and cool tomorrow.
Temperatures Yesterday—Max., 88; Min., 72
Details today, 6:22 A. M.; Sunset, 7:28 P. M.

Section
1

VOL. XCIV. No. 31,998.

Entered as Second-Class Matter,
Postoffice, New York, N. Y.

Copyright, 1945, by The New York Times Company.

NEW YORK, SUNDAY, SEPTEMBER 2, 1945.

TEN CENTS
New York City and Suburban Areas (15c Elsewhere)

JAPAN SURRENDERS TO ALLIES, SIGNS RIGID TERMS ON WARSHIP; TRUMAN SETS TODAY AS V-J DAY

HOLIDAY TRAFFIC NEAR 1941 LEVEL; 'GAS' IS PLENTIFUL

Exodus From City Is Greatest Since Pre-War Days but Congestion Is Avoided

GOOD WEATHER PROMISED

Near-by Resorts Do Capacity Business—3 Persons Die in Queens Accidents

America's millions, deprived since 1941 of the chance to cruise the highways of their nation, hit the road in traditional Labor Day week-end style yesterday.

There was a plentiful supply of gasoline, the sun shone warm out of blue skies, and everyone felt free from war worries. This combined to roll up traffic that continued heavy all day.

New York City's heat-ridden population took to car, train, bus and plane. The exodus to near-by mountain and seashore resorts was the greatest since that of 1941.

The weather formed a perfect lure. Not even the thunder showers predicted by the Weather Bureau for late afternoon took place. Today's prediction is for clearing weather early, followed by cooler, with the highest temperature around 80 degrees, and with fresh to strong northwest winds. A clear and cool Monday is forecast by the bureau. The temperature yesterday reached 88 degrees at 3:30 P. M. with the humidity at 52 per cent. The all-time high for the date was set in 1924 with 92.5 degrees and the low in 1872 with 51.

Many Cars Come Into City

Travel in the city was two-way. As cars streamed out of the city over bridges, on ferries and through tunnels, out-of-towners poured in. The main idea for Labor Day seemed to be change of scenery.

Thousands of automobiles, many of them looking as though they had just been taken off the jacks for the first time in years, formed a continuous procession along the main highways leading up-State, out on Long Island and to the South Jersey shore.

The Port of New York Authority reported that 60,000 automobiles had crossed the George Washington Bridge into New Jersey. Forty-five thousand cars passed through the Holland Tunnel during the sixteen hours preceding 6 o'clock last night. Lincoln Tunnel police said traffic was heavier than usual.

Few serious accidents were reported. "Maybe it's because the cars just don't have the pep," remarked a Westchester County parkway policeman.

Sights along the parkways bore out his contention. Many cars became pathetically silent as their drivers resignedly hauled them over to the side of the road to patch up tires or to fume over engine repairs.

Gasoline Supplies Abundant

Assured of as much gasoline as they wanted, motorists traveled leisurely and did not cause congestion. Filling station pumps received their heaviest workout in years. Station operators estimated that demands for gasoline ranged from 10 to 30 per cent over last week-end, but they reported there was no difficulty in obtaining supplies.

The Cities Service Oil Company said it was having difficulty in meeting orders for premium gasoline, ordinarily accounting for 25 per cent of sales, as the supply was limited, but no company reported shortages of non-premium gasoline. No motorist was forced to stay in town because of lack of fuel.

Trains, buses and airlines were crowded, as they have been all through the day war. The exodus

Continued on Page 30, Column 2

Times Sq. Takes V-J News Quietly

Times Square throngs, which had greeted Japanese capitulation explosively last month, took the formal signing of terms in much calmer fashion last night.

Two hundred policemen, including twenty-five mounted patrolmen, who had been assigned to the area in case of another outburst of feeling, reported that the street crowds took the flashing of the bulletin from Times Tower at 10:04 P. M. with a few cheers and good-natured remarks, and did not attempt to start a celebration.

In numbers the crowd was no larger than an average Saturday night, and of the persons present perhaps half or more were out-of-town visitors here for the Labor Day week-end. Other parts of the city were similarly quiet.

Mayor La Guardia had said earlier that the people "have had their big time and are satisfied." He decided not to hold a celebration in Central Park today as had been planned.

PRESIDENT STRESSES LABOR DAY OF PEACE

But He Warns That After Six Holidays of Hostilities Great New Problems Lie Ahead

Special to The New York Times.

WASHINGTON, Sept. 1.—President Truman hailed the first Labor Day of peace in six years today and declared a grateful world would always remember the workers of all free nations for their contribution to victory.

Secretary Forrestal and J. A. Krug, chairman of the War Production Board, also lauded the men and women of labor, and Philip Murray, chairman of the Congress of Industrial Organizations, told a radio audience that America's vast war plant must be put to work on peacetime products which would give prosperity unlimited to this country.

Mr. Truman's statement said that six years ago today the workers of the United States, and of the world, awoke to a Labor Day in a world at war, and added:

"We in the United States had two years of grace, but the time was squarely joined at that hour, as we now know. There was to be no peace until tyranny had been outlawed.

"Today we stand on the threshold of a new world. We must do our part in making this world what it should be, a world in which the bigotries of race and class and creed shall not be permitted to warp the souls of men.

"We enter upon an era of great problems, but to live is to face problems. Our men and women did not falter in the task of saving freedom. They will not falter now in the task of making freedom

Continued on Page 24, Column 3

Public Gets Big Army Food Stocks; Whipping Cream Is Freed of Bans

Special to The New York Times.

WASHINGTON, Sept. 1.—The national food situation continued its steady improvement today as the Department of Agriculture, with four orders, increased the supplies of butter, canned salmon and ice cream and signalled the return of whipping cream.

This action was a direct consequence of the sharp reduction of military requirements of these foods. With the discontinuance of butter purchases by the armed forces, the Department explained, it is now possible to revoke the limitations on the sale of heavy cream and the use of butter fat in the production of all frozen dairy products. Both these rulings will make

whipping cream and ice cream of a higher butter fat content readily available.

In a simultaneous direction, the agency ordered released for civilian use all butter currently held by creameries and receivers for the armed forces and other Government buyers. Although as much as 20,000,000 pounds of butter may be returned to civilian consumers under this ruling, ration values will not be changed, it was indicated.

"At the time ration point values were established for September, the Office of Price Administration recognized the possibility of these

Continued on Page 35, Column 1

HAILS ERA OF PEACE

President Calls On U.S. to Stride On Toward a World of Good-Will

SALUTES HEROIC DEAD

Cautions Jubilant Nation Hard Jobs Ahead Need Same Zeal as War

Text of the President's address proclaiming V-J Day, P. 4.

By WILLIAM S. WHITE
Special to The New York Times.

WASHINGTON, Sept. 1.—President Truman hailed the memory of all who have fallen and in an appeal to all Americans to go forward now in hope and fraternity toward "a new and better world of peace and international good-will," tonight solemnly proclaimed tomorrow to be V-J Day.

The moment that he began to speak was, in the official and historical sense, the first moment of peace since a December day nearly four years ago, when, at a sudden, a harsh and an incredible blow into the whole of the Pacific world went into flames.

Into the human calendar of great American holidays, like the Fourth of July and the Eleventh of November, the President thus entered another date, the Second of September, that does not technically signify the end of the "duration" and will have no basis as a legal end of the war. The termination of hostilities, for purposes of computing military service, for setting the limit to war agencies and for all other like formalities, will be set only by final decision of Congress.

Japanese Surrender Signaled

But Mr. Truman's speech was a speech to the heart of a country that had had the skill to make the atomic bomb and could now "use the same skill and energy and determination to overcome all the difficulties ahead," rather than to the keepers of its books of law.

It was notice from the White House, so long awaited, that nearly four years of war, a struggle of sacrificial grandeur such as the United States had never known, had come to an end, and that the terrible ledger that was opened at Pearl Harbor had now been balanced and closed.

The President spoke in this mood, a mood of valedictory and of dedication, as he proclaimed "this . . . victory of more than arms alone . . . this . . . victory of liberty over tyranny." He had just received the signal from across the world that the Japanese had signed, aboard the great battleship Missouri, the last, humiliat-

Continued on Page 4, Column 1

JAPANESE FOREIGN MINISTER SIGNING SURRENDER ARTICLES

Mamoru Shigemitsu (right, seated), on behalf of Emperor Hirohito, affixes his signature to document as Gen. Douglas MacArthur (left) and Lieut. Gen. Richard K. Sutherland (center) look on during ceremony aboard the Missouri in Tokyo Bay.
Associated Press Wirephoto (via Navy Radio from U. S. S. Iowa)

BYRNES FORESEES A PEACEFUL JAPAN

Says People Are Expected to Force Development—World Amity Vital, Hull Warns

Special to The New York Times.

WASHINGTON, Sept. 1.—Secretary of State James F. Byrnes declared tonight that with Japan's surrender we have entered the second phase of our war—"what might be called the spiritual disarmament of that nation, to make them want peace instead of wanting war."

The intention of this Government

Continued on Page 5, Column 1

Japan's Surrender Ordered Over Militarist Opposition

By FRANK L. KLUCKHOHN
By Wireless to The New York Times.

TOKYO, Sept. 1.—In the rubble of this once-proud imperial capital the story of how the Japanese Army opposed the surrender and how the Emperor made the final decision to capitulate after having heard the opinions of all his advisers, and how War Minister Korechika Anami had committed suicide was unfolded today by one of a handful of those in a position to know without bias what occurred.

It was also learned how the Japanese reacted step by step to wartime developments and how propaganda that Japan could win last time been continued to the last moment, thus leaving the industrious long-

Continued on Page 7, Column 1

World News Summarized

SUNDAY, SEPTEMBER 2, 1945

The rulers of Japan, who set the Pacific ablaze nearly four years ago with their surprise attack on Pearl Harbor and hoped to culminate that assault with a peace dictated in the White House, formally signed their unconditional surrender to the Allied powers in Tokyo Bay. Foreign Minister Shigemitsu signed the historic document for his country in the shadow of the sixteen-inch gun muzzles of the battleship Missouri. General MacArthur, who signed in behalf of the Allies, said mankind hoped a better world would result from the solemn occasion. [1:8; map P. 12.]

President Truman proclaimed today as V-J Day. He urged the nation to observe the day of victory over Japan in a spirit of dedication and as a symbol of "victory of liberty over tyranny." He also asked his countrymen to remember "our departed gallant leader, Franklin D. Roosevelt." [1:2.]

Japan's decision to surrender was dictated by Emperor Hirohito after he had overruled a strong faction within the Cabinet and the army that wanted to keep on with the war in the

belief that the Japanese could defeat an invasion of the homeland, according to well-informed observers in Tokyo. [1:5-6.]

Medical "experiments" recalling medieval sadism were carried out on dying American prisoners of war by young Japanese Army doctors, two American physicians interned with their compatriots said aboard a United States hospital ship. [1:6-7.]

With the Foreign Ministers' Council scheduled to meet in London next week to begin consideration of peace terms, it was learned that a serious division of opinion over the disposition of the Italian colonies had developed in the State Department. [1:8.]

Former Secretary of State Stettinius said in London that the development of the atomic bomb emphasized the need for the "speedy creation of the United Nations Organization to keep the peace of the world" and predicted that as soon as the organization began functioning it would appoint a military staff to deal with the use of atomic bombs, as well as all other types of force, in preserving peace. [12:2.]

Enemy Tortured Dying Americans With Sadist Medical 'Experiments'

By ROBERT TRUMBULL
By Wireless to The New York Times.

ABOARD THE HOSPITAL SHIP BENEVOLENCE, in Tokyo Bay, Sept. 1 — Seriously ailing American prisoners at Shinagawa, the only hospital serving 8,000 prisoners of war held in the Tokyo area, were guinea pigs for fantastic experiments recalling the sorcery and sadism of the middle ages, Drs. Mack L. Gottlieb and Harold W. Keschner, both of New York, told this correspondent today.

Dr. Gottlieb, who had his home and office at 207 East Forty-fourth Street, was a Naval officer captured at Guam. Dr. Keschner, of 451 West End Avenue, was taken with an Army force in the Philippines. Both are in good physical

Continued on Page 14, Column 1

WAR COMES TO END

Articles of Capitulation Endorsed by Countries in Pacific Conflict

M'ARTHUR SEES PEACE

Emperor Orders Subjects to Obey All Commands Issued by General

The texts of the surrender documents and statements, P. 3.

By The Associated Press.

ABOARD THE U. S. S. MISSOURI in Tokyo Bay, Sunday, Sept. 2—Japan surrendered formally and unconditionally to the Allies today in a twenty-minute ceremony which ended just as the sun burst through low-hanging clouds as a shining symbol to a ravaged world now done with war.

[A United Press dispatch said the leading Japanese delegate signed the articles at 9:03 A. M. Sunday, Tokyo time, and that General MacArthur signed them at 9:07 A. M.]

Twelve signatures, requiring only a few minutes to inscribe on the articles of surrender, ended the bloody Pacific conflict.

On behalf of Emperor Hirohito, Foreign Minister Mamoru Shigemitsu signed for the Government and Gen. Yoshijiro Umezu for the Imperial General Staff.

MacArthur Voices Peace Hope

Gen. Douglas MacArthur then accepted in behalf of the United Nations, declaring:

"It is my earnest hope and indeed the hope of all mankind that from this solemn occasion a better world shall emerge out of the blood and carnage of the past."

One by one the Allied representatives stepped forward and signed the document that blighted Japan's dream of empire built on bloodshed and tyranny.

First was Admiral Chester W. Nimitz for the United States, then the representatives of China, the United Kingdom, the Soviet, Australia, Canada, France, the Netherlands and New Zealand.

The flags of the United States, Britain, the Soviet and China fluttered from the veranda deck of the famed superdreadnaught, polished and scrubbed as never before. More than 100 high-ranking military and naval officers watched.

Pledges Justice and Tolerance

"As Supreme Commander for the Allied powers," General MacArthur told the Japanese, "I announce it my firm purpose, in the tradition of the countries I represent, to proceed in the discharge of my responsibilities with justice and tolerance, while taking all necessary dispositions to insure that the terms of surrender are fully, promptly and faithfully complied with."

All through this dramatic half hour, only those aboard the battleship knew of what was taking place, because the Missouri has no broadcasting facilities.

But recordings were rushed to the near-by communications ship Ancon, and the solemn words of General MacArthur beginning the ceremony—"We are gathered here, representatives of the major warring powers"—were flashed around the world.

The Japanese representatives were present at the command of Emperor Hirohito contained in a proclamation issued by order of the Emperor Supreme Allied Commander. The Emperor further commanded his officials "to issue general orders to the military and naval forces in accordance with the direction of the Supreme Commander

Continued on Page 2, Column 3

TOKYO AIDES WEEP AS GENERAL SIGNS

Imperial Staff Chief Hastily Scrawls His Signature— Shigemitsu Is Anxious

ABOARD U. S. S. MISSOURI in Tokyo Bay, Sunday, Sept. 2—The solemn surrender ceremony, on this battleship today, marking the final defeat in Japan's 2,600-year-old semi-legendary history, required only a few minutes as twelve signatures were affixed to the articles.

Surrounded by the might of the United States Navy and Army, and under the eyes of the American and British commanders they so ruthlessly defeated in the Philippines and Malaya, the Japanese representatives quietly made the marks on paper that ended the bloody Pacific period.

The Japanese delegation came aboard at 8:55 A. M., 7:55 P. M. Saturday, E. W. T., as scheduled. They reached the Missouri in personnel speed boats flying the American flag.

Foreign Minister Mamoru Shigemitsu climbed stiffly up the ladder and limped forward on his right leg, which is artificial. His was wounded by a bomb tossed by a Korean terrorist in Shanghai many years ago.

On behalf of Emperor Hirohito, Mr. Shigemitsu signed first for

Continued on Page 9, Column 1

U. S. CHIEFS DIVIDED ON ITALY'S COLONIES

State Department Split Over Russia and Influence Zones Is Projected by Issue

By JAMES B. RESTON
Special to The New York Times.

WASHINGTON, Sept. 1.—A fundamental issue has developed in the Department of State over the future of the Italian colonies, particularly Eritrea, Libya and Italian Somaliland.

The issue is whether these colonies should go back to Italy as part of her sovereign territory, be taken from her and administered by the United States, Britain, France and the Soviet Union under the United Nations Organization or be administered by a neutral international commission under the United Nations.

With the Foreign Ministers' Council scheduled to meet in London next week to begin consideration of peace terms, it was learned that a serious division of opinion over the disposition of the Italian colonies had developed in the State Department. [1:8.]

The major powers that defeated Germany are soon to start draft-

Continued on Page 15, Column 1

"All the News
That's Fit to Print"

The New York Times.

LATE CITY EDITION
Cloudy with showers today. Considerable cloudiness tomorrow.

Temperatures Yesterday—Max., 75; Min., 66
Sunrise today, 6:36 A. M.; Sunset, 7:06 P. M.

Copyright, 1945, by the New York Times Company.

VOL. XCIV. No. 32,011.   Entered as Second-Class Matter, Postoffice, New York, N. Y.   NEW YORK, SATURDAY, SEPTEMBER 15, 1945.   THREE CENTS NEW YORK CITY

M'ARTHUR PLEDGES IRON RULE, REBUKES CRITICS ON POLICY; CURBS DOMEI NEWS AGENCY

FIRM GRIP MAPPED

General Says All Terms of Surrender Will Be Imposed on Japan

HOMMA READY TO GIVE UP

Japanese Premier Asks U. S. to 'Forget Pearl Harbor' in Interests of Peace

By GEORGE E. JONES
By Wireless to The New York Times.

YOKOHAMA, Japan, Saturday, Sept. 15—Gen. Douglas MacArthur took cognizance yesterday of criticism of his so-called "soft policy" toward Japan. In an extraordinary statement defining his problems and policies, he emphasized that the surrender terms imposed on the beaten empire would be carried out in a stern, uncompromising fashion.

At the same time the Supreme Commander for the Allied Powers admitted that it was difficult for him to "exercise that degree of patience which is unquestionably demanded if the long-time policies which have been decreed are to be successfully accomplished without repercussions which would be detrimental to the well being of the world."

This was General MacArthur's rebuttal to the criticism, particularly that of the American press, of his policy of working to the fullest possible extent through the existing Japanese government.

Domei Curbed, Put Under Censor

General MacArthur's patience evidently had worn thin as he ordered the suspension of Domei, the Japanese news agency, which had been foremost in propagating stories of American "brutalities" toward Japanese civilians.

Today Supreme Headquarters rescinded the suspension and permitted Domei to reopen at noon after a shutdown of nearly eighteen hours.

Henceforth, however, Domei must use for its foreign news only what it receives from the United States Office of War Information broadcasts and its local news will be subjected to strict American censorship. Presumably the censorship will be applied also to local news matter gathered by the Japanese newspapers.

This backdown from General MacArthur's original order ended a news drought for Tokyo's large papers that sent them scurrying to American press associations and syndicates seeking to arrange for reception of foreign news from American sources.

The shutdown order was rescinded after conversations between headquarters and Domei representatives in which the Japanese agency was reminded sharply that Japan was a defeated nation and that Domei would take its orders from the occupation authorities without "ifs" and "buts." General MacArthur has been displeased at the tendency of the Japanese press, particularly Domei, to assume that Japan enjoyed equal status with other nations and as such possessed prerogatives of sovereignty in dealings with the American occupation forces.

Still in First Phase of Action

In effect General MacArthur stated that we were still in the first phase, which is primarily one of military considerations—that of deploying sufficient American troops onto Japanese soil and demobilizing Japanese forces. It promised that when this phase had been completed "no one need have any doubt about the prompt, complete, entire fulfillment of the terms of the surrender."

He added that Japan was in a state of utter collapse industrially and militarily and said that her existing structure was controlled completely by the American occupation forces. This amounts in effect to an explanation of his present policy in terms of promises for a stern policy in the future where military conditions permit.

[Lieut. Gen. Masaharu Homma, held responsible by General MacArthur for the Bataan death march, arrived in Tokyo and said he was preparing to surrender himself, The Associated Press reported.]

[Earlier Premier Prince Naru-
Continued on Page 4, Column 3]

POLAND DENOUNCES VATICAN CONCORDAT

Asserts Holy See Violated It—Arrests and Deportations of Clerics Reported

By Wireless to The New York Times.

LONDON, Sept. 14—The Warsaw Government has denounced the concordat that has governed relations between Poland and the Holy See since 1925. It became known here today. The decision was taken on Sept. 4, with fifteen Cabinet Ministers voting in favor against.

It also was reported in Catholic circles here that two Polish priests were arrested this week on charges that are not known. They are Dr. Albert Sztajer, who was attached to Cardinal Hlond's cathedral at Poznan, and Father Kuhn, a German priest of the Danzig diocese. Dr. Sztajer will be put on trial shortly. Father Kuhn already has been sentenced to death.

These arrests followed alleged deportations to Russia of the Bishop of Luck and to Central Poland of the Archbishop of Vilna and the arrest of the Bishop of Danzig, all of which were reported to Warsaw.

In an article on religious conditions in Poland, the Catholic weekly Tablet will say tomorrow that these events "confirm the view already forced upon us that the present limited freedom enjoyed by Polish Catholics is only temporary and will end when it is decided that no more Poles abroad can be inveighed back."

Father Piotr Kruszynski, Vicar General of the diocese of Lublin,
Continued on Page 3, Column 2

ARGENTINE REPLY FOUND MISLEADING

Many Errors Shown in Answer to U. S. Charges of Failure to Live Up to Obligations

By ARNALDO CORTESI
By Wireless to The New York Times.

BUENOS AIRES, Sept. 14—On Tuesday the Foreign Ministry published a 10,000-word document to prove that the Argentine Government had complied faithfully with the commitments it assumed when it signed the final Act of Chapultepec. A careful study of this document shows that it contains so many hiatuses and makes so many erroneous or misleading statements that it can confidently be described as a very poor attempt to justify the Government's far from brilliant position.

Far from proving that Argentina carried out her commitments, it convicts the Government of the most astonishing laxness in almost all matters of fundamental importance. Since the Argentine document was provoked by former Assistant Secretary of State Nelson Rockefeller's charges that Argentina had not taken the measures necessary to eliminate Axis firms, it perhaps would be best to start from this point.

The Argentine Government substantially confirms Mr. Rockefeller's figures. To date the Government has eliminated only two small subsidiaries of the Trans Lamental Company and two German banks, while six German insurance companies are in the process of liquidation. Bids also have been requested for the sale of merchandise belonging to about a
Continued on Page 16, Column 1

Chinese Communists Claim Gains Ranging From Yangtze to Peiping

By TILLMAN DURDIN
By Wireless to The New York Times.

CHUNGKING, China, Sept. 14—Sweeping territorial gains from the Yangtze Valley to areas north and west of Peiping are claimed for the Communist armies in a communiqué issued today from Communist headquarters in Chungking. The communiqué summarized Communist army activities of the last week.

The Communists claim to have "fairly complete control of everything but points on the railways" in an area stretching from Kalgan to the mouth of the Yangtze River and from the Shantung Peninsula to east of Shansi and including northern and northwest Shansi. The communiqué said "puppet armies" in the big cities were strong enough to resist attacks.

At a meeting with the press in Chungking today Mao Tze-tung,
Continued on Page 5, Column 2

chairman of the Central Executive Committee of the Communist party, said the Communists were still fighting because "the Japanese and the puppets are fighting us, and since they are fighting us, we are still fighting them."

He claimed the important Hopei port of Chinwangtao north of Tientsin, had been taken by the Communists in addition to Shanhaikwan, where the Great Wall meets the sea, and the capital of Jehol Province.

Gen. Chou En-lai, Communist military leader, who also attended the press conference, stated that the Japanese had attacked the Communists in Chahar Province and, after recovering two important towns, had turned them over to

---

Storm Races to Florida; 2 Subways Flooded Here

6th and 8th Ave. Lines Tied Up 3 Hours as Half Inch of Rain Falls in 10 Minutes—Boy Drowned on Newark Street

A torrential rainstorm that began at the start of the rush hour last evening halted service on the Sixth and Eighth Avenue subways through midtown Manhattan for three hours last night, flooded thousands of cellars and delayed millions on their way home. In New Jersey it was responsible for two deaths, one by electrocution, the other by drowning, in addition to uprooting trees and tearing the roof from a home in Elizabeth.

Half an inch of rain fell in Manhattan in the ten minutes between 5 and 5:10 P. M., according to Weather Bureau measurements. This was not a record fall. Last year .76 inches fell in ten minutes on Aug. 16 and .85 inches in ten minutes on Sept. 13, the eve of last year's hurricane.

There was no connection between yesterday's storm and the hurricane moving toward Miami out of the Carribean, according to the Weather Bureau. The local storm, it was explained, was part
Continued on Page 30, Column 6

Exposed Areas Are Prepared as Hurricane With 150-Mile Winds Moves Toward Coast—Bahamas Await Big Blow

By The Associated Press.

MIAMI, Fla., Sept. 14—A tropical hurricane which is reported to have created great havoc in Turks Island with 150-mile winds swirled toward the Florida Keys tonight and at 11 o'clock was about 210 miles southeast of Miami.

Thousands of persons began to move from exposed areas under Coast Guard, Red Cross and Weather Bureau urgings. Schools, police stations and other public buildings were thrown open to refugees throughout south Florida.

The Federal storm warning service estimated that squalls would be felt in this area tomorrow morning, building up to gales and then howling hurricane winds as the center passed, probably over the Florida Keys, tomorrow afternoon.

The red and black flags of the hurricane warning signal were up from Fort Lauderdale to Key West and Dry Tortugas.

Army, Navy and commercial airplanes sped out of the danger
Continued on Page 30, Column 2

TROLLEY CARS HERE ON WAY TO OBLIVION BY NEXT YEAR'S END

700 New Buses to Assume Travel Burden on Lines in Manhattan and Bronx

The antiquated, clangorous and slow trolley car is to disappear from the streets of Manhattan and most of the Bronx by the end of next year, according to an announcement made yesterday by the Third Avenue Transit Corporation.

As replacements for 450 trolleys that are to be scrapped, 700 new buses will travel the seventy-five miles of surface lines scheduled for abandonment in Manhattan and the Bronx, and thirty miles in Yonkers, New Rochelle and Mount Vernon. Most of the buses already have been ordered from General Motors Corporation.

Announcement of the company's program, involving $11,000,000 of financing, was made by its president, Victor McQuistion. The buses, he said, would cost an average of $15,000 each.

In Manhattan the street car lines hat will mark the passing of an .ra are those running up Broad-
Continued on Page 11, Column 5

VALENTINE RETIRES; LA GUARDIA DELAYS NAMING SUCCESSOR

Mayor Tells Police at Promotion Ceremonies New Head Will Come From Ranks

The Police Department is operating today without a commissioner, as the resignation of Lewis J. Valentine, its chief for almost eleven years, became effective at midnight without the appointment of a successor by Mayor La Guardia.

As the time drew near for Mr. Valentine to perform his last official act by presiding at departmental promotion ceremonies at noon yesterday, Centre Street gossip predicted confidently that the climax of the proceedings would be the naming of a new commissioner. The 500 members of the force present in the line-up room sat up expectantly as the Mayor walked to the rostrum, waited eagerly for him to broach the subject and then relaxed as he made it clear that he would take his legal time about swearing in a Presidential nomination.

Plainly, the Mayor was having fun. With Mr. Valentine out of the department after forty-two years
Continued on Page 11, Column 1

World News Summarized

SATURDAY, SEPTEMBER 15, 1945

General MacArthur pledged that Japan would be made to carry out her terms of unconditional surrender in a stern, uncompromising manner. Taking note of criticism of the occupation as indicating "a soft policy," he said this was an "erroneous concept." He emphasized that the occupation was still in its first phase and that when this phase was completed "no one need have any doubt about prompt, complete, entire fulfillment of the terms of surrender." The Allied commander also curbed the Domei agency, foremost Japanese news outlet. [1:1.]

Premier Higashi-Kuni asked Americans to "forget Pearl Harbor" and declared a new Japan would emerge after reconstruction that would be abhorrent of militarism and would be "as peace-loving as the United States." [4:1.]

General Homma, Japanese commander in the Philippines during the Bataan "death march," arrived in Tokyo to surrender as a war criminal. [4:6.]

A Communist communiqué issued from Chungking reported large-scale territorial gains and said the Chinese Communists had "fairly complete" control between Kalgan and the mouth of the Yangtze River and from the Shantung Peninsula to east of Shansi. [1:2-3.]

Japanese forces surrendering on Nauru Island were said to have resorted to cannibalism. [5:2.]

On the eve of Viceroy Wavell's return the All-India Congress party working committee voted to contest all elections in India and to continue the program of negotiation and cooperation with

seeking independence. [6:2.]

The Foreign Ministers' Council in London began detailed discussions of the treaty with Italy and made encouraging progress. All nations that were at war with Italy will be asked to submit their views. The council also set up a joint secretariat consisting of the secretaries of the five delegations to speed its work. [1:2-3.]

Exchange of operational information between the Red Army and the American-British forces during the war was called "wholly satisfactory" by General Deane, head of the American military mission in Moscow. [9:4.]

Poland denounced its concordat with the Vatican. [1:2.]

A study of a 10,000-word document issued by the Argentine Foreign Ministry led to the conclusion that it was a poor attempt to justify the Argentine Government's position and tended to convict that Government of laxity in carrying out its commitments under the Act of Chapultepec. [1:3.]

The tempo of reconversion suffered a serious setback as the Ford Motor Company shut down after hitting out at "unauthorized" strikes that were interfering with its supplies. [1:8.]

The British Trades Union Congress adopted a resolution urging a general forty-hour week in industry and a government housing program. [9:2.]

The Pearl Harbor disaster will be investigated by a joint Senate-House committee of five Democrats and four Republicans.

Big 5 Invite Other Powers To Present Views on Italy

Evatt Is Credited With Winning Voice for Smaller Allies on Peace Treaty—Parley Picks Up Speed, Forms Secretariat

By HERBERT L. MATTHEWS
By Cable to The New York Times.

LONDON, Sept. 14—The Council of Foreign Ministers of the great powers, pushed by internal and external pressure, suddenly came to its majority today as a full-fledged organization to settle the peace problems of the world.

The Foreign Ministers began their detailed discussions of a treaty with Italy and found surprisingly easy going. The Council called in a number of other powers for discussions, established a joint secretariat to carry on through the coming months and in general adopted methods of procedure that show that this body, which began as a council of five powers, is really a world organization.

If any one man deserves the credit for forcing this issue so quickly it is the fiery Australian Minister for External Affairs, Dr. Herbert V. Evatt, who came to London last week brimming with a determination that the smaller powers would have their say, and today's development was his triumph. The essential points were set forth in two communiqués, one from the Council and the other from Dr. Evatt himself.

The first communiqué begins by saying that there were two meetings today, one presided over by Foreign Minister Wang Shih-chieh of China and the other by Secretary of State James F. Byrnes of the United States, in accordance with the rotation decided upon on the first day. Encouraged by their progress today, the Foreign Ministers decided to forget about the traditional British week-end and to work tomorrow and perhaps Sunday.

"The Council began its discussion of terms for the peace settlement with Italy," says the communiqué. "It was agreed all the United Nations at war with Italy would be invited to submit if they wished, their views in writing on this subject. It was also decided that the president of the session,
Continued on Page 7, Column 4

FORD ENDS ALL PRODUCTION, BLAMES CRIPPLING STRIKES; ALL AUTO INDUSTRY MENACED

Labor Rows Worry Capital; Detroit Situation 'Ominous'

Officials Fear Crisis Before Peace Parley of Unions and Management, and Want Early Meeting—Congress Ponders Steps

By LOUIS STARK
Special to The New York Times.

WASHINGTON, Sept. 14—A national labor-industry crisis, which might even precede President Truman's scheduled "industrial peace" meeting, was regarded as a possibility today by labor officials, who felt that Detroit labor developments were "ominous."

Secretary Schwellenbach called for reports from the Conciliation Service, which has had a commissioner in close touch with the Detroit labor situation.

Other officials felt that the piling up of wage demands by unions and the comparative slowness in settling problems of reconversion may touch off a series of strikes and disputes that will keep the Labor Department and the War Labor Board as busy as at some periods during the war.

The difficulty facing the board, however, is that neither labor nor industry fears any possible "sanctions." To labor the no-strike agreement is no longer binding. While high international union of-
Continued on Page 2, Column 6

50,000 ARE LAID OFF

Company Head Charges Irresponsible Groups Balk Reconversion

UNION PLANS CAMPAIGN

UAW-CIO Leaders Insist on 30% Auto Pay Rise Under Sweeping Strike Plan

The Ford Motor Company halted all production at its plants throughout the country and laid off 50,000 workers, blaming "irresponsible labor groups" for strikes against its supplies. [1:8.]

Meanwhile at Flint the Automobile Workers Union's executive board moved to demand a 30 per cent nation-wide pay rise under threat of strikes, and a labor-management showdown loomed. [2:5.]

Washington feared a labor crisis before the labor-management conference, with Detroit situation called ominous. [1:6-7.]

A CIO Electrical Workers Union began an enrollment drive among 12,000 striking "white-collar" workers at Westinghouse Electric. [1:6-7.]

AFL railway unions will demand a thirty-six hour week with no pay cut. [2:7.]

Benjamin Fairless, president of the United States Steel Corporation, said a union demand for $2 a day wage increase cannot be granted without a sharp rise in steel prices. [2:8.]

Company in Blunt Attack

By JAMES B. RESTON

DETROIT, Sept. 14—The Ford Motor Company halted virtually all production in its plants throughout the country today and laid off 50,000 workers, basing its action upon "crippling and unauthorized strikes" against companies supplying it with parts.

The company's action, set forth in a statement signed by Henry Ford 2d, executive vice president, applied to all plants except its Lincoln and Rouge steel factories. The statement said that "continued outbreaks by irresponsible labor groups are impeding the regular progress of reconversion."

The development came as the entire automotive industry appeared heading for a labor-management showdown after the International Executive Board of the CIO United Automobile Workers Union had demanded earlier today a 30 per cent wage increase throughout the industry under a threat of strikes to enforce the demand.

Period of Tension Starts

A period of tension in the automotive capital began this morning when the 22-man Executive Committee of the UAW, largest CIO union in the country with a membership of about 1,250,000, announced at a union meeting in Flint that the UAW would either get its 30 per cent raise or call a series of concentrated strikes, against one of the Big Three auto companies and its suppliers and then against another, but on a basis of one at a time so that the full force of the international union could be thrown against each individual of the Big Three.

In outlining this "divide and conquer" policy, R. J. Thomas, international president; Walter Reuther, vice president, and George F. Addes, secretary - treasurer, stated that their new drive would be carried out under the law, and that the union would "crack down" on wildcat strikes.

The Ford company statement, coming soon afterward, was blunt. It read as follows:

"After several weeks operations in the face of crippling and unauthorized strikes against many of our suppliers, the Ford Motor Company is being forced to halt virtually all of its production operations late today.

"We have considered all angles of the situation. We wanted to keep men at work. We had hoped that by this time we would be hiring more men. Instead we are telling 50,000 of our employes to stay off their jobs indefinitely.
Continued on Page 2, Column 3

COLLEGES CHART 2 BILLION OUTLAY

Survey Discloses a Building Program Marking Greatest Expansion in Their History

By BENJAMIN FINE

Colleges and universities in all parts of the United States face the greatest period of expansion in their history, involving a post-war building program of possibly more than $2,000,000,000, a survey conducted by The New York Times has disclosed.

After four years of war-enforced delay, the colleges report that new dormitories, laboratories, classrooms, gymnasiums and other necessary buildings will be constructed as soon as materials and priorities can be obtained. Almost every one of them needs repair and reconstruction work.

A sampling of forty representative institutions of higher learning showed that blueprints have been prepared for buildings and development that will cost $256,000,000. This sampling, which is less than 10 per cent of the 600 recognized liberal arts institutions and State universities, did not cover the professional schools or junior colleges, where an even greater expansion is planned.

Plainly, the college heads are preparing for a substantial rise in enrollment. Many institutions predict that their students will increase by 50 to 100 per cent. As a result, building must start at once. Since Pearl Harbor little, if any, work has been done on the campuses. Almost every college and university reported that buildings
Continued on Page 16, Column 2

BRADLEY REVAMPS VETERANS' SERVICE

Sweeping Decentralization to Give 13 Districts Controls—Hospital Changes Planned

By CHARLES HURD
Special to The New York Times.

WASHINGTON, Sept. 14—The modernized Veterans Administration ordered by President Truman took shape today when Gen. Omar N. Bradley, new administrator, announced a decentralization program for the organization together with innovations in medical service designed to meet criticisms.

General Bradley made public his reorganization program less than twenty-four hours after it was announced to tabular form, cautioning reporters that for the most part it existed as yet only on paper. But he said he hoped to be able to show accomplishment soon.

"Don't get the idea," he said at a news conference, "that we think this plan will perform a miracle, or get things done right now. But we hope it will show definite improvement in the work of the Veterans Administration."

General Bradley plans to:

1. Decentralize supervision and control over veterans' facilities into thirteen branch offices that will have absolute control over the facilities and offices in their areas.

2. Raise the medical establishment to rank equal to other departments, add a planning section and break insurance away from general finance.

3. Separate vocational training from other activities and make it a specialized project equal in importance to medical care.

4. Reform veterans' hospitals to
Continued on Page 3, Column 5

Ten Lawyers in Congress Named To Conduct Pearl Harbor Inquiry

By WILLIAM S. WHITE
Special to The New York Times.

WASHINGTON, Sept. 14—A joint Congressional committee of ten members, all lawyers, was appointed today to investigate the Pearl Harbor disaster.

For the Senate, Senator McKellar of Tennessee, the presiding officer, chose Senators Barkley of Kentucky, the majority leader; George of Georgia and Lucas of Illinois, Democrats, and Brewster of Maine, and Ferguson of Michigan, Republicans. Senator George withheld a final acceptance, potentially, and had given great amount of work was pending before his committee but promised his cooperation but later would make a decision by early next week.

On the part of the House, Speaker Rayburn, who has made it plain that he requested Congressional insistence on an inquiry and

The selection of some of the most widely known and veteran members of the Senate caused some comment that the investigating group would be "a Senate committee."

Speaker Rayburn, too, had followed no precise criterion in appointing the House members of the committee. He disclosed that he had sought the recommendations of Representative Martin of Massachusetts, the House Republican leader, in selecting the minority members.

The Speaker, who has made it plain that he requested Congressional insistence on an inquiry and
Continued on Page 5, Column 2

"All the News That's Fit to Print"

The New York Times.

LATE CITY EDITION

Sunny, warm today. Sunny, with increasing cloudiness tomorrow
Temperatures Yesterday—Max., 70; Min., 49
Sunrise today, 5:48 A. M.; Sunset, 6:15 P. M.
Full U. S. Weather Bureau Report, Page 31

Copyright, 1946, by The New York Times Company

VOL. XCV..No. 32,205.

Entered as Second-Class Matter,
Postoffice, New York, N. Y.

NEW YORK, THURSDAY, MARCH 28, 1946.

THREE CENTS IN NEW YORK CITY

RUSSIAN, DEFEATED ON IRAN, WALKS OUT OF UNO; TEHERAN'S ENVOY PUTS PLEA BEFORE COUNCIL; SAYS SOVIET ASKED OCCUPATION AND OIL RIGHTS

REUTHER ELECTED PRESIDENT OF UAW BY NARROW MARGIN

8-Year Reign of Thomas Is Ended in Balloting Marked by Fist Fights, Near-Riots

VICTOR MAKES UNITY PLEA

Plans Campaign Among Farm Equipment Makers, Pledges Assistance to Murray

By WALTER W. RUCH
Special to The New York Times.

ATLANTIC CITY, N. J., March 27—The United Automobile Workers, CIO, crowned ten years of trade unionism today by electing the 38-year-old red-head to the union presidency that had been held for eight years by R. J. Thomas.

In an election that was as close as it was bitter, the delegates at the tenth convention of the huge union elevated the fiery leader from his post of vice president to one of the most powerful positions in the labor movement by a majority of only 124.4 votes.

The final tabulation, under a system of fractional voting, gave Reuther 4,444.8 and Thomas 4,320.4.

Mr. Reuther's first gesture was one of friendliness toward the Left Wing element that had battled furiously to keep him from office, and his first promise was one that he would exercise every power at his command to bring unity into an organization that has, admittedly, been disintegrating at the top level.

Plans Membership Drive

As for the "common enemy," he immediately outlined plans to expand the membership through drives to organize the farm machinery workers, the white collar workers and the engineers and technicians of the automotive industry as part of the UAW.

In his first address as president, Mr. Reuther sought to scotch, once and for all, rumors of dissension between him and Philip Murray, president of the Congress of Industrial Organizations, by extending full cooperation and expressing an anxious desire to walk at Mr. Murray's side to help bear "his heavy burden."

In a word, Mr. Reuther stepped into the presidency with a plea for unity that he might bind up the factionalism that abounds in a union harboring virtually every breed of political faith in the nation.

The man he had defeated, who had lost in a seventh attempt at re-election, was on the verge of tears as he gave up the office he held since Homer Martin, the first president, was ousted in 1938. He accepted a hearty handshake from the winner, who was heard to say: "Well, Tommy, now we can work together for a better union."

Mr. Thomas was understood reliably to be slated for appointment by Mr. Murray to serve as representative of the CIO on the newly formed World Federation of Trade Unions.

A movement was under way late tonight, however, to draft Mr. Thomas as a candidate for one of the two vice-presidential posts, which will be filled tomorrow. Among those urging such action were a number of Reuther delegates, who called at the Thomas headquarters to express their personal good-will toward the defeated candidate. Mr. Thomas promised an answer in the morning.

Fights Enliven Voting

Fist fights and near-riots enlivened the voting session, which began with nominations at noon and ended at 4:30 P. M., with the most tumultuous demonstration of the convention. So near exhaustion were the frenzied partisans as a result of the narrow margin separating the candidates throughout the day that an overnight recess was taken before proceeding with the election of a secretary-treasurer and two vice presidents.

His red locks flecked with red,

Continued on Page 31, Column 5

When You Think of Writing
Think of Whiting.—Advt.

U. S. Tutor Sought For Hirohito's Son

By Wireless to The New York Times.

TOKYO, March 27 — Emperor Hirohito has asked the members of the American education mission at present here under the chairmanship of Dr. George D. Stoddard, New York State Commissioner of Education, to recommend an American tutor for the 12-year-old Crown Prince Akihito, it was learned in palace circles today.

The report came as members of the mission were received in audience this afternoon, later attended a tea party and witnessed court dances in the presence of the Emperor and his younger brother, Prince Nobushito Takamatsu.

Prince Akihito now is enrolled in the Peers School, of which his father also is a graduate. He also has the tutorial services of R. H. Blythe, an Englishman long resident in Japan, who is teaching him English. It is understood that an American tutor is being sought to supplement Mr. Blythe's teachings.

DRASTIC PROGRAM ON FOOD ADOPTED

UNRRA Resolution Outlines Steps, Including Rationing, to Meet Famine Crisis

UNRRA resolution outlining world food policy, Page 14.

By BESS FURMAN
Special to The New York Times.

ATLANTIC CITY, N. J., March 27—The eleven-nation special food committee, which has been hard at work since Friday on ways of meeting the famine crisis, recommended today rigorous food-saving measures. It also called for a recess in this United Nations Relief and Rehabilitation Administration Council to permit assessing the scarce supply situation, with provision to reconvene in Washington as soon as the director general can report.

With a few slight word changes, the resolution of the food committee was adopted unanimously at a session of the committee of the whole on policy held tonight to close the two weeks debate here on world food.

The expectation here was that the Council would reconvene in Washington in two or three weeks. In the interim the UNRRA director general would be requested under the resolution of the food committee "to consult immediately and continuously with representatives of the supplying Governments and with the combined food board to consider the effectiveness of steps being taken and to report thereon to the Central Committee and the Council." This duty no doubt will devolve on Fiorello La Guardia, slated to succeed Director General Herbert H. Lehman, although Mr. Lehman earlier had agreed to serve through the Council, not anticipating a recess.

Dallas W. Dort, second alternate of the American delegation, who served as chairman of the commit-

Continued on Page 14, Column 2

10c Fare Resolution Withdrawn; Defeat by Board Was Indicated

By PAUL CROWELL

Cornelius A. Hall, Borough President of Richmond, withdrew yesterday, "pending further conferences with Mayor O'Dwyer," the ten-cent subway fare resolution submitted by him to the Board of Estimate on March 14.

Mr. Hall's announcement came soon after the committee of the whole of the Board of Estimate ended a three-hour executive meeting at City Hall. Mayor O'Dwyer and the other Democratic members of the board declined to discuss Mr. Hall's announcement, but it was reliably reported that he decided to withdraw the higher-fare resolution after his colleagues had indicated that they would vote it down today and would not agree

to lay it over for consideration at some future meeting.

The resolution called for a ten-cent fare on all transit lines owned and operated by the city, with free transfers for any single continuous trip. It also provided for a one-cent fare on the Staten Island ferries, with free transfers to subways and certain bus lines. Another provision called for retention of a five-cent fare for school children traveling to and from school.

Mr. Hall declined to discuss details of the proceedings at the executive meeting, but did say that "it was a lengthy discussion."

"I am withdrawing my resolution pending further conferences with Mayor O'Dwyer," he declared. Mayor O'Dwyer recently indi-

Continued on Page 29, Column 5

HOTEL GROSSMAN
In the Beautiful Pine Belt
at Lakewood, New Jersey.—Advt.

IRAN'S STORY TOLD

Ambassador Ala Says He Does Not Know of Any Agreement in Force

DISCLOSES DEMANDS

Byrnes Asks That Case Be Confined to Purely Procedural Issue

Iranian Ambassador's statement of his country's case, P. 9.

By WILL LISSNER

In relief at becoming a participant in the deliberations of the United Nations Security Council on Iran's case, Ambassador Hussein Ala of Iran took a place at the Council table at 5:50 o'clock yesterday afternoon and disclosed demands made by the Soviet Union upon his country in secret Soviet-Iranian negotiations between Feb. 19 and March 3 of this year.

The Iranian Ambassador plunged almost at once to one of the most vigorously discussed points, the question of whether or not there was a Soviet-Iranian agreement, as both Marshal Stalin and the Soviet delegate had indicated, when he stated:

"May I say once and for all that I know of no agreement or understanding, secret or otherwise, having been entered into between my Government and the Soviet Union with respect to any of the matters involved in the dispute now referred to this Council."

Mr. Ala, a short, spare man of quiet dignity, moved on the invitation of the chairman, Dr. Quo Tai-chi, from the seat in the front row of the Council chamber, where for two days he had been a mute witness of the Council's proceedings, to a seat on the extreme right of the table next to Dr. Oskar Lange, Polish representative, after the Council had voted to hear him.

"It was a relief," he said at the close of the session. "Imagine being obliged to watch all this discussion and not being able to begin making a statement."

Keen Interest Shown

While the members of the Council listened with keen interest, Mr. Ala began his presentation of Iran's reasons for opposing delay in consideration of her case.

"The issue between Iran and the Soviet Union was that the latter was interfering in the internal affairs of Iran through the medium of Soviet officials and armed forces," he asserted.

When Prime Minister Ahmad Ghavam of Iran went to Moscow on Feb. 19 to negotiate, as directed by the Security Council in its resolution of last Jan. 30, Mr. Ala continued, the Soviet officials "would not agree to withdraw their troops from Iran or to refrain from interfering in the internal affairs of Iran."

Instead, he said, the Soviet officials made a series of proposals. Soviet troops were to continue to stay in some parts of Iran indefi-

Continued on Page 11, Column 2

IRAN AGAIN DENIES NEW SOVIET PACT

Premier Reiterates No Written or Oral Accord Was Reached in Talks in Moscow

By GENE CURRIVAN
By Wireless to The New York Times.

TEHERAN, Iran, March 27—Official sources here reiterated today that there was no new agreement with the Soviet Union despite all the clamoring for details from other parts of the world. Premier Ahmad Ghavam has not altered his position one degree since he returned from his conference with Moscow.

He said then that he had failed

Continued on Page 11, Column 5

World News Summarized

THURSDAY, MARCH 28, 1946

The Soviet Union walked out of the UNO Security Council session late yesterday afternoon after the Russian proposal to defer consideration of the Iranian question until April 10 had been defeated, 9 to 2. Only Russia and Poland voted for it. When it became evident that Iranian Ambassador Ala would be invited to the table to present his case, Ambassador Gromyko announced he was unable to participate further in the discussions or remain present, picked up his papers and departed. [1:8.]

Mr. Gromyko's withdrawal was in conformity with strict instructions from Moscow and he is expected to attend any sessions before April 10 at which the merits of the Iranian question are not discussed. [1:5-6.] Oskar Lange, Poland's delegate, defended Mr. Gromyko's action and declared that Poland would continue in attendance. [2:2.]

Russia, at the Moscow conferences with Premier Ghavam, instead of agreeing to withdraw from Iran, made counter-proposals that were unacceptable, Mr. Ala disclosed to the Council. The Russians wanted Soviet troops to remain in some parts of Iran "for an indefinite period"; they demanded recognition of Azerbaijan's autonomy and formation of a joint Soviet-Iranian oil company in which Russia would hold 51 per cent of the stock. There have been no further discussions or agreements, he said, and he had not been authorized to agree before Mr. Ala finished. [1:3.] Official sources in Teheran confirmed the lack of any agreement. [1:4.]

The day of debate was marked by frequent sharp exchanges. The Council will meet in executive session this afternoon. [4:2.]

The Military Staff Committee began work on the international police force to maintain world security and peace through the UNO. [10:2.]

Russian Naval Lieutenant Redin was held in $25,000 bail in Portland, Ore., on espionage charges that United States officials called a "frame-up" to damage Russian prestige. He was accused of having induced some unnamed person to obtain data about the destroyer-tender Yellowstone, described as a "floating shipyard." [6:3.]

The British Labor party attacked Communists and dissident left-wingers in a manifesto rejecting a proposal to affiliate with the Communist party, which was accused of harboring fifth columnists. [10:3-4.]

In this country, observers saw a rebuke to leftists in the labor movement [31:2] in the defeat of R. J. Thomas for president of the United Auto Workers Union, CIO. [1:1.]

All nations were urged to their greatest efforts to cut food consumption and increase production to meet the world famine crisis in an UNRRA resolution. [1:2.]

Yugoslavia was warned in a sharp Allied communiqué that American and British occupation troops would oppose any sudden attempt by Marshal Tito's men to seize part of the Venezia Giulia area. [1:7; map P. 15.] Russia presented new draft peace treaties for Bulgaria and Hungary designed to meet Anglo-American objections. [15:2.]

León Blum told American negotiators that France would have to spend at least $17,000,-000,000 in five years to re-establish her economic position and to permit her to play her full part in collective security. [1:6.]

Gromyko Is Stern and Silent As He Leaves UNO Chamber

By W. H. LAWRENCE

With grim, stony-faced determination, young Andrei A. Gromyko took a fateful walk out of the United Nations Security Council at 5:19 P. M., yesterday. He went because the Kremlin had told him that under no circumstances would the Soviet Union present to the Council before April 10 a defense of its actions in Iran. The Council had just rejected, 9 to 2, his motion to postpone the case for two weeks.

He did not wait for his opponent to begin to speak. He did not wait even until the Council had decided the issue affirmatively by inviting his opponent, Hussein Ala, Iranian Ambassador to the United States, to join the Council table.

But Mr. Gromyko will be back.

Continued on Page 3, Column 5

SOVIET DELEGATE WALKS OUT OF UNO—IRAN'S ENVOY TAKES A SEAT

Ambassador Andrei Gromyko is flanked by newspaper men as he leaves the chamber after the delegates refused to postpone discussion of the Iranian dispute until April 10.
The New York Times.

Ambassador Hussein Ala addressing the delegates. At the left is an assistant to Dr. Oskar Lange, Poland's representative, and at the right is Akbar Daftari of the Iranian Embassy. Associated Press

COUNCIL PROCEEDS

Soviet Departure Fails to Swerve Body in Hearing of Issue

SOVIET COURSE HAZY

She Will Be Present at a Meeting Today—Poland Backs Her

Transcript of UNO proceedings on Iran question, Page 8.

By JAMES B. RESTON

The Soviet Union took a walk at the United Nations Security Council meeting yesterday, but it will be represented at the Council's Committee of Experts today, and it will come back to the Council when it feels like it, which will probably be on April 10.

This action, which broke, temporarily, the rule of Big Five unanimity, which the Russians have supported from the start, was not a break with the UNO. It was not to be compared, as some observers have been comparing it, with the German, Italian and Japanese departures from the League of Nations; nor was it an indication that the coalition that produced victory had been dissolved.

It is a decision by the Soviet Government, carried out by its Ambassador to Washington, Andrei A. Gromyko, to leave the Council for two weeks while the question of Red Army troops in Iran is being discussed. It is a parliamentary maneuver. It is an expression of protest against the Council.

Not a Break With Council

But it is not a break with the Council. In fact, not only do the Soviet representatives say they will be in the meeting of the Committee of Experts today, but in addition it is reported that if today's closed session of the Council deals only with the procedural aspects of the Iranian question, they may even attend that, though this is not at all certain.

At 5:04 yesterday afternoon, at the end of what began to look strangely like a filibuster by the Soviet Union, the Council defeated the Soviet Union's motion to postpone discussion of the Iranian case until April 10. Only the U.S.S.R.

At 5:19, before the Council had voted to invite the Iranian Ambassador to sit at the Council table and tell why he thought the case of the Soviet troops in Iran was urgent, the youthful, pokerfaced Soviet delegate, Ambassador Gromyko, raised his hand and addressed the chair.

Soviet Statement on Withdrawal

As he was recognized, the spotlights in the chamber room went on slowly. The chamber was crowded. The delegates, weary of endless argument on legal points, frustrated by the lack of any rules of procedure and frankly out of patience with the Soviet Ambassador's repetitive argument, turned indulgently toward him and settled down for what looked after another long speech. But he was brief and to the point.

"For reasons which I explained clearly enough in our meeting of yesterday and in today's meeting, Mr. Chairman," he said in Russian, "I, as representative of the Soviet Union, am not able to take part further in the discussions of the Security Council because my proposal has not been accepted by the Council, nor am I able to be present at the meeting of the Council, and I therefore leave the meeting."

For a few minutes the audience did not understand the meaning of this, for when he finished speaking he waited expressionless in his chair until the translators and

Continued on Page 3, Column 1

ALLIES WARN TITO ON VENEZIA GIULIA

Issue Blunt Statement Against Any Yugoslav Move to Invade Disputed Zone at Trieste

By SAM POPE BREWER
By Wireless to The New York Times.

ROME, March 27—The Allied Governments issued a firm warning tonight to the Yugoslavs against any effort to stage a sudden invasion of the disputed Zone A of Venezia Giulia, now occupied by Anglo-American forces.

In the most blunt statement made on the subject in many months, Lieut. Gen. William D. Morgan, Supreme Allied Commander in the Mediterranean theatre, from his headquarters in Caserta, speaking in the names of the American and British Governments, said: "Public order will be enforced with justice, and in our zone we shall tolerate no attempt to prejudge in any way the final disposition of the territory.

"To this end, the American and British Governments have authorized me to declare that it is their firm intention to maintain their present position in Venezia Giulia until an agreed settlement of the territorial dispute has been reached and put into effect."

Allied Forces Reduced

This is the first time since the agreement was signed with Marshal Tito last June for the present division of Venezia Giulia into Zones A and B that such action has been necessary by the British and Americans.

[Zone A constitutes about a quarter of the area on the western side of the peninsula against the Italian frontier, and includes

Continued on Page 15, Column 2

BLUM PUTS NO TOP ON SIZE OF U. S. LOAN

Emissary Says France Needs $5,000,000,000 of Our Goods to Modernize Industry

By JOHN H. CRIDER
Special to The New York Times.

WASHINGTON, March 27—Léon Blum, special French emissary to the United States, opened the current financial negotiations by painting a pitiable picture of France as "a nation twice ruined in thirty years," but citing the post-war accomplishments of her people as evidence of their courage and determination to recover.

The release today by the French Embassy of excerpts from M. Blum's lengthy presentation at the opening session on Monday was the first of a series of official releases under the rule of liberal public information adopted yesterday by the negotiators.

M. Blum opened on a note of "great solemnity" to stress the unity of all French political parties in supporting the "principles of democracy" and the "unconditional and unqualified" acceptance by France and all her constituent parties of the "principles of collec-

Continued on Page 17, Column 2

Braden Bars a Break With Peron; Says Europe Needs Argentine Aid

Spruille Braden, Assistant Secretary of State and leading exponent of a firm policy in dealing with Argentina, indicated yesterday that there was nothing we could do at the moment about the Perón regime, recently victorious in the election held there.

In a frank discussion here, Mr. Braden ruled out the breaking of diplomatic relations as "silly," and any attempt to impose sanctions as futile, because neither France nor Britain would back us, nor would we, in this country, want to assume the responsibility of depriving the starving of Europe of the food Argentina could supply.

Mr. Braden was the principal speaker at a seminar for women's clubs, arranged by THE NEW YORK TIMES in cooperation with the General Federation of Wom-

en's Clubs, held at Times Hall, 240 West Forty-fourth street.

Other speakers on the program, the first of three scheduled, included Turner Catledge, assistant managing editor; Foster Hailey, editorial writer; James B. Reston, national correspondent; Anne O'Hare McCormick, editorial correspondent, all of THE TIMES; John J. McCloy, former assistant Secretary of War; Mrs. William Dick Sporborg of the General Federation of Women's Clubs and Mrs. Arthur Hays Sulzberger, who welcomed the guests.

Mr. Braden's exposition of our present attitude toward Argentina came during the question and answer period. The question to which he addressed himself was:

"If the United States applies

Continued on Page 3, Column 1

PURE WATER is vital to health. Drink Great Bear Ideal Spring Water. GR. 5-3810.—Advt.

The New York Times.

Copyright, 1946, by The New York Times Company.
VOL. XCV..No. 32,239.
Entered as Second-Class Matter. Postoffice, New York, N. Y.
NEW YORK, WEDNESDAY, MAY 1, 1946.
THREE CENTS NEW YORK CITY

LATE CITY EDITION
Partly cloudy and mild today. Occasional showers tomorrow.
Temperature Yesterday—Max., 64; Min., 61
Full U. S. Weather Bureau Report, Page 31

WARSHIP BLOWS UP AT MUNITIONS PIER IN PORT, KILLING 5

60 on Escort Vessel Injured —Blasts Shake New Jersey Towns Near Big Depot

BOMBS ASHORE SET OFF

Sailor Is Only Slightly Hurt as Depth Charge Explodes as He Is Carrying It

By MEYER BERGER
Special to The New York Times.

LEONARDO, N. J., April 30—One officer and four sailors of the destroyer escort Solar's complement of fourteen officers and 136 enlisted men vanished utterly before noon today in an ammunition explosion that tore away one-third of the 306-foot ship's forward structure.

About sixty of the ship's crew were injured, but only thirty-five were hospitalized, and of them only a handful remained tonight for further treatment. The Navy withheld the names of the five missing men and the names of the injured because not all their families had been officially notified.

The explosion happened as the Solar's crew was unloading her ammunition supply in preparation for an overhaul. Normally she carries about fifteen tons of assorted ammunition, including depth bombs and smaller charges, torpedoes and shells for her cannon. Only one-third of this amount was still aboard when the blast occurred.

Tons of Explosives Near By

Near by, when the detonation shook the New Jersey coast in and around the Raritan Bay district, were a number of other vessels preparing to unload ammunition. It was unofficially estimated here that these vessels held, all told, about 25,000 tons of explosives. Tugs dragged these craft out of the danger zone.

Burning fragments from the Solar, hurled at tremendous force against freight cars on the pier, started other explosions. One car in a freight string, filled chiefly with depth charges, blew up and all but vanished in dust and smoke, scattering its parts in all directions. Three strings of cars were hauled shoreward by their locomotive crews, at great risk.

No one seemed certain tonight what had caused the explosion, but what seemed like a possible explanation came from Jack Horne, fireman second class, of Charlotte, N. C. He thought a piece of ammunition carried by Joseph Stuchinski, seaman, of Baltimore, might have done it.

"Ski," the fireman said, "was carrying a 'hedgehog' from the forward magazine. While he was holding it, it just went off. He must have bumped it against something, because those things go off when anything touches them."

Seaman Stuchinski, oddly enough, was not seriously injured. He was deafened, a few minor scratches showed on his chest when he got to the first-aid station and his dungarees were split.

"It went off. The thing just went off," he said.

The "hedgehog" Stuchinski carried was an anti-submarine depth charge. Metal-cased, weighing about sixty pounds, it is generally cylindrical, about thirty inches long and between four and five inches in diameter.

Bow Like Elephant's Trunk

The Solar lay at the northern, or bay end, of the easternmost of the three great piers that jut out from the Navy's Earle Ammunition Depot, when she blew up. She was approximately one and one-half miles from the beach end of the depot. The blast curled her bow in much the same shape as an elephant's back-bent trunk.

The concussion was felt twenty to thirty miles around. The detonation rushed across Raritan Bay to shake homes in Tottenville, Richmond Valley, Pleasant Plains, Princess Bay, Great Kills, Oakwood and New Dorp, all on Staten Island and shattered panes in some of those communities.

Ground tremors were felt to the west and to the southwest. These were some freakish effects. Residents in Middletown Township, including Rumson, Fair Haven, Red Bank and Little Silver, for example, seemed certain the explosion was local. Several frightened housewives called the police to say, "the boiler just blew up in my cellar."

Dogs raced away from the beach

Continued on Page 2, Column 3

AFTER EXPLOSIONS RIPPED DESTROYER ESCORT

The wrecked U. S. S. Solar at the Navy Ammunition Depot in Earle, N. J., yesterday
The New York Times (U. S. Navy)

BAN BY MUSICIANS BLOW TO TELEVISION

Petrillo Plans to Prolong the Refusal of Union Men to the Industry Indefinitely

By JACK GOULD

The American Federation of Musicians, headed by James C. Petrillo, plans to forbid its members to work in television until some indefinite date in the future when the union can determine the effects of video's advent on present-day radio, it was learned yesterday.

Television broadcasters were agreed that Mr. Petrillo's stand would retard the immediate development of video programs, since it could be a matter of months if not years before anyone could determine to what extent television would supplant or complement sound broadcasting.

Use of "live" musicians was first denied the television industry in February, 1945, by the international executive board of the federation, but yesterday was the first time that Mr. Petrillo explained the action and indicated that the ban would be of prolonged duration.

Musical Films Already Banned

Last week Mr. Petrillo's union and the Hollywood motion picture producers entered into an agreement not to permit films containing music to be used in television, a move leaving the telecasters with only records as a possible source of music. Beginning July 1, under a rule of the Federal Communications Commission, the television stations are scheduled to offer twenty-eight hours of programs a week, but under Mr. Petrillo's edicts they will be able to rely primarily on talks, sporting events and other non-musical fare.

Coincidentally with stating the union's position on television, Mr. Petrillo also reiterated his stand against permitting standard radio programs containing music to be presented simultaneously on frequency modulation outlets. The union is insisting on double crews of musicians in the event of such duplication.

The re-statement of the union's views on FM were regarded with

Continued on Page 28, Column 2

Stalin Warns of War Plot By 'International Reaction'

By The Associated Press.

LONDON, April 30—Generalissimo Stalin promised tonight that the Soviet Union would be true to a policy of peace and security but charged that what he described as "international reaction" was "hatching plans of a new war." In an order of the day broadcast by the Moscow radio the Russian leader also declared that it was necessary to be constantly vigilant, "to protect as the apple of one's eye the armed forces and defensive power of our country."

TEXT OF STALIN ORDER

His broadcast order, issued in connection with the Soviet Union's May Day celebration, was heard in London by the Soviet monitor, who issued the following text:

Comrades, Red Army and Red Navy men, sergeants and petty officers, comrade officers, generals and admirals, working people of the Soviet Union:

Today, for the first time since the victorious termination of the Great Patriotic War we celebrate May 1—the international holiday of working people—in conditions of peaceful life, won in a hard struggle against the enemies at the cost of heavy sacrifices and privations.

One year ago the Red Army hoisted the banner of victory over Berlin and completed the defeat of fascist Germany. Within four months after the victorious termination of the war against Germany, imperialist Japan downed her arms. The Second World War, prepared by the forces of international reaction and unleashed by the chief fascist states, ended in a full victory of the freedom-loving nations. The smashup and liquidation of the main hotbeds of fascism and world aggression resulted in changes in the political life of the nations of the world, in a wide growth of the democratic movement of the nations.

Taught by the experience of war, the popular masses realized that the destinies of states cannot be entrusted to reactionary leaders, who pursue the narrow caste and selfish anti-popular aims. It is for this reason that nations, which no longer wish to live in the old way, take destinies of their states into their own hands, establish democratic order and actively fight against the forces of reaction, against instigators of a new war. The nations of the

Continued on Page 5, Column 4

INQUIRY FINDS 'PERIL' TO SECRETS OF WAR

Senators Hear Radar Makers on Russian Buying and Urge Law Tightening

By C. P. TRUSSELL
Special to The New York Times.

WASHINGTON, April 30—Need for a tightening of the laws to provide protection for wartime secrets against attempts to gather in the electronics and other fields was declared by Senate investigators today to be "very definite." The statement came after a closed-session inquiry into negotiations for sales of radar and similar equipment to Russia.

Members of a special Senate Judiciary subcommittee, conducting the investigation, said that there was no evidence that "classified,"

Continued on Page 4, Column 2

World News Summarized

WEDNESDAY, MAY 1, 1946

Palestine should become neither a Jewish state nor an Arab state, the Anglo-American Committee of Inquiry declared in its report made public simultaneously last night in Washington and London. Admission of 100,000 Jews this year and virtual abrogation of the 1939 British White Paper with its restrictions on land holdings were recommended. Other suggestions included continuation of the present mandate until establishment of a United Nations trusteeship and resolute suppression of violence and terrorism by Jews or Arabs. [1:8.]

Although President Truman expressed pleasure over certain parts of the report, it was felt in Washington that neither the Jews nor Arabs would be satisfied. [13.1.] In fact, Arab leaders threatened to combat any additional Jewish immigration [13:3] and Zionists expressed their opposition. Bartley C. Crum, a member of the committee, predicted that a directive authorizing the entry of 100,000 Jews into Palestine would "issue forthwith." [1:6-7.] British reaction counted heavily upon American support in whatever was done, but rejected the absence of any long-term solution. [1:1.]

Italy will be permitted to retain most of southern Tyrol despite Austrian claims, the Foreign Ministers tentatively agreed at their conference in Paris, but they were as wide apart as ever on what to do about Trieste and the Venezia Giulia area. It was decided to invite Yugoslavia and Italy to present their cases anew. [1:5.]

Britain tried to meet French desires by suggesting internationalization of either the Ruhr or both the Ruhr and the left bank of the Rhine for fifty years. [2:1.] Secretary Byrnes' proposed four-power treaty to keep Germany disarmed was favorably received in the Senate Foreign Affairs Committee. [2:2.] The United Nations Security Council subcommittee opens its investigation into Franco Spain this afternoon. [1:7.] Europe's ruined industries should be restored before attempts to eradicate world unemployment, the Economic and Employment Commission heard [8:5], while the Transport and Communications Commission debated the relative merits of free enterprise and government control of shipping. [7:1.] The Commission on Human Rights may seek a new international bill of rights and ask authority to supervise its implementation. [8:2.]

Tabriz, capital of Azerbaijan, has been formally evacuated by Russian troops, the Tabriz radio reported. [3:6.] Premier Stalin declared that, while the world must remain vigilant against reaction, it had "no reason to doubt" that Russia would remain steadfast in her devotion to international peace and security. [1:3-4.]

Japan was shocked at the plot to assassinate General MacArthur and the Government offered its apologies. No arrests have been announced. [1:6-7.]

Ammunition being unloaded from the destroyer-escort Solar in Raritan Bay exploded, killing an officer and four sailors. [1:1.]

John L. Lewis served notice that anthracite miners intended to strike on May 31 unless they obtained the same demands that led to the soft-coal strike. Negotiations will start in New York on May 10. No progress was made toward settling the bituminous dispute. [1:1.]

Further restrictions were placed on the use of grain by distillers in order to make more food available for world famine relief. [1:2-3.]

General Motors was authorized by the OPA to raise prices on its cars from $16 to $60 to cover wage increases. [27:6-7.] House members returned to Washington still opposed to extending price control without heavy restrictions. [30:5.]

BIG FOUR RULE OUT AUSTRIA'S DEMAND FOR SOUTH TYROL

Paris Conference Rejects Any Major Frontier Revision In That Region of Italy

NO PROGRESS ON TRIESTE

Rome and Belgrade Are Asked to Send Delegates—Report of Experts Confusing

By C. L. SULZBERGER
By Cable to The New York Times.

PARIS, April 30—Now that Italy's retention of most of the Province of Bolzano [South Tyrol], which is claimed by Austria, was virtually assured tonight after the Council of Foreign Ministers had agreed that no requests for a major frontier change would be accepted in that area so valuable in hydroelectric power.

At the same time, after examining a verbose and confused report on Trieste and Venezia Giulia, submitted at long last by the special commission sent by the Foreign Ministers' deputies to investigate the Italian-Yugoslav border area, the Ministers agreed to invite the Yugoslav and Italian Governments to send delegates here on Friday to present once again their views on this hotly disputed and vitally important region.

The report showed a complete divergence in opinion between the Soviet investigator and the three other participants on the value of a census taken in 1945 by a Yugoslav, Professor Rodlich. The Soviet member of the commission said the census was fine and the three others said it was just the opposite. Since this census is of vital importance in deciding the ethnic basis for a decision, that leaves everything up in the air.

Suggested by Molotov

The move to widen the scope of the Foreign Ministers' meeting by inviting in the Italians and Yugoslavs was suggested by Vyacheslav M. Molotov. The Soviet Foreign Minister recalled that the Potsdam decisions, the "bible" under which the peace treaties are being drafted, provided that the interested parties should be included when necessary. Thus, the doors have been opened to permit entry of those delegations—Greek, Italian, Yugoslav, Hungarian and Bulgarian—now clamoring for a

Continued on Page 3, Column 4

Sharp Restrictions in Distilling Ordered in Food Conservation

By CHARLES E. EGAN
Special to The New York Times.

WASHINGTON, April 30—World famine is more than a short term problem, and plans to meet its reappearance next winter should be drafted immediately, Chester C. Davis, chairman of the President's Special Famine Emergency Committee, asserted today.

Mr. Davis, who conferred with President Truman, later said that emergency measures, taken to insure larger relief shipment of grains and other foods to faminestricken areas in the next few weeks, could not be considered as final, but were merely "the first sprint" in a continuing race to avert death for millions who otherwise would starve.

Meanwhile, Secretary Anderson issued an order restricting distilleries who operated for five days at full mashing capacity in April to three capacity days in May.

The order also limited the use of grain by the entire distilling industry to 2,000,000 bushels a month, based on use of wheat in the

manufacture of spirits and restricted distillers to the use of corn which is unsuitable for human consumption.

In January, distillers were permitted ten capacity mashing days, but were cut to seven and one-half in February and to five days in March and April.

Brewers, operating on a 30 per cent reduction of grain, were not included in today's order.

"Every report coming before us makes it plain that the present famine is not a short run emergency that ends on July 1," Mr. Davis' statement said, adding:

"The present food shortages have been seriously aggravated by drought in many parts of the world, but even with good weather the wartime destruction of agricultural facilities will be felt for a long time.

"Farm animals and farm machinery have been destroyed. The strength of farm workers has

Continued on Page 22, Column 3

JOINT PALESTINE BODY BARS A JEWISH STATE, BUT URGES ENTRY OF 100,000 REFUGEES

Arabs 'Outraged' by Report; Jews Are Far From Satisfied

Rival Agencies Reiterate Their Arguments — U. S., British Talks Are Forecast on Easing Burden Too Big for London

By HERBERT L. MATTHEWS
By Wireless to The New York Times.

LONDON, April 30—Now that the report of the Anglo-American Committee of Inquiry on Palestine has been published, one can safely predict tonight that the next step will be for the British to consult the United States Government about it. The British have reached the point at which they consider that Palestine is far too great a burden for them to be forced to handle alone.

No Government spokesman would say anything about the report tonight because the Cabinet and other officials have not had time to study it. One must keep in mind that the members of the committee had a mandate only to make recommendations, which do not in any sense involve Governmental responsibility.

The Arab Office in London has lost no time in issuing a scorching statement condemning the report, lock, stock and barrel. The Jewish Agency for Palestine gave the report a mixed reception. It was happy about the proposal to allow 100,000 Jewish refugees to enter Palestine but asserted that without the formation of a Jewish state there could be no solution to the problem of homeless Jews.

On all sides one hears dubious comment about the fact that the committee's report makes no suggestion in terms of any sort of finality nor does it even offer any kind of long-term solution to the Palestinian problem. It is feared that even moderate elements among the Arabs will be more disturbed about that feature of the report than any other.

In their present mood of shocked disgust over the murder of seven British soldiers in Tel Aviv last Thursday the British are inclined to place the most prominence on that part of the report dealing with security and with making it clear that violence and terrorism will be resolutely repressed. The state-

Continued on Page 14, Column 3

Truman Said to Plan Start Of Jewish Entry 'Forthwith'

By LAWRENCE RESNER

Bartley C. Crum, one of the six United States members of the Joint Anglo-American Committee of Inquiry on Palestine, predicted here yesterday, on the basis of a discussion he had with President Truman at the White House on Monday, that the directives authorizing the admission of 100,000 European Jews into Palestine would "issue forthwith."

Mr. Crum, a San Francisco lawyer, also expressed the belief that most Jewish groups would endorse the affirmative aspects of the report, although reserving their right to continue a fight for the achievement of their own ideological tenets, principally a Jewish state.

An immediate endorsement of the recommendation to obtain the admission of the 100,000 European Jews came from Joseph M. Proskauer, president of the American Jewish Committee, who said the provisions for immediate action were "obviously based on the highest considerations of statesmanship and humanity."

The World Zionist Emergency Council, which speaks for some of the largest and most active Zionist groups in the United States, is in motion the first formal investigation by the United Nations, authorized Monday by a 10-to-0 vote of the Security Council, in which Russia did not participate but refrained from exercising an asserted right to veto the inquiry.

The initial negative response by a Jewish group came from the Political Action Committee for Palestine, whose executive vice chairman, Dr. Baruch Korff, said that despite the report's few fine points, the commission had proved

Continued on Page 15, Column 6

U. N.'S SPAIN INQUIRY COMMENCES TODAY

5-Man Subcommittee to Meet Here in Secret—No Outside Witnesses at First Session

By W. H. LAWRENCE

The Franco regime in Spain goes on trial today on charges that it is a cause of international friction and a threat to world peace.

Meeting privately at 3 P. M., representatives of Australia, China, France, Poland and Brazil will set in motion the first formal investigation by the United Nations, authorized Monday by a 10-to-0 vote of the Security Council, in which Russia did not participate but refrained from exercising an asserted right to veto the inquiry.

How, where and when the Council subcommittee will function presumably will be decided in the early part of today's meeting, and the members then will turn to analyzing the evidence now before them, listing the specific charges

Continued on Page 7, Column 3

MacArthur Plot Alarms Japanese; They See Possible Repercussions

By The Associated Press.

TOKYO, April 30—News of a frustrated assassination plot against General Douglas MacArthur tonight shocked the Japanese.

The first reaction was two-fold: A feeling that their country had lost face; fears that repercussions might be felt in every household.

The Government officially apologized. Katsuo Okazaki, representing Foreign Minister Shigeru Yoshida, visited General MacArthur's office two hours after Allied Headquarters had announced discovery of the plot. He did not see the general personally, but delivered a verbal message to aides.

Mr. Okazaki expressed "deep regret and concern" and said that Government was "greatly embarrassed." He asked if there was anything his Government could do. Barker, Premier Kijuro Shidehara, Mr. Yoshida and Home Minister Chuzo Mitsuchi conferred.

Japanese reporters speculated that they discussed tighter precautions than previously were planned for the May Day demonstrations.

Many Japanese immediately asked, "Will this create more anti-Japanese feeling in America?" They linked this with fear that adverse American reaction might complicate American efforts to obtain food and might mean a longer, harsher occupation.

They also expressed regret that the incident might mar the occupation and change the attitude of General MacArthur, whom the Japanese generally respect.

Allied headquarters had previously given some details of the plot. One conspirator was seized and a nation-wide hunt was launched for the die-hard Japanese militarist named as the arch plotter.

The accused and hunted plot leader was Hideo Tokagama, former member of the Kempeitai or "thought police." In the

Continued on Page 13, Column 6

TRUMAN FOR ACTION

Inquiry Upholds His Visa Proposal, Urges End of White Paper

WOULD GUARD ARAB RIGHTS

Report for Change in Holy Land Property Curbs—Demands a Firm Stand on Violence

The text of the report of the Anglo-American Committee of Inquiry on Palestine, Pages 15 to 21, inclusive.

By FELIX BELAIR Jr.
Special to The New York Times.

WASHINGTON, April 30—The Anglo-American Committee of Inquiry on problems of Jews in Europe and Palestine, reporting to the two Governments today on its four-month investigation, urged the admission of 100,000 European Jews into the Holy Land as soon as possible, but flatly rejected the idea of a Jewish state, together with Arab claims for dominance. It asserted Christendom's own interest in the area.

Released simultaneously for publication in Washington and London, the report drew from President Truman an expression of satisfaction that his proposal for the admission of 100,000 Jews into Palestine had been recommended. He added that "the transference of these unfortunate people should now be accomplished with the greatest dispatch."

The President declared it significant that the report aimed at guarantees for Arab civil and religious rights and urged measures to improve Arab cultural, educational and economic positions.

Land Changes Asked

"I am also pleased," he said, "that the committee recommends, in effect, the abrogation of the White Paper of 1939."

The report repudiated the 1939 White Paper principles, which made further Jewish immigration dependent on Arab consent and banned Jewish land purchases in a major part of Palestine.

Dependent for its final effect on adoption by both Governments, the report covered a wide range of controversial subjects on which President Truman gave no hint of his attitude except to say that he was taking them under advisement.

However, Mr. Truman seemed to have embraced the major policy statement rejecting "once and for all the exclusive claims of Jews and Arabs to Palestine," which the committee enunciated as follows:

"(I. That Jew shall not dominate Arab and Arab shall not dominate Jew in Palestine. (II.) That Palestine shall be neither a Jewish state nor an Arab state. (III.) That the form of government ultimately to be established shall, under international guarantees, fully protect and preserve the interests in the Holy Land of Christendom and of the Moslem and Jewish faiths."

Stress on Unique Status

With deliberate emphasis, the Committee of Inquiry declared that "Palestine is a Holy Land, sacred to Christian, to Jew and to Moslem alike; and because it is a Holy Land, Palestine is not, and can never become, a land which any race or religion can justly claim as its very own."

With equal emphasis, the committee said the same considerations set Palestine apart from other lands, and dedicated it to the precepts and practices of the brotherhood of man rather than to those of narrow nationalism.

The 42,000-word report was signed in Lausanne, Switzerland, by Judge Joseph C. Hutcheson, United States chairman, Sir John E. Singleton, British chairman, Frank Aydelotte, Frank W. Buxton, Bartley C. Crum, James G. McDonald and William Phillips, American members, and W. F. Crick, R. H. S. Crossman, Frederick Leggett, R. E. Manningham-Buller and M. Morrison for Britain. For the immediate future the

Continued on Page 14, Column 2

"All the News
That's Fit to Print"

The New York Times.

LATE CITY EDITION
Mostly sunny today. Fair and
warmer tomorrow.

Temperature Yesterday—Max., 54; Min., 4:
Sunrise today, 6:58 A. M.; Sunset, 6:17 P. M.
Full U. S. Weather Bureau Report, Page 20

Copyright, 1946, by The New York Times Company

VOL. XCVI...No. 32,393.

Entered as Second-Class Matter,
Postoffice, New York, N. Y.

NEW YORK, WEDNESDAY, OCTOBER 2, 1946.

THREE CENTS NEW YORK CITY

12 NAZI WAR LEADERS SENTENCED TO BE HANGED; GOERING HEADS LIST OF THOSE TO DIE BY OCT. 16; HESS GETS LIFE, SIX OTHERS ORDERED TO PRISON

SHIP OFFICERS QUIT, PARALYZING PORT 2D TIME IN MONTH

Never Before Have Masters Been Called From Bridges —Engineers Also Strike

WASHINGTON PLEAS FAIL

But Efforts to Settle Dispute Over Wages and Working Conditions Are Continued

By GEORGE HORNE

The cogs of the nation's merchant marine slowed to a standstill yesterday for the second time in a month as the unprecedented strike of licensed officers got under way.

It was unprecedented because never before in the country's shipping history have shipmasters—captains earning as much as $500 and $600 a month—been called from their bridges in a union action to enforce wage and working demands. But they were leaving their ships on order, along with brother engineer officers of the Marine Engineers Beneficial Association.

Reaction among the captains was mixed, and the situation affecting them at a late hour last night was obscure, after a welter of messages to and from the negotiating headquarters in Washington, where Government authorities were still trying to effect a settlement before the walkout could settle down to a long-term affair.

Many Captains Not in Union

Many captains are not members of the National Organization of Masters, Mates and Pilots (AFL), even on such ships as have MMP contracts. Shipping operators said the captains, who are the owners' supreme representatives aboard, and as such considered beyond the call of strike action, were "being threatened."

They declared that Capt. Harry Martin, East Coast president of the MMP, had agreed in Washington yesterday to leave security watches aboard all ships, including a captain and a day and night mate for stand-by duty. But they said the pledge was not being honored.

At a special meeting of the AFL Maritime Trades Department at the office of the International Longshoremen's Association last night it was announced that "the status quo" remains. That meant that captains were being called off, whether they agreed or not. The AFL spokesman said the response among all MMP officers was excellent.

Ship operators took the position that the masters were "in the middle" and "behind the eight-ball," and they agreed that many would have to leave their ships at the union's call.

The MMP leaders have stood by their original conception of the walkout as being no strike. It was, the union leaders said, simply a case of the men not working in

Continued on Page 4, Column 3

Cards Beat Dodgers In First Game, 4-2

Despite a muscle ailment, Howie Pollet pitched the Cardinals to a 4-2 victory over the Dodgers at St. Louis yesterday in the first of a three-game play-off series for the National League pennant. The Cards meanwhile routed Ralph Branca, first of five Brooklyn pitchers, with three runs in as many innings.

Howie Schultz momentarily tied the score for the Dodgers with his homer in the third and also batted in their second run with a single in the seventh. The play-offs, first such in the history of major league baseball, will be resumed tomorrow at Ebbets Field, and the third contest, if necessary, will be played there Friday.

(Complete details on Page 35.)

Write "SKY-RITE" for sample free air-mail envelopes. 76 Varick St., N. Y.—Advt.

12 Inches of Snow Blanket Several Up-State Areas

Flurries Are Reported as Far South as the Pennsylvania Line—Temperature Here Is Near Record Low for Date

By The Associated Press.

ALBANY, Oct. 1 — Canadian-border areas of upper New York dug out tonight from more than a foot of snow as high winds churned the tail-end of the season's first storm into near-blizzard fury.

It was still snowing early tonight, but a United States weather forecaster described the pre-winter blast as a one-day storm. He predicted low temperatures for another 48 hours.

The storm, whipping across the Adirondack area from Canada, forced some schools to close, blocked secondary highways and disrupted power and communications lines in northern New York.

Although the brunt of the storm was felt in the upper Adirondacks, its effect was State-wide. Temperatures plummeted toward the freezing mark and snow flurries were reported in western and southern New York, along the Pennsylvania line.

Syracuse, reporting its earliest

snow in forty-four years of official records, had a half-inch.

New York City's 45-degree temperature early this morning was within three degrees of the 1916 record low for the date.

Some up-State areas without snow had steady rain. Saratoga Springs reported a twenty-four-hour fall of 1.5 inches and Schenectady had 2.08 inches in the thirty-six hours ending at 8 A. M.

The villages of Malone in Franklin County and Potsdam in St. Lawrence apparently were hardest hit, with traffic crippled and heavy damage caused by falling trees and branches. Malone had 13 inches of snow and Potsdam a foot. Both were without electric power.

Malone's gas service was cut partly when a falling tree damaged an iron culvert. The Alice Hyde Memorial Hospital was without electricity all morning and gas most of the day. Power was re-

Continued on Page 27, Column 2

LEHMAN 'STRADDLE' CHARGED BY IVES

Says Rival Evades Wallace Foreign Policy Issue With Aim to Placate Left

Special to THE NEW YORK TIMES.

ALBANY, Oct. 1—Irving M. Ives, Republican candidate for United States Senator, charged tonight that former Governor Herbert H. Lehman, his Democratic opponent, had issued a "shadow doctrine" on foreign policy designed to placate both mid-line Democrats and left-wing groups.

Mr. Lehman, he declared, straddled the issue and took a "vague and insecure" stand which had something to please "each of the political organizations and splinter parties he represents in this campaign."

In a State-wide radio broadcast he challenged Mr. Lehman to tell the people whether he agreed with Secretary of State James F. Byrnes or with former Secretary of Commerce Henry A. Wallace. He declared it impossible to side with both.

Challenge on "Enslavement"

"Mr. Wallace believes in drawing an iron curtain across eastern Europe," he said, adding:

"We have seen that wars arise when people are enslaved and the truth kept from them. Does my opponent favor a policy which would permit this condition to ex-

Continued on Page 3, Column 3

HULL, 75, STRICKEN AFTER PEACE PLEA

United Nations' 'Father' Calls on Powers to Renew Zeal —His Condition Serious

Text of Mr. Hull's statement appears on page 18.

By BERTRAM D. HULEN

WASHINGTON, Oct. 1—Cordell Hull, former Secretary of State, suffered a stroke in the United States Naval Hospital at Bethesda, Md., last night, a few hours after he had completed a statement appealing to the Great Powers to compose their differences for the sake of world peace.

The stroke was officially described at first as "slight," but the hospital announced later that Mr. Hull's condition had become "more serious during the day." Friends meanwhile had described him as extremely weak and had expressed grave concern. They considered his condition to be critical.

A hospital bulletin issued at 10 o'clock tonight said Mr. Hull remained in serious condition. "No improvement has been noted in his condition since the last bulletin," it said. "No change" was reported at midnight.

Nevertheless, the former Secretary's statement for world peace was issued on his behalf tonight, carrying out his instructions. It

Continued on Page 18, Column 3

11,236-MILE RECORD SET AS NAVY PLANE LANDS IN COLUMBUS

Truculent Turtle Smashes Old Mark by 3,300 Miles in Non-Stop Flight From Australia

UP 55 HOURS 15 MINUTES

Four-Man Crew, Fresh Despite Rough Hop, Is Disappointed at Not Finishing in Washington

By FREDERICK GRAHAM
Special to THE NEW YORK TIMES.

COLUMBUS, Ohio, Oct. 1—A non-stop flight distance record that surpassed the previous mark by more than 3,300 miles was set today when the Truculent Turtle, the Navy's new twin-engine, land-based patrol bomber, landed here to complete an 11,236-mile flight that started Sunday morning in Perth, Australia.

The plane touched down here at 12:25 P. M., Eastern standard time.

The time for the flight, which started in the warm spring weather of Australia and ended in chilly winds here, was 55 hours 15 minutes. Despite a heavy load of fuel and constant headwinds that averaged 11.5 miles an hour for the entire trip, the average speed of the plane was 203.4 miles an hour.

The old distance record, set by the four-motored Dreamboat, a Superfortress, in a flight from Guam to Washington, was 7,916 miles.

Like "Long Patrol Mission"

"You might say it was no tougher than a good, long patrol mission," Comdr. Thomas D. Davies, chief of the four-man crew of the Truculent Turtle, said after the plane had completed the 11,236-mile flight.

Davies, chief of the four-man crew, Hjalmar Schacht asked for chocolate for his two children tonight. When the three men acquitted by the International Military Tribunal appeared before 200 representatives of the world press.

Schacht got his candy bars and all reaped a harvest of cigarettes

Continued on Page 12, Column 3

World News Summarized

WEDNESDAY, OCTOBER 2, 1946

Twelve high Nazi conspirators were sentenced by the International Military Tribunal in Nuremberg yesterday to death by hanging for the supreme crime of aggressive war; three received life sentences in prison, four received lesser terms and three were acquitted.

The men who will be executed not later than Oct. 16 are Goering, von Ribbentrop, Kaltenbrunner, Rosenberg, Frank, Frick, Streicher, Sauckel, Seyss-Inquart, Keitel and Jodl. Bormann was sentenced to death in absentia. Hess, Funk and Grand Admiral Raeder received life sentences, von Schirach and Speer twenty years, von Neurath fifteen years and Grand Admiral Doenitz ten years. Schacht, von Papen and Fritzsche were acquitted. [All the foregoing 1:8.]

The verdicts on Hess, and the exoneration of the General Staff, Cabinet and Storm Troops as organizations brought a strong dissent from the Russian Justice, Maj. Gen. Nikitchenko. The chief American prosecutor, Justice Jackson, said he was "disappointed" in the liberation of von Papen and Schacht, because it would adversely affect further prosecution of industrialists and militarists. [1:6-7.]

Russia accused the United States at a commission session of the Conference of Paris of attempting to change agreements reached by the Foreign Ministers Council on Trieste, and the Slav bloc succeeded in delaying a vote. [1:7.]

Former Secretary of State Hull, who is 75 years old today, suffered a stroke in Bethesda Naval Hospital shortly after completing a statement urging the Great Powers to compose their differences for the sake of peace. His condition is serious. "Incalculable disaster" would follow any

irreconcilable division in this "most perilous juncture in history," Mr. Hull said. [1:3.]

A House committee, it was disclosed, has been quietly laying the basis for early Congressional approval for this country's first integrated, permanent worldwide espionage and counterespionage service. [13:1.]

Iran, rejecting Britain's disavowals, has asked for the recall of a British Embassy secretary accused of conspiring to bring about a revolt of southern tribesmen. [11:1.]

Dmitri Shostakovich's new Ninth Symphony has been condemned in the Soviet press for ideological weakness and failing to reflect the true spirit of the Russian people. [31:3-4.]

Bernard M. Baruch characterized as "either misinformation or complete distortion" charges at a political rally by supporters of former Secretary Wallace that the United States expected other nations to give up their atomic energy secrets while this country withheld all information. [1:6-7.]

The American Merchant Marine was almost completely tied up by the strike of engineers and dock officers that began at midnight yesterday. Federal conciliation efforts continued without result. [1:1.]

No progress was made toward ending the Pittsburgh power walkout that has halted production on vital materials [2:2], and a strike of CIO warehouse and office workers threatens to paralyze the dress manufacturing industry in New York. [2:4.] Thirty-seven persons were injured in a picketing riot at Hollywood studios. [3:1.]

The Navy bomber Truculent Turtle landed at Columbus, Ohio, establishing a new world distance record of 11,236 miles in its non-stop flight from Perth, Australia. [1:4; map P. 12.]

City's Search for Meat Supplies Fails to Uncover Any Hoarding

A meat search by three city departments was three-quarters finished yesterday and disclosed holdings in local slaughterhouses, storage plants and railroad cars of 13,312,880 pounds—not much compared to New York's normal consumption of 3,800,000 pounds a day.

With fewer than fifty of the city's 400 major repositories of meat still to be visited by the task force of 225 policemen and inspectors of the Health and Market departments, Mayor O'Dwyer said he saw nothing in the findings so far to warrant municipal action.

Meat supplies in retail stores, meanwhile, continued to shrink, and the Office of Price Administration reported that the black market was shrinking even faster than the supply of available meat. This did not seem any great victory to housewives, since the race was in the direction of a zero supply.

OPA enforcement agents, continuing their daily check on prices and, incidentally, supply, found

only one out of ten butcher shops with meat to sell. Many were shut and many others sold only poultry. There was more sausage meat than any other kind. Last week the district OPA had reported one shop out of five selling meat.

Yesterday's report by the district enforcement staff was to the effect that only 5 per cent of the meat being offered for sale was at black market prices, whereas the same office had estimated last week that 20 to 35 per cent of the local sales were at over-ceiling prices.

The City Council, in a majority resolution sent to its rules committee, called upon the Federal Government to seize all cattle and meat in the country and blamed the meat industry for "open defiance to the American people by the creation of a meat famine." The resolution, which also urged that the Government make available meat to the public as an emergency health measure, the meat so

Continued on Page 33, Column 3

RECEIVING THEIR FREEDOM FROM NUREMBERG COURT

Col. Burton C. Andrus, who headed the prison where the defendants were confined during their trial, handing out letters certifying their liberty to Hans Fritzsche (left), Franz von Papen (second from right) and Hjalmar Schacht (right).

Associated Press Radiophoto

GERMANY NOT FREE, SCHACHT COMPLAINS

Von Papen Says He Has Given Up Politics—Austria Seeks Extradition for Trial

By DANA ADAMS SCHMIDT
Special to THE NEW YORK TIMES.

NUREMBERG, Germany, Oct. 1—Franz von Papen said that his political career was "absolutely ended," Hans Fritzsche asked to be tried again by a German court and Hjalmar Schacht asked for chocolate for his two children tonight when the three men acquitted by the International Military Tribunal appeared before 200 representatives of the world press.

Schacht got his candy bars and all reaped a harvest of cigarettes

Continued on Page 20, Column 3

Russian and Jackson Object; Schacht Called a Swindler

By The Associated Press.

NUREMBERG, Germany, Oct. 1—Soviet Justice J. I. Nikitchenko tonight assailed the acquittal of three high Nazis by the International Military Tribunal, asserting that the opinion freeing Hjalmar Schacht, banker, was in "obvious contradiction to the evidence." [Justice Nikitchenko also declared Schacht a "swindler," according to a Reuters dispatch.]

The Russian Major General also dissented from the acquittal for the German General Staff, the Reich Cabinet and the decision imprisoning Rudolf Hess for life instead of giving him the death penalty.

Justice Robert Jackson of the United States, speaking for what he called the prosecutors of all nations, declared the decisions on individuals were of secondary importance compared to the fact that the principle was established making aggressive war a crime punishable by death. However, Justice Jackson also assailed the Schacht verdict.

Justice Nikitchenko said Fritzsche, as a radio propagandist, "had a most basic relation to the preparation and conduct of aggressive warfare." The most detailed dissent was in the case of the German General Staff and High Command, of which Justice Nikitchenko said:

"Without their advice and active cooperation, Hitler could not have solved [his] problems. In the majority of cases their opinion was decisive. * * * The General Staff issued most brutal decrees and orders for relentless measures against unarmed, peaceful population and prisoners of war."

Justice Nikitchenko said bluntly

Continued on Page 24, Column 6

Baruch Rebukes Wallace Groups For Distorting U. S. Atom Plan

By A. M. ROSENTHAL
Special to THE NEW YORK TIMES.

LAKE SUCCESS, N. Y., Oct. 1—In a sharp reply to followers of former Secretary of Commerce Henry A. Wallace, Bernard M. Baruch, American representative on the United Nations Atomic Energy Commission, categorically denied tonight that this country was asking the rest of the world to stop nuclear research and reveal its uranium resources while the United States retained complete freedom of action.

Mr. Baruch's strongly worded denial was the result of statements made in Chicago on Saturday at a conference of the National Citizens Political Action Committee, Independent Citizens Committee of the Arts, Sciences and Professions, and the Congress of Industrial Organizations' Political Action Committee. It was sent as a telegram addressed to Henry Morgenthau, Harold Ickes and Philip Murray, president of the CIO, who were speakers at the conference.

After noting that the conference had gone on record as saying that the United States was trying to have other nations accept "binding agreements" while keeping its technical knowledge to itself as long as it saw fit, Mr. Baruch declared:

"I say without reservation that this is either misinformation or complete distortion. Nowhere does any such statement occur in the American proposal."

Mr. Baruch followed his denial with a pointed request for a correction.

"I am sending this to you," he said in the telegrams, "in order that you may see that this is corrected immediately."

The Baruch statement was issued by the American delegation at 7 P. M., on the eve of a meeting tomorrow morning of the Atomic Energy Commission's Committee 2, which will discuss the

Continued on Page 16, Column 2

50-MINUTE SESSION

Tribunal Dooms Keitel, Ribbentrop, Streicher, Rosenberg, Jodl

SIX SAID TO APPEAL

Allied Council in Berlin Last Resort—Doenitz Gets Lightest Term

Verdicts in the Nuremberg trials are on pages 22, 23, 24.

By KATHLEEN McLAUGHLIN
Special to THE NEW YORK TIMES.

NUREMBERG, Germany, Oct. 1—Death by hanging was decreed this afternoon for twelve of the original twenty-two defendants indicted in the Nuremberg war crimes trials. Three others—Dr. Hjalmar Schacht, Franz von Papen and Dr. Hans Fritzsche—were acquitted by the International Military Tribunal over the dissent of the Soviet member of the court, Maj. Gen. Iola T. Nikitchenko.

Those who will die by the noose within fifteen days, unless reprieved through an appeal within four days to the Allied Control Council in Berlin, are Hermann Goering, Joachim von Ribbentrop, Field Marshal Gen. Wilhelm Keitel, Ernst Kaltenbrunner, Dr. Alfred Rosenberg, Hans Frank, Wilhelm Frick, Julius Streicher, Fritz Sauckel, Col. Gen. Alfred Jodl and Arthur Seyss-Inquart.

Martin Bormann, who succeeded Rudolf Hess as Deputy Fuehrer and who was tried in absentia, owing to the lack of conclusive evidence that he is dead, also was sentenced to death by hanging if and when he ever is apprehended.

Mitigation in von Neurath Case

Life imprisonment was meted out to Hess, Walther Funk and Grand Admiral Erich Raeder. General Nikitchenko dissented likewise from his colleagues' judgment on Hess, expressing the opinion that he had merited death by hanging.

Baldur von Schirach, formerly supreme leader of the Hitler Jugend, and Albert Speer, Reich Minister for Armament and Munitions and chief of the Todt Organization, received twenty years.

Possibly in consideration of his advanced years, Baron Constantin von Neurath, former Foreign Minister, although adjudged guilty on all four counts, received the comparatively mild sentence of fifteen years' imprisonment. He is 73. The Tribunal said in mitigation that he had been dismissed by Adolf Hitler for having been too lenient in his administration as Protector for Bohemia and Moravia and that he had intervened to obtain the release of many Czechoslovaks and had been arrested.

The mildest punishment of all fell to Grand Admiral Karl Doenitz, once Commander in Chief of the German Navy and, during the last days of the war, successor to Hitler as head of the German Government. He must serve ten years in prison.

[Six of those convicted—von Ribbentrop, Frank, Seyss-Inquart, von Schirach, Speer and Doenitz—have appealed their sentences, the British Broadcasting Company said, quoting official sources. The broadcast was recorded by the National Broadcasting Company.]

Pattern Is Similar

In the courtroom, which over the last ten months has echoed unceasingly to the testimony of the unprecedented horrors precipitated upon the world through the Nazi hierarchy, the profound drama of the concluding phase of the trial lasted only fifty minutes. Lord Justice Sir Geoffrey Lawrence, as presiding jurist, announced all the sentences to the eighteen convicted men as they were summoned singly before the tribunal. An atmosphere of utter solemnity prevailed throughout this grim interval.

Beginning with Goering, former

Continued on Page 21, Column 3

"All the News
That's Fit to Print"

The New York Times.

LATE CITY EDITION
Fair and continued cold today
and tomorrow.
Temperature Range Today: Max.: 38; Min.: 26
Temperature Yesterday—Max.: 45; Min.: 30
U. S. Weather Bureau Report, Page 10; Sect. 1

Section
1

NEWS INDEX, PAGE 79, THIS SECTION

VOL. XCVII..No. 32,817.

Entered as Second-Class Matter,
Postoffice, New York, N. Y.

NEW YORK, SUNDAY, NOVEMBER 30, 1947.

Including Magazine
and Book Review.

FIFTEEN CENTS

Copyright, 1947, by The New York Times Company.

SCHUMAN BARS DISCUSSION OF FRENCH LABOR OVERTURE; COMMUNIST PAPERS SEIZED

VAST GI HOUSING TO RISE NEAR SITE OF WORLD'S FAIR

21 14-Story Apartment Units to Form Nation's Largest Veterans' Cooperative

ASSEMBLY VOTES PALESTINE PARTITION; MARGIN IS 33 TO 13; ARABS WALK OUT; ARANHA HAILS WORK AS SESSION ENDS

PREMIER ADAMANT

Strikers Must Go Back on Regime's Terms— Labor Curbs Urged

ASSEMBLY SPLIT ON CODE

324 Saboteurs Are Arrested— Paris to Expel Aliens Who Help Ruin Economy

By HAROLD CALLENDER
Special to The New York Times.

PARIS, Sunday, Nov. 30—Premier Robert Schuman refused early today to meet the leaders of the Confederation of Labor to discuss a strike settlement different from that offered by the French Government.

Meanwhile, the Premier pressed hard for immediate passage by the Assembly of a law to strengthen the Government's hand by enlarging its police force and enabling it to imprison those who sought to force men to strike or who committed or urged sabotage.

As intense activity continued throughout the night inside and outside the Assembly, it became clear that the labor leaders who had encouraged the strikes had at last taken the initiative in seeking to end them, and that the Cabinet was divided regarding the policy the Government should adopt.

Early last evening Paris police surrounded the plants of the two Communist newspapers, l'Humanité and Ce Soir, entered the buildings and seized the plates of special editions whose publication had been forbidden. No papers were allowed to leave the plants. Later the police vacated the premises.

The special edition of l'Humanité, in large headlines printed in red ink, proclaimed: "They wish to assassinate the Republic!"

Minister Begins Parley

Shortly after that M. Schuman had placed his proposed law before the Assembly early yesterday, Pierre Lebrun, a Communist secretary of the confederation, issued a statement urging renewed negotiations and mentioning that the striking workers would have a hard time when the Dec. 1 pay day came on Monday without pay envelopes.

At the same time, Daniel Mayer, Socialist Minister of Labor, who understood to have opposed the law that M. Schuman actually opened negotiations with the executive committee of the confederation, which sat most of the night in his office while the Cabinet met in the Falais Bourbon. Through M. Mayer the committee asked to see M. Schuman, but the Premier refused his request and denied that the Government was negotiating with the strike leaders.

A sharp divergence of view—

Continued on Page 46, Column 3

Major Sports Results

FOOTBALL

With Rip Rowan passing for the first touchdown and dashing ninety-two yards for the second, Army beat Navy yesterday for the fourth straight year. N.Y.U. rallied to beat Fordham. Scores of leading games:

Alabama ..21	Miami, Fla... 6
Army 23	Navy 0
Florida 25	Kansas State 7
Fordham ...13	N. Y. U. 12
Ga. Tech.. 7	Georgia 0
Holy Cross .20	Boston Coll.. 6
Maryland .. 0	N. C. State.. 19
Mich. State .58	Hawaii 19
Mississippi ..33	Miss. State ..14
N. Carolina .40	Virginia 7
Oklahoma ..21	Okla. A.&M..13
Oregon St. ..27	Nebraska ... 6
Rice 34	Baylor 6
S. M. U. 13	T. C. U. 19
Tennessee ..12	Vanderbilt .. 7
Texas Tech..14	Hardin-Sim.. 6
West Va....17	Pittsburgh . 2

CROSS COUNTRY

Curtis Stone of Philadelphia won the National A.A.U. championship at Van Cortlandt Park, but the New York A. C. took the team title for the third successive time.

HORSE RACING

Incline outran Gallorette to capture the Bryan and O'Hara Memorial Handicap at Bowie on the last day of the major Eastern season.

(Full details in Section 5.)

U. S. Troops to Stay in Italy Beyond Dec. 3 Sailing Date

Change in Plans Is Linked to Disturbances Led by Communists—Milan Is Calm Following Compromise on Prefect

By ARNALDO CORTESI
Special to The New York Times.

ROME, Nov. 29—The United States Army Department today ordered Maj. Gen. Lawrence Jaynes, commanding the Mediterranean Theatre of Operations, and his entire staff to postpone their departure from Italy. With them will remain about 2,500 officers and men who are leading specialists of the United States Army in Italy.

The order is believed to reflect the anxiety with which the Government in Washington views the Communist-fomented disturbances in Italy.

General Jaynes and his officers and men had planned to leave from Leghorn on Dec. 3 aboard the Admiral Sims. Washington ordered a postponement of departure until Dec. 14, the deadline set by the Italian peace treaty. No explanation was given for the change of plans and this strengthened the impression that it was dictated by

preoccupation over Italy's political outlook.

The officers and men with General Jaynes form the skeleton organization for a large army. They include highly trained specialists, familiar with conditions in Italy. They belong to the Engineer, Signal, Ordnance, Secretariat, Quartermaster, Medical and Military Police Corps and other auxiliary services.

Washington's change of plans came after General Jaynes had said farewell to Pope Pius and President Enrico de Nicola. Ambassador James C. Dunn called on Premier Alcide de Gasperi two days ago, and it is presumed that he informed the Italian Government then of the postponement of the American troops' departure.

Though the American troops should, under present plans, leave

Continued on Page 45, Column 3

No-Parking Area Is Created From City Hall to Canal St.

After a two-hour conference with Mayor O'Dwyer at Police Headquarters, Police Commissioner Arthur W. Wallander announced yesterday two further moves in the department's efforts to ease traffic congestion in the city.

Commissioner Wallander added the section of Manhattan north of City Hall as far as Canal Street and west to but not including West Street to the restricted parking areas already established in a large part of the borough below Fifty-ninth Street.

He also said that a survey was being made throughout the city in an effort to discover additional sites for municipal parking lots like the one established at the old World's Fair parking lot in Flushing, Queens. The lot set up experimentally there "looks promising," he said, reporting that 746 motorists had used it on Friday.

Mayor Explains Needs

The Commissioner announced the moves at a press conference at the end of his talk with the Mayor. Mr. O'Dwyer sat in on the press conference and added some comments of his own after his aide had made the announcement.

About forty traffic policemen will be needed to enforce the parking restrictions in the new area, Mr. O'Dwyer said. Commissioner Wallander has asked for 200 additional men for the Police Department to take care of this and other needs, which would add $6,000,000 to the department's budget, he continued.

Together with $4,000,000 of the men added to the force last July, this would amount to a total of $10,000,000 that would have to be appropriated for the Police Department next year in addition to

Continued on Page 27, Column 1

WAR PAY 'RACKET' HUNTED BY TRUMAN

Gen. Vaughan Says President Wants Army, Navy, Air House-Cleaning on Disability Cases

Special to The New York Times.

WASHINGTON, Nov. 29—The armed services are preparing to turn over to President Truman at his request the records of 28,000 wartime Army officers who have been retired for disability on tax-free pay normally amounting to three-fourths of their active service remuneration.

This became known as an aftermath of the case against Maj. Gen. Bennett E. Meyers and was confirmed today by Maj. Gen. Harry H. Vaughan, the President's military aide, who said at Philadelphia that Mr. Truman was determined to "wipe out any possible 'racket'" in tax-free disability retirement pay.

The President has already spoken about the matter to James Forrestal, Secretary of Defense, and it is expected that a formal directive will be received soon.

Presumably the order will apply also to naval officers retired for disability so that once the President has the records in hand he

Continued on Page 75, Column 2

Congress Action Lags on Aid Bill Despite Warnings Need Is Urgent

By JOHN D. MORRIS
Special to The New York Times.

WASHINGTON, Nov. 29—Congress set aside the troublesome problems of European aid and domestic inflation today and attended the Army-Navy game practically en masse, while pressures for accelerated action on the legislative problems awaited members' return to work Monday.

Despite repeated representations of urgency in both fields, the Congressional machinery faced a slowdown in production of the authorization for winter relief for France, Italy and Austria.

Formulation of anti-inflation legislation still had hardly begun, and completion of the task was far out of sight.

The Senate was prepared to resume consideration Monday of the foreign relief bill, but earlier expectations of passage on that day had been diminished by failure yesterday to dispose of four amendments proposed by Senator

James P. Kem, Republican, of Missouri.

While some of them are acceptable to the bill's managers, at least one is expected to cause considerable discussion and possible delay of a vote on the bill itself until Tuesday.

This would require detailed, written acknowledgement by every recipient of relief supplies that the goods were gifts of the United States.

Senator Kem successfully proposed action on the amendments yesterday, asserting that he wanted Thanksgiving holiday absentees to be present when the votes were taken. He thus disrupted leaders' plans for accelerated action so that the bill might be disposed of Monday.

Hope for a final vote Monday

Continued on Page 26, Column 1

COST PUT AT $58,000,000

Occupancy on Tenant-Owner Basis—Work Will Start Before End of Year

By LEE E. COOPER

On a fifty-five-acre tract overlooking the site of the World's Fair of 1939, the country's largest veterans' cooperative apartment community soon will begin to take form, it became known last night.

After nearly a year of negotiations, and with the official blessing of the city and of the Veterans Administration, plans for the $58,000,000 project were revealed by Frederick Briggs, chairman of the board of the Communities Redevelopment Corporation, which is sponsoring the enterprise.

The new Queens housing center, which will occupy a large part of the former Arrowbrook Golf Club grounds, will be for occupancy exclusively by veterans of World War II and their families on a tenant-ownership basis.

Plans call for the erection of twenty-one fourteen-story apartment houses of the fireproof type, to accommodate 5,699 families. Each building will have its own garage facilities, to be rented separately, for tenants' automobiles.

Shopping Centers Will Rise

In furtherance of the plan to create a self-contained community, the builders will erect shopping centers at the edges of the property, which is bounded by Main Street, Jewel Avenue and Park Drive East, within the boundaries of Forest Hills. A promenade, with stores beneath it, will be constructed on the hillside overlooking Flushing Meadow Park. The residential buildings will be set amid winding tree-lined walks and landscaped park spaces.

The Board of Estimate gave its unanimous sanction to the over-all plan for the project at a special closed session last Wednesday, after receiving a favorable report on it from Robert Moses, City Construction Coordinator who had been in consultation with the sponsors.

The city's cooperation will be limited to street changes and zoning aids permitting stores and the erection of fourteen-story houses on the site. No municipal financial

Continued on Page 12, Column 2

World News Summarized

SUNDAY, NOVEMBER 30, 1947

The General Assembly of the United Nations yesterday approved the plan for the partition of Palestine by a vote of 33 to 13 with ten abstentions and one absence. After the vote there were repeated statements of bitterness and disillusion from the Arab representatives. One after another they asserted that the Charter had been violated and that their nations would not be bound by the action and would reserve "freedom of action." The Arabs then walked out of the Assembly. [1:8.]

The Arabs subsequently pronounced the United Nations "dead," and disavowed any intention of playing a part under the partition plan. They went on to say, however, that this did not mean their retirement from the United Nations. Zionist leaders were jubilant over the outcome. [1:6-7.]

Zionists attending the Assembly expressed their joy with tears and excited laughter. Dr. Oswaldo Aranha praised the public for its good behavior. [1:7.]

The Palestine debate concluded the business of the current session of the General Assembly, and Dr. Aranha of Brazil gave his closing address. He declared that this second meeting had made a notable contribution to world peace, and after the delegates had risen to applaud him the session adjourned. [1:5.]

In London, Soviet Foreign Minister Molotov demanded the early establishment of a German government to speed the peace treaty. The other Ministers, seeing this as a move to commit them against any possible partition of Germany, opposed him. [1:6-7.] Secretary Marshall plans next week to achieve the economic unification of Germany through the removal of all

sonal barriers in what is expected to be the most important United States proposal at the conference. [50:3.]

In the deputies' meeting the Soviet delegation continued to study the French proposals on Austria and refused to agree on principle at any point. Action was delayed, but it was felt the Russians might accept. [51:1.]

In Paris, Premier Schuman declined to discuss with leaders of the Confederation of Labor any strike settlement on terms other than the Government's. He asked for police powers to suppress Communist agitators and moved against Communist newspapers. They had charged that a "revolutionary coup" was planned for midnight and that "assassination of the Republic" was its objective. The editions were suppressed. [1:1.]

In Italy, the United States commander and 2,500 American troops were ordered by Washington to postpone departure, presumably because of the troubled situation. The general strike in Milan, however, was ended. [1:2-3.]

The Rome Expedition in the Antarctic announced the exploration and mapping of a vast area of about 100,000 square miles of territory in the name of the United States. [56:3.]

A scientific advance that may be of importance in insect pest control was announced by the United States Army. Ultrasonic waves have been developed that are lethal to mice and small insects. [14:1.]

Defense Secretary Forrestal has been instructed by President Truman to turn over the records of 28,000 wartime Army officers who have been retired for disability on tax-free pay, in the determination to wipe out any possible "racket." [1:2.]

PEACE GAINS NOTED

Brazilian Says Contacts Inspired No Forecast of Imminent War

CITES ROLE OF MINORITY

Lie Regrets That Economic Issues Were Sidetracked —Others Hail Aranha

By MARSHALL E. NEWTON

It is the mission of the United Nations to achieve world peace and the General Assembly made a memorable contribution in that direction, Dr. Oswaldo Aranha of Brazil, president of the Assembly, told the delegates of the fifty-seven member nations yesterday in his speech closing the second regular session at Flushing Meadows.

When he finished his address the delegates rose and applauded Dr. Aranha, whose talents and statesmanlike handling of the difficult task of presiding at the international assembly had been lauded by several preceding speakers.

Dr. Aranha pointed out that the present post-war period had not been marked by the armed conflicts that followed the Peace of Versailles and he said that we lived today in a different era, in which our minds must turn to the future and not the past.

Calls for Foresight

"But close contact with international political life leads to no forecast of world war in the near future," he said. "The world seeks, however, new forms of political, economic and social integration in which the contest of ideas will supersede the clash of arms. But it was obvious that the Soviet delegation is no longer possible. A new reality is rising in sour days, to which we must impart the spirit of the United Nations, the only conception capable of insuring peace, solidarity, dignity and equality for all peoples.

"Our action should not be post factum. Our task is one of foresight and of organized prevention to eliminate the elements and factors capable of disturbing world

Continued on Page 67, Column 3

Arabs See U. N. 'Murdered,' Disavow Any Partition Role

Angry Delegates Stalk From Assembly Hall Before Formal Closing—Silver Voices Gratification, Offers Friendship

By A. M. ROSENTHAL

Bitter Arab delegates walked out of the General Assembly hall at Flushing Meadow last night after the vote for the partition of Palestine and solemnly announced that in their eyes the United Nations had died.

"No, not died," said Faris el-Khouri of Syria. "Murdered."

The representatives of the Arab states swept out of the building without waiting for the formal end of the Assembly and the farewell speeches. But before they announced that they would have absolutely nothing to do with the United Nations Commission for Palestine, nothing to do with the transitional period after the end of the mandate and nothing to do with partition.

There was an open thread of warning running through all the Arab delegates' comments on the Assembly's action. They spoke of bloodshed to come and said that

responsibility would not be theirs, but would be on the shoulders of the countries that had pressed for partition.

On the other side of the quarter-century Arab-Zionist dispute there was jubilance and hope for the future. Dr. Abba Hillel Silver, chairman of the American section of the Jewish Agency for Palestine, expressed his gratitude to the Assembly and especially to the United States and the Soviet Union.

Dr. Silver's statement follows:

"We are deeply grateful for the action of the General Assembly of the United Nations. It marks a turning point in Jewish history. It is an impressive reaffirmation of the just claim of the Jewish people to rebuild its national life in its ancestral home.

"This noble decision to re-establish the Jewish state and restore

Continued on Page 60, Column 1

Molotov Insists on Regime Before Treaty on Germany

By DREW MIDDLETON
Special to The New York Times.

LONDON, Nov. 29—Soviet Foreign Minister Molotov urged with new fervor in the Council of Foreign Ministers today the early establishment of a central German government as a precondition of the peace treaty.

Mr. Molotov's argument was based on the futility of completing a German peace treaty with no German government to sign it or assist in its preparation. But it was obvious that the Soviet delegate was moved by fears that the Western Allies, at this Council meeting failed, would make their own arrangements for a German government and treaty.

With a stridency that surprised an otherwise decorous meeting, Mr. Molotov declared the Soviet Union would never recognize a peace signed by Western Germany and the Western powers. No government set up in the United States zone and no "ersatz government for Bizonia" will be an adequate substitute for the Soviet proposal, he asserted.

Secretary of State Marshall and French Foreign Minister Bidault both flatly opposed any tendency to make the establishment of a German government a precondition of signing the German peace treaty.

A compromise proposal presented by British Foreign Secretary Bevin was as abruptly turned down by Mr. Molotov, who said it did not go far enough. Then he proceeded to add a clause that made the British proposal an echo of the Soviet suggestion.

This brisk exchange of German participation in the peace making followed an encouraging agreement by the Big Four on the main

Continued on Page 54, Column 3

ZIONIST AUDIENCE JOYFUL AFTER VOTE

Tears, Excited Laughter Mark Tension—Aranha Commends Public's Good Behavior

By WALTER S. SULLIVAN

The attention of the entire Arab and Jewish worlds focused on Flushing Meadow yesterday to hear the verdict of the United Nations General Assembly on the future of Palestine.

The reaction in the packed hall to the decision for partition typified that of listeners far and near. While members of the Arab delegations walked out, Zionists in the audience rejoiced.

It was a rejoicing that started with silence and grew as the meeting neared its end. In the public lobby there were kisses and tears and excited laughter. In the delegates' lounge a rabbi cried, "This is the day the Lord hath made! Let us rejoice in it and be glad!"

The initial silence resulted from a call to order by the Assembly's president, Dr. Oswaldo Aranha. A burst of applause that greeted the surprise vote of France in favor of partition, and it was this that had

Continued on Page 67, Column 2

Company Asks Rise in Gas Rate From $1.15 to $2 Sliding Scale

The Consolidated Edison Company of New York, Inc., announced yesterday it had applied to the State Public Service Commission for permission to increase the maximum charge for gas from $1.15 a thousand cubic feet to $2 with declining rates after the first thousand.

The company proposed an immediate schedule of temporary rates which it estimated would increase its annual revenues approximately $8,239,700 on the basis of estimated gas sales for 1947.

The petition said that neither Consolidated Edison nor any of its predecessor companies has increased its rates since Oct. 1, 1922, and that existing rates were confiscatory of the company's property. It was estimated that the company would lose $1,498,500 in 1947 through its gas operations.

According to the company, 57 per cent of the gas it supplies is sold at the maximum rate of $1.15 a thousand cubic feet. The company's rates ranged from $1.15 a thousand cubic feet for those who have been retired for disability on tax-free pay, in the

Island City, Flushing, College Point, Whitestone, Douglaston, Bayside, Little Neck and Bellerose.

The company proposed an immediate schedule of temporary rates which it estimated would increase its annual revenues approximately $8,239,700 on the basis of estimated gas sales for 1947.

If this increase had been in effect through 1947, the company said, it would have provided the company with a net return after taxes of $4,300,000 in connection with its gas operations.

If approved by the Public Service Commission, the new classifications would provide a minimum charge of $2 for the first thousand cubic feet or less of gas consumed in any bi-monthly billing period.

For the first 4,000 cubic feet over the initial 1,000-foot block, residential customers would be charged 12 cents a hundred; 10 cents a hundred

Continued on Page 12, Column 1

U. N. REJECTS DELAY

Proposal Driven Through by U. S. and Soviet Will Set Up Two States

COMMISSION IS APPOINTED

Britain Holds Out Hand to It— Arabs Fail in Last-Minute Resort to Federal Plan

By THOMAS J. HAMILTON

The United Nations General Assembly approved yesterday a proposal to partition Palestine into two states, one Arab and the other Jewish, that are to become fully independent by Oct. 1.

The vote was 33 to 13 with ten abstentions and one delegation, the Siamese, absent.

The decision was primarily a result of the fact that the delegations of the United States and the Soviet Union, which were at loggerheads on every other important issue before the Assembly, stood together on partition.

Andrei A. Gromyko and Herschel V. Johnson both urged the Assembly yesterday not to agree to further delay but to vote for partition at once.

The Assembly disregarded last-minute Arab efforts to effect a compromise. Although the votes of a dozen or more delegations seesawed to the last, supporters of partition had two votes more than the required two-thirds majority, or a margin of three.

How Members Voted

The roll-call vote was as follows:

For (33)—Australia, Belgium, Bolivia, Brazil, Canada, Costa Rica, Czechoslovakia, Denmark, Dominican Republic, Ecuador, France, Guatemala, Haiti, Iceland, Liberia, Luxembourg, the Netherlands, New Zealand, Nicaragua, Norway, Panama, Paraguay, Peru, Philippines, Poland, Sweden, the Ukraine, South Africa, Uruguay, the Soviet Union, the United States, Venezuela, White Russia.

Against (13)—Afghanistan, Cuba, Egypt, Greece, India, Iran, Iraq, Lebanon, Pakistan, Saudi Arabia, Syria, Turkey, Yemen.

Abstentions (10) — Argentina, Chile, China, Colombia, El Salvador, Ethiopia, Honduras, Mexico, United Kingdom, Yugoslavia.

Absent (1)—Siam.

All other questions before the Assembly were disposed of a week ago, and it ended its second regular session at 6:37 P. M. after farewell speeches by Dr. Oswaldo Aranha, its President, and Trygve Lie, the Secretary General. The Assembly's third regular session is to open in a European capital on Sept. 21.

The vote on partition was taken at 5:35 P. M. Representatives of Iraq, Saudi Arabia, Syria and Yemen, four of the six Arab member states, announced that they would not be bound by the Assembly's decision and walked out of the Assembly Hall at Flushing Meadow. The Egyptian and Lebanese delegates were silent and walked out too.

Briton Seeks Contact

Sir Alexander Cadogan, representative of Britain, which is to terminate the League of Nations mandate over Palestine and withdraw all British troops by Aug. 1, made a brief statement after the vote. He requested the United Nations Palestine Commission to establish contact with the British Government about the date of its arrival in Palestine and the coordination of its plans with the withdrawal of British troops.

The United Nations commission, which will be responsible to the Security Council in the event that the Arabs carry out their threats to fight rather than agree to partition, will be composed of representatives of Bolivia, Czechoslovakia, Denmark, Panama and the Philippines.

This slate, which is understood to have the backing of the United Nations Commission, was proposed by Dr. Aranha and approved without opposition after the Arab delegates had walked out.

The commission, as proposed by the partition subcommittee, comprised

Continued on Page 85, Column 2

147

The New York Times.

LATE CITY EDITION

Increasing cloudiness, cold today. Snow, not so cold tomorrow.
Temperature Range Today—Max.,16; Min.,6
Temperatures Yesterday—Max.,24; Min.,5.5
Full U. S. Weather Bureau Report, Page 31

Copyright, 1948, by The New York Times Company

VOL. XCVII No. 32,879.　Entered as Second-Class Matter, Postoffice, New York, N. Y.　NEW YORK, SATURDAY, JANUARY 31, 1948.　THREE CENTS NEW YORK CITY

MANY HOMES WITHOUT HEAT AS ZERO COLD IS DUE HERE; U. S. CUTS OIL EXPORTS 18½%

FUEL CRISIS GROWS

Hundreds of Families Reported Suffering in City Area

BAY STATE SEIZES PLANT

Bradford Acts When Walkout Threatens Boston Gas—Oil Diversion Denied Here

By WILL LISSNER

Hundreds of families in the city were reported by their landlords to be in cold homes for lack of fuel oil last night as temperatures dropped toward zero in Manhattan and toward subzero levels in the suburbs.

At 3 A. M. today the temperature dropped to 2.2 degrees, establishing a new low record for the season. The previous record was 5 degrees, registered last Saturday.

The winter's coldest weather gripped not only New York but the whole Northwest. The Midwest and South, however, got some relief yesterday from the protracted cold spell. The fuel situation was reported acute in many cities throughout the East.

Temperatures, after falling to points between zero and 5 degrees above in Manhattan and zero and 10 degrees below in the suburbs, are expected to rise today to 20 degrees. The cold is due to continue, according to the United States Weather Bureau, but whereas yesterday was sunny, increasing cloudiness was expected today. More snow is threatened tomorrow. The lowest temperature yesterday was 5.5 degrees at 9:50 A. M.

Yesterday's hourly temperatures were:

1 A. M.	23	2 P. M.	12
2 A. M.	23	3 P. M.	12
3 A. M.	22	4 P. M.	11
4 A. M.	18	5 P. M.	10
5 A. M.	13	6 P. M.	9
6 A. M.	9	7 P. M.	11
7 A. M.	7	8 P. M.	8
8 A. M.	7	9 P. M.	9
9 A. M.	6	10 P. M.	7
9:50 A. M. ..	5.5	11 P. M.	7
10 A. M.	6	12 P. M.	5
11 A. M.	7	1 A. M.	5
Noon	9	2 A. M.	4
1 P. M.	10	3 A. M.	2.2

Petroleum Exports Cut

As the fuel shortage produced critical conditions for many apartment and home owners in this and other cities, officials took steps to relieve the situation.

The Commerce Department announced in Washington that it had ordered exports of petroleum products cut 18½ per cent from 11,850,000 to 9,650,000 barrels during the first quarter of the year. Oil exports to Japan and the Ryukyus were cut from 1,600,000 barrels to 100,000. Exports will be allowed from areas where fuel can be spared best, the department said.

In Massachusetts Gov. Robert F. Bradford ordered the seizure of a gas plant in Everett where a walkout of 900 workers was threatened that would have affected service to sixty-four municipalities and 1,500,000 residents of Greater Boston. After seizure and issuance of a temporary injunction, union leaders ordered their employes to remain at work.

In Tennessee, Governor James McCord proclaimed a state of emergency and announced a voluntary fuel conservation program.

In Rochester, Sheriff's deputies and city policemen were organized to make emergency deliveries of fuel oil in extreme cases.

In Endicott, Mayor E. Raymond Lee declared an emergency due to the gas shortage and urged residents to conserve fuel. Many homes there and in Binghamton and Johnson City were without heat and residents sought emergency shelter.

Philadelphians Warned

Residents of Philadelphia were warned of a gas shortage caused by the oil shortage and were urged to restrict use of gas to the absolute minimum.

Police Commissioner Arthur W. Wallander of this city, regional fuel coordinator, sent telegrams asking eighty-six terminal dealers here to remain open today and tomorrow, because of the expected severe cold, to supply fuel oil to hardship cases.

Mayor O'Dwyer declared during the afternoon that it was not necessary at this time to proclaim a state of emergency and to divert

Continued on Page 12, Column 5

Petroleum Shipment Abroad Is Curbed to Ease Shortage

Department of Commerce Orders Quotas Reduced From 11,850,000 to 9,650,000 Barrels for Quarter—Slashes Japan

Special to THE NEW YORK TIMES.

WASHINGTON, Jan. 30—The Department of Commerce announced today that "in view of the serious shortage of fuel oils," in this country it had ordered an 18½ per cent cut in exports of petroleum products during the first quarter of this year. Its action will reduce from 11,850,000 to 9,650,000 the barrels of petroleum designated for overseas.

The Department also announced that it would limit licenses for export of petroleum products to shipments for those areas of the United States where the fuel can best be spared during the emergency.

In addition, it was disclosed that a separate quota of gas oil and distillate fuel oil had been established for the first quarter for shipments to Japan and the Ryukyus, drastically cutting their supply from 1,600,000 barrels to 100,000. The Department said that the difference would be met from oil production

---

ing areas outside the United States.

Proposals had been made in Congress to stop all shipments abroad except those going to American military forces. Bills designed to accomplish this end have been introduced in the House and the Senate.

Walter S. Hallanan, chairman of the National Petroleum Council, said today that the petroleum industry had taken "prompt and forthright action to alleviate the shortages of some petroleum products which have been rendered acute in certain sections by the severe cold weather." The industry "takes pride in the fact that it was the first to develop a voluntary agreement under the recent authorization of Congress," he added.

Canada Is Not Affected

WASHINGTON, Jan. 30 (AP)—The action today of the Department of Commerce—

Continued on Page 11, Column 4

Hope Wanes in Sea Search For 28 Aboard Lost Airliner

By FREDERICK GRAHAM

The Atlantic area northeast of Bermuda was being searched last night for survivors of a British South American Airways plane that disappeared in the area early yesterday morning with a crew of six and at least twenty-two passengers, but hope had almost been abandoned.

The thirty-two-passenger plane, which listed among those aboard Air Marshal Sir Arthur Coningham, Royal Air Force, who commanded the Second Tactical Air Force of the Allies at the invasion of Normandy, was out of London and on the Azores-to-Bermuda leg of the flight when last heard from about 1 A. M. (EST) yesterday.

At least sixteen United States Air Force, Navy and Coast Guard planes plus three Coast Guard cutters, two commercial steamers and a British South American Airways plane worked over a large area about 400 miles northeast of Bermuda without success. More aircraft are scheduled to continue the search today.

The plane, a converted Lancaster bomber of the type used by the RAF for saturation bombing of Germany, had stopped in Santa Maria in the Azores to refuel. An Associated Press dispatch from Bermuda said the plane, believed to have been commanded by Capt. David Colby, radioed to Bermuda that it would arrive there at midnight Thursday, an hour and a half late. One hour later it reported to Bermuda again, saying it was 440 miles northeast of Bermuda and that there was a moderate sea swell and that it was bucking strong headwinds. Nothing more has been heard from the plane.

The only other report that might

Continued on Page 10, Column 2

ORVILLE WRIGHT, 76, IS DEAD IN DAYTON

Co-Inventor With His Brother, Wilbur, of the Airplane Was Pilot in First Flight

Special to THE NEW YORK TIMES.

DAYTON, Ohio, Jan. 30—Orville Wright, who with his brother, the late Wilbur Wright, invented the airplane, died here tonight at 10:40 in Miami Valley Hospital. He was 76 years old.

Mr. Wright, who had been confined to a hospital in October, collapsed in his office on Tuesday. He was suffering from lung congestion and coronary arteriosclerosis.

At the bedside when Mr. Wright died were Horace A. Wright, a nephew; Mrs. H. S. Miller, a niece, and Delyle Myers, a nurse. The announcement that he was dead was made by Dr. A. B. Brower, family physician.

Engrossing Amusement

In the early fall of 1900 fishermen and Coast Guardsmen dwelling on that lonely and desolate spot of sand dividing Albemarle Sound from the Atlantic Ocean on the coast of North Carolina called

Continued on Page 12, Column 2

Arms Get Atomic Energy Priority In Policy Set by Congress Group

By WILLIAM S. WHITE

Special to THE NEW YORK TIMES.

WASHINGTON, Jan. 30—The Joint Committee on Atomic Energy laid down today a firm policy that the production of atomic weapons, rather than work on peacetime applications of atomic energy, must be the "vital business" of the United States for the foreseeable future.

It declared also that "uninterrupted operation" of the "critical," or military, facilities of the Atomic Energy Commission was so essential to national security that an investigation was in motion to find a formula to assure "continuity of work" under all labor eventualities.

In its first report to Congress, the committee indicated some dissatisfaction "in a number of cases" with certain aspects of the handling of internal security with the personnel of the Atomic Energy Commission.

"Until such time as an effective, enforceable and reliable program for the international control of atomic energy is in successful operation, the most vital business of the Atomic Energy Commission must be the meeting of the atomic requirements of national defense."

The joint committee has been assured that those charged with these responsibilities are keenly aware thereof. This phase of the atomic energy program is of para-

Continued on Page 7, Column 1

Record 799-Million Budget Is Asked by Dewey for State

He Estimates Actual Outlay at 753 Millions for Next Fiscal Year, but Says No Rise in Taxes Is Needed—Warns on Inflation

By LEO EGAN

Special to THE NEW YORK TIMES.

ALBANY, Jan. 30—Governor Dewey submitted another record-breaking budget to the Legislature tonight, calling for appropriations of $799,600,000, including deficiencies for the current year, but estimating expenditures in the new budget year at a figure of $753,500,000. The Governor regards the lower figure as his "budget" total.

Appropriations recommended are $128,200,000 higher than those carried in last year's budget message but, because of supplemental grants for teacher pay, veterans' housing, college housing, central schools and rent control, only $53,400,000 higher than actual appropriations, which were $746,200,000.

The expenditures of $753,500,000 contemplated in Mr. Dewey's message compare with an actual total of $707,500,000 in the current year, according to revised estimates. The revised figure reflects increased relief contributions and higher food prices for inmates of state institutions which are being provided for in deficiency appropriations.

Allowing for continuance of the reductions made in 1946, which he recommended, the Governor estimated that existing regular taxes would produce $758,800,000 in the new budget year, enough to balance expenditures and leave a $5,000,000 surplus.

The regular tax structure does not include the additional one-cent-a-package levy on cigarettes or the 20 per cent increase in existing income tax rates which were voted to finance the $400,000,000 veterans' bonus. If the present return from these special levies continued, Mr. Dewey said, the bonus bonds might be retired in eight or

Continued on Page 9, Column 1

Text of Gov. Dewey's budget message will be found on pages 8 and 9.

REALTY VALUATIONS RISE $745,775,468 IN CITY FOR 1948-49

Higher Accrued Value Is Chief Factor in $17,684,240,921 Total, Biggest Since '33

By LEE E. COOPER

New York's land and buildings, regarded as the richest segment of real estate in the world, have risen in value to $17,684,240,921 on the city's tax books for the coming fiscal year.

Municipal assessors have chalked up a tentative increase of $745,775,468 over current figures on taxable properties for the year beginning July 1, 1948, to carry the aggregate valuations to the highest level since 1933.

A report submitted to Mayor O'Dwyer yesterday by Harry B. Chambers, president of the Tax Commission, showed an average rise of about 4½ per cent for the five boroughs, accounted for largely by an "upswing in "accrued value" rather than by addition of new construction to the assessment rolls.

The report set the following tentative

Continued on Page 11, Column 3

GOP GROUP SHAPES SHARP ERP REVISION WITH FUND REDUCED

A Proposal to Sell U. S. Goods to Latin America for Food for Europe Wins Favor

By FELIX BELAIR Jr.

Special to THE NEW YORK TIMES.

WASHINGTON, Jan. 30—A fighting nucleus of eighteen Senate Republicans agreed late tonight to press for important changes in the Administration's European Recovery Program as the party's legislative leaders brushed aside President Truman's demand for approval of the full $6,800,000,000 asked for the first fifteen months of operations.

The group of eighteen Senators, in which Westerners predominated, called for a complete shift in emphasis of the Marshall Plan "from the underwriting or trade deficits to the support of specific production programs" in which financial aid would be contingent on increased output of food, coal, steel and transportation facilities.

Senator Joseph H. Ball of Minnesota said the principles agreed

Continued on Page 6, Column 2

World News Summarized

SATURDAY, JANUARY 31, 1948

Mohandas K. Gandhi, 78-year-old spiritual leader of hundreds of millions of Indians, was shot in New Delhi yesterday as he walked toward a pergola to lead 1,000 of his followers in evening prayer. He died twenty-five minutes later. His assassin, a Hindu, was seized after he had fired three quick shots into the frail leader, who only recently had ended a hunger strike in protest against communal strife. [1:8.]

News of the tragedy shocked the world. In Bombay, it ignited a new outburst of rioting. [2:3.] United Nations officials at Lake Success feared this might be the beginning of a new wave of violence throughout India. [2:4-5.] President Truman said the whole world would mourn and expressed hope that the assassination would "not retard the peace of India and the world." [2:1.] Similar expressions of regret were voiced in London, where the King and the Queen and Prime Minister Attlee were among the many leaders to pay tribute to Mr. Gandhi. [1:6-7.]

The French National Assembly approved, 308 to 242, the Government's program to establish a free gold market and to allow Frenchmen to repatriate foreign assets by paying a tax. The Socialists reversed their previous stand and voted for the program. [1:6-7.]

Two recent Russian notes protesting the reopening for American use of an airfield in Tripolitania and the presence of American naval craft in Italian ports will be rejected by the State Department. [6:5.] The Navy announced that another 1,000 marines would go to the Mediterranean soon to replace an equal number now serving in that area. [6:4-5.]

The United States consulate in Jerusalem declared American citizens participating in the fighting would lose their passports and right to protection. [1:7.] Britain announced at Lake Success before the Palestine Commission that she could not allow the formation of any armed militia in Palestine before her mandate ends. [4:3.]

In Washington a group of eighteen Senate Republicans urged a change in the European Recovery Program to support specific production goals and brushed aside the Administration's request for approval of the full initial $6,800,000,000. [1:5.]

An 18½ per cent reduction in exports of petroleum products was ordered by the Commerce Department "in view of the serious shortage" of oil in this country. [1:2.3.]

Also in Washington, the Joint Committee on Atomic Energy declared this nation must concentrate for the foreseeable future on the "uninterrupted" production of atomic weapons in preference to the peaceful utilization of atomic energy. [1:2.3.]

Governor Dewey asked the Legislature to appropriate $799,600,000 as he submitted another record-breaking budget. Appropriations last year totaled $746,200,000. [1:4-5.]

Winter's coldest weather hit the metropolitan area, with the thermometer hovering near zero in the city. In the suburbs the temperature was expected to fall to sub-zero levels during the night. Some homes suffered from a shortage of fuel oil. [1:1.]

A thirty-passenger British plane was feared lost on its way to Bermuda. [1:2-3.]

Orville Wright, air pioneer, died in Dayton, Ohio, at 76. [1:2.]

GANDHI IS KILLED BY A HINDU; INDIA SHAKEN, WORLD MOURNS; 15 DIE IN RIOTING IN BOMBAY

MOHANDAS K. GANDHI
The New York Times

THREE SHOTS FIRED

Slayer Is Seized, Beaten After Felling Victim on Way to Prayer

DOMINION IS BEWILDERED

Nehru Appeals to the Nation to Keep Peace—U. S. Consul Assisted in Capture

By ROBERT TRUMBULL

Special to THE NEW YORK TIMES.

NEW DELHI, India, Jan. 30—Mohandas K. Gandhi was killed by an assassin's bullet today. The assassin was a Hindu who fired three shots from a pistol at a range of three feet.

The 78-year-old Gandhi, who was the one person who held discordant elements together and kept some sort of unity in this turbulent land, was shot down at 5:15 P. M. as he was proceeding through the Birla House gardens to the pergola from which he was to deliver his daily prayer meeting message.

The assassin was immediately seized.

He later identified himself as Nathuran Vinayak Godse, 36, a Hindu of the Mahratta tribes in Poona. This has been a center of resistance to Gandhi's ideology.

Mr. Gandhi died twenty-five minutes later. His death left all India stunned and bewildered as to the direction that this newly independent land would take without its "Mahatma" (Great Teacher).

The loss of Mr. Gandhi brings this country of 300,000,000 abruptly to a crossroads. Mingled with the sadness in this capital tonight was an undercurrent of fear and uncertainty, for now the strongest influence for peace in India that this generation has known is gone.

[Communal riots already swept Bombay when news of Mr. Gandhi's death was received. The Associated Press reported that fifteen persons were killed and more than fifty injured before an uneasy peace was established.]

Appeal Made By Nehru

Prime Minister Pandit Jawaharlal Nehru, in a voice choked with emotion, appealed in a radio address tonight for a sane approach to the future. He asked that India's path be turned away from violence in memory of the great peacemaker who had departed.

Mr. Gandhi's body will be cremated in the orthodox Hindu fashion according to his often expressed wishes. His body will be carried from his New Delhi residence on a simple wooden cot covered with a sheet at 11:30 tomorrow morning. The funeral procession will wind through every principal street of the two cities of New and Old Delhi and reach the burning ghats on the bank of the sacred Jumna River at about 4 P. M. There the remains of the greatest Indian since Gautama Buddha will be wrapped in a sheet, laid on a pyre of wood and burned. His ashes will be scattered on the Jumna's waters, eventually to mingle with the Ganges where the two holy rivers meet at the temple city of Allahabad.

These simple ceremonies were announced tonight by Pandit Nehru in respect to Mr. Gandhi's wishes, although many of the leaders desired that his body be embalmed and exhibited in state. India will see the last of Mr. Gandhi as it saw him when he lived—a humble and unassuming Hindu.

News Spreads Quickly

News of the assassination of Mr. Gandhi—only a few days after he had finished a five-day fast to bring about communal friendship—spread quickly through New Delhi. Immediately there was spontaneous movement of thousands to Birla House, home of G. D. Birla, the multimillionaire industrialist, where Mr. Gandhi and his six secretaries had been guests since he came to New Delhi in the midst of the disturbances in India's capital.

While walking through the gardens to this evening's prayer meeting when Mr. Gandhi had just reached the top of a short flight of brick steps, his slender brown arms

Continued on Page 2, Column 6

All Britain Honors Gandhi; Truman Deplores Tragedy

By HERBERT L. MATTHEWS

Special to THE NEW YORK TIMES.

LONDON, Jan. 30—Mohandas K. Gandhi, in death, has won the unanimous tribute of Britons—something he never hoped for or expected during his life. Nowhere outside of India has the shock of his assassination contained the feelings and emotions evident here today because Britain and Mr. Gandhi have been linked for good or evil over the last forty years.

In a special broadcast to the British people tonight the Prime Minister said:

"The voice which pleaded for peace and brotherhood has been silenced, but I am certain that his spirit will continue to animate his fellow countrymen and will plead for peace and concord."

[President Truman and Secretary Marshall expressed their grief and condolences in messages to India. Members of Congress were apprehensive. Leaders of many other lands joined in paying tribute and in deploring the manner of Mr. Gandhi's death.]

The sincerity of today's expressions of grief, which came from the King and Queen, the Prime Minister, the political parties—even the Communist—and from many humble Londoners who filed silently into India House this afternoon to pay tribute, cannot be doubted.

Those many quarrels when Mr. Gandhi fought with his passive resistance against the imperial power of Britain are truly things of the past. Mr. Gandhi himself paid high tribute to Britain for her policy of freeing India and of trying to help to keep the two dominions at peace with each other. The British, on their side, have

Continued on Page 3, Column 2

U. S. WARNS CITIZENS IN PALESTINE FIGHT

Consulate General Says They Face Loss of Passports and All Protective Rights

By SAM POPE BREWER

JERUSALEM, Jan. 30—United States citizens fighting in the armed services of the Jews or the Arabs will lose their protection, the United States Consulate General warned Americans in Palestine tonight. Furthermore, naturalized citizens, it was said, would lose their American nationality if they fought for a foreign power.

[Zionist hopes for getting United Nations help in arming a Jewish militia in Palestine were dimmed by the statement of Sir Alexander Cadogan, chief British representative, that the British Government would not allow formation of such forces before the end of the mandate.]

The consular warning is being twisted by Arab sources into a promise that those fighting for the Jews may have their passports back when the fighting ends. The relevant passage reads: "American passports valid only for direct

Continued on Page 4, Column 4

France Votes Free Gold Market, Legalizes Hidden Assets by a Tax

By HAROLD CALLENDER

PARIS, Jan. 30—Parliamentary sanction was given today for the Government's devaluation of the franc and its accompanying monetary policy.

By a vote of 308 to 242, the National Assembly passed the Government's bill to create a free gold market and to legalize the hitherto illegal possession of gold market bill, which they had opposed bitterly Wednesday, although their Ministers had apparently accepted it in the Cabinet meeting last Saturday. They were not reluctant to switch, for they did not desire to upset the Government and wreck the "Third Force," hostile though they were to the Government's departure from a planned economy.

The freezing measure, taken when the Socialists had precipitated a Cabinet crisis by their opposition to the gold market bill, was considered mainly a political move. But René Mayer, Finance Minister, told the

Continued on Page 5, Column 2

The New York Times.

Copyright, 1948, by The New York Times Company.

VOL. XCVII..No. 32,984.

Entered as Second-Class Matter.
Postoffice, New York, N. Y.

NEW YORK, SATURDAY, MAY 15, 1948.

THREE CENTS NEW YORK CITY

LATE CITY EDITION
Fair and warmer today and tomorrow.

Temperature Range Today—Max.: 65; Min.: 46
Temperature Yesterday—Max.: 53; Min.: 45
Full U. S. Weather Bureau Report, Page 21

ZIONISTS PROCLAIM NEW STATE OF ISRAEL; TRUMAN RECOGNIZES IT AND HOPES FOR PEACE; TEL AVIV IS BOMBED, EGYPT ORDERS INVASION

NAVY PUSHES PLAN FOR CONSTRUCTION OF MISSILE VESSELS

Sullivan Asks House Committee to Approve Halting Work on Battleship, Destroyer Types

WANTS 65,000-TON CARRIER

Floating 'Submarine Killers' Are Also Stressed in Plea for Diverting $300,000,000 Fund

By C. P. TRUSSELL
Special to THE NEW YORK TIMES.

WASHINGTON, May 14—The Navy asked Congress today for authority to shift sharply its construction of fighting craft from battleship, cruiser and destroyer types to guided missile vessels, a 65,000-ton carrier able to base, far at sea, planes with an operating radius of 1,700 miles, better still and floating "enemy submarine killers."

Such new ships, John L. Sullivan, Secretary of the Navy, told the House Armed Services Committee, must have a higher priority "because of the more immediate need for them in the event of an emergency." The immediate reaction of the committee appeared to favor prompt action.

For such a shift in construction, Secretary Sullivan brought out, the Navy wanted to halt the building of thirteen naval vessels, a 65,000-ton carrier able to base, far at sea, planes with an operating radius of 1,700 miles, floating "enemy submarine killers."

the large cruiser Hawaii, seven destroyers, two destroyer escorts and two submarines. To date about $197,000,000 has been spent on them.

However, this money was not to be abandoned, Mr. Sullivan emphasized. These craft could be converted now to the new program, he explained, or be put aside for a fitting-out later as new weapons were developed.

New Aims for $300,800,000 Fund

What the Navy wanted, Secretary Sullivan asserted, was Congressional permission to divert some $300,000,000 remaining in the present ship construction account to these purposes:

Starting the 65,000-ton aircraft carrier (the biggest ones now are the two of the Midway class, at 45,000 tons), which might cost around $124,000,000.

Building, for reproduction later, of a "submarine killer." (Hearings on the defense program have indicated that Russia has made great progress in the submarine field.) A "killer" machine, it is indicated, is developing in new work on the cruiser type of seacraft.

The construction of four submarines of types advanced beyond those now building.

In addition, there was under plan a conversion in an unidentified way of a carrier and two submarines.

Secretary Sullivan told the committee that the Kentucky and the Hawaii would not have to stand by for the development of new weapons. It is planned, he disclosed, that they be converted into guided missile ships. Apparently to allay fears in Congress that larger aircraft carriers make easier targets for enemy bombers, Mr. Sullivan drew upon experience in the second World War and the results of atom-bomb tests at Bikini.

Speed Held Bomb Defense

"The experiments at Bikini," Mr. Sullivan said, "have proved that a fast-moving fleet is an unprofitable target for an atomic bomb."

Members of the committee interpreted this as a Navy Department conclusion that even though a potential enemy might acquire the atomic bomb, the revised construction program proposed today promised a maximum of safety. Mr. Sullivan recalled that the Navy lost three large and two light carriers in the Pacific, but none was sunk by aircraft though each, equipped to latest model, would discourage the spending of atomic bombs, even if an enemy had some.

Today, the Senate Republican

Continued on Page 7, Column 4

Heaviest Trading in 8 Years Marks Stock Market Spurt

3,840,000 Shares Change Hands as Wave of Bullish Enthusiasm Increases Securities 1 to 7 Points

The hectic days of the Nineteen Twenties were re-enacted yesterday on the floor of the New York Stock Exchange when the most turbulent session in recent years produce increases of 1 to 7 points in the share list. Accompanied by a burst of bullish enthusiasm not witnessed in almost a decade, the deluge of buying orders so taxed the facilities of the Exchange that the reporting ticker tape lagged behind floor transactions by five minutes.

The cracking of the 1947 high level at the approach of mid-day served as the signal for a buying rush. Public participation suddenly enlarged and buying orders pressed floor traders to the utmost. This condition existed for forty-five minutes in the final hour when 1,350,000 shares were traded.

Accompanied by the broadest market on record with a total of 1,151 issues dealt in, volume on the Stock Exchange spiraled to 3,840,000 shares, the largest since May 21, 1940, in contrast to the Thursday turnover of 2,030,000 shares.

Brokers termed it the "wildest" bull market in twenty years on the premise that at no time in the interval had the industrials and rails advanced with such a unity of force.

While the ground had been well laid for a movement of such scope earlier this week, it was the piercing of the 1947 resistance point that confirmed the presence of a bull market to those who act by the charts, or averages. Early in the day, telegrams were sent by several advisory services to their clients urging the purchase of securities. The response to this advice showed primarily in the final

Continued on Page 23, Column 4

Truman Sees His Election; Calls GOP 'Obstructionist'

By ANTHONY LEVIERO
Special to THE NEW YORK TIMES.

WASHINGTON, May 14—President Truman asserted tonight that there would be a Democrat in the White House during the next four years and that he would be the man. He made the statement to a cheering audience of 1,000 young Democrats at their meeting here.

The President's speech was a fighting one in the true Truman manner. He spoke extemporaneously, resorting to whimsy and irony and using forceful gestures of his arms to underscore his points.

Mr. Truman accused the Republican party of stealing Democratic platform planks. "You know," he said, "it has been their habit since 1936 of taking a few planks out of the old Democratic platforms and building a platform and then saying, 'Me, too.'"

[The text of President Truman's speech is on Page 7.]

"What have the Republicans done in the last fifteen and a half years?" Mr. Truman asked, then said:

"They have been obstructionists. They spent most of their time while I was in the Senate—and I was there for ten years—in obstructing progressive legislation that was for the welfare of the common man, and throwing bricks and mud at the greatest President that ever sat in the White House."

Mr. Truman was interrupted by applause at this obvious allusion to President Roosevelt.

"That has been their record," he continued, "and they haven't changed a bit. They were against Social Security. They were against TVA. They were against wages

Continued on Page 16, Column 3

MINNESOTA'S GUARD OUT IN MEAT STRIKE

Governor Acts After 200 Raid Cudahy Newport Plant, Attack 60 Workers and Abduct 25

Special to THE NEW YORK TIMES.

ST. PAUL, Minn., May 14—National Guard troops were ordered to South St. Paul and Newport, towns on opposite banks of the Mississippi River near here, by Governor Luther Youngdahl today following violent disorders at strike-bound packing plants in the area and the statement of the local sheriffs that their forces could not maintain law and order.

The Governor did not proclaim martial law but said the troops would take their orders from the civil authorities.

The Governor's action followed a serious outbreak at the Cudahy packing plant in Newport shortly before last midnight in which a group of about 200 men raided the plant with clubs, knives and hammers. In South St. Paul on Thursday strikers forced back police who tried to open a way through picket lines at the Swift & Co. plant in

Continued on Page 7, Column 2

Princess Elizabeth, in Paris Talk, Asks Common Effort of 2 Nations

By LANSING WARREN

PARIS, May 14—Speaking 'n faultless French with just the touch of a British accent to delight French ears, Princess Elizabeth today asked France and Britain to make a common effort to lead Europe to moral and intellectual as well as economic reconstruction.

Her well-worded and discerning speech was cheered, but she went straight to the hearts of the Parisian throng when, with disarming frankness, she avowed her joy that her first foreign trip since her marriage had brought her here to Paris.

"For a long time," she said, "I have wanted to come to France. More fortunate than I, my husband already knew your admirable capital and he is all the happier to return. This trip is all the more important and agreeable for the warmth of your welcome which has touched us both."

From the time they stepped down from the train at the Gare du Nord early today, Princess Elizabeth and Prince Philip, Duke of Edinburgh, were the center of admiring attention from the throngs that lined the streets and from all the French officials who received them throughout the day.

President Vincent Auriol voiced the general feeling when in a statement issued tonight he said:

"I have been personally struck by her grace, her charm, her modesty and her nobility. I feel sure that the sentiments that she has expressed went straight to the hearts of all the French."

Elizabeth's address, broadcast to the French nation, was delivered from the top of the monumental entry to the Galliera Museum, where she came to open the British Government's exhibition of relics and souvenirs of famous Brit-

Continued on Page 6, Column 3

AIR ATTACK OPENS

Planes Cause Fires at Port—Defense Fliers Go Into Action

BORDER IS BREACHED

Cairo Vanguard Takes Colony—Trans-Jordan Reports a Movement

By The Associated Press.

TEL AVIV, Palestine, Saturday, May 15—Air raiders bombed this all-Jewish city at about dawn today.

First reports said there were "some casualties" near the power and light station.

[Cairo reported that Egyptian armed forces had been ordered to enter Palestine. Arab armies moved from Trans-Jordan at 12:01 A. M. Saturday to "liberate the Holy Land from Zionism," said a Trans-Jordan communiqué reported by The United Press from Amman.]

Tel Aviv was under complete blackout all night but no sirens were sounded during the raid. Civil guards were alerted and fifteen to twenty ships in the port area moved out to sea.

The planes swooped over Tel Aviv little more than twelve hours after Jewish leaders proclaimed the existence of a new Hebrew state of Israel.

Some bombs fell in the vicinity of the power station along the Yarkum River near Tel Aviv.

Persons at the scene said there was one hit on or near the power station, causing "some casualties."

TEL AVIV, Saturday, May 15 (UP)—Some tiny bombs were dropped on Tel Aviv by two aircraft described as bombers and accompanied by two small fighters. One Jew was killed and three were hospitalized. Jewish Army aircraft took to the skies a few minutes after the enemy planes whizzed over rooftops at an estimated altitude of 300 feet.

Several fires could be seen north

Continued on Page 2, Column 3

U. S. MOVES QUICKLY

President Acknowledges de Facto Authority of Israel Immediately

TRUCE AIM STRESSED

Soviet Gesture to New Nation Anticipated— Others Due to Act

By BERTRAM D. HULEN
Special to THE NEW YORK TIMES.

WASHINGTON, May 14—President Truman announced early tonight recognition by the United States of the new Jewish State of Israel. The President acted instantly upon being informed that the new nation had been proclaimed.

"This Government," he announced, "has been informed that a Jewish state has been proclaimed in Palestine and recognition has been requested by the provisional government thereof.

"The United States recognizes the provisional government as the de facto authority of the new State of Israel."

These two paragraphs constituted the text of the President's statement.

Coupled with the announcement was an expression of hope for peace in Palestine. This was made known through a separate White House statement issued by Charles G. Ross, Presidential press secretary.

"The desire of the United States to obtain a truce in Palestine," this said, "will in no way be lessened by the proclamation of a Jewish state.

"We hope that the new Jewish state will join with the Security Council Truce Commission in redoubled efforts to bring an end to the fighting—which has been throughout the United Nations' consideration of Palestine a principal objective of this Government."

[Pending stabilization of the Palestine situation and indications that the State of Israel had

Continued on Page 3, Column 2

AT HELM OF THE JEWISH STATE

David Ben-Gurion
Premier

Moshe Shertok
Foreign Minister
The New York Times

U. N. Votes for a Mediator; Special Assembly Is Ended

By THOMAS J. HAMILTON

After hearing both the Soviet Union and the Arab delegates denounce the United States for its sudden recognition of the new Jewish state in Palestine, the United Nations General Assembly decided last night to send a Mediator to the Holy Land to do what he could to arrange a truce and carry on public services.

The vote was 31 to 7, with sixteen abstentions and four delegates absent, and the General Assembly, which was called into special session at Flushing Meadow on April 16 at the request of the United States, adjourned for good at 8:32 P. M.

The failure of the General Assembly either to repeal the partition resolution of last November or to provide military force to keep the peace means that the fate of Palestine will be decided by the impending war between Jews and Arabs, not by any United Nations action.

The mediation resolution conforms substantially with a United States proposal announced last Wednesday, after it had become obvious that the General Assembly would not accept the original United States plan for a temporary trusteeship.

However, the General Assembly refused to accept a United States plan for a temporary trusteeship over Jerusalem, which was rejected earlier in the evening by a vote of 20 to 15, less than the necessary two-thirds majority.

Two other proposals regarding Jerusalem were rejected, but presumably the provisions of the partition resolution on Jerusalem, which was to have been established as an international enclave under the administration of the Trusteeship Council, still stand.

In addition, the Assembly de-

Continued on Page 4, Column 4

CUNNINGHAM GOES AS MANDATE ENDS

British Commissioner Boards Cruiser Off Haifa — Jews Take Down Union Jack

By The Associated Press.

HAIFA, Palestine, Saturday, May 15—Britain ended her mandate over the Holy Land last midnight. Lieut. Gen. Sir Alan Cunningham, the last British High Commissioner, sailed from Haifa port, finishing British mandate guidance.

Sir Alan's departure from Palestine's richest port caused little excitement among the Jews, who control most of the city.

The British fired a few rockets and searchlights spotlighted the cruiser as it steamed from the harbor.

Wearing the uniform of a British Army general, Sir Alan walked down a few steps of dock into a launch that took him to the cruiser Euryalus.

Upon getting into the launch, he turned and looked soberly up across the docks. There stood an honor guard of Grenadier Guards and Royal Marine commandos.

The launch pulled away amid the

Continued on Page 2, Column 7

U. N. Bars Jerusalem Trusteeship; Vote Follows Mandate Deadline

By MALLORY BROWNE

The United Nations General Assembly rejected yesterday the United States plan for a temporary trusteeship regime in Jerusalem.

Solidly opposed by the Arab States and the Russian bloc, the plan to set up a United Nations Commissioner authorized to protect the Holy City and its holy places failed to obtain the necessary two-thirds majority at the closing session at Flushing Meadow.

The vote, which came just after the bombshell of the United States recognition of the new Jewish State had burst in the Assembly, was 20 in favor, 13 against and 19 abstentions. The balance was turned by the hostility of Britain and most of the Dominions.

The United States fought hard all day, first in the Political and Security Committee of the Assembly, sitting at Lake Success, and then in the evening session of the Assembly, to get the trusteeship plan adopted before the end of the

mandate at 6:01 P. M., New York time.

An Arab filibuster, aided by the Soviet bloc, defeated this effort. It was well past the zero hour when a roll-call vote showed that the Assembly preferred to leave Harold Evans, newly appointed Jerusalem municipal Commissioner, in sole charge of the Holy City and its treasures.

As one Arab after another filed up to the tribune and took up the maximum five-minute period allowed in repeating the arguments against a trusteeship plan, 6:01 o'clock went by.

At once Awni Khalidy of Iraq, who had led the Arab fight against the trusteeship plan, rushed up to the tribune and exclaimed that the mandate was at an end, and that, since, as Francis B. Sayre of the United States had said, the measure must

Continued on Page 3, Column 5

THE JEWS REJOICE

Some Weep as Quest for Statehood Ends —White Paper Dies

HELP OF U. N. ASKED

New Regime Holds Out Hand to Arabs—U. S. Gesture Acclaimed

Text of declaration setting up new Jewish state, Page 2.

By GENE CURRIVAN
Special to THE NEW YORK TIMES.

TEL AVIV, Palestine, Saturday, May 15—The Jewish state, the world's newest sovereignty, to be known as the State of Israel, came into being in Palestine at midnight upon termination of the British mandate.

Recognition of the state by the United States, which had opposed its establishment at this time, came as a complete surprise to the people, who were tense and ready for the threatened invasion by Arab forces and appealed for help by the United Nations.

In one of the most hopeful periods of their troubled history the Jewish people here gave a sigh of relief and took a new hold on life when they learned that the greatest national power had accepted them into the international fraternity.

Ceremony Simple and Solemn

The declaration of the new state by David Ben-Gurion, chairman of the National Council and the first Premier of reborn Israel, was delivered during a simple and solemn ceremony at 4 P. M., and new life was instilled into his people, but from without there was the rumbling of guns, a flashback to other declarations of independence that had not been easily achieved.

The first action of the new Government was to revoke the Palestine White Paper of 1939, which restricted Jewish immigration and land purchase.

In the proclamation of the new state the Government appealed to the United Nations "to assist the Jewish people in the building of its state and to admit Israel into the family of nations."

The proclamation added:

"We offer peace and amity to all neighboring states and their peoples, and invite them to cooperate with the independent Jewish nation for the common good of all. The State of Israel is ready to contribute its full share to the peaceful progress and reconstruction of the Middle East."

World Jews Asked to Aid

The statement appealed to Jews throughout the world to assist in the task of immigration and development and in the "struggle for the fulfillment of the dream of generations — the redemption of Israel."

Plans for the ceremony had been laid with great secrecy. None but the hundred or more invited guests and journalists was aware of the meeting until it started, and even the guests learned of the site only ten minutes before. It was held in the Tel Aviv Museum of Art, a white, modern-design two-story building. Above it flew the Star of David, which is the state's flag, and below, on the sidewalk, was a guard of honor of the Haganah, the army of the Jewish Agency for Palestine.

As photographers' bulbs flashed and movie cameras ground out reels of the scene, great crowds gathered and cheered the Ministers and other members of the Government as they entered the building. The security arrangements were perfect. Sten guns were brandished in every direction and even the roots stood by.

The setting for the reading o the proclamation whose hall held paintings by prominent Jewish artists. Many of them depicted the sufferings and joys of the people of the Diaspora, the dispersal of the Jews. The thirteen Ministers of the

Continued on Page 8, Column 6

World News Summarized

SATURDAY, MAY 15, 1948

Several hours after the state of Israel, the first Hebrew nation in 2,000 years, had been proclaimed in a Zionist declaration of independence in Tel Aviv, [1:8.], President Truman announced that the United States recognized the "provisional government" of Israel as "the de facto authority of the new state." A second White House statement expressed the hope that the new regime would cooperate with United Nations efforts to bring about peace in Palestine. [1:5.] The British High Commissioner departed from Palestine and boarded a cruiser at Haifa as Britain's rule over the Holy Land formally ended. [1:7.]

The special session of the United Nations General Assembly ended last night after it had agreed to send a mediator to Palestine to try to arrange a truce. [1:6-7.] The trusteeship plan for Jerusalem sponsored by the United States was rejected by the Assembly, with the Arab states and the Soviet bloc opposed to the measure. [1:6-7.]

Tel Aviv was bombed at dawn. Egypt ordered her troops to invade Palestine. Trans-Jordan reported her army on the move also. [1:4.] Haganah claimed

that its forces captured Acre in the north. [2:3.]

In Moscow the newspaper Pravda, in the first editorial comment on the recent exchange between Washington and Moscow, accused the United States of double-dealing. [4:8.]

Paris crowds gave an enthusiastic welcome to Princess Elizabeth and the Duke of Edinburgh when they arrived for a visit. [1:2-3.]

Congress received a request from the Navy for authority to shift the emphasis in its construction of fighting craft to guided-missile vessels. [1:1.] President Truman predicted that he would be re-elected next November. [1:2-3.]

Minnesota National Guard troops were rushed to South St. Paul and Newport after 200 persons had raided the Cudahy meat packing plant at Newport, where a strike is in progress, attacking about sixty workers and abducting twenty-five of them. [1:2.]

The New York Stock Exchange enjoyed one of its biggest days in recent years as an avalanche of buying orders sent stocks up from 1 to 7 points. Trading reached a total of 3,840,000 shares, the largest since May 21, 1940. [1:2-3.]

Winston Churchill's War Memoirs

See Page 17 for today's installment, in which Mr. Churchill describes the invasion of Norway and the clash of the British and German fleets.

The New York Times.

7 A.M. EDITION

Partly cloudy today with occasional rain tonight and tomorrow.

Temperature Range Today—Max. 54; Min. 41
Temperature Yesterday—Max. 54; Min. 43
Full U. S. Weather Bureau Report, Page 34

Copyright, 1948, by The New York Times Company.

VOL. XCVIII No. 33,156.

Entered as Second-Class Matter, Postoffice, New York, N. Y.

NEW YORK, WEDNESDAY, NOVEMBER 3, 1948.

Three Square, New York 18, N. Y. Telephone LAckawanna 4-1000

THREE CENTS

TRUMAN LEADS DEWEY IN LATE RETURNS; THURMOND GETS 40 VOTES; WALLACE TRAILS; DEMOCRATS GAIN IN HOUSE AND SENATE

SHIFT IN CONGRESS

Democrats Win Control of Senate by Wresting Six Seats From GOP

LEADING FOR 3 MORE

Republicans' House Rule Endangered as Rivals Surge in East, West

By C. P. TRUSSELL

Democratic control of both the Senate and House of the Eighty-first Congress was probable at 6 A. M. today from yesterday's dramatic and surprise-laden election.

From the Senate returns it had been made certain that Democrats had wrested Republican seats from Illinois, Iowa, Oklahoma, West Virginia. Minnesota and Wyoming. It requires a net gain of only four for the Democrats to acquire a majority from the present division of 51 to 45 in favor of the Republicans.

The Democratic sweep, however, had not ended there. They were riding to indicated victory over Republicans in three other states, Kentucky, Delaware and Idaho.

This, it appeared, was a virtual promise to the Democrats that they would have a bare majority, plus four and thus remove, or at least lessen, doubts that they could reorganize the Senate.

Republican Holds Broken

The Republicans also were in desperate danger, despite a sweep by Democrats of thirty-one Republican-held seats to conquer, of having the House also torn from their grasp. Republicans already had lost many seats in the industrial East and the Democratic sweep was pressing westward.

In the Senate race the Democrats, while breaking into Republican territory, appeared to be holding solidly in those areas and preserving their present seats. In addition they were causing not only surprises but shocks at many points.

There remained a situation, however, which injected concern into the jubilation that reigned in Democratic camps. Even a "safe" majority in the upper House would make for Democratic harmony as a question left for future developments to answer. The Democratic party split had carried forty Southern electoral votes for the States' Rights candidate, J. Strom Thurmond of South Carolina—possibly sufficient to throw the whole Presidential and Vice-Presidential election into the hands of the Congress itself.

It was believed by experienced observers that Democratic voting in the Senate on many occasions would distinctly not follow the party line. Whether or to what extent the proved bitterness might delay or block a reorganization of the Senate, if it should be in order in the light of indicated returns, also remained to be seen.

Meanwhile, the completed returns and trends of others appeared to be taking persistent courses.

One of the most spectacular surprises of the Senate returns was in

Continued on Page 8, Column 2

Marshall Will Quit Jan. 20, Paris Says

By The Associated Press

PARIS, Wednesday, Nov. 3.—Secretary of State Marshall will resign next Jan. 20 regardless of the outcome of the Presidential election, an informed source in the American United Nations delegation said today.

The source said that there had been many recent reports that Secretary Marshall might resign.

Secretary Marshall, the source said, planned to retire to his farm.

Senators Elected

Democrats—19

Alabama	*John J. Sparkman
Arkansas	*John L. McClellan
Colorado	*Edwin C. Johnson
Georgia	*Richard B. Russell
Illinois	†Paul H. Douglas
Iowa	‡Guy M. Gillette
Louisiana	*Allen J. Ellender Sr.
Louisiana	‡Russell B. Long
Minnesota	†Hubert H. Humphrey
Mississippi	*James O. Eastland
North Carolina	§J. Melville Broughton
Oklahoma	†Robert S. Kerr
Rhode Island	*Theodore F. Green
South Carolina	*Burnet R. Maybank
Tennessee	*Estes Kefauver
Texas	†Lyndon B. Johnson
Virginia	*A. Willis Robertson
West Virginia	†Matthew M. Neely
Wyoming	*Lester C. Hunt

Republicans—8

Kansas	†Andrew F. Schoeppel
Maine	§Margaret Chase Smith
Massachusetts	*Leverett Saltonstall
Nebraska	*Kenneth S. Wherry
New Hampshire	*Styles Bridges
New Jersey	*Robert C. Hendrickson
Oregon	*Guy Cordon
South Dakota	†Karl E. Mundt

In Doubt—6

Delaware	Michigan
Idaho	Montana
Kentucky	New Mexico

*Re-elected Tuesday for full term ending Jan. 3, 1955.
†Elected Tuesday for full term ending Jan. 3, 1955.
‡Elected Tuesday for unexpired term ending Jan. 3, 1951.
§Elected Tuesday for unexpired term ending Jan. 3, 1949, and for full term ending Jan. 3, 1955.
§Elected Sept. 13, 1948.

MARCANTONIO WINS BY NARROW MARGIN

His Vote of 35,937 Beats Ellis, Morrissey—Isacson and Pressman Defeated

By WARREN MOSCOW

Representative Vito Marcantonio last night squeaked through to a narrow victory for re-election to Congress over John P. Morrissey, Tammany Democrat, and John Ellis, Republican, in his first contest as a candidate on the American Labor party line alone.

Facing a divided opposition and with the loyal support of thousands who live in the slums of East Harlem to overcome a more conservative vote lower down in Yorkville, the peppery Representative, who has been denounced consistently for being a close adherent of the Communist party line, won by a thin margin. His victory was a minor political miracle on the surface, yet somewhat expected by those familiar with the political conditions in the area.

He was the only leftist to win in the metropolitan area, however, and middle-of-the-road Democrats had a field day as rightist Republicans, elected in the 1946 GOP landslide, also went down in a consistent pattern of Congressional defeat.

Final figures in the contest, with no election districts missing, gave Mr. Marcantonio 35,937, Mr. Morrissey 31,184 and Mr. Ellis 31,482. Mr. Ellis polled 26,518 Republican votes, and 4,964 on the Liberal Party line.

In one of the closest contests, attracting almost as much interest as the Marcantonio one, Representative Jacob K. Javits, Liberal and Republican nominee in the Twenty-first District, Washington Heights, overcame the normal Democratic voting tendencies in the area for the second time to win re-election. He defeated Paul O'Dwyer, brother of the Mayor, and candidate of the Democratic and American Labor parties, by a vote of 66,455 to 64,297.

When the returns showed him the winner, Mr. Javits issued the following statement:

"The victory in our district is a victory for the people of the district, and I have had the honor of carrying the fight for them in beating down an unprincipled political deal. In carrying out my functions in the Congress, I will continue to be the people's Congressman."

On the debit side for the leftists was the defeat of the incumbent Leo Isacson, ALP member from the Bronx, who won a surprising victory in a by-election last spring. Yesterday, the Democratic candi-

Continued on Page 5, Column 5

DEWEY WINS STATE

Piles Up 525,042 Lead Outside City, Loses by 489,047 Here

LABOR IS BIG FACTOR

Wallace Total 503,404 —Liberals Poll 222,217 for the President

By JAMES A. HAGERTY

Governor Dewey, Republican nominee for President, carried his home state of New York in yesterday's election by a plurality of about 37,000 over President Truman, his Democratic opponent, and won New York's important forty-seven electoral votes.

With fifteen election districts missing out of 5,592 outside New York City, and with the city complete, the vote on the two major-party candidates was:

	Dewey	Truman
New York City	1,108,054	1,597,101
Rest of State	1,720,223	1,195,181
Totals	**2,828,277**	**2,792,281**

This gave Governor Dewey an actual plurality in the state of 35,996, which probably will be increased by about 1,500 by returns from the missing up-state districts, probably all Republican. Mr. Dewey carried the state outside New York City by 525,042 on the tabulated returns. Mr. Truman's New York City plurality was 489,047.

Henry A. Wallace, Progressive candidate for President, received a larger vote in the state than had been generally expected. With fifteen up-state election districts missing, he polled 503,404 votes, of which 423,424 were in New York City and 79,980 elsewhere in the state.

The Liberal party polled 222,219 votes for President Truman, of which 194,449 were cast in New York City and 27,770 in the rest of the state.

President Truman's strong showing, which held the plurality for his Republican opponent to several hundred thousand less than most pre-election estimates, was due to strong support from members of

Continued on Page 11, Column 2

THE TRUMANS AND THE DEWEYS VOTING IN YESTERDAY'S ELECTION

The President placing his ballot in the box at the polling place in his home town of Independence, Mo. Waiting their turn to vote are Mrs. Truman and their daughter, Margaret.
Associated Press Wirephoto

Governor Dewey signing the register at the polling place in public school at 121 East Fifty-first Street. Mrs. Dewey is standing beside her husband, and the registrar is Mrs. E. V. Hough.
The New York Times

JERSEY FOR DEWEY BY 70,000 MARGIN

Governor Overtakes Truman —Hendrickson Wins, Party Loses 3 House Seats

By RUSSELL PORTER

With only 101 out of 3,707 election districts unreported at 6 o'clock this morning, New Jersey's sixteen electoral votes went to Governor Dewey by an indicated plurality of about 70,000.

This was a surprisingly small margin over President Truman, in view of claims by Republican managers as late as last night that the Dewey margin would be 234,000.

State Treasurer Robert C. Hendrickson, Republican, of Woodbury defeated Archibald S. Alexander, Democrat, of Bernardsville by

Continued on Page 6, Column 2

Wallace Vote Is Far Short Of His Party's Expectations

By WILL LISSNER

No signs of the 10,000,000 vote that the Progressive party leaders were counting upon for their Presidential candidate, Henry A. Wallace, appeared in returns early today from roughly half the country's projected popular vote in yesterday's election.

As the returns rolled in, it became clear that Mr. Wallace would not get even half the vote his campaign managers expected, and probably not even a quarter of it. Of 25,431,641 votes counted, Mr. Wallace polled 618,705, or about 3 per cent. Undoubtedly this figure was influenced by the failure to count minority party polls in some states in the early counting.

In New York, however, Mr. Wallace's vote was decisive, and in several other states, such as California, it made serious inroads on the Democratic showing for President Truman.

In forty of the forty-five states in which the Progressive party was on the ballot, Mr. Wallace was running better than half of 1 per cent in seventeen and at fractions of 1 per cent, some of them infinitesimal, in twenty-three.

The states that were giving Mr. Wallace better than 1 per cent were California, Connecticut, Florida, Idaho, Iowa, Maryland, Massachusetts, Minnesota, Montana, Nevada, New Jersey, New York, North Dakota, Oregon, Pennsylvania, South Dakota and Wisconsin.

The states that were giving him less than 1 per cent of the vote

Continued on Page 15, Column 2

40 ELECTORAL VOTES TO STATES RIGHTERS

Alabama, Mississippi, South Carolina, Louisiana Won, but Popular Vote Is Short

By CLAYTON KNOWLES

The States Rights Democratic ticket, headed by Gov. J. Strom Thurmond of South Carolina, was romping off this morning with forty electoral votes in five Southern states, an electoral total that had been as good as conceded to it even before the balloting began. With about half the projected national vote recorded, the Thurmond-Wright ticket had polled 552,417 popular votes. It was on the ballot in only thirteen states.

Not beyond the realm of possibility was the prospect that neither President Truman nor Governor Dewey would win a clear majority of the electoral vote. States Righters hoped for such an eventuality in launching their party last July. In such a situation, the election is thrown into the House of Representatives, where each state delegation casts one vote.

The forty States Rights electoral votes were made up of Alabama's eleven, South Carolina's eight, Mississippi's nine, Louisiana's ten and two of Tennessee's twelve.

Two electoral candidates, pledged to the Thurmond-Wright ticket, were running on the Democratic slate which was leading in latest tabulations in Tennessee. They were running on the States' Rights slate which was showing up a poor third in latest reports.

The forty-vote indication fell far below the predictions of Governor Thurmond and other States' Rights leaders, who forecast that the ticket would win more than 100 electoral votes.

This, the fourth party in the national election, while living up to advance estimates in point of electoral votes, was not polling the great popular vote in the South that had been expected. It did not appear to be making large enough inroads in a number of key Southern states to throw these states to the Republican ticket as some persons had expected.

Among those that had been placed in this category were North Carolina

Continued on Page 7, Column 2

FORECASTS UPSET

President Surprises by Taking Early Popular Vote Lead, Holds It

AHEAD ON ELECTORS

Truman Has Indicated 227, Governor 176— 88 Are Doubtful

By ARTHUR KROCK

At 6 A. M. today, after a night in which his political fortunes waxed and waned with every passing hour, President Harry S. Truman took an impressive lead over his Republican opponent, Gov. Thomas E. Dewey of New York, in both the popular and electoral vote of the nation which went to the polls yesterday in the forty-eight states of the Union to choose a President, a Vice President, and the Eighty-first Congress and thirty-two Governors.

Ahead in the popular vote at all times during the counting, the President gained the electoral lead when Illinois was conceded to him at 5 A. M. and his chance of gaining Ohio steadily improved. At 6 A. M. the division of electoral votes between him and Governor Dewey that appeared to be established was as follows:

Truman, 227; Dewey, 176; doubtful, 88.

The remaining 40 of the total of 531 electoral votes apparently had been won by the Presidential candidate of the Democratic States Rights party, Gov. J. Strom Thurmond of South Carolina.

Truman Needs 39 More

Only thirty-nine more electoral votes were needed by the President to attain the majority of 266 that would give him a full term in the White House in his own right. And fifty-three were in sight—in the doubtful states of Iowa, Nevada, Washington, Iowa and California. However, in the last named, with a block of twenty-five, Governor Dewey was holding the lead.

If California ends with a Dewey victory, Ohio, with twenty-five electors, can overcome that loss, and Ohio went definitely into the doubtful column in the early hours of today. Therefore the possibility that the election would end without a decision, and the choice of a President would devolve on the House of Representatives in the Eighty-first Congress, remained within the area of strong possibility, with the Senate empowered to choose the next Vice President. But Governor Dewey's chances to win the election were fading fast at dawn today.

The possibility of an election by the House is the consequence of the capture of forty electors in the South by the States' Rights Democratic party, whose nominees were Govs. J. Strom Thurmond of South Carolina and Fielding Wright of Mississippi. And, if this is the eventual outcome, the President will have been defeated by the revolt of Southern Democrats against his "civil rights" program of Federal laws to enforce anti-segregation and a "fair employment practices" act in the states.

The returns at 6 A. M. however, further upset the earlier indication that the Progressive party candidacy of Henry A. Wallace had not proved as costly to the President, or more so, than the Southern Democratic insurrection. For if Mr. Dewey's pluralities in New York and in Ohio are as narrow as was indicated early today, Mr. Truman can attribute his failure to carry them both to the Wallace votes that was subtracted from the normal Democratic following.

The Congressional returns were more definite. Democratic candidates for the Senate appear certain to win the four crucial contests that will give the two wings of the party a numerical Senate

Continued on Page 2, Column 3

BOWLES IS ELECTED IN GOVERNOR RACE

He Wins Connecticut by 1,400 Votes, While Dewey Carries State for GOP by 15,000

Special to The New York Times.

NEW HAVEN, Conn., Nov. 2.— With only one town unreported, Chester A. Bowles, Democrat, leading by 1,322 votes, is certain of election as Governor of Connecticut over the incumbent, James C. Shannon.

Governor Dewey, the first Republican to carry the state since Herbert Hoover won it in 1932, has carried the state over President Truman by about 15,000 votes.

The Democrats also disrupted the Republican domination in Congress, which included all six Representatives in the last House. Abraham A. Ribicoff, a lawyer of Hartford, and John A. McGuire, both Democrats, upset the Republican incumbents in the First and Third Districts.

Representatives John Davis Lodge and James T. Patterson, respectively, are the only Republicans assured of re-election. Both candidates of the party trail in close contests for the Second District seat and Congressman-at-Large.

In the large cities of New Haven, Hartford and Waterbury, Mr. Bowles piled up a majority of 40,-

Continued on Page 2, Column 4

12,000 See Start of Horse Show; Mexican and French Officers Win

By JOHN RENDEL

New York's wealth and fashion and a large number of plain citizens divided their interest between the election returns and the annual visitations of the horse as a medium for sport and the exchange of social amenities last night. The occasion was the formal opening of the Sixtieth National Horse Show, launched again on an election "ternoon for a run of eight days of matinee and evening performances in Madison Square Garden.

In some ways it was the biggest national held since the war stopped. There were more horses, the number exceeding 500 from this country, Canada, Mexico and France. The Royal Canadian Mounted Police, in scarlet and blue, were back with their eye-catching ride to music for the first time since 1936. France was represented by a military contingent, also for the first time since 1934. Mexico and Canada were in the same in-

International jumping competition, as they had been a year ago.

Horse and man combined for exciting hunter and jumper contests. There were slick saddle horses, flashy harness rigs to remind the metropolis that a lot of country life still existed where the horse had a place.

The void in the refulgent panoply was in the absence of a United States Army team, disbanded soon after last summer's Olympic Games because the horse, isn't what he was in war any more. America's military riders, always hitherto present as far as memory served, were missed by the 12,000 on hand in the seats around the arena floor to honor the horse and participate, vicariously or otherwise, in the spectacle of society on parade.

There was another parade, too, that was a lot more stirring. It was the traditional one of the in-

Continued on Page 38, Column 1

World News Summarized

WEDNESDAY, NOVEMBER 3, 1948

President Truman at 7 o'clock this morning, was within sight of an electoral majority that would keep him in the White House for four years more. Maintaining an early lead in the popular vote he gradually won more and more states in a close race with Governor Dewey [1:8.] Governor Thurmond carried four Southern states on the States' Rights ticket [1:5], but the vote for Henry A. Wallace was only a fraction of what his supporters had expected. [1:5-6.]

It was Mr. Wallace's half-million votes in New York State that enabled Mr. Dewey to win by a narrow margin. [1:3.] The New York Governor also carried New Jersey by a close vote. [1:4.] Mr. Dewey won in Connecticut, but Chester Bowles, Democrat, was elected Governor. [1:7.]

Control of Congress passed from the Republicans to the Democrats, unofficial and incomplete returns indicated. The Democrats easily won enough seats to take over the Senate [1:1] and apparently defeated more than enough Republicans to control the House. [9:3.]

In this city Representative Marcantonio was re-elected, but Representative Isacson and other American Labor party candidates were defeated. [1:2.] For the first time since 1938 the Democrats made gains in the State Legislature. [18:3.] The coveted post of Surrogate in New York County was won by George Frankenthaler, Republi-

can, who had a plurality of 644 over Judge John A. Mullen, Democrat. [7:1.]

Chairman Spaak of the United Nations General Assembly's Political Committee admonished Soviet Deputy Foreign Minister Vishinsky during debate on the Balkan question to stop "insulting other delegates." [21:3-4.] Poland asked in the Economic Committee that action be taken against the United States for alleged economic sanctions under the Marshall Plan. [21:2.]

The Benelux countries have been asked for their detailed information on their four-year recovery plans. The Belgians fear pressure to impose a planned economy. [30:4-5.]

Plans to ban collective disobedience of taxation laws and other Communist moves will be considered by the French Cabinet today. Numerous casualties resulted from clashes between miners and American forces seizing strike-bound mines. [24:2.]

Although it was denied that peace talks between Israel and Trans-Jordan had begun, it was reported authoritatively that King Abdullah had decided that such talks should be held. [23:4.]

Chinese planes continued to bomb Mukden, occupied by the Communists. [24:3-4.]

Washington took two steps affecting national defense. The inactive National Guard was re-established [54:2] and Selective Service recommended that qualified medical and other Southern students receive draft deferment until graduation. [54:5.]

"All the News That's Fit to Print"

The New York Times.

LATE CITY EDITION
Partly cloudy and mild today; fair tonight and tomorrow.
Temperature Range Today—Max., 65; Min., 47
Temperature Yesterday—Max., 60; Min., 48
Full U. S. Weather Bureau Report, Page 51

Copyright, 1949, by The New York Times Company.

VOL. XCVIII..No. 33,346.   Entered as Second-Class Matter, Postoffice, New York, N. Y.   NEW YORK, THURSDAY, MAY 12, 1949.   Times Square, New York 18, N. Y. Telephone LAckawanna 4-1000   THREE CENTS NEW YORK CITY

ISRAEL WINS A SEAT IN U.N. BY 37-12 VOTE

ARABS INDIGNANT

Quit the Assembly Hall After Poll—9 Nations Abstain in Ballot

59TH COUNTRY IN BODY

Israel's Foreign Chief Sharett Pledges Peace Effort—Debate Brings Polish Attack

By THOMAS J. HAMILTON

The General Assembly admitted Israel to membership in the United Nations at 7:28 last night by a vote of 37 to 12, with nine abstentions.

The delegations of the six Arab states—Egypt, Iraq, Lebanon, Saudi Arabia, Syria and Yemen—walked out of the Assembly Hall at Flushing Meadow in protest before the applause over the election of Israel as the fifty-ninth member of the United Nations had died away. They indignantly refused to make any statement to correspondents regarding their intentions, but drove away to New York.

The Arab delegates, who also walked out when the General Assembly adopted the resolution recommending the partition of Palestine on Nov. 29, 1947, gave no hint of their impending action in their speeches in the General Assembly in the afternoon.

Charge Israeli Violation

They protested bitterly, however, that Israel had refused to comply with the provisions of a General Assembly resolution adopted on Dec. 11, 1948, calling for an international regime in Jerusalem and the repatriation of Arab refugees. Also, they challenged the validity of a Security Council recommendation for the admission of Israel, since Britain, a permanent member of its Council, had abstained.

The Charter requires the concurring votes of the Big Five on all except procedural questions, and the Arab delegates insisted that the Assembly should first get a ruling from the International Court of Justice. This procedure was contained in a resolution presented by Iraq yesterday afternoon, but Dr. Evatt ruled it out of order on the ground that the General Assembly could not examine the decision of another United Nations body.

The Yemen delegation returned shortly after 10 o'clock for the night session of the Assembly, and an Egyptian delegate came back a few minutes later, but the other desks remained vacant.

Immediately after the vote Dr. Evatt summoned to the platform Moshe Sharett, Israeli Foreign Minister, who had arrived by plane from Tel Aviv early yesterday to hear the final speeches.

"We enter this Assembly, which represents the collective statesmanship of the world, in a spirit of humility, anxious for guidance and enlightenment," said Mr. Sharett, who re-stated the Israeli policy of "loyalty to the fundamental principles of the United Nations' Charter and friendship with all peace-loving states, especially with the United States of America and the Union of Soviet Socialist Republics."

Now a Working Member

Mr. Sharett took his seat at the desk that had previously been prepared for the Israeli delegation in the back of the Assembly hall, between the Iraqi and Lebanese delegations. United Nations officials said no additional formalities were required, and that Israel would have the right to participate in all further proceedings of the General Assembly on the same basis as the fifty-eight other members.

The vote came too late to permit the Israeli flag to be raised in the area in front of the main delegates' entrance. A flag pole, however, had been prepared in advance, and there will be a ceremony at Lake Success at 10:30 A. M. today. The General Assembly took up the application at its afternoon session and the debate concluded at 7:30 as a result of the fact that additional time was taken up with the protests of the Arab delegates.

Continued on Page 15, Column 1

When You Think of Writing Think of Whiting.—Advt.

KENNY TO ASK COURT FOR ORDER TO SEIZE JERSEY CITY BOOKS

Mayor-Elect Seeks to Prevent Any Alterations of Records to Shield Old Regime

FULL INQUIRY IS PLANNED

'It's All Right With Me,' Says Hague of Defeat—Fight for State Rule Likely

By LEO EGAN

The political coalition that dethroned Frank Hague as boss of Jersey City has decided to seek a court order barring the outgoing city administration from destroying or altering official records before it leaves office next Tuesday.

John V. Kenny, who headed the coalition and who will become Mayor in the new administration, said a formal application for an order impounding city books and records would be submitted tomorrow to Judge William Brennan in Hudson County Superior Court.

One of the first acts of the new regime, Mr. Kenny added, will be to order a full-scale audit of the records and accounts of the outgoing administration, headed by Mayor Frank Hague Eggers, nephew of the 73-year-old former Mayor, who was one of the last of the old-time bosses in the United States to yield up his political power.

Drive to End State Rule Seen

While the new regime was making its plans for sifting city records for evidence of illegal acts and misuse of public funds on behalf of the Hague machine, Democrats in other parts of New Jersey were contemplating a drive to strip Mr. Hague of his control of the Democratic party in the state.

In any reorganization of the state Democratic organization, the state elections will result in an overwhelming victory for the Republican State ticket, headed by Gov. Alfred E. Driscoll.

The action was taken by the House Veterans Affairs Committee at a closed meeting that had been scheduled merely to formalize its action yesterday in approving pensions on a weekly basis.

The committee voted, 14 to 8, to confine the $72-a-month payments to unemployable veterans. By a voice vote, it then cleared the measure formally to the House.

Approval of the limitation was prompted by Veterans Administration estimates, drawn up overnight, that without it the bill would add $65,000,000,000 to the cost of veterans' benefits over the next fifty years. Yesterday's action had been based on a $12,000,000,000 estimate.

As finally approved, the measure's fifty-year cost was estimated at $8,693,000,000 by Guy H. Birdsall, assistant veterans administrator.

Mr. Rankin was joined by Representative A. Leonard Allen, Democrat, of Louisiana, in voting against reporting the bill. Shortly afterward the Mississippi legislator arose in the House to protest the action of the committee, of which he is chairman.

The employability clause, he asserted, would bar pensions from taking over. Mr. Kenny said that

Continued on Page 25, Column 2

WAR PENSION BILL IS SHARPLY LIMITED

House Group Confines Benefit to Unemployable and Reports Measure as Rankin Protests

By JOHN D. MORRIS

WASHINGTON, May 11 — The new veterans pension bill was further watered down in committee today—to such an extent that its author, Representative John E. Rankin, Democrat, of Mississippi, voted, though in vain, against reporting it to the House.

Continued on Page 32, Column 4

Johnson Approves Air Force Plan To Distribute Negroes Among Units

Special to The New York Times.

WASHINGTON, May 11—Latest proposals by the Air Force to conform to armed service policy on racial equality were approved today by Louis Johnson, Secretary of Defense.

W. Stuart Symington, Secretary of the Air Force, wrote to Secretary Johnson on April 30 and assured the defense chief that his directive of April 6 asking equality of treatment and opportunity "without regard to race, color, religion, or national origin" would be put into effect.

One of the principal moves in this direction is an Air Force order disbanding the all-Negro 332nd Fighter Wing at Lockbourne Air Force base at Columbus, Ohio. Its 2,000 officers and men will be distributed throughout the service in non-segregated units, it was stated.

Another assurance given to Mr. Johnson, it was learned, was that "key" positions would be open to Negroes who are individually qualified to hold them.

Letters from Kenneth C. Royall,

Secretary of the Army at that time, and Dan A. Kimball, Assistant Secretary of the Navy, answering the same April 6 directive, were in effect rejected by Mr. Johnson on the ground that they were too general. The Secretary of Defense asked the two officials to "clarify" the information contained in their responses. Both letters, it was learned, told Mr. Johnson that his policy was already in effect, and did not indicate that additional changes would be made.

In his reply to the Army and Navy, Mr. Johnson fixed a deadline of May 25 by which the two services are to provide more details of their plans to conform to the equality policy. The services were instructed to make their replies through Thomas R. Reid, chairman of the National Military Establishment's Personnel Policy Board.

Mr. Johnson made his April 6 directive to the armed service public on April 20, at which time he stated that he intended to

Continued on Page 54, Column 1

BERLIN LAND BLOCKADE IS LIFTED; FIRST TRAIN, AUTOS REACH CITY; ZONE TROOP RETIREMENT STUDIED

U.S. PLAN WEIGHED

Big 3 Would Withdraw to Ports in the North Under Proposal

FRENCH WOULD GO HOME

Presentation of Suggestion Will Depend on Soviet Stand in Paris Talks

By JAMES RESTON
Special to The New York Times.

WASHINGTON, May 11—The United States was reported today to have under consideration a plan under which all occupation troops in Germany would be withdrawn into restricted areas at the North German ports.

Under this plan, which is being discussed with Britain and France, Soviet troops would be situated on the West Bank of the Oder in Stettin, British troops would be restricted to the area of Hamburg, and United States troops would be concentrated in Bremen.

[Stettin was included in the Soviet zone in the Potsdam pact, but under a separate agreement reached Sept. 20, 1947, the Russians turned over control of the former German port to Poland. Bremen is a United States enclave in the British zone.]

These troops, it is understood, would be obliged, under this plan, to use only sea communications, and France, which has a common frontier with Germany, would withdraw her occupation troops into her own territory.

An understanding apparently already has been reached among the Western powers to reject any Soviet proposal at the forthcoming meeting of the Council of Foreign Ministers in Paris for the complete evacuation of all occupation troops from all of Germany.

It is felt here that total withdrawal of these troops would be detrimental to the economic recovery and sense of security of Western Europe.

However, if Soviet Foreign Minister Andrei Y. Vishinsky should demonstrate in Paris that his Government was now prepared to establish a central government in Germany along the lines laid down by the Western powers for the

Continued on Page 3, Column 2

IT'S A REAL HOLIDAY FOR THESE BERLIN YOUNGSTERS

Joyous children hold their lunch boxes over their heads as they get news that there will be no school in celebration of the end of the blockade. The sign reads "blockade free."
Associated Press Radiophoto

ACHESON STILL BARS FRANCO AS FASCIST

Says Spanish Regime Denies Basic Rights in the Pattern of Hitler and Mussolini

Secretary Acheson's remarks on Spanish regime, Page 10.

By BERTRAM D. HULEN
Special to The New York Times.

WASHINGTON, May 11—Secretary of State Dean Acheson declared today that the question of restoring full diplomatic relations with Spain turned primarily upon the attitude of Western European countries that were still opposed to bringing her back into their international family for military and economic cooperation.

This attitude, the Secretary told his weekly news conference, was conditioned by the absence of fundamental freedoms under the Franco regime which, he said, originally and still was patterned on Nazi Germany and Fascist Italy. At an-

Continued on Page 10, Column 1

Eisler Reported Stowaway; Seizure in Britain Is Asked

By WILL LISSNER

A man who has identified himself as Gerhart Eisler, native of Germany, is fleeing from the United States aboard the Gdynia-America liner Batory, it became known yesterday. The fugitive is believed to be the former Comintern agent named by the House Un-American Activities Committee as America's No. 1 Communist, jumping $23,500 bail to escape serving a year in jail and other penalties, but his identity has not yet been definitely established.

The Federal Bureau of Investigation and the Immigration and Naturalization Service of the Department of Justice moved yesterday to fix the identity of the fugitive. If the man aboard the Batory is the German-born Communist leader Eisler, he will be placed in custody for eventual return.

The fugitive is bound for Gdynia, but the ship, which sailed last Saturday, will put into Southampton Saturday. To make sure that Polish Communists aboard the ship do not balk a return, the State Department, at the request of the Department of Justice, notified Scotland Yard of the incident and asked that top investigators meet the ship on her arrival in the English port. Scotland Yard was asked to hold the suspect.

If Eisler, the convicted Communist agent, has fled the jurisdiction of the Federal District Court, his bail would be forfeited even though the English authorities return him, it was said at the Federal building.

The forfeiture of the $23,500 bail would be a blow to the Civil Rights Congress and the American Committee for the Protection of the Foreign Born. For a good part of

Continued on Page 4, Column 3

FIRST BERLIN TRAIN FROM WEST SEALED

Officials Lock Doors and Draw Shades to Keep Russians Out and Reporters In

By The United Press.

BERLIN, Thursday, May 12—The first western passenger train since last year arrived in Berlin at 5:11 A. M. today (11:11 P. M. Wednesday, Eastern Daylight Time)—hauled by a Soviet zone locomotive.

A combined British-American train of twelve cars, it carried approximately 140 Western nationals, including seventy-three British troops and at least a score of reporters.

Anglo-American officials ordered the doors locked and the shades drawn soon after the train left Helmstedt at 1:23 A. M., the first train to make the West-East run on the Helmstedt-Berlin road since last year.

The train officials said that the "sealing" of the cars was necessary "to keep the Russians out and to keep you newsmen in." The reporters peeked anyway but saw only a moonlit plain landscape during the eventless three hours

Continued on Page 2, Column 2

U.S. Reds Liken Pact to Hitler Axis; Norman Thomas Urges Ratification

By WILLIAM S. WHITE
Special to The New York Times.

WASHINGTON, May 11 — The Communist party of the United States, through a statement filed by its general secretary, Eugene Dennis, likened the North Atlantic treaty today to "Hitler's Axis," and demanded that the Senate withhold any action toward its ratification until after the Big Four Foreign Ministers' conference.

However, Norman Thomas, Socialist leader, supported ratification of the treaty before the Senate Foreign Relations Committee, but stressed that he did so with much anxiety because of the "dangers" that might lie in it.

He expressed belief that the pact should not be ratified unless it was "absolutely plain" that Spain would not be included in it, and equally plain that proposed American military aid should not be used against colonial peoples.

Senator Tom Connally, Democrat, of Texas, committee chair-

man, said that Spain's inclusion was "highly improbable" since it could be done only by unanimous consent of the twelve countries that signed the treaty.

Above all, Mr. Thomas recommended that before ratification this country issue "a mighty appeal for an end of the armament race under effective international controls which would make the pact unnecessary."

The Communist party proposal that the pact be held back, first advanced last week by Henry A. Wallace, was offered also by representatives of the National Council of American-Soviet Friendship and the National Council of the Arts, Sciences and Professions.

Witnesses for these organizations appeared before the committee and further urged Soviet-United States conferences looking toward resolving differences between the two countries.

Their recommendations for de-

Continued on Page 7, Column 2

SIEGE ON 328 DAYS

Leading Car Speeds 102 Miles From the British Zone in 1½ Hours

AIRLIFT PLANES CONTINUE

West Concerned as Russians Turn Back Some Trucks— City's Lights Turned On

By DREW MIDDLETON
Special to The New York Times.

BERLIN, Thursday, May 12—Just as the morning sun rose over the jagged skyline of this broken but defiant city a Soviet zone locomotive chugged wearily into the Charlottenburg Station in the British sector hauling the first train to reach Berlin from the West in 328 days.

Arrival of the train completed the relief of the city from the iron vise of the Soviet blockade.

At one minute after midnight [6:01 P. M. Wednesday, Eastern daylight time] two jeeps and a convoy of cars, buses and trucks roared out of the city for the Western zones. An hour and three quarters later the first cars of a flotilla that simultaneously had left Helmstedt, in the British zone at the border of the Soviet zone, swept into Berlin to re-establish the land link with the West broken since the Soviet Military administration established a complete blockade of the city last June.

By morning it was evident that the Russians had observed the letter if not the spirit of the East-West agreement reached in New York. Traffic was flowing freely along the Autobahn.

Although there had been some difficulty over locomotives, the Russians had promised to send sixteen freight trains and one passenger train into Berlin each day. Pending settlement of the dispute the trains would be pulled by Soviet zone locomotives.

Western Officials Disturbed

To Berliners who awoke in the night to find lights burning in the streets and in their homes and intersector barriers dismantled, the action indicated that the Russians had returned to the West-East agreement reached in New York.

Americans and British in Military Government offices, however, were distinctly disturbed by the turning back at Soviet checkpoints of trucks bound for the Western zones with Western sector exports.

This refusal to permit trucks to pass stems from a Soviet order of January, 1948. Hence it is not affected by the New York agreement on ending the blockade. But the Western Powers felt that the action indicated that the Russians would not give an inch more than called for by that agreement.

The first railroad train since June of 1948 passed through the checkpoint at Helmstedt, in the British zone at the border of the Soviet zone, at 1:23 A. M., bound for Berlin.

The first car from Helmstedt, driven by Walter G. Rundle, United Press manager for Germany, arrived at the American checkpoint outside Berlin at 1:44. Mr. Rundle had driven the distance, which the British declare is 102 miles, in an hour and thirty-seven minutes. He said that the bridge across the Elbe at Magdeburg was in good condition.

Aide's Wife Enters City

The first woman to enter Berlin after lifting of the blockade was Adelaide de Neufville, wife of Lawrence de Neufville, consultant to the civil affairs division of the United States Military Government.

The first two railroad trains to start across the Soviet zone for Berlin since June 17, 1948, left Russian control early this morning. The first of these was a passenger train carrying correspondents. It moved into the moonlit landscape of the Russian zone at 1:55 after an eleven-minute wait at the checkpoint.

Eight minutes later a freight train of forty-two cars carrying coal from the Ruhr for Berlin passed through the checkpoint en route to Berlin, symbolizing the end not only of the Russian block-

Continued on Page 2, Column 2

ARABS INDIGNANT

Protesters in Tripoli Tear U. S. Flag to Bits

By The United Press.

TRIPOLI, LIBYA, May 11—Demonstrators tore to shreds a United States flag in front of the United States Consulate in Tripoli today and set fire to a number of Italian establishments.

The demonstrators, demanding full independence for this former Italian colony, shouted "Long live Russia! Down with America and the United Nations!"

Special to The New York Times.

LAKE SUCCESS, May 11—A United Kingdom proposal that Eritrea, except for the western province, be incorporated into Ethiopia was approved in a subcommittee of the Political Committee this morning by a vote of ten to three with two abstentions.

A second United Kingdom proposal that the western province be incorporated in the adjacent Sudan also was approved by a vote of seven to two with six abstentions.

World News Summarized

THURSDAY, MAY 12, 1949

The 328-day Soviet blockade of Berlin ended on schedule at 12:01 o'clock this morning, Berlin time, and approximately an hour and one-half later the first vehicles from the Western zones of Germany entered the city followed by the first train. [1:8; maps P. 2.]

The first Western passenger train to Berlin was sealed; a jeep led the road convoy [1:7.] Russian guards at Berlin ignored automobiles going to Helmstedt; people watched on the Autobahn. [3:1.]

Secretary of State Acheson warned that the end of the blockade did not, in itself, solve the German problem. He said Russia's willingness at the forthcoming Big Four meeting in Paris to consider proposals that would not erase the progress made in Germany by the Western powers would determine the outcome. Explaining this country's position, he discussed the draft constitution for a West German state. [4:2.] The United States was said to be considering a plan for withdrawal of all occupation troops to North German ports, except for French forces, which would return to France. [1:4.]

Guarded optimism was expressed by Moscow's New Times in an editorial on the Big Four meeting. The editorial said the talks could be a "turning point" in East-West relations. [4:6.]

Communists, urging at a Senate hearing in Washington that ratification of the North Atlantic treaty be deferred until after the Paris meeting, likened the pact to "Hitler's Axis." [1:6-7.]

Victorious anti-Hague forces in Jersey City will seek a court order impounding all public records until an audit can be made. [1:3.]

Israel became the fifty-ninth member of the United Nations when the General Assembly voted, 37 to 12, to admit her. The six Arab states left the hall in protest. [1:1.] Foreign Minister Sharett, the first Israeli delegate to the United Nations, pledged his country to work for peace with its Arab neighbors and to remain friendly with both the United States and Russia. [12:3.]

Japan is not what she was ten years ago, Premier Yoshida said in appealing for proper understanding by the world. He asked access to materials and markets to enable Japan to become self-supporting. [19:1.]

Representative Rankin disowned his veterans' pension bill when a "watered-down" version was reported by a House committee. [1:2.]

Labor leaders and President Truman were said to have agreed on pressing passage of the Administration's labor bill with some amendments. [24:2.]

A man who identified himself as Gerhart Eisler, this country's No. 1 Communist, was reported secretly on a Polish liner now at sea. [1:6-7.]

The United States will abstain from a United Nations vote to

Index to other news appears on Page 32.

The New York Times.

Copyright, 1949, by The New York Times Company

LATE CITY EDITION
Fair and quite cool today
and tomorrow.

Temperature Range Today—Max. 62; Min. 49
Temperature Yesterday—Max. 66; Min. 50
Full U. S. Weather Bureau Report, Page 27

VOL. XCIX..No. 33,481.

Entered as Second-Class Matter.
Postoffice, New York, N. Y.

NEW YORK, SATURDAY, SEPTEMBER 24, 1949.

Times Square, New York 18, N. Y.
Telephone LAckawanna 4-1000

THREE CENTS NEW YORK CITY

SMALL STEEL MILL SETS PENSION PLAN, A POSSIBLE PATTERN

Proposal by Employer of 1,200, With Workers Sharing Costs, Is Held Poser for Union

---

LIMITS CAUSE FOR STRIKE

Murray Is Firm for 'Package' Urged by Panel — Wildcat Walkout Hits Another Plant

By A. H. RASKIN
Special to The New York Times.

PITTSBURGH, Sept. 23—The first hint at the strategy the steel industry may employ to head off a threatened strike of 500,000 steel workers Oct. 1 came today from one of the smallest companies in the industry.

While the United States Steel Corporation and other big companies marked time on the first day of their renewed negotiations with the United Steel Workers of America, CIO, the Follansbee Steel Corporation made a proposal to the union that was widely regarded here as the forerunner of similar offers to be made by the rest of the industry.

The company, which has 1,200 employes at plants in Follansbee, W. Va., and Toronto, Ohio, informed the union that it was prepared to commit itself to pay 6 cents an hour for pensions, provided its workers put up an additional 3 cents an hour.

Employes Pay for Insurance

The company already has a contributory program of social insurance, to which it gives, about 4 cents an hour and the workers 2 cents.

The proposal would bring the company's outlay for pensions and welfare into line with the 10-cent "package" recommended by President Truman's fact-finding board. At the same time it would make an end run around the union's insistence that employers pay the whole cost of industrial social security.

The Truman panel endorsed the idea that employers should meet the bill for pensions and social insurance, but opened the door for supplementary payments by workers to increase the amount of protection that could be provided. The board said such arrangements could be effected through collective bargaining.

If other steel companies subscribe to the 6-cent figure for pensions and 4 cents for health, hospital and other forms of social insurance, on condition that their workers also contribute, the union would be maneuvered into the position of having to decide whether or not to strike solely for establishment of the non-contributory principle.

Philip Murray, president of the union, has stressed the union's belief that the most important element in the Truman board's report was its recommendation that care for the "human machine" should be as much a charge on industry as care of plant equipment. The union has barred any compromise on that issue.

Murray Also Threatening Strike

At a two-hour conference with representatives of United States Steel this afternoon, Mr. Murray reiterated the union's determination to strike unless the company agreed to shoulder the full cost of pensions and welfare on the 6-cent and 4-cent basis suggested by the fact-finders.

The company made no immediate reply. Subcommittees were set up by both sides to continue negotiations Monday, five days before the strike deadline.

There was nothing to indicate that "Big Steel" had abandoned the opposition it expressed in public statements last week to exemption of workers from any direct share of financial responsibility for their own pensions and insurance.

The company has committed itself to give 4 cents an hour for welfare, provided workers made an additional payment of the same sum, but it has declined to set any specific figure for pensions until a joint study of retirement benefits is completed next March 31.

Negotiations between the union and other large steel companies took place today in a dozen cities, but none of the companies gave any new indication of its position. In virtually all cases the talks were recessed until Monday without any sign of a break in the deadlock that has existed since the first negotiations got under way in June.

Union negotiators warned that the patience of the men in the steel mills was wearing thin at the lack of progress toward employer—

Continued on Page 28, Column 1

Cancer Patient Slain; Daughter Detained

Special to The New York Times.

STAMFORD, Conn., Sept. 23—Carol Paight, 20 years old, was placed under police guard in Stamford Hospital tonight pending investigation of whether she shot her police-sergeant father in pity after learning that he had an inoperable cancer.

The father, Carl Paight, 52, died seven hours after he was shot with his own service pistol at 5:45 P. M. He had been in the hospital since Sept. 15, suffering from the effects of an operation that showed he had cancer.

The daughter, who had been alone with him, became hysterical. Sedatives were administered before she could be questioned by the police and a psychiatrist. Father and daughter had been deeply attached, friends said. Police who knew both because of Sergeant Paight's twenty-eight years of service here, said that she had declared upon being told of the cancer that she did not want her father to suffer.

RED DEFENSE RESTS; REBUTTAL WAIVED

Jury in 9-Month Trial Excused Till Summaries Begin Oct. 4, May Get Case Week Later

By RUSSELL PORTER

The defense rested in the nine-month Communist trial yesterday, and the Government waived its right of rebuttal. Federal Judge Harold R. Medina gave counsel until 2 o'clock Tuesday afternoon to submit requests for instructions to be included in his charge to the jury and announced that arguments on closing motions would be heard at 10:30 o'clock Wednesday morning.

Judge Medina excused the jury until Tuesday morning, Oct. 4, when, if he denies the usual defense motions to throw out the case, summaries will begin. In the absence of unexpected developments, the case should go to the jury by the week beginning Monday, Oct. 10.

Eleven members of the Communist party's American Politburo or national board have been on trial since January 17, for criminal conspiracy to teach and advocate overthrow of the Government and destruction of American democracy by force and violence. Government witnesses have testified that the defendants reorganized the party for this purpose in 1945 on orders from Moscow.

The defense took roughly six months to present its case, including a two-month preliminary challenge to the Federal jury system. The Government introduced its evidence in two months.

The defense called thirty-five witnesses and the Government fifteen. The defense offered 429 exhibits, the Government 332.

Of the 158 trial days, the defense used 109—eighty-two in the trial proper and twenty-seven in the jury challenge. The Government spent thirty-seven days in the presentation of evidence. Ten days were devoted to picking the jury and two days to opening statements by opposing counsel.

The Government called its first witness on March 23 and rested on May 19. The defense began to present evidence on May 23, four months ago yesterday.

Nearly 20,000 pages of testimony

Continued on Page 7, Column 2

CIO SEES LEFTISTS QUITTING TO FORM OWN ORGANIZATION

High Officers Say Such Action Is Called for by New Line of Communist Party

---

FIGHT AT CONVENTION DUE

National Body Plans to Set Up Rival Right-Wing Unions if Pro-Red Groups Depart

By LOUIS STARK
Special to The New York Times.

WASHINGTON, Sept. 23—High officers of the Congress of Industrial Organizations expressed the view today that the new Communist party line was to split all pro-Communist unions from the CIO and to form a new labor federation. This belief is supported by the following developments:

1. A factional struggle within the CIO Teachers Union in New York, in which the pro-Communists are demanding that the union leave the CIO, though their opponents proclaim loyalty to the parent body.

2. The decision of pro-Communist unions to carry the fight on autonomy and wage policies to the right wing, led by Philip Murray, president of the CIO.

3. The "impossible" demands decided on several days ago by the convention of the United Electrical Radio and Machine Workers that will be served on Mr. Murray.

4. Refusal of the Farm Equipment Workers Union to obey the CIO mandate to merge with the United Automobile Workers. The Murray forces are prepared for a possible split. If it occurs, they will charter right-wing groups to form the nucleus of new organizations supplanting the dissidents.

Eleven Affiliates Involved

Eleven CIO affiliates may be affected by the possible schism. While they have been generally credited with a membership of 1,000,000 members, informed officials say that their total is more nearly 600,000.

The largest of the dissidents is the UE, which says it bargains for 600,000 members. This union, however, is reported by right-wing officers to be paying to the CIO on about 350,000 members. Some of the leftist-led unions have been in arrears in payments to the national organization for some months.

The largest nut that the CIO has to crack is the UE, its third largest affiliate. This union, well entrenched in General Electric, Westinghouse and other large radio and electrical manufacturing companies, is a strong, well-disciplined organization.

Despite its strength, CIO officials indicated that they would meet any challenge of the UE's re-elected officers. If the union should decide to leave the CIO, the latter's officers feel confident of winning adherence of the workers in the big General Electric and Westinghouse plants as the nucleus of a new electrical union.

Mr. Murray's associates are impatient for the battle because daily evidences of leftist dissidence convinces them that the latter have made up their minds to split the CIO and to put the blame on the right wing.

The latest aspect of the leftist attack on the CIO leadership is

Continued on Page 28, Column 1

ATOM BLAST IN RUSSIA DISCLOSED; TRUMAN AGAIN ASKS U.N. CONTROL; VISHINSKY PROPOSES A PEACE PACT

ADDRESSING U. N.

Andrei Y. Vishinsky
The New York Times

VISHINSKY SAYS U.S. PLOTS ATOMIC WAR

Calls for Great Power Treaty to Strengthen World Peace in Assembly Speech

Text of Vishinsky address to U. N. Assembly is on Page 4.

By THOMAS J. HAMILTON

Andrei Y. Vishinsky, the Soviet Foreign Minister, accused the United States and Britain yesterday of planning an atomic war, and introduced a resolution at Flushing Meadow proposing that the United Nations General Assembly request the five Great Powers to conclude "a pact for the strengthening of peace."

The resolution also would call on all nations to settle their disputes without resorting to the use or threat of force, and would take note "of the unbending will and determination of peoples to ward

Continued on Page 4, Column 1

CAPITOL FOR ACCORD

Lucas Says 'Future of Civilization' May Rest on Atom Control

AIRING OF VIEWS URGED

McMahon Holds U. S. Should 'Demand Right' to Put Case Before Russians Via Radio

By WILLIAM S. WHITE
Special to The New York Times.

WASHINGTON, Sept. 23—In a great anxiety that passed soon into a positive response—demands for fresh tries at international control of the atomic bomb—Congress heard today the news that an atomic explosion had occurred in the Soviet Union.

The atmosphere at the Capitol almost everywhere was consciously quiet and restrained. Some of the most responsible members of Congress issued statements saying that the American people could have confidence, in any possible crisis, in the military leadership and the military power of this country.

Beyond this, Administration Congressional spokesmen said in substance that the implications of the President's disclosure of what had happened in Russia were beyond the scope of any Congressional action. They looked toward the United Nations as the forum for this matter.

Senator Scott W. Lucas of Illinois, the Democratic leader of the Senate, and Senator Brien McMahon, Democrat, of Connecticut, the principal Congressional authority on atomic energy, came out almost at once for another attempt at bringing the bomb under the world's seal.

"I believe," said Senator Lucas, "that nothing could give the world greater confidence in survival than for the delegates at the United Nations to reconsider the question of atomic energy control, and arrive at an agreement acceptable to all.

"The world knows that our rep-

Continued on Page 3, Column 5

World News Summarized

SATURDAY, SEPTEMBER 24, 1949

President Truman issued yesterday a terse statement containing this dramatic disclosure: "We have evidence that within recent weeks an atomic explosion occurred in the U. S. S. R."

His announcement, indicating that United States monopoly in atomic weapons had ended, added that "ever since atomic energy was first released by man, the eventual development of this new force by other nations was to be expected." He said the news would not lead to any shift in the United States position on international atomic control. [1:7.]

New efforts to achieve an acceptable plan for international control of atomic weapons were urged in Congress, where Mr. Truman's announcement was received with restrained anxiety. [1:5.] Reassuring statements were urged by General Eisenhower and Maj. Gen. Leslie R. Groves, wartime chief of the atomic bomb project. General Eisenhower said he saw no reason why "a development that was anticipated years ago should cause any revolutionary change in our way of thinking or 'n our actions." [2:2.] One r ult expected by Washington officials was a spur to the North Atlantic defense program. Closer cooperation among the United States, Britain and Canada in atomic development was also seen. [2:3-4.]

Scientists who had generally predicted that the Russians would eventually succeed in discovering the secret of setting off an atomic explosion saw the Russian development as having come at least three years earlier than had been expected. [1:6-7.]

Soviet Foreign Minister Vishinsky said nothing about Russian possession of an atomic bomb in his eagerly awaited address to the United Nations General Assembly. He accused the United States and Britain of planning an atomic war. Mr. Vishinsky introduced a resolution calling for "the unconditional prohibition of atomic weapons" and another asking the five major powers to make "a pact for the strengthening of peace." [1:4.]

Renewed negotiations by the Big Four Foreign Ministers' deputies on an Austrian state treaty got off to a bad start. Russian refusal to reconsider the controversial issues forced an indefinite adjournment. [6:2.]

The British Labor Government will ask for a vote of confidence after Parliament convenes next week to debate the Government's devaluation of the pound. [6:3.]

In China the battle for the important seaport of Amoy reached new intensity. [5:1; with map.]

In a move that might set the pattern for the big companies in the steel industry to stave off a threatened strike by 500,000 steelworkers, the Follansbee Steel Corporation offered a pension plan under which the company would pay 6 cents an hour and the employes an additional 3 cents an hour. [1:1.]

High CIO officials were reported to believe that the new Communist party line was to try to split all pro-Communist unions from the CIO to organize a new labor federation. [1:3.]

Index to other news appears on Page 14.

Truman Statement on Atom

By The United Press.

WASHINGTON, Sept. 23—The text of President Truman's statement today announcing a recent atomic explosion in the Soviet Union:

I believe the American people to the fullest extent consistent with the national security are entitled to be informed of all developments in the field of atomic energy. That is my reason for making public the following information.

We have evidence that within recent weeks an atomic explosion occurred in the U.S.S.R.

Ever since atomic energy was first released by man, the eventual development of this new force by other nations was to be expected. This probability has always been taken into account by us.

Nearly four years ago I pointed out that "scientific opinion appears to be practically unanimous that the essential theoretical knowledge upon which the discovery is based is already widely known. There is also substantial agreement that foreign research can come abreast of our present theoretical knowledge in time." And, in the three-nation declaration of the President of the United States and the Prime Ministers of the United Kingdom and Canada, dated Nov. 15, 1945, it was emphasized that no single nation could, in fact, have a monopoly of atomic weapons.

This recent development emphasizes once again, if indeed such emphasis were needed, the necessity for that truly effective and enforceable international control of atomic energy which this Government and the large majority of the members of the United Nations support.

Soviet Achievement Ahead Of Predictions by 3 Years

By WILLIAM L. LAURENCE

President Truman's announcement that we have evidence of the occurrence of an "atomic explosion" in the Soviet Union within recent weeks ranks only next to his original announcement of the explosion of the first atomic bomb over Hiroshima on Aug. 6, 1945. It marks the end of the first period of the atomic age and the beginning of the second.

The momentous event is bound to have profound repercussions the world over. Though the scientists have predicted its coming, it came at least three years sooner than was expected. This was largely the result of an erroneous assumption that Russian scientists could know nothing about developing an atomic bomb until after we informed them about it following Hiroshima. The fact of the matter is that scientists everywhere recognized the tremendous potentialities of atomic energy for war and peace as soon as the discovery of uranium fission was announced to the world in January, 1939.

While it is likely that Soviet scientists tested the first and only bomb they had, it would be dangerous to assume that they are four years behind us and that it would take them that long to catch up with us. It would be much more reasonable to assume that they have geared their plants to produce at the rate of one bomb a week, so that they will have a stockpile of at least fifty bombs a year from now, enough to destroy fifty of our cities with 40,-000,000 of our population.

On the other hand, it is also likely that the latest event will make possible a better understanding between us and Russia, leading toward an agreement for the international control of atomic energy. Bargaining between equals is more likely to produce desirable results than bargaining between two principals, one of which holds

Continued on Page 2, Column 6

ACHESON RULES OUT SHIFT IN U. S. PLANS

Western Diplomats and Atomic Experts at U. N. Agree to Uphold Control Program

Text of Secretary Acheson's statement is printed on Page 2.

By A. M. ROSENTHAL

Secretary of State Dean Acheson said yesterday that he assumed the explosion in Russia reported by President Truman had been caused by an actual atomic weapon. He insisted, however, that the news had come as no shock and would not change the United States-sponsored plan for international control of atomic energy.

Other Western diplomats and atomic control specialists at the United Nations Assembly at Flushing Meadow took the same line. Unanimously, they said that the majority of the members of the United Nations would stick to the plan that had been fought by the Soviet Union for more than three years.

United Nations officials took it for granted that the President's announcement had pushed the world organization back into the center of the atomic picture despite the long deadlock on control negotiations. Secretary General Trygve Lie summed up the Secretariat attitude by saying that the

Continued on Page 2, Column 5

U.S. REACTION FIRM

President Does Not Say Soviet Union Has an Atomic Bomb

PICKS WORDS CAREFULLY

But He Implies Our Absolute Dominance in New Weapons Has Virtually Ended

By ANTHONY LEVIERO
Special to The New York Times.

WASHINGTON, Sept. 23—President Truman announced this morning that an atomic explosion had occurred in Russia within recent weeks. This statement implied that the absolute dominance of the United States in atomic weapons had virtually ended.

"We have evidence that within recent weeks an atomic explosion occurred in the U.S.S.R.," said President Truman.

These words stood out in red-letter vividness in a brief undramatic statement in which the Chief Executive said that the United States always had taken into account the probability that other nations would develop "this new force."

He pleaded once again for adoption of the system of international control of atomic energy promulgated by the United States and supported by the large majority of countries now assembled in the United Nations General Assembly at Flushing Meadow.

McMahon Reveals News

Mr. Truman announced the discovery to the Cabinet, assembled in the White House at 11 A. M. for the usual Friday meeting. Simultaneously on Capitol Hill Senator Brien McMahon, Democrat, of Connecticut, stood before the members of the Joint Congressional Atomic Energy Committee and gave them the news, which Mr. Truman had passed on to him at 3:15 P. M. yesterday.

White House correspondents had their usual conference with Charles G. Ross, the President's secretary, at 10:30 A. M. It was routine, but they filed out his secretary, Miss Myrtle Bergheim, asked them not to go away. A moment before 11 A. M. Miss Bergheim entered the press room and said: "Press!"

The news men filed into Mr. Ross' office. He said he wished the door closed, and a secret service man took his post there. Then Mr. Ross said that he would pass out an announcement and that nobody was to leave the room until everyone present had a copy. Then he began passing around the President's mimeographed statement.

Tass Correspondent Attends

One of the first reporters to scan his copy exclaimed, "Russia has the atomic bomb!" There was a wild rush through the door and to the telephones in the near-by press room. One of the news men who sprinted out was the correspondent of Tass, the official Soviet news agency.

"The President has just given it to the Cabinet," said Mr. Ross as they went.

Thus the President did not personally appear, and there was no opportunity then or later to put questions to him.

Secretary of Defense Louis Johnson came out of the Cabinet meeting soon afterward. He came shaking his head as the questions came. Reporters literally clutched his arms as he headed for his limousine.

"Have we made any change in the disposition of our forces since this happened?" This question was asked twice.

"No," Mr. Johnson finally said.

"Does the Cabinet know any more about this than is contained in the President's statement?"

"The Cabinet knows all about it," Mr. Johnson replied to this. "I was fully informed."

"Do you have any reason to believe this was the first atomic explosion in Russia?" asked another reporter.

This time Mr. Johnson smilingly shook his head, negatively.

"Don't overplay it," remarked Mr. Johnson, departing. In the cir-

Continued on Page 2, Column 3

Auto Crash Kills Publisher's Wife As He Reaches for Spilling Cup

Special to The New York Times.

HARRISON, N. Y., Sept. 23—Marvin Pierce, president of the McCall Corporation, magazine and fashion publishers, at 230 Park Avenue, New York, was driving to the Rye railroad station this morning when he tried to prevent a cup of coffee from spilling on his wife's clothes. In an accident that followed, his wife, Mrs. Pauline Robinson Pierce, 53 years old, was killed and Mr. Pierce was injured.

The couple left their Purchase Street home, adjoining the Westchester Country Club, soon after 8 A. M. Mr. Pierce, who is 56, was at the wheel and his wife was beside him, ready to drive home from the station after her husband had boarded a commuters' train for New York.

Mrs. Pierce held in her hands a cup of coffee that she had carried from the breakfast table. After sipping the fluid, she placed the cup for a moment on the seat between her husband and herself. From a corner of his eye Mr. Pierce saw the cup tipping toward his wife.

As Mr. Pierce reached for the cup, the auto swerved to the left side of the road, hit a soft shoulder, plunged 100 feet down a moderate embankment, slid between a pole and a tree and crashed into a tree and a stone wall. Striking the windshield, Mrs. Pierce died of a fractured skull. The accident occurred on Highland Road near Purchase Street.

Taken to the United Hospital in Port Chester, Mr. Pierce told his story to the police. Detectives found the coffee cup, done China of English manufacture, unbroken in the wreckage of the car. It was taken to police headquarters. Physicians listed Mr. Pierce's injuries as a cerebral concussion, fractured nose, four broken ribs and several bruises. His condition tonight was improving.

Besides her husband, Mrs. Pierce leaves two sons, James R. and Scott Pierce of Rye, and two daughters, Mrs. Walter G. Rafferty of West Hartford, Conn., and Mrs. G. H. W. Bush of Bakersfield, Calif.

Couple Held in Quebec Air Crash; Woman Said to Have Planted Bomb

By The Associated Press.

QUEBEC, Sept. 23—Police reported tonight that a drug-dazed woman confessed to carrying a package, believed to have contained dynamite, which was placed aboard an ill-fated Quebec Airways plane that blew up Sept. 9, killing all twenty-three persons aboard.

Police said the woman, identified as Mrs. Arthur Pitre, admitted taking the package to the Quebec Airport where it was placed aboard the plane, but she insisted that she did not know the contents of the package.

Royal Canadian Mounted Police said the woman was recovering from sleeping pills she took at the suggestion of her lover, whose wife was aboard the plane.

Provincial police detained as a material witness J. A. Guay, a young Quebec jeweler, whose 28-year-old wife was one of the passengers who lost their lives when the plane was ripped open by an blast in the luggage compartment. The plane smashed into a mountain near Sault au Cochon, forty miles northeast of here.

Mrs. Pitre was also being held as a material witness.

Police also are reported to have questioned a third person in connection with the case.

Police described the third person as a 26-year-old "pretty waitress." They said she was a close acquaintance of Guay.

The crash took the lives of three New York executives of the Kennecott Copper Corporation. They were President E. T. Stannard, President-designate Arthur D. Storke and Vice President R. J. Parker.

Quebec Provincial police detained Mrs. Pitre at her home in Quebec. Persons living near by saw police enter the woman's Gauvreau Street home, an apartment. Crowds gathered outside and police were called to keep the curious on the move.

Police Inspector René Belec told

Continued on Page 26, Column 2

1950 - 1959

"All the News That's Fit to Print"

NEWS INDEX, PAGE 79, THIS SECTION

The New York Times.

Copyright, 1950, by The New York Times Company.

LATE CITY EDITION
Cloudy, mild today and tomorrow, followed by clearing and colder.

Temperatures Range Today—Max., 50; Min., 34
Temperature Yesterday—Max., 40; Min., 24
Full U. S. Weather Bureau Report, Page 12

Section 1

VOL. XCIX..No. 33,601.

Entered as Second-Class Matter,
Postoffice, New York, N. Y.

NEW YORK, SUNDAY, JANUARY 22, 1950.

Including Magazine
and Book Review.

FIFTEEN CENTS
New York City and
30 Mile Zone | Elsewhere
Twenty Cents

TRUMAN, ACHESON DEMAND CONGRESS VOTE AID TO KOREA

Rayburn Says Bill Will Come to Floor Again, and It Is 'Going to Be Passed'

SPEEDY ACTION IS SOUGHT

Secretary of State Expresses 'Concern and Dismay' — Sees Threat to U. S. Policy

By JOHN D. MORRIS
Special to THE NEW YORK TIMES.

WASHINGTON, Jan. 21—President Truman today deplored the House of Representatives' rejection of the Korean aid bill and called for "speedy rectification."

In a statement released by the White House along with a letter in which Dean Acheson, Secretary of State, expressed "concern and dismay" over the development, the President said he would take up the matter with Congressional leaders and urge immediate action.

Even before he spoke out, however, Speaker Sam Rayburn told reporters that a bill would be brought to the floor again, and "the House is going to pass it."

The measure authorizing $60,000,000 of appropriations to continue the $120,000,000 economic aid program for the infant Korean Republic, was killed in the House Thursday by a surprise vote of 193 to 191. The Senate had passed a separate bill last year.

"Important Foreign Policy"

President Truman called for early reversal of the House action "in order that important foreign-policy interests of this country may be properly safeguarded."

He expressed his entire concurrence in the views expressed by Mr. Acheson in a letter to the President dated yesterday.

The Secretary said the House action, if not quickly reversed, would have "the most far-reaching adverse effects upon our foreign policy, not only in Korea but in many other areas of the world" where "our encouragement is a major element in the struggle for freedom."

Mr. Acheson said our conduct in Korea was regarded by the world "as a measure of the seriousness of our concern with the freedom and welfare of peoples maintaining their independence in the face of great obstacles."

He suggested that failure to provide further aid would imperil Korea's survival as a free nation and be "disastrous" for this country's foreign policy.

Dr. John Myun Chang, the Korean Ambassador, said tonight he was gratified and "very much encouraged" by the Truman and Acheson statements.

The envoy expressed "deep gratitude" for the statements and added the hope that the United States could find a way to continue aid to Korea, which, he said, is "absolutely essential to the recovery of its domestic economy."

Parley on Another Vote

Congressional leaders had already conferred with Mr. Acheson and other State Department officials on the question of obtaining another House vote on the question.

They are now seeking to determine the best way of doing so. To bring the defeated measure up for reconsideration would require a two-thirds majority vote. Consequently, it is believed that some other method must be found.

The prevailing view appeared to be that the quickest way would be to take the Senate-approved Korean aid bill to the House floor. It would have to be reported first by the Foreign Affairs Committee, after being amended there to conform with the House bill.

Speaker Rayburn, indicating that he favored this method, said an attempt could then be made to obtain Rules Committee clearance and, if this failed, the measure could be called up under the "by-passing" procedure that the House retained yesterday.

Senator Tom Connally, Democrat, of Texas, chairman of the Senate Foreign Relations Committee, voiced his readiness to help with the problem, if necessary, by putting through a bill linking Korean aid with continuation of the authority to provide economic assistance to Nationalist China.

He said this might be done by revising a bill sponsored by Senators H. Alexander Smith of New Jersey and William F. Knowland of California, Republicans, now pend-

Continued on Page 4, Column 4

The New York Times Five Cents Tomorrow

Because of continued increasing costs in all phases of the operation of this newspaper, the newsstand price of THE NEW YORK TIMES on weekdays in New York City will be five cents beginning tomorrow. The new price of THE TIMES will be the same as that of other standard-sized newspapers in New York and, generally throughout the country.

FULL ASIA VICTORY IS SEEN IN MOSCOW

Lenin Memorial Orator Says Capitalism Cannot Halt the Revolutionary Movement

By HARRISON E. SALISBURY
Special to THE NEW YORK TIMES.

MOSCOW, Jan. 21—Top figures of the Soviet Government and the Communist party were told tonight that capitalism and imperialism were no longer capable of halting the mass revolutionary movement of millions of Asiatic peoples inspired by successes of communism in China and the Soviet Union.

This analysis of the contemporary situation in Asia was placed before leaders of the Soviet Union and Chinese Communist chiefs at the important annual memorial meeting held at the Bolshoi Theatre on the anniversary of Lenin's death twenty-six years ago.

The Lenin memorial oration is one of the year's most important Communist party declarations. Tonight as last year, it was given by P. N. Pospelov, editor of the party's newspaper Pravda.

[The Associated Press stated that among those reported present at the Bolshoi Theatre were Chinese Communist leader Mao Tse-tung and the regime's Premier and Foreign Minister, Chou En-lai. Mr. Mao received a special ovation at mention of his name by Mr. Pospelov.]

Chinese Leaders' Presence Cited

The leaders of the new Chinese Communist regime are in Moscow conferring upon the broadest kind of understandings with the Soviet leadership. Mr. Mao has been in Moscow for nearly five weeks. Last night he was joined by Mr. Chou, accompanied by a distinguished delegation including top figures in the new Northeast China Government established in Manchuria and most of the leading specialists of the new Chinese regime in trade, commerce and industry.

Mr. Pospelov's analysis of the revolutionary successes and possibilities in Asia was coupled with the sharpest denunciation of United States imperialism and a frank prediction that "capitalism will unavoidably be replaced by socialism."

"The great victory of the Chinese people already has proved that imperialism is incapable of suppressing the forces of the people, that this struggle awakens and attracts into the struggle millions of toilers," he said. "The great teaching of Leninism shows the people of all countries the road of the fight against the unheard of calamities of imperialism, shows the road of liberation from the yoke of imperialism, the road to a new Socialist life."

He declared that the United

Continued on Page 5, Column 1

BERLIN RAIL OFFICE IS RETURNED BY U. S. TO EAST GERMANS

Commandant Says He Yielded to Avoid New Hardships in the Western Sectors

HITS SOVIET 'PROVOCATION'

Difficulties Following Seizure Outweighed the Gain of 600 Rooms, He Asserts

Special to THE NEW YORK TIMES.

BERLIN, Jan. 21—Maj. Gen. Maxwell D. Taylor, United States Commandant in Berlin, this afternoon ordered the State Railway Administration building in the American sector restored to East German custody. Western sector police were withdrawn at 5 o'clock.

At a press conference called simultaneously with the release of the building, General Taylor made it clear that the basis of his action was the reprisals already taken against the population of the Western sectors and the threats of further hardships through nonpayment of wages to railway employes living in those sectors.

Confiscation of the Reichsbahn structure had been ordered. General Taylor said, as part of a program to obtain the maximum use of office and housing space in the United States sector of this badly damaged city; only forty of its 600 rooms had been used recently.

"Far from sympathizing with this purpose," his prepared statement said, "the Soviet authorities have seized upon the affair as an excuse to harass the residents of West Berlin, to threaten fresh reprisals against Reichsbahn workers and generally to disturb the peace of the city. They have not attempted to conceal their intention to discharge additional railway workers, and to threaten to make further reductions in their West mark salary payments.

Claim Termed Absurd

"On Jan. 20, representatives of the Berlin press were given a tour of the Reichsbahndirektion building, where they verified the absurdity of the claim that the communications of the Reichsbahn were being interfered with. They found the usual communications personnel on the job, coming and going in the same way as during the Reichsbahn occupation. Furthermore, they verified the extent of the building space standing vacant.

"It was the American intention to put this space to use for the benefit of Berlin. Unfortunately, the unreasonable and provocative attitude of the Soviets and of the Reichsbahn makes it appear probable that the hardships which they intend to impose outweigh the benefits arising from the American plan.

"Having regretfully reached this conclusion, I am suspending the notice of custody and withdrawing the West sector police from the interior of the building.

"We now know the facts about it and shall watch to see whether the Reichsbahn puts it to a remunerative use in providing transportation service to the city.

"If our action accomplishes this, it will have served its purpose."

Obviously taken by surprise, Communist propaganda agencies were unprecedentedly brief in their comment tonight on General Taylor's move. The Soviet-controlled Radio Berlin said that the United States had succumbed to "thousands of protests by workers."

Continued on Page 12, Column 3

CHURCHILL WARNS OF SOCIALIST DRIFT, ASKS END TO CURBS

Defines Big Election Issue as More Regimentation or a Return to Freedom

LABOR CLAIMS FLOUTED

Conservative Leader Credits Full Employment to Loans From U. S. and Dominions

By RAYMOND DANIELL
Special to THE NEW YORK TIMES.

LONDON, Jan. 21—Striking the first blow for the Conservatives in the election campaign, Winston Churchill called upon the nation's voters to set Britain free of Socialist controls and restrictions.

"The main reason why we are unable to earn our own living and make our way in the world is because we are not allowed to do so," he declared in a radio speech from his home at Westerham in Kent.

The former Prime Minister's radio address was described as a "political" but not an "election" speech. The fact is that the campaign does not officially begin until Feb. 3 when Parliament is dissolved.

As the first step toward its dissolution, taken in the orderly process of British electoral machinery, King George VI issued a proclamation today postponing the next meeting of Parliament until after Jan. 24, the date on which it had been called to reconvene. This means that this Parliament, elected in 1945, will not meet again.

It was a good Churchillian speech, which "pinked" the Laborites where it hurt, on spending, housing and the high cost of living, but possibly because of the high standard of oratorical leadership that the wartime leader had set, it fell a little flat on British ears.

The first few persons this correspondent talked to after its delivery found it "disappointing." But Mr. Churchill was under the handicap of sounding a keynote for his party before his party has made known its election program. That will be issued in the coming week.

It would have been a tactical blunder for him to anticipate any surprises that this Conservative manifesto will contain. So his address to the electorate tonight was necessarily primarily a critique rather than a statement of policy, but he did manage to get across the idea that between the Laborites and the Conservatives there is no dispute about the virtue of a country's whole labor force being usefully employed.

The choice before the people of

Continued on Page 30, Column 1

HISS GUILTY ON BOTH PERJURY COUNTS; BETRAYAL OF U. S. SECRETS IS AFFIRMED; SENTENCE WEDNESDAY; LIMIT 10 YEARS

PRINCIPAL FIGURES IN THE HISS PERJURY TRIAL

Alger Hiss leaving Federal Building.

Mrs. Ada Condell, foreman of the jury.

Judge Henry W. Goddard, who presided.
The New York Times

JURY OUT 24 HOURS

Verdict Follows a Call on Judge to Restate Rulings on Evidence

CHAMBERS STORY UPHELD

Defendant Is Impassive—His Counsel Announces That an Appeal Will Be Taken

By WILLIAM R. CONKLIN

Alger Hiss, a highly respected State Department official for ten of his forty-five years, was found guilty on two counts of perjury by a Federal jury of eight women and four men yesterday.

Nearly twenty-four hours after receiving the case, the jury reported its verdict at 2:50 P. M. The middle-aged jurors had begun their deliberations at 3:10 P. M. on Friday after ten weeks of testimony in the second perjury trial.

By convicting Hiss on both counts, the jury found that he had betrayed his trust by passing secret State Department documents to Whittaker Chambers. The former courier for a Communist spy ring was the Government's key witness against the former official. The verdict meant that the jury believed Mr. Chambers and the corroborating evidence produced by the Government.

The convicted defendant faces maximum penalties of five years' imprisonment and $2,000 fine on each count, a combined total of ten years and $4,000. Federal Judge Henry W. Goddard continued his bail at $5,000 and set Wednesday at 10:30 A. M. for sentencing. Sentence will be passed in the same thirteenth floor courtroom of the United States District Court where Hiss was tried.

Lapsing of Espionage Charge

The case of "The United States of America versus Alger Hiss" rested on a two-count perjury indictment. Thomas F. Murphy, Government prosecutor, had taxed Mr. Hiss with treason and espionage against his country. However, any possible prosecution for espionage had been ruled out by a three-year statute of limitations, which conferred immunity after March, 1941.

Hiss was thus brought to trial on one count of perjury for denying that he ever gave secret documents to Mr. Chambers. The second count charged perjury for denying that he had seen the Government contended after Jan. 1, 1937. The Government contended that the documents were passed in February and March, 1938.

By its verdict the jury upheld the Government's contention that Priscilla Hiss, 46-year-old wife of the defendant, had typed copies of the documents for Mr. Chambers on the Hisses' Woodstock typewriter.

Mr. Chambers had told the jury that he had been a paid functionary of the Communist party in Washington and had collected secret information for Russia from 1935 to April, 1938.

Basis Laid for Appeal

Claude B. Cross and Edward C. McLean, defense attorneys, would not say at first whether they would appeal the verdict. They had established a basis for an appeal by taking exception to a part of the charge of Judge Henry W. Goddard.

"There won't be any statement," Mr. McLean said. "I do not wish to discuss the possibility of an appeal now. There is just no statement." But later Mr. Cross said that "you can be sure the verdict will be appealed."

After the jury had convicted on both counts, Mr. Murphy asked that Hiss' bail of $5,000 be increased in conformity with the custom for "all convicted defendants." After Mr. Cross protested, Judge Goddard permitted Hiss to remain at liberty under the same bail. Mr. Cross said he would make some motions on Wednesday, the day set for sentencing.

Should defense attorneys file an appeal, it would act as an automatic stay of sentence. If an appeal should reach the United States

Continued on Page 56, Column 1

EARLY 'RIGHTS' VOTE APPEARS UNLIKELY

Items of 'Unfinished Business' May Get Precedence Despite House Action on Rules

Special to THE NEW YORK TIMES.

WASHINGTON, Jan. 21—Chances for consideration by the House of Representatives on Monday of the Administration's bill to establish a Federal Fair Employment Practices code were evaluated as practically nil at the Capitol today. Some proponents of the legislation had hoped a vote on it might be taken on that day.

Being the fourth Monday in the month, it will be in order for chairmen of committees that have favorably-reported bills pending before the Rules Committee for more than twenty-one days to move on the floor to proceed to their consideration. Such discharge motions

Continued on Page 37, Column 3

Senate to Sift R. F. C. Loans With View to Writing Curbs

By H. WALTON CLOKE
Special to THE NEW YORK TIMES.

WASHINGTON, Jan. 21—The stage has been set for a full-scale Congressional investigation of the lending policy of the billion-dollar Reconstruction Finance Corporation. As a result of the inquiry, Congress is expected to set forth, once and for all, the terms on which it wants the RFC's lending operations to function.

Irritated by recent big loans that the RFC granted to several corporations, as well as some that were made in the earlier days of the agency, members on both sides of the aisle in Congress have been demanding a clarification of policy.

Leading this group is Senator J. William Fulbright, Democrat, of Arkansas, who recently lost a battle with the RFC over a loan to the Kaiser-Frazer Corporation.

The Senator, who has not forgotten the rather sharp rebuff, has started the wheels of Congressional investigation turning. On Tuesday he will ask the Senate Banking and Currency Committee, of which he is a member, to inquire into the RFC's action in granting the following loans:

Kaiser-Frazer Corporation ...$44,000,000
Northwest Air Lines ... 12,000,000
Waltham Watch Co. ... 6,000,000
Texmass Petroleum Co. ... 15,100,000

Financial observers have foreseen nothing that would block the Senator's request for action. As head of the Senate Banking and Currency subcommittee on the RFC, he conducted a three-day inquiry into the loan policy of the agency last summer. It was at that time that the Senator questioned the wisdom of advancing additional funds to the Lustron Corporation, Columbus, Ohio, which is now in default on $37,500,000 of RFC loans.

Once the full committee approves

Continued on Page 43, Column 3

MAYOR RIDICULES IDEA OF RESIGNING

Telephones From Florida That He Is Getting Rid of Virus and Will Return to Job

By JAMES A. HAGERTY

In a telephone message to THE NEW YORK TIMES from Key Largo, Fla., Mayor O'Dwyer declared yesterday that he had no intention of resigning.

In his telephone conversation, the Mayor appeared to be hearty of voice and very cheerful. Questioned about a report that he contemplated retirement, he said: "It is utterly ridiculous. It touches my sense of humor."

The Mayor then laughed heartily and continued:

"I am down here to get the virus out of my system. I am going to stay till I've got it licked and I think I am well on the way to doing that. I feel much better. I want to get completely well so that I can return to the city and stay at my desk in City Hall to work as efficiently on my program."

The Mayor said that Dr. Edward M. Bernecker, who left Newark Airport by plane on Friday, had not arrived but was expected to reach Key Largo today. It is understood that he will have a series of talks with the Mayor and that

Continued on Page 37, Column 4

350,000,000-Gallon Water Loss In 24 Hours Largest Since Dec. 12

By PAUL CROWELL

The city's water storage reservoirs suffered a loss of 350,000,000 gallons in the twenty-four hours ended at 8 A. M. yesterday.

It was the first storage loss since Dec. 26 and the largest since Dec. 12. Officials of the Department of Water Supply, Gas and Electricity, attributed the loss to a slightly increased consumption of water, coupled with the absence of appreciable rain or snowfall in the up-state watershed areas.

The city's reservoirs lost 102,600,000 gallons in the twenty-four hours ended at 8 A. M. on Dec. 27. In the twenty-four hours ended at 8 A. M. on Dec. 13 the storage loss was 662,000,000 gallons.

The reversal of the upward trend in water storage gave city officials serious concern and boosted to 1,121,600,000 gallons the average

Continued on Page 47, Column 1

The Water Situation

The following figures as of 8 A. M. yesterday give the number of gallons of water in the city's reservoirs. The difference in the two days is the net after intake and the day's consumption:

Friday 106,662,000,000
Yesterday 106,312,000,000
Net loss 350,000,000

Average daily storage gain needed to fill reservoirs by June 1 1,121,600,000

Watershed snowfall:
Schoharie ...... .02 inch.
Esopus ...... .04 inch
Croton ...... .02 inch

At present consumption there remains about ninety days' supply before pressure fails.

Catskill and Croton reservoirs at capacity hold 253,136,000,000 gallons.

World News Summarized

SUNDAY, JANUARY 22, 1950

The jury of eight women and four men in the Alger Hiss trial yesterday found the former State Department official guilty of perjury on two counts. The jury reached this verdict nearly twenty-four hours after receiving the case and its decision meant that it had accepted the testimony of Whittaker Chambers, confessed former spy, over the denials by Mr. Hiss of having passed secret documents to Mr. Chambers. Federal Judge Goddard will pass sentence Wednesday. [1:8.]

Mayor O'Dwyer characterized as "utterly ridiculous" rumors that he might resign his office because of ill health. [1:7.] •

Although some supporters of the Truman Administration's Federal Fair Employment Practices code had hoped that the House might vote on it tomorrow, there was little likelihood the measure would get to the House floor by that time. [1:5.]

Congress planned a sweeping inquiry into the lending policy of the Reconstruction Finance Corporation as a preliminary to fixing the terms on which the organization's lending may operate in the future. [1:6-7.]

President Truman urged "speedy rectification" of the House of Representatives' rejection by a narrow margin of the bill providing $60,000,000 for aid to Korea. Secretary of State Acheson asserted that failure to assist Korea would jeopardize her survival as a free nation. [1:1.]

The journey to Moscow of Communist China's Foreign Minister, Chou En-lai, was seen as an indication that the negotiations between the Chinese Communists and the Soviet Union had reached the decisive stage. Peiping vigorously denied Russia was

"detaching" four north China areas as charged by Mr. Acheson. [7:1.]

The annual Lenin memorial meeting in Moscow was told that the mass revolutionary movement in Asia could not be stopped by capitalism. [1:2.]

Winston Churchill set the keynote for the campaign of the Conservative party for next month's general election by telling British voters that the "main reason why we are unable to earn our own living and make our way in the world is because we are not allowed to do so." Mr. Churchill said the choice was to regain freedom or plunge the nation deeper into socialism. [1:4.]

General Taylor, the United States commander in Berlin, ordered the seized Railway Administration building in the United States sector restored to East German custody. [1:3.]

Franco - German rapprochement was seen as announcement by the West German republic that it was suspending trade talks with France. German officials cited France's attitude over the Saar as a reason for the suspension and proposed an international Saar statute similar to that in the Ruhr. [3:1.]

The Allied High Commission, in a move intended as a public wisdom of the Bonn regime for "impudent" behavior, will demand that the Germans withdraw their announcement that gas rationing would end the end of this month. [2:2.]

Finland virtually rejected Moscow's demand that she extradite 300 "war criminals" who are said by the Russians to have found refuge among the Finns. [24:2.]

Bonn Halts French Trade Talks After Clash Over Policy on Saar

By HAROLD CALLENDER
Special to THE NEW YORK TIMES.

PARIS, Jan. 21—A diplomatic crisis between France and Western Germany developed suddenly today when the French learned that, after challenging France's policy in the Saar, the Bonn regime had suspended negotiations for the trade treaty with France that was to have been signed a week ago.

French officials were angered by these German actions, which they considered as endangering the faint beginnings of a French-German rapprochement in the field of economic relations.

[In Bonn, Mrs. reported that Chancellor Konrad Adenauer, in a parting conference with High Commissioner John J. McCloy, had proposed the creation of an international statute for the Saar similar to the Ruhr statute now in force.]

When asked by the French For-

eign Office for an explanation of their suspension of the negotiations, Bonn officials replied that they did not mean to go back on the trade pact but they must postpone its signature because of internal difficulties raised by German farmers and because of the positions taken on the Saar question.

French officials said this reply surprised them because they considered the treaty would contribute to development of intra-European trade and desired to sign it as soon as possible.

This move by Bonn was regarded here as a maneuver to force reconsideration of the status of the Saar. Such was considered the purpose likewise of the statement that Dr. Konrad Adenauer, Chancellor

Continued on Page 3, Column 5

153

"All the News That's Fit to Print"

The New York Times.

LATE CITY EDITION

A little rain and cold today. Cloudy, continued cold tomorrow.
Temperature Range Today—Max., 38 ; Min., 31
Temperatures Yesterday—Max., 37 ; Min., 42
Full U. S. Weather Bureau Report, Page 35

Copyright, 1950, by The New York Times Company.

VOL. XCIX..No. 33,611.

Entered as Second-Class Matter.
Postoffice, New York, N. Y.

NEW YORK, WEDNESDAY, FEBRUARY 1, 1950.

Times Square, New York 18, N. Y.
Telephone Lackawanna 4-1000

RAG PAPER EDITION
SEVENTY-FIVE CENTS

PRESIDENT SEEKS 70-DAY COAL TRUCE, FACT-FINDING BOARD

He Ignores Taft Law in Asking 5-Day Week at Old Wages Pending Study of Dispute

AVOIDS WORD 'EMERGENCY'

Operator Acceptance Is Seen Likely, but the Plan Holds Disadvantages for Lewis

Text of announcement by White House on coal, Page 22.

By JOSEPH A. LOFTUS
Special to The New York Times.

WASHINGTON, Jan. 31—President Truman moved into the soft coal dispute today with a proposal that John L. Lewis and the operators call a seventy-day truce and submit their arguments to a fact-finding board. He asked for an answer by 5 P. M. Saturday.

Under the truce "normal" production of coal would be resumed. This was understood to mean a return to the five-day work week by the members of the United Mine Workers, headed by Mr. Lewis. The wage scale of the expired union contract would be paid. A board of three would make recommendations in sixty days, but the recommendations would not be binding.

President Truman thus used the approach he used in the steel dispute last summer. This avoids use of the Taft-Hartley Law and its injunctive authority, although the President said in November that if he acted in the coal case he would use that law.

"Grave Concern" Voiced

The President's message to Mr. Lewis and the operators spoke of the "grave concern" about the dispute, but avoided Taft-Hartley words, such as "emergency" and "health and safety."

The dispute in the anthracite industry was omitted from the proposal.

The President said that in the final analysis the parties themselves must write their own agreement. "Voluntary action, not compulsion, in these matters is not only my personal conviction but the national policy," he declared.

Aware that the miners and operators were to meet at 2 P. M. tomorrow to try bargaining again, the President said he did not want to interfere with that. He told them that if they could reach an agreement to resume full production next Monday they should disregard his proposal and let him know about it by noon Saturday.

Mr. Lewis' attorneys are due in court at 10 A. M. tomorrow to answer a petition for an injunction filed by Robert N. Denham, general counsel of the National Labor Relations Board. Mr. Lewis and the other officers of the union filed affidavits in the case today. They denied violating the Taft-Hartley Law in the coal negotiations which began last May and accused the operators of refusing to bargain.

Surmise on Board Make-Up

The make-up of the fact-finding board, if the President's truce proposal goes into effect, is a matter of conjecture. When the proposal was under consideration at the White House in November the three men who had been asked if they were available were David L. Cole, who was a member of the fact-finding steel panel; John Dunlop, Harvard economics professor, and Willard Wirtz of Northwestern University, former chairman of the National Wage Stabilization Board. Neither side would say tonight

Continued on Page 22, Column 2

Melchior Threatens To Quit Opera Here

Lauritz Melchior stepped into the Metropolitan Opera dispute last night by saying that he would not return next season "unless indicated plans change materially." He would make no comment on the possible return of Kirsten Flagstad but, like Helen Traubel, as reported resentment at not being approached sooner by Rudolf Bing, who will be the general manager for 1950-1951.

"I would have assumed," Mr. Melchior said, "that the natural courtesy of the management or the Metropolitan would dictate a call to any leading artist who had appeared regularly with the company for twenty-four years to determine his position with

Continued on Page 24, Column 2

By Winston Churchill:
The Second World War

Volume III—The Grand Alliance
Book I—Germany Drives East
INSTALLMENT 6:
THE JAPANESE ENVOY

THE New Year had brought disturbing news from the Far East. The Japanese Navy was increasingly active off the coasts of Southern Indo-China. Japanese warships were reported in Saigon harbour and the Gulf of Siam. On January 31 the Japanese Government negotiated an armistice between the Vichy French and Siam. Rumours spread that this settlement of a frontier dispute in South-east Asia was to be the prelude to the entry of Japan into the war. The Germans were at the same time bringing increased pressure to bear upon Japan to attack the British at Singapore.

* * *

About this time several telegrams arrived from our Commander-in-Chief in the Far East urging the reinforcement of Hong Kong. I did not agree with his views.

Prime Minister to General Ismay   7 Jan 41

This is all wrong. If Japan goes to war with us there is not the slightest chance of holding Hong Kong or relieving it. It is most unwise to increase the loss we shall suffer there. Instead of increasing the garrison it ought to be reduced to a symbolical scale. Any trouble arising there must be dealt with at the Peace Conference after the war. We must avoid frittering away our resources on untenable positions. Japan will think long before declaring war on the British Empire, and whether there are two or six battalions at Hong Kong will make no difference to her choice. I wish we had fewer troops there, but to move any would be noticeable and dangerous.

Later on it will be seen that I allowed myself to be drawn from this position, and that two Canadian battalions were sent as reinforcements.

* * *

IN the second week of February I became conscious of a stir and flutter in the Japanese Embassy and colony in London. They were evidently in a high state of excitement, and they chattered to one another with much indiscretion. In these days we kept our eyes and ears open. Various reports were laid before me which certainly gave the impression that they had received news from home which required them to pack up without a moment's delay. This agitation among people usually so reserved made me feel that a sudden act of war upon us by Japan might be imminent, and I thought it well to impart my misgivings to the President.

Former Naval Person to President Roosevelt   15 Feb 41

Many drifting straws seem to indicate Japanese intention to make war on us or do something that would force us to make war on them in the next few weeks or months. I am not myself convinced that this is not a war of nerves designed to cover Japanese encroachments in Siam and Indo-China. However, I think I ought to let you know that the weight of the Japanese Navy, if thrown against us, would confront us with situations beyond the scope of our naval resources. I do not myself think that the Japanese would be likely to send the large military expedition necessary to lay siege to Singapore. The Japanese would no doubt occupy whatever strategic points and oilfields in the Dutch East Indies and thereabouts they covet, and thus get into a far better position for a full-scale attack on Singapore later on. They would also raid Australian and New Zealand ports and coasts, causing deep anxiety in those Dominions, which have already sent all their best-trained fighting men to the Middle East. But the attack which I fear the most would be by raiders, including possibly battle-cruisers, upon our trade routes and communications across the Pacific and Indian Oceans. We could by courting disaster elsewhere send a few strong ships into these vast waters, but all the trade would have to go into convoy and escorts would be few and far between. Not only would this be a most grievous additional restriction and derangement of our whole war economy, but it would bring altogether to an end all reinforcements of the armies we had planned to build up in the Middle East from Australasian and Indian sources. Any threat of a major invasion of Australia or New Zealand would of course force us to withdraw our Fleet from the Eastern Mediterranean, with disastrous military possibilities there, and the certainty that Turkey would have to make some accommodation, for reopening of the German trade and oil supplies from the Black Sea. You will therefore see, Mr. President, the awful enfeeblement of our war effort that would result merely from the sending out by Japan of her battle-cruisers and her twelve 8-inch-gun cruisers into the Eastern oceans, and still more from any serious invasion threat against the two Australasian democracies in the Southern Pacific.

Some believe that Japan in her present mood would not hesitate to court or attempt to wage war both against Great Britain and the United States. Personally I think the odds are definitely against that, but no one can tell. Everything that you can do to inspire the Japanese with the fear of a double war may avert the danger. It however they come in against us and we are alone, the grave character of the consequences cannot easily be overstated.

The agitation among the Japanese in London subsided as quickly as it had begun. Silence and Oriental decorum reigned once more.

Former Naval Person to President Roosevelt   20 Feb 41

I have better news about Japan. Apparently Matsuoka is visiting Berlin, Rome, and Moscow in the near future. This may well be a diplomatic sop to cover absence of action against Great Britain. If Japanese attack which seemed imminent is now postponed, this is largely due to fear of United States. The more these fears can be played upon the better, but I understand thoroughly your difficulties pending passage of [Lend-Lease] Bill on which our hopes depend. Appreciation given in my last Personal and Secret of naval consequences following Japanese aggression against Great Britain holds good in all circumstances.

* * *

Behind the complex political scene in Japan three decisions seem to emerge at this time. The first was to send the Foreign Secretary, Matsuoka, to Europe to find out for himself about the German mastery of Europe, and especially when the invasion of Britain was really going to begin. Were the British forces so far tied up in naval defence that Japan could not afford to reinforce her Eastern possessions if Japan attacked them? Although he had been educated in the United States, and Secret of naval consequences anti-American. He was deeply impressed by the Nazi movement and the might of embattled Germany. He was under the Hitler

Continued on Page 31

FRANCE PROTESTS SOVIET RECOGNITION OF HO CHI MINH RULE

Note to Russia Asserts Action Could 'Gravely Impair' Paris-Moscow Ties

U. S. AND BRITAIN INFORMED

Government of North Korea Announces Acceptance of Viet Nam Rebel Regime

By LANSING WARREN
Special to The New York Times.

PARIS, Jan. 31—France tonight delivered to the Soviet Embassy here a vigorous protest against Soviet recognition of Ho Chi Minh, the enemy of France in Indo-China. The note charged that the Soviet action was of a nature "gravely to impair French-Soviet relations."

In diplomatic circles here the Soviet Union's action was considered as a threat not only to the French position in Indo-China but as an effort to prevent the United States from building a policy of containment in Asia such as has been successful in Europe.

The text of the French note follows:

The French Government has learned through publication of a communiqué by the Tass Agency that the Government of the U.S.S.R. has taken the decision of recognizing as the Government of the Viet Nam the insurrectional government of Ho Chi Minh. Such a decision violates the principles of international law, since the only regular government of the Viet Nam is the government constituted by His Majesty Bao Dai, to whom the French Government has transferred the rights of sovereignty which it previously held.

In encouraging, as is the obvious intention of the Soviet Government, the insurrectional movement of Ho Chi Minh, this decision can only render more difficult the restoration of peace in Viet Nam. In taking the initiative which it has just announced, the Government of the U.S.S.R. is committing with regard to France an act whose character and consequences cannot be underestimated.

For all these reasons the French Government raises a solemn protest against a decision which is of a nature gravely to impair Franco-Soviet relations.

The note was delivered by Alexander Parodi, general secretary of the French Foreign Ministry, after Soviet Ambassador Alexandre Bogomolov, who was invited to the Quai d'Orsay, had replied he could not come today but would present himself tomorrow.

Copies of the French protest to

Continued on Page 11, Column 1

TRUMAN ORDERS HYDROGEN BOMB BUILT FOR SECURITY PENDING AN ATOMIC PACT; CONGRESS HAILS STEP; BOARD BEGINS JOB

DISCUSSING PLANS FOR MAKING HYDROGEN BOMB

Members of the Joint Congressional Atomic Energy Committee talk with Sumner T. Pike, right, acting head of the Atomic Energy Commission, after President Truman gave his approval. Seated are Chairman Brien McMahon, Representatives Carl T. Durham, Chet Holifield and W. Sterling Cole. Standing are Senator John W. Bricker, Representatives Paul J. Kilday, Melvin Price, Carl Hinshaw and Charles H. Elston.

The New York Times (by George Tames)

STIKKER IS NAMED E. R. P. CONCILIATOR

Council in Paris Accepts Dutch Leader Supported by Britain —E. C. A. Goals Unmet

By HAROLD CALLENDER
Special to The New York Times.

PARIS, Jan. 31—Dr. Dirk U. Stikker, Foreign Minister of the Netherlands, was named today to the post of "political conciliator" of the European Marshall Plan Council instead of Paul-Henri Spaak, former Premier of Belgium, whose appointment was vetoed by the British Government. Paul G. Hoffman, Economic Cooperation Administrator, and W. Averell Harriman, ECA Ambassador in Europe, had desired that M. Spaak be chosen.

Dr. Stikker was elected by the Council. He was the candidate of the British who had first suggested Dr. Halvard M. Lange, Nor-

Continued on Page 14, Column 4

Truman Asks Utility Leader To Head Top Research Body

By JAMES RESTON
Special to The New York Times.

WASHINGTON, Jan. 31—President Truman has offered the Government's top scientific job—chairmanship of the Research and Development Board in the Department of Defense—to William Webster of Boston, a vice president of the New England Electric System, it was learned today.

Mr. Webster, 49 years old, a graduate of the United States Naval Academy and former chairman of the Defense Department's Military Liaison Committee with the Atomic Energy Commission, would be largely responsible for preparing an integrated military research and development program so that weapons such as the new hydrogen bomb would take their proper place in a well-balanced defense policy.

The chairmanship of the Research and Development Board was held by Dr. Vannevar Bush from 1947 to 1948 and by Dr. Karl T. Compton, former president of the Massachusetts Institute of Technology, from 1948 until Nov. 3, 1949. Since then the work of the board has been supervised by Dr. Robert F. Rinehart as deputy chairman.

Coincidental with his offer of the Government's principal scientific position to Mr. Webster, President Truman was reported to be working actively on selection of a successor to David E. Lilienthal as chairman of the Atomic Energy Commission. One person said to be under consideration is Carroll Wilson, present general manager of the AEC.

Mr. Lilienthal is reliably reported to have proposed that control of

Continued on Page 5, Column 3

City Realty Values Up for 6th Year; Assessment Total $18,493,559,079

By LEE E. COOPER

New York's taxable realty wealth increased on the city's books for the sixth consecutive year, with the result that property owners are due to pay levies on the highest aggregate valuation in seventeen years, according to official figures made public yesterday.

In a report to Mayor O'Dwyer's office, William E. Boyland, president of the Tax Commission, set the total tentative assessed valuation of real estate in the five boroughs for 1950-51 at $18,493,559,079. This is $381,337,900 above the final valuation for 1949-50, which was $18,112,233,179.

A House committee reported, 17 to 1, a bill for economic aid to Korea and Nationalist China.

This state paid $557,000,000 in jobless benefits last year, nearly twice the 1948 total, Albany reported. [21:1.]

this year of $316,525,750 in "ordinary" real estate, to $16,120,113,875, and of $64,802,150 in the holdings of utility corporations, which were listed tentatively for the new tax year at $1,655,893,290.

Added to these sums was $717,551,914 for special franchises, the exact amount of which will not be set by the State Tax Commission for another month. The figure used by the city officials is based on the 1949-50 records.

Although no particular area was found by the field assessors to have increased generally in value—in contrast to last year when sharp gains were listed for the land around Stuyvesant Town and the United Nations site—there were decreases in the city as a whole.

Largely for purposes of "equalization," to bring properties in line with neighboring valuations, in-

The report showed a net rise for this city's tentative realty value for tax purposes was set at $18,493,559,079. [1:6-7.]

HISTORIC DECISION

President Says He Must Defend Nation Against Possible Aggressor

SOVIET 'EXPLOSION' CITED

His Ruling Wins Bipartisan Support on Capitol Hill—No Fund Request Due Now

By ANTHONY LEVIERO
Special to The New York Times.

WASHINGTON, Jan. 31—President Truman announced today that he had ordered the Atomic Energy Commission to produce the hydrogen bomb.

The Chief Executive acted in his role of Commander in Chief of the Armed Forces, ordering an improved weapon for national security. Thus, from the domestic standpoint, he removed the question of producing the super-weapon as an issue that might be argued on moral grounds.

As for international statecraft, Mr. Truman, by treating the hydrogen bomb as an addition to the American armory, also removed it as an issue that might be interpreted as an advanced threat or inducement in seeking international control of atomic weapons. Nevertheless, Mr. Truman said that his perseverance in providing for national defense would be matched by his efforts to seek international control of atomic weapons.

New Phase of Atomic Age

In his announcement, Mr. Truman regarded the hydrogen bomb as a "progressive outgrowth of the nation's production of this uranium-plutonium atomic bomb. He put it this way: the commission was "to continue its work on all forms of atomic weapons, including the so-called hydrogen or super-bomb."

His use of the word "continue" was understood to imply that with national security the over-riding consideration, the chief factor guiding his decision was whether it was practicable to make the bomb. Scientists have said that it is.

In effect, the President's decision, which won wide acclaim in Congress, marked the advent of a new phase of the atomic age and a surge ahead of Russia in the race to retain military supremacy.

The bombs that visited destruction on Hiroshima and Nagasaki split the atom. The new bomb would fuse atoms instead, but with a power 100 to 1,000 times greater than the improved fission bombs that have been developed since the Japanese cities were struck.

The President's Statement

The President explained his decision in the following brief statement:

"It is part of my responsibility as Commander in Chief of the Armed Forces to see to it that our country is able to defend itself against any possible aggressor. Accordingly, I have directed the Atomic Energy Commission to continue its work on all forms of atomic weapons, including the so-called hydrogen or super-bomb.

Continued on Page 3, Column 2

IT'S A TRITON BOMB, MIGHTIEST POSSIBLE

Would Release Energy More Than Seven Times '45 Type —No Critical-Mass Limit

By WILLIAM L. LAURENCE

What President Truman referred to yesterday as the "so-called hydrogen bomb" is not a hydrogen bomb at all in the true scientific meaning of the term.

This, the most powerful superbomb that can be built on earth, it can now be revealed, actually is the triton bomb, in which the basic element used is tritium, a hydrogen isotope (twin) of atomic mass 3. It is an element hardly known to the public but well known to nuclear physicists. A triton is the nucleus of tritium, composed of one proton and two neutrons.

The term hydrogen, as used by scientists, refers strictly to the common form of hydrogen of atomic mass 1, a mass that cannot be made into a bomb.

While the process responsible for the vast amounts of energy released by the sun every second in

Continued on Page 4, Column 4

Air Defense Mapped For Atom Projects

By AUSTIN STEVENS
Special to The New York Times.

WASHINGTON, Jan. 31—The Air Force disclosed tonight that it planned to throw a protective aerial "wall" around key atomic installations of the country.

Under a plan worked out today at the Pentagon, the Air Force will insist on the positive identification of any airplane flying within 100 miles of three atomic plants and, failing to be advised of an aircraft's identity will send fighter planes aloft to observe its character and course.

The plan in effect is a revival of a wartime measure whereby in combat zones any aircraft picked up by radar or other means of detection was consid-

Continued on Page 3, Column 6

World News Summarized

WEDNESDAY, FEBRUARY 1, 1950

President Truman, acting in his capacity as Commander in Chief of the Armed Forces, yesterday directed the Atomic Energy Commission "to continue its work on all forms of atomic weapons, including the so-called hydrogen or super-bomb." The work, he said, would go forward "on a basis consistent with the over-all objectives of our program for peace and security" and "until a satisfactory plan for international control of atomic energy is achieved." [1:8.]

Congressional opinion heavily supported the President, and demands for speeding the work were made. The Atomic Energy Commission reported to Congress that atomic weapons now were being made by the "industrial type" of production and stockpiles were growing rapidly. [3:5.]

New defense safeguards were thrown about the atomic plants at Oak Ridge, Tenn.; Los Alamos, N. M., and Hanford, Wash. Any plane approaching within 100 miles of the plants without prior identification and clearance will be intercepted by Air Force fighters. [1:4.]

The hydrogen bomb, it was disclosed, is really a triton bomb, the basic element of which is tritium, a hydrogen isotope. [1:7.]

William Webster has been asked to head the Research and Development Board of the Department of Defense as successor to Dr. Karl T. Compton who resigned. [1:6-7.]

Dealing with the major domestic problem of coal, President Truman asked John L. Lewis and the operators to call a seventy-

day truce and to submit the issues to a nonstatutory fact-finding board such as he had named in the steel dispute. The President asked for a full five-day week in the soft-coal mines during the truce. [1:1.] Leaders of more than 100,000 striking miners were divided over urging the men to return. Operators indicated an inclination to accept the plan. [22:5.]

France, in a strong note of protest, told Moscow that Soviet recognition of Ho Chi Minh in Indo-China "gravely" impaired French-Soviet relations. Washington called Moscow's action proof that the Ho regime was Communist. [1:4.]

Senator Connally said Britain's policy of extending her embargo on dollar oil to the Commonwealth was "an act of hostility to our economy." [15:2.]

Britain won a victory in the European Marshall Plan Council when Foreign Minister Stikker of the Netherlands was elected "political conciliator." [1:5.]

French Premier Bidault won five close votes of confidence on the budget. [14:3.]

This city's tentative realty value for tax purposes was set at $18,493,559,079. [1:6-7.]

FIGHT TOOTH DECAY. Use PER-AMMO ammoniated tooth paste for more effective mouth lasting dental care. Triple-guaranteed to give complete satisfaction. 49c, 42c—Advt.

Index to other news appears on Page 30.

"All the News That's Fit to Print"

The New York Times.

LATE CITY EDITION

Drizzle and fog early today, fair later. Cloudy tomorrow.

Temperature Range Today—Max.,42; Min.,34
Temperatures Yesterday—Max.,41; Min.,33
Full U. S. Weather Bureau Report, Page 51

VOL. XCIX..No. 33,617.

Entered as Second-Class Matter.
Postoffice, New York, N. Y.

NEW YORK, TUESDAY, FEBRUARY 7, 1950.

Copyright, 1950, by The New York Times Company

Times Square, New York 18, N. Y.
Telephone Lackawanna 4-1000

FIVE CENTS

G. O. P. POSES ISSUE FOR '50 AS LIBERTY VERSUS SOCIALISM

FAIR DEAL IS TARGET

Republicans Want Cuts in Spending and Taxes, Revised Taft Law

BACK FOREIGN POLICY AID

But Hit Conduct of Program—Party Declaration Fails to Win United Support

Text of Republican party statement is printed on Page 29.

By W. H. LAWRENCE
Special to The New York Times.

WASHINGTON, Feb. 6—The Republican party policy makers today proclaimed "Liberty against Socialism" to be the major domestic issue of the 1950 Congressional elections.

But the party failed to achieve complete unity, either in its denunciation of the Truman Administration's program at home and abroad, or on the alternatives which it promised.

In all-day separate and closed meetings members of the Republican National Committee and the House and Senate Republican conferences finally gave their approval to a "statement of principles and objectives" designed to serve as a national platform for the months between now and the November elections.

Party chieftains had hoped that the declaration would demonstrate party unity and purpose and bring a new flow of financial contributions to defray campaign expenses, but a group led by Senator Henry Cabot Lodge Jr. of Massachusetts, Senator Margaret Chase Smith of Maine, Representative Jacob K. Javits of New York and Representative James C. Fulton of Pennsylvania promptly made known its dissatisfaction.

"Fair Deal" Vigorously Opposed

As was to be expected, the party declaration approved by the majority was vigorous in its opposition to enactment of the most of the Fair Deal program put before Congress by President Truman.

On foreign policy questions it found a middle ground, advocating continuance of a bipartisan attitude but sharply criticizing the administration of foreign policy with particular reference to "secret agreements" made at Yalta and Potsdam "which have created new injustices and new dangers throughout the world."

An effort was made by Werner Schroeder, Illinois national committeeman, to put the party on record as opposed to continuance of the bipartisan foreign policy, but was overwhelmingly defeated in the national committee. Members said that a voice vote showed support for Mr. Schroeder from only one or two others.

The party statement declared:

"We advocate a strong policy against the spread of communism or fascism at home and abroad, and we insist that America's efforts toward this end be directed by those who have no sympathy either with communism or fascism."

It asserted that "basic American principles are threatened by the Administration's program for a planned economy modeled on the Socialist Governments of Europe, including price and wage control, rationing, socialized medicine, regional authorities and the Brannan Plan with its controls, penalties, fines and jail sentences."

The Republican program "to rebuild a prosperous and progressive America" included these major planks:

A return to a balanced budget

Continued on Page 28, Column 3

By Winston Churchill:
The Second World War

Installment 11 of the excerpts from Mr. Churchill's memoirs of the war will be found today on Page 29

McCloy Warns the Germans Against a Revival of Nazism

At Opening of Amerika Haus in Stuttgart He Clarifies U. S. Policy, Declaring Its Chief Concern Is to Build Democracy

By DREW MIDDLETON

STUTTGART, Germany, Feb. 6—The United States will use all its power to fight a revival of nazism in Germany, John J. McCloy, United States High Commissioner, asserted today.

The western Germans were bluntly warned to concentrate on internal problems, avoid "agitation" on foreign issues and to build democracy toward "unification of all Germany."

Speaking before an audience of 1,600 in the Stuttgart Opera House, Mr. McCloy turned the dedication of this city's Amerika Haus, an information center, into what was at once a major declaration of United States policy in Germany and an admission that the progress of Germany toward democracy had been neither as

fast nor as complete as some officials had believed.

Mr. McCloy flatly told the Germans they would not be allowed a political position endangering the peace of Europe and "there will be no German army or air force."

Later at a press conference he declared he was not contemplating any changes in the occupation statute that defines the Allied powers at present and did not talk about such changes on his recent trip to Washington.

Shortly after his speech the High Commissioner intervened sharply and perhaps decisively in the denazification scandal currently shaking the government of Wuerttemberg-Baden by publicly

Continued on Page 4, Column 3

The text of the McCloy address is on Page 4.

WORLD ARMS TALK URGED BY TYDINGS TO END 'NIGHTMARE'

Senator Asks Call by Truman to Ease Fears by Reducing All Weapons Down to the Rifle

By WILLIAM S. WHITE
Special to The New York Times.

WASHINGTON, Feb. 6—Senator Millard E. Tydings, Democrat, of Maryland, appealed to President Truman today to call a world conference for disarmament, in conventional as well as atomic weapons, to "end the world's nightmare of fear."

Mr. Tydings, a powerful figure as chairman of the Senate's Armed Services Committee and a member of its Foreign Relations Committee and the Joint Congressional Committee on Atomic Energy, asked the Senate to approve a resolution "authorizing and requesting" the President to summon such a meeting.

Lacking some such "fundamental" approach to peace, he asserted, "we are up against the possible extinction of all the human beings of this earth."

It would be "difficult" for Marshal Stalin or any other ruler, he argued, to "refuse an appeal by the President openly made on an honest and fair basis."

Senator Tydings' speech reopened a Senate debate on atomic policy, and weapons policy generally, which had been set off last week by Senator Brien McMahon, Democrat, of Connecticut, with the recommendation that this country at "almost any cost" seek an international arrangement neutralizing atomic and hydrogen weapons.

It appeared to reflect a considerable Congressional dissatisfaction at the fact that President Truman's recently announced decision to go ahead with the hydrogen bomb development was accompanied by no new approach to the Soviet Union toward atomic control.

Mr. Tydings contended that strict international inspection of

Continued on Page 2, Column 6

JAPAN SAID TO BACK GIVING BASES TO U.S.

Visit by Joint Chiefs Is Held to Have Convinced Most Party Heads on Move

By LINDESAY PARROTT
Special to The New York Times.

TOKYO, Feb. 6—Leaders of Japan's major political parties with the exception of the extreme left have become convinced as a result of the visit here by the Joint Chiefs of Staff that this nation should grant air, naval and army bases to the United States in return for a protective guarantee under the peace treaty. There are indications they believe that the view would be supported by a large majority of the post-war Japanese electorate.

The conviction of the Japanese leaders, the importance of which it is difficult to overstress, comes as a result of the emphasis they believe was placed by the Joint Chiefs on big American installations already existing here.

The three generals and one admiral who compose the Joint Chiefs left Japan today for Okinawa after visiting the naval base at Yokosuka, Army installations in the Osaka region and the large Air Force base at Itazuke in Kyushu. They were prevented from inspecting the newly built major air base at Misawa in northeast Honshu by weather conditions.

Though no information was forthcoming, either from the chiefs or local United States military authorities, the Japanese were inclined to believe the principal point of the visit was evaluation of these and other bases and the

Continued on Page 11, Column 2

WEST GERMANS CUT SHIPMENT OF STEEL INTO RUSSIAN ZONE

Act After East Drops Far Below Pact Figure on Sending Grain to Western Areas

By JACK RAYMOND
Special to The New York Times.

FRANKFORT, Germany, Feb. 6—The West German Government has decided to curtail steel shipments from the Ruhr to the Soviet zone, it became known today.

The reason to be given the East zone regime, will be that terms of the interzonal trade agreement are in danger of being broken by Soviet zone failure to provide adequate shipments of grain. It may be assumed that recent transport difficulties imposed by the Soviet zone regime had no little to do with it.

[Monday night the Russians again blocked traffic at Helmstedt without explanation, slowing down the entry of Berlin-bound trucks to the point where a waiting line was established again, The Associated Press said. By midnight, with the entry rate cut to four or five trucks an hour, there was a line of fifteen trucks, the first such

Continued on Page 6, Column 5

WORLD ARMS TALK (continued)

World News Summarized

TUESDAY, FEBRUARY 7, 1950

President Truman invoked the Taft-Hartley Act yesterday and named a three-man fact-finding board in the soft-coal dispute. The board was instructed to report not later than Monday, and if negotiations have not been resumed the President may seek an eighty-day injunction. It was the eighth time Mr. Truman had invoked the Taft-Hartley Act, the third time against the coal union. John L. Lewis made no comment. [1:8.] The miners, who went on a general strike, expressed defiance of an injunction. [1:5.]

Leaders of the CIO telephone union, who have called a nationwide strike for tomorrow, were voting on a Government proposal to delay action sixteen days while Federal mediators sought a peace formula. [1:6-7.]

In this city, a State fact-finding board opened hearings on demands by the transit workers for a pay increase, shorter hours and other changes in working conditions. [1:6.] The Continental Paper Company announced it was closing its $16,000,000 Ridgefield Park, N. J., plant, which has been strike-bound seven months. [17:1.]

Concern was expressed over the growing danger to peace resulting from the inability of the United States and the Soviet Union to agree on atomic control. Senator Tydings introduced a resolution calling on the President to convoke a world conference for disarmament of conventional as well as atomic weapons under inspection. [1:3.] A Senate group heard pleas for a "tyranny-proof" United Nations police force to be set up with or with-

out Soviet consent. [3:4.] Some United Nations observers held direct Washington-Moscow talks might prove of value. [3:2-3.]

The FBI told a Congressional committee that Dr. Fuchs, British atomic scientist who had worked on bomb research in this country, had transmitted "vital secret information" to the Russians and had a long record of "sympathy with Communist ideology." Dr. Fuchs is under arrest in Britain. [3:1.] A Justice Department official told the jury in the Coplon-Gubitchev espionage trial how a decoy message had led to the arrest of the defendants. [14:2.]

Republican policy conference, with distinct rumblings of discontent, adopted a statement proclaiming "liberty against socialism" the keynote of this year's Congressional elections. [1:1.] In New Jersey, William B. Widnall, Republican, was elected representative to succeed J. Parnell Thomas. [1:2-3.]

"We Americans are not here exclusively to feed the German people and promote economic recovery, but to help the Germans establish a political democracy, regain economic health, rejoin the democratic world and stamp out every vestige of nazism," United States High Commissioner McCloy said in Stuttgart. [1:2-4.] His blunt speech, which was welcomed by the British and French, was said to reflect accurately this country's new policy of straight talking. [5:3.]

Western Germany has decided to cut steel shipments to the Soviet zone. [1:4.]

Premier Bidault formed a new French Cabinet without any Socialist Ministers. [7:1.]

Index to other news appears on Page 25.

Widnall, Jersey Republican, Wins Thomas Seat in Congress by 2 to 1

Special to The New York Times.

HACKENSACK, N. J., Feb. 6—William B. Widnall, a Republican lawyer from Saddle River, tonight won a two-to-one victory in the special Seventh Congressional District election to choose a successor to J. Parnell Thomas, Republican, jailed for payroll padding.

Mr. Widnall received 31,754 votes against 15,370 for his Democratic opponent, former Mayor George T. English of East Paterson, a textile manufacturer.

The 42-year-old victor, a State Assemblyman from Bergen County, took the lead as soon as returns began to come in when the polls closed at 8 P. M. and maintained a wide margin from that time on.

A little more than two hours later Mr. English, who had predicted a "resentment vote" growing out of the Thomas scandal, conceded victory to Mr. Widnall.

"The victory is yours," he said at 10:10 P. M. in a telephone call to Mr. Widnall at the Republican campaign headquarters in Ridgewood. "My congratulations to you.

Your support in the Seventh Congressional District apparently goes beyond partisan politics at this time."

On Mr. Widnall's invitation, Mr. English, accompanied by Mrs. English, then visited his opponent's headquarters, where a victory party was in the making. A momentary silence that greeted the Democrat and his wife when they walked in gave way immediately to a heavy burst of applause and cheers.

Mr. Widnall introduced his opponent to the gathering and read the message conceding victory.

The Republican who had hoped to offer a "constructive program toward a better United States.

"It is my hope," he continued, "that this Republican victory is a forerunner of great Republican victories in November."

Mr. Widnall entered the primary fight for the candidacy without a

Continued on Page 28, Column 3

TRUMAN INVOKES TAFT-HARTLEY ACT IN COAL STRIKE, NAMES FACT BOARD; 370,000 MINERS OUT, VOICING DEFIANCE

BITUMINOUS TIE-UP

Only 30,000 of 400,000 Diggers Stay on Job in Soft Coal Fields

TAFT ACT 'CLUB' ASSAILED

But Owners Hold Strikers Will Obey Writ to Work—Anthracite Mines Busy

By A. H. RASKIN
Special to The New York Times.

PITTSBURGH, Feb. 6—A general strike in the country's soft coal fields was the reply given by members of the United Mine Workers today to President Truman's request for voluntary restoration of "normal" coal production.

Two hundred and seventy thousand miners who had been working a three-day week put aside their tools and joined 100,000 others who have been on a "no-day week" for the last month. Their walkout left some 30,000 UMW members at work in bituminous mines that have signed new contracts with John L. Lewis, president of the union, and in a handful of mines west of the Mississippi.

News that President Truman had put in motion the machinery for an eighty-day injunction under the national emergency provisions of the Taft-Hartley Act brought fresh expressions of defiance from the strikers. In Pennsylvania and West Virginia, where the tie-up has been in effect for a full month, local union leaders asserted that their men did not intend to go back without a contract, even if Mr. Lewis ordered them to do so.

Sabotage Is Predicted

These statements were discounted by mine owners. They voiced certainty that the miners would go back on Mr. Lewis' signal when an injunction was issued. However, some operators said they expected many locals might be slow to return and that the injunction period would be marked by "sabotage, slowdowns and sporadic stoppages" in many areas.

The first hint that the union would instruct its members to comply with a back-to-work order

Continued on Page 19, Column 4

Ching Asks a 16-Day Delay In Call for Telephone Strike

Union, Polling Leaders Across Nation, Will Reply Today—Mediator Gravely Warns the 320,000 Set to Quit Tomorrow

A sixteen-day postponement of the threatened strike affecting 320,-000 telephone workers hung in the balance last night. Acting on a proposal of Cyrus S. Ching, Federal Mediation and Conciliation Service director, the executive board of the Communication Workers of America, CIO, was being polled across the country on whether to accept the delay.

The walkout, scheduled for 6 A. M. tomorrow, would affect directly 100,000 telephone workers represented by the CWA. Another 220,000 telephone employes probably would refuse to cross picket lines. The postponement sought by Mr. Ching would delay the strike call until Feb. 24.

Before the union can answer Mr. Ching, nine members of the executive board must indicate their position to Joseph A. Beirne, president of the CWA.

These include, beside Mr. Beirne, John J. Moran, John Crull and A. T. Jones, all vice presidents of the national union; C. W. Werkau, secretary-treasurer, and four re-

gional directors, Mrs. Mary Hansen, Eastern region, Newark; Ray Hackney, Southwestern, St. Louis; Joseph Deirdroff, Western, Denver, and Ray Dreyer, Central, Chicago.

Mr. Ching will receive the union leaders' decision in Washington this morning. He formulated his proposal for delay while in New York, where he sought vainly for a break in the deadlocked negotiations between the CWA and the American Telephone and Telegraph Company. The negotiations resume at 10 A. M. today in the New Yorker Hotel.

Mr. Ching warned of the grave impact should the strike take place. He told both union and company spokesmen that "many of the freedoms which both sides presently enjoy, and are enjoyed by employers and unions generally, will be endangered by a demonstration of an absence of sound and stable management-labor relations in the critical communications industry." Despite this warning, a gen-

Continued on Page 18, Column 5

TRANSIT INQUIRY ON; QUILL LEADS FIGHT

Mayor's Committee Hearings Open With Union Vigorously Pressing Its Demands

By ALEXANDER FEINBERG

The Transport Workers Union, CIO, got its long-sought opportunity yesterday to start presenting its demands for a wage increase of 21 cents an hour across the board for all of the city's 43,000 transit workers, along with forty-eight hours' pay for a five-day, forty-hour week. Other salient points among its demands called for the setting up of a grievance committee with recourse to impartial arbitration, and improved pension, vacation and holiday benefits.

John F. O'Donnell, union counsel, introduced voluminous exhibits tending to show that New York's transit workers were the lowest paid of any in twelve major cities, several of them with municipally operated systems. Other exhibits sought to show that they were paid less than railroad employes and truck drivers.

Through still other exhibits he sought to make the contrasting point that New York took good care of its policemen, firemen and

Continued on Page 17, Column 4

RESORT TO THE LAW

President Acts Against Lewis, Chooses Inquiry Body Headed by Cole

ASKS A REPORT BY MONDAY

Injunction Move Is Due Then if the Operators and Miners Have Not Resumed Talks

By ANTHONY LEVIERO
Special to The New York Times.

WASHINGTON, Feb. 6—President Truman invoked the Taft-Hartley Act against John L. Lewis and the United Mine Workers today as the soft-coal strike became almost complete and virtually ended bituminous production.

Simultaneously the Chief Executive appointed an emergency board of three seasoned labor arbitrators to study the dispute and report to him on or before next Monday.

This move under the law allowed the mine owners and the miners six days in which to seek again a basis for negotiation. Failing that, the real showdown should follow next week. Under the Taft-Hartley Law, the Government is compelled to apply for a court injunction that would require the miners to go back to work for eighty days pending a renewed search for a settlement.

David L. Cole, a lawyer of Paterson, N. J., and a veteran arbitrator with experience in coal disputes, was appointed chairman of the board. The other members were William Willard Wirtz, a Professor of Law at Northwestern University and former chairman of the National Wage Stabilization Board, and John Dunlop, associate professor of economics at the Harvard School of Business Administration.

Board Holds First Meeting

The board members arrived here tonight and had a session with Peter Seitz, general counsel of the United States Conciliation Service, who briefed them on the background of the dispute. Then they held an organization meeting and planned to begin their proceedings tomorrow.

Through a spokesman, Mr. Lewis blanketed the President's dramatic action with a "no comment" that then lapsed into silence. What his course might be was a riddle. There was no assurance that he would cooperate with the board or that his miners would heed the eighty-day injunction, if the proceedings went that far.

All that appeared certain tonight was that Mr. Lewis had created an imposing dilemma for his old antagonist, President Truman, who has made the repeal of the Taft-Hartley Act a major political issue for this year's Congressional election.

Unlike this unsuccessful action of last Tuesday, when he issued a conciliatory statement and sought to bring the operators and the miners before an extralegal board, Mr. Truman today said nothing. He did what the law required—issued an executive order creating the board.

In the order, phrased in legal language, Mr. Truman expressed the opinion that if the strike were allowed to continue it "will imperil the national health and safety." He acted under Section 206 of the Taft-Hartley Act, which provides for Presidential action when a strike threatens to reach emergency proportions.

Action Forecast for Days

His action was announced by Charles G. Ross, White House press secretary. It had been forecast for several days, and a large number of reporters had gathered in the lobby of the Executive offices. Mr. Ross called them in a little after noon and said:

"The President at 11:35 this morning signed an Executive order creating a board to inquire into a dispute in the bituminous coal industry. This board is to report not later than Feb. 13. Of course, it could report earlier, but that is the terminal date."

Earlier the reporters got an intimation of this action from Speak-

Continued on Page 15, Column 1

WATER SUPPLY DIPS 3D SUCCESSIVE DAY

Officials Call On the Public to Reduce Consumption in 'Every Possible Way'

By CHARLES G. BENNETT

As water shortage in the city's Catskill and Croton reservoirs dipped by 134,000,000 gallons yesterday, the third successive day of storage losses, water officials issued an urgent appeal to the public to reduce water use "in every possible way."

The new appeal was underscored by the weekly consumption report. This showed that last week's water consumption averaged 868,000,000 gallons daily, an increase of 8,000,-000 gallons daily over that for the previous week. It was the first week since mid-November that consumption had not declined or at least done no worse than in the preceding week.

Stephen J. Carney, Commissioner of Water Supply, Gas and Electricity, noted that in spite of the one-week rise, New Yorkers still had maintained an over-all average daily reduction of 324,000,000 gallons in water consumption since the "base" week, Oct. 2 to 8, 1949.

The new series of daily storage losses, coming at a time of the year when normally the reservoirs are rising, Mr. Carney said, made it imperative that the public make even further savings.

Mr. Carney said that he thought

Continued on Page 17, Column 2

Port Body Urges Helicopter Lines; Offers Field Atop Its Bus Terminal

By FREDERICK GRAHAM

The Port of New York Authority told the Civil Aeronautics Board yesterday that it strongly recommended mail, passenger and express service by helicopters in the metropolitan area. It offered to provide a landing area atop the new bus terminal it is building on Eighth Avenue between Fortieth and Forty-first Streets.

The recommendation and offer were made by Fred M. Glass, director of airport development for the bi-state agency, at the opening session of a CAB hearing to determine whether the New York area is to have helicopter shuttle service. The hearing was held in the assembly room of the Commerce and Industry Association, 233 Broadway.

In addition to the Port Authority, representatives of five communities in New Jersey, Connecticut and New York appeared before the CAB examiner, Ferdinand M. Moran, CAB examiner, to urge authorization of helicopter shuttle service.

Representatives of helicopter manufacturing companies also testified as to the types, performance and availability of their equipment. The sum of their testimony was that dependable helicopters were now flying and had been extensively tested both by the armed services and in commercial operations. They added that larger and better helicopters were coming along.

After explaining that the Port Authority was appearing at the hearing because of its obligation to promote the full, efficient and economical development of transportation in the Port District, Mr. Glass said:

"With our greater population and more intensified commercial life, the New York-New York Port District, more than any other area in the country, requires the best transportation services. The helicopter, with its unique ability to take off and land on small spaces, and to move passengers and

Continued on Page 25, Column 4

"All the News
That's Fit to Print"

The New York Times.

LATE CITY EDITION
Sunny with pleasant temperatures today. Fair tomorrow.
Temperature Range Today—Max.,80; Min., 60
Temperatures Yesterday—Max.,90.3; Min., 69
Full U. S. Weather Bureau Report, Page 55

Copyright, 1950, by The New York Times Company.

VOL. XCIX..No. 33,758.

Entered as Second-Class Matter
Post Office, New York, N. Y.

NEW YORK, WEDNESDAY, JUNE 28, 1950.

Times Square, New York 18, N. Y.
Telephone LAckawanna 4-1000

RAG PAPER EDITION
SEVENTY-FIVE CENTS

TRUMAN ORDERS U. S. AIR, NAVY UNITS TO FIGHT IN AID OF KOREA; U. N. COUNCIL SUPPORTS HIM; OUR FLIERS IN ACTION; FLEET GUARDS FORMOSA

114 RESCUED HERE AS LINER GROUNDS AFTER COLLISION

Excalibur, With Hole 15 Feet Wide in Side, Settles on Mud Flat Off Brooklyn

FIRES START ON FREIGHTER

One Person Slightly Injured—Responsibility for the Crash Still to Be Decided

By WILLIAM R. CONKLIN

Thirty-five minutes after a gay departure for a Mediterranean cruise, the American Export Line's Excalibur was disabled in a collision yesterday in the Narrows, but all her 114 passengers were taken off safely.

The confetti-speckled cruise ship left Pier 4, Jersey City, at noon for a forty-three-day voyage. At 12:35 P. M. the collision with the inbound Colombia occurred off Sixty-ninth Street, Brooklyn.

The impact crushed the bow of the freighter and tore a hole fifteen feet wide in the port side of the Excalibur forward of the bridge. Fire broke out in a paint storeroom.

While passengers and both crews remained calm, water quickly flooded the forward holds of the cruise ship. The Excalibur settled with her bow on a midstream mud bank, with her screw lifted in the air.

Passengers Taken Off by Tugs

Passengers on the sinking ship donned bright orange life preservers and were taken off by two tugs of the Moran Towing Company. Except for one woman who bruised three fingers of her left hand, all passengers were uninjured. They were returned to Pier 4, and the ship line arranged for hotel accommodations for them.

No official on the scene would assess responsibility for the collision. The Coast Guard required both captains to file written reports on the crash today. Under usual procedure, a Coast Guard board of inquiry hears evidence and fixes blame. Unofficially, it was said that a misunderstanding of whistle signals was the probable cause of the accident.

Capt. S. N. Groves of Brooklyn, a veteran of twenty-five years at sea, commanded the Excalibur, a ship of 9,644 gross tons with a top speed of seventeen knots. The Colombia, owned by the United Steamship Lines of Denmark, was commanded by Capt. Christian Mikkelsen of Copenhagen. The freighter was operated by the Scandinavian-American Steamship Company of 25 Broadway. Carrying cotton, wool and lubricating oils, she was bound from Philadelphia to Pier 24 at Congress Street, Brooklyn.

When the collision occurred there was good visibility despite a light haze over the lower bay. Persons in Shore Road Park saw the collision clearly, half a mile off the Brooklyn waterfront.

As the Excalibur's forward holds filled, her nose dropped into a mudbank and she swung to face upstream on the incoming tide.

2 Fireboats Help Freighter

The fireboats William J. Gaynor and Firefighter put lines on the 5,146-ton freighter to fight the fire on board. With the help of the ship's forty-two crewmen they subdued a fire in the forward hold. A collision bulkhead between that point and the forecastle prevented them from tackling another fire in the peak.

With Army, Navy, Coast Guard and Moran tugs helping, the burning vessel was moved into the north side of the Sixty-ninth Street ferry pier. John L. Holian, Deputy Fire Chief commanding the Marine Division, summoned a hook and ladder company to pour streams into the burning peak from the pier. Within an hour, the fire was extinguished.

Joseph H. Boggs, senior assistant purser of the Excalibur, said it was fortunate that the collision had occurred in shoal water.

"Immediately after the crash we

Continued on Page 29, Column 2

SANCTIONS VOTED

Council Adopts Plan of U. S. for Armed Force in Korea, 7 to 1

THE SOVIET IS ABSENT

Yugoslavia Casts Lone Dissent—Egypt and India Abstain

Mr. Austin's statement to the United Nations is on Page 6.

By THOMAS J. HAMILTON
Special to THE NEW YORK TIMES.

LAKE SUCCESS, June 27—The Security Council adopted tonight a United States resolution recommending that members of the United Nations use armed force in repelling the invasion of southern Korea and restoring international peace and security.

The vote on the resolution, which amounted to Security Council authorization for President Truman's decision to use United States naval and air units to the defense of the Republic of Korea, was 7 to 1, with Yugoslavia voting against.

The representatives of India and Egypt did not vote because they had not received instructions from their Governments. The Soviet Union was absent.

Representatives of Britain, France, Nationalist China, Cuba, Ecuador and Norway announced this afternoon that they would vote for the United States resolution without change. However, the Council recessed at 5:12 P. M. to permit Sir Benegal Rau and Mahmoud Bey Fawzi, the representatives of India and Egypt, to try to reach their Governments by telephone.

The vote was finally taken at 10:45 P. M. after both said they had been unable to establish communication with responsible authorities. With Egypt and India again not participating, the Council then rejected, seven to one, a Yugoslav resolution proposing that the Council renew its appeal for compliance with the cease-fire resolution it adopted Sunday and request the two sides to agree to United Nations mediation.

The Council then recessed again while Sir Benegal and Fawzi Bey attempted to obtain instructions. Apparently Fawzi Bey did so, but neither he nor Sir Benegal made any further statement, and the Council adjourned at 11 P. M.

Both Security Council members and other delegates who crowded around their table showed their realization that a historic decision for the United Nations and the world was being taken tonight. Warren R. Austin, the United States representative, was determined to avoid postponing a decision until tomorrow, and the Indian and Egyptian representatives cooperated by not requesting a postponement because of their failure to receive instructions.

Mr. Austin said after the meeting that the immediate effect of the resolution "should be to stop

Continued on Page 7, Column 1

President Takes Chief Role In Determining U. S. Course

Truman's Leadership for Forceful Policy to Meet Threat to World Peace Draws Together Advisers on Vital Move

By ARTHUR KROCK

WASHINGTON, June 27—Some of those who participated in the meetings Sunday and Monday nights, at which the momentous decisions were taken to resist further Communist aggressions, beginning in the Far East, with the combat air and naval power of the United States, described today to associate this writer as determined from the outset to adopt the forceful policy which was announced this morning.

As soon as the first meeting assembled, they said, it was plain that these were to be the bases of his decision:

1. The situation created by Communist tactics at various points of the world, culminating in the attack of North Korea on South Korea, had been allowed to drift too long.

2. The entire Far East was deteriorating in a manner to threaten the peace of the world, a line had to be drawn at once, and the United States had to draw it.

3. National security was the primary interest, but embedded in this were world peace and the prestige and future effectiveness of the United Nations, which was the architect of the South Korean Government.

4. It was a time for courage, even boldness, and calculated risk, which other members of the United Nations would be invited to share as they saw fit.

5. It was not a time to give the slightest consideration to previous policies or to individuals associated with those policies. If, for example, the fundamental change in the Far Eastern situation

Continued on Page 4, Column 3

MAINLAND ATTACKS ENDED BY FORMOSA

Chinese Nationalists Halt Air, Navy Forays in Accordance With Request by Truman

By The Associated Press

TAIPEI, Formosa, Wednesday, June 28—The Chinese Nationalists today ordered their Air Force and Navy to cease attacks on the Communist mainland in accordance with a President's request.

President Truman had ordered United States warships to protect Formosa against Communist attack and at the same time asked the Nationalists to cease offensive operations.

Nationalist Foreign Minister George Yeh hailed the President's order for warship protection as "a most welcome sign of comradeship in the fight against communism."

Generalissimo Chiang Kai-shek and his Cabinet had met after the United States note was delivered to the United States Embassy. It was understood the note carried with it instructions to see that it was brought personally to Generalissimo Chiang's attention.

Mr. Yeh translated the text to the Generalissimo last night in the presence of United States Charge d'Affaires Robert Strong.

Mr. Strong was with Generalissimo Chiang for about twenty minutes. After his departure the latter consulted with Mr. Yeh, Premier Chen Cheng and other officials.

The decision was announced after Generalissimo Chiang conferred with Gen. Chou Chih-jou, Chief of the Joint General Staff, and other top Nationalist commanders.

The Nationalists were believed to have agreed to Washington's re-

Continued on Page 8, Column 4

HOUSE VOTES 315-4 TO PROLONG DRAFT

Korea Crisis Breaks Deadlock —Bill Expected to Be Sent to White House Tonight

Special to THE NEW YORK TIMES.

WASHINGTON, June 27—The House of Representatives today passed, by a vote of 315 to 4, an extension of the draft for another year.

The bill added authority for President Truman to call to active duty members of the National Guard and the reserve forces for periods not exceeding twenty-one months.

The Senate agreed to vote on the bill tomorrow afternoon. Swift passage is expected there so that the bill may reach President Truman for his signature tomorrow night.

As recently as yesterday the Senate and the House appeared to be in a hopeless deadlock over the manner in which the selective service system could be kept alive without much leeway for the President to put it to use. Today when

Continued on Page 16, Column 5

U. S. FORCE FIGHTING

MacArthur Installs an Advanced Echelon in Southern Korea

FOE LOSES 4 PLANES

American Craft in Battle to Protect Evacuation —Seoul Is Quiet

By LINDESAY PARROTT
Special to THE NEW YORK TIMES.

TOKYO, Wednesday, June 28—The United States is now actively intervening in the Korean civil war, an announcement from Gen. Douglas MacArthur's headquarters here made clear this morning.

[Gen. Douglas MacArthur announced Wednesday that the forces of South Korea now were holding the Communist Korean invaders, a United Press dispatch from Tokyo said. At the same time he reported that United States fliers had begun bombing and strafing missions against North Korean forces. Seoul was reported quiet.]

General MacArthur revealed that a "small advanced echelon" from his headquarters had been established in Korea, presumably cooperating with the United States Military Advisory Group, which has been in Korea since the Republic was established there under President Syngman Rhee two years ago.

The MacArthur announcement stated that Far East air forces and elements of the naval forces under the general's command were "conducting" combat missions south of the Thirty-eighth Parallel—the dividing line between Communist North Korea and the United States-recognized Korean Republic. These operations, it was officially stated, are "in support of the Korean Republic," whose Government has now been reinstalled in the capital, Seoul, after withdrawal of the Northern armored spearheads that had penetrated to the outskirts of the city yesterday.

The announcement said United States planes, which were providing air cover for the evacuation of women and children and dependents of various United States missions, had shot down four North Korean fighters that were interfering with the operation of the

Continued on Page 17, Column 3

Statement on Korea

By The Associated Press

WASHINGTON, June 27—The text of President Truman's statement today on Korea:

In Korea the Government forces, which were armed to prevent border raids and to preserve internal security, were attacked by invading forces from North Korea. The Security Council of the United Nations called upon the invading troops to cease hostilities and to withdraw to the Thirty-eighth Parallel. This they have not done, but on the contrary have pressed the attack. The Security Council called upon all members of the United Nations to render every assistance to the United Nations in the execution of this resolution.

In these circumstances I have ordered United States air and sea forces to give the Korean Government troops cover and support.

The attack upon Korea makes it plain beyond all doubt that communism has passed beyond the use of subversion to conquer independent nations and will now use armed invasion and war.

It has defied the orders of the Security Council of the United Nations issued to preserve international peace and security. In these circumstances the occupation of Formosa by Communist forces would be a direct threat to the security of the Pacific area and to United States forces performing their lawful and necessary functions in that area.

Accordingly I have ordered the Seventh Fleet to prevent any attack on Formosa. As a corollary of this action I am calling upon the Chinese Government on Formosa to cease all air and sea operations against the mainland. The Seventh Fleet will see that this is done. The determination of the future status of Formosa must await the restoration of security in the Pacific, a peace settlement with Japan, or consideration by the United Nations.

I have also directed that United States forces in the Philippines be strengthened and that military assistance to the Philippine Government be accelerated.

I have similarly directed acceleration in the furnishing of military assistance to the forces of France and the associated states in Indo-China and the dispatch of a military mission to provide close working relations with those forces.

I know that all members of the United Nations will consider carefully the consequences of this latest aggression in Korea in defiance of the Charter of the United Nations. A return to the rule of force in international affairs would have far-reaching effects. The United States will continue to uphold the rule of law.

I have instructed Ambassador Austin, as the representative of the United States to the Security Council, to report these steps to the Council.

NORTH KOREA CALLS U. N. ORDER ILLEGAL

Declares Security Council's 'Cease Fire' Invalid Without Assent of China and Russia

Special to THE NEW YORK TIMES.

HONG KONG, June 27—The North Korean Government issued a statement today saying that it regarded the cease fire order of the United Nations Security Council illegal for two reasons. It said these were, one, because the Democratic Peoples Republic of North Korea was not represented when its affairs were discussed and, two, because the Soviet Union and (Communist) China did not participate.

On the latter point it cited the United Nations Charter, which requires unanimity of five permanent members of the Security Council on questions of substance. China and Russia are both permanent members. [But the Communist rulers of China have not been recognized by the United Nations as representing that country.]

Drastic measures were taken in North Korea yesterday to organize

Continued on Page 18, Column 5

LEGISLATORS HAIL ACTION BY TRUMAN

Almost Unanimous Approval Is Voiced in Congress by Both Sides—House Cheers

By HAROLD B. HINTON

WASHINGTON, June 27—President Truman's announcement today that United States air and sea power would be employed to expel the Communist invaders from South Korea evoked almost unanimous support in Congress. His statement was read by the majority floor leaders in both houses.

In the House of Representatives, the members rose to their feet and cheered as the reading was completed by Representative John W. McCormack of Massachusetts. In the Senate, the reading by Senator Scott W. Lucas, of Illinois, brought immediate declarations of support from several Republican Senators.

Showing the same spirit of solidarity in the face of crisis, as the present situation was frequently described, Senate and House conferees agreed on legislation to ex-

Continued on Page 5, Column 1

BID MADE TO RUSSIA

President Asks Moscow to Act to Terminate Fighting in Korea

CHIANG TOLD TO HALT

U.S. Directs Him to Stop Blows at Reds—Will Reinforce Manila

By ANTHONY LEVIERO

WASHINGTON, June 27—President Truman announced today that he had ordered United States air and naval forces to fight in South Korea's Army. He said this country took the action, as a member of the United Nations, to enforce the cease-fire order issued by the Security Council Sunday night.

Then acting independently of the United Nations, in a move to assure this country's security, the Chief Executive ordered Vice Admiral Arthur D. Struble to form a protective cordon around Formosa to prevent its invasion by Communist Chinese forces.

Along with these fateful decisions, Mr. Truman also ordered an increase of our forces based in the Philippine Republic, as well as more speedy military assistance to that country and to the French and Vietnam forces that are fighting Communist armies in Indo-China.

After he had started these moves that might mean a decided turn toward peace or a general war, the President sent Ambassador Alan G. Kirk to the Russian Foreign Office in Moscow to request the Soviet Union to use its good offices to end the hostilities. This was an obvious proffer of an opportunity for Russia to end the crisis before her own forces might get involved.

Door Opened for Russia

In the capital this was regarded as being at once a possible face-saving device for Russia in a showdown crisis and a feeler to determine her intentions.

The decisions amounted to a showdown in the "cold war" with Russia, in which this country has at last decided to begin shooting in a limited area. Yet all the decisions followed a carefully worked out formula of action within the framework of the United Nations, as well as unilateral moves that avoided any direct provocation of the Soviet Union.

Mr. Truman based the decision to fight for the South Koreans entirely on the Security Council resolution which called upon all members of the United Nations to help carry it out. And at the Pentagon it was explained that our air and naval forces would fight only below the Thirty-eighth Parallel that divides South Korea from the Russian-sponsored North Korea.

"The Security Council called upon all members of the United Nations to render every assistance to the United Nations in the execution of this resolution." Mr. Truman stated. "In these circumstances I have ordered United States air and sea forces to give the Korean Government troops cover and support."

Russia Is Not Mentioned

Mr. Truman carefully avoided mentioning Russia in his great shift in United States foreign policy on a conclusion that the "cold war" had passed from an uneasy passive stage to "armed invasion and war." He blamed "communism."

"The attack upon Korea makes it plain beyond all doubt that communism has passed beyond the use of subversion to conquer independent nations and will now use armed invasion and war," he said. "It has defied the orders of the Security Council of the United Nations issued to preserve international peace and security, In these circumstances the occupation of Formosa by Communist forces would be a direct threat to the security of the Pacific area and to United States forces performing

Continued on Page 2, Column 3

City, T.W.U. in 2-Year Peace Pact; Mayor Signs Fare Rise Resolution

Officials of the Transport Workers Union, C. I. O., the members of the Board of Transportation and Mayor O'Dwyer signed at City Hall yesterday a memorandum of understanding seeking to guarantee two years of peace in the city-owned rapid transit system.

The accord closely followed recommendations made on May 31 by the Mayor's Transit Fact-Finding Board, granting an 11-cent-an-hour increase to 35,929 operating employes, a third week of vacation after ten years and an additional holiday each year. The cost of the changes recommended by the fact-finders amounts to $13,188,515 a year.

The union bound itself not to engage in any strike or other interference with transit operations and not to seek any basic changes

in the accord before July 1, 1952. It agreed to resolve all disputes in accordance with the grievance machinery set up in the pact. The union obligated itself also to recognize the board's managerial authority and to "cooperate in the attainment of efficient operations."

The Board of Transportation agreed to retain competent industrial engineers to report on a program for achieving a five-day, forty-hour work week for all employes now having a scheduled work-week in excess of forty hours.

Mayor O'Dwyer also signed yesterday afternoon a resolution of the Board of Transportation, effective Saturday, increasing fares on the city-owned surface lines

Continued on Page 28, Column 2

World News Summarized

WEDNESDAY, JUNE 28, 1950

United States air and sea forces were ordered by President Truman yesterday to give Korean troops "cover and support." Moving directly to meet Communist "armed invasion and war" in Asia, the President instructed the Seventh Fleet to "prevent any attack on Formosa," called on the Chinese Nationalists to halt all attacks on the mainland, ordered United States forces in the Philippines strengthened and moved to speed military assistance to those islands and to Indo-China. He instructed Ambassador Kirk in Moscow to urge the Soviet Union to help end hostilities. [1:8; map P. 2.]

Naval and air elements are "conducting combat missions south of the Thirty-eighth Parallel of Korea in support of the Seoul Government, General MacArthur announced. An advance echelon of his General Headquarters has been set up in Korea, he added. Conflicting reports of the fighting showed positions little changed during the day. [1:5; maps P. 17.] In Washington it was said that General MacArthur had sufficient forces to give the South Koreans air and sea preponderance. [13:3.]

This country's new Far East policy was set at conferences during which the President's positive program and leadership convinced his top aides that his decisions "were both inevitable

and right." [1:3-4,1. He dropped unity to an Administration that had been split on many vital policy issues. [4:6-7.]

Governor Dewey, speaking as head of the Republican party, pledged full support to the President [4:3] and Congress was almost unanimous in its endorsement. [1:7.] The House 315 to 4, passed a one-year extension of the draft with broad new powers for the President; the Senate will vote today. [1:4.] Senate Republicans, however, blocked a vote today on the foreign arms aid bill. [14:3.] The National Security Resources Board has ready for introduction a sweeping bill authorizing the President to freeze prices, wages, manpower and materials. [15:2.]

The United Nations Security Council, with Russia absent and Yugoslavia voting no, approved a United States motion to permit member nations to send armed forces to help repel the Korean invasion. [1:2.]

British parties united in supporting President Truman's program. The Labor Government won concessive votes on its refusal to join talks on pooling Europe's heavy industry. [19:4.]

John S. Service, a key figure in Senator McCarthy's charges of communism in the State Department, has been cleared by the department's Loyalty Security Board. [22:3.]

Index to other news appears on Page 28.

Stocks Rally After Big New Losses In War Scare; Sales Near 5 Million

By ROBERT H. FETRIDGE

Securities markets the world over were subjected yesterday to wide fluctuations as the "Korean situation approached a crisis of universal concern.

Calmer thinking emerged successful on the New York exchanges, but only after prices encountered terrific battering. Losses that at one time ranged to 5 points and even more in standard issues on the New York Stock Exchange were either trimmed or eliminated. Quotations were definitely on the recovery side at the close, with the final composite rate down only 0.75 point. As pictured by THE NEW YORK TIMES index, the market was midway between the highs and lows of the day at the final bell.

London was the worst sufferer among the major exchanges, while the Canadian markets followed the lead of New York.

It was a wild day on the trading floor of the Stock Exchange. Business almost reached the 5,000,000-share mark, the reporting ticker tape was constantly thrown behind actual transactions and at one time was twenty-seven minutes late. This necessitated "flash" prices on the ticker to keep brokerage offices at least abreast of the price changes in the stocks.

The trend changed with such rapidity that selling orders were still being executed after the price direction changed for the better.

Continued on Page 41, Column 6

"All the News That's Fit to Print"

The New York Times.

LATE CITY EDITION
Some cloudiness early today, fair and warmer later. Mild tomorrow.

Temperature Range Today—Max.,75; Min.,60
Temperature Yesterday—Max.,65; Min.,57
Full U. S. Weather Bureau Report, Page 53

VOL. XCIX.—No. 33,837.

Entered as Second-Class Matter,
Post Office, New York, N. Y.

NEW YORK, FRIDAY, SEPTEMBER 15, 1950.

Times Square, New York 18, N. Y.
Telephone LAckawanna 4-1000

Copyright, 1950, by The New York Times Company.

FIVE CENTS

U. N. FORCES LAND BEHIND COMMUNISTS IN KOREA; SEIZE INCHON, PORT OF SEOUL; MOVE INLAND; U. S. WILL PRESS FOR A JAPANESE PEACE TREATY

2 GARMENT UNIONS ASK 15% WAGE RISE IN POLICY REVERSAL

Nation-Wide Demand Drafted by Big A.F.L. and C.I.O. Units to Match Costs of Living

KOREAN WAR EFFECT CITED

Long Reluctance on Economic Grounds Dropped—Mills in Northeast Grant 10%

The two largest garment unions in the United States announced yesterday that they would seek an immediate, country-wide general wage increase of 15 per cent for their thousands of members.

In this city the International Ladies Garment Workers Union, A. F. L., held a special meeting of its general executive board to formulate wage policy for 425,000 members. Locally, the union has received no pay rise since 1948, and its 80,000 dressmakers have been at the same wage level since 1947.

By a coincidence a subcommittee of the general executive board of the Amalgamated Clothing Workers of America, C. I. O., meeting in Asbury Park, N. J., drafted a similar plan to be presented to the full board today for ratification. This union will try to win higher wages for 150,000 men's clothing workers and 80,000 others engaged in the making of shirts and cotton garments.

Both organizations, which are among the most powerful and responsible in the country in wage matters, based their new demands on the rise in living costs since the start of the Korean war. Amalgamated members received their last rise, $5, in 1947.

Turnabout in Attitude

In recent years the two unions, facing poor conditions in their industries, have pursued a cautious pace in moving on the wage question. Now with nearly full employment, rising prices for textiles and mark-ups on finished products, they have come to the conclusion that pay rises are both necessary and justified.

The Amalgamated, which has a total membership of 400,000—50,000 of whom are in New York—had operated on the theory that wage rises would force up clothing prices in a period of slack demand and increase unemployment among the union's members. However, it won increases in pension and medical benefits, involving no rise in employer payroll contributions.

Amalgamated officials estimated yesterday that their full 15 per cent demand would raise the cost of making a suit by less than $1. Average clothing pay ranges from $1.50 to $1.62½ an hour. The new demand would add 22½ to 24½ cents to those rates. Cotton wages run from $1.02 to $1.10. These would be brought up by 15 to 16½ cents an hour.

Unlike the Amalgamated, which bargains on a national level with employer associations, the Ladies Garment Workers will try to win its demands on a local basis. Word has already gone out to the union's 400 locals over the country to press for increases in talks for new contracts, under wage-reopening clauses and through requests for voluntary adjustments.

Agreement for Conference

Officials of the Amalgamated said that the United States Clothing Manufacturers Association had agreed to confer with the union's bargaining committee, but that no date had been set for the first meeting. Wage talks with shirt manufacturers will begin next week in this city and other shirt centers.

The move by the Ladies Garment Workers, fifth largest affiliate of the American Federation of Labor, represented the first such attempt by a major A. F. L. union. In the C. I. O., of which the Amalgamated is the fourth largest unit, the United Automobile Workers

Continued on Page 19, Column 3

Excess Profits Tax Now Asked by House

By JOHN D. MORRIS
Special to The New York Times.

WASHINGTON, Sept. 14—The House went on record today, 331 to 2, as favoring action this session on an excess profits tax that would be retroactive to July 1, or Oct. 1.

The vote came on a motion by Representative Herman P. Eberharter, Democrat of Pennsylvania, to amend the pending general tax-increase bill in such a way as to require the House Ways and Means and Senate Finance Committees to bring out a separate excess profits measure before adjournment. The opposition votes were cast by Representative E. E. Cox, Democrat of Georgia, and D. W. Nicholson, Republican of Massachusetts.

The directive will not be binding however, unless it is contained in the final draft of the general tax bill, which now goes to a House-Senate conference committee for adjustment of differences between versions originally passed by the two chambers

As passed by the Senate, the bill contained a provision direct-

Continued on Page 20, Column 2

TAFT AND WHERRY OPPOSE MARSHALL

Favoritism to Chinese Reds Is Charged—Senate Puts Off Action Until Today

Special to The New York Times.

WASHINGTON, Sept. 14—A small band of Republican Senators gathered today in opposition to the bill to waive existing law and permit General of the Army George C. Marshall, a professional soldier, to serve as Secretary of Defense.

The Republican leaders, however, made no attempt to declare it an all-party issue, and the Senate's passage of the measure, probably tomorrow, was thus assured.

It had been intended to put debate tonight, but unexpected difficulties intervened in other aspects of the Administration's final "must" list for this Congress.

At length, soon after 9 P. M., Senator Scott W. Lucas of Illinois, the Democratic Senate leader, not only put over "the Marshall bill" until tomorrow but abandoned hope of bringing this Congress to a close, as had been planned, by Saturday night.

Preliminary action by the House of Representatives was expected tomorrow on the bill. The House Armed Services Committee will meet at 10 A. M. to give its approval. The House Rules committee, which governs the legislative traffic in that chamber, will meet at 11 A. M. to give it a right of way for the floor.

The bill simply specifies that the Military Unification Act notwithstanding, "General of the Army Gen. George C. Marshall" is to be permitted to serve as Secretary of Defense.

The act forbids the office to a

Continued on page 9, Column 2

3 Robbers Shoot 2 Payroll Guards, Flee With $23,436 in Madison Ave.

Three robbers shot down two armed payroll messengers as the victims stepped into the lobby of 625 Madison Avenue early yesterday and fled with $23,436.

There were no outside witnesses to the crime and no nearby witnesses. Two small blood stains near the curb outside 35 East Fifty-eighth Street, the service entrance through which the thugs escaped, were reported as of little value but an alarm describing the getaway car with the notation that it might be blood-stained was broadcast. One robber might have been accidentally wounded by a companion, according to the police.

Fifty detectives were assigned to cover the East Side and to make a search through the city for the gunmen's car and to check hospitals and offices of physicians for evidence of anyone treated for a gunshot wound. By last night detectives had questioned thirty per-

sons, including a number employed in the vicinity of the crime, in their search for clues.

The thugs fired five shots as they ambushed the couriers, Harold F. O'Connor, 43 years old, of 883 Columbus Avenue, and Joseph E. Gilgar, 54, of 34-50 Twenty-eighth Street, Long Island City, Queens. Although Mr. O'Connor managed to get his pistol from his holster as the last of the attackers sped out the side door he did not return the fire.

Herman Siegal, an employe of a laundry service, entered the building soon after the shooting and sounded the alarm. The elevator operator and a porter, the only two building service workers on duty at the time, also heard the shots but their policemen were arriving when they came from the cellar. Mr. Gilgar, critically wounded

Continued on Page 22, Column 2

SENATE UNANIMOUS FOR BIG ARMS FUND BUT VOTES AID CURB

Approval of 17 Billion Bars Economic Help if Ally Ships War Goods to Russia

MOVE IS AIMED AT BRITISH

Proposal Would Give Defense Secretary Authority Superior to That of E. C. A. Director

By WILLIAM S. WHITE
Special to The New York Times.

WASHINGTON, Sept. 14—The Senate passed unanimously tonight an urgent and supplemental appropriation bill of $17,192,000,000. Nine dollars of every ten in it would go to strengthening the defense of the United States and its associates of the western world.

Added to this big measure was a rider intended to halt all Marshall Plan economic aid, but not military help, to any benefiting nation that shipped to the Soviet Union or any of its satellites any commodity or article deemed to be useful in the manufacture of "arms, armament, or military matériel."

This stipulation was offered by Senator Kenneth S. Wherry of Nebraska, the Republican Senate leader. It was approved by a voice vote, in which not a dissent was heard.

It would leave it to the Secretary of Defense to determine what commodities ought to fall under the ban. Once he had defined them, the Marshall Plan administrator, Paul G. Hoffman, would have no option but to cut off from that plan any offending country.

The stipulation was aimed mainly at the British, who long have been accused by the Republicans of sending to Russia or to Soviet friends articles that might be used in a war.

The effect was to put the Secretary of Defense in the great and delicate area of determining what would be useful to the Soviet war potential, far above the Marshall Plan agency, the Economic Cooperation Administration. Admittedly, it would give him a sort veto power over the trade practices of the European nations if he wanted to use it.

The prospective Secretary of Defense is the author of the Marshall Plan itself, General of the Army George C. Marshall.

The Senate's insistence upon this limitation over Mr. Hoffman as yet to meet the approval of the House of Representatives, as does the whole of the appropriations bill. That measure, when it passed the House in August, had been for $16,771,356,077, or some $421,000,-000 less than it stood tonight as it came from the Senate.

The additions made by the Senate were largely military, as the Korean war since August, but there were other new sums, too. There was, for example, $60,000,-

Continued on Page 4, Column 3

World News Summarized

FRIDAY, SEPTEMBER 15, 1950

United Nations forces have struck in strength against the North Koreans with landings on both coasts behind the enemy's lines. A major amphibious blow was at Inchon, the port of Seoul, where United States and British warships had shelled the area Wednesday. At least two other landings were on the east coast north of Pohang. Army First Korean claims to have sunk landing craft were disputed. Along the United Nations defense perimeter in the south relatively light action was reported, except north of Taegu. [1:8; maps Pages 1 and 2.]

Observers with United States Marines on the way to a landing looked to a quick knock-out effect on the North Koreans. [1:6-7.]

The Commission on Korea reported to the United Nations Security Council that, as week before the invasion, American officers rejected South Korean warnings of an attack. The report blamed North Korea for an unprovoked aggression. [1:7.]

President Truman directed the State Department to try again to obtain a Japanese peace treaty and to seek some way to end the technical state of war with Germany. [1:5.] The State Department is studying a $250,-000,000 economic aid program for South Asia and the Middle East. [4:5.]

Foreign ministers of the United States, Britain and France discussed the "serious situation" affecting Europe and Asia. The British and French ministers agreed to seek new instructions on rearming Western Germany. France and France feel no military aid should go to the Germans until the North At-

lantic nations are armed. [1:6-7.] The North Atlantic Council will consider this subject at meetings opening today. [16:2.] Britain's Defense Minister predicted that a unified command would result from the talks. He disclosed that France planned to try again to obtain a Western Big Three discussion and ten men next year and ten more later. [16:3-4.]

Britain's Labor government announced it would take over the steel industry in January. The Conservatives immediately demanded a no-confidence vote and the Commons will decide the issue next week. [1:4.]

The Senate unanimously passed a $17,192,000,000 money bill, mostly for defense, with a rider designed to end all Marshall Plan economic aid to nations shipping "arms, armament or military matériel" to the Soviet Union or its satellites. [1:3.]

The House sent the interim tax bill to conference, but voted 331 to 2 for Congress to stay in session until an excess profits tax was passed. [1:2.]

A Republican fight led by Senator Taft against enabling General Marshall to become Secretary of Defense delayed a Senate vote until today. [1:2.]

The A. F. L. and C. I. O. garment unions asked an immediate 15 per cent pay increase for their 655,000 members to meet higher living costs. [1:1.]

There will be no more 1 or 2 days or water curbs in this city unless the situation again gets critical, but water must not be wasted, officials said. [27:3.]

NEWS BULLETINS FROM THE TIMES

Every hour on the hour
7 A. M. through Midnight
WQXR AM 1560
WQXR FM 96.3

Index to other news appears on Page 26.

Backbone of Attack On Taegu 'Broken'

Special to The New York Times.

TAEGU, Korea, Sept. 14—Maj. Gen. Hobart Gay, commanding the United States First Cavalry Division, said today he believed "we have the backbone" of the North Korean attack on the key United Nations advance base at Taegu.

This, General Gay said, is the situation, at least, "at the moment," after four days of seesaw fighting north and west of the city. The Communists put an estimated three divisions into the attack, with a fourth behind the lines.

General Gay said he might have to change his mind but all indications today were that the situation at Taegu had considerably bettered.

ATTLEE RISKS FATE ON STEEL QUESTION

Conservatives Offer Censure Motion on Labor's Decision to Implement Nationalization

Special to The New York Times.

LONDON, Sept. 14—The British Conservatives precipitated a Parliamentary crisis today by calling for a vote of censure after an announcement by the Labor Government that it intended to implement its authority to nationalize the country's steel industry.

The matter will be debated on Tuesday. If the Government, with its slim majority, is defeated it will resign and there will be a general election.

This is how the issue arose: There is on the statute books a law enabling the Government to take over the steel industry next January and appoint a board to do it by October. The Opposition asked today what the Government proposed to do about it. George Strauss, the Minister of Supply, said the Government intended to carry out the law, which Parliament had enacted when Labor had a bigger majority than it has now. Those were fighting words. They ended the political truce that Winston Churchill had proffered

Continued on Page 16, Column 5

ACTION BY TRUMAN

Right to Move Forces at Will in Islands Is Held U. S. Aim

MAY IGNORE SOVIET

Factors in Ending State of War With Germany Studied, He Says

By ANTHONY LEVIERO
Special to The New York Times.

WASHINGTON, Sept. 14—President Truman announced today that he had directed the State Department to begin a new effort to obtain a Japanese peace treaty. Behind the move was this country's resolve to produce a peace agreement, with or without Soviet participation.

[The Associated Press said Secretary of State Acheson had informed British Foreign Secretary Bevin and French Foreign Minister Schuman that the United States was ready to begin informal talks on the development of a Japanese peace treaty.]

Our policy with respect to Japan, said the Chief Executive, was in harmony with our general aim to "end all war situations," including the deadlocks over Germany and Austria.

The President opened his news conference by reading a formal statement, announcing the new effort on the Japanese treaty, which would be made informally in discussions with members of the Far Eastern Commission. He said this would be done "in the first instance," leaving the implication that the U. S. would proceed further if the deadlock created by the Soviet Union in the commission persisted.

Informed sources said afterward that this country was determined to make some kind of peace settlement with Japan, without the Soviet Union if that country continued its obstructive tactics. The same sources said the United States would seek the right not

Continued on Page 15, Column 1

U. N. TROOPS MAKE LANDINGS IN KOREA

United States and South Korean forces landed at Inchon (1) and drove inland, while other South Korean troops landed near Pohang (4) and at another point on the east coast about twenty-five miles north of Pohang. A fourth landing was reported made at Kunsan (3) on the west coast. Earlier, United Nations naval planes had battered targets from Pyongyang (2) and southward (points are indicated by bomb devices). South Koreans already hold islands marked by stars. The diagonally shaded area is the United Nations' southern beachhead.

The New York Times   Sept. 15, 1950

'This Is Our Sunday Punch,' Task Force Observer Says

By ROBERT C. MILLER
United Press Correspondent

WITH UNITED STATES MARINES, at Sea, Friday, Sept. 15 —This is the one we have been waiting for. Within a few hours ships of this blacked-out task force will begin a shore bombardment to pave the way for landing craft that will carry the Marines in for what we hope to be the final battle of the Korean war.

This is our Sunday punch. We will know by tonight whether it will knock out the North Koreans.

There are no excuses for this one—everything has been planned and worked out for weeks. The supplies are adequate, the men are trained and the plans drawn down to the merest detail.

Everything that can be done to insure the success of this operation has been done.

This ship is like a tightly trained boxer during those dreadful last hours before the bell, when the long weeks of training camp ordeal are finished and there is nothing to do but wait.

We are crammed with men who have been stacked into every corner of this assault ship. In the holds are the deadliest weapons we possess to arm them for the attack.

Every marine aboard is a combat veteran who came to a South Korean port directly from the front lines. They are loaded at the same port at which they arrived

Continued on Page 4, Column 3

U. S. SHUNNED SIGNS ON KOREA, U. N. TOLD

Inquiry Report Says Republic Warned General an Invasion From North Was Near

Excerpts from findings of Commission are on Page 6.

By A. M. ROSENTHAL
Special to The New York Times.

LAKE SUCCESS, Sept. 14—The United Nations Commission on Korea reported today that six weeks before the start of the war United States officers denied South Korean warnings that invasion from the north was imminent.

From January, 1950, to May 12, the commission reported, defense officials of the Korean Republic had warned that the Communist army was strong and getting stronger and that it was just a

Continued on Page 7, Column 2

Bevin and Schuman Agree to Seek Instructions on Arming of Germans

By THOMAS J. HAMILTON

Foreign Minister Robert Schuman of France and Foreign Secretary Ernest Bevin of Britain agreed yesterday to ask their governments for instructions regarding Mr. Acheson's proposal on Monday, after the meeting today and tomorrow of the foreign ministers of the twelve countries that are parties to the North Atlantic Treaty.

This decision was hedged with many conditions, but it is believed that it may open the door—if only partly—to acceptance of Secretary of State Dean Acheson's contention that Western German soldiers are absolutely essential for the defense of Western Europe against Soviet aggression.

According to well-informed sources, M. Schuman and Mr. Bevin agreed to send cablegrams to their Governments on the German rearmament with certain blanks. If these blanks were filled

Continued on Page 14, Column 5

3 LANDINGS MADE

Allies Strike at Western Port and Two Points North of Pohang

4TH PUSH REPORTED

Units of U. S. Marines Join Blow Behind the Front Lines of Foe

By The Associated Press.

TOKYO, Friday, Sept. 15—United Nations invasion forces landed today at Inchon, the port city for Seoul on Korea's west coast—150 miles with the 130,000-man North Korean Army at the fighting front.

Covered by planes and warships, United States troops stormed ashore on the island of Wolmi, linked to Inchon by a causeway. South Korean Marines landed at Inchon.

In a simultaneous operation other United States forces landed immediately behind the Communist lines on the east coast. They made two landings—one two miles northeast of Communist-held Pohang, the other at Yongdok, more than twenty-five miles north of Pohang.

[Sources in Washington said the United States forces involved were units of the Second Marine Division.]

The west coast invasion, preceded by cruiser and destroyer bombardments and sweeping carrier plane strikes, swung the United Nations to the offensive for the first time since the Reds began the war last June 25.

Close to 38th Parallel

The invasion at Inchon, putting United Nations forces close to the Thirty-eighth Parallel which the North Koreans crossed June 25, was announced by the South Korean Commander in Chief, Maj. Gen. Chung Il Kwon.

He said that heavy pressure was quickly exerted by the invasion forces on the Communists near Kimpo airfield, Seoul's big air base. Kimpo is twelve miles northwest of Seoul and ten miles north of Inchon.

A report from Pusan said that still other United Nations forces had gone ashore at Kunsan, a west coast city 100 miles south of Seoul. The report came from the South Korean National Assembly man, who said a warship bombardment had supported the landing.

One thousand South Korean commandos went ashore on the east coast near Pohang, striking at a coastal road that would bar the way to any retreat by the North Korean forces defending the port. The commandos quickly called for air support.

A big United States battleship was reported Thursday to be off the east coast in the Pohang-Yongdok sector.

Invasion Follows Naval Attack

The North Koreans had been expecting an invasion at Inchon since Rear Adm. John M. Hoskins, commander of Task Force 77, sent British and United States cruisers and destroyers close in to bombard Inchon Wednesday. The targets included Wolmi Island.

While their shells hit the area, carrier planes for the second straight day ranged 210 miles from Kunsan to Pyongyang, capital city of the North Koreans, hitting at airfields.

B-29's coordinated these blows, blowing up an underground arsenal north of Pyongyang and severing rail lines from Pyongyang for 100 miles south to Seoul and for 200 miles southeast to Kumchon.

[Gen. Douglas MacArthur's headquarters announced at noon today, Friday, that United Nations forces were again in the walled city of Kasan, ten miles north of Taegu, from which they had been forced to retreat last week. The United Press reported.]

The Pyongyang radio broadcast claimed down today that had sunk three United States destroyers and four landing craft Wednesday. The officials in Washington quickly said the three destroyers had suffered

Continued on Page 2, Column 5

The New York Times.

Copyright, 1950, by The New York Times Company.

VOL. C..No. 33,885.

Entered as Second-Class Matter, Post Office, New York, N. Y.

NEW YORK, THURSDAY, NOVEMBER 2, 1950.

Times Square, New York 18, N. Y. Telephone LAckawanna 4-1000

RAG PAPER EDITION
SEVENTY-FIVE CENTS

KOREAN REDS HIT U. S. UNIT; NOW USE JETS

REGIMENT TRAPPED

Foe Employing Rockets Against First Cavalry Division at Unsan

U. N. TROOPS FORCED BACK

Only 24th Division Makes Gain and Then It Is Told to Halt Its Advance

By LINDESAY PARROTT
Special to The New York Times

TOKYO, Thursday, Nov. 2—North Korean Communist, reinforced by troops of the Chinese Red Army, savagely attacked today advance guards of the United States First Cavalry Division thrown into action near the west coast of Korea to reinforce the weakening South Korean troops.

The attack made north and west of Unsan, where the Communists had concentrated their strength during the last few days and had driven back South Korean spearhead as much as thirty miles in some sectors. Using tanks, artillery and heavy mortar fire, the North Koreans cut off one regiment of the United States Cavalry Division. Other units of the division were reported to be attempting to fight their way through to reach the isolated troops.

The fighting was in progress between Unsan and Taechon, but a spokesman for the United States First Cavalry said the situation was too vague and confused to locate the positions to which the United States troops had been forced to retreat.

Admits Chinese Are Fighting

For the first time a corps spokesman officially admitted that "Chinese" troops" were launching an assault.

"We don't know whether they represent the Chinese Government," he said, and added that it also was unknown whether or not Chinese reinforcements made up the bulk of the new strength that had enabled the shattered North Korean Army to take the offensive again—at least locally—against the United Nations move toward the Manchurian border.

The Communists launched their attack in the morning. According to reports from Korea, they used heavy rocket bombardment for the first time in the war. The latest accounts said the enemy had overrun several First Cavalry positions, capturing weapons and turning them against Americans who had been hurriedly brought up to the combat line after all but one United States division—the Twenty-fourth Infantry, farther to the west—had been out of the contact with the enemy and behind the Korean Republican army being driven in by the enemy counter-attack.

This morning the North Koreans were reported to be within one half mile of Unsan.

Rockets Launched on Ground

The use of the rockets, fired from launchers on the ground, represented the second new weapon introduced on the North Korean side within the last two days. Yesterday for the first time the enemy flung jet-propelled fighter planes into combat.

Meanwhile, the ground advance of the Allied forces halted at Chongko, where the United States Twenty-fourth Infantry Division stood within eighteen miles of the border city of Sinuiju, reported to be the new capital of the North Korean Communist Government.

All along the rest of the front South Korean divisions were in retreat or on the defensive against enemy attacks strengthened by contingents of Chinese Communist soldiers trained in the Chinese Red Army.

Six enemy jet fighters made their appearance yesterday over Sonchon on the west coast, fought a brief dogfight with Mustangs of the United States Fifth Air Force and then flashed back toward the Manchurian border without casualties on either side. Observers said the jet-propelled planes resembled the Soviet model MIG-15, with swept back wings and a speed of 600 miles an hour. On the previous occasion jet planes were believed to have been seen over North Korea, but this was the

Continued on Page 3, Column 1

PLAYWRIGHT DIES

George Bernard Shaw
The New York Times

BERNARD SHAW, 94, DIES IN HIS HOME

Famous Irish Wit Had Been in Coma for Day—Broken Thigh Led to Final Illness

By The Associated Press

AYOT ST. LAWRENCE, England, Thursday, Nov. 2—George Bernard Shaw, one of the modern age's greatest dramatists and its most caustic critic, died today at the age of 94. The white-bearded Irish-born sage, whose wit was renowned throughout the world for half a century, succumbed at 4:59 A. M. (11:59 P. M. Wednesday, Eastern standard time).

His death was announced to newsmen by his housekeeper, Mrs. Alice Laden. Wearing black, she appeared at the gates of the cottage, Shaw's Corner, and told the reporters: "Mr. Shaw is dead."

A few minutes after her announcement, Dr. Thomas Probyn, Shaw's physician, hurried into the house. Twenty minutes later, Shaw's longtime biographer, F. E. Loewenstein, told newsmen that the playwright died peacefully without regaining consciousness. Only two nurses were with him when death came.

The famed dramatist, who professed himself both a Communist and an atheist, was visited in his last hours by an Anglican clergyman, who said final prayers for the old sage's soul.

"It is wrong to say that he was an atheist," said the minister, the Rev. R. G. Davies. "He believed in God."

Shaw lapsed into his final coma yesterday morning at 3 o'clock (10 P. M. Tuesday, Eastern standard time) and never regained consciousness. Operated on seven weeks ago for a broken thigh suffered when he slipped and fell in his garden, he grew steadily weaker. A bladder ailment aggravated his condition.

Lights burned for two nights in Shaw's Corner, the red brick

Continued on Page 28, Column 2

Pope Affirms Dogma of Assumption Of Mary to Heaven 'Body and Soul'

By CAMILLE M. CIANFARRA
Special to The New York Times

ROME, Nov. 1—Pope Pius proclaimed today the dogma of the Assumption to heaven of the Virgin Mary.

"We pronounce, declare and define to be a dogma revealed by God that the Immaculate Mother of God, Mary, ever virgin, when the course of her life on earth was finished was taken up body and soul into heaven," the Pope declared.

The Pontiff spoke ex cathedra as supreme pastor of the church and teacher of Roman Catholic doctrine during an open air ceremony of pomp and magnificence to an audience of thirty-five Cardinals and 480 Archbishops and Bishops in the grandiose setting of St. Peter's Square.

A throng of 200,000 faithful, including Holy Year pilgrims from so many countries that they could be said truly to represent the

Vatican texts on dogma and speech by Pope are on Page 12.

whole Catholic world, packed every inch of space of the oval-shaped square that had been transformed for the occasion into a vast Christian temple.

Beginning today 400,000,000 members of the Catholic religion must believe explicitly and without reservation—otherwise they will incur excommunication as heretics—the Catholic tradition of the Assumption now defined as a dogma or as article of faith. The Catholic Church holds that dogmas are truths revealed directly by God or through the apostles and contained in the two sole fonts of Catholic doctrine—the Bible and tradition.

As such they are irrevocably binding on all Catholics and may be defined by the Pope either alone or as a matter of faith, through the apostles and contained in the Ecumenical Council represented.

Continued on Page 13, Column 1

LIE TERM EXTENDED AS U. N. SECRETARY FOR 3 YEARS, 46 TO 5

Assembly Vote Continues Him in Office Despite Bitter Attacks by Russians

ARAB BLOC, CHINA ABSTAIN

Australia Also Shuns Support —Final Move by Vishinsky to Block Step Fails

The text of Secretary Lie's address is printed on Page 3.

By THOMAS J. HAMILTON

Overriding last-ditch Soviet opposition, the General Assembly yesterday extended the term of Trygve Lie as Secretary General of the United Nations for another three years. The vote was 46 to 5, with only the five members of the Soviet bloc opposed.

However, Australia, Nationalist China and six members of the Arab bloc—Egypt, Iraq, Lebanon, Saudi Arabia, Syria and Yemen—abstained. Haiti was absent.

Mr. Lie, whose present five-year term will expire next Feb. 1, told the Assembly when it reconvened for the afternoon session that he interpreted the extension of his term as a vote of confidence and a reaffirmation of the independence and integrity of the position.

Mr. Lie did not refer to his stand in favor of United Nations action for the defense of South Korea, which had led the Soviet Union to veto his re-election. But he said that he had worked hard for the past five years to reconcile "the conflicting interests that divide the world" and that he would continue to do so.

Iraq Explains Abstention

Immediately after the vote Dr. Fadhil Jamali of Iraq explained that he had not been able to vote for the extension of Mr. Lie's term because he felt that, despite Mr. Lie's "many fine qualities," he had not been "entirely impartial" in the Palestine question. He added that "Mr. Lie did not react toward recent Jewish aggressions in Palestine with anything like the zeal which he displayed on the question of Korea."

"With due respect to Mr. Lie, we do not believe that he helped enough to make the United Nations bring about peace and justice to the Arabs of Palestine," Dr. Jamali said.

Nasrollah Entezam of Iran, President of the Assembly, who had given Dr. Jamali the floor to explain his vote, then pounded his gavel, declaring that this was not an explanation, and that Dr. Jamali could not "continue this way in attacking a person who is not present here and who has received the confidence of the General Assembly by forty-six votes in his favor."

Dr. Jamali then stepped down from the rostrum with the statement that "it would certainly have been a betrayal of Arab public opinion and sentiment if we had not abstained."

Sir Keith Officer, who then was recognized to explain that Australia shared the view that Mr. Lie must not be punished for doing "his clear duty as regards the action of the United Nations in Korea," but that Australia had "genuine doubts" about the legality of the extension of Mr. Lie's term, which

Continued on Page 5, Column 5

CAPITAL STARTLED

Police Swiftly Cordon Blair House as Shots Attract Big Crowds

PHOTOGRAPHERS NEAR BY

Leap From Their Auto, Halted by Traffic Light, Into Action —Passers-by See Fight

By PAUL P. KENNEDY
Special to The New York Times

WASHINGTON, Nov. 1—This city, which has heard the sound of assassins' guns before, reacted with electric suddenness today as shots exploded before the front door of President Truman's own residence. Within a few moments after the firing had stopped in front of Blair House hundreds of spectators were straining at police cordons almost magically thrown up at the intersecting streets bounding the block in which the President's temporary residence is situated.

Street cars, which run along Pennsylvania Avenue in front of the White House and Blair House, were backed up three blocks from Jackson Place, which bounds the Blair House block on the east, and for as many blocks from Seventeenth Street, which bounds Blair House block on the west.

Automobile traffic snarls blocked the approach of a number of ambulances and police squad cars, and wailing sirens heightened the confusion.

Approaching the scene of the shooting from the outer fringe of the crowd, one picked up at least a dozen accounts of what had happened. The accounts grew less lurid toward the core of the trouble.

Rumors Fly Among Throngs

These reports were received from spectators, at least a half block from the Blair House, and from newspaper men scurrying from the scene to the nearest telephones. On the outer reaches of the crowd the rumor was that two or three persons had entered Blair House with submachine guns firing and that the President had been assassinated or wounded.

Even among the reporters and photographers directly in front of the Blair House, the early accounts were confusing. It was not until fully fifteen minutes after the firing that it was clearly estab-

Continued on Page 16, Column 6

ASSASSINATION OF TRUMAN FOILED IN GUN FIGHT OUTSIDE BLAIR HOUSE; PUERTO RICAN PLOTTER, GUARD DIE

WOULD-BE ASSASSIN OF PRESIDENT SHOT DOWN

Oscar Collazo lying at the bottom of the steps to the Blair-Lee House as White House guard is putting his revolver back in his holster. This picture was made by a photographer of The New York Times, who was waiting to accompany Mr. Truman to a dedication ceremony at Arlington Cemetery.

The New York Times (by Bruce Hoertel)

PUERTO RICO'S HEAD LINKS TWO ATTACKS

Governor Says Nationalist Forces Sparked by Reds Shot at Truman, Himself

By The United Press

SAN JUAN, Puerto Rico, Nov. 1—Gov. Luis Muñoz Marin said tonight that Puerto Rican Nationalists were being used by the Communists both in the attempt to assassinate President Truman and in the abortive revolt here, in which he also was a target.

"This further crime—the Washington attempt—further confirms me in my conviction that the Nationalists are having their lunacy, fanaticism and irresponsibility manipulated for the benefit of Communist propaganda and strategy," the Governor said.

"We all feel deeply relieved that no tragic consequences resulted from this criminal act.

"The people are profoundly

Continued on Page 19, Column 2

Assassins' Kin and Friends Are Rounded Up in Bronx

By MEYER BERGER

Thirteen Puerto Ricans—six women and seven men—were taken to the offices of the United States Secret Service at 90 Church Street last night for questioning about the attempt yesterday on President Truman's life in Washington.

Policemen said they were the families and friends of the two assassins. Unofficially, Oscar Collazo of 173 Brook Avenue, the Bronx, one of the men who fired a gun at Blair House, was described as treasurer of the Puerto Rican branch of the Puerto Rican Nationalists, bitter enemies of the United States.

Collazo, wounded, is in the Emergency Hospital in Washington. The second gunman, tentatively identified by Secret Service men as Griselio Torresola of 1259 Ward Avenue in the East Bronx, was killed by police bullets.

Mrs. Rose Collazo, 42 years old, the wounded man's wife, was taken into custody. She was arraigned at 2 o'clock this morning in Federal Court before United States Commissioner Edward M. McDonald on a charge of having conspired with the two assassins and two unnamed persons to harm a member of the Government. Commissioner McDonald held her in $50,000 bail for a hearing next Thursday.

Following the arraignment Secret Service men took her to the Federal House of Detention.

At the request of Assistant United States Attorney Irving H. Saypol, Commissioner McDonald issued John Doe warrants for the two unidentified persons named in the conspiracy complaint.

Earlier Mrs. Collazo had told officials and newspaper men:

"I am Oscar Collazo's wife. He

Continued on Page 18, Column 3

PRESIDENT RESTING

Awakened by Shots, He Sees Battle in Which Three Are Wounded

HE KEEPS APPOINTMENTS

Documents Link 2 Assassins, Who Lived Here, to Puerto Rican Extremist Leader

By ANTHONY LEVIERO
Special to The New York Times

WASHINGTON, Nov. 1—Quick-shooting White House guards cut down two assassins this afternoon when they attempted to invade Blair House in a Puerto Rican Nationalist plot to assassinate President Truman.

Tonight one assassin and one policeman were dead, and two policemen were wounded, one critically. The other assassin, seriously wounded, told the United States Secret Service that he and his companion had come down from New York two days ago to kill Mr. Truman.

On the body of the dead assassin was found a letter and a "memorandum," both cryptic but indicative of conspiracy. The missives were in the same handwriting and on the same stationery. They bore in the form of a signature, the name of Pedro Albizu Campos, leader of the Puerto Rican Nationalist extremists who carried out the uprising in Puerto Rico Monday.

U. E. Baughman, chief of the Secret Service, cautioned reporters, however, that he had no proof that Albizu Campos was the author of the two documents.

THE DEAD

COFFELT, Pvt. Leslie, of Arlington, Va., White House guard.

TORRESOLA, Griselio, of 1259 Ward Avenue, New York, assassin.

THE INJURED

COLLAZO, Oscar, of 173 Brook Avenue, New York, assassin; shot in the chest.

DOWNS, Pvt. Joseph, of Silver Spring, Md., White House guard; in critical condition with multiple wounds.

BIRDZELL, Pvt. Donald T., of Washington, White House guard; in "fair" condition with knees shattered by bullets.

All three wounded are expected to recover.

Taking his usual afternoon nap and roused by a fury of shooting, Mr. Truman looked down from an upstairs bedroom of Blair House. In the bright sun of Pennsylvania Avenue was terror and confusion. At the foot of the stoop leading in to Blair House lay one of the assassins, alive, blood flowing from the middle of his chest and staining his blue shirt.

"A President has to expect those things," Mr. Truman said, later.

Truman Keeps to Schedule

Serene, a man of good conscience, for he had told the people of Puerto Rico unequivocally that they were free to work out their own political destiny, Mr. Truman punctiliously kept his remaining appointments of the day.

The outrage, however, made the Federal police agencies increasingly alert, and new safeguards were put around the President and his family. Meanwhile, the Secret Service began to trace back the plot through New York, where the apparent source in the island possession of the Caribbean, which is

Continued on Page 16, Column 2

PRESIDENT IS CALM AT DILL DEDICATION

Speaks, After Attempt to Kill Him, at Unveiling of Statue of British Field Marshal

By The Associated Press

WASHINGTON, Nov. 1—Less than an hour after an attempt had been made to assassinate him, President Truman calmly dedicated a memorial to Britain's Field Marshal Sir John Dill at Arlington National Cemetery today.

"It is important to the peace of the world that peoples understand each other and have full faith in each other's sincerity," he said.

He made no reference to the gunfight in front of his Blair House residence. Many of the 600 dignitaries present at the unveiling wondered why Mr. Truman was surrounded by such an unusually heavy guard of Secret Service men.

The President in his address said that he welcomed "this opportunity to remind my countrymen that the maintenance of a perfect understanding between the people of Great Britain and the United States is of great importance.

Continued on Page 17, Column 2

November Heat Record of 81° Set; Zoo and Parks Draw Big Crowds

By IRA HENRY FREEMAN

November came in like a lamb yesterday, a spring lamb.

On the fourth day of an unseasonably warm wave extending over the eastern third of the country, the temperature in this city climbed to 81 degrees at 1:15 P. M. It dropped one degree for an hour, but at 2:15 again reached 81, and the latter time was officially accepted as the record.

This was not only the warmest for any Nov. 1 but also higher than ever reached in November since the Weather Bureau began keeping records here in 1871. The previous record for Nov. 1 was 70 degrees in 1946, while the previous high for any November day was 80 on Nov. 6, 1948.

The coolest it got during the day was 59 degrees from 6 to 7 o'clock in the morning. That was two degrees above the normal maximum for Nov. 1. Col. James W. Osmun, chief assistant meteor-

ologist in charge of the New York Weather Bureau, pointed out.

During the luncheon period when the mercury was rising 4 and 5 degrees an hour, throngs of office workers and shoppers on the midtown streets were uncomfortably warm. In Bryant Park the benches were jammed with men in shirt sleeves and girls in summer blouses.

Some air-cooled restaurants and offices turned the refrigeration back on temporarily. Women shoppers in Fifth Avenue and Fifty-seventh Street strolled along with their suit jackets over their arms.

The retail clothing business, incidentally, was slackened temporarily by the weather, Thomas A. Terry, executive vice president of the Fifth Avenue Association, reported.

The brass Prometheus bringing

Continued on Page 22, Column 1

Campos Captured In San Juan Home

By The United Press

SAN JUAN, Puerto Rico, Thursday, Nov. 2—National policemen poured five heavy volleys of rifle and pistol fire into the home of Pedro Albizu Campos early today and captured the Nationalist party leader when he fled into the street.

The Puerto Rican Governor, Luis Muñoz Marin, earlier had accused the Nationalist extremist leader of responsibility for the attempt against President Truman yesterday. The would-be assassins were said to be members of the Nationalist party.

World News Summarized

THURSDAY, NOVEMBER 2, 1950

Two assassins, identified as Puerto Rican Nationalists, attempted to kill President Truman yesterday while he was taking an afternoon nap in Blair House. One assailant was killed and the other badly wounded in a gun fight outside the house with guards, one of whom died. Two policemen were seriously wounded. The President went to the window to see what has happened and was shooed to safety by alert agents. [1:8.] Later he dedicated a memorial in Arlington Cemetery honoring Sir John Dill, British Field Marshal. [1:7.]

Secret Service agents listed the two Puerto Ricans as Bronx residents, and last night six women and five men were taken to 90 Church Street for questioning. [1:6-7.] Just before the Blair House attack an unidentified man threw two bottles of ignited gasoline into the Puerto Rican labor office in this city, but they did not explode. [17:7.] In Puerto Rico, which has been torn by Nationalist uprisings, the Government spurred its hunt for revolutionary leaders. [1:5.]

Washington, electrified by the attack, the sixth attempt on a President's life [16:8], crowded to the scene. Eyewitness reports were confusing and conflicting. [1:4.] An ironic twist to the assassination attempt was the fact that President Truman was a strong advocate of Puerto Rican independence. [16:1.]

Chinese and North Korean troops, using rockets and heavy guns, drove back United States troops in the Unsan area, trapping one regiment. Other United

States forces were ordered to halt their advance 18 miles from the border. [1:1; map Page 2.]

India expressed "keen disappointment" in answering Communist China's rejection of her concern over the invasion of Tibet. [9:2.]

The United Nations General Assembly, 46 to 5, extended the term of Secretary General Lie for three years. Only the Soviet bloc voted no, but Australia, Nationalist China and the Arab states abstained. [1:3.]

France is ready to contribute half of forty divisions planned for Western Europe by 1953, Defense Minister Moch said. Secretary Acheson declared it was agreed there should be no German general staff, national army or war industries. [8:3.]

Pope Pius proclaimed as dogma the Assumption of the Virgin Mary into heaven. [1:2-3.]

George Bernard Shaw died at his home in England. He was 94 years old. [1:2.]

Theodore Roosevelt, Woodrow Wilson, Alexander Graham Bell, Dr. William C. Gorgas, Josiah Willard Gibbs and Susan B. Anthony were elected to the Hall of Fame. [34:3.]

The City Planning Commission approved a record $478,761,756 capital budget for 1951 and a $1,235,850,237 five-year program. [33:1.]

NEWS BULLETINS FROM THE TIMES
Every hour on the hour
7 A. M. through Midnight
WQXR AM 1560
WQXR FM 96.3

Index to other news appears on Page 32.

"All the News That's Fit to Print"

The New York Times.

NEWS INDEX, PAGE 87, THIS SECTION

VOL. C..No. 33,930.

Entered as Second-Class Matter.
Post Office. New York. N. Y.

NEW YORK, SUNDAY, DECEMBER 17, 1950.

Including Magazine and Book Review.

LATE CITY EDITION
Mostly fair and cold today. Fair and continued cold tomorrow.

Temperature Range Today—Max. 35; Min. 27
Temperature Yesterday—Max. 42; Min. 32

U. S. Weather Bureau Report, Page 7: Sect. 1

Section 1

FIFTEEN CENTS New York City / Elsewhere

Copyright, 1950, by The New York Times Company.

PRESIDENT PROCLAIMS A NATIONAL EMERGENCY; AUTO PRICES ROLLED BACK; RAIL STRIKE ENDS; ALLIES GIVE UP HAMHUNG; WU REJECTS TRUCE

U.N. 'TRAP' ALLEGED

Peiping Representative Says He Will Start Home Tuesday

BIDS U. S. QUIT KOREA

'Volunteers' to Withdraw if Formosa Also Is Yielded, He States

Text of press statement by Mr. Wu is printed on Page 12.

By A. M. ROSENTHAL

LAKE SUCCESS, Dec. 16—Communist China rejected today the United Nations plan for a cease-fire in Korea as a "trap," and Peiping's representatives here said they would leave for home here on Tuesday.

The Chinese Communists warned that the great problems of the world could not be settled peacefully unless Peiping got a seat in the United Nations and a major voice in Asia. They made it clear that their conditions for peace in Korea remained United States withdrawal from the country and an end to American "aggression" in Formosa. On those conditions, they implied, Communist China would withdraw its "volunteer troops" from Korea.

Peiping's stand was outlined in a special press conference here called by its chief representative at the United Nations, the impassive Wu Hsiu-chuan. Before coming to the press conference Mr. Wu informed United Nations officials that he would leave for Peiping on Tuesday by air.

Wu Complains to Lie

Mr. Wu was reported to have told Secretary General Trygve Lie last night that his delegation had come to New York weeks ago to discuss Soviet charges of United States aggression against China and had not been invited to testify before the General Assembly's Political and Security Committee. The committee has opened debate on the item but recessed the discussion to take up the problem of Chinese intervention in Korea. Mr. Wu complained to Mr. Lie that there was no purpose in his staying if the committee did not discuss the Soviet charges, which are centered on Formosa and Korea.

The Secretary General immediately got in touch with the three-man cease-fire committee set up by the Assembly to sound out the United States and Communist China on the possibility of a cease-fire and efforts were said to have been made to persuade Mr. Wu to change his mind about leaving. But the Chinese still were planning to leave Tuesday.

Delegation May Stay

Some diplomats said that developments Monday would decide whether the Chinese Communists would leave. The Political Committee is to map its remaining work on Monday and the Chinese Communists may attend in the visitors' section. If the committee votes to resume talk on Formosa immediately, as it was believed, the Chinese may stay for a while.

For its part, the cease-fire committee announced that it would present an interim report to the Assembly on Monday, and stressed the word interim. The committee released a statement saying that it intended to go ahead with its efforts for a Korean cease-fire. It was reported that the three diplomats—Lester B. Pearson of Canada, Sir Benegal N. Rau of India and Nasrollah Entezam of Iran—would now try to make direct contact with Chinese Communist leaders in Peiping.

The committee met with Mr. Lie today before the Wu press conference. In another room, a little while later, Mr. Lie met with Mr. Wu and introduced him to Mr. Entezam, who is president of the Assembly. Sometime over the weekend, there will be another

Continued on Page 12, Column 5

TURNING DOWN CEASE-FIRE PLAN

Wu Hsiu-chuan, right, outlining Communist China's stand at special press conference he called at Lake Success. With him are Miss Kung Pu-sheng and Chiso Kuan-hua.

The New York Times (by Ernest Sisto)

Paris and London Void Pacts In Arming Bonn, Soviet Says

By HAROLD CALLENDER

PARIS, Dec. 16—The Soviet Government handed to the French and British Ambassadors in Moscow yesterday a note accusing France and Britain of violating their treaties with the Soviet Union by sponsoring rearmament of the Germans.

[Text of the Soviet note to France and Britain, Page 18.]

The step was considered an effort to hamstring defense discussions due to begin in Brussels Monday among the Foreign and Defense Ministers of the North Atlantic Treaty nations.

The new note was a sequel to that of Oct. 18 to France, Britain and the United States in which Moscow said it would not "tolerate" measures of the Western powers aimed at reviving the German Regular Army.

The treaties that Moscow now charges were violated are Britain's pact with the Soviet Union of May 26, 1942, and France's similar treaty signed Dec. 10, 1944. The principal content of both treaties was an agreement not to make a separate peace with Germany or to make any alliance against either of the signatories.

Both treaties were made when the Soviet Union was aligned with but not formally allied with the Western powers in the war against Germany, and when both France and Britain sought to insure against a revival of German power, which then seemed to them the greatest possible future menace.

A warning of yesterday's note was given to the French by Jacques Duclos, French Communist leader, who, in a speech at Brest last Sunday, said that in accepting rearmament of the Germans "the French Government repudiates the signature of France and deliberately violates" the French-Soviet treaty.

M. Duclos specified that the violation

Continued on Page 19, Column 1

RED CHINA'S ASSETS IN U. S. ARE FROZEN

Washington Takes Unilateral Action—Tightens Ban on Shipping to Mainland

By WALTER H. WAGGONER
Special to THE NEW YORK TIMES.

WASHINGTON, Dec. 16—The United States, in actions believed to have fallen just short of a war declaration, froze Chinese Communist funds in United States territory tonight and prohibited United States ships from calling at Chinese ports.

These steps, taken less than twelve hours after President Truman had proclaimed a national emergency, completed an economic embargo characteristic of a state of war.

The State, Treasury and Commerce Departments acted in concert on the moves.

The United States took this action alone. That the Government had consulted other friendly powers was not denied, and the fact that the United States acted unilaterally indicated disapproval by the other nations.

The State Department said that the freezing of Communist China's assets and the barring of United States ships from her ports had been "forced upon us" by the in-

Continued on Page 16, Column 2

Nyack Area Fears the Thruway Means Razing of 250 Buildings

NYACK, N. Y., Dec. 16—Fear was widespread here today that the proposed Thruway crossing of the Tappan Zee would require the razing of 250 homes and other buildings and remove half the property in the village of South Nyack from local tax rolls.

Unpopular in this area from the time it was first contemplated, the Tappan Zee bridge project aroused fresh demonstrations of hostility as a relatively detailed map of the property needed for the bridge and approaches became available.

After examining the map, some residents asserted that the project would obliterate South Nyack almost as if it had been the target of an atomic bomb.

The villages of Nyack, South Nyack and Grandview, which are in the path of the Thruway, are planning a joint suit to enjoin the State Thruway Authority from proceeding with its plans. They are also arranging to send delegations to Governor Dewey and the Legislature to voice their demand for a change in plans.

Harold A. Williams, supervisor of the town of Orangetown, in which Grandview, South Nyack and Nyack are situated, received by messenger last night a copy of the new map from Bertram D. Tallamy, State Superintendent of Public Works and chairman of the Thruway Authority.

It showed the Rockland bridgehead of the Tappan Zee crossing in the northeast corner of Grandview. From that point the approach highway is sketched cutting diag-

Continued on Page 75, Column 2

BEACHHEAD IS CUT

U.N. Troops Forced Back to Narrowed Area as Foe Perils Lines

NAVY SHELLS REDS

MacArthur Aides Report Chinese Build-Up for Attack in West

By LINDESAY PARROTT
Special to THE NEW YORK TIMES.

TOKYO, Sunday, Dec. 17—United Nations forces pulled back yesterday from the wrecked industrial city of Hamhung on the beleaguered northeast Korean beachhead to form a tight perimeter around the seaport of Hungnam. Off that port lay Allied warships to pour fire on advancing columns of Chinese Communists.

Hamhung was evacuated in mid-afternoon yesterday as Chinese troops began to pour into the city's northeastern suburbs. United States engineers blew bridges across the Tongsonchon River and smaller tributaries to delay the pursuit.

Reports this morning said the enemy occupied the city and in this area was about seven miles from the Hungnam beaches. Attacks from the northeast and northwest continued and at the deepest penetration the Reds were only three or four miles from the port.

The withdrawals came after heavy Chinese attacks on the northern and western faces of the United Nations area around the Hungnam beaches had made some penetrations south of Oro on a mountain highway down from the Changjin Reservoir and toward Chigyong where the Chinese were thrusting toward the important Yonpo airfield.

Indications were that the Communist invaders had massed ten to twelve divisions — more than 100,000 men — north and west of Hamhung in an attempt to drive

Continued on Page 3, Column 1

STRIKERS RETURN

Workers Heed Request of President—Freight Jam Is Melting

MAILS MOVING AGAIN

Pay Dispute Settlement Is Expected Quickly in Washington

By GEORGE ECKEL
Special to THE NEW YORK TIMES.

CHICAGO, Dec. 16—Railroad transportation services were returning rapidly to normal today, as more than 10,000 switchmen ended their mushrooming three-day wildcat strike at the behest of President Truman.

The strikers were going back to work in fourteen of fifteen cities to which the walkout had spread. They did so without a settlement of the wage-hour dispute between the carriers and their union, the Brotherhood of Railroad Trainmen. The union, however, had not authorized the walkout.

[In Washington it was believed a quick settlement of the pay dispute underlying the strike would be effected, probably on terms long available to the union.]

[In New York, mountains of mail and freight began to melt as virtually normal railroad service was restored.]

The last of the strikers to return were those at the Illinois Central yards in Birmingham, Ala. Strikers returned at the yards of the Southern Railroad in Birmingham a few hours earlier.

The Postoffice Department lifted its thirty-nine-hour embargo at 11:15 A. M., E. S. T., today, resuming "normal service" at once, and workers began the attack on mountains of backlogged Christmas parcels in the nation's key transport centers and in Chicago, St. Louis, Washington and Pittsburgh began to

Continued on Page 44, Column 1

Recent Auto Rises Canceled By First Price-Freeze Edict

'Ceiling Regulation No. 1' of Economic Stabilization Agency Holds Schedules to Dec. 1 Levels—Wage Study Set

By CHARLES E. EGAN
Special to THE NEW YORK TIMES.

WASHINGTON, Dec. 16—The first price freeze and roll-back actions to result from the present national emergency were announced today by the Economic Stabilization Agency.

Under orders effective at once prices of passenger automobiles are frozen as of Dec. 1, and companies that have increased quotations for their 1951 lines are ordered to "roll them back" to that date or face Federal penalties.

Today's order, which came soon after President Truman's action declaring a national emergency, was regarded here as a forerunner of a variety of similar edicts to issue from the agency beginning Monday.

[In Detroit, a Ford executive said the company would "conform promptly." The head of the automobile workers' union opposed "pin-prick" controls.]

The order was studied closely by representatives of the automobile industry, since it was setting a pattern for ensuing regulations. There was a general feeling that

Dec. 1 would be selected as the terminal date for price increases and that ceilings declared by the Economic Stabilization Agency over the coming month would use quotations of that date as determining factors in industries affected.

The price action in the auto industry is based upon the authority granted under the President's declaration of a national emergency. It is the first order also to affect the economy since the office of Price Administration exercised its powers in World War II.

According to officials the order was issued to enable the Economic Stabilization Agency to make a comprehensive analysis of the effect of cost increases upon the profit position of the companies affected and to ascertain whether cost increases actually incurred justified the recent price increases. If the study justifies the price advances, it was added, the agency will make whatever changes in

Continued on Page 59, Column 3

U. S. Urges Defense Parley By All American Republics

Special to THE NEW YORK TIMES.

WASHINGTON, Dec. 16—The United States proposed today an emergency meeting of the foreign ministers of the twenty-one American republics for tightening the defenses of this hemisphere against the threat of international communism.

Secretary of State Dean Acheson instructed the United States representative to the Council of the Organization of American States to request such a meeting, and he said he was acting under the direction of President Truman.

In making his request known today, Mr. Acheson declared:

"The United States, having embarked on urgent mobilization for the common defense, wishes to consult its fellow members in the inter-American community with respect to the situation which we all face and on the coordination of the common effort required to meet it."

He asserted that "the aggressive policy of international communism, carried out through its satellites, has brought about a situation in which the entire free world is threatened."

The Secretary added that the United States, after consultations with leaders of Congress and the other American Governments, would propose a time and place for the meeting and set forth an agenda for consideration.

Edward G. Miller Jr., Assistant Secretary of State for Inter-American Affairs, said it was the hope

Continued on Page 35, Column 3

Hanley to Get $16,000 State Job; Dewey Makes Good His Promise

By WARREN WEAVER Jr.
Special to THE NEW YORK TIMES.

ALBANY, Dec. 16—The appointment of Lieut. Gov. Joe R. Hanley as special counsel to the State Division of Veterans Affairs at an annual salary of $16,000 was announced today by Leo V. Lanning, director of the division. Mr. Hanley will assume his new post on Jan. 1.

Mr. Lanning said he had made the appointment "at the suggestion of Governor Dewey." Thus the Governor made good on a three-month-old pledge to give Mr. Hanley a state position, if the 74-year-old official would fail to win his Senatorial campaign against Senator Herbert H. Lehman.

The question of Mr. Hanley's future was one of the issues raised in the political storm that followed release Oct. 16 of the now-

famed Hanley letter, which was written Sept. 5. In the letter to representative W. Kingsland Macy, the Lieutenant Governor wrote:

"I have an iron-clad, unbreakable arrangement whereby I will be given a job with the state which I would like and enjoy (I have been told what it is) at sufficient compensation to make my net income more than I now have."

Subsequently both the Governor and Mr. Hanley denied that any specific post had been discussed between them. Both men reported, however, that Mr. Dewey had expressed reluctance to see Mr. Han-

Continued on Page 68, Column 1

TRUMAN SETS DRIVE

Gives Wilson Sweeping Powers, Asks 'Mighty Production Effort'

U. S. RALLIES TO CALL

Congress Speeds Action —Stand of President Praised in Europe

Texts of proclamation and executive order are on Page 30.

By ANTHONY LEVIERO
Special to THE NEW YORK TIMES.

WASHINGTON, Dec. 16—President Truman proclaimed a state of emergency this morning and delegated many of his own war powers to Charles E. Wilson, the new Mobilization Director. Soon afterward the defense program moved into higher gear.

Today was a day of action in the White House, in Congress and elsewhere in the Government, as officials moved to implement the President's declaration to the nation and the world last night that the United States would meet the challenge of communism.

The Economic Stabilization Agency cancelled the price increases made by Ford, General Motors and Chrysler in the last few days, and this was merely the harbinger of many new controls that eventually will encompass the entire economy.

Industry evinced its readiness to accept any war production goals, striking railroad men returned to work, and the general response from the public indicated an acceptance of the austerity program suggested by the President.

Proclamation Is Signed

Mr. Truman had pleaded with unity, like past Presidents coping with crises, and as in 1917 and 1941 the country was rallying with vigor.

In the free countries of Western Europe Mr. Truman was applauded for his no-appeasement speech in which he pledged to create an "arsenal of freedom" to strengthen all free countries. From Russia, which the President blamed directly for the postwar troubles of the world, came a typical blast that this country was warmongering.

Mr. Truman took two actions this morning to start a drastic increase of the mobilization program. He signed the proclamation of emergency, which unleashed scores of additional executive powers, and issued an executive order granting virtually blanket authority to Mr. Wilson to carry out all aspects of war production and economic control he deemed necessary. This authority received by Mr. Wilson is subject in the Executive Branch of the Government only to the veto of President Truman.

Threat to Freedoms Cited

In his proclamation President Truman declared that conquest of the world was the objective of "Communist imperialism." He said this now constituted a threat to the freedoms guaranteed by the Bill of Rights, to the free enterprise system and to other rights, like collective bargaining, that free people had chosen for themselves. These were the elements of a "full and rich life" that could be lost by the triumph of the Communist way of life, Mr. Truman said, calling for "a mighty production effort" for defense.

Mr. Truman called for sacrifices, for cooperation by state and local officials, for loyalty to the principles on which the nation was founded, and faith in which our friends

Continued on Page 28, Column 2

DISASTER SERVICES PUT ON ALERT HERE

Wallander Orders Agencies to Be in Condition of Readiness on 24-Hour-a-Day Basis

By DOUGLAS DALES

City agencies that would have functions to perform in the event of an enemy attack were ordered yesterday to be maintained in a condition of readiness on a twenty-four-hour-a-day basis.

The order was issued by Arthur W. Wallander, Civil Defense Director, with the approval of Mayor Impellitteri after the declaration of a state of emergency by President Truman.

Twenty-two municipal divisions, including the five borough presidents' offices, were directed by Mr. Wallander to maintain at least skeleton staffs throughout the day and night. Some of the departments affected already operate on a twenty-four-hour schedule be-

Continued on Page 39, Column 2

World News Summarized

SUNDAY, DECEMBER 17, 1950

President Truman followed his Friday night message to the people that the nation was in grave danger by proclaiming today a state of emergency. He delegated most of his own wartime powers to Charles E. Wilson, Director of the Office of Defense Mobilization, whose unparalleled controls over the country's economy will be subject only to Presidential veto. [1:8.] Shortly afterward, the Economic Stabilization Agency, in its first price-fixing action, ordered auto prices frozen at Dec. 1 levels. [1:6-7.]

In this city the declaration of emergency led to orders to twenty-two municipal departments that would have duties in the event of an attack to maintain around-the-clock vigil. [1:7.]

In response to the President's appeal to end their wildcat strike, railroad switchmen returned to work. [1:5.]

Shortly before leaving for Brussels, Secretary of State Acheson, acting with Mr. Truman's approval, proposed an emergency meeting of the foreign ministers of the twenty-one American republics to consider the strengthening of hemispheric defenses. [1:6-7.]

The United Nations' plan for a cease-fire in Korea was rejected by the Chinese Communist delegation as a United Nations "trap." The Chinese accused this country of "aggression" in Korea and Formosa, but indicated that if this "aggression" were terminated Peiping would be willing to advise the Chinese "volunteers" in Korea to quit fighting. [1:1.]

Two drastic steps directed against the Peiping regime were taken by Washington: all Chinese Communist funds in United

States territory were frozen and all American ships were told to avoid Red China's ports. [1:2.]

Hamhung, in northeastern Korea, was abandoned to the enemy, as the defenders withdrew toward Hungnam. About 100,000 Chinese were reported pressing upon the shrinking beachhead. [1:4; maps, P. 2.]

The United Nations' plan for a cease-fire in Korea was rejected by the Chinese Communist delegation as a United Nations "trap." The Chinese accused this country of "aggression" in Korea and Formosa, but indicated that if this "aggression" were terminated Peiping would be willing to advise the Chinese "volunteers" in Korea to quit fighting. [1:1.]

Soviet Foreign Minister Vishinsky left Lake Success for home, expressing optimism and "wishes for peace, well-being and happiness" to the people of the United States. [5:1.] According to documents made public in Washington, Moscow's slave labor system has been a major factor in the economic organization of the Soviet Union. [20:1.] In new notes to France and Britain, the Soviet Government charged that London and Paris, by supporting the rearmament of Western Germany, were guilty of violating their agreements with Moscow not to participate in anti-Soviet alliances. [1:2-3.]

Prime Minister Attlee said there was no basis for the fear of wanton use of the atomic bomb by the United States. He warned Britons, however, that the future held disagreeable things in store for them, including a curb on improvements in their standard of living. [10:1.]

At the suggestion of Governor Dewey, Lieut. Gov. Joe R. Hanley has been named special counsel to the State Division of Veterans Affairs. [1:6-7.]

NEWS BULLETINS FROM THE TIMES
Every hour on the hour
8 A. M. through Midnight
Except at Noon, 4 and 9 P. M. today
WQXR AM 1560
WQXR FM 96.3

"All the News That's Fit to Print"

The New York Times.

LATE CITY EDITION

Fair and cold; cloudy later today. Fair and cold tomorrow.

Temperature Range Today—Max.,33; Min.,22
Temperature Yesterday—Max.,33; Min.,22
Full U. S. Weather Bureau Report, Page 61

Copyright, 1950, by The New York Times Company.

VOL. C...No. 33,933.

Entered as Second-Class Matter,
Post Office, New York, N. Y.

NEW YORK, WEDNESDAY, DECEMBER 20, 1950.

Times Square, New York 18, N. Y.
Telephone LAckawanna 4-1000

FIVE CENTS

DEWEY ORDERS CUT IN STATE'S EXPENSES NOT TIED TO DEFENSE

He Says No New Jobs Can Be Created Except in Health and Mobilization Agencies

NO DISMISSALS PLANNED

Crisis Calls for All Possible Economy in Civil Government, Governor Tells Aides

By WARREN WEAVER Jr.
Special to The New York Times.

ALBANY, Dec. 19—Governor Dewey moved today to cut the expenditure of all state departments and agencies not contributing directly to mobilization or defense. In a step aimed at achieving an "austerity economy" for the state, he ordered a reduction in all services non-essential to defense.

The Governor froze expansion of many segments of the state government by directing that "no new positions, however desirable or even necessary in ordinary times, be allowed in any department or agency."

He specified, however, that exceptions would be made in the case of defense facilities, mental and tuberculosis hospitals and health services and "the opening of other new essential facilities."

Mr. Dewey also said that he expected to save substantial amounts by not filling vacancies that existed or might appear later in the state service. Such savings, he indicated, could be diverted to parts of the state economy that would require expansion because of the national emergency.

"There are presently vacancies in many state departments, and there will be more," the Governor wrote in a directive to all department heads. "I expect that the additional services required by the international crisis will be provided by cutting back existing positions from among the vacancies which now exist and will occur."

Salary Rise Under Study

Mr. Dewey reassured the state employes that the economy policies would "not involve the dismissal of any existing personnel, nor will it affect such salary adjustments as the study already under way may call for."

Two committees under the direction of Controller Frank C. Moore are studying the possibility of pay rises for Civil Service employes and school teachers. During his fall campaign, Mr. Dewey virtually promised the state's teachers an increase in 1951.

"The present international crisis, in my judgment, requires that every service provided by all units of government, except those relating to the defense of the United States and those essential to the maintenance of the home front, be kept at an absolute minimum and reduced if possible," the Governor said.

"During each of the last two years, budget requests have not only been sharply cut back but, actually, reduced operating budgets have been achieved in most departments. I recognize that most departments have been cut to the bone. We shall have to cut further."

Some Services Will Expand

Mr. Dewey emphasized that the manpower demands of the armed forces and industry would soon decrease the number of persons in the state service, but, he added, the existing personnel in state defense and health programs would have to handle even more work as a result of the emergency.

"With the expansion of the military forces of the United States. there will be a serious drain of manpower from both government and industry," Mr. Dewey predicted. "At the same time civil and military defense and health services will need expansion.

"This expansion must come from within the existing personnel and that therefore existing services, however desirable in normal times, and the personnel which provide them, must be reduced."

The Governor said that he had arrived at these economy measures after a series of conferences with T. Norman Hurd, State Budget Director.

Despite Mr. Dewey's efforts to reduce expenditures, state officials expect that the budget to be presented to the Legislature by Feb. 1 would exceed the $867,760,632 figure set for this fiscal year, which began April 1.

Hutchins, C. C. Davis Join the Ford Fund

Special to The New York Times.

LOS ANGELES, Dec. 19—Paul G. Hoffman, president of the $238,000,000 Ford Foundation, announced today the appointment of Robert M. Hutchins, chancellor of the University of Chicago, and Chester C. Davis, president of the Federal Reserve Bank of St. Louis, as associate directors of the foundation.

Mr. Hoffman declared in a statement:

"The great opportunity open to the Ford Foundation is dramatically illustrated by the willingness of Mr. Davis and Mr. Hutchins to leave their important posts to work with the foundation."

Pasadena. Mr. Hoffman's home, will be the planning and grant-distributing center of the foundation, which will finance study and endeavor in five basic fields: peace, education, strengthening of democracy, economics and human relations.

Mr. Hutchins will take leave of absence Jan. 1 from his university post and will resign June 30. He will make his home in Pasadena. Mr. Davis will retain his bank post.

AUTO EDICT STANDS, TRUMAN DECLARES

He Upholds Price Orders Issued by Stabilization Agency—Contracts Worry Reuther

By LOUIS STARK
Special to The New York Times.

WASHINGTON, Dec. 19—President Truman made it clear today that price edicts issued by the Economic Stabilization Agency would be made to stick.

The law will be enforced, the President said, when asked at a news conference what General Motors would have to conform to the agency's price freeze and roll-back on 1951 cars to Dec. 1 levels.

General Motors, which declared the price order discriminatory yesterday, suspended sales of all 1951 model Chevrolet, Pontiac and Cadillac cars.

The company's request today for modification of the order issued by Alan Valentine, Economic Stabilizer, is understood to have been rejected by the agency.

The Ford Motor Company today voluntarily informed Mr. Valentine that it had rescinded its price increases effective midnight Dec. 17 and would also refund to dealers increased charges on cars still in their hands.

Mr. Valentine immediately wired the Ford Company commending it for "patriotic compliance with Ceiling Price Regulation No. 1." He assured the company that "prompt compliance with a regulation will never be permitted to operate to the disadvantage of any seller."

"The price rollback order was issued by Mr. Valentine under his authority conveyed in the defense production act of 1950. This law grants him authority to freeze or roll back prices and wages.

At his news conference today the President, in reply to a question, said that the price of General Motors cars would be set at whatever level the stabilization director said they should be. As for Government action to lift the sales ban the President remarked that his officials would cross that bridge when they got to it.

Meanwhile Walter P. Reuther, president of the United Automobile Workers of America, C. I. O.,

Continued on Page 22. Column 3

GOVERNMENT SEEKS VOLUNTARY FREEZE AT PRICES OF DEC. 1

Such a Ceiling Would Confine Profits Within Scope of '46-'49 Average Return

'AVOID MANDATORY CURBS'

20 Per Cent Cutback in Tin Ordered Starting Feb. 1— Wage Controls Studied

By CHARLES E. EGAN
Special to The New York Times.

WASHINGTON, Dec. 19—Business and industry today were asked to observe a voluntary price ceiling that would confine profits within the scope of the average 1946-49 returns and keep prices to consumers in the neighborhood of the Dec. 1 levels of this year.

In an outline of "pricing standards" the Economic Stabilization Agency asked nation-wide compliance on a voluntary basis "to avoid the necessity of further mandatory price controls."

The voluntary regulations, it was added, are sufficiently elastic to allow for normal profits and to encourage initiative in industry.

The price agency, which cannot invoke a formal and general price freeze without also imposing ceilings on wages, made no request for voluntary wage ceilings today. Spokesmen for the agency said, however, that the Wage Stabilization Board of the agency was now at work on a wage control announcement.

Agencies Adjust Plans

The tempo of enforcement orders increased visibly yesterday as various governmental defense agencies adjusted their operations to President Truman's declaration of a national emergency Saturday.

The E. S. A. turned down its request to West Coast oil refineries to rescind a recent price increase of 25 cents a barrel for crude oil, summoned representatives of the companies to Washington to meet with agency officials Thursday to justify the increase.

The summons recalled that sent to the Ford Motor Company and General Motors recently to suspend the effectiveness of price rises averaging 5 per cent on 1951 lines. The motor people, who also refused, were summoned to Washington, and when they still declined to give ground were ordered by the agency to roll back their quotations to Dec. 1 levels.

The National Production Authority announced today that it had ordered users of tin to cut back the amount of that scarce metal used for civilian products by 20 per cent commencing Feb. 1. The mandatory curtailment, it was said, presages other orders from the same agency barring the use of tin in such items as canned beers, lubricating oil cans, salted nuts and similar items.

Representatives of the food industry said the order, although milder than the tin cutbacks in the last war could conceivably bring on rationing of canned foods. In the last war, it was declared, the shortage of tin rather than peaches, pears and other tinned products, forced the rationing of such canned goods.

In its appeal for a voluntary price ceiling today the E. S. A. served notice on business and industry generally that it would scrutinize any price increases made since Dec. 1 to see if they were permissible as follows:

"1. Prices may not be increased if

Continued on Page 25, Column 1

Jane's Says Soviet Speeds War Fleet

Special to The New York Times.

LONDON, Dec. 19—Soviet Union is hastening to increase its naval strength, which, according to Jane's Fighting Ships for 1950-51, is "far in excess of the normal requirements of defense."

According to the naval annual published tomorrow the Soviet Union last March launched a sister ship to the 35,800-ton battleship Sovyetski Soyuz. This ship has six 16-inch guns, sixty small anti-aircraft guns and two batteries for guided missiles fired from towers, according to Jane's. A third new battleship, slightly larger, is still on the stocks, Jane's said.

The Soviet target of 1,000 submarines in service by the end of 1951 is regarded here as alarming. Jane's estimates that the Soviet Union now has between 350 and 370 submarines.

PRESIDENT REFUSES TO DISMISS ACHESON

He Stoutly Defends Secretary as Foremost Foe of Reds— Republicans Attacked

Special to The New York Times.

WASHINGTON, Dec. 19—President Truman asserted today that Secretary of State Dean Acheson was the foremost anti-Communist in the Government and made a sharp attack on his Republican critics. He said that he had no intention of dismissing the Secretary.

This was the President's reply to the Republicans in the Senate and the House who formally called last week for the ousting of Mr. Acheson. Mr. Truman delivered it at a news conference.

He denounced Mr. Acheson's opponents for what he said were slanderous and vicious attacks on the Secretary during the election campaign. This was not the way that a two-party system should work, he added.

Mr. Truman likened the demand for Mr. Acheson's dismissal to one made by a group of Republicans on President Lincoln for the removal of his Secretary of State, William H. Seward. Lincoln refused, and Mr. Truman asserted

Continued on Page 9, Column 1

BEACHHEAD IS HELD

Regrouped Korean Foes Battered by Navy Fire —Airfield Yielded

CENTRAL SECTOR FLARES

Eighth Army Reports Enemy Is Attacking Both North and South of Parallel

By LINDESAY PARROTT
Special to The New York Times.

TOKYO, Wednesday, Dec. 20—Despite the commitment of reconstituted North Korean forces, Communist attempts to breach the United Nations lines around the Hungnam beachhead failed yesterday.

The Chinese were believed to have pushed the North Koreans forward after having taken enormous losses since the beginning of the northeast campaign around the Changjin Reservoir where the United States First Marine Division staged its epic breakout. Some estimates placed the Chinese dead as high as 30,000 to 40,000—possibly one-third of the total invading force in this area.

Reports from the front said three North Korean divisions were aligned along the shrinking beachhead around Hungnam where United States soldiers fought with their backs to the Sea of Japan.

The North Koreans thrust small-scale but aggressive attacks against the northeastern sector of the Allied salient. All attacks were reported to have been beaten off under the fire of naval guns, massed artillery on the ground and repeated air attacks.

Fighting in Kaesong Area

In the West, South Korean troops were in "strong contact" with "identified" units of the new North Korean army north and south of the Thirty-eighth Parallel along a thirty-mile front north of Chunchon, near the center of the peninsula, an Eighth Army spokesman said.

Thirty miles north of Seoul a two-hour firefight occurred along the Imjin River, one of the few natural barriers in the region of the Parallel. [An Associated Press dispatch from Korea said the firefight had taken place about fifteen miles east of Kaesong and that the

Continued on Page 9, Column 1

EISENHOWER HEADS WEST'S ARMY; ALLIED PRODUCTION BOARD SET UP; NEW RED BLOWS IN KOREA PARRIED

AN ALLIED COMMANDER ONCE MORE

Gen. Dwight D. Eisenhower in St. Louis yesterday after his appointment as supreme commander of the Allied Army to defend Western Europe.

Associated Press Wirephoto

Truman Will Send More Men To Europe as Soon as He Can

By ANTHONY LEVIERO
Special to The New York Times.

WASHINGTON, Dec. 19—President Truman, in designating Gen. Dwight D. Eisenhower as supreme commander of the Western forces in Europe, declared today that additional United States troops would be sent there as soon as possible.

The historic action will take the victor of World War II to the old battlefields early in January. His mission will be to build a force much like the one that triumphed on V-E Day in a concerted effort by the North Atlantic Treaty nations to prevent World War III by being strong.

The White House announced the appointment at 6:30 o'clock this morning—an hour selected to permit the announcement's issuance simultaneously in Western Europe at an hour that would have maximum publicity effect.

[General Eisenhower, in St. Louis on his way to Denver for the holidays, said he was "hopeful of preserving the peace" in the European defense post, which, he added, was unlike his World War II job because the new command had "no belligerent purpose."]

Mr. Truman acted after he had been informed in a telegram from Dean Acheson, Secretary of State, in Brussels, that the North Atlantic Council meeting there had "completed arrangements for the establishment of an integrated European defense force." Mr. Acheson said the member nations had expressed "their earnest hope" that General Eisenhower would be selected for the top leadership role. In his reply, Mr. Truman said: "Pursuant to the request of the

Continued on Page 6, Column 3

WU FLIES FOR HOME AFTER ACCUSING U.N.

Chinese Red Wishes Americans Merry Christmas, Happy New Year but Charges 'Plot'

By WALTER SULLIVAN
Special to The New York Times.

LAKE SUCCESS, Dec. 19—Wu Hsiu-chuan, Communist China's first envoy to the Western world, abandoned his efforts at the United Nations today and flew home with his eight aides. Thus he bracketed Formosa with the Korean problem. Any "device" that reversed the process, requiring a Korean cease-fire first, was "nothing but a trickery and a plot," he said.

Mr. Wu saw one of the three

Continued on Page 14, Column 5

ATLANTIC PLAN SET

Western Big 3 Will Ask Bonn Tomorrow to Join Nations in Defense

NOTES TO SOVIET DRAFTED

Allies to Agree to Four-Power Talks if Not Restricted to All-German Agenda

By C. L. SULZBERGER
Special to The New York Times.

BRUSSELS, Belgium, Dec. 19—The North Atlantic Council appointed Gen. Dwight D. Eisenhower today as commander of the defense force of the Western world.

Before the council ended its sixth session, it also established a new production board to supervise the economic aspects of the West's productive measures. It agreed to study means for the allocation of available raw materials in the world and for insuring a fair distribution among the democratic powers.

In other words, the groundwork for the "total defense" of peace in Europe was laid down.

The Federated Republic of Western Germany will be approached Thursday by the Allied High Commissioners on its attitude toward associating itself with the North Atlantic Treaty powers in the common defense of Europe.

This was decided tonight at a meeting of Secretary of State Dean Acheson, Foreign Secretary Ernest Bevin and Foreign Minister Robert Schuman. Immediately afterward they asked the political advisers of their commissioners to arrange technical details for this week's discussion.

3 Ministers' Talks Harmonious

The Western Big Three talk was briefer than had been expected and certainly was more harmonious than some participants had foreseen. It activated the accords previously approved by the Atlantic council, specifying the terms under which the Bonn regime would be invited to contribute to continental defense.

These include revision of the existing Occupation Statute, permission for Germany to organize infantry units in brigade-group form up to 6,000 men and supported by some tactical air power, and a general equalization of Germany's political status in the direction of contractual relationships.

A communiqué published after the Western Big Three talks said the High Commissioners had been asked, together with the Bonn Government, to "explore this problem" of joining on the Atlantic Council's terms, "as well as any changes in the present occupation arrangements which might logically attend a German defense contribution."

Unofficial German observers here regard the choice of the word "explore" as especially happy and implying more equality between victor and vanquished than had previously been acknowledged.

Moscow Notes Agreed On

It is clear that the West intends to offer Germany a swift equality with the Western Allied powers if, in turn, Bonn pledges full cooperation.

Meanwhile, the three Western Ministers also agreed on the text of their notes to Moscow replying to a Soviet request for a four-party foreign ministers' meeting on Germany. It is not yet known what the wording of the answer is, but it is thought that agreement in principle is given on condition that the agenda items will not be strictly limited to Germany.

Thus end forty-eight hectic hours of international talks in Brussels. Secretary Acheson hopes to be able to leave for Washington early tomorrow, depending on the weather. Mr. Bevin and M. Schuman will remain here tomorrow to discuss with the Belgian, Netherland and Luxembourg delegations on an national basis the structure of General Eisenhower's over-all defense command.

Many of the more important participants in the mass discussions have left Brussels to start

Continued on Page 16, Column 3

Fire Delays 55,000 on 2 Railroads As Truck Dives to Tracks in Bronx

Fifty-five thousand persons, all but 10 per cent of them commuters, were delayed from five minutes to nearly two hours yesterday morning after a twenty-ton meat truck plunged thirty feet from the street level onto the tracks of the New York Central and New York, New Haven & Hartford Railroads in the Bronx.

The tie-up was caused when the aluminum-covered truck apparently went out of control just before 5 A. M. on a 30 to 45 degree slope of St. Paul's Place between Washington and Park Avenues. The police believe that the driver, whom they identified as Fred Davidson of Philadelphia, was lost, since St. Paul's Place is not a street on the regular route he was traveling.

As the story was reconstructed, the driver found himself out of control on the slope and in attempting to halt his vehicle skidded 100 feet and virtually demolished two parked automobiles.

The truck sped west toward Park Avenue, it was said, the

to Grand Central from the junction in the Woodlawn section of the Bronx. Twelve of the incoming trains were said to be long distance trains.

The accident, in which the truck driver was burned to death, affected travelers aboard 103 rush-hour trains—thirty outbound from Grand Central Terminal and seventy-three inbound, carrying passengers from upper New York State, Connecticut, Rhode Island, Massachusetts and Maine.

Officials of the New York Central System estimated that aboard the inbound trains were 45,000 persons on their way to business. Thirty-four rush trains were operated by the New York Central and the others by the New Haven, which uses the New York Central tracks

Continued on Page 60, Column 1

World News Summarized

WEDNESDAY, DECEMBER 20, 1950

General Eisenhower was appointed Commander of Allied forces in Europe by the North Atlantic Council, which also decided to create an international defense production board to supervise economic aspects of Continental defense and agreed to study a fair allocation of raw materials. West Germany will be approached tomorrow on how Germany "might assume" a role in Europe's defense. Secretary Acheson, British Foreign Secretary Bevin and French Foreign Minister Schuman agreed on a note to Moscow in reply to its suggestion for a Big Four conference. [1:8.]

The appointment came after President Truman had designated General Eisenhower for the post. He will have full command of all United States forces in Europe, including reinforcements promised by the President, and operational command over the other North Atlantic forces in Europe. [1:6-7.] The general named Lieut. Gen. Gruenther his Chief of Staff and will leave in ten days for a preliminary trip to Paris. [12:3.] General Eisenhower was granted an indefinite leave of absence as president of Columbia University. [13:3.]

The British expected the Eisenhower appointment to spur Europe's rearming [11:3-4.] and the French hoped it would clarify the role to be played by the Germans. [20:3.] The cautious tone of the North Atlantic Council's communiqué disappointed United States officials in Germany and the German Socialist leader. [11:2.]

Greatly strengthened North Korean forces took up battle posts on all fronts. Allied troops maintained their Hungnam beachhead and gave up the Yonpo airfield. [1:5; map P. 2.] Peiping's representative to the United Nations, having received no instructions to negotiate a cease-fire, left for home after wishing the "American people" a Merry Christmas and denouncing Anglo-American "aggression." [1:6.]

President Truman defended Secretary Acheson against Republican attacks and again refused to dismiss him. [1:4.]

General Motors will sell its cars at whatever levels the Stabilization Director says they should be sold, the President said. [1:2.] The Government asked business to adopt voluntary price ceilings based on a 1946-49 average profit or fixed mandatory controls. [1:3.]

Five more Air National Guard groups have been called to Federal duty. [1:6-7.]

Governor Dewey ordered curbs on nonessential services and in filling new posts to put the state on an emergency basis. [1:1.]

The Senate passed and sent to the White House the Yugoslav famine-aid bill. [12:5.]

This city's $415,141,303 capital budget was approved by the City Council. [35:1.]

NEWS BULLETINS FROM THE TIMES
Every hour on the hour
7 A.M. through Midnight
WQXR AM 1560
WQXR FM 96.3

Index to other news appears on last page of this section.

Five Air Guard Groups Called Up For Active Duty Beginning Feb. 1

By AUSTIN STEVENS
Special to The New York Times.

WASHINGTON, Dec. 19—The Air Force today ordered five additional Air National Guard groups to Federal duty, presumably for assignment to defense of the continental United States.

Five more Air National Guard groups have been called to Federal duty. [1:6-7.]

Guard air groups at full strength number about 1,500 men and have either forty-eight or seventy-five planes, depending on whether they are light bomber or fighter units.

Gen. Hoyt S. Vandenberg, Air Force Chief of Staff, announced that the call-up was effective Feb. 1. An Air Force spokesman said later that an effort would be made to notify the guardsmen involved by Jan. 1.

Security considerations prevented release of the designations of the groups, their present bases or where they would be assigned. However, it has been known that Air Force planners have contemplated using the Guard increasing-

ly to bolster the nation's air defense network—the combination of radar detection and fighter planes based in areas believed most subject to attack.

Air National Guard fighter groups, totaling at the start of the Korean fighting twenty-seven, are at somewhat better than 75 per cent of authorized strength on a national basis. The tactical units had some 2,700 aircraft, ranging from World War II fighters and medium bombers to F-80 jet fighters and the later type F-84 jet fighter.

A typical fighter group at full strength would consist of three squadrons of twenty-five planes each with added "spares." The 1,500-personnel strength would include communications sections, servicing, base squadron, main-

Continued on Page 29, Column 1

100TH ANNIVERSARY
"All the News
That's Fit to Print"
1851   1951

The New York Times.

LATE CITY EDITION
Fair today, increasing cloudiness
tomorrow and mild both days.
Temperatures Range Today—Max., 60; Min., 45
Temperatures Yesterday—Max., 45; Min., 48
Full U. S. Weather Bureau Report, Page 50

Copyright, 1951, by The New York Times Company.

VOL. C. No. 34,045.

Entered as Second-Class Matter,
Post Office, New York, N. Y.

NEW YORK, WEDNESDAY, APRIL 11, 1951.

Times Square, New York 18, N. Y.
Telephone LAckawanna 4-1000

RAG PAPER EDITION
SEVENTY-FIVE CENTS

TRUMAN RELIEVES M'ARTHUR OF ALL HIS POSTS; FINDS HIM UNABLE TO BACK U. S.-U. N. POLICIES; RIDGWAY NAMED TO FAR EASTERN COMMANDS

HOUSE VOTES U. M. T. ONLY AS A PROGRAM; MARSHALL WORRIED

Chamber Accepts Compromise Setting Up Commission to Draft Details of Plan

FUTURE LAW IS REQUIRED

Congress' Approval Is Needed to Start Universal Training— General Sees Risk in This

By JOHN D. MORRIS
Special to The New York Times.

WASHINGTON, April 10—Concessions offered by advocates of Universal Military Training to save the program from outright rejection were approved today by the House of Representatives, but it remained to be seen whether the aim had been achieved.

General of the Army George C. Marshall, Secretary of Defense, meanwhile voiced the fear that current maneuvering in the House might "largely emasculate" the training features of the pending draft and training bill.

It was not clear, however, whether he was concerned over the main fight, expected later this week, over a proposal to eliminate all Universal Military Training provisions from the bill.

It was to head this off that the bill's managers headed by Representative Carl Vinson, Democrat of Georgia, offered the concessions that were approved today. The House accepted them on a voice vote.

Further Action Necessary

Consequently, as the bill now stands, little more than the principle of Universal Military Training is retained. A commission to draw up a detailed U. M. T. plan would be created. A "National Security Training Corps" would also be established, at least on paper.

But before anyone could be drafted to serve in the proposed corps, there would have to be another formal act of Congress, subject to Presidential approval or veto like any other bill, authorizing details of the training program.

At the same time, however, the revised bill retains safeguards against future pigeon-holing of U. M. T. in the House Rules Committee or elsewhere. The planning commission, which also would administer the program once Congress had authorized its institution, would be required to submit a detailed training plan to Congress within six months. The House and Senate Armed Services Committees would be required to report out a bill or resolution within forty-five days of receiving the plan. The measure then could be called up at any time.

Opponents Withhold Attack

In the House, bills ordinarily must be cleared by the Rules Committee before they can be considered on the floor. The Rules Committee bottled up a Universal Military Training Bill in the Eightieth Congress.

Opponents of any form of U. M. T. legislation did not fight the concessions approved in the House today, explaining that the proposals would make the bill less obnoxious although still unacceptable to them.

They were still hoping for approval of a substitute sponsored by Representative Graham A. Barden, Democrat of North Carolina, that would retain only what they regard as the "emergency" features of the pending draft measure. These include a three-year extension of authority to draft men 19 through 26 years of age for actual military service.

The Barden bill would eliminate authority to lower the draft age to 18½ as well as all long-range training features of the pending measure.

The Senate has already passed a draft and training bill adhering closely to the Administration's recommendations. It would authorize the drafting of men at the age of 18 and permit the President to put Universal Military Training

Continued on Page 18, Column 4

Tobey Asserts He Recorded R. F. C. Talks With Truman

President Said to Withdraw Fee Accusation—Niles Held Attempting to Aid Dawson

By C. P. TRUSSELL
Special to The New York Times.

WASHINGTON, April 10—Senator Charles W. Tobey, Republican of New Hampshire, was represented tonight as having told the Senate (Fulbright) subcommittee investigating the Reconstruction Finance Corporation that President Truman had charged in a telephone conversation with him that members of Congress had accepted fees for obtaining R. F. C. loans for constituents.

The Senator was said to have reported also that in a later telephonic communication the President had said that he had been mistaken.

Both telephonic conversations were said to have been recorded on disks in Mr. Tobey's possession. The date, or dates, were not made public. The Senator declined to discuss the matter and members of the investigating group also were silent.

In another development in the R. F. C. inquiry, former Senator Burton K. Wheeler, Democrat of

Burton K. Wheeler
Associated Press

Montana, said today that he had asked Senator Tobey to "go easy on" Donald S. Dawson, a White House aide, during the Senate investigation of the agency. Mr. Wheeler asserted that he acted as

Continued on Page 25, Column 3

Sterling Hayden Was a Red; 'Stupidest Thing I Ever Did'

Special to The New York Times.

WASHINGTON, April 10—Sterling Hayden, motion picture actor and decorated former United States Marine, told the House Committee on Un-American Activities today that he had been a member of the Communist party from June to December of 1946.

"It was the stupidest and most ignorant thing I ever did in my life," he said. "I went into it with an emotional and very unsound approach, but I don't mean to imply that I was dragged into it. I went in voluntarily."

Mr. Hayden, a native of Montclair, N. J., said there were thousands of others like him, who should come in and tell their stories.

He added that shortly after the invasion of South Korea his attorney had written to J. Edgar Hoover, director of the Federal Bureau of Investigation, giving his Communist case history and seeking a means of eliminating any prejudice against his recall to the service.

Under questioning for more than three hours, the former husband of Madeleine Carroll, screen star, told of a restless life that started with his quitting high school at the age of fifteen and going to sea, and winding up in Hollywood. A Capt. Warwich Tompkins, described by him as an "open and avowed Communist," ran through his story.

He identified Captain Tompkins as an employe of Amtorg, the of-

Continued on Page 14, Column 5

PRICE AIDE RESIGNS, CONDEMNS DI SALLE

M. E. Thompson, Ex-Governor of Georgia, Hits 'Kansas City Crowd' in Administration

Special to The New York Times.

WASHINGTON, April 10—With bitter words for Price Stabilizer Michael V. DiSalle, and for the "Kansas City crowd" he said was in the saddle in the national Administration, M. E. Thompson, former Governor of Georgia, resigned today as a consultant to the Office of Price Stabilization.

Mr. Thompson, once a power in Georgia politics, and who asserted that he battled successfully against the States Righters there who tried to keep President Truman's name off the ballot in 1948, declared that he would not support the Democratic party in 1952 if the "Kansas City crowd" still held control.

"If this be political treason,

Continued on Page 20, Column 1

Navy Suspends Explosives Expert; State Department Then Bars Wife

Special to The New York Times.

WASHINGTON, April 10—The Navy Department suspended Dr. Stephen Brunauer today as a "security risk," giving the 47-year-old high explosives expert thirty days in which to answer the charges.

The State Department meanwhile suspended Mrs. Esther Caukin Brunauer, wife of the Navy scientist, pending the outcome of the investigation of her husband. The State Department made it plain in a statement that the action against Mrs. Brunauer was based not on information about her, but only as a result of the Navy suspension.

Both of the Brunauers were named by Senator Joseph R. McCarthy, Republican of Wisconsin, in the course of his charges last year of Communist infiltration of the Government.

The announcement of Dr. Brunauer's suspension, effective immediately, was made while he was on a trip to New England for the Navy. Questioned by reporters at LaGuardia Field, on his way back to the capital, he said:

"I do not know for what reason I was suspended. I think some one made a mistake. I telephoned Washington and a Navy spokesman said he did not know the reason for the suspension. I do not want to comment further on anything."

Mrs. Brunauer issued a stout denial of the McCarthy charges on March 13, 1950, defending herself and her husband against the allegations they were Communists.

The Navy announcement of her suspension of Dr. Brunauer followed the disclosure by the State Department that the action had already taken place. The Navy gave no details of the charges, but said that Dr. Brunauer would have thirty days to answer the charges and request a hearing.

The decision of Francis P. Matthews, Secretary of the Navy, will be final, it was said.

Asked whether the suspension of Mrs. Brunauer in response to charges against her husband was

Continued on Page 16, Column 3

RISE IN SALES TAX EXPECTED TO PASS CITY COUNCIL TODAY

Finance Committee Studies Bill at Length—Fight Against Measure Goes On

RUML A FISCAL ADVISER

Mayor Declines Challenge to Debate With Hoving—Joseph Suggests State-Wide Levy

The finance committee of the City Council spent an inconclusive three-hour executive session at City Hall yesterday afternoon weighing the merits of the proposed increase in the retail sales tax from 2 to 3 per cent, but when the meeting ended nothing had changed the prospect that the tax rise would be approved.

It was indicated that today the committee, after further behind-closed-doors deliberations, would favor the sales impost rise by a vote of 8 to 2, or possibly 9 to 3, and that later today the full City Council would adopt the measure by something like 19 to 6.

If the tax bill clears the Council hurdles today, as is indicated, it is expected that the Board of Estimate, whose members are committed to it, will give its approval at tomorrow's regular meeting.

Meanwhile, Controller Lazarus Joseph announced the appointment of Beardsley Ruml, business consultant, financier and economist, as a special deputy controller to advise Mr. Joseph on fiscal matters. Mr. Ruml, whose appointment was for an "indefinite" tenure, will serve without pay.

Mr. Ruml was at one time connected with the Federal Reserve Board and also with the New York Stock Exchange. He is a

Continued on Page 32, Column 4

U. S. PRODS NATIONS

Suggests U. N. Members Send More Troops to Fight in Korea

3 AVENUES ARE LISTED

Contributions Sought From Nations Not Yet Committed

By A. M. ROSENTHAL
Special to The New York Times.

UNITED NATIONS, N. Y., April 10—The United States has been quietly suggesting that members of the United Nations increase, or at least maintain, their contributions of troops for the Korean war effort.

Informed sources here report that for some time the United States has been keeping in touch with members of the world organization to see if non-United States representation in the international army could be increased.

[Chinese Communist troops in Korea clung to their positions along the Hwachon Reservoir in the face of daylong United Nations attacks. Eighth Army headquarters clamped a stringent security blackout on news from the front as a major battle seemed to impend in the reservoir area.]

So far there has been no general appeal to the United Nations members to contribute more troops; it has all been on a country-to-country basis. Diplomats said that there was no indication that a new general request for troops in Korea was in the making.

But on a longer-range basis, the question of more troops may be considered by the committee set up by the General Assembly on Feb. 1 to plan possible sanctions

Continued on Page 5, Column 3

World News Summarized

WEDNESDAY, APRIL 11, 1951

President Truman relieved General of the Army MacArthur of his command in the Pacific because the United Nations commander had been unable to give his "wholehearted support" to United States and United Nations policies. The Presidential ouster has forced the general from all his commands, including his role in the occupation of Japan. Lieut. Gen. Matthew B. Ridgway has been designated to take over all the Far Eastern commands. [1:8.]

The United States has been asking other United Nations members to increase, or at least maintain, their forces fighting in Korea and asking for troops from countries that have sent none. [1:5.]

Enemy resistance increased in the Hwachon Reservoir area of Korea. The Communists still held the dam although Hwachon itself appeared deserted. [3:1; map P. 2.] Mao Tse-tung was said to have been officially reported ill and Liu Shao-chi was said to be acting in his place at the head of the Chinese Communist regime. [9:2.]

Britain has suggested that the United States invite Communist China to the discussions on a Japanese peace treaty and send Peiping a draft of the proposed pact. The treaty, Britain holds, should include the return of Formosa to China. [1:6-7.]

Senator Tobey was said to have disclosed that he had recorded telephone talks with President Truman about the Senate R. F. C. inquiry. [1:2-3.]

The Navy suspended Dr. Stephen Brunauer, a scientist, as a "security risk" and the State Department dropped his wife, Esther, until the husband's case was settled. [1:2-3.]

chose to increase taxes, already heavy, rather than cut social welfare funds. [1:7.]

The bill giving West German labor equal rights with management in the operation of the steel and coal industries was passed by the lower house. [14:2.]

The House passed and sent to the Senate a supplemental defense money bill 43 per cent below Administration requests [29:1] and cut from the draft bill a provision for Universal Military Training in favor of a Presidential commission to draw detailed plans. [1:1.] Defense Secretary Marshall ordered all three armed services to share equitably drafters of superior standing. [19:3.]

Mobilization Director Wilson called for an end to complacency, selfishness and partisanship if we are to beat down the "dreadful shadow" of history's most "absolute and ruthless" dictatorship. [23:1.] M. E. Thompson resigned as consultant to the Price Stabilizer in protest against "political" control and general wastefulness. [1:2.]

Organized baseball was ordered not to raise players' salaries above a club's 1950 highest. [33:2-3.] The Army ruled certain pay rises for nonoperating rail workers until a special panel ruled in the case. [33:1.]

The days of "easy and automatic" relations between the United States and Canada are over, Canada's External Affairs Minister declared. "There will be frictions," he said, "that can be settled easily, he said, if the United States recognizes that Canadian leadership does not mean she is willing to be merely an echo of somebody else's voice." [1:6-7.]

A "severe, but not crippling" budget was presented to Britain by the Labor Government, which

NEWS BULLETINS FROM THE TIMES
Every hour on the hour
7 A.M. until Midnight
WQXR AM 1560
WQXR FM 96.3

Index to other news appears on last page of this section.

DISMISSED BY THE PRESIDENT

General of the Army Douglas MacArthur

Britain Asks That Red China Have Role in Japanese Pact

By WALTER H. WAGGONER
Special to The New York Times.

WASHINGTON, April 10—Britain has suggested to the United States that Communist China be brought into the negotiations for a Japanese peace treaty. The British proposal also specifically asked that the United States send a copy of its treaty draft to the Peiping regime for its consideration and, further, that the treaty provide for the ultimate if not immediate return of Formosa to "China."

By "China" the British mean the regime of Mao Tse-tung, since that is the China now recognized by London.

These suggestions have been made in the course of recent conversations between the two Governments. They represent another difference of opinion that has developed between London and Washington on both the procedure for negotiating a Japanese treaty and the form the settlement should have.

The basis for the British request that Peiping be given a look at the United States treaty draft is to enable the Chinese Communists to reject the proposal if they want to, as the Soviet Union is expected to do.

At the same time, it is vigorously denied here that Britain would refuse to sign any treaty draft that Communist China rejects. Reports that such an "or else" position has

Continued on Page 8, Column 5

BUDGET INCREASES BRITONS' TAX LOAD

Income, Profit, Purchase, Auto and Gasoline Imposts Rise —Social Services Uncut

By RAYMOND DANIELL

LONDON, April 10—The already heavily burdened British people were called upon today to pay even higher taxes to preserve their welfare state. Hugh Gaitskell, Chancellor of the Exchequer, introducing his first budget, told the House of Commons that there were only two ways of meeting the extra cost of rearmament. One, which brought cheers from the Conservative Opposition, was by reducing expenditures for social welfare.

The alternative he adopted was a sharp rise in both direct and indirect taxes. This brought cheers

Continued on Page 8, Column 5

PRESIDENT MOVES

Van Fleet Is Named to Command 8th Army in Drastic Shift

VIOLATIONS ARE CITED

White House Statement Quotes Directives and Implies Breaches

Texts of statements and orders in MacArthur dispute, Page 8.

By W. H. LAWRENCE
Special to The New York Times.

WASHINGTON, Wednesday, April 11—President Truman early today relieved General of the Army Douglas MacArthur of all his commands in the Far East and appointed Lieut. Gen. Matthew B. Ridgway as his successor.

The President said he had relieved General MacArthur "with deep regret" because he had concluded that the Far Eastern Commander "is unable to give his wholehearted support to the policies of the United States Government and of the United Nations in matters pertaining to his official duties.

General MacArthur, in a message to House Minority Leader Joseph W. Martin Jr. of Massachusetts, made public by Mr. Martin last Thursday, had publicly challenged the President's foreign policy, urging that the United States concentrate on Asia instead of Europe and use Generalissimo Chiang Kai-shek's Formosa-based troops to open a second front on the mainland of China.

The change in command is effective at once. General Ridgway, who has been in command of the Eighth Army in Korea since the death in December of Gen. Walton H. Walker, assumes all of General MacArthur's titles—Supreme Commander, United Nations Forces in Korea, Supreme Commander for Allied Powers, Japan, Commander-in-Chief, Far East, and Commanding General U. S. Army, Far East.

Commanded in Greece

The Eighth Army command will pass to Lieut. Gen. James A. Van Fleet whose most recent important command was as head of the American military mission in Greece, when that country was repelling a Communist-directed guerrilla attack under the Truman doctrine.

In ousting General MacArthur for his public disagreement with American policy designed to localize the Asiatic war, the President said:

"Full and vigorous debate on matters of national policy is a vital element in the Constitutional system of our free democracy.

"It is fundamental, however, that military commanders must be governed by the policies and directives issued to them in the manner provided by our laws and Con-

Continued on Page 8, Column 1

News Stuns Tokyo; MacArthur Is Silent

By The Associated Press

TOKYO, Wednesday, April 11—A small brown envelope with "flash" printed on it in red carried the news that he had been discharged from his commands by President Truman.

It was delivered by a senior aide, Col. Sid Huff, who said that the General received the news without comment. Colonel Huff indicated that the General had no forewarning that he was being relieved.

The General announced that he would have no statement immediately.

The message came as a Signal Corps communication about the time and Army radio announced the news.

General MacArthur got the word while at lunch with his wife, Senator Warren G. Mag-

Continued on Page 8, Column 4

Canada Bars a 'Yes' Role to U. S.; Pearson Sees Unity Despite Friction

By The United Press

TORONTO, April 10—Lester B. Pearson, Canadian Secretary for External Affairs, said today that "easy and automatic" relations between Canada and the United States were a thing of the past.

In a speech apparently aimed at United States consumption, Mr. Pearson said that Canada was not willing to be "merely an echo of somebody else's voice" and reserved the right to criticize "our great friend, the United States."

Mr. Pearson said that Canada would march forward with the United States "in the pursuit of objectives which we share."

"Nevertheless, the days of relatively easy and automatic relations with our neighbor are, I think, over," he added.

Mr. Pearson indicated that one of the "angry waves" that could weaken relations between Canada and the United States was the controversy over General of the Army Douglas MacArthur's statement on the war in Korea.

Later, in a second speech, Mr. Pearson made an indirect reference to General MacArthur when he said that a successful foreign policy must work toward goals accepted by the majority of the people, and it would have a better chance of "reaching these goals if we abandon what has been discribed "hoop-la diplomacy" at Lake Success, at Ottawa, or, I hasten to add, at Tokyo."

He said that the free nations stood in danger of "nothing less

Continued on Page 6, Column 3

100TH ANNIVERSARY
"All the News
That's Fit to Print"
1851   1951

The New York Times.

LATE CITY EDITION
Partly cloudy, mild today; cooler tonight. Rain likely tomorrow.
Temperature Range Today—Max., 70 ; Min., 55
Temperatures Yesterday—Max., 70 ; Min., 47
Full U. S. Weather Bureau Report, Page 33

Copyright, 1951, by The New York Times Company

VOL. CI . No. 34,244.

Entered as Second-Class Matter,
Post Office, New York, N. Y.

NEW YORK, SATURDAY, OCTOBER 27, 1951.

Times Square, New York 18, N. Y.
Telephone LAckawanna 4-1000

RAG PAPER EDITION
SEVENTY-FIVE CENTS

TRUMAN PLEA TO PIER MEN IS UNHEEDED

TAFT LAW IGNORED

President Rejects Move by Industry After Talk With the Cabinet

BASES CALL ON DEFENSE

Insurgents Say No National Emergency Was Declared—Attack 'Unfair Verdict'

By GEORGE HORNE

President Truman appealed to New York waterfront strikers last night to return to work in behalf of the defense effort but the defiant strike committee immediately rejected th> plea and called for widening of the costly stoppage.

The President, to whom Cyrus S. Ching, director of the Federal Mediation and Conciliation Service, had referred the dispute, discussed it with the Cabinet before making his decision not to accede to the demands of industrial leaders to invoke the procedure of the Taft-Hartley Act.

Mr. Truman said he had been informed that defense activity was being hampered and that "in the national interest" the employes ought to get back to their tasks.

The twelve-day strike started in a handful of locals on Oct. 15 and snowballed under pressure of roaming wildcat squads until it paralyzed the vast Port of New York, spread to Boston, halted work on military shipments and piled up cargoes entrained in value at nearly $300,000,000.

Demanded Pact Reopening

The intransigent strikers demanded reopening of a contract that had been negotiated through weeks of discussion with employers and was finally ratified by a 2-to-1 vote of the union's membership.

The new contract of the International Longshoremen's Association, A. F. L., and the New York Shipping Association, provided a 10-cent increase to make the basic hourly wage $2.10. It stipulated improvements in vacation terms, a single shape-up or work-call a day and other benefits which the majority of the union's 125-man wage committee approved and recommended.

Announcement of the plea from the White House was followed within ten or fifteen minutes by the insurgent rejection. John J. (Gene) Sampson, business agent of Local 791, spearhead local in the strike, said that the strikers would not accept the President's proposal since he had not seen fit to declare a national emergency. The President could have invoked the Taft-Hartley Act despite the fact that the walkout involved an intra-union matter and not a labor-management dispute in which no contract existed. Moreover, he could have used a Wage Stabilization Board dispute procedure on a matter affecting national defense.

He had been urged by industrial and business associations and individuals in New York and New Jersey to apply the former procedure on the grounds that the stoppage was causing the layoff of thousands of workers other than the 30,000 affected longshoremen and immobilizing ships, cargo and investments mounting into millions of dollars.

Two-Day Intercession Failed

Mr. Ching had sent the dispute to the White House following withdrawal of the Federal mediation agency after a boisterous and futile two-day intercession in New York.

Clyde M. Mills, No. 1 Ching aide and a trouble-shooter for the agency, had headed a commissioner's panel in New York in efforts to end the union's "family quarrel." The mediation men called it an "intolerable situation," a phrase that heightened the bitter feeling of recalcitrant strike leaders who described the Mills withdrawal announcement as unfair and tantamount to a verdict of guilt.

The text of Mr. Truman's statement follows:

"I have been informed by Mr. Charles E. Wilson, of the Office of Defense Mobilization, that because of the work stoppages in the ports of New

Continued on Page 22, Column 2

Marciano Knocks Out Louis in 8th Round

Rocky Marciano, 27-year-old Brockton, Mass., boxer, became a leading contender for the world heavyweight championship when he knocked out Joe Louis, former holder of the title, in the eighth round of their scheduled ten-round bout in Madison Square Garden last night.

The defeat marked the end of the 37-year-old Louis' hopes of becoming the first ex-titleholder to regain the crown. Marciano dropped Louis for a count of eight before he sent him through the ropes with a right to the jaw at 2:36 of the eighth. Referee Ruby Goldstein disdained a count. It was Marciano's thirty-eighth triumph in a row, thirty-three of them by knockouts.

Louis showed no signs of weakening until the seventh round. He weighed 212¾ pounds to Marciano's 187.

Details on Page 12.

FLATH'S VICE SQUAD UPSET BY MONAGHAN

Entire Personnel Transferred —Step May Foreshadow Clean Sweep of Plainclothes Men

By ALEXANDER FEINBERG

The entire personnel of the Chief Inspector's plainclothes squad, the top police unit assigned to the task of suppressing vice and gambling, was transferred yesterday by Police Commissioner George P. Monaghan.

Sixteen of the seventeen members of the squad were sent back to uniform a week after the retirement of August W. Flath as Chief Inspector and Mr. Monaghan's collateral declaration that all plainclothes squads would be reconstituted. The other member, formerly attached to the detective division, was reassigned there.

A year ago—on Sept. 29, 1950—Thomas F. Murphy, then Police Commissioner, on his fourth day in office ordered all of the 336 men in the plainclothes division back into uniform. He replaced them with selected patrolmen, "neither besmirched nor tainted," from the ranks of recruits and newly appointed policemen.

New Sweep Is Seen

Yesterday's action by Mr. Monaghan was believed to be the forerunner of a second clean sweep of all plainclothes personnel. In the shift, two acting lieutenants were reduced to sergeant, and an inspector, who headed the squad, a deputy inspector, an acting captain, two lieutenants and ten patrolmen were affected. Eight of the ten plainclothes men will take a loss of $240 a year in extra compensation.

Inspector Francis W. Lent, head of the squad under Chief Flath, who last week was succeeded by Chief Inspector Conrad H. Rothen-

Continued on Page 2, Column 5

Error in Race Placing at Jamaica Costs $15,655, Helps Cancer Fund

By JAMES ROACH

The Damon Runyon Fund for Cancer Research was the winner in the third race on the Jamaica City-at-Jamaica program yesterday—a horse race that the placing judges never will forget.

The placing judges made a $15,655 mistake. Perhaps the fund will profit by as much as $10,000 from it.

A horse named Swing Cheer finished first, with Air Service second by a nose over Sao Paulo. The mutuel-ticket numbers, in order, were 11, 13 and 5. But the numbers didn't go up in the proper order on the result board.

The three placing judges, in the unhappiest moment of their racing careers, reversed the place and show horses, and put up 11, 5 and 13.

They soon discovered their error, but not in time to prevent the flashing of the "official" sign, which set in motion the pay-offs. Apparently there were no complaints from any of the 19,355

Continued on Page 14, Column 1

racegoers. One reason: the photo was not put on public display. It showed that Air Service, on the outside, had beaten the on-the-rail Sao Paulo by six or eight inches. Place payoffs on Sao Paulo were made at the rate of $5.10 for each $2. By the time the stewards had notified the Empire City Racing Association management of the error almost all of the payoffs had been made.

What to do?

James Butler, Empire City president, conferred with other officials. There was no precedent in New York racing for their problem.

The management had an "out" in that the first general rule of New York racing reads that "final decision of the racing officials upon the running and results of races shall be conclusive." They could wash their hands of it. The management didn't want that "out." It wanted to pay off those who had

KOREAN FOE DROPS DEMAND FOR TRUCE ON 38TH PARALLEL

But Enemy's Plan for 15-Mile U.N. Retreat From the Front Is Termed Unacceptable

REDS WOULD YIELD IN PART

Communists Propose to Move Out of Last Area They Hold South of Old Boundary

By LINDESAY PARROTT
Special to THE NEW YORK TIMES.

TOKYO, Saturday, Oct. 27—Although a Communist proposal for a fifteen-mile retreat by Allied forces in Korea was unacceptable to the United Nations Command, the negotiators for a truce were closer to geographical agreement on a cease-fire line today than at any time since the conferences started last July.

The enemy's proposal, providing for a United Nations withdrawal in the east and center, and for evacuation by the Communists of the last ground they hold in South Korea, was an abandonment of the Communist demand for a cease-fire based on the political boundary of the Thirty-eighth Parallel.

The plan was announced to Allied representatives at a ninety-minute meeting yesterday of subcommitteemen of both sides at their tent village near Panmunjom. There the United Nations on the day before had advanced its own proposal for a truce line and buffer zone close to the battle positions won by the Allied forces still grinding forward slowly into North Korea.

[The Associated Press said the third subcommittee session was held from 11 A. M. to 1 P. M. Saturday (9 to 11 P. M. Friday, Eastern standard time). The United Nations negotiators, Maj. Gen. Henry I. Hodes and Rear Admiral Arleigh A. Burke, failed to make any progress with the Communist representatives on the truce line issue. An afternoon session was scheduled for 3 o'clock.]

'Unilateral' Retreat Cited

Thus far, there has been no formal Allied rejection of the enemy proposal. But an official United Nations bulletin pointed out yesterday afternoon that the Chinese and North Korean plan required a "unilateral" withdrawal by United Nations forces from militarily important positions along virtually the present battle line.

Among these would be hard-won ground at "Heartbreak Ridge" and the "Punchbowl" in the rugged mountains of the peninsula's eastern watershed, and the "Iron Triangle" in the center. It was estimated that the retreat would extend along a 100-mile front, ceding almost all of the territory gained by Gen. James A. Van Fleet's summer and autumn offensives, staged since the armistice talks began.

In exchange, the Communists offered to yield the Ongjin Peninsula and an area around Yonan. There, tongues of land thrust down into the Yellow Sea below the Thirty-eighth Parallel.

But this territory generally is considered indefensible, except by a force that also could hold an enclave to the north above the old boundary, and the United Nations in the present campaign never has made any serious attempt to challenge this.

Continued on Page 3, Column 1

MOSES SEEKS STEEL OF FOREIGN MAKERS

Would Meet Needs for Roads by Dealing Directly With Mills in Germany and Belgium

The quest of Robert Moses, City Construction Coordinator, for imported steel to fill the construction needs of traffic relief projects in the city has been frustrated thus far by soaring prices that far exceed the limitations of the public purse, he said yesterday.

Now he is seeking ways to get the essential metal directly from German and Belgian manufacturing bases without paying a middleman's profit to the importers in this country.

Mr. Moses pointed out that the Federal allocation system had seriously restricted domestic steel for city use.

The difficulties encountered in attempts to get foreign steel were

Continued on Page 34, Column 2

CHURCHILL IS RETURNED TO POWER WITH A MARGIN OF 26 OVER LABOR; WASHINGTON EXPECTS VISIT SOON

THE NEW PRIME MINISTER CONGRATULATED BY HIS WIFE

Winston Churchill as he appeared yesterday after late returns had assured his party of victory in the British elections
Associated Press Radiophoto

Gain for U. S.-British Ties Seen by Congress Members

By WILLIAM S. WHITE
Special to THE NEW YORK TIMES.

WASHINGTON, Oct. 26—The return of the Conservatives to power in Britain will improve British-American relations as far as both parties in Congress are concerned. The success of the ticket headed by Winston Churchill likewise will tend to ease the way for any future programs in aid of Britain, be they economic or military, other things being equal.

Washington generally expected Mr. Churchill to come to this country soon for consultation with President Truman on the coordination of United States and British foreign policy. The Prime Minister and the President are old friends, their previous meetings having included the Potsdam conference of July, 1945.

There was much speculation here that Mr. Churchill would time his visit to coincide with the President's extended vacation at Key West, Fla., which starts Nov. 8.

Continued on Page 3, Column 7

World News Summarized

SATURDAY, OCTOBER 27, 1951

Winston Churchill, as the leader of the victorious Conservative party, was asked by King George VI to become the new British Prime Minister in place of Clement R. Attlee, who resigned. With four districts still unreported, the Conservatives had an overall majority of eighteen and a majority of twenty-six over Labor in the newly elected Parliament. [1:8.]

Mr. Churchill and his aides will face many heavy tasks, including the fulfillment of their pledge to "denationalize" the iron and steel industry and to decentralize the administration of the nationalized coal industry and of the rail and road transport systems. [1:7.] Mr. Churchill, reflecting the sober mood in which the Conservative victory was accepted on all sides, said, "We shall do our very best." [3:1.]

The majority of the remnants of the once mighty Liberal party backed the Conservatives and this support was the major factor in the Conservative capture of twenty-one of the twenty-four seats won from Labor. [3:8.]

Congressional members of both parties foresaw an improvement in British-United States relations, particularly in the field of foreign policies. [1:5-6.]

In Paris European observers also were optimistic of greater Allied unity as a result of the British election. [4:3.]

Yugoslavia will receive a larger amount of military aid from the United States and a pact was agreed to be signed in Belgrade

next week by representatives of the two countries. [1:6.]

In the Korean truce negotiations the Communists abandoned their demand that the demarcation line between the opposing armies be set along the Thirty-Eighth Parallel, but their newer proposal, calling for a fifteen-mile retreat by Allied forces, was unacceptable to United Nations officials. [1:3.]

Allied fliers shot down two enemy jet planes and damaged three others in another air battle over Northwest Korea. [2:8; with map.]

The peace treaty signed at San Francisco was ratified by the lower house of the Japanese Diet, which also approved the security pact allowing the maintenance of a United States garrison in Japan. [2:1.]

President Truman, emphasizing the serious effect on the defense program of the wildcat dock walkout here, appealed to the strikers to return to work, but his plea was promptly rejected. [1:1.]

Thomas H. White, Cleveland industrialist, and his wife and daughter-in-law were killed when their private plane, piloted by Mr. White, crashed as it approached a landing at the Washington airport. [1:6-7.]

NEWS BULLETINS FROM THE TIMES
Every hour on the hour
7 A.M. through Midnight
WQXR AM 1560
WQXR FM 96.3

Index to other news appears on last page of this section.

ATTLEE STEPS DOWN

King Then Calls on War Leader to Take Over at Time of Crisis

LABOR TOPS POPULAR VOTE

Party Polls 48.8% to Rival's 48.1 While Losing Out on Seats by 293 to 319

By RAYMOND DANIELL
Special to THE NEW YORK TIMES.

LONDON, Oct. 26—For the second time in both their lifetimes, George VI today called upon Winston Churchill to form a government at a time of national crisis.

A little earlier the King, who is convalescing from a serious operation, received Clement R. Attlee and accepted his resignation as Prime Minister because the verdict of the people of Britain had gone against the Labor party in yesterday's general election. Therefore, Mr. Churchill, leader of the Conservative party, now takes his place at the helm of the ship of state that Mr. Attlee has sailed according to Socialist navigation rules for the past six years, and with a depleted crew for nineteen months.

After the 1950 election Mr. Attlee's Labor Government never had a majority of more than seven. It seems now that Mr. Churchill in the skipper's role will not be much better off.

Over-all Margin Now 18

As matters stand now the Conservatives have a majority over all others of eighteen, and twenty-six more seats than the Labor party alone. The majority may increase or decrease but not enough to make any real difference.

There are only four constituencies remaining to be heard from in the present count. In addition there is a seat to be filled in a delayed election. If the Conservatives won all the remaining seats, which is unlikely, their over-all majority would be twenty-three. However, if these seats did not change the Conservative majority would be seventeen.

The present party standings follow:

Conservatives 319
Labor 293
Liberals 5
Independents 3

All of the Independents are Irish, two of them probably will not ever vote, and one of them leans toward Labor.

This accounts for 620 of the 625 seats in the House of Commons. The four constituencies remaining to be heard from, two have been held in the past by Conservatives, one by Labor and one by the Liberals.

Seat Held Safe for Labor

The 625th seat was vacant because one of the candidates died during the campaign. It, however, is a safe seat for Labor and when the election is held it should add one more seat to Labor's strength in the House.

Mr. Attlee probably was right in ascribing his downfall to the way the Liberals voted. At party headquarters after he had taken leave of the House he said:

"I don't think there is any reason to dispute that our loss of seats has been due to the fact that when it came to the point more Liberals voted Conservative than Labor."

How many more Liberals voted

Continued on Page 3, Column 2

MANY CHANGES SET BY CONSERVATIVES

'Denationalization' of Steel, Tax Revision and Broad Housing Program Listed

By CLIFTON DANIEL

LONDON, Oct. 26 — Former Prime Minister Attlee said in his recent ill-starred election campaign that his Labor Government could not be expected to clear up in six years, the mess of Labor's six years.

Next week the Conservatives will set about tidying up what they regard as the mess of Labor's six years. They have promised many changes, although not as many as the ideological differences between the two parties might indicate, and they have years of legislative work ahead of them.

Their program is not as ambitious as that of the 1945 Labor Government, which came to power with plans to remake the whole economic and social structure of Britain. Among the tasks that the Conservatives have set themselves are these:

1. To "denationalize" the iron and steel industry, the last enterprise taken under public ownership by the Labor Government last March.

2. To decentralize the administration of the Nationalized Coal Industry and of the state-owned railroad and road transport systems.

3. To build more houses, 300,000 a year being the stated target, and

Continued on Page 3, Column 4

U. S. WILL INCREASE ARMS TO YUGOSLAVS

Heavy Weapons Will Help Tito Resist Aggression—Pact to Be Signed Next Week

By WALTER H. WAGGONER
Special to THE NEW YORK TIMES.

WASHINGTON, Oct. 26—The United States and Yugoslavia will sign a military aid agreement in Belgrade next week to assure new and larger shipments of American arms to Marshal Tito's anti-Soviet armed forces.

The agreement will bring to a close negotiations between the two Governments that formally got under way here last June, with plans to remake the whole economic and social structure of inspection trip to Yugoslavia early this month by Gen. J. Lawton Collins, United States Army Chief of Staff.

Arms that can then be expected to start flowing to the only Government holding out in Eastern Europe against Russian domina-

Continued on Page 5, Column 4

Industrialist Flying to See Marshall Killed as Plane Crashes in Potomac

Special to THE NEW YORK TIMES.

WASHINGTON, Oct. 26—Thomas H. White, Cleveland industrialist, his wife, the former Miss Kathleen York, and his daughter-in-law, Mrs. Robert White, were killed here this morning when a plane piloted by Mr. White fell into the Potomac River while approaching National Airport. Mr. White was on the way to keep a luncheon appointment with General of the Army George C. Marshall, former Defense Secretary.

Thomas H. White, Cleveland industrialist, and his wife and daughter-in-law were killed when their private plane, piloted by Mr. White, crashed as it approached a landing at the Washington airport. Mr. White, 57 years old, a grandson of the founder of the White Motor Company and White Sewing Machine Company, was piloting the plane, a single-engine Beechcraft Bonanza, from Hunting Valley Village, a Cleveland suburb, to Washington.

The plane had made a routine stop at Youngstown, Ohio, and was scheduled to arrive here at 10:15 A. M. The crash occurred at 10:12 A. M.

There was no immediate expla-

nation as to the cause of the accident. Radio tower operators said that the plane, given landing clearance, was apparently making a normal approach when at about 200 feet altitude it suddenly nosed down and fell into the river's edge where the water was shallow.

Crash boats were at the scene within a few minutes and their crews recovered the bodies from the plane. The nose and engine of the plane were pushed into the passenger compartment.

The Civil Aeronautics Administration and police began an investigation.

Mr. White's purpose in visiting General Marshall could not be learned. He was going to talk with him about Nato, an Elkhound which the children of Norway recently presented to the General, General Marshall, long an acquaintance of Mr. White, had exchanged some correspondence about the dog. It was indi-

Continued on Page 34, Column 4

Churchill in Office: A Wartime Study

The energy, versatility and qualities of mind that Mr. Churchill brings to the Prime Ministership are vividly illustrated in today's installment of his war memoirs. His ideas on diplomacy, his attitude toward Americans, his views on how to handle the Russians are set forth in a series of wartime minutes.

See Page 21

The New York Times.

LATE CITY EDITION
Light snow this morning followed
by clearing. Fair tomorrow.
Temperature Range Today—Max., 43; Min., 35
Temperatures Yesterday—Max., 43; Min., 33
Full U. S. Weather Bureau Report, Page 55

VOL. CI..No. 34,347.

Entered as Second-Class Matter,
Post Office, New York, N. Y.

NEW YORK, THURSDAY, FEBRUARY 7, 1952.

Copyright, 1952, by The New York Times Company.

Times Square, New York 36, N. Y.
Telephone LAckawanna 4-1000

FIVE CENTS

KING GEORGE VI DIES IN SLEEP AT SANDRINGHAM; ELIZABETH, QUEEN AT 25, FLYING FROM AFRICA; PRESIDENT AMONG WORLD LEADERS IN TRIBUTE

2½% INTEREST RATE FOR SAVINGS BANKS APPROVED BY STATE

85% of Institutions Expected to Adopt 'Permissive' Rule Lifting 17-Year Ceiling

NEW U. S. TAXES A FACTOR

Board Adjusts Payments on Commercial Deposits, Acts to Clear Extra Dividends

By GEORGE A. MOONEY

New York's thrifty received a new incentive yesterday.

Terminating a policy that dates to 1935, the State Banking Board acted to raise its ceiling on interest-dividends paid on savings and thrift deposits from a 2 per cent maximum to 2½ per cent. Eighty-five per cent of the state's 130 savings banks are expected to put the increase in effect at an early date.

Last night the Dime Savings Bank of Brooklyn became the first in this area to announce it would pay 2½ per cent for the current quarter ending March 31.

Trustees of the Roosevelt Savings Bank announced they would meet today to increase the rate from 2 to 2½ per cent on account balances and deposits for the three-month period starting Jan. 1.

Other savings banks and competitive commercial banks, where possible, are likely to take similar action soon.

Responding to the higher level of prevailing rates, and especially to Federal taxes imposed at the beginning of this year, several savings banks asked permission some weeks ago to pay larger dividends. Under the new tax law, savings institutions are made liable for income taxes at the regular corporate rate on all earnings after surplus and reserves total 12 per cent of deposits.

Regulation Is "Permissive"

William A. Lyon, Superintendent of Banks, in announcing the board's action yesterday said the new 2½ per cent rate was "permissive."

"Banks are permitted under the regulation to pay any rate up to that maximum which directors and trustees believe to be advisable in the light of the earning power and the capital or surplus position of their institutions," he explained.

Two other important amendments also were made in General Regulation No. 3, the dividend and interest rate regulation, Mr. Lyon said. In the first of these, relating to commercial banks' special interest and thrift deposits, the board approved a limit on interest payments at the maximum rate of 2½ per cent on the first $10,000 of any account and setting a ceiling on the 1½ per cent on that portion of any special and thrift account in excess of $10,000.

The largest individual account that may be accepted by savings banks is $10,000, the maximum

Continued on Page 55, Column 6

Truman 'Shows Off' New White House

By W. H. LAWRENCE
Special to The New York Times.

WASHINGTON, Feb. 6—Ducking nimbly around and under scaffolding, President Truman today took a few correspondents on a conducted tour of the White House, which is being reconstructed. He said it was still his hope that the First Family would be able to move into it early in April after three and one-half years in Blair House.

Mixing history and comment about the tribulations of a tenant who decides to get a house done over, Mr. Truman led the reporters through the building for forty minutes, answering questions and volunteering observations about nearly every room.

The hum of power saws as workmen went ahead with their jobs sometimes drowned his

Continued on Page 23, Column 1

1-Way Traffic Signs Due Soon in Times Sq.

By JOSEPH C. INGRAHAM

Conversion of Seventh and Eighth Avenues to one-way operation has been decided upon by Acting Traffic Commissioner T. T. Wiley despite objections of the New York City Omnibus Corporation.

Preparations for the new traffic pattern were well under way yesterday, with new guideposts rising in Times Square and the fittings all set to hold the one-way arrows. Work on the other sections of the one-way routes, which extend from Columbus Circle to below Canal Street, also was progressing. Seventh Avenue-Varick Street will handle southbound flow and Hudson Street-Abingdon Square-Eighth

Continued on Page 17, Column 5

CHARGES OF WASTE IN DEFENSE DENIED

Pentagon Aides Tell Senators of Savings—Admiral Calls Himself 'Oyster Fork Fox'

By HAROLD B. HINTON
Special to The New York Times.

WASHINGTON, Feb. 6—Officials of the Department of Defense underwent a period of criticism before a Senate Appropriations subcommittee today and did not seem to like it. They were appearing in support of defense budget estimates of more than $52,000,-000,000.

The principal witness was Vice Admiral Charles W. Fox, Chief of Naval Supplies, who told the Senators of the progress the Navy had made in simplifying the cataloguing of its supplies. When his presentation was interrupted by questions about allegations of waste and extravagance, the Pentagon contingent moved to the counter-offensive.

"I stand before you as Oyster Fork Fox," the admiral asserted, as the Senators and spectators laughed. "I am supposed to have bought 11,000,000 oyster forks for the Navy, and I had nothing more to do with it than you did."

He said that the Navy last

Continued on Page 4, Column 3

RED TRAPS FEARED IN FOE'S PROPOSAL FOR KOREA PARLEY

Communist Demand for Airing of Status of Formosa Viewed as Bar to U. N. Accord

TRUMAN CITED AS A GUIDE

Nam Il Argues Stand Taken by President on Blockading China Widens Issues

Text of Gen. Nam Il's statement is printed on Page 2.

By LINDESAY PARROTT
Special to The New York Times.

TOKYO, Thursday, Feb. 7—The United Nations Command began today a detailed study of the Communist proposal for a top-level political conference three months after the armistice in the Korean war to deal with related issues in the Far East.

This morning no hint of Allied reaction had come from the advance camp at Munsan, where the United Nations representatives took the Communist program after it had been delivered to them at a plenary session of the truce delegations at Panmunjom, on the way to headquarters of the United Nations Commander, Gen. Matthew B. Ridgway, in Tokyo.

The enemy proposal was made by North Korean Gen. Nam Il, head of the Chinese and North Korean delegation, who drove to the meeting place in a big American limousine with whitewall tires. He nodded curtly to the senior United Nations representative, Vice Admiral Charles Turner Joy, and then launched into his prepared introductory remarks — considerably more extensive, it turned out, than the brief formal proposal for a governmental conference for "peaceful settlement of the Korean question and other questions related to peace in Korea."

Before the session adjourned it was agreed that a new plenary sitting should be held by the delegates of both sides after the United Nations study had been com-

Continued on Page 2, Column 6

World News Summarized

THURSDAY, FEBRUARY 7, 1952

King George VI died in his sleep at Sandringham Palace yesterday morning; his daughter was proclaimed Queen Elizabeth II. The King, who seemingly had recovered from an operation for the removal of a growth on his lung, had felt so well he had been out shooting the day before. [1:8.] The British people were stunned by their sudden loss. [1:7.]

King George became the British ruler in 1936 when his brother, King Edward VIII and later Duke of Windsor, abdicated. He saw little peace during his reign. Threats of war, armed conflict and the "cold war" marked his tenure. [10:1.] During the bombing of London he refused to take special precautions or leave Buckingham Palace. [13:7-8.]

The new Queen started for London by plane when she learned of her father's death. She had been touring East Africa with her consort, the Duke of Edinburgh. [1:6-7.] She is the first to ascend to Britain's throne since 115 years ago, when Queen Victoria was crowned. [1:5-6.] The Duke of Windsor sails from New York tonight, alone, to attend his brother's funeral. [14:3.]

President Truman, Secretary Acheson and others expressed the sorrow of the United States [1:5] as did former President Hoover, Mayor Impellitteri and others in this city. [14:5.] United Nations flags were flown at half-staff. [15:1.]

The Soviet Union, for the fifth time, vetoed Italy's membership in the United Nations. [1:4.] The Russians did not join forty-seven other countries in pledging funds for expanded technical assistance this year. [3:4.]

Allied officers studied the Communist proposal for a political conference three months after a Korean armistice. [1:3.]

West German leaders were unmoved by American and British pleas to cool their anger over French moves in the Saar and not to endanger plans for West Europe's defense. [6:3.]

A masked witness told a House committee he had seen Russians kill hundreds of Polish officers in Katyn Forest in 1939. [4:3.] Defense Department heads, testifying on the military budget before a Senate group, vigorously defended their spending. [1:2.] Mobilization heads also were under attack for plans to spread defense contracts to unemployment areas. [39:4.]

The slow-down in the military aircraft production rate will have little immediate effect on consumer goods but will avoid more stringent curbs later, a survey showed. [3:1.]

Governor Byrnes of South Carolina blamed "Negro politicians of the North" for the Democratic party's shift from a State's Rights program. [21:1.]

This state authorized banks to pay up to 2½ per cent on savings and thrift accounts. [1:1.] Columbia University will increase tuition fees up to 25 per cent next fall and adjust faculty salaries upward. [29:1.]

SOVIET AGAIN BALKS ITALY'S U. N. ENTRY

Russia for Fifth Time Vetoes Application—Is Beaten on En Bloc Admission Bid

By THOMAS J. HAMILTON
Special to The New York Times.

PARIS, Feb. 6—Italy's application for membership in the United Nations was vetoed by the Soviet Union tonight for the fifth time. Ten of the eleven members of the Security Council voted for a French resolution recommending the admission of Italy.

Jacob A. Malik, the Soviet representative, based his action on the refusal of the United States to accept a Soviet proposal for en bloc admission of fourteen applicants, including five Communist governments.

The Soviet resolution afterward was rejected by a vote of six to two. The United States, Brazil, Nationalist China, Greece, the Netherlands and Turkey voted against the resolution, while Pakistan joined the Soviet Union in supporting it. Britain, France and Chile abstained.

Mr. Malik accused the United States of blocking Italy's admission. He declared that "the Italian people will note that it is the United States, with the help of the United Kingdom" that had "provoked" the Soviet veto. He added that if the Western powers had wanted to get Italy admitted, and, indeed, had been the first British king to visit the country.

Gross Protests "Horsetrade"

Ernest A. Gross, the United States delegate, retorted that on the contrary the Italian people would hardly be grateful for being made a part of the proposed "horsetrade." He asked whether Mr. Malik really believed that Italy would "be put in the same basket" with such "a shadow state" as Outer Mongolia, one of the Communist candidates included in the Soviet resolution.

Mr. Gross also expressed regret that the new state of Libya, which came into existence on Christmas Day, 1951, had been included in the Soviet en bloc proposal—which presumably meant that it likewise would encounter a Soviet veto unless the Western powers agree to the Soviet mass entry proposal.

Mr. Malik replied that Outer Mongolia deserved to be admitted. He said that its participation in the war against Japan "along with that of the Soviet Union" saved 1,000,000 American lives. He said he based his statement on statements by the United States high command.

Reconsideration today of Italy's long-standing application was the result of a General Assembly resolution last fall requesting the Security Council to consider, in the light of Italy's responsibilities as a member of the General Assembly resolution last fall requesting the Security Council to consider, in the light of Italy's responsibilities

Continued on Page 3, Column 5

THE NEW QUEEN AND THE LATE KING

ELIZABETH II   GEORGE VI   Associated Press

Ruler Becomes Elizabeth II; Her Son, 3, Is Crown Prince

By CLIFTON DANIEL
Special to The New York Times.

LONDON, Feb. 6—Britain entered a new Elizabethan era today. Upon the death of King George VI, Princess Elizabeth Alexandra Mary, his elder daughter, automatically became Queen of the United Kingdom and the Dominions Overseas at the age of 25.

Tonight at the first meeting of her Privy Council she was formally styled Queen Elizabeth II.

[Text of the Privy Council's proclamation is on Page 14.]

Thus, for the first time in 115 years, a woman ascended the world's most exalted and stable throne. At the Gloucester Assizes, as in other law courts of the land, the judges marshal closed the court with words not heard since the end of Queen Victoria's sixty-three-year reign in 1901: "God save the Queen and my lords the Queen's justices."

For the first time in British history the sovereign was abroad in the Empire at the moment of accession.

Already bearing the full responsibility of the crown, the new Queen will return here by air from Kenya in Africa tomorrow accompanied by her consort, the Duke of Edinburgh.

They were to have boarded the liner Gothic at Mombasa tomorrow to sail for Ceylon, Australia and New Zealand on a five-month ceremonial tour deputizing for the late King, whose illness prevented him from going.

With the accession of the Queen, her son Prince Charles, three years and two months old, became the Crown Prince and heir to the

Continued on Page 14, Column 3

TRUMAN EXPRESSES SORROW OF NATION

Voices Sympathy for British Over Loss of King—Acheson and Others Pay Tribute

Special to The New York Times.

WASHINGTON, Feb. 6—President Truman and the nation paid tribute to King George VI today in extending this country's sympathy to the British people on his death.

"He played his part nobly and with full understanding of the responsibility which was his," the President said in a formal statement.

All official Washington responded in kind following the surprise and shock at the news of the monarch's passing early this morning. Highest officials in the Government and leaders of both House of Congress joined in expressions of sympathy and praise for the man who had been a steadfast friend of the United States and, indeed, had been the first British King to visit the country. Secretary of State Dean Acheson commented on the courage with which King George had borne his physical suffering and noted: "It is a characteristic English spirit and the King possessed it in abundance."

Envoy Calls on Acheson

Sir Oliver Franks, British Ambassador, accompanied by seven representatives of the British Commonwealth, called on Secretary Acheson shortly after noon to inform him formally of the King's death.

"A world personage who maintained the highest tradition of the English constitutional monarchy passes in the death of His Majesty King George VI," President Truman said in his statement.

"From his accession to the throne through all the ills which beset the world throughout the years of his reign—including the most disastrous war in history—he played his part nobly and with full understanding which was his. His heroic endurance of pain and suffering during these past few years is a true reflection of the bravery of the British people in adversity.

"The King was ever conscious of his obligations as sovereign of a nation which through centuries has been the champion of personal liberty and those free institutions

Continued on Page 14, Column 5

Elizabeth Weeps at News of Death, But Is Calm in African Take-Off

By The United Press.

NAIROBI, Kenya, Feb. 6—the local populace to spare the new Young Queen Elizabeth II left hurriedly for home by plane tonight only a few hours after her husband had broken the news to her of her father's death.

The 25-year-old former Princess, after having broken down in tears, was composed when she departed early tonight on the long flight to London.

With Prince Philip she left the hunting lodge where the royal couple had been staying and drove in a closed automobile eight miles to a small airport near the East African town of Nunyuki. She took off in an East African Airways C-47 for Entebbe in Uganda, where the British Overseas Airways craft that had flown her to Africa waited to take her back to Britain.

The royal couple landed at Entebbe airport at 9:10 P. M. (1:10 P. M., Eastern standard time), but news of her arrival was kept from

Queen a further ordeal.

A tropical thunderstorm at Entebbe delayed the departure of the Queen's plane for more than two hours, but it finally took off at 11:47 P. M. for Libya as the weather cleared.

[The plane made a stop at the Royal Air Force base at El Adem, Libya, landing there at 1:15 A. M., Thursday, Eastern standard time, The United Press reported.]

At El Adem and Malta the Royal Air Force had planes standing by to escort the Queen's plane over the Mediterranean. It is scheduled to reach London at 4:30 P. M. Thursday, Greenwich time (11:30 A. M., E. S. T.)

Crowds of silent, sorrowful persons of all races lined the main street of Nunyuki as the Queen's party passed through. The Queen, her face showing the strain of the

Continued on Page 13, Column 8

15-YEAR REIGN ENDS

British Monarch's Death at 56 Follows a Lung Operation Last Fall

PARLIAMENT HALTED

Churchill Conveys News to Commons—Attlee Suspends Party Strife

By RAYMOND DANIELL
Special to The New York Times.

LONDON, Feb. 6—In the early hours of this morning George VI died peacefully in his sleep at the royal estate at Sandringham. As night fell upon this mourning capital of a still great family of nations, his elder daughter was proclaimed Queen of this realm and its dependencies, head of the British Commonwealth and the Defender of the Faith, and the title of Elizabeth II.

She is flying home tonight from her tragically interrupted visit to East Africa with her consort, the Duke of Edinburgh, and is expected back tomorrow to assume her royal duties as the wearer of the crown that somewhat mystically binds the British Commonwealth together.

Like the Elizabeth of England's golden age, she takes the throne at the age of 25.

Operated On 4 Months Ago

The King's death occurred just a little more than four months after an operation for the removal of a growth in his right lung. This operation resulted in the loss of the lung. His recovery seemed assured and in recent days he had been seen publicly at the theatre and at London Airport when he bade good-by to his daughter, now the Queen, as she set out with Prince Philip, her husband, on a journey that was to take her to East Africa, Australia and New Zealand. Only yesterday he was out shooting, his favorite sport.

It was assumed that the King had died as a result of a heart attack, probably caused by coronary thrombosis.

Tributes to the late monarch poured into London from leading world figures and from persons of humbler station.

His death came in his 57th year. It was the beginning of the sixteenth year of an unhappy reign. He never wanted or expected to throne of Britain, but he ascended to it when his brother Edward VIII abdicated to marry the "woman I love," Wallis Simpson.

Six years of his reign were war years when he and Elizabeth, his Queen, who now becomes Queen Mother, endeared themselves to their people by their bravery and devotion to their predestined role.

When he was crowned King on May 12, 1937, he was King-Emperor but the title of Emperor went with the granting of independence to India. His reign marked the end of an era of British power.

Parliament Is Suspended

His death also brought to an end this session of Parliament in the midst of a bitter and acrimonious debate on how far this country should go in aligning itself with United States policy in the Far East lest it be dragged into war. That debate, which began yesterday, was left in mid-air as Parliament put aside its controversies to swear allegiance to the new Queen and deferred its partisan arguments on controversial issues until a more seemly time.

At Sandringham when the King died there were his two grandchildren, whom he adored, Prince Charles and Princess Anne; Sir Alan Lascelles, his private secretary; Sir Harold Campbell, his equerry, and Lady Hyde, lady-in-waiting to his Queen. Soon after his death was discovered by a servant bringing early morning tea, Dr. James Ansell, "Surgeon Apothecary" to the royal household at Sandringham, was called.

He said that the King had died in his sleep without pain.

News of the King's death went out over the news tickers at the 10:45 A. M. at 11:15 it was broad-

Continued on Page 13, Column 2

LONDON IS STILLED AS BRITONS MOURN

All Amusements Closed, Lights Dimmed, Streets Nearly Empty After News Stuns People

By FARNSWORTH FOWLE
Special to The New York Times.

LONDON, Feb. 6—This was a silent city tonight, with bright lights dimmed and all places of entertainment closed, as Londoners went home shocked by the death of their King.

The news reached most office workers at noon when they went out for lunch and found venders of early editions of afternoon papers shouting "The King's dead!"

"What King?" was a typical first reaction. It was hard to believe that it was indeed their own monarch, even though it had been generally realized since the King's operation last September that he might not have many years to live. Only a week ago tonight he attended a performance of "South Pacific" at the Drury Lane Theatre.

The suddenness of the news contrasted with the memory of how the public had been prepared during the final illness of the King's father, George V, with a broadcast communiqué saying, "The King's life is moving peacefully to its close."

Flags at half-staff appeared on public buildings and many private ones by noon. Theatres, cinemas and night clubs all shut down, as did the Stock Exchange and other markets.

The laughter of silent, cheerful office girls was muted as

Continued on Page 13, Column 6

NEWS BULLETINS FROM THE TIMES
Every hour on the hour
7 A.M. to Midnight
Except at 4 P.M. Today
WQXR AM 1560
WQXR FM 96.3

Index to other news appears on last page of this section.

"All the News
That's Fit to Print"

The New York Times.

LATE CITY EDITION
Mostly fair today and tonight.
Chance of showers tomorrow.
Temperature Range Today—Max., 54; Min., 40
Temperature Yesterday—Max., 53; Min., 41
Full U. S. Weather Bureau Report, Page 55

Copyright, 1952, by The New York Times Company.

VOL. CI. No. 34,409.

Entered as Second-Class Matter,
Post Office. New York, N. Y.

NEW YORK, WEDNESDAY, APRIL 9, 1952.

Time, Square, New York 36, N. Y.
Telephone Lackawana 4-1000

FIVE CENTS

TAFT SWEEPS ILLINOIS TEST BY MAJORITY

STASSEN IS SECOND

Eisenhower, Off Ballot, Is Third—Stevenson Write-In Is Light

KEFAUVER HAS STRENGTH

But Governor's Popular Vote for State Office Exceeds Tally for Tennessean

By RICHARD J. H. JOHNSTON
Special to The New York Times.

CHICAGO, Wednesday, April 9 —Senator Robert A. Taft of Ohio, running far ahead of his opponents for the support of Illinois's fifty elected national convention delegates, emerged victor by a wide margin today in this state's Presidential preference primary election.

For President

Returns from 4,880 of 9,610 precincts gave:

REPUBLICANS

Sen. Robert A. Taft	366,977
Harold E. Stassen	61,252
Gen. Dwight D. Eisenhower	*50,877
Riley A. Bender	10,946
Gen. Douglas MacArthur	*3,092
Gov. Earl Warren	*119

(* Write-in.)

DEMOCRATS

Sen. Kefauver (4,576 pcts.)	275,553
Gov. Stevenson (783 pcts.)	*4,531

(* Write-in.)

The write-ins for Gov. Adlai E. Stevenson of Illinois were from downstate counties. Cook County, which includes Chicago, delayed write-in reports.

The tally for Senator Taft far exceeded the total votes of his rivals, Mr. Stassen, ex-Governor of Minnesota; General Eisenhower, a write-in candidate, and Mr. Bender, a Chicago Hotel operator.

The indications were that Mr. Taft was winning forty-eight of the state's fifty elected delegates. General Eisenhower appeared to have two.

Senator Estes Kefauver of Tennessee, unopposed for the Democratic Presidential nomination, rolled up a strong vote. However, Governor Stevenson ran ahead of the Tennessean in the total popular vote in his unopposed bid for the Gubernatorial nomination.

In the Illinois Republican Gubernatorial race, William G. Stratton, State Treasurer, outstripped his opponents.

For Governor

Returns from 5,366 of 9,610 precincts gave:

REPUBLICANS

William G. Stratton	297,409
Park Livingston	110,285
Richard Y. Rowe	95,184
W. N. Erickson (withdrawn from race)	36,287
Anthony A. Pelley	16,120

DEMOCRATS

Returns from 4,450 of 9,610 precincts gave:

Gov. Stevenson (unopp'sed)	356,209

On the basis of returns from about half of the state's 9,610 precincts in the Presidential popularity vote, it appeared that Mr. Taft would run 7 to 1 over Mr. Stassen

Continued on Page 20, Column 3

Halley Lists 'Waste' For 'Raucous' Critics

Specific illustrations of waste in the city government were offered yesterday by Rudolph Halley, President of the City Council, to support his argument that the only real cure for New York's recurring financial crises would be a complete overhaul of its system of administrative management.

In a speech at a luncheon arranged by the Citizens Budget Commission at the Roosevelt Hotel, Mr. Halley, self-styled "watchdog" of the city, gave these examples from the Department of Hospitals:

¶Bellevue Hospital ordered thirty-seven new refrigerators in 1948 at a cost of $35,183. They were delivered in 1948 and 1949. Last February they were not yet installed because they operated on alternating current while the hospital system used direct current.

¶A total of $45,000 of X-ray

Continued on Page 22, Column 5

COSTELLO RECEIVES 18 MONTHS, IS FINED $5,000 IN CONTEMPT

Judge Ryan Says He 'May Well Have Prevented Important Disclosures' to Senators

F. B. I. CHECKS ON 2 JURORS

Blaikie, to Whose Club Ousted Foreman Belongs, Charges 'Funny Politics' Go On

By CHARLES GRUTZNER

Frank Costello was sentenced yesterday to eighteen months in prison and fined $5,000—the heaviest penalty ever imposed here for contempt—by Federal Judge Sylvester Ryan, who declared that the gambler's balkiness before the Senate Crime Investigating Committee "may well have prevented important disclosures."

The bigtime racketeer, who has kept out of prison since he served ten months on a pistol-carrying conviction in 1915, remained free in $5,000 bail as the result of filing a notice of appeal with the United States Court of Appeals. A hearing will be held tomorrow to determine whether bail should be continued pending outcome of the appeal, expected to be heard next month.

Developments that followed quickly upon the sentencing of the well-dressed, gravel-voiced racket boss cleared up some of the mystery that had clouded the case since last Friday, when Judge Ryan had dismissed two jurors before giving Costello's fate into the hands of a jury reinforced by alternates.

Checking on Dismissed Jurors

United States Attorney Myles J. Lane announced that he and the Federal Bureau of Investigation were checking on Mrs. Helen Louise Mason, who had been jury foreman during four days of the trial, and Julius A. Fox, original Juror No. 9. The two jurors allegedly concealed from the court circumstances that may have prejudiced them in reaching a verdict.

The F. B. I., it was learned, is searching for a man who was brash enough and stupid enough to try to shake down Costello's attorney, George Wolf, for $250 with a crude offer of jury-fixing. The bid for $250 had nothing to do with the dismissal of either juror.

Judge Ryan, who had withheld all details on Friday, instructed Mr. Lane yesterday to make public the record of conversations the judge had held in his chambers with Mrs. Mason, Mr. Fox and the prosecution attorneys. The record made it clear that Mrs. Mason was removed from the jury because of her political activity in the Democratic club headed by Robert Blaikie, Tammany leader who crossed party lines to support Rudolph Halley, former chief counsel to the Senate Crime Committee, in his successful race for City Council President last fall.

Mr. Fox was removed because of two civil actions for treble damages brought by the Office of Price

Continued on Page 18, Column 6

Pinay Wins 10 Tests On French Finances

By LANSING WARREN
Special to The New York Times.

PARIS, April 8—Premier Antoine Pinay, breaking through Opposition hostility and garnering support from both Gaullist and Popular Republican groups, won a victory today for his plan of financing France's budget.

The Premier, an independent, was successful in the National Assembly in a series of ten votes of confidence, which provided additional evidence of the shaping of a new right-wing majority in France.

The crucial vote was on the provision aiming to bring out hidden capital in France by an unconditional amnesty for all past tax delinquencies, which was adopted by 259 votes to 210. The program as a whole was approved by a vote of 311 to 206. Most of the other ballots gave the Government more than 400

Continued on Page 6, Column 3

FOE'S 'PHONY' ISSUE ON KOREA SCORNED

U. N. Accuses Reds at Parley of Setting Up Soviet Question for Airfield Bargaining

By LINDESAY PARROTT
Special to The New York Times.

TOKYO, Wednesday, April 9—The United Nations negotiators at Panmunjom accused the Communists today of introducing a "phony issue" in the negotiations for an armistice in Korea with the demand that the Soviet Union be included as a "neutral" nation to police a cease-fire.

The Allied representative on the committee of generals discussing conditions for the enforcement of a truce, Maj. Gen. William K. Harrison, told correspondents that the United Nations Command would not agree to the bargain hinted at by the Chinese and North Koreans. The enemy delegates had indicated that they might be prepared to withdraw the Soviet nomination if the Allies would agree to permit the construction and rehabilitation of airfields north of the Thirty-eighth Parallel during an armistice.

"They are trying to equate something for nothing," General Harrison said after an enemy spokesman, for the third time, had urged the two outstanding questions be settled as a joint item.

General Harrison said he was convinced that the Russian issue had been raised "only to bargain

Continued on Page 3, Column 2

NEW PARLEY TODAY

Both Sides Will Confer With Steelman as Talks Shift to Washington

TO COOPERATE WITH U. S.

Union and Owners Promise to Run Mills After Truman Acts in Pay Deadlock

By A. H. RASKIN

The United Steelworkers of America, C. I. O., called off last night its national steel strike and directed its 600,000 members to stay at work under President Truman's seizure order.

The instructions were issued by Philip Murray, president of the union, even before the President had finished his radio speech announcing the takeover of the mills. The union leader expressed certainty that the workers would comply "as patriotic Americans."

High Government officials reported that they had assurances of industry cooperation in running the mills, even though the companies will fight the legality of the seizure in the Federal courts. A boycott by executive and supervisory personnel would have made it impossible for the Government to maintain steel production.

The industry, angered by the criticism Mr. Truman heaped on its position in the dispute over steel wages and prices, decided to wait until today before issuing formal comment. Privately company spokesmen denounced the seizure as "confiscation" and asserted that it could lead to the socialization of all American industry unless the courts upset the President's order.

Last-Minute Efforts Fail

The Federal takeover was ordered thirty minutes after frantic attempts to effect a last-minute agreement between the major steel producers and the union had collapsed in New York.

More than 400,000 steel workers already had been laid off and the fires were down in blast furnaces from Pittsburgh, Pa., to Pittsburg, Calif., when the President acted.

The Federal action warded off a full-fledged strike of the members of the steel union at 12:01 o'clock this morning, but the time required to reheat the furnaces will entail a minimum loss of 1,000,000 tons of steel this week.

Dr. John R. Steelman, Acting Director of Defense Mobilization, will make a new effort to settle the wage-price dispute at the White House this afternoon. He will be assisted by Nathan P. Feinsinger, Chairman of the Wage Stabilization Board, who sought unsuccessfully to effect an agreement in five days of talks with company and union officials here.

Two-Year Contract Proposed

Mr. Feinsinger, who gave up the New York conferences at 10 P. M., said he still hoped the suggestions he made would provide the basis for an eventual settlement. He disclosed that he had proposed that the parties agree on a two-year contract, instead of the eighteen-month pact originally recommended by the Wage Board.

Under the Feinsinger plan, the union would get the same wage increases and other benefits the board had proposed but they would be spaced over a longer period. This would assure the nation of a longer period of strike-free steel production and would give the companies a longer time before the union would be in a position to demand a new rise in wages.

The Wage Board's proposals called for a wage increase of 12½ cents an hour, retroactive to Jan. 1; a further increase of 2½ cents July 1 and a third increase of 2½ cents next Jan. 1. In addition, the board urged a union shop and fringe benefits that would cost 5.4 cents an hour this year and 3½ cents an hour next year. Steel wages now average $1.88 an hour.

The union insisted that the industry accept all of the board's recommendations in a new eighteen-month contract. The industry countered with an offer of a pay increase of 12½ cents an hour, retroactive to March 1 and 5.4

Continued on Page 14, Column 1

TRUMAN SEIZES STEEL; STRIKE OFF; HE SCORES INDUSTRY AS RECKLESS; COMPANIES START FIGHT IN COURTS

TAKES OVER STEEL INDUSTRY

Associated Press Wirephoto
President Truman speaking from the new White House communications room last night for the first time.

Sawyer, Taking Over Steel, Plans No Pay Changes Now

By JOSEPH A. LOFTUS

WASHINGTON, April 8—Charles Sawyer, Secretary of Commerce, who has become the nominal operator of most of the nation's steel industry, said tonight that he planned "no change of any kind at this moment" in the wages and working conditions of the industry's employes.

As to the legal justification for President Truman's seizure of the industry tonight, Mr. Sawyer said he understood the President had acted under his "general Constitutional powers, but I prefer not to bind the Attorney General."

"If the matter is taken to court the legal phases will be handled wholly by the Attorney General," he added. "He prepared the papers. I did not participate in it."

Reminded that the Attorney General, J. Howard McGrath, had just resigned, the Secretary said, "There's quite a department over there; a lot of competent men."

The Secretary held a news conference in his office a few minutes after Mr. Truman had finished his broadcast announcement that the Government was taking over the steel mills in order to continue production in the face of the impending strike.

Will Await Bargaining

Replying to questions about the wage increases recommended by the Wage Stabilization Board and rejected by the industry, Mr. Sawyer said he would "await the results of the collective bargaining negotiations Dr. [John R.] Steelman [Acting Director of Defense Mobilization] will carry on in accordance with the President's directive."

Pressed on whether present wage terms and conditions would continue, he declared: "I said for the time being they would; I don't commit myself for the long pull."

The Secretary answered without hesitation all questions fired at him, although qualifying some answers with statements that he was subject to the orders of the President and the legal interpretations of the Attorney General.

He issued a formal statement saying:

"I neither requested nor wanted this job, but when our men at the front are taking orders in the face of great danger those of us far back can do no less.

"The President has given me what I realize is a difficult assignment. I accept it.

"I dislike as much as anyone to witness, let alone participate in, the seizure of property. We are, however, facing a situation of great peril where continued production of steel is essential to our national welfare.

"The President has made his decision and has made clear to me his reasons for the seizure. I hope that both industry and labor will accept the statements I make in good faith and will co-

Continued on Page 16, Column 7

Two Hisses Termed Soviet Agents in '39

By CLAYTON KNOWLES
Special to The New York Times.

WASHINGTON, April 8—William C. Bullitt, former United States Ambassador to France and to Russia, asserted today that he was advised on the highest French authority late in 1939 that "two brothers named Hiss," both officers in the State Department, were "Soviet agents."

Testifying before the Senate Internal Security subcommittee, the ex-Ambassador said that this information was given to him by Edouard Daladier, then French Premier, who attributed it to the French Intelligence Service.

Mr. Bullitt said that at the time he did not know either Alger or Donald Hiss or that they were in the department. The former envoy added that he laughed at the

Continued on Page 15, Column 6

PRESIDENT IN PLEA

Address on Air Charges Industry With Greed for High Profits

SAWYER WILL RUN MILLS

Washington Judge Signs Order Setting Hearing for Today on Legality of Action

The President's broadcast and his Executive order, Page 16.

By CHARLES E. EGAN
Special to The New York Times.

WASHINGTON, April 8—President Truman tonight ordered seizure of the steel mills to avert a strike of their 600,000 workers. An order directing that the Government take over the mills was issued effective at midnight, one minute before the scheduled strike was to take place.

Under the terms of tonight's order, which the President said had been issued "in the public interest," Charles Sawyer, Secretary of Commerce, will take over the operation of the steel mills.

In moving against the giant of American industries the President was believed to have touched off one of the sharpest legal battles in a generation. The steel mill owners are insistent that the President does not have power, under the Constitution or under his emergency grants of authority, to take possession of the mills. Counsel for steel mills were prepared to challenge the President's action in a half dozen Federal district courts in the country tomorrow, according to reports.

[Federal Judge Walter M. Bastian signed an order early Wednesday in Washington calling a hearing for 11:30 A. M. on a suit filed by two of the major steel companies—Republic and Youngstown Sheet and Tube—challenging the Government's seizure. The Associated Press reported.]

Steelman Sets Meeting

In compliance with the President's request, Dr. John R. Steelman, Acting Director of Defense Mobilization, telephoned representatives of the six big steel companies and Philip Murray, president of the United Steelworkers of America, C. I. O. Dr. Steelman asked the operators and Mr. Murray to come to Washington for a meeting with him at 3 P. M. tomorrow.

In addition, Dr. Steelman talked by telephone with Nathan Feinsinger, chairman of the Wage Stabilization Board, who has been in New York advising in the steel-wage dispute. Mr. Feinsinger will meet with Dr. Steelman at noon to give the Defense Mobilizer a complete report on the discussions that have been in progress in New York.

Also in response to the President's orders, Secretary Sawyer immediately designated the presidents of the steel companies as "operating managers" on behalf of the United States.

In a statement issued after the President's broadcast Mr. Sawyer

Continued on Page 16, Column 3

Phone Talks Stalled; Service Is Still Good

By STANLEY LEVEY

Substantial sections of the nation's communications systems still were beset by strikes yesterday, but telephone and telegraph service did not appear to be suffering much.

Attempts by Federal mediators to settle the telephone strikes began Monday by 67,250 workers in forty-three states and the District of Columbia were unavailing. There were no such efforts in the six-day-old strike of 31,000 employes of the Western Union Telegraph Company, however, though the company reported some restoration of service in many parts of the country.

Chances that the Western Union strike would spread to New York were reduced last night when the striking union lost a National

Continued on Page 17, Column 4

Mayor, 'Run Down,' Plans Florida Rest

Mayor Impellitteri announced yesterday at City Hall that on the advice of his physician he would leave the city late tomorrow afternoon by plane for a two-week vacation at Palm Beach, Fla.

According to the Mayor, his physician, Dr. James G. Robilotti, told him he was "run down" and "needed a rest." Mr. Impellitteri said that for about two months he had had a "recurring cold" from which he had not been able to recover completely, and he hoped the two-week sojourn in the South would provide a cure.

While in Palm Beach, the Mayor said, he will be the guest of City Commerce Commissioner and Mrs. Walter T. Shirley at the Shirley home in the Florida resort city.

Mr. Impellitteri said he would

Continued on Page 22, Column 4

WARREN DISAVOWS AN 'AGAINST' POLICY

Governor in Opening Speech Here Asks for Nomination of Sound Progressive

Gov. Earl Warren of California, making his first major address to a New York audience as a Republican Presidential contender, appealed last night for the nomination of a progressive candidate who would not "turn back the clock" in the nation's affairs, even if he could do so.

Governor Warren addressed an attentive gathering of more than 1,000 persons at the annual $100-a-plate dinner of the New York County Republican Committee in the Waldorf-Astoria Hotel. Governor Dewey, whose running mate in the 1948 Presidential campaign was Governor Warren, introduced Governor Warren without reference to the latter's 1952 ambition to head the slate, and Governor Warren in turn refrained from mentioning himself as a candidate.

Governor Warren, while attacking the Truman administration as graft-ridden and incompetent, summed up his philosophy by saying:

"We cannot rely upon an 'against' campaign to win the election in November. We must convince the American people that we are thinking in terms of forward action for their welfare. We must not be afraid of the word 'welfare.' We must not shrink from the known needs for social progress that we can make our candidate.

Continued on Page 23, Column 2

TRUMAN SEES PERIL WORSE THAN SOVIET

In Point 4 Speech He Attacks Imperialism—Ties Liberty to Scientific Advance

Text of the President's address on Point Four, Page 4.

By FELIX BELAIR Jr.
Special to The New York Times.

WASHINGTON, April 8—President Truman told a national conference tonight that the Point Four concept of improving the lot of the neglected people of the earth would surely fail "unless scientific progress is linked with political freedom."

Mr. Truman declared he feared that the crescendo of imperialism in the recent history of the world might swell to even greater proportions, if it were not silenced now, than the menace of the Soviet Union today.

The President's speech was delivered at a night session of the National Conference on International Economic and Social Development, given by Dean Acheson, Secretary of State, who substituted for Mr. Truman to allow the President to make a speech to the nation on the steel situation.

"Mass suffering," the President

Continued on Page 4, Column 3

Baruchs Praised at Site of Housing

Officials of City and U. S. Join in Tribute at Groundbreaking

City and Federal officials paid tribute yesterday to the Baruch family at a groundbreaking ceremony for the Baruch Houses, the East Side's biggest public housing project. Tenancy is to begin in the summer of 1953.

Bernard M. Baruch and his brother, Dr. Herman B. Baruch, former Ambassador to the Netherlands, were at the ceremony. The project, bounded by Delancey, East Houston and Columbia Streets and Franklin D. Roosevelt Drive, is named for their father, Dr. Simon Baruch.

In behalf of the family Mr. Baruch expressed appreciation for "naming this great enterprise after my father." He was "deeply interested in the human side of people," the son said.

Robert Moses, City Construction Coordinator, told how Dr. Simon Baruch, a Confederate Army physician, was instrumental in setting up in 1901 the city's first public bath, named for him. A bust of his noted son will be placed there, Mr. Moses said, adding: "Probably it's against his wishes, but we'll put it up anyway."

The speaker took time out for

Continued on Page 25, Column 4

The New York Times (by Meyer Liebowitz)
Dr. Herman Baruch and Bernard M. Baruch with Diane and Irving Siegel, neighborhood children, after ground-breaking for the Baruch Houses on the lower East Side yesterday.

The New York Times.

VOL. CI..No. 34,464.

Entered as Second-Class Matter,
Post Office, New York, N. Y.

NEW YORK, TUESDAY, JUNE 3, 1952.

Copyright, 1952, by The New York Times Company.

Times Square, New York 36, N. Y.
Telephone Lackawanna 4-1000

FIVE CENTS

LATE CITY EDITION

Fair today; some cloudiness tonight. Becoming fair tomorrow.

Temperature Range Today—Max., 72; Min., 60
Temperatures Yesterday—Max., 81; Min., 58
Full U. S. Weather Bureau Report, Page 39

SUPREME COURT VOIDS STEEL SEIZURE, 6 TO 3; HOLDS TRUMAN USURPED POWERS OF CONGRESS; WORKERS AGAIN STRIKE AS MILLS ARE RETURNED

SWIFT SENATE VOTE ON BONN ACCORDS IS ASKED BY TRUMAN

Message Calls Defense Moves in Europe 'Great Forward Stride' Toward Peace

ACHESON REPORTS TO U. S.

Both President and Secretary Declare Soviet Measures Will Not Deter the West

Truman message and Acheson address are on Page 8.

By WALTER H. WAGGONER
Special to The New York Times.

WASHINGTON, June 2—President Truman urged the Senate today to approve two agreements putting West Germany on a footing of equality among nations and binding an enemy of World War II to the free world's defense alliance.

Asking for "early and favorable" action on the two pacts, signed by the diplomats of the Western Governments in Europe last week, the President said in a message to the Senate that the documents taken together "constitute a great forward stride toward strengthening peace and freedom in the world."

Accompanying his message were the so-called peace contract with West Germany, an arrangement just short of a formal treaty, and an amendment to the North Atlantic Treaty that would extend its defense guarantees to the Bonn Government in return for reciprocal pledges. Both require approval by the Senate to become effective.

European Pact Also Sent

For the Senate's information, Mr. Truman also attached a number of other documents signed in either Paris or Bonn, the major one being the treaty constituting the six-nation European Defense Community that would bring West German troops into a European army.

In Bonn, Germany, Dr. Kurt Schumacher, Social Democratic leader, began the Opposition's campaign against ratification of the defense arrangements. He said that under the present terms the Germans would bear the brunt of the burdens involved in those accords while the Western Allies would enjoy the benefits.

Even before the President's message arrived, Senator Tom Connally, the Texas Democrat who heads the Senate Foreign Relations Committee, predicted that the Senate would give Mr. Truman the approval he sought.

The Senator's forecast was made on the basis of two hours of discussion, at a joint session of the Senate Foreign Relations and House Foreign Affairs Committees, with Secretary of State Dean Acheson.

Mr. Connally said that Mr. Acheson had assured the committees that "no secret or undisclosed commitments or guarantees" were made while he was on his European mission that produced the agreements.

Connally to Speed Action

The Senate's foreign policy spokesman said it was important that the treaties "go into effect as soon as possible" and he made it plain that he would do his part in speeding Senate action.

"In my view it is essential that Western Germany be accorded its proper place in the family of nations without delay so that we can proceed with the task of building the joint defense of the free world as rapidly as possible," he said in a statement.

Secretary Acheson, meanwhile, went directly to the American people for understanding and support of the new agreements, addressing the nation by radio and television this evening on the need and necessity of the new line-up of allies.

As President Truman had done, Mr. Acheson stressed the "very great stake" held by the United States in helping support and

Continued on Page 8, Column 3

Red Leader Named Premier of Rumania

By The United Press.

BUCHAREST, Rumania, June 2—The National Assembly proclaimed Gheorghe Gheorghiu-Dej as new Premier of Rumania today to succeed Dr. Petru Groza, who was named President of the republic.

M. Gheorghiu-Dej was named Premier by a unanimous vote. Dr. Groza, who had been Premier since March 6, 1945, was elected President of the Assembly, a post tantamount to President of the republic. On the Assembly, a post tantamount to President of the republic. The Government changes followed a request from the former President, Dr. Constantin Parhon, that he be relieved of his functions so he could dedicate himself entirely to his scientific work.

The Assembly took no action regarding Mme. Ana Pauker.

[The Bucharest radio revealed last week that Mme. Pauker, Rumanian Foreign Minister, had

Continued on Page 13, Column 2

ALLIES TERM TRUCE UP TO FOE IN KOREA

Reds Are Told World Opinion Will Judge Refusal to Agree to New Poll of Captives

By LINDESAY PARROTT
Special to The New York Times.

TOKYO, Tuesday, June 3—Maj. Gen. William K. Harrison Jr., senior United Nations truce delegate, told the Communists today: "The entire future of the armistice negotiations is now up to your side."

He warned the Chinese and North Koreans that the "court of world opinion" would judge their refusal to entertain the United Nations proposal that prisoners of war should be questioned by an impartial body in the presence of Communist representatives after a truce to determine how many wished to return to their former command.

General Harrison spoke during a thirty-minute session in the gravest warning given so far that the world would hold the Communists responsible for a delay in the truce and the failure of prisoners to return to their homes.

Outlining the proposal for "re-screening" of the prisoners, made after the enemy had challenged the result of an Allied poll that showed fewer than half the total

Continued on Page 3, Column 3

Another Prisoner on Koje Is Killed; Clark Set to Use Force on Captives

By GEORGE BARRETT
Special to The New York Times.

KOJE ISLAND, Korea, Tuesday, June 3—The accidental firing by an Allied soldier of a heavy machine gun near a prison stockade on this island killed one North Korean captive and wounded another today.

This mishap followed a statement yesterday by the new Far East Commander, Gen. Mark W. Clark, that Allied camp authorities were prepared to use "maximum force" to restore uncontested control over Communist captives.

An Army spokesman said that the North Korean who was killed had been standing near the barbed wire of Compound 78 when the machine gun went off. Other prisoners dragged the body farther inside the enclosure and refused to surrender it to United Nations medical personnel. They also refused to yield the wounded man for treatment on the active list.

An Army spokesman said that Brig. Gen. Haydon L. Boatner, camp commander, expressed concern over the accidental shooting the second within a week at Koje.

Meanwhile, the prisoners resumed their demonstrations inside the enclosures, to which the camp command had attempted to put an end. In Compound 76 captive North Koreans held a mock funeral, presumably commemorating the five prisoners who were killed there last Friday. They hung black crepe

on a flagpole and draped an ominous coffin with paper wreaths while General Boatner looked on from outside the barbed wire.

In Compound 602, according to pooled dispatches, the prisoners again erected the flagpole knocked down yesterday in a tank-led raid by United Nations guards, after the flying of the North Korean emblem had been forbidden. General Boatner told correspondents: "It will not be there very long."

Making his first visit to the troubled prison island yesterday, General Clark made it clear that the new United Nations policy of firmness might have taken so much starch out of the "die-hard" Communists that not much real fight was left in them.

Gen. James A. Van Fleet, Eighth Army commander, who came with General Clark, compared the atmosphere in seventeen compounds with the captives' mood of only a few weeks ago and happily summed up the situation that way.

In a late development last night there was a sudden flare-up of resistance from Compound 60, when a group of North Koreans—there are about 200 prisoners in this compound on war crimes charges—shouted taunts at a South Korean officer walking past the enclosure. The South Korean listened at first to the taunting, but was fi-

Continued on Page 4, Column 2

EISENHOWER YIELDS PAY IN RETIREMENT; FREE TO CAMPAIGN

He Leaves Army Duties Today —Waives $19,541 a Year to Avert Any Criticism

DECORATED BY PRESIDENT

Truman Hails Him as Symbol of Nation's Aim—General to Leave for Abilene

By JAMES RESTON
Special to The New York Times.

WASHINGTON, June 2—General of the Army Dwight D. Eisenhower has asked to be placed on the Army's retired list without pay, starting tomorrow. This request, which the Army said today had been approved by Secretary of Defense Robert A. Lovett, will release the general from the Army's regulations against political campaigning.

The current military appropriations legislation does not permit officers under the age of 62 to retire with pay unless the Department of Defense finds that this would cause personal hardship or be bad for the service.

[In South Dakota and California the final primaries will be held Tuesday, with the Dakota contest between General Eisenhower and Senator Robert A. Taft of Ohio attracting major attention. On the Democratic side, Senator Estes Kefauver is seeking delegates in both primaries. The Missouri Republican convention completed the formalities of naming a twenty-six-member delegation.]

General Eisenhower wrote to Mr. Lovett on May 28, asking that no special certification be made in his case, because his name was "directly involved in the national political campaign." The general, who is 61, would have been entitled to $19,541 a year in pay and allowances if, like General of the Army Douglas MacArthur, he had remained on the active list.

From his European headquarters, General Eisenhower wrote:

"There are a number of delegates already pledged to seek my nomination as the Republican Presidential candidate and, in the normal course of events, I will be talking to some of these delegates prior to the National Convention. As an officer on the retired list, I would feel free to engage in such

Continued on Page 19, Column 1

TWO IMPORTANT STEPS YESTERDAY IN THE STEEL DISPUTE

Secretary of Commerce Charles Sawyer signing formal order returning nation's steel plants to owners.

Philip Murray, C. I. O. and steel union president, making call that sent 600,000 workers on strike.

Associated Press Wirephotos

REALTY TAX TO RISE 12 TO 15 POINTS HERE

Final Valuations Show Record City Rate of $3.08 Probably Will Soar to $3.21

By PETER KIHSS

A rise of twelve to fifteen points in the city's basic real estate tax rate of $3.08, already the highest in history, was forecast unofficially yesterday when the final valuations of taxable real estate and special franchises were set at $19,425,499,087 for the fiscal year beginning July 1.

The revised valuations were $58,392,794 less than the tentative valuations made public Feb. 1, but $648,742,541 above the final figure of $18,776,756,546 for the current tax year. The total was the second highest in the city's history, exceeded only by 1932's $19,616,-915,429.

While no city official would go on record with a tax forecast, pending a revised estimate of general fund revenues due from Comptroller Lazarus Joseph on June 20, the pencils flew at City Hall to make some approximations based on Mayor Impellitteri's budget message of April 1.

Mayor's Estimate of Need

The Mayor had estimated then that the new $1,469,265,102 expense budget would need a yield of $622,804,788 from real estate taxes. The Mayor reported that this was practically the maximum that could be levied on real estate within constitutional limitations.

Dividing this proposed yield by the final realty valuations would give a basic tax rate of nearly $3.21 for each $100 of assessed valuation, or thirteen points above the rate that has prevailed this year and last. Above this come borough rates, which this year have varied from 18 to 21 cents.

Municipal fiscal experts indicated this $3.21 basic tax rate approximation might still vary slightly, depending on revisions in the general fund. But they noted that the original general fund estimate had included $12,500,000 from an overnight parking tax, which the Mayor has been unable to get.

The main hopes in fiscal quarters appeared to be for rises in other general fund sources that might at least make up the loss from the parking tax estimate. In round numbers, each point in the real estate tax levy yields not quite $2,000,000.

The final realty valuations were transmitted to the Mayor by William E. Boyland, president of the seven-member Tax Commission. They showed ordinary real estate at $16,846,784,544, up $553,300,800 from last year; real estate of utility corporations at $1,738,-555,835, up $54,008,315, and special

Continued on Page 45, Column 1

600,000 Quit Steel Mills; Industry Offers to Bargain

By A. H. RASKIN
Special to The New York Times.

PITTSBURGH, June 2—The steel industry got its mills back today, but they were producing no steel. Six hundred thousand members of the United Steelworkers of America, C. I. O., quit work as soon as they learned that the Supreme Court had ruled against Government seizure of the steel plants.

Many did not wait even for formal strike orders from their union president, Philip Murray. They simply put aside their tools and streamed out of mills that normally produce 95 per cent of the country's steel. All who stayed were supervisors and maintenance men engaged in the orderly cooling of blast furnaces to prevent permanent damage to equipment.

Mr. Murray got word of the court's decision at luncheon in a hotel across from his Pittsburgh headquarters. He rushed back and wired all union locals to stop work.

His message said: "The act of the court leaves the members of the United Steelworkers of America without the benefit of a collective bargaining agreement. In the absence of a wage agreement, our members have no alternative other than to cease work."

Mr. Murray also called upon the major steel companies to renew contract negotiations on the basis of the wage increases and other benefits recommended by the Wage Stabilization Board.

In a joint reply tonight, six of the largest companies said they were prepared to sit down with the union at once but that bargaining would have to proceed on a

Continued on Page 24, Column 2

CONGRESS HAILS END OF STEEL SEIZURE

Some Demand Constitutional Curb on President—Censure of Truman Is Hinted

By C. P. TRUSSELL
Special to The New York Times.

WASHINGTON, June 2—Congress generally hailed today the Supreme Court's 6-3 decision holding President Truman's seizure of the steel industry unconstitutional.

Many at the Capitol held to the view that Mr. Truman still had ample legal power to invoke the Taft-Hartley Act, which he has sought unsuccessfully to have repealed, and to let its injunctions against strikes settle the problem. There was much speculation as to whether the President now would invoke that law.

Prompt Congressional action to meet the problem of the steel walkout was in doubt, however.

Demands were made that the court's verdict be clinched, either by giving the President the powers he thought he had, or by writing into the Constitution a prohibition against the use of seizure powers without specific backing in law.

Committee Meets Tomorrow

A House Judiciary subcommittee that has on its docket a dozen or so measures to impeach Mr. Truman, to censure him or to give him powers or deprive him of them was scheduled to meet Wednesday. It appeared tonight that it might recommend a censure on top of today's court decision.

On the Senate calendar today was a bill that would amend the Constitution to bar the President from seizing any private property except under specific law.

Its sponsor, Senator Pat McCarran, Democrat of Nevada and chairman of the Senate Judiciary Committee, obtained Senator Homer E. Ferguson, Republican of Michigan, granted the Senate's unanimous consent for the McCarran bill to remain on the calendar with no prejudice.

A single objection, under the rules of the calendar, could block a proposed Constitutional amendment under this procedure.

Another measure, sponsored by Senator Wayne Morse, Republican of Oregon, would provide Constitu-

Continued on Page 23, Column 1

BLACK GIVES RULING

President Cannot Make Law in Good or Bad Times, Majority Says

VINSON IS DISSENTER

Rejects Idea Executive Is 'Messenger Boy' in Crisis—Steel Curbed

The majority opinion, Page 22; others in part, Pages 22 and 23.

By JOSEPH A. LOFTUS
Special to The New York Times.

WASHINGTON, June 2—The Supreme Court of the United States ruled, 6 to 3, today that President Truman's seizure of the steel industry to avert a strike violated the Constitution by usurping the legislative powers reserved to Congress.

The President bowed promptly by directing Secretary of Commerce Charles Sawyer to release the properties to their private owners, and the United Steelworkers of America, C. I. O., went on strike.

As a result of the walkout the Government ordered a halt in deliveries of steel from retail warehouses to consumer goods producers in an effort to conserve steel for defense needs.

Authorities said the action was directed at preventing a drain on warehouses by buyers who usually got their steel at the mills. Manufacturers who ordinarily receive steel from warehouses will continue to do so, they added. No order was issued against steel exports.

The Supreme Court justices who voted to uphold District Judge David A. Pine's order dispossessing the Government were: Hugo L. Black, Felix Frankfurter, William O. Douglas, Robert H. Jackson, Harold H. Burton and Tom C. Clark.

Dissenting were: Chief Justice Fred M. Vinson and Justices Stanley F. Reed and Sherman Minton.

Founding Fathers' Action Cited

The court ruled in effect that when the President seized the steel mills he seized the lawmaking power, because only Congress could authorize the taking of private property for public use.

"The Constitution did not subject this law-making power of Congress to Presidential or military supervision or control," said the opinion of the court, written by Justice Black.

"The founders of this nation entrusted the lawmaking power to the Congress alone in both good and bad times," it added. "It would do no good to recall the historical events, the fears of power and the hopes for freedom that lay behind their choice. Such a review would but confirm our holding that this seizure order cannot stand."

Chief Justice Vinson, writing a vigorous dissent, declared that the President's action to keep steel flowing was warranted by the world emergency.

"History bears out the genius of the founding fathers who created a Government subject to law but not left subject to inertia when vigor and initiative are required," the Chief Justice wrote.

Vinson Criticizes Majority

"As the district judge stated this is no time for 'timorous' judicial action," he declared. "But neither is this a time for timorous executive action."

Chief Justice Vinson said the majority of the court, not the minority, was seeking to amend the Constitution.

"The broad Executive power granted by Article II to an officer on duty 365 days a year cannot, it is said, be invoked to avert disaster.

"Instead, the President must confine himself to sending a message to Congress recommending action. Under this messenger-boy concept of the office, the President cannot even act to preserve legislative programs from destruction so that Congress will have something left to act upon.

"The court, contrary to a widely

Continued on Page 23, Column 5

NEXT MOVE IN CRISIS IS CALLED TRUMAN'S

President Could Use Taft Act or Appeal to Congress—No Word From White House

By ANTHONY LEVIERO
Special to The New York Times.

WASHINGTON, June 2—With steel workers walking out of mills all over the country in the wake of the decision of the United States Supreme Court today nullifying the President's seizure of the industry, the next move was held to be up to Mr. Truman.

There was no indication from the White House tonight, however, as to what we might do. Meanwhile, Mr. Truman and his advisers were studying the seven opinions of the high tribunal.

Two obvious steps were presumably being considered by Mr. Truman.

The first would be to invoke the Taft-Hartley Act, which would require the union men to return to work for eighty days while a fact-finding board investigated the wage dispute. The other move might be a renewal of the plea that Mr. Truman addressed to Congress soon after the decision for specific statutory authority to deal with labor disputes in major industries in time of emergency.

In the courts and in Congress Mr. Truman has been severely criticized for not having used the Taft law that labor hates before he resorted to seizure. His answer has been that the steel workers had waited ninety-nine days while the Wage Stabilization Board studied the wage dispute. Further-

Continued on Page 23, Column 7

Speedy Action by a Teller Foils Hold-Up in East 42d Street Bank

A would-be bank robber who escaped although three armed guards were near by was foiled yesterday in an attempt to hold up the Irving Trust Company at 100 East Forty-second Street by an alert 27-year-old teller, described by his superiors in the bank as a "guy with real guts."

This was the story as it was pieced together from accounts by the police of the East Thirty-fifth Street station and H. G. Brownson, vice president in charge of the bank's Forty-second Street office at Pershing Square:

At 2:50 P. M., an hour and ten minutes before the bank's closing time, a man about 45 years old, dressed in a gray suit and wearing a dark felt hat, approached a teller's cage about 100 feet from the Forty-second Street entrance to the bank.

There were 125 employes on duty, including the armed guards, and fifteen persons on the bank

floor, which is in the second story of the Continental Can Building.

The cage the man approached was occupied by Charles Lehanka of 460 Audubon Avenue, who had worked in the bank for a little more than a year.

Without a word, the man handed to Mr. Lehanka a two-page note. The writing was a combination of lettering and script and was done in pencil on unlined paper.

Mr. Lehanka read only the first couple of sentences of the 138-word message. They said: "Don't press the alarm button if you value your life. Give me all the folding money you have in that cage."

At this point, Mr. Lehanka made a swift and courageous decision. He dropped to the floor and pressed the alarm, which sounded at Police Headquarters

Continued on Page 26, Column 4

The New York Times.

LATE CITY EDITION
Fair and warm today and tomorrow.
Temperature Range Today—Max., 85 ; Min., 64
Temperatures Yesterday—Max., 85 ; Min., 65
Full U. S. Weather Bureau Report, Page 29

VOL. CI..No. 34,503.
Entered as Second-Class Matter,
Post Office, New York, N. Y.

NEW YORK, SATURDAY, JULY 12, 1952.

Copyright, 1952, by The New York Times Company

Times Square, New York 36 N. Y.
Telephone Lackawanna 4—1000

FIVE CENTS

EISENHOWER NOMINATED ON THE FIRST BALLOT; SENATOR NIXON CHOSEN AS HIS RUNNING MATE; GENERAL PLEDGES 'TOTAL VICTORY' CRUSADE

LONG U. N. AIR RAID POUNDS PYONGYANG AND REDS' BUILD-UP

Three-Wave Daylight Attack Is Followed by Smashing B-29 Blows at Night

NORTH'S CAPITAL AFLAME

Allied Land, Navy and Marine Fighter-Bombers Strike as Korea Truce Talks Drag On

By LINDESAY PARROTT
Special to The New York Times.

TOKYO, Saturday, July 12—Allied aircraft of many nations smashed yesterday at the North Korean capital at Pyongyang and the Communists' military build-up in western Korea in one of the largest and most devastating raids of the war.

Attacking in waves from 10 A. M. until late in the afternoon, the planes flew 1,200 sorties from ground bases and from the decks of United States and British carriers at sea.

Almost 600 tons of bombs fell on the daylight targets at Pyongyang and at Hwangju and Sariwon, on the rail line south of Pyongyang, where for months the Communist armies have stockpiled supplies of arms and munitions and placed military headquarters, communications centers and repair shops.

Meanwhile, the truce talks at Panmunjom continued, the brief sessions on the vexed question producing no indicated progress. A brief sitting was held this forenoon and another meeting was set for tomorrow.

Mass Night Strike

Last night, in what headquarters of the Far East Air Forces here called the "largest night air strike of the Korean conflict," B-29 Superforts from Japanese and Okinawan bases returned to the Communist capital in a new blow. The medium bombers also fanned out over North Korea, hitting supply concentrations at Hamhung, on the east coast; Kyomipo, near Pyongyang, and Sinmak, to the north.

Fifty-four of the B-29's unloaded 540 tons of high explosives over Pyongyang, still blazing from the attack of the fighter-bombers during daylight. Industrial plants, vehicle parks and repair shops were reported hit, with "excellent" results.

Sixty-five bombers participated in the attacks throughout North Korea, with major concentration over selected targets at Pyongyang. The clouds that moved in over the Pyongyang area cleared at night and the bombardiers saw their projectiles fall in direct hits.

[Later, Far East Air Forces said one F-84 Thunderjet was lost in the day and night attacks. The Associated Press reported all the Superforts returned safely to base. The F-84 was shot down by Communist ground fire. The report did not cover Navy or Marine or other Allied planes.]

Reds' Radio Makes Claim

The Reds' Pyongyang radio, on the air a few hours after the daylight strikes, claimed ten Allied aircraft shot down.

No official estimate of the damage done in the day and night attacks had been made pending the study of aerial photographs taken from reconnaissance planes that followed close on the tails of the bombers.

Returning pilots spoke of huge secondary explosions that followed hits by bombs and rockets and big islands of fire raging last evening where hundreds of gallons of napalm—jellied gasoline—fell.

Pyongyang, the biggest railroad junction in North Korea, around which the enemy had built air-fields, anti-aircraft positions and supply dumps and where some of the few remaining industrial targets north of the Thirty-eighth Parallel remained, was a mass of flames, observers said.

Pilots flying in the second wave of attack said smoke was rising thousands of feet from the Red

Continued on Page 2, Column 3

O'Dwyer Considers Staying in Mexico

By SYDNEY GRUSON
Special to The New York Times.

MEXICO CITY, July 11—Ambassador William O'Dwyer is seriously considering taking up permanent residence in Mexico when his job comes to an end.

All the Ambassador will say for public quotation at this time is that he has "made no definite plans" for the future. But he has recently told persons inquiring about his plans that settling down in Mexico is high among the possibilities.

The former New York Mayor celebrated his sixty-second birthday last Monday and in discussing the future, he has expressed concern for the financial security of his wife, the former Sloan Simpson, in the event of his death.

On his retirement from the mayoralty of New York to become Ambassador to Mexico, Mr.

Continued on Page 11, Column 5

STEEL LEADERS SEE UNION, THEN CONFER

Murray Awaits New Industry Offer in Pittsburgh—Talks Expected to Go On Today

By A. H. RASKIN
Special to The New York Times.

PITTSBURGH, July 11—Negotiations to end the crippling national steel strike waited on a new industry offer today.

After a ninety-minute meeting this morning with Philip Murray, president of the United Steelworkers of America, C. I. O., a committee representing the major steel and iron ore producers went to the headquarters of the United States Steel Corporation where they spent the afternoon in private conference with other steel company officials.

No report came from the closely guarded industry session, but there was hope that the committee would emerge with a new peace proposal to put before the union tomorrow.

Mr. Murray announced at 8:30 P. M. that no further joint meetings would be held today but that it was "reasonable" to expect there would be an industry-union meeting tomorrow.

"We did meet with the industry today, and that's that," the union leader said.

Leaders on both sides refrained

Continued on Page 23, Column 6

$445,560,000 SOUGHT FOR NEW SUBWAYS BY TRANSIT BOARD

Second Avenue Network and 2 Brooklyn Extensions Put Before Estimate Body

BENEFITS DESPITE DEFICIT

Traffic Relief Seen—Costs of Operation 17 to 20% Above Revenue Conceded

By PAUL CROWELL

The Board of Transportation authorized yesterday, subject to approval of the Board of Estimate, eight subway construction projects in Manhattan, Brooklyn, Queens and the Bronx with a total estimated cost of $445,650,000.

The projects listed were six routes of the Second Avenue trunk line, with connections with existing subway lines, and the proposed extensions of the Utica Avenue and Nostrand Avenue I. R. T. subway lines in Brooklyn. The cost of the Second Avenue project was estimated at $363,500,000, including $41,000,000 for equipment. The two Brooklyn extensions were estimated to cost $82,150,000, including $13,990,000 for equipment.

The proposals would include also a subway link-up in the form of a new line from Fifty-third Street and Avenue of the Americas to East Seventy-sixth Street and Second Avenue and thence running under the East River to Woodside and Thirty-eighth Avenue in Queens.

Not in Use Before 1957-58

In a report to the Board of Estimate that ground for the eight projects could not be broken before next fall. It was indicated that the operation of the Second Avenue trunk line and its connections could not begin before 1958 and that of the two Brooklyn extensions before 1957.

The transit agency's report admitted that audition of the Second Avenue line and the two Brooklyn extensions to the existing rapid transit system would create an enlarged subway network unable to yield a 10-cent fare.

"The most desirable benefits to be derived from the proposed routes," the report said, "are those which will be realized by the mil-

Continued on Page 29, Column 3

THE 1952 STANDARD-BEARERS OF THE REPUBLICAN PARTY

Gen. Dwight D. Eisenhower, for President

Associated Press Wirephoto
Senator Richard M. Nixon, for Vice President

TAFT GIVES WINNER HIS PLEDGE OF AID

Pair Exchange Compliments in Cordial Chat but Supporters of Ohioan Are Bitter

By LEO EGAN

CHICAGO, July 11—General of the Army Dwight D. Eisenhower and Senator Robert A. Taft today had their first face-to-face meeting since the Republican convention opened and exchanged mutual professions of esteem and respect in an obvious effort to allay factional bitterness within the Republican party.

Senator Taft, his brother, Charles P. Taft, Republican candidate for Governor of Ohio, and David S. Ingalls, who managed the Senator's pre-convention campaign, all pledged themselves during the day to use their full influence to persuade the Senator's friends to give full support to the convention winner.

Usually it is the loser who calls upon the winner, but General Eisenhower reversed the custom to make a personal call on Senator Taft soon after the nomination and to bespeak the Ohioan's help in the campaign ahead.

Senator Taft, with three of his four sons standing beside him, received the general in his headquarters' suite at the Conrad Hilton Hotel and offered his congratulations. Later the two fought their way, with the help of a detail of Chicago police, into the entrance hall of the Taft headquarters where television and newsreel cameras had been set up and newspaper reporters and photographers were waiting.

General Praises Taft

As soon as he could make himself heard, Senator Taft stepped before the microphones and said:

"I want to congratulate General Eisenhower. I shall do everything possible in the campaign to secure his election and to help in his Administration."

General Eisenhower, flashing the grin he has made famous, then turned to the crowd, jammed shoulder-to-shoulder in the hall, and said:

"I came over to pay a call of friendship on a very great American. His willingness to cooperate is absolutely necessary to the success of the Republican party in the campaign and in the Administration to follow."

General Eisenhower's statement brought a chorus of cheers from Taft followers, who slightly outnumbered the reporters and television crews in the hall. Earlier, when the general first arrived, he had been greeted by a mixture of cheers and boos, followed by a "We want Taft" chant.

Others who contributed largely to the convention victory were Herbert Brownell Jr. of New

Continued on Page 6, Column 1

Nominee Asks Unity at Home And Just, Sure Peace Abroad

By JAMES RESTON
Special to The New York Times.

CONVENTION BUILDING in Chicago, July 11—General of the Army Dwight D. Eisenhower accepted the Republican Presidential nomination tonight and summoned this great "crusade" for "total victory" over the Democrats in November.

[Text of Eisenhower speech of acceptance is on Page 4.]

Likening his new assignment to the historic "crusade" he led against Nazi Germany, the 61-year-old retired five-star general pledged himself to "a program of progressive politics" designed to produce unity at home and peace abroad.

To the obvious delight of a convention audience, many of whose members have feared that he would not conduct a fighting campaign against the Administration, General Eisenhower defined his first aim:

"To sweep from office an Administration which has fastened on every man of us the wastefulness, the arrogance and corruption in high places; the heavy burdens and anxieties which are the bitter fruit of a party too long in power."

VICTORS' STRATEGY OUTPACED RIVALS'

Action on Doubtful Delegate Issue and on TV Ban Took Lead From Taft's Men

By JAMES A. HAGERTY
Special to The New York Times.

CHICAGO, July 11—General of the Army Dwight D. Eisenhower won the Republican nomination for President because the members of his board of strategy completely outmaneuvered the supposedly adroit group of politicians who managed the campaign of Senator Robert A. Taft of Ohio.

The initial break that started the chain of events that led to the nomination of General Eisenhower came even before the convention opened last Monday when the Taft-dominated Republican National Committee and its pro-Taft chairman, Guy George Gabrielson, refused to permit television, radio and motion picture coverage of the committee's hearing on delegate contests. The committee had even barred newspaper photographers from the hearings as previous Republican conventions.

The result was that every television and radio chain in the country filled the air with protests against what they called an "Iron Curtain" on the committee's proceedings, demanded free access to the hearings and stressed that it was supporters of Senator Taft who had imposed the ban over the objection of supporters of General Eisenhower. This television and radio barrage proved very damaging to Senator Taft's candidacy.

With supporters of Senator Taft in control of the National Committee and its Committee on Arrangements for the convention, the Eisenhower campaign managers not only overcame this handicap but scored in test votes involving contests in Georgia, Louisiana and Texas, took control of the convention and went on to nominate General Eisenhower.

Heading the Eisenhower group and entitled to major credit for directing the Eisenhower campaign was Senator Henry Cabot Lodge Jr., campaign manager.

Continued on Page 6, Column 4

Remembering at the same time the acrimonious arguments and sharp divisions that preceded his nomination on the first ballot this morning, General Eisenhower appealed for an end of squabbling at home and torment abroad in these terms:

"It is our aim to give to our country a program of progressive policies drawn from our finest Republican traditions; to unite us

Continued on Page 5, Column 1

NIXON, ACCEPTING, URGES G.O.P. SWEEP

Senator Was Selected Without Opposition—His Record and Youth Strong Factors

Text of acceptance speech by Senator Nixon, Page 4.

By WILLIAM S. WHITE
Special to The New York Times.

CONVENTION BUILDING in Chicago, July 11—Senator Richard Milhous Nixon of California was nominated without opposition as the Republican candidate for Vice President of the United States.

The whole proceeding required less than half an hour.

Senator Nixon, who is 39 years old, was the choice of all the leaders who supported his senior on the 1952 Republican ticket, General of the Army Dwight D. Eisenhower, and was, of course, acceptable to the general.

Accepting the nomination in a short speech to the Republican National Convention tonight, Senator Nixon put in a strong appeal for the election of a Republican Congress.

Control by the G. O. P. was vital, he said, and especially to put in places of power such men as Senator Robert A. Taft of Ohio, General Eisenhower's defeated antagonist for the Presidential designation.

It was only with a Republican Congress, Mr. Nixon declared, that the Republicans could consolidate

Continued on Page 6, Column 2

Bitterly Divided Convention

General Eisenhower won in a bitterly divided Republican convention. In the last week the general had taken leadership in the contest from Senator Robert A. Taft of Ohio, the chief party spokesman in Congress, who was making his third unsuccessful bid for nomination to the office once held by his father, William Howard Taft.

Victory came for General Eisenhower on the first ballot. The official results were 845 for General Eisenhower, 280 for Senator Taft, 77 for Gov. Earl Warren of California, and 4 for General of the Army Douglas MacArthur.

But that figure did not represent truly the voting sentiments of these delegates as they faced the crucial and final showdown between General Eisenhower and Senator Taft.

When the first roll-call of the states was completed, General Eisenhower had 595 votes—nine short of the required majority of 604—and Senator Taft had 500. The balance of power rested with favorite-son candidates, such as Governor Warren, who had 81 votes, and Harold E. Stassen, former Minnesota Governor, with 20. General MacArthur had received only 10 votes.

Others Then Changed

While Governor Warren's California delegation held firm for him in the hope of a deadlock, Mr. Stassen's Minnesota delegates, now that a victory for General Eisenhower was in the offing, broke away and cast nineteen votes for General Eisenhower before a first ballot result could be announced.

The nineteen, added to the General's previous total, gave him 614, or ten more than a majority. Then other states began to change their votes in order to be recorded on the side of the winner.

Thus, the choice of General Eisenhower's nomination later was made unanimous on the motion of principal backers of Senator Taft and Governor Warren, who pledged their support for the principals to the nominee, it was made clear that General Eisenhower was the choice of a divided convention, and the chance of one of his first tasks would be to restore party unity and heal the deep wounds inflicted during the

Continued on Page 7, Column 1

REVISED VOTE 845

Minnesota Leads Switch to Eisenhower and Others Join Rush•

BUT SOME HOLD OUT

First Call of the States Gave General 595 to 500 for Taft

First ballot with revised vote is printed on Page 6.

By W. H. LAWRENCE
Special to The New York Times.

CONVENTION BUILDING in Chicago, July 11—General of the Army Dwight D. Eisenhower won a hard-fought first-ballot nomination today as the Republican candidate for President and Senator Richard M. Nixon of California was chosen by acclamation as his running mate for the Vice Presidency.

The former Supreme Allied Commander in Europe went before the 1,206 Republican delegates tonight to accept the nomination and pledge that he would lead "a great crusade" for "total victory" against a Democratic Administration he described as wasteful, arrogant and corrupt and too long in power. He said he would have "nothing in reserve" in his drive to put a Republican in the White House for the first time since March 4, 1933.

The Republican convention adjourned finally at 9:21 P. M., Central daylight time (9:21 New York time) after it had heard Senator Nixon accept the Vice-Presidential nomination. He pledged a "fighting campaign" to insure election not only of a Republican President, but also a House and Senate controlled by his party.

Democrats Respond to Eisenhower By Urging Liberal as His Opponent

Democratic party leaders in various parts of the country reacted yesterday to the Presidential nomination of General of the Army Dwight D. Eisenhower on the Republican ticket by emphasizing the need for a liberal nominee to oppose the general.

Although many prominent Democrats, including Averell Harriman, Senator Estes Kefauver of Tennessee and Senator Richard B. Russell of Georgia, were outspoken in their views, President Truman, who stayed close to his television set in Washington watching the Republican proceedings in Chicago, maintained silence.

Mr. Truman had only one scheduled engagement yesterday afternoon, setting aside most of his time for studying the Republican situation.

At Springfield, Ill., Gov. Adlai E. Stevenson said he had no comment on the nomination of General Eisenhower. He reiterated his assertion that he was not a candidate for the Democratic nomination.

The labor plank in the Republican platform adopted in Chicago yesterday came under attack from the International Association of Machinists, an independent union. A. J. Hayes, the president, sent telegrams, before General Eisenhower was nominated, to the four leading Republican candidates denouncing the plank as "unfriendly to labor" and adding:

"The Republican party has long had the reputation of being the

Continued on Page 10, Column 2

as did [Wendell] Willkie and [Thomas E.] Dewey before him that no matter how hard he tries to escape it the Republican party's record will be a handicap greater than he can overcome. After Nov. 4 he will be a sadder but wiser general."

Continued on Page 7, Column 2

Freed American Tells of Drugging With 'Truth Medicine' in China

By HENRY R. LIEBERMAN
Special to The New York Times.

HONG KONG, July 11—Robert T. Bryan, China-born American lawyer who was held incommunicado for sixteen and a half months as a political prisoner in a Shanghai jail, said today that his Communist captors had drugged him with two injections of "truth medicine" in an attempt to extract an acceptable "confession" and a separate statement denouncing the United States State Department.

Mr. Bryan, who served as municipal advocate for the Shanghai International Settlement from 1928 to 1941, was arrested Feb. 14, 1951.

He was subsequently accused of espionage and illegal attempts at responsibility for extradition proceedings in which Communist political operatives had been turned over to the Nationalist Government during the days of extraterritoriality.

"They blindfolded me, put me on a table and stuck something in my spine," he said in describing the first drug injection. "After about ten or twenty minutes when they sat me down, I felt I was sitting in mid-air.

"I wrote something, but I do not remember what happened. It took my volition away. I awoke the next morning with a terrific hangover."

This was the first report by a released political prisoner that he had been drugged by the Chinese Communists to elicit a "confes-

Continued on Page 2, Column 3

sion." It raised immediate speculation about the "confessions" of Lieut. John Quinn and Lieut. Kenneth L. Enoch, the captured American fliers who were represented by the Peiping Government as having admitted the dropping of "germ bombs" in Korea.

In addition to the American military advisers captured by the Chinese Reds in Korea, thirty-seven American civilians are officially listed here as being imprisoned in China. Thirteen more are reported to be under house arrest.

Mr. Bryan, who has resided in China about forty-five of his fifty-nine years, and who was also interned during World War II, said he underwent his first drug injection last April, after two of his "confession" drafts had been pronounced unacceptable. He said the second was administered last month, when he again failed to satisfy his interrogators after having received the option of "establishing merit" either by denouncing his friends or criticizing the State Department.

He subsequently accused of the Foreign Service Act of 1946, that they did not like that, so I was blindfolded and doped again," he recalled. "Later, when they showed me my signature, I told them I would repudiate anything obtained by drugs. They said no, this could

Continued on Page 2, Column 4

"All the News That's Fit to Print"

The New York Times.

Copyright, 1952. by The New York Times Company.

LATE CITY EDITION
Fair and continued pleasant today and tomorrow.
Temperature Range Today—Max.: 84; Min.: 66
Temperatures Yesterday—Max.: 82; Min.: 66
Full U. S. Weather Bureau Report. Page 2

VOL. CI..No. 34,517.

Entered as Second-Class Matter,
Post Office, New York, N. Y.

NEW YORK, SATURDAY, JULY 26, 1952.

Times Square, New York 18 N. Y.
Telephone LAckawanna 4-1000

FIVE CENTS

STEVENSON IS NOMINATED ON THE THIRD BALLOT; PLEDGES FIGHT 'WITH ALL MY HEART AND SOUL'; TRUMAN PROMISES TO 'TAKE OFF COAT' AND HELP

MOSSADEGH HINTS AT NEW ENDEAVOR TO SOLVE OIL ISSUE

Iranian Premier Tells Nation That 'Solution of Problem' Has Now Become 'Easier'

EARLY REFORMS PLEDGED

Government Leader Confers With Communists—Feeling Against U. S. Mounts

Special to THE NEW YORK TIMES.

TEHERAN, Iran. July 25.— Premier Mohammed Mossadegh told the nation in a radio broadcast tonight that the tangled oil problem had taken a turn for the better and that therefore he was resolved to initiate and carry out reform measures and to take fundamental speedy steps he believed the country direly needed now.

[The Associated Press reported that the Premier made his statement in these words: "In view of the fact that a solution to the oil problem now is easier, I intend to institute reforms which the country needs. These reforms can take place only in a calm atmosphere. So long as there is disorder, there is no opportunity for any kind of improvements."]

Dr. Mossadegh summoned George Middleton, British Chargé d'Affaires, to his office. They conferred for more than two hours. The purpose of the visit has not been disclosed but Mr. Middleton said that a guess that it concerned oil would not be far wrong.

Dr. Mossadegh's internal authority is now unchallenged and the decision of the International Court of Justice that the Anglo-Iranian oil complaint was outside its jurisdiction improved considerably his international situation in approaching the oil issue. Speculation naturally is to the effect that, starting from this position, he may seek again some type of solution of the oil problem.

Mossadegh Sees Communists

Dr. Mossadegh received the leaders of the Tudeh Communist organization, which now calls itself the Association to Combat Imperialism. The subject obviously was the relation between the Government and the National Front on one hand and Communist leaders on the other after their cooperation in last Monday's violent events, which drove Ahmad Ghavam from power.

In his radio address to the nation the Premier said:

"My dear compatriots, you will admit that no social reforms can be carried out without the existence of security forces. The maintenance of peace and security is the first condition of positive acts of the Government.

"The offenses and encroachments of some members of the security forces may have induced you to look askance on the entire security forces, but with the formation of a national government there is no reason why this suspicion should continue to exist.

Continued on Page 3, Column 5

U. S. Olympian Sets Steeplechase Mark

By ALLISON DANZIG
Special to THE NEW YORK TIMES.

HELSINKI, Finland, July 25.— Horace Ashenfelter won today the fastest 3,000-meter steeplechase race ever run for the United States' twelfth gold medal in track and field and the first Olympic victory ever in this event.

In the remarkable time of 8 minutes 45.4 seconds, 18.4 seconds under the Olympic record that has stood in the books since 1936, the 29-year-old Penn State graduate from Glen Ridge, N. J., ran away from the world's best to win by thirty yards as the first eight to finish excelled the old mark.

Vladimir Kazantsev of Russia, the favorite, who shadowed the special agent of the Federal Bureau of Investigation virtually all the way until he stumbled in the

Continued on Page 16, Column 1

Snag on Iron Ore Pay Blocks Order to Reopen Steel Mills

600,000 Union Men Await Pact for Miners —Fairless and Murray Plan to Visit Plants to Promote Labor Harmony

By A. H. RASKIN
Special to THE NEW YORK TIMES.

WASHINGTON. July 25.—The longest and most costly steel strike in the country's history was officially called off today, but an unexpected snag over wage rates for 23,000 iron ore miners blocked the sending of union back-to-work orders to 600,000 striking steel workers.

The last-minute difficulty, which both sides hoped would blow over in a few hours, cast a shadow over settlement arrangements that had indicated the steel dispute might provide a foundation for a new era of cooperative labor-management relations in the industry that represents the backbone of the American economy.

With only one dissenting vote, the 175-man Wage Policy Committee of the United Steelworkers of America, C. I. O., voted this afternoon to accept the settlement terms agreed upon at the White House yesterday by Philip Murray,

president of the union, and Benjamin F. Fairless, president and chairman of the United States Steel Corporation.

The agreement, which was personally announced by President Truman, provided a wage increase of 16 cents an hour, retroactive to last March 1; paid holidays, higher shift differentials and other "fringe" benefits that would cost 5.4 cent an hour more, and a modified union shop.

The agreement specified that iron-ore miners were to get all the same benefits, plus additional wage increases intended to bring their pay scales up to the steel level.

It was this provision that caused the difficulty today.

Under the agreement part of the difference in wage rates was to be made up at once and the rest at the end of the first year of the new contract.

Continued on Page 30, Column 5

U. N. Truce Team Walks Out Of Korea Talks for a Week

By LINDESAY PARROTT
Special to THE NEW YORK TIMES.

TOKYO, Saturday, July 26.—The United Nations delegates walked out of the new plenary sessions at Panmunjom today and told the Communists they would return in a week for further discussion of an armistice in the Korean war.

The senior Allied delegate, Maj. Gen. William K. Harrison Jr., led the United Nations representatives out of the conference tent after much of the first of a new series of meetings to a violent repetition of charges against the United Nations Command. The two sides agreed, however, that during the week's adjournment staff officers would meet to see what could be done to draft new tentative armistice terms as a basis for further discussion.

Pooled dispatches from Korea said General Harrison was shaking with anger as he left the road-side tent, where the Chinese and North Koreans, after the breakdown of the last three weeks' sessions,

Continued on Page 2, Column 3

6 AIDES OF FAROUK RESIGN AFTER COUP

5 High-Ranking Police Officials Jailed as Maher Cabinet Acts Speedily in Egypt

By The Associated Press.

CAIRO, July 25.—Gen. Mohammed Naguib Bey's Army-backed governmental house-cleaning with anger as he left the road reached to King Farouk's own palace today. Six of the monarch's top aides resigned.

At the same time Egypt's new strong man moved anew to crush opposition to the military coup by which he had installed the anti-corruption Government of Premier Aly Maher Pasha.

Maher Pasha's new Cabinet took over today, pledged to try to end the crisis that has swept this Middle East country for six months. The Cabinet hopes to end the corruption that, according to Maher Pasha, had brought the crisis about and to settle Egypt's dispute with Britain over the Suez Canal and the Sudan.

Police Officials Arrested

General Naguib Bey flew to Alexandria for a conference with Maher Pasha, leaving behind him a series of arrests. Among those held were five high-ranking political and police officials who were accused of conspiring against the public safety, an army communiqué said. Twelve generals of the Egyptian Army also were in custody.

The officials held included Maj. Gen. Mounif Mahmoud Pasha, Under Secretary of the Interior Ministry; the commandant of the Cairo police, the director of a special section of the Interior Ministry and two high officers of the political section of the police.

The communiqué said: "Although we have detained these few people * * * a much larger number of army men have been arrested."

Maj. Gen. Sirry Amer Bey, commander of Egypt's frontier corps, was arrested at Salum, on the Egyptian-Libyan border, and returned to Cairo.

General Naguib Bey received an ovation when he called on the new Premier. While they conferred for an hour, a crowd outside cheered and called the general "Protector of Egypt."

After the conference he told newsmen that his first aim was to assure the people of Alexandria

Continued on Page 3, Column 3

PRESIDENT IN FORM

Talks in 'Whistle Stop' Manner, Predicting Ticket's Victory

HITS AT EISENHOWER

Says 'People Will Not Choose Man Without Faith in People'

Text of the President's speech at the Convention, Page 4

Special to THE NEW YORK TIMES.

CONVENTION BUILDING in Chicago, Saturday, July 26—President Truman told a cheering Democratic National Convention early this morning that it had nominated a winner in Gov. Adlai E. Stevenson of Illinois.

The President promised that he would "take off my coat and go out to help him win."

In a direct attack upon Gen. Dwight D. Eisenhower, the Republican Presidential nominee, Mr. Truman declared that the "people won't choose a leader who does not have faith in the people." He said he did not think the country would be turned over to men "who are more concerned with cutting the budget than with the security of the United States."

This was a reference to General Eisenhower's pre-nomination pledge to reduce the Federal budget by $40,000,000,000 under certain conditions.

How to Win Elections

Mr. Truman started to speak at 1:42 A. M., after a four minute ovation. He reminded the delegates that four years ago at about the same hour in the morning he had predicted victory for the ticket headed by himself and Senator Alben W. Barkley of Kentucky for Vice President.

"But you didn't believe me," said the President with a grin.

"I'm telling you now that Adlai Stevenson will win in 1952."

The President said that the real reason Democrats won elections "is perfectly simple—it is because they give the American people the kind of Government they want."

"The Republicans," he declared, "are going to throw millions of dollars into an attempt to confuse

Continued on Page 5, Column 8

GOVERNOR ACCEPTS

Humility Marks Speech by Nominee Before Cheering Delegates

HE HAILS PLATFORM

Illinoisan in Tribute to Losing Candidates— Bids for Unity

Text of the acceptance speech by Mr. Stevenson, Page 5.

By JAMES RESTON

CONVENTION BUILDING in Chicago, Saturday, July 26—Gov. Adlai E. Stevenson of Illinois, in a speech marked both by humility in the face of the high honor and by a vigorous determination in the face of its challenge, early today accepted the Democratic nomination for President.

"I will fight to win that office with all my heart and soul," he told the cheering delegates. "With your help, I have no doubt that we will win."

Earlier, the "no" man from the Lincoln country, had for the first time said "yes."

"I did not want it," he said a moment after he had been nominated by the Democratic National Convention.

"But to shirk it would be to repay honor with dishonor," he added.

The call, he continued, "asked of me nothing except that I give such talents as I have to the services of my country. That I will do."

"I feel no exaltation or sense of triumph whatever, nothing but humility. I shall go on my knees and I shall ask my God to give me strength and courage and to nourish my spirit for this great undertaking in this great hour of history."

At the outset, he said, he had never been "more conscious of the appalling responsibility of office."

He went immediately to the convention hall from the home on Chicago's "Gold Coast" where he made his short statement.

The 52-year-old Governor developed this same solemn theme after he had been driven at breakneck speed through the late night traf-

Continued on Page 5, Column 4

THE DEMOCRATIC STANDARD-BEARER

ADLAI E. STEVENSON

Associated Press Wirephoto

300-VOTE SWITCH DECIDES CONTEST

Harriman's Withdrawal Swings Big State Blocs on Third Ballot to the Governor

Harriman statement, Kefauver and Russell talks, Page 4

By FELIX BELAIR Jr.
Special to THE NEW YORK TIMES.

CONVENTION BUILDING in Chicago, Saturday, July 26.—A sudden switch of more than 300 votes gave Gov. Adlai E. Stevenson of Illinois a third-ballot victory and the Democratic Presidential nomination here early today after Averell Harriman had announced his withdrawal from the contest and New York, Pennsylvania, Massachusetts, Michigan and Arkansas had swung in behind the choice of President Truman.

The race came out just as predicted by the managers of Governor Stevenson's floor campaign. Paul E. Fitzpatrick, the state party chairman, took the speaker's platform after a dinner recess to announce Mr. Harriman's withdrawal. Massachusetts' favorite son, Gov. Paul A. Dever, followed with the announcement to the convention that he, too, was withdrawing in favor of Governor Stevenson.

Mr. Fitzpatrick's statement in behalf of Mr. Harriman was followed much later in the session by speeches by Senator Estes Kefauver of Tennessee and Senator Richard B. Russell of Georgia, both conceding the nomination to the Illinoisan.

With the Harriman and Dever switches there were more than 100 votes right there to be added to Governor Stevenson's second ballot total of 423½. When Michigan switched its 40 votes from Senator Estes Kefauver it remained only for Pennsylvania to bring along the stragglers by giving the Governor all its 70 votes, a net gain of 30.

Texas held out with its big 52-vote bloc, as did other delegations favoring Senator Russell but the die was already cast.

Senator Kefauver came up the center aisle of the auditorium on the arm of Senator Paul H. Douglas of Illinois in an attempt to gain the platform to announce his plan to nominate Senator Douglas, who was not in nomination but who would then have withdrawn and urged all Kefauver delegates to vote for Governor Stevenson. But Speaker Sam Rayburn, the convention's permanent chairman, ruled that the balloting must proceed.

Governor Stevenson was within a few votes of the required 615½ majority when the roll-call of the states ended and Speaker Rayburn gave to Tennessee the first oppor-

Continued on Page 5, Column 1

LEADERS IN HUDDLE ON VICE PRESIDENCY

Balloting Is Postponed Until Noon Today as Kefauver Foes Present Objections

Special to THE NEW YORK TIMES.

CONVENTION BUILDING in Chicago, Saturday, July 26.—Democratic party leaders went into a huddle early today immediately following the Presidential nomination of Gov. Adlai E. Stevenson for talks on the Vice Presidency.

The National Convention put off its choice until a noon session. The original program had called for selection of Governor Stevenson's running mate after his acceptance speech.

It was understood that the delay stemmed principally from some objections to Senator Estes Kefauver of Tennessee, who forged to the top of the "guess" list after he dramatically yielded in the Presidential race.

A late starter among the possibilities was Representative John W. McCormack of Massachusetts. Others mentioned were Vice President Alben W. Barkley, Senator John J. Sparkman of Alabama, Secretary of the Interior Oscar L. Chapman and Senator Richard B. Russell of Georgia.

Among those in the huddle at the near-by Stockyards Inn were Averell Harriman, who last night withdrew from the Presidential race, and Jake Arvey of Chicago, Governor Stevenson's principal backer in Illinois.

Regarding the possibility of taking the post, Senator Kefauver said:

"I haven't been offered the place and I really don't believe I would want to accept it. I haven't talked

Continued on Page 8, Column 7

Two Coalitions Won Stevenson's Victory

By JAMES A. HAGERTY
Special to THE NEW YORK TIMES.

CHICAGO, Saturday, July 26— The strategy used by supporters of Gov. Adlai E. Stevenson to get him the Democratic nomination for President, like the horns of a dilemma, had two prongs.

First, by a coalition with supporters of Senators Richard B. Russell of Georgia and Robert S. Kerr of Oklahoma they brought about the seating of the Virginia, Louisiana and South Carolina delegations, members of which had declined to take the loyalty pledge imposed by the Credentials Committee as a condition of participation in the convention.

Continued on Page 5, Column 1

RIVALS DROP OU

Withdrawal of Harrima Starts States' Rush to the Governor

ILLINOISAN TRAILE

But Picked Up Strengt From Larger States— Got C. I. O. Backing

The three ballots of Convention are printed on Page 6.

By WILLIAM S. WHITE
Special to THE NEW YORK TIMES.

CONVENTION BUILDING i Chicago, Saturday, July 26— Go Adlai E. Stevenson of Illinois wa nominated early today on the thir ballot for President of the Unite States by the thirty-first Democratic National Convention.

President Truman came here t salute him and to stand with hi before the delegates.

Mr. Truman, cheerful and smiling, declared to the Convention:

"I'm telling you now Adlai Stevenson is going to win in 1952 * * * I am going to take my coat off an do everything I can to help him win."

Governor Stevenson told the delegates that he could never have sought such an honor, and adding:

"I have asked the merciful Father of us all to let this cup pass from me. But from such dread responsibility now does no shrink in fear, in self-interest, or in false humility."

"So," he went on, quoting from the Bible, "if this cup may no pass away from Me, except I drink it, Thy will be done."

Huge Demonstration

Mr. Truman walked, as an enormous demonstration beat the walls of this hall, the length of the platform to greet Mr. Stevenson an take him to face the crowd.

The convention adjourned at 2:35 A. M. (3:35 A. M. New York time), to meet again at 11 A. M.

Governor Stevenson's nomination—the first genuine draft, since the Republicans demanded and James A. Garfield in 1880—came after the withdrawal of Averell Harriman of New York had turned the great bulk of that delegation to the Governor's standard.

Then Senator Estes Kefauver of Tennessee put over the Stevenson selection. Tennessee cast its 28 votes for the Governor, who was then a handful short of the required 615½, needed for a majority in a total of 1,230.

'Did Best We Could'

Senator Richard B. Russell of Georgia, after Mr. Stevenson's nomination, pledged to join in efforts for a party victory in November.

Senator Kefauver told the convention that it had been "quite apparent" that someone here had to yield. His intention, he said, had been to nominate Senator Paul H. Douglas of Illinois and Senator Douglas had intended in turn to give his favor to Governor Stevenson.

But this had been made impracticable by the Stevenson rush, Mr. Kefauver said, in effect, so he was simply retiring. It had been a good fight, he observed, "and we did the best we could."

Senator Kefauver, it appeared, was heading instead for the Vice Presidential nomination. The selection for Vice President is scheduled to be made today.

Four aggressive aspirants—Mr. Harriman, Senator Russell and Senator Robert S. Kerr of Oklahoma—had struggled with the Stevenson draft movement until it became apparent that there was to be no stopping it. Senator Kerr had retired early—before dinner-time last night— when his own Oklahoma delegation had left him, obviously with his consent, though he did not make it formal until nearly midnight.

Mr. Harriman's announcement of retirement from the race came after Mr. Truman, a Stevenson backer, had arrived here. The

Continued on Page 5, Column 1

CONVENTION-BOUND PRESIDENT VOTES BY PROXY

At the precise moment Mr. Truman was waving farewell at the Washington Airport before starting for Chicago in his plane . . .

. . . Thomas J. Gavin was casting his vote as the President's alternate on the convention floor in support of Adlai E. Stevenson.

Associated Press Wirephoto

"All the News That's Fit to Print"

The New York Times.

Copyright, 1952, by The New York Times Company.

VOL. CII No. 34,619.

Entered as Second-Class Matter.
Post Office, New York, N. Y.

NEW YORK, WEDNESDAY, NOVEMBER 5, 1952.

Times Square, New York 36, N. Y.
Telephone Lackawanna 4-1000

FIVE CENTS

ELECTION EXTRA

Fair, warmer today. Some cloudiness and turning cooler tomorrow.
Temperature Range Today—Max., 62; Min., 38
Temperatures Yesterday—Max., 52; Min., 39
Full U. S. Weather Bureau Report, Page 54

EISENHOWER WINS IN A LANDSLIDE; TAKES NEW YORK; IVES ELECTED; REPUBLICANS GAIN IN CONGRESS

G.O.P. HOUSE LIKELY

But the Senate Margin Hangs in the Balance of Two Close Races

LODGE TRAILING RIVAL

President Eisenhower May Lack a Working Majority in Congress

By JAMES RESTON

It appeared at 4:30 this morning that control of the United States Senate could be determined by the outcome of the Senatorial races in Michigan and Massachusetts.

At that time the Republicans appeared to have picked up five new seats and lost three others, thus enabling them to wipe out the two-seat advantage held by the Democrats at the end of the Eighty-second Congress.

To assure the power to organize the Senate and place their Republicans at the head of its important committees, however, Senator Henry Cabot Lodge Jr., Republican of Massachusetts, would have to overcome an advantage of more than 15,000 held by Representative John F. Kennedy, his opponent.

And Representative Charles E. Potter, Republican of Michigan had to retain the 47,000 lead he held over the Democratic incumbent, Senator Blair Moody of Michigan.

Morse May Be Vital

So close was the Senate race that there was a possibility that control of the upper chamber could be determined by the decision of Senator Wayne Morse of Oregon, who was elected as a Republican, but who broke with his party during the campaign, and announced that hereafter he was an "independent."

Though it appeared that the Republicans had won control of the House, one thing was certain: that President Dwight D. Eisenhower would not have a comfortable working majority in either house and would require all his gifts of persuasion to win consent for his policies on Capitol Hill.

Several factors in the Senate race were noteworthy.

Of the ten so-called isolationist or extremist Republicans who went before the voters yesterday, seven seemed fairly sure of victory. These were Senators Joseph R. McCarthy of Wisconsin; John W. Bricker of Ohio; William E. Jenner of Indiana; Edward Martin of Pennsylvania; Arthur V. Watkins of Utah, George W. Malone of Nevada and Hugh Butler of Nebraska.

Three other Republicans in this same category, however, were in serious trouble if they had not actually been defeated. They were:

Continued on Page 15, Column 1

M'Carthy Is Winner, But Is Last on Ticket

By RICHARD J. H. JOHNSTON
Special to The New York Times.

MILWAUKEE, Wednesday, Nov. 5—Wisconsin went to the Republicans today for the third time in a national election since 1920.

The predicted Republican sweep of the state and capture of its twelve electoral votes became a certainty a few minutes after midnight.

Gen. Dwight D. Eisenhower, the Republican Presidential nominee ran second on the G. O. P. ticket with Gov. Walter J. Kohler Jr. leading the slate in his bid for re-election.

As the returns neared the final count, Gen. Dwight D. Eisenhower vote indicated he would emerge as leader of the G. O. P. slate in Wisconsin. With 2,036 of the state's 3,224 voting precincts reported, his vote was 554,369 to Gov. Adlai E. Stevenson's 356,218.

Gov. Walter J. Kohler, seeking

Continued on Page 22, Column 6

Electoral Vote by States

	Eisenhower's no		Eisenhower's no
Ala.	— 11	Neb.	— 6
Ariz.	4	Nev.	— 3
Ark.	— 8	N. H.	4
Calif.	32	N. J.	16
Colo.	6	N. M.	4
Conn.	8	N. Y.	45
Del.	3	N. C.	— 14
Fla.	— 10	N. D.	4
Ga.	— 12	Ohio	25
Idaho	4	Okla.	8
Ill.	27	Ore.	6
Ind.	13	Pa.	32
Iowa	10	R. Isl.	4
Kan.	8	S. C.	— 8
Ky.	— 10	S. D.	4
La.	— 10	Tenn.	— 11
Me.	5	Texas	24
Md.	9	Utah	4
Mass.	16	Vt.	3
Mich.	20	Va.	12
Minn.	11	Wash.	9
Miss.	— 8	W. Va.	— 8
Mo.	— 13	Wisc.	12
Mont.	4	Wyo.	3
		Total..	442 89

*Trend.

EISENHOWER TAKES JERSEY BY 300,000

Senator Smith Is Re-elected—Bond Issues Supported in Record Balloting

By RUSSELL PORTER

With more than three-quarters of New Jersey's vote counted early this morning, Gen. Dwight D. Eisenhower appeared headed toward a plurality of close to 300,-000 in the state over Gov. Adlai E. Stevenson. This far exceeded Governor Dewey's 1948 plurality of 85,669 over President Truman.

United States Senator H. Alexander Smith, Republican candidate for re-election, won a sweeping victory over his Democratic opponent, Archibald S. Alexander, though Mr. Smith ran behind the head of his ticket. His indicated plurality was about 200,000.

The returns were:

PRESIDENT
3,461 precincts out of 3,840:
Eisenhower 1,203,120
Stevenson 921,375

UNITED STATES SENATOR
3,399 precincts out of 3,840:
Smith 1,089,863
Alexander 903,533

The Republicans appeared to have retained their majority of nine to five in New Jersey's delegation in the House of Representatives.

Both bond issues on the ballot

Continued on Page 23, Column 2

Hill Battle Spurts in Korea; Allies Press 'Triangle' Fight

By LINDESAY PARROTT
Special to The New York Times.

TOKYO, Wednesday, Nov. 5—The hard-fighting South Korean infantry, driving for the third time in three days up the slopes of the central Korean ridges, drove a penetration today into the Communist lines on the western flank of "Triangle Hill," a strategic position north of Kumhwa.

Early this afternoon, the Republic of Korea (R. O. K.) troops had captured one of the twin peaks that project from "Triangle," named "Jane Russell Hill." The sharp, indecisive combat continued.

The attack on the twin peaks was tied in with a new drive against the central pyramid of "Triangle Hill." The South Koreans again thrust within yards of the crest.

The Chinese Reds struck again just to the east in a new attempt to capture the summit of "Sniper Ridge," flanking "Triangle" on the United Nations' right.

The crest of "Triangle" had been lost to the Chinese Communists after the United Nations limited objective offensive took it last month. The South Koreans pushed up southern slopes today to within fifty yards of the Reds' crest.

Some reports said the fighting again today was as furious as dur-

Continued on Page 3, Column 3

STATE LEAD 850,000

General's Upstate Edge Tops Million—He Loses City by Only 362,674

PROTEST VOTE SEEN

Albany County, Other Areas in Democratic Column Switch

By JAMES A. HAGERTY

Gen. Dwight D. Eisenhower, Republican nominee for President, carried New York State with its forty-five electoral votes with a plurality of landslide proportions that will reach nearly 850,000.

With 33 election districts missing, all outside this city, General Eisenhower led Gov. Adlai E. Stevenson, his Democratic opponent, by an actual plurality of 846,029 and an indicated plurality of 840,-034.

To carry his adopted state by this astounding plurality, General Eisenhower held Governor Stevenson down to an actual plurality of 362,674 in this city, far less than the supporters of the Democratic candidate expected.

With the 33 election districts missing, General Eisenhower carried the state outside the city by an actual plurality of 1,265,789 and, assuming that his vote held up in the missing districts, by an indicated plurality of about 1,270,-000.

Governor Stevenson carried Manhattan by 147,633, the Bronx by 151,597 and Brooklyn by 209,-130, all far below Democratic expectations. General Eisenhower carried Queens by 117,872 and Richmond by 27,834, well above

Continued on Page 24, Column 3

State Presidential Vote

CITY SUMMARY

	Eisenhower (Rep.)	Stevenson (Dem.-Lib.)
Manhattan	300,234	447,877
Bronx	241,545	393,052
Brooklyn	447,148	656,278
Queens	449,505	331,633
Richmond	55,981	28,247
Total	1,494,413	1,857,087
Upstate	2,413,299	1,147,510
*Grand total.	3,907,712	3,104,597

*4,394 election districts out of 4,394 in the city reporting and 5,222 out of 5,954 upstate.

New President and Vice President

DWIGHT D. EISENHOWER

RICHARD M. NIXON

The New York Times

IVES IS RE-ELECTED BY RECORD MARGIN

Defeats Cashmore by Biggest Plurality of Any Republican —Harding Mark Topped

By LEO EGAN

Senator Irving M. Ives won re-election in a three-cornered race yesterday by the largest plurality ever obtained by a Republican candidate in New York State, topping President Warren G. Harding's record-setting margin of 1,089,929 in 1920 by more than 200,000 votes.

The former majority leader of the State Assembly and co-sponsor of New York's law against racial discrimination in employment that became the first Republican Senator to win re-election in New York since the late James W. Wadsworth performed that feat in the Harding landslide of 1920.

Not only did Senator Ives carry the normally Republican upstate area by a plurality that may reach 1,297,972, but he came within 118 votes of capturing normally Democratic New York City as well.

The complete Senate vote in the city gave Senator Ives 1,416,250 to 1,416,968 for Borough President John Cashmore of Brooklyn, the Democratic candidate. Thus Mr. Cashmore's plurality within the city was held to 718 votes.

With 5,854 of the 5,954 districts outside the city tolaled, Senator Ives had an actual plurality of 1,299,928. On this basis, his final upstate margin should reach 1,300,000.

Dr. George S. Counts, the Liberal party candidate, polled 454,042 votes in the same districts tabulated for Senator Ives and Mr. Cashmore. On this basis his final vote could reach 460,000. Corliss Lamont, the American Labor can-

Continued on Page 21, Column 3

Vote for Senator

CITY SUMMARY

	Ives (Rep.)	Cashmore (Dem.)	Counts (Lib.)
Man'n	303,040	322,157	88,797
Bronx	233,548	277,506	101,014
B'klyn	398,498	522,751	147,370
Queens	429,225	265,812	62,558
Rich'd	51,939	28,742	2,044
Total	1,416,250	1,416,968	401,783
Up-state	2,399,770	1,099,842	52,259
Gr Totl	3,816,020	2,516,810	454,042

4,394 election districts out of 4,394 in the city reporting and 5,854 out of 5,954 up-state.

Eisenhower Cracks South, Heads for Victory in Texas

By WILLIAM S. WHITE

Gen. Dwight D. Eisenhower, the Republican Presidential candidate, has smashed the traditionally Democratic Solid South in his national victory over Gov. Adlai E. Stevenson. He has carried outright Florida and Virginia, with their twenty-two electoral votes. This morning unofficial observers gave him the greatest Southern prize of all—Texas and its twenty-four electoral votes, the sixth biggest bloc in the United States.

Confirmation of this indicated loss would involve a Democratic disaster.

Apart from all this and from receiving the greatest popular ballot ever given a Republican in the South, General Eisenhower was first narrowly leading and then narrowly trailing this morning in normally Democratic Tennessee, which has eleven electoral votes. In Tennessee, the position was so close that the result probably will not be known until late this afternoon.

In Louisiana and South Carolina Governor Stevenson had slight leads after trailing often in the early returns.

Only the hardest of the hard core of the Old South has remained wholly faithful to the old Democratic tradition.

Mississippi, Arkansas, North

Continued on Page 22, Column 3

CONNECTICUT G. O. P. SEATS 2 IN SENATE

Benton and Ribicoff Concede to Purtell and Bush While Eisenhower Sweeps State

HARTFORD, Conn., Wednesday, Nov. 5—Gen. Dwight D. Eisenhower swept to an amazing landslide victory in Connecticut yesterday, winning by a margin of nearly 130,000 votes over Gov. Adlai E. Stevenson in final returns from the 169 cities and towns in the state.

The victory astounded Republicans as well as Democrats. Prior to the election, Republican leaders had made cautious claims of victory by about 25,000 or 30,000 votes, while Democrats privately thought they had a chance to win the state.

The tremendous Eisenhower sweep carried two Republican United States Senators into office with him. Senator William A. Purtell of West Hartford defeated William Benton, Democrat, for the full six-year term by a margin of 90,286, and Prescott S. Bush, Greenwich banker, defeated Representative Abraham A. Ribicoff of Hartford, Democrat, by 30,373 votes. Mr. Ribicoff made a spectacular uphill run but was edged out by Mr. Bush's lead in the small towns that are traditionally Republican.

Final returns:

PRESIDENT
169 precincts out of 169:
Eisenhower 610,989
Stevenson 481,482

UNITED STATES SENATOR
(For six-year Term)
169 precincts out of 169:
Purtell (R.) 575,445
Benton (D.) 485,159
(For Four-year Term)
Bush (R.) 559,586
Ribicoff (D.) 529,213

The Eisenhower sweep enabled the Republicans to win five of the six seats from Connecticut in the House of Representatives, a gain

Continued on Page 23, Column 5

RACE IS CONCEDED

Virginia and Florida Go to the General as Do Illinois and Ohio

SWEEP IS NATION-WIDE

Victor Calls for Unity and Thanks Governor for Pledging Support

By ARTHUR KROCK

Gen. Dwight D. Eisenhower was elected President of the United States yesterday in an electoral vote landslide and with an emphatic popular majority that probably will give his party a small margin of control in the House of Representatives but may leave the Senate as it is—forty-nine Democrats, forty-seven Republicans and one independent.

Senator Richard M. Nixon of California was elected Vice President.

The Democratic Presidential candidate, Gov. Adlai E. Stevenson of Illinois, shortly after midnight conceded his defeat by a record turnout of American voters.

At 4 A. M. today the Republican candidate had carried states with a total of 431 electors, or 165 more than the 266 required for the selection of a President. The Democratic candidate seemed sure of 59, with 31 doubtful in Kentucky, Louisiana and Tennessee.

General Eisenhower's landslide victory, both in electoral and popular votes, was nation-wide in its pattern, extending from New England—where Massachusetts and Rhode Island broke their Democratic voting habits of many years—down the Eastern seaboard to Maryland, Virginia and Florida and westward to almost every state between the coasts, including California.

General Wins Illinois

The Republican candidate took Illinois, Governor Stevenson's home state. In South Carolina, though he lost its electors on a technicality, he won a majority of the voters. And, completing the first successful Republican invasion of the States of the former Confederacy, the General carried Texas and broke the one-party system in the South.

The personal popularity that enabled him to defeat Senator Robert A. Taft of Ohio in the Republican primaries in Texas, and present him with the issue on which he defeated the Senator for the Republican nomination, crushed the regular Democratic organization of Texas that was led by Speaker Sam Rayburn of the House of Representatives and had the blessing of former Vice President John N. Garner.

The tide that bore General Eisenhower to the White House, though it did not give him a comfortable working majority in either the national House or the Senate (the Democrats may still nominally control the machinery of that branch), probably increased the number of Republican governors beyond the present twenty-five.

Continued on Page 14, Column 3

GENERAL APPEALS FOR UNITED PEOPLE

He Vows Not to Give 'Short Weight' as President — Thanks Rival for Pledge

By WILLIAM R. CONKLIN

A jubilant Gen. Dwight D. Eisenhower accepted his election as President early this morning with a pledge to the American people that he would not give "short weight" in the execution of his new responsibilities in Washington.

With his wife by his side, the Republican President-elect told 2,000 campaign supporters in the grand ballroom of the Commodore Hotel at 2:05 A. M. that he would take the support of a united people to carry his Administration to success in its efforts to build a "better future for America."

His remarks were carried by radio and television to all parts of the country.

He read a message he had sent a few minutes before to his defeated rival, Gov. Adlai E. Stevenson of Illinois, thanking him for his promise of assistance. General Eisenhower expressed hope that Americans of both parties would speedily forget campaign bitter-

Continued on Page 20, Column 2

Stevenson Concedes the Victory As Weeping Backers Cry 'No, No'

By WILLIAM M. BLAIR
Special to The New York Times.

SPRINGFIELD, Ill., Wednesday, Nov. 5—Gov. Adlai E. Stevenson conceded defeat early today to his Republican opponent, Gen. Dwight D. Eisenhower, and pledged the support "he will need to carry out the great tasks that lie before him."

The Governor came from the Executive Mansion to the Democratic Headquarters in the Leland Hotel to make his announcement before a jammed ballroom of supporters, many of whom broke into tears and cried, "No, no."

Governor Stevenson said:

"General Eisenhower has been a great leader in war. I know him to be a vigorous and valiant opponent in the campaign. These qualities will now be dedicated to the next four years.

"It is traditionally American to fight hard before an election. It is equally traditional to close ranks as soon as the people have

Continued on Page 16, Column 2

spoken. From the depths of my heart I thank all of my party, and all of those independents and Republicans who supported Senator Sparkman and me."

The Governor said he was dispatched to General Eisenhower in New York a telegram which he read. It said:

"The people have made their choice and I congratulate you. You may be the servant and, as guardian of peace and make the dale of trouble a door of hope is my earnest prayer. Best Wishes.

Adlai E. Stevenson."

Governor Stevenson did have a grin, however, for the crowd and displayed his ever-present humor to reporters. Asked how about 1956, he echoed in a loud voice and with mock surprise "56! Examine that man's head."

As for his immediate plans, he

"All the News
That's Fit to Print"

The New York Times.

Copyright, 1953, by The New York Times Company.

VOL. CII...No. 34,709.   Entered as Second-Class Matter.
Post Office, New York, N. Y.   NEW YORK, TUESDAY, FEBRUARY 3, 1953.   Times Square, New York 36, N. Y.
Telephone Lackawanna 4-1000   FIVE CENTS

LATE CITY EDITION
Cloudy, becoming fair this after-
noon. Some cloudiness tomorrow.
Temperature Range Today-Max., 40; Min., 29
Temperature Yesterday-Max., 39.6; Min., 14.5
Full U. S. Weather Bureau Report, Page 40

EISENHOWER FREES CHIANG TO RAID MAINLAND; BIDS CONGRESS VOID ALL 'SECRET' PACTS ABROAD; WOULD END CONTROLS; OPPOSES TAX CUTS NOW

EUROPE STORM TOLL EXCEEDS 1,400 DEAD AS FLOODS SUBSIDE

296 Die Along British Coast —Thousands Still Missing as Help Is Speeded

DUTCH COUNT 955 KILLED

Million in Netherlands Affected —Belgian Area Battered —Dunkirk Hard Hit

By TANIA LONG
Special to The New York Times.

LONDON, Tuesday, Feb. 3—As the gales abated and the raging waters of the North Sea began to recede, three nations counted their dead today and assessed the damage resulting from their worst flood disaster in recent history.

Hard hit were Britain, the Netherlands and Belgium where huge waves swept across large sections of the coast Saturday night and early Sunday, breaking through dikes and seawalls and swallowing entire towns and villages.

[The Associated Press said the known dead in the storm area totaled more than 1,400 early Tuesday. In the Netherlands, 955 persons drowned. The toll in Britain stood at 443, including 296 killed in floods along the east coast, 132 who lost their lives in the sinking of the ferry Princess Victoria in the Irish Sea and fifteen lost on a missing trawler. Belgium had twenty-two dead.]

Several thousand persons were still missing, and it was feared that the death roll would mount heavily at Britain and the Netherlands was realized, the full resources of the two countries were quickly mobilized to give aid in the emergency. At the same time, assistance was sped to the Netherlands from France, Belgium and Denmark, and the United States forces in Europe, which also had its casualties.

The Swiss Red Cross Society announced it would begin an immediate collection of money to aid the British and Dutch flood victims, and there were offers of assistance, financial or material, from many other European countries and the United States.

In the meantime, the two nations worst affected put into action emergency plans to deal with the thousands rendered homeless by the floods. In Britain, civil defense plans prepared against a possible atomic attack were put into operation to shelter and feed the dispossessed.

Government Sends Help

The Government ordered its storehouses opened and sent thousands of blankets, mattresses, and other items to the distressed areas, while the women's voluntary services brought out their trucks and set into motion the Flying Food Convoys, organized during World War II and kept in reserve against the possible outbreak of another conflict.

While examination of many thousands was being carried on, engineers in Britain and the Netherlands began their battle to restore the broken dikes and sea walls. Using sandbags, logs and other material readily available, they filled the gaps in an effort to halt a further influx from the sea.

There was still danger that the combination of winds and high tides that caused the original disaster might bring further flood

Continued on Page 4, Column 5

Ships Arrive, Depart On Own in Tug Strike

Cargo and passenger vessels berthed and departed on their own power yesterday in New York, Philadelphia and Norfolk as the three-port strike of towboat crews continued without signs of a break.

Mild winds and calm waters here made it possible for most ships to dock or leave the harbor without the aid of tugs. A few inbound vessels, however, were held up at anchorage and several scheduled to leave were unable to do so.

Longshoremen shaped up and worked as usual. It had been feared that they might abstain from work in sympathy with the 3,500 strikers, who are members of Local 333 of the Marine Division of the International Longshoremen's Association, A. F. L.

One result of the strike was an interference with garbage dis-

Continued on Page 20, Column 4

A.F.L. ACTS TO END PIER UNION ABUSES

Breaking Traditional Policy, Its Council Orders Inquiry— Hogan Subpoenas Ryan

By A. H. RASKIN
Special to The New York Times.

MIAMI BEACH, Feb. 2—Acting to stamp out racketeering in its ranks, the American Federation of Labor made two sharp breaks today with its tradition of noninterference in the internal affairs of its affiliated unions.

Its executive council set up a committee of three federation vice presidents to consider means of cleaning up the gang-infested International Longshoremen's Association. The committee began its work at once and it was indicated that it would submit its report in forty-eight hours.

[District Attorney Frank S. Hogan announced in New York Monday night that he had issued a grand jury subpoena for the appearance at 2 o'clock Tuesday afternoon of Joseph P. Ryan, president of the International Longshoremen's Association.]

The council also called on another affiliated union, the United Automobile Workers, to revoke the charter of a New York local headed by a convicted extortionist. If the automobile union refuses to comply, the council has the power to recommend that it be expelled from the federation at the next annual convention.

In a third action of the opening of its mid-winter meeting at the Monte Carlo Hotel here, the executive council set Feb. 24 as the date for resumption of formal peace talks between the A. F. L. and the

Continued on Page 20, Column 1

Southeast Britain's Coast Lifeless And Awash as Seen From Plane

By THOMAS F. BRADY
Special to The New York Times.

LONDON, Feb. 2—A vast coastal region of southeastern Britain lay submerged by salt water today, as the Romans found it 2,000 years ago. Seen from the air the land was awash and lifeless.

The plane's pilot, Capt. Theodore W. Morton, had been over Canvey early in the morning. Then a convoy of army trucks was splashing through the town getting out the last survivors. The trucks had towed rowboats, and other small boats had moved slowly in the canals between rows of brick houses. Captain Morton had seen one rescue—a man taken by a boat from the window of a house.

Miles of glistening gray water were broken by brown roofs of houses, telephone poles still tied together by wires, the gun barrels of an anti-aircraft battery, and along the course of the Thames reminders of industry and commerce—black oil tanks, stretches of raised railroad track, a long factory roof with a smokeless stack.

Above the Thames Estuary, thirty-five miles from London, the plane circled low over Canvey Island, where forty-eight hours earlier 13,000 persons had had their homes. Canvey is separated from the mainland by a narrow stream, but today its housetops were isolated in the new swollen estuary of the Thames. The roofs

Continued on Page 4, Column 6

BRITAIN IS ANXIOUS

Makes Representations to U. S. on the Effects of Formosa Policy

PARLIAMENT AROUSED

Churchill Defers Debate Till Today, When Eden Will State Policy

By JAY WALZ
Special to The New York Times.

WASHINGTON, Feb. 2—Britain has made representations to the United States about President Eisenhower's decision to allow the Chinese Nationalists to raid the China mainland.

Anthony Eden, British Foreign Secretary, who is to make a statement on the subject before the House of Commons tomorrow, communicated with the State Department today.

It is understood that he advised diplomatic officials here that the British Government believed the new order to the Seventh Fleet would greatly complicate the political situation both in Europe and in the Far East.

In his communication, Mr. Eden is believed to have argued that the Chinese civil war, raise the fears of a general war in the Far East and thus make any general settlement in the Far East even more difficult.

Bradley Discounts Risk

General of the Army Omar Bradley, chairman of the Joint Chiefs of Staff, said tonight that President Eisenhower's new policy on Formosa did not increase greatly the chances of the United States' becoming involved in a "big war" in the Far East.

The Eisenhower Administration contends that the United States, while intending no aggressive move, cannot permit its Navy, as the President put it, "to serve as a defensive arm of Communist China" by continuing its neutralizing function between the Nationalists and the Communists.

Some diplomatic sources feel that Britain's concern over developments may reflect general uneasiness among United States Allies in Europe over the direction of United States foreign policy.

Among these were British Embassy officials, who withheld comment pending Mr. Eden's statement in Parliament tomorrow.

However, F. B. Tomlinson, an Embassy counselor, called on Assistant Secretary of State John M. Allison last Saturday to express "concern" over reports of President Eisenhower's decision about

Continued on Page 11, Column 2

DELIVERS FIRST STATE OF UNION MESSAGE: President Eisenhower addressing a joint session of Congress yesterday. In background are Richard M. Nixon, Vice President, and Speaker of the House Joseph W. Martin Jr.
The New York Times (by Bruce Hoertel)

RED BLOW STOPPED BY SOUTH KOREANS

650-Man Attack on the Eastern Front Repulsed — Sabres Down Two Enemy Jets

By The Associated Press.

SEOUL, Korea, Tuesday, Feb. 3—North Koreans launched a 650-man attack on the eastern front today, but stout South Korean defenders repulsed the assault and pursued the Communists across the craggy No Man's Land in below-zero cold.

The Korean Communists attacked at 12:45 A. M. across one mile of the mountainous front. They threw three companies into this attack and mounted two diversionary attacks of platoon size to the east.

Moving up under cover of a 680-round artillery and mortar barrage, the main force drove within forty yards of the main South Korean defenses.

The bitterly resisting South Koreans mounted a counter-attack at 2 A. M., drove off the Reds and chased them back across the snow-clad hills. An Eighth Army staff officer reported an estimated fifty-five of the enemy were killed.

Sabres Down Two MIG's

TOKYO, Tuesday, Feb. 3—Sabre jets of the United States Fifth Air Force shot down two Soviet-designed MIG jet fighters over northwest Korea yesterday, probably destroyed another and damaged two more, while fighter-bombers and high-velocity tank-mounted guns hammered at the enemy-entrenched line across the peninsula.

Twelve Sabres clashed with eight MIG's in dogfights that ranged from 50,000 feet to 500 feet altitude, and from the Yalu River to Changchon on the west coast. The two kills were credited to Col. James K. Johnson and Maj. Foster L. Smith.

Meanwhile, more than 100 fighter-bombers, continuing the pattern of saturation raids on selected targets, plastered a big enemy troop concentration and storage area south of Chinnampo, seaport of the North Korean Communist capital at Pyongyang and import-ant routes to the western front. The planes hauled forty buildings, returning pilots said, and set off six large secondary explosions, indicating that ammunition storage areas had been hit.

Other fighter-bombers flying along the front lines knocked out

Continued on Page 5, Column 2

Capehart Moves to Retain Controls on Stand-By Basis

By CLAYTON KNOWLES
Special to The New York Times.

WASHINGTON, Feb. 2—Opposition cropped up today in an influential Republican quarter to President Eisenhower's proposal to let price and wage controls die on April 30 without maintaining stand-by machinery to reimpose them if needed.

Senator Homer E. Capehart, chairman of the Senate Banking and Currency Committee, introduced a bill to set up such machinery within a few minutes after the President made his position known in his State of the Union Message.

He did not challenge the President's belief that price-wage controls had outlived their present usefulness but he did question the possibility of enacting a controls law quickly if one should be needed again.

"It is the height of impracticability," Mr. Capehart said, "to expect that the Congress can do a proper job of legislating a good controls law into effect in a period of less than three months, and for such a law to begin properly functioning within seven months from the incidence of the request for the legislation."

He maintained that inaction during this enforced waiting period would promote hoarding, scare buying and indiscriminate spending, all of which contribute to inflation. He said this was precisely what happened after the outbreak of hostilities in Korea. Before a

Continued on Page 15, Column 4

Convicted Communists Snub Offer To Go to Russia Instead of Prison

By EDWARD RANZAL

Thirteen secondary Communist leaders got the chance yesterday to go to Russia as an alternative to going to prison for criminal conspiracy to teach and advocate the overthrow of the United States Government by force and violence. The offer was made by Federal Judge Edward J. Dimock.

Defense counsel and several of the defendants emphatically rejected the proposal, terming it "intolerable" and "unpalatable." Elizabeth Gurley Flynn, one of the thirteen, declared:

"We feel we belong here and have a political responsibility here. We feel we would be traitors to the American people if we turned our backs on them just to escape jail."

Judge Dimock also said he would not impose the maximum sentence of five years and $10,000 fine on the thirteen. However, United States Attorney Myles J. Lane recommended that the max-

imum sentence be imposed on each.

The actual sentencing was postponed until today by Judge Dimock after oral hearings by twelve of the thirteen defendants. At 4:40 P. M., after the court had been advised that in addition to the remaining defendant four defense attorneys would add to the voluminous record of the nine-and-a-half month trial, Judge Dimock adjourned court.

The first suggestion that Judge Dimock had an alternative plan came when the jurist asked Mr. Lane what he thought of the idea of permitting the defendants to go voluntarily to Russia rather than serve a prison sentence. Mr. Lane said he had no objection if he defendants first served their prison terms, then headed for the Soviet Union.

Then, after Miss Flynn had ad-

Continued on Page 8, Column 2

CONGRESS PRAISES EISENHOWER TALK

But 7th Fleet Decision Brings Fear of War Extension and Deeper U. S. Involvement

By C. P. TRUSSELL
Special to The New York Times.

WASHINGTON, Feb. 2—President Eisenhower's first message on the State of the Union, delivered personally today to a joint session of Congress in the packed House of Representatives chamber, got a rousing reception.

However, as the new President made his exit, arms linked with Senator Robert A. Taft of Ohio, Senate Majority Leader, whom he defeated for the Republican Presidential nomination, the speech appeared to leave in its wake a trail of issues that spelled Congressional controversy to come.

Although the President's speech brought praise from Democrats as well as Republicans, President Eisenhower's decision to end the United States Seventh Fleet's role as a barrier against raids by the Chinese Nationalists on the Communist-held mainland seemed to overshadow concern to many Congressmen. It was difficult to determine whether the Republican view that the action would end the stalemate in Korea outweighed fear, expressed largely by Democrats, that it might extend the Korean conflict and involve the United States more deeply in Asia.

Resentment Expressed

Senators and Representatives repeatedly asked whether releasing Chiang Kai-shek's Formosa force to attack the Chinese mainland would imply that the United States would have to back up such actions with American men and planes. This, they contended, would mean deeper involvement and perhaps another world war.

Influential Democrats in Congress expressed resentment over the section of the President's address in which he contended, as former President Truman, constituted a protection for the Communist mainland while other Communists were fighting United Nations troops, mostly American, in Korea.

Representative John W. McCormack, Democrat of Massachusetts and House Whip, called it "hitting below the belt." He charged that President Eisenhower, while asking for bipartisan foreign policy, was acting "to destroy it."

Opponents contended the Sev-

Continued on Page 17, Column 1

CIVIL RIGHTS PLANS GET WIDE SUPPORT

Challenge to McCarthy Seen on Security Issues — Duel Over Immigration Looms

By WILLIAM S. WHITE
Special to The New York Times.

WASHINGTON, Feb. 2—President Eisenhower appeared to please nearly all the political Center in Congress today with the civil rights, loyalty and immigration policies laid down in his State of the Union Message.

The Left Wing at some points and the Right Wing at other points were made far from happy, for varying reasons.

The prospect raised was that the President could count upon at least as much Democratic support as Republican support—and perhaps more—for his approach in these fields, which encompass some

Continued on Page 17, Column 1

STATE OF THE UNION

President Sees No 'Logic or Sense' in Sea Patrol Helping Chinese Reds

HIS 'POSITIVE POLICY'

Reciprocal Trade Pacts, Aid to Europe Backed in Congress Message

Text of the State of the Union Message, Pages 14 and 15.

By ANTHONY LEVIERO
Special to The New York Times.

WASHINGTON, Feb. 2—President Eisenhower today ended the United States Seventh Fleet's protective screening of Red China, thus permitting the Nationalist forces of Generalissimo Chiang Kai-shek on Formosa to attack the Communist-held mainland.

The President also called upon Congress to repudiate any secret concessions made to the Russians at the World War II conferences at Teheran, Yalta and Potsdam.

Roars of applause greeted General Eisenhower's twin enunciations of a "new, positive foreign policy," made in his first State of the Union Message delivered before a joint session of Congress.

The first Republican President to chart a course for the nation in two decades, General Eisenhower also dwelt on domestic affairs in his address, proposing a program that would turn the country toward a freer enterprise system and "natural" economic law.

His Program Detailed

In outlining his policies for the new Administration the President made these points:

¶There no longer was any "sense or logic" in the use of the Seventh Fleet to shield Red China.

¶The Government "recognizes no kind of commitment contained in secret understandings of the past with foreign governments which permit * * * enslavement."

¶Aid to Europe would be continued with the Allies required to be full partners matching United States contributions according to their capabilities.

¶The new foreign policy would be the true product of bipartisanship and cooperation between the President and Congress and it would be coherent and global.

¶Incontrovertible evidence is at hand of Russian possession of atomic weapons and therefore civil defense preparedness is a "sheer necessity."

¶The reciprocal trade treaties should be continued, American investments abroad should be encouraged and customs procedures simplified.

¶The Secretary of Defense would take steps to obtain the maximum in national security at minimum cost.

¶The first order of domestic business should be to balance the budget, after which a reduction in taxation would be in order.

¶Wage-price controls should not

Continued on Page 15, Column 1

To Suburban Readers

The strike of newspaper deliverymen against suburban wholesalers has curtailed distribution of The New York Times outside New York within a 50-mile radius. Distribution of The Times to newsstands will be continued, however, at all newsstands within the New York City line. Suburbanites in New York during the evening are advised to get their copies before going home. Temporary mail subscriptions may be ordered for the duration of the emergency at no increase over the regular newsstand price by telephoning The Times. Information on how and where to get The Times is given at the end of The New York Times News Bulletins, which are broadcast every hour on the hour over WQXR, 1560 on the AM dial, and WQXR-FM, 96.3 on the FM dial.

"All the News That's Fit to Print"

The New York Times.

Copyright, 1953, by The New York Times Company

VOL. CII..No. 34,740.

Entered as Second-Class Matter,
Post Office, New York, N. Y.

NEW YORK, FRIDAY, MARCH 6, 1953.

Times Square, New York 36, N. Y.
Telephone LAckawanna 4-1000

FIVE CENTS

LATE CITY EDITION
Fair, little temperature change today. Mostly fair tomorrow.
Temperature Range Today—Max.: 47; Min.: 29
Temperature Yesterday—Max.: 44; Min.: 33
Full U. S. Weather Bureau Report, Page 47

STALIN DIES AFTER 29-YEAR RULE; HIS SUCCESSOR NOT ANNOUNCED; U.S. WATCHFUL, EISENHOWER SAYS

WORST CITY CRISIS SINCE 1933 IS SEEN IN STATE TAX PLAN

Moore and McGovern Demand Payroll Levy and Transit Unit Mandated to Raise Fares

MAYOR CALLS DEMOCRATS

Estimate Board to Get Report on Views of County Leaders —Bus Reduction Directed

By PAUL CROWELL

The city Government is facing the most serious financial and political crisis to confront any Administration since 1933, when leading banking houses rescued a Democratic regime from fiscal disaster.

This was the consensus last night of top city officials to whom Lieut. Gov. Frank C. Moore and State Controller J. Raymond McGovern had indicated earlier in the day that a sound fiscal program for 1953-54 and succeeding years should include both a city payroll tax and a transit authority with a duty to increase fares to meet operating deficits of the municipal lines.

That the city Government realized the political dangers inherent in the adoption of the suggested fiscal program was indicated later in the day when Mayor Impellitteri, without consulting the Board of Estimate, asked the five Democratic county leaders to confer with him at noon today at City Hall. Among those invited was Tammany leader Carmine G. De-Sapio, the only member of the group who is at loggerheads with the Mayor on matters of patronage.

Leaders' Views Important

After a two-hour conference with Mr. Moore and Mr. McGovern at Mr. McGovern's office, 270 Broadway, the Mayor and Board of Estimate held an even longer closed meeting at City Hall, which will be resumed at 3 o'clock this afternoon. At today's session an important factor will be the attitude of the five Democratic county leaders, as reported by the Mayor, toward the proposals upon which the two state officials apparently are insisting.

In another municipal development, the Mayor's Transit Advisory Commission demanded that the eight privately owned bus companies involved in the recent bus strike and Michael J. Quill's Transport Workers Union, C. I. O., take immediate steps to wipe out excess bus lines and to reduce the number of buses on lines that were needed. City tax relief was made dependent on such action.

The conference with Mr. Moore and Mr. McGovern was a continuation of last Monday's talks at Albany on the city's $218,700,000 fiscal program, which in effect already had been rejected by the two state officials in their joint memorandum of Feb. 22.

At the outset of the meeting the

Continued on Page 19, Column 1

F.B.I. Agents Depict Rebuff by Monaghan

By LUTHER A. HUSTON

WASHINGTON, March 5—Leland V. Boardman, special agent in charge of the New York office of the Federal Bureau of Investigation, asserted today that Police Commissioner George P. Monaghan had notified him that he would not make New York City policemen available to any Federal law enforcement agency for questioning and that they would respond only to summonses from a Federal grand jury.

This policy, Mr. Boardman said, was founded upon a purported agreement between the New York Police Department and the Criminal Division of the Department of Justice to "block out F. B. I. investigators from cases involving police brutality in civil rights cases."

Another agent quoted Commis-

Continued on Page 16, Column 2

Eisenhower Plans to Pare Policy-Level Civil Service

Directive Will Repeal 2 That Truman Issued Anchoring Some Democrats in Their Jobs —Organization of Administration Object

By PAUL P. KENNEDY
Special to THE NEW YORK TIMES.

WASHINGTON, March 5—Several hundred persons face the possibility of losing Civil Service status and probably their Government jobs under an Executive Order to be issued by President Eisenhower next week.

In announcing the forthcoming order, James C. Hagerty, White House press secretary, said that all those affected would not necessarily lose their jobs. The announcement was generally interpreted, however, to mean that the Administration was preparing to clear out holdover Democrats in high policy-making and administrative positions in order to replace them with personnel of the Administration's own choosing.

President Eisenhower's order, which he directed to be drafted immediately, will repeal two Executive Orders of former President Truman in 1947 and 1948 in which certain persons on Schedule A of Civil Service rules would receive Civil Service protection against separation from the Government. The President's order will emphasize that the rights of veterans, specified in the Veterans Preference Act of 1944 in order to re-spected.

Schedule A is a list of positions to which appointments may be made without reference to Civil Service rules or regulations. The appointees may assume their positions without Civil Service examinations and their classifications are not subject to review by Civil Service Boards.

Mr. Hagerty said the "several hundred" persons to be affected by the order were employed in all departments and agencies of the Government. The order, he said, applied to people who had been put under Civil Service in the last twenty years.

The new Administration, since coming into office Jan. 20, Mr.

Continued on Page 15, Column 2

President May Take a Hand If Inquiries Imperil Amity

By C. P. TRUSSELL
Special to THE NEW YORK TIMES.

WASHINGTON, March 5—President Eisenhower indicated today that if the Senate investigation into the Voice of America, being conducted by Senator Joseph R. McCarthy, or other Congressional inquiries, reached a point of inviting international misunderstanding and difficulties he might intervene.

This, he emphasized at a news conference, would mean that he would have to desert his long-held conviction that the Congress had an inherent right to investigate as it pleased. He was still hoping, he said, to avoid a situation in which a spokesman for the Executive Branch of the Government would have to take issue with actions of the coordinate Legislative Branch.

The question that prompted these responses was based upon largely upon television, by the Judiciary subcommittee headed by Senator McCarthy, Republican of Wisconsin.

The group is inquiring into the management and personnel of the Voice, the Government's radio program for telling the story of America. Broadcasts are beamed to eighty-seven countries in nearly forty languages.

At yesterday's hearing Reed Harris, deputy director of the State

Continued on Page 14, Column 6

EISENHOWER PRAISES RESTRAINT IN PRICES

Asserts There Has Been Little Evidence of Gouging—More Controls Are Removed

By CHARLES E. EGAN

WASHINGTON, March 5—President Eisenhower today complimented business for what he termed the admirable restraint it had shown in pricing policies since the removal of most price controls.

General Eisenhower said at his news conference that since the program of removing major segments of the economy from price regulation got under way Feb. 6, there had been little discernible evidence of attempts to gouge consumers.

The President's observations came immediately before an announcement from the Office of Price Stabilization that it had removed price ceilings on another wide range of items, including bread and bakery products, new and used cars, major household appliances, dry cleaning and diaper services.

Hopes for a New Climate

Another development was a Senate committee hearing at which Charles R. Sligh Jr., president of the National Association of Manufacturers, attacked proposals to establish stand-by controls authority. With such authority, the President could declare a ninety-day "freeze" of all prices and wages in event of all-out war or other critical emergency.

About the only major price increase that has occurred since the Office of Price Stabilization began implementing his orders for relaxation of price ceilings, the President said, has been an expected rise of 6 to 7 cents a pound in copper.

The absence of price gouging, the President added, confirms his belief that the American people are ready to be considerate and moderate. He added that he hoped it would be established—harmonious labor-management relations, for instance—that would minimize harmful pressures on the economy.

Continued on Page 15, Column 3

VISHINSKY LEAVING

Foreign Minister Called to Moscow to Report —Will Sail Today

U. N. TO LOWER FLAG

Lie Praises Premier as Statesman—Pearson Hails Fight on Nazis

By THOMAS J. HAMILTON
Special to THE NEW YORK TIMES.

UNITED NATIONS, N. Y., March 5—Soviet Foreign Minister Andrei Y. Vishinsky, who was reported to have been informed of the death of Premier Stalin before the public announcement by the Moscow radio, plans to leave for Moscow tomorrow.

Mr. Vishinsky and a party of Soviet officials are scheduled to sail aboard the French liner Liberté tomorrow at 4 P. M. Plans for the sailing were disclosed at Police Headquarters. The police said they had been informed that the party would travel in seven automobiles from Glen Cove, L. I., where the Soviet delegation to the United Nations has headquarters, to Pier 88, Hudson River at Forty-eighth Street. The liner will call at Plymouth and Le Havre.

Mr. Vishinsky has a heart condition and therefore avoids air travel whenever possible.

Valerian A. Zorin, Soviet representative to the United Nations, revealed this afternoon Mr. Vishinsky's plans to leave tomorrow. Mr. Vishinsky's decision was taken after he had received a telephone call from Moscow earlier in the day.

Disclosure by Consulate

There was no indication whether this telephone call had given any indication of Mr. Stalin's death. The news that Mr. Vishinsky had been informed prior to the public announcement came from a telephone inquiry at the Soviet Consulate at 680 Park Avenue.

Earlier inquiries at the headquarters of the Soviet delegation to the United Nations had brought repeated denials that Mr. Vishinsky was there. The consulate revealed, however, not only that Mr. Vishinsky was actually at the delegation headquarters but also that he had been informed of the news earlier.

According to United Nations protocol, the only flag that will fly at the United Nations flagpole tomorrow is the banner of the United Nations itself, and it will be at half-staff. The same procedure will be followed during the day of the funeral of Premier Stalin.

Informed of the death of Mr.

Continued on Page 13, Column 2

CONDOLENCES SENT

President Orders Terse Formal Note on Stalin Dispatched to Soviet

TRIBUTE IS OMITTED

Eisenhower Still Ready to Confer on Peace With the Kremlin

By JAMES RESTON
Special to THE NEW YORK TIMES.

WASHINGTON, March 5—President Eisenhower authorized John Foster Dulles, Secretary of State, tonight to send the United States' "official condolences" to the Soviet Government on the death of Premier Stalin.

Earlier the President had told reporters at his press conference that he could not tell what affect the illness of the Premier would have on the "cold war." A definite watchfulness is our policy for the moment, the President added.

The President announced the statement of condolences less than an hour after he had been informed of Mr. Stalin's death by James C. Hagerty, press secretary, at 4:25 P. M. The statement was as follows:

The President authorized the Secretary of State to send the following message to the American Embassy in Moscow: The Government of the United States tenders its official condolences to the Government of the Union of Socialist Soviet Republics on the death of Generalissimo Joseph Stalin, Prime Minister of the Soviet Union.

Dulles Informed by Hagerty

Mr. Hagerty notified Mr. Dulles, who was a guest at the British Embassy, immediately after the President had been informed.

The press secretary said the President's message would be transmitted to the Soviet Government through by Jacob-D. Beam, Chargé d'Affaires in Moscow.

The terse wording of the message was noted here, especially the phrase "official condolences." Diplomatic circles suggested that the wording was about as brief and formal as possible under diplomatic protocol.

They recalled, however, that the President previously had expressed condolences. In the first White House statement issued after word had been received of the serious illness of Mr. Stalin, General Eisenhower directed his words to the Soviet people rather than the Premier or the Government.

Indications were that the President's official condolences would stand in so far as the Government

Continued on Page 12, Column 5

PREMIER JOSEPH STALIN
A portrait released by Sovfoto, Soviet picture agency

Soviet Fear of an Eruption Discerned in Call for Unity

By HARRY SCHWARTZ

The fact that appeals for "monolithic unity" and "vigilance" have now become the main theme of Soviet domestic propaganda appears to be a clear indication that the present Soviet rulers fear Premier Stalin's death may result in an explosive resolution of the major tensions now repressed in the Soviet Union.

The unity theme dominates the official announcement of Stalin's death. It was first voiced in the initial communiqué regarding Stalin's illness issued by the highest Government and Communist party authorities. Unity and vigilance were the central ideas in the long leading editorials that appeared yesterday morning on the front pages of both Pravda and Izvestia.

The same theme may also have given the first hint that Georgi M. Malenkov is leading in the succession race, but this hint seemed far from conclusive. The editorial mentioned by name only Lenin, Premier Stalin, and Mr. Malenkov, quoting the latter's speech last October when he said, "The prospects and ways of our progress are based on the laws of the national economy, on the science of the Communist social structure which have been evolved by Comrade Stalin."

The apparent contradiction of Moscow has announced that Nikita S. Khrushchev will head the committee preparing

Continued on Page 12, Column 2

AMMUNITION SHORT, VAN FLEET ASSERTS

He Affirms Scarcity in Korea and Byrd Writes to Wilson Demanding Explanation

By HAROLD B. HINTON
Special to THE NEW YORK TIMES.

WASHINGTON, March 5—Gen. James A. Van Fleet, former Commander of United Nations ground forces in Korea, told the Senate Armed Services Committee today that he had been handicapped during the entire twenty-two months he had had the command by shortages of ammunition and manpower. He specified hand grenades, and mentioned "other types" of ammunition as having been seriously short all the time and critically short on all occasions.

Praised by Symington

So much the general said before a public meeting of the committee. Senator Stuart Symington, Democrat of Missouri and former Secretary of the Air Force, praised General Van Fleet for his intelligence and courage in reporting these matters to the public. If other military figures would emulate the example, he declared, "we won't send our youth out to fight with these shortages, even if we have fewer television sets."

[In the Korean war action, Air Force Thunderjet fighter-bombers made a record 1,000-mile raid on a Communist industrial center on the northeast coast sixty miles from Siberia. Navy carrier bombers made heavy attacks in North Korea. Ground action was light.]

In a later closed session with the committee, General Van Fleet apparently amplified his discussion of the shortages. The amplification prompted Senator Harry F. Byrd, Democrat of Virginia, to write a letter to Charles E. Wil-

Continued on Page 2, Column 2

PREMIER ILL 4 DAYS

Announcement of Death Made by Top Soviet and Party Chiefs

STROKE PROVES FATAL

Leaders Issue an Appeal to People for Unity and Vigilance

Text of official announcement of Stalin's death, Page 8.

By HARRISON E. SALISBURY
Special to THE NEW YORK TIMES.

MOSCOW, Friday, March 6—Premier Joseph Stalin died at 9:50 P. M. yesterday [1:50 P. M. Thursday, Eastern standard time] in the Kremlin at the age of 73, it was announced officially this morning. He had been in power twenty-nine years.

The announcement was made in the name of the Central Committee of the Communist party, the Council of Ministers and the Presidium of the Supreme Soviet.

Calling on the Soviet people to rally firmly around the party and Government, the announcement asked them to display unity and the highest political vigilance "in the struggle against internal and external foes." [No announcement was made of a successor to Premier Stalin.]

The Soviet leader's death stemmed from general circulatory and respiratory deficiency occurred just short of four days after he had been stricken with a brain hemorrhage in his Kremlin apartment.

Accompanying the death announcement was a final medical certificate issued by a group of ten physicians, headed by Health Minister A. F. Tretyakov, who attended Mr. Stalin in his last illness under the direct and closest supervision of the Central Committee and the Council of Ministers.

Pulse Rate Was High

The medical certificate revealed that in the last hours Mr. Stalin's condition grew worse rapidly, with repeated heavy and sharp circulatory and heart collapses. His breathing grew superficial and sharply irregular. His pulse rate rose to 140 to 150 a minute and at 9:50 P. M., "because of a growing circulatory and respiratory insufficiency, J. V. Stalin died."

[The news of Mr. Stalin's death was withheld by Soviet officials for more than six hours.]

Pravda appeared this morning with broad black borders around its front page, which was devoted entirely to Mr. Stalin. The layout included a large photograph of the Premier, the announcement by the Government, the medical bulletins and the announcement of the formation of a funeral commis-

Continued on Page 8, Column 2

Treaties Manifesto Shelved in Congress

By WILLIAM S. WHITE

WASHINGTON, March 5—President Eisenhower's proposed United States declaration against "perversion" of the wartime Yalta and Potsdam agreements into instruments for enslaving peoples was put on the shelf in Congress today.

The announced Congressional reason was that the manifesto would be inopportune now in view of Premier Stalin's fatal illness, though the President himself indicated at his news conference that he thought this need not delay action. The Congressional developments came before the announcement of Mr. Stalin's death.

The Republican leaders in Congress could not take the resolution to the floor of either house

Continued on Page 6, Column 5

Pole Flies to Denmark in First Intact Russian MIG-15 to Reach West

A young Polish pilot seeking political asylum flew this Soviet-made MIG-15 into a Danish airport at Bornholm yesterday, making it the first fighter plane of its type acquired undamaged by the West. Name of pilot (center figure) was withheld.

Special to THE NEW YORK TIMES.

COPENHAGEN, Denmark, March 5—The first intact Russian-built MIG-15 jet fighter—the newest known type of Russian jet fighter—to land west of the Iron Curtain came down this morning at Roenne airport on the Danish island of Bornholm. It came from a Polish Baltic base.

The 21-year-old Polish lieutenant who had left with the fighter gave himself up to Danish authorities as a political refugee and asked for asylum. Very little is known about his story. Danish authorities are keeping it secret for the time being.

The young Pole performed a fantastic maneuver in landing the jet fighter on the grass-covered airstrip at Roenne, only 1,200 meters (3,937 feet) long. Jet fighters normally require a 3,000-meter (9,843 feet) concrete runway to start and land.

At the farther end of the air-

Continued on Page 3, Column 2

"All the News That's Fit to Print"

The New York Times.

LATE CITY EDITION

Mostly fair and cold today. Increasingly cloudy and cold tomorrow.

Temperature Range Today—Max., 38 ; Min., 32
Temperature Yesterday—Max., 41 ; Min., 32
Full U. S. Weather Bureau Report, Page 21

VOL. CII..No. 34,741.

Entered as Second-Class Matter.
Post Office, New York, N. Y.

NEW YORK, SATURDAY, MARCH 7, 1953.

Copyright, 1953, by The New York Times Company.

Times Square, New York 36, N. Y.
Telephone Lackawanna 4-1000

FIVE CENTS

MALENKOV IS NAMED NEW SOVIET PREMIER; WIDE CHANGES DISCLOSED TO AVOID 'PANIC'; THRONGS PASS STALIN BIER; RITES MONDAY

MAJORITY OF BOARD BARS STATE TERMS FOR CITY FISCAL AID

Stands on Mayor's Plan After Democratic Leaders Report Price Politically Ruinous

VOTE ON DECISION IS 5 TO 3

New York's Legislators Held Unwilling to Support Fare Rise or Payroll Impost

By PAUL CROWELL

A majority of the Board of Estimate decided yesterday to stand firm on Mayor Impellitteri's $218,700,000 fiscal program for 1953-54, refusing to purchase substantial financial aid from Governor Dewey's Republican Administration at a price considered politically ruinous by the Democratic leaders of the city's five counties.

At an executive meeting of the board, five members holding a majority of its sixteen votes refused to modify the Mayor's program by including, at the virtual insistence of Lieut. Gov. Frank C. Moore and State Controller J. Raymond McGovern, a city payroll tax and a transit authority mandated to increase the fare on municipal subway and surface lines to meet operating deficits.

The Moore-McGovern position was outlined to the Mayor and the Board of Estimate on Thursday at a conference in Mr. McGovern's New York office. The Mayor and his colleagues were told that a number of major items in the city's program, including the Mayor's plan for a transit authority designed to preserve the 10-cent fare by subsidizing operating deficits with an income tax on business, were unacceptable to the state.

Tax Request Discounted

The city officials also were informed that their requested increase of power to tax real estate, estimated to yield an additional annual revenue of $100,000,000, had little chance of approval at Albany unless the payroll tax and the "higher-fare" transit authority were made part of the city program.

The state spokesmen asked for the city's decision by the end of the week. It was made known to Mr. McGovern by telephone late yesterday afternoon. Mr. McGovern, it was learned, would discuss it with Mr. Moore over the week-end and possibly with Governor Dewey tonight.

Thursday's conference between city and state officials was followed by a long meeting of the Board of Estimate, at which no decision was reached. After the meeting, the Mayor invited State Democratic Chairman Richard H. Balch, the five Democratic county leaders and Assemblyman Eugene F. Bannigan, minority leader at Albany, to a luncheon meeting yesterday at the National Democratic Club, 233 Madison Avenue. The state's virtual ultimatum was discussed at this meeting, after

Continued on Page 21, Column 4

Rowdy Pupils Cause A School Bus Strike

Special to The New York Times.

ATLANTIC CITY, March 6—Drivers of school buses serving this resort's north side went on "strike" today against high school students because they were "fed up" with the youths' rowdy, "almost savage" antics.

The drivers, who operate four special school buses for the Atlantic City Transportation Company in the morning and afternoon, reported to work but refused to make the school trips. They made regular passenger runs, however, during other parts of the day.

Roy L. Foley, president of Local 1358, Amalgamated Association of Street Electric Railway and Motor Coach Employes of America, said the union was supporting the "striking" drivers.

"We will not permit our men

Continued on Page 32, Column 5

Ammunition Ample to Repel Reds in Korea, Says Wilson

He Will Give 'Facts' to Senators Tuesday on Issue Raised by Van Fleet's Report —Clark Also Denies Shortage

By HAROLD B. HINTON
Special to The New York Times.

WASHINGTON, March 6—Charles E. Wilson, the Secretary of Defense, assured the public today that "there is sufficient ammunition available in the Far East Command to counter any enemy attack in Korea."

The statement was contained in a letter to Senator Leverett Saltonstall, Republican of Massachusetts and chairman of the Senate Armed Services Committee. Most members of the committee had been aroused yesterday by testimony from Gen. James A. Van Fleet, former commander of the United Nations ground forces in Korea, that he had been handicapped during his entire twenty-two months of command by shortages of men and ammunition.

The Far East Command was mentioned by Secretary Wilson includes Japan as well as Korea.

[In Korea, on an inspection, Gen. Mark W. Clark, the United Nations commander, said that "certain types" of artillery

shells had been rationed but that there was "ample" ammunition to repel any all-out Communist offensive.]

The Senate committee, after hearing General Van Fleet in two closed sessions, decided to invite Mr. Wilson, Robert T. Stevens, the Secretary of the Army, and Gen. J. Lawton Collins, the Army Chief of Staff, to give their views on the matter. Some members hoped that General Van Fleet could attend the closed hearing at which the other officials would appear next Tuesday morning.

Senator Saltonstall said he had also invited General of the Army Omar N. Bradley, Chairman of the Joint Chiefs of Staff, but that General Bradley would be in Europe on Tuesday.

The Pentagon officials, he said, will be asked "to place the rather confusing and conflicting views which have been laid before us in

Continued on Page 2, Column 6

HALLEY DEMANDS RENT LAW BE KEPT

He Proposes That Council Ask Legislature to Let City Control as Alternative

A demand that the Legislature extend the present State Rent Law or permit the city to enact its own controls was made yesterday by City Council President Rudolph Halley. At the same time he accused the State Administration of a "rent grab."

Acting jointly with Councilman Earl Brown, Manhattan Democrat, Mr. Halley placed in the City Council hopper for introduction next Tuesday a resolution setting forth his rent law proposals.

The proposed rent control now before the Legislature, as submitted by the Temporary State Commission on Rents and Rental Conditions, Mr. Halley charged, "permits a rent grab in that it authorizes blanket increases without regard to the nature or condition of the accommodations, without a showing of landlord need and without regard to the hardship of the tenants."

There is no proof that acute housing shortage in the city has been relieved, Mr. Halley asserted, and "no evidence to show that the low and middle-income families who make up the bulk of the tenants of the city can afford to pay increases."

Hardship Is Predicted

The Council President predicted that the proposed new state law would work a "serious hardship" on the majority of low and middle-income tenants here, "many of whom live in substandard dwellings and most of whom can ill afford to pay rent increases at this time."

"The clear evidence is," he declared, "that if a blanket increase either in rent or percentage of rent is authorized, the great majority of tenants in New York City will have no choice but to pay oppressive rents because of the unavailability of apartments by reason of the housing shortage."

He added that the proposed state bill "ignores the problems and the needs of a great majority of the people of the city."

The resolution to be put before the City Council by Mr. Halley and Mr. Brown set forth:

"That the Legislature of the State of New York either extend the existing rent control law without change for another two years or, in the alternative, that it authorize the City of New York to enact its own rent control laws so that those who know the facts and understand the problems of the people of the City of New

Continued on Page 21, Column 7

POLICE ALTER PLAN TO FIGHT GAMBLING

One Officer in Each Borough to Be in Charge—Brooklyn Clean-Up Discussed

The Police Department is planning to place the enforcement of gambling and vice laws in the hands of individual commanders for each of the five boroughs in a move to "concentrate responsibility."

This plan, and another to cope with assaults on the public in Brooklyn, were announced yesterday after Commissioner George P. Monaghan conferred for an hour with District Attorney Miles F. McDonald, County Judge Samuel S. Leibowitz, Raymond H. Chadayne, foreman of the Brooklyn rackets grand jury, and Assistant District Attorney Julius Helfand.

The meeting took place in Judge Leibowitz' chambers in the Central Court Building at the request of Mr. Monaghan.

Judge Leibowitz explained that Mr. Monaghan had asked for the meeting "so that we could sit down informally and see what we can do to correct, to clean up, the conditions that need cleaning up in the Borough of Brooklyn."

Judge Leibowitz, who acted as

Continued on Page 32, Column 2

VISHINSKY DEPARTS

Pays a Tearful Tribute to Stalin and Sails— Silent on Shake-Up

GROMYKO SENT HERE

U. N. Hears Indonesian Appeal for Eisenhower and Malenkov to Talk

By THOMAS J. HAMILTON
Special to The New York Times.

UNITED NATIONS, N. Y., March 6—Andrei Y. Vishinsky, in what turned out to be his last official act as Foreign Minister of the Soviet Union, delivered a tearful tribute here this morning to "the great Stalin," and sailed on the Liberté this afternoon for home and possibly an uncertain future.

He said just before the Liberté sailed that he had had no advance knowledge of the election of Georgi M. Malenkov as Premier, and declined to comment.

During the day's debate, Dr. L. N. Palar, chief Indonesian delegate, urged the United Nations to call for a direct meeting between President Eisenhower and Premier Malenkov as a move to ease world tensions and prepare the way for a settlement in Korea.

Andrei A. Gromyko, now Soviet Ambassador to London, who was permanent Soviet representative at the United Nations from 1946 until 1948, will come to New York to take over temporarily as representative to the United Nations. Mr. Gromyko left London hastily by air tonight. Headwinds forced his plane, a British Overseas Airways Stratocruiser, to stop at Shannon Airport in Ireland.

Speech Precedes Shake-Up

Mr. Vishinsky's statement in the Political and Security Committee of the General Assembly was made five hours before the Moscow radio announced the government changes, which included the appointment of Vyacheslav M. Molotov as Foreign Minister and the demotion of Mr. Vishinsky to Deputy Foreign Minister and permanent Soviet representative to the United Nations.

[Aboard the Liberté last night A. A. Soldatov, a member of the Soviet delegation to the United Nations, said that Mr. Vishinsky had been informed of his new job, but that he declined to comment for publication.]

Mr. Vishinsky showed so plainly the effect of strain and grief during his United Nations appearance this morning that a delegate remarked, after Mr. Vishinsky had returned to the Soviet delegation's

Continued on Page 3, Column 6

HUGE FUNERAL SET

Body to Be Placed With Lenin's in Red Square After Ceremonies

MEMORIAL PLANNED

New Pantheon Is Due —Mourners in Moscow Offer Quiet Homage

Special to The New York Times.

MOSCOW, Saturday, March 7—Thousands of grieving Moscow citizens have filed past Stalin's bier in the Hall of Columns through the night. A Government announcement early today said that the body of the late Premier would be taken Monday to lie beside that of Lenin in the famous tomb in Red Square.

The funeral services will be held in Red Square at noon Monday. Hundreds and hundreds of thousands of Muscovites, possibly as many as 2,000,000, will have passed Stalin's bier before the funeral services.

Like that of Lenin, Stalin's body will be subjected to the embalming process developed by Soviet scientists to preserve it in its unchanged condition indefinitely, the announcement added.

The Government also announced plans for the construction of what it described as "a monumental building—pantheon—memorial."

After this building has been completed, the bodies of Lenin and Stalin and those of other famous party figures and leaders, which now lie buried in the Kremlin wall, will be transferred, the Government said. Then the building will be opened for visitation by "wide masses of workers," the announcement said.

Meanwhile, the body of Stalin lay in state in the same chamber where his co-revolutionist lay in state on his death in January, 1924.

Throngs Fill City Streets

Mourners filled the streets for block after block around the Hall of Columns yesterday and lines stretched back as far as Moscow's Garden Circle Boulevard about a mile distant.

No man knew how many mourners would pass through the chandelier-hung funeral rooms during the period of lying-in-state. But it was evident that the total would be numbered in the millions—two or three.

In the hour of deep tragedy over Stalin's death, government functions operated with efficiency.

The death of Stalin, was announced at 4 A. M. By 3 P. M. Stalin's body had been brought

Continued on Page 5, Column 2

NEW SOVIET LEADER: Georgi M. Malenkov, 51, who succeeded Joseph V. Stalin yesterday as Premier of Soviet Union.
Sovfoto

Britain Agrees to Step Up Economic War on Peiping

By JAMES RESTON
Special to The New York Times.

WASHINGTON, March 6—President Eisenhower declined to comment today on the selection of Georgi M. Malenkov as Premier of the Soviet Union. He concentrated instead on unifying British-American policies in the war against Communist aggression and apparently made some progress, particularly in the economic war against Communist China.

Secretary of State John Foster Dulles and the British Foreign Secretary, Anthony Eden, made a tour of the world political horizon this morning, while the President was discussing the Stalin crisis with his Cabinet. Mr. Eden then had a private talk with the President and stayed on at the White House for lunch.

Results of Conversations

The results of these and yesterday's political conversations with the British were understood to be as follows:

¶The British undertook to adopt new measures to reduce the flow of strategic materials to Communist China. These measures will include adding to the present list of goods on the "forbidden" list and supervising more closely the operations of British-owned and registered ships.

¶Agreement was reached on the advisability of disengaging United States, British and French armed forces in the Korean, Malayan and Indo-China wars as fast as dependable native troops. There was acceptance of the principle that these three wars were all part of a single campaign against the Communist aggressors and that strategy should be coordinated as much as possible.

¶Mr. Eden also made clear that his Government had no intention of withdrawing recognition from the Chinese Communists. The United States also maintained its position on that subject; namely, that it would not recognize Mao Tse-tung, but continue to recognize Chiang Kai-shek.

¶However, it was reported that there was agreement on both sides that the death of Stalin and the selection of Mr. Malenkov as Soviet Premier increased the chances of a split between Moscow and Peiping, since Mr. Mao, the Chinese Communist dictator, has often regarded himself as the leading theoretician of the Communist world, next to Premier Stalin.

¶Both sides reached agreement on the policies that were being followed in trying to reach a new understanding with Egypt, but found themselves far apart once more in their estimates of what would happen if the current negotiations collapsed in Iran. The United States position was that the British approach to the Iran-

Continued on Page 8, Column 3

FOUR TO HELP RULE

Beria, Molotov, Bulganin and Kaganovich Are Deputy Premiers

TEN-MAN PRESIDIUM

Molotov Is Again Foreign Minister—Vishinsky Demoted to U. N.

Text of announcement of Soviet changes is on Page 3.

By HARRISON E. SALISBURY
Special to The New York Times.

MOSCOW, March 6 — Georgi Maximilianovich Malenkov was named head of the Soviet Government tonight in place of the late Joseph Stalin in a series of changes in the highest Soviet leadership.

Mr. Malenkov has assumed the post of Chairman of the Council of Ministers, which was held by Stalin.

At the same time he was named as first in the list of the Presidium of the Central Committee of the Communist party, which is composed of ten members and four alternates.

Standing beside him in the chief and most responsible posts of Government and party in this reorganized structure are four veteran Soviet leaders and co-workers of Stalin—Lavrenti P. Beria, Vyacheslav M. Molotov, Nikolai A. Bulganin and Lazar M. Kaganovich. Those four become the First Deputy Chairmen of the Council of Ministers and with Mr. Malenkov constitute its Presidium.

The announcement over the Moscow radio at 11:30 o'clock tonight was made in the name of the Central Committee of the Communist party, the Council of Ministers and the Presidium of the Supreme Soviet.

Changes to Avoid 'Panic'

The changes in the directing bodies of the Government were made, it was announced, with the purpose of maintaining uninterrupted and correct leadership and avoiding "any kind of disarray and panic."

The announcement said the changes would secure the nation from any kind of interruption in directing the activity of state and party organs and "unconditionally secure" the execution of party and Government policies both internally and abroad.

The chief impression given by the Government both in tonight's announcement and in the proclamation of Stalin's death was one of firmness and the highest political vigilance, a sense of the rallying together of party and Government forces to withstand any threats from within or from without.

The Government was acting with the greatest resolution and with marked vigor. Mr. Malenkov lost no time in demonstrating his will and determination to prove a worthy custodian of the policies of monolithic unity and steel resolu-

Continued on Page 3, Column 2

EUROPE IS CAUTIOUS ON SOVIET FUTURE

London Shuns Predictions but Asks Vigilance—Paris, Rome Pay Stalin Formal Tribute

By RAYMOND DANIELL
Special to The New York Times.

LONDON, March 6—Persons here whose business it is to forecast the course of Soviet policy received little indication of its trend from the appointment of Georgi M. Malenkov as the successor to Premier Stalin.

The elevation of Mr. Malenkov was not entirely unexpected but British betting odds were about even between him and Vyacheslav M. Molotov who, at 63—twice a year's Mr. Malenkov's senior—again becomes Soviet Foreign Minister.

To that extent the death of Stalin is regarded here as something to regret, if not to mourn over, because in the course of years, this dictator with the power of final decision had followed a pattern of action that made intelligent prediction possible.

[Elsewhere in Europe the news of Stalin's death caused some apprehension regarding future developments in Soviet policy.]

Malenkov's Mind Unknown

Nobody here—not even those charged with the responsibility of knowing—knows how Mr. Malenkov's mind works, what are his ideas of foreign policy, nor, least of all, what real power lies behind his new title.

There had been some idea that Mr. Malenkov might be Stalin's heir. It is believed that his age ruled him out but there is a question about whether he is old enough to be ruled out for the future.

Will Lavrenti P. Beria, an aspirant for national leadership, be content to remain in what amounts to third place, in charge of home affairs?

The appointment of Marshal Nikolai A. Bulganin, who is 57, to the Ministry of War and of 72-year-old Marshal Kliment Y. Voroshilov to succeed Nikolai M. Shvernik as chairman of the Supreme Council of the Presidium, also attracted attention.

In any struggle for power that

Continued on Page 6, Column 5

'Voice' Aide Charges Chief Parroted 'Reds'

By C. P. TRUSSELL
Special to The New York Times.

WASHINGTON, March 6—Howard Maier, a political specialist for the Voice of America, testified today that he had received a reprimand from the State Department for having written a script for a counter-propaganda radio broadcast that had been denounced in what he termed the Communist-controlled press.

It appeared from the reprimand, Mr. Maier told the Senate investigating subcommittee, headed by Senator Joseph R. McCarthy, Republican of Wisconsin, that in investigating the Voice, the State Department group agreed with the denunciation.

Foremost among the inquiry's exhibits was a column in The Daily Compass of New York, now out of

Continued on Page 10, Column 4

Half-Staff Flags Here Stir Confusion

Most of Them Flown for the Late Head of Staten Island

Many flags flew at half staff here yesterday, but most were not a mark of respect for Premier Stalin of the Soviet Union. Only a few were.

Flags on public buildings, including the City Hall, were ordered flown at half staff by Mayor Impellitteri as a mark of respect for Cornelius A. Hall, retired Borough President of Richmond. Mr. Hall died Thursday, too.

At United Nations headquarters the United Nations flag was at half staff too, but this was out of respect for Stalin.

There were other tributes to the Premier. The national red ensign of Britain was at half staff on the Queen Elizabeth, and the tricolor of France was flown similarly on the Liberté.

Officers of the Queen Elizabeth said the red ensign had been lowered in respect to the Premier. French Line officials refused explanation. However, Andrei Y.

Continued on Page 4, Column 4

The New York Times
At City Hall for Mr. Hall

The New York Times
At U. N. for Premier Stalin

The New York Times.

Copyright, 1953, by The New York Times Company.

VOL. CII..No. 34,828.

Entered as Second-Class Matter,
Post Office, New York, N. Y.

NEW YORK, TUESDAY, JUNE 2, 1953.

Times Square, New York 36, N. Y.
Telephone LAckawanna 4-1000

FIVE CENTS

AUTHORITY LEASES CITY TRANSIT LINES; FARE RISE IN SIGHT

Estimate Board Votes, 11-5, for 10-Year Pact Including Terms Asked by Joseph

EFFECTIVE DATE IS JUNE 15

New Agency Seeking Tokens From Mint, Indicating New Charge May Not Be 15c

Digest of lease signed by city and Transit Authority, Page 32.

By LEO EGAN

The Board of Estimate voted 11 to 5 yesterday to lease the city's $1,700,000,000 transit system to the newly created New York City Transit Authority for a period of ten years, during which the authority will be obligated to raise enough revenue from fares and incidental charges to meet operating costs.

By approving the lease, the board is almost certain that the authority will raise transit fares by July 30 in an amount sufficient to overcome a prospective operating deficit of $47,000,000 for the fiscal year beginning July 1. A first step in this direction was taken by the authority within a few hours after the board acted when it decided to explore the possibility of obtaining from the United States Mint at Philadelphia an emergency supply of tokens, to be used on all three divisions of the rapid transit lines in the collection of a higher fare.

Casey Tells of Token Plans

The decision to request the Federal Government's help in obtaining enough tokens to put a fare change into effect by July 30, the statutory deadline, was announced by Maj. Gen. Hugh J. Casey, authority chairman, after a special authority meeting at the offices of the Board of Transportation, 370 Jay Street, Brooklyn.

Sidney H. Bingham, chairman of the Board of Transportation, will confer with the Director of the Mint at Philadelphia today on the possibility of obtaining 20,000,000 tokens, General Casey said. Subsequent additions to the supply would be obtained from private suppliers, he added.

To speed the negotiations with the Mint, the authority has requested Governor Dewey to intervene with the Secretary of the Treasury. General Casey said.

A design for the token was officially approved by the authority yesterday. It is a perforated coin, somewhat smaller than a dime.

By exploring the possibility of obtaining enough tokens for use on all three divisions, the authority indicated it might reject Mr. Bingham's recommendation for a 15-cent fare in favor of a smaller charge, perhaps 12 or 12½ cents a ride. The present fare is 10 cents.

A major justification for the Bingham recommendation was that it would involve the use of tokens on only the I.R.T. division, which has electrically operated turnstiles. On the B.M.T. and IND divisions, which have mechanical turnstiles, two coins—a dime and a nickel—would be used to pay the fare.

General Casey emphasized in announcing the authority action that no decisions on a fare increase had been reached. It will not be possible to arrive at a conclusion, he said, until all pertinent facts are studied.

City Fiscal Problem Eased

The Board of Estimate's decision yesterday automatically relieved the city of the necessity of meeting the prospective operating deficit out of tax revenues in the new fiscal year that starts July 1. It likewise vested the city with power to collect $50,000,000 a year in additional taxes from real estate for general municipal purposes, plus, for the next four years, enough to liquidate an accumulated deficit of $39,000,000 in the transit pension system.

Moreover, in accordance with special laws enacted by the Legislature earlier this year on the recommendation of Governor Dewey, transfer of the deficit-ridden transit system to the authority gives the city power at any time in the future to impose a one-half of 1 per cent payroll tax, payable in equal parts by employers and employes, estimated to raise $60,-600,000 a year.

The city's budget for the new fiscal year, already approved by the Board of Estimate and City Council, contemplates full use of the additional real estate taxing powers, but no use of the payroll tax.

As had been forecast, Rudolph

Continued on Page 28, Column 2

Eisenhower Moves to Limit State Department to Policy

New Reorganization Plans Would Transfer Present Operating Functions to 2 Special Agencies, Information and Foreign Aid

By ANTHONY LEVIERO
Special to THE NEW YORK TIMES.

WASHINGTON, June 1—President Eisenhower proposed today to restore the State Department to its traditional pre-war policy-making role and to transfer virtually all its operating functions to new organizations—the United States Information Agency and the Foreign Operations Administration.

A far-reaching reorganization of the department that was requested by the President in two plans submitted to Congress today, with a promise of further changes to be sought early next year.

Today he stressed two objectives:

1. To divest the department of the functional tasks that had involved it in political controversy during the post-war era.

2. To make the Secretary of State supreme, next to the President, in the policy supervision of all foreign information and aid programs.

The controversial Voice of America and other information programs would be swept out of the State Department, the Mutual Security Agency and other agencies and concentrated in the new Information Agency. The Mutual Security Agency itself would become the nucleus around which would be built the new Foreign Operations Administration to take over various other programs for technical, economic and military assistance.

Of operating programs, all that would be left in the State Department would be the programs for the educational exchange of persons.

The two new agencies would have administrative autonomy, just as the Mutual Security Agency has today. But a new idea in Government organization was introduced. The directors of the two agencies would not only be subject to close

Continued on Page 24, Column 4

Text of message on propaganda and aid plans, Page 24.

MRS. HOBBY WARNS DOCTORS ON TASKS

Social-Economic Problems in the Field Must Be Solved by A.M.A. or Others, She Says

Mrs. Oveta Culp Hobby, Secretary of Health, Education and Welfare, declared at the annual meeting of the American Medical Association, which opened yesterday, that organized medicine must find solutions to the social-economic problems facing medicine today or the solution would be taken out of its hands. She expressed confidence that the American Medical Association "will meet this challenge."

Addressing the House of Delegates, policy-making body of the association, at the Waldorf-Astoria Hotel, Mrs. Hobby said the social and economic demands on the medical profession "are only the continuing challenge in this long history of constant adaptation to a changing society, but never have these problems been more onerous and critical than today."

The association opened its 102d annual meeting yesterday. For five days progress in all branches of medicine will be reviewed in 400 reports by leaders in their fields.

The sessions are being held in seven hotels and in Town Hall while 635 scientific and technical exhibits are being displayed on four floors of Grand Central Palace. The exhibits are open only to doctors and their guests.

Mrs. Hobby in her speech to the delegates said she agreed fully

Continued on Page 26, Column 5

HUMPHREY OPPOSES REVENUE LOSS NOW

He Calls Cut Gamble With U.S. Security—Asks House Unit to Extend Excess Profit Tax

By JOHN D. MORRIS
Special to THE NEW YORK TIMES.

WASHINGTON, June 1—George M. Humphrey, Secretary of the Treasury, told Congress today that only "full mobilization" would justify tax increases to produce any more revenue than the Administration was now seeking.

The Government's chief fiscal officer so testified in opening the Administration's case before the House Ways and Means Committee for a six-month extension of the excess profits tax and the cancellation of automatic cuts in regular corporation and excise (sales) levies slated for next April 1.

The Administration, he said, wants those three phases of its tax program carried out in a single bill this year, though the committee has limited its present deliberations to extension of the excess profits law, which is due to expire June 30.

The Secretary asserted that losses in Federal revenue now would be an unsafe gamble with the country's security.

Mr. Humphrey also made the following points:

¶ That he was "very strongly opposed" to any change in the excess profits tax during the extension period.

¶ That he would fight any continuation of the levy beyond Dec. 31.

¶ That tax relief starting next

Continued on Page 47, Column 2

Harvard Elects Dr. N. M. Pusey, Midwest Educator, as President

Lawrence College Head, 46, Has 3 Degrees From University— Favors Humanities Study

By JOHN H. FENTON
Special to THE NEW YORK TIMES.

CAMBRIDGE, Mass., June 1—Dr. Nathan Marsh Pusey, president of Lawrence College in Appleton, Wis., was elected the twenty-fourth president of Harvard by the Harvard Corporation today.

Dr. Pusey, who is a native of Council Bluffs, Iowa, and 46 years old, is a scholar in Greek history, and holds three degrees from Harvard: Bachelor of Arts, magna cum laude, 1928; Master of Arts, 1932, and Doctor of Philosophy, 1937. He prepared for college at Abraham Lincoln High School in Council Bluffs.

The Iowa educator will succeed Dr. James Bryant Conant, who will become president-emeritus of Harvard University on Sept. 1. Dr. Conant, now on leave, is serving as United States High Commissioner for Germany.

Dr. Pusey's election by the Harvard Corporation is subject to the confirmation of the Board of Overseers. This confirmation, customarily a formality, is scheduled to be voted on June 10, the day before the Harvard commencement. On only one occasion, in 1868, have the overseers refused the corporation permission to elect a president.

Associated Press
Dr. Nathan M. Pusey

The occasion of the only refusal was in the election of Dr. Charles W. Eliot, the original choice of the corporation, as the twenty-first president. The corporation prevailed after a delay of six months, and Dr. Eliot became president in 1869.

Dr. Pusey, reached by telephone at Appleton, said that he considered the corporation's action "a tremendous honor." But he con-

Continued on Page 27, Column 5

RHEE BOWS TO U.S.; SAYS KOREA AGREES TO EISENHOWER AIMS

Statement on Message From Washington Hints Opposition to Truce Plans Is Easing

By The Associated Press.

SEOUL, Korea, June 2—President Syngman Rhee disclosed today he had received a three-point message from President Eisenhower, and added: "We must accept anything that the United States President wants.

"Common sense and wisdom require that we cooperate with the United States at any cost," Dr. Rhee said, without saying what President Eisenhower had told him.

The statement of the 78-year-old leader of the Republic of Korea indicated that South Korean opposition to the secret proposal by the United Nations Command for bringing an armistice in Korea was lessening.

Dr. Rhee also said he was looking for some one to take the place of Maj. Gen. Choi Duk Shin as the South Korean delegate on the United Nations armistice negotiation team.

Dr. Rhee declined to elaborate on his apparently conciliatory statement. He spoke to correspondents at a parade of the British Commonwealth Division honoring the Coronation of Elizabeth II. Nor did he make it precisely clear whether he was ready now to accept the Allied truce proposal, to which he and his Government had expressed vigorous opposition.

South Korea's acting Premier, Pyun Yun Tae, threatened yesterday a break with the Allies and a go-it-alone policy for South Korea but deferred action until after next Thursday's critical truce session.

The Communists are expected to reply to the Allied proposal at Thursday's meeting.

Rhee Said to Seek Treaty

By JAY WALZ
Special to THE NEW YORK TIMES.

WASHINGTON, June 1—The Eisenhower Administration was reported today to have had a new request from President Syngman Rhee of South Korea for the pledge of a mutual defense pact and of military and economic help as a basis for the Seoul Government's support of present Allied truce proposals.

These conditions were said on good authority to be important features of a four-point program outlined in a letter forwarded to President Eisenhower through Ellis O. Briggs, United States Ambassador at Seoul.

The principal point in the still-secret United Nations proposal to the Communists for disposition of Korean war prisoners who refuse to return home was understood to be that final determination of the captives' fate would be up to the General Assembly of the United Nations.

Officially, the White House and State Department were silent on developments on Korea, and offered "no comment" even on reports that a letter from President Rhee might have been received.

Had Asked Pledge in Writing

The South Korean request for a mutual defense pact with the United States is not new. Dr. You Chan Yang, the Korean Ambassador here, has made repeated representations to the State Department for such a pledge of defense help in the event of future Communist aggression.

He has made the point that, while President Eisenhower has said publicly that the United States will never desert Korea, it would be more satisfying from the Korean standpoint to have "something down in black and white."

Dr. President Rhee's four points were reported to be (1) a pledge to sign a mutual defense pact with Korea; (2) a promise by the United States to provide military and financial help to Korea on a large scale; (3) withdrawal of all foreign troops on both sides as soon as a truce has started and prisoners have been exchanged, and (4) agreement that the United States would not stand in the way of South Korea in efforts to unite that country at some future time.

As far as the last point is concerned, sources felt South Korea did not have in mind the use of military force to bring together North and South Korea.

Meanwhile, some Capitol Hill leaders spoke out on recent Korea developments.

Senator William F. Knowland of California, who is chairman of the Senate Republican Policy Committee, said the United States should "risk" war with Russia to expand the fighting, if truce negotiations with the Communists collapsed at ....

In another ...., Senator H. Alexander ...., Republican of New Je...., thought

Continued ...., Column 5

---

2 OF BRITISH TEAM CONQUER EVEREST; QUEEN GETS NEWS AS CORONATION GIFT; THRONGS LINE HER PROCESSION ROUTE

CROWDS DEFY RAIN

Face a Day of Showers After All-Night Vigil to Hail Their Sovereign

By RAYMOND DANIELL
Special to THE NEW YORK TIMES.

LONDON, Tuesday, June 2—This is the day that all London, all Britain, all the Commonwealth and half the world have been awaiting. It is the day on which the crown of one of this old country's radiantly lovely young Queen Elizabeth II whose reign, it is hoped, will usher in another golden age.

The weather for the day was uncertain. By early morning the wind still blew, but rains that fell during the night had ceased, at least temporarily. The weather forecaster, however, was not optimistic about the prospects for the day, which was chosen originally because rain had not fallen on June 2 for many years. The forecast was for cool weather and showers, with sunny intervals.

Last night's gusts and rain discomfited the hundreds of thousands of persons who squatted the whole length of the royal way but if these hardships dislodged any it was unnoticeable because there were others waiting to take their places.

Some of these squatters, lacking reserved seats in the stands to accommodate 250,000 persons, began staking out their claims as early as midnight Sunday.

Squatters Sit on Curbs

By noon yesterday they were sitting on the curbs at Trafalgar Square and were packed two and three deep on the sidewalks along the Mall leading from Admiralty Arch to Buckingham Palace. By dinner time last night the East Carriage Drive in Hyde Park was filled with men, women and even young children with raincoats, blankets, lunch baskets and inflatable mattresses prepared to defend their little vantage points until the Queen's ornate gilded coach, with its eight gray horses, one named Eisenhower, had passed late in the afternoon.

During the day Queen Mother Elizabeth, accompanied by Princess Margaret, visited the palace to see the Queen on the eve of her coronation. By the time they left, an hour later, the crowd outside Buckingham Palace numbered nearly 50,000. The police, who had let the crowd swarm over the roadway, had to make strenuous efforts to clear a path for their car.

Later Princess Margaret made a visit to Westminster Abbey, where she was received by the Earl Marshal. Again the police had trouble clearing a way for her to return to the palace.

Even Oxford Street, that busy shopping center, was taken over by sidewalk squatters almost as soon as the big stores closed. Trafalgar Square, through which the Queen will pass three times on her way from Buckingham Palace to Westminster Abbey, and again back to the palace, was filled with curbstone sitters even at midday. Some of them had been there twelve hours then with an additional twenty-four in front of them. The litter they made of sodden

Continued on Page 8, Column 1

The New York Times
June 2, 1953
AT THE TOP: Solid black line shows route of British expedition, the first to reach Mount Everest's summit.

Abbey, Bedecked and Aglow, Awaits the Coronation Hour

By TANIA LONG
Special to THE NEW YORK TIMES.

LONDON, Tuesday, June 2—As one enters Westminster Abbey, where Elizabeth II is to be crowned in a few hours, a magnificent scene greets the eye. The austere gray interior has been converted into a rich and glowing setting for the young Queen's coronation. Carpeting and hangings in warm tones of blue and gold, banners of white embroidered with the royal coats of arms, and the deep rose of the throne and the royal chairs blend into a splendid symphony of color.

In the pale light of early morning a hush lies over the Abbey. Only a few of the great assemblage of 7,000 guests have arrived, and there is little movement in the vast edifice.

From the great west door, where the Queen will enter, a thick carpet of deep azure blue reaches through the nave to the choir stalls. Hangings of blue silk with royal emblems embroidered in gold are draped over the edges of the stands and balconies, giving warmth to the gray fabric of the church.

From the choir to the altar in that area known as the Coronation Theatre the floor is covered in rich gold pile, against which the deep rose-covered throne and chairs, and the opulent blue hangings on the walls stand out in sharp contrast.

Under a huge chandelier in the center of the Coronation Theatre and raised on a dais stands the throne. Five steps lead up to it. It faces the altar and because the Queen will be facing away from the majority of the guests, its back is low so that they too may see the Queen's crowned head during the latter part of the ceremony.

The throne chair is late ....

Continued on Page 6, Column 1

Notables File Past Empty Thrones On Way to Offer Homage to Queen

By C. L. SULZBERGER
Special to THE NEW YORK TIMES.

LONDON, Tuesday, June 2—At 6 o'clock this morning the most distinguished men in Britain began filing past an empty throne. Within a few brief hours, seated upon it and wearing the heavy crown of St. Edward the Confessor, a young Queen will receive their homage.

For Britain and for her still vast empire, this is a significant moment. A new Elizabethan age of challenge and uncertainty has started.

Westminster Abbey, in its fullest splendor, with gold plate and regalia spread out on the altar, containing two thrones today. The first is that of King Edward I, a gnarled oaken chair having beneath it the Stone of Scone from the Scotland he had conquered.

Upon it the Queen is crowned. From it she will hear the acclaim of her subjects, the distant booming of her cannon and the solemn

prayer of her primate, the Archbishop of Canterbury, exhorting:

"God crown you with a crown of glory and righteousness, that, having a right faith and manifold fruit of good works, you may obtain the crown of an everlasting kingdom by the gift of Him whose Kingdom endureth forever. Amen."

Only then, when she is fully consecrated and acclaimed, will the Queen, assisted by her lay and clerical peers, mount the royal throne on its dais.

Since the early dawn crept over the stirring city of London, pushing its light across gray Whitehall and through the soft rose and amber windows of this Holy Church of St. Peter, which is its rightful name, the Abbey has come to life for one of those great occasions when it nurtures royal monarchs.

Finely attired lords and ladies are sweeping into their places, bear-

Continued on Page 12, Column 5

HIGHEST PEAK WON

New Zealander and a Guide Made the Final Climb to Top Friday

By Reuters.

KATMANDU, Nepal, Tuesday, June 2—The British expedition has conquered Mount Everest, a message flashed from Namche Bazar to the British Embassy here said today.

The message said Edmund Hillary, a New Zealand beekeeper and mountaineer, and Tensing Norkay, the famous Sherpa guide, had reached the hitherto unscaled summit from Camp Eight last Friday.

The news of this success had to be rushed by runner from the British expedition's base camp on Khumbu Glacier to the radio post at Namche Bazar.

It is understood here that this was the expedition's third attack on the last slopes leading to the summit, a first double attempt having failed.

Experts here said the success was largely due to the fine weather, combined with properly acclimatized climbers and the excellent organization and leadership of Col. H. C. J. Hunt.

Full details of the exploit are not expected to reach here for some days.

It is believed here that the news was transmitted specially to London by diplomatic channels so Queen Elizabeth could be told.

Queen Told at Palace

LONDON, Tuesday, June 2 (Reuters)—The Times of London reported the news of the scaling of Mount Everest in a copyrighted message today.

The news was published in a special edition of The Times at its early sale among coronation crowds in London.

Queen Elizabeth, resting at Buckingham Palace, was told on the eve of her coronation that the British expedition had conquered Mount Everest. The news was brought to her as she spent a quiet evening "at home." The British climbers had succeeded in their plan to give her a world-shaking coronation present.

Mount Everest, the 29,002-foot giant, was the last main outpost of the world unknown to man.

The thirteen members of the expedition formed the eleventh team to try to conquer the mountain in the past thirty years. Many climbers have died in the high ice and snow of the Himalaya giant.

The Sherpa guide, Tensing Norkay, a 42-year-old native veteran of more assaults on Mount Everest than any other man.

With 362 porters, twenty Sherpa guides and 10,000 pounds of baggage the expedition left the Nepalese base of Katmandu on March 10. Thus it took sixty days from start to finish.

The climbers carried three flags—the Union Jack, the United Nations flag and the Nepalese flag—to plant on the summit.

They made an approach to the "Goddess Mother of the Snows" from the south, or Nepalese, side.

It was the route reconnoitred by Sir Eric Shipton, who led a British

Continued on Page 14, Column 7

Tito Abolishes Rank Of Army Commissar

By JACK RAYMOND
Special to THE NEW YORK TIMES.

BELGRADE, Yugoslavia, June 1—President Tito abolished today the system of political commissars in the Yugoslav armed forces, asserting that present conditions no longer required them.

Not mentioned in Marshal Tito's order was the fact that this will undoubtedly make it easier for Yugoslavia to carry on with growing plans for integrating their military establishment with Western defense projects.

"It will be much easier to deal with Yugoslav military people now," said a Western military liaison expert here.

The political commissars, who wore uniforms and were equal in rank with military commanders in the Yugoslav Army, were introduced in imitation of Soviet military practice in the early days of partisan warfare against Germany. Even after the break with the

Continued on Page 13, Column 3

DULLES SAYS U.S. AIM IS TO GAIN FRIENDS

Report on Near East-Asian Trip Urges 'Impartial' Approach to Arab-Israeli Dispute

Text of Secretary Dulles' talk about recent trip, Page 4.

Special to THE NEW YORK TIMES.

WASHINGTON, June 1—John Foster Dulles, Secretary of State, said tonight that it was the policy of the Eisenhower Administration to develop goodwill among the nations of the Near East and South Asia to thwart the Kremlin's desire to exploit their many differences.

To this end, he urged an "impartial" approach to Israeli-Arab disputes so as to win the support of both sides against the "common threat"—communism. He said the United States must make clear to all nations concerned with independence that the North Atlantic Treaty alliance was in no way related to a desire to help colonial powers keep or win back their colonies.

In a country-wide radio and television report on his twenty-day tour of the Middle East and South Asia, Mr. Dulles urged the strategic importance of that rich and populous area and said its problems could not be ignored without dangerous consequences.

'Primary Purpose' Stressed

The Secretary's half-hour address was carried over the radio and television networks of the American Broadcasting System and by the Du Mont television network, and the National Broadcasting Company radio network rebroadcast it. The Secretary gave a country-by-country account of the trip, on which he was accompanied by Harold E. Stassen, Director for Mutual Security. They made stops all the way from Egypt to Pakistan and India.

Mr. Dulles declared that the "primary purpose of the trip "was to show friendliness and to develop understanding," and he added: "These people we visited are all proud peoples who have a great tradition and, I believe, a great future."

The Eisenhower Administration, he continued, plans to make "friendship—not fault-finding—the basis of its foreign policy."

Addressing himself to problems of the troubled Holy Land, Mr. Dulles said he had come back to Washington convinced that the Arabs were "more fearful of Zionism than of communism."

On the other hand, he added,

Continued on Page 5, Column 6

The New York Times.

Copyright, 1953, by The New York Times Company.

VOL. CII.—No. 34,846.
Entered as Second-Class Matter,
Post Office, New York, N. Y.
NEW YORK, SATURDAY, JUNE 20, 1953.
Times Square, New York 36, N. Y.
Telephone LAckawanna 4-1000
RAG PAPER EDITION
SEVENTY-FIVE CENTS

REDS INSIST U.N. RECAPTURE ALL RELEASED PRISONERS; TRUCE TALKS RECESS AGAIN

FOE WRITES CLARK

Questions if Allies Can Control South Korean Leaders and Army

Text of the Communist note to General Clark is on Page 3.

By LINDESAY PARROTT
Special to The New York Times.

TOKYO, Saturday, June 20—Communist armistice delegates at Panmunjom demanded today that the United Nations recapture all 25,000 anti-Communist prisoners of the Korean war released by the order of Dr. Syngman Rhee, South Korean President.

The demand was made in the course of a twenty-five-minute meeting of the full truce delegations called for this morning by the senior Communist truce representative, Lieut. Gen. Nam Il of North Korea.

The Communist high command sent a strong protest to Gen. Mark W. Clark, United Nations commander, asserting that the Allies, equally with Dr. Rhee, must bear "serious responsibility" for the incident. The message was signed by the top enemy commanders, Marshal Kim Il Sung, North Korean Premier, and Chinese Gen. Peng Teh-huai.

The Communist protest was an angry one, and it was significant that it was made directly to the Allied commander. Yet it seemed to indicate that the enemy was not prepared to completely end the negotiations for an armistice.

The letter to General Clark repeated many of the old charges of American coercion and duplicity, but did not slam the door to further conversations.

[The Associated Press said that Pyun Yun Tae, Acting South Korean Premier, demanded Saturday in a letter to General Clark that all anti-Communist North Korean prisoners remaining in Allied stockades be turned over to the Republic for immediate release.

[Soon afterward, in Tokyo General Clark's United Nations headquarters made public a scorching letter to the South Korean President, saying General Clark could "not at this time estimate the ultimate consequences" of President Rhee's "precipitous and shocking" release of the 25,000 anti-Communist war captives, General Clark accused Dr. Rhee of breaking a "persona commitment" not to take action.]

At the armistice conference, the Communists in effect demanded that the Allied command assume full control over the fiery South Korean President from acting on his own. Pointedly, the Communists asked:

"Is the United Nations Command able to control the South Korean Government and Army? If not, does the armistice in Korea include the Syngman Rhee clique.

"If it is not included, what assurance is there for implementation of the armistice agreement on the part of South Korea?

"If it is included, then your side must be responsible for recovering immediately all the 25,000 prisoners of

Continued on Page 3, Column 4

U. S. SEES POSITION IN KOREA AS GRAVE

Dulles Meets With Both Parties and Envoys of U. N. Allies in Atmosphere of Urgency

By WILLIAM S. WHITE
Special to The New York Times.

WASHINGTON, June 19—The United States Government worked in haste today to save a Korean truce that some responsible men regarded as all but lost through South Korea's angry defiance of the United Nations.

According to an authoritative source in the Prisoner-of-War Command here, officials in Tokyo had been warned that such a measure might be taken by the Government of the Republic of Korea. However, the Prisoner-of-War Command was assured by higher headquarters that Dr. Rhee was "bluffing."

As a result, South Korean security guards were not replaced by American soldiers and other precautionary measures were insufficient.

However, the freeing of the prisoners came as no surprise to those who have been close to President Rhee these last few weeks. Nor was it a surprise to diplomatic circles in Pusan, the temporary South Korean capital.

They knew how defiant the President's attitude has been from the start, and they regard him as a rather unpredictable individual, apt to go off on a desperate tangent at almost any time.

Some Americans farther away from the scene, however, have had a tendency to underestimate what Dr. Rhee might do and to grasp at any straw that indicated that he was yielding ground in his fight. That was why the repeated threats to free the prisoners on the spot and the ample information available indicating that the South Korean Government was taking concrete steps along these lines were virtually ignored by those in a position to do something about it.

One reason for this reluctance to recognize the facts in the matter is that it is difficult for an American to understand Dr. Rhee's reasoning. The Korean leader feels that to accept a truce agreement is tantamount to inviting self-destruction.

He is not only worried about the surrender of the employes in North Korea but has been forced earlier in the day when a group of leading tanker operators submitted to the demands of the N. M. U. on the basis of similar wage rises and other terms. After this agreement was reached, it was a foregone conclusion that the rest of the industry would follow.

President Rhee and those close

Continued on Page 2, Column 3

U. N. OFFICERS FELT RHEE WAS BLUFFING

Warnings Unheeded, Prisoner Command Took No Steps to Prevent Mass Escape

By ROBERT ALDEN
Special to The New York Times.

SEOUL, Korea, June 19—The United Nations Command was not prepared for the precipitate action taken by Dr. Syngman Rhee, President of South Korea, in freeing non-Communist prisoners of war.

HIS ATTEMPT TO ESCAPE FAILS: A U. S. Marine, right, escorts a wounded prisoner at Ascom City, near Inchon, where about 500 anti-Communists escaped. Marines and other troops prevented a larger break-out.

AID BILL APPROVED AS DEMOCRATS SAVE MEASURE IN HOUSE

G.O.P. Split on Cutting Funds, but 280-108 Vote Prevails —4.9 Billion Authorized

By FELIX BELAIR Jr.
Special to The New York Times.

WASHINGTON, June 19—The House of Representatives authorized today an appropriation of $4,995,732,500 for military, economic and technical aid to fifty-six free governments and dependencies resisting communism. The vote sending the measure to the Senate was 280 to 108, with one Representative merely voting "present."

Throughout the afternoon, a smoothly functioning bipartisan majority shouted down repeated attempts to cut the authorization items below the recommendations of the Foreign Affairs Committee. But it was the Democrats under Representative Sam Rayburn of Texas, the minority leader, who provided the margin of victory.

Republicans by the score deserted the leadership of Speaker Joseph W. Martin Jr. to vote for economy amendments. There was no record vote on any of the attempts to slash the measure and, although the foreign policy prestige of President Eisenhower had been thrown into the debate by the Republican leadership, it was the Democrats who gave him his vote of confidence.

On the final vote, 160 Democrats joined with 119 Republicans and an Independent, Frazier Reams of Ohio, to provide the 280 majority for the bill. A total of eighty-one Republicans and twenty-seven Democrats voted against the measure. Representative Harold A. Patten, Democrat of Arizona, was the one who voted "present."

Members Rally to Vote

The high tide of opposition to the authorization—which is $476,-000,000 less than the Administration had requested—came shortly before the final vote. Representative Hamer H. Budge, Republican of Idaho, offered an amendment to cut all the items by 10 per cent, but it was rejected by a standing vote of 132 to 101.

The same amendment had lost by a narrower margin a few minutes earlier when, on a count, the vote was put at 132 to 102. But when a vote by tellers was demanded, members burst from the cloakrooms on either side of the House to provide the extra votes.

An even earlier attempt to accomplish the same result and cut the authorization by $498,000,000 was made when Representative William M. Colmer, Democrat of Mississippi, sought to place a ceiling on the total authorization of $4,500,000,000. This move was rejected, 204 to 83.

The pattern of unrecorded voting on the amendments had been set shortly after the House met for business an hour before noon.

Representative Lawrence Smith, Republican of Wisconsin, proposed to cut $329,186,000 from the section providing military aid to Western Europe. The amendment would have eliminated military aid totaling $216,906,000 for Yugo-

Continued on Page 18, Column 4

4-Day Seamen's Strike Ends As Wage Demands Are Met

By GEORGE HORNE

The four-day-old seamen's strike, which immobilized 125 vessels and threatened to paralyze one-half of the nation's fleet of 1,500 ships, came to an end at 12:45 A. M. today.

National Maritime Union seamen, who struck on Tuesday when the operators refused to accede to wage demands, signed with the dry-cargo shipping employers at the headquarters of the Federal Mediation and Conciliation Service, winning wage rises ranging from 2 to 6 per cent. The settlement terms constituted a complete capitulation by the operators.

A few minutes earlier, the striking American Radio Association, also an affiliate of the Congress for Industrial Organizations, signed for a 4 per cent wage increase with a group of tanker operators.

But the accord of the employes in both cases had been foretold earlier in the day when a group of leading tanker operators submitted to the demands of the N. M. U. on the basis of similar wage rises and other terms. After this agreement was reached, it was a foregone conclusion that the rest of the industry would follow.

The new contract for the dry-cargo men will run for only a year, with a wage reopening in the fall. Union leaders called the wage terms "the best increases won by any industry this year." They were preparing to send out telegrams releasing the immobilized ships throughout the nation, including the superliner United States, tied up in New York.

Commissioners Harry Winning and Sidney Steiner, who have been serving under Frank Brown, co-ordinating director of the Federal Mediation and Conciliation Service, in seeking to settle the costly walk-

Continued on Page 22, Column 2

ROSENBERGS EXECUTED AS ATOM SPIES AFTER SUPREME COURT VACATES STAY; LAST-MINUTE PLEA TO PRESIDENT FAILS

SIX JUSTICES AGREE

President Says Couple Increased 'Chances of Atomic War'

Texts of related documents in case are printed on Page 7.

By LUTHER A. HUSTON
Special to The New York Times.

WASHINGTON, June 19—President Eisenhower and the Supreme Court refused today to save Julius and Ethel Rosenberg from death in the electric chair.

The high court vacated the stay granted to the atomic spies on Wednesday by Justice William O. Douglas. It upheld the legality of the death sentence imposed by Federal Judge Irving R. Kaufman.

Less than an hour after the court had announced its verdict, President Eisenhower refused Executive clemency for the second time. He had denied a similar petition on Feb. 11.

"I can only say that, by immeasurably increasing the chances of atomic war, the Rosenbergs may have condemned to death tens of millions of innocent people all over the world," the President said. "The execution of two human beings is a grave matter. But even graver is the thought of the millions of dead whose deaths may be directly attributable to what these spies have done."

He was convinced, the President said, that the Rosenbergs had received "the fullest measure of justice and due process of law."

"When in their most solemn judgment the tribunals of the United States have adjudged them guilty and the sentence just, I will not intervene in this matter," the President declared.

Vinson Reads Court's Ruling

The prevailing opinion setting aside Justice Douglas' stay of execution was read by Chief Justice Fred M. Vinson and was concurred in by Associate Justices Stanley F. Reed, Robert H. Jackson, Harold H. Burton, Sherman Minton and Tom C. Clark.

Justices Douglas and Hugo L. Black dissented. Justice Felix Frankfurter announced neither a concurrence nor a dissent. In a brief separate opinion he said the questions raised were "complicated and novel" and that he felt the application of the Attorney General for revocation of the stay should not be disposed of until more time had been afforded for study and argument. He promised to set forth more specific[al]ly in due course the ground for this position.

Also read from the bench were a concurring opinion by Justice Clark, in which he was joined by Justices Vinson, Reed, Jackson, Burton and Minton, and a concurring opinion by Justice Jackson.

Continued on Page 8, Column 5

Their Death Penalty Carried Out

[Photographs of Julius Rosenberg and Ethel Rosenberg]
Associated Press
Julius Rosenberg   **Ethel Rosenberg**

Eisenhower Is Denounced To 5,000 in Union Sq. Rally

Sympathizers of Julius and Ethel Rosenberg bombarded judges with new appeals last night and staged rallies in a desperate, last-minute flurry of efforts to save the condemned atom spies from the electric chair.

As time ran out for the doomed couple, lawyers and sympathizers tried every avenue of appeal and protest in a feverish evening that included:

¶An order by Police Commissioner George P. Monaghan to all police commands to maintain a special city-wide vigil against any disorder or violence in connection with the execution.

¶Three separate appeals to Federal Judge Irving R. Kaufman, who sentenced the Rosenbergs, to stay their execution. He rejected all.

¶Two separate appeals to two Federal Circuit Court judges to grant a stay. These also were denied.

¶A rally by an estimated 5,000 persons in Seventeenth Street, west of the north end of Union Square, where members of the New York Clemency Committee of the National Committee to Secure Justice in the Rosenberg Case denounced President Eisenhower as "bloodthirsty."

Final Pleas to Kaufman

Judge Kaufman, for whom the police ordered a reinforced fifteen-man guard at his Park Avenue apartment, was importuned by attorneys making frantic new legal maneuvers to save the Rosenbergs.

Daniel C. Marshall, a Los Angeles lawyer who had pleaded with the Supreme Court for a stay, begged Judge Kaufman to telephone the prison and delay the execution for one hour so that Mr. Marshall could elaborate his argument. But Judge Kaufman refused about twenty minutes before the executions began.

Milton H. Friedman, a lawyer representing the Rosenberg defense counsel, asked Judge Kaufman to throw out the scheduled executions on the ground that they would constitute "an outrageous insult to world Jewry" if they were carried out on the Jewish Sabbath. Judge Kaufman rejected the plea, saying he had been assured the executions would not be within the Sabbath period.

Frank Scheiner, another lawyer representing the defense, asked Judge Kaufman to throw out the convictions of the couple on the same grounds argued yesterday before the Supreme Court. Judge Kaufman rejected this motion without any opinion.

Another defense lawyer, Arthur Kinoy, went to New Haven, Conn., in an unsuccessful effort to induce Judges Jerome N. Frank and Thomas W. Swan of the Court of Appeals to block the executions.

Prayer Meeting' Denunciation

In Seventeenth Street, more than 5,000 persons assembled for a prayer meeting for the Rosenbergs heard President Eisenhower denounced as "bloodthirsty."

He was linked with Attorney General Herbert Brownell Jr., Senator Joseph R. McCarthy, Republican of Wisconsin, and Senator William E. Jenner, Republican of Indiana, in a plot "to destroy the rights and liberties of the American people.

A premature announcement that the Rosenbergs had been put to death created a wave of hysteria at

Continued on Page 6, Column 6

PAIR SILENT TO END

Husband Is First to Die —Both Composed on Going to Chair

By WILLIAM R. CONKLIN
Special to The New York Times.

OSSINING, N. Y., June 19—Stoic and tight-lipped to the end, Julius and Ethel Rosenberg paid the death penalty tonight in the electric chair at Sing Sing Prison for their war-time atomic espionage for Soviet Russia.

The pair, first husband and wife to pay the supreme penalty here, and the first in the United States to die for espionage, went to their deaths with a composure that astonished the witnesses.

Julius, 35 years old, was first to enter the glaringly lighted, white-walled death chamber. He walked slowly behind Rabbi Irving Koslove, a chaplain at Sing Sing, who was intoning the Twenty-third Psalm, "The Lord is my shepherd, I shall not want." As Rosenberg neared the brown-stained oak chair he seemed to sway from side to side.

Guards quickly placed him in the chair. He was clean-shaven, no longer wearing his mustache, and wore a white T-shirt. At 8:04 o'clock the first shock of 2,000 volts, with its ten amperes, coursed through his body. After two subsequent shocks his life ended at 8:06½ P. M.

Dr. H. W. Kipp and Dr. George McCracken applied stethoscopes to his chest, and Dr. Kipp said: "I pronounce this man dead."

Wife Kisses Matron

Ethel Rosenberg, the 37-year-old wife, entered the death chamber a few minutes after the body of her husband had been removed. She wore a dark green print dress with white polka dots, and, like her husband, was shod in loafer-type cloth slippers. Her hair was close-cropped on top to permit contact of an electrode.

Just before she reached the chair the five-foot, 100-pound woman held out her hand to Mrs. Helen Evans, a matron. As Mrs. Evans grasped her hand, Mrs. Rosenberg drew her close and kissed her lightly on the cheek. Rabbi Koslove, standing about ten feet from the chair, was intoning the Fifteenth and Thirty-first Psalms.

Mrs. Evans choked up at the final farewell and left the room quickly. Mrs. Lucy Many, a former matron who is now a prison telephone operator, also shook hands with the doomed woman.

Mrs. Rosenberg sat in the electric chair "with the most composed face of the state executioner, in an alcove.

She winced a bit as the electrode came in contact with her head, but her arms remained relaxed under their binding straps. Silent, she walked while the guards dropped a leather mask over her face. To her right stood Joseph P. Francel, the state executioner, in an alcove.

The first of three successive shocks was applied at 8:11½ P. M. After the third shock the two doctors applied their stethoscopes and two more applications of the cur-

Continued on Page 6, Column 2

7 IN HAWAII GUILTY OF RED CONSPIRACY

Director of Bridges' Union and Six Others Convicted of Violating the Smith Act

Special to The New York Times.

HONOLULU, June 19—A Federal jury today found Jack W. Hall, regional director in Hawaii for the International Longshoremen's and Warehousemen's Union, and six other defendants guilty of a Communist conspiracy to teach and advocate the overthrow of the United States Government by force and violence.

Immediately after the verdict, stevedores halted work on all island docks in the possible forerunner of a general protest strike. The United Press reported. Within two hours after the verdict was announced Hall's union suspended negotiations on a new contract and longshoremen began walking off the jobs at Castle and Cook Pier 32. By 3:30 P. M., Hawaii time, all Honolulu docks were abandoned and stevedores had walked off the only two ships in the port of Hilo on the island of Hawaii.]

The all-male, multi-racial jury returned its verdict shortly before 1 P. M. Hawaii standard time (7 P. M., Eastern daylight time) after having deliberated for sixteen hours. Six men defendants sat in sports or aloha shirts and one woman heard the verdict read without any show of emotion as they stood behind the defense counsel's table.

A defense request for a poll of the jury revealed that the verdict was unanimous in each case.

The defense attorney, Richard

Continued on Page 5, Column 3

West Asks Soviet to Bar Firearms In Keeping Order in East Berlin

By WALTER SULLIVAN
Special to The New York Times.

BERLIN, June 19—The three Western powers in Berlin urged the Soviet Union today to forbid the use of firearms by its troops and by the East German police in the Soviet sector of the city to prevent further bloodshed.

An announcement said that Brig. Gen. Pierre Manceaux-Demiau, French Commandant in Berlin and this month's chairman of the Allied Kommandatura, had made repeated vain attempts to see high Soviet authorities to discuss the problem. It added that finally he had gone to Soviet headquarters in East Berlin to leave in person a note stating the point of view of the Western Commandants.

Meanwhile, as the eastern part of the city continued to appear quiet, United States authorities delivered Otto Nuschke to Soviet officers. Herr Nuschke, East German Deputy Premier, was forced into the United States sector of Berlin by the rioters Wednesday.

Herr Nuschke, 70 years of age, was questioned thoroughly by both United States and West Berlin officials before being returned to the Soviet sector. According to an official announcement by the United States mission, he was asked whether he wanted political asylum in the West and said no.

The West Berlin police sought to determine whether he could be linked with a "kidnapping." Possibly this referred to the case of Dr. Walter Linse, anti-Communist leader, who was abducted from the United States sector last year.

East Germany's leading Communist newspaper, Neues Deutschland, conceded today that the work stoppages and disorders of the last few days had reached into the remote corners of that region. It expressed

Continued on Page 4, Column 6

Professor Loses Fulbright Award After Wife Balks at Red Inquiry

By FREDERICK GRAHAM

A Fulbright award granted last April to Dr. Naphtali Lewis of Brooklyn College to study in Italy during the next academic year has been canceled by the State Department. Senator Joseph R. McCarthy, Republican of Wisconsin, said yesterday.

"I think it [the cancellation] is an excellent idea," the Senator asserted at the end of a thirty-seven-minute hearing of the Senate Permanent subcommittee on Investigations into the background of Dr. Lewis and his wife, Helen B. Lewis, who once held a teaching post at Brooklyn College.

The formal title of Fulbright award is the United States Educational Exchange Award. The awards are granted to educators and students for study abroad and are named for Senator J. William Fulbright, Democrat of Arkansas, who pioneered the program.

Senator McCarthy, who sat as a one-member subcommittee at the Federal Courthouse in Foley Square, said that the purpose of the inquiry was to learn whether Mrs. Lewis was now or ever had been a member of the Communist party.

Because she planned to go abroad with her husband for the coming year at the expense of the Federal Government, Senator McCarthy declared that he believed it was very important to know if she now or ever had been a Communist. Unable to elicit an answer on this point from Mrs. Lewis, Senator McCarthy asserted that her refusal to answer on the ground it might tend to incriminate her was the same as saying that "I am a member of the party."

Mrs. Lewis steadfastly refused to answer questions on whether she had held Communist cell meet-

Continued on Page 5, Column 4

"All the News That's Fit to Print"

The New York Times.

LATE CITY EDITION

Warm, humid, showers likely late today. Fair, not so warm tomorrow.
Temperature Range Today—Max., 88; Min., 68
Temperatures Yesterday—Max., 77; Min., 62
Full U. S. Weather Bureau Report, Page 35

Copyright, 1953, by The New York Times Company.

VOL. CII..No. 34,883.   Entered as Second-Class Matter.
Post Office, New York, N. Y.   NEW YORK, MONDAY, JULY 27, 1953.   Times Square, New York 36, N. Y.
Telephone LAckawanna 4-1000   FIVE CENTS

TRUCE IS SIGNED, ENDING THE FIGHTING IN KOREA; P.O.W. EXCHANGE NEAR; RHEE GETS U. S. PLEDGE; EISENHOWER BIDS FREE WORLD STAY VIGILANT

GEROSA AND STARK PICKED BY WAGNER TO COMPLETE SLATE

Bronx Contractor to Run for Controller, Brooklyn Clothier for Council President

DESAPIO PRAISES CHOICE

Tammany Head Sees Approval This Week by Party Leaders Opposed to Impellitteri

By PAUL CROWELL

Lawrence E. Gerosa, a Bronx contractor, and Abe Stark, a Brooklyn merchant, were selected as running mates yesterday by Manhattan Borough President Robert F. Wagner Jr., who was chosen last week by the Democratic organizations of Bronx and New York Counties as their candidate for Mayor.

Mr. Gerosa was named as a candidate for Controller and Mr. Stark for President of the City Council. The slate headed by Mr. Wagner will wage a primary contest against the ticket headed by Mayor Impellitteri, whose running mates are City Councilman Charles E. Keegan of the Bronx for Controller and Julius Helfand, assistant district attorney of Kings County, for Council President.

The Impellitteri-Keegan-Helfand ticket has the backing of the Democratic organizations of Brooklyn, Queens and Staten Island.

At the Biltmore Hotel Mr. Wagner said that Mr. Gerosa and Mr. Stark were his personal choices but that he expected the Bronx and Tammany Hall executive committees to approve them without hesitation.

Wagner Voices Confidence

"I was given a free hand in picking my running mates," Mr. Wagner said. "I chose them after consulting with representatives of civic organizations, labor and business and the Bronx and Manhattan county leadership.

"I am confident that the Bronx and New York County executive committees will approve my choices. Speaking for myself and my running mates I am sure that we will win the primary contest next September and go on to win the November election."

Carmine G. DeSapio, the leader of Tammany Hall, expressed confidence that the executive committee of the Bronx and Manhattan organizations would approve Mr. Wagner's selections at a meeting to be held early this week. He described Mr. Gerosa and Mr. Stark as "outstanding representative business men who will make a great contribution to public service."

Mr. Gerosa, who was born in Milan, Italy, Aug. 10, 1894, lives at 615 West 252d Street in the Riverdale section. He is married and has three children.

He was designated in 1945 by four of the five Democratic county leaders as a candidate for Controller on a ticket headed by former Mayor William O'Dwyer, but withdrew in favor of Lazarus Jo-

Continued on Page 20, Column 4

Arizona Raids Polygamous Cult; Seeks to Wipe Out Its Community

By GLADWIN HILL
Special to The New York Times.

SHORT CREEK, Ariz., July 26—Arizona authorities, under an unusual proclamation of insurrection, raided this remote farming hamlet on the state's northern border at dawn today and placed virtually the entire adult population under arrest in an effort to wipe out the nation's last remaining center of organized polygamy.

The defendants, thirty-six men and eighty-six women, constituted the principal membership of a professed Fundamentalist sect — disowned by the Church of Jesus Christ of Latter Day Saints (Mormon) in 1939—that has continued to practice the plural marriages renounced by the Mormon church in 1890.

Separated from the outside world by the towering cliffs and arid gorges of Arizona's wild and inaccessible "Strip" between the Grand Canyon and the Utah border, members of the cult, organized on a communal economic basis, allegedly have been maintaining as many as a half-dozen wives and thirty children, and have fostered child marriages.

In addition to 122 adults and child brides named in warrants held by a raiding force of 120 peace officers, the colony included some 263 children.

The state's avowed objective is to wipe out the community, imprison the adult ringleaders, and find new homes and lives for the children and for the numerous

Continued on Page 36, Column 1

Clark Ready to Start Release Of Red Captives in Few Days

But Allied Commander Says It May Be Two or Three Weeks Before Americans Freed by the Communists Arrive in U. S.

By JAMES RESTON
Special to The New York Times.

SOMEWHERE IN KOREA, July 26—Gen. Mark W. Clark said tonight he was prepared to start shipping Communist prisoners of war to North Korea and Communist China within a "few days," but he thought it would be two or three weeks before American prisoners would reach the United States.

The United Nations commander told several reporters aboard his plane en route to the signing of the truce agreement at Munsan, Korea, that while the Communists had comparatively few prisoners to send back, United Nations procedures for handling captives were undoubtedly faster.

The United Nations Command now holds 68,000 North Koreans and 5,000 Chinese Communists who want to return to their native lands, and 8,000 North Korean and about 15,000 Chinese Commu-

nists who have refused to return home.

In contrast, the Communists hold only 12,000 United Nations prisoners, of whom 3,000 are Americans.

Nevertheless, General Clark said, he thought it would be unwise for the Americans to expect that United States prisoners would be sent back as fast as the United Nations Command would return the Communists.

He said he expected the Communists to return the American captives at the rate of about 400 daily, while the Allies were in position to return as many as 1,500 Communists every day.

In accordance with plans that are now ready, General Clark asserted, the Communist captives would be put aboard small naval

Continued on Page 9, Column 2

Accord on plans for prisoners of war is on Page 7.

Eisenhower Accepts Aid Cut; Drive to Adjourn Advances

Special to The New York Times.

WASHINGTON, July 26—The drive for adjournment of Congress by Saturday appeared more certain of success today as the Eisenhower Administration privately indicated it could operate

under the $4,562,664,000 foreign aid fund bill approved yesterday by the Senate Appropriations Committee.

The Administration decision, already conveyed to Senate leaders, was said to represent an understanding, reluctantly reached, that little improvement could be hoped for on the committee action, which restored half the $1,115,050,000 reduction made last week in the House of Representatives.

The Administration leaders in the Senate are being asked to do no more than "hold the line" when the Mutual Security money bill comes to the floor for debate, and possibly a vote, on Wednesday.

For the record, the Administration still sought passage of the House aid bill before adjournment of the postal rate increase bill, designed to produce an additional $240,500,000 in revenue, but the pressure for the proposal did not seem very great.

Summerfield Is Doubtful

Postmaster General Arthur E. Summerfield, guest on the National Broadcasting Company's "Meet the Press" television interview, said tonight he thought Congress should stay in session to pass the bill but conceded he did not know whether it would.

"I know they've had a busy six months," he said.

The House Post Office and Civil Service Committee, which has been conducting hearings for two weeks, has given no indication when a postal bill will be reported. The House leadership tentatively has scheduled the measure for midweek consideration on the floor. There have been no formal hearings.

Continued on Page 11, Column 2

55 REPORTED KILLED IN CUBAN REBELLION

Batista Voids Constitutional Guarantees, Hits Partisans of Ex-President Prio

By R. HART PHILLIPS
Special to The New York Times.

HAVANA, July 26—Fifty-five persons were reported killed and many more wounded in a rebellion today at Santiago de Cuba and near-by Bayamo. Martial law was imposed in Santiago following the uprising and military authorities began to round up members of revolutionary groups.

President Fulgencio Batista and his Cabinet in a special session tonight suspended constitutional guarantees for a period of ninety days, according to an official note from the Presidential Palace. The action was taken to enable the Government to cope with revolutionary activities following the revolt earlier in the day.

"Mercenaries in the service of those who became rich during the regime of Prio [former President Carlos Prio Socarras], in conjunction with Communist elements" were accused of the attacks on the military posts at Santiago and Bayamo in a joint statement signed by the Ministers.

Continued on Page 13, Column 2

TALK CONDITION SET

U. S. to Boycott Political Parleys After 90 Days if It Finds Foe Stalls

By W. H. LAWRENCE

WASHINGTON, July 26—The United States was willing to join the projected Korean political conference ninety days after it begins if this Government is convinced that the Communists are not negotiating in good faith and that further sessions would be futile.

But, this Government has not promised to resume hostilities in Korea at that time, nor has it promised to give South Korea any moral or material support if that Government carries out its threat to attempt to unify divided Korea by military force.

The conditional pledge to quit the Korean political conference after ninety days—if this Government believes it is futile—has been given to Dr. Syngman Rhee, South Korean President, who has already announced publicly that his agreement to cooperate in the armistice extends for only ninety days after the political conference convenes. Under the truce terms the conference will convene within ninety days after the armistice.

The Communists have not been told heretofore of this American intention to quit the political talks in any specified period if they seem to this Government to be fruitless. The United States contends that a walkout from the political talks would not violate the armistice.

U. S. to Make Decision

This Government is not committed to walk out of the peace talks simply if Dr. Rhee and the South Koreans walk out. The United States will make its own decisions as to whether the political negotiations are being carried on in good faith.

There is not, so far as is known, any agreement by the other principal members of the United Nations to walk out at the same time that the United States might decide to leave the conference.

Observers here did not feel that the assurances given to Dr. Rhee were necessarily in conflict with the guarantee given the Communists by Lieut. Gen. William K. Harrison Jr., chief United Nations negotiator, that there would be no time limit on the political conference.

It was pointed out that the armistice agreement included no time limitation for success or failure of the political conference—but it also imposed no requirement on either the Communists or the Allies to continue negotiations if it

Continued on Page 3, Column 2

U. N. Assembly Meets Aug. 17 To Plan Post-Truce Parley

Special to The New York Times.

UNITED NATIONS, N. Y., July 26—Promptly upon receiving formal notification of the signing of the Korean armistice, Lester B. Pearson of Canada, President of the General Assembly, issued a call tonight to member delegations for resumption on Aug. 17 of the suspended seventh Assembly session. The Assembly will decide details of the Far Eastern political conference scheduled to take place within ninety days of the signing of the truce agreement.

Official notification that the truce agreement had been signed was given orally to Secretary General Dag Hammarskjold and to Mr. Pearson by the permanent representative of the United States, former Senator Henry Cabot Lodge Jr., in the same committee room at headquarters that the General Assembly question some months ago.

Mr. Lodge then handed to Mr. Pearson a copy of the text of the communication, addressed to the Secretary General and issued by the United States Mission earlier.

United Nations Command and the commanders of the Communist forces in Korea, i. e., the Korean People's Army and the Chinese People's Volunteers. The agreement was signed for the United Nations Command at 1000 hours [10 A. M.] on July 27, 1953, Korean time, and becomes effective at 2200 hours [10 P. M.], July 27, 1953, Korean time. [The actual signing was at 10:01 A. M., Korean time, or 9:01 P. M., Sunday, Eastern daylight time.]

"A report of the Unified Command transmitting the official text of the armistice agreement will be sent to you shortly."

Telegrams to the delegates which had been prepared earlier, were dispatched to the delegations summoning them to report for the reconvened session in mid-August.

In a joint broadcast from the committee room, which followed that of President Eisenhower from Washington, all three of the United Nations principals repeated for radio and television audiences statements issued earlier.

"The whole world is thankful that the negotiations at Panmunjom have brought the fighting in Korea to an end by the signature of an armistice agreement," Mr.

Continued on Page 4, Column 5

PRESIDENT IS HAPPY

But Warns in Broadcast That Global Peace Is Yet to Be Achieved

Texts of Eisenhower and Dulles talks are on Page 4.

Special to The New York Times.

WASHINGTON, July 26—President Eisenhower greeted the news of the Korean armistice tonight with prayers of thanksgiving but warned the nation that the Allies had won an armistice only on a single battleground and had not achieved peace in the world.

The President spoke over radio and television networks about an hour after the official cease-fire documents had been signed.

General Eisenhower said the United States and all the free world must not relax its guard, or fail to be vigilant against "the possibility of untoward developments."

After the President had spoken, Charles E. Wilson, Secretary of Defense, issued a statement warning against any relaxation in the country's defense program because of the truce. He advised, too, that it would be a "long time" before American troops could be withdrawn from Korea "with safety."

"We must not be misled into the same demobilization which followed World Wars I and II," he said. "Such a demobilization would inevitably again tempt an aggressor."

Dulles Sees U. N. Victory

John Foster Dulles, Secretary of State, described the armistice as a great victory for the United Nations because "for the first time in history an international organization had stood against an aggressor and has marshaled force to meet force."

President Eisenhower spoke from the White House, across Pennsylvania Avenue, and about a block east from Blair House, where President Truman asked thirty-seven months ago to commit United States forces to the defense of South Korea, then being overrun by the Communist armies from the north.

The President said he hoped that the coming of peace to Korea would at last convince all nations of the wisdom of composing their differences by negotiation before—rather than after—"various resorts to brutal and futile battle."

He closed his brief speech by quoting from the final paragraph of Lincoln's Second Inaugural Address, which he said expressed the resolution and dedication of all Americans, now as in 1865.

These were Lincoln's words: "With malice toward none, with

Continued on Page 4, Column 2

REPORTS ON TRUCE: President Eisenhower making nationwide television broadcast from the White House last night.
The New York Times (by Fred J. Sass)

DEFENSE CHIEFS SEE BILLION CUT IN ARMS

Wilson Tells Quantico Parley Our Gain in Might Makes Any Attack on Us 'Foolhardy'

By AUSTIN STEVENS

QUANTICO, Va., July 26—Defense officials attending the high-level defense conference at the Marine Corps base here predicted today that with any kind of "decent" Korean truce defense spending could be trimmed by as much as $1,000,000,000 in the next twelve months.

Secretary of Defense Charles E. Wilson told the conference that "we have attained a strength which should make any attack upon us foolhardy in the extreme, and we are increasing our strength daily."

The previously stated defense spending figure for the fiscal year that started July 1 was $43,200,-000,000. Official announcement was made two days ago that W. J. McNeil, Assistant Secretary of Defense in charge of the budget, had told the conference, which included high military leaders, that cuts were expected in that figure. He did not indicate where the cuts were to be made.

In their prediction today the defense officials said that the post-truce reductions would not be greater than $1,000,000,000 in the year because so many fixed costs would continue.

The immediate economies would come in ammunition, trucks and other "consumption items" of war. Over-all military manpower gradually would be cut back from the present 3,500,000 by 200,000 per-haps more. One item mentioned today as an example was the immediate ending of combat pay, which is budgeted at $56,000,000.

However, defense officials stated, some other costs would rise. Assuming, for instance, that large numbers of United States troops would remain in Korea for some time, it was said, it would become necessary to build barracks and other semi-permanent installations.

The three-day highly secret conference called by Secretary Wilson to have the armed services present their situations and problems and also to get members of his new defense "team" to know

Continued on Page 9, Column 1

MARINES STOP REDS IN LAST-HOUR FIGHT

Chinese Foe's Dawn Attacks Hit U. S. Units on West and South Koreans in Center

By The United Press

TOKYO, Monday, July 27—Chinese Communist troops threw "last hour propaganda" attacks at Allied forces on the central and western fronts of the rain-swept Korean battle line today, only a few hours before the armistice was signed at Panmunjom.

An estimated two enemy companies smashed into United Nations lines at the bend of the Kumsong River on the central front. South Korean forces fought the Reds hand-to-hand for more than an hour.

Allied troops all along the 155-mile line across the peninsula were ordered to hold casualties to a minimum and not to pick fights with the Reds.

The Allied orders were issued as Chinese Red shock troops just before dawn attacked United States Marines on a western front outpost for the fourth consecutive day. The Reds hit the hilltop positions northeast of Panmunjom in forces up to 200 men.

First Marine Division officers said the first wave of the attack was turned off without casualty among the Americans. The marines

Continued on Page 2, Column 1

CEREMONY IS BRIEF

Halt in 3-Year Conflict for a Political Parley Due at 9 A. M. Today

Armistice text, on Pages 6, 7; Clark and Taylor statements, 9.

By LINDESAY PARROTT
Special to The New York Times.

TOKYO, Monday, July 27—Communist and United Nations delegates in Panmunjom signed an armistice at 10:01 A. M. today [9:01 P. M., Sunday, Eastern daylight time]. Under the truce terms, hostilities in the three-year-old Korean war are to cease at 10 o'clock tonight [9 A. M., Monday, Eastern daylight time].

[President Syngman Rhee of South Korea promised in a statement at Seoul Monday to observe the armistice "for a limited time" while a political conference tried to unify Korea by peaceful means, The United Press said.]

The historic document was signed in a roadside hall the Communists built specially for the occasion. The ceremony, attended by representatives of sixteen members of the United Nations, took precisely eleven minutes. Then the respective delegations walked from the meeting place without a word or handshake between them.

The matter-of-fact procedure underlined what spokesmen of both sides emphasized: That though the shooting would cease within twelve hours after the signing, only an uneasy armed truce and political difficulties, perhaps even greater than those of the armistice negotiations, were ahead.

Signers Are Expressionless

The representatives of the two sides were expressionless as they put their names to a pile of documents, providing for an exchange of prisoners, establishment of a neutral zone for the cease-fire and a later political conference that would attempt to settle the tragic Korean questions, unsolved by three years of fighting that caused hundreds of thousands of casualties.

According to the latest figures, revealed July 21 by the Department of Defense, the United States had suffered a total of 139,272 casualties. This included 24,965 dead, 101,368 wounded, 2,938 captured, 8,476 missing and 1,525 previously reported captured or missing, but since returned to military control.

Early this afternoon the Allied part in conclusion of the armistice was completed at advance headquarters near Munsan, where Gen. Mark W. Clark, United Nations commander, put his name to the documents the Communists signed at Panmunjom.

General Clark signed in the presence of some of his high-ranking officers, Vice Admiral Robert P. Briscoe, commander of the naval forces in the Far East; Gen. Otto P. Weyland, head of the Far East Air Forces; Gen. Maxwell D. Taylor, Eighth Army commander; Lieut. Gen. Samuel Anderson of the Fifth Air Force, and Vice Admiral J. J. Clark, heading the Seventh Fleet.

Also present at Munsan as

Continued on Page 2, Column 3

Skeptical G. I.'s Finally Convinced; Most Take News With Little Elation

By GREG MacGREGOR

SEOUL, Korea, July 26—Tonight, on the eve of the armistice, the front-line G. I.'s faced their last full night of fighting in the thirty-seven-month-old Korean war.

"It will never happen," a Marine private manning the line on the central front said with a laugh as his sergeant told him the war would end tomorrow.

Not until the Armed Forces Radio Service was picked up at 6 P. M. tonight by portable receivers along the front were the men willing to believe the news. Then the announcer's voice and a bolt of lightning.

Some G. I.'s stared dumbly at each other and others broke out in smiles.

As news of the armistice filtered down to the men at the front, it was met with an atmosphere of mingled disbelief and temporary confusion in its wake. In many cases the soldiers flatly refused to accept the word of their own officers and noncommissioned officers. The men had had so many disappointments over cease-fire reports in the past that they were slow to accept the truth.

"Didja hear that—didja hear that?" one man kept shouting over and over as he ran from his tent then.

"Wait'll they sign it—who knows what's going to happen?" a skeptic

Continued on Page 2, Column 4

ENGINEERS (also women math majors)—See G. E. this week about a future in jet aircraft details in today's Classified Section.—Advt.

The New York Times.

Copyright, 1954, by The New York Times Company.

VOL. CIII..No. 35,101.

Entered as Second-Class Matter, Post Office, New York, N. Y.

NEW YORK, TUESDAY, MARCH 2, 1954.

Times Square, New York 36, N. Y. Telephone LAckawanna 4-1000

FIVE CENTS

HIDDEN OWNERSHIP OF RACEWAY STOCK BARED AT HEARING

Former Legislator, Intimate of O'Dwyer, Erickson Kin and Ex-Convict Are Identified

HOLDINGS PUT AT MILLION

Moreland Inquiry Opens Public Sessions, Gets Details of Yonkers Track Purchase

By EMANUEL PERLMUTTER

Politicians and persons with underworld backgrounds or friendships were found yesterday to have been the hidden owners of close to a million dollars' worth of stock in several New York harness racing tracks.

These disclosures were made as the Moreland Act Commission opened public hearings here on the scandal-ridden raceways. The proceedings are being held in the Criminal Court Building, 100 Centre Street.

Among those who were shown to have struck it rich secretly on the trotting tracks were former Assemblyman Elmer J. Kellam of Hancock, N. Y.; Irving Sherman, political intimate of former Mayor William O'Dwyer and admitted friend of gangsters; Frank J. Erickson, son of the convicted gambler, and Samuel J. Stirratt, an ex-convict with a long police record.

Additional testimony was introduced indicating that loans from racketeers had helped the original incorporators of the Algam Corporation to purchase Yonkers Empire City Race Track —now Yonkers Raceway—for $2,400,000 in 1949.

Named a Racing Steward

Mr. Kellam, who served in the Assembly from Delaware County between 1943 and 1950, admitted on the witness stand that he had transferred 10,000 shares in Mid-State Raceway, near Syracuse, to a "dummy" owner after he had been appointed as a state racing steward last year.

The former Republican legislator said that he became the beneficiary of the stock, which was listed in the name of Marvin Wynkoop of Downesville, N. Y., and that he intended to sell it but had been unable to do so because of the pressure of his duties as a steward at Roosevelt Raceway, Westbury, L. I. He described the duties of a steward as "protecting the public, to see if the races are on the level."

"Did you think it was proper for a steward to own stock in a track?" Bruce Bromley, the commission chairman, asked him.

Mr. Kellam, a sandy-haired, florid-faced man, shook his head apologetically. "I don't think it's good judgment," he conceded. "But I never performed any duties at a track where I was a stockholder."

Still Owns Track Stock

The witness said he now owned 9,500 shares in the upstate track. He said he assumed he still held the job as racing steward.

At this point, Harness Racing Commissioner George P. Monaghan, sitting as a member of the Moreland Commission, interrupted to point out that stewards served for one year and that they had to be reappointed each racing season.

The testimony involving Irving Sherman, who was referred to as the contact man for Frank Costello during Mayor O'Dwyer's administration, was given by Sam Sherman, a raincoat manufacturer, of 30 West Fifty-fourth Street. He is not related to Irving Sherman.

Sam Sherman testified that although he was the listed owner of 22,500 shares of stock and $50,000 worth of bonds in the Algam Corporation, holding company for the Yonkers track, Irving Sherman actually owned 80 per cent of the investment.

In October, 1953, soon after the Moreland Commission was appointed, Algam purchased 20,000 shares from him, Mr. Sherman said. He said the purchase price was $298,000, a total of $30 a share. Of this sum, he testified, he gave $145,000 to Irving Sherman, the remainder of the latter's share being tied up in litigation.

In addition, Mr. Sherman said, the 2,500 shares of voting stock that he and his secret partner owned were sold at the same time for $75,000 to M. Duke Manacher, a stockholder in Algam. He said he gave $60,000 of this sum to Irving Sherman.

The $50,000 worth of bonds

Continued on Page 12, Column 2

Jarka, Big Stevedore, Quits Port Under Fire

By A. H. RASKIN

The Jarka Corporation, one of the world's largest stevedoring enterprises, decided yesterday to stop operating in the Port of New York.

The company and its president, Frank W. Nolan, are awaiting trial in Special Sessions on charges of having paid out $119,859 in bribes to shipping executives for steering contracts to Jarka. The Waterfront Commission has been conducting an investigation to determine whether the company should be barred from doing business here.

The Jarka decision to withdraw its application for a stevedoring license was the highlight of another hectic day on the strife-swept waterfront. Other developments included:

¶A request by Charles T.

Continued on Page 11, Column 1

UNITY PLEA OPENS CARACAS MEETING

Hemisphere Accord Founded on Sovereignty and Equality Is Urged on Delegates

By SAM POPE BREWER
Special to The New York Times.

CARACAS, Venezuela, March 1—President Marcos Perez Jimenez of Venezuela opened the tenth Inter-American Conference today with a plea for closer unity among the American States on the basis of sovereignty and equality.

There is explosive material on the agenda in questions such as Communist infiltration in Latin America and rules for granting political asylum. Yet all indications today were that most of the delegates were in a conciliatory mood and that means would be sought to avoid heated clashes.

The elaborate security precautions taken for the conference seemed to grow in importance when word of the shooting in the United States Congress was received.

[Guatemala lost her first test at the parley on a procedural question, while at home President Jacobo Arbenz Guzman denied any Soviet intervention in the country's internal affairs.]

Speaking at the first session in the great modernistic assembly hall of University City, President Perez emphasized that the idea of continental unity had existed from the day the American nations won their independence.

"The existence of basic factors of a type common to all the continent, and the desire to obtain and preserve independence were the fundamental reasons for which there appeared almost simultaneously in the greater part of the peoples of America the idea of unity among them," he said.

He added, however, that "the unity of our peoples should be based on comprehension, the feeling of reciprocal assistance and mutual respect."

"We shall understand each

Continued on Page 9, Column 1

---

31 KILLED IN SUDAN IN NATIVES' CLASH AS NAGUIB ARRIVES

117 Hurt in Battle at Khartum Palace Between Tribesmen and Pro-Egyptian Group

Dispatch of The Times, London.

KHARTUM, the Sudan, March 1—The arrival in the Sudan today of Maj. Gen. Mohammed Naguib, Egyptian President, revived factional passions of this nascent state in a clash in which at least twenty-two persons were killed. [The Associated Press placed the toll at thirty-one.]

Among the dead were eight of the police force, including the British police commandant of Khartum, H. S. McGuigan, and the superintendent, Mustapha el Mahdi. One hundred seventeen were wounded, of whom thirty-two were seriously injured.

The factional struggle was of a primitive nature. The dead and wounded were seen to bear the marks of clubs and spears, not gunshot wounds.

[Meanwhile, a spokesman for the ruling junta in Egypt said in Cairo Monday that General Naguib owed his reinstatement as President to agitation begun by eight Communist army officers.]

The tragedy here was enacted outside the Governor General's palace, which stands on the site of the residency where Gen. Charles G. Gordon, then Governor General, died from the thrusts of tribesmen's spears during the historic Khartum siege in 1885. Inside the residency, General Naguib, Sir Robert Howe, Governor General, and Selwyn Lloyd, Minister of State of the British Foreign Office, were at lunch during today's events.

Parliament Opening Put Off

In view of the passions aroused by the rioting, the Governor General postponed a meeting of the Sudanese Parliament, scheduled for this afternoon, until March 10.

It seemed today as though the army of Mohammed Ahmed, the Mahdi, or Moslem leader who defeated General Gordon, were on the march again. The rioters massed outside the Khartum airport, turbaned and robed in shining white, with their hundreds of banners waving above the throng. They were supporters of the patron of the Sudanese independence movement, Sir Abdel Rahman el Mahdi, mainly Baggara tribesmen from the provinces who gathered to greet General Naguib with chanted slogans demanding independence for the Sudan.

"No Egypt, No Britain!" they cried as they surged up to Sudanese Defense Force troops who barred their way to the airport.

This was no unkempt rabble; their banners were of trim red, green and black stripes, superimposed with a white spear cutting a white crescent.

General Naguib left his aircraft at Khartum airport at 10 A. M. He was accompanied by Maj. Salah Salem, Egyptian Minister of National Guidance and Minister of State for Sudanese Affairs. Sir Robert, Ismail el Azhary, Prime Minister of the

Continued on Page 2, Column 2

FIVE CONGRESSMEN SHOT IN HOUSE BY 3 PUERTO RICAN NATIONALISTS; BULLETS SPRAY FROM GALLERY

Associated Press Wirephoto

SEIZED IN SHOOTING: Capitol police hold three Puerto Rican Nationalists after they fired from gallery seats into House chamber, wounding five Representatives. Prisoners, left to right, are Lolita Lebron, Rafael C. Miranda and Andres Cordero.

CAPITOL IN UPROAR

Woman, Accomplices Quickly Overpowered —High Bonds Set

By CLAYTON KNOWLES
Special to The New York Times.

WASHINGTON, March 1 — Five members of the Congress of The United States were shot down on the floor of the House of Representatives today.

Their assailants, at least three Puerto Rican Nationalists, shouted for freedom of their homeland as they fired murderously although at random from a spectators' gallery just above the House floor. Possibly twenty-five shots were fired.

Bullets rained down from two German Lugers and other pistols of lesser caliber. They crashed through the table of the majority leader and chairs around it, and struck near the table of the Minority Leader beyond. The time was 2:32 P. M.

House members at first thought the sounds were of firecrackers. But as their colleagues fell or took cover as they heard the slugs hit around them, all realized what was happening.

The wounded House members:

ALVIN M. BENTLEY, 35 years old, multimillionaire Michigan Republican, shot through lung, liver and intestine. Condition critical.

BEN F. JENSEN, 61, Republican of Iowa, shot in back. Condition serious.

CLIFFORD DAVIS, 56, Democrat of Tennessee, shot in the leg. Condition good.

GEORGE H. FALLON, 51, Democrat of Maryland, leg wound. Condition good.

KENNETH A. ROBERTS, 41, Democrat of Alabama, leg wound. Condition good.

Assailants Subdued

Within a matter of minutes, the episode, which threw the Capitol and most of official Washington into an uproar, was at an end. Gallery attendants, aided by spectators, Capitol police and even one House member, quickly overcame and disarmed the three gun wielders.

The three Puerto Ricans, all residents of New York, were booked at police headquarters on charges of assault with intent to kill. They gave their names and addresses as:

LOLITA LEBRON, 34, 315 West Ninety-fourth Street.

RAFAEL C. MIRANDA, 25, 120 South First Street, Brooklyn.

ANDRES CORDERO, 29, of 108 East 103d Street.

A fourth Puerto Rican, also named in the shooting, many years ago I was irked by eyewitnesses who had heard shots only as "backfiring automobiles," "blowouts" and "firecrackers." But this time I too thought that firecrackers were going off, and I thought it was a Latin demonstration.

But only for a moment. I saw two men and a woman, in the second row of the Ladies Gallery, pumping at pistols. The two men appeared to be aiming at the desk of Representative Charles A. Halleck of Indiana, the Republican floor leader.

The woman had her pistol high.

Continued on Page 16, Column 7

M'LEOD AUTHORITY IS CUT BY DULLES

Friend of McCarthy Loses Personnel Duties, Keeps His Security Office

Special to The New York Times.

WASHINGTON, March 1 — The Eisenhower Administration stripped Scott McLeod today of his authority over "department personnel." It left him in charge of security matters.

This action, which was announced on the authority of John Foster Dulles, the Secretary of State, was widely interpreted as a thrust by the Administration at the McCarthy wing of the Republican party.

Mr. McLeod is a close friend of Senator Joseph R. McCarthy, Republican of Wisconsin. He went to the State Department last January from the office of Senator Styles Bridges, Republican of New Hampshire.

He had served as administrative assistant to Senator Bridges and at one time was an agent of the Federal Bureau of Investigation.

Mr. McLeod made five speeches for the Republican party in the recent Lincoln Week series of partisan addresses, and there were Democratic protests that he was improperly using his office. A Republican member of the Civil Service Commission, George Moore, said informally that such political activity was forbidden by the Hatch Act, which limits the partisanship of certain Federal officials and employees.

The counsel of the State Department ruled that Mr. McLeod was not under the Hatch Act.

Policies Criticized

On Jan. 16, five former United States Ambassadors charged in an open letter that State Department personnel and security policies might be "laying the foundations for a Foreign Service competent to serve a totalitarian government rather than the Government of the United States as we have heretofore known it."

They did not mention Mr. McLeod by name, but both the personnel and security policies were under his direction.

In a speech on Feb. 18 in Larchmont, N. Y., Mr. McLeod described as "scandalous libel" any suggestion that he was attempting to destroy the diplomatic service by spreading fear among its people.

The State Department an-

Continued on Page 15, Column 1

McCarthy, Dirksen Suggest Labor Camps for Army Reds

By W. H. LAWRENCE
Special to The New York Times.

WASHINGTON, March 1—Senators Joseph R. McCarthy and Everett M. Dirksen suggested today "disagreeable" labor camps for armed services personnel who were Communists or who invoked the Fifth Amendment when asked about Communist associations.

Their suggestion grew out of new disclosures by the Senate Permanent Subcommittee on Investigations of "contradictions" in the Army system of handling officers and enlisted men who are alleged Communists or admitted former Communists.

Senator McCarthy, Republican of Wisconsin, is chairman of the subcommittee, and Senator Dirksen, an Illinois Republican, is a member.

The subcommittee accepted an Army suggestion that it question Robert T. Stevens, Secretary of the Army, at a closed session on Thursday or next Monday. All advance indications on both sides were that it would be a "friendly" hearing and not a controversial showdown such as was threatened but called off last week.

With four Republicans and one Democrat present, the subcommittee today questioned in secret an Army private and a former private in considering a problem of fundamental importance to all the armed forces. Stated broadly, the subcommittee raised these questions:

¶Should admitted Communists,

Continued on Page 14, Column 2

U. S. Dismissed 355 In Subversive Cases

Special to The New York Times.

WASHINGTON, March 1—The Civil Service Commission reported today that 355 Federal employees whose personnel files contained some allegations of subversive associations had been separated from the Government payroll between May 28 and Dec. 31, 1953.

The report was the first overall breakdown provided by the Administration to Congress since the controversy over the 2,200 persons said by President Eisenhower to have been separated as "security risks."

Philip Young, commission chairman, said the "security" separations totaled 2,224, of whom 983 were dismissed and 1,241 resigned. These figures included 124 dismissals and 231 resigna-

Continued on Page 13, Column 2

WITNESS DESCRIBES SHOOTING, CAPTURE

Reporter Sees Firing in House —Struck on Cheek by Chip Torn Loose by Bullet

By C. P. TRUSSELL
Special to The New York Times.

WASHINGTON, March 1 — Until the shooting in the House of Representatives today things were somewhat dull.

So dull, in fact, that a short time before members had been summoned by bells to the floor to listen to the issue at hand, whether they wanted to or not. It concerned admittance of Mexican farm laborers.

The quorum bell was answered by 243 members, most of whom were still on the floor when the shooting started in what is called the Ladies' Gallery.

As a police reporter

Continued on Page 16, Column 1

EISENHOWER TARGET FOR FANATICS ALSO

Secret Service Men Detected Puerto Rican Plot Against President in November

Special to The New York Times.

WASHINGTON, March 1—Puerto Rican extremists who have been conspiring to harm President Eisenhower if they got the opportunity, according to the Federal Secret Service.

Henry Cabot Lodge Jr., chief of the United States delegation to the United Nations, was put under twenty-four-hour guard last November for the same reason.

U. E. Baughman, chief of the Secret Service, was asked tonight about the reports of a conspiracy against the President.

"Three or four months ago," he replied, "the Secret Service obtained information indicating the Puerto Rican Nationalists were still possibly interested in harming the President in their fight for independence."

This statement from the head of the agency charged with protecting the President reflected the close watch that the Secret Service had kept on the Nationalist movement ever since two of its members tried to kill President Truman on Nov. 1, 1950.

Truman Case Still 'Open'

Although one assassin was killed in the gun battle in front of Blair House and Oscar Collazo, his companion, is serving a life sentence, the Secret Service still carries the attempted assassination of Mr. Truman as an "open case." It does this because it has not given up the possibility of rounding up the conspirators who directed the assassins.

Mr. Baughman said that the Secret Service had obtained information about designs on President Eisenhower last November. That coincided with the threats on Mr. Lodge. It was indicated tonight that there was an apparent link between the threats to Mr. Lodge and the designs on the President.

A police guard was put around

Continued on Page 17, Column 2

Nehru Decries U. S. Policy On Asia and the 'Cold War'

By ROBERT TRUMBULL
Special to The New York Times.

NEW DELHI, India, March 1—Prime Minister Jawaharlal Nehru scathingly condemned virtually the entire United States policy in Asia and in the "cold war" today. His most outspoken speech among many on this subject, delivered to the House of the People, the lower chamber of Parliament, was repeatedly interrupted by thunderous applause. He was given a prolonged ovation at its end.

Mr. Nehru was commenting on President Eisenhower's personal letter last week informing the Indian leader of Washington's intention to furnish military aid to Pakistan and offering the same assistance to India.

Mr. Nehru scorned General Eisenhower's tender with the statement that "in making this suggestion, the President has done less than justice to us or to himself."

"If we object to military aid being given to Pakistan, we would be hypocrites and unprincipled opportunists to accept such aid ourselves," he added.

The Prime Minister told the cheering House that United States members of the United Nations cease-fire observer team

Continued on Page 8, Column 2

in Kashmir should be removed. He said that "these American observers can no longer be treated by us as neutrals" in India's dispute with Pakistan over possession of the strategic northern state.

[At United Nations Headquarters a spokesman said no action would be taken pending an official communication from India. In Washington a State Department spokesman said India would have to complain to the United Nations if she wanted the United States members withdrawn.]

In his tersely formal reply to the United States note, which he read out, Mr. Nehru coldly thanked the President for his "assurances," but dismissed them with this curt statement: "You well known, aware of the views of my Government and our people in regard to this matter. We shall continue to pursue that policy."

The Indian note ignored the offer of arms.

Mr. Nehru, in his speech, took especially heated exception to the version of United States policy in Asia as quoted from testimony by Walter S. Robertson, Assistant Secretary of State, before a

Continued on Page 8, Column 2

Atom Blast Opens Test in Pacific; No Hint of Hydrogen Plans Given

Special to The New York Times.

WASHINGTON, March 1—The Atomic Energy Commission today announced the first in a new series of test explosions at its Pacific proving ground in the Marshall Islands.

The commission did not make clear whether the "atomic device" was of the fission or thermonuclear (hydrogen) type. There have been unofficial indications, however, that a variety of hydrogen weapons or devices will be tested during the next several weeks.

The most powerful of these is expected to be an actual hydrogen bomb with perhaps twice the explosive power of the experimental device that disintegrated an island of Eniwetok atoll on Nov. 1, 1952.

[Rear Admiral] Lewis L. Strauss, chairman of the Atomic Energy Commission, announced today that Joint Task Force Seven had detonated an atomic device at the A. E. C.'s Pacific proving ground in the Marshall Islands. This was the first in a series of tests.

The language of Admiral Strauss' statement did not make

Continued on Page 6, Column 5

The New York Times.

LATE CITY EDITION

Increasingly cloudy today. Rain tonight and tomorrow.

Temperature Range Today—Max., 45; Min., 31
Temperature Yesterday—Max., 46; Min., 31
Full U. S. Weather Bureau Report, Page 42

VOL. CIII..No. 35,111.

Entered as Second-Class Matter.
Post Office, New York, N. Y.

Copyright, 1954, by The New York Times Company.

NEW YORK, FRIDAY, MARCH 12, 1954.

Times Square, New York 36, N. Y.
Telephone LAckawanna 4-1000

FIVE CENTS

HALF OF DOCKMEN IN BROOKLYN JOIN OUTLAW WALKOUT

Huge Food Cargoes Reported in Danger of Spoiling—Trade Losses Mounting

COURT IS PICKETED AGAIN

Rally Backs a Tie-Up Until I. L. A. Is Certified—Jersey Strikers Pledge Return

By A. H. RASKIN

The outlaw dock strike got worse yesterday.

Half of the longshoremen in Brooklyn, the only section of the port that had been operating normally, joined the week-old walkout.

Importers notified the National Labor Relations Board that millions of dollars worth of fruit and vegetables were in danger of rotting on piers and in the holds of strike-stalled ships.

The tie-up turned into a blockade when Philadelphia locals of the old International Longshoremen's Association refused to unload passenger or cargo vessels diverted from New York. Rank-and-file leaders of the local stoppage sought to make the boycott coast-wide, but received no immediate assurances of help from other ports.

The Commerce and Industry Association reported that the turbulent dock labor situation was causing many large corporations to shunt their import and export schedules to other cities. The group predicted that 10 per cent of the lost trade never would be recovered.

The one bright spot in the waterfront picture was a promise by Jersey City strikers to go back to their jobs this morning. The promise was given by spokesmen for both of the warring dock unions—the I. L. A. and its American Federation of Labor rival—at a conference with Commissioner Lawrence A. Whipple in Jersey City.

Picket Line Is Crossed

The federation union, which has been opposing the walkout, mobilized 100 longshoremen to pierce an I. L. A. picket line at a Manhattan wharf of the United Fruit Company. Ignoring the jeers of several hundred members of the old union, five gangs of A. F. L. dock workers walked onto Pier 3, just north of the Battery, to unload coffee and miscellaneous cargo from Guatemala and Honduras. The cargo was aboard the freighter Loveland.

Two hundred and fifty I. L. A. strikers renewed the picketing of the United States Court House in Foley Square. It was the second time they had marched outside the building in protest against two anti-strike court orders.

One was an injunction forbidding the I. L. A. to strike or to interfere with waterfront truck movements. The other was a $100,000 contempt action against the union and three officers of its West Side locals.

The strike has been carried on in defiance of the two orders and in disregard of back-to-work appeals by Capt. William V. Bradley, president of the I. L. A. Strike leaders say the walkout will continue until the old union is certified as the sole bargaining agent for the port's 24,000 dock workers.

The threat to keep the port tied up for all the months that may

Continued on Page 43, Column 2

Wilson Aide Named Secretary of Navy

Charles S. Thomas, Assistant Secretary of Defense, after he was named the successor to Robert B. Anderson, right.

Associated Press Wirephoto

Special to The New York Times.

WASHINGTON, March 11—Charles Sparks Thomas, Assistant Secretary of Defense, was nominated by President Eisenhower today to be Secretary of the Navy. Mr. Thomas, if confirmed by the Senate, will suc-

ceed Robert B. Anderson, who will become Under Secretary of Defense when Roger B. Kyes vacates the post on May 1. A successor to Mr. Thomas has not yet been chosen. The

Continued on Page 8, Column 4

'Direct' Warning to Reds Urged by U. S. at Caracas

By SYDNEY GRUSON
Special to The New York Times.

CARACAS, Venezuela, March 11—The United States called on the Tenth Inter-American Conference today to issue a "simple, clear and direct" warning to the leaders of international communism to keep hands off the Americas.

The best way to do this, John Foster Dulles, United States Secretary of State, said, is to adopt the United States anti-Communist resolution without crippling amendments. These, he said, would "alter the heart" of the proposed denunciation of international communism as a threat to the hemisphere.

After a week of general debate the Communist issue was joined late today in the Political Committee when consideration of the resolution began. The Secretary made his third major speech on the question in an effort to block a series of crippling amendments submitted by Mexico.

Mr. Dulles sought to eliminate the fears of some delegates that the resolution could in his own words, "be interpreted as intervention or justifying intervention in the genuinely domestic affairs of an American state."

'Natural Historical Fears'

"This concern is, we believe, due to natural historical fears rather than to any language in the United States proposal," the Secretary said.

Delegates of Argentina, Guatemala and Mexico, all of whom spoke in the wind-up of the general debate this morning, had expressed this fear. The spokesmen for Guatemala, where the Communists have won high positions in the Government, have charged that the United States was seeking to cloak interventionist ideas in the guise of collective action against Guatemala.

Mexico's delegate spoke twice today, in the general debate and in answer to Secretary Dulles' rejection of Mexico's amendments. On both occasions Roberto Cordova of Mexico emphasized that his country was not trying to defend international communism but only the right of any people to choose their own form of government and political institutions.

Mexico, he said, would willingly subscribe to the United States proposal if his delegation were convinced that it did not represent a backward step regarding intervention. But later he brushed aside Mr. Dulles' assurances on this point and in fact took no note of the Secretary's announcement that the United States was itself proposing an addition to the declarative portion of the resolution to declare:

"This declaration of foreign policy made by the American republics in relation to the dangers originating outside this hemisphere is designed to protect and not to impair the inalienable right of each American state freely to choose its own form of government and economic system and to live its own social and cultural life."

As the resolution stood before,

Continued on Page 6, Column 4

SCHWABLE TELLS OF P. O. W. ORDEAL

Tells How His Mental Torture by Reds Almost Made Him Believe Germ 'Confession'

By ELIE ABEL
Special to The New York Times.

WASHINGTON, March 11—Col. Frank H. Schwable described today how a mature man could be conditioned to accept as real the fictions he had invented to appease the Communists.

Taking the witness chair for the first time, the lean, nervous Marine aviator talked for six hours before a court of inquiry. He tried to explain how it felt to have his brain washed, how reality became a blur in the mind, how the judgment could be fogged and the will destroyed.

He did not quite believe his own story that the United States had waged bacteriological warfare in Korea, Colonel Schwable told the court, which is investigating his false "confession."

"I was never convinced in my own mind that we in the First Marine Air Wing had used bug warfare," he testified. "I knew we hadn't. But the rest of it [the fraudulent confession] was real to me—the conferences, the planes and how they would go about their missions."

Rear Admiral Thomas J. Cooper, who was questioning the

Continued on Page 5, Column 3

SENATE COMBINES STATEHOOD PLANS BY VOTE OF 46-43

Ignores Eisenhower's Wishes for Action on Hawaii Alone —Democrats Score Victory

By CLAYTON KNOWLES
Special to The New York Times.

WASHINGTON, March 11—The Senate disregarded Administration wishes in voting today to put Hawaiian and Alaskan statehood proposals in a single bill.

The decision to join the proposals carried by a vote of 46 to 43 and came a day after President Eisenhower had urged separate consideration of the statehood measures. He had asked for immediate statehood for Hawaii only. This is the Republican party position.

The Senate's vote was mainly along party lines, with the Democrats winning. However, the plan to combine the bills prevailed by the margin of the votes of three Republican who broke with their party on the question. They were Senators William Langer of North Dakota, John M. Butler of Maryland and George W. Malone of Nevada.

Forty-two Democrats and the Senate's one independent, Wayne Morse of Oregon, cast the other votes for a combined bill.

Forty-one Republicans and two Democrats, Spessard L. Holland of Florida and Russell B. Long of Louisiana, opposed the merger plan.

Knowland to Back Bill

The issue in the three-day debate preceding the vote was whether statehood aspirations of Hawaii and Alaska would be hurt or helped by putting them together. Senator William F. Knowland of California, Republican Senate leader, contended it would hurt. Senator Clinton P. Anderson, Democrat of New Mexico and sponsor of the one-package proposal, asserted it would help.

After the Senate action, Senator Knowland, conceding a chance to pass a combined bill, said he would vote for it. So did other Republicans in opposition on the vote today. Senator Hugh Butler of Nebraska, Interior Committee chairman who fought the Anderson amendment, said the Senate "might fool some people by passing the bill now before us."

The Nebraska Republican alluded to the fact that a group of Southern Democrats, numbering fifteen to twenty, had supported the Anderson amendment in the hope of defeating both statehood proposals. Senator George A. Smathers, Democrat of Florida, frankly conceded during debate

Continued on Page 13, Column 3

ARMY CHARGES M'CARTHY AND COHN THREATENED IT IN TRYING TO OBTAIN PREFERRED TREATMENT FOR SCHINE

SENATOR ATTACKS

Hits Back at Stevenson, Murrow and Flanders in Radio Broadcast

Special to The New York Times.

WASHINGTON, March 11—Senator Joseph R. McCarthy struck back tonight at criticism of him by Adlai E. Stevenson, Edward R. Murrow and Senator Ralph E. Flanders.

The Wisconsin Republican said that Mr. Stevenson's assertion that only one alleged active Communist had been found in the Government in the last year was "absolutely false."

He called Mr. Murrow, Columbia Broadcasting System commentator, one of the "extreme Left Wing bleeding-heart elements of television and radio." He cited an article in The Pittsburgh Sun-Telegraph of Feb. 18, 1935, to charge that Mr. Murrow had been on the advisory council for a summer session of Moscow University, where overthrow of the existing social order was taught.

[Three and a half hours after Mr. McCarthy's broadcast, Mr. Murrow issued a statement in which he said that in 1935, in his capacity as assistant director of the Institute of International Education, he was a member of the advisory committee for a summer school in Moscow. He added, however, that "in actual fact the summer school was canceled by Russian authorities before it began."]

McCarthy Quotes Lincoln

Mr. McCarthy said he would rather stand with Abraham Lincoln, who said during Civil War times the danger to the United States was from within and not from without, rather than with Senator Flanders, a Republican of Vermont, who said the danger today is from without rather than from within.

Appearing on a question and answer radio broadcast with Fulton Lewis Jr., over the Mutual Broadcasting System, Senator McCarthy struck back at Messrs. Stevenson, Murrow and Flanders but made no mention of the implied criticism voiced by President Eisenhower at his news conference yesterday.

He also made no mention of his quarrel with the National Broadcasting Company and the Columbia Broadcasting System because they refused him free time for a reply to Mr. Stevenson and gave it instead to the Republican National Committee, which designated Vice President Nixon to make the official reply Saturday night.

Mr. Murrow had devoted a thir-

Continued on Page 11, Column 1

Cohn Scored When Woman Denies McCarthy's Charges

Mrs. Moss Counters Accusation as Red While Senators Decry 'Innuendo'— Crowd Applauds Hearing Scene

Special to The New York Times.

WASHINGTON, March 11—Mrs. Annie Lee Moss, suspended Army Signal Corps employe, softly but flatly denied all Communist party activities or membership today.

The crowded caucus room of the Senate Office Building, where the Senate Permanent Subcommittee on Investigation was in session, rang with repeated applause as Democratic members struck at "convicting people by rumor and hearsay and innuendo."

The target of Democratic resentment was Roy Cohn, chief counsel for the subcommittee headed by Senator Joseph R. McCarthy, Wisconsin Republican. Mr. Cohn had countered Mrs. Moss' testimony by saying the subcommittee had still secret evidence that she was a Communist.

Three hours later, the Senate found that "no member made any" evidence or refrain from public mention of it.

Senator McCarthy, in the original hearing at which the charges against Mrs. Moss were produced, had suggested she would "run the risk of indictment for perjury" when she appeared before the committee.

Senator McCarthy was absent from the committee room today when the scene over Mrs. Moss' testimony took place. He had gone to his office to prepare for his radio appearance later in which he answered criticism of him and the Republican party by Adlai E. Stevenson, the 1952 Democratic Presidential nominee.

No effort was made by the presiding officer, Senator Karl E. Mundt, South Dakota Republican, to check the crowd's applause or to interfere with the Democrats in their vigorous denunciation of Mr. Cohn's tactics.

Senator Mundt ordered the

Continued on Page 10, Column 3

STEVENS A TARGET

Report Quotes Counsel As Saying Secretary Would Be 'Through'

The text of the Army's report is printed on Page 9A.

By W. H. LAWRENCE
Special to The New York Times.

WASHINGTON, March 11—The Army reported today it had been subjected to direct threats by Senator Joseph R. McCarthy and his chief counsel, Roy Cohn.

The threats, the Army said, were made in an effort to obtain preferential treatment for G. David Schine, now a private in the Army but formerly an investigator for the McCarthy subcommittee.

In a thirty-four-page report sent to each member of Senator McCarthy's Permanent Subcommittee on Investigations and some members of the Armed Services Committee, the Army declared the Wisconsin Republican and Mr. Cohn first had sought a direct commission for Private Schine.

Failing in that, the report said, they had then demanded for him an assignment in the New York area so he could study alleged subversive material in West Point textbooks.

In the period between Oct. 13 and Nov. 3, before Senator McCarthy began his open fight with the Army, John G. Adams, Army Counsel, reported he had told Mr. Cohn that it would not be in the national interest to give preferential treatment to Private Schine.

"Mr. Cohn replied that if the national interest was what the Army wanted, he'd give it a little and then proceeded to outline how he would expose the Army in its worst light and show the country how shabbily it is being run," the report declared.

Threat to Stevens Cited

The report quoted Mr. Cohn as threatening on one occasion to "wreck the Army" and make certain that Robert T. Stevens was "through" as the Secretary of the Army. At another time, the report said, "Mr. Cohn stated to Mr. Adams that he would teach Mr. Adams what it meant to go over his head."

The report is expected to spur growing demands for Mr. Cohn's ouster.

Senator McCarthy made it clear in answer that he would rather battle with "one or two" in the Army with high command on the Cohn-Schine case. He said he had instructed his own committee staff to pull out of its files everything bearing on the case and give them to him so they could be "made available to the American public."

"I don't like to do it," he told a New York Times correspondent. "The deeper I get into it, I'm convinced the Army as a whole is damn clean. What some people in the Army do doesn't mean the entire Army."

He said he had sought at a luncheon with Charles E. Wilson, Secretary of Defense, and

Continued on Page 9-B, Col 2

SENATE UNIT ASKS OUSTER OF CHAVEZ

Cites Election Irregularities in '52 but Does Not Accuse New Mexico Democrat

By WILLIAM S. WHITE
Special to The New York Times.

WASHINGTON, March 11—A Senate showdown on a long-forecast Republican effort to unseat Senator Dennis Chavez because of alleged election irregularities in 1952 drew near today. A Republican-controlled Senate subcommittee formally filed its expected report recommending that the New Mexico Democrat's seat be held vacant.

It also urged that the Senate find that "no member was elected from New Mexico in the 1952 general election."

The Republicans asserted that there had been no free expression of the will of the people, in part because of the alleged denial of the right of secret ballot. Senator Chavez nowhere was charged with fraud.

The Republican subcommittee chairman, Senator Frank A. Barrett of Wyoming, said there had been "no intention to cast aspersions" on Mr. Chavez. It simply had been impossible to determine whether Senator Chavez or his Republican opponent, Brig. Gen. Patrick J. Hurley, retired, actually had won, Mr. Barrett said.

Senator Chavez asserted the Republicans had delivered a "tremendous insult to the officials and people of New Mexico."

Democrats Are Confident

The Democrats, who had insisted on clearing the issue without further delay, plainly were confident he would be sustained. Disinterested observation seemed to support their confidence.

If Senator Chavez should be ousted and the Republican Governor of New Mexico, Edwin L. Mechem, should appoint a Republican as temporary successor, the Republican party would gain actual, as distinguished from the present nominal, control of the Senate.

The improbability of such an outcome, however, was reflected by the fact that there now were more Democrats in the Senate than Republicans and in the fact that it was the Democrats who were demanding decisive action.

The Democratic member of the subcommittee, Senator Thomas C. Hennings Jr. of Missouri, gave notice that he would file a dissenting report upholding Mr. Chavez' right to his seat.

The whole issue will go next week, probably on Tuesday, to the full Senate Rules Committee. The universal expectation in the Senate was that the full committee would sustain the Repub-

Continued on Page 14, Columns 2

SHOWDOWN NEARS ON TAX EXEMPTION

Martin Admits Some Votes of Democrats Are Needed to Defeat Increase Plan

Special to The New York Times.

WASHINGTON, March 11—The Administration will need the votes of some Democrats to win a showdown battle next week against higher personal income tax exemptions.

This was conceded by the Speaker of the House of Representatives, Joseph W. Martin Jr., Republican of Massachusetts. He said he realized some members of his party would break ranks on the issue but added:

"I am of the opinion that there will be enough responsible members of the Democratic party to more than offset what losses we may have."

His analysis was in response to a prediction by Representative Sam Rayburn of Texas, House minority leader, that the Democrats would win the fight for a $100 increase in present exemptions of $600 each for taxpayers and dependents.

Mr. Rayburn said after a caucus of House Democrats that he knew of none who would vote against the proposal. In that case, defection of half a dozen or so Republicans, depending on the absentee situation when the vote was taken, could bring victory for the Democrats.

Parliamentary preliminaries for the fight were completed this afternoon when the Rules Com-

Continued on Page 8, Column 6

White Meets Backers of Young; Denies Central Compromise Bid

By ROBERT E. BEDINGFIELD

William White, president of the New York Central Railroad Company, had two important visitors in his offices at 230 Park Avenue yesterday: Clint W. Murchison and Sid W. Richardson.

They are the Texas millionaires who bought 800,000 shares of Central stock—one-eighth of the outstanding shares—last month from the Chesapeake and Ohio Railway Company to help their friend Robert R. Young in his attempt to wrest control of the $2,600,-000,000 New York Central System from its present management.

Versions of the events leading to the meeting differed sharply. Mr. White said Mr. Murchison had arranged it in his own room. But the Texans said it had been requested by John J. McCloy, chairman of the Chase National Bank, of which Percy J. Ebbott is president.

Mr. Ebbott is a Central director. The Chase National Bank was the trustee for the 800,000 shares of Central stock before they were sold by the C. & O.

Mr. McCloy, through a spokesman, said last night that the request for the meeting had originated with Mr. Murchison. But a spokesman for Mr. Young insisted yesterday that the visit had been in response to an appeal from the Central forces for a Young representative to discuss settlement of their differences.

Mr. White branded as a "plain lie" intimations that the Central management might be seeking a compromise with Mr. Young.

Mr. White summoned reporters late yesterday afternoon to deny the "compromise" rumors that had spread through Wall Street and the Grand Central Terminal area after it was dis-

Continued on Page 36, Column 3

264 Exposed to Atom Radiation After Nuclear Blast in Pacific

By The Associated Press.

WASHINGTON, March 11—The Atomic Energy Commission said tonight that twenty-eight Americans and 236 natives were "unexpectedly" subjected to "some radiation" during the recent atomic test in the Marshall Islands but all those exposed were "reported well."

The commission announced on March 1 that the first of a series of nuclear tests had started in the Pacific proving grounds.

The commission announcement today said:

"During the course of a routine atomic test in the Marshall Islands, twenty-eight United States personnel and 236 residents were transported from neighboring atolls to Kwajalein Island according to plans as a precautionary measure.

"The individuals were unexpectedly exposed to some radia-

tion. There were no burns. All are reported well.

"After completion of the atomic tests, they will be returned to their homes."

The commission made no immediate amplification of this announcement. However, it seemed probable that a "fall-out" of radioactive waste and activated moisture from a cloud drifting from the explosion probably descended on the Americans and natives on the atoll to which they had been moved.

Atomic test officials try to make careful forecasts of wind directions but sometimes miscalculate.

Exposure to mild radiation last spring were within two miles of an atomic explosion at the Nevada proving grounds and later walked to "Ground

Continued on Page 8, Column 4

Lasting Prevention of Polio Reported in Vaccine Tests

Dr. Salk Says Discovery Fights Off All 3 Kinds of Crippling Disease

By WILLIAM L. LAURENCE
Special to The New York Times.

NEW ORLEANS, March 11—The latest tests on children with the anti-polio vaccine have revealed that the vaccine provides the body with lasting defensive powers against the three types of viruses causing the disease, it was reported tonight.

This was described as the long-sought answer to a vital question, making it practically certain not only that the vaccine will produce effective immunity against all the three types of polio but also that the immunity will be of the lasting type, possibly for the individual's lifetime.

This could mean that within the next three to five years polio, crippler of young and old alike, will join diphtheria, smallpox, typhoid and other formerly dreaded infectious diseases as plagues finally tamed and conquered by man.

The newest findings were described here tonight before the New Orleans Graduate Medical Assembly by Dr. Jonas E. Salk, of the Virus Research Laboratory, University of Pittsburgh School of Medicine.

Associated Press

Dr. Jonas E. Salk

Dr. Salk developed the vaccine against the three types of polio-producing viruses, using viruses that had been rendered incapable of producing the disease while they still retained their power to produce immunity.

The whole issue will go next week, probably on Tuesday, to the full Senate Rules Committee.

Replying to remarks made this morning in Detroit by Dr. Albert

Continued on Page 22, Column 2

"All the News That's Fit to Print"

The New York Times.

LATE CITY EDITION
Clearing and continued cold today; fair tonight and tomorrow.
Temperature Range Today—Max., 45; Min., 32
Temperatures Yesterday—Max., 44; Min., 32
Full U. S. Weather Bureau Report, Page 63

VOL. CIII. No. 35,131.

Entered as Second-Class Matter.
Post Office, New York, N. Y.

NEW YORK, THURSDAY, APRIL 1, 1954.

Times Square, New York 36, N. Y.
Telephone LAckawanna 4-1000

Copyright, 1954, by The New York Times Company.

FIVE CENTS

SOVIET IN BID TO JOIN NATO; U.S. SAYS 'NO'

OFFER BY MOLOTOV

He Urges West to Enter All-European Pact—Deplores 'Cold War'

Text of Soviet note to West on European security, Page 4.

By HARRISON E. SALISBURY
Special to The New York Times.

MOSCOW, March 31—The Soviet Union has proposed that the United States and West European states join a Soviet-sponsored general European security treaty. In return the Soviet Union is prepared to examine the question of assuming membership in the North Atlantic Treaty Organization.

The Soviet diplomatic move was contained in a note Vyacheslav M. Molotov, Soviet Foreign Minister, handed to Charles E. Bohlen, United States Ambassador, and his British and French diplomatic colleagues, Sir William Hayter and Louis Joxe.

There were qualifications and provisos, both written and implied, in Mr. Molotov's proposal, which was transmitted by the Western Ambassadors to Washington, London and Paris.

But the essence of what Mr. Molotov suggested was plain—that as soon as possible the "cold war," should be called off.

The United States rejected the Soviet proposals. A State Department spokesman said the Soviet Government simply was continuing its effort to block the development of West European security. Paris sources called the Soviet note an attempt to spread confusion on the European Defense Community Treaty and to undermine the Atlantic alliance. British sources termed the Soviet suggestion of joining the alliance "just a Trojan horse."]

Defense Plan Main Target

The Soviet Foreign Minister made it plain that his immediate target was the European Defense Community.

But Mr. Molotov said the Atlantic alliance was another matter.

Mr. Molotov suggested that his proposed all-European organization and the Atlantic alliance be placed in balance. He proposed that all European powers, plus the United States, could join the Soviet - sponsored organization while the Soviet Union might become a member of the Atlantic alliance.

Mr. Molotov noted that the world was facing the peril of a war in which atomic and hydrogen bombs threatened "incalculable disaster," including the annihilation of peaceful peoples, the wiping out of whole cities, of contemporary industry, culture and science, of "ancient centers of civilization" as well as "the great capitals of the states of the world."

Mr. Molotov asserted that at this moment all the world powers bore an especially great responsibility and said the Soviet Union

Continued on Page 5, Column 3

Reds in Mass Attack Against Dienbienphu

By TILLMAN DURDIN
Special to The New York Times.

SAIGON, Vietnam, March 31—Vietminh forces last night launched a new mass attack against the French defenses at Dienbienphu.

[The French High Command in Hanoi said three Vietminh divisions were assaulting Dienbienphu, The United Press reported.]

During a night of savage fighting the Communist-led Vietminh troops established a foothold within the French positions. However, they were pushed back this morning at some points by desperately resisting French Union contingents.

A late bulletin from French headquarters here said violent combat continued today. Bad weather yesterday hastened the beginning of the Vietminh assault, but as the clouds cleared

Continued on Page 7, Column 1

France Ousts Juin For Anti-Pact Talk

The New York Times
Marshal Alphonse P. Juin

Special to The New York Times.

PARIS, Thursday, April 1—Marshal Alphonse-Pierre Juin was disciplined by the French Cabinet at a special meeting early this morning for his speech against the European army treaty and for a snub to Premier Joseph Laniel. The

Continued on Page 7, Column 3

PRESIDENT BACKS FIRM ASIA POLICY

Supports 'United Action' Plan of Dulles—Senator Douglas Urges Facing War Risk

By WILLIAM S. WHITE
Special to The New York Times.

WASHINGTON, March 31—President Eisenhower made it plain today that this Government was deeply committed to "united action" against any Communist effort to overrun Southeast Asia.

He underwrote every word uttered by his Secretary of State, John Foster Dulles, in proclaiming that policy in a speech two nights ago.

[The Soviet Foreign Ministry in Moscow denied Mr. Dulles' assertion that Foreign Minister Molotov had agreed the Geneva conference would not be a five-power meeting.]

The President defined "united action" as primarily the responsibility of the free peoples directly under threat. He declared also that, speaking generally, the United States could put itself under no greater disadvantages than by spreading its ground forces and other forces about the

Continued on Page 12, Column 4

I.L.A. INSURGENTS REJECT PAY RISE, STALL PIER PEACE

Eisenhower, Putting Local Action First, Says U.S. Is Prepared to Cooperate

By A. H. RASKIN

Insurgent elements in the old International Longshoremen's Association yesterday killed a union-inspired move to end their strike, the longest and costliest in the port's history.

The union's sixty-two-member wage-scale committee spurned an employer pay offer and demanded a contract that would make the I. L. A. sole bargaining agent for the 24,000 workers on New York and New Jersey piers.

The shipping industry retorted that it could not legally sign such an agreement until the National Labor Relations Board decided whether the old union or its American Federation of Labor rival was entitled to speak for the dock workers.

The only remaining hope for a quick end to the twenty-seven-day tie-up was the possibility that the union might order the strikers back to the piers after the labor board in Washington had ruled on a new election. A ruling is expected before the end of this week.

At a City Hall conference with Deputy Mayor Henry Epstein, I. L. A. leaders authorized a statement that the sooner the board handed down its ruling the sooner the men would be back on the job. However, they shied away from any clear-cut promise that the strike would be called off as soon as the board acted.

President Watching Strike

In Washington, President Eisenhower said the Government was alert to the strike situation and was prepared to take whatever action might be necessary to cope with it, in cooperation with state and city authorities. The President added that the White House would be guided by this rule: Everything is handled locally as long as it can be.

The collapse of the back-to-work effort here speeded Federal plans to obtain a blanket injunction banning pickets and "loiterers" from the waterfront. Charles T. Douds, regional director of the National Labor Relations Board, laid the groundwork for such an injunction by issuing a sweeping complaint against the I. L. A. last night.

The complaint, described by members of Mr. Douds' staff as the most drastic ever issued by the board, accused the old union and its locals of having intimidated dock workers through mass picketing, blocking pier entrances, physical assaults, overturning automobiles, slashing tires and congregating in large groups" to harass non-strikers.

Labor board attorneys are expected to go into Federal Court today to ask for an injunction based on the Douds complaint. Its purpose would be to halt all picketing and other interference

Continued on Page 47, Column 4

NEW PLANS NEEDED

Defense Experts to Go to Work at Once on Factory Shifts

Special to The New York Times.

WASHINGTON, March 31—Dispersal plans for defense production plants in major cities will have to be redrawn in the light of today's hydrogen bomb disclosures.

Plans for dispersing defense production plants to date have been based upon a ten-mile radius of "immediate danger," which officials conceded was outdated.

Reliable sources indicated the Administration's defense planners were scheduled to go to work at once to draw a new set of criteria for plant dispersal.

The aim of the plant dispersal program is to get new key production plants outside probable target areas. To make this attractive, the Government offers builders of such plants accelerated tax amortization certificates permitting them to write off the cost of the plants for tax purposes in five instead of the normal twenty or more years.

Another plan, effective tomorrow, to insure control of materials and production in event of atomic or hydrogen-bomb attack, was announced by the Government today. Nominal account will be kept of available materials and production facilities so that an orderly but rapid expansion for military atomic production and construction will be possible in an emergency.

Eighty-nine Surveys Undertaken

The industry dispersal program is under the supervision of the Office of Defense Mobilization but is handled by the Area Development Division of the Business and Defense Services Administration within the Department of Commerce.

The Area Development group so far has organized committees to make dispersal plans in many key communities. Of eighty-nine committees that have undertaken such surveys, thirty-five have reported and their plans have been approved by the Office of Defense Mobilization. Among these is the committee for the New York City 'metropolitan area, which completed its work last month.

Officials predicted that the New York City survey, as well as the others, probably would have to be redone in the light of the facts learned about the destructiveness of the hydrogen bomb.

In announcing the new Defense Materials System, the Business and Defense Services Administration explained it would

Continued on Page 23, Column 2

H-BOMB CAN WIPE OUT ANY CITY, STRAUSS REPORTS AFTER TESTS; U.S. RESTUDIES PLANT DISPERSAL

The New York Times
April 1, 1954

Extent to which a hydrogen bomb explosion could devastate New York and its environs

(Map of New York area showing concentric damage-radius circles: 50 MILES DIAMETER, 32 MILES DIAMETER, 26 MILES DIAMETER, 16 MILES DIAMETER, 8 MILES DIAMETER. Legend:)
A — TOTAL DESTRUCTION
B — SEVERE DAMAGE
C — MODERATE DAMAGE
D — PARTIAL DAMAGE
E — LIMIT OF INCENDIARY ACTION

Senate Unit Votes Changes President Asked in Taft Act

By JOSEPH A. LOFTUS
Special to The New York Times.

WASHINGTON, March 31—The Senate Labor Committee approved a Taft-Hartley revision bill today with the Democrats crying "steamroller." The vote was 7 to 6 along party lines. The bill deals only with President Eisenhower's recommendations, minus an Administration proposal to require Federally conducted elections among workers before a strike could be called.

Another Administration proposal, for standards to conserve union welfare funds, will be dealt with separately after an inquiry. The House Labor Committee expects to report a bill on the same subject next week. It will contain many more revisions than the Senate bill.

Two provisions dealing with state powers were added to the Senate committee draft today just before the final vote to report a bill. They are certain to be fought vigorously.

One of these new sections deals with state emergencies. As finally approved, it reads:

"Nothing in this act shall be construed to interfere with the enactment and enforcement by the states of laws to deal in emergencies with labor disputes which, if permitted to occur or continue, will constitute a clear and present danger to the health or safety of the people of the state; provided, that no state shall be authorized by this subsection to take action in any labor dispute in which the Federal Government is acting pursuant to Sections 206 to 210, inclusive, of this act."

Sections 206 to 210 are the national emergency provisions of the Taft-Hartley Act. When these were invoked, state action would be superseded, but the

Continued on Page 34, Column 3

HOUSING BAN FOES CLAIM A 'VICTORY'

G.O.P. House Chiefs Foresee 33,000 Units in Fiscal '55 —Eisenhower 'Delighted'

Special to The New York Times.

WASHINGTON, March 31—What had been intended as a defeat for the Eisenhower Administration developed as a probable victory today as a parliamentary tangle over public housing legislation began unraveling.

President Eisenhower himself said he was delighted at the outcome.

Republican leaders of the House claimed a victory by interpreting the mix-up, which occurred in the House yesterday, as meaning that the Public Housing Administration is now to go ahead with plans for construction of 33,000 to 35,000 new low-rent public housing units.

Today, the leaders moved to provide authority for an additional 35,000 units in the year starting July 1, 1955, by supporting an amendment to a general housing bill that comes before the House tomorrow.

Their aim is to give the President a legislative green light to carry out the first two years of his four-year program for 35,000 new units a year.

Action by Opposition

Yesterday's confusion in the House resulted from the attempt of public housing opponents, led by Representative Howard W. Smith, Democrat of Virginia, to kill the entire program by striking from a pending appropriations bill a "rider" allowing construction of 20,000 new units in the year starting next July 1.

The rider was eliminated from the bill on a point of order raised by Mr. Smith, who successfully challenged it as legislation on an appropriations bill in violation of House rules.

Killing the rider, according to Mr. Smith, would leave the Government without authority to start any new projects after next July 1. He based this position on an existing law, enacted as a rider on the same appropriations bill last year, limiting new construction to 20,000 units in the present fiscal year and prohibiting any further commitments without Congressional authorization.

As soon as Mr. Smith had

Continued on Page 34, Column 4

Calm in Middle East Urged by President

By The United Press.

WASHINGTON, March 31—President Eisenhower called on Israel and the Arab states today to restrain their extremists and permit other nations to help them settle their disputes.

He declined to answer a question at his news conference as to whether he believed the bitter Arab-Israeli feud, which recently erupted into new violence, should be referred to the United Nations Security Council. However, he said the United Nations had the full support of the United States in its plan to seek harmony in the Middle East.

General Eisenhower said the United States has been giving strong support to the plan to develop the resources of the area, including the water resources of the Jordan River, and hoped the plan would be successful.

He said the Israeli-Arab issue was so charged with emotional

Continued on Page 2, Column 3

VAST POWER BARED

March 1 Explosion Was Equivalent to Millions of Tons of TNT

Text of Strauss statement and conference transcript, Page 20.

By WILLIAM L. LAURENCE
Special to The New York Times.

WASHINGTON, March 31—The United States can now build a hydrogen bomb big enough to destroy any city.

In revealing this today, Rear Admiral Lewis L. Strauss, chairman of the United States Atomic Energy Commission, hinted that such a bomb could be delivered by plane.

The bomb tested at the Eniwetok proving grounds on March 1, Admiral Strauss announced, provided "a hydrogen blast in the megaton range." He said it was "double that of the calculated estimate." A megaton is equivalent to 1,000,000 tons of TNT.

The explosive power attained in the test was reported by a member of the Joint Congressional Committee on Atomic Energy as twelve to fourteen megatons. This represents an explosive force 600 to 700 times the power of the bombs that destroyed Hiroshima and Nagasaki.

No Limit to Bomb Size

Admiral Strauss made his statement at the President's news conference. He declared that the hydrogen bomb could be made as large as desired—"large enough to take out a city, to destroy a city."

"How big a city?", he was asked.

"Any city?"

"New York?"

"The metropolitan area, yes," he replied.

Admiral Strauss explained later that by "metropolitan area" he meant the heart of Manhattan and not the actual metropolitan area, which covers 3,550 square miles.

[Prime Minister Churchill, yielding to Opposition pressure, agreed to debate the Government's policy on the hydrogen bomb in the House of Commons Monday.]

Despite the hydrogen bomb's enormous power, Admiral Strauss said, the test was "at no time out of control." Furthermore, he gave the nation and the world the assurance given to him by scientists that it was "impossible for any such test or series of tests to get out of control."

Admiral Strauss' appearance at the President's press conference was at President Eisenhower's request. He made available to the American people portions of the report he had made to President Eisenhower yesterday on the hydrogen bomb tests in the Pacific.

The tests of hydrogen weapons on March 1 and 26, he said, have "added enormous potential to our military posture." He later amplified this remark with a statement that "the results of these

Continued on Page 21, Column 4

EISENHOWER SIGNS TAX CUT MEASURE

Excise Reductions Effective Today—President Voices Hope of Business Gain

By JOHN D. MORRIS
Special to The New York Times.

WASHINGTON, March 31—President Eisenhower signed the $999,000,000 excise tax reduction bill into law today. He voiced hope that the damage to Federal revenues would be offset to some degree by the resulting stimulation of business.

Federal sales taxes on a long list of items, from pocketbooks to household appliances, consequently will be reduced sharply as of 12:01 A. M. tomorrow. The savings are expected to be passed along to consumers, at least in part, by most of the industries affected. On a majority of items covered, the tax cut amounts to 50 per cent.

Enactment of the bill adds an estimated $999,000,000 to the Federal deficit of $2,928,000,000 projected by President Eisenhower for the 1955 fiscal year, which starts next July 1.

On the ground that the Government could not afford such revenue losses in addition to those involved in other recent and pending tax cuts, the Administration had opposed any broad-scale reduction of excises at this time.

The President told his news conference that, nevertheless, he was accepting the bill wholeheartedly. From the beginning, he explained, there was a difference of opinion on the revenue effects. One school of thought, he noted, believes that the reductions can stimulate business to

Continued on Page 16, Column 7

Color Film of First H-Bomb Test Is Previewed by Press in Capital

Special to The New York Times.

WASHINGTON, March 31—The world's most fearsome weapon, the fusion bomb, was shown in action for the first time here in public today before an audience of representatives of the press and other information media.

They saw a reproduction in color film of the phenomena that followed the explosion of the first full-scale hydrogen weapon on the Pacific proving grounds in the Marshall Islands in November, 1952.

The event marked the entry of mankind into the Hydrogen Age, taking the fateful step from the kiloton (thousands of tons) to the megaton (millions of tons) of explosive power in terms of TNT.

The film was released by the Atomic Energy Commission and the Department of Defense for public issuance by the Federal Civil Defense Administration. It was intended for general release at 6 P. M. April 7, and reviews

The test in November, 1952, was known as Operation Ivy and the device tested was known as Mike. At the time it was the greatest explosion in history. Since then, however, it has been greatly exceeded by the test explosions on March 1 and 26.

The film opens with an introduction by President Eisenhower, who recites an excerpt from his historic address before the United Nations on Dec. 8, 1953, relating to the need of the peoples of

of it were to be embargoed until then.

However, a descriptive review by a syndicated columnist appeared in newspapers a few hours after the showing. Because of this The Times is publishing its review now.

Continued on Page 23, Column 2

10 Pupils Burned to Death in School Near Buffalo

Associated Press Wirephoto
Smoke and flames billow from frame annex of an elementary school in Cheektowaga, N. Y.

Special to The New York Times.

BUFFALO, March 31—Ten sixth grade pupils in the Cleveland Hill elementary school died today in a fire that trapped them in a room of the school's one-story frame annex on Mapleview Drive in suburban Cheektowaga. Twenty-two other persons, nineteen of them children, were burned or injured and taken to hospitals. The school has an enrollment of more than 1,200. Hundreds of pupils of the adjoining Cleveland Hill High School were sent home. The fire followed a blast that was described variously as an explosion and

Continued on Page 34, Column 3

"All the News That's Fit to Print"

The New York Times.

LATE CITY EDITION
Cloudy, scattered showers today.
Partly cloudy, cool tomorrow.
Temperature Range Today—Max., 58; Min., 47
Temperatures Yesterday—Max., 60; Min., 46
Full U. S. Weather Bureau Report, Page 21

Copyright, 1954, by The New York Times Company.

VOL. CIII..No. 35,168.   Entered as Second-Class Matter, Post Office, New York, N. Y.   NEW YORK, SATURDAY, MAY 8, 1954.   Times Square, New York 36, N. Y. Telephone LAckawanna 4-1000   FIVE CENTS

PLEAS FOR SCHINE LACED BY THREATS, STEVENS TESTIFIES

Phone Calls Mingled Them, He Tells Jenkins, Who Brings Army Case to Sharp Focus

OFFICIAL DENIES 'BANTER'

Mundt Asserts Subcommittee Hit a 'Security Roadblock' on Monitored Conversations

Excerpts from transcript of the hearing are on Page 8.

By W. H. LAWRENCE
Special to The New York Times.

WASHINGTON, May 7—The Secretary of the Army testified today that Senator Joseph R. McCarthy and his key aides had mixed, in the same conversations, repeated requests for favored treatment for Pvt. G. David Schine with "threats" of continued exposure of alleged Communists in the Army.

Ray H. Jenkins, special counsel for the Senate subcommittee, propounded the queries to Army Secretary Robert T. Stevens that brought into sharp focus the heart of the Army case.

This was that the Senator and his staff had used the investigative power of the Senate to back up their demands for special favors for Private Schine, who, until he was drafted, was an unpaid subcommittee consultant.

As Mr. Stevens, on his twelfth day on the stand, neared the end of his testimony, Mr. Jenkins propounded a series of climactic questions.

"I'll ask you," he said, "whether or not * * * many telephone calls were either transmitted to you or Mr. Adams [John G. Adams, Army Counsel] with reference to Mr. Schine."

"Yes sir," the Secretary replied.

Subjects Intertwined

"I'll ask you," Mr. Jenkins continued, "whether or not in those t_____ _____s ____ _____ were discussions not only with reference to Schine but also with reference to the McCarthy investigating committee's work at Fort Monmouth. Were those two subjects discussed in the same conversations, on numerous occasions or on a few occasions, or on no occasions?"

"Yes, they were discussed on a number of occasions," Mr. Stevens declared.

"So that the conversations," Mr. Jenkins went on, "with reference to the investigation of Monmouth and with reference to Schine were intertwined, so to speak, in one telephone conversation. Is that right, Mr. Secretary?"

"Yes sir," the answer came.

"And did you not regard that," the counsel pursued, "as being a combination of a request for preferences for Schine, on the one hand, and correlated with a discussion or a threat of continued investigation of Fort Monmouth?"

"Yes. I couldn't separate the two," was Secretary Stevens' conclusion.

Mr. Stevens then coldly rejected suggestions by Senator Everett M. Dirksen, Illinois Republican, that the remarks taken as threatening might have been good-natured "banter." The Army Secretary said he regarded the threats as a "very serious matter."

Other major developments in

Continued on Page 8, Column 3

Seaway Bill Passed, Sent to Eisenhower

Special to The New York Times.

WASHINGTON, May 7—The Senate gave final Congressional approval today to the St. Lawrence Seaway bill.

It now goes to the White House where President Eisenhower has said he will sign the measure every President since Warren G. Harding has sought.

The Senate action was by voice vote. The Senate concurred in two minor changes made by the House of Representatives yesterday in giving approval of the bill by a vote of 241 to 158. The Senate had passed the measure, 51 to 33, on Jan. 20.

The bill, which authorizes the United States to join with Canada in constructing the project, calls for the establishment of a St. Lawrence Seaway Development Corporation to act for the United States subject to the supervision of the President.

General Eisenhower will name

Continued on Page 18, Column 5

State to Get $113,000,000 Under New U.S. Road Law

Grants Will Be Allocated Over 2 Years—4 Classes of Highways to Benefit—City Expected to Gain $5,000,000

Special to The New York Times.

ALBANY, May 7—The Public Works Department estimated today that New York would get $113,000,000 of the $1,932,000,000 in Federal highway grants authorized by President Eisenhower yesterday.

The figure in the new law represented an increase of $41,600,000 over New York's grants under the old Federal-aid highway measure. The new amounts will be spread over a period of two years, starting July 1, 1955.

The new Federal grants, as under the old law, will have to be matched by an equal amount of state funds. This represented no problem for the state since it already was planning a huge expansion in state highway construction funds.

At this year's legislative session alternative constitutional amendments to authorize state bond issues of either $500,000,000 or $750,000,000 for highway construction received initial approval. One of the two will be taken up for final legislative approval and submission to the voters next year.

The Public Works Department analysis put the state's share at roughly $56,500,000 a year for the fiscal years 1956 and 1957. The first of these starts July 1, 1955, and the second July 1, 1956.

Four classes of roads will share in this amount: primary highways, secondary highways, urban arterial highways and interstate highway routes. More than $14,700,000 a year is provided for primary highways. This is $3,200,000 a year more than New York has been getting.

For secondary roads the new annual allocation is $5,900,000, an increase of $1,300,000. For urban arterial highways the new allowance is more than $22,900,000, an increase of almost $5,000,000. For interstate routes the new allocation is $12,700,000, an increase of $11,600,000.

Since New York City usually

Continued on Page 36, Column 3

Steel Workers Set to Snub Union Anti-Raiding Accord

By A. H. RASKIN
Special to The New York Times.

PITTSBURGH, May 7 — The 1,250,000-member United Steelworkers of America, C. I. O., intends to boycott the no-raiding pact between the American Federation of Labor and the Congress of Industrial Organizations.

The decision of David J. McDonald, president of the giant steel union, to withhold his signature from the peace plan represents as crippling a blow to the pact's effectiveness as the refusal of Dave Beck, an A. F. L. vice president, to bring his 1,300,000-member International Brotherhood of Teamsters under the agreement.

Word of the steel union's plans leaked out here just one week after Mr. McDonald had forged an informal alliance with Mr. Beck and John L. Lewis, president of the United Mine Workers, independent, at a luncheon conference in Washington.

Close associates of the steel union head said his decision had been formed well before the meeting. Mr. McDonald is a member of the joint A. F. L.-C. I. O. committee that drafted the no-raiding pact last summer. The agreement won unanimous approval from the 1953 conventions of both organizations.

However, Mr. McDonald was understood to feel his own union should not commit itself until specific questions relating to the union's jurisdiction had been settled to its satisfaction.

Mr. McDonald is eager to integrate into his organization dock workers employed at Great Lakes ports through which iron ore is shipped to steel mills from the Mesabi range in upper Minnesota. The steel union recently won control over the crews on most of the ore boats and it feels

Continued on Page 10, Column 4

BUSINESS TO OFFER 3% TAX SUBSTITUTE

'Top Committee' Representing 67 Groups Seeks a Meeting With Mayor Wednesday

By PAUL CROWELL

Mayor Wagner was asked yesterday to discuss with a "top committee" of outstanding business men next Wednesday a "sound nonpartisan" proposal for added city revenue. The adoption of it would make unnecessary the extension of the 3 per cent sales tax to commercial services, the civic group said.

It was expected that the Mayor, or, in line with his announced policy of discussing major city problems with all responsible organizations seeking conferences, would grant the request, although the meeting might take place later in the week if the Mayor's office commitments prevented a Wednesday conference.

The request for the meeting was made in a telegram sent the Mayor by Harold W. McGraw and John T. Clancy, co-chairmen of the Joint Conference for Better Government in New York City. This organization, claiming to represent sixty-seven business and taxpayers groups, is one of the leading opponents of the proposal to tax commercial services.

Asked Business to Join Plea

The telegram was in reply to the Mayor's letter of last Thursday in which he declared that extension of the sales tax to commercial services was "seemingly" inevitable unless a special session of the Legislature gave the city an acceptable substitute method of raising the $30,000,000 the broadened sales tax would yield in 1954-55.

In his letter the Mayor asked for the cooperation of the sixty-seven business and taxpayer groups in "a genuine non-partisan appeal to Albany." The McGraw-Clancy telegram assured today that the proposal to be presented for his consideration would represent "the high level non-partisan business thinking" of the "top committee," which would begin on Monday a series of executive meetings from which the plan would emerge.

The telegram expressed confidence that the plan would talk the "ruinous" sales tax proposal if the Mayor would "move sincerely" in cooperation with the business group.

The Mayor was informed that four members of the "top committee" had been chosen earlier in the day at a special meeting called to consider his letter.

They were Percy I. Ebbott, president of the Chase National Bank; Warren Lee Pierson, chairman of the board of Trans World Airlines, Inc.; Clinton W. Blume, president of the Real Es-

Continued on Page 23, Column 5

Housing Unit Counsel Ordered To Answer Charges or Be Ousted

Acting Commissioner Directs Bovard, Now on Leave, to Act in 14 Days

By The United Press.

WASHINGTON, May 7—Norman P. Mason, acting Federal Housing Administrator, charged today that the agency's counsel, Burton C. Bovard, had failed to do his job "satisfactorily" and gave him fourteen days to answer the charges or be dismissed.

Mr. Mason, named to clean up alleged widespread housing scandals, said he had "no evidence of illegal activity" by Mr. Bovard. The charges involve his "failure to satisfactorily carry out the duties of general counsel of the F. H. A.," he explained.

While he gave Mr. Bovard fourteen days to show cause why he should not be removed, he said he might extend that time. If counsel fails to answer the charges, Mr. Mason added, he will be "removed from office" within thirty days.

Mr. Mason also offered to give Mr. Bovard a public hearing within twenty-one days if he agreed to testify under oath and be subject to cross-examination.

Associated Press
Burton C. Bovard

Meanwhile, Senator Harry F. Byrd, Democrat of Virginia, said he had sent to the Justice Department information that might be "helpful" in pinning down responsibility for Government hous-

Continued on Page 15, Column 7

TAFT ACT CHANGES KILLED BY SENATE; DEMOCRATS SOLID

Party Prevails in 50-42 Vote to Return Bill — President Rebuffed on Program

Special to The New York Times.

WASHINGTON, May 7—The Senate today killed amendments to the Taft-Hartley Law for the 1954 session of Congress.

A vote of 50 to 42 sent the Administration bill to revise the labor act back to ____.

The Democrats engineered this with solidarity, something they had not achieved on a roll-call vote in the modern cycle of labor legislation going back to the Norris-LaGuardia Act of 1932. Three Republicans joined them, but their votes did not affect the result.

Forty-six of the Senate's forty-eight Democrats were for returning the bill and the two others were paired for recommittal.

Just before the tally, Senator William F. Knowland of California, the Republican leader, sternly told his colleagues what nearly everybody understood:

"A motion to recommit this bill is a motion to kill this bill as far as this session is concerned."

Nobody challenged this on or off the Senate floor.

Senator H. Alexander Smith, Republican of New Jersey, confirmed such a conclusion after the vote. As chairman of the Labor Committee, he was in charge of the bill on the floor, and though he lost he appeared happy that the fight was over.

Feels Sense of Relief

"I feel a sense of relief," he commented. "I'm just as cheerful as a dickey bird."

He said he did not think the issue of state's rights in labor matters should be opened again at this session by his committee, and he did not think the House of Representatives would produce a bill on the subject, either. The House Labor Committee has been writing a bill, but was deferring a final vote until the Senate acted.

The Republican Senators who voted to recommit were: William Langer and Milton R. Young of North Dakota and George W. Malone of Nevada. Senator Wayne Morse of Oregon, an Independent, also voted this way.

The stated reason for the Democrats' solid vote to recommit the bill was the fact that the Republican majority on the Labor Committee would not consider amendments outside the area of President Eisenhower's recommendations.

This was not considered the final reason, however, at least not the sole reason.

The Northern Democrats, mostly friendly to labor, had been persuaded that the Administration bill would make the Taft-Hartley Law more undesirable to them and that they might fare better by waiting until the next Congress was elected.

The Southern Democrats felt that some of the President's recommendations undesirably weakened some of the labor controls. Also, if the bill were not recommitted, they would face

Continued on Page 11, Column 2

DIENBIENPHU IS LOST AFTER 55 DAYS; NO WORD OF DE CASTRIES AND HIS MEN; DULLES SAYS UNITY CAN CHECK REDS

ASIA PACT PUSHED

Secretary Rules Out Armed Action Without Congress' Approval

Text of the Dulles address is printed on Page 4.

By WILLIAM S. WHITE
Special to The New York Times.

WASHINGTON, May 7—John Foster Dulles, Secretary of State, predicted tonight that the current efforts toward collective defense in Southeast Asia ultimately would halt Communist aggression short of its aims.

Reporting in a broadcast on the Geneva conference on the Far East, Mr. Dulles made two points plain.

1. That the possibility of ultimate United States military intervention in Indo-China, in association with other free nations, was real.

2. That there was no intention, in any event, of committing United States forces without the sanction of Congress.

The French Union fortress of Dienbienphu in Indo-China fell only at the cost of "staggering losses" to the Communists, Mr. Dulles noted.

"An epic battle has ended but great causes have, before now, been won out of lost battles," he added.

Steps Proposed for U. S.

He declared that the Eisenhower Administration regarded as important the following steps for a solution of the Indo-China crisis:

¶The French should give greater reality to their intention to grant full independence to Vietnam, Laos and Cambodia, the three Associated States of the country. This would take away from the Communists their false claim to be leading the fight for independence.

¶There should be greater reliance upon the national armies that would be fighting in their own homeland. He believed this could be done if the peoples felt that they had a good cause for which to fight and if better facilities for training and equipment were provided for them.

¶There should be greater free-world assistance. France is carrying on a struggle that is over-burdening her economic resources. "Much progress" has been made toward all those goals, the Secretary asserted.

As to the current negotiations for creating a free-world alliance in Asia, Mr. Dulles reported that progress had been made and that "unity of purpose persists."

The fall of Dienbienphu will only "harden, not weaken, our purpose to stay unified," he added.

Geneva Hopes Stand

While "present conditions" in Indo-China do not "provide a suitable basis" for armed intervention by the United States, the possibility under other circumstances of "serious commitments" by the United States nevertheless exists, Mr. Dulles said.

The Geneva conference, he went on, may yet find a settlement by which an honorable armistice can be arranged, but the United States "would be gravely concerned" if the outcome should "provide a road to a Communist takeover and further aggression."

"If this occurs, or if hostilities continue, then the need will be even more urgent to create the conditions for united action in defense of the area," he said.

"In making commitments which might involve the use of armed force, the Congress is a full partner," Mr. Dulles continued. "Only the Congress can declare war." President Eisenhower has repeatedly emphasized that he would not take military action in Indo-China without the consent of Congress.

"Furthermore, he has made clear that he would not seek that unless, in his opinion, there would be an adequate collective effort based upon genuine mutuality of purpose in defending vital interests.

"This declaration took on added significance in light of the fact that earlier in the day Mr. Dulles had gone over with President Eisenhower for an hour and a

Continued on Page 4, Column 4

WEST STILL PLANS ARMISTICE TALKS

Negotiations on Indo-China Set to Open in Geneva, Subject to Paris Action

By THOMAS J. HAMILTON
Special to The New York Times.

GENEVA, May 7—The United States, Britain and France decided tonight to go ahead with the opening of the Indo-China negotiations here tomorrow in spite of the capture of Dienbienphu. Their decision, however, was made subject to the action of the French Cabinet.

The three Western powers had previously agreed to adjourn the conference on Far Eastern affairs a proposal for an armistice over which the Vietminh would withdraw from southern Vietnam and the Red River delta in northern Vietnam.

This is the program that Foreign Minister Georges Bidault proposed had been made and that "unity of purpose persists."

The fall of Dienbienphu will only "harden, not weaken, our purpose to stay unified," he added.

However, if the Cabinet over-rules M. Bidault and orders him to propose a simple cease-fire, the new-found unity of the Western powers will be destroyed and it will be necessary to postpone the opening of the conference while a new formula is negotiated.

Gen. Walter Bedell Smith, Under Secretary of State, busied himself

Continued on Page 4, Column 7

FRANCE IS SENDING MORE MEN TO WAR

No Protest Greets Laniel's Statement—Shock of Loss Seems to Unify Deputies

By LANSING WARREN
Special to The New York Times.

PARIS, May 7—The French Assembly heard Premier Joseph Laniel's statement on the fall of Dienbienphu in utter silence and adjourned for half an hour late this afternoon as a sign of mourning and respect for the valiant dead.

The shock was evidently great and most of the Deputies, as they discussed it, seemed to have been drawn together in a renewed determination that they would not now give up the fight. Even those members of the Assembly who had most strongly urged an end to the conflict were disposed today to show that France would not capitulate.

No one protested when the Premier made the announcement that more troops were on the way to Indo-China so that the expeditionary corps would not be weakened.

The Cabinet, in unison, decided upon military steps to aid the troops in the other parts of Vietnam to hold out.

The Vietminh tactics of overwhelming Dienbienphu on the eve of the opening of the Geneva conference on Indo-China seemed in a fair way to result in bolstering French resistance and in

Continued on Page 3, Column 2

ASSAULT SUCCEEDS

Fort Falls After 20-Hour Fight — Last Strong Point Is Silent

Special to The New York Times.

PARIS, May 7—The fall of Dienbienphu was announced today by Premier Joseph Laniel.

The news of the worst military defeat that the French have suffered since the Indo-China war began in December, 1946, came suddenly.

It was received with confused emotion. The heroic defense of Dienbienphu, besieged for fifty-five days, had been followed in screaming headlines since March 13, when the Vietminh launched its first attack — as if for the first time in more than seven years the public had fully realized that the country was fighting an enormously bloody and costly war.

M. Laniel told the Assembly that the heroic stronghold had been taken after twenty hours of fighting and continuous alertness for the last two months. He could not issue any information on the fate of the commander, Brig. Gen. Christian de Castries, or of the defenders or the wounded who have wasted underground for several weeks.

Final Concentration

All that he knew, the Premier said, was that the southern resistance point called Isabelle was still defended under the command of Col. André Lalande. French artillery with some tanks were concentrated at that center.

[Contact with the Isabelle outpost has been lost, according to an Associated Press dispatch from Saigon.]

"The Vietminh now are only a few meters away," were the last words heard from General de Castries over the radio-telephone, the French Cabinet was told. The last dispatch received from the battle was that the central strong point had been submerged.

For the defenders of Dienbienphu there was French pride in their heroism and sadness over their fate. There was also some grim anger against those who had engulfed them in defeat and, if not anger, at least unkindly feelings for those responsible for French political and military policy.

Before last March the name of Dienbienphu, now solidly entrenched in French military annals, was unknown here, but not in Indo-China, where it had some importance.

The Vietminh had taken Dienbienphu, a peaceful community of 9,000 persons, who grew rice and poppy for opium, in February, 1953, and used it to help launch operations against Laos in the following April.

French Seizure Nov. 21

Last November when a Vietminh column was spotted heading northwest in the Thai country to the French base of Laichau, the French decided to evacuate Laichau and seize Dienbienphu, using parachutists from the Tonkin area.

A successful operation was launched Nov. 21 and after the Laichau garrison moved in the French began daily efforts to strengthen it by building underground fortifications, improving the airfield and setting up barbed wire.

The establishment of the Dienbienphu base had strategic and political reasons. Close to the Laotian border, it helped fend off Vietminh attacks southward into Laos and against the capital of Luang Prabang by threatening the Vietminh rear and blocking supply lines.

The fact that the Vietminh withdrew from Laos and did not attack Luang Prabang is attributed to French control of Dienbienphu. The French also wished to remain in the Thai tribal country to encourage and help the T'ai guerrillas hostile to the Vietminh.

Finally, Dienbienphu, because of its geographical position, was expected to require a large Vietminh force to attack it, thus relieving pressure on French defenses in the much more vital Tonkin delta area.

This is precisely what happened. The French garrison num-

Continued on Page 2, Column 4

Associated Press Radiophoto
REVEALS MILITARY DEFEAT: Premier Joseph Laniel after he told French Cabinet of the fall of Dienbienphu.

U. S. Rejects Soviet Note Seeking European Pact and Role in NATO

By DANA ADAMS SCHMIDT
Special to The New York Times.

WASHINGTON, May 7—The United States rejected today the Soviet Union's proposal of March 31 that it should join in the formation of a new European security organization and its suggestion for Soviet admission to the North Atlantic Treaty Organization.

A State Department spokesman had rejected the Soviet proposal the day it was made as a transparent maneuver to upset Western security arrangements.

In the note delivered by United States Embassy in Moscow to the Soviet Foreign Ministry, John Foster Dulles, Secretary of State, spelled out the United States rejection and proposed instead that the Soviet Union demonstrate its good intentions in a

step by step elimination of the outstanding sources of international tension.

Possibly in response to criticism in Europe of the State Department's original out-of-hand rejection of the Soviet note of March 31, the new note emphasized that this reply had been worked out in consultation with the British and French Governments.

Mr. Dulles suggested that the Soviet Government join with France, Britain and the United States in a five-point program:

1. To find a speedy settlement of the Austrian question "that will restore to Austria its full sovereignty and independence."

He noted that at the Berlin conference, after the Western powers had offered to accept the Soviet text of proposals, the Soviet Union demonstrated its

Continued on Page 6, Column 4

"All the News
That's Fit to Print"

The New York Times.

Copyright, 1954, by The New York Times Company.

LATE CITY EDITION
Fair and cool today. Mostly sunny,
continued cool tomorrow.
Temperature Range Today—Max., 65; Min., 52
Temperature Yesterday—Max., 69; Min., 52
Full U. S. Weather Bureau Report, Page 61

VOL. CIII...No. 35,178.

Entered as Second-Class Matter,
Post Office, New York, N. Y.

NEW YORK, TUESDAY, MAY 18, 1954.

Times Square, New York 36, N. Y.
Telephone Lackawanna 4-1000

FIVE CENTS

HIGH COURT BANS SCHOOL SEGREGATION; 9-TO-0 DECISION GRANTS TIME TO COMPLY

McCarthy Hearing Off a Week as Eisenhower Bars Report

SENATOR IS IRATE

President Orders Aides Not to Disclose Details of Top-Level Meeting

President's letter and excerpts from transcript, Pages 24, 25, 26.

By W. H. LAWRENCE
Special to The New York Times.

WASHINGTON, May 17—A secrecy directive by President Eisenhower resulted today in an abrupt recess for at least a week of the Senate's Army-McCarthy hearings.

Democratic and Republican Senators, some publicly and some privately, predicted that the investigation might never resume in earnest. However, there were other Senators who insisted that the investigation would go on to completion.

The recess was voted after Herbert Brownell Jr., the Attorney General, disclosed formally that criminal prosecutions might be instituted against those involved in the "preparation and dissemination" of an altered, condensed but still confidential Federal Bureau of Investigation report. This was offered in evidence last week by Senator Joseph R. McCarthy, Republican of Wisconsin.

Republicans outvoted Democrats 4 to 3 on the Senate Permanent Subcommittee of Investigation to recess the hearings until 10 o'clock next Monday morning. They acted amid charges and denials that the way was being prepared for a "whitewash."

Constitutional Division Cited

President Eisenhower cited the constitutional separation of powers between the Executive and Legislative branches in directing that details and conversations at a "high level" Administration meeting on Jan. 21 must be withheld from the committee.

Testimony already has been given that top White House, Justice and Defense officials had made plans at that conference to deal with Senator McCarthy.

The Presidential order served effectively to seal the lips of John G. Adams, the Army's regular counselor, about what Sherman Adams, the chief Presidential assistant, said to him in advising that a written report be prepared on how Senator McCarthy and his chief counsel, Roy M. Cohn, persistently sought preferential treatment for Pvt. G. David Schine.

Before his induction, Mr. Schine was an unpaid consultant to the McCarthy subcommittee, the same group that is now conducting the hearings under the temporary chairmanship of Senator Karl E. Mundt, Republican of South Dakota.

Senator McCarthy angrily denounced today's Eisenhower order as "an Iron Curtain." His ire was shared, but in more restrained fashion, by all the Republican and Democratic members of the investigating committee.

The week's postponement of

Continued on Page 24, Column 1

Communist Arms Unloaded in Guatemala By Vessel From Polish Port, U. S. Learns

State Department Views News Gravely Because of Red Infiltration

Special to The New York Times.

WASHINGTON, May 17—The State Department said today that it had reliable information that "an important shipment of arms" had been sent from Communist-controlled territory to Guatemala.

It said the arms, now being unloaded at Puerto Barrios, Guatemala, had been shipped from Stettin, a former German Baltic seaport, which has been occupied by Communist Poland since World War II. The Guatemalan regime has been frequently accused of being influenced by Communists.

"Because of the origin of these arms, the point of their embarkation, their destination and the

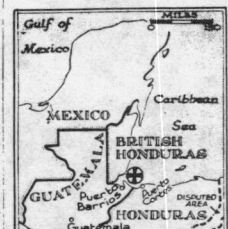

The New York Times   May 18, 1954.
Site of arms arrival (cross)

quantity of arms involved, the Department of State considers that this is a development of gravity," the announcement said.

A freighter arrived at Puerto

Embassy Says Nation of Central America May Buy Munitions Anywhere

Barrios last Saturday, the State Department reported, carrying a large shipment of armament consigned to the Guatemalan Government.

The State Department did not divulge the exact quantity of the arms, their nature or where they had been manufactured.

Reliable sources told The New York Times, however, that ten freight car loads of goods listed in the manifest as "hardware" had been unloaded from this ship and sent to the city of Guatemala since Sunday. Guatemala is 150 miles from Puerto Barrios.

Continued on Page 10, Column 5

REACTION OF SOUTH

'Breathing Spell' for Adjustment Tempers Region's Feelings

By JOHN N. POPHAM
Special to The New York Times.

CHATTANOOGA, Tenn., May 17—The South's reaction to the Supreme Court's decision outlawing racial segregation in public schools appeared to be tempered considerably today.

The time lag allowed for carrying out the required transitions seemed to be the major factor in that reaction.

Southern leaders of both races in political, educational and community service fields expressed comment that covered a wide range. Some spoke bitter words that verged on defiance. Others ranged from sharp disagreement to predictions of peaceful and successful adjustment in accord with the ruling.

But underneath the surface of much of the comment, it was evident that many Southerners recognized that the decision had laid down the legal principle rejecting segregation in public education facilities.

They also noted that it had left open a challenge to the region to join in working out a program of necessary changes in the present bi-racial school systems.

Three of the most illustrative viewpoints were those expressed by Gov. James F. Byrnes of South Carolina and Herman Talmadge of Georgia, and Harold Fleming, a spokesman for the Southern Regional Council, the most effective interracial organization in the South.

Byrnes Sees Reversal

Governor Byrnes, who has vigorously defended the doctrine of separate but equal facilities in education, said that he was "shocked to learn that the court has reversed itself" with regard to past rulings on that doctrine.

However, Governor Byrnes, a former Associate Justice of the Supreme Court, noted that the tribunal had not yet delivered its final decree setting forth the time and terms for ending segregation in the schools.

Pointing out that South Carolina, a party in the litigation before the court, had until October to present arguments on how the Supreme Court should order the implementation of the decision, Governor Byrnes declared: "I urge all of our people, white and colored, to exercise restraint and preserve order."

Governor Talmadge repeatedly has vowed there "will never be mixed schools while I am Governor" and has warned that school integration would lead to "bloodshed."

Continued on Page 20, Column 1

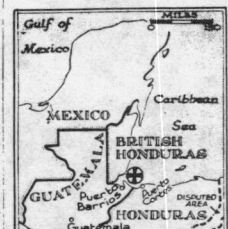

LEADERS IN SEGREGATION FIGHT: Lawyers who led battle before U. S. Supreme Court for abolition of segregation in public schools congratulate one another as they leave court after announcement of decision. Left to right: George E. C. Hayes, Thurgood Marshall and James M. Nabrit.
Associated Press Wirephoto

1896 RULING UPSET

'Separate but Equal' Doctrine Held Out of Place in Education

Text of Supreme Court decision is printed on Page 15.

By LUTHER A. HUSTON
Special to The New York Times.

WASHINGTON, May 17—The Supreme Court unanimously outlawed today racial segregation in public schools.

Chief Justice Earl Warren read two opinions that put the stamp of unconstitutionality on school systems in twenty-one states and the District of Columbia where segregation is permissive or mandatory.

The court, taking cognizance of the problems involved in the integration of the school systems concerned, put over until the next term, beginning in October, the formulation of decrees to effectuate its 9-to-0 decision.

The opinions set aside the "separate but equal" doctrine laid down by the Supreme Court in 1896.

"In the field of public education," Chief Justice Warren said, "the doctrine of 'separate but equal' has no place. Separate educational facilities are inherently unequal."

He stated the question and supplied the answer as follows:

"We come then to the question presented: Does segregation of children in public schools solely on the basis of race, even though physical facilities and other 'tangible' factors may be equal, deprive the children of the minority group of equal educational opportunities? We believe that it does."

States Stressed Rights

The court's opinion does not apply to private schools. It is directed entirely at public schools. It does not affect the "separate but equal doctrine" as applied on railroads and other public carriers entirely within states that have such restrictions.

The principal ruling of the court was in four cases involving state laws. The states' right to operate separated schools had been argued before the court on two occasions by representatives of South Carolina, Virginia, Kansas and Delaware.

In these cases, consolidated in one opinion, the high court held that school segregation deprived Negroes of "the equal protection of the laws guaranteed by the Fourteenth Amendment."

The other opinion involved the District of Columbia. Here schools have been segregated since Civil War days under laws passed by Congress.

"In view of our decision that the Constitution prohibits the states from maintaining racially segregated public schools," the Chief Justice said, "it would be unthinkable that the same Constitution would impose a lesser duty on the Federal Government.

"We hold that racial segregation in the public schools of the District of Columbia is a denial

Continued on Page 14, Column 6

SOVIET BIDS VIENNA CEASE 'INTRIGUES'

Envoy Warns Austrian Chief on Inciting East Zone—Raab Denies Charges

By JOHN MacCORMAC
Special to The New York Times.

VIENNA, May 17—The Soviet Union warned Austria today to put an end to "hostile and subversive intrigues" against the Soviet occupation forces, or Soviet authorities would do it themselves.

Ivan I. Ilyichev, Soviet High Commissioner, reverted to a practice of early post-war days by summoning Chancellor Julius Raab and Vice Chancellor Adolf Schaerf to give them this warning. The Chancellor denied the Soviet charges.

Mr. Ilyichev said the Austrian Government had been guilty of staging actions hostile to the Soviet while the Austrian press had published daily slanderous and inciting announcements about the Soviet Union and Soviet occupation troops.

The cessation of Soviet control over the movement of freight, said the High Commissioner, was abused to smuggle militarist literature and provocative incitements into the Soviet zone with the connivance of the Austrian Minister of Interior.

When Soviet authorities ordered the removal of anti-Soviet placards in their zone, the minister instructed his subordinates to disregard the order and the Government approved his action, said Mr. Ilyichev.

He added that the Government, and particularly the Minister of Interior, had tolerated militarist propaganda by former soldiers' organizations and dissemination of propaganda for another Anschluss (union) with Germany.

The High Commissioner reminded the Government leaders that since Austria had not obtained

Continued on Page 9, Column 3

City Colleges' Board Can't Pick Chairman

The Board of Higher Education was unable to elect a chairman at its annual meeting last night at Hunter College.

A spokesman said it was the first time "within memory of board officials" that such a situation had occurred.

Nineteen of the twenty-one members of the board, which governs the four municipal colleges, attended.

Two members nominated for the one-year-term were unable to attain the required majority of eleven votes. They were Joseph B. Cavallaro, who was up for re-election as chairman, and Dr. Harry J. Carman, who was restored to the board on March 2 by Mayor Wagner.

The election was laid over until June 15.

INDO-CHINA PARLEY WEIGHS TWO PLANS

French and Rebel Peace Bids Will Be Studied Jointly as a Basis for Settlement

By THOMAS J. HAMILTON
Special to The New York Times.

GENEVA, May 17—The Far East conference decided today to take up French and Vietminh proposals jointly as a basis for settlement of the war in Indo-China.

The secret session, which lasted three and a half hours, was generally recognized as the opening round in what may turn out to be a long process of negotiation. Another secret meeting will be held tomorrow.

Western delegates felt that Vyacheslav M. Molotov, Soviet Foreign Minister, was continuing to give the impression that in the end he might throw Moscow's influence on the side of an agreed settlement.

However, the West failed to obtain answers to the two fundamental questions that are expected to determine whether the negotiations here will have any chance of success: Will the Communists agree to a separate settlement for Laos and Cambodia, and will they agree to an armistice in Vietnam without at the same time requiring a political settlement?

The conference will address itself tomorrow to the issue of Laos and Cambodia. The two Indo-Chinese states are relatively free from Communist infiltration, and their leaders contend, with the support of the French, that the only thing that needs to be done is the withdrawal of the Communists.

The Laos-Cambodia and Vietnam issues were discussed inconclusively today after the delegates had devoted the first part of their meeting to the intricate dispute over evacuation of French Union wounded from Dienbienphu, seized by the Communist-

Continued on Page 2, Column 2

2 TAX PROJECTS DIE IN ESTIMATE BOARD

Beer Levy and More Parking Collections Killed—Payroll Impost Still Weighed

By CHARLES G. BENNETT

Two possible new revenue sources were definitely eliminated yesterday by the Board of Estimate in executive session. They were the proposed 1-cent-a-glass tax on beer and the suggestion to extend metered parking into hours now "free."

In a three-hour City Hall parley the board failed once more to decide on a new impost or imposts to balance the 1954-55 budget of $1,639,438,325. Mayor Wagner said after the meeting that the highly controversial 3 per cent sales tax on commercial services was "still one of the taxes at the top of the list."

Saying he felt the Board of Estimate was close to a decision on the knotty tax question, the Mayor added that "there's no decision to discard any tax" except the two mentioned above, and that at the same time "no tax is inevitable."

The board will wrestle with the tax question again in executive session on Thursday at 2:30 P. M. The Mayor said the City Council, which is holding up a bill to impose the sales tax extension, would be invited to send a delegation to the Thursday session.

Continued on Page 32, Column 5

MORETTIS' LAWYER MUST BARE TALKS

Jersey Court Orders Counsel to Racketeers in Bergen to Divulge Data to Grand Jury

By GEORGE CABLE WRIGHT
Special to The New York Times.

TRENTON, May 17—The New Jersey Supreme Court today ordered a lawyer who once had represented top Bergen County racketeers to divulge to a grand jury the substance of confidential talks with those clients.

The four-to-three decision reversed the rulings of two lower courts. Involved was the refusal more than a year ago of John E. Selser, Hackensack attorney, to answer four questions put to him by the Bergen County grand jury.

Mr. Selser told the jury that two of his clients, Willie Moretti, slain gambler, had given him the names of persons connected with Walter G. Winne who had received protection money from syndicate gamblers. Mr. Winne, superseded prosecutor of Bergen County, was acquitted last week of nonfeasance in office.

But the attorney balked when asked to reveal these and the names of other persons who, his clients alleged, had paid for protection money or who had received political contributions from the state and county level. He pleaded that his lips were sealed by the duty of "nondisclosure of confidential communications between client and attorney."

Represented Morettis, Others

Mr. Selser had represented Moretti, who was murdered in Cliffside Park in October, 1951, and his brother, the late Salvatore Moretti, for many years. He also was the attorney of record for Joe Adonis, Arthur Longano and James (Piggy) Lynch. The last four were among five men convicted and sent to prison in May, 1952, as the leaders of the Bergen gambling syndicate.

Mr. MacMahon contended that Adonis and the two Morettis visited his home in November, 1950, and that Willie told him then that $225,000 in protection money had been paid to Harold

Continued on Page 36, Column 3

RULING TO FIGURE IN '54 CAMPAIGN

Decision Tied to Eisenhower—Russell Leads Southerners in Criticism of Court

By WILLIAM S. WHITE
Special to The New York Times.

WASHINGTON, May 17—Congress as a whole grappled gingerly today with the profound political implications of the Supreme Court's anti-segregation decision.

It became clear at once—and by both parties was accepted in private as inevitable—that the court's action would figure importantly in the coming Congressional election campaigns.

Publicly, however, the Republicans and the non-Southern Democrats on the whole maintained silence. The Southerners, all angry or sorrowing in one degree or another, were quickly articulate and split among themselves into at least three factions.

One Southern group, by all the indications not a large one, was openly defiant of the court, as typified by the comment of Senator James O. Eastland of Mississippi.

"The South," Mr. Eastland said, "will not abide by nor obey this legislative decision by a political court."

A second Southern group, while not openly challenging the court, began to threaten efforts to force an alteration of its view, as illustrated by the comment of

Continued on Page 20, Column 2

Churchill Asks Negotiated Peace With Guarantees for Indo-China

By DREW MIDDLETON
Special to The New York Times.

LONDON, May 17—Britain will seek effective international guarantees for any peace settlement in Indo-China, Prime Minister Churchill declared today.

Negotiation of an "acceptable" settlement at the Geneva conference remains the immediate task of the British Government, Sir Winston emphasized in a statement to the House of Commons.

Until the outcome of that conference is known, he added, "final decisions" cannot be taken by the Government about the establishment of a collective defense system in Southeast Asia and the Western Pacific.

Peace by negotiation as urged from Sir Winston's cautious statement as the only policy that

the Cabinet was ready to apply to the problem of Indo-China. Observers were struck by the fact that, aside from the Prime Minister's reference to the necessity of backing a settlement there with guarantees, the British position was substantially the same as when the Geneva conference began.

[Indonesia is considering asking India and Burma to join her in a nonaggression treaty with Communist China as a means of offsetting United States plans for a Southeast Asian alliance.]

Sir Winston's adherence to negotiation is acceptable to both major parties in the Commons, but

Continued on Page 4, Column 3

Costello Is Sentenced to 5 Years, Fined $30,000 in U. S. Tax Case

By EDWARD RANZAL

Frank Costello was sentenced yesterday by Federal Judge John F. X. McGohey to five years in jail and fined $30,000 for income tax evasion.

The dapper, 61-year-old gambler was remanded immediately. Later Judge Harold R. Medina in the United States Court of Appeals refused to set bail pending appeal. Costello, who listened to the sentencing in icy-calm manner, was taken to the Federal House of Detention, 427 West Street.

Besides the jail sentence and the fines, Judge McGohey also assessed Costello for court costs. Lloyd F. MacMahon, chief assistant United States Attorney, said the costs would be about $5,000, only a fraction of what it cost the Government in its investigation, which began in earnest in 1952.

Costello was convicted Thursday night by a Federal court jury of five women and seven men of three counts of a four-count indictment. They found the gambler guilty of evading a total of $51,095 in taxes from 1947 through 1949.

In 1947 Costello evaded $22,-

563; in 1948, $13,786, and in 1949, $14,746. He was acquitted of the charge of evading taxes in 1946. Costello's attorney, Leo C. Fennelly, told Judge McGohey that the acquittal on this count meant that the gambler was entitled to a refund for that year.

Before the sentencing Mr. MacMahon said that for years Costello had schemed to cheat the Government out of taxes. He added that the gambler had concealed at least $140,000 of his income from 1947 through 1949, more than half his income.

Mr. MacMahon contended that Costello, by devious means, had concealed the receipt of his income as well as the source by using cash in every transaction where it was possible.

Evidence at the six-week trial, the prosecutor said, showed that from 1937 through 1945 Costello deliberately underestimated his income by at least $202,000. The statute of limitations, he added, bars prosecution for the earlier years.

"Costello has spent a lifetime making money on the shady side

Continued on Page 36, Column 4

'Voice' Speaks in 34 Languages To Flash Court Ruling to World

Within an hour after the Supreme Court decision on school segregation yesterday afternoon, the Voice of America sent a news broadcast by shortwave to Eastern Europe.

The decision came in time for the regularly scheduled "Worldwide English Broadcast" at 2 o'clock. The broadcast was written in English on the Voice's central desk and was sent by teletype to the thirty-four language desks.

There it was translated and sent out in various foreign tongues all over the world as broadcast time arrived for each.

"Chief Justice [Earl] Warren, reading the court's findings, said that the doctrine of providing separate but equal facilities has no place in public education. Separation of children solely because of race, he said, generates feelings in their hearts and minds which might never be undone."

"The ruling in effect outlaws all segregation in public schools throughout the United States. The court held that to separate students is a denial of the due process of law guaranteed by the Fifth Amendment to the Constitution and equal opportunity

Continued on Page 15, Column 4

"All the News That's Fit to Print"

The New York Times.

LATE CITY EDITION
Some cloudiness with a few showers today. Fair tomorrow.
Temperature Range Today—Max., 86; Min., 70
Temperature Yesterday—Max., 88.3; Min., 68.8
Full U. S. Weather Bureau Report, Page 47

VOL. CIII No. 35,242.

Entered as Second-Class Matter,
Post Office, New York, N. Y.

NEW YORK, WEDNESDAY, JULY 21, 1954.

Times Square, New York 36, N. Y.
Telephone Lackawanna 4-1000

FIVE CENTS

M'CARTHY ACCEPTS COHN RESIGNATION, TRANSFERS SURINE

Puts the Assistant Counsel on Own Payroll—Panel Defers Any Action on La Venia

CONFIRMS REST OF STAFF

Carr Among 22 Approved—Senator Calls Loss of Cohn 'Great Victory' for Reds

Texts of Cohn letter, McCarthy statement are on Page 10.

By ANTHONY LEVIERO
Special to The New York Times.

WASHINGTON, July 20—Senator Joseph R. McCarthy yielded today to the insistent demand for a staff housecleaning from a majority of the members of the Senate Permanent Subcommittee on Investigations.

The results, as the subcommittee met over a steak luncheon in the old Supreme Court chamber in the Capitol, were these:

¶Senator McCarthy reluctantly accepted the resignation of Roy M. Cohn, the subcommittee's chief counsel, denouncing those who had sought it and saying the result was a "great victory" for communism.

¶Mr. McCarthy transferred the controversial assistant counsel Don Surine, from the subcommittee staff to his personal payroll, also with a vigorous defense of him.

Action on La Venia Deferred

Both these changes were personal actions of Senator McCarthy as chairman taken before the subcommittee met. In this way he headed off inevitable defeat on a staff housecleaning demanded by a majority of four of the seven members of the subcommittee led by Senator Charles E. Potter, Republican of Michigan.

The subcommittee itself then voted unanimously to withhold "without prejudice" confirmation of Thomas La Venia in his position as office manager and investigator until further consideration of his personal record.

The subcommittee then voted to confirm twenty-two other employes of the subcommittee in their present jobs. Among them were two others who had come under fire during the thirty-six days of the Army-McCarthy hearings that ended on June 17.

One was Francis P. Carr, staff director, who had been named as a principal in the controversy but was removed from that category before the hearings ended.

Juliana Approved

The other was James N. Juliana, a staff investigator, who assumed full responsibility during the hearings for cropping an Army colonel out of a photograph introduced in evidence. As produced by the McCarthy side, this photograph showed only Robert T. Stevens, Secretary of the Army, and Pvt. G. David Schine.

There was no discussion by the subcommittee on whether to oust Mr. Carr, who said he was staying "unless I am voted out." Senator McCarthy said that all votes today were unanimous.

On Capitol Hill the staff changes were regarded as one of the few reversals ever suffered by Mr. McCarthy in his Senatorial career which began in 1946. The action today was a direct

Continued on Page 10, Column 3

Miss Connolly Breaks Leg, Out of U.S. Play

By The Associated Press.

SAN DIEGO, Calif., July 20—Maureen Connolly, the tennis queen, was so seriously injured when she was crushed against a big cement truck while riding her horse here today that she will be unable to defend her national title next month at Forest Hills, Queens.

Surgery and X-rays administered that the small bone in her lower right leg was broken and that muscles and tendons of the calf were damaged by a deep gash.

This definitely ends her hope of winning the United States championship for the fourth straight time.

She will hardly be able to get around, doctors said, by the start of the tournament on Aug. 28.

"Little Mo," who will be 20 on Sept. 17, was wheeled into surgery within an hour after reaching the hospital.

She was conscious when she

Continued on Page 21, Column 2

House Inquiry Asked Into a House Inquiry

By C. P. TRUSSELL
Special to The New York Times.

WASHINGTON, July 20—The House of Representatives was urged today to investigate one of its investigations.

At issue was the inquiry into tax-free educational and philanthropic foundations that began in May.

Early this month the investigators decided to hold no more public hearings. At that point the witnesses, including two committee researchers, had been eleven to one in criticism of foundations. The foundations were given permission to file sworn statements in rebuttal.

A resolution was introduced in the House this afternoon by Representative Jacob K. Javits, Republican of Manhattan. It called on the Rules Committee,

Continued on Page 30, Column 7

SHOWDOWN TODAY ON T. V. A. CURB SET

Democrats Decide to Permit Vote on President's Order for Power Contract

By WILLIAM M. BLAIR
Special to The New York Times.

WASHINGTON, July 20—A band of Senate Democrats agreed tonight to a showdown tomorrow afternoon in their fight against President Eisenhower's order to the Atomic Energy Commission to carry out a private power contract.

They intimated, however, that if defeated they would renew what Senate Republican leaders have called a filibuster against the important atomic energy bill.

The President's order directed the commission to negotiate a contract with a private utilities group to supply the Tennessee Valley Authority with power.

The Senate recessed at 9:37 P. M. after Senator William F. Knowland, the Republican Floor Leader, had said he hoped for a vote in the power fight tomorrow and completion of the bill by the same time tomorrow night.

He announced that he had instructed the Sergeant at Arms to set up cots in the Senate wing of the Capitol in the event it was necessary to work through the night to complete the entire atomic energy bill.

The Democrats' decision at a strategy meeting ended temporarily seven days of unlimited talking in the Senate that stalled the Administration's program.

Backed up behind the atomic

Continued on Page 8, Column 2

EISENHOWER LOSES ON PUBLIC HOUSING BY VOTE OF 234-156

House Rejects Plan to Build 140,000 Units in 4 Years —35,000 in One Voted

By CLAYTON KNOWLES
Special to The New York Times.

WASHINGTON, July 20—The House of Representatives killed the last real hope today to enact President Eisenhower's public housing program at this session of Congress.

By a vote of 234 to 156, it rejected a proposal sponsored by Democrats to write the President's request for 140,000 public housing units over a four-year period into the compromise housing bill that emerged last week from Senate-House conference.

Arrayed against the proposal were 155 Republicans and 79 Democrats. Supporting the President's position in the vote were 105 Democrats, 50 Republicans and one Independent.

Soon after this test, the House approved, 358 to 30, terms of the omnibus compromise on housing. It contained provision for only 35,000 units in a one-year extension of the public housing program. Many asserted that this authorization was meaningless because of restrictions in the provision. Some said not 10,000 units could be built under it.

Action Regarded as Final

The House action, which promises to create a major political issue for the Congressional campaign, was as good as final even though the Senate still has to ratify the conference report. The original Senate bill carried the President's public housing program, but it was pared, almost beyond recognition, in conference.

The general belief was that the Senate would not even attempt to reinstate the President's program since today's vote was the second in which the House had rejected it. On April 2 the House, then considering the bill for the first time, turned down the 140,000-unit program, 211 to 176.

Representative Brent Spence, Democrat of Kentucky, made the motion to reinstate the President's program, on the ground that, without it, individuals of low income could only gravitate to the slums.

Representative Jesse P. Wolcott, Republican of Michigan, defending the proposition that a unit of slum housing must be razed before a unit of public housing could be built, declared: "With these limitations, we conferees believe we have done a masterful job on public housing

Continued on Page 16, Column 4

INDOCHINA ARMISTICE IS SIGNED; VIETNAM SPLIT AT 17TH PARALLEL; U. S. FINDS IT CAN 'RESPECT' PACT

CAPITAL CAUTIOUS

Accepts in Principle— Bars Any Guarantee Except by Alliance

Special to The New York Times.

WASHINGTON, July 20—The United States Government will issue a unilateral statement tomorrow accepting in principle the terms of the Indochina cease-fire accord. It also will acknowledge its "ability to respect" such terms under the United Nations Charter, diplomatic officials disclosed tonight.

The decision to state the United States Government's position on the agreement—probably by President Eisenhower at his regular news conference tomorrow—was disclosed after diplomatic intelligence established the terms contained a clause permitting a free exchange of populations between northern and southern Vietnam.

For a period of one year, according to this understanding, no effort would be made to prevent movement between the two areas. Diplomatic officials attached the greatest importance to this clause, which they considered would avert the swallowing up of the anti-Communist and predominantly Catholic population of parts of northern Vietnam by the Red regime.

Interruption Is Temporary

Of only slightly less importance is a provision in the agreement whereby the right of the free areas of the partitioned Indochina States to receive foreign military assistance would be interrupted only temporarily, so that no interference with their sovereignty would be entailed.

It was understood the temporary restriction on the receipt of military assistance from the United States and other free nations would end after a period of "disengagement" during which forces would be withdrawn from existing front-line areas.

Diplomatic officials conversant with its terms held that the cease-fire generally came within the terms of the seven principles that President Eisenhower and Prime Minister Churchill laid down three weeks ago.

These included division of

Continued on Page 3, Column 3

AGREE ON TRUCE: Pierre Mendès-France, French Premier, as he appeared yesterday with Pham Van Dong, Vietminh Foreign Minister, left, at French headquarters in Geneva. Behind them are Guy de la Tournelle, wearing eyeglasses, and Georges Boris, aides to French leader.
Associated Press Radiophoto

SENATORS TO PUSH GERMAN REARMING

Leading Republicans Will Urge Action This Year in Addition to Granting Sovereignty

By WILLIAM S. WHITE
Special to The New York Times.

WASHINGTON, July 20—Powerful Senate Republicans will advise the Eisenhower Administration that West German rearmament and sovereignty should be pushed this year.

They are prepared to suggest to the Administration that the United States-British plan to give sovereignty without the right to rearm, as an alternative to the faltering European Defense Community project, would not be realistic.

They will argue that implicit in sovereignty is the right of self-defense and that the two concepts cannot be separated validly, as John Foster Dulles, Secretary of State, has proposed to do.

Senator Homer Ferguson of Michigan, chairman of the Senate Republican Policy Committee, who is one of the leaders in this movement, expects some sort of Congressional resolution backing both German sovereignty and German rearmament to be offered before Congress adjourns this month or early next month.

Others, among them Senator William F. Knowland of California, Republican Senate floor leader, are taking a more reserved line pending a study by the State Department of the legal situation.

Mr. Dulles has adopted the position that the question of rearmament must be deferred un-

Continued on Page 5, Column 3

38 Jersey Forgeries Charged to Hoffman

Special to The New York Times.

TRENTON, July 20—The preliminary report of a handwriting expert released here today said that former Gov. Harold G. Hoffman apparently concealed his $300,000 defalcations by forging thirty-eight bank certifications in six years.

Attorney General Grover C. Richman made public the findings of Albert D. Osborne of Montclair, who for a month has been studying the signatures on the certifications from the South Amboy Trust Company.

The certifications of general state treasury funds deposited at the South Amboy bank cover a period from June 30, 1947, to Dec. 31, 1953. They all had the signature of George A. Kress, a vice president of the bank. No breakdown of the amount was

Continued on Page 48, Column 1

French Call Pact No Victory But See Gains for Europe

By HAROLD CALLENDER

PARIS, July 20—The terms of agreement for the truce in Indochina were regarded here as presaging a peace without victory. Some called it a peace that would confirm a defeat for the West in Asia and would mark the most notable loss in battle of French territories since Louis XV lost Canada in the eighteenth century.

But it was expected that this ill wind in Asia might blow some good for France and the Atlantic alliance in Europe.

The truce seemed likely to give great prestige to Premier Pierre Mendès-France, and to enable him to stay in office to seek a decision on the European army treaty and to press for a program to stimulate the French economy.

It appeared probable tonight that the Premier would submit the treaty to the National Assembly early in August with suggested modifications that would not require further action by the parliaments of the other signatories. The West German Chancellor, Dr. Konrad Adenauer, has indicated that he would consider changes that could be made without resort to parliaments.

New Unity a By-Product

Removal of the uncertainty that has surrounded the treaty for two years would clear up the question of West Germany's sovereignty and rearmament and permit in this sphere a unity among the United States, Britain and France that has not yet existed. Such a gain in Europe might be considered as offsetting to some extent the failure of Western policy in Indochina.

A severe blow to French prestige in Asia and probably in North Africa was foreseen in the truce. In North Africa that prestige is far more important than in Asia because France's African territories are more important to her. But M. Mendès-France's argument has been that France must cut her losses in Asia in order to conserve her strength in Europe; and if she revamps her economy, as he desires, the net result may be to increase her influence and even her prestige in Europe and Africa.

M. Mendès-France has urged that the failure to reconcile Vietnam with the French Union by a prompt grant of independence should not be repeated in North Africa, where nationalist movements now are menacing.

The truce in Indochina will mark the frustration of a prolonged Western effort to resist the conquest of Vietnam, Laos and Cambodia by a nationalist movement that was anti-Western and Communist-led. Against it were employed unsuccessfully a French army, a native force and United States aid that was to amount to $800,000,000 this year.

The truce will mark an advance of communism in the sense that

Continued on Page 2, Column 4

LONG WAR ENDING

2 Accords Completed —One on Cambodia Due Later Today

By THOMAS J. HAMILTON
Special to The New York Times.

GENEVA, Wednesday, July 21 —Armistice agreements bringing the fighting in Vietnam and Laos to a halt were signed this morning by representatives of the French and Communist Vietminh forces.

A French spokesman said the armistice would take effect forty-eight hours later.

The signing ceremony, witnessed by representatives of the nine delegations participating in the Far Eastern conference here, began at 3:42 A. M. (9:12 P. M. Tuesday, Eastern daylight time). It brought to a close the eight-year struggle for Indochina.

The armistice in Cambodia will not be signed until later this morning. The Far Eastern conference will hold its final session this afternoon to complete work on the political settlement. Under it Laos and Cambodia will be neutralized and elections to create a unified government in Vietnam will be held within two years from the date of the armistice.

Pierre Mendès-France, French Premier, who had set July 20 as his deadline to obtain an armistice or resign, had missed it by a few hours. He canceled a radio speech to the French people and went to bed before the two agreements were signed at the Palais des Nations, former headquarters of the League of Nations, where conference sessions have been held since the Indochina negotiations began last May.

Rebels Get Northern Part

Under the Vietnamese agreement, Vietnam is to be divided into two parts, about equal in area and population, between the Communist-led Vietminh rebels who will hold northern Vietnam, north of a line along the Seventeenth Parallel, and the French-sponsored Government of Bao Dai.

The partition line thus is far enough north to preserve Hue, the ancient capital of Annam; Tourane, an important port and naval and air base, and the only major highway leading to Laos from the coast.

The French will not give up Hanoi and Haiphong, in the Red River delta area, in the north, for approximately a year, which will give them time to evacuate personnel of the French expeditionary force in the territory remaining to them in the delta, plus civilians fearing persecution by the Communists.

Under the armistice agreements, the Communists recognize the Governments of Laos and Cambodia. However, regrouping areas for Communist troops were authorized in Laos, The forces of the Communist "resistance government" in Laos will be concentrated in two provinces near the frontier with Vietminh territory. (Some sources identified the two provinces as Samneua and Phongsaly.)

The Cambodian delegation held out against the provision, and prolonged sessions of the "drafting committee" of the Vietminh and Cambodian representatives

Continued on Page 2, Column 5

HANOI PREPARING FOR TRUCE PERIOD

French Study Plans Designed to Preserve Calm in Delta and Effect Evacuation

By HENRY R. LIEBERMAN
Special to The New York Times.

HANOI, Vietnam, July 20—Two kinds of preparations were being made here to cope with problems related to the surrender of North Vietnam to the Vietminh under a cease-fire. Hanoi will eventually be taken over by the Vietminh under a truce agreement.

French authorities were preparing security measures to "maintain calm" in this city of 340,000. Plans originally drawn up to evacuate French, foreign and a number of Vietnamese civilians under battle conditions were also being restudied in terms of a more leisurely evacuation.

It was being taken for granted today in this city, which is seven hours ahead of Geneva time, that the seven-and-a-half-year-old Indochinese war was drawing to a close.

Geneva reports aroused considerable interest in Hanoi but created no public excitement. In fact, despite a demonstration against partition yesterday by several thousand Vietnamese, there has been no major agitation

Continued on Page 2, Column 2

Reds Have Margin in Indochina Despite Even Split Under Truce

By TILLMAN DURDIN
Special to The New York Times.

GENEVA, July 20—In statistical terms, a balanced settlement on Indochina seems to have been reached.

The Communist Vietminh has gained the northern half of Vietnam, inhabited by about 12,000,000 persons. If the Vietminh forces evacuate other areas according to the terms, the southern half of Vietnam and the states of Laos and Cambodia will remain in non-Communist hands. Approximately 10,000,000 Vietnamese, 4,000,000 Cambodians and 1,400,000 Laotians live in the territories to remain outside Communist control. Northern Vietnam is somewhat smaller, both in population and area, than

Continued on Page 3, Column 2

But the sum of the parts of Indochina due to be non-Communist.

However, the Communists will have advantages not reflected by comparative figures. The Vietminh rebels will control the northern Vietnamese, who are more tough and vigorous than the southern Vietnamese and the easygoing Buddhists of Laos and Cambodia. North Vietnam will envelop northern and eastern Laos and will be in a commanding strategic position with relation to Vietnam's western neighbor.

The Vietminh will have a disciplined, well-organized government and a powerful army,

Arrests Here Bare 'Sure Thing' Racing Fraud by Radio

Pocket transmitter at left sends race results to receiver near track, whence an agent phones data to an associate posted near a betting parlor. This man, using transmitter built into suitcase at right, relays result to a bettor, who gets electronic impulses through concealed dimes on receiver shown in left hand above. Agent then bets on horse that won.
The New York Times

The police cracked down yesterday on a gambling ring that has been using Dick Tracy techniques, complete with purse-size transmitters and ankle-shock radio receivers, to flash race results far in advance of official returns. Twenty-eight persons were rounded up in fast-hitting raids in Manhattan, Brooklyn and Queens. Fifty detectives and policemen, under the command of Supervising Assistant Chief Inspector James Nidds, fanned out through the three boroughs at 8 A. M. After the half-hour round-up, when the twenty-eight captives were paraded before Queens Assistant District Attorney Lawrence Peirez, a crime-comics story on the use of ingenious electronic devices was unfolded. Race-track plotters were pictured tapping

Continued on Page 28, Column 3

"All the News That's Fit to Print"

The New York Times.

LATE CITY EDITION
Fair and cold today and tonight.
Fair and milder tomorrow.
Temperature Range Today—Max., 40; Min., 25
Temperature Yesterday—Max., 37.4; Min., 28.5
Full U. S. Weather Bureau Report, Page 51

Copyright, 1954, by The New York Times Company.

VOL. CIV.No. 35,377. Entered as Second-Class Matter, Post Office, New York, N. Y.

NEW YORK, FRIDAY, DECEMBER 3, 1954.

Times Square, New York 36, N. Y.
Telephone LAckawanna 4-1000

FIVE CENTS

POPE IN COLLAPSE, BUT REST FOLLOWS A DIFFICULT NIGHT

Morning Announcement Tells of the 78-Year-old Pontiff's Battle Against Illness

KIN CALLED TO BEDSIDE

Trouble Laid to a Perforated Ulcer and Physicians Study Possibilities of Operation

By The Associated Press

ROME, Friday, Dec. 3—The Vatican announced this morning that Pope Pius XII, gravely stricken, had survived the night. A spokesman said a more detailed bulletin would be issued later today.

The Pope suffered a severe collapse yesterday.

The first word this morning on his condition was given by Dr. Luciano Casimiri, spokesman for the Vatican press office, at 8:05 o'clock [2:05 A. M., Eastern standard time.]

"After a difficult night, the Holy Father is now resting," the spokesman said.

There were unconfirmed reports that the Pope had suffered a heart attack in the night, accompanied by more of the intense gastritis, nausea and hiccups for which he has been under treatment. There are indications also that the Pope's condition may be aggravated by a gastric ulcer.

His personal physician, Dr. Riccardo Galeazzi-Lisi, spent the entire night at his bedside, after making emergency X-rays yesterday and calling in a surgeon for consultation.

Grave Fears Felt

By ARNALDO CORTESI
Special to The New York Times.

ROME, Friday, Dec. 3—Pope Pius XII suffered a collapse at 3:30 o'clock yesterday afternoon due, it is believed, to a perforated ulcer.

The Pope fell into a coma and the gravest fears for his life were felt. He is 78 years old and has been weakened because for the last four days his feeding has been by artificial means.

Extreme unction was administered and Pius' nearest relatives —three nephews—were called to his bedside.

Five hours later, the Pope had overcome the crisis and his archiater, or chief physician, Prof. Riccardo Galeazzi-Lisi, said there was no immediate cause for alarm.

The Pope was stated to be resting as easily as could be expected under the circumstances, although breathing heavily and reduced to exhaustion.

It was learned that the possibility of an abdominal operation sometime today or in the next few days was being considered. The exact nature of the operation under consideration was not stated but it is understood that a noticeable swelling of the Pope's abdomen developed yesterday afternoon, accompanied by cramps and excruciating pain. Radioscopic and clinical tests were made late in the evening to ascertain both the exact nature of the Pope's ailment and whether he is in condition to undergo surgery.

From the time he fell seriously ill in January of this year, Pope Pius had refused to take the barium meal necessary if full X-ray examination of his stomach

Continued on Page 4, Column 1

Rio Conference Ends With Major Accords

By SAM POPE BREWER
Special to The New York Times.

PETROPOLIS, Brazil, Dec. 2 —The twenty-one American republics ended tonight their first general economic conference with agreements on many major points and plans to hold another such meeting within two years.

Antonio Carrillo Flores, Minister of Finance of Mexico, said in the principal address at the closing session that public opinion of this hemisphere would find on studying results of the conference that its work "was not sterile."

Carlos Lleras Restrepo of Colombia introduced a dissenting note into the general air of agreement. He said at this final session that his country did not feel the conference had gone far enough toward increasing international banking facilities and stabilizing commodity prices. An

Continued on Page 10, Column 5

President Rejects Blockade Of China Now as Act of War

But He Pledges No Let-Up in Efforts to Free 13 Americans Jailed by Peiping—Holds Truce Obligates U. N. to Act

By JOSEPH A. LOFTUS
Special to The New York Times

WASHINGTON, Dec. 2—President Eisenhower asserted today he was not going to be pushed emotionally into an act of war—such as a naval blockade of Communist China.

Neither, he said, is he going to let Peiping get away with the imprisonment of thirteen Americans on spy charges.

He insisted that the United Nations act for the release of at least eleven of the Americans because they were uniformed veterans of the Korean war and as such the United Nations was obligated to act in their behalf.

[At the United Nations, the United States said it wanted the world body to condemn the imprisonment by Red China of eleven American airmen shot down during the Korean war.]

"We are yet far from exhausting all of our resources" to liberate these men, the President

said at his news conference: "I mention only one of those that is available to us."

He asserted that Red China deliberately timed its announcement of the imprisonment to divide the people of the United States as well as the United States from its allies. He added that the United States must be forever on its guard against this divide-and-conquer technique.

His personal feelings of anger, resentment and frustration were as great as any American's, he said, but he believed that restraint in public expression was the wiser course. To respond with patience rather than with truculence does not mean appeasement, he declared.

The President was clearly reading a lesson in the behavior of public officials to Senator Wil-

Continued on Page 2, Column 4

East Bloc Says Joint Army Will Counter Bonn in NATO

By CLIFTON DANIEL
Special to The New York Times.

MOSCOW, Dec. 2—In a declaration signed in the Kremlin tonight, eight European Communist regimes gave notice that if the Atlantic powers enlisted West Germany in their alliance, an East European defense organization would be created.

Representatives of eight governments concluding a four-day conference here said a further meeting would be called to plan defense measures should the London and Paris agreements for West German armament and sovereignty be finally ratified.

The envisioned defense organization would have combined military forces under a joint command like that of the North Atlantic Treaty Organization. It would be in addition to the existing framework of treaties concluded long ago among the eight powers.

Communist China's complete approval of the declaration and the measures envisioned in it was signified at the final meeting of the representatives of the eight European powers today. China's endorsement was given by Chang Wen-tien, Peiping's Deputy Foreign Minister and Ambassador to Moscow.

Having in mind the combined strength of Communist China, the Soviet Union and seven other units in the East bloc conference, the delegates declared:

"Never before have the forces of peace and socialism been so mighty and so consolidated as now. Any attempts to attack, launch a war and interfere with the peaceful life of our peoples will meet with a shattering rebuff."

The declaration, bound in a red Morocco folder with ribbons

Continued on Page 5, Column 5

ATOM POWER SEEN AS COMMON IN 1976

Half of All Electric Plants Then Building Will Use It, G. E. Head Tells N.A.M.

By A. H. RASKIN

By 1976 atomic energy will be used to fuel half of all the electric generating plants then being built, it was predicted yesterday. This forecast was put before the National Association of Manufacturers by Ralph J. Cordiner, president of General Electric.

His estimate of the speed with which nuclear power would come into widespread use as a source of electric power was considerably more optimistic than most official calculations. Mr. Cordiner made his prediction as part of a plea to industrialists to shun "creeping conservatism" in their approach to business planning.

The head of the country's biggest electrical manufacturing company advised his fellow-executives to make their plans on a twenty-year basis, instead of limiting themselves to the ups and downs of the immediate sales market.

West Called Stronger

Other highlights at the second session of the association's fifty-ninth annual Congress of American Industry in the Waldorf-Astoria Hotel included:

¶An assertion by Gen. Walter Bedell Smith that the United States and its allies had built up a sufficient superiority over the Communist countries to "deter aggression and maintain peace." The former Under Secretary of State emphasized, however, that the balance of power was still "rather tenuous."

¶A report by a Dutch industrialist that five of his employes, who spent three months working in a Pennsylvania linoleum factory, had come home convinced that "America is a working man's world."

¶An attack by Charles R. Sligh Jr., N. A. M. board chairman, on union proposals for a guaranteed annual wage. He contended that wage guarantees would destroy business, rather than stabilize employment.

¶An assertion by Prof. Leo Wolman of Columbia University that the Taft-Hartley Act represented no substantial improvement over the old Wagner Act in curbing union power and preventing encroachment on management rights.

¶Election as N. A. M. president of Henry G. Riter 3d of Montclair, N. J., president of Thomas A. Edison, Inc., and chairman of the board of Copperweld Steel. Mr. Riter, who was an investment banker before he became an industrialist, succeeds H. C. McClellan of Los Angeles.

General Smith, who quit the State Department two months

Continued on Page 24, Column 2

EISENHOWER WARNS G. O. P. RIGHT WING; CHIDES KNOWLAND

Insists Party Must Follow a Progressive Course or Face Loss of Influence

Transcript and summary of the news conference, Page 18.

By WILLIAM S. WHITE
Special to The New York Times.

WASHINGTON, Dec. 2—President Eisenhower, reasserting leadership for his concept of a progressive Republican party, rebuked today the Senate Republican floor leader, William F. Knowland of California, and the party's right wing generally.

The President did not seek to disclaim the existence of a split in the party. He said instead that the party would not long be a force in American life unless it followed a course of progressivism.

As before, he defined this progressivism as a liberal attitude in the Government's relationship with the individual and a conservative attitude concerning the national economy and the individual's pocketbook.

It was the first time since he entered the White House two years ago that General Eisenhower publicly and without apology had criticized a leading member of his party in Congress. Always before, he had avoided such criticism, relying frequently on the fact that the Constitution made Congress an independent branch of Government.

Even this time, the President somewhat softened his language toward the end, with the comments that while Senator Knowland sometimes made statements that certainly did not conform with the Administration's approach these normally affected method rather than principle.

China Blockade Urged

He made it clear, nevertheless, that distinctions in methods were important, suggesting that the methods of Senator Knowland might mean the difference between peace and war in Asia.

Senator Knowland, in the face of rejections from John Foster Dulles, Secretary of State, and the President himself, has been calling for a blockade of Communist China to force the liberation of United States citizens in Communist prisons.

Yesterday, moreover, Mr. Knowland broke with the Administration on another sensitive issue, coming out against a Senate censure of Senator Joseph R. McCarthy, Republican of Wisconsin. The President said little about the issue, observing only that it was up to the Senate to determine what was required for the preservation of its dignity.

On the point of the profound difference within the Republican party over policy toward Red China, however, the President spoke extensively and voluntarily. He took up Senator Knowland's

Continued on Page 18, Column 1

'Copter Saves 5 Plane Survivors Down 45 Hours on Mountainside

Two Perish in Crash of DC-3 in New Hampshire—Work of Stewardess Praised

By JOHN H. FENTON
Special to The New York Times.

BOSTON, Dec. 2—Five survivors of the crash of a Northeast Airlines plane were plucked by helicopter today from a bleak mountainside near the Maine-New Hampshire border. They had spent forty-five hours on the snow-covered spot in bitter cold.

The two others aboard the DC-3 died of injuries a few hours after the plane had fallen into a stretch of pine woods.

The dead were George McCormick, 37 years old, of Kingston, N. Y., co-pilot, and John McNulty, 39, of Boston, flight supervisor.

First to be rescued was the pilot, Capt. W. Peter Carey, 37, of Swampscott, Mass. He suffered severe head injuries. He and Miss Mary McEttrick, 23, of Boston, the stewardess, were flown here for medical treatment. Miss McEttrick suffered from shock and exposure.

The survivors praised Miss McEttrick for her cooperation throughout the ordeal during which they huddled in the wrecked plane for nearly two days. Her cheerful attempts to make them com-

Stewardess Mary McEttrick in Berlin (N. H.) hospital.

fortable and her care of the injured prompted them to agree that "she's quite a girl."

Seventy-five Northeast employes, who were flown to Berlin,

Continued on Page 29, Column 4

FINAL VOTE CONDEMNS M'CARTHY, 67-22, FOR ABUSING SENATE AND COMMITTEE; ZWICKER COUNT ELIMINATED IN DEBATE

RANCOR CONTINUES

Welker Refuses to Let Flanders Apology Go Into the Record

By JAMES RESTON

WASHINGTON, Dec. 2—The McCarthy debate ended as it began in a spasm of rancor and vindictiveness that will divide the Senate and the country for a long time to come.

Though there were some lighthearted semantics at the close over whether Senator Joseph R. McCarthy was "censured" or "condemned," the underlying feeling among the principals ranged from uneasiness to sullen anger.

The junior Senator from Wisconsin himself produced almost the only hint of humor all day. Asked whether he thought the Senate had passed a resolution of "censure" or "condemnation," he replied:

"I wouldn't say it was a vote of confidence."

He then announced that he was "very happy to get this circus over" and would get back to "the job of digging Communists 'out of the Government" on Monday.

Controversy Continues

Even after the vote was over, the controversy went on.

Senator Ralph E. Flanders, Republican of Vermont, arose and said he wanted to apologize to the Senate for some remarks he had made about Senator McCarthy some months ago. He added that he had told the Wisconsin Senator that he proposed to do so and had asked him to remain in the chamber, but Senator McCarthy had declined.

Then Senator Flanders asked for unanimous consent to have the Congressional Record amended to show that he had apologized for some of his remarks. This was blocked by Senator Herman Welker, Republican of Idaho, who angrily refused to give consent.

The usual lavish courtesy of the upper chamber gave way to biting sarcasm at the close. Senator J. William Fulbright, Democrat of Arkansas, said he would try to answer a question by Senator Welker, who "very surprised that a distinguished Rhodes scholar could not answer any question."

The End of a Phase

The main significance of the special session was that it ended that phase of the McCarthy controversy in which the Senate of the United States was hesitant to take action against the Wisconsin Senator.

For most of the five years Senator McCarthy launched his anti-Communist crusade, the Senate of the United States has led a double life—critical of the Senator in private, and afraid of his political power in public.

During most of this period there has been a kind of political paralysis among the anti-McCarthy faction, and it was never entirely clear who was for him and who was against him. This doubt has now been removed.

The Senator from Wisconsin will remain for a month as chairman of the Government Operations Committee. He will lose none of his rights. He will have the power of subpoena and he will wield his gavel.

What has changed is not Mr. McCarthy but his opponents. They are in the open now, willing and in some cases eager to match his criticisms with their own. In short, the balance of criticism, dominated for so long by Senator McCarthy, has been restored.

Behind this, too, is a decision by the Executive Branch of the Government to take a firmer position against his efforts to persuade Federal employes to give him documents they are not authorized to disclose.

So long as Congress hesitated to take action against Mr. McCarthy, the Executive itself was divided about how to defend its own classified files, but today is called—has stiffened the anti-McCarthy element in the Administration.

Thus, while he can exercise all

Continued on Page 16, Column 7

CONDEMNED ON TWO COUNTS: Senator McCarthy as he left the Senate floor last night after members adopted a resolution condemning his conduct. The vote was 67-22.
Associated Press Wirephoto

PRESIDENT ALERTS MAYORS ON ATTACK

Cities Are Front-Line Targets, He Warns—Asks Teamwork in Federal-Local Defense

By ELIE ABEL
Special to The New York Times.

WASHINGTON, Dec. 2—President Eisenhower warned today that United States cities were front-line targets for modern weapons 'capable' of such destruction as to appall the imagination.'

The President called for closer municipal-Federal cooperation in civil-defense planning as he welcomed about 240 mayors, city manager and other local officials to a two-day conference in the State Department auditorium.

Val Peterson, Federal Civil Defense Administrator, expanded on the President's warning in a guarded discussion of radioactive "fall-out," a phenomenon that adds a new dimension to the terror of thermonuclear (hydrogen) bombs.

The idea that only city dwellers need to worry about bombing is obsolete today, Mr. Peterson said. If a hydrogen bomb is detonated on or close to the ground, he explained, tremendous amounts of earth and debris are sucked up into the fireball and made radioactive.

Although the heavy particles will not travel far, he said, the lighter ones may be wafted away by winds of the upper air, at alti-

Continued on Page 19, Column 1

SENATORS CLEARED ON M'CARTHY MAIL

Inquiry Indicates Request for Check Was Handled by Staff as Routine Matter

By WILLIAM M. BLAIR
Special to The New York Times.

WASHINGTON, Dec. 2—A special Senate committee apparently will report to the Senate that a check of Senator Joseph R. McCarthy's mail in 1952 was handled as a routine matter by a subcommittee's staff member.

Senator Walter F. George, Democrat of Georgia, indicated as much to Senator McCarthy this afternoon as the special two-member committee completed its overnight inquiry into how the mail check was authorized.

"There's nothing to be gained from pursuing the matter further," Senator McCarthy told Senator George, who replied, "I don't think so."

Senator George and Senator Homer Ferguson, Republican of Michigan, spent the day in closed session to hear testimony from persons on the staff of the Senate subcommittee on Privileges and Elections, which had inquired into Senator McCarthy's finances in 1952.

Mr. Ferguson said that a written report would be filed with the Senate. The report is expected to be filed with the secretary of the Senate tomorrow.

The two Senators were named by the Senate last night to in-

Continued on Page 15, Column 3

REPUBLICANS SPLIT

Democrats Act Solidly in Support of Motion Against Senator

Excerpts from transcript of Senate debate, Pages 12, 13

By ANTHONY LEVIERO
Special to The New York Times.

WASHINGTON, Dec. 2—The Senate voted 67 to 22 tonight to condemn Joseph R. McCarthy, Republican Senator from Wisconsin.

Every one of the forty-four Democrats present voted against Mr. McCarthy. The Republicans were evenly divided—twenty-two for condemnation and twenty-two against. The one independent, Senator Wayne Morse, of Oregon, also voted against Mr. McCarthy.

In the ultimate action the Senate voted to condemn Senator McCarthy for contempt of a Senate Elections subcommittee that investigated his conduct and financial affairs, for abuse of its members, and for his insults to the Senate itself during the censure proceeding.

Lost in a day of complex and often confused parliamentary maneuvering was the proposal to censure Senator McCarthy for his denunciation of Brig. Gen. Ralph W. Zwicker as unfit to wear his uniform.

This proposal was defeated by a parliamentary device that avoided a direct vote on the merits of the issue. Inquiry among influential Senators indicated they considered the Zwicker proposal a dilemma they wished to avoid.

Amendment Substituted

They said they wished to censure because the facts warranted it. If they failed to do so, they believed large elements of the public would feel the Senate took notice of offenses only against itself and not against ordinary citizens.

But also if they did censure for this, then Senator McCarthy could exploit the decision, contending he was being punished for his effort to expose former Maj. Irving Peress, the Army dentist who was promoted and honorably discharged, and who was denounced by Mr. McCarthy as a "Fifth Amendment Communist."

Mr. McCarthy's denunciation of General Zwicker, who was commanding officer at Camp Kilmer, N. J., when Dr. Peress was discharged, occurred when the Senator interrogated General Zwicker on the question of who had promoted Dr. Peress.

The direct test on the Zwicker issue was avoided by the substitution of the amendment to condemn Senator McCarthy for having insulted the Senate during his censure trial.

McCarthy Loses Three Tests

Thus in its final form the resolution of condemnation was in two parts, covering the offenses against the Elections subcommittee and its members in the first part, and against the Senate in the second. Three test votes were all lost by Mr. McCarthy before the final condemnation.

First was a motion to table the Zwicker proposal, made by Senator Styles Bridges, Republican of New Hampshire, the president pro tem of the Senate, who assumed the leadership of the effort to save Mr. McCarthy yesterday.

Such a motion, if it had succeeded, might have led to a situation that would have prolonged the debate.

But amid signs that the Zwicker issue would have tough sledding, Senator Wallace F. Bennett, Republican of Utah, served notice that if Mr. Bridges' move were defeated he would attempt to substitute for the Zwicker issue his amendment for abuse of the Senate. The significance of this was that an amendment by substitution would require no time out for debate.

Then the voting proceeded. The motion to table the Zwicker proposal was defeated 55 to 33. Mr. Bennett's motion to substitute passed by 64 to 23 and in the next vote his amendment was adopted by the same tally.

The final vote placing Mr. Mc-

Continued on Page 14, Column 3

G.O.P. Weighs End of Rent Curb Outside of the Metropolitan Area

By LEO EGAN

Republican legislative leaders are giving serious consideration to relaxing state rent controls outside of the metropolitan area, which includes Nassau and Westchester counties as well as New York City.

Such a proposal could set the stage for a major clash between Governor-elect Averell Harriman, Democrat-Liberal, and Republican majorities in the Senate and Assembly.

The Democratic platform on which Mr. Harriman was elected favors tightening rather than relaxing 'rent control. Moreover, Mr. Harriman affirmed his full support of this position on several occasions during the campaign. One proposal favored by some Republicans calls for decontrolling all rents outside of the New York metropolitan area. This is politically impossible or unacceptable they favor decontrolling

all one and two-family houses outside of the metropolitan area, leaving controls in effect only on apartments and tenements.

Both suggestions were formally advanced at a recent closed-door meeting of the Temporary State Commission on Rents and Rental Conditions, headed by Assemblyman Joseph F. Carlino of Long Beach, L. I.

As a result, Joseph D. McGoldrick, State Rent Administrator, was instructed by the commission to prepare a report and recommendations on both proposals covering the probable effect of such a relaxation of controls, the number of dwelling units in volved, and the ratio of vacancies to dwelling units affected at present.

Major up-state cities that would be affected by such a

Continued on Page 24, Column 5

"All the News That's Fit to Print"

The New York Times.

LATE CITY EDITION
Fair and cold today. Increasing cloudiness, cold tomorrow.
Temperature Range Today—Max., 22; Min., 16
Temperature Yesterday—Max., 23; Min., 12
Full U. S. Weather Bureau Report, Page 29

Copyright, 1955, by The New York Times Company

VOL. CIV..No. 35,434.

Entered as Second-Class Matter,
Post Office, New York, N. Y.

NEW YORK, SATURDAY, JANUARY 29, 1955.

Times Square, New York 36, N. Y.
Telephone LAckawanna 4-1000

FIVE CENTS

ATOMIC COMMITTEE RESCINDS SUPPORT FOR DIXON-YATES

Party-Line Vote in Congress Group Would Cancel Pact —Victory for Democrats

G. O. P. WAIVER 'VOIDED'

But Case Is Expected to Go to the Courts as Experts Doubt Action's Legality

By WILLIAM M. BLAIR
Special to The New York Times.

WASHINGTON, Jan. 28—On a party line vote of 10 to 8 the Joint Congressional Committee on Atomic Energy recommended today that the Administration cancel the Dixon-Yates contract.

The major point of the resolution adopted by the Democratic vote was rescission of a waiver voted last fall by the committee, then Republican-controlled, to speed action on the contract. The waiver set aside a provision of atomic law that such contracts lie before the Joint Committee for thirty days while Congress is in session.

This apparent repudiation of the action by the old committee set up the legal tangle that Democrats were sure would toss the issue into court. They felt this was true unless their action today forced the Administration to back down on its decision, directed by President Eisenhower, to feed private power into the Tennessee Valley Authority.

Republican contended that the Democratic action was "meaningless." They agreed, however, that a court test was the ultimate outcome.

New Phase in Dispute

Within Administration circles the first private reaction was that the new Democratic move to kill the contract was just another phase of the running fight. It was also believed that the Administration was standing firmly behind its decision.

Lewis L. Strauss, Chairman of the Atomic Energy Commission, which made the contract, said he had no comment at this time.

Republicans on the Joint Committee futilely raised their arguments and points of order against the Democratic resolution at the lively closed session. The one-hour-and-forty-minute meeting was attended by thirteen of the committee. Proxy votes were cast for the absent members.

Senator Clinton P. Anderson, New Mexico Democrat and committee chairman, said the matter now rested in the hands of the A. E. C.

The $107,250,000 contract was made with two private southern utilities, Middle South Utilities, Inc., and the Southern Company. These companies, headed by Edgar H. Dixon and Eugene A. Yates, respectively, have formed the Mississippi Valley Generating Company to construct a private steam plant at West Memphis, Ark. This plant would transmit power to the T. V. A. as "replacement" for some 600,000 kilowatts of energy that T. V. A. now supplies to atomic operations at Paducah, Ky.

The arrangement was made by the Administration to avoid a Federal outlay of $100,000,000 that the T. V. A. had requested for a new steam plant to meet

Continued on Page 7, Column 8

Nichols of A. E. C. Reported Resigning

Special to The New York Times.

WASHINGTON, Jan. 28—Maj. Gen. Kenneth D. Nichols is understood to have resigned as general manager of the Atomic Energy Commission.

His resignation was submitted last September to Lewis L. Strauss, commission chairman, but has not been acted upon for several reasons. Among the reasons, it was said, is the split that developed within the commission between Mr. Strauss and other members and the fight over the Dixon-Yates private power contract.

R. W. Cook, assistant general manager, is said to be Mr. Strauss' choice to succeed General Nichols. Mr. Cook carried the burden of the negotiations in the Dixon-Yates contract.

Informed sources said that General Nichols was leaving to accept a post in private industry controlled by the family of An-

Continued on Page 7, Column 6

7 Women Questioned In Rubinstein Slaying

By MILTON BRACKER

Intense police activity that began early yesterday and continued until early today failed to indicate that any major progress had been made toward solving the murder of Serge Rubinstein.

The 46-year-old financial manipulator and convicted draft dodger was strangled in his home at 814 Fifth Avenue some time between 2 and 7 A. M. on Thursday.

Detectives questioned a prisoner in Sing Sing who thought he had vital information. They left Ossining with strong doubts that he had. The bulk of the inquiry centered on hundreds of names in six letter-sized loose-leaf books that Rubinstein secretaries regarded as private telephone lists.

All day, and late last night, a series of women—at least seven of them—were interrogated in

Continued on Page 30, Column 1

PAY RISE ASSURED FOR CITY TEACHERS

Beame, at Budget Hearing, Cautions Full Increase May Take 2 or 3 Years

By CHARLES G. BENNETT

The city's teachers were assured yesterday of adequate pay increases even if it should take more than a year to achieve them.

At a departmental hearing on the Board of Education's $314,149,116 budget request for 1955-56, Budget Director Abraham D. Beame outlined a plan for increasing the teachers' salaries by stages.

Under the formula described by Mr. Beame, the Wagner Administration would set a maximum increase and seek to attain it as quickly as possible. However, it would be spread over two or three years if necessary, the proposition for this year would be as generous as possible, depending upon the city's success with its fiscal program in Albany.

Last Monday Mayor Wagner said that teacher salary increases would be provided by the city in 1955-56, but he did not indicate an amount. On Wednesday, he earmarked $24,400,000 for education in the $104,779,335 of proposed fund increases he submitted to Governor Harriman and legislative leaders.

The Board of Education's budget was presented by Vito F. Lanza, member of the board; Dr. William Jansen, Superintendent of Schools, and Charles Gilman, the

Continued on Page 16, Column 3

ECONOMY OF WEST TOPS SOVIET BLOC, CONGRESS IS TOLD

U. S. Expected to Widen Gap in the Next Two Decades, Survey of Trends Shows

By JOHN D. MORRIS
Special to The New York Times.

WASHINGTON, Jan. 28—The economic capacity of the United States, Canada and Western Europe has been found to be "significantly greater" than the combined strength of the Soviet bloc.

Moreover, a study made public today by a Congressional committee held that there were "strong grounds" for expecting the United States to widen in the next two decades the gap between the size of its economy and that of the Soviet Union.

This forecast was hedged, however, with the observation that "the rate of growth in the Soviet Union might be somewhat higher than the rate of growth in the United States."

These and other conclusions, largely favorable to the West but with many qualifications, were set forth in a 339-page report on comparative trends of economic growth between the Western Powers and the Soviet bloc, exclusive of Communist China.

Federal Document

The document was prepared under the direction of Dr. Howard S. Piquet, international economics specialist of the Legislative Reference Service of the Library of Congress for the Joint Committee on the Economic Report. It was a compilation and analysis of material gathered by various agencies of the United States and foreign governments.

From 1938 through 1953, Dr. Piquet found, the gross national product of the United States—total output of goods and services—increased almost twice as rapidly as that of the Soviet Union and three times as rapidly as that of independent Europe.

But from 1948, he reported, its growth was only two-thirds as fast as the Soviet's and not quite 30 per cent faster than Western Europe's.

Western Europe, according to the report, has been growing economically "somewhat more slowly" since 1938 than the Soviet Union but more rapidly than satellite countries. Dr. Piquet said expansion of international trade was indispensable to the free European countries to prevent their growth from falling further behind that of Soviet Russia.

The slow economic progress of the satellites was attributed in major part to "the tremendous

Continued on Page 7, Column 2

SENATE VOTES FORMOSA PLAN, 85-3; U. N. TO ACT, MAY INVITE RED CHINA; BRITISH BID SOVIET CURB PEIPING

MEETING MONDAY

New Zealand Calls on Council to Consider Offshore Fighting

By THOMAS J. HAMILTON
Special to The New York Times.

UNITED NATIONS, N. Y., Jan. 28—The United Nations Security Council will meet Monday to try to stop the fighting between Nationalist and Communist China over the small islands off the mainland.

New Zealand, with the support of the United States and Britain, asked the Security Council to take up the question, which does not directly affect Communist China's threats to "liberate" Formosa, the Nationalist stronghold, and the near-by Pescadores Islands.

Sir Leslie Knox Munro, the New Zealand representative, said at a press conference that he would support an invitation to Communist China to take part in the debate, and that he believed this would be the principal business at the session Monday.

A British spokesman said that Britain also would support an invitation. It was learned the United States would not oppose it.

Nationalist Delegate Cool

Dr. T. F. Tsiang, who as the representative of Nationalist China has the right of veto in the Council, said that he did not object to a Security Council discussion but that he would oppose an invitation to Communist China.

Dr. Tsiang did not say whether he would carry his fight against an invitation to Communist China to the point of trying to invoke the "double veto." On Nov. 1950, when the Council, despite his negative vote, invited Communist China to take part in the debate on its charge that the United States had committed "aggression" in Korea.

Under the "double veto," a great power delegate can use his veto to compel the Council to consider a matter veto-able. He then may cast a second veto to consider technicalities would prevent. However, some delegates believe that other technicalities would prevent Dr. Tsiang from making the attempt. Communist China, of course, is

Continued on Page 7, Column 2

A PLEA TO KREMLIN

Envoy Asks Molotov to Prevent Hostilities in the Far East

By CLIFTON DANIEL
Special to The New York Times.

MOSCOW, Jan. 28—Britain asked the Soviet Union today to use its influence with Communist China to prevent any incident that might lead to "general hostilities" in the Far East.

At the same time the Ambassador said that with United States approval an invitation might be issued for the Peiping Government to attend the United Nations Security Council for the first time to discuss the issues that were threatening the peace.

London's extraordinary appeal was delivered to Vyacheslav M. Molotov in the Kremlin by Sir William Hayter, the British Ambassador.

The Foreign Minister made no immediate response to the proposals presented by the Ambassador but remarked that if the United States would "cease its aggressive actions in the area of Formosa this would help to decrease international tension."

Mr. Molotov at the same time said the Soviet Government was ready to give support to measures really directed toward the preservation of peace and reduction of international tension and would consider the British proposals.

Britain specifically requested that the Soviet Union support New Zealand's motion to submit the Formosa dispute to the United Nations Security Council and urge the Peiping Government to accept an invitation to attend the council meeting that the New Zealand delegation proposes to extend.

Danger to Peace Seen

The Ambassador said that not only Britain and New Zealand but the United States was supporting such an invitation.

In general Sir William told Mr. Molotov that the British Government believed that the present situation in the Formosa area "represents serious danger to peace" and that it behooved everyone to "show maximum restraint in their actions as well as their public statements."

Sir William, at his own request, called on Mr. Molotov at 1 o'clock and remained for half an hour. Delivering an oral statement, the Ambassador informed Mr. Molotov that Humphrey Trevelyan, British chargé d'affaires at Peiping, was informing the Chinese Communist Government of New Zealand's intention to raise the Formosa issue in the Security Council.

Later the Foreign Ministry's secretary informed the British Embassy that an account of the interview would be published tomorrow in the Soviet press. The embassy thereupon gave out its own story of the meeting.

The two versions agreed very closely with each other but the Soviet version released tonight by Tass was longer and if anything presented the British argu-

Continued on Page 2, Column 4

Beck Bids President Study Welfare Funds

By A. H. RASKIN
Special to The New York Times.

MIAMI BEACH, Jan. 28—A top union official recommended today that President Eisenhower appoint a special commission to investigate welfare fund abuses.

The suggestion came from Dave Beck, president of the International Brotherhood of Teamsters, A. F. L., in a news conference at the final session of the mid-winter meeting of the union's executive board.

The union, largest in the country, has been a major target in recent Congressional and state investigations into welfare racketeering by unions, employes and insurance companies.

Mr. Beck charged that all these inquiries had been conducted by "politicians playing football with welfare programs for their own personal interests." "I favor the selection of

Continued on Page 16, Column 4

Britain's Formosa Solution Is Two Chinas, Both in U. N.

Eden's Conciliatory Tone to Reds Held to Presage Ultimate Policy Aim

By DREW MIDDLETON
Special to The New York Times.

LONDON, Jan. 28—Sir Anthony Eden spoke in a conciliatory vein toward Communist China tonight in urging United Nations action on the Formosa issue.

The tone of the Foreign Secretary's remarks reflects the Government's fear that the Communists will refuse to attend a discussion of a cease-fire in the Formosa area. This discussion, to prevent "a spread of hostilities and the outbreak of war," is the "immediate" purpose of British policy, Sir Anthony said.

The United Nations will not ask Peiping to surrender what it considers to be its rights in the Far East crisis, he said.

The Foreign Secretary asserted that this conflict in Asia against the United Nations forces would weigh against it in a discussion of the crisis with the Security Council.

The ultimate purpose of British policy, it is understood, is the establishment of a State of Formosa under President Chiang Kai-shek and the inclusion of

Associated Press
Sir Anthony Eden

both Communist and Nationalist Chinese states in the United Nations.

Sir Anthony, in his attempt to induce the Communists to attend the Security Council meeting has gone too far, some observers said.

For instance, Peiping regards

Continued on Page 2, Column 4

Air and Sea Forces of U. S. On War Basis in Far East

Planes Are Redeployed

By ROBERT TRUMBULL
Special to The New York Times.

TOKYO, Jan. 28—It has become apparent that the United States Air Force has gone onto a full war basis in this area.

It is ready to strike anywhere with all the weapons at its command if the Communists attack. The Air Force has redeployed its strength in the Far East, including the dispatch of a potent fighter-bomber wing to bolea-guered Formosa. So it is natural that the boys who may have to fight are thinking of their weapons. The atomic bomb figures prominently in this thought.

The most responsible opinion holds that there is not going to be any war, but no chances are being taken.

It is a popular opinion here that if the United States really wants to stop an enemy's air force, the way to do it is to lay an atomic bomb on each of his bases.

South Korea as a Base

Since the Red Chinese Air Force would have to operate largely from the complex of airfields surrounding Shanghai, it occurs to an American flier that the thing to do in the event of hostilities is to strike with atomic weapons from South Korea, the nearest place from which to hit Shanghai and other inviting Communist targets.

Short of using atomic bombs, veterans foresee another long, hard war of attrition before the enemy can be bested in the air with conventional weapons. This is in spite of the fact that United States airmen are confident that their jet fighters, which proved their superiority over Russian types in Korea, can handle the odds against them in number of planes now available to both sides in the Far East.

It is estimated on good authority that the United States Far East Air Force, consisting of fourteen wings, has immediately nearly 900 fighters and about 120 bombers, or 1,000 battle types. Against this the Red Chinese, Russians and North Koreans together are thought to have based in this area more than 5,000 - third types.

The Air Force figures exclude planes of the Strategic Air Command and 300 to 400 on Seventh Fleet carriers.

Numerous moves have been made in readiness for whatever kind of war might come. It is already known to the Neutral Nations Supervisory Commission and therefore presumably also to the Communists, that the Far East Air Force recently dispatched a squadron of F-86 Sabrejet fighters and another squad-

Continued on Page 4, Column 3

The Navy Is Confident

By ALLEN DRURY
Special to The New York Times.

WASHINGTON, Jan. 28—Secretary Charles S. Thomas said today the Navy could handle "the situation in the Formosan Straits or any other emergency."

And he declared that if a major war should occur "now, or in the future," the Navy could withstand the initial onslaught and build rapidly to full mobilization.

Mr. Thomas appeared before the House Armed Services Committee to testify on proposed budget cuts. These would reduce the fleet 100 ships and reduce the Navy by 62,000 men and the Marine Corps by 31,000 by the end of 1956.

"To be specific in regard to the current and urgent issue," the Secretary told the committee, "the Navy at present strength can, in my opinion, adequately cope with any local naval actions with respect to the limited area of the Formosan Straits.

"If a major conflict should occur now or in the future, this naval program is still designed to withstand the initial onslaught, to contribute immediately to the nation's retaliatory power, and to provide a base for full and rapid mobilization."

Expanding on his testimony,

Continued on Page 4, Column 3

Soviet Offers Japan End to State of War

Special to The New York Times.

TOKYO, Saturday, Jan. 29—Moscow has made overtures to the Japanese Government for ending the state of war between the two countries.

A note said to be from Vyacheslav M. Molotov, Soviet Foreign Minister, to Japanese Premier Ichiro Hatoyama, delivered Tuesday by the head of the unofficial Soviet mission here, is understood to have raised for a peace settlement.

These issues include title to the Habomai and Shikotan Islands off the northernmost main Japanese island of Hokkaido. The Soviet has occupied these outposts since the end of World War II.

A Foreign Ministry official said the note as received in English translation was undated and unsigned. As such,

Continued on Page 2, Column 7

CURBS ARE BEATEN

Fail by Big Margins— President Will Sign Resolution Today

By ELIE ABEL
Special to The New York Times.

WASHINGTON, Jan. 28—The Senate tonight overwhelmingly authorized President Eisenhower to take war action, if need be, in defense of Formosa.

The vote was 85 to 3. Only Senators Herbert H. Lehman, Democrat of New York, William Langer, Republican of North Dakota, and Wayne Morse, Oregon Independent, were recorded against the resolution. Forty-three Democrats and 42 Republicans voted for it.

The Senate struck down three attempts to limit the President's powers. It then completed Congressional action on the joint resolution, passed 409 to 3 by the House of Representatives last Tuesday.

President Eisenhower will sign the measure in the White House at 8:30 A. M. tomorrow, James C. Hagerty, White House press secretary, said there would be no comment from the White House before that time.

Eight Senators not voting were announced as for the resolution. They were Dennis Chavez of New Mexico, J. Allen Frear of Delaware, John F. Kennedy of Massachusetts, Matthew M. Neely of West Virginia and Lyndon B. Johnson of Texas, Democrats, and Charles E. Potter of Michigan, Ralph E. Flanders of Vermont and John W. Bricker of Ohio.

Provisions of Resolution

Tonight's roll-call vote endorses the President's authority to:

¶Order United States armed forces into action "as he deems necessary for the specific purpose of securing and protecting Formosa and the Pescadores against armed attack."

¶Use the force of United States arms to deny the Chinese Communists possession of "such related positions and territories of that area now in friendly hands" such as the Quemoy and Matsu island groups.

The Senate went along with the President's request after three days of debate, in which opponents of the measure warned that the United States was risking open war with Communist China by extending its protective shield to disputed islands off the Chinese mainland.

Although the Senate's endorsement was overwhelming, many who voted "aye" did so with misgivings and doubt about the wisdom of the course President Eisenhower had charted last Monday in his message to Congress.

The outcome was certain from the start of the debate. President Eisenhower helped to shrink the opposition when he announced yesterday that he had delegated to no one the power of decision and would keep a tight rein on the use of sea and air forces for strictly defensive purposes.

Some Senators Persuaded

The assurance from the President helped persuade some of the worried Senators to back the resolution. Another factor was their fear that a "nay" would be interpreted abroad as signifying a lack of united determination in the United States Government.

The temper of the Senate was reflected in the overwhelming majorities with which it mustered against attempts to vote President Eisenhower less authority than he had asked.

First to be defeated, 83 to 3, was the amendment offered by Senator Langer to forbid the sending of United States armed forces onto the Chinese mainland or nearer than twelve miles from the coast.

The only Senators to vote for this limitation were Senators Langer, Lehman and Morse.

The Senate also rejected, 75 to 11, a substitute resolution by Senator Estes Kefauver, Democrat of Tennessee.

The Senate then struck down a third amendment, offered by Senator Hubert H. Humphrey, Democrat of Minnesota, 74 to 13. This proposal, taken over by Senator Lehman after Mr. Humphrey

Continued on Page 3, Column 3

A Subtropic Bittern Braves City Cold

Bittern on East Eighty-first Street fire escape. An Audubon view: "Almost unbelievable."

Marsh Recluse, Far Off Trail, Sleeps on Fire Escape Here

By JACK ROTH

A bird that ought to be in a marsh in Florida or Georgia amid pickerel weed and water lilies was seen yesterday in mid-Manhattan. It was watched for two and a half hours before it flew away.

After careful inspection from a respectful distance, two members of the National Audubon Society excitedly agreed they were looking at "an almost unbelievable sight"—an American bittern on an East Eighty-first Street fire escape on the winter's coldest day.

The society was called to the scene by Miss Babette New, of 23 East Eighty-first Street, between Madison and Fifth Avenues. Miss New, who has a terrace apartment, opened a door at 9:30 A. M. to let her dog out.

The New York Times (by Ernest Sisto)
The inveterate hermit of the heron family leaves urban perch.

There on a fence was a two-foot, drab brown bird with green legs, standing stiff as a rod.

The bird flew to the fire escape when it saw the dog. There it remained motionless, apparently asleep, long after the Audubon people began watching it.

Andrew Bihun Jr., advertising manager of the society's maga-

Continued on Page 16, Column 5

"All the News That's Fit to Print"

The New York Times.

LATE CITY EDITION
Partly cloudy today. Considerable cloudiness and milder tomorrow.
Temperature Range Today—Max., 41; Min., 33
Temperatures Yesterday—Max., 38; Min., 27
Full U. S. Weather Bureau Report, Page 55

Copyright, 1955, by The New York Times Company.

VOL. CIV..No. 35,445.

Entered as Second-Class Matter.
Post Office, New York, N. Y.

NEW YORK, WEDNESDAY, FEBRUARY 9, 1955.

Times Square, New York 36, N. Y.
Telephone Lackawanna 4-1000

FIVE CENTS

BULGANIN IS PREMIER AS MALENKOV RESIGNS, BUT KHRUSHCHEV IS VIEWED AS REAL LEADER; MOLOTOV, WARNING U. S., CLAIMS H-BOMB LEAD

EISENHOWER ASKS 7 BILLION PROGRAM TO BUILD SCHOOLS

Message to Congress Urges Federal-State-Local Plan for Grants and Loans

DEMOCRATS DECRY SCOPE

Leaders Denounce Proposal as 'Makeshift' — Demand Far Larger Expenditures

Text of the President's message is printed on Page 20.

By W. H. LAWRENCE
Special to The New York Times.

WASHINGTON, Feb. 8—President Eisenhower proposed today a three-year $7,000,000,000 Federal-state-local school construction program.

He asked Congress to make available $220,000,000 in Federal grants and about $900,000,000 in loans to meet a current deficit of more than 300,000 school classrooms.

The message went to a Democratic-controlled Congress. Leaders in the education field in both the Senate and the House called it inadequate and "makeshift."

Some critics declared the Presidential program would be ineffective in about one-fourth of the states, which have constitutional limitations on incurring or increasing debts.

Indirectly, President Eisenhower also suggested higher pay for school teachers, but his message advanced no concrete proposals on this. He said low pay was a factor in the shortage of teachers, which he declared was "less obvious but ultimately more dangerous than the classroom shortage."

"Because of the magnitude of the job, but more fundamentally because of the undeniable importance of free education to a free way of life, the states must take to provide our children with proper classrooms must be weighed most carefully," the President said, continuing:

"The phrase 'free education' is a debatable choice. For unless education continues to be free—

Continued on Page 20, Column 1

A. E. C. WON'T DROP DIXON-YATES PACT

2-1 Vote Disclosed by Board —Congress Plea Rejected

By WILLIAM M. BLAIR

WASHINGTON, Feb 8—By a 2 to 1 vote, the Atomic Energy Commission has turned down a Democratic demand that the Dixon-Yates private power contract be canceled.

The split vote, taken on Saturday, followed the lead of President Eisenhower, who asserted three days before the vote that he would not withdraw the controversial contract to feed private power into the Tennessee Valley Authority.

Lewis L. Strauss, A. E. C. chairman, and Dr. Willard Frank Libby, a new member, voted to stick by the contract. Thomas E. Murray voted for cancellation.

As Mr. Strauss disclosed the decision today, Mr. Murray went before the Joint Congressional Committee on Atomic Energy to renew his charge that the Dixon-Yates controversy had interfered with the commission's primary job of developing atomic weapons and peacetime uses of the atom.

His main concern, he testified, was "whether we will in the future maintain our present position of world leadership in the nuclear field." He concluded:

"The attention the commission today gives to making policy de-

Continued on Page 37, Column 6

President Appeals For Satellite People

Special to The New York Times.

WASHINGTON, Feb. 8—President Eisenhower urged tonight a continuing effort to "intensify the will for freedom in the satellite countries behind the Iron Curtain."

He spoke from the White House on a closed-circuit television program in behalf of the Crusade for Freedom, which operates Radio Free Europe and the Free Europe Press. The crusade hopes to raise $10,000,000 this year.

He took no cognizance of the resignation of Georgi M. Malenkov as Soviet Premier and his replacement by Marshal Nikolai A. Bulganin. His prepared text was left unchanged after the Moscow developments had become known.

The President emphasized that the masses imprisoned behind the Iron Curtain would remain potential deterrents to

Continued on Page 6, Column 6

HOUSE, 394-4, BACKS DRAFT EXTENSION

Four-Year Continuance Finds the Democrats Unanimous —New Features Added

By C. P. TRUSSELL
Special to The New York Times.

WASHINGTON, Feb. 8—The House of Representatives voted 394 to 4 today to continue the draft for four years.

This extension, the fourth since 1940, was urged by President Eisenhower. The Administration concluded that the international situation generally required the maintenance of the United States armed forces of 2,850,000 officers and men. Such a force, experience had shown, could not be mobilized through voluntary enlistments.

The four who voted against draft extension were Republicans. Democrats supported the move unanimously. The four dissenters were Representatives Noah M. Mason of Illinois, Usher L. Burdick of North Dakota; Clare E. Hoffman of Michigan, and Wint Smith of Kansas.

The extension measure now goes to the Senate. There it is expected to win approval, with its opponents again on the Republican side. No one predicted that the extension would be approved finally in Congress long before the present draft authorization expires June 30.

In granting the continuance of Selective Service the House added new features to the law. They included:

¶If the selective draft continued it should include all the benefits and allowance given to present draftees to aid their dependents. Also continued for four

Continued on Page 16, Column 4

Private Atom Reactor In This Area Planned

By PETER KIHSS

A plan for the nation's first nuclear reactor entirely owned and operated by private industry was announced here yesterday by the American Machine and Foundry Company. It would use radiations for confidential experiments for co-operating companies.

Gen. Walter Bedell Smith, retired, vice chairman of the foundry concern's board, said invitations to join the scheme had gone to companies in the fields of electronics, petroleum, food, pharmaceutical and chemical products, ceramics, rubber, metals, textiles, agriculture, machinery and others.

The project would occupy 250 acres somewhere in the New York area. A so-called swimming pool reactor would use uranium fuel surrounded by water serving as a moderator, cooler and shield.

The atomic furnace would

Continued on Page 19, Column 3

MIGHT IS STRESSED

Foreign Minister Says Soviet Force Is on Par With West

Excerpts from Molotov speech are printed on Page 6.

Special to The New York Times.

MOSCOW, Feb. 8—Claiming superiority for the Soviet Union in hydrogen weapons, Foreign Minister Vyacheslav M. Molotov delivered to the United States today a warning of the strength of the world Communist forces.

His declaration reiterating the might of the Communist camp was made at a joint session of the Supreme Soviet, the national legislature of the Soviet Union. He spoke immediately following the change in Soviet Premiership that placed Marshal Nikolai A. Bulganin at the head of the Government.

[According to The Associated Press, the Soviet Parliament resumed its joint session at 2 A. M. Wednesday, New York time, and immediately began debating Mr. Molotov's speech. Laughter and applause greeted Mr. Molotov's taunts at, and defiance of, the United States, which he singled out as the leader of the "aggressive" Western coalition. He also called on the United States once again to evacuate Formosa.

Balance 'Quite Established'

In one of his most outspoken passages, Mr. Molotov declared that it must be understood that the balance of forces between the Soviet Union and the United States had been "quite established."

Comparing the two and taking into account the vast human and material resources of this country, the strength of its allies, and the justness of its cause, Mr. Molotov declared, "it will become clear that the Soviet Union is no weaker than the United States."

As for atomic strength, he said in an earlier passage that "the aggressive circles of the United States miscalculated again." They thought it would take ten or fifteen years for the Soviet Union to catch up with official holiday from all important business of ten days while Republican speakers celebrate the birthday of Abraham Lincoln.

but "the Soviet people have achieved such success that not the Soviet Union but the United States finds itself in the position of being behind."

In this belittling and challeng-

Continued on Page 6, Column 4

CHANGE IN HIGH SOVIET COUNCILS: The scene yesterday in Supreme Soviet at Moscow after Marshal Nikolai A. Bulganin was elected to succeed Georgi M. Malenkov. Front row, from left, are Lazar M. Kaganovich, Marshal Bulganin, Nikita S. Khrushchev, Mr. Malenkov and Marshal Kliment E. Voroshilov. At far right in rear is Anastas I. Mikoyan.

Associated Press Radiophoto

SENATE UNIT VOTES FORMOSA TREATY

Committee Ballot Is 11 to 2 —Whole Chamber May Adopt Pact by Tomorrow Night

By WILLIAM S. WHITE
Special to The New York Times.

WASHINGTON, Feb. 8—The Senate Foreign Relations Committee approved today the defense treaty with Nationalist China on Formosa. The vote was 11 to 2.

The committee's chairman, Senator Walter F. George, Democrat of Georgia, will take the pact to the Senate tomorrow in the hope that it can be cleared there by Thursday night.

Failing final action by then, there can be none before the week after next.

Beginning Friday, the Senate, by old custom, will have an un-

Continued on Page 14, Column 3

Khrushchev Comes to Fore In Compromise on Bulganin

The following article is by a member of The Times staff who is a specialist on Soviet affairs.

By HARRY SCHWARTZ

Nikita S. Khrushchev appeared to have emerged yesterday as the most powerful single person in the Soviet Union, the heir to Stalin's mantle.

Stalin ruled the Soviet Union during most of his reign without holding any Government post, content to be general secretary of the Communist party.

It was as first secretary, the new name for general secretary, of the party that Mr. Khrushchev nominated Nikolai A. Bulganin to be Premier. But the largest ovation went to the first secretary, not to the new Premier.

Even before yesterday, Mr. Khrushchev had given abundant testimony that he, not some amorphous "collective leadership," is the leader.

It may be that his power is subject still to the majority of his colleagues in the Presidium of the Central Committee or to the rest of the army leaders. But since last December the public image has been of a Mr. Khru-

Continued on Page 4, Column 5

This article is by a reporter of The Times who returned last fall after five years in Moscow.

By HARRISON E. SALISBURY

Marshal Nikolai A. Bulganin almost certainly is a compromise choice as Soviet Premier. He apparently represents a coalition of the party forces of Nikita S. Khrushchev and the army group headed by Marshal Georgi G. Zhukov.

The heralded showdown between Mr. Khrushchev and former Premier Georgi M. Malenkov has occurred more quickly than this observer had expected.

Apparently the army threw its backing to Mr. Khrushchev.

Regardless of the fire and vigor of Foreign Minister Vyacheslav M. Molotov's address yesterday, Soviet power in the international arena will remain weakened for a considerable time. The crisis that resulted in the execution of Deputy Premier Lavrenti P. Beria left little outward signs of cracks in the Kremlin wall. However, it seemed certain the Soviet Government would be a longer time in over-

Continued on Page 4, Column 7

U. S. SEES STRUGGLE AS FAR FROM OVER

Experts on Moscow Conclude It Is Too Early to Decide About Effect of Change

By JAMES RESTON
Special to The New York Times.

WASHINGTON, Feb. 8—The United States Government, concentrating on its plans for blocking Communist expansion, refused to comment today on the battle of the dictators in the Soviet Union.

The capital hummed with speculation all day. But after hours of cooperative guesswork the official experts on the Soviet Union decided to let events interpret the Moscow changes.

Ambassador Charles E. Bohlen's first official cablegram on the news came in at 7:49 A. M. It was discussed briefly by Secretary of State Dulles at his 9:15 staff conference.

Thereafter the official advisers on the Soviet Union were in less dogmatic than most opinion facts. Their conclusions—far apart in the capital—were as follows:

¶There is trouble in the Soviet "paradise." Premier Georgi M. Malenkov was dismissed not because everything was going well; the dramatic news was a sign, not of Communist strength, but of weakness.

¶Nikita S. Khrushchev, the Communist party boss, is probably the most powerful figure for the moment. But the fierce struggle over succession, always a problem in Russia, even in the time of the czars, is far from over.

¶It is too early to reach any

Continued on Page 7, Column 1

U. S. Plane Downed By Reds in Tachens

By The Associated Press.

WITH UNITED STATES SEVENTH FLEET, in the Tachens, Wednesday, Feb. 9—Red anti-aircraft batteries shot down a United States AD Skyraider plane twenty miles southwest of the Tachen Islands today, the Navy said.

The pilot and two crew members of the carrier-based plane were rescued by the destroyer Isbell, the Navy said.

The Navy released a terse message from Vice Admiral Alfred M. Pride:

"Vice Admiral Pride learned during the last day of evacuation that three small holes were discovered in one wing during inspection after returning to base."

MOSCOW SHAKE-UP

Malenkov Avows Guilt for Shortcomings in Agriculture

Texts of Malenkov statement and Khrushchev speech, Page 2.

By CLIFTON DANIEL
Special to The New York Times.

MOSCOW, Feb. 8—On nomination by Nikita S. Khrushchev, first secretary of the Communist party, Marshal Nikolai A. Bulganin became head of the Soviet Government today. He replaced Georgi M. Malenkov, who had been Premier since the death of Stalin March 5, 1953.

Reproaching himself for inadequate leadership, Mr. Malenkov offered his resignation this afternoon to the Supreme Soviet, national legislature of the Soviet Union.

[News of the resignation was published in a Late C..y Extra of The New York Times on Tuesday.]

Mr. Malenkov said he would fulfill "with greatest scrupulousness" the duties that would now be assigned to him. Those duties were not stated at once.

In resigning Mr. Malenkov took on himself the "guilt and responsibility" for the present state of Soviet agriculture, which had been roundly criticized by Mr. Khrushchev.

To Support Party Line

Mr. Malenkov also proclaimed his understanding of the Communist party line that forced development of heavy industry must be the basis for increasing agricultural production and all other branches of the Soviet economy. That line has recently been re-emphasized with new firmness by the Central Committee of the party and its propaganda organs.

The Central Committee's decision, taken in the last days of January on the initiative of Mr. Khrushchev, gave orders for still further efforts to increase Soviet agricultural output and Mr. Malenkov said today the decision had revealed to him his shortcomings as an administrator.

The change in the Premiership, accomplished in barely ten minutes of swift political action, left two major questions unanswered for the moment:

What will be Mr. Malenkov's future position and who will be Defense Minister of the Soviet

Continued on Page 2, Column 3

TUNIS LEADER AIDS PINAY ON CABINET

U.S. Bipartisan Idea Adapted by Premier-Designate

By LANSING WARREN
Special to The New York Times.

PARIS, Feb. 8—Premier-designate Antoine Pinay obtained some help today from the Tunisian Premier in his efforts to form a French Cabinet.

After their conference the Tunisian Premier, Tahar ben Ammar, said he had found that he and M. Pinay had similar ideas and that "I hope we shall continue the negotiations that were started with the Government of Mendès-France." M. ben Ammar declared that he was going full of optimism to Tunis to inform the Bey, Sidi Mohammed el Amin, about the consultations.

The statement will be used by M. Pinay in trying to convince the party groups that his Cabinet can handle the crisis in Tunisia.

In dealing with those groups today M. Pinay obtained support from M. Mendès-France's Radical group, but met a rebuff from the Socialists. The Radical executive voted, 81 to 67, to participate in the Pinay Cabinet. This opposed the invitation of the seventy-six Radical Deputies, who never vote in unison.

The Socialists, through Christian Pineau, former Minister of Finance, declined the invitation to join the Cabinet. M. Pinay had

Continued on Page 11, Column 3

All Civilians Off Upper Tachen; First U. S. Ship Returns to Formosa

American and Chinese military personnel, in the foreground, observe the evacuation operation on Upper Tachen Island.

Associated Press Wirephoto via Radio From Taipei

Special to The New York Times.

KEELUNG, Formosa, Wednesday, Feb. 9—The first United States Navy ship with Chinese Nationalist civilians evacuated from the Tachen Islands docked here this morning. She was an 8,000-ton transport with 3,816 civilians on board. Vice Admiral Alfred M. Pride, Commander of the United States Seventh Fleet, announced last night that the evacuation of civilians from Upper Tachen Island was completed at 5:17 P. M. yesterday. [In Washington, the Navy announced early Wednesday that the Seventh Fleet had reported that the last "organized group" of civilians had been evacuated from South Tachen Island, The

"All the News That's Fit to Print"

The New York Times.

LATE CITY EDITION
Chance of some showers and mild today, tonight and tomorrow.
Temperature Range Today—Max.: 65; Min.: 47
Temperature Yesterday—Max.: 65; Min.: 43
Full U.S. Weather Bureau Report, Page 20

VOL. CIV. No. 35,501.

Entered as Second-Class Matter,
Post Office, New York, N. Y.

NEW YORK, WEDNESDAY, APRIL 6, 1955.

Times Square, New York 36, N. Y.
Telephone LAckawanna 4-1000

FIVE CENTS

Copyright, 1955, by The New York Times Company.

MANPOWER SLASH IN MARINES, NAVY BACKED WITH 'IFS'

Carney and Shepherd Call Reduced Budget Adequate if No Emergency Occurs

DEMOCRATS CONCERNED

But They Are Assured Corps' Ability to Strike Quickly in an Attack Won't Suffer

By C. P. TRUSSELL
Special to The New York Times.

WASHINGTON, April 5—Top uniformed officers of the Navy and Marine Corps supported the President's reduced armed services budget today. At points, they appeared to be salting loyalty to the Commander in Chief with reservations.

The $34,000,000,000 budget for the fiscal year starting July 1, it seemed, was all right as of now. It was evident, however, that if the "international situation worsened, more money would be requested in a hurry.

Those testifying before a Senate Appropriations subcommittee were Gen. Lemuel C. Shepherd Jr., Commandant of the Marine Corps, and Admiral Robert B. Carney, Chief of Naval Operations.

Meanwhile, more civilian heads of the armed services continued to support the reduced budget. They included Charles S. Thomas, Secretary of the Navy, and Harold E. Talbott, Secretary of the Air Force.

A spokesman for Robert T. Stevens, Secretary of the Army, is expected to back the other civilian leaders tomorrow. Mr. Stevens is out of the country.

Frank Answers Sought

Democrats of the subcommittee, which is headed by Senator Dennis Chavez, Democrat of New Mexico, continued to search for blunt answers from the uniformed officers as to how they felt about the military cuts.

The Democrats do not like proposed cuts in Marine Corps forces. General Shepherd was asked how he squared his support of a reduction in the armed forces with the mission of the Marine Corps to be the first to fight in case of an attack.

"It is manifest," he replied, "that reductions of the magnitude with which we are confronted [a cut from 215,000 to 193,-000] involve some sacrifice.

"However, we are determined that the sacrifice will not be made in readiness of our basic striking forces. The reduction will be absorbed primarily by disbanding certain reinforcing combat and logistic units and by reducing the manning levels of other supporting units.

"Operationally, the effect of these actions will be to diminish somewhat the striking power of

Continued on Page 14, Column 2

JERSEY SEIZES 62 IN HOT-ROD TRAP

Racers Caught on Unlighted Road Used as Speedway

Special to The New York Times.

CHATSWORTH, N. J., April 5—It's a rare man who can lay hands on a will-o'-the-wisp, especially if it's motor-powered. Yet that's what State Trooper Leonard Miller did under a bright moon last night.

For weeks now, nocturnal travelers through the lonely pine lands of Burlington County have been frightened almost off the highway by dabs of light whooshing past them at breakneck speed.

The police, who had their suspicions about the souped-up will-o'-the-wisp, were hard put to track them down. One night the reports came from here, the next from there. Always the apparition appeared from unlighted stretches along Route 72, which runs from the center of the state to the coast. Among other attractions for hot-rodders it has a fourteen-mile stretch that is almost ruler-straight.

Last night the state troopers set a trap along a section that was without highway lamps but bright in the moonlight.

Local chapters may work out their own program, headquarters said. They may get all their funds from the United Drive, merely retaining the "right" to their own drive.

Since most United Fund Drives

Continued on Page 22, Column 2

Harriman and Wagner Plan Own City-State Fiscal Study

Financing by a Private Foundation May Be Sought for Project Ignored by the Legislature, Mayor Announces

By CHARLES G. BENNETT

Governor Harriman and Mayor Wagner will go ahead soon with the appointment of a committee to make a long-range study of state-city fiscal relationships. It is possible that funds will be sought from a private foundation for the study.

Mayor Wagner announced this yesterday as he discussed the city's fiscal situation in an interview in his office, 63 Park Row, and later before 300 members of the Bond Club at a luncheon at 120 Broadway. He forecast that Republicans as well as Democrats would be invited to serve on the fiscal study committee.

The Mayor expressed hope that the committee would find a formula for taking the whole city-state financial problem "entirely out of politics." He predicted that the prestige of the study committee members would be so great that the state Legislature could not afford to ignore its suggestions.

At its session just ended, the Legislature failed to take any action creating a legislative commission to make the state-city financial study. Mayor Wagner, backed by the Governor, had called for such a survey in an effort to end the recurring crises that send the Mayor and his aides to Albany each year seeking state aid and authorizing new tax increases.

At his interview yesterday Mayor Wagner commented that the city had had more cooperation than usual from the Legislature in approval of city bills.

At the same time he noted that the Legislature had helped to solve city fiscal woes for "this year only" and that the city financial measures did "not call

Continued on Page 21, Column 3

Canada Cuts Income Taxes In a Bid to Spur Prosperity

By RAYMOND DANIELL
Special to The New York Times.

OTTAWA, April 5—The Canadian Government decided tonight to cut taxes. The national debt will be increased in the interest of national prosperity. Indirect and direct personal and corporate income taxes were cut to increase purchasing power and investment capital, with the advance knowledge that the Government would be collecting less than it plans to spend.

This is in accord with the expressed Liberal policy of taxing for surpluses in good and prosperous times and accepting a deficit when business, agriculture and industry run into trouble. The Canadian economy is not in serious trouble, but unemployment, a slowing down of industry and a drop in farm income have raised danger signals.

Tonight, in presenting his first budget as Minister of Finance, Walter Harris, in spite of an un-expected deficit of nearly $150,-000,000 last year, proposed new tax cuts that will reduce the Government's revenues by about $207,000,000 in a full year based on normal expectations of increased prosperity.

Mr. Harris proposed a new schedule of rates to reduce the personal income tax by 12 to 13 per cent for 85 per cent of the country's taxpayers. There are 3,800,000 persons in this category in this country of 15,000,-000 inhabitants.

This, of course, will add to the country's national debt. This, Mr. Harris asserted, should be no cause for alarm. He was taking into account an expected rise in the country's revenues as a product of about 5 per cent, Mr. Harris said, in reducing the scale of taxes. With more wealth being produced, he said, it was possible to reduce

Continued on Page 12, Column 5

RED CROSS EASES FUND DRIVE RULES

Permits Chapters to Join in Community Campaigns Under Some Conditions

By The Associated Press.

WASHINGTON, April 5—The American National Red Cross announced today that it had relaxed its rules so that under certain conditions local chapters could participate in Community or United Fund raising drives.

Most Red Cross chapters have refused to become a part of fund-raising campaigns such as Community Chest and United Fund Drives. In these, welfare agencies are grouped. Each receives a percentage of the funds raised.

E. Roland Harriman, national Red Cross chairman, said the board of governors had adopted the policy yesterday.

With the changes, he said, Red Cross chapters will be able to plan in a more direct and helpful manner with other agencies and community leaders in matters of united or federated fund raising."

The board said the United States Government had established the American National Red Cross as this nation's official volunteer agency under the Geneva conventions. It added that this "unique and official" status made certain conditions of fund-raising necessary.

Units Control Own Budgets

The board said each local Red Cross chapter would keep its rights:

"To determine and control its budget and goal.

"To conduct a roll-call for members and funds in the month designated by the board of governors.

"To conduct emergency campaigns in disaster, war or other unforeseen need when authorized by the board of governors.

"To issue a membership card to each person from whose contribution the Red Cross received $1 or more.

The amended policy keeps the provision that all chapters will "participate in annual campaigns for members and funds for the purpose of enrolling members and obtaining adequate voluntary contributions to finance the budgetary requirements of the chapters and the national organization."

Red Cross headquarters here said it would be possible for a local chapter to participate in a United Fund Drive and also conduct its own campaign later if needed to reach its goal.

Local chapters may work out

Continued on Page 12, Column 5

---

3 Hefty Councilmen in Small Cab Say Rule on Front Seat Must Go

Six hundred and thirty-five pounds of City Councilmen found themselves uncomfortably squeezed recently into the back seat of one of the new small taxicabs. In front, the seat next to the driver beckoned, empty and inviting. Under the law, nothing could be done about it. The Councilmen had to stay put. The Councilmen—there were three—decided "there ought to be a law." So now there probably will be.

The legislation authorizing the stock-car five-passenger cabs (driver and four fares, maximum) specifies that a passenger may legally ride in front with the driver only if there is a full complement of three in back. The law says nothing about the sizes and weights of these back-seat riders.

Yesterday, "Fat Man's Amendment" was introduced in the City Council to distribute the small-taxi fare weight more evenly.

The amendment, referred to the Council's General Welfare Committee, would permit a passenger to ride in front with either two or three passengers on the back seat. The sponsors of the amendment were Edward A. Cunningham, Bronx Democrat, and John J. Merli, Manhattan Democrat.

Mr. Cunningham, who weighs 225 pounds, was one of the three Councilmen who took the back-seat ride in discomfort. The others were James J. Murphy, Staten Island Democrat, weighing in at 216 pounds, and James J. Boland, Manhattan Democrat, a mere 200-pounder.

There was no ready explanation as to why Mr. Merli, who tips the beam at substantially less than 200 pounds, was a co-sponsor of the amendment. Other Councilmen guessed that he was "just going along for the ride."

Councilman Cunningham, in explaining his bill after yesterday's Council session, said that the proposed amendment would be of aid not only to overweight passengers but also to women burdened with bundles. Referring to the plight of Mr. Murphy, Mr. Boland and himself, Mr. Cunningham said:

"When three fat guys like us try to squeeze into the back seat of one of these small-sized cabs it is a tight fit, and something has to give."

Since Mr. Boland was not at yesterday's Council session and Mr. Cunningham and Mr. Murphy left City Hall soon after the meeting, it was impossible to

Continued on Page 26, Column 5

WEST BIG 3 BAR AUSTRIAN ACCORD WITH SOVIET ONLY

Joint Declaration Advises Both Vienna and Moscow Big 4 Approval Is Needed

Special to The New York Times.

WASHINGTON, April 5—The Western Big Three cautioned Austria and the Soviet Union today against making bilateral commitments on the terms of an Austrian state treaty.

The United States, Britain and France issued a joint declaration noting that conclusion of the long-pending pact was of concern to all of the "Big Four powers as well as Austria.

If the Soviet Union should offer "proposals which hold clear promise of the restoration of freedom and independence to Austria, these would appropriately be discussed by the four Ambassadors in Vienna with the participation of the Austrian Government," the joint declaration said. It was made public simultaneously here and in London and Paris.

While it was not specifically directed to either the Moscow or Vienna Government, the statement was interpreted here as advice to both on the Western Big Three's attitude toward the Soviet-Austrian meeting scheduled for next week in Moscow.

West Wary on Concessions

The Western Big Three were understood to be particularly concerned lest Julius Raab, the Austrian Chancellor, make concessions to the Soviet Union that would be unacceptable to them.

Chancellor Raab and a delegation of Austrian officials will fly to Moscow Monday to discuss new ways of arriving at a treaty. The mission is being undertaken at the March 24 invitation of Vyacheslav M. Molotov, Soviet Foreign Minister.

One way a guarantee of Austrian independence that would prevent another Anschluss, or union, between Austria and Germany.

The other was an expression of Austria's willingness to guarantee that she would not join any military alliance or allow her territory to be used for foreign military bases.

The West has never opposed military neutrality for Austria and never has planned to include Austria in the North Atlantic alliance. The concern is more over a possible attempt by the Soviet Union to insist on unacceptable guarantee terms with respect to either or both of Mr. Molotov's points.

In the past, one of the main barriers to a pact restoring Austria's freedom and ending the four-power occupation has been the Soviet Union's insistence on the maintenance of occupation troops until a German treaty has been completed.

The text of today's three-power declaration follows:

"For many years the Governments of the United Kingdom, the United States and France have sought to conclude an Austrian state treaty. They have made ceaseless efforts thus to bring about the restoration of

Continued on Page 12, Column 3

DULLES SAYS U. S. WON'T START WAR

Holds Any Conflict in Formosa Area Would Be Reds' Doing —Restates Quemoy Stand

By DANA ADAMS SCHMIDT
Special to The New York Times.

WASHINGTON, April 5—Secretary of State Dulles said today that if there was war in the Formosa Strait it would be the Communist Chinese who started it.

The United States, he asserted, has made "perfectly clear" its desire for a cease-fire and peace in the strait. But the Chinese Communists, he declared, unfortunately do not seem to be much under the influence of the peace propaganda they disseminate.

The Secretary made his observations in reply to a request for an assessment of the prospects for war or peace in the Formosa Strait at the first news conference he has held since March 15.

"To answer that question would require me to read the minds of people to whom I have no access, that is, the Communist leaders in Peiping," Mr. Dulles observed.

The Secretary was asked about continuing demands in Congress that the United States make known now whether it will defend Quemoy and Matsu Islands against Communist attack. Mr. Dulles said he knew the answer to that one by heart. There was no commitment of any kind, sort or description, expressed or implied, he declared, binding the United States to the defense of anything except Formosa and the Pescadores.

'Very Difficult Ground'

The suggestion that the United States should announce now it proposed to fulfill its treaty commitments entered onto "very difficult ground," he said. He did not see how it could be done.

The Secretary observed that the United States also had a commitment to defend the United States of America but no one had yet asked for a commitment as to how that would be done.

Asked whether that meant the United States would not fight for the defense of Quemoy and Matsu for the sake of the morale of Chinese Nationalist troops in Formosa, he replied that it would not, "unless that was vital for the defense of Formosa and the Pescadores. It all comes back to that."

President Eisenhower has told Congress that he and he alone would make the decision whether the United States should help defend Quemoy and Matsu. He said his decision would depend on whether the invasion of the offshore islands was a preliminary to invasion of Formosa or the Pescadores.

While Mr. Dulles was speaking to the press, Secretary of the

Continued on Page 7, Column 5

ON WAY TO RETIREMENT: Sir Winston Churchill moist-eyed as he arrived in auto yesterday at Buckingham Palace to tender resignation as Prime Minister to Queen Elizabeth.
Associated Press Radiophoto

CHURCHILL QUITS AS PRIME MINISTER; DECLINES DUKEDOM TO STAY AN M. P.; EDEN TAKES OVER LEADERSHIP TODAY

President Declares Allies Still Will Heed Churchill

By W. H. LAWRENCE
Special to The New York Times.

WASHINGTON, April 5—President Eisenhower declared today that leaders of the free world were bound to seek Sir Winston Churchill's counsel and advice, even in retirement.

Democrats and Republicans joined the President in personal tributes to the retiring British Prime Minister.

There were formal statements from John Foster Dulles, Secretary of State; Vice President Richard M. Nixon, and from a host of Senate and House members.

The President went into the White House Rose Garden to record for newsreels and television cameras his personal tribute to his long-time associate in war and peace.

It is not usual for the head of the United States Government to express himself so feelingly when the head of another government resigns from office.

But Sir Winston's departure changed all the rules. The President spoke into the cameras in the obvious hope that the British statesman himself would see the pictures and hear the words.

"We have just had editorial word that my old and very dear friend, Sir Winston Churchill, has retired from his position as head of Her Majesty's Government in the United Kingdom," the President said.

"Naturally, an event such as this recalls to my mind many stirring incidents both of war and peace. I have greatly respected and valued my associations with a man so great as Winston Churchill.

"And now, if I dare, I should like to address a word directly to Sir Winston.

"All of us in the free world

Continued on Page 11, Column 7

Vietnam Dissidents Give Warning to U.S.

By ROBERT ALDEN
Special to The New York Times.

SAIGON, Vietnam, April 5—The groups fighting Vietnam's Government warned tonight that continued United States support of Premier Ngo Dinh Diem might lead to civil war.

They said that as far as they were concerned the truce was ended and that "all responsibility for bloodshed—Vietnamese and foreign—would rest on Ngo Dinh Diem."

It was further charged that the United States had turned over four tanks to the Government. As far as can be determined, the United States should help defend Quemoy and Matsu. He said his decision would depend do not have any tanks in Vietnam.

The Ngo Dinh Diem Cabinet voted today to stand firm in the face of the Opposition's threat. As the situation in Saigon grew more tense by the hour, officials made it known that the Government had

Continued on Page 12, Column 3

BRITISH ERA ENDS

Aged Statesman Tells Queen of Decision— Cabinet Shifts Due

By DREW MIDDLETON
Special to The New York Times.

LONDON, April 5—Sir Winston Churchill resigned as Prime Minister today. Age has done what Britain's enemies and his political rivals could not accomplish.

Tomorrow Queen Elizabeth II will summon Sir Anthony Eden to Buckingham Palace and ask him to form a new Government. Sir Anthony's accession as Prime Minister will mark the passing of the Churchill era.

While shadows lengthened on the palace lawns, Sir Winston stood talking with the Queen at her study window. Their business was his resignation. When the audience ended he passed out of the palace, through cheering ranks of his countrymen.

The most important change in British political life since the end of World War II was announced from Buckingham Palace in a single sentence:

"The Right Honorable Sir Winston Churchill had an audience of the Queen this evening and tendered his resignation as Prime Minister and First Lord of the Treasury, which Her Majesty was graciously pleased to accept."

Transition to Eden Era

Thus Sir Winston, Knight of the Garter, Privy Councilor, Order of Merit and Companion of Honor, left the office he has held at two different times for a total of eight years, seven months and twenty-five days.

While Sir Winston, who is 80 years old, bowed beaming to crowds shouting "Good old Winnie!" in Downing Street tonight, political London bubbled with anticipation.

When Sir Anthony is asked by the Queen tomorrow to form a Government, all, the Ministers will place their offices at his disposal. This will open the way to changes that, immediately or after the election, will change the Churchill Government into the Eden Government.

The decision on the date of a general parliamentary election is Sir Anthony's. Polls conducted by newspaper men in the House of Commons indicate that a great majority of the Members of Parliament expect that election will take place May 26.

If this date is chosen, the new

Continued on Page 11, Column 2

CHURCHILL BARS OFFER OF PEERAGE

Prefers to Stay Commoner. He Replies to Queen's Bid —Britons Acclaim Him

By BENJAMIN WELLES
Special to The New York Times.

LONDON, April 5—Sir Winston Churchill declined a dukedom today to remain in the House of Commons.

In an audience with Queen Elizabeth II in her study in Buckingham Palace, he tendered his resignation to his sovereign. The Queen accepted it and then offered him the highest titular dignity in the land. But Sir Winston, a grandson of the seventh Duke of Marlborough, humbly yet firmly declined it.

He had been a "House of Commons man" for almost fifty years, he recalled, and he preferred to remain one rather than accept a peerage and enter the House of Lords.

The decision showed that Sir Winston, after laying down the cares and responsibilities of high office, would continue as an elder statesman in the Commons, which he has loved—and which has intermittently loved him—during that half century.

Had Declined Earldom

It was not the first time Sir Winston, had turned down the offer of a peerage to remain in the lower but more powerful legislative chamber. In the aftermath of victory in 1945 he was offered an earldom, but refused it.

The 28-year-old Queen and the 80-year-old statesman each knew what was in the other's mind when they met today. He knew in advance what she would offer and she knew what his reply would be. But Elizabeth and Sir Winston, both exemplars of a tradition in tradition-loving land, observed the forms and courtesies due between the sovereign and a retiring counselor and friend.

The last non-royal dukedom was given to the Marquess of Westminster in 1874, the year of Sir Winston's birth. There are now twenty-six dukes in the United Kingdom peerage, in addition to the royal dukes—Edinburgh, Cornwall, Gloucester, Kent and Windsor.

Sir Winston's refusal of the proffered peerage means that his name will remain as it is. His resignation, as it affected His knighthood, acquired in 1953

Continued on Page 11, Column 5

SOUTH AFRICA OUT OF UNESCO RANKS

Quits United Nations Agency Over Racial Issue

By LEONARD INGALLS
Special to The New York Times.

JOHANNESBURG, South Africa, April 5—South Africa has withdrawn from the United Nations Educational, Scientific and Cultural Organization.

Eric H. Louw, Minister of External Affairs, said today in Capetown that it had been decided to terminate this country's participation in the United Nations agency because of its "interference in South Africa's racial problems."

He reported that the South African Ambassador in Paris had been instructed to inform the director of the United Nations agency of the Union's action. The decision to withdraw, Mr. Louw said, was made recently.

The Minister announced also that South Africa would not participate in deliberations in May before the International Court of Justice on its administration of the territory of South-West Africa under the League of Nations mandate. The territory was incorporated into South Africa in 1949.

This step of incorporation was not approved by the United Nations, which sought to have South Africa accept trusteeship of South-West Africa under United Nations supervision. South Africa ignored the United

Continued on Page 2, Column 3

"All the News That's Fit to Print"

The New York Times.

LATE CITY EDITION
Fair and seasonably warm today.
Fair, quite warm tomorrow.
Temperature Range Today—Max., 86; Min., 67
Temperature Today—Max., 77.9; Min., 66.5
Full U. S. Weather Bureau Report, Page 36

Copyright, 1955, by The New York Times Company

VOL. CIV. No. 35,616.

Entered as Second-Class Matter,
Post Office, New York, N. Y.

NEW YORK, SATURDAY, JULY 30, 1955.

Times Square, New York 36, N. Y.
Telephone Lackawanna 4-1000

FIVE CENTS

TALBOTT QUITTING, PERHAPS AT ONCE, G.O.P. SOURCES SAY

But the White House Asserts 'There's Nothing Before Us' —Secretary 'Sits Tight'

ANOTHER INQUIRY LOOMS

Democrats Charge He Misled Them on Chrysler Stock by Giving It to Children

By ALLEN DRURY
Special to The New York Times.

WASHINGTON, July 29—Republican Senators high in Administration councils said tonight that the resignation of Harold E. Talbott as Secretary of the Air Force was "imminent."

The Senators, who declined to be quoted by name, said the resignation might be announced over the weekend. At the White House, the Presidential press secretary, James C. Hagerty, would say only, "There is nothing before us."

Mr. Talbott said he was "sitting tight" and "has no more idea than a jackrabbit" of resigning.

He said he would be at his office in the morning and that he was "going ahead and try and run the Air Force as I have tried to do through all of this."

[A possibility, at least, that the Secretary would resign was discerned by The Associated Press, which quoted him as having said later, "I will do nothing at any time to embarrass President Eisenhower, and I will do whatever the President wishes me to do."]

The embattled Cabinet officer, already under investigation for his activities in connection with business for a management consultant corporation in which he was a partner, appeared to be headed for still another inquiry.

Senators Differ With Him

This one would revolve around a promise he made at the time of his appointment in 1953 to divest himself of 2,000 shares of Chrysler stock.

The new investigation, it was indicated, might be instigated by Democratic members of the Senate Armed Services Committee, which handled the Talbott nomination two years ago. They charged today that he had "improperly misled" them at that time concerning his plans for the stock.

Mr. Talbott testified Wednesday before the Senate Permanent Subcommittee on Investigations that he had given the stock to his four children, two of them minors. The Secretary said he had made it clear to the Armed Services Committee that he might give the stock away instead of selling it outright. But members of that committee said today they had had no such understanding.

Senator Harry F. Byrd, Democrat of Virginia, with whom Mr. Talbott said he had had an informal understanding that he might give the stock to members of his family, said he had no recollection of such a conversation. The Senator said he had understood the stock would be sold.

Senator Richard B. Russell, Democrat of Georgia, chairman of the Armed Services Committee, said today it was his "distinct impression from what Mr.

Continued on Page 6, Column 7

President Sees Party In Control 'Forever'

Special to The New York Times.

WASHINGTON, July 29—President Eisenhower said today that a properly unified Republican party could retain control of the national Administration "forever."

Addressing a Republican pre-adjournment breakfast rally, the President urged Republican legislators to get behind the principles he advocates.

He gave no sign whether he intended to lead the party again next year, but Republicans who have been urging him to run for re-election appeared encouraged.

Reporters were not invited to the meeting this morning. It was attended by all but a few of the Republicans in the Senate and House of Representatives, and members of the Cabinet and several members of the White House staff. James C. Hagerty, White House press secretary, gave a summary of

Continued on Page 6, Column 5

Court Rejects Plea To Deport Bridges

Special to The New York Times.

SAN FRANCISCO, July 29—Federal Judge Louis E. Goodman today refused to strip Harry Renton Bridges, Pacific Coast labor leader, of his United States citizenship.

Judge Goodman, in the Government's fourth attempt to deport Mr. Bridges to his native Australia, ruled the prosecution had not proved its charges that the longshore leader had been a member of the Communist party before he was naturalized Sept. 17, 1945.

United States Attorney Lloyd H. Burke and Lynn J. Gillard and Robert H. Schnacke, assistant Federal attorneys, prosecuted the case. They said a decision to appeal would depend on the outcome of consultation with Department of Justice officials in Wash-

Continued on Page 10, Column 6

J. E. HOOVER SHUNS CITY POLICE POST

Declines Mayor's Bid to Be Commissioner—Wagner Is Said to Seek Outsider

By PAUL CROWELL

J. Edgar Hoover, director of the Federal Bureau of Investigation, has declined an invitation by Mayor Wagner to become the city's next Police Commissioner.

The offer of appointment to the $25,000 post now held by Francis W. H. Adams was made by the Mayor early this week through an unidentified emissary described at City Hall as a close friend of the F. B. I. chief.

Mr. Adams announced his resignation last Sunday but is remaining at his post until the Mayor appoints a successor.

The first announcement of Mr. Hoover's rejection of the Mayor's offer came from Washington. It was made by Louis B. Nichols, an assistant director of the F. B. I., after he had talked on the telephone with his chief. Mr. Nichols said Mr. Hoover was traveling "somewhere on the West Coast."

"Mr. Hoover has no plans to leave the F. B. I. and has declined Mayor Wagner's kind offer," Mr. Nichols said. He then telephoned the same announcement to William R. Peer, the Mayor's executive secretary. Mr. Peer passed the word along to the Mayor, who is spending the week-end at his summer home in Islip, L. I. The Mayor had no comment.

A report that Carmine G. De Sapio, head of Tammany Hall, was a guest at the Islip home, presumably to discuss the appointment of a new Police Commissioner, was spiked by the Mayor. Mr. DeSapio, he said, was not there and was not expected.

"I'll name the Police Commissioner myself without consultation with anybody," the Mayor declared.

The Mayor did receive visits

Continued on Page 34, Column 6

CONGRESS CHIEFS ABANDON PLANS TO ADJOURN TODAY

House to Meet on Monday —Fuel Gas Bill Sidetracked —Public Housing Set Back

Special to The New York Times.

WASHINGTON, July 29—Congress was caught tonight in the traditional minor frenzy of the eleventh hour as the controlling Democrats labored urgently toward bringing this session to an end.

All hope for an adjournment by tomorrow night, as had long been planned, was abandoned.

The Senate was in position to finish its work by then but the House of Representatives had a solid docket of work still ahead. Late in the day the House Democratic floor leader, Representative John W. McCormack of Massachusetts, officially announced that there would be a House meeting on Monday.

He prepared a calendar of business that will result in carrying Congress into next week.

The House quit for the night at 6:17 P. M. and will reassemble at 10:30 tomorrow morning.

Pressing to meet the original quitting date as nearly as they could, the Senate leaders officially cast aside until next year the most controversial single measure remaining on that side.

Defeat for President

This was a bill, passed 209 to 203 last night by the House, to exempt natural gas producers from Federal price control.

The decision was in a modified sense a blow to the President, who had expressed support in principle for the bill.

It was a much heavier blow, however, to the leading Democrats of Congress, including Sam Rayburn of Texas, Speaker of the House of Representatives, and the ailing Senate Democratic chieftain, Senator Lyndon B. Johnson of Texas.

While many Republicans had gone along with the bill, its essential backers were these and other Southern and Southwestern Democratic members of Congress from the gas-producing states.

Adamantly against the project was the great bulk of the Northern wing of the Democratic party in Congress, especially the members from urban consumer areas.

The President, too, was suffering setbacks, however provisional some might turn out to be. For the White House was understood to be appealing privately for some aspects of his program.

The House, with the encouragement of the Republican Administration leadership, by 217 to 188 knocked all public housing out of an omnibus housing bill.

The President had requested authority for the construction of 35,000 public housing units a year for two years.

One hundred fifty-one House Republicans voted with sixty-six Democrats to deny even this much public housing, though for complicated reasons not necessarily

Continued on Page 6, Column 4

U.S. TO LAUNCH EARTH SATELLITE 200-300 MILES INTO OUTER SPACE; WORLD WILL GET SCIENTIFIC DATA

MAN-MADE SATELLITE: Artist's renditions of the earth-circling satellite, based on a concept of Prof. S. F. Singer of the University of Maryland. Professor Singer's specifications—diameter of about two feet, weight 100 pounds and speed 17,280 miles an hour—conform closely with those of the announcement from the White House.

Associated Press Wirephoto (from Popular Science)

R.A.F. IS RETURNING 400 U.S. SABRE JETS

Set to Replace Fighters With British-Made Aircraft, to Be Paid For in Aid Funds

Special to The New York Times.

LONDON, July 29—Britain announced today she was returning 400 Sabre Jet fighters to the United States and replacing them with British-made Hawker Hunters.

The British jets will be paid for by the United States under the Mutual Defense Assistance Program. The contract for the planes totals $140,000,000. It was signed more than a year ago, but the Hunter has been haunted by production delays.

Today's announcement indicates both the United States and Royal Air Forces are confident that the Hunter's time of trial is over, and that the planes are being produced in satisfactory numbers.

"Several" Royal Air Force squadrons are already equipped with them, an Air Ministry spokesman said.

The Hunter, which is comparable in performance with the Sabre Jet, or North American F-86F, flies about 650 miles an hour in operational trim.

The 400 Sabre Jets are being replaced not because they are

Continued on Page 3, Column 3

Russians Already Striving To Set Up Space Satellite

By HARRY SCHWARTZ

The United States and the Soviet Union now appear to be in a race for the glory of making the first major step toward interplanetary flight—the launching of an earth satellite in space. Soviet determination to achieve this objective was announced last April 15 in the newspaper Vechernaya Moskva (Evening Moscow).

The newspaper revealed then that a committee of top Soviet scientists, including the renowned physicist Prof. Peter Kapitsa, had been set up to devise a satellite in space somewhat similar to that outlined in Washington.

The announced objective of the Soviet space satellite was to photograph cloud and ice formations above the earth as an aid to weather forecasting.

[In Moscow, sources said Saturday that the Soviet Union was preparing to launch an earth satellite similar to the one planned by the United States, The United Press reported.]

Intense Soviet interest in achieving priority over all other nations in regard to all aspects of interplanetary flight has been evident for some years. The most authoritative Soviet statement of the practicability of such efforts was made in January, 1954, by the President of the Soviet Academy of Sciences, Alexander N. Nesmeyanov.

He said then: "Science has

Continued on Page 7, Column 4

A. E. C. CITES GAINS IN H-BOMB FIELD

Designs of New Arms Based on '54 Tests—Reactors for Plane Engines Advanced

Special to The New York Times.

WASHINGTON, July 29—Hydrogen weapons, apparently of several types, have been produced for the United States atomic arsenal in the first six months of this year.

The atomic energy commission disclosed this today in its eighteenth semiannual report. The design of the new weapons was based on the results of the spectacular 1954 hydrogen bomb tests in the Pacific.

The weapons advance was one of several major developments reported by the commission. Others were:

¶The commission's program for developing reactors for industrial and military electric power and for naval and aircraft propulsion "made greater strides during the first six months of 1955 than in any earlier half-year."

On the aircraft problem it

Continued on Page 15, Column 4

U. S.-Peiping Trade Of Shows Proposed

By THOMAS F. BRADY
Special to The New York Times.

PARIS, July 29—A Chinese Communist theatrical company and an American theatrical company have exchanged invitations to appear in each other's country.

The reciprocal invitations are subject to Government approval on both sides, but it is known that both Governments are aware of the project.

The participants, whose cultural olive branches may add another bit of greenery to the signs of post - "cold - war" spring, are the Peiping Opera, which is now touring Europe, and the Everyman Opera, which has presented George Gershwin's "Porgy and Bess" in most major European cities west of the Iron Curtain.

On the Chinese side the project has at least semi-official approval already. The invitation was extended to by

Continued on Page 10, Column 5

PACE 18,000 M.P.H.

Rocket to Start Object Size of a Basketball in 1957 or 1958

Texts of press conference and documents, Pages 8 and 9.

By RUSSELL BAKER
Special to The New York Times.

WASHINGTON, July 29—This country plans to launch history's first man-made, earth-circling satellite into space during 1957 or 1958.

Tentative plans envision an unmanned globular object about the size of a basketball. The satellite will flash around the earth about once every ninety minutes at a speed of 18,000 miles an hour in a fixed path 200 to 300 miles above the ground.

These plans were announced this afternoon at an extraordinary White House news conference attended by a battery of prominent scientists.

James C. Hagerty, White House press secretary, joined the scientists in stressing the satellite's immense scientific value to all nations and minimizing its threat as a potential instrument of war.

All nations, including the Communist countries, will have complete access to all scientific data gathered beyond the earth's known frontier, Mr. Hagerty said.

American scientists also will give the world the plot of the satellite's orbit, or course through space, so that scholars of all countries may study it.

Data Available to All

If the object carries radio equipment for transmitting scientific data to the earth, other nations will receive the broadcasting frequencies so they can tune in.

The satellite will girdle the earth "entirely for scientific purposes," Mr. Hagerty said.

"Do you mean as distinct from war-making purposes?" he was asked.

"If you wish, yes," he replied. The scientists said they were convinced that the satellite was now "feasible" with available technological methods and materials.

Once aloft, they said, it is expected to produce new information about the unexplored outer atmosphere that is necessary before human travel in space can be undertaken.

As the scientists depicted it, the satellite would be hurled into space under rocket power. The rocket, in several stages, would fall away piece by piece as each stage burnt out its fuel load.

At a point somewhere between 200 and 300 miles above the earth, the satellite—or "the bird," as the scientists call it—would get one final mighty blast from the rocket's last stage.

This would end its hurtling into orbit at a speed of 18,000 miles an hour. A man standing on earth could perhaps barely

Continued on Page 7, Column 1

NO MILITARY ROLE FOR GLOBAL BALL

Device Cannot Survey Land Nor Can It Drop Bomb— Its Goal Is Defined

By ANTHONY LEVIERO
Special to The New York Times.

WASHINGTON, July 29—The earth satellite will have no practicable military application in the foreseeable future. However, it will help man come to a better understanding of the natural laws of the universe.

Research scientists in the Pentagon said the man-made satellite, whizzing around the earth with a tumbling motion, would give them valuable information. This could be applied to flight studies for the intercontinental ballistics missile, a threat atomic weapon now being developed for wars between the continents.

There are two important things that the satellite will not be able to do:

1. It will have no utility for gaining terrestrial data that might be used as part of President Eisenhower's Geneva plan for inspecting the military establishments of the United States and Russia.

2. It will not be able to drop nuclear weapons, or anything else for that matter, back on earth for use against a hostile country.

The first satellite may have a mouse aboard, but scientists said they could not foresee the time when human beings would be able to go into outer space as passengers.

The Return Expected

The greatest return the scientists expect from the first satellite will be knowledge of conditions in the outer atmosphere—for instance, the density of it at different altitudes, a field of knowledge with large gaps in it.

The first satellite is expected to provide new information about:

¶The nature of the sun.
¶Solar radio noise.
¶Cosmic radiation.
¶Magnetic noises and their causes.
¶The aurora, or luminous, static - producing phenomenon that radiates from the north and south magnetic poles.

Defense Department research scientists pleaded with reporters to repress any tendency to exploit speculations that have been popularized in recent years by fiction writers. They said the possibility of human passengers in a man-made satellite and its use for military purposes were so remotely in the future that speculations about it were practically useless.

In stressing that all the data they will gain will be in abstract and basic science, the military

Continued on Page 7, Column 6

Sofia Offers Israel Air Crash Damages

Special to The New York Times.

TEL AVIV, July 29—The Bulgarian Government has agreed to pay at least part compensation for the shooting down of an Israeli airliner Wednesday. Fifty-eight persons, including twelve New Yorkers, died in the crash.

A Foreign Office spokesman said today the Bulgarian promise was made yesterday in a note to Baruch Nir, Israeli chargé d'affaires in Sofia.

[Bulgaria will permit three Israeli aircraft investigators, who have been waiting in Greece, to go to the scene of the crash, Athens reported Friday.]

The Bulgarian note expressed the Sofia Government's "profound regret" and notified Israel of the appointment of a special Government commission to inquire into the circumstances of what it called "the deplorable accident." The Bul-

Continued on Page 2, Column 5

Three Ex-G. I. Turncoats Land in San Francisco and Are Jailed by Army

Associated Press Wirephoto
Capt. Walter E. Leahy, right, reads a summary of court-martial charges against the turncoats before formally taking them into custody. The prisoners are, from left, Otho G. Bell, William C. Cowart and Lewis W. Griggs.

By LAWRENCE E. DAVIES
Special to The New York Times.

SAN FRANCISCO, July 29—Three dishonorably discharged soldiers who renounced America two years ago for life in Communist China came home today to

an emotional greeting from relatives and to an Army stockade. They promised to "gladly accept whatever punishment is coming to us." When the American President liner President Cleveland docked this afternoon after a

trip from the Orient military policemen promptly arrested William C. Cowart, 22 years old, of Dalton, Ga.; Lewis W. Griggs, 22, of Jacksonville, Tex., and Otho G. Bell, 24, formerly of Hillsboro, Miss. They listened intently and so-

berly while Capt. Walter R. Leahy of the provost marshall's office at the San Francisco Presidio read a 400-word summary of court - martial charges based on their alleged

Continued on Page 10, Column 3

The New York Times.

LATE CITY EDITION

Conditions of U.S. Weather Bureau forecast:
Mostly fair and somewhat milder
today. Partly cloudy tomorrow.
Temp. range today: 42-25; yesterday: 35-23
Full U. S. Weather Bureau Report, Page 48

VOL. CV..No. 35,831.

Entered as Second-Class Matter,
Post Office, New York, N. Y.

© 1956, by The New York Times Company.

NEW YORK, THURSDAY, MARCH 1, 1956.

Times Square, New York M, N. Y.
Telephone Lackawanna 4-1000

FIVE CENTS

EISENHOWER SAYS HE WILL SEEK A 2D TERM; CONFIDENT OF HEALTH; BARS 'BARNSTORMING'; PRAISES NIXON BUT DOES NOT ENDORSE HIM

U.S. JUDGE ORDERS ALABAMA CO-ED TO BE REINSTATED

Bids School Admit Miss Lucy by Monday—Bars Contempt Action Against Trustees

CITES THEIR 'GOOD FAITH'

He Finds That Reaction Was Underestimated—Negro Says She Will Return

By WAYNE PHILLIPS
Special to The New York Times.

BIRMINGHAM, Ala., Feb. 29
—The University of Alabama
was ordered today to reinstate
Autherine J. Lucy, its first Negro student, by Monday morning.

Miss Lucy, 26 years old, of
Birmingham, was enrolled at the
university Feb. 1 after a three-
year court fight. She was suspended five days later after a
series of campus disorders protesting her presence.

Federal Judge Hobart H.
Grooms also vacated a contempt
motion, sought by Miss Lucy,
against the board of trustees
and officials of the university.
He said the trustees had acted
in good faith in suspending Miss
Lucy. If they had not done so,
he ruled, "she might have suffered great bodily harm."

Miss Lucy sat tense and nervous today in the Federal District Court here as a succession
of witnesses recounted the
events leading to her suspension.
Some said that if she returned
to the campus she might be
killed.

Feared for Life, She Says

She said on the witness stand
that while she was a virtual
prisoner in a classroom building
held in a state of siege by a
howling mob outside, she feared
that she might be killed. She
said she had prayed.

With deliberation and occasional flashes of dry wit she
answered the questions of the
university's attorney, Andrew J.
Thomas. Beside her, when she
sat at the counsel table, was a
well-worn copy of the Bible.

After she heard the decision
of Judge Grooms readmitting
her, she said again that she
would return to the campus.

"That girl sure has guts," her
attorney, Thurgood Marshall,
chief counsel for the National

Continued on Page 28, Column 1

TEAMSTERS UNION FACES SUSPENSION

Meany Weighs Tie to I. L. A. —Internal Strife Rises

By A. H. RASKIN

The International Brotherhood
of Teamsters, most powerful unit
in the merged labor movement,
is facing possible suspension
over its alliance with the exiled
International Longshoremen's
Association.

The possibility of punitive action by the parent federation
arose yesterday amid fresh out-
croppings of internal strife within the 1,300,000-member truck
union. The uprisings were designed to prevent domination of
the union by James R. Hoffa,
international vice president and
chairman of the Central States
Conference of Teamsters.

The Detroit unionist announced
Monday that the teamsters
would deposit $400,000 to the
credit of the I. L. A. to enable
it to pay its debts and to participate in a joint organizing drive.
The pier union was expelled
from the American Federation of
Labor in 1953 on charges of
gang domination.

In Washington, George Meany,
president of the united labor
movement, announced that he
had begun an investigation into
the teamster-longshore pact. He
pledged that he would take

Continued on Page 28, Column 2

Testimony Clashes At Gas Gift Inquiry

By RUSSELL BAKER
Special to The New York Times.

WASHINGTON, Feb. 29—
Senate investigators were told
today that John M. Neff had
offered a $2,500 campaign con-
tribution in Iowa for the chance
to talk with Senator Bourke
B. Hickenlooper about the
natural gas bill.

However, Mr. Neff, an at-
torney for the Superior Oil
Company of California, denied
the story under oath. The conflicting testimony will be sent
to the Department of Justice
for possible perjury action.

The witness who testified
that the offer had been made
was Robert K. Goodwin, a
Des Moines manufacturer and
banker and Republican Committeeman for Iowa.

The two men, smiling wanly,
confronted each other under
the great glass chandeliers in
the Senate caucus room, then

Continued on Page 13, Column 3

G.O.P. TAX CUT BILL VOTED AT ALBANY

Legislature Acts in Face of Veto Threat—Committees Propose Budget Slash

By LEO EGAN
Special to The New York Times.

ALBANY, Feb. 29—Republi-
can majorities rammed their
$50,000,000 income tax cut bill
through both Senate and Assembly this afternoon. They did
this despite warnings the bill
would be vetoed by Governor
Harriman, a Democrat.

In the Senate the vote was 35
to 23. In the Assembly it was
54 to 58. All the Democrats
voted against the measure in
both houses.

The Senate deliberately voted
down the Governor's plan today.
The vote was 36 to 22, one Democrat, Joseph Zaretski of Manhattan, voting with the Republicans in opposition. He explained he was opposed to any
tax cut this year.

While the bill was under discussion, the Republican controlled Senate Finance and Assembly Ways and Means Committees proposed reductions totaling $23,528,072 in Governor
Harriman's record high $1,494,-
700,000 state-spending program
for next year.

Democrat Hits Action

Among the suggested cuts
were the elimination of a $9,900,-
000 appropriation to give New
York City a share in motor vehicle license fees and the elimination of a $2,400,000 item for
state subsidies for child day-
care centers, most of which
would have gone to New York
City.

Passage of the Republican income tax cut bill today represented an abrupt termination of
negotiations between the Governor and legislative leaders for a
compromise on this subject.

Assemblyman Eugene F. Bannigan, the Democratic minority
leader, charged on the floor that
Republicans were courting a
veto of the tax-cut bill to justify a refusal to increase gasoline
and Diesel fuel taxes. Such increases have been recommended
by the Temporary Highway Finance Commission to support a
$500,000,000 highway bond is-
sue and an expanded highway
construction program.

Lacking the two-thirds majorities needed in each House to
repass a bill over the Governor's
veto, the Republicans are expected to abandon their efforts
for an income tax cut after today.

Mr. Harriman announced that
he was still willing to resume
compromise tax-reduction negotiations. But his offer is unlikely to be accepted.

The Republican bill as passed
today would give all taxpayers
a credit of 20 per cent on the
first $100 of taxes due on April
15 and a 10 per cent credit on
the next $400, with a limit of $60
to any one taxpayer. Governor
Harriman had proposed a re-

Continued on Page 25, Column 4

DULLES SUGGESTS SOVIET MAY FAVOR CUT IN ARMS COST

Tells Senate Unit, However, U. S. Will Not Be Misled Into Weakening Defenses

By ELIE ABEL
Special to The New York Times.

WASHINGTON, Feb. 29 —
Secretary of State Dulles suggested today that the Soviet Union might welcome some reduction in the present burden of
armaments.

Testifying before a special
Senate Foreign Relations subcommittee on disarmament, Mr.
Dulles qualified this statement
with assurances that the Administration would not jeopardize
the nation's security by accepting at face value Soviet promises to disarm.

"We do not minimize the difficulties of dealing in these matters with a potential enemy who
is untrustworthy and who in
manifold ways has demonstrated
that he is a past master of the
art of evasion and secretiveness," the Secretary of State
said.

"However, there is some reason to believe that the Soviet
Union itself would welcome relief from the present burden of
armament," he added.

Russians Called Dissatisfied

Mr. Dulles said this assessment was based on the "logic"
of the present situation within
the Soviet Union. He depicted
the Russian people as being "in
a state of very considerable dissatisfaction" with their low
standard of living.

It would be logical for the Soviet leaders to agree to spend
less on armaments so they could
apply an increased share of their
production to raising the living
standards of their own people,
Mr. Dulles said. In addition,
the Soviet Union would thus
have more to spend on its new
program of economic aid to underdeveloped countries in South
Asia and the Middle East, he
added.

The Secretary of State, who
leaves for Pakistan Friday afternoon to attend the council
meeting of the Southeast Asian
Collective Defense Treaty in
Karachi March 6 to 8, appeared
before a subcommittee headed
by Senator Hubert H. Humphrey,
Democrat of Minnesota, which
is surveying the whole disarmament problem.

Senator Leverett Saltonstall,
Republican of Massachusetts,
asked Mr. Dulles whether "face-
to-face" meetings with the Soviet leaders offered the best hope
of achieving a disarmament accord.

"I don't know any other way,"
Mr. Dulles replied. "I don't get

Continued on Page 6, Column 3

9,000 Jam Court as Scofflaws Rush to Beat Amnesty Deadline

By JACK ROTH

The last day of the amnesty
period for scofflaws found 9,000
persons in the Criminal Courts
Building at 100 Centre Street
yesterday. The worst jam in
Manhattan Traffic Court history
ensued.

About 6,000 persons waited in
long lines in the lobby to pay
their fines at the court clerk's
windows. Three thousand of
these were scofflaws. At one
point the lines backed up a stairway leading to the second floor.
In addition, another 3,000
repentant drivers crowded about
the Traffic Summons Control
Bureau on the third floor. Tables
were supplied in the corridors for
the scofflaws to fill out forms.

Mr. Harriman announced that
he was still willing to resume
Magistrate John M. Mur-
tagh called the amnesty a "great
success" and estimated that of
the 20,000 persons categorized as
scofflaws all but about 6,000
had appeared.

He predicted that when all the
scofflaw tickets of the amnesty
period had been processed, the
accounting would show that the
city had collected nearly $750,-
000 in fines on long-ignored
traffic summonses.

"Because of the last-minute
influx of scofflaws," Mr. Murtagh said, "there will be a delay
of perhaps a week before we can
turn over the warrants to the
police for the arrest of the remainder. We must make certain
that none of the warrants apply
to people who appeared at the
last minute.

"But early next month the
police will carry out its action. Our
goal is 100 per cent compliance
with every summons issued since
1950."

He reiterated an earlier statement that this amnesty for
scofflaws would be the last such
grace period, because "motorists
must be taught to answer summonses on time." There were two
previous amnesties.

Concerning the last-minute
rush, which was marked by
confusion and grumbling, Mr.
Murtagh admitted such great
numbers had not been anticipated.

The confusion was caused by
the fact that five patrolmen,
suddenly called to keep the lines

Continued on Page 25, Column 4

Gronchi in Congress Discounts Arms Tie

By DANA ADAMS SCHMIDT
Special to The New York Times.

WASHINGTON, Feb. 29—
President Giovanni Gronchi of
Italy urged Congress today to
lead the Western world away
from military alliances and
toward economic cooperation
to counter Communist expan-
sionism.

"The reorganization of the
Western world is the central
problem of the day," he declared in an address before a
joint session of the Senate
and the House of Representatives.

As an early step he proposed
that the North Atlantic Treaty
Organization be "brought into
line" with today's realities, in
which "military imbalance has
been reduced," but in which,
none the less, "the world is no
more secure than it was one
or two years ago."

The North Atlantic alliance,

Continued on Page 5, Column 3

PARIS ARMY CHIEF QUITS ON ALGERIA

Guillaume Out After Policy Dispute—Special Powers Asked by Government

By ROBERT C. DOTY
Special to The New York Times.

PARIS, Feb. 29—The French
Government reorganized its high
military command today and
asked for special powers to deal
with the Algerian revolt.

Gen. Augustin Guillaume was
replaced as Chief of the General Staff following disagreement
with his civilian chiefs over military policy in North Africa. He
was succeeded by Gen. Paul Ely,
a member of the high council of
the armed forces.

Late today, Premier Guy Mollet submitted to Parliament a
request for extensive powers in
the fields of administration, economic and social affairs, and
security for Robert Lacoste, Minister Residing in Algeria.

Details were not revealed, but
the special powers were reported
to include authority to reinstate
the "state of urgency" in Algeria or even, if events should
warrant it, full martial law.

Debate on this measure, probably early next week, was expected to present the left-of-
center Republican Front Cabinet
with its first serious political test.
Some observers doubted that the
National Assembly would grant
the Government's request.

Neither here nor in Algeria
has M. Mollet's appeal to the
rebels to lay down their arms
and accept the arbitration of
new elections aroused any enthusiasm.

Conservatives, including most

Continued on Page 3, Column 2

2D SPOT IN DOUBT

Foes of Vice President Now May Push Drive to Block Him

By W. H. LAWRENCE
Special to The New York Times.

WASHINGTON, Feb. 29—
President Eisenhower passed up
today two opportunities to give
an automatic immediate endorsement to renomination of Vice
President Richard M. Nixon.

General Eisenhower said he
properly could not speak out on
the choice of a running mate
until after the Republican National Convention itself had
picked its Presidential nominee.

He mixed repetition of previous high praise for Mr. Nixon
with what sounded at least like
indirect criticism of the Vice
President for his recent effort
to continue a Republican party
label on Chief Justice Earl
Warren. The President said he
personally would admit that
any Supreme Court justice
continued to have a political
designation while on the high
court.

President Eisenhower's failure
to call at once for Vice President
Nixon's renomination undoubtedly will put new steam behind an
effort already under way by
some influential Republicans to
select another running mate.
These anti-Nixon men argue
that the 1956 campaign involving a President who has suffered
a heart attack will place new
emphasis with voters on the Vice
Presidential nominee.

Silent on Running Mate

In his radio-television address
to the nation, the President
made no mention at all of Mr.
Nixon or any other possible running mate.

The omission by the President
may not be meaningful, however.
General Eisenhower is assured
of renomination by acclamation,
and the convention unquestionably will nominate any man he
favors for Vice President. So he
could speak up for Mr. Nixon
even at the last minute and insure his renomination.

The Nixon question was
raised in two ways immediately
after the President had disclosed
he would be available for renomination and re-election if the
Republican party and a majority
of the people wanted him.

He was asked directly whether
he would again want Mr. Nixon
as his running mate.

"As a matter of fact," President Eisenhower responded, "I
wouldn't mention the Vice Presidency, in spite of my tremendous admiration for Mr. Nixon,
for this reason: I believe it is
traditional that the Vice President is not nominated until after a * * * Presidential candidate is nominated; so I think
that we will have to wait and
see whom the Republican convention nominates, and then it will
be proper to give an expression
on that point."

Respect 'Unbounded'

Asked whether, if nominated,
he would have a personal preference for Mr. Nixon's renomination, the President responded:

"I will say nothing more about
it. I have said that my admiration and my respect for the Vice
President Nixon is unbounded.
He has been for me a loyal and
dedicated associate, and a successful one.

"I am very fond of him, but
I am going to say no more about
it."

The indirect criticism came
when President Eisenhower was
asked his own reaction to the
Vice President's characteriza-
tion of Mr. Warren as a Republican Chief Justice.

The President said he would
not comment, and never had, on
a comment by someone else. He
added:

"But I will say this: Once a
man has passed into the Supreme Court as an American
citizen and nothing else in my
book until he comes out of that
court, and I believe that it would
be—I would never admit that
he was—longer had a political
designation."

There has been sharp political
controversy over the Vice President's recent contention in a
New York newspaper that the Su-

Continued on Page 14, Column 3

EXPLAINS DECISION: President and Mrs. Eisenhower at
the White House last night, before his TV-radio speech.

Associated Press Wirephoto

Butler Questions Fitness; Republicans Hail Decision

By JOHN D. MORRIS
Special to The New York Times.

WASHINGTON, Feb. 29—The physical fitness of President Eisenhower to serve another term was challenged
sharply today within minutes of his announcement that he
was willing to run. "The
American people will never
elect a President who, at
65, has had a serious heart
attack and who is unable to
be a full-time Chief Executive,"
Paul M. Butler, the Democratic
National Chairman, declared.

While Mr. Butler raised the
issue of health, other leaders of
both parties publicly hailed the
President's decision.

The prevailing Democratic line
was one of gratification that
General Eisenhower considered
his recovery sufficient to permit
him to stand the rigors and pressures of four more years in the
White House. But warnings of
a hard campaign "on the issues,"
requiring vigorous activity by
both candidates and ending in a
Democratic victory, also came
from leading party spokesmen.

Republicans responded to the
announcement with enthusiasm
that promised the President's renomination without a dissent by
the national convention at San
Francisco next August.

Predictions that the delegates
would choose him by acclamation
came from Vice President Richard M. Nixon and Senator Wil-

Continued on Page 17, Column 1

Two Senators Ask Inquiry on Benson

By WILLIAM M. BLAIR
Special to The New York Times.

WASHINGTON, Feb. 29 —
Two Senate Democrats sug-
gested today that the special
lobby investigating committee
explore what they charged
were efforts by the Secretary
of Agriculture to influence
Southern Senators to vote
against rigid farm-price supports.

Senator Hubert H. Hum-
phrey of Minnesota said that
Ezra Taft Benson, the Secretary, appeared to have
violated a law prohibiting
lobbying with Federal appropriations. The situation "is
close enough to make it appear necessary for our own
committee on lobbying to look
into it most carefully," he declared.

Senator Allen J. Ellender
of Louisiana accused Mr. Benson of "trying to buy votes of

Continued on Page 19, Column 2

CAN 'LAST 5 YEARS'

President Finds 'Not Slightest Doubt' of Fitness for Duty

*Conference transcript, Page 14;
text of speech, Page 15.*

By JAMES RESTON
Special to The New York Times.

WASHINGTON, Feb. 29—He
said "yes."

Dwight David Eisenhower, the
thirty-third President of the
United States, agreed this morning to a second-term nomination. He explained why in a
television-radio report to the
nation tonight.

Speaking slowly and in a
slightly hoarse voice, General
Eisenhower said tonight: "After
the most careful and devoutly
prayerful consideration * * * I
have decided that if the Republican party chooses to renomi-
nate me, I shall accept."

The 65-year-old President
frankly told his party tonight,
however, that because of his
heart attack last Sept. 24, he
must restrict his activities in the
conduct of his office and in the
Presidential campaign.

The President had raised personally the problems created by
his heart attack at a crowded
news conference this morning at
which he said: "I assure you of
this: My answer would not be in
the affirmative unless I thought
I could last out the five years."

Can Perform His Duties

And he told the nation
tonight:

"As of this moment, there is
not the slightest doubt that I
can perform as well as I ever
have all the important duties
of the Presidency. This I say because I am actually doing so
and have been doing so for many
weeks."

Speaking of the Presidential
campaign, General Eisenhower
warned that "neither for renomination nor re-election would I
engage in extensive traveling
and in whistle-stop speaking—
normally referred to as 'barn-
storming.'" He added:

"I had long ago made up my
mind, before I ever dreamed of
a personal heart attack, that I
could never, as President of all
the people, conduct the kind of
political campaign where I was
personally a candidate. The first
duty of a President is to discharge to the limit of his ability
the responsibilities of his office."

General Eisenhower did not
mention the Vice-Presidency in
his radio address. He was cautious about committing himself

Continued on Page 15, Column 6

STEVENSON CALLS DECISION PROPER

Bids President 'Set Terms of Debate' on His Health —Sees 'Vigorous' Drive

By CLAYTON KNOWLES

Adlai E. Stevenson called
upon President Eisenhower yesterday to "set the terms of the
debate" on the issue of his
health, now that he has declared
his availability for a second
term.

Most active of the Democratic
candidates for the Presidency,
the former Illinois Governor
stressed that it was General
Eisenhower who had "drawn the
distinction between the private
matter of his personal health
and the public question of how
the office of President shall be
administered."

In Washington, it was felt that
President Eisenhower's decision
would help Mr. Stevenson's
chances for the Democratic
nomination.

Mr. Stevenson said it was fitting that President Eisenhower,
before whom he went to defeat
in 1952, should be the candidate
and thus defend the policies and
record of his Administration.

This view, given in a brief
statement, was echoed by other
Democrats across the country
and by leading Republicans, too,
with a noticeable change in inflection. And Mr. Stevenson
noted also that the President
must look forward to carrying
the "burden of what will be a
very vigorous campaign."

This was a point that other
Democratic candidates, announced and unannounced,
stressed as well.

Expectations that the President would announce his decision
jammed the two galleries of the
New York Stock Exchange well
before its opening at 10 A. M.
In Albany, Governor Harriman
asserted that the President "can
no longer shift responsibility to
associates and subordinates."
Mr. Harriman asserted that the
President must now answer for
his actions to the domination of
one group in our country—the
big interests"—and for policies
abroad that have "undermined
our prestige and shaken the confidence in us of the people of the
free world."

And at Milwaukee, Senator
Estes Kefauver, like Mr. Steven-

Continued on Page 15, Column 3

MARKET SURGES, THEN FALLS BACK

News Sets Off Buying Wave, but Stocks End Lower

By BURTON CRANE

Wall Street had its day of anti-
climax yesterday. The President's
announcement that he would
seek re-election brought a boiling market of 3,900,000 shares, a
ticker tape that ran nineteen
minutes behind the floor for a
single hour—and a net loss on
the day.

More stocks fell than rose.
Seven of the ten most heavily
traded issues closed lower. The
New York Times combined average of fifty stocks fell 2.62
points to 322.96, a drop of more
than 4/5 of 1 per cent.

This was a point that other
dent would announce his decision
jammed the two galleries of the
The east gallery was largely reserved for reporters, photographers and newsreel and television cameramen. The general
public thronged the west gallery.

At the opening, the market
was active and strongly higher,
starting with gains of 1 and 2
points to close, for example.
United States Steel, for example,
was up ⅝ on 10,000 shares.
Volume continued heavy and

Continued on Page 41, Column 2

"All the News That's Fit to Print"

The New York Times.

LATE CITY EDITION
Heavy rain and high winds today; clearing tonight. Fair tomorrow.
Temperature Range Today—Max., 79; Min., 71
Temperatures Yesterday—Max., 78.6; Min., 67
Full U. S. Weather Bureau Report, Page 61

Copyright, 1955, by The New York Times Company.

VOL. CV. No. 35,668.

Entered as Second-Class Matter,
Post Office, New York, N. Y.

NEW YORK, TUESDAY, SEPTEMBER 20, 1955.

Times Square, New York 36, N. Y.
Telephone LAckawanna 4-1000

FIVE CENTS

GALES MOVE ON THE CITY; SOUTH IS HIT

DAMAGE IS SEVERE

New York Area Due to Feel the Effects of Hurricane Today

By PETER KIHSS

Hurricane Ione tore wide destruction in coastal North Carolina when it roared in from the Atlantic Ocean early yesterday morning.

Then it slowed down and became a tricky problem that kept the entire Eastern Seaboard worried.

In Washington the United States Weather Bureau said at 3 o'clock this morning that the tropical twister was centered about twenty miles southeast of Norfolk, Va., with winds of over thirty-five miles an hour swirling outward 200 miles to the north and east.

Swirling northeastward at eight to ten miles an hour, it is expected to pick up speed and intensity as it swings out to sea. It was expected to be off the Delaware coast this morning and southeast of Long Island in the afternoon.

Ernest J. Christie, in charge of the Weather Bureau here, said at 3 o'clock this morning that New York City would feel the worst effects of the storm later today.

The center of the storm, he said, would pass southeast of the city during the day. New York City, on the northern fringe of the storm, would have heavy rain at times with wind velocities of forty to fifty miles an hour and gusts possibly up to sixty miles an hour. Clearing weather was forecast for tonight.

Forecasts Are Qualified

Hurricane force is seventy-five miles an hour or more, according to the Weather Bureau scale.

But meteorologists were qualifying all their forecasts, warning that Ione—whose name comes from the Greek word meaning "go"—was an erratic personality.

Ione, hatched last Wednesday east of Puerto Rico, did millions of dollars worth of damage as it roared overland across the coastal areas of North Carolina with winds up to 107 miles an hour.

Communications lines were down, roads and bridges washed out, crops destroyed, large areas of cities flooded and hundreds made homeless.

Reports of the damage were fragmentary, but mounting rapidly as communications were restored. Four persons were reported dead at New Bern, N. C., and three at Beaufort, N. C. The Red Cross said it was providing shelter for 1,800 persons in the state.

New Bern, a city of 15,000 persons, was jammed before the hurricane with hundreds of refugees from tidal river lowlands. Forty blocks of the city were flooded and for fifteen hours the community was without power, communications and without water.

Continued on Page 24, Column 1

Hilda Rips Tampico In 'Worst Disaster'

By The United Press

MEXICO CITY, Sept. 19.—President Adolfo Ruiz Cortines tonight ordered unlimited Government aid for storm-lashed Tampico as Hurricane Hilda sent a flood of "catastrophic proportions" over three-quarters of the port city.

The President said Tampico, cut off by winds and water from the outside world, was confronted with "the worst disaster in its history."

[The Associated Press said Monday that Gov. Horacio Teran reported the hurricane had killed twelve persons and injured 350 in Tampico. The Governor of Tamaulipas State said 90 per cent of the buildings in the city had been damaged and 15,000 were homeless. A state of emergency was ordered.]

A medical brigade of 200

Continued on Page 24, Column 7

CITY IS PREPARED FOR STORM'S FURY

Lines Kept Open From Center at Police Headquarters to Waiting Emergency Men

Residents of the metropolitan area battened down for Hurricane Ione yesterday while Government and welfare agencies made elaborate plans to mitigate the fury of wind, rain and high tides.

New York and surrounding communities, long forewarned, appeared to be prepared as never before to weather a big storm.

The focal point of relief, rescue and damage control activities was Mayor Wagner's board of planning and operations sitting at Police Headquarters.

A communications center in the line-up room, staffed by 114 policemen, maintained open lines to all city departments and welfare agencies. Representatives of each organization were posted there at nightfall ready to flash orders to emergency crews and speed throughout the city.

Police Commissioner Stephen P. Kennedy urged the public, in event of emergency, to telephone available information to the Police Department.

The Civil Defense Administration, on alert since Sunday night, had its 149 fire and rescue units ready for instant action. At T. M. Robert E. Condon, City Director of Civil Defense, ordered his top personnel to remain on duty until further notice.

Two thousand Red Cross workers were standing by in the city and neighboring communities. The city's Department of Welfare was similarly prepared to staff 100 relief centers in the five boroughs.

In Albany three units of the New York National Guard, including the Forty-second Division stationed here, were alerted

Continued on Page 24, Column 8

Democratic Farm Experts Call Republicans' Program Ruinous

By RICHARD J. H. JOHNSTON

CHICAGO, Sept. 19.—The nation's farmers face a grim future unless action is taken immediately to relieve them of economic stress, a Democratic agricultural advisory committee said today.

Under the chairmanship of Claude R. Wickard, former Secretary of Agriculture, the fourteen-man committee met here in the Conrad Hilton Hotel to "explore all aspects of our agricultural problems."

This was the first meeting of the group that was formed to guide the Democratic farm policy fight. It was created on Aug. 31 at the behest of Paul M. Butler, chairman of the Democratic National Committee.

[Meanwhile, Democrats in Washington opened a drive to goad the Administration into unveiling its farm plans before Congress reconvenes in

Continued on Page 23, Column 4

HARRIMAN READY TO COMPETE IN '56, ADVISER DECLARES

Prendergast Says Governor Would Oppose Stevenson if Party Wanted Him

By WARREN WEAVER Jr.
Special to The New York Times.

ALBANY, Sept. 19.—Governor Harriman will seek the Presidential nomination next year if "convinced the convention wanted him," the Democratic State Chairman said today.

The chairman asserted the Governor would do this even in the event of a floor fight with Adlai E. Stevenson.

Michael H. Prendergast, the Governor's chief political lieutenant, declared that under such conditions Mr. Harriman would take the nomination "regardless of whether Stevenson stepped aside or not."

This was the first public indication from within his official political family that Mr. Harriman's repeated expressions of support for Mr. Stevenson might be weakening in the face of insistence that he seek the nomination.

Charles Van Devander, the Governor's press secretary, said tonight there would be no comment from his office on the Prendergast statement. He said the Governor was in New York City. The Governor's aides in New York likewise said there would be no comment.

For the last year whenever Presidential politics were discussed, Mr. Harriman has said "I'm for Stevenson," smiled broadly and declined to discuss any other possibilities.

Says Democrats Can Win

Mr. Prendergast was the Governor's personal choice to succeed Richard H. Balch as head of the Democratic State Committee last July.

The Democratic chairman characterized as "a lot of nonsense" Republican assertions that no opponent could beat President Eisenhower.

"I don't give a damn who they run," Mr. Prendergast declared. "We can win next year with the right man, and I think Harriman is the right man. Regardless of who he says he's for, I'm representing the Democratic party—the rank and file of it—when I say I'm for Harriman."

Although Mr. Prendergast said he could not speak for the Governor, he described Mr. Harriman indirectly as a man who was thinking now in terms of his own candidacy, rather than Mr. Stevenson's or anyone else's.

"I know Mr. Harriman well enough to know that he is so definitely interested in a Democratic victory in 1956 that if he felt someone else, other than himself, were stronger and had a better chance of winning, he would be for him regardless," the state chairman declared.

Mr. Prendergast's analysis of the situation was made at a press conference. He called the session to announce that former President Harry S. Truman would speak at the state-wide Democratic candidate's rally here on Oct. 7.

The state chairman was generally deprecatory of Mr. Stevenson's chances. He said that the former Illinois Governor's announcement of his plans in November "isn't going to stampede anybody." He predicted that getting the nomination would be "no walkover for Stevenson."

Sees Swing to Harriman

On the contrary, Mr. Prendergast said, prospects that the national convention might look favorably on Mr. Harriman appear to be increasing daily.

"I think we're going into the convention with a lot of sentiment in our favor," he asserted. "Unless something unforeseen happens, I don't see how we can miss."

He later amended this to say he believed that the Governor has "a better than even chance of getting the nomination."

Mr. Prendergast was asked if the Governor had requested him to "soft-pedal" his Harriman-for-President campaign, inasmuch as Mr. Harriman was on record for Mr. Stevenson.

"No, he's said nothing about that," the chairman replied.

Mr. Prendergast also announced that he would open an upstate office for the State Committee in the Sheraton Ten Eyck Hotel here on Oct. 1. It will include offices for Miss Mary Louise Nice of Tonawanda, state committee vice chairman, and Carmine G. DeSapio, the party's national committeeman.

The Democratic leader said he was particularly glad to have

Continued on Page 23, Column 3

Governor Calls for Federal Aid To Save Nation's Ailing Schools

But Royall Tells Conference That the Education System Should Be Contracted

By BENJAMIN FINE

A sweeping program of Federal aid to education, on both school and college levels, was advocated yesterday by Governor Harriman.

Speaking before 800 community, labor, business and school leaders at the New York State Conference on Education, the Governor said that nothing but Federal support could solve the critical problem in American education.

The two-day meeting at the Biltmore Hotel is a preliminary to the White House Conference on Education in Washington from Nov. 28 to Dec. 1. Major school issues are on the agenda, for both the New York and the Washington sessions.

Unexpectedly, the conference opened on a controversial note. The chairman of the New York State committee, Kenneth C. Royall, who was the keynote speaker, told the delegates they should be thinking of ways to contract, not expand, the educational system. Mr. Royall, who was Secretary of War under

Continued on Page 25, Column 6

PERON'S REGIME IS OVERTHROWN; JUNTA WILL MEET WITH REBELS; CROWDS HAIL FALL OF DICTATOR

U. S. TIES HINTED

Will Grant Recognition to Insurgents as They Take Over Nation

By DANA ADAMS SCHMIDT
Special to The New York Times.

WASHINGTON, Sept. 19.—Administration officials said tonight that the United States would undoubtedly recognize any new Argentine Government that showed it was in control of the country.

The State Department, insisting that any comment at this time would be a form of interference, declined to discuss the attitude the United States might take toward a new Argentine Government.

However, other officials of the Administration pointed out that the United States had followed the practice of recognizing Latin-American revolutionary governments as soon as they exercised full authority. In some cases there has been preliminary discussion with other Latin-American governments.

The fact that relations between the United States and President Juan D. Perón were frequently strained during his nine years as President made it unlikely the United States would hesitate, these officials said.

Hostile Attitude Cited

For several years after President Perón had taken power his attitude toward the United States was hostile, thus playing upon popular antipathies toward the "Yankee imperialists." However, in recent years relations between Washington and Buenos Aires have been correct, although "hardly warm," in the view of one diplomatic student of Latin-American affairs.

President Perón has sought and obtained from the United States a number of loans that have helped his Government through the difficulties that followed the application of "Perónist economics." This consisted of building up industry at the expense of agriculture.

As to whether the United States has ever "supported" the Peronist regime, there are strong differences of opinion among officials. The prevailing view is that the United States Government's attitude has been carefully "objective."

While avoiding anything that would look like official interference, State Department officials told a Congressional committee after the unsuccessful June 16 rising in Argentina that they were seeking to use United States influence quietly to prevent persecution of the Roman Catholic Church.

Catholic groups in the United States at that time complained that the United States openly

Continued on Page 2, Column 6

COMMAND VAGUE

Rebels Believed to Be in 3 Groups, With No Over-All Chief

By TAD SZULC
Special to The New York Times.

SANTIAGO, Chile, Sept. 19.—Broadcasts from Argentina indicated today that the rebel forces were operating with at least three separate commands and that no over-all chief of the movement had yet emerged.

Admiral Issac Rojas was in charge of the naval operation along the Argentine coast and of the marine units ashore. There were contradictory reports as to the identity of the leaders of the insurgent army forces operating inland.

In a telephone interview from the headquarters of the rebel-directed Second Army in Mendoza, in the foothills of the Andes, a general who identified himself as the chief of the revolutionary command said that Gen. Eduardo Leonardi was the top military leader of the movement.

He said that General Leonardi was in Cordoba, where attacks along the Argentine forces had been fought off for several days.

General About 52 Years Old

He described General Leonardi as a "respected" officer who had served at one time as an Argentine military attaché abroad. He said General Leonardi was about 52 years old. No other data about General Leonardi were available here.

A virtually independent command in Mendoza, embracing the provinces of Mendoza, San Juan and San Luis, was held by Gen. Julio Alberto Lagos.

In an earlier telephone interview General Lagos identified himself as the chief of the revolution. But his chief of staff said later that General Lagos meant he was merely in charge of the three western provinces.

The chief of staff said that the coordination among the various commands was still deficient and he refused to say what plans the rebels had to take over the Government of Argentina. He declined to say what form of revolutionary government was being established.

He declared that communication among the various commanders was by radio and courier planes.

Broadcasts picked up in Santiago told the series of dramatic events that culminated today in the virtual surrender of the man who for twelve years had ruled Argentina as a dictator.

It came on the fourth day of the bloody rebellion against President Juan D. Perón by the Navy and sections of the Army as the insurgent fleet stood off

Continued on Page 2, Column 3

GEN. JUAN D. PERON

MOSCOW TO INSIST ON BONN-RED TALK

Soviet Will Shun Any Voice in German Domestic Rifts in Treaty Due Today

By CLIFTON DANIEL
Special to The New York Times.

MOSCOW, Sept. 19.—Measures to force West Germany to deal directly with the East German Communist Government were being planned today in Moscow.

Walter Ulbricht, East German Deputy Premier and Communist party chief, declared that in the future there would be no other way of settling questions in dispute between the two parts of Germany.

He said that under the treaty to be concluded with the Soviet Union here tomorrow the East German Government would control the border with West Germany and communications between West Germany and West Berlin.

"The sooner the politicians of Bonn and West Berlin realize that they cannot undermine the East German regime, the better it will be for the populace of West Berlin," Herr Ulbricht said ominously.

His implication seemed to be that the East German Government would be in a position to impose a new blockade on Berlin and that on such matters the Bonn Government would have to negotiate not with mere officials or technicians but with the East German Government itself.

Sovereign Status Due

Herr Ulbricht spoke during the negotiations with Soviet leaders on a treaty that will give to the East German regime the same sovereign status the Western Allies gave West Germany.

Upon conclusion of the treaty the Soviet Government will abolish the office of High Commissioner in Germany, Marshal Nikolai A. Bulganin, Soviet Premier, disclosed in a speech.

Henceforth, the Soviet Ambassador to East Germany will deal with United States, British and French representatives in West Germany on questions concerning Germany as a whole and on questions arising from four-power agreements, the Soviet Premier declared.

In addition, Marshal Bulganin said all laws, decrees and directives promulgated by the four-power Allied Control Council for Germany would be annulled on the territory of East Germany. Those regulations were enacted between 1945 and 1948, when the Soviet representative, Marshal Vassily D. Sokolovsky, withdrew and the Allied Control Council ceased to function.

The treaty between the Soviet Union and East Germany will provide that East Germany is free in all internal and external affairs, including relations with West Germany, Herr Ulbricht

Continued on Page 8, Column 3

FINNS AND SOVIET RENEW ALLIANCE

Moscow Agrees to Withdraw Its Military and Naval Forces Within 3 Months

Special to The New York Times.

MOSCOW, Sept. 19.—Finland and the Soviet Union renewed their mutual defense alliance today for a period of twenty years.

At the same time the Soviet Government formally agreed to withdraw its military and naval forces from their base on Finnish territory within three months.

Those were the results of the Soviet-Finnish negotiations concluded here today and they gave "great joy" to the witty and lively old man who is President of Finland, Juho K. Paasikivi.

"I am here in Moscow for the seventh time for negotiations on affairs of state concerning Finland and the Soviet Union," the President said this evening at a party held in the Kremlin to celebrate the signing of the two agreements.

"But this is the first time that I return to our capital satisfied," he said. "Usually I have returned unsatisfied."

His audience laughed and applauded.

Exactly eight years ago today President Paasikivi was here on one of those unsatisfying missions. He signed a fifty-year lease that gave to the Soviet Union a naval and military base on the Porkkala Peninsula as provided by the truce agreement that ended the war between the two countries in 1944.

Tonight President Paasikivi observed that the Porkkala base now to be handed back to Finland was situated only twelve

Continued on Page 6, Column 3

PEACE IS SOUGHT

Government Orders Its Forces to End Fight —Port Is Shelled

Texts of the Government and Perón statements, Page 3.

By EDWARD A. MORROW
Special to The New York Times.

BUENOS AIRES, Tuesday, Sept. 20.—The Government of President Juan D. Perón fell last night.

A four-man junta of army generals assumed command of the forces that had fought unsuccessfully to keep General Perón in power. He had been master of Argentina since Oct. 17, 1945, and its President for nine years.

[A loyalist military junta told the rebels that General Perón had officially resigned the Presidency, The Associated Press reported.]

The junta quickly entered into negotiations to end the four-day civil war. Army and Navy units had joined in the rebellion and forced the resignation of the President, the Cabinet and other authorities.

Among those who tended their "irrevocable" resignations was the Minister of the Army, Gen. Franklin Lucero. On June 16 he had quelled a navy-led revolt.

There was no news about the whereabouts of President Perón tonight. Some reports had him in asylum at the Paraguayan Embassy in Buenos Aires. The embassy denied these.

Perón Statement Read

The low ceiling prevented any planes from leaving the city's army airport and seemed to cast doubt on other reports that the President had fled to Paraguay.

General Perón offered his resignation yesterday afternoon in a statement read for him over the state radio. He suggested that he had made a somewhat similar offer to resign Aug. 31 but withdrew it after "protests" from his followers.

It was widely rumored that General Perón had committed suicide. There was no official announcement to this effect, and well-informed diplomats doubted the report.

[A rebel radio broadcast from Bahia Blanca said the Argentine Confederation of Labor was planning a general strike for dawn Tuesday in an effort to restore General Perón to power, The Associated Press reported.]

The Government ordered troops that still remained loyal to it to cease fighting. It asked the rebels to do likewise to prevent further bloodshed after the Navy had shelled the seaside city of Mar del Plata and the rebels had shown other signs of strength throughout the country.

Large sections of the Buenos Aires population braved a light rain this afternoon to stage joyous demonstrations in the city's streets. The Plaza de Mayo, scene of many mass Perónist demonstrations in the past, had a small number of the Perón

Continued on Page 3, Column 5

U.N. Opening in Harmony Today; Chilean Next Head of Assembly

By THOMAS J. HAMILTON
Special to The New York Times.

UNITED NATIONS, N. Y., Sept. 19.—A noncontroversial start is assured for the 1955 session of the United Nations General Assembly, which will convene tomorrow afternoon.

The only important business scheduled for tomorrow is the election of José Maza, a veteran Chilean diplomat, as President of the Assembly.

Dr. Eelco N. van Kleffens, Dutch Minister to Portugal, the election of vice presidents and committee chairmen will take place Wednesday and the opening debate will begin Thursday.

Some delegates believe that Vyacheslav M. Molotov, the Soviet Foreign Minister, will immediately put forward the standard Soviet demand for the seating of Chinese Communist representatives.

Should he do so, it would not cause more than a short flurry, since the Assembly is ready with its equally standard counter-proposal that the question of Chinese representation should not be taken up at the current session. The United States is known to have enough votes to assure the adoption of its resolution.

Dr. Joseph M. A. H. Luns, co-Foreign Minister of the Netherlands, will call the Assembly to order in the absence of Dr. Eelco N. van Kleffens, Dutch Minister to Portugal, as President of the 1954 session.

In any event, the speeches by Mr. Dulles and Mr. Molotov are expected to set the keynote for

Continued on Page 12, Column 1

Kenneth C. Royall

President Truman, told that too many young people were attending college who should not be there.

He deplored the "widespread feeling" among educators that every high school boy and girl should go to college. He urged

Continued on Page 25, Column 6

"All the News That's Fit to Print"

The New York Times.

© 1956, by The New York Times Company.

7:30 A. M. EXTRA
Condensation of U. S. Weather Bureau forecast:
Mostly cloudy and warm today.
Mostly fair and warm tomorrow.
Temperature range today: 84—69.
Temperature range yesterday: 85.2—67.
Full U. S. Weather Bureau Report, Page 56.

VOL. CV No. 35,978.   Entered as Second-Class Matter, Post Office, New York, N. Y.   NEW YORK, THURSDAY, JULY 26, 1956.   Times Square, New York 36, N. Y. Telephone: LAckawanna 4-1000   FIVE CENTS

ANDREA DORIA AND STOCKHOLM COLLIDE; 1,134 PASSENGERS ABANDON ITALIAN SHIP IN FOG AT SEA; ALL SAVED, MANY INJURED

STASSEN SUGGESTS EISENHOWER STATE IF HE IS FOR NIXON

Aide to End Pro-Herter Drive If the President Gives Nod to the Vice President

GETS NO G.O.P. BACKING

Says Hall Tries to Foreclose Choice of Delegates in Advance of Convention

By JAMES RESTON
Special to The New York Times.

WASHINGTON, July 25 — Harold E. Stassen, the loneliest man in Washington, said today he would abandon his anti-Nixon campaign if President Eisenhower personally expressed a preference for Vice President Richard M. Nixon on the 1956 election ticket.

In the absence of such a statement from the President, the White House disarmament aide made it clear that he would continue to advocate the Vice-Presidential nomination of Gov. Christian A. Herter of Massachusetts.

The President has let it be known that he was "delighted" that Mr. Nixon was available for the Vice - Presidential nomination. But he has not expressed a clear preference for him over other possible candidates.

Takes Aim at Hall

However, a reliable source informed The New York Times today that Governor Herter agreed to nominate Mr. Nixon for the Vice Presidency yesterday after a telephoned message from the White House saying that it was the President's wish that he do so.

Mr. Stassen was left today without the cooperation of Governor Herter or the public support of a single influential Republican politician.

Nevertheless, he took dead aim both at Mr. Nixon and the chairman of the Republican National Committee, Leonard W. Hall.

The 43-year-old Vice President, Mr. Stassen said, ran last in a private poll he (Stassen) conducted on eight potential Republican Vice - Presidential candidates. He did not say who was polled, or who did the polling, or what questions were asked—only that Mr. Nixon, Governor Herter and Mr. Stassen himself were among the eight.

He also wrote a letter in the middle of last night to Repre-

Continued on Page 8, Column 5

Jordanian Group Attacks U. N. Palestine Truce Unit

Villagers' Fire Wounds One Observer —Burns Scores Incident — Amman Puts the Blame on Israelis

By HOMER BIGART
Special to The New York Times.

JERUSALEM, July 25—Jordanian villagers attacked a team of United Nations military observers today near Jerusalem. Lieut. Col. E. H. Thalin of Sweden was seriously wounded by the Jordanian fire, United Nations sources said.

They reported that the villagers "went berserk" after an exchange of fire with Israelis in which several Jordanians were wounded. During the engagement the Israelis employed mortar fire. There were no Israeli casualties.

[Jordanian sources in Amman said Israeli fire had been responsible. The Amman reports said ten Jordanians were wounded.]

Colonel Thalin was the third United Nations casualty in two days. Yesterday two Canadian officers were seriously wounded

in a mine explosion on Mount Scopus.

Maj. Gen. E. L. M. Burns of Canada, United Nations truce supervisor, said tonight that he was "astonished and deeply concerned by the attack by the Jordanian villagers."

He had already made arrangements to confer tomorrow with Maj. Gen. Ali Abu Nuwar, Chief of Staff of the Jordanian Army, on measures to be taken by Jordan to reduce the number of provocative incidents along the Israeli frontier. Israel's Premier, David Ben-Gurion, has threatened punitive action unless the provocations cease.

The current trouble spot on the frontier is in the Judean hills only five miles from Jerusalem where raw, new houses

Continued on Page 2, Column 3

DOWNTOWN TO GET 4TH NEW BUILDING

25-Story Structure Is Slated on Broad Street Site of R. C. A. Communications

By GLENN FOWLER

Another large office building is soon to rise in the downtown Manhattan financial district.

The building, the fourth large structure to be planned in the area within the last two years, will be twenty-five stories high. It will cover the block front on Beaver Street between Broad and New Streets, near Bowling Green.

It will stand on a plot of 48,000 square feet, running back 215 feet along Broad Street and 200 feet along New Street.

To be known as 60 Broad Street, the building will have an aluminum facade and a beacon light atop the roof. It will be fully air-conditioned, will have acoustic ceilings and will be equipped with operatorless elevators. Garage space will be provided in the basement. There will be 650,000 square feet of floor space above the ground floor.

The property on which the structure will be built is owned by R. C. A. Communications.

Continued on Page 41, Column 2

CONFEREES VOTE 3.7 BILLION IN AID

Reappropriated Fund Lifts Total to $4,006,570,000— Curb on Tito Supported

Special to The New York Times.

WASHINGTON, July 25—Conferees from the Senate and House of Representatives agreed today on a compromise foreign aid appropriation of $3,766,570,-000.

This sum to carry the Mutual Security Program for another year would be increased by $240,000,000 of reappropriated money to a total of $4,006,570,-000.

The bargain struck by the conferees amounted to a substantially even split between the $4,110,920,000 in new money originally allocated by the Senate and the $3,425,120,000 provided originally by the House.

President Eisenhower initially had asked for $4,900,000,000 for the fiscal year that opened July 1, although the appropriation for the fiscal year just ended was only $2,700,000,000.

Retained by the conferees was a rider in the Senate bill directing President Eisenhower not to give new military assistance funds to Communist Yugoslavia except for spare parts and replacements.

This stipulation was primarily the work of the Senate Republican leader, William F. Knowland of California. It did not affect $100,000,000 in military aid to Yugoslavia that already is "in the pipeline," nor did it

Continued on Page 12, Column 3

CRAFT RUSH TO AID

Terse Radio Messages of the Rescue Vessels Depict Operations

Help for the stricken liners Andrea Doria and Stockholm flowed almost instantly from all points of the compass to the spot at which they collided last night.

Ships large and small, Coast Guard vessels, luxury liners, Gloucester fishing boats, coastal steamers, all headed for the spot off Nantucket Lightship where the lives of some 2,500 persons were in danger.

It was 11:22 last night when the ships collided in a dense fog. The Andrea Doria, luxury liner of the Italian Line, shaken dangerously despite a double hull and other special safety features, sent out the first SOS less than a minute later.

The Coast Guard, with stations at Cape Ann, Cape Cod, Boston and other near-by points, sent out every available craft as soon as the position of the crash had been determined. Then came reassuring promises of help from the Ile de France and other craft within quick reach of the spot.

The Search and Rescue Division of the Coast Guard in New York received its first alert at 11:25 last night. It was then that the Coast Guard radio station at East Moriches, L. I. notified New York headquarters:

"Andrea Doria and Stockholm collided 11:22 local time Lat. 40:30 N., Long. 69:53 W."

Coast Guard Cutters Aid

The East Moriches radio had picked up simultaneous SOS messages from the ships a minute or two before. The next hour was spent verifying positions and notifying all Coast Guard and merchant ships of the disaster and calling on them for help. The Coast Guard sent out ten cutters from New York, Boston and New London, Conn., and diverted three other ships cruising in that area.

The stark drama being played on the open ocean in darkness and fog was pictured in tense, taut radio messages recorded by the wireless room of The New York Times. They read:

12:21 A.M.—S. S. Stockholm says: Badly damaged. The whole bow crushed and No. 1 hold filled with water. Have to stay in our position. If you [Andrea Doria] can lower your lifeboats we can pick them up.

12:21 A. M.—S.S. Andrea Doria replied: You have to come to us.

12:38 A. M.—S. S. Cape Ann reports: Now between the two ships and her boats are ready. Has two lifeboats.

12:45 A. M. Coast Guard boat says: Ten miles away; leave lifeboats.

1:12 A. M. Andrea Doria says: Needs more lifeboats still.

1:13 A. M. Unidentified ship, when queried, says: We have twelve lifeboats.

Stricken Ship's Boats Useless

1:21 A. M. Cape Ann asks Doria: How close do you want our ship to come to you?

1:24 A. M. Cape Ann reports: We have two boats for Andrea. Now proceeding to get close to her.

1:26 A. M. Andrea Doria reports: Danger immediate, need lifeboats, as many as possible. Can't use our lifeboats.

1:30 A. M. Stockholm gives position: Lat. 40:34 N.; Long. 69:45 W.

1:33 A. M. Cape Ann asks Andrea: Want Cape Ann to move in any closer than Cape Ann is now?

1:34 A. M. Ile de France says: We are nine miles from you. Will launch as many boats as possible.

1:43 A. M. Doria repeats earlier message: Here danger immediate. Need lifeboats, as many as possible. Can't use our lifeboats.

1:46 A. M. Unidentified ship notifies Andrea: Two lifeboats on way over to you.

1:53 A. M. S.S. Manaqui radios both ships: Will arrive yours at .0900 Q. M. T. (5 A. M., E. D. T.) Have two lifeboats.

1:54 A. M. Andrea replies: O. K. Thanks.

1:56 A. M. Unidentified Nor-

Continued on Page 15, Column 1

The 29,000-ton Italian Line vessel, the Andrea Doria, which carried 1,134 passengers   *The New York Times*

The 12,644-ton Swedish American liner Stockholm, largest liner ever built in Sweden

SHIPS' PIERS QUIET IN NEW YORK PORT

Crowds Expected at Andrea Doria's Docks—Relatives Begin Calling Lines

The sea disaster had not early today awakened the pier at West Forty-fourth Street where the Andrea Doria had been scheduled to dock later in the morning.

This pier, as well as the terminal at West Fifty-seventh Street, where the Stockholm had left just before noon yesterday in a gala sailing, remained dark and quiet.

However, unaccustomed night lights began blinking on at the Italian Line's office at 24 State Street before 4 o'clock when reports of the company's staff began arriving.

They had been rounded up from their scattered homes around the Metropolitan area by officials of the line under Rosmino Pernigotti, assistant general manager of the company here.

The company officials were making plans to handle expected crowds at West Forty-fourth Street during the morning. Several thousand visitors were expected to begin gathering there by 8 o'clock, some not knowing about the collision.

It is an axiom in the harbor that every arriving passenger attracts five or more relatives and friends as welcomers, and the Italian Line officials were preparing to give them the tragic news and to forestall a rush by worried relatives on the line's downtown office.

Many of the relatives already knew of the crash at sea, and the office and pier of the com-

Continued on Page 14, Column 3

Many Notables Are Listed Aboard the Andrea Doria

Persons prominent in business, the theatre, politics, journalism and government were among the passengers aboard the Andrea Doria when she collided last night with the Stockholm. Two directors of the Standard Oil Company (New Jersey) were on the passenger list. They were Stewart Coleman, traveling with his family, and Marion W. Boyer, accompanied by his wife. Mr. Coleman, 57 years old, lives at 365 Barrett Road, Cedarhurst, L. I. Mr. Boyer, 54, lives in Greenwich, Conn.

Another passenger was Richardson Dilworth, Mayor of Philadelphia, and his wife. Mr. Dilworth, a lawyer by profession, is 57. He served as a Marine in both World Wars, and received the Purple Heart in World War I and the Silver Star in World War II.

Ruth Roman, Hollywood motion picture star, and her son Richard Hall, were on the Andrea Doria. Miss Roman recently divorced Mortimer Hall, owner of a Los Angeles radio station.

Two refugees from behind the Iron Curtain, the dancers Istvan Rabovsky and his wife Nora Kovach, also were passengers. They are natives of Hungary. In May, 1953, they fled to the West from East Berlin, where they had gone for a dancing engagement. In 1954, they came to this country.

Also on board were Camille M. Cianfarra, Madrid correspondent of The New York Times, and his family. A native of New York, Mr. Cianfarra joined The Times in 1935 in Rome. He became a specialist in Vatican affairs, and has written two books about the Vatican. He became Madrid correspondent in 1951.

Others on board included Ferdinand M. Thieriot, circulation manager of The San Francisco

Continued on Page 15, Column 2

2D VESSEL IS SAFE

Ile de France In Today With Survivors From Crash Off Nantucket

By MAX FRANKEL

The trans-Atlantic liners Andrea Doria and Stockholm collided in a heavy Atlantic fog at 11:22 o'clock last night, forty-five miles south of Nantucket Island.

The Andrea Doria ordered her 1,134 passengers aboard to abandon ship. All were reported to have been rescued at 4:58 A. M. There was no immediate word, however, on the fate of her crew of 575.

At 5:15 A. M. today, however, the Ile de France reported from the scene that no more help was needed.

The French Liner estimated at 7 A. M. that she would arrive in New York shortly after 6 o'clock this afternoon with 1,000 survivors from the Andrea Doria. It was not clear to which ports the other survivors would be taken.

The Stockholm, although it had taken water through a crushed bow, was able to keep her 550 passengers and crew of 200 aboard. She was waiting for an escort to attempt to return to New York at a slow speed.

Many survivors of the Italian ship were said to have been seriously injured. The Stockholm said she had five "critical" cases aboard. Desperate and repeated calls for medical assistance were radioed from the score of rescue vessels in the area.

Deck Dips into Water

The Andrea Doria lay helpless in the thick fog. The black-and-white ship reported she was listing "very badly." She gave no other indication of the extent or nature of her damage nor was there word whether she could remain afloat.

The Stockholm reported at 6 A. M. that the Andrea Doria's main deck was dipping to the surface of the water.

The 29,000-ton Italian Line vessel apparently was listing so severely that she could launch no more than two of her lifeboats. Her lifeboats can carry 2,000 persons.

The French Ile de France had the largest of the rescue vessels on hand, and the Stockholm apparently recovered the bulk of the Andrea Doria's passengers. At one time as many as 100 lifeboats probably were in the water. It was not clear how the passengers were loaded into the lifeboats.

At 4:58, the master of the Ile de France told the Stockholm: "All passengers rescued." "Proceeding to New York full speed."

The Ile de France left New York yesterday bound for Le Havre.

Since shortly after the collision, the Andrea Doria had run her lights and radio on emergency power and said she did not know much longer she could keep in touch with rescue craft. Her hull was so weak the Stock-

Continued on Page 14, Column 5

SHIP BUILT TO TAKE COLLISION SAFELY

Andrea Doria Hull Divided to Give Stability—Lifeboats Could Carry 2,000

The Andrea Doria was specially built to give her more stability in case of just such a collision as she had last night with the Stockholm.

The hull was subdivided into eleven watertight compartments extending the entire length of the ship. Bulkheads parallel with her engine rooms were designed to lessen the effect of a collision.

The ship carried lifeboats with a capacity of 2,000 persons. Some of these boats were made of light metal alloy and were hung from davits operated by motor-driven winches. Two of the boats were motor-driven and fitted with radios.

Luxurious to the last detail, the ship was completely fireproofed and radar-equipped.

The ship has two groups of turbines capable of generating 50,000 horsepower to turn its three blade propellers, each weighing sixteen tons. They are nineteen feet in diameter and turn 143 revolutions a minute.

The Andrea Doria and the Stockholm had been the prides of the Italian and Swedish merchant marines.

The Stockholm, when launched in 1948, was the largest passenger vessel ever to have been built in Swedish yards. The Andrea Doria, when launched in 1951, was the last word in modern design and comfort. It was flagship of its line until supplanted by new vessels a few years later.

When she went into service as flagship of the Swedish American Line, the Stockholm had a capacity of 364 passengers and 150 officers and crew. Alterations in 1953 increased the capacity to nearly 600 passengers with a proportionate increase in the size of the crew.

The Stockholm had an over-all length of 510 feet and a beam of

Continued on Page 15, Column 6

Cause of the Crash Puzzles Radar Men

Experts on radar said today they could not explain how the collision between the Andrea Doria and the Stockholm could have taken place when both vessels were equipped with radar equipment.

They said that even with the "visibility nil" conditions reported in the vicinity each ship should have been able to observe the other for distances up to fifty miles.

The experts declared that, even without knowing precisely what systems the vessels carried, they almost certainly were equipped with highly flexible installations such as are standard on large passenger vessels. They should have been able to use two types of operation—generalized scanning all around the vessel, and a narrower type of observation of a restricted sector of the horizon.

They should also have been

Continued on Page 14, Column 4

Eisenhower's Four Years

An Analysis of Agriculture Policy And Steps Taken to Meet Problems

This is the fifth of a series of articles analyzing the record of the Eisenhower Administration at the start of the Presidential election campaign.

By WILLIAM M. BLAIR
Special to The New York Times.

WASHINGTON, July 25—President Eisenhower has faced a number of stubborn dilemmas in the last four years but no other problem on the home front has been comparable to the one on farms.

Like the Communist problem overseas, it has absorbed his attention. From time to time it has been mitigated by his policies. Always, however, it has returned to plague him in one form or another.

In his home town of Abilene, Kan., in mid-1952 the President began formulating his program to reconcile freedom and prosperity for the American farmer. As he put it later, "full parity in the market place" and a minimum of Government regulation were his aims.

It has been a long, perplexing struggle for the President. But despite a notable effort, success has eluded him. The farmer still is tied up in Government con-

Continued on Page 12, Column 1

Ailing Millikin Plans To Leave the Senate

By WILLIAM S. WHITE
Special to The New York Times.

WASHINGTON, July 25—Senator Eugene D. Millikin of Colorado, a powerful member of the Republican leadership, said a farewell today in the Senate.

He was compelled by long and agonizing illness to announce that he would not seek re-election in the fall.

The decision was a heavy blow to the Republican party generally, and to its conservative wing in particular.

Mr. Millikin as a well campaigner would have been a formidable favorite to keep his seat safe for the Republicans. Even as an ailing prospective campaigner he had been greatly feared by the Democrats.

His retirement seemed plainly to forward Democratic prospects for retaining control

trols and has considerably less cash in his pockets.

Every new Administration inherits the past. Thus twenty years of Democratic and often bipartisan farm policies have failed, despite high Federal subsidies, to solve the boom and bust ills that have beset agriculture in the midst of an expanding industrial economy and national prosperity.

Indeed, President Eisenhower and his embattled Secretary of Agriculture, Ezra Taft Benson, have blamed those policies and the last two wars for the surpluses that have resisted their remedies and have depressed farm prices.

From a peak of $15,943,000,000 in 1948, farm income fell to $12,-851,000,000 in 1950, before the Korean war. It climbed to $14,-801,000,000 in 1951, slipped to $14,051,000,000 in the Presiden-

Continued on Page 12, Column 1

Continued on Page 10, Column 3

SCENE OF THE COLLISION: The liners Andrea Doria and the Stockholm stricken off Nantucket Island (cross).

The New York Times   July 26, 1956

"All the News That's Fit to Print"

The New York Times.

LATE CITY EDITION
Condensation of U. S. Weather Bureau forecast:
Warm, humid, chance of afternoon or evening showers today and tomorrow.
Temperature range today: 85—72
Temperature range yesterday: 87.1—72.5
Full U. S. Weather Bureau Report, Page 41.

VOL. CV..No. 36,000.

Entered as Second-Class Matter,
Post Office, New York, N. Y.

NEW YORK, FRIDAY, AUGUST 17, 1956.

Times Square, New York, N. Y.
Telephone Lackawanna 4-1000

FIVE CENTS

© 1956, by The New York Times Company.

STEVENSON NOMINATED ON THE FIRST BALLOT; OVERWHELMS HARRIMAN BY 905½ VOTES TO 210; PUTS RUNNING MATE UP TO THE CONVENTION

DULLES PROPOSES A BOARD FOR SUEZ WITH LINK TO U. N.

Agency Would Include Egypt —Shepilov Conciliatory As Meeting Opens

Texts of Dulles and Shepilov statements are on Page 3.

By HAROLD CALLENDER
Special to The New York Times.

LONDON, Aug. 16—Secretary of State Dulles presented to the Suez Canal conference today what was, in effect, a United States-British-French plan for the future of the waterway.

His proposal, made on the first day of the conference of twenty-two nations, was that the operation of the canal should be entrusted to an international board established by treaty and "associated" with the United Nations. Egypt would be represented on the board.

From the Soviet Union, represented by its Foreign Minister, Dmitri T. Shepilov, came a long comment, not on the conference. Mr. Shepilov's speech reiterated the criticisms and reservations lengthily expressed in the Soviet note of Aug. 9 questioning the composition and competence of the conference. But it ended in an ostensible offer to cooperate to make the conference a "first step" in a negotiation on the Suez problem.

Nasser Aide Is Firm

But negotiation seemed to be rejected by an apparent spokesman for President Gamal Abdel Nasser of Egypt, who arrived here tonight by plane from Cairo. He was Wing Comdr. Ali Sabry, political adviser to the President.

To reporters who met him at London Airport he said President Nasser would not acknowledge any independent authority over the canal, which must be under Egypt's sole control. He said: "There will be no compromise that interferes with the independence and sovereignty of Egypt."

It was assumed here that Wing Commander Sabry would speak for President Nasser in the informal talks that will take place outside the conference, which decided today to meet only in the afternoons.

In a short speech welcoming the conference to London, Prime Minister Eden said the occasion

Continued on Page 3, Column 3

POLAND TO WIDEN PRIVATE BUSINESS

To Encourage Limited Group of Service Industries

By SYDNEY GRUSON
Special to The New York Times.

WARSAW, Aug. 16—The Polish Communist party has started to encourage limited private enterprise. Thus it is reversing one of the basic tenets of its economic philosophy.

The Government has decreed a number of inducements to rebuild small service industries where a minimum of materials is required and the main value is in the labor. Included under the decree are bakers, tailors, cobblers, plumbers, blacksmiths, mechanics and producers in the traditional cottage industries such as embroidery and woodworking.

It is not likely that this will lead to an immediate increase in retail shopkeeping because manufactured goods still will have to be bought by shopkeepers from Government stores at retail prices.

All other East European Communist countries have a small number of private shops. These are the remains of the campaign against private enterprise. But no other satellite has permitted the opening of new shops or the encouragement of small industries as Poland is now going to.

The Polish moves to encourage

Continued on Page 5, Column 2

AP Correspondent Freed by Hungary

By JOHN MacCORMAC
Special to The New York Times.

VIENNA, Aug. 16—Dr. Endre Marton, Hungarian correspondent of The Associated Press imprisoned since February, 1955, on charges of spying, was released from prison today. Word of his release came from Budapest.

His wife, Ilona Nylas Marton, who was arrested on similar charges four months later, was set free last April when accusations against her were said to have been found baseless. She had worked as United Press correspondent in Budapest.

The arrest of the Martons came shortly after the return of Matyas Rakosi to complete power in Hungary as Communist boss.

WIDE ARAB STRIKE PROTESTS PARLEY

Egypt Virtually at Standstill but Canal Is Unaffected— Violence in Libyan City

By OSGOOD CARUTHERS
Special to The New York Times.

CAIRO, Aug. 16—Cairo, the greatest metropolis in Africa and the Middle East, was virtually a dead city today.

A Government-sponsored twenty-four hour strike throughout Egypt brought the nation almost to a standstill. The strike was in protest against the opening today of the London conference on the status of the Suez Canal.

Reports from the rest of the Arab world said similar protest demonstrations in various forms had been staged in support of Egypt's opposition to the conference.

Among the few operations unaffected by the Egyptian strike was the passage of the daily convoys of ships through Suez Canal. The state authority that has taken over control of the canal since President Abdel Gamal Nasser nationalized the Suez Canal Company ordered that work go on there as usual.

Public utilities also were kept in operation.

Cairo Airport Is Closed

The international airport at Cairo was closed. All airlines using it had canceled their flights for the day.

Shops in Cairo, Port Said, Ismailia, Suez and Alexandria were shuttered. The streets of these usually teeming cities were virtually deserted.

No incidents were reported throughout the country. The Government had issued orders against either rallies or street demonstrations. Security measures imposed by Colonel Nasser's police force were totally effective.

Streets approaching foreign embassies were heavily guarded by policemen on foot, on horseback and in radio cruise cars. Ordinary Government offices were closed. However, top officials stayed at their posts and continued intensive diplomatic and political activities in connection with the Suez Canal crisis. They studied reports from London on the progress of the Suez conference.

The Soviet Union's Cairo Embassy was reported to have kept open direct telephone and telegraph lines to London throughout the day. Western embassies worked at full pace, although some of their Egyptian employes stayed away for the day.

Tear Gas Used in Tripoli

CAIRO, Aug. 16 (Reuters)—Among the incidents reported today in the Moslem world were the arrest of several Libyan demonstrators in Tripoli.

Policemen there broke up a pro-Egyptian demonstration with tear gas. Also in Tripoli, a small boy threw a stone through a window of a United States cultural affairs center.

In Casablanca, Morocco, crowds thronged the streets shouting anti-British and anti-French slogans and "Vive Nas-

Continued on Page 2, Column 4

TRUCE IN CYPRUS URGED ON BRITISH BY UNDERGROUND

Leaflet by Pro-Greek Force Proposes Negotiations— London Awaits Word

By The United Press.

NICOSIA, Cyprus, Aug. 16—The Greek Cypriote underground organization, blamed for much of the terrorism that has swept this Mediterranean island in the last year and a half, offered Britain a military truce today.

The appeal for the truce by the National Organization of Cypriote Fighters, known as E. O. K. A., was made in leaflets distributed on the streets of Nicosia.

The leaflets said that E. O. K. A. was asking for a cease-fire to test the British Government's good faith. If the truce call was ignored, "operations will be resumed on a fiercer and more intensive scale."

Observers said the proposed truce might indicate the first sign of a take-over of underground activities by Amargyros Karadimas, who has been reported as successor of the long-hunted Col. George Grivas.

The Underground Leadership

The truce leaflets were signed by "Dighenis," the traditional name for a Cypriote nationalist, ethnic Greek outlaw leader. Since E. O. K. A. began its anti-British terrorism April 1, 1955, Dighenis is believed to have been Colonel Grivas, a 58-year-old former Greek Army officer.

The truce offer came shortly after Field Marshal Sir John Harding, the British Governor of Cyprus, outlined his terms in an interview with the English-language Times of Cyprus:

"Let the murderers make the first move if there is to be a stopping of violence and its consequences on this island," Governor Harding said.

The "consequences" to which he referred were a British crackdown on terrorism with added military and police force, as well as the recent hanging of at least five convicted extremists.

Governor Harding said the pro-Greek terrorists had committed more than forty murders before the first hanging took place. In July, he said, the illegal underground group committed seventeen murders.

"If we have to look for responsibility for the deaths of these men [the executed extremists], we must look back to the people who started the terrorist movement and persuaded them to take up murder," the Governor added.

The E. O. K. A. leaflets said that, awaiting a reply by the British, the underground had halted its operations. "But," the leaflets added, "E. O. K. A. is

Continued on Page 4, Column 5

Russians Exporting New Bible to U. S.

By HARRISON E. SALISBURY

Godless Russia is now exporting Bibles to God-fearing America.

In the newest twist of Communist policy the Soviet state book monopoly is shipping Bibles, in the Russian language, to the United States. They are now on sale in New York at $10 a copy.

The Russian Bibles are published in excellent type on good quality paper by the Moscow Patriarchy of the Russian Orthodox Church. They are distributed abroad, however, by Mezhdunarodnaya Kniga, the Soviet state book monopoly.

An initial shipment of fifty copies of the new Bible was received by the Four Continent Book Corporation, 821 Broadway. It was said to be selling well.

The American shipment is part of a first printing of 25,000 Bibles. A second printing, numbering 75,000, is expected soon. In view of the

Continued on Page 11, Column 1

GEROSA REBUFFED IN ECONOMY PLEA

City Units Ask $408,335,704 More in New Capital Than His Report Had Advised

By PAUL CROWELL

City departments and agencies have asked the City Planning Commission to allocate in its 1957 capital budget $589,035,704 of new funds chargeable against the municipal debt limit. The over-all total of capital budget requests is $1,064,452,161.

The $589,035,704 in requests for new funds is $408,335,704 more than Controller Lawrence E. Gerosa believes the city can borrow for public works projects without having to impose new nuisance taxes to help balance its expense budget for 1957-58.

On Wednesday Mr. Gerosa warned the Board of Estimate and other city agencies that borrowing for public works projects must be curtailed if new nuisance taxes were to be avoided. He estimated that it would be unsafe for the city to borrow more than $180,300,000 within the debt limit for 'such projects in 1957.

In Chicago, where he is attending the Democratic national convention, Mayor Wagner said he was confident that the city would be 'able to produce a balanced budget for 1957-58 without recourse to any new nuisance taxes. The Mayor took issue with

Continued on Page 12, Column 1

4 Israelis on Bus Killed, 7 Hurt In an Ambush in Southern Negev

Attackers Said to Have Come From Jordan—Land Mine Blast Injures Five

Special to The New York Times.

ELATH, Israel, Aug. 16—Gunmen who were believed to have infiltrated from Jordan killed four Israelis today in an ambush of a bus and its military escort in the Negev. Seven others were wounded in the attack on the road to this frontier town on the shore of the Red Sea.

Elsewhere in the bleak Negev today three civilians also were hurt when the truck in which they were riding north of Sde Boker was blown up by a land mine.

A Government spokesman said the Foreign Ministry had apprised Maj. Gen. E. L. M. Burns of Canada, chief of the United Nations truce team in Palestine, "of the particular gravity of the situation."

Today's dead were three soldiers who had traveled in a jeep as a vanguard, and one bus pas-

The New York Times   Aug. 17, 1956

A bus fell into an ambush in the Negev (1) as a truck was blown up by a land mine to north of Sde Boker (2).

RACE IS LEFT OPEN

Humphrey, Kefauver Leading in Contest for Vice President

Text of Stevenson talk after nomination is on Page 7.

By JAMES RESTON
Special to The New York Times.

CHICAGO, Aug. 16—Adlai E. Stevenson, the Democratic party's Presidential nominee, made a dramatic personal appeal to the convention tonight to make a free and solemn choice of his Vice-Presidential running-mate.

In a move designed to point up the controversy in the Republican party over the nomination in San Francisco next week of a running-mate for President Eisenhower, Mr. Stevenson told the convention that he would not try to hand-pick the Democratic Vice-Presidential nominee.

President Eisenhower has been challenged by Harold E. Stassen, his special assistant on disarmament, to give the Republican convention a similar free choice. The President has indicated that he would be "perfectly satisfied" with Vice President Richard M. Nixon on the Republican ticket this year, but has also said he wants an open convention.

"The choice will be yours." Mr. Stevenson told the delegates shortly after 11 o'clock. "The profit will be the nation's."

Great Care Urged

Mr. Stevenson emphasized that seven of the thirty-four Presidents in the history of the United States had reached the White House as a result of the death of the President.

This, he said, placed an especially heavy obligation on the convention to choose the Vice-Presidential nominee tomorrow with great care.

There was a prolonged back-stage dispute this afternoon and night over whether Mr. Stevenson would make his acceptance speech tonight immediately after he was nominated for the second time by acclamation.

Mr. Stevenson wanted to accept tonight rather than tomorrow, when he was scheduled to come before the convention and share the platform with former President Harry S. Truman, who waged an open campaign to defeat him here this week.

The chairman of the convention, Speaker Sam Rayburn, and the chairman of the Democratic National Committee, Paul M. Butler, insisted, however, that the original program be followed even if it was distasteful to the nominee.

Mr. Stevenson then asked and was granted permission to make his appeal on the Vice Presidential question.

No Mention of Truman

Unlike most of the speakers before the convention, Mr. Stevenson did not address Mr. Truman as he opened his remarks before the jammed convention hall.

Mr. Truman sat in a box on his right, but Mr. Stevenson merely addressed the chairman, Mr. Rayburn, and the delegates.

"The responsibility of the Presidency has grown so great," he said, "that the nation's attention has become focused as never before on the office of the Vice Presidency. The choice for that office has become almost as important as the choice for the Presidency."

Mr. Stevenson then added that "each political party" had the "solemn obligation" to offer the country a person fully equipped first to assist in the discharge of the duties of the most exacting job in the world, and second, "to himself assume, if need be, this highest responsibility."

"I have decided," Mr. Stevenson said, "that the selection of the Vice-Presidential nominee should be made through the free processes of this convention so that the Democratic party's candidate for this office may join me before the nation not as one man's selection but as one chosen by our great party even as I have been chosen."

Continued on Page 7, Column 2

High Police Press Delinquency Drive

By CLAYTON KNOWLES

An unusual meeting at Police Headquarters, called to intensify the city's war against juvenile delinquency, last night produced demands for funds fo. 5,000 more patrolmen.

The department's entire approach to the juvenile problem was reviewed in the light of a 41.3 per cent rise in crimes by youths for the first six months of the year over the comparable period of 1955.

Commissioner Stephen P. Kennedy, conceding that the police "cannot do this job alone," appealed to leaders of the Youth Councils to step up their efforts as the new school year started. The councils are citizen groups that work with the police at the precinct level. All precinct captains and the youth officers who work with them were present.

Notably absent were represen-

Contin. ed on Page 44, Column 1

Associated Press Wirephoto

THE WINNER: Adlai E. Stevenson as he appeared last night at the convention hall, after he had been nominated.

Stevenson Pledges to Fight 'All the Way' in Campaign

By WILLIAM M. BLAIR
Special to The New York Times.

CHICAGO, Aug. 16—Adlai E. Stevenson, the Democratic nomination in his pocket, lost no time tonight in starting the long hard race against President Eisenhower. "This is the end of a long journey," he told his cheering campaign workers, "but it is also the beginning of a long journey. And I'm going to fight all of it the way."

The Democratic candidate addressed his supporters at the Conrad Hilton Hotel less than an hour after he told the Democratic National Convention that would have a free choice of the Vice-Presidential candidate.

This action, together with his other activities throughout the day, was a clear indication that he had been thinking ahead and planning his campaign against the Republican President who is considered certain of renomination at San Francisco next week.

In a number of statements earlier in the day, Mr. Stevenson showed solicitude for the big-city voters, with their concern over civil rights, and the traditionally Democratic states of the South.

First of all, he had said that he would have preferred a "specific endorsement" of the Supreme Court's decision against school segregation in the platform.

But he had balanced this with friendly words for the South. He called the Democratic party "a truly national party" and was outspoken in his preference for harmony over division in party ranks.

Continued on Page 7, Column 3

HARRIMAN PLANS '58 ALBANY RACE

Governor Also Pledges Aid to Stevenson in Drive to 'Put Him Over'

By LEO EGAN
Special to The New York Times.

CHICAGO, Aug. 16—Governor Harriman of New York pledged his help to Adlai E. Stevenson tonight less than half an hour after the former Illinois Governor had defeated him for the Democratic nomination for President.

Earlier, in a television appearance on the Columbia Broadcasting System, Mr. Harriman made it unmistakably clear that he intended to seek in 1958 a second term as Governor.

In the broadcast Mr. Harriman said he expected to remain as Governor of New York "for many, many years" if he failed to win the Presidential nomination. He remarked that "you know there's another election in 1958." That is the year in which the next state election of a Governor takes place.

The Governor said he intended to call on Mr. Stevenson following his television concession of the nomination to congratulate the winner in person. "We are old friends, you know," he observed.

The Governor said he would campaign from one end of the state to the other because he regarded Democratic victories in the national election and in Congressional and legislative races as important.

The Governor kept score on the balloting in an air-conditioned room off the main convention hall. With him as the roll was called and his fate sealed were George Backer, a personal associate; Charles Van Devander, his press secretary; Walter Mordaunt, an assistant press secretary; Theodor Tannenwald, a friend; Daniel E. Gutman, his counsel, and Mrs. India Edwards, chairman of the women's division of his campaign committee.

Mrs. Harriman and the Governor's two daughters, Mrs. Stanley Mortimer and Mrs. Shirley

Contin. ed on Page 7, Column 7

VICTOR IS CHEERED

Wins by Acclamation Upon Motion of the Harriman Camp

Texts of Kennedy and Gary speeches are on Page 8.

By W. H. LAWRENCE
Special to The New York Times.

CHICAGO, Aug. 16—Adlai E. Stevenson won renomination for President on the first ballot at the Democratic National Convention tonight.

The roll-call gave Mr. Stevenson 905½ votes, with only 686½ required for victory. Governor Harriman of New York ran a poor second with only 210 votes despite all the help that former President Harry S. Truman could give him.

Gov. Raymond Gary of Oklahoma, who had placed Governor Harriman in nomination, moved to give Mr. Stevenson the unanimous support of the convention.

Speaker Sam Rayburn, the Permanent Chairman, put the question as one of choosing the nominee by acclamation. There was an ear-splitting roar of "ayes."

"There are no 'noes,'" announced Speaker Rayburn without asking whether there was any opposition.

Mr. Stevenson announced at once that he wanted the convention to have a free-and-open choice of his Vice-Presidential running mate without his indicating in advance any preference. That vote will be taken tomorrow afternoon.

Cheered by Delegates

The Presidential nominee received a tremendous ovation when he appeared before the convention to express his thanks and to make his suggestion that the delegates themselves choose the Vice-Presidential nominee.

He did not say so, but it was obvious that the purpose of his move was to contrast the Democratic method of choosing a Vice-Presidential nominee with that of the Republican party. The top G. O. P. leadership has joined in slating renomination of Vice President Richard M. Nixon as President Eisenhower's running mate.

Upon receiving news of the nomination, Mr. Stevenson said: "I feel relieved and happy." Later he told the delegates:

"My heart is full and I did deeply grateful but I did not come here to speak of the action you have just taken. That I shall

Continued on Page 6, Column 3

DE SAPIO SUFFERS LOSS OF PRESTIGE

But Wagner Gains Stature as Backer of Stevenson

Special to The New York Times.

CHICAGO, Aug. 16—Adlai E. Stevenson's nomination for President raised tonight the possibility of major power shifts in the Democratic party in New York State.

Carmine G. De Sapio's prestige as a state and national political leader has suffered a setback because of Governor Harriman's failure to make a better showing, in the opinion of many New York delegates.

As the leader of Tammany Hall, national committeeman for New York and unofficial manager of Mr. Harriman's campaign, Mr. De Sapio came to the convention as a prospective kingmaker. He will leave as a local politician.

Mayor Wagner, on the other hand, will leave with more prestige and, possibly, political power than when he entered it. From the start, Mr. Wagner was outspoken in his preference for Mr. Stevenson over Governor Harriman. His one concession to party "unity" was an agreement to waive this preference for one ballot to give Mr. Harriman a courtesy vote.

Should Mr. Stevenson be elected, it is the view of most

Continued on Page 9, Column 1

"All the News That's Fit to Print"

The New York Times.

LATE CITY EDITION
Condensation of U.S. Weather Bureau forecast:
Cloudy, cool with rain today.
Fair and milder tomorrow.
Temperature range today: 56—48.
Temperature range yesterday: 55.4—45.4.
Full U. S. Weather Bureau Report, Page 41.

© 1956, by The New York Times Company.

VOL. CVI. No. 36,071.
Entered as Second-Class Matter,
Post Office, New York, N. Y.
NEW YORK, SATURDAY, OCTOBER 27, 1956.
Times Square, New York 36, N. Y.
Telephone Lackawanna 4-1000
FIVE CENTS

HUNGARIAN REVOLT SPREADS; NAGY TOTTERS; THOUSANDS IN ARMY FIGHT SOVIET TROOPS; U. S. CONSULTS ALLIES ON TAKING U.N. ACTION

STEVENSON ASKS EISENHOWER POLICY ON A COBALT BOMB

Inquires in Illinois Whether President Plans a Further Step in Nuclear Arms

Text of Stevenson speech will be found on Page 14.

By HARRISON E. SALISBURY
Special to The New York Times.

ALBUQUERQUE, N. M., Oct. 26—Adlai E. Stevenson challenged President Eisenhower today to state whether he proposed to develop the cobalt bomb or some more terrible weapon that might thrust the earth off its axis.

Mr. Stevenson suddenly renewed his nuclear offensive with an unexpected peroration to an address at Rock Island, Ill. He flew to Albuquerque later.

Tonight, in a speech here, he raised the question whether President Eisenhower had abandoned a move to halt hydrogen bomb tests "because his political opponents dared propose such a course."

The Rock Island audience of 1,300 filled the Fort Theatre, largest in the industrially depressed farm equipment center. The Democratic Presidential nominee renewed the cobalt bomb in a new indictment of General Eisenhower's policies and position on the hydrogen bomb.

Sees Fundamental Wrong

Mr. Stevenson asserted that he had evidence provided only yesterday by four scientists that already radiation "in certain areas of the world" had passed the danger point. Mr. Stevenson did not specify the areas.

Members of Mr. Stevenson's staff identified the scientists as Walter Selove, Brookhaven National Laboratories; Louis Osborn and R. M. Weinstein of the Massachusetts Institute of Technology, and Herman P. Epstein of Brandeis University.

Mr. Stevenson charged that the President was fundamentally wrong in basing national security on reliance upon the "deterrent effect of our lead in nuclear weapons." He recalled that ten years ago similar reliance had been placed upon the original atom bombs and that "to our surprise" the Russians had caught up with the United States in no time.

"And they'll do it again in the hydrogen field," he said. "Maybe they have already."

"What does Mr. Eisenhower propose then?" Mr. Stevenson

Continued on Page 14, Column 2

U. N. Delegates Sign Atomic Energy Agreement Here

For United States, James J. Wadsworth

The New York Times (by Edward Hausner)
For Soviet Union, Georgi N. Zaroubin

STEVENSON LIKELY TO WIN IN VIRGINIA

Second Survey Finds States' Rights Bloc and Powell's Activity Hurt G. O. P.

A Times Team Report

Teams of New York Times reporters have recently surveyed political trends in twenty-seven closely contested states. They are now resurveying the most doubtful of those states. This is the first such resurvey. It comes from Clarence Dean, Tillman Durdin, Max Frankel, John D. Morris and William S. White.

By WILLIAM S. WHITE

RICHMOND, Va., Oct. 26—If visible trends and measurable data have their accustomed meaning, Adlai E. Stevenson should win Virginia's twelve electoral votes on Nov. 6.

On nearly every traditional basis of calculation, the Democratic Presidential nominee is ahead in the state, and should remain ahead at the decisive hour when the votes are counted on election night.

It is nevertheless necessary to put in a qualification that is both a cliché and a fact of political life in Virginia. This is that racial and other social currents run so deeply and are so unreadable that President Eisenhower might, after all, repeat his 1952 victory in this state—one of four Southern states that he carried.

A tragic, and in some degree hopeless, bitterness suffuses both the white and Negro races here. The issue of segregation versus integration is aflame, and it throws into doubt all the generally reliable political indexes.

Conclusions Indicated

These indexes, as far as they go, suggest the following conclusions:

¶The Eisenhower movement of 1952 has lost a good deal of its urgency; there is little now of the spirit of "crusade" in it. The social pressures for voting Republican are far less powerful than in 1952.

¶The President will lose some of his 1952 strength in every area of Virginia. Mr. Stevenson thus should be able to surmount the 80,000-vote plurality, out of a total of about 619,000, that General Eisenhower ran up here four years ago.

¶The third-party candidacy of T. Coleman Andrews, States' Rights Presidential aspirant, although certainly will take more votes from President Eisenhower than from Mr. Stevenson.

This is the conclusion of a New York Times team that has just made a resurvey of this state. The team reported on Oct. 8 from Richmond that Mr. Stevenson seemed to have whatever edge there was then.

At that time there was some uncertainty about the most "Southern" part of Virginia. This

Continued on Page 13, Column 6

EISENHOWER ADDS TENNESSEE SPEECH

Expands Campaign Again— Check-Up Begins Today

By ALVIN SHUSTER
Special to The New York Times.

WASHINGTON, Oct. 26—President Eisenhower expanded his campaign plans again today. They now include a speech next week in Tennessee, one of the four Southern states he carried in 1952.

The White House announced that the President would add Memphis to a schedule that already included Texas, Florida and Virginia, the three other traditionally Democratic states that "liked Ike" four years ago.

In addition, he will speak in Oklahoma and Pennsylvania. On Monday he will go to Miami, Jacksonville and Richmond; on Wednesday, Oklahoma City, Memphis and Dallas, and on Thursday, Philadelphia.

The decision to broaden the President's schedule came on the eve of his pre-election physical examination. The President will enter Walter Reed Army Medical Center shortly after noon today. He will stay there until after the results of the "head-to-toe" examination will be made known. The President announced plans

Continued on Page 13, Column 1

U.S. to Give Atom Agency 11,000 Pounds of Uranium

By LINDESAY PARROTT
Special to The New York Times.

UNITED NATIONS, N. Y., Oct. 26—President Eisenhower promised today to make available 11,000 pounds of Uranium 235 to the newly established International Atomic Energy Agency. The pledge was made in a message read this morning to the closing session of an eighty-two-state conference that debated and approved the statute of the new world organization.

Representatives of seventy of these states formally signed the statute just before noon at ceremonies in the newly decorated General Assembly Hall of the United Nations.

The President's message was read from the rostrum by Lewis L. Strauss, Chairman of the United States Atomic Energy Commission.

The message said in part:
"To enable the international atomic agency—upon its establishment by appropriate governmental actions—to start atomic research and power programs without delay, the United States will make available to the international agency, on terms to be agreed with the agency, 5,000 kilograms of a nuclear fuel, Uranium 235."

This is one-quarter of the 20,000 kilograms (about 44,800 pounds) earmarked by the United States last February for use by friendly nations in the development of peaceful atomic programs.

In addition, the President pledged that the United States later would match the contributions of all other nations to the agency's nuclear materials "bank."

These additional supplies will become available between the establishment of the agency, after the ratification of the statute by eighteen powers, and July 1, 1960. They will be furnished on

Continued on Page 12, Column 3

CITY WARNS UNION ON SUBWAY STRIKE

Mayor Scores M.B.A. Threat as 'Political Blackmail'— Transit Board to Act

By RALPH KATZ

Mayor Wagner and the Transit Authority warned the Motormen's Benevolent Association yesterday against taking strike action on the city's subways.

In a telegram to Theodore Loos, president of the independent union, the Mayor asserted that he would not "tolerate" a strike. The authority said that if a strike vote was taken in violation of a Supreme Court injunction, "we shall take steps to meet it."

Both messages resulted from a report on Thursday by a union executive committee member that job action was planned for Nov. 5. The union official, who declined to permit the use of his name, said that the strike vote would be taken next Wednesday.

The union says it represents

Continued on Page 18, Column 6

Rioting in Singapore Takes Mounting Toll

Special to The New York Times.

SINGAPORE, Oct. 26—Rioting resulting from a strike of students spread to many parts of Singapore today. The official casualty toll reached seven dead and fifty-one injured.

The seriousness of the situation caused 27,000 police reserves and policemen to be held ready in the Federation of Malaya to be airlifted to Singapore if the violence in the Crown Colony got out of hand.

[More British troops were being moved into Singapore early Saturday as the number of dead rose to eleven, according to Reuters. Ninety-nine persons were officially listed as injured, and 219 have been arrested in two days of fighting.]

Malaya's Chief Minister

Continued on Page 16, Column 3

WEST SEEKS WAY

France, Britain, Others Study How to Appeal Russian Intervention

By EDWIN L. DALE Jr.
Special to The New York Times.

WASHINGTON, Oct. 26—The State Department disclosed today that the United States was consulting with Britain, France and other friendly governments on "the feasibility and advisability of bringing the situation in Hungary before the United Nations."

This was revealed by Lincoln White, the State Department spokesman. Officials said later that the United States was making no proposals, but was exploring various possibilities.

The Governments being consulted, other than Britain and France, were not identified.

[In Paris, Foreign Minister Christian Pineau warned the West against attempts to exploit the uprisings in Poland and Hungary.]

Mr. White said that among the questions under consideration was that of the legality of the presence of Soviet troops in Hungary under the Warsaw pact. Statements by President Eisenhower and Secretary of State Dulles on this point have appeared to be in conflict.

Troop Use Questioned

The Warsaw Pact of May 14, 1955, is a Soviet version of the North Atlantic Treaty Organization. Under the pact's provisions, Soviet troops have remained in Hungary, a member nation, to "safeguard" her security.

The view in the State Department is that there is little doubt that the troops have a right to be there. But a question might be raised about the legitimacy of their use to put down an internal rebellion.

Even this raises a problem, however. The Soviet troops are being used at the request of the Hungarian Government. There is little effort in Washington to deny that United States forces abroad could be used in the same way if there were a Communist-led revolution in, say, Italy.

In 1944 and 1945, for example, British troops, on the request of the Athens Government, fought Communist rebels in Greece.

Furthermore, any possible United Nations approach is at the moment clouded by French threats to use force in Morocco and Tunisia to protect European there.

The United Nations situation.

Continued on Page 5, Column 3

Reporter in Budapest Tells How Protest Grew Into War

Account From the Embattled City Says Soviet's Massed Tanks Slowed Revolt, Which the Massacre Then Rekindled

By JOHN MacCORMAC
Special to The New York Times.

BUDAPEST, Hungary, Oct. 26—What began here Tuesday as a demonstration turned that same night into a revolt, and yesterday became a war that was still raging today.

It is war by Soviet troops and Hungarian political policemen against the mass of the Hungarian people. The war is being waged on behalf of the Soviet Union and in support of the Hungarian Communist Government, which would fall in ten minutes if it were not for the presence of Soviet tanks in Budapest.

The Soviet troops were called in by the Hungarian Government. It still was dominated by Erno Gero, who had succeeded Matyas Rakosi as First Secretary of the Hungarian Working People's (Communist) party. Imre Nagy, for whose appointment as Premier

the insurgent masses had been calling, did not take office until after the invitation to the Soviet troops had been sent, although by doing so he countenanced it.

Mr. Gero's removal from power did not occur until Mikhail A. Suslov, a member of the Soviet Presidium, and Anastas I. Mikoyan, a Soviet First Deputy Premier, who had successively visited Hungary when the fall of M. Rakosi was imminent, arrived in Budapest yesterday for a brief visit.

As late as last night the insurgents still were calling for a democratic government headed by Mr. Nagy, but one that would accede to demands that no Communist regime anywhere had yet accepted. But they were saying that Mr. Nagy already had demonstrated he was no Gomulka. This was a reference to

Continued on Page 2, Column 3

Poles, Quiet, Watch Revolt in Hungary But Get Little News

By HENRY GINIGER
Special to The New York Times.

WARSAW, Oct. 26—For the first time in almost a week Poland was reported completely quiet today.

As the ferment that accompanied changes in the country's Communist leadership died down, considerable attention was turned to events in Hungary.

Warsaw newspapers announced that in response to an appeal by the Hungarian Red Cross a special plane flew to Budapest today with blood plasma and other supplies for the victims of the fighting there. Later it was understood the plane was unable to land in Budapest and returned here with its cargo.

Of the fighting itself there were virtually no news here. Communications between Warsaw and Budapest, by private phones at least, had been cut. Two regularly scheduled plane flights were canceled today.

From its "fragmentary information," Trybuna Ludu, the Polish Communist official organ, said this morning it had concluded that "the peaceful demonstration of the Hungarian

Continued on Page 3, Column 6

FIGHTING EXTENDS TO AUSTRIAN LINE

Hungarian Physicians Cross Border With Medical Plea in the Rebels' Behalf

By PAUL HOFMANN
Special to The New York Times.

VIENNA, Saturday, Oct. 27—Rebellion has spread to westernmost Hungary and has sent casualties and refugees across the border into Austria.

Shortly after 8 o'clock last night a Hungarian ambulance with three physicians appeared near the Austrian frontier village of Nicklesdorf on the main Vienna-Budapest highway and asked to see the Austrian authorities. The physicians said they were acting for the rebels and urgently requested medical supplies for their injured. They said seventy persons had been killed and 200 wounded in fighting in the Hungarian town of Magyarovar, seven miles east of the border.

The atmosphere in Vienna late yesterday was that of a city behind battle lines. Plasma and medical supplies were hurriedly assembled and Red Cross am-

Continued on Page 3, Column 4

NEW PEACE PLEA

Shake-Up of Regime and Revision of Tie to Moscow Vowed

By ELIE ABEL
Special to The New York Times.

VIENNA, Saturday, Oct. 27—The battle of Budapest was still in doubt early today, with Soviet troops on one side and a fiercely hostile Hungarian populace on the other.

The insurrection had spread over a large part of the country. The desperate regime of Premier Imre Nagy was struggling to maintain itself in a few scarred Government buildings along the Pest embankment with the aid of Soviet tanks and artillery.

The bulk of the Hungarian Army had given up the fight, according to reports reaching Vienna, and thousands of officers and soldiers had joined the insurrection, now in its fifth day.

[The Budapest radio said at dawn Saturday that Soviet and Hungarian troops had launched new attacks throughout Hungary against the rebels, the Associated Press reported from Vienna. The broadcast said fighting must continue because rebel elements had defied an ultimatum to surrender. No further word had been received up to 4 A. M., New York time.]

A Rebel Government

Rebel forces controlling the industrial town of Gyor in West Hungary, proclaimed their own "independent Hungarian Government." Western reporters managed to establish contact with this group from the Austrian frontier.

The anti-Communist Hungarians said they were expecting an early attack on Gyor by Soviet Army forces. The rebels told newsmen they had a number of tanks some of them captured and the rest surrendered voluntarily by Hungarian Army units.

The indication during the night was that Premier Nagy could count only on the support of the Hungarian Red Security Police and the Soviet Army. The weakness of his three-day-old Government was plain.

The Central Committee of the Hungarian Working People's (Communist) party made a fresh appeal for peace and order yesterday afternoon under the new First Secretary, Janos Kadar.

Communists' Program

The committee outlined a program virtually identical with that of the Polish United Workers (Communist) party led by Wladyslaw Gomulka. A new relationship with the Soviet Union will be worked out, the Hungarian committee promised, on the principles of "national independence, complete equality and non-interference."

The party leadership pledged that it would seek a withdrawal of Soviet forces from strongpoints as soon as order was restored, and offered an unconditional amnesty for all insurrectionists.

Continued on Page 3, Column 2

Sultan Strengthens Moroccan Cabinet

By THOMAS F. BRADY
Special to The New York Times.

RABAT, Morocco, Saturday, Oct. 27—A new Moroccan Cabinet of fourteen ministers, headed by Premier M'barek Bekkai, was sworn in at 3 A. M. today before Sultan Mohammed V. The Cabinet change gave predominance to the strongly nationalist Istiqlal (Independence) party.

The Sultan told his new Ministers they were chosen "to confront the difficulties" in which the country finds itself.

These difficulties are the result of the breach with France over the seizure of five Algerian nationalist rebel leaders from a Moroccan plane Monday night. The Algerians were the Sultan's guests and were en

Continued on Page 16, Column 2

SOVIET ARMORED VEHICLES PROWL STREETS OF BUDAPEST: A tank and a smaller vehicle moving somewhere along Kossuth Street in the embattled Hungarian capital. This picture was taken by a Western traveler, just before he left the city for Vienna. It was sent here by radio. The fighting that had started on Tuesday still continued.

Associated Press Radiophoto

The New York Times.

LATE CITY EDITION
Condemnation of U. S. Weather Bureau forecast:
Mostly fair today
and tomorrow.

Temperature range today: 65—48.
Temperature range yesterday: 62.2—48.1.
Full U. S. Weather Bureau Report, Page 74.

VOL. CVI—No. 36,074.   Entered as Second-Class Matter, Post Office, New York, N. Y.   NEW YORK, TUESDAY, OCTOBER 30, 1956.   Times Square, New York 36, N. Y. Telephone Lackawanna 4-1000   FIVE CENTS

© 1956, by The New York Times Company.

ISRAELIS THRUST INTO EGYPT AND NEAR SUEZ; U.S. GOES TO U.N. UNDER ANTI-AGGRESSION PACT

Budapest Rebels Refuse to Yield Until Soviet Troops Leave

EISENHOWER BIDS SOUTH FIGHT BIAS ON A 'LOCAL BASIS'

In Miami He Stresses Roles of States—Hails Byrd in Speech in Virginia

Texts of Eisenhower speeches are on Pages 24 and 25.

By RUSSELL BAKER
Special to The New York Times.

RICHMOND, Va., Oct. 29—President Eisenhower, campaigning in the South today, urged that the problem of achieving racial equality be handled largely "on a local and state basis."

He told a Miami Airport audience he was "convinced that progress today in equality of opportunity and equality before the law had "to be achieved finally in the hearts of men rather than in legislative halls."

The President was applauded lightly when he said that "there must be intelligent understanding of the human factors and emotions involved if we are to make steady progress in the matter rather than simply to make political promises never intended to be kept."

In the field of civil rights, he added, he had tried to bring "reason, good sense and good judgment to the performance of clear duty."

Makes 1,800-Mile Trip

Though he delivered three airport speeches in an 1,800-mile aerial campaign in Florida and Virginia, he touched on the civil rights issue only once.

That was in Miami, in the President's first speech today.

In Jacksonville, Fla., and Richmond, Va., where the southern tradition is stronger than in Miami, he did not discuss the racial theme. Nor did he refer directly in any of his speeches to the controversial school integration issue or the Supreme Court decision.

He concentrated instead on three matters: peace, prosperity and attacks on the Democratic ticket.

And at Miami General Eisenhower tried for the first time the handshaking style of campaigning developed to a high art by Senator Estes Kefauver.

Surrounded by several hundred rabid admirers on his way to his plane after speaking, he shook hands by the score with a zest rarely matched by Senator Kefauver and a folksiness as impressive as the Senator's own.

"Hi ya, folks," he said, and

Continued on Page 24, Column 4

PRESIDENT GIVEN MINNESOTA LEAD

Resurvey Finds Him Moving Ahead in a Close Contest

A Times Team Report

Teams of New York Times reporters have recently surveyed political trends in twenty-seven closely contested states. They are now rechecking the most doubtful states. Following is a resurvey report from Leonard Buder, Donald Janson and W. H. Lawrence.

By DONALD JANSON
Special to The New York Times.

MINNEAPOLIS, Oct. 28—President Eisenhower appears to hold a tenuous lead in the race for Minnesota's eleven electoral votes.

A month ago New York Times reporters found the President and Adlai E. Stevenson running neck and neck in this state. The Eisenhower victory margin of four years ago—155,000 out of 1,379,000 votes cast—had buckled under the impact of defections by farmers who were caught in a cost-price vise.

The farm revolt remains strong today in some areas.

Continued on Page 28, Column 2

Stevenson Says U. S. Gets 'Less Than Truth' on Strife

Charges President Endangered the Nation by 'Good News' From the Mideast— Boston Crowds Hail Candidate

By HARRISON E. SALISBURY
Special to The New York Times.

BOSTON, Oct. 29—Adlai E. Stevenson charged tonight that President Eisenhower had given the nation reassurances about the Middle East that had been "tragically less than the truth."

"The Government has not been

Texts of Stevenson statement and speech, Page 28.

telling us the whole truth," Mr. Stevenson said.

"As a campaigning politician there is none better. It is as a performing politician, as a President who knows how to control his own party, who knows how to grasp the reins of Government that he fails."

Several times Mr. Stevenson's partisan audience booed references to the President. The chorus of boos every time he mentioned Vice President Richard M. Nixon started the moment the crowd sensed that Mr.

The Presidential nominee addressed an overflow Democratic throng of more than 8,000 in Mechanics Hall in the climax of his drive for Massachusetts' sixteen electoral votes.

Mr. Stevenson's address was televised nationally by the American Broadcasting Company. After the telecast was completed, Mr. Stevenson appended one of his sharpest challenges to

Continued on Page 29, Column 3

POLAND'S LEADERS BACK HUNGARIANS

Support Demands for Exit of Soviet Troops—Call for End of Strife

By SYDNEY GRUSON
Special to The New York Times.

WARSAW, Oct. 29—The Polish Communist party, differing sharply once again with the Soviet Union, came out formally today in support of Hungarian demands for the withdrawal of Soviet troops from Hungary.

Yesterday the new leadership of the Polish United Workers (Communist) party rejected the Soviet allegation that foreign agents and counter-revolutionaries were responsible for the Hungarian tragedy. Today the Poles stood up again on the side of the Hungarians.

An appeal to those on both sides of the barricades in Hungary to halt fratricidal strife was issued by Wladyslaw Gomulka, the Polish party's First Secretary, and by Premier Jozef Cyrankiewicz.

Emphasizing the growing insistence here for independence in foreign as well as internal affairs, the party statement ignored the Soviet charges of Western interference in Hungary.

For the Poles the statement of solidarity was a means of publicly expressing their appreciation for Hungarian help when Poland was threatened by the Soviet leaders a week ago. Poland escaped Hungary's fate

Continued on Page 22, Column 1

Russians Befriend One Hungarian City

By HOMER BIGART
Special to The New York Times.

GYOR, Hungary, Oct. 29—The small Soviet garrison of this industrial city here retired to a near-by wood, giving the townspeople free rein to rally and shout against the Nagy Government and demand democratic national elections.

The Russians here must be credited with sensible behavior. They abandoned their barracks a few days ago under no pressure and took to the wood.

There the Soviet officers are living with their wives and children in tents. They have not shot anyone. The townspeople show their gratitude by taking the Russians eggs and milk.

And although Gyor has

Continued on Page 13, Column 1

Patrols in Budapest Are Trigger-Happy From Propaganda

By JOHN MacCORMAC
Special to The New York Times.

BUDAPEST, Hungary, Oct. 29—The seventh day of the Hungarian revolution has dawned with Soviet soldiers still patrolling the Budapest stree's despite a promise by Hungary's new Government that they would be withdrawn. The Government had qualified its announcement yesterday with the condition "as soon as order has been completely restored."

As far as could be learned, armed resistance in Budapest has ceased, even in the Maria Theresa barracks in Ulloi Ut which was holding out late yesterday. But that order can ever be completely restored in Budapest as long as the Russians are here seems unlikely because of the fears and propaganda with which the Soviet troops seem to be filled.

At 10 o'clock last night, for instance, a Soviet soldier guarding an area known as Szent Istvan Ut shot and seriously wounded Noel Barber, London Daily Mail correspondent. Mr. Barber had been making a tour of inspection to get the public's reaction to Premier Imre Nagy's announcement that there would be no further firing and that the insurrection had been recognized by his Government as

Continued on Page 15, Column 2

FIGHTING PERSISTS

Russians Still Pulling Out, With Hungarian Units Taking Over

Text of editorial in Communist newspaper on Page 10.

By ELIE ABEL
Special to The New York Times.

VIENNA, Tuesday, Oct. 30—Soviet troops remained in control of Budapest this morning while the Government of Imre Nagy pleaded with the stubborn revolutionaries to lay down their arms.

But the rebels refused to give up the fight until Mr. Nagy had made good on his promise that the Soviet forces would evacuate the battered city, monitored reports from the Hungarian capital said.

This morning the Budapest radio broadcast the following communiqué:

"While Soviet forces are being withdrawn from Budapest, Hungarian police and armed youth units are maintaining order. Such armed groups as are still resisting will lay down their arms at 9 A. M. [3 A.M. New York time] and will then take part in maintaining order."

[Up to 6 A. M. New York time there had been no further reports on the situation in Hungary.]

Appeal Is Pressed

Earlier this morning the Budapest radio broadcast an appeal by Karoly Janda, Defense Minister, to the rebels to lay down their arms before 9 A. M.

In spite of the gradual Soviet withdrawal, fighting in Budapest flared up again last night. Soviet tank forces engaged in heavy combat in several parts of the city. Latest reports said artillery fire was heard in Budapest all night.

Rebels from eastern Hungary and from the region of Gyor in the west were understood to have joined the insurgents in the capital.

The rebel-held Miskolc radio in northeast Hungary, in a broadcast monitored here, urged anti-Communists in Budapest not to lay down their arms before the last Soviet soldier had left the country.

A general strike called by the rebel leaders appeared to be continuing in many parts of Hungary for the fifth day. Most factory workers, railroad men and miners stayed away from their jobs again this morning despite pressing appeals from Mr. Nagy's Government to resume work.

Nearly complete was an unofficial school strike. Instead of attending classes many teenagers in Budapest did courier work for the rebels and even

Continued on Page 10, Column 2

1950 PLEDGE CITED

White House Recalls Promise to Assist Victim of Attack

By DANA ADAMS SCHMIDT
Special to The New York Times.

WASHINGTON, Oct. 29—The United States will take the movement of Israeli forces into Egypt to the United Nations Security Council tomorrow morning.

The planned appeal to the United Nations was announced by the White House tonight after President Eisenhower had held an emergency meeting there with Secretary of State Dulles and six other high officials.

[An emergency meeting of the Security Council was set for 11 A. M. Tuesday.]

The White House statement follows:

"At the meeting, the President recalled that the United States under this and prior Administrations has pledged itself to assist the victim of any aggression in the Middle East. We shall honor our pledge.

"The United States is in consultation with the British and French Governments, parties with us to the tripartite declaration of 1950, as it contemplated by that declaration that the situation shall be taken to the United Nations Security Council tomorrow morning.

Special Session in Abeyance

"The question of whether and when the President will call a special session of the Congress will be decided in the light of the unfolding situation."

The statement was read by James C. Hagerty, Presidential press secretary. He said it had the full authority of the President and the other conferees.

Others at the meeting, in addition to Mr. Dulles, were Charles E. Wilson, Secretary of Defense; Admiral Arthur W. Radford, Chairman of the Joint Chiefs of Staff; Sherman Adams, Assistant to the President; Herbert Hoover Jr., Under Secretary of State; Allen W. Dulles, director of the Central Intelligence Agency, and Wilton B. Persons, deputy assistant to the President.

Leaves Are Canceled

The high command of the Egyptian armed forces recalled all officers and enlisted men on leave to meet the Israeli threat. Orders broadcast by the Cairo radio said all must "report immediately to their units." Reservists were not affected.

The Egyptian communiqué identified the three frontier checkpoints where it said the Israeli raiders had been halted at Kuntilla, Nekhet and El Mimet. All are on the eastern side of the rocky Sinai Peninsula. [No additional details on the fighting were received up to 5

Suez Canal authorities in Cairo said the situation along the waterway was normal. They said no blackout has been imposed and no emergency alert sounded.

[In the United Nations Security Council, France formally charged Egypt with gunrunning for the Algerian rebels.]

Continued on Page 6, Column 2

The New York Times   Oct. 30, 1956

ISRAELIS OPEN DRIVE: The advance into Egypt was reported made at and below Kuntilla, with a thrust near the Suez Canal. There was a flare-up in Gaza area (cross).

Cairo Says Egyptian Units Have Engaged the Israelis

By The United Press.

CAIRO, Tuesday, Oct. 30—The Egyptian Army said today it had begun "liquidating" an Israeli force that had thrust deep into Egyptian territory toward the Suez Canal. Egyptian army headquarters announced that the Israeli force was being suffered "heavy casualties" in the night-long fighting. It gave no precise figures.

"The enemy's plan to penetrate deep inside Egyptian territory failed," the Egyptian communiqué, said. "Egyptian armed forces early this morning started liquidating the enemy forces."

[Iraq informed Egypt early Tuesday that Iraqi troops were ready to offer immediate assistance against the Israeli thrust, The Associated Press said. The offer was announced after an urgent morning meeting of Premier Nuri as-Said's Cabinet in Baghdad.]

The one-and-a-half-hour-meeting at the White House took place immediately after the President's return by air from a campaign trip in Florida and Virginia.

The State Department said Americans "not performing essential services" would be asked to leave the Middle East. Among the first to leave was a group that flew from Israel to Athens.

Earlier, Secretary of State Dulles had initiated the joint steps with Britain and France. The State Department an-

Continued on Page 3, Column 1

FRANCE ACCUSES FIVE OF TREASON

Files Formal Charges Against Algerians Seized in Plane —Sends Aide to Tunisia

By ROBERT C. DOTY
Special to The New York Times.

PARIS, Oct. 29—Five leaders of the Algerian rebellion, seized a week ago, were formally charged today with treason against France. The offense is punishable by death.

The five are Mohammed ben Bella, Mohammed Khider, Mustafa Lachraf, Monammed Boudiaf and Hossein Ait Ahmed, all members of the Algerian National Liberation Front, who has directed the two-year rebellion against France from headquarters in Cairo.

Their arrest Oct. 22, while aboard a Moroccan plane flying to a conference of North African leaders in Tunis, set off a wave of anti-French protest and violence. Arab anger was based on the theory that the five men were under the protection of Sultan Mohammed V of Morocco, with tacit French consent, at the time of their arrest.

In the United Nations Security Council, France formally charged Egypt with gunrunning for the Algerian rebels.]

As Algerians, the five seized rebel leaders are French citizens, hence subject to a treason

Continued on Page 10, Column 2

Maria Callas Bows At Opening of 'Met'

By ROSS PARMENTER

Bellini's "Norma" has never been notably popular in this country. But last night, when it opened the Metropolitan Opera's seventy-second season, it established a record box-office record. Never have so many Americans tried to pay so much money to hear an opera.

The actual sum paid by those who managed to crowd into the opera house was $75,510.50. This exceeded by more than $10,000 the previous box-office record of $45,336, which was set with the opening night "Faust" in 1953. The larger sum, though, was not paid by a larger number of persons. After all, sell-outs have been customary on first nights, and fire regulations re-

Continued on Page 43, Column 2

DEEP DRIVE MADE

Tel Aviv Declares Aim Is to Smash Egyptian Commando Bases

Text of Israeli statement will be found on Page 4.

By MOSHE BRILLIANT
Special to The New York Times.

TEL AVIV, Israel, Oct. 29—An Israeli military force thrust into the Sinai Peninsula of Egypt today. It was reported to have reached within twenty miles of the Suez Canal.

Army sources said the Israelis were west of the crossroads where the road to Kuntilla branches off from the Suez-Quseima highway.

The Israelis were said to have halted there and to have dug in.

A Foreign Ministry statement said the operation had been started "to eliminate the Egyptian fedayeen [commando squad] bases in the Sinai Peninsula."

Army sources said the Israelis had smashed the Egyptian position at "Kuntilla and Ras el Naqb at the southern end of the international border. The forces then advanced more than seventy-five miles.

No fighting was reported on the northern end of the border or in the Gaza Strip, which is heavily populated.

'Too Big for a Reprisal'

Reports from the Sinai area described the fighting as "too big for a reprisal and too small for a war." Details of the fighting were not available tonight, but reliable sources said there had been no aerial bombardment of Egyptian positions.

It was not clear tonight whether the Israelis proposed to push on to the Suez Canal or withdraw to Israeli territory, as they have done after reprisal raids. A high official said: "I do not know. It depends on developments."

Yesterday the Israeli Government attributed its decision to call up reserves to what it said was a renewal of commando activities, to the Egyptian-Jordanian-Syrian military alliance negotiated last Wednesday, to Arab declarations that "their principal concern is a war of destruction against Israel" and to the movement of Iraqi forces to Jordan's border.

According to information here, the Egyptians have a considerable part of their Army in the Sinai Peninsula. Their land forces are reported equipped with the

Continued on Page 5, Column 5

CITY SCHOOL AIDES SPUR INTEGRATION

District Lines Are Shifted in Some Brooklyn Areas

By BENJAMIN FINE

Without any public announcement, the Board of Education has quietly begun a program to integrate white and Negro pupils in areas where a segregation pattern has existed in the past.

A score of schools in the Bedford-Stuyvesant area of Brooklyn have become interracial since the fall term opened. Children are taken from the all-Negro schools and put into the formerly all-white schools.

At the same time, fairly large groups of children—ranging from fifty to 200—have been taken from a number of all-white schools and placed into the all-Negro schools. In doing this, the board has amended or discarded the old district and school zoning regulations.

This step is part of a "positive program" on integration, Charles H. Silver, Board of Education president, said yesterday. The board has forty assistant superintendents to do everything possible to place Negro and white children in the same schools.

The superintendents are doing

Continued on Page 30, Column 3

AMERICANS LEAVE ISRAEL: Wives and children of State Department personnel boarding Air Force transport plane last night at Lydda Airport near Jerusalem. They were flown to Athens. More dependents are to follow today.

"All the News That's Fit to Print"

The New York Times.

LATE CITY EDITION

Condensation of U. S. Weather Bureau forecast:
Partly cloudy, little temperature change today and tomorrow.

Temperature range today: 65–51.
Temperature range yesterday: 68.3–51.
Full U. S. Weather Bureau Report, Page 46.

VOL. CVI—No. 36,078.

Entered as Second-Class Matter,
Post Office, New York, N. Y.

NEW YORK, SATURDAY, NOVEMBER 3, 1956.

Times Square, New York 36, N. Y.
Telephone Lackawanna 4-1000

FIVE CENTS

BRITISH AND FRENCH PUSH TOWARD LANDING; ISRAELIS CAPTURE GAZA AND CONTROL SINAI

Hungary Protests to Soviet Against New Troop Moves; West Urges Action by U. N.; Tension Is Rising in Poland

---

STEVENSON OFFERS A PROGRAM TO END STRIFE IN MIDEAST

Calls for a Cease-Fire and Israel's Security—Detroit Crowd Boos President

Speech at Detroit and remarks at Cleveland, Page 20.

By HARRISON E. SALISBURY
Special to The New York Times

DETROIT, Nov. 2—Adlai E. Stevenson offered tonight a program to restore peace in the Middle East, based on the security of Israel and restoration of the Western Alliance.

Mr. Stevenson submitted his program to an enthusiastic overflow audience at the Fox Theatre.

He charged that President Eisenhower did not know what had been happening in the Middle East and that "someone had misled him."

Mr. Stevenson's program called for these steps:

¶A cease-fire in the Middle East.

¶Restoration of the Western grand alliance of the United States, France and Britain.

¶Security for Israel against Arab attack.

¶Establishment of the principle of international concern for the Suez Canal and an end of one-man or one-country control.

¶An all-out attack on resettlement of 900,000 Arab refugees in Middle Eastern lands.

¶A joint program for improvement of economic conditions in the Middle East.

Mr. Stevenson's address was carried on a state TV network. Several thousand persons were unable to gain admission to the theatre.

Earlier today, Mr. Stevenson spoke in Cleveland's Public Square. A huge throng heard him demand United Nations action in behalf of the new Hungarian regime.

Democratic officials put the crowd at 65,000. Newspaper reporters estimated it at closer to 30,000. There was agreement, however, that it was larger than General Eisenhower drew in the same place and time three weeks ago.

Tonight Mr. Stevenson asserted that the first task in the

Continued on Page 20, Column 5

COUNCIL HEARING ON QUINN SLATED

Mayor Backs Tenney Report on Official's Carting Job

By CHARLES G. BENNETT

The City Council will hold hearings soon to consider charges against Councilman Hugh Quinn, Queens Democrat.

In a report to Mayor Wagner on Thursday, Investigation Commissioner Charles H. Tenney found that Mr. Quinn had committed an "apparent" violation of the City Charter and had given grounds for his removal from office.

Yesterday Mayor Wagner said he agreed with the Investigation Commissioner's conclusions.

Council Majority Leader Joseph T. Sharkey, Brooklyn Democrat, said he would call the Councilmen together next week, probably Wednesday, to arrange for hearings in the Quinn case. A question for the Councilmen to determine, Mr. Sharkey said, is whether the hearings will be public or private.

The Council, under the Charter, is the judge of the qualifications of its members. It may expel a member by a two-thirds vote.

Mr. Sharkey said he thought

Continued on Page 48, Column 3

HUNGARIAN PREMIER Imre Nagy, Communist who took office during national anti-Soviet uprising, addressing nation by radio. Date when photograph was taken was not given.

Associated Press Radiophoto

Eisenhower Sees Victory, Leaves Campaign to Nixon

By RUSSELL BAKER
Special to The New York Times

WASHINGTON, Nov. 2—President Eisenhower now is so confident of re-election Tuesday that he is treating Adlai E. Stevenson's driving campaign finish with a show of indifference. This was emphasized last night in Philadelphia when he indicated that, from his point of view, the campaign was over and that henceforth he would address the nation only in the non-partisan role of President.

It was pointedly driven home today when the White House noted that Vice President Richard M. Nixon, rather than the President, had been selected to reply tonight to the Democratic nominee's attack on foreign policy.

James C. Hagerty, White House press secretary, said the President's discussion of the Middle Eastern and Central European crises Wednesday had been "nonpolitical." Mr. Stevenson's reply last night, he added, "was strictly political."

Mr. Hagerty's implication was that the President no longer intended to trouble with replies to Mr. Stevenson's "political" charges and that this chore now could be handled adequately by Mr. Nixon.

The President, he added, knew in advance the substance of the Vice President's speech. The White House staff had helped Mr. Nixon get "the facts to refute a lot of misstatements that Mr. Stevenson made last night," Mr. Hagerty said.

The White House also an-

Continued on Page 19, Column 6

PRESIDENT LEADS IN PENNSYLVANIA

Slim Edge Not Widened Yet by Crises Abroad—Clark's Margin for Senate Cut

A Times Team Report

Teams of New York Times reporters have now completed a survey of political trends in twenty-seven states. They have rechecked eight of those states—the most doubtful ones. Following is a final resurvey report by Leonard Buder, Donald Janson and Wayne Phillips.

By WAYNE PHILLIPS
Special to The New York Times

PHILADELPHIA, Nov. 2—President Eisenhower is clinging to a lead in this state so insubstantial that it could be washed away by a heavy rain on election day.

Depending upon developments in the Middle East crisis, he may be able to increase that lead in the four days remaining before the election. But at the moment the world crisis has served only to create doubts in the minds of voters on both sides of the race. Those doubts have not yet crystallized in favor of either candidate.

Two weeks ago a New York Times team found the Pennsylvania Democrats well organized and confident. They were fighting an uphill battle against the appeal of the President's personality, but the odds were on their side in a state that once was a bastion of Republicanism.

They appeared to have made the public—and most Republican newspapers, too—to their Senatorial candidate, Joseph S. Clark Jr. Clark had created a substantial indecision among the 1952 supporters of President Eisenhower, and had won over enough of them to give some hope of carrying the state for Adlai E. Stevenson.

For Mr. Stevenson this state is the keystone in any arch of triumph he may hope to build. Its thirty-two electoral votes, with various combinations of states, could carry him to a

Continued on Page 15, Column 2

Nixon Hails Break With Allies' Policies

By WILLIAM M. BLAIR
Special to The New York Times

HERSHEY, Pa., Nov. 2—Vice President Richard M. Nixon hailed tonight this country's break with Anglo-French policies as a "declaration of independence that has had an electrifying effect throughout the world."

Speaking with the full backing of President Eisenhower, he assailed Adlai E. Stevenson for charging that the Administration's foreign policy was a failure and that the President should have averted the Middle East crisis.

He said that the United Nations General Assembly vote gave "the lie to [Mr. Stevenson's] preposterous charge" that the United States stood alone "in an unfriendly world."

The General Assembly early

Continued on Page 19, Column 1

TROOPS REPORTED CROSSING POLAND

Soviet Movement Is Said to Be to East Germany—Panic Buying in Warsaw

By SYDNEY GRUSON

WARSAW, Nov. 2—Reports reaching Warsaw tonight of large-scale Soviet troop movements across Poland from Russia to East Germany. No details were available.

The purpose and the meaning of the troop movements were not disclosed. But even before they had been reported the situation in Poland had reached a point of extreme tension.

All through the day the Polish radio repeated its broadcast of an appeal for "calm, discipline and a sense of responsibility" within the nation.

In Warsaw panic buying began. People bought up all the foodstuffs in the stores and then after withdrawing their money from the banks began to buy jewelry and valuables.

Word came from various parts

Continued on Page 14, Column 4

U. S. Protests Refusal by Soviet To Let Americans Quit Hungary

Special to The New York Times

WASHINGTON, Nov. 2—The United States protested tonight to the Soviet Union against the action of Soviet troops who prevented a convoy of Americans from leaving Hungary.

A report of the incident from the United States Legation in Budapest reached the State Department in early evening. Deputy Under Secretary of State Robert Murphy called in Georgi N. Zaroubin, the Soviet Ambassador, at once.

Mr. Zaroubin told Mr. Murphy he would get in touch with his Government in Moscow about the matter.

A State Department spokesman said Mr. Murphy spoke "energetically" against the Soviet Ambassador against the "interference with American official personnel."

According to the official report, the convoy consisted of dependents—wives and children of United States legation staff in Budapest as well as French, British and American correspondents was turned back from the Austrian border by Soviet troops at 4:30 P. M. today.

"Polemics are useless," said a Soviet officer told them. "It is requested that you turn around tomorrow.

"We had a report from Budapest that a convoy of our lega-

Continued on Page 16, Column 4

NEW PLEA BY NAGY

Premier Asks That U. N. Defend Neutrality of Hungary

By JOHN MacCORMAC
Special to The New York Times

BUDAPEST, Hungary, Saturday, Nov. 3—The Hungarian Government made three oral protests yesterday to the Soviet Ambassador in Budapest, complaining that Russian reinforcements were still pouring across the frontier.

[Soviet tanks sealed the main crossings of the Austrian - Hungarian border Friday. This was regarded as a preliminary to dealing sternly with the insurgents.]

Premier Imre Nagy also sent a new appeal to the Secretary General of the United Nations to guarantee Hungary's neutrality and to bring her case before the General Assembly.

Similarly Joseph Cardinal Mindszenty, primate of Hungary, appealed to the West for political support of the revolutionaries and relief for the needy.

Soviet Forces Approaching

Early today, forces at the command of the Revolutionary Council of the Hungarian Army occupied the Parliament Building and took up posts on and near all bridges spanning the Danube. These measures were prompted by information that Soviet forces were approaching the capital.

In his plea to the Secretary General of the United Nations, Premier Nagy said that Hungary's first demand for the withdrawal of Soviet troops had been received favorably by Moscow. In spite of this, he went on, fresh Soviet troops were brought in to Hungary on Tuesday and Wednesday.

The Hungarian Government then denounced the Warsaw Pact, proclaimed Hungary a neutral state and demanded the withdrawal of all Soviet troops. Budapest also proposed that an agreement for the reappointment of two joint Hungarian-Soviet committees, one political and one military, to discuss the terms and set the timetable for this withdrawal.

The Premier said that he had protested against any further influx of Soviet soldiers, pointing out to the United Nations that new Soviet units had entered

Continued on Page 15, Column 1

Eisenhower Offers Relief to Hungary

Special to The New York Times

WASHINGTON, Nov. 2—President Eisenhower late today offered $20,000,000 worth of food and medical supplies to relieve the suffering in Hungary resulting from the revolt against Soviet domination.

The White House announcement of this offer followed a conference between the President, Secretary of State Dulles, and Under Secretary of State Herbert Hoover Jr.

The aid would consist of $15,000,000 in surplus foodstuffs and $5,000,000 in specially purchased meats, oils, fats, and medical supplies.

The President urged the American people to continue sending their contributions to the American Red Cross, which is pouring relief supplies into

Continued on Page 16, Column 7

Israelis Are Mopping Up; Egypt Braces for Landing

12,000 Prisoners Taken

By HOMER BIGART
Special to The New York Times

TEL AVIV, Israel, Saturday, Nov. 3—Israel's lightning conquest of Egypt's Sinai Peninsula and the Gaza Strip is complete except for minor mopping-up operations. The ancient Philistine capital of Gaza was the last town to fall.

In its drive, Maj. Gen. Moshe Dayan's tough Army had killed, captured or put to flight 30,000 Egyptian troops east of the Suez Canal.

With Israel's southern flank secure after only four days of operations, the Government faced with calm confidence reinforced by Syrian troops and that the Syrian-Jordanian-Egyptian defense pact was about to become operative.

Gaza collapsed after a three-hour fight yesterday morning. A United Nations truce aide,

Continued on Page 3, Column 5

Cairo Defense Held Ready

By The United Press

CAIRO, Nov. 2—Waves of British and French bombers and fighters blasted Cairo and outlying villages today. An Egyptian communiqué said 100 persons had been killed in one town alone.

Simultaneously, President Gamal Abdel Nasser announced that Egyptian forces in the Sinai desert had "completed their withdrawal safely."

"Now we are waiting for the British and French in the delta," he said. Only "suicide commandos" had been left in Sinai to harass the advancing Israeli forces, he added.

The communiqué asserted that fourteen British and French planes had been shot down in today's raids. An earlier communiqué had claimed three kills in addition to six reported downed yesterday morning. This would

Continued on Page 3, Column 2

U. N. SPEAKERS ASK HELP FOR HUNGARY

Override Soviet Objections as Security Council Argues International Action

Excerpts from Security Council debate are on Page 16.

By LINDESAY PARROTT
Special to The New York Times

UNITED NATIONS, N. Y., Nov. 2—The Western powers override Soviet objections today and called on the United Nations to take measures against Soviet military action in Hungary.

An emergency meeting of the Security Council heard all nations that spoke, except the Soviet Union, appeal for international action against the reinforcement of Soviet troops in Hungary, where rebel nationalists appear to have taken control. Premier Imre Nagy, the United Nations yesterday to guarantee the country's neutrality.

No decision was reached at the two-hour session of the Council tonight. The members will meet again tomorrow afternoon in an attempt to decide on a course of action.

The meeting was sparked by a new message from Mr. Nagy distributed to Council members tonight.

The letter, couched in terms similar to the one Mr. Nagy sent to the United Nations yesterday, charged that "large" Soviet military units had crossed the Hungarian border. Moving toward

Continued on Page 16, Column 1

PARIS ACTS TO BAR CEASE-FIRE NOW

Fears That Immediate Halt in Military Operations Would Save Nasser

By HAROLD CALLENDER
Special to The New York Times

PARIS, Nov. 2—The French Government moved fast today to prevent a United Nations cease-fire in the Suez Canal Zone.

It feared a halt in military operation now would save Gamal Abdel Nasser, President of Egypt, whose regime the French and British seek to topple date. In that case the French would feel deprived of a victory they regard as already within their grasp.

This was the explanation of the hurried trip to London during the day by Christian Pineau, French Foreign Minister, that was given by high political authorities here tonight.

In London, M. Pineau, Prime Minister Eden and Selwyn Lloyd, British Foreign Secretary, were reported to have agreed they would not accept a cease-fire at least until British-French troops had landed. They were expected to land tomorrow.

Action by U. N. Noted

The United Nations General Assembly voted early today for a cease-fire in the Middle East but the question was how it could be carried out.

[Prime Minister Eden rejected a Laborite demand that he order an immediate end to British attacks on Egypt. This was in response to Laborite pressure that he comply with the resolution of the United Nations General Assembly calling for a cease-fire.]

The fear that took possession of French officials was that Prime Minister Eden might agree to a premature cease-fire.

If so, he would do it, according to these officials, because he is harried by the British Labor party to call off the French-British military expedition to Egypt, and because he is pressed by Secretary of State Dulles, who is credited here with desiring a cease-fire before the United States election Tuesday.

It was even suggested that the United States Sixth Fleet, now in the Mediterranean, might be mandated by the General Assembly to occupy the Suez Canal zone, instead of the French-British forces now preparing to occupy it.

Continued on Page 2, Column 3

BOMBING PRESSED

Planes Center Attacks on Army After Cairo Loses Airpower

By DREW MIDDLETON
Special to The New York Times

LONDON, Nov. 2—The neutralization of the Egyptian Air Force, a primary condition to successful landing operations, was claimed tonight by British and French airpower.

More than a hundred Egyptian planes have been destroyed or damaged at airfields by bombers and fighters of Royal Air Force and French Air Force. A high proportion of these were Soviet-built MIG-15 jet fighter planes and Ilyushin-28 twin-jet bombers, R. A. F. sources said.

At the outset of the operations the Egyptian Air Force had ninety MIGs and fifty Ilyushins. Since not all of them were airworthy Wednesday when the attack began, the allies' claim to have neutralized Egypt's airpower appears valid.

Transit Camp Bombed

The British-French air attack is shifting away from air bases onto the Egyptian Army's central forces, now known to be moving slowly northward and northeastward away from the Cairo area.

British air reconnaissance reported the movement of tanks and infantry into the area around Port Said, one of the three sites chosen by the allies for occupation.

One target successfully attacked was a military transit camp, around which tanks and guns were concentrated, about fifteen miles northeast of Cairo in the El Khanka area.

[The British reported that the Egyptians had sunk seven ships in an effort to block the Suez Canal. It was not known in London whether the Egyptian effort had succeeded. No word of an allied landing in Egypt had been received up to 4 A. M., New York time.]

Information that the Syrian Government was placing its armed forces under the commander in chief of the Egyptian forces has not altered British or French planning for forthcoming operations.

As part of the psychological preparation for the allied landing operations the Cairo Radio, the Voice of Arabia, was silenced

Continued on Page 2, Column 3

ARABS SAID TO PUT TROOPS IN JORDAN

Syrian and Iraqi Forces Are Reported on March

By DANA ADAMS SCHMIDT
Special to The New York Times

WASHINGTON, Nov. 2—Syrian and Iraqi troops are marching into Jordan, according to information telephoned from Cairo, the Egyptian Embassy press counselor announced tonight.

The official, Mohammed Habib, reported also that Lebanese workers had cut one of the pipelines that carry Arabian oil to the Mediterranean.

The report of the troop movements followed announcement by Syria, in a formal note to the State Department, that she had placed her armed forces under Egyptian command. This was done under terms of the Syrian-Egyptian defense pact, the Syrian Chargé d'Affaires, Mamun Jamul, informed the State Department.

The Syrian armed forces are now taking orders from the Egyptian Commander in Chief, Gen. Abdel Hakim Amer, Mr. Jamul said, continuing, "Syria

Continued on Page 3, Column 3

The New York Times.

LATE CITY EDITION
Continuation of U.S. Weather Bureau forecast:
Considerable cloudiness, seasonably cool today and tomorrow.
Temperature range today: 56—48. Temperature range yesterday: 52.8—44.2.
Full U. S. Weather Bureau Report, Page 96.

NEWS SUMMARY AND INDEX, PAGE 96

SECTION ONE

VOL. CVI.. No. 36,079. Entered as Second-Class Matter, Post Office, New York, N. Y.

NEW YORK, SUNDAY, NOVEMBER 4, 1956.

© 1956, by The New York Times Company

TWENTY-FIVE CENTS

SOVIET ATTACKS HUNGARY, SEIZES NAGY; U. S. LEGATION IN BUDAPEST UNDER FIRE; MINDSZENTY IN REFUGE WITH AMERICANS

U. N. Assembly Backs Call to Set Up Mideast Truce Force

STEVENSON HOLDS PRESIDENT LACKS 'ENERGY' FOR JOB

In Last Big Address, He Asks if Nation Is Prepared to Accept Nixon as Leader

Stevenson statement, Page 72; text of speech, Page 73.

By HARRISON E. SALISBURY
Special to The New York Times.

CHICAGO, Nov. 3—Adlai E. Stevenson charged tonight that President Eisenhower "now lacks the energy" to cope with world problems such as the present crisis in the Middle East.

He asked the nation whether it was prepared to accept Richard M. Nixon "as Commander in Chief to exercise power over peace and war."

"Every consideration," Mr. Stevenson said, "the President's age, his health and the fact that he cannot succeed himself make it inevitable that the dominant figure in the Republican party under a second Eisenhower term would be Richard Nixon."

This was the first time that Mr. Stevenson in direct fashion had raised the question of General Eisenhower's health, his physical strength and his ability to survive his full term if re-elected.

It placed—on the eve of the election—the question of General Eisenhower's age and his health directly in the forefront of the campaign.

Nixon Draws Boos

Mr. Stevenson's every reference to Mr. Nixon brought forth a hurricane of boos that was equaled only by several waves of boos for General Eisenhower's foreign policy and references to the asserted errors of John Foster Dulles, Secretary of State.

Mr. Stevenson's remarks, which were carried to the nation by television, were cut off the air on a chorus of boos for Mr. Nixon. The conclusion of his address ran over the allotted air time.

General Eisenhower is 66 years old. Mr. Stevenson had foresworn any discussion of the President's health, insisting that this was a matter for each individual voter.

However, in charging tonight that the crisis in world affairs had stemmed directly from the President's "part-time conduct" of his office, Mr. Stevenson took a look into the future.

The fact is, he asserted, General Eisenhower "in the next years would inevitably recede more and more from the picture."

The President, Mr. Stevenson

Continued on Page 73, Column 2

Major Sports News

FOOTBALL

Yale, Navy, Syracuse, Columbia and Army won major Eastern contests yesterday. Scores of leading games:

Amherst .... 6 Tufts 0
Army ...... 55 Colgate 46
Columbia ..25 Cornell 19
Georgia Tech 7 Duke 0
Illinois ... 7 Purdue 7
Michigan ..17 Iowa 14
Michigan St..33 Wisconsin . 0
Minnesota .. 7 Pitt 6
Navy .....33 Notre Dame. 7
Ohio State.. 6 Northwestern 2
Oklahoma ..27 Colorado ..19
Penn ......28 Harvard ...14
Princeton ..21 Brown 7
Rutgers ...20 Lafayette ..19
Syracuse ...13 Penn State.. 9
Tennessee ..20 N. Carolina. 0
T. C. U. .... 7 Baylor 0
U. C. L. A...14 Stanford ...13
W. Virginia .14 Cl. Wash'ton 0
Yale ......17 Dartmouth . 0

HORSE RACING

Summer Tan took the Gallant Fox Handicap in track record time at Jamaica.

Details in Section 5.

London, Paris Bar Truce; Eden Pledges Israeli Exit

U. N. Occupation Offered

By HAROLD CALLENDER
Special to The New York Times.

PARIS, Nov. 3—Britain and France rejected today the United Nations call for a cease-fire in the Suez area.

At the same time they made a counter-proposal designed to bring their independent military action under the authority of the United Nations. They thus sought to heal the breach between the two powers on the one hand and the United Nations and the United States on the other.

The United Nations General Assembly recommended the cease-fire Thursday by adopting a resolution introduced by the United States.

The two European powers de-

Continued on Page 18, Column 1

Prime Minister Speaks

By DREW MIDDLETON
Special to The New York Times.

LONDON, Nov. 3—The British Government will insure the withdrawal of Israeli forces from Egyptian territory once British and French troops have occupied

Eden's text and Gaitskell excerpts are on Page 28.

key points on the Suez Canal, Sir Anthony Eden declared tonight.

The objective of his policy of intervention in the Middle East is a lasting settlement in the area and a stronger United Nations, able "to act as well as to talk," the Prime Minister told

Continued on Page 28, Column 6

President Expected to Win; Democratic Congress Seen

New York Times Team Reports

Following are summaries of the apparent voting trends for President and the United States Senate and House of Representatives. They are based on the reports of New York Times teams that have surveyed twenty-seven closely contested states and of correspondents in twenty-one other states.

Presidential Race

By W. H. LAWRENCE

Surveys indicate that President Eisenhower and Vice President Richard M. Nixon will be re-elected on Tuesday by comfortable majorities of both the popular and electoral votes.

Reports from New York Times correspondents who have investigated political sentiment in the forty-eight states indicate these probable results:

For President Eisenhower—A minimum of twenty-seven states with 285 electoral votes, or nineteen votes more than required for a majority of the 531-member Electoral College.

For Adlai E. Stevenson—A minimum of seven states with seventy-six electoral votes.

Leaning toward President Eisenhower—Eight states with ninety-nine electoral votes.

Leaning toward Mr. Steven-

Continued on Page 69, Column 1

Congressional Races

By WILLIAM S. WHITE

The Democrats appear likely to hold Congress in Tuesday's national elections in spite of the prospect that President Eisenhower will retain the White House for the Republicans.

The outlook thus is for a continuation of the divided form of national political sentiment in the forty-eight states that has guided the country since 1954.

A landslide for President Eisenhower would, of course, alter every present prospect. The weight of all current evidence suggests clearly, however, these approximate results:

¶The Democrats should at least retain their present thin margin of control in the Senate—49 Democrats to 47 Republicans.

¶There should be a Democratic House of Representatives again with no less than the

Continued on Page 68, Column 5

EISENHOWER PLANS TALKS TOMORROW

To Make 2 Short Speeches on TV—Mitchell Reports Advances by Labor

By CHARLES E. EGAN
Special to The New York Times.

WASHINGTON, Nov. 3 — Politics held an active, if subordinate, role in White House operations on this Saturday before election.

While the President was closeted with advisers in discussions of events in the Middle East and Europe, his top aides found time:

¶To consult with Leonard W. Hall, chairman of the Republican National Committee, on campaign strategy.

¶To issue a special report by James P. Mitchell, Secretary of Labor, detailing aid given to workers by his department under the present Administration.

¶To give a preliminary outline of the President's two Election Eve television appearances on Monday.

The announcement was made by a State Department spokesman, Lincoln White, at Walter Reed Army Hospital. It said Mr. Dulles, 68 years old, probably would be in the hospital for two to three weeks and that he "should be able to return to his desk in approximately six weeks." Mr. Dulles' pulse was reported to be 76, his blood pressure 126/75.

Continued on Page 78, Column 4

DULLES IS GAINING AFTER OPERATION

Part of His Large Intestine Is Removed—He Will Stay in Hospital 2 Weeks

By EDWIN L. DALE Jr.
Special to The New York Times.

WASHINGTON, Nov. 3—John Foster Dulles, Secretary of State, underwent successful surgery today for removal of a perforated portion of his large intestine.

It was announced after the two-and-one-half-hour operation that Mr. Dulles had "left the operating table in good condition" and that he was "resting comfortably."

The announcement was made by a State Department spokesman, Lincoln White, at Walter Reed Army Hospital. It said Mr. Dulles, 68 years old, probably would be in the hospital for two to three weeks and that he "should be able to return to his desk in approximately six weeks." Mr. Dulles' pulse was reported to be 76, his blood pressure 126/75.

The surgery was performed by Maj. Gen. Leonard D. Heaton, commanding officer of Walter Reed, who had operated on President Eisenhower in June for ileitis. He was assisted today by James C. Hagerty, White House press secretary.

Continued on Page 78, Column 3

Mideast Oil Lines Reported Blown Up

By SAM POPE BREWER
Special to The New York Times.

BEIRUT, Lebanon, Nov. 3—Pipelines carrying more than half a million barrels of oil daily from Iraq to the Mediterranean coast have stopped operating as a result of the fighting in Egypt.

Reports circulating here were that the Iraq Petroleum Company's three pumping stations in Syria known as T-2, T-3 and T-4 had been blown up and burned.

[At the United Nations an Egyptian spokesman was quoted by The United Press as having said all oil pipelines in every Middle East country except Saudi Arabia had been blown up or shut down.]

No oil installations in Lebanon were damaged up to tonight. Reports abroad that the effect was incorrect, according

Continued on Page 17, Column 4

BID TO U. N. CHIEF

Canada's Motion That He Plan Suez Unit Adopted, 59 to 0

Texts of draft resolutions and debate excerpts, Page 29.

By KATHLEEN TELTSCH
Special to The New York Times.

UNITED NATIONS, N. Y., Sunday, Nov. 4—The General Assembly voted early today to ask the Secretary General to submit a plan for creation of a United Nations police force to obtain and supervise a cease-fire in the Middle East.

The policing proposal, sponsored by Canada, was adopted 57 to 0, at 2:17 A. M. at an emergency session of the Assembly.

Nineteen states abstained, among them Israel, France and Britain. The latter two earlier had rejected an Assembly call for a cease-fire and said they would keep on with their "police action" in Egypt to safeguard the Suez Canal.

The proposal, made by Lester B. Pearson, Canada's Secretary for External Affairs, calls on Secretary General Dag Hammarskjold to submit blueprints within forty-eight hours for an "emergency international United Nations force."

New Truce Plan Adopted

No details were suggested by Mr. Pearson, but such a police force presumably would have to include several thousand men. The Canadian spokesman said he would recommend Canada's participation. His proposal, however, left all arrangements to the Secretary General.

Within minutes, the emergency session adopted a second resolution, co-sponsored by nineteen Asian and African countries. This renewed the cease-fire appeal made two days ago and asked Mr. Hammarskjold to report within twelve hours on whether the states had complied.

The second resolution was approved, 59 to 5, with twelve abstentions. Among the abstainers were France, Britain, Israel, Australia and New Zealand.

[Washington indicated that the Administration, after initial anger at the British-French and Israeli moves, was taking a more moderate, hopeful and understanding attitude.]

Weary United Nations delegates approved the new proposals at an event-filled emergency session, at which the United States presented a new Middle East plan. This seeks a long-range settlement of the Palestine problem and also of the current Suez Canal dispute.

In warmly supporting the Ca-

Continued on Page 29, Column 8

SOVIET ROAD BLOCK IN HUNGARY: Soviet tank obstructs road near Magyarovar.
Associated Press Radiophoto

ISRAELI PATROLS REACH SUEZ BANK

Penetrate Zone at 3 Points as Eden Disclosed in British-French Landings Irks Regime

By HOMER BIGART
Special to The New York Times.

TEL AVIV, Israel, Sunday, Nov. 4—Israeli patrols reached the east bank of the Suez Canal yesterday.

A Government spokesman said Israeli columns had penetrated at three places the ten-mile buffer zone east of the canal that Britain and France wanted kept clear of warring Israeli and Egyptian forces.

Meanwhile, the Cabinet of Premier David Ben-Gurion studied reports that Syrian and Iraqi troops had entered Jordan. The developments in Jordan were being followed with "concern and alertness," according to a Foreign Ministry source.

[In Moscow, Marshal Kliment Y. Voroshilov, Soviet chief of state, told President Shukry al-Kuwatly of Syria at a farewell reception that the Soviet Union was prepared to give Syria the "necessary assistance "to reinforce her independence against foreign threats."]

2-Nation Plan Criticized

The Government spokesman offered no reason why the Israelis had entered the proscribed zone. But the Israelis are increasingly disturbed over the slowness of British and French forces in occupying the canal.

The announcement that Israelis were within ten miles of the canal at three points—opposite El Qantara in the north, Ismailia in the center and Suez at the southern terminus—may have been timed to coincide with reports here that the British-French invasion also had been put off because of United States pressure.

Continued on Page 17, Column 1

British Bomb Raids On Egypt Continued In Landing Prelude

Texts of the communiqués are printed on Page 26.

By LEONARD INGALLS
Special to The New York Times.

LONDON, Nov. 3—British bombers turned their heaviest attack today on airfields in Egypt to ammunition dumps, barracks and armored weapons depots of the Egyptian Army.

There were indications that the landing by British and French forces in the Suez Canal Zone would be made by paratroopers and seaborne invasion units within the next forty-eight hours.

The Beirut radio, quoting an Egyptian communiqué, reported that a British-French force attempted to land at the southern entrance to the canal, but was driven off with heavy losses.

The Egyptians said they had sunk four British naval vessels and captured three troop landing craft at Suez with fire from shore batteries and torpedo boats. One British ship was sunk by gunfire, and a British destroyer, a troop carrier and another British naval unit were said to have been sunk by torpedoes.

The Egyptians also reported they had shot down seventeen British-French planes over the Suez Canal area.

[There was little detailed information on the military situation in announcements or dispatches from Cairo.]

An Admiralty spokesman said "there is no information in London to support the Egyptian

Continued on Page 26, Column 3

Nutting Quits Post; Churchill For Eden

The text of Churchill letter will be found on Page 24.

Special to The New York Times.

LONDON, Sunday, Nov. 4—Anthony Nutting, Minister of State in the Foreign Office, resigned from the Government tonight because he strongly disagreed with its policy of armed intervention in Egypt.

But Israel has insisted that no firm deal was made with the French on where the advance would be halted.

Meanwhile, the Israelis reported they were rapidly occupying all key points on the occupied Sinai Peninsula.

Lieut. Col. Moshe Pearlman, Government and Army spokesman, said that the whole area was "relatively quiet" and that "the entire peninsula in very short time will be in Israeli hands."

British Embassy sources said

Continued on Page 24, Column 5

SOVIET VETO BARS ACTION IN COUNCIL

Censure Move in U. N. Over New Attack on Hungary Carried to Assembly

Excerpts from statements in Security Council, Page 35.

By LINDESAY PARROTT
Special to The New York Times.

UNITED NATIONS, N. Y., Sunday, Nov. 4—The Soviet Union early today vetoed a United States resolution proposing Security Council censure of the Russian military attack on Hungary.

Nine nations favored the United States proposal and one abstained, Yugoslavia.

The veto was the seventy-ninth cast by the Soviet Union since the world organization was born. Henry Cabot Lodge Jr., United States representative, immediately moved for an emergency session of the General Assembly to take up the Hungarian crisis. The Assembly already was in permanent special session over the French-British intervention in the Suez Canal area.

Council's Will 'Thwarted'

Angrily, Mr Lodge told the Council that the will of the world organization had been "thwarted" by the Soviet veto and that the eleven-nation body had been prevented from fulfilling its responsibilities. In this "grave situation," he said, Assembly action was required.

The Council adopted the United States resolution for reference to the Assembly by a vote of 40 to 1. This ballot came at 5:21 A. M.

The Assembly meeting was set for 8 o'clock tonight.

The Council adjourned at 5:24 A. M.

The Council's action, marking the Soviet Union's seventy-ninth veto, was taken after the United States had called the group together at 3 A. M. to protest against the reoccupation of Budapest by Soviet troops. According to the latest reports from early today, the Hungarian capital was in the hands of Soviet troops after Russian tanks earlier had ringed the city.

The United States legation was understood to have been under fire. Mr. Lodge also reported that Joseph Cardinal Mindszenty and his staff had taken refuge in the legation.

The Security Council had adjourned shortly after midnight.

Continued on Page 35, Column 4

This section consists of 140 pages divided into three parts. The news summary and index will be found on Page 95. Society news begins on Page 90 and obituary articles will be found on Pages 86 and 87.

CAPITAL STORMED

Freedom Radios Fade From Air as Russians Shell Key Centers

By PAUL HOFMANN
Special to The New York Times.

VIENNA, Sunday, Nov. 4—Soviet troops started attacking Budapest and other Hungarian cities, towns and key military installations at dawn today.

At 9 A. M., local time (3 A. M. Eastern standard time) four hours after Budapest had been awakened by Russian artillery fire, overpowering Soviet tanks and infantry forces had stormed the Parliament Building and made Premier Imre Nagy and most members of his government prisoners.

Fighting in Budapest and many other parts of the country was continuing, but the prospects for the free Hungarian Government forces were nearly hopeless in the face of crushing Soviet superiority.

The Budapest radio and other Hungarian freedom stations went off the air one after another.

Before going silent, they directed desperate pleas to the West, especially to the United States, and to the United Nations for help to save the Hungarian people from "annihilation."

Mindszenty in U. S. Legation

Joseph Cardinal Mindszenty, Roman Catholic primate of Hungary, who had been freed from detention last week, and his secretary had taken refuge in the building of the United States Legation.

The United States legation, near the Parliament Building, was under fire at 9:30 A. M.

A fierce battle was raging in the immediate surroundings.

At 7 A. M. "several hundred" Soviet heavy tanks were reported attacking key Hungarian Army positions on the outskirts of Budapest and attempting to penetrate the city. The main thrust of the Soviet forces came apparently from the southeast.

Shortly before 7 A. M. the Budapest radio repeated Premier Nagy's announcement of the Soviet attack. It directed an appeal to Dag Hammarskjold, Secretary General of the United Nations. At the same time the M. T. I. Hungarian news agency reported:

"Russian troops have suddenly attacked Budapest and the entire country. They have opened fire on everyone in Hungary. It is a general attack.

"Janos Kadar [since Oct. 24 secretary of the Hungarian Communist party], Gyorgy Marosan and Sandor Ronai have formed a new Government and started crushing the counter-

Continued on Page 34, Column 6

Pravda Denounces Nagy for 'Reaction'

By Reuters.

LONDON, Sunday, Nov. 4—The Soviet Communist party newspaper Pravda attacked Premier Imre Nagy of Hungary today "in strong terms," according to the Moscow radio.

Pravda said that of barring the way to reaction in Hungary has to be carried out without the slightest delay—such is the course dictated by events.

The broadcast quoted Pravda as saying: "Imre Nagy turned out to be, objectively speaking, an accomplice of the reactionary forces. Imre Nagy cannot and does not want to fight the dark forces of reaction."

Pravda asserted that it was Mr. Nagy who had requested bringing Soviet troops into Budapest, "as it was vital for the interests of the Socialist regime."

Continued on Page 15, Column 1

"All the News That's Fit to Print"

The New York Times.

LATE CITY EDITION
Combination of U. S. Weather Bureau forecast:
Some cloudiness today; cloudy to-night. Clearing, cooler tomorrow.
Temperature range today: 66—50.
Temperature range yesterday: 65.4—52.2.
Full U. S. Weather Bureau Report, Page 42.

© 1956, by The New York Times Company.

VOL. CVI.—No. 36,082.

Entered as Second-Class Matter,
Post Office, New York, N. Y.

NEW YORK, WEDNESDAY, NOVEMBER 7, 1956.

Times Square, New York 36, N. Y.
Telephone Lackawanna 4-7000

FIVE CENTS

EISENHOWER BY A LANDSLIDE; BATTLE FOR CONGRESS CLOSE; JAVITS VICTOR OVER WAGNER

Suez Warfare Stopped Under British-French Cease-Fire

MAYOR CONCEDES

Javits, Swept In With the Eisenhower Tide, Wins Stiff Contest

Vote for Senator

CITY SUMMARY

	Javits (Rep.)	Wagner (Dem.-Lib.)
Manhattan ...	270,146	393,462
Bronx	218,895	374,810
Brooklyn ...	398,088	605,002
Queens ...	400,832	372,505
Richmond ..	49,694	32,881
Total ...	1,337,655	1,778,660
Upstate ...	2,362,618	1,478,238

Grand total 3,700,273 3,256,898
All E. D.'s of 4,607 in city and 6,522 of 6,525 upstate.

By DOUGLAS DALES

Attorney General Jacob K. Javits was swept to victory yesterday in the Eisenhower Republican landslide in his race against Mayor Wagner for the United States Senate.

Mayor Wagner conceded defeat in a statement at 1:22 A. M. after the trend to Javits' victory became unmistakable.

Mr. Wagner carried three boroughs in the city—Manhattan, Brooklyn and the Bronx—but lost in Queens and Richmond.

The city-wide complete totals gave Mr. Javits 1,337,655 votes to 1,778,660 for Mayor Wagner. The Mayor's total include 233,560 on the Liberal party line. The Liberal line attracted 404,769 votes in the city four years ago, when the party ran its own candidate for the Senate, George S. Counts.

The victor's margin was expected to reach 444,000 with the final results. With all city districts and 6,522 of 6,525 districts upstate reported, Mr. Javits had an edge of 443,375.

Mayor Wagner carried two of the fifty-seven upstate counties, Erie and Albany. Eisenhower carried both.

Everywhere outside the city, Mr. Javits ran substantially behind the President's vote. On the other hand, Mayor Wagner ran well ahead of Adlai E. Stevenson, the Democratic candidate for President.

In view of the size of the

Continued on Page 26, Column 2

PRESIDENT SCORES NEW HIGH IN STATE

Plurality Tops 1,500,000 as He Cuts Rival's City Edge

State Presidential Vote

CITY SUMMARY

	Eisenhower (Rep.)	Stevenson (Dem.-Lib.)
Manhattan ..	299,929	378,018
Bronx	256,009	343,656
Brooklyn ...	459,703	558,187
Queens ...	471,144	313,311
Richmond ..	64,236	196,653
Total ...	1,551,921	1,614,825
Upstate ...	2,766,183	1,127,403

Grand total 4,318,104 2,742,228
All E. D.'s of 4,607 in city and 6,522 of 6,525 upstate.

By LEO EGAN

President Eisenhower swept New York yesterday by a plurality that dwarfed all previous records.

With sixty-one of the state's 11,132 election districts still to report this morning, General Eisenhower's margin exceeded 1,500,000.

The previous record for a Presidential plurality in New York was established in 1920, when the late Warren G. Harding, Republican, defeated James M. Cox, Democrat, by 1,139,927.

All the missing districts are in Republican territory upstate.

Continued on Page 28, Column 1

An International Summary:
The Mideast and Hungary

Following are summaries of the leading developments in the Middle East and Europe. The full foreign news report begins on the first page of the second part.

Cease-Fire Is On

Britain and France put a cease-fire into effect and halted their advance in Egypt. Prime Minister Eden told Commons that conditions had been established for an international police force under the United Nations to promote settlement of Middle Eastern issues.

Invaders Hold Canal

The invasion forces claimed control of the Suez Canal Zone. They took Port Said and drove south before the cease-fire became effective.

Egyptians Halt Fight

The Egyptians decided to hold their fire at the deadline in the hope that the United Nations resolution of Nov. 2, providing for withdrawal of all forces behind armistice lines, would be carried out.

Soviet May Send 'Volunteers'

Indications in Moscow were that Soviet "volunteers" who began applying for service with Egyptian forces might go to the Middle East despite the cease-fire. Moscow broadcast a Cairo appeal for aid.

Troop Withdrawal Asked

Asian and Arab states drafted a United Nations resolution calling on Britain, France and Israel to withdraw their troops from Egypt immediately. A special session of the General Assembly called for last night was postponed until this morning.

Hungarian Battle Persists

Stubborn Hungarian revolutionary forces are continuing to fight the Soviet army in Budapest, according to diplomatic reports received in Vienna. Women and children were said to be fighting alongside the men in a house-to-house struggle. The General Assembly scheduled a special session this afternoon to consider Soviet intervention in Hungary.

EISENHOWER SETS RECORD IN JERSEY

Margin of 700,000 Carries All 21 Counties—G. O. P. Wins 2 Hudson Seats

By GEORGE CABLE WRIGHT

President Eisenhower yesterday scored the greatest victory in New Jersey political history.

With most of the state's ballots tallied early this morning, his margin over Adlai E. Stevenson had soared above 700,000, almost double that of 1952. He became the first candidate in modern times to carry all twenty-one counties.

The President's margin was expected to reach 444,000 with the final results. With all city districts and 6,522 of 6,525 districts upstate reported, Mr. Javits had an edge of 443,375.

This county gave the President a majority of 76,554. In 1952 Mr. Stevenson had carried Hudson by 7,886 votes.

In fact, Republicans swept every county contest. When residents of Hudson awake this morning it is certain that many will find it hard to believe that for the next two years they will be represented in Congress by not one, but two, Republicans. There was no precedent there for that.

A third Democratic incumbent, Representative Harrison A. Williams Jr., went down to defeat in Union County.

Thus, the Democratic representation of six in the House was cut in half. All eight Republican incumbents were re-elected.

Continued on Page 28, Column 5

BUSH RE-ELECTED IN CONNECTICUT

Plurality for Eisenhower of 303,036 Biggest in State in a Presidential Race

By RICHARD H. PARKE
Special to The New York Times.

HARTFORD, Nov. 6—President Eisenhower scored an easy victory in Connecticut today. He carried to victory with him Senator Prescott S. Bush, the Republican incumbent.

The President's plurality of 303,036 votes over Adlai E. Stevenson, Democratic candidate, was the greatest margin the State ever has given a Presidential candidate. The previous high figure was 136,138 votes, achieved by President Coolidge in 1924.

The President, whose 1952 plurality of 129,363 was considered of landslide proportions, defeated Mr. Stevenson today by 708,995 votes to 405,959, according to complete but unofficial returns.

The Republican sweep was general throughout the state. It carried in Senator Bush by a plurality of 129,544 votes. He defeated his Democratic opponent, Representative Thomas J. Dodd, by 607,330 to 477,876.

The Republicans also retained

Continued on Page 28, Column 5

Coudert Wins in Close Contest; Vote in Queens 7th Rechecked

By CLAYTON KNOWLES

The Republicans emerged yesterday from a hard-fought Congressional campaign early today with a possible net gain of one in the state delegation to the House of Representatives.

At 4:20 A. M. a final decision rested on the outcome of the race in the Seventh district of Queens. Here Representative James J. Delaney, Democratic incumbent, claimed victory at 4:15 A. M. by forty votes, but a final tally was unavailable.

An hour and a half earlier, Delaney supporters were conceding the election of Joseph Stockinger, a Republican, but the contest was so close that all 217 districts were being rechecked.

The announced vote for 202 districts was 72,186 for Mr. Stockinger to 72,112 for Mr. De-

---

SENATE IN DOUBT

Democrats Lag in East on War Issue but Gain in the West

By WILLIAM S. WHITE

The Democrats and Republicans fought along a swaying electoral battle line early today for control of the oncoming Eighty-fifth Congress.

Not all the power of President Eisenhower's landslide victory had been enough to put his Republican Congressional colleagues in front.

The Senate race, in which the Republicans were attempting to overturn a present 49-to-47 Democratic margin of control, was an affair of hairbreadth drama. Small net Republican gains for the House of Representatives were indicated. But whether these would continue or would be enough remained wholly in doubt.

The Republicans needed a net gain of 15 House seats, and the capture of 2 additional and now vacant seats that had been Republican.

The pattern of the Congressional contest was this: The East, more sensitive than other sections to the last-minute issue involved in the Middle Eastern and Central European war crises, on the whole was hitting the Democrats hard. The appeal of "don't change horses in midstream" was strong in this area. In the interior, however, Democratic organizational strength, farm discontent and other factors were turning up great Democratic strength.

Cooper Wins in Kentucky

The position on the Senate in some critical states was this:

KENTUCKY—A gain of one Republican seat in former Senator John Sherman Cooper's defeat of his Democratic challenger, Lawrence Wetherby, for the seat made vacant by the death of Senator Alben W. Barkley.

The possibility of another gain for the Republicans in the fact that the assistant Democratic leader of the Senate, Earle C. Clements, was running behind Thruston B. Morton, a former assistant Secretary of State in the Eisenhower Administration.

NEW YORK—A Republican gain in the victory of Jacob K. Javits over Mayor Wagner for the seat being vacated by Senator Herbert H. Lehman, Democrat-Liberal.

OHIO—A Democratic gain in the defeat by Gov. Frank J. Lausche of Senator George H. Bender.

ILLINOIS—Senator Everett M. Dirksen, Republican, ran ahead of his Democratic opponent, Richard Stengel.

PENNSYLVANIA—Joseph S.

Continued on Page 3, Column 1

PRESIDENT EISENHOWER   VICE-PRESIDENT NIXON

G. O. P. MAKES BID TO CAPTURE HOUSE

Picks Up 9 Seats in East, but Drive Eases in West —Midwest to Decide

By JOHN D. MORRIS

Republicans got off to a fast start in their bid to recapture control of the House of Representatives, but appeared to lose steam early today as returns trickled in from the West.

As of 3 A. M., results from yesterday's Congressional races indicated a decided Republican trend, with some major upsets for the Democrats. However, with control of nearly two-thirds of the 435 seats still in doubt, victory for either party was far from certain.

The undecided contests were almost entirely in the Midwest, where the issue of declining farm income was a factor favoring the Democrats, and in the Far West.

G. O. P. Gains in East

Such returns as were available from those areas indicated possible Democratic gains in Iowa, California and South Dakota. Eastward, where the only decisive tallies were available, Republicans had picked up nine seats held by Democrats in the Eighty-fourth Congress while holding their own in all other contests where returns were conclusive. One, in New York City, was subject to a recount. Democrats had failed to capture any Republican seat except one that they took in the Maine election on Sept. 10.

Republican incumbents were easy victors in a number of contests that had promised to be close.

The most outstanding upsets were in New Jersey, where the Hudson county Democratic stronghold of the late Mayor Frank Hague of Jersey City unseated its two Democratic Representatives, T. James Tumulty and Alfred D. Sieminski, in the Thirteenth and Fourteenth Congressional Districts.

Mr. Sieminski lost to Norman M. Roth, Republican. Mr. Tumulty, a 300-pound legislator, was defeated by Vincent J. Dellay, Republican.

A third Democratic incumbent in New Jersey, Harrison A. Williams, lost to Florence P. Dwyer, Republican.

Republicans also picked up easy victories at Connecticut, one in Delaware, one in Pennsylvania, one in Indiana and

Continued on Page 3, Column 2

Stevenson Concedes Defeat and Wishes President Success

Stevenson and Kefauver talks appear on Page 13.

By HARRISON E. SALISBURY
Special to The New York Times.

CHICAGO, Wednesday, Nov. 7—Adlai E. Stevenson conceded the election of President Eisenhower in a statement made public at 12:25 A. M. Central standard time today (1:25 Eastern standard time).

In a telegram to President Eisenhower, the Democratic candidate expressed his understanding of "grave difficulties" that the Administration faced and wished all success to General Eisenhower in the years ahead.

Mr. Stevenson coupled his telegram of congratulations to the President with an appeal to his followers to carry forward in the "crusade for what he called a "New America."

He called on America's leaders to recognize that the nation "wants to face up squarely to the facts of today's world."

"We don't want to draw back from them," Mr. Stevenson said. "We can't. We are ready, for the test that we know history has set for us."

Mr. Stevenson in his statement took note of the troubled conditions of the world.

"Beyond the seas, in much of the world, in Russia, in China, in Hungary, in all the trembling satellites, partisan controversy is forbidden and dissent suppressed," Mr. Stevenson said.

Mr. Stevenson also took note

Continued on Page 13, Column 3

Electoral Vote by States

	Eisen-hower	Steven-son		Eisen-hower	Steven-son
Ala. ...		11	Nev. ...	3	
Ariz. ..	4		N. J. ..	16	
Ark. ...		8	N. M. ..	4	
Calif. ..	32		N. Y. ..	45	
Colo. ..	6		N. C. ...		14
Conn. ..	8		N. D. ..	4	
Del. ...	3		Ohio ..	25	
Fla. ...	10		Okla. ..	8	
Ga. ...		12	Ore. ...	6	
Idaho ..	4		Pa. ...	32	
Ill. ...	27		R. I. ...		4
Ind. ...	13		S. C. ...		8
Iowa ..	10		S. D. ..	4	
Kan. ...	8		Tenn. ..	11	
Ky. ...	10		Texas ..	24	
La. ...	10		Utah ..	4	
Me. ...	5		Vt. ...	3	
Md. ...	9		Va. ...	12	
Mass. ..	16		Wash. ..	9	
Mich. ..	20		W. Va. ..	8	
Minn. ..	11		Wisc. ..	12	
Miss. ..		8	Wyo. ..	3	
Mo. ...		13			
Neb. ...	6		Total 457	74	

EISENHOWER VOWS TO TOIL FOR PEACE

Hails Landslide Re-election as Proof Nation Wants 'Modern Republicanism'

Texts of the Eisenhower and Nixon talks on Page 12.

By RUSSELL BAKER
Special to The New York Times.

WASHINGTON, Wednesday, Nov. 7—President Eisenhower hailed his landslide re-election victory today as proof that his "modern Republicanism" has now proved itself and America has approved of modern Republicanism.

He pledged in a victory statement early this morning to work with "whatever talents the good God has given me for 168,000,000 Americans here at home and for peace in the world."

Addressing a jubilant crowd of party workers at Republican election headquarters here and the nation, over television, the President declared that so long as the G.O.P. pursued the "ideals, the hopes and aspirations" of the people, it would continue to flourish.

"If it is anything less," he said, "it is only a conspiracy to seize power. And the Republican party is not that."

'Looks to the Future'

Thus, in his moment of triumph, General Eisenhower claimed a sweeping triumph for what his Administration's philosophers had styled the "new Republicanism" and what he himself termed this morning "modern Republicanism."

"Modern Republicanism," he said, "looks to the future and this means it will gain constantly new recruits." So long as it continued to remain "modern," he added, it would "continue to increase in power and influence for decades to come."

So long as it clings to its "modern" ideals, the President declared, it would "point the way to peace among nations and prosperity, advancing prosperity, advancing prosperity here at home in which everyone will share."

The President delivered his victory statement at 1:45 A. M. about fifteen minutes after this restive crowd gathered in the mammoth ballroom of the Sheraton-Park Hotel had heard Adlai E. Stevenson concede defeat in Chicago.

General Eisenhower had been waiting upstairs in a third-floor suite for three and a half hours

Continued on Page 13, Column 1

---

41 STATES TO G.O.P.

President Sweeps All the North and West, Scores in South

By JAMES RESTON

Dwight David Eisenhower won yesterday the most spectacular Presidential election victory since Franklin D. Roosevelt submerged Alfred M. Landon in 1936.

The smiling 66-year-old hero of the Normandy invasion, who was in a Denver hospital recuperating from a heart attack just a year ago today, thus became the first Republican in this century to win two successive Presidential elections. William McKinley did it in 1896 and 1900.

Adlai E. Stevenson of Illinois, who lost to Mr. Eisenhower four years ago, thirty-nine states to nine, conceded defeat at 1:25 this morning.

At 4:45 A. M. President Eisenhower had won forty-one states to seven for Mr. Stevenson. His electoral lead at that time was 457 to 74 for Stevenson, and his popular vote was 25,071,331 to 18,337,434—up 2 per cent over 1952. Two hundred and sixty-six electoral votes are needed for election.

Victory in All Areas

This was a national victory in every conceivable way. It started in Connecticut. It swept every state in New England. It took New York by a plurality of more than 1,500,000. It carried all the Middle Atlantic states, all the Midwest, all the Rocky Mountain states and everything beyond the Rockies.

More than that, the Republican tide swept along the border states and to the South, carried all the states won by the G.O.P. there in 1952—Virginia, Texas, Tennessee and Florida—and even took Louisiana for the first time since the Hayes-Tilden election of 1876.

For the President and his 43-year old Vice Presidential running mate, Richard M. Nixon of California, who carried much of the Republican campaign, it was a more impressive victory than for the Republican party.

So close were many races for

Continued on Page 2, Column 3

CLARK LEADS DUFF IN PENNSYLVANIA

Democrat's Edge Dropping —President Takes State

By WILLIAM G. WEART
Special to The New York Times.

PHILADELPHIA, Wednesday, Nov. 7—Joseph S. Clark Jr., former Mayor of Philadelphia, was running ahead of Senator James H. Duff early today.

But his margin was ebbing as returns from rural areas and small towns began to offset the lead he piled up in large cities.

President Eisenhower won the state's thirty-two electoral votes by a plurality that was steadily mounting.

Mr. Clark expressed disappointment at the defeat of his party's standard-bearer. He attributed General Eisenhower's victory to his "personal popularity." Mr. Clark's campaign manager, Mayor Richardson Dilworth of Philadelphia, said the President's re-election was due to the "emotion caused by the war situation."

In the event the final tally in the Senatorial race is close, an estimated 50,000 absentee votes cast by servicemen and hospitalized veterans may decide the outcome. Under the law, absentee ballots are mailed to county

Continued on Page 13, Column 1

"All the News
That's Fit to Print"

The New York Times.

© 1957, by The New York Times Company.

VOL. CVI..No. 36,146.

Entered as Second-Class Matter,
Post Office, New York, N. Y.

NEW YORK, THURSDAY, JANUARY 10, 1957.

Times Square, New York 36, N. Y.
Telephone Lackawanna 4-1000

LATE CITY EDITION

Condensation of U. S. Weather Bureau forecast:
Rain changing to snow today; much
colder tonight. Fair tomorrow.
Temperature range today: 30—25.
Temperature range yesterday: 40—30.2.
Full U. S. Weather Bureau Report, Page 58.

FIVE CENTS

HARRIMAN URGES NEW WELFARE AID AND CUT IN TAXES

DELIVERS MESSAGE

G. O. P. Calls Program 'Moderate'—State's Revenues Increase

Text of Harriman's message is on Pages 17, 18 and 19.

Special to The New York Times.

ALBANY, Jan. 9—Governor Harriman proposed today an increase in state social welfare benefits and an expansion of state services in several fields. He also asked, to the degree warranted, cuts in personal income and unincorporated business taxes.

His program was contained in an 18,000-word annual message, which he delivered in person at the opening session of the 180th Legislature. A good part of the program had been disclosed unofficially in advance.

Of the proposals revealed today for the first time, the most startling was a suggestion that up to $150 for hospital expenses be provided as an additional benefit for 4,653,000 wage-earners covered by the state's Disability Benefits Law.

The Governor's message provided no additional details. His staff is preparing legislation on the subject.

Program Jointly Financed

This law provides for disability payments up to $49 a week for those whose wages are suspended because of an illness or disability not related to their employment. The benefits are financed by joint contributions of employers and employes.

Hospital benefits under the Governor's program would be financed without any additional employe contribution. Their cost has been estimated roughly at $15,000,000 a year. The plan has strong support from organized labor.

Democratic legislators acting on Mayor Wagner's behalf introduced fourteen measures today designed to aid the city administration in one form or another. The most important measure would provide the city with $100,000 a year in new revenue by revising the system of bidding for public contracts.

One of the notable omissions in the Governor's message was any discussion of Mayor Wagner's proposals for revising financial relations between the state and city governments. At various times in the past Mr. Harriman has endorsed, partly at least, the Mayor's repeated assertion that the city is receiving less than it deserves. This

Continued on Page 16, Column 4

Rise in Meat Prices Predicted by U. S.

By WILLIAM M. BLAIR
Special to The New York Times.

WASHINGTON, Jan. 9—The Department of Agriculture forecast today that consumers would pay higher prices for meat this year.

Total meat production will be less than in 1956 to raise prices, particularly on pork. Retail prices on choice beef will stay above 1956 levels throughout the winter, and spring and likely climb again in the fall, but at a slower rate.

There are ample supplies of beef, the department reported, but it cast a wary eye on the drought in the Great Plains states. Persistent drought could lead to still higher prices

Continued on Page 30, Column 1

STATE G. O. P. SPLIT; SPRAGUE IS TARGET

Leader's Policies Opposed—Appointment of Lefkowitz Brings Revolt Into Open

By LEO EGAN

ALBANY, Jan. 9—A deep split in the Republican party has been brought into the open by the controversy that preceded today's election of Louis J. Lefkowitz as state Attorney General.

Substantial forces are in revolt against what they regard as the domination of the party by J. Russel Sprague, Republican leader of Nassau County.

This was behind the severe criticism heaped on L. Judson Morhouse, state chairman, at last night's caucus of Republican members of the Assembly. Mr. Sprague was not mentioned, but it was apparent that he and not Mr. Morhouse had been the real target.

Few Republicans will dispute that Mr. Sprague is the dominant party leader in the state. Many hold that his leadership is sound and constructive and has been responsible for improving the party's position.

Even though it was later repudiated, an implied criticism of Mr. Lefkowitz' selection by Senator Jacob K. Javits appeared

Continued on Page 20, Column 2

2 SENATE LEADERS BACK COMPROMISE ON CLOSURE RULE

Johnson Supports Knowland in Resolution for Easier Curb on Filibusters

By JOHN D. MORRIS
Special to The New York Times

WASHINGTON, Jan. 9—Leaders of both parties and thirty other Senators joined today in sponsoring a "middle-ground" proposal to strengthen the Senate's hand in dealing with filibusters.

The Republican leader, Senator William F. Knowland of California, introduced a resolution changing Senate rules to permit closure, or limitation of debate, by two-thirds of the Senators present and voting. Two-thirds of the entire membership, or sixty-four Senators, now is required.

In a surprise move, Senator Lyndon B. Johnson of Texas, the Democratic leader, signed up as a co-sponsor. Nine other Democrats and twenty-one Republicans promptly added their names.

Hope for Action Revived

Today's development revived hope that something would be done this session to curb the power of Senate minorities to block action on legislation by the filibuster—the tactic of unlimited dilatory debate to prevent a vote.

The resolution must be approved by the Committee on Rules and Administration, but leaders spread the word privately that they would use their full influence to clear that and other prospective obstacles to early Senate action.

It was said they were even prepared to break a probable filibuster against the resolution when it reached the floor. This would be attempted, according to tentative plans, by holding the Senate in round-the-clock session to wear down filibustering opponents.

Alternatives Proposed

Alternatives to the Knowland-Johnson proposals were introduced today by two Republican Senators, Irving M. Ives of New York and Prescott S. Bush of Connecticut.

In addition, Senator Hubert H. Humphrey, Democrat of Minnesota, introduced a resolution to declare "void and of no further effect" the present rule's provision that closure cannot be invoked in debate on a motion to consider rules changes.

This so-called "built-in filibuster clause" would be repealed by the Knowland resolution without testing its constitutionality as contemplated by Senator Humphrey. Vice President Richard M. Nixon held it to be unconstitutional in an advisory

Continued on Page 21, Column 1

DULLES OPPOSES MOVE TO WEAKEN PLAN ON MIDEAST

Rejects Substitute Proposal as Violating U. N. Charter —Gordon Supports Him

By JOSEPH A. LOFTUS
Special to The New York Times.

WASHINGTON, Jan. 9—The Eisenhower Administration took a firm stand today against a move to water down its proposals for meeting Communist penetration of the Middle East.

John Foster Dulles, Secretary of State, raised detailed objections to a resolution drafted by an anonymous author as a possible substitute for the Administration's proposals.

Substance of Proposal

The proposed substitute, which Speaker Sam Rayburn said had been prepared by a former high official of the Government, would simply state:

"The United States regards as vital to her interest the preservation of the independence and integrity of the states of the Middle East and, if necessary, will use her armed forces to that end."

Secretary Dulles said the substitute would call for military action that would violate the United Nations Charter and the position the United States took in opposing British and French military efforts "to overthrow the Nasser regime."

Mr. Dulles said the substitute also would have required the United States to fight Israel, Britain and France last November.

Representative Thomas S. Gordon, Democrat of Illinois and chairman of the House Foreign Affairs Committee, agreed with Mr. Dulles.

Democrats Surprised

However, other Democrats on the committee expressed shock and surprise at what one called the "baldness" of the Secretary's comment that the British and French sought to overthrow the regime of Gamal Abdel Nasser, President of Egypt.

Despite the fact that no one has confessed parenthood of the "short form" approach to the Middle East problem, Secretary Dulles was considerably exer-

Continued on Page 5, Column 2

EDEN RESIGNS, PLEADING ILL HEALTH; BUTLER OR MACMILLAN TO GET POST; EISENHOWER AND DULLES IN TRIBUTE

REACTION IS MIXED

Both Regret and Relief Expressed in Capital —Cairo Jubilant

By DANA ADAMS SCHMIDT
Special to The New York Times.

WASHINGTON, Jan. 9—Washington heard the news of Prime Minister Eden's resignation with a mixture of regret and relief.

President Eisenhower and Secretary of State Dulles, overlooking the sharp differences they had had with Sir Anthony over the Suez Canal and the invasion of Egypt, issued friendly tributes to the British leader.

Some Administration officials observed privately that Sir Anthony's departure might hasten the repair of the British-United States alliance as a main pillar in the foreign policies of both countries.

[Sir Anthony's resignation brought jubilation in Cairo, where it was felt his departure would make negotiations on resumption of relations easier. Paris regarded Sir Anthony as a belated casualty of the military action in Suez.]

Butler's Suez View Cited

Those Washington officials who thought relations with London would be strengthened noted reports that R. A. Butler, who might succeed Sir Anthony, had opposed the invasion of Egypt.

Others, however, expressed concern that the resignation might lead to elections in Britain and a Labor Government that might agree with the United States on Middle East policy but prove more difficult in other respects.

Washington was by no means surprised at the resignation. It had been foreseen by highly placed officials as the ultimate consequence of the Suez Canal venture.

They had watched the Prime Minister's difficulties increasing since his visit to Washington just a year ago in a vain attempt to gain backing for his Middle Eastern and other policies.

Only a few weeks ago, while Sir Anthony was convalescing in Jamaica, B. W. I., the White House rejected British suggestions that he again visit President Eisenhower.

Today, however, the President expressed hope that his "old and good friend," Sir Anthony, would soon recover and enjoy "many useful years of happiness."

James C. Hagerty, White House press secretary, made public the following statement from the President:

"I have just been informed of

Continued on Page 4, Column 4

PRESIDENT PLANS OATH IN PRIVATE

Only His Family and Nixon's to See Jan. 20 Swearing-In

Special to The New York Times.

WASHINGTON, Jan. 9—The White House reversed itself today and ruled that President Eisenhower and Vice President Richard M. Nixon would take their second term oaths on Sunday, Jan. 20, at a private, family ceremony in the White House.

Earlier plans had called for live telecasting and other reporting of the first ceremony.

The formal public inauguration will be held in front of the Capitol Building beginning at noon on Monday, Jan. 21. This ceremony will be televised and broadcast nationally.

The decision on the private ceremony was announced as the Cabinet met to review the State of the Union Message that General Eisenhower will deliver in person before a joint session of the House of Representatives and Senate at 12:30 P. M. tomorrow.

The second version from the White House was that the message would not contain any major legislative surprises and would include few specific legislative proposals. The program of legislation will be reserved for the Budget Message, which also was reviewed at the Cabinet

Continued on Page 22, Column 6

Associated Press Wirephoto

STEPS DOWN: Sir Anthony Eden going to Buckingham Palace yesterday to resign as Prime Minister of Britain.

Europeans See U.S. As Bypassing Allies In Mideast Policy

By HAROLD CALLENDER

PARIS, Jan. 9—President Eisenhower's plan to defend the Middle East against Communist aggression is regarded by some foreign affairs experts as a policy not of isolationism but of isolation.

It is seen as a move by the United States alone, even though in conformity with the United Nations Charter.

Much discussion has taken place among diplomats and students of the area since President Eisenhower formulated his doctrine Saturday in a speech published and studied here this week. He proposed that Congress authorize him to use the armed forces of the United States, if necessary, against any Communist or Communist-dominated aggression in the Middle East.

Although this doctrine is regarded as new by some Americans, the impression in Europe is that it amounts to a reassertion and geographical extension of the policy of containment of Soviet power. This policy was formed under the Truman Administration when Dean Acheson was Secretary of State, and a Republican, the late Senator Arthur H. Vandenberg, then chairman of the Senate Foreign Relations Committee, cooperated in a bi-partisan foreign policy.

But the containment policy, as applied in Europe, took the form of the North Atlantic alliance, which was extended to Asia when Turkey joined it. So the alliance has a flank in the Middle East.

At the meeting in December of the North Atlantic Council, which directs the alliance, it

Continued on Page 6, Column 3

FRENCH AGAIN BID U. N. SHUN ALGERIA

Premier Presents France as a Plaintiff Against Arab Nations—Defines Aims

By HENRY GINIGER
Special to The New York Times.

PARIS, Jan. 9—The French Government told the United Nations today to keep hands off Algeria. The issue is expected to be discussed at this session of the General Assembly.

A 5,000-word document, reiterating the French contention that the United Nations is incompetent to deal with the Algerian problem and explaining how France proposed to handle it, was read by Premier Guy Mollet to a large group of newsmen in his office.

Approved at a special meeting of the Cabinet in the morning, the document constituted the first major reply to the anti-French offensive launched by the Arab nations. It presented France not as a defendant but as a plaintiff against Egypt and other nations, accusing them of interference in an internal French matter.

The text contained almost nothing that had not been said before. The Premier said as much, declaring he would not be showing much consideration for the United Nations if he were to announce some radical change in the French attitude. To many observers the Government's Algerian policy appeared to be at the point where it was when the Cabinet took office in February of last year. Then, as now, it could offer no specific assurances

Continued on Page 6, Column 4

SUEZ KEY FACTOR

Queen Is Expected to Appoint New Prime Minister Today

By DREW MIDDLETON
Special to The New York Times.

LONDON, Jan. 9—Sir Anthony Eden resigned tonight as Prime Minister of Britain, pleading ill health.

His health and his spirit both have broken under the pressures aroused in Britain and abroad by his policy of intervention in Egypt.

Queen Elizabeth II is expected to choose his successor tomorrow. The choice lies between Richard Austen Butler, Lord Privy Seal and leader of the House of Commons, and Harold Macmillan, Chancellor of the Exchequer.

Political circles late tonight seemed to be swinging to the support of Mr. Butler as Sir Anthony's successor. But there is as yet no firm indication that "Rab," as he is known, can command a majority of the Conservative members of the House of Commons.

The new Conservative Prime Minister will face a Laborite Opposition clamoring for a general election and a national situation in which Britain's economic and international position has deteriorated sharply from the bright prospects that prevailed when Sir Anthony assumed office 644 days ago on April 6, 1935.

Bids Colleagues Good-by

A career that was thirty-three years in the making ended in Sir Anthony's forty-minute interview at Buckingham Palace with the Queen. Then he returned to 10 Downing Street to announce his decision and to say good-by to his colleagues in the Cabinet and other members of his Ministry. Later, with Lady Eden, he drove to Chequers, the country residence of British Prime Ministers.

After Sir Anthony returned from the palace the following statement was issued:

"It is announced from Buckingham Palace that the Right Honorable Sir Anthony Eden, M. P. (Prime Minister and First Lord of the Treasury) had an audience of the Queen this evening and tendered his resignation as Prime Minister and First Lord of the Treasury, which Her Majesty was pleased to accept."

The Prime Minister himself followed this announcement with a personal statement from 10 Downing Street. The statement said:

"When I returned to this

Continued on Page 2, Column 3

GAITSKELL SEEKS BRITISH ELECTION

Laborite, at Harvard, Says Eden Did 'the Right Thing'

Special to The New York Times.

CAMBRIDGE, Mass., Jan. 9—Hugh Gaitskell, leader of the British Labor party, called today for a general election. He indicated his belief that his party might win such a test.

The 50-year-old party chairman, who would be Britain's Prime Minister in the event of a Labor victory, said at a news conference at Harvard University he was "sorry that Sir Anthony Eden's health has not recovered despite his trip to Jamaica."

"He has done the right thing in resigning," Mr. Gaitskell added. "But as the whole Cabinet has publicly identified themselves completely with the foreign policy pursued by the late Government in the last three months I consider that there ought now to be a general election in Britain so that the country can have an opportunity to choose a new Government.

Mr. Gaitskell is at Harvard to give three lectures. He delivered the second tonight, calling for greater cooperation among the countries of the North Atlantic Treaty Organization. He is

Continued on Page 4, Column 6

RIBICOFF PROGRAM AVOIDS RISE IN TAX

More Pay for Teachers and Court Reforms Are Urged

By RICHARD H. PARKE

HARTFORD, Jan. 9—Gov. Abraham A. Ribicoff outlined today a broad legislative program that he said could be achieved without new taxes or increases in current levies.

He recommended additional expenditures in fields ranging from atomic energy to mental health. The proposals were designed, he declared, to "allow the state to live within its budget."

The Governor, a Democrat, offered his program to the opening session of the Thirty-sixth Biennial General Assembly. Republicans control the Legislature by the largest majority they have held in thirty years.

Among the Governor's major recommendations were these:

¶A $60 increase in the $180-a-year cost-of-living pay rise for state workers.

¶A $21-a-pupil increase in state aid for education, to be used exclusively for "underwriting desperately needed pay raises for 15,500 school teachers."

¶A court reform plan that would replace the local court system with a system of state courts staffed by full-time judges.

¶The construction of a $1,000,-

Continued on Page 21, Column 2

Javits Takes Oath and Brings Senate to Full Strength

Associated Press Wirephoto

Jacob K. Javits and Vice President Nixon re-enacting the induction ceremony yesterday

Special to The New York Times.

WASHINGTON, Jan. 9—Jacob K. Javits, Republican of New York, took the oath of office today and thus brought the Senate to its full complement of ninety-six members.

The new Senator had delayed taking his oath until after New York State Republican leaders named a man to succeed him as State Attorney General. They selected Louis J. Lefkowitz.

Senator Javits was sworn in by Vice President Richard M. Nixon. He received a standing round of applause by the Senate and spectators, including Mrs. Javits, two of their children, Joy, 8 years old, and Joshua, 7, and his brother and a nephew.

Later the Senator told re-

was engaged in one of its favorite pastimes, the eulogizing of a member.

The member in this case was Senator William F. Knowland of California, the Republican leader, who yesterday announced his intention to retire two years from now at the end of his present term.

Senator Javits was sworn in by Vice President Richard M. Nixon. He received a standing round of applause by the Senate and spectators, including Mrs. Javits, two of their children, Joy, 8 years old, and Joshua, 7, and his brother and a nephew.

Senator Javits said he had not been a novice in Congress, having served eight years in the House, and had great respect for the Senate's procedures.

Freshman Senators traditionally are assigned to the less desirable committees, and such was the case with Mr. Javits. In recent years the Democrats have operated to give new Senators one good committee post, but Republicans usually have operated on the last-come last-served basis

Continued on Page 20, Column 1

porters that he was "certainly not happy" with his assignments to the District of Columbia and Rules Committees. But he said he was not a novice in Congress, having served eight years in the House, and had great respect for the Senate's procedures.

Senator Javits resignation became effective in Albany at 12:56 P. M. today. He appeared on the Senate floor promptly at 1 P. M., but was not sworn in until 1:22 because the Senate

Asia-Africa Bloc Will Ask U. N. To Call on Israelis to Quit Egypt

By THOMAS J. HAMILTON
Special to The New York Times.

UNITED NATIONS, N. Y., Jan. 9—The Asian-African group decided today to seek another resolution by the General Assembly calling for the withdrawal of Israeli forces "behind the armistice demarcation lines."

However, Israel still holds the Gaza Strip, the rest of the Sinai Peninsula, including the southernmost tip, where Egyptian coastal guns commanded the channel leading into the Gulf of Aqaba, and two small islands at the mouth of the gulf that belong to Saudi Arabia but that previously were administered by Egypt.

Mrs. Golda Meir, Israeli Foreign Minister, returned to Israel yesterday. She left the impression that Israel would not evacuate the remaining territory unless the United Nations provided guarantees against the resumption of Egyptian guerrilla raids and against the revival of the blockade of the Israeli port of Elath, on the Gulf of Aqaba.

No information on the nature of the guarantees Israel wants

Continued on Page 6, Column 6

195

"All the News That's Fit to Print"

The New York Times.

LATE CITY EDITION
U. S. Weather Bureau report (Page 48) forecast:
Rain, drizzle early today; brightening
later. Fair and warm tomorrow.
Temp. range: 64-54.   (Yesterday) at 58.6-55.01

VOL CVI..No. 36,252.   © 1957, by The New York Times Company.   NEW YORK, FRIDAY, APRIL 26, 1957.   Times Square, New York 36, N. Y.
Telephone LAckawanna 4-1000   FIVE CENTS

EISENHOWER ASKS FULL DISCLOSURE OF LABOR FUNDS

Administration Calls for Laws to Wipe Out 'Abomination' of Union Racketeering

RANK AND FILE PRAISED

President and Mitchell Put Stress on Moves to Block 'Punitive' Legislation

Text of Eisenhower statement appears on Page 14.

By W. H. LAWRENCE
Special to The New York Times.

AUGUSTA, Ga., April 25—The Eisenhower Administration decided today to ask Congress for full public disclosure of union receipts and expenditures.

James P. Mitchell, Secretary of Labor, reported the interim legislative program for labor after a ninety-minute conference with President Eisenhower at the President's temporary office at the Augusta National Golf Club.

Mr. Mitchell said the legislative proposals had grown out of evidence of improper practices already developed by the Senate Select Committee on Improper Activities in the Labor or Management Field. The committee is headed by Senator John L. McClellan, Democrat of Arkansas.

Secretary Mitchell warned against a "headlong" rush "impelled by the hysteria of the moment to secure punitive legislation aimed at undermining or weakening the general body of organized labor."

A Request Renewed

He said the Administration proposals were designed to strengthen the rights of the union rank and file and to "help the American labor movement to clean house in those areas where they need help."

Specifically, the President and the Secretary of Labor renewed their three-year-old request to Congress that it pass laws providing for the registration, reporting and disclosure of funds deposited under welfare and pension plans.

In addition, Secretary Mitchell said the President also had approved a proposal that Congress authorize the Labor Department to make public the reports now filed with it concerning union funds in general under the Taft-Hartley Act. Those reports now are not made public.

Secretary Mitchell indicated that the Administration later might ask Congress for Federal review and audits of the union financial statements.

Continued on Page 14, Column 3

CITY BARS HOUSING AT CANCER CENTER

Relocation Problems Cited —Bridge Routes Filed

By CHARLES G. BENNETT

After months of hearings, the Board of Estimate yesterday rejected a proposal to build a $6,500,000 middle-income housing project in Yorkville.

The proposal had been made by the Memorial Center for Cancer and Allied Diseases, the Sloan Kettering Institute and the Rockefeller Institute for Medical Research.

The board acted on two other major items of city business.

It received and referred to city agencies the plans for Brooklyn and Staten Island approach routes to the Narrows Bridge and for the Queens and Bronx approaches to the Throgs Neck Bridge. Robert Moses, chairman of the Triborough Bridge and Tunnel Authority, submitted the plans.

The board approved $25,000 to put under way initial studies of the rehabilitation of the downtown area of Brooklyn, including the feasibility of a sports center that would serve as a home for the Brooklyn Dodgers baseball team.

In the case of the rejected Yorkville project, the sponsoring institutions had sought permission for nearly two years to construct two buildings. One would be for nurses and would contain 287 apartments. The other was for technical, research and professional personnel. It was to have 180 apartments.

The site for the proposed institutions

Continued on Page 17, Column 5

Associated Press Wirephoto
CONFER IN GEORGIA: President Eisenhower with James P. Mitchell, Secretary of Labor, in Augusta yesterday. They drew plans for laws dealing with labor unions.

M'CLELLAN WARNS OF 'GANGSTERISM'

Tells Publishers Momentum of Rackets Perils U. S.— Mrs. Luce Chides Press

Text of McClellan's speech will be found on Page 16.

The chairman of the Senate committee investigating union rackets said last night that it intended to continue its exposures of wrongdoing until Congress had enough information to "clean up the mess."

Senator John L. McClellan, Democrat of Arkansas, made his statement at a dinner of the Bureau of Advertising of the American Newspaper Publishers Association. He predicted that the investigation, which he said was still in its early stages, would produce legislation to protect union members, management and the public.

The committee chairman, speaking at the Waldorf-Astoria Hotel, warned that racketeering now had enough momentum to bring about a "gangsterism economy" and threaten liberty in the United States if it were not stopped.

'Shock Troops' of Diplomacy

Mrs. Clare Boothe Luce, former Ambassador to Italy, urged the press and public to support the American Foreign Service. Mrs. Luce spoke of the "shock troops of our diplomatic front lines" and termed them a vital instrument for the preservation of world peace.

The occasion, the Bureau of Advertising's forty-fourth annual dinner, marked the end of the seventy-first annual convention of the bureau's parent organization, the American Newspaper Publishers Association. It also marked the end of New York's annual Press Week.

As Senator McClellan spoke, preparations were made for a closed hearing on labor-management abuses in the New York area at the United States Court House today. Three officials of one of the union locals under investigation were indicted by a New York County grand jury yesterday on charges of steal-

Continued on Page 16, Column 2

De Sapio Leadership Extolled by Wagner Before Party Chiefs

By CLAYTON KNOWLES

Ringing praise for Carmine G. De Sapio and predictions of a great victory for Mayor Wagner this fall marked speeches at the annual dinner of the New York County Democratic Committee last night.

The Mayor, a candidate for reelection, was lavish in proclaiming the "forceful, dynamic, political brilliance" of Mr. De Sapio, leader of the Tammany organization for the last eight years.

About 2,200 persons attended the $50-a-plate dinner, which was held at the Commodore Hotel.

In his text Mr. Wagner said also that Mr. De Sapio had set "an example of undivided allegiance to the principles of good government—of government devoted exclusively to the needs and the welfare of the people."

Called Friend of Decency

Extemporizing in delivery, he added that Mr. De Sapio had been the "stalwart friend of decency, honesty and integrity in government." He said he was "proud to call him my friend."

The extent of the accolade took on significance in view of the start next Monday of public hearings by the Republican-dominated legislative committee into the Joseph (Socks) Lanza parole case.

Lanza has Tammany connections. And there has been reference to aid sought from "the man with the glasses." Mr. De Sapio, who wears dark tinted glasses, has scoffed at the suggestion that the reference might have been to him.

In his own speech last night, Mr. De Sapio said that he still felt, as he had when he as-

Continued on Page 12, Column 4

Recording by Lanza Is Reported Missing

By LEO EGAN

A tape recording of one conversation between Joseph (Socks) Lanza and his wife and others in the Westchester County jail was reported missing yesterday.

The disclosure was made by Arthur L. Reuter, Acting State Commissioner of Investigation. The Commissioner is conducting one of two investigations into the dismissal of parole violation charges against Lanza, a convicted extortionist.

The missing recording was made a half-hour before Lanza's release on Feb. 20. He had been arrested as a parole violator on Feb. 5. His release followed the dismissal of the charges against him by the Parole Board while being questioned about his decision by Commissioner Stone.

Commissioner Stone subsequently resigned from the Parole Board while being questioned about his decision by

Continued on Page 15, Column 2

PRESIDENT PLANS OIL IMPORT STUDY; SEES PERIL TO U.S.

Gets O.D.M. Report Warning of Rise in Foreign Fuel —Quotas May Result

By RICHARD E. MOONEY
WASHINGTON, April 25—President Eisenhower announced today he would order an investigation to determine whether imports of crude oil threatened national security. He asserted "there is reason for the belief" that such a threat exists.

The President, in Augusta, Ga., acted after receiving advice from Gordon Gray, Director of the Office of Defense Mobilization. Mr. Gray said that the trend of imports and forecasts for coming months had given reason to believe there was a threat. Mr. Gray released his and the President's memoranda at a news conference here.

If the President finds a threat to national security, he is required by law to take action that will reduce imports. This presumably would be done by placing them under quota limitations or by raising the tariff.

Independents Skeptical

General Eisenhower asked Mr. Gray to explore the possibility of limiting imports by voluntary action. This would be done while the Presidential investigation was under way.

Major importers might prefer voluntary restrictions, rather than legal quota limitations or higher tariff charges. But the independent producers in this country, with no overseas operations, feel efforts for voluntary curtailment are futile.

The question of import limitation has been introduced by the appeal of a number of independent companies. They contend that national security is being threatened because increased oil imports discourage exploration for new oil resources in this country—resources on which the United States would depend in time of war.

Voluntary Pact Sought

The Office of Defense Mobilization has tried for two years to get voluntary agreement among importers. Mr. Gray's certification to the President that a threat exists is the most forceful step that has been taken so far. In fact, it is the first such action under the law—Section 7 of the Trade Agreements Extension (Reciprocal Trade) Act of 1955.

The actual Presidential order for an investigation awaits the selection of a group to make the study, and the preparation of necessary papers.

The United States produced more than 2,600,000,000 barrels (forty-two gallons a barrel) of crude oil last year, or an average of more than 7,100,000 barrels a day. Refineries consumed a little more than 2,900,000,000 barrels.

On the basis of pure physical capacity, the nation's wells

Continued on Page 5, Column 4

KING SCORES CAIRO

Installs a New Cabinet —Vows Fight to the Finish on Reds

By OSGOOD CARUTHERS
Special to The New York Times.

AMMAN, Jordan, April 25—King Hussein proclaimed today a fight to the finish against a conspiracy to overthrow him. He imposed martial law and formed a new Government.

The 21-year-old monarch charged openly for the first time that the conspiracy was getting its support from Egypt.

Moving swiftly, the King placed the principal cities of Amman, Jerusalem, Ramallah, Nablus and Irbid under a total curfew. He also placed the Jordanian police force under direct command of the Army.

[The Associated Press reported from Amman that King Hussein had abolished Jordan's ten political parties.]

The monarch appeared to have emerged as a mature and grimly determined fighter, defending his throne against efforts by Egypt and Syria to turn Jordan into their anti-Western satellite.

His imposition of an armored fist on the Palestinian part of Jordan and his warning, in a pre-dawn broadcast, that "conspiracies might take away the remaining part of Arab Palestine" made clear that he would fight to prevent cession of the west bank and would be ready against possible Israeli attack.

Plans Carefully Laid

Events moved swiftly last night, but it was evident that the King's plans had been carefully laid. During the early evening the Government of Premier Hussein Fakhri Khalidi finally carried out an earlier decision to quit.

The Khalidi Government had been formed on the basis of support of all parties, including the National Socialists, the left-wing Baath (Resurrection) party and their pro-Communist supporters. That support was withdrawn the day before yesterday and these parties, encouraged by the Cairo radio, called the people out on a general strike and ineffective riots.

King Hussein was ready for these developments. He kept the rioters tightly confined and there was no bloodshed. In addition the monarch had a new Cabinet at his palace, ready and waiting to take over as soon as the Khalidi Government resigned.

The new Government is headed by Ibrahim Hashem, 69 years

Continued on Page 3, Column 3

U. S. ORDERS 6TH FLEET TO MIDEAST, SAYS COMMUNISTS MENACE JORDAN; HUSSEIN PROCLAIMS MARTIAL LAW

The New York Times   April 26, 1957
NAVAL MOVEMENT: Ships of the United States Sixth Fleet left Cannes (1) and Naples (2) to deploy in the eastern Mediterranean, perhaps from Egypt to Turkey (3), in a measure to help Jordan (4) remain independent.

Nasser Sees Syria's Leader On Mounting Jordan Crisis

By HOMER BIGART
Special to The New York Times.

CAIRO, April 25—In an atmosphere of deepening crisis, President Gamal Abdel Nasser conferred again tonight with President Shukri al-Kuwatly of Syria on what to do about Jordan. The Egyptian President is reported eager to avoid any break with King Hussein of Jordan.

But the formation of an avowedly pro-Western government in Amman has sharpened Egyptian suspicions of some grand strategic design by the Western powers to bring Jordan into the Baghdad Pact.

In an apparent effort to patch up relations with King Saud of Saudi Arabia, who has been backing Hussein, President Nasser will send a three-man mission to Riyadh tomorrow. Mr. al-Kuwatly will accompany the Egyptian team and it was reported that he would later go to Amman for a talk with King Hussein.

President Nasser's decision to send a special mission to Saudi Arabia came after he had received a message from King Saud, the contents of which were not disclosed. The Egyptian mission will consist of President Nasser's political adviser, Col. Ali Sabry, Sheikh Hassan el Bakouri, Minister of Works, and Anwar el Sadat, head of the Islamic Congress and publisher of the newspaper Al Gomhouria.

Chief Aides at Talks

Mr. al-Kuwatly arrived unexpectedly this morning from Damascus and for several hours Egypt tried to keep his arrival secret. The Cairo radio finally broke the news at 2:30 P. M. after Damascus had announced Mr. al-Kuwatly's departure for Egypt.

President Nasser and President al-Kuwatly conferred for three hours and met again tonight in another emergency session. The Egyptian Commander in Chief, Gen. Abdel Hakim Amer, and the Syrian Chief of Staff, Gen. Tewfik Nizam el-Din, attended both meetings.

Also present were Colonel Sabry, the Syrian Foreign Minister, Salah Bitar, and the Syrian Minister of Public Works, Fakhir Kayyali.

No communiqué was issued. Diplomatic sources speculated that neither President Nasser

Continued on Page 4, Column 1

MOSCOW ACCUSES U. S. OF MEDDLING

Broadcast Attacks 'Blatant Interference' in Jordan— Hussein Also Scored

By The Associated Press.

LONDON, April 25—Moscow accused the United States tonight of "blatant interference" in the internal affairs of Jordan.

An anonymous commentator on the Moscow radio's home service said the Jordanian situation remained tense amid an "atmosphere of deep internal political crisis."

The Moscow radio said the United States, "by means of behind-the-scenes machinations, is trying to set up a Jordanian Government that would adopt the aggressive Eisenhower doctrine and give up the policy of protecting the national interests and [Jordan's] unity with other free Arab countries."

Later tonight, an Arabic-language broadcast from Moscow said, "One is surprised, to say the least, at what King Hussein said about international communism seeking to destroy Jordan." King Hussein, in interviews yesterday, attributed Jordan's troubles to international Communist propaganda and subversion.

U. S. Agitation Alleged

The commentator went on: "We cannot but see in this statement an unsuccessful attempt to stir up suspicions against the Soviet Union. It is well known that the Soviet Union has never interfered in the internal affairs of Jordan. On the contrary, the Soviet Union has always firmly supported the struggle of the Jordanian people against all imperialists to build up their free and independent country.

"We must also point out that this statement is but a repetition of the false allegations that are being used by American propaganda to lay responsibility and consequences on others."

The broadcast said "the interlude" of United States diplomacy in the internal affairs [of Jordan] is getting more open and brazen."

Dulles' Speech Criticized

By WILLIAM J. JORDEN
Special to The New York Times.

MOSCOW, April 23—The Soviet Union's leaders insisted tonight they were not trying to export the Communist revolution. They said they could not understand why Secretary of State Dulles insisted on advocating a policy of "liberation" from communism for the countries of Eastern Europe.

The Kremlin roundly castigated Mr. Dulles for the speech he made before a gathering of American editors three days ago. A statement criticizing his speech and attributed to "leading circles of the Soviet Union"

Continued on Page 5, Column 3

A SHOW OF FORCE

British Also Say a Free Jordan Is Essential to Mideast Peace

By DANA ADAMS SCHMIDT
Special to The New York Times.

WASHINGTON, April 25—The United States deployed its military and political power today to assure the survival of an independent Jordan.

It sent the Sixth Fleet, with the aircraft carrier Forrestal, hurrying back from the western Mediterranean to the eastern Mediterranean so suddenly that 150 sailors were left stranded on leave in Paris.

[A British Foreign Office spokesman said that Jordan's independence and integrity were "essential elements" in maintaining Middle East peace.]

The United States also began to set out the political justification for any future intervention. This justification is, in the Administration's view, that Jordan is menaced by the forces of international communism.

A State Department declaration to this effect, following a similar statement by King Hussein of Jordan yesterday, seemed designed to make the Eisenhower Doctrine applicable in the struggle over Jordan.

Statement Expanded

The declaration expanded President Eisenhower's statement yesterday in Augusta, Ga., that preservation of Jordan's independence was "vital to the national interest."

Lincoln White, press officer of the State Department, read this statement:

"The statement issued in Augusta, Ga., represented a view by the world by the President that a finding had been made in the Joint Resolution of the Congress on the Middle East [the Eisenhower Doctrine] that the preservation of the independence and integrity of the nations of the Middle East was vital to the national interest of the United States and to world peace.

"This reminder was appropriate because of the threat to the independence and integrity of Jordan by international communism as King Hussein himself stated."

Generally, according to Administration experts, international communism works indirectly in Jordan through the left-wing and extremist nationalist

Continued on Page 2, Column 4

U. N. CHIEF LOOKS TO COURT ON SUEZ

Hammarskjold Says It Could Settle Israeli Ship Issue

By THOMAS J. HAMILTON
Special to The New York Times.

UNITED NATIONS, N. Y., April 25—Dag Hammarskjold suggested today that the question whether Israeli ships had the right to use the Suez Canal be decided by the International Court of Justice.

The Secretary General of the United Nations asserted at a news conference that "Governments concerned" could decide. He added, however, that "as a reasonably well-informed observer," he saw a possibility that the issue could be resolved under procedures set forth in the Egyptian declaration yesterday on operation of the canal.

The declaration provided that any unresolved differences among the signatories over the meaning of the Constantinople Convention of 1888, guaranteeing freedom of navigation, would be referred to the International Court.

Egypt apparently promised to accept compulsory jurisdiction. However, Israel and the United States, which were not parties to the convention, could not take the issue to the Court.

Further questions brought out the contradictory language of the declaration, which provides that while the canal should be open to the shipping of all nations, both in war and peace, Egypt is entitled to take action to guard her security. Reminded that this right was qualified by

Continued on Page 4, Column 5

N. Y. U. Hospital Is Planned, With Research Chief Goal

By ROBERT K. PLUMB

Plans for a new hospital to make the New York University-Bellevue Medical Center a pioneering scientific research institution were announced yesterday. The plans call for a nineteen-story building of

This is a drawing of the new nineteen-story hospital building that will rise at New York University-Bellevue Medical Center. The architects are Skidmore, Owings & Merrill.

white brick and glass just south of Thirty-fourth Street and east of First Avenue. But the plans tell only part of the story. For it is the intention of New York University medical men to use the new $20,000,000 institution to find out

how to reduce the time lag between laboratory science and bedside medical practice. Other possible improvements in medicine may in part be "built into" the new hospital.

Continued on Page 18, Column 3

A. E. C. Aide Says Dr. Schweitzer Errs

By EDWARD L. DALE Jr.
Special to The New York Times.

WASHINGTON, April 25—The scientist member of the Atomic Energy Commission sharply disputed today the contention of Dr. Albert Schweitzer that nuclear weapons tests were creating "a danger for the human race."

Dr. Willard F. Libby, the commission member, wrote to Dr. Schweitzer "as a scientist, to present data bearing on a scientific fact." He made his letter public two days after a broadcast from Oslo of Dr. Schweitzer's warning.

After paying tribute to Dr. Schweitzer, humanitarian and winner of the Nobel Peace Prize, Dr. Libby said he feared Dr. Schweitzer's appeal was not based on the latest information on radioactive fall-out. Dr. Libby added: "I know you have the intellectual strength

Continued on Page 3, Column 2

"All the News That's Fit to Print"

The New York Times.

LATE CITY EDITION
U. S. Weather Bureau Report (Page 26) forecast:
Some cloudiness, warm today.
Partly cloudy, humid tomorrow.
Temp. range: 88—70. Yesterday: 86.4—61.4.

VOL. CVI..No. 36,321.   © 1957, by The New York Times Company, Times Square, New York 36, N. Y.   NEW YORK, THURSDAY, JULY 4, 1957.   10c beyond 100-mile zone from New York City   FIVE CENTS

PRESIDENT BARS BALLOT ON RIGHTS; WOULD HEAR FOES

Rejects Proposal by Russell to Hold Referendum, but Plans to Study Bill

CITES COURT'S DECISIONS

'Ready to Listen' to South's Arguments — Senator Welcomes the Offer

News conference transcript and summary, Page 13.

By WILLIAM S. WHITE
Special to The New York Times.

WASHINGTON, July 3—President Eisenhower made it plain today that he was taking another and a closer look at the implications of the Administration's civil rights bill in the wake of vehement Southern attacks on it.

At the same time, he rejected a proposal from the Southern opposition that the bill be submitted directly to the people in a national referendum.

He declared at his news conference, however, that he was "ready to listen" to any presentation of their side from the embattled Southerners.

Their chief spokesman, Senator Richard B. Russell, Democrat of Georgia, denounced the bill yesterday as so "cunningly contrived" that it could be questioned whether the President himself understood its full scope.

Opponents Map Strategy

Senator Russell was holding a strategy meeting at the Capitol with fellow Senators while the President was speaking. By coincidence, they themselves about that time were discussing the possibility of going to him in a group to offer their views.

Some were at first disposed not to attempt this course, lest it be interpreted as a sign of weakness.

Told later of the President's remarks, however, Senator Russell said:

"If the President wishes to talk to us on this matter, his wish—as would be the wish of any President of the United States—will be to us a command. I should be glad to meet with him in any circumstances he might prefer—alone or with others as he might wish."

From the Senate floor, Senator Russell charged yesterday that the Attorney General, Herbert Brownell Jr., had prepared a "deceptive piece of legislation" that would amount to "an unlimited grant of powers to the Attorney General to govern by injunction and Federal bayonet."

Bill Passed by House

As passed by the House of Representatives, the bill would:

¶Permit the Justice Department to intervene in behalf of any individual, with or without his consent, whose civil rights had been denied or were under threat of denial. This would be done by obtaining a Federal court injunction against the violator or imminent violator. If he refused to obey this writ, he could be held in contempt by a judge, sitting without a jury, and fined or imprisoned.

¶Set up a special civil rights division within the Justice Department.

¶Create a Federal civil rights commission to investigate and attempt to rectify cases of racial discrimination.

The civil rights advocates, Mr. Russell contended, are pretending that their main concern is to protect the right to vote, but in fact are seeking means to force racial integration in the South, in the schools and elsewhere, even to the point of possible use of Federal troops.

Russell Sees Pretense

The President at his news conference today showed that he had been disturbed by the comments of Senator Russell, with whom he had had many agreeable relationships.

During his military career, General Eisenhower often appeared before the Senate Armed Services Committee, of which Mr. Russell is chairman.

On Senator Russell's suggestion of a referendum, the President said he doubted that there was any constitutional basis for such a step; that Congress itself had the responsibility to enact legislation, and that in any case the issue would not make "a very good subject for a referendum, even if you could have one."

On Mr. Russell's denunciation of the bill, however, President Eisenhower did

Continued on Page 26, Column 7

Eisenhower Raises Atomic Fuel Quota

By JOHN W. FINNEY
Special to The New York Times.

WASHINGTON, July 3—The White House more than doubled today the amount of nuclear fuel the United States would make available for atomic power plants at home and abroad.

President Eisenhower announced that he was allocating an additional 59,800 kilograms—or 131,560 pounds—of uranium 235 for peaceful purposes in domestic and foreign nuclear power projects.

Including its previous allocations, the United States has now pledged to make 100,000 kilograms—or 220,000 pounds—of uranium fuel available for peaceful purposes. At current atomic energy commission prices, the value of this fuel is $1,700,000,000.

The 100,000 kilograms will

Continued on Page 12, Column 3

CITY BUILDING UNIT STUDIED BY STATE

Heck Announces Watchdog Inquiry—Step Welcomed by Mayor and Aides

By EMANUEL PERLMUTTER

The Republican - controlled legislative watchdog committee has begun an investigation of the New York City Department of Buildings.

This was disclosed yesterday by Assemblyman Oswald D. Heck, Republican Speaker of the Assembly. He said the committee was checking reports of "graft, corruption and 'extortion'" in the department.

Confirmation was given by Senator William F. Horan, Republican of Tuckahoe, chairman of the Joint Legislative Committee on Government Operations, the official name of the watchdog unit.

Mr. Horan said the committee's staff was making "preliminary investigations into those and other matters."

Mayor Gives His Views

Mayor Wagner said his Administration welcomed the watchdog committee's investigation.

"I have said time and again that we would welcome any investigation of any city department," he declared. "We have nothing to hide. If there is wrongdoing no one is more important than I to root it out and take swift, decisive action.

"I have already asked those with complaints against the Department of Buildings to come in and state their complaints. I have promised full protection to all who cooperate in this fashion."

Charles H. Tenney, the City Investigation Commissioner who has begun his own inquiry into rumors that building inspectors were shaking down property-owners guilty of violations and those seeking building permits,

Continued on Page 37, Column 3

G.O.P. Picks 3-War Marine To Oppose Jack in Borough

By RUSSELL PORTER

Melvin L. Krulewitch, 61-year-old lawyer and twice-wounded Marine Corps Reserve veteran of three wars, was designated yesterday as the Republican candidate for Borough President of Manhattan. He will oppose Hulan E. Jack, the Democratic incumbent in the November election.

Mr. Krulewitch, who is a major general in the Reserve, was the only Republican named for Borough President or District Attorney at meetings of the executive committees of the New York and Kings County Republican Committees.

The following three Democrats, who already had their own party designations, were re-endorsed by the Republicans for re-election as Borough President or District Attorney:

Borough President John Cashmore of Brooklyn.

District Attorney Frank S. Hogan of New York County (Manhattan).

District Attorney Edward S. Silver of Kings County (Brooklyn).

Both executive committees formally approved the recent designation of three Republican city-wide candidates by the five county leaders. These candidates are Robert K. Christenberry for Mayor, Mrs. Caroline K. Simon for President of the City Council and State Senator Walter

Continued on Page 29, Column 7

DEMOCRATS BACK EASING OF CURBS ON ALIEN QUOTAS

Key Legislators in Agreement on Compromise to Bring in 140,000 More in 2 Years

By JOHN D. MORRIS
Special to The New York Times.

WASHINGTON, July 3—Key Democrats in Congress have quietly reached substantial agreement on a compromise plan for easing restrictions on immigration.

The compromise, described as acceptable in nearly all major respects to legislators most interested in the problem, is embodied in a bill introduced last Thursday by Senator John F. Kennedy, Democrat of Massachusetts.

The measure has the backing of Lyndon B. Johnson of Texas, the Senate Democratic leader, Representative Francis E. Walter, Democrat of Pennsylvania, who holds the key to action by the House of Representatives, also participated in the unpublished negotiations that preceded its introduction. Sponsors look for his cooperation.

The bill would permit the entry over a two-year period of 140,000 to 150,000 regular immigrants and refugees who otherwise would be excluded.

Eisenhower Plan Included

While it includes features of the Soviet system suggested the Jan. 31 in a special message to Congress, asked authority to bring in 190,000 more persons a year.

The annual quota under present law is 154,857, of which 60,-000 quota numbers expire unused each year. Total entrances, including unrestricted immigration from Western Hemisphere countries, amounted to 321,625 in 1956.

Democratic strategists hope to obtain Republican help in steering the Kennedy bill through Congress toward the end of the session without public hearings.

The tentative plan, similar to one that failed in the last hours of the 1956 session, is to attach the measure to a minor immigration bill passed by the House and now pending on the Senate calendar.

Tactic Failed Last Year

Senate passage of the combined bill would send it to a Senate-House conference committee for agreement on the final version.

The tactic failed last year when Representative Walter, chairman of the House Judiciary Subcommittee on Immigration, invoked a parliamentary technicality to keep a similar bill from going to conference.

This time, according to Senator Kennedy, Mr. Walter "has

Continued on Page 11, Column 1

WIDE SHAKE-UP IN KREMLIN OUSTS MOLOTOV, MALENKOV, KAGANOVICH AS KHRUSHCHEV TIGHTENS REINS

U. S. IS GRATIFIED

State Department Says Ousters Show Strain in Soviet System

By JAMES RESTON
Special to The New York Times.

WASHINGTON, July 3—Official Washington tried hard to conceal its pleasure over the latest shake-up in the Soviet Union today but didn't quite succeed.

"No comment," said James C. Hagerty, White House press secretary, grinning broadly, and the grin was the most tangible and significant act in a day devoted mainly to gleeful speculation.

¶News of the official Soviet announcement of the dismissal of Vyacheslav M. Molotov, Lazar M. Kaganovich, Georgi M. Malenkov and Dmitri T. Shepilov was brought to President Eisenhower during a meeting of the National Security Council in the afternoon. Reports of developments were rushed to the White House from the State Department and the Central Intelligence Agency throughout the day.

Mr. Hagerty told the press in midafternoon that the Administration had advance indication of the ouster. He noted that Nikita S. Khrushchev, First Secretary of the Soviet Communist party, and Marshal Nikolai A. Bulganin, Soviet Premier, had recently postponed a visit to Czechoslovakia, and that an aerial demonstration over Moscow, to which Communist bloc leaders had been invited, had suddenly been canceled.

Beyond that, however, he would not comment.

White Reads Statement

The State Department was more explicit. In answer to reporters' questions, Lincoln White, press officer, read the following statement:

"It has long been known that the Soviet system operates under stresses and strains. Arbitrary and abrupt dismissals without public discussion of the issues are also characteristic of the system.

"The official Soviet press has at various times suggested there have been disagreements over basic policies in such fields as Government organizations, agriculture, heavy industry, consumer goods and satellite affairs.

"The serious nature of the divergence of views is clearly shown by the number and importance of the persons dismissed or shifted. We are naturally following these developments closely for the effect they may have on Soviet basic policy."

Effect on U. S. Policy Seen

The Soviet changes have come at a critical time in the development of United States foreign policy and is expected to have some influence on that policy, particularly as it affects Communist China and the Soviet Union.

Both the Executive and Legislative branches of the United States Government have been divided about how to deal with Moscow and Peiping. Some legislators and officials have favored making a major effort to reach a disarmament agreement with the Soviet Union and acquiescing in an accommodation with the Chinese Communists.

Others have been opposing this on the ground that the whole Communist world was in ferment. They have been going along reluctantly with the current United States policy in the disarmament talks in London, but insisting that the way to break up the Communist alliance between Moscow and Peiping was to maintain the economic pressure.

Secretary of State Dulles, who left for his Great Lakes retreat on Duck Island today, and only yesterday that he was opposed to making concessions to the Chinese Communists, and regarded dictatorial communism in both Peiping and Moscow as a "passing phase."

Today's developments in Moscow, coming on top of a new debate in Peiping over ideological questions, were expected to strengthen those who have concluded that the thing to do was to keep the pressure on, not to grow weary of the long struggle, not to make risky conces-

Continued on Page 3, Column 2

Vyacheslav M. Molotov
The New York Times

Georgi M. Malenkov
Associated Press

Lazar M. Kaganovich
Sovfoto

U. S. MAY SPREAD 'CLEAN' BOMB DATA

President Weighs Proposal to Give Others Knowledge on Eliminating Fall-Out

By JACK RAYMOND
Special to The New York Times.

WASHINGTON, July 3—President Eisenhower said today he was thinking of sharing with the Soviet Union and other countries the knowledge of how to produce "clean" hydrogen bombs.

Such a step would require legislation, he said. But he disclosed that he had asked his scientific advisers about the possibility of sharing, and they had suggested such a course might be adopted as soon as they had proved they could produce a bomb totally free of dangerous radioactive fall-out.

The President said that in the meantime he intended to invite foreign countries to make their own measurements of the percentage of radioactivity on the site of the next United States hydrogen bomb detonation.

This should serve as an appropriate test by doubters of the contention that even now only 4 per cent radioactivity results from the explosion of United States hydrogen bombs, the President declared.

U-235 Given to Others

President Eisenhower opened his news conference with an announcement that the United States was making more uranium-235 available in the peaceful uses of atomic power.

In response to questions about United States policy on disarmament and the effects on that policy of reduced radioactive fall-out in bomb explosions, the President emphasized:

¶The United States stands firm on its position at the London disarmament conference, agreeing to a temporary suspension of nuclear arms tests if it will lead to an end of bomb-making.

¶The United States disarm-

Continued on Page 12, Column 2

Moscow Ousters Termed Victory for 'Liberal' Policy

By HARRISON E. SALISBURY

Nikita S. Khrushchev, First Secretary of the Soviet Communist party, appears to have won a smashing victory for his "New Look" policies of easing tensions at home and abroad. This was the initial reaction of competent specialists in Soviet affairs to the dramatic decisions of the latest meeting in Moscow of the party's Central Committee.

With the firm support of the Soviet Army, the Communist party apparatus and the Government bureaucracy, Mr. Khrushchev has ousted from the Soviet ruling group a powerful bloc of Stalinist oppositionists.

Mr. Khrushchev's ability to remove from the party's Presidium and Central Committee such veteran party chieftains as Vyacheslav M. Molotov, Lazar M. Kaganovich and Georgi M. Malenkov was testimony to the power he had now mustered behind his leadership.

Indictment Is Stressed

Of great importance in international relations was the nature of the indictment placed against them, Mr. Khrushchev and his victorious Central Committee majority charged Mr. Molotov, Mr. Kaganovich, Mr. Malenkov and their supporters with persistent and deliberate efforts to sabotage every effort to ease international tensions, improve the life of Soviet citizens at home and destroy the vestiges of Stalinist excesses.

The communiqué announcing the dismissals outlined a platform of the Khrushchev faction, which promised to continue striving for better international relations.

While the main force of the Khrushchev indictment was directed against Mr. Molotov, Mr. Kaganovich and Mr. Malenkov, they were not the only targets. In effect Mr. Khrushchev made a clean sweep.

He also ousted Dmitri T. Shepilov, the former Pravda editor and Foreign Minister who was identified with the "Young Turk" faction of the party. Mr.

Continued on Page 3, Column 4

Holiday Traffic Exodus Begins; 952 Police Cars Will Patrol City

Police Commissioner Stephen P. Kennedy yesterday declared "all-out war" on reckless drivers, in a move to help law-abiding citizens survive the Fourth of July holiday week-end.

Fifty-two unmarked cars and 900 regular radio patrol cars were assigned to watch traffic from 4 P. M. yesterday until 8 A. M. Monday.

The holiday exodus began yesterday afternoon. It was estimated that 1,000,000 cars would carry 3,500,000 persons out of the city during the four-day week-end.

Most of the nation was promised generally fair and warm weather today which to celebrate the 181st anniversary of the adoption of the Declaration of Independence by the Continental Congress.

The Weather Bureau said temperatures here which climbed to 86.4 degrees at 6:40 P. M. yesterday — might reach 85 to 90 degrees today. Yesterday was the first day to exceed 80 degrees since last Friday. The outlook for tomorrow and Saturday is partly cloudy, warm and humid.

The National Safety Council estimated that 45,000,000 motor vehicles would be on the roads. It feared a possible record Independence Day toll of 535 highway deaths between 6 P. M. yesterday and midnight Sunday.

The council warned that eight of every ten fatal accidents occur in rural areas; speed is involved in seven out of ten, and drinking is a factor in almost half. Indiana and Iowa detailed National Guardsmen to aid road patrols; Kentucky and Georgia planned road blocks to check drivers, and New Mexico ordered jail for reckless drivers until their records could be checked.

In the city, 120 police cars will operate in a safety-chain plan, with cars patrolling back and forth on a single side of the major parkways and highways. Six cars of the accident investigation unit will work around-the-clock duty. Two police helicopters will be used.

The major delays yesterday affected traffic leaving the city over the George Washington Bridge. Between 5 and 6:30 P. M. cars on the West Side

Continued on Page 26, Column 2

3 STALINISTS OUT

Shepilov Also Dropped for Opposing Current Policies of Soviet

Texts of communiqué, Pravda editorial, Pages 2 and 4.

By WILLIAM J. JORDEN
Special to The New York Times.

MOSCOW, Thursday, July 4—The Soviet Communist party has accused Vyacheslav M. Molotov, Georgi M. Malenkov and Lazar M. Kaganovich of anti-party activities and has ousted them from the country's leadership.

They were removed both from the Presidium of the party's Central Committee and from the Central Committee itself. However, they remained as members of the party.

Dmitri T. Shepilov, who was said to have joined them in working against the majority, was also ousted from alternate membership in the Presidium, from the Central Committee and from his job as one of the party secretaries.

Three Linked With Stalin

The three Communist leaders, all known for their connections with Stalin, were accused of having tried to restore "methods of leadership that were condemned by the Twentieth Party Congress," an allusion to the system prevailing in Stalin's time. They were said to have tried to form an anti-party faction to achieve their aims.

The action against them was taken during an eight-day meeting of the Central Committee from June 22 through 29. The text of the committee's resolution was released by Tass, the Soviet news agency, last night.

Of the former eleven members of the party Presidium only six remained. They are Nikita S. Khrushchev, Nikolai A. Bulganin, Kliment Y. Voroshilov, Anastas I. Mikoyan, Mikhail A. Suslov and Alexei I. Kirichenko.

Zhukov Is Elevated

Marshal Georgi K. Zhukov, the Defense Minister, and Miss Yekaterina A. Furtseva, the only woman on the Presidium, were among five alternate members who were raised to full rank. Four other regular members were newly added to the Presidium.

In addition to the four leading figures who were singled out for severe criticism and ousted from the Presidium, Mikhail G. Pervukhin and Maxim Z. Saburov also were dropped from the group.

Mr. Pervukhin was demoted to the position of alternate member of the Presidium, but nothing was known of Mr. Saburov's present position. He was not mentioned as having been dropped from the Central Committee itself.

Messrs. Molotov, Malenkov and Kaganovich were said to have opposed all the major policy moves of recent years that have come to be associated with the name of Mr. Khrushchev. The Central Committee's indictment

Continued on Page 2, Column 3

SOVIET EXPECTED TO EASE BLOC TIE

Shift in Leadership Viewed as Move to Consolidate the Communist Orbit

By SYDNEY GRUSON
Special to The New York Times.

PRAGUE, Czechoslovakia, July 3—The changes in the Soviet Communist party's leadership, announced in Moscow tonight, may usher in a significant period of readjustment in relations between the Soviet Union and other Communist countries.

The changes, and the Pravda editorial accompanying them, were considered of such basic importance that people here and in Warsaw hesitated to comment until a more thorough study became possible. But among their first impressions were these:

¶Nikita S. Khrushchev had consolidated his position as the first among equals in the new Presidium of the Soviet party.

¶Mr. Khrushchev was bent on a determined effort to narrow the steadily widening gap between the Soviet party and some of the other Communist parties, particularly that of Communist China.

To Lessen Antagonism

The dismissal of Vyacheslav M. Molotov would be bound to lessen the sharp antagonism between Moscow and Belgrade, Yugoslavia, and the differences between Moscow and Warsaw as well. In both Belgrade and Warsaw Mr. Molotov had been considered the prime architect of a tough policy toward parties straying from the Soviet line.

The section of the Pravda editorial concerning the failure of "sectarians and dogmatists" [Stalinists] to understand the necessity of consolidating the Socialist camp was read here as aimed against Mr. Molotov.

Through the Pravda editorial the Soviet Union was assuming a posture that had already been taken by elsewhere in the Communist camp. Editorial strictures against Stalinists on the one hand and revisionists on the other echoed the "struggle on two fronts" adopted as the Polish party's major ideological line months ago.

One paragraph in Pravda particularly sounded like dozens of recent editorials in Trybuna Ludu, the newspaper of the Polish party's Central Committee. Pravda described "sectarians and dogmatists" as people "divorced from life" who have "backward conceptions."

"They do not see new situations," Pravda declared. "They stubbornly cling to obsolete forms and methods of work and reject that which is born by life. They would like to turn the party back to those incorrect methods of leadership rejected by the Twentieth Party Congress."

Thus at long last the Russians conceded that Marshal Tito had

Continued on Page 3, Column 7

Italy Holds TV Aide In Give-Away Fraud

By PAUL HOFMANN
Special to The New York Times.

ROME, July 3—One of Italy's best-known television personalities was in prison today, charged with rigging give-away shows.

Giuseppe Ruggiero, 42 years old, never spoke a line before television cameras and never was introduced to watchers. But his sternly benevolent face is familiar to millions because it used to appear on the screen whenever something was to be won.

In his wordless way Signor Ruggiero was quite a performer. To the unseen audience he was fair play personified. As chief of the promotion department of the state broadcasting and television system Signor Ruggiero presided over the distribution of thousands of television sets, record players, refrigerators and automobiles.

Now he is accused of having

Continued on Page 37, Column 1

"All the News That's Fit to Print"

The New York Times.

LATE CITY EDITION
U. S. Weather Bureau Report (Page 50) forecasts:
Mostly fair and seasonable today and tomorrow.
Temp. range: 70—57. Yesterday: 67.7—55.9.

VOL. CVII . No. 36,404.   © 1957, by The New York Times Company.   NEW YORK, WEDNESDAY, SEPTEMBER 25, 1957.   10c beyond 100-mile zone from New York City   FIVE CENTS

PRESIDENT SENDS TROOPS TO LITTLE ROCK, FEDERALIZES ARKANSAS NATIONAL GUARD; TELLS NATION HE ACTED TO AVOID ANARCHY

WEST AGAIN BARS SOVIET PROPOSAL ON MIDEAST TALK

U. S. Says Latest Moscow Note 'Cynically Distorts' American Actions

Text of U. S. note to Soviet will be found on Page 5.

By DANA ADAMS SCHMIDT

WASHINGTON, Sept. 24—The United States, Britain and France rejected today the latest in a series of Soviet bids for recognition of the Soviet Union's role in the Middle East.

A brief United States reply delivered in Moscow today said "offensive in tone and cynically distorts" United States objectives and actions in the Middle East."

It accused the Soviet Union of setting in motion "a chain of events leading to the present dangerous situation" by shipping large quantities of arms into the area.

U. S. Affirms Doctrine

The note warned the Soviet Union that the United States Government intended to carry out the national policy laid down in the Eisenhower Doctrine, which "regards the preservation of the independence and integrity of the nations of that region as vital to world peace and as vital, therefore, to its own national interests."

The doctrine, proclaimed in a Joint Resolution of the House of Representatives and the Senate on March 9, 1957, also affirmed the President's authority to use United States forces to aid any Middle East state that asked for help against aggression by a power controlled by international communism.

The Soviet Union's note also accused the United States of seeking to overthrow the Syrian Government and of generally fomenting trouble in the Middle East.

3d Rejection of Soviet Bid

It had proposed, for the third time, a four-power declaration renouncing the use of force in the area. Earlier Soviet proposals for such a declaration, all rejected by the West, were made Feb. 11 and April 19.

As interpreted by United States experts on the Middle East, these notes were meant to convey the idea that the four powers should meet to negotiate a settlement of their rivalries in the Middle East. The first of the notes even went into detail with a proposal for an embargo on shipment of arms to the area.

Because the Soviet Union has asserted its presence in Syria, and because there seems to be little the Western powers can do to reverse developments in

Continued on Page 5, Column 3

Rebel Chief Seized In Algiers Gunfight

By THOMAS F. BRADY
Special to The New York Times.

ALGIERS, Algeria, Sept. 24—The chief of the nationalist terrorist organization in Algiers was in the hands of French parachute troops today. The rebel leader, Saadi Yacef, 29 years old, had eluded capture in the crowded Casbah for more than two years.

With him was 24-year-old Miss Zorah Drif, an Algerian revolutionary, who was condemned to death in absentia by a French military tribunal.

A parachute colonel told reporters this evening that Mr. Yacef and Miss Drif had surrendered at 5:30 A. M. after the terrorist chief had wounded a lieutenant colonel and a master sergeant of a Foreign Legion parachute regiment. The colonel then took reporters to a hideout high in the Casbah where he described how the

Continued on Page 4, Column 3

London and Bonn Rule Out Any Currency Revaluation

Britain Tells Monetary Fund Session She Will Draw $500,000,000 in Stand-By Credit From Export-Import Bank

By EDWIN L. DALE JR.
Special to The New York Times.

WASHINGTON, Sept. 24—British and West German spokesmen and the Managing Director of the International Monetary Fund said today that the question of exchange rates for the pound and the mark was "definitely settled." There will be no change.

At the same time, Britain, through Peter Thorneycroft, Chancellor of the Exchequer, announced she would draw "over the coming weeks" the $500,000,000 stand-by credit she arranged last winter with the United States Export-Import Bank.

In his speech at the annual meeting of the fund, Mr. Thor-neycroft indicated that Britain was drawing the money to demonstrate to speculators that she had the resources to defend the pound.

Both the British and the West Germans emphasized that the recent huge flow of gold and dollars out of Britain and into West Germany had been based solely on speculation, not on basic factors in their foreign trading accounts.

Per Jacobsson, the Fund's Managing Director, said: "The growing knowledge that there will be no alteration in the value of either the Deutsche

Continued on Page 8, Column 5

SOVIET ASSAILED BY LLOYD AT U. N.

Briton Suggests Arms Sent Arabs May Be Stocks for Future Bases

Excerpts from Lloyd's speech are printed on Page 4.

By THOMAS J. HAMILTON
Special to The New York Times.

UNITED NATIONS, N. Y., Sept. 24—Britain denounced today Soviet arms shipments to Arab countries. Selwyn Lloyd, British Foreign Secretary, suggested that the purpose might be to "pre-stock forward bases for the Soviet Union itself."

Mr. Lloyd told the General Assembly that Soviet arms had been delivered "on such a scale as to give some color to this suggestion." He added that Britain viewed the Syrian situation "with grave concern." In addition, he criticized Soviet policy throughout the area.

Mr. Lloyd devoted most of his speech to the Middle East and to disarmament. He did not say what action the Assembly should take on either subject.

However, he declared that Secretary of State Dulles, in

Continued on Page 4, Column 3

City Approves Plan By Wiley to Build Midtown Garages

By JOSEPH C. INGRAHAM

The Board of Estimate has approved in principle the program of Traffic Commissioner T. T. Wiley for garage construction in the heart of lower and mid-Manhattan.

The decision clears the way for a start on $24,000,000 of garages. It also settles a three-year dispute between Mr. Wiley and other city executives that had stymied off-street parking relief.

As a result, the first of the projects—a garage in the Herald Square area—will be on the board's calendar on Oct. 9. Eight other garages are to be centrally located in Manhattan and two in the busiest parts of the Bronx.

The Herald Square garage will be east of the Avenue of the Americas between West Thirty-fifth and Thirty-sixth Streets with entrances and exits on both streets. There will be space for 610 cars on eight levels accessible by ramps. Rates will be geared to "meet the heavy unsatisfied demand for short-time parking," Mr. Wiley said.

Rates proposed by the Commissioner would be 25 cents a

Continued on Page 25, Column 1

SOLDIERS FLY IN

1,000 Go to Little Rock —9,936 in Guard Told to Report

The texts of Executive orders on troops are on Page 16.

By JACK RAYMOND
Special to The New York Times.

WASHINGTON, Sept. 24—The Army ordered all Arkansas National Guardsmen to report for Federal duty tonight and rushed 1,000 airborne troops of the Regular Army into Little Rock to preserve order.

The Regulars were members of the 101st Airborne Division, which won fame in World War II under the command of Gen. Maxwell D. Taylor, now Chief of Staff of the Army.

Maj. Gen. Edwin A. Walker, a much-decorated combat commander with a reputation for toughness, was put in command of the Regular Army contingent and the federalized Arkansas National Guard. He is the commander of the Arkansas Military District.

General Walker's mission is to make sure that no one frustrates Federal Court orders that nine Negro pupils be admitted to Central High School.

Wilson Carries Out Order

Charles E. Wilson, Secretary of Defense, carrying out President Eisenhower's mandate, earlier had called the entire Arkansas Army and Air National Guard, totaling 9,936 men, into Federal service.

The Secretary of Defense and Wilber M. Brucker, Secretary of the Army, acted two hours after President Eisenhower's executive order authorizing "all appropriate steps" to make school attendance possible for the Negroes who had been admitted to the high school.

However, an Army spokesman said that it was planned to make "the absolute minimum demonstration of force necessary."

Immediately after Secretary Wilson signed the federalization call to the Arkansas Guard at 2:25 P. M., Secretary Brucker telephoned the office of Gov. Orval E. Faubus in Little Rock.

At the same time he sent a telegram to the Governor, explaining that President Eisenhower "desires" the personnel of the Arkansas Army and Air National Guard organizations

Continued on Page 14, Column 2

Associated Press Wirephoto
SOLDIERS IN LITTLE ROCK: Residents of Arkansas capital looking on last night as men of the 101st Airborne Division took positions outside the Central High School.

GOVERNORS URGE WHITE HOUSE TALK

Southerners Move to Set Up Mediation Machinery in Use of Federal Troops

By JOHN N. POPHAM
Special to The New York Times.

SEA ISLAND, Ga., Sept. 24—Southern Governors moved tonight to establish mediation machinery that would remove Federal troops from the South. The Governors acted a few hours after the President had federalized the Arkansas National Guard.

Gov. Luther Hodges of North Carolina, chairman of the Southern Governors Conference in session here, announced that two proposals would be submitted to the resolutions committee of the conference for formal consideration tomorrow.

One is a proposal of Gov. Frank G. Clement of Tennessee to establish an informal committee of Southern Governors to seek a meeting with President Eisenhower in a search for a solution to the Little Rock school integration crisis.

The other is a request to the President to hold off the use of Federal troops and to agree

Continued on Page 16, Column 2

Troops on Guard at School, Negroes Ready to Return

By BENJAMIN FINE
Special to The New York Times.

LITTLE ROCK, Ark., Sept. 24—Troops from the Army's crack 101st Airborne Division, carrying carbines and billy clubs, took posts around Central High School tonight. They were here to see that court-ordered integration is carried out.

With police sirens wailing and headlights flashing, Army trucks loaded with a quarter of the contingent of 1,000 crack troops of the division that was ordered to Little Rock by President Eisenhower to prevent mob riots and violence.

The first group of 500 airborne soldiers came to the city this afternoon from Fort Campbell, Ky., and a second group of 500 arrived by plane this evening. The bulk of the two groups bivouacked for the night in areas away from the school.

General Issues Order

Maj. Gen. Edwin A. Walker, commander of the Arkansas Military District, issued a formal order to the people of Little Rock not to collect in crowds and to let Central High School be integrated peaceably.

With the arrival of Federal troops, including some Negro soldiers who were not expected to be on duty at the school, Negro students were ready to try again to enter the high school.

A mob of 1,000 persons yesterday forced the city and school authorities to withdraw nine Negro students who had attended integrated classes for 3 hours and 13 minutes. The students did not try to enter the school today.

Mrs. L. C. Bates, president

Continued on Page 15, Column 1

Price Index Up .2%; Sets Another High

By RICHARD E. MOONEY
Special to The New York Times.

WASHINGTON, Sept. 24—The United States Consumers' Price Index rose two-tenths of a per cent in August, setting another record. It was the twelfth consecutive monthly increase, but among the smallest of the twelve.

The Labor Department's Bureau of Labor Statistics reported today that the index rose in August to 121, taking the average in the 1947-49 period as a comparison base of 100. All major categories of prices increased, but food and housing were the strongest factors.

The August index was 3.8 per cent higher than that of a year earlier. This meant that a typical city family paid $1.03 3/5 in August of 1957 for the goods and services that cost $1 in August of 1956.

The Commerce Department

Continued on Page 24, Column 3

EISENHOWER ON AIR

Says School Defiance Has Gravely Harmed Prestige of U. S.

Text of President's address appears on Page 14.

By ANTHONY LEWIS
Special to The New York Times.

WASHINGTON, Sept. 24—President Eisenhower sent Federal troops to Little Rock, Ark., today to open the way for the admission of nine Negro pupils to Central High School.

Earlier, the President federalized the Arkansas National Guard and authorized calling the Guard and regular Federal forces to remove obstructions to justice in Little Rock school integration.

His history-making action was based on a formal finding that his "cease and desist" proclamation, issued last night, had not been obeyed. Mobs of pro-segregationists still gathered in the vicinity of Central High School this morning.

Tonight, from the White House, President Eisenhower told the nation in a speech for radio and television that he had acted to prevent "mob rule" and "anarchy."

Historic Decision

The President's decision to send troops to Little Rock was reached at his vacation headquarters in Newport, R. I. It was one of historic importance politically, socially, constitutionally. For the first time since the Reconstruction days that followed the Civil War, the Federal Government was using its ultimate power to compel equal treatment of the Negro in the South.

He said violent defiance of Federal Court orders in Little Rock had done grave harm to "the prestige and influence, and indeed to the safety, of our nation and the world." He called on the people of Arkansas and the South to "preserve and respect the law even when they disagree with it."

Guardsmen Withdrawn

Action quickly followed the President's orders. During the day and night 1,000 members of the 101st Airborne Division were flown to Little Rock. Charles E. Wilson, Secretary of the Defense, ordered into Federal service all 10,000 members of the Arkansas National Guard.

Today's events were the climax of three weeks of skirmishing between the Federal Government and Gov. Orval E. Faubus of Arkansas. It was three weeks ago this morning that the Governor first ordered National Guard troops to Central High School to preserve order. The nine Negro students were prevented from entering the school.

The Guardsmen were gone yesterday, withdrawn by Governor Faubus as the result of a

Continued on Page 14, Column 6

CONGRESS IS SPLIT ON USE OF TROOPS

Johnston Calls for Faubus to Resist President but Others Hail His Move

By JOHN W. FINNEY
Special to The New York Times.

WASHINGTON, Sept. 24—Congressional reaction to President Eisenhower's decision to use troops in the Little Rock integration crisis ranged from angry denunciation to outright praise today.

Southern Senators sharply criticized the President and suggested he had exceeded his legal authority. Northern Senators supported the President, but some of them expressed reservations that the action was rather belated.

Expects Faubus to Act

Senator Olin D. Johnston, Democrat of South Carolina, suggested that Gov. Orval E. Faubus of Arkansas "stand up for states' rights" and force a showdown with the President by calling out the Arkansas National Guard on his own.

Senator Johnston, a former Governor of South Carolina, said if he were Governor Faubus, "I'd proclaim a state of insurrection down there, and I'd call out the National Guard and I'd then find out who's going to run things in my state."

Asked by reporters whether he believed Governor Faubus would take such steps, Senator Johnston said, "I think he will and I hope he will."

Aiken Defends Move

Senator John L. McClellan, Democrat of Arkansas, said he believed such use of military force by the Federal Government was "without authority of law."

He said he was "very apprehensive that such action may precipitate more trouble than it will prevent."

Senator Richard B. Russell, Democrat of Georgia, and leader of Southern opposition to the Civil Rights Bill in the last session, said that President Eisenhower's use of troops might "put Negro children in the white schools," but that it would "have a calamitous effect on race relations and on the cause of national unity."

On the other side of the issue, Senator George D. Aiken, Republican of Vermont, said the President "is undoubtedly with-

Continued on Page 17, Column 3

U. S. Cutters Conquer Northwest Passage

3 Coast Guard Craft First of the Nation to Make Transit

By JOHN H. FENTON
Special to The New York Times.

BOSTON, Sept. 24 — Two Coast Guard cutters were saluted in Boston Harbor today at the end of a successful mission to find a practical Northwest Passage—a route around the top of the North American Continent.

A third cutter, the Spar, proceeded directly to her home port at Bristol, R. I., to be welcomed there as the first United States vessel to circumnavigate the continent.

The cutters Storis, from Juneau, Alaska, and the Bramble, from Miami, Fla., put in here for their welcoming. They will continue their homeward voyages later in the week.

The three cutters were the first United States vessels to make the passage.

The shrill sirens of water-spouting fireboats and the deeper-throated whistles of other craft sounded a "well done" as the two bulky cutters made their way up the harbor.

Ranking Coast Guard officers and civil officials joined the crews in a dockside welcome as the cutters tied up at

Continued on Page 19, Column 1

Coast Guardsmen on the stern of the Spar view her sister cutters, Bramble, left, and Storis, during the transit of Simpson Strait. This was a difficult part of the voyage.

Textile Union Gets 30 Days to Reform

By A. H. RASKIN

A scandal-tainted textile union was ordered yesterday to oust its two oldest officers within thirty days or face possible suspension from the merged labor federation.

The ultimatum was given to the 40,000-member United Textile Workers by the executive council of the American Federation of Labor and Congress of Industrial Organizations.

It foreshadowed the fixing of a similar clean-up deadline today for the 1,400,000-member International Brotherhood of Teamsters, and the 140,000-member Bakery and Confectionery Workers International Union.

The federation's Ethical Practices Committee has found all three unions guilty of violating the anti-racketeering code of the A. F. L.-C. I. O. constitution. The findings were based

Continued on Page 18, Column 3

"All the News That's Fit to Print"

The New York Times.

LATE CITY EDITION
U. S. Weather Bureau Report (Page 33) forecasts:
Cloudy and cool today and tonight.
Mostly fair tomorrow.
Temp. range: 65—53. Yesterday: 62.4—49.2.

VOL. CVII..No. 36,414.

© 1957, by The New York Times Company.
Times Square, New York 36, N. Y.

NEW YORK, SATURDAY, OCTOBER 5, 1957.

10c beyond 100-mile zone from New York City

FIVE CENTS

SOVIET FIRES EARTH SATELLITE INTO SPACE; IT IS CIRCLING THE GLOBE AT 18,000 M. P. H.; SPHERE TRACKED IN 4 CROSSINGS OVER U. S.

HOFFA IS ELECTED TEAMSTERS' HEAD; WARNS OF BATTLE

Defeats Two Foes 3 to 1 —Says Union Will Fight 'With Every Ounce'

Text of the Hoffa address is printed on Page 6.

By A. H. RASKIN
Special to The New York Times.

MIAMI BEACH, Oct. 4—The scandal - scarred International Brotherhood of Teamsters elected James R. Hoffa as its president today.

He won by a margin of nearly 3 to 1 over the combined vote of two rivals who campaigned on pledges to clean up the nation's biggest union.

Senate rackets investigators and Hoffa critics in the union rank-and-file immediately opened actions to strip the 44-year-old former warehouseman from Detroit of his election victory.

A jubilant Hoffa exhibited, however, greater concern over the possibility that his union might be ousted from the American Federation of Labor and Congress of Industrial Organizations. He appealed for time to prove that he could make the teamsters "a model of trade unionism."

The parent organization has ordered the 1,400,000-member Teamsters Union to get rid of corrupt leadership by Oct. 24 or face suspension. Hoffa said he felt actions by the union at its week-long convention here should satisfy the federation.

Warns Union Will Fight

He made it plain to the 1,700 cheering delegates that he did not intend to go before the convention in the role of supplicant. He felt expulsion would not destroy the teamsters. He warned that the union would fight "with every ounce of strength we possess" if it found itself outside.

In such a civil war the teamsters would start with a war chest of $38,000,000 in the hands of the international union and much more at the disposal of its locals. The teamsters also could count on their strategic power over other unions through their control of trucks and warehouses.

The Hoffa victory brought warnings of repressive legislation from James P. Mitchell, Secretary of Labor, and Senator John L. McClellan, Democrat of Arkansas. The Senator heads the Select Committee on Improper Activities in the Labor or Management Field, which has accused Hoffa of gangster associations and questionable financial practices.

Winner on First Ballot

A three-hour roll-call gave Hoffa the $50,000-a-year union presidency on the first ballot. His machine, in full command of the convention since it opened Monday, registered 1,208 votes for Hoffa.

William A. Lee of Chicago, the union's seventh vice president, was second with 313 votes. Thomas J. Haggerty of Chicago, secretary - treasurer of Milk Wagon Drivers Union, Local 753, trailed with 140 votes.

The Hoffa forces then began providing the new leader with a rubber stamp board. It elected five of thirteen vice presidents and would have elected the rest today if time had permitted completion of the cumbersome balloting procedure.

Hoffa repeatedly indicated his irritation that some of the old vice presidents marked for elimination had refused to give up without the formality of a roll-call.

Even before the voting, the McClellan committee subpoenaed the full records of the convention's credentials committee. A United States marshal served the subpoena on Joseph Konowe of New York, the committee secretary. He was directed to turn over all

Continued on Page 6, Column 7

IN TOKEN OF VICTORY: Dave Beck, retiring head of the Teamsters Union, raises hand of James R. Hoffa upon his election as union's president. At right is Mrs. Hoffa.
Associated Press Wirephoto

FAUBUS COMPARES HIS STAND TO LEE'S

Says He Will Remain Loyal to People of Arkansas— All Is Quiet at School

By HOMER BIGART
Special to The New York Times.

LITTLE ROCK, Ark., Oct. 4 —Gov. Orval E. Faubus said today that he had made a decision as painfully difficult as the one that had confronted Robert E. Lee at the outset of the Civil War.

"Lee was offered command of the Federal Army in 1861," Governor Faubus recalled. "Lee decided to remain loyal to the people of his state.

"The Democratic party of the North wants me to go along with them on the integration issue. I will remain with the People of Arkansas."

Governor Faubus said he had come under no local pressure to change his stand on integration at Little Rock Central High School. It was a stand that forced President Eisenhower to send Federal troops into this city to uphold Federal Court decisions and to safeguard the nine Negro students registered at Central High.

3,000 Teachers Absent

About 3,000 teachers out of some 39,000 were not in their classrooms yesterday, compared with 2,700 absent on Thursday.

The city's acting Health Commissioner, Dr. Roscoe P. Kandle, said he expected that the total number of people affected by the highly infectious disease would run closer to 800,000 rather than 1,600,000 as predicted in some quarters.

It was estimated Thursday that 200,000 persons in New York had contracted the respiratory infection, and the total yesterday was believed to be somewhat higher.

Commissioner Kandle explained that any attempt to project the ultimate number of cases would involve conjecture

Continued on Page 8, Column 1

Flu Widens in City; 10% Rate Predicted; 200,000 Pupils Out

By ROBERT ALDEN

Asian influenza continued to spread through the city yesterday.

Commissioner of Hospitals Morris A. Jacobs reported that there were ten times more respiratory infections than during the comparable period a year ago.

Attendance in the city's schools fell again. The Board of Education said that close to 200,000 of the city's 941,000 pupils were not in their classrooms yesterday. On Thursday 160,000 pupils were absent.

The attendance estimates were based on a sampling of the schools by the board. The sampling showed that in some schools in the Harlem area—the section hardest hit by the epidemic—more than 50 per cent of the pupils were absent. The board estimated that the overall city absence rate was 20 per cent.

ARGENTINA TAKES EMERGENCY STEPS

State of Siege Proclaimed in Buenos Aires Region —Arrests Reported

By Reuters.

BUENOS AIRES, Oct. 4— A state of siege, suspending constitutional guarantees, was proclaimed tonight in Buenos Aires city and Province.

The Under Secretary of the Ministry of Interior, Garcia Puente, announced the state of siege at a news conference.

He said the emergency move suspended for thirty days the constitutional guarantees in the capital and the Province of Buenos Aires, but not in the remainder of the nation.

He said the measure was aimed exclusively "at defending the normal development of the Government's political plan, jeopardized through sabotage and social unrest."

The proclamation of the state of siege followed the arrest of scores of labor leaders during the day. The number arrested was estimated by observers as 100 to 200.

Bankers, telephone workers, oilworkers, seamstresses and other unions reported tonight that their leaders had been detained and were taken aboard

Continued on Page 5, Column 6

COURSE RECORDED

Navy Picks Up Radio Signals—4 Report Sighting Device

By WALTER SULLIVAN
Special to The New York Times.

WASHINGTON, Saturday, Oct. 5—The Naval Research Laboratory announced early today that it had recorded four crossings of the Soviet earth satellite over the United States.

It said that one had passed near Washington. Two crossings were farther to the west. The location of the fourth was not made available immediately.

It added that tracking would be continued in an attempt to pin down the orbit sufficiently to obtain scientific information of the type sought in the International Geophysical Year.

[Four visual sightings, one of which was in conjunction with a radio signal, were reported by early Saturday morning. Two sightings were made at Columbus, Ohio, and one each from Terre Haute, Ind., and Whittier, Calif.]

Press Reports Noted

Soviet newspapers reported several weeks ago that the Soviet satellites would broadcast on frequencies in the neighborhood of twenty and forty megacycles. More exact frequencies were given by Soviet scientists at a conference on rockets and satellites that took place here this week.

Presumably the Naval Research Laboratory, which is responsible for the United States satellite program under the National Academy of Sciences, immediately set up receivers on those frequencies.

Deception Ruled Out

American scientists believe this was because of a shortage of Soviet receivers capable of handling the higher frequency. It was not thought to be designed to hide the satellite since the Soviet signals are within easy reach of American listeners.

This was demonstrated last night as amateur and commercial radio stations, as well as the Naval Research Laboratory, reported hearing them.

Teams of visual observers at 150 stations in the United States and other Western nations were alerted during the

Continued on Page 3, Column 6

The New York Times   Oct. 5, 1957
The approximate orbit of the Russian earth satellite is shown by black line. The rotation of the earth will bring the United States under the orbit of Soviet-made moon.

Device Is 8 Times Heavier Than One Planned by U.S.

Special to The New York Times.

WASHINGTON, Oct. 4—Leaders of the United States earth satellite program were astonished tonight to learn that the Soviet Union had launched a satellite eight times heavier than that contemplated by this country.

Dr. Joseph Kaplan, chairman of the United States program for the International Geophysical Year, described the 184-pound weight as "fantastic."

The heaviest American satellites are to weigh twenty-one and a half pounds.

The actual launching, nevertheless, did not take the American scientists by surprise. At the end of working sessions on the International Conference on Rockets and Satellites, which has been taking place here, some said they thought the pitching of a Soviet satellite into the sky was imminent.

The satellite must fly at a speed of about 18,000 miles an hour to counteract the force of gravity at an altitude of 560 miles. The initial announcement in Moscow did not make it clear whether or not the rocket that placed it in orbit was aimed north or south.

Its Direction in Doubt

This would determine whether or not the satellite's initial crossing of the United States was northbound or southbound. Since the earth rotates within the orbit of the satellite should in one day traverse almost all nations of the world.

With an orbit inclined 65 degrees to the equator, its sweep would cover virtually the entire region between the Arctic circle and the Antarctic circle.

William A. Holaday, special assistant to the Secretary of Defense for guided missiles, said the launching was not evidence of Soviet technological superiority in missile and rocket developments.

Mr. Holaday noted that Project Vanguard, the United States satellite program, had been an "open" project as part of the International Geophysical year and there has been no

Continued on Page 3, Column 7

SATELLITE SIGNAL BROADCAST HERE

Impulse Carried on Radio and TV—First Reported by Long Island Station

By ROY SILVER

Radio signals from the first satellite launched yesterday were broadcast to radio and television audiences here last night.

The first word that the signals had been received in this country was reported by RCA Communication, Inc. It said that its receiving station at Riverhead, L. I., had picked up what it believed to be radio signals from the Soviet satellite.

The National Broadcasting Company and the Columbia Broadcasting System broke their radio and television programs to enable their audiences to hear the pinging sound of the moon's signal. The British Broadcasting Corporation in London also had tuned powerful receivers to the Soviet earth satellite frequencies. Reuter's radio station north of London reported hearing the signals.

RCA Communications, a subsidiary of Radio Corporation of America, said the first signal had been received at 8:07 P. M. on a frequency of 20.005 megacycles on the 15-meter wave length.

One hour and twenty-nine minutes later, at 9:36 P. M., the receiving station, situated about eighty miles from the city, reported that the satellite was making another round of the earth. Other approaches by the

Continued on Page 2, Column 4

560 MILES HIGH

Visible With Simple Binoculars, Moscow Statement Says

Text of Tass announcement appears on Page 3.

By WILLIAM J. JORDEN
Special to The New York Times.

MOSCOW, Saturday, Oct. 5—The Soviet Union announced this morning that it successfully launched a man-made earth satellite into space yesterday.

The Russians calculated the satellite's orbit at a maximum of 560 miles above the earth and its speed at 18,000 miles an hour.

The official Soviet news agency Tass said the artificial moon, with a diameter of twenty-two inches and a weight of 184 pounds, was circling the earth once every hour and thirty-five minutes. This means more than fifteen times a day.

Two radio transmitters, Tass said, are sending signals continuously on frequencies of 20.005 and 40.002 megacycles. These signals were said to be strong enough to be picked up by amateur radio operators. The trajectory of the satellite is being tracked by numerous scientific stations.

Due Over Moscow Today

Tass said the satellite was moving at an angle of 65 degrees to the equatorial plane and would pass over the Moscow area twice today.

"Its flight," the announcement added, "will be observed in the rays of the rising and setting sun with the aid of the simplest optical instruments, such as binoculars and spyglasses."

The Soviet Union said the world's first satellite was "successfully launched" yesterday. Thus it asserted that it had put a scientific instrument into space before the United States. Washington has disclosed plans to launch a satellite next spring.

The Moscow announcement said the Soviet Union planned to send up more and bigger and heavier artificial satellites during the current International Geophysical Year, an eighteen-month period of study of the earth, its crust and the space surrounding it.

Five Miles a Second

The rocket that carried the satellite into space left the earth at a rate of five miles a second, the Tass announcement said. Nothing was revealed, however, concerning the material of which the man-made moon was constructed or the site in the Soviet Union where the sphere was launched.

The Soviet Union said its sphere circling the earth had opened the way to interplanetary travel.

It did not pass up the opportunity to use the launching for propaganda purposes. It said in its announcement that people now could see how "the new socialist society" had turned the boldest dreams of mankind into reality.

Moscow said the satellite was the result of years of study and research on the part of Soviet scientists.

Several Years of Study

Tass said:

"For several years the research and experimental designing work has been under way in the Soviet Union to create artificial satellites of the earth.

"It has already been reported in the press that the launching of the earth satellites in the U. S. S. R. had been planned in accordance with the program of International Geophysical Year research.

"As a result of intensive work by the research institutes and design bureaus, the first artificial earth satellite in the world has now been created. This first satellite was successfully launched in the U. S. S. R. on October four."

The Soviet announcement said that as a result of the tremendous speed at which the satellite was moving it would

Continued on Page 3, Column 3

Ex-Premier Mollet Accepts Bid To Form a New French Cabinet

Socialist Leader Agrees With Reluctance and Without Giving Much Hope

By ROBERT C. DOTY
Special to The New York Times.

PARIS, Oct. 4—Former Premier Guy Mollet agreed reluctantly and without much hope today to try to form a new French Cabinet.

M. Mollet's pessimism, shared by many observers here, was based on the fact that both he and his party, the Socialists, still hold strongly to the policies that caused the defeat of the last two Cabinets, M. Mollet's own and that of Premier Maurice Bourgès-Maunoury, a Radical.

Thus the Socialists still support the views on economic and social questions, including the demand for extensive governmental decree powers in those domains, that brought M. Mollet's Government down last May after a record-breaking sixty-eight weeks in office. The average Cabinet's life span has been twenty-nine weeks.

At the same time the Socialists regard as a minimum of reform the program for limited

Continued on Page 5, Column 6

Guy Mollet
Associated Press

Warsaw Crushes New Protest; Clubs, Tear Gas Rout Students

By SYDNEY GRUSON
Special to The New York Times.

WARSAW, Oct. 4—Policemen and students clashed again in the streets of Warsaw tonight.

Security chiefs, seemingly nervous, threw a guard of several hundred workers' militia around the downtown headquarters of the ruling United Workers (Communist) party.

For the second successive night the police broke up demonstrations by firing tear gas and beating students and others with rubber truncheons.

What began last night as a protest against the closing of one newspaper was turning tonight into a general clamor against police brutality and the suppression of free speech. By midnight the city had calmed

down and the people had left the streets.

Among those clubbed tonight was Franco Fabiani, permanent correspondent here of the Italian Communist paper L'Unita. He suffered two minor head wounds.

Signor Fabiani was caught in crowds charged by the police after about 3,000 students had met in the Polytechnic and adopted a resolution protesting both the closing of the newspaper Po Prostu and the "brutal interference" of the police at last night's meeting.

Tonight's trouble centered on the Polytechnic, the huge advanced technical school near the heart of Warsaw. It was

Continued on Page 5, Column 3

City Sifts Charge That Schupler, Brooklyn Councilman, Sold a Job

By PAUL CROWELL

The city is investigating a complaint that Councilman Philip J. Schupler accepted a $500 fee last year in exchange for a promise to get a job for a Brooklyn business man.

William R. Peer, secretary to Mayor Wagner, said yesterday that the inquiry was started several weeks ago after the complaint had been made by Sol L. Hoffman of 1934 Sixty-third Street, Brooklyn.

At the office of Investigation Commissioner Charles H. Tenney, who is making the investigation, it was said that no findings or conclusions had been reached.

The charge was denied by Mr. Schupler, a Democrat-Liberal, in a telephone interview.

He said that he had received a $500 check from Mr. Hoffman in May, 1956, but that it was given to him as a campaign contribution. Mr. Schupler was then a candidate for re-election as a Democratic district leader. He was defeated in the primary election a month later.

Disclosure of the investigation brought from Robert K. Christenberry, the Republican candidate for Mayor, the charge that "corruption and scandal in our City Council is symptomatic of the Wagner administration."

In a formal statement concerning the Schupler case Mr. Christenberry called upon the city's voters to support his

Continued on Page 15, Column 2

199

The New York Times.

LATE CITY EDITION
U.S. Weather Bureau Report (Page 95) forecast:
Rain early today; cloudy later; rain late tonight and tomorrow.
Temp. range: 65—55. Yesterday: 62.0—55.2.

NEWS SUMMARY AND INDEX, PAGE 95

VOL. CVII—No. 36,443.   © 1957, by The New York Times Company. Times Square, New York 36, N. Y.   NEW YORK, SUNDAY, NOVEMBER 3, 1957.   25c beyond 100-mile zone from New York City   SECTION ONE   TWENTY-FIVE CENTS

SOVIET FIRES NEW SATELLITE, CARRYING DOG; HALF-TON SPHERE IS REPORTED 900 MILES UP

Zhukov Ousted From Party Jobs; Konev Condemns Him

MEYNER'S VICTORY IS SEEN IN SURVEY OF JERSEY VOTERS

Democratic Governor Likely to Win Re-election Over Senator Forbes Tuesday

A Times Team Report

A team of New York Times reporters has just completed a survey of political trends and issues in New Jersey. Reports on the election campaign there come from George Cable Wright, Milton Honig, Alfred E. Clark, Leonard Buder, John W. Slocum and Layhmond Robinson.

By GEORGE CABLE WRIGHT

The curtain will descend tomorrow night on the New Jersey Governorship campaign. The contest—on the surface, at least—appears to have been enacted before a relatively bored audience.

Neither Gov. Robert B. Meyner, the Democratic incumbent, nor State Senator Malcolm S. Forbes, the Republican candidate, has exhibited the ability to rouse the voting public markedly from its apparent apathy.

Beyond the Hudson and the Delaware, however, far greater interest is being manifested in the contest.

The Eisenhower Administration has staked its prestige on the results of the balloting as never before in a state-wide race. Republicans and Democrats alike at the national level are eagerly awaiting the vote tally. Each party hopes to gain from it a trend in its favor.

Surprise Possible

The apparent lack of interest locally may well be misleading. It is not an uncommon trait of the state's electorate, as witness 1953, 1954 and 1956. In those years, the pre-election temper turned out to be a "sleeper." The voters, from Cape May to High Point, set their alarms for election morn, and flocked to the polls.

As the present campaign progressed, it became increasingly evident that, in all probability, it would be decided on the basis of personality rather than on issues. This was verified by a team of New York Times reporters in the field.

On the basis of findings of The Times' survey team, victory for Mr. Meyner is definitely indicated.

Continued on Page 60, Column 6

Major Sports News

FOOTBALL

Navy beat Notre Dame in the nation's top college contest yesterday. Scores of leading games:

Alabama .....14 Georgia 13
Amherst .....19 Tufts 6
Army ....53 Colgate 6
Auburn ......13 Florida 0
Cornell ......8 Columbia 0
Dartmouth ...14 Yale 14
Delaware ....23 Rutgers 19
Georgia T. ..13 Duke 6
Harvard .....13 Penn 0
Iowa ....21 Michigan 21
Michigan St.21 Wisconsin 7
Minnesota ...14 Indiana 0
Missouri ....9 Colorado 6
Navy ....20 Notre Dame....6
N. C. State..19 Wake Forest...6
Ohio State...47 Northwestern .6
Oklahoma ....13 Kansas St.....0
Oregon ......27 Stanford 26
Oregon St....39 Wash. St.....25
Penn St......27 W. Virginia...6
Princeton ....7 Brown 0
Purdue ......21 Illinois 6
Syracuse ....24 Pittsburgh ...21
T. C. U. .....19 Baylor 1
Tennessee ...35 N. Carolina...0
Texas A.&M...7 Arkansas 0
Vanderbilt ...7 L. S. U. 0

HORSE RACING

Eddie Schmidt won the $86,900 Gallant Fox Handicap at Jamaica by half a length. Bold Ruler was first in the Benjamin Franklin Handicap.

HOCKEY

The Rangers routed the Boston Bruins, 5—0.

Details in Section 5.

President and Class Honor Academy

The New York Times (by Arthur Brower)
The President drinks from fountain he and other members of 1915 class gave to academy. Mrs. Eisenhower watches.

By W. H. LAWRENCE
Special to The New York Times.

WEST POINT, N. Y., Nov. 2—President Eisenhower watched Army defeat Colgate today as the climax to a nostalgic reunion with his 1915 Military Academy classmates. Like any other old grad, the President leaped to his feet and cheered whenever Army threatened or scored—and he had many opportunities this afternoon as the West Point

Continued on Page 45, Column 1

DEMOCRATS COUNT ON PARTY VICTORY

Believe Wagner Can Win Without Liberal Votes in Mayoral Race

By LEO EGAN

Democratic leaders were counting confidently yesterday on obtaining enough votes on their party's line alone to insure the re-election of Mayor Wagner and his running mates next Tuesday. If they can do so, it will be the first time since 1932 that a Democrat has received a majority of all the votes in a New York City Mayoral election.

Four years ago Mr. Wagner won by virtue of a split in the opposition between Harold Riegelman, Republican, and Rudolph Halley, Liberal and independent. Mr. Wagner received just over 45 per cent of the total vote cast.

This year the Democratic party is backing Mayor Wagner and his two city-wide running mates, Controller Lawrence E. Gerosa and City Council President Abe Stark. But Democratic leaders would like to be able to say they could have won without the Liberal endorsement.

Alex Rose, state vice chairman and spokesman for the Liberal party, referred to this Democratic attitude yesterday in appealing for a large Wagner-Gerosa-Stark vote on the Liberal party line.

"A large vote on the Liberal line is a vote with a special message to the city administration to be independent and is the best guarantee for a clean and effective administration at all levels of city government," he said.

"A large vote on the Liberal line will continue the Liberal party as the political conscience

Continued on Page 53, Column 3

Voters Will Settle 7 State Questions; Issues Are Listed

Special to The New York Times.

ALBANY, Nov. 2—Voters who go to the polls on Tuesday will have a chance to pass on six proposed amendments to the State Constitution and whether a constitutional convention should be held.

If performance runs true, only about half those voting will bother to answer the seven questions across the top of every ballot.

The type on the ballot is small and the questions do not always express in the limited space the impact of the proposition.

Following is a description of each proposal, what it would do and the arguments for and against it:

The ballot asks:

"Shall there be a convention to revise the Constitution and amend the same?"

Approval would mean the voters would elect delegates on a party basis in 1958 and those elected would hold a convention the following year, probably in the summer. The convention

Continued on Page 62, Column 4

British and French, a Year After, Say Suez Invasion Was Justified

London Reconciled

By DREW MIDDLETON
Special to The New York Times.

LONDON, Nov. 2—In the view of some of those who planned the British-French invasion of Egypt, the situation obtaining in the Middle East a year later justifies that attempt to halt the march of Arab nationalism and its ally, Soviet communism, in the area.

A year ago the Soviet Union had one client and ally in the Middle East, Egypt. Today it has two, Egypt and Syria. The withdrawal of the British and French forces from Suez at the behest of the United Nations has been interpreted by Arab nationalism as a victory and the index against a power vacuum into which Soviet imperialism has moved, it is noted.

The view that the French

Continued on Page 33, Column 3

Paris Still Bitter

By ROBERT C. DOTY
Special to The New York Times.

PARIS, Nov. 2—The weekend of the first anniversary of the British-French invasion of Egypt finds most Frenchmen, including those who planned the operation, convinced that it was a good idea.

There is no tendency here to push such an idea aggressively. On the contrary, French high officialdom seeks to liquidate as speedily and unobtrusively as possible the remaining economic, political and diplomatic consequences of last fall's events. This is regarded as the logical prerequisite to a restoration of complete interallied confidence and effective action to repair the Western position in the Middle East.

Furthermore, as the French

Continued on Page 33, Column 6

A.F.L.-C.I.O. TARGET RESIGNS AS CHIEF OF TEXTILE UNION

Valente Voices Hope Group Will Stay in Federation —2 More Actions Taken

Special to The New York Times.

WASHINGTON, Nov. 2—The president of the United Textile Workers, Anthony Valente, resigned today. He said he was acting to help his union retain its membership in the American Federation of Labor and Congress of Industrial Organizations.

The 44,000-member union was one of three cited for corruption last month by the executive council of the parent labor organization. Mr. Valente was declared ineligible to hold office.

Tonight, the leadership of the union accepted the resignation of Mr. Valente and announced other steps to conform with demands by the A. F. L.-C. I. O. to "clean up" the textile workers operations.

Francis Schaufenbil, secretary-treasurer of the union, told reporters at the end of an all-day meeting of the organization's executive board that "we certainly hope" the actions taken would keep the textile workers in the parent body.

2 Other Measures

The board meeting was called today to answer charges brought by the A. F. L.-C. I. O. council.

In addition to accepting Mr. Valente's resignation, the board took these two actions to comply with the council's demands:

1. It agreed to call a special convention "as soon as possible" to elect new officers. The session will be in Washington, New York or Philadelphia.

2. The board "rescinded" a $104,000 severance pay deal for Lloyd Klenert, resigned secretary-treasurer, and "has not obligated" the union on any financial arrangement with any other resigned officers. This was, presumably, a reference to Mr. Valente. Senate investigators have accused Mr. Valente and Mr. Klenert of buying their homes with union funds and using devious bookkeeping to cover their tracks.

Criticizes Members of Council

Mr. Valente resigned at a meeting of the Textile Workers Executive Board, called to answer the council's charges. Talking with reporters during a recess, he loosed bitter criticism against twelve of the twenty-nine members of the A. F. L.-C. I. O. council.

He said the twelve had pledged him their support, but "they reneged on their commitments." He did not name the twelve.

This development in the labor

Continued on Page 44, Column 3

ZHUKOV HUMBLED

He Admits 'Mistakes' —Accused of 'Cult' in Armed Forces

Text of Soviet communiqué is printed on Page 4.

By WILLIAM J. JORDEN
Special to The New York Times.

MOSCOW, Sunday, Nov. 3—Marshal Georgi K. Zhukov, dismissed a week ago as Defense Minister of the Soviet Union, has been removed from all his top posts in the Soviet Communist party.

The party's Central Committee announced last night that Marshal Zhukov had lost his place on the party's central policy-making group, the Presidium, as well as on the Central Committee itself. The principal charge against the hero of World War II was that he had tried to eliminate the Communist party's direction and control of the Soviet armed forces.

The Communist party newspaper Pravda reported this morning that Marshal Zhukov had admitted his "mistakes" during the Central Committee meeting at which he was expelled from the party leadership.

Anti-Stalin Phrase Used

He tempered that acceptance somewhat by telling his party comrades that he accepted their criticism of him as being "in the main correct." He also was said to have accepted the attack on his leadership of the armed forces as being of "comradely" party assistance to me personally and to other military workers."

The barrel-chested, square-jawed soldier was charged with promoting his own "cult of personality" in the army. This is the phrase used here in reference to Stalin's one-man rule, which was vigorously condemned by the Twentieth Congress of the Communist party last year.

"With the help of sycophants and flatterers," the Central Committee said, "he was praised to the sky in lectures and reports, in articles, films and pamphlets, and his person and role in the Great Patriotic War [World War II] were overglorified."

The result, the Central Committee charged, was that the whole history of the war had been "distorted." It said that by building himself up Marshal Zhukov had belittled the efforts of the Soviet people, of the

Continued on Page 3, Column 1

Marshal Is Linked to Stalin In Blame for '41 Reverses

Konev Charges Ex-Chief Distorted History to Create Hero's Role

Special to The New York Times.

MOSCOW, Sunday, Nov. 3—Marshal Ivan S. Konev, long companion and subordinate of Marshal Georgi K. Zhukov, condemned the former Defense Minister today for "errors in military science."

Marshal Konev's attack was the first derogatory statement leveled against Marshal Zhukov on military grounds.

Soviet commander of the Warsaw Pact forces, Marshal Konev issued his condemnation in an article in today's Pravda, the Communist party organ.

The Konev article said that Marshal Zhukov was responsible along with Stalin for lack of preparedness in the Soviet Union to meet the imminent German attack in June, 1941. It belittled Marshal Zhukov's role in the victories at Stalingrad and Berlin and accused Marshal Zhukov of undue pride and of twisting historical fact.

Associated Press
Marshal Ivan S. Konev

Marshal Konev's attack on Marshal Zhukov was bitter and extensive. Marshal Konev noted that his former comrade in

Continued on Page 3, Column 4

SOVIET 'STRESSES' SEEN BY THE U. S.

Washington Expects Strain Behind the Iron Curtain From Zhukov Disgrace

State Department statement will be found on Page 6.

By RUSSELL BAKER
Special to The New York Times.

WASHINGTON, Nov. 2—The State Department said tonight that the downgrading of Marshal Georgi K. Zhukov showed the "strains and stresses" present in the Soviet Union and the countries dominated by the Soviet Communists.

In a brief formal statement, the department noted that Marshal Zhukov's "disgrace" followed only by a short time the expressed desire of Nikita S. Khrushchev, First Secretary of the Soviet Communist party, to send the military leader on a special mission to the United States.

The department said this, following so closely "similar action against" other one-time Soviet leaders, demonstrated the polit-

Continued on Page 7, Column 1

ORBIT COMPLETED

Animal Still Is Alive, Sealed in Satellite, Moscow Thinks

By The Associated Press

LONDON, Sunday, Nov. 3—The Soviet Union announced today it had launched a second space satellite—this one carrying a dog. Radio signals indicated that the animal was living, the Russians said.

A satellite six times as heavy as the one sent up Oct. 4 now is circling the earth every hour and forty-two minutes at a height of 937 miles, Moscow said. This means that the speed is nearly 18,000 miles an hour for the 1,110-pound satellite.

The dog has been reported hermetically sealed in a container equipped with an air-conditioning system.

Moscow Radio said data received from the second satellite indicated the "functioning of scientific instruments and control of the living activities of the animal are taking place normally."

First Trip Reported

The new satellite carries transmitting equipment and apparatus for measuring cosmic rays, temperature and pressure. It also carries equipment for reporting the condition of the dog.

It first passed over the Soviet capital at 11:20 P. M. Eastern Standard Time last night and then completed its first trip around the earth over Moscow at 1:05 A. M. today, the Soviet Union reported.

The announcement said the second satellite was "dedicated to the fortieth anniversary of the great October revolution," which the Communist world will celebrate in Moscow beginning next Thursday.

The new earth satellite is completing its orbit in about seven minutes more than the original Sputnik, still circling the earth.

Japan Receives Signals

Moscow said the second sphere was sending out two radio signals.

One, like the "beep" signal transmitted by the first satellite, is on a frequency of 20.005 megacycles. The other signal, at 40.002 megacycles, is a continuous note.

The perigee (minimum altitude) probably is about 140 miles, the same as the first satellite, Dr. Hynek said. "It seems like a repetition of the orbit of the first satellite," he added.

The Soviet launching of the

Continued on Page 26, Column 4

SATELLITE SIGNAL RECEIVED AT M.I.T.

Scientists Believe That Orbit Repeats First Sphere— Trackers Are Alerted

By The United Press

CAMBRIDGE, Mass., Sunday, Nov. 3—The first American pick-up of the new Soviet satellite's radio signal was reported early today to the Smithsonian Astrophysical Observatory.

Leon Campbell at the observatory said that the report was received from William S. Cooper of the Massachusetts Institute of Technology. Mr. Cooper said that he heard the signal at 2:02 A. M., between 20 and 20.5 megacycles.

Dr. J. Allen Hynek of the observatory staff said that the satellite apparently was in roughly the same path of 65 degrees as the first Soviet satellite.

Continued on Page 26, Column 2

Mao Is in Moscow; He Hails Soviet Tie

By MAX FRANKEL
Special to The New York Times.

MOSCOW, Nov. 2—Mao Tse-tung, leader of Communist China, arrived in Moscow today. He is probably the most important of the gathering here to show the unity and might of international communism.

Virtually all the reigning heads of Communist nations and parties, with the notable exception of President Tito of Yugoslavia, will make the pilgrimage here to join in next week's celebrations of the fortieth anniversary of the Bolshevik Revolution.

Expected in addition to Mr. Mao, who is the Chinese Communist chief of state and party chairman, are Poland's party leader, Wladyslaw Gomulka, and Premier Jozef Cyrankiewicz; Premier Janos Kadar of Hun-

Continued on Page 27, Column 3

Associated Press Radiophoto
CHINESE COMMUNIST LEADER GREETED IN MOSCOW: Mao Tse-tung, left, the chief of state and Communist party chief, as he arrived yesterday at the capital airport. Welcoming him were Nikita S. Khrushchev, center, Soviet Communist chief, and Premier Nikolai A. Bulganin. Mr. Mao will take part in commemorating the Bolshevik Revolution.

"All the News That's Fit to Print"

The New York Times.

LATE CITY EDITION
U. S. Weather Bureau Report (Page 45) forecast:
Fair, breezy, less humid today; clear
and cool tonight. Fair tomorrow.
Temp. range: 78—60. Yesterday: 79.3—64.8.

VOL. CVII..No. 36,654.   © 1958, by The New York Times Company. Times Square, New York 36, N. Y.   NEW YORK, MONDAY, JUNE 2, 1958.   10c beyond 100-mile zone from New York City. Higher in air delivery cities.   FIVE CENTS

DE GAULLE NAMED PREMIER IN 329-224 VOTE; ASKS 6-MONTH DECREE RULE; LEFTISTS RIOT; ALGIERS IS DISPLEASED BY CABINET CHOICES

CRASHES KILL 344 ON 3-DAY HOLIDAY; RAIN CURBS TOLL

Auto Deaths Below Forecast —Temperature Climbs to 79.3 Degrees Here

By LAWRENCE O'KANE

Traffic fatalities climbed yesterday in the final, homebound hours of the Memorial Day week-end.

Bad weather over much of the nation dampened the outing spirits of many. But it also induced motorists to drive carefully.

By 2 A. M. today 344 persons had died in traffic accidents since 6 P. M. Thursday, according to The Associated Press. Altogether there were 554 accident deaths, including 122 drownings and eight-eight from miscellaneous causes.

In New York City, three persons were killed and 556 injured in 387 road accidents, according to Police Department figures covering the period from 8 A. M. Thursday to 4 P. M. yesterday. Only property was damaged in 487 other accidents.

Cautious Optimism

Late yesterday the National Safety Council began to express cautious optimism that traffic deaths would not exceed the peak three-day Memorial Day week-end toll of 369 recorded in 1955.

Last week the council had predicted 350 deaths for the 1958 holiday week-end, but after a series of multi-death accidents Saturday it began to voice fears of a new record.

The council said rain and slippery highways had restricted short-distance travel as picnics and beach outings were canceled. Showers and thunderstorms were reported yesterday from the Gulf states to southern New England. Squalls ranged the Great Lakes and tornado alerts were issued for parts of the South and Midwest.

Rain Avoids City

In New York City, the warmest day of the year sent hundreds of thousands to beaches and parks. Afternoon rains had been predicted, but failed to materialize. The threat kept crowds from swelling to record proportions, however, and chilly offshore winds kept most beachgoers out of the water.

The year's highest temperature here—79.3 degrees—was registered at 4:20 P. M.

Today is expected to be fair but not as warm or humid as yesterday. Afternoon temperatures are expected to be in the 70's. The prediction for Tuesday is fair with pleasant temperatures and low humidity.

As yesterday drew to a close, city-bound traffic increased on highways and bridges and in tunnels. Most reports described the flow as heavy, but moving freely.

A 22-year-old airman was injured fatally early yesterday when his automobile struck a

Continued on Page 18, Column 2

Mahoney Wins Upstate Support As G.O.P.'s Choice for Governor

By DOUGLAS DALES

Support for State Senator Walter J. Mahoney of Buffalo as the Republican nominee for Governor spread eastward over the week-end. Heretofore backing for the Senate leader was concentrated in western New York.

In a joint statement, county chairmen of four Hudson Valley - Catskill counties declared that no suggested candidate had Senator Mahoney's experience in state government or his capacity to present issues in a forthright and intelligent fashion.

The statement was issued by Neal Brandow of Greene, Dr. Odgen Bush of Delaware, Harold Cole of Sullivan and Kenneth L. Wilson of Ulster.

These counties, with six others whose leaders or party organizations have endorsed Mr. Mahoney, will have 181 of the 586 delegates needed for nomination at the convention Aug. 25 and 26 in Rochester.

Previously the Buffalo Senator has been assured publicly of the backing of Erie, Niagara, Chautauqua, Oneida, Madison and Herkimer Counties. In addition, he has received private assurances of support in at least ten other counties, according to close associates.

Neither of the two other potential candidates—Nelson A. Rockefeller and Leonard W. Hall—has received such firm delegate support. Mr. Hall

Continued on Page 15, Column 2

Ernst Report on Galindez Clears Dominican Dictator

Inquiry for Trujillo Hints That Missing Columbia Scholar May Be Alive—Anti-Franco Activities Cited

By PETER KIHSS

Morris L. Ernst has filed a report in effect clearing Generalissimo Rafael L. Trujillo and his Dominican dictatorship of any role in the two-year-old disappearance here of Jesús de Galindez, a Basque scholar.

The New York lawyer's report, made after a ten-month investigation for the Dominican Republic, implied that the anti-Trujillo writer might be alive. It suggested that Dr. Galindez' disappearance March 12, 1956, might be related "to his substantial and perhaps carefully confused fiscal operations and his profound interest in Spain after Franco."

Dr. Galindez, a Spanish exile, had reported to the Department of Justice a total of $1,024,-118.24 in contributions he raised as agent for the anti-Franco Basque Government - in - exile from May, 1949, through January, 1956.

The Ernst report also rejected a theory that Gerald Lester Murphy, an American pilot who vanished in the Dominican Republic Dec. 3, 1956, might have flown Mr. Galindez to that country as a kidnap victim.

Mr. Ernst asserted that the Cuban Government had "reliable reports" that Mr. Murphy landed his plane in Cuba on March 13, 1956—before setting it down later that day in Miami.

The lawyer charged that Mr. Murphy had been "engaged in an illegal operation for hire." He recalled the pilot's reputed statements that he had flown arms and funds to Cuba for opponents of Cuban President Fulgencio Batista.

While formal comment by Government investigators in the United States was unavailable,

Continued on Page 14, Column 4

Hospital Deficits Increase With Advance in Medicine

By EMMA HARRISON

Voluntary hospitals in the New York area reported an operating loss of $23,500,000 for 1957, the United Hospital Fund disclosed yesterday. This is an increase of $3,550,000 over the 1956 figure of $19,950,000.

The operating loss for the seventy-four voluntary hospitals and convalescent homes is exclusive of the hospitals' receipts from philanthropic support and income from investment. But the figure also excludes hospital depreciation, interest on indebtedness and money spent on research and medical education, the fund noted.

The fund estimated the hospitals' net loss after all income at $6,000,000. This estimate includes an allowance of 5 per cent for plant depreciation.

However, operating income, including revenue from patients and from auxiliary activities such as nursing schools and cafeterias, went up 6.8 per cent to $176,000,000. Operating costs, meanwhile, climbed 8 per cent to $199,500,000.

Thus, with operating costs increasing partly because of better care for patients, the voluntary hospitals are faced with a paradox: The more

Continued on Page 20, Column 2

187 MILLION URGED FOR CITY SCHOOLS

73 Projects Are Planned Over Three Budgets to House 74,740 Pupils

By GENE CURRIVAN

An extraordinary capital budget estimate of $187,600,000 for the city's school building program was announced yesterday. It would require financing in three successive budgets.

It includes seventy-three projects with an enrollment capacity of 74,740 pupils.

The proposed budget for next year is $108,200,000 for thirty-one projects.

Last year the Board of Education asked for $106,800,000 and received a little less than $96,000,000.

This year's unusual proposal was put forth by the Committee on Building and Sites headed by Charles J. Bensley. It may be predicated on the hope that a constitutional amendment giving the city the right to borrow $500,000,000 for spending on buildings will eventually be adopted. The amendment has been approved by the Legislature but must be reapproved at the next session and then sub-

Continued on Page 19, Column 4

Soviet Fishing Fleet Off Canada Causing Concern in Washington

Vessels Anchored Near Grand Banks — Each Departing Craft Always Replaced

By ALLEN DRURY

WASHINGTON, June 1—A half-dozen Soviet fishing ships riding at anchor 100 miles off the east coast of Canada have the United States Navy and Air Force puzzled.

The vessels, stationed near an area marked off with buoys flying small Soviet flags, are in international fishing waters near the Grand Banks.

Moscow recently lodged a vigorous protest with the United States Embassy, charging that a United States military plane had flown over one of the vessels at masthead height. The accusation has been denied by a high Washington official. He told newsmen that planes - in the area normally flew at several thousand feet altitude.

According to this source, the United States Government recently received from Canada a photograph of one of the buoys made by a helicopter. The photograph appeared to indicate the buoy was a conventional type, with no signs of electronic gear that might be

vessel is always replaced and causing some concern.

The New York Times   June 2, 1958
Soviet fishing vessels are anchored 100 miles off east coast of Canada (cross).

Continued on Page 5, Column 4

JUNTA AIDE BITTER

'Not the Government We Hoped For,' Civil Leader Declares

By THOMAS F. BRADY
Special to The New York Times.

ALGIERS, June 1 — Léon Delbecque, vice president of the All-Algerian Committee of Public Safety, said tonight that the de Gaulle Cabinet was "not yet the Government of Public Safety we hoped for."

Looking at the list of ministers of Premier Charles de Gaulle, he said to reporters: "You call that a Government? Who is Minister of the Interior? A civil servant. Who is Minister of Foreign Affairs? A civil servant."

Emile Pelletier, the new Interior Minister, is a former Prefect. Maurice Couve de Murville, the Foreign Minister, is a career diplomat. Both are considered non-political "technicians."

Moderation Is Target

M. Delbecque was expressing the bitter disappointment that is felt among civilian insurgent leaders here at the liberal moderation shown thus far in General de Gaulle's assumption of power. No one associated with the Public Safety movement appears on the Cabinet list.

Although M. Delbecque did not appear to approve of career civil servants in the Cabinet, he expressed his confidence in Premier de Gaulle and said he regarded the Cabinet as a step toward the ultimate goal.

M. Delbecque denied a report that he had written Premier de Gaulle protesting against the make-up of the new Cabinet. The Algerian leader said he had written to the general every day for the last three days but did not indicate the contents except to say that he had informed General de Gaulle of the situation in Algeria. M. Delbecque added that he had not received any response.

Salan Aide Sees Victory

Col. Charles Lacheroy, spokesman for Gen. Raoul Salan, military ruler of Algeria, hailed General de Gaulle's assumption of power as a victory.

But outside the Government General Building, scene of regular mass demonstrations since the civil-military insurrection May 13, there was only a scattering of persons and no sign of rejoicing.

Asked why there was no celebration, Lucien Neuwirth, official spokesman for the Public Safety Committee, said: "Today is Sunday. People are at home." Last Sunday, however, the peo-

Continued on Page 3, Column 1

Associated Press Radiophoto
DE GAULLE STATES HIS TERMS: The general speaking in Paris yesterday to the French National Assembly before it approved the wartime leader as the nation's Premier.

U. S. IS 'GRATIFIED' AT FRENCH ACTION

White House Gives de Gaulle Warm Welcome—Capital Hopes He Can Visit Soon

By DANA ADAMS SCHMIDT
Special to The New York Times.

WASHINGTON, June 1—The White House welcomed Gen. Charles de Gaulle as Premier of France today in a warmly worded statement issued only two hours after the news of his investiture had reached Washington.

Administration officials said unofficially that they would be glad to see General de Gaulle visit the United States soon.

They said they assumed, however, that he would be too preoccupied with French internal affairs during his first six months to make such a trip unless it were required to prepare for a summit meeting with the Soviet Union.

The White House statement was issued from Gettysburg, where President Eisenhower is spending the week-end. It read as follows:

"We have been witnessing with sympathy and understanding the difficult days through which France has passed recently, and we are gratified that the French crisis is now being resolved.

"General de Gaulle has assumed heavy responsibilities at a critical juncture in French history. Our thoughts go out to the great French nation, wish-

Continued on Page 6, Column 6

Red-Led Demonstrators Clash With Paris Police

By W. GRANGER BLAIR
Special to The New York Times.

PARIS, June 1—Communist-inspired riots erupted in Paris today a few hours before the National Assembly voted to install Gen. Charles de Gaulle as Premier. The outbreaks started at 3 P. M. in working-class quarters in northern, eastern and southern sections of the city.

At almost the same moment the general rose to deliver his investiture speech in a jammed and tense Parliament ringed by armed security guards.

For the next three hours thousands of policemen, crowded into heavy vans, rushed to trouble spots to clash with about 10,000 demonstrators.

Many persons were injured—several dozen, according to the police. The injured included twenty-five members of the security force. The police arrested 190 rioters.

Crowds Arrive From Suburbs

Besides Leftists ready for action in town, the mobs were replenished by Leftists from industrial suburbs. Even before they arrived, the police descended on key train, bus and subway exits to intercept them.

The first clash between security forces and rioters came in northern Paris near the Porte de Clignancourt. Several hundred demonstrators tried to force their way south toward the center of the city through four vanloads of policemen.

Both sides struck out with clubs. After fifteen minutes of confused fighting, the Leftists retreated northward.

These rioters, like their fellows elsewhere in the city, car-

Continued on Page 5, Column 1

DE GAULLE SHUNS ASSEMBLY DEBATE

Strides Out After He Makes Brief Statement — Anger and Fear Mark Session

By HENRY GINIGER
Special to The New York Times.

PARIS, June 1—In anger, defiance, fear and resignation, the National Assembly held today one of the last sessions of France's present parliamentary Government.

The Fourth Republic may go on—many Deputies fear its end—but it will not be the same one that France has known since it began functioning in 1947.

This was the consensus of those who were able to fight their way into the Assembly building on the Left Bank of the Seine to witness the strangest and most memorable session the Assembly has ever had.

That France had turned a page of her history was evident in the way the session ran its course. It took the Assembly a little more than four hours to accept Gen. Charles de Gaulle by a vote of 329 to 224 and during that time the man the Deputies were debating was not present.

General Scorns System

In the past, lesser aspirants to the Premiership—those willing to work within the established system General de Gaulle has always scorned—have made the investiture speeches, then have sat down alone on the front-center benches of the semi-circular chamber to follow the debate, take notes and answer questions put to them.

When General de Gaulle, looking tired and slightly hunched in his gray, double-breasted suit, finished his seven-minute speech, he strode out and was not seen again. From about 3:45 P. M. to shortly after 7:30, the Deputies seemed to be addressing a phantom or to be arguing with each other.

It appeared to many that for General de Gaulle the dialogue between him and the Republic's representatives had ended with the

Continued on Page 4, Column 5

GENERAL IS HEARD

Assembly Postpones Voting on Reforms Urged by Regime

Text of de Gaulle's speech to the Assembly, Page 4.

By ROBERT C. DOTY
Special to The New York Times.

PARIS, Monday, June 2—Gen. Charles de Gaulle has become Premier of France. The National Assembly voted last night, 329 to 224, to invest the 67-year-old leader of the wartime French liberation movement.

Approved at the same time was a fifteen-member Cabinet, including three former Premiers, representatives of seven parties on the Left, Right and Center, and five nonpolitical technicians. The most noteworthy of the latter was the choice of Maurice Couve de Murville, a career diplomat, as Foreign Minister.

General de Gaulle returns to power twelve years after renouncing the Provisional Presidency and at a moment when France faces the threat of civil war by civilians and military leaders dissatisfied with governmental efforts toward ending the rebellion in Algeria.

Terms Implicitly Accepted

By investing General de Gaulle as Premier, the Deputies implicitly accepted the terms he outlined in a seven-minute speech to the packed, breathless Assembly. He demanded:

¶Six months of full decree power, free from Parliamentary interference.

¶Immediate action to revise the Constitution in a manner to permit a popular referendum on sweeping reforms, transforming the Parliamentary regime into a Presidential one.

¶Authority to submit to a referendum reforms of the French Union, permitting a new basis of association with such overseas territories as Algeria and Central and West Africa. This was widely interpreted as opening the possibility even of full independence for some areas.

Breakdown of Vote

General de Gaulle had the almost solid support of the Center and Right wing, nearly half of the Socialist votes and more than half of the Radical votes. Voting against him were the Communists, the rest of the Socialists and Radicals, and scattered Deputies of other parties.

From Algiers came reports that the inclusion in the Cabinet of men of such liberal repute in colonial matters as former Premiers Antoine Pinay, an Independent, and Pierre Pflimlin, the Popular Republican who preceded General de Gaulle, had caused disappointment among ultra-colonialists in the dissident Committees of Public Safety there.

Soon after the Assembly vote was announced General de Gaulle met with President René Coty and the new Cabinet at the Elysée Palace while a violent thunderstorm lashed the capital. During the meeting a bolt struck the palace.

At the end of the meeting,

Continued on Page 4, Column 6

Tunisian Units Fire At 3 French Planes

By Reuters.

TUNIS, June 1—Tunisian troops fired today on three French planes that "violated Tunisian air space" in the Gabès region, a Government spokesman said tonight.

No further details were given and there was no immediate comment by French sources here.

The Tunisians reported yesterday that their troops had "apparently" hit a French plane that flew over Tunisian positions in the Gabès area. Gabès, the site of a French air base, is about 200 miles south of Tunis.

Government sources still withheld official comment on French political developments. But the

Continued on Page 4, Column 3

Supporters of Foreign Aid Hope For Senate Passage This Week

Special to The New York Times.

WASHINGTON, June 1—Administration supporters hope to see the $3,068,900,000 authorization for foreign aid safely through the Senate this week. They will then concentrate on getting the five-year foreign trade extension through the House of Representatives.

The prospects for the first appeared somewhat brighter today than prospects for the second. Passage of the aid bill without major change may come by Thursday.

Senate debate on the aid bill started last week with major speeches by the chairman of the Foreign Relations Committee, Senator Theodore Francis Green, Democrat of Rhode Island, and a top-ranking Republican, H. Alexander Smith of New Jersey. On the controversy, it was indicated, may center around an amendment authorizing aid to Communist-bloc nations.

This amendment would permit a broader interpretation of the Battle Act. That act now prohibits aid to Communist lands except when the President certifies to Congress that it is necessary for national defense.

Passage of the trade bill may not come in the House until well into the following week, and then only with drastic changes that could provoke a Presidential veto if concurred in by the Senate.

Continued on Page 16, Column 4

"All the News That's Fit to Print"

The New York Times.

LATE CITY EDITION
U. S. Weather Bureau Report (Page 43) forecasts:
Mostly fair and continued warm today, tonight and tomorrow.
Temp. range: 86—68. Yesterday: 83.2—66.5.

VOL. CVII—No. 36,683.   © 1958 by The New York Times Company. Times Square, New York 36, N. Y.   NEW YORK, TUESDAY, JULY 1, 1958.   30¢ beyond 100-mile zone from New York City. Higher in air delivery cities.   K   FIVE CENTS

ALASKA TO JOIN UNION AS THE 49TH STATE; FINAL APPROVAL IS VOTED BY SENATE, 64-20; BILL SENT TO EISENHOWER, WHO WILL SIGN IT

2 MORE AMERICANS ABDUCTED IN CUBA BY REBEL FORCES

44 From U. S. and Canada Now Held—Officials of Nickel Plant Latest

Special to The New York Times.

HAVANA, June 30 — Two more Americans were kidnapped today by the Cuban rebels, bringing to forty-four the number of North American servicemen and civilians seized since last Thursday.

Those kidnapped today are officers of the Nicaro nickel plant, on the north coast of Oriente Province.

Oriente is the center of operations of the rebels, led by Fidel Castro and his brother Raul, against the Government of President Fulgencio Batista. The rebels say they have carried out the kidnappings to bring pressure on the United States Government to halt military aid and assistance to the Batista regime.

Among the United States citizens seized—three of the victims are Canadians — are twenty-eight sailors and marines from the United States Naval Base at Guantanamo Bay, on the south coast of Oriente.

U. S. Denies Rebel Charge

Replying to a rebel charge that the base had been used by Cuban military planes operating against the insurgents, the United States Ambassador, Earl E. T. Smith, issued a statement yesterday saying that the base was not open to planes on combat operations.

The rebels told a sailor whom they did not abduct that his kidnapped colleagues would be released today.

United States officials have been in contact with the rebels in an attempt to negotiate the release of the naval and marine personnel as well as the ten Americans and two Canadians seized last Thursday. All twelve are employes of the Moa Bay Mining Company, on the north coast of Oriente. Two civilians, an American and a Canadian, were kidnapped last night.

The Mine Is Not Guarded

The Americans seized today are Sherman Avery White and J. Andrew Poll, administrator general and assistant administrator, respectively, of the Nickel Processing Company, which leases the Nicaro plant from the United States Government. They were carried off at 8:30 this morning by a group of eight rebels, according to the announcement of the United States Embassy.

No details are available, but it is supposed that the two officials went to the mine, about twelve miles from the small town of Nicaro, where 6,000 workers and officials live, to check on operations. Presumably there were abducted there. The entrance of the town is guarded by an army detachment.

Continued on Page 3, Column 6

Soviet Offers Talk On Yugoslav Credit

By United Press International.

LONDON, Tuesday, July 1 — The Soviet Union proposed negotiations with Yugoslavia today on $285,000,000 in credits that the Kremlin had suspended.

The Moscow radio said the proposal was contained in a Soviet note sent to Yugoslavia June 28 and published today in Moscow newspapers.

In the note the Soviet Union said an earlier note to Yugoslavia had suggested revisions in existing economic agreements, including the postponement of one loan for several years. The Soviet Union received no reply to the suggestions, today's note said.

"The Soviet Government suggests that talks of representatives of both Governments should be held as soon as possible"

Continued on Page 2, Column 5

Russians to Attend Geneva Talk Today

By JOHN W. FINNEY
Special to The New York Times.

GENEVA, June 30—The Soviet Union agreed today to enter into technical talks with the West on the detection of tests of nuclear weapons. As a result, talks between scientists of four Western and four Communist nations will begin here tomorrow afternoon in a conference room in the Old League of Nations headquarters.

The Soviet agreement was announced by Dr. Yevgeni K. Fedorov, head of the Soviet delegation of scientists, following a two-hour conference with Dr. James B. Fisk, chairman of the Western scientific group.

Dr. Fedorov said at a news conference later it had been agreed that the talks would begin tomorrow and that discussions would be limited to two.

Continued on Page 5, Column 1

BEIRUT USES JETS TO CHECK REBELS

Bombards Force—Imperiling Airport—U. N. Questions Suspected Syrians

By United Press International.

BEIRUT, Lebanon, June 30—The Government sent rocket-firing jet fighters against rebels in the hills only seven miles from Beirut International Airport today. At the same time, the Tripoli command reported it had cut the main rebel supply line into that city.

On their side, the rebels declared they had cut the main highway between Beirut and Damascus.

Druse tribesmen under the leadership of rebel chieftain Kamal Jumblatt were in the hills overlooking the airport. Jumblatt's army of 500 to 1,000 men appeared also to be poised for a night attack on Chemlan, fifteen miles southeast of the capital which had been emptied of civilians.

[At the United Nations, Secretary General Dag Hammarskjold said United Nations observers in Lebanon had begun to question prisoners, "said to be Syrians," on their possible connection with the Lebanese uprising.]

A rebel spokesman said the Druse forces were astride the main highway to Damascus. There was no Government confirmation, but former Premier

Continued on Page 6, Column 2

N. A. ROCKEFELLER ENTERS G.O.P. RACE FOR GOVERNORSHIP

Promises Strong Fight—Mahoney and Hall Top Him in Delegate Votes

Text of Rockefeller statement is printed on Page 36.

By CLAYTON KNOWLES

Nelson A. Rockefeller announced his candidacy for Governor yesterday. He said that if nominated he would "leave no stone unturned" to win election.

The announcement, expected for some weeks, brought the declared candidates in Republican ranks to two.

Leonard W. Hall of Oyster Bay, L. I., former Republican national chairman, announced his candidacy several weeks ago and has been campaigning vigorously. State Senator Walter J. Mahoney of Buffalo has promised to announce his position "some time in August."

In promising an "aggressive campaign," Mr. Rockefeller declared that New York's status as the Empire State had been put in jeopardy by a "complacent administration" in Albany that evaded, rather than dealt with, serious fiscal and social problems.

New Approach Held Needed

His decision to make the race, he explained, was rooted in the "deep conviction that a new approach to government must be taken in New York State." He said "new energy and efficiency, vision, courage and imagination" would be needed to enable the state "to regain its traditional pre-eminence."

Mr. Rockefeller asserted that "a lifetime spent in administration, both in government and in private and philanthropic activities," qualified him to provide the "progressive, imaginative leadership" that state conditions required.

"If nominated, I will accept the challenge and wage an aggressive campaign on the issues," he said. "If elected, I shall serve with the full awareness of the responsibility such confidence places upon me."

A member of one of America's wealthiest families, the youthful-looking board chairman of Rockefeller Center, Inc., will celebrate his fiftieth birthday next Tuesday. He is the first Rockefeller to seek elective office.

A grandson of the late John D. Rockefeller, who founded the oil dynasty, he said his family

Continued on Page 36, Column 4

DISMISSAL RULING CURBS PRESIDENT

High Court Holds He Lacks Power to Oust Wiener of War Claims Agency

By RUSSELL BAKER
Special to The New York Times.

WASHINGTON, June 30—The Supreme Court tightened today the limitation on the President's power to remove officials of Federal quasi-judicial bodies.

Where Congress has not defined justifiable causes for dismissal, the court held, it must be assumed that Congress does not want to hang a "Damocles' sword" over these officials by permitting the President to remove them solely to substitute "men of his own choosing."

The opinion, written for a unanimous court by Justice Felix Frankfurter, upheld Myron Wiener's contention that he was wrongfully dismissed from the War Claims Commission in 1953 so that President Eisenhower could administer the agency with personnel of his own selection.

1935 Ruling Recalled

The last significant Supreme Court ruling in the historic debate over Presidential power to dismiss was rendered in 1935. Then, in a case closely paralleling the Wiener case, the court ruled that the President could not dismiss an officer of a Federal regulatory agency for any reason except those stipulated in law.

In the 1935 case, Humphrey's Executor v. United States, President Roosevelt dismissed a member of the Federal Trade Commission on the ground that the "aims and purposes" of his Administration could be "carried out most effectively with personnel of my own selection."

The court overruled him, holding that a President could dismiss only for reasons speci-

Continued on Page 20, Column 2

Narcotics Agent Warns Inquiry Mafia Seeks to Invade Industry

By JOSEPH A. LOFTUS
Special to The New York Times.

WASHINGTON, June 30—An expert on the Mafia told Senators today that the secret criminal organization was making a "concerted effort" to penetrate unions and management.

They are "the same people who are active in the narcotics traffic," Martin F. Pera, a Federal narcotic agent, told the Select Committee on Improper Activities in the Labor or Management Field.

Mr. Pera was the second witness as the committee laid the groundwork for extensive hearings on what the chairman, Senator John L. McClellan, said "appears to be a close-knit, clandestine criminal syndicate."

The Arkansas Democrat, in his opening statement, said the committee "has become convinced that the relationship of

the national criminal syndicate with legitimate labor and business is far more critical than has heretofore been revealed."

The first witness was Sgt. Edgar D. Croswell of the New York State police, who broke up a gangland meeting last Nov. 14 at the home of Joseph Barbara in Apalachin, N. Y. Barbara has a serious heart condition and will not testify.

Mr. Pera had barely touched on the labor-management angle when the committee recessed for the day. Photographs of him were barred because of the nature of his work.

The agent, who has worked on the narcotics problem in several foreign countries, told the committee about the origins of

Continued on Page 14, Column 6

Alabama Is Denied Access To Rolls of N. A. A. C. P.

Special to The New York Times.

WASHINGTON, June 30—A $100,000 contempt fine imposed by Alabama when the National Association for the Advancement of Colored People refused to disclose its list of members in the state was struck down today by the Supreme Court.

The court held unanimously that compulsory disclosure under the circumstances in Alabama would violate constitutional guarantees of free speech and association, Justice John Marshall Harlan writing for the court, said:

"Inviolability of privacy in group association may in many circumstances be indispensable to preservation of freedom of

Text of the opinion will be found on Page 18.

association, particularly where a group espouses dissident beliefs.

"Petitioner [the N. A. A. C. P.] has made an uncontroverted showing that on past occasions revelation of the identity of its rank-and-file members has exposed these members to economic reprisal, loss of employment, threat of physical coercion and other manifestations of public hostility."

A Major Victory

The decision was a major victory for the N. A. A. C. P. in a fight to continue operations in the South. Its activities include helping to bring suits to end school segregation.

Seven Southern states have passed legislation aimed at the association or have acted against it through state courts. Included are several statutes to require disclosure of members' names and others to restrict any financial help to Negro plaintiffs in lawsuits.

The organization has carried most of the legal burden of pushing for compliance with the Supreme Court's decision of 1954 holding school segregation unconstitutional.

In 1956 Alabama accused the N. A. A. C. P. of failing to obey a law requiring out-of-

Continued on Page 18, Column 1

HIGH COURT BARS LITTLE ROCK PLEA

Suggests Appeals Bench Set Integration Stay Review Before School Term

Text of the opinion will be found on Page 19.

By ANTHONY LEWIS
Special to The New York Times.

WASHINGTON, June 30—The Supreme Court refused today to review on an emergency basis the order suspending school integration in Little Rock until January, 1961.

But the high court strongly suggested that the case be reviewed by the United States Court of Appeals for the Eighth Circuit before the next school term begins in September. That court has recessed for the summer.

"We have no doubt," the Supreme Court said in a short unsigned order, "that the Court of Appeals will recognize the vital importance of the time element in this litigation, and that it will act upon the application for a stay or the appeal in ample time to permit arrangements to be made for the next school year."

Summer Review Asked

Lawyers of the National Association for the Advancement of Colored People had asked the Supreme Court to by-pass the Eighth Circuit and hear the case this summer to assure early and final review.

A notice of appeal from District Judge Harry J. Lemley's suspension decision has been filed with the Eighth Circuit. So has an application for a stay of the decision pending its appeal. Judge Lemley denied a stay.

If the Eighth Circuit were to grant the stay, the need for speed would be gone, from the N. A. A. C. P.'s viewpoint. Little Rock Central High School would open with a handful of Negro children among the whites, as this last year, while the appeal was argued.

Chief Justice Earl Warren read the order to a packed courtroom at the end of a busy and dramatic day—the last in the high court's 1957-58 term.

Twenty-one cases that had been argued earlier in the term were decided today—with forty opinions. The Chief Justice announced that the court had disposed of all its pending business before recess-

Continued on Page 19, Column 1

ALASKANS APPEAR STUNNED BY NEWS

Civil Defense Whistles in Anchorage Signal Vote to Crowds in the Streets

By LAWRENCE E. DAVIES
Special to The New York Times.

ANCHORAGE, Alaska, June 30—Alaskans were stunned today by the realization that Congress had finally invited them to become "first class citizens."

Here in the territorial metropolis, the center of much of the agitation for statehood, it took them a while to get their bearings.

Long after the civil defense whistles had blown, signaling the Senate's action preparing the way for a forty-ninth star on the flag, unbelieving crowds almost silently walked the streets amid the tooting of automobile horns.

Texas Car Is 'Shot'

Stores did business as usual. A woman traffic policeman rode her motorcycle down Fourth Avenue putting tickets on cars that were parked overtime. Some amateur photographers gleefully "shot" a passing car bearing a Texas license plate, emblematic of a state that would have to give up its much-loved stories of bigness as Alaska completes the transition to statehood.

Rita Martin, queen of the annual Fur Rendezvous, climbed a fire truck ladder and pinned a huge silver star—the forty-ninth—to a 60-by-40-foot flag hurriedly draped over the front wall of the Federal Building. Miss Orah Dee Clark, 83 years old, who in 1915 was the first school principal here, stood watching the star-pinning ceremony on an automobile-jammed street.

It was an emotion-packed moment for her. She had come to the territory in 1906, and to

Continued on Page 16, Column 2

OPPOSITION WILTS

A Bipartisan Coalition Defeats All Efforts to Amend Plan

By C. P. TRUSSELL
Special to The New York Times.

WASHINGTON, June 30—The Senate approved tonight the admission of Alaska as the forty-ninth state in the Union. The vote was 64 to 20.

Only President Eisenhower's signature, which is assured, and approval in a territorial referendum remain before statehood is formally achieved. Test votes indicate that the issue will carry by an overwhelming majority.

The Senate accepted the statehood bill passed by the House of Representatives word for word, beating down every effort to change it. Thus the bill goes directly to the White House.

Any change in the language would have sent the bill back to the House and invited further delays and possible death.

Final Senate action came after five days and evenings of battle, some of it bitter. The vote crossed party lines. The South fought admission, but not solidly. Senators from other sections of the country were also divided.

Stepovich in Gallery

Thirty-three Republicans and thirty-one Democrats voted in favor of admission. Opposed were seven Republicans and thirteen Democrats.

Gov. Michael A. Stepovich of Alaska sat tensely in the Senate gallery while the vote was being taken. When the result was announced he shouted:

"Thank God!"

As well-wishers surrounded him he made a prediction:

"I believe that we will show the United States of America that we will be one of the greatest states in the Union within the next fifty years," he said.

It is expected that Alaska will assume full statehood by autumn or early winter. Its two Senators and one member of the House of Representatives could take their Congressional posts when the Eighty-Sixth Congress convenes next January.

Amendments Defeated

Before the final vote tonight, the Senate rejected by a vote of 62—22 a point of order entered by Senator James O. Eastland, Democrat of Mississippi.

He noted that Alaska Constitution provided that in the election of the first two Senators, one be given a six-year term and the other two or four years, to permit the staggering of Senatorial incumbencies.

Mr. Eastland said that this violated the United States Constitution's provision that all Senators be elected for six years.

But the Senate decided that this was not a valid objection and overrode it.

Senator John Stennis, Democrat of Mississippi, moved that the bill be referred to the Sen-

Continued on Page 16, Column 1

Rayburn Bars G.O.P. Demand For Inquiry on Fox Testimony

By WILLIAM M. BLAIR
Special to The New York Times.

WASHINGTON, June 30—Speaker Sam Rayburn rejected today a Republican attempt to have the House of Representatives investigate the conduct of the subcommittee that has been investigating the relations of Sherman Adams and Bernard Goldfine.

The Democratic Speaker ruled out of order a resolution proposed by Representative Thomas B. Curtis, Republican of Missouri. Mr. Curtis argued that the testimony of John Fox of Boston, a lawyer and industrialist, should have been taken in executive session, in accordance with House rules.

His move was another effort by Republicans to smother the inquiry, which they contend has developed into a "smear" of Mr. Adams and others and to stem the political fears of Republican

candidates up for re-election. Mr. Adams is the assistant to President Eisenhower.

Meanwhile, Mr. Fox announced that he had instructed his lawyers to file libel suits against Mr. Adams and four other persons for what he called "scurrilous" statements about his veracity. He said he would ask $1,000,000 damages from each.

Besides Mr. Adams, he named Roger Robb of Washington and Samuel P. Sears of Boston, lawyers for Mr. Goldfine, New England industrialist; Robert B. Choate, publisher of The Boston Herald and Boston Traveler; William J. Dempsey, counsel for the Boston Herald-Traveler Corporation, and the corporation itself.

As the political atmosphere

Continued on Page 14, Column 4

SEEKS NOMINATION: Nelson A. Rockefeller at news conference at which he discussed his candidacy for nomination for Governor of New York on Republican slate.

The New York Times

ALASKA: Heavy lines define area approved for statehood. The symbols denote its present and potential resources.

The New York Times   July 1, 1958

"All the News That's Fit to Print"

The New York Times.

LATE CITY EDITION
U.S. Weather Bureau Report (Page 30) forecasts:
Fair and pleasant today;
fair tonight and tomorrow.
Temp. range: 83—67. Yesterday: 83.0—70.0.

VOL. CVII..No. 36,722.   © 1958, by The New York Times Company.
Times Square, New York 36, N. Y.   NEW YORK, SATURDAY, AUGUST 9, 1958.   10c beyond 100-mile zone from New York City.
Higher in air delivery cities.   FIVE CENTS

CHIEF OF U.N. GIVES A PLAN FOR MIDEAST

ASSEMBLY MEETS

Hears Call for Step-Up of Its Economic and Political Efforts

Hammarskjold and Munro statements are on Page 2.

By THOMAS J. HAMILTON
Special to The New York Times.

UNITED NATIONS, N. Y., Aug. 8—Secretary General Dag Hammarskjold proposed today that the United Nations step up its political and economic activities in the Middle East to stabilize the area.

Mr. Hammarskjold took the floor at the opening of the General Assembly's emergency special session on the Middle East to put forward his program. He had intended to present this proposal if there was a meeting of heads of government within the framework of the United Nations Security Council.

The principal provisions of his plan are:

¶A declaration by the Arab states reaffirming their adherence to the principles of mutual respect for each other's territory, non-aggression and non-interference in each other's internal affairs.

¶The continuation and extension of present United Nations activities in Lebanon and Jordan.

¶Joint action by the Arab states, with the support of the United Nations, in economic development. This would include arrangements for cooperation between "oil-producing and oil-transiting countries" and joint utilization of water resources.

Session Is Adjourned

Mr. Hammarskjold's statement was the outstanding development of the opening session, which lasted thirty-five minutes until 10:30 A. M. Wednesday to give foreign ministers of some of the eighty-one member nations time to get here.

Contrary to the general expectation, Arkady A. Sobolev, Soviet delegate, did not demand the admission of Chinese Communist representatives. However, he took the floor to repeat his denunciation of the presence of United States forces in Lebanon and British forces in Jordan, and again demanded their immediate withdrawal.

Henry Cabot Lodge of the

Continued on Page 2, Column 3

U.S. MAY REDUCE FORCE IN LEBANON

Token Removal of Marine Battalion Planned

By W. H. LAWRENCE
Special to The New York Times.

BEIRUT, Lebanon, Aug. 8—The United States tentatively plans to reload a marine battalion on ships next week in a "symbolic" gesture of withdrawal from Lebanon.

A responsible source said the decision to reduce the force on shore by about 2,000 men had been communicated to the Lebanese Government and to Gen. Fouad Chehab, armed forces commander and President-elect.

Before the marine unit is pulled out, a small detachment of Army engineers and truck personnel will be moved from Lebanon to the Turkish port of Iskenderun to improve facilities at the Atlantic alliance base at Adana, an important center of air striking power and supply for the United States operation in Lebanon.

The moves will have both political and military effects, it is believed. The political aims are both local and international.

Locally, leaders of the continuing insurrection against the Government of President Camille Chamoun have been insisting on speedy removal of United States troops as a condition for a cease-fire now that General Chehab has been elected. He will succeed Mr. Chamoun Sept.

Continued on Page 3, Column 2

HOUSE VOTES BILL TO AID EDUCATION IN SCIENCE FIELD

Student Loans Raised in Place of Scholarships by 900 Million Measure

By BESS FURMAN
Special to The New York Times.

WASHINGTON, Aug. 8—The House of Representatives adopted today a four-year, $900,000,000 bill to aid science education.

No money was shorn from the bill. But the scholarship provision, on which a compromise had already been made with President Eisenhower, was deleted.

The scholarship funds were shifted to the bill's loan provisions. This was accomplished in a standing vote of 109 to 78, on a motion offered by Representative Walter H. Judd, Republican of Minnesota.

The loan provisions of the bill were increased from $40,-000,000 in the first year to $60,-000,000 and from $60,000,000 in each of the three succeeding years to $80,000,000.

The final adoption was by voice vote, after a motion to kill the bill by sending it back to committee had been defeated in a roll-call vote of 233 to 139. The motion was offered by Representative Ralph W. Gwinn, Republican of Westchester.

The legislation now goes to the Senate, which has already scheduled to consider on Monday its own broader science-aid bill, sponsored by Senator Lister Hill, Democrat of Alabama.

Scholarships in Senate Bill

The Senate bill includes a four-year program totaling $70,-000,000 for college scholarships. If that survives on the Senate floor, some compromise on scholarships will have to be worked out by House and Senate conferees.

As adopted, the House bill would cost an estimated total of $147,000,000 in the first year of operation.

It would provide:

¶Loans averaging $600 to more than 90,000 needy students, of which the Federal Government would pay a total of $60,000,000.

¶One thousand fellowships of $2,000 each to train graduate teachers, with reimbursement to universities for additional costs to expand graduate schools.

¶Grants to the states for scientific teaching equipment and laboratory improvement, totaling $60,000,000.

¶Grants to states to improve testing and guidance programs, $15,000,000, and $6,000,000 to set up teacher-training institutes in this field.

¶Grants to institutions to set up short-term institutes for foreign language teachers, to pay half the cost of permanent foreign language centers and stipends for those attending. This was estimated at a total of $4,-500,000.

¶For research under the United States Office of Education on better educational use

Continued on Page 5, Column 3

U.S. LEADERS SPLIT ON MIDEAST AIMS

Eisenhower Action May Be Needed to Fix Policy for Assembly Debate

By E. W. KENWORTHY
Special to The New York Times.

WASHINGTON, Aug. 8—High-level differences of opinion have developed within the Administration over the strategy and tactics to be used in the United Nations debate on the Middle East crisis, officials indicated today.

The differences are being argued out thoroughly and amicably, and a concerted position will almost certainly be arrived at during the week-end, these officials said. Nevertheless, it was considered possible that President Eisenhower might have to make the final decision on the United States approach.

Dulles Remark Recalled

The differences were said to have become apparent soon after Secretary of State Dulles' news conference a week ago Thursday. At that conference he made it clear that the United States intended to meet the Soviet charge of United States and British aggression in Lebanon and Jordan with a counter-arraignment against the Soviet Union and the United Arab Republic on "indirect aggression."

Until the problems of indirect aggression are met directly and dealt with it will not be possible to create the atmosphere of political stability in the Middle East necessary for any attack on economic problems, Mr. Dulles said.

Almost immediately some

Continued on Page 3, Column 1

Glennan, Ohio Educator, Named To Direct New U. S. Space Unit

Case Tech President Served on A.E.C. Under Truman— Dryden Picked as Aide

Special to The New York Times.

WASHINGTON, Aug. 8—T. Keith Glennan, a Cleveland educator and former member of the Atomic Energy Commission, is President Eisenhower's choice to head the new civilian space agency.

The President sent Mr. Glennan's nomination to the Senate today along with that of Dr. Hugh L. Dryden as Deputy Administrator of the agency.

Mr. Glennan is president of the Case Institute of Technology. Dr. Dryden is director of the National Advisory Committee for Aeronautics.

The National Aeronautics and Space Administration was created by an Act of Congress signed by the President ten days ago.

Mr. Glennan's appointment is believed to be noncontroversial. There may be some objection to the choice of Dr. Dryden, however, and this could delay Senate confirmation of the nominees.

Members of the House Space Committee have criticized Dr. Dryden as presenting a program for the conquest of space that lacked "boldness, imagina-

Continued on Page 4, Column 3

Peronists Win Rule Of Argentine Labor

By JUAN de ONIS
Special to The New York Times.

BUENOS AIRES, Aug. 8—The Argentine Senate adopted today a controversial union organization law that virtually hands the labor movement back to Peronist control.

President Arturo Frondizi's Senate majority approved the text of a bill, passed by the Chamber of Deputies, without changing a word. It did so despite formal opposition from the Roman Catholic Church, business and professional organizations, and nearly all of the press and the anti-Peronist labor unions.

The bill, which re-establishes the single General Labor Confederation, with the official right to speak for labor, awaits the President's signature only.

In eighteen of the bill's fifty-

Continued on Page 4, Column 7

The New York Times
CALL TO ACTION: Dag Hammarskjold addressing the General Assembly.

NAUTILUS SAILS UNDER THE POLE AND 1,830 MILES OF ARCTIC ICECAP IN PACIFIC-TO-ATLANTIC PASSAGE

U. S. Navy, from Associated Press
TIME OF DECISION: Officers of the Nautilus choose a place to submerge below ice for undersea voyage across Arctic regions. Standing at the right in the conning tower of the submarine is her skipper, Comdr. W. R. Anderson.

FOUR-DAY VOYAGE

New Route to Europe Pioneered—Skipper and Crew Cited

Text of Navy fact sheet, Page 6. The Citation, Page 7.

By FELIX BELAIR Jr.
Special to The New York Times.

WASHINGTON, Aug. 8 — History's first undersea voyage across the top of the world, a distance of 1,830 miles under the polar icecap, was disclosed at the White House today.

The trip was made in four days by the Nautilus, the world's first atomic submarine. The voyage pioneered a new and shorter route from the Pacific to the Atlantic and Europe — a route that might be used by cargo submarines. It also added to man's knowledge of the subsurface of the Arctic basin.

The voyage took the Nautilus under the North Pole. The overall trip began at Pearl Harbor July 23 and ended at Iceland Aug. 7.

Dives at Point Barrow

The Nautilus went under the icecap at Point Barrow, Alaska, and surfaced four days later at a point in the Atlantic between Spitsbergen and Greenland. She is now on her way to Western Europe.

The feat of the Nautilus, with 116 crewmen and scientific observers aboard, was revealed as President Eisenhower decorated the submarine's skipper, Comdr. W. R. Anderson, with the Legion of Merit. A Presidential Unit Citation—the first ever conferred in peacetime—went to the submarine, with a ribbon and special clasp in the form of a golden "N" to all who participated in the cruise.

The Presidential citation to Commander Anderson said that the Nautilus under his leadership had pioneered a submerged sea lane between the Eastern and Western Hemispheres. It added:

"This points the way for further exploration and possible use of this route by nuclear powered cargo submarines as a new commercial seaway between the major oceans of the world."

Skipper Tells Story

A few minutes after the award, Commander Anderson, admittedly "a little dazed" by the speed of events that brought him here overnight by helicopter and jet plane from Arctic waters, was telling his story of "Operation Northwest Passage."

News of the voyage reached the Capitol with electrifying effect. William F. Knowland of California, the Senate Republican leader, read a brief dispatch to the Senate and remarked:

"This should give us courage and remind us to have faith. It shows that this is no time to sell America short."

Senator Mike Mansfield of Montana, the Democratic acting

Continued on Page 6, Column 1

VETO THREATENED ON PENSIONS BILL

Social Security Rate Rise Backed by White House but State Plan Is Fought

By JOHN D. MORRIS
Special to The New York Times.

WASHINGTON, Aug. 8—The Eisenhower Administration raised the threat of a veto today against a bill to increase Social Security benefits.

The measure, approved by the House, calls for a 7 per cent increase in Old Age and Survivors Insurance benefits and higher Social Security taxes to finance it. Those provisions were endorsed by Arthur S. Flemming, Secretary of Health, Education and Welfare.

But the Administration is "strongly opposed," Mr. Flemming told the Senate Finance Committee, to provisions that would increase the Federal Government's share in the cost of state relief programs.

Would Recommend Veto

"Suppose we passed the House bill, would you recommend a veto?" asked Senator Paul H. Douglas, Democrat of Illinois.

"I would," Mr. Flemming replied.

Mr. Flemming was the first witness at the opening of two days of hearings on the measure, which is scheduled for Senate action before Congress adjourns. He told the Senators that his views were those of the Administration.

The bill calls for increases in monthly cash benefits under the insurance program starting

Continued on Page 5, Column 2

NEW PASSAGE: Heavy line traces the Nautilus' route from Pacific to Atlantic Oceans

The New York Times   Aug. 9, 1958
NEW PASSAGE: Heavy line traces the Nautilus' route from Pacific to Atlantic Oceans

---

Hogan Is Expected To Enter the Race For Senate Monday

By DOUGLAS DALES

A statement circulated yesterday by the New York Young Democratic Club indicated that District Attorney Frank S. Hogan had made up his mind to enter the race for the Democratic Senate nomination nearly a month ago.

Mr. Hogan yesterday scheduled a news conference for Monday noon to "issue a statement."

If, as expected, he then announces his entry, he will become the fifth declared candidate in the field.

Mr. Hogan's intentions were forecast in a summary of an interview conducted by a committee of the Young Democratic Club with Mr. Hogan on July 17. The summary was submitted to Mr. Hogan for revisions before its circulation among club members.

The summary indicated that Mr. Hogan was already making plans for the future operation of his office and that he expected to have a say in the selection of a successor.

His views on this were given as follows:

"When queried as to the

Continued on Page 14, Column 5

Rackets Unit Asks Prosecution for 13

By ALLEN DRURY
Special to The New York Times.

WASHINGTON, Aug. 8—Senate rackets investigators voted unanimously today to ask the Senate to approve contempt-of-Congress citations against thirteen witnesses.

They include the president of the Carpenters Union and the reputed heir to Al Capone's gangland empire.

The action was taken by the Select Committee on Improper Activities in the Labor or Management Field. It acted in a closed meeting between morning and afternoon public sessions at which it heard witnesses give further testimony on associates of James R. Hoffa, president of the International Brotherhood of Teamsters.

Senator John L. McClellan, Democrat of Arkansas, the com-

Continued on Page 5, Column 6

POLAR TRIP OPENS DEFENSE FRONTIER

U.S. Strategic Advantage Is Seen as Temporary— Soviet Effort Expected

By HANSON W. BALDWIN

A new ocean — the frozen wastes of the Arctic — has been opened to navigation and hence to naval utilization.

This is the meaning of the transpolar, under-ice voyage from Alaska to the Greenland Sea of the nuclear-powered submarine Nautilus.

The newest achievement of the Nautilus, which had already broken all records in submarine history, has immense strategic implications.

Last year the Nautilus made a five-and-one-half-day, 1,000-mile trip under the Arctic ice pack and clearly foreshadowed the shape of things to come.

The Arctic ice pack has hitherto prevented penetration of the Arctic Ocean except, with great difficulty, by foot or by air.

Ships Skirt Land

In certain seasons of the year when the ice pack recedes from the land, or thins out, surface ships have skirted the land masses bordering the Arctic, but their cruises have been short and difficult and they have never penetrated deep into the pack.

The submerged navigation of the Nautilus under the Pole and from Pacific to Atlantic means that utilization of the Arctic Ocean for military purposes is now possible for the first time in history.

Three military capabilities for Arctic submarine operations are immediately foreseeable.

Potentially the most important —in a strategic sense—is the utilization of the Arctic for the launching of guided missiles from submarines. The fleet ballistic missile, Polaris, a two-stage, solid-fuel rocket with a range of 500 to 1,500 miles, and a powerful thermonuclear warhead, is now under development. It has been designed for launching from a submerged submarine at considerable depths.

Nine nuclear-powered submarines, each much larger than the Nautilus and each capable

Continued on Page 6, Column 3

Nautilus' Skipper Helps to Mitigate A Snub to Rickover

By ANTHONY LEWIS
Special to The New York Times.

WASHINGTON, Aug. 8—The man largely responsible for construction of the world's first nuclear-powered submarine was not asked to the White House today to share her moment of triumph.

Some thought was given to inviting Rear Admiral Hyman G. Rickover to the ceremony for the Nautilus, White House officials said. But only "top brass" had been asked and it was decided no exception could be made for him.

The skipper of the Nautilus, Comdr. W. R. Anderson, proved in the circumstances to be as bold a navigator in Navy politics as in the waters under polar ice.

Commander Anderson went directly from the White House to Admiral Rickover's office in the Navy Building, a few blocks away. There he paid his personal respects on the slight, frail figure whose tough-minded drive made the Nautilus a reality.

For Admiral Rickover the ci-

Continued on Page 7, Column 2

Associated Press
T. Keith Glennan

before Congress adjourns, both can be installed under recess appointments.

---

479 Get Jaywalking Summonses But Public Is Hailed on Response

By BERNARD STENGREN

Pedestrians waited for traffic lights and motorists waited for pedestrians yesterday as the police began enforcing New York's new safety law.

High officials of the Traffic and Police Departments said they were gratified at the extent of compliance by drivers and walkers.

Traffic Commissioner T. T. Wiley said:

"My hat is off to New York. The reaction is wonderful."

He spoke after a tour of midtown Manhattan during which turning trucks waited for pedestrians and cab drivers not only waited but also shouted warnings to pedestrians starting to cross against lights.

John J. King, assistant Chief Inspector and head of the Safety Division, said that although some persons had argued that

The new law went into effect yesterday. Between 8 A. M., when enforcement began, and 4 P. M., when the police day shift ended, 479 summonses returnable for $2 were issued to pedestrians.

These included 255 in Manhattan, ninety-three in Brooklyn, ninety-eight in Queens, thirty-one in the Bronx and two in Richmond—where there is only one "Don't Walk" signal.

Twenty-two motorists who failed to give the right of way to pedestrians received summonses for that infraction, which was added Thursday to violations subject to "rigid enforcement."

In Manhattan, five were is-

Continued on Page 15, Column 5

"All the News That's Fit to Print"

The New York Times.

LATE CITY EDITION
U. S. Weather Bureau Report (Page 73) forecasts
Partly cloudy and mild today and tomorrow.
Temp. range: 72—59. Yesterday: 68.5—52.5.

VOL. CVIII..No. 36,783. © 1958, by The New York Times Company. Times Square, New York 36, N. Y.

NEW YORK, THURSDAY, OCTOBER 9, 1958.

10c beyond 100-mile zone from New York City. Higher in air delivery cities.

FIVE CENTS

YANKEES WIN, 4-3, IN TENTH AND TIE BRAVES IN SERIES

McDougald's Homer Ignites 2-Run Rally and Starts Spahn to Defeat

DUREN VICTOR IN RELIEF

But Turley Collects Final Out After Losers Score and Get Two Men On

By JOHN DREBINGER
Special to The New York Times.

MILWAUKEE, Oct. 8—The Yankees kept going today in the 1958 world series. They did it by bringing down the Braves in ten innings with the sixth game, 4 to 3.

Thus the Yankees, who only a few days ago trailed at three games to one, now are all squa re, with the seventh and deciding encounter coming up tomorrow.

Gil McDougald, with a home run in the tenth inning, brought to an end a heroic effort by the Milwaukee southpaw, Warren Spahn, to gain his third straight triumph of the series.

The blow broke a 2-all tie. In its wake the Bombers completed the rout of Spahn with singles by Elston Howard and Yogi Berra, a second tally coming home as Bill Skowron greeted the incoming Don McMahon with a single.

Braves Fight Back

The Yanks were ahead, 4—2, but the show was far from over for the crowd of 46,367. The Braves kicked up an uproar in the last of the tenth that just missed plunging the battle into another deadlock.

They routed Ryne Duren, whose blinding fast ball had baffled them in the four previous innings. They pushed across a run and got the tying run to third, with still another runner on first. But Casey Stengel, pulling out all the stops to maintain what was left of the lead, called on his other fireballing ace, Bob Turley.

Bullet Bob, who on Monday in New York had kept the Bombers in contention by winning the fifth game with a shutout, faced Frank Torre, a left-handed pinch hitter.

Torre sent a soft fly toward right and it looked every inch a single.

But McDougald, the Yankee second baseman and the hero apparent because of his homer, tore back on the grass. He leaped high in the air and pulled down the ball, which suddenly

Continued on Page 51, Column 5

MAN IN A BALLOON GIVES SPACE DATA

But Descends Prematurely After Going Up 19 Miles

By The Associated Press.

ALAMOGORDO, N. M., Oct. 8—An Air Force balloon exploring the fringe of space returned to earth early tonight after it had carried its pilot, Lieut. Clifton McClure 3d, to 99,600 feet.

The balloon, launched today, began an unexpected and unexplained descent late this afternoon. A spokesman at Holloman Air Force Base said "it must be an emergency or they wouldn't be bringing him down."

The balloon landed on the desert ranges west of here, near the San Andres Mountains about thirty miles away.

The Air Force sent a helicopter to the site of the landing to pick up the pilot and the instruments the gondola carried to the stratosphere.

[Failure of the cooling system forced the balloon down, United Press International reported. Lieutenant McClure walked out of the gondola and was taken to an Air Force hospital for a physical examination.]

At 11:05 A. M. Mountain standard time (2:05 P. M., New York time) the balloon reached an altitude of 99,600 feet—just 400 feet short of the planned goal. The balloon was launched at 5:55 A. M.

Lieutenant McClure started his descent about 4 P. M.

During his flight the 25-year-old jet pilot, who became a

Continued on Page 5, Column 3

Final Registration Is Starting Today

By LEO EGAN

The final registration period for this year's election starts today in New York City and Nassau and Westchester Counties. It will continue tomorrow and end on Saturday.

Democratic and Republican party officials are making strenuous efforts to persuade potential voters who have not registered yet to do so. Only those who have registered by Saturday night will be permitted to vote.

Those who registered for last year's municipal elections in New York City and Westchester are automatically registered for this year unless they have moved outside of their election districts. All others are required by law to register to qualify as voters.

In New York City 4,613

Continued on Page 31, Column 5

FAUBUS EXPANDS SCHOOL FUND PLEA

Letters With Seal of State Going Throughout Nation in Bid for Donations

Special to The New York Times.

LITTLE ROCK, Oct. 8—Gov. Orval E. Faubus opened a nation-wide appeal today for funds to help educate Little Rock's teen-agers in a system of private high schools.

The Governor said copies of a letter appealing for contributions would be mailed to persons who had written him pledging their support in his fight against school integration.

The letters will go out on official stationery displaying the official seal of the state. They will be signed by Governor Faubus and by Dr. T. J. Raney, president of the Little Rock Private School Corporation.

For the last ten days the corporation has been accepting donations for the operations of private high schools for Little Rock's white students.

No Date Announced

The corporation has not announced an opening date for its schools, although Dr. Raney has promised it would begin operation "as soon as we can get things rolling." The classes would be held in donated buildings.

Governor Faubus revealed the contents of his appeal letter in which he said donations would benefit "all freedom-loving citizens of this nation."

He said thousands of the letters would be printed. An extra staff of thirteen stenographers was at work filing addresses gleaned from the mail received by the Governor this fall. A secretary said there were between 20,000 and 30,000 pieces of mail and telegrams.

It was the first time that the Governor had asked for money in the fight to maintain segregated schooling in the state. But Mr. Faubus had earlier pledged his support to those who had appealed for financial support.

The Governor's Letter

The appeal letter said:

"The plan set up by action of the extraordinary session of the General Assembly provided for the use of state funds, to be allocated on a per-student basis, for the student's education in whatever school he chose to attend.

"At the request of the N. A. A. C. P. [National Association for the Advancement of Colored People] and the Justice Department, the Federal courts have enjoined all public officials, including school teachers, from using the state funds, as provided by law.

"The acts have been challenged in the courts of the state, where they have already been upheld as constitutional. At the present time the schools are closed through the injunctive process of the Federal courts.

"For this reason it appears necessary that the Little Rock Private School Corporation should proceed with its plan to set up private schools in private facilities, to be operated by private funds.

"It is urgent that the students re-enter school at the earliest possible date. We would, therefore, appreciate your assistance in providing contributions to our school funds.

Continued on Page 38, Column 5

'PRIVATE' CLASSES DIRECTED TO STOP USING VIRGINIA AID

U. S. Judge Paul Says White Units Must Drop Public Teachers or Integrate

By ANTHONY LEWIS
Special to The New York Times.

HARRISONBURG, Va., Oct. 8—Federal District Judge John Paul ruled today that "private" classes set up to replace closed Virginia schools must stop using public funds and teachers or else end segregation themselves.

"It is the opinion of the court," Judge Paul said, "that these so-called private schools are an obvious evasion of the mandate of the Supreme Court."

His order affects Charlottesville, where 1,700 children have been shut out of a high school and an elementary school, and Warren County, where 1,000 students are out of the county's only high school.

A state anti-integration law requires the closing of any public school where white and Negro children are enrolled.

Court to Rule on Norfolk

About 10,000 children are out of school in Norfolk. Judge Walter E. Hoffman will consider that case on Friday of this week.

In Charlottesville, public school teachers have been giving classes in private homes and churches and lodge halls. A similar plan for Warren County is scheduled to start tomorrow.

Attorneys for the National Association for the Advancement of Colored People had asked Judge Paul in effect to make the two school boards reopen their schools. This was the burden of "motions for further relief" that they filed in the two cases.

Judge Paul said he did not think he had the right to direct the reopening of schools. He noted particularly that a suit to test the school closing law has been filed by state authorities in the Virginia Supreme Court of Appeals, and said he recognized the "propriety" of letting the issue be fought out there.

Asks State's Good Faith

But the judge said the state authorities, if they are in good faith, should not try to enforce the challenged acts until the results of the legal test are in.

"The state is not pursuing that course," he said. "It has closed these schools, and it is continuing to assist education in what are called private schools but are really public. All that has happened is that they've closed the school buildings but are continuing to operate the schools in other buildings.

"If the state is going to discontinue public education in these localities," he added, "it must be a complete abandonment and not a pretext."

Judge Paul's decision was based on the doctrine—re-emphasized by the Supreme Court in its Little Rock opinion last week—that no institution can be maintained to the extent militarily neces-

Continued on Page 27, Column 1

President Completes His Staff, Naming Counsel as No. 2 Aide

Gerald D. Morgan   David W. Kendall

By FELIX BELAIR Jr.
Special to The New York Times.

WASHINGTON, Oct. 8 — President Eisenhower completed the reorganization of the White House staff today by designating Gerald D. Morgan as No. 2 aide.

The promotion of another "old hand" on the White House staff served to emphasize President Eisenhower's continued main reliance on the staff system rather

—companied by the appointment of David W. Kendall, Washington attorney, to succeed Mr. Morgan as special counsel.

Mr. Morgan, who is 49 years old, has been special counsel to the President since February, 1955. The announcement of the designation of Mr. Morgan was ac-

Continued on Page 61, Column 1

POPE, 82, DIES AFTER 2D STROKE; MILLIONS OFFER THEIR PRAYERS; CARDINALS TO NAME SUCCESSOR

Announcement Of Pope's Death

By United Press International.

CASTEL GANDOLFO, Italy, Thursday, Oct. 9—Following is the official announcement of the death of the Pope:

The Supreme Pontiff, Pope Pius XII, is dead. Pius XII, the most esteemed and venerated man in the world, one of the greatest Pontiffs of the century, with sanctity passed away at 3:52 A. M., Oct. 9, 1958.

Eugenio Pacelli was born March 2, 1876, and elected Pope on March 2, 1939. He was therefore 82 years 7 months 7 days, and his pontificate was nineteen years 7 months and 7 days.

The Catholic Church and the whole world, for whose profit he spent his brilliant, intellectual energies, his heart and his actions, now gather in mourning around his body and memory, grateful for the immense and valid work he carried out to re-establish among men, children of God, the force of justice, law and peace.

Let the unanimous prayers for the repose of his lofty soul, which today passed into eternal bliss, rise from the hearts of all faithful and the entire Christianity.

Fastest Travel Urged

Fifteen Cardinals were present in or near Rome early this morning. Of these, thirteen are Italians. The other two are Cardinal Tisserant and Gregory Peter XV, Cardinal Agagianian, a Russian-born Armenian who has risen to prominence in the Roman Curia, or central church administration.

Italian Cardinals heading Archdioceses in various parts of the country are due to reach the capital later today. Cardinals outside Italy are expected and indeed requested to come to Rome by the fastest possible means.

With aviation just entering the jet age, it may be foreseen that members of the Sacred College will gather here much quicker than at the death of Pius XI in 1939.

Will Meet Daily

As the "Senate of the Church," the Cardinals will hold a plenary meeting later today and they will reconvene every day until they enter the conclave.

One of the first items on the agenda of the Cardinals' meeting later today will be the transfer of Pius XII's body from his death bed at Castel Gandolfo to Rome.

As if he had had a premonition, the late Pontiff in his apostolic constitution of 1945 concerning the vacancy of the Holy See inserted a provision contemplating the possibility of a Pope's death outside Rome. This had not occurred since the end of the eighteenth century. The provision was that the Cardinals must see to it 'that the dead Pontiff is moved to St. Peter's Basilica in Rome in a "decorous and dignified manner.'

Some of the powers of the Sacred College will be wielded in its name by the Cardinal Camerlengo, or chamberlain of the church. This dignitary will be elected by the cardinals in their first plenary meeting later today.

Now 55 Cardinals

The Sacred College now has fifty-five members, fifteen short of its full complement of seventy. Fifteen are in Rome. Most of the remaining forty will proceed here immediately for the exercise of the college's interim powers.

Most of these men are aged—in their seventies and eighties. Some are behind the Iron Curtain.

Jozsef Cardinal Mindszenty, Primate of Hungary, has been told that he will be allowed to go to Rome, but he has indicated that he probably will not do so, because he fears that the government might not readmit him.

The Cardinal is a refugee in the United States Legation in Budapest.

Others who may not reach Rome are Stefan Cardinal Wyszynski, Primate of Poland, and Aloysius Cardinal Stepinac, Primate of Yugoslavia. Cardinal

Continued on Page 24, Column 1

COLLEGE IS CALLED

55 Princes of Church Rule Pending Vote in 15 to 18 Days

Special to The New York Times.

ROME, Thursday, Oct. 9 — The death of Pope Pius XII today opened the interregnum, or régime of the Holy See's vacancy. It will last until a new Pontiff is elected by the Cardinals in a secret conclave, to be convened not sooner than Oct. 24 or later than Oct. 27.

During the next few weeks the Church will be governed by the Sacred College of Cardinals. As dean of this body, Eugene Cardinal Tisserant immediately instructed the Vatican Secretariat of State to notify all his colleagues that the Apostolic See had become vacant, and to summon them to Rome.

Later today, the French-born, bearded Cardinal, who is 74 years old, is to make the formal announcement of the Pope's death to the diplomats accredited to the Holy See and, through them or through apostolic nuncios in world capitals, to heads of state.

City Pays Homage On Receiving News Of Pontiff's Death

The news of the death of Pope Pius XII was received with varying manifestations in the New York area last night.

As the news became known in Times Square, many Roman Catholics paused and then continued on their way. A few inclined their heads briefly as they gave a prayer for the repose of the Pope's soul. Others made the sign of the cross unobtrusively.

With aviation just entering the jet age, it may be foreseen that members of the Sacred College will gather here much quicker after the death of Pius XII in 1939.

Will Meet Daily

As the "Senate of the Church," the Cardinals will hold a plenary meeting later today and they will reconvene every day until they enter the conclave.

One of the first items on the agenda of the Cardinals' meeting later today will be the transfer of Pius XII's body from his death bed at Castel Gandolfo to Rome.

Three days ago the Communists announced in a broadcast directed at the Nationalists that the bombardment had been ordered suspended for a week on condition that the United States stopped escorting Nationalist convoys.

Today the State Department said that the escort activity had been undertaken at the request of the Nationalist Government, and had been ordered "to the extent militarily neces-

Continued on Page 7, Column 5

U. S. ORDERS HALT IN QUEMOY ESCORT

Set to Resume Operations if Reds End Cease-Fire—Chiang Was Consulted

By E. W. KENWORTHY
Special to The New York Times.

WASHINGTON, Oct. 8—The United States announced today that its naval vessels in the Taiwan Strait had stopped escorting Chinese Nationalist convoys supplying Quemoy.

At the same time the United States made clear that it would resume the escort operations if the Chinese Communists resumed their artillery attacks on the Quemoy group.

Three days ago the Communists announced in a broadcast directed at the Nationalists that the bombardment had been ordered suspended for a week on condition that the United States stopped escorting Nationalist convoys.

Today the State Department said that the escort activity had been undertaken at the request of the Nationalist Government, and had been ordered "to the extent militarily neces-

Continued on Page 7, Column 5

POPE PIUS XII
Associated Press

ROME HEARS TOLL OF BELLS FOR PIUS

Some Citizens in Prayer Before St. Peter's Basilica as End Is Announced

By PAUL HOFMANN
Special to The New York Times.

ROME, Thursday, Oct. 9 — When Rome's many church bells started tolling before dawn today to announce the death of Pius XII, a few persons were still praying in St. Peter's Square and in the city's churches that had remained open all night.

They had remained from the throngs gathered yesterday in the Square and at the churches.

Many Catholics walked to the nearest Roman Catholic church, some of which had been kept open beyond their usual 10 P. M. closing, aware that the Pope's death was imminent. There, prayers were said and impromptu services were held informally as the communicants offered prayers to the effect that Pope Pius' soul reach Heaven.

Some Churches Reopened

As some of the Catholic churches reopened their doors and their lights streamed out onto the sidewalks, patrolling policemen, many of whom had not heard of the Pope's death, stopped to investigate. Some of them stayed to pray.

As if he had had a premonition, not all of Catholic faith, felt the hard-to-describe emotion experienced when the news of the death of one of the great world figures comes to them.

The Pope's death found Cardinal Spellman, Archbishop of the Diocese of New York aboard the Greek liner, Olympia, bound for New York from Cannes, France. He had been accompanying a group of 450 Catholics visiting the Holy Places of Europe. He received an audience with the late Pope several days ago.

Attention Concentrated

At midnight thousands had still been thronging in front of St. Peter's Basilica. Among them were a group of pilgrims who had come from Germany in a dozen buses.

Although the streets and open squares of Rome had gradually emptied about 2 A. M., many Romans stayed up at their homes to follow transmissions of the Vatican radio from Castel Gandolfo.

Listeners said they were deeply impressed and moved by the post-midnight mass said at the dying Pope's bedside by one of his former closest aides, Archbishop Domenico Tardini. The homely Roman accent with which the popular prelate flavors his Latin for once sounded solemn and grave as he recited the prayers of the dying.

After the end of the mass, the Vatican radio urged listeners to keep their sets tuned in and to pray for the Pontiff while waiting that "God's will be done."

The announcement to Rome of Pius XII's death was made in a brief bulletin by the Vatican radio at 3:56 A. M. (10:56 P. M., Wednesday, New York time.) Sacred music followed.

Pilgrims at Castel Gandolfo

CASTEL GANDOLFO, Italy, Oct. 8—Thousands of Romans and pilgrims gathered in this hill town today to be near the dying Pope and to pray for him. They will fill the vacancies that occur when the terms of Sweden, Iraq and Colombia expire at the end of 1958.

Continued on Page 21, Column 4

PONTIFF 19 YEARS

End Comes Quietly in Papal Bedroom at Summer Palace

By ARNALDO CORTESI
Special to The New York Times.

CASTEL GANDOLFO, Italy; Thursday, Oct. 9—Pope Pius XII, the 260th successor of the Apostle Peter on the Pontifical throne of Rome, died at 3:52 A. M. today (10:52 P. M. New York time, Wednesday).

The Pontiff's death came as millions prayed for him throughout the world.

The 82-year-old Pontiff did not regain consciousness after a cerebral stroke he suffered yesterday morning.

It was the second stroke he had suffered in forty-seven hours. The first occurred at 8:30 A. M. Monday and he seemed to be recovering from it.

The second stroke struck him at 7:30 A. M. yesterday. After it the Pope sank gradually until the moment of his death.

Death occurred in a simple and unadorned bedroom on the second floor at the back of the papal palace of Castel Gandolfo.

End Comes Quietly

The Pope was passing the summer in the cooler atmosphere of the Alban Hills as he had done every year. He had planned to return to the Vatican at the end of November in time for the spiritual exercises before Christmas.

Pius XII had been Pope for nineteen years, seven months and seven days since his elevation to the pontificate March 2, 1939. He was born in Rome March 2, 1876. He was, therefore, elevated to the pontificate on his 63rd birthday and was a week more than 82 years and seven months of age when he died.

Since the Pope had been unconscious for many hours before his death he had left no last words in the generally accepted meaning of this term. The last recorded words that he uttered were: "Pray, pray, pray that this unhappy situation for the Church may end."

At the moment of his death Pius XII was completely paralyzed and incapable of any movement. He had been un-

Continued on Page 21, Column 1

WASHINGTON SEES LEBANON SECURE

Plans to Recall All Troops —Karami Said to Quit

By DANA ADAMS SCHMIDT
Special to The New York Times.

WASHINGTON, Oct. 8 — United States troops will be "totally withdrawn from Lebanon" by the end of this month, the State Department announced today.

The department said this decision was based on improvement in "international aspects of Lebanon's security situation" and progress toward "more stable international conditions in the area."

[Reports from Beirut said Premier Rashid Karami had resigned after thirty-one of the sixty-six Deputies in Parliament said they would not support him. United States Marines were patrolling Beirut after a band disarmed three military policemen.]

State Department officials explained that Lebanon's security situation had improved mainly as a result of the election of a new President and the tapering off of the United Arab Republic's "indirect aggression" against Lebanon.

Interference in the life of Lebanon by infiltration of arms and men was apparently ceasing, they said. Inflammatory broadcasts against the Government of Lebanon also have diminished, although broadcasts against the Government of Jordan have tapered off only a little, the officials reported.

In this connection the officials

Continued on Page 5, Column 1

---

3 Countries Named To Security Council

By KATHLEEN TELTSCH
Special to The New York Times.

UNITED NATIONS, N. Y., Oct. 8—Italy, Tunisia and Argentina were elected to Security Council membership today. They will fill the vacancies that occur when the terms of Sweden, Iraq and Colombia expire at the end of 1958.

The three new members were elected at a session of the General Assembly. The voting by secret ballot was a formality since the three nations were unchallenged candidates.

The six nonpermanent seats on the Council are traditionally allotted to nations of six broad geographic areas. There have been exceptions, the latest in 1957 when Japan was elected to

Continued on Page 14, Column 3

"All the News That's Fit to Print"

The New York Times.

LATE CITY EDITION
U.S. Weather Bureau Report (Page 46) forecast:
Mostly cloudy today; mostly fair tonight and tomorrow.
Temp. range: 56—44. Yesterday: 47.2—44.6.

VOL. CVIII..No. 36,803. © 1958, by The New York Times Company. Times Square, New York 36, N. Y.   NEW YORK, WEDNESDAY, OCTOBER 29, 1958.   10c beyond 100-mile zone from New York City. Higher in air delivery cities.   FIVE CENTS

PRESIDENT CALLS FOR VICTORY HERE TO AID HIS POLICY

Tells G. O. P. Workers That Democrats Lack Honest and Sane Principles

HE LAUDS ROCKEFELLER

Asks Special Aid to Keating—Meets Kean and Zeller—Talks at Sports Fete

By HARRISON E. SALISBURY

President Eisenhower yesterday attacked the "dominant wing" of the Democratic party as lacking "straightforward, honest, sound and sane principles, which make America great."

The President leveled the charge in urging Republican campaign workers here to make every effort to elect Nelson A. Rockefeller and Representative Kenneth B. Keating, the party's candidates for Governor and Senator.

The President spent the day in New York largely in political endeavors connected with the campaign. He spoke at two rallies of campaign workers and conferred with several candidates.

He traveled by bubble-topped car through midtown Manhattan streets. A persistent drizzle cut down street crowds. The police estimated that 30,000 persons saw the President.

Attends Football Dinner

The President spent just one minute less than twenty-four hours in the city. He arrived at La Guardia Airport at 11:14 P. M. Monday and departed last night at 11:13 o'clock after attending the first annual Football Hall of Fame dinner, sponsored by the National Football Foundation and the Football Hall of Fame at the Astor Hotel.

The President landed in Washington at 12:14 A. M. and went directly to the White House.

While the President's day was largely devoted to political tasks the partisan note was firmly sounded only once. This was during a brief talk he gave to workers at Republican campaign headquarters at the Roosevelt Hotel.

In making only one such call President Eisenhower generally followed the emphasis on an appeal to the independent, nonparty voter that has been stressed by Mr. Rockefeller in his gubernatorial bid.

All Deny a Split

President Eisenhower did not repeat the harsh language he employed on the Pacific Coast in characterizing Democratic "radicals" or in calling for a "fumigation" of labor unions whose leaders had been found unworthy. Mr. Rockefeller has dissociated himself from these remarks of the President.

James A. Hagerty, the President's press secretary, vigorously denied that Mr. Rockefeller had indicated a negative attitude toward campaign efforts in New York City by the President.

Mr. Hagerty did say, however, that the state Republican committee had not, to his knowledge, requested the President to come to New York.

Mr. Rockefeller went out of his way to make clear that

Continued on Page 25, Column 1

R.C.A. Yields in Trust Suit; Will Ease Patent Licensing

Consent Action to Aid Competitors and Inventors in Radio Field—Company Fined $100,000 in Monopoly Case

By EDWARD RANZAL

The Government's antitrust suits against the Radio Corporation of America ended yesterday in Federal court with a consent judgment and a fine.

R. C. A. declined to defend itself against the charges of criminal monopoly in the licensing of electronic radio equipment patents and was fined $100,000.

At the same time, the Government's civil action was ended with the consent judgment. Competitors will now be able to obtain R. C. A. electronic radio patents under a relaxed licensing agreement.

The decree also will assure patent owners of a competitive market for their inventions and will permit them to exploit the fruits of their own research, according to Victor R. Hansen, assistant attorney general in charge of the Antitrust Division.

A statement issued by David Sarnoff, chairman of the board, and John L. Burns, president of R. C. A., declared that the terms of the decree dealt primarily with apparatus for radio purposes and did not affect the company's activities in automation, electronic computers, medical electronics and other aspects of the new industrial field.

The criminal indictment was filed Feb. 1. R. C. A. pleaded no defense to the four counts—restraint of commerce in radio

Continued on Page 35, Column 3

Survey Finds Ohio Divided Over 'Right-to-Work' Issue

A Times Team Report

This is a report from a New York Times team that surveyed political sentiment in Ohio. Team members were Wayne Phillips, Edith Evans Asbury, Stanley Levey, Joseph A. Loftus and William G. Weart. Eleven pivotal states have been surveyed previously and other reports, including some state rechecks, will continue until the elections next Tuesday.

By WAYNE PHILLIPS

COLUMBUS, Oct. 27—With barely a week to go before the election, Ohio is a divided and confused state.

The presence on the ballot of a proposed "right-to-work" amendment to the State Constitution has become the dominant political issue, overshadowing contests for Governor and United States Senator.

The amendment would outlaw the union shop provision contained in 82 per cent of Ohio labor-management contracts. The provision makes union membership after a stated period a requisite of employment.

Members of a New York Times team, talking to voters from the Ohio River to Lake Erie, from the Pennsylvania to the Indiana border, found people thoroughly confused on how to vote on the amendment.

Unusual Interest in Off-Year

Republican Gov. C. William O'Neill appeared to be running behind his Democratic opponent, Michael V. DiSalle, former Mayor of Toledo and former Federal Price Administrator.

Senator John W. Bricker, a Republican, seemed to be safe in his bid for a third term unless the controversy over the "work" amendment brought out a disproportionately heavy Democratic vote.

If that happened, any of nine Republican-held Congressional seats might be in danger. Otherwise, the team saw little prospect of a change in the state's present Congressional line-up of seventeen Republicans and six Democrats.

Proponents of the amendment argue that it would help to clean up union corruption and make unions more responsive to the will of members. Opponents argue that it would destroy unions, reduce wages and undermine social benefits for which unions had fought.

The proposed amendment has created deep and bitter disputes

Continued on Page 26, Column 1

RECORD HIGH SET BY NATIONAL DEBT

Total at $280,851,429,657 Under Deficit Borrowing as Revenue Declines

By United Press International

WASHINGTON, Oct. 28—The national debt, with larger spending and a decline in Government income as factors, has reached a record high, it was disclosed today.

The Treasury's daily financial statement showed that it was $280,851,429,657.13 on Oct. 23. Included are some non-Treasury securities the Government guarantees. The previous high was $280,821,613,238.96 on Dec. 31, 1955.

Based on the population of about 175,000,000, the new figure represents a debt of $1,604.87 for every man, woman and child in the nation. This per capita figure, however, is not a record. In the fiscal year 1946, before the post-war upsurge in the population, the per capita debt was $1,905.42. The debt then was $269,422,099,173.

The latest rise in the debt reflected recent Treasury borrowing to finance the record peacetime budget deficit of $12,000,000,000 expected for the current fiscal year. The deficit results

Continued on Page 39, Column 6

DULLES ASSAILS REDS' HALF-TRUCE AS POLITICAL STEP

Says Alternate-Day Shelling of Quemoy Results in 'Promiscuous Killing'

Transcript of the Dulles news conference is on Page 18.

By E. W. KENWORTHY
Special to The New York Times.

WASHINGTON, Oct. 28—Secretary of State Dulles said today that the intermittent shelling of Quemoy by the Chinese Communists had no military purpose and amounted to promiscuous killing for political ends.

Asked at his news conference what he thought of "the idea of having war every other day," Mr. Dulles replied:

"If you have a military purpose, you carry on your shooting for military objectives and your purpose is to destroy the capacity of your enemy to resist. When you do it only every other day and say, in between times, you can bring in supplies * * * that shows the killing is done for political purposes and promiscuously." [Question 5, Page 18.]

Red Conditions Recalled

The Chinese Communists have announced that they will not shell key military objectives on even-numbered days to enable the Nationalists to bring in supplies.

Mr. Dulles said he knew of no precedent for the alternate-day cease-fire, but he did have an explanation for what he called this "outlandish and rather uncivilized" procedure.

After seven weeks of trying to interdict resupplying of the islands, Mr. Dulles said, the Communists discovered that "the islands could not be cut off and made to wither on the vine."

"Therefore," he continued, "they had to confront a new situation. They knew that we could resupply the island, so in order to save face, they said, 'We will let you resupply the island every other day.'" [Questions 6 and 7.]

No General War Seen

In view of their failure to reduce the island or cut it off, Mr. Dulles said he doubted that the Chinese Communists would now "engage in a level of military effort which is likely to provoke a general war." [Question 7.]

Unquestionably, Mr. Dulles said, Peiping's real objective is not the offshore islands but Taiwan itself. The Communists, he indicated, hope to achieve that objective through a longrange propaganda campaign designed "to split the inhabitants of Taiwan away from cooperation with the Americans."

To that end, he suggested, the Chinese Communists are refurbishing the pre-World War II Japanese propaganda theme of a "co-prosperity sphere of Asia for the Asians."

The Chinese Communists, he declared, are now saying, "Let us work together and get rid of these Americans; they are the

Continued on Page 18, Column 4

CARDINAL RONCALLI ELECTED POPE; VENETIAN, 76, REIGNS AS JOHN XXIII; THOUSANDS HAIL HIM AT ST. PETER'S

THE NEW PONTIFF, Pope John XXIII, raising his hand in blessing yesterday on a balcony of St. Peter's Basilica. He appeared before throng an hour after he was elected.
Associated Press Radiophoto

DULLES IS GLOOMY ON A NUCLEAR BAN

Doubts Test Suspension Can Be Negotiated as Soviet Finds It Is 'Behind'

By DANA ADAMS SCHMIDT
Special to The New York Times.

WASHINGTON, Oct. 28—Secretary of State Dulles said today that prospects for negotiating a ban on nuclear tests were dim because the Soviet Union had discovered it was "considerably behind" the United States in nuclear weapons development.

Soviet realization of inferiority grew out of the meetings of experts at Geneva last summer on technical means of controlling a suspension of nuclear tests, he said at his news conference.

As a result, he continued, the Soviet Union has "lost interest in the suspension" of tests, which is the subject of negotiations to begin in Geneva Friday. [Question 11, Page 18.]

The Secretary opened his conference by reading a statement denouncing Soviet "insincerity" on the test issue. This, he said, was "clearly exposed" by the Soviet rejection yesterday of the proposal of the United States and Britain to suspend tests for at least one year beginning Oct. 31.

After years of propaganda designed to show the Soviet Union's "high humanitarian purposes" and "concern for the effect of testing upon human

Continued on Page 6, Column 3

3 Russians and Briton Win Nobel Awards for Science

By WERNER WISKARI
Special to The New York Times.

STOCKHOLM, Sweden, Oct. 28—Three Soviet physicists and a British biochemist were named today as winners of Nobel Prizes in science. The 1958 physics prize is to be shared by Dr. Pavel A. Cherenkov, Prof. Ilya M. Frank and Academician Igor Y. Tamm, all members of the Physics Academy of the Soviet Academy of Sciences.

They were cited for research beginning in the Nineteen Thirties that is credited with having opened the way to recent discoveries of atomic particles, such as the antiproton, and with spurring the study of cosmic radiation.

[In Moscow, it was indicated that the three Soviet scientists would go to Stockholm to receive their prize.]

Briton Is Chemistry Winner

The 1958 chemistry prize goes to Dr. Frederick Sanger of Cambridge University's department of biochemistry. He was honored for developing a method for studying the structure of proteins and especially for isolating and identifying the components of the insulin molecule.

The prizes were announced this afternoon by the Royal Swedish Academy of Science, designated to make the annual awards under the will of Alfred Nobel, the Swedish inventor of dynamite. Each of the Nobel awards this year amounts to the equivalent of $41,420.

Like Tuesday's literature award to the poet and novelist Boris Pasternak, this year's prize constitutes a Soviet first. The only Soviet citizen to win a Nobel award before this year was Nikolai N. Semenov, who shared the 1956 chemistry prize with Sir Cyril Norman Hinshelwood of Britain.

Two Russians, Ivan P. Pavlov

Continued on Page 10, Column 2

U.S. WON'T OPPOSE CHANGES IN NATO

However, Washington Aides Shun de Gaulle Plan for 3-Power Directorate

By JACK RAYMOND
Special to The New York Times.

WASHINGTON, Oct. 28—United States officials indicated today that the organizational structure of the North Atlantic alliance was as good as could be expected, but said they would not oppose some changes.

The proposal by Premier Charles de Gaulle of France for a United States-British-French political executive has found little sympathy here, regardless of whether the group is set up within NATO or outside it.

The proposal was contained in letters sent by the French leader to President Eisenhower and Prime Minister Harold Macmillan.

The chief reason for United States coolness toward the proposal is that most of the fifteen countries in the alliance have made clear that they are against it.

NATO Base Broadened

The majority, it was observed, is composed of the small countries. They have, in recent years, forced changes that broaden rather than narrow the base of military and political responsibility in the organization.

The United States is interested in proposals for broadening the area of NATO responsibility. However, officials here are wary of any extension that would make NATO more than a "regional" organization as approved by the United Nations.

Nevertheless, peripheral problems, such as those developing in the Middle East, are recognized as having a great impact on the Western alliance. United States officials are prepared to discuss this.

At the same time it was made evident here that the United States wants to avoid participating in the formation of a Big Three political arrangement that commits this country to consultation on its world obligations.

The United States has agreed at past NATO meetings to discuss its affairs, but only as a matter of agreement rather than formal obligation.

Premier de Gaulle's proposal, which became known last week

Continued on Page 6, Column 2

Diefenbaker Sees Gain in Ties to U.S.

By RUSSELL PORTER

Prime Minister John Diefenbaker of Canada said last night that relations between Canada and the United States had improved in the last year, but that problems remained in the field of trade and economic affairs.

He urged that trade relations between the two countries be based on Canadian as well as American rights. Against the Soviet economic offensive, he declared, freedom cannot afford to allow the economic weakening of any free nation.

Mr. Diefenbaker spoke here at a dinner of the Pilgrims of the United States in his honor at the Waldorf-Astoria Hotel.

Secretary of State Dulles joined in the tribute to Mr. Diefenbaker and stressed the importance of Canadian-Ameri-

Continued on Page 18, Column 1

11 BALLOTS TAKEN

New Pontiff Elevates Conclave Secretary to Cardinalate

By ARNALDO CORTESI
Special to The New York Times.

ROME, Oct. 28—Angelo Giuseppe Cardinal Roncalli, Patriarch of Venice, was elevated to the Papacy this afternoon. He will be 77 years old Nov. 25.

He will sit on the throne of St. Peter as the 262d Supreme Pontiff of the Roman Catholic Church and will rule the Church as sovereign under the name of John XXIII. No Sovereign Pontiff has used the name since 1334, when John XXII died.

The successor to Pope Pius XII, who died Oct. 9, was elected on the eleventh ballot. He was named as the third day of the voting in a walled enclosure in the Vatican was drawing to a close.

The conclave that elevated him was one of the fifteen shortest held since the Papacy returned to Rome from Avignon, France, in the second half of the fourteenth century. Fifty-nine conclaves have been held since then.

Coronation Likely Nov. 9

Cardinal Roncalli became Supreme Pontiff at the very moment when he replied affirmatively on being asked by the Dean of the Sacred College of Cardinals whether he accepted his election. He uttered the Latin word "Accepto" ("I accept") a few minutes before 5 P. M. [11 A. M. New York time]. He was invested with the full powers of the Papacy from that instant, though his reign will be counted from the day of his coronation, expected to be Nov. 9.

One hour after his election, the new Pope appeared on the outer balcony of St. Peter's Basilica and gave his first blessing to the thousands gathered in St. Peter's Square. Before and after the blessing the crowd sang hymns. The hymns sung were "Christus Vincit" (Christ Conquers) and the Te Deum.

New Cardinal Named

As the first act of his Pontificate, Pope John XXIII conferred the Cardinal's red hat on Msgr. Alberto di Jorio, who had acted as secretary of the conclave. The new Pope did so by removing his own Cardinal's biretta from his head and placing it on that of Msgr. di Jorio.

This was a return to tradition, since in the past all Popes went out to reward the secretary of the conclave. However, Pius XII omitted to do so.

The new Pope also asked all Cardinals to remain in conclave until tomorrow morning, which they did.

That the Catholic Church again had a head was conveyed to watchers in St. Peter's Square by the white smoke emanating from a stovepipe above the roof of the Sistine Chapel, where the voting took

Continued on Page 14, Column 1

New Pontiff Faces Difficult Problems

By PAUL HOFMANN
Special to The New York Times.

ROME, Oct. 28—Pope John XXIII was a successful Vatican diplomat before he became the new Supreme Pontiff of the Roman Catholic Church.

His great experience and skill in two distant fields of work for the church should enable the former Angelo Giuseppe Cardinal Roncalli to cope with the formidable problems confronting the Papacy at present, high ecclesiastics said tonight.

In choosing the Patriarch of Venice and former Apostolic Nuncio to France the Sacred College of Cardinals overcame great wisdom its initial uncertainty whether to place on the Throne of St. Peter a "pastoral" or a "diplomatic" Pontiff, the churchmen remarked. The personality of

Continued on Page 15, Column 1

Airliner Takes Dive To Avoid Collision

By The Associated Press

MIAMI, Fla., Oct. 28—A Panagra airliner with forty-five persons aboard dived to safety last night after a formation of an Air Force refueling tanker and two jet fighters.

The pilot of the airliner said that he was flying at an assigned altitude on a recognized airway when the incident took place over Wilmington, N. C., at 6:47 P. M.

The Air Force said that the tanker had a Civil Aeronautics Administration clearance within a 100-mile radius of Florence, N. C. The three Air Force craft were eighty-two miles from Florence when the incident took place.

The airliner was bound from New York to Peru, with stops at Washington and Miami.

The plane was manned by a

Continued on Page 19, Column a

HIGH HOPES are expressed by President Eisenhower as he leaves the Astor Hotel here. With the President yesterday were Kenneth B. Keating, left, and Nelson A. Rockefeller, the Republican candidates for Senator and Governor.
The New York Times

"All the News That's Fit to Print"

The New York Times.

LATE CITY EDITION
U.S. Weather Bureau Report (Page 57) forecasts:
Partly cloudy, warmer today; cloudy milder, chance of rain tomorrow.
Temp. range: 42—25. Yesterday: 35.3—27.9.

VOL. CVIII..No. 36,938.   © 1959, by The New York Times Company. Times Square, New York 36, N. Y.   NEW YORK, FRIDAY, MARCH 13, 1959.   10 cents beyond 50-mile zone from New York City except on Long Island. Higher in air delivery cities.   FIVE CENTS

HAWAII IS VOTED INTO UNION AS 50TH STATE; HOUSE GRANTS FINAL APPROVAL, 323 TO 89; EISENHOWER'S SIGNATURE OF BILL ASSURED

ADENAUER IS FIRM AGAINST TROOP CUT IN MIDDLE EUROPE

Gets Assurance in Talks With Macmillan That the British Seek No Disengagement

By SYDNEY GRUSON
Special to The New York Times.

BONN, Germany, March 12 —Chancellor Konrad Adenauer restated to Prime Minister Harold Macmillan today West Germany's opposition to any reduction of Allied forces in Central Europe except within a general disarmament agreement.

The British leader came to Bonn today to give the Chancellor a personal report on his recent conversations in Moscow and to reassure the West Germans that Britain was not seeking the disengagement of Eastern and Western forces in Germany.

Nor, said a British Foreign Office spokesman, does London favor even a controlled limitation of forces if this would result in disequilibrium between the troops and armaments of East and West in Central Europe.

Trip Is Second of Three

Mr. Macmillan's trip here was the second of his three planned journeys to brief other Western leaders about his talks with Premier Nikita S. Khrushchev of the Soviet Union. Mr. Macmillan was in Paris earlier this week and he will cross the Atlantic for separate meetings with President Eisenhower and Prime Minister John Diefenbaker of Canada next week.

The first session between Mr. Macmillan and Dr. Adenauer, who were accompanied by their foreign ministers and two advisers each, lasted three hours. The talks were resumed tonight after a dinner in Mr. Macmillan's honor. They will continue tomorrow in the Chancellor's Palais Schaumburg offices.

The differences in outlook between the Prime Minister and the Chancellor were evident in their remarks at the airport on Mr. Macmillan's arrival.

Mr. Macmillan said the West was firm and united on the prin-

Continued on Page 3, Column 4

ROCKEFELLER ASKS A DRIVE ON CRIME

In Message to Legislature, He Urges Tighter Laws

By WARREN WEAVER Jr.
Special to The New York Times.

ALBANY, March 12—Governor Rockefeller called on the Legislature today to join him in prosecuting a war against organized crime "more vigorously than ever before."

The Governor sent a special message to the lawmakers, with a dozen recommendations for tightening the existing criminal law and making law-enforcement organizations more powerful and better trained.

In his election campaign last fall, Mr. Rockefeller was outspoken in his criticism of the increase in criminal activity during the Harriman Administration. He pledged swift action against racketeers and law violators if he should be elected.

Mr. Rockefeller urged today that the Legislature:

¶Make it a misdemeanor to defy a subpoena from the State Commission of Investigation or engage in obstructive or contemptuous conduct before the crime panel.

¶Set up a municipal police training council that would establish minimum training standards for all members of police forces.

¶Increase the statute of limitations for prosecution for tax evasion from two to five years, thus giving the state more time

Continued on Page 16, Column 2

Governor Taking Charge Of Meeting City Tax Needs

Orders Report on Costs and Resources for Conference With Mayor Tomorrow —Wants an Agreement Next Week

By DOUGLAS DALES
Special to The New York Times.

ALBANY, March 12.—With his own program for higher state taxes out of the way, Governor Rockefeller has decided to take personal command of the Albany action needed to help New York City balance its budget for the fiscal year starting July 1.

The decision was made at a meeting with Republican legislative leaders today, called to discuss the conference to be held with Mayor Wagner Saturday morning on the city's budget problem.

The task force was designated at a meeting attended by Mr. Rockefeller, Tax Commissioner Joseph H. Murphy, Budget Director T. Norman Hurd, Majority Leader Walter J. Mahoney of the Senate and Majority Leader Joseph F. Carlino of

In preparation for the meeting, Governor Rockefeller hastily named a task force to examine New York City's needs and the resources that might be tapped to meet them. A report has been asked by tomorrow night in time to be digested before the meeting with the Mayor.

The meeting will be held at the Executive Mansion and will be attended by Republican and Democratic legislative leaders.

Continued on Page 16, Column 4

Snowfall of 5 to 10 Inches Delays All Transit in Area

By PETER KIHSS

With spring only nine days away, the city got its heaviest snowfall of the season yesterday—5.3 inches. It was perhaps nature's way of marking the seventy-first anniversary of the famous blizzard of '88.

On March 12, 1888, that storm hurled 16.5 inches of snow on the city, and in two more days brought the total to 20.9 inches.

Rockland and Fairfield Counties reported ten inches of snow yesterday; Westchester, seven to nine; Bergen, six to seven; Long Island, five to six; Elizabeth, N. J., 5.4, and New Brunswick, N. J., two to three.

Rain and warming temperatures turned the snow into slush in the city. Temperatures dropped during the night, however, and turned the slush to ice on some roadways. The less heavily traveled roads in the suburbs and upstate were reported especially dangerous.

The forecast for today was for partly cloudy and warmer. The temperature may reach the low forties and cause the ice and snow to melt.

Yesterday's storm was caused by two low-pressure areas moving in from the Midwest and from the Virginia coast. Snow fell throughout the Northeast. Depths ranged up to fourteen inches in Chautauqua County on Lake Erie, the Schoharie Valley west of Albany and in western Maryland.

Seven deaths were attributed to the storm in New York, New Jersey and Ohio.

The city's public schools had only 70 per cent attendance. Radio station WOR, which gathers and broadcasts news of

Continued on Page 22, Column 1

GOVERNOR NAMES COMMERCE HEAD

Appoints McHugh, President of New York Telephone — Utility Picks Successor

Governor Rockefeller completed his Cabinet in Albany yesterday with the appointment of Keith S. McHugh to head the Department of Commerce.

Mr. McHugh, who is 64 years old, will retire as president of the New York Telephone Company on April 30 to accept the appointment.

Governor Rockefeller said he was looking to Mr. McHugh to "invigorate" the department so that its full potential to stimulate business in the state would be realized.

Mr. McHugh is leaving a $150,000-a-year job for one that pays $18,500. However, within a year, he will qualify for a company pension as a forty-year man. A company spokesman said a pension arrangement would be worked out by the board of directors.

Meanwhile, the directors of the telephone company elected Clifton W. Phalen to succeed

Continued on Page 16, Column 2

CITY VOTES DEAL ON POWER PLANTS WITH CON EDISON

But Contract Is Changed to Permit New Bids When Final Auction Is Held

By PAUL CROWELL

Contracts for the sale of the city's three rapid-transit power plants to the Consolidated Edison Company at a gross price of $125,840,000 were approved unanimously by the Board of Estimate last night.

The vote was taken after the language of the contracts had been changed slightly to make certain that bidders other than Consolidated Edison could submit offers when the power plants are disposed of at public auction, as required by the City Charter.

The changes were made after Harvey M. Spear, counsel for unidentified "substantial New York interests," had complained that his clients might not be able to submit bids technically admissible under the terms of the agreements.

Clients Not Identified

Mr. Spear declined to tell the board the names of his clients, saying that they would be disclosed when bids were received.

Mr. Spear said his clients, while preferring to submit an offer to purchase the power plants for lease back to the Transit Authority, would also be prepared to submit a bid for purchase and operation.

The contracts approved by the board paved the way for transfer of the plants to Consolidated Edison by July 1, assuming that the company was the successful bidder.

The company's bid was for at least $99,382,871 in cash in addition to concessions that would bring the total minimum purchase price up to $125,840,000. The company also offered to supply the three divisions of the city subway system with power under a ten-year contract at uniform rates.

Company Supplies IND

The company now supplies all power for the IND division. The IRT and BMT divisions obtain power from the three city plants that are on Kent Avenue, Brooklyn, and West Fifty-ninth Street and East Forty-seventh Street in Manhattan.

By its vote the Board of Estimate authorized the Mayor to execute, subject to specified conditions, a contract for selling the three plants and one plant for purchasing power from the three divisions of the city subway system now operated by the Transit Authority.

The board also authorized the Commissioner of Marine and Aviation, Vincent A. G. O'Connor, to execute waterfront leases in connection with the transfer

Continued on Page 15, Column 2

STATEHOOD!

STATEHOOD!

THE BIG NEWS: Chester Kahapea, 13, offering copies of The Honolulu Star-Bulletin yesterday in the Hawaiian capital. The flag on the front page contains fifty stars.
Associated Press Wirephoto

3 OF JOINT CHIEFS WILL BE RENAMED

Twining, Burke and White Slated for New Terms— Lemnitzer to Get Post

By HANSON W. BALDWIN
Special to The New York Times.

WASHINGTON, March 12—The reappointments of three members of the Joint Chiefs of Staff will be announced soon.

Those who will be reappointed to new two-year terms starting this summer are Gen. Nathan F. Twining, chairman of the Joint Chiefs of Staff; Gen. Thomas D. White, Chief of Staff of the Air Force, and Admiral Arleigh A. Burke, Chief of Naval Operations.

Gen. Lyman L. Lemnitzer, Vice Chief of Staff of the Army, will succeed Gen. Maxwell D. Taylor, present Army Chief of Staff, whose second two-year term ends June 30. General Taylor is expected to retire.

The second two-year term of Gen. Randolph McC. Pate, as Commandant of the Marine Corps, does not expire until next Dec. 31, and as far as is known his successor has not yet been selected. General Pate also expects to retire.

The names of Lieut. Gen. Merrill B. Twining, a brother of the chairman of the Joint Chiefs, and of Lieut. Gen. Edwin A. Pollock have been mentioned in connection with the

Continued on Page 4, Column 2

U. S. and Canada List Seaway Tolls, Effective on April 1

By RICHARD E. MOONEY
Special to The New York Times.

WASHINGTON, March 12—The United States and Canada announced St. Lawrence Seaway tolls today, to take effect April 1.

They are identical to those proposed last June after negotiations by committees of both nations. The differences are primarily in definitions, mostly for the types of cargo that would qualify for the low rate applying to "bulk" shipments.

[Opposition to the toll setup came from port, rail, shipping and civic interests. They called the rates unrealistically low and the estimated revenue too high. The Port of New York Authority feared a loss of 3,500 waterfront jobs because of "unfair competition" resulting from the tolls.]

Railroads Competing

The Seaway links the Great Lakes and the Atlantic for deepwater ships. Part of it was opened last summer, and the full length is scheduled to be working soon.

Interests that would benefit from the new water route and those against whom it would compete had been fighting over the toll issue.

The fight was moving into a new phase. Major railroads are considering a 20 to 25 per cent reduction of rates they charge for transporting grain for export. This would enable them better to compete with the price for shipping via the waterway.

Seaway tolls are intended to

Continued on Page 10, Column 2

HOUSE UNIT CUTS JOBLESS AID BILL

Restricts Extension of U. S. Assistance to 3 Months Instead of One Year

Special to The New York Times.

WASHINGTON, March 12—The House Ways and Means Committee approved today a bill for a three-month tapering-off of emergency Federal aid to the unemployed.

The measure falls far short of earlier plans by Democratic leaders for a year's extension of the program beyond its present expiration date of March 31.

The effect would be to prevent an abrupt cut-off of payments to about 300,000 jobless workers expected to be drawing the emergency benefits at the end of this month.

Instead, these workers would stay on the rolls until they had exhausted the benefits to which they would have been entitled in the absence of a March 31 termination date.

The committee acted in closed session by what was reported as a one-sided voice vote. The House is expected to pass the bill early next week.

Democratic sources reported that the one-year extension plan had been set aside in the interest of assuring quick enactment of a bill. President Eisenhower and House Republican leaders had voiced strong opposition to the earlier Democratic proposal.

Another factor was the apparent lack of enthusiasm with which the proposed one-year

Continued on Page 18, Column 4

MEASURE SPEEDED

A Short-Cut Sends It Direct to President, Who Is 'Delighted'

By C. P. TRUSSELL
Special to The New York Times.

WASHINGTON, March 12—The Territory of Hawaii was voted into the Union today as the fiftieth state.

The House of Representatives gave its approval by a vote of 323 to 89. Yesterday the Senate approved the Hawaii bill, 76 to 15.

President Eisenhower's approval is assured. The White House said today he was "delighted" and noted that "he has been urging it for some time."

Thus, after one of the fastest actions by Congress in years, only the mechanics of admitting a new state remain before Hawaii joins the Union.

The question arose as to whether the island territory some 2,000 miles from continental United States would seek to put its fiftieth star into the flag July 4 of this year when Alaska adds its forty-ninth. There is barely enough time to do so and island leaders doubted that it would be done.

Governor Gives Word

With the galleries filled, the House started its long roll-call in midafternoon. Among the spectators was the Governor of Hawaii, William F. Quinn. When the roll-call began he quietly left the gallery and went to the office of Sam Rayburn, Speaker of the House.

At the Speaker's office Governor Quinn telephoned Acting Gov. Edward E. Johnston at Honolulu and asked him to hold the line. When he was notified that the roll-call had recorded 219 ayes—a majority of the House—Governor Quinn sent off a celebration in the islands by shouting:

"Sound the sirens, close the schools and get going."

A little later he added a note of caution:

"Keep the lid on a little, Ed."

Before Hawaii can attain statehood it must hold a referendum on whether it wants to assume the burdens at this time. Besides agreeing at the polls with provisions of the new law,

Continued on Page 13, Column 2

HAWAIIANS START 2 DAYS' FESTIVITY

Alaska Sends First 'Aloha' to Celebrating Islanders

By LAWRENCE E. DAVIES
Special to The New York Times.

HONOLULU, March 12—The kamaaina and the malihini celebrated today Congressional assurance that the nation was ready to welcome Hawaii as the fiftieth state.

That is to say, the oldtimer—the Hawaiian version of the Alaskan sourdough—joined with the newcomer — the Hawaiian counterpart of the Alaskan cheechako — in opening a two-day demonstration of gratitude over the prospective ending of territorial status for the islands.

The celebration got off to a restrained start. It picked up momentum as the day wore on toward a climax here on the island of Oahu with huge bonfires, aerial and offshore military pyrotechnics and hula dancing.

At the beginning everyone seemed to be waiting for someone else to show the way. Within a half-hour after word came from Washington of the action in the House of Representatives, the Waikiki area was clogged with horn-tooting automobiles. Bands and colorfully clad marchers took over at midafternoon.

Colored paper streamers were flung from downtown office buildings along King and Merchant Streets. Hands were thrust forward with a "happy statehood" salutation. Mayor Neal Blaisdell of Honolulu was so

Continued on Page 13, Column 1

There Are Times When Bad Weather Brings Out the Best in a Man

It was such a time yesterday at Vesey St. and Broadway   And a man came forward to lend a gallant, helping hand
The New York Times (by Neal Boenzi)

Fulton Street Widening Dropped By Jack on Protest of Merchants

The highly controversial proposal to widen part of Fulton Street in lower Manhattan was withdrawn from further consideration yesterday by Borough President Hulan E. Jack of Manhattan.

The action by the Board of Estimate permitting Mr. Jack to drop the project constituted a victory for a group of Fulton Street merchants.

Opponents have fought the proposal as threatening hardship to "hundreds of business men and thousands of their employes." They have also argued that the widening would not materially relieve the area's traffic situation.

Mr. Jack said he favored studies of the possibility of both an eastbound and a westbound artery in lower Manhattan.

Pending such studies, he said, it would be better to withdraw the Fulton Street proposal. In the meantime, he added, he hoped all of those who have been involved in the widening dispute would have a better understanding of the problem.

The proposal that Mr. Jack withdrew called for widening Fulton Street on its south side from Broadway to Water Street. The project was intended as the first stage of an eventual widening of Fulton Street from South Street to West Street.

Two major slum clearance cooperative housing projects totaling $61,000,000 in cost in the Rockaways, Queens, were approved by the board. One was Hammels-Rockaway,

Continued on Page 22, Column 6

The New York Times.

LATE CITY EDITION
U. S. Weather Bureau Report (Page 43) forecasts:
Considerable cloudiness today and tonight. Chance of showers tomorrow.
Temp. range: 79—66; yesterday: 76.8—63.8.

VOL. CIX..No. 37,137. © 1959, by The New York Times Company. Times Square, New York 36, N. Y. NEW YORK, MONDAY, SEPTEMBER 28, 1959. 10 cents beyond 50-mile zone from New York City except on Long Island. Higher in air delivery cities. FIVE CENTS

PRESIDENT AND KHRUSHCHEV IN AGREEMENT ON NEW BERLIN TALKS AND MORE EXCHANGES; EISENHOWER DEFERS VISIT; PREMIER LEAVES

TYPHOON DEATHS IN JAPAN AT 1,132; 1,457 ARE MISSING

Damage Tops $100,000,000 as Storm Heads North— 927,700 Lose Homes

By The Associated Press

TOKYO, Sept. 27—Battered Japan, struck by the worst typhoon in a quarter of a century, counted more than 2,500 dead or missing today.

As Typhoon Vera headed toward Soviet territory, the national police reported 1,132 known dead, 1,457 missing, 4,668 injured and 927,700 homeless. Damage was unofficially estimated at more than $100,-000,000.

Officials feared the toll would rise when word was received from villages isolated by floods, landslides, washed-out roads and rail lines or broken telephone lines.

Nagoya Hit Hard

The harbor of the industrial city of Nagoya, one of the hardest hit, was described as a "sea of dead." Seven ocean-going ships lay grounded like beached whales in the harbor. The harbor was choked with debris. In other regions, parts of villages were swept away by floods.

Typhoon Vera, the fifth to strike Japan this year, formed in the southwest Pacific, off Iwo Jima. It struck Kii Peninsula in south-central Honshu Saturday night with maximum winds of 160 miles an hour.

The storm swept across the industrial heart of central Honshu over Mie, Nara, Gifu and Aichi prefectures and into the Sea of Japan.

The typhoon then moved up the Sea of Japan along the west coast of Honshu, crossed northern Honshu and southeastern Hokkaido, the northern-most island, and was last reported

Continued on Page 3, Column 4

STRIKE-BREAKING FACES STATE CURB

Registering of Job Agencies Asked in Panel Report

By RUSSELL PORTER

A state investigating committee yesterday recommended legislation to compel registration of professional strike-breaking agencies and public disclosure of their activities.

It also urged that all employment agencies be required to inform job applicants if they are to take jobs of striking workers.

The committee was appointed in 1958 by Isidor Lubin, then State Industrial Commissioner, to investigate concerns reported to be supplying out-of-state strikebreakers to New York employers.

Mr. Lubin's action followed charges by the International Typographical Union that the Macy chain of newspapers in Westchester County had imported to break a printers' strike.

Charges Strike Is Illegal

The Macy chain has charged the strike is illegal and that the union's demands violated the Taft-Hartley law.

Two other publishers were also involved in the investigation. They were the Griscom chain of weekly papers in Nassau County and The Lockport Union-Sun and Journal, a daily newspaper in Niagara County.

The committee in its report said it had discovered only one commercial agency engaged in supplying strikebreakers to newspapers.

It is said this firm was the Schleppey-Klein Agency, owned and operated by Bloor Schleppey of Zionsville, Ind., with the help of Miss Shirley Klein, now an executive of the Macy chain.

According to the committee, this agency is exclusively engaged in recruiting and supply-

Continued on Page 12, Column 2

Red Chinese Harass Indians on Frontier

By United Press International

PAURI, India, Sept. 27—Chinese Communist troops from Tibet are taking over land previously considered India's and have reinforced their garrisons along the border, reports received here said today.

The reports said Chinese forces oppose the frontier of Uttar Pradesh were harassing Indian business men and confiscating their goods and money on the slightest pretext.

Traders and villagers said the Chinese had moved more troops into Tibetan areas facing Uttar Pradesh and had built new roads and six airstrips to supply them. Chinese planes frequently violate Indian airspace, they said.

The reports reached this

Continued on Page 3, Column 2

LAOTIANS RETAKE BORDER FORTRESS

Bastion Near North Vietnam Captured in Night Raid— Fighting Is Fierce

By GREG MacGREGOR

VIENTIANE, Laos, Sept. 27—Muong Het, a strongly defended rebel-held fortress about eight miles from the North Vietnamese border, was reported recaptured by Government troops at dawn today in one of the sharpest encounters of the current strife.

The thrust to retake the position, which was seized by the rebels Aug. 30, began yesterday, according to informed sources. It was estimated that about 500 "Lao-Viets," the name now used in Laotian military circles to describe non-North Vietnamese troops, had been encircled in Muong Het and forced to fight. Chinese tactics adopted by both sides had been to withdraw in the face of heavy onslaught.

The size of the Government attacking force was not given. Casualties on both sides were described as heavy.

It was stated that Xieng Kho, another position in the northern part of Samneua Province near Muong Het, was still in enemy hands. Other positions along the border still held by the rebels were named

Continued on Page 2, Column 2

Dodgers and Braves End in Tie; Pennant Play-Off Starts Today

Fred Haney | Walter Alston

The New York Times | Associated Press Wirephoto

The Dodgers and the Braves finished the National League season yesterday tied for the pen....ant. The two clubs will meet at Milwaukee this afternoon in the first of a three-game play-off series.

Manager Walter Alston's Dodgers defeated the Cubs, 7–1, and Manager Fred Haney's Braves downed the Phils, 5–2, in their final regularly scheduled games. The Giants, who had a chance for a tie in the event the Braves and Dodgers lost, bowed twice to the Cardinals.

Originally scheduled to open on Wednesday in Chicago with the White Sox, the American

League pennant winner, as the home team, the world series will start either Thursday or Friday. There will be a one day rest after the play-off, with the second game scheduled for tomorrow in Los Angeles and the third game, if necessary, the third game Wednesday.

Sandy Koufax will pitch for Los Angeles today. Lew Burdette will hurl for the Braves.

The play-off is the third in National League history. The Dodgers lost to the Cards in two games in 1946 and to the Giants in three in 1951.

Details on Page 40

VIEWS UNCHANGED

But Both Sides Retain Reliance on Parleys to Solve Problems

By JAMES RESTON
Special to The New York Times.

WASHINGTON, Sept. 27—The main result of Premier Khrushchev's visit to the United States is that it produced agreement to talk some more. This, at least, is the general view here.

It avoided the danger of personal injury. It ended without any break in the policy of settling international differences by negotiation, and it extended the negotiating period well into the middle of President Eisenhower's last year in office.

The President and his guest reached few agreements, but apparently they were impressed with each other's determination to avoid war, and to continue talking to that end.

Arms Control Urged

If there was any change in the policies of the United States and the Soviet Union, it was in the emphasis on the principle of "the strictest comprehensive control" over any disarmament agreement.

This was Mr. Khrushchev's phrase in his television address to the American people tonight. This is the principle Washington has been trying to get Moscow to accept for years. The question now is whether this principle can now be applied in specific terms to all disarmament talks coming up or only to the Soviet Union's ambitious plan of "total disarmament."

The talks on the future of Germany and Berlin did not go well. They produced more heated conversation at Camp David than anything else.

Neither Side Budges

Neither side budged from the position it held in the nine weeks of fruitless negotiation at the Big Four foreign ministers conference at Geneva this summer. And Mr. Khrushchev went away saying that his way of settling the problem was the only way he knew of reaching a settlement.

Nevertheless, there was agreement to reopen talks on the Berlin question if the other nations concerned agreed, and a curiously worded agreement to fix President Eisenhower's return visit to the Soviet Union for "next spring."

There has been some hope

Continued on Page 20, Column 1

FAREWELL: President Eisenhower wishes Premier Khrushchev a safe voyage home on steps of Blair House in Washington. At right is Andrei A. Gromyko, Soviet Foreign Minister. Oleg A. Troyanovsky, an interpreter, is in the center.
Associated Press Wirephoto

RUSSIAN EXPECTS NO QUICK CHANGE

In Talks on Last Day He Says 'Effort and Patience' Are Needed to Erase Enmity

By WILLIAM J. JORDEN
Special to The New York Times.

WASHINGTON, Sept. 27—Premier Khrushchev said tonight it was "impossible to count on a sudden change" in United States-Soviet relations.

He said the main obstacle to an easing of tensions lay in certain influential forces in this country that opposed efforts to end the "cold war." He expressed confidence that common sense would prevail, but said "great effort and patience" would be required to erase the suspicions and enmity of recent years.

In his farewell appearances in this country, a news conference and a television speech, the visiting Premier repeated his assertion that it was the Soviet Union that was working hardest for better relations.

U. S. Desire for Peace Seen

Mr. Khrushchev said he had no doubt that President Eisenhower shared his desire for an improvement in relations. He declared, too, that he was sure the American people wanted peace as much as the Soviet people.

He accused those who questioned the sincerity of Soviet proposals of standing in the way of agreements. Progress is being frustrated by certain people in the United States, the Premier commented, but he did not, name them or say more than that they were "still influential."

If Mr. Khrushchev was influenced in any way by his visit to the United States and his first-hand look at its wealth and variety, he gave no sign of it.

Soviet Progress Depicted

He said that what he had seen here had not shaken his "faith that the political, economic and social system in the Soviet Union is the fairest and most progressive." In fact, he spent most of the forty-five minutes of his television speech telling of the progress his country had made under the leadership of the Communist party.

Mr. Khrushchev's news conference, held earlier in the main ballroom of the National Press Club, was a light-hearted occasion unmarred by any display of temper such as marked his previous appearance here on Sept. 16, the day after his arrival in the United States.

Five minutes before the conference was to begin at 4 P. M.,

Continued on Page 19, Column 7

Grandchildren Key To President's Trip

By ANTHONY LEWIS
Special to The New York Times.

WASHINGTON, Sept. 27—Premier Khrushchev said today that it was because President Eisenhower's four grandchildren would accompany him to Russia that the President's projected Soviet visit had been postponed until next spring.

"I would like to reveal a secret," the Premier said at his news conference when he was asked the reason for the postponement. With a happy but sly smile, like a cozy grandpa, he told the story.

"Yesterday the President was kind enough to invite me to his farm, where I met his wonderful grandchildren," Mr.

Continued on Page 16, Column 2

U.S.-Soviet Communique

Special to The New York Times.

WASHINGTON, Sept. 27—Following is the text of the joint United States-Soviet communique issued today:

The Chairman of the Council of Ministers of the U. S. S. R., N. S. Khrushchev, and President Eisenhower have had a frank exchange of opinions at Camp David.

In some of these conversations the United States Secretary of State Herter and Soviet Foreign Minister Gromyko, as well as other officials from both countries, participated.

The Chairman of the Council of Ministers of the U. S. S. R. and the President have agreed that these discussions have been useful in clarifying each other's position on a number of subjects. The talks were not undertaken to negotiate issues.

It is hoped, however, that their exchanges of views will contribute to a better understanding of the motives and position of each, and thus to the achievement of a just and lasting peace.

The Chairman of the Council of Ministers of the U. S. S. R. and the President of the United States agreed that the question of general disarmament is the most important one facing the world today. Both Governments will make every effort to achieve a constructive solution of this problem.

A Discussion of Germany

In the course of the conversations an exchange of views took place on the question of Germany, including the question of a peace treaty with Germany, in which the positions of both sides were expounded.

With respect to the specific Berlin question, an understanding was reached, subject to the approval of the other parties directly concerned, that negotiations would be reopened with a view to achieving a solution which would be in accordance with the interests of all concerned and in the interest of the maintenance of peace.

In addition to these questions, useful conversations were held on a number of questions affecting the relations between the Union of Soviet Socialist Republics and the United States. These subjects included the question of trade between the two countries. With respect to an increase in exchanges of persons and ideas, substantial progress was made in discussions between officials and it is expected that certain agreements will be reached in the near future.

The Chairman of the Council of Ministers of the U. S. S. R. and the President agreed that all outstanding international questions should be settled not by the application of force but by peaceful means through negotiation.

Finally, it was agreed that an exact date for the return visit of the President to the Soviet Union next spring would be arranged through diplomatic channels.

Bonn Is Agreeable To Talks on Berlin

By SYDNEY GRUSON
Special to The New York Times.

BONN, Germany, Sept. 27—Government sources said tonight that West Germany would undoubtedly be agreeable to another foreign ministers' conference on the Berlin question.

News of the communique issued in Washington today by President Eisenhower and Premier Khrushchev arrived too late in European capitals for high-level government comment.

Although the Eisenhower-Khrushchev communique did not specify at what level the Berlin negotiations should be resumed, it was assumed here that the foreign ministers were meant and that the nine weeks of dis-

Continued on Page 19, Column 6

PEACE IS STRESSED

President Will Report His Views Today at News Conference

Khrushchev news conference and speech and U. S. news conference, Pages 18-19.

By HARRISON E. SALISBURY
Special to The New York Times.

WASHINGTON, Sept. 27—Premier Khrushchev brought his historic thirteen-day visit to a conclusion today by reaching a series of understandings with President Eisenhower designed to ease "cold war" tensions.

The extent of these understandings was not immediately revealed. However, they were of a scope that suggested that the Khrushchev-Eisenhower conversations had produced at least a limited armistice in the "cold war."

High Points Delineated

The high points of the discussions held by the Soviet and United States leaders, as outlined by a communique, and by Mr. Khrushchev at a news conference and by United States statements, were:

¶An agreement that new talks will be held on the Berlin question. These talks may be held by the foreign ministers, or at a lower level, or possibly at a summit conference.

¶Discussion of a possible summit conference. Mr. Khrushchev said the Soviet Union felt that the time was ripe for such a meeting and that Geneva might be a suitable place. The United States position on this point was not entirely clear.

¶An agreement for President Eisenhower to postpone his trip to the Soviet Union until spring or summer. Mr. Khrushchev said he had proposed the postponement because the weather would be better at that time.

¶An understanding to broaden the present program of exchanges between the United States and the Soviet Union and to undertake explorations of questions relating to trade.

¶An agreement to reopen the long-stalemated negotiations over the World War II Lend-Lease settlement.

¶A joint declaration that "all outstanding international questions should be settled not by the application of force but by peaceful means through negotiation."

The results of the three days

Continued on Page 16, Column 1

KHRUSHCHEV OFF WITH 21-GUN POMP

Nixon Bids Him Farewell at Airport—Both Stress Need for Negotiation

Remarks by Khrushchev and Nixon at airport, Page 17.

By W. H. LAWRENCE
Special to The New York Times.

ANDREWS AIR FORCE BASE, Md., Sept. 27—Premier Khrushchev took off for the Soviet Union at 10 o'clock tonight.

He flew in the giant TU-114 turbo-prop airliner that brought him here about noon Sept. 15. The flight to Moscow was scheduled to be non-stop.

Vice President Richard M. Nixon substituted for President Eisenhower in farewell ceremonies. With him were Secretary of State Christian A. Herter and Gen. Nathan F. Twining, Chairman of the Joint Chiefs of Staff.

The final ceremony at this air base about twelve miles from Washington included all the official honors usually paid a chief of state as Mr Khrushchev had been termed by the Soviet Foreign Ministry for this journey. Previously he had been considered a head of government.

Ceremonies At Airfield

Just before departure a twenty-one-gun salute from a 75-mm. howitzer boomed out after a fifty-six-piece Army band had played the anthems of the Soviet Union and the United States.

The ceremonies began shortly after 9:15 P. M., when Mr. Khrushchev arrived by car from Blair House, official guest house of the President, where he had had a quiet dinner with his family and fellow officials after a hectic day.

At the airfield he was greeted by a 128-member honor guard, including representatives of the Army, Air Force, Navy and Marines.

Mr. Nixon and Mr. Khrushchev did not, however, troop the guard, as the President and Mr. Khrushchev had done after the Premier's daylight arrival.

Continued on Page 17, Column 1

PRESIDENT URGED TO MEET SENATORS

Mansfield Asks Consultation on Khrushchev Talks

By WILLIAM M. BLAIR
Special to The New York Times.

WASHINGTON, Sept. 27—President Eisenhower was called upon today to consult as soon as possible with Senate Democratic and Republican leaders on his conversations with Premier Khrushchev.

Such a consultation would be a demonstration to Mr. Khrushchev and the world of the "basic unity of the American people," Senator Mike Mansfield, Democrat of Montana, declared in a statement.

The Senate's assistant Democratic leader asserted the conference also should be called "because if there is to be progress toward peace beyond the President's exchange of views with Prime Minister Khrushchev any actions to that end ultimately will require the advice and consent—the sanctions of the Senate."

The President might also discuss the "significance" of his conversations with leaders of the House as well as of the Senate, Senator Mansfield said.

He suggested that the meeting might be held at Camp David, the Maryland mountain retreat where the President and the So-

Continued on Page 17, Column 3

The New York Times.

LATE CITY EDITION
U. S. Weather Bureau Report (Page 63) forecasts
Mostly cloudy, mild, some rain today. Mostly cloudy tomorrow.
Temp. range: 50—37; yesterday: 41.6—34.5

NEWS SUMMARY AND INDEX, PAGE 63

SECTION ONE

VOL. CIX....No. 37,227.

© 1959, by The New York Times Company
Times Square, New York 36, N. Y.

NEW YORK, SUNDAY, DECEMBER 27, 1959.

35c outside New York City. Its suburban area and Long Island. Higher in air delivery cities.

TWENTY-FIVE CENTS

WEST TO CONFER SPEEDILY TO SET DATE OF SUMMIT

Mid-May Is Still Favored in Washington After Reply from Khrushchev

SWIFT AGREEMENT SEEN

President Must Also Act on the Expiration of Ban on Nuclear Weapons Tests

By JACK RAYMOND
Special to The New York Times.

WASHINGTON, Dec. 26—A speedy round of consultations among the Western powers was in prospect today to set a date for summit talks in Paris with the Soviet Union.

New instructions are expected to be sent to the United States, British and French Ambassadors in Moscow some time next week to discuss the subject with Andrei A. Gromyko, the Soviet Foreign Minister.

A date in mid-May was still favored in the speculation here. Much of the speculation centered on what President Eisenhower's preference might be, although no hint of his intentions was available. The President, who visited his grandchildren at his Gettysburg farm this morning, received no official visitors at the White House.

Two Urgent Issues at Hand

The summit date is one of two urgent issues awaiting President Eisenhower's action. The other is the expiration Thursday night of the fourteen-month-old ban on nuclear-weapons testing.

The prevailing belief is that the President will order an extension of the prohibition, possibly for an indefinite period. Officials said no decision had been made.

Even if an extension is ordered, the President is expected to remind the Russians, who also have unilaterally suspended nuclear-weapons tests, that further observation of the moratorium by the United States would depend upon progress in the Geneva negotiations toward a formal agreement.

Inspection Is Obstacle

The United States, Britain and the Soviet Union have failed thus far in the talks that began at Geneva fourteen months ago to get over the stumbling block of an acceptable inspection system.

This undoubtedly will be a major matter for discussion at the projected summit meeting.

President Eisenhower joined with the British and French leaders this week in inviting Premier Khrushchev to meet them in Paris April 27. The Soviet leader suggested that the proposed date was inconvenient, apparently because of his expected presence at the traditional May Day celebration in Moscow. Mr. Khrushchev suggested April 21 or May 4 instead.

The Paris summit meeting, slated to be the forerunner of

Continued on Page 2, Column 4

Soviet Party Orders Tightened Controls Over the Collectives

By MAX FRANKEL
Special to The New York Times.

MOSCOW, Dec. 26—Tighter party control was decreed today for Soviet collective farms.

The Central Committee of the Communist party ordered the organizational changes to spur agricultural production, which it said had been good in 1959, but not good enough.

The committee's decrees were made public this evening after the close of a four-day meeting of the group devoted almost exclusively to agriculture. Although the final statement contained a serious indictment of the farm leadership in Kazakhstan, no high-level personnel changes were announced.

The party said the production of 62,000,000 tons of milk this year would exceed the gross milk output of the United States. It also expect-

Continued on Page 3, Column 2

TRIBE WAR PERILS LIBERTY FOR CONGO

Barbaric Fighting Dismays Africans Who Seek Early Withdrawal by Belgians

By HOMER BIGART
Special to The New York Times.

MUTOTO STATION, Belgian Congo, Dec. 26—A barbaric civil war in the heart of the Belgian Congo may wreck Congolese plans for speedy independence.

The savagery of the fighting has upset even some militant nationalists, who are beginning to dread what might happen if the restraining influence of Belgian authority were suddenly lifted.

Equally macabre has been the discovery by Belgian authorities of the mass poisoning of scores of members of the Bushongo tribe, which has been neutral in the fighting.

The Belgians say investigations revealed that 226 tribesmen were poisoned during a recent series of tschipapa, or occult ceremonial trials in which whole villages participate. Drinking bouts are held in which the contents of some cups are poisoned. Those who receive them are presumed to have been guilty of some offense.

Old Customs Revived

The Belgians have outlawed tschipapa. But the agitation for independence apparently has encouraged the Bushongo to revert to old customs. Cynics believe that the tschipapa are rigged by witch doctors who slip poison into the cups of tribesmen of whom the chief wants to be rid.

The war, cruder and more horrible than the tschipapa, involves two closely related tribes, the Lulua and the Baluba.

They are wrestling for control of Kasai Province, which is fertile, well populated and the world's biggest producer of industrial diamonds. Here the aggressive Lulua are trying to cast out the more docile and more advanced Baluba.

King Baudouin of the Belgians, who is touring the Congo, arrived this morning in Luluabourg, the provincial capital. He received a dignified, restrained

Continued on Page 8, Column 1

MEYNER, RIBICOFF GET STUDY HITTING TAX BY NEW YORK

Levy Tied to Services Used Is Called Fairest System— Parley Set for Tuesday

Excerpts from report on tax will be found on Page 46.

By GEORGE CABLE WRIGHT
Special to The New York Times.

TRENTON, Dec. 26—A report to Gov. Robert B. Meyner and Gov. Abraham A. Ribicoff said today that New York State should aim at taxing nonresidents only in proportion to the services it provided them.

It also suggested that nonresidents be permitted to deduct from their New York income taxes the levies they paid on residential properties in their home states.

If New York refuses to do this at present, the report continued, it should at least earmark 30 per cent of the nonresidents' taxes for aid to distressed commuter rail lines.

To Talk With Rockefeller

Governor Meyner of New Jersey and Governor Ribicoff of Connecticut will meet with Governor Rockefeller of New York on Tuesday in an attempt to solve the controversy over the taxing of out-of-state residents who work in New York.

The report was prepared by William C. Warren, interstate tax consultant to Mr. Meyner and Roswell F. Magill, who acts in a similar capacity for Mr. Ribicoff. It comprised a detailed analysis of the effect on nonresidents of New York State's income tax.

Mr. Warren, who lives in Ridgewood, N. J., is Dean of the Columbia University Law School. Mr. Magill, a tax lawyer, lives in Westport, Conn.

The report argued that unless about $15,000,000 was cut annually from nonresident taxes there would be no equity among the states' taxpayers.

New York Plan Scored

It assailed the Rockefeller administration's plan for settling the thirty-year-old interstate tax dispute, characterizing the plan as "inherently defective and no solution to the problem." It warned that the New York proposal, if adopted, might result in still "greater injustice and disparity" than under the present law.

The Rockefeller administration's proposal would permit nonresidents who worked in New York to take exemptions proportional to the share of their incomes earned in New York.

If approved by the New York Legislature, it would become effective only when neighboring states authorized their employers to withhold taxes on employes who live in New York or to furnish Albany with data

Continued on Page 46, Column 3

ROCKEFELLER GIVES UP '60 RACE, CLEARING THE PATH FOR NIXON; DEMOCRATS' HOPES ARE BUOYED

LEADERSHIP WARY

But Top Democrats Appear Pleased by the Decision

By JAMES RESTON
Special to The New York Times.

WASHINGTON, Dec. 26—Leading Democrats were publicly canny but privately pleased tonight by Governor Rockefeller's decision not to seek the Republican Presidential nomination.

Adlai E. Stevenson of Illinois expressed regret that the Republicans had been left "with no other choice than Mr. Nixon" as their Presidential candidate.

Representative Sam Rayburn, the Democratic Speaker of the House of Representatives, who is an old friend of the New York Governor and who recently greeted the Governor in Dallas, said he "never commented on Republican candidates" though he "sometimes commented on Republican policies."

Senator Hubert H. Humphrey of Minnesota, one of the most loquacious member of his party, in the most surprising reaction of the day, said "no comment."

Private Opinions Given

Nevertheless, the Democrats expressed in private these reasons for being pleased with Governor Rockefeller's withdrawal:

¶They could beat Vice President Nixon more easily than Mr. Rockefeller because, they said, the New York Governor had more support among independent and Democratic voters.

¶They now knew where they stood. They had to nominate a Presidential candidate before the Republicans, on July 11 in Los Angeles, and they could now assume in advance that Mr. Nixon would be their opponent.

¶The Rockefeller announcement revived the conservative-liberal issue between the parties, because it gave the impression that the Republican party did not want "competition" from a liberal candidate. Mr. Nixon, who is now expected to get the Republican nomination without a contest, issued the following statement after being notified of the Governor's decision:

"Governor Rockefeller has made an excellent impression in the states he has visited in the past few months.

"People throughout the nation have recognized him as a leader of national and international stature.

"Regardless of the decision he

Continued on Page 38, Column 6

GOVERNOR ROCKEFELLER

VICE PRESIDENT NIXON
Associated Press

ROCKEFELLER SAYS IT WAS 'GREAT FUN'

Relaxed Governor Discusses a Variety of Subjects on Train to Philadelphia

By MILTON BRACKER
Special to The New York Times.

PHILADELPHIA, Dec. 26—Governor Rockefeller sat back with one leg over a table in a Pullman drawing room on his way here tonight, a few hours after announcing that he would not seek the Republican nomination for President.

He said "it" had been a "very invigorating business" and "great fun."

There was no particular antecedent for "it" and none was needed. The Governor had determined not to add a word of comment to his withdrawal statement, until he holds a news conference in Albany, probably next week.

He stuck to that decision but, in an informal conversation, he could not conceal some amusement at the surprise his action had caused.

He seemed to be saying, "I told them that I hadn't made up my mind—but they wouldn't believe me." Many people had insisted on making up his mind for him, he mused; well, that was their prerogative. An ironic

Continued on Page 37, Column 5

Mitchell and Halleck Gain Backing for Vice President

By W. H. LAWRENCE
Special to The New York Times.

WASHINGTON, Dec. 26—Secretary of Labor James P. Mitchell and Representative Charles A. Halleck emerged tonight as the two most talked of possibilities for the Republican Vice - Presidential nomination.

Republican interest in the Vice-Presidency quickened in the wake of the surprise decision by Governor Rockefeller not to seek the Presidential nomination.

This act, virtually insuring the nomination of Vice President Richard M. Nixon, took most of the steam and interest out of the Republican convention. Delegates will meet in Chicago next July 25.

This left only a campaign for the Vice-Presidential spot to add interest to the pre-convention Republican maneuvering. But, in the final analysis, the Presidential nominee will be free—openly or by indirection—to pick whomever he wants as a running mate and the convention quickly will ratify the selection.

Many Factors in Choice

Geography, party background, and, perhaps, religion may all have a bearing on the Republican Vice-Presidential choice next year. This will be true especially if the Democrats, meeting first, put a Roman Catholic like Senator John F. Kennedy of Massachusetts or Gov. Edmund G. Brown of California on the ticket.

One likely result of Governor Rockefeller's decision will be to increase the pressure on him to stand as Mr. Nixon's running mate. This will persist despite the New York Governor's firm reaffirmation of earlier statements that he would not be a candidate for Vice President under any conceivable circumstances. But many Republican leaders insist

Continued on Page 36, Column 6

GOVERNOR FACING EASIER STATE JOB

Expected to Gain a Stronger Hand in Pressing Broad Program in Legislature

Special to The New York Times.

ALBANY, Dec. 26 — Governor Rockefeller's withdrawal from the Republican Presidential race will shift the national political spotlight away from the 1960 session of the State Legislature.

The result will undoubtedly be a more orderly meeting of the lawmakers. It will probably also enhance Mr. Rockefeller's prospects of winning approval of more of his first large-scale legislative program.

The Governor will have top-heavy Republican majorities in both houses of the Legislature, as have all his predecessors, Republican and Democratic, for the last twenty years.

His problem in winning support for his new programs, of which there will be plenty next year, involves the danger that conservative Republicans in the Senate and Assembly may fall off and join the Democrats in opposition.

Help for Governor Seen

Some of these upstate Republican lawmakers have made no bones about their preference for Mr. Nixon for the Presidential nomination. Mr. Rockefeller's graceful withdrawal is not likely to injure his position with this group.

Others, more sensitive to legislative prerogative than opposed to a Rockefeller candidacy, had expressed resentment over the possibility that the Governor might attempt to "use" the Legislature as a demonstration of what a strong and progressive President he would make. This is no longer a factor, as of today.

There had been talk that Mr. Rockefeller would attempt to speed the session, which normally runs from early Janary to mid-March or later, in an effort to free himself to participate in some of the Presidential primary contests in other states.

With the Governor no longer a candidate, there is no question of limiting the length of the session. This might even strengthen Mr. Rockefeller's hand, "making him willing to stay in the capital indefinitely if the lawmakers should balk at his proposals.

Paradoxically, Mr. Rockefel-

Continued on Page 4, Column 6

DECISION IS 'FINAL'

Governor Explains He Wishes to Avert a 'Massive' Fight

Text of Rockefeller statement is printed on Page 37.

By WARREN WEAVER Jr.
Special to The New York Times.

ALBANY, Dec. 26—Governor Rockefeller withdrew abruptly today from competition for the Republican Presidential nomination in 1960. He said his decision was "definite and final."

He also announced an "absolutely definite" resolve not to be the party's candidate for Vice President. It was a stand he had adopted from the beginning when it appeared he might seek the Presidential nomination.

The Governor's action, unforeseen and almost inexplicable to many observers, appeared to clear the way for the unanimous nomination of Vice President Richard M. Nixon by the Republican National Convention next July.

Nixon Gets Free Hand

It also left Mr. Nixon free to select any Vice-Presidential running mate he saw fit, without reference to any Rockefeller sentiment that might have built up in recent months.

Mr. Rockefeller said he had reached the decision because an attempt to challenge Mr. Nixon would have involved "a massive struggle" and thus have forced him to slight his duties as Governor.

This was the only explanation Mr. Rockefeller offered for withdrawing at a time when virtually every political figure in the state—including many of his close associates—had become convinced he was about to become a declared candidate for President.

Obligations are Stressed

The Governor did not say he could not defeat the Vice President in open competition in the primaries. He did not say that the Republican cause would be injured by such an intra-party contest. All he said was that the effort would "make impossible the fulfillment of my obligations as Governor of New York."

Mr. Rockefeller based his prediction that any Nixon-Rockefeller competition would be "massive" on a conclusion that "the great majority of those who will control the Republican convention stand opposed to any contest for the nomination."

This was a barely veiled method of saying that almost every leading Republican he had met in his tours of fifteen states

Continued on Page 37, Column 1

Sports News

FOOTBALL

The New York Giants will play the Baltimore Colts in Baltimore's Memorial Stadium today in the National Football League championship play-off. The game will be seen by a sellout crowd of 57,557 and will be telecast and broadcast nationally. The Colts are favored by 3½ points. The Colts beat the Giants, 23 to 17, in the title game last year.

In college football, the Blue defeated the Gray, 20 to 8, yesterday in their annual all-star game at Montgomery, Ala. The North beat the South, 27 to 17, in their annual all-star contest at Miami. The passing of Joe Caldwell of Army was the major factor. The National All-Stars downed the Southwest All-Stars, 21 to 6, in the Copper Bowl at Tempe, Ariz.

BASKETBALL

Cincinnati trounced St. Bonaventure, 96 to 56, in the first round of the Holiday Festival tournament at Madison Square Garden. Oscar Robertson of Cincinnati scored 47 points. In other Festival games, New York University downed Dartmouth, 78 to 68; Iowa topped St. John's of Brooklyn, 91 to 84, and St. Joseph's of Philadelphia won from Manhattan College, 84 to 70.

Details in Section 5.

Deaths Exceed 350 In Holiday Driving

A rising toll of death on the highways marred celebration of the Christmas holiday during the long week-end.

By 2 o'clock this morning at least 355 persons had died in traffic accidents over the nation. In the only three persons were injured early today in an accident in the rain on the lower level of the Queensboro Bridge. Seven vehicles were involved. Two tow trucks had responded after an accident between an automobile and a taxi, and three other cars crashed into the tow trucks.

The injured were taken to Grand Central Hospital. Their names were not immediately available. One was reported in critical condition.

Before the three-day holiday

Police Drop a Historic Whistle

Order Here Scraps SOS Device That Dates to 1889

By IRA HENRY FREEMAN

Another note of New York—the famous police whistle—is passing into history.

In an order dated Dec. 24, Police Commissioner Stephen P. Kennedy told his approximately 18,500 patrolmen and 1,500 sergeants that they would no longer be required to carry the tubular whistle.

The tubular whistle is a long, nickel-plated instrument with its own stimulating tone. It takes vigor to blow. Its sound can be heard for four or five blocks on a quiet night. For at least seventy years, it had been used by patrolmen and sometimes by civilians—to call other policemen on post to aid.

Today, Commissioner Kennedy's order said, the whistle is rarely used to call aid. The policeman uses the call-box telephone connected to his precinct, or the radio of his prowl car, or ever a public telephone.

If there is no time to make telephone calls, the policeman in need can blow his traffic whistle, or bang his nightstick on the curb, or fire his revolver into the air, the Commissioner said.

The traffic whistle is that

Continued on Page 47, Column 3

Tubular whistle is dropped

Traffic whistle will stay
The New York Times

But Traffic Variety Will Still Pierce Ears of City

incorporated in 1652. For that reason, the watchmen were called the rattle watch. The watchmen would walk their posts, swinging their rattles to scare off "evil doers," Mr. Irving said.

In 1691, under the English, the first uniformed policeman patroled the streets of New York. Instead of a rattle, he swung a bell. The rattles, however, persisted.

Wooden whistles were used at least as early as 1854. Mr. Irving has one said to have belonged to George Washington Walling, a Police Commissioner of that period. In 1860, the pea whistle, a lead casting in which a dried pea vibrated, was used by policemen to call others from near-by posts. It is similar to the dreaded traffic whistle of today.

The practice of banging the baton, truncheon or nightstick on the curbstone or a wall or railing, and of discharging a firearm in the air, is, of course, as old as those police weapons themselves.

According to Jay Irving, a cartoonist, whose hobby is collecting the history and lore of the New York Police Department, the present-day police whistle's duties date from about 1889.

The watchmen in New Amsterdam carried rattles, not whistles, after the town was

Continued on Page 28, Column 3

T. W. U. Chiefs Vote Full Tie-Up Jan. 1

By STANLEY LEVEY

The leadership of the Transport Workers Union voted yesterday to recommend a New Year's Day strike on New York's private and public transit lines to support demands for a wage rise.

The vote was taken among members of the executive board of the union's Local 100, representing 35,000 bus and subway workers. The recommendation, which was unanimous, will go before a mass union rally this afternoon at Manhattan Center.

Michael J. Quill, international union president, and Matthew Guinan, head of Local 100, said weeks of negotiations with the Transit Authority had been "fruitless" and that discussions had reached a "complete deadlock."

Today's membership meeting is expected to accept the rec-

Continued on Page 4, Column 4

1960 - 1969

The New York Times.

LATE CITY EDITION
U. S. Weather Bureau Report (Page 61) forecast:
Fair today; mostly fair tonight.
Partly cloudy and warm tomorrow.
Temp. range: 74–54; yesterday: 69.1–52.5.

VOL. CIX..No. 37,358.   © 1960, by The New York Times Company.
Times Square, New York 36, N. Y.   **NEW YORK, FRIDAY, MAY 6, 1960.**   10 cents beyond 50-mile zone from New York City
except on Long Island. Higher in air delivery cities.   **FIVE CENTS**

A. M. A. DENOUNCES EISENHOWER PLAN FOR CARE OF AGED

Says Proposal Takes False Tack That Most Over 65 Are Medically Indigent

OTHERS JOIN IN ATTACK

Goldwater Sees 'Socialized Medicine'—Labor Assails Measure as Unsound

By AUSTIN C. WEHRWEIN
Special to The New York Times.

CHICAGO, May 5 — The American Medical Association assailed today the Eisenhower Administration's health-care plan for the aged.

A statement issued through the association's headquarters here in the name of its president, Dr. Louis M. Orr of Orlando, Fla., said the Administration plan was "based on the false premise that all persons over 65 need health care and cannot afford it."

"This is not a fact," the statement declared.

"The truth is that a majority of our older people are capable of continuing a happy, healthy, and in many cases, productive life.

"Of the more than 15,000,000 persons in the nation over 65 years of age, only 15 per cent are on old age assistance.

Rejects 2 Proposals

"An undetermined number, although able to finance other costs, find it difficult to withstand the additional burden of the cost of illness.

"It is for these people that something should be done. Neither the Forand advocates nor the Administration proposal is tailored to meet these problems."

[In Washington, the Administration's proposal was attacked by Senator Barry Goldwater as "socialized medicine" and by the merged labor federation as unsound and politically inspired.]

The medical association's reference to "Forand" alluded to a bill sponsored by Representative Aime J. Forand, Democrat of Rhode Island. It would extend the Social Security system, and increase Social Security taxes, to provide medical care for persons over 65.

The Administration's proposal, offered yesterday, calls for Federal and state subsidies of insurance systems to be set up by the states. The estimated annual cost of $1,200,000,000

Continued on Page 32, Column 3

O'DWYER'S NIECE NAMED TO BENCH

Mayor Appoints Her Despite Bar Groups' Opposition

By LAYHMOND ROBINSON

Mayor Wagner named Joan O'Dwyer O'Neill, 33-year-old niece of former Mayor William O'Dwyer, a city magistrate yesterday, despite the objections of two of the three bar groups to whom he had submitted her name.

He reported, however, that five bar groups, including the third one asked to pass on her, had given her "unanimous approval."

The Mayor also made it clear that he regarded Mrs. O'Neill as qualified for the $16,000-a-year post on the Magistrate's Court, which basically has jurisdiction over minor crimes.

10-Year Term Slated

The appointment, which needs no further approval, is to fill out two months of a term of a magistrate who resigned. Mrs. O'Neill will then be appointed for a full ten-year term.

In commenting on the division of the bar associations over the designation, the Mayor said he had "always sought bar association approval for bench nominees," but had "never intended or pretended that such support had to be unanimous."

He emphasized that he regarded Mrs. O'Neill, "whom I know quite well," as qualified for the position.

The opposition has stemmed largely from the feeling by some lawyers that Mrs. O'Neill had not

Continued on Page 14, Column 5

West Virginia Poll Finds Kennedy Gain

By W. H. LAWRENCE
Special to The New York Times.

CHARLESTON, W. Va., May 5 — Substantial voting gains for Senator John F. Kennedy were reported today in West Virginia.

Politicians and polls alike brought reports of a strong, well-financed and well-organized Kennedy drive to wrest victory from Senator Hubert H. Humphrey of Minnesota, considered the favorite in next Tuesday's Democratic Presidential preferential primary here.

One politician, who classified himself as neutral but formerly pro-Humphrey, admiringly called the Kennedy effort "a blitz." But what he and other politicians, including many in the Kennedy camp, questioned was whether the indicated gains in the southern coal fields were

Continued on Page 13, Column 1

RIBICOFF ASSAILS NEW HAVEN LINE

'This Is Not the Way to Run a Business,' He Says in Calling 4-State Parley

By RICHARD H. PARKE
Special to The New York Times.

GREENWICH, Conn., May 5 — Gov. Abraham A. Ribicoff accused the New Haven Railroad today of "shabby and shoddy" bookkeeping, of "wasting 'great sums'" and of employing "scare words, false issues, emotional appeals and misrepresentations."

"Clearly," he said, "this is not the way to run a business which must count so heavily on public goodwill, public support, public respect and, yes, even public affection."

Governor Ribicoff delivered his attack in announcing that he was inviting the Governors of New York, Rhode Island and Massachusetts and the Mayor of New York to confer with him on the New Haven's future. No date has been set for the conference.

Tax Relief Proposed

Mr. Ribicoff said he would ask them to consider taking action on the recommendations in the report issued on the New Haven yesterday by the Connecticut Public Utilities Commission.

The report, which was also critical of the railroad management, proposed several measures to aid the line. They included a joint tax-relief program by the four states and an interstate authority that would cooperate with the railroad in providing commuter service in the New York area.

Governor Ribicoff, who disclosed the railroad at a meeting here of the First Selectman's Association of Fairfield County, also said he was prepared to recommend a railroad

Continued on Page 20, Column 1

DILLON CONSULTS A. F. L.-C. I. O. AIDE IN ARAB SHIP CASE

Seeks Way to End Picketing Here as Mideast Boycott of U. S. Vessels Spreads

By DANA ADAMS SCHMIDT
Special to The New York Times.

WASHINGTON, May 5—Under Secretary of State Douglas Dillon conferred today with Arthur J. Goldberg, special counsel of the American Federation of Labor and Congress of Industrial Organizations, on possible ways of ending the picketing of the United Arab Republic ship Cleopatra in New York.

Union and State Department officials spoke of the possibility of working out a statement of United States policy that would lead the Seafarers International Union to call off its pickets.

But State Department officials were emphatic in pointing out that they had no means of forcing the United Arab Republic to give up its practice of blacklisting ships that put in at Israeli ports. This boycott precipitated the picketing.

Meanwhile, concern grew at the State Department over indications that the blockade of the Cleopatra and the Arab counter-blockade were reversing the trend toward better United States relations with the Arab world.

Blockade May Spread

"From almost every post we have had laments that the diplomatic efforts of years are being upset by this affair," an official of the department said.

If the blockade continues the impact on commerce would deepen and might next spread to airlines, he added.

The reports included the following points:

¶In Khartoum, capital of the Sudan, the press for the first time in two years assumed an anti-United States tone.

¶The Bombay Port Workers Union telegraphed President Eisenhower protesting the blockade of the Cleopatra and declaring that its continuance would result in a boycott of United States ships seeking to enter the Bombay port. This was the first sign that the counter-blockade might spread beyond the Arab world.

¶A Libyan Government official suggested informally to United States diplomats that "it would be better" if United States ships avoided Libyan ports while the Cleopatra was being picketed.

¶The American Export liner Excalibur, due today in Alexandria, the United Arab Republic port, was diverted by its owners to a destination not yet disclosed. The United States freighter Exchequer began un-

Continued on Page 2, Column 3

SOVIET DOWNS AMERICAN PLANE; U.S. SAYS IT WAS WEATHER CRAFT; KHRUSHCHEV SEES SUMMIT BLOW

CAPITAL EXPLAINS

Reports Unarmed U-2 Vanished at Border After Difficulty

Text of the U. S. statement on plane is on Page 7.

By JACK RAYMOND
Special to The New York Times.

WASHINGTON, May 5—The United States said today an American weather-observation plane flown by a civilian apparently went astray near the Turkish-Soviet border Sunday when the pilot's oxygen supply failed.

This was the official explanation of the incident described by Premier Khrushchev when he said an American "invader" had been shot down over the Soviet Union.

According to the official statement, the pilot was in a heavily instrumented U-2 single-engine plane, chartered from the Lockheed Aircraft Corporation by the National Aeronautics and Space Administration.

The pilot was identified later as Francis G. Powers, 30 years old, a Lockheed employee.

Plane Used in Research

The plane was flying at an altitude close to 55,000 feet, making weather observations over the Lake Van area of Turkey as part of a world-wide research program begun in 1956, a spokesman for the civilian space agency said.

The spokesman emphasized that the plane was unarmed and carried no military equipment of any kind. He said it was marked with the letters N. A. S. A. in black on a gold-yellow band and with an N. A. S. A. seal, a globe within calipers. [Premier Khrushchev said the plane shot down bore no identification marks.]

Can Text Radioactivity

The U-2, in addition to its use for weather observation, was developed by Lockheed originally for the Air Force in a secret program initiated in 1954 to study radioactivity resulting from nuclear tests.

The U-2 can maintain flight at altitudes up to 55,000 feet for as long as four hours. It is powered by a single Pratt & Whitney J-57 turbojet engine. In the high-altitude sampling program, U-2 aircraft have taken samples of radioactive fall-out by exposing filter paper to the atmosphere.

The agency spokesman denied that the U-2 missing in Turkey carried any radioactivity-detection instruments.

The incident occurred in one

Continued on Page 7, Column 1

ANNOUNCES DOWNING OF U. S. PLANE: Premier Khrushchev speaking yesterday during opening session of the Supreme Soviet (parliament) at the Kremlin in Moscow.
Associated Press Radiophoto

U. S. ASKS DETAILS OF PLANE INCIDENT

Data Sought From Envoy in Moscow as Washington Reacts With Restraint

By WILLIAM J. JORDEN
Special to The New York Times.

WASHINGTON, May 5 — Washington reacted with restraint today to Premier Khrushchev's announcement that a United States plane had been shot down Sunday on Soviet territory.

There were some angry words on Capitol Hill—including a suggestion that President Eisenhower refuse to go to the summit meeting with Mr. Khrushchev in Paris May 16. But the Administration would say little more than that additional information was being sought from Moscow.

A message went to Ambassador Llewellyn E. Thompson Jr. in Moscow this afternoon instructing him to request more details from the Soviet authorities.

Text Made Available Late

The text of Mr. Khrushchev's long speech to the Supreme Soviet became available to officials only late this afternoon. Their first reaction was that he seemed to be preparing the way for placing the blame for a summit failure on the Western powers.

He also seemed to be giving advance warning that the Allied leaders could expect little softness from him at the Paris meeting. The consensus was that the Khrushchev address was the latest move in pre-summit maneuvering, but that it had not altered measurably his outlook for the summit meeting.

Mr. Khrushchev said that the Governments of the United States, Britain and France did not seem to be looking forward

Continued on Page 7, Column 6

Soviet Will Revalue Ruble; Income Tax to End by '65

By MAX FRANKEL
Special to The New York Times.

MOSCOW, May 5—Premier Khrushchev proclaimed a complex fiscal reform today. The changes will bring a new and more costly ruble into Soviet circulation next year and an abolition of most personal income taxes by 1965.

The Premier pledged greater take-home pay to lower-paid industrial workers and office employes and said that this would be matched by increased stocks of consumer goods in the stores.

In fact, he promised a great new drive for the production of consumer goods once his ambitious seven-year economic plan is fulfilled in 1965.

Mr. Khrushchev proposed the currency revaluation and tax revisions to the Supreme Soviet, the national Parliament. Enabling legislation as requested by the Soviet leader is expected after a day or two of comment from the Deputies. It is expected to be some time, however, before everyone here, including experts, understands the ramifications of the program.

Unanimous Adoption Seen

There is little doubt that the changes will be unanimously adopted essentially as outlined by Mr. Khrushchev in a broadcast speech. He asked that all the arithmetic complications of the new formulas be tirelessly explained to the Soviet people, together with assurances that the country will gain by the changes and that no one will suffer.

Premier Khrushchev also promised that the currency reform would not affect the Soviet Union's foreign economic dealings or contracts. The official value of the ruble is four to $1. American tourists in the Soviet Union, however, receive a premium payment that brings them a total of ten rubles a dollar.

There was no suggestion in Moscow that the reform was a prelude to free convertibility of

Continued on Page 8, Column 3

PREMIER IS BITTER

Assails 'Provocation Aimed at Wrecking' May 16 Parley

Excerpts from Khrushchev's remarks are on Page 6.

By OSGOOD CARUTHERS
Special to The New York Times.

MOSCOW, May 5 — Premier Khrushchev said today that a United States plane on a mission of "aggressive provocation aimed at wrecking the summit conference" invaded Soviet territory May 1 and was shot down.

The Premier, in the most blistering speech against American policies he had made since his meetings with President Eisenhower last autumn, declared that the incursion, as well as declarations by United States policy makers, cast gloom on the prospects for the success of the summit meeting in Paris eleven days hence.

He expressed anger over the fact that President Eisenhower had supported declarations against Soviet foreign policies by Vice President Richard M. Nixon, Secretary of State Christian A. Herter, Under Secretary of State Douglas Dillon and others.

He Seems to Bar Nixon

He surmised, Mr. Khrushchev said, that General Eisenhower, while wanting peace, was a victim of tight restrictions by "imperialists and militarists" around him.

Mr. Khrushchev expressed regret that the President wanted to limit the summit meeting to one week and he virtually rejected a proposal to sit at the table with Mr. Nixon if the Vice President was delegated to take over for General Eisenhower in case the session went over the time limit.

The most sensational section of Mr. Khrushchev's three-and-a-half-hour speech, made before the opening session of the Supreme Soviet, the nation's version of a parliament, was that concerning the charges of United States violations of Soviet airspace.

Foreign Policy to Fore

Mr. Khrushchev actually had been called upon to open the Supreme Soviet session to deal exclusively with sweeping new domestic policies that will affect every Soviet worker: gradual abolition of income taxes by 1965 and by next year, reduction of the work day to seven hours and an upward revaluation of the ruble.

However, the Soviet leader seized the occasion to discuss foreign policy and the summit conference. He apparently had determined to tell the Soviet people that recent Western actions and statements had darkened his previous optimism.

The Premier predicted to foreign diplomats earlier this week that his talk on foreign and domestic policies would contain major surprises. Indeed, his report of the plane incident came as a shock to Westerners and

Continued on Page 6, Column 4

ANKARA STUDENTS JOSTLE MENDERES

Turkish Premier Is Caught in Street Demonstration —Escapes Amid Jeers

By JAY WALZ

ISTANBUL, Turkey, May 5—Premier Adnan Menderes was jostled and jeered in Ankara today when he was caught by surprise in a student demonstration.

Anti-Menderes students mingled with a crowd of the Premier's supporters. They crowded around him shouting "Freedom! Freedom!" as he walked among them on his way to a political club.

One student clutched Premier Menderes' arm and asked, "How long do we suffer at your hands?" The Premier angrily called a policeman to take the young man away.

After a few minutes Mr. Menderes escaped unharmed in a small car that had been parked near by. It pushed through the crowd with witnesses estimated at about 3,000. A Government spokesman maintained that only 250 were demonstrators. The rest were bystanders, he said.

Police and Cavalry Busy

About 300 policemen and a troop of cavalry dispersed the crowd, which witnesses estimated at about 3,000. A Government spokesman maintained that only 250 were demonstrators. The rest were bystanders, he said.

A few shots were fired into the air but no one was reported injured. The disturbance lasted for about an hour and a half.

Before the demonstrations in Ankara, a group of students allied with Mr. Menderes' Democratic party were waiting to greet him as he drove to the political club in Kizilay Square in the new section of Ankara. Soldiers lined his route along Ataturk Boulevard.

The anti-Menderes students had passed the word to infiltrate the throng, using the watchword "Five, Five, Five, K.," meaning "Be at Kizilay Square at 5:55 P. M."

The outbreak marked the

Continued on Page 4, Column 5

London in Gala Mood for Princess' Wedding Today

Princess Margaret and Antony Armstrong-Jones as they arrived at Clarence House, the Princess' home, after rehearsing for their wedding in Westminster Abbey.
Associated Press Radiophoto

By DREW MIDDLETON
Special to The New York Times.

LONDON, May 5 — The Church of England stressed the spiritual aspects of tomorrow's royal wedding in a brave but unavailing attempt to modify the carnival mood that has gripped the heart of this dignified capital tonight.

Outside Westminster Abbey crowds gaped at decorations hailing the marriage of Princess Margaret to Antony Armstrong-Jones. Inside, the Very Rev. Eric Symes Abbott, Dean of Westminster, emphasized that "here are two people — a man and a woman — for whom it is the greatest day of their lives." Westminster Abbey, the Dean observed,

Continued on Page 26, Column 3

---

23 Are Killed and Scores Injured As Twisters Hit East Oklahoma

By The Associated Press.

WILBURTON, Okla., May 5—At least twenty-three persons were killed by tornadoes that slashed across eastern Oklahoma tonight. At least eleven were killed and scores injured in this college town.

A witness, Mrs. Denny Jones, said the tornado hit Wilburton about 6:45 P. M. with a "freight-train" roar.

All communications were cut and travel and rescue efforts were hampered by torrential rains.

The highway patrol and newsmen listed the Wilburton victims as:

Gordon Mote, 70 years old; Mrs. James Reeves, wife of an instructor at Eastern Oklahoma A&M Junior College; a Mrs. Porter and a Mrs. McGee; James Parks, about 70; Mr. and Mrs. Mike Brady, both about 70; Truman Clark, about 45;

Wildon Raines; Margie Bark, and one unidentified man.

Several of the older victims were killed when the twister leveled the Calvary Baptist Church where services were being held.

More than seventy-five persons were reported injured.

Ambulances raced over slick roads to hospitals at McAlester, Poteau, Hartshorne and Heavener.

A newsman on the scene said about 1,000 rescue workers rushed into the city of 2,000 in reply to a call for help.

Tornadoes killed two in the area around Moffett and Roland two small communities nestled against the Arkansas border near Fort Smith.

Sheriff Prentice Maddux of Fort Smith said four bodies

Continued on Page 62, Column 7

Harvey Firestone 3d Dies in Havana Fall

Special to The New York Times.

HAVANA, May 5—Harvey S. Firestone 3d plunged to his death from the twentieth floor of a Havana luxury hotel tonight, six hours after arriving here from Miami. The victim, who was 32 years old, was the son of Harvey S. Firestone Jr., chairman of the board of the Firestone Tire and Rubber Company.

[Cuban authorities ruled the death a suicide, The Associated Press reported.]

The Cuban police said David Morgan Firestone, 29, a cousin of the dead man, had told them that Harvey Firestone had attempted suicide on a previous occasion in the United States.

The victim had been crippled since birth by cerebral palsy.

Mr. Firestone arrived in Havana today accompanied by his

Continued on Page 62, Column 5

The New York Times.

LATE CITY EDITION
U. S. Weather Bureau Report (Page 82) forecasts:
Early showers, clearing later today;
mostly fair tonight and tomorrow.
Temp. range: 78—62; yesterday: 77.0—61.5.

VOL. CIX..No. 37,370.   © 1960, by The New York Times Company. Times Square, New York 36, N. Y.   NEW YORK, WEDNESDAY, MAY 18, 1960.   10 cents beyond 50-mile zone from New York City except on Long Island. Higher in air delivery cities.   FIVE CENTS

SUMMIT CONFERENCE BREAKS UP IN DISPUTE; WEST BLAMES KHRUSHCHEV'S RIGID STAND; HE INSISTS ON EISENHOWER SPYING APOLOGY

PASSENGER GAINS AND CITY SUBSIDY END TRANSIT LOSS

Board Expects $4,000,000 Surplus June 30 Instead of Deficit of $116,000

By STANLEY LEVEY

Thanks to more riders and city subsidies, the Transit Authority expects to end the present fiscal year on June 30 with a surplus of $4,000,000 instead of a deficit of $116,000.

Most of the help from the city had been anticipated in planning for 1959-60. But the sharp upturn in passenger revenues had not.

While the agency was pleased with the development, it had no explanation for it yesterday beyond the suggestion that new buses and subway cars were responsible.

"We just have more riders," Charles L. Patterson, chairman of the authority, said happily.

The prospect of a big surplus apparently made firm a previous pledge by the authority that the present 15-cent bus and subway fare would be held at least until July 1, 1962. On that date contracts between the agency and the Transport Workers Union expire.

City Subsidies Counted On

The projected $4,000,000 surplus was based on the record for the first nine months of the fiscal year. From last July 1 to March 31 the authority's revenues exceeded its expenses by $2,865,021. In the same period of the preceding year the agency had a $7,822,803 deficit and it finished that fiscal year with a total deficit of $19,200,000.

Last spring, when the authority drew up its 1959-60 operating budget, it expected to end the year with a deficit of $116,000. The officials knew then that they could count on the

Continued on Page 21, Column 3

2 NETWORKS FIGHT FREE TV DEBATES

But Would Give Candidates Time Under Own Plans

By TOM WICKER

Special to The New York Times.

WASHINGTON, May 17—Adlai E. Stevenson's idea for a series of television debates between the major Presidential candidates encountered still opposition today from the TV industry and the opposition party.

Dr. Frank Stanton, president of the Columbia Broadcasting System, and David C. Adams, senior vice president of the National Broadcasting Company, resisted Mr. Stevenson's proposal that the networks be required by law to grant free time to the candidates.

However, both said that their networks would make free time available voluntarily, under certain circumstances.

Bill Before Senate Unit

Mr. Stevenson's "great debate" plan is embodied in S. 3171, a bill pending before the Communications Subcommittee of the Senate Interstate and Foreign Commerce Committee. The group heard and questioned the former Governor of Illinois yesterday and Dr. Stanton today.

It also received today a written statement from Mr. Adams and took written testimony against the bill from Vice President Nixon, former President Herbert Hoover and Thomas E. Dewey, twice a Republican Presidential candidate.

Mr. Adams will be questioned at an afternoon session tomorrow. In his statement he described S. 3171 as "the wrong way to go about doing the right thing." The bill, he said, is "discriminatory" and "confiscatory." It is not needed, he went on, because N. B. C. already proposes to "invite the major Pres-

Continued on Page 29, Column 3

U. S. Sues to Open Biloxi Beach to All

Special to The New York Times

WASHINGTON, May 17—The Justice Department sued Biloxi, Miss., today in a move to open the Gulf coast beach there to Negroes.

Three weeks ago, on the week-end of April 23, a group of about forty Negroes tried to swim at the beach. They were chased by white men with clubs. It has been reported that Negroes are not permitted to swim anywhere on the twenty-six-mile beach.

Gunfire and street fights in Biloxi followed the episode. Two white men and eight Negroes were wounded by bullets. Several Negroes who had tried to use the beach were arrested and fined $25 each for "disturbing the peace."

The Justice Department suit was based on the fact that

Continued on Page 22, Column 1

KENNEDY SWEEPS MARYLAND'S VOTE

Gets 70% of Total in Routing Morse for Sixth Straight Primary Triumph

By W. H. LAWRENCE

Special to The New York Times.

BALTIMORE, May 17—Senator John F. Kennedy won a landslide victory in Maryland's Democratic primary today to enlarge his claim to the Presidential nomination.

The young Massachusetts contender polled about 70 per cent of the vote and picked up twenty-four first-ballot delegate votes at the national convention opening in Los Angeles July 11.

There was no contest in the Republican preferential primary.

Senator Kennedy overwhelmed Senator Wayne Morse of Oregon and Maryland politicians who had urged a vote for an uninstructed delegation to demonstrate support for the Presidential aspirations of Senator Stuart Symington of Missouri, and Senators Lyndon B. Johnson of Texas and Adlai E. Stevenson of Illinois.

Returns from 1,354 of 1,356 precincts gave:

Kennedy 199,362
Morse 49,323

Mr. Kennedy jumped far ahead in the first precinct to report, and built his lead steadily in every contest.

Mr. Morse took his worst beating in Baltimore, which casts about half the Democratic vote, trailing his rival by a plurality in excess of 73,000.

The Oregonian received about 17 per cent of the vote, or 50 per cent less than the expectation he voiced Sunday, when he conceded defeat in advance.

For Senator Kennedy this was his sixth straight primary victory and an impressive show of strength before his final

Continued on Page 30, Column 4

Vatican Paper Proclaims Right Of Church to Role in Politics

Special to The New York Times.

ROME, May 17—L'Osservatore Romano, the Vatican newspaper, declared today that the Roman Catholic hierarchy had "the right and the duty to intervene" in the political field to guide its flock. It rejected what it termed "the absurd split of conscience between the believer and the citizen."

The pronouncement was in a front-page editorial prepared by the Vatican Press Service and described as "authoritative." It deplored "the great confusion of ideas that is spreading, especially in some nations, among Catholics with regard to the relations between Catholic doctrine and social and political activities, and between the ecclesiastical hierarchy and

where some left-of-center elements in the dominant Christian Democratic party, which enjoys Vatican backing, have recently advocated collaboration with Left-Wing Socialists, against some elements of the Roman Catholic Episcopacy.

However, L'Osservatore Romano made it plain that the pronouncement was valid for Roman Catholic laymen everywhere. It referred to the situation in Italy,

Continued on Page 31, Column 1

SOVIET SHIFT SEEN

'Warmed-Up Cold War' Awaited—Khrushchev Will Stop in Berlin

By SYDNEY GRUSON

PARIS, May 17—Western diplomats here expressed the belief today that Premier Khrushchev's break with President Eisenhower signaled a major change in Soviet policy. One Frenchman suggested that this tended toward a "warmed-up cold war."

The change will become apparent quickly, these diplomats believe, perhaps even in a session of the Supreme Soviet, the parliament in Moscow, that Mr. Khrushchev is expected to summon on his return home.

Meanwhile, the Soviet Premier plans to stop in Berlin on his way back to Moscow. His meetings in Berlin with East Germany's Communist leaders are expected by Western diplomats to open some new phase in the Soviet campaign to resolve the Berlin issue.

Soviet-Bloc Parley Predicted

Soviet sources here said Mr. Khrushchev would also call together the Soviet Union's Eastern European allies to consider the consequences of the rupture with President Eisenhower and the failure of the Paris summit conference.

The Russians have been threatening to sign a separate peace treaty with East Germany and place access to West Berlin in East German hands unless the West negotiates a Berlin settlement.

Bits and pieces purporting to show the Soviet leader's plans and intentions were being dropped here all day by Communist sources. But nothing was forthcoming to answer clearly the major question bedeviling Allied diplomats:

What led the Soviet Premier to torpedo the summit conference before it ever got going?

Internal Pressures Seen

Two theses are being exchanged among the diplomats. They are essentially contradictory, but a common thread runs through them. It is that Mr. Khrushchev is under stronger pressure from his political opponents throughout the Communist bloc and not only in the Soviet Union than at any time since he won power.

The favored thesis was that Premier Khrushchev, with his position frozen, that a decision had been taken in Moscow beforehand to prevent any conference by posing what were patently inacceptable conditions to the President of the United States.

The minority view was that something happened to force a policy switch on Mr. Khrushchev during the week.

Mr. Khrushchev made what was generally regarded as a conciliatory statement on arriving here Saturday but utterly abandoned that attitude the next day.

In that connection some

Continued on Page 15, Column 5

TRANQUIL INTERLUDE: President Eisenhower and Prime Minister Macmillan stroll about the grounds of the villa in Marnes-la-Coquette, where the President lived in 1951 and 1952 as the commander of the North Atlantic Treaty Organization forces in Europe.

United Press International Radiophoto

WIELDING THE AXE: Premier Khrushchev chops wood near Sézanne, France.

Radiophoto to The New York Times (by Erich Lessing—Magnum)

DEMOCRATS HINT 'BLUNDERS' PROBE

But Mansfield and Johnson Emphasize United Front During Crisis in Paris

By RUSSELL BAKER

Special to The New York Times.

WASHINGTON, May 17—Democratic Congressional leaders created a temporary united front behind President Eisenhower today for the duration of the summit crisis but hinted at possible investigations to come.

Senator Mike Mansfield of Montana, the Senate's deputy Democratic leader, said that questions about Administration "blunders" preceding the Paris conference "must be asked," but only "at the proper time."

While the President is still in Paris and the Soviet Union is threatening to create a fresh German crisis that could bring "all peoples to the edge of catastrophe" is not the right time, he told the Senate.

Lyndon B. Johnson of Texas, the Democratic Senate leader, agreed that first priority should be given to maintaining a united national front behind the President in the present period of uncertainty.

Johnson Bars Division

"If there have been mistakes, responsibility will be assessed coolly and objectively," he said. "But one mistake that we cannot afford to make right now is to weaken the free world by division within our own ranks."

Behind these speeches by the Senate's two Democratic leaders was the conviction that to permit a great national debate at this point might strengthen Premier Khrushchev's indictment of the United States Government and further embarrass President Eisenhower.

By tacit agreement with the leadership, most Congressional Democrats suspended criticism of the Administration and waited nervously for further developments in Paris.

Many Republicans were conceding today that even if the Administration got out of Paris without additional trouble, the party had been politically hurt for the election campaign ahead.

Moreover, the calm that even if Senators Johnson and Mansfield

Continued on Page 14, Column 5

The Western Communique

By the Associated Press

PARIS, May 17—Following is a joint communiqué issued tonight by Britain, France and the United States:

The President of the United States, the President of the French Republic and the Prime Minister of the United Kingdom take note of the fact that because of the attitude adopted by the Chairman of the Council of Ministers of the Soviet Union it has not been possible to begin, at the summit conference, the examination of the problems which it had been agreed would be discussed between the four chiefs of state or government.

They regret that these discussions, so important for world peace, could not take place. For their part, they remain unshaken in their conviction that all outstanding international questions should be settled not by the use or threat of force but by peaceful means through negotiation. They themselves remain ready to take part in such negotiations at any suitable time in the future.

PRELATE IN CUBA DENOUNCES REDS

Archbishop Urges Fight— Stand Could Bring Death

By R. HART PHILLIPS

Special to The New York Times.

HAVANA, May 17—A pastoral letter attacking communism and urging Cuban Roman Catholics to combat this "enemy within our gates" has been issued by the Archbishop of Santiago de Cuba, Msgr. Enrique Pérez Serantes.

The letter, which the Archbishop ordered read in churches of his archdiocese of Oriente Province, was published in Havana today by Información and El Crisol, Cuba's only independent newspapers. The Government press and radio ignored the pastoral.

This letter has special significance since anti-communism has been declared by the Government of Premier Fidel Castro to be synonymous with "counter-revolutionary activities," punishable by death before a firing squad or long imprisonment.

Castro's Ranks Split

The letter caused a sensation in the island, particularly since Archbishop Pérez Serantes has long been a close friend of Premier Castro and is credited with having saved the life of the revolutionary leader in 1953.

At that time, following an unsuccessful attack by Dr. Castro and a group of young revolutionaries on the Moncava army post of Santiago de Cuba, the Archbishop protected Dr. Castro and obtained assurances for his life from the authorities while others of the group were being hunted down and killed.

Communism is a major issue in Cuba and has split the ranks of Premier Castro's own revolutionary followers. The issue has

Continued on Page 5, Column 3

LUMUMBA RISING AS A CONGO RULER

Defies Belgians as He Builds Power in Interior Region

By HOMER BIGART

Special to The New York Times.

STANLEYVILLE, Belgian Congo, May 17—Belgian authority is collapsing in part of the Congo.

Patrice Emergy Lumumba, Congolese nationalist leader, is taking over as virtual dictator of this city and much of the Stanleyville and Eastern Provinces.

Not even the arrival of Belgian troop reinforcements is likely to halt the rapid erosion of the colonial administration's authority. Forty-five days before Congolese independence the Belgian administration already seems subservient to the nationalists.

Ban on Meetings Defied

M. Lumumba saw reports of troops arrivals at the Kamina military base in Katanga Province as an "attempt to intimidate the voters and influence the election in favor of Belgian selected candidates." He said he had sent a telegram to King Baudouin of the Belgians demanding the recall of the troops. He did not seem unduly worried, however.

Yesterday, in a moment of painful humiliation for the Belgian settlers, M. Lumumba defied a ban on public meetings. He did it in the heart of the city that jailed him last October for inciting riots.

The incident marked the beginning of a triumphal tour by M. Lumumba of the region north of Stanleyville. There, in villages deep in the equatorial forest, he demanded and received assurances from Belgian officials that watchers from his party, the National Congolese Movement, would be allowed at

Continued on Page 6, Column 3

CHARGES TRADED

Allies Leave the Door Open to New Talk— Soviet Scores U.S.

By DREW MIDDLETON

Special to The New York Times.

PARIS, May 17—The summit conference died tonight. The leaders of the West said Premier Khrushchev had killed it. The Russians blamed the United States.

President Eisenhower, Prime Minister Macmillan and President de Gaulle feel "complete disgust" at the attitude of the Soviet delegation has taken over in the last two days, James C. Hagerty, White House press secretary, reported.

In a communiqué issued this evening, the three Western chiefs declared that the Soviet leader's attitude had made it impossible to begin examination of the problems that it had been agreed should be discussed.

Apology Was Demanded

Premier Khrushchev had refused to meet with the Western leaders, on the invitation of President de Gaulle, unless President Eisenhower apologized for United States espionage flights over the Soviet Union. This the President "was not prepared to do.

The meeting, so long prepared and so anxiously awaited, expired in an atmosphere of gloomy foreboding. Diplomats of the three Western powers feared the world situation would deteriorate.

The Western leaders pledged their support to a settlement of all outstanding international issues by negotiation rather than by the use or threat of force. France, Britain and the United States remain ready for such negotiations "at any suitable time in the future," a communiqué said.

Soviet in Sharp Attack

A few minutes after the communiqué had been made public, a group of leading Soviet editors answered it with a sharp denunciation of the United States. The conference foundered, a Soviet statement said, because "aggressive actions" of the United States Government and the Administration's failure to accept responsibility had "torpedoed the conference which the peoples of the whole world were awaiting with such hopes."

The Western leaders will meet again tomorrow afternoon at a preliminary conference between their foreign ministers, Christian A. Herter, Selwyn Lloyd and Maurice Couve de Murville. These meetings, Western diplomats said, will review

Continued on Page 14, Column 1

COLLAPSE FEARED FOR GENEVA TALK

Summit Breakdown Likely to Affect Nuclear-Test and Arms Discussion

By A. M. ROSENTHAL

Special to The New York Times.

PARIS, May 17—The East-West negotiations in Geneva on disarmament and on a nuclear test ban were collapsing today.

Premier Khrushchev's decision to boycott the summit meeting convinced Western diplomats that the chances for agreement on disarmament and the ending of nuclear tests had been blown to bits and would take considerable time to paste together again.

The West was going on the assumption that the Soviet Union would not immediately call off the two sets of negotiations.

Russians were saying that the Khrushchev tactics at the summit did not mean that the Geneva talks would be called off. But the opinion of diplomats here was that the political foundation for agreement had been smashed.

American sources said tonight that the prospects for both conferences had been pushed back, if not destroyed.

Foreign Secretary Selwyn Lloyd of Britain said the breakdown at the summit need not wreck the two Geneva meetings.

The Western delegations were expecting the Soviet Union to take the issue of the U-2 reconnaissance plane to Geneva and make it their political centerpiece at the disarmament negotiations. Moscow has repeatedly said the West is more interested in espionage than dis-

Continued on Page 15, Column 7

KHRUSHCHEV STEP REKNITS NATO TIE

Allies Feel Premier Carried U-2 Exploitation Too Far

By ROBERT C. DOTY

Special to The New York Times.

PARIS, May 17—Soviet intransigence, applied this time to bringing the summit conference to a halt, has again served to restore the cohesion of the North Atlantic Treaty Organization.

The conclusion of NATO secretariat officials of the United States and of smaller powers today was that Premier Khrushchev had again played his hand badly in exploitation of Soviet grievances arising from the downing of the United States U-2 reconnaissance plane over the Soviet Union May 1.

The same officials were unwilling to predict the long-term effects on the Atlantic alliance of the events since Sunday. New, heavy Soviet pressure on Berlin—one of the possibilities—would reimpose severe strains on the military and political resources of NATO.

But for the present at least, resentment of Soviet tactics here has largely overshadowed the

Continued on Page 14, Column 7

Jovial Khrushchev Has Rural Holiday

By OSGOOD CARUTHERS

PARIS, May 17—Premier Khrushchev spent a happy day outdoors in France today despite all the efforts of the Western leaders to get him indoors for a session of the summit conference.

With seeming abandon, the leader of the Soviet Union spent the day doing the things he wanted to do when he came to France on a state visit two months ago. Meanwhile, the tense and anxious leaders of the West waited for him to save his summit from catastrophe.

Mr. Khrushchev held sidewalk and barnyard news conferences. He dashed up to startled Frenchmen and shook their

Continued on Page 14, Column 7

210

The New York Times.

LATE CITY EDITION

U. S. Weather Bureau Report (Page 54) forecasts:
Cloudy, chance of showers today. Fair, cooler, less humid tomorrow.
Temp. range: 84—72; yesterday: 83.2—70.
Temp.-Hum. Index: high 70's; yesterday: 78.

VOL. CIX—No. 37,427.   © 1960, by The New York Times Company. Times Square, New York 36, N. Y.   NEW YORK, THURSDAY, JULY 14, 1960.   10 cents beyond 50-mile zone from New York City except on Long Island. Higher in air delivery cities.   FIVE CENTS

KENNEDY NOMINATED ON THE FIRST BALLOT; OVERWHELMS JOHNSON BY 806 VOTES TO 409

Security Council Authorizes U. N. Force to Aid Congo

PEACE UNIT VOTED

U. S. and Soviet Clash in Debate—Belgians Asked to Pull Out

Congolese texts, resolution, debate excerpts, Page 4.

By THOMAS J. HAMILTON
Special to The New York Times.

UNITED NATIONS, N. Y., Thursday, July 14 — The Security Council authorized Secretary General Dag Hammarskjold today to organize and send a United Nations force to the Congo.

The vote was eight in favor and none against, with Britain, France and Nationalist China abstaining.

The vote was taken at 3:03 A. M., nearly six and a half hours after the Security Council, at the request of Mr. Hammarskjold, began its urgent night session. The decision was delayed by bitter exchanges between the United States and Soviet representatives, Henry Cabot Lodge and Arkady A. Sobolev. The Council adjourned at 3:21 A. M.

Outcome Was Uncertain

The outcome remained uncertain until the last. It was known that Britain, France and Nationalist China would abstain. They objected to a provision in the resolution, which was introduced by Tunisia, calling for the withdrawal of Belgian troops from the Congo.

The withdrawal recommendation was included on the demand of the Soviet Union and the African states. However, word was passed during the long meeting that the Soviet Union and Poland had not received instructions on the Tunisian proposal, and would therefore abstain if the United States insisted upon a vote at this meeting.

This belief was strengthened after Walter Loridan, the Belgian representative, announced that Belgian troops would be withdrawn from the Congo when the United Nations force is able to provide "effective" maintenance of order.

Mr. Sobolev termed this statement unsatisfactory. He introduced amendments condemning Belgian "armed aggression" in the Congo, stating that the Belgian forces must be withdrawn "immediately," and limiting participation in the United Nations force to the other African states.

The first two amendments were rejected 7 to 2, with only the Soviet Union and Poland

Continued on Page 4, Column 3

HOGAN WILL PRESS A NEW JACK TRIAL

Fall Date to Be Asked Today in Borough Chief's Case

By PETER FLINT

A date for a new trial for Borough President Hulan E. Jack of Manhattan on charges of conflict of interest and conspiracy will be requested by District Attorney Frank S. Hogan today in the Court of General Sessions.

Since the court is now in summer recess, with only three of the nine judges sitting, the prosecutor is expected to ask for a date in the fall.

Mr. Jack's first trial ended last Thursday night when the jury failed to agree on a verdict after two days of deliberation and was discharged.

Mr. Jack's lawyer, Carson DeWitt Baker, said he would request an immediate trial. But he expressed the view that Mr. Hogan would "have his way as usual," and that the new trial probably would begin in October.

Mr. Baker also expressed "firm conviction" that the Borough President would continue his self-suspension from office until the case was resolved. Mr.

Continued on Page 25, Column 5

Belgian Commandos Rout Congo Troops at Airport

Bunche Meets With Both Sides to Try to Halt Clashes—Congolese Open Fire on Convoy of Refugees

By HENRY TANNER
Special to The New York Times.

LEOPOLDVILLE, the Congo, July 13—Belgian commandos occupied Leopoldville's airport today and then clashed with Congolese troops. At least six Congolese and two Belgians were killed.

Belgian forces occupied the airport at midmorning. They went into action after Congolese soldiers had moved into the airport and had threatened to interfere with the evacuation of Belgian civilians by Sabena, the Belgian airline.

[Leopoldville was reported by press associations to be under the control of Belgian troops, but there was uncertainty over the extent of control. Congolese troops opened fire on Wednesday night on a convoy of 300 Belgians heading for the airport. Reuters said the Congo Government had declared that a "state of war" existed with Belgium. The Congo has asked Ghana to send troops.

[In Brussels, the Belgian Government said it would keep troops at key points in the Congo.]

Dr. Ralph J. Bunche, United Nations Under Secretary, met with Congolese authorities and Ambassador Jean van den Bosch of Belgium this afternoon in an effort to halt the clashes. He left the United States Embassy, where he has an office, in the early afternoon with the blue United Nations flag flying

Continued on Page 3, Column 2

KISHI IS STABBED AT HOME IN TOKYO

Japan's Premier Is Reported Not Badly Hurt—Ikeda Chosen His Successor

By RICHARD J. H. JOHNSTON
Special to The New York Times.

TOKYO, Thursday, July 14—Premier Nobusuke Kishi was attacked by an assassin and stabbed in the thigh within an hour after his apparent successor had been elected by his party.

The Premier was attacked at a reception in his official residence. The attacker was identified by the authorities as Taizo Aramaki, a Rightist, about 45 years old.

Mr. Kishi was removed to a nearby hospital, where it was announced that his condition was not serious.

His assailant was arrested.

The police established the time of the attack at 2:30 P. M. This would be within forty minutes of Mr. Kishi's departure from Hibiya Hall in Downtown Tokyo, where the Liberal-Democratic party convention had been held.

The reception at the Premier's home was arranged to honor Hayato Ikeda, who, less than an hour before had been elected in the convention of the governing party as its new president, replacing Mr. Kishi, who had resigned in the convention a short time before.

Mr. Ikeda, now Trade Minister, backs the Kishi policies.

The attack on the 63-year-old Premier was an ironic twist in the turbulent politics of recent months in Japan.

On June 23 he had announced

Continued on Page 11, Column 2

Peru Urges O.A.S. Debate Red Threat; U. S. Favors Parley

Special to The New York Times.

WASHINGTON, July 13 — Peru has suggested that the foreign ministers of the American nations meet soon to consider the Soviet threat to inter-American unity and democracy in the Western Hemisphere.

Informed sources said the Peruvian initiative was welcomed by the United States and that Washington would support the proposal. It is believed that the Peruvian suggestion will be considered at a meeting this week of the Council of the Organization of American States.

The Peruvian suggestion was circulated today among representatives of the twenty-one members of the O.A.S. It was also the subject of urgent consultation at embassies and in the State Department.

Peru's proposal was couched in careful diplomatic language, but its meaning was clear. The message stressed the necessity for the continued solidarity of the countries of this hemisphere. It called for the defense of the regional system in inter-American affairs and of democratic principles.

There was no specific refer-

Continued on Page 12, Column 5

2 Planes Down Off Philippines; 86 of 88 Aboard Saved From Sea

Two Lost as U. S. Airliner Ditches—Island DC-3 Also Crashes, 30 on It Safe

By United Press International.

MANILA, Thursday, July 14—An American airplane and a Philippine passenger plane went down at sea in separate accidents today with a total of eighty-eight persons aboard. But eighty-six were reported safe after swift, dramatic rescue from shark-dangerous waters.

At least thirty-four Americans were aboard one of the planes, a Northwest Orient Airlines DC7-C on the last leg of a New York-to-Manila flight with fifty-one passengers and a crew of seven.

United States air force amphibious planes from Clark Field reported the rescue of fifty-two passengers and crew of the Northwest plane. One person was reported killed and one missing.

The Northwest plane, which had come from New York via Seattle, Anchorage, Tokyo and Okinawa, crash-landed near the little island of Jimalog, of the Potillo group about 150 miles northeast of Manila, after a propeller "ran away" and fell off and a wing caught fire.

Capt. David Rall, 53 years old of Seattle, deliberately put the plane down at sea after the radio cut out at 4:20 A. M. [4:20 P. M.

Passengers on the Northwest

Continued on Page 12, Column 4

Union Forcing Plant To Return to City

By A. H. RASKIN

An arbitrator has ordered a New York clothing manufacturer to reopen his closed factory here and to pay the Amalgamated Clothing Workers union more than $200,000 in damages for having moved his work to Mississippi.

The employer, who lost a court fight to block arbitration, made it clear yesterday that he would resist the unusual award through new litigation.

The union is confident that recent decisions of the United States Supreme Court strengthening the power of arbitrators and limiting the right of judges to upset their awards will bar a successful challenge.

Jacob S. Potofsky, president of the Amalgamated, hailed the award as proof that "runaway

Continued on Page 55, Column 4

MOSCOW BIDS U. N. CONVENE AT ONCE ON RB-47 INCIDENT

Says Flights by U. S. Planes With Reconnaissance Aim Are Threat to Peace

By OSGOOD CARUTHERS
Special to The New York Times.

MOSCOW, July 13—The Soviet Union called today for an urgent meeting of the United Nations Security Council to discuss its charges of United States "aggressive actions."

The Soviet complaint derived from the shooting down of a United States RB-47 reconnaissance plane off the Soviet coast in the Barents Sea on July 1.

[In a statement from the summer White House at Newport, R. I., the United States backed a full investigation by the United Nations of the "wanton shooting down" of the plane.]

Moscow called for the United Nations meeting in a cablegram sent by Foreign Minister Andrei A. Gromyko today to the president of the Security Council, José A. Correa of Ecuador.

Hammarskjold Gets Copy

The message, a copy of which was sent to Secretary General Dag Hammarskjold, charged that the United States flights constituted "a serious threat to the preservation of peace."

The United States has denied that the RB-47 plane had violated Soviet territorial waters as alleged by the Kremlin.

The Soviet request came on the heels of a statement yesterday by Premier Khrushchev that his Government might take the matter of the plane before the Security Council.

He said he did not expect that the Security Council, which he described as an "instrument" of the United States, would take any action satisfactory to the Soviet Union. However, he said he thought it was necessary to raise the question there anyway if only to "discredit the dishonest judges once more."

Mr. Gromyko's cablegram, which he said would be followed by an explanatory letter, noted that the Security Council had discussed the previous plane incident, in which a U-2 reconnaissance jet was shot down deep inside Soviet territory on May 1.

The message asked the Security Council to "take such measures as appear necessary to put an end to these dangers

Continued on Page 6, Column 5

AFTER THE VICTORY: Senator John F. Kennedy of Massachusetts heads for rostrum at Los Angeles Memorial Sports Arena to address the Democratic National Convention.

Associated Press Wirephoto

JOHNSON PLEDGES HELP TO KENNEDY

He Assures Candidate of His Full Support and Issues a Call for Party Unity

By JOHN D. MORRIS
Special to The New York Times.

LOS ANGELES, July 13—Senator Lyndon B. Johnson accepted tonight "with all my heart" Senator John F. Kennedy's nomination for President.

The Texan, who had watched the convention proceedings by television in his suite at the Biltmore Hotel, issued a four-paragraph statement just as the first ballot ended. It had been prepared in anticipation of a Kennedy victory.

"The delegates have made their decision and I accept it with all my heart.

"Senator Kennedy has my sincere congratulations, and my solemn assurance that in the coming months of this campaign, no one will be more dedicated than I—no one will work harder than I to make doubly sure of what all Democrats here and throughout the country know must come about for America and the free world—that John F. Kennedy will be elected the next President of the United States.

"We have a winner—he has proved it here.

"Now, let our party unite behind our candidate—let us sweep the country this November, so that in January Democrats

Continued on Page 15, Column 6

Plan to End Strike On L.I.R.R. Offered

Governor Rockefeller's fact-finding board proposed an arbitration plan last night to bring an immediate end to the Long Island Rail Road strike.

The plan was rejected almost at once by the union's negotiating committee. It charged that most arbitrators had been "so brainwashed by the propaganda of the Association of American Railroads and the National Association of Manufacturers" that labor could not trust them.

The rejection will be reviewed by the 1,350 strikers at a meeting this morning, but union leaders said they would "bet a million dollars that the men will turn the idea down unanimously."

The company said the union's reaction made further study of the plan seem academic. It

Continued on Page 20, Column 2

Symington Heavy Favorite For Second Place on Ticket

By LEO EGAN
Special to The New York Times.

LOS ANGELES, July 13 — Senator Stuart Symington became a heavy favorite for the Vice-Presidential nomination tonight following Senator John F. Kennedy's first-ballot nomination for President. The Missouri delegation was the first to swing into line behind Senator Kennedy after the New Englander had clinched the nomination for first place.

At the Kennedy headquarters in the Biltmore Hotel it was announced that the Presidential nominee would meet with those under consideration for Vice President and with party leaders from all sections of the country before going to bed.

Before the convention opened, he had promised the New York delegation, which was an important factor in his victory, that he would consult with its leaders before making a choice on second place.

Senator Symington parried questions about the Vice-Presidential nomination with the comment that the matter was entirely up to Senator Kennedy.

Good Word for Jackson

Although the Missouri Senator was regarded as the front runner for the Vice-Presidential nomination, two others were receiving serious consideration. They were Gov. Orville L. Freeman of Minnesota, who had placed the New Englander in nomination, and Senator Henry M. Jackson of Washington State.

At a meeting of the Washington delegation today, Robert F. Kennedy, the Senator's brother and floor manager, said that Senator Jackson was his (Robert's) personal choice for the place but that political considerations might force his brother to turn elsewhere.

Governor Freeman had also been informed that those around Senator Kennedy had a high regard for him and that he would be acceptable as a Vice-Presidential candidate.

Up to the hour of Senator Kennedy's nomination, Senator Symington and Representative Charles A. Brown of Missouri, his campaign manager, were declaring that Senator Symington was not a candidate. But few delegates accepted this at

Continued on Page 15, Column 2

STEVENSON GIVEN A WILD RECEPTION

His Nomination Touches Off Roaring Demonstration— It Lasts 25 Mintues

By WILLIAM M. BLAIR
Special to The New York Times.

LOS ANGELES, July 13—A wild, emotional demonstration for Adlai E. Stevenson shook the Democratic National Convention tonight.

As the name of the man who led the Democrats in 1952 and 1956 was placed before the convention, the galleries erupted in a screaming roar that dwarfed all that went before.

A rip-roaring nominating speech by Senator Eugene J. McCarthy, an "egghead" from Minnesota, set off the nearest thing to hysteria that this convention has seen.

Although the demonstrators obviously were full of enthusiasm, it was also obvious that the demonstration was at least partly contrived.

It took the convention chairman, Gov. LeRoy Collins of Florida, twenty-five minutes to slow down the stamping, shouting show to get seconding speeches.

Supporters Storm Floor

Stevenson supporters from outside the convention stormed the floor, some apparently gaining entrance by ruses, to call for the man who said he did not come West to seek the nomination.

Chanting, placard - waving demonstrators jammed the aisles while the galleries suddenly came alive with thousands of placards and hundreds of demonstrators going round and round in a deafening din.

The bobbing, weaving demonstrators on the floor, many of them young persons, caused many delegates to cover their ears. And many covered their heads with their hands as the Stevenson rooters bounced a giant, white papier-mâché ball through the air. The ball represented a snowball intended to dramatize today's third attempt at a "Draft Stevenson" effort.

For the most part, the delegates appeared unmoved by the

Continued on Page 15, Column 2

LONG DRIVE WINS

Wyoming's Vote Puts Bostonian Over Top Before Acclamation

Kennedy's talk on Page 14; nominating speeches, 16.

By W. H. LAWRENCE
Special to The New York Times.

LOS ANGELES, Thursday, July 14—Senator John F. Kennedy smashed his way to a first-ballot Presidential nomination at the Democratic National Convention last night and won the right to oppose Vice President Richard M. Nixon in November.

The 43-year-old Massachusetts Senator overwhelmed his opposition, piling up 806 votes to 409 ballots for his nearest rival, Senator Lyndon B. Johnson of Texas, the Senate majority leader. Senator Kennedy's victory came just before 11 o'clock last night [2 A. M. Thursday, New York time].

Then the convention made it unanimous on motion of Gov. James T. Blair Jr. of Missouri, who had placed Senator Stuart Symington of Missouri in nomination.

'We Shall Win'

Senator Kennedy, appearing before the shouting convention early today, pledged he would carry the fight to the country in the fall "and we shall win."

He thanked his defeated rivals for their generosity and appealed to all of their backers to keep the party strong and united in a tremendously important election. He spoke directly of Senators Johnson and Symington and the favorite sons, but made no reference to Adlai E. Stevenson.

The third session of the national convention adjourned after his speech. The next session will convene at 5 P. M. today.

Little Wyoming, well down the roll-call, provided the decisive fifteen votes that gave victory to Senator Kennedy. Two favorite-son states, Minnesota and New Jersey, waited in vain to give the on-rushing Kennedy bandwagon the final shove.

When Wyoming came in with its vote, the Kennedy total had mounted to 765 votes, or four more than the 761 votes required for nomination.

It was a tremendous victory for Senator Kennedy. Mr. Johnson, the Senate majority leader, had fought desperately to reverse a Kennedy tide that had been running for months. But Senator Johnson quickly telephoned his congratulations to

Continued on Page 14, Column 1

F.H.A. INVESTMENT OPENED TO PUBLIC

Individuals Invited to Deal in U. S.-Insured Mortgages

By RICHARD E. MOONEY
Special to The New York Times.

WASHINGTON, July 13—The Government invited individuals today to invest in mortgages insured against loss by the Federal Housing Administration.

It was, in effect, an offer of a long-term investment that could earn the investor more than 5 per cent and would be paid off by the Government if the mortgage went into default.

The yields of representative stocks and bonds currently are lower than 5 per cent.

Investment in an F. H. A.-insured mortgage is not riskless. The investor would have to hold his investment until the mortgage was paid off in full in the event that he did not sell it before, then he might be at a loss.

Besides being an attractive offer, and a break with policy of twenty-five years' standing, the Federal Housing Administration's third stimulant to today's action was the Government's third attempt to stimulate sagging activity in home building in many months.

In April, the F. H. A. reduced

Continued on Page 55, Column 4

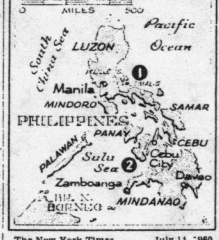

Sites of crash of U. S. plane (1) and Philippines plane (2)

The New York Times   July 14, 1960

The New York Times.

LATE CITY EDITION
U. S. Weather Bureau Report (Page 54) forecasts:
Mostly fair and warm today,
tonight and tomorrow.
Temp. range: 84—65; yesterday: 72.9—68.9.
Temp.-Hum. index: 76; yesterday: 71.

VOL. CIX..No. 37,441. © 1960, by The New York Times Company. NEW YORK, THURSDAY, JULY 28, 1960. 10 cents beyond 50-mile zone from New York City except on Long Island. Higher in air delivery cities. FIVE CENTS

NIXON IS GIVEN NOMINATION BY ACCLAMATION AFTER GOLDWATER GETS 10 LOUISIANA VOTES; CANDIDATE PICKS LODGE FOR SECOND PLACE

SANITATION UNION QUITS IN PROTEST; GARBAGE PILES UP

5,000 March on City Hall as Wage Talks Break Off —Walkout May Go On

By LAYHMOND ROBINSON

Thousands of tons of refuse were left lying on city streets yesterday when angry sanitation workers suddenly stopped work to protest a breakdown in wage negotiations with the city.

The Sanitation Department reported that at least 4,600 of the 5,000 garbage collectors, street cleaners and incinerator employes on the day shift had failed to report for duty at 7 A. M. They may not report today, either.

Instead, the shouting, chanting city employes, augmented by 1,000 fellow workers who were on vacation or had days off, marched to City Hall.

They besieged the building for several hours, created a traffic jam and gave a 100-man police detail some anxious moments in holding the surging crowd behind barricades. However, there was no violence, though the police took the precaution of locking the doors of City Hall.

Meeting Collapses

Later in the day, a collapse of a hastily arranged meeting between union and city negotiators brought predictions that the walkout, which the union has denied is a strike, might last for some time.

Last night, as a result of the walkout, Traffic Commissioner T. T. Wiley announced that alternate-side parking rules would be lifted here today. Motorists may ignore signs that normally prohibit parking on Thursdays between 8 A. M. and 11 A. M. and 11 A. M. and 2 P. M. The department has not decided yet what it will do about parking regulations tomorrow.

City Demands Return

At the meeting between union and city negotiators, the spokesmen for the city, acting under instruction from the Board of Estimate, demanded that the men return to work before negotiations were resumed. Union negotiators rejected the demand and vowed to stay out until the city came up with a better offer on wages and fringe benefits.

The state's Condon-Wadlin Law prohibits strikes by Civil Service employes but Mayor Wagner would not say yesterday whether he viewed the stoppage as a strike, nor would he say whether the law would be invoked for the first time here.

Union members did not report for the night shift. The Sanitation Department said only a handful had showed up for night duty, which begins at 4 P. M. Usually about 700 men work the night shift in the summer.

The Sanitation Commissioner warned the men involved that they would be docked a day's pay for each day they refused

Continued on Page 11, Column 4

Iran Cuts Cairo Tie In Dispute on Israel

By Reuters.

TEHERAN, Iran, July 27—Iran severed diplomatic relations with the United Arab Republic today and gave Cairo's Ambassador here twenty-four hours to get out of the country.

The severance was announced by Foreign Minister Abbas Aram after he had served the expulsion order on the Ambassador, Mahmoud Hammad.

Mr. Aram said the move to oust Mr. Hammad was made after President Gamal Abdel Nasser attacked Shah Mohammed Riza Pahlevi of Iran yesterday in a speech at Alexandria. President Nasser said the Shah for his statement Saturday that Iran had recognized Israel.

The Iranian Foreign Minister described President Nasser as

Continued on Page 5, Column 1

Stock Margin Rate Is Cut To 70% by Reserve Board

Officials Deny Reduction From 90% Is Aimed at Shoring Up the Market— Economic Significance Minimized

By TOM WICKER
Special to The New York Times.

WASHINGTON, July 27—The margin requirement for purchases of stocks was reduced from 90 to 70 per cent today by the Federal Reserve Board.

The reduction is effective tomorrow. It reflects the belief of the board of governors of the Federal Reserve that stock market credit is relatively stable at this time.

The margin requirement governs the minimum cash payment a stock buyer must make. As an example, today's action will reduce from $900 to $700 the amount of cash that must be put up for each $1,000 of stock.

The reduction also applies to short sales, in which a trader borrows stock and sells it in the hope of buying it back later at a lower price and thus making a profit.

The margin requirement is a device by which the Federal Re-serve attempts to prevent excessive use of credit in the stock market. A spokesman said today the board of governors "just thinks 70 per cent will do it" under today's conditions.

The price of common stocks has declined recently. But the spokesman denied that today's action was an attempt to shore up prices or to stimulate credit and speculative activity.

He conceded, however, that since a trader could pick up more stock with the same amount of money, beginning tomorrow, the reduction might have an initial effect on the volume of transactions.

Despite the fact that the latest change before today's in margin requirements—an advance from 70 to 90 per cent on Oct. 16, 1958—came when the

Continued on Page 37, Column 1

FRENCH 'SLIGHTS' ANGER ADENAUER

He Will Leave for Week-End Paris Talks Only Because His Hand Was Forced

By SYDNEY GRUSON
Special to The New York Times.

BONN, Germany, July 27—Chancellor Adenauer will fly to Paris for talks with President de Gaulle Friday, but in a furious mood and only because the French forced his hand.

Both Paris and Bonn announced the meeting this afternoon and said the main subject of the talks would be the political integration of Western Europe.

But the background to this laconic announcement was far more dramatic. The Chancellor had been infuriated by a number of what he considers slights to West Germany by France and had determined not to go through with the meeting this week-end.

The French, aware of his mood, let it be known last night to West German reporters in Paris and to some French newspapers that the meeting was on. Apparently rather than permit a crack for all the world to see in the painfully restored French-German friendship, the keystone of his European policy.

Continued on Page 2, Column 5

British Earl Named Foreign Secretary In Cabinet Shuffle

By DREW MIDDLETON
Special to The New York Times.

LONDON, July 27 — Prime Minister Macmillan chose the Earl of Home as Britain's new Foreign Secretary today in a major reconstruction of the Conservative Government.

Selwyn Lloyd leaves the Foreign Office to become Chancellor of the Exchequer. A successful tenure there would improve Mr. Lloyd's prospects as the future Prime Minister.

Lord Home (whose name is pronounced Hume) is the first peer to be Foreign Secretary since Lord Halifax held the office twenty years ago. The official announcement of his appointment this evening brought to a climax the mounting criticism of the last five days.

Mr. Macmillan will be forced to defend his choice against the Labor party's censure in a House of Commons debate tomorrow night.

The objections to the appointment of Lord Home were based on two points. First, the critics said, the Foreign Secretary should be a member of the House of Commons and answerable if the House to any questions on foreign policy. Second, the objectors maintained, there was nothing in Lord Home's career to justify the appointment.

The first newspaper comment

Continued on Page 2, Column 2

CHIEFS CONSULTED

Bricker Is Expected to Place U.N. Aide in Nomination

By LEO EGAN

CHICAGO, Thursday, July 28—Henry Cabot Lodge, delegate to the United Nations, was picked today by Vice President Richard M. Nixon to be his running mate.

Mr. Nixon revealed his preference a few hours after he himself had been nominated for President by the Republican convention.

Mr. Nixon came out of his room and made this announcement:

"I have reached a decision that I shall recommend to the convention Henry Cabot Lodge."

He said he would call Mr. Lodge at his New York home and ask if he would accept. He said he expected the decision to be affirmative.

Mr. Nixon made the announcement at 2:20 A. M. Central daylight time (3:20 A. M. New York time).

This decision all but assured Mr. Lodge's nomination for Vice President when the convention votes tonight on that post.

Mr. Nixon made the selection in consultation with leading Republicans in a meeting that began at his hotel about a half hour after the adjournment of last night's session of the convention.

Choice Not Unanimous

New York was represented at the meeting by L. Judson Morhouse, its Republican State Chairman.

The choice of Mr. Lodge was far from unanimous. However, Mr. Nixon insisted upon the Presidential nominee's right to choose his running mate.

Earlier yesterday, Mr. Nixon listed the 58-year-old former Massachusetts Senator as one of the four front runners for the vice-presidential nomination.

The three others were:

Senator Thruston B. Morton of Kentucky, the 52-year-old Republican National Chairman.

Representative Walter R. Judd of Minnesota, now 61 years old, who delivered the keynote address to the convention on Monday.

Robert B. Anderson, the 50-year-old Secretary of the Treasury, a former Texas Democrat who became an Eisenhower Republican in 1952.

To offset Midwest opposition to Mr. Lodge, an arrangement was reported to have been made to have former Senator John W. Bricker of Ohio place his name in nomination. And Representative Gerald Ford of Michigan, a

Continued on Page 12, Column 5

AFTER THE DELEGATES VOTED: Vice President and Mrs. Nixon at their hotel in Chicago last night with their daughters, Patricia, left, 14 years old, and Julie, 12.

NIXON BOLSTERS ROCKEFELLER TIE

New York Delegation Greets Him Warmly — Governor to Campaign Anywhere

By WARREN WEAVER Jr.
Special to The New York Times.

CHICAGO, July 27—At political sword points only a week ago, Governor Rockefeller and Vice President Nixon joined today in a powerful demonstration of concord.

Mr. Nixon made a special morning trip two miles up Michigan Avenue to visit his new-found supporters in the New York delegation. The delegation endorsed him unanimously, if belatedly, yesterday.

The Governor went to the Sheraton Towers lobby to greet Mr. Nixon, like classmates at a reunion. Beaming, he escorted him to the closed caucus. They posed for pictures with arms around each other.

Mr. Rockefeller said the Vice President's visit had given the New Yorkers "a final inspiration and emotional lift."

"We're with you all the way," he promised.

Mr. Nixon was hardly less enthusiastic about the Governor. He pleaded with the New York

Continued on Page 14, Column 5

13 Dead in Chicago Crash Of 'Copter on Airport Run

By The Associated Press.

CHICAGO, July 27—A helicopter carrying passengers between airports suddenly lost power and plunged in a mass of flames into a suburban cemetery tonight. All thirteen persons aboard were killed. Wreckage was scattered over a wide area.

A swath of clipped tree tops almost 600 feet long indicated that the pilot had tried to gain altitude.

Witnesses said the craft, an S-58, carrying eleven passengers and a crew of two, stopped in air, zigzagged a moment and then plummeted, shooting flames.

The helicopter, owned by Chicago Helicopter Airways, Inc., was on an eleven-minute trip from Midway Airport on the Southwest side to O'Hare International Airport on the Northwest side.

Falls Near River

It plunged into the Forest Home Cemetery north of Roosevelt Road near the Des Plaines River. The crash site is between suburban Maywood and Forest Park.

An officer of the helicopter company landed near the crash scene and said that the pilot of the downed craft was Capt. Robert Meyer, 37 years old. The names of the other victims were not immediately available.

However, a company spokesman said "no one of national importance was known to be aboard." He apparently referred to the fact the Republican National Convention is meeting in Chicago.

The helicopter, which has a capacity of fourteen, including

Continued on Page 55, Column 2

Key Issues in Congo Awaiting U.N. Chief

By HENRY TANNER
Special to The New York Times.

LEOPOLDVILLE, the Congo, July 27—Secretary General Dag Hammarskjold is likely to be successful in paving the way for the peaceful entry of United Nations forces into Katanga Province, diplomatic observers here predict.

Mr. Hammarskjold is scheduled to arrive here tomorrow from Brussels. Katanga, which has declared its independence of the Congo, is expected to be the dominant issue in his consultations here. He will spend four or five days talking with Congolese, Belgian and United Nations officials.

Katanga is now controlled by Belgian forces that went there at the request of the provincial Premier, Moise Tshombe. Mr.

Continued on Page 2, Column 6

UNITY IS STRESSED

Goldwater Withdraws and Asks Backing for the Nominee

Hatfield's speech, Page 12; Goldwater text, Page 14.

By W. H. LAWRENCE
Special to The New York Times.

CHICAGO, Thursday, July 28—Vice President Richard M. Nixon swept to a first-ballot Republican Presidential nomination last night and the right to face Democratic Senator John F. Kennedy in the November election.

Early today, Mr. Nixon chose Henry Cabot Lodge, chief United States delegate to the United Nations, as his Vice-Presidential running mate.

Mr. Nixon received 1,321 votes on the polling of state delegations. Senator Barry Goldwater of Arizona received ten votes, cast by members of the twenty-six-vote Louisiana delegation even after the Arizonan had asked withdrawal of his name from consideration.

At the end of the roll-call, Louisiana moved to make Mr. Nixon's choice unanimous, but balked at changing its ten votes from the Goldwater to the Nixon column without a poll. When the roll-call vote was announced as 1,321 to 10, the Arizona delegation then moved to make the nomination unanimous, and this was done by acclamation.

Goldwater Asks Unity

The convention decision pits the 47-year-old Vice President against the 43-year-old Senator from Massachusetts. Mr. Nixon is the first Vice President in the history of the modern two-party system to win a Presidential nomination in his own right.

Senator Goldwater made the dramatic appearance of the night, calling upon all conservatives to back Mr. Nixon in November and avoid any party split or stay-at-home nonvoting attitude that would help Democrats "dedicated to the destruction of this country."

Withdrawing his own name from consideration for the Presidency, the Arizona Senator, an avowed conservative, said he had been campaigning for Mr. Nixon's nomination for the last six years and would fight for his election in November.

Lecture to Conservatives

"Let us put our shoulders to the wheel of Dick Nixon and push him over across the line," Senator Goldwater said.

He lectured conservatives sternly, telling them they must "grow up" and get to work "if we want to take this party back some day—and I think we can."

He said the Democratic party no longer was the party of Jefferson, Jackson and Wilson but now was ruled by "Bowles, Galbraith and Reuther." His references were to Representative Chester Bowles of Connecticut; Kenneth Galbraith, Harvard economist, and Walter P. Reu-

Continued on Page 12, Column 1

ROBERT KENNEDY EASES SPLIT HERE

Candidate's Brother Wins Prendergast's Approval of Independent Group

By CLAYTON KNOWLES

Robert F. Kennedy came to New York yesterday and brought Michael H. Prendergast around to an agreement that an independent citizens' committee could work effectively in the state for the election of Senator John F. Kennedy as President.

Mr. Prendergast, the Democratic state chairman, reversed his earlier opposition to such an auxiliary campaign unit during a two-and-a-half hour luncheon meeting with Mr. Kennedy, who is the manager of his brother's campaign for the Presidency.

Carmine G. De Sapio, Democratic national committeeman, who sat in on the session at the Hampshire House, asked if he, too, was satisfied. "One hundred per cent!" he said with emphasis.

The conference was one of five important meetings that Mr. Prendergast had during a busy day with representatives of virtually every shade of thinking within the Democratic party.

The session with Mr. Prendergast was of particular importance because Mr. Prendergast had understood originally that the campaign would be run strictly through the Democratic state organization.

Later, when the Senator agreed to establishing a Citizens for Kennedy committee here, Mr. Prendergast viewed the enterprise as competitive with the regular organization's work. He also viewed the individuals

Continued on Page 16, Column 1

Eisenhower Is Firm For Middle of Road

By DONALD JANSON
Special to The New York Times.

CHICAGO, July 27—President Eisenhower emphasized today the superiority of a middle political course over right or left extremes.

He denounced the Socialist philosophy of a "fairly friendly European country" he said he had been reading about in the last few weeks.

"The experiment of almost complete paternalism there, he said, has resulted in a sharp rise in the suicide rate, "more than twice our drunkenness," and a "lack of moderation discernible on all sides."

It was believed that he had alluded to Sweden. Its suicide rate is 19.9 for every 100,000 persons, compared with ten in

Continued on Page 14, Column 4

NEWS INDEX

	Page		Page
Books	25	Music	19-20
Bridge	24	Obituaries	27
Business	34-35	Real Estate	51
Buyers	43	Screen	19-20
Crossword	25	Ships and Air	54
Editorial	24	Society	31
Fashions	20-21	Sports	21-25
Financial	32-43	TV and Radio	53
Food	30-31	Theaters	19-20
Letters	24	U. N. Proceedings	12
Man in the News	14	Weather	54

News Summary and Index, Page 29

PROTEST AT CITY HALL: Employes of the Department of Sanitation rally against the breakdown of wage talks

The New York Times.

LATE CITY EDITION
U. S. Weather Bureau Report (Page 95) forecast:
Fair and warm today; fair tonight.
Chance of thunder showers tomorrow.

Temp. range: 83—68; yesterday: 82.3—63.4.
Temp.-Hum. index: near 77; yesterday: 76.

NEWS SUMMARY AND INDEX, PAGE 95

VOL. CIX . No. 37,465.   © 1960, by The New York Times Company.
Times Square, New York 36, N. Y.   NEW YORK, SUNDAY, AUGUST 21, 1960.   25c outside New York City, its suburban area and Long Island, 35c in 17 Western states, Canada; higher in air delivery cities.   SECTION ONE   THIRTY CENTS

NIXON ENDORSES NEW JAVITS PLAN FOR CARE OF AGED

Backs Contributory Medical Insurance Based on Aid From U. S. and States

MEANS TEST RULED OUT

Senator's Proposal Faces a Showdown With Kennedy's Social Security Set-Up

By TOM WICKER

WASHINGTON, Aug. 20—Vice President Nixon lent his support, today to a new program of contributory health insurance as the Senate opened a politically charged debate on the issue of medical care for the aged.

The new plan was introduced and strongly advocated by Senator Jacob K. Javits, the New York Republican.

It will be offered, he told reporters later, as an amendment to the relief-payments bill approved by the Senate Finance Committee. It will also be offered as a substitute for the Social Security plan backed by the Democratic Presidential candidate, Senator John F. Kennedy of Massachusetts.

Mr. Nixon, the Republican nominee, made no statement on the matter. Senator Javits said he had his support and a Nixon spokesman later asserted that the Vice President had helped the Senator to prepare the insurance program.

Similar Plan Recalled

Mr. Javits noted that he had introduced a similar plan in the House of Representatives in 1949. Mr. Nixon and Christian A. Herter, now Secretary of State, were among the co-sponsors.

The Javits plan is along the lines of the Eisenhower Administration's "medicare" voluntary insurance plan but offers considerably wider benefits. It is also more liberal in its not requiring a means test for beneficiaries and in being less costly for participants.

For these reasons, Senator Javits said he could not say he had the support of President Eisenhower. The Nixon spokesman said, however, that Arthur S. Flemming, Secretary of Health, Education and Welfare had also helped prepare the Javits program.

Saltonstall Backs Plan

Among Senator Javits' co-sponsors is Senator Leverett Saltonstall of Massachusetts, who introduced the Medicare scheme. Seven other Republicans also joined the New Yorker.

This program would make about 11,000,000 persons over 65 years of age eligible for health insurance, but not those with incomes over $3,000 for individuals or $4,500 for couples. The Federal and state governments would share in the cost of the insurance.

Senator Javits put the annual

Continued on Page 44, Column 1

Sports News

BASEBALL

The Yankees beat the Washington Senators, 9—5, yesterday with four runs in the eleventh inning — two on a homer by Bill Skowron. The victory kept the Yankees a game and a half ahead of the second-place White Sox. The White Sox defeated the Athletics, 3—0, on Herb Score's two-hit pitching. The Red Sox won from the Orioles, 8—6, in the afternoon. The Orioles won their night game, 6—0, in the National League, the first-place Pirates topped the Reds, 10—7.

HARNESS RACING

Hairos II, representing the Netherlands, won the $50,000 International Trot at Roosevelt Raceway. He paid $11.90 for $2. Crevalcore of Italy was second and Silver Song of the United States third.

HORSE RACING

Tompion, the $83,100 Travers Stakes at Saratoga. One-Eyed King took the Arlington Handicap at Chicago.

TENNIS

Rod Laver of Australia and Earl (Butch) Buchholz of St. Louis gained the final of the Newport Casino tournament.

Details in Section 5.

MEETING IN INDEPENDENCE: Senator John F. Kennedy with former President Truman at the Truman Library in the Missouri city. At rear is Senator Stuart Symington.

United Press International Telephoto

Kennedy Calls on Truman; Gets a Forecast of Victory

By W. H. LAWRENCE
Special to The New York Times.

INDEPENDENCE, Mo., Aug. 20—Former President Harry S. Truman joined Senator John F. Kennedy today in what he forecast would be a winning campaign for the Democratic Presidential nominee.

The former President conferred for forty minutes with the Massachusetts Senator, whose nomination he opposed when he boycotted the Democratic National Convention at Los Angeles.

Laughing in recollection of his upset victory in 1948 over Gov. Thomas E. Dewey of New York, Mr. Truman said he had "no use" for pollsters. He added that he put no stock in a recent Gallup poll that showed Vice President Nixon leading Senator Kennedy 50 to 44 per cent.

"The Democrats are going to win," Mr. Truman said.

Talked by Telephone

The Truman-Kennedy conference was their first meeting since the Democratic convention, but they had talked earlier by telephone. At that time Mr. Truman gave assurances that he would support the ticket actively.

The groundwork for this session had been laid ten days ago when Gov. Abraham A. Ribicoff of Connecticut came as Senator Kennedy's peacemaking emissary to talk with the former President.

From all appearances, the meeting was jovial and cordial, although Mr. Truman got a little edgy when he was reminded of the harsh things he had said about Senator Kennedy before his nomination.

He was reminded that he had expressed doubts that Senator Kennedy was ready for the Presidency because he was too young and inexperienced, and that he had also asserted that the convention had been "prearranged" to produce Senator Kennedy's nomination.

To most of these, the former

Continued on Page 46, Column 1

NIXON GIVES IDEAS ON RED CHALLENGE

Says Knowledge of Ideology Is Needed to Meet It— Report First in Series

By WILLIAM J. JORDEN
Special to The New York Times.

WASHINGTON, Aug. 20—Vice President Nixon released today a thirty-page analysis of the meaning of communism. It was the first of a series of reports setting forth the thinking of the Republican Presidential candidate on major issues facing the American people.

Mr. Nixon wrote that a "major weakness" in the struggle against "the militant aggressiveness of international communism" was a prevailing lack of understanding of the character of the challenge. He said that "nothing less than a knowledge in depth of the Communist idea is necessary if we are to deal with it effectively."

The Vice President offered his study of communism as an aid to the kind of knowledge he said was necessary. It did not pretend to be an original contribution to the vast collection of studies on Communist theory. Rather it was a summation of Mr. Nixon's thoughts on some of the main features of earlier studies.

Mr. Nixon said the American people recognized that "we must retain our present military and economic advantage over the Communist bloc." He said the United States would "keep the lead that we have gained" in rocket technology and space exploration.

Sees Battle of Ideas

"What we must realize, "is that this struggle probably will not be decided in the military, economic, or scientific areas, important as these are. The battle in which we are engaged is primarily one of ideas. The test is one not so much of arms but of faith."

The Republican candidate then explored what he considered some of the main elements of Communist thought and attacked them variously as misleading, immoral or of demonstrated ineffectuality.

He stressed that the principal appeal of Communist ideas today was not to broad masses of people but "more often to an intelligent minority in newly developing countries who are trying to decide which road to progress."

Introducing his discussion of

Continued on Page 40, Column 1

Wagner Will Press Extra Registration

By DOUGLAS DALES

Mayor Wagner voiced regret yesterday at Governor Rockefeller's rejection of his plea for a special session of the Legislature to revise voter registration dates. He reaffirmed his intention to provide additional registration time.

The four days fixed by the Legislature for registration, Oct. 12 through 15, conflict with Jewish religious observances. The Mayor had requested the special session to substitute Oct. 10 and 11 for Oct. 13 and 14.

Mayor Wagner said he could not understand why the Governor had turned down his request in view of its endorsement by the bipartisan Board of Elections, composed of two Democrats and two Republicans. He noted he had asked for the

Continued on Page 42, Column 4

CHELSEA—Only Months City Beachfront Kosher Hotel, under the (U). WO 6-1137.—Advt.

SOUTH FACES TEST IN SCHOOLS FIGHT

New Orleans Desegregation Ruling Sparks a Crisis— Election Adds Pressure

By CLAUDE SITTON
Special to The New York Times.

ATLANTA, Aug. 20—The deep South faces new steps toward desegregation of its public schools this fall under the complex pressures of a Presidential election year.

The area's response, according to the Southern Regional Council, may well affect both the election and the future pace of desegregation elsewhere.

The council, which is made up of white and Negro leaders in the South, released a study to-day of progress in the field since 1954, when the Supreme Court issued its decision on desegregation. The study also treated the outlook for this fall.

Its report noted that, after an initial surge of compliance in the border states, "desegregation has been a campaign fought by laws and lawyers over the careers of a few amazingly staunch Negro children."

As a result of a Federal court order directing New Orleans' schools to begin desegregation in September, the council said, "the deep South at last faces the demand that it comply with the law."

The outcome of that test will have far-reaching implications, the organization contended.

"Perhaps the truth has been," it said, "that desegregation cannot move more rapidly in the

Continued on Page 65, Column 3

Mali Alliance in Africa Splits; Senegal-Sudan Strife Feared

De Gaulle Invites Contending Premiers to Paris—Dakar Under Senegalese Rule

By HENRY GINIGER

PARIS, Aug. 20—The Mali Federation in West Africa broke up suddenly today. A civil war between its component states, Senegal and Sudan, was threatened.

The uneasy eighteen-month partnership between the former French territories, which are members of the French Community, broke down early this morning in Dakar when the Senegalese Government headed by Mamadou Dia announced its withdrawal.

The Senegalese thus struck back at the Mali Premier, Modibo Keita, who also is Premier of Sudan. Late last night Mr. Keita canceled Mr. Dia's defense and external-security powers and proclaimed a state of emergency.

Shortly after the Senegalese Government had declared its independence, Senegalese forces took over control of Dakar, the west-coast port that is Senegal's chief city. Mr. Keita was said

Continued on Page 8, Column 1

DOMINICANS QUIT AMERICAS PARLEY; SANCTIONS VOTED

O. A. S. Ministers Condemn Trujillo Regime—Call for Severing of Relations

Text of O. A. S. resolution on Dominican Republic, Page 3.

By TAD SZULC
Special to The New York Times.

SAN JOSE, Costa Rica, Aug. 20—Dominican delegates abandoned the conference of the American foreign ministers today as it unanimously voted precedent - setting sanctions against the Dominican Republic.

The foreign ministers' meeting this afternoon as a general commission, approved by a roll-call vote a resolution "emphatically" condemning the Dominican Republic for "acts of aggression and intervention" against Venezuela, including an attempt to assassinate Venezuela's President, Dr. Romulo Betancourt.

The resolution also called for an immediate break in diplomatic relations with the Dominican regime by members of the Organization of American States and for "partial interruption of economic relations."

The afternoon action on the Dominican issue was final; the resolution now goes to the O. A. S. Council in Washington, which will ask member nations to carry out the terms.

New Sessions on Cuba

Next week the ministers will convene in new sessions to deal with Caribbean tensions and Soviet interests in Cuba.

The parting gesture of the Dominican delegation was to demand a fight against "American imperialism," apparently prompted by the firm position taken by the United States against the Dominican dictatorship of Generalissimo Rafael Leonidas Trujillo Molina.

As a result of a legal maneuver by Venezuela late last night, the conference members did not take any practical steps to provide for a peaceful transition to democracy in the Dominican Republic. Secretary of State Christian A. Herter had advocated the formation of a special mechanism to avert the danger of possible chaos if the Trujillo regime should crumble.

Herter States U. S. View

Speaking tonight at a formal closing session of this week's conference, Mr. Herter said that the United States, while supporting the resolution that was adopted, would have preferred to see the appointment of a special committee with power to foster true democracy in the Dominican Republic. The United States, he added adjusted its views "to maintain the solidarity and common approach of our community."

The Dominican Foreign Minister, Porfirio Herrera Baez, and several others in his delegation left San José late this afternoon for Panama en route to Ciudad Trujillo. They departed from their hotel through

Continued on Page 3, Column 1

Senegal (1) broke her tie to the Sudan Republic (2).
The New York Times Aug. 21, 1960

said to be virtually a prisoner in his palace.

Communications between Dakar and the outside world were cut about 4 A. M. and news reaching Paris was sketchy. Both Dakar and Bamako, capital of Sudan, were reported to be calm.

Acting swiftly early this evening to prevent an irreparable breach in the French Community, President de Gaulle

Continued on Page 8, Column 1

TWO SOVIET DOGS IN ORBIT RETURNED TO EARTH ALIVE AS SATELLITE IS RETRIEVED

Mrs. Powers Plans Appeal For Moscow's Clemency

Will Send a Letter Directly to Brezhnev —Wife of Pilot Is Unable to Leave 'Without Trying to Do Everything'

Special to The New York Times.

MOSCOW, Aug. 20—Mrs. Francis Gary Powers said today she would begin her fight to obtain clemency for her husband by appealing to President Leonid I. Brezhnev of the Soviet Union.

"I cannot leave Moscow without trying to do everything in the world for him," Mrs. Powers said. "But my impression on seeing Gary was that he did not think anything would help."

The wife of the U-2 pilot, who was shot down near Sverdlovsk May 1, spoke with reporters in her suite at the Ukraine Hotel.

She had been present yesterday in the Hall of Columns of Trade Union House when the Soviet's highest military tribunal found her husband guilty of espionage and sentenced him to a loss of freedom for ten years.

Mr. Powers will spend three

years in prison, the court decreed. The remaining seven presumably will be in a penal colony, or working in a remote section of the Soviet under close supervision of the authorities.

Mrs. Powers, who is 25 years old, was pale but composed as she answered questions. She sat on a striped blue sofa beside her widowed mother, Mrs. Monteen Beck Brown.

Mrs. Powers and the pilot's parents, Mr. and Mrs. Oliver W. Powers, expect to deliver early next week a letter to the office of Mr. Brezhnev, President of the Presidium of the Supreme Soviet (Parliament).

Mikhail I. Grinyov, state-appointed defense attorney for the 31-year-old pilot, said this afternoon that Mr. Brezhnev prob-

Continued on Page 71, Column 4

Soviet Opposes U. N. Plan; Bunche Will Leave Congo

By JAMES FERON
Special to The New York Times.

UNITED NATIONS, N. Y., Aug. 20—The Soviet Union told Secretary General Dag Hammarskjold today it opposed the week-old United Nations technical assistance program in the Congo. Vasily V. Kuznetsov, a First Deputy Foreign Minister, also demanded the immediate withdrawal of

Statements at U. N. on the Congo appear on Page 16.

"armed groups from Canada" from the African republic "because they are allies of Belgium, which is guilty of aggression in the Congo."

[In Leopoldville, Premier Patrice Lumumba abandoned his demand for the withdrawal of all white United Nations troops.]

It was also announced here that Dr. Ralph J. Bunche, who has been in charge of all United Nations operations in the Congo, would be replaced shortly by Rajeshwar Dayal, India's High Commissioner to Pakistan. United Nations officials denied the change had been prompted by any diminishing effectiveness in Dr. Bunche's relations with Congolese officials.

They also denied the shift was prompted by rising tension between Gen. Carl Carlsson von Horn, head of the United Nations force, and Maj. Gen. Henry T. Alexander, head of the Ghanaian contingent.

The discord within the United Nations force in regard to the Ghanaian troops was brought out in documents made public by Mr. Hammarskjold. These included criticism by the Secretary General of actions of the Ghanaians and a reply by Gen-

Continued on Page 15, Column 1

LOYAL LAOS UNITS MARCH ON REBELS

Five Battalions Heading for Vientiane—Opposition to New Regime Growing

By JACQUES NEVARD
Special to The New York Times.

SAVANNAKHET, Laos, Aug. 20—Five battalions of loyal Laotian troops are moving on the rebel center of Vientiane from the north and south, it was learned here today from sources close to Maj. Gen. Phoumi Nosavan.

It was not known whether their orders were to attack the capital or to lay siege to it in an effort to starve the rebels into submission.

[About 200 American women and children have been evacuated from Laos to neighboring Thailand to escape the threats of civil war and floods. Planes flying from Vientiane to Bangkok completed the airlift of nearly 500 foreigners Saturday.]

Deputies Joining General

The original battalion of paratroopers headed by Capt. Kong Le, which seized Vientiane Aug. 9, was reported yesterday to have been joined by two companies of pro-Communist Pathet Lao rebels.

Meanwhile, General Phoumi Nosavan, pro-Western chairman of the "Committee to Counter the Coup d'Etat in Laos," was rapidly organizing a regime here in the south of Laos. Thus far twenty out of fifty-eight Deputies elected to the National Assembly last April have arrived and others are expected.

Under Laotian law thirty Deputies are required for a quorum, and if that figure is reached it is expected that the Assembly will repudiate its action in voting against the Government of Premier Tiao Somsanith and setting up the present Vientiane regime of Prince Souvanna Phouma. It took the action under the guns of Captain Kong Le's troops with a mob howling outside the door of the National Assembly.

Three of the Deputies now here escaped from Vientiane

Continued on Page 19, Column 1

Salt Inquiry Shows How Roy Cohn Lost

By CHARLES GRUTZNER

An account of how Roy M. Cohn and William Fugazy, rival boxing promoters, lost a fight with Fortune Pope to control the supply of Dominican rock salt for this city is scattered through the files of the State Investigation Commission.

It depicts Joseph V. Spagna, who resigned Thursday as Purchase Commissioner, as the man who decided in favor of Mr. Pope, his friend of twenty-five years.

The state commission reported Wednesday that it had found contract-rigging, collusive bidding, bribery, shortweighting and other dishonesty in this city's annual purchase of $700,-000 in rock salt for snow and ice removal. It accused Mr. Spagna of having rigged contract procedures to favor Mr. Pope, who had a financial inter-

Continued on Page 55, Column 1

ANIMALS UNHURT

Capsule Comes Down After 17 Circuits in 24-Hour Flight

By SEYMOUR TOPPING
Special to The New York Times.

MOSCOW, Aug. 20—Living creatures have returned safely to earth from an orbit in space for the first time in history, the Soviet Union announced today.

It said its "second cosmic space ship" landed on target today after circling the earth for twenty-four hours with its cargo of two dogs, some rats and mice, flies, plants, seeds and fungi.

On its eighteenth circuit of the earth at an altitude of about 200 miles, the five-ton space ship responded to a signal from the ground and began to descend, detaching the capsule containing the animals en route.

Announced by Tass

Tass, the Soviet press agency, said:

"The space ship's control system and braking device operated with great accuracy and ensured the ship's descent to the fixed spot. The deviation from the calculated spot amounted to some ten kilometers [6¼ miles].

"The space ship, weighing 4,600 kilograms (not counting the last stage of the carrier rocket), provided as it was with a special thermal shield, safely passed through the earth's atmosphere. The space ship and the jettisoned capsule containing the experimental animals landed safely."

[In Washington, T. Keith Glennan, head of the National Aeronautics and Space Administration, saluted the Soviet Union for "a fine job." He added, however, that he did not regard the accomplishment as "a major first" in space exploration but rather as "just another step" toward meeting "the problems we all face."]

Television in Cabin

The space ship was launched yesterday with what was described as a cabin equipped with "everything necessary for the future flight of a man."

In the cabin, under the lenses of television cameras, were the dogs Strelka and Belka (feminine forms of the words Little Arrow and Squirrel).

Tass said scientists on the ground watched the dogs on their television screens during the flight, observed their behavior, and even saw one of the dogs take food."

Meanwhile, other apparatus was recording and transmitting the animals' heart beats, blood pressure, respiration and movements, and the functioning of equipment designed to maintain

Continued on Page 33, Column 1

Today's Sections

Index to Subjects

GOING-TO-COLLEGE HANDBOOK, 32, full of head and heart—practical help for the college-bound young man and woman. At your bookstore. Atheneum. Vo.—Advt.

The New York Times.

LATE CITY EDITION
U. S. Weather Bureau Report (Page 93) forecasts:
Cloudy, periods of rain today.
Partly cloudy, colder tomorrow.
Temp. range: 55—41; yesterday: 53.8—40.4.

VOL. CX..No. 37,546.   © 1960 by The New York Times Company. Times Square, New York 36, N. Y.   NEW YORK, THURSDAY, NOVEMBER 10, 1960.   10 cents beyond 50-mile zone from New York City except on Long Island. Higher in air delivery cities.   FIVE CENTS

KENNEDY'S VICTORY WON BY CLOSE MARGIN; HE PROMISES FIGHT FOR WORLD FREEDOM; EISENHOWER OFFERS 'ORDERLY TRANSITION'

DEMOCRATS HERE SPLIT IN VICTORY; LEHMAN ASSAILED

De Sapio Accepts Challenge for Party Control—Mayor Claims Leadership

Text of De Sapio statement appears on Page 43.

By LEO EGAN

Less than twenty-four hours after the polls closed, the political coalition that gave Senator John F. Kennedy New York's forty-five electoral votes began coming apart at the seams.

Its disintegration was signaled by Carmine G. De Sapio in a statement assailing former Gov. Herbert H. Lehman, key figure in the Democratic reform group, and Alex Rose, Liberal party master of strategy.

The statement accepted Mr. Lehman's election night challenge to a finish fight for control of the party organization in the city and state.

At the same time it appeared to rule out any chance of a Democratic-Liberal party coalition for next year's Mayoral election in New York City and for the Governorship election in the state in 1962 if Mr. De Sapio remains in control of the party machinery.

Kennedy's Delicate Problem

Mr. De Sapio, leader of Tammany and Democratic National Committeeman for New York; Michael H. Prendergast, the Democratic State Chairman, and a number of party leaders in the city and upstate before issuing his statement.

The collapse of the coalition so soon after it achieved its goal gave President-elect Kennedy a delicate political problem before he takes office. At some stage soon he will have to decide whom in New York to consult about appointments for the new Administration.

Thus, in so far as New York is concerned, the election appeared to raise as many questions as it settled. Control of the Democratic party machinery is one of them. Among the others are: What is Mayor Wagner's political future? And what is Governor Rockefeller's?

When told of Mr. De Sapio's statement last night, Mayor Wagner commented that he in-

Continued on Page 43, Column 1

ATOM BILL BEATEN IN FRENCH SENATE

Debre to Push Compromise on Nuclear Force Plan

By W. GRANGER BLAIR
Special to The New York Times.

PARIS, Thursday, Nov. 10—The Senate early today rejected President de Gaulle's project for an independent French nuclear striking force.

By a vote of 186 to 83, with seventeen abstentions, this conservative Upper House approved a procedural motion to table the national nuclear deterrent bill that had been passed to it by the National Assembly Oct. 27.

Although the Senate's action was a stinging blow to President de Gaulle and a sharp indication of mounting parliamentary opposition, it did not mean that the Government's measure would not eventually become law.

It was announced after the vote that Premier Michel Debre would call for the creation of a mixed committee of Senators and Deputies to work out a compromise measure. Should this conference committee fail to find a compromise, the Government would resubmit its measure to the Assembly for a second reading, and virtually certain approval. The measure would then become law with or without the Senate's approval.

The Senate motion to table

Continued on Page 8, Column 1

Registration Set-Up Called Faulty Here

By DOUGLAS DALES

Political leaders voiced dissatisfaction yesterday over the way permanent personal registration functioned here Tuesday in its first test in a Presidential election.

Charges were made that thousands of persons had been disfranchised because they were unable to convince election inspectors that they had registered and were eligible to vote.

How many voters may have been so affected was conceededly a guess. But a check of the Supreme Courts in the five boroughs indicated that more than 1,500 persons had gone before the justices for orders directing the inspectors to permit them to vote.

"There was a minimum of 10,000 denied the right to vote," Abraham Gellinoff,

Continued on Page 43, Column 5

ASSEMBLY DELAYS U.N. CONGO DEBATE

Postpones It Indefinitely, 48-30, as Soviet Backs Step—U. S. Move Fails

By KATHLEEN TELTSCH
Special to The New York Times.

UNITED NATIONS, N. Y., Nov. 9—The General Assembly voted tonight to postpone the debate on the Congo indefinitely.

The 48-to-30 vote, with eighteen abstentions, was on a surprise move made by Ghana with the help of Guinea and Nigeria and the enthusiastic support of the Soviet bloc.

The United States tried to avoid the adjournment vote by asking for a suspension of the session until delegates could ponder the unexpected request.

Western sources said privately that Ghana's initiative appeared to have been presented in part by the presence here of President Joseph Kasavubu of the Congo and the likelihood that the Assembly's Credentials Committee would agree to his request for the seating of a Congolese delegation of his supporters.

A Two-Hour Wrangle

Ghana, Guinea, India and five other states had joined in sponsoring a resolution that aims instead at having the Assembly seat a delegation designated by the deposed Congolese Premier, Patrice Lumumba.

The Assembly acted after a two-hour wrangle marked by two table-thumping demonstrations by the Soviet bloc and also by Ghana, both in protest against the efforts of Foreign Minister Pierre Wigny of Belgium to defend his country's position on the Congo issue.

The adjournment request was made by Alex Quaison-Sackey, Ghana's chief delegate. He appealed to the Assembly to hold off any further debate pending the efforts of a fifteen-member Asian-African commission to reconcile the clashing political factions in the Congo and restore some governmental stability.

He said that the commission probably would leave the Congo in a week and that further acrimonious debate in the Assembly would only hamper the conciliation effort.

However, the adjournment as voted did not stipulate how long the debate should be suspended. United States sources said tonight they understood this to mean that discussion could

Continued on Page 3, Column 1

WINNER'S PLEDGE

Family Is With Him as He Vows to Press Nation's Cause

Text of Kennedy's statement is printed on Page 36.

By HOMER BIGART
Special to The New York Times.

HYANNIS, Mass., Nov. 9—Senator John F. Kennedy accepted in solemn mood today his election as President.

He pledged all his energy to advancing "the long-range interests of the United States and the cause of freedom around the world."

He made this pledge inside the flag-decked Hyannis Armory at 1:45 P. M., an hour after Vice President Nixon, his Republican opponent, had conceded defeat.

His wife, Jacqueline, stood at his side as the 43-year-old President-elect faced 300 newsmen and massed batteries of TV cameras and gave his victory statement to the nation.

Behind him were arrayed the Kennedy family: his father, former Ambassador Joseph P. Kennedy; his mother, three sisters and three brothers.

No Sign of Jubilation

The Kennedys showed no evidence of jubilation. All were expressions of solemnity. Mr. Kennedy's margin of victory was too slender to stir much elation. Some of his aides acknowledged disappointment over the startlingly narrow gap in the popular vote.

Mr. Kennedy, after responding to applause with a diffident bow and a smile, first read the telegram from Mr. Nixon conceding defeat and extending congratulations. The Senator had stayed up until 3:50 A. M. awaiting this concession and had gone to bed disappointed when the Vice President withheld it.

Replies to Nixon

Mr. Nixon wired the President-elect that all the nation would give him "united support" in the next four years.

Mr. Kennedy replied to Mr. Nixon:

"I know that the nation can continue to count on your unswerving loyalty in whatever effort you undertake, and that you and I can maintain our long-standing cordial relations in the years ahead."

Mr. Kennedy then read a congratulatory message from President Eisenhower.

In his message the President informed Mr. Kennedy that he would shortly receive suggestions from the President as to the change-over of responsibilities for national leadership.

To this Senator Kennedy had replied:

"I am grateful for your wire and good wishes. I look forward to working with you in the near future. The whole country is hopeful that your long ex-

Continued on Page 36, Column 7

THE MESSAGES WERE CONGRATULATORY: Senator John F. Kennedy displaying telegrams at Hyannis, Mass. With him are Mrs. Kennedy, his parents and Robert F. Kennedy, left, and R. Sargent Shriver, a brother-in-law.

United Press International Telephoto

KHRUSHCHEV NOTE SALUTES KENNEDY

Message of Congratulations Asks for Negotiations on Tensions in World

Text of Khrushchev message will be found on Page 42.

By The Associated Press.

MOSCOW, Nov. 9—Soviet Premier Khrushchev congratulated Senator John F. Kennedy today for his Presidential victory.

He expressed hope that Soviet-United States relations would "again follow the line along which they were developing in Franklin Roosevelt's time."

He urged negotiations aimed at easing the international situation.

[In Bonn, Chancellor Konrad Adenauer said he planned to go to Washington early next year for conferences with Mr. Kennedy.]

Mr. Khrushchev's statements in a congratulatory message to Mr. Kennedy coincided with Moscow's insistence that the policies of President Eisenhower had suffered a rebuff in the election.

The Soviet press contended that the election proved "the American people have blackballed the policy of the 'cold war' and the arms race, that they want changes and expect Washington to pursue a reasonable course in international affairs, a course dictated by life and the balance of forces now prevailing in the world." Mr.

Continued on Page 42, Column 3

Electoral Vote by States

	Rep. Dem.		Rep. Dem.		Rep. Dem.
Alabama	5*	Louisiana	10	Ohio	25
Alaska	3	Maine	5	Oklahoma	8
Arizona	4	Maryland	9	Oregon	6
Arkansas	8	Mass.	16	Penna.	32
California	32	Michigan	20	Rhode Island	4
Colorado	6	Minnesota	11	So. Carolina	8
Conn.	8	Mississippi	**	So. Dakota	4
Delaware	3	Missouri	13	Tennessee	11
Florida	10	Montana	4	Texas	24
Georgia	12	Nebraska	6	Utah	4
Hawaii	3	Nevada	3	Vermont	3
Idaho	4	New Hamp.	4	Virginia	12
Illinois	27	New Jersey	16	Washington	9
Indiana	13	New Mexico	4	W. Virginia	8
Iowa	10	New York	45	Wisconsin	12
Kansas	8	No. Carolina	14	Wyoming	3
Kentucky	10	North Dakota	4	Total	185 300

*Five electors are pledged to Kennedy and six unpledged.
**Eight electors not pledged to vote for party candidates.

LIBERALS SUFFER SETBACK IN HOUSE

G. O. P. Picks Up 22 Seats to Aid Conservative Bloc

By JOHN D. MORRIS

The House of Representatives will have a more conservative tinge in the Eighty-seventh Congress.

Inroads into the present House Democratic majority of 283 to 154 scored by the Republicans in Tuesday's elections promised to strengthen their conservative coalition with Southern Democrats.

The liberal legislative program to be submitted early next year by the new Democratic President, John F. Kennedy, may consequently face handicaps in the new Congress, which convenes Jan. 3.

In the Senate, Republicans cut the Democratic margin by two seats, to 64 to 36. That chamber remains predominantly liberal in membership, although conservatives dominate key committee posts.

Gubernatorial Shifts

The Democrats achieved a net gain of one governorship and now control thirty-four of the fifty state houses. In twenty-seven gubernatorial contests the Democrats won fifteen and the Republicans twelve, with an exchange of party control in thirteen.

In the House races, nearly complete unofficial returns showed that the Democrats had elected 257 House candidates and the Republicans 175, with five contests still in doubt.

The Republicans captured twenty-nine seats held by Democrats and lost seven of their own, for a net gain of at least twenty-two. For a bare numerical majority of 219 they would have had to achieve a net gain of sixty-five.

Among the eleven states of the Old Confederacy the Republicans maintained their seven seats in the Eighty-

Continued on Page 38, Column 4

10 Irish Soldiers Slain in Congo When U.N. Patrol Is Ambushed

By PAUL HOFMANN
Special to The New York Times.

LEOPOLDVILLE, the Congo, Nov. 9—A patrol of eleven Irish soldiers of the United Nations force in the Congo was ambushed in the northern part of Katanga Province yesterday. The bodies of four men were sighted.

[The United Nations Command said that ten soldiers had been slain in the ambush, Reuters reported. The Irish Army announced in Dublin that one private had survived the attack. Reports received by the United Nations in New York said the surviving soldier was "badly wounded," according to United Press International.]

The patrol belonged to the Irish Thirty-third Battalion, which has headquarters in the industrial city of Albertville. The battalion, with a strength of about 550 men, is responsible for maintaining order in a vast area of North Katanga. The region has been the scene of intertribal warfare and clashes between Baluba tribesmen and the gendarmerie controlled by Moise Tshombe, President of Katanga.

United Nations officials here were unable to say who had attacked the Irish patrol. The ambush occurred south of Niemba, a village between Albertville and Kabalo. The zone is inhabited by Baluba tribesmen but it is not known whether Baluba tribesmen were responsible for the assault.

Announcing the loss, a United Nations spokesman said it brought the toll of dead in the international force in the Congo to about thirty since the world organization's troops arrived

Continued on Page 2, Column 3

RESULTS DELAYED

Popular Vote Almost Even—300-185 Is Electoral Tally

By JAMES RESTON

Senator John F. Kennedy of Massachusetts finally won the 1960 Presidential election from Vice President Nixon by the astonishing margin of less than two votes per voting precinct.

Senator Kennedy's electoral vote total stood yesterday at 300, just thirty-one more than the 269 needed for election. The Vice President's total was 185. Fifty-two additional electoral votes, including California's thirty-two, were still in doubt last night.

But the popular vote was a different story. The two candidates ran virtually even. Senator Kennedy's lead last night was little more than 300,000 in a total tabulated vote of about 66,000,000 cast in 165,826 precincts.

That was a plurality for the Senator of less than one-half of 1 per cent of the total vote—the smallest percentage difference between the popular vote of two Presidential candidates since 1880, when James A. Garfield outran Gen. Winfield Scott Hancock by 7,000 votes in a total of almost 9,000,000.

End Divided Government

Nevertheless, yesterday's voting radically altered the political balance of power in America in favor of the Democrats and put them in a commanding position in the Federal and state capitals unknown since the heyday of Franklin D. Roosevelt.

They regained control of the White House for the first time since 1952 and thus ended divided government in Washington. They retained control of the Senate and the House of Representatives, although with slightly reduced margins. And they increased their hold on the state governorships by one, bringing the Democratic margin to 34—16.

The President-elect is the first Roman Catholic ever to win the nation's highest office. The only other member of his church nominated for President was Alfred E. Smith, who was defeated by Herbert Hoover in 1928.

Faces Difficult Questions

Despite his personal triumph, President-elect Kennedy is confronted by a number of hard questions:

¶In the face of such a narrow victory how can he get through the Congress the liberal program he proposed during the campaign?

¶Can so close an election produce any impetus for loosening the conservative coalition of Republicans and Southern Democrats which has blocked most liberal legislation in the House?

¶Will the new President be successfully to claim a mandate for legislation such as the $1.25 minimum wage, Fed-

Continued on Page 35, Column 1

PRESIDENT SENDS WIRE TO KENNEDY

He Felicitates Senator and Orders Agency Chiefs to Cooperate With Him

By FELIX BELAIR Jr.
Special to The New York Times.

AUGUSTA, Ga., Nov. 9—President Eisenhower congratulated President-elect John F. Kennedy today on his election and then invited him to designate representatives to participate in all Federal policy discussions to assure an "orderly transition" to the new Administration.

The text of the President's telegram was withheld here at the request of Mr. Kennedy. But President Eisenhower is understood to have told the President-elect that he had instructed all heads of Federal departments and agencies to "cooperate fully" with Mr. Kennedy's representatives.

President Eisenhower arrived here for his customary fall holiday in midafternoon after a two-hour flight from Washington.

The President's message of congratulation to Mr. Kennedy was sent from the White House just before he took off for his favorite vacation retreat here at Augusta National Golf Club.

He also sent messages to the defeated Republican candidate, Vice President Nixon, and his running mate, Henry Cabot Lodge, as well as Vice President-elect Lyndon B. Johnson.

In his telegram to Mr. Nixon

Continued on Page 42, Column 7

NIXON WIRE GIVES HIS 'BEST WISHES'

Sends Kennedy a Message —500 in Capital Hail Him

By BILL BECKER

LOS ANGELES, Nov. 9—Vice President Nixon conceded today the Presidential election to his Democratic opponent, Senator John F. Kennedy.

About twelve hours after the polls had closed, the Vice President sent the following telegram to Senator Kennedy at Hyannis Port, Mass.:

"I want to repeat through this wire the congratulations and best wishes I extended to you on television last night. I know that you will have the united support of all Americans as you lead the nation in the cause of peace and freedom in the next four years."

Read by Aide

The telegram was read to newsmen by Mr. Nixon's press secretary, Herbert G. Klein, at 9:45 A. M., Pacific standard time (12:45 P. M., Eastern standard time).

The Vice President did not make a personal appearance. Mr. Klein said Mr. Nixon was resting with Mrs. Nixon and their two daughters in their suite at the Ambassador Hotel.

It was obvious that the Vice President had considered his remarks late on election night a virtual concession.

[A crowd of several hundred greeted Mr. Nixon when he arrived Wednesday night at Andrews Air Base, near Washington, after a flight of four and a half hours from Los Angeles.]

Mr. Nixon remained in seclusion most of the morning although Mr. Klein said he was up about 6 A. M. after little more than three hours of sleep. The secretary said Mr. Nixon

Continued on Page 42, Column 1

Vatican Calls Kennedy Election Proof of American Democracy

By ARNALDO CORTESI

ROME, Nov. 9—The election of Senator John F. Kennedy, a Roman Catholic, to the Presidency was received with keen satisfaction in the Vatican today.

During the campaign the Vatican remained neutral. Its newspaper, L'Osservatore Romano, abstained from all comment lest it be accused of siding with one candidate against the other.

Today the editor of the newspaper, former Italian Deputy Raimondo Manzini, said:

"Kennedy's victory strengthens the appreciation for the high democratic principles of freedom that guide American public life and assure access to the highest office to every citizen regardless of race, or religion.

"The effective support given by large numbers of Protestant

Continued on Page 38, Column 7

"All the News That's Fit to Print"

The New York Times.

LATE CITY EDITION
U.S. Weather Bureau Report (Page 46) forecast:
Cold, chance of snow flurries today;
fair and cold tonight and tomorrow.
Temp. range: 35—22; yesterday: 40.1—30.

VOL. CX .. No. 37,583.
© 1960 by The New York Times Company.
Times Square, New York 36, N. Y.

NEW YORK, SATURDAY, DECEMBER 17, 1960.

10 cents beyond 50-mile zone from New York City
except on Long Island. Higher in air delivery cities.

FIVE CENTS

127 DIE AS 2 AIRLINERS COLLIDE OVER CITY; JET SETS BROOKLYN FIRE, KILLING 5 OTHERS; SECOND PLANE CRASHES ON STATEN ISLAND

STATEN ISLAND: Wreckage of Trans World Airlines Super Constellation in New Dorp

BROOKLYN: Rescue workers gather near ruins of United Air Lines DC-8 jet in Seventh Avenue at Sterling Place, in the Park Slope section

The New York Times

ETHIOPIAN REVOLT SAID TO COLLAPSE; SELASSIE HAILED

Envoys in U. S. and Britain Report Rebels Seized —Emperor in Asmara

Special to The New York Times.

WASHINGTON, Dec. 16 — The Ethiopian Embassy here reported today that the attempt by the Imperial Guard to overthrow Emperor Haile Selassie I had "ended in complete failure early this morning."

Ambassador Mikael Imru issued a statement saying that the army and air force, which had remained loyal to the Emperor, had captured Addis Ababa, the capital, and "overpowered and seized" the "disgruntled officers" of the Imperial Guard. The rebels had seized the city Wednesday.

[The Emperor arrived in Asmara, Ethiopia, Friday and received a tumultuous welcome from his loyal subjects there. He was told that the palace rebellion had failed.]

Prince Not Mentioned

The rebel group was reported at first to have been led by the Emperor's son, Crown Prince Asfa-Wossen. Later reports suggested that the Crown Prince might have acted "under duress."

The Ambassador's statement this morning made no mention of the part played by the Crown Prince and threw no light on his fate or his whereabouts.

Nor did the Ambassador say anything about his father, Ras Imru, the 68-year-old cousin of the Emperor, who was reported to have been appointed Premier of the government formed by the rebels.

The Ambassador stated that the loyal forces had been led by Maj. Gen. Merod Mengsha, Chief of Staff; Maj. Gen. Kebede Guebre, army commander.

Continued on Page 2, Column 4

New Pact to Expand Cuban-Soviet Trade

By MAX FRANKEL
Special to The New York Times.

HAVANA, Dec. 16 — Cuba and the Soviet Union plan to exchange goods valued at $168,000,000 next year, the Ministry of Commerce disclosed here today.

The expanded trade dealings will be in addition to exchanges of sugar and other products for Soviet oil that had been agreed upon last February.

Although no details about the new arrangements were disclosed, it appeared almost certain that the Soviet Union would purchase considerably more Cuban sugar than it originally had planned.

Whatever the terms of the new trade agreement, it will

Continued on Page 6, Column 2

Dillon Appointed Secretary of Treasury; Kennedy's Brother Is Attorney General

By W. H. LAWRENCE

WASHINGTON, Dec. 16 — President-elect John F. Kennedy designated a Republican, Douglas Dillon, as his Secretary of the Treasury today and named his brother, Robert F. Kennedy, as Attorney General.

Mr. Dillon, now serving the Eisenhower Administration as Under Secretary of State, dis-

Second Republican Gets Post in New Cabinet— President Approves

Senator Kennedy said he would complete his Cabinet tomorrow by naming his Postmaster General from the family where he is planning a prolonged holiday through Christmas and New Year's Day.

He left little doubt that his choice would be J. Edward Day, a California insurance executive, who flew in by jet from Los Angeles during the night and then flew South with the President-elect this afternoon.

The President-elect left Washington aboard his private twin-engine Convair, Caroline, at 4 P. M. Also aboard the airplane for the flight to Palm Beach were his brother, Robert, and two of Robert's children, Bobby and Joseph.

In two news conferences from the front stoop of his Georgetown home just after noon, Senator Kennedy announced first

closed that he had sought the assent of President Eisenhower this morning and of Vice President Nixon earlier.

"Neither of them had any objection if I felt that this was something that would be in the national security interest of the country, and if we were to work toward a sound fiscal policy as is the case," Mr. Dillon said.

Both appointments long had been forecast. But the choice of Robert Kennedy, 35 years old, is expected to provoke a political storm. Senator Kennedy set a precedent by naming his brother to the Cabinet.

the choice of Mr. Dillon and then of his brother, Robert.

At the same time, he said Byron R. White, Denver attorney and former All-America football star at the University of Colorado, would be Deputy Attorney General. Harry J. Anslinger, Commissioner of Narcotics in the Treasury Department, has agreed to stay in that position, Senator Kennedy said.

Appointments Forecast

Highly placed Democrats forecast the following other major appointments by Senator Kennedy shortly:

¶Mrs. Elizabeth Smith, California's Democratic national committeewoman, as Treasurer of the United States, replacing Mrs. Ivy Baker Priest.

¶Fred Dutton of California as secretary of the Kennedy Cabinet. He is a former executive secretary to Gov. Edmund G. Brown of California.

Mr. Dillon, 51 years old, becomes the Cabinet's second Republican. He will serve with

Continued on Page 14, Column 6

The texts of Kennedy's news conferences are on Page 14.

PRO-WEST FORCES TAKE VIENTIANE

New Premier Enters Laos Capital as Fighting Ends

By DREW MIDDLETON
Special to The New York Times.

PARIS, Dec. 16 — The United States offered Western Europe a mighty new nuclear armory today for defense against the Communist bloc.

Secretary of State Christian A. Herter announced what he termed a new concept for operation of medium-range ballistic missiles to the Ministerial Council of the North Atlantic Treaty Organization late this afternoon.

The offer was conditional upon agreement by the European allies on political control of the weapons, which were described by Mr. Herter as offering the best means for providing a common defense in the field of medium-range ballistic missiles.

The offer calls for commitment to the Atlantic alliance before the end of 1963 of five ballistic missile submarines armed with eighty Polaris missiles. The step would enlarge the alliance's military capabilities and reaffirm the United States' commitment to Europe's defense, he said.

The United States would then expect other members of the

Continued on Page 13, Column 4

Because of communications difficulties, the following dispatch was filed jointly by correspondents in Vientiane.

VIENTIANE, Laos, Dec. 16—Prince Boun Oum, the new Premier of Laos, and the rightist pro-Western general, Phoumi Nosavan, drove into Vientiane at dusk today and announced the liberation of this shattered administrative capital.

At the same time, Capt. Peng, a cheerful Laotian tank officer, was busy cleaning from hold-out positions at the Vientiane airport the stubborn remnants of Capt. Kong Le's pro-Communist paratroops and guerrillas of the Communist-led Pathet Lao movement.

The seventy-six-hour battle for Vientiane ended at 5 P. M. local time [5 A. M., Friday, Eastern Standard Time].

Rightist Troops Hold City

By JACQUES NEVARD
Special to The New York Times.

VIENTIANE, Dec. 16—The troops of Gen. Phoumi Nosavan held the center of Vientiane this morning eighteen hours after they had captured it for a second time in a seesaw battle with tenacious pro-Communist defenders.

Mortar, machine-gun and small-arms fire could still be heard as tanks and armored cars cruised through the streets.

After a night lull the battle broke out hot and fierce again. The heart of this usually somnolent

Continued on Page 6, Column 2

U.S. Offers NATO A Nuclear Arsenal And 5 Submarines

A PILOT OFF ROUTE, U.S. OFFICIALS HINT

C.A.B. and F.A.A. Open Wide Inquiries—Tape Records of Flights to Be Studied

By RUSSELL PORTER

A preliminary investigation of the air disaster here yesterday suggested that the two planes collided because one was off its course.

An extensive inquiry was opened by the two Federal agencies concerned with civilian aviation, the Civil Aeronautics Board and the Federal Aviation Agency.

E. R. Quesada, Administrator of the Federal Aviation Agency, which is responsible for the operation of the airways, said last night that it was "very probable" that there had been a collision.

Alan S. Boyd, a member of the C. A. B., which investigates air accidents, was present when Mr. Quesada made his statement at New York International Airport. The two officials held a joint news conference.

They said that the investigation was just starting and little had been learned, but that the Trans World Airlines plane had fallen in three parts in Staten Island in a way indicating that it could not have been broken up by hitting the ground.

They said this made it appear likely there had been a collision, but there was as yet no positive evidence of a collision.

"All we know is that two planes crashed eleven miles apart," they said.

Shortly before the disaster, they said, the T. W. A. plane flew over the Linden, N. J., area

Continued on Page 10, Column 1

WIDE U.N. POWER IN CONGO IS URGED

100-Day Blanket Authority Sought for Hammarskjold

By LINDESAY PARROTT
Special to The New York Times.

UNITED NATIONS, N. Y., Dec. 16—An urgent meeting of the General Assembly heard a proposal tonight to grant blanket emergency powers to Secretary General Dag Hammarskjold for 100 days to settle the growing crisis in the Congo.

Francisco Milla Bermudez of Honduras read the text of a proposed resolution that would give effect to the plan.

Because of the series of recurring emergencies in the new African state, he said, full interim powers for the Secretary General might be the best way to bring peace and order to the country under the terms of the Charter.

The Assembly adjourned at 10:35 P. M. to meet again at 10:30 A. M. tomorrow, with the United States delegate scheduled as the first speaker.

Latin-American sources said that some other Latin-American nations had been consulted on the Honduran proposal, though none joined in sponsoring the plan.

Señor Milla Bermudez announced that he was prepared to consider changes in his text and would introduce it formally when all members agreed.

The proposal would permit the Assembly to revoke the Secretary General's special authority if necessary or extend it beyond the 100-day period if Mr. Hammarskjold seemed to be succeeding.

The Honduran proposal was

10 Brooklyn Houses Burn After Plane Hits a Church

By JOHN F. MURPHY

Ten four-story tenement buildings and an empty church were set afire when the United Air Lines DC-8 jet crashed and exploded in the populous Park Slope district of Brooklyn yesterday. More than 250 firemen and about fifty pieces of apparatus rushed to the seven-alarm blaze, which took more than two hours to bring under control.

There were several hundred persons in the buildings when the airliner plummeted through one tenement on Sterling Place and rammed into the Pillar of Fire Church across the street.

A rapid-fire series of small explosions followed, igniting roofs and spraying wreckage over a wide area.

Tenants Race From Homes

As soon as the plane crashed, women, children and elderly persons came pouring out of the buildings into the street, dressed in housecoats, sweaters and pajamas. They ran panic-stricken from the smoldering wreckage.

Aside from those on the plane who were killed, five persons on the ground died. These five presumably included three persons known to be missing. The police said even more bodies might be found beneath the fuselage.

The one victim identified was Charles J. Cooper, 34 years old, a sanitation worker, who had been shoveling snow. Those missing were Wallace E. Lewis, 90, the caretaker of the church at 123 Sterling Place; Joseph Colacano, 29, and John Opperisano, 35. Mr. Colacano Mr. Opperisano had been selling Christmas trees on the sidewalk.

The first fire alarm was sounded at 10:36 A. M. When

Continued on Page 9, Column 1

S. I. HOMES SPARED BY FALLING DEBRIS

Parts of Airliner Land in Backyards—No One on Ground Is Injured

By THOMAS BUCKLEY

Distances that can be paced off quickly—50 feet, 150 feet, 200 yards—were the measure of life and death on quiet streets on Staten Island yesterday.

Men, women and children saw the flaming wreckage of a Trans World Airlines Super-Constellation plunge toward them and fall short. And although all forty-four persons on board were killed, no one on the ground was even scratched by the fall of the shattered airliner.

The flaming forward section of the craft, from which twenty-nine bodies were taken, smashed to earth on the northwest corner of Miller Army Air Field, less than 150 feet from the eight-room frame home of Edward Brody, at 324 Boundary Lane, Midland Beach. Dozens of other homes on tree-lined streets stood near by.

"I saw it coming right at us," Mrs. Brody said. "I ran upstairs to get my daughters.

Continued on Page 11, Column 1

DISASTER IN FOG

DC-8 Plunges Into Park Slope Street, Missing School

By HOMER BIGART

Two airliners collided over New York harbor yesterday in fog and sleet, killing 127 passengers and crewmen. One plane crashed in Brooklyn, killing five more persons on the ground, and the other fell on Staten Island.

A United Air Lines DC-8 jet from Chicago plunged into the crowded Park Slope section of Brooklyn shortly after 10:30 A. M. All but one of its seventy-seven passengers and the crew of seven were killed. The survivor was an 11-year-old boy.

The plane demolished a church and killed a Department of Sanitation worker on the ground. Burning debris caused a seven-alarm fire, destroying ten brownstone apartment buildings, several shops and a funeral home. Nine persons were injured on the ground.

Three Unaccounted For

Three persons were unaccounted for, including the 90-year-old custodian of the Pillar of Fire Church, 123 Sterling Place, a Gothic structure that was leveled by flames.

At almost the same instant as the Brooklyn disaster, a Trans World Airlines Lockheed Super - Constellation crashed near Miller Army Air Field, New Dorp, S. I., eleven miles to the southwest.

This plane, out of Dayton and Columbus, Ohio, apparently exploded in the air just before the crash. All thirty-nine passengers and the crew of five were killed or fatally injured.

Parts of the plane fell in the Lower Bay and parts on the northwest corner of Miller Field.

Three victims were taken by Coast Guard helicopter to the Public Health Service Hospital.

Continued on Page 8, Column 1

4 Cardinals Named; One Is an American

By ARNALDO CORTESI
Special to The New York Times.

ROME, Dec. 16 — The Most Rev. Joseph Elmer Ritter, Archbishop of St. Louis, and three other prelates were named today by Pope John XXIII to be created Cardinals Jan. 16.

The elevation of Archbishop Ritter will return the number of American Cardinals to six, as it was up to the death of John F. Cardinal O'Hara, Archbishop of Philadelphia, less than four months ago.

The present American Cardinals are Archbishops Francis Spellman of New York, James F. McIntyre of Los Angeles, Richard Cushing of Boston, Albert G. Meyer of Chicago and Aloysius J. Muench of Milwau-

Continued on Page 2, Column 1

Boy, 11, Only Survivor of Crash

Steven Baltz is comforted by persons at scene of crash.
© New York Journal-American

Condition Is Critical —Parents and Sister at His Bedside

By ROBERT CONLEY

An 11-year-old boy, flying here to meet his mother and sister, was the only survivor of yesterday's airliner collision.

He was thrown from the tail section of a United Air Lines jet and found in a Brooklyn snowbank, his clothes aflame.

The youngster, Steven Baltz of Wilmette, Ill., regained consciousness last night, but was still in critical condition early today with burns and broken bones.

His mother and sister were at his bedside when he awoke at Methodist Hospital in Brooklyn. They had flown here from Chicago and met him there. His father, William S. Baltz, flew in late in the day and reached the bedside just after dark.

"He's coming along quite well, very well," the father said after

Continued on Page 11, Column 6

NEWS INDEX

	Page		Page
Art	47	Music	19-20
Books	21	Obituaries	29
Bridge	20	Real Estate	29
Business	30-31	Screen	19-20
Churches	47	Ships and Air	43
Crossword	21	Society	42
Editorial	22	Sports	27-29
Fashions	24	TV and Radio	47
Financial	30-41	Theatres	19-20
Food	25	U. N. Proceedings	3
Letters	22	U. S. Weather	46
Man in the News	2	Wash. Proceedings	25
		Events Today	28

News Summary and Index, Page 25

The New York Times.

LATE CITY EDITION
U. S. Weather Bureau Report (Page 66) forecasts:
Mostly fair, seasonably cold today and tonight. Fair, warmer tomorrow.
Temp. range 38—25; yesterday: 35—31.

VOL. CX..No. 37,601.   © 1961 by The New York Times Company. Times Square, New York 36, N. Y.   NEW YORK, WEDNESDAY, JANUARY 4, 1961.   10 cents beyond 50-mile zone from New York City except on Long Island. Higher in air delivery cities.   FIVE CENTS

U. S. BREAKS ITS DIPLOMATIC TIES WITH CUBA AND ADVISES AMERICANS TO LEAVE ISLAND; EISENHOWER CITES 'VILIFICATION' BY CASTRO

CONGRESS OPENS WITH CONFLICTS ON PROCEDURES

Filibuster Curbs Sought in Senate—Colmer's Purge Is Believed Certain

By RUSSELL BAKER
Special to The New York Times.

WASHINGTON, Jan. 3—The Eighty-seventh Congress convened today amid clashes in both houses over rules of procedure.

In the Senate, proponents of tighter curbs on the rules of debate opened a battle to make it easier to cut off filibusters. The skirmishes ended inconclusively with a decision to postpone further action until tomorrow.

In the House of Representatives. Speaker Sam Rayburn was reported to have completed arrangements for removing Representative William M. Colmer. Democrat of Mississippi, from the Rules Committee and replacing him with a member who would reinforce the Texas Democrat's leadership.

Pledges by Leaders

The Senate session was marked by a clash between Vice President Nixon and Richard B. Russell. The Georgia Democrat, leader of the Southern bloc, normally gets deference from the chair. Twice, however, Mr. Nixon used his gavel against him with authority.

In the House's traditional opening procedures, Mr. Rayburn and Charles A. Halleck of Indiana, the Republican minority leader, made pledges to work for responsible government.

Behind the scenes, however, a liberal-conservative fight for control of the Rules Committee continued unabated. Mr. Rayburn was assured of the necessary votes in the Democratic Committee on Committees to help purge Mr. Colmer.

This presumably would create a Rules Committee majority favoring critical parts of President-elect John F. Kennedy's program. Capitol observers described the Rayburn plan as "replacing a 'no' man with a 'yes' man."

Friction in Caucus

Meanwhile, Senate Republicans joined Democrats in a standing ovation for the new and only woman member on the Democratic side, Mrs. Maurine Neuberger of Oregon.

Mr. Nixon's duty on the rostrum was to administer the oath to each Senator elected in November.

A Senate Democratic caucus this morning brought more friction. As expected, Mike Mansfield of Montana was elected to succeed Vice President-elect Lyndon B. Johnson as majority leader, and Hubert H. Humphrey of Minnesota was named assistant leader.

Mr. Mansfield, however, created a surprise when he announced that he wanted the

Continued on Page 24, Column 2

I.T.T. Voices Hopes On H-Bomb Power

By GENE SMITH

Experiments that might lead to a "low-cost nuclear fusion process" were announced here yesterday by the International Telephone and Telegraph Corporation.

No details were given, but the experiments apparently dealt with a concept that many nuclear experts have not considered promising. The company said the experiments had been conducted "for a number of years" but made no claim of success.

The problem of producing a controlled and sustained nuclear fusion, and thus harnessing the reaction of the hydrogen bomb, is the goal of many experiments being conducted both here and abroad.

Temperatures of millions of degrees Centigrade are neces-

Continued on Page 18, Column 3

Legislators Choose Mahoney, Carlino

By WARREN WEAVER Jr.
Special to The New York Times.

ALBANY, Jan. 3—Senators and Assemblymen descended on the capital tonight to prepare for the opening of the 1961 legislative session here tomorrow.

The Republican majorities in the Senate and Assembly held separate caucuses to choose their leaders and housekeeping officers for the next two years.

The Democrats chose their own nominees at separate sessions, but since the Republicans control both houses their nominations were equivalent to election.

There were no surprises. Senator Walter J. Mahoney of Buffalo was chosen temporary President of the Senate, the official title of the majority leader, a post he has held for the last seven years. In the Assembly, Joseph F.

Continued on Page 14, Column 1

L.I.R.R. SEEKS AID TO AVERT 'CRISIS'

Says It Will Be Unable to Meet April Payroll—Two Rail Walkouts Cited

By CLARENCE DEAN

The Long Island Rail Road appealed yesterday for financial help to avert what it said was an impending crisis.

A statement by Thomas M. Goodfellow, president of the line, declared that unless the help was forthcoming the railroad would be unable to meet its payroll by the last week in April.

The present indications, Mr. Goodfellow said, are that the carrier's deficit by the end of this year will exceed $4,000,000.

If there is no financial help, Mr. Goodfellow said, three alternatives will arise: "a whopping fare increase," a cut in maintenance "to rock bottom" or "an arbitrary 12 per cent slash in the number of commuter trains." He declined to suggest specifically what kind of financial help the road wanted.

He attributed the railroad's predicament to unforeseen emergencies, chiefly a twenty-six-day strike on the Long Island last summer and a subsequent twelve-day shutdown of Pennsylvania Station as a result of a strike against the Pennsylvania Railroad.

For last October and Novem-

Continued on Page 67, Column 2

U.S. SAYS SOVIET AND RED VIETNAM AID LAOS REBELS

Asserts 180 Air Drops Were Made in Nineteen Days— President Sees Advisers

Text of the State Department statement is on Page 8.

By WILLIAM J. JORDEN
Special to The New York Times.

WASHINGTON, Jan. 3—The United States Government charged today that the Soviet Union and North Vietnam were guilty of "extensive participation" in military operations against the Government of Laos.

To bolster its charge, the State Department released a listing of Communist supply flights over Laos, serial numbers of Soviet planes engaged in the airlift, dates and places of air drops to the anti-Government rebels and other details.

The department said the two Communist powers had carried out more than 180 air sorties into Laos in the nineteen days from Dec. 15 through Jan. 2 to drop supplies and personnel to pro-Communist forces. It said that "substantial numbers" of North Vietnamese had been parachuted into Laos to help the rebels.

Elaboration Is Declined

A department spokesman would not elaborate on the numbers. Nor would he use the term "aggression" to describe the Communists' activities.

The charges against the Communist states were attributed to "hard evidence," however. Today's bill of particulars detailed earlier general charges of Communist intervention in Laos.

The catalogue of Communist involvement should be read, officials said, with the strong statement issued by the United States Government three days ago in mind. On Saturday the State Department warned that the Government would take "the most serious view" of intervention in Laos by the Chinese Communists, North Vietnamese "or others" in support of the anti-Government rebels.

Today's Government statement on Laos was issued soon after a special briefing on the Laos situation for President Eisenhower by his top diplomatic, military and intelligence advisers. It was the third White House conference on Laos in four days.

On Capitol Hill a group of House members also received an up-to-date report on developments in Laos. John M.

Continued on Page 8, Column 5

NO ENTRY: Portion of the crowd in front of the U. S. Embassy in Havana as Cubans sought visas yesterday. When they discovered that the visa section of the embassy had been closed, there were cries of protest and dismay.

Associated Press Radiophoto

Belgian Assembly Defeats Socialists; Violence Continues

By HARRY GILROY
Special to The New York Times.

BRUSSELS, Belgium, Jan. 3—The Belgian House of Representatives rejected today a motion to withdraw the proposed new law to raise taxes and tighten up the social security administration, against which 500,000 Socialist workers are striking.

Leo Collard, president of the Socialist party, and Achille van Acker, a former Premier, presented the motion. It was defeated by a vote of 121 to 83 with 1 abstention.

The House gave the Government three votes of confidence before adjourning at 8 P. M. until 2 P. M. tomorrow. The votes followed three critical speeches by Socialists and one by a Communist member on the conduct of public affairs and on the treatment of strikers.

The votes were taken in a calm parliamentary atmosphere that contrasted with an unruly session in which the measure was last discussed Dec. 23, and even more with the street demonstrations that turned up new

Continued on Page 12, Column 3

CASTRO'S CABINET DRAFTING A REPLY

Emergency Session Called After U. S. Acts—Premier Says 'Cuba Is Alert'

By R. HART PHILLIPS
Special to The New York Times.

HAVANA, Jan. 3—Premier Fidel Castro, President Osvaldo Dorticós Torrado and members of the Cuban Cabinet met in the Presidential Palace tonight at 10:30 to draft a reply to the United States' break in diplomatic relations with Cuba.

The reply will be delivered here soon, according to a statement by Dr. Carlos Olivares, Cuba's Foreign Under Secretary. The Cabinet meeting ended without any announcement.

The Cuban people learned of the United States move tonight when the announcement was made over all radio stations.

The announcer said that "according to cables received President Eisenhower had broken off diplomatic relations with Cuba on the pretext of the order of the Revolutionary Government that he withdraw his 300 spies in the embassy from Cuba."

"Being discovered in his criminal plans of terrorism Eisenhower has responded with the habitual shamelessness of imperialism," the announcer declared.

The announcer said the radio would keep the people informed

Continued on Page 3, Column 5

U. S. Will Help Evacuate Its Citizens Living in Cuba

Special to The New York Times.

HAVANA, Wednesday, Jan. 4—The United States Embassy last night urged all Americans in Cuba to leave the island. A statement issued by the press attaché said that "all American citizens are urged to depart from Cuba immediately unless compelling reasons oblige them to remain."

The embassy has arranged for a ferry of the West Indies Fruit and Steamship Company to sail from Havana to West Palm Beach today and Friday to evacuate the Americans.

Additional extra flights to Miami from the José Marti International Airport will augment the facilities for departure today and tomorrow.

Cuba Guarantees Safety

The Castro regime, in a note delivered this morning to the United States Chargé d' Affaires, Daniel M. Braddock, pledged the "most absolute guarantees" for the safety of all American citizens in Cuba, including diplomatic or consular officials "as well as residents or tourists."

Meanwhile, thousands of Cubans who for months have been seeking visas to the United States were dismayed yesterday by the Cuban-United States crisis.

A long line of Cubans appeared as usual at the United States Embassy early in the morning after Premier Fidel Castro had ordered a cut in the embassy staff. They found the

Continued on Page 3, Column 6

KENNEDY AVOIDS ROLE IN DECISION

Rusk Turns Down Herter Move to Link Democrats to Break With Cuba

By JAMES RESTON
Special to The New York Times.

WASHINGTON, Jan. 3—The Eisenhower Administration took full responsibility tonight for the diplomatic break with Cuba.

Secretary of State Christian A. Herter yesterday informed Dean Rusk, who will succeed him in less than three weeks, of the President's decision, but he did not seek the advice of the leaders of the incoming Administration on what should be done.

Mr. Herter asked Mr. Rusk whether the incoming Democratic Administration would like to associate itself with the break. Mr. Rusk replied after consultations with President-elect John F. Kennedy that in the absence of complete information on all the relevant factors the new Administration did not feel that it could participate in the decision.

Both parties thus found themselves in an extremely delicate position. The Republicans were well aware of the fact that they were taking a decision that would greatly complicate the problems of the Kennedy Administration in the early days of its responsibility after the inauguration Jan. 20.

At the same time, they did not feel that they could avoid responsibility for reacting quickly to Premier Fidel Castro's demand that the United States diplomatic mission in Cuba should be reduced to eleven persons.

The Democrats were equally

Continued on Page 4, Column 3

REGIME IS SCORED

People Suffer Under 'Yoke of Dictator,' President Says

Texts of President's statement and notes are on Page 3.

By E. W. KENWORTHY
Special to The New York Times.

WASHINGTON, Jan. 3—The United States formally terminated diplomatic and consular relations with Cuba tonight.

President Eisenhower announced the break with the Government of Premier Fidel Castro in a statement issued at the White House at 8:30 o'clock.

The break came a day and a half after the Cuban Government had delivered a note to the United States Embassy in Havana demanding that the staff of the embassy and the consulate there be reduced to eleven persons within forty-eight hours.

The President said in his statement:

"There is a limit to what the United States in self-respect can endure. That limit has now been reached."

Normal Situation 'Impossible'

The action of the Castro Government, the President said, "can have no other purpose than to render impossible the conduct of normal diplomatic relations with that Government."

Therefore, the President said, he had instructed the Secretary of State to deliver a note to the Cuban Embassy here announcing the formal ending of relations.

The President added that "this calculated action on the part of the Castro Government is only the latest of a long series of harassments, baseless accusations and vilification."

President Eisenhower said in his statement that the friendship of the United States for the Cuban people "is not affected" by the breaking of diplomatic relations with the Castro regime.

Sympathy Expressed

"It is my hope and my conviction," the President said, "that in the not too distant future it will be possible for the historic friendship between us once again to find its reflection in normal relations of every sort."

"Meanwhile," his statement said, "our sympathy goes out to the people of Cuba now suffering under the yoke of a dictator."

The United States requested the Government of Cuba, in turn, to withdraw "as soon as possible" the entire Cuban personnel in the Cuban Embassy in Washington and in all Cuban consular offices in the United States.

In a note to the Cuban Government, Secretary of State Christian A. Herter stated that it was requesting the Government of Switzerland to assume

Continued on Page 3, Column 1

Cuban U.N. Charge To Get Stern Reply

By LINDESAY PARROTT
Special to The New York Times.

UNITED NATIONS, N. Y., Jan. 3—The United States will follow up its break in relations with Cuba by sharply rejecting before the Security Council tomorrow Cuban charges of American "aggressive intentions."

Representatives of Western delegations here tonight expressed some surprise at the United States severance of relations. The American delegation, during the day, had been in contact with allied nations over the Cuban charges. It was understood, however, that the question discussed was largely whether opposition should be offered to Cuba's request to put the issue on the agenda.

The Council is to meet at 10:30 A. M. at the request of Foreign Minister Raul Roa of

Continued on Page 4, Column 4

Hammarskjold Flying to Congo To Try to End Factional Strife

By JAMES FERON
Special to The New York Times.

UNITED NATIONS, N. Y., Jan. 3—Secretary General Dag Hammarskjold left for the Congo today in an attempt to end the civil disorders threatening the work of the United Nations force there.

His departure, which had been delayed a day by party disorders in Kivu Province, remained uncertain until two hours before he left because of the changing situation in Laos.

At New York International Airport, Mr. Hammarskjold said he did not intend to visit Laos on this trip but that he might return to the United Nations earlier than he had planned if the Laotian situation required his presence here.

for Leopoldville at 5:55 P. M.

He will spend two days in the Congo and will talk with members of the eleven-nation United Nations Conciliation Commission, the Congo Government and United Nations force leaders. Technically, the visit is only a side trip on the way to South Africa, where the Secretary General will spend eight days studying racial segregation.

However, United Nations sources suggested that Mr. Hammarskjold's principal concern now was the "developing civil war" in the Congo. They felt that continuing strife between opposing Congolese factions could put the United Nations force in an untenable

Continued on Page 12, Column 5

WELCOME TO WASHINGTON: Lyndon B. Johnson, right, Vice President-elect, ... A. Mickey, ... With them at ... A. Smith 3d of ...

"All the News That's Fit to Print"

The New York Times.

LATE CITY EDITION
U.S. Weather Bureau Report (Page 81) forecasts:
Increasing cloudiness today; chance of rain tonight and tomorrow.
Temp. range: 54—40; yesterday: 52—43.

VOL. CX . No. 37,699.   © 1961 by The New York Times Company. Times Square, New York 36, N.Y.   NEW YORK, WEDNESDAY, APRIL 12, 1961.   10 cents beyond 50-mile zone from New York City except on Long Island. Higher in air delivery cities.   FIVE CENTS

SOVIET ORBITS MAN AND RECOVERS HIM; SPACE PIONEER REPORTS: 'I FEEL WELL'; SENT MESSAGES WHILE CIRCLING EARTH

HEAD OF RESERVE URGES PRICE CUTS TO RELIEVE SLUMP

Martin Asserts Reductions Would Mean More Jobs and Demand for Goods

By RICHARD E. MOONEY
Special to The New York Times

WASHINGTON, April 11—The chairman of the Federal Reserve Board made a strong appeal today for price reductions as a means of solving the nation's economic problems.

"Throughout our country, we must not only increase our productivity but also pass some of the gains on to the consumer in the form of lower prices, rather than having all of it go exclusively to labor in higher wages or to management in higher profits," he said.

The chairman, William McC. Martin Jr., said that price cuts could stimulate buying demand that would "provide more jobs for those who are now unemployed, keep the economy moving to higher levels, and [provide] still greater job opportunities in the future."

Some Gains Reported

The Labor Department reported, meanwhile, a modest increase in the factory work week and factory pay for March.

Mr. Martin spoke at the annual meeting of the Association of Reserve City Bankers at Boca Raton, Fla. Copies of his talk were made available here.

It was not the first time that a voice from Washington had been raised in favor of price cuts. It is a point that gets lost, however, in the debates most often heard here, over what the Government should or should not do. In the form presented, it is simply an exhortation. Neither Mr. Martin nor the Kennedy Administration advocates price or wage controls.

Addressing himself to the domestic economy, Mr. Martin said that "at the moment we have pressing need to reduce unemployment and to promote economic growth at the maximum sustainable speed." The way to meet the need, he said, is "a judicious blend" of specific actions, monetary and fiscal policies, and wage-price policies.

Answers Critics of Policy

In such a setting, he said, interest rates need not rise so high nor fall so low as they have in past business cycles.

Mr. Martin used his speech to answer critics who have said that recent Federal Reserve strategy cannot work and has already failed. Seven weeks ago the reserve system abandoned its established policy of buying and selling only the shortest-term securities—Treasury bills—when it sought to impose its influence on credit conditions

Continued on Page 25, Column 5

Realtor Is Indicted In Expense Padding

By EDWARD RANZAL

The president of Pease & Elliman, Inc., a leading real estate concern here, was indicted yesterday on charges of income tax evasion through fraudulent claims for entertainment and travel expenses.

The indictment against the executive, Robert Neaderland, by a Federal grand jury was said to be the first of its kind in the Southern District of New York. It was expected to break ground for future prosecutions for overstatement of business expenses.

Mr. Neaderland, 53 years old, lives at 160 Central Park South. His concern is one of the leading developers of apartments on the East Side. He is charged with attempting to evade $27,550 in income taxes in 1954 and 1955, according to

Continued on Page 38, Column 3

Wide College Aid Is Adopted by State

By WARREN WEAVER Jr.
Special to The New York Times

ALBANY, April 11—A higher-education program that will make $12,300,000 in new financial assistance available to college and university students in New York State this year was approved by Governor Rockefeller today.

He said the program gave assurance that "no young man or woman with the ability and desire for a higher education need be deprived of that opportunity for lack of funds."

The seven higher education measures that were signed included a bill that gave New York City permission to establish a city university to consist of the four municipal colleges and the community colleges in the five boroughs. One of the bills provides

Continued on Page 48, Column 3

COUNCIL APPROVES OWN CHARTER BILL

Rebuffs Mayor by Spurning State Law Under Which He Named Commission

By CHARLES G. BENNETT

The City Council passed its own bill yesterday calling for the appointment of a commission to draft a new City Charter. The vote was 21 to 3.

Council officers immediately prepared to send the measure directly to Mayor Wagner for his signature or veto. This would be based on a contention by the Council's high command that since the bill merely calls for the appointment of a commission, it does not require Board of Estimate action.

The Council's stand constituted a challenge to the new state law under which Mayor Wagner already has appointed an eleven-member Charter commission to revise the Charter.

Majority Leader Joseph T. Sharkey, who is also Democratic leader of Kings County, repeated his charge that Governor Rockefeller and Mayor Wagner had been "playing together" on Charter revision. Mayor Wagner supported the state bill.

Mr. Sharkey also said he "hoped and expected" that there

Continued on Page 26, Column 3

Population Center Moves West; Census Puts It at Centralia, Ill.

The New York Times   April 12, 1961
United States center of population, which was near Portsmouth, Ohio, a hundred years ago, has continued moving west and by 1960 was just northwest of Centralia, Ill.

By The Associated Press

WASHINGTON, April 11—The population center of the United States has moved again. Secretary of Commerce Luther H. Hodges announced today that the new center, based on the 1960 census, was near Centralia, Ill., fifty-seven miles west of its 1950 location.

In general, the population center is the point through which a straight line can be drawn in any direction dividing the country's population in half. As many people would live on one side of the line as on the other.

Mr. Hodges had another def-

Continued on Page 77, Column 5

ISRAEL DEFENDS TRIBUNAL'S RIGHT TO TRY EICHMANN

Ex-Nazi Is More Confident as Jerusalem Hearing Enters Its 2d Day

By HOMER BIGART
Special to The New York Times

JERUSALEM (Israeli Sector), Wednesday, April 12—The Attorney General of Israel, Gideon Hausner, resumed this morning his defense of the right of his country to try Adolf Eichmann for the murder of millions of Jews.

The defendant, as he entered his bulletproof glass cage on the second day of his trial seemed more confident. For the first time, he looked out at the audience. Then he sat down and engaged in an animated conversation with his German lawyer, Dr. Robert Servatius through a microphone in the glass cage. Eichmann smiled at his lawyer and seemed at ease.

On the first day of the trial, Eichmann, stonily impassive, heard his lawyer challenge the court's right to try the former Nazi leader on charges of delivering millions of Jews to Nazi annihilation camps.

The debate over Israel's right to try Eichmann was expected to continue through today's session. The court will not meet tomorrow, Holocaust Day, a day of mourning in Israel for the victims of Nazi terror.

Indictment Is Read

For seventy minutes Eichmann remained standing while the presiding judge, Justice Moshe Landau of the Israeli Supreme Court, read in Hebrew a fifteen-count indictment charging him with crimes against the Jewish people and crimes against humanity. The indictment was translated into German for Eichmann's benefit.

Rigidly erect, his head tilted back and his thin lips tightly compressed, the one-time chief of the Gestapo's Jewish Affairs Section betrayed no emotion during the opening day of trial.

His thin, hawklike visage with its large, sharply pointed nose was fixed intently on the proceedings. Not once did Eichmann turn to gaze on the throng of newsmen, foreign observers and Israeli citizens in the 750 seats in the Beit Haam (House of the People), the converted

Continued on Page 16, Column 1

Former Nazi Hears Indictment Read as Trial Begins in Jerusalem

Adolf Eichmann, charged with crimes against the Jewish people and against humanity, standing in special booth in Beit Haam courtroom yesterday. Justices at bench are, from left, Benyamin Halevi, Moshe Landau, Yitzhak Raveh.

U.S. IS DISTURBED BY DELAY ON LAOS

Soviet Lag on Cease-Fire and Increase in Supplies Regarded as Ominous

By WILLIAM J. JORDEN
Special to The New York Times

WASHINGTON, April 11—Officials said today the United States Government was disturbed by Moscow's delay in accepting a Western plan for an immediate cease-fire in Laos.

A spokesman for the State Department said that continued delay would be regarded here as "a matter of very serious concern."

Adding to the worries of Administration leaders were intelligence reports of a general increase in the flow of Soviet-bloc military supplies to the Pathet Lao movement in recent days. This was regarded as an ominous sign of Soviet intentions in Laos.

Rusk Voices Hope

High officials continued to be hopeful, however, that Moscow would soon give a favorable answer to the cease-fire plan advanced by the British several weeks ago.

That hope was voiced on Capitol Hill today by Secretary of State Dean Rusk. The Secretary told Senators that he expected a Soviet answer "within a very few days."

The presumption here is that continued fighting in Laos contains the seeds of a possibly enlarged conflict and that the Soviet bloc does not want to

Continued on Page 12, Column 4

Centennial of War Rocked by Dispute

By The Associated Press

CHARLESTON, S. C., April 11—New Jersey accused the National Civil War Centennial Commission of "pathetic mismanagement" tonight and asked that President Kennedy remove Maj. Gen. Ulysses S. Grant 3d as chairman.

Joseph Dempsey, vice chairman of the Jersey Centennial Commission, made the charge at a news conference after General Grant had turned down the state's request for time to rebut a dinner speaker who had criticized its civil rights practices.

General Grant and Donald Flamm, Jersey chairman, engaged in an unscheduled standing debate at the crowded dinner at the Charleston Naval Base, General Grant, too loud applause, insisted that New

Continued on Page 2, Column 3

Eichmann peers intently at tribunal during proceedings
Associated Press Radiophoto

FRANCE DECLARES ANTI-U.N. 'STRIKE'

De Gaulle Bars Any Role in Armed Ventures — Warns Algerians on Partition

By HENRY GINIGER
Special to The New York Times

PARIS, April 11—France proclaimed today a virtual strike against the United Nations.

In one of the harshest indictments he has ever made against the organization, President de Gaulle said France "did not wish to participate either by her men or her money in any present or possible enterprise of this organization—or of this disorganization" at his news conference.

The President, in response to a question, confirmed his country's refusal to contribute to the costs of the United Nations force in the Congo. A Foreign Ministry spokesman said that in this context the President's statement referred to present or future military enterprises, although the word "military" did not occur in the text of his news conference.

On another issue, President de Gaulle offered a mixture of incentives for Algerian rebel cooperation with France. He warned anew that a "rupture" might result in the partitioning of Algeria to protect those Algerians who wished to remain under French control.

The President called for reform of the United Nations as well as of the Atlantic Alliance. He said that his confidence in the free people of the world will overcome those dangers if they are united and resolute.

Continued on Page 3, Column 5

BRITISH CONSIDER TRADE UNITY STEP

Kennedy Hopes London Will Enter Common Market

By JAMES RESTON
Special to The New York Times

WASHINGTON, April 11—President Kennedy now has the impression that the British Government is seriously thinking about joining the European Economic Community, or Common Market.

This impression is based on the fact that during the President's conversations with Prime Minister Macmillan here last week the British leader asked what the United States Government would think if Britain decided to reverse her policy and join the Western European nations now working toward economic and political integration.

Administration to Cooperate

President Kennedy's reply was that the United States would regard this as a major advance toward the unity of the West.

The President did not in any way imply that the United States was thinking of joining the Common Market itself, but he did stress his Government's determination to cooperate fully with its allies in the Organization for Economic Cooperation and Development.

On a recent trip to London it is known that George Ball, United States Under Secretary of State for Economic Affairs, urged upon Viscount Hailsham, the British Lord President of the Council, that Britain give the most serious consideration

Continued on Page 2, Column 3

ADENAUER IN U.S. TO SEE KENNEDY

Arrives for First Talks With President—Stresses Unity

Special to The New York Times

WASHINGTON, April 11—Chancellor Adenauer of West Germany arrived here tonight for his first meetings with President Kennedy.

He alighted at Andrews Air Force Base from the Lufthansa jet airliner that brought him without stop from Bonn.

In an arrival statement the 85-year-old Chancellor said the German people had already developed "great confidence" in the new President of the United States. He said he was looking forward to establishing personal contact with Mr. Kennedy.

Dr. Adenauer pledged that his country's considerable energy and ability would be devoted to the cause of peace and freedom. He said that his Government realized that its share of responsibility for the future of the world grew "in proportion with our efficiency and capacity."

"Our times are filled with threats and dangers," the Chancellor said, "but I feel sure that the free people of the world will overcome those dangers if they are united and resolute."

The West German leader and his party, including his daughter, Frau Libeth Werhahn, were

Continued on Page 6, Column 5

187-MILE HEIGHT

Yuri Gagarin, a Major, Makes the Flight in 5-Ton Vehicle

Text of the Tass statement is printed on Page 22.

By United Press International

MOSCOW, Wednesday, April 12—The Soviet Union announced today it had won the race to put a man into space. The official press agency, Tass, said a man had orbited the earth in a spaceship and had been brought back alive and safe.

A brief announcement said the first reported space man had landed in what was described as the "prescribed area" of the Soviet Union after a historic flight.

A Moscow radio announcer broke into a program and said in emotional tones:

"Russia has successfully launched a man into space. His name is Yuri Gagarin. He was launched in a sputnik named Vostok, which means 'East.'"

Reports on Landing

Tass said that, on landing, Major Gagarin said: "Please report to the party and Government, and personally to Nikita Sergeyevich Khrushchev, that the landing was normal, I feel well, have no injuries or bruises."

He landed at 10:55 A. M. Moscow time [2:55 A. M. New York time].

Earlier, the major reported: "Flight is proceeding normally, I feel well."

After orbiting the earth the major applied a braking device, and the vehicle space landed in the Soviet Union, Tass said.

Major Gagarin, 27 years old, is an industrial technician, and married. He was reported to have received pre-flight training similar to that of the astronauts who will man the United States' first space ships.

Soared to 187 Miles

The announcer said the Sputnik reached a minimum altitude of 175 kilometers (109½ miles) and a maximum altitude of 302 kilometers (187¾ miles).

He said the weight of the Sputnik was 10,395 pounds, or slightly over five tons.

It said the time of the launching came at 2 A. M. New York time.

It said everything functioned normally during the flight. Constant radio contact was maintained between earth and the sputnik, the Moscow radio said.

The announcer said the duration of each revolution around the earth was 89.1 minutes.

The title of the announcement was "The First Human Flight into the Cosmos."

The radio, which was quoting a Tass press agency statement on the launching, said that Maj.

Continued on Page 22, Column 1

White House Confirms Firing; Feat Hailed by U. S. Scientists

By JOHN W. FINNEY
Special to The New York Times

WASHINGTON, Wednesday, April 12—Pierre Salinger, White House press secretary, announced early today that "American tracking stations have confirmed the fact that the Soviet Union has launched a satellite today."

"We are keeping in close touch with the situation but have no additional comment at this time," he said.

The Soviet success in orbiting the first man into space left United States officials in a resigned mood of congratulations.

The United States has no chance of equaling the Soviet feat until perhaps late this year.

The Soviet announcement did not take them by surprise, since there had been advance information from United States tracking stations that a satellite had been launched.

James E. Webb, head of the National Aeronautics and Space Administration, described the feat as "a significant accomplishment" that "demonstrates great technical capacity."

"I hope that they can find it possible to make the benefits of this event available to the rest of the world," he said.

Dr. Hugh L. Dryden, deputy administrator of the space agency, commented, "This is something we have been expecting for some time."

"It is only the beginning of man's continued effort of manned exploration of space," he said, "and I think we should continue as rapidly as we can with our own program."

In appraising the achieve-

Continued on Page 24, Column 1

The news story that did not see light
HEID ONLY when three men went into space—Page 45

217

"All the News That's Fit to Print"

The New York Times.

LATE CITY EDITION
U.S. Weather Bureau Report (Page 74) forecasts:
Mostly fair today.
Fair tonight and tomorrow.
Temp. range: 56—42; yesterday: 55—42.

VOL. CX..No. 37,705.
© 1961 by The New York Times Company.
Times Square, New York 36, N. Y.

NEW YORK, TUESDAY, APRIL 18, 1961.

10 cents beyond 50-mile zone from New York City except on Long Island. Higher in air delivery cities.

FIVE CENTS

SUPREME COURT UPHOLDS UNIONS AGAINST N.L.R.B.

It Upsets Board's Ruling That Contracts Illegally Force Membership

MAILERS' PACTS BACKED

New York Printers' Local and California Teamsters Win on Agreements

By ANTHONY LEWIS
Special to The New York Times.

WASHINGTON, April 17—A series of decisions by the National Labor Relations Board designed to prevent the compelling of union membership was struck down today by the Supreme Court.

The court disposed of a group of major labor cases that will affect dozens of others pending in the lower courts and before the labor relations board. The court did the following things in its principal rulings:

¶It upheld, 6 to 2, contracts of the International Typographical Union with newspapers that provided that the foreman of the composing room or mail room must be an I. T. U. member and must handle all hiring in his operations.

¶By the same vote, it upheld a provision in I. T. U. contracts that made the I. T. U. "general laws" applicable unless in conflict with Federal or state laws.

¶By the same vote, it held there was nothing illegal in bargaining agreements that provided that casual workers, both union and nonunion, be hired through a union-operated hiring hall.

¶It killed, 7 to 1, an N. L. R. B. ruling making labor and management refund to employes all union dues collected under an agreement found to constitute an illegal closed shop.

Douglas Writes Opinion

Justice William O. Douglas wrote the opinion of the court in all the cases. There was an eight-man court because Justice Felix Frankfurter took no part in the decisions.

Two cases settled long disputes over standard contracts sought by the typographical union. The first of these involved the New York Mailers' Union 6, which is affiliated with the I. T. U., and The New York Daily News and The Wall Street Journal.

The contract specified that mail room foremen must be members of the I. T. U. and must do the hiring. The N. L. R. B. had ruled that the foremen clause was a coercive device to make sure that only union members were hired and that it was thus a violation of the Taft-Hartley Law.

Justice Douglas wrote today that first, the contract said no foreman should be disciplined by the union for carrying out the publisher's instructions, and he concluded that the foreman remained the employer's agent despite his union membership.

Second, Justice Douglas said, the court would "not assume" that the foreman clause would produce discrimination in favor of union members in the absence of actual proof of discrimination. The N. L. R. B. was thus left free to bring a case to show that

Continued on Page 27, Column 3

Jersey Votes Today In Primary Election

By GEORGE CABLE WRIGHT
Special to The New York Times.

TRENTON, April 17 — New Jersey residents will nominate major party candidates for Governor tomorrow, along with candidates for ten of twenty-one State Senate seats and for all sixty seats in the Assembly.

Also at stake will be the nominations for scores of county and local posts.

The polls will open at 7 A. M. and close at 8 P. M.

Interest will center on the balloting in the Republican nomination for Governor. A bitter three-way contest for the nomination came to a close tonight with television and radio appeals by the participants.

They are James P. Mitchell, the former Secretary of Labor, and State Senators Walter H. Jones of Bergen county and

Continued on Page 38, Column 1

U.S. Finds Soviet's Reply On Laos Is Unsatisfactory

Rusk Says Note Is Unclear on Timing and Verification of Cease-Fire— Calls Issue 'Very Critical'

By E. W. KENWORTHY
Special to The New York Times.

WASHINGTON, April 17—Secretary of State Dean Rusk said today that the new Soviet note on Laos did not satisfy the United States on the timing and verification of a cease-fire.

This, Mr. Rusk said at his news conference, is a "very critical matter" in any attempt to bring "the situation to a peaceful and satisfactory conclusion." [Introductory statement, Page 18.]

The Soviet note "clarifying" Moscow's first reply to the British proposals of March 23 was delivered to Sir Frank Roberts, the British Ambassador, yesterday. The British Embassy informed Mr. Rusk of the contents of the reply last night.

The British had proposed a three-step procedure; a call for a cease-fire by Britain and the Soviet Union, the co-chairmen of the 1954 Geneva Conference that brought the Indochinese

war to an end; verification of the cease-fire by the three-nation International Control Commission, which observed the carrying out of the Geneva accord in Laos, and a fourteen-nation conference to set up a neutral, independent Laotian Government.

It was the British intention that these steps should take place in quick order. But Britain and the United States have made clear that there could be no conference until a cease-fire was in effect.

In one respect the Soviet note represented an advance over the earlier response, according to informed sources here. Previously Moscow had indicated that the cease-fire and the conference must take place simultaneously—or very nearly so.

In yesterday's note, these

Continued on Page 2, Column 1

HIGH COURT VOIDS CAFE'S NEGRO BAN

Holds Private Restaurant on State Land in Delaware Cannot Refuse Service

Special to The New York Times.

WASHINGTON, April 17—The Supreme Court held today that a privately operated restaurant situated in a publicly owned parking garage in Wilmington, Del., could not refuse to serve Negroes.

Six justices agreed on that result. The three others thought the case should have been sent back to the Delaware Supreme Court for clarification of its views on state law.

The decision is a significant one because of the light it throws on the established doctrine that only "official action" is covered by the Fourteenth Amendment. The Constitution does not prohibit racial discrimination by private persons or enterprises.

The court concluded that the Government of Delaware was sufficiently involved in this private enterprise, the restaurant, to bring it under the Constitution. In the view of observers here, the court broke at least some new ground in reaching that conclusion.

Justice Tom C. Clark wrote the opinion for the court. He was joined by Chief Justice Earl Warren and Justices Hugo L. Black, William O. Douglas and William J. Brennan Jr.

A separate concurring opinion, resting on quite different grounds, was filed by Justice Potter Stewart. Dissents suggesting that the court should

Continued on Page 26, Column 1

HAUSNER ATTACKS EICHMANN'S PLEA

Israeli Prosecutor Details His Charges After Ex-Nazi Says He Is Not Guilty

Text of decision and Hausner excerpts are on Page 23.

By HOMER BIGART
Special to The New York Times.

JERUSALEM (Israeli Sector), April 17 — Attorney General Gideon Hausner began an attack today on Adolf Eichmann's plea of innocence at his trial for responsibility in the killing of millions of Jews.

Earlier in the day Eichmann lost a challenge to the court's jurisdiction and entered his not-guilty plea when the trial was resumed after the week-end recess. Eichmann's plea for a hearing, on his kidnapping from Argentina was rejected by the court.

"In the sense of the indictment I am not guilty," Eichmann had told the three Israeli judges.

He made his statement of innocence in a precise but toneless voice in reply to charges that he had planned the annihilation of 6,000,000 European Jews for the Nazis during World War II.

From the qualified nature of his plea, it was clear that Eichmann's defense would be based on the contention that he was a mere cog in the machinery of genocide and that he was bound by higher orders when he delivered the Jews to death camps.

Standing rigidly erect and

Continued on Page 23, Column 7

GIZENGA OFFICERS ACCEPT MOBUTU AS ARMY'S CHIEF

Kasavubu Agrees to Reform Troops—Signs Accord on Congo-U.N. Cooperation

By HENRY TANNER
Special to The New York Times.

LEOPOLDVILLE, the Congo, April 17—Congolese Army headquarters announced tonight that field commanders operating under the control of the Leftist regime of Antoine Gizenga had recognized the authority of Maj. Gen. Joseph D. Mobutu as military commander in chief.

General Mobutu is the commander of the Central Government's forces.

The announcement said officers of the Gizenga regime had recognized General Mobutu during a conference at Bundoki, on the border of Eastern Province. The province is controlled by Mr. Gizenga.

The announcement also said a cease-fire had been ordered all along the border of Eastern and Equator Provinces.

Here in Leopoldville President Joseph Kasavubu and representatives of Secretary General Dag Hammarskjold signed an agreement on reorganization of the Congolese Army and the withdrawal of some foreign advisers.

Resolution 'Accepted'

The Congolese President and his Government "accepted" the Security Council resolution of Feb. 21 with the "understanding" that the United Nations, in implementing the resolution, respected the sovereignty of the Congo Republic.

The announcement on the military agreement did not say whether Gen. Victor Lundula, who has been commanding Mr. Gizenga's forces, took part in the conference.

Despite rumors of rivalry between him and Mr. Gizenga, General Lundula has consistently stressed his loyalty to his civilian superiors in Stanleyville, capital of Eastern Province.

General Mobutu left Leopoldville a week ago for the border area where the military conference took place. Talks between the two sides had continued intermittently for several weeks with and without his participation.

Kasavubu Plan Backed

In accepting the Security Council resolution the Leopoldville Government "recognized" the necessity for reorganizing the Congolese National Army. It reaffirmed President Kasavubu's earlier proposal that the reorganization take place with United Nations assistance, but under his personal authority as chief of state.

The agreement called for the United Nations to give assistance to the President so that "all foreign civil officials, military and paramilitary mercenaries and political advisers who have not been engaged under his authority" will be re-

Continued on Page 4, Column 3

ANTI-CASTRO UNITS LAND IN CUBA; REPORT FIGHTING AT BEACHHEAD; RUSK SAYS U. S. WON'T INTERVENE

April 18, 1961

CARIBBEAN STRIFE: Rebel forces attacking Cuba landed in Las Villas Province in the area of Bahia de Cochinos (1, and A on the inset map). Other anti-Castro landings were said to have taken place in area of Santiago de Cuba (2) and in Pinar del Rio (3).

The New York Times

ROA CHARGES U.S. ARMED INVADERS

Tells U.N. That C.I.A. Aided Attacks—'Aggression' Is Denied by Stevenson

Excerpts from Stevenson and Roa statements, Page 16.

By THOMAS J. HAMILTON
Special to The New York Times.

UNITED NATIONS, N. Y., April 17—Dr. Raul Roa, Foreign Minister of Cuba, charged today that his country had been invaded this morning "by a force of mercenaries, organized, financed and armed by the Government of the United States."

Dr. Roa told the General Assembly's Political Committee that the attack had been launched from points in Florida and Guatemala under the direction of the Central Intelligence Agency, which he called the "Gestapo." The Gestapo was the Nazi security police force.

He continued to use terms made familiar to nazism by calling Dr. José Miró Cardona, head of the anti-Castro Cuban Revolutionary Council, the "gauleiter." Gauleiters were regional party leaders under the Nazis.

Florida Launching Denied

Adlai E. Stevenson, chief United States delegate, said in reply that "the United States has committed no aggression against Cuba and no offensive has been launched from Florida or from any other part of the United States."

[In Guatemala, the Government denied that it had participated in any attack on Cuba.]

Just before the debate ended late this evening Dr. Roa charged that two jet planes from a United States carrier had escorted a Cuban rebel plane to safety this afternoon. He also alleged that forces from the United States Naval Base at Guantanamo had entered Oriente Province, where

Continued on Page 17, Column 1

Rusk Declares Sympathy Of Nation for Castro Foes

By JAMES RESTON
Special to The New York Times.

WASHINGTON, April 17—Secretary of State Dean Rusk expressed today the sympathy of the American people for those who struck against Castroism in Cuba, but emphasized "there is not and will not be any intervention there by United States forces."

The Administration did not deny that it was giving material support to the raiding parties, but this aid was undoubtedly on a much smaller

Transcript of Rusk's news conference is on Page 18.

scale than originally planned here and the landings in Cuba were much smaller than excited reports of "invasion" suggested.

No more than 200 to 300 men were involved in the week-end landings on the vast coastline of Cuba, according to reliable information reaching here.

In fact, the landings of the last forty-eight hours were not designed to get a lot of fighting men on the ground, but to provide supplies for the anti-Castro underground already operating there as a result of at least six other landings that have taken place over the last few months.

Refugees Assume Control

In the last ten days, the Cuban refugees have assumed control of the operations against Premier Fidel Castro. Accordingly, official Washington could not be sure of the fate of all the small parties that went ashore. Secretary Rusk was extremely cautious in his remarks on the situation at his news conference this morning. What happens in Cuba, he said, is for the Cuban people to decide. He added, however, that the Administration was "not indifferent" to the intrusion of the "Communist conspiracy" into this hemisphere and promised to "work together with other governments of this hemisphere to meet efforts by this conspiracy to extend its penetration." [Opening statement, Page 18.]

On this point, considerable attention was being paid here

Continued on Page 18, Column 1

PREMIER DEFIANT

Says His Troops Battle Heroically to Repel Attacking Force

The texts of Castro appeals are printed on Page 14.

By TAD SZULC
Special to The New York Times.

MIAMI, Tuesday, April 18—Rebel troops opposed to Premier Fidel Castro landed before dawn yesterday on the swampy southern coast of Cuba in Las Villas Province.

The attack, which was supported from the air, was announced by the rebels and confirmed by the Cuban Government.

After fourteen hours of silence on the progress of the assault, the Government radio in Havana broadcast early today a terse communiqué signed by Premier Castro announcing only that "our armed forces are continuing to fight the enemy heroically."

The announcement, made shortly before 1 A. M., said that within the next few hours details of "our successes" would be given.

The communiqué came amid a wave of rebel assertions of victories, new landings and internal uprisings. The rebel spokesmen were acclaiming important progress in new landings in Oriente and Pinar del Rio Provinces, but none of these reports could be confirmed.

Government Reports Battle

The Government communiqué said a battle had been fought in the southeastern part of Las Villas Province, where yesterday morning's landings occurred.

Although the communiqué was signed by Premier Castro, the Cuban leader has not spoken since the attack began. An earlier communiqué issued yesterday, reported the rebel landings.

In a communiqué issued last night, the Revolutionary Council, the top command of the rebel forces, said merely that military supplies and equipment were landed successfully on the marshy beachhead. The communiqué added that "some armed resistance" by supporters of Premier Castro had been overcome.

Premier Castro was reported to have escaped injury in an early-morning air raid yesterday near the beachhead.

The Revolutionary Council's announcement spoke of action in Matanzas Province, indicating that the rebels might have

Continued on Page 14, Column 1

MOSCOW BLAMES U. S. FOR ATTACK

Izvestia Asserts 'American Hirelings' Invade Cuba— Khrushchev Confers

By SEYMOUR TOPPING
Special to The New York Times.

MOSCOW, April 17—The Soviet Union charged tonight that the United States was responsible for the landing in Cuba by what it described as "American hirelings."

Izvestia, the Soviet Government newspaper, contended that plans for landing anti-Castro forces in Cuba have been worked out and inspired by "American imperialists."

"On all continents voices now are crying out determinedly for an end to the armed aggression against Cuba and for the defense of the freedom and independence of the Cuban people," Izvestia said.

At his vacation retreat in Sochi on the Black Sea, Premier Khrushchev conferred on the Cuban crisis with Foreign Minister Andrei A. Gromyko. A formal Government statement is expected tomorrow.

Atmosphere Is Tense

An atmosphere of tension gripped the Soviet capital after the announcement at 4 P. M. by the Moscow radio that "an armed intervention against Cuba" had begun.

It was felt by most Western experts that the Soviet reaction would be confined to strong diplomatic representations, complaints in the United Nations and a propaganda onslaught against the United States.

Some observers recalled that in a speech here July 10, Mr. Khrushchev had declared: "Figuratively speaking, if need be, Soviet artillerymen can support the Cuban people with their rocket fire, should the aggressive forces in the Pentagon dare to start intervention against Cuba."

The Soviet leader also had noted that the United States was no longer out of range of Soviet missiles.

Western experts said that Mr. Khrushchev's statement seemed to have more applicability to an invasion of Cuba than to an attack of the type being undertaken

Continued on Page 17, Column 2

CHANTING CUBANS BACK CASTRO HERE

1,000 in Midtown March Dispersed by Police

Nearly 1,000 chanting, sign-bearing pro-Castro Cubans demonstrated last night outside the United Nations and the United States Mission to the United Nations and in the Times Square area.

Heavy police details had kept the crowds behind barriers most of the day and no violence erupted until a smaller group of pro-Castro Cubans blocked pedestrian traffic in Times Square area. The police made two arrests and two policemen were injured during a brief scuffle with the demonstrators.

Many of the demonstrators carried Cuban flags and pictures of Dr. Castro as they marched from the United Nations Plaza along Forty-second Street to the corner of Eighth Avenue and Forty-third street.

An emergency police signal brought ten radio cars and ten mounted policemen to that area. The crowd then broke up into four sections and departed in different directions.

A few minutes later, at 8 P. M., a smaller group of demonstrators formed on the sidewalk on Broadway between

Continued on Page 14, Column 5

Eisenhowers Are Welcomed Home to Pennsylvania

General and Mrs. Eisenhower in Harrisburg with Gov. David L. Lawrence of Pennsylvania
United Press International Telephoto

By The Associated Press.

HARRISBURG, Pa., April 17—Thousands of persons welcomed former President Dwight D. Eisenhower and Mrs. Eisenhower home to Pennsylvania today. The gathering was the state's official

welcome for General Eisenhower, who left the White House Jan. 20. The former President, looking tanned and fit after a six-week vacation in California, was obviously touched by Gov. David L. Lawrence, a Democrat, headed

the state and city officials on the platform. The Eisenhowers have a farm home in Gettysburg, thirty-five miles southwest of this capital city. It is the only home they have ever owned. They left for home by car after the ceremonies.

Walker Is Relieved of Command While Army Checks Birch Ties

Special to The New York Times.

WASHINGTON, April 17—The Army said today that Maj. Gen. Edwin A. Walker had been relieved of his command in Germany while an investigation was made into reports that he had been indoctrinating his troops with the views of the John Birch Society.

The announcement said that Secretary of the Army Elvis J. Stahr Jr. had ordered General Walker transferred immediately from command of the front-line Twenty-fourth Division "pending the outcome of an official investigation."

The investigation will involve "certain published statements and actions of General Walker," the Army said.

The announcement did not mention the Birch Society. However, officials acknowledged that the transfer and investigation had been prompted by allegations that the 51-year-old general had been urging the views of the Right-Wing group upon his troops for the last six months.

The Overseas Weekly, a privately owned newspaper distributed among American troops in Europe, reported last week that General Walker had instituted a special troop-indoctrination program using materials and publications of the society.

General Walker accused the newspaper yesterday of being "immoral, unscrupulous, corrupt and destructive." The newspaper stood by its report and said that his charges

Continued on Page 24, Column 6

"All the News That's Fit to Print"

The New York Times.

LATE CITY EDITION
U. S. Weather Bureau Report (Page 62) forecast:
Cloudy, warm, chance of rain late today or tonight and tomorrow.
Temp. range: 61—48; yesterday: 70—47.

VOL. CX..No. 37,723.   © 1961 by The New York Times Company. Times Square, New York 36, N. Y.   NEW YORK, SATURDAY, MAY 6, 1961.   10 cents beyond 50-mile zone from New York City except on Long Island. Higher in air delivery cities.   FIVE CENTS

JOHNSON TO MEET LEADERS IN ASIA ON U.S. TROOP USE

President Says Decision on South Vietnam Action Will Await Report

TALKS SET IN CAPITALS

Ngo Dinh Diem Is Expected to Seek American Units to Deter Red Attack

Transcript of news conference and summary, Page 14.

By WILLIAM J. JORDEN
Special to The New York Times.

WASHINGTON, May 5—President Kennedy said today that the assignment of United States armed forces to South Vietnam would be one of several important matters Vice President Lyndon B. Johnson would discuss on his coming trip to Asia. [Opening statement and Question 4, Page 14.]

The President confirmed that the possibility of sending United States troops to Southeast Asia was under study. He indicated that the final decision would depend on the results of Mr. Johnson's talks in Saigon with President Ngo Dinh Diem and others.

Mr. Kennedy said at a news conference that a special task force in the Government was working on problems related to helping South Vietnam maintain its independence. The question has been considered by the National Security Council as well, he said.

Vital Assignment

Mr. Johnson is expected to leave next Tuesday for the Far East. He also will meet with top Government officials in Bangkok, Thailand; Manila, and other capitals.

The President today described the Johnson mission as "an extremely important assignment."

It is widely assumed here that President Ngo will ask for the assignment of at least a token force of United States troops and regard it as a guarantee of United States' involvement should his country be attacked in force by the Communist North.

Mr. Kennedy did not touch on the matter today, but it is known that the Government is also considering the possibility of sending a similar token force to Thailand. The latter is allied to the United States in the

Continued on Page 3, Column 4

NIXON ASKS DRIVE TO OFFSET SOVIET

Bids Kennedy Rally America to a Fresh Foreign Policy

Excerpts from Nixon speech are printed on Page 2.

By AUSTIN C. WEHRWEIN
Special to The New York Times.

CHICAGO, May 5—Former Vice President Richard M. Nixon urged President Kennedy today to rally the American people for a new start in American foreign policy.

Mr. Nixon called for a "searching reappraisal of the free world's ability, particularly America's ability, to deal with the kind of aggression in which Communists are now engaging."

He further revealed that he had given President Kennedy the "assurance that I will support him to the hilt in backing positive action he may decide is necessary to resist Communist aggression."

[President Kennedy, meanwhile, sent his nuclear testban negotiator back to Geneva with an implied warning that the United States might not continue the talks much longer without some prospect of a safeguarded treaty.]

To meet such threats, the former Vice President said that the United States was prepared to act alone if swift action were needed while machinery for collective action was being set up.

The lesson of Cuba and Laos, he said, is this:

"We must never talk bigger than we are prepared to act.

"When our words are strong and our actions are timid, we

Continued on Page 2, Column 3

Continued on Page 3, Column 2

Talks Open in Laos On Truce Details; Meeting 'Friendly'

By JACQUES NEVARD
Special to The New York Times.

HIN HEUP, Laos, May 5—Military representatives of the pro-Western Laotian Government and the pro-Communist Pathet Lao rebels held a preliminary conference here today on machinery for continuing the cease-fire that became effective Wednesday.

The conference lasted one hour and five minutes and was described as "friendly."

According to a Laotian Army spokesman, Col. Oudom Sananikone, the meeting did not take up any political questions.

There appeared to be few tangible results of the talks, but Colonel Oudom Sananikone stressed that the meeting was a preliminary one.

He said that the first Pathet Lao request was that the next meeting take place at Namone, thirty-five miles north of here

2 BILLION AID PLAN FOR BRAZIL IS NEAR

U. S. Presses World-Wide Program of New Loans and Debt Deferments

By TAD SZULC
Special to The New York Times.

WASHINGTON, May 5—An international financial rescue package worth more than $2,000,000,000 is being prepared for Brazil. Negotiations, already well advanced, involve the United States, six Western European countries, Japan and the International Monetary Fund.

The agreements, which may be announced late next week, call for new loans totaling nearly $630,000,000. About $340,000,000 of this is to be provided by the United States. The remainder will take the form of a postponement in the repayment of much of Brazil's huge foreign debt.

This international financial operation, the largest ever involving a Latin-American country and one of the largest anywhere in postwar years, is designed to provide President Janio Quadros with extra time and resources to reorganize his economy.

Broad Effort in View

The United States is playing a key role in putting together the Brazilian package. It will also supply separate smaller loans to bolster the economies of Venezuela and Bolivia. Venezuela, which is facing serious budget difficulties, expects to receive soon an initial loan of $50,000,000.

Besides these emergency measures to assist the economies of individual Latin-American republics, the United States moved today to call a special inter-American conference to blueprint long-range economic and social development programs.

President Kennedy announced at his news conference that the United States' delegation to the Council of the Organization of American States would be named

Continued on Page 17, Column 1

Kennedy Plans Aid To Retrain Jobless And Spur Recovery

By PETER BRAESTRUP
Special to The New York Times.

WASHINGTON, May 5—The Kennedy Administration expects to ask Congress for at least $75,000,000 to provide retraining for the long-term unemployed. Other new anti-recession measures also are being considered.

The key question that President Kennedy has yet to decide is whether to break the Administration's self-imposed limit on Federal spending in an effort to stimulate the economy and spur employment.

The $75,000,000 program for retraining workers who have been laid off by technological change and by the decay of their own industries will not materially affect the budget. Nor will the President's orders to the Pentagon to channel more defense contracts to small

Continued on Page 19, Column 2

U. S. HURLS MAN 115 MILES INTO SPACE; SHEPARD WORKS CONTROLS IN CAPSULE, REPORTS BY RADIO IN 15-MINUTE FLIGHT

RETURN: Astronaut rides in one of helicopters carrying his Mercury capsule to the Lake Champlain

LAUNCHING: Rocket lifts the capsule

SAFE ABOARD: On the Lake Champlain's deck, Comdr. Alan B. Shepard Jr. views capsule he occupied

Associated Press Wirephotos

ASTRONAUT: Commander Shepard removes space suit.

IN FINE CONDITION

Astronaut Drops Into the Sea Four Miles From Carrier

Excerpts from radioed reports by Shepard, Page 8

By RICHARD WITKIN
Special to The New York Times.

CAPE CANAVERAL, Fla., May 5—A slim, cool Navy test pilot was rocketed 115 miles into space today.

Thirty-seven-year-old Comdr. Alan B. Shepard Jr. thus became the first American space explorer.

Commander Shepard landed safely 302 miles out at sea fifteen minutes after the launching. He was quickly lifted aboard a Marine Corps helicopter.

"Boy, what a ride!" he said, as he was flown to the aircraft carrier Lake Champlain four miles away.

Extensive physical examinations were begun immediately. Tonight doctors reported Commander Shepard in "excellent" condition, suffering no ill effects.

Major U. S. Step

The near-perfect flight represented the United States' first major step in the race to explore space with manned space craft.

True, it was only a modest leap compared with the once-around-the-earth orbital flight of Maj. Yuri A. Cagarin of the Soviet Union.

The Russian's speed of more than 17,000 miles an hour was almost four times Commander Shepard's, 4,500. The distance the Russian traveled was almost 100 times as great.

But Commander Shepard maneuvered his craft in space—something the Russians have not claimed for Major Gagarin.

All in all, the American flight was welcomed almost rapturous-

Continued on Page 8, Column 1

MAYOR IS UPHELD ON CHARTER LAW

But Court Reverses Ban on Action by Council, Opening Way to Rival Proposals

By RONALD MAIORANA

Mayor Wagner's right to appoint a Charter Revision Commission was upheld by Justice Irving Saypol yesterday in State Supreme Court.

However, Justice Saypol ruled invalid part of the law under which the Mayor had acted. This part excluded the City Council from Charter-revision activity.

Lawyers said the ruling appeared to make possible the enactment of the City Council's own plan for a Charter Revision Commission. Thus, it is conceivable, they said, that two competing Charters—one drawn by the Mayor's commission and the other by a commission created by the Council—could be submitted to the voters Nov. 7.

In a twenty-two-page decision that caused confusion at City Hall, Justice Saypol ruled that the section of the state law that had the effect of bypassing the City Council was invalid because it was an improper delegation of legislative power. He said: "The newly enacted au-

Continued on Page 22, Column 1

Shepard Had Periscope: 'What a Beautiful View'

By JOHN W. FINNEY
Special to The New York Times.

CAPE CANAVERAL, Fla., May 5—"All systems go * * * Everything A-O.K. * * * Mission very smooth * * * What a beautiful view! * * * Coming in for a landing."

These were the reports of Comdr. Alan B. Shepard Jr. as he rode the capsule Freedom 7 115 miles up into space today in the United States' first step toward manned exploration of space. His "A-O.K." is a rocket engineer term meaning double O.K. or perfect.

In a calm, methodical way he reported back by radio on every detail of his fifteen-minute flight, even during the moments of greatest stress as his capsule accelerated from the launching pad and then quickly decelerated upon re-entering the earth's atmosphere.

And there were moments of excitement in his voice, such as when he viewed much of the Eastern Coast of the United States through a periscope from 115 miles up in space.

"What a beautiful view!" he exclaimed into a microphone inside his visored space helmet and then, according to instructions, he returned to scientific observations to report that the cloud cover was three- to four-tenths and was obscuring much of the coast up through Cape Hatteras.

Three-to-four-tenths cloud cover is a description used by

Continued on Page 10, Column 1

NATION TO WIDEN ITS SPACE EFFORTS

Kennedy Wants More Funds —He Telephones Shepard to Offer Congratulations

Texts of Kennedy statement and call to Shepard, Page 11.

By DAVID HALBERSTAM
Special to The New York Times.

WASHINGTON, May 5—An even greater effort in the exploration of space was promised today by President Kennedy.

On the day of this country's first manned space flight, he told a news conference that he would make an additional request for appropriations for its space program this year.

"We are going to make a substantially larger effort in space," he declared. [Question 1, Page 14.]

Earlier in the day the President telephoned his personal congratulations to Comdr. Alan B. Shepard Jr., the nation's first space traveler, in a call from the White House to the aircraft carrier Lake Champlain.

The President also congratulated the commander's wife and his six fellow-astronauts.

Commander Shepard will visit Washington Monday. There will be a ceremony at noon on

Continued on Page 11, Column 7

PRESIDENT TO ASK INCOME TAX CUTS

Drop Next Year Is Planned, Dillon Tells House Unit

By JOHN D. MORRIS
Special to The New York Times.

WASHINGTON, May 5—The Kennedy Administration plans to lay before Congress next year a tax reform program that will include reduction of individual income taxes.

Secretary of the Treasury Douglas Dillon told the House Ways and Means Committee of the plan today but gave no details. He made it clear, however, that taxpayers with high incomes would probably be among the chief beneficiaries of a proposed reduction in rates.

"I think those in high brackets deserve relief," he said.

Mr. Dillon was questioned for nearly three hours, mainly by Republican committee members, as he completed three days of testimony on 'tax-revision legislation being sought now by the Administration.

The pending proposals include $1,700,000,000 a year in special tax credits for business enterprises to encourage modernization and expansion of plant and equipment. Tax laws on foreign income, business expense accounts and stock dividends

Continued on Page 23, Column 3

Nation Exults Over Space Feat; City Plans to Honor Astronaut

By ROBERT CONLEY

The successful flight of America's first astronaut, Comdr. Alan B. Shepard Jr., roused the country yesterday to one of its highest peaks of exultation since the end of World War II.

The achievement brought relief from the strain of fears about the Soviet Union's success in orbiting a man, feelings of new hope for the future from Maine to Hawaii and dancing in the streets at New York's Columbus Circle.

"Wonderful." "Tremendous." "The greatest thing that ever happened," thousands of persons said as the reaction took hold across the country.

Knots of people crowded sidewalks to watch television screens in store windows. Others jumped up to cheer, pounded friends on the back, ran into neighbors' houses or fell silent.

"He made it," a woman gasped in Chicago, then broke into tears. "He made it."

New York City laid plans for the "most fabulous" ticker tape welcome ever given—one that a city official said would be "even bigger than the one for Charles Lindbergh."

In Washington, Congressmen moved to bestow the nation's

Continued on Page 11, Column 5

Elizabeth Visits Pope in Vatican

By ARNALDO CORTESI
Special to The New York Times.

ROME, May 5—Pope John XXIII received Queen Elizabeth II and Prince Philip in a private audience today with traditional pomp and ceremony. The meeting was marked by extreme cordiality.

Addressing the Queen in French, the Pope said that relations between Britain and

Continued on Page 19, Column 6

Pope John XXIII in private audience with Queen Elizabeth

Associated Press Wirephoto

14 Dead, 57 Hurt by Tornado; 2 Towns in Oklahoma Hard Hit

By The Associated Press.

POTEAU, Okla., May 5—A vicious tornado tore through two tiny eastern Oklahoma communities near here tonight, killing at least fourteen persons and injuring fifty-seven.

Ten were reported dead at Howe and four at Reichert. The death toll could go higher as rescue workers dug into the debris.

There was a report that a light plane—trying to avoid the massive storm cloud—crashed after a wing tore off. The highway patrol said that a woman who lived in the area reported she saw the plane go down west

It was a grim anniversary for this rolling, wooded area some 200 miles southeast of Oklahoma City. Just one year ago twelve were killed when a twister destroyed most of the downtown area of Wilburton.

Tornadoes had plagued Oklahoma for two days, but until tonight there had been only one fatality from the scores of funnels sighted.

Two of the dead were babies. One father died with his 3-month-old son and a mother with her 14-month-old boy.

Tiny farms are scattered throughout the twister-pounded

Continued on Page 62, Column 6

NEWS INDEX

"All the News That's Fit to Print"

The New York Times.

LATE CITY EDITION
U. S. Weather Bureau Report 'Page 70; forecast:
Partly cloudy, showers today, tonight and tomorrow.
Temp. range: 79–56; yesterday: 79–47

VOL. CX...No. 37,749.

© 1961 by The New York Times Company.
Times Square, New York 36, N. Y.

NEW YORK, THURSDAY, JUNE 1, 1961.

10 cents beyond 50-mile zone from New York City
except on Long Island. Higher in air delivery cities.

FIVE CENTS

KENNEDY AND DE GAULLE AGREE TO DEFEND BERLIN; DISCUSS ASIA AND AFRICA

GUARD OF HONOR: President Kennedy and President de Gaulle are accompanied by Republican Guard as they ride from Orly Airport to the Quai d'Orsay in French capital.

PRESIDENTS MEET

Stand Firm on Soviet Threat—Parisians Hail Kennedys

Statements by de Gaulle and Kennedy are on Page 11.

By ROBERT C. DOTY
Special to The New York Times.

PARIS, May 31 — President Kennedy and President de Gaulle proclaimed today their "complete identity of views" on Western action to counter any threat to Berlin by the Soviet Union.

In view of the position on Berlin authoritatively attributed to General de Gaulle on the question, this meant that the two leaders apparently had reached agreement to go to war if necessary to maintain Western rights in the divided city.

Pierre Salinger, White House press secretary, and Pierre Baraduc, spokesman for the French Foreign Ministry, reported agreement on Berlin as a result of the thirty-seven-minute conversation between the two leaders just before they lunched together today.

In an hour-and-fifty-minute conversation after lunch, Mr. Kennedy and General de Gaulle began discussions of problems in Southeast Asia, notably Laos, and in Africa.

Welcome Is Colorful

The state visit by President and Mrs. Kennedy got off to a colorful start.

After their arrival at Orly Airport at 10:20 A. M. (5:20 A. M. Eastern Daylight Time), they rode in a motorcade through flag-decked streets.

The morning was bright and sunny and 500,000 or 1,500,000 cheering Parisians—depending on whether skeptical professional estimates or enthusiastic official figures were followed—lined the streets.

The two Presidents had three occasions to exchange complimentary words in public—at the airport, at luncheon toasts, and in a final exchange at a formal state dinner at the Elysée palace tonight.

At the dinner, Mr. Kennedy made a strong statement on the interdependence of France and the United States. He declared that "American forces will remain in Europe as long as they are required, ready to meet any threat with whatever response is needed."

Taken in the context of the earlier talks on Berlin, this seemed to be a preliminary to going all the way—including, ap-

Continued on Page 10, Column 1

Western Big Three Confer On Tough U.S. Berlin Plan

By SYDNEY GRUSON
Special to The New York Times.

BONN, Germany, May 31—The United States, Britain and France have begun consultations in Washington on American proposals to strengthen plans to meet a new Berlin crisis. A White House group headed by Dean Acheson, former Secretary of State, worked on the proposals on President Kennedy's orders, reliable sources here said.

The President was reported to have been dissatisfied with the need, under the current plans, for the Western Big Three to consult at almost every step of their reaction to Soviet or East German moves against West Berlin.

The sources said the United States now was seeking agreement for a whole series of measures that the Allies might have to take. Britain has always resisted this kind of advance commitment, it was said.

The French Attitude

Diplomats here believe that France is unlikely to oppose the new American proposals. President de Gaulle is known to advocate the most uncompromising front to the Russians on the Berlin question. When he was here ten days ago, he assured Chancellor Adenauer he would urge this view on President Kennedy.

As they have been from the start of the Berlin crisis in 1958, when Premier Khrushchev first proposed the transformation of West Berlin into a demilitarized

Continued on Page 10, Column 2

BEN-GURION FIRM ON IMMIGRATION

Reiterates View on Zionism in Cordial Meeting Here With U. S. Leaders

By IRVING SPIEGEL

Premier David Ben-Gurion spoke to American Zionist leaders here yesterday in a congenial atmosphere and held fast to his view that Zionism means nothing less than "aliyah"—immigration to Israel.

The Zionist leaders included Dr. Nahum Goldmann, president of the World Zionist Organization, and Rabbi Irving Miller, chairman of the American Zionist Council, the representative body of all Zionist groups in the country.

The setting was 515 Park Avenue, site of the offices of the Zionist Council and the executives of the agency, the Jewish Agency for Israel and various other groups. Before delivering two talks in the building, Mr. Ben-Gurion exchanged warm greetings with Dr. Goldmann and other Zionist leaders.

Free Exchange Stressed

Speaking first at a joint session of leaders of the Council and the executives of the agency, the Israeli leader said that the Zionist movement could not be the only link between Jews in America and Israel. He added that Israel welcomed close relationships between the Jewish people and other groups.

Mr. Ben-Gurion stressed the right of a free exchange of opinions between himself and Zionist leaders. He said this could only be accomplished in such nations as the United States and Israel with strong adherence to democratic ideals and practices.

"Such differences can be conducted in a friendly spirit," he asserted.

On frequent occasions Mr. Ben-Gurion has said that a good Zionist is one who goes to Israel. Zionist leaders in the United States have replied that the role of the world Zionist movement was not only to aid

Continued on Page 19, Column 1

Jobless Total Falls But Rate Hits 6.9%

Special to The New York Times.

WASHINGTON, May 31—A high unemployment rate of nearly 7 per cent continued in May for the sixth straight month despite seasonal rises in jobs, the Labor Department reported today.

Between mid-April and mid-May employment rose seasonally by 1,044,000 to 66,778,000. This total was 400,000 below that for May, 1960.

The number of unemployed Americans declined, also seasonally, by 194,000 to 4,768,000, as farm and construction work picked up last month.

But the seasonally adjusted unemployment rate increased from 6.8 to 6.9 per cent.

Asked if these May statistics

Continued on Page 19, Column 1

FRENCH GENERALS GET 15-YEAR TERM IN ALGERIA MUTINY

Challe and Zeller Sentenced for Leadership of Rising— Stripped of Decorations

By HENRY GINIGER
Special to The New York Times.

PARIS, May 31 — Former Gens. Maurice Challe and André Zeller were sentenced today to fifteen years in prison for their leadership of the military mutiny in Algeria last month.

A high military tribunal of nine distinguished jurists, generals and admirals thus ended a three-day trial. The relative leniency of their decision contrasted with the furor and anger that the generals had provoked when they seized power in Algiers early in the morning of April 22. Four days later their mutiny collapsed.

Both men had been liable to the death sentence, but the state prosecutor, Antonin Besson, said he could not see his way clear to demand it. Instead he asked for twenty years for each on the ground that there were extenuating circumstances.

Indulgence for the Army

To a large extent the indulgence shown was for the French Army itself, personified by the two generals on trial.

The three days of hearings gave the impression of a conscience-stricken military arm now living in despair because it had promised the Algerian people that it would keep Algeria French. Now it is the instrument of a policy that seeks a settlement with the Moslem rebels on the basis of Algeria's independence.

Challe and Zeller listened to their sentences without expression and their partisans in the courtroom remained silent.

The prison terms were accompanied by a court decision stripping the two men of all their decorations, including that of the Legion of Honor. They had already been deprived of their rank of full general by President de Gaulle during the mutiny.

Appeals Not Possible

The sentences cannot be appealed, but they can be commuted by the President. Challe, who is 55 years old, and Zeller, who is 63, will live their years of disgrace probably in a fort or fortress where they will be able to receive visits, newspapers and mail.

Tonight they were taken in a pouring rain back to their cells in Santé prison in Paris. Challe smoked a pipe on the way out of the Palace of Justice and appeared relaxed, as did Zeller.

Before M. Besson began his summation, the court clerk read a letter from Paul Delouvrier, who was Delegate General in Algeria during 1959 and 1960 when Challe was supreme commander.

M. Delouvrier said he still had esteem for Challe because of his high motives in acting

Continued on Page 4, Column 3

New Submarine-Finder Project Could Blunt the Role of Polaris

Mid-Atlantic Laboratory Acts to Trace Undersea Craft Through Their Sounds

By WALTER SULLIVAN

A program to develop what may become the underwater equivalent of the North American radar-warning system was announced today.

The effort under way in secret for a considerable time, is known as Project Artemis. Its success would be a mixed blessing.

If, as now seems possible, the United States can develop equipment to locate a submarine under the pack ice of the Arctic Ocean, so, eventually, can the Soviet Union. The deterrent effect of nuclear-powered submarines carrying Polaris missiles would be greatly reduced if they could no longer move in secret.

At present, however, it is thought that the Soviet Union lags far behind the United States in this field of research.

The prime contractor for the study is the Hudson Laboratories, operated by Columbia University at Yonkers in behalf of the Office of Naval

Sketch of the Project Artemis tower near Bermuda.

Research. Thirty university, industrial and government scientific groups are taking part.

Columbia and other participants in the project were permitted by the Navy to announce the program.

Among the project's chief tools are a midocean laboratory on a tower thirty miles from Bermuda and a 17,000-ton tanker modified so that it can raise and lower an immense sound generator into the sea. This "sound transducer" is five stories high and weighs

Continued on Page 16, Column 4

RUSK DELAYS TRIP

He Stays in Capital to Follow Events— Coup Is Doubted

By WILLIAM J. JORDEN
Special to The New York Times.

WASHINGTON, May 31—Secretary of State Dean Rusk delayed his departure for Europe today at President Kennedy's request. The President asked Mr. Rusk to follow developments in the wake of the assassination of the Dominican dictator, Generalissimo Rafael Leonidas Trujillo Molina.

The President talked by telephone from Paris with Secretary Rusk.

Officials here said they presumed the Secretary of State would be able to leave Washington in time to participate in the Vienna conference between President Kennedy and Premier Khrushchev. Those talks open Saturday.

Mr. Rusk and his top aides were studying reports from every available source on General Trujillo's death. The more important questions being asked were:

Who planned and carried out the Trujillo assassination? What group or individual now holds political power? Does the death of General Trujillo mean a shift in the Dominican Republic's political orientation? If so, in which direction, Left or Right?

Balaguer Reports Death

There were reports that the assassination was carried out by military elements as part of an attempted coup d'état. But the glowing tribute to the dead ruler broadcast by Caribe radio in Ciudad Trujillo indicated that anti-Trujillo forces were not in control in the Dominican capital.

The decree reporting General Trujillo's death was issued in the name of President Joaquin Balaguer. Officials took this as a further indication that there had been no overthrow of the Government.

President Balaguer's statement that "the Dominican Army is in control of the situation" was open to a variety of interpretations. It could mean that the army has seized power. Or it could indicate that there had been an unsuccessful armed effort by Dominican or foreign elements to capture the capital. Officials here said it was not yet clear what the situation was in the Dominican capital, although available evidence indicated there had been no important changes in the Government.

The first report that Trujillo had been murdered reached Washington early this morning.

Continued on Page 14, Column 5

TRUJILLO SHOT DEAD BY ASSASSINS; HIS REGIME REPORTS ARMY RULES; DOMINICAN CRISIS STUDIED BY U. S.

Associated Press
ASSASSINATED: Generalissimo Rafael Leonidas Trujillo Molina, the dictator of the Dominican Republic.

Foes of Trujillo Riot Here, Wrecking Consulate Room

By EMANUEL PERLMUTTER

Enemies of the Trujillo regime rioted yesterday at the Dominican Consulate offices in Rockefeller Center. As a result of the disorders, thirty-one men were taken to the West Forty-seventh Street police station and charged with disorderly conduct.

Despite the violence that took place in the consulate and in the street, no one was injured.

Most of the men arrested were part of a group that had forced its way into the third floor reception room seeking confirmation of General Trujillo's death from Consul General Luis R. Mercado. The men announced their intention to take possession of the offices at 1270 Avenue of the Americas.

When Dr. Mercado said he had no information for them and returned to the consulate's inner offices, the Trujillo foes began their disturbances.

Outer Room Wrecked

They tore pictures from the wall, broke a water cooler, overturned a small telephone switchboard and threw books around the room. They were prevented from entering the third floor reception room to ransack the inner suite by Detective Walter Maidhof and Patrolman Joseph De Rosa, who had been assigned to guard the consulate.

The approximately twenty-five men who entered the consulate reception room were part of a crowd of about 200 enemies of the Trujillo regime who had gathered outside the building at 5 P. M.

The disorders inside brought more than fifty policemen to the scene. More than 2,600 pedestrians, homeward bound at rush hour, stopped to watch. The police kept the Trujillo foes in the street until two patrol wagons arrived.

The police reinforcements also prevented thirty Trujillo foes who had made their way to the third floor room from entering the reception room to aid their associates.

Dr. Mercado said after the disturbance that he would cooperate with the police in any action they took against the rioters. He said he had no comment to make about General Trujillo's death or his own plans.

Police Commissioner Michael Murphy went to the consulate and conferred with Dr. Mercado for twenty minutes. The Consul General left his office at 7:40 P. M. with a police bodyguard. The men who took part in

Continued on Page 15, Column 2

MAYOR DEMANDS SCHOOL REPAIRS

Tells Board to Act 'or Else' as He Institutes Drive on Red-Tape Procedures

By LEONARD BUDER

An angry Mayor Wagner told the Board of Education yesterday to speed school repairs "or else."

After a ninety-minute meeting at City Hall with top school and other city officials, the Mayor declared:

"I do not intend to let bureaucratic red tape make our school problem look bad. I do not intend to let this kind of red tape make our schools actually bad."

Mr. Wagner announced he had ordered school officials to embark on an emergency program to expedite necessary repairs, and he promised that the funds would be found to finance such a program.

"There will be no red tape; we'll get action or else," the Mayor said in issuing his order. He indicated that disciplinary action would be taken against anyone found derelict in duty.

He also indicated that he did not consider the nine-member school board responsible for the situation, but rather administrative red tape and a "slowness" in procedure. The Mayor has the power to remove board members, after bringing charges and holding a

Continued on Page 27, Column 1

U. S. Fails to Enjoin Birmingham Police

By The Associated Press.

MONTGOMERY, Ala., May 31—A Federal judge rejected today a request by the Justice Department for a no-violence injunction against the Birmingham, Ala., police, but warned sternly against further violence toward Freedom Riders.

In its action the Government sought to prohibit the police from allowing mobs to interfere with Freedom Riders and other interstate passengers.

Still pending before United States District Judge Frank M. Johnson Jr. in Montgomery is a Government request for a con-

Continued on Page 23, Column 3

NEWS HELD A DAY

Murder of Dictator Laid to a General Seeking Revenge

Texts of the proclamation and decree are on Page 14.

By PETER KIHSS

Generalissimo Rafael Leonidas Trujillo Molina, dictator of the Dominican Republic since 1930, was assassinated Tuesday night.

The death of the 69-year-old Caribbean strongman was announced over the signature of Dr. Joaquin Balaguer, who became President last August. The announcement of the assassination by the Dominican Caribe radio at 5:45 P. M. yesterday, New York time, gave no details.

Dr. Balaguer also is reported to have said the army was in control.

From San Juan, P. R. The Associated Press said information reaching there from responsible sources was that the generalissimo had been shot.

Seven persons in an automobile were said to have attacked him at 10 P. M. Tuesday as he was driving to Ciudad Trujillo from his home in San Cristobal.

Killing Laid to Revenge

The National Broadcasting Company reported last night that a disgruntled army general seeking revenge had carried out the assassination.

In a telephone call from Ciudad Trujillo, NBC's John Hlavacek said General Trujillo had been shot from ambush by a band of seven men headed by Gen. Juan Tomas Diaz.

One of the assassins was killed and several others captured, Mr. Hlavacek reported. The general and several survivors escaped into the mountains, where 1,000 troops were reported waiting.

The general was believed to have acted to avenge some wrong done to his family.

The Associated Press reported that the police went at 4:30 A. M. to the home of Roman Catholic Bishop Thomas F. Reilly, a United States citizen who has been under house arrest in the capital as a result of his quarrels with the regime. Bishop Reilly was reported to have been taken away but later

Continued on Page 14, Column 1

PUPIL PLAN GIVEN TO NEW ROCHELLE

Integration Method Set— Town Official Sees Chaos

Text of Kaufman decree is printed on Page 24.

By EDWARD RANZAL

Federal Judge Irving R. Kaufman ordered New Rochelle yesterday to let any child transfer out of the predominantly Negro Lincoln Elementary School.

He had previously ruled that the school had been deliberately created and maintained as a segregated institution.

His order yesterday, outlining principles to be followed in desegregation, rejected a plan submitted under protest by a majority group of the New Rochelle Board of Education. This plan would have offered temporary transfers to selected pupils.

Judge Kaufman said no administrative measures could be allowed to preserve segregation. "There is no room in the Constitution for any concept of inferior citizenship," he said.

In New Rochelle, Merryle Stanley Rukeyser, president of the Board of Education, said compliance would cause "chaos" in the school system. He said the board would appeal to the United States Court of Appeals.

The court refused to stay its order pending an appeal. Un-

Continued on Page 24, Column 1

The New York Times.

LATE CITY EDITION
U. S. Weather Bureau Report (Page 40) forecasts:
Considerable cloudiness today;
occasional rain tonight, tomorrow.
Temp. range: 72—59; yesterday: 71—49.
Temp.-Hum. Index: middle 60's; yesterday: 66.

VOL. CXI . No. 37,859.   © 1961 by The New York Times Company.
Times Square, New York 36, N. Y.   NEW YORK, TUESDAY, SEPTEMBER 19, 1961.   10 cents beyond 50-mile zone from New York City, except on Long Island. Higher in air delivery cities.   FIVE CENTS

HAMMARSKJOLD DIES IN AFRICAN AIR CRASH; KENNEDY GOING TO U.N. IN SUCCESSION CRISIS

MAYOR APPOINTS 9 CIVIC LEADERS AS SCHOOL BOARD

Group Is Due to Be Sworn Today but Injunction Is Sought to Bar Change

By PAUL CROWELL

Mayor Wagner named a new nine-member Board of Education yesterday to replace the present board, which goes out of existence tomorrow.

The new board, which like the old one is unsalaried, is scheduled to be sworn in at City Hall today at 3:30 P. M., but there may be a last-minute hitch.

Two members of the outgoing board moved in Supreme Court yesterday to have the Legislature's recent action dismissing the old board declared illegal and to prevent Mayor Wagner, in the meantime, from swearing in the members of the new board this afternoon.

A legal representative of the city will appear at the Brooklyn court at 10 o'clock this morning to contest both the complaint and the appeal for an injunction against the Mayor.

'Red Letter Day'

For his own part, before the legal action was instituted, Mayor Wagner expressed the hope that the swearing-in ceremony scheduled for the new board members this afternoon would mark "a red letter day for the City of New York for all the days to come."

He expressed the belief that "this can be the best board our city has ever had, possibly the best board any city ever had."

The board has seven members from Manhattan, and one each from Brooklyn and Queens.

The board was chosen from a list of twenty-six recommended by an eleven-man panel set up by the state on Aug. 21. A special session of the Legislature had passed a law to dissolve the present board and pave the way for a new one.

Appointees Listed

The Mayor's appointees are:

Brendan Byrne, public relations man, 85-19 118th Street, Kew Gardens, Queens.
James B. Donovan, lawyer, 35 Prospect Park West, Brooklyn.
Lloyd K. Garrison, lawyer, 133 East Sixty-fourth Street.
John F. Hennessy, engineer, 144 East Thirty-ninth Street.
Morris Iushewitz, labor leader, 386 Park Avenue South.
Samuel R. Pierce, lawyer, 2225 Fifth Avenue.
Anna M. Rosenberg, relations consultant, 1136 Fifth Avenue.
Max J. Rubin, lawyer, 101 West Fifty-fifth Street.
Clarence O. Senior, economist and sociologist, 15 Claremont Avenue.

In announcing the appointments, the Mayor said that he had chosen the board "without regard to politics."

"I do not even know the political affiliations of those I have selected," he said, "except in the cases where I have had previous personal knowledge." It was

Continued on Page 30, Column 6

Militia Seizes 176 In Cuban Outbreak

Special to The New York Times.

HAVANA, Sept. 18—Militiamen in plainclothes who had mingled with the crowd arrested 176 persons last night after a demonstration had broken out during a religious procession near here.

Eighteen demonstrators were injured, three seriously, when the militiamen swung clubs they had hidden in their clothing.

The outburst occurred one week after a larger anti-Government demonstration before a Havana church. Seven were injured, one fatally, by the militia and many were arrested in that demonstration.

The new incident took place a few hours after 136 priests had been deported from Cuba

Continued on Page 13, Column 1

New Group Seeks Funds to Purchase And Repair Slums

By MARTIN ARNOLD

A nonprofit organization has been set up here to offer inducements to private investors to buy and improve slum tenements.

The organization, headed by former Deputy Mayor Paul T. O'Keefe, would select the buildings, find buyers and repair, operate and maintain the tenements.

Private investors would own the buildings and would collect profits agreed upon between them and the organization.

8 to 10 Per Cent Profit

The profits usually would be 8 to 10 per cent. Many unimproved slum tenements now bring profits up to 25 per cent.

Laurance S. Rockefeller, son of the late John D. Rockefeller Jr., has agreed to invest up to $750,000 in tenements to get the program started.

Mr. Rockefeller will not be part of the organization. A spokesman said last night that Mr. Rockefeller had agreed to help the program because he felt it was "a way to get responsible private money that will be reasonably rewarded into such housing."

The Rockefeller spokesman and other supporters of the program emphasized that the project would not be charitable or philanthropic. Rather,

Continued on Page 25, Column 1

3 STATES TO GET U. S. TRANSIT AID

New Committee Wins Pledge of Support From 2 Bodies at Orientation Meeting

By LLOYD GARRISON

Special to The New York Times.

WASHINGTON, Sept. 18—The newly created Tri-State Transportation Committee won Government support today for its plans to improve transport and commuter service in the New York metropolitan area.

Committee members from New York, New Jersey and Connecticut met for more than three hours with representatives of the Housing and Home Finance Agency and the Bureau of Public Roads.

Dr. William J. Ronan, secretary to Governor Rockefeller, said the meeting had been called to explain the aims of the group and to seek Federal cooperation. He described the session as "very heartening."

The committee did not ask for specific amounts of money, he added, but would undoubtedly seek financial support "sometime soon."

Government participants in the meeting indicated funds would be made available if requested.

Anxious to Aid

"This is the kind of program we would like to assist," said Morton J. Schussheim, assistant administrator for program policy at the Housing and Home Finance Agency. The agency is involved in transportation problems through its urban renewal program.

His enthusiasm was echoed by another Federal representative, Edward H. Holmes, assistant commissioner of the Bureau of Public Roads.

Dr. Ronan acted as regional chairman at the meeting. The New Jersey delegation was led by Highway Commissioner Dwight R. G. Palmer and the Connecticut by Carl LaLumia, executive aide to Gov. John Dempsey.

Roger H. Gilman, on leave from the Port of New York Authority to serve as executive director of the committee, attended the meeting but deferred immediately after it had ended.

The tri-state committee was established three weeks ago to study and make recommendations on improving commuter service and to attack also problems of motor traffic, air travel and freight distribution. Its

Continued on Page 18, Column 3

Rescue workers study wreckage of the Secretary General's plane in Northern Rhodesia.
Associated Press Radiophoto

Secretary General Dag Hammarskjold
The New York Times

Adenauer Begins Efforts To Form Coalition in Bonn

By SYDNEY GRUSON

Special to The New York Times.

BONN, Germany, Sept. 18—Chancellor Adenauer began fighting for his political life today as a result of his party's heavy losses in the West German elections.

With the Christian Democratic Union's parliamentary majority wiped out yesterday, the 85-year-old Chancellor lost no time in seeking a coalition with the Free Democratic party led by Dr. Erich Mende. The Free Democrats made the biggest gain in the election.

Dr. Adenauer rejected the bid of Willy Brandt, West Berlin's Mayor, for a national coalition embracing the Social Democrats as well as the two other parties. A coalition with the Socialists, the Chancellor said at a news conference, "would not correspond with our democratic feeling."

The big question was not whether Dr. Adenauer could set the terms for a coalition but whether he could survive the demands for his retirement and his replacement as Chancellor by Dr. Ludwig Erhard, the 64-year-old Minister of Economics.

There was considerable speculation that the Free Democrats would agree to Dr. Adenauer's continuing as Chancellor for a limited period—just long enough to carry the onus for accepting the hard decisions facing West Germany.

With the long, bitter campaign and the vote at last out of the way, a beginning was in sight for the long-awaited public discussion of these decisions.

The Free Democrats' news service, commenting on the election results, which left the party holding the balance of power, said:

"An epoch of German postwar history has ended. The coming months and years will destroy many illusions and place extraordinary demands on our people."

The statement reflected a continuing but decreasing reluctance to specify the demands. Two are accepted by almost all West German officials as inevitable: the acceptance of the Oder-Neisse border as Germany's frontier with Poland and some form of de facto recognition for Communist East Germany, with all that means to the loss of hope for the reunification of Germany.

No one here is yet sure whether the West Germans are

Continued on Page 3, Column 5

2D SOVIET ROCKET FIRED 7,500 MILES

Lands in Same Pacific Area as Shot Last Wednesday

By THEODORE SHABAD

MOSCOW, Sept. 18 — The Soviet Union fired a second rocket 7,500 miles into the central Pacific yesterday.

An announcement today by Tass, the Soviet press agency, said that the dummy of the rocket's last stage had landed "in the immediate proximity" of the spot where the first rocket of the current series hit the water last Wednesday.

Today's brief Tass statement emphasized the accuracy of the Soviet shots. It referred to the "high-precision control system" of the rocket and called it "another big achievement of Soviet rocketry."

[In Washington, the Atomic Energy Commission announced that the Soviet Union on Monday exploded its thirteenth nuclear device since it resumed testing Sept. 1. The yield of the atmospheric explosion was "on the order of a megaton" and the site was "in the vicinity of Novaya Zemlya," the commission said.]

The present series of test shots was announced on Sept. 10. Ships and planes were advised to keep away from the target area, 1,000 miles southwest of Hawaii, during the

Continued on Page 8, Column 1

VIETNAM REBELS BURN CITY IN RAID

Regime Says 1,000 Reds Took Part in Attack

By The Associated Press.

SAIGON, Vietnam, Tuesday, Sept. 19—More than 1,000 Communist rebels attacked and burned the capital of Phuoc Vinh Province, sixty miles north of Saigon early yesterday, the Government said today.

It was believed to be the largest rebel assault so far in South Vietnam's civil war.

The province chief, an army major, and his deputy and a large number of Government civil guardsmen were killed.

About fifty wounded were rushed to Saigon hospitals after the rebels withdrew under attack.

The Government announced that the Viet Cong guerrillas stormed the capital at 1 A. M. yesterday in a move to liberate rebels taken prisoner. The Viet Cong held the town for several hours in pre-dawn darkness, burning and ransacking several provincial buildings.

One source estimated 1,500 Viet Cong took part in the attack, the first on a provincial capital.

It also marked a new height in violence in the areas north of Saigon where the rebels were said to be gaining in strength.

Phuoc Thanh is a newly created province in a largely upland forest and rubber-growing

Continued on Page 3, Column 7

ACTING SECRETARY IS SOUGHT AT U. N.

Delegates Favoring Proposal to Appoint Mongi Slim— Assembly Meets Today

By THOMAS J. HAMILTON

Special to The New York Times.

UNITED NATIONS, N. Y., Sept. 18—On the eve of the opening of the United Nations General Assembly session, a move was developing to have Mongi Slim of Tunisia take over the coordination of the Secretariat until the election of a successor to Dag Hammarskjold.

The death of Mr. Hammarskjold saddened delegates to the General Assembly, which will open its sixteenth session tomorrow afternoon.

Delegates and members of the Secretariat mourned the death of an able diplomat who had helped bring about compromise solutions of dangerous issues in an age of nuclear stalemates.

Long Struggle Feared

There were grave forebodings of a long struggle over the choice of a Secretary General who would be acceptable to both the Soviet Union and the Western powers.

The interim plan to address the United Nations crisis was made known after he had paid a tribute to Mr. Hammarskjold, in which he said:

"I am hopeful that the members of the United Nations, recognizing his untiring labors, will attempt in the coming sessions and in the years to come to try to build the United Nations into the effective instrument for peace which was Dag Hammarskjold's great ambition."

Interim Plan Sought

As for the crisis at the United Nations, the United States believes that an interim arrangement must be made quickly, with the concurrence of the Soviet Union if possible, to enable the office of the Secretary General to carry out the past instructions of the world organization.

This is an urgent matter in the Congo, where United Nations troops in secessionist Katanga Province have been under fire and must be reinforced quickly.

Officials here and in New York were in constant consultation today about how this could be done in the face of the Soviet Union's opposition to the

Continued on Page 16, Column 2

President to Assure U. N. U. S. Backs a Single Chief

By JAMES RESTON

WASHINGTON, Sept. 18—President Kennedy decided tonight to intervene personally in the constitutional crisis created at the United Nations by the death of Secretary General Dag Hammarskjold.

The White House announced that the President would address the General Assembly in New York, probably Friday. His purpose in doing so is to reassure the delegates and Secretariat that the United States supports the United Nations and is determined to do everything possible to maintain the executive authority of the office of the Secretary General.

The President's plan to address the United Nations session will open its sixteenth session

KATANGA IMPERILS MAIN U. N. AIR BASE

Loss Would Be Second Big Defeat—Tshombe Units Claim Capture of 500

Special to The New York Times.

ELISABETHVILLE, the Congo, Sept. 18—United Nations troops guarding the big air base at Kamina, in Katanga Province, were reported under heavy fire today and in danger of being overwhelmed by their Katangan attackers.

[According to The Associated Press, Katangan military radio messages reported the capture of the Kamina base and the surrender of its 500 Irish and Swedish defenders.]

The loss of the air base would be the second major defeat for the United Nations in the six days of fighting here. This morning, the surrender of a garrison of 158 Irish troops was completed at Jadotville, sixty-five miles north of Elisabethville.

With the military situation deteriorating, United Nations forces here spent an anxious morning waiting for news of Secretary General Dag Hammarskjold. Word of his death brought sorrow to the already grim band of United Nations soldiers and officials.

Outside this capital of Katanga, the secessionist forces are more numerous than those

Continued on Page 14, Column 6

French to End the Occupation Of Bizerte City, Starting Today

By THOMAS F. BRADY

TUNIS, Sept. 18—French and Tunisian representatives agreed today on a plan for the withdrawal of French troops from the city of Bizerte and its environs.

The withdrawal will start tomorrow morning and continue through Saturday.

Negotiations leading to the troop pullback began after a proposal by President Habib Bourguiba of Tunisia Sept. 7 to permit the French to maintain their naval-air base for the duration of the Berlin crisis if they would agree to a timetable for the eventual evacuation of the base.

A Soviet spokesman said today that his delegation would press this demand, which was submitted to the General Assembly by Premier Khrushchev a year ago, at the impending session.

Although the Soviet delegate, Valerian A. Zorin, refused to join other members of the Security Council in praising Mr.

entrance. Fighting had broken out July 19 after France declared a Tunisian demand for a promise to evacuate the base.

In return for ending of the city's occupation, the Tunisians have guaranteed to the French the right of circulation among the scattered military installations in the Bizerte region and freedom of movement westward from the entrance of the city of Bizerte, on which the installations are situated.

The first concrete step toward a solution of the Bizerte dispute was an exchange of prisoners Sept. 10.

The second step was the agreement just achieved in a military withdrawal to the positions held before the July

Continued on Page 2, Column 3

12 OTHERS KILLED

Lone Survivor Reports Explosions on Flight to Tshombe Talks

By DAVID HALBERSTAM

Special to The New York Times.

NDOLA, Northern Rhodesia, Sept. 18—Secretary General Dag Hammarskjold of the United Nations was killed today with twelve others in the crash of a plane carrying him to a meeting with President Moise Tshombe of Katanga Province. The meeting had been called in an effort to end the fighting in Katanga.

The bodies of the Secretary General and his staff were found about four miles from the Ndola airport in Northern Rhodesia. The plane had been scheduled to land at the airport last night.

[The Associated Press said that mistaken identity and tight security led it to report erroneously Sunday night that Mr. Hammarskjold's plane had reached Ndola.]

The site of the crash is close to the border of the Congolese province of Katanga. The Congo is an area that has demanded much of Mr. Hammarskjold's time and patience in the last fifteen months.

Crash Stuns U. N. Aides

The news of the crash stunned this area. Earlier today United Nations officials at Elisabethville seemed dazed as they kept hearing reports that Mr. Hammarskjold had not arrived in Ndola.

[The Associated Press reported that the lone survivor, Harold M. Julian, a United Nations security guard, said that a series of explosions had preceded the crash. He also said that the plane had turned away from a landing, apparently on Mr. Hammarskjold's orders.]

At near-by Kitwe, in Northern Rhodesia, President Tshombe was holding a news conference and was saying that he hoped to meet in a few minutes with the Secretary General and end the war when a newsman said:

"President Tshombe, Mr. Hammarskjold is dead. His body lies not far away in the wreckage of his airplane."

Mr. Tshombe's face reflected shock and horror seemed to show in his eyes.

Tshombe Expresses Regret

"I regret it very much if what you say is true," he said. "He was a man who enjoyed the respect of many African nations and I had hoped to reach a settlement with him that would leave Katanga free."

Earlier in his news conference Mr. Tshombe had attacked United Nations policy in the Congo.

Mr. Hammarskjold's plane was a United Nations DC-6B. It left Leopoldville yesterday. Much concerning the crash remains inexplicable.

The Secretary General's plane apparently crashed after it had circled the Ndola airport twice and had been waved in. No one here could offer any explanation for the crash.

It was believed that the plane might have taken a circuitous route to avoid the Katanga area, which is patrolled by one Katanga jet fighter. This might account for the plane's late arrival here and it might account for some fatigue on the part of the pilot.

There apparently was only one survivor, a man who was found severely burned and in a delirious state near the plane. He was taken to a hospital.

Those who have been trying to end the Katanga fighting believe that Mr. Hammarskjold's death was a terrible blow to hopes for a truce.

Mr. Tshombe has refused to meet with United Nations officials in Elisabethville, the Ka-

Continued on Page 14, Column 1

"All the News That's Fit to Print"

The New York Times.

LATE CITY EDITION
U. S. Weather Bureau Report (Page 90) forecasts:
Increasing cloudiness today.
Snow, rain tonight. Rain tomorrow.
Temp. range: 38—26; yesterday: 37—30.

VOL. CXI. No. 38,014.

© 1962 by The New York Times Company.
Times Square, New York 36, N. Y.

NEW YORK, WEDNESDAY, FEBRUARY 21, 1962.

10 cents beyond 50-mile zone from New York City
except on Long Island. Higher in air delivery cities.

FIVE CENTS

GLENN ORBITS EARTH 3 TIMES SAFELY; PICKED UP IN CAPSULE BY DESTROYER; PRESIDENT WILL GREET HIM IN FLORIDA

CARLINO CLEARED IN SHELTER CASE BY ETHICS PANEL

Lane Scored in Unanimous Report, Which He Calls 'Cynical and Callous'

Text of concluding sections of report is on Page 50.

By WARREN WEAVER Jr.
Special to The New York Times.

ALBANY, Feb. 20—The Assembly Committee on Ethics and Guidance exonerated Speaker Joseph F. Carlino today of charges of conflict of interest made by Assemblyman Mark Lane.

In a unanimous report submitted to the Legislature, the bipartisan committee said:

¶Mr. Carlino did not "betray the public trust" by serving as a director of a company manufacturing home fall-out shelters while helping to pass school-shelter legislation last November.

¶The Speaker was not influenced in his official actions in behalf of the bill by the fact that he was a member of the board of directors of Lancer Industries, Inc.

¶He did not receive any special benefit from the passage of the legislation.

Charges Unsubstantiated

"The committee concludes with respect to each and every accusation contained in the charges filed," the report said, "that Assemblyman Lane and those who testified in their support failed to submit credible evidence to substantiate them."

In submitting the report, the Ethics Committee requested that the full 150-member lower house vote "with respect to the conclusions reached herein" in the light of the fact that "the charges were directed against its [the Assembly's] highest ranking official."

Assemblyman Donald A. Campbell, Republican of Amsterdam, who is chairman of the committee, said he would move in the Assembly tomorrow for acceptance of the report. Mr. Carlino is expected to be absent during the debate and vote.

Assemblyman Lane, a Democrat of Manhattan, had charged that the Speaker was guilty of

Continued on Page 50, Column 1

ROCKEFELLER BARS KOREA WAR BONUS

Voices Opposition in Face of Legislators' Backing

By LAYHMOND ROBINSON
Special to The New York Times.

ALBANY, Feb. 20—Governor Rockefeller expressed strong opposition tonight to a state bonus for veterans of the Korean war.

Mr. Rockefeller told the New York State Department of the American Legion that he could not "as a responsible leader of government" support the demand for a bonus. The veterans' group had been campaigning for a $100,000,000 bonus for the 482,000 Korean war veterans or their next-of-kin in the state.

The Governor said his stand was backed "unanimously" by the "Republican leadership of the state." This was a reference to the leaders of the Republican-controlled Legislature.

He said that demands for funds for education, mental health, narcotics control and other state services were too great to admit a diversion of money for a veterans' bonus.

Mr. Rockefeller thus took a position in direct opposition to that of most of the Republican and Democratic members of the Legislature, who have been pushing for the bonus. The issue

Continued on Page 51, Column 1

Jersey Bus Strike Settled; Service Is Due Tomorrow

By PETER KIHSS

An agreement to end the New Jersey bus strike was reached last night. The agreement, subject to ratification by the striking employes, was announced by Gov. Richard J. Hughes. The pact will be submitted to the union members at their garages starting at 7 A. M. today.

Union and management men expressed hope that buses could begin operating tomorrow at 4:30 A. M.

The strike against Public Service Coordinated Transport started at 12:01 A. M. Monday and halted 2,511 buses providing 1,000,000 rides a day. The company's 200 routes serve all of New Jersey's twenty-one counties except Warren and Hunterdon and go into New York City and Philadelphia. The Newark subway system was also shut.

Carlin Gets Credit

Governor Hughes credited Mayor Leo P. Carlin of Newark with having "sparkplugged" the successful negotiations. Mayor Carlin flew back from a Miami Beach vacation yesterday and arranged the talks with both sides and with Daniel F. Fitzpatrick, a Federal mediator, and the Governor and himself. The meeting started in Newark at 8:30 P. M., and the agreement was announced at 11:28 P. M.

Earlier, David L. Yunich, president of Bamberger's New Jersey, had asserted that the strike was having a "devastating * * * almost catastrophic" effect on retail business in Newark and elsewhere in the state. A Camden department store reported sales had fallen nearly 50 per cent on Monday, although not that far yesterday.

Despite the drop in shopping, most commuters managed to get to work by alternate means and with a minimum of confusion.

The agreement reached last night provides for a wage increase of 10 cents an hour retroactive to Feb. 1 and extending to next Feb. 1; 4 cents more an hour from then until Aug. 1, 1963, and another 4 cents an hour from then until

Continued on Page 39, Column 3

ROSENTHAL WINS QUEENS ELECTION

But Democrat-Liberal Has Margin of Only 193 Votes—Machines Guarded

By CLAYTON KNOWLES

Benjamin S. Rosenthal, a Democrat-Liberal backed by President Kennedy, squeaked through to victory last night in a special Congressional election in Queens' Sixth District.

By the slim margin of 193 votes, Mr. Rosenthal, a lanky 38-year-old Elmhurst lawyer, edged past Thomas F. Galvin of Flushing, the Republican candidate, to win a three-way race. Emil Levin of Flushing, a Democrat running as an independent, finished far behind.

The unofficial final tally, delayed as the early vote was hastily rechecked for errors, was: Rosenthal, 16,032; Galvin, 15,839, and Levin, 4,216.

Republicans immediately challenged the result and, while Mr. Galvin did not immediately ask for a recount, he sent a telegram demanding that the voting machines be impounded. All voting machines, normally put

Continued on Page 48, Column 3

McNamara Reports Gains by Vietnamese

By JACK RAYMOND
Special to The New York Times.

WASHINGTON, Feb. 20—Secretary of Defense Robert S. McNamara returned to the capital today and reported improvement in the South Vietnamese effort against Communist insurgents.

He had presided at a meeting of United States military and civilian officials yesterday at the headquarters in Hawaii of Admiral Harry D. Felt, commander of United States forces in the Pacific. The meeting was the third in a series of monthly talks on the hostilities in South Vietnam.

A spokesman for Mr. McNamara said that the forces of South Vietnam, supported by the United States, "are hitting

Continued on Page 8, Column 5

READY: Lieut. Col. John H. Glenn Jr. walks to the van to take him to the launching site at Cape Canaveral, Fla.

N.A.S.A. via Associated Press Wirephoto

LIFT-OFF: The Atlas rocket booster bearing the Project Mercury spacecraft roars aloft with 360,000-pound thrust.

N.A.S.A. via United Press International Telephoto

RECOVERY: Crewmen of destroyer Noa secure capsule carrying astronaut before lifting it out of the Atlantic.

N.A.S.A. via Associated Press Wirephoto

KENNEDY PRAISES 'WONDERFUL JOB'

Tells Glenn Nation Is 'Really Proud of You'—Welcome at White House Planned

By TOM WICKER
Special to The New York Times.

WASHINGTON, Feb. 20—President Kennedy phoned Lieut. Col. John H. Glenn Jr. today immediately after the astronaut's successful orbital flight and arranged to meet him at Cape Canaveral Friday morning.

The President also set in motion plans for bringing Colonel Glenn to Washington on Monday or Tuesday, for reception at the White House and the Capitol and a parade down Pennsylvania Avenue.

A television set in his office and an open telephone line to Cape Canaveral had kept Mr. Kennedy informed of Colonel Glenn's progress all through the day.

The astronaut's three orbits around the earth, Mr. Kennedy said in a statement, have embarked the United States on a "new ocean"—that of space.

"I believe the United States must sail on it and be in a position second to none," the President said within minutes of Colonel Glenn's safe emergence from his Mercury capsule.

Colonel Glenn, he said, is the "kind of American of whom we are most proud." Mr. Kennedy also praised "all those who participated" in making the astronaut's flight successful.

Then, at 4:10 P. M., Mr. Ken-

Continued on Page 23, Column 7

The President's Statement

Special to The New York Times.

WASHINGTON, Feb. 20—*Following is the text of President Kennedy's statement on Colonel Glenn's flight:*

I know that I express the great happiness and thanksgiving of all of us that Colonel Glenn has completed his trip, and I know that this is particularly felt by Mrs. Glenn and his two children.

A few days ago Colonel Glenn came to the White House and visited me, and he is—as are the other astronauts—the kind of American of whom we are most proud.

Some years ago, as a Marine pilot, he raced the sun across this country—and lost. And today he won.

I also want to say a word for all those who participated with Colonel Glenn in Canaveral. They faced many disappointments and delays—the burdens upon them were great—but they kept their heads and they made a judgment, and I think that judgment has been vindicated.

We have a long way to go in this space race. We started late. But this is the new ocean, and I believe the United States must sail on it and be in a position second to none.

Some months ago I said that I hoped every American would serve his country. Today Colonel Glenn served his, and we all express our thanks to him.

ADENAUER WANTS PARLEY ON BERLIN

Suggests Foreign Ministers of Big Four Meet 'Soon'

By SYDNEY GRUSON
Special to The New York Times.

BONN, Germany, Feb. 20—Chancellor Adenauer suggested today that a Big Four foreign ministers' conference on Berlin should be convened "soon." He was speaking to the Parliamentary group of the Christian Democratic Union.

He said that it might be "expedient" to "take a pause" in the Berlin talks now going on between Andrei A. Gromyko, the Soviet Foreign Minister, and Llewellyn E. Thompson Jr., the United States Ambassador to Moscow.

Ambassador Thompson should not continue "negotiating" endlessly, Dr. Adenauer added. There have been four meetings in the last seven weeks between Mr. Gromyko and Mr. Thompson without any advance toward a Berlin settlement.

Continued on Page 2, Column 2

URBAN PLAN VOTE PUT OFF IN SENATE

Administration Rebuffed on Forcing Issue to Floor

By RUSSELL BAKER
Special to The New York Times.

WASHINGTON, Feb. 20—President Kennedy affronted the Senate's dignity today and got a political rebuff for it.

In a surprising repudiation of the Administration's voting form sheets, the elders turned on the White House and rejected a leadership move to get a quick floor test of the President's urban affairs proposal. The vote was 58 to 42.

Thus, the White House lost its chance to get a favorable Senate vote on the plan before the House could vote to kill it. The Democrats also lost their chance to get the Senate's Republicans clearly on record for or against the plan to create a Cabinet-level Department of Urban Affairs and Housing.

Today's test came on the dusty parliamentary question whether the Senate should take the plan away from the Government Operations Committee and bring it to an immediate floor vote. This is known as "discharging" the committee. It is an extraordinary procedure that is rarely used because it is repugnant to Senate traditions.

Today it became the instrument of the President's defeat.

The move to discharge the committee was undertaken with misgivings yesterday by Mike Mansfield of Montana, Senate Democratic leader. The reason was a sudden threat by the

Continued on Page 16, Column 4

81,000-MILE TRIP

Flight Aides Feared for the Capsule as It Began Its Re-Entry

Transcript of conversations with Glenn, Pages 25 and 26.

By RICHARD WITKIN
Special to The New York Times.

CAPE CANAVERAL, Fla., Feb. 20—John H. Glenn Jr. orbited three times around the earth today and landed safely to become the first American to make such a flight.

The 40-year-old Marine Corps lieutenant colonel traveled about 81,000 miles in 4 hours 56 minutes before splashing into the Atlantic at 2:43 P. M. Eastern Standard Time.

He had been launched from here at 9:47 A. M.

The astronaut's safe return was no less a relief than a thrill to the Project Mercury team, because there had been real concern that the Friendship 7 capsule might disintegrate as it rammed back into the atmosphere.

There had also been a serious question whether Colonel Glenn could complete three orbits as planned. But despite persistent control problems, he managed to complete the entire flight plan.

Lands in Bahamas Area

The astronaut's landing place was near Grand Turk Island in the Bahamas, about 700 miles southeast of here.

Still in his capsule, he was plucked from the water at 3:01 P. M. with a boom and block and tackle by the destroyer Noa. The capsule was deposited on deck at 3:04.

Colonel Glenn's first words as he stepped out onto the Noa's deck were: "It was hot in there."

He quickly obtained a glass of iced tea.

He was in fine condition except for two skinned knuckles hurt in the process of blowing out the side hatch of the capsule.

The colonel was transferred by helicopter to the carrier Randolph, whose recovery helicopters had raced the Noa for the honor of making the pickup. After a meal and extensive "de-briefing" aboard the carrier, he was flown to Grand Turk by submarine patrol plane for two days of rest and interviews on technical, medical and other aspects of his flight.

The Noa, nearest ship to the

Continued on Page 20, Column 1

COL. GLENN FLOWN TO ISLE FOR CHECK

He Feels Tired but Elated —Goes to Grand Turk for Report and Examination

By JOHN W. FINNEY
Special to The New York Times.

GRAND TURK ISLAND, Feb. 20—An elated but tired John H. Glenn Jr. returned to earth tonight and reported that he "couldn't feel better."

The 40-year-old astronaut also reported that he had felt no sickness or discomfort during his five-hour, three-orbit flight around the earth, even during the extended period of weightlessness.

Colonel Glenn landed at this small British possession at 9:11 P. M. in a Navy S-2-F submarine patrol plane. He was clad in light blue coveralls. He had co-piloted the plane from the carrier Randolph, where he spent several hours after being retrieved from the Atlantic ocean.

Around his ears were the marks of the earphones that he had worn while piloting a plane that traveled at about one-hundredth the speed of his Friendship 7 space capsule.

Asked how he felt, the redheaded marine replied: "Fine, wonderful, I couldn't feel better."

And he was also happy. His first comment on stepping into the small hospital arranged for him was: "First I want something to eat—I am hungry." A steak dinner was promptly ordered.

Continued on Page 23, Column 2

NEW YORK PAUSES TO 'WATCH' GLENN

Millions Rivet Attention on Astronaut in Flight

By NAN ROBERTSON

The thoughts of millions of New Yorkers were riveted for hours yesterday on one man alone in space.

Minute by minute, they followed the orbital flight of Lieut. Col. John H. Glenn Jr. three times around the earth, waiting in agonizing suspense for his safe return. The life of New York almost stood still during the dramatic countdown.

From then on until Colonel Glenn scrambled "hale and hearty" out of his capsule into the destroyer Noa, people carried on absent-mindedly and in spurts. Millions of working men lost during the day, but no one could have begrudged this. Employers and the employed alike were drawn irresistibly to radio and television sets.

The most spectacular display of interest occurred in Grand Central Terminal, where throngs of up to 9,000 persons massed before a huge television screen. The police described it as the largest static crowd in the station's history. The terminal manager said those who

Continued on Page 22, Column 6

Moscow, Unmoved, Gives News of Orbit

By THEODORE SHABAD
Special to The New York Times.

MOSCOW, Feb. 20—The Russians voiced congratulations tonight on hearing of Lieut. Col. John H. Glenn Jr.'s orbital space flight.

But they showed no enthusiasm on the successful launching and landing of the spacecraft Friendship 7.

These reactions were reported from Moscow University to United States exchange students who had been listening with Russians to radio reports of Colonel Glenn's progress.

"They congratulated us in friendly fashion but were oddly reserved," an American said. Soviet radio and television were unusually prompt in reporting the flight. The first bul-

Continued on Page 22, Column 5

Leaders of Algeria Back Peace Terms

By THOMAS F. BRADY
Special to The New York Times.

TUNIS, Feb. 20—The Algerian nationalist Provisional Government met today and gave full approval to peace accords negotiated with the French by four members of the rebel regime.

One Algerian said afterward: "All twelve members of the Government are in unanimous agreement." This was a reference to five ministers who are prisoners in France, the four negotiators and three ministers who remained in Tunis during the secret talks last week on the French-Swiss border.

The negotiators were Belkacem Krim, M'Hammed Yazid, Saad Dahlab and Lakhdar Ben Tobbal. They met here today

Continued on Page 11, Column 2

The New York Times.

LATE CITY EDITION
U.S. Weather Bureau Report (Page 50) forecasts:
Partly cloudy, windy. Possible rain
then fair tonight and tomorrow.
Temp. range: 50—38; yesterday: 43—38

VOL. CXI..No. 38,066.   © 1962 by The New York Times Company.
Times Square, New York 36, N. Y.   NEW YORK, SATURDAY, APRIL 14, 1962.   10 cents beyond 50-mile zone from New York City
except on Long Island. Higher in air delivery cities.   FIVE CENTS

NEW U. S. PLAN ON BERLIN ASKS PEACE PLEDGES

PACKAGE OFFER

Proposal to Be Made to Soviet on Monday if Allies Approve

By SYDNEY GRUSON
Special to The New York Times.

BONN, Germany, April 13—The United States has given its allies the outline of a package offer it wants to submit to the Soviet Union for a settlement of the Berlin crisis.

According to reliable sources here, West Germany and France have expressed serious reservations about the proposal. The West German reservations are based on the belief that it would too greatly enhance Communist East Germany's international position.

The United States, it is reported, hopes for quick Allied approval to enable Secretary of State Dean Rusk to make the offer to the Soviet Ambassador, Anatoly I. Dobrynin, at the resumption of talks on the Berlin issue in Washington next Monday.

Principal Proposals

The main points of the proposal are the following:

¶A United States-Soviet undertaking to prevent the spread of nuclear weapons.

¶An exchange of nonaggression declarations between the North Atlantic Treaty Organization and the Warsaw Pact, the Soviet bloc's military alliance.

¶The establishment of a number of committees composed of equal numbers of West and East Germans to handle "technical" contacts between the two Germanys.

¶The formation of an international authority to supervise travel between West Berlin and West Germany.

The United States is also said to have suggested the establishment of a conference of deputies of the foreign ministers of the Big Four—the United States, the Soviet Union, Britain and France—to meet regularly on the Berlin situation.

The United States proposal envisions no change in the status of West Berlin as an occupied city or in the presence there of American, British and French garrisons. The Soviet Union insists on making West Berlin a demilitarized, "free city."

The end of the occupation and

Continued on Page 2, Column 5

ATOMIC IMPASSE

Khrushchev Rebuffs West's Final Appeal for Test Ban Pact

By SEYMOUR TOPPING
Special to The New York Times.

MOSCOW, Saturday, April 14—Premier Khrushchev has spurned what appeared to be the final offer by the United States and Britain to sign a nuclear test-ban treaty that would avert the renewal of Western testing in the atmosphere later this month.

In a message sent yesterday to Prime Minister Macmillan, Mr. Khrushchev again branded the Western call for a treaty that would be enforced through international inspection as an attempt to expose the Soviet Union to espionage.

The Soviet leader asserted that President Kennedy and the Prime Minister already had decided to go ahead with nuclear testing in the Pacific as planned.

Motives Are Questioned

Referring to the joint statement by the United States and Britain last Monday appealing to him to obviate the need for Western testing by agreeing to international verification, Mr. Khrushchev said:

"Frankly speaking, I am confident that the Governments of the United States and Britain do not believe that their demands would be accepted. They only need to make a show before public opinion, to make the impression of being worried about how to liquidate tensions and strengthen trust."

Mr. Khrushchev's statement seemed to indicate that the United States and Britain would hold their test series as scheduled and that, as a result, the Soviet Union would conduct another series of its own.

"In the future your holding of nuclear weapons tests underground or in the atmosphere, in space or under water, will force the Soviet Union to hold tests of its own nuclear weapons so that the defense of the countries of socialism against the aggressive forces that do not heed reason and pursue a challenging policy will be at an appropriate level," the Premier said.

Kennedy Announced Step

President Kennedy announced the intention of the United States to resume testing after an evaluation of the massive series of tests carried out by the Soviet Union in the atmosphere late last year. These tests were in violation of a three-year moratorium.

In his statement March 2, Mr. Kennedy said that the Soviet series had given Moscow a technical advantage that endangered the security of the United States.

The Khrushchev message was a reply to a brief private message Mr. Macmillan had addressed to the Premier Monday, supplementary to the joint statement by the United States and Britain. Mr. Macmillan appealed for earnest consideration and acceptance of the principle of international verification

Continued on Page 2, Column 2

CITY CONSIDERING ISSUE OF PENALTY IN SCHOOL STRIKE

State May Be Asked to Help Decide Whether Teachers Forfeited Their Jobs

By LEONARD BUDER

The Board of Education may ask the State Education Commissioner to help decide what, if any, penalties should be imposed on the teachers who took part in Wednesday's school strike.

An informal meeting of the school board has been called for Monday to discuss this and other issues stemming from the strike.

The board's problem concerns these questions:

Did the 20,000 public school teachers who failed to report to work Wednesday automatically lose their jobs under the state's Condon-Wadlin Act?

If the teachers did lose their jobs legally, can the board rehire them as provided in the act without imposing the specified penalties on the teachers?

Allen Stand Cited

School sources noted yesterday that the State Education Commissioner, Dr. James E. Allen Jr., said last Sunday that if the teachers struck "those in positions of authority have no choice but to enforce the law."

It was also recalled that in 1960, when 5,000 city teachers staged a one-day work-stoppage, the school board checked with the Commissioner before allowing the teachers to return to work without any penalties. However, at that time, the board did not call the teachers' action a strike.

Charles Cogen, president of the United Federation of Teachers, said last night he was confident there would be no reprisals against teachers.

At the same time, he said that any teacher subjected to reprisal should bring the matter to the union's attention. Mr. Cogen appeared on a fifteen-minute broadcast on WNBC-TV.

Court Action Dropped

With the strike over, the board did not bother yesterday to file its petition for an injunction to bar the federation from picketing and otherwise interfering with the schools.

After the strike had developed Wednesday, the board obtained a restraining order from State Supreme Court Justice William C. Hecht Jr. The order also directed Charles Cogen, president of the federation, and other officers to appear yesterday to show cause why an injunction should not be granted.

When the case was recalled

Continued on Page 16, Column 1

INLAND IS THE KEY

Its Refusal to Adopt Higher Prices Sets Off Cancellations

By KENNETH S. SMITH

Steel prices figured in high drama yesterday, with Inland Steel Company furnishing the prologue and United States Steel Corporation the dénouement.

The action shuttled from coast to coast, with some key scenes in the midlands. The actors in the price drama ranged from dour steel company accountants around the country to jubilant aides of the Kennedy Administration in Washington.

The audience ranged from Wall Street financiers and stock brokers to Main Street housewives who wondered vaguely if all the talk about higher steel prices would affect the cost of the things they buy.

Their worries were academic as the curtain fell in early evening. United States Steel rescinded the $6-a-ton price increase it posted on Wednesday, laying to rest the short-lived steel price rise.

Bethlehem Steel Yields

Bethlehem Steel Corporation, the nation's second largest steel producer, was the first to rescind its price increases in reaction to the refusal of Inland to raise its prices.

Immediately, the New York Stock Exchange reacted sharply to the news. Stock prices rose steadily after 3:15 P. M., following the Bethlehem announcement.

The rise in security prices during the final thirty minutes of trading was greater than that gain for the whole day.

The shares of United States Steel, which did not make its rescinding announcement until after the stock market had closed, declined 62⅝ cents, finishing at $66.75. It was the only major steel issue to show a loss on the day.

The action started when Inland Steel's board of directors announced that the Chicago-based giant of the mid-continent steel markets would not make any adjustments in its steel mill products at this time.

"The company has long recognized the need for improve-

Continued on Page 10, Column 5

STEEL GIVES IN, RESCINDS RISES UNDER PRESSURE BY PRESIDENT; HE SAYS DECISION SERVES NATION

BALK AT STEEL PRICE RISE: John F. Smith, seated, president of Inland Steel Company, and Philip D. Block Jr., vice chairman, at company offices yesterday in Chicago. Mr. Block announced Inland would not make adjustments in prices at this time.
United Press International Telephoto

FARM BILL TESTS LOST BY KENNEDY

Senate Unit Knocks Out Key Curbs—House Committee Defers Showdown Vote

By WILLIAM M. BLAIR
Special to The New York Times.

WASHINGTON, April 13—President Kennedy suffered a double setback today in his fight for farm legislation providing stiff controls to curb surplus crop production.

The Senate Agriculture Committee approved late today a farm bill stripped of the Administration's key control proposals. Earlier, the House Agriculture Committee postponed a show-down vote on the Administration's bill despite the President's efforts to get it approved.

President Kennedy was understood to have sought to line up for the House measure two votes would have permitted approval of it. He failed, and the committee's Democratic leaders were forced to postpone action on the bill until after the Easter recess. The recess begins Thursday.

The House committee voted 19 to 16 to postpone action on the bill, which proposes some of the stiffest production controls in history. The vote was taken on motion of the Democratic majority because, as the committee chairman, Representative Harold D. Cooley of North Carolina, said, "we didn't have the votes" for approval.

The Senate committee voted 14 to 4 to report its bill to the Senate. On the key vote in the day-long session, the committee divided 9 to 8 to substitute a program now in effect for corn and other livestock feed

Continued on Page 12, Column 3

---

54 Million Nonfarm Jobs Establish a March Record

By JOHN D. POMFRET
Special to The New York Times.

WASHINGTON, April 13—The number of workers on nonfarm payrolls and the average weekly earnings of factory production workers rose to March records last month, the Department of Labor said.

But side by side with these figures were others that showed less than the expected increase last month in the number of construction workers and no improvement in the number who have been unemployed for half a year or more.

Today's report, a department spokesman said, indicated a "sharpening" in the disparity between the circumstances of those who have jobs and those who do not.

The spokesman, Seymour L. Wolfbein, Deputy Assistant Secretary of Labor, said that "the big push on the employment side isn't making the dent we'd like on the unemployment side."

Factory Employment Up

The department had announced its March labor force estimates in summary last week. These showed a rise in total civilian employment to 66,300,000, a record for the month. But they showed virtually no change in the employment rate. Today's figures from the department gave details.

Nonfarm payroll employment moved up in March by 160,000 to 54,000,000. That was 500,000 more than the previous record for March, set in 1960. Manufacturing employment, which usually declines somewhat in March, rose by 60,000 to 16,500,000. That was about 650,000 more than in March, 1961.

The industries mainly responsible for the improvement in both the month and the year were metals, electrical equip-

Continued on Page 12, Column 4

HOUSE UNIT VOTES RECORD ARMS BILL

47.8 Billion Total Is Biggest for Peacetime Year—Cut in Reserves Opposed

By JACK RAYMOND
Special to The New York Times.

WASHINGTON, April 13—The House Appropriations Committee voted a military funds bill totaling $47,839,491,000, a peacetime record, today for the fiscal year beginning July 1.

The committee called for acceleration of the controversial RS-70 airplane project. But it left to the Administration's discretion the decision whether to expand the program as the Air Force has requested.

The committee rejected, however, Administration plans for a cutback in the National Guard and Army Reserve forces. It provided money to maintain these at 700,000 despite plans for a 58,000-man reduction.

Although the House panel recalled past refusals by Congress to accept cuts in Reserve strength, it did not resort to the mandatory language that it has in the past effectively preserved existing National Guard and Reserve force levels.

Housing Aid Backed

In a separate action the House Armed Services Committee approved a bill that would provide increased housing allowances for military men. The increase, the first since 1952, would add $291,000,000 in military costs.

Housing allowances for military men will cost about $1,300,000 in the current fiscal year.

The House Aeronautics and Space Committee, meanwhile, was reported to be considering a $100,000,000 cut in President Kennedy's $3,800,000,000 space budget.

The relatively small space cut was said to indicate caution on the part of committee members in contrast to enthusiasm last year for virtually any space effort to compete with Russia.

The defense appropriations measure, which is expected to

Continued on Page 2, Column 1

KENNEDY IS VICTOR

Uses His Full Powers for 72 Hours to Subdue Industry

Text of McNamara statement is printed on Page 10.

By RICHARD E. MOONEY
Special to The New York Times.

WASHINGTON, April 13—President Kennedy triumphed today over the titans of the steel industry.

Almost precisely seventy-two hours after the United States Steel Corporation's announcement of a price increase, the corporation backed down and rescinded the increase late this afternoon.

The action by United States Steel, the nation's largest steel producer, followed announcements by the Inland Steel Company and the Kaiser Steel Corporation that they would not increase their prices, and a statement by Bethlehem Steel Corporation, the nation's second largest producer, that it was canceling its rises.

By early evening seven of the eight companies that had raised their prices in the last three days had canceled them. The eighth, Wheeling Steel Corporation, said it would announce its decision tomorrow.

Many Forms of Pressure

For three days the great forces at the command of the President of the United States had been brought to bear on the steel industry.

Some of the effort was exerted in the open—the President's open denunciation of the companies, calculated to arouse public opinion against them; the opening of grand jury proceedings leading to possible antitrust action, and the threat to divert orders to companies that had not raised prices.

But privately as well, the President and his advisers were bringing every form of persuasion to bear on the industry, trying to hold back the companies that had not yet raised prices and induce the others to roll back the price increase.

Kennedy's Statement

President Kennedy was informed of the actions by United States Steel and Bethlehem off Norfolk, Va., where he was aboard a cruiser observing naval maneuvers. He issued this statement:

"The people of the United States are most gratified by the announcements of Bethlehem and United States Steel Company that their proposed price increases are being rescinded.

"In taking the action at this time, they are serving the public interest and their actions will assist our common objective of strengthening our country and our economy."

Even during this dramatic day, as the steel industry started to weaken, the Administration pressed on with the actions that the price increase had started.

Secretary of Defense Robert S. McNamara continued to

Continued on Page 10, Column 1

SYRIAN PRESIDENT RETURNS TO RULE

Army Frees el-Kodsi From a Prison Hospital

By DANA ADAMS SCHMIDT
Special to The New York Times.

BEIRUT, Lebanon, April 13—Syria's army chief announced today the return to office of President Nazem el-Kodsi. The President had been in a prison hospital.

The army commander, Maj. Gen. Abdel Karim Zahreddin, announced the return over the Damascus radio. He indicated that the new Government would follow a more Leftist course than its predecessor.

It was understood that the army agreed to a condition set by the President—that the Constituent Assembly be reconstituted. However, a majority of the 172 Assembly members are reported to have promised the army that they would resign. Their resignations would clear the way for a new election.

It was reported that President el-Kodsi, with the army's approval, would ask Rashad Barmada, Minister of Defense, to form a new Cabinet. He would replace Premier Maarouf Dawalibi, whose Rightist leanings were a key factor that provoked a coup d'état by the Syrian Army on March 28.

General Zahreddin said the army had dropped its plan to establish a transition Cabinet before constitutional life was re-established because "such a government would be responsible to the army and would thereby contradict the principles of constitutional life."

Continued on Page 7, Column 2

Jouhaud Sentenced to Die As No. 2 Secret Army Head

'This King Business' A Headache to Shah

By MAX FRANKEL
Special to The New York Times.

WASHINGTON, April 13—Mohammed Riza Pahlevi, Shah of Iran, declared here today that "this king business has given me personally nothing but headaches."

The Western-educated ruler of the 2,500-year-old monarchy of Persia said he had lived under constant "strain and stress," suffered vilification and attempts on his life and, in twenty years on the throne, had presided over the liquidation of almost the entire royal fortune.

But the monarchy itself will not be given away, he asserted in an address to the National Press Club. Though the country is looking toward a "type of democracy peculiar to ourselves" and toward rapid economic progress in the next two decades, he said, the in-

Continued on Page 6, Column 5

Edmond Jouhaud, right, arrives at Paris court for trial
United Press International Telephoto

By W. GRANGER BLAIR
Special to The New York Times.

PARIS, April 13—Edmond Jouhaud, second in command of the terrorist Secret Army Organization in Algeria, was condemned to death by a high military tribunal tonight.

The verdict against the former air force general was handed down after two hours and fifteen minutes of deliberation by five civilian jurists, three lieutenant generals and a vice admiral.

There is no appeal from the

tribunal's sentence. Only President de Gaulle can commute it and Jouhaud's attorneys said today that the former general's "honor" would not permit him to beg for mercy.

Although the defense indicated that Jouhaud faced the guillotine as an officer who had been stripped of his rank during the short-lived generals' coup in Algiers last April, some legal

Continued on Page 4, Column 4

High Agriculture Aide Resigns Over Links to Billie Sol Estes

Special to The New York Times.

WASHINGTON, April 13—A high official of the Department of Agriculture resigned today after he had been linked with the gift-giving activities of Billie Sol Estes, Texas financier who has been indicted for fraud.

Emery E. Jacobs, deputy administrator of the Agricultural Stabilization and Conservation Service, said that he was resigning to "face these accusations." He denied receiving favors from Mr. Estes.

The board has been investigating Mr. Estes' financial dealings in West Texas agricultural mortgages. Six elevators that Mr. Estes controls have contracts for the storage of 33,000,000 bushels of Government grain sorghums and wheat valued at $36,000,000.

An Agricultural spokesman said that a check of the storage

facilities Tuesday showed everything in proper order.

The inquiry board heard yesterday that Mr. Jacobs had been in the Nieman-Marcus store in Dallas last September and that he had ordered a suit and other clothing mailed to the apartment of his secretary, Mrs. Margaret S. Campbell, here. A salesman testified that a "Mr. Jacobs" and other men were with Mr. Estes and that the two men were Agriculture Department officials.

Reports from Dallas said that sales slips introduced at the board of inquiry hearings showed that the three men had made purchases totaling $1,433.20. But there was confusion here as to how much was for Mr. Jacobs.

One report quoted one of four Nieman-Marcus employes as

Continued on Page 12, Column 3

Hamburger Fat Law Challenged by Judge

By SAMUEL KAPLAN

The constitutionality of the city's law limiting the amount of fat in hamburger was questioned by Magistrate Louis S. Wallach in Brooklyn Municipal Term Court yesterday.

He told two defendants who had pleaded guilty to violating the law that they should change their plea and make a test case of it. He said that if they did not he would fine them $50. They did not and were fined $50.

Magistrate Wallach said that people should be allowed to buy hamburger that contained more than 30 per cent fat if they want ed to.

He allowed the Sumner Project Meat Market, Inc., to be substituted as the defendant in the case. The original defendants were Daniel and Paul Esposito of the Money Worth Meat Market, 568

Continued on Page 16, Column 5

The New York Times.

LATE CITY EDITION
U. S. Weather Bureau Report (Page 66) forecasts:
Partly cloudy today. Fair tonight.
Sunny and warm tomorrow.
Temp. range: 80—61; yesterday: 85—61.

VOL. CXI. No. 38,107. © 1962 by The New York Times Company Times Square, New York 36, N. Y. NEW YORK, FRIDAY, MAY 25, 1962. 10 cents beyond 50-mile zone from New York City except on Long Island. Higher in air delivery cities. FIVE CENTS

CARPENTER ORBITS EARTH 3 TIMES SAFELY, BUT OVERSHOOTS LANDING AREA 250 MILES; FATE IN DOUBT AN HOUR, HE IS FOUND IN RAFT

STIFF GRAIN CURB VOTED AS SENATE UPHOLDS KENNEDY

Tightest Controls in History Are Added to Farm Bill— Committee Reversed

By RUSSELL BAKER
Special to The New York Times.

WASHINGTON, May 24— The Senate gave President Kennedy a victory on the farm bill today by voting the strictest controls in history on the production of wheat and feed grains.

Voting largely along party lines, the Senate reversed its Agriculture Committee and put the Administration's production curbs on wheat and livestock feed grains back into the farm bill.

Final Senate action on the measure is expected tomorrow after work is completed on its less controversial sections. The action will then shift to the House, where the Kennedy control program has been approved by the Agriculture Committee. The House has delayed action to see what the Senate would do.

Democrats See Victory

House Democrats predict another victory there for the President. Republican leaders contend that the production curbs will be rejected. The outlook is for a bitter, closely fought floor battle.

The President's fight in the Senate was led by Allen J. Ellender of Louisiana, Democratic chairman of the Agriculture Committee. He received important help from Senator Richard B. Russell, Democrat of Georgia, leader of the Southern bloc.

The two important votes came on Mr. Ellender's moves to write into the bill the Administration plans on wheat and feed grains.

The vote for adopting the wheat program was 53 to 36. The majority consisted of fifty-one Democrats and two Republicans—Senators John Sherman Cooper and Thruston B. Morton, both of Kentucky. Opposing it were thirty Republicans and six Democrats.

Cooper Cites Failure

Mr. Cooper said he had supported the program because "no new principle is involved." He said that wheat had been under control since 1935 and was in the heaviest surplus of all crops under Government price supports. "The present wheat program is a failure," he declared.

The vote to adopt the feed-grain program was 46 to 37. Again, it was cast largely along party lines after the Senate had beaten attempts to weaken the program. The feed-grain program applies to corn, barley, grain sorghums, rye and oats.

Broadly, the two provisions would give the farmer a choice of limiting production and receiving high Federal price supports, or of rejecting the curbs and having price-support levels

Continued on Page 20, Column 3

4.6 Billion Aid Bill Voted by House Unit

By FELIX BELAIR Jr.
Special to The New York Times.

WASHINGTON, May 24—A foreign aid authorization of $4,668,500,000 was approved today by the House Foreign Affairs Committee for the year beginning July 1.

The authorization was $210,000,000 less than President Kennedy had requested.

It included $600,000,000 for the Alliance for Progress, the program of aid to Latin-American republics other than Cuba. The legislation provided $1,500,000,000 more for economic development loans under the alliance at the rate of $500,000,000 in each of the three fiscal years beginning July 1, 1963.

The committee's action on the bill confirmed its $600,-000,000 cutback in long-term authorization of funds for the alliance. President Kennedy's

Continued on Page 5, Column 3

TORNADO INJURES 25 IN WATERBURY

One Man Killed, 45 Homes Destroyed — Jersey and L. I. Lashed by Storms

A tornado swept through Waterbury, Conn., yesterday, killing one man and injuring at least twenty-five other persons. Forty-five houses were destroyed and 150 others damaged.

The tornado was one of a series of storms that battered the East with lightning, hail, high winds and heavy rain.

Falling trees toppled power lines in many parts of Brooklyn, Queens and Long Island. Eleven thousand homes were without electricity for varying periods.

A tornado also struck in central New Jersey, north of Trenton, flipping a truck on its side and uprooting trees. Other parts of the state were hit by hail, heavy rains and winds.

Commuters Drenched

In New York City, commuters on the way home from work were drenched by a sudden rainstorm. The skies quickly cleared, but at about 9 P. M. a new thunderstorm struck, accompanied by a downpour that lasted about an hour. The Weather Bureau forecast partly cloudy and mild weather for today.

A Weather Bureau spokesman said the thunderstorms were the result of an encounter between relatively cool and dry air moving in from the West, and warm, moist air in the East.

The effects were felt as far north as Montreal, where a tornado tore off most of the roof of the Seminary College of Holy Apostles. Nearly 200 persons were in the building, but the casualties were three students who suffered slight cuts and bruises.

Similar storms, not directly related to those in the East, struck scattered sections of the Middle West. Hutchinson, Kan.,

Continued on Page 42, Column 6

DE GAULLE ANGRY OVER SALAN CASE; COURT IS REBUKED

Joxe Says Tribunal's Ruling Could Hurt French Forces Fighting Algeria Terror

Special to The New York Times.

PARIS, May 24 — An angry Government expressed concern today over the effect that the sentence of life imprisonment for former General Raoul Salan would have on the morale of the Government forces fighting the Secret Army Organization.

Louis Joxe, Minister for Algerian Affairs, told the Cabinet that the judgment, which has stunned the nation, could constitute a "blow to the morale" of the security forces.

President de Gaulle was understood to have expressed his anger at the judgment in the strongest terms during the Cabinet session. At the meeting, the Government took a first step to restore public liberties in Algeria after more than seven years of war restrictions.

In preparation for the self-determination vote scheduled in Algeria for July 1, the Ministers approved an ordinance allowing free formation of parties and other political groups. Some restrictive police measures also will be abrogated.

Rightist Defeat Sighted

At the same time, the Government expressed its belief that the Secret Army Organization, which is still attempting to disrupt the Algerian ceasefire accords and prevent independence, was on its way to defeat.

Confidence was expressed that voting would be possible everywhere in Algeria on the scheduled date. The vote is expected to approve independence for Algeria in association with France.

The heaviest casualties, inflicted by the Secret Army Organization have been among the gendarmerie, the republican security companies and the special undercover police units.

Salan, former chief of the terrorist underground, escaped the death penalty last night when a high military tribunal, after finding him guilty on all five counts involving his activities in Algeria, ruled that there were extenuating circumstances in his case. The judgment was expected to encourage the Secret Army organization to continue its terrorism.

Strongest Action Possible

The statement by M. Joxe at the Cabinet meeting at which General de Gaulle presided was reported by Alain Peyrefitte, Secretary of State for Information.

It clearly represented the strongest rebuke that the Government felt it could publicly deliver against the judgment, in view of the independence of judicial institutions in France.

Other elements of public life were unrestrained in their reactions to the Salan ruling. In general, the political Left was outraged and the Right was delighted.

But virtually everyone was amazed, since it had not appeared possible that the chief of the terrorist movement would get a lesser sentence than his second in command, Edmond Jouhaud, who was condemned to death by the same high tribunal slightly more than a month ago.

M. Peyrefitte disclosed after the Cabinet meeting that the Government had "envisaged the consequences that" this

Continued on Page 6, Column 2

RECOVERY AND CONGRATULATIONS: Lieut. Comdr. M. Scott Carpenter is hoisted aboard a Navy helicopter from beside floating capsule after his orbital trip. Later, on the carrier Intrepid, he talks with President Kennedy. N.A.S.A. via Associated Press Wirephoto

Dean to Join Zorin In Plan to Condemn War Propaganda

By Reuters.

GENEVA, May 24—Arthur H. Dean, chief United States delegate at the seventeen-nation disarmament conference, said today that the United States and the Soviet Union planned to present a joint declaration condemning war propaganda.

Mr. Dean said that the two countries, as co-chairmen of the conference had been working on the text of the declaration in private and, barring unforeseen problems, they would submit it to the full conference tomorrow.

He stressed that the declaration was not a ban on war propaganda, but simply a statement against it.

During earlier discussion of the question by the full conference, the West objected to the Soviet Union's proposal for a ban on war propaganda, calling it undesirable and unenforceable under American constitutional guarantees of freedom of speech and of the press.

As a counter-proposal, the United States suggested that East and West open avenues of communication and encourage the exchange of information to counter propaganda.

Mr. Dean said today that the chief Soviet delegate, Valerian A. Zorin, had submitted the

Continued on Page 4, Column 4

U.S. OFFERS PLAN FOR NEW GUINEA

Suggests Gradual Transfer From Dutch to Jakarta, Then a Plebiscite

By MAX FRANKEL
Special to The New York Times.

WASHINGTON, May 24 — The United States' proposals to settle the Dutch-Indonesian dispute over Netherlands New Guinea call for a rigidly supervised plebiscite in the indefinite future, but only after Indonesians have taken over administration of the area.

This feature of the plan and the fact that Washington has taken more than an intermediary's interest in the problem seem to be resented by the Dutch and appear to account for their refusal to reopen negotiations with the Indonesians.

[In The Hague, the lower House of the Netherlands Parliament rejected Thursday night a resolution calling on the Government to accept the United States plan as the basis for a New Guinea settlement.]

Both U Thant, Acting Secretary General of the United Nations, and President Kennedy appealed yesterday for new talks to settle the issue before the current fighting in New Guinea

Continued on Page 2, Column 2

Entire Nation Gives Thanks When Astronaut Is Sighted

A sigh of relief went up across the nation yesterday following the news that Lieut. Comdr. M. Scott Carpenter had been found in a life raft in the Atlantic after his triple orbit of the earth. Until it became known that radio contact with Commander Carpenter's space capsule had been lost, the flight had aroused less interest than that of Lieut. Col. John H. Glenn Jr. last February.

The general assumption seemed to be that Commander Carpenter would safely follow Colonel Glenn's path.

In Congress and state legislative bodies, procedure was interrupted to announce the news of the astronaut's rescue. The Massachusetts House of Representatives halted for a moment of prayerful thanks.

Cheers Greet News

"Have they found him yet?" was the question asked across the country. In a restaurant in Toledo, Ohio, two dozen patrons cheered at Commander Carpenter's rescue.

"Thank God," one said.

Here, about 7,000 persons stood silently in Grand Central Terminal in front of a huge television screen when it was announced that radio contact had been lost.

They broke into cheers when word came that the 37-year-old astronaut had been sighted in the Atlantic.

Subway riders received the word over loudspeakers in stations. A storm of ticker-tape descended from buildings in Rockefeller Center. An anonymous person gave expression to his feelings by writing "Bravo Carpenter" on the typewriter in front of the Longine-Wittnauer Building on Fifth Avenue.

Mayor Sends Wire

In the ballroom of the Biltmore Hotel, Francis Cardinal Spellman opened a reception in honor of his seventy-third birthday by asking 800 women guests to give thanks in prayer for the successful flight.

At City Hall, Mayor Wagner invited Commander Carpenter to a parade up Broadway, the city's traditional welcome to heroes.

"All New York City joins in paying you deserved tribute," he said in a telegram. "Your dramatic flight and rescue have thrilled all of us."

In Washington, the Senate interrupted debate on a farm bill to applaud the news that Commander Carpenter had been found. Senator Hubert H. Humphrey of Minnesota, assistant Democratic leader, paid tribute to the astronaut and those who had participated in the launching.

Senator Everett McKinley Dirksen of Illinois, the Repub-

Continued on Page 17, Column 4

ON OCEAN 3 HOURS

Capsule Picked Up— Nose of Craft Too High on Re-entry

Excerpts from Project Mercury record are on Page 16.

By RICHARD WITKIN
Special to The New York Times.

CAPE CANAVERAL, Fla., May 24 — M. Scott Carpenter became today the second American astronaut to orbit the earth.

His three-orbit trip ended, however, with a global audience suffering almost an hour's anxiety about his safe return.

It was three hours from the time his space capsule landed until he was plucked from a life raft by a rescue helicopter. And it was hours later before the capsule was picked up by the destroyer Pierce.

Tonight, on Grand Turk Island in the British West Indies, Commander Carpenter had an emotional reunion with two fellow-astronauts, John H. Glenn, who made the first orbital flight, and Walter M. Schirra.

Carried Beyond Goal

Coming down from orbit, the 37-year-old Navy test pilot was carried 250 miles beyond the intended Caribbean landing point and the recovery ships waiting to pick him up.

[In Washington, President Kennedy termed Commander Carpenter's courage and the skill of his rescuers "heart-warming to all of us." The President authorized the National Aeronautics and Space Administration to award its Distinguished Service Medal to Commander Carpenter.]

The overshoot was said to have been caused by the fact that the nose of the Aurora VII capsule was pointed too high at the time the retro or braking rockets fired to slow its speed and bring it out of orbit.

Radio communication blacked out, as it was expected to, part way in the descent. But because the capsule was beyond its target point, voice communication did not resume, as it normally would, after a gap of four or five minutes.

Millions Await Word

Project Mercury officials had immediate indications from two seconds of radar reception as the capsule disappeared over the horizon, that it had survived the searing re-entry into the atmosphere, though the astronaut's fate was unknown.

The millions following the flight by television and radio did not even have this reed to lean on, since word of the radar reception was not relayed to them by Mercury officials.

It was only after thirty-five minutes of bleak silence following the initial blackout that the public had a reassuring word.

It was announced that an automatically transmitted signal had been picked up by a Navy search plane. But even this carried no clue, for the public or officials, as to whether the capsule's parachute had popped

Continued on Page 14, Column 1

RESCUE TECHNIQUE PLANNED 3 YEARS

Project Mercury Provided for Emergency Pick-Ups Outside Target Area

By JOHN W. FINNEY
Special to The New York Times.

CAPE CANAVERAL, May 24—Three years of "contingency planning" by Project Mercury paid off today by assuring the safe rescue of Lieut. Comdr. M. Scott Carpenter after he had overshot his landing area by 250 miles.

In drafting plans for sending men into space, project officials attempted to develop a course of action to meet any emergency.

One of these, which became a momentarily frightening reality today, was that the astronaut and his capsule would return outside of the selected landing areas and beyond the immediate reach of the Navy recovery task force.

To meet this contingency, plans were developed for emergency rescue by airborne teams of Air Force men who would parachute to the aid of the astronaut.

This plan was put into effect today when the Aurora VII capsule landed beyond the Navy task force stationed in the prime

Continued on Page 15, Column 8

Maryland Calls Special Session As Court Orders Redistricting

By The Associated Press

ANNAPOLIS, Md., May 24 — Gov. J. Millard Tawes called a special session of the Maryland Legislature today after a court order had invalidated the distribution of seats in the House of Delegates.

Judge O. Bowie Duckett in Anne Arundel County Circuit Court that the present distribution of House seats, weighed in favor of small counties, was "invidious discrimination" against the voting rights of residents of three metropolitan counties.

Governor Tawes summoned the Legislature to meet in special session at 10 A. M. tomorrow to fill "an acute constitutional void" resulting from the court order.

In anticipation of the court ruling, legislation already has been prepared by the administration to give nineteen more seats to metropolitan areas in the November election and take nineteen away from less populated areas in 1966. The present membership of the House is 123.

The Governor also had alerted legislators earlier in the week to be ready for the special session, which is expected to enact stop-gap legislation before the June 1 deadline for passage of simple bills. New jobs cannot be created in an emergency act in Maryland.

Judge Duckett did not disturb the make-up of the State

Continued on Page 18, Column 2

Model Penal Code Is Approved By the American Law Institute

By ANTHONY LEWIS
Special to The New York Times.

WASHINGTON, May 24 — The American Law Institute gave final approval today to a model penal code that has been under preparation for ten years.

The code is regarded by many authorities as one of the most important recent projects in legal scholarship. Even before its completion it had begun to influence the criminal law of the states and the Federal Government.

The code is intended to take a fresh look at all of criminal law—its philosophical underpinnings, its definitions of crimes, its provisions for sentencing and correction of offenders.

The principal work on the code was done by two law professors—Herbert Wechsler of Columbia University and Louis B. Schwartz of the University of Pennsylvania. They received a standing ovation from institute members after the final vote on the code.

The Law Institute is an association of the country's most distinguished judges, law professors and practitioners. It works to codify and modernize the law. It has completed such other projects as a uniform commercial code that has been adopted by many states, including New York.

Under the institute's procedure, sections of a work such as the model penal code are prepared by the principal draftsmen, then debated in various committees and before the full membership at the annual meetings here in Washington. Then further drafts are written and rewritten until the language is finally approved.

The late Judge Learned Hand was one of the many eminent figures who took part, under this procedure, in the shaping of the penal code.

One of his arguments was that the criminal law should not punish any kind of sexual relations, normal or abnormal, between consenting adults in private. The institute adopted

Continued on Page 50, Column 2

Attempt to Fly Balloon in Space To Test Vision Is Part Success

By HAROLD M. SCHMECK Jr.
Special to The New York Times.

CAPE CANAVERAL, Fla., May 24—Lieut. Comdr. M. Scott Carpenter's attempt to fly a balloon in space today was only partly successful.

The experiment was one of the most important conducted during the three-orbit flight. It was intended to show how well a person can perceive various colors in space and also was a test of ability to judge distances and sizes against the unfamiliar black sky of the space environment.

There are points of considerable importance to the nation's moon exploration program because they could offer hints concerning the difficulties to be expected in rendezvous of a

space vehicle with another object in space.

The balloon, thirty inches in diameter totally inflated, had panels of different hues—yellow, orange, flat white and phosphorescent, so that a comparison of visibility of different colors could be made. It was expected to produce a drag of only one one-hundredth on the space craft. Commander Carpenter found that an orange color called "Day Glow" showed up the best when sunlight was on it.

Rendezvous in space is expected to be important in Proj-

Continued on Page 15, Column 3

The New York Times.

LATE CITY EDITION
U.S. Weather Bureau Report (Page 95) forecasts:
Sunny today; fair and cool tonight.
Mostly fair and pleasant tomorrow.
Temp. range: 70—50; yesterday: 68—54.
Temp.-Hum. Index: 64; yesterday: 65.

NEWS SUMMARY AND INDEX, PAGE 95

VOL. CXII..No. 38,235.
© 1962 by The New York Times Company.
Times Square, New York 36, N. Y.

NEW YORK, SUNDAY, SEPTEMBER 30, 1962.

15c beyond 50-mile zone
beyond 200-mile zone
from New York City, except on Long Island
from New York City, higher in air delivery cities.

SECTION ONE

THIRTY CENTS

KENNEDY FEDERALIZES MISSISSIPPI'S GUARD; MOBILIZES TROOPS, ORDERS STATE TO YIELD; ADDRESSES NATION TODAY ON RACIAL CRISIS

PRESIDENT CALLS RUSK AND BRITON TO DISCUSS BERLIN

Lord Home and Envoys Will Fly to Capital Today as German Crisis Grows

By E. W. KENWORTHY

WASHINGTON, Sept. 29—President Kennedy will meet here tomorrow with high United States and British officials to discuss the Berlin situation and other foreign policy questions.

The luncheon at the White House will be attended by Secretary of State Dean Rusk; the Earl of Home, the British Foreign Secretary; David K. E. Bruce, the United States Ambassador in London, and Sir David Ormsby Gore, the British Ambassador in Washington.

[Mr. Rusk said in New York that assertions by the Communists that they had no troops in Laos were "nonsense and the world knows it."]

Newport Trip Called Off

President Kennedy had planned to fly to Newport this afternoon and have luncheon there with the British and American officials, however, at 3 P.M. the White House said he had called off the trip.

Andrew T. Hatcher, associate press secretary, was reticent at the time about saying that the trip cancellation was related to the integration crisis in Mississippi.

The ministers and ambassadors will fly here tomorrow from New York, where they are attending sessions of the United Nations General Assembly.

The White House did not say what would be discussed. But officials here said it was obvious that Berlin and increasing tensions there would demand much of the meeting's attention.

High Administration officials have not disguised their deep concern over the lack of interest on the part of the Soviet Union in various proposals by the United States and Britain to reduce tension over Berlin. For example, Soviet officials

Continued on Page 26, Column 1

GIANTS AND COLTS SPLIT TWO GAMES

Dodgers Clinch at Least a Tie for First Place

The league-leading Los Angeles Dodgers lost to the St. Louis Cardinals yesterday but remained a game ahead of the San Francisco Giants who split a double-header with the Houston Colts. The results assured the Dodgers of at least a tie for first place.

FOOTBALL

Army and Columbia won major college football contests in New York. Scores of leading games:

Army . . . . . 9* Syracuse . . . 2
Auburn . . . 22 Tennessee . . .21
Boston Coll..28 Villanova . .13
California . .21 San Jose St. . 8
Colgate . . .23 Cornell 12
Columbia . .27 Brown 20
Dartmouth .27 Mass. 3
Duke . . . . .21 S. Carolina. . 8
Ga. Tech ..17 Florida 0
Harvard . .27 Lehigh 7
Holy Cross..16 Buffalo 7
Iowa . . . . .28 Oregon St. . 8
Minnesota . 0 Missouri . . . 0
Mississippi .14 Kentucky . . 0
Navy . . . . .21 W. & M. . . .16
Nebraska ..25 Michigan . .13
Notre Dame.13 Oklahoma. . 7
Ohio State..41 N. Carolina . 7
Oregon . . .13 Utah 8
Penn. . . . .13 Lafayette . .11
Penn State.20 Air Force. . 6
Princeton . .15 Rutgers 6
Stanford . .16 Mich. St. .13
Washington .18 Illinois 7
Yale . . . . .18 Conn. 14

HORSE RACING

Kelso won the $115,200 Woodward Stakes as the Aqueduct meeting ended. Jaipur was a distant second to the favorite.

Details in Section 5

Brandt, Rockefeller and Wagner Lead Steuben March

The New York Times

Mayor Willy Brandt of West Berlin joins Mayor Wagner and Governor Rockefeller at the head of about 25,000 marchers during annual Steuben Day parade up Fifth Avenue.

By DAVID BINDER

The Bavarians yodeled, the Cologners danced a two-step, the Rhinelanders sang, the Hamburgers cried "Hummel Hummel" and the bands played Berliner melodies as 25,000 German-Americans marched up Fifth Avenue yesterday.

The occasion was the fifth annual Steuben Parade, honoring Baron Friedrich Wilhelm von Steuben, the general from Magdeburg who helped George Washington drill the Continental Army during the American Revolution. Mayor Willy Brandt of West Berlin was the honored guest. German touches were everywhere —in black corduroy carpenter costumes, gymnastic stunts

Continued on Page 52, Column 3

KENNEDY WISHES BEN BELLA WELL

'Warmest Congratulations' Sent as U. S. Recognizes New Algerian Regime

By PETER BRAESTRUP
Special to The New York Times

WASHINGTON, Sept. 29—President Kennedy today sent "warmest congratulations" to Ahmed Ben Bella, Premier of independent Algeria's newly formed Government.

Mr. Kennedy, who as a Senator endorsed Algerian self-rule in 1957, wished Mr. Ben Bella "every success" and said that "my Government and my people share my earnest desire to foster and extend the cordial relations that exist between our two countries."

The President's message coincided with the State Department's announcement of formal diplomatic recognition of the newly established Government of Algeria.

New Premier to Visit Here

Yesterday Mr. Ben Bella announced his Cabinet and pledged a "neutralist and non-engaged" foreign policy in a speech before the week-old National Assembly. The Assembly subsequently approved the Cabinet list, 159 to 1 with 19 abstentions.

Secretary of State Dean Rusk sent congratulations to the Algerian Foreign Minister, Mohammed Khemisti, saying that he looked forward to a meeting "in the near future."

Informed sources said today that President Kennedy and Secretary Rusk would meet with Mr. Ben Bella sometime after the Algerian Premier's arrival in the United States, possibly late next week, to head

Continued on Page 4, Column 1

Norway Criticizes Paris Plan to Build National A-Forces

By HENRY GINIGER
Special to The New York Times

PARIS, Sept. 29—The four-day state visit by King Olav V of Norway ended today with a strong attack by the Norwegian Foreign Minister, Dr. Halvard M. Lange, on national atomic striking forces in Europe such as that planned by France.

King Olav took leave of President de Gaulle this morning before flying to Oslo. He had been warmly received and responded with the same warmth in a recorded message of thanks that was broadcast over the French radio and television.

It was left to Dr. Lange, who had accompanied the King, to underline the serious divergences between the Norwegian and French Governments on Western defense. He did so in a statement to the French News Agency.

Reliance Placed on the U. S.

Dr. Lange said the Western alliance must rest on confidence among its members, for "otherwise it has no sense." He said that Norway, placing her confidence in the United States' assumption of the burden and responsibility for the West's nuclear armament, was hostile to national atomic forces in Europe.

President de Gaulle has often said that France must assume responsibility for her defense, and he and his aides have left the widespread impression that they are not wholly confident of the United States' ability or willingness to defend Western Europe.

Dr. Lange said Western Europe should assume greater shares of the burden of conventional armaments and of help to underdeveloped nations, a

Continued on Page 23, Column 2

U.N. Says Katanga Still Recruits Troops in Violation of Promise

By SAM POPE BREWER
Special to The New York Times

UNITED NATIONS, N. Y., Sept. 29—The United Nations has accused the Government of Katanga of continuing to recruit mercenaries in spite of repeated promises not to do so.

The charges were made in a letter from the chief United Nations officer in the Congo, Robert K. A. Gardiner, to President Moise Tshombe of Katanga Province, dated last Tuesday and made public here last night.

[In Elisabethville President Tshombe likened the United Nations charges to "the stories of sea serpents or the abominable snowman." He said such charges always precede an attack on Katanga.]

Mr. Gardiner charged that recruiting was still being carried on through newspaper advertisements, especially in

Continued on Page 6, Column 1

He said: "I am worried to see that in spite of your affirmations that there would be no more mercenaries serving the Katangese Gendarmerie, bodies of Europeans killed in combat between the National Congolese Army and the Gendarmerie have been found."

In further support of the charges, Mr. Gardiner said that the United Nations organization in the Congo had a complete file of the names, addresses and photographs of mercenaries who had arrived in Katanga in recent months. It also has copies of payrolls signed by the

Mr. Gardiner charged that recruiting was still being carried on through newspaper advertisements, especially in time both in the form of troops and material"

Continued on Page 8, Column 1

JOHNSON IS FINED

Barnett's Lieutenant Is Liable to a Penalty of $5,000 a Day

Text of court order finding Johnson guilty, Page 66.

By HEDRICK SMITH
Special to The New York Times

NEW ORLEANS, Sept. 29—Lieut. Gov. Paul B. Johnson Jr. of Mississippi was held in civil contempt of Federal court orders today in his state's integration crisis.

A three-judge panel of the United States Court of Appeals for the Fifth Circuit tried Mr. Johnson in absentia. He was found guilty of defying court orders forbidding any official interference with the desegregation of the University of Mississippi.

The court gave Mr. Johnson until 11 A.M. Tuesday to purge himself of contempt or face a fine of $5,000 a day. The fine is to start building up immediately, but no money is to be collected until Tuesday.

The opinion closely followed the language used in a contempt ruling yesterday against Gov. Ross R. Barnett except that Mr. Johnson is not initially subject to arrest.

Fine Might Increase

However, the court ruled that if Mr. Johnson became Acting Governor and refused to comply with its orders, he would face the same penalties as Mr. Barnett.

This means that, in such a situation, Mr. Johnson could face arrest and a fine of $10,000 a day unless he retreated and ordered Mississippi officials to comply with the court's desegregation orders.

Like Governor Barnett, Mr. Johnson did not appear at the court hearing.

There were no attorneys in court to represent him. However, the two attorneys for the state of Mississippi were in the courtroom—Charles Clarke of Jackson and John C. Satterfield of Yazoo City.

They entered no pleadings or arguments in Mr. Johnson's behalf. However, they submitted

Continued on Page 66, Column 1

U.S. TELLS SOVIET TO OUST 2 AS SPIES

Says Aides at U. N. Bought Secrets From Sailor, Held Here in $100,000 Bail

By EMANUEL PERLMUTTER

The United States yesterday demanded the expulsion of two members of the Soviet delegation to the United Nations who were involved with an American sailor in an espionage plot.

In a sharply worded note to the Soviet mission, the United States said: "As host to the United Nations, the Government of the United States strongly protests the espionage activities directed against the internal security of the United States."

The Russians countered a few hours later with a note charging that Federal agents had illegally arrested, manhandled and questioned the two

Continued on Page 29, Column 1

Principals in Naval Secrets Case

Nelson Cornelious Drummond, a Navy petty officer, sitting between Federal officers after his arrest early yesterday.

Ivan Y. Vyrodov, member of Soviet mission to the U. N.

Associated Press

Yevgeny M. Prokhorov, second secretary of mission.

Federal Troops Massing At a Base Near Memphis

Soldiers Landed by Army Helicopters for Possible Duty in Mississippi Crisis —Engineers Ordered Into State

Special to The New York Times

MEMPHIS, Tenn., Sept. 29—Hundreds of Army troops and about 500 United States marshals were in the huge Memphis Naval Air Station near here tonight.

The Government kept flying men in during the day for a showdown next week with Gov. Ross R. Barnett of Mississippi over the court-ordered desegregation of the University of Mississippi.

[President Kennedy ordered an Army Engineer battalion to move into Mississippi and set up a tent city for 700 United States marshals, according to United Press International.]

Large Army helicopters landed 200 to 250 soldiers during the day. Newsmen were barred from the air station, 18 miles north of Memphis, but they counted 16 helicopters as they landed and discharged troops. The Pentagon in Washington admitted that the helicopters were here.

Earlier, about 400 men had been flown in by Navy transport planes. The armed soldiers were confined to the base.

Sailors leaving the base on weekend liberty told newsmen about the soldiers' being here.

The Department of Defense denied that any paratroop units had been sent to Memphis. So did Gen. C. W. G. Rich, commander of Fort Campbell, Army base in Kentucky. It was from there that 110 men of the 70th Battalion of Engineers were sent to the air station yesterday.

Gen. H. H. Howze, commander of Fort Bragg, Army base in North Carolina, would not confirm that paratroopers had been

Continued on Page 68, Column 5

Longshore Walkout Scheduled Tonight; Ships Rush to Sea

By EDWARD A. MORROW

A steady stream of ships sailed out of New York and other Atlantic and Gulf ports yesterday to avoid being caught in a longshoremen's strike that appeared certain to begin at 12:01 A.M. tomorrow.

Work on the piers continued at a record level as shipowners filed unusual weekend calls for labor with the Waterfront Commission.

The bistate agency said that 17,459 men had been hired to work 101 ships at 80 piers at time-and-a-half pay. On a normal Saturday the waterfront force is 2,000 to 3,000 men.

Sixty-two ships passed the quarantine station outbound yesterday. This number would have been even higher had not some operators decided to postpone the sailing of 12 ships until today to accept all the tonnage that could be moved off the piers before the deadline.

Cruise Liner Held Up

The 591 passengers aboard the Queen of Bermuda, which was scheduled to sail at 3 P.M. for Hamilton, Bermuda, found their cruise departure delayed until 8 A.M. this morning so the vessel could load cargo.

While the peak of the effort to get ships out has passed, a Sunday hiring record is expected to be broken today, a Waterfront Commission spokesman said.

The agency has received calls for 8,500 men to work 35 piers at double their regular pay of $3.02 an hour. The normal Sunday work force averages 1,000.

Federal mediators failed yes-

Continued on Page 44, Column 5

ACTS AT MIDNIGHT

President Holds Talks With Gov. Barnett but to No Avail

Text of Kennedy proclamation is printed on Page 68.

By ANTHONY LEWIS
Special to The New York Times

WASHINGTON, Sunday, Sept. 30.—President Kennedy committed the full weight of the Federal Government at midnight last night to end Mississippi's defiance of the Union.

He called the state's National Guard into Federal service.

He sent troops of the United States Army to Memphis, Tenn., to stand in reserve if more force were needed.

And he issued a proclamation calling on the Government and people of Mississippi to abandon what had become the most serious challenge to Federal authority since the Civil War.

Addresses Nation Tonight

Tonight, the President goes on the air to explain the situation to the American people. He will speak over all national television and radio networks at 7:30 New York time.

The President took one official action—his "irrevocable steps"—after three telephone conversations yesterday with Governor Ross R. Barnett of Mississippi.

In a statement issued at five minutes before midnight, the acting White House press secretary, Andrew T. Hatcher, said that in the conversations "the President was unable to receive from Governor Barnett satisfactory assurances that law and order could, or would, be maintained in Oxford, Miss. during the coming week."

Crisis Over Negro Student

Oxford is the seat of the University of Mississippi. Mississippi's defiance of Federal court orders to admit a Negro, James H. Meredith, to the university, has provoked the Federal-state crisis.

Mr. Hatcher said the action was being taken at that late hour—and telegrams dispatched to the guard commanders—so that the units "will be available for service Monday." Most Guardsmen are one-day-a-week soldiers, and it will take time to mobilize them.

The regular Army troops sent to Memphis comprised 900 military policemen, especially

Continued on Page 68, Column 1

SUPREME COURT OPENS TOMORROW

Legislative Districting Still Among Major Problems— Goldberg to Be Sworn

Special to The New York Times

WASHINGTON, Sept. 29—The Supreme Court convenes Monday for a new term that promises to be one of high drama and significance.

Two issues that dominated the last term—legislative districting and prayers in the schools—will be back in new and difficult guises.

The court will consider such other controversial problems as restaurant segregation, contempt of Congress and censorship of books and movies.

Goldberg to Take Oath

The presence of two new justices on the bench will heighten interest. In a court that has so frequently been divided 5-to-4 in recent years, two changes in membership could shift the balance of judicial philosophies.

Arthur J. Goldberg, appointed to replace Felix Frankfurter on his retirement, is scheduled to take the oath of office Monday. Byron R. White succeeded Charles E. Whittaker last April, too late to permit any real appraisal of his views last term.

Seldom, if ever, have new members of the Supreme Court faced questions so intellectually challenging or with so great a potential impact on

Continued on Page 74, Column 3

Traffic Overhaul at Lincoln Sq. Called Basic to Orderly Growth

By JOSEPH C. INGRAHAM

The city was urged yesterday to overhaul traffic patterns around Lincoln Center before approving any future construction.

The proposal was submitted in a report by Day & Zimmermann, Philadelphia consulting engineers.

The firm was hired by the city on April 23 to conduct a $30,000 study of the effects of future developments on traffic and mass transit, with "particular emphasis on the impact that the proposed Litho City housing development would impose."

Among the principal recommendations were the following:

¶Widening and rebuilding parts of the West Side Highway.

¶Changing the traffic pattern in local streets.

¶Adding crosstown express streets and rebuilding existing ones.

¶Changing the traffic pattern within the Lincoln Center for the Performing Arts.

The Litho City project, sponsored by Local 1, Amalgamated Lithographers of America, is planned along the Hudson River between 60th and 70th Streets.

Consisting of 17 buildings of 23 and 33 stories over the New York Central's freight yards, the project would tower above the western side of Lincoln Center.

The consultants stressed that their broad traffic study was predicated largely on the Litho City project. They noted that the original plans had called for 6,000 apartments for 15,000 to 20,000 persons, but said

Continued on Page 85, Column 3

"All the News That's Fit to Print"

The New York Times.

LATE CITY EDITION
U. S. Weather Bureau Report (Page 77) forecasts:
Mostly sunny today. Fair tonight and tomorrow.
Temp. range: 75—54; yesterday: 74—52.

VOL. CXII.No. 38,237.
© 1962 by The New York Times Company.
Times Square, New York 36, N. Y.

NEW YORK, TUESDAY, OCTOBER 2, 1962.

10 cents beyond 50-mile zone from New York City except on Long Island. Higher in air delivery cities.

FIVE CENTS

3,000 TROOPS PUT DOWN MISSISSIPPI RIOTING AND SEIZE 200 AS NEGRO ATTENDS CLASSES; EX-GEN. WALKER IS HELD FOR INSURRECTION

SENATE REJECTS AID CUTS AND BAN ON HELP FOR REDS

Upholds Kennedy's Authority to Assist Nations That Do Business With Cuba

By FELIX BELAIR Jr.
Special to The New York Times.

WASHINGTON, Oct. 1—The Senate decided for the Administration today in preliminary votes on the foreign aid appropriation bill, due for passage tomorrow.

It voted, 47 to 28, against cutting $785,000,000 from the $792,400,000 of military and economic aid funds that its Appropriations Committee restored to the bill the House had cut heavily.

The effect of the vote was to hold the appropriation at $4,422,800,000, as recommended by its Appropriations Committee. The Administration had requested the full amount of the authorized ceiling of $1,-754,800,000 but the House cut this back to $3,630,400,000.

On a later vote, the Senate confirmed this action by rejecting a proposal by Senator Allen J. Ellender, Democrat of Louisiana, to adopt the House cut of $150,000,000 for military aid.

Votes Become Narrow

By increasingly narrow margins, however, it supported other Administration goals. For instance, it voted, 39-36 to continue the President's discretion to aid countries doing business with Cuba. Then it decided, 39-37, to give the President similar discretion to waive the ban on aiding Communist nations such as Yugoslavia and Poland.

All three proposals were sponsored by Senator William Proxmire, Democrat of Wisconsin.

They were intended, first, to cut back the separate money items in the bill to the low levels voted by the House. Second, they would have approved the House's ban on aiding any Communist countries or free nations that help the Castro regime or allow their ships to deliver cargo to Cuba.

Only with the help of Republican members was the Democratic leadership able to turn back the Proxmire attack on the President's discretionary powers on the proposal to ban aid to nations shipping to Cuba, 12 Republicans voted with 27 Democrats to defeat the move, while 22 Democrats and 14 Re-

Continued on Page 16, Column 1

MOSCOW FOCUSING ON BLOC IN EUROPE

Rift With Chinese Believed Behind New Emphasis

By SEYMOUR TOPPING
Special to The New York Times

MOSCOW, Oct. 1—The Soviet Union has decided to pursue its program of rapprochement with Yugoslavia even at the risk of a further deterioration in relations with Communist China.

Diplomatic officials here have found evidence of this development in a comparative study of Soviet and Chinese Communist documents.

These officials believe that the ideological quarrel with Peking has caused Moscow to resolve to concentrate its resources on the consolidation of the European Communist economic bloc.

Pravda, the Communist party newspaper, published today an edited version of the communiqué issued by the Central Committee of the Communist party at the conclusion of its plenary session Friday.

The Soviet summary, which covered half a page in Pravda, omitted the strong attacks on President Tito of Yugoslavia for his so-called "modern revision-

Continued on Page 3, Column 1

Associated Press Wirephoto
PRISONERS ARE MARCHED TO ARMORY IN OXFORD: Army men escort a group of prisoners to National Guard Armory. The group had participated in a disturbance and was apprehended after the soldiers were ordered to fire at the feet of the rioters.

United Press International Telephoto
WALKER IS STOPPED BY TROOPS: Former Maj. Gen. Edwin A. Walker is detained by soldiers near the courthouse in Oxford. He was turned over to U.S. marshals and being held in $100,000 bail on charges stemming from his role in Sunday's campus riots.

Home Urges West to Help East's Coexistence Moves

By ARNOLD H. LUBASCH

The Earl of Home, Britain's Foreign Secretary, urged last night that the West pursue policies designed to help the Soviet bloc move toward genuine coexistence. He suggested that nuclear war was no longer a useful instrument of policy, that Communist doctrine was changing because of this and that Soviet society was changing even faster.

The West should recognize these facts, he said, and adapt its policies to them.

In addition, Mr. Spaak appealed to the entire world to understand the "new Europe" and its goal of "world cooperation."

Mr. Spaak's policy statement in the General Assembly was addressed in the first instance to 18 newly independent African states, all former possessions of France, Belgium or Italy.

Some of the states have asked the European Economic Community, or Common Market, for status as associates.

The six members of the market — Belgium, France, West Germany, Italy, the Netherlands and Luxembourg—are negotiating with the African states in Brussels.

Success Is Predicted

Mr. Spaak predicted that these talks would be concluded successfully by the end of 1962.

He also predicted that the negotiations with Britain for her admission to the market would be successful. He said the market would then have about the same productive capacity as the United States, and more than the Soviet Union.

The Belgian Foreign Minister, who was one of the leaders in the formation of the Common Market, defended it against two charges: that it is a manifestation of "neo-colonialism," and that it is merely intended to provide economic support for the North Atlantic Treaty Organization.

Mr. Kalonji, self - styled "king," virtually seceded from the central Government shortly after the Congo became independent two years ago. He escaped recently from a prison near Leopoldville and returned to his capital of Bakwanga.

A United Nations spokesman

Continued on Page 5, Column 2

SPAAK REASSURES AFRICA ON TRADE

Tells Newer U.N. Members That Common Market Will Aid Their Development

By THOMAS J. HAMILTON
Special to The New York Times

UNITED NATIONS, N. Y., Oct. 1—Paul-Henri Spaak, the Foreign Minister of Belgium, assured underdeveloped countries today that they could count on the cooperation of the members of the European Economic Community in the fight for economic advancement.

Lord Home's remarks were made at a dinner in the Waldorf - Astoria Hotel. The dinner was given by the Pilgrims of the United States, a friendship society devoted to cultivating understanding between this country and the nations of the British Commonwealth.

The organization, composed of 1,000 prominent persons, was founded in 1903. A sister organization across the Atlantic is known as the Pilgrims of Great Britain. The groups give dinners in honor of leading statesmen to promote understanding and brotherhood among nations.

Cites Soviet Ingenuity

Lord Home observed that the Russians exercise great ingenuity to reconcile their propaganda about peaceful coexistence with a program that permits limited force in certain regions to further the cause of Communist domination.

The West must be on guard against this technique, he said, and against the force that backs it up. He mentioned Berlin and South Vietnam as two areas of particular concern.

"I pray," he added, "that Cuba may never become a third."

Communist doctrine has begun to change, Lord Home

Continued on Page 2, Column 2

Congo Flies Troops To End Kasai Revolt

By Reuters

LEOPOLDVILLE, the Congo, Oct. 1—Reliable sources said today that the central Congolese Government was flying troops to Luluabourg to put down a new revolt by supporters of Albert Kalonji in South Kasai. Luluabourg is the Government army base nearest to the diamond-rich province.

The troop movement followed the declaration by the Government of a state of emergency in South Kasai. No immediate action was planned by the United Nations.

Continued on Page 5, Column 2

KENNEDY MOVING TO END PIER TIE-UP

He Names Board of Inquiry as First Step in Obtaining Taft-Hartley Injunction

By JOHN D. POMFRET
Special to The New York Times

WASHINGTON, Oct. 1—President Kennedy took the first step today toward getting an injunction to end the Atlantic and Gulf Coast longshoremen's strike for 80 days.

Declaring that continuation of the strike would imperil the national health and safety, the President issued an Executive order naming a three-man board of inquiry to investigate the dispute and to report to him by Thursday.

[Meanwhile in New York, leaders of the nation's seven major maritime unions abandoned inter-union battling to plan support for the striking longshoremen. American seamen and officers started leaving their ships, while other unions made plans to avoid servicing foreign-flag ships entering Atlantic and Gulf ports.]

The strike, which began at 12:01 A.M. today, has tied up all ports from Searsport, Me., to Brownsville, Tex. About 75,-000 members of the International

Continued on Page 78, Column 5

Columbia Study Scores Doctors; Says Quality of Care Lags Here

Financial Sanctions Under Blue Shield Suggested in Trussell Report

By FARNSWORTH FOWLE

The medical profession is "doing little" about the quality of medical care in the metropolitan area, the state was told yesterday in an experts' report.

The report warned that the first reaction of many laymen to poor medical care "is to demand firm and drastic government action—and indeed this may occur." It said that "strong medical, hospital, community and government leadership must be asserted in the public interest."

The conclusions were contained in the final volume of the Trussell-van Dyke Report, an independent study for the state by the Columbia University School of Public Health and Administrative Medicine. It was directed by Dr. Ray E. Trussell, chairman of the school, now on leave from the school while serving as New York City's Commissioner of Hospitals, and Frank van Dyke, an associate professor at the school.

The report called on the medical profession to welcome cur-

The New York Times
Dr. Ray E. Trussell

rent efforts of management and labor toward improving medical care.

"The organized purchasers of medical and hospital care can be the strongest arm of the community in upgrading standards, and it is to the best interest of organized medicine and hospitals to work with them,"

Continued on Page 63, Column 3

WALKER IS FACING 4 FEDERAL COUNTS

Flown to Medical Center in Missouri to Await Trial— Bail Put at $100,000

Special to The New York Times

OXFORD, Miss., Oct. 1 — Former Maj. Gen. Edwin A. Walker was arrested today on four charges, including insurrection, for his role in last night's rioting at the University of Mississippi.

The man who commanded Federal forces during the school integration crisis at Little Rock in 1957 was held in $100,000 bail.

Unable to put up the bail, he was flown to the United States Medical Center for Federal Prisoners at Springfield, Mo., to await his trial.

[Mr. Walker, accompanied by marshals, arrived at the medical center Monday night, The Associated Press said.]

"They don't have a thing on me," Mr. Walker said after his arrest. He dictated a message to Gov. Ross R. Barnett, which said:

"Mr. Walker hopes his efforts were in your behalf and in behalf of the stand for freedom everywhere. Do nothing based on my status that is not in support of your own objectives.

Continued on Page 27, Column 3

Bidwell's Tax Trial Ends in Hung Jury

By DAVID ANDERSON

The tax-evasion trial of J. Truman Bidwell, former chairman of the New York Stock Exchange, ended early today with a hung jury.

The jury, which had been deliberating since 1 P.M., filed into the courtroom shortly after midnight and told Federal Judge Thomas F. Murphy that it was "hopelessly deadlocked."

Judge Murphy, who two hours earlier had rejected a similar report and had instructed the jurors to try once more, now said:

"I declare a mistrial. Unhappy as I am, I guess there is nothing else we can do."

The prosecutor, Assistant United States Attorney Stephen E. Kaufman, said the Government would now consider

Continued on Page 18, Column 3

Mississippi Aides Blamed By U.S. Officials for Riot

By ANTHONY LEWIS
Special to The New York Times

WASHINGTON, Oct. 1 — The Federal Government asserted today that the failure of Mississippi officials to keep their word led to the bloody rioting in Oxford, Miss., last night. Attorney General Robert F. Kennedy and other spokesmen said that Gov. Ross R. Barnett and his aides had repeatedly given as-

Statements by Robert Kennedy and Eastland, Page 25.

surances that they could and would maintain order when James H. Meredith, a Negro, entered the University of Mississippi last night.

Instead, the Federal spokesmen said, the state police were withdrawn at the crucial moment of the developing mob scene. Federal troops were called in, but two men were dead and many were injured by the time they arrived.

The report, read by Mr. Eastland this morning sought to put the blame for the rioting on "amateurism by untrained marshals." It said that the 300 marshals at the university last night had "provoked" the crowd of 2,500 persons gathered on the campus.

The university officials also

Continued on Page 25, Column 1

BARNETT CHARGES MARSHALS ERRED

Says 'Trigger-Happy' U.S. Officers Are Responsible for Campus Bloodshed

Text of Barnett statement appears on Page 25.

By HEDRICK SMITH
Special to The New York Times

JACKSON, Miss., Oct. 1 — Gov. Ross R. Barnett tonight attributed the fatal rioting at the University of Mississippi last night to "inexperienced, nervous and trigger-happy Federal marshals."

The Governor made the statement in a recorded broadcast carried by the National Broadcasting Company. In a later recorded broadcast, carried by the Columbia Broadcasting System, Mr. Barnett directly assailed President Kennedy.

"The responsibility for this unwarranted breach of the peace and violence in Mississippi rests directly with the President of the United States," he said. "He ordered armed forces to invade Mississippi and their actions were directly responsible for violence, bloodshed and death."

People Are "Enraged"

In his earlier statement, the Governor said that the people of Mississippi "are enraged, incensed—and rightly so."

"Free men do not submit meekly to the kind of treatment Mississippians received," he said.

The Governor also said that the only solution to the Mississippi integration crisis was for the Federal Government to remove James H. Meredith, a 29-year-old Negro student, from the university.

"The Federal authorities alone have the power to stop bloodshed in Mississippi," he said.

Continued on Page 25, Column 5

SHOTS QUELL MOB

Enrolling of Meredith Ends Segregation in State Schools

By CLAUDE SITTON
Special to The New York Times

OXFORD, Miss., Oct. 1—James H. Meredith, a Negro, enrolled in the University of Mississippi today and began classes as Federal troops and federalized units of the Mississippi National Guard quelled a 15-hour riot.

A force of more than 3,000 soldiers and guardsmen and 400 deputy United States marshals fired rifles and hurled tear-gas grenades to stop the violent demonstrations.

Throughout the day more troops streamed into Oxford. Tonight a force approaching 5,000 soldiers and guardsmen, along with the Federal marshals, maintained an uneasy peace in this town of 6,500 in the northern Mississippi hills.

[There were two flareups tonight in which tear gas had to be used, United Press International reported. A small crowd of students began throwing bottles at marshals outside Baxter Hall, where Mr. Meredith was housed. They were quickly dispersed by tear gas. Soldiers also broke up a minor demonstration at a downtown intersection.]

200 Are Seized

The troops seized approximately 200 persons.

They were seized in the mobs of students and adults that besieged the university administration building last night and attacked troops on the town square this morning.

Among those arrested was former Maj. Gen. Edwin A. Walker, who resigned his commission after having been reprimanded for his ultra-rightwing political activity. He was charged with insurrection.

The university's acceptance of Mr. Meredith, a 29-year-old Air Force veteran, followed Gov. Ross R. Barnett's retreat from his defiance of Federal court orders that the Negro be enrolled.

Mr. Meredith's admission marked the first desegregation of a public educational institution in Mississippi. It reduced the Deep South bloc of massive-resistance states to two—

Continued on Page 24, Column 6

CAMPUS A BIVOUAC AS NEGRO ENTERS

2,000 Troops Stand Guard —Meredith Eats Alone

By McCANDLISH PHILLIPS
Special to The New York Times

OXFORD, Miss., Oct. 1—The University of Mississippi campus was under military occupation today as James H. Meredith, its first Negro student, registered and attended two classes.

Two thousand of the more than 3,000 Army and National Guard troops here made the tree-studded, rolling campus look like a cross between a bivouac and a prisoner-of-war camp. More olive drab uniforms were evident on campus than student casual dress.

Mr. Meredith, who did not get his first meal on campus until supper was served to him privately tonight, was housed in an end room in Baxter Hall, a male residence dormitory. The room next door was occupied by Federal marshals.

The 29-year-old Negro was taken from his dormitory room under guard at 7:45 A. M. and marched to the Lyceum, the administration building. There he was registered in 45 minutes—

Continued on Page 1, Column 1

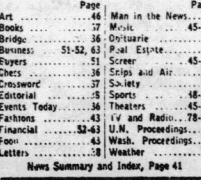

"All the News
That's Fit to Print"

The New York Times.

LATE CITY EDITION
U.S. Weather Bureau Report (Page 74) forecasts:
Partly cloudy, breezy, cool today.
Fair and cool tonight and tomorrow.
Temp. range: 54—45; yesterday: 66—44.

VOL. CXII..No. 38,258.   © 1962 by The New York Times Company.
Times Square, New York 36, N. Y.   NEW YORK, TUESDAY, OCTOBER 23, 1962.   10 cents beyond 50-mile zone from New York City except on Long Island. Higher in air delivery cities.   FIVE CENTS

U.S. IMPOSES ARMS BLOCKADE ON CUBA ON FINDING OFFENSIVE-MISSILE SITES; KENNEDY READY FOR SOVIET SHOWDOWN

U.S. JUDGES GIVEN POWER TO REQUIRE VOTE FOR NEGROES

High Court Upholds Order Forcing the Registration of 54 in Alabama County

Special to The New York Times

WASHINGTON, Oct. 22 — The Supreme Court held today that Federal judges have the power to make state registrars put specific Negroes on the voting rolls.

Alabama had challenged an order by Federal District Judge Frank M. Johnson Jr. requiring the registration of 54 specific Negroes in Macon County, Ala. The order was upheld by the United States Court of Appeals for the Fifth Circuit.

Today the Supreme Court unanimously affirmed the disputed order. And it did so in a way that indicated once again its mood of impatience with Southern efforts to maintain denials of Negro rights.

One-Sentence Ruling

All that was before the court was an application for review of the Fifth Circuit decision. The usual alternatives would have been to deny the petition or to grant it and hear oral argument later.

Instead, the court granted review and then, summarily, affirmed the lower courts. It did so in a single sentence, with just one citation in the way of explanation.

The citation was to a decision in 1960 upholding a Federal Court order in a Louisiana voting case. There, a district judge had told Louisiana registrars to put back on their books 1,377 Negroes whose names had been removed in a purge by the segregationist Citizens Council.

Action by Congress

The Macon County case was one of the first brought by the Department of Justice under the Civil Rights Act of 1957. It is especially significant because the county is in the so-called Black Belt, with a predominantly Negro population.

In 1958, when the suit was started, virtually all of the 3,000 white persons of voting age in the county were registered. But only about 1,000 of the 12,000 potential Negro voters were actually eligible.

In a further move, the registrars resigned, and this was held to leave no defendants to be sued. Congress in 1960 handled this problem by providing

Continued on Page 24, Column 4

102 SAVED AT SEA AS PLANE DITCHES

Rescue Is Made off Alaska Minutes After Accident

By The Associated Press.

SITKA, Alaska, Oct. 22—A military-charter airliner ditched in the ocean near here today, but all 102 persons aboard were saved in a quick rescue operation.

The plane, a DC-7C of Northwest Airlines, was going from McChord Air Force Base in Washington to Anchorage, Alaska. It carried 95 passengers and a crew of seven.

The rescue was reported by Northwest and the Alaska Coastal-Ellis Airline at Sitka, which also reported that there apparently were no serious injuries.

The plane went down shortly after the Federal Aviation Agency got word that it was being ditched because of propeller trouble.

A Coast Guard plane alighted on the water nearby; the Air Force sent two rescue planes, and small boats from Sitka, about seven miles north of the

Continued on Page 6, Column 2

Chinese Open New Front; Use Tanks Against Indians

Nehru Warns of Peril to Independence —Reds Attack Near Burmese Border and Press Two Other Drives

Special to The New York Times

NEW DELHI, Oct. 22—Prime Minister Jawaharlal Nehru told the people of India tonight that the Chinese Communist attack was a threat to their liberty.

His grave warning followed word that the advancing Chinese had opened a third front in the Himalayas, near the Burmese border and had used tanks for the first time. Five more Indian posts fell to the Chinese on the third day of savage fighting.

[A bid for negotiations for a peace accord was broadcast by the Chinese Communist radio early Tuesday, The Associated Press reported from Tokyo.]

In a broadcast, Mr. Nehru denounced the Peking regime as "a powerful and unscrupulous

Continued on Page 3, Column 1

U.S. Bids U.N. Bar China; Denounces Attack on India

By SAM POPE BREWER

Special to The New York Times

UNITED NATIONS, N. Y., Oct. 22—Adlai E. Stevenson told the General Assembly today that Communist China's "naked aggression" against India was new proof that it was unfit for membership in the United Nations.

The chief United States representative at the United Nations spoke as the Assembly took up the perennial question of admitting Peking.

Mr. Stevenson told the members that by their actions in the Indian frontier the Chinese Communists "again show their scorn for the Charter of this organization."

U.S. SAID TO EASE KATANGA POLICY

Reported Willing to Put Off Any Economic Sanctions —Congolese Disturbed

By LLOYD GARRISON

Special to The New York Times

LEOPOLDVILLE, the Congo, Oct. 22 — Authoritative sources said today that the United States was no longer insisting that Katanga Province strictly meet the deadlines of the United Nations plan to end its secession from the Congo.

This has alarmed Congolese officials. They say that the United States shift is reflected in United Nations policy.

The United Nations plan, introduced Aug. 2 by U Thant, Acting Secretary General, was said to have been conceived largely by the United States.

As outlined by Mr. Thant, the plan's first stage called for the following timetable:

Within thirty days a program was to be decided on for the reintegration of Katanga's army into the Congolese National Army. Sixty days were to be allowed for the program to be carried out.

Recall of Missions

All Katangese foreign missions were to be recalled immediately, and all Katanga's foreign currency reserves were to be put under the control of the central Government, with 50 per cent of these reserves rebated to Katanga.

Unification of the Congo's currency was to have begun within 10 days.

Katanga was to have started immediately to give 50 per cent of her tax revenues to the central Government.

Not one of these conditions has been met.

Last week Cyrille Adoula, Premier of the central Government, declared that "the deadline for the first stage has passed." He said that it was now time for the United Nations to consider the second stage — economic sanctions.

A shift in United States policy became apparent over the weekend after the departure of George C. McGhee, Under Secretary of State for Political Af-

Continued on Page 3, Column 6

SHIPS MUST STOP

Other Action Planned If Big Rockets Are Not Dismantled

By JAMES RESTON

Special to The New York Times

WASHINGTON, Oct. 22—President Kennedy drew the line tonight, not with Cuba, but with the Soviet Union. After almost a generation of trying to keep the "cold war" from reaching a direct confrontation between United States and Soviet power, a decision has been made to force Soviet missile bases from this hemisphere at the risk of war.

This is the official interpretation of President Kennedy's speech tonight, and to point to American forces bear it out. On the highest authority, it can be said that these orders include the following:

¶Ships carrying to Cuba weapons capable of striking the continental United States must either turn back or submit to search and seizure, or fight. If they try to run the blockade, a warning shot will be fired across their bows; if they still do not submit, they will be attacked.

¶This applies not only to ships but to any planes suspected of carrying additional offensive weapons to Cuba. There is no evidence that there are nuclear warheads in Cuba, but long-range aircraft suspected of carrying these or any other offensive weapons, will be intercepted, and instructions have been issued to do everything possible to check all Communist-bloc planes en route to Cuba via Newfoundland or Africa.

Prepared to Risk War

Even this will not satisfy the new policy announced by President Kennedy. Not only must new offensive weapons be stopped, under the President's orders, but those already in Cuba must be dismantled, or the United States will take whatever additional action is necessary, beginning with a much more rigorous blockade of such things as Cuba's essential oil supplies, to force compliance.

If this leads to Soviet retaliation, such as a counter-blockade of Berlin, the United States is prepared to risk a major war to defend its present position in the former German capital. Accordingly, American forces, not only in Berlin and West Germany but all over the world, have been placed on emergency alert. The new policy has been defined in a private communi-

Continued on Page 19, Column 1

TRAFFIC DELAYED AT BERLIN BORDER

Reds Start Intensive Check of Civilian Trucks an Hour Before Kennedy Speech

By SYDNEY GRUSON

Special to The New York Times

BONN, Oct. 22—The East German police began to slow down civilian traffic between West Berlin and West Germany late tonight.

About an hour before President Kennedy announced the United States countermeasures against the Soviet build-up in Cuba, the police started intensive examination of the papers of trucks moving into East German territory.

The connection, if any, between the two actions was not immediately clear. Similar harassment of civilian traffic has occurred periodically over the years. The immediate reaction in West Berlin was to consider tonight's harassment as part of the regular order of things, rather than as an advance countermeasure to the American moves against Cuba.

Nevertheless, there was deep anxiety that the Soviet Union would retaliate by causing trouble on the West's access lines to the city.

The outcome of tomorrow's meetings between Andrei A. Gromyko, the Soviet Foreign Minister, and East German Communist leaders was awaited with concern.

Continued on Page 17, Column 3

Canada Asks Inspection of Cuba; Britain Supporting Quarantine

Diefenbaker Comments

By RAYMOND DANIELL

Special to The New York Times

OTTAWA, Oct. 22 — Prime Minister John Diefenbaker of Canada declared tonight the time had come for an impartial inspection of what is happening in Cuba by eight of the "nonaligned nations."

Interrupting debate of the Canadian economic crisis in the House of Commons, Mr. Diefenbaker described President Kennedy's speech on Cuba as "somber and challenging."

"Naturally," he said, "there has been little time to give consideration to positive action that might be taken. But I suggest that if there is a desire—and I am sure there is on the part of the U.S.S.R.—to have the facts, if a group comprising the unaligned members of the 18-nation disarmament committee, were given the opportunity of making an on-site inspection of Cuba to ascertain what the facts are, a major step forward would be taken."

Meanwhile it was disclosed that Canada has barred the use of her airfields, including that

Continued on Page 21, Column 2

British Note Peril

By DREW MIDDLETON

Special to The New York Times

LONDON, Oct. 22—Qualified sources said today that approval for President Kennedy's military quarantine of Cuba could be expected from the British government.

A Foreign Office spokesman declared, "Revelation of the Soviet build-up in Cuba will come as a shock to the whole civilized world."

Official comment cannot be given until after Prime Minister Macmillan and his Cabinet have discussed the President's statement.

Initial reaction among diplomats was that the President had taken the most reasonable course to frustrate what military circles regard as evident danger to the United States: a buildup of Soviet nuclear capacity in Cuba.

The danger that war might result from a Soviet attempt to break what amounts to a military blockade of Cuba is accepted. But one experienced airman expressed the general feeling this way: "War can come from any one of a number of causes.

Continued on Page 21, Column 1

ANNOUNCES HIS ACTION: President Kennedy speaking to the nation last night on radio and television. He told of moves to keep offensive equipment away from Cuba.
Associated Press Wirephoto

Moscow Says U.S. Holds 'Armed Fist' Over Cuba

By SEYMOUR TOPPING

Special to The New York Times

MOSCOW, Tuesday, Oct. 23—In a broadcast before President Kennedy's speech on the missile build-up in Cuba, the Moscow radio said that the unusual activity in Washington indicated that the United States "once again was raising its armed fist over Cuba." The broadcast said there was "real hysteria" in Washington.

A Soviet reply to the United States note on Cuba that was given last night to Anatoly F. Dobrynin, the Soviet Ambassador to Washington, was expected to be delivered in 24 hours. It was expected that the reply would take the form either of a diplomatic communication or a message to President Kennedy from Premier Khrushchev.

Western observers said it appeared inevitable in view of recent Soviet statements that the reply would be a denial of any offensive Soviet intent and a charge of United States aggression against Cuba.

Veracity Questioned

The veracity of the Soviet Government was directly questioned in President Kennedy's speech, which was given after delivery of the note. The President said evidence had been obtained that Moscow was constructing offensive missile bases on Cuban territory.

The Soviet Government statement of Sept. 11, which warned the United States that an attack on Cuba would mean war, contended that the Soviet weapons supplied to Cuba were of a defensive nature.

Western observers said the crisis over Cuba would enter a critical phase when and if United States war vessels sought to halt and search a Soviet ship bound for Cuba. A number of Soviet vessels carrying civilian goods and pos-

Continued on Page 18, Column 3

BIG FORCE MASSES TO BLOCKADE CUBA

Armada Is Under Orders to Open Fire if Necessary— All Troops Are Alerted

By JACK RAYMOND

Special to The New York Times

WASHINGTON, Oct. 22—American ships and planes began preparing tonight to impose a blockade of Cuba. United States forces are under orders to thwart any attempt to deliver offensive weapons to Havana.

A Defense Department spokesman said that a large force of ships and planes concentrating in the Caribbean area had instructions to use force if necessary, including sinking of ships, to carry out President Kennedy's orders for a "quarantine" of Cuba.

The Pentagon said also that United States military units throughout the world, including the garrison in Berlin and the nuclear-armed Strategic Air Command, had been placed "on alert."

Dependents of servicemen at the Guantanamo Bay Naval Base in Cuba have been evacuated, the department said.

Forces at Base Doubled

It added that the military forces there, which were previously put at 3,300 naval officers and men and several hundred Marines, have been doubled.

Air defense units in the United States, particularly radar warning stations, interceptor aircraft and ground-to-air missiles, "have been redeployed," the department spokesman said.

The orders for additional defense precautions were taken the spokesman continued, on the basis of aerial photographs evidence of long-range ballistic missile bases and the arrival of Soviet Ilyushin-28 bombers in Cuba.

The spokesman displayed some of the aerial photographs and pointed to some missiles sites that, he said, had been established only in the last 10 or 15 days.

He said some of the missile

Continued on Page 20 Column 1

PRESIDENT GRAVE

Asserts Russians Lied and Put Hemisphere in Great Danger

Text of the President's address is printed on Page 18.

By ANTHONY LEWIS

WASHINGTON, Oct. 22—President Kennedy imposed a naval and air "quarantine" tonight on the shipment of offensive military equipment to Cuba.

In a speech of extraordinary gravity, he told the American people that the Soviet Union, contrary to promises, was building offensive missile and bomber bases in Cuba. He said the bases could handle missiles carrying nuclear warheads up to 2,000 miles.

Thus a critical moment in the cold war was at hand tonight. The President had decided on a direct confrontation with — and challenge to — the power of the Soviet Union.

Direct Thrust at Soviet

Two aspects of the speech were notable. One was its direct thrust at the Soviet Union as the party responsible for the crisis. Mr. Kennedy treated Cuba and the Government of Premier Fidel Castro as a mere pawn in Moscow's hands and drew the issue as one with the Soviet Government.

The President, in language of unusual bluntness, accused the Soviet leaders of deliberately "false statements about their intentions in Cuba."

The other aspect of the speech particularly noted by observers here was its flat commitment by the United States to act alone against the missile threat in Cuba.

Nation Ready to Act

The President made it clear that this country would not stop short of military action to end what he called a "clandestine, reckless and provocative threat to world peace."

Mr. Kennedy asked the United States was asking for an emergency meeting of the United Nations Security Council to consider a resolution for "dismantling and withdrawal of all offensive weapons in Cuba."

He said the launching of a nuclear missile from Cuba against any nation in the Western Hemisphere would be regarded as an attack by the Soviet Union against the United States. It would be met, he said, by retaliation against the Soviet Union.

He called on Premier Khrushchev to withdraw the missiles from Cuba and so "move the

Continued on Page 18, Column 1

KENNEDY CANCELS CAMPAIGN TALKS

He and Johnson Take Step to Concentrate on Crisis

By CABELL PHILLIPS

Special to The New York Times

WASHINGTON, Oct. 22—The White House announced tonight that President Kennedy and Vice President Johnson would make no further political appearances in the Congressional campaign because of the Cuban crisis.

The move by the Administration was considered evidence not only of the seriousness of the situation but also of the desire of the President to unify the country behind his blockade order and keep the issue out of partisan politics.

In this connection, the White House said the President personally informed former Republican Presidents Dwight D. Eisenhower and Herbert Hoover, as well as former Democratic President Harry S. Truman, of his decision.

And the White House announced that John J. McCloy, former disarmament adviser to the Kennedy Administration and a Republican, had been as-

Continued on Page 18, Column 7

Stocks Plunge Early On Crisis, but Rally

By RICHARD RUTTER

An already badly battered stock market was hit by massive selling yesterday as talk of a new international crisis spread in Wall Street.

The selling was of dimensions reminiscent of late May when the market experienced its worst break in a generation. Yesterday, the tape ran as much as 19 minutes late before a half-hearted recovery set in that cut losses by about one-third.

Both tape lateness and volume were the greatest since July 10. Two million shares were traded in the first two hours. Stock markets in London, Frankfurt and Brussels, following Wall Street's lead, also took large losses.

A shift in United States policy became apparent over the weekend after the departure of George C. McGhee, Under Secretary of State for Political Af-

Continued on Page 3, Column 6

All Military Forces Mobilized by Castro

By The Associated Press.

KEY WEST, Tuesday, Oct. 23 —All of Cuba's military forces have been mobilized as a result "of the news from the United States," the Havana radio said today.

The broadcast said the order was issued by Premier Fidel Castro, who will address the nation later today.

"Our combat units rapidly placed themselves on a fighting basis," said the Havana broadcast.

"Hundreds of thousands of men were mobilized in the course of a few hours," added the broadcast, which followed by some hours President Kennedy's announcement of a naval blockade against Cuba.

During the evening, Havana appeared slow to react to President Kennedy's broadcast.

Continued on Page 20. Column 6

"All the News That's Fit to Print"

The New York Times.

LATE CITY EDITION
U.S. Weather Bureau Report (Page 57) forecasts:
Chance of rain, then cloudy today,
tonight. Chance of rain tomorrow.
Temp. range: 58—46; yesterday: 57—41.

VOL. CXII..No. 38,264.   © 1962 by The New York Times Company. Times Square, New York 36, N. Y.   NEW YORK, MONDAY, OCTOBER 29, 1962.   10 cents beyond 50-mile zone from New York City except on Long Island. Higher in air delivery cities.   FIVE CENTS

U.S. AND SOVIET REACH ACCORD ON CUBA; KENNEDY ACCEPTS KHRUSHCHEV PLEDGE TO REMOVE MISSILES UNDER U.N. WATCH

DE GAULLE WINS 61% OF BALLOTS; ABSTENTIONS HIGH

46% of the Eligible Voters Support President's Plan on Choosing Successor

By ROBERT C. DOTY
Special to The New York Times

PARIS, Monday, Oct. 29—President de Gaulle won his referendum battle in nationwide balloting yesterday, but he suffered substantial losses of support in comparison with previous tests.

On the basis of complete unofficial returns early this morning, 61.76 per cent of the valid ballots cast were in favor of the President's proposal to elect his eventual successor by popular vote instead of by the limited college of 80,000 "notables" specified in the present Constitution.

But, with abstentions running at about 24 per cent of the electorate, General de Gaulle had only a minority—about 46 per cent—of the registered voters backing him.

Tally of Voting

Of 27,579,424 registered voters, 21,306,123 went to the polls and 20,740,649 cast valid ballots. Of these, 12,808,196 were "yes" votes and 7,932,453 were "no" votes. A total of 565,474 voters invalidated their ballots.

Most political observers, including those of the traditional French parties united against the President, indicated the belief that this was just sufficient backing to dissuade the President from carrying out his threat to resign if the voters expressed only "vague and doubtful" confidence in him.

The result, on which General de Gaulle must ponder, was that of every 100 potential voters, 46 said "yes" to the President and his proposal, 29 said "no" and 25 either did not care enough to vote or spoiled their ballots.

Gaullist and Opposition interpretations of the results varied widely, however. Premier Georges Pompidou called the "yes" vote a "massive" one.

Ballots Subtracted

By subtracting the Communist and extreme Right-Wing votes, he reached the conclusion that the traditional parties aligned against the President had been able to swing only 10 to 12 per cent of the voters into the "no" column.

Bertrand Motte, president of the Independent (Conservative) group in the dissolved National Assembly and one of the leaders of the Opposition coalition, found, however, that "the regime has been hurt." The "no" vote, he said, represented "a very important percentage of Frenchmen."

One section of the country—the southwest—deserted General deGaulle and voted "no" by varying margins. His backing

Continued on Page 3, Column 1

MCA Will Finance Shows on Broadway

By MURRAY SCHUMACH

HOLLYWOOD, Oct. 28—MCA, Inc., already a major power in movies, television and records, will become one of the nation's most important financiers of Broadway shows.

The aim of MCA is to finance entire shows. It will back musicals as well as dramas.

The plan to expand into Broadway became known this weekend after conferences between the president of the corporation, Lew R. Wasserman, and Milton R. Rackmil, who is president of Universal Pictures and vice chairman of MCA.

In disclosing the plan to finance shows, Mr. Wasserman explained that MCA did not intend to produce them. This approach to Broadway is novel, for MCA is not interested pri-

Continued on Page 37, Column 5

Associated Press Radiophoto
DE GAULLE VOTES IN REFERENDUM: President de Gaulle casting ballot in Colombey-les-deux-Eglises.

Castro Asks Guantanamo; Strives to Repair Prestige

By TAD SZULC
Special to The New York Times

WASHINGTON, Oct. 28 — Premier Fidel Castro demanded today that the United States evacuate its naval base at Guantanamo Bay. This was taken here tonight as a major point in evidence that Cuba's revolutionary leader was struggling to salvage his prestige at home and in the rest of Latin America.

United States officials and Latin-American diplomats believed the provisional accord between Washington and Moscow on the withdrawal of nuclear missiles from Cuba left the Castro regime a substantial loser in the crisis.

Therefore, it was believed here that Premier Castro would try

Text of the Castro statement appears on Page 19.

his best to inject such sensitive issues as the fate of the Guantanamo base into the negotiations at the United Nations.

The United States is not prepared to discuss the status of Guantanamo with Cuba, officials said.

Officials considered the possibility that, in the light of his reactions last night and today to the United States-Soviet settlement over the bases in Cuba, he might seek to block a final agreement unless his conditions were met.

There was agreement here tonight that the realities of East-West relationships and the close danger of war in recent days had forced a solution of the bases dispute over Dr. Castro's head.

Whether or not he was fully consulted by Moscow on the

Continued on Page 19, Column 1

WARFARE ALTERS INDIA PROFOUNDLY

Nonalignment Views Are Re-examined—Many Call Menon Career Ruined

By A. M. ROSENTHAL
Special to The New York Times

NEW DELHI, Oct. 28 — The Chinese Communist invasion of India's northern frontiers has brought about profound changes in this country — in politics, in thought, in international attitudes and in the lives of the men in power.

It has, in the opinion of New Delhi's tightly knit political community, wrecked the political future of Defense Minister V. K. Krishna Menon.

At a rally today Mr. Menon said India had been forced to yield territory and that the people had to be prepared for more sacrifices and losses. The Indian Government said Chinese forces had opened an attack in a new section in the frontier region of Ladakh and had forced Indian troops out of one post by overwhelming numbers.

Chinese Drive into Ladakh

The attack today and those of the last week are apparently designed to plant the Chinese flag all across Ladakh. In the North East Frontier Agency, 800 miles to the east, there was a lull in the fighting.

Before the Chinese attacks, Mr. Menon was at the height of his career. He had won a smashing victory at the polls in Bombay and had created a well-financed political foundation that he and his followers hoped would one day help make him Prime Minister.

Now Mr. Menon is being blamed bitterly and widely for two things—for failing to foresee the invasion and for failing to prepare Indian armed forces to meet it.

Heavy pressure is being put on Prime Minister Jawaharlal Nehru to remove Mr. Menon from the Defense Ministry. Some politicians here believe his resignation is a matter of time. Others say that his power is already being whittled away gradually by Mr. Nehru, but that the Prime Minister will

Continued on Page 13, Column 1

Caracas Guards Oil After 4 Red Blasts

By United Press International

CARACAS, Venezuela, Oct. 28—The Government declared the rich oil-producing region around Lake Maracaibo a zone of military operations tonight and sent marines to protect oil installations. The action was taken after dynamite attacks last night by Communist terrorists.

A Government spokesman said, however, that the attacks against four electric power stations of the United States-controlled Creole Petroleum Corporation were not so serious as first feared. Creole is an affiliate of the Standard Oil Company of New Jersey.

Venezuelan authorities said earlier that the blasts, part of the Communist war of nerves and destruction against the Government of President Rom-

Continued on Page 19, Column 1

THANT SETS VISIT

He Will Go to Havana Tomorrow to Seek Castro Consent

Text of Thant note to Castro is printed on Page 18.

By THOMAS J. HAMILTON
Special to The New York Times

UNITED NATIONS, N.Y., Oct. 28—U Thant, the Acting Secretary General, will fly to Cuba Tuesday with his top assistants to discuss arrangements for a United Nations check on the dismantling of Soviet missiles and the halting of the building of bases.

Mr. Thant plans to stay in Cuba only long enough to obtain Premier Fidel Castro's acceptance of the Thant plan to send observer teams to inspect and be sure Premier Khrushchev's agreement to dismantle the missiles is complied with.

According to reliable sources, once the Acting Secretary General makes these arrangements, he will return to obtain authorization from the Security Council for the inspection program.

Mahmoud Riad of the United Arab Republic, who on Thursday will take over the monthly presidency of the Security Council from the Soviet delegate, had a talk with Mr. Thant today. Mr. Riad said he saw no need for a Council meeting until Mr. Thant returned—perhaps Thursday or Friday.

Outcome Awaited

The Council suspended its debate Thursday night to await the outcome of messages exchanged by President Kennedy and Premier Khrushchev.

Premier Castro's consent will be necessary under the precedent set in the Suez crisis of 1956.

At that time the late Secretary General, Dag Hammarskjold, ruled that President Gamal Abdel Nasser would have to agree to all arrangements for stationing United Nations forces in the United Arab Republic, including which countries might supply the troops.

Premier Castro offered to provide a Cuban plane to transport the Acting Secretary General and his aides, who are expected to include Brig. Indar Jit Rikhye of the Indian Army, a military adviser.

Mr. Thant told Premier Castro, however, that he preferred to charter his own plane. An

Continued on Page 18, Column 1

The President's View

Kennedy Rejects Thesis That Outcome On Cuba Shows 'Tough Line' Is Best

By JAMES RESTON
Special to The New York Times

WASHINGTON, Oct. 28 — President Kennedy is looking at the Cuban crisis not as a great victory but merely as an honorable accommodation in a single isolated area of the "cold war."

War has been avoided, but the Communists retain a sanctuary in the Western Hemisphere. The Russians have withdrawn rather than fight, but this was done in an area

News Analysis

strategically disadvantageous to them and does not mean that they would do the same in many other areas where the battlefield is disadvantageous to the West. This, at least, is the official view here.

The President is not even drawing general conclusions from this special case about the tactics of dealing with the Soviet Union in the future. To be specific, while he may be equally bold again in risking conflict in support of vital national interests, he is rejecting the conclusion of the traditional "hardliners" that the way to deal with Moscow everywhere in the world is to be "tough," as in Cuba.

In other circles there seems to be general agreement about these three more optimistic conclusions:

¶In modern weaponry, the Soviet Union does not feel itself the master of the United States. If Moscow did, it would not have insisted on ending the ban on nuclear testing and it would not have taken the long gamble to establish medium and intermediate missiles in Cuba where they would be effective against the United States.

¶In the Western alliance, President Kennedy has enhanced his leadership by defying the Soviet challenge and achieving at least part of his main objectives without war.

¶In his dealings with the Russians, he has probably removed the Soviet illusion that America would not fight and thus reduced the chances of miscalculation in Moscow.

¶In the perpetual propaganda dialogue of the "cold war," it has been demonstrated that the United States did not make a deal with the Soviet Union at the expense of Turkey, while the same thing can scarcely be said about the

Continued on Page 17, Column 7

RUSSIAN ACCEDES

Tells President Work on Bases Is Halted —Invites Talks

Texts of Khrushchev notes to Kennedy and Thant, Page 16.

By SEYMOUR TOPPING
Special to The New York Times

MOSCOW, Oct. 28—Premier Khrushchev agreed today to end the construction of Soviet bases in Cuba and to dismantle Soviet rockets there, both under United Nations supervision.

In a message to President Kennedy, the Soviet leader said that he already had issued instructions for this and for crating and returning the rockets to the Soviet Union.

This was said to have been done in return for the commitments offered in a letter sent to Mr. Khrushchev yesterday by President Kennedy. The letter expressed the United States' readiness to lift the naval quarantine of Cuba and join with other nations of the Western Hemisphere in providing assurances against an invasion of the island.

Offer of Talks Welcomed

Mr. Khrushchev's message, which was broadcast at 5 P.M. Moscow time, indicated unconditional acceptance of the measures stipulated by the President to bar offensive Soviet weapons from Cuba.

The Premier also welcomed the readiness of President Kennedy to discuss a détente, or relaxation of tension, between the nations of the North Atlantic Treaty Organization and its East European Communist counterpart, the Warsaw Pact organization.

The Russian leader insisted that Soviet weapons had been introduced in Cuba solely for the defense of the island. He added that, in view of the assurances of the President "the motives which induced us to render assistance of such a kind to Cuba would disappear."

There was no mention in the Khrushchev message of the proposal made in the Premier's letter of yesterday to communication of yesterday to Mr. Khrushchev. Mr. Khrushchev then offered to withdraw Soviet weapons from Cuba, but in exchange for similar action by the United States in respect to Turkey, where a missile base of the North Atlantic Treaty Organization is maintained.

Western observers here be-

Continued on Page 16, Column 5

United Press International Teletophoto
PRESIDENT ATTENDS MASS: Mr. Kennedy at St. Stephen's Roman Catholic Church in Washington yesterday before receiving Premier Khrushchev's message.

Plane Veers Over Soviet, Kennedy Voices Regrets

By ANTHONY LEWIS
Special to The New York Times

WASHINGTON, Oct. 28—A United States plane flew over Soviet Far Eastern territory today, but both President Kennedy and Premier Khrushchev sought to avoid tension over the incident. The President told Mr. Khrushchev that the incursion resulted from a navigational error.

"I regret this incident and will see to it that every precaution is taken to prevent recurrence," Mr. Kennedy declared.

Premier Khrushchev disclosed the incident in his letter to President Kennedy on the Cuban crisis. He recalled previous flights by U-2 reconnaissance planes over Soviet territory but used language much less bristling than the Russians had employed in earlier protests.

Plane Said to Be Unarmed

The President, for his part, went into much greater detail than usual on the reasons for the flight and adopted a reassuring tone. He gave the explanation in his response to Mr. Khrushchev's letter on the Cuban crisis.

Mr. Kennedy said the plane "without arms or photographic equipment," was on a mission to sample the atmosphere in connection with Soviet nuclear tests. Its course was from Eielson Air Force Base in Alaska to the North Pole and back.

In turning at the pole, the President said, "the pilot made a serious navigational error that carried him over Soviet territory."

He immediately made an emergency call on open radio for navigational assistance and

Continued on Page 17, Column 8

U.S. Looks for Hint Of Shift at Kremlin

By MAX FRANKEL
Special to The New York Times

WASHINGTON, Oct. 28—President Kennedy and his advisers weighed every word and step in the climactic moments of the Cuban blockade crisis today for possible signs of confusion and division in the Kremlin.

There was satisfaction here about the promise of an early settlement. But there was no celebration, no talk yet of an American victory or of a Russian capitulation to Moscow.

Two considerations dictated the Administration's caution tonight.

On the one hand, the Presi-

Continued on Page 18, Column 1

CAPITAL HOPEFUL

Plans to End Blockade as Soon as Moscow Lives Up to Vow

Texts of the Kennedy statement and message are on Page 16.

By E. W. KENWORTHY
Special to The New York Times

WASHINGTON, Oct. 28—President Kennedy and Premier Khrushchev reached apparent agreement today on a formula to end the crisis over Cuba and to begin talks on easing tensions in other areas.

Premier Khrushchev pledged the Soviet Union to stop work on its missile sites in Cuba, to dismantle the weapons and to crate them and take them home. All this would be done under verification of United Nations representatives.

President Kennedy, for his part, pledged the lifting of the Cuban arms blockade when the United Nations had taken the "necessary measures," and that the United States would not invade Cuba.

U. S. Conditions Met

Essentially this formula meets the conditions that President Kennedy set for the beginning of talks. If it is carried out, it would achieve the objective of the President in establishing the blockade last week: the removal of the Soviet missile bases in Cuba.

While officials were gratified at the agreement reached on United States terms, there was no sense either of triumph or jubilation. The agreement, they realized, was only the beginning. The terms of it were not nailed down and Soviet negotiators were expected to arrive at the United Nations with a "bag full of fine print."

Although Mr. Khrushchev mentioned verification of the dismantling by United Nations observers in today's note, sources here do not consider it unlikely that the Russians may suggest that the observers be under the procedures of the Security Council.

This would make their findings subject to a veto by the Soviet Union as one of the 11 members of the Council.

No Big Gains Envisioned

United States officials did not expect a Cuban settlement, if it materialized, to lead to any great breakthroughs on such problems as inspection for a nuclear test ban and disarmament.

On the other hand, it was thought possible that a Cuban settlement might set a precedent for limited reciprocal concessions in some areas.

The break in the crisis came dramatically early this morning after a night of steadily mounting fears that events were running ahead of diplomatic efforts to control them.

The break came with the arrival of a letter from Premier Khrushchev in which the Soviet

Continued on Page 16, Column 1

PATROLS MAINTAIN BLOCKADE OF CUBA

Pentagon Says Its Military Precautions Continue—Air Reconnaissance Goes On

By JACK RAYMOND
Special to The New York Times

WASHINGTON, Oct. 28—The Defense Department said today that the United States was continuing its military precautions against Cuba.

A department spokesman said that reconnaissance flights were still being carried out, presumably to verify Premier Khrushchev's announcement that he had ordered the dismantling of ballistic missiles in Cuba and a cessation of work on bases on the island.

The spokesman said also that air and sea patrols in the blockade of Cuba were being maintained. For the first time in a week of crisis, the Pentagon official referred to the military build-up carried out to meet the emergency, describing it as "quite a development of power."

Reserve Units Called Up

The Pentagon, which announced last night that 24 Air Force Reserve troop carrier squadrons were being ordered to active duty, issued implementing instructions that went into effect at 9 A.M.

The mobilization of the reserve units, which operate C-119 and C-23 troop and cargo aircraft, will affect 14,214 reservists, the Pentagon estimated.

Under special legislation that Congress passed in its last session at President Kennedy's request, the reservists may be held on active duty for a period up to one year.

The Pentagon refused to comment on a statement by Senator Kenneth Keating that he had unconfirmed reports that submarine bases were being built

Continued on Page 17, Column 1

Relief Felt in NATO At Cuba Relaxation

Special to The New York Times

PARIS, Oct. 28—There was great relief today within the North Atlantic Treaty Organization at Premier Khrushchev's pledge to remove Soviet missiles from Cuba. Some Governments, however, notably that of France, tended to take a cautious attitude toward the Soviet move.

The relief followed reports that concern was expressed this morning at a secret meeting of the North Atlantic Council that NATO might be drawn into conflict if the United States moved against Cuba either through invasion or bombardment.

The concern had been caused by a message from Premier Khrushchev to President Kennedy that seemed to imply the threat of

Continued on Page 16, Column 4

TONIGHT at 9:05 PM!
"Kismet" Complete Score
Radio Station WNCN 650 AM-100.3 FM-Advt.

"All the News That's Fit to Print"

The New York Times.

LATE CITY EDITION

U. S. Weather Bureau Report (Page 78) forecasts:
Cloudy with chance of showers today; clear tonight. Fair, warm tomorrow.
Temp. range: 80—63; yesterday: 69—58.
Temp.-Hum. index: high 60's yesterday: 67.

VOL. CXII..No. 38,482.

© 1963 by The New York Times Company.
Times Square, New York 36, N.Y.

NEW YORK, TUESDAY, JUNE 4, 1963.

TEN CENTS

ARIZONA UPHELD OVER CALIFORNIA ON WATER RIGHTS

Supreme Court's 7-1 Ruling Caps 40-Year Fight on Use of the Colorado River

WIDE EFFECT FORESEEN

3 Justices Strongly Oppose Provision Allowing U. S. to Apportion Supplies

By WILLIAM M. BLAIR
Special to The New York Times

WASHINGTON, June 3 — Arizona won in the Supreme Court today its 40-year struggle with California over how much water each state can take from the Colorado River.

The Court, voting 7 to 1, upheld a special master's recommendations on division of the water. The decision is of great economic significance to the Southwest, for the Colorado and its tributaries are the major water sources in that rapidly growing area.

The Court split, 5 to 3, however, on the majority ruling that the Secretary of the Interior had the power to apportion mainstream water among users in the lower basin states, particularly in periods of shortage.

Oppose Federal Role

The dissenters on this issue were Justices John Marshall Harlan, William O. Douglas and Potter Stewart. They sharply challenged the majority view that Congress intended a "single appointed Federal official" to have the authority to apportion mainstream waters, whether in shortage or surplus. They found this delegation of power "extraordinary." And they argued that state law was intended to control apportionment among users within a single state and that this principle had been established by the Court in earlier water rights cases.

The majority opinion said California was entitled to 4,-400,000 acre feet of water annually from the mainstream of the Colorado, Arizona 2,800,000 acre feet and Nevada 300,000 acre feet. An acre foot is the amount of water that will cover one acre to a depth of one foot —about 325,850 gallons.

The division was confined to the area's mainstream. The Court rejected California's effort to include the Colorado's tributaries, principally the Gila in Arizona, in any water allo-

Continued on Page 23, Column 1

AGENCY SHOP WINS COURT'S APPROVAL

Ruled Permissible by U. S. Law, Optional in States

By JOSEPH A. LOFTUS
Special to The New York Times

WASHINGTON, June 3—A labor contract requiring nonmembers to pay service fees to a union is permissible under Federal law, but may be prohibited by state law, the Supreme Court ruled today.

The agency shop, as this type of contract is called, was reviewed in two decisions. There was no dissent. Associate Justice Arthur J. Goldberg did not participate.

Where the state's prohibition is enforceable—in state courts or before the National Labor Relations Board—was a question reserved for later decision. That point was set for argument in the next term.

In two other labor decisions, the Court reversed damage verdicts won by individuals against unions in the state courts of Texas and Ohio. The vote in each was 6 to 2. Justices William O. Douglas and Tom C. Clark dissented. Justice Goldberg did not participate.

The central point in all four cases was the extent of state jurisdiction in the field of labor-management relations. Under the Court's doctrine of Federal pre-emption, the states have no jurisdiction except where Congress has specifically conceded it, or where the N.L.R.B. can afford no remedy, or where there is an overriding state in-

Continued on Page 24, Column 5

Douglas Upbraids Black From Bench

Special to The New York Times

WASHINGTON, June 3—Justice William O. Douglas made an unusually sharp attack today on a major opinion by his colleague on the Supreme Court, Hugo L. Black.

The tenor of Justice Douglas's extemporaneous remarks from the bench startled those in the courtroom. His strong language was the more surprising because the two men have served together for 24 years and have been regarded as extremely close in judicial philosophy.

Justice Douglas's dissent was in the Colorado River water case. Justice Black wrote the opinion of the court deciding generally against California's claims and in favor of Arizona's.

From the bench Justice

Continued on Page 22, Column 8

PRESIDENT DELAYS RIGHTS MESSAGE

Plans Conferences in Fight on Public Discrimination —G.O.P. Offers a Bill

By E. W. KENWORTHY
Special to The New York Times

WASHINGTON, June 3—President Kennedy decided tonight to delay for a week his civil rights message to Congress proposing legislation to outlaw discrimination in public accommodations.

He had hoped to get new legislative proposals to Congress tomorrow. He leaves on Wednesday for a Western trip and will stay out of Washington the rest of the week.

One factor in tonight's decision was that last-minute tinkering with the draft labin and the accompanying Presidential message was still going on. It was deemed wise not to rush so important a matter.

The President believed also that it would help the legislation to go ahead first with scheduled conferences. He will meet tomorrow, for example, with business executives who have large holdings in the South. His brother, Attorney General Robert F. Kennedy, will meet other groups.

Democrats Briefed

The week will also be used to try to create a favorable climate at the Capitol. Democratic Congressional leaders, who were briefed on civil rights by the President today, will discuss the legislation with others in both parties.

The decision to delay the message was especially difficult for the President because 24 House Republicans introduced today their own legislation to bar racial discrimination in public accommodations. They were plainly intent on beating the Administration in offering a measure.

One of two main proposals of the Administration's legislation would deal with racial discrimi-

Continued on Page 27, Column 1

PUPIL TRANSFERS TO DIVIDE RACES VOIDED BY COURT

Supreme Bench Says Plan in Two Tennessee Areas Slows Desegregation

By ANTHONY LEWIS
Special to The New York Times

WASHINGTON, June 3 — The Supreme Court held unconstitutional today a school desegregation plan that allows pupils to transfer out of schools where their race is in the minority.

Justice Tom C. Clark said that the plan was invalid because it based transfers "solely on racial factors" and led to "perpetuation of segregation." He spoke for a unanimous Court.

The transfer plan was at issue in cases from Knoxville, Tenn., and from Davidson County, adjoining Nashville. Similar provisions are in use in Memphis and some Virginia communities.

Five other Southern states have statutes saying that no child may be compelled to attend a school where he would be in a racial minority. They are Alabama, Arkansas, Florida, Louisiana and North Carolina.

Broad Impact Likely

Thus today's decision can be expected to have a major impact on the South. It will remove the legal basis for a device widely used to cushion the effect of school desegregation.

In practice, the Tennessee provisions — and those in other areas — worked as follows:

School boards, in response to the Supreme Court's desegregation decision, abolished the former separate school maps for whites and Negroes. New school districts were drawn for a single, nonracial system.

But any white student who thereupon found himself in the district of "a school previously serving colored students" could automatically transfer to another school. So could a Negro zoned into a school formerly serving whites.

Transfers Made Easy

The plan also, significantly, permitted automatic transfers "when a student would otherwise be required to attend a school where the majority of students of that school or in his or her grade are of a different race."

A student in such a minority situation had only to ask and he would be transferred. Others who wanted to switch schools had to persuade the school board there was "good cause."

The provision was generally regarded as a way of assuring white families that their children would not be placed in a mostly Negro school. It was defended as necessary to reduce opposition to desegregation.

Negroes, on the other hand, said the transfer provision had made true integration of the schools impossible. They especially criticized the fact that there was no automatic right of a pupil to transfer from a school entirely or mostly of his

Continued on Page 25, Column 3

DC-7 With 101 Lost in Alaska; 95 Military Men and Kin Aboard

Vast Air-Sea Hunt Pressed for Chartered Craft After Radio Contact Breaks Off

By The Associated Press

JUNEAU, Alaska, June 3—A military-chartered airliner carrying 101 persons—men, women and children — vanished off southeastern Alaska today under circumstances suggesting sudden disaster.

The Northwest Airlines DC-7, a piston-engined aircraft, last radioed 30 to 40 miles at sea off Prince of Wales Island, requesting a change of altitude from 14,000 to 18,000 feet. Air traffic men trying to reply minutes later got no answer.

The last confirmed message from the plane was at 10:06 A.M., about two and a half hours after it had left McChord Air Force Base, Wash., with 95 military passengers, including dependents, and a crew of six.

An intensive search by planes and vessels was made in the deteriorating weather.

The Coast Guard said later tonight that a Canadian plane had reported a sighting that appeared to be wreckage near Graham Island, in northern British Columbia.

The only detailed information concerning the sighting came

Continued on Page 13, Column 1

Fairbanks
ELMENDORF
ALASKA
YUKON
CANADA
Pacific
Whitehorse
PRINCE OF WALES ISLAND
B.C.
COLUMBIA
VANCOUVER ISLAND
WASH.

The New York Times
June 4, 1963
Cross shows where plane last reported its position.

Army May Release Ft. Tilden for Park

By CHARLES G. BENNETT

There is a "very, very good possibility" that the Army might make Fort Tilden available to the city for the Breezy Point park development, Mayor Wagner said yesterday.

"We learned last week," the Mayor said at an impromptu press conference, "that there is a good possibility that the Army might move its installations and Nike bases from there in the near future, and then we can start negotiations."

An Army spokesman said in Washington last night that the Army had been reviewing the situation but had not made any decision.

Fort Tilden is on 317 acres next to the 236-acre Jacob Riis Park. The city proposes ultimately to have in all 1,362

Continued on Page 43, Column 5

POST AWAITS VOTE

Archbishop of Milan a Possible Choice as New Pontiff

By PAUL HOFMANN

ROME, June 3—Amid the drama of Pope John XXIII's final hours, Romans speculated whether his successor would be an Italian or a "foreigner."

At the same time, ecclesiastics and laymen debated whether the next Pontiff would show the conciliatory, progressive attitude of Pope John or lead the Roman Catholic Church back to a more conservative position.

An Italian prince of the church, Giovanni Battista Cardinal Montini, 65-year-old Archbishop of Milan, was widely mentioned as the leading candidate.

Cardinal Montini is regarded as a prominent representative of the "progressive" wing of the world episcopacy, which revealed its strength with the manifest encouragement of Pope John during the first session of the Ecumenical Council in the Vatican last autumn.

A Close Aide to Pius XII

As monsignor, the present Cardinal Montini was for many years a close aide to the late Pope Pius XII, Pope John's predecessor, in the Vatican Secretariat of State. The slim, ascetic-looking churchman, who is credited with a prodigious capacity for hard work, became Archbishop of Milan, one of the largest Catholic dioceses in the world, in 1954, but was still not a Cardinal when Pope Pius XII died in 1958.

The Archbishop of Milan then already had such a reputation that some commentators suggested that the Cardinals would depart from a 600-year-old tradition and elect a prelate who was not one of their number.

Instead the Cardinals elevated one of their number, Angelo Giuseppe Cardinal Roncalli, Patriarch of Venice. As Pope John XXIII he conferred on Archbishop Montini the red hat of Cardinal in his first consistory in December, 1958. Cardinal Montini also rose to Pope John throughout his pontificate and if he is elected as his successor he is expected to continue his policies.

Cardinals Take Over Rule

Soon after Pope John died tonight, the Cardinals present in the Vatican started taking over the interim government of the church on behalf of the 82 members of the Sacred College of Cardinals. The Cardinals will unite jointly until their vote in conclave results in the election of the new Pope.

Prominent among conservative Italian Cardinals thought to be of papal timber is Giuseppe Cardinal Siri, Archbishop of Genoa. He is 57 years old.

The leader of the conservative wing at the Ecumenical Council, Alfredo Cardinal Ottaviani, a 72-year-old Vatican theologian and guardian of

Continued on Page 18, Column 6

HAITIAN CONTACTS RESUMED BY U.S.

Duvalier Regime Regarded as Firmly in Power Even if Not Constitutional

By TAD SZULC
Special to The New York Times

WASHINGTON, June 3 — The United States resumed "normal diplomatic business" with Haiti today after nearly three weeks of a suspension of contacts intended to underline Washington's disapproval of President François Duvalier.

The decision to return to normal relations and to remove a Navy task force from the vicinity of Haiti appeared to reverse last month's undisguised policy efforts aimed at Dr. Duvalier's removal.

At the peak of the Haiti crisis, the Kennedy Administration is known to have convinced itself that President Duvalier's regime was on the brink of collapse because of mounting United States pressures.

It was then expected that Dr. Duvalier would voluntarily give up office and leave Haiti on May 15. The United States regarded that date as the end of his legal term.

Marine Landing Envisaged

Accordingly, the Administration secretly prepared with at least three Latin-American governments a plan that might have involved a landing in Haiti by United States marines, it has been disclosed. An inter-American "police action" in support of a new regime in Haiti was also envisaged.

The details of this planned operation were disclosed by diplomats who participated in its preparation last month.

The operation was abandoned on May 15, however, after an all-night vigil here by officials of the Organization of American States. It then became clear that Dr. Duvalier did not intend to leave Haiti.

The State Department later that day instructed Ambassador Raymond L. Thurston in Port-au-Prince to suspend immediately his contacts with the Haitian Government. The move was made secretly and the Administration confirmed it indirectly only after it was published in press dispatches from Haiti.

Regime Still Held Illegal

Today, Lincoln White, the State Department spokesman, announced that the United States chargé d'affaires in Port-au-Prince, Glion Curtis Jr., was being instructed "to resume normal diplomatic business with the Government of Haiti."

Administration officials insisted that the lifting of the short-lived diplomatic sanctions did not imply any change in the United States view that the Duvalier regime was unconstitutional. It was made clear, however, that the United States had concluded that the Haitian Government was firmly in power.

Therefore, officials said, a re-

Continued on Page 6, Column 5

Africans Complain Of Bias in Moscow

By SEYMOUR TOPPING
Special to The New York Times

MOSCOW, June 3 — A sharp controversy has arisen between Soviet authorities and African students who have complained of discrimination fostered by a Moscow newspaper article.

The article, published by Komsomolskaya Pravda, the newspaper of the Communist Youth League, purported to tell the experiences of a Russian girl who was sold into a harem by a Moslem student she had married.

African students here interpreted the article as a warning to Russian girls against association with Moslems. It was published on Oct. 27 after a number of Africans had complained of being attacked by Russians and appeared publicly in the company

Continued on Page 5, Column 1

POPE JOHN XXIII IS DEAD AT 81, ENDING 4½-YEAR REIGN DEVOTED TO PEACE AND CHRISTIAN UNITY

Associated Press
POPE JOHN XXIII

Washington Mourns Loss Of Great Force for Peace

By M. S. HANDLER

WASHINGTON, June 3—President Kennedy paid high tribute today to the statesmanship and moral leadership of Pope John XXIII. The President said of the Pontiff: "His compassion and kindly strength have bequeathed humanity a new legacy of purpose and courage for the future."

Mr. Kennedy led official Washington in mourning the passing of Pope John as a great loss to mankind. Members of both houses of Congress and churchmen of various faiths joined in expressing the belief that the Pontiff had made an immense contribution to the reconciliation of all Christian faiths, to the reconciliation of his church with Judaism, and to the preservation of peace.

President Kennedy said the Pope had "brought compassion and understanding drawn from wide experience to the most divisive problems of a tumultuous age."

Statement by President

The President's statement said:

"The highest work of any man is to protect and carry on the deepest spiritual heritage of the race. To Pope John was given the almost unique gift of enriching and enlarging that tradition. Armed with humility and calm which surrounded his earliest days, he brought compassion and an understanding drawn from wide experience to the most divisive problems of a tumultuous age.

"The ennobling precepts of his encyclicals and his actions drew on the accumulated wisdom of an ancient faith for guidance in the 'most' complex and troublesome problems of the modern age. To him the divine spark which unites all men would ultimately prove more enduring than the forces which divide. His wisdom, compassion and kindly strength have bequeathed humanity a new legacy of purpose and courage for the future."

The reference to Pope John's encyclicals marked the second such praise. At Boston College

Continued on Page 21, Column 1

A LIBERAL PONTIFF

Church Council and Encyclical on Amity Marked Tenure

By ARNALDO CORTESI
Special to The New York Times

ROME, June 3 — Pope John XXIII, champion of world peace and a tireless fighter for the union of all Christian churches, died in the Vatican tonight while Cardinals and other prelates and several of his relatives prayed around his sickbed. He was 81 years old.

John XXIII was the 261st Pope to sit on the throne that was first occupied by the Apostle Peter.

In the four years, seven months and six days of his reign he conquered the hearts of people throughout the world. Few other Popes before him were so universally admired.

The Pope's death came at 7:49 P.M. (2:49 P.M. Eastern daylight time.)

After a long struggle the Pope developed peritonitis, brought on by a stomach tumor. The tumor was discovered last November.

Doctors Gave Up Hope

His doctors had given up hope at the onset of the peritonitis, an inflammation of the lining of the abdominal cavity, which was given as the cause of his death. Much of the intervening period was passed in a state of coma or semicoma. The Pope was lucid most of yesterday, however, but in great pain, which he bore with remarkable fortitude. Early yesterday afternoon he suffered a "new crisis."

Before entering his last state of coma, he repeatedly said in Latin: "Into Thy hands, O Lord, I commit my soul."

The Pope had dedicated much of his pontificate to promoting Christian unity and the unity of all men as brothers under a common God.

Pope's Last Words

In his last words, addressed to the assembled Cardinals and prelates around his sickbed, the Pope said:

"Ut unum sint." They are Latin words meaning "That they may be one."

The words were originally spoken by Jesus after the Last Supper.

The night of May 25 the Pope suffered a hemorrhage that brought him close to death. A series of blood transfusions saved his life. He had been improving when peritonitis developed.

John XXIII was elected Pope Oct. 28, 1958. He was born in the village of Sotto il Monte in northern Italy Nov. 25, 1881. He was thus 81 years, six months and nine days old at his death.

Pope John passed his last days in his bedroom on the top floor of the Vatican Palace. A small crowd of ecclesiastics and laymen had congregated there when they were told that the Pope was near death.

Washington will not accord the Pope the flag tribute he will receive in New York. The State Department explained that flags in Washington are

Continued on Page 18, Column 1

WAGNER ORDERS FLAGS LOWERED

Leads City in Mourning and Picks 2 Representatives to Attend Pope's Funeral

Mayor Wagner yesterday ordered flags on all city buildings flown at half-staff until the burial of Pope John. The Mayor led the city in mourning the Pope.

"Pope John XXIII symbolized faith, goodness, courage and compassion," Mayor Wagner said, adding, "He appealed always to the best in the human heart and all humanity is uplifted by the noble example which he set."

Mayor Wagner also designated Commissioner of Public Events Richard C. Patterson Jr. and Thomas J. Deegan, chairman of the World's Fair executive committee, as official city representatives at the Pope's funeral.

Both are in Rome on other business.

Continued on Page 18, Column 4

St. Peter's Throng Silenced by Grief

Special to The New York Times

ROME, June 3—A vast throng in the piazza in front of St. Peter's Basilica heard the news of the death of Pope John this evening in sad and resigned silence.

Many knelt in quiet prayer and crossed themselves as several hundred surged toward the bronze doors leading into Vatican City to watch as one of the two portals was swung shut as a traditional sign that the Pope was dead.

The Pope's death came only minutes after a brief offering brought to an end a mass celebrated for the Pontiff on the steps of the Basilica by Luigi Cardinal Traglia, pro-vicar of the Diocese of Rome.

More than 35,000 Romans, visitors, pilgrims, nuns and clergymen gathered to hear the mass, which started at 7 PM. By the time the last sacred

Continued on Page 21, Column 2

Those at Bedside

Those around the bedside included Eugene Cardinal Tisserant, the bearded French dean of the Sacred College; Benedetto Cardinal Aloisi Masella, who as Cardinal Camerlengo, or Chamberlain, heads the interim administration of the Roman Catholic Church; the Pope's three brothers—Giuseppe, Alfredo and Zaverio Roncalli—and his widowed sister, Assunta; three nephews, several members of the Papal household, such as his sacristan, his confessor and his Master of the Chamber.

A larger crowd, including ambassadors and ministers, waited in an adjacent room.

Swiss guards kept all others out of the Papal apartment.

About 30 minutes before the Pope died it became clear from his labored breathing and his falling pulse rate that he was near death. The Pope's personal physician, Prof. Antonio Gasbarrini, warned Cardinal Aloisi Masella that the Pope had not long to live.

The mass for the Pope was said at an altar in an adjoining room

Continued on Page 18, Column 1

The New York Times.

LATE CITY EDITION
U. S. Weather Bureau Report (Page 50) forecasts:
Sunny and cool today; clear tonight.
Sunny and warmer tomorrow.
Temp. range: 74—55; yesterday: 70—55.
Temp.-Hum. Index: 70; yesterday: 69.

VOL. CXII...No. 38,500. © 1963 by The New York Times Company. Times Square, New York 36, N. Y.   NEW YORK, SATURDAY, JUNE 22, 1963.   TEN CENTS

---

18 UNION CHIEFS ACT TO END BIAS IN CONSTRUCTION

Bid Locals Admit Qualified Negroes as Apprentices and as Members

PROGRAM NOT BINDING

N.A.A.C.P. Aide Says Plan Sounds Good, but Notes It Must Be Implemented

Special to The New York Times

WASHINGTON, June 21—The presidents of the 18 building trades unions adopted today a program to eliminate racial discrimination in apprenticeship, union membership and assignment to job openings.

At the same time, they warned that they would fight any effort by the Government to determine qualifications necessary for admission into the industry and into union membership.

The building trades unions have been the most criticized segment of the labor movement on discrimination. The National Association for the Advancement of Colored People has long contended that most building trades locals practice systematic exclusion of Negroes. Recently, the association picketed construction projects in New York and Philadelphia.

Government Pressure

This activity and increased pressure on them by the Government to eliminate discriminatory practices prompted the building trades presidents to discuss the situation. Today's statement, adopted unanimously, was the result.

The union leaders said they recognized the Government's interest and its duty to correct economic injustice and pledged their "good faith to work toward the goal."

The program consists of the following points:

¶Local unions are urged to accept any applicant for membership who meets the required qualifications regardless of his race, creed, color or national origin.

¶If a local operates an exclusive hiring hall or a work referral system, applicants for employment are to be referred to work without discrimination as to race, creed, color or national origin.

¶Locals shall also accept and refer applicants for apprenticeship without discrimination.

Adoption of the statement does not automatically bind the local unions to abide by it.

A spokesman for the Building

Continued on Page 8, Column 1

STATE DEMOCRATS MAY SHIFT POWER

Change in Rules Proposed to Move Control Upstate

By RICHARD P. HUNT

State Democratic leaders are considering a reorganization plan that would for the first time give upstate Democrats a major, if not dominant, role in party affairs.

The plan, which is contained in a proposed set of rules of the state committee, implies that the traditional control of the party machinery by New York City Democrats will be limited or ended.

The rules have been proposed after a year of study by a nine-member committee appointed by William H. McKeon, the Democratic state chairman. They will be submitted for ratification at a state committee meeting in Albany on Tuesday.

The most important change proposed is the creation of a 38-member executive committee, which would be empowered to carry on the party's business in behalf of the full 300-member state committee.

Democrats from the 57 coun-

Continued on Page 24, Column 5

Lawyers Promise Kennedy Aid in Easing Race Unrest

Leaders of Bar Agree to Form Working Group Across Nation — President to See Negro Officials Today

By MARJORIE HUNTER
Special to The New York Times

WASHINGTON, June 21—Many of the nation's leading lawyers promised President Kennedy at a conference today that they would help open the lines of communication between the races. But they were told by a participant at the conference that they faced "a long hot summer."

At a meeting in the White House, the lawyers acceded to a Presidential request that they set up a committee that would try to ease racial tensions and provide national and local leadership.

Today's meeting was one in a series that the President has held in recent weeks with religious leaders, businessmen, Governors and labor leaders. So far, the President has conferred with several thousand persons on civil-rights matters.

Heading the lawyers' racial communications committee will be Harrison Tweed of New York and Bernard G. Segal of Philadelphia. All of the 244 lawyers attending today's meeting were invited to serve on the committee.

Another committee, also dealing with racial communications, will be established by the American Bar Association. This was announced during the White House meeting by Sylvester C. Smith Jr. of Newark, N. J., the association's president.

Joining the President in meeting the lawyers in the East Room were Vice President Johnson and Attorney General Robert F. Kennedy. Of the lawyers present, 66 were from Southern states. There were 23

Continued on Page 8, Column 3

Wagner to Help Negroes Get More Building Jobs

By CHARLES G. BENNETT

Mayor Wagner said yesterday that he would appoint "in a day or two" a panel of three qualified persons to induce construction unions to take in more Negroes. The panel will be given a week to examine employment records, talk with all groups concerned and make recommendations.

At the same time the Mayor said he had been assured by Peter Brennan, president of the Building Trades and Construction Council, that "technically qualified" members of minority groups would be put to work "right away" if job opportunities existed.

The Mayor spoke at a news conference in City Hall a few hours after his return from two weeks in Hawaii and Tokyo. Beforehand he had conferred at Gracie Mansion with Mr. Brennan and with Harry Van Arsdale Jr., president of the Central Labor Council.

Asks Special Session

Mr. Wagner dashed from the City Hall news interview back to Idlewild Airport, where he had landed early in the morning, to fly to Lake Placid, N.Y., to attend the New York State Conference of Mayors.

At the Lake Placid conference last night, Mayor Wagner called on Mayors throughout the state to join him in a request to Governor Rockefeller and the legislative leaders to summon a special session to deal with racial discrimination.

New state laws, Mr. Wagner proposed, should include financial aid to municipalities to speed desegregation in jobs, housing, education and other fields.

At City Hall the Mayor said of Mr. Brennan's promise to bring more Negroes into construction jobs as fast as possible:

"During the week the panel is preparing its recommendations, my office staff will be

Continued on Page 9, Column 2

MAYOR TO OPPOSE RACE BY DE SAPIO

Indicates He May Campaign in 'Village' in an Effort to Block Comeback Drive

Mayor Wagner made it clear yesterday that he would actively oppose Carmine G. De Sapio's attempted political comeback.

The Mayor was asked at a wide-ranging City Hall news conference about Mr. De Sapio's announcement Wednesday that he would be a candidate for the Democratic leadership of the First Assembly District South. This Greenwich Village area was the base of his former statewide political power.

"This is a free country," the Mayor replied. Then he added grimly, "My position on Mr. De Sapio has not changed."

Pressed as to whether he would actually go into Greenwich Village to oppose a De Sapio comeback, Mr. Wagner said a Mayor did not generally have time to go into the districts in district campaigns. But he conceded that he had done so, and indicated he might do so again.

He was asked, "No one should expect any encouragement from you for Mr. De Sapio?"

"That is the understatement of the year," the Mayor shot back.

Then the Mayor said: "I'll wait until the campaign begins

Continued on Page 24, Column 3

JUDICIAL INQUIRY ON PROFUMO SET; LABOR ASSAILS IT

Macmillan Announces Study of Security Aspects, but Foes Call It 'Cover-Up'

By SYDNEY GRUSON
Special to The New York Times

LONDON, June 21 — Prime Minister Macmillan announced today that a judicial inquiry would be held into the security aspects of the Profumo scandal. The form of the inquiry was immediately criticized by the Opposition Labor party as a "cover-up."

Mr. Macmillan told the House of Commons that Lord Denning, as Master of the Rolls, the third-highest judicial official in Britain, would conduct the inquiry. The Prime Minister also gravely took note of continuing rumors about the involvement of "all sorts of people" in the affair.

Asked by Harold Wilson, Labor's leader, whether he was satisfied that nothing more remained to be disclosed, Mr. Macmillan replied:

"I know of no things which I have not told the House, but I have heard these terrible things being said now of all sorts of people which, if allowed to go on, will destroy not only one side of the House of Commons but the other side of the House of Commons."

Chamber Is Crowded

To a chamber unusually crowded for a Friday session, Mr. Macmillan said that the rumors "affect the honor and integrity of public life" in Britain "and if they were true such a situation might point to a security risk."

Pressing for the appointment of a select committee of Members of Parliament to conduct the inquiry, Mr. Wilson said that Lord Denning would have no power to compel the attendance of witnesses or compel proof.

"Is the Prime Minister aware that some of the evidence required will be collected from some of the most unmitigated liars in this country?" Mr. Wilson asked.

He also referred to the rumors. In a judicial inquiry, he said, they "cannot be dissipated and the men concerned enabled to clear their names, as they have every right to do."

Blackmail Linked to Case

The rumors are boundless on Fleet Street, the home of the British press, and in Westminster, the home of Parliament. Not even the royal family has escaped.

One of the rumors has linked blackmail to the case of Dr. Stephen Ward, 50-year-old society osteopath. Dr. Ward is in custody on charges of living off the earnings of prostitution.

He introduced Christine Keeler, 21-year-old self-styled model, to John Profumo when Mr. Profumo was Secretary of State for War and to Capt. Yevgeni E. Ivanov, a Soviet deputy naval attaché until his recall last December. Miss Keeler had simultaneous affairs with the two men.

Another rumor involves the identity of a man said to be

Continued on Page 7, Column 1

FRENCH NAVY ENDS NATO ATLANTIC TIE

Paris Announces Resuming of Unrestrained Control of Virtually Whole Fleet

By DREW MIDDLETON
Special to The New York Times

PARIS, June 21—France announced today that she would resume unrestrained control of virtually the whole of the nation's naval fighting force.

A curt bulletin issued by the semiofficial French Press Agency said that "the French Government has decided to withdraw from the NATO Fleet in the North Atlantic." The bulletin cited official sources.

The Government's decision was described here as a logical consequence of France's action in 1959. In that year she withdrew her Mediterranean fleet from the alliance's control.

Effect of New Move

Earlier this year the squadrons of that fleet were transferred from the Mediterranean base of Toulon to the North Atlantic base of Brest in Brittany.

As a consequence of today's announcement, the bulk of the powerful French forces hitherto earmarked for training and planning under the ultimate command of the Supreme Allied Commander Atlantic have now been withdrawn.

[In Washington officials were distressed by the French action. The Administration was embarrassed by its timing on the eve of President Kennedy's departure for Europe.]

Allied diplomats almost universally deplored the psychological shock that the action

Continued on Page 20, Column 5

World Labor Parley Bars South African

Special to The New York Times

GENEVA, June 21 — United States Government and American worker delegates voted today for the expulsion of a South African from the International Labor Organization conference.

The credentials of the South African, a worker delegate, were rejected by a vote of 135 to 3, with 57 abstentions. His credentials had been issued by his Government.

The member states of the 108-nation organization, a United Nations specialized agency, are represented by two government delegates, a representative of employer groups and a trade unionist. Each has separate voting rights. The worker repre-

Continued on Page 4, Column 2

CARDINAL MONTINI ELECTED POPE; LIBERAL, 65, WILL REIGN AS PAUL VI; LIKELY TO CONTINUE JOHN'S WORK

POPE PAUL VI in his first public appearance gives his blessing to the crowd that had gathered outside St. Peter's Basilica. Holding missal is Msgr. Salvatore Capoferri.

United Press International Radiophoto

5TH VOTE DECISIVE

New Pontiff Gives His Blessing to Crowd— Coronation June 30

By ARNALDO CORTESI
Special to The New York Times

ROME, June 21 — Giovanni Battista Cardinal Montini, 65-year-old Archbishop of Milan, was elected Supreme Pontiff of the Roman Catholic Church today. He will reign as Pope Paul VI.

The man who had been described as the most likely prince of the church to succeed Pope John XXIII manifested his intention of continuing his predecessor's policies by confirming Amleto Giuseppi Cardinal Cicognani as Apostolic Secretary of State. Cardinal Cicognani held the post under John XXIII.

Pope Paul was elected on the fifth ballot conducted in the Sacred College of Cardinals. He and 79 other Cardinals from 29 nations — both figures were records — went into conclave Wednesday evening.

The news that the more than 500,000,000 Roman Catholics in the world had a new spiritual leader was given at 11:22 A.M. by a white puff of smoke from a stovepipe on the roof of the Sistine Chapel in Vatican City.

262d on Papal Throne

The new pope, a native of the Lombardy region, who was 65 last Sept. 26, will be, according to Catholic tradition, the 262d occupant of the throne of St. Peter.

The coronation of Paul VI will take place in St. Peter's Basilica early in the morning of June 30, the day President Kennedy is to arrive in Europe during his 10-day tour of Europe. In the Western church the day is the Feast of St. Paul, the apostle who was the first in the church to bear the name. The last Pope to use it, Paul V, a Borghese, died in 1621.

An hour after his election, Pope Paul appeared on a balcony of St. Peter's Basilica to impart an apostolic benediction to a huge crowd. There were emotional scenes as most people dropped to their knees to receive the blessing. Some women wept and others held infants toward the Pope.

Acceptance at 11:15 A.M.

The conclave that elected Pope Paul lasted 11 hours. It ranks as the sixth shortest in the last four centuries. In the last century there were been only two that were shorter, the one that elected Pius XII in 1939, which lasted 30 hours, and the one that elected Leo XIII in 1878, which lasted 36 hours. Pope John was elected in 1958 on the 11th ballot on the third day.

Paul VI assumed all papal prerogatives and rights at 11:15 A.M. (6:15 A.M., Eastern daylight time) when, after protesting that he felt unworthy, he gave his acceptance to the dean of the Sacred College, Eugène Cardinal Tisserant. The coronation is a formality and the

Continued on Page 2, Column 1

Rome Believes New Pope Will Press for Reforms

Clear-cut Decision Seen

By PAUL HOFMANN
Special to The New York Times

ROME, June 21 — Pope Paul VI began his pontificate today amid general forecasts that it would bring an energetic continuation of the progressive course charted by Pope John XXIII.

The consensus in Rome was that the conclave, by elevating the 65-year-old Archbishop of Milan to the papacy, had made a clear decision for a liberal pontificate—and one hopefully expected to last a long time.

First responses from world centers showed international agreement with this evaluation.

The general belief here was that Pope Paul had been elected with the understanding that he would soon reopen the church's Ecumenical Council in the Vatican, suspended by the death of his predecessor. Ecclesiastics who had served in the past with the new Pontiff predicted that he would press for enactment

Continued on Page 3, Column 5

Choice Widely Hailed

By GEORGE DUGAN

Both Protestant and Jewish leaders said yesterday that the election of Pope Paul VI showed that the reform and renewal so close to the heart of Pope John would be emphasized in the days to come.

The new Pope, who was given the red hat of a cardinal by his predecessor, was deeply involved in the Ecumenical Council, which had been scheduled to reconvene on Sept. 8.

The election of Pope Paul aroused great interest in Washington, which is curious about the political effects the choice of a liberal will have on the European left. President Kennedy, who will visit the new Pope July 2, sent the Pontiff his "heartiest congratulations."

J. Irwin Miller, president of

Continued on Page 3, Column 3

HOUSE UNIT VOTES DEFENSE FUND CUT

Reduction of 1.9 Billion Is Protested by McNamara

By JACK RAYMOND
Special to The New York Times

WASHINGTON, June 21—The House Appropriations Committee approved a $47,092,209,-000 defense fund measure today, with only relatively small changes in the Administration's original request.

But even these changes drew an immediate protest from Secretary of Defense Robert S. McNamara. He said the cuts in airplane procurement money "would deny us necessary tactical support for our combat-ready Army divisions."

President Kennedy last January requested $49,014,237,000 in defense appropriations for the fiscal year 1964, beginning July 1. The committee cut the total by $1,922,028,000.

The committee noted that more than $500,000,000 of the cut represented bookkeeping shifts.

"The accompanying bill," the committee said in its report, based on four months of closed hearings, "will support programs which will promote the security of the United States and assure the continuation of the policy of military supremacy."

According to the report, the bill would provide armed forces totaling 2,695,000 officers and

Continued on Page 20, Column 2

TAX DISCLOSURE AROUSES OTTAWA

Minister Admits Plan Was Known to 3 Businessmen

By HOMER BIGART
Special to The New York Times

OTTAWA, June 21 —Walter L. Gordon, the harassed Minister of Finance in the minority Liberal Government, gave fresh ammunition to his critics in Parliament today.

He admitted that the three Toronto businessmen who helped write his budget knew in advance of the withdrawal Wednesday of a controversial tax proposal. The tax had been aimed at halting the take-over of Canadian companies by foreigners.

The proposal would have placed a 30 per cent tax on the seller of a large block of shares in a Canadian company to a foreigner. Its withdrawal was announced while the stock markets of Canada were still open, and caused frenzied speculation. Members of the Opposition have demanded an investigation to determine whether the leakage of budget secrets permitted "insiders" to make windfall profits on the markets.

Mr. Gordon had been under fire all week for employing three financial experts from Toronto, two of whom had re-

Continued on Page 14, Column 7

Brezhnev Advances As Khrushchev Heir

By SEYMOUR TOPPING
Special to The New York Times

MOSCOW, June 21—Leonid I. Brezhnev, a member of the ruling Presidium of the Soviet Communist Party, emerged tonight after plenary meetings of the Central Committee as a rising political heir of Premier Khrushchev.

Mr. Brezhnev, who is 57 years old and a protégé of Mr. Khrushchev, has been appointed to the Secretariat of the Central Committee. The Secretariat is the chief executive body of the party.

Western analysts note that Mr. Brezhnev now holds an array of party and Government positions that make it appear that he is being groomed to assume the roles of Frol R.

Continued on Page 5, Column 3

The New York Times

PROMISES ACTION: Mayor Wagner at City Hall news conference where he announced plans to eliminate racial discrimination in the city's construction-industry unions.

"All the News That's Fit to Print"

The New York Times.

LATE CITY EDITION
U. S. Weather Bureau Report (Page 58) forecast:
Cloudy with scattered showers today;
partly cloudy tonight and tomorrow.
Temp. range: 77—62; yesterday: 81—61.
Temp.-Hum. Index: 70 to 75; yesterday: 72.

VOL. CXII. No. 38,568.
© 1963 by The New York Times Company.
Times Square, New York 36, N. Y.

NEW YORK, THURSDAY, AUGUST 29, 1963.

TEN CENTS

KENNEDY SIGNS BILL AVERTING A RAIL STRIKE

PRECEDENT IS SET

Arbitration Imposed by Congress—Vote in House 286-66

Text of Kennedy's statement will be found on Page 13.

By JOHN D. POMFRET
Special to The New York Times

WASHINGTON, Aug. 28 — Congress passed today a bill that prevented a national railroad strike scheduled for midnight. President Kennedy signed it immediately.

The House completed the Congressional action. It adopted by a standing vote of 286 to 66 the same joint resolution passed yesterday by the Senate. The measure provides for arbitration of the two principal issues in the railroad work rules dispute and bars a strike for 180 days.

The action was without Federal precedent. Never before in the history of peacetime labor relations has Congress imposed arbitration in a labor-management dispute.

The failure of the railroads and the five train operating unions to resolve their dispute, and the Congressional action this made necessary, is considered by many to represent a major failure for the collective bargaining system.

Many Are Reluctant

Even many Congressmen who voted for the measure, convinced that the economic consequences of a national railroad strike made action to head it off essential, did so with great reluctance. They said they feared that their action might set a precedent detrimental to collective bargaining.

An arbitration board was created by Congress to consider the two key issues. These are whether diesel locomotive firemen are necessary in freight and yard service and the size of train-service crews.

Congress ordered negotiations on the remaining issues on the theory that with the two main issues disposed of, the presumably less important matters could be settled by traditional collective bargaining.

But some well-informed Government sources do not believe the remaining issues will be

Continued on Page 13, Column 1

LODI KILLER SLAIN; 2D MAN GIVES UP

Ex-Convict Is Shot 7 Times in a Midtown Hotel

One of the killers of two New Jersey policemen was shot to death early yesterday by New York detectives during a violent struggle in his midtown hotel room. Sixteen hours later, the second man wanted in the slayings quietly surrendered.

The slain killer, 25-year-old Frank Falco, was asleep in his underwear when the police, using a passkey, entered his room at the Manhattan Hotel, Eighth Avenue and 44th Street. Although awakened with a revolver pressed to his throat, he fought desperately before being killed by seven bullets. He died snarling at the police and cursing them.

Thomas (Rabbi Tom) Trantino, 27, the second man, walked into the East 22d Street station house at 9:10 P.M., accompanied by a lawyer. He was neatly dressed and clean-shaven.

The men, both ex-convicts, had been the object of a grim police hunt since Detective Sgt. Peter Voto and Gary Tedesco, a police appointee, were gunned down early Monday morning in the Angel Lounge on Route 46 in Lodi, N. J. Mr. Tedesco was to have officially joined the Lodi force today.

A tip led the New York detectives to the hotel, where Falco had checked in at 8 P.M. Tuesday under the name of J. Rello of Newport, R. I.

Lieut. Thomas Quinn, a 53-year-old police veteran with 16 citations for bravery, entered Falco's 23d-floor room first, his

Continued on Page 35, Column 2

U. S. PRESSES U. N. TO CONDEMN SYRIA ON ISRAELI DEATHS

Stevenson Deplores Killing of Youths—Thant Assures Council on Cease-Fire

Text of Stevenson statement appears on Page 2.

By KATHLEEN TELTSCH
Special to The New York Times

UNITED NATIONS, N. Y., Aug. 28 — Adlai E. Stevenson declared today that the recent slaying of two Israeli farmers by Syrians was "wanton murder" deserving the strongest condemnation by the Security Council.

The United States delegate, followed by the British representative, gave forceful support to Israel's charges arising from the Aug. 20 ambush killing of two 19-year-old Israelis at the Almagor farm settlement.

Mr. Stevenson rejected Syria's countercharges against Israel as "not corroborated" by United Nations investigations.

The United States policy statement drew a favorable reaction from Michael S. Comay of Israel, who said it encouraged him to expect the Council to take "firm and vigorous action."

Syrian Disapproves

However, there was disapproval from Dr. Salah el-Tarazi of Syria, who criticized Mr. Stevenson as "not particularly objective." He added that Mr. Stevenson in past years had not deplored Syrian losses with equal feeling.

The Council, resuming its airing of the new crisis, was told by the Secretary General, U Thant, that United Nations inspection showed "no evidence of a military build-up on either side" of the armistice line.

Mr. Thant reported that both parties were heeding the United Nations cease-fire achieved last Friday after the ambush and subsequent exchanges of shooting greatly increased tension in the area. Bullets collected at one shooting site were on exhibit in the Council chamber.

Both Mr. Stevenson and Roger W. Jackling of Britain urged Syria and Israel to accept the suggestion by the United Nations truce chief, Lieut. Gen. Odd Bull, for avoiding new eruptions along their border, including an exchange of prisoners. Mr. Comay indicated a favorable Israeli reaction.

Evidence Questioned

Dr. Tarazi, in his turn, insisted that Israel's allegations remained unproved and that some evidence could have been faked. He noted photographs of footgear found at the ambush scene and said Syrian soldiers did not wear such shoes.

He was supported by Sidi Baba of Morocco, who accused Israel of making a "great superficial fuss" over the Almagor incident to create a climate for pressuring the Arabs into signing a peace treaty.

The United States and Britain are understood to be drafting a resolution that would condemn the killings and rebuke Syria by implication, rather than by outright condemnation, as Israel has been asking. Similar formulas have been used in the past.

Such an indirect condemnation might be blocked by a veto from the Soviet Union, however, which in the past has rejected resolutions opposed by the Arabs.

Mr. Stevenson told the 11-nation Council that General Bull's information was admitted

Continued on Page 2, Column 3

2 Girls Murdered In E. 88th St. Flat

Two young women, one the daughter of a writer and the other of a prominent surgeon, were bound and stabbed to death yesterday in their apartment at 57 East 88th Street.

The victims, Janice Wylie, 21 years old, and Emily Hoffert, 23, had been stabbed repeatedly. Three bloodstained kitchen knives were found in the five-room apartment, which the girls shared with another young woman. The suite had been ransacked.

The bodies were found on a bedroom floor by Janice's father, the writer Max Wylie, and by Patricia Tolles, 23, the third roommate.

Mr. Wylie, who lives nearby, at 55 East 86th Street, is a

Continued on Page 35, Column 5

U.S. SPURNS DENIAL BY DIEM ON CRISIS

Absolves the Army Again in Vietnam Pagoda Raids and Points Toward Nhu

By TAD SZULC
Special to The New York Times

WASHINGTON, Aug. 28 — The United States reaffirmed today its belief that the South Vietnamese Government had violated pledges on the Buddhist crisis and that Vietnamese military chiefs were innocent of responsibility for assaults on pagodas.

This was the reaction of the Administration to communiqués issued in Saigon in the last 24 hours by the Government of President Ngo Dinh Diem in the name of the Vietnamese Joint General Staff.

The communiqués charged that Washington's public statements on the crisis reflected "totally erroneous information."

[In Saigon, youths loyal to the secret police were reported to be warning the population against anti-Government demonstrations.]

Change Is Held Vital

With the Vietnam crisis already regarded by the United States as extremely grave, this public dispute seemed to pull it toward an unpredictable showdown.

The quarrel over who smashed pagodas and who arrested leaders of the Buddhist protest movement is understood to affect deeply the Kennedy Administration's evolving policy of encouraging Vietnamese military chiefs to reach for power.

This policy, still tentative, is that a fundamental change is required in the structure of the Saigon Government, Washington sources explain. They say the goal is national harmony that would let Vietnam concentrate again on the war against the Communist guerrillas of the Vietcong.

Specifically, Washington is said to deem internal peace out of the question as long as Ngo Dinh Nhu, chief of secret police and brother of the President, retains his vast power.

Mr. Nhu is considered almost a symbol of the friction between Vietnam's Buddhists and the Roman Catholic Ngo Government.

It is reported that in searching for an alternative to the regime—a course that was unthinkable here before the Buddhist crisis—the United States has almost openly been advanced

Continued on Page 3, Column 4

NEWS INDEX

200,000 MARCH FOR CIVIL RIGHTS IN ORDERLY WASHINGTON RALLY; PRESIDENT SEES GAIN FOR NEGRO

VIEW FROM THE LINCOLN MEMORIAL: The scene during the march looking toward the Washington Monument
Associated Press

VIEW FROM THE WASHINGTON MONUMENT: Marchers assembling around Reflecting Pool at the Lincoln Memorial
United Press International Telephoto

CONGRESS CORDIAL BUT NOT SWAYED

Leaders of March Pay Calls of Courtesy at Capitol

By WARREN WEAVER Jr.
Special to The New York Times

WASHINGTON, Aug. 28 — The civil rights demonstration that swept more than 200,000 people through the capital today appeared to have left much of Congress untouched — physically, emotionally and politically.

In the morning, 13 demonstration leaders drove quietly up Capitol Hill and paid courtesy calls on Congressional leaders of both parties. The atmosphere was cordial, but there were no conversions.

In the afternoon, about 75 Senators and Representatives went from Capitol Hill to the Lincoln Memorial to be introduced, sit on the steps and listen to Gospel singing and speeches on civil rights.

A few demonstrators violated marching orders and went up to the Capitol to visit legislators in their offices. A few Senators welcomed trainloads and busfuls of constituents in person.

Otherwise, there was really evidence that the demonstration, however large and fervent, would play a material role in advancing civil rights legislation.

Senator Hubert H. Humphrey, one of the most enthusiastic

Continued on Page 17, Column 1

'I Have a Dream . . .'

Peroration by Dr. King Sums Up A Day the Capital Will Remember

By JAMES RESTON

WASHINGTON, Aug. 28 — Abraham Lincoln, who presided in his stone temple today above the children of the slaves he emancipated, may have used just the right words to sum up the general reaction to the Negro's massive march on Washington. "I think," he wrote to Gov. Andrew G. Curtin of Pennsylvania in 1861, "the necessity of being ready increases. Look to it." Washington may not have changed a vote today, but it is a little more conscious tonight of the necessity of being ready for freedom. It may not "look to it" at once, since it is looking to so many things, but it will be a long time before it forgets the melodious and melancholy voice of the Rev. Dr. Martin Luther King Jr. crying out his dreams to the multitude.

News Analysis

It was Dr. King who, near the end of the day, touched the vast audience. Until then the pilgrimage was merely a great spectacle. Only those marchers from the embattled towns in the Old Confederacy had anything like the old crusading zeal. For many the day seemed an adventure, a long outing in the late summer sun—part Coney Island, part Disneyland, part political convention, and part July-fry.

But Dr. King brought them alive in the late afternoon with a peroration that was an anguished echo from all the old

Continued on Page 17, Column 6

PRESIDENT MEETS MARCH LEADERS

Says Bipartisan Support Is Needed for Rights Bill

Rights statement and Labor Day proclamation, Page 16.

By TOM WICKER
Special to The New York Times

WASHINGTON, Aug. 28 — President Kennedy served tea and sympathy and blunt political advice late today to the tired but proud leaders of the march on Washington.

In an hour-long conference, the President told the 10 leaders that "very strong bipartisan support" would be needed to get civil rights legislation enacted this year.

In a statement issued immediately after the conference, Mr. Kennedy said that "the cause of 20,000,000 Negroes has been advanced" by the orderly demonstration, "conducted so appropriately before the nation's shrine to the Great Emancipator."

Earlier, in a Labor Day statement released in advance of the holiday, the President called on the nation to speed up its efforts to achieve equal rights for all in jobs, education and voting.

The main discussion between the march leaders and the President concerned prospects for civil rights legislation, the leaders said after the White House meeting. They talked with Mr. Kennedy around the long table in the Cabinet Room, where the leaders were served tea, coffee

Continued on Page 16, Column 1

ACTION ASKED NOW

10 Leaders of Protest Urge Laws to End Racial Inequity

Excerpts from talks at rally are printed on Page 21.

By E. W. KENWORTHY
Special to The New York Times

WASHINGTON, Aug. 28 — More than 200,000 Americans, most of them black but many of them white, demonstrated here today for a full and speedy program of civil rights and equal job opportunities.

It was the greatest assembly for a redress of grievances that this capital has ever seen.

One hundred years and 240 days after Abraham Lincoln enjoined the emancipated slaves to "abstain from all violence" and "labor faithfully for reasonable wages," this vast throng proclaimed in march and song and through the speeches of their leaders that they were still waiting for the freedom and the jobs.

Children Clap and Sing

There was no violence to mar the demonstration. In fact, at times there was an air of hootenanny about it as groups of schoolchildren clapped hands and swung into the familiar freedom songs.

But if the crowd was good-natured, the underlying tone was one of dead seriousness. The emphasis was on "freedom" and "now." At the same time the leaders emphasized, paradoxically but realistically, that the struggle was just beginning.

On Capitol Hill, opinion was divided about the impact of the demonstration in stimulating Congressional action on civil rights legislation. But at the White House, President Kennedy declared that the cause of 20,000,000 Negroes had been advanced by the march.

The march leaders went from the shadows of the Lincoln Memorial to the White House to meet with the President for 75 minutes. Afterward, Mr. Kennedy issued a 400-word statement praising the marchers for the "deep fervor and the quiet dignity" that had characterized the demonstration.

Says Nation Can Be Proud

The nation, the President said, "can properly be proud of the demonstration that occurred here today."

The main target of the demonstration was Congress, whose committees are now considering the Administration's civil rights bill.

At the Lincoln Memorial this afternoon, some speakers, knowing little of the ways of Congress, assumed that the passage of a strengthened civil rights bill had been assured by the moving events of the day.

But from statements by Congressional leaders, after they had met with the march committee this morning, this did not seem certain at all. These statements came before the demonstration.

Senator Mike Mansfield of Montana, the Senate Democratic leader, said he could not say whether the mass protest

Continued on Page 16, Column 1

Capital Is Occupied By a Gentle Army

By RUSSELL BAKER
Special to The New York Times

WASHINGTON, Aug. 28 — No one could remember an invading army quite as gentle as the 200,000 civil rights marchers who occupied Washington today.

For the most part, they came silently during the night, and early morning, occupied the great shaded boulevards of the Mall, and spread through the parklands between the Washington Monument and the Potomac.

But instead of the emotional horde of angry militants that many had feared, what Washington saw was a vast army of quiet, middle-class Americans

Continued on Page 17, Column 7

The New York Times.

LATE CITY EDITION
U.S. Weather Bureau Report (Page 52) forecasts:
Cloudy, cool and windy today; fair and colder tonight. Fair tomorrow.
Temp. range: 52—42; yesterday: 53—48.

VOL. CXIII..No. 38,633. © 1963 by The New York Times Company. Times Square, New York 36, N.Y.   NEW YORK, SATURDAY, NOVEMBER 2, 1963.   TEN CENTS

RUSSIANS REPORT LAUNCHING CRAFT THAT SHIFTS ORBIT

Major Advance Is Claimed for Rendezvous in Space —More Shots Predicted

KHRUSHCHEV JUBILANT

He Expresses Support for a U.S.-Soviet Lunar Trip if Tensions Are Eased

By THEODORE SHABAD
Special to The New York Times

MOSCOW, Nov. 1—The Soviet Union announced the launching today of a new type of maneuverable satellite in a major step toward perfecting rendezvous techniques in space. Shortly afterward Premier Khrushchev indicated support for a joint Soviet-American moon project.

The unmanned earth-controlled spaceship, called Polyot 1, or Flight 1, appeared to have the same capability as that sought in the United States Gemini project, which is still under development.

It reportedly performed extensive horizontal and vertical maneuvers that moved it from its initial nearly circular orbit with an apogee (maximum distance from earth) of 368 miles to a greatly elongated orbit with an apogee of 862 miles.

There was no indication whether the satellite was being guided by telemetry from the ground or had been programed before its launching.

Stresses Joint Flights

As the teletype machines of Tass, the Soviet press agency, clattered out the communique on the launching, Premier Khrushchev announced the news at a reception for Premier Prince Souvanna Phouma of Laos.

Smiling and triumphant, with his hands folded in a characteristic pose across his stomach, the Soviet leader said that the new vehicle offered "unlimited" possibilities in space exploration.

"Man is now no longer a prisoner of his ship, but can make the ship obey his will," Mr. Khrushchev said.

Noting that the Soviet Union had studied "with attention" President Kennedy's proposal for a joint United States-Soviet manned moon flight, Mr. Khrushchev said:

"What could be better than to send a Russian and an American to the moon together, or better yet, a Russian man and an American woman?"

Anastas I. Mikoyan, a First Deputy Premier, who was standing behind Mr. Khrushchev in his first public appearance after a recent illness, joined in the general laughter that followed Soviet propagandists have made

Continued on Page 9, Column 1

WOODS REOPENED IN MOST OF STATE

Rain Permits Hunting Again —Water Still Short

Governor Rockefeller reopened virtually all the state's woodlands for recreational use yesterday after intermittent rains had reduced the danger of forest fires. His order also meant, in most counties, the reinstatement of the hunting season, which had been halted Oct. 23.

However, the trace of rain that fell on New York City's watershed did little or nothing to replenish its reservoirs. Commissioner Armand D'Angelo of the Department of Water Supply, Gas and Electricity said that at 8 A.M. yesterday the city's water supply was at only 29.1 per cent of capacity.

Mr. D'Angelo pointed out that a year ago on this date, the city's six upstate reservoirs were at 42.7 per cent of capacity and that two years ago they contained 67.7 per cent of capacity.

Appealing for conservation of water, city officials said that care could save 100 billion gallons of water by next June, or about one-fifth of the reservoirs' capacity.

More rain fell here in the first day of November than in the entire month of October. The weather bureau said it had recorded 0.59 inches of rain during the 24-hour period. The

Continued on Page 53, Column 2

14 Indicted on L. I. In Party Vandalism

Special to The New York Times

RIVERHEAD, L. I., Nov. 1 —Thirteen young men and one young woman were indicted today for $3,202 worth of damage at a Southampton mansion after a debutante party on the night of Aug. 31. Several are members of prominent families in New York and Philadelphia.

A Suffolk County grand jury charged them with destruction of property, a misdemeanor carrying upon conviction a maximum penalty of six months in jail and a $250 fine.

District Attorney Bernard C. Smith said the 14 would be permitted to surrender voluntarily next Friday. But, he said, he will seek to extradite any of those living outside the state who do not

Continued on Page 12, Column 2

INSURRECTION LAW IN GEORGIA VOIDED

U.S. Court Prohibits, 2 to 1, Trial of 4 in Americus— Integrationists Bailed

By CLAUDE SITTON
Special to The New York Times

AMERICUS, Ga., Nov. 1 — A Federal court handed down an injunction today prohibiting the prosecution of four civil rights workers on state insurrection charges.

It declared, in a 2-to-1 decision, the insurrection statute unconstitutional.

The three-judge panel also directed local authorities to set reasonable bail on unrelated state and city charges against the four and two other persons.

The six were freed immediately on bonds totaling $11,150.

Officials of the state, Sumter County and Americus were given until next January by the court to prepare their defense against charges that they had engaged in a conspiracy to suppress the civil rights movement here.

Two Laws Affected

The injunction against these officials applies to prosecution of the insurrection charges, which carry a maximum penalty of death, and charges of unlawful assembly. Both statutes were held unconstitutional by the court.

Lawyers said the actions marked the first time that the Federal judiciary had halted a state court proceeding in a civil rights case at the request of a private party.

The court held that it had the power to do so under the Civil Rights Act of 1870 and an amendment to the Civil Rights Act of 1957.

The act of 1870 gives district courts jurisdiction over civil actions initiated by a person to end a denial of his constitutional rights by a state or its officials. It also entitles him to recover damages or obtain equitable relief under any Congressional act providing for the protection of civil rights.

The amendment of 1957 makes the statutory authority to enjoin a state court proceeding

Continued on Page 12, Column 5

SENATE REFUSES TO ASK DEEP CUT FOR FOREIGN AID

Turns Back, 46-29, Motion by Morse Urging Revision of Bill by Committee

By FELIX BELAIR Jr.
Special to The New York Times

WASHINGTON, Nov. 1—The Senate rallied behind its leaders today and blocked a move by dissident Democrats to return the $4.2 billion foreign aid authorization to the Foreign Relations Committee for possibly heavy pruning.

In a 46-29 vote it rejected a recommittal motion by Senator Wayne Morse and set the stage for a favorable vote next week on a proposal to cut the authorization by $385 million.

The proposal, designed to head off even deeper cuts on the floor, was lampooned by Mr. Morse, Democrat of Oregon, as the "powerhouse amendment."

The plan was put before the Senate late yesterday by Senators Mike Mansfield and Everett McKinley Dirksen, the Democratic and Republican leaders, respectively. It was co-sponsored by the two top-ranking members of both parties on the Foreign Relations Committee.

Morse Is Ridiculed

Senator Dirksen mocked and ridiculed Senator Morse and his recommittal motion with mimicry and sarcasm. Although Mr. Dirksen left the Senators and gallery spectators rocking with laughter, Mr. Morse appeared more determined than ever to prolong consideration of the bill.

Assuming an attitude of high moral rectitude, and using the familiar gestures of the Oregon Senator, Mr. Dirksen recalled Mr. Morse's blanket objection to any agreement limiting debate and added that "he can just stew in his own juice."

Mr. Dirksen invoked a vision of Senators in red flannels, sitting around Christmas trees with their grandchildren, and then held his head in his hands as he enacted the frustration and despair at having to return to the Senate to resume consideration of the foreign assistance authorization.

Margin Nearly 2 to 1

He said, "The clock and the calendar are running out on this session of the Senate" and noted the important measures on which the Senate had yet to act. But he added:

"With a decent approach and with no Senator feeling that all the wisdom reposes in him alone, we can get out of here on schedule."

Winding up his performance, the Republican leader said the motion to return the bill to committee "comes with poor grace from the senior Senator from Oregon who, because of his personal frustration and because he doesn't like it, wants to take another whack at it."

In the voting that followed, 29 Democrats were joined by 13 Republicans to provide a margin of nearly 2 to 1 against the motion, while 21 Democrats and 8 Republicans were recorded in its support.

Normally, the unwritten rules of senatorial courtesy require that a member be notified when

Continued on Page 12, Column 5

Czechs, Malaysians To Split U.N. Term

By ALEXANDER BURNHAM
Special to The New York Times

UNITED NATIONS, N. Y., Nov. 1—The General Assembly gave its approval today to a gentlemen's agreement whereby Czechoslovakia and Malaysia would split a two-year term on the Security Council. It then elected Czechoslovakia for the first year.

The approval followed 11 ballots by the Assembly on Oct. 18 and Oct. 25 in an effort to choose between the two.

After two weeks of consultations with other countries, the Czechs and Malaysians agreed to share the term.

Before today's secret vote the Assembly president, Dr. Carlos Sosa Rodriguez, said that if the delegations agreed to the arrangement Czechoslovakia would be the sole candidate for election.

Czechoslovakia then received

Continued on Page 6, Column 6

MOROCCANS SAY TRUCE IS VIOLATED

Accuse Algeria of 2d Attack at the Border—Ben Bella Denies Earlier Charge

By Reuters

RABAT, Morocco, Saturday, Nov. 2—Moroccan military officials said early today that Algeria broke the cease-fire in border fighting a few minutes after it became effective at midnight.

The officials said Algerian forces launched a "violent attack" toward the Sahara town of Figuig.

The Moroccan announcement came shortly after the Algerian News Agency had reported that Algerian forces on the desert frontier ceased fire at midnight in accordance with the agreement reached Wednesday in Bamako, Mali, by President Ahmed Ben Bella of Algeria and King Hassan II of Morocco.

A local Moroccan Army command said firing was still heard from the heights above Figuig more than 45 minutes after the cease-fire time.

Yesterday King Hassan reported that Moroccan forces withdrew from Figuig earlier in the day, because of the conditions of the agreement.

[In Algiers, President Ben Bella said the accusation by King Hassan was a ruse. He countered with a charge that the Moroccans had shelled a village in Algerian territory.]

The Algerian agency said President Ben Bella's troops would remain on guard against provocations and that the country would strictly observe the conditions of the agreement.

The truce agreement was

Continued on Page 5, Column 3

OPTIMISM VOICED

American Complicity Denied but a Key Role Is Acknowledged

By MAX FRANKEL
Special to The New York Times

WASHINGTON, Saturday, Nov. 2—The Administration welcomes the coup d'état in South Vietnam, assumes that its policies helped to bring it about and is confident of greater progress now in the war against the Communist guerrillas.

There were, of course, no public statements to this effect even after the success of the coup appeared certain this morning. Officials denied any direct involvement in the military plot and are likely to deplore the deaths of President Ngo Dinh Diem and his brother Ngo Dinh Nhu if reports of their deaths are confirmed.

It is conceded here, however, that the United States Government had created the atmosphere that made the coup possible. This had been done by President Kennedy's denunciation of President Ngo Dinh Diem and by constant pressure from Washington for changes in his regime.

The belief here has been that Washington's hostility and the political unrest in Saigon had virtually paralyzed the Ngo Dinh Diem regime and seriously impaired its conduct of the guerrilla war, to which the United States is deeply committed.

Useful if Not Essential

A change of government, therefore, was regarded as useful if not essential, and of benefit to both the people of South Vietnam and United States policy.

Administration leaders are confident that a new civilian government could quickly restore order in Saigon and turn its attentions back to the war effort. They believe the ouster of President Ngo Dinh Diem, of his brother and principal political adviser, Ngo Dinh Nhu, and of only a few of their principal adherents will bring an end to internal repression and recurrent political turmoil.

Because the Administration here so obviously welcomed the coup and had come close in recent weeks to inviting it, there was widespread discussion of the extent of Washington's involvement.

High officials insisted with

Continued on Page 3, Column 3

POLES TRY TO END SOVIET-CHINA RIFT

Tell Envoys to Use Every Chance for Mediation

By PAUL UNDERWOOD

WARSAW, Nov. 1 — Poland's Communist leadership was reported today to be trying to mediate the ideological quarrel between the Soviet Union and Communist China.

Many of the world's Communist parties, including the Polish, have made repeated calls for an end to the bitter polemics.

Diplomatic sources report that the Polish Ambassadors in Moscow and Peking have been told by Warsaw to make themselves available if any opportunity for peace-making efforts arises. It is assumed that other Polish officials have received similar instructions.

The whole weight of Polish influence within the Communist world is being directed toward calming tempers on both sides.

The chances for a truce in the dispute seems to have improved as a result of Premier Khrushchev's call last Saturday for both sides to halt public denunciations.

This move was widely interpreted in the West as an effort by the Soviet leader to absolve himself of responsibility in advance of a gathering of world Communist figures in Moscow this month to celebrate the an

Continued on Page 10, Column 5

REBELS IN VIETNAM OUST DIEM, REPORT HIM AND NHU SUICIDES; SHARPER FIGHT ON REDS VOWED

Ngo Dinh Diem   Ngo Dinh Nhu

The New York Times   Nov. 2, 1963

Heavy fighting was reported at the Presidential Palace (1) in Saigon. Anti-Government forces seized the Defense Ministry (2) and police and navy headquarters (3 and 4).

U.S. Fleet Sent to Vietnam To Safeguard Americans

By JOHN W. FINNEY
Special to The New York Times

WASHINGTON, Nov. 1 — The Defense Department ordered ships of the Seventh Fleet to the vicinity of South Vietnam today to protect any American lives in South Vietnam who might be endangered by disorders accompanying the overthrow of President Ngo Dinh Diem.

The Pentagon emphasized that the order was strictly a "precautionary measure" and did not signify any intention to intervene militarily in the Vietnamese crisis.

"This order has been given should it be necessary to protect American lives in South Vietnam," a brief Pentagon announcement said.

The order was issued by Secretary of Defense Robert S. McNamara shortly before 11 A.M. —about eight hours after Washington learned of the military revolt.

The first word of the outbreak of fighting in Saigon came shortly before 3 A.M., Eastern standard time, in a report from the United States Embassy in Vietnam teletyped to the White House situation room, a command center in the White House basement that receives diplomatic and intelligence reports from around the world.

Kennedy Notified Quickly

The report set off a flurry of early-morning activity that turned on the lights in the White House, the State Department, the Pentagon and the Central Intelligence Agency.

Watch officers in the situation room called McGeorge Bundy, the President's special assistant for national security affairs, as soon as the embassy's report arrived. Mr. Bundy awakened President Kennedy with a 3 A.M. telephone call. During the predawn hours, the President kept informed on developments by telephone. At 6 A.M. Mr. Bundy went to the President's bedroom to give him a briefing on the uprising.

Mr. Kennedy did not go to his office until 9:20 A.M., shortly before he received the credentials of the new Ambassador from Norway. Until then he

Continued on Page 2, Column 2

PALACE BESIEGED

Army, Air Force and Marines Combine to Oust President

Communiques by coup leaders will be found on Page 4.

By HEDRICK SMITH
Special to The New York Times

WASHINGTON, Saturday, Nov. 2—The South Vietnamese Government of President Ngo Dinh Diem has fallen in a swift military coup d'état.

The insurgents reported over the Saigon radio this morning that Ngo Dinh Diem and his powerful brother Ngo Dinh Nhu had committed suicide.

High officials here confirmed that President Ngo Dinh Diem surrendered to the rebels at 6:05 this morning, Saigon time (5:05 P.M. Friday, New York time), and that the brothers were arrested. There was no official confirmation of the suicide report, which was relayed by the United States Embassy in Saigon.

Anti-Red Drive Promised

All indications were that the military committee that staged the coup was firmly anti-Communist and pro-Western. It was viewed as eager to eliminate the repressive features of the Ngo Dinh Diem Government, which had so frustrated the United States recently.

The insurrectionists pledged to intensify the country's struggle against the Communist guerrillas—the cause that the United States had feared must suffer from Ngo Dinh Diem's loss of popular support.

According to the Saigon radio, the brothers escaped the rebel forces after their surrender and sought asylum in a church. Then, the radio added, they were recaptured. The time of their suicide was given as 10:45 this morning (9:45 P.M., Friday, New York time).

Officials said that Vice President Nguyen Ngoc Tho, a Buddhist highly regarded in Washington, was expected to become Premier of a caretaker civilian government.

Discrimination Was Issue

Vu Van Mau, who resigned as South Vietnam's Foreign Minister last August, was also expected to play a prominent role. His resignation protested the Government's Aug. 21 destruction of Buddhist pagodas, which intensified the religious crisis that led to the coup.

Since last May South Vietnam's Buddhists had been charging the Government of the Roman Catholic Ngo family with religious discrimination.

The military leaders were reported to have assured Ambassador Henry Cabot Lodge that they intended to turn over control of the Government to responsible civilian officials.

This made it likely that the United States would extend diplomatic recognition to the

Continued on Page 2, Column 1

MRS. NHU CHARGES U.S. INCITED COUP

Says Revolt Could Not Occur Without American Help— Won't Stay in Country

By JACK LANGGUTH
Special to The New York Times

BEVERLY HILLS, Calif., Nov. 1—Mrs. Ngo Dinh Nhu bitterly accused the United States Government today of inciting and backing the military revolt in South Vietnam.

Uncertain whether her husband, the brother of South Vietnam's President, was alive or dead, Mrs. Ngo Dinh Nhu was angry and distracted during her first appearance since receiving news of the uprising in Saigon.

Later in the day she received reports that the Government of her family had been deposed. Secluded in her hotel room, with a policeman on guard at her door, she told aides that she would have no further comment until information was more definite.

Previous Attempts Alleged

She met reporters as she left her hotel for an All Saints Day noon mass at the nearby Church of the Good Shepherd. Mrs. Ngo Dinh Nhu began calmly by observing that "it was not the first time" that the American Government had tried to overthrow President Ngo Dinh Diem, her brother-in-law.

She became more agitated when asked whether the United States had played a role in the military coup. "Definitely," she replied. "No coup can erupt without American incitement and backing."

Asked whether she might seek political asylum in the United States, Mrs. Ngo Dinh Nhu replied: "Never," she added. "I cannot stay in a country with people who have stabbed my Government.

"I believe that all the devils of the hell are against us," she said before being escorted to a limousine. "But we shall triumph."

She did not explain what she meant by triumph, but presumably she was alluding to the fight against the Communists. Accompanied by her 18-year-old daughter, Ngo Dinh Le

Continued on Page 3, Column 1

Dominicans Arrest Presidential 'Heir'

Special to The New York Times

SANTO DOMINGO, Dominican Republic, Nov. 1—Dr. Juan Casasnovas Garrido, a former president of the Senate who contends he is the rightful Provisional President of the Dominican Republic, was seized today by forces of the civilian junta.

Dr. Casasnovas was injured in the left arm as he attempted to escape arrest—a block from the home in which he had been hiding for two days, according to Mrs. Dunia D. Garrido, a relative of Dr. Casasnovas. He was hiding in her home in the Sánchez-Luperón district.

Another relative living in the house was also arrested.

At police headquarters this afternoon Dr. Casasnovas indicated that his arm had been injured by a tree branch, not a

Continued on Page 8, Column 5

NEWS INDEX

News Summary and Index, Page 27

Dwight D. Eisenhower's 'The White House Years' appears on Page 27.

FREED IN GEORGIA: Donald Harris, right, receives an enthusiastic welcome after he, Ralph Allen, left background, and Thomas McDaniel, center foreground, were released on bond following a precedent-setting decision by a three-man Federal court in Americus.

Associated Press Wirephoto

"All the News That's Fit to Print"

The New York Times.

LATE CITY EDITION
U. S. Weather Bureau Report (Page 58) forecasts:
Cloudy, windy, chance of showers today and tonight. Cold tomorrow.
Temp. Range: 62—54; yesterday: 64—51.

VOL. CXIII...No. 38,654. © 1963 by The New York Times Company. Times Square, New York 36, N. Y.

NEW YORK, SATURDAY, NOVEMBER 23, 1963.

TEN CENTS

KENNEDY IS KILLED BY SNIPER AS HE RIDES IN CAR IN DALLAS; JOHNSON SWORN IN ON PLANE

TEXAN ASKS UNITY

Congressional Chiefs of Both Parties Promise Aid

By FELIX BELAIR Jr.
Special to The New York Times

WASHINGTON, Nov. 22 — Lyndon B. Johnson returned to a stunned capital shortly after 6 P.M. today to assume the duties of the Presidency.

The new President asked for and received from Congressional leaders of both parties their "united support in the face of the tragedy which has befallen our country." He said it was "more essential that ever before that this country be united."

Partisan differences disappeared in the chorus of assurances with which the Congressional leaders responded.

Mr. Johnson was described by those who talked with him as "stunned and shaken" by the assassination of President Kennedy.

Discusses U.S. Security

But he moved quickly from problems of national security and foreign policy to funeral arrangements for Mr. Kennedy.

Across the street from the West Wing of the White House, the President conferred with officials in his old Vice-Presidential offices in the Executive Office Building.

Senator George A. Smathers, Democrat of Florida, a personal friend of the dead President, was one of those who described Mr. Johnson as shaken.

"Everyone is," he added. "But the President is the more so because he was right there when the tragedy occurred."

While flying to Washington aboard the Presidential plane, Mr. Johnson arranged for a meeting with Cabinet members to ask that they remain at their posts. He made the same request of staff members in the executive offices.

Meets With Harriman

"Calm and contained" was the way Senator J. W. Fulbright described the President's manner during a discussion of foreign-policy matters with Under Secretary of State W. Averell Harriman. The Arkansas Senator said the President had been working on "what looked like a statement"—presumably an assurance of continuity of the nation's foreign policy.

The new President's first conference was aboard the helicopter that flew him the 15 miles from Andrews Air Force Base

Continued on Page 11, Column 3

Henry Grossman

"This is a sad time for all people. We have suffered a loss that cannot be weighed. For me it is a deep personal tragedy. I know the world shares the sorrow that Mrs. Kennedy and her family bear. I will do my best. That is all I can do. I ask for your help —and God's."—President Lyndon Baines Johnson.

PRESIDENT'S BODY WILL LIE IN STATE

Funeral Mass to Be Monday in Capital After Homage Is Paid by Public

By JACK RAYMOND
Special to The New York Times

WASHINGTON, Nov. 22 — The body of John F. Kennedy will lie in state in the rotunda of the Capitol Sunday and then will be borne to St. Matthew's Roman Catholic Cathedral for a pontifical requiem mass at noon Monday.

The President's body was returned to Washington tonight in the same Air Force jet that carried him to Texas. The airliner, with Mrs. Kennedy, the new President, Lyndon B. Johnson, and Mrs. Johnson aboard, arrived at Andrews Air Force Base at 5:58 P.M.

It was announced later that Mr. Kennedy's body would lie in the White House tomorrow from 10 A.M. to 6 P.M., during which time Government and diplomatic officials will pay their respects.

The coffin will be taken from the White House to the Capitol rotunda Sunday morning, where

Continued on Page 9, Column 3

PARTIES' OUTLOOK FOR '64 CONFUSED

Republican Prospects Rise —Johnson Faces Possible Fight Against Liberals

By WARREN WEAVER Jr.
Special to The New York Times

WASHINGTON, Nov. 22 — President Kennedy's assassination threw the American political scene into turmoil today.

It removed at a single blow the man who would have been renominated for a second term in the White House by acclamation nine months from now.

It elevated into the Presidency and the leadership of the Democratic party an older, more conservative man still emerging from his Southern heritage.

It increased immeasurably for the leaders of the Republican party prospects of electing a President next November.

The shock of the President's death stilled the official voices of politics in the capital, But so profound was the potential effect on the government and leadership that private consideration could not be silenced.

Before, there had been facts and strong probabilities on the

Continued on Page 6, Column 3

LEFTIST ACCUSED

Figure in a Pro-Castro Group Is Charged— Policeman Slain

By GLADWIN HILL
Special to The New York Times

DALLAS, Tex., Nov. 22—The Dallas police and Federal officers issued a charge of murder late tonight in the assassination of President Kennedy.

The accused is Lee Harvey Oswald, a 24-year-old former marine, who went to live in the Soviet Union in 1959 and returned to Texas last year.

Capt. Will Fritz, head of the Dallas police homicide bureau, identified Oswald as an adherent of the left-wing Fair Play for Cuba Committee.

Oswald was arrested about two hours after the shooting, in a movie theater three miles away, shortly after he allegedly shot and killed a policeman on a street nearby.

He was arraigned tonight on a charge of murdering the police officer. The charge related to the Kennedy killing was made later.

Appears in Line-Up

After the arraignment, the suspect, a slight, dark-haired man, was taken downstairs to appear in a line-up, presumably before witnesses of the Kennedy assassination.

While being escorted, handcuffed, through a police building corridor, he shouted: "I haven't shot anybody."

Captain Fritz said Oswald was employed—the exact job was unknown—at the Texas School Book Depository, a warehouse from which the assassin's bullets came. The captain said some witnesses had placed Oswald in the building at the time of the assassination.

The sequence of events leading to his arrest was as follows:

As a citywide manhunt began during the hour following the assassination, an unidentified man notified police headquarters, over a police-car radio, that the car's officer had been

Continued on Page 4, Column 1

NEWS INDEX

John Fitzgerald Kennedy
1917-1963

Henry Grossman

Why America Weeps

Kennedy Victim of Violent Streak He Sought to Curb in the Nation

By JAMES RESTON
Special to The New York Times

WASHINGTON, Nov. 22—America wept tonight, not alone for its dead young President, but for itself. The grief was general, for somehow the worst in the nation had prevailed over the best. The indictment extended beyond the assassin, for something in the nation itself, some strain of madness and violence, had destroyed the highest symbol of law and order.

The City Goes Dark

By ROBERT C. DOTY

The center of New York, the restless night city, wore darkness and went in near silence after the murder of President Kennedy last night.

In and around Times Square, the normal, frenetic Friday night pulse slowed as near to a halt as it ever comes. Most legitimate and night theaters, night clubs and dance halls closed their doors and darkened their marquees.

As dusk came, automatic devices turned on the huge, gaudy display signs that normally blot out the night. Then, one by one, the lights blinked out, turning the great carnival strip into what was almost a mourning band.

There were exceptions, of course. Restaurants, by decision of their trade associations, remained lighted and open as a

Continued on Page 5, Column 2

Gov. Connally Shot; Mrs. Kennedy Safe

President Is Struck Down by a Rifle Shot From Building on Motorcade Route— Johnson, Riding Behind, Is Unhurt

By TOM WICKER
Special to The New York Times

DALLAS, Nov. 22—President John Fitzgerald Kennedy was shot and killed by an assassin today.

He died of a wound in the brain caused by a rifle bullet that was fired at him as he was riding through downtown Dallas in a motorcade.

Vice President Lyndon Baines Johnson, who was riding in the third car behind Mr. Kennedy's, was sworn in as the 36th President of the United States 99 minutes after Mr. Kennedy's death.

Mr. Johnson is 55 years old; Mr. Kennedy was 46.

Shortly after the assassination, Lee H. Oswald, described as a one-time defector to the Soviet Union, active in the Fair Play for Cuba Committee, was arrested by the Dallas police. Tonight he was accused of the killing.

Suspect Captured After Scuffle

Oswald, 24 years old, was also accused of slaying a policeman who had approached him in the street. Oswald was subdued after a scuffle with a second policeman in a nearby theater.

The shooting took place at 12:30 P.M., Central standard time (1:30 P.M., New York time). Mr. Kennedy was pronounced dead at 1 P.M. and Mr. Johnson was sworn in at 2:39 P.M.

Mr. Johnson, who was uninjured in the shooting, took his oath in the Presidential jet plane as it stood on the runway at Love Field. The body of the President was aboard. Immediately after the oath-taking, the plane took off for Washington.

Standing beside the new President as Mr. Johnson took the oath of office was Mrs. John F. Kennedy. Her stocking was saturated with her husband's blood.

Gov. John B. Connally Jr. of Texas, who was riding in the same car with Mr. Kennedy, was severely wounded in the chest, ribs and arm. His condition was serious, but not critical.

The killer fired the rifle from a building just off the motorcade route. Mr. Kennedy,

Continued on Page 2,

THE NEW PRESIDENT: Lyndon B. Johnson takes oath before Judge Sarah T. Hughes in plane at Dallas. Mrs. Kennedy and Representative Jack Brooks are at right. To left are Mrs. Johnson and Representative Albert Thomas.

Capt. Cecil Stoughton via United Press International

WHEN THE BULLETS STRUCK: Mrs. Kennedy moving to the aid of the President after he was hit by a sniper yesterday in Dallas. A guard mounts rear bumper. Gov. John B. Connally Jr. of Texas, also in the car, was wounded.

Associated Press

The New York Times.

LATE CITY EDITION
U. S. Weather Bureau Report (Page 38) forecasts:
Sunny and cool today; fair, milder tonight. Cloudy, milder tomorrow.
Temp. Range: 46—32; yesterday: 53—37.

VOL. CXIII..No. 38,656.

© 1963 by The New York Times Company.
Times Square, New York 36, N. Y.

NEW YORK, MONDAY, NOVEMBER 25, 1963.

TEN CENTS

PRESIDENT'S ASSASSIN SHOT TO DEATH IN JAIL CORRIDOR BY A DALLAS CITIZEN; GRIEVING THRONGS VIEW KENNEDY BIER

FAREWELL: Kneeling with her mother at John Fitzgerald Kennedy's coffin in the Capitol, Caroline touches the flag

Associated Press Wirephoto

Mrs. Kennedy Leads Public Mourning

By MARJORIE HUNTER
Special to The New York Times

WASHINGTON, Nov. 24 — Mrs. John F. Kennedy, firmly holding the hands of her two children, followed the coffin bearing the body of her husband as it left the White House today for the last time.

Her eyes swollen, she moved quietly to the edge of the steps of the North Portico and paused to watch the coffin placed in the caisson by military bearers.

Her son, John Jr., tugged at her hand and pointed to a black, riderless horse, part of the ceremonial procession. She leaned down and spoke to him.

Mrs. Kennedy wore a simple black suit and black lace mantilla. John Jr., who will be 3 years old tomorrow, and Caroline, who will be 6 on Wednesday, wore similar pale blue coats, white anklets and red shoes.

As the three stood there framed against the black-draped doorway, there was an eerie silence. It was broken only by the occasional sound of hoofs of the restless gray horses that were to pull the caisson up Pennsylvania Avenue to the Capitol.

Later, after the tributes had been spoken, Mrs. Kennedy walked slowly to the coffin, touched it with her fingertips, knelt and kissed it. Caroline was by her side. They were rejoined by John Jr. at the door.

Shortly after 9 o'clock tonight Mrs. Kennedy returned to the Capitol and again kneeled before the coffin and kissed it.

Mrs. Kennedy walked into the Rotunda on the arm of her husband's brother, Robert, who stopped at the rope holding

Still holding the hands of her children, Mrs. Kennedy followed the flag-draped coffin into the Capitol Rotunda. She

stared straight ahead as the coffin was placed on the catafalque, a simple funeral bier draped in black broadcloth.

John Jr., wide-eyed and bewildered, was restless. Clutching a tiny flag, he was led away by a military aide.

Continued on Page 2, Column 8

BUSINESS OF CITY WILL HALT TODAY

Mayor Says Only Essential Services Will Be Provided

Changes in events here are listed on Page 9.

By LEONARD INGALLS

Normal public, business and social activity in the city will be almost completely suspended today out of respect for President Kennedy.

Mayor Wagner announced yesterday that the city would continue in full mourning throughout the day. Only essential city services will be maintained, he said.

"Those city employes not engaged in activities imperative to the health, safety and welfare of our citizens are to be released from duty and their offices closed through Monday," Mr. Wagner said at City Hall.

Proclamation of the day as a legal holiday by Governor Rockefeller in observance of Mr. Kennedy's funeral permits banks and other institutions to close.

Classes at schools and colleges will be suspended. Department stores and specialty shops will be shut. Securities exchanges and commodity markets will not operate. Most places of entertainment will be closed. There will be no deliveries of mail and post offices will be shut.

Special memorial services for the murdered President have been scheduled at churches and synagogues.

At St. Patrick's Cathedral

Continued on Page 9, Column 1

Pope Paul Warns That Hate and Evil Imperil Civil Order

Special to The New York Times

ROME, Nov. 24 — Pope Paul VI, alluding to the assassination of President Kennedy, said today that it showed how much "capacity for hatred and evil still remains in the world."

Without mentioning Mr. Kennedy by name, the Pontiff spoke of "the crime that has aroused in these days the deploration of the whole world." He said it illustrated "how great the threat to civil order and peace still is."

The Pope was addressing thousands of people gathered in St. Peter's Square for his usual Sunday-noon benediction.

"We cannot, at this moment of prayer together, take our thoughts from the crime that has aroused in these days the deploration of the whole world," he said.

"After dwelling upon the man who is no longer with us and after comforting those who still live in mourning and grief, our thoughts show us how much the capacity for hatred and evil yet remains in the world, how great the threat to civil order and peace still is, and how great is the need for the grace of

Continued on Page 4, Column 7

JOHNSON AFFIRMS AIMS IN VIETNAM

Retains Kennedy's Policy of Aiding War on Reds — Lodge Briefs President

By E. W. KENWORTHY

WASHINGTON, Nov. 24 — President Johnson reaffirmed today the policy objectives of his predecessor regarding South Vietnam. He called upon all Government agencies to support that policy with full unity of purpose.

This was disclosed by White House sources after a meeting between President Johnson and Henry Cabot Lodge, United States Ambassador to South Vietnam.

The meeting lasted nearly an hour. It was described as being devoted to a full review of the conclusions reached by participants in a strategy conference on South Vietnam held in Honolulu last Wednesday.

In another move today that emphasized the President's desire to convey at home and abroad the impression of continuity, Mr. Johnson asked all members of the White House staff to remain at their jobs. This was announced by Pierre Salinger, White House press secretary.

Some Expected to Leave

Mr. Salinger said the President would leave up to the officials involved how long they wished to arrive him.

Inevitably some of these officials — especially those from the universities and foundations — will decide to leave their posts after an interval.

But the President's request today would seem to insure that during the difficult days of adjustment and transition he would continue to have the benefit of the experience of key policy figures.

Attending the meeting between the President and Ambassador Lodge today were Secretary of State Dean Rusk, Secretary of Defense Robert S. McNamara, Under Secretary of State George W. Ball, John A. McCone, director of the Central Intelligence Agency, and McGeorge Bundy, special assistant to the President for national security affairs.

Secretaries Rusk and McNamara, Ambassador Lodge and Mr. Bundy all took part in the Honolulu conference.

As a result of the meeting, White House informants said, President Johnson laid down a

Continued on Page 5, Column 1

JOHNSON SCORED BY CHINESE REDS

Views Called 'Reactionary' —Taiwan Aid Attacked

By United Press International

TOKYO, Nov. 24 — Communist China bitterly criticized President Johnson today and termed him a supporter of the late President Kennedy's "trickery policy."

"Since the emergence of the Kennedy regime," the Chinese Communist press agency Hsinhua said, "Johnson has positively supported various reactionary policies of the Kennedy Administration and participated in formulating and promoting such policies.

"Johnson has supported Kennedy's trickery policy and has called for the maintenance of such a policy in a series of his speeches."

The Chinese Communists reported the assassination of President Kennedy in a four-paragraph dispatch eight hours after it occurred. But they made no comment.

Hsinhua said Mr. Johnson "was one of the central figures in the Kennedy Government and has made frequent trips abroad."

The Chinese statement added that Mr. Johnson believed "the United States, in making two-faced antirevolutionary policies, must maintain a strong position on the basis of strong force."

"He also looks toward Cuba with animosity and has called for the elimination of the Cuban revolutionary Government," it

Continued on Page 7, Column 6

NEWS INDEX

CROWD IS HUSHED

Mourners at Capitol File Past the Coffin Far Into the Night

Texts of eulogies spoken in Washington, Page 4.

By TOM WICKER
Special to The New York Times

WASHINGTON, Monday, Nov. 25—Thousands of sorrowing Americans filed past John Fitzgerald Kennedy's bier in the Great Rotunda of the United States Capitol yesterday and early today.

Mr. Kennedy's body lay in state in the center of the vast, stone-floored chamber. Long after midnight the silent procession of mourners continued.

Some wept. All were hushed. As the two lines moved in a large circle around either side of the flag-covered coffin, almost the only sounds were the shuffle of feet and the quiet voices of policemen urging the people to "keep moving, keep moving right along."

By 2:45 A. M. today 115,000 persons had passed the bier.

Yesterday afternoon a crowd estimated at 300,000 lined Pennsylvania and Constitution Avenues to watch the passage of the caisson bearing the body of the 35th President of the United States, slain in the 47th year of his life by an assassin's bullet.

A Riderless Horse

Behind the caisson, following military tradition, came a riderless bay gelding, with a pair of military boots reversed in the silver stirrups.

The horse was Sardar, the thoroughbred that belongs to Mrs. John F. Kennedy.

Mrs. Kennedy, her two children, President and Mrs. Johnson and Mr. Kennedy's brother, Attorney General Robert F. Kennedy, rode in the first car of a 10-car procession that followed the caisson.

The procession moved at a funeral pace, to the sound of muffled drums, from the White House to Pennsylvania Avenue. It was a journey Mr. Kennedy had made formally four times.

At the Capitol, brief ceremonies of eulogy were held in the Rotunda before the admission of the waiting thousands who swarmed over the plaza and stretched in a long line up East Capitol Street.

At the conclusion of the cere-

Continued on Page 2, Column 1

World's Leaders to Attend Requiem Today in Capital

Mrs. Kennedy Will Walk Behind the Caisson to Mass at Cathedral

By JACK RAYMOND
Special to The New York Times

WASHINGTON, Nov. 24 — Mrs. John F. Kennedy, joined by world and national leaders, will walk behind the horse-drawn caisson that bears her husband's body from the White House to St. Matthew's Roman Catholic Cathedral tomorrow.

Following a requiem mass, John Fitzgerald Kennedy, the 35th President of the United States, will be escorted in a solemn state procession to Arlington National Cemetery to be buried with military honors.

The gravesite, on a beautiful grassy knoll, provides a sweeping view of the capital city and it is itself easily in view from the Memorial Bridge approach to the national burial ground.

The state funeral procession will begin at 10:30 A.M. at the Capitol, where the closed, flag-draped coffin of the President

Continued on Page 6, Column 8

Officials of Nearly 100 Lands in U.S.—They Will Meet Johnson

By MAX FRANKEL
Special to The New York Times

WASHINGTON, Nov. 24 — An emperor, a king, a queen, princes, presidents, premiers and ministers from every continent converged on Washington this evening to pay final tribute to President Kennedy and to make the acquaintance of President Johnson.

List of leaders expected at the funeral, Page 6.

Representing nearly 100 nations, the foreign dignitaries will include the largest assembly of ruling statesmen ever gathered in the United States for any event.

Their arrival here, through the night, virtually overwhelmed an already tense and overburdened capital. Nonetheless, each visitor received the protocol deference and police protection of more normal

Continued on Page 6, Column 1

Millions of Viewers See Oswald Killing On 2 TV Networks

By JACK GOULD

The fatal shooting of Lee H. Oswald, who was held as the assassin of President Kennedy, was seen as it occurred yesterday by millions of television viewers.

The National Broadcasting Company telecast the dramatic happening live. Less than a minute later the Columbia Broadcasting System telecast it by means of tape, made as the shooting occurred.

C. B. S. headquarters recorded the pictures from Dallas as they were received here over a closed circuit. Officials, upon seeing the contents of the Dallas relay, put the tape out over the network instantly.

The incident marked the first time in 15 years of television around the globe that a real-life homicide had occurred in front of live cameras. The closest parallel occurred in October, 1960, when Inejiro Asanuma, Japanese political leader, was knifed on a public stage in

Continued on Page 10, Column 8

ONE BULLET FIRED

Night-Club Man Who Admired Kennedy Is Oswald's Slayer

By GLADWIN HILL
Special to The New York Times

DALLAS, Nov. 24 — President Kennedy's assassin, Lee Harvey Oswald, was fatally shot by a Dallas night-club operator today as the police started to move him from the city jail to the county jail.

The shooting occurred in the basement of the municipal building at about 11:20 A.M. central standard time (12:20 P.M. New York time).

The assailant, Jack Rubenstein, known as Jack Ruby, lunged from a cluster of newsmen observing the transfer of Oswald from the jail to an armored truck.

Millions of viewers saw the shooting on television.

As the shot rang out, a police detective suddenly recognized Ruby and exclaimed: "Jack, you son of a bitch!"

A murder charge was filed against Ruby by Assistant District Attorney William F. Alexander. Justice of the Peace Pierce McBride ordered him held without bail.

Detectives Flank Him

Oswald was arrested Friday after Mr. Kennedy was shot dead while riding through Dallas in an open car. He was charged with murdering the President and a policeman who was shot a short time later trying to question Oswald.

As the 24-year-old prisoner, flanked by two detectives, stepped onto a basement garage ramp, Ruby thrust a .38-caliber, snub-nose revolver into Oswald's left side and fired a single shot.

The 52-year-old night-club operator, an ardent admirer of President Kennedy and his family, was described as having been distraught.

He spoke with the director of the F.B.I., J. Edgar Hoover, and ordered the redoubled investigation.

The action came as official Washington was showing increasing concern about the entire handling of the aftermath of President Kennedy's assassination.

Officials were convinced that Oswald was the assassin. But their concern was over the public impression of the criminal proceedings.

Tonight they were consider-

Continued on Page 11, Column 3

JOHNSON SPURS OSWALD INQUIRY

President Orders F. B. I. to Check Death — Handling of Case Worries Capital

By ANTHONY LEWIS
Special to The New York Times

WASHINGTON, Nov. 24 — President Johnson directed the Federal Bureau of Investigation tonight to look into "every aspect" of the murder of Lee H. Oswald.

[District Attorney Henry Wade said he understood that the police were looking into the possibility that Oswald had been slain to prevent him from talking, The Associated Press reported. Mr. Wade said that so far no connection between Oswald and Ruby had been established.]

Oswald slumped to the concrete paving, wordlessly clutching his side and writhing with pain.

Oswald apparently lost con-

Continued on Page 10, Column 1

OSWALD IS SHOT: Lee Harvey Oswald cringes as Jack Ruby attacks him at Dallas jail. Policeman is J. R. Leavelle.

Copyright 1963—Dallas Times-Herald and Photographer Bob Jackson, from United Press International Telephoto

The New York Times.

VOL. CXIII.—No. 38,864.
© 1964 by The New York Times Company
Times Square, New York, N.Y. 10036

NEW YORK, SATURDAY, JUNE 20, 1964.

LATE CITY EDITION
U. S. Weather Bureau Report (Page 52) forecasts:
Fair and hot today and tomorrow.
Chance of late showers each day.
Temp. Range: 91—71; yesterday: 80—65.
Temp.-Hum. Index: 80 to 85; yesterday: 74.

TEN CENTS

U.S. STRESSING IT WOULD FIGHT TO DEFEND ASIA

WARNING TO REDS

Commitment to Laos and South Vietnam Called Unlimited

By MAX FRANKEL
Special to The New York Times

WASHINGTON, June 19—The Administration is saying more emphatically each day that North Vietnam and its closest ally, Communist China, must leave their neighbors alone or face a war with the United States.

In the minds of officials here the United States commitment to the security of Southeast Asia is now unlimited and comparable with the commitment to West Berlin.

In diplomatic terms this means the officials think themselves unable to negotiate with anything except the threat of force to persuade the Asian Communists to stop the efforts to "liberate" South Vietnam and Laos.

Thus far, the Administration is not sure that the Asian Communists have accurately interpreted the warning signals from Washington. It is not sure that its allies in Europe appreciate the gravity of the United States commitment. And it is not sure that the American people understand the reasons for it.

Decision Publicized

Accordingly, the word is being passed with increasing vigor to the Congress, to the Washington press corps and to the Western allies.

These official assertions suggest that the decision to deny Southeast Asia to Communism was, in effect, taken a long time ago through circumstance and a cumulative series of lesser decisions.

The view that Laos can somehow be handled separately from South Vietnam has been abandoned. The earlier emphasis on limited involvement in South Vietnam's guerrilla warfare has been replaced by unlimited pledges of support for the whole region.

The hope here is that Hanoi and Peking are alert to this hardening of attitudes and that they have been properly forewarned by the less direct as well as public utterances of Administration leaders and, particularly, by the recent involvement of United States military planes in Laos.

Compromise Doubted

The subtleties of the situation have made the Administration reticent to discuss future military moves beyond hints that every violation of past agreements in Southeast Asia and every change in the forms of contest will draw a firm response.

All the comments here stress that the choice between war and peace lies in the hands of the Asian Communists because Washington sees no way of negotiating a compromise. It will not sit down with Peking and Hanoi until recent violations of past agreements for Laos are redressed because it could have no confidence in any new agreement.

To some extent, the Adminis-

Continued on Page 7, Column 1

Yanks Woo Cabbies With 20,000 Tickets

By ROBERT LIPSYTE

The New York Yankees, long lordly and aloof atop baseball's corporate standings, have gone down to the street to wage promotional warfare.

They have given away more than 10,000 reserved tickets worth $25,000 to more than 5,000 city cab drivers, on the sidewalk along Broadway at 50th and 61st Streets in the last two days. Today, they expect to give away 10,000 more.

The Yankees' first mass giveaway program is the latest in a series of gimmicks to figure lagging attendance and combat the Mets at the box office.

"The idea," said Robert O. Fishel, the Yankees' public relations director, "is to make

Continued on Page 15, Column 2

SENATOR KENNEDY HURT IN AIR CRASH; BAYH INJURED, TOO

Both Are in Fair Condition in Massachusetts Hospital —Pilot of Plane Killed

By The Associated Press

SOUTHAMPTON, Mass., Saturday, June 20—Senator Edward M. Kennedy, younger brother of President Kennedy, and Senator Birch Bayh were injured in the crash of a private plane last night while on the way to the Massachusetts Democratic Convention.

The pilot was killed and two other persons were injured. Mr. Kennedy was semiconscious.

Both Senators were reported in fair condition at Cooley Dickinson Hospital in nearby Northampton.

Also injured were Mrs. Bayh, reported in good condition, and Edward Moss of Andover, administrative aide to Mr. Ken-

Associated Press
Senator Edward M. Kennedy

nedy, who was reported in critical condition.

The pilot was identified as Edwin J. Zimny, 48 years old, of Lawrence, a last-minute substitute for the regular Kennedy pilot.

Senator Kennedy, Democrat of Massachusetts, was treated in an emergency room for back and chest injuries. His wife, Joan, visited him after he was transferred to an intensive-care unit.

Senator Bayh, Democrat of Indiana, suffered a hip injury. Mrs. Bayh was reported suffering from shock.

Mr. Kennedy's parents, Mr. and Mrs. Joseph P. Kennedy, who were vacationing at their summer home in Hyannis Port, were not told of the plane crash.

Attorney General Robert F. Kennedy, brother of the Senator, boarded the family plane with an aide and was reported on the way to Boston.

Two Civil Aeronautics Board investigators were sent from

Continued on Page 54, Column 1

North Katanga City Is Seized By Rebels, the Congo Reports

Europeans Flee Albertville, Crossing Lake Tanganyika to Nearby Burundi

By J. ANTHONY LUKAS
Special to The New York Times

LEOPOLDVILLE, the Congo, June 19—Albertville, the capital of North Katanga Province, was reported today to have fallen to anti-Government rebels.

According to messages reaching here, rebels striking south along the shore of Lake Tanganyika entered the city about midday. It is not known whether there was any resistance from Congolese soldiers there.

Many of the city's Europeans have fled in steamers across the lake. At least 150 women and children left on two steamers last night for Bujumbura, the capital of Burundi.

Another steamer, with 350 persons aboard, was scheduled to leave early this afternoon, but it was not whether it got away.

Meanwhile, the United States Embassy here said that two American civilian pilots who had been flying combat missions for the Congolese Army had voluntarily decided to halt the flights. An embassy official said the pilots made their decision after they learned that they might be subject to penalties under United States law.

The embassy spokesman adhered to the official United States position that the two men were "individual Americans on contract to the Congolese Government."

He said the United States Government had neither authorized their contract nor directed their activities here.

Mr. Dearborn and planned to return to the United States soon. However, he said Mr. Coney would answer no other questions.

CIVIL RIGHTS BILL PASSED, 73-27; JOHNSON URGES ALL TO COMPLY; DIRKSEN BERATES GOLDWATER

PRESIDENT'S PLEA

He Declares the Task Now Is to Change Law Into Custom

Special to The New York Times

SAN FRANCISCO, June 19—President Johnson called the Senate passage of his civil rights bill today a "challenge to men of good will in every part of the country to transform the commands of our law into the customs of our land."

Mr. Johnson said it was now the nation's task "to reach beyond the content of the bill to conquer the barriers of poor education, poverty, and squalid housing which are an inheritance of past injustice and an impediment to future advance."

He said that he did not "underestimate the depth of the passions involved in the struggle for racial equality."

But he also spoke of "a large reservoir of goodwill and compassion, of decency and fair play which seeks a vision of justice without violence in the streets."

Johnson Statement

If these forces, the President said, "do not desert the field, if they can be brought to the battle, then the years of trial will be a prelude to the final triumph of a land with liberty and justice for all.'"

The President issued his statement on the rights bill here, while he was beginning a two-day tour of California. The full text of the statement follows:

"Senate passage of the civil rights bill is a major step toward equal opportunities for all Americans. I congratulate Senators of both parties who worked to make passage possible.

"I look forward to the day, which will not be long forthcoming, when the bill becomes law. That will be a milestone in America's progress toward full justice for all her citizens.

"No single act of Congress can, by itself, eliminate discrimination and prejudice, hatred and injustice.

Broad National Consensus

"But this bill goes further to invest the rights of man with the protection of law than any legislation in this century.

"First, it will provide a carefully designed code to test and enforce the right of every American to go to school, to get a job, to vote, and to pursue his life unhampered by the barriers of racial discrimination.

"Second, it will, in itself, help educate all Americans to their responsibility to give equal treatment to their fellow citizens.

"Third, it will enlist one of the most powerful moral forces of American society on the side of civil rights—the moral obligation to respect and obey the law of the land.

"Fourth, and perhaps most important, this bill is a renewal and a re-enforcement, a symbol and a strengthening of that abiding commitment to human dignity and the equality of man which has been the guid-

Continued on Page 11, Column 3

United Press International Telephoto
ON HAND FOR THE VOTE: Visitors waiting outside the Capitol yesterday for admittance to the Senate Chamber, before the vote on the civil rights bill was registered.

ARIZONAN TARGET OF G.O.P. LEADER

Illinoisan, in Speech on the Senate Floor, Scores View Bill Is Unconstitutional

By ANTHONY LEWIS
Special to The New York Times

WASHINGTON, June 19—The Republican leader in the Senate, Everett McKinley Dirksen of Illinois, closed the civil rights debate tonight with a biting attack on his party's leading Presidential prospect, Senator Barry Goldwater.

Senator Goldwater's announced opposition to the bill brought on the attack. He said yesterday that he could not "in good conscience" vote for the bill because he thought it was "unconstitutional" and would lead to a "police state."

Earlier, it was reported that former President Dwight D. Eisenhower had indicated to Mr Goldwater that the general would not hold a negative vote on the bill against the Arizonan.

On the floor of the Senate, Mr. Dirksen ridiculed the Goldwater constitutional argument and moral position.

Looking often at Senator Goldwater, though never mentioning him by name, Mr. Dirksen in effect challenged the likely nominee of his party on what may be the chief issue at the Republican National Convention next month.

Dirksen Cites Legislation

First, Senator Dirksen mentioned many past pieces of legislation that had first been denounced as "unconstitutional." He listed the child labor prohibition, the Pure Food and Drug Act, the Minimum Wage Law and Social Security.

"It required no constitutional amendment," Senator Dirksen said, "to bring about all these forward thrusts in the interests of the people.

"It leads me to one conclusion: in the history of mankind, there is an inexorable moral force that moves us forward.

"No matter the resistance of people who do not fully understand, it will not be denied."

At this point, Senator Dirksen turned and looked directly at Senator Goldwater, who sat at his desk at the side of the chamber. Thrusting his right arm in Senator Goldwater's direction, he said:

"Utter all the extreme opin-

Continued on Page 11, Column 6

Erhard Bars Visit To the Soviet Union

Special to The New York Times

BONN, June 19 — Chancellor Ludwig Erhard turned down today an unofficial but urgent Soviet invitation to go to Moscow for an attempt at improving Soviet-West German relations.

He suggested instead that the Soviet Premier ask for an official invitation to Bonn if he thought the trip would be worthwhile.

At his first news conference here in six months, Dr. Erhard carefully held open the door for an eventual encounter with Premier Khrushchev while dashing cold water on the prospects of settling soon any of the fundamental questions that divide Bonn and Moscow.

As he spoke, Bonn's Western allies were putting the final

Continued on Page 2, Column 4

Region's Reaction Varied

By United Press International

ATLANTA, June 19 — Deep South politicians and businessmen lashed out angrily at passage of the civil rights bill today and an elderly Negro said, "I'll believe it when I see it."

There was little indication that the Senate's action would reduce the number of demonstrations in the immediate future.

James L. Farmer, national director of the Congress of Racial Equality, said that CORE would press for implementation and enforcement of the bill's provisions.

"There will be no breathing spell on demonstrations," Mr. Farmer said. "We breathe easier when the pressure is on.

"The passage of the civil rights bill may well be the single most important act of our Congress in several decades," Mr. Farmer said. "It gives hope to Negroes that the American people and Government mean to redeem the promises of the Declaration of Independence and the Emancipation Proclamation."

Mr. Farmer also saw the bill

Continued on Page 12, Column 6

JOHNSON IS FIRM

Vows in California to Oppose Violators of Freedom in World

By TOM WICKER
Special to The New York Times

SAN FRANCISCO, June 19—President Johnson promised tonight to open an "offensive in the pursuit of peace" based on an overwhelming military power that "makes it possible to seek agreement without fearing loss of liberty."

The President, addressing an audience of nearly 2,500 at a Democratic party fund-raising dinner, also pledged stern American opposition to "those who believe they can violate their neighbor's borders and steal their neighbor's freedom."

At the end of a day in California during which he gave several indications that he expected to be President for at least four more years, Mr. Johnson said he wanted to double the size of the Peace Corps, pursue what he called the "great society" with "the vision and value of pioneers" and achieve "full equality for all our people."

Earlier in the day, after an enthusiastic welcome from more than 300,000 San Franciscans who lined Market Street to see his motorcade, the President came as near as he ever has to predicting his election in November.

Predicts the Good Life

"A Government which can get things done and knows where it is going," he said, is "the kind of Government you have had for the past four years—and that is the kind of Government you are going to get for the next four years."

Mr. Johnson's remarks were made at the dedication of a new Federal office building in downtown San Francisco. Before he came here, he also spoke at Edwards Air Force Base in the Mojave Desert and broke ground for a new Oakland Bay area rapid transit system at ceremonies in Concord.

It was not until tonight, when he attended the $100-a-plate fund-raising dinner, that Mr. Johnson played an openly political role.

At every stop he voiced his prophecies of the good life for every American, promising Californians the lion's share.

At the party dinner, he shifted his emphasis somewhat, detailing the increases since 1960 in American military might. He declared:

"We have used that strength not to intimidate others, but to

Continued on Page 6, Column 4

ACTION BY SENATE

Revised Measure Now Goes Back to House for Concurrence

By E. W. KENWORTHY
Special to The New York Times

WASHINGTON, June 19 — The Senate passed the civil rights bill today by a vote of 73 to 27.

The final roll-call came at 7:40 P.M. on the 83d day of debate, nine days after closure was invoked.

Voting for the bill were 46 Democrats and 27 Republicans. Voting against it were 21 Democrats and six Republicans. Except for Senator Robert C. Byrd of West Virginia, all the Democratic votes against the bill came from Southerners.

Senator Barry Goldwater of Arizona voted against the bill, as he said yesterday he would. The five other Republicans opposing it all support Mr. Goldwater's candidacy for the Republican Presidential nomination.

They were Bourke B. Hickenlooper of Iowa, chairman of the Senate Republican Policy Committee; Norris Cotton of New Hampshire, Edwin L. Mechem of New Mexico, Milward L. Simpson of Wyoming and John G. Tower of Texas.

2 Pledge Acceptance

The bill will now go back to the House for concurrence in the changes that the Senate made in the measure the House passed last Feb. 10 by a vote of 290 to 130.

Tonight, Representatives Emanuel Celler, Democrat of New York, and William M. McCulloch, Republican of Ohio, who are the chairman and ranking minority member of the House Judiciary Committee, said that they would accept the Senate version of the bill.

"We believe that the House membership will take the same position," they said.

With the support of these two men, who were responsible for the House bill, acceptance of the Senate bill in the House is assured.

President Johnson hopes to have the bill on his desk by July 3 at the latest so that he can sign it on the Fourth of July.

Powers of the Bill

The bill passed by the Senate outlaws discrimination in places of public accommodation, publicly owned facilities, employment and union membership and Federally aided programs. It gives the Attorney General new powers to speed school desegregation and enforce the Negro's right to vote.

The Senate bill differs from the House measure chiefly in giving states and local communities more scope and time to deal with complaints of discrimination in hiring and public accommodations. It allows the Attorney General to initiate suits in these areas where he finds a "pattern" of discrimination, but does not permit him, as did the House bill, to file suits on behalf of individuals.

After the roll-call, several thousand people gathered in the plaza before the floodlit Capitol to applaud the Senate Democratic leader, Mike Mansfield of Montana, and the Republican leader, Everett McKinley Dirksen of Illinois. Mr. Dirksen was instrumental in shaping the compromise that the Senate passed.

Burke Marshall, the Justice Department's civil rights chief, said after the bill was passed tonight that the department would move promptly to enforce the measure.

"I think there is going to be compliance with this bill," Mr. Marshall said. "That's the first thing."

"But where there is a pattern

Continued on Page 10, Column 1

Rights Bill Roll-Call Vote

By The Associated Press

WASHINGTON, June 19—Following is the 73-27 vote by which the Senate passed the civil rights bill tonight:

FOR PASSAGE—73

Democrats—46

Anderson (N.M.)	Hayden (Ariz.)	Monroney (Okla.)
Bartlett (Alaska)	Humphrey (Minn.)	Morse (Ore.)
Bayh (Ind.)	Inouye (Hawaii)	Moss (Utah)
Brewster (Md.)	Jackson (Wash.)	Muskie (Me.)
Bible (Nev.)	Kennedy (Mass.)	Nelson (Wis.)
Burdick (N.D.)	Lausche (Ohio)	Neuberger (Ore.)
Cannon (Nev.)	Long (Mo.)	Pastore (R.I.)
Church (Idaho)	Magnuson (Wash.)	Pell (R.I.)
Clark (Pa.)	Mansfield (Mont.)	Proxmire (Wis.)
Dodd (Conn.)	McCarthy (Minn.)	Randolph (W. Va.)
Douglas (Ill.)	McGee (Wyo.)	Ribicoff (Conn.)
Edmondson (Okla.)	McGovern (S.D.)	Symington (Mo.)
Engle (Calif.)	McIntyre (N.H.)	Williams (N. J.)
Gruening (Alaska)	McNamara (Mich.)	Yarborough (Tex.)
Hart (Mich.)	Metcalf (Mont.)	Young (Ohio)
Hartke (Ind.)		

Republicans—27

Aiken (Vt.)	Dirksen (Ill.)	Morton (Ky.)
Allott (Colo.)	Dominick (Colo.)	Mundt (S. D.)
Beall (Md.)	Fong (Hawaii)	Pearson (Kan.)
Bennett (Utah)	Hruska (Neb.)	Prouty (Vt.)
Boggs (Del.)	Javits (N. Y.)	Saltonstall (Mass.)
Carlson (Kan.)	Jordan (Idaho)	Scott (Pa.)
Case (N. J.)	Keating (N. Y.)	Smith (Me.)
Cooper (Ky.)	Kuchel (Calif.)	Williams (Del.)
Curtis (Neb.)	Miller (Iowa)	Young (N. D.)

AGAINST PASSAGE—27

Democrats—21

Byrd (Va.)	Hill (Ala.)	Russell (Ga.)
Byrd (W. Va.)	Holland (Fla.)	Smathers (Fla.)
Eastland (Miss.)	Johnston (S. C.)	Sparkman (Ala.)
Ellender (La.)	Jordan (N. C.)	Stennis (Miss.)
Ervin (N. C.)	Long (La.)	Talmadge (Ga.)
Fulbright (Ark.)	McClellan (Ark.)	Thurmond (S.C.)
Gore (Tenn.)	Robertson (Va.)	Walters (Tenn.)

Republicans—6

Cotton (N. H.)	Hickenlooper (Iowa)	Simpson (Wyo.)
Goldwater (Ariz.)	Mechem (N. M.)	Tower (Tex.)

Negro Leaders Hail Passage; Some Southerners Voice Anger

CORE Plans Tests

By MARTIN ARNOLD

Leaders of national civil rights groups last night hailed the Senate passage of the civil rights bill, and vowed that the measure would be quickly tested.

There was little indication that the Senate's action would reduce the number of demonstrations in the immediate future.

Gov. George C. Wallace of Alabama declared that "this is a sad day for individual freedom and liberty," but a Chattanooga housewife said, "I firmly believe in it."

Reaction differed sharply between stanchly segregationist areas and areas where there has been desegregation.

Many Negroes approached on the streets in the South had little, if any comment.

"I just don't know much about it. I'm afraid to say," said a Negro in Nashville.

"It is good. I am glad," said George Thomson, a 40-year-old Negro cab driver in Montgomery, Ala.

Jefferson Johnson, an elderly Negro selling ice cream on a street in Birmingham, Ala. said:

"I'll believe it when I see it. I hope it'll do good, but—well,

Continued on Page 10, Column 4

"All the News That's Fit to Print"

The New York Times.

LATE CITY EDITION
U. S. Weather Bureau Report (Page 48) forecast:
Sunny and pleasant today; clear, cool tonight. Sunny tomorrow.
Temp. Range: 82—62; yesterday: 81—62.
Temp.-Hum. Index: high 60's; yesterday: 71.

VOL. CXIII..No. 38,906.
© 1964 by The New York Times Company
Times Square, New York, N. Y. 10036

NEW YORK, SATURDAY, AUGUST 1, 1964.

TEN CENTS

RANGER TAKES CLOSE-UP MOON PHOTOS REVEALING CRATERS ONLY 3 FEET WIDE; DATA GAINED ON LANDING SITE FOR MAN

Associated Press Wirephoto

THREE MILES FROM THE MOON: This view of lunar surface was transmitted by the Ranger 7 spacecraft 3.2 seconds before it crashed. The lens gridmarks are scale references to calibrate amount of distortion. Smallest craters shown are about 30 feet in diameter and about 10 feet in depth.

1,000 FEET FROM THE MOON: Upper photo was the last. At right it merges into blur caused by static after the Ranger 7 crashed. Below, photo taken from 3,000 feet.

U.S. STEEL WEIGHS MIDTOWN PROJECT

$100 Million Industrial and Housing Complex May Be Built Above Rail Yard

By ROBERT E. BEDINGFIELD

The United States Steel Corporation has acquired the air rights over a 40-acre railroad yard in mid-Manhattan and is considering erecting a $100 million housing and industrial complex over the site.

U.S. Steel's board of directors has approved the purchase of Webb & Knapp's lease of the air rights over the New York Central Railroad's freight yard that lies between West 30th and West 37th Streets and extends from 10th to 12th Avenue.

Webb & Knapp realized about $7 million on the deal.

It is understood that the plan being considered calls for the construction of nine apartment buildings of about 30 stories each that would provide middle-income housing for 12,000 families. The project also envisages numerous adjoining industrial buildings of several stories each.

Plan Still Studied

Last night a spokesman for U.S. Steel confirmed that the directors had authorized the acquisition of the air rights from Webb & Knapp.

He said, however, that no definite plan had yet been decided for utilization of the area. If the corporation decides to go ahead with the proposed housing development, he added, it would be for the purpose of demonstrating the company's contention that steel is useful as a prime material in middle-income housing.

Webb & Knapp has held a leasehold on the air rights to the part of the Central yard that lies between West 30th and West 37th Streets and extends from 11th to 12th Avenue and West 30th to West 33d Street between 10th and 11th Avenues.

Webb & Knapp since Dec. 15, 1961, has held a leasehold on the air rights to the part of the Central yard that lies between West 30th and West 37th Streets and extends from 11th to 12th Avenue and West 30th to West 33d Street between 10th and 11th Avenues.

Webb & Knapp will net $3 million on the deal since $4 million of the proceeds will be applied to its repayment of a note of that amount owed the steel company.

The proposed U.S. Steel plans

Continued on Page 34, Column 4

Wagner Rejects Demands For Civilian Police Board

By R. W. APPLE Jr.

Mayor Wagner refused yesterday to appoint an independent civilian police review board sought by civil rights leaders.

In a long statement released at City Hall, the Mayor omitted any mention of another key demand of Negro leaders—the suspension of Police Lieut. Thomas R. Gilligan, who shot and killed a 15-year-old Negro on the East Side on July 16.

Instead, Mr. Wagner proposed a seven-point program whose main thrust was economic.

Text of Wagner's statement is printed on Page 11.

M'KESSON TO CUT ANTIBIOTIC PRICE

Plans to Sell Tetracycline at Third of Present Cost— Pfizer Says It Will Sue

By MARTIN ARNOLD

The nation's largest wholesale drug distributor announced yesterday that it would manufacture and sell tetracycline at about one-third the price at which it is sold by other manufacturers in the United States.

Tetracycline is a broad-spectrum antibiotic that is effective against a variety of bacterial infections. Yearly sales in the country total about $100 million, or about a third of the total sale of antibiotics.

The announcement was made by McKesson & Robbins, which said that it would offer pills for about 6 cents each wholesale, or about $6 for 100 250-milligram tablets. A spokesman for the company said that other drug concerns that manufacture tetracycline in the United States sell it for "slightly more than $17 a hundred tablets wholesale."

Chas. Pfizer & Co., one of the discoverers of tetracycline, immediately announced that it would file suit against McKesson & Robbins for patent infringement.

There are a number of small distributing concerns that buy tetracycline abroad, notably in Italy, and sell it for a low price here.

The importance of the McKesson & Robbins move, observers point out, is that the company's product will be American made and therefore, justifiably or not, druggists and doctors will be less hesitant

Continued on Page 24, Column 6

calling for the creation of about 1,500 temporary and permanent city jobs for unemployed young people.

The Mayor also set up a committee to review the findings of Deputy Mayor Edward F. Cavanagh Jr., who had been directed earlier to review the actions of the Police Department's review board.

King Voices Regret

Mr. Wagner's statement was his first since he began last Monday a series of conversations with the Rev. Dr. Martin Luther King Jr., president of the Southern Christian Leadership Conference, following racial riots here two weeks ago.

Dr. King said in a telephone interview from Atlanta that he was "very sorry" the Mayor had not ordered the creation of an independent board to evaluate allegations of police brutality. He said he had pressed the issue again and again during his talks with Mr. Wagner.

L. Joseph Overton, president of the Unity Council of Harlem Organizations, condemned the Mayor's actions and demanded again the creation of a review board composed of persons associated with neither the city government nor the police.

"I believe the Mayor has made my position untenable," Mr. Overton said. "He has made it virtually impossible for me to guarantee continued peace on the streets of Harlem."

Mr. Overton's organization was set up in an attempt to restore order in Harlem after the riots touched off by the Gilligan incident. The council was insisted that only the creation of a review board would solve the city's racial crisis.

Police Commissioner Michael

Continued on Page 11, Column 5

PAKISTAN ACCEPTS LOAN FROM CHINA

$60 Million, Interest Free, to Be Used for Imports of Industrial Goods

Special to The New York Times

KARACHI, Pakistan, July 31 — Pakistan announced today that she would accept a "generous offer" by Communist China of a $60 million long-term, interest-free loan.

It is the first loan offered by Peking to Pakistan, which is allied with the West in the Central Treaty Organization and the Southeast Asia Treaty Organization, both aimed at preventing Communist aggression.

Commerce Minister Wahid-uz-Zaman, who recently returned from a tour of Communist China, said at a news conference in Rawalpindi that the loan would be used to pay for imports of machinery, cement and sugar mills.

Mr. Zaman said the Chinese Government would not even place a service charge on the loan.

United States loans offered to Pakistan are repayable in United States dollars in 40 years, including a 10-year grace period during which no payment is

Continued on Page 3, Column 2

Johnson Is Said to Have Asked Kennedy to Manage Campaign

Offer Being Considered

By The Associated Press

WASHINGTON, Saturday, Aug. 1—President Johnson has asked Attorney General Robert F. Kennedy to manage his Presidential campaign, informed sources said today.

They said the offer was made Wednesday at the same time Mr. Johnson told Mr. Kennedy he was eliminating him from consideration as a Vice-Presidential candidate.

"I don't want to get into that," Mr. Kennedy said yesterday when asked about reports of the offer before he left for Hyannis Port, Mass., for the weekend. And Kennedy

Continued on Page 6, Column 2

Rusk Post Desired

By CABELL PHILLIPS

Special to The New York Times

WASHINGTON, July 31 — Attorney General Robert F. Kennedy would like to be Secretary of State now that the Vice Presidency has been foreclosed to him.

This is the consensus of several close friends and associates of Mr. Kennedy after President Johnson's statement yesterday that the Attorney General and others of Cabinet rank had been eliminated from consideration for the second spot on the Democratic ticket.

Mr. Kennedy, his friends say, is exerting no pressure to obtain the State Department post. But they say he has let it be

Continued on Page 6, Column 5

Attitude on Soviet Is Upheld by Rusk In Policy Warning

By MAX FRANKEL

Special to The New York Times

WASHINGTON, July 31 — Secretary of State Dean Rusk, in an oblique jab at Senator Barry Goldwater, said today that it was "unrealistic" to think the Soviet Union would "roll over and play dead" if its vital interests were threatened by the United States.

In answering several political questions at a news conference, Mr. Rusk said the Administration had "eminently demonstrated" that it was "just as tough and just as stubborn as is necessary" to protect its vital interests and those of the Western allies.

But he cautioned that the Soviet Union, too, would be stubborn in defending its interests. Therefore, he said, conflicts of interest must be approached with care and persistence to find ways in which the vital parts of the world can live together.

Mr. Rusk did not refer directly to Mr. Goldwater, the Republican candidate for President, or his views, but the Secretary's questioners did, leaving no doubt about the meaning of their inquiries.

Secretary Rusk said he

Continued on Page 2, Column 3

PRESIDENT HAILS NEW LUNAR FEAT

Calls Ranger Flight 'Basic Step' to Manned Landing —Praises Scientists

By JOHN D. POMFRET

Special to The New York Times

WASHINGTON, July 31 — President Johnson congratulated today the scientists and technicians responsible for the successful flight of Ranger 7 to the moon.

The President was in the White House living quarters when Dr. William H. Pickering, director of the Jet Propulsion Laboratory at Pasadena, Calif., telephoned to inform him that the shot was a success.

The President felicitated Dr. Pickering and Dr. Homer E. Newell, assistant administrator for space science and application of the space agency, then had the White House issue a statement praising those who participated in the flight.

Mr. Johnson called the flight "a basic step forward in our orderly program to assemble the scientific knowledge necessary for man's trip to the moon."

Guide in Planning Trip

"The pictures obtained of the lunar surface should prove extremely useful," the President said, continuing:

"They will be a guide in constructing the lunar excursion module and in planning the trip.

"We shall now be able to better map out our descent route. We'll be able to build our lunar landing equipment with greater certainty and knowledge of the conditions which our astronauts will encounter on the moon.

"I recognize that this great success has come only after a number of failures and partial failures in our efforts to send probes to the moon. This success would spur us on to added effort in the future.

"The fact that our Soviet competitors have had many unpublicized failures to the moon and the planets also confirms the complexity of today's success.

"On behalf of a grateful nation, let me again congratu-

Continued on Page 8, Column 3

Craft Hits Target Area; 4,000 Pictures Sent Back

Details of Lunar Region Seen Thousand Times Clearer Than Before—Feat Hailed as Leap in Knowledge

By RICHARD WITKIN

Special to The New York Times

PASADENA, Calif., July 31—Ranger 7 radioed to earth today the first close-up pictures of the moon—a historic collection of 4,000 pictures one thousand times as clear as anything ever seen through earth-bound telescopes.

Scientists here were hailing the achievement, which exceeded all expectations, as by far the

Text of the news conference will be found on Page 10.

greatest advance in lunar astronomy since Galileo.

They said the pictures not only represented a great leap in man's knowledge of the moon, but also, on a more practical level, lent encouragement that the lunar surface was suitable for Project Apollo's manned lunar landings.

Taken in 17 Minutes

The still pictures were snapped and transmitted in the last 17 minutes before the spacecraft crashed into an area northwest of the Sea of Clouds.

They meant in effect that the 240,000 mile distance to the moon had been shrunk by man's ingenuity to a mere half-mile in terms of what he could see of its topography. They showed craters three feet in diameter and a foot to a foot and a half deep.

The best earthbound telescopes, handicapped by the shimmering mantle of the atmosphere, can shrink the lunar distance only to 500 miles and reveal features no smaller than about one-mile across.

The startling disclosures of what Ranger 7 had wrought were made at a packed news conference here by a team of scientists headed by Dr. Gerard P. Kuiper of the University of Arizona.

The conference, televised nationally, was held in the auditorium of the Jet Propulsion Laboratory of the National Aeronautics Space Administration.

"This is a great day for science," the eminent astronomer

said at the start, "and a great day for the United States.

"What has been achieved is truly remarkable. We have made progress in resolution [clarity of pictures] not by a factor of 10 . . . not by a factor of 100, which would have been remarkable, but by a factor of 1,000."

As a series of ten samples of the Ranger 7 photographs were flashed on a screen, Dr. Kuiper pointed out some of the more interesting features. Among the highlights of his recital and of answers both he and another member of the scientific panel made were these:

¶A few hours' quick study of Ranger 7's massive output had not revealed that there were any totally unforeseen problems on the moon. But the numberless new details opened a region of knowledge that would keep scientists in deep study for three or four years or more.

¶There was evidence that the white rays around some major craters were caused not by light fluffy material tossed up from the moon but by sizable rocks thrown off in the formation of these large craters. The rocks made numerous secondary craters deep enough to represent an extreme hazard for a manned lunar landing in the area. Such areas were to be avoided like poison, Dr. Kuiper said.

¶The tentative impression of the scientific team was that the lunar surface dust or other substance was not thick enough to swallow an astronaut landing craft. Dr. Eugene Shoemaker

Continued on Page 8, Column 1

"All the News That's Fit to Print"

The New York Times.

LATE CITY EDITION
U.S. Weather Bureau Report (Page 66) forecast:
Variable cloudiness today; clear tonight. Fair and cool tomorrow.

Temp. Range: 86—65; yesterday: 81—57.
Temp.-Hum. Index: low 70's; yesterday: 73.

VOL. CXIII—No. 38,910.

© 1964 by The New York Times Company.
Times Square, New York, N.Y. 10036

NEW YORK, WEDNESDAY, AUGUST 5, 1964.

TEN CENTS

U.S. PLANES ATTACK NORTH VIETNAM BASES; PRESIDENT ORDERS 'LIMITED' RETALIATION AFTER COMMUNISTS' PT BOATS RENEW RAIDS

F.B.I. Finds 3 Bodies Believed to Be Rights Workers'

GRAVES AT A DAM

Discovery Is Made in New Earth Mound in Mississippi

By CLAUDE SITTON
Special to The New York Times

JACKSON, Miss., Aug. 4—Bodies believed to be those of three civil rights workers missing since June 21 were found early tonight near Philadelphia, Miss.

Federal Bureau of Investigation agents recovered the bodies from a newly erected earthen dam in a thickly wooded area about six miles southwest of Philadelphia, in east-central Mississippi.

The dam is several hundred yards off State Highway 21, near the Neshoba County fairgrounds.

Fulton Jackson, the county coroner, made a preliminary examination at the scene. The bodies were then sealed in plastic bags and brought by ambulance to the University of Mississippi Medical Center in Jackson, 70 miles to the southwest.

Pledge by Governor

Roy K. Moore, special agent in charge of the Jackson F.B.I. office, said physicians and fingerprint experts would seek to make positive identification and establish the cause of death.

[In Washington, authoritative sources said that President Johnson had telephoned Gov. Paul B. Johnson Jr. of Mississippi after having learned of the discovery of the bodies. However, this could not be confirmed immediately.]

Governor Johnson said in a statement:

"If these are the bodies of the three civil rights workers who have been missing several weeks, the investigative forces of the State of Mississippi will exert every effort to apprehend those who may have been responsible."

Area Searched Earlier

Mr. Johnson said he understood F.B.I. agents had searched the area once before and had noticed the new dam. Later, when they saw that the dam had collected no water despite heavy showers, they returned for a further investigation.

Excavation uncovered the bodies in the fill of the dam, the Governor said.

Sheriff L. A. Rainey, who had just returned from a vacation, visited the scene a short while after the discovery.

The missing men were Michael H. Schwerner, 24 years old, and Andrew Goodman, 20, both white and both from New York City, and James E. Chaney, 21, a Negro of Meridian, Miss.

All three had been taking part in the Mississippi Summer Project, a state-wide civil rights drive, which began on the week

Continued on Page 27, Column 2

Scattered Violence Keeps Jersey City Tense 3d Night

400 Policemen Confine Most of Rioters to 2 Sections—Crowds Watch in Streets Despite Danger

By FRED POWLEDGE
Special to The New York Times

JERSEY CITY, Aug. 4—Scattered violence broke out again here tonight as roving groups of Negroes hurled crude Molotov cocktails in the streets. There was some gunfire but no injuries were reported.

About 400 city policemen contained most of the young rioters to two predominantly Negro neighborhoods. There were at least ⁓⁓ arrests.

Although it was dangerous to be on the streets on this third night of violence, many people watched from sidewalks and front porches as police cars, their red lights flashing, sped from one pocket of violence to another.

On Ocean Avenue the police trained spotlights on the roof of a three-story block of apartments. A man had been seen on the roof, and it was feared that he was armed with a rifle, tire bombs, or both. Yet on the sidewalk below, a woman walked her dog, apparently without concern, through throngs of helmeted policemen. From a front porch across the street, a baby cried.

Since the rioting started Sunday night, more than 30 persons have been injured, two of them with gunshot wounds. None of the wounds was critical. More than three dozen persons have been arrested.

Five hundred more Jersey City policemen stood ready to

Continued on Page 36, Column 1

JOHNSON SEEKING EXTREMISM PLANK

Favors a Stand Against Far Left and Right Without Naming Any Groups

Special to The New York Times

WASHINGTON, Aug. 4—President Johnson wants the Democratic platform to take a stand against extremism of the right and the left, without naming any particular organization.

Mr. Johnson, at the moment, plans to attend the party's national convention in Atlantic City only on Thursday night, Aug. 27, when he is scheduled to make his acceptance speech. But his wish on the platform is likely to be enough to make his views effective.

As yet, however, he has had no detailed discussions with the platform drafters.

The President is also planning to follow a somewhat unusual procedure in having himself placed in nomination. This is to be done by "co-nominators" — Governors Edmund G. Brown of California and John B. Connally Jr. of Texas.

These and other fairly well-advanced plans of the President have been learned from high Democratic sources.

However, on the question of most current interest, Mr. Johnson's choice for a Vice-Presidential candidate, no decision has yet been made.

Senator Hubert H. Humphrey

Continued on Page 14, Column 6

Rockefeller to Join Goldwater's Parley On Campaign Unity

Special to The New York Times

ALBANY, Aug. 4—Governor Rockefeller has accepted the invitation of Senator Goldwater to attend a meeting of Republican Governors at Hershey, Pa., on Aug. 12.

The invitation was extended by the Republican Presidential nominee in telegrams last Saturday to the 16 Republican Governors.

Mr. Rockefeller, who was a candidate for the Presidential nomination until after his defeat in the California primary, June 2, was one of Senator Goldwater's severest critics through the Republican National Convention last month in San Francisco.

Mr. Goldwater has called the Hershey gathering in an effort to promote unity within the Republican party behind his candidacy.

The prospects for success of

Continued on Page 16, Column 1

REDS DRIVEN OFF

Two Torpedo Vessels Believed Sunk in Gulf of Tonkin

By ARNOLD H. LUBASCH

WASHINGTON, Aug. 4—The Defense Department announced tonight that North Vietnamese PT boats made a "deliberate attack" today on two United States destroyers patrolling in international waters in the Gulf of Tonkin off North Vietnam.

The attack came two days after North Vietnamese torpedo boats attacked the Maddox, one of the destroyers in today's incident.

The destroyers and covering carrier-based aircraft fired on the vessels in today's attack, drove them off and apparently sank at least two of them, according to the announcement. The Pentagon said there were no United States casualties or damage.

The attack was made by an "undetermined number of North Vietnamese PT boats" during darkness about 65 miles from the nearest land, the Pentagon reported. It said the attack came at 10:30 P. M., North Vietnamese time, or 10:30 A. M., Washington time.

'Fabrication,' Reds Say

[The North Vietnamese regime said Wednesday that the report of another attack on United States ships was a "fabrication."]

The second attack was described in Washington as much fiercer than the first one, which was said to have lasted half an hour. The second battle was understood to have lasted about three hours in rough seas, with bad weather and low visibility.

"We are in a very serious situation," a Government official said.

The attack came shortly before the State Department made public a stern protest about the North Vietnamese attack Sunday on the Maddox. It was then patrolling about 30 miles off North Vietnam, also in international waters in the Gulf of Tonkin.

The protest over the first incident was announced shortly after noon here, when the

Continued on Page 3, Column 1

2 CARRIERS USED

McNamara Reports on Aerial Strikes and Reinforcements

By JACK RAYMOND

WASHINGTON, Wednesday, Aug. 5 — Secretary of Defense Robert S. McNamara said at a postmidnight news conference that the United States planes that attacked North Vietnam yesterday and today had come from the carriers Constellation and Ticonderoga in the Gulf of Tonkin.

He said that the attacks had been directed against the bases used by the North Vietnamese PT boats that attacked two United States destroyers in international waters yesterday.

The Secretary added that the naval planes, believed to have included propeller-driven as well as jet-powered craft, had also conducted strikes against "certain other targets directly supporting the operation of the PT boats."

The United States planes used conventional weapons.

Separate Targets

Mr. McNamara, who held his news conference shortly after President Johnson had addressed the nation on television, emphasized in his report that the PT boat bases and the supporting facilities in North Vietnam had been separate targets.

He offered a guess, based on incomplete reports, that in the exchange of fire between the attacking PT boats and the United States destroyers and aircraft in international waters, at least two and possibly four of the North Vietnamese Soviet-made PT boats had been sunk.

The Defense Secretary disclosed that at one point in the Vietnamese PT boat attack, the Maddox observed an unidentified aircraft on radar, but that there was no air attack and the radar image was soon lost.

The hostilities that provoked United States retaliation began Sunday with an attack by North Vietnamese PT boats on the United States destroyer Maddox in the Gulf of Tonkin.

Hanoi Not Attacked

The first United States reaction was a note of protest and warning. But, as announced by the President and the Secretary of Defense, the second PT boat attack on the destroyers Maddox and C. Turner Joy yesterday precipitated the counteraction.

The Secretary of Defense said at the news conference that the retaliatory strikes were still under way at that time.

He made clear, in response to questions, that no targets outside North Vietnam had been attacked by the United States warplanes. He specifically re-

Continued on Page 4, Column 3

FORCES ENLARGED

Stevenson to Appeal for Action by U.N. on 'Open Aggression'

By TOM WICKER
Special to The New York Times

WASHINGTON, Aug. 4—President Johnson has ordered retaliatory action against gunboats and "certain supporting facilities in North Vietnam" after renewed attacks against American destroyers in the Gulf of Tonkin.

In a television address tonight, Mr. Johnson said air attacks on the North Vietnamese ships and facilities were taking place as he spoke, shortly after 11:30 P.M.

State Department sources said the attacks were being carried out with conventional weapons on a number of shore bases in North Vietnam, with the objective of destroying them and the 30 to 40 gunboats they served.

The aim, they explained, was to destroy North Vietnam's gunboat capability. They said more air strikes might come later, if needed. Carrier-based aircraft were used in tonight's strike.

2 Boats Believed Sunk

Administration officials also announced that substantial additional units, primarily air and sea forces, were being sent to Southeast Asia.

This "positive reply," as the President called it, followed a naval battle in which a number of North Vietnamese PT boats attacked two United States destroyers with torpedoes. Two of the boats were believed to have been sunk. The United States forces suffered no damage and no loss of lives.

Mr. Johnson termed the North Vietnamese attacks "open aggression on the high seas."

Washington's response is "limited and fitting," the President said, and his Administration seeks no general extension of the guerrilla war in South Vietnam.

Goldwater Approves

"We Americans know," he said, "although others appear to forget, the risks of spreading conflict."

Mr. Johnson said Secretary of State Dean Rusk had been instructed to make this American attitude clear to all nations. He added that Adlai E. Stevenson, chief United States delegate, would raise the matter immediately in the United Nations Security Council. [The Council was expected to meet at 10:30 A.M. Wednesday.]

The President said he had informed his Republican Presidential rival, Senator Barry Goldwater, of his action and

Continued on Page 2, Column 3

DECISION: President Johnson, in a nationwide broadcast, tells of action he ordered taken against North Vietnam.

Associated Press Wirephoto

The President's Address

Following is the text of the President's address on Vietnam last night, as recorded by The New York Times:

My fellow Americans:

As President and Commander in Chief, it is my duty to the American people to report that renewed hostile actions against United States ships on the high seas in the Gulf of Tonkin have today required me to order the military forces of the United States to take action in reply.

The initial attack on the destroyer Maddox on Aug. 2 was repeated today by a number of hostile vessels attacking two U.S. destroyers with torpedoes.

The destroyers and supporting aircraft acted at once on the orders I gave after the initial act of aggression.

We believe at least two of the attacking boats were sunk. There were no U.S. losses.

The performance of commanders and crews in this engagement is in the highest tradition of the United States Navy.

But repeated acts of violence against the armed forces of the United States must be met not only with alert defense but with positive reply.

Action 'Now in Execution'

That reply is being given, as I speak to you tonight. Air action is now in execution against gunboats and certain supporting facilities in North Vietnam which have been used in these hostile operations.

In the larger sense, this new act of aggression aimed directly at our own forces again brings home to all of us in the United States the importance of the struggle for peace and security in Southeast Asia.

Aggression by terror against the peaceful villages of South Vietnam has now been joined by open aggression on the high seas against the United States of America.

The determination of all Americans to carry out our full commitment to the people and to the Government of South Vietnam will be redoubled by this outrage. Yet our response for the present will be limited and fitting.

We Americans know—although others appear to forget—the risk of spreading conflict. We still seek no wider war. I have instructed the Secretary of State to make this position totally clear to friends and to adversaries and, indeed, to all.

I have instructed Ambassador Stevenson to raise this matter immediately and urgently before the Security Council of the United Nations.

Congressional Resolution Asked

Finally, I have today met with the leaders of both parties in the Congress of the United States and I have informed them that I shall immediately request the Congress to pass a resolution making it clear that our Government is united in its determination to take all necessary measures in support of freedom and in defense of peace in Southeast Asia.

I have been given encouraging assurance by these leaders of both parties that such a resolution will be promptly introduced, freely and expeditiously debated, and passed with overwhelming support.

And just a few minutes ago I was able to reach Senator Goldwater and I am glad to say that he has expressed his support of the statement that I am making to you tonight.

It is a solemn responsibility to have to order even limited military action by forces whose over-all strength is as vast and as awesome as those of the United States of America.

But it is my considered conviction, shared throughout your Government, that firmness in the right is indispensable today for peace.

That firmness will always be measured. Its mission is peace.

Auto Collision Insurance Rates In State Increased 4.3 to 25%

By JOSEPH C. INGRAHAM

Higher auto damage in-own car, is optional. The rate su.ance rates — with increases from 4.3 to 25 per cent—will go into effect today for private passenger car owners in the state.

The increases were disclosed yesterday by the National Automobile Underwriters Association, which said that sharp rises in auto thefts and in the cost of repairs had made them necessary.

The association said that although the statewide rise would be the lesser amount, the rates in most of the metropolitan areas had been increased as much as 25 per cent.

Physical damage insurance, which reimburses a car owner for loss of or damage to his

revisions apply to collision insurance and to comprehensive coverage, which protects motorists against loss due to theft, fire, windstorm, glass breakage and other hazards.

While each of these coverages can be bought separately, the National Automobile Underwriters Association, rating organization for more than 400 companies here, lumps the vari

Continued on Page 67, Column 2

Salinger Appointed to the Senate

Pierre Salinger, left, with Gov. Edmund G. Brown of California after the announcement yesterday in Sacramento.

United Press International Telephoto

By WALLACE TURNER
Special to The New York Times

SAN FRANCISCO, Aug. 4—Pierre Salinger was appointed to the Senate today by Gov. Edmund G. Brown of California to fill the unexpired five months of the term of the late Senator Clair Engle. Mr. Salinger is scheduled to be sworn in tomorrow about noon. He will be escorted to the rostrum by Senator Thomas H.

Kuchel of California, the assistant Senate Republican leader. Governor Brown will be present in the Senate galleries when the new Senator takes his oath. Mr. Salinger, who was White House press

Continued on Page 16, Column 3

Congolese Battling Inside Stanleyville

By J. ANTHONY LUKAS
Special to The New York Times

LEOPOLDVILLE, the Congo, Aug. 4—Rebels of the "Popular Army" and Government troops battled tonight in the streets of Stanleyville, the chief city in the northern Congo.

Messages from the United States consul there said heavy fighting was going on early this evening in front of the consulate, about half a mile from the center of the city.

At 6:15 P. M. Stanleyville time, the consul, Michael P. E. Hoyt, telegraphed that the army was "advancing across front lawn of consulate" and seemed to be "pushing rebels back."

Eight minutes later he said that the army troops were "advancing rapidly and in numbers beyond consulate on road to Wanie Rukula." He said that

Continued on Page 8, Column 4

Khanh Is Fighting Threat of a Coup

By SEYMOUR TOPPING
Special to The New York Times

SAIGON, South Vietnam, Aug. 4—Premier Nguyen Khanh struggled today to strengthen the political stability of his Government as his aides privately warned of plots to drive him from office. United States officials were concerned about the political deterioration in Saigon.

The malaise in the capital was attributed more to a clash of rival political and military personalities than to pressure from the Vietcong insurgents. United States sources said reports from provinces indicated that conditions there were generally better than in Saigon.

Once again, rumors of a coup d'état were circulating in Sai-

Continued on Page 4, Column 7

The New York Times.

LATE CITY EDITION
U. S. Weather Bureau Report (Page 45) forecasts.
Cloudy, then fair today; fair and
cooler tonight. Fair tomorrow.
Temp. Range: 70—55; yesterday: 73—59.

VOL. CXIV..No. 38,964.   © 1964 by The New York Times Company.
Times Square, New York, N. Y. 10036   NEW YORK, MONDAY, SEPTEMBER 28, 1964.   Today's Issue Contains 96 Pages in Two Sections   TEN CENTS

WARREN COMMISSION FINDS OSWALD GUILTY AND SAYS ASSASSIN AND RUBY ACTED ALONE; REBUKES SECRET SERVICE, ASKS REVAMPING

F.B.I. IS CRITICIZED

Security Steps Taken by Secret Service Held Inadequate

By FELIX BELAIR Jr.
Special to The New York Times

WASHINGTON, Sept. 27 — A sweeping revision of the organization and basic operating practices of the United States Secret Service was recommended today by the Warren Commission.

The commission sharply rebuked the Secret Service for failure to make adequate preparation for the visit of President Kennedy to Dallas last November. It reprimanded the Federal Bureau of Investigation for failure to supply the Secret Service with information concerning the presence of Lee Harvey Oswald in Dallas.

The commission deplored the fact that "there was no fully adequate liaison" between the F.B.I. and the Secret Service before the Dallas trip. It noted that some improvements had occurred since then but it insisted that, ultimately, Presidential protection required improvement in working arrangements of all Federal agencies concerned, including the Central Intelligence Agency, the State Department and the military intelligence branches.

Scrutiny Is Urged

The State Department was admonished to scrutinize more carefully requests for return to the United States of defectors

The report's appendix on Presidential protection will be printed in tomorrow's Times.

like Oswald "who have evidenced disloyalty or hostility to this country or who have expressed a desire to renounce their citizenship."

The brunt of the commission's indictment was directed at the century-old agency responsible for the safety of the President and his family. Its chief charge was that the Secret Service had not checked buildings along the route of the Presidential motorcade in Dallas nor asked the local police to do so.

The commission called for the appointment of a new special assistant to the Secretary of the Treasury with general supervisory authority over the Secret Service.

The commission found, however, that the conduct of the Secret Service agents in the Presidential motorcade "demonstrates that the President and the nation can expect courage and devotion to duty from agents of the Secret Service."

It acknowledged that whatever the human and material resources at the command of the Secret Service, a President can only be made as safe as he wants to be.

The report declared that its recommendations were "compelled by the facts disclosed in this investigation." It noted that

Continued on Page 15, Column 1

JOHNSON NAMES 4 TO ACT ON REPORT

Commission Calls for Action to Increase the Security of the Presidency

By The Associated Press

JOHNSON CITY, Tex., Sept. 27—President Johnson appointed a four-man committee today to advise him "on the execution of the recommendations of the Warren Commission."

The commission, which investigated the assassination of President Kennedy, recommended action to tighten the protection of Presidents and to make the killing of a President or a Vice President a Federal crime.

[Mike Mansfield of Montana, the Senate majority leader, said in Washington that Congress, which has been aiming at adjournment at the end of this week, "should stay here and act, if the President sends us any recommendations."]

Members of the committee are Secretary of the Treasury Douglas Dillon, Acting Attorney General Nicholas deB. Katzenbach, John A. McCone, director of the Central Intelligence Agency, and McGeorge Bundy, Special Assistant to the President for National Security Affairs.

The President named no chairman for the committee, but it was understood that Secretary Dillon, as ranking member, would have general supervision over the group.

The group will presumably

Continued on Page 17, Column 3

A New Chapter Unfolds in the Kennedy Legend

By JAMES RESTON
Special to The New York Times

WASHINGTON, Sept. 27 —The Warren Commission has fulfilled its primary assignment. It has tried, as a servant of history, to discover truth. But the assassination of President Kennedy was so symbolic of human irony and tragedy, and so involved in the complicated and elemental conflicts of the age, that many vital questions remain, and the philosophers, novelists and dramatists will have to take it from here.

News Analysis

The commission has not concluded the Kennedy mystery so much as it has opened up a whole new chapter in the Kennedy legend.

It has provided the greatest repository of Presidential political history, drama and fiction since the murder of Mr. Lincoln and since legend is often more powerful than history, this may be the commission's most significant achievement.

Now the central mystery of who killed the President has been answered by the commission only in the process of raising a new catalogue of mysteries. Now the main characters in the play have been surrounded by a host of new characters, each of whom appears briefly at a critical moment with some vital testimony, only to disappear without our really knowing much about who they are.

The whole story is full of the mystery of life. Lee Harvey Oswald's motive for murdering the President remains obscure. The distinguished members of the commission and their staff obviously gave up on it.

The "might-have-beens" are maddening. If only he had been given that visa to go to Cuba and thence to the Soviet Union just before the assassination! If he had not been allowed to come back from there in the first place! Who was "the neighbor" who got him the job in the Texas Book Depository, from where he

shot the President? And what were the details of Oswald's attempted suicide in Moscow?

The wild accidents are equally intriguing. There is, for example, the case of Mrs. Bledsoe, who rented Oswald a room in Dallas and then, on a 10,000-to-1 chance, just happened to be on the bus he boarded when he was running away from the crime.

Then there are the consoling yearnings and kindnesses in the midst of tragedy: Ruth Paine, who was also "alienated" and "isolated," and frustrated like Oswald, but who nevertheless "befriended" Marina Oswald in her time of

Continued on Page 15, Column 6

'MYTHS' OF CASE DENIED IN DETAIL

Panel Says Misinformation on the Assassination Led to 'Distorted' Views

By PETER KIHSS

The Warren Commission rejected in detail yesterday a number of charges suggesting that Lee Harvey Oswald had not acted alone in the assassination of President Kennedy.

The commission said that "publicizing of unchecked information" had led to "myths" and "distorted" interpretations. While each inaccuracy could be explained, it went on, "the number and variety of misstatements issued by the police" in Dallas would have "greatly assisted a skillful defense attorney."

On the other hand, Mark Lane, chairman of a Citizens Committee of Inquiry here, contended that if the report contained all the available evidence, "Oswald would have been acquitted" of both the President's assassination and the murder of the Dallas patrolman, J. D. Tippit.

In a news conference, Mr. Lane, a former Assemblyman, said his group would continue its efforts to "answer the unanswered questions." He said it had more than 250 workers here, with other committees in England, France and Denmark, and interested groups on 20 college campuses. His group estimated that it had raised and

Continued on Page 16, Column 4

PANEL UNANIMOUS

Theory of Conspiracy by Left or Right Is Rejected

The text of the report begins on the first page of the second section.

By ANTHONY LEWIS
Special to The New York Times

WASHINGTON, Sept. 27 — The assassination of President Kennedy was the work of one man, Lee Harvey Oswald. There was no conspiracy, foreign or domestic.

That was the central finding in the Warren Commission report, made public this evening. Chief Justice Earl Warren and the six other members of the President's Commission on the Assassination of President John F. Kennedy were unanimous on this and all questions. The commission found that Jack Ruby was on his own in killing Oswald. It rejected all theories that the two men were in some way connected. It said that neither rightists nor Communists bore responsibility for the murder of the President in Dallas last Nov. 22.

Why did Oswald do it? To this most important and most mysterious question the commission had no certain answer. It suggested that Oswald had no rational purpose, no motive adequate if "judged by the standards of reasonable men."

A Product of His Life

Rather, the commission saw Oswald's terrible act as the product of his entire life—a life "characterized by isolation, frustration and failure." He was just 24 years old at the time of the assassination.

"Oswald was profoundly alienated from the world in which he lived," the report said. "He had very few, if any, close relationships with other people and he appeared to have had great difficulty in finding a meaningful place in the world. He was never satisfied with anything.

"When he was in the United States, he resented the capitalist system. When he was in the Soviet Union, he apparently resented the Communist party members, who were accorded special privileges and who he thought were betraying Communism, and he spoke well of the United States."

The commission found that Oswald shot at former Maj. Gen. Edwin A. Walker in Dallas on April 10, 1963, narrowly missing him. It cited this as evidence of his capacity for violence.

It listed as factors that might have led Oswald to the assassination "his deep-rooted resentment of all authority, which was expressed in a hostility toward every society in which he lived," his "urge to try to find a place in history" and his "avowed commitment to Marx-

Continued on Page 14, Column 1

THE WARREN COMMISSION: President's Commission on the Assassination of President Kennedy at commission offices at Veterans of Foreign Wars Building, Washington. From left: Representative Gerald R. Ford, Representative Hale Boggs, Senator Richard B. Russell, Chief Justice Earl Warren, Senator John Sherman Cooper, John J. McCloy, Allen W. Dulles, and J. Lee Rankin, commission counsel. Portraits are of President Johnson, President Kennedy and Joseph J. Lombardo, head of Veterans of Foreign Wars.

Harris & Ewing

High Clerics to Ask Stronger Statement By Council on Jews

Special to The New York Times

ROME, Sept. 27—A powerful array of Roman Catholic prelates, including at least three American Cardinals, are preparing to speak out for a strong statement by the Ecumenical Council on the Jews, clerical sources said today.

The sources said that Richard James Cardinal Cushing, Archbishop of Boston, is known to have prepared an address to be given at the Council when the issue is debated.

The draft of the declaration was introduced last Friday by Augustin Cardinal Bea, the German Jesuit, who heads the Council's Secretariat for the Promotion of Christian Unity.

The group will presumably

Other Cardinals Named

The earlier statement, among other things, made plain that the Jews of Christ's time and of today bore no responsibility for the Crucifixion. The weakened declaration declares only that Jews of today cannot be blamed.

Among those expected to attack the newer version are two other American Cardinals—Joseph Elmer Ritter, Archbishop of St. Louis, and Albert Gregory Meyer, Archbishop of Chicago.

Cardinal Spellman of New York has also said that he favors the more forceful state-

Continued on Page 7, Column 1

2 CITIES DENY REIN ON POLICE IN RIOTS

Civilian Review Units Hold F.B.I. Criticism Unfounded

By FRED POWLEDGE

Officials of civilian police advisory boards in Rochester and Philadelphia disagreed yesterday with a statement by the Federal Bureau of Investigation that boards such as theirs had "virtually paralyzed" the police during the summer riots.

The Rev. William H. Gray Jr., executive secretary of Philadelphia's eight-member review board, said: "It's over-simplifying the situation to say that the board has an effect on the rioting or the police behavior."

Ross J. Guglielmino, the executive director and legal counsel of the Rochester board, said he did not feel the F.B.I. criticism applied to Rochester.

What the F.B.I. Found

The two men commented in telephone interviews on a report released Saturday by President Johnson. The President had asked the F.B.I. to collect its investigations of summer riots in New York City, Rochester, Dixmoor, Ill.; Philadelphia, Seaside, Ore., Hampton Beach, N. H., and Jersey City, Paterson, and Elizabeth, N. J., and advise him if there were any pattern in the outbreaks.

The report, submitted by F.B.I. Director J. Edgar Hoover, concluded that the riots were not basically racial, although large numbers of Negroes took part; that they were not organized on a national basis, and that none of them was planned by any one group or individual.

Among the several points

Continued on Page 48, Column 1

Congress Will Act On Appalachia Aid And Medical Care

Special to The New York Times

WASHINGTON, Sept. 27 — The fate of two key Administration programs—health insurance for the aged and aid to Appalachia—may be decided this week as Congress pushes toward adjournment.

"We could finish up Saturday; that's my most optimistic guess," Senator Mike Mansfield of Montana, the majority leader, said today. "But I have my fingers crossed."

The health insurance issue, currently in House-Senate conference, could delay adjournment until the following week, some legislative leaders believe.

Prospects for conference approval of some form of health insurance for the aged under Social Security have ranged from bright to gloomy in recent days.

The House passed a bill this summer to increase Social Security taxes as well as cash

Continued on Page 18, Column 4

CAMPAIGN IMPACT BELIEVED LIKELY

'Kennedy Legacy' Could Aid Democrats at the Polls

By TOM WICKER
Special to The New York Times

WASHINGTON, Sept. 27 — The effects of the Warren Commission's report are sure to extend far beyond its conclusion that Lee Harvey Oswald, acting alone, killed President Kennedy last Nov. 22.

The massive document could have repercussions on the 1964 elections, on the present conduct of President Johnson, and ultimately on the availability of college campuses. His group estimated that it had raised and

Other Agencies Affected

The assignments and powers of other agencies such as the Federal Bureau of Investigation and even the Central Intelligence Agency might be revamped and independent review of their activities and efficiency might be increased.

In the field of legislation, the report might produce—as recommended by the commission—a law making it a Federal crime to kill or attempt to kill a President, a Vice President or any officer next in line to the Presidency and the President-elect and Vice President-elect. Other legislation, particularly relating to security and investigative agencies and to the protection of Presidents, could also grow from the report.

Although the State Department was generally cleared of

Continued on Page 15, Column 5

G.I.'s Rescue Vietnam Captives; Uprising Stirs Mistrust of U.S.

By PETER GROSE
Special to The New York Times

SAIGON, South Vietnam, Sept. 27 — United States Army helicopters rescued 60 Vietnamese hostages today from a camp of rebel tribesmen in the central highlands.

The release of the prisoners met a Government condition for negotiations with the armed mountain tribesmen. It appeared to reduce the danger of a violent clash.

Nevertheless, the revolt is having serious political consequences, involving growing suspicion between the United States mission and the Premier, Maj. Gen. Nguyen Khanh. The rebellion has intensified Saigon's feeling that the United States, which has supported General Khanh, is undergoing a change of policy.

[About five persons were reported shot dead when security forces fired on a crowd in Quinhon, 270 miles north of Saigon. Later a mob stormed a radio station and troops were called in to evict the demonstrators, Reuters reported.]

Officials around General Khanh say he no longer believes he can count on American help to stay in power and he feels he must seek firmer support from

Continued on Page 2, Column 1

Scientific Police Work Traced Bullets to Rifle Oswald Owned

By JOHN W. FINNEY
Special to The New York Times

WASHINGTON, Sept. 27 — The Warren Commission's conclusion that Lee Harvey Oswald killed President Kennedy rests in large part on scientific evidence painstakingly established through modern technology.

On the basis of the scientific evidence alone it was possible to establish that the shots were fired by a rifle owned and possessed by Oswald, that the shots were fired from the sixth floor window of a building in which Oswald worked, and that the fatal wound could have been caused by the bullets from the high-powered rifle.

These crucial points were established through scientific detective work that combined the techniques of handwriting, ballistics, and fiber and wounds analysis. Among the devices used were microscopes, spectroscopes, X-rays, surveying instruments and skulls filled with gelatin.

Even nuclear science was employed. Paraffin casts from Oswald's hands and face were put into a nuclear reactor at the Oak Ridge (Tenn.) National Laboratory in an unsuccessful attempt to see if radiation would show up traces of gunpowder. One major question still

Continued on Page 16, Column 3

"All the News That's Fit to Print"

The New York Times.

LATE CITY EDITION
U.S. Weather Bureau Report (Page 74) forecast:
Cloudy and cooler today; chance of
rain tonight and tomorrow.
Temp. Range: 68—53; yesterday: 64 48

VOL. CXIV. No. 38,982.

© 1964 by The New York Times Company.
Times Square, New York, N. Y. 10036

NEW YORK, FRIDAY, OCTOBER 16, 1964.

TEN CENTS

KHRUSHCHEV OUSTED FROM TOP POSTS; BREZHNEV GETS CHIEF PARTY POSITION AND KOSYGIN IS NAMED NEW PREMIER

Labor Party Is the Apparent Victor in British Election

JOHNSON DENIES JENKINS COVER-UP; SETS F.B.I. INQUIRY

Praises His Aide's Service, but Says He Requested Resignation From Post

By TOM WICKER
Special to The New York Times

WASHINGTON, Oct. 15—President Johnson said tonight that until late yesterday he had had no information of any kind that "had ever raised a question" about the personal conduct of Walter W. Jenkins, his friend and special assistant.

The President made the statement, his first public comment on the Jenkins case, as he flew back here from a day of campaigning in New York.

In effect, he was denying Republican allegations that he had covered up knowledge of Mr. Jenkins's two arrests on morals charges. The disclosure of these arrests yesterday has shaken the Johnson Administration and the Democratic Presidential campaign.

Mr. Johnson's resignation as special assistant to the President was announced in New York last night after the disclosure of his police record.

Mr. Johnson also disclosed in his statement tonight that he had requested the resignation of Mr. Jenkins.

'Dedication' Is Cited

The text of Mr. Johnson's statement follows:

"Walter Jenkins has worked with me faithfully for 25 years. No man I know has given more personal dedication and tireless labor.

"Until late yesterday no information or report of any kind to me had ever raised a question with respect to his personal conduct. Mr. Jenkins is now in the care of his physician and his many friends will join in praying for his early recovery. For myself and Mrs. Johnson I want to say that our hearts go out with the deepest compassion for him and for his wife and six children—and they have our love and prayers.

"On this case as on any such case, the public interest comes before all personal feelings. I have requested and received Mr. Jenkins's resignation.

"Within moments after being notified last night, I ordered Director J. Edgar Hoover of the F.B.I. to make an immediate and comprehensive inquiry and report promptly to me and the American people."

The incident apparently is regarded by the Republicans as a major development in their

Continued on Page 20, Column 1

Cole Porter Is Dead; Songwriter Was 72

By The Associated Press

SANTA MONICA, Calif., Oct. 15 — Cole Porter, the world-famed composer and lyricist, died at 11:05 P.M. today at a Santa Monica hospital, where he underwent kidney surgery last Tuesday. He was 72 years old.

Mr. Porter wrote the lyrics and music for his songs, and to both he brought such an individuality of style that a genre known as "the Cole Porter song" became recognized.

The hallmarks of a typical Porter song were lyrics that were urbane or witty and a melody with a sinuous, brooding quality. Some of his best-known songs in this vein were "What

Continued on Page 29, Column 1

"OH WHAT A LOVELY WAR"
Broadhurst Theatre W. 44th St.—Advt.

G.O.P. Hopes Rise, But Jenkins Effect On Race Is Cloudy

By EARL MAZO

The Walter W. Jenkins case inspired high hopes in the camp of Senator Barry Goldwater yesterday and dismay among supporters of President Johnson.

But by nightfall, reports from Moscow that Premier Khrushchev has been replaced led many political observers to speculate that the possible anti-Johnson impact of the Jenkins disclosure might be nullified by the effect of an international crisis upon the voters.

A leading Republican put it this way:

"That Lyndon Johnson is lucky. The arrest of his man Jenkins accented the whole Bobby Baker corruption mess, which is Barry Goldwater's strongest issue. But then comes this Khrushchev thing, taking the headlines and accenting Barry's greatest weakness.

Continued on Page 21, Column 1

JOHNSON HAILED AT LIBERAL RALLY

Asserts 'Great Society' Is a Practical Goal—He Is Acclaimed Upstate

By HOMER BIGART

President Johnson received a frenzied ovation last night from 20,000 persons who packed Madison Square Garden for a Liberal party rally.

The President expounded to the Garden audience his vision of the "Great Society" and insisted it was a practical goal —"not some vague, dreamlike utopia."

He said he would present a series of proposals dealing with the total needs of a metropolitan area.

These proposals, he said, would be built on the cooperation of government with industry—"the same sort of cooperation that has built our national defense and allowed us to explore the stars."

Campaigns With Kennedy

The President went to the Garden after stumping the state with Robert F. Kennedy, the Democratic-Liberal candidate for the Senate, and receiving tumultuous welcomes from huge crowds on a 22-mile tour of Brooklyn.

Despite the Walter Jenkins scandal, no lessening of enthusiasm was apparent in the throngs that greeted the President in Brooklyn or jammed the Garden for the Liberal party's climactic demonstration.

Roaring applause greeted the President and Mrs. Johnson when they entered the Garden at 8:20 P.M.

The President read his speech in a matter-of-fact voice and the subject matter—the "Great Society"—inspired no cheers.

But when he turned to the day's dramatic developments in the Soviet Union, the crowd's interest was stimulated. A crescendo of applause followed his remark: "We do not intend to bury anyone anywhere and we do not intend to be buried ourselves."

The President warned that this was no time for impulsive leadership. He said "an impulsive thumb can move up toward a button," resulting in the destruction of millions of lives in a matter of moments.

Recalling the Cuban missile crisis, he declared that President Kennedy "had the steadiest thumb, the greatest heart and

Continued on Page 22, Column 1

SLIM EDGE LIKELY

Wilson Aide Defeated in Campaign Marred by a Racial Issue

By SYDNEY GRUSON
Special to The New York Times

LONDON, Friday, Oct. 16—Britain apparently elected a Labor Government in yesterday's general election and sent the Conservatives, who have governed for 13 years, into opposition.

However, all indications pointed to the closest result since the Conservatives won with a majority of 17 in 1951. There is still a chance that Labor will not get a working majority.

With counting finished for the night, the standing of the parties from the results in 430 of the 630 constituencies was:

Labor—247
Conservative—181
Liberal—2

But this Labor lead of 66 House of Commons seats was misleading. Most of the results were from urban areas and the Conservatives are expected to cut deeply into the lead when counting in the rural Conservative strongholds resumes later this morning.

Labor Gains 52 Seats

The computers of the British Broadcasting Corporation and of Press Association, the cooperative newsgathering agency, both forecast an ultimate Labor majority over the Conservatives of 17.

Labor gained 52 seats, two from the Liberals and the rest from the Conservatives. The Conservatives lost 50 seats and took four from Labor.

Sir Alec Douglas-Home, the Conservative leader and Prime Minister, would not concede. He did not emerge from 10 Downing Street, his London office and residence, where he watched the election results on television.

So long as he did not concede, Harold Wilson, Labor's leader, refused to claim victory. Mr. Wilson would be Prime Minister in a Labor Government.

Patrick Gordon Walker, slated to be Foreign Secretary in a Labor Cabinet, lost the Smethwick constituency of industrial Birmingham to Peter Griffiths, a Conservative.

It was at Smethwick that a bitter campaign had been waged

Continued on Page 18, Column 1

Cards Win World Series, Defeating Yankees, 7 to 5

By JOSEPH DURSO
Special to The New York Times

ST. LOUIS, Oct. 15—The St. Louis Cardinals completed their melodramatic climb from the depths of the National League to baseball's pinnacle today when they defeated the New York Yankees, 7—5, and captured the World Series.

They won it in the seventh and final game before a roaring crowd of 30,346 persons in Busch Stadium after they had won the National League pennant in the final game of the regular season. And they won it in the same way—behind the fast-ball pitching of 28-year-old Bob Gibson, who struck out nine Yankees and survived three late home runs that knocked in all the Yankees' runs.

Five pitchers struggled against Gibson to withstand the Cardinals. But the Redbirds scored three runs in the fourth inning, three in the fifth and one in the sixth to bring St. Louis its first championship in 18 years and the second straight loss of the World Series.

The Yankees had not lost two years in a row since 1921 and

Nikita S. Khrushchev
Relieved of political posts

Leonid I. Brezhnev
Named as the leader of the party

Aleksei N. Kosygin
Appointed as the Soviet Premier
Associated Press

Cholesterol Studies Bring Nobel Award To Two Biochemists

By The Associated Press

STOCKHOLM, Oct. 15—The 1964 Nobel Prize in Physiology or Medicine was awarded jointly today to Prof. Konrad E. Bloch of Harvard University and Prof. Feodor Lynen of the University of Munich.

The two were honored for their discoveries concerning the mechanism and regulation of cholesterol and fatty acid metabolism. They will share prize money equivalent to about $54,000.

In its citation, the prize-awarding body, the Royal Caroline Institute, said the therapy against circulatory diseases and related disturbances in altered hormone metabolism would in the future rest upon the work of today's Nobel Prize winners.

Dr. Bloch, a 52-year-old naturalized American born in Germany, is Higgins Professor of Biochemistry at Harvard. He was credited with "brilliant investigations" showing how cholesterol is built up from acetic acid.

Cholesterol, a fatty substance

Continued on Page 3, Column 1

THREATENED SUIT HALTS STATE LOAN

Deals to Borrow $17 Million Delayed by Challenge to Rockefeller Financing

By PETER KIHSS

Two state agencies have had to postpone the closing of deals to borrow $17.3 million because of a threatened court suit by Teamsters Joint Council 16 against financing methods of the Rockefeller administration.

The Governor's office declined yesterday to say why the closing had been held up. But a high state official said the purchasers of bond-anticipation notes required standard certificates assuring that they would not become involved in litigation, and he said that such statements could not be given because of the threatened teamsters suit.

Governor Rockefeller was reported to have sought through intermediaries to get the union council president, John J. O'Rourke, to drop the threatened suit. The Governor's view was said to have been that "thousands" of jobs of currently employed construction workers would be endangered if the financing were held up.

But Nicholas M. Kisburg, legislative and research director of the teamsters' council, said last night that the state could lose $806 million to carry on construction through bond issues already approved by the voters but not yet invoked by the Governor.

Governor Rockefeller's office said that $13.8 million in bond-anticipation notes of the State Housing Finance Agency had first been sold to five buyers Oct. 8, with delivery scheduled for yesterday. Yesterday, the agency "postponed delivery of the notes," the Governor's office said.

Similarly, it said, $3.5 million in bond-anticipation notes of the State Dormitory Authority had been sold Oct. 8, but delivery had to be "postponed" on Wednesday.

The purchasers of the Housing Finance Agency notes were

Continued on Page 31, Column 1

U.S. Surprised but Expects No Radical Shift in Policy

By MAX FRANKEL
Special to The New York Times

WASHINGTON, Oct. 15—The Administration was surprised but not alarmed by the change of leadership in Moscow today. Analysts of Soviet affairs were almost unanimous in the view that Premier Khrushchev had suddenly been forced to step down for reasons of personality and policy, not merely age and health.

But the survival and promotion of prominent Khrushchev lieutenants, officials said, seemed to preclude any radical policy changes in the near future, at least in East-West relations.

In New York, President Johnson said that the shift in the Kremlin "may or may not be a sign of deep turmoil or a sign of changes to come." He commented at the end of his prepared remarks at a Liberal party rally.

Peace Is the Mission

"For ourselves, the need is clear—we should keep steady on our goals," he said. "Peace is the mission of the American people and we are not about to be deterred. We will be firm and restrained. We can meet any test but our quest is always for peace."

In Milwaukee, Senator Hubert H. Humphrey expressed doubt that the Soviet change would bring about a "quick" meeting of Soviet and United States leaders. Talking to newsmen

Continued on Page 15, Column 1

STOCKS PLUMMET IN HECTIC TRADING

Changes in Kremlin Set Off Sharpest Drop in Prices Since Kennedy's Death

By RICHARD PHALON

Rumors of impending changes in the Kremlin swept Wall Street yesterday. By 1:30 P.M. a rolling tide of uneasiness had driven prices on the New York Stock Exchange to their deepest loss since the assassination of President Kennedy last Nov. 22.

Trading volume ran to 6.5 million shares, well below the record of 14.7 million shares churned up in the big market break of May 29, 1962, but much of it came in a concentrated burst after the noon hour. By 2:30 P.M. the tape lagged 27 minutes behind activity on the floor of the stock exchange.

Many brokers felt yesterday's market break followed a classic pattern. As one diagnosed it, the small investors were doing much of the selling. "They can't see anything, they can't touch anything and they're nervous. They're selling and the professionals are bargain-hunting," he observed.

Losses Cut in Half

The first tangible sign that bargain-hunters were on the move came at 2:30 P.M. when market losses were cut in half. By 3 P.M. reports that Premier Khrushchev was retiring were confirmed and the news spread rapidly across the floor of the stock exchange.

At the close of trading, the stock market was down 6.74 points as measured by the Dow-Jones industrial average. The New York Times combined average of 50 stocks closed with a loss of 5.79 points.

Despite the late rally, it was the biggest loss since Aug. 4 when the stock prices plummeted after the Gulf of Tonkin naval action.

Boardroom habitués at midtown brokerage houses glared at the dancing symbols on the big Trans-Lux tapes with a frown-

Continued on Page 53, Column 7

American Motors Struck by U.A.W.

By DAVID R. JONES
Special to The New York Times

DETROIT, Friday, Oct. 16—The United Automobile Workers struck the American Motors Corporation this morning after failure to reach a new labor agreement.

Edward L. Cushman, American Motors vice president and top labor negotiator, announced at 1:05 A.M. today that the parties had agreed to retain a profit-sharing plan in a new contract. But he said the strike deadline arrived before they could resolve other differences.

The strike affects about 23,000 workers at four plants in two Wisconsin cities. The company makes Rambler automobiles.

The walkout widened labor strife in the industry, where nearly 300,000 workers already have been made idle by an auto

Continued on Page 40, Column 1

MOSCOW IS QUIET

Pravda Says Change Won't Bring Return of Harsh Policies

By HENRY TANNER
Special to The New York Times

MOSCOW, Friday, Oct. 16 — Premier Khrushchev has been deprived of political power in the Soviet Union.

He was replaced by Leonid I. Brezhnev, 57 years old, as First Secretary of the Communist party and by Aleksei N. Kosygin, 60, as Premier.

Mr. Khrushchev, who is 70, even lost his seat in the Presidium of the Central Committee of the party, the third most important position he held in the leadership.

This indicated that he had fallen into disgrace.

[Dispatches did not mention if Mr. Khrushchev had been removed from the Central Committee itself. Under normal procedure such action would come at a meeting of the Soviet Communist party Congress.]

Adzhubei Reported Ousted

The changes were announced by Tass, the Soviet press agency, a few minutes after midnight. The Tass statement did not contain a single word of praise for the ousted leader.

Unofficial but reliable sources later reported that Aleksei I. Adzhubei, Mr. Khrushchev's son-in-law, had been deposed as chief editor of the Government newspaper Izvestia.

Mr. Khrushchev's whereabouts was not known. Nor was it known whether he was at liberty or under surveillance. Western diplomats assumed, however, that the changeover had been made peacefully.

Diplomats Voice Assurance

Moscow's streets were quiet. There were no signs of movements by either the army or police. Some of the smaller Western embassies, which had been without a police guard for the last several months, reported yesterday that the policemen were back in front of the gates.

Western diplomats said they did not expect the new leaders to change basic Soviet policy toward the West.

Mr. Brezhnev and Mr. Kosygin can be expected to continue Mr. Khrushchev's policy of "peaceful coexistence" with the West, the diplomats said.

The Soviet Communist party newspaper Pravda indicated today that the party would continue to carry out policies of de-Stalinization and economic improvements under its new leadership.

The paper printed the same bare announcement that had been carried in the English-

Continued on Page 14, Column 1

The TFX Unveiled; McNamara Hails It

By RICHARD WITKIN
Special to The New York Times

FORT WORTH, Tex., Oct. 15 —The TFX, the plane that launched 3,000 pages of Congressional inquiry, rolled out the factory door into public view today.

The twin-jet plane, which has revolutionary movable wings and now is called the F-111, is scheduled to make its first flight by the end of the year. The rollout ceremony was attended by a dais full of civilian and military dignitaries, headed by Secretary of Defense Robert S. McNamara.

Mr. McNamara has been at the center of the political storm over the TFX—now the F-111—program since his office overruled the unanimous judgment

Continued on Page 11, Column 1

"OH WHAT A LOVELY WAR"
Broadhurst Theatre W. 44th St.—Advt.

SOMETHING NEW IN APARTMENT ADS.
Exclusive new feature! See actual floor plans when you check Apartment Directory ads in today's World-Telegram.—Advt.

NEWS INDEX

	Page		Page
Art	77	Music	30-34
Books	36-37	Obituaries	39
Bridge	36	Real Estate	53
Business	55, 62-63	Screen	30-34
Buyers	45	Ships and Air	74
Crossword	37	Society	42-43
Editorial	38	Sports	44-52
Events Today	36	Theaters	30-34
Fashions	42-43	TV and Radio	79
Financial	53-63	U. N. Proceedings	12
Food	46	Weather	74
Man in the News	20	World's Fair	31

News Summary and Index, Page 41.

"All the News That's Fit to Print"

The New York Times.

LATE CITY EDITION
U. S. Weather Bureau Report (Page 78) forecasts:
Sunny today; clear tonight.
Fair and milder tomorrow.
Temp. Range: 63—48; yesterday: 60—49.

VOL. CXIV.... No. 39,001. © 1964 by The New York Times Company. Times Square, New York, N. Y. 10036. NEW YORK, WEDNESDAY, NOVEMBER 4, 1964. TEN CENTS

JOHNSON SWAMPS GOLDWATER AND KENNEDY BEATS KEATING; DEMOCRATS WIN LEGISLATURE

KENNEDY EDGE 6-5

Keating's Defeat Is Termed a 'Tragedy' by Rockefeller

New York Vote

PRESIDENT
Johnson, Dem.... 4,509,514
Goldwater, Rep.... 2,089,113
11,330 of 12,439 E.D.'s rptg.

SENATOR
Kennedy, Dem.... 3,479,976
Keating, Rep.... 2,857,023
11,318 of 12,439 E.D.'s rptg.

By R. W. APPLE Jr.

Robert F. Kennedy was elected to the United States Senate from New York yesterday in his first bid for elective office, overwhelming Republican Senator Kenneth B. Keating.

With more than 80 per cent of the vote counted, Mr. Kennedy held a 6-to-5 lead. Because most of the untallied vote was in heavily Democratic New York City, it appeared that the former Attorney General's plurality might reach 650,000.

Mr. Keating conceded defeat at 11:39 P.M. with the announcement at the Roosevelt Hotel that he had sent a congratulatory telegram to Mr. Kennedy.

Governor Rockefeller, standing beside the white-haired Rochester legislator, said Mr. Keating's defeat was "a tragedy for the state and nation."

Runs Behind Johnson

"Senator Keating, one of the great Senators in the history of New York, has been rolled under by a national landslide," the Governor added. "He waged a magnificent campaign."

Mr. Kennedy ran well behind President Johnson, who seemed to be headed for a record margin of 2.5 million votes or more in the state. The President won all of the state's 62 counties.

It thus appeared that about a million New York voters had split their ticket to cast votes for Mr. Johnson and Mr. Keating — but even this wasn't enough to make the Senate contest close.

A major surprise was the showing of the Liberal party, which had expected to deliver

Continued on Page 27, Column 4

STATE DEMOCRATS GAIN SIX IN HOUSE

Lindsay and Other Liberal Republicans Keep Seats

By WARREN WEAVER Jr.

Democrats swept through the New York Congressional delegation in yesterday's election, unseating six Republican Representatives and threatening the House seat of a seventh.

In the wake of the Johnson victory, the Democrats increased their strength in the delegation from 20 to 26 while the number of Republicans dropped from 21 to 14, with one district in doubt.

Although they failed to dislodge any of the three New York City Republican congressmen, Democratic candidates scored victories elsewhere across the state. They took two seats in Nassau County, one in Westchester, one in the Hudson Valley and two in Western New York.

Among the chief Republican survivors was Representative John V. Lindsay of Manhattan, who won by a 65,000-vote margin in his East Side district.

Other Republicans to retain their seats were Representative Seymour Halpern of Queens, who like Mr. Lindsay had opposed Senator Barry Goldwater, and, Representative Ogden R.

Continued on Page 24, Column 3

"OH WHAT A LOVELY WAR" IS A HILARIOUS MUSICAL.—New York Times. Broadhurst Theatre, W. 44 St.—Advt.

The Election at a Glance

President

	Number of States	Electoral Votes
Johnson	45	486
Goldwater	6	52
*includes Dist. of Columbia

President—New York		Senator—New York	
Johnson	4,509,514	Kennedy	3,479,976
Goldwater	2,089,113	Keating	2,857,023
*incomplete		*incomplete	

The Senate

Newly Elected Senators		Make-up of New Senate	
Democrats	25	Democrats	65
Republicans	5	Republicans	30
In doubt	5	In doubt	5

The House

Democrats elected	261
Republicans elected	127
In doubt	47

JOHNSON CRUSHES RIVAL IN JERSEY

Lead Near 900,000, Topping Eisenhower's Record— Williams Re-elected

New Jersey Vote

PRESIDENT
Johnson, Dem.... 1,645,844
Goldwater, Rep.... 853,708
4,001 of 4,603 E.D.'s rptg.

SENATOR
Williams, Dem.... 1,474,523
Shanley, Rep.... 891,425
4,001 of 4,603 E.D.'s rptg.

By GEORGE CABLE WRIGHT

President Johnson won New Jersey's 17 electoral votes yesterday in the biggest political victory ever scored in the state.

With 91 per cent of the vote tallied, the President held a record lead of nearly 900,000 votes over his Republican opponent, Senator Barry Goldwater.

Until yesterday, the record plurality for a Presidential candidate in New Jersey was the 756,605-vote margin rolled up by President Eisenhower, a Republican, in 1956.

In sweeping at least 19, and possibly all of the state's 21 counties, Mr. Johnson carried to victory with him incumbent Democratic Senator Harrison A. Williams Jr. Democrats also captured a majority of the state's 15 seats in the House of Representatives for the first time since 1912.

In the present Congress, Republicans hold eight of the seats. On the basis of incomplete returns from yesterday's balloting, Democrats won at least 10 seats.

The Democratic candidate James J. Howard also held a narrow lead over his Republican opponent, Marcus Daly, in an

Continued on Page 32, Column 4

G.O.P. Grip Broken In Suburban Voting

By JOHN SIBLEY

Traditional Republican bastions in the suburbs crumbled before the Johnson onslaught yesterday, and the President carried with him many local Democratic candidates in nearby New York and New Jersey.

Widespread ticket-splitting showed, however, that Republican suburbanites were not forsaking their party so much as they were renouncing their Presidential nominee, Senator Barry Goldwater.

Westchester County, for the first time since 1912, gave a plurality to a Democratic Presidential candidate. Rockland County went Democratic for the first time since Franklin D. Roosevelt carried the county in 1936 and for only the fourth time in 100 years.

Long Island's suburbs, too, which helped make the President, became the first Democratic Presidential candidate in modern

Continued on Page 23, Column 2

Connecticut Votes 2-1 for President; All Democrats Win

Connecticut Vote

PRESIDENT (Complete)
Johnson, D.... 825,416
Goldwater, R.... 392,556

SENATOR
Dodd, D.... 779,252
Lodge, R.... 425,376

By RICHARD H. PARKE

President Johnson led a sweeping Democratic victory in Connecticut yesterday.

His better than 2-to-1 margin over Senator Barry Goldwater eclipsed the previous record plurality in a Presidential race in the state. Mr. Johnson's plurality was 432,860. The earlier record had been set by President Dwight D. Eisenhower in 1956 when he defeated Adlai E. Stevenson by 306,758 votes.

Senator Thomas J. Dodd, the Democratic incumbent, also triumphed easily over his Republican opponent, former Gov. John Davis Lodge. But the 57-year-old Senator ran about 45,000 votes behind the President.

One result of President Johnson's landslide was the defeat of the state's only Republican Congressman, Representative Abner W. Sibal of the Fourth (Fairfield County) District. Mr. Sibal lost the normally Republican district to former Representative Donald J. Irwin, a

Continued on Page 32, Column 1

ROMNEY IS VICTOR; PERCY'S BID FAILS

Democrats Likely to Achieve Gain in Governorships

By JOSEPH A. LOFTUS

Democrats gave a good account of themselves in 25 contests for Governor yesterday, but it was a Republican who produced the spectacular.

Gov. George Romney, running afoul from Senator Barry Goldwater, set off a Michigan ticket-splitting spree to win re-election and thereby planted himself firmly in the thin front line of 1968 Presidential possibilities.

While Senator Goldwater gathered barely a third of Michigan's votes, the Governor defeated Neil Staebler with more than 55 per cent of the tally.

Strong Goldwater supporters "cut" Governor Romney, but the latter improved on his own 1962 vote totals in the labor-Democratic areas of Detroit and Flint-Saginaw.

The Republicans failed to capture a major prize, the Illinois governorship. The defeated nominee, Charles H. Percy, had figured in Presidential talk for the future.

Gov. Otto J. Kerner won a second term in Illinois despite the failure of Mayor Richard Daley's organization to deliver Chicago majorities as big as those Mr. Kerner won there four years ago.

Nationally the Democrats seemed likely to score a

Continued on Page 24, Column 4

UPSET AT ALBANY

Carlino and Mahoney Defeated—Special Session Expected

By LAYHMOND ROBINSON

A surge of Democratic votes swept the Republicans from control of the State Legislature yesterday for the first time in more than a quarter of a century.

The massive victory gave the Democrats a probable working majority of a dozen seats in the Assembly and a half dozen in the Senate.

Not since 1935, in the sweep of Franklin D. Roosevelt's New Deal, had the Democrats had control of both the houses. Not since 1938 had they held control of the Senate.

Toppled from their powerful posts in stunning upsets were Assembly Speaker Joseph F. Carlino of Long Beach, L. I., and Senate Majority Leader Walter J. Mahoney of Buffalo.

Beaten by Outsiders

Both suffered defeat at the hands of virtually unknown Democrats.

Mr. Carlino, the top Republican in the lower house for six years and an Assemblyman representing Nassau's Second and Assembly District for 20 years, was beaten by Jerome R. McDougal Jr., a car salesman making his first race for public office.

Senator Mahoney, often called the most powerful man in the Legislature, was unseated by John H. Doerr of Buffalo in Erie County's 55th Senate District.

Another high-ranking Republican who lost was Senator MacNeil Mitchell of Manhattan, the most influential New York City member of the two houses.

In some districts in the suburbs and in upstate counties, Democrats captured Assembly and Senate seats for the first time in this century.

Districting Fight Due

At the last session, the G.O.P. had a 10-vote edge over the Democrats in the Assembly, holding 85 seats to 65 for the Democrats. In the Senate they had a 33-25 edge.

Although the Democrats ended this G.O.P. domination, the battle for control could be resumed again in December.

The Governor is expected to call a special session of the Legislature soon to adopt a new plan for reapportioning seats in the two houses.

This reapportionment session will be controlled by the present members, with the Republicans in control.

Members elected yesterday do not take their seats until the

Continued on Page 33, Column 3

Summary of International News: Wilson Acts to Nationalize Steel

Following is a summary of foreign news. A full report begins on the first page of the second part.

Labor Offers Program

Britain's new Labor Government offered a program of controversial legislation to Parliament. Headed by a demand for renationalization of the steel industry, the proposals indicate one of the bitterest sessions in parliamentary history.

French Explain Aim

Foreign Minister Maurice Couve de Murville told the French Parliament that the United States and Europe should develop separate, but not necessarily hostile, policies. In Washington, he predicted that a major crisis for Atlantic unity would arise at a NATO meeting in December.

Bolivian Troops Revolt

A military revolt broke out in Bolivia and appeared to be spreading across the country. A truce designed to open the

LYNDON BAINES JOHNSON

The New York Times
HUBERT HORATIO HUMPHREY

SOUTH REVERSES VOTING PATTERNS

Goldwater Makes Inroads, but Most Electoral Votes Go to the President

By JOHN HERBERS
Special to The New York Times

ATLANTA, Nov. 3 — President Johnson carried a majority of Southern states tonight by turning the normal voting patterns inside out.

The rural Deep South, solidly Democratic in the past, voted for Senator Barry Goldwater of Arizona on the Republican ticket. The states on the border of the region, which had gone Republican in recent Presidential elections, returned to the Democrats.

But so strong was the Goldwater tide in the Deep South that seven Republican congressional candidates rode to victory on the Senator's coattails from districts that had been Democratic since Reconstruction.

The Republicans made their biggest gains in Alabama, where five candidates for Congress defeated Democratic opponents.

President Johnson carried Virginia, North Carolina, Florida, Tennessee, Arkansas and Texas with a total of 81 electoral votes. Senator Goldwater carried Louisiana, Mississippi, Alabama, Georgia and South Carolina with a total of 47 electoral votes.

South Carolina and Mississippi had not voted for Repub-

Continued on Page 24, Column 2

Democrats Are Assured Of Majorities in Congress

House Gain for Democrats

By JOHN D. MORRIS

Democrats strengthened their control of the House of Representatives in yesterday's election, scoring substantial gains in all regions except the South.

With returns from Congressional races still incomplete early this morning, the trend indicated a Democratic pickup of at least 20 seats and possibly 3, or more.

The Republicans nevertheless scored spectacular breakthroughs in the South, winning five of Alabama's eight seats, one of Mississippi's five and at least one of Georgia's 10.

Those gains were more than offset, however, by the loss of both of their Texas seats and heavy Democratic gains in other parts of the country.

The House division in the expiring 88th Congress is 257 Democrats and 178 Republicans. This credits five vacancies to the parties last holding the seats. Three were occupied by Democrats and two by Republicans.

With 218 needed for a major-

Continued on Page 21, Column 1

WHITE BACKLASH DOESN'T DEVELOP

Vote in Suburbs in North Is Strong for President

By ANTHONY LEWIS

Rich and poor, Protestant and Roman Catholic and Jew, farmer and city-dweller and suburbanite all showed marked shifts toward President Johnson in yesterday's extraordinary election.

Only in the Deep South did Senator Barry Goldwater score any significant gains for the Republican ticket over four years ago. Riding the crest of the racial issue there, he swung Mississippi, Alabama, Georgia, South Carolina and Louisiana to his party.

The white backlash, on which Mr. Goldwater had counted so strongly, failed to materialize in most parts of the North. Only among voters of Polish and other East European origins were there signs of this resentment toward Negroes, and even this phenomenon was scattered.

Continued on Page 26, Column 1

3 G.O.P. Senators Lose

By E. W. KENWORTHY

The Democrats appeared virtually certain today of maintaining a nearly 2-to-1 majority in the United States Senate.

At 3 A.M. the Democrats had won 25 of the 35 contests in yesterday's elections. These, added to their 40 holdovers, assured them of 65 seats when the Eighty-ninth Congress convenes in January.

The Republicans, at the same hour, had won only five seats—in Vermont, Nebraska, Delaware, Arizona and Hawaii—all of which were won by incumbent Senators. These, added to 25 holdovers, assured the Republicans of at least 30 seats.

The party line-up when Congress adjourned last month was 66 Democrats and 34 Republicans.

By 3 A.M. the Democrats had captured three seats from the Republicans.

In New York, Robert F. Kennedy, former Attorney General, a brother of President Kennedy,

Continued on Page 20, Column 1

PRESIDENT SEES A UNITY MANDATE

In Victory Talk, He Pays Tribute to Predecessor

The text of Johnson's talk will be found on Page 22.

By CHARLES MOHR
Special to The New York Times

AUSTIN, Tex., Wednesday, Nov. 4—President Johnson said early this morning that his election was a "mandate for unity" and for a "government that provides equal opportunity for all and special privilege for none."

Mr. Johnson, obviously deeply moved by his landslide victory, told a crowd at the Municipal Auditorium here that it was a tribute to "the program begun by our beloved President John F. Kennedy."

Of the returns, Mr. Johnson said, "I doubt there have ever been so many people seeing so many things alike" on an Election Day.

Earlier, Mr. Johnson had said of Senator Barry Goldwater's refusal to concede that it was "purely a matter for the individual involved—whatever reasons he may have, I don't know."

He also said that the election was going "about as we expected."

Mr. Johnson appeared on the Municipal Auditorium stage with his wife and two daughters to a long ovation.

He said that no words are

Continued on Page 22, Column 6

TURNOUT IS HEAVY

President Expected to Get 60% of Vote, With 44 States

By TOM WICKER

Lyndon Baines Johnson of Texas compiled one of the greatest landslide victories in American history yesterday to win a four-year term of his own as the 36th President of the United States.

Senator Hubert H. Humphrey of Minnesota, Mr. Johnson's running mate on the Democratic ticket, was carried into office as Vice President.

Mr. Johnson's triumph, giving him the "loud and clear" national mandate he had said he wanted, brought 44 states and the district of Columbia, with 486 electoral votes, into the Democratic column.

Senator Barry Goldwater, the Republican candidate, who sought to offer the people "a choice, not an echo" with a strongly conservative campaign, won only five states in the Deep South and gained a narrow victory in his home state of Arizona. Carrying it gave him a total of 52 electoral votes.

Senator Plans Statement

A heavy voter turnout favored the more numerous Democrats.

In Austin, Tex., Mr. Johnson appeared in the Municipal Auditorium to say that his victory was "a tribute to men and women of all parties."

"It is a mandate for unity, for a Government that serves no special interest," he said.

The election meant, he said, that "our nation should forget our petty differences and stand united before all the world."

Mr. Goldwater did not concede. A spokesman announced that the Senator would make no statement until 10 A.M. today in Phoenix.

Johnson Carries Texas

But the totals were not the only marks of the massive Democratic victory. Traditionally Republican states were howled over like tenpins—Vermont, Indiana, Kansas, Nebraska, Wyoming, among others.

In New York, both houses of the Legislature were headed for Democratic control for the first time in years. Heralded Republicans like Charles H. Percy, the gubernatorial candidate in Illinois, went down to defeat.

Former Attorney General Robert F. Kennedy, riding Mr. Johnson's long coattails, overwhelmed Senator Kenneth B. Keating in New York.

But ticket splitting was widespread. And in the South, Georgia voted Republican; never

Continued on Page 22, Column 1

Salinger Is Losing; Johnson Wins State

By LAWRENCE E. DAVIES
Special to The New York Times

SAN FRANCISCO, Wednesday, Nov. 4—President Johnson captured California's 40 electoral votes in his triumph over Senator Barry Goldwater in yesterday's election.

On the basis of the incomplete count of ballots, however, the President's former press secretary, Senator Pierre Salinger, apparently lost his Senatorial battle to George Murphy, the Republican nominee.

Mr. Salinger late last night refused to concede defeat but said he "would be less than candid if I didn't say the vote doesn't look good." Some of his campaign strategists agreed that the results "looked bad" but declared they expected developments for a few hours before leaving anything definite to say.

Mr. Salinger, who has been

Continued on Page 34, Column 4

EAT, DRINK and enjoy buying foods in season, reasonably this week. Read food news features in The New York Times—Advt.

NEWS INDEX

	Page		Page
Books	36–37	Music	44–47
Bridge	38	Obituaries	39
Business	56	Real Estate	63
Buyers	40	Ships and Air	78
Chess	38	Society	30–31
Crossword	39	Sports	52–58
Editorial	42	Theaters	44–47
Fashions	39	TV and Radio	79
Financial	55–61	U. N. Proceedings	12
Food	39–41	Wall Street	56
Man in the News	43	Weather	78

News Summary and Index, Page 41

WORLD'S LEADING PRODUCER of Folk Music on Records. Write for Free Xmas catalog. Folkways, 116 W. 46 St., N.Y.C.—Advt.

"All the News
That's Fit to Print"

The New York Times.

LATE CITY EDITION
U. S. Weather Bureau Report (Page 70) forecasts:
Cloudy and foggy, then partly cloudy
today; cloudy tonight and tomorrow.
Temp. range: 42—38; yesterday: 40—35.

VOL. CXIV..No. 39,136.   © 1965 by The New York Times Company
7 Times Square, New York, N. Y. 10036   NEW YORK, FRIDAY, MARCH 19, 1965.   TEN CENTS

RUSSIAN FLOATS IN SPACE FOR 10 MINUTES; LEAVES ORBITING CRAFT WITH A LIFELINE; MOSCOW SAYS MOON TRIP IS 'TARGET NOW'

JOHNSON OFFERS TO CALL UP GUARD IF WALLACE WON'T

Rejects Governor's Bid for U.S. 'Civilian Forces' to Protect Rights March

Excerpts from address by Gov. Wallace are on Page 20.

By CABELL PHILLIPS
Special to The New York Times

WASHINGTON, March 18 — President Johnson offered tonight to mobilize the Alabama National Guard to protect the Selma-to-Montgomery marchers next week.

In rejecting a request by Gov. George C. Wallace for "federal civilian forces" to police the demonstration, the President pointed out that the Governor could mobilize the Guard if he felt such protection was needed.

He then said that if the Governor did not do so, and conditions warranted, he would call up the Guard himself.

[In Montgomery, Governor Wallace told a joint session of the Alabama Legislature of his request to President Johnson. After he spoke, the Legislature adopted a resolution calling the protest march "asinine and ridiculous." Page 20.]

Delays Ranch Trip

The President's statement was made to a hastily summoned news conference in his White House office at 10:15 o'clock tonight. He had delayed his departure for a weekend at his ranch in Texas because of the developments in the Alabama situation.

The President first read reporters a telegram he had received from Governor Wallace at 8:48 tonight.

The Governor said that in order to maintain maximum security for the march which had been authorized by a Federal Court the state would need the services of more than 6,000 men, 489 vehicles, 15 buses and necessary supporting units.

The President's statement said:

"The questions raised by the Selma-Montgomery march were submitted to the court in Montgomery, Ala.

Cites Court's Ruling

"That court, with an Alabama judge sitting, after hearing all of the evidence, including evidence as to the problems of protecting marchers, determined that a march should be permitted and that the marchers should be protected.

"The Federal Government does not have civilian personnel approaching the figure suggested by Governor Wallace. However, Governor Wallace has at his disposal over 10,000 trained members of the Alabama National Guard which he could call into service.

"If he is unable or unwilling to call up the Guard, and to maintain law and order in Alabama——

Continued on Page 20, Column 7

FOWLER IS NAMED DILLON SUCCESSOR

President Nominates Former Under Secretary to Head Treasury Department

By CHARLES MOHR
Special to The New York Times

WASHINGTON, March 18 — President Johnson announced today that he had nominated Henry H. Fowler to succeed Douglas Dillon as Secretary of the Treasury.

Mr. Dillon, who has wanted to leave the Government for some time, is expected to resign soon. Mr. Fowler, 56 years old, a corporate lawyer, is a former Under Secretary of the Treasury. He returned to the practice of law in April of 1964.

Mr. Johnson left tonight for a long weekend at his ranch in Texas. His press secretary, George E. Reedy, said Mr. Johnson would hold a news conference at the ranch at noon Saturday, Eastern standard time.

Shortly before the President's departure, reporters were summoned into his Oval Office, where they found Mr. Fowler, a short, dapper man with carefully groomed white hair.

Different Choice Rumored

Only about an hour earlier, press associations had carried a report asserting that the House Ways and Means Committee had been told by its chairman, Wilbur D. Mills, that the President planned to name David Kennedy, president of the Continental Bank of Chicago, to the Treasury post.

That report may have had some bearing on the unexpected timing of Mr. Fowler's nomination. Mr. Mills, Democrat of Arkansas, denied having made the remark about Mr. Fowler.

It was known that for several weeks Mr. Johnson had attempted to persuade Donald C. Cook, a New York utility executive, to take the Treasury job. Mr. Cook, a close personal and political friend of the President——

Continued on Page 17, Column 2

LEAVING SPACESHIP: Lieut. Col. Aleksel A. Leonov emerges from Voskhod 2 to become first man to float freely in space. Photos were made from videotape broadcast.
Tass via Associated Press Cablephoto

ALONE IN SPACE: Colonel Leonov outside the ship traveling at nearly five miles a second. He is attached by a lifeline. The projection at right carries movie equipment.
Tass via Associated Press Cablephoto

WEIGHTLESS: Colonel Leonov turning behind his craft. Balance between forces of his orbital motion and the pull of gravity produces the condition of weightlessness.
Tass via United Press International Cablephoto

BEFORE THE FLIGHT: Colonel Leonov in space suit before launching. He spent 10 minutes outside the craft.
Tass via Associated Press Cablephoto

2D MAN FLIES SHIP

TV in Soviet Shows Astronaut Turning Slow Somersault

Text of Soviet announcement is printed on Page 14.

By HENRY TANNER
Special to The New York Times

MOSCOW, Friday, March 19 — A Soviet Air Force officer, who yesterday became the first man to leave an orbiting spacecraft and float in space, was still circling the earth early today in the capsule with a fellow astronaut.

Lieut. Col. Aleksel A. Leonov, 30 years old, left the two-man Voskhod 2 as it passed over the Soviet Union while completing its first orbit and beginning its second. He stayed outside the cabin for 10 minutes, according to Tass, official Soviet press agency.

The spaceship, piloted by Col. Pavel I. Belyayev, 39, was launched at 10 A.M. Moscow time yesterday, 2 A.M. Eastern standard time. The launching site, not announced at first, was later said to be the cosmodrome Baekonur in Kazakhstan. All previous Soviet manned space shots have originated there.

[Vasily Seleznev, a leading Soviet space official, said on Moscow television Thursday that "the target before us now is the moon, and we hope to reach it in no distant future," The Associated Press reported.]

New Shot Rumored

There was widespread speculation that a second spaceship might be launched sometime today in an attempt to effect for the first time a link-up of two crafts in space.

As Colonel Leonov traveled through space tethered to his ship at a speed of nearly five miles a second, he was shielded by a specially equipped space suit. This protected him from the intense heat of the sun.

Specialists said that even the slightest penetration of his suit by the sun's rays would have caused instant death.

If the five-yard pole lifeline that connected him with the ship had broken, he could have been lost, orbiting the earth as a human satellite. His body would have burned up on re-entry after a week or perhaps months of orbiting.

No Steering Devices

His space suit was not equipped with any devices by which he could have steered his way back to the spacecraft. Voskhod 2 was orbiting every 90.9 minutes. The apogee, or highest point, of its orbit was approximately 309 miles, higher than any previous manned space flight. Its perigee, or low point, was given as approximately 108 miles.

American space experts said they thought the launching was performed by the same vehicle used in earlier Soviet space flights, developing a thrust of about 900,000 pounds. The fact

Continued on Page 14, Column 1

Court Denies Police Need To Tell Suspect of Rights

By SIDNEY E. ZION

The New York Court of Appeals has ruled that the police do not have to advise a suspect of his right to remain silent and his right to have a lawyer before taking his confession.

Legal observers consider the decision of great importance because the courts had appeared to be moving in the direction of requiring the police to inform suspects of their constitutional rights before questioning them.

In fact, the California Supreme Court reversed a conviction in January because the defendant had not been told of his right to have a lawyer and his right to remain silent before confessing.

Thus the two largest states in the country are in direct conflict on what lawyers agree to be one of the most important criminal-law questions of the day.

In the New York case, People v. Gunner, the defendant

Continued on Page 26, Column 1

ALLEN IS UPHELD IN MALVERNE CASE

Court Rules He Has Right to Order Shifts of Pupils

By R. W. APPLE Jr.
Special to The New York Times

ALBANY, March 18 — The Court of Appeals affirmed today the right of the Commissioner of Education to order the reorganization of school districts to promote integration.

By a 5-to-2 vote, the court upheld the order of the Commissioner of Education, James E. Allen Jr., that the elementary schools of Malverne, L. I., be brought into better racial balance. The Malverne situation has been considered an integration test case.

The court's decision was narrowly based. It dealt only with the Commissioner's authority—not with the nature of his order or with this goals.

"Disagreement with the sociological, psychological and educational assumptions relied upon by the Commissioner cannot be evaluated by this court," the decision said. "Such arguments can only be heard in the Legislature, which has endowed the Commissioner with all but absolute power, or by the board of regents, who are elected by the Legislature and make policy."

The Appellate Division of the State Supreme Court, whose decision the Court of Appeals affirmed, had endorsed "the judgment of the Commissioner that correction of racial imbalance is an educational aid to a minority group in attaining the skills and level of education

Continued on Page 21, Column 8

CITY AGAIN FACES WATER SHORTAGE

D'Angelo Says Reserves Are Far Below Normal—Light Snowfall Upstate Cited

By CHARLES G. BENNETT

New York City is facing a possible "serious situation" in its water supply this year, and a summer conservation program will probably be necessary.

Armand D'Angelo, Commissioner of Water Supply, Gas and Electricity, said yesterday that he was concerned that the city's reservoirs were only at 38.1 per cent of their capacity yesterday, a level far below normal for this time of year.

A prime factor in determining whether the city will be short of water this year will be the rainfall between now and June. Mr. D'Angelo said he was heartened that the supply had risen from an all-time low percentage of 24.8 last Feb. 5, but he said the rise was not so great as it should be for this time of year.

Total Capacity Rises

Although the Feb. 5 supply was a record low on a percentage basis, the reserves have been lower because total capacity has increased over the years.

For instance, the 33 per cent of capacity low point reached during the water shortage of 1949-50 represented far less water in storage than the 24.8 per cent of last Feb. 5 because the total capacity of the reservoirs in 1950 was 253 billion gallons, compared with 476.5 billion gallons now.

In mid-February, predictions of heavy storms in the watershed areas had led water authorities to expect that spring runoffs to the reservoirs would raise water levels to normal measurements—near capacity—by June 1, when the summer depletion usually begins.

On Feb. 18 a spokesman for Mr. D'Angelo accordingly said

Continued on Page 28, Column 1

Cypriotes Said to Install Soviet-Supplied Missiles

By MAX FRANKEL
Special to The New York Times

WASHINGTON, March 18—The Johnson Administration has acquired apparently convincing evidence that Soviet-made antiaircraft missiles are about to be installed on Cyprus by the Cypriote Government.

Some reports suggest that some of the missiles are already in place.

United States officials, fearing a major crisis, are said to be applying strong pressure upon Greece in a last-minute effort to halt the emplacements.

Although Athens is pledged to give military and diplomatic support to the Greek Cypriote majority on the island, there is some doubt about the extent of its influence over the Government of President Makarios.

Greek-Turkish Clash Feared

Turkey, which has been supporting the Turkish Cypriote minority, has threatened to attack the missile sites from the air.

Some sources feared that preventive raids would be made within the next few days, reviving the danger of war between Greece and Turkey, both members of the North Atlantic Treaty Organization.

The Administration refused today to say anything about its evidence, except to note "press reports" of missile shipments.

A guarded State Department comment betrayed some concern, however. It said that "now more than ever" the parties involved in the Cyprus dispute ought to handle their problem

Continued on Page 4, Column 4

INDONESIAN REDS HARRY AMERICANS

Cut Power for Residences— Try to Seize Oil Plants

By NEIL SHEEHAN
Special to The New York Times

JAKARTA, Indonesia, March 18 — Communist labor unions cut off gas and electricity at a United States Embassy apartment building and the home of the American naval attaché here today and attempted to seize control of United States-owned oil installations in southern Sumatra.

The Jakarta offices of the Indonesian-American Friendship Society, an activity of The Associated Press were also deprived of electricity.

Antara, the Government press agency, announced that Communist oil workers had actually taken control of the Standard Vacuum Oil Company's refinery at Sungei Gerong near the Sumatran port of Palembang.

However, a company spokesman here said that "the plant was not taken over and operations are normal."

Informed sources said the Communist workers had demonstrated at the refinery and demanded that the American manager hand it over to them.

When he refused, the workers hung posters on the walls of the refinery buildings declaring the installation the property of the Indonesian Government and returned to work. The posters were later removed by the Indonesian police.

A similar demonstration and

Continued on Page 2, Column 3

Senate Defeats Southern Move To Delay Bill on Voting, 67-13

By E. W. KENWORTHY
Special to The New York Times

WASHINGTON, March 18 — The bipartisan voting-rights bill started on its legislative journey through both houses of Congress today amid displays of overwhelming support that seemed to augur relatively quick enactment.

In the Senate, Southerners began efforts to delay the bill as soon as it was introduced jointly by the Democratic leader, Mike Mansfield of Montana, and the Republican leader, Everett McKinley Dirksen of Illinois, with 56 co-sponsors from both parties. Later, more Senators joined, bringing the total sponsorship to 66.

The Southerners were overwhelmed on a roll-call vote, 67 to 13.

Continued on Page 21, Column 1

In the House, where the bill was introduced yesterday, Attorney General Nicholas deB. Katzenbach was the first witness before the Constitutional Subcommittee of the Judiciary Committee.

When the Attorney General completed his explanation of the bill and defense of its constitutionality, Representative William M. McCulloch of Ohio, the ranking Republican on the committee, said that Mr. Katzenbach had made "one of the best statements I have heard in my 17 years in the House."

The Southern case came on a motion by Mr. Mansfield to send the bill to the Senate

Continued on Page 21, Column 8

L.I.R.R. 'Slowdown' Delays Thousands

By PETER MILLONES

Thousands of commuters on the Long Island Rail Road were delayed up to several hours last night when engineers refused to move trains until headlights were inspected.

The railroad called the engineers' action a "wildcat slowdown." At its height the slowdown became a full stop as virtually all trains were halted on the line from Manhattan to Montauk.

But shortly after midnight, as the slowdown reached Pennsylvania Station, trains were reported running normally again. There were no indications that service would be affected this morning for the line's 200,000 commuters.

The engineers began calling

Continued on Page 18, Column 6

Kennedy Will Join Mt. Kennedy Climb

By WARREN WEAVER Jr.
Special to The New York Times

WASHINGTON, March 18—Senator Robert F. Kennedy is flying to the Yukon this weekend to join in an attempt to scale for the first time a 13,900-foot peak named after President Kennedy.

The Senator, although an outdoor enthusiast and experienced hiker, has never climbed a mountain. The five other members of the expedition are all experts; one of them is James W. Whittaker, the first American to climb Mount Everest.

The goal of the expedition, Mount Kennedy, is in the St. Elias Mountains, 25 miles north of the Yukon-British Columbia line and just east of the Alas-

Continued on Page 24, Column 1

NEWS INDEX

	Page		Page
Art	27, 32	Music	27-31
Books	33-35	Obituaries	35
Bridge	32	Real Estate	55
Business	48-49, 57	Screen	27-31
Buyers	46	Ships and Air.	69-70
Crossword	33	Society	40-47
Editorial	36	Sports	46-47
Events Today	38	Theaters	27-31
Fashions	48	TV and Radio	71
Financial	48-56	U. N. Proceedings	11
Food	47	Wash. Proceedings	35
Man in the News	14	Weather	70

News Summary and Index, Page 37

"All the News
That's Fit to Print"

The New York Times.

NEWS SUMMARY AND INDEX, PAGE 95

LATE CITY EDITION
U.S. Weather Bureau Report (Page 95) forecasts:
Mostly sunny, hot and humid today;
fair, warm tonight and tomorrow.
Temp.—Range: 92—68; yesterday: 87—63.
Temp.—Hum. Index: high 70's; yesterday: 77.

SECTION ONE

VOL. CXIV—No. 39,285. © 1965 by The New York Times Company Times Square, New York, N.Y. 10036 THE NEW YORK TIMES, SUNDAY, AUGUST 15, 1965. 50c beyond 50-mile zone from New York City, except Long Island, higher in air delivery cities THIRTY CENTS

U.S. ADDING 6,400 TO MARINE FORCE IN SOUTH VIETNAM

Step Goes Beyond Increase Announced by Johnson— Advance Units Arrive

DANANG STRENGTHENED

Company There Carries Out Attack by Copter Against Vietcong-Held Village

By CHARLES MOHR
Special to The New York Times

SAIGON, South Vietnam, Sunday, Aug. 15—A few thousand more United States marines landed in South Vietnam today as advance elements for a total of 6,400 Marine Corps reinforcements expected within days.

A military spokesman said that headquarters units of the Seventh Regimental Landing Team, of the First Marine Division, with a battalion of troops, had come ashore in landing craft at Chulai, 350 miles north of Saigon, yesterday. Another regiment of marines has been stationed there for several months.

The spokesman did not disclose the size of the newly arrived group, but a battalion landing team numbers 1,500 to 1,800 men.

Another Battalion Lands

This morning another battalion of marines began landing at Danang, north of Chulai. Danang is the main headquarters of the Marine forces in South Vietnam.

The spokesman said the full regimental strength of 6,400 would soon be on hand.

The Marine landings were not part of the planned increase of 50,000 American troops announced by President Johnson on July 28, the spokesman added. Instead, he said, they represent a "supplement."

As of Aug. 8, there were 82,400 American servicemen in South Vietnam, 25,700 of them marines. Mr. Johnson has said that the total will soon reach at least 125,000.

In the Danang area before dawn, United States marines engaged in an unorthodox night helicopter-assault operation. A rifle company was landed near the village of Phoan under the illumination of aerial flares of 1.5 million candlepower dropped

Continued on Page 2, Column 3

Earl Brown Rejects Spot on Beame Slate

The New York Times
Earl Brown

By RICHARD L. MADDEN

Earl Brown, chairman of the city's Commission on Human Rights, declined yesterday to run for Manhattan Borough President on the slate of Controller Abraham D. Beame in the Democratic primary.

Mr. Brown said that "overriding personal considerations have left me no choice." He did not elaborate.

The Beame forces circulated petitions to put Mr.

Continued on Page 43, Column 1

MOSCOW REPORTS NEW MOON PHOTOS

Pictures of Far Side Said to Fill In the Gap of Earlier Survey by Spacecraft

By PETER GROSE
Special to The New York Times

MOSCOW, Aug. 14—An unmanned spacecraft has transmitted high-definition television pictures of hitherto unphotographed areas on the side of the moon opposite the earth, Tass, the Soviet press agency, said today.

The pictures were not made public.

Combined with the first photographs ever of the far side of the moon, taken in October, 1959, the new pictures give a complete pictorial record of the side of the moon that is never turned toward the earth. Tass said.

The pictures announced today were taken July 20 from a point much closer to the moon than the earlier series, less than 7,000 miles above the surface against about 40,000 in 1959.

The new pictures show surface features three miles or less across, according to Grigory Leikin, a senior researcher of the Astronomical Society at the Soviet Academy of Sciences.

A complete atlas of the

Continued on Page 41, Column 1

PAPANDREOU BLOC SPLIT BY WALKOUT IN HIS OWN PARTY

Two of Ex-Premier's Aides Claim Enough Support to Form New Greek Regime

Special to The New York Times

ATHENS, Aug. 14—Two of former Premier George Papandreou's principal aides announced today that they had decided to break away from his majority Center Union party at the head of an undisclosed number of Members of Parliament.

The declaration by Stephanos Stephanopoulos, Deputy Premier in the Papandreou Government ousted July 15, and Elias Tsirimokos, its Interior Minister, raised hopes that a Greek Government would be formed Monday.

A spokesman for the two leaders said they had "the support of more Center Union Deputies than is needed to swing a parliamentary majority in their favor."

Third Aide May Defect

A third Papandreou aide, Savros Papapolitis, who heads a group of 10 Center Union Deputies, asserted that he was reconsidering his allegiance to the former Premier and might join the defectors.

The spokesman and Mr. Tsirimokos, both of whom were expected to be candidates for Premier, said a formal declaration of secession from the Papandreou party would be sent to Parliament Monday.

Today's development was a direct result of former Premier Papandreou's stiffening attitude in his conflict with King Constantine, who forced him out of power July 15 in a clash over political influence in the Greek army. The King was opposed to a Papandreou plan to replace the Defense Minister and to purge right-wing army officers.

Novas Cabinet Failed

Constantine promptly appointed a Papandreou aide, George Athanasiadis-Novas, Speaker of Parliament, to form a new government. But Mr. Athanasiadis-Novas managed to get the support of only 25 Center Union deputies.

He was overthrown in a stormy session of Parliament early on Aug. 5 by the combined Papandreou forces and 22 pro-Communist Deputies while Athens was in the grip of riots and street fighting between Papandreou supporters and the police.

A week ago, King Constantine asked another Papandreou aide, Mr. Stephanopoulos, to form a government. But the Premier-designate gave up the attempt after having been rebuffed at a Center Union caucus by a majority still loyal to Mr. Papandreou.

At a 90-minute audience at the palace Friday, Mr. Papan-

Continued on Page 42, Column 1

---

21 DEAD IN LOS ANGELES RIOTS; 600 HURT; 20,000 TROOPS CALLED; PRESIDENT CONDEMNS VIOLENCE

JOHNSON SHOCKED

He Calls Disturbances 'Tragic' and Appeals for Order on Coast

By ROBERT B. SEMPLE Jr.
Special to The New York Times

AUSTIN, Tex., Aug. 14—President Johnson described the Los Angeles riots today as "tragic and shocking." He warned the rioters that their rights could not be won and their grievances remedied "through violence."

The President appealed to "every person in a position of leadership" in Los Angeles to make "every effort to restore order."

He also instructed two high Administration officials to meet with Gov. Edmund G. Brown of California in New York and to place themselves at the Governor's disposal in an effort to stop the riots. Mr. Brown stopped in New York before returning to California from an interrupted overseas vacation.

The two officials were Lee C. White, special counsel to the President, and LeRoy Collins, Under Secretary of Commerce. Mr. Collins is former director of the Community Relations Service, which is charged with encouraging voluntary compliance with the Civil Rights Act of 1964.

Report on Troops Denied

A report from California said that the Administration had also promised to provide Federal troops if necessary to quell the disturbance. This report was quickly denied by a Presidential aide, Joseph A. Califano Jr.

Reached in Washington, Mr. Califano pointed out that California had 21,000 National Guardsmen on whom it could call and said that there was no need to involve Regular Army troops.

Mr. Johnson's appeal for speedy restoration of order was read to reporters by his press secretary, Bill D. Moyers. The President, spending the weekend at his ranch 65 miles west of Austin, has been keeping in close touch with the situation through the Justice Department and members of his staff in Washington.

The President's statement did not speculate on the causes of the disturbances and White House aides here were reluctant to do so. One aide said that the riots had happened so quickly there had been little opportunity to examine the reasons for them. He said that he

Continued on Page 77, Column 3

GUARDSMEN SWEEP AREA: Mobilized National Guardsmen move in convoy formation through Negro section of Los Angeles where looting and arson continued into fourth day.

SCENE OF DESTRUCTION: Deserted after another night of violence in the city, 103d Street is littered with debris. Estimates of damage ranged up to $100 million.

United Press International Telephoto

2,000 GUARDSMEN ON CHICAGO ALERT

Kerner Notifies Units After 2d Night of Racial Riots— Negroes Get Appeal

By DONALD JANSON
Special to The New York Times

CHICAGO, Aug. 14—Gov. Otto Kerner placed 2,000 National Guardsmen on stand-by alert at armories here today in the wake of two nights of Chicago's worst racial rioting in 13 years.

The action was taken at the request of Orlando W. Wilson, Chicago's superintendent of police, to forestall any resumption of the bottle-throwing violence that injured 60 persons last night.

Mr. Wilson warned residents of the largely Negro West Side neighborhood where the rioting occurred that unless they did "all in their power" to help the police prevent lawlessness the situation could deteriorate into uncontrolled strife such as Los Angeles has suffered the last few days.

He spoke at a solemn news conference in the office of Mayor Richard J. Daley. The Mayor, by his side, appealed to Chicagoans to stay off the street in the West Side neighborhood so that the police could isolate troublemakers and prevent any recurrence of last night's eight-hour riot.

The area, 40 blocks west of downtown Chicago, was quiet tonight. Taverns that ordinarily would have been jammed on a Saturday night were closed. Pulaski Road between Madison Street and the Eisenhower expressway was littered with broken glass, and stores with their windows hit by rocks and bottles were boarded up to prevent looting.

By the time the police restored order shortly before dawn today 104 persons had been arrested, primarily on charges of disorderly conduct and resisting arrest. Most of

---

Discontent and Hate Viewed as Factors In Coast Violence

By WALLACE TURNER
Special to The New York Times

LOS ANGELES, Aug. 14—Negroes in a depressed area of Los Angeles were swept up into an emotional tide of hate and bitterness that caused them to beat and burn property here today.

One worker for the Congress of Racial Equality, Cornell Henderson, a Negro, declared, "There were a lot of young hoods and agitators. But there were a lot of others who were just discontented and took advantage of the situation for emotional release."

There also was a heavy overlay of hate preaching, said Mr. Henderson.

"I saw the Black Muslims in the area," he said. "They were preaching resistance and 'down with the police brutality' and the usual thing that they talk about. They wanted to have the white men driven away. They chanted 'go away, whitey' at any white people they saw."

Psychiatrists, examining an

Continued on Page 80, Column 1

Policeman Kills One, Shoots 2d in Beating

By THEODORE JONES

A 23-year-old Brooklyn laborer was fatally shot and a 15-year-old youth was wounded early yesterday by an off-duty patrolman who went to the aid of a man being beaten and robbed by six youths.

The police said both the youth and the laborer had attacked the patrolman with knives after he had identified himself and sought to halt the beaten man in front of a five-story apartment house at the corner of Nostrand and Vernon Avenues. The patrolman and all others involved were Negroes.

However, a witness to the shooting gave a different version. He said the slain man, identified as Willie James

---

GOV. BROWN VOWS TO RESTORE ORDER

Arrives in Los Angeles Aboard White House Plane—Cut Short Holiday in Greece

Special to The New York Times

LOS ANGELES, Aug. 14—Gov. Edmund G. Brown returned to California tonight and pledged "to restore law and order in Los Angeles."

In a news conference alongside the White House jet that flew him from New York, he said that he did not plan to accept President Johnson's offer of Federal help now.

"I don't want to federalize the National Guard—that's a major step—unless I have to," Governor Brown said.

"But if I have to, I will. I intend to restore law and order to Los Angeles."

"I will go down to the area as soon as I can," he said.

In a brief stopover in New York, the Governor referred to the Negro rioting here as "a state of insurrection."

Governor Brown arrived at the Los Angeles international airport just before 10 P.M. Pacific daylight time (1 A.M. Sunday, Eastern daylight time). He was met by Lieut. Gov. Glenn Anderson, who ordered the National Guard to riot control duty Friday afternoon.

The Governor appeared on the steps of the Air Force Jetstar after a four-minute conference inside the cabin. Other participants were the state Attorney General, Thomas Lynch; Hale Champion, the State Director of Finance, one of the Governor's chief advisers, and Jack Burby, the Governor's press secretary. Mrs. Brown accompanied her husband.

The Governor said he had returned to California to "give what aid the Governor can give" to the Mayor and police officials of Los Angeles.

"However, a witness to the shooting gave a different version. He said the slain man," "I said: 'I want to see this catastrophe ended.' The Governor sidestepped

---

CURFEW ORDERED

Outbursts Spread to New Areas—Disaster Zone Is Proclaimed

By GLADWIN HILL
Special to The New York Times

LOS ANGELES, Aug. 14—Rioting, looting and burning spread today for the fourth day in the Negro district of southwestern Los Angeles. The disorders continued despite the rifle fire of National Guard troops and local peace forces.

The death toll from the hoodlum-instigated lawlessness rose tonight to 21. Nineteen of the victims were rioters, one was a sheriff's deputy and one a fireman. The last two were white men, as was one of the victims officially classed as a rioter.

The number of injured reached about 600, most of them rioters. Arrests totaled 1,409. Estimates of property damage ranged from $30 million to $100 million.

The number of California guardsmen called up rose to 20,000, according to Lieut. Gen. Roderick Hill, the state's National Guard adjutant. Some 4,000 were on patrol today. More than 1,000 policemen and deputies were in the area.

Curfew Hours

Tonight Lieut. Gov. Glenn Anderson proclaimed a curfew in a 35-square-mile area where the rioting has centered. From 8 P.M. to sunrise, he decreed, anyone on the streets except law-enforcement officers and newsmen will be seized.

Mr. Anderson, serving as acting Governor until Gov. Edmund G. Brown returned tonight from a European vacation, also proclaimed the riot zone a disaster area. This permitted policemen to be brought in as needed from surrounding cities in four counties.

Local authorities said help might have to be sought from the Federal Government.

"It's a mess, and it's getting progressively worse," General Hill said. "It started with a few square blocks, and today it was spreading over 21 square miles."

Sniping Increases

There were signs late tonight of some diminution in the disorders. Reports of new outbreaks of looting and fires were less frequent. But there was an increase in sniping from roofs and buildings.

Two sheriff's deputies were wounded in one exchange with snipers.

The depredations in the fourday rampage, triggered by the arrest last Wednesday night of a Negro on charges of drunken driving, spread despite a massive sweep operation. Block by block, the troops and civilian officers removed everyone from the streets who could give no

Continued on Page 79, Column 1

Sports News

GOLF

Dave Marr shot a one-under-par 70 yesterday to tie Tommy Aaron for first place in the Professional Golfers Association tournament in Ligonier, Pa. Each has 209 for 54 holes. Gardner Dickinson shot a 69 for 210 and Jack Nicklaus and Billy Casper shared fourth place at 211.

BASEBALL

Hector Lopez's single with the bases loaded in the ninth inning yesterday gave the New York Yankees a 3-2 victory over the Kansas City Athletics in the second Bat Day at the Stadium. The victory gave the Yanks 59-59 won-lost mark, the first time they have been at .500 since they were 7-7. The Cleveland Indians beat the league-leading Minnesota Twins, 3-1, behind the three-hit pitching of Sam McDowell, who struck out 11 to run his total to 227, best in the league.

The New York Mets beat the Astros, 1-0, in 10 innings at Houston and ended an 11-game losing streak. The victory was the Mets' first in the Astrodome. The Los Angeles Dodgers beat the Pittsburgh Pirates, 1-0, in the 10th inning for Sandy Koufax's 21st victory.

FOOTBALL

The New York Giants opened their exhibition season by absorbing a 44-7 trouncing from the Packers at Green Bay.

HORSE RACING

What a Treat scored a neck victory in the 85th Alabama Stakes for 3-year-old fillies at Saratoga. Discipline was second and Terentia third in the $63,200 race, but their order was reversed after a foul claim by Larry Adams. Terentia's jockey. Eighteen fillies started. Mister Judge, $21, won the $22,950 Longport Handicap at Atlantic City by a neck.

164-Year-Old Brooklyn Navy Yard Launches Last Ship

The New York Times (by Jack Manning)
Mrs. Bruce Solomonson, daughter of Vice President and Mrs. Humphrey, christens the amphibious transport Duluth, the last ship to be launched at the Brooklyn Navy Yard.

By DOUGLAS ROBINSON

The 164-year-old Brooklyn Navy Yard launched its last ship yesterday amid the blare of martial music, the boom of cannon and the fluttering of flags. The installation, formally known as the New York Naval Shipyard, was ordered closed last year by Defense Secretary Robert S. McNamara as part of an economy move. Despite the gay trappings of the launching, an air of sadness hung over the assembled workers and their families and officials who joined Navy officers and officials to see the amphibious transport Duluth float into the East River. "It's not a happy day, especially for the younger workers," commented Vincent DiNovi, who has been a machinist at the yard for 25 years. "It's not a happy day and it's the last launching and it's the last

"All the News That's Fit to Print"

The New York Times.

LATE CITY EDITION
U. S. Weather Bureau Report forecasts:
Mostly sunny, cool today; increasing cloudiness tonight and tomorrow.
Temp. Range: 45—30; yesterday: 57—45.

VOL. CXV....No. 39,372.   © 1965 by The New York Times Company Times Square, New York, N.Y. 10036   NEW YORK, WEDNESDAY, NOVEMBER 10, 1965   TEN CENTS

POWER FAILURE SNARLS NORTHEAST; 800,000 ARE CAUGHT IN SUBWAYS HERE; AUTOS TIED UP, CITY GROPES IN DARK

To Our Readers

Because of the power blackout, the mechanical facilities of The New York Times were put out of operation last night and early today. Through the courtesy of The Newark Evening News this issue of The Times was set into type and printed in The Evening News's plant from The Times's own news reports. The financial tables are those of The Evening News.

Johnson Restates Goals in Vietnam

By The Associated Press
JOHNSON CITY, Tex., Nov. 9—President Johnson has restated broad American goals in Viet Nam and proclaimed Nov. 28 as "a day of dedication and prayer" for all members of the anti-Communist forces there.

The United States Government, he said, "remains ready without condition for the international discussions that can lead to lasting peace."

Mr. Johnson's proclamation, which followed a cue from Congress, was made public today though he actually signed it three days ago.

The Presidential document sidestepped one potential source of direct friction between Americans who support and oppose the Vietnam war.

Nov. 27 Suggested

Congress had suggested Nov. 27 as the day of prayer. However, a series of antiwar demonstrations, including a march on Washington, had been planned for that day.

Mr. Johnson, who had authority to fix the timing of the tribute to fighting forces in Vietnam, decided on the following day, a Sunday. In so doing, he is reported to have wanted to avoid a direct confrontation between backers and critics of American policy in Vietnam.

As the President has said on many occasions, he believes the great majority of Americans support his policy on Vietnam.

'Honored Tradition' Cited

The President proclaimed Nov. 28 "as a day of dedication and prayer, honoring the men and women of South Vietnam, and of the United States, and of all other countries, who are risking their lives to bring about a just peace in South Vietnam."

He had this to say about American war aims:

"In assisting the people of South Vietnam to resist unprovoked aggression, the United States and other nations are carrying on the honored tradition of defending a people's right to freedom ... the purpose of the United States in Vietnam is to help open the way for social justice in place of unprovoked aggression, and peace instead of war."

Mr. Johnson noted that both the Senate and the House had passed resolutions saying "it would be fitting for the President to set aside a national day of remembrance dedicated to those Americans who are committing their lives, blood and energies in the defense of world peace."

During the evening Mr. Johnson talked by telephone with Governor Rockefeller and Mayor

(Continued on Page 3, Column 3)

G.I.'s Score Big Victory

Vietcong Force Almost Wiped Out by U.S. Airborne Unit

By R. W. APPLE JR.
Special to The New York Times
BIENHOA, South Vietnam, Nov. 9—The toll of almost 400 Vietcong killed in a battle 30 miles northeast of Saigon yesterday marked a decisive victory for troops of the US 173d Airborne Brigade.

The American paratroopers, members of one battalion, tired into waves of enemy troops at point-blank range in the eight-hour battle.

The United States troops suffered substantial casualties in the battle in a dense tropical thicket, but only at the battle of Chulay had an American unit inflicted heavier losses on the Vietcong.

Most of the fighting tok place at such close range that American M-79 grenades, which explode only after they have traveled 12 yards, bounced harmlessly off the guerrillas.

Assaults Thrown Back

The Americans were surrounded several times, but each time they threw back enemy assaults and held their positions. The Vietcong, using flame throwers and molten-metal thermite grenades for the first time in the war, attacked until they were almost wiped out.

This afternoon, with the battle over, the United States troops were returned by helicopter to their base camp at the sprawling installation here.

Sunday night, two platoons from the 173d, moving through the underbrush on patrol in the jungle area where they had been operating since Nov. 5, found fresh footprints and heard the frightened cackling of chickens.

At 7:30 A.M. two platoons moved out again, clawing their way through the brush in the jungle gloom, and began climbing a pair of rocky hills. Both platoons were from C Company of the First Battalion, 503d Infantry.

'Right on Their Path'

Suddenly the platoon on the right, about 50 men, found itself in a circle of mud and thatch huts. The huts were invisible from the air because of the palmetto trees arching overhead and almost invisible from the ground because of the underbrush.

The company's commanding officer, Capt. Henry B. Tucker of Columbus, Ohio, said later:

(Continued Page 5, Column 3)

CITY IN DARKNESS: Except for scattered independent lighting this is how the city looked from the Jersey side.

ON A TRAIN GOING NOWHERE: Commuters waiting on subway in Times Square area. Picture was made in
The New York Times

U.S. Orders An Inquiry

President Calls for a Study of Power Failure in East

By JOHN D. POMFRET
Special to The New York Times
AUSTIN, Tex., Nov. 9—President Johnson ordered today an immediate and complete investigation of the power failure that blacked out a large section of the East.

The President issued the order in a memorandum to Joseph C. Swidler, chairman of the Federal Power Commission.

Within minutes after the investigation was ordered, Mr. Swidler sent telegrams to all power companies in the affected areas, requesting their assistance. He also telephoned Defense Secretary Robert S. McNamara and Attorney General Nicholas de B. Katzenbach, telling them to coordinate the inquiry with them.

During the evening Mr. Johnson talked by telephone with Governor Rockefeller and Mayor

(Continued on Page 3, Column 3)

Miss Liberty Shines Through Blackout

The Statue of Liberty maintained its illumination throughout last night's long blackout.

Residents of lower Manhattan saw clearly the floodlit base of the statue on Liberty Island and the lighted torch. Except for an occasional passing river craft, the statue appeared to be the only beacon of light in the harbor.

Power for statue's lights was supplied by the New Jersey Public Service Company.

City's Glitter Goes But Not Its Poise

By FRED POWLEDGE
Broadway, Manhattan and the rest of the city lost their glitter last night. Yet New Yorkers, who are used to living in crises, seemed to take the blackout in stride.

By the thousands they calmly stored over this human tragedy, wait for office buildings and stores soon after the blackout started.

They grabbed every taxicab in sight. Some cab drivers turned on their "off duty" signs and headed for home themselves. Then the New Yorkers grabbed every bus in sight. Although many merchants feared looting and violence, the police reported little such trouble. Many New Yorkers even seemed merry. There was the same air of revelry that often accompanies a heavy snowstorm.

Time to Admire Skyline

Commuters stuck in Manhattan with the prospect of a long wait, before getting to their homes found time to admire the unexpected sight of a moonlit Manhattan skyline, with stars, clouds and no neon.

Below ground, subway riders who waited in stalled trains sat quietly, resigned and goodhumored.

At the Piccadilly Hotel on 45th Street in the heart of the theater district, a guest sat behind the desk helping the management dispense candles. No one seemed panicky, although a woman at the cigarette counter refused to sell anything to anyone who didn't have the correct change. Her cash register would not open.

Huckster Sells Flashlights

A huckster on Broadway sold flashlights, complete with batteries, for $1 apiece. A few doors away, in one of the shops that specializes in imported transistor radios and tape recorders, a salesman got rid of dozens of flashlights at $3 each.

Brief Thought of Disaster

A young actress who lives in Greenwich Village was caught in a bath when the lights went out. She said that her first thoughts were "this is an atomic attack," but that she quickly dismissed such an idea and poured herself a drink.

In Times Square, pedestrians

(Continued on Page 3, Column 6)

ers gathered to listen to portable radios and wait for some form of transportation home.

Some did not wait. Thousands walked across the Queensboro and Brooklyn Bridges, where the stunning night views of the city were strangely missing. The Brooklyn Bridge has a pedestrian walkway, above the automobile roadway, but the Queensboro does not. The Queens bound pedestrians walked across the south lane of the auto roadway four and five abreast. Cars crawled along behind them.

Cross Streets Jammed

Although many offices and stores closed immediately after the blackout began, some essential services stayed open.

Hospitals, using emergency power supplies, stayed lighted. Newspapers did too, but the light came from candles.

Manhattan's crosstown streets became unbroken ribbons of white light as automobiles, the brightest sources of light, jammed the narrow roadways.

Police cars turned on their red blinking lights. Buses crawled down the streets, their interior lamps lighting the faces of crowded passengers.

A Woolworth's store on Lexington Avenue reported a "landoffice business" in candles. People stood in lines that stretched into the street, waiting for a chance to buy a candle.

A street repair crew worked on, filling a hole in the pavement as their supervisor held a flashlight.

Bars filled quickly. The Astor Bar in Times Square, always a popular place, was more popular than ever. The candles planted in ashtrays seemed to produce more than enough light for drinkers.

Another bar in Times Square locked its doors, leaving contented drinkers within a good excuse to remain inside, but angering those who wanted to get in.

On street corners, New York-

Food Is Sent To Subways

10,000 Are Stranded Long After Most Are Led Out

By SAMUEL KAPLAN
Subway trains sputtered to a halt in tunnels, on elevated tracks and in stations yesterday, stranding about 800,000 rush hour riders—10,000 of whom were still stuck at midnight.

The Transit Authority and the Police Department worked into the early hours of the morning attempting to remove passengers from crowded, stalled cars.

At midnight, food was sent to the passengers who were still waiting to be escorted out along the narrow catwalks in dark tunnels and high above rivers and streets.

Despite the anxious condition, no panic was reported, although there was confusion and fear in some of the 600 trains when they first stalled on the city's tracks.

The most difficult evacuation took place on the Williamsburg

(Continued Page 2, Column 8)

Snarl at Rush Hour Spreads Into 9 States

10,000 in the National Guard and 5,000 Off-Duty Policemen Are Called to Service in New York

By PETER KIHSS
The largest power failure in history blacked out nearly all of New York City, parts of nine Northeastern states and two provinces of southeastern Canada last night. Some 80,000 square miles, in which perhaps 25 million people live and work, were affected.

It was more than three hours before the first lights came back on in any part of the New York City area. When they came on in Nassau and Suffolk Counties at 9 P.M., overloads plunged the area into darkness again in 10 minutes.

Striking at the evening rush hour, the power failure trapped 800,000 riders on New York City's subways. Railroads halted. Traffic was jammed. Airplanes found themselves circling, unable to land. But the Defense Department reported that the Strategic Air Command and other defense installations functioned without a halt.

National Guard Called Out

Five thousand off-duty policemen were summoned to duty here. Ten thousand National Guardsmen were called up in New York City alone. Other militiamen were alerted in Rhode Island and Massachusetts, as well as upstate New York.

The lights and the power went out first at 5:17 P.M. somewhere along the Niagara frontier of New York state. Nobody could tell why for hours afterward.

The tripping of automatic switches hurtled the blackout eastward across the state—to Buffalo, Rochester, Syracuse, Utica, Schnectady, Troy and Albany.

Within four minutes the line of darkness had plunged across Massachusetts all the way to Boston. It was like a pattern of falling dominoes—darkness sped southward through Connecticut, northward into Vermont, New Hampshire, Maine and Canada.

Sputtering at 5:27

At 5:27 P.M. the lights began sputtering in New York City, and within seconds the giant Consolidated Edison system blacked out in Manhattan, the Bronx, Queens and most of Brooklyn—but not in Staten Island and parts of Brooklyn that were interconnected with the Public Service Electric and Gas Company of New Jersey.

The darkness probed outward into northern New Jersey, up into Westchester and Rockland Counties, eastward into Long Island.

As far south as Washington. a Potomac Electric Power Company spokesman reported a power "dip" at 5:30 P.M., lasting less than a minute and virtually unnoticed in the nation's capital.

In Pennsylvania, the blackout spread through Pittsburgh and Reading into parts of Philadelphia and then into New Jersey along the coast above Atlantic City.

President Johnson, in Austin, Tex., ordered the full resources of the Federal Government thrown into an investigation by the Federal Power Commission. The Federal Bureau of Investigation, the Defense Department and other agencies were ordered to report "at the earliest possible moment."

Some Fear Sabotage

Asked whether there was any belief that sabotage might have been involved, Bill D. Moyers, the President's Press Secretary, would say only that "all of the resources of the Government" were being invoked in the investigation.

Later Mr. Johnson was advised that utility officials were "pretty well agreed upon the belief that there is substantially no chance of sabotage." Mr. Moyers said one theory was that the failure had been in automatic frequency control equipment.

Power companies, stripped of the protection of interconnected grids that would guard against minor failures on their own. This is how the Ontario Hydro Electric Commission. a Government-owned utility, cut away after loss of power for six million persons. It began bringing power back at 6:15 P.M.

In New York City, the Ravenswood plant in Queens, which provides 1.8 million kilowatts out of the 7.6 million produced by the city's Consolidated Edison plants, began sending smoke up from its stacks, as auxiliary steam power began to build up for its generators.

At 7:15 P.M. smoke began curling up also from the Hudson Avenue station in Brooklyn. It was from Hudson Avenue that the first power was restored here: Five feeder cables of 27,000 volts each sent light back into Coney Island at 8:42 P.M.

An hour later Consolidated Edison reported 17 of the

(Continued on Page 2, Column 1 and 2)

Man, 22, Immolates Himself In Antiwar Protest at U.N.

By THOMAS BUCKLEY
A 21-year-old former seminarian soaked himself with gasoline and then set himself aflame in front of the United Nations at dawn yesterday, as a protest against "war, all war."

Guards from the organization and city patrolmen beat out the flames that enveloped him as he sat crosslegged on First Avenue and then rushed him to Bellevue Hospital.

He was drifting near death in the emergency ward last night, with second and third-degree burns covering 95 per cent of his body. The hospital staff said he had almost no chance of surviving.

The youth, Roger Allen LaPorte, was a member of the Catholic Worker movement, a charitable and pacifist organization with headquarters at 175 Chrystie Street on the Lower East Side. He lived in a tenement apartment leased by the

organization at 58 Kenmare Street, a few blocks away.

Mr. LaPorte's self-immolation was the second in seven days attributable, at least in part, to continued United States' involvement in the war in Vietnam. Last Monday, Norman R. Morrison, a 32-year-old Quaker from Baltimore, burned himself to death in front of the Pentagon in Washington.

U Thant, the Secretary General of the United Nations, which has been seeking a solution to the Asian conflict, and Arthur Goldberg, the chief United States delegate to the world body, reacted with shock and horror to Mr. LaPorte's action.

Questioned at a city reception Mr. Goldberg said that while the youth had undoubtedly been impelled by "the highest principles and motives," his action was "terribly unfortunate and terribly unnecessary."

"Perhaps there has been a

failure on our part." he went on. "Perhaps we are not sufficiently communicating to the people of the world our dedication, our attachment and commitment to the idea that peace is the only way for mankind in the nuclear age."

A spokesman said that Mr. Thant was "deeply grieved over this human tragedy, whatever the motivation might be. U Thant regards human life as very sacred."

Attended Union Sq. Protest

Friends of Mr. LaPorte said that he had been melancholy but not obviously emotionally disturbed since Saturday, when he attended the demonstration at Union Square at which five other youths burned their draft cards.

Robert Steed, a fellow member of the Catholic Workers, said that Mr. LaPorte had been unable to make up his mind to

(Continued on Page 5, Column 1)

How City Met the Emergency: Off-Duty Men Are Mobilized

The city's emergency services were mobilized last night to deal with the sudden power blackout.

Five thousand off-duty policemen were summoned by a message broadcast over WNYC, the city's radio station. They joined the 7,000 who were on duty when the lights went out and were held on for the emergency.

The Fire Department, too, brought in off-duty firemen because their overloaded telegraphic communications made it difficult to keep contact with scattered fire apparatus in the field.

The Fire Department radio was out of service from 5:30 p.m. to 8:30 p.m. and the dispatchers had to keep in touch with the firehouses and vehicles by telephone. They had the radio system back in operation at 8:30 and were able to communicate with men in the field from that hour.

Hospitals were generally able to carry on with the generating

systems that they have for such emergencies. Operations were performed in some of them by lights provided by these auxiliary systems.

The switchboard in the Communications Bureau at Police Headquarters was swamped by calls from puzzled and frightened persons. So many calls came in for radio cars to help persons trapped in stalled elevators, in the subways and to deal with fires and other emergencies that no count was kept of their errands or destinations.

Ice Looting Is Reported

Detectives were sent to West 123d Street in Harlem where they were told there had been looting. When they got there, they found one store window broken.

At Bellevue Hospital, the 2,300 patients were treated by several hundred nurses and doctors in candlelight. Although the city hospital has an auxiliary generating system, it is too

small to service the massive enclave of buildings and was not used. However, in the operating and emergency rooms, the Fire Department set up emergency lights powered by small generators. One operation was finished just before the blackout occurred.

The major problems at Bellevue involved reassuring mentally disturbed patients and mildly medicines in dimly lighted pharmacies. Quantities of dry ice was obtained to keep blood plasma from spoiling.

Car Battery Used

One Bellevue employee brought an iron lung set at Bellevue since 1962, was transferred to a Bird Respirator, which is operated by compressed air. No ill effects were reported.

Louis Lobo, who has been in an iron lung at Bellevue since 1962, was transferred to a Bird Respirator. He set it up on a wheelchair and powered emer-

(Continued on Page 2, Column 7)

"All the News That's Fit to Print"

The New York Times.

LATE CITY EDITION

U. S. Weather Bureau Report (Page 94; Forecast)
Light rain and snow, then clearing today; becoming cloudy tomorrow.
Temp. range: 46–57; yesterday: 48–42.

VOL. CXV..No. 39,408.

© 1965 by The New York Times Company
Times Square, New York, N. Y. 10036

NEW YORK, THURSDAY, DECEMBER 16, 1965.

TEN CENTS

TWO GEMINIS FLY 6 TO 10 FEET APART IN MAN'S FIRST SPACE RENDEZVOUS; CREWS, FACE TO FACE, TALK BY RADIO

U.S. JETS SMASH BIG POWER PLANT OUTSIDE HAIPHONG

Cut Nation's Current 15% —Generators Supported Industries in Hanoi

By NEIL SHEEHAN
Special to The New York Times

SAIGON, South Vietnam, Dec. 15—United States jet fighter-bombers destroyed a large power plant today 14 miles from Haiphong, North Vietnam's chief port, in the first American air strike against a North Vietnamese target of major industrial importance.

A military spokesman said the planes, flown by Air Force pilots, had struck the Uongbi thermal power plant, northeast of Haiphong. The plant has a capacity of 24,000 kilowatts, about 15 per cent of North Vietnam's total electric-power output. It supplies some of the power needs of both Hanoi and Haiphong.

The center of the plant, housing steam turbines, generators and other sensitive equipment, was smashed at 11 A.M. with 12 tons of 3,000-pound bombs. A single flight of F-105 Thunderchief fighter-bombers — apparently four to six craft—made the raid.

Secondary Blasts Sighted

A spokesman said that the pilots had encountered bad weather and heavy antiaircraft fire but reported having destroyed the plant. Several secondary explosions—detonations of explosives on the ground—were observed during the raid.

This was the first time United States aircraft had struck so close to North Vietnam's two major cities—Hanoi and Haiphong. The closest previous strike was a recent raid against a firing site for Soviet-made surface-to-air missiles, 22 miles from Hanoi.

Secretary of Defense McNamara, who arrived back in Washington shortly after midnight from the North Atlantic Alliance meeting in Paris, said the bombing of the power plant near Haiphong "is representative of the type of attack we have carried out and will continue to carry out." The Associated Press reported Thursday. Page 3.]

Many Homes Darkened

According to military spokesmen here, the destruction of the power plant was certain to affect North Vietnamese civilians much more directly than have previous strikes, almost all of which have been aimed at road, rail and river networks and military installations.

The power-station raid will probably cut off electricity in large numbers of civilian homes as well as significantly reduce the amount of power available for industries in the Hai-

Continued on Page 3, Column 1

U.S. Said to Caution Latins on Moscow

By HENRY RAYMONT
Special to The New York Times

MONTEVIDEO, Uruguay, Dec. 15—The United States is warning Uruguay and other Latin - American countries against underestimating the continued aggressiveness and subversive potential of Soviet Communism, qualified sources said today.

The diplomatic initiative is directed against what United States authorities consider to be undue complacency among Latin-American leaders.

These authorities think that the split between Moscow and Peking has led to the assumption among Latins that pro-Soviet Communists no longer threaten republican institutions in the Western Hemisphere.

According to United States officials, this assumption ignores the deterioration in East-West

Continued on Page 17, Column 1

Gemini 7 Crew

Lieut. Col. Frank Borman

Comdr. James A. Lovell Jr.

Major Steps From Launching to Rendezvous

The New York Times
Dec. 16, 1965

Major steps of yesterday's rendezvous of the Gemini 6 and Gemini 7 spacecraft are shown, from the launching of Gemini 6 to its meeting with Gemini 7, orbiting about 185 miles above the earth. At rendezvous two craft were nose to nose within 10 feet of each other.

McNamara Warns NATO Of Chinese Atom Threat

By PETER BRAESTRUP
Special to The New York Times

PARIS, Dec. 15—Defense Secretary Robert S. McNamara urged the United States' Western European allies today to start worrying now about the threat posed by Communist China's growing nuclear strength.

At the same time, he pledged that the mounting United States effort in Vietnam would not require the withdrawal of "major combat units" from American forces in Western Europe.

Mr. McNamara addressed ministers of the 15-nation North Atlantic Treaty Organization in their year-end meeting, which began yesterday.

Behind Closed Doors

The Defense Secretary spoke behind closed doors. His remarks, like those of other speakers, were summarized by a delegation spokesman.

Mr. McNamara said that the Chinese Communists, having already detonated two test nuclear devices, would produce enough fissionable material in the next two years to start a small stockpile of atomic weapons.

Moreover, he continued, the Chinese, despite a "near-famine" economy, are spending 10 per cent of their gross national product on defense.

He said Peking's new mili-

Continued on Page 8, Column 3

JOHNSON AND AYUB CALL PEACE VITAL

Say Dispute With India Must Cease So Efforts Can Be Turned to Key Problems

By JOHN D. POMFRET
Special to The New York Times

WASHINGTON, Dec. 15 President Johnson and President Mohammad Ayub Khan of Pakistan said today that they agreed on the need for a peaceful resolution of all outstanding differences between India and Pakistan.

This is necessary, they said, "so that the energies and resources of the peoples of the subcontinent would not be wastefully diverted from their efforts to meet their vitally important social and economic problems."

The two leaders issued a joint communiqué at the conclusion of two days of meetings at the White House. It described the discussions as "frank, wide-ranging and productive."

Kashmir Main Issue

The main dispute between India and Pakistan is over Kashmir. This dispute led to a short war last summer.

There was no expressed agreement between the two Presidents on the specific lines along which the dispute over Kashmir should be settled.

They both were said to believe that the working out of such specific arrangements must await the outcome of further conferences that already have been scheduled.

President Ayub and India's Prime Minister, Lal Bahadur Shastri, are to meet Jan. 4 at the invitation of the Soviet Union to discuss their differences. They will confer at the Soviet Central Asian city of Tashkent.

Prime Minister Shastri and President Johnson will meet in Washington Feb. 1 and 2.

Continued on Page 6, Column 3

47-CENT FARE SEEN IN QUILL DEMANDS

Transit Authority Warns It Would Be Needed to Meet Union Pay Proposals

By EMANUEL PERLMUTTER

The Transit Authority said yesterday that if it granted the contract demands of its unions it would have to raise the 15-cent fare to 47 cents.

It asserted that a fare increase that great would lead to such a loss of riders that "the reduced use of the system would be financially catastrophic."

Mr. McNamara addressed The authority has estimated that demands of the Transport Workers Union would cost it $680 million in a two-year contract.

"Adding an increased labor cost of $340 million annually to the T.A. budget would, in the absence of other sources of revenue, increase the present 3-cent deficit incurred for each passenger carried by 19 cents, creating a 22-cent operating deficit per ride," the authority asserted. "The fare would have to be increased to not less than 47 cents."

The authority said that granting the demands would also result in increasing the "basic wage rate per hour alone

Continued on Page 58, Column 4

Staggered Working Hours Urged to Cut Transit Jam

By JOSEPH C. INGRAHAM

The chronic morning and evening subway crushes can be eliminated by staggering working hours, according to a plan made public by Mayor Wagner yesterday. The success of the proposal hinges on whether employers and employes can be persuaded to alter their traditional 9-to-5 work pattern, the Mayor said.

Only the conclusions of the eight-volume, 200,000-word report, based on a six-year study that cost $200,000, were released by the Mayor. The study was directed by Prof. Lawrence B. Cohen of the department of industrial engineering at Columbia University.

Principal Finding

The principal finding was that "work staggering is a feasible way of relieving subway congestion into and out of Manhattan's central business district during the rush hours so that standing passengers might be reasonably comfortable."

Professor Cohen held that the idea was technically and economically feasible and, within limits, which he defined very generally, was sociologically acceptable to management and labor.

In Professor Cohen's view, rush-hour crowding would be markedly alleviated if a 25 per cent spread of the peak loads

Continued on Page 58, Column 3

Gemini 6 Crew

Capt. Walter M. Schirra Jr.

Maj. Thomas P. Stafford

Craft in Formation Orbit 185 Miles Up

Officials of Space Agency Are Jubilant at Success — Maneuver Is Vital to a Manned Landing on Moon

By JOHN NOBLE WILFORD
Special to The New York Times

HOUSTON, Dec. 15—Four American astronauts steered Gemini 6 and Gemini 7 today to man's first rendezvous in the vastness of outer space.

In a spectacular performance of space navigation, the astronauts brought their craft within six to ten feet of each other about 185 miles above the earth. The two capsules then circled the earth nearly two times on a four-hour formation flight before Gemini 6 broke away to a lower orbit.

The pilots of the pursuing Gemini 6 were Capt. Walter M. Schirra Jr. of the Navy and Maj. Thomas P. Stafford of the Air Force. Pilots of the Gemini 7 target ship were Lieut. Col. Frank Borman and Comdr. James A. Lovell Jr. of the Navy.

The crews came close enough to see into each other's cabins, trade gibes and inspect details on the exteriors of their funnel-shaped spacecraft. The Gemini 6 astronauts could see Commander Lovell's beard and could tell that Colonel Borman was chewing gum.

"We have company tonight!" radioed Colonel Borman from Gemini 7, which has been in orbit 11 days of its record 14-day mission. Gemini 6, launched from Cape Kennedy at 8:37 A.M., Eastern standard time, today, is expected to splash down near the Bahamas at 10:29 A.M. tomorrow.

Officials Jubilant

The success of the mission brought jubilation at the space center here.

"It's the biggest milestone since the flight of John Glenn," Christopher C. Kraft Jr., the flight director, said. Colonel Glenn's Mercury flight on Feb. 20, 1962, was the first orbital mission by an American.

The two Geminis today proved that two spacecraft can find each other, rendezvous and presumably link up.

Such a maneuver is necessary if astronauts are to land on the moon and are to return to their mother ship, which would be circling in a lunar orbit. Space officials are aiming for such a manned landing in 1969.

Today's rendezvous also opens the way to operations in which men and supplies can be ferried out to orbiting stations, such as the Air Force's planned Manned Orbiting Laboratory.

'Made It Look Easy'

"These crews made it look easy," said Dr. Robert Gilruth, director of the Manned Spacecraft Center here, praising all those who had made the mission a success.

Just before final rendezvous, there was an anxious moment of silence. Radio contact between the craft and the ground was lost. Then a relay tracking station off Hawaii reported in. The two Gemini had drawn within 120 feet of each other.

"There just seems to be a lot of traffic up here," Captain Schirra commented.

"Call a policeman," Colonel

Continued on Page 28, Column 1

AT LAST, GEMINI 6 HAS A PERFECT DAY

Even Sun Comes Out in Time to Dispel Last Doubt of Jubilant Ground Staff

By EVERT CLARK
Special to The New York Times

CAPE KENNEDY, Fla., Dec. 15—After twice having had its wings clipped by failure, the Gemini 6 finally climbed to its space rendezvous today in a most spectacular way.

For 15 years, missiles have flown from this sandy point of land. But no one today could recall a flight of greater beauty.

It left behind a sense of exhilaration missing since Mercury capsules took the first American astronauts into space four years ago.

On top of the triumph, plans were quickly made to have Gemini 6 splash down about 800 miles east of here at 10:29 o'clock tomorrow morning. The pilots will return here on Friday for the first of many days of debriefing.

A splendid sunrise had created the perfect backdrop and set the mood for the day. It dispelled a worrisome ground fog that had clung to the scrubby palmetto like the doubts that had hung over Gemini 6 in recent days.

Attitude Was Cautious

Through last night the members of two recent false starts was so fresh that the attitude was one of caution and crossed fingers.

Yet today, from the beginning, a cockiness and almost a jubilance seemed to run through the pilots, the overworked ground crews and official observers.

It was typified by the reaction of James S. McDonnell, the 67-year-old engineer whose factory in Missouri makes the Gemini capsules.

He overslept. Awakened at 6:30 A.M. as the sun began to turn the high, scattered clouds the color of a tea rose, he looked at the sky and cried out:

"You see! I told them I'd bring them good weather from St. Louis!"

It became a day for enthusiasm.

"She looks like a dream," Navy Capt. Walter M. Schir-

Continued on Page 28, Column 8

NASA CUTS BACK SCIENCE PROGRAM

Orbiting Solar Observatory Canceled in Move to Hold Down Expanding Budget

Special to The New York Times

WASHINGTON, Dec. 15— The National Aeronautics and Space Administration, caught in a tight budgetary squeeze, canceled today one of its most ambitious scientific projects.

"Budgetary considerations" were cited by the agency in explaining a halt in further work on the Advanced Orbiting Solar Observatory. The observatory, capable of making detailed observations of the sun, had been planned for launching in 1969.

Behind the cryptic explanation was the deliberately unpublicized fact that the agency was faced with a budgetary dilemma. It has been attempting to finance its expanding program and still heed White House directives to hold down nonmilitary spending.

Some Delays Foreseen

The present expectation is that the civilian space budget for the fiscal year 1967, beginning next July 1, will be held by the White House to about $5.17 billion, equal to the appropriation for this year, and perhaps even less. This would be about $500 million less than the space agency considered necessary to maintain the momentum of its expanding program and sought from the White House.

Enough money will be provided in the budget next year to keep Project Apollo on its schedule of landing a manned expedition on the moon before 1970. But to keep within the budgetary confines imposed by the White House, there will have to be some curtailment in the

Continued on Page 29, Column 4

Johnson Calls Feat Step Toward Moon

By JACK RAYMOND
Special to The New York Times

WASHINGTON, Dec. 15— President Johnson hailed the Gemini satellite rendezvous today as a step toward the moon. The President congratulated the astronauts and all those who had anything to do with the space feat.

"You have all moved us one step higher on the stairway to the moon," he said exuberantly.

The President conveyed his feelings in a message to James E. Webb, administrator of the National Aeronautics and Space Administration. He had watched the progress of the launching and flight anxiously throughout the day.

Bill D. Moyers, the President's press secretary, said Mr. Johnson watched the Gemini 6 launching over his bedroom television set. Then, throughout the

Continued on Page 28, Column 8

Somerset Maugham Is Dead at 91

Novelist, Short Story Writer, Playwright Succumbs in Nice

By The Associated Press

NICE, France, Thursday, Dec. 16—W. Somerset Maugham died early today at his Riviera villa, La Mauresque. The world-famous novelist, playwright and short-story writer was 91 years old.

Maugham fell last Friday and then suffered a stroke. He was taken to the British-American Hospital Saturday. After a medical consultation on Sunday, physicians gave him only hours to live.

He rallied slightly but weakened yesterday. When all hope was gone, he was taken from the hospital to die in his Moorish-style villa at nearby Cap Ferrat, his secretary and companion of many years, Alan Searle, said in announcing Maugham's death.

A prolific author, Maugham turned out 30 plays, 21 novels and 120 short stories. His mas-

Pictorial Parade
W. Somerset Maugham

terpiece was "Of Human Bondage," published in 1915 when he was 41 years old. It centered

Continued on Page 50, Column 1

"All the News That's Fit to Print"

The New York Times.

LATE CITY EDITION
U. S. Weather Bureau Report (Page 34) forecast:
Partly cloudy and cold today; fair, cold tonight. Fair, warmer tomorrow.
Temp. Range: 39–32; yesterday: 44–37.

VOL. CXVI..No. 39,816.

© 1967 by The New York Times Company.
Times Square, New York, N. Y. 10036

NEW YORK, SATURDAY, JANUARY 28, 1967.

10 CENTS

500,000 IN THE CITY GO WITHOUT HEAT IN HOUSING STRIKE

Elderly Are the Hardest Hit in Public Developments Affected by Dispute

6,000 EMPLOYEES ARE OUT

'Real Progress' Is Reported by Union as Negotiations With Officials Resume

By DAMON STETSON

Nearly all of the 500,000 residents in public housing developments here were left without heat or hot water yesterday by a strike of 6,000 employes of the City Housing Authority.

Elderly persons, mothers and small children huddled around gas stoves in their kitchens in an effort to keep warm. School children and workers returning home through the drenching rain and wind found their apartments cold and cheerless.

A housewife at Riis Houses on East 10th Street summed up her feelings with the comment, "Got no heat, no hot water—they don't get my rent."

The temperature during the day remained close to 40 degrees but dropped to the mid-30's last night.

Governor Rockefeller, taking note of the plight of the thousands of dwellers in public housing without heat in all state armories in the city opened last night to accommodate residents without heat.

'Cold and Damp'

"We've got no hot water or nothing," said Mrs. Ruth Bradley, an elderly tenant in Red Hook Houses in Brooklyn. "It's cold and damp in here anyway, but now it's really cold, and it hurts my arthritis."

The strike by members of Local 237 of the International Brotherhood of Teamsters began officially at 11 A.M. Thursday, but most tenants didn't feel its impact until they got up yesterday morning and found they had no hot water and that their apartments were becoming increasingly chilly.

A spokesman for the authority said that the fuel tanks had been filled to capacity and that the strikers had been requested to set boilers on automatic controls. But Barry Feinstein, vice president of Local 237, said that the union had instructed its members to avoid a possibly dangerous situation that might result from untended boilers and to shut them down.

The authority said that the automatic controls were equipped with safety devices and could have operated for several days without attention. But an official conceded that in 90 per cent of the authority's 147 developments, the boilers had been shut down and that tenants were without heat or hot water.

Negotiations aimed at ending the strike were resumed yesterday afternoon by Mr. Feinstein and his committee and by Walter E. Washington, the chairman, and other officials of the authority. The talks were continuing early this morning.

A union spokesman said that

Continued on Page 24, Column 4

Chicago Is Crippled By a 23-Inch Snow; Police Kill Looter

By DONALD JANSON
Special to The New York Times

CHICAGO, Jan. 27—A city accustomed to snowstorms succumbed to one today.

Chicago is not easy to fell. The nation's third largest city takes in stride weather that makes winter hurt.

But this time wind and snow combined with paralyzing fury in a two-day onslaught that brought Chicago to its knees. It was the worst storm in history here, dumping more than 23 inches of snow on the city and 26 inches on its southern suburbs.

[The Chicago police shot and killed a 10-year-old girl who they said was helping loot a store in the snow-filled streets of the West Side Friday, according to The Associated Press. The storm thundered toward the East during the day and snow warnings were posted as far east as Maine, Vermont and New York.]

Chicagoans trooped to work yesterday, ignoring the heavy

Continued on Page 16, Column 1

LINDSAY ORDERS O'DWYER OUSTED

But Procaccino Says Board Counsel Will Stay On in Transit Subsidy Suit

By SETH S. KING

Mayor Lindsay dismissed Paul O'Dwyer yesterday as a special corporation counsel.

He acted after Mr. O'Dwyer had summoned the Mayor and the Transit Authority to court to explain why they refused to use $84.3-million to subsidize the transit system.

[Controller Mario A. Procaccino immediately declared that Mr. O'Dwyer would go right on representing the Board of Estimate in the case.

A Conspicuous Exception

The board is trying to force the Republican Mayor to use the $84.3-million for a transit subsidy as the Democratic-controlled City Council had directed.

Mr. Procaccino said the dismissal of Mr. O'Dwyer was "an incredible step" in a politically inspired move to thwart the board, which the Democrats also control.

"The Mayor really wants to use $84-million of the taxpayers' money for other purposes," the controller declared. "That money was specifically appropriated to keep the subway fare where it is and not to help the Mayor balance his budget."

The latest phase in the battle over the proposed transit subsidy began Thursday when the board overruled the Mayor and directed Mr. O'Dwyer to go into court for a ruling on whether the city had the right to subsidize the transit system.

Last November, at the insistence of the board, Mr. O'Dwyer, a brother of former Mayor William O'Dwyer and a former Democratic City Councilman, had been appointed by Corporation Counsel J. Lee Rankin to pursue the question

Continued on Page 25, Column 6

NATION'S BANKS SET 5¾% RATE; REBUKING CHASE

Prime Borrowing Cost Falls From 6% but Not to Level of 5½%, Kept by Leader

By H. ERICH HEINEMANN

Business borrowing costs dropped yesterday as banks across the country reduced their prime interest rate to 5¾ per cent from 6 per cent.

The reduction contrasted with the drop to 5½ per cent announced on Thursday by the Chase Manhattan Bank. The question immediately arose whether Chase would adjust its rate to conform to the new industry standard. Late yesterday, a spokesman for Chase said the bank had "no present intention" of doing so.

Meanwhile, it was learned yesterday that there had been discussions between the Chase Bank and the Johnson Administration prior to the bank's announcement of the reduction to 5½ per cent.

Well-informed sources in Washington said last night that the Government "was not taken by surprise" by Chase's action.

Prime Rate Defined

A spokesman for Chase confirmed last night that "as a matter of courtesy" both the Federal Reserve Bank of New York and the Treasury Department had been notified of the decision to lower the rate shortly before the bank's public announcement.

The prime rate, or minimum business-lending rate, according to one major New York bank, "applies to short-term loans to substantial depositors with the highest credit ratings."

[The Bank of Canada announced a reduction in its lending rate to 5 per cent from 5¼ per cent, effective Monday. The rate had remained unchanged since last March 14 when it was raised to 5¼ per cent from 5 per cent.]

A Conspicuous Exception

The general reduction in the prime rate by banks in the United States was the first since Aug. 23, 1960, when it dropped to 4½ per cent from 5 per cent. The new reduction is only the fifth decline since the custom of a prime rate was established in the nineteen-thirties.

The rate reduction was interpreted by bankers and economists as further evidence of the trend toward lower interest rates that started last fall. In time, they said, credit should become more plentiful and its cost should continue to decline—not only for business but for consumers as well, particularly on home mortgages.

The move to 5¾ per cent was led by the First National City Bank of New York. The bank announced its decision about 11 A.M. By the end of the day practically every other large bank in the country had joined in the decision to post a 5¾ per cent rate.

Chase, of course, stayed at 5½ per cent.

Other bankers, though, voiced the opinion that sooner or later

Continued on Page 32, Column 1

3 APOLLO ASTRONAUTS DIE IN FIRE; GRISSOM, WHITE, CHAFFEE CAUGHT IN CAPSULE DURING A TEST ON PAD

BEFORE AN EARLIER TEST: Lieut. Col. Virgil I. Grissom, left, Air Force Lieut. Col. Edward H. White 2d, center, and Navy Lieut. Comdr. Roger B. Chaffee in front of the launching pad. Photograph was released Tuesday.

United Press International

NASA, via Associated Press Wirephoto

HOURS BEFORE THE TRAGEDY: Colonel Grissom walking to the Apollo spacecraft ahead of Commander Chaffee, yesterday, some 5½ hours before the fire broke out. The capsule was atop a Saturn 1-B rocket, 218 feet above pad.

TRAGEDY AT CAPE

Rescuers Are Blocked by Dense Smoke—Cause Is Studied

Excerpts from news parley on accident, Page 10.

By The Associated Press

CAPE KENNEDY, Fla., Jan. 27—The three-man crew of astronauts for the Apollo 1 mission were killed tonight in a flash fire aboard the huge spacecraft designed to take man to the moon.

Those killed in the blaze on a launching pad were:

VIRGIL I. GRISSOM, 40 years old, Air Force lieutenant colonel, one of the seven original Mercury astronauts.

EDWARD H. WHITE 2d, 36, a lieutenant colonel in the Air Force, the first American to "walk" in space.

ROGER B. CHAFFEE, 31, a Navy lieutenant commander, who had been awaiting his first space flight.

The astronauts were the first American spacemen to be killed on the job and, ironically, died while on the ground. The bodies were removed hours later and a space agency spokesman said death was "instantaneous."

Three other astronauts died in airplane crashes, in the line of duty, but today's tragedy involved the first "on premises" deaths in the American space program—the first time anyone was killed while in space hardware.

Simulation Under Way

The fire broke out at 6:31 P.M. while the three men were taking part in a full-scale simulation of the scheduled Feb. 21 launching that was to take them into the heavens for 14 days of orbiting the earth.

They were trapped behind closed hatches, according to the National Aeronautics and Space Administration.

[Officials said an electrical spark must have ignited the pure oxygen inside the cabin, United Press International reported.]

Paul Haney, spokesman for America's astronauts, said he understood there had been a fire aboard. He said monitors had received no word from the astronauts during the fire.

Mr. Haney said 26 members of the launching pad crew were treated for smoke inhalation. He said 24 were released and two were hospitalized in good condition.

Space agency officials were alerted by someone on the ground that the fire had broken out, Mr. Haney reported. He said emergency crews tried to reach the astronauts but were blocked by the dense smoke that rolled out of the cockpit.

Officials at Cape Kennedy said that the three astronauts were seated abreast in the rocket in the exercise, just as they would be in actual

Continued on Page 10, Column 1

TOWAWAY POLICY IS EASED FOR U.N.

City to Extend Parking Area for Diplomats and Chase Other Motorists Out

The city joined with United Nations officials yesterday in an effort to meet the complaints of diplomats about the towaway crackdown on cars illegally parked in midtown.

The program worked out at a private meeting seeks to reduce the towing away of diplomatic vehicles by the police and provides for various cooperative measures. Specific measures include plans to supply the diplomats with more on-street parking spaces and to chase "squatters" out of parking areas already reserved for the diplomats.

The move to provide more space for diplomats' cars followed similar action regarding handicapped drivers and physicians. On Thursday, the city said that it would designate as many as 700 new special parking places for invalids. A study was also ordered to provide similar spaces for physicians.

The city, however, reserved the right to tow away illegally parked diplomatic vehicles that create a hazard.

Henry A. Barnes, city Traffic Commissioner, said that the city hoped to supply 100 or more reserved on-street parking places—designated by blue traffic signs—for the diplomats. That would raise their midtown total to about 700.

Diplomats have not been carried away by Mayor Lindsay's "no exceptions" towaway program against illegal midtown parking—but a number of their cars have been.

Since the tough policy went into effect Monday—and up to 11:30 P.M. yesterday—998 vehicles have been towed to the "pound" on Pier 74 at the Hudson River and 34th Street. This number includes 22 diplomatic or foreign consular cars.

About a dozen foreign delegations have been affected. Although the diplomats are exempt from the $40 fee—$25 for towing and the $15 fine—they

Continued on Page 28, Column 1

62 Nations Sign Treaty To Curb Arms in Space

By MAX FRANKEL
Special to The New York Times

WASHINGTON, Jan. 27—President Johnson presided today over a White House ceremony at which the United States, the Soviet Union and 60 other countries signed a treaty to limit military activities in outer space.

Mr. Johnson hailed it as an "inspiring moment in the history of the human race" and described the treaty as a "first, firm step toward keeping outer space free forever from the implements of war."

The ceremony took place before the accident at Cape Kennedy, Fla., in which three American astronauts lost their lives.

Treaty-signing ceremonies were held earlier today in Moscow and London, but the pact will not take effect until it is ratified by the United States, the Soviet Union, Britain and two other countries.

For most nations, that is a mere formality, but in the United States, the Senate must give its consent by a two-thirds vote.

Eventual ratification here is expected, because the treaty does not prohibit any present or planned American military activities in space.

It prohibits the placing of nuclear weapons or other weapons of mass destruction in orbit, on the moon or on other celestial bodies. It also bars all military installations and maneuvers from the moon and other planets.

It does not, however, prohibit the orbiting of military spacecraft without large weapons or the use of unmanned satellites for military purposes, such as reconnaissance.

Some opposition here may focus on the difficulties of inspecting Soviet satellites for the presence of nuclear weapons. But American officials expressed confidence that the treaty posed no threat to national security.

They predicted that the treaty

Continued on Page 6, Column 2

APOLLO PROGRAM DEALT HARD BLOW

The Slim Margin for Failure Believed Jeopardizing a Moon Landing by '70

By EVERT CLARK
Special to The New York Times

WASHINGTON, Jan. 27—Tonight's accident at Cape Kennedy is expected to deal a serious blow to the Apollo program, which has struggled hard to stay on schedule in the face of annual budget cuts.

Space officials have warned for several years that their margin of operation was thin, that continual economy by the Administration and Congress had left no room for failures if the moon was to be reached by 1970.

Since they first raised this cry, the mishaps have gradually accumulated.

Although it will be some time before the full impact of the accident can be assessed, it means more than the loss of a carefully selected, highly competent crew.

It probably means the loss of a spacecraft and possibly parts of the launching rocket. It also may mean damage to the launching pad that could delay a flight using the backup rocket. A backup crew flew the Gemini 9 after the original Gemini 9 pilots were killed in a plane crash.

Last March, President Johnson reaffirmed the goal laid down by President Kennedy when he announced the Apollo program in May of 1961. The United States, Mr. Johnson said, still intends "to land the first man on the surface of the moon" by 1970.

Mr. Johnson's words were interpreted at the time as an answer—and a bit of a reprimand—to the National Aeronautics and Space Administration, which had been complaining to Congress about budget cuts made within the Administration.

On the same day, Vice President Humphrey reminded the space leaders that the program "cannot be exempt" from tight budgetary discipline.

Following the ceremony at

Continued on Page 10, Column 2

ARMY OPPOSITION TO MAO REPORTED

Troops in 2 Regions Said to Resist Orders to Help in Ousting Party Officials

By CHARLES MOHR
Special to The New York Times

HONG KONG, Jan. 27—Disunity and confusion in the Chinese Army seemed apparent today in the wake of an order to the army to stamp out resistance to Mao Tse-tung's political purge.

There was no immediate confirmation of Peking wall posters reporting that troops in the far western autonomous region of Sinkiang and in Inner Mongolia were opposing orders by Mr. Mao, who is Chairman of the Chinese Communist party, to help oust entrenched party officials.

[Reacting to clashes in Moscow in which Chinese students were hurt, Peking declared that the Soviet Union's leaders were "swine" in the same category as the last Czar, Hitler and the Ku Klux Klan. Page 2.]

The analysts here noted that the troop commander in the Sinkiang military region, Wang Enmao, was concurrently the head of the Communist party's Provincial Committee there. He could hardly be expected to use his troops to oust himself and his comrades from office, the analysts said.

A similar situation prevailed in Inner Mongolia, where Ulanfu, a Mongol, was both military commander and head of the party committee. Whether he is in

Continued on Page 2, Column 4

Einstein Relativity Theory Challenged

By WALTER SULLIVAN

A leading physicist reported yesterday an observation that, if true and correctly interpreted, would invalidate Albert Einstein's theory of relativity.

Dr. Robert H. Dicke, professor of physics at Princeton University, told a conference on astrophysics here that his observations of the sun last summer showed that its shape was flattened at the poles.

The effect of this flattening, or oblateness, is sufficient, he said, to explain a significant portion of the orbital behavior of Mercury, the planet closest to the sun, without recourse to relativity. It was the precise conformity of Mercury's orbit to Dr. Einstein's predictions that was the chief pillar of his theory.

If Dr. Dicke is correct, this pillar has been undermined.

However, he struck a cautious note in his report to the astrophysical conference. "It wouldn't surprise me," he said, "if general relativity is just plain wrong."

General relativity deals with gravity and its manifestations

Continued on Page 12, Column 4

Sun's image
Spinning wheel with 2 notches
Mirror
Rotating wheel
Mirror
Disk
Photocell
Schematic drawing

The New York Times (Daniel Brownstein)   Jan. 28, 1967

Instrument used by Dr. Robert H. Dicke to determine the sun's shape was based on notched spinning wheel, as shown in upper schematic diagram. As the wheel spun, light of sun passing through notches varied with sun's shape. Light variations during each spin were detected by photocell.

Fire on Spacecraft Captured on Film

By MARTIN WALDRON
Special to The New York Times

HOUSTON, Jan. 27—The flash fire that killed three astronauts in a spacecraft at Cape Kennedy tonight was filmed, an official of the National Aeronautics and Space Administration said today.

However, the film and recordings made of the astronauts' voices, which were being monitored at Cape Kennedy and at Houston during the test, were sealed immediately after the accident.

Paul P. Haney, director of public affairs for the Manned Spacecraft Center here, said the film and the recordings would be turned over to a board of inquiry that has been given the task of finding out exactly what happened.

The board of inquiry, which will include top officials of the space program, will be appointed tomorrow, Mr. Haney said.

Space officials from Houston

Continued on Page 10, Column 5

"All the News
That's Fit to Print"

The New York Times

LATE CITY EDITION
Weather: Sunny and warm today;
fair tonight and tomorrow. Temp.
range: today 83-61; Monday 81-62.
Temp.-Hum. Index: 75; Monday
61-72. Full U.S. report on Page 93.

VOL. CXVI..No. 39,945   © 1967 The New York Times Company.   NEW YORK, TUESDAY, JUNE 6, 1967   10 CENTS

ISRAELI AND ARAB FORCES BATTLING; BOTH CLAIM LAND AND AIR VICTORIES; CEASE-FIRE EFFORTS STALLED IN U.N.

4 States Hit by Blackout

JERSEY HURT MOST

13 Million Affected—Power Back Quickly in Philadelphia

By PETER KIHSS

A massive electrical failure along an interconnected system shut off power at midmorning yesterday for 13 million persons in 1,000 square miles — three-fourths of New Jersey, much of eastern Pennsylvania and eastern Maryland and the northern half of Delaware.

It was more than three hours before power started to come back on in Newark. The restoration of power started in Philadelphia, the nation's fourth largest city, about a half hour after the failure occurred.

Not until 8:15 P.M. did Russell B. Williams, vice president for public relations for the Public Service Electric and Gas Company of New Jersey, report all sections served by his company had regained their electricity.

New York City escaped with only some flickering of lights in Brooklyn and Staten Island and a slight voltage drop when, according to the Consolidated Edison Company, a sensor device at 10:18 A.M. automatically cut off a tie-in to New Jersey across the Arthur Kill.

Source and Cause Sought

Last night, the Federal Power Commission said the precise source and cause — human, mechanical or just too much demand — were still being sought. But Lee C. White, its chairman, said the commission had been worrying for some time about the ability of the Pennsylvania-New Jersey-Maryland grid to meet this summer's demand.

The failure — this time fortunately during sunshine, in contrast to the historic Nov. 9, 1965, blackout in New York City and the Northeast—spread with thunderbolt speed from the New Jersey-New York border and Wilkes-Barre, Pa., on the north, to south of Dover, Del., and west to Harrisburg, Pa.

Ingenuity, imagination and a gentle sense of resignation followed in the path of the blackout. Housewives sighed wearily and put away their irons. Subway riders took buses and elevator riders walked.

People sitting in front of radio and television sets listening to the news of the crisis in the Middle East felt new bewilderment as the sets faded out.

One of the last communities to have its power restored, about 7:30 P.M., was Montclair, N. J. During the day stores in the main business area closed —including a barber who finished his last haircut on the sidewalk outside his shop—and residents made thousands of calls to the police asking advice on "everything under the sun.

Continued on Page 42, Column 1

Traffic Is Snarled As Signals Go Out

By PAUL HOFMANN

Motorists blew their horns in self-defense and drove gingerly through intersections where traffic lights were out. 1,500 persons were stranded in the Philadelphia subway and railroad trains in four states rolled to a halt in yesterday's power blackout.

Air traffic over the Northeast generally suffered only little delay and disruption, but Newark Airport was severely crippled for the first hour or so after the power failure started and before emergency equipment could restore partial power.

The Newark control tower was cut off from aircraft on the ground and in the air.

Continued on Page 42, Column 7

HIGH COURT CURBS HOME INSPECTIONS

Backs Right to Deny Entry Not Supported by Warrant —Also Protects Business

By FRED P. GRAHAM
Special to The New York Times

WASHINGTON, June 5 — Property owners may refuse to open their homes or businesses to health, fire and other administrative inspectors unless they have search warrants, the Supreme Court ruled today.

In extending the search warrant requirement beyond law enforcement officials to the routine inspections of administrative authorities, the Court relaxed the traditional standards for the issuance of search warrants.

It ruled that inspectors may obtain warrants to enter premises without having cause to believe that evidence of an ordinance violation would be found inside.

The 6-to-3 opinion by Justice Byron R. White said that such warrants might be obtained for an entire city area simply by showing that a certain period of time had passed since the last inspection, or by showing that the buildings were in a rundown condition.

This provoked a strong dissent

Continued on Page 32, Column 3

U.S. PLANES DOWN 3 MIG'S NEAR HANOI IN RAID ON BRIDGES

Foe Mounts Heavy Defense —Soviet Rejects American Denial of Ship Attack

By United Press International

SAIGON, South Vietnam, June 5 — United States planes bombed North Vietnam's war industry today and shot down three MIG interceptors near Hanoi. Military spokesmen said that the North Vietnamese had put up heavy air defenses.

F-105 Thunderchiefs flew into the heart of North Vietnam's industrial triangle and bombed railroad bridges around the Thainguyen manufacturing complex. Other United States planes bombed a manufacturing complex near the Phucyen MIG base about 20 miles north of Hanoi.

Officials said that all three MIG's had been shot down by Phantoms flying protective cover for the Thunderchiefs. There were no reports of American air losses.

[In Moscow, the Soviet Government rejected a United States denial that American planes had attacked a Soviet merchant ship in a North Vietnamese port Friday. Page 3.]

MIG Total Reaches 77

The enemy losses brought to 77 the total number of MIG's shot down by American aircraft over North Vietnam.

The Soviet press agency, Tass, said that two United States planes were shot down over North Vietnam today, but there was no American confirmation.

Maj. Durward K. Priester, 36 years old, of Hampton, S.C., and Capt. John Pankhurst, 27, of Midland, Mich., both of the Air Force, were credited with one of the MIG's.

Pilots Fly 98 Missions

SAIGON, June 5 — Although poor weather covered most of North Vietnam yesterday, pilots flew 98 missions in the Southern Panhandle, the narrow stretch of North Vietnam just north of the border.

Two United States planes were lost: an F-105 Thunder-

Continued on Page 3, Column 5

WAR IN MIDEAST: Israelis reported they seized El Arish (1) and Tarakumbasis (2). Fighting was heavy in Jerusalem (3) and Gaza Strip (4). Cairo said it repulsed foe at Kuntilla (5) and Khan Yunis (A on inset), but Israel said she took latter and Rafah (B).

Egypt, Backed by Soviet, Blocks U.N. Call for Truce

By DREW MIDDLETON
Special to The New York Times

UNITED NATIONS, N. Y., June 5—The Security Council recessed tonight after 12 hours of futile effort to frame a resolution calling for a cease-fire and a withdrawal of forces in the Arab-Israeli war.

The refusal of the United Arab Republic to obey any resolution that demanded the withdrawal of its forces beyond the positions they occupied Sunday was the chief reason for the deadlock.

The Egyptian intransigence was strengthened, qualified sources said, by the support of the Soviet Union and India. On the other hand, there were indications Nikolai T. Fedorenko of the Soviet Union had asked his Government for further instructions.

"It is quite evident," a Western delegate said, "that the Russians do not like the prospect of another 'eyeball-to-eyeball' confrontation with the United States over what to tell them is a sideshow."

Denmark's representative on the 15-member Council, Hans Tabor, who is 'his month's President, announced the recess. He said that the consultations were still going on and would continue tomorrow, and he set 11:30 A.M. as the time for the next meeting.

Mr. Tabor asked members to be available from 10:30 A.M. He had hoped, he said, that when he recessed the first of today's meetings this morning that recess would be shorter than it was.

During the interval between the two brief meetings, the United Arab Republic, backed

Continued on Page 17, Column 3

MOSCOW DEMANDS ISRAEL QUIT EGYPT

Soviet Bids U.N. Condemn 'Aggression' and Repeats Support of Arabs

By PETER GROSE

MOSCOW, Tuesday, June 6—The Soviet Union demanded today that Israel "immediately and unconditionally" halt military operations and pull her troops back from Egyptian territory.

A Government statement condemned "Israeli aggression," asserted the Soviet "right to take all steps that may be necessitated by the situation" and called on states, specifically including the major powers, to work for peace.

The United Nations "must discharge its direct duty: condemn Israeli actions and promptly take steps to restore peace in the Middle East," the statement said.

It expressed the hope that other governments "will do, for their part, everything in their power to extinguish the military conflagration in the Middle East."

This was the first official reaction from the Soviet Government

Continued on Page 18, Column 6

U.S. SEEKS TO HOLD A NEUTRAL STANCE

Presses for a Cease-Fire— Many in Congress Oppose a Unilateral Move in Area

By JOHN W. FINNEY
Special to The New York Times

WASHINGTON, June 5—The Administration sought today to maintain a neutral role in the Middle East without formally committing itself to be neutral.

The White House, warning that "tragic consequences" would result if the fighting continued, called on both sides to accept an immediate cease-fire. The dominant Congressional reaction was that the United States should take no unilateral action in the Middle East.

In an attempt to bring about a cease-fire, the Administration deliberately refrained from fixing any blame for the outbreak of fighting.

[In London, the Foreign Secretary said that Britain's policy was "not to take sides." France suspended all deliveries of military equipment to the Middle East. Page 18.]

Confusion Develops in U.S.

The Johnson Administration, in attempting to maintain a position for mediation, became entangled in some confusion over how "neutral" it was.

The State Department spokesman, Robert J. McCloskey, started the confusion by declaring that "our position is neutral in thought, word and deed."

The Administration then spent the rest of the day attempting to tone down the McCloskey declaration by emphasizing that the United States was not neutral in terms of long-standing obligations to support the political independence and territorial integrity of Israel and of the Arab nations.

As it cast around for some way to bring the fighting to an end, the Administration announced that travel by American citizens to Israel and 13 Arab countries was being banned, unless the traveler had the specific permission of the State Department.

As of today, the State Department announced, United

Continued on Page 18, Column 1

Fighting Is Raging In Gaza and Sinai; Action in Air Heavy

Major Mideast Developments

On the Battlefronts

Israel and the Arab nations were locked in full-scale war yesterday along the borders of Israel and in the skies.

Fighting raged from Syria, on the north, to the Sinai Desert, on the south, and on the Jordanian-Israeli border.

Israel claimed major victories in the Sinai Desert and the Gaza Strip, reporting that her troops and tanks had taken El Arish and Khan Yunis, key towns, and asserting that the fall of Gaza city was imminent. In other sectors, the Israelis reported the capture of the Jordanian town of Jenin and said that Syrian land forces had entered the conflict for the first time with an attack on a border village.

Israel also said her pilots had shattered the Egyptian, Syrian and Jordanian Air Forces. Israeli pilots were reported to have destroyed 374 enemy planes, with an additional 34 probably destroyed. Israel put her losses at 19 aircraft.

The United Arab Republic said, however, that Arab land forces had repulsed invading Israeli armor on the Gaza Strip and at two points in the Sinai Peninsula.

In Jerusalem, Jordanian and Israeli troops exchanged machine-gun and mortar fire across no man's land.

In the Capitals

In Tel Aviv, Israeli leaders declared that their goals did not include the conquest of Arab territory.

In Cairo, President Gamal Abdel Nasser said the Arabs sought to "eliminate the shadow of Zionism from Palestine."

In Washington, the Johnson Administration sought to maintain a neutral role in the conflict and, calling on both sides to accept an immediate truce, avoided placing blame.

In Moscow, the Government issued a statement denouncing "Israeli aggression" and demanding withdrawal.

Nasser Exhorts Arabs

By ERIC PACE
Special to The New York Times

CAIRO, Tuesday, June 6—The Cairo radio announced last night that the United Arab Republic's forces had invaded Israel after having "wiped out" enemy attacks" in Egyptian territory on the Sinai Peninsula.

The United Arab Republic had declared earlier that its forces had retaliated on land, sea and in the air after Israel carried out surprise ground and air attacks on Egyptian border areas and airbases this morning.

President Gamal Abdel Nasser declared in a statement relayed by the Egyptian Government news service that all Arabs were now fighting to "eliminate the shadow of Zionism from Palestine and to restore its Arabism."

Progress of Fighting Unclear

The over-all progress of the conflict was unclear from the series of military communiqués issued throughout the day by the Cairo radio. But these reported that the United Arab Republic had destroyed 86 Israeli planes by nightfall while they acknowledged only two Egyptian planes lost to the Israelis.

They said that United Arab Republic and Palestinian land forces had repulsed Israeli invaders at Khan Yunis on the Gaza Strip and at Kuntilla and El Aguila on the Sinai Peninsula. Egyptian forces were said

Continued on Page 16, Column 5

Israel Depicts Gains

By JAMES FERON
Special to The New York Times

JERUSALEM (Israel), Tuesday, June 6—The Israeli Air Force indicated early today that it had decimated the Egyptian, Syrian and Jordanian air forces in a sweeping series of air battles and ground attacks.

Israeli pilots reported that they had destroyed 374 enemy planes, and that 34 other aircraft probably had been destroyed.

The Israelis put their losses at 19 planes. Eight pilots were reported killed and 11 were reported missing, including some known to have been captured.

Movement on Sinai

Striking gains were also reported on the Sinai Peninsula where the hostilities began, according to the Israelis, with the shelling of Israeli settlements along the Gaza border at dawn yesterday.

The Israeli Chief of Staff, Maj. Gen. Itzhak Rabin, said in a statement issued at a post-midnight news conference in Tel Aviv that Israeli armor had captured El Arish and was moving along the El Arish-Abu Aweigila road.

The Gaza town of Rafah was reported captured as well as the junction of Khan Yunis in the disputed Gaza Strip. The fall of Gaza itself was considered imminent.

The Air Force chief, Mordechai Hod, said that most of the damage had been done to the Egyptians, who lost 286 aircraft.

Continued on Page 16, Column 1

Speck Is Sentenced To Chair on Sept. 1

By DONALD JANSON
Special to The New York Times

PEORIA, Ill., June 5—Richard F. Speck was sentenced to death in the electric chair today for the murders last summer in Chicago of eight young nurses.

The 25-year-old drifter stood mute and expressionless a foot in front of the bench as Circuit Court Judge Herbert C. Paschen ordered the execution for Sept. 1.

Before sentence was passed, the public defender, Gerald W. Getty, told the judge that the lanky, itinerant seaman had nothing to say in his own behalf.

A jury of seven men and five women found Speck guilty of each of the murders last April

Continued on Page 28, Column 4

U.S. Military Analysts Expect Short War, With Israel Winning

By WILLIAM BEECHER
Special to The New York Times

WASHINGTON, June 5 — A number of American military analysts while admitting that the situation is still very confused say the war in the Middle East, were of the opinion that the war would probably be short and that Israel would prevail.

Analysts at the Pentagon said that the Egyptian Army was a lot stronger today than in 1956, when Israeli forces swept through the Sinai Peninsula, but that Israel still was believed to have a better-balanced, better-trained, better-led military force.

Several experts, while conceding that predictions are treacherous, said they believed Israel might want to fight holdings should be able to "punch

through" Egyptian forces in one of two directions in Sinai and elsewhere in a week to 10 days.

In 1956, Israel was able to overwhelm opposition in Sinai in 100 hours, but at that time Egypt was fighting on two fronts, with a British - French force pressing in from the north along the Suez Canal.

"Nobody, of course, knows how much better the Egyptian Army has become," said one general, "but we don't think they've had time enough to become a first-class fighting force."

Analysts speculated that Israel might want to fight holdings

Continued on Page 19, Column 4

Troops and Armor Clash in Jerusalem

By TERENCE SMITH

JERUSALEM (Israel), June 5 — War came to this divided city today at 11:20 A.M., a little more than three hours after the first announcement of the fighting at the Sinai border to the south.

Within minutes of the first shots, Arabs and Israelis were firing at each other with rifles, machine-guns, mortars, tanks and artillery from positions along an eight-mile border through the city.

The fighting continued into the night. In the darkness, the Jordanians threw up a shower of antiaircraft fire as jets swept overhead.

In early fighting, Jordanian

Continued on Page 16, Column 7

Israeli Planes Raid Airports in Jordan

By DANA ADAMS SCHMIDT
Special to The New York Times

AMMAN, Jordan, June 5—Clouds of black smoke rose over the Amman airport today as four Israeli jet bombers circled and dived, apparently more or less at will. Only light antiaircraft and machine-gun fire appeared to be opposing them as they bombed and strafed aircraft and installations in four attacks.

The Israeli Air Force also was reported to have bombed Jordan's airport in El Mafraq.

Civilians fled the streets as air-raid sirens wailed. Most residents of the leading hotel, the Intercontinental, made for an air-raid shelter in the nightclub. But some watched

Continued on Page 16, Column 8

HOSPITAL DIMMED: A nurse comforting a patient in a dark corridor of Jersey City Medical Center yesterday.

NEWS INDEX

	Page		Page
Art	52	Obituaries	44, 47
Books	45	Real Estate	77
Bridge	45	Screen	53-55
Business	63-64, 73-76	Ships and Air	82
Buyers	74	Society	56
Crossword	45	Supreme Court	33, 61
Editorials	46	Theaters	53-55
Fashions	51	TV and Radio	94-95
Financial	63-76	U. N. Proceedings	17
Food	51	U. S. Proceedings	17
Man in the News	17	Wash. Proceedings	17
Music	53-55	Weather	93
		News Summary and Index, Page 49	

A group of Florida executives are in N.Y. today seeking to meet a group of N.Y. V.I.P.'s. See adv. pg. 75.—Advt.

The New York Times

VOL. CXVI..No. 39,947   © 1967 The New York Times Company.   NEW YORK, THURSDAY, JUNE 8, 1967   10 CENTS

ISRAELIS ROUT THE ARABS, APPROACH SUEZ, BREAK BLOCKADE, OCCUPY OLD JERUSALEM; AGREE TO U.N. CEASE-FIRE; U.A.R. REJECTS IT

JOHNSON WILL USE CABINET TO COURT STATES' OFFICIALS

Aides Will Seek to Tighten Ties Between Governors and the White House

By WARREN WEAVER Jr.
Special to The New York Times

WASHINGTON, June 7—President Johnson has decided to use the members of his Cabinet as diplomatic agents in his campaign to improve relations between the Administration and state governments.

The President has approved a plan under which each member of the Cabinet would be assigned four or five states as his personal responsibility, with instructions to maintain personal contact between the Governors and the White House.

As part of the same effort, each of the 50 states will be given a "day" in Washington next fall and winter, when a planeload of its key officials will fly here to hold conferences all over the capital, capped by a meeting of the Governors with the President.

Bryant's Work Continued

Both projects reflect Mr. Johnson's continuing determination to build domestic as well as foreign bridges by working to sort out the tangled Federal-state relations that have been increasingly complicated by the administration of the Great Society programs.

Both are attempts to give some permanency to the contacts established during the last four months by Farris Bryant, the President's envoy to the states, on visits to 40 capitals with a squad of Federal experts.

Mr. Bryant, a former Governor of Florida who is now the director of the Office of Emergency Planning, plans to leave his White House post this summer, possibly to return to politics in his home state, and he is eager to help establish more permanent lines of communication before his departure.

As now envisioned, each Cabinet officer would visit all of the President.

Continued on Page 29, Column 2

CONFEREES BLOCK A DRAFT LOTTERY

Compromise Bill Continues Deferment of Students

By United Press International
WASHINGTON, June 7 — Senate and House negotiators reached agreement today on a new military draft bill that rules out, for the present, any lottery-like random selection system to determine the order of induction.

The bill was a compromise of differing bills that the Senate and House had passed. It would guarantee the continuance of educational deferments for college undergraduates and students enrolled in apprentice and job training programs.

Senator Richard B. Russell, Democrat of Georgia, who is chairman of the Senate conferees, said the Senate might act on the four-year draft extension bill tomorrow. House action must await approval by the Senate.

Congressional action will clear the way for President Johnson, under current discretionary powers, to reverse the order of induction and take 19-year-olds first from the Selec-

Continued on Page 3, Column 1

NEWS INDEX

	Page		Page
Books	44-45	Obituaries	47
Bridge	46	Real Estate	78
Business	..67, 76, 78	Screen	50-53
Buyers	66	Ships and Air	93
Crossword	46	Society	57
Editorials	46	Sports	50-53
Fashions	57	Theaters	50-53
Financial	64-78	TV and Radio	95
Food	...37	U. N. Proceedings	4
Man in the News	16	Wash. Proceedings	31
Music	50-53	Weather	93

News Summary and Index, Page 49

Rise in Debt Ceiling Rejected in House; Johnson Rebuffed

Special to The New York Times
WASHINGTON, June 7—The House of Representatives dealt the Johnson Administration a sharp setback today by rejecting a bill to increase the ceiling on the national debt $29-billion, to $365-billion.

The vote against passage was 210 to 197, with Republicans voting solidly to kill the bill. Enough Democrats, mostly Southerners, voted with them to turn the tide.

About six Northern Democratic "doves"—opponents of the war in Vietnam—also joined the opposition.

In all, 34 Democrats joined with 176 Republicans to defeat the measure.

Today's action raised the possibility—though a slim one—of financial chaos after June 30. At that time the debt limit reverts to its "permanent" ceiling of $285-billion, though the debt, at $330-billion, is already far above that level. The legal authority of the Treasury to pay its bills would be in doubt.

However, the Ways and

Continued on Page 30, Column 4

U.S. VOWS TO SEEK A DURABLE PEACE

Johnson Recalls Bundy for New Mideast Planning Unit — 'Real Chance' Is Seen

By MAX FRANKEL
Special to The New York Times

WASHINGTON, June 7 — President Johnson pledged today to do his best to help translate the new Middle Eastern situation into a more lasting settlement between Israel and her Arab neighbors.

Apparently hoping to exploit Israel's lightning military success—which has surprised but not displeased the White House—Mr. Johnson ordered the drafting of special policies for a "new peace" and set up new machinery to deal with the situation.

The President said that the United States, which had worked hard to avoid the war, felt that "there is now a real chance" to turn from "the frustrations of the past to the hopes of a peaceful future."

But Mr. Johnson said the handling of the crisis and the preparations for a lasting settlement would require the most careful consideration in the United States Government. To organize that effort he recalled McGeorge Bundy to temporary duty at the White House as executive secretary to a special subcommittee of the National Security Council.

Mr. Bundy will seek a temporary leave from the presidency of the Ford Foundation, which he assumed last year after serving as special assistant for

Continued on Page 19, Column 1

Dorothy Parker, 73, Literary Wit, Dies

By ALDEN WHITMAN

Dorothy Parker, the sardonic humorist who purveyed her wit in conversation, short stories, verse and criticism, died of a heart attack yesterday afternoon in her suite at the Volney Hotel, 23 East 74th Street. She was 73 years old and had been in frail health in recent years.

In print and in person, Miss Parker sparkled with a word or a phrase, for she honed her humor to its most economical size. Her rapier wit, much of it spontaneous, gained its early renown from her membership in the Algonquin Round Table, an informal luncheon club in the nineteen-twenties, where some of

Continued on Page 28, Column 1

EBAN SEES THANT

Says Acceptance Is Based on Enemy's Reciprocal Action

Excerpts from debate at U.N. are printed on Page 18.

By DREW MIDDLETON
Special to The New York Times

UNITED NATIONS, N. Y., June 7—The Security Council unanimously adopted a Soviet resolution today calling on the combatants in the Middle East to "cease fire and all military activities" at 4 P.M., New York time today.

The Government of Israel shortly thereafter announced that she had accepted the call for the Council for a cease-fire, provided her Arab foes agreed.

In the evening, reports from the Middle East indicated rejection of the call by the United Arab Republic, Syria, Iraq, Saudi Arabia, Algeria and Kuwait. Jordan told Secretary General Thant that she would abide by the cease-fire, except in self-defense.

Says It's in Effect

Abba Eban, the Foreign Minister of Israel, told the Secretary General that a cease-fire was already in effect between Jordan and Israel.

In presenting the resolution, the Soviet delegate, Nikolai T. Federenko, made it clear that if Israel failed to heed the Security Council's demands, Moscow would consider severing diplomatic relations. The original Security Council resolution, adopted yesterday, simply called for a cease-fire.

But the reports from the Arab capitals indicate, diplomatic sources here said, that military operations will continue.

According to diplomats, the best hope lies in a draft resolution presented by George Ignatieff, the Canadian delegate. This proposes that the President of the Security Council and the Secretary General take measures to insure compliance with the resolutions.

Today's resolution demanded that the combatants "cease fire and all military activities on 7 June 1967 by 2000 hours Greenwich mean time." The resolution was adopted less than an hour before this time, which is 4 P.M. New York time, 10 P.M. in Jordan and Israel and 11 P.M. in the United Arab Republic and Syria.

The Council adjourned without voting on the Canadian draft largely because Milko Ta-

Continued on Page 18, Column 2

OLD JERUSALEM IS NOW IN ISRAELI HANDS: Israeli soldiers in prayer at the Wailing Wall yesterday
United Press International Radiophoto

Major Mideast Developments

On the Battlefronts

Israel claimed victory in the Sinai Desert after three days of fighting. Sharm el Sheik, guarding the entrance to the Gulf of Aqaba, fell after a paratroop attack, and the Israelis said the blockade of the gulf was broken. Other Israeli units were within 20 miles of the Suez Canal, and one Israeli report placed them in the eastern section of Ismailia, on the canal itself.

In Jerusalem, for the first time in 19 years, Israeli Jews prayed at the Wailing Wall as their troops occupied the Old City. Israeli troops captured Jericho, in Jordan, and sped northward to take Nablus, giving them control of the west bank of the Jordan.

The Egyptian High Command reported that its forces had fallen back from first-line positions in the Sinai Peninsula and were fighting fiercely from unspecified secondary positions. It announced that Egyptian troops had pulled back from Sharm el Sheik to join main defense units.

In the Capitals

In the United Nations, Israel accepted the call for a cease-fire, provided the Arabs complied. Jordan announced that she would accept and ordered her troops to fire only in self-defense. But Baghdad declared that Iraq had refused. There were indications that Syria, Algeria and Kuwait were opposed.

In Cairo, an Egyptian official said the United Arab Republic would fight on.

In Moscow, the Soviet Union threatened to break diplomatic relations with Israel if she did not observe the cease-fire.

In Paris, the French proposed an international agreement for free passage in the Gulf of Aqaba similar to the one governing the Dardanelles in Turkey.

In Washington, President Johnson promised to seek a settlement that would assure lasting peace in the Mideast.

In London, the British urged the Israelis to halt before they aroused more turmoil in the Arab world and diminished the chances for a settlement.

Israelis Weep and Pray Beside the Wailing Wall

By TERENCE SMITH
Special to The New York Times

JERUSALEM, June 7—Israeli troops wept and prayed today at the foot of the Wailing Wall—the last remnant of Solomon's Second Temple and the object of pilgrimage by Jews through the centuries.

In battle dress and still carrying their weapons, they gathered at the base of the sand-colored wall and sang Hallel, a series of prayers reserved for occasions of great joy.

They were repeating a tradition that goes back 2,000 years but has been denied Israeli Jews since 1948, when the first of three wars with the Arabs ended in this area.

The wall is all that remains of the Second Temple, built in the 10th century before Christ and destroyed by the Romans in A.D. 70.

The Israelis, trembling with emotion, bowed vigorously from the waist as they chanted psalms in a lusty chorus. Most had submachine guns slung over their shoulders and several held bazookas as they prayed.

Among the leaders to pray at the wall was Maj. Gen. Moshe Dayan, the new Defense Minister. He told the troops:

"We have returned to the holiest of our holy places, never to depart from it again."

General Dayan, who was at the

Continued on Page 17, Column 1

AQABA GULF OPEN

Dayan Asserts Israel Does Not Intend to Capture the Canal

By The Associated Press
TEL AVIV, June 7 — Israel proclaimed victory tonight in the Sinai Peninsula campaign against the United Arab Republic. On the eastern front, both the Old City of Jerusalem and Bethlehem were captured from the Jordanians.

"The Egyptians are defeated," said Maj. Gen. Itzhak Rabin, the Israeli Chief of Staff.

"All their efforts are aimed at withdrawing behind the Suez Canal, and we are taking care of that. The whole area is in our hands. The main effort of the Egyptians is to save themselves."

Israel Losses 'Not Great'

Describing the developments through the third day of this third Arab-Israeli war in 19 years, General Rabin made these claims:

¶Sinai, the Egyptian territory between Israel's Negev Desert and the Suez Canal, is taken.

¶Most of the Jordanian territory on the west bank of the Jordan River, including Jericho, is in Israeli hands, and most of Jordan's army has been captured.

¶Relative to what was done, the number of Israeli casualties was "not great."

The Israelis were reported to have swept to the Suez Canal.

[An Israeli delegation source at the United Nations said Israeli troops had seized that part of the canal city of Ismailia that is on the eastern side of the waterway. But this was denied by an army source in Tel Aviv who said, according to Reuters, that the Israelis had not taken any point along the canal.

[Maj. Gen. Moshe Dayan, the Israeli Defense Minister, declared that there was "no intention" of taking the canal, United Press International reported.]

'Never to Depart'

After the fall of the Old City of Jerusalem, Defense Minister Moshe Dayan said there that the Israelis had reunited their capital and would never "depart from it again."

Israel reported that paratroops aided by naval units had captured Sharm el Sheik, commanding the entrance to the Gulf of Aqaba, and said the blockade that the Egyptians had mounted from that position had been broken.

"The Strait of Tiran is now open," General Rabin said.

Israel's chief of staff said his men had taken on the United Arab Republic, Jordan, Syria and Iraq, knocked out their air forces and overrun their armor and infantry.

"All this the armed forces of Israel did alone," he declared.

The general then turned over the briefing to Brig. Gen. Mordecai Hod, commander of the air force, who announced 441 Arab

Continued on Page 16, Column 1

CAIRO ANNOUNCES A SINAI PULLBACK

Blames Foreign Aid to Foe, but Says Troops Fight On in Secondary Positions

By ERIC PACE
Special to The New York Times

CAIRO, June 7—An Egyptian military communiqué reported today that forces of the United Arab Republic had fallen back from some first-line positions on the Sinai Peninsula and were engaged in fierce fighting against Israeli troops from secondary positions.

Another statement of the High Command, broadcast four hours later by the Cairo radio, said Egyptian troops at Sharm el Sheik, guarding the entrance to the Gulf of Aqaba, had joined other Egyptian forces "now concentrated in the Sinai Peninsula."

There was no elaboration, but the communiqué, broadcast about 5:30 P.M., appeared to confirm Israeli reports that the Egyptians had been forced to retreat from Sharm el Sheik.

At night, the High Command reported that Israeli paratroops had dropped over the "second-line Egyptian front" but had been "completely wiped out."

The communiqué also said the Israelis had tried another drop at Sharm el Sheik after the

Continued on Page 17, Column 6

Pentagon Believes Israeli Jets Struck From Sea, Eluded Radar

By WILLIAM BEECHER
Special to The New York Times

WASHINGTON, June 7 — At least a part of the Israeli Air Force that caught large numbers of Egyptian aircraft on the ground in the early hours of the war may have slipped through gaps in the United Arab Republic's radar net by flying in over the Mediterranean.

This possibility was raised today by Pentagon analysts. If correct, it would help to explain how Israeli pilots were able to surprise so many Egyptian jets before they could get into the air.

It might also serve to provide part of the explanation behind insistent Arab assertions that carrier-based United States and British jets participated in the raids.

Shortly after the raids, the Jordanian radio charged that Jordanian radar

Continued on Page 18, Column 8

CONQUEST IN THE MIDEAST: Israeli troops took Sharm el Sheik (1), drove on to the Suez Canal (2) and seized control of the Old City in Jerusalem (3). Photo was taken in September, 1966, during the flight of Gemini II.

"All the News That's Fit to Print"

The New York Times

LATE CITY EDITION
Weather: Fair and warm today, tonight and tomorrow. Temp. range: today 85-63; Thurs. 85-64. Temp.-Hum. Index: today 70 to 75; Thurs. 77. Full U.S. report on Page 89.

VOL. CXVI..No. 39,948   © 1967 The New York Times Company.   NEW YORK, FRIDAY, JUNE 9, 1967   10 CENTS

EGYPT AND SYRIA AGREE TO U.N. CEASE-FIRE; ISRAEL REPORTS TROOPS REACH SUEZ CANAL; JOHNSON, KOSYGIN USED HOT LINE IN CRISIS

SENATE APPROVES A TIGHTENED RULE ON REDISTRICTING

33 States Ordered to Bring Population Variant Down to 10% by 1968 Election

By JAMES F. CLARITY
Special to The New York Times

WASHINGTON, June 8—The Senate approved today a bill requiring that by the 1968 election no state have a population variance of more than 10 cent between its largest and smallest Congressional districts.

The approval, which came in a surprise vote of 57 to 25, was a result of a fight by Senator Edward M. Kennedy, Democrat of Massachusetts, to amend a measure that would have permitted a variance of 35 per cent until the 1972 election.

The Kennedy amendment, which was soundly defeated in committee two weeks ago, is intended, according to the Senator, to make Congressional redistricting conform with the Supreme Court's one-man, one-vote ruling of 1964. The amendment also deleted language giving the states power to determine when the compactness of a district was "practicable."

An Altered Version

The measure, before it was amended today, was an altered version of a bill already passed by the House. The House bill provided for a population variance of 30 per cent, as was amended by the Senate Judiciary Committee to cover four additional states.

The version passed today, which now goes to a Senate-House conference, would apply to 33 states having variances of more than 10 per cent. Nine of these states are under Federal court orders to redistrict.

The 17 states not covered by today's Senate action either elect Representatives at large or have variances lower than 10 per cent.

Mr. Kennedy's proposal was approved, first in a crucial 44-to-89 vote as an amendment, then in the final vote on the bill as amended, 57 to 25.

"We knew it would be close."

Continued on Page 26, Column 1

Arms Cost Stress Scored by Rickover

By EVERT CLARK
Special to The New York Times

WASHINGTON, June 8—Vice Adm. Hyman G. Rickover has denounced the cost-effectiveness approach to weapons development as an "ism," a "new religion" and a "fog bomb" that is keeping the nation from gaining technology that would save lives.

In Congressional testimony released today, the head of the nuclear-powered ship program attacked present management techniques in the Pentagon.

By Presidential order, many of these techniques—including the mathematical analysis of cost vs. effectiveness—are now being spread throughout the executive branch of

Continued on Page 2, Column 4

JURY FINDS LAXITY IN BUILDINGS UNIT

Graft, Shirking and Lack of Personnel Training Are Cited—Moerdler Agrees

By JACK ROTH

A New York County grand jury criticized yesterday longstanding conditions in the Buildings Department that it said had resulted in corruption among housing inspectors and landlords.

The jury also said the situation permitted some inspectors and their supervisors to quit work as early as 10:30 A.M. and go to bars and racetracks for the rest of the day.

The jury, in a presentment handed up to Supreme Court Justice Mitchell D. Schweitzer, charged that the department suffered from lack of financial and manpower resources.

It asserted that inspectors were not properly trained for their jobs, that they were unaware of their department's rules and regulations, that there was duplication in inspections, that electronic processing equipment was failing to do its job and that unauthorized persons had access to file rooms and private departmental offices.

The Buildings Commissioner,

Continued on Page 31, Column 1

ALL SINAI IS HELD

U.A.R. Loses 50 Tanks in Actions Termed Fiercest of War

By Reuters

TEL AVIV, Friday, June 9—Israeli troops have reached the bank of the Suez Canal and have taken control of the entire Sinai Peninsula, the Israeli radio reported this morning.

The radio broadcast the text of a message from the commander in the southern front, to the Chief of Staff, Gen. Yitzhak Rabin. The message said:

"Happy to inform you that our forces are stationed on the bank of the Suez Canal and the Red Sea. The Sinai Peninsula is in our hands. Greetings to you and to the whole defense forces of Israel."

Battle reports yesterday indicated that the remnants of two Egyptian armored divisions and four infantry divisions were trapped in the western part of that Sinai Desert.

50 Tanks Reported Wrecked

The news of Cairo's acceptance of the United Nations cease-fire coincided with an announcement by an Israeli spokesman that three battles in the desert yesterday had been "the fiercest in this war."

The Israelis said they had shot down eight Egyptian planes and destroyed at least 50 Egyptian tanks during the fighting.

Other tanks were wrecked and left on the road to Qantara, about 30 miles north of Ismailia, about midway along the 100-mile Suez Canal.

Among the Egyptian planes downed were a Soviet-made Ilyushin bomber and several Soviet-built Sukhoi-7's. Israeli planes also struck Soviet-made missile sites in the Suez Canal zone during daylight raids, the spokesman added.

Despite the continuation of heavy fighting, the Israeli spokesman said that all escape routes for Egyptian armored units had been closed.

He added that Israeli forces had captured oilfields at Ras Sudar, south of the port of Taufiq on the western coast of the Sinai Peninsula. Israeli soldiers said the wells were afire

Continued on Page 17, Column 6

AFTER THE BATTLE: Egyptian prisoners, prone on the sand, their hands behind their heads, are guarded in a compound by Israeli troops at El Arish in the northern Sinai Peninsula. El Arish was taken by Israel Tuesday.

United Press International Cablephoto

EGYPTIANS TOLD OF TRUCE DECISION

Cairo Broadcast Is Terse—Syrians Also Announce Approval of Cease-Fire

By ERIC PACE
Special to The New York Times

CAIRO, Friday, June 9—The Government told the Egyptian people this morning that it had conditionally accepted a cease-fire in the war with Israel.

There was no immediate popular reaction because the Cairo radio waited until early morning before announcing, more than three hours after the fact, that the United Arab Republic had told Secretary General Thant of the United Nations that it would agree to a truce if Israel did so.

[The Damascus radio announced that Syria, too, had accepted the cease-fire, Reuters reported. Page 17.]

Cairo was blacked out as protection against possible Israeli air raids when the news came, but nocturnal strollers reported that policemen were already taking down at least some of the anti-Israeli banners that have festooned the city for the last few weeks.

An early edition of a popular Cairo newspaper, Al Akhbar, put the news on the front page but made no comment. There was also no elaboration from the radio, which broadcast a military communiqué saying that the battle against Israel was continuing at all points along the Egyptian front.

The terse announcement of the cease-fire contrasted with

Continued on Page 17, Column 2

U.S. Planes Batter MIG Base in North

Special to The New York Times

SAIGON, South Vietnam, June 8 — American fighter-bombers knocked out a MIG base near Hanoi yesterday and wrecked a surface-to-air missile storage area 50 miles southwest of the capital, the United States Command reported today.

At the same time, new fighting broke out just south of the demilitarized zone at the border between North Vietnam and South Vietnam, where a fierce battle raged for control of three hills last month.

Navy carrier pilots attacked the Kep Airfield, 37 miles northeast of Hanoi, for the seventh time since April 24. A headquarters spokesman said the airfield is "closed tempo-

Continued on Page 3, Column 4

Major Mideast Developments

In the Capitals

The United Arab Republic accepted a United Nations cease-fire. Israel had previously agreed to stop hostilities if her enemies were willing to go along.

In Damascus, after a series of militant vows to fight on, the Syrians announced that they would also accept the cease-fire.

President Johnson welcomed the cease-fire agreement and urged prompt action to solve the "many more fundamental" questions in the Middle East.

An emergency declaration on oil was being considered by the Johnson Administration after major oil companies reported that a worldwide transportation problem had resulted from the war.

The hot line between Washington and Moscow was used this week for the first time during a crisis.

On the Battlefronts

Before the cease-fire went into effect, Israeli planes and torpedo boats mistakenly attacked a United States communications ship about 15 miles off Sinai. The Pentagon reported that 10 Americans had been killed and 100 wounded. Israel sent an apology.

Israel reported that her troops had reached the bank of the Suez Canal and that the entire Sinai Peninsula was under her control. Earlier Israel reported three fierce desert battles in which at least 50 Egyptian tanks had been destroyed.

The United Arab Republic announced that its air force had inflicted heavy damage on Israeli armored columns trying to advance westward from El Arish in the Sinai Peninsula.

At the Strait of Tiran, a Soviet freighter bound for the Jordanian port of Aqaba was the first ship to pass since Israel declared the waterway open to shipping on Wednesday. Two Israeli ships prepared to follow.

DONATIONS POUR IN FOR ISRAELI FUND

Many Give All They Have—Some Gifts in Millions

By M. S. HANDLER

"You have got it all now," said a brief letter containing a check for $25,000.

The message was from a professor at the Jewish Theological Seminary who said he had gladly stripped himself of his worldly goods and sent the proceeds to the United Jewish Appeal for the Israel Emergency Fund.

The owner of two gas stations arrived at the appeal's offices and turned over the deeds to the stations as his contribution to the multi-million fund drive.

Other Jews walked in with the cash-surrender values of their life insurance policies. Still others, deeply moved by the Arab-Israeli war, sold real estate and securities and sent the money to the fund's headquarters, on the Avenue of the Americas at 51st street.

These were some examples of the dramas being played out in Jewish communities across the United States, U.J.A. officials said yesterday.

The contributions, appeal of-

Continued on Page 11, Column 1

ISRAEL, IN ERROR, ATTACKS U.S. SHIP

10 Navy Men Die, 100 Hurt in Raids North of Sinai

By WILLIAM BEECHER
Special to The New York Times

WASHINGTON, June 8 —An American naval vessel was mistakenly attacked by Israeli planes and torpedo boats today in international waters about 15 miles north of the Sinai Peninsula. Reports tonight listed the toll as 10 dead and 100 wounded. Twenty of the wounded were hurt critically.

The vessel, the Liberty, was on a peaceful, though war-related mission. Pentagon sources said she had been dispatched from Spain to the war zone to provide additional communications to facilitate the evacuation of American citizens from the Middle East and North Africa.

Pentagon officials said it was too early to tell whether indemnification would be asked from Israel for the loss of life and the damage to the Navy ship.

President Johnson, in a letter to the Senate majority leader, Mike Mansfield, noted that the

Continued on Page 19, Column 1

A SHIFT BY CAIRO

Thant Notifies Council in Middle of Debate on Resolutions

Excerpts from the U.N. debate are printed on Page 16.

By DREW MIDDLETON
Special to The New York Times

UNITED NATIONS, N. Y., June 8—The United Arab Republic, the leader of the anti-Israel coalition, today accepted the Security Council's demand for a cease-fire in the Middle East provided Israel did the same.

Yesterday, the delegate of Israel said his country accepted the cease-fire provided Israel's foes agreed to it. Reports here yesterday indicated rejection by Cairo.

Syria gave notice tonight that she would comply, informing the Secretary General after the Security Council recessed.

This afternoon, in his dry, precise voice Secretary General Thant read to the Council a brief letter from Mohamed Awad el-Kony, the U.A.R. delegate, disclosing that President Gamal Abdel Nasser's Government had "decided to accept the cease-fire" called for in the two Council resolutions "on the condition that the other party ceases fire."

He Scraps Long Speech

Mr. el-Kony wrote the letter after a long telephone conversation with Cairo shortly before the Council meeting began. After the call, he scrapped a 20-page speech he had prepared and wrote the note to Mr. Thant.

The Israeli Foreign Minister, Abba Eban, hailed the immediate prospect of a cease-fire as "a notable step" and called on other Arab governments to follow the Egyptian lead.

Cairo's acceptance of the Council resolutions adopted unanimously on Tuesday and Wednesday raised rather than lowered the heat of the debate between the United States and the Soviet Union over the resolutions each submitted to the Council.

Arthur J. Goldberg, the United States delegate, saying he hoped for a peace "stable and just to all concerned," submitted a draft of a resolution calling for the "withdrawal and disengagement of armed personnel," the renunciation of force, "the maintenance of vital international rights" and the establishment of a peace in the area.

The Administration was said

Continued on Page 17, Column 1

JOHNSON PLEASED BY GAINS ON TRUCE

Looks to a Stable Peace—White House Discloses Use of the Hot Line

Texts of the Mansfield letter and Johnson reply, Page 18.

By MAX FRANKEL
Special to The New York Times

WASHINGTON, June 8—President Johnson welcomed spreading acceptance of a cease-fire agreement in the Middle East today, but urged all parties to move promptly toward the "many more fundamental" questions bearing on a stable peace.

While thus pressing for more than merely another frail armistice, the White House also disclosed that its hot-line connection with Moscow had been used for the first time this week in an international crisis.

The United States used the teletype link this morning when it heard of an attack on an American communications ship off the Sinai Peninsula. At the time, the source of the attack was not known.

The Soviet Government, whose warships have been observing the movements of the United States Sixth Fleet in the eastern Mediterranean, was advised that the carrier-based American planes were scrambling into action for the sole purpose of assisting the distressed vessel.

It was later learned that Israeli forces had attacked the American ship in error.

The announcement of quick exchanges to prevent misunder-

Continued on Page 18, Column 1

Russians Continue To Harass 6th Fleet

By NEIL SHEEHAN

ABOARD U. S. S. AMERICA in the Eastern Mediterranean, June 8—Two Soviet warships, a destroyer and a small, highly maneuverable patrol craft, moved into the formation of this Sixth Fleet carrier task force group this morning and began systematically harassing the American ships.

The harassment was undertaken despite a warning to another Soviet destroyer yesterday from Vice Adm. William I. Martin, the Sixth Fleet commander. Admiral Martin warned from the area of the American formation. He said the Soviet vessel must withdraw from the area of the American ship, while following the carrier

Continued on Page 15, Column 1

SOVIET SHIP SAILS INTO AQABA GULF

Passage Is First Since Israel Lifted Arab Blockade

By Reuters

ELATH, Israel, June 8—A Soviet freighter bound for the Jordanian port of Aqaba passed through the Strait of Tiran today, the first ship to do so since Israel declared the passage an international waterway yesterday.

Two outgoing Israeli freighters were preparing to pass through the strait since the Egyptians blockaded the Gulf of Aqaba on May 23.

A report from Sharm el Sheik, which dominates the strait, dis-

Continued on Page 17, Column 2

CRUSHING OFFENSIVES: Israelis thrust westward across northern Sinai (1) to the Suez Canal after sharp fighting at Bir Gifgafa and Mitla Pass, and routed Egyptians at Nakhl and Thamad in drive farther south (2). Soviet ship passed through Strait of Tiran (3), now under Israeli control. Meanwhile Israeli attack on U.S. ship in Mediterranean (4) killed 10 men. Israelis held west bank of the River Jordan as far north as Jenin (5).

"All the News That's Fit to Print"

The New York Times

LATE CITY EDITION

Weather: Snow likely today, tonight. Partly cloudy tomorrow. Temp. range: Today 35-31; Tuesday 41-32. Full U.S. report on Page 90.

VOL. CXVII..No. 40,177

© 1968 The New York Times Company.

NEW YORK, WEDNESDAY, JANUARY 24, 1968

10 CENTS

MILLS TURNS DOWN AIDES OF JOHNSON ON TAX SURCHARGE

Says They Did Not Convince Him They Had Done Their Best to Cut Spending

'ANOTHER LOOK' URGED

House Leader's Stand Hints at Delay Until March in Acting on New Levy

By EILEEN SHANAHAN
Special to The New York Times

WASHINGTON, Jan. 23 — Representative Wilbur D. Mills told the Administration "no" again today on the tax increase.

At the end of two days of hearings before the House Ways and Means Committee, of which he is chairman, the Arkansas Democrat told Administration officials that they had "not yet established" to his satisfaction that "you've done the best you can" to hold down Government spending.

Mr. Mills asked the officials to "take another look" at next year's planned Government spending of $147.4-billion, on the basis of the traditional administrative budget, while the committee turns its attention to another issue. That is the Administration's proposals to reduce the deficit in the United States' balance of international payments.

Date Left Undecided

Just how long the committee might take with the balance-of-payments program and when it might get back to the tax bill, Mr. Mills did not say. It seemed unlikely that the committee could resume consideration of the proposed 10 per cent tax surcharge before early March, at the soonest.

Meanwhile, the Gallup Poll reported that President Johnson faces a difficult test in trying to sell American voters on a tax increase at this time, and that the opposition comes as much from the rank and file of his own party as from others.

In addition to dealing with the balance-of-payments problem, Mr. Mills indicated that the committee might also consider, ahead of any new look at the tax surcharge, both the extension of excise taxes on automobiles and telephone service and a further step up in corporate tax collections.

Excise Action Favored

He said that an extension of the excise taxes "has to be done." Under present law they would go down on April 1 from 7 to 2 per cent on automobiles and from 10 to 1 per cent on telephone service.

In addition, he said it "might be possible, without a great deal of argument, to do some part" of what the Administration has asked to bring corporations closer to a pay-as-you-go tax basis.

Mr. Mills's reference to approval of only "part" of the corporate tax collection speed-up reflected his belief that the smallest corporations — those with tax liabilities of $25,000 or less — should probably not be put on a full pay-as-you-

Continued on Page 25, Column 1

Jersey Sues State On Price for PATH

By FRED P. GRAHAM
Special to The New York Times

WASHINGTON, Jan. 23 — New Jersey sued New York in the Supreme Court today in an unusual legal move designed to bar New York courts from approving an excessive land condemnation judgment against the Port of New York Authority.

In a suit filed directly in the Court, Attorney General Arthur J. Sills of New Jersey contended that the New York Court of Appeals violated an agreement between the two states when it ruled that the Port Authority would pay $30-million for the assets of the Hudson Rapid Tubes Corporation.

The assets of the Hudson & Manhattan Railroad

Continued on Page 30, Column 3

City Council Votes A One-Year Trial Of Group Cab Rides

By SETH S. KING

A year-long experiment in group taxi riding was approved yesterday by the City Council.

As soon as Mayor Lindsay signs the bill his task force on taxis will be allowed to organize and supervise such rides from the Eastern Airlines Shuttle Terminal at La Guardia Airport to four zones in Manhattan.

The Council also passed a bill eliminating a requirement that cab drivers be residents of the city.

It also adopted a resolution calling upon the Police Department's Hack Bureau to require each taxi to be equipped with an exterior switch, or similar device, instead of an interior switch, to operate its off-duty sign.

This was aimed at preventing a driver from suddenly turning on his off-duty sign with an interior switch when he saw a fare he did not want to pick up. The

Continued on Page 35, Column 1

JOHNSON PROGRAM INDICTED BY G.O.P.

In TV Reply, Party Charges His Policies Led to Riots, Crime Rise and Inflation

Excerpts from the statements will be found on Page 28.

By JOHN HERBERS
Special to The New York Times

WASHINGTON, Jan. 23 — Republicans in Congress told the American people tonight that President Johnson's policies had led to riots, crime and inflation at home and loss of influence and prestige abroad.

In a one-hour telecast over the Columbia Broadcasting System from the auditorium of the new Senate Office Building, eight Senators and nine Representatives delivered a harsh indictment of the Administration's record and said that President Johnson had vastly underestimated the extent of discontent in the country.

America, they said, needs a new leader who would seek a military victory in Vietnam, take a strong stand against worldwide Communism, move decisively to stamp out crime and violence at home and hold down Government spending.

The broadcast, entitled "The State of the Union—the Republican Appraisal," was a reply to President Johnson's State of

Continued on Page 28, Column 3

3,600 Drugs Facing Relabeling To List Ailments They Combat

By United Press International

WASHINGTON, Jan. 23 — Virtually every drug originally manufactured in America between 1938 and 1962 will have to be relabeled to tell exactly what ailments it is effective against, the Government told the drug industry today.

Some of the 3,600 drugs — sold in as many as 18,000 different combinations — are going to be ordered off the market, and the advertising of nearly all the drugs will have to be changed, William W. Goodrich, assistant general counsel for the Food and Drug Administration, said.

He spoke at a two-hour conference of drug manufacturers called to explain the agency's study of the effectiveness of all prescription and nonprescription drugs marketed in that 24-year period.

The review had been ordered under the Kefauver-Harris Act of 1962, which requires that all drugs sold domestically be proved effective as well as safe for their intended uses. Prior to the new rules, the drugs had only to be found safe.

The first step toward removal from the market of a group of drugs was taken today

with publication in the Federal Register that there was no evidence that the drugs rutin, quercetin, hesperidin or bioflavonoids "are effective for use in man for any conditions." The listed drugs have been promoted for years as agents for the control of hemorrhage and in dietary food supplements.

Manufacturers of such drugs licensed by the drug agency and manufacturers of similar products — called "me too" products—were invited by the agency to a hearing Jan. 31 to discuss the ruling.

Robert Giles, a member of the Pharmaceutical Manufacturers Association, rose at the meeting to criticize Mr. Goodrich and other officials of the drug agency for public estimates that 10 per cent of the drugs under study would be found totally ineffective and ruled off the market.

In New York last month, Dr. James L. Goddard, Food and Drug Commissioner, estimated that 10 per cent of prescription and over-the-counter drugs would have to be withdrawn from the market because of the efficacy reviews.

Officials of the agency said

Continued on Page 32, Column 1

PRESIDENT OFFERS PROJECT TO SPUR HIRING OF JOBLESS

$2-Billion Manpower Plea Stresses Industrial Effort to Assist 'Hard Core'

Text of President's message is printed on Page 24.

By MAX FRANKEL
Special to The New York Times

WASHINGTON, Jan. 23 — President Johnson asked Congress today for quick action to help him mount the first large-scale effort to induce private industry to train and hire the hard-core cases among the urban unemployed.

In the first of more than a dozen special messages covering his major legislative proposals for the year, the President urged the expansion of all Government manpower efforts by 25 per cent, from a budget of $1.65-billion in the current fiscal year, ending June 30, to $2.09-billion in the year starting July 1.

Total Is Expanding

He suggested spending the bulk of the $442-million increase on programs to find, train and employ the most disadvantaged citizens, most of whom have given up the search for work because of inadequate training, discrimination, discouragement and a general despair.

There are more than a million such persons, the Administration believes, including a still expanding total of 500,000 in 50 major cities. The President would try to place 100,000 of these in jobs in the next 18 months and aim for a target of 500,000 by mid-1971.

"It is a waste that an enlightened nation should not tolerate," Mr. Johnson said in his message. "It is a waste that a nation concerned by disorders in its city streets cannot tolerate."

National Organization

Existing manpower programs have not reached the hard-core jobless effectively, Mr. Johnson reported. Therefore he proposed the expansion of promising experiments with direct subsidies to private employers who incur the extra costs of training and making jobs available to hitherto unqualified persons.

He said he was creating a national organization of leading businessmen, headed by Henry Ford 2d, chairman of the Ford Motor Company, to enlist the cooperation of industry and to work with Government officials in the regions and cities.

At the same time, the President proposed a significant expansion of the year-old Government program to train the

Continued on Page 24, Column 1

Danish Socialists Beaten in Election; Krag Will Resign

By ALVIN SHUSTER
Special to The New York Times

COPENHAGEN, Denmark, Jan. 23 — The Social Democratic party, in power for the last 15 years, was defeated tonight in a huge protest vote.

The Danes, upset over rising prices and taxes, turned to the right in their national elections. Three non-Socialist parties won enough seats in Parliament to enable them to form a new government.

Premier Jens Otto Krag, the Social Democratic Premier, said he would resign tomorrow.

Emerging as victors today were the Radical Liberals, the Conservatives and the Agrarian Liberals. The three parties had indicated strongly before the election that if they won a parliamentary majority they would form a government.

Social Democrats Largest

Between them, with about 95 per cent of the votes counted, they had 101 seats, the Radical Liberals going from 13 to 28, the Conservatives from 34 to 38 and the Agrarian Liberals remaining unchanged at 35.

The Social Democrats will remain the largest single party in Parliament with 63 seats, a loss of six. The extreme leftist Socialist People's party, which had won 20 seats in the last elections in 1966, dropped to 11.

The voting was heavy. The final count may show that 90 per cent of the 3.3 million eligible voters cast ballots.

Mr. Krag appeared on television tonight and made a last-minute appeal to save his

Continued on Page 7, Column 1

RADIATION FOUND WHERE B-52 FELL

It Suggests Hydrogen Bombs Did Not Go Through Ice Off Greenland Base

By JOHN W. FINNEY
Special to The New York Times

WASHINGTON, Jan. 23 — Air Force search teams have reported today to have detected small amounts of radiation from some or all of the four hydrogen bombs missing after a B-52 bomber crashed on the ice off northwest Greenland.

After two days of hunting with dog sleds and helicopters, teams from the Thule Air Force Base in Greenland still had not found the unarmed thermonuclear weapons. But the detection of the radiation was taken as an encouraging sign that the bombs were scattered across the surface and had not plunged through the ice with parts of the bomber into about 800 feet of water.

If the bombs are still on the surface, recovery operations will be easier. It was first thought that the bombs had sunk to the bottom of North Star Bay, about seven miles southwest of the Thule base, raising the problem of underwater recovery operations through the sea ice.

The radiation suggested that some of the bombs might have broken apart in the impact of the crash and during the subsequent explosion in the bomber as it careened several hundred feet across the ice. If the bombs have split and

Continued on Page 6, Column 4

NORTH KOREA SEIZES NAVY SHIP, HOLDS 83 ON BOARD AS U.S. SPIES; ENTERPRISE IS ORDERED TO AREA

Pueblo, seized off North Korea and taken to Wonsan, is an intelligence collection vessel of the United States Navy

Associated Press

The American vessel was seized off Wonsan (cross)

The New York Times
Jan. 24, 1968

4 CREWMEN HURT

Rusk Says Efforts Are Under Way to Obtain Vessel's Release

U.S. statement and Pyongyang broadcast are on Page 15.

By NEIL SHEEHAN
Special to The New York Times

WASHINGTON, Jan. 23 — North Korean patrol boats seized a United States Navy intelligence ship off Wonsan today and took the ship and her 83 crew members into the North Korean port.

The Defense Department, reporting the incident, said the ship had been in international waters about 25 miles off the eastern coast of North Korea when she was boarded by armed North Korean sailors at 1:45 P.M. (11:45 P.M. Monday, Eastern Standard time).

But North Korea, in a Pyongyang radio broadcast, asserted that the Pueblo had "intruded into the territorial waters of the republic and was carrying out hostile activities." The broadcast called the Pueblo "an armed spy boat of the United States imperialist aggressor force."

Matter of 'Utmost Gravity'

Secretary of State Dean Rusk called the seizure of the Pueblo "a matter of the utmost gravity." He said the United States was negotiating with North Korea "through the channels that are available to us to obtain the immediate release of the vessel and her crew."

The incident forced a sudden confrontation between the United States and an Asian Communist government that has long been calling for diversionary assaults against "United States imperialism" to distract American energies from the war in Vietnam.

The Defense Department said four crewmen of the Pueblo had been wounded, one critically. One report said a crew member had lost a leg. The Pentagon declined to say how the men had been wounded.

North Korean Report

Later—on Wednesday morning, Korean time—the North Vietnamese said at an armistice meeting in Panmunjom that several of the Pueblo's crew were "killed or wounded" in the incident, and a North Vietnamese broadcast monitored in Tokyo said the vessel resisted seizure. The Pentagon declined to comment.

The Pueblo carried 6 officers, 75 enlisted men and 2 civilians, whom the Defense Department identified as Navy civilian hydrographers performing oceanographic research.

Military sources said the nuclear-powered aircraft carrier Enterprise and two destroyers

Continued on Page 14, Column 5

5,000 MEN MASSED AT KHESANH BY U.S.

Marines Rushed In as Foe Builds Up Force in Area— Supply Planes Fired On

By CHARLES MOHR
Special to The New York Times

KHESANH, South Vietnam, Jan. 23 — More than 5,000 United States marines have been concentrated at Khesanh amid indications that one of the major battles of the Vietnam war may be in the offing.

The marines were rushed in because of an increasingly obvious concentration of North Vietnamese troops in the area.

The nearness of the enemy forces made itself evident when the unmistakable sound of a bullet striking a fuselage rang out as a transport plane glided in to land at the Marine base here. The fat-bellied C-123 Loadmaster landed, safe despite the bullet hole.

The crew pushed pallets of 155-mm. artillery ammunition off the plane and then turned to four large wooden crates addressed to "Fifth Graves

Continued on Page 3, Column 1

RETURN OF PUEBLO ASKED BY U.S. AIDE

Immediate Action Sought at Meeting in Panmunjom of Armistice Group

By Reuters

PANMUNJOM, Korea, Wednesday, Jan. 24—The American commander of the United Nations Command demanded at a meeting of the Mixed Armistice Commission today that the Pueblo and her crew of 83 be returned immediately by North Korea.

Rear Adm. John V. Smith also told the chief North Korean delegate, Maj. Gen. Chung Kook Pak, that the United States reserved the right to demand compensation for the capture of the vessel by the North Korean Navy yesterday.

[The North Koreans said the ship "will remain in our hands," United Press International reported.]

General Pak said North Korean naval vessels fired at the Pueblo yesterday and "several of her crew members were killed or wounded." The Defense Department in Washington had said no one was killed.

Admiral Smith also protested what he said was an intrusion by a band of 31 North Korean agents into Seoul, the South Korean capital, Sunday night. The intrusion resulted in the death of 11 persons.

The meeting today in the demilitarized zone between North and South Korea was called by the United Nations Command Monday, before the Pueblo was taken, because of the infiltration incident.

The United Nations had asked that the meeting take place yesterday, but the North Koreans wanted it held today

Continued on Page 14, Column 1

Seizure of Vessel Scored in Capital

By United Press International

WASHINGTON, Jan. 23 — North Korea's seizure of the United States intelligence-gathering ship Pueblo was condemned in Congress today as an act of war. Some lawmakers demanded a quick military response.

Senator Richard B. Russell, chairman of the Senate Armed Services Committee, said that the action was "a breach of international law amounting to an act of war."

The Georgia Democrat added that "it certainly behooves our Government to take a very strong position in demanding release of the ship and of the men."

Representative Bob

Continued on Page 14, Column 1

U.S. Resumes Normal Relations With Greece's Military Regime

By PETER GROSE
Special to The New York Times

WASHINGTON, Jan. 23 — The United States resumed "normal" diplomatic relations with Greece today, six weeks after King Constantine failed in his attempt to oust the military regime.

The State Department said that Ambassador Phillips Talbot had been instructed to make an official call on the Greek Foreign Minister, Panayotis Pipinelis, and thus signal the resumption of formal contacts between the two governments.

The department spokesman, Robert J. McCloskey, swept aside a maze of protocol and political considerations by stating, "The United States Government continues to regard King Constantine as the Greek chief of state—relations between the King and the Government in Athens are an in-

on a pragmatic basis, for they fear that the Greek forces in the North Atlantic Treaty Organization are being weakened by lack of heavy matériel.

Small arms, ammunition, spare parts and other maintenance stocks continue to be supplied to the Greek forces by the United States. This kind of military aid was not suspended after the April coup.

Shipments of large-scale military supplies from the United States remain embargoed, the department added, as they have been since last April when the junta seized power.

This is causing concern among Administration officials

Continued on Page 8, Column 1

"All the News That's Fit to Print"

The New York Times

LATE CITY EDITION

Weather: Clearing today, turning cold tonight. Fair, cool tomorrow. Temp. range: today 62-44; Thurs. 73-52. Full U.S. report on Page 92.

VOL. CXVII.No. 40,249   © 1968 The New York Times Company.   NEW YORK, FRIDAY, APRIL 5, 1968   10 CENTS

MARTIN LUTHER KING IS SLAIN IN MEMPHIS; A WHITE IS SUSPECTED; JOHNSON URGES CALM

JOHNSON DELAYS TRIP TO HAWAII; MAY LEAVE TODAY

President Spends a Hectic Day Here and in Capital —Sees Thant at the U.N.

By MAX FRANKEL
Special to The New York Times

WASHINGTON, April 4—President Johnson postponed his trip to Hawaii at least until tomorrow after he heard of the death of the Rev. Dr. Martin Luther King Jr. tonight.

The news, which visibly shocked the President, came at the end of one of the most extraordinary days in perhaps the most extraordinary week of his Administration.

Mr. Johnson was to have flown from Washington at about midnight for a series of strategy conferences with his military and diplomatic leaders stationed in South Vietnam. On the way, he had planned a breakfast meeting in California with former President Dwight D. Eisenhower.

Instead, the President telephoned Mrs. King in Atlanta, made a brief appeal for calm on television and went to his office to follow the reports of unrest and disturbance given him periodically by Attorney General Ramsey Clark.

Cancels Dinner Appearance

Mr. Johnson also canceled an appearance before a Democratic party fund-raising dinner here —the final event of a hectic schedule that became ever more hectic as the day unfolded.

The President began the day by making final arrangements for the Hawaii meeting. It had been tentatively planned before his order Sunday to curtail the bombing of North Vietnam and the news yesterday that Hanoi was interested in establishing direct contact.

[The new United States peace moves are producing a quiet but bitter reaction in the South Vietnamese Government that is causing increasing concern among United States officials in Saigon. Page 14.]

But the diplomatic development, though not the principal subject of the Honolulu meetings, added special weight to his conversations with Gen. William C. Westmoreland, the American commander in South Vietnam, and other officials.

Mr. Johnson was careful not to arouse false hopes of peace, but he appeared encouraged and in buoyant spirit as he decided before noon to fly first to New York to attend the investiture of the Most Rev. Terence J. Cooke as Archbishop of New York.

Then, while in New York,

Continued on Page 12, Column 1

Hanoi Charges U.S. Raid Far North of 20th Parallel

By EVERT CLARK
Special to The New York Times

WASHINGTON, April 4 — North Vietnam charged in a broadcast today that United States planes had bombed a "populated area" in northwestern Vietnam far north of the 20th parallel. The Defense Department said it knew of no such raid but was investigating.

President Johnson has ordered that there be no attacks on North Vietnam north of the 20th Parallel as a step toward de-escalating the war.

[In South Vietnam, United States marines beat off an attack by about 400 North Vietnamese soldiers charging up a hill near Khesanh, killing 93, The Associated Press reported. Meanwhile, an American relief column was nearing the besieged base. Page 15.]

The Hanoi radio, in a broadcast monitored and translated here, said three waves of United States planes dropped more than 50 bombs on a "populated area" about 30 miles west of Laichau, capital of Laichau Province, this morning.

The nearest village to that

Continued on Page 15, Column 1

The New York Times   April 5, 1968
Hanoi said that area near Laichau (cross) was target.

HUMPHREY HINTS HE'LL ENTER RACE

Tells Unionists in Pittsburgh He Will Act Soon—Abel and Wirtz Back Him

By ROY REED
Special to The New York Times

PITTSBURGH, April 4 — Two thousand labor representatives, including the head of the United Steel Workers union, clamorously urged Vice President Humphrey today to run for President.

The Vice President left little doubt that he would oblige them, but he indicated that he would wait until President Johnson returned from his Hawaii conference before making an announcement.

"I know what your request is, and I know what your thoughts are," he told the delegates to the Pennsylvania A.F.L.-C.I.O. convention. "I am most grateful. I am not one to walk away from a decision, and a decision will come in due time."

But nothing he does should interfere with President Johnson's peace mission, he said.

Several other political leaders urged Mr. Humphrey today to enter the race for the Democratic Presidential nomination. The most prominent among them was Secretary of Labor W. Willard Wirtz, who was addressing a union convention at Miami Beach.

I. W. Abel, president of the steelworkers Union, rose as Mr.

Continued on Page 32, Column 1

Johnson Shuns Role Of '68 'Lame Duck,' Kennedy Was Told

By JOHN HERBERS
Special to The New York Times

WASHINGTON, April 4—In his meeting with Senator Robert F. Kennedy yesterday President Johnson said he would remain out of the political fight this year because he did not believe it was appropriate for a "lame duck" President to try to pick his successor.

This and other details of the Johnson-Kennedy meeting were learned today from knowledgeable sources.

The meeting, which Senator Kennedy had requested in the interest of "national unity," was described as an extraordinarily friendly one, with both the Senator and the President speaking in a conciliatory manner.

President Johnson was pictured as the "elder statesman" of the party who had decided to remain aloof from this year's scramble for the Presidency in an effort to keep the party as strong as possible and retain his own dignity and effectiveness as President.

At one point, it was reported, the President said he did not want to make a spectacle of himself as a lame duck President attempting to dictate to the party who should be nominated at the national convention.

In this regard, he pointed out that in 1956 former President Harry S. Truman went to the

Continued on Page 31, Column 4

DISMAY IN NATION

Negroes Urge Others to Carry on Spirit of Nonviolence

By LAWRENCE VAN GELDER

Dismay, shame, anger and foreboding marked the nation's reaction last night to the Rev. Dr. Martin Luther King Jr.'s murder.

From the high offices of state to the man in the street, news of the moderate civil rights leader's violent death in Memphis yesterday drew, for the most part, stunned and sober statements.

Most major Negro organizations and Negro leaders, lamenting Dr. King's death, expressed hope that it serve as a spur to others to carry on in his spirit of nonviolence. But some Negro militants responded with bitterness and anger.

Roy Wilkins, executive director of the National Association for the Advancement of Colored People, said his organization was "shocked and deeply grieved by the dastardly murder of Dr. Martin Luther King."

"His murderer or murderers must be promptly apprehended and brought to justice," Mr. Wilkins said.

'A Man of Peace'

"Dr. King was a symbol of the nonviolent civil rights protest movement. He was a man of peace, of dedication, of great courage. His senseless assassination solves nothing. It will not stay the civil rights movement; it will instead spur it to greater activity."

Whitney M. Young Jr., executive director of the National Urban League, said:

"We are unspeakably shocked by the murder of Martin Luther King, one of the greatest leaders of our time. This is a bitter reflection on America. We fear for our country.

"The only possible answer now is for the nation to act immediately on what Dr. King has been fighting for—passage of the civil rights and antipoverty bills and a true and just equality for all men. Those of us who have remained loyal to his concept of nonviolence have been dealt a mortal blow."

Mayor Richard G. Hatcher of Gary, Ind., a Negro, termed the death of Dr. King "every man's loss."

"Men who care for humankind and struggle for its salvation through reason and faith have lost a leader of monumental stature," he said. "A man of his magnitude will not soon pass this way again."

At his home in Stamford, Conn., the former baseball star Jackie Robinson called the

Continued on Page 26, Column 1

PRESIDENT'S PLEA

On TV, He Deplores 'Brutal' Murder of Negro Leader

Statements by Johnson and Humphrey are on Page 24.

Special to The New York Times

WASHINGTON, April 4—President Johnson deplored tonight in a brief television address to the nation the "brutal slaying" of the Rev. Dr. Martin Luther King Jr.

He asked "every citizen to reject the blind violence that has struck Dr. King, who lived by nonviolence."

Mr. Johnson said he was postponing his scheduled departure tonight for a Honolulu conference on Vietnam and that instead he would leave tomorrow.

The President spoke from the White House. At the Washington Hilton Hotel, where Democratic members of Congress had gathered to honor the President and the Vice President, Mr. Humphrey, his voice strained with emotion, said:

"Martin Luther King stands with our other American martyrs in the cause of freedom and justice. His death is a terrible tragedy."

The dinner was canceled 10 to 15 minutes after the Vice President spoke. Mr. Johnson, who was scheduled to appear at the dinner, canceled his plans to attend.

F.B.I. Inquiry Ordered

Attorney General Ramsey Clark ordered an immediate inquiry by the Federal Bureau of Investigation into the shooting of Dr. King in Memphis.

He said the purpose of the investigation would be to determine whether any Federal law had been violated.

One provision of the law that could be invoked makes it a crime to engage in a conspiracy to deprive a person of his civil rights.

In addition to F.B.I. agents, Department of Justice civil rights representatives were on the scene in Memphis and were in touch with the Attorney General.

Military sources said that no National Guard units had yet been Federalized and no Regular Army troops had been alerted yet for possible movement to cities where violence had broken out.

National Guard troops, such as the 4,000 men who have been called into Memphis, remain under state control until the responsible Governor requests help and the President

Continued on Page 24, Column 7

Associated Press
THE REV. DR. MARTIN LUTHER KING Jr.

Scattered Violence Occurs In Harlem and Brooklyn

12 Are Arrested Here

By THOMAS A. JOHNSON

Sporadic violence erupted in Harlem and Brooklyn's Bedford-Stuyvesant section last night after news of Dr. Martin Luther King's assassination spread in the two predominantly Negro communities.

Mayor Lindsay, who went to Harlem in an effort to quiet the outbreaks, was caught in the midst of an unruly crowd and had to be hustled into a limousine by bodyguards.

Police reinforcements, including elements of the riot-trained Tactical Patrol Force, were rushed into both communities.

Two arrests were reported in Brooklyn and 10 in Harlem. A television crewman was said to have been injured by flying glass.

There were numerous instances of rock-throwing, looting and arson reported both in Brooklyn and in Harlem, starting around 11 P.M. and continuing early today.

Gangs of youth in both areas were reported roaming through the streets, now and then taunting policemen and firemen on duty.

The police fired several volleys of shots in the air to disperse crowds along Brooklyn's Fulton Street and Harlem's

Continued on Page 26, Column 2

Widespread Disorders

Disorders broke out in scattered parts of the nation last night after the slaying of the Rev. Dr. Martin Luther King Jr. The National Guard was called out or alerted in several cities.

In Washington, scattered but persistent looting and vandalism erupted, led for a time by Stokely Carmichael, former head of the Student Nonviolent Coordinating Committee. All available policemen were being called to duty.

About 4,000 Tennessee National Guardsmen were ordered to duty in Nashville because of disorders.

In North Carolina, Gov. Dan K. Moore alerted the Guard in Greensboro at the request of Mayor Carson Bain. State Highway patrolmen were dispatched to Raleigh.

There were riotous outbursts

Continued on Page 26, Column 5

GUARD CALLED OUT

Curfew Is Ordered in Memphis, but Fires and Looting Erupt

By EARL CALDWELL
Special to The New York Times

MEMPHIS, Friday, April 5— The Rev. Dr. Martin Luther King Jr., who preached nonviolence and racial brotherhood, was fatally shot here last night by a distant gunman who then raced away and escaped.

Four thousand National Guard troops were ordered into Memphis by Gov. Buford Ellington after the 39-year-old Nobel Prize-winning civil rights leader died.

A curfew was imposed on the shocked city of 550,000 inhabitants, 40 per cent of whom are Negro.

But the police said the tragedy had been followed by incidents that included sporadic shooting, fires, bricks and bottles thrown at policemen, and looting that started in Negro districts and then spread over the city.

White Car Sought

Police Director Frank Holloman said the assassin might have been a white man who was "50 to 100 yards away in a flophouse."

Chief of Detectives W. P. Huston said a late model white Mustang was described as the killer's getaway car. Its occupant was described as a bareheaded white man in his 30's, wearing a black suit and black tie.

The detective chief said the police had chased two cars near the motel where Dr. King was shot and had halted one that had two out-of-town men as occupants. The men were questioned but seemed to have nothing to do with the killing, he said.

Rifle Found Nearby

A high-powered 30.06-caliber rifle was found about a block from the scene of the shooting, on South Main Street. "We think it's the gun," Chief Huston said, reporting it would be turned over to the Federal Bureau of Investigation.

Dr. King was shot while he leaned out over a second-floor railing outside his room at the Lorraine Motel. He was chatting with two friends just before starting for dinner.

One of the friends was a musician, and Dr. King had just asked him to play a Negro spiritual, "Precious Lord, Take My Hand," at a rally that was to have been held two hours later in support of striking Memphis sanitationmen.

Paul Hess, assistant adminis-

Continued on Page 24, Column 1

Archbishop Cooke Installed; President Looks On

By EDWARD B. FISKE

The Most Rev. Terence J. Cooke was installed as the seventh Roman Catholic Archbishop of New York yesterday in a historic pageant attended by the President of the United States and highlighted by prayers for the success of his peace efforts in Vietnam.

"Let us pray with all our hearts that God will inspire our President," the 47-year-old Archbishop said in his homily at St. Patrick's Cathedral.

"In the last few days, we have all admired his heroic efforts in the search for peace in Vietnam. We ask God to bless his efforts with success. May God inspire not only our President, but also other leaders and the leaders of all nations of the world to find a way to peace."

Then the Archbishop, speaking from a white marble pulpit and surrounded by a blaze of purple, gold and scarlet robes, addressed himself directly to Mr. Johnson, who sat below him in a front pew.

The President, sitting with his hands clasped and his legs crossed, listened with obvious intensity to the Archbishop's words.

"Mr. President," he said, "our hearts, our hopes, our continued prayers go with you."

Mr. Johnson, accompanied by his daughter, Mrs. Patrick J. Nugent, led a festive congregation of about 5,000 cardinals, bishops, priests, laymen, nuns, civic leaders

Continued on Page 38, Column 1

The New York Times (by Neal Boenzi)
President Johnson and his daughter, Mrs. Patrick J. Nugent, right, listening during yesterday's ceremonies. At left are Mrs. John F. Kennedy and Lieut. Gov. Malcolm Wilson. Security personnel are in the row between them.

Archbishop Luigi Raimondi, Apostolic Delegate to the U.S., speaking after Archbishop Terence J. Cooke was enthroned

The New York Times

LATE CITY EDITION

Weather: Sunny and mild today;
fair tonight. Sunny, mild tomorrow.
Temp. range: today 50-35. Friday
62-46. Full U. S. report on Page 78.

VOL. CXVII..No. 40,250   © 1968 The New York Times Company.   NEW YORK, SATURDAY, APRIL 6, 1968   10 CENTS

ARMY TROOPS IN CAPITAL AS NEGROES RIOT; GUARD SENT INTO CHICAGO, DETROIT, BOSTON; JOHNSON ASKS A JOINT SESSION OF CONGRESS

SIEGE OF KHESANH DECLARED LIFTED; TROOPS HUNT FOE

Relief Column, Within Mile of Base, Presses Search —Helicopters Kill 50

By The Associated Press

KHESANH, South Vietnam, Saturday, April 6—The 76-day North Vietnamese siege of the Marine base at Khesanh was officially declared lifted yesterday.

United States marines and helicopter-borne Army troops today pushed toward what was described as North Vietnamese regimental headquarters south of the base.

The 20,000-man relief column reached the base and then fanned out on three sides in search of the vanishing enemy soldiers. Army helicopter units entered the base.

The sweep could take the Americans all the way to the Laotian border. less than 10 miles away, in the effort to root out the 7,000 men said to remain in an enemy force once estimated at 20,000. North Vietnam uses Laos as a staging area for attacks along South Vietnam's borders.

Gunships Attack Near Town

The United States command said that helicopter gunships of the First Cavalry Division (Airmobile), criscrossing the skies ahead of the ground troops, killed 50 North Vietnamese late yesterday near the town of Khesanh, which is two miles south of the base.

Earlier, United States forces fought about 150 enemy soldiers four miles east of the town. Nine enemy soldiers and one American were reported killed.

The town was made an enemy command post after South Vietnamese troops and a small unit of United States marines abandoned it in January under a heavy siege.

Ten thousand civilians, mostly montagnard tribesmen, fled the town when fighting broke out. Many are in refugee camps in the coastal lowlands.

The relief column made no immediate attempt to enter the Khesanh base. Enemy gunners zeroed in on the outpost with 110 rounds of artillery and mortar fire.

Before the pressure on the

Continued on Page 2, Column 4

Hanoi Voices Doubt Over U.S. Sincerity

By Agence France-Presse

HANOI, North Vietnam, April 5—Hanoi protested today against what it called "savage bombings" of North Vietnam and "intensification of the war in South Vietnam" since President Johnson's announcement Sunday of restriction on attacks on the North.

Under the signature "Commentator," a pseudonym customarily indicating official authorship, an editorial in the party newspaper, Nhan Dan, questioned the sincerity of Mr. Johnson's avowed desire for peace.

[Despite the tone of the Hanoi editorial, Administration officials saw no indication that North Vietnam was backing away from talks with the United States. Page 5.]

The Nhan Dan editorial said: "The decision of the United

Continued on Page 3, Column 1

SOVIET ENDORSES ASSENT BY HANOI

Moscow Mentioned as Site of Talks With U.S.—China Urges Continued War

By RAYMOND H. ANDERSON
Special to The New York Times

MOSCOW, April 5 — The Soviet Government today endorsed the agreement by North Vietnam to start discussions with the United States toward a complete halt of bombing to open the door to full-scale negotiations.

The statement came amid speculation that Moscow might be the site for a meeting between United States and North Vietnamese representatives.

Premier Aleksei N. Kosygin is cutting short his trip to Iran and will return to Moscow Sunday, one day early.

[Communist China, however, termed President Johnson's peace overture as a smokescreen and urged the North Vietnamese and the Vietcong to continue fighting.]

The United States Embassy denied that it had any knowledge of arrangements for a meeting here. The United States, it was understood,

Continued on Page 4, Column 3

PRESIDENT GRAVE

Sets Day of Mourning for Dr. King—Meets Rights Leaders

President's statement and his proclamation, Page 23.

By MAX FRANKEL
Special to The New York Times

WASHINGTON, April 5 — President Johnson asked today to address a joint session of Congress no later than Monday evening so that he could propose "constructive action instead of destructive action in this hour of national need."

Gravely imploring Americans to "stand their ground to deny violence its victory" in the reaction to the slaying of the Rev. Dr. Martin Luther King Jr., the President set out to arouse the nation's conscience and to win quick action on the long-stalled major items of his domestic program.

He proclaimed Sunday a national day of mourning for Dr. King, who was shot yesterday in Memphis and died later in a hospital.

Meanwhile, Congressional leaders said that Dr. King's murder could assure passage next week of a landmark civil rights bill.

Conference Canceled

To deal with the divisiveness that he said was "tearing this nation apart," Mr. Johnson canceled the already delayed conference he had planned for this weekend in Hawaii with American military and diplomatic officials stationed in South Vietnam.

Gen. William C. Westmoreland, the American commander in the war zone, was flying to Washington instead and will probably see Mr. Johnson tomorrow morning.

The President spent almost the entire day working "to avoid catastrophe." He met with moderate Negro leaders and members of Congress and of his Administration to find ways of containing the violence, arson and looting that threatened many big cities and that spread here to within a few blocks of the White House.

He also conferred all day with officials of the District of Columbia and gave them Federal troops this evening to help restore order.

Mr. Johnson's demeanor all

Continued on Page 23, Column 1

ON DUTY IN WASHINGTON: A soldier with a machine gun and another with a rifle, left, stand guard on the steps outside the Senate chamber. Flag was lowered to half-staff in tribute to the Rev. Dr. Martin Luther King Jr.
Associated Press

New York Volatile As Anger and Fear Set a Tense Mood

By MICHAEL STERN

A volatile mood of deep sorrow, fist-shaking anger and undefined fear settled on the city yesterday as it absorbed the impact of the death of the Rev. Dr. Martin Luther King Jr.

Many schools, colleges, offices and shops closed early partly out of respect for the memory of the slain civil rights leader, and partly because of reports that new outbreaks of violence would erupt.

Half of the armed guardsmen, in fatigues and riot helmets, began patrolling glass-littered West Side streets about 10 P.M. The rest stood by in armories.

The city's bustling waterfront grew still at noon as seamen and longshoremen stopped work as a tribute to Dr. King. The stoppage was announced by the International Longshoremen's Association and the National Maritime Union.

Seven thousand to eight thousand high school and college students released from classes assembled at a memorial rally for Dr. King at the

Continued on Page 26, Column 5

OUTBREAKS HERE RELATIVELY MILD

Negro Areas Are Quiet, but Bands of Young Vandals Roam Midtown Streets

By SYLVAN FOX

The streets of Harlem and Bedford-Stuyvesant were generally calm last night after a burst of violence and looting early yesterday in the wake of the assassination of the Rev. Dr. Martin Luther King Jr. in Memphis.

Mayor Lindsay, appearing on television at 11:30 P.M., praised New Yorkers for keeping the peace and said: "We can work together again for progress and for peace in this city and in this nation."

Earlier in the evening, bands of youths—mostly Negro teenagers—swarmed into mid-Manhattan, engaged in scattered violence and some looting and were dispersed by a massive show of police force.

The police arrested 27 adults on minor charges, and nine youths were charged with juvenile delinquency. Two persons were reported seized at Columbus Circle, where seven shop windows were smashed and

Continued on Page 27, Column 1

7 Die as Fires and Looting Spread in Chicago Rioting

By DONALD JANSON
Special to The New York Times

CHICAGO, Saturday, April 6—Six thousand National Guard troops were called up yesterday as rioters pillaged stores along a two-mile stretch of Madison Street in the Negro West Side. Seven Negroes were killed and about 350 arrested, the police reported, as the violence and ransacking tapered off late last night.

About 100 city buses were damaged by bricks and rocks. Drivers, passengers, policemen, firemen, motorists and pedestrians were among at least 75 persons injured.

Mother Beaten

Mrs. Bernadine Laskow, mother of three children, was pulled from her car by Negro youths and beaten. Some white pedestrians who were in the Negro slum suffered the same treatment.

Dozens of automobiles that entered the 12-square-mile riot zone emerged with smashed windows and dented hoods. In some blocks all store windows were boarded or broken. Cab drivers refused to enter

Continued on Page 23, Column 8

EUROPE DISMAYED; FEARFUL FOR U.S.

Murder of Dr. King Evokes Doubts Over Stability of the American Society

By ANTHONY LEWIS
Special to The New York Times

LONDON, April 5—The murder of the Rev. Dr. Martin Luther King Jr. evoked in Europe today a reaction of intense horror at the deed and of fear for the stability of American society.

In governments, in the press and among the public, there were expressions of sympathy that went beyond formalities. Dr. King was deeply admired in Europe and held up as a symbol of hope for America.

'A Common, Tragic Link'

All the concerns about the United States and its leadership that have grown here in recent years—concerns especially about the war in Vietnam and the violence in America—were fed by the killing of the civil rights leader in Memphis last night.

Everywhere in Europe, people linked Dr. King's death with the assassination of President Kennedy in 1963. That two men so admired here could so similarly be killed intensified doubts about the character of America today.

"From John Fitzgerald Kennedy to Martin Luther King,"

Continued on Page 28, Column 3

MANY FIRES SET

White House Guarded by G.I.'s—14 Dead in U.S. Outbreaks

Text of proclamation and Executive order, Page 22.

By BEN A. FRANKLIN
Special to The New York Times

WASHINGTON, April 5—President Johnson ordered 4,000 regular Army and National Guard troops into the nation's capital tonight to try to end riotous looting, burglarizing and burning by roving bands of Negro youths. The arson and looting began yesterday after the murder of the Rev. Dr. Martin Luther King Jr. in Memphis.

The White House announced at 5 P.M. that because the President had determined that "a condition of domestic violence and disorder" existed, he had issued a proclamation and an Executive order mobilizing combat-equipped troops in Washington. Some of the troops were sent to guard the Capitol and the White House.

Reinforcements numbering 2,500 riot-trained soldiers — a brigade of the 82d Airborne Division from Ft. Bragg, N. C. — were airlifted to nearby Andrews Air Force Base. to be held in reserve this weekend.

Guard Called in Other Cities

The National Guard also was called out in a half-dozen other cities in an effort to stem disorders or guard against them—Chicago, Detroit, Boston, Jackson, Miss., Raleigh, N. C., and Tallahassee, Fla.

The death toll from the violence stemming from Dr. King's assassination stood at a total of 14 tonight. Besides five deaths in Washington, they included seven in Chicago, one in Detroit and one in Tallahassee.

Mayor Walter E. Washington, who is a Negro, declared a 13-hour curfew, from 5:30 P.M. to 6:30 A.M. The Mayor's emergency order halted the sale of liquor and forbade the sale, transportation or possession of firearms, explosives or flammable liquids.

At midnight, the police reported five dead, all but one of them Negroes, in 28 hours of disorders in this city of about 800,000, 63 per cent of them Negroes. Four Negroes were killed today, including two suspected looters, one of them 14 years old, who were shot to death by policemen in separate isolated encounters across the Anacostia River far from the areas of general disorders. The two other Negro deaths today were described as apparently the result of accidents.

The white man, George Fletcher, 28, of suburban Wood-

Continued on Page 22, Column 1

Clark Is Sure Killer Will Soon Be Seized

By MARTIN WALDRON
Special to The New York Times

MEMPHIS, Tenn., April 5—Attorney General Ramsey Clark said today that he was "confident" of a quick solution to the assassination here yesterday of the Rev. Dr. Martin Luther King Jr.

A source close to the intensive manhunt said that agents of the Federal Bureau of Investigation were close to making an arrest.

The Attorney General, who flew here this morning at the order of President Johnson with other top officials of the Justice Department, told a news conference that the F.B.I. was searching for the killer in several states.

He said that the killer, who was believed to have escaped in a white Mustang automobile,

Continued on Page 24, Column 1

Negroes Strive to Ease Tensions; False Rumors Raise City's Fears

Militants Join Effort

By THOMAS A. JOHNSON

At the height of the violence in Harlem early yesterday morning, about 30 young Negro militants fanned out from Jay's Bar and Grill on 125th Street near Eighth Avenue and tried to persuade other Negroes to stop breaking windows, looting and setting fires.

This particular group was made up of members of Harlem CORE, and they were only a part of the many hundreds of Negroes living in the violence-torn areas of Harlem and Brooklyn who worked actively to stop the disorders.

The volunteer peace-keepers tried to end the violence by a variety of methods and for a variety of reasons.

Some were church groups.

Continued on Page 26, Column 1

Racial Unrest Exaggerated

By MURRAY SCHUMACH

The city was flooded yesterday with wild and unfounded rumors that exceeded the amount of violence and heightened widespread fears of racial riots.

In some instances, the reports became so persistent that corporations allowed employes, particularly women, to leave for home early in the afternoon.

The untrue reports included subway disruptions, bombings, mass assaults and imposition of a citywide curfew. Almost any kind of holdup, apparently, was associated in the minds of some rumor-mongers with racial disturbances and was then exaggerated.

Barry H. Gottehrer, the head

Continued on Page 26, Column 6

The New York Times by Barton Silverman

MARCHING DOWN BROADWAY: Demonstrators protesting the slaying of the Rev. Dr. Martin Luther King Jr. crossing 23d Street on the way to City Hall yesterday. The march began after a memorial ceremony in Central Park.

If you live North of 14th St. you'll
like LOOIT Upper Biltmore Twn—Adv't

251

The New York Times

LATE CITY EDITION
Weather: Sunny, warm today; fair, continued warm tonight, tomorrow. Temp. range: today 88-62; Wed. 83-59. Temp.-Hum. Index 75; Wed. 74. Full U.S. report on Page 94.

VOL. CXVII..No. 40,311   © 1968 The New York Times Company.   NEW YORK, THURSDAY, JUNE 6, 1968   10 CENTS

KENNEDY IS DEAD, VICTIM OF ASSASSIN; SUSPECT, ARAB IMMIGRANT, ARRAIGNED; JOHNSON APPOINTS PANEL ON VIOLENCE

MARCUS TESTIFIES DE SAPIO HAD ROLE IN A CON ED DEAL

Says Itkin Sought Delay of Permit to Aid Own Scheme With Ex-Tammany Head

By BARNARD L. COLLIER

Former Water Commissioner James L. Marcus testified yesterday that he had been asked to delay approval of a permit to Consolidated Edison while the former Tammany Hall leader, Carmine G. De Sapio, was trying to make a deal with the utility company.

Marcus testified that the request came last September from his business partner, Herbert Itkin, who was in turn trying to negotiate a deal with Mr. De Sapio.

The testimony was elicited from Marcus under cross-examination on the third day of a Federal bribery conspiracy trial that has been marked by the mention in Marcus's testimony of several prominent members of both the Republican and Democratic parties.

Marcus was asked if there was a time when he, as Commissioner of Water Supply, Gas and Electricity, had "done business" with Con Edison. His answer was yes.

Says Itkin Asked Delay

"Itkin came to me," he said, "and said that Con Ed wanted a permit to increase the voltage on one of their power lines for 20 miles." He added that his approval as Commissioner was needed.

"Itkin said I should hold up for a while because he was negotiating with Carmine De Sapio, who was negotiating with Con Ed."

Marcus said that Mr. Itkin asked him to delay the approval for "a few weeks."

At that point in the trial, which came at about 4:40 P.M., Herman Zoloto, a lawyer representing Henry Fried, a contractor, and Mr. Fried's company, S. T. Grand, Inc., shouted:

"You're way ahead of your story, Mr. Marcus!"

Judge Edward Weinfeld broke in and scolded Mr. Zoloto for "a highly improper re-

Continued on Page 41, Column 1

TRANSIT PACKAGE SUBMITTED TO CITY

M.T.A. Seeks Approval of 8 New Subway Routes

By EMANUEL PERLMUTTER

A $1.27-billion package of subway and commuter railroad additions and improvements was submitted to the Board of Estimate and Mayor Lindsay yesterday.

The program was presented by the Metropolitan Transportation Authority and the New York City Transit Authority with a request for speedy city agreement on the new routes and engineering designs.

The over-all plan, which would take 10 years to complete, consists of eight new subway routes, including a Second Avenue subway, and Long Island Rail Road connections to the East Side of Manhattan and to Kennedy International Airport.

City approval of the routes and designs is a first step before application can be made for $60-million set aside by the Legislature for the engineering design of the mass transportation program presented by the Metropolitan Transportation

Continued on Page 55, Column 1

France Will Meet Tariff Deadline; Strikes Dwindling

By HENRY TANNER
Special to The New York Times

PARIS, June 5 — Maurice Couve de Murville told France's partners in the Common Market today that despite the nationwide strike now coming to a close, the Government would honor the July 1 deadline for the abolition of remaining tariffs in the European trade bloc.

Today workers in the nationalized railroad company, the Paris transit system, the post and telegraph offices and other public administrations voted to go back to work. Trains are expected to start running tomorrow on several major national lines and the Paris subways.

By the end of the week, it is expected, the nationwide strike, now in its 18th day, will be all but ended. Mr. Couve de Murville, who is the new Minister of Economy and Finance, also reassured his countrymen

Continued on Page 15, Column 1

JERUSALEM POLICE CLASH WITH ARABS

Israelis Halt Procession on Anniversary of War—U.N. Council Meets on Fighting

Special to The New York Times

JERUSALEM, June 5—A silent Arab procession commemorating the first anniversary of the Arab-Israeli war erupted into a violent clash today when Isareli policemen intercepted the marchers at the edge of the walled Old City of Jerusalem.

The clash was the most violent aspect of a widespread protest in which Arabs shuttered shops and other businesses here and elsewhere on the west bank of the Jordan and in the occupied Gaza Strip. It came after a day-long battle yesterday across the Jordan between the Israelis and Jordanians, in which aircraft and artillery were used.

[The United Nations Security Council met Wednesday at the urgent request of Israel and Jordan to consider recurrent hostilities along their cease-fire line. It postponed debate, probably until Thursday. Page 3.]

In the west-bank towns of Nablus, Jenin and Tulkarm, all centers of Arab nationalism, the general strike was 100 per cent effective. All stores, cafes and offices were closed, public transportation ceased and the streets were virtually devoid of traffic and pedestrians. Schools throughout the west bank and Gaza Strip had no

Continued on Page 2, Column 4

Italy's Cabinet Quits As Parliament Opens

By ROBERT C. DOTY

ROME, June 5—Premier Aldo Moro and his center-left coalition Government, which has ruled Italy for four and a half years, resigned tonight with the convening of the new parliament, the fifth since World War II.

President Giuseppe Saragat asked Mr. Moro and his ministers to remain in office as a caretaker government while the search for a new government, which may be arduous, goes on.

Resignation of the government with the convening of a new parliament is automatic. But any hope that the Moro

Continued on Page 14, Column 3

6 IN RACE GUARDED

Secret Service Given Campaign Security Task by President

Text of the Johnson speech is printed on Page 23.

By MAX FRANKEL
Special to The New York Times

WASHINGTON, June 5—For the second time in five years, Lyndon B. Johnson undertook today, amid national shock and outrage, to offer protection, prayer, comfort and assistance to his political rivals in the Kennedy family and then to try to heal the country's political and psychological wounds.

The President's first reaction to the shooting of Senator Robert F. Kennedy this morning was that "there are no words equal to the horror of this tragedy."

But tonight, in an emotional and at times even angry statement on television, he pleaded with all Americans to end the violence in their midst once and for all, to tolerate neither hatred nor the preaching of violence and to resolve to live under the law.

A Guard for Candidates

Mr. Johnson said he was appointing a commission of distinguished citizens to investigate both the circumstances and the causes of physical violence of all kinds in the United States, in the hope that the nation can learn "how we can stop it".

Earlier he had moved swiftly to provide protective Secret Service details to the six announced Presidential candidates of major parties, other than Vice President Humphrey, who already has such protection because of his office.

Meanwhile, in the House of Representatives, a vote of 317 to 60 cleared the way for the House to accept the Senate version of an anticrime bill, including controls over the interstate sale of hand guns. The vote rejected a move to send the legislation to a Senate-House conference.

Members of Commission

To the commission Mr. Johnson named Milton Eisenhower, former president of Johns Hopkins University; Archbishop Terence J. Cooke of New York; Albert Jenner, Chicago lawyer who worked for the commission that investigated the assassination of President Kennedy; former Ambassador Patricia Harris; Eric Hoffer, the longshoreman-turned-philosopher; Senators Philip Hart, Democrat of Michigan, and Roman L. Hruska, Republican of Nebraska; Representatives Hale Boggs, Democrat of Louisiana, majority whip in the House; Representative William M. McCulloch, Republican of Ohio, and Federal Judge Leon Higginbotham of Philadelphia.

The President described himself as shocked, dismayed and deeply disturbed, as he knew all Americans were, by the shooting, which he described as the "latest spectacular example" of lawlessness and violence.

"So let us, for God's sake, re-

Continued on Page 23, Column 1

AFTER THE SHOOTING: Senator Kennedy's wife, Ethel, bends over him as a man checks pulse to determine condition

HANOI INSISTS U.S. HALT ITS BOMBING

Aides Call Talks Response to Johnson—Suspicion Voiced of a Plot Against Kennedy

By HEDRICK SMITH
Special to The New York Times

PARIS, June 5—North Vietnamese negotiators contended today that Hanoi had responded to President Johnson's restriction of American air attacks on the north by entering official talks here. They asserted that the next move, a total halt in bombing, was up to the United States.

The North Vietnamese argument, put forward in the seventh negotiating session between the two sides since May 13, exchanged one of the sharpest exchanges since the Vietnam talks began here.

The North Vietnamese made no direct comment on the shooting of Senator Robert F. Kennedy, but circles close to the delegation voiced suspicions in private, asking if the attack was not part of a conspiracy by the Johnson Administration. [Page 33.]

Near the end of today's session at the former Majestic Hotel, Hanoi's chief representative, Xuan Thuy, leaned across the negotiating table and asked the American delegates bluntly:

"When will the United States unconditionally cease the bombing and all other acts of war against the Democratic Republic of Vietnam so that other questions can be discussed?"

In response, Mr. Averell Har-

Continued on Page 8, Column 4

Big Board Weighs 4 Special Closings

By VARTANIG G. VARTAN

A securities industry panel recommended yesterday that the New York Stock Exchange, the American Stock Exchange and the over-the-counter market close down for four days over the next month to cope with the deluge of paperwork in brokerage offices.

The panel proposed closing the securities markets for three Wednesdays—June 12, 19 and 26—as well as Friday, July 5. The board of governors of the New York Stock Exchange will meet this afternoon to consider the proposal. Wall Street sources said that in view of the critical situation the governors are expected to accept the pro-

Continued on Page 73, Column 1

ROBERT F. KENNEDY
The New York Times (by George Tames)

A Pall Over Politics

Murder Raises Grave Questions for Presidency Races Now and in Future

By TOM WICKER
Special to The New York Times

WASHINGTON, June 6—The murder of Robert F. Kennedy shattered the 1968 Presidential campaign and lowered a pall of uncertainty over American politics now and in the years to come. For the immediate future, it may well have assured the nominations by the Democrats and Republicans of the present front-running candidates—Vice President Humphrey and Richard Nixon. It raised grave questions, however, about the personal dangers of political campaigning in the United States. It added a tragic new dimension to the near-martyrdom of the Kennedy family, which has now lost two sons to assassins' bullets.

It removed forever one of the most promising young political leaders in recent American history, one with particular appeal for the poor, the downtrodden and the alienated inhabitants of the Negro slum. That appeal had been proved in all of Robert Kennedy's primary victories this year.

These elements of society also revered the Senator's brother, President Kennedy,

News Analysis

who was assassinated on Nov. 22, 1963. How they would react to Robert Kennedy's murder—both in the immediate future and for the long political pull—was a crucial question.

The murder added sorrowful emphasis to one of Robert Kennedy's major political themes—the necessity for orderly and just redress of grievances, in place of violent action.

Ultimately, Mr. Kennedy's death—the first assassination of an American Presidential candidate—might lead to changes in campaigning practices, even to the fundamental manner in which the nation chooses its President.

The most immediate effect, however, was that for the third —and most harrowing—time a shock wave of unexpected events had completely altered the shape of the 1968 campaign.

The first came on March 12 when Senator Eugene J. McCarthy of Minnesota won 42 per cent of the Democratic vote in the New Hampshire primary, and Mr. Kennedy immediately thereafter became an active candidate.

The second transformation

Continued on Page 8, Column 1

SURGERY IN VAIN

President Calls Death Tragedy, Proclaims a Day of Mourning

Texts of the medical reports appear on Page 22.

By GLADWIN HILL
Special to The New York Times

LOS ANGELES, June 6—Senator Robert F. Kennedy, the brother of a murdered President, died at 1:44 A.M. today of an assassin's shots.

The New York Senator was wounded more than 20 hours earlier, moments after he had made his victory statement in the California primary.

At his side when he died today in Good Samaritan Hospital were his wife, Ethel; his sisters, Mrs. Stephen Smith and Mrs. Patricia Lawford; his brother-in-law, Stephen Smith; and his sister-in-law, Mrs. John F. Kennedy, whose husband was assassinated 4½ years ago in Dallas.

In Washington, President Johnson issued a statement calling the death a tragedy. He proclaimed next Sunday a national day of mourning.

The Final Report

Hopes had risen slightly when more than eight hours went by without a new medical bulletin on the stricken Senator, but the grimness of the final announcement was signaled when Frank Mankiewicz, Mr. Kennedy's press secretary, walked slowly down the street in front of the hospital toward the littered gymnasium that served as press headquarters.

Mr. Mankiewicz bit his lip. His shoulders slumped.

He stepped to a lectern in front of a green-tinted chalkboard and bowed his head for a moment while the television lights snapped on.

Then, at one minute before 2 A.M., he told of the death of Mr. Kennedy.

Following is the text of the statement from Mr. Mankiewicz:

"I have a short announcement to read which I will read at this time. Senator Robert Francis Kennedy died at 1:44 A.M. today, June 6, 1968. With

Continued on Page 20, Column 1

NOTES ON KENNEDY IN SUSPECT'S HOME

Cite 'Necessity' to Murder Senator Before June 5, Anniversary of War

By PETER KIHSS

A notebook found in the Pasadena home of Sirhan Bishara Sirhan had "a direct reference to the necessity to assassinate Senator Kennedy before June 5, 1968," Mayor Samuel W. Yorty of Los Angeles said last night.

The date was the first anniversary of the six-day war, in which Israeli forces smashed those of the United Arab Republic, Syria and Jordan.

Sirhan, a 24-year-old Christian Arab, who has described himself as a Jerusalem-born Jordanian, is being held in the shooting of the New York Senator.

Justice Department records indicated that Sirhan came to the United States with his family in January of 1957 as immigrants, less than three months after the Suez war in 1956. Sirhan was 12 at the time.

The family quickly broke up in discord, the father staying in New York to work as a plumber and then going back to their former Palestine home, the mother taking five children to California, where a sixth child immigrated later.

Sirhan was described yesterday by Police Chief Thomas Reddin of Los Angeles as "very cool, very calm, very stable and quite lucid."

He was quoted as having said,

Continued on Page 21, Column 8

Father of Suspect 'Sickened' by News

By TERENCE SMITH
Special to The New York Times

ET TAIYIBA, Israeli-Occupied Jordan, Thursday, June 6—Bishara Sirhan's hands trembled as he talked about his son Sirhan Bishara Sirhan, the accused assailant of Senator Robert F. Kennedy.

Mr. Sirhan dwelled on the tragedy of the shooting. He became angry as he talked, and finally said: "This news made me sick when I heard it. If my son has done this dirty thing, then let them hang him."

Mr. Sirhan's memories of his five sons are those of 10 years ago, when he last saw them and their mother. After years of fierce family quarrels, Bishara

Continued on Page 21, Col an 4

KUCHEL UNSEATED AS RAFFERTY WINS

Conservative Beats Senator in California's Primary

By LAWRENCE E. DAVIES
Special to The New York Times

LOS ANGELES, June 5—Dr. Max Rafferty, State Superintendent of Public Instruction, defeated Senator Thomas H. Kuchel in the Republican Senatorial primary in California yesterday, cutting short Mr. Kuchel's 15-year career in the Senate.

Returns from 20,714 of 21,-301 precincts gave:

Rafferty	1,056,038	50%
Kuchel	985,097	47%

As the vote count continued today, it became apparent that the conservative Republicanism of Southern California had carried Dr. Rafferty to victory over the heretofore unbeatable Republican whip in the Senate.

Mr. Kuchel, an outspoken liberal-moderate who had made his targets in recent years, was beaten by the voters in Los Angeles, San Diego and Orange Counties, after having led Dr. Rafferty last night and early today.

Dr. Rafferty, who has become

Continued on Page 28, Column 3

NEWS INDEX

"All the News That's Fit to Print"

The New York Times

LATE CITY EDITION
Weather: Sunny, warm today; fair, seasonable tonight and tomorrow. Temp. range: today 89-73; Tuesday 91-72. Temp.-Hum. Index yesterday 81. Complete U.S. report on Page 90.

VOL. CXVII.No. 40,387   © 1968 The New York Times Company.   NEW YORK, WEDNESDAY, AUGUST 21, 1968   10 CENTS

CZECHOSLOVAKIA INVADED BY RUSSIANS AND FOUR OTHER WARSAW PACT FORCES; THEY OPEN FIRE ON CROWDS IN PRAGUE

13 INDICTED HERE IN RIGGING OF BIDS ON UTILITY WORK

Contracts Worth 49-Million Involved—14 Construction Companies Also Named

By MARTIN TOLCHIN

Fourteen, major construction companies, 12 top corporate executives and one employe were indicted here yesterday on charges of rigging bids on utilities contracts totaling $49.8-million.

The defendants were accused of deciding among themselves who would be low bidder in the contracts with Consolidated Edison, the Brooklyn Union Gas Company, and the Empire City Subway Company—the latter a subsidiary of the New York Telephone Company.

The indictments charge that the defendants then accommodated the selected low bidder by submitting higher bids.

The companies included such important contractors as Lipsett, Inc., a leading demolition company that razed Pennsylvania Station, the Savoy Plaza Hotel and the Third Avenue El; the Slattery Contracting Company, which held the general contract for excavating the site of United Nations Headquarters and built subway spurs and the Lincoln Center reflecting pool, and the Thomas Crimmins Contracting Company, which did the excavation for numerous skyscrapers.

1959 Activities Covered

The companies received contracts to dig trenches for electrical conduits and gas mains and for paving work. The contracts totaled $49,788,165.

The four indictments, with a total of 28 counts, were an outgrowth of the investigation of James L. Marcus, former City Water Commissioner, who pleaded guilty in Federal court to receiving a $40,000 kickback on a city reservoir cleaning contract.

"Our interest in Marcus and [Herbert] Itkin led us to the inquiry that led to these indictments," Frank S. Hogan, New York County District Attorney, said.

He noted that the indictments alleged activities that began in 1959, "before the community at large was aware of Marcus and Itkin," and

Continued on Page 35, Column 3

OUTLOOK GUARDED FOR EISENHOWER

His Condition Still Critical Despite 'Favorable Trend'

By FELIX BELAIR Jr.
Special to The New York Times

WASHINGTON, Aug. 20 — Former President Dwight D. Eisenhower clung resolutely to life today, but with a fragile grip that his doctors acknowledged could loosen at any time.

The condition of the 77-year-old General of the Army still was listed as "critical" and the outlook for his survival as "guarded." His doctors have used this term to mean uncertain or unpredictable.

A bulletin issued at Walter Reed Army Medical Center about 11 A.M. mentioned the development of a "favorable trend" in the pattern of abnormal heart rhythm.

The episodes of rapid irregularity in the heartbeat have persisted, the doctors reported, but they were isolated and did not involve the sustained fibrillating, or fluttering, reported prior to last night.

At the time of the morning

Continued on Page 13, Column 1

Democrats Debate Position on the War in Vietnam

The New York Times
Secretary of State Rusk defended the Administration's policies at the hearing.

Associated Press
Senator George S. McGovern of South Dakota was critical of the Administration.

The New York Times (by George Tames)
Kenneth P. O'Donnell, left, who was an aide to President Kennedy, talks with Senator J. W. Fulbright, standing right, at the platform hearing. The Senator spoke against the war.

NIXON INCREASES GALLUP POLL LEAD

Tops Humphrey, 45% to 29, and Maintains His Margin Over McCarthy, 42 to 37

Special to The New York Times

PRINCETON, N. J., Aug. 20 —Richard M. Nixon stretched a slim mid-July edge over Vice President Humphrey to a 45-to-29 per cent lead in voter preference immediately following the Republican National Convention, according to the latest Gallup Poll.

Against Senator Eugene J. McCarthy—Mr. Humphrey's chief rival for the Democratic Presidential nomination—Mr. Nixon held a 42-to-37 per cent lead, almost the same margin he had in the previous test in mid-July.

Mr. Nixon's improved advantage over the Vice President was caused more by Mr. Humphrey's losses than by gains by Mr. Nixon. The Republican nominee was 5 percentage points higher than the pre-convention survey, while Mr. Humphrey was 9 points lower.

Support for the independent candidacy of George A. Wallace of Alabama held up. He polled 18 per cent in the Nixon-Humphrey-Wallace test and 16 per cent in the Nixon-McCarthy-Wallace post-convention survey.

In interviewing between Aug. 8 and 11, the following question was asked of a representative sample of 1,526 adults in over 320 localities:

"Suppose the Presidential election were being held today. If Hubert Humphrey were the Democratic candidate, running against Richard Nixon, the Republican candidate, and George Wallace of Alabama were the candidate of a third party, which would you like to see

Continued on Page 34, Column 2

Guard Is Called Up To Protect Chicago During Convention

By DONALD JANSON
Special to The New York Times

CHICAGO, Aug. 20—Gov. Samuel H. Shapiro called up the National Guard today to keep order in the city during the Democratic National Convention.

At the request of Mayor Richard J. Daley, the Governor ordered 5,649 Illinois National Guardsmen to round-the-clock duty in Chicago beginning Friday to head off threats of "tumult, riot or mob disorder."

Meanwhile, an Army spokesman in Washington confirmed in a telephone interview that about 6,000 regular Army troops received rigorous riot-control training at Fort Hood, Tex., last week as a precautionary measure.

That exercise, he said, was called Operation Jackson Park, after the park in Chicago

Continued on Page 32, Column 2

Democrats to Seat Mississippi Rebels

By MAX FRANKEL
Special to The New York Times

CHICAGO, Aug. 20—Mississippi's regular delegation to the Democratic National Convention was barred from its seats tonight by an overwhelming vote of the Credentials Committee on the ground that it had failed to meet national standards to assure the full participation of Negroes in the political process.

A biracial delegation including many members who have fought many years for this moment will be seated in place of the regulars.

At the same time, the Credentials Committee rejected by various votes the delegate

Continued on Page 32, Column 6

SOVIET EXPLAINS

Says Its Troops Moved at the Request of Czechoslovaks

By RAYMOND H. ANDERSON
Special to The New York Times

MOSCOW, Wednesday, Aug. 21 — Moscow announced this morning that troops from the Soviet Union and four other Communist countries had invaded Czechoslovakia at the request of the "party and Government leaders of the Czechoslovak Socialist Republic."

The announcement followed unofficial information here that Alexander Dubcek, the reform leader of the Czechoslovak party Presidium, had been overthrown.

In a statement authorized by the Soviet Government, the official press agency, Tass, declared at 7:30 A.M. Moscow time (12:30 A.M., New York time) that Czechoslovakia had come under a threat from "counterrevolutionary forces" involved in a collusion with foreign forces hostile to socialism.

Friendship Stressed

Tass said that troops from Bulgaria. East Germany, Hungary, Poland and the Soviet Union, acting from motivations of "inseverable friendship and cooperation," entered Czechoslovakia early this morning.

The troops will be withdrawn as soon as the threat to Czechoslovakia and neighboring Communist countries has been eliminated, according to Tass.

"The actions that are being taken are not directed against any state and in no measure infringe state interests of anybody," the statement said. "They serve the purpose of peace and have been prompted by concern for its consolidation."

"The fraternal countries firmly and resolutely counterpose their unbreakable solidarity to any threat from outside," the Soviet explanation continued. "Nobody will ever be allowed to wrest a single link from the community of Socialist states."

Polemics Resumed

The handwriting was on the wall for the Czechoslovak reform regime last Friday when the Soviet press abruptly resumed its bitter polemics against the country.

Czechoslovakia's seven-month-old experiment with democracy under Communist rule was explicitly doomed yesterday when the Soviet Communist party warned in an editorial that imperial intrigues must be "nipped in the bud."

Rumors swept Moscow yesterday that the Soviet party's Central Committee had met in secret session, presumably to endorse intervention. Official sources insisted, however, that

Continued on Page 14, Column 6

13 Points in Delta Are Shelled by Foe

By JOSEPH B. TREASTER
Special to The New York Times

SAIGON, South Vietnam, Wednesday, Aug. 22 — The Vietcong shelled 13 cities and military installations in the Mekong Delta this morning, extending their latest wave of attacks into South Vietnam's southern-most region.

Seven of the shellings were followed by ground attacks.

Initial reports were sketchy, but a United States military spokesman said that allied casualties and damage in all of the attacks appeared to be light.

To the north, allied troops are making an increasing number of forays into the southern

Continued on Page 4, Column 3

KENNEDY BACKERS OFFER WAR PLANK

But McCarthy Group Balks at Compromise—Rusk Is for General Statement

Text of plank and excerpts from statement, Page 33.

By JOHN W. FINNEY
Special to The New York Times

WASHINGTON, Aug. 20 — Supporters of the late Senator Robert F. Kennedy circulated in the Democratic platform committee today a compromise dovish plank on Vietnam calling for a halt in the bombing of North Vietnam, a cease-fire and negotiations between the Saigon Government and the National Liberation Front, the political arm of the Vietcong.

In the bitter fight developing within the platform committee, the proposed plank is designed to provide a common front for supporters of Senator Eugene J. McCarthy, Senator George S. McGovern and Senator Kennedy.

For the moment, however, some difficulty was being encountered in winning the approval of some McCarthy partisans, who were holding out for a plank that would be more critical of the Administration.

As the doves began to mount a concerted attack on the Administration's Vietnam policy, Secretary of State Dean Rusk was called in to defend the Administration position. Mr. Rusk,

Continued on Page 33, Column 2

NEWS INDEX

SOVIET EXPLAINS (map section)

The New York Times   Aug. 21, 1968
FIVE-POWER INVASION: Soviet planes carried troops into Prague (cross). Ground forces of bloc crossed Czechoslovak borders that are indicated by heavy line.

Versions of the Two Sides

Following are the texts of the Prague radio announcement of the Soviet-bloc invasion of Czechoslovakia, as monitored in Washington, and of a Soviet statement distributed in New York by Tass, the Soviet press agency.

Czechoslovak Radio Broadcast

To the entire people of the Czechoslovak Socialist Republic: Yesterday, on 20 August, around 2300 [11 P.M.], troops of the Soviet Union, Polish People's Republic, the G.D.R. [East Germany], the Hungarian People's Republic and the Bulgarian People's Republic crossed the frontiers of the Czechoslovak Socialist Republic.

This happened without the knowledge of the President of the Republic, the Chairman of the National Assembly, the Premier, or the First Secretary of the Czechoslovak Communist party Central Committee.

In the evening hours the Presidium of the Czechoslovak Communist party Central Committee [had] held a session and discussed preparations for the 14th Czechoslovak Communist party congress.

The Czechoslovak Communist party Central Committee Presidium appeals to all citizens of our republic to maintain calm and not to offer resistance to the troops on the march. Our army, security corps and people's militia have not received the command to defend the country.

The Czechoslovak Communist party Central Committee Presidium regard this act as contrary not only to the fundamental principles of relations between Socialist states but also as contrary to the principles of international law.

All leading functionaries of the state, the Communist party and the National Front: Remain in your functions as representatives of the state, elected to the laws of the Czechoslovak Socialist Republic.

Constitutional functionaries are immediately convening a session of the National Assembly of our republic, and the Presidium is at the same time convening a plenum of the Central Committee to discuss the situation that has arisen.

PRESIDIUM OF THE CZECHOSLOVAK COMMUNIST PARTY CENTRAL COMMITTEE.

Announcement by Moscow

Tass is authorized to state that party and Government leaders of the Czechoslovak Socialist Republic have asked the Soviet Union and other allied states to render the fraternal Czechoslovak people urgent assistance, including assistance with armed forces. This request was brought about by the threat which has arisen to the Socialist system existing in Czechoslovakia and to the statehood established by the Con-

Continued on Page 14, Column 2

Soviet Turns Back Clock

By JAMES RESTON

The Soviet invasion of Czechoslovakia has transformed world and American politics.

It occurred in the middle of the American Presidential election of 1968, as the Soviet invasion of Hungary took place during the Eisenhower-Stevenson Presidential election of 1956. The Soviet Union moved on Prague while the United States was preoccupied in Vietnam, as they moved on Budapest in 1956 while the British and French were preoccupied with the invasion of Suez.

News Analysis

The latest move by Moscow startled Washington just as officials there were convening on new moves to reach an agreement with the Soviet Union on Vietnam.

Washington was prepared for a dramatic move by the Soviet Union against the new liberal regime in Prague, but not for anything quite so bold as an invasion by the Red Army.

It had been observing closely the increasingly violent attacks on the Czechoslovak Government in the Soviet press, and. Under Secretary of State Charles E. Bohlen, former United States Ambassador to the Soviet Union and France, and warned of the possibility of a coup d'état, followed by Soviet military intervention in Czechoslovakia. But a direct invasion at this time was discounted.

In fact, the Johnson Administration, under attack on its Vietnam policy just before the Democratic Presidential nominating convention next week in Chicago, was discussing new moves to enlist the help of the Soviet Union when the Red Army moved.

The first impression of the crisis was that this Soviet intervention in Czechoslovakia, like the first one at the end of World War II, would increase

Continued on Page 15, Column 1

TANKS ENTER CITY

Deaths Are Reported --Troops Surround Offices of Party

By TAD SZULC
Special to The New York Times

PRAGUE, Wednesday, Aug. 21—Czechoslovakia was occupied early today by troops of the Soviet Union and four of its Warsaw Pact allies in a series of swift land and air movements.

Airborne Soviet troops and paratroopers surrounded the building of the Communist party Central Committee, along with five tanks. At least 25 tanks were seen in the city.

Several persons were reported killed early this morning. Unconfirmed reports said that two Czechoslovak soldiers and a woman were killed by Bulgarian tank fire in front of the Prague radio building shortly before the station was captured and went off the air.

[Soviet troops began shooting at Czechoslovak demonstrators outside the Prague radio building at 7:25 A.M., Reuters reported. C.T.K., the Czechoslovak press agency, was quoted by United Press International as having said that citizens were throwing themselves in front of the tanks in an attempt to block the seizure of the city.]

Move a Surprise

The Soviet move caught Czechoslovaks by surprise, although all day yesterday there were indications of new tensions.

Confusion was caused in the capital by leaflets dropped from unidentified aircraft asserting that Antonin Novotny, the President of Czechoslovakia who was deposed in March by the Communist liberals, had been pushed out by a "clique." The leaflets said that Mr. Novotny remained the country's legal President.

At 5 A.M. the Prague radio, still in the hands of adherents of the Communist liberals, broadcast a dramatic appeal to the population in the name of Alexander Dubcek, the party

Continued on Page 14, Column 1

JOHNSON SUMMONS SECURITY COUNCIL

Calls Emergency Session After Seeing Soviet Envoy

By B. DRUMMOND AYRES JR.
Special to The New York Times

WASHINGTON, Aug. 20—President Johnson met with the National Security Council in an emergency session tonight to discuss developments in Czechoslovakia after he received a visit from the Soviet Ambassador.

The Council meeting, which was held in the Cabinet Room in the West Wing of the White House, began at 10:15 P.M. and lasted for 55 minutes.

It was followed by a 15-minute meeting at the State Department between the Soviet Ambassador, Anatoly F. Dobrynen, and Secretary of State Dean Rusk.

There was no indication after either of the meetings of what course the United States would take in the crisis, which clearly came as a stunning surprise here.

During the recent weeks of tension around Czechoslovakia, the Administration has insistently maintained a hand-off attitude, arguing that any gestures of support from Washington would only complicate the Prague regime's status in the Communist camp. Any move to exploit the Soviet di-

Continued on Page 15, Column 1

"All the News
That's Fit to Print"

The New York Times

LATE CITY EDITION

Weather: Rain today and tonight.
Cloudy, showers likely tomorrow.
Temp. range: today 52-48; Wed.
54-45. Full U.S. report on Page 93.

VOL.CXVIII..No.40,465   © 1968 The New York Times Company.   NEW YORK, THURSDAY, NOVEMBER 7, 1968   10 CENTS

NIXON WINS BY A THIN MARGIN, PLEADS FOR REUNITED NATION

NIXON'S ELECTION EXPECTED TO SLOW PARIS NEGOTIATION

Allied Diplomats Suggest All Sides May Adopt a Wait-and-See Stance

By HEDRICK SMITH
Special to The New York Times

PARIS, Nov. 6—Allied diplomats suggested tonight that Richard M. Nixon's election victory would add, at least temporarily, to the delays and complications of getting meaningful Vietnam peace negotiations under way.

The American, the North Vietnamese and the National Liberation Front delegations here had no comment on the election results.

But allied diplomats close to the talks suggested that the Republican victory would probably bring eventual changes in the American negotiating team, encourage delays by the South Vietnamese Government, and induce a wait-and-see attitude by all sides until Mr. Nixon's own approach to the talks became clearer.

The uncertainty about the future relationship between the outgoing Johnson Administration and Mr. Nixon is considered the primary complicating factor.

Eyes on Saigon

"Everybody has to see how Nixon and Johnson are going to handle this period," said one Western diplomat.

The Saigon Government is reported to feel that the Johnson Administration pressed it too rapidly toward expanded talks embracing the Vietcong. It now is expected to use the change-over period in the United States to play for time.

South Vietnamese officials here made no secret that they consider Mr. Nixon more sympathetic than Mr. Johnson to their position.

They have recently dropped hints that they expect no active negotiating on issues of substance until early next year.

Western diplomats now speculate that President Nguyen Van Thieu may delay sending a delegation to the talks here until he has learned Mr. Nixon's views.

But a more common opinion is that Saigon will send a delegation soon and then try to stall until the Republicans take office in January.

The Republican victory,
Continued on Page 13, Column 1

POLICE SEIZE 125 ON C.C.N.Y. CAMPUS

AWOL Soldier Taken From Student Center 'Sanctuary'

About 250 members of the Tactical Patrol Force moved onto the City College campus early today at the request of the administration and arrested more than 100 students and the AWOL soldier they had been guarding in a student center.

Under the direction of Police Commissioner Howard R. Leary, Chief Inspector Sanford Garelik and a number of other high police officials, the arrests were carried out without violence following a warning from the administration to vacate the building.

In all, about 125 persons were arrested, including supporters of the peace movement and Pvt. William Brakefield, who had been in the Finley Student Center, at 133d Street and Convent Avenue, since last
Continued on Page 4, Column 4

SHE KNEW IT ALL ALONG: President-elect Richard M. Nixon holding crewelwork, a facsimile of Presidential seal embroidered by his daughter Julie, who stands beside her fiancé, David Eisenhower. Mrs. Nixon and daughter Patricia completed the family group at the Waldorf-Astoria yesterday.

The New York Times (by Neal Boenzi)

Soviet Bids U.S. Confer; Calls for 'Normalization'

By HENRY KAMM
Special to The New York Times

MOSCOW, Nov. 6—The Soviet Union greeted the election of a new President of the United States today with a call for the "normalization" of relations between Moscow and Washington for the sake of world peace.

The demand was put forward in a speech on behalf of the ruling Politburo of the Communist party by First Deputy Premier Kirill T. Mazurov as election returns in the United States showed that Richard M. Nixon had won the Presidency. The occasion was the traditional speech in the Kremlin on the eve of the anniversary of the Bolshevik Revolution.

To underline the importance Moscow attaches to relations with the United States, Mr. Mazurov raised the issue twice. In the speech he called for mutual limitations on nuclear weapons and delivery systems, the official said:

"It is relevant to recall in this connection that we have expressed readiness to conduct negotiations with the United States on the entire range of these problems. But their positive solution does not depend on the Soviet Union alone."

Review of Soviet Actions

After a review of Soviet actions on the international scene, Mr. Mazurov returned to Soviet-American relations. He said:

"We have always attached great importance to the normalization of relations between the Soviet Union and the United States, which would be important not only to both of our countries but also to world peace."

Continued on Page 14, Column 1

POSITION ON SINAI DEFINED BY ISRAEL

Note to Jarring Links Issue of Boundaries to Security Needs and Tiran Rights

By DREW MIDDLETON
Special to The New York Times

UNITED NATIONS, N. Y., Nov. 6—Israel has told the United Arab Republic that her attitude toward the boundary question will be governed by her security needs and the maintenance of full protection of Israeli navigation in the Strait of Tiran.

This is the first time that Israel has defined with any precision her interest in the Sinai Peninsula.

Western diplomats inferred that if Israel's security requirements were fulfilled, including protection of shipping in the Strait of Tiran, the Government would not reject an arrangement that returned a demilitarized Sinai to Egypt. The peninsula has been occupied by Israel since the Israeli-Arab war of June, 1967.

This information was in a memorandum that Foreign Minister Abba Eban gave yesterday to Dr. Gunnar V. Jarring, the United Nations intermediary. Mr. Eban went over the text of the memorandum with Dr. Jarring at meetings yesterday afternoon and last night.

Ambassador Jarring was asked to transmit the memorandum to Mahmoud Riad, the Egyptian Foreign Minister. The clarification of Israel's approach to the boundary problem apparently was intended to rebut Mr.
Continued on Page 2, Column 3

REPUBLICANS GAIN SAFE ALBANY EDGE

Lead in Assembly Put at 77-73 and in Senate at 33-24 Unofficially

By JAMES F. CLARITY

Republican officials said yesterday that they expected to have clear majorities in both houses of the 1969 Legislature.

The Republicans, on the basis of unofficial but reliable vote-counts in the elections for the 150 Assembly and 57 Senate seats, will probably control the Assembly by 77 to 73, and the Senate by 33 to 24.

The official counts of several close Assembly races were not expected to affect lower house control, which the Republicans appeared almost certain to have wrested from the Democrats in Tuesday's election.

Official Count Delayed

The official count of the close races was expected to be completed early next week. The G.O.P. Senate majority was assured, regardless of the final count in a few close races.

But the Republicans' control of the Assembly, which they had lost in 1964, did not appear to give G.O.P. leaders assurance that their programs and legislation or those proposed by Governor Rockefeller would necessarily sail through the Legislature because of the majorities in both houses.

Among the Republicans who captured Democratic seats in the Assembly were several conservatives who, by combining with conservative Democrats, could obstruct, if not defeat, legislation they considered liberally oriented, or objectionable for other reasons.

Three of the newly elected Republican Assembly members
Continued on Page 40, Column 5

Senate's Liberal Coalition Survives Gains by G.O.P.

By DAVID E. ROSENBAUM

Republicans made a net gain of at least four Senate seats in Tuesday's election, but the balance between liberals and conservatives did not appear to have changed substantially from the present Senate.

One Senate race remained in doubt last night. In Oregon, Wayne Morse, a Democrat, who served four terms, was running a close race with State Representative Robert W. Packwood, a Republican. Observers said it might be days before the outcome was certain.

Depending on the Oregon race, the Democrats will hold 58 or 59 seats in the new Senate to 41 or 42 for the Republicans. In the present Senate there are 63 Democrats and 37 Republicans.

Four conservative Republicans and one conservative Democrat were elected to seats that had been held by liberals or moderates. On the other hand, there was a shift in favor of liberals in at least two states.

Thus it appeared that a majority could still be formed from liberal Northern Democrats and moderate Republicans to pass legislation on such issues as
Continued on Page 29, Column 2

Election Tables

Tables reporting the vote in national, state and local contests in Tuesday's election are now scheduled for publication in The New York Times tomorrow.

The Times had expected to print them today, but breakdowns in the News Election Service's national and regional computers made a total recheck of the election results necessary. This recheck is expected to be concluded today.

civil rights and aid to education.

The Republicans' net gain of only four seats in the new Senate to 41 or 42 for the Republicans dashed the party's hopes of capturing control of that body.

In the Senate the Republicans picked up seats that had been held by Democrats in Arizona, Florida, Maryland, Ohio, Oklahoma and Pennsylvania. Democrats took Republican-held seats in California and Iowa.

Among the new conservatives was Barry Goldwater, the Republican Presidential nominee in 1964. He defeated Roy L. Elson for the Arizona
Continued on Page 21, Column 1

GOAL IS HARMONY

President-Elect Vows His Administration Will Be 'Open'

By ROBERT B. SEMPLE Jr.

President-elect Richard M. Nixon turned yesterday from the business of winning elections to the business of assembling an Administration.

Weary but thankful, he appeared before an elated band of supporters gathered in the ballroom of the Waldorf-Astoria at 11:35 A.M. He expressed his gratitude for their

Transcript of Nixon's remarks will be found on Page 21.

efforts and his admiration for the "gallant and courageous fight" of his opponent.

He also extended the hand of friendship to the disappointed partisans of Mr. Humphrey's cause—particularly the young.

Near the end of his eight-minute talk, Mr. Nixon took note of the division in the nation and pledged, in these words, to bend every effort to restore racial peace and social harmony:

"I saw many signs in this campaign. Some of them were not friendly and some were very friendly. But the one that touched me the most was one that I saw in Deshler, Ohio, at the end of a long day of whistle-stopping, a little town, in the dusk, almost impossible to see — but a teen-ager held up a sign, 'Bring Us Together.'

"And that will be the great objective of this Administration at the outset, to bring the American people together. This will be an open Administration, open to new ideas, open to men and women of both parties, open to critics as well as those who support us.

"We want to bridge the generation gap. We want to bridge the gap between the races. We want to bring America together. And I am confident that this task is one that we can undertake and one in which we will be successful."

Several hours later the campaign entourage began to disassemble, its members heading home for a brief but long-overdue rest. The candidate himself flew southward for a three-day vacation in Key Biscayne, a peninsula just south of Miami where he rested occasionally during the campaign.

Although he has been urged
Continued on Page 21, Column 1

ELECTOR VOTE 287

Lead in Popular Tally May Be Smaller Than Kennedy's in '60

By MAX FRANKEL

Richard Milhous Nixon emerged the victor yesterday in one of the closest and most tumultuous Presidential campaigns in history and set himself the task of reuniting the nation.

Elected over Hubert H. Humphrey by the barest of margins—only four one-hundredths of a percentage point in the popular vote—and confronted by a Congress in control of the Democrats, the President-elect said it "will be the great objective of this Administration at the outset to bring the American people together."

He pledged, as the 37th President, to form "an open Administration, open to new ideas, open to men and women of both parties, open to critics as well as those who support us" so as to bridge the gap between the generations and the races.

Details Left for Later

But after an exhausting and tense night of awaiting the verdict at the Waldorf-Astoria Hotel here, Mr. Nixon and his closest aides were not yet prepared to suggest how they intended to organize themselves and to approach these objectives. The Republican victor expressed admiration for his opponent's challenge and reiterated his desire to help President Johnson achieve peace in Vietnam between now and Inauguration Day on Jan. 20.

The verdict of an electorate that appeared to number 73 million could not be discerned until mid-morning because Mr. Nixon and Mr. Humphrey finished in a virtual tie in the popular vote, just as Mr. Nixon and John F. Kennedy did in 1960.

With 94 per cent of the nation's election precincts reporting, Mr. Nixon's total stood last evening at 29,726,409 votes to Mr. Humphrey's 29,677,152. The margin of 49,257 was even smaller than Mr. Kennedy's margin of 112,803.

Meaning Hard to Find

When translated into the determining electoral votes of the states, these returns proved even more difficult to read, and the result in two states—Alaska and Missouri—was still not final last night. But the unofficial returns from elsewhere gave Mr. Nixon a minimum of 287 electoral votes, 17 more than the 270 required for election. Mr. Humphrey won 191.

Because of the tightness of the race, the third-party challenger, George C. Wallace, came close to realizing his minimum objective of denying victory to the major-party candidates and then somehow forcing a bargain for his sup-
Continued on Page 20, Column 1

A Loser Concedes and Tries to Smile

By R. W. APPLE Jr.
Special to The New York Times

MINNEAPOLIS, Nov. 6—It was probably Hubert Horatio Humphrey's last hurrah in Presidential politics.

He had lost once before, in 1960, and had been crushed by the superb organization of John F. Kennedy in the West

Transcript of the Humphrey statement is on Page 22.

Virginia primary. Now he had lost again, this time to the man whom John Kennedy had defeated, in an agonizingly close finish.

The Vice President—a hearty, sentimental man, given to laughter and to tears—tried to smile as he stood on the stage in the Leamington Hotel's ballroom this morning and listened to his faithful followers shout, "We Want Humphrey!" But what he brought forth was more a grimace than a grin. "Thank you very much," he said in a quavering voice. "It's nice to know."

Mr. Humphrey went through
Continued on Page 22, Column 1

Vice President Humphrey with his wife after conceding

Johnson Vows Aid In Power Transfer

By NEIL SHEEHAN
Special to The New York Times

SAN ANTONIO, Tex., Nov. 6—In a telegram of congratulations this morning, President Johnson informed President-elect Richard M. Nixon that he would do "everything in my power to make your burdens lighter on that day when you assume the responsibilities of the President."

Even as Mr. Johnson's telegram was being transmitted to Mr. Nixon from the President's ranch 65 miles north of here, the machinery had been set in motion for an orderly transition from the old Administration to the new.

Lawson Knott, the administrator of the General Services
Continued on Page 20, Column 3

254

The New York Times

LATE CITY EDITION

Weather: Mostly sunny, cold today; fair, warmer tonight and tomorrow. Temp. range: today 30-20; Tuesday 34-24. Full U.S. report on Page 62.

VOL. CXVIII—No. 40,513   © 1968 The New York Times Company.   NEW YORK, WEDNESDAY, DECEMBER 25, 1968   10 CENTS

3 MEN FLY AROUND THE MOON ONLY 70 MILES FROM SURFACE; FIRE ROCKET, HEAD FOR EARTH

PUEBLO CREWMEN GREETED ON COAST; CAPTORS ASSAILED

Relatives Weep and Scream —Captain Asserts North Koreans Are Inhuman

By BERNARD GWERTZMAN
Special to The New York Times

SAN DIEGO, Dec. 24 — The crew of the intelligence ship Pueblo returned to the United States today in time for Christmas with many of their families.

Led by Comdr. Lloyd M. Bucher, the 82 survivors arrived at the Miramar Naval Air Station outside this city and were met immediately by emotional, sometimes hysterical, greetings and embraces of wives, mothers, fathers and children.

The one man who did not return alive, Duane D. Hodges, was carried from one of the C-141 transports in a flag-draped coffin while the air station band played the Navy hymn.

Commander Bucher, apparently overwrought with emotion, spoke in a low voice as he told the more than 250 relatives, the 300 newsmen and the national television audience about the 11 months his crew spent in North Korean captivity.

Calls Captors Inhuman

He described North Korea as a land "completely devoid of humanity, completely devoted to enslavement of men's minds."

[In Washington, the Navy named Vice Adm. Harold S. Bowen to head a court of inquiry into the Pueblo incident.]

Commander Bucher said that, during the months in North Korea, "the thought that preyed on my mind was the embarrassment to my country because of the loss of one of its fine ships."

At a news conference held in the base theater at Navy Hospital here, Rear Adm. Edwin Rosenberg, the representative of the Commander in Chief, Pacific Fleet, in charge of the Pueblo's repatriation, repeated his past praise

Continued on Page 2, Column 1

At Least 22 Survive Pennsylvania Crash Of Plane With 45

Special to The New York Times

BRADFORD, Pa., Wednesday, Dec. 25—An Allegheny Airlines jetprop plane with 45 persons aboard crashed last night in rugged terrain during a heavy snowstorm while attempting to land at Bradford Regional Airport 15 miles south of here.

There were at least 22 survivors.

The twin-engine plane was Allegheny Flight 736, bound from Detroit to Washington. It had stopped in Erie, Pa., and had been scheduled to stop in Bradford and Harrisburg, too.

The wreck, about three miles southeast of the airport, was reported shortly before 9 P.M. by Allegheny Flight 734 out of Cleveland, which said it saw a fire.

It took rescue teams an hour to reach the scene on snowmobiles in freezing temperatures. Several inches of snow had fallen during the day in the heavily wooded area and

Continued on Page 62, Column 1

Pope Paul Says Mass In a Huge Steel Mill

By ROBERT C. DOTY
Special to The New York Times

TARANTO, Italy, Wednesday, Dec. 25—Pope Paul VI celebrated Christmas midnight mass here for 15,000 workers and members of their families in a huge, echoing mill.

The Pontiff chose the vast Italsider steel plant at this developing industrial center in the heel of the Italian boot as the place to express "the fraternal and radiant presence of Christ among workers throughout the world."

Even while the Pope said mass at an altar consisting of a four-ton slab of steel supported on two broad sections of steel pipe, work continued elsewhere throughout the 2,000-acre plant, the largest in Europe.

Blast furnaces poured plumes of flame into a rainy

Continued on Page 34, Column 1

VIOLATIONS MAR TRUCE IN VIETNAM

80 Incidents Are Reported —22 Enemy Soldiers and an American Killed

By B. DRUMMOND AYRES Jr.
Special to The New York Times

SAIGON, South Vietnam, Wednesday, Dec. 25—The allies and the Vietcong put separate cease-fires into effect yesterday to mark Christmas, but not all the guns fell silent.

At 9 o'clock this morning, the American military command said there had been at least 80 "incidents" involving military contact since the allied cease-fire, scheduled to run 24 hours, went into effect at 6 P.M. yesterday.

The enemy cease-fire began at 1 A.M. yesterday and was scheduled to run for 72 hours. Allied military spokesmen said there were at least eight incidents involving military contact during the first hours of that stand-down.

In about 30 of the incidents, casualties were suffered by one or both sides. The allied spokesmen said that overall South Vietnamese losses had been light. United States losses were broken down as one soldier killed and 38 wounded.

At least 22 enemy soldiers died.

It was not known whether North Vietnamese troops in South Vietnam were complying with the Vietcong cease-fire order. During previous holiday

Continued on Page 5, Column 3

Christmas Day

Today is Christmas Day. Following is a list of services that are affected:

Public and Parochial Schools —Closed.

Post Office—Closed except for special delivery.

Stores—Most retail and department stores closed.

Banks—Closed.

Stock Exchanges—Closed.

Sanitation—No regular refuse collection.

Parking—Sunday parking regulations in force, permitting parking in alternate-side parking zones and at most parking meters.

Libraries—Closed except for the Main Reading Room of the Library at Fifth Avenue and 42d Street, which will be open from 1 to 10 P.M.

Col. Frank Borman

Maj. William A. Anders

Capt. James A. Lovell Jr.

Moon pictures taken through the window of the Apollo 8 spacecraft that were telecast to earth last night. In picture at left Sea of Crises area, the larger crater is 30 to 40 miles wide. The picture at right was last transmitted.

FUEL DELIVERIES FALL SHORT HERE

City's Health Chief Warns of Danger to Sick—Flu Vaccine and Blood Low

By ARNOLD H. LUBASCH

A shortage of heat, vaccine and blood plagued the city yesterday as the Hong Kong flu epidemic continued, and the Health Commissioner warned that many sick people might die unless emergency fuel deliveries were made.

Mayor Lindsay, who said most drivers had stopped fuel deliveries for the holiday, joined Health Commissioner Edward O'Rourke in appealing for fuel deliveries today even though it was Christmas.

With the temperature dropping into the low twenties last night, hundreds of homes, apartment houses and commercial buildings remained without fuel, although oil companies sought to catch up on deliveries delayed by last week's strike.

The city's supply of flu vaccine ran out yesterday as efforts were made to arrange for further shipments before Jan. 2, when 40,000 more doses are scheduled to arrive.

A critical shortage of blood was reported by the Greater

Continued on Page 21, Column 1

Orbit Shows Lunar Interior Is 'Lumpy'

By WALTER SULLIVAN
Special to The New York Times

HOUSTON, Dec. 24—For the first time human beings took a close look today at the earth's nearest celestial neighbor, viewing it from many angles to seek out clues to the events that formed its awesomely rugged terrain.

Until now man has always been forced to look at the moon from a single direction at a great distance, although in the last few years spacecraft have provided glimpses of the far side and close-up views of the earth-facing side.

Today the three Apollo astronauts sailed serenely over the giant craters, looking down their throats, marveling at their crumbling walls and countless strange features that have long puzzled astronomers.

They reported seeing many freshly formed craters, indicating that the cataclysmic events that have pocked the moon and sprinkled it with rubble are continuing. Some of the craters, the astronauts said, looked as

Slight Wobbles Observed in Spacecraft's Course

though a giant pick had been hacking at a concrete surface, producing fine dust as well as other debris.

They became the first men to witness a lunar sunrise and found it a strange and unexpected experience. According to Capt. James A. Lovell Jr., about two minutes before sunrise a fine white haze appeared over the horizon where the sun was about to appear.

"It takes the fan shape," he said, "unlike the sunrise on earth, where the atmosphere affects it."

Meanwhile, analysis of the orbital flight by radio antennas on earth showed that, from time to time, the spacecraft wobbled slightly in its path. This confirmed earlier indications that the interior of the moon is "lumpy."

Some scientists, notably Dr. Harold C. Urey of the University of California, San Diego, a Nobel laureate, have suggested that the moon is like a giant raisin cake with lumps of dense iron embedded in material that is far less dense. Such a body could have been formed from a cloud of dust and smaller objects, including chunks of iron, during the formation of the solar system.

If the moon were uniformly dense and perfectly spherical, the gravitational field surrounding it would be perfectly symmetrical. It was this field that held the Apollo spacecraft in orbit. The fact that the spacecraft's road was slightly bumpy, so to speak, revealed an uneven distribution of mass within the moon. In particular, this was noted as the astronauts sailed over Copernicus, one of the largest and most spectacular craters on the moon. It was in darkness but was dimly illuminated by ghostly earthshine—sunlight reflected by the earth. The lumpiness of the moon

Continued on Page 38, Column 1

Astronauts Examine 'Vast, Lonely' Place; Read From Genesis

By JOHN NOBLE WILFORD
Special to The New York Times

HOUSTON, Wednesday, Dec. 25—The three astronauts of Apollo 8 yesterday became the first men to orbit the moon. Early today, after flying 10 times around that desolate realm of dream and scientific mystery, they started their return to earth.

They fired the spacecraft's main rocket engine at 1:10 A.M. to kick them out of lunar orbit

Excerpts from messages to and from Apollo, Page 36.

and to carry them toward a splashdown in the Pacific Ocean on Friday.

Through the static of 231,000 miles, as Apollo 8 swung around from behind the moon and started for earth, one of the astronauts dispelled any doubts, saying, "Please be informed there is a Santa Claus."

57-Hour Return Trip

It would be a 57-hour return trip from the most far-reaching voyage of the space age thus far—or of any other previous age. The astronauts had seen, as no other men had, the ancient lunar craters, plains and rugged mountains from as close as 70 miles.

At 4:59 A.M. yesterday, about 20 hours before the return trip, Col. Frank Borman of the Air Force, Capt. James A. Lovell Jr. of the Navy and Maj. William A. Anders of the Air Force, swept into an orbit of the moon by firing the spacecraft's main rocket. This occurred after they flew around the leading edge of the moon and were directly behind the earth's only natural satellite.

"We got it! We've got it!" exclaimed a mission commentator of the National Aeronautics and Space Administration as the spacecraft emerged from behind the moon 24 minutes later, and was clearly flying a safe and smooth orbit.

Businesslike Report

The calm and laconic Apollo explorers, however, were all business. Captain Lovell's first message to earth was simply: "Go ahead, Houston. Apollo 8. Burn complete. Our orbit is 169.1 by 60.5—169.1 by 60.5."

The astronauts flew twice around the moon in the egg-shaped orbit, then dropped to a circular orbit nearly 70 miles above the ancient craters, plains and rugged mountains of the lunar surface.

As they beamed their first live television from orbit on Christmas Eve morning, they described the surface of the moon as a colorless gray, "like

Earth Like on 'Oasis'

Colonel Borman described the moon as a "vast, lonely and forbidding sight," adding that it was "not a very inviting place to live or work."

Captain Lovell saw the earth as a "grand oasis in the big vastness of space."

Major Anders was most impressed by "the lunar sunrise and sunsets."

As the telecast neared its end, Colonel Borman said, "Apollo 8 has a message for you." With that, Major Anders began reading the opening verses from the Book of Genesis about creation of the earth.

"In the beginning," Major Anders read, "God created the heaven and the earth.

"And the earth was without form and voice; and darkness was upon the face of the deep . . ."

Captain Lovell then took up with the verse beginning, "And God called the light day, and the darkness He called night."

Colonel Borman closed the reading with the verse that read:

"And God called the dry land Earth; and the gathering together of the water called He Seas; and God saw that it was good."

Sends Holiday Greetings

After that Colonel Borman signed off, saying:

"Good-by, good night. Merry Christmas. God bless all of you, all of you on the good earth."

Glynn S. Lunney, one of the flight directors here, told reporters earlier, "we have a completely 'go' spacecraft."

George M. Low, the spacecraft manager at the Manned Spacecraft Center, said he was "altogether happy" with the mission — the most ambitious and daring thus far in the nation's $24-billion Apollo project to land men on the moon next year.

Although the mission's object was not primarily scientific, Dr. John Dietrich of the space center's geology and geochemistry branch, said that the television pictures and advance

Continued on Page 38, Column 1

NEWS INDEX

Merry Christmas, Mlle. Richmond Love, Josh.—Advt.

A Reflection: Riders on Earth Together, Brothers in Eternal Cold

By ARCHIBALD MacLEISH

MEN'S conception of themselves and of each other has always depended on their notion of the earth. When the earth was the World—all the world there was—and the stars were lights in Dante's heaven, and the ground beneath men's feet roofed Hell (at least no Hell beneath the feet)—men began to see themselves, not as God-directed actors at the center of a noble drama, but as helpless victims of a senseless farce where all the rest were helpless victims also, and millions could be killed in world-wide wars or in concentration camps without a thought or reason for the killing—for we call it one—of force.

And when, centuries later, the earth was no longer the World but a small, wet, spinning planet in the solar system of a minor star off at the edge of an inconsiderable galaxy in the immeasurable distances of space—when Dante's heaven had disappeared and there was no Hell (at least no Hell beneath the feet)—men began to see themselves, not as God-directed actors at the center of a noble drama, but as helpless victims of a senseless farce where all the rest were helpless victims also, and millions could be killed in world-wide wars or in concentration camps without a thought or reason for the killing—for we call it one—of force.

Now, in the last few hours, the notion may have changed again. For the first time in all time men have seen the earth: seen it not as continents or oceans from the little distance of a hundred miles or two or three, but seen it from the depths of space; seen it whole and round and beautiful and small as even Dante—that "first imagination of Christendom"—had never dreamed of seeing it; as the Twentieth Century philosophers of absurdity and despair were incapable of guessing that it might be seen. And seeing it so, one question came to the minds of those who looked at it.

"Is it inhabited?" they said to each other and laughed—and then they did not laugh. What came to their minds a hundred thousand miles and more into space—"half way to the moon" they put it—what came to their minds was the life on that little, lonely, floating planet; that tiny raft in the enormous, empty night. "Is it inhabited?"

THE medieval notion of the earth put man at the center of everything. The nuclear notion of the earth put him nowhere—beyond the range of reason even—lost in absurdity and war. This latest notion may have other consequences. Formed as it was in the minds of heroic voyagers who were also men, it may remake our image of mankind. No longer that preposterous figure at the center, degraded and degrading victim off at the margins of reality and blind with blood, man may at last become himself.

To see the earth as it truly is, small and blue and beautiful in that eternal silence where it floats, is to see ourselves as riders on the earth together, brothers on that bright loveliness in the eternal cold—brothers who know now they are truly brothers.

The New York Times

LATE CITY EDITION
Weather: Rain, warm today; clear
tonight. Sunny, pleasant tomorrow.
Temp. range: today 80-66; Sunday
71-56. Temp.-Hum. Index yesterday
69. Complete U.S. report on P. 50.

VOL. CXVIII . No. 40,721   © 1969 The New York Times Company.   NEW YORK, MONDAY, JULY 21, 1969   10 CENTS

MEN WALK ON MOON

ASTRONAUTS LAND ON PLAIN; COLLECT ROCKS, PLANT FLAG

Voice From Moon: 'Eagle Has Landed'

EAGLE (the lunar module): Houston, Tranquility Base here. The Eagle has landed.

HOUSTON: Roger, Tranquility, we copy you on the ground. You've got a bunch of guys about to turn blue. We're breathing again. Thanks a lot.

TRANQUILITY BASE: Thank you.

HOUSTON: You're looking good here.

TRANQUILITY BASE: A very smooth touchdown.

HOUSTON: Eagle, you are stay for T1. [The first step in the lunar operation.] Over.

TRANQUILITY BASE: Roger. Stay for T1.

HOUSTON: Roger and we see you venting the ox.

TRANQUILITY BASE: Roger.

COLUMBIA (the command and service module): How do you read me?

HOUSTON: Columbia, he has landed Tranquility Base. Eagle is at Tranquility. I read you five by. Over.

COLUMBIA: Yes, I heard the whole thing.

HOUSTON: Well, it's a good show.

COLUMBIA: Fantastic.

TRANQUILITY BASE: I'll second that.

APOLLO CONTROL: The next major stay-no stay will be for the T2 event. That is at 21 minutes 26 seconds after initiation of power descent.

COLUMBIA: Up telemetry command reset to re-acquire on high gain.

HOUSTON: Copy. Out.

APOLLO CONTROL: We have an unofficial time for that touchdown of 102 hours, 45 minutes, 42 seconds and we will update that.

HOUSTON: Eagle, you loaded R2 wrong. We want 10254.

TRANQUILITY BASE: Roger. Do you want the horizontal 55 15.2?

HOUSTON: That's affirmative.

APOLLO CONTROL: We're now less than four minutes from our next stay-no stay. It will be for one complete revolution of the command module.

One of the first things that Armstrong and Aldrin will do after getting their next stay-no stay will be to remove their helmets and gloves.

HOUSTON: Eagle, you are stay for T2. Over.

Continued on Page 4, Col. 1

VOYAGE TO THE MOON

By ARCHIBALD MacLEISH

Presence among us,

      wanderer in our skies,

dazzle of silver in our leaves and on our
waters silver,

O

silver evasion in our farthest thought—
"the visiting moon" . . . "the glimpses of the moon" . . .

and we have touched you!

      From the first of time,
before the first of time, before the
first men tasted time, we thought of you.
You were a wonder to us, unattainable,
a longing past the reach of longing,
a light beyond our light, our lives—perhaps
a meaning to us . . .

  Now
our hands have touched you in your depth of night.

Three days and three nights we journeyed,
steered by farthest stars, climbed outward,
crossed the invisible tide-rip where the floating dust
falls one way or the other in the void between,
followed that other down, encountered
cold, faced death—unfathomable emptiness . . .

Then, the fourth day evening, we descended,
made fast, set foot at dawn upon your beaches,
sifted between our fingers your cold sand.

We stand here in the dusk, the cold, the silence . . .

and here, as at the first of time, we lift our heads.
Over us, more beautiful than the moon, a
moon, a wonder to us, unattainable,
a longing past the reach of longing,
a light beyond our light, our lives—perhaps
a meaning to us . . .

    O, a meaning!

over us on these, silent beaches the bright
earth,

    presence among us

Neil A. Armstrong moves away from the leg of the landing craft after taking the first step on the surface of the moon

The New York Times from C.B.S. News
Col. Edwin E. Aldrin Jr. climbing down the ladder. The television camera was attached to a side of the lunar module.

Associated Press
Mr. Armstrong, right, and Colonel Aldrin raise the U.S. flag. A metal rod at right angles to the mast keeps flag unfurled.

A Powdery Surface Is Closely Explored

By JOHN NOBLE WILFORD
Special to The New York Times

HOUSTON, Monday, July 21—Men have landed and walked on the moon.

Two Americans, astronauts of Apollo 11, steered their fragile four-legged lunar module safely and smoothly to the historic landing yesterday at 4:17:40 P.M., Eastern daylight time.

Neil A. Armstrong, the 38-year-old civilian commander, radioed to earth and the mission control room here:

"Houston, Tranquility Base here. The Eagle has landed."

The first men to reach the moon—Mr. Armstrong and his co-pilot, Col. Edwin E. Aldrin Jr. of the Air Force—brought their ship to rest on a level, rock-strewn plain near the southwestern shore of the arid Sea of Tranquility.

About six and a half hours later, Mr. Armstrong opened the landing craft's hatch, stepped slowly down the ladder and declared as he planted the first human footprint on the lunar crust:

"That's one small step for man, one giant leap for mankind."

His first step on the moon came at 10:56:20 P.M., as a television camera outside the craft transmitted his every move to an awed and excited audience of hundreds of millions of people on earth.

Tentative Steps Test Soil

Mr. Armstrong's initial steps were tentative tests of the lunar soil's firmness and of his ability to move about easily in his bulky white spacesuit and backpacks and under the influence of lunar gravity, which is one-sixth that of the earth.

"The surface is fine and powdery," the astronaut reported. "I can pick it up loosely with my toe. It does adhere in fine layers like powdered charcoal to the sole and sides of my boots. I only go in a small fraction of an inch, maybe an eighth of an inch. But I can see the footprints of my boots in the treads in the fine sandy particles.

After 19 minutes of Mr. Armstrong's testing, Colonel Aldrin joined him outside the craft.

The two men got busy setting up another television camera out from the lunar module, planting an American flag into the ground, scooping up soil and rock samples, deploying scientific experiments and hopping and loping about in a demonstration of their lunar agility.

They found walking and working on the moon less taxing than had been forecast. Mr. Armstrong once reported he was "very comfortable."

And people back on earth found the black-and-white television pictures of the bug-shaped lunar module and the men tramping about it so sharp and clear as to seem unreal, more like a toy and toy-like figures than human beings on the most daring and far-reaching expedition thus far undertaken.

Nixon Telephones Congratulations

During one break in the astronauts' work, President Nixon congratulated them from the White House in what, he said, "certainly has to be the most historic telephone call ever made."

"Because of what you have done," the President told the astronauts, "the heavens have become a part of man's world. And as you talk to us from the Sea of Tranquility it requires us to redouble our efforts to bring peace and tranquility to earth.

"For one priceless moment in the whole history of man all the people on this earth are truly one—one in their pride in what you have done and one in our prayers that you will return safely to earth."

Mr. Armstrong replied:

"Thank you Mr. President. It's a great honor and privilege for us to be here representing not only the United States but men of peace of all nations, men with interests and a curiosity and men with a vision for the future."

Mr. Armstrong and Colonel Aldrin returned to their landing craft and closed the hatch at 1:12 A.M., 2 hours 21 minutes after opening the hatch on the moon. While the third member of the crew, Lieut. Col. Michael Collins of the Air Force, kept his orbital vigil overhead in the command ship, the two moon explorers settled down to sleep.

Outside their vehicle the astronauts had found a bleak

Continued on Pages 2, Col. 1

Today's 4-Part Issue of The Times

This morning's issue of The New York Times is divided into four parts. The first part is devoted to news of Apollo 11 and includes Editorials and letters to the Editor (Page 16). Poems on the landing on the moon appear on Page 17.

General news begins on the first page of the second part. The News Summary and Index is on the first page of the third part, which includes sports news, obituaries (Page 51) and transportation news and weather reports (Pages 50 and 52).

Financial and business news begins on the first page of the fourth part.

Following is the News Index for today's issue:

1970 - 1975

"All the News That's Fit to Print"

The New York Times

LATE CITY EDITION
Weather: Cloudy but clearing today.
Fair tonight. Cloudy, mild tomorrow.
Temp. range: today 51-43; Tuesday 48-42. Full U.S. report on Page 85.

VOL. CXIX..No. 40,989   © 1970 The New York Times Company.   NEW YORK, WEDNESDAY, APRIL 15, 1970   10 CENTS

CREW OF CRIPPLED APOLLO 13 STARTS BACK AFTER ROUNDING MOON AND FIRING ROCKET; MEN APPEAR CALM DESPITE LOW RESERVES

Judge Blackmun of Minnesota Is Named To Supreme Court Seat by the President

Nominee, 61, Is Regarded as a Scholarly Jurist

By ROBERT B. SEMPLE Jr.
Special to The New York Times

WASHINGTON, April 14—President Nixon today nominated Harry Andrew Blackmun of Minnesota to the Supreme Court.

Judge Blackmun, a member of the United States Court of Appeals for the Eighth Circuit, is regarded in the legal profession as a scholarly and mildly conservative judge.

Mr. Nixon's third choice for the vacancy created by the resignation of Abe Fortas was announced by Ronald L. Ziegler, the White House press secretary, late this afternoon. The President did not appear and did not issue a statement. Mr. Ziegler made the announcement while standing on the same small platform in the new White House press head-

United Press International
Judge Harry A. Blackmun in St. Louis yesterday.

quarters where Mr. Nixon last Thursday accused the Senate of hypocrisy and regional bias for refusing to approve his first two nominees for the vacancy.

The two men, both Southern-

A Prolonged Examination by Senate Panel Seen

ers, were Clement F. Haynsworth Jr. and G. Harrold Carswell. The Senate rejected Judge Haynsworth last November and Judge Carswell last Wednesday.

Judge Blackmun will also require Senate confirmation, but early reaction to his nomination on Capitol Hill was inconclusive. On the basis of the Senate's recent performance, however, it seemed likely that Judge Blackmun would be subjected to prolonged and searching examination by the Senate Judiciary Committee. Until that time, there may be a reluctance on the part of many Senators to commit themselves.

Senator Sam J. Ervin Jr., Democrat of North Carolina and a senior member of the Judiciary Committee, refused to

Continued on Page 34, Column 3

RISE OF 30% URGED IN CITY REALTY TAX

G.O.P. Leaders in Albany Call On Mayor to Accept $440-Million Package

By RICHARD PHALON
Special to The New York Times

ALBANY, April 14 — Mayor Lindsay arrived here tonight for talks with Republican legislators on the city's financial problems facing the possibility that he might have to adopt a $440-million package of real estate tax increases.

The package, which some Republican leaders are urging as a part-answer to the $630-million the Mayor says he needs to balance the budget next fiscal year, would raise the real estate tax rate from $5.52 per $100 to around $7 per $100 of assessed valuation —an increase of almost 30 per cent.

City budget officials said about $200-million of the package would go into effect next year through normal growth of assessed valuations and an expected increase in the equalization rate designed to iron out variations in assessment practices throughout the city.

The Mayor's mission here tonight is to persuade the Republican leaders that the city is entitled to more state aid on the basis of the tax effort it is already making and on the basis of the additional "do it yourself" revenue measures he has had introduced here in the closing days of the session.

Continued on Page 36, Column 4

Adm. Moorer Named To Head Joint Chiefs

Special to The New York Times

WASHINGTON, April 14 — President Nixon today named Adm. Thomas H. Moorer, Chief of Naval Operations, as chairman of the Joint Chiefs of Staff, the nation's highest ranking military officer.

If confirmed by the Senate and no obstacles to confirmation are foreseen here—Admiral Moorer will be the second Navy man to hold the post. Adm. Arthur W. Radford was chairman from 1953 to 1957, in the Eisenhower Administration.

Mr. Nixon also disclosed his intention to nominate Vice Adm. Elmo R. Zumwalt Jr., commander of naval forces in Vietnam and chief of the Naval Advisory Group, United States Military Assistance Command

Continued on Page 14, Column 4

Brezhnev Says Soviet Aim Is 'Reasonable' Arms Pact

By BERNARD GWERTZMAN
Special to The New York Times

MOSCOW, April 14—Leonid I. Brezhnev, the Soviet Communist party leader, said today that the Soviet Union would welcome "a reasonable agreement" with the United States on limiting strategic arms when the second round of Soviet-American talks begins in Vienna on Thursday.

After loud and prolonged applause, Mr. Brezhnev added: "We cannot act otherwise."

His wide-ranging foreign policy speech covered the Middle East, Vietnam and Europe, in which he broke no new ground, and relations with China, which he said were being harmed by what he called continuing anti-Soviet war hysteria in Peking.

Last night's speech was devoted entirely to economic problems and reflected his view that the Soviet Union must adopt technological advances and rally the people to overcome its mediocre economic showing of recent years.

His critical words on how the

Excerpts from Brezhnev talk are printed on Page 17.

military superiority over the Soviet Union "we will reply with the necessary increase in military might that guarantees our defense."

Continued on Page 17, Column 1

U.S. Arrests Russian Skipper In Alaska Gulf for Spilling Oil

By ROBERT M. SMITH
Special to The New York Times

WASHINGTON, April 14—A Coast Guard cutter sent a boarding party aboard a Soviet tanker in the Gulf of Alaska last night and arrested the ship's master on charges of spilling a mile-long oil slick near Kodiak Island.

The master of the Soviet vessel, V. C. Sherstobitov, has been flown to Anchorage where he is awaiting arraignment under the Refuse Act of 1899. His ship, the 345-foot motor vessel Mozyr, is still standing by near Kodiak Island.

In response to questions about an unconfirmed report that became available here, the State Department said the Soviet captain had been arrested.

According to information obtained by telephone from the scene, the American boarding party—consisting of a young operations officer, a representative of the Bureau of Fisheries and a seaman-photographer—encountered no resistance.

The Americans spent several hours on board the Soviet vessel while Captain Sherstobitov waited for his fleet commander in Vladivostok to tell him whether he should go with the Americans.

Comdr. John H. Byrd Jr. of New London, Conn., was the captain of the Coast Guard cutter involved, the Storis. Commander Byrd was reached today by telephone on Kodiak

Continued on Page 74, Column 4

Cambodia Appeals To World for Arms

By HENRY KAMM
Special to The New York Times

PNOMPENH, Cambodia, April 14—Premier Lon Nol issued an urgent appeal tonight for arms from any country that wanted to provide them.

[The State Department said the United States had received no request. Other sources expected one and predicted that it would be granted.]

In a broadcast statement in French and Cambodian, the Premier declared:

"The Salvation Government has the duty to inform the nation that in view of the gravity of the present situation, it finds it necessary to accept all unconditional foreign aid, wherever it may come from, for the salvation of the nation."

The Premier underlined the

Continued on Page 3, Column 1

VOYAGE OF A STRICKEN SPACESHIP: Apollo 13, its hopes for America's third lunar landing dashed by a ruptured oxygen tank, arced around the moon last night on a course that would bring it back to earth on Friday.

BEFORE FLIGHT: Capt. James A. Lovell Jr., Fred W. Haise Jr. and John L. Swigert Jr.

SENATE APPROVES TV CAMPAIGN CURB

Limit in Spending on Races for Federal Offices Voted Over G.O.P. Opposition

By JOHN W. FINNEY
Special to The New York Times

WASHINGTON, April 14 — Over Republican opposition, the Senate approved today campaign reform legislation designed to limit and perhaps reduce the mounting spending on political broadcasts over television and radio.

The legislation would place a ceiling on how much a candidate for Federal office could spend on television and radio broadcasts. In addition, it would reduce the rates at which broadcasting stations sell air time to political candidates.

The spending limitations were incorporated in legislation repealing the so-called "equal time" provision in the communications act, thus permitting the television and radio networks to provide free broadcast time for the Presidential and Vice-Presidential candidates in the 1972 elections without giving comparable time to every minor candidate. Whether or not this free time is to be used for debates, as it was in the 1960 Presidential elections, or for some other format is to be worked out by the candidates and the networks.

The campaign reform legislation, first proposed two years ago, passed the Senate with unexpected ease after only one day of debate. It now goes to the House, where, as in the Senate, the Democratic majority is expected to prevail over Republican opposition.

The legislation is designed to

Continued on Page 86, Column 4

Plight of 3 Crewmen Stirs World Interest and Prayer

By MARTIN ARNOLD

Suddenly, in the moment it takes an oxygen tank to spring a leak, the flight of Apollo 13 was no longer something everybody took for granted and was even slightly bored with.

For all around the world yesterday, during the Apollo 13 emergency, there was a surge of interest in the flight and there were prayers, and anguish also, for the three men who were fighting to get their crippled spaceship home.

The world-wide shift in interest in Apollo 13 was best summed up in two printed lines—one in an Italian newspaper, the other in a French paper.

Before the bad news broke, Milan's Il Giorno commented in a headline: "Too Perfect; the Public Is Getting Bored."

Yesterday morning, in Paris, Le Monde said: "The whole human race is participating with them in the agony of their return."

In the United States there was an outpouring of prayer, and here and there some expression of bitterness, too, that man was reaching toward space without

Continued on Page 29, Column 4

having first solved the problems on earth.

Both the Senate and House passed resolutions yesterday asking all Americans to pray at 9 o'clock Eastern standard time last night, for the safe return of their countrymen. And they urged businesses and communications media to pause briefly, if they could, for the prayers at that hour.

Special services and masses were called for in thousands of churches and synagogues around the country — at St. Patrick's Cathedral and St. Thomas Episcopal Church and Temple Emanu-El in New York City, for example.

Rabbi Abraham Gross, president of the Rabbinical Alliance of America, called on all clergymen to pray for the safe return of Apollo 13, and, in Baltimore, Frank Gunter Jr., Maryland chairman of the National Conference of Christians and Jews, asked all residents of the state to observe a minute of silent prayer at 4 P.M. yesterday.

In Montgomery, Ala., T.R. Hennessey, a retired Air Force

Continued on Page 29, Column 7

TARGET IS PACIFIC

Chance of Safe Return Deemed 'Excellent' Despite the Risks

Excerpts from conversations with spacecraft, Page 28.

By JOHN NOBLE WILFORD
Special to The New York Times

HOUSTON, Wednesday, April 15—With the lives of its three astronauts hanging in the balance, the crippled spaceship Apollo 13 swung around the moon last night and rocketed toward an emergency splashdown in the Pacific Ocean Friday.

After the craft looped the moon, a crucial four-minute and 24-second rocket firing sent the astronauts on a fast and more accurate course — a drastic change of plans caused by Monday night's massive power failure aboard the moon-bound spacecraft.

The rocket blast started at 9:41 P.M. Eastern standard time as the astronauts, depending on their attached lunar landing craft as a back-up return craft, pulled away about 6,000 miles from the right side of the moon.

"That was a good burn," Mission Control radioed after the lunar module's descent rocket shut down on schedule.

Though its success sent the first ripple of relief through Mission Control in the three-man crew, Capt. James A. Lovell Jr. of the Navy and Fred W. Haise Jr. and John L. Swigert Jr., both civilians, were still a long way from home and not yet out of trouble.

A Race With Time

The three astronauts were calm, despite the fact that they were racing time, trying to reach the earth before their severely limited reserves of oxygen, electricity and water ran out.

Grim-faced flight directors here called it "the most critical situation" in the history of the American space program. But, barring any further trouble, they said the chances of the astronauts' safe return were "excellent."

A rising carbon-dioxide level in the spacecraft stirred new concern late last night for the astronauts' safety. The amount rose to the point where it triggered an alarm light, but Mission Control said it was prepared to have it go to twice that level to conserve the lithium hydroxide chemical used to cleanse the cabin atmosphere.

Laboratory tests have shown that triple the present level can be tolerated without signs of organic damage, space agency doctors said.

NASA scientists were de-

Continued on Page 28, Column 3

NIXON IS BRIEFED ON APOLLO CRISIS

Meets With Space Experts During Unannounced Visit to Center in Maryland

By RICHARD D. LYONS
Special to The New York Times

GREENBELT, Md., April 14—President Nixon, looking taut and tired, met with technical experts of the space agency here for 45 minutes this afternoon and was briefed about the past and future problems of the Apollo 13 mission.

Dr. John F. Clark, director of the National Aeronautics and Space Administration's Goddard Space Flight Center here, said that the President was deeply concerned and that he asked "many knowledgeable questions" about the mission's problems and "the contingencies that have been planned."

This center is the eyes, ears and touch of Apollo 13. It is here that all the information transmitted by the spaceship is collected from 17 tracking stations around the world and sent on to the Manned Spacecraft Center in Houston for analysis.

Unannounced Visit

Hatless and dressed in a tan raincoat, dark blue suit and blue striped tie, Mr. Nixon made an unannounced visit to the center, driving from the White House, 13 miles away.

The President had been briefed by his aides three times during the night and early this morning about the sudden power loss in the Apollo 13 spaceship as it was heading toward the moon. According to Ronald L. Ziegler, the White House press secretary, Mr. Nixon was informed about 4 A.M. today that the corrective firing of the lunar module's engine would bring the space craft on a free return to earth.

"The President will be receiving reports throughout the day

Continued on Page 29, Column 7

The New York Times (by Edward Hausner)
PRAY FOR ASTRONAUTS: Worshippers at a special mass at St. Patrick's Cathedral for the crew of Apollo 13

"All the News That's Fit to Print"

The New York Times

LATE CITY EDITION

Weather: Partly sunny today; fair tonight. Partly cloudy tomorrow. Temp. range: today 75-59; Friday 85-66. Temp.-Hum. Index yesterday 77. Full U.S. report on Page 56.

VOL.CXIX...No. 41,055

© 1970 The New York Times Company.

NEW YORK, SATURDAY, JUNE 20, 1970

15 CENTS

COMMISSION ASKS CANADA TO REDUCE DRUG PENALTIES

Report to Government Calls for End to Prison Terms in Cases of Possession

OTTAWA WEIGHS ACTION

Indicates Marijuana May Be Removed From Narcotic List but Not Legalized

Excerpts from the commission's report are on Page 6.

By JAY WALZ
Special to The New York Times

OTTAWA, June 19—An official commission recommended today that Canada radically relax her laws banning or restricting the use of narcotics.

It called for the abolition of prison terms for those convicted of possessing any mind-altering drugs. The category includes marijuana, opium, heroin and LSD.

It said simple possession of these drugs should be considered a minor offense subject to a fine of not more than $100.

At present marijuana smokers, as narcotics users, may come before criminal courts and on conviction. receive fines ranging to $2,000 and jail sentences up to seven years. Many first offenders, however, come before magistrates, authorized to impose fines or jail sentences of five days, often suspended.

The commission said it was not prepared to recommend that the use of marijuana be legalized. but had decided the Cannabis group. including marijuana and hashish, should be moved from the jurisdiction of the severe Narcotics Control Act to that of the more permissive Food and Drugs Act.

These recommendations came from the five-member Commission on Nonmedical Use of Drugs. led by Gerald LeDain, law dean at York University in Toronto. which has been study-

Continued on Page 6, Column 1

U.S. Withdraws Backing Of Loan to Penn Central

By ROBERT E. BEDINGFIELD

The Nixon Administration, in a reversal of plans, decided yesterday not to guarantee up to $200-million of bank loans for the financially troubled Penn Central Company and its huge railroad subsidiary, the Penn Central Transportation Company.

Daniel Z. Henkin, Assistant Secretary of Defense for Public Affairs, said the Defense Department had refused to sign a guarantee of the borrowing "in the light of growing uncertainty regarding the enactment of legislation," which the White House has asked, that would give railroads guarantees for 15 years of loans up to $750-million.

The White House was "aware that the Department of Defense has made this decision and concurred in it," according to Ronald L. Ziegler, the President's press secretary. When asked where the Defense Department's decision. left the railroad, Mr. Ziegler said details would have to come from the Defense Department. He said only that it was his under-

standing that the Penn Central loan is no longer under consideration.

The withdrawal of the Government's promised guarantee of the Penn Central's credit was a complete surprise to railroad observers, who are aware that the Penn Central is in desperate need of funds to meet its millions of dollars' worth of commercial paper (short-term notes) maturing daily.

"Oh my God!" exclaimed a senior officer of one of the Penn Central's principal bank creditors when he was informed of the Defense Department's decision.

"We had been led to believe they would guarantee the loan," the banker said. "This is totally disturbing."

He added that his bank is in

Continued on Page 44, Column 3

Melville Sentenced To 13 to 18 Years In Bombings Here

By CRAIG R. WHITNEY

Samuel J. Melville, who a month ago admitted a plot to bomb eight Manhattan office buildings last fall, began a 13-to-18-year prison term yesterday after being sentenced in heavily guarded Federal and state courtrooms.

The 34-year-old engineering technician, who by his own admission became a bomb-throwing radical, gave a clenched-fist salute after Federal Judge Milton Pollack gave him 13 years—the second of two sentences he received yesterday—and went off to the Tombs.

Judge Pollack imposed the maximum sentence—10 years—for Melville's. confessed bombing of the Federal office building at 26 Federal Plaza, and said: "Congress could well

Continued on Page 18, Column 1

MITCHELL SPURS JACKSON INQUIRY

Calls a Special Grand Jury After Mississippi Ignores Ultimatum in Shootings

By FRED P. GRAHAM
Special to The New York Times

WASHINGTON, June 19—A special Federal grand jury will be convened in Jackson, Miss., on June 29 to investigate the fatal shooting of two students last month at Jackson State College, Attorney General John N. Mitchell announced today.

Mr. Mitchell warned, during a visit to the campus of the predominantly Negro college last month, that he would take "appropriate action" to get the facts if state officials failed to cooperate with the Justice Department's investigation of the incident.

Today's announcement suggested that Mr. Mitchell's patience had worn thin. The special grand jury will convene only a week before the formation on July 6 of a regular Federal grand jury, which had been expected to undertake the investigation of the incident.

Meeting of Jury Noted

Mr. Mitchell took note in his statement of the forthcoming meeting of the regular grand jury. But he said that nonetheless he had dispatched Assistant Attorney General Jerris Leonard to Jackson last Tuesday to urge Chief Judge William Harold Cox to call the special grand jury.

The special jury "will make a detailed investigation of what actually happened on this occasion" to determine whether or not any Federal laws were violated, Mr. Mitchell said.

Judge Cox called state and Federal officials before him on Tuesday and ordered them "to fully cooperate and coordinate their efforts," Mr. Mitchell said.

A state grand jury is also scheduled to convene on July

Continued on Page 18, Column 1

Prosecutor Scores City Police On Delays in Detective's Trial

By LESLEY OELSNER

Alfred J. Scotti, chief assistant district attorney of Manhattan, scored the Police Department yesterday for having failed to finish its departmental trial of a detective accused of dishonesty before that detective's retirement, and right to a police pension, became final.

"I'm outraged, I'm really angry." said Mr. Scotti, who until yest day had firmly defended the Police Department's efforts to investigate and regulate itself. "How are we going to deter these crooks, these certain corrupt police, from being corrupt when they can always get their pensions?"

The police allowed Detective Michael Martin "to slip through their hands," Mr. Scotti said, by the "unnecessarily protracted manner" in which it han-

died his trial on charges of selling confidential police information to banks, airlines, detective agencies and other companies.

The Police Department did not finish Detective Martin's trial within the 30-day period following his submission of retirement papers. Under the city's administrative code, a conviction must be obtained within 30 days if a policeman is to be barred from his pension rights.

According to Mr. Scotti, the trial of Detective Martin should have been a "simple matter" and could have been completed "far before the 30-day period ended." on midnight Thursday.

Mr. Scotti said that his office would now seek an indictment

Continued on Page 25, Column 1

SOYUZ 9 RETURNS AFTER 17-DAY TRIP SETS SPACE MARK

2 Russian Astronauts Well Following Test of Ability to Man Orbiting Stations

By BERNARD GWERTZMAN
Special to The New York Times

MOSCOW, June 19—Two Soviet astronauts, Col. Andrian G. Nikolayev and Vitaly A. Sevastyanov, landed safely on the earth today after the longest manned flight in history aboard the Soyuz 9 spacecraft.

Tass, the Soviet press agency, announced that the command capsule carrying Colonel Nikolayev, 40 years old, and Mr. Sevastyanov, 34, made a soft landing about 47 miles west of the city of Karaganda, in Soviet Kazakhstan, at 2:59 P.M., Moscow time (7:59 A.M. Eastern daylight time).

"A quick medical checkup of the astronauts showed that they had withstood the prolonged space flight well," Tass reported.

U.S. Held Previous Record

In all, the Soyuz 9 was orbiting the earth for 17 days 16 hours and 59 minutes. The previous endurance record was 13 days 18 hours and 35 minutes by two Americans, Col. Frank Borman and Capt. James A. Lovell Jr., aboard Gemini 7 in December, 1965.

The main goal of the Soviet flight was to test the astronauts' ability to withstand long periods of weightlessness. This is important, scientists have stressed, because men will be called upon to spend long periods, perhaps months, in permanent earth-orbiting stations, which both the Soviet Union and the United States plan to build in this decade.

A congratulatory message sent Colonel Nikolayev and Mr. Sevastyanov by the Soviet Communist party and Government underscored this aim. The message termed the flight "a new, important step in astronautics."

'Basis for Future Flights'

"It marks the beginning of long manned space flights," the message said, and "will serve as the basis for future space flights and will bring closer the time of building permanent orbital stations."

Leonid I. Brezhnev, the Communist party General Secretary, announced last October that space stations were the Soviet goal, and Mstislav V. Keldysh, president of the Soviet Academy of Sciences, has predicted that about five years of work would be needed before a station could be placed into orbit.

These stations would have the dual function of serving as launching pads for flights into outer space and as laboratories for conducting scientific work dealing with the cosmos and the earth.

As usual with Soviet manned flights, there was no advance word that the Soyuz 9 mission was reaching its end, although an article this morning in Pravda, the Communist party newspaper, about the craft's parachute system led to speculation that a landing was near.

First word of the touchdown was broadcast as a bulletin about 3:45 P.M., about 45 min-

Continued on Page 8, Column 4

Edward Heath leaving 10 Downing Street after courtesy call on Harold Wilson yesterday

A short time later, Mr. Wilson and his wife moved out of the official London residence

Associated Press

HEATH BECOMES PRIME MINISTER; MAKES A PLEDGE TO UNITE BRITAIN; CONTROLS COMMONS BY 30 SEATS

WILSON DISPLACED

Liberals Are Crushed and Labor's Seats Decline by 59

Special to The New York Times

LONDON, June 19—Edward Heath moved into 10 Downing Street tonight as the new Conservative party Prime Minister of Britain.

A tide of votes from up-country areas, as forecast by computers during the night, carried his party to victory in the general election yesterday. It will have a margin of 30 seats in the new Parliament.

From the steps of the historic house where he will live and work, Mr. Heath, who is a 53-year-old bachelor, told a crowd that his purpose would be "not to divide but to unite." In the phrase of his great Tory predecessor Disraeli, he said he would k to create "one nation."

Dispelling Divisive Image

His first statement as Prime Minister was plainly intended to dispel the divisive image of Enoch Powell, the right-wing Conservative, who won by a big majority. Mr. Powell caused a national uproar by campaigning on issues of race and disorder.

The final results for the 630 seats in the House of Commons, compared with those for the last Parliament just before dissolution, are as follows:

	New	Old
Conservative	330	262
Labor	287	346
Liberal	6	13
Other	7	7
Vacant	—	2

That gave the Conservatives a margin of 30 over all others in the House, a workable figure, in the opinion of most experts. The Tories governed from 1951 to 1955 with a margin of 17.

Today, after 7 P.M., Queen Elizabeth II gave Mr. Heath his commission to form a Government. He kissed her hands and had the job.

Harold Wilson, Labor party Prime Minister since October, 1964, had gone to Buckingham Palace a few minutes earlier. After many visits as the Queen's principal adviser, he went this time to tender his

Continued on Page 12, Column 1

BRITISH MARKETS BUOYED BY TORIES

Election Victory Sets Off 'Colossal' Buying Surge

By JOHN M. LEE
Special to The New York Times

LONDON, June 19—Champagne corks popped in some London brokerage offices today as financial markets gave Britain's new Conservative Government a huge vote of confidence.

The London Stock Exchange opened with a burst of buying that brokers described as "colossal." The Financial Times industrial share index scored a record rise of 22.6 points in the first hour of trading. Profit taking brought the gain back to 16.9 points at the closing figure of 351.5.

The demand for British Government securities was so great that dealers complained they could get only 25 per cent to 50 per cent of the bonds ordered.

The pound sterling reflected support by international bankers—the oft-decried "gnomes of Zurich" — and rose smartly

Continued on Page 39, Column 1

In West Cambodia, Weak Army Waits

By SYDNEY H. SCHANBERG
Special to The New York Times

SISOPHON, Cambodia, June 19—The flies that swarm through the tilting barracks seem to be in control of the decaying army garrison in this town in Cambodia's northwest.

This is the headquarters of four battalions, but three and a half of them consist of raw recruits. Most of the officers and noncommissioned officers apparently have been called up from the reserves.

The situation at the Sisophon garrison is indicative of the Cambodian Army's condition throughout this area. It is weak, unprepared and highly vulnerable to enemy assault.

An 800-mile drive through the western part of the coun-

try revealed key bridges unguarded. New troops sent out on operations against the North Vietnamese and Vietcong enemy sometimes do little more than march up and down the main road. Most of the Government checkpoints and guard posts are manned by teen-age students, some of them girls, all eager but totally untrained. Many long stretches of road leading to major towns and installations have no Government military presence at all.

The commandant at Sisophon, Lieut. Col. Suos Chea, told some visitors that the railway and highway bridges from his garrison to the border with Thailand, 30 miles away, were of major concern, but he seemed pessimistic about his ability to protect

them effectively against Communist attacks or sabotage.

Like every military commander one meets in Cambodia these days, the colonel lamented his lack of modern arms, equipment and even uniforms and boots.

The colonel, who sat on the rickety front porch of his quarters, oblivious to the flies that buzzed around him and on him, said the only thing his troops had enough of was food.

Only a handful of the colonel's troops are in the garrison now. They could be seen peering out the windows of their peeling, cracking barracks, waiting for a monsoon downpour.

The others have been sent

Continued on Page 3, Column 2

Air Force Deploys Multiple Warheads on Missiles

Special to The New York Times

WASHINGTON, June 19—The United States reached an important milestone today in the important development of arms technology by announcing that it had deployed multiple warheads on some American intercontinental missiles.

In a 70-word statement, the Air Force announced: "We can now say that the Strategic Air Command has assumed responsibility for the first flight of these missiles at Minot Air Force Base, North Dakota."

The statement said the first flight consisted of 10 missiles and one launching control facility, but avoided stating explicitly that the triple warhead had been mounted on the missile. It was made clear, however, that the S.A.C. would not assume responsibility for missiles that were not operational.

In the view of most weapons experts, the deployment of these multiple, independently targeted re-entry vehicles, known as MIRV's, which were originally developed in re-

sponse to antiballistic missiles by the Soviet Union, heralds the opening of a new era in the strategic arms race.

Heretofore, nuclear missiles have been equipped with one warhead to each missile. But with MIRV's, each side in the arms race can now increase greatly the number of thermonuclear warheads it can launch without adding to the number of missiles.

The Minuteman 3 missiles for example, are replacing in underground silos the older generation Minuteman 2, a more conventional weapon. The Minuteman 3 is armed with three warheads.

To its supporters, the MIRV represents an important advance in nuclear weaponry, primarily as a means to penetrate missile defenses. The deployment at Minot Air Force Base is the first step in the planned replacement of 500 Minuteman 1 and 2 missiles with MIRV's.

To its critics, the multiple warhead represents a dangerous new stage in the escalating arms race, a road-

block on the path to an agreement on the limitation of strategic arms, and an irreversible step in the direction of more nuclear weapons.

Critics in the Senate and elsewhere have argued that the continued testing and deployment of the MIRV after a 22-month testing program will induce the Russians to continue their own tests.

This, in turn, is expected to harden the bargaining positions of both sides at the strategic-arms limitation talks in Vienna, although Administration and Defense Department officials have said that the MIRV missiles can be scrapped if a pact to that effect is reached with the Soviet Union. On June 4, for example, Dr. John S. Foster Jr., the Pentagon's director of defense research and engineering, suggested to a Senate subcommittee that this country's development of MIRV and antiballistic missiles could be halted if the Russians agreed.

But the limitation or banning

Continued on Page 2, Column 3

AFTER RETURN TO EARTH: Vitaly I. Sevastyanov, left, and Col. Andrian G. Nikolayev eating their first meal after the Soyuz 9 spacecraft landed in Kazakhstan Their space endurance record was 17 days and almost 17 hours.

Tass via Associated Press

The New York Times

LATE CITY EDITION

Weather: Sunny, cool today; clear, cool tonight. Fair, mild tomorrow. Temp. range: today 60-48; Monday 66-52. Full U.S. report on Page 85.

VOL.CXX..No.41,156
© 1970 The New York Times Company.
NEW YORK, TUESDAY, SEPTEMBER 29, 1970
15 CENTS

VATICAN CITY: President Nixon with Pope Paul VI during special audience yesterday. Later, he flew by helicopter to U.S.S. Saratoga, with Sixth Fleet in the Mediterranean.
United Press International

NASSER DIES OF HEART ATTACK; BLOW TO PEACE EFFORTS SEEN; NIXON CANCELS FLEET EXERCISE

A GESTURE BY U.S.

President Terms Loss Tragic—He Joins Fleet Off Italy

By Reuters

ABOARD U.S.S. SARATOGA, in the Mediterranean, Tuesday, Sept. 29—President Nixon last night ordered cancellation of today's exercises of the United States Sixth Fleet in the Mediterranean because of the death of President Gamal Abdel Nasser of Egypt.

The President, who arrived aboard this aircraft carrier last night, had planned to watch a demonstration of Sixth Fleet firepower, including the launching and recovery of aircraft.

Officials said: "Upon hearing of the death of President Nasser, the President ordered the cancellation of the firepower demonstration, which were to be held in conjunction with his visit to the Sixth Fleet."

They said that Mr. Nixon's conferences with Sixth Fleet commanders aboard the flagship Springfield would go on as scheduled.

The President flew to this carrier off the coast of Italy by helicopter after a day in which he had conferred in Rome with the President and the Premier of Italy and with Pope Paul VI.

'Tragic Loss'

The President in a statement said that the death of President Nasser was a tragic loss of an outstanding Arab leader.

"I was shocked to hear of the sudden death of President Nasser," Mr. Nixon said. "The world has lost an outstanding leader who tirelessly and devotedly served the causes of his countrymen and the Arab world.

"This tragic loss requires that all nations, and particularly those in the Middle East, resume their efforts to calm passions, reach for mutual understanding and building lasting peace.

"On behalf of the American people I extended deep sympathy to his family and to his people."

Stresses Role of Fleet

Earlier Mr. Nixon had told the men of the Saratoga that never had American military and diplomatic power been used more effectively than in the latest Middle East crisis.

Chatting with sailors who greeted his helicopter on the flight deck, Mr. Nixon spoke of "a hard two or three weeks," which he said had been capped by success. He referred to the Jordanian truce and recovery of the hostages from the hijacked airliners.

"The fact that we were successful is the fact that you were there," he told the sailors. He mentioned their

Continued on Page 19, Column 1

President Gamal Abdel Nasser bidding good-by to King Hussein of Jordan after meeting in Cairo yesterday. From ceremony, he returned home where he died of heart attack.
United Press International

U.S. Officials See Period Of Instability in Mideast

By TERENCE SMITH
Special to The New York Times

WASHINGTON, Sept. 28 — United States officials, startled by the death of Gamal Abdel Nasser, tended to view it today as a blow to peace-making efforts in the Middle East.

A ranking State Department official described the Egyptian President's death as a "critical loss at a decisive moment in history."

The immediate reaction of officials here was that it would bring a period of instability in the Arab world and would therefore reduce the already-thin prospects for negotiating an early resolution of the Arab-Israeli dispute.

[In Moscow, Western diplomats expected the Soviet leaders to assure the United Arab Republic that President Nasser's death would not affect Soviet support for the Arab cause. Page 17.]

An hour before the Cairo radio announcement, a cable from Donald C. Bergus, the senior United States representative in Cairo, reported a

rumor that the Egyptian leader was critically ill or perhaps dead. The message was being decoded as the public announcement came.

Six hours earlier Rodger P. Davies, the Acting Assistant Secretary of State for Near Eastern and South Asian Affairs, had told a closed session of the House Foreign Affairs Committee that the Nixon Administration was "leaning toward optimism" about the prospects of getting the United States-sponsored peace initiative in the Middle East back on the track.

The Senate was informed of the news by Senator John C. Stennis, Democrat of Mississippi, who interrupted a debate on election relations. He described Mr. Nasser, the leader in Cairo since 1952, as "superior to most anyone who might have been in power."

"I hope his death does not mean upheaval and turmoil in

Continued on Page 19, Column 1

Arab Truce Observers Arrive In Generally Peaceful Amman

By ERIC PACE
Special to The New York Times

AMMAN, Jordan, Sept. 28—One hundred foreign Arab officers arrived here today to serve on the peace-keeping observer teams that will be deployed in Amman under the agreement reached yesterday in Cairo to end hostilities between the Jordanian Government and the Palestinian commandos.

The cease-fire instituted last Friday after nine days of civil

populous area around the Hussein Mosque at the heart of the city, where gunfire was occasionally heard during the day.

Despite a further provision of the Cairo agreement for a release of detainees, scores were still visible this morning at the army prison camp on the way to the airport. As their women peered in through the barbed-wire fence, they were seated in orderly rows, apparently being indoctrinated by their Jordanian Army captors.

The army appeared generally to be trying to finish its clean-up of Ashrafiyeh, once a commando stronghold. Aside from that, no wide-scale military operations were known to be under way. The general calm this morning followed radio broadcasts of the 14-point agreement signed by King Hus-

Continued on Page 18, Column 5

ARAB-WORLD HERO

Vice President Sadat Takes Over as the Interim Leader

Obituary article will be found on Page 16.

By RAYMOND H. ANDERSON
Special to The New York Times

CAIRO, Tuesday, Sept. 29—President Gamal Abdel Nasser, leader of Egypt for 18 years and hero of much of the Arab world, died here yesterday.

The Government radio said the 52-year-old President was the victim of a heart attack.

The death was announced on Cairo's television and radio stations shortly before 11 P.M. by Vice President Anwar Sadat. An hour earlier, regular programs on television and radio were abruptly suspended and replaced with chanting of verses from the Koran. Official mourning was proclaimed for 40 days.

The President suffered the heart attack at 3 P.M. and died three hours later.

No obvious successor to Mr. Nasser was in sight, and no Egyptian seemed in a mood tonight to speculate about the matter.

Funeral Will Be Thursday

Vice President Sadat took over as interim ruler. He reported that emergency meetings had been held by the higher executive committee of the Arab Socialist Union, the political organization created by Mr. Nasser, and the Council of Ministers.

President Nasser's funeral will be held Thursday.

The impact of Mr. Nasser's death will be felt throughout the Arab world. Despite controversies and rivalries during his long years of power, he was the strongest figure of leadership among the Arabs.

Since the battlefield defeat of three Arab armies by Israel in June, 1967, Mr. Nasser was the leader who rallied the Arabs to rebuild their forces for a war of liberation if other means to recover the lands failed.

Favored Political Solution

But he repeatedly emphasized that he favored a political solution of the conflict with Israel if one could be achieved.

Although Mr. Nasser gained a reputation as a fire-breathing radical in his early years in power as a force for moderation and pragmatism.

Even on the emotional issue of Israel, he was able to swing much of the Arab world behind his acceptance in July of a United States initiative for a cease-fire and he revived efforts for a negotiated settlement. The outlook for pursuing

Continued on Page 17, Column 1

THE ARAB WORLD IS GRIEF-STRICKEN

Moslems Fire Rifles Into Air as Sign of Mourning —Koran Read on Radio

By JOHN L. HESS
Special to The New York Times

BEIRUT, Lebanon, Sept. 28—The Arab world went into mourning tonight over the loss of its major international figure. Arab distress was heightened by the fear that instability would increase in the area and diminish the already slender prospect of peace.

Television stations went off the air and radio programs were replaced by chants and readings from the Koran. In Beirut, Moslems fired thousands of shots into the air as a sign of emotion for the loss of Gamal Abdel Nasser. Men walked in the streets in impromptu procession declaiming "Allah Akbar!"—"God is great."

Security forces reacted to thwart rioting of the kind that followed President Nasser's offer of resignation after the six-day war of June, 1967.

Youths started bonfires of automobile tires and a crowd began collecting outside the United States Embassy.

[A senior Cabinet minister in Israel said that the Israelis now appeared to face an indefinite stalemate on peace negotiations. Page 18.]

Observers here said that President Nasser was the only Arab

Continued on Page 17, Column 7

Fourth Group of Hostages Here After Seeing President in Rome

By ROBERT D. McFADDEN

Thirty-three travel-weary Americans, whose ordinary lives became the focus of international concern during three harrowing weeks while they were hostages in Jordan, arrived at Kennedy International Airport last night and were met by loved ones, friends and a clamoring throng of newsmen.

The passengers—26 men, 6 women and an infant—were the fourth group of Americans brought home safely from an ordeal that began with multiple hijackings Sept. 6. All but two of the 33 were released in Amman over the weekend and flown home through Nicosia, Cyprus, and Rome.

Their faces were haggard but smiling and their clothes rumpled after a 12-hour flight from Rome, where they met President Nixon in the morning. They stepped off a chartered flight at the Trans World Airlines terminal shortly after 6 P.M. They were quickly ushered through Customs and led into a private room for a reunion with 175 relatives.

Nearly 1,000 friends greeted them in the corridors and public waiting rooms as they emerged.

Six Americans are still being held of the original group on three hijacked planes. They are someplace in Jordan.

Contrary to the confused reports at three previous returning flights, passengers who were reluctant to talk were not besieged by newsmen trusting cameras and microphones into

Continued on Page 18, Column 2

50,000 FLEE BLAZE IN SAN DIEGO AREA

Brush Fire, 30 Miles Long, Is California's Biggest Yet —5 Die in Copter Crash

By United Press International

LOS ANGELES, Sept. 28—The largest brush fire in California history raged today through mountain canyons near the Mexican border, driving thousands of persons from their homes as the flames advanced.

In the San Gabriel Mountains to the north, a helicopter being used by the United States Forest Service to fight another fire crashed late today, killing the five persons aboard.

More than 50,000 persons were evacuated from small communities in San Diego County. The 200-acre fire there erupted in the Cleveland National Forest on Saturday when a falling tree severed a power line. At least 250 structures have been destroyed.

Decreasing winds tonight and a forecast of scattered showers in mountain areas raised hopes that the blaze could be contained tomorrow.

Arson Arrests Made

The enormous blaze, 30 miles from tip to tip, eclipsed in size the Matailaja fire of 1930, which burned 125,000 acres in Kern and Los Angeles Counties.

"We've barely kept up with the situation," said Arlen B. Cartwright of the State Division of Forestry. "The problem seems to come from the fact that fire nuts run around and see flames and smoke and this makes them want to set more fires—which they do."

Arson was suspected in two other major blazes in San Diego County, and five arrests were made in Los Angeles County.

More than 5,000 men worked 36-hour shifts on the fire lines and the neighboring county of San Bernardino was stripped of all but five of its fire engines.

Continued on Page 10, Column 2

Malpractice Suits Reported Soaring

By LAWRENCE K. ALTMAN

Witnesses at a State Senate public hearing testified here yesterday that a steep rise in medical malpractice suits was forcing physicians to practice "defensive medicine" shirk hazardous modes of treatment that could be of benefit to patients, and pass along the costs of skyrocketing insurance premiums to patients.

"One physician of every six has been sued for malpractice," State Senator Norman F. Lent told the hearing. And more than 10,000 Americans will initiate medical malpractice suits this year, Senator Lent, who is chairman of the Senate Committee on Health, added.

Because some insurance companies find medical malpractice insurance unprofitable, wit-

Continued on Page 32, Column 1

Intrepid Wins Series, 4-1, And Keeps America's Cup

By STEVE CADY
Special to The New York Times

NEWPORT, R.I., Sept. 28 — The longest series in 100 years of America's Cup challenges came to a desperately dramatic close today with Intrepid completing a 4-1 conquest of Gretel II.

Once again, the defender of yachting's most famous prize had to fight off almost constant pressure by the chunky Australian challenger.

Until a wind shift put Intrepid in clover starting the final leg of the 24.3-mile race, the action had been about as close as a boat race can produce. The cynics say watching two yachts is like watching grass grow, but the grass was on fire again today, as it was so often during this controversial series.

Stage Set for Upset

When Gretel II closed to within two boat lengths at the fifth mark, the stage was set for another upset of the kind the Australian sloop brought off last Thursday. Then the wind shifted from north to east, Intrepid hit it on the right tack and the suspense evaporated.

With the final windward leg turned into a race, the redesigned 1967 defender opened up

and came home safely, 1 minute 44 seconds ahead.

As Intrepid swept majestically across the line about 250 yards ahead of her dangerous rival, the familiar dream of another successful Cup defense began unfolding. Horns, whistles and sirens aboard some 150 spectator boats and Coast Guard patrol vessels cut loose with a noisy salute to the American yacht—the second ever to defend the Cup twice.

A Triumphant Allusion

Bill Ficker, the 42-year-old Californian with the bald head and the bold starting-line maneuvers, shook hands with his young crew. They, in turn, hoisted a "Ficker Is Quicker" flag to the top of Intrepid's mast, a triumphant allusion to the tactical swiftness of their skipper.

In today's race, Ficker and his young stalwarts had to be quicker. Jim Hardy gave Gretel II a slight lead at the start but Ficker took it away early on the opening windward leg. He spent the rest of a cold, overcast afternoon desperately keeping the Aussies from breaking through in the fluky

Continued on Page 53, Column 1

John Dos Passos Is Dead at 74; Acclaimed for 'U.S.A.' Trilogy

Special to The New York Times

BALTIMORE, Sept. 28—John Dos Passos, the novelist of the post-World War I generation who wrote more than 30 books, including the trilogy "U.S.A.," died today in his apartment.

Mr. Dos Passos, who was 74 years old, had been troubled by a heart ailment in recent years and was released only Saturday from Good Samaritan Hospital. When not away on his extensive travels, he divided his time between his apartment here and a home in Westmoreland, Va.

Mr. Dos Passos is survived by his widow, the former Elizabeth Hamlin Holdridge; their daughter, Lucy, and a stepson, Christopher Holdridge.

A funeral service will be held Thursday at 10 A.M. at the William Cook-Brooks Funeral Home in the nearby town of Towson, Md.

Gil Friedberg-Pix
John Dos Passos

Fame From Early Books

By ALDEN WHITMAN

The life and writings of John Dos Passos were marked by a progression from left to right. "Every day I become more Red," he said in his youth. "My one ambition is to be able to sing 'The International.'" But in middle and old age, he turned against his former ideas, berating liberals, Socialists and Communists with zeal. The one-time writer for The New Masses became a contributor to The National Review; the friend of Ernest Hemingway became that of William F. Buckley Jr.; and the supporter of

William Z. Foster turned into the backer of Barry Goldwater.

His novels, too, marched rightward. The trilogy "U.S.A.," completed in 1936 and generally recognized as one of the hinges of modern fiction, was a painstakingly detailed and angry portrait of industrial America between 1898 and 1929. It concluded with the heroine's joining the Communist party in revulsion over what she believed were the injustices of the Sacco-Vanzetti case.

His subsequent trilogy, "District of Columbia," completed in 1949, acerbically chronicled what the author clearly viewed as the failure of the New Deal.

Continued on Page 47, Column 1

Anti-Arab Jet Plot Laid to Seized Pair

By MORRIS KAPLAN

An Israeli Army veteran and his wife, accused of trying to board a London-bound plane here with a live hand grenade and four loaded guns hidden in their clothing, were reported yesterday to have planned to hijack an Arab airliner and take it to Israel.

Law - enforcement sources said that the couple reportedly had planned to board a United Arab Airlines plane bound for Cairo at the London airport and divert the flight to Israel "in retaliation" for a recent attempted hijacking of an El Al airliner in London.

The sources said that the veteran, Avraham Hershkovitz, had worked as a "manager" here for the Jewish Defense

Continued on Page 12, Column 3

war seemed generally effective this morning. There were no fires along the capital's skyline, although a few bursts of firing resounded in the center of Amman and on Jebel Luweibida and Jebel Amman, two of the city's seven hills.

Law - enforcement sources reported that shelling or shooting was continuing in part of the Palestinians' Ashrafiyeh quarter, where many of the airline hostages had been held.

There was no sign that either the army or the commandos had abandoned their positions in Amman, as the Cairo agreement called for. The guerrillas are entrenched in a

---

The New York Times

LATE CITY EDITION

Weather: Partly sunny, mild today;
fair tonight. Cloudy, mild tomorrow.
Temp. range: today 49-35; Friday
40-26. Full U.S. report on Page 58.

VOL.CXX..No. 41,286   © 1971 The New York Times Company.   NEW YORK, SATURDAY, FEBRUARY 6, 1971   15 CENTS

2 ASTRONAUTS WALK AND WORK FOR HOURS ON MOON'S SURFACE

U.S. OFFICIALS FEEL NIXON HAS DECIDED ON STRIKE IN LAOS

Timing of South Vietnamese Drive Is Said to Depend on Pace of Build-up

By TERENCE SMITH
Special to The New York Times

WASHINGTON, Feb. 5 — Strong indications emerged here today that the Nixon Administration had decided to go ahead with a strike by South Vietnamese troops against enemy supply lines in southern Laos.

The Administration's official spokesmen continued, for the seventh consecutive day, to refuse any public comment on the possibility of such a strike, but officials not directly concerned with the planning said they believed the White House had decided within the last 48 hours to go ahead.

Roads and Bridges Rebuilt

The timing of the strike, the officials said, would depend upon how quickly the nearly 30,000 allied soldiers massed along the Laotian border could complete "stage one" of the new operation, called Dewey Canyon II.

In the initial stage, which began early last Saturday, the troops have swept westward across the northernmost tip of South Vietnam, scouring the countryside for enemy troops, rebuilding roads and bridges and reoccupying long-deserted allied outposts such as Khesanh and Langvei.

According to reports from the field, this work was still under way today. [Page 4.]

Army engineers were working around the clock to rehabilitate the airstrip at Khesanh and strengthen the bunkers that 6,000 American Marines occupied during a 77-day siege at the outpost three years ago.

Secure Base Sought

Little enemy resistance has been encountered in the first stage of the operation, despite intelligence reports that up to nine regiments of North Vietnamese regulars were in the rugged mountains along the border.

According to a White House source, the operation was conceived as a two-stage project, with the final decision to go into Laos hinging, among other considerations, on the amount of fighting encountered in the first stage.

The military planners reportedly considered it necessary to establish a secure base in the northwestern corner of South Vietnam before deciding whether to begin the second stage of the operation.

At least one intelligence report indicated that American

Continued on Page 5, Column 1

A Laotian General Cool to Bigger War

By HENRY KAMM
Special to The New York Times

DONG HENE, Laos, Feb. 5 — The commander of Laotian combat troops in the center of the panhandle of Laos said at his beleaguered forward command post today that the situation was critical and he did not expect to be able to hold out under mounting North Vietnamese pressure.

But the commander, Brig. Gen. Nouphet Deoheuong, said nobody had told him that less than 100 miles eastward in the northwest corner of South Vietnam, a large force of American and South Vietnamese troops was driving the enemy in his direction. His meagerly equipped, ragtag forces had received no reinforcements from the Laotian Government.

Continued on Page 6, Column 4

MAN ON MOON: Capt. Alan B. Shepard Jr. steps off module ladder onto lunar surface.

FOR THE RECORD: Captain Shepard, right, stands by the U.S. flag as Comdr. Edgar D. Mitchell snaps his picture. A TV camera transmitted the scene. At left, behind Commander Mitchell, are an umbrella-like communications antenna and, rear, the module.

C.B.S. News

2D WALK IS BEGUN

Hike to Crater Planned —Men Are to Rejoin Mother Ship Today

By JOHN NOBLE WILFORD
Special to The New York Times

HOUSTON, Saturday, Feb. 6 — Two American astronauts walked the gentle slopes of Fra Mauro yesterday, setting up instruments, collecting rocks and probing subsurface reaches in search of clues to the moon's earliest history.

While earthbound scientists eagerly watched their every televised step, Capt. Alan B. Shepard Jr. and Comdr. Edgar D. Mitchell of the Navy, the Apollo 14 explorers, spent more than four and one-half hours outside their landing craft, Antares.

Shortly before 3:30 A.M. today, the men began their second moon exploration.

The 47-year-old Captain Shepard opened the hatch at 9:49 A.M. Eastern standard time yesterday and stepped out on the "porch" at the top of the ladder.

The hatch remained open for four hours and 40 minutes, until 2:29 P.M.

"It certainly is a stark place here at Fra Mauro," he remarked, looking out at the undulating hills and ridges, the gray and brown soil, the distant craters and the black sky above.

Nuclear-Powered Station

During the moon walk, Captain Shepard and Commander Mitchell established a nuclear-powered scientific station to record moonquakes, measure electrically charged particles and detect the composition and energies of solar wind. The first signals from the seismometers were of the astronauts' own footsteps.

The two men also "thumped" the ancient moon surface with small explosive charges that sent vibrations to depths of 70 feet for indications of the rubble-like structure below the surface. In addition, the astronauts gathered soil and rocks, two of which were as big as footballs.

It was the first of the two scheduled moon excursions by the two astronauts, who landed early yesterday in the Fra Mauro highlands for a planned 33½-hour visit.

Their explorations are considered the most intensive and ambitious made thus far on the moon. Scientists are especially interested in Fra Mauro because it may have rocks as old as the solar system itself.

Men Awaken Early

The second moon walk had originally been scheduled for 5:30 this morning, but the two astronauts awoke from a nap sooner than expected and received permission to begin their walk of up to five hours.

"We're up and running this morning," Commander Shepard reported at 12:23. "The shape of the crew is excellent."

A hike out to a boulder-rimmed crater about 2,000 feet from Antares was planned.

After the second walk, the astronauts are to fire the ascent engine of Antares at 1:47 P.M. to leave the moon and rejoin the command ship, Kitty Hawk.

Maj. Stuart A. Roosa of the Air Force, the third crew member, is piloting Kitty Hawk in a 70-mile-high lunar orbit. Fra Mauro lies near the lunar equator at the eastern edge of the Ocean of Storms.

Continued on Page 12, Column 1

JURY CALLS POLICE IN GAMING INQUIRY

Looks Into Charges That 30 Were Involved With Major Gambler in Brooklyn

By DAVID BURNHAM

A Brooklyn grand jury is investigating reports of corrupt links among more than 30 policemen and former policemen, a judge and a gambling empire allegedly operated by a Brooklyn figure with a long criminal record.

The investigation is based on evidence collected during the last year by the office of District Attorney Eugene Gold and the internal affairs division of the Police Department.

More than 50 known gamblers, policemen and former policemen already have been subpoenaed. One of the first subpoenas was handed on Thursday to Thomas Marino, 72 years old, reportedly the operator of the gambling ring.

In another development involving possible corruption, the State Supreme Court yesterday upheld the legality of the subpoenas for 14 policemen,

Continued on Page 14, Column 4

Court Upholds Patrolmen On Retroactive Pay Claim

By DAMON STETSON

State Supreme Court Justice Irving H. Saypol ruled yesterday that the Patrolmen's Benevolent Association had a valid contract with the city requiring a $100-a-month retroactive pay increase for 27,000 patrolmen.

The contract that the judge ruled "enforceable" ran from Oct. 1, 1968, to Dec. 31, 1970, so that the total of retroactive pay that the patrolmen claim is $2,700 each for the 27-month period.

The increase is based on a pay-parity provision in the contract saying the patrolmen should be paid at a rate of $3 for every $3.50 paid to sergeants.

Issue Not Settled

The issue, which has been in the courts for nearly a year and spurred a strike by the policemen last month, is still not settled, however.

A spokesman for Mayor Lindsay said that on advice of the Corporation Counsel, J. Lee Rankin, the city was going to appeal Judge Saypol's decision. The Mayor, the spokesman said, has asked the Corporation Counsel to expedite

the appeal on the decision, which could cost the city hundreds of millions of dollars.

The appeal to the Appellate Division and then, perhaps, to the State Court of Appeals could take weeks or even months, lawyers said.

Edward J. Kiernan, president of the P.B.A., said the decision of Justice Saypol "reaffirmed my confidence in the court system."

Dissidents Noted

In an oblique reference to dissident members of the association who led last month's strike of policemen without P.B.A. sanction, Mr. Kiernan said the ruling should restore the faith of all policemen in the court structure. He recalled that the P.B.A. leadership had urged the strikers to get back on the job and trust the courts to deal fairly with the patrolmen's suit.

The policemen struck after the Court of Appeals ruled last month that a trial must be held to determine the validity of the contract.

John J. Loflin Jr., who represented the city in the trial be-

Continued on Page 14, Column 4

DEFECTIVE SWITCH POSED A PROBLEM

A Short Circuit That Could Have Aborted the Landing Required New Program

By RICHARD WITKIN

It took some ingenious rewriting of a computer program and about 60 rapid-fire punches on a cockpit keyboard to clear the way for the Apollo lunar landing yesterday.

The difficulty, described by officials as a "very serious" problem, was apparently in a cockpit switch that was producing intermittent short circuits.

The two astronauts aboard the lunar module were never endangered by the trouble. But it threatened to delay the landing attempt for one, two, or even three more lunar orbits. And there was an outside chance it could have canceled the landing attempt altogether.

Other Problems Cited

There were other technical aberrations that cropped up during the descent from lunar orbit to the Fra Mauro landing site, notably the distressing delay in proper functioning of the landing radar. However, it was the misbehaving switch that caused the day's biggest commotion.

The difficulty turned up at 1:30 a.m., less than three hours before the landing ship Antares was to start its final descent to the moon.

At the space agency's control center in Houston, engineers monitoring the operations of every spacecraft system saw a "spurious" number turn up on a console. The num-

Continued on Page 12, Column 2

Direct From Moon

Following are conversations between flight controllers in Houston and Capt. Alan B. Shepard Jr. and Comdr. Edgar D. Mitchell of the Navy, as recorded by The New York Times. The conversations occurred during the first moon walk yesterday, when the astronauts left the lunar lander, Antares.

ANTARES (9:49 A.M.)—Forward hatch the rest of the way open. O.K., forward hatch is open.

MITCHELL—I'll get your antenna as you go out.

SHEPARD — All righty, starting out the door.

HOUSTON—Shortly Shepard will be throwing the equipment conveyor belt.

MITCHELL — While he's working on the LEC [lunar equipment conveyor] let me comment that it certainly is a stark place here. I think it's quite all the more stark by the fact that the sky is completely black.

SHEPARD—Starting down the ladder.

HOUSTON—Roger . . . O.K. Al, beautiful. We see you coming down the ladder now. It looks like you're about on the bottom step—and on the surface. How's that for an old man?

SHEPARD — O.K., you're right. Al is on the surface. It's been a long way, but we're here. Now I can see

the reason we have a tilt is we landed on a slope. The landing gear struts appear to be about evenly depressed. Moving around, getting familiar with the surface. The surface in which the forward footpad landed is extremely soft. As a matter of fact, it's in a small depression. The soil is so soft that it comes up all the way to the top of the footpads.

HOUSTON—Roger.

SHEPARD—O. K., we'll move on over and take a look at Fra Mauro. Take a look at Cone Crater, which is right where it should be and is a very impressive sight.

HOUSTON—Antares, this is Houston. You are go for two-man EVA [extravehicular activity]. Over.

MITCHELL—Roger, Houston. Thank you.

SHEPARD—Continuing, we can see the boulders on the rim. It looks as though we have a good traverse route

Continued on Page 12, Column 6

Unemployment Rate Down For First Time in 7 Months

By EILEEN SHANAHAN
Special to The New York Times

WASHINGTON, Feb. 5—The statistics for last year changed somewhat in January, its first decline in seven months, the Labor Department reported today.

The actual number of people out of work rose, however, as it generally does in January, to 5.4 million, the largest number in 10 years.

The unemployment rate is adjusted to eliminate the effects of normal seasonal changes, a procedure designed to make the underlying trend clearer.

Secretary of Labor James D. Hodgson attributed "great significance" to the downturn in the unemployment rate in January, coupled with other developments in the labor market.

On the other hand, Harold Goldstein, the Assistant Commissioner of Labor Statistics, described the change as "marginally significant." Mr. Goldstein is a career civil servant and the Bureau of Labor Statistics, where he works, is a traditionally nonpartisan division of the Labor Department.

The January statistics also present a somewhat confusing picture, partly because a routine revision in some of the

unemployment rate dropped the basis for comparison.

The unemployment rate for December, originally reported as 6 per cent, was revised upward to 6.2 per cent.

On the revised basis, the January rate was 6 per cent, a drop of two-tenths of a percentage point from the December level.

As it turned out, a drop of two-tenths of a percentage point would have been recorded if the revisions had not taken place. On the unrevised basis, the January rate would have been 5.8 per cent.

These revisions, which are made annually, incorporate the most up-to-date information on the adjustments in the raw figures that are needed to eliminate purely seasonal influences. The idea of revising the figures and the process by which they are revised are accepted as valid by all economists and statisticians in the field.

The differing interpretations of the figures made by Secretary Hodgson and Mr. Goldstein were unrelated to the revision in the seasonal adjustments, although some seasonal developments figured in the

Continued on Page 22, Column 1

City Seeks New Unit To Finance Housing

By STEVEN R. WEISMAN

Mayor Lindsay yesterday announced a bipartisan drive to seek the creation of a city housing finance agency that would float $700 million in bonds to provide mortgages for 25,000 new and rehabilitated apartments here in two years.

The push to gain approval of the measure by the Legislature, Mr. Lindsay said, will be "the city's No. 1 state legislative priority."

Under the bill, bonds of the proposed New York City Housing Development Corporation would be backed up by the "moral obligation," but not the full faith and credit, of New York City. In this manner, the corporation could be created without changing the city's debt limit, which is imposed by the

Continued on Page 16, Column 5

WARNING!
NO U.S. PERSONNEL
BEYOND THIS POINT

Associated Press

NEAR THE LAOTIAN BORDER: G.I.'s posting a warning near Langvei in South Vietnam. U.S. ground forces are forbidden to cross into Laos, about 200 yards beyond the sign.

NEWS INDEX			
	Page		Page
Antiques	33	Movies	20-21
Art	24-25	Music	20-21
Books	27	Obituaries	5
Bridge	26	Op-Ed	31
Business	39, 47	Society	31
Churches	34	Sports	33-37
Crossword	27	Theaters	20-21
Editorials	30	Transportation	58
Financial	39-47	TV and Radio	55
Letters	30	U.S.	
Man in the News	5	Women's News	23

News Summary and Index, Page 31

The New York Times

LATE CITY EDITION
Weather: Chance of showers today,
tonight. Partly sunny tomorrow.
Temp. range: today 74-94; Wed.
72-91. Temp. Hum. Index yesterday
82. Full U.S. report on Page 94.

VOL. CXX...No. 41,431   © 1971 The New York Times Company   NEW YORK, THURSDAY, JULY 1, 1971   15 CENTS

SUPREME COURT, 6-3, UPHOLDS NEWSPAPERS ON PUBLICATION OF THE PENTAGON REPORT; TIMES RESUMES ITS SERIES, HALTED 15 DAYS

Nixon Says Turks Agree To Ban the Opium Poppy

By JOHN HERBERS
Special to The New York Times

WASHINGTON, June 30—President Nixon announced today that Turkey had agreed to eliminate within a year her production of opium poppies, which account for about two-thirds of the illegal heroin reaching the United States.

Mr. Nixon, in a brief announcement delivered in the White House press room, said that as a result of negotiations between the United States and Turkish Governments, Premier Nihat Erim had agreed to ban altogether the cultivation of opium poppies by June, 1972.

He said the joint announcement, made simultaneously in Washington and Ankara, "represents by far the most significant breakthrough that has been achieved in stopping the source of supply of heroin in our worldwide offensive against dangerous drugs."

Two weeks ago, Mr. Nixon sent a message to William J. Handley, the United States Ambassador in Turkey, saying that the time for talk had passed and the United States must have action by the Turkish Government in ending poppy cultivation.

Today, the President praised Premier Erim for "courageous, statesmanlike action" and said the United States would provide money and technical assistance in helping Turkish farmers shift to other crops.

Officials would not say how much American money would be involved, but the United States has made a $3-million commitment to Turkey on the heroin problem.

Secretary of State William P. Rogers, who helped work

Continued on Page 22, Column 1

Soviet Starts an Inquiry Into 3 Astronauts' Deaths

By BERNARD GWERTZMAN
Special to The New York Times

MOSCOW, June 30—The Soviet authorities appointed a special commission tonight to investigate the deaths of their three astronauts who perished this morning when their Soyuz 11 craft was returning to earth after the longest manned space flight in history.

News of the astronauts' deaths shocked many Soviet people. And Western specialists predicted that their deaths would retard development of the Salyut space station program. The three astronauts had spent more than three weeks working and exercising aboard the Salyut craft, described as the world's first space laboratory.

[In the United States, American officials said the Soviet space disaster had probably been caused by a failure in the oxygen supply. They also said the accident should not delay United States space flights. Articles on Page 30.]

Tonight, the Soviet people seemed caught up in the human aspects of the disaster and the mystery of what caused the deaths of Lieut. Col. Georgi T. Dobrovolsky, the flight commander, Vladislav N. Volkov, the flight engineer, and Viktor I. Patsayev, the test engineer.

Were their deaths caused by the weakened state of their bodies after nearly 24 days of weightlessness? Were they

Continued on Page 30, Column 3

PRESIDENT CALLS STEEL AND LABOR TO WHITE HOUSE

He Asks Both Sides to Meet With Him Tuesday Before Contract Talks Start

By PHILIP SHABECOFF
Special to The New York Times

WASHINGTON, June 30—President Nixon has called the negotiators of the steel companies and steelworkers union to meet with him next Tuesday before they sit down to begin contract negotiations, a White House spokesman announced today.

It will be the first time that the President will have met with labor and management in any industry prior to nationwide contract negotiations, according to Ronald L. Ziegler, the White House press secretary.

Discussion Issues Listed

Mr. Ziegler said that the President had called the meeting to discuss general economic developments and trends in the world steel markets.

Earlier today, the chairman of the Federal Reserve Board, Arthur F. Burns, told a Congressional committee that the "first priority" should be given to a new Government move to try to moderate price and wage increases and expressed his concern over the spread of "inflationary psychology" in this country.

The Administration has repeatedly warned that excessive increases in steel wages and prices would severely retard efforts to control inflation. Hints have been dropped that import quotas that protect domestic steel from foreign competition will be eased or lifted if prices go too high.

President Nixon has been in-

Continued on Page 38, Column 1

Pentagon Papers: Study Reports Kennedy Made 'Gamble' Into a 'Broad Commitment'

By HEDRICK SMITH

The Pentagon's study of the Vietnam war concludes that President John F. Kennedy transformed the "limited-risk gamble" of the Eisenhower Administration into a "broad commitment" to prevent Communist domination of South Vietnam.

Although Mr. Kennedy resisted pressures for putting American ground-combat units into South Vietnam, the Pentagon analysts say, he took a series of actions that significantly expanded the American military and political involvement in Vietnam but nonetheless left President Lyndon B. Johnson with as bad a situation as Mr. Kennedy inherited.

"The dilemma of the U.S. involvement dating from the Kennedy era," the Pentagon study observes, was to use "only limited means to achieve excessive ends."

Moreover, according to the study, prepared in 1967-68 by Government analysts, the Kennedy tactics deepened the American involvement in Vietnam piecemeal, with each step minimizing public recognition that the American role was growing.

The expansion of that role, over three decades, is traced in the 3,000 pages of the Pentagon's study, which is ac-

companied by 4,000 pages of documents on the Vietnam era. Previous articles in The Times's presentation of this material have recounted President Johnson's movement to war in 1964 and 1965.

President Kennedy made his first fresh commitments to Vietnam secretly. The Pentagon study discloses that in the spring of 1961 the President ordered 400

> The Times today resumes its series of articles on the Pentagon's secret study of the Vietnam war. The study was obtained through the investigative reporting of Neil Sheehan, and the articles were researched and written over three months by Mr. Sheehan and other staff members. The fourth and fifth articles, both by Hedrick Smith, are published today and form an account of decisions in the Kennedy Administration.
> Three pages of documentary material covering the Kennedy policy begin on Page 3, and documents on the 1963 coup begin on Page 9. A summary of the three earlier articles, covering the Johnson Administration, appears on Page 15.

Special Forces troops and 100 other American military advisers sent to South Vietnam. No publicity was given to either move.

Small as the numbers seem in retrospect, the Pentagon study comments that even the first such expansion "signaled a willingness to go beyond the 685-man limit on the size of the U.S. [military] mission in Vietnam, which, if it were done openly, would be the first formal breach of the Geneva agreement." Under the interpretation of that agreement in effect since 1956, the United States war limited to 685 military advisers in Vietnam. Washington, while it did not sign the accord, pledged not to undermine it.

On May 11, 1961, the day on which President Kennedy decided to send the Special Forces, he also ordered the start of a campaign of clandestine warfare against North Vietnam, to be conducted by South Vietnamese agents directed and trained by the Central Intelligence Agency and some American Special Forces troops. [See text, action memorandum, May 11, 1961, Page 3.]

The President's instructions, as quoted in the documents, were, "In North Vietnam . . . [to] form networks of resistance, covert bases and teams for

Continued on Page 6, Column 1

U.S. and Diem's Overthrow: Step by Step

The Pentagon's secret study of the Vietnam war discloses that President Kennedy knew and approved of plans for the military coup d'état that overthrew President Ngo Dinh Diem in 1963.

"Our complicity in his overthrow heightened our responsibilities and our commitment" in Vietnam, the study finds.

In August and October of 1963, the narrative recounts, the United States gave its support to a cabal of army generals bent on removing the controversial leader, whose rise to power Mr. Kennedy had backed in speeches in the middle nineteen-fifties and who had been the anchor of American policy in Vietnam for nine years.

The coup, one of the most dramatic episodes in the history of the American involvement in Vietnam, was a watershed. As the Pentagon study observes, it was a time when Washington—with the Diem regime gone—could have reconsidered its entire commitment to South Vietnam and decided to disengage.

At least two Administration officials advocated disengagement but, according to the Pentagon study, it "was never

seriously considered a policy alternative because of the assumption that an independent, non-Communist SVN was too important a strategic interest to abandon."

The effect, according to this account, was that the United States, discovering after the coup that the war against the Vietcong had been going much worse than officials previously thought, felt compelled to do more—rather than less—for Saigon. By supporting the anti-Diem coup, the analyst asserts, "the U.S. inadvertently deepened its involvement. The inadvertence is the key factor."

According to the Pentagon account of the 1963 events in Saigon, Washington did not originate the anti-Diem coup, nor did American forces intervene in any way, even to try to prevent the assassinations of Mr. Diem and his brother Ngo Dinh Nhu, who, as the chief Diem political adviser, had accumulated immense power. Popular discontent with the Diem regime focused on Mr. Nhu and his wife.

But for weeks—and with the White House informed every step of the way—

the American mission in Saigon maintained secret contacts with the plotting generals through one of the Central Intelligence Agency's most experienced and versatile operatives, an Indochina veteran, Lieut. Col. Lucien Conein. The colonel, who is now in retirement, first landed in Vietnam in 1944 to parachute for the Office of Strategic Services, the wartime forerunner of the C.I.A.

So trusted by the Vietnamese generals was Colonel Conein that he was in their midst at Vietnamese General Staff headquarters as they launched the coup. Indeed, on Oct. 25, a week earlier, in a cable to McGeorge Bundy, the President's special assistant for national security, Ambassador Lodge had occasion to describe Colonel Conein to the C.I.A.—referring to the agency, in code terminology, as C.A.S.—as the indispensable man:

"C.A.S. has been punctilious in carrying out my instructions. I have personally approved each meeting between General Don [one of three main plotters] and Conein who has carried out my

Continued on Page 12, Column 1

BURGER DISSENTS

First Amendment Rule Held to Block Most Prior Restraints

Decision, concurring opinions, dissents start on Page 17.

By FRED P. GRAHAM
Special to The New York Times

WASHINGTON, June 30 — The Supreme Court freed The New York Times and The Washington Post today to resume immediate publication of articles based on the secret Pentagon papers on the origins of the Vietnam war.

By a vote of 6 to 3 the Court held that any attempt by the Government to block news articles prior to publication bears "a heavy burden of presumption against its constitutionality."

In a historic test of that principle — the first effort by the Government to enjoin publication on the ground of national security — the Court declared that "the Government has not met that burden."

The brief judgment was read to a hushed courtroom by Chief Justice Warren E. Burger at 2:30 P.M. at a special session called three hours before.

Old Tradition Observed

The Chief Justice was one of the dissenters, along with Associate Justices Harry A. Blackmun and John M. Harlan, but because the decision was rendered in an unsigned opinion, the Chief Justice read it in court in accordance with long-standing custom.

In New York Arthur Ochs Sulzberger, president and publisher of The Times, said at a news conference that he had "never really doubted that this day would come and that we'd win." His reaction, he said, was "complete joy and delight."

The case had been expected to produce a landmark ruling on the circumstances under which prior restraint could be imposed upon the press, but because no opinion by a single Justice commanded the support of a majority, the unsigned opinion will show as little precedent.

Uncertainty Over Outcome

Because it came on the 15th day after The Times had been restrained from publishing further articles in its series mined from the 7,000 pages of material—the first such restraint "in the name of "national security" in the history of the United States—there was some uncertainty whether the press had scored a strong victory or whether a precedent for some degree of restraint had been set.

Alexander M. Bickel, the Yale law professor who had argued for The Times in the case, said in a telephone interview that the ruling placed the press in a "stronger position." He maintained that no Federal District Judge would henceforth temporarily restrain a newspaper on the Justice Department's complaint that "this is what they have printed and we don't like it" and that a direct threat of irreparable harm would have to be alleged.

However, the United States Solicitor General, Erwin N. Griswold, turned to another lawyer shortly after the Justices filed from the courtroom and remarked: "Maybe the newspapers will show a little

Continued on Page 15, Column 1

CHOU TIES U.N. SEAT TO TAIPEI'S OUSTER

Also Says Peking Must Have Permanent Council Post if It Is to Be Member

By TAKASHI OKA
Special to The New York Times

TOKYO, June 30 — Premier Chou En-lai of China said in an interview published here today that for his country to join the United Nations it was necessary not only that all membership rights be "restored," including a permanent seat in the Security Council, but that the Nationalists be ousted from the United Nations.

Mr. Chou made the comment in a meeting with Yoshikatsu Takeiri, chairman of Komeito, the Clean Government party, who is visiting Peking with eight of his followers. The Premier's comments were published today in the party newspaper Komei Shimbun as well as in other major Japanese newspapers.

"What Steps Are Necessary"

Mr. Chou's comments, which are consistent with the line Peking has taken on prospective United Nations membership, apparently weakened attempts by the United States, Japan and other interested members of the United Nations to safeguard at least a General Assembly seat for the Nationalists while admitting the Chinese Communists to the Security Council as well as the Assembly.

"What steps do you think are necessary in order to get China back into the United Nations?" Mr. Chou was asked.

Continued on Page 32, Column 4

Jim Garrison Is Arrested; U.S. Says He Took Bribes

By ROY REED
Special to The New York Times

NEW ORLEANS, June 30 — District Attorney Jim Garrison was arrested by Federal agents today and charged with taking bribes to protect illegal pinball gambling in New Orleans.

The Justice Department said that the last payment, $1,000, was delivered to Mr. Garrison at his home last night in marked $50 bills. The payment, the department said, was handed to him by a once-trusted confidant who had secretly gone to work for the Government's agents.

Mr. Garrison, 50 years old, who attempted to prove a conspiracy in the 1963 assassination of President Kennedy,

was taken into custody at his home. He was fingerprinted and placed under $5,000 bond by a Federal magistrate.

The Justice Department said that Mr. Garrison had taken up to $1,500 a month in bribes.

According to the Government, Mr. Garrison had received the bribes from pinball operators since 1962.

"I've never accepted a dollar in my life," the District Attorney told reporters as he walked into the French Quarter Courthouse to face the magistrate.

Mr. Garrison was one of 10 men arrested. The others in-

Continued on Page 55, Column 3

Cousin Asserts Jerome Johnson Told of Job With Italian League

By BARBARA CAMPBELL

A cousin of Jerome A. Johnson, who was shot to death at the site of a rally in Columbus Circle after allegedly firing three bullets into Joseph A. Colombo Sr., said yesterday that Johnson told him "several months ago" he was working for the Italian-American Civil Rights League as a photographer.

This latest development raised a series of questions for investigators. If Johnson was working for the league, was he known there? Was he an employe or a hanger-on, perhaps a temporary called in on occasion?

Chief of Detectives Albert A. Seedman said last night only that the telephone-number switch, if true, "certainly puts

a check by The New York Times disclosed yesterday that the number had been recently changed. The operator said the number had been switched to a new number, that of the Italian-American League.

About three months before the shooting, Johnson gave his cousin a telephone number where he could be reached and

Continued on Page 53, Column 1

THE STATES RATIFY FULL VOTE AT 18

Ohio Becomes 38th to Back the 26th Amendment

By R. W. APPLE Jr.
Special to The New York Times

WASHINGTON, June 30—The 26th Amendment to the Constitution, lowering to 18 years the minimum voting age in local and state as well as Federal elections, was ratified tonight.

Ohio became the 38th state to approve the Amendment when the state's House of Representatives, meeting in extraordinary evening session, gave its assent, 81 to 9. The Ohio Senate had approved the measure yesterday, 30 to 2.

The ratification of at least 38 states, or three-quarters of the total, is required for constitutional amendments.

An atmosphere of near-panic attended Ohio's climactic vote. The Republican chairman of the House, Charles F. Kurfess, had planned to let a number of members, both Republicans and Democrats, speak on the issue before calling for a vote.

But after only three short speeches, the Republican floor leader, Robert E. Leavitt, interrupted to warn:

"I've just been informed that the Legislature of Oklahoma

Continued on Page 43, Column 1

Conferees Cut Military Pay Rise As Authority to Draft Runs Out

By DAVID E. ROSENBAUM
Special to The New York Times

WASHINGTON, June 30 — The Nixon Administration suffered a major budgetary victory today in the House-Senate conference on the draft extension bill.

The conference agreement also appeared to represent a setback for supporters of an all-volunteer Army, who had sought larger pay increases than those cleared by the conferees.

The conferees accepted a figure for military pay and allowances that was more than $900-million below what the Senate and House had approved. The raises voted by the conferees would cost about $1.8-billion in the fiscal year starting tomorrow and would go into effect Oct. 1.

The figure approved by the conference was still $800-million above what President Nixon sought in his budget, but the House and Senate had passed increases of about $1.7-billion over the budget.

The Nixon Administration had argued that so large an increase would force severe and possibly dangerous reductions in other parts of the defense budget.

The Government's basic authority to draft men into the

military expires at midnight tonight.

The conferees completed action on all provisions of the draft bill today except the Senate-passed amendment that calls for the withdrawal of United States troops from Indochina within nine months if prisoners of war are first

Continued on Page 29, Column 1

False Advertising Laid to H&R Block

By JOHN D. MORRIS
Special to The New York Times

WASHINGTON, June 30 — H & R Block, Inc., which says it prepares income tax returns for eight million American annually, was accused by the Federal Trade Commission today of false advertising and illegally using confidential information supplied by customers.

The commission published similar but separate citations against H & R Block and the Beneficial Corporation, which offers income tax services on a smaller scale through a subsidiary, the Beneficial Management Corporation. In radio and television advertisements, the name

Continued on Page 57, Column 2

ACTION BY GRAVEL VEXES SENATORS

But No Disciplinary Action Against Him Is Expected

By JOHN W. FINNEY
Special to The New York Times

WASHINGTON, June 30 — Many Senators privately expressed dismay, shock and chagrin today at Senator Mike Gravel's release of parts of the Pentagon's secret study of the Vietnam war. But it appeared that no disciplinary action would be taken against the Alaska Democrat.

Last night Senator Gravel tried to read the documents to the Senate in an all-night speech and, when he was blocked for lack of a quorum, proceeded to call an impromptu meeting of his Senate Public Works subcommittee. He read from the study for three and one-half hours, with his voice sometimes breaking into sobs, and tears occasionally rolling down his face.

His action incurred the displeasure of many of his colleagues, who felt that it reflected on the dignity and composure of the Senate. But in the clublike atmosphere of the Senate, there was a widespread reluctance, extending down from the leadership, to take any formal disciplinary

Continued on Page 16, Column 2

"All the News That's Fit to Print"

The New York Times

LATE CITY EDITION

Weather: Variable cloudiness, mild today; fair tonight and tomorrow. Temp. range: today 70-78; Monday 71-75. Full U.S. report on Page 81.

VOL. CXX...No. 41,506

© 1971 The New York Times Company

NEW YORK, TUESDAY, SEPTEMBER 14, 1971

15 CENTS

BUSINESS FAVORS U.S. PANEL TO RULE PAY-PRICE POLICY

Leaders Urge President to Give the Private Sector Only an Advisory Role

MEET AT WHITE HOUSE

Oppose Curb on Profits in Phase Two of Program— Nixon Offers No Plan

By ROBERT B. SEMPLE Jr.
Special to The New York Times

WASHINGTON, Sept. 13— Spokesmen from the business community told President Nixon today that the next phase of the new economic strategy should be managed by the Federal Government, with the private sector playing essentially an advisory role.

Last Friday, union leaders who met with the President recommended the creation of a tripartite board representing labor, management and the general public to control wages and prices, without governmental interference, after the current 90-day freeze.

Confer Two Hours

This morning Mr. Nixon met for nearly two hours with 11 corporate executives and leaders of business associations in the second of a series of meetings designed to solicit ideas from various interest groups on what ought to be done to manage the economy after the current wage-price-rent freeze expires at midnight, Nov. 13.

Meanwhile, Secretary of the Treasury John B. Connally indicated that price controls in some form would be continued after the expiration of the freeze.

At today's meeting, according to the public statements of some participants and the private comments of others, most of the businessmen present told Mr. Nixon that the basic decisions on wage and price policy should remain with some kind of Government board.

They felt, however, that business, labor, agriculture and other groups should be consulted extensively before such decisions are made.

Typical Comment

It was not totally clear whether the business group thought that the private sector should have veto power over the decisions made by the Government board. But sources said that the consensus of the group was that business, labor and other groups should restrict themselves to offering suggestions and making recommendations, leaving ultimate wage-price decisions in the Government's hands.

A typical comment came from James M. Roche, chairman of General Motors, who was asked to address himself to labor's suggestion that a tripartite board draw up its own rules on what specific wages and prices should be controlled, rather

Continued on Page 26, Column 4

Common Market Agrees To Resist U.S. on Dollar

6 Finance Ministers Ask America to Devalue

By CLYDE H. FARNSWORTH
Special to The New York Times

BRUSSELS, Sept. 13—The European Common Market, in an assertive mood, temporarily buried its internal quarrels today to confront the United States with a uniform set of demands, including devaluation of the dollar, to resolve the monetary crisis.

Finance ministers of the six member countries of the trade bloc took the position that the United States would not get the multilateral upward revaluation of major foreign currencies that it is seeking until it agreed to eliminate its import surcharge and raise the official price of gold.

Stand Is Prepared

The six nations, which will probably be joined by other European powers (including Britain) and by Japan as well, were preparing the stand they will take at key monetary meetings later this month in London and Washington.

Observers said the effect of today's decision was to throw the ball back at President Nixon, who imposed the surcharge on Aug. 15 as a weapon to force currency valuations upward, a greater sharing of defense decisions in the Atlantic

Continued on Page 25, Column 5

Basic Payments Deficit Hits $9-Billion Rate

By PHILIP SHABECOFF
Special to The New York Times

WASHINGTON, Sept. 13— Paul A. Volcker, Under Secretary of the Treasury, disclosed publicly today that the United States' basic balance-of-payments deficit reached an annual rate of $9-billion in the first half of 1971.

It had been reported earlier that the basic deficit was so large that Mr. Volcker had shocked representatives of the group of 10 major trading nations at a meeting in Paris last week when he described its dimensions.

A $9-billion deficit for the year would be almost three times higher than the highest previous such deficit in recent American history.

Panel Hears Testimony

The basic balance of payments refers to all trade and monetary transactions with foreign countries except for erratic short-term capital flows. It is often regarded as the best measure of a country's true international payments position.

Mr. Volcker told the International Trade Subcommittee of the Senate Finance Committee today, "At the heart of this deterioration in our basic accounts was a severe decline in our merchandise trade balance."

In the years 1960-1969 the

Continued on Page 25, Column 1

Text of the finance ministers' agreement is on Page 25.

9 HOSTAGES AND 28 PRISONERS DIE AS 1,000 STORM PRISON IN ATTICA; 28 RESCUED, SCORES ARE INJURED

Elmer Huehn, released hostage, being greeted by his wife — *The New York Times*

Guard, who had been held, still dazed after being released — *Associated Press*

Relatives of hostages in Attica prison after being told that at least 15 of the men being held had been set free — *The New York Times/Michael Evans*

'LIKE A WAR ZONE'

Air and Ground Attack Follows Refusal of Convicts to Yield

By FRED FERRETTI
Special to the New York Times

ATTICA, N. Y., Sept. 13— The rebellion at the Attica Correctional Facility ended this morning in a bloody clash and mass deaths that four days of taut negotiations had sought to avert.

Thirty-seven men — 9 hostages and 28 prisoners — were killed as 1,000 state troopers, sheriff's deputies and prison guards stormed the prison under a low-flying pall of tear

Text of Oswald's statement is printed on Page 28.

gas dropped by helicopters. They retook from inmates the cellblocks they had captured last Thursday.

In this worst of recent American prison revolts, several of the hostages — prison guards and civilian workers — died when convicts slashed their throats with knives. Others were stabbed and beaten with clubs and lengths of pipe.

Most of the prisoners killed in the assault fell under the thick hail of rifle and shotgun fire laid down by the invading troopers.

Doctor Fears More Deaths

A volunteer doctor who worked among the wounded after the assault said the prison's interior was "like a war zone." Standing in front of the prison in a blood-stained white coat, he said that many more of the wounded "are likely to die."

Late today a deputy director of correction, Walter Dunbar, said that two of the hostages had been killed "before today" and that one had been stabbed and emasculated.

Of the remaining seven, five were killed instantly by the inmates and two died in the prison hospital.

Mr. Dunbar said that in addition to the 28 dead inmates, eight other convicts of the total of 2,237 were missing. Two of the dead prisoners, he said, were killed "by their own colleagues and lay in a large pool of blood in a fourth-tier cellblock."

Oswald Orders Attack

He said he considered the state's recapture of the prison an "efficient, affirmative police action."

The action was ordered with "extreme reluctance" by State Correction Commissioner Russell G. Oswald after consultation with Governor Rockefeller. It followed an ultimatum to the more than 1,000 rebellious prisoners that they release the hostages they held and return to their cells.

Most of the 28 hostages rescued by the invaders and scores of prisoners were treated for wounds and the effects

Continued on Page 28, Column 2

NIXON PANEL ASKS FREE TRADE MOVES

Urges Negotiations to End All Barriers in 25 Years— Labor Members Dissent

By EDWIN L. DALE Jr.
Special to The New York Times

WASHINGTON, Sept. 13—A Presidential commission, calling for a "new realism" in the nation's foreign economic and trade policy, said today that "the time has come to begin immediately a major series of international negotiations" with the long-term aim of "elimination of all barriers to international trade and capital movements within 25 years."

The basic thrust of the report of the 27-member Commission on International Trade and Investment Policy was in the direction of freer trade here and abroad. The two members from organized labor dissented from the entire report, calling for controls on the inflow of goods and the outflow of capital and technology.

The report, consisting of 307 pages and 147 recommendations, was presented to President Nixon today by the commission chairman, Albert L.

Continued on Page 24, Column 1

A summary of the panel's recommendations, Page 24.

Knowles Will Head Rockefeller Fund; Lost Out on U.S. Job

By M. A. FARBER

Dr. John H. Knowles, the 45-year-old Massachusetts hospital administrator who was a controversial candidate for the nation's top health post in 1969, was named president of the Rockefeller Foundation yesterday.

He will succeed Dr. J. George Harrar next July as head of the second wealthiest foundation in the country, a multipurpose philanthropic enterprise with assets of more than $800-million and activities throughout the world. The Ford Foundation has assets of more than $2.5-billion.

Dr. Harrar, an early leader in the "green revolution" in food production in developing nations, will reach the Rockefeller Foundation's mandatory retirement age of 65 next December.

Dr. Knowles, an outspoken liberal on social as well as specifically medical issues, has been general director of the Massachusetts General Hospital in Boston since 1962.

In 1969 Dr. Knowles was proposed by Robert H. Finch as Assistant Secretary for Health and Scientific Affairs, in the Department of Health, Education and Welfare. Mr. Finch, who is now on the White House staff, was then Secretary of the

Continued on Page 37, Column 3

4 Days of Attica Talks End in Failure

By TOM WICKER
Special to The New York Times

ATTICA, N. Y., Sept. 13— At 9:43:28 this morning the power went off in the small littered steward's room on the second floor of the Attica Correctional Facility's administration building.

The hands of an electric clock on the wall pointed to that second for almost two hours, while state policemen and other officers put a bloody end to a massive uprising by about 1,500 inmates —mostly black and Puerto Rican.

To the 17 men in the room, the hands marked the moment of truth—the second when the end came for four days of emotional and exhausting effort to avoid the bloodshed that every one of them feared from the beginning. For 28 of the prisoners with whom they had vainly "negotiated" and for nine of the hostages the prisoners had been holding, death had been signaled.

At 9:48 A.M., five minutes after the lights went out, armed troopers moved behind fire hoses down the littered, gasoline-smelling corridor the 17 men and their colleagues had used in a series of harrowing visits to the prisoners' stronghold in Cellblock D and its exercise yard.

Other assaulting forces came over the walls that surrounded the exercise yard. By about 11 A.M., the prison authorities said that the institution was virtually "secure," although some cell block areas remained to be finally cleared. Active resistance had ceased.

Some members of the unusual group of 17 citizen "observers," summoned by the prisoners and authorized by the state authorities to try to find a peaceful solution, had believed all along that none could be devised. Others had hoped to the last. All had drained themselves emotionally and physically, when failure put an end to their efforts and to the lives of 37 men.

Gazing out the window of the steward's room at the helmeted troopers and the drifts of gas floating across the prison grounds, two of the 17-member group, Representative Herman Badillo of New York City and this correspondent, assured each

Continued on Page 29, Column 1

ROCKEFELLER SEES A PLOT AT PRISON

'Revolutionary Tactics' Led to Uprising, He Says— Investigation Planned

By WILLIAM E. FARRELL

Governor Rockefeller said yesterday that the uprising at Attica Prison was brought on by the "revolutionary tactics of militants" and that he had ordered "a full investigation of all the factors leading to this uprising, including the role that outside forces would appear to have played."

The Governor's comments were contained in a statement issued by his office here following one of the most critical moves of his 13 years in office —his sanctioning of the decision of State Commissioner of Correction Russell G. Oswald to storm the prison.

The action taken by the state was the subject of a telephone conversation yesterday afternoon between the Governor and President Nixon in which the President expressed support for the Governor's response to the prisoner rebellion, and in particular for his refusal to grant the amnesty demand.

Spokesmen for the Governor and the President agreed on the substance of the conversa-

Continued on Page 30, Column 1

A Hostage Says Threats Left Him 'Scared Silly'

By JOSEPH LELYVELD
Special to The New York Times

ATTICA, N. Y., Sept. 13—"I laid there on the floor and knew I was going to bleed to death right there."

As he said this, the only signs that Ron Kozlowski had been one of the hostages whose throats had been slit in the first fierce instants of the assault on the rebellious prisoners here were a small two-inch bandage at the base of his neck and a visible shakiness in his knees.

"They told us, 'As soon as the first shot is fired, you white blankety-blanks have had it.' I was scared silly up there. I really didn't want them to shoot."

Mr. Kozlowski, a 23-year-old accounts clerk at the prison, said he was one of a small group of hostages who were led this morning, bound and blindfolded, out of the jerrybuilt pen in the center of the prison yard where all the hostages had been held for four days. The 30 others left in the pen were also bound and blindfolded soon after State Correctional Commissioner Russell G. Oswald delivered the ultimatum to the more than 1,000 rebellious prisoners.

First, Mr. Kozlowski said, his group was taken to a pit that was doused with gasoline and told they would be burned alive

Continued on Page 29, Column 3

BID FAREWELL TO HUSBAND AND FATHER: Nina Khrushchev paying her last respects as rain fell yesterday in Novodevichye Monastery's Cemetery in Moscow. Daughters, Yelena, right, and Rada, behind mother, stand with friends and relatives at flower-covered bier. Cemetery is three miles from Kremlin. Dispatch is on Page 10. — *Associated Press*

GAVE ORDER: Russell G. Oswald, State Correction Commissioner, after action. — *Associated Press*

"All the News That's Fit to Print"

The New York Times

LATE CITY EDITION

Weather: Cloudy today and tonight. Partly sunny and milder tomorrow. Temp. range: today 60-67; Monday 58-62. Full U.S. report on Page 82.

VOL. CXXI.. No. 41,548   © 1971 The New York Times Company   NEW YORK, TUESDAY, OCTOBER 26, 1971   15 CENTS

U.N. SEATS PEKING AND EXPELS TAIPEI; NATIONALISTS WALK OUT BEFORE VOTE; U.S. DEFEATED ON TWO KEY QUESTIONS

Tanzanian and Albanian delegations applaud defeat of "important question" resolution

United Press International

WASHINGTON CALM

Officials Uncertain of Effect of Defeat on Future Relations

Special to The New York Times

WASHINGTON, Oct. 25—Official Washington reacted with outward calm tonight to the crushing American defeat in the United Nations on the China issue. But there was uncertainty as to the effect the historic vote would have on future United States relations with Taiwan, the United Nations and the Peking Government.

Although the defeat was a distinct public setback for the Administration, most knowledgeable officials here had concluded in the last 48 hours that the weeks of arm twisting and private pressure in foreign capitals would fail to save Taiwan's seat and were therefore not surprised by the outcome.

At the time the vote was being held on the "important question," many prominent Administration and Congressional figures were unaware that it was taking place. On this Veterans Day holiday, most people here had assumed that the crucial voting would not take place until tomorrow. And with a heavy rain falling all day in Washington, many officials had retired early.

No television station in Washington carried the initial phases of the debate live tonight, contributing to the lack of awareness. Washington's public television station, WETA, carried the later parts of the debate, after the crucial vote.

U.S. Withholds Comment

Even James C. H. Shen, the Ambassador of Nationalist China, was caught by surprise by the vote tonight. He was in New Haven for a speaking engagement at Yale and had gone to sleep without knowing of the events at the United Nations. When awakened by a reporter's call, he said he would have no comment.

Both the State Department and the White House said there would be no immediate official comment, but privately some officials wondered aloud about the significance of what they called the most important defeat ever suffered by the United States in the world organization.

Senator James L. Buckley, Conservative-Republican of New York, reacted sharply. He said he had asked his staff to prepare legislation for "a major reduction" in the American financial contribution to the United Nations, which runs about one-third of the annual $200-million budget.

"The action taken by the General Assembly tonight," he said, "may well be recorded as the beginning of the end of the United Nations, as marking

Continued on Page 16, Column 6

Liu Chieh, right, Nationalists' chief U.N. delegate, and delegation walk out of the hall

United Press International

CHOW SAYS PEKING WILL SUBVERT U.N.

Nationalist Minister Sees Change to 'Maoist Front' As Result of Defeat

By SAM POPE BREWER

UNITED NATIONS, N.Y., Oct. 25—Nationalist China's Foreign Minister, Chow Shu-kai, walked with his delegation out of the United Nations tonight and declared bitterly that Communist China, in his nation's place, would subvert the world organization.

"Once it has been seated both in the General Assembly and in the Security Council," Mr. Chow said of Peking, "it will surely transform the United Nations into a Maoist front and a battlefield for international subversion."

Mr. Chow, grave but unflinching in the glare of batteries of television lights, stood with Taiwan's delegate, Liu Chieh, at his side in a hallway outside the General Assembly Hall, where the overwhelming defeat for his Government had been voted. He declared:

"There are those who think that participation of the Communist regime will enhance the prospect of peace. The idea is to subject the aggressive regime to the discipline of international public opinion. This is dangerous nonsense—it is like tying a tiger with a straw rope."

Asked if he had had a foreboding of defeat when he wrote the document, Mr. Chow said, quietly: "When you are fighting a war, you prepare for

Continued on Page 11, Column 1

SESSION IS TENSE

Washington Loses Its Battle for Taipei by 76 to 35

By HENRY TANNER

Special to The New York Times

UNITED NATIONS, N. Y., Tuesday, Oct. 26—In a tense and emotion-filled meeting of more than eight hours, the General Assembly voted overwhelmingly last night to admit Communist China and to expel the Chinese Nationalist Government.

Moments before the vote, Liu Chieh, the Chinese Nationalist representative, announced from the rostrum that his Government would take no further part in the proceedings of the Assembly. He received friendly applause from most delegations, and then led his delegation out of the hall.

Texts of U.N. resolutions will be found on Page 10.

The vote, which brought delegates to their feet in wild applause, was 76 in favor, 35 opposed, and 17 abstentions. The vote was on a resolution sponsored by Albania and 20 other nations, calling for the seating of Peking as the only legitimate representative of China and the expulsion of "the representatives of Chiang Kai-shek."

Voting Is Sudden

Thus, the United States lost—in the 22d year—its battle to keep Nationalist China in the United Nations. This development, which came with dramatic suddenness, was denounced by the chief American delegate as a "moment of infamy."

The key decision that signaled the United States defeat came an hour and a half earlier, when the Assembly voted, 59 to 55 with 15 absentees, to reject the American draft resolution that would have declared the expulsion of the Nationalists an "important question" requiring a two-thirds majority for approval.

The United States had successfully used such a resolution since 1961 to keep the Chinese Communists out and the Chinese Nationalists in. Before that time, a simple majority would have admitted Peking, but no majority could be mustered.

Pandemonium Breaks Out

Last night as the electrical tally boards flashed the news that the "important question" proposal had failed, pandemonium broke out on the Assembly floor. Delegates jumped up and applauded.

The American delegation, also in the front row, sat in total dejection. George Bush, the United States delegate, who had

Continued on Page 10, Column 2

LINDSAY DEFENDS KNAPP HEARINGS

Tells P.B.A. Head the Inquiry is in 'The Best Interest' of Everyone' on Force

By DAVID BURNHAM

Mayor Lindsay said yesterday that while the Knapp Commission hearings meant "discomfort and shock" for many policemen and citizens, dealing decisively with police corruption was in "the best interest of every member of the police force."

Mr. Lindsay made the statement in a letter to Edward J. Kiernan, president of the Patrolmen's Benevolent Association.

The Mayor also said he intended to use the recommendations of the Knapp Commission, expected in a written report by the end of the year, "as the basis for a major campaign to build public confidence in the Police Department and the integrity of our law enforcement processes."

The Mayor's letter was in response to charges made last week by Mr. Kiernan that the Knapp Commission's hearings

Continued on Page 31, Column 5

Powell Is Seeking To Avoid Clashes Over Court Seat

By JAMES M. NAUGHTON

Special to The New York Times

WASHINGTON, Oct. 25 — Lewis F. Powell Jr., the third Southern conservative nominated to the Supreme Court by President Nixon, is attempting to avoid the collisions over ethics and racial attitudes that contributed to the Senate's rejection of his two predecessors.

Mr. Powell, aware that his life, professional record and judicial philosophy are about to undergo rigorous examination, discussed his background with unusual candor in an interview at his Richmond law office this weekend.

He pledged to do "whatever is necessary and proper" to separate himself from corporate directorships and financial holdings that might constitute potential conflicts of interest.

Mr. Powell sought to place in what he regards as the proper context the comparatively minor chinks that have appeared in his image as a racial moderate — membership in two segregated clubs in Richmond and authorship of a brief filed by

Continued on Page 22, Column 4

Pakistanis Report 501 of Foe Killed In Eastern Area

By MALCOLM W. BROWNE

Special to The New York Times

KARACHI, Pakistan, Oct. 25 — The Government reported tonight that its forces had killed 501 "enemy troops"—defined as "Indians and Indian agents"—in heavy fighting in East Pakistan.

The Government, here in Pakistan's western wing, uses the term "Indian agents" to refer to all of its adversaries in East Pakistan, including the Pakistanis there who have been battling for Bengali independence since March with Indian support.

U.N. Observers Suggested

Today the Government said some of the bodies bore identification tags of the Indian Army. If the casualties are indeed Indians and if the toll even approaches the figures given, that would indicate that the fighting has reached its greatest intensity since the brief Indian-Pakistani conflict in 1965.

[In New Delhi, Defense Minister Jagjivan Ram reiterated that India would not pull her troops back from her borders "as long as the Pakistani threat continues." Page 17.]

Meanwhile, the Government announced that President Agha Mohammad Yahya Khan had asked for the intercession of Secretary General U Thant of the United Nations in the dispute.

According to the Pakistani radio, President Yahya Khan proposed that United Nations observers be posted on both sides of the border between East Pakistan and India to supervise a mutual withdrawal

Continued on Page 17, Column 1

BREZHNEV IN PARIS, BACKED ON TALKS

Pompidou Agrees to a Quick Start on Preparations for Europe Security Parley

By HENRY GINIGER

PARIS, Oct. 25 — President Pompidou and Leonid I. Brezhnev, leader of the Soviet Communist party, agreed quickly today to begin active preparation for a European security conference.

The agreement was made known at a state dinner in Versailles that marked the end of the first day of a six-day visit by Mr. Brezhnev. The Soviet leader was received this afternoon with the honors of a chief of state, and only a few discordant notes marred the friendly atmosphere of Mr. Brezhnev's first visit to a Western country since he became party leader in 1964.

[In Washington it was reported that Mr. Brezhnev had signaled Western leaders that he had officially assumed over-all responsibility for Moscow's relations with the United States and Western Europe. Page 5.]

In toasts this evening, Mr. Pompidou and Mr. Brezhnev spoke in similar terms of the need to end hostility between blocs.

Mr. Brezhnev said that France and the Soviet Union were close "on a fundamental problem—that of ending the division of the world into political-military blocs." Mr. Pompidou declared such blocs carried within them "the certainty of

Continued on Page 6, Column 4

U.N. Roll-Calls on China

Special to The New York Times

UNITED NATIONS, N. Y., Oct. 25—Following are two roll-call votes taken in the General Assembly tonight on seating Communist China and expelling Nationalist China.

On Two-Thirds Requirement

Resolution declaring the expulsion of Nationalist China an "important matter" and thus requiring a two-thirds vote rather than a simple majority for passage.

On Seating Peking

Resolution to seat Communist China and expel Nationalist China.

IN FAVOR—55

Argentina, Australia, Bahrain, Barbados, Belgium, Bolivia, Brazil, Cent. Afr. Rep., Chad, Chile, China, Colombia, Costa Rica, Dahomey, El Salvador, Fiji, Gabon, Gambia, Guatemala, Haiti, Honduras, Indonesia, Israel, Ivory Coast, Jamaica, Japan, Jordan, Lesotho, Liberia, Madagascar, Malawi, Mauritius, Mexico, New Zealand, Nicaragua, Niger, Panama, Paraguay, Philippines, Saudi Arabia, Spain, Swaziland, Thailand, United States, Upper Volta, Uruguay, Venezuela

OPPOSED—59

Afghanistan, Albania, Algeria, Bhutan, Bulgaria, Burma, Burundi, Byelorussia, Cameroon, Canada, Ceylon, Chile, Congo (Brazza), Czechoslovakia, Denmark, Ecuador, Egypt, Eth. Guinea, Ethiopia, Finland, France, Ghana, Guinea, Hungary, Iceland, India, Iran, Iraq, Ireland, Kenya, Kuwait, Laos, Libya, Malaysia, Mali, Mauritania, Mongolia, Morocco, Nepal, Nigeria, Norway, Pakistan, Peru, Poland, Romania, Sierra Leone, Somalia, Soviet Union, Sudan, Sweden, Syria, Tanzania, Trinidad-Tobago, Uganda, Ukraine, U.S.S.R., Yemen, Yugoslavia, Zambia

ABSTENTIONS—15

Austria, Bahrain, Belgium, Botswana, Cyprus, Italy, Luxembourg, Malta, Morocco, Netherlands, Qatar, Senegal, Togo, Tunisia, Turkey

Absent—Maldives, Oman.

IN FAVOR—76

Afghanistan, Albania, Algeria, Australia, Austria, Belgium, Bhutan, Botswana, Bulgaria, Burma, Burundi, Byelorussia, Cameroon, Canada, Ceylon, Chile, Congo (Brazza), Congo (Kinsh.), Czechoslovakia, Dahomey, Denmark, Ecuador, Egypt, Eth. Guinea, Ethiopia, Finland, France, Ghana, Guinea, Guyana, Hungary, Iceland, India, Iran, Iraq, Ireland, Israel, Kenya, Kuwait, Laos, Libya, Malaysia, Mali, Mauritania, Mexico, Mongolia, Morocco, Nepal, Netherlands, Nigeria, Norway, Pakistan, Peru, Poland, Portugal, Romania, Rwanda, Senegal, Sierra Leone, Singapore, Somalia, Soviet Union, Sudan, Sweden, Syria, Tanzania, Togo, Trinidad-Tobago, Tunisia, Turkey, Uganda, Ukraine, United States, Yemen, Yugoslavia, Zambia

OPPOSED—35

Australia, Bolivia, Brazil, Cent. Afr. Rep., Chad, Congo (Kinsh.), Costa Rica, Dominican Rep., El Salvador, Gabon, Gambia, Guatemala, Haiti, Honduras, Ivory Coast, Japan, Lesotho, Liberia, Madagascar, Malawi, Malta, New Zealand, Nicaragua, Niger, Paraguay, Philippines, Saudi Arabia, South Africa, Swaziland, United States, Upper Volta, Uruguay, Venezuela

ABSTENTIONS—17

Argentina, Bahrain, Barbados, Colombia, Cyprus, Fiji, Greece, Indonesia, Jamaica, Jordan, Lebanon, Luxembourg, Mauritius, Panama, Qatar, Spain, Thailand

Absent—China, Maldives, Oman.

End of China's Isolation

Peking Victory Held Likely to Speed Series of International Realignments

By MAX FRANKEL

Special to The New York Times

WASHINGTON, Oct. 25—With the vote at the United Nations tonight, China burst fully and finally from the isolation first impos on her by the United States a generation ago and periodically preferred by her own Communist Government.

Though Washington was calm or simply asleep at the symbolic moment, its rear-guard effort to save Taiwan in the world organization only heightened the drama of Peking's entry onto the world stage and deepened some of the resentments in conservative circles here.

President Nixon will undoubtedly show some sympathy for those resentments. He considers his projected journey to China as far more significant than most actions of the United Nations, and he sincerely hoped that his gesture would win a more gentle handling for the Chinese Nationalists.

But there was obviously a

Continued on Page 10, Column 7

News Analysis

Peking's Backers Jubilant Over Vote

By TAD SZULC

Special to The New York Times

UNITED NATIONS, N. Y., Oct. 25—Salim Ahmed Salim, the young chief delegate from Tanzania, jumped to his feet tonight and led his colleagues in a victory jig in front of the Tanzanian delegation in the front row of the General Assembly.

At the opposite end of the hall, where the United States delegation occupies a front-row seat, George Bush, the American chief delegate, slumped dejectedly in his chair.

It was exactly 9:47 P.M. and the United Nations General Assembly had just finished its roll-

Continued on Page 10, Column 2

By Lyndon B. Johnson: First Steps Toward Peace

INSTALLMENT X

Following is the 10th of 11 installments of excerpts from Lyndon Baines Johnson's memoirs of his Presidential years, which will be published by Holt, Rinehart & Winston on Nov. 1 under the title "The Vantage Point: Perspectives of the Presidency, 1963-1969":

Wednesday, April 3, 1968, began most days in the White House. I was up early and read through the morning papers over breakfast. I listened to the radio news and glanced again at the front pages. One item, which I had heard broadcast the previous afternoon, was receiving considerable attention. In a speech on Tuesday Senator J. William Fulbright had told the Senate that the partial bombing halt I had ordered three nights before added up to only "a very limited change in existing policy." He forecast that the halt would not move

Hanoi in the direction of peace talks.

I was surprised by Fulbright's reasoning and by his timing. We had stopped bombing over more than three-fourths of North Vietnam, an area where 9 out of every 10 North Vietnamese lived. That was much more than a "limited change" in our actions. Moreover, I believed Hanoi was not yet ready to judge the significance of our move without advice from Americans.

In the Senate discussion following Senator Fulbright's speech, Majority Leader Mike Mansfield and other Senators spoke up strongly in defense of our action and disputed Fulbright's charges. Senator Mansfield recalled the long talk ke and I had had on the evening of March 27 and he disclosed that I had informed him on that occasion that we were going to stop bombing north of the 20th parallel.

To my mind, the principal issue was not where the precise line marking the no-bombing area was drawn but rather how Hanoi would react to our self-imposed restriction. The key question in the Senate discussion, I believed, was raised by Senator Frank Lausche of Ohio: "How can Ho Chi Minh give any affirmative action when the Senator from Arkansas and others attack the Government before Ho can respond?"

While Fulbright's allegations dominated the news stories and headlines, Lausche's pertinent question received scant attention. I saw it mentioned only once, in The New York Times on April 3, and then only in the 30th and last paragraph on Page 14.

These reflections put me in a bad mood as I prepared to leave for the

Continued on Page 34, Column 1

"All the News That's Fit to Print"

The New York Times

LATE CITY EDITION

Weather: Cloudy and ... day, colder tonight. Sunn ... ow Temp. range: today 4 ... day 52-63. Full U.S. report ... age 82.

VOL. CXXI...No. 41,600

© 1971 The New York Times Company

NEW YORK, FRIDAY, DECEMBER 17, 1971

15 CENTS

INDIA ORDERS CEASE-FIRE ON BOTH FRONTS AFTER PAKISTANIS' SURRENDER IN THE EAST

CONGRESS BREAKS FOREIGN AID JAM; SEEKS TO ADJOURN

House Rejection of Vietnam Amendment Sets Stage for Conferees' Accord

By JOHN W. FINNEY
Special to The New York Times

WASHINGTON, Dec. 16 — Congress apparently broke today the impasse on foreign aid legislation that has ben holding up adjournment as the House unexpectedly met Senate demands for a vote on an amendment on Vietnam troop withdrawal.

The House rejected, by a vote of 130 to 101, the withdrawal amendment offered by the Senate majority leader, Mike Mansfield, and incorporated by the Senate in the foreign aid authorization legislation. But the net effect of the House action was to reopen Senate-House negotiations on the foreign aid legislation that had been deadlocked for weeks in a conference committee.

With the foreign aid issue apparently on the way to resolution, Senate and House leaders were optimistic that the first session of the 92d Congress could adjourn by tomorrow.

Ryan Breaks Impasse

With Senate and House leaders caught up in a power struggle over foreign aid, the impasse was broken in a surprise move by Representative William Fitts Ryan, Democrat of Manhattan.

Independently of the Congressional leaders who were meeting in the Senate Appropriations Committee room seeking a way to continue the foreign aid program, Mr. Ryan unexpectedly stood up on the House floor to offer a motion instructing the House conferees to accept the Mansfield amendment.

He had found a provision in the House rules permitting such a motion to be made if a Senate-House conference committee had been deadlocked for 20 days.

Motion to Table

A surprised Representative Thomas E. Morgan, of Pennsylvania, chairman of the House Foreign Affairs Committee, promptly moved to table, or lay aside, the Ryan motion, a move that carried by the 29-vote margin.

Technically, the House did not have the specific vote on the Mansfield amendment that Senate conferees had been demanding in the conference on the foreign aid legislation. It was the refusal of the House conferees to yield to this demand by Senator Mansfield

Continued on Page 45, Column 4

City Speeds Repair On Garbage Trucks

By PAUL L. MONTGOMERY

Sanitation Department officials here believe they are on the way to solving one of their most persistent problems—the inordinate number of collection trucks awaiting repairs in the department's shops.

The solution, something of a revolution in city administration, is embodied in a single sheet of statistics distributed to department mechanics this week. It lists the times the mechanics are expected to spend to complete 18 routine tasks.

The revolution is that the times listed are an average of 46 per cent less than those that had prevailed.

The new productivity standards, reached after consultation with the mechanics' union, are frequently mentioned by city officials as an example of

Continued on Page 72, Column 1

Monthly Record Set For Housing Starts

By JACK ROSENTHAL
Special to The New York Times

WASHINGTON, Dec. 16 — Home building reached a monthly high in November, practically insuring that 1971 will be a record year, George Romney, Secretary of Housing and Urban Development, announced today at an odd, hastily called news conference.

The seasonally adjusted annual rate of housing starts in November was 2,316,000 units, Mr. Romney said, the highest figure ever. The actual 1971 figure is now likely to approach 2.1 million units, probably the highest ever.

The November figure compares with a downward revised October figure of 2,008,000 units and with 1,693,000 units for November, 1970.

The gain in housing starts,

Continued on Page 69, Column 3

REVAMPING URGED FOR BANK SYSTEM

Hunt Commission Proposes Change in U.S. Regulation of Money Institutions

By H. ERICH HEINEMANN
Special to The New York Times

WASHINGTON, Dec. 16 — The nation's financial structure and the Federal agencies that regulate it require a complete overhaul, a Presidential commission has concluded.

If adopted, the commission's recommendations should result in sharper competition, possibly lower prices for consumers and — over time — the gradual disappearance of the present sharp legal distinctions between different types of financial institutions.

The group is formally called the Presidential Commission on Financial Structure and Regulation and informally known as the Hunt Commission (for its chairman, Reed O. Hunt, retired chairman of the Crown Zellerbach Corporation). The commission is due to present its report to the White House in a few days. A copy of its recommendations, but not the report itself, was obtained today.

The key problem that led

Continued on Page 65, Column 1

Nixon Pledges to Seek Release Of Skipper of Ship Cuba Seized

Mr. Nixon consoles wife of José Villa, ship's captain

Associated Press

By JAMES M. NAUGHTON

KEY BISCAYNE, Fla., Dec. 16 — President Nixon pledged today that he would do what he could to seek the release of José Villa, the captain of a Miami-based freighter attacked by a Cuban gunboat and seized yesterday in the Bahamas.

The President met with Captain Villa's wife, Isabel, and three children for 10 minutes at the Florida White House. The family of the captain, a Cuban exile who is now a naturalized United States citizen, had gone there to deliver a letter pleading for Mr. Nixon's intervention.

Ronald L. Ziegler, the White House press secretary, that after the meeting that the Administration deplored the Cuban attack as an "unconscionable act" and that the United States had asked the Swiss Embassy in Havana to demand the "immediate" release of Captain Villa.

Earlier, before the captain's family saw the President, Mr. Ziegler used milder terms to

Continued on Page 12, Column 3

WEST TO FIGHT ON

Yahya Calls for Help, but Vows to Battle 'Alone if We Must'

By MALCOLM W. BROWNE
Special to The New York Times

RAWALPINDI, Pakistan, Dec. 16 — President Agha Mohammad Yahya Khan acknowledged tonight that his forces in East Pakistan had been overwhelmed but pledged to continue the war against India until final victory.

In a radio speech to the nation, he also urgently called for

Text of Yahya's speech will be found on Page 17.

help from the community of nations in Pakistan's struggle, but added: "We shall fight alone if we must."

Later, Pakistan formally acknowledged that India now controls what had been East Pakistan.

A communiqué issued here in West Pakistan said:

"Latest reports indicate that following an arrangement between the local commanders of India and Pakistan in the Eastern theater, fighting has ceased in East Pakistan, and Indian troops have entered Dacca."

No Details Are Given

The communiqué said nothing more about East Pakistan and gave no details of the "arrangement."

But it indicated that fighting in West Pakistan was continuing.

For the first time since the war began, military and diplomatic spokesmen failed to hold their daily evening briefing and correspondents here had no access to Pakistani officials.

The air war in the west was apparently still in progress. Indian air raids were reported on Karachi, Sialkot and other cities with significant numbers of civilian casualties.

Continued on Page 17, Column 4

BHUTTO SUGGESTS ACCORD ON BENGAL

Pakistani Urges Cease-fire and Negotiations With Both Indians and Insurgents

By HENRY TANNER
Special to The New York Times

UNITED NATIONS, N. Y., Dec. 16 — Pakistan's Deputy Prime Minister and Foreign Minister, Zulfikar Ali Bhutto, declared today that Pakistan should accept a cease-fire with India and should prepare to negotiate a permanent settlement with the insurgents in East Bengal as well as with the Government of India.

Mr. Bhutto, in an interview, also said that Pakistan, which is now ruled by a military government, should return to civilian democratic government "very soon." His remarks appeared to put him at odds with President Agha Mohammad Yahya Khan of Pakistan, who pledged today in a speech to continue the war against India.

Mr. Bhutto announced that he would return to Pakistan in a few days to start laying the groundwork for sweeping internal and external reform as well as for negotiation with the insurgents.

Mr. Bhutto, who is the leading civilian figure in West Pakistan, stressed that he did not concede the final loss of East Pakistan.

The Security Council, meanwhile, was close to agreement when it adjourned tonight on a resolution calling for an im-

Continued on Page 17, Column 1

Walsh at Hearing: Forgot Graft Report

By DAVID BURNHAM

Former First Deputy Police Commissioner John F. Walsh admitted in sworn testimony yesterday that he had received a report of widespread police corruption in the Bronx at least six months before any police investigation was begun.

Mr. Walsh, the second-ranking New York police official for almost four years, told the Knapp Commission that the detailed report he had received on corruption among plainclothes men "left my mind."

Months later, without any orders to initiate it from Mr. Walsh, an investigation was begun by police officials in the Bronx that "eventually led to criminal indictments against 10 policemen and department charges against 11 others, in-

Continued on Page 46, Column 1

SIGNING THE SURRENDER AGREEMENT: Lieut. Gen. Jagjit Singh Aurora, left, commander of India's eastern forces, and Lieut. Gen. A. A. K. Niazi, Pakistani commander in East Pakistan, during surrender ceremony in Dacca yesterday.

United Press International

The Surrender Document

By Reuters

NEW DELHI, Dec. 16—Following is the text of the instrument of surrender signed today by the Pakistani and Indian commanders in East Pakistan:

The Pakistani Eastern Command agree to surrender all Pakistani armed forces in Bangladesh to Lieut. Gen. Jagjit Singh Aurora, general officer commanding in chief of the Indian and Bangladesh forces in the eastern theater.

This surrender includes all Pakistani land, air and naval forces as also all paramilitary forces and civil armed forces.

These forces will lay down their arms and surrender at the place where they are currently located to the nearest regular troops in the command of Lieut. Gen. Jagjit Singh Aurora.

Pakistani Eastern Command shall come under the orders of Lieut. Gen. Jagjit Singh Aurora as soon as this instrument has been signed. Disobedience of orders will be regarded as a breach of the surrender terms and will be dealt with in accordance with accepted laws and usages of war.

The decision of Lieut. Gen. Jagjit Singh Aurora shall be final should any doubt arise as to the meaning or interpretation of surrender terms.

"Lieut. Gen. Jagjit Singh Aurora gives his solemn assurance that personnel who surrender shall be treated with dignity and respect that soldiers are entitled to in accordance with the provisions of the Geneva convention and guarantees safety and well-being of all Pakistan military and paramilitary forces who surrender.

Protection will be provided to foreign nationals, ethnic minorities and personnel of the West Pakistan region by the forces in the command of Lieut. Gen. Jagjit Singh Aurora.

The March Into Dacca: Last Clash and Victory

2 Men at a Table

By SYDNEY H. SCHANBERG
Special to The New York Times

DACCA, Pakistan, Dec. 16—On a broad grassy field in central Dacca known as the Race Course, the Pakistani forces formally surrendered today, 13 days after the Indian Army began its drive into East Pakistan.

It was at the Race Course on March 7 that Sheik Mujibur Rahman, in a speech to thousands of Bengalis, called for the end of martial law and the transfer of power to his autonomy-minded Awami League, which had won a majority in national elections.

Today there were no speeches —just two men sitting at a single table on the grass—Lieut. Gen. Jagjit Singh Aurora, chief of India's Eastern Command, and Lieut. Gen. A. A. K. Niazi, commander of the 70,000 Pakistani troops in East Pakistan—who signed the formal papers of Pakistani surrender in the East.

The final hours of the Indian drive, which ended with the ceremony at the Race Course, were punctuated by artillery and machine-gun fire as the troops pushed across the Lakhya River, just outside Dacca proper.

Seven Western journalists, in-

Continued on Page 16, Column 3

Joy and Marigolds

By JAMES P. STERBA
Special to The New York Times

DACCA, Pakistan, Dec. 16—Shouting "Joi Bangla!" and waving the Bangladesh flag, Indian troops in trucks and buses poured into the Pakistani military camp north of town today just after the Pakistanis had accepted an ultimatum to surrender.

Indian soldiers with marigolds passed armed Pakistani soldiers in great traffic jams within the camp. Pakistani officers saluted Indian officers. Officers of both armies, many of whom attended the same schools under the British, shook hands and asked about mutual friends.

In Dacca itself, there were spontaneous eruptions of joy and celebration in the streets. Bengalis kissed Indian Punjabi soldiers, tossing flowers at them and at the rebels who accom-

Continued on Page 16, Column 2

DACCA CAPTURED

Guns Quiet in Bengali Area but War Goes On at Western Front

By CHARLES MOHR
Special to The New York Times

NEW DELHI, Dec. 16—India today ordered a complete cease-fire in the war with Pakistan after seizing Dacca, the East Pakistani capital, and accepting the surrender of Pakistan's forces there.

With guns stilled by the surrender in the East, the cease-

Statements by Mrs. Gandhi appear on Page 16.

fire on the western front, more than a thousand miles away, was set—without any agreement from Pakistan—to begin at 8 P.M. tomorrow, Indian time (9:30 A.M. Friday, New York time).

After 14 days of bitter warfare over the status of the Bengalis in East Pakistan, Prime Minister Indira Gandhi of India said, "It is pointless in our view to continue the present conflict."

Pakistani Shortages Seen

But President Agha Mohammad Yahya Khan of Pakistan asserted in a nationwide radio broadcast that the war was still on "and we will continue to fight."

Pakistan is believed by independent observers, however, to have grave supply-line problems, so that their stockpiles of fuel and ammunition may not permit a prolonged war.

A major tank battle—the largest of the war—has erupted on the western front near the little Pakistani town of Shakargarh, in the Punjab. Indian officials said India had lost 15 tanks and claimed the destruction of 45 Pakistani tanks.

Continued on Page 16, Column 1

CHINESE CHARGE INDIAN INCURSION

Protest May Foreshadow Use of Military Pressure in Support of Pakistan

By TILLMAN DURDIN
Special to The New York Times

HONG KONG, Dec. 16—China, in a formal Government statement today on the Indian-Pakistani war, predicted a turbulent future for India. At the same time, the Chinese pointed toward a possible trouble zone by filing a strong protest in New Delhi over alleged Indian incursions from Sikkim into Tibet.

Even as India celebrated her quick victory in the East, China accused her of violating the border between the Indian protectorate of Sikkim and Tibet, terming the action "a grave encroachment" on Chinese territory.

The statement and the protest were reported here in quick

Text of Chinese statement is printed on Page 18.

succession tonight from Peking by Hsinhua, the Chinese press agency.

The protest could foreshadow military pressure from China, a strong supporter of Pakistan, along sections of the eastern Himalayan border between India and China.

The 1,600-word statement warned India that "he who plays with fire will be consumed by fire" and asserted that "henceforth there will be no tranquillity" for the Indian people.

Calling attention to India's own problems with minority nationalities, which it likened to the Bengali situation in East Pakistan, the statement said: "It may be asked how

Continued on Page 18, Column 2

Chinese Charge Denied

Indian officials said there had been no fighting on the Chinese border, and a Foreign Ministry spokesman described the accusation by Peking—a supporter of Pakistan—as "totally without foundation." Nonetheless, the protest raised apprehensions here that the conflict might be widened.

India's offensive in East Pakistan, which began in the early hours of Dec. 4, ended at 4:31 P.M. today in the total surrender of the four divisions of West Pakistani troops there.

The surrender agreement was signed in Dacca by Lieut. Gen. Jagjit Singh Aurora, who commands India's eastern forces, and Lieut. Gen. A. A. K. Niazi,

Continued on Page 16, Column 1

Mrs. Gandhi Writes President: U.S. Could Have Averted War

By FOX BUTTERFIELD
Special to The New York Times

NEW DELHI, Dec. 16—Prime Minister Indira Gandhi has written to President Nixon, in a letter released today, that the war between India and Pakistan could have been avoided if the United States had used its

Text of Mrs. Gandhi's letter is printed on Page 17.

"power, influence and authority" to achieve a political solution to the crisis in East Pakistan.

Mrs. Gandhi wrote that despite advice that she gave in August to Henry A. Kissinger, the President's adviser on national security affairs, only "lip service was paid to the need for a political settlement, but not a single worthwhile step was taken to bring it about."

Mrs. Gandhi said she was

Continued on Page 17, Column 3

writing at a time of deep anguish over the "unhappy turn" which relations between India and the United States have taken." The letter was sent to Mr. Nixon yesterday.

Relations between the two countries, which have been strained because the United States did not denounce Pakistan for her repression of the Bengali movement for autonomy last spring, deteriorated sharply this week with the news that the nuclear-powered aircraft carrier Enterprise and seven other American Navy ships were heading for the Bay of Bengal.

"India was deeply hurt," Mrs. Gandhi wrote, "by the innuendoes and insinuations that it was she who had precipitated

"All the News That's Fit to Print"

The New York Times

LATE CITY EDITION

Weather: Rain today; mostly cloudy tonight. Fair and milder tomorrow. Temp. range: today 51-55; Monday 53-66. Full U.S. report on Page 82.

VOL. CXXI..No. 41,744

© 1972 The New York Times Company

NEW YORK, TUESDAY, MAY 9, 1972

15 CENTS

NIXON ORDERS ENEMY'S PORTS MINED; SAYS MATERIEL WILL BE DENIED HANOI UNTIL IT FREES P.O.W.'S AND HALTS WAR

Governor Reported Irked By Nixon's Abortion Views

Rockefeller Indicates Plan to Veto Bill Stands Despite President's Support for Repeal of Present State Law

By JAMES F. CLARITY
Special to The New York Times

ALBANY, May 8 — Governor Rockefeller was reliably reported today to be angered by President Nixon's intervention in the issue of elective abortions, now pending in the Legislature.

One of the highest elected Republican officials in the state described Mr. Rockefeller as "very upset" about the President's action.

The Governor's office said that despite the President's announced support for repeal of the state's liberal abortion law, Mr. Rockefeller would veto the repeal if it was approved by the Legislature. Relations between the Governor and the President, which had improved greatly in the last several months, with Mr. Rockefeller agreeing to serve as the President's campaign manager in the

Continued on Page 26, Column 2

PAY BOARD TRIMS EAST COAST RAISE OF LONGSHOREMEN

Votes, 6-1, to Permit Rises of 9.8 to 12% Instead of 15 —Fitzsimmons Dissents

By EDWARD COWAN
Special to The New York Times

WASHINGTON, May 8—The Pay Board directed East and Gulf Coast shippers and longshoremen tonight to roll back their agreed wage increase of 70 cents an hour to 55 cents.

About 49,000 longshoremen will be allowed increases ranging from 9.8 per cent to 12 per cent under the decision, which scaled back an agreement that had contemplated an increase calculated by the board at 15 per cent.

George H. Boldt, chairman of the seven-member board, said that he expected the International Longshoremen's Association "to look it over, be disappointed and go along with what's now the law of the land."

Boldt Declines to Predict

However, Judge Boldt, in a brief corridor meeting with newsmen, declined to prognosticate when asked if he thought the dock workers would strike.

Judge Boldt issued a summary of the decision after a difficult four-hour board meeting that ended with a vote of 6 to 1. The dissenter was Frank E. Fitzsimmons, president of the International Brotherhood of Teamsters, who is the only labor leader still on the board.

Four other union leaders quit the board in March after it scaled back the longshore settlement on the West Coast to 14.9 per cent from a proposed 20.9 per cent. Only Mr. Fitzsimmons remained.

President Nixon then reconstituted what had been a 15-member tripartite group as a panel of seven public members. In New York, Thomas G. Gleason, president of the Inter-

Continued on Page 17, Column 1

New Vega Recall

The General Motors Corporation yesterday recalled 350,000 of its 1971 and 1972 Vegas to correct a safety defect. It was the second major recall of Vegas in a month. Details on Page 16.

Associated Press
VIETNAM ADDRESS: President Nixon speaking last night

The New York Times/May 9, 1972
NEW TARGETS: Ports (underlined), rail lines from China

HIGH MEAT PRICES LAID TO RACKETS

City Consumers Squeezed by 15% Inflation of Costs, Law Officials Report

By LACEY FOSBURGH

The infiltration of organized crime into key positions in the New York City meat industry has artificially inflated the retail prices for fresh meat in supermarkets by 15 per cent, according to information developed by the Manhattan District Attorney's Office and other law-enforcement agencies here and in Washington.

Consumers buying meat in the New York-New Jersey area, they say, are putting at least a million dollars a week directly into the coffers of organized crime.

Years of Collusion Alleged

Racketeers — both in the industry and in the unions that service it — have reportedly been in collusion for at least two years "systematically" extorting "week by week, month by month," as one source put it, "vast sums of money" from the supermarket chains and the wholesale suppliers.

"This is the price they pay to stay in business," another source said, "the price of labor peace."

This picture of extortion, bribery and the ultimate victimization of the consumer

Continued on Page 66, Column 1

Local School Units Defended by Mayor

By LEONARD BUDER

Mayor Lindsay declared yesterday that the city's decentralized school boards had brought "a new vigor to the whole process of achieving quality public education."

Mr. Lindsay said that while it is "much too soon to make a final judgment on decentralization" he felt that "the community school boards have made important advances since the inception of decentralization a little less than two years ago."

The Mayor made the statement in commenting on the assertion Sunday by Dr. Kenneth B. Clark, a member of the State Board of Regents, that the school

Continued on Page 53, Column 5

State Senate Votes To Liberalize Curbs In Rape Testimony

By ALFONSO A. NARVAEZ
Special to The New York Times

ALBANY, May 8—The Senate gave overwhelming approval today to a bill modifying the extent to which a rape victim's testimony must be corroborated to convict an alleged attacker.

The measure, which passed by a vote of 56 to 1, removes the need for testimony corroborating the identity of the alleged assailant and the fact that penetration actually took place. The bill, passed with no debate, now goes to the Governor, who is expected to sign it.

In other action today as the Legislature continued its push for adjournment:

¶Three city officials—Controller Abraham D. Beame, City Council Majority Leader Thomas J. Cuite and the Council's finance chairman, Mario Merola—met here with state budget officials on legislation affecting the city's proposed $9.9-billion budget. The meet-

Continued on Page 27, Column 1

Ruling Party Leads In Italian Election; Neo-Fascists Gain

By PAUL HOFMANN
Special to The New York Times

ROME, Tuesday, May 9—The governing Christian Democrats achieved a remarkable comeback in Italy's general elections Sunday and yesterday, receiving a clear mandate to continue leading the Government as they have been doing since 1945.

At the same time, however, the neo-Fascists advanced and the Communists won gains in the Chamber of Deputies and suffered losses in the Senate. With most of the votes counted early today, increasing polarization between left and right in Italian politics became apparent.

The Christian Democrats apparently raised their share of the total popular vote close to 40 per cent again and were confirmed once more as the nation's strongest political force.

But no party was anywhere near winning a majority in the 630-seat Chamber or among the 315 elected members of the Senate. The prospects, therefore, appeared to be for another period of coalition governments and, possibly, protracted instability.

Italian commentators attributed the rightist gains and

Continued on Page 3, Column 1

CONGRESS IS SPLIT ON NIXON'S ACTION

Republicans Acclaim His Leadership—Democrats Call Him Reckless

By JOHN W. FINNEY
Special to The New York Times

WASHINGTON, May 8—President Nixon was alternately praised tonight by members of Congress for his firm leadership and accused of setting the nation on a dangerous confrontation with the Soviet Union that could lead to world war.

Republicans praised him on both political and military grounds for his decision to mine North Vietnam's harbors. Representative Gerald R. Ford, the House Republican leader, described Mr. Nixon as "generous in his bid for peace but firm in his determination that we will not surrender."

"The only way left to end the Vietnam war is to deprive the enemy of the supplies he needs to continue the invasion," Mr. Ford said.

Senator Robert P. Griffin of Michigan, the assistant Republican leader in the Senate, said "it was using medicine but necessary."

Democrats, however, used

Continued on Page 19, Column 1

President Urges Soviet To Avoid Confrontation

By BERNARD GWERTZMAN
Special to The New York Times

WASHINGTON, May 8—President Nixon's speech tonight appealed to the Soviet Union not to let its support of Hanoi lead it to a confrontation with the United States over his decision to try to cut off supplies to North Vietnam.

In carefully chosen language, Mr. Nixon appeared anxious to avoid turning the Vietnam war into a direct Soviet-American clash.

But some diplomats feel the mining of North Vietnam's ports has raised the possibility of cancellation of Mr. Nixon's scheduled trip to Moscow two weeks from today and even of a military confrontation if Soviet naval forces try to thwart Mr. Nixon's actions.

Dobrynin Informed

Officially, the Nixon Administration said tonight that plans for Mr. Nixon's visit to the Soviet Union were still going ahead. But a high official added that the chances that it would take place had sharply lessened because of the tensions sure to be raised as the result of the effort to prevent supplies from arriving in North Vietnam.

Anatoly F. Dobrynin, the Soviet Ambassador to the United States, was informed of Mr. Nixon's speech about an hour beforehand at a White House meeting with Henry A. Kissinger, President Nixon's adviser on national security.

Mr. Dobrynin was also the Soviet envoy in October, 1962, when President John F. Kennedy ordered a quarantine of offensive Soviet weapons being shipped to Cuba. This led to the so-called Cuban missile crisis.

Continued on Page 19, Column 5

SPEAKS TO NATION

He Gives the Ships of Other Countries 3 Days to Leave

By ROBERT B. SEMPLE Jr.
Special to The New York Times

WASHINGTON, May 8 — President Nixon announced tonight that he had ordered the mining of all North Vietnamese ports and other measures to prevent the flow of arms and other military supplies to the enemy.

Mr. Nixon told a nationwide television and radio audience

The text of Nixon's speech is printed on Page 18.

that his orders were being executed as he spoke.

From the President's somber and stern speech and from explanations by other Administration officials, the following picture of the American action emerged:

¶All major North Vietnamese ports would be mined, ships of other countries in the harbors, most of which are Russian, would have three "daylight periods" in which to leave. After that the mines will become active and ships coming or going will move at their own peril.

¶United States naval vessels will not search or seize ships of other countries entering or leaving North Vietnamese ports, thus avoiding a direct confrontation with the Russians.

¶American and South Vietnamese ships and planes would take "appropriate measures" to stop North Vietnam from unloading matériel on beaches from unmined waters.

¶United States and South Vietnamese forces would interdict, presumably by bombing, the movement of matériel in North Vietnam over rail lines originating in China.

There was much confusion tonight about whether the United States and South Vietnam had proclaimed a blockade. The President did not use the word and Pentagon spokesmen denied that a blockade existed in the technical sense. But some observers felt that the practical effect on North Vietnam of the President's actions would be the same as a blockade.

[In Saigon, the United States command announced Tuesday that Navy planes had completed the initial phases of the mining operations in North Vietnamese harbors ordered by President Nixon.]

Two Basic Conditions

Mr. Nixon said the mining, the attacks on the rail lines within North Vietnam, and the efforts to interdict the movement of supplies by water would cease the moment the enemy agreed to two basic conditions: the return of American prisoners of war, and an internationally supervised cease-fire.

"Then," he said, "we will stop all acts of force throughout Indochina and proceed with the complete withdrawal of all forces within four months."

The White House would not say tonight whether, in effect, words, Mr. Nixon was in effect making the North Vietnamese a new peace proposal.

But observers here noted that he mentioned no political requirements for American withdrawal. Until now he has always insisted on some form of

Continued on Page 18, Column 5

HANOI SAYS RAIDS STRUCK AT DIKES

But U.S. Asserts Military Installations Were Hit in Attacks on North

By CRAIG R. WHITNEY
Special to The New York Times

SAIGON, South Vietnam, Tuesday, May 9—United States Navy fighter-bombers struck at North Vietnamese storage facilities, barracks and training facilities in an area about 15 miles west of Hanoi yesterday in the closest strikes to the North Vietnamese capital since April 16, the American command announced.

The command's announcement said the planes attacked "military heartland targets" that "are helping to support the Communist invasion" of South Vietnam.

The Hanoi radio, in a broadcast at noon, said American planes "deliberately struck at the dike system in Namha Province" southeast of Hanoi.

[The United States command denied that American jets had bombed the dikes, United Press International reported.]

The dikes support an elaborate system of irrigation and

Continued on Page 19, Column 7

4 Armed Arab Hijackers Hold Jet and 101 Hostages in Israel

By The Associated Press

TEL AVIV, May 8—Despite a tip-off and a security search, four armed Arabs hijacked an Israel-bound Belgian Sabena jetliner carrying 101 persons today.

After landing in Tel Aviv, they threatened to blow up the plane and its passengers unless Israel freed 300 Palestinian guerrilla prisoners and flew them to Cairo. A senior Israeli Army officer told the hijackers that freeing hundreds of prisoners within a few hours was impossible.

The Israelis, speaking to the hijackers by radio, were reported to have offered to free 15 or 20 military prisoners of war "as a gesture of goodwill."

The gunmen, who seized the plane after it left Vienna, set a deadline of 10 P.M. Tel Aviv time to make a deal, but the

deadline passed with no explosion or other evident action.

As negotiations were being carried on by radio, the pilot, Captain Reginald Levy, said that the plane was unfit to take off. The hijackers said that it must be made ready to leave by 5:30 A.M. or that it would be blown up. They later extended the deadline again but stipulated no time.

The Arabs also demanded to talk with a representative of the International Committee of the Red Cross.

"If the plane is not refueled I think they will blow it up," Captain Levy said by radio. "They are serious."

The police in Brussels said that they had been told by tele-

Continued on Page 7, Column 1

The New York Times/William E. Sauro
CITY OFFICIALS IN ALBANY: Foreground, from left: Controller Abraham D. Beame and Councilmen Thomas J. Cuite, majority leader, and Mario Merola, finance committee chairman. City budget was topic. Rear, from right, State Senator John J. Marchi, Assemblyman Alexander Chananau, almost hidden; Senator Warren M. Anderson.

DO YOU KNOW ANY IMPORTANT MAN IN BUSINESS WHO DOES NOT READ FORBES MAGAZINE?—ADVT.

"All the News
That's Fit to Print"

The New York Times

LATE CITY EDITION

Weather: Cloudy, mild with chance of showers today, tonight, tomorrow. Temp. range: today 59-73; Monday 57-74. Full U.S. report on Page 86.

VOL.CXXI..No.41,751   © 1972 The New York Times Company   NEW YORK, TUESDAY, MAY 16, 1972   15 CENTS

WALLACE IS SHOT; CONDITION SERIOUS; A SUSPECT SEIZED AT MARYLAND RALLY

AFTER SPEECH: Gov. George C. Wallace takes off jacket and goes to shake hands. At front is Secret Service agent.
Associated Press

DURING SHOOTING: Man at right with light hair and sun glasses holds gun as person in crowd tries to shake his arm
C.B.S. News via United Press International

Saigon's Forces Reoccupy Bastogne Base Near Hue

By MALCOLM W. BROWNE
Special to The New York Times

SAIGON, South Vietnam, Tuesday, May 16 — South Vietnamese troops, led by a platoon of 30 soldiers flown in by helicopters, reoccupied Fire Base Bastogne yesterday on the southwesterly approaches to Hue.

The five helicopters carrying the soldiers reportedly encountered no enemy fire as they landed at the base, which the South Vietnamese abandoned April 28 under heavy attack. The base had fallen after the North Vietnamese who had besieged it for more than three weeks sent commandos storming in to penetrate the barbed-wire defenses.

But after routing the defenders at the end of April, the North Vietnamese did not move their long-range 130-mm. artillery into Bastogne to shell Hue, the former imperial capital of Vietnam on the coast 15 miles away.

[The United States com-

mand announced the arrival of the carrier Saratoga off the Vietnamese coast Monday, bringing to six the number of attack carriers there. United Press International reported. The United States Seventh Fleet was now said to have 60 ships in the area.]

[In Washington, Secretary of State William P. Rogers angrily defended the mining of North Vietnam's harbors and said that if the Johnson Administration had taken the step earlier, the war might have ended long ago. Page 14.]

Allied officers in the Hue area said that if the re-entry into Fire Base Bastogne appeared to have been easy, this was only because it had capped more than a week of slow, hard fighting and more days of heavy air and artillery bombardment.

South Vietnamese spokes-

Continued on Page 14, Column 3

Court Exempts the Amish From Going to High School

By FRED P. GRAHAM
Special to The New York Times

WASHINGTON, May 15—The Supreme Court ruled 7 to 0 today that the Amish religious sect is exempt from state compulsory education laws that require children to attend school beyond the eighth grade.

The Amish—the rural "plain people" who cling to a horse-and-buggy way of life—believe that education teaches worldly values at odds with the simple life required by their creed.

With this in mind, the Court held that state laws requiring children to attend school until they are 16 years of age violate the constitutional rights of the Amish to free exercise of religion.

The decision specifically applied to Wisconsin, but it was written in terms broad enough to apply to all states that require attendance in public or private schools beyond the eighth grade. Mississippi and South Carolina are the only states that do not have compulsory school attendance laws.

The opinion, written by Chief Justice Warren E. Burger, was the first by the Court holding a religious group immune from

compulsory attendance requirements.

The Court stressed the 300-year resistance of the Amish to modern influences and served notice that faddish new sects or communes that reject formal education would probably not be granted similar exemptions.

"It cannot be overemphasized," Justice Burger wrote, "that we are not dealing with a way of life and mode of education by a group claiming to have recently discovered some 'progressive' or more en-

Continued on Page 20, Column 1

PRESSURE GROUPS ANGER ROCKEFELLER

He Asserts Judges Blocked Court Reform and Lawyers Stymied 'No-Fault' Bill

By JAMES F. CLARITY
Special to The New York Times

ALBANY, May 15—Governor Rockefeller charged today that "inordinate pressures" placed on legislators by judges and lawyers had blocked two of his "vital programs"—court reform and no-fault insurance—in the 1972 Legislature.

Mr. Rockefeller, commenting on the action of the Legislature three days after it had adjourned for the year, said the

The no-fault insurance bill was defeated through the lobbying efforts of one small group of men—the New York State Trial Lawyers Association. Article on Page 31.

judges had stymied most of his court-reform program. The lawyers, Mr. Rockefeller said, had blocked the no-fault automobile accident insurance bill he had supported.

The Governor pledged to continue to fight for passage of the two programs next year. He said undue pressure had also been exerted on the legislators to repeal the state's liberalized abortion law. The Governor vetoed the repeal measure Saturday.

"My pledge is to make an all-out fight for no-fault automobile insurance and court reform in 1973," Mr. Rockefeller said at a news conference in the Red Room of the Capitol. "Some headlines have interpreted the failure of the Legislature to enact these two vital programs as a setback for me. The truth is that they marked a setback for the people of New York State.

"At no time," the Governor

Continued on Page 38, Column 2

Hogan Drops Jay Kriegel Case; Reports He Can't Prove Perjury

By DAVID BURNHAM

The question of whether one of Mayor Lindsay's closest aides, Jay L. Kriegel, committed perjury during his testimony before the Knapp Commission will not be presented to a grand jury, District Attorney Frank S. Hogan announced yesterday.

Mr. Hogan said his office was dropping the case because "the people would not be able to establish beyond a reasonable doubt that there was a willful, irreconcilable inconsistency" between Mr. Kriegel's testimony before the Knapp Commission on June 17, 1971, and Dec. 20, 1971.

The commission was created by Mayor Lindsay on the

recommendation of a special committee that included Mr. Hogan—to investigate allegations of widespread police corruption and of failure by officials in the Lindsay administration to follow up on information about cases of corruption brought to their attention.

Mr. Hogan, in a two-and-a-half-page statement, said another reason for not proceeding with the case was that "there is substantial doubt concerning the authority of the Knapp Commission to administer the oath" at the December hearings.

Whitman Knapp, the chairman of the commission, said in

Continued on Page 28, Column 2

NEWS INDEX

	Page		Page
Art	48	Movies	48-51
Books	41	Music	48-51
Bridge	40	Obituaries	42
Business	57, 64	Op-Ed	43
Chess	41	Real Estate	62
Crossword	41	Ships and Air	32-53
Editorials	42	Theaters	48-51
Family/Style	52	TV and Radio	55
Financial	57-71	U. N. Proceedings	
Going Out Guide	49	Washington Record	18
Letters	42	Weather	86

News Summary and Index, Page 45

GUNMAN'S ATTACK CLOUDS CAMPAIGN

Uncertainty Created Both by Wallace's Status and Impact of Shooting

By MAX FRANKEL
Special to The New York Times

WASHINGTON, May 15—The bullets that felled George C. Wallace on the eve of his greatest achievements in national politics will also upset both the conduct and the calculations of the 1972 Presidential campaign.

If he could recover in time to resume some form of campaigning, and his press secretary says he will, the Alabama Governor may find an even more aroused constituency rallying to his cause. And some degree of sympathy vote may further swell his expected victories tomorrow in the Democratic primaries of Michigan and Maryland.

The Governor had 210 delegate votes of the 1,509 needed for nomination when he was struck down.

If he is forced out of the campaign, there is no one now in sight to pick up the banner of populism, tinged with an overtone of segregation, that brought the Governor 9.9 million votes, or 13.5 per cent of the total cast for President, in 1968 and seemed to promise him an equally strong following this year.

No one has ever quite

Continued on Page 34, Column 7

KNEELING OVER HUSBAND: Mrs. Cornelia Wallace bending over the Governor after he was shot at close range
C.B.S. News via Associated Press

Shooting Suspect Shouted: 'Hey, George! Over Here!'

By WARREN WEAVER Jr.
Special to The New York Times

LAUREL, Md., May 15 — George C. Wallace was shot while standing at the new crossroads of middle America today, between the drive-in bank and variety store of a suburban shopping center.

The suspected assailant, a young white man, called the Alabama Governor over to him after Mr. Wallace had stepped from behind his bullet-proof speaking stand and came down to shake hands with the crowd of about 1,000.

"Hey, George! Hey, George! Come over here! Come over here!" the man shouted insistently, according to several witnesses. The man had been standing against the ropes that cleared a space for security guards and reporters between the crowd and the small parking lot speaking stand.

Mr. Wallace heard the shouts and veered to his left, working his way down the line of admirers. He came first to Mrs. Brigitte Howkins of Hyattsville, who reached over a man, took Mr. Wallace's hand and said: "Good luck, Governor Wallace."

"He smiled at me," Mrs. Howkins recalled later, "dropped my hand and reached out for another when the man who had been standing on my right lifted his right arm and suddenly shot me."

Mr. Wallace fell to the asphalt parking surface and lay

on his back in the brilliant sunshine. Witnesses said he was bleeding from the chest and appeared also to have been struck in the right arm.

Val Hymes, a columnist for several Maryland newspapers, saw the Governor sprawled on the pavement, a large red splotch spreading across his shirt front. "I thought at first he was dead," she said.

Mrs. Wallace ran to his side,

Continued on Page 34, Column 4

Kennedy Guarded By Secret Service

By BEN A. FRANKLIN
Special to The New York Times

WASHINGTON, May 15—Shortly after Gov. George C. Wallace of Alabama was shot today, President Nixon ordered Secret Service protection for Senator Edward M. Kennedy of Massachusetts, Representative Shirley Chisholm of Brooklyn and Representative Wilbur D. Mills of Arkansas.

Senator Kennedy, who has declared repeatedly that he is not a candidate for President, accepted the offer, and an unspecified number of agents were guarding his home tonight in nearby McLean, Va. Agents joined Mrs. Chisholm in Detroit, where she was stay-

Continued on Page 35, Column 1

MILWAUKEE MAN HELD AS SUSPECT

Seized on Weapons Charge Last October in Wisconsin —Many Paradoxes Seen

By JAMES T. WOOTEN
Special to The New York Times

WASHINGTON, May 15—The young white man arrested as a suspect today in the shooting of Gov. George C. Wallace is a 21-year-old resident of Milwaukee who pasted Wallace bumper stickers on his car and his apartment door and was exuberantly cheering the Democratic Presidential candidate only moments before the shots rang out.

Those apparent contradictions are but a small part of the paradoxical picture now being sketched of Arthur Herman Bremer, the man accused by Federal authorities today of having tried to kill the Alabama Governor at a shopping center in Laurel, Md.

It was reported that he was arrested on a charge of carrying a concealed weapon last Oct. 18 and was subsequently convicted of disorderly conduct.

A Justice Department spokesman said that the .38-caliber snub-nosed revolver used at Laurel had been purchased in Milwaukee Jan. 13 and fired five times today.

From descriptions supplied

Continued on Page 34, Column 2

3 MORE WOUNDED

Legs of Governor Are Paralyzed but Hope Is Voiced by Doctor

By R. W. APPLE Jr.
Special to The New York Times

LAUREL, Md., Tuesday, May 16—Gov. George C. Wallace of Alabama, seemingly on the verge of his greatest electoral triumphs, was shot and gravely wounded yesterday afternoon as he campaigned for President at a shopping center in this suburb of Washington.

Late last night, after the 52-year-old Governor emerged from almost five hours of emergency surgery at the Holy Cross Hospital in nearby Silver Spring, Md., one of his surgeons said that he expected Mr. Wallace "to make a full recovery."

The surgeon, Dr. Joseph Schanno, said that Mr. Wallace had suffered at least four wounds and the doctors had removed one bullet. He said that another bullet was lodged near the spine and that the Governor's legs were paralyzed as a result.

Will Continue Campaign

The Governor's wife, Cornelia, said she was "very happy that he's alive and has a sound heart and a sound brain." Billy Joe Camp, his press secretary, reported this morning, after Mrs. Wallace had talked with the Governor, that he would continue his Presidential campaign and "will be at the Democratic convention as a strong, viable candidate."

The state and local police arrested a suspect, who was identified by the Justice Department as Arthur Herman Bremer, a 21-year-old white man from Milwaukee. The department said that the Secret Service had taken custody of a .38-caliber, snub-nosed, five-shot revolver allegedly used by Mr. Bremer in the shooting. Weapons and state charges were filed against him.

Held in $200,000 Bond

Mr. Bremer was taken before United States Magistrate Clarence Goetz in Baltimore last night and was ordered held under $200,000 bond.

Three persons who were with Governor Wallace as he plunged into the crowd at the Laurel Shopping Center were also hit by the four or five bullets fired by the attacker.

The shooting occurred after the Governor, having finished a speech here, shed his coat and stepped from behind the bullet-proof speaking stand.

A young man wearing sunglasses and a red, white and blue shirt bedecked with Wallace buttons thrust his right hand between two other people

Continued on Page 34, Column 1

IF YOU KNOW ANY IMPORTANT MAN IN BUSINESS WHO DOES NOT READ FORBES MAGAZINE?—ADVT.

"All the News
That's Fit to Print"

The New York Times

LATE CITY EDITION
Weather: Mostly sunny, mild today.
Fair and mild tonight, tomorrow.
Temp. range: today 54-71; Friday
46-67. Full U.S. report on Page 58.

VOL.CXXI...No.41,762   © 1972 The New York Times Company   NEW YORK, SATURDAY, MAY 27, 1972   15 CENTS

U.S. AND SOVIET SIGN TWO ARMS ACCORDS TO LIMIT GROWTH OF ATOMIC ARSENALS; TRADE PACT DELAYED, TALKS TO GO ON

Joint Commission Set Up To Resolve Trade Issues

By ROBERT B. SEMPLE Jr.
Special to The New York Times

MOSCOW, May 26—The United States and the Soviet Union announced the formation of a joint commission today to devise a comprehensive trade agreement that has proved impossible to reach during President Nixon's visit to Moscow.

The announcement, not altogether unexpected, represented an admission by both sides that the two countries had been unable to reconcile differences on the trade issue, and it constituted the first disappointment of the Moscow summit meeting.

Under the terms of the agreement, announced to reporters here by Peter M. Flanigan, Assistant to President Nixon, the joint commission will have these assignments:

¶To negotiate an over-all trade agreement including reciprocal "most favored nation" treatment—meaning, essentially, that imports from the Soviet Union will receive the same tariff advantages given most other United States trading partners.

¶To devise arrangements under which credits will be provided to finance sales by each nation to the other.

¶To set up an arbitration mechanism for settling commercial disputes arising from trade.

U.S. TRADE DEFICIT BIG AGAIN IN APRIL

Imports Exceeded Exports by $699-Million, Second Largest Gap on Record

By EDWIN L. DALE Jr.
Special to The New York Times

WASHINGTON, May 26—The United States recorded another huge deficit in its foreign trade in April, the Commerce Department reported today. Imports exceeded exports by $699-million, the second largest deficit for a month on record. The high was set last October, at $821-million.

In the first four months of the year the total trade deficit was $2.2-billion, almost guaranteeing that the year as a whole will see a larger deficit than last year's $2-billion, which was the first trade deficit in this century.

However, officials continue to expect some improvement as 1972 proceeds and the delayed effects of devaluation of the dollar begin to be felt.

Exports in April, seasonally adjusted, were $3.760-billion, down from $3.891-billion in March and the lowest export total of the year so far. A drop in exports of large jet aircraft was partly responsible.

Imports in April were $4.46-billion, down slightly from the figure of $4.475-billion in March. Both figures were above April a year ago—indicating a continued expansion of trade—but the rise in imports was much bigger than that for exports.

For the first four months of the year, exports were running

Continued on Page 35, Column 1

Lindsay Aide Says Council Must Raise Taxes on Property

By FRANCIS X. CLINES

Mayor Lindsay's office insisted yesterday that the City Council had no choice but to approve up to $89-million in higher property taxes to close an expected budget gap, regardless of the continuing opposition of Council members.

Councilman Matthew J. Troy Jr., the leader of the tax revolt, agreed with Deputy Mayor Edward K. Hamilton that there was such an obligation in the City Charter's mandate to approve real-estate taxes by June 25. But he said he would violate it rather than vote aye.

"I'm prepared to go to jail," Mr. Troy declared.

The Mayor's press spokesman, Thomas Morgan, immediately commented: "We've alerted the Corrections Department to prepare a padded cell with a view."

Thus, a farcical tone was added to the considerable confusion as the Mayor's office tried to decide what to do next in completing a balanced budget.

Continued on Page 12, Column 5

NEWS INDEX

AFTER SIGNING: President Nixon and Leonid I. Brezhnev exchange treaty copies at Kremlin. In center, Soviet President Nikolai V. Podgorny.

United Press International

FOE PUSHES FIGHT IN TWO KEY AREAS

Losses Heavy, but Enemy Clings to Small Gains at Kontum and Hue

Special to The New York Times

SAIGON, South Vietnam, Saturday, May 27—North Vietnamese soldiers hurled themselves against Government defenses in the Central Highlands city of Kontum and near the northern city of Hue through the day yesterday.

They suffered many casualties and lost 16 tanks, 13 at Kontum and three near Hue, according to American and South Vietnamese military spokesmen. But at nightfall they reportedly continued to hold small pockets of ground taken from the South Vietnamese.

In Kontum, North Vietnamese infiltrators still occupied pockets in the southeastern and northeastern parts of town and continued to keep the airport closed to traffic, according to American sources.

In the northernmost part of South Vietnam, Communist forces were said to hold small bulges of territory about 20 miles northwest of Hue, having penetrated Government defenses along the Mychanh River.

Informed sources said that at one point four North Vietnamese tanks rolled into a de-

Continued on Page 6, Column 2

A First Step, but a Major Stride

By MAX FRANKEL
Special to The New York Times

MOSCOW, Saturday, May 27—The nuclear age gained its first strategic arms limitation treaty in the Kremlin last night. Its awkward name—commonly shortened to SALT
—is needed because the accord involves no disarmament. Its purpose is to freeze the balance of terrifying weapons and to make sure the terror works by preventing any effective defense against them.

News Analysis

It is a major step forward in the already long history of nuclear arms negotiation. But it is also only a beginning.

Both President Nixon and the Soviet Party chief, Leonid I. Brezhnev, vowed to press ahead toward further limitations and perhaps eventually even some reductions in arms. So this treaty is likely to be known as SALT I.

It is a beginning, achieved after seven years of effort and 30 months of negotiation in one of those fleeting moments when the two superpowers felt themselves strategic equals, despite inequality in the quality and number of their arms, and when their two leaders felt themselves strong enough politically to make the agreements stick.

The arms race will go on, not only in the regular army, navy and air force weaponry that is unaffected by the accord but also in the quality of nuclear warheads—that is, their size and accuracy and evasive skills—and in the arts of antisubmarine warfare and even in the technology of the missile defense systems that the treaty is to limit severely at inadequate levels.

Indeed, under certain conditions or political pressures, the treaty itself may stimulate further competition in these uncovered areas. And because the accord renounces those weapons that both sides think they now possess in sufficient number, it may not even save much money in future budgets.

Continued on Page 9, Column 7

CEILINGS ARE SET

Nixon and Brezhnev Pledge to Abide by Treaty at Once

By HEDRICK SMITH
Special to The New York Times

MOSCOW, Saturday, May 27—President Nixon and the Soviet Communist party leader, Leonid I. Brezhnev, signed two historic agreements last night that for the first time put limits on the growth of American and Soviet strategic nuclear arsenals.

In a brief televised ceremony in the Great Hall of the Kremlin, the two leaders put their

Arms accord texts, Page 8, and toasts on Page 9

signatures to a treaty that establishes a ceiling of 200 launchers for each side's defensive missile systems and commits them not to try to build nationwide antimissile defenses. The treaty, which is for an indefinitely, requires ratification by the Senate in Washington, but both sides pledged to abide by it at once.

Applause After Signing

They also signed an interim accord on offensive systems that freezes land-based and submarine-based intercontinental missiles at the level now in operation or under construction.

After signing the two accords, Mr. Brezhnev and Mr. Nixon walked toward each other, smiling broadly, and shook hands vigorously amidst applause from a gathering of senior officials, including negotiators who had worked through the day to put the final touches on the agreements. Mr. Nixon then said:

"We want to be remembered by our deeds, not by the fact that we brought war to the world, but by the fact that we made the world a more peaceful one for all peoples of the world."

Can Improve Quality

Mr. Kosygin said in reply: "This is a great victory for the Soviet and American peoples in the matter of easing international tension. This is a victory for all peaceloving people, because security and peace is the common goal."

Later, American officials reported that the two leaders had resolved several deadlocks in their talks here this week.

In a toast at a dinner he gave for the Soviet leaders at Spaso House, the American Ambassador's residence, the President hailed the agreements as "enormously important."

Gerard C. Smith, the chief American negotiator, told reporters that today's two agreements were "not the end of the road by any means, but they

Continued on Page 8, Column 1

LAIRD DISCOUNTS BIG ARMS SAVINGS

Reaction to Pact in Capital Mostly Favorable but Some Conservatives Are Critical

By JUAN M. VASQUEZ
Special to The New York Times

WASHINGTON, May 26—Defense Secretary Melvin R. Laird today hailed the United States arms agreements with the Soviet Union but warned against the expectation of major cost savings.

Returning to the capital after several days of discussions with Atlantic alliance defense ministers in Brussels, Mr. Laird declared that the agreements to limit strategic arms "will enhance the national security of the United States."

He asserted, however, that "we still need to keep up our guard" and that the United States must "maintain a technological superior position."

He added, "There will be no savings as far as the request for offensive strategic weapons which have been presented to the Congress in the 1973 budget."

Specifically, he cited the Air Force B-1 bomber program and submarine construction as areas in which Congress might seek reductions, according to reports he had heard. "That just cannot be," he said.

Mr. Laird, a former Congressman from Wisconsin, told

Continued on Page 10, Column 3

Court Throws Out Jersey Law Barring Primary Cross-Voting

Special to The New York Times

NEWARK, May 26—New Jersey's primary election law prohibiting enrolled voters from casting ballots in other party contests was declared unconstitutional today by a three-judge Federal panel.

The decision specifically threw out the provisions that require enrolled voters to sit out two consecutive primary elections before switching parties. The court declared this waiting period "unreasonable and excessive."

The court directed Attorney General George F. Kugler Jr. to notify local election boards that they must permit voters to choose in which primary they want to vote on June 6 without reference to their party enrollment.

A spokesman for the Attorney General said he would not comment on whether the decision would be appealed until he had had time to study it.

If the decision stands for the coming primary, it could affect the outcome of the contests for 109 Democratic convention delegates between Senators Hubert H. Humphrey and George McGovern. Republican voters could tip the scales in favor of the man they consider the weaker candidate against President Nixon, who is unopposed on the Republican primary ballot.

The Democratic state chairman, Salvatore A. Bontempo, said he did not know how the decision would affect the primary balloting but said he was

Continued on Page 23, Column 2

U.S. AND SOVIET NUCLEAR ARSENALS

THE ARMS RACE	WHAT ACCORDS ALLOW (Basically present levels)	WARHEADS (Not covered by accords)

MISSILE IN SILO: Above photograph, from a Czech source, is said to show a Soviet emplacement. Soviet arms totals on chart include weapons that are under construction.

Photograph from Gamma/Photoreporters

The New York Times/May 27, 1972

Von Braun Will Leave NASA For Job in Aerospace Industry

By HAROLD M. SCHMECK Jr.
Special to The New York Times

WASHINGTON, May 26—Dr. Wernher von Braun, one of the chief architects of man's first landing on the moon, is retiring from the National Aeronautics and Space Administration.

The German-born rocket expert, who has worked for the United States Government since the end of World War II, will leave the space agency July 1 to become corporate vice president for engineering and development of Fairchild Industries, a major aerospace company.

"Dr. von Braun's decision to retire from NASA is a source of great regret to all of us at the agency," said Dr. James C. Fletcher, NASA's administrator.

"For more than a quarter of a century, he has served the United States as the leader in space rocket development," Dr. Fletcher said in the announcement. "His efforts first put the United States in space with Explorer I. As director of the Marshall Space Flight Center for over 10 years, he directed the development of the world's most powerful rocket, the Saturn 5—which has taken 10 American astronauts to the surface of the moon."

Two of those astronauts, Neil A. Armstrong, the first man to set foot on the moon, and Edwin E. Aldrin Jr., his companion on the historic Apollo 11 moon landing, have al-

Continued on Page 59, Column 1

The New York Times

LATE CITY EDITION

Weather: Rain today; showers likely
tonight. Fair and milder tomorrow.
Temp. range: today 68-74; Thursday
66-76. Temp.-Hum. Index yesterday
71. Full U.S. report on Page 70.

VOL. CXXI . No. 41,796   © 1972 The New York Times Company   NEW YORK, FRIDAY, JUNE 30, 1972   15 CENTS

SUPREME COURT, 5-4, BARS DEATH PENALTY AS IT IS IMPOSED UNDER PRESENT STATUTES

Party Panel Strips McGovern of 151 California Delegates

SENATOR SET BACK

He Deplores Move by Coalition of Rivals— State Law Ignored

By WARREN WEAVER Jr.
Special to The New York Times

WASHINGTON, June 29—The Democratic National Convention's Credentials Committee stripped Senator George McGovern today of 151 delegates he thought he had won in the California primary, disregarding state law in a display of political power.

Accomplished by a coalition of his rivals for the Presidential nomination, the move abruptly slowed the momentum of the South Dakotan's campaign and heavily clouded his prospects for tying up the nomination before the convention meets July 10.

The committee ended nearly four hours of debate by voting, 72 to 66, to divide the 271-member California delegation among all the Presidential candidates who competed in the June 6 primary, instead of following the California statute, which allots all the delegates to whoever gets the most votes.

Move Called 'Outrageous'

In an unusually bitter news conference at the Capitol, Senator McGovern called the committee decision "an incredible, cynical, rotten political steal" and "an outrageous way to treat the American people."

Informed at a National Press Club luncheon about the committee action, Senator Hubert H. Humphrey said that his chances for the nomination had been "markedly improved."

"I'm not going to say any more—I've got the votes," the Minnesotan said.

Authoritative sources said, meanwhile, that Senator McGovern, if he ultimately won the nomination, viewed Senator Edward M. Kennedy of Massachusetts as his first choice for a running mate. [Details on Page 20.]

Appeal Is Planned

The Credentials Committee decision will be appealed to the convention when it opens in Miami Beach, but it may prove difficult for the McGovern forces to reverse because the 151 delegates at issue—or perhaps the entire 271 from California—will not be able to vote on their own case.

This dramatic recoup for Senator McGovern was achieved by a tight, well-disciplined coalition of committee members who were either uncommitted or favored Senator Humphrey, Senator Edmund S. Muskie of Maine, Senator Henry M. Jackson of Washington or Gov. George C. Wallace of Alabama.

The development provoked angry protests from Mr. McGovern's supporters, who main-

Continued on Page 26, Column 3

Press Loses Plea to Keep Data From Grand Juries

Special to The New York Times

WASHINGTON, June 29—The Supreme Court held 5 to 4 today that journalists have no First Amendment right to refuse to tell grand juries the names of confidential sources and information given to them in confidence.

The decision overturned a lower Federal court ruling on behalf of Earl Caldwell, a reporter for The New York Times.

Excerpts from Supreme Court action are on Page 15.

in San Francisco, who had refused to enter a Federal grand jury room to be questioned on information given him by the Black Panther party.

In two related cases, the Court held that Paul M. Branzburg, an investigative reporter for The Louisville Courier-Journal at the time his case arose, and Paul Pappas, a television newsman in New Bedford, Mass., must tell state grand juries names and other information given them in confidence or face imprisonment for contempt.

The sweeping decision by Justice Byron R. White, supported by President Nixon's four appointees, contained a firm rejection of the theory that the First Amendment shields newsmen under certain circumstances from having to testify when the result would be to cut off news sources and deprive the public of news.

This theory has never been considered before today by the Supreme Court. But in recent years, as a wave of subpoenas issued from grand juries for newsmen's notes, radio stations' tapes and television companies' films, some lower courts began to construe the First Amendment as giving journalists some protection against being compelled to disclose confidences.

The courts usually reasoned that if forcing a newsman to testify would cut off future information, he should be excused unless the Government could show a compelling need for his testimony.

"We cannot accept the argu-

Continued on Page 15, Column 4

Gravel Is Denied Immunity In Case of Pentagon Papers

By ROBERT M. SMITH
Special to The New York Times

WASHINGTON, June 29—The Supreme Court ruled today, by a 5-to-4 vote, that Congressional immunity did not prevent a grand jury from asking Senator Mike Gravel or his aides certain questions about his version of the Pentagon papers—including the question where had he obtained the papers.

In a second case that turned on the same constitutional issue, the Court held, 6 to 3, that legislative privilege did not shield Daniel B. Brewster, a former Democratic Senator from Maryland, from prosecution on bribery charges.

Both decisions were handed down, with several others, on the last day of the Court's current term. The Gravel decision was written by Justice Byron R. White, who was joined by the four men President Nixon named to the Court—Chief Justice Warren E. Burger and Associate Justices Harry A. Blackmun, Lewis F. Powell Jr. and William H. Rehnquist.

Senator Gravel, Democrat of Alaska, reacted by issuing a

Continued on Page 16, Column 4

FUND MISUSE LAID TO 4 L.I. UNIONISTS

U.S. Says They Used Money in Labor-Industry Pool to Pay Ball Team's Debt

By DAVID K. SHIPLER

Four officials of a Long Island construction union were charged yesterday with using employer funds to pay off a union debt of $11,245.

The charges, filed by the Federal Organized Crime Strike Force in Brooklyn, came just hours after city officials discharged a veteran inspector in the Buildings Department who was accused of taking a $100 bribe from the owner of a Park Avenue cooperative apartment.

The two cases, while unrelated, continued to focus attention on the widespread corruption in the construction industry described early in the week by a New York Times report. According to the articles in The Times, based on a six-week investigation, builders pay at least $25-million a year here in bribes to inspectors, policemen, union

Continued on Page 28, Column 1

U.S. Copters Ferry 1,000 To Quangtri Battleground

By MALCOLM W. BROWNE
Special to The New York Times

SAIGON, South Vietnam, Friday, June 30—About 1,000 South Vietnamese marines were flown by United States helicopters yesterday into an area between the city of Quangtri and the South China Sea to join in the drive to retake the Communist-held province.

With the South Vietnamese offensive in the northernmost part of the country broadened, heavy fighting was reported from the area today. The thrust was begun Wednesday by a task force of more than 10,000 South Vietnamese marines and paratroopers.

During the night, South Vietnamese troops reported that they killed 225 enemy soldiers in various enemy sectors. Two enemy tanks were reported destroyed by artillery fire near Hailang, in the southern part of Quangtri province, while the bulk of the South Vietnamese tank force was fighting.

The helicopter-borne assault yesterday brought two battalions of South Vietnamese ma-

Continued on Page 3, Column 4

rines into two landing zones in a region east of the city of Quangtri. That city was abandoned to Communist forces on May 1 and the present drive is intended to oust the North Vietnamese from the whole province within three months.

The main South Vietnamese force, which began a northward drive Wednesday from positions along the Mychanh river line, northwest of the city of Hue, consists of elements of South Vietnamese marine and airborne divisions.

A United States Navy spokesman said that American marine helicopters took four hours to complete the landings. While a South Vietnamese spokesman said there had been no enemy opposition, another American spokesman said enemy ground fire had been encountered in both of the landing zones east of the city.

After heavy naval bombard-

Continued on Page 3, Column 4

NIXON DISCLOSES VIETNAM PARLEY RESUMES JULY 13

He Says U.S. Is Returning on Assumption Hanoi Will Negotiate Constructively

By ROBERT B. SEMPLE Jr.
Special to The New York Times

WASHINGTON, June 29—President Nixon disclosed tonight that the United States and North Vietnam would resume the Paris peace talks on the Vietnam war on July 13.

In a nationally televised news conference—his first in more

Transcript of Nixon news conference is on Page 2.

than a year—Mr. Nixon said the United States was returning to the negotiating table "on the assumption that the North Vietnamese are prepared to negotiate in a constructive and serious way."

He said that if both sides were prepared to engage in serious talks the war could be ended by next year. He also left open the opposite possibility—that the North Vietnamese might not proceed "on that basis," in which case he vowed to continue American bombing and other forms of military pressure. [Question 1, Page 2.]

Talks 'Without Conditions'

Though Mr. Nixon seemed pleased to announce the resumption of the talks, which were suspended by the United States on May 4, he gave no hint in his remarks that his intense diplomacy in Moscow and Peking in recent weeks had produced assurances that Hanoi was now prepared to move closer to the American position. The most he could or would say was that both sides had agreed to resume negotiating "without conditions."

The President also used the news conference to offer an unusually strong defense of his bombing policy and to give that policy an expanded rationale. In previous statements he has described the bombing as an essentially military tactic designed to protect the shrinking American ground forces in Vietnam and to compensate for the North Vietnamese attacks launched at the end of March.

Tonight he emphasized that

Continued on Page 3, Column 1

SPARED: Elmer Branch, 19, sentenced to die for nonfatal assault, in Huntsville, Tex., jail. He was one of condemned men whose sentences were upset by Supreme Court.

PRESIDENT WIDENS FOOD PRICE CURBS

Applies Controls to Produce After It Leaves the Farm —Seafood Also Covered

Special to The New York Times

WASHINGTON, June 29—President Nixon extended controls today to the retail and wholesale prices of such unprocessed food products as eggs, fresh vegetables, fresh fruits and all raw seafood products.

But he stopped short of the far more drastic step of placing direct controls on the prices farmers receive for these products.

The action was the President's second effort this week to impose some restraint on rising food prices, which could be a crucial issue next fall in the Presidential campaign. His reluctance to act directly on farm prices, however, appeared to reflect his concern about antagonizing the farm vote in an election year, as well as fears among some officials that direct controls might be difficult to enforce and might result in shortages.

Officials conceded at a White House briefing that the action might have little immediate effect on prices. But they expressed hope that it would exert some restraint on mark-ups and profit margins at each stage of the food distribution chain that, in time, could stem the

Continued on Page 16, Column 4

$502,000 Hijacking Laid to Jobless Man

By JERRY M. FLINT
Special to The New York Times

DETROIT, June 29—Martin Joseph McNally, 28 years old, was arrested last night in front of his home in Wyandotte, Mich., outside Detroit, by agents of the Federal Bureau of Investigation and charged with air piracy in connection with an airline hijacking in the Midwest last week in which $502,000 ransom was paid. He was held today in $100,000 bond.

The hijacker bailed out over Peru, Ind., but dropped the money, which was later recovered.

Government attorneys said Mr. McNally, an unemployed

Continued on Page 9, Column 2

Nixon Backs Death Penalty For Kidnapping, Hijacking

By WILLIAM ROBBINS
Special to The New York Times

WASHINGTON, June 29—President Nixon said tonight he hoped that the Supreme Court's decision restricting the death penalty "does not go so far as to rule out capital punishment for kidnapping and hijacking."

Asked about the Court's 5-to-4 decision, issued today, Mr. Nixon said that "any punishment is cruel and inhuman which takes the life of man or woman." He added that the death penalty had actually saved lives by deterring such major crimes as kidnapping. [Question 15, Page 2.]

The President acknowledged, however, that he had not had time to study all nine opinions. He said that he had read only the opinion of Chief Justice Warren E. Burger, a dissent from the majority ruling.

The words of the Chief Justice as well as those of another dissenter, Justice Powell, clearly bar capital punishment under both Federal and state laws as presently written.

"Not only does it [the ruling] invalidate hundreds of state and Federal laws," Justice Powell wrote in his dissenting opinion, "it deprives those jurisdictions of the power to legislate with respect to capital punishment in the future, except in a manner consistent with the cloudily outlined views of those Justices who do not purport to undertake total abolition."

And Chief Justice Burger himself said: "It is clear that if state legislatures and the Congress wish to maintain the availability of capital punishment, significant statutory changes will have to be made."

On other domestic questions, the President did the following:

¶He declined to say whether Vice President Agnew would be his choice as a running-mate in the next election.

¶He voiced support for legislation specifically restricting the possession of handguns.

¶He said former Secretary of

Continued on Page 14, Column 5

Parole in Capital Offenses Less Likely, Officials Say

By MARTIN ARNOLD

Governors and high state officials said yesterday that the Supreme Court's ruling that capital punishment was unconstitutional could profoundly change the structure of criminal penalties in the country.

Officials in many areas said it might become much more difficult, if not impossible, to get parole in cases that were until yesterday capital offenses. Thus, when a person is sentenced to life in prison, it may mean just that, they said.

Gov. Preston Smith of Texas said that the state legislature would be called upon to pass mandatory life prison sentences for certain crimes, barring any parole.

Gov. Jimmy Carter of Georgia said:

"This decision clears the way for us to re-examine all our laws in Georgia. I still don't think seven years is long enough for a man to serve in prison who has committed premeditated murder and is given a life sentence."

Gov. Ronald Reagan of California said he believed that the ruling would allow his state to

reinstate the death penalty in certain cases — "cold-blooded, premeditated, planned murder" —if the voters approved a death penalty referendum that will be on the ballot in November.

Brendan Ryan, St. Louis Circuit Attorney, said: "We will have to re-examine our statutes and perhaps make a life sentence really mean life. Perhaps we should now redefine our homicide laws so as to make some eligible for parole after a given time, but others only parolable through executive clemency, if at all."

Prof. Yale Kamisar of the University of Michigan Law School, considered one of the nation's leading constitutional authorities, expressed surprise and delight with the ruling, but was fearful that there might be a reaction against it.

"There will be increased attention given life sentencing,"

Continued on Page 15, Column 1

COURT SPARES 600

4 Justices Named by Nixon All Dissent in Historic Decision

By FRED P. GRAHAM
Special to The New York Times

WASHINGTON, June 29—The Supreme Court ruled today that capital punishment, as now administered in the United States, is unconstitutional "cruel and unusual" punishment.

The historic decision, came on a vote of 5 to 4.

Although the five Justices in the majority issued separate opinions and did not agree on

Excerpts from Court decision on death penalty, Page 14.

a single reason for their action, the effect of the decision appeared to be to rule out executions under any capital punishment laws now in effect in this country.

The decision will also save from execution 600 condemned men and women now on death rows in the United States, although it did not overturn their convictions. Most will be held in prison for the rest of their lives, but under some states' procedures some of the prisoners may eventually gain their freedom.

Eighth Amendment Cited

The decision pitted the five holdovers of the more liberal Warren Court against the four appointees of President Nixon, who dissented. The ruling came as the Supreme Court handed down its final decisions of the year and recessed until Oct. 2.

Three Justices in the majority, William O. Douglas, William J. Brennan Jr. and Thurgood Marshall, concluded that executions in modern-day America necessarily violate the Eighth Amendment's prohibition against "cruel and unusual punishments."

The other two in the majority, the two "swing men" of the Court, Justices Potter Stewart and Byron R. White, reasoned that the present legal system operates in a cruel and unusual way, because it gives judges and juries the discretion to decree life or death and they impose it erratically.

As Justice Stewart put it, the death penalty is "so wantonly and so freakishly imposed" that those who are sentenced to death receive excessively harsh treatment.

View of Chief Justice

"These death sentences are cruel and unusual in the same way that being struck by lightning is cruel and unusual," he said.

As the dissenters pointed out, this alignment means that no death sentence can pass muster before the present Supreme Court unless it satisfies the objections voiced by Justices Stewart and White.

Chief Justice Warren E. Burger suggested that legislatures could attempt to do this in two ways. One is to state in statute books in detail the conditions under which a judge or jury can impose the death penalty—such as rape accompanied by a vicious assault, or a convict's murder of a prison guard.

The second would be to revert to the practice of more than a century ago, and impose mandatory death sentences for

Continued on Page 14, Column 4

Senate Votes Antipoverty Bill, Including Plan for Legal Aid

By The Associated Press

WASHINGTON, June 29—The Senate passed a $9.6-billion antipoverty bill today that included a provision to put the Legal Services program for the poor under an independent corporation.

The bill, passed by a vote of 74 to 16 after a week of debate, authorizes funds for two additional years for programs designed to help 26 million Americans officially defined as poor.

The Senate vote sent the legislation back to the House, which passed a somewhat different version last February.

The conference to try to settle the differences between the two measures will be held after Congress returns July 17 from

its recess for the Democratic National Convention.

The bill authorizes sums well beyond President Nixon's recommendations for many programs of the Office of Economic Opportunity, the antipoverty agency. And the bill does not give the President the complete free hand he sought in handling or transferring the programs.

In addition, Administration officials indicated that they still found unacceptable the form of the Legal Services Corporation set out in the bill. For these reasons, there is reason to believe that Mr. Nixon

Continued on Page 10, Column 4

"All the News
That's Fit to Print"

The New York Times

LATE CITY EDITION

Weather: Partly sunny, warm today;
fair, warm tonight. Sunny tomorrow.
Temp. range: today 64-84; Monday
66-71. Temp.-Hum. Index yesterday
70. Full U.S. report on Page 69.

VOL.CXXI .. No. 41,828   © 1972 The New York Times Company   NEW YORK, TUESDAY, AUGUST 1, 1972   15 CENTS

EAGLETON QUITS AT REQUEST OF M'GOVERN; SAYS HE DOES NOT WANT TO 'DIVIDE' PARTY

6 KILLED BY BOMBS AFTER TROOP PUSH ON I.R.A. IN ULSTER

Blasts in Village Wound 30 as Soldiers Move Through Urban Catholic Areas

By BERNARD WEINRAUB
Special to The New York Times

BELFAST, Northern Ireland, July 31 — Six persons were killed in terrorist bomb blasts today following a predawn operation by British troops that smashed the barricades of Roman Catholic areas in Belfast and Londonderry.

As thousands of soldiers, backed by armored convoys and bulldozers, moved through silent Catholic neighborhoods this morning, three bombs exploded without warning in automobiles in the center of the tiny village of Claudy, 10 miles southeast of Londonderry. The six victims included a 9-year-old girl. Among the 30 wounded, five are in critical condition.

Most Barricades Gone

By tonight, almost all the barricades in Londonderry and Belfast had been swept aside. Weary British soldiers, gripping automatic weapons, were deployed beside schools, apartment houses and empty pubs in Catholic areas.

"The position now is that anyone can go anywhere at any time," Maj. Gen. Robert Ford, the commander of land forces here, said this evening.

Belfast and Londonderry are under virtual siege. Flak-jacketed soldiers — some of them with faces blackened with charcoal—patrolled such Irish Republican Army strongholds as Andersonstown, Falls Road and the Ardoyne in Belfast as well as the Bogside in Londonderry. Troop carriers, tanks and armored cars, equipped with twin Browning machine guns, rumbled down the center of Belfast.

'Army Now in Control'

"The army are now in occupation and control throughout Northern Ireland," William Whitelaw, the British administrator for Ulster, said this morning after the assault into so-called "no-go" areas established by the Catholics. It was the biggest military operation ever mounted in Northern Ireland.

For nearly three years, areas of Londonderry and Belfast, Northern Ireland's two principal cities, have been effectively barricaded to the army and the police, creating a haven for the I.R.A. Mr. Whitelaw had hesitated in the past to dismantle the barricades and deploy troops into these areas, fearing bitter gun-

Continued on Page 3, Column 4

Ellsberg's Lawyers Ask Rehnquist Ban

By FRED P. GRAHAM
Special to The New York Times

LOS ANGELES, July 31—The tangled court proceedings in the Pentagon papers case were further complicated today when the defense sought to disqualify Justice William H. Rehnquist from taking part in the Supreme Court's consideration of the case.

The request that Justice Rehnquist excuse himself came in response to a Justice Department application, filed with the Supreme Court today, that asked the full Court to overturn Justice William O. Douglas's stay of the Pentagon papers trial.

Justice Rehnquist was asked, in a telegram to the Court, to excuse himself from any action on the stay because of his alleged connection with aspects of the Pentagon papers contro-

Continued on Page 16, Column 4

Lend-Lease Debts Blocking A Soviet-U.S. Trade Pact

By HEDRICK SMITH
Special to The New York Times

MOSCOW, July 31—Persisting differences over Soviet repayment of a World War II lend-lease debt have prevented Secretary of Commerce Peter G. Peterson and top-level Soviet officials from achieving an over-all Soviet-American trade agreement in 10 days of talks here, diplomatic sources reported tonight.

Mr. Peterson, who had a three-hour meeting with the Communist party general secretary, Leonid I. Brezhnev, in the Crimea yesterday and a four-hour negotiating session here today with the Soviet Union's Foreign Trade Minister, Nikolai S. Patolichev, leaves for Poland tomorrow en route home.

Diplomatic sources said the joint Soviet-American Economic Commission would issue a communiqué on its work tomorrow, probably announcing plans for another meeting in Washington to make a final effort at achieving the elusive trade agreement before the November election.

The commission was established during President Nixon's May summit meeting with Soviet leaders when, despite efforts, they failed to reach a trade agreement.

Diplomatic sources said tonight that the two sides were still deadlocked over terms of Soviet repayment of the lend-lease debt. The Soviets are demanding a 2 per cent interest rate on the outstanding debt, and the Americans are asking for 6 per cent.

"We began at zero and came back to zero," was the way one negotiator described the 10 days of talks. But other officials, both Soviet and American, insisted that progress had been made, that the results had been about as expected, and that the warm atmosphere of the May summit meeting persisted.

Neutral diplomats have suggested that the White House is hesitant to make trade concessions to Moscow until it sees

Continued on Page 52, Column 1

European Families Feel The Bite of Rising Costs

By CLYDE H. FARNSWORTH
Special to The New York Times

PARIS, July 31—Inflation, which seems to be the inevitable accompaniment of life in a modern industrial society, is changing the habits and attitudes of Europeans.

Strikes in Britain, France, Italy and elsewhere are one sign of the frustrations the working man feels in trying to keep up with the ever-mounting cost of living.

In Britain, the industrial strife is on a scale not seen since the nineteen-twenties. And Italy is already feeling the tremors heralding the quakes that will come this fall when the latest wage contracts expire.

The more prosperous European middle classes, while less afflicted, have not been spared. They are squeezed right and left, but their problem is not so much earning enough to live as keeping what they've got. The 16th century French writer Montaigne put it succinctly. "I find it more trouble to watch over money than to get it."

No issue—whether soccer or Bobby Fischer's chess antics, the topless fad at St. Tropez or new ministers in Paris, Bonn

and Rome—can quite compete with the inexorable march of prices as a topic of conversation in the pubs and municipal flats of England, around the wooden kitchen tables of France, in the winehouses of Germany and Austria, in the tulip-decked living rooms of the Netherlands or in the crammed Fiat of a Neapolitan family rolling on the ramp of the ferry to the island of Ischia.

What exactly is happening to prices? How are they affecting the daily lives of Europeans? What are the Europeans doing about them? What are the attitudes of governments and the financial authorities?

Here is what the raw statistics show for latest annual inflation rates in some nations: the Netherlands, 8 per cent; Switzerland, 6.3 per cent; Britain, 6.2 per cent; France, 5.4 per cent; West Germany, 5.1 per cent; Japan, 4.5 per cent, and the United States, 3.2 per cent.

But the statistics don't tell anything like the full story. Things like this are left out:

¶Bus fares have doubled in

Continued on Page 2, Column 1

HATCH ACT UPSET; U.S. COURT FINDS CURBS TOO VAGUE

Civil Service Unit Enjoined From Enforcing Bars on Political Activity

By ROBERT M. SMITH
Special to The New York Times

WASHINGTON, July 31 — A three-judge panel of the United States District Court here ruled today that the Hatch Act's prohibitions on political activity by Federal civil service employees are so vague and broad that they are unconstitutional.

By a vote of 2 to 1, the panel enjoined the Civil Service Commission from enforcing the 33-year-old act. The court stayed its injunction, however, until the Supreme Court can decide the issue.

It was not clear whether the Civil Service Commission would continue to enforce the act. A spokesman for the commission said its lawyers were still analyzing the decision. Similarly, a Justice Department spokesman said that Government lawyers had not decided whether to appeal the case to the Supreme Court.

Letter Carriers Sue

The suit against the Civil Service Commission was brought by the National Association of Letter Carriers, six local Democratic and Republican committees and six Federal employees as a class action on behalf of all Federal and state employees covered by the Hatch Act.

The court held that the political committees had not shown that they adequately represented state employes and therefore limited its ruling to Federal employes.

In his opinion for the court, District Judge Gerhard A. Gesell took note of a 1947 decision by the Supreme Court, United Public Workers v. Mitchell, which upheld the act, but it contended that the present case was different.

Judge Gesell said that this case "focuses not on the merits of the objective of the Hatch Act but on the manner in which Congress defined the conduct it purported to prohibit." He held the Congressional definition "ambiguous and unsatisfactory."

He pointed out that the Congressional definition "incorporates by reference over 3,000

Continued on Page 25, Column 4

Senator George McGovern announcing the withdrawal of Senator Thomas F. Eagleton

OTTAWA REJECTS LEGAL MARIJUANA

But Asks End to Jail Terms for Possession and to Criminal Citations

By JAY WALZ
Special to The New York Times

OTTAWA, July 31 — The Canadian Government today rejected recent recommendations that it legalize the simple possession of marijuana and hashish. However, under a new policy to be proposed to Parliament, first offenders would be treated far more leniently than in the past.

"The Government has no intention to legalize possession of cannabis in any form," Health Minister John C. Munro declared in a statement, "nor does it intend to legalize the cultivation of cannabis for personal use."

At the same time, Mr. Munro continued, the Government recognizes the need to amend laws to reduce their "impact" on users not involved in the trafficking or cultivation of the illegal drugs. To make this possible, the Government will seek to transfer all controls relating to cannabis, the group of drugs that includes marijuana and hashish, from the Narcotic

Continued on Page 6, Column 1

Eagleton Tells McGovern It Was 'the Only Decision'

By DOUGLAS E. KNEELAND
Special to The New York Times

WASHINGTON, July 31—A little after 8:30 tonight, Senator Thomas F. Eagleton left the Marble Room just off the Senate floor for the long walk down the underground corridor to his office building. At his side was Senator George McGovern, the Democratic candidate for the Presidency. When they went into the Marble Room, Senator Eagleton was McGovern's running mate. When they left, Senator Eagleton knew it was all over.

The 42-year-old Missourian was gaunt, red-eyed and visibly nervous. But as they walked down the corridor, he had his arm draped over Mr. McGovern's shoulder.

Over and over he said to the man who had just convinced him to resign from the ticket that it was "the correct decision, the only decision—it will prove to be the right one in the long run."

Hands Held High

As they reached a fork in the tunnel, they parted ways with hands held high in waves as Mr. Eagleton went to his office in one building and Mr. McGovern moved toward his in another.

A little more than an hour later, the two men thrust their way, with the aid of Secret Service agents, through the crush of newsmen and campaign aides jamming Room 318—the Caucus Room in the Old Senate Office Building.

The chamber was electric with excitement, expectant yet somehow sad about the announcement that most of those

Continued on Page 24, Column 4

5 THUGS AT PLAZA GET $45,000 GEMS

21 Employees Held Captive as Gunmen Break Open 5 Safe-Deposit Boxes

By ERIC PACE

Five dapper robbers smashed open five safe-deposit boxes at the Plaza Hotel early yesterday, the police said, and escaped with more than $45,000 worth of jewelry belonging to jewelers who had come here for a convention.

Waving pistols, the robbers herded 21 hotel employees and bystanders into a 10-by-11-foot office. Then, crouching under a crystal chandelier, they broke open the boxes, scooped up an emerald tiara and other pieces of jewelry and drove off.

"If somebody pulls a gun on you, you don't argue with him," said Jack Craver, the hotel manager, who went to the hotel at Fifth Avenue and Central Park South soon after the hour-long rain ended at 5 A.M.

He said that the two hotel security men on duty had been patrolling upstairs during the holdup and that the other employees had not sounded alarms. No one was hurt, and no ar-

Continued on Page 70, Column 1

Paul-Henri Spaak Is Dead at 73; An Architect of European Unity

By ROBERT D. McFADDEN

Paul-Henri Spaak, the Belgian statesman who was one of the chief architects of European unification and Western solidarity in the postwar era, died of kidney failure yesterday in Brussels. He was 73 years old.

Mr. Spaak, who came to be known as "Mr. Europe" for his international vision and towering efforts to integrate the continent, became ill while on vacation in the Azores on Saturday. He was flown home in a United States Air Force plane, entered Brugmann Hospital on Sunday and died shortly after midnight.

Although Mr. Spaak retired from political life in 1966, he had remained active, traveling, writing and speaking frequently about the institutions and peoples he loved, and was generally believed to have been in good health in recent years, apart from regular attacks of gout.

Paul-Henri Spaak

After the announcement of his death yesterday, flags were ordered flown at half-staff throughout Belgium and in many parts of Europe, and there were scores of tributes for the man with a global vision from leaders around the

Continued on Page 38, Column 2

SUCCESSOR SOUGHT

O'Brien and Muskie in Running — Dakotan to Address Nation

By JAMES M. NAUGHTON
Special to The New York Times

WASHINGTON, July 31 — Senator Thomas F. Eagleton, yielding to a request from Senator George McGovern, withdrew tonight from his campaign for the Vice-Presidency. He said that he did not wish to "divide the Democratic party" by continuing as its nominee.

Eighteen days after choosing Mr. Eagleton as his running

Statements and excerpts are printed on Page 25.

mate, Senator McGovern, the Democratic Presidential nominee, announced that they had agreed that the "best course" would be for Mr. Eagleton to step aside and thereby terminate a national debate over his health.

Thus Mr. Eagleton became the first Vice-Presidential nominee ever to withdraw from candidacy, other than by death. Democratic leaders across the country, after learning of Mr. Eagleton's withdrawal, said that while the action was sad personally, it would strengthen the party's chances in the November election.

May Pick O'Brien

Senator McGovern said that he did not have a new nominee in mind, but there were reports that he would recommend to the Democratic National Committee that it select its former chairman, Lawrence F. O'Brien, to take Mr. Eagleton's place.

Among other names mentioned was that of Senator Edmund S. Muskie of Maine, whose associates said that he would be available if Mr. McGovern were to ask him to become the new Vice-Presidential nominee.

Mr. McGovern said at a news conference at which he and Mr. Eagleton announced the decision that "health was not a factor" in making it. But he added that Senator Eagleton's disclosure, six days ago, that he had been hospitalized in 1960, 1964 and 1966 for treatment of nervous exhaustion and fatigue had "dominated the political dialogue of the country" and threatened to obscure the real issue of the campaign.

Committee to Choose

Mr. Eagleton said he would write a letter in the morning officially informing Mrs. Jean Westwood, the chairman of the national committee, of his decision. Mrs. Westwood will then convene a meeting of the committee, which has the responsibility of choosing a new candidate.

Mr. McGovern announced that he would go on nationwide television at 9 P.M. tomorrow "to discuss the events of the campaign to date." But he said he did not expect to announce a Vice-Presidential nominee tomorrow.

It was clear that Senator Eagleton had yielded to Senator McGovern in agreeing to withdraw at a two-hour private meeting in the Marble Room off the United States Senate chamber earlier tonight.

"I would have preferred to remain on the ticket," Mr. Eagleton said at a news conference an hour later in the high-ceiling Caucus Room of the Old Senate Office Building.

He said that he had "marshaled my arguments in lawyer-like fashion" in seeking to

Continued on Page 24, Column 3

3 Hijack Jet, Collect $1-Million and Fly to Algeria

By RICHARD WITKIN

Three hijackers commandeered a Delta Air Lines jet yesterday, collected a major portion of the $1-million they had demanded and forced the crew to head for Algeria.

Accompanied by three women and two or three children, the hijackers released the 86 other passengers at Miami after the extortion money, stuffed in a blue suitcase, had been hauled into the cockpit by rope.

A Delta spokesman said that he could not say precisely how much money had been turned over but that it was believed to be the largest amount ever paid in a hijacking in this country. The previous high was slightly over $500,000.

Refueled in Boston

Having obtained the money, the hijackers, who are black, ordered the DC-8 flown to Boston to refuel and to pick up a navigator for the over-water flight. At 8:50 P.M. the plane headed out over the ocean on a nonstop flight for Algiers, which has become a haven for some black militants.

The plane was expected to reach Algiers at 3:23 A.M., Eastern daylight time.

In another hijacking to Algeria in early June, the $500,000 in extortion money collected by the two hijackers was later re-

Continued on Page 69, Column 5

An F.B.I. agent lugging a suitcase containing ransom money demanded by hijackers to the Delta Air Lines DC-8 at Miami Airport. As directed by the hijackers, presumably to show that he was unarmed, the agent wore only a swimsuit.

News Summary and Index, Page 17

The New York Times

VOL. CXXI...No. 41,864   © 1972 The New York Times Company   NEW YORK, WEDNESDAY, SEPTEMBER 6, 1972   15 CENTS

9 ISRAELIS ON OLYMPIC TEAM KILLED WITH 4 ARAB CAPTORS AS POLICE FIGHT BAND THAT DISRUPTED MUNICH GAMES

A copter making a test run before picking up Arabs involved in the attack on Israelis. At rear is the Olympic Tower. Sign in German says, "Olympic Village, Gate 6."

MRS. MEIR SPEAKS

A Hushed Parliament Hears Her Assail 'Lunatic Acts'

By TERENCE SMITH
Special to The New York Times

JERUSALEM, Sept. 5—Her voice heavy and trembling with emotion, Premier Golda Meir today denounced "these lunatic acts of terrorism, abduction and blackmail, which tear asunder the web of international life."

Speaking to a hushed and somber parliament before the fate of the Israeli hostages held captive in Munich was known, she said, "It is inconceivable that the Olympic events should continue as long as our citizens are under the threat of being murdered in the Olympic Village."

She called on all the nations participating in the Olympics to do "whatever is necessary" to rescue the nine Israelis taken hostage by Arab guerrillas in an early-morning attack in which two other Israelis were killed.

[Official sources in Jerusalem said early Wednesday that the Cabinet would meet later in the morning and that there would be no statement on the deaths of the hostages until then.]

Cabinet Still Firm

Although she was not explicit, Mrs. Meir left the impression that Israel would continue to refuse the guerrillas' demands for the release of 200 Palestinian commandos held in this country. Cabinet sources said the Government remained committed to its hard-line policy of neither dealing with nor making concessions to the guerrillas.

Most Israelis seemed stunned by the news of the bizarre attack on the Israeli athletes, which was first reported here on a radio broadcast at 9 A.M. (3 A.M. Tuesday, New York time). Although Israeli citizens traveling abroad have been attacked by Palestinian guerrillas before, the Olympics seemed to many an unlikely setting.

"The games were going so well," one Jerusalem news dealer said, "and now this."

In parliament, where the members had gathered in an extraordinary session to confirm the Justice Minister, the attack was the sole topic of conversation.

Cabinet Ministers and members of parliament sat in the building's modern, sun-washed dining room waiting for additional news from Munich. Each hour on the hour, the large room grew silent and the ministers gathered four deep around a radio as the Israeli radio summarized the developments.

The tension was greatest at

Continued on Page 20, Column 2

752 Air-Conditioned Cars Ordered for City Subways

By EDWARD RANZAL

Mayor Lindsay announced yesterday that 752 new air-conditioned subway cars had been ordered for $210.5-million. He said the contract was the largest ever signed in the country for the purchase of passenger railroad cars.

The first group of cars, which will be manufactured by the Pullman-Standard Company, are to be delivered by 1973.

The cars will provide a quieter ride than present equipment, according to Dr. William J. Ronan, chairman of the Metropolitan Transportation Authority.

The new equipment, which will be used on the IND and BMT lines, will enable the authority to phase out more than 1,200 pre-World War II cars, which are smaller than the new ones. A study is being made, Dr. Ronan said, to produce an air-conditioned unit that can be used in cars in the smaller tunnels of the IRT system.

20% of Fleet by '75

Each car will cost more than $273,000. The city will provide one-third of the total funds—the money has been provided in the city's 1972-73 capital budget—and the Federal Urban Mass Transportation Administration will supply the rest.

By 1975 more than 20 per cent of the city's fleet of nearly 7,000 subway cars will consist of new air-conditioned cars.

The first order under the contract will be for 454 cars at a cost of $127.4-million. Some of them will be delivered in

Continued on Page 91, Column 2

Berrigan and a Nun Get Prison Terms In Letter Smuggling

By JOHN KIFNER
Special to The New York Times

HARRISBURG, Pa., Sept. 5—The Rev. Philip F. Berrigan—cleared of charges that he led a plot to kidnap President Nixon's adviser on national security affairs, Henry A. Kissinger—was sentenced in Federal District Court here today to four concurrent two-year terms for smuggling letters out of the Lewisburg Penitentiary.

Sister Elizabeth McAlister, also cleared of the plot charges, was sentenced to one year in jail and three years' probation for smuggling letters.

Moments after the sentences were announced, Government attorneys moved to dismiss the first three substantive counts of their indictment, confirming that the Justice Department would not seek a retrial of the controversial "Harrisburg Seven" case.

The Government charged Father Berrigan, Sister Elizabeth, two other Roman Catholic priests, a former priest, a former nun and a Pakistani scholar with conspiracy to kidnap Mr. Kissinger as ransom to force a halt to the bombing in Viet-

Continued on Page 16, Column 1

West German policemen talking with a spokesman, right, for Arabs who invaded Israeli quarters at Olympic Village

A West German Army ambulance passing through the heavily guarded gate at the military airfield in Fürstenfeldbruck, near Munich, after the commandos and the hostages landed in three helicopters.

PARLEY REJECTS HIJACKING TREATY

U.S.-Canadian Project for Penalizing Nations Aiding Air Pirates Rebuffed

By ROBERT LINDSEY
Special to The New York Times

WASHINGTON, Sept. 5—Delegates to a 17-nation conference here rejected today United States-Canadian efforts to negotiate an international antihijacking treaty based on a draft proposed by the two nations.

The move for nonacceptance was led by France and Britain and supported by the Soviet Union and Egypt.

Faced with what appeared to be certain defeat if it came to a vote, the two North American nations acquiesced in a French proposal to start writing a new treaty from scratch, after debates on what "principles" should be included.

The delegates have eight working days before the conference is scheduled to end. Today's rejection was a significant setback for the United

Continued on Page 91, Column 2

Nixon Tightens Security In U.S. Against 'Outlaws'

By TAD SZULC
Special to The New York Times

WASHINGTON, Sept. 5—President Nixon said today that "extra security measures" would be taken in the United States to protect American citizens as well as visiting Israelis from possible attacks by Palestinian guerrillas.

Mr. Nixon, speaking to newsmen in San Francisco, left it unclear, however, whether he meant that this new protection would cover prominent American Jews or only those whom he described as "Americans of Israeli background, American citizens."

Speaking before the gunfight at a military airport in Munich, in which the Israeli hostages were killed, Mr. Nixon discussed the capture of Israeli Olympic team members by Palestinian guerrillas and the slaying of two Israelis. He said:

"Since we are dealing with international outlaws who are unpredictable, we have to take extra security measures to protect those who might be the targets of this kind of activity in the future. That might include Americans of Israeli background, American citizens."

Late tonight, after word was received in Washington of the death of the Israeli hostages and West German policemen,

Continued on Page 20, Column 1

Reports First Said Israelis Were Safe

Contradictory reports last night about the fate of the Israeli hostages seized by Arab terrorists in the Olympic Village threw the public into confusion all over the world.

Throughout the day, as the tragedy in Munich unfolded, millions of viewers throughout the world watched on live television, which employed circuits that had been intended for the Games. But in the evening, when the events reached their climax, viewers could get no definitive word for hours on how the hostages fared.

[Page 20.]

A 23-HOUR DRAMA

2 Others Are Slain in Their Quarters in Guerrilla Raid

By DAVID BINDER
Special to The New York Times

MUNICH, West Germany, Wednesday, Sept. 6—Eleven members of Israel's Olympic team and four Arab terrorists were killed yesterday in a 23-hour drama that began with an invasion of the Olympic Village by the Arabs. It ended in a shootout at a military airport some 15 miles away as the Arabs were preparing to fly to Cairo with their Israeli hostages.

The first two Israelis were killed early yesterday morning when Arab commandos, armed with automatic rifles, broke into the quarters of the Israeli team and seized nine others as hostages. The hostages were killed in the airport shootout between the Arabs and German policemen and soldiers.

The bloodshed brought: the suspension of the Olympic Games and there was doubt if they would be resumed. Willi Daume, president of the West German Organizing Committee, announced early today that he would ask the International Olympic Committee to meet tomorrow to decide whether they should continue.

Policeman Killed

In addition to the slain Israelis and Arabs, a German policeman was killed and a helicopter pilot was critically wounded. Three Arabs were wounded.

There were some reports that two of the hostages said to have been killed might still be alive. "It is a dim hope," said Dr. Bruno Merk, the Interior Minister of Bavaria, "but I am skeptical on this point."

The bloodbath at the airport that ended at 1 A.M. today, came after long hours of negotiation between German and Arabs at the Israeli quarters in the Olympic Village where the Arabs demanded the release of 200 Arab commandos imprisoned in Israel.

Finally the West German armed forces supplied three helicopters to transport the Arabs and their Israeli hostages to the airport at Fürstenfeldbruck. From there all were to be flown to Cairo.

A Boeing-707 provided by the Lufthansa German Airlines was waiting.

Two of the terrorists, carrying their automatic rifles, walked about 170 yards from the helicopters to the plane. And then they started back to pick up the other Arabs and the hostages.

Positions Cited

As the Arabs were returning, German sharpshooters reportedly opened fire from the darkness beyond the pools of light at the airport. The Arabs returned fire.

The torment of the entire event was heightened by confusion created in the public mind by contradictory reports from German and Olympic officials after the gunfire erupted at the airport.

Dr. Merk, in a press conference at 3 o'clock this morning said:

"In this situation our task was made more difficult by the lack of agreement from Israel and goal to free the hostages to free prisoners or to get guarantees from the Arabs not to take action against the hos-

Continued on Page 18, Column 1

GAMES SUSPENDED; RITES IN ARENA SET

Halt Is the First Since 1896, When the Classic Resumed
—Egypt Team in Forfeit

By NEIL AMDUR

MUNICH, West Germany, Wednesday, Sept. 6—The Olympic Games were suspended yesterday for the first time since competition in the modern era began in 1896.

Late-afternoon and evening events were called off in the wake of an attack staged by Arab guerrillas before dawn on the Olympic Village in which two Israelis were killed and nine others taken hostage. The hostages were later killed.

After the attack, Mark Spitz, the American swimmer who won seven gold medals in the Munich Olympics and who is Jewish, flew hurriedly to London on his way back to the United States. There were fears before his departure that he too might become a victim.

Continued on Page 18, Column 4

Elizabeth City Hall Under Investigation

By RONALD SULLIVAN
Special to The New York Times

TRENTON, Sept. 5—Law enforcement authorities reported here today that the administration of Mayor Thomas J. Dunn of Elizabeth was the target of a Union County grand jury investigation of alleged municipal corruption.

Mayor Dunn, a Democrat running for a third term, said in an interview that he had "no knowledge of any investigation involving me or my administration." But he said he volunteered last spring to appear before a Union County grand jury.

According to official sources, the grand jury is investigating charges of payoffs and kickbacks involving city officials, contracts and businessmen. City

license officials have already been subpoenaed, as have a number of city records and contracts.

Karl Asch, the county prosecutor, refused to comment on the nature of the reported investigation. He did say his staff had been instructed to seek indictments before the Nov. 7 elections.

Last week two of Mr. Dunn's three mayoral opponents were indicted in separate matters by a Union County grand jury.

Matthew J. Nilsen, a Republican freeholder in the county, was indicted on charges of atrocious assault in August in a case involving an alleged extortion.

In the other indictment, Michael J. DeMartino, a Dem-

ocratic City Councilman in Elizabeth, was charged with misconduct in office in a case involving a $3,000 bribe in 1968.

Mayor Dunn recently endorsed President Nixon for re-election. Political observers in Union County noted that the indictments of two of his opponents were sought by a Republican prosecutor, and were seen as aiding the Mayor's re-election chances.

However, Mr. Asch, who has obtained indictments against prominent Union County political figures in recent months, contended today that his anti-corruption drive was "absolutely nonpolitical" and that the investigation of the Dunn

Continued on Page 40, Column 6

IF YOU'RE NOT DRINKING WILLIAM PENN'S SCOTCH, DRINK DEWAR'S William Lawson 86.8 Proof Blended Scotch Whiskies. Imported by Palmer & Lord, Ltd., Syosset, N.Y.—Advt.

"All the News That's Fit to Print"

The New York Times

LATE CITY EDITION

Weather: Cloudy, mild today; cool tonight. Chance of rain tomorrow. Temp. range: today 43-63; Thursday 42-56. Full U.S. Report on Page 82.

VOL. CXXII..No. 41,915   © 1972 The New York Times Company   NEW YORK, FRIDAY, OCTOBER 27, 1972   15 CENTS

KISSINGER ASSERTS THAT 'PEACE IS AT HAND'; SAIGON SAYS IT WILL AGREE TO A CEASE-FIRE

BOARD REVERSES SCRIBNER, ORDERS 32 INTO J.H.S. 211

Minority Pupils Are Upheld Despite Parental Protests That Shut the School

By LEONARD BUDER

The City Board of Education yesterday overruled Chancellor Harvey B. Scribner and directed that 32 black and Puerto Rican children be admitted to John Wilson Junior High School 211 in Canarsie — the school they had been barred from entering last week when protesting white parents took over the building and shut it down.

Last Monday night, in what turned out to be a futile effort

Texts of Scribner and board statements, Page 36.

to resolve the long-boiling controversy, Dr. Scribner reversed an order he had issued that had assigned the 32 Brownsville children to the Wilson school. Instead, Dr. Scribner assigned them—over the objections of the Brownsville parents — to Isaac Bildersee Junior High School 68, a virtually all-white Canarsie school.

The city board, at a 5 P.M. news conference attended by Dr. Scribner, announced that it had directed the Chancellor to reinstate his original order, issued on Oct. 11.

Date of Entry Open

The order of the city board did not specify when the children were to be admitted. When Dr. Scribner was asked later when they would go to J.H.S. 211, he replied:

"When I think it is most appropriate for these children to attend. I am not prepared to say if it will be tomorrow morning or a week from tomorrow morning."

Yesterday morning, when they were still in defiance of Dr. Scribner's earlier ruling, the Brownsville youngsters were turned away by school officials and policemen when they sought to enter the heavily guarded Wilson school.

Last night Mrs. Joan Boatright, a leader of the Brownsville group, along with the Rev. Wilbert B. Miller, a spokesman for the blacks, said she was "very happy" over the Board of Education's new order. She added that the par-

Continued on Page 36, Column 3

Sherwin and 2 Are Guilty Of Conspiracy in Road Bid

By JOSEPH F. SULLIVAN
Special to The New York Times

FREEHOLD, N. J., Oct. 26—Paul J. Sherwin, New Jersey's Secretary of State, and two co-defendants were found guilty today of conspiring to influence the award of a $600,000 highway contract in return for a $10,000 contribution to the state Republican finance committee.

Sherwin, who was Governor Cahill's closest personal friend and chief political adviser, sat stoically in the front row of the courtroom with his wife and six children as Mrs. Virginia Cappello, the Englishtown housewife who served as jury foreman, read the verdict.

But his wife, Elva, and their three daughters sobbed uncontrollably as the guilty findings were read and as Superior Court Judge Francis X. Crahay polled the jury of seven men and five women.

"Daddy, you didn't do it!" cried Mrs. Jean Mooney, the couple's oldest daughter, as she clung to her father's arm. Their youngest daughter, 15-year-old Caroline, shook her head in disbelief and cried openly as she stared at the jury.

Judge Crahay set Nov. 10 for sentencing the 53-year-old Sherwin and his co-defendants, a contractor, Michael J. Manzo, 53, and a Republican fund raiser, William C. Loughran, 43. Each man was found guilty on conspiracy and bribery counts and faces a maximum penalty of six years in jail and a $2,000 fine.

Governor Cahill declined to comment on the conviction, but a number of officials in Trenton, both Republican and Democratic, said that the case could be harmful to the Governor should he run for a second term next year.

Mr. Cahill based his first campaign on a strong anticrime, anticorruption position.

"This kind of thing makes

Continued on Page 45, Column 1

MacGregor Identifies Four Who Guided Special Fund

By NICHOLAS GAGE
Special to The New York Times

WASHINGTON, Oct. 26—Clark MacGregor, chairman of the Committee for the Re-election of the President, acknowledged today that selected members of the re-election effort had held control of a special cash fund but he insisted that it had not been used to underwrite sabotage against the Democrats.

He said that the money had been used for preliminary planning of President Nixon's campaign and to determine if there had been any organized efforts to disrupt "the presentation of the President's case" in the New Hampshire primary in March.

Mr. MacGregor said the money had been under the control of Jeb Stuart Magruder, a deputy director of the re-election committee; Maurice H. Stans, chairman of the Finance Committee to Re-elect the President; G. Gordon Liddy, the finance committee counsel, who has been indicted in the alleged bugging at the Democratic headquarters here, and Bart Porter, an advance man with the re-election committee.

He said that some of the money had been left over from the 1968 political campaign and the rest had been collected before last April 7, when the new law governing campaign financing went into effect.

Continued on Page 13, Column 1

Nixon Aide Discards Idea of Jobless Goal

By EILEEN SHANAHAN

WASHINGTON, Oct. 26—Herbert Stein, chairman of the President's Council of Economic Advisers, formally abandoned today the idea of a maximum unemployment rate of 4 per cent as a national goal.

In testimony before the Joint Economic Committee of Congress, he said that the setting of any specific target for unemployment would be "counterproductive."

The reason, he said, is that by setting a numerical goal, the nation might make one of two policy errors, or both. It might take steps that were too

Continued on Page 25, Column 4

DOUBT IS VOICED

South Vietnam Resists Any Accord Against People's Interests

By CRAIG R. WHITNEY

SAIGON, South Vietnam, Friday, Oct. 27—The South Vietnamese Foreign Ministry issued a statement this morning that said South Vietnam was "ready to accept a cease-fire" but "would never accept a political settlement which goes against the interests and aspirations of the 17 million South Vietnamese people."

The statement, in reaction to yesterday's broadcast by the Hanoi radio that the United States and North Vietnam had agreed to a cease-fire to begin Oct. 31, was the first official reaction in Saigon to disclosures about the recent negotiations.

The statement appeared to be designed to emphasize that the main obstacle to an accord and a cease-fire was President Nguyen Van Thieu's doubts about what the details of the political settlement would be, not any general objection.

Trick Is Seen

Hanoi's statement yesterday was vague and somewhat sketchy on those details, and the Saigon statement said of the broadcast: "This is just a North Vietnamese Communist trick to create suspicion between the Republic of Vietnam and our United States ally and to create public pressures for an early end to the bombing and blockade."

The statement said, "The South Vietnamese people's right to self-determination should be respected in any solution to the Vietnam war."

As the possibility of a peace settlement soon finally began to become a reality this week, the critical problem remaining is President Thieu's willingness to accept the one hammered out by Henry A. Kissinger and the North Vietnamese in Paris. So far President Thieu has not expressed himself clearly on this.

U.S. Friendship Cited

The American Ambassador, Ellsworth Bunker, met with President Thieu, the man who, Hanoi implied, stands in the way of a settlement, for an hour at noon yesterday and for half an hour early last night. The embassy was silent on what was discussed, but it is an open secret here that President Thieu and Mr. Kissinger had basic differences of opinion when they met to discuss the peace negotiations.

There was no word either from the Presidential Palace, except that one official said, "We are keeping cool."

An earlier Government radio commentary said: "Self-determination for the people cannot result from secret agreements.

Continued on Page 17, Column 7

Henry A. Kissinger discussing peace plans yesterday. Speaking of provisions for supervision of elections in Vietnam, he said they were so complex it seemed that only his colleague, Ambassador William H. Sullivan, left, understood them completely.
Associated Press

McGovern Says He Hopes Nixon View Is Confirmed

By DOUGLAS E. KNEELAND
Special to The New York Times

IOWA CITY, Oct. 26—Senator George McGovern expressed hope here today that the Nixon Administration's confidence of an imminent cease-fire in the Vietnam war was well founded. But he refused, in a carefully worded speech to 15,000 people on the campus of the University of Iowa, to credit the Nixon Administration for the prospect of peace, saying that those who had opposed the war deserved "much of the credit."

Senator McGovern learned of the White House briefing on the Vietnam peace situation by Dr. Henry Kissinger, President Nixon's national security adviser, as he was leaving Detroit.

Despite the efforts of his senior staff members to appear to take the possibility of a settlement in stride, their faces were serious and it seemed obvious that they were worried about the political effects of Dr. Kissinger's announcement.

In his speech in Iowa City, Senator McGovern implied, without saying so directly, that the President's search for a settlement had been timed to the Nov. 7 election.

"The question that haunts my mind this afternoon," he told the cheering audience "is

Continued on Page 24, Column 6

COMMUNISTS INSIST U.S. SIGN ON OCT. 31

In Paris, They Demand That It Honor a Commitment on Date on 9-Point Pact

By FLORA LEWIS
Special to The New York Times

PARIS, Oct. 26—North Vietnamese and Vietcong delegates here demanded today that the United States observe what they said was a firm agreement to sign a Vietnam cease-fire accord in Paris next Tuesday, Oct. 31.

Nonetheless, they said they would be back again next Thursday for the 165th session of the formal Paris conference on Vietnam. Hanoi's chief delegate, Xuan Thuy, avoided a question about whether private negotiations would continue with the United States if the draft agreement were not signed as it stood.

"Wait and you will see," he said, grinning broadly.

[The Hanoi radio said Friday that North Vietnam's National Assembly had adopted a resolution demanding that the United States meet the Oct. 31 deadline, United Press International reported.]

Mr. Thuy conducted a news conference personally after the formal session, instead of leaving it to his spokesman, as is

Continued on Page 17, Column 1

NEW TALK NEEDED

U.S. Breaks Silence on Efforts and Urges Further Session

By BERNARD GWERTZMAN
Special to The New York Times

WASHINGTON, Oct. 26—Henry A. Kissinger said today that "peace is at hand" in Indochina and that a final agreement on a cease-fire and political arrangement could be reached in one more negotiating session with the North Vietnamese "lasting not more than three or four days."

The remaining details, he said, would not halt the rapid

The text of Kissinger news conference is on Page 18; Text by Hanoi, Page 19; Saigon statement, Page 17.

movement toward an end to the war.

"We must remember that, having come this far, we cannot fail and we will not fail over what still remains to be accomplished," he said during an hour-long briefing for newsmen.

Inspection a Factor

These remaining problems include last-minute American desires to strengthen the machinery for international inspection, a wish to make sure that South Vietnam can sign the draft agreement along with Hanoi and Washington, and a number of questions arising from linguistic differences in the English-language and Vietnamese versions.

Some of these, although minor on the surface, could lead to some delay in reaching a final agreement, despite Mr. Kissinger's definite effort to present a hopeful picture.

Breaking the Administration's silence on the intensive secret peace efforts of the past few weeks, Mr. Kissinger confirmed North Vietnam's announcement broadcast by the Hanoi radio this morning that a breakthrough had occurred at the Paris talks on Oct. 8 and that the two sides had reached over-all agreement on a nine-point plan to end the fighting and establish a new political order in South Vietnam.

Timing Is Disputed

But Mr. Kissinger, who has conducted the negotiations for President Nixon for nearly four years, disputed Hanoi's contention in that broadcast that the United States had consented, as a condition of the agreement, to sign the accord by Oct. 31. He acknowledged, however, that the Administration had made "a major effort" to sign by that date.

Mr. Kissinger, President Nixon's adviser on national security, sought to convey, in the jammed White House news-briefing room, a sense of optimism for the settlement of the war. He tended to minimize the differences that remained with Hanoi and the problems that had arisen last week in his talks in Saigon.

Summary by Kissinger

He seemed eager to assure the American people and the North Vietnamese Government that the Administration was seeking a settlement along the tentative lines already reached. He also seemed intent on keeping relations with Saigon steady in this stormy period.

"We will not be stampeded into an agreement until its provisions are right," he said, aiming his remarks at Hanoi; "we will not be deflected from an agreement when its provisions are right," in an allusion to

Continued on Page 16, Column 1

NIXON OPTIMISTIC ABOUT CEASE-FIRE

President, on Political Trip to Appalachia, Says Goal Is 'Peace With Honor'

By LINDA CHARLTON
Special to The New York Times

ASHLAND, Ky., Oct. 26—President Nixon said tonight he was confident that difficulties blocking a Vietnam cease-fire and peace settlement "can and will be worked out."

At an airport rally in Huntington, W. Va., before coming here in a political swing into Appalachia, the President said, "I can say to you in confidence that we shall succeed in achieving our objective, which is peace with honor and not peace with surrender."

"There are still difficulties to be worked out," he added. "I am confident that they can and will be worked out."

This was Mr. Nixon's first public statement about what he described as "a significant breakthrough" in the negotiations to end the Vietnam war. It came on the first of two stops in a brief campaign foray into West Virginia and Kentucky and was repeated in a speech here.

The remarks were made a few hours after his adviser for

Continued on Page 24, Column 1

U.S. May Speed Shipments Of War Material to Saigon

By WILLIAM BEECHER
Special to The New York Times

WASHINGTON, Oct. 26—Pentagon sources said today that the Defense Department was considering a significant acceleration of arms shipments to South Vietnam to insure that most of the jets, tanks and artillery previously scheduled for delivery arrive before any cease-fire closes off reinforcement.

Already, these sources disclosed, there has been some step-up in the movement of war material over the last few weeks as the prospects of a cease-fire brightened.

"We had carefully worked out a list of equipment necessary to enable South Vietnam to defend itself," one Defense official said. "Nothing has happened to suggest it can get by with less."

At the same time, officials said, the Pentagon is preparing plans to neutralize the mines blocking North Vietnam's ports and inland waterways and is planning an airlift of remaining American military personnel from South Vietnam once truce arrangements have been completed.

Pentagon officials stressed that the acceleration of shipments would involve only

Continued on Page 24, Column 4

equipment previously scheduled to be sent to South Vietnam.

"The other side is not stopping its supplies either," one official declared. "They're still moving things through the DMZ every day."

The tentative agreement outlined to newsmen today by Henry A. Kissinger, the President's national security adviser, would permit both sides to replace military equipment inside South Vietnam with "comparable" equipment, but not additional or significantly better weapons.

But the problem, officials said, is that some key items of equipment, especially jet aircraft, have been approved and funded by Congress but will not come off production lines for some time.

Specifically, this includes a squadron, or 24, Cessna T-37 jet close-support fighters and three squadrons, or 72, Nor-

Continued on Page 16, Column 3

Igor Sikorsky, Helicopter Pioneer, Dies

By ALDEN WHITMAN

The New York Times
Igor I. Sikorsky

Igor I. Sikorsky, the legendary aviation pioneer who developed the world's first practical helicopter, died yesterday of a heart attack in his home in Easton, Conn. He was 83 years of age, and until recently had visited his office several times a week in the Sikorsky plant in nearby Stratford.

Mr. Sikorsky's helicopter achieved reality only when he was in middle life. The craft was simply a seeming grab bag of steel tubing, gears and drive belts topped by a single three-blade rotor and a two-blade rotor at its tail. Into its open cockpit climbed the 50-year-old Igor Ivanovich Sikorsky, dapperly clad in a black overcoat

and a jaunty Homburg. He started the 75-horsepower engine, pulled on the pitch control and inched the plane off the ground until it hung clear for 10 seconds.

The date was Sept. 14, 1939, the place was Stratford, Conn., and the occasion was the first flight of the VS-300, a helicopter that its designer had been dreaming about since he was a boy in imperial Russia. It was the prototype, moreover, of more than 5,000 such craft, many of them highly sophisticated, that were to be produced by the Sikorsky plant before his death.

"I constructed the helicopter

Continued on Page 27, Column 1

Lincoln Center Forum Curtailing Season, and Jules Irving Resigns

By MEL GUSSOW

Because of insufficient funds, the season of the Forum Theater at Lincoln Center will be canceled after the coming Samuel Beckett festival, according to Jules Irving, artistic director of the Repertory Theater of Lincoln Center.

As a result, Mr. Irving has submitted his resignation to the board of directors of the Repertory Theater.

Mr. Irving's resignation and the future use of the Forum will be considered at the board's monthly meeting Monday.

During the seven years of Mr. Irving's directorship, there have been recurrent rumors of his replacement, and he has been repeatedly beleaguered by financial crises. But he said yesterday that the resignation was entirely his own decision and

was completely based on the cancellation of the Forum season. He refused to comment further until the board meeting, except to say: "If the Forum has to be curtailed, I don't wish to stay here."

Mr. Irving made his decision known to Clarke Coggeshall, president of the board of the Repertory Theater of Lincoln Center.

"I am terribly distressed personally at Mr. Irving's decision to submit his resignation as artistic director effective at the end of this season," said Mr. Coggeshall in a prepared statement. "Mr. Irving has been an exceptionally imaginative and resourceful artistic director for the past seven years and he has steadily developed the Reper-

Continued on Page 34, Column 1

Associated Press
Mr. Sikorsky, flying one of his early helicopters, hovered close to the ground as an aide hurried up to hand him a package. The field is at Stratford, Conn.

"All the News That's Fit to Print"

The New York Times

LATE CITY EDITION

Weather: Cloudy, rain likely today and tonight. Cloudy, cool tomorrow. Temp. range: today 48-60; Tuesday 45-61. Full U.S. report on Page 93.

VOL. CXXII..No. 41,927   © 1972 The New York Times Company   NEW YORK, WEDNESDAY, NOVEMBER 8, 1972   15 CENTS

NIXON ELECTED IN LANDSLIDE; M'GOVERN IS BEATEN IN STATE; DEMOCRATS RETAIN CONGRESS

President Loses in City By 81,920-Vote Margin

By FRANK LYNN

President Nixon swept New York State yesterday, but lost to Senator McGovern in New York City by a total of 81,920 votes.

Mr. Nixon's statewide plurality was expected to be about a million votes.

With 11,521 of the 12,948 districts in the state reporting, the tally was:

Nixon 3,712,113
McGovern 2,539,326

With all of the 4,219 districts in the city reporting, the tally was:

Nixon 1,259,244
McGovern 1,341,164

The President's strong showing in the state rivaled the 1956 victory of President Dwight D. Eisenhower, who first brought Mr. Nixon to the national ticket 20 years ago.

The Nixon victory did not appear to carry too far down the Republican line. The Legislature remained Republican, but with no indication of sub-

stantially increased Republican majorities.

Three Republican candidates for the Court of Appeals held slight leads but returns were still inconclusive.

The President's capture of the state was only the third time a Republican Presidential candidate had won New York since 1928.

Dozens of sample districts showed last night that the President substantially improved his 1968 showing in virtually all ethnic groups and geographic areas in the state and city.

In many cases, particularly in the cities, Mr. Nixon surpassed Governor Rockefeller's victory margins of two years ago.

In New York City, Senator McGovern carried districts that were predominantly black, Puerto Rican and Jewish. But in the Jewish areas, Mr. Nixon doubled his showing of four years before. In a middle class

Continued on Page 36, Column 2

Nixon Has a Big Plurality In Jersey and Connecticut

Case an Easy Winner

By RONALD SULLIVAN

President Nixon won the overwhelming victory predicted for him in New Jersey in yesterday's Presidential election, defeating Senator George McGovern by a 2-to-1 margin.

At the same time, Senator Clifford P. Case, the liberal Republican, won a fourth term and one of the biggest election victories in New Jersey's history, defeating Paul J. Krebs, the Democratic candidate.

However, incumbent Democratic Representatives survived the G.O.P. onslaught in the top of the ballot in what political leaders described as a remarkable display of ticket-splitting. The Presidential tally, with 4,142 districts of 5,212 reporting, was:

Nixon 1,440,420
McGovern 862,582

The tally in the race for the Senate, with 3,657 of 5,212 districts reporting, was:

Case 1,112,754
Krebs 627,352

With both Mr. Nixon and Senator Case piling up 2-to-1 margins throughout the state, Republican leaders predicted that the President's margin would rival the 800,000-vote plurality achieved by Dwight D.

Continued on Page 37, Column 3

Hartford Assembly G.O.P.

By LAWRENCE FELLOWS
Special to The New York Times

HARTFORD, Nov. 7—President Nixon carried Connecticut today in a landslide victory.

The President swept the state's eight electoral votes with a plurality of 252,289, approaching the 306,758-vote margin by which the late President Dwight D. Eisenhower carried the state in 1956.

The Republicans also took control of the General Assembly, winning the State Senate by 23 to 13 and the House of Representatives by 93 to 58.

But widespread ticket-splitting enabled three of the four incumbent Democratic Representatives to keep their seats in Washington.

With all of the 169 towns in the state reporting, the Presidential tally was:

Nixon 799,249
McGovern 546,960
Representative John G. Schmitz of California, the

Continued on Page 37, Column 7

Reid Wins as Democrat; Bella Abzug Easy Victor

By RICHARD L. MADDEN

Representative Ogden R. Reid, a former Republican, was reelected yesterday as a Democrat in Westchester County, and Representative Bella S. Abzug, a one-term Democrat, won a decisive re-election in Manhattan.

In another key Westchester race, Representative Peter A. Peyser, a freshman Republican, claimed victory over his predecessor in the House, Richard L. Ottinger, a Democrat-Liberal, who was seeking to recapture his former seat.

Mrs. Abzug defeated by about a 2-to-1 margin Mrs. Priscilla M. Ryan, a Liberal and widow of the late Representative William F. Ryan, who had defeated Mrs. Abzug in the Democratic primary in the 20th Congressional District last June.

With about 85 per cent of the vote reported in Westchester, but with large numbers of absentee ballots still to be counted, Mr. Reid led Carl A. Vergari, a Republican-Conservative and the county's District Attorney, by more than 8,000 votes.

Despite the strong vote for

Mrs. Smith Defeated For Senate in Maine

By BILL KOVACH
Special to The New York Times

PROVIDENCE, R. I., Wednesday, Nov. 8—The 34-year Congressional career of Senator Margaret Chase Smith, the Senate's only woman member, ended last night in a major upset as Democrats showed unexpected strength in New England Senate and Gubernatorial races.

William D. Hathaway, the Democrat who gave up his Second District Congressional office to challenge the 74-year-old Mrs. Smith despite her near-legendary standing in Maine, won the seat in a hard-fought contest.

Mr. Hathaway's stunning victory was part of a Democratic surge that overcame the general New England sweep by President Nixon, and reflected stubborn ticket-splitting by

Continued on Page 21, Column 1

MANY VOTES SPLIT

G.O.P. Loses Senate Seats in 6 States and Picks Up 4 Others

By R. W. APPLE Jr.

The Democratic party withstood President Nixon's landslide yesterday to retain control of both houses of Congress.

With voters in all parts of the nation splitting their tickets in huge numbers, the Democrats brought off a series of startling upsets in Senate contests to gain at least two seats, similar to their feat in the face of Dwight D. Eisenhower's sweep of 1956.

The Democrats captured previously Republican Senate seats in six states—Delaware, Iowa, Kentucky, Maine, Colorado and South Dakota. Those pickups more than offset Republican gains in the two Southwestern states of Oklahoma and New Mexico and the two Southern states of Virginia and North Carolina.

Two Races Open

Two Senate races remained in doubt this morning—in Alaska and Nebraska. Both seats were held by the Republicans in the last Congress.

The figures for the House were far less complete, but the Republicans were not making the gains they expected to take control. It appeared that they would pick up somewhere in the neighborhood of a dozen seats; they had already gained seven.

At present, the Senate lineup is 54 Democrats, 44 Republicans, one Conservative-Republican and one independent who votes with the Democrats. In the House it is 255 Democrats, 177 Republicans and three vacancies.

Mr. Nixon's coattails proved relatively short this year, as they had in 1968. In state after state, he swept to massive vic-

Continued on Page 34, Column 7

Olympic Fund Barred

Voters in Colorado cut off public funds for the 1976 Winter Olympics yesterday. Without the tax money, the International Olympic Committee was all but forced to move the games to another site. Page 31.

M'GOVERN TO BACK MOVES FOR PEACE

But Says He Will Continue to Oppose Policies He Had Deplored in Campaign

By JAMES M. NAUGHTON

SIOUX FALLS, S.D., Nov. 7 — Senator George McGovern conceded defeat of his Presidential candidacy here tonight but said that he would "shed no tears" because of the effort his campaign had made to draw the nation close to peace.

The Democratic nominee told 1,200 cheering enthusiasts at 10:40 P.M., Central standard time, that he had sent a telegram to President Nixon pledg-

Text of McGovern's comments appears on Page 3

ing support for "peace abroad and justice at home."

He said the President had his "full support" in efforts toward such goals.

But he added in his speech, which was televised, that he would, as the leader of the "loyal opposition," continue to oppose any policies that he had deplored during his long campaign.

"Now, the question is to what standards does the loyal

Continued on Page 3, Column 3

A Rockefeller Loses West Virginia Race

By BEN A. FRANKLIN
Special to The New York Times

CHARLESTON, W. Va., Wednesday, Nov. 8—Secretary of State John D. Rockefeller 4th suffered a sharp defeat yesterday in a bid for the West Virginia governorship. The loss appeared, at least, to have postponed a possible role for him in national Democratic politics in 1976.

Gov. Arch A. Moore Jr., a Republican former Congressman who is the first Governor here who has been constitutionally able to succeed to a second

Continued on Page 23, Column 1

President and Mrs. Nixon and Vice President Agnew at the Republican celebration in Washington early today

The Election at a Glance

President
Needed for Election—270 Electoral Votes

	*Number of States	Electoral Votes
Nixon	49	521
McGovern	2	17

The Senate

Newly Elected Senators		Make-up of New Senate	
Democrats	16	Democrats	57
Republicans	15	Republicans	41
In Doubt	2	In Doubt	2

The House

Democrats Elected	218
Republicans Elected	154
In Doubt	63

*Includes District of Columbia.

Victory, 10 Years Later

Spectacular Nixon Vote Considered Vindication in Light of Past Defeats

By JAMES RESTON

It was a spectacular personal victory for Richard Nixon, 10 years to the day, and almost to the hour, after his most humiliating defeat by Pat Brown in the 1962 election for the governorship of California.

Beaten by John Kennedy by the narrowest of margins in the Presidential election of 1960, beaten again for the control of his own state in 1962, finished with American politics by his own angry proclamation exactly a decade ago, here he is now, not only vindicated but triumphant in one of the most decisive victories in the history of American Presidential politics.

In a few days before he will take the oath of office for a second term as President of the United States (Jan. 9), he will be 60 years old. His thirties were a political surprise, even to himself, his forties were an agony of controversy and self-doubt, his fifties were a struggle and at the end a triumph. What now will he do with his sixties? This is the question that even his most intimate associates in Washington cannot answer.

In the world, he has to achieve not only the cease-fire, but the peace he has promised this decade in a record coal-mining state. These also suffered a setback through his defeat in a race that splintered all others here.

News Analysis

Japan and the Common Market countries of Europe, who are now challenging the American economic leadership of the modern world.

At home, Mr. Nixon has to deal also now with the minorities who failed to support him in the election: the poor and the blacks who have been left behind in the general prosperity of the nation, the young in the universities who have been over-run but not persuaded of his philosophy.

Continued on Page 34, Column 3

NIXON ISSUES CALL TO 'GREAT TASKS'

At Victory Celebration, He Vows to Make Himself 'Worthy' of Victory

By ROBERT B. SEMPLE Jr.
Special to The New York Times

WASHINGTON, Wednesday, Nov. 8 — President Nixon summoned the nation last night "to get on with the great tasks that lie before us" and, in a later statement to a crowd of cheering supporters, pledged to make himself "worthy of this victory."

Mr. Nixon made two statements, both televised.

The first of these was a brief statement from his desk

Text of Nixon's remarks is printed on Page 34

in the Oval Office of the White House in which he pledged himself to secure not only "a peace with honor in Vietnam" but also "a new era of peace throughout the world; to "prosperity without war and without inflation" at home, and to an America in which all citizens will have "an equal chance."

"I would only hope," he said, "that in these next four years we can so conduct ourselves in

Continued on Page 34, Column 3

MARGIN ABOUT 60%

Massachusetts Is Only State to Give Vote to the Dakotan

By MAX FRANKEL

Richard Milhous Nixon won re-election by a huge majority yesterday, perhaps the largest ever given a President.

Mr. Nixon scored a stunning personal triumph in all sections of the country, sweeping New York and most other bastions of Democratic strength.

He was gathering more than 60 per cent of the nation's ballots and more than 500 electoral votes. He lost only Massachusetts and the District of Columbia.

The victory was reminiscent of the landslide triumphs of Franklin D. Roosevelt in 1936 and Lyndon B. Johnson in 1964, although it could fall just short of their record proportions.

Tickets Are Split

Despite this drubbing of George Stanley McGovern, the Democratic challenger, the voters split their tickets in record numbers to leave the Democrats in control of both houses of Congress and a majority of the nation's governorships. Mr. Nixon thus became the first two-term President to face an opposition Congress at both inaugurals.

The turnout of voters appeared to be unusually low, despite jams at many polling places. Projections indicated a total vote of 76 million out of a voting-age population of 139.6 million, or only about 54 per cent. If accurate, that would be the lowest proportion since 51.4 per cent in 1948. The percentage had been over 60 per cent in every election since then.

May Claim Mandate

The President seemed certain, however, to claim a clear mandate for his policies of gradual disengagement from Vietnam, continued strong spending on defense, opposition to busing to integrate the schools and a slowdown in Federal spending for social programs. These are the issues he stressed through the campaign.

The 59-year-old Mr. Nixon, who will be 60 before inauguration on Jan. 20, could also claim a resounding personal vindication against the strong charges of corruption brought against him personally by the opposition.

By coincidence, the greatest triumph of his 26 years in national politics came on the 10th anniversary of his defeat for Governor of California—the time he told newsmen they would not have Nixon to kick around anymore.

McGovern Concedes

Mr. McGovern, 50, conceded defeat before midnight in the East with a telegram of support for the President if he leads the nation to peace abroad and justice at home.

The South Dakotan took credit for helping to push the Administration nearer to peace in Indochina and assured his cheering supporters at the Sioux Falls Coliseum that their defeat would bear fruit for years to come.

The President responded in a brief address from the White

Continued on Page 34, Column 1

Summary of Other News

Following is a summary of major nonelection news. A full report begins on the first page, second part.

Canarsie School Boycott

Leaders of Canarsie parents who have kept their children out of school for two weeks declared yesterday that "the boycott is over" and called on parents to return their children to school. But the prospect of full classes today remained in doubt since more than 1,000 parents shouted down the same call Monday night.

Bid by Vietcong

Agents of the National Liberation Front have made several recent contacts with Saigon's anti-Government, non-Communist opposition, according to opposition sources.

Britons Protest Price Rises

British Government offices were swamped with complaints of price increases on the first full day of Prime Minister Heath's anti-inflation freeze. But a check of London shops found no wide pattern of violations. Most of the increases involved noncontrolled items.

Soviet Parades Its Arms

The Soviet Union, marking the 55th anniversary of the Bolshevik Revolution, paraded its military might in low-key fashion. The unusually deliberate movements of Leonid I. Brezhnev, the party leader, reinforced speculation that he had been ill.

The New York Times

VOL. CXXII...No. 41,976   © 1972 The New York Times Company   — NEW YORK, WEDNESDAY, DECEMBER 27, 1972 —   15 CENTS

U.S. SAYS BOMBING IS BACK AT LEVEL PRECEDING PAUSE

Warplanes From Thailand, Guam and Carriers Take Off for North Vietnam

HALT LASTED 36 HOURS

Hanoi Reports 8 B-52's Shot Down in Day—Pentagon Calls Loss Rate Normal

By JOSEPH B. TREASTER
Special to The New York Times

SAIGON, South Vietnam, Wednesday, Dec. 27—With its 36-hour pause in the bombing of North Vietnam ended, the United States command said yesterday that the planes were once again operating as they had last week, when the raids were the heaviest of the war.

Maj. Jere K. Forbus, a spokesman for the command, announced yesterday afternoon that the Christmas pause in bombing had ended three hours earlier, at 1 P.M. (midnight Monday, New York time). At that time, warplanes started taking off from aircraft carriers in the South China Sea and from bases in Thailand and Guam.

Informed officers had said before the pause that about 100 B-52's and several hundred smaller fighter-bombers had been participating in the attacks.

57 Listed as Missing

Many officers in Saigon said yesterday that despite denials from the Pentagon, B-52 losses since the raids began Dec. 18 have been much higher than had been expected.

As of last evening the command had acknowledged having lost 11 of the heavy eight-engine bombers, which each carry more than 24 tons of bombs and which usually fly in formations of three. The command has also reported six fighter-bombers down.

Altogether, the command says, 57 American airmen are missing in action. Hanoi says it has captured more than 100.

The Hanoi radio said today that eight more B-52's and an F-4 Phantom fighter-bomber were shot down yesterday. The North Vietnamese now maintain that they have destroyed a total of 62 American aircraft, including 26 of the heavy bombers, which are valued at $8-million each, since the raids began Dec. 18.

[The Pentagon had no comment on the Hanoi radio report, but it said earlier that the loss rate of B-52's was not materially greater than in raids last spring though now "there are more B-52's involved."]

'Brutal and Barbaric Act'

In a statement condemning the resumption of the bombing, the North Vietnamese Foreign Ministry said over the Hanoi radio this morning that many B-52's and "scores of other aircraft" struck urban and suburban areas in Hanoi, Haiphong, Thai Nguyen — the site of the nation's principal steel mill—and other cities last night.

"This is a brutal and barbaric act aimed at killing civilians, an act that surpasses Hitler's war crimes in scope and intensity," the Foreign Ministry

Continued on Page 10, Column 1

Jury Begins Investigation Into Drug Losses by Police

Judge Threatens Murphy With Contempt for Refusal to Cooperate in Inquiry as Two Officers Fail to Appear

By EMANUEL PERLMUTTER

A grand jury began taking testimony yesterday in the recently disclosed theft of 300 pounds of heroin and cocaine from the Police Department, and a judge threatened Police Commissioner Patrick V. Murphy and two of his aides with contempt for refusing to cooperate with the jury.

Gene L. Gruppuso, the police property clerk, testified before the jurors in the morning in the Manhattan Criminal Court Building. However, Assistant Chief Inspector John Guido, who is in charge of the inspection division, and Inspector Howard A. Metzdorff of the internal affairs division, were not present to testify when their names were called.

The subpoenaing of the policemen by the grand jury was a rebuff to Maurice H. Nadjari, the special state prosecutor, and to Governor Rockefeller. Last October, the Governor had directed Commissioner Murphy to send information about possible criminal-justice corruption

only to Mr. Nadjari. The city's District Attorneys and Mr. Nadjari are fighting over who should investigate the narcotics thefts.

A subpoena had been served on Commissioner Murphy last Friday, calling for the three witnesses to appear before the grand jury yesterday. Mr. Murphy was also directed to turn over to the jurors department records on the stolen narcotics that had been held as evidence by the police.

At the request of Mr. Rogers, Supreme Court Justice Sidney A. Fine issued the subpoenas last week.

In a hearing yesterday before Justice Fine, Mr. Rogers contended that the grand jury

Continued on Page 25, Column 6

School Board Plans Offer To Buy Scribner Contract

By GENE I. MAEROFF

The Board of Education was drafting a letter yesterday that it intends to send to School Chancellor Harvey B. Scribner, outlining a proposal to buy up his contract. A board member, who declined to be identified, said that there "had been no dissent" at a meeting Friday at which the five members decided to offer to pay Dr. Scribner for the remaining six months of his three-year contract and relieve him of his $53,000-a-year post.

Dr. Scribner, who was reported to be out of town and unavailable for comment, announced at a news conference Thursday that he intended to leave his post June 30. He blamed his decision on a "confidence gap" that he said had developed between him and the Board of Education.

The names of possible successors have not been mentioned by the board, but speculation centered on Irving Anker, the deputy chancellor.

Once Headed System

Mr. Anker headed the 1.1-million-pupil New York City school system on an interim basis in 1970, before Dr. Scribner assumed the job. Mr. Anker is seen as someone who could again serve on an acting basis until a permanent chancellor is named.

Should Dr. Scribner refuse to accept a settlement, the board—if it continues to seek his removal—would have to bring departmental charges against him, which is regarded as an unlikely possibility.

"We would rather not have to think about this aspect," one board member said yesterday.

Prior to his announcement last week, Dr. Scribner's reappointment was by no means assured, but he was regarded as still being in contention.

However, he apparently

Continued on Page 27, Column 3

GRAND JURY GETS POLICE SHOOTING

Defendant Is Central Figure in $500 Bail Dispute Involving Two Judges

By RALPH BLUMENTHAL

A grand jury here began an investigation yesterday of the holdup shooting of a patrolman—a case that has stirred controversy because of the release of the suspect in $500 cash bail.

Among the first to testify was another man shot in the holdup. He said he had told the grand jury he could identify the holdup man.

The witness, Edward M. Blagden, then returned to his hospital bed, from where he made public an open letter berating Criminal Court Judge Bruce McMarion Wright for having released the suspect in $500 cash bail.

Judge Wright indicated yesterday that the case was under review by the Appellate Division and a spokesman said the judge was under the division's orders not to discuss the matter publicly.

Other judicial authorities, meanwhile, said they had no jurisdiction and indicated they were not now preparing any

Continued on Page 25, Column 1

Appraisal of the Arts

The second half of an assessment of the year in art and culture by nine critics for The New York Times appears on Page 29.

CITY AIDES TO LOSE APPROVAL POWER ON NEW BUILDING

Owners to Be Responsible Under Antigraft Plan— Delays Seen Curbed

By ROBERT E. TOMASSON

In a major move aimed at reducing "graft-inducing situations" in the construction industry, the city will shift authority for initial building approval next month from its 75 plan examiners to individual owners, architects and engineers.

The "sharp departure from tradition" was announced by Joseph Stein, Commissioner of the Department of Buildings, who said the move was taken in response to the industry's complaint of excessive delays in obtaining building permits that "created graft-inducing situations to obtain expeditious approval."

Instead of the months that were often required to obtain the necessary building permits, they will be issued within days under the new system, Commissioner Stein said.

Builder Cites 'Ways'

Owners will still be held accountable for meeting requirements of the building code, Mr. Stein said, but will no longer have to suffer delays because of objections raised by individual examiners.

Building plans have often had to be submitted several times before their approval, and there has been widespread talk in the industry that there "were ways," as one major builder phrased it yesterday, to expedite approval.

One alleged widespread abuse was the consideration of plans out of sequence in which they were submitted.

In a series of articles in The New York Times last summer, it was estimated that the construction industry paid out at least $25-million in bribes annually to officials and others in connection with virtually every phase of building.

Rise of the 'Expediter'

The complexity of the city's 371-page building code has given rise to creation of the position of men known in the trade as "expediters" whose essential function is to cultivate plan examiners.

One chief executive of a large construction firm here said yesterday that plan approval was often obtained "on what amounts to a scale system, with so much graft for each apartment" in a proposed project.

John Tudda, an architect whose firm has functioned as a consultant to expedite city approval on projects including the Ruppert Brewery Urban Renewal site in the Yorkville area of Manhattan and Lincoln

Continued on Page 18, Column 4

TRUMAN, 33D PRESIDENT, IS DEAD; SERVED IN TIME OF FIRST A-BOMB, MARSHALL PLAN, NATO AND KOREA

HARRY S. TRUMAN, 1884-1972

The Truman home in Independence, Mo., yesterday
United Press International

Funeral to Be Tomorrow In Independence Library

By B. DRUMMOND AYRES Jr.
Special to The New York Times

KANSAS CITY, Mo., Dec. 26—Harry S. Truman, the 33d President of the United States, died this morning. He was 88 years old.

Mr. Truman, an outspoken and decisive Missouri Democrat who served in the White House from 1945 to 1953, succumbed at 7:50 A.M., central standard time, in Kansas City's Research Hospital and Medical Center.

He had been a patient there for the last 22 days, struggling against lung congestion, heart irregularity, kidney blockages, failure of the digestive system and the afflictions of old age.

In the more than seven years he was President, from the time Franklin Delano Roosevelt's death suddenly elevated him from the Vice-Presidency until he himself was succeeded by Dwight David Eisenhower, Mr. Truman left a major mark as a world leader.

He brought mankind face to face with the age of holocaust by ordering atomic bombs dropped on Japan, sent American troops into Korea to halt Communist aggression in Asia, helped contain Communism in Europe by forming the North Atlantic Treaty Organization and speeded the postwar recovery of Europe through the Marshall Plan.

His domestic record was

somewhat less dramatic, for his proposals and ideas were often premature. He ended up on the losing side of fights other Presidents later won — Federal health care, equal rights legislation, low income housing.

His other legacies were perhaps less tangible but no less remembered — the morning walk, the "give 'em hell" campaign that nipped Thomas E.

An obituary article appears on Pages 46-49. An appraisal by the late Dean Acheson, written in 1964, will be found on Page 45.

Dewey at the wire, the desk plaque that proclaimed "The buck stops here!" and the word to the timid and indecisive: "If you can't stand the heat, you better get out of the kitchen."

Toward the end of his struggle for life, the former President weakened steadily. Early yesterday, his doctors warned that death might come "within hours."

When it came, the doctors announced that the cause was "a complexity of organic failures causing a collapse of the cardiovascular system."

A state funeral will be held Thursday in nearby Independence, Mr. Truman's home

Continued on Page 44, Column 1

National Day of Mourning Proclaimed by President

By JACK ROSENTHAL
Special to The New York Times

WASHINGTON, Dec. 26—President Nixon today declared Thursday a national day of mourning for former President Harry S. Truman and made plans to pay his personal respects tomorrow in Independence, Mo.

In a proclamation issued before leaving the vacation White House in Key Biscayne, Mr. Nixon ordered all Federal of-

Text of Nixon's proclamation will be found on Page 44.

fices to close Thursday and urged that the nation pay homage to the late President in worship services.

As he returned to Washington, Mr. Nixon announced that he and Mrs. Nixon would fly to Independence tomorrow to lay a wreath at the Truman Presidential Library, where Mr. Truman's body will lie in state. Officials said that the Nixons hoped to have the opportunity to offer their condolences in person to Mrs. Truman.

The Nixons plan to return to Washington after the wreath-laying, indicating that they will not attend the funeral in Independence on Thursday.

The reason, it appeared, was the desire of the Truman family to have a private funeral.

It was announced in Austin,

Continued on Page 44, Column 2

Tex., that former President and Mrs. Lyndon B. Johnson and members of their family would also go to Independence tomorrow to pay their final respects. They planned to return to Texas in the late afternoon.

In a proclamation that he signed Thursday, all stock exchanges will be closed Thursday. Most banks, with the exception of those in Connecticut, will be open. Post offices will be closed, and there will be no regular delivery of mail. [Details on Page 59.]

A memorial service for Mr. Truman here will be held in the Washington Cathedral, for Federal and foreign dignitaries. No date has been set, but the State Department said it would be within two weeks.

As a Senator and as Vice-Presidential candidate in 1952, Mr. Nixon had been bitterly critical of Mr. Truman, but today, the President voiced warm and unstinting praise.

In a statement issued an hour after word of Mr. Truman's death reached the vacation White House in Florida, Mr. Nixon said:

"Harry S. Truman will be remembered as one of the most courageous Presidents in our history, who led the nation and the world through a critical period with exceptional vision

Tug of War Strains West Side Housing

By DEIRDRE CARMODY

An empty brick-strewn lot on the Upper West Side, first scheduled for middle-income housing and now slated for low-income housing, has become the symbol of controversy between groups in the neighborhood that are dedicated to preserving the ethnic and economic mix in the area but that cannot agree on how to do it.

The site, on Columbus Avenue between 90th and 91st Streets, is also a symbol of the pitfalls of the ambitious West Side Urban Renewal Project, which celebrates its 10th anniversary next month.

It is caught in a tug-of-war between those who believe there is an urgent need for middle-income housing to keep the area from becoming a slum

and those who say that the urgent need is for low-income housing to relocate the hundreds of residents who have been uprooted by the urban renewal project.

One of the major complaints about the housing change from middle-income to low-income is Trinity School, which is directly across 91st Street from the lot. The private coeducational school, which has been on its present site since 1893, has filed suit against the city in Federal Court for allegedly having reneged on an agreement with the school that provided for a middle-income apartment house on the site across the street.

According to school officials, Trinity has long considered moving the entire institution to

Pawling, N.Y., where it owned land. As the area around the school became shabbier and increasingly less attractive to prospective parents (who today pay from $1,600 for a first-grader to $2,500 for a 12th-grader), the decision to move became more imminent.

By the mid-nineteen sixties the area, in the words of the lawsuit, was "deteriorated, substandard unsanitary" with "dilapidated and crumbling structures" and a high incidence of crime.

At this time, however, the city was completing its fourth revision of the West Side Urban Renewal Project, which envisioned the refurbishing of the area from 87th Street to

Continued on Page 16, Column 4

Study Finds Incomes More Unequal

By PHILIP SHABECOFF
Special to The New York Times

WASHINGTON, Dec. 26—A changing population and a changing industrial structure are producing a persistent trend toward inequality in the distribution of income among wage and salary earners in the United States, a study published by the Labor Department has found.

The trend is toward a concentration of an increasingly large share of wage and salary income among people in jobs and professions that already bring higher pay, and it is likely to continue for some time, Peter Henle, author of the study, says.

The study, in the department's current Monthly Labor Review, departs from the widely accepted view that there has been little change in the distribution of income in America since World War II. Most studies of income distribution examine earnings comes, which include such nonearned incomes as welfare and Social Security payments. Family incomes also reflect the growing trend toward more than one wage earner per family.

The study by Mr. Henle

senior specialist on labor for the Library of Congress, examines only the money earnings, wages and salaries of male workers, so as to obtain a view of shifts in the distribution of payments for work performed.

Male Workers Studied

In the period examined, 1958-1972, average earned income was steadily rising throughout the economy as a whole. But in the distribution of that income Mr. Henle found "a slight persistent trend toward inequality." This trend toward inequality was found between various occupations and industries and was also found within several occupations and industries.

For example, using unpublished data from the Bureau of the Census, Mr. Henle found that from 1958 to 1970 the share of aggregate wage and salary income earned by the

lowest fifth of male workers declined to 4.60 per cent from 5.10. At the same time, the share of the highest fifth of male wage and salary earners rose to 40.55 per cent from 38.15.

This trend did not necessarily affect the very highest-paid and lowest-paid workers on the earned income scale, Mr. Henle said. For example, he noted that, while there had been a marked increase in the number of professionals earning $40,000 to $50,000 a year, there had been little change in the number of executives earning $200,000 or more.

Denies 'Scheme Against Poor'

In a telephone interview, he stressed that the inequality in income distribution was not caused by any "nefarious scheme against poor people." Rather, the trend reflects a tendency in the economy to produce more higher-paying jobs without reducing the number of lower-paid workers, he said.

One reason has been a heavy flow of young people into the labor force as a result of the

Continued on Page 22, Column 4

Navy Buys $1.7-Million in Stock Of Ailing Defense Plant on L.I.

By DAVID A. ANDELMAN
Special to The New York Times

HAUPPAUGE, L.I., Dec. 26—The Navy has purchased all 17,414 shares of preferred stock in the Gap Instrument Corporation here as a means of helping the company, which has been experiencing heavy cost overruns. This has made the Department of Defense the largest single stockholder in the company.

The arrangement, believed to mark the first time that the Department of Defense has purchased stock in a private corporation, provides that no dividends be paid on the $1.7-million in nonvoting, nonconvertible shares and that the stock be redeemed beginning in 1976 but only out of the company's af-

ter-tax profits.

The company has not shown a profit in the last four years, and in 1968 showed a profit of only $10,700.

Last week, Senator William Proxmire criticized the Navy for acting as "Grumman's banker" because the Navy delivered a $26-million loan at 6¼ per cent interest to that aerospace company for the F-14, a plane that has also experienced cost overruns.

Gap first ran into trouble nearly three years ago on a contract to manufacture 31 fire-control consoles for Navy destroyers. The company had

Continued on Page 29, Column 4

Love to Emil & Clara Lane the world's best parents. Happy anniv. Busi. Advt.

"All the News That's Fit to Print"

LATE CITY EDITION
Weather: Partly sunny, mild today; cold tonight. Fair, mild tomorrow. Temp. range: today 36-49; Tuesday 45-58. Full U.S. report on Page 81.

The New York Times

VOL. CXXII .. No. 42,004   © 1973 The New York Times Company   NEW YORK, WEDNESDAY, JANUARY 24, 1973   15 CENTS

VIETNAM ACCORD IS REACHED; CEASE-FIRE BEGINS SATURDAY; P.O.W.'S TO BE FREE IN 60 DAYS

THE SITUATION IN INDOCHINA

Areas Generally Under Control of Allied Governments
Communist-Controlled Areas
Disputed Areas
Communist Base Areas
Air Base

Map shows approximate areas held by Communist and Government forces in South Vietnam, Laos and Cambodia. While Communists control large regions, population concentrations are mostly in Government-dominated areas.

The New York Times/Daniel Brownstein/Jan. 24, 1973

THIEU IS CAUTIOUS

Says the Agreement Doesn't Guarantee Lasting Peace

By SYLVAN FOX
Special to The New York Times

SAIGON, South Vietnam, Wednesday, Jan. 24—President Nguyen Van Thieu, joining in announcing the Paris accord on Vietnam, declared today that he considered it only as a cease-fire and not as a guarantee of "a stable, long-lasting peace."

While contending the agreement demonstrated that Communist aggression against the

Excerpts from Thieu speech are printed on Page 16.

South had "been smashed," President Thieu said:

"Let me say frankly of the peace accord to be signed in three days that I consider it only as a cease-fire agreement. As to whether or not we will have real peace, we must wait and see.

'Not More or Less'

"I say this is only a cease-fire agreement, not more or less. In the days to come, we'll see if the Communists will observe the agreement."

President Thieu made his declarations in a 40-minute speech broadcast to the South Vietnamese people this morning. The beginning of his speech was timed to coincide with the radio and television address by President Nixon, which was broadcast on the armed forces radio here, but Mr. Thieu continued long after Mr. Nixon had finished his talk.

Like President Nixon, Mr. Thieu announced that a cease-fire would go into effect throughout South Vietnam at 8 A.M. Sunday Saigon time.

Mr. Thieu did not indicate whether his Government had signed or would sign the peace

Continued on Page 16, Column 5

Transcript of the Speech by President on Vietnam

Following is a transcript of President Nixon's televised address to the nation last night on the Vietnam war, as recorded by The New York Times:

Good evening. I have asked for this radio and television time tonight for the purpose of announcing that we today have concluded an agreement to end the war and bring peace with honor in Vietnam and Southeast Asia.

The following statement is being issued at this moment in Washington and Hanoi:

"At 12:30 Paris time today, Jan. 23, 1973, the agreement on ending the war and restoring peace in Vietnam was initialed by Dr. Henry Kissinger on behalf of the United States and Special Adviser Le Duc Tho on behalf of the Democratic Republic of Vietnam.

"The agreement will be formally signed by the parties participating in the Paris Conference on Vietnam on Jan. 27, 1973, at the International Conference Center in Paris. The cease-fire will take effect at 2400 Greenwich mean time, Jan. 27, 1973. The United States and the Democratic Republic of Vietnam express the hope that this agreement will insure stable peace in Vietnam and contribute to the preservation of lasting peace in Indochina and Southeast Asia."

Essential Conditions 'Have Been Met'

That concludes the formal statement.

Throughout the years of negotiations, we have insisted on peace with honor.

In my addresses to the nation from this room on Jan. 25 and May 8, I set forth the goals that we considered essential for peace with honor. In the settlement that has now been agreed to, all the conditions that I laid down then have been met—a cease-fire internationally supervised will begin at 7 P.M. this Saturday, Jan. 27, Washington time. Within 60 days from this Saturday all Americans held prisoners of war throughout Indochina will be released.

There will be the fullest possible accounting for all of those who are missing in action.

During the same 60-day period all American forces will be withdrawn from South Vietnam.

The people of South Vietnam have been guaranteed the right to determine their own future without outside interference.

By joint agreement, the full text of the agreement and the protocols to carry it out will be issued tomorrow.

Throughout these negotiations we have been in the closest consultation with President Thieu and other representatives of the Republic of Vietnam.

This settlement meets the goals and has the full support of President Thieu and the Government of the Republic of Vietnam as well as that of our other allies who are affected.

The United States will continue to recognize the Gov-

Continued on Page 16, Column 3

President Nixon during his White House speech.
C.B.S. News

TROOPS TO LEAVE

On TV, Nixon Asserts 'Peace With Honor' Is Aim of Pact

By BERNARD GWERTZMAN
Special to The New York Times

WASHINGTON, Jan. 23—President Nixon said tonight that Henry A. Kissinger and North Vietnam's chief negotiator, Le Duc Tho, had initialed an agreement in Paris today "to end the war and bring peace with honor in Vietnam and Southeast Asia."

In a televised report to the nation, a few hours after Mr. Kissinger returned to Washington, Mr. Nixon said a cease-fire in Vietnam would go into effect on Saturday at 7 P.M., Eastern standard time.

Simultaneous announcements were made in Hanoi and Saigon.

Mr. Nixon said that under the terms of the accord—which will be formally signed on Saturday—all American prisoners of war would be released and the remaining 23,700-man American force in South Vietnam would be withdrawn within 60 days.

Wider Peace Indicated

He referred to "peace" in Southeast Asia, suggesting that the accord extended to Laos and Cambodia, which have also been engaged in the war. But there was no direct mention of those two nations today, and it is not known if the cease-fire extends to them as well.

Obviously pleased by the long-awaited development, ending the longest war in American history, Mr. Nixon said the Hanoi-Washington agreement "meets the goals" and has the "full support" of President Nguyen Van Thieu of South Vietnam.

Earlier Mr. Thieu had expressed strong reservations about the draft agreement worked out by Mr. Kissinger and Mr. Tho in October.

Tonight Mr. Nixon sketched only the outline of the accord. The full text of the agreement and accompanying protocols will be issued tomorrow by joint agreement with Hanoi, he said.

It was not possible, for instance, to determine from Mr. Nixon's 10-minute address what changes had been made in the agreement since October.

In his brief description of the accord, Mr. Nixon said that the cease-fire would be "internationally supervised," a refer-

Continued on Page 16, Column 1

CONGRESS UNITED IN VOICING RELIEF

Some Worry Is Expressed on Permanence of Peace by Critics of War

By JAMES M. NAUGHTON
Special to The New York Times

WASHINGTON, Jan. 23—Members of Congress, after years of bitter debate over the war in Vietnam, united tonight in voicing relief and gratitude that the conflict appeared to be at an end.

At the same time, however, some supporters and critics of the Vietnam policies of two Administrations sought to draw from President Nixon's announcement fresh justification for their opposite viewpoints in the long dispute that divided Congress and the nation.

"Peace has come, may peace remain," said Hugh Scott of Pennsylvania, the Senate Republican leader and one of those who had steadfastly defended Mr. Nixon's four-year search for a negotiated truce.

"This is a day for which each of us should be thankful to the Lord," he said.

Senator Edward W. Brooke, a Massachusetts Republican who had been among leaders of an unsuccessful attempt to legislate a United States withdrawal from Indochina, expressed elation that "in four days, a decade of death and destruction will end."

But Mr. Brooke said that the nation had "waited so long for this day that, instead of joy,

Continued on Page 17, Column 7

MITCHELL LINKED TO $199,000 FUND

Watergate Witness Asserts He and Stans Approved of Payments to Liddy

By WALTER RUGABER
Special to The New York Times

WASHINGTON, Jan. 23—A witness said today that $199,000 was paid to a defendant in the Watergate trial during last year's campaign with the approval of former Attorney General John N. Mitchell and former Commerce Secretary Maurice H. Stans.

The money was said to have gone to G. Gordon Liddy, an attorney for President Nixon's campaign organization last year who had been assigned to establish what another witness described as "an intelligence gathering operation."

For the second consecutive day, Chief Judge John J. Sirica indicated dissatisfaction with the prosecution's examination of a witness, excused the jury, and posed a series of questions himself.

It was the United States District Court judge who elicited from Hugh W. Sloan Jr., former treasurer of the Finance Committee to Re-elect the President, the names of Mr. Nixon's two former Cabinet officers.

Mr. Sloan told Judge Sirica

Continued on Page 15, Column 1

Envoy Held Captive

The United States Ambassador to Haiti, Clinton E. Knox, was being held at gunpoint early today by at least two men in his residence in Port-au-Prince. Details on Page 8.

Thousands at Johnson Bier

By ROY REED
Special to The New York Times

AUSTIN, Tex., Wednesday, Jan. 24—Thousands of persons of all ages and from all walks of life filed past the coffin of former President Lyndon B. Johnson yesterday and throughout the night as his body lay in state in the huge library bearing his name at the University of Texas.

The flag-draped coffin of Mr. Johnson, who died Monday, had been brought from the Weed Corley Funeral Home here to the library at noon. It was placed at the top of a long stairway in front of a long metal wall etched with scenes of Mr. Johnson's life.

His widow, Lady Bird, and their two daughters and sons-in-law, Mr. and Mrs. Charles

S. Robb and Mr. and Mrs. Patrick J. Nugent, arrived with the coffin. Mrs. Johnson was escorted by Brig. Gen. James Cross, retired, pilot of the Presidential plane while Mr. Johnson was President.

Once during a brief service around the coffin, Mrs. Johnson glanced at a group of reporters nearby and beckoned to Norma Milligan of Newsweek's Washington bureau, whom she had known in Washington. The two women embraced, both with moist eyes, and after a few words of consolation Mrs. Johnson smiled and said, "Oh, but didn't he live well!"

The former President's body

Continued on Page 22, Column 6

Trinity's Bells Ring Out News of Accord

As soon as President Nixon ended his Vietnam peace announcement last night, Larry King, the organist at Trinity Church, went to an octave-and-a-half keyboard in the sanctuary and began pealing the 10 bells in the tower of the historic church at Broadway and Wall Street.

Mr. King was one of many persons in New York and its environs who, in one way or another, to express their joy, their relief—and some their cynicism—at the official word from the

President that peace in Vietnam had been tentatively agreed upon.

For 15 minutes the sound of Trinity's bells, which weigh up to 3,000 pounds apiece and include the oldest bells still in use in New York City, resounded off the walls of the skyscrapers in the financial district. Mr. King called the bell-ringing "a symbolic gesture of the gratitude all of us at Trinity Church feel that this war is being ended."

By the Episcopal church's original charter given by

King William III of England in 1697 the bells can be rung only by the specific direction of the rector. The current rector, the Rev. Robert R. Parks, said that other than normal use preceding and following services, they are rung only on "great occasions," such as the conclu-

Continued on Page 17, Column 1

War Leaves Deep Mark on U.S.

By JAMES RESTON
Special to The New York Times

WASHINGTON, Jan. 23—America is moving out of Vietnam after the longest and most divisive conflict since the War Between the States. But Vietnam is not moving out of America, for the impact of the war there is likely to influence American life for many years to come. Though it is probably too early to distinguish between the temporary and the enduring consequences, one thing is fairly clear: There has been a sharp decline in respect for authority in the United States as a result of the war—a decline in respect not only for the civil authority of government but also for the moral authority of the schools, the universities, the press, the church and even the family.

There was no cease-fire on

News Analysis

this front. Vietnam did not start the challenge to authority, but it weakened respect for the executives who got the nation involved in the war in the first place, for the Congress that let it go on for more than a decade and for the democratic process of debate, which failed to influence the course of battle for years and which finally declined into physical combat and sporadic anarchy.

Even after a cease-fire, there will still be considerable contention in the country over whether the challenges to authority are good or bad.

Many Americans have maintained that it was precisely the

dissent and the defiance that forced social reform at home and a settlement abroad.

Others have argued that the war produced a whole new revolutionary climate in America, which encouraged the Communists to prolong the conflict and disrupted the nation's unity and the previously accepted attitudes, standards and restraints in American public and private conduct. But few Americans challenge the proposition that for good or bad, something has happened to American life—something not yet understood or agreed upon, something that is different, important and probably enduring.

Even at the moment of the Vietnam compromise, for example, there was a rash of teacher strikes in several of the great cities of the nation; one-time members of the Central Intelligence Agency, some of them

Continued on Page 17, Column 3

Mrs. Lyndon B. Johnson near coffin of the former President as a clergyman delivered a eulogy. With her at the Johnson Library in Austin, Tex., are her elder daughter, Mrs. Charles S. Robb and Mr. Robb, left.
Associated Press

The New York Times

LATE CITY EDITION
Weather: Rain late today, tonight
becoming light snow early tomorrow.
Temp. range: today 40-45; Friday
40-44. Full U.S. report on Page 59

SECTION ONE

VOL.CXXII..No. 42,008   © 1973 The New York Times Company   NEW YORK, SUNDAY, JANUARY 28, 1973   75c beyond 50-mile zone from New York City, except Long Island. Higher in air delivery cities.   **50 CENTS**

VIETNAM PEACE PACTS SIGNED; AMERICA'S LONGEST WAR HALTS

Nation Ends Draft, Turns to Volunteers

Change Is Ordered Six Months Early— Youths Must Still Register

By DAVID E. ROSENBAUM
Special to The New York Times

WASHINGTON, Jan. 27—Defense Secretary Melvin R. Laird announced today that the military draft had ended.

As a result of the announcement, men born in 1953 and afterward will not be subject to conscription, and men born before 1953 but not yet drafted will have no further liability to the draft.

These men will be the first in two generations to have no prospect of being drafted. Except for a brief hiatus in 1947 and 1948, men have been conscripted regularly since 1940.

President Nixon's authority to conscript troops into the military expires June 30. Since no one has been drafted since December, the President achieved his goal of turning the military into an all-volunteer force six months ahead of the deadline.

The President and Mr. Laird had promised repeatedly that the June 30 deadline would be met. But Mr. Laird had held out the possibility that as many as 5,000 men would be drafted this year from March through June.

Message From Laird

But, in a message to senior defense officials that was made public today, Mr. Laird said:

"With the signing of the peace agreement in Paris today, and, after receiving a report from the Secretary of the Army that he foresees no need for further inductions, I wish to inform you that the armed forces henceforth will depend exclusively on volunteer soldiers, sailors, airmen and marines.

"The use of the draft has ended."

Although no one will be drafted, the Selective Service machinery will most likely remain on the books for standby use in an emergency. Men will continue to have to register for

the draft when they turn 18, and young men will still be assigned lottery numbers based on their birthdays.

Congress has mandated, however, that the Government call up Reserves and National Guardsmen before it turns to a reinstatement of the draft to meet future emergencies.

A spokesman for the Selective Service System said that men who had refused to report for induction would still be subject to criminal prosecution. But, he said, men with induction postponements that were due to expire before June 30 will not be drafted.

"We will draft nobody," the spokesman said.

Hopes Senate Will Act

Mr. Laird's single qualification about ending the draft applied to doctors and dentists. The Nixon Administration has asked Congress to approve sizable bonuses for doctors and dentists in an effort to attract enough volunteers in those professions.

The House of Representatives passed such legislation last year, and Mr. Laird said in his message today:

"I am particularly hopeful that the Senate will promptly follow the lead of the House and enact legislation giving added incentives for service from members of the health professions, so that the requirements for health services personnel can also be put on a volunteer basis."

The House is almost certainly willing to pass the bill again this year, but Representative F. Edward Hébert, chairman of the House Armed Services Committee, has said that his committee will not act until the Senate passes the legislation.

Mr. Laird also urged Congress to approve bonuses to attract men to the National Guard and

Continued on Page 28, Column 1

In the morning ceremony at the Hotel Majestic in Paris were, from the left, the Vietcong, North Vietnamese, South Vietnamese and U.S. delegations

Signing, from left, William P. Rogers for U.S., Nguyen Duy Trinh for Hanoi, Mrs. Nguyen Thi Binh for the Vietcong, Tran Van Lam for Saigon
Associated Press, United Press International and C.B.S. News

Hanoi Lists of P.O.W.'s Are Made Public by U.S.

By BERNARD GWERTZMAN
Special to The New York Times

WASHINGTON, Jan. 27—The State Department tonight released the list of American civilians acknowledged by North Vietnam as having been captured in South Vietnam during the Vietnam war. The list left about half the 51 Amer-

ican civilians believed missing or captured unaccounted for.

The list that the North Vietnamese turned over to American officials in Paris today named 27 American civilians as prisoners of the Vietcong, and listed seven other Americans as having died in captivity.

At the same time, the Defense Department began releasing, in batches, the names of the military prisoners in Communist hands who were on the list turned over in Paris along with the civilians.

2 Diplomats Listed

The United States, in Paris, provided a list of 26,000 Communist prisoners held by South Vietnam in exchange. The lists were turned over following the formal signing of the Vietnam cease-fire agreement.

Frank A. Sieverts, the State Department official charged with prisoner affairs, said that Hanoi apparently did not in-

Continued on Page 24, Column 2

The Toll: 12 Years of War

Military
United States—45,933 killed, 303,616 wounded, 587 captured, 1,335 missing (up to Jan. 13, 1973).
South Vietnam—183,528 killed and 499,026 wounded.
North Vietnam and Vietcong—924,048 (an estimate by Saigon; figures on wounded not available.)

Civilian
415,000 South Vietnamese killed and 935,000 wounded in combat (1965 through 1972).
31,463 South Vietnamese killed and 49,000 abducted as result of Vietcong actions against civilians.
20,587 killed by Saigon actions against civilian Vietcong.
North Vietnamese—Casualties not known.

Nation Celebrates Peace In Prayer and Muted Joy

By MICHAEL KNIGHT

President Nixon, like millions of other Americans, watched the signing of the Vietnam cease-fire agreement on television yesterday and then, like many others, took part in a modest and somber celebration of the end of a tragic war.

The President, relaxing in his home at Key Biscayne, Fla. had proclaimed 7 P.M. yesterday as a "national moment of prayer and thanksgiving" and the 24-

hour period thereafter as a day of prayer.

Throughout the country, in cities and in hamlets, church bells tolled, fire companies sounded their horns, and small, quiet gatherings were held in homes and in public places.

Some Voice Caution

Some of those who celebrated the end of the American war did so cautiously. The executive secretary of the Washington, D. C., Council of Churches said, "The reason many of us are not throwing our hats in the air is that we are just so stunned and ashamed because the war went on so long, so needlessly."

In Elmira, N. Y., Mrs. Lucielle Cesari did not turn on the lights of a Christmas tree in her yard, lights she had lit every night for five years in a "vigil" remembering the war.

In Longmeadow, Mass., a bell forged by Paul Revere, the silversmith and patriot, was sounded in its steeple at the First Church of Christ. The bell was first sounded to signal the end of the War of 1812.

In Key Biscayne, the President attended a special service at the Key Biscayne Presbyterian Church about a mile from his home.

The minister, the Rev. John A. Huffman, Jr., borrowed from a song by two antiwar activists

Continued on Page 20, Column 3

CEREMONIES COOL

Two Sessions in Paris Formally Conclude the Agreement

By FLORA LEWIS
Special to The New York Times

PARIS, Jan. 27—The Vietnam cease-fire agreement was signed here today in eerie silence, without a word or a gesture to express the world's relief that the years of war were officially ending.

The accord was effective at 7 P.M. Eastern standard time. Secretary of State William P. Rogers wrote his name 62 times on the documents providing—after 12 years—a settlement of the longest, most divisive foreign war in America's history.

The official title of the text was "Agreement on Ending the War and Restoring Peace in Vietnam." But the cold, almost gloomy atmosphere at two separate signing ceremonies reflected the uncertainties of whether peace is now assured.

The conflict, which has raged in one way or another for over a quarter of a century, had been inconclusive, without clear victory or defeat for either side.

Involvement Gradually Grew

After a gradually increasing involvement that began even before France left Indochina in 1954, the United States entered into a full-scale combat role in 1965. The United States considers Jan. 1, 1961, as the war's starting date and casualties are counted from then.

By 1968, when the build-up was stopped and then reversed, there were 529,000 Americans fighting in Vietnam. United States dead passed 45,000 by the end of the war.

The peace agreements were as ambiguous as the conflict, which many of America's friends first saw as generous aid to a weak and threatened ally, but which many came to consider an exercise of brute power against a tiny nation.

Built on Compromises

The peace agreements signed today were built of compromises that permit the two Vietnamese sides to give them contradictory meanings and, they clearly hope, to continue their unfinished struggle in the political arena without continuing the slaughter.

The signing took place in two ceremonies. In the morning, the participants were the United States, North Vietnam, South Vietnam and the Vietcong. Because the Saigon Government does not wish to imply recognition of the Vietcong's Provisional Revolutionary Government, all references to that government were confined to a second set of documents. That set was signed in the afternoon.

Continued on Page 24, Column 7

BATTLES CONTINUE AFTER CEASE-FIRE

U.S. Copter Sent to Pick Up Vietcong Officers Said to Have Been Shot Down

By FOX BUTTERFIELD
Special to The New York Times

SAIGON, South Vietnam, Sunday, Jan. 28—A cease-fire officially went into effect throughout Vietnam at 8 A.M. today, but widespread fighting continued and there were reports that an unarmed American helicopter sent to pick up a Vietcong delegation and bring it to Saigon had been shot down over Tay Ninh Province.

The helicopter, which was painted white and which is normally used for medical evacuation flight, was to bring the Vietcong's delegation to the four-power Joint Military Commission that will oversee the cease-fire. There was no immediate word on the fate of the crew.

[North Vietnam issued a statement Sunday informing its people of the cease-fire, saying, "Today, the 28th of January, war completely ends in both zones of our country," Reuters reported from Hong Kong.]

334 Incidents Reported

The South Vietnamese command reported this morning that in the 24 hours ending at dawn, North Vietnamese and Vietcong troops initiated 334 incidents throughout the country. According to Government officers, that is the highest number since they began keeping a record. However, more Communist troops were probably involved during the 1968 Tet offensive, they said.

Only an hour and a half before the cease-fire began, Communist gunners struck Tan Son Nhut airport on the outskirts

Continued on Page 18, Column 1

A Reluctant G.I.'s Life and Death

By JON NORDHEIMER
Special to The New York Times

ST. JOSEPH, Mo.—The house on Penn Street where Charley Stockbauer used to live sits near a historic crossroads of America.

It was from St. Joseph that the pioneers who won the West

a century ago set out across the prairie in rough wagons drawn by mules and oxen and gritty conviction.

They came here by railroad and steamboat in the waning days of winter and huddled in muddy encampments on the gray bluffs above the Missouri River, waiting with mounting excitement for the floodwaters to recede from the Kansas plain.

As with most American school children, the seeds of patriotism were planted deep in Charley Stockbauer, and he grew to manhood in St. Joseph surrounded by the ghosts of 19th-century heroes and the legends of the days when men strode boldly toward an uncertain horizon, enduring hardship and fear on the impulse of duty or national destiny.

Values Questioned

These values are still enshrined, but they have been questioned as never before by Charley Stockbauer's generation during the turbulent years when the vagaries of the war in Vietnam challenged traditional American attitudes about sacred abstractions such as patriotism.

Charley Stockbauer was a confused and reluctant warrior in a conflict that almost nobody fully understands, and that confusion and reluctance are mirrored here in the town that was his home before he died in Vietnam. Patriotism here, but here, as else-

where across the country in these days when the war has at last come to an end, there is a reticence about it all, a nervous hesitance about parading the flag.

The myths and the legends persist. Buffalo Bill and Wild Bill Hickok were raw-boned riders from the Overland Pony Express, and the mail they carried westward started out from a brick building that still stands on Penn Street. Indian fighters purchased, with leather pouches

Continued on Page 24, Column 1

Today's Sections

COLLECT Russian Stamps? See SEYMOUR CO. classified Stamp ad today.—Advt.

SIZZLING steak-complete-defts. to your door in 1 hour. DIAL-A-STEAK. 203-1888—Advt.

Other News About Accords

CAMBODIA — The exiled Cambodian head of state said in Peking that his guerrilla forces would fight on despite the cease-fire in Vietnam. Cambodia announced a suspension of offensive activities tomorrow. [Page 26.]

TRUCE OBSERVERS — Teams of officers from Poland and Canada left for Vietnam to join with others expected from Hungary and Indonesia. [Page 24.]

INTERNATIONAL CONFERENCE—The United States proposed Feb. 26 as the date for 12-nation meeting on guaranteeing peace. [Page 16.]

LAOS—The head of the pro-Communist negotiating team returned from Hanoi and gave no indication that a cease-fire could be arranged quickly in Laos. [Page 21.]

President and Mrs. Nixon and their daughter, Mrs. David Eisenhower, attending a memorial service in Key Biscayne Presbyterian Church, near the Florida White House.
United Press International

"All the News
That's Fit to Print"

The New York Times

LATE CITY EDITION

Weather: Partly sunny today; fair tonight. Chance of rain tomorrow. Temp. range: today 50-54; Monday 45-68. Full U.S. report on Page 86.

VOL. CXXII...No. 42,101   © 1973 The New York Times Company   NEW YORK, TUESDAY, MAY 1, 1973   15 CENTS

NIXON ACCEPTS ONUS FOR WATERGATE, BUT SAYS HE DIDN'T KNOW ABOUT PLOT; HALDEMAN, EHRLICHMAN, DEAN RESIGN; RICHARDSON PUT IN KLEINDIENST POST

Biaggi Testimony to Jury Ordered Released in Full

U.S. Judge Criticizes Candidate's Petition —Delays Disclosure Pending Appeal —Troy Out as Campaign Chief

By JOHN CORRY

A Federal judge yesterday ordered the release of Mario Biaggi's testimony before a grand jury but held up the order when the mayoral candidate's lawyer said he would appeal to block disclosure.

In issuing the order, Judge Edmund L. Palmieri denied a motion by the Bronx Congressman for a panel of three judges to look over his testimony and state whether he had taken the Fifth Amendment "solely" on questions about his personal finances.

In the past, Mr. Biaggi had told leaders of the Conserva-

ROGERS DEFENDS CAMBODIA RAIDS

Facing Fulbright Committee, He Says the Constitution Justifies the Bombing

By BERNARD GWERTZMAN
Special to The New York Times

WASHINGTON, April 30 — Secretary of State William P. Rogers said today that the continued American bombing in Cambodia was legally justified by the Constitution and was "a meaningful interim action" to force the Communist-backed insurgents there to agree to a cease-fire.

Mr. Rogers, testifying before the Senate Foreign Relations

Text of Rogers memorandum will be found on Page 10.

Committee, presented the Administration's long-awaited legal justification for the Cambodian bombing, an issue that has aroused considerable criticism from members of the committee, including its chairman, Senator J. W. Fulbright.

They have argued that President Nixon has no legal basis for the bombing, now that all American troops have been withdrawn from South Vietnam.

Though the committee members generally accorded Mr. Rogers friendly treatment, his arguments, both in his comments to the committee and in a 13-page legal memorandum, failed to sway the most vocal critics such as Senators Ful-

Continued on Page 11, Column 1

Egyptian Air Bases Reported Equipped For Libyan Planes

Special to The New York Times

BEIRUT, Lebanon, April 30— Diplomatic sources report that ground equipment has been installed at some Egyptian air bases for French-built fighter-bombers from Libya and British-built planes from other Arab countries, and that it has been tested by the aircraft during brief visits.

Israel has been charging that French-built Mirage jets from Libya and British-built Hunter interceptors from Iraq have been transferred to Egyptian bases, but there has been no comment in Cairo. A French Government spokesman said last week that French inquiries about the charges had brought denials from Libya and Egypt.

According to informed diplomats here, however, several embassies are known to have reported to their governments that ground equipment for Mirages was installed several weeks ago. These embassies are said to believe that the

Continued on Page 6, Column 1

WERE you in Seattle during the last 10 days of History? 17 m., color 18 mm. color—Quick Prints—Same day service. Paramount Pictures. (212) 281-1167.—Advt.

Elliot L. Richardson, named Attorney General, yesterday

United Press International

President Nixon in White House press room after address

CONTROLS VOTED FOR ANOTHER YEAR

President Reluctantly Signs Compromise Bill Extending Wage and Price Curbs

By EDWARD COWAN
Special to The New York Times

WASHINGTON, April 30— With the reluctant support of the Administration, both houses of Congress approved today, and President Nixon signed, a compromise bill extending for another year the President's authority to regulate wages and prices.

Mr. Nixon signed the bill tonight, just after making a nationwide television and radio speech. The existing law, called the Economic Stabilization Act, was scheduled to expire at midnight.

The vote in the House was 267 to 115, a larger margin for passage than appeared likely before the Easter recess. The voice vote in the Senate was unrecorded.

Voting for the bill were 153 Democrats and 114 Republicans; opposed were 58 Democrats and 57 Republicans.

Meanwhile, the Department of Agriculture reported that prices increased by farmers fell by 1.5 per cent in April, the first decline in a year. [Page 55.]

Mr. Nixon had sought a simple one-year extension of the act. But with the public frustrated

Continued on Page 17, Column 1

Ellsberg Judge Demands Affidavits on Bugging Tie

By MARTIN ARNOLD
Special to The New York Times

LOS ANGELES, April 30 — The judge in the Pentagon papers trial today ordered four figures connected to the Watergate affair to produce affidavits concerning any link between that break-in and the trial here.

Federal District Judge William Matthew Byrne Jr. said that he was not foreclosing the possibility of summoning the four men here to testify, although he denied, for now, a defense request for an immediate hearing.

The affidavit order was directed to John W. Dean 3d, former special counsel to President Nixon; L. Patrick Gray 3d, former acting director of the F.B.I., and G. Gordon Liddy and E. Howard Hunt Jr., conspirators in the Watergate bugging.

Judge Byrne indicated that he also would probably require affidavits and perhaps testimony from former Attorney General John N. Mitchell, Richard G. Kleindienst, the present Attorney General; John

D. Ehrlichman, until today the President's chief for domestic affairs; H. R. Haldeman, Mr. Nixon's chief of staff who also resigned today; Charles W. Colson, former Presidential special counsel, and Robert C. Mardian, former Assistant Attorney General.

Today's court session began with the judge announcing from the bench that about a month ago he met with Mr. Ehrlichman and President Nixon, "for approximately one minute or less," at Mr. Ehrlichman's suggestion.

At that time, he said, he was offered a new Government position, but he said he told Mr. Ehrlichman that he could not consider it "until this case is concluded." He did not say what the position was, but his name has been mentioned as a possible director of the Federal Bureau of Investigation.

Then, in response to demands from two defense lawyers,

Continued on Page 33, Column 6

Nixon Asks Tax Law Shift To Ease Filing on Income

By EILEEN SHANAHAN
Special to The New York Times

WASHINGTON, April 30— The Nixon Administration proposed today changes in the tax laws and tax forms that would make it easier for millions of individuals to figure out their Federal income taxes.

The Administration did, however, recommend enactment of two new provisions that would limit the ability of wealthy individuals to combine different preferential sections of the tax laws in ways that permit them to escape all or most Federal income tax.

The proposals were submitted to the House Ways and Means Committee by the Secretary of the Treasury, George P. Shultz, in the form of a 175-page booklet called "Proposals for Tax Change."

The committee chairman, Wilbur D. Mills, Democrat of Arkansas, said he thought the proposals did not go far enough and criticized particularly the lack of any proposed changes in the taxation of capital gains and in the estate and gift taxes.

The plan for simplifying the

Summary of proposed changes is printed on Page 34.

ing to capital gains, depreciation, the depletion allowance and so on — would remain untouched under the Administration's plan.

All the basic provisions of the laws that reduce taxes for those who invest in business or property—the provisions relat-

Continued on Page 35, Column 7

Kissinger Is Going to Moscow For Talks on Brezhnev's Visit

Special to The New York Times

WASHINGTON, April 30 — Henry A. Kissinger will fly to Moscow this week for talks with Leonid I. Brezhnev, the Soviet Communist party leader, on plans for Mr. Brezhnev's expected visit to the United States late in June.

While in Moscow with his top staff aides, Mr. Kissinger will also discuss Vietnam, arms control negotiations, trade questions and other matters with Mr. Brezhnev and other top officials, a senior Administration official said.

No date for Mr. Brezhnev's trip has been announced, but an Administration official said that both sides were planning on late June—around June 25.

It will be Mr. Brezhnev's first journey to the United States and the first by a top Soviet

Continued on Page 4, Column 4

range of bilateral problems and matters of mutual interest."

But a senior Administration official said that the primary mission of the President's adviser for national security would be to discuss the details and likely agenda for Mr. Brezhnev's visit to the United States, which will return Mr. Nixon's visit to the Soviet Union last spring.

2 AIDES PRAISED

Counsel Forced Out —Leonard Garment Takes Over Job

By R. W. APPLE Jr.
Special to The New York Times

WASHINGTON, April 30 — Four top Nixon Administration officials resigned today as a consequence of the Watergate case, one of the most widespread scandals in American Presidential history.

H. R. Haldeman, the austere and secretive White House

Texts of Nixon announcement and resignations, Page 30.

chief of staff, and John D. Ehrlichman, the President's chief adviser on domestic affairs, maintained their innocence in letters submitting their resignations. Both said their ability to carry out their daily duties had been undermined.

The President chose Elliot L. Richardson, the Secretary of Defense, to succeed Richard G. Kleindienst as Attorney General and placed Mr. Richardson in charge of the Watergate investigation.

Mr. Kleindienst said he had quit because close friends had become Watergate suspects and "impartial enforcement of the law" ruled out such 'intimate relationships."

Dean's Departure Asked

Mr. Nixon also announced that he had "requested and accepted" the resignation of John W. Dean 3d, the White House counsel, who had threatened to implicate superiors. Leonard Garment, a special Presidential consultant, was named to replace Mr. Dean temporarily.

No replacements for the two key aides were named, and the President gave no hint as to whom he might choose.

In a related development, the United States Information Agency announced tonight that Gordon Strachan had resigned as general counsel "after learning that persons with whom he had worked closely at the White House had submitted their resignations today." The statement said Mr. Strachan "stressed that he had no complicity in the Democratic National Committee break-in or in any alleged attempt to cover it up."

Mr. Haldeman's and Mr. Ehrlichman's departures strip the White House of its central operating mechanism at a time when far-reaching decisions must be made on inflation, Indochina policy and American relations with Europe.

The actions were announced

Continued on Page 30, Column 1

NEW DATA CITED

President Tells How He Changed Mind About Charges

By JOHN HERBERS
Special to The New York Times

WASHINGTON, April 30 — President Nixon told the nation tonight that he accepted the responsibility for what happened in the Watergate case even though he had had no knowledge of political espionage or attempts to cover it up. The President went on na-

The text of Nixon's speech is printed on Page 31.

tionwide television and radio to discuss the case after he received the resignations of three top staff members who have been implicated—H. R. Haldeman, John D. Ehrlichman and John W. Dean 3d. He also accepted the resignation of Attorney General Richard G. Kleindienst.

Wrongdoing Alleged

While the President accepted the responsibility and pledged every effort to achieve justice in the case, he alleged wrongdoing or cover-up attempts on the part of those he had delegated to run his 1972 Presidential campaign and those he appointed to investigate the matter during the campaign.

And he implied that his own election officials, in the Watergate espionage, were attempting to stop wrongdoing by the Democrats.

Mr. Nixon also said that hereafter the investigation of the Watergate matters would be delegated to his new Attorney General, Elliot L. Richardson, while he, the President, turned his attention to grave foreign and domestic matters. He added that he would leave it up to Mr. Richardson whether to appoint a special prosecutor.

Weeks of Tension

The speech, which came after weeks of growing tension as the White House as developments in the Watergate scandal implicated Administration figures, was an emotional appeal to save the integrity of his Presidency for the 1,361 days, by Mr. Nixon's count, that remain in his term. This was the 100th day of his second term.

"Tonight I ask for your prayers to help me in everything that I do," Mr. Nixon said at the end. "God bless America and God bless each and every one of you."

He accepted responsibility for Watergate with these words:

"In any organization the man

Continued on Page 31, Column 5

SHAKE-UP LAUDED BY CONGRESSMEN

But Many Warn That Step Is Not Enough to Restore Faith in Administration

By JAMES M. NAUGHTON
Special to The New York Times

WASHINGTON, April 30 — Members of Congress joined in widespread, bipartisan praise today for President Nixon's shake-up of his Administration's high command.

But many Senators and Representatives coupled their commendations with warnings that a housecleaning of the White House staff would not be sufficient to restore faith in the Nixon Administration or the Government as a whole.

Furthermore, Representative John E. Moss of California urged House Democratic leaders to open a formal inquiry into the possible impeachment of President Nixon.

The suggestion by the longtime Democratic Congressman—which key leaders of both parties in the House described as "premature" — was the most severe reaction on Capitol Hill to the latest developments in the Watergate conspiracy case.

At Huron, Ohio, the nation's Democratic Governors joined in the call for appointment of a special prosecutor in the Watergate case.

Mark O. Hatfield, Republican

Continued on Page 33, Column 6

End of Era in Nixon Presidency

By ROBERT B. SEMPLE Jr.
Special to The New York Times

WASHINGTON, April 30 — The resignations of H. R. Haldeman and John D. Ehrlichman from President Nixon's senior staff clearly mark the end of one era of the Nixon Presidency and the beginning of another. Things simply will not be the same. The question is how much different they will be.

The few men who remain in the President's suddenly shrunken entourage do not believe that the scandals of the moment will have much impact on Mr. Nixon's own personality. His habits are well entrenched, and 'any future White House operation will reflect the style of its master.

But there are some here

now, in the White House and on Capitol Hill, who hope that Mr. Nixon will seize what they sense to be a rare opening to redesign his relationships with Congress, the bureaucracy, and even the press.

They hope to increase his access to others and theirs to him, to replace the closed corporation that the White House had become with the "open Presidency" to which he once aspired, and to return to his own first principles by decentralizing some of the power that has steadily flowed from the Government agencies to a few Government-makers in the White House.

Mr. Haldeman and Mr. Ehrlichman helped design that system, ran the system and, in time, came to symbolize the system. Their Teutonic names

News Analysis

and mutual zeal for efficient execution gave rise to many jokes. Their enemies called them Hans and Fritz; their friends simply teased them.

In Mr. Ehrlichman's office on the second floor of the White House is a copy of Daniel P. Moynihan's "Understanding Poverty," which carries this inscription: "For John Ehrlichman. Achtung! D.P.M."

But their power was no joke. They were met with long ties and easy access to the President, men of loyalty, men who transmitted Mr. Nixon's orders to the bureaucracy and to whom, with few exceptions, Mr. Nixon's Cabinet members were forced to report before winning humble access to the Oval Office.

In all areas other than for-

Continued on Page 33, Column 4

"All the News That's Fit to Print"

The New York Times

LATE CITY EDITION

Weather: Partly cloudy today; cool tonight. Partly sunny tomorrow. Temp. range: Today 57–69; Friday 55–75. Full U.S. report on Page 66.

VOL. CXXII...No. 42,112   © 1973 The New York Times Company   NEW YORK, SATURDAY, MAY 12, 1973   15 CENTS

PENTAGON PAPERS CHARGES ARE DISMISSED; JUDGE BYRNE FREES ELLSBERG AND RUSSO, ASSAILS 'IMPROPER GOVERNMENT CONDUCT'

White House Says Attacks Will Continue in Cambodia

By BERNARD GWERTZMAN
Special to The New York Times

WASHINGTON, May 11 — The White House said today that the United States would continue with "the right policy" of bombing in Cambodia in support of President Lon Nol's government, despite the vote yesterday in the House of Representatives blocking the transfer of military funds for such raids.

Ronald L. Ziegler, the White House press secretary, made the statement and also announced — jointly with North Vietnam—that Henry A. Kissinger and Le Duc Tho, Hanoi's chief negotiator, would resume talks on Thursday in Paris to seek ways of achieving "strict implementation" of the three-and-a-half-month-old cease-fire agreement.

In its insistence on the bombing program, the Nixon Administration is apparently heading for a possible constitutional conflict with Congress, if the Senate, as expected, supports the House action next week.

The Senate majority leader, Mike Mansfield, told reporters today: "If the will of the Congress and the intention of the Congress — the representatives

GRAY CALL TO NIXON

Said to Inform Inquiry It Came 3 Weeks After Watergate

By ANTHONY RIPLEY
Special to The New York Times

WASHINGTON, May 11 — L. Patrick Gray 3d has told Senate investigators that he talked by telephone with President Nixon about three weeks after the Watergate burglary last June 17 to express concern over White House obstacles in his path and confusion that was hampering his investigation, committee sources said today.

Mr. Gray, at the time acting director of the Federal Bureau of Investigation, was concerned over the action of White House aides, these sources said.

The sources would not comment on how Mr. Gray said the President reacted to the telephone complaint. The sources did not specify the nature of the obstacles that Mr. Gray said he had faced.

Talks To Prosecution

Mr. Gray, who resigned as acting director of the F.B.I. in the wake of the Watergate scandals, was questioned by the Senate investigators last night. He spent most of today talking to the prosecution team from the Justice Department but apparently did not appear before the grand jury, which gathered at 4:30 P.M. in the Federal courthouse.

There were a flurry of news reports tonight that Mr. Gray had told the President of an attempt to impede the Watergate investigation. Mr. Gray received "no reaction" from the President, according to The Baltimore Sun.

Committee sources here said such reports were "out of focus" and did not fully reflect Mr. Gray's position.

Sought to End Confusion

"There was confusion," one source said. "Gray felt things should be straightened out so that he could carry out his investigation."

In past statements to investigators and testimony before Congress, Mr. Gray has repeatedly described his troubles with the White House staff.

Mr. Gray said that the President's counsel, John W. Dean 3d, had sat in while F.B.I. agents were interviewing persons at the White House and that Mr. Dean had "probably" lied to agents. Mr. Gray also said that he had turned over raw F.B.I. investigation files to Mr. Dean. At the time the Presidential counsel was conducting a separate investigation of the

United Press International

Judge William Matthew Byrne Jr., above, threw out the Pentagon papers case and, left, defendants were freed. They are Anthony J. Russo Jr., left, and Dr. Daniel Ellsberg.

Air of Expectancy, Then Tears, Shouts, Embraces

By JUDITH KINNARD
Special to The New York Times

LOS ANGELES, May 11— Her tears of joy had dried, but cheers still filled the courtroom when Patricia Ellsberg embraced one of many friends and said:

"I could never believe the scene of waiting for the jury to come in. I just knew it would never happen."

Federal District Court Judge William Matthew Byrne Jr. had just closed the Pentagon

papers trial with a broad decision that harshly admonished the Government for misconduct.

Dr. Ellsberg, looking gaunt as much from loss of weight as from the pressure of the last two years, spoke to a cheering crowd on the steps of the courthouse after the verdict.

Almost crushed by newsmen as he stood with his arm around his wife, he said: "This trial is not over until

that bombing is over in Cambodia." And he added that he intended to sue for damages specific individuals in the Government, perhaps the President himself.

Like every other major decision in the case since it went to trial in January, the final dramatic ruling came amid an air of expectancy that had pervaded the proceedings all week.

By 7 A.M., when the smog had already descended on

Los Angeles, spectators had begun lining up in the corridor outside the dark brown door to the courtroom for the limited passes for access to the trial, which ended almost two years after Dr. Daniel Ellsberg and Anthony J. Russo Jr. were indicted.

Photographers waited for the judge, whose latest pictures, showing shorter and fuller hair, were taken three

NEW TRIAL BARRED

But Decision Does Not Solve Constitutional Issues in Case

By MARTIN ARNOLD
Special to The New York Times

LOS ANGELES, May 11—Citing what he called "improper Government conduct shielded so long from public view," the judge in the Pentagon papers trial dismissed today all charges against Dr. Daniel Ellsberg and Anthony J. Russo Jr.

And he made it clear in his ruling that the two men would not be tried again on charges

The text of Judge Byrne's decision is on Page 14.

of stealing and copying the Pentagon papers.

"The conduct of the Government has placed the case in such a posture that it precludes the fair, dispassionate resolution of these issues by a jury," he said.

David R. Nissen, the chief prosecutor, said, "It appears that the posture is such that no appeal will be possible."

Defendants Not Vindicated

But the decision by United States District Court Judge William Matthew Byrne Jr. did not vindicate the defendants; it chastised the Government. Nor did it resolve the important constitutional issues that the case

The end of the trial, on its 89th day, was dramatic. The courtroom was jammed; the jury box was filled with news reporters; defense workers in the Ellsberg-Russo cause, mostly young people, sat in chairs lining the courtroom wall.

Dr. Ellsberg and Mr. Russo, surrounded by their lawyers, stared intently as Judge Byrne quickly read his ruling.

The Government's action in this case, he said, "offended a sense of justice," and so "I have decided to declare a mistrial and grant the motion for dismissal." The time was 2:07 P.M.

The courtroom erupted in loud cheering and clapping. The judge, barely hiding a smile, quickly strode out the door behind his bench.

Tension had been building

Continued on Page 14, Column 5

NIXON AGAIN ASKS LEGAL AID TO POOR

Independent Agency Would Replace O.E.O. Unit

By LINDA CHARLTON
Special to The New York Times

WASHINGTON, May 11—President Nixon resubmitted to Congress today, in slightly revised form, his proposals for providing free legal assistance to the poor through the creation of an independent Legal Services Corporation.

A program to make available legal aid in civil matters to those unable to afford it otherwise is now a part of the Office of Economic Opportunity, which is scheduled to go out of existence July 1. Efforts to establish the program as an independent entity date back more than two years through a history of disagreement, compromise and veto. Today's bill is apparently a compromise reached after much internal Administration battling.

The new proposal would create an independent, federally funded Legal Services Corporation with an 11-member board of directors appointed by the President—a focal point of controversy in previous versions—but subject to confirmation by the Senate. Not more than six members could be of the same political party, and a majority would be lawyers.

It also includes very specific

Continued on Page 31 Column 3

Sudan Puts Off Trying 8 Who Killed U.S. Envoys

By HENRY TANNER
Special to The New York Times

CAIRO, May 11—President Gaafar al-Nimeiry of the Sudan has decided to postpone indefinitely the trial of the eight Palestinian guerrillas who killed three diplomats, two Americans and a Belgian, while holding the Saudi Embassy in Khartoum last March 2, informed Sudanese sources said here today.

After the slayings General Nimeiry and other leading officials publicly pledged an early trial. They said that the guerrillas would be charged with murder, a capital offense in the Sudan.

Now the same officials say that the Israeli force that thrust into the heart of Beirut, the Lebanese capital, last month and killed three leading mem-

bers of the Palestinian resistance made it impossible for General Nimeiry—or any other Arab statesman—to convict Palestinian guerrillas of a crime that in Arab eyes was as much a patriotic deed as the raid into Beirut was in Israeli eyes.

The recent fighting between Lebanese troops and Palestinians is another reason why no public trial of the eight guerrillas should be held, Sudanese officials say. The trial, they maintain, would be interpreted throughout the Arab world as another instance of "fratricide."

The outlook now is for a lengthy confinement of the eight without trial, informed sources say.

General Nimeiry's decision is likely to renew friction between the Sudan and the United States, which resumed diplomatic relations less than a year ago.

The State Department is known to have served notice that no new ambassador will be sent to Khartoum unless the slayers of Ambassador Cleo A.

Continued on Page 11, Column 3

2-GERMANY PACT IS VOTED IN BONN

Parliament Also Approves Joining United Nations

By DAVID BINDER
Special to The New York Times

BONN, May 11 — The treaty that will establish formal relations between the two Germanys after more than two decades of hostile nonrecognition was ratified by the lower house of the West German Parliament today by a vote of 268 to 217.

By a second vote, 365 to 121, the lower house also gave its approval to the prospective entry of West Germany into the United Nations along with East Germany.

The treaty, regarded as the crowning achievement of Chancellor Willy Brandt's policy of normalizing relations with Eastern Europe, was concluded last November. It is expected to go into effect later this month after the ratification process is completed here and in East Germany.

The upper house of the West German Parliament is expected to approve the treaty next week and send it to President Gustav Heinemann for signature. Ratification by the East German Parliament is also expected next week, with ceremonial approval by the State Council to follow.

The treaty will greatly enlarge the opportunities for the Germans of the two states to

Continued on Page 10, Column 1

A New Grand Jury Reported Planning To Summon Biaggi

By NICHOLAS GAGE

Representative Mario Biaggi, who appeared twice before a Federal grand jury in 1971, will be called before another jury for further questioning, authoritative sources said yesterday.

On Thursday night Mr. Biaggi admitted that he had refused to answer questions before the 1971 jury after repeatedly denying it for several months.

The Bronx Representative had been scheduled to be called before a Federal grand jury on April 27, but the appearance was postponed pending resolution of the court battle—that was just then beginning—over release of his 1971 testimony. That testimony is to be released today.

The United States Attorney's office has received new information

Continued on Page 15, Column 1

CONNALLY TO TAKE LEAVE FROM FIRM

New Adviser to President Will Also Resign From All Corporate Boards

By JOHN HERBERS

WASHINGTON, May 11—John B. Connally announced today that he would take a leave of absence from his law firm and resign from all corporate boards during the time he will serve as special adviser to President Nixon.

Mr. Connally's announcement, issued by his office in Houston, came after disclosure that the firm in which he is a senior partner is representing the Gulf Resources and Chemical Corporation, now under investigation by a Federal grand jury in connection with campaign contributions sent to the Committee for the Re-election of the President. The disclosure was made today in Newsday and other newspapers.

"I am today taking a leave of absence from my law firm for the period during which I will serve as a special adviser to the President," said the former Secretary of the Treasury and former Texas Governor.

"I am also resigning from all corporate boards on which I serve," he continued. "Notwithstanding that my service will be on an intermittent and voluntary basis and without any operational role, I will not engage in any legal practice nor participate in any dividends or revenues or as a partner of the firm during this advisory period."

Continued on Page 16, Column 3

Congress Ascending

Watergate Seen as Altering Balance Between Executive and Capitol Hill

By JAMES M. NAUGHTON
Special to The New York Times

WASHINGTON, May 11—The White House is slipping and Congress is rising as the balance of power in Washington is being altered perceptibly by the Watergate conspiracy case. For the first time in six years the House of Representatives went on record yesterday, by a vote of 219 to 188, in opposition to White House policies in Indochina. For the second time in five weeks, the Senate declared yesterday, 66 to 24, that the White House was obligated to adhere to the directions of Congress on Government spending.

"Both houses are beginning to see eye to eye on Congres-

News Analysis

sional responsibility," the Senate Democratic leader, Mike Mansfield, said today in an interview.

A senior associate of President Nixon predicted privately today that the White House and the Nixon Cabinet would abandon their attitude of disregard for those on Capitol Hill and become, in the official's words, "more receptive" to Congressional viewpoints.

The change is only beginning to be visible. Much of it is atmospheric. It remains for Congress, long a slumbering giant, to take steps to "even the balance," as Mr. Mansfield put it, but he and others are becoming

Continued on Page 13, Column 1

Norton Simon Bought Smuggled Idol

By DAVID L. SHIREY

Norton Simon, the West Coast industrialist and art collector, said yesterday that he had paid $1-million for a bronze sculpture of a Hindu deity that Indian Government officials say was stolen from a South Indian temple and smuggled out of India.

"Hell, yes, it was smuggled," said Mr. Simon in a telephone interview. "I spent between $15-million and $16-million over the last two years on Asian art, and most of it was smuggled. I don't know whether it was stolen."

Indian Government officials, who have for two years been seeking the return of the 44-inch sculpture representing the deity Siva, known in its region of discovery as Nataraja, say that it was one of several stolen from a temple in Sivapuram, in southern India and smuggled out of the country. They also say that the original works were replaced in the temple by modern fakes.

The New York Times/Meyer Liebowitz

The bronze statue of the Hindu deity Siva, dancing

86th St. Toonerville Tale: 3 Flee From a Police Van

By LESLEY OELSNER

Three prisoners, two of them handcuffed together, leaped from the back of a police van yesterday and ran off along West 86th Street to freedom.

The van continued on its precinct-to-precinct morning rounds and then, 40 minutes later, at 79th Street and Lexington, two more prisoners jumped out. This time by standers shouted and policemen jumped from the vehicle, quickly capturing the fugitives—and learning for the first time of the disappearance of the other three.

Capt. Alexander Davis of Manhattan North, said, "How's that for a Toonerville tale?"

Captain Davis, who is in charge of investigating how the escapes occurred, reported late yesterday afternoon that the fugitives—all alleged robbers—were still at large. "Four or five detec-

tives," he said, as well as the police officer who had arrested them the night before, Daniel Traynor of the 28th Precinct, were looking for the men.

The route to freedom, the captain said, appeared to have been facilitated by a defective lock on the van door.

The van began its trip early yesterday at the 28th Precinct station at 229 West 123d Street. It was to go from precinct to precinct picking up men who had been arrested the night before and then take them to the Criminal Courts Building at 100 Centre Street.

Among the men it picked up at the 28th were the three escapees—Edward McBride, 24 years old, of 215 West 101st Street, and Vincent Perry, 19, and Tony Grant,

Continued on Page 21, Column 1

"All the News That's Fit to Print"

The New York Times

LATE CITY EDITION
Weather: Very hot again today; very warm tonight. Hot tomorrow. Temp. range: today 78-96; Wed. 76-95. Temp.-Hum. Index yesterday 83. Full U.S. report on Page 66.

VOL. CXXII ..No. 42,222   © 1973 The New York Times Company   NEW YORK, THURSDAY, AUGUST 30, 1973   15 CENTS

JUDGE SIRICA ORDERS NIXON TO YIELD TAPES TO HIM FOR A DECISION ON GRAND JURY USE; PRESIDENT DECLARES HE 'WILL NOT COMPLY'

PEKING DISCLOSES 5-DAY CONGRESS OF CHINESE PARTY

Meeting Ousted Lin, Named Central Committee and Adopted a Constitution

By TILLMAN DURDIN
Special to The New York Times

HONG KONG, Aug. 29—China disclosed today that the 10th Congress of her Communist party was held in Peking last Friday through yesterday.

The announcement was made in a dispatch of Hsinhua, the

Text of the communiqué is printed on Page 14.

official press agency. It said the Congress formally expelled Defense Minister Lin Piao and Chen Po-ta from the party. Mr. Lin was designated Chairman Mao Tse-tung's successor during the last Congress in 1969, and is reported to have been killed in 1971 after attempting to assassinate Chairman Mao. Both he and Mr. Chen, a former Politburo member, were denounced as renegades and traitors.

Political Report by Chou

The Congress also adopted a revised party constitution, selected a new Central Committee and approved a political report delivered by Premier Chou En-lai.

It is assumed that the new Central Committee will hold its first meeting in a day or two and name members of the all-important Politburo and the standing committee of the Politburo. These bodies run China on a day-to-day basis.

The Central Committee members were reported to include the old, middle-aged and young, which the communiqué said showed that the party "has no lack of successors."

Mao Presided

The Congress, at which Chairman Mao presided, was the briefest in the history of the Chinese party.

Attended by 1,249 delegates, the Congress was held in the greatest secrecy and confounded foreign newsmen and diplomats in Peking.

Obviously, hard decisions on sharing of power and position between factions had to be made before the Congress was held and this probably delayed its convening. The result is an apportioning of positions between the civilian moderates, represented by Premier Chou, and important career party members, military leaders and the so-called leftists generally associated with Chiang Ching, Mr. Mao's wife.

The 10th Congress appeared to have been even more of a

Continued on Page 14, Column 1

Sadat and Qaddafi Act on Unification

By HENRY TANNER
Special to The New York Times

CAIRO, Aug. 29—President Anwar el-Sadat of Egypt and the Libyan leader, Col. Muammar el-Qaddafi, tonight proclaimed the "birth of a new unified Arab state" but made it emphatically clear that actual unification of their two countries was still a long way off.

A declaration issued in the name of the two leaders satisfied every point of the Egyptian Government's wish for a slow, gradual approach that could be broken off at any stage. It fell far short of the immediate full union that Colonel Qaddafi had urgently demanded.

Mr. Sadat and Colonel Qaddafi agreed in August, 1972, to work toward "complete unity." The process, to take a year,

Continued on Page 5, Column 1

180,000 Hit by Blackout In Four Areas of Queens

By FRANK J. PRIAL

About 180,000 Queens residents were left without electrical power last night when a group of Consolidated Edison Company cables burned out at 6:15 P.M. The blackout, the first major power failure of the summer, also darkened passenger terminals and hangars at La Guardia Airport.

The cables, and the entire Con Edison network, had been running at full capacity because of the unrelenting, record-breaking heat. Yesterday New Yorkers plodded through their second day of above 90-degree temperatures and high humidity, and there was no relief in sight.

High for the day was 95 degrees at 2:35 P.M., three degrees below Tuesday's high of 98, the record for the summer —so far.

The burned-out cables, 27,000-volt feeder cables supplying all of Jackson Heights and parts of Corona, Woodside and

Elmhurst, as well as the airport, had been strained by a day of fires and breakdowns.

At about 11:30 P.M., at least 5,000 Con Edison customers were left without power on Staten Island, when seven feeder cables were knocked out in the Great Kills and Richmondtown sections. Full power was restored to 795 customers in Richmondtown after 65 minutes. Scattered areas of Great Kills were still blacked out at 2:30 A.M.

The power failure in Queens came just as Con Edison was about to end its second day of a 5 per cent system-wide power reduction. The cutback, which also affected the rest of the state's power companies, which are members of the New York State Power Pool, lasted from 10 A.M. to 6:25 P.M.

Throughout the day, the situation had been more serious in Jackson Heights than anywhere else in the Con Edison area, and the company had asked its Jackson Heights customers to be particularly careful about using power when they came home from work last night.

Four of eight feeder cables serving the area had burned out at about 3 A.M. yesterday. One

Continued on Page 27, Column 1

Official Temperatures

Wed. Tues.		2 P.M.	94 95
3 A.M. 81 79		3 P.M.	94 97
4 A.M. 80 79		4 P.M.	93 96
5 A.M. 77 79		5 P.M.	93 94
6 A.M. 77 79		6 P.M.	90 93
7 A.M. 76 77		7 P.M.	89 93
8 A.M. 78 78		8 P.M.	88 89
9 A.M. 81 81		9 P.M.	86 87
10 A.M. 83 83		10 P.M.	86 87
11 A.M. 85 84		11 P.M.	85 85
Noon 89 85		Midnight	84 84
1 P.M. 92 93		2 A.M.	82 82
		Thurs. Wed.	
		1 A.M.	84 83
		2 A.M.	83 81

The Soviet Dissidents

Moscow Showing It Will Maintain Ideological War and Internal Curbs

By THEODORE SHABAD
Special to The New York Times

MOSCOW, Aug. 29—The sudden upsurge in news of dissidence from Moscow has brought into sharp focus the Soviet leaders' determination to pursue their policy of improved relations with the West without giving an inch to domestic pressures for liberal reforms.

There appear to be some elements of coincidence in the timing of the current trial of two dissidents and the rash of moves and countermoves in the cases of two of the most outspoken advocates of change in the Soviet system—Andrei D. Sakharov, the physicist, and Aleksandr I. Solzhenitsyn, the novelist.

But the pattern of events of the last two weeks also fits in neatly with the intensification of ideological warfare that has become increasingly evident in

News Analysis

the Soviet Union since the meeting between President Nixon and Leonid I. Brezhnev, the Soviet Communist party chief.

It seems a far cry from the smiles-and-sweetness atmosphere that was being conveyed by the Soviet mass media in those June days to the rapid-fire sequence of recent Soviet denunciations of supposedly subversive threats, foreign and domestic.

First, after a moratorium of several months coinciding with the summit period, the United States again became fair game in the Soviet media. Radio listeners were warned against writing to the Voice of America, which was presented as an intelligence-gathering organization, and "Sesame Street" was described as the kind of program that should be kept off Soviet living room screens if

Continued on Page 9, Column 1

APPEAL UNCERTAIN

White House Hints at Possible Defiance of Court Ruling

By JOHN HERBERS
Special to The New York Times

SAN CLEMENTE, Calif., Aug. 29—The White House said today that President Nixon would not comply with Judge John J. Sirica's order to turn over his Watergate tape recordings to the court.

In a terse statement issued by its press office, the White House said the President was considering the possibility of appeal or "how otherwise to sustain the President's position."

This left open the clear possibility that the President might simply refuse to obey the order without first resorting to appeal.

Compromise Ruled Out

White House spokesmen would not elaborate on the statement, but it was plain that it was another assertion by President Nixon that he would not compromise on the issue.

In his news conference last Wednesday, Mr. Nixon said his right to withhold the tapes as a point of executive privilege was absolute.

"Let me explain the principle of confidentiality exists or it does not exist," he said. "Once it is compromised or it is known that a conversation that is held with the President can be subject to a subpoena by a Senate committee, by a grand jury, by a prosecutor, and be listened to by anyone, the principle of confidentiality is thereby irreparably damaged."

Confidentiality Needed

To conduct the affairs of the Presidency, in both foreign and domestic matters, Mr. Nixon said, "he must be able to do so with the principle of confidentiality intact."

The President seems more determined now to resist compromise on the tapes than he was a few weeks ago. Last month, Gerald L. Warren, the deputy White House press secretary, said Mr. Nixon would

Continued on Page 21, Column 6

Union Aides Indicted

Peter Ottley, president of the 20,000-member Local 144 of the Hotel, Hospital, Nursing Home and Allied Service Employes Union, and Peter Byrne, its secretary-treasurer, were indicted here yesterday by a Federal grand jury on charges of embezzling union funds. Page 44.

Judge John J. Sirica, who ruled on the Presidential tapes, in his chambers.
The New York Times/George Tames

NIXON'S LAWYERS ASSAIL COMMITTEE

In Paper Filed in Court, His Counsel Rejects Demand of Senators for Tapes

Special to The New York Times

WASHINGTON, Aug. 29—President Nixon's lawyers charged today that the Senate Watergate committee had conducted a "criminal investigation and trial" that exceeded the authority granted to Congress by the Constitution.

In papers filed in Federal District Court, the White House attorneys rejected the committee's demand for tape recordings of Nixon conversations on the ground that the Senators were illegally attempting to determine "whether or not criminal acts have been committed and the guilt or innocence of individuals."

The President's lawyers also contended that the court had no jurisdiction over their client, either as an individual or as President, and that Mr. Nixon "owes no duty," in either capacity, to the Senate committee to provide it with recordings of his confidential meetings or other related documents.

In a legal countermove, the Senate committee filed with Chief Judge John J. Sirica a motion for summary judgment in the same case, a request that the judge enforce two subpoenas already served on the President with a minimum of further court proceedings.

The motion by the committee

Continued on Page 21, Column 3

Judge Sirica's Order

This matter having come before the court on motion of the Watergate special prosecutor made on behalf of the June, 1972, grand jury of this district for an order to show cause, and the court being advised in the premises, it is by the court this 29th day of August, 1973, for the reasons stated in the attached opinion,

Ordered that respondent, President Richard M. Nixon, or any subordinate officer, official or employe with custody or control of the documents or objects listed in the grand jury subpoena duces tecum of July 23, 1973, served on respondent in this district, is hereby commanded to produce forthwith for the court's examination in camera, the subpoenaed documents or objects which have not heretofore been produced to the grand jury; and it is

Further ordered that the ruling herein be stayed for a period of five days in which time respondent may perfect an appeal from the ruling; and it is

Further ordered that should respondent appeal from the ruling herein, the above stay will be extended indefinitely pending the completion of such appeal or appeals.

JOHN J. SIRICA
CHIEF JUDGE

White House Reply

As Mr. Wright pointed out in his oral argument before the court, in camera inspection of these tapes is inconsistent with the President's position relating to the question of separation of powers as provided by the Constitution and the necessity of maintaining the precedent of confidentiality of private Presidential conversations for this President and for Presidents in the future.

The President consequently will not comply with this order.

White House counsel are now considering the possibility of obtaining appellate review or how otherwise to sustain the President's position.

Nadjari Studying Charge Of Plan to Bribe a Justice

By C. GERALD FRASER

Special Prosecutor Maurice H. Nadjari's office disclosed yesterday that it was investigating an alleged conspiracy to pay a $50,000 bribe to a State Supreme Court justice.

Although details of the conspiracy were not disclosed, sources close to the investigation said that it grew out of a case involving the Citizens Casualty Company of New York, which was declared insolvent in 1970 after fighting a long court battle to stay in business.

In that battle, the company, whose lawyer was Representative Mario Biaggi, won a brief victory before Acting Supreme Court Justice Adolph C. Orlando, an interim appointee, who is now sitting in the Court of Claims. But Judge Orlando was reversed and the company was ordered dissolved.

Biaggi Received $240,000

Mr. Biaggi was paid $240,000, but was later ordered to return $100,000 of the fee. The court order said that the $100,000 was contingent on Mr. Biaggi's winning complete victory for the company while Mr. Biaggi maintained that he was obligated only to win the aspect of the case that came before Judge Orlando.

Yesterday in State Supreme Court, Justice John M. Murtagh refused to quash a sub-

poena issued by Mr. Nadjari to the Century National Bank and Trust Company. Joseph A. Phillips, the chief assistant special prosecutor, said that bank records would be able to shed light on "the sources of moneys used to pay the bribe and to account for moneys obtained as a result of the case."

Mr. Phillips told Justice Murtagh yesterday that "in the course of that investigation, the evidence developed by the grand jury indicates that the principal officers of the Century Bank have information and evidence" relating to the alleged bribery.

Inquiry Leads to Bank

In this way, the special prosecutor got into transactions involving the Century National Bank and Trust Company of 1372 Broadway.

In an affidavit filed yesterday, Mr. Phillips said: "As a result of the alleged bribe, the conspirators obtained substantial sums of moneys due to the determination of the case."

And he said to Justice Murtagh: "Where did the money as a result of the bribe go?... all of the leads we have produced point to Century National Bank."

The executive officers of the bank are Vincent F. Albano, Republican county chairman.

Continued on Page 33, Column 3

A HISTORIC RULING

President First Since Jefferson Directed to Give Up Records

By WARREN WEAVER Jr.
Special to The New York Times

WASHINGTON, Aug. 29—President Nixon was ordered today by Judge John J. Sirica to make tape recordings of White House conversations involving the Watergate case available to him for a decision on their use by a grand jury.

Presidential aides announced, however, that Mr. Nixon "will

Text of Judge Sirica's opinion will be found on Page 20.

not comply with the order."

A White House statement said that the President's lawyers, led by Prof. Charles Alan Wright, were considering appealing the decision by Judge Sirica, who is chief judge of the United States District Court here, but it also hinted that they might find some other method of sustaining the President's legal position.

If faced with a refusal by Mr. Nixon to accept the court's ruling or to challenge it by an appeal, Archibald Cox, the special prosecutor, might initiate contempt proceedings or begin an appeal of his own, based on the court's refusal to give him the tapes directly.

Serious Consequences

It was only the second time in the nation's history that a court had required a President, against his will, to produce his personal records as evidence, and the decision was certain to have serious political, governmental and legal consequences, both immediate and long-range. The first case involved President Jefferson.

At San Clemente, where President Nixon is vacationing, officials announced that he would not comply with the court order on the ground that inspection of the tapes by a judge "is inconsistent with the President's position relating to the question of separation of powers as provided by the Constitution and the necessity of maintaining precedents of confidentiality of private Presidential conversations . . ."

The White House statement said that the President's lawyers were considering an appeal "or how otherwise to sustain" Mr. Nixon's legal position.

The last phrase raised the possibility that the President might ignore the court order rather than appeal it, thus precipitating another constitutional clash between the executive and judicial branches.

Authority Upheld

Judge Sirica said that he was "simply unable" to decide whether the President's refusal to release the tapes and related documents was valid without inspecting the recordings himself. He upheld the authority of the court to take such action.

If he finds evidence relating to criminal activity in the tapes, and it can be successfully separated from the privileged statements dealing with the President's official duties, the judge said, he will excise the privileged portions and pass the unprivileged portions along to the Watergate grand jury. Archibald Cox, the special prosecutor, is presiding over the panel.

"If privileged and unprivi-

Continued on Page 21, Column 1

NEWS INDEX

	Page		Page
Books	31	Music	24-26
Bridge	30	Obituaries	36
Business	44-54	Op-Ed	35
Chess	30	Society	29
Crossword	31	Sports	38-43
Editorials	34	Theaters	24-26
Family/Style	28	Transportation	66
Financial	44-54	TV and Radio	66
Letters	34	U. N. Proceedings	3
Man in the News	21	Weather	66
Movies	24-26		

News Summary and Index, Page 35

BEREAVED BY EARTHQUAKE: A woman and the only one of her four children who survived sit in ruins of home in Orizaba, Mexico. Incomplete reports put the toll of Tuesday's quake at more than 600. Details, Page 12.
United Press International

The New York Times

LATE CITY EDITION
Weather: Partly sunny today; fair tonight. Partly sunny tomorrow. Temp. range: today 53-75; Saturday 53-73. Additional details on Page 91.

SECTION ONE

VOL.CXXIII..No. 42,260   © 1973 The New York Times Company   NEW YORK, SUNDAY, OCTOBER 7, 1973   75c beyond 50-mile zone from New York City, except Long Island. Higher in air delivery cities.   50 CENTS

ARABS AND ISRAELIS BATTLE ON TWO FRONTS; EGYPTIANS BRIDGE SUEZ; AIR DUELS INTENSE

Associated Press
REDS, ORIOLES WIN PLAYOFF OPENERS: Johnny Bench after his homer won National League game for Cincinnati from New York, 2-1. Sparky Anderson, manager, is at lower left. Baltimore beat Oakland, 6-0, in the American League. Details in Section 5.

U.S. ASKS A HALT

Pleas by Kissinger to Prevent the Fighting Prove Fruitless

By BERNARD GWERTZMAN
Special to The New York Times

WASHINGTON, Oct. 6—The United States appealed to Israel and Egypt today to halt the fighting.

Secretary of State Kissinger, who was in New York, was caught by surprise when the crisis developed. He made a last-minute effort by telephone with Foreign Minister Abba Eban of Israel and Foreign Minister Mohammed H. el-Zayyat of Egypt to prevent the fighting from breaking out, but it proved fruitless.

Both men had had routine talks with Mr. Kissinger in the last two days without giving any indication that fighting was about to erupt, Administration officials said.

Kissinger Urges 'Restraint'

On instructions from President Nixon, who was in Key Biscayne, Fla., for the weekend, Mr. Kissinger "urged restraint to avoid the undermining and violation of the cease-fire" in effect since August, 1970, "and to avoid any escalation and continuation of the fighting," Robert J. McCloskey, a State Department spokesman, said in New York before Mr. Kissinger returned to Washington this afternoon.

In addition, Mr. Kissinger sent cables to King Faisal of Saudi Arabia and King Hussein of Jordan, both friendly to the United States, expressing the hope that they would "use their good office to urge restraint where they have the influence to do so," Mr. McCloskey said.

Call to Waldheim

Mr. Kissinger telephoned Secretary General Waldheim of the United Nations and Sir Laurence McIntyre of Australia, this month's President of the Security Council, to discuss possible Council action. He also called the Soviet Ambassador, Anatoly F. Dobrynin, in Washington, Mr. McCloskey said, presumably to urge Soviet restraint as well.

The crisis struck Washington without much warning. American intelligence had routinely reported signs of military build-ups in Egypt and Syria in recent weeks, but the analysts believed these were either

Continued on Page 14, Column 1

CAB DRIVER SLAIN IN TENSE BOSTON

Found Stabbed to Death in Roxbury Area Following Two Previous Killings

By JOHN KIFNER
Special to The New York Times

BOSTON, Oct. 6—The body of a young white taxi driver who had been stabbed to death was found today in the predominantly black Roxbury neighborhood as this uneasy city tried to come to grips with its racial fears.

The police identified the driver as Kirk Miller, a student at Clarkson College, who was working for the Boston Cab Company. His body was found hidden in some bushes in a vacant lot in Roxbury.

Detectives said that he had multiple stab wounds in his back and head. They said that they "had to assume" that robbery was a possible motive although they could not discount other factors. They said that no money was found on the body.

Mr. Miller was discovered by his sister Sally and a friend, Jeffrey Carter.

Tuesday night, a young white woman was burned to death by six youths in Roxbury, and less than 48 hours later an elderly white man was slain near a housing project. There

Continued on Page 77, Column 3

Tax Agents Compile Data On Net Worth of Agnew

By MARTIN WALDRON
Special to The New York Times

BALTIMORE, Oct. 6—Agents of the Internal Revenue Service are apparently compiling a statement on Vice President Agnew's net worth as part of the continuing investigation into his financial affairs.

Although the purpose of the revenue service's investigation is not known, the service often uses the technique of the net worth audit in an attempt to show that a defendant accused of evading taxes is worth more than the amounts on which he paid taxes.

Earlier this week, the Federal grand jury investigating Mr. Agnew indicted N. Dale Anderson, who succeeded Mr. Agnew as Baltimore County Executive, on income tax charges after revenue agents compiled a net worth statement on Mr. Anderson.

By law, the revenue service is prohibited from commenting on individual income tax reports or on investigations it may have under way.

But in the last few weeks its agents have been collecting data dealing with Mr. Agnew's affairs, even minor transactions, according to sources knowledgeable about the investigations.

On Oct. 3, agents from the Charlotte, N. C., intelligence office of the service subpoenaed records in Asheville, N. C., showing a gift of four yards of homespun cloth worth $16 to Mr. Agnew in 1967 at the time of the Southern Governors Conference, the sources said.

Such gifts are sometimes considered as income for tax purposes.

In making a case charging income tax evasion against an individual, the revenue service sometimes alleges failure to pay tax on specific income items, which it then seeks to prove were received by the individual.

The revenue agents and agents of the Federal Bureau of Investigation are apparently checking every financial transaction that the Vice President

Continued on Page 33, Column 1

United Press International
Army boots slung over his shoulder, an Israeli reservist reports for duty in Tel Aviv

U.N. COUNCIL AIDES CONFER ON CRISIS

President of Body Seeks Views on Calling Meeting to Deal With Fighting

By ROBERT ALDEN
Special to The New York Times

UNITED NATIONS, N. Y., Oct. 6—The President of the Security Council, Sir Laurence McIntyre of Australia, opened formal consultations tonight with other members of the Council to seek their views on calling a Council meeting to deal with the fighting in the Middle East.

The Western powers generally favored calling such a meeting, but not prematurely. They said that a premature meeting would result in little more than invective, charge and counterclaim.

Another proposal the Council members were discussing was for the President of the Council to appeal to both sides in the Middle East to halt the fighting. While Western powers generally supported such an appeal, the Chinese and the Russians held back endorsement; the French said they would have to study the idea.

Neither the Israelis nor the Arab states called for an urgent meeting of the Council today, though the Egyptian Foreign Minister, Dr. Mohammed H. el-Zayyat, said he wanted to

Continued on Page 8, Column 1

Israelis and Egyptians Tell Of Beginnings of Conflict

Jerusalem's Report
By TERENCE SMITH
Special to The New York Times

JERUSALEM, Sunday, Oct. 7 —Heavy fighting erupted yesterday between Israeli and Arab forces along the Suez Canal and Golan heights cease-fire lines, a military spokesman announced.

The forces were still fighting early this morning in what Defense Minister Moshe Dayan described as "all-out war."

The fighting began at 2 P.M. yesterday, Israeli time (8 A.M. New York time). Egyptian forces managed to cross the Suez Canal during the afternoon and establish bridgeheads at several points on the Israeli-held eastern bank, but Israeli military spokesmen said last night that Israeli forces had moved into position to block them.

On the occupied Golan heights, a large-scale Syrian force including armor and artil-

Mrs. Meir's address, Page 5; Dayan excerpts, Page 6.

Continued on Page 4, Column 1

Cairo Communiques
By HENRY TANNER
Special to The New York Times

CAIRO, Oct. 6 — The Egyptian Government announced today that Israeli ground, sea and air forces attacked Egypt and Syria early this afternoon along the entire length of their front lines with Israel.

In a succession of communiqués read on the Government-controlled Cairo radio, Egypt said that her forces had crossed the Suez Canal in several places and had placed Egyptian flags on the Israeli-held eastern bank.

The radio said that the Egyptians had crossed the canal—the cease-fire line since the 1967 war—after repelling Israeli landing attempts on the Egyptian-held western bank.

The radio interrupted its regular program just after 2 P.M. Cairo time (8 A.M., New York time) saying that the Israeli action had started at 1:30 local time with air attacks on Ain Sukhna, 30 miles south of the town of Suez on the Egyptian shore of the Red Sea, and

Continued on Page 7, Column 1

SYRIANS IN CLASH

Fighting Along Canal and Golan Heights Goes On All Night

By ROBERT D. McFADDEN

The heaviest fighting in the Middle East since the 1967 war erupted yesterday on Israel's front lines with Egypt along the Suez Canal and Syria in the Golan heights.

Official announcements by Israel and Egypt agreed that Egyptian forces had crossed the Suez Canal and established footholds in the Israeli-occupied Sinai Peninsula.

A military communiqué issued in Cairo said that Egyptian forces had captured most of the eastern bank of the 100-mile canal. An Israeli military communiqué said the Egyptians had attempted to cross the canal at several points by helicopters and small boats and had succeeded in laying down pontoon bridges at two points. Armored forces were pouring across them into Sinai, it said.

Fighting All Night

A communiqué issued early today in Tel Aviv said fighting had raged all night along the canal's eastern bank and along the entire cease-fire line with Syria.

Each side accused the other of having started the fighting. But military observers posted by the United Nations reported crossings by Egyptian forces at five points along the Suez, and said Syrians had attacked in the Golan heights at two points.

Israeli and Syrian artillery dueled in the Golan heights, and on both battlefronts there were air clashes. The Cairo radio said Egyptian forces had shot down 11 Israeli planes and lost 10 of their own in battles over the Sinai and the Gulf of Suez. The Israeli spokesman did not comment on losses but said Israeli planes had shot down 10 Egyptian helicopters carrying troops into the southern Sinai.

Shelling by Syrians

In Damascus, the military command said that Syrian pilots and ground fire had shot down 10 Israeli aircraft in renewed action over the Golan heights this morning.

Syrian artillery was reported by the Israelis to have shelled a number of settlements in the occupied Golan heights and the Hula Valley area.

The Damascus radio said that Syrian forces had reoccupied Mount Hermon in the Golan heights for the first time since 1967, and said Syrian troops were fighting on the ground with Israeli forces along the entire cease-fire line.

An Israeli spokesman said today that Israeli planes had sunk an Egyptian vessel and that the navy had sunk three troop-carrying Egyptian craft during the night.

Gunboats Reported Sunk

As fighting continued into the night, Syrian and Israeli gunboats clashed in the Syrian harbor of Latakia, 110 miles north of Beirut. An Israeli communiqué said that five Soviet-built Syrian vessels were sunk by Israeli sea-to-sea missiles being used for the first time.

In Damascus, however, a military spokesman said that Syrian forces had sunk four Israeli naval vessels and shot down two Israeli helicopters in the sea battle.

No military action involving Jordan or Lebanon was reported, but King Hussein of Jordan placed his armed forces on full alert and conferred by telephone with President Anwar el-Sadat of Egypt and President Hafez al-Assad of Syria. Jordan was a belligerent in the 1967 war won by Israel.

The Government radio stations in Cairo and in Damascus

Continued on Page 2, Column 3

Queens Sports Center Proposed

By EMANUEL PERLMUTTER

Creation of a $275-million sports complex on air rights over the Sunnyside, Queens, railroad yards of the Penn Central was proposed yesterday by the State Racing and Wagering Board.

The project, which would be competitive with the proposed athletic complex in the New Jersey Meadows, would include two race tracks, an 80,000-seat stadium for football and other entertainments, a 1,000-room resort and convention hotel and parking for 20,000 cars.

No housing or other buildings would have to be demolished for the project since it would be built on a platform over the 300-acre yard site, which is less than a mile east of the Queensboro Bridge at the junction of Queens and Northern Boulevards and just a few minutes from Times Square by subway.

Under the proposal, the project would be financed by a bond issue and proceeds from the sale of Aqueduct Race Track. The air rights would be purchased by the Metropolitan Transportation Authority from the Penn Central and leased to the State Urban Development Corporation, which would build the necessary facilities.

Emil Mosbacher Jr., chairman of the Racing and Wager-

Continued on Page 49, Column 1

Race track is flanked by Northern Boulevard at right and Skillman Avenue, left. Hotel rises at center, next to stadium. Queensboro Bridge leads to Manhattan.

Gas Pipeline Contest Develops in Alaska

By GLADWIN HILL
Special to The New York Times

PRUDHOE BAY, Alaska, Sept. 29 — Another Alaskan pipeline dispute is brewing.

While the oil companies with the big petroleum deposits here on the North Slope await a final Congressional go-ahead to build a controversial 789-mile pipeline to Alaska's south coast, a consortium of United States and Canadian concerns is pushing plans to tap the region's rich natural gas reserves via a different but equally controversial 2,000-mile route.

Current exploratory activities of the gas consortium, pointing toward a possible major incursion into the Arctic National

Continued on Page 74, Column 3

The New York Times/Oct. 7, 1973
Heavy arrows (upper right) indicate drive by Syrians and (lower left) crossing of Suez Canal by Egyptians.

GRADE A SALE! Berman's Endless Markdown is the fastest of the Month; these are new a lot of opportunities at a low price. WHO really killed Robert Kennedy? "THE SECOND GUN" TODAY T L 3—ADVT.

"All the News That's Fit to Print"

The New York Times

LATE CITY EDITION

Weather: Partly sunny today; cool tonight. Fair and milder tomorrow. Temp. range: today 54-68; Wed. 58-75. Additional details on Page 90.

VOL. CXXIII...No. 42,264

© 1973 The New York Times Company

NEW YORK, THURSDAY, OCTOBER 11, 1973

15 CENTS

AGNEW QUITS VICE PRESIDENCY AND ADMITS TAX EVASION IN '67; NIXON CONSULTS ON SUCCESSOR

U.S. Believes Moscow Is Resupplying Arabs by Airlift

Soviet Could Spur Move to Aid Israel

By JOHN W. FINNEY
Special to The New York Times

WASHINGTON, Oct. 10—Administration officials said today that they believed the Soviet Union was airlifting military equipment to resupply the forces of Egypt and Syria.

The State Department said that if the Russians were in fact engaged in a huge resupply effort, this would put a "new face" on the Middle East conflict. Speaking for the department, Robert J. McCloskey said, however, that he was "not in a position to confirm that any of this is taking place at this time."

But other officials, apparently acting upon instructions laid down by the State Department, readily volunteered this information. They did so, however, on a basis that precluded their identification.

The fact that officials who until today had been extremely reluctant to discuss any detail of the Middle East war were now willing to talk openly about indications of a Soviet resupply effort prompted immediate speculation that the Nixon Administration might be laying the groundwork for resupplying the forces of Israel.

There were reports that Israel was flying military supplies from the United States and from American bases in Britain and West Germany, but it was not clear whether the supplies referred to had previously been ordered. Asked about the reports, the Defense Department refused to confirm or deny them.

The exact nature of the reported Soviet airlift remains unclear, United States officials said. All that is known, according to officials, is that in the last day or so, an unusually large number of Western transports have been observed landing at Egyptian and Syrian airports. The presumption is that the planes are carrying military equipment.

The airlift, officials reported, was being staged primarily from Hungary, with the planes

Continued on Page 18, Column 1

A 10-Mile Egyptian Gain

By HENRY TANNER
Special to The New York Times

IN THE SINAI PENINSULA, Oct. 10 — Egyptian soldiers, tanks and equipment are continuing to pour across the Suez Canal, a group of Western correspondents confirmed from the battle area today.

On a three-and-a-half-mile tour into the Sinai Peninsula, this correspondent also saw evidence that Egyptian forces had reached positions 10 miles or more east of the canal in some parts of the sector.

[In the air war the Egyptians said they had shot down six more Israeli planes. Egyptian aircraft were said to have attacked Israeli command headquarters, units and administrative installations on the northern Sinai coast.]

The Egyptian soldiers in the area toured by the correspondents were in high spirits, often jubilant, and seemed oblivious to Israeli artillery shells bursting near them.

"Don't worry, God is with us!" one of three young soldiers shouted laughingly to the correspondents, who ducked for cover when a shell burst too close for comfort. The Egyptians remained where they were, standing atop a ridge.

Shells fell every few moments but caused no casualties during a half-hour visit to the particular sector. An Egyptian officer said they were from an Israeli battery 15 miles away that was trying to hit a military bridge.

More than 50 trucks interspersed with antiaircraft guns were lined up in open country on the west bank, waiting for their turn to cross the canal. Waved onto the bridge by a young soldier with a yellow flag, they moved quickly, often with three or four vehicles on the bridge simultaneously.

On one truck two young soldiers were dancing. Others clapped their hands rhythmically.

The elation and excitement of returning to Egyptian territory occupied for more than six years by Israel was everywhere.

The loose boards and pontoons that made up the bridge

Continued on Page 18, Column 5

Israel Claiming Heights

By CHARLES MOHR
Special to The New York Times

TEL AVIV, Thursday, Oct. 11—Israel said last night that the Syrian Army on the Golan heights had been driven back to the 1967 cease-fire line, but Israeli forces fighting the Egyptians clearly seemed to have suspended a counterat-

Text of Mrs. Meir's address is printed on Page 19.

tack aimed at pushing them from the eastern bank of the Suez Canal.

A highly informed source said that Israel estimated the Egyptian invasion force at five divisions, which could be close to 75,000 men. The force, he said, crossed with about 600 tanks, and 300 to 400 of these

GARVEY WALLBANG'S PARTY AT NATE.—Adv.

may still be operational.

The Israeli Air Force bombed two air fields in the Nile delta as well as a naval headquarters, fuel installation and power plant in Syria in a day of slackening air action.

The Israeli command announced this morning that for the first time in the war Israeli forces had struck against the opposite bank of the Suez Canal. The command spokesman said that an Israeli force of unannounced size had raided convoys and rear echelon installations of the Egyptian Army.

The wording of the communiqué indicated that the operation was not an attempt to gain a foothold on the other side and that the raiding force

Continued on Page 19, Column 3

CONGRESS TO VOTE

Opposition Is Hinted if Choice Is Possible 1976 Candidate

Special to The New York Times

WASHINGTON, Oct. 10—President Nixon began his search today for a successor to Vice President Agnew amid indications that he will face stiff resistance from Congress if he chooses anyone who might qualify as a strong Republican candidate in 1976.

The Senate majority leader, Mike Mansfield, Democrat of Montana, said the choice of either John B. Connally, the former Treasury Secretary and Texas Governor, or Gov. Ronald Reagan of California—both presumed contenders for the Republican Presidential nomination in 1976—would provoke a fight from Senate Democrats. Similar warnings had come from Democratic leaders in the House.

Quick Action Indicated

Mr. Nixon's first moves today indicated that he wished to move quickly but with some show of bipartisan consultation. Senator Mansfield said after meeting the President that Mr. Nixon had indicated he would submit the name of his nominee to Congress "at the end of this week or the first of next week."

"President Nixon intends to move expeditiously in selecting a nominee and he trusts the Congress will then act promptly to consider the nomination," Ronald L. Ziegler, the President's press secretary, announced shortly after word that the President had accepted Mr. Agnew's resignation spread through the White House.

Mr. Nixon then began meeting with Congressional leaders of both parties and with George Bush, chairman of the Republican National Committee, to reach an understanding on the procedures he will follow in selecting a Vice President under

Continued on Page 34, Column 2

Mets in World Series; Defeat Reds for Flag

By JOSEPH DURSO

The New York Mets completed their six-week odyssey from last place to the National League pennant yesterday when they overpowered the favored Cincinnati Reds, 7-2, in a tumultuous game that rocked and almost ruined Shea Stadium.

In a riotous scene that brought back memories of their "miracle" of 1969, they decided the field after delaying the game in the ninth inning and clawed huge chunks of fence, sod and fixtures from the arena.

Professional sports may have had more clamorous moments. But New York baseball has had none since the Mets won the World Series four years ago after eight seasons as the comic relief of the leagues.

Their rise this summer car-

ried them from medical history to baseball history, and their public responded yesterday by mobbing Willie Mays, Pete Rose and the 340 police officers struggling to prevent panic.

Repairs on the stadium were started immediately after the crowd had dispersed shortly after 5 o'clock, while the Mets celebrated their victory in champagne and prepared for the next milestone.

They will open the World Series on Saturday in the home park of the Oakland A's or Baltimore Orioles, who will decide the American League pennant this after-

Continued on Page 61, Column 4

Associated Press
Spiro T. Agnew speaking to reporters after appearing at court in Baltimore yesterday

Agnew Plea Ends 65 Days Of Insisting on Innocence

By BEN A. FRANKLIN
Special to The New York Times

BALTIMORE, Oct. 10—Vice President Agnew ended today 65 days of defiant insistence that he was innocent of any wrongdoing by pleading no contest to a charge of cheating the Government of $13,551.47 on his Federal income tax pay-

Richardson, Agnew, Hoffman statements on Page 35.

ment for 1967, his first year as Governor of Maryland. Then he resigned his Federal office.

At a dramatic, surprise appearance here before United States District Court Judge Walter E. Hoffman after two days of secret negotiations, Mr. Agnew was confronted in open court by Attorney General Elliot L. Richardson.

The Attorney General said

Continued on Page 35, Column 1

I.R.S. Sees Nothing to Prevent New Tax Cases Against Agnew

By EILEEN SHANAHAN
Special to The New York Times

WASHINGTON, Oct. 10—Former Vice President Agnew's plea of "no contest" today in the income-tax evasion case against him could mark only the beginning of difficulties for him with the Internal Revenue Service.

An official spokesman for Internal Revenue said that so far as the agency is aware, there was nothing in the agreement leading to Mr. Agnew's resignation that would prohibit Internal Revenue from attempting to collect taxes on every payment to Mr. Agnew that could be documented as having been made but not reported on his tax returns.

The charge of tax evasion to

which Mr. Agnew pleaded "nolo contendere" involved $29,500. But a document released by the Justice Department detailing the evidence against the former Vice President alleges payments from contractors and others totaling as much as $100,000. The precise figure is not clear, because some of the allegations of illegal payments are stated in terms of percentages of the value of construction contracts awarded, and the figures for the contracts themselves are not given.

The Internal Revenue spokesman said, however, that it was common in tax-evasion cases for a charge of criminal tax evasion to be made involving

Continued on Page 33, Column 3

Judge Orders Fine, 3 Years' Probation

By JAMES M. NAUGHTON
Special to The New York Times

WASHINGTON, Oct. 10—Spiro T. Agnew resigned as Vice President of the United States today under an agreement with the Department of Justice to admit evasion of Federal income taxes and avoid imprisonment.

The stunning development, ending a Federal grand jury investigation of Mr. Agnew in Baltimore and probably terminating his political career, shocked his closest associates and precipitated an immediate search by President Nixon for a successor.

"I hereby resign the office of Vice President of the United States, effective immediately," Mr. Agnew declared in a formal statement delivered at 2:05 P.M. to Secretary of State Kissinger, as provided in the Succession Act of 1792.

Minutes later, Mr. Agnew stood before United States District Judge Walter E. Hoffman in a Baltimore courtroom, hands barely trembling, and read from a statement in which he pleaded nolo contendere, or no contest, to a Government charge that he had failed to report $29,500 of income received in 1967, when he was Governor of Maryland. Such a plea, while not an admission of guilt, subjects a defendant to a judgment of conviction on the charge.

Tells Court Income Was Taxable

"I admit that I did receive payments during the year 1967 which were not expended for political purposes and that, therefore, these payments were income taxable to me in that year and that I so knew," the nation's 39th Vice President told the stilled courtroom.

Judge Hoffman sentenced Mr. Agnew to three years' probation and fined him $10,000. The judge declared from the bench that he would have sent Mr. Agnew to prison had not Attorney General Elliot L. Richardson personally interceded, arguing that "leniency is justified."

In his dramatic courtroom statement, Mr. Agnew declared that he was innocent of any other wrongdoing but that it would "seriously prejudice the national interest" to involve himself in a protracted struggle before the courts or Congress.

Mr. Agnew also cited the national interest in a letter to President Nixon saying that he was resigning.

"I respect your decision," the President wrote to Mr. Agnew in a "Dear Ted" letter made public by the White House. The letter hailed Mr. Agnew for "courage and candor," praised his patriotism and dedication, and expressed Mr. Nixon's "great sense of personal loss." But it agreed

Continued on Page 33, Column 1

EVIDENCE SHOWS GIFTS TO AGNEW

Cites Requests and Receipt of Over $100,000—Denial Also Entered in Record

By ANTHONY RIPLEY
Special to The New York Times

BALTIMORE, Oct. 10—Spiro T. Agnew, in three elective offices including the Vice-Presidency, asked for and accepted cash payments totaling more than $100,000, according to the evidence gathered against him by the United States Attorneys in Baltimore.

That evidence, denied by Mr. Agnew, was entered into the

Charge and jury information are on Pages 36, 37 and 38.

record of the case in Federal District Court today as part of the agreement between the Justice Department and Mr. Agnew's lawyers.

It became a permanent part of the record in the case, along with Mr. Agnew's denial and other terms of the agreement that included his resignation and a plea of no contest to a tax charge.

A long list of other charges, involving perhaps $100,000 in payoffs by Maryland contrac-

Continued on Page 38, Column 1

Agnew-Nixon Exchange

October 10, 1973

Dear Mr. President:

As you are aware, the accusations against me cannot be resolved without a long, divisive and debilitating struggle in the Congress and in the courts. I have concluded that, painful as it is to me and to my family, it is in the best interests of the nation that I relinquish the Vice Presidency.

Accordingly, I have today resigned the office of Vice President of the United States. A copy of the instrument of resignation is enclosed.

It has been a privilege to serve with you. May I express to the American people, through you, my deep gratitude for their confidence in twice electing me to be Vice President.

Sincerely,
SPIRO T. AGNEW

October 10, 1973.

Dear Ted:

The most difficult decisions are often those that are the most personal, and I know your decision to resign as Vice President has been as difficult as any facing a man in public life could be. Your departure from the Administration leaves me with a great sense of personal loss. You have been a valued associate throughout these nearly five years that we have served together. However, I respect your decision, and I also respect the concern for the national interest that led you to conclude that a resolution of the matter in this way, rather than through an extended battle in the courts and the Congress, was advisable in order to prevent a protracted period of national division and uncertainty.

As Vice President, you have addressed the great issues of our times with courage and candor. Your strong patriotism, and your profound dedication to the welfare of the nation, have been an inspiration to all who have served with you as well as to millions of others throughout the country.

I have been deeply saddened by this whole course of events, and I hope that you and your family will be sustained in the days ahead by a well-justified pride in all that you have contributed to the nation by your years of service as Vice President.

Sincerely,
RICHARD NIXON

NEWS INDEX

	Page		Page
Art	42	Man in the News	33
Books	43	Movies	56-59
Bridge	42	Music	56-59
Business	67-75	Obituaries	50
Chess	42	Op-Ed	43
Crossword	43	Sports	61-66
Editorials	42	Theaters	56-59
Family Style	54	Transportation	84
Financial	67-75	TV and Radio	94-95
Going Out Guide	58	U.N. Proceedings	20
Letters	42	Weather	90

News Summary and Index, Page 47

AUGUST FRESH feels 30% APX.—Adv. with BOB CORCORAN for Girls—Adv.

WILLCOX & GIBBS sells mens suits for bigger men? (t's a match's.—WG-Ann Adv.)

"All the News That's Fit to Print"

The New York Times

LATE CITY EDITION

Weather: Mostly sunny, mild today; cloudy, chance of rain tonight. Temp. range: today 56-73. Friday 51-71. Additional details on Page 70.

VOL. CXXIII....No. 42,266   © 1973 The New York Times Company   NEW YORK, SATURDAY, OCTOBER 13, 1973   15 CENTS

GERALD FORD NAMED BY NIXON AS THE SUCCESSOR TO AGNEW

Appeals Court Agrees President Should Give Up Tapes

Israelis Drive Syrians Back Within 18 Miles of Damascus

Capture of Capital Thought Unlikely

By CHARLES MOHR
Special to The New York Times

EL QUNEITRA, on the Golan Heights, Oct. 12—Parts of the Syrian Army appeared to be in full retreat today as the Israeli Army advanced to within 18 miles of the Syrian capital of Damascus.

But an Israeli officer said: "We won't be having dinner together tomorrow in Damascus."

[In Tel Aviv, a well-informed Israeli source said that "the latest thinking is that we will not capture Damascus, which would be a terrible headache." An Israeli military spokesman said that Israeli forces had encountered Iraqi troops in the Golan heights for the first time.]

In at least one area of the Syrian front, northeast of the town of El Quneitra, it was apparent that Syrian forces were in retreat, although still fighting delaying actions.

Reporters following the Israeli Army and clocking distances on the odometers of their rented sedans—could see that the Israeli forward elements were at least 30 kilometers, or 18 miles, past the old 1967 cease-fire line—and thus about 30 kilometers from Damascus.

It was apparent to neutral foreign observers that, in this

one area at least, the main Syrian line of resistance had been smashed. The heavy fortifications constructed by Syria on the 1967 cease-fire line were abandoned and many of its bunkers damaged or destroyed.

Great plumes of brown dust rose in the air as Israeli tank companies moved forward over the rolling, hill-dotted terrain east of the cease-fire line.

A heavy Syrian artillery barrage came in on an area about four miles within Syria this afternoon, but journalists had no clear idea what was happening at the spearhead of the Israeli advance and how determined Syrian resistance was in the most forward areas.

On a brief visit to what is now the Israeli rear area on the route of advance, there were

Continued on Page 14, Column 5

To Our Readers

Distribution of this issue of The New York Times was delayed by the printers' union in defiance of a court order. The stoppages also made it necessary to reduce coverage of the news. Details, Page 24.

3 Freighters Sunk

By JUAN de ONIS
Special to The New York Times

DAMASCUS, Syria, Oct. 12 — Syrian air defenses today shot down 35 Israeli planes that attacked military air bases around this capital and other targets, according to a military spokesman.

Three freighters, one Soviet, one Japanese and one Greek, were sunk during attacks by Israeli missile boats on the ports of Latakia and Tartus, an official announcement said today. The Syrian spokesman said eight of the attacking Israeli craft were sunk by Syrian missile boats.

[In Cairo, military communiqués said that Egyptian forces were continuing to pour across the Suez Canal. Page 15.]

On the ground, "fierce fighting" continued all along the Syrian front, said the spokesman. He said more than 40 Israeli tanks and 20 armored vehicles had been destroyed. There was no figure on Syrian losses.

The front, along the occupied Golan Heights, was 24 miles southeast of this city of 840,000 people, which was calm tonight under a nearly full moon.

Traffic in the blacked-out streets consisted mainly of

Continued on Page 15, Column 1

JUDGES RULE 5-2

Historic Decision Finds President Not Above Law's Commands

By LESLEY OELSNER
Special to The New York Times

WASHINGTON, Oct. 12—In what it called an "unavoidable" and "extraordinary" ruling, the United States Court of Appeals held tonight that President Nixon must turn over to the Federal District Court here the disputed White House tape recordings possibly bearing on Watergate crimes.

By a 5-to-2 vote, the appeals court said that the District Court could then give the Watergate grand jury any relevant material, unless it felt that there was some public interest to be served by withholding "particular" statements or information.

Excerpts from court opinions will be found on Page 21.

"Though the President is elected by nationwide ballot, and is often said to represent all the people, he does not embody the nation's sovereignty," the court said. "He is not above the law's commands."

Order Is Upheld

Participants in today's decision were David L. Bazelon, chief judge, and J. Skelly Wright, Carl McGowan, Harold Leventhal, Spottswood W. Robinson, 3d, George E. MacKinnon and Malcolm R. Wilkey.

The court's ruling, issued at 6 P.M. through the clerk's office on the fifth floor of the Federal Courthouse here, thus substantially upheld the order last August of Federal District Judge John J. Sirica, although it appeared to take an even tougher stance against the President than Judge Sirica had.

The appellate court made its ruling in response to requests by both Mr. Nixon and Archibald Cox, the special Watergate prosecutor, to reverse Judge Sirica. Mr. Cox, who had initiated the proceedings when he had a subpoena issued for the tapes, asked the appeals court to order that the tapes be turned over directly to the grand jury.

Mr. Nixon, for his part, asked

Continued on Page 20, Column 4

Gerald R. Ford with President, after Mr. Nixon nominated him for Vice President
United Press International

Amtrak Will Double Fleet Of 'Corridor' Metroliners

By EDWARD C. BURKS

Amtrak, the nationwide rail passenger system, announced yesterday that it would virtually double its fleet of Metroliner cars and extend high-speed Metroliner service from New York to Boston.

It signed contracts in Washington for new equipment valued at $63.5-million including the following:

¶Fifty-seven new Metroliner-type coaches, capable of operation in trains pulled by either electric or diesel locomotives, for service in the Washington-New York-Boston "Northeast Corridor."

¶Eleven new 6,000-horsepower electric locomotives (added to 15 ordered earlier this year) to replace the famed but ancient Penn Central GG-1 electrics that have operated in the corridor since the nineteen-thirties.

¶Seventy new diesel passenger locomotives for other Amtrak routes around the nation.

In Philadelphia, Judge John P. Fullam, who is in charge of the Penn Central Railroad's bankruptcy case in Federal District Court, said he believed

Continued on Page 20, Column 4

there was no immediate need for the carrier to cease its operations. [Details Page 47.]

With the award of yesterday's contracts, Amtrak has now committed more than $110-million this year to new locomotives and passenger cars.

Started in 1969, the high-speed Metroliner service between New York and Washington has been expanded to a train every hour in each direction from early morning until evening on weekdays.

There are somewhat fewer services on the weekends. In addition, some Metroliners go on through New York as far as New Haven.

Although very-high speed service on the New York-Boston line must await the day of extensive track realignment on the curving route, new equipment ordered yesterday can substantially reduce present running times, according to Amtrak.

Bryan Duff, Amtrak's news director, said that the first of the new Metroliner-type coaches with airliner interiors should be delivered in 15 months. They are to be built by the Budd Company at Red Lion, Pa.

The 61 Metroliner cars now in operation are self-propelled and equipped with pantographs on the roof. Their use is thus limited to the relatively short stretches in this country with overhead catenary installations. The new cars will have the

Continued on Page 70, Column 5

P.S.C. Certifies Shortage Of Fuel Oil on Long Island

First in the State

By DAVID A. ANDELMAN

The State Public Service Commission certified yesterday that a major shortage in home and industrial fuel oils existed for Long Island—the first region in the state to be declared an "oil insufficient area."

According to the certification, between now and Jan. 15 Long Island will face a shortage of at least 150.1 million gallons of No. 2 home heating oil and 39.5 million gallons of Nos. 4 and 6 industrial fuel oils.

The certification was made to Henry L. Diamond, the State Environmental Conservation Commissioner, who must now decide whether to lift the regulations prohibiting use of high-sulphur fuel oil to ease the anticipated shortage.

Yesterday's certification applies only to fuels distributed through Northville Industries, the largest distributor on Long Island, but reportedly not the only one finding supplies short. As a result, a senior official of the Public Service Commission noted, "there may be other

Continued on Page 36, Column 3

Federal Controls Ordered

By The Associated Press

WASHINGTON, Oct. 12—The Nixon Administration reluctantly adopted today a mandatory allocation program governing the wholesale distribution of home heating oil.

At the same time, Congress moved steadily closer to forcing a mandatory program for all petroleum products.

The Administration's limited program, which will take effect Nov. 1, requires suppliers to distribute home heating oil, jet fuel, kerosene, diesel fuel, range oil, stove oil and gas oil to their customers in proportion to purchases made in the calendar year 1972.

On Oct. 2, the Administration imposed a similar allocation program on propane gas, but so far there is no Government control over the distribution of crude oil or of gasoline and other petroleum products.

Legislation now before Congress would require mandatory allocation of all petroleum products and crude oil.

The House Rules Committee

Continued on Page 36, Column 5

Fumes and smoke rise as Israeli artillerymen, on the Syrian border, fire 155-mm. guns
United Press International

Israel Is Accused in U.N. Of Sinking a Soviet Ship

By ROBERT ALDEN
Special to The New York Times

UNITED NATIONS, N. Y., Oct. 12—The Soviet Union accused Israel today of "barbarous" attacks on nonmilitary targets and demanded that they be stopped at once.

Yakov A. Malik, the Soviet delegate, read to the Security Council a dispatch from Tass, the Soviet press agency, that said the Soviet merchant ship Ilya Mechnikov had been sunk in Tartus, a Syrian port, by an Israeli attack.

Tass demanded "an immediate stop to the bombings of peaceful towns in Syria and Egypt, and the strict observance by Israel of the norms of international law."

"The continuation of criminal acts by Israel will lead to grave

consequences for Israel itself," the Tass article added.

Yosef Tekoah, the Israeli representative, said his information on the basis of a news dispatch was that the Soviet merchant ship had been damaged as a result of a naval battle that took place between Syrian and Israeli naval vessels outside the port. He termed the damage "unfortunate."

Reports from Damascus said that the ship had subsequently been sunk, as had a Greek and a Japanese merchant ship during attacks made by Israeli missile boats on the ports of Tartus and Latakia.

"We regret the sinking of

Continued on Page 14, Column 2

Rival Stadium Plans Stir a Bistate Furor

By FRANK LYNN

A bitter behind-the-scenes struggle has developed between New York and New Jersey over a proposed Sunnyside, Queens, sport complex that has the strong backing of Governor Rockefeller and that could effectively kill a similar New Jersey race track and football stadium.

High New York State sources said that the Governor had approved the announcement of the Queens sports complex last Saturday that forced postponement of the sale of a $280-million bond issue to finance the New Jersey race track and stadium for the New York Football Giants in the Hackensack Meadows.

"We were signaling investors of New York's interest in its

Continued on Page 24, Column 5

MOVE IS SURPRISE

House G.O.P. Leader Would Be the 40th Vice President

By JOHN HERBERS
Special to The New York Times

WASHINGTON, Oct. 12—Gerald Rudolph Ford of Michigan, the 60-year-old minority leader of the House of Representatives, was nominated by President Nixon tonight to be the 40th Vice President of the United States.

Mr. Nixon, making the surprise announcement on national television and radio shortly after 9 P.M., said that he would

Texts of Nixon and Ford remarks are on Page 19.

send the nomination to Congress tomorrow. Because of Mr. Ford's long service in that body, 25 years, he was expected to be easily confirmed.

Under the 25th Amendment, ratified in 1967 and never used before tonight, the nomination must be approved by simple majorities of both the House and the Senate before he can take office.

Mr. Ford's selection came two days after Spiro T. Agnew, who had served in the office almost five years, resigned, pleaded no contest to income tax evasion, was fined $10,000 and was placed on probation for three years.

Move Toward Unity

In a brief announcement speech in the East Room of the White House, Mr. Nixon made it clear that he had chosen a respected memb of Congress for the post because he considered it essential for national unity to select a person who would not be the subject of a protracted and bitter fight in Congress.

It was learned that Mr. Nixon had given strong consideration to former Treasury Secretary John B. Connally but that leaders in the Democratic-controlled Congress had served notice they would oppose him. They opposed Mr. Connally because he recently switched to the Republican party and because it would have appeared that Mr. Nixon was setting him up for the Presidency in the 1976 elections.

Mr. Ford, the President said, "has earned the respect of both Democrats and Republicans."

'Unwavering' on Vietnam

"He is a man also who has been unwavering in his support of the policies that brought peace with honor for America in Vietnam and in support of the policies for a strong national defense," Mr. Nixon said.

Several score Congressional leaders, Cabinet members and other high Government officials burst into cheers and surrounded the baldish, tanned Republican and offered congratulations even before Mr. Nixon uttered his name. They knew he was the nominee when Mr. Nixon said his choice "is a man who has served for 25 years in the House of Representatives with great distinction."

Mr. Ford, the President said, met the three criteria he had set for the nominee—that "the

Continued on Page 19, Column 1

CHOICE IS PRAISED BY BOTH PARTIES

Widespread Enthusiasm Is Expressed in Congress— Fast Confirmation Seen

By RICHARD L. MADDEN
Special to The New York Times

WASHINGTON, Oct. 12—Congressional Democrats and Republicans received President Nixon's choice of Gerald R. Ford to be Vice President with widespread enthusiasm tonight.

The reaction indicated that the nomination of Mr. Ford of Michigan, who has been the House Republican leader since 1965, would be confirmed relatively quickly by both houses, barring some unforeseen development.

However, it was expected that the Senate would take more time than the House in considering the nomination.

"My own feeling is Gerry will probably be confirmed," said Speaker Carl Albert of Oklahoma, he added:

"I think I was the first in Congress to tell the President that Gerry would be the easiest candidate to sell to the House. He's a very fine man to work with. I think he's earned this."

Senator Robert C. Byrd of West Virginia, the Democratic majority whip and member of the Senate Rules Committee, which will probably handle Mr. Ford's nomination, said he did not think it would be proper

Continued on Page 19, Column 5

Agnew Prosecution Took Pains To Prepare a 'Locked-Up Case'

By AGIS SALPUKAS
Special to The New York Times

BALTIMORE, Oct. 12 — It started modestly.

When George Beall, the United States Attorney for Maryland, asked that a grand jury be impaneled last Dec. 4, he recalled in an interview today, the thought was: "If we ended up bringing criminal charges against a couple of building inspectors in Baltimore it would have been justified."

And the inquiry remained focused on lesser political figures, with no hint that it would lead higher, until the beginning of June when several key witnesses were given favored treatment from the prosecutors by telling them what they knew about making payments to the then Vice President Agnew.

By the beginning of July, Mr. Beall was convinced that the case against the Vice President was serious and on July 3 he called Attorney General Elliot L. Richardson to inform him of the explosive turn of events.

Mr. Beall comes from a long line of prominent Republicans in Maryland. He is the son of J. Glenn Beall, the former Republican United States Senator, and the brother of J. Glenn Beall Jr., who won election to the Senate in 1970. Today he recalled his feelings at that point last summer when he realized the implication of the inquiry.

"I was turning somersaults," he said as he sat at his neat

Continued on Page 18, Column 2

The New York Times

VOL. CXXIII..No. 42,274   © 1973 The New York Times Company   NEW YORK, SUNDAY, OCTOBER 21, 1973   The beyond 50-mile zone from New York City, except Long Island. Higher in air delivery cities.   50 CENTS

NIXON DISCHARGES COX FOR DEFIANCE; ABOLISHES WATERGATE TASK FORCE; RICHARDSON AND RUCKELSHAUS OUT

Kissinger Meets Brezhnev on Mideast Cease-Fire Plan

Secretary of State Kissinger with Leonid I. Brezhnev yesterday in Moscow

OUTCRY IN HOUSE

Impeaching Nixon Is Openly Discussed by Leadership

By RICHARD L. MADDEN
Special to The New York Times

WASHINGTON, Oct. 20—For the first time tonight, members of the Democratic and Republican leadership of the House of Representatives began talking publicly and seriously about impeaching President Nixon.

Within minutes after the White House announced a drastic shake-up of the Justice Department, House leaders acknowledged that resolutions calling for impeachment would be pouring into the House when Congress reconvened after the Veterans Day holiday.

Representative John J. McFall of California, the Democratic whip, said that the House "must now go ahead and seriously consider beginning impeachment."

Representative John B. Anderson of Illinois, the Chairman of the House Republican Conference, said that it was "very difficult" to forecast the outcome, but predicted that "obviously, impeachment resolutions are going to be raining down like hailstones."

Originates in House

Under the Constitution, impeachment proceedings must begin in the House. If the House, by a majority vote, decides that a President should be impeached—or brought to trial—then the case goes to the Senate. The House vote functions as something like a grand jury indictment.

The Senate converts itself into a court to hear the case against the President, and the Chief Justice of the United States presides over the Senate's deliberations.

The Senate has sat as a court of impeachment only 12 times in the nation's history, mostly in cases involving Federal judges. Only one case involved a President, in 1868 when Andrew Johnson was acquitted. A motion to convict him, requiring a two-thirds majority

Continued on Page 62, Column 4

The New York Times
Ex-Deputy Attorney General
William D. Ruckelshaus.

United Press International
Attorney General Elliot L. Richardson introducing Archibald Cox, left, as special Watergate prosecutor last May.

BORK TAKES OVER

Duties of Prosecutor Are Shifted Back to Justice Dept.

By DOUGLAS E. KNEELAND
Special to The New York Times

WASHINGTON, Oct. 20 — President Nixon, reacting angrily tonight to refusals to obey his orders, dismissed the special Watergate prosecutor, Archibald Cox, abolished Mr. Cox's office, accepted the resignation of Elliot L. Richardson, the Attorney General, and discharged William D. Ruckelshaus, the Deputy Attorney General.

The President's dramatic action edged the nation closer to the constitutional confrontation he said he was trying to avoid.

Senior members of both parties in the House of Representatives were reported to be

White House's statement and
letters, excerpts from Cox
conference, Pages 60-61.

seriously discussing impeachment of the President because of his refusal to obey an order by the United States Court of Appeals that he turn over to the courts tape recordings of conversations about the Watergate case, and because of Mr. Nixon's dismissal of Mr. Cox.

The President announced that he had abolished the Watergate prosecutor's office as of 8 o'clock tonight and that the duties of that office had been transferred back to the Department of Justice, where his spokesman said they would be "carried out with thoroughness and vigor."

Events Listed

These were the events that led to the confrontation between the President and Congress and the Government's top law enforcement officers:

¶Mr. Cox said in a televised news conference that he would return to Federal court in defiance of the President's orders to seek a decision that Mr. Nixon had violated a ruling that the tapes must be turned over to the courts.

¶Attorney General Richardson, after being told by the President that Mr. Cox must be dismissed, resigned.

¶Deputy Attorney General Ruckelshaus was ordered by Mr. Nixon to discharge Mr. Cox. Mr. Ruckelshaus refused and was dismissed immediately.

¶The President informed

Continued on Page 60, Column 4

TALKS BEING SPED

U.S. Responds Quickly to Personal Appeal by Soviet Leader

By HEDRICK SMITH
Special to The New York Times

MOSCOW, Oct. 20—Secretary of State Kissinger arrived in Moscow today and quickly entered into talks with Leonid I. Brezhnev on the two-week-old Middle East war.

Less than two hours after his blue-and-white Air Force jet touched down at Vnukovo Airport, Mr. Kissinger and top aides met with Mr. Brezhnev, the Soviet Communist party leader, at the Kremlin. An American spokesman disclosed that it was Mr. Brezhnev's wish that the talks start at once.

[In Washington, President Nixon was reported to have sent another message to Mr. Brezhnev. The White House refused to provide details. Page 26. American maritime union leaders, meeting in Miami, said they would boycott handling of all cargo and ships involved in trade with the Soviet Union. Page 31.]

Personal Appeal by Brezhnev

The initial round of talks lasted for two hours. Negotiations are expected to resume tomorrow morning.

Mr. Kissinger reached Moscow only slightly more than 24 hours after Premier Aleksei N. Kosygin returned here from Cairo. Mr. Brezhnev's personal appeal for Mr. Kissinger to come here was seen as a deliberate effort by the Soviet leader to demonstrate his interest in not letting the events in the Middle East disrupt Soviet-American accommodation.

Strangely, Mr. Kosygin was not listed as a participant in the talks, which began at 9:15 P.M. (2:15 P.M., New York time) at the Kremlin. Mr. Brezhnev was joined by Foreign Minister Andrei A. Gromyko, who had personally greeted Secretary Kissinger at the airport.

With Mr. Kissinger in the talks were Joseph J. Sisco, Assistant Secretary of State for Near Eastern and South Asian Affairs, his chief deputy, Alfred L. Atherton, Helmut Sonnenfeldt, the senior staff member of the National Security Council, and Winston Lord, another

Continued on Page 26, Column 7

2 Thrown to Deaths

Two young women, sisters from the Caribbean island of Grenada, were thrown to their deaths from a Manhattan hotel window yesterday. Their suspected killer, a musician from Trinidad, apparently walked in front of a subway train later and was killed. Details on Page 73.

Israel Reports Enlarging Of Foothold on West Bank

By TERENCE SMITH
Special to The New York Times

TEL AVIV, Oct. 20 — Israeli forces on the west bank of the Suez Canal pushed out in three directions today, "enlarging and deepening" their foothold on Egyptian territory, a military spokesman said here.

The spokesman, Maj. Gen. Uzi Narkiss, said the reinforced Israeli units now occupied a square-shaped area south of Ismailia and had largely cleared it of surface-to-air missile batteries.

He said forward Israeli units had penetrated some 20 miles into Egypt and had cut the road leading south from Ismailia to Suez. The Israelis would then be within artillery distance of the main Ismailia-Cairo road, along which fresh Egyptian tank units have been pushed into the fighting during the last 48 hours.

[The Egyptian command said that 85 Israeli tanks and 56 halftracks were destroyed in fighting on the western bank of the Suez Canal and on the central front in the Sinai. In Damascus, Syria announced that her planes had bombed an Israeli oil refinery at Haifa. This was denied by the Israelis. Page 26.]

General Narkiss described the Israeli force west of the canal as "much stronger, more important and secure" than it was yesterday. Reliable Western sources said it now included more than 200 tanks and 10,000 men and was being reinforced continually.

Today the Israeli force reportedly pushed out to the west, north and south, knocking out SAM batteries, artillery positions and fighting running battles with Egyptian tank units. General Narkiss said about 60 to 70 Egyptian tanks had been destroyed during the day.

Retreat a Possibility

In addition, Israeli warplanes are now operating freely over the entire central sector of the canal, Israeli military sources said. In dogfights over the area today, 10 Egyptian planes were reported shot down. No Israeli losses were announced.

The Israeli objective seems to be to push north and south from the central sector, destroying missile and artillery batteries along the way, and to sever the Egyptian supply lines to the forces on the eastern bank.

If the Egyptians were cut off

Continued on Page 26, Column 3

Saudi Oil Is Cut Off

Saudi Arabia has decided to stop all oil exports to the United States "in view of the increase in American support for Israel," the Government radio reported. Algeria announced similar action. Details on Page 28.

Ervin at First Renounces, Then Accepts Tapes Plan

Special to The New York Times

WASHINGTON, Oct. 20—Senator Sam J. Ervin Jr. renounced today and then reaccepted President Nixon's proposal to release an authenticated summary of the Watergate tapes.

Out of the day-long confusion and dispute over the offer extended last night by President Nixon came, however, a White House guarantee to Senator Ervin that the summary would contain "verbatim language" from conversations recorded on the tapes.

Senator Ervin, chairman of the Senate Watergate committee, renounced the agreement this morning after reaching the conclusion that he had misunderstood what Mr. Nixon had offered to turn over to the committee.

The North Carolina Democrat said that he had left the White House last night believing that the committee would get partial, verbatim transcripts of the Watergate conversations. But this morning, he said, it appeared that the Senators would be given only a summary of what the tapes contained.

"I would not accept any summary," he said. "I would not accept anybody's interpretation of what the tapes contain."

The comments appeared to observers here to threaten to scuttle the President's compromise proposal, coming on top of the rejection of the offer by Archibald Cox, the special Watergate prosecutor.

Late today, however, at a news conference in Asheville, N.C., Senator Ervin said that he had "just been in communication with the White House," and that he had been advised that "my interpretation of the agreement is identical with that of the White House."

A White House official subsequently explained that Mr. Ervin had been assured that the report on the tapes that would be issued to the committee and to the Federal courts by the President would include portions of the verbatim conversations held in Mr. Nixon's office with key Watergate figures.

The official, who asked that

Continued on Page 51, Column 1

RICHARDSON QUITS OVER ORDER ON COX

Attorney General Says He Couldn't Oust Prosecutor —Cites Autonomy Vow

By JOHN M. CREWDSON
Special to The New York Times

WASHINGTON, Oct. 20—Elliot L. Richardson resigned as Attorney General tonight, saying that he could not carry out President Nixon's order to discharge Archibald Cox, the special Watergate prosecutor, in the light of his earlier pledge to provide Mr. Cox with "full authority" to contest Presidential claims of executive privilege.

During his confirmation hearings before the Senate Judiciary Committee in May, Mr. Richardson promised that Mr. Cox would have unimpeded authority to subpoena potential evidence from any source, including the President himself.

The resignation of Mr. Richardson, who has held four major posts in the Nixon Administration since the President first took office in January, 1969, ended a week of negotiations involving the Attorney General, Mr. Cox and the White House.

Tonight, Mr. Richardson, sounding as exhausted over the telephone as he said he was, had nothing to add to his letter to the President.

In the letter, Mr. Richardson made clear his feelings that Mr. Nixon's directive to Mr. Cox

Continued on Page 59, Column 1

Oakland Defeats Mets, 3-1, to Even World Series; Final Game Is Today

United Press International
A's Reggie Jackson hitting his second double of the game against the Mets off Tom Seaver in the third inning. Jackson knocked in Sal Bando, for his second run batted in. Jerry Grote is catching. Details in Section 5.

The Quality of Life Here Is Rated High in Survey

By PETER KIHSS

Tops in mental health and racial equality, and even in low-cost transportation—that was the New York metropolitan area at the end of the nineteen-sixties, according to efforts to measure some important aspects of the "quality of life" in 18 major urban areas.

But the New York metropolitan area was "least desirable" in indicators of "public order" and "community concern" and next to costliest in its housing.

These are among findings being published by the State Labor Department. They come from an ongoing project by the Urban Institute of Washington seeking "social indicators" to compare different areas.

The metropolitan area was defined in the project as New York City, Nassau, Suffolk, Westchester and Rockland Counties. The others were similar "standard metropolitan statistical areas" selected because of availability of comparative yearly data.

As analyzed by the state agency, the latter years of the sixties saw "apparent improvement" in eight indicators for the New York area—reduction of poverty, increase in individual income, health in terms of infant mortality, mental health as indicated by suicide rates, racial equality, based on unemployment rates, community concern as measured by charitable contributions, me-

Continued on Page 71, Column 1

The New York Times

LATE CITY EDITION

Weather: Chance of rain today; mild tonight. Fair, mild tomorrow. Temp. range: today 53-68; Thursday 51-68. Additional details on Page 86.

VOL.CXXIII..No.42,279   © 1973 The New York Times Company   NEW YORK, FRIDAY, OCTOBER 26, 1973   15 CENTS

U.S. FORCES PUT ON WORLDWIDE ALERT LEST SOVIET SEND TROOPS TO MIDEAST; CRISIS EASED AS U.N. SETS UP A PATROL

ACTION BY COUNCIL

Unit Will Be Made Up of Soldiers From Smaller Nations

By KATHLEEN TELTSCH
Special to The New York Times

UNITED NATIONS, N. Y., Oct. 25—The Security Council voted today to establish a United Nations emergency force to insure a cease-fire in the Middle East, using troops from smaller countries.

The vote was 14 to 0, with China not participating in the adoption of the resolution,

Excerpts from Malik remarks are printed on Page 19.

which asked Secretary General Waldheim to report back within 24 hours on proposals for carrying out the Council's decision.

The vote came in a meeting that was delayed as delegates watched Secretary of State Kissinger's news conference on television amid concern over a possible big-power confrontation in the Middle East.

Threat May Be Averted

The importance of the Security Council's action, as seen by some Western diplomats, was that it could head off the possibility that the Soviet Union might unilaterally send troops to the Middle East.

One Western official said that while the creation of a United Nations peace-keeping force might "be a can of worms," it might also prevent a major-power confrontation.

A quick dispatch of United Nations forces, said a European, "could get all of us off a very painful hook."

Yesterday Egypt had asked that Soviet and American forces be sent to the Middle East to compel Israel to pull back to the positions she occupied Monday when the first cease-fire was ordered. The United States rejected Cairo's appeal that American troops be sent.

Resolution Revised

During the delay this morning, at the insistence of the United States, the eight non-aligned countries sponsoring the resolution agreed to revise it to exclude the five permanent Council members—the Soviet Union, the United States, China, France and Britain—from participation in the emergency force. The original resolution, introduced in a meeting that ended at 12:35 o'clock this morning, did not exclude the major powers.

The willingness of the Soviet

Continued on Page 19, Column 7

FORD BACKS STUDY ON IMPEACHMENT

Says He'll Support Congress if It Insists on Another Watergate Prosecutor

By JAMES M. NAUGHTON
Special to The New York Times

WASHINGTON, Oct. 25—Gerald R. Ford, President Nixon's nominee for Vice President, said today that the House of Representatives should "carry on" with an inquiry into the question of impeaching the President.

Moreover, Mr. Ford said in response to questions that he would support demands for creation of a new Watergate special prosecutor's office if a majority of the Congress insisted on it.

Mr. Ford, who is the minority leader of the House, outlined his views minutes after the House Republican Conference implored three White House officials to persuade Mr. Nixon to name a new special prosecutor and to make public the contents of the secret Watergate tape recordings.

Bryce N. Harlow, a counselor to the President, told newsmen that the Republican requests would be conveyed to Mr. Nixon and that the President would decide "very shortly" whether to name a successor to Archibald Cox, the special prosecutor who was discharged Saturday.

But Democrats in the Senate and the House pressed ahead with plans to enact legislation that would grant Chief Judge John J. Sirica of the United

Continued on Page 24, Column 5

Text of U.N. Resolution

Special to The New York Times

UNITED NATIONS, N.Y., Oct. 25—Following is the resolution adopted by the Security Council today:

The Security Council,

Recalling its Resolutions 338 (1973) of 22 October, 1973, and 339 (1973) of 23 October, 1973,

Noting with regret the reported repeated violations of the cease-fire in noncompliance with Resolutions 338 (1973) and 339 (1973),

Noting with concern from the Secretary General's report that the United Nations military observers have not yet been enabled to place themselves on both sides of the cease-fire line,

1. Demands that immediate and complete cease-fire be observed and that the parties return to the positions occupied by them at 16:50 hours G.M.T. on 22 October, 1973;

2. Requests the Secretary General, as an immediate step, to increase the number of United Nations military observers on both sides;

3. Decides to set up immediately under its authority a United Nations emergency force to be composed of personnel drawn from states members of the United Nations except permanent members of the Security Council, and requests the Secretary General to report within 24 hours on the steps taken to this effect;

4. Requests the Secretary General to report to the Council on an urgent and continuing basis on the state of implementation of this resolution as well as Resolutions 338 (1973) and 339 (1973);

5. Requests all member states to extend their full cooperation to the United Nations in the implementation of this resolution as well as Resolutions 338 (1973) and 339 (1973).

Smoke Fells 150 on IRT In Crash in South Bronx

By ROBERT D. McFADDEN

More than 150 subway riders suffered smoke inhalation and other minor injuries and hundreds more were trapped in a dark smoky tunnel in the South Bronx for an hour or more last night after an IRT express train struck the rear of another that had been stalled by a fire.

Passengers recounted scenes of confusion, crying, and even instances of hysteria as a northbound train with flames and smoke pouring from a middle car stalled just north of the Longwood Avenue station on the Pelham Bay Park line and was hit by a following train.

The impact of the collision was described by Transit Authority spokesmen as light, but riders on both trains said many had been hurled to the floor. The collision occurred on the express track—the center of three tracks—at the north end of the station, at about 7:20 P.M.

More than a dozen ambulances from hospitals in the Bronx converged on Longwood Avenue and Southern Boulevard in Hunts Point, along with Manhattan and Queens hospital disaster units, a dozen pieces of Fire Department apparatus

Continued on Page 14, Column 3

Beame Recruiting Unit

Controller Abraham D. Beame is so confident of victory in the mayoral election that he is forming a "recruiting" committee to seek out prospective top-level appointees for a Beame administration. Details, Page 31.

U.S. Says Mafia Informer Gave Evidence Against Rep. Brasco

By NICHOLAS GAGE
Special to The New York Times

WASHINGTON, Oct. 25—The indictment of Representative Frank J. Brasco on Tuesday came as a result of information given to the Justice Department by John A. Masiello, a Mafia captain who was involved in the case, according to Federal sources.

Masiello is the highest ranking member of the crime syndicate known to have been "turned"—converted into a Government informer or witness.

The sources told The New York Times that Mafia leaders had already learned about

Masiello's cooperation with the Government and reportedly had issued a "contract" on his life. He is currently under heavy Government protection in New York.

Representative Brasco was indicted on charges of conspiring to receive $27,500 in illegal payoffs in 1968 for helping Masiello's trucking concern get contracts to haul mail for the Post Office. Masiello was named as co-conspirator with the 41-year-old Democrat and his uncle, Joseph Brasco, but not as a defendant.

Masiello was listed by the Justice Department as a captain

Continued on Page 29, Column 2

Members of a Texas Air National Guard group are briefed at Ellington Air Force Base
Associated Press

President Nixon sees Secretary of State Kissinger off for his Washington news session
Associated Press

EGYPT SAYS ISRAEL CONTINUES FIRING

Sadat's Aide Reports Road From Cairo to Suez City Was Cut During Day

By HENRY TANNER
Special to The New York Times

CAIRO, Oct. 25—Egypt accused Israel today of continuing to violate the cease-fire agreement and said Israeli troops had fired on Egyptian forces wherever they were found.

A foreign-policy adviser to President Anwar el-Sadat said at a news conference that the Israelis cut the vital road from Cairo to the city of Suez at the southern end of the canal during the day.

The adviser, Ashraf Ghorbal, expressed deep bitterness over the shipment of United States matériel to the Israeli forces, "some of it straight to the battlefield." This, he said, enables the Israelis to continue to violate the truce.

Meanwhile, United Nations truce teams took up positions on the Cairo-Suez road 63 miles from Cairo and 12 miles west of Ismailia on the Cairo-Ismailia road. Egyptian officials charged that the Israelis had prevented United Nations observers from taking up a position at the canal site at which Israeli

Continued on Page 21, Column 5

Moscow Exhibits Tension, But No Intent to Intervene

By HEDRICK SMITH
Special to The New York Times

MOSCOW, Oct. 25—The Soviet Union showed new signs of tension with the United States today, but gave no public indication that it was preparing to intervene in the Middle East.

The Soviet leader, Leonid I. Brezhnev, abruptly postponed a scheduled address to 3,000 delegates at the opening session of the World Peace Congress here, in which many had expected him to emphasize the benefits of reconciliation and of Soviet-American cooperation in defusing the Middle East conflict.

He was seen leaving his balcony box for urgent consultations during other speeches and then circulating papers to President Nikolai V. Podgorny. Afterward, Foreign Minister

Andrei A. Gromyko left the box.

Moscow signaled acute concern over the fate of Egyptian forces on the east side of the Suez Canal with a string of dispatches by Tass, the official press agency, charging Israel with repeated violations of the Middle East cease-fire and with attempts to capture the city of Suez.

This was in keeping with Soviet efforts to shield Egyptian forces from further defeats along the Suez Canal. The sharpened Soviet line against Washington suggested disillusion with the American moves. It could also have been read as an effort by Moscow to convey

Continued on Page 21, Column 3

Trapped Egyptian Force Held Key Factor in Crisis

By CHARLES MOHR
Special to The New York Times

TEL AVIV, Oct. 25 — The Egyptian III Corps, estimated to number 15,000 to 30,000 men, remained trapped by the Israelis today, unable to acquire fresh supplies of water and food.

It was generally felt here that the plight of the Egyptian force

was at the root of the increasingly tense international situation, in which the United States, citing concern that the Soviet Union was planning to introduce troops into the Middle East.

Israeli spokesmen said that there was no fighting or violation of the cease-fire by either side during the day on either the Egyptian or the Syrian fronts and that the United Nations Truce Supervision Organization's observer teams were moving into position.

Egypt's III Corps is cut off in a narrow pocket on the eastern bank of the Suez Canal south of the Great Bitter Lake and in a small enclave embracing the city of Suez at the southern end of the canal.

If the isolation of the Egyptian force is very much prolonged, the III Corps might be forced to surrender or ask for free passage through Israeli lines.

The surrender of a cease-fire of such a substantial part of the Egyptian armed forces might constitute a stinging political humiliation for the Egyptian Government.

Such a move would reduce Egypt's holdings on the eastern bank of the canal, all of which she had seized soon after the war began on Oct. 6, to a narrow strip running from Qantara to a point opposite

Continued on Page 21, Column 2

KISSINGER SPEAKS

He Cites Ambiguous Signs by Moscow as the Cause

By BERNARD GWERTZMAN
Special to The New York Times

WASHINGTON, Friday, Oct 26—The United States ordered its military forces on a worldwide "precautionary alert" early yesterday morning, citing concern that the Soviet Union was planning to introduce military forces into the Middle East. But the crisis seemed to abate when the Soviet Union joined later in a United Nations Security Council resolution barring big powers from participating in a Middle East peacekeeping force.

Secretary of State Kissinger said at a news conference in

Transcript of the Kissinger news conference, Page 19.

Washington that the United States was not seeking a confrontation with the Soviet Union.

And a State Department spokesman, noting that Mr. Kissinger had said that such a Security Council vote would ease tensions, termed the United Nations action "a step in the right direction." As of early today the precautionary alert was still in effect.

Other officials said that because of the Council vote some military units might be taken off alert later this morning.

Alert in Soviet Union

The alert was instituted after the Soviet Union gave what Mr. Kissinger called "ambiguous" signs that it might intervene to help out Egyptian forces caught behind Israeli lines and faced with destruction or surrender despite the cease-fire.

Military officials cited an alert of airborne troops within the Soviet Union as one cause of the American alert. [Detail on Page 20.]

Intervention by the big powers, Mr. Kissinger warned, could cause major tensions in the world.

The sudden developments unforeseen yesterday when the White House was reporting that the Middle East cease-fire was taking effect, shocked the nation's capital and led President Nixon to postpone his scheduled news conference last evening in which he was expected to defend his actions in the Watergate tapes controversy.

Denial by Kissinger

The crisis, caused by uncertainty in Washington about the ability of the superpowers to avoid a direct confrontation over the Middle East, also produced some speculation that Mr. Nixon might have ordered the alert to distract domestic criticism.

Mr. Kissinger denied such allegations strongly, saying: "It is a symptom of what is happening to our country that it could even be suggested that the United States would alert its forces for domestic reasons."

He added, in his televised news conference, that "the President had no other choice as a responsible national leader" than to follow the advice

Continued on Page 19, Column 1

The Newspaper that likes New York.

U.N. observers, in vehicles towing supply trailers, moving to posts in Egypt yesterday
United Press International

"All the News That's Fit to Print"

The New York Times

LATE CITY EDITION

Weather: Mostly sunny today; cold tonight. Sunny and cold tomorrow. Temp. range: today 36-46; Thursday 45-62. Additional details on Page 81.

VOL. CXXIII...No. 42,321   © 1973 The New York Times Company   NEW YORK, FRIDAY, DECEMBER 7, 1973   15 CENTS

Governor to Quit and Seek Presidency, His Aides Say

Expected to Announce the Move Before Christmas — Wilson Would Succeed Him and Address New Legislature

By FRANK LYNN

Governor Rockefeller will resign the governorship and turn it over to Lieut. Gov. Malcolm Wilson so Mr. Rockefeller can devote full time to his Presidential quest, his closest associates said yesterday.

The resignation will be announced before Christmas, to give Mr. Wilson time to prepare a State of the State message when the Legislature convenes Jan. 9, the informants said in interviews with The New York Times.

The decision of the 65-year-old Mr. Rockefeller to resign after 15 years ended months of soul-searching in which he weighed, first, whether to seek a fifth term next year, and, then, whether to resign before his fourth term ends, to give Mr. Wilson maximum exposure and the advantages of an incumbent in next year's gubernatorial election.

The decision appeared to be final, although one Rockefeller associate cautioned that he could change his mind. But even this informant agreed that the Governor's actions pointed to resignation. He said Mr. Rockefeller's demeanor at the Tuesday meeting of his newly formed National Commission on Critical Choices convinced him that "the Governor has something entirely viable with the commission and something he's going to throw himself into heavily."

The Governor, who was in Washington yesterday for a meeting of the National Commission on Water Quality, which he heads, was unavailable for comment, but his press secretary, Ronald Maiorana, said that "there is no point in my speculating on any of the options that Governor has before him."

The Governor himself had signaled a decision to resign at a news conference Tuesday when, speaking of the commis-

Continued on Page 49, Column 5

Wholesale Index Up 1.8% On Soaring Prices of Fuel

By EDWIN L. DALE Jr.
Special to The New York Times

WASHINGTON, Dec. 6—Soaring prices for oil products and other fuels were the main element in another big increase in the Government's wholesale price index in November, the Labor Department reported today.

The index rose 1.8 per cent after adjustment for normal seasonal changes in some prices. The increase occurred despite a third consecutive monthly decline for farm and food prices — a decline that may now be over.

The wholesale price index was 17.5 per cent above a year earlier, an unheard of rate of inflation for peacetime in the modern era. This huge rise reflected chiefly an explosion in prices of raw commodities of all kinds, agricultural and non-agricultural, plus the more recent burst in the energy area.

Labor Doubts Data

Today's index showed an almost unbelievable increase of 34.7 per cent in prices of refined petroleum products in a single month — but the Labor Department indicated that it doubted its own statistics in this case.

The department said it based its index on prices in "spot markets" which now "appear to represent a declining portion of the transactions taking place in domestic markets." Petroleum products sold on a long-term or medium-term contract basis undoubtedly rose

Continued on Page 61, Column 6

ARABS CUT FUNDS AT BANKS OF U.S.

Transfers May Be Spurred by Accord in Cairo to Use Money for Development

By CLYDE H. FARNSWORTH
Special to The New York Times

PARIS, Dec. 6—Arab states are stepping up their economic offensive against the United States by withdrawing funds from American banks.

"The French and Swiss banks ought to be very happy because they are getting the deposits," one American commented.

The transfers may be accelerated as a result of actions by Arab League economic ministers meeting for the last three days in Cairo. They agreed "in principle" that funds should be withdrawn from Western banks to finance development projects in Arab countries.

Mahmoud Riad, secretary general of the Arab League, said that a "gradual withdrawal of deposits" had been agreed on.

"Special planning committees will meet to discuss what percentages would be withdrawn, and how the money would be invested," a spokesman for the league was quoted as having said.

Arab sources in Cairo said that Egypt and Syria would get priority in the development program.

The Arabs, in both official

Continued on Page 63, Column 3

M.T.A. TO PROVIDE TWO SUNDAY RIDES FOR PRICE OF ONE

5-Week Plan on All Subway, Bus and Train Routes Is Aimed at Luring Riders

By DEIRDRE CARMODY

In a dramatic experiment to lure people to public transportation on "gasless Sundays," the Metropolitan Transportation Authority will provide round-trip transportation for the price of a normal one-way fare on all public transportation in New York City and on all M.T.A. commuter lines for five consecutive Sundays beginning Dec. 16.

"We are really pioneering," said Dr. William J. Ronan, chairman of the authority, when he announced the plans at a news conference yesterday. "As far as I know, it's the first move of its kind that has been made in the country in response to the energy crisis."

Under the plan, which will be in effect from 6 A.M. Sundays to 1 A.M. Mondays, subway riders will be given a token and a return coupon for their 35 cents. The coupon will be good only on that day. Bus riders will be given similar return passes that the coupons may not be used interchangeably on subways and buses.

Connecticut Accord

Riders on the M.T.A. commuter lines—Long Island Rail Road and the Harlem, Hudson and New Haven lines of the Penn Central—will be issued round-trip tickets for the price of single fares. These return tickets also will be good only on the date of purchase.

Under an agreement with Gov. Thomas J. Meskill of Connecticut, the special fares will also apply to the Connecticut portion of the New Haven line. Governor Meskill said the plan included the New Canaan, Waterbury and Danbury branches.

The plan will also include Nassau County buses that are operated by the Metropolitan Suburban Bus Authority, a subsidiary of the M.T.A.

Also included in the program is the Staten Island Rapid Transit Operating Authority, a subsidiary of the M.T.A. However, the Staten Island ferry, which is operated by the city's Department of Marine and Aviation and which charges 10 cents

Continued on Page 46, Column 4

Air Travelers Delayed

Thousands of air travelers were delayed here yesterday as employes of Trans World Airlines, on strike for a month, picketed at the terminals of American Airlines and Pan American World Airways. Operations resumed last night when pickets were removed in compliance with a court order. Page 81.

Con Ed Announces 'Dramatic' Cut Here In the Use of Power

By RICHARD SEVERO

Consolidated Edison yesterday reported a "dramatic decrease" in the electricity, natural gas and steam used by its customers during November, and a company executive hailed it as "strong indication that customers in New York and Westchester County are cooperating in conserving energy."

Con Edison said its November electric output was 0.6 per cent below November, 1972, when a 4 per cent increase would normally have been expected. Natural gas was down 2.1 per cent, compared with a company projection of an 8 per cent increase for "normal" times, and steam output was down 8.4 per cent, compared with an original expectation of a 2.7 per cent increase.

Louis H. Roddis, company vice chairman, added that it was the first time in more than 30 years that electric sales had declined.

Shortly before Con Edison announced the November figures, a fire broke out in its Ravenswood, Queens, plant, knocking out "Big Allis," the giant generator that can produce 10 per cent of the company's total capacity of 10 million kilowatts.

A spokesman said that there was "no immediate problem"

Continued on Page 47, Column 2

WHITE HOUSE BARS ROLE ON TRUCKERS

Nixon Aide Says Halting of Interstate Road Blockades Is 'Matter for the States'

By PHILIP SHABECOFF
Special to The New York Times

WASHINGTON, Dec. 6—The White House avoided today responsibility for halting the truck driver blockades of interstate highways and instead called on the state Governors to take action.

Asked at a White House briefing why President Nixon was not using the power of the Federal Government against truck drivers illegally snarling traffic on interstate highways in protest over higher fuel prices and lower speed limits, the deputy press secretary, Gerald L. Warren, replied that it was "a matter for the states."

Meanwhile widespread concern by truck drivers took a new form as the blockades that paralyzed traffic at several points for three days were called off and a bid to shut down the entire trucking industry was started.

Mr. Warren was also asked why the Federal Government was able to act against civil rights and peace demonstrators who blocked traffic but not against the wildcatting truckers. He was specifically asked about the mass arrest, without warrants, of more than 10,000 peace demonstrators in May, 1971, by Washington D.C. police acting under the supervision of the then Attorney General, John N. Mitchell.

Mr. Warren, in reply, reiterated that the blockade of the interstate highways was for the

Continued on Page 46, Column 3

FORD SWORN AS VICE PRESIDENT AFTER HOUSE APPROVES, 387-35; HE VOWS EQUAL JUSTICE FOR ALL

Gerald R. Ford being sworn in as Vice President of the United States as his wife, Elizabeth, held Bible and Chief Justice Warren E. Burger administered oath. Observing were President Nixon, at right, and at rear, Carl Albert, left, Speaker of the House, and James O. Eastland, right, who is the President pro tem of the Senate.

The New York Times/George Tames

A Watershed for Nixon

Some Republicans in Congress Hope Ford Will Soon Be the 38th President

By JAMES M. NAUGHTON
Special to The New York Times

WASHINGTON, Dec. 6—Now that Gerald R. Ford has become the nation's 40th Vice President, a number of Republicans in Congress hope that he will soon become the 38th President.

News Analysis	They expect and desire the resignation of President Nixon. His resignation would relieve them of the need to face up to an eventual vote on his impeachment.

But if Mr. Nixon does not step down voluntarily by next spring or somehow restore widespread public confidence in his Administration, some of Mr. Ford's old colleagues in the House of Representatives are likely to join in any impeachment move against the President.

The reason, outlined privately in the last few days by typical Republicans, is a basic one:

"Their own political future is at stake.

"You'd like him to resign, wouldn't you?" a senior Democrat said tauntingly to a Republican colleague in the Speaker's lobby just off the House floor. "The President's an albatross around your neck."

"At least that," the Republican replied.

Similar conversations have become increasingly commonplace as Congress, resolving the issue of Presidential succession, has begun to focus on the question of Presidential conduct. Republicans, though a minority in Congress, are central to any determination of Mr. Nixon's fate. A month ago, they were demanding a verdict on Mr. Ford's nomination. Now, they

Continued on Page 27, Column 5

Nixon-Dean Tape Will Go To Mitchell Trial Judge

By ARNOLD H. LUBASCH

Federal prosecutors disclosed last night that the White House had agreed to provide the tape recording of a conversation between President Nixon and John W. Dean 3d for the trial of two former Cabinet officers.

The tape recording of the conversation last Feb. 28 between the President and former White House counsel was demanded yesterday by Judge Lee P. Gagliardi, who is presiding over the trial of former Attorney General John N. Mitchell and former Secretary of Commerce Maurice H. Stans that is scheduled to begin Jan. 9 in Federal District Court here.

Mr. Mitchell and Mr. Stans were indicted last May 10 for allegedly obstructing an investigation of the financial operations of Robert L. Vesco in return for the fugitive financier's secret $200,000 cash contribution to President Nixon's 1972 election campaign.

Meanwhile, Mr. Vesco was granted permission yesterday to live in Argentina and will not be liable to extradition, Reuters reported. (Page 20.)

Two prosecutors in the Mitchell-Stans trial, James W. Rayhill and Kenneth R. Feinberg, told Judge Gagliardi yesterday after his request that J. Fred Buzhardt Jr., a special White House counsel, had informed them that the tape would be provided no later than next Friday for the judge to examine in private.

Judge Gagliardi had indicated earlier that he would not permit Mr. Dean to testify as a

Continued on Page 27, Column 2

Level of South Vietnam Fighting Is Fiercest Since Truce Accord

By JAMES M. MARKHAM
Special to The New York Times

SAIGON, South Vietnam, Dec. 6—In the last month, the fighting in South Vietnam has reached its fiercest levels since the January signing of the cease-fire, which has since been shattered.

The North Vietnamese and their Vietcong allies have taken the initiative in most of the actions—though the South Vietnamese Air Force has been bombing at a scorching pace. But it is not clear that the Communists have struck the opening blows of a much-predicted dry-season offensive.

In the eyes of some military analysts here, the intentions of the Communists for

1974 remain uncertain. "They are still looking for a strategy that works," one authority on the Indochinese Communist movement observed.

But there is almost universal agreement that the new year will see more and probably heavier fighting. A few months ago some people were talking about "a momentum to peace." Now they, too, are talking about momentum in the other direction.

South Vietnam's President, Nguyen Van Thieu, himself a former general, has been the most persistent and outspoken on an upcoming all-out Communist

Continued on Page 8, Column 3

LOYALTY TO NIXON

1,500 Hear Ford Give His Full Support to President

By MARJORIE HUNTER
Special to The New York Times

WASHINGTON, Dec. 6 — Gerald R. Ford, pledging "equal justice for all Americans," took office just after dusk tonight as the 40th Vice President of the United States. With President Nixon standing right behind him, he was sworn into office in the 116-

Transcript of the ceremony and speech are on Page 27; a page of pictures, 26.

year-old House chamber, which has been his political home for the last 25 years.

Only an hour earlier, the House completed action on his nomination by voting 387 to 35 for confirmation. He was confirmed Nov. 27 by the Senate by a vote of 92 to 3.

Mr. Ford, 60 years old, resigned his House seat before assuming the Vice-Presidency. He has been minority leader of the House since 1965.

Jerry Ford's Day

It was clearly Jerry Ford's day, and not even President Nixon's appearance overshadowed the new Vice President. The waves of applause and the smiles of his colleagues were seemingly beamed at him alone as he stood, in a trim navy blue suit, his right hand held high in recognition of old friends.

And, as he spoke, it was the Jerry Ford many of them had listened to through the years, speaking in a flat tone, declaring his love for his wife and his country and pledging his loyalty to his President.

The historic ceremony ended a Vice-Presidential vacancy that had existed since the resignation on Oct. 10 of Spiro T. Agnew just before he pleaded no contest to a charge of income tax evasion.

First Use of Amendment

This is the first time that a Vice President was chosen under the 25th Amendment to the Constitution. The amendment, ratified by the states in 1967, provides for Presidential succession and for filling Vice-Presidential vacancies.

The 25th Amendment was adopted to deal with situations such as that which existed following the assassination of President Kennedy in 1963. At that time, the Vice-Presidency stood vacant 13 months after Vice President Johnson succeeded to the Presidency.

Mr. Ford heard none of today's five hours of House debate, nor did he vote. He arrived in the chamber just minutes after the final vote had been cast and was greeted by thunderous cheers and applause—the first of many such

Continued on Page 27, Column 2

Stock Prices Score Sixth Biggest Rise

The stock market bounded ahead yesterday in a dynamic recovery that saw the sixth biggest point advance ever for the Dow-Jones industrial average. The blue-chip indicator soared 25.81 points to 814.12.

Wall Street labeled the action a technical rally in the absence of any significant news developments. A similar rally with a gain of 22 points occurred on Nov. 28.

The market's latest recovery followed a drop of 198 points in the Dow average within a six-week period. Trading was heavy on the New York Stock Exchange, where 23.26 million shares changed hands.

In the glamour group, Kodak rose 7 points and McDonald's advanced 7½.

Details on Page 61.

Vizzini Is Indicted In Firemen's Strike

By JOHN SIBLEY

Richard J. Vizzini, president of the Uniformed Firefighters Association, and two other top union officials were arrested yesterday on charges stemming from the first strike by the city's 10,900 firemen exactly one month earlier.

An eight-count indictment handed up by a Manhattan grand jury charges the three with reckless endangerment of life and property, attempted coercion of city officials during bargaining negotiations, obstructing governmental administration and conspiring to commit each of these crimes.

Mr. Vizzini's co-defendants are John O'Sullivan, the U.F.A.'s financial and recording secretary, and Dominick Gentiluomo, sergeant at arms.

All three pleaded not guilty

Continued on Page 14, Column 4

"Big Allis," the million-kilowatt turbine that was damaged by a fire in Con Edison's Ravenswood, Queens, plant, giving off steam, a normal procedure during shutdown. At right are firemen who put out fire. Assessment of damage will take at least two days.

The New York Times/Neal Boenzi

The New York Times

LATE CITY EDITION
North: Rainy, windy and cold today and tonight. Temp. range 38-47. South: Rain today. Temp. range 35-42. Additional details on Page 91.

SECTION ONE

VOL. CXXIII...No. 42,323   © 1973 The New York Times Company   NEW YORK, SUNDAY, DECEMBER 9, 1973   75c beyond 50-mile zone from New York City, except Long Island. Higher in air delivery cities.   50 CENTS

PAPAL EXAMPLE FOR SAVING FUEL: Pope Paul VI waving from horse-drawn carriage while passing through St. Peter's Square in Rome yesterday, a public holiday in Italy. All private traffic was banned and the Pope did not use his limousine. Details, Page 7.

Associated Press

NIXON REVEALS FINANCIAL FILE, ASKS CONGRESS PANEL TO DECIDE IF HE OWES $267,000 MORE IN TAX

President Agrees to Abide By Committee's Judgment

By EILEEN SHANAHAN
Special to The New York Times

WASHINGTON, Dec. 8—The White House conceded today that there were serious questions about the legality of two separate aspects of President Nixon's recent tax returns and said that he and Mrs. Nixon might owe as much as $267,000 in additional Federal income tax if both of his original contentions were reversed.

Mr. Nixon, in a move believed to be without precedent, announced that he would let the Congressional Joint Committee on Internal Revenue Taxation decide whether he should pay any additional tax because of the two disputed items.

"I will abide by the committee's judgment," he said in a written statement.

Wilbur D. Mills of Arkansas, chairman of the Joint Committee, said Mr. Mills had seen him, in a brief telephone conversation on Thursday, to take on the job, and that he agreed. He said that he did not yet know how the committee would proceed and could not guess whether it would hold public hearings.

The Joint Committee is made up of the five senior members —three Democrats and two Republicans—of the House Ways and Means Committee and the Senate Finance Committee. A majority of the members are conservative.

The committee has statutory authority to look at any tax return, but no explicit authorization to audit returns or order any changes in what a taxpayer claimed.

It is allowed to examine tax returns primarily as a means of studying how well the tax laws, or their administration, are working.

The documents concer ,g the President's finances that were made public by the White House today showed that one of his own accountants believed he should have paid a capital gains tax on the sale, in 1970, of land adjacent to his oceanside house in San

Continued on Page 62, Column 7

Nixon Friend Gave Tricia $25,000 Trust Fund in '58

By DAVID E. ROSENBAUM
Special to The New York Times

WASHINGTON, Dec. 8—When Richard M. Nixon was Vice President, a wealthy friend established a trust fund of more than $25,000 for Mr. Nixon's older daughter, Tricia, according to information released today by the White House.

The trust fund was set up in 1958 by Elmer H. Bobst, who was then chairman of the Warner-Lambert Pharmaceutical Company, and the gift consisted primarily of Warner-Lambert stock, White House officials said.

At the time of the gift, the late Estes Kefauver, then a Democratic Senator from Tennessee, was preparing for extensive hearings into prices and related matters in the drug industry. When he ran for the Presidency in 1960, Mr. Nixon, like his opponent, John F. Kennedy, took a strong stand against one of the key proposals that evolved from the Kefauver hearings—legislation that would establish Federal regulation of drug prices.

The officials said that President Nixon's younger daughter, Julie, now Mrs. David Eisenhower, had no such trust fund, but they could not explain why a gift was made to one daughter and not the other.

When Tricia, now married to Edward F. Cox, reached the age of 21 in 1967, she received the proceeds from the trust fund and shortly afterward lent $20,-000 to her father to buy two undeveloped lots in Key Biscayne, Fla.

The Nixons got a bargain price on the lots and sold them five years later for nearly four times what they paid for them.

Newsweek magazine reported last month that investigators were checking reports that, to minimize the capital-gains taxes on the profit from the sale, the President claimed the entire capital gain on his own tax return last year. Since Mr. Nixon had established such large deductions last year, the Newsweek article said, he would have had to pay lower taxes than his daughter on her share of the profit.

Documents released by the White House today indicated that the allegation reported by Newsweek was incorrect and

Continued on Page 63, Column 1

Nixon Income and Outgo

Special to The New York Times

WASHINGTON, Dec. 8—The following is a summary of cash received and spent by President and Mrs. Nixon from Jan. 1, 1969, to May 31, 1973, as released today:

SOURCE OF CASH

Salary and allowances	$1,090,635
Sale of New York residence	311,023
Redemption of Fisher's Island, Inc., stock	371,782
Sale of interest in two unimproved lots on Key Biscayne	134,350
Payment of share of undivided profits from Mudge, Rose, Guthrie & Alexander for period prior to Jan. 1, 1969, and repayment of capital	128,611
Interest on bank accounts, rents from Whittier property, book royalties and interest on capital with law firm	65,240
Principal from estate of Hannah Nixon	13,577
Borrowings	725,000
Refund from Baltusrol Golf Club	1,500
Collection of miscellaneous accounts	1,218
Reimbursement of expenses for maintenance of Golf Club by Golfing Friends of the President	4,800
Collection of insurance claim for fire loss damage	11,954
	$2,859,690

APPLICATION OF CASH

Payments for residence operating expenses		$172,835
Personal expenses		300,206
Official expenses		63,029
Rental and investment property expenses		24,382
Interest paid		271,350
Income taxes:		
Income taxes 1969 through 1972, inclusive	$78,651	
Federal income tax paid in 1969 and 1970 on 1968 income	38,646	
New York State income tax paid in 1969 on 1968 income	7,351	
1973 withholding of Federal income tax	30,816	155,464
Payments for improvements, furnishings, and other capital costs at residences		293,691
Repayment of debt incurred to acquire residences		385,592
Payments for purchase of residences		419,663
Repayment to Mrs. P. N. [Tricia Nixon Cox] Cox		65,000
Repayment of other debt		296,396
Deposit C. G. Rebozo		10,000
Acquisition of savings bonds		3,975
Purchase of furniture—Wash., D.C.		7,186
Payment of accounts payable owing at Jan. 1, 1969		5,845
Payments to contractors, vendors and Treasurer of U.S. for fire damage		11,954
		$2,486,568

INCREASE IN CASH

Cash received		$2,859,690
Cash disbursed		2,486,568
Increase		373,122
Cash on hand, Jan. 1, 1969		59,752
Cash on hand, May 31, 1973		$ 432,874

Ultimate Issue Remains

Public Reaction Called Key to Whether Disclosure Will Affect Nixon's Future

By R. W. APPLE Jr.
Special to The New York Times

WASHINGTON, Dec. 8—By releasing his personal financial records today, President Nixon sought, as he himself said, to "put to rest" most of the "questions outstanding in the public mind" about his business affairs. But neither the President nor his battery of lawyers and accountants can answer the ultimate question: Will this latest Presidential initiative head off impeachment or resignation, or will it fall short? The answer to that lies with the American people, and their response is less than certain.

Mr. Nixon has convinced most politicians in Washington that he has no intention of resigning, although many believe that he might do so if his conviction by the Senate seemed imminent. Likewise, it is taken for granted here that impeachment and conviction are unlikely unless the members of Congress feel tremendous election-year pressure from the voters.

Thus the public impact of today's disclosures and those to follow — not so much the detail but the general impression of the President's culpability or innocence — becomes central. Mr. Nixon sems to understand this, and it is to the public jury that he is appealing.

Certainly no one can complain that the disclosure is incomplete; for a President, it was the most complete ever. But it covered only one part of the controversy that has swirled about Mr. Nixon since the Watergate scandal broke.

News Analysis

What people think of the President's probity will be affected by dozens of other issues. These include the conversations the White House says were never recorded and the partly erased tapes, for example, about which there has been no full explanation.

Perhaps more important, there is the matter of the timing of the financial disclosure. From the beginning of his time of troubles, Mr. Nixon has seemed to make gestures to public indignation at precisely the point when those gestures had lost their power to soothe.

Had he forced the resigna-

Continued on Page 62, Column 5

VOLUMINOUS DATA

President Concedes Material May Raise More Controversy

By JOHN HERBERS
Special to The New York Times

WASHINGTON, Dec. 8—President Nixon made public today a voluminous amount of information, including his income tax returns for his first four years in office, which he said should lay to rest "false rumors" about his personal financing.

The extensive disclosures, unprecedented for an American President, came after several months of persistent reports

Documents relating to Nixon report, Pages 62, 64 and 65.

that the President had profited improperly from his high office. Previously, he had maintained that he was entitled to the same privacy as every other American.

At the same time, however, he acknowledged that more "questions and controversies" might result from his disclosures.

Two of the major controversies—whether he realized a capital gain on a sale of land in San Clemente, Calif., and his large deduction for his gift of papers to the National Archives—involved material he submitted to the Congressional Joint Committee on Internal Revenue Taxation. He promised to abide by the committee's ruling, even if it meant paying $267,000, plus interest, in additional taxes.

Emergency Preparation

The statistics and documents, put together on an emergency basis over the last three and a half weeks, were designed to show, as the President said at Disney World, Fla., on Nov. 17, that he was "no crook"—that he had no hidden $1-million investment portfolio, that he had not illegally sheltered income on which his daughter Tricia should have paid taxes, that campaign funds had not been used in the purchase of his San Clemente home.

The material included the following:

¶During four years as President, Mr. Nixon became a millionaire by more than tripling his net worth, which was $307,141 when he entered office, with virtually all his income deriving from his $200,000-a-year salary and $50,000 expense allowance.

¶By taking advantage of a wide assortment of deductions and exemptions, Mr. Nixon paid about the same income tax for three years as the typical wage earner making $5,-969. In his statement today, Mr. Nixon said: "I have proceeded in a manner I thought both prudent and in the best

Continued on Page 62, Column 1

The President and the Plumbers: A Look at 2 Security Questions

By SEYMOUR M. HERSH
Special to The New York Times

WASHINGTON, Dec. 8—For months President Nixon has been citing national security as the reason for authorizing establishment of the secret White House investigation unit known as the plumbers and as justification for restricting some aspects of the Watergate inquiry.

The President has never given any details of his national security concerns, noting that they were "highly sensitive" matters.

Interviews over the last month by The New York Times with dozens of past and present Administration officials, including men who were closely involved with the plumbers, have suggested that at least two principal national security fears, neither of which has ever

This is the first of two articles on the former secret White House investigative unit known as the plumbers.

been substantiated, motivated the President.

One was a fear—nourished in part, some sources said, by Henry A. Kissinger, then the President's national security adviser—that Daniel Ellsberg, who said he turned over the Pentagon papers to the press, might pass on to the Soviet Union secrets far more important than any information contained in the Pentagon study of the Vietnam war.

Specifically, the sources said, the White House feared that Dr. Ellsberg, a former Rand Corporation and Defense Department official, may have been a Soviet intelligence informer who, in the weeks after

publication of the Pentagon papers in June, 1971, was capable of turning over details of the most closely held nuclear targeting secrets of the United States, which were contained in a highly classified document known as the Single Integrated Operation Plans, or S.I.O.P.

The second major concern was that a highly placed Soviet agent of the K.G.B., the Soviet intelligence agency, operating as an American counterspy, would be compromised by continued inquiry by the special prosecutor and the Senate Watergate committee into the Ellsberg case. The agent informed his F.B.I. contacts that a set of the Pentagon papers had been delivered to the Soviet Embassy in Washington shortly after a Federal court had ordered The Times to stop

Continued on Page 76, Column 1

Arab Oil Aides Indicate End to Embargo in 1974

By DAVID BINDER
Special to The New York Times

WASHINGTON, Dec. 8—Two of the conference of oil ministers Arab oil ministers indicated today that they believed that at the height of the fourth Middle East war, the embargo on petroleum shipments to the United States and the Netherlands would be lifted some time in 1974.

The ministers, Sheik Ahmed Zaki al-Yamani of Saudi Arabia and Belaid Abdessalam of Algeria, have been in Washington since Wednesday representing nine Arab countries in talks with United States officials.

Speaking to newsmen of the embargo that was initiated at Kuwait on Oct. 17 at the fourth Middle East war, Sheik Yamani said, "I think we can change some time in 1974."

Mr. Abdsalam, in an interview in his heavily guarded suite at the Madison Hotel, said that he had been "encouraged to a certain degree," by what he had heard from Secretary of State Kissinger, that the United States would influence Israel to accede to a peace settlement that would lead to a lifting of the embargo and restoration of oil production.

"We are hopeful that the United States approach will be such as to make it possible to reconsider our position," he said in French. "The United States is extremely well placed to exert pressure to bring about a cessation by Israel of its aggressive policy and its policy of annexation."

Mr. Abdessalam added that although he and Sheik Yamani had heard "statements" on United States policy "nothing concrete" in the way of commitments had been made by Mr. Kissinger.

Saudi Arabia was unreservedly behind the idea of an embargo against countries favoring Israel, he said, but initially resisted the idea of a cutback in production. Algeria was also

Continued on Page 4, Column 1

GASOLINE SUPPLY DROPS ACROSS U.S.

Concern Mounting as Curbs Nixon Asked Fail to Stem E-risk Run on Stations

By DAVID A. ANDELMAN

Service-station owners and their spokesmen throughout the country expressed concern yesterday over a gasoline drought brought on by tight supplies and a run on their pumps.

The situation has developed despite gasless Sundays, for which American motorists again began preparing themselves yesterday.

"Our stations' December allotments have been cut from 10 to 20 per cent," said Sebastian Gaeta, president of the 1,500-member Long Island Gasoline Retailers Association.

The tendency to sell has been overcoming the tendency to spread out these smaller supplies for the whole month. Around the Christmas holidays will be the worst week. A lot of stations just won't have any to sell at all."

Maximums Imposed

Many stations already were running dry yesterday—some closing down as early as 9:30 A.M., after runs on their supply cleaned them out.

Others reacted to what they said were disclosures made to them yesterday that the gasoline suppliers were cutting out all Sunday deliveries to conserve some stocks for Monday morning. Still more imposed strict maximums on the amount of gasoline they would sell to any one driver and tried to care for their regular customers first.

David Greenberg, owner of

Continued on Page 30, Column 1

Ballet Strike Ends

The 25-day strike by dancers of the New York City Ballet ended yesterday, and the company said performances of "The Nutcracker" would begin Wednesday. Details, Page 41.

Love Asserts He Lacked Means to Do Energy Job

By WALLACE TURNER
Special to The New York Times

DENVER, Dec. 8—Last June, Gov. John A. Love took a telephone call from the White House asking him to be the Administration's energy czar. This week, forced out of his job, he returned to Denver as an out-of-work lawyer, bewildered by five months in Richard M. Nixon's Washington.

Mr. Love's account is one of a puzzled man who gave up the governorship of Colorado to become the White House energy adviser but was never able to get a definition of his authority or to persuade the Administration to accept his proposals for a tougher energy program.

He says he was never able to talk alone with the President, was given an inadequate staff of eight or nine strangers, and then found himself mysteriously faced with a reorganization proposal that left him in a superfluous job.

And while some in Washington say that Mr. Love was squeezed out because he failed

John A. Love
United Press International

Continued on Page 31, Column 1

Retired Policeman and Druggist Help Thwart Brooklyn Holdup

By EMANUEL PERLMUTTER

An attempted robbery in a Brooklyn drugstore was frustrated yesterday through the combined efforts of a former policeman who left the force three days ago because of a serious injury, a pharmacist who kept his wits after a pistol had been held to his head and two detectives specially trained in negotiating with gunmen holding hostages.

The 30-minute drama ended after a shootout in which one of the two holdup men was slightly wounded by a police bullet and stunned by the druggist who struck him on the head with a stick and escaped. A young woman who allegedly served as a lookout was cap-

It all started at 9:45 A.M. when, the police said, Joseph Marino, 34 years old, and Patrick Parascand, 30, both of 3013 Brighton Sixth Street in the Brighton Beach section of Brooklyn, entered the drugstore.

Fergus Walsh, a 72-year-old pharmacist, was alone behind the counter of the store at 8002 Fifth Avenue, in the Bay Ridge district. The man speaking to him vaguely about needing a prescription and Mr. Walsh, who had been robbed twice before, said later, "I knew it was trouble."

The two holdup men allegedly

Continued on Page 80, Column 3

Today's Sections

Index to Subjects

"All the News That's Fit to Print"

The New York Times

LATE CITY EDITION
Weather: Chance of showers later today, tonight. Milder tomorrow. Temp. range: today 36-46; Friday 43-49. Additional details on Page 62.

VOL. CXXIII...No. 42,406
© 1974 The New York Times Company

NEW YORK, SATURDAY, MARCH 2, 1974

20¢ beyond 50-mile radius of New York City, except Long Island. Higher in air delivery cities.

15 CENTS

FEDERAL GRAND JURY INDICTS 7 NIXON AIDES ON CHARGES OF CONSPIRACY ON WATERGATE; HALDEMAN, EHRLICHMAN, MITCHELL ON LIST

John N. Mitchell
Former Attorney General

H. R. Haldeman
Headed White House staff

John D. Ehrlichman
Was Presidential adviser

Charles W. Colson
Former White House lawyer

Robert C. Mardian
1972 campaign coordinator

Kenneth W. Parkinson
Lawyer for campaign unit

Gordon C. Strachan
Assisted Mr. Haldeman

COLSON IS NAMED

A Question of Veracity of the President Is Indirectly Raised

By ANTHONY RIPLEY
Special to The New York Times

WASHINGTON, March 1—A Federal grand jury today indicted seven men, all former officials of President Nixon's Administration of his 1972 re-election campaign, on charges of covering up the Watergate scandal.

Never before have so many close and trusted advisers of an American President faced criminal accusations in a single indictment.

All were charged with conspiracy — a conspiracy, the grand jury said, that continued

Five pages of Watergate material with indictment text begin on Page 14.

"up to and including" today; six were charged additionally with obstruction of justice; two with perjury and three with false statements to the Federal Bureau of Investigation, the grand jury or both.

The indictment accused one defendant, H. R. Haldeman, the former White House chief of staff, of lying when he quoted the President as saying "it would be wrong" to raise hush money for the perpetrators of the original Watergate burglary—a break-in June 17, 1972, at the Democratic National Committee headquarters.

Endorsed Statement

This indirectly raised a question about Mr. Nixon's veracity because he endorsed Mr. Haldeman at a news conference last Aug. 22. The President recalled a meeting at the White House at which clemency for the Watergate defendants and financial support for their families was discussed. Mr. Nixon said he had told his White House counsel, John W. Dean 3d, "John it, is wrong, it won't work."

With the indictment, the grand jury handed to Chief Judge John J. Sirica of the Federal District Court here a sealed report, accompanied by a bulky briefcase reportedly containing evidence of Mr. Nixon's role in the Watergate affair.

This information was presumably intended for the House Judiciary Committee, which is considering a motion to impeach the President and put him on trial before the Senate.

The defendants and the charges against them are as follows:

John N. Mitchell, former Attorney General and director of Mr. Nixon's 1968 and 1972 Presidential campaigns—conspiracy, obstruction of justice, false statements to the F.B.I, false statements to the grand jury and perjury.

Mr. Haldeman—conspiracy, obstruction of justice and perjury.

John D. Ehrlichman, former assistant to the President for domestic affairs—conspiracy, obstruction of justice, false statements to the F.B.I, and false statements to the grand jury.

Charles W. Colson, former special counsel to the President—conspiracy and obstruction of justice.

Robert C. Mardian, former aide to Mr. Mitchell in the 1972 campaign—conspiracy.

Kenneth W. Parkinson, attorney for the Committee for the Re-election of the President—conspiracy and obstruction of justice.

Gordon C. Strachan, former aide to Mr. Haldeman—conspiracy, obstruction of justice and false statements to the grand jury.

The , key conspiracy count

Continued on Page 16, Column 1

Heath, Trailing Labor Party In Britain, Declines to Resign

Special to The New York Times

LONDON, March 1—Prime Minister Heath, deprived of his majority in Parliament by Britain's voters, declined to resign tonight. His action raised the prospect that Mr. Heath's Conservatives, outnumbered by the Labor party in the new House of Commons, would try to remain in power.

Thus Britain faced one of the gravest crises in her modern political history. The last time when neither main party won an over-all majority was in 1929.

There was no official word. But sources close to Mr. Heath said that he had told Queen Elizabeth tonight that he wanted to stay in office despite his party's failure to win an over-all majority in the general election yesterday.

Wilson Prepared to Govern

A few hours earlier, Harold Wilson, the leader of the Labor party, said that he was prepared to form a new Cabinet. Labor also failed to win a majority, but it holds five more seats than the Conservatives.

With the virtual stalemate between the two big parties, the balance of power in the new House would be held by smaller ones, including the Liberals, Scottish and Welsh

Nationalists and the Members from Northern Ireland.

If Mr. Heath carries on with a minority government, despite his campaign bid for a "fresh mandate" and a "strong" majority, the question is for how long. He could go down to defeat quickly in the new House of Commons if a majority voted "no confidence" on some issue that arose for debate.

If that occurred, it is expected that he would ask the Queen to call for Mr. Wilson to form a new Government. Any call for a new election is regarded as unlikely until sometime later after the party leaders have a chance to try to win support in the House.

It was Mr. Heath, on Feb. 7, who used his power as Prime Minister to order Parliament dissolved and to call yesterday's election.

His goal was a mandate to settle a strike in the Government-owned coal mines that

British Pound Plunges

The value of the British pound fell 1.85 cents and prices of stocks went down 24 points in hectic trading in London yesterday in reaction to the setback for Britain's Conservative Government. Details on Page 41.

had crippled the country's production and forced it onto a three-day work week. Yesterday that mandate from the voters eluded him.

Tonight this was the standing of the parties in the new House of Commons, compared with their standings in the old one:

	New	Old
Labor	301	287
Conservative	296	322
Liberal	14	11
Others	23	10
Undecided	1	..

Mr. Heath, after a day of meetings with his advisers at 10 Downing Street, emerged shortly after 7:30 P.M. local time (3:30 P.M., New York time) for his meeting with the Queen, who had interrupted a visit to Australia to return here.

Statement Is Issued

A statement from 10 Downing Street said:

"The Queen has granted the Prime Minister's request to her to grant him an audience at 7:45 P.M. so that he can report on the current political situation."

If Mr. Health had submitted his resignation, the announcement would have come quickly. But it was clear that he had

Continued on Page 10, Column 1

MITCHELL JUDGE HALTS TRIAL HERE

Weighs Motion for Mistrial Over 'Apparent Excesses' in Prosecutor's Speech

By RALPH BLUMENTHAL

Federal Judge Lee P. Gagliardi abruptly suspended yesterday the conspiracy-perjury trial of John N. Mitchell and Maurice H. Stans for what he called "apparent excesses" by the chief Government prosecutor in his opening statement.

Judge Gagliardi said that he would rule Monday on demands by defense attorneys for a mistrial. He ordered the prosecutor, Assistant United States Attorney James W. Rayhill, to submit a "documented response" with his "excuses."

While neither side would comment on the surprising development, some observers in the court believed it unlikely that the judge would decide to discharge the newly picked jury, which had been carefully isolated from news of yesterday's Watergate indictments naming Mr. Mitchell along with six others.

Conspiracy Charged

The historic trial was interrupted just after the Government had told the jury that it would prove that the defendants had conspired to quash a Federal investigation of Robert L. Vesco, the fugitive financier, in exchange for his secret $200,000 cash contribution to President Nixon's re-election campaign, that the defendants covered up the scheme and lied about it when questioned under oath.

At the close of his hour and 50 minutes presentation in the fifth-floor courtroom in the

Continued on Page 18, Column 6

Nixon Urges Quick Trials, Cautions on Prejudgment

By JOHN HERBERS

WASHINGTON, March 1 — President Nixon expressed the hope today that trials arising out of the new Watergate indictments "will move quickly to a just conclusion." He also cautioned the nation to remember that the accused are presumed innocent unless proved guilty.

"The indictments indicate the judicial process is finally moving toward resolution of the matter," Gerald L. Warren, the White House deputy press secretary, said in a statement approved by Mr. Nixon. The statement, read to newsmen, added:

"It is the President's hope that the trials will move quickly to a just conclusion. The President is confident that all Americans will join him in recognizing that those indicted are presumed innocent unless proof of guilt is established in the courts."

The statement also declared that the President had "always maintained that the judicial system is the proper forum for the resolution of the questions

concerning Watergate."

Two of the seven men accused in today's indictment, Charles W. Colson and Kenneth W. Parkinson, issued personal statements of innocence on the charges. The other five relied on their attorneys to issue brief formal statement a short time later. [Details, Page 16.]

Word of the Watergate indictments reached the Oval Office today via the news tickers and the President—busy with policy meetings, ceremony and entertaining of Congressmen—reacted with his brief formal statement about an hour later.

Gen. Alexander M. Haig Jr. and Ronald L. Ziegler, the President's chief assistants, informed Mr. Nixon of the charges against his former high associates just as the President was ending a meeting with his economic and energy advisers and was preparing to welcome the Mayor of Meridian, Miss., Tom Stuart, who had gotten 20,000 names on a petition to

Continued on Page 17, Column 3

SIRICA SAID TO GET FINDINGS ON NIXON

Grand Jury Reported to Ask Him to Give Evidence on Watergate to House

By JAMES M. NAUGHTON
Special to The New York Times

WASHINGTON, March 1—The Watergate grand jury reportedly asked Chief Judge John J. Sirica of the United States District Court today to give the House impeachment inquiry evidence relating to President Nixon's role in the Watergate case.

The grand jury issued a sealed "report" to the judge, and investigative sources said that they understood the document contained a description of the grand jury's findings about Mr. Nixon's possible involvement in the Watergate cover-up.

Moments later, the special Watergate prosecutor's office gave Judge Sirica a large briefcase said to contain a mass of documents and other evidence sought by the House Judiciary Committee for its investigation of the President's conduct in

Continued on Page 17, Column 1

The Scene in Sirica's Court: A Historic 13 Minutes

By LINDA CHARLTON
Special to The New York Times

WASHINGTON, March 1—At 10 A.M. today, Judge John J. Sirica was sitting in his chambers, reminiscing about his 16 years on the bench, whiling away the time until he could put a black robe over his gray suit and walk into Courtroom 2 to preside over history.

At the close of his hour and 50 minutes presentation in the fifth-floor courtroom in the nial phrases, ending with the prayer for the country and for "this honorable court." Some 13 minutes and surprisingly few words later, it was over.

The small, wood-paneled courtroom, with a checkerboard cork floor, an American flag and seal and two maroon ceramic water pitchers as the only decorations, was filled—with lawyers, Watergate task force staff members and reporters. The long line of would-be specta-

tors that had started forming two hours before the 11 A.M. hearing was exiled to the corridor.

The prosecution's table was crowded with lawyers and papers. At the defense table, on the right side of the courtroom, sat a lone figure, Paul Murphy of the law firm of Hundley & Gacheris, representing John N. Mitchell.

The focus of attention was a group of 21 distributed

Continued on Page 18, Column 3

RED CROSS VISITS 65 ISRAELI P.O.W.'S

Sees Prisoners in Syria— Kissinger Confers With Assad in Damascus

By BERNARD GWERTZMAN
Special to The New York Times

DAMASCUS, Syria, March 1—Israeli prisoners held by Syria, long the focus of a dispute that prevented troop-pullback negotiations, received their first visit from Red Cross inspectors today.

The visit was arranged as part of the latest round of Middle East diplomacy, which carried Secretary of State Kissinger today from Egypt to Israel and then to Syria. He immediately began talks here with President Hafez al-Assad to convey ideas on troop disengagements that he had just received from Premier Golda Meir and other top Israeli officials.

At the end of the session between President Assad and the Secretary of State, both American and Syrian spokesmen indicated that talks on the separation of forces would continue after Mr. Kissinger left here tomorrow on his way to return to the United States. There was no announcement that any firm agreement had been reached on how negotiations between Israel and Syria would take place.

The Syrian spokesman said that Mr. Assad had not accepted the Israeli position offered to him by Mr. Kissinger and had offered one in return, which Mr. Kissinger "will study

Continued on Page 4, Column 3

Two-Way Radios in Taxis To Help City Fight Crime

By WILL LISSNER

The city officially began a program yesterday to put on the streets thousands of cruising taxicab drivers trained in the observation and reporting of crime and who are in radio communication with the police.

The new auxiliary arm of the police is the Civilian Radio Motor Patrol, which, Mayor Beame said, already has 500 crime watchers at work — 350 in the Bedford Park section of the Bronx and 150 in communities in Brooklyn operating from a Sheepshead Bay base.

Many taxicabs are dispatched by radio, the dispatcher having the transmitter and the cab the receiver. These one-way systems cannot be used in this program. The patrol system in use links the dispatcher and the driver by a two-way radio.

Under the system, telephone lines link the dispatcher to the switchboard operator in the police station. When necessary, the desk sergeant can then talk directly to the taxicab driver.

Two similar networks are to be opened soon in Queens, one in Long Island City and one in Richmond Hill, according to Stanley Bakalar, president of the Associated Radio Metered

Taxi Owners Council.

"Eventually Manhattan and Staten Island will be covered, too," he added.

"This is another example of how we can use the city's greatest asset—its citizens—in attacking its number one problem, crime," Mayor Beame said. He and Police Commissioner Michael J. Codd and a group of Bronx officials joined in inaugurating the system at a ceremony at the Bedford Park station in the Bronx.

The program costs the city only the services of the coordinator, Lieut. John Higgins, and the training officers. In the Bronx the cost of installing the tie-lines between the taxi dispatchers and the police was paid for by the First National City Bank and the $12 monthly service charge for the tie-line phones is paid by the taxi cooperatives—the All City Radio Taxi Association and the Bronx Two-Way Radio Metered Taxi Company. Each taxi will display a yellow and black decal announcing its participation in "Civilian Radio Patrol, Community Service."

The city's police have a number of programs in operation using civilians to supplement the department's professional manpower. A primary one is the Auxiliary Police, whose members patrol the streets and perform other police functions under the supervision of police officers.

Another is the Blockwatcher Program, in which civilians act as the eyes of the police on their own block.

NEWS INDEX

Assistant U.S. Attorney James W. Rayhill, standing, making his opening statement to the jury in the trial of John N. Mitchell, seated foreground, and Maurice H. Stans. Judge Lee P. Gagliardi is at upper left.
The New York Times/Marilyn Church

"All the News That's Fit to Print"

The New York Times

LATE CITY EDITION
Weather: Showers likely today and tonight. Clearing, mild tomorrow. Temp. range: today 52-65; Wed. 50-71. Additional details on Page 82.

VOL.CXXIII..No.42,439
© 1974 The New York Times Company

NEW YORK, THURSDAY, APRIL 4, 1974

20c beyond 50-mile radius of New York City, except Long Island. Higher in air delivery cities.

15 CENTS

NIXON TO PAY $432,787 IN BACK TAXES; CONGRESS PANEL STAFF AND I.R.S. FIND UNDERPAYMENTS IN 4 YEARS IN OFFICE

Miss Hearst Says She Joins Terrorists

In a Broadcast Message, Kidnapping Victim Vows to Fight for 'Oppressed'

By EARL CALDWELL
Special to The New York Times

SAN FRANCISCO, April 3—Patricia Hearst said in a tape-recorded message received today that she had chosen to join the forces of the Symbionese Liberation Army and fight for "the freedom of oppressed people."

She said that she had been offered the choice of being released or the chance to join the underground terrorist group.

"I have chosen to stay and fight," she said.

The message, delivered to Berkeley radio station KPFA, came one day after the group that calls itself the Symbionese Liberation Army had announced that it was planning to release the 20-year-old daughter of the newspaper executive, Randolph A. Hearst. The police say she was abducted from her apartment at gunpoint last Feb. 4.

In a brief meeting with reporters several hours after the message from his daughter was broadcast, Mr. Hearst said he did not believe that his

Continued on Page 21, Column 1

United Press International
Patricia Hearst holding a submachine gun in front of an S.L.A. symbol, in photo sent by the group yesterday.

Queen Elizabeth 2 Transfers Passengers

By ALLAN M. SIEGAL

After two days adrift in the Atlantic Ocean, 1,648 passengers abandoned the crippled liner Queen Elizabeth 2 yesterday in slightly choppy seas. Then, climbing gangplanks and crowding aboard the Norwegian cruise ship Sea Venture, which had dashed to their rescue overnight, the passengers headed for Bermuda, en route to New York.

The mid-ocean shuttle, scheduled to last three hours, stretched from 10 A.M. to 4 P.M. Many elderly passengers had to be helped into and out of the launches, and two Sea Venture crewmen steadying a gangway were injured slightly when the sea rolled. But all passengers were reported safe.

"It was a great adventure," said Mrs. Arthur R. Bray of Stonington, Conn., the first passenger to reach the Sea Venture. As she spoke, crewmen ladled out hot soup, and loudspeakers squawked direc-

tions to the showers for QE2 vacationers who had done without them for 48 hours.

"It's going magnificently, thank heaven," said the QE2's skipper, Capt. Peter Jackson, who was reached by radiotelephone midway through the shuttle operation.

At a London news conference, Cunard's chairman, Victor Matthews, was asked about the possibility that sabotage had caused the breakdown. "I think it's most unlikely," he said, "but we don't know how it happened."

Insurance covers the breakdown and repair costs, but not the refunds or the rescue arrangements and not any loss of business if future cruises are

But Captain Jackson said he doubted that repairs could be made soon, and he expected the vessel to be towed into port by tugs. Most of her 940 crewmen stayed aboard.

Cunard Line officials in London said they still hoped the Queen Elizabeth 2 could soon repair at least one of her three boilers, which broke down Monday morning, and make the 270 miles northeast to Bermuda partly under her own steam. Another cruise might depart from Bermuda in a week, they said.

Continued on Page 46, Column 4

Israeli War Report Broadly Criticized

By TERENCE SMITH
Special to The New York Times

JERUSALEM, April 3—The initial findings of the official commission investigating the October war were attacked from both the left and right today as overly severe on the military command and overly lenient toward the political leadership.

Calls on the Cabinet of Premier Golda Meir to resign came from dovish elements in the governing Labor party, the right-wing opposition and the editorial columns of leading newspapers.

The commission's initial report, which was issued late last night after four months of testimony, assigned to the military command the primary blame for Israel's unprepared-

Continued on Page 13, Column 1

Carriers Ask U.S. Aid

Pan American World Airways and Trans World Airlines asked yesterday for huge Federal subsidies because of soaring fuel prices. The Penn Central Railroad is to seek $40-million in Government aid to maintain service for the next five months. Page 61.

TORNADOES STRIKE 9 STATES, CANADA; MORE THAN 200 DIE

Hundreds Are Hurt in the South and Middle West—Damage Put in Millions

By The Associated Press

Tornadoes struck nine states in the Middle West and South last night, then swirled into Canada. More than 200 people were killed.

Hundreds of injuries were also reported as the twisters struck parts of Ohio, Illinois, Indiana, Kentucky, Tennessee, Alabama, Michigan, Georgia, North Carolina and Canada's Ontario Province. Damage totaled millions of dollars. Half the town of Xenia, Ohio, a community of 25,000 people, was destroyed, according to the county sheriff. Authorities estimated that 25 persons died in the Xenia area alone.

The authorities counted 213 deaths and gave this breakdown: Kentucky, 66 deaths; Indiana, 37; Ohio, 36; Illinois, 2; Alabama, 19; Tennessee, 31; Georgia, 15; Michigan, 2; North Carolina, 3; and Windsor, Ontario, 8.

The eight persons in Windsor were killed and more than 20 injured when a tornado ripped off the roof of the local curling rink.

A police broadcast in Xenia said:

"You wouldn't believe what this town looks like. We are begging for all kinds of medical assistance, manpower and other assistance."

Tales of horror filtered in from other areas in the storm belt, which was for the most part without communication. "There have been bodies in fields and everything else, people with injuries," said a report from Harrison County, Indiana.

Some states called up their National Guard.

The tornadoes struck cities of

Continued on Page 23, Column 1

French Name Poher Interim President

By NAN ROBERTSON
Special to The New York Times

PARIS, April 3—Alain Poher, centrist president of the Senate, was officially proclaimed the Acting President of France today in an atmosphere of grave uncertainty and political confusion.

The death of President Georges Pompidou last night produced a virtually universal mood of shock despite national concern over a long and debilitating illness that had forced him to relinquish many duties in the last few months. His death, and doubts about a successor, raised economic fears and started a rush into gold. [Page 61.]

Mr. Poher will preside over

Continued on Page 16, Column 1

ASSEMBLY VOTES TO SAVE PENSIONS

Would Guarantee Benefits of All in Private Industry After 15 Years in Plan

By DAVID A. ANDELMAN
Special to The New York Times

ALBANY, April 3—The Assembly voted today to protect the pensions of all workers in private industry in the state by guaranteeing their rights to benefits after 15 years in a pension plan. Also, the State Superintendent of Insurance would be required to audit periodically every pension fund.

The bill, which now goes to the Senate, is the first such legislation in the country, according to its sponsor, Assemblyman John G. McCarthy, a Republican of Huntington, L.I. It is a product of more than two years of hearings throughout the state.

What it means is that all workers who change companies after 15 years in a pension plan and all those who, after 15 years, are left behind when

Continued on Page 25, Column 1

WATERGATE JURY INDICTS REINECKE FOR LIES ON I.T.T.

California Official Accused on Remarks to Mitchell in Antitrust Dispute

By E.W. KENWORTHY
Special to The New York Times

WASHINGTON, April 3—Ed Reinecke, the Lieutenant Governor of California, was indicted by a Watergate grand jury today on three counts of lying to the Senate Judiciary Committee.

The charges stemmed from the investigation in March and April, 1972, into possible political influence in the settlement of three antitrust suits against the International Telephone and Telegraph Corporation.

The two principal charges alleged that Mr. Reinecke lied when he told the committee that he had not discussed with former Attorney General John N. Mitchell an I.T.T. pledge of money for the Republican convention until Sept. 17, 1971. This was six weeks after the antitrust suits were settled.

These charges immediately aroused speculation here over whether Mr. Mitchell would be indicted in the case, since his testimony was the same as Mr. Reinecke's.

Mr. Reinecke, a 50-year-old Republican, has been a leading candidate for the Governorship, and the front-runner against Houston Flournoy, the state Controller, in the Re-

Continued on Page 31, Column 1

Laotian Coalition Near

The Premier of Laos, Prince Souvanna Phouma, announced yesterday that the long-expected coalition government with the Communist-led Pathet Lao would be presented to the King tomorrow. The Prince met yesterday with his half-brother, Prince Souphanouvong, the leader of the Pathet Lao. Page 3.

President Decides Not to Contest Case

Nixon Vow Is Cited

By JOHN HERBERS
Special to The New York Times

WASHINGTON, April 3—The White House said tonight that while President Nixon would pay the full amount of back taxes requested by the Internal Revenue Service, he could have, and perhaps should have, contested the finding.

His decision not to appeal

Text of White House statement is printed on Page 28.

the request in the courts, the White House statement said, was made because he had promised earlier to abide by the judgment of the Joint Congressional Committee on Internal Revenue Taxation.

The statement, issued by the White House press office, disclosed that the Internal Revenue Service had ruled that the President owed $432,787.13, plus interest. The White House added, however, that the I.R.S. had also ruled that there was no question of fraud on the part of the President.

There was no immediate word from the I.R.S.

Defense Is Outlined

In the statement, the White House said that the President's lawyers had advised him that they sought to present to the joint committee "valid and compelling" reasons as to why the findings by the staff committee were incorrect.

Although the statement did not make clear how many items the lawyers believed were improperly judged against the President, the focus was on the large deduction that Mr. Nixon took for the gift of his pre-Presidential papers to the National Archives.

"His intent to give the papers was clear," the statement said. "Their delivery was accomplished in March, 1969, four months before the July deadline. His intent as to the

Continued on Page 28, Column 1

Interest to Be Paid

By EILEEN SHANAHAN
Special to The New York Times

WASHINGTON, April 3—President Nixon announced tonight that he would pay $432,-787.13 in back taxes plus interest after Congressional investigators and the Internal Revenue Service both concluded that he had underpaid his taxes by more than $400,000 for his first four years in the White House.

The White House said that the President would pay the

Introduction and summary of recommendations, Page 28.

sum assessed by the Internal Revenue Service. Details of the delinquencies discovered by the Revenue Service were not made public.

Congressional investigators, in finding underpayments totaling $444,022, said that they had found five different categories of taxable income that Mr. Nixon should have reported and failed to report and six different categories of deductions that they said he took without being entitled to do so.

Fraud Is Not Alleged

The White House said that the revenue service did not allege that fraud had been committed. The Congressional investigators said that they had not attempted to reach a conclusion on the matter of fraud because that was an issue that might come before the House Judiciary Committee, which is considering whether to recommend impeachment of Mr. Nixon.

The Congressional investigators, members of the staff of the Joint Committee on Internal Revenue Taxation, found improprieties connected with nearly every one of the controversial items in Mr. Nixon's tax returns that have been widely discussed in recent months. These include the big deduction for his gift of his pre-Presidential papers to the National Archives and his not reporting capital gains on two real estate sales.

The staff also reported adversely on some other matters that had received little or no previous public notice.

In the last category were Mr. Nixon's not reporting as taxable income certain expenditures, made out of public funds, that the committee staff said solely benefited him or his family, and not the public.

$5,391 for 'Masqued Ball'

Among these expenditures were $5,391 for a "masqued ball" given by his daughter Tricia in 1969; $27,015 worth of purely personal airplane travel by the Nixon family and friends; and $92,298 in improvements to the Nixons' houses in San Clemente, Calif., and Key Biscayne, Fla.

The staff also found two instances, totaling $1,284, in which it said Mr. Nixon could have taken larger deductions than he claimed.

The White House made no attempt to explain the relatively small difference between the deficiency found by the joint committee's staff and that found by the revenue service.

The tone of the White House statement was one of argument with the conclusions of the

Continued on Page 29, Column 2

Document Reporting Undeclared Nixon Income and Impermissible Deductions

RECOMMENDED DEFICIENCY AND INTEREST, 1969-72

SCHEDULE A	1969	1970	1971	1972
1. Income as reported on return (AGI)	$328,162	$262,943	$262,385	$268,778
2. Additions to income	142,367	85,994	13,592	18,011
a. Gain on sale of New York apartment (50% of NLTCG)	$75,924			
b. Improvements to San Clemente and Key Biscayne properties	62,442	$17,800	$8,956	$3,101
c. Personal use of government airplanes by family and friends	4,001	9,276	4,636	9,102
d. Gain on sale of San Clemente property (50% of NLTCG)		56,918		5,808
e. Gain on sale of Florida lots (50% of NLTCG)				
3. Deductions from income improperly taken as itemized deductions (item 6)	−6,294	−5,510	−5,517	−5,332
4. Corrected income (AGI) (1+2−3)	378,535	464,235	307,182	343,427	255,677	270,460	247,570	281,457
5. Deductions reported on return				
6. Deductions improperly taken as itemized deductions but allowable in arriving at AGI (item 3)	−6,294	−5,510	−5,517	−5,332
7. Deductions not allowable:				
a. Charitable contribution deduction for gift of papers	$117,184	$140,976	$152,102	$157,303
	95,298	123,959	128,668	134,093
b. Amounts treated on return as business deductions	21,833	16,954	23,402	23,210
i. San Clemente residence	4,700	7,808	10,237	9,422
ii. Key Biscayne residence	292	646	614	583
iii. Depreciation of White House furniture	1,347	7,153	1,095	889
iv. Guest fund deductions	16,841	63	11,456	12,316
c. Gasoline tax	53		42	
8. Additional deductions allowed:				
a. Sales tax	1,274			
b. Gasoline tax			10	
9. Allowable itemized deductions (5−6−7+8)	56,331	160,696	98,058	84,945
10. Corrected taxable income (4−9−personal exemptions)	406,104	180,856	171,052	195,012
11. Ordinary tax determined on corrected taxable income	137,394	58,820	90,545	86,927
12. Alternative capital gain tax (if applicable)	84,185	32,512		7,261
13. Total corrected ordinary income tax liability (11+12)	243,737	94,203	90,545	94,188
14. Total tax (13 plus minimum tax)	243,737	94,203	90,545	94,188
15. Tax as shown on return	72,682	793	878	4,298
16. Deficiency (14−15)	171,055	93,410	89,667	89,890
17. Interest	(*)	16,638	10,547	5,224
18. Total deficiency and interest	171,055	110,048	100,214	95,114

¹ Not long term capital gain.
² This amount represents those deductions claimed because of the business use of the Key Biscayne residence. The President had claimed these expenses as itemized deductions, but the committee staff believes that they should be allowed as expenses incurred in connection with maintaining investment property (sec. 212). This means that it now is a deduction to arrive at AGI, rather than an itemized deduction and is treated accordingly.

³ Personal exemptions for 1969 totaled $1,800 ($600X3); $1,875 for 1970 ($625X3); $1,350 for 1972 ($675X2), and $1,500 for 1972 ($750X2).
⁴ Includes $22,158 of income tax surcharge.
⁵ Includes $2,283 of income tax surcharge at 2.5 percent and minimum tax of $588.
* Since 1969 is a closed year, and any payment by the President would be voluntary, the staff did not include an interest payment for the deficiency in this year. However, if interest were to be included, the amount would be $40,732.

Table prepared by Congressional investigators lists President Nixon's adjusted gross income (AGI) as reported by him on Line 1. It shows calculations made by the Congressional staff and, on Line 16, deficiencies found, totaling $444,022. Of this, Mr. Nixon agreed to pay $432,787.13, or $11,234.87 less, not counting the interest listed on Line 17.

NEWS INDEX

	Page		Page
Art	54	Movies	50-54
Books	39	Music	50-54
Bridge	38	Obituaries	44, 55
Business	61-71	Op-Ed	39
Chess	38	Sports	53-60
Crossword	38	Theaters	50-54
Editorials	38	Transportation	85
Family/Style	48	TV and Radio	83
Financial	61-71	U. N. Proceedings	3
Going Out Guide	52	Weather	82
News Summary and Index, Page 43			

WILLCOX & GIBBS with premier on sale for the apparel trade (WG-AMEX—ADVT.)

The New York Times

LATE CITY EDITION
Weather: Cloudy, warm, showers likely today through tomorrow. Temp. range: today 56-80. Sunday 49-80. Additional details on Page 66.

VOL. CXXIII...No. 42,464   © 1974 The New York Times Company   NEW YORK, MONDAY, APRIL 29, 1974   20c beyond 50-mile radius of New York City, except Long Island. Higher in air delivery cities.   15 CENTS

MITCHELL AND STANS ARE ACQUITTED ON ALL COUNTS AFTER 48-DAY TRIAL

The New York Times/Joyce Dopkeen
Some of thousands who participated in "Solidarity Day" rally at Hammarskjold Plaza

100,000 IN MARCH FOR SOVIET JEWS

5th Ave. Parade Followed by Rally Asks Freedom of Emigration to Israel

By IRVING SPIEGEL

With priests, ministers and rabbis in the vanguard, a crowd estimated by the police at more than 100,000 paraded down Fifth Avenue yesterday to demonstrate solidarity with Soviet Jews denied the right to emigrate to Israel.

The parade reached a high point when the outpouring of men, women and children filled Dag Hammarskjold Plaza on East 47th Street for the event, titled "Solidarity Sunday for Soviet Jewry."

Governor Wilson, in a proclamation on Soviet Jews, read by Attorney General Louis J. Lefkowitz, said that Solidarity Day served "to remind us that the basic human rights which all Americans enjoy are still being denied to peoples in other parts of the world."

At Hammarskjold Plaza, the throngs stood from building wall to building wall, with little room to move, on 47th Street from First Avenue almost to Third Avenue.

Sponsored by the Greater New York Conference of Soviet Jewry, composed of 79 agencies and headed by Stanley H. Lowell, the parade began at 11:30 A.M. at 68th Street and Fifth Avenue. Men, women and children had arrived by chartered bus from Pennsylvania, New Jersey and New York.

Leading the parade was a 17-

Continued on Page 4, Column 4

31 Are Seized in 21 Raids Here On $189-Million Gambling Ring

By ROBERT D. McFADDEN

Teams of rackets investigators simultaneously raided 21 alleged gambling "wire rooms" across the city yesterday, arresting 31 persons and dismantling what authorities described as a $189-million-a-year sports- and horse-betting operation.

Carrying search warrants, crowbars and battering rams, the investigators invaded apartments, private homes and social clubs in Brooklyn, Queens, the Bronx and Staten Island about 1:15 P.M.

About 110 men, investigators were said to have seized betting records indicating that the 21 establishments had been handling $518,000 a

Continued on Page 23, Column 2

KISSINGER MEETS GROMYKO TO SEEK MIDEAST BACKING

In Geneva at Start of Trip, He Tries to Get Soviet Help for Israeli-Syrian Pact

By BERNARD GWERTZMAN
Special to The New York Times

GENEVA, April 28 — Secretary of State Kissinger arrived here tonight and met with Soviet Foreign Minister Andrei A. Gromyko to discuss Soviet-American issues and to try to get Soviet help in his efforts for an Israeli-Syrian accord.

An hour after his arrival here, the first stop in a journey aimed at persuading Israel and Syria to compromise on an agreement to separate their troops in the Golan Heights, Mr. Kissinger went to the Soviet mission for talks with Mr. Gromyko.

Mr. Kissinger planned to pursue with Mr. Gromyko the full range of agenda items for President Nixon's trip to Moscow set for late June.

Mr. Kissinger and Mr. Gromyko plan to go into detail on the Middle East situation—the main reason for Mr. Kissinger's stop here—at tomorrow's meeting in Mr. Kissinger's suite in the Inter-Continental Hotel.

Newsmen aboard Mr. Kissinger's Air Force 707 jet were told that Mr. Kissinger viewed this trip as the most difficult of his five Middle East journeys since November. Failure to get Israel and Syria to bridge the large gap between their negotiating stances could lead to a resumption of all-out hostilities, a senior American official said.

After tomorrow's meeting

Continued on Page 3, Column 1

Leftists Plan Lisbon Role; Socialist Leader Returns

By HENRY GINIGER
Special to The New York Times

LISBON, April 28 — Mario Soares, the leader of the Socialist party, returned here in triumph today from five years of exile in Paris as Portuguese leftists began organizing themselves for the possibility of a role in a provisional government.

Power is now held by a seven-man military junta that toppled the country's right-wing authoritarian rulers last Thursday. The junta has promised to form a provisional government within the next few weeks. But it was not known what political elements would be admitted into the government or what policies it would pursue, particularly on the war against black rebels in Africa.

Amid the carnival atmosphere here, surface unity prevailed both among the disparate political forces in the coun-

try and between them and the armed forces. The holiday mood is expected to reach a high point on Wednesday with a huge May Day demonstration by leftists.

Mr. Soares, who had been in jail a dozen times for opposing the previous rulers, received an emotional welcome from thousands of suporters as he arrived by train after an overnight journey from Paris.

An exuberant crowd chanted "A united people cannot be vanquished" and sang the national anthem over and over again. There were also a few tears as fallen heroes of the long fight against a seemingly impregnable regime were cited.

Appearing on a balcony of the railroad station, the 49-year-old Mr. Soares paid tribute to the armed forces and appealed

Continued on Page 14, Column 4

Blacks Building a Nation While Battling Portugal

The following dispatch by a New York Times correspondent was written in the rebel-controlled area of Portuguese Guinea shortly before the military coup in Lisbon.

By THOMAS A. JOHNSON
Special to The New York Times

A JUNGLE CAMP, Portuguese Guinea — For 14 years, African rebels in this malaria-ridden jungle territory have been carrying on an armed struggle against Portuguese rule.

They claim control now over nearly three-fourths of the territory of Portuguese Guinea.

which is about twice the size of New Jersey, and over more than half the population of 600,000 farmers, herdsmen and fishermen. The rebels in Portugal's two other much larger African territories—Angola and Mozambique — make no such claims.

The rebels here, who call the territory they control Guinea-Bissau, have named their movement the African Party for the Independence of Guinea-Bissau and Cape Verde Islands. The short version is either the African party, or P.A.I.G.C.—the initials of its name in Portuguese.

Last September the African party, which was founded in 1956 by the late Amilcar Cabral and began its armed struggle in 1959, proclaimed the independence of Guinea-Bissau. Although the proclamation was ignored by Lisbon, the African party — or African government as its leaders now refer to it — has been recognized by 82 nations as the legal government of Guinea-Bissau, even though it has no official capital.

My 10-day trip through territory controlled by this African

Continued on Page 12, Column 4

Photographs for The New York Times by TYRONE DUKES
Maurice H. Stans, left, and John N. Mitchell talking to newsmen after they were acquitted

Verdict Dims a Key Impeachment Issue; Value of Tapes Stressed; Nixon 'Pleased'

By JAMES M. NAUGHTON
Special to The New York Times

WASHINGTON, April 28 — The acquittal verdict today in the Mitchell-Stans trial heartened the White House, virtually eliminated a key issue in the House impeachment inquiry and underscored the importance of the Watergate tape recordings in other criminal and impeachment proceedings.

"The President was very pleased for the two men and their families," a White House spokesman said of the acquittal in New York of former Attorney General John N. Mitchell and former Commerce Secretary Maurice H. Stans.

The reaction, in a White House apparently involved in a counteroffensive against the impeachment proceedings, was probably understated. Well-

placed Administration officials said that the verdict might play a crucial role in President Nixon's dealings with the House Judiciary Committee.

The key issue affected by the acquittal of Mr. Mitchell and Mr. Stans was the committee's investigation of the secret $200,000 gift to the President's 1972 re-election campaign by Robert L. Vesco. It is now believed that the committee's staff will downgrade or abandon the in-

vestigation of the donation, which was at the heart of the Mitchell-Stans trial.

The acquittal was the first development in almost a year-since the resignations of H. R. Haldeman and John D. Ehrlichman and the dismissal of John W. Dean 3d from the White House staff last April 30—to offer encouragement for Mr. Nixon in the Watergate affair.

Beyond a change in atmosphere, however, the verdict may have significant practical impact on the President's future course of action.

In finding Mr. Mitchell and Mr. Stans not guilty of obstructing justice and perjury in the tangled affairs of Mr. Vesco, the fugitive financier, the trial jury in New York in

Continued on Page 38, Column 6

Nixon Talk on Tapes

President Nixon will go on television tonight with a report on his planned response to the House Judiciary Committee's subpoena of 42 taped conversations, White House sources reported. Details on Page 19.

JURY OUT 26 HOURS

Ex-Nixon Aides Cleared of Acting Illegally in S.E.C.-Vesco Case

By MARTIN ARNOLD

John N. Mitchell and Maurice H. Stans were acquitted yesterday of all charges in their criminal conspiracy case, thus ending the first trial of former Cabinet officials since the Teapot Dome scandal.

A jury of nine men and three women deliberated 26 hours over four days to reach a verdict, which came on the 48th day of the trial.

Mr. Mitchell and Mr. Stans, former leaders of President Nixon's re-election campaign, were charged with conspiracy, obstruction of justice and perjury.

The Government had alleged that the defendants attempted to impede a Securities and Exchange Commission investigation of Robert L. Vesco, a financier, in return for a secret $200,000 cash contribution that Mr. Vesco made to Mr. Nixon's re-election campaign.

Embraces Lawyer

After the 16th "Not guilty" was solemnly pronounced by Sybil Kucharski, a Westchester bank teller who served as the jury's foreman, Mr. Stans embraced one of his lawyers, then fell forward on the defense table and cradled his head in his arms. He appeared to be near tears.

"My heart stopped for 30 seconds, I feel reborn," the former Secretary of Commerce said moments later, amid pandemonium in the dark, rather old Federal courtroom that had been the scene of many historic moments.

Mr. Mitchell was all smiles and appeared to take the verdict somewhat more calmly. The former Attorney General said he had been confident of acquittal from the beginning, adding:

"The truth will out. We got to the jury system, and that always works. Our fate was resting with a very fine jury—a cross section of Americans."

Jurors' Explanation

The jurors said in interviews later that they had not found the key government witnesses credible. But they did forward a note to Judge Lee P. Gagliardi praising the chief prosecutor, John R. Wing, for "performing brilliantly."

In a waste basket in the deserted jury room, a piece of paper from a yellow legal tablet was found with these words written by a juror, "Nixon and Vesco is needed for proof."

Presumably this referred to President Nixon, since both of his brothers, F. Donald Nixon and Edward C. Nixon, were witnesses at this trial. A third Nixon in the case was Donald A. Nixon, the President's nephew, who is now with Mr. Vesco. The financier, also indicted in this case, has fled the country.

Judge Is Notified

The end came at 12:57 P.M., seven minutes after the jury foreman, Miss Kucharski, notified the judge by note that a verdict had been reached. Word swept through the Federal Court House at Foley Square, empty on a Sunday afternoon except for guards, the defendants, their lawyers, the press and the courthouse buffs who spent the hot, sunny morning inside waiting for a possible verdict.

When the jury filed in, the courtroom was jammed. The defendants and their lawyers

Continued on Page 38, Column 3

Jurors in the Mitchell-Stans trial after the trial ended. Front row, from left: Andrew Choa, bank executive; Sybil Kucharski, foreman, bank teller; Clarence Brown, letter carrier, and Rolando DeTouche, engineering technician.

Rear: King D. Kinson, subway conductor; Raymond Crowe, shipping foreman, and Leonard Eppler, medical service supervisor. They are standing at the Skyline Motel on Tenth Avenue, where they were sequestered.

Jurors Couldn't Believe Federal Witnesses

By MARCIA CHAMBERS

The jurors in the Mitchell-Stans trial said yesterday that they had voted to acquit the two former Cabinet officers of all criminal charges because they could not believe the testimony of crucial Government witnesses.

Again and again, in interview after interview at the Skyline Motel where they had been sequestered for the last eight days, the jurors used the words "incredible" or "unbelievable."

They used the words when they talked about John W. Dean 3d, G. Bradford Cook, William J. Casey, Harry L. Sears and Laurence Richardson Jr., all key prosecution witnesses.

"I don't want to say Mr.

Dean was lying, but he was often unbelievable," said Sybil Kucharski, the 21-year-old foreman of the jury.

And at the same time, Miss Kucharski said of the defendants: "We didn't feel they had any reason to lie. We didn't feel they had the need. They were credible men."

The jurors did not, however, start out by believing the defendants.

Miss Kucharski, who is a bank teller in Westchester County, said that shortly after the deliberations began last Thursday afternoon, the jury was split 8 to 4 for conviction, though no formal vote was taken at that time.

While Miss Kucharski refused to say which jurors

emerged as the leaders who conceivably helped turn around the conviction verdict which they then began, she did say that the prosecution had not presented enough "hard evidence." Moreover, she said the judge's charge helped them to get the facts on the law "and to think things out logically."

The Government's case centered on an alleged misuse of power. Telephone calls were made from John N. Mitchell, then the Attorney General, to Mr. Dean, then the White House counsel, to Mr. Casey, then the chairman of the Securities and Exchange Commission, regarding the "status" of Robert L. Vesco, the financier who is now a fugitive.

But Miss Kucharski and five other jurors who were inter-

viewed said they did not see the Government's case that way.

"We didn't put them above the law," Miss Kucharski said. "But we felt they were doing things in the course of the normal working day. They weren't sneaking around or anything."

The man who was sneaking around was Mr. Vesco, another juror said. Mr. Vesco, named as a defendant in this case, fled the United States to Costa Rica and Nassau, the Bahamas. Attempts by the Government to extradite him failed.

"I think Vesco was the real culprit of this whole thing," said Clarence Brown, a letter carrier from Ossining. "He may

Continued on Page 38, Column 1

WILLCOX & GIBBS 1938 sales were 30% higher than 1972 (WG-AMEX)—Advt.

The New York Times

LATE CITY EDITION

Weather: Fair today; rain likely tonight. Chance of rain tomorrow. Temp. range: today 61-77; Wed. 62-84. Additional details on Page 82.

VOL.CXXIII...No. 42,481

© 1974 The New York Times Company

NEW YORK, THURSDAY, MAY 16, 1974

20c beyond 50-mile radius of New York City, except Long Island. Higher in air delivery cities.

15 CENTS

Busing of Pupils Upheld In a Senate Vote of 47-46

Ban Urged by Gurney Fails After 6 Hours of Debate—Revision in Aid Formula May Cost Schools Here $23-Million

By RICHARD D. LYONS
Special to The New York Times

WASHINGTON, May 15—The Senate in effect upheld today the busing of children to end school segregation by a vote of 47 to 46.

The victory for the Senate liberals came only seven weeks after the House of Representatives by a vote of 293 to 117 approved a provision to prohibit Federal courts from ordering long-distance busing of children.

Today's vote followed six hours of often emotional debate. The critical Senate vote tabled an antibusing amendment offered by Senator Edward J. Gurney, Republican of Florida, to the Federal aid to education bill that has been on the Senate floor all week.

The motion to table was made by Senator Jacob K. Javits, Republican of New York. In a radio address in March, President Nixon supported the antibusing language of the Gurney amendment, which was introduced in the House by Representative Marvin L. Esch, Republican of Michigan.

After defeating the Gurney amendment, the Senate approved, by a vote of 56 to 36, a more limited provision prohibiting the busing of pupils from one school district into another unless it has been found that discrimination is practiced in both districts or that district lines in both districts were drawn for the purpose of maintaining segregation.

The amendment is aimed at situations such as that in Detroit, where a Federal court has ordered busing between city schools and those in affluent white suburbs. The Detroit case

Continued on Page 9, Column 1

HOUSE UNIT ISSUES 2 NEW SUBPOENAS TO NIXON FOR DATA

Some on the Judiciary Panel Charge Transcripts Omit Significant Material

By JAMES M. NAUGHTON
Special to The New York Times

WASHINGTON, May 15—The House Judiciary Committee issued today two new subpoenas for White House tape recordings and other documents amid charges by some committee members that significant portions of President Nixon's Watergate conversations had been omitted from edited White House transcripts.

In a series of votes on the two subpoenas, the committee

Text of two memorandums on tape subpoenas, Page 26.

demanded this morning that the President turn over to its impeachment inquiry the tape recordings of 11 Watergate-related conversations as well as diaries of Mr. Nixon's White House meetings over more than eight months in 1972 and 1973. The committee has not received any of this material, either in tape or other documentary form.

Two White House recordings previously obtained by the Judiciary Committee were played for the panel members this afternoon, prompting several Democrats to increase their resolve to obtain tapes, and not transcripts, of the relevant Watergate conversations.

Significance Disputed

Two Democratic members of the panel, Representatives Robert F. Drinan of Massachusetts and Jerome R. Waldie of California, told reporters after hearing the tape of a Sept. 15, 1972, White House conversation that material had been omitted from the White House transcripts not because it was inaudible but, as Mr. Waldie stated it, "because of the content."

Both Democrats declined to specify the nature of the missing material, however, and some Republicans on the committee said that they did not regard the omissions as serious or deliberate.

"The only thing that was deleted was the expletives, nothing of substance," Representative Delbert L. Latta, Republican of Ohio, said after the four-hour closed hearing at which recordings were played for about 40 minutes.

Renewed Effort by Panel

The new subpoenas, which "commanded" Mr. Nixon to supply the recordings and diaries by next Wednesday, were the first step in a renewed and bipartisan effort by the Judiciary Committee to obtain tapes and documents that Mr. Nixon has so far refused to yield.

John M. Doar, the committee's special counsel on impeachment, said that he would meet tomorrow with White House lawyers to get a final answer on whether Mr. Nixon would voluntarily supply recordings of 66 other conversations bearing on pledges of large political contributions to the President's re-election campaign by dairy industry groups and the International Telephone

Continued on Page 26, Column 1

Beame Asks $11.1-Billion For an 'Austerity' Budget

By GLENN FOWLER

Mayor Beame formally presented his first operating budget as the city's chief executive yesterday, labeling it an "austerity" blueprint that calls for spending $11.1-billion

OIL DEPLETION AID FACES HOUSE VOTE

Democrats Mandate Action on Proposal to Repeal 22% Allowance Now

By EILEEN SHANAHAN
Special to The New York Times

WASHINGTON, May 15—Democratic members of the House of Representatives voted overwhelmingly today to force a straight yes-or-no vote in the House on immediate termination of the 22 per cent depletion allowance for the oil industry.

The action by the House Democratic Caucus, though technically only on a procedural matter, brought repeal of the depletion allowance closer than it has ever been in its 50-year history.

The vote in the caucus came about after weeks of intensive strategy planning, lobbying and nose-counting masterminded by three organizations: the American Federation of Labor and Congress of Industrial Organizations, Ralph Nader's tax reform research group and Common Cause, the citizens' lobby.

Rep. Green Is Key

The action of the caucus also brought into prominence a new leader on tax issues among the liberal Democrats in the House, Representative William J. Green of Pennsylvania.

In addition, the vote marked the first time that the new rules of the Democratic Caucus had been used to make sure that the House got to vote on a specific issue. The rules were adopted in February, 1973.

The action was deplored by Frank N. Ikard, president of the American Petroleum Institute. He said that the caucus had displayed a "lynch mob attitude" and predicted that the nation would "suffer a devastating setback in its efforts to attain a reasonable degree of energy self-sufficiency" if the ultimate victory in Congress went to those who, as he put it, "are demanding punitive tax action aimed at petroleum producers."

The caucus voted to permit

Continued on Page 17, Column 1

to run the municipal government in the fiscal year beginning July 1.

Declaring that he intended to provide "little in the way

Excerpts from Mayor Beame's budget are on Page 34.

of new money for new programs," Mr. Beame detailed in a 67-page message accompanying the basic document his financial acrobatics in overcoming a threatened $1.5-billion gap between income and outgo, enabling him finally to bring the budget into balance, as required by law.

The projected 1974-75 spending level, which is almost 8 per cent higher than the current fiscal year's actual outlay, spreads most of the available money among the areas of concern that have come to absorb much of the municipal treasury: public schools ($2.7-billion), welfare and related programs ($2.6-billion), public safety ($1.3-billion for police and fire) and health services ($1.2-billion).

One unusually large item is $1.5-billion for debt service — money to pay interest and amortization on the city's mounting debt — representing in the new budget a 63 per cent increase over the cost in the current fiscal year.

Mr. Beame placed the blame for the city's financial condition on his predecessor, John V. Lindsay, and he had harsh words for the

Continued on Page 34, Column 1

Police-Killing Mistrial

A mistrial was declared here yesterday in the trial of five reputed members of the Black Liberation Army who were charged with murdering two policemen. Page 45.

Haig Said to Testify Simon Warned of Hughes Inquiry

By JOHN M. CREWDSON
Special to The New York Times

WASHINGTON, May 15—Gen. Alexander M. Haig Jr., reportedly told a closed-door session of the Senate Watergate committee today that he was warned a year ago by William E. Simon, then Deputy Secretary of the Treasury, that a Federal investigation of a $100,000 political contribution from Howard R. Hughes had reached the point where it could eventually prove an embarrassment to President Nixon.

Sources familiar with his testimony said General Haig, the White House chief of staff, had identified Mr. Simon, who was confirmed last week as Secretary of the Treasury, as the individual who told him in the spring of 1973 that an Internal Revenue Service inquiry into the trail of the Hughes

money had led to Charles G. Rebozo, Mr. Nixon's close friend.

General Haig's testimony about his knowledge of the Hughes-Rebozo matter was given under oath during an hour-and-a-half session before the Watergate committee members and lawyers, after the President had agreed to waive a claim of executive privilege invoked earlier this month before the committee by the general.

The committee voted unanimously today to ask the full Senate to extend its mandate in the Watergate case through the end of June. Senate Resolution 60, which authorizes the select committee's investiga

Continued on Page 28, Column 4

16 YOUNG ISRAELI HOSTAGES DIE AS TROOPS KILL 3 ARAB CAPTORS; KISSINGER TALKS DELAYED A DAY

Young victims being carried from school in Maalot after the clash between Arab guerrillas and Israeli troops

United Press International

A student, wounded in chest and arm, is carried from the Natia Meir school building

Associated Press

CHAPIN SENTENCED TO 10-30 MONTHS

Former Nixon Aide Appeals Prison Term for Lying to Watergate Grand Jury

By ANTHONY RIPLEY
Special to The New York Times

WASHINGTON, May 15—Dwight L. Chapin, President Nixon's former appointments secretary, was sentenced today to a minimum of 10 months in prison for lying to a Watergate grand jury about political sabotage in the 1972 campaign.

Judge Gerhard A. Gesell imposed two concurrent sentences of 10 to 30 months each, calling it "a punishment sentence for a man who is not likely to repeat and needs no rehabilitation."

When Judge Gesell read the sentence, Mr. Chapin was apparently unmoved as he stood before the bench in United States District Court here. On April 5, he was convicted by a jury on two counts of lying about his dealings with Donald H. Segretti, an old college friend. Mr. Chapin was acquitted on a third count, and a fourth count was dismissed during the trial.

"It appears to the court that your resort to the convenience of swearing falsely when called before a grand jury cannot be condoned," Judge Gesell told the 33-year-old defendant. "I have therefore decided you

Continued on Page 27, Column 4

Threats by Nixon Reported on Tape Heard by Inquiry

By DAVID E. ROSENBAUM
Special to The New York Times

WASHINGTON, May 15—The tape recording of President Nixon's Sept. 15, 1972, conversation with H. R. Haldeman and John W. Dean 3d, which was heard today by members of the House Judiciary Committee, contains at least one long passage that does not appear in the edited White House transcript of that tape, according to a committee source.

In the passage cited by the source, President Nixon threatens to punish The Washington Post and its attorney, Edward Bennett Williams, and notes specifically that The Post owns television stations.

There is the clear implication, according to the source, that the President hoped to take Government action to deprive The Post of its television licenses.

The Post won a Pulitzer Prize last year for its many disclosures about the Watergate case and other scandals in the Nixon Administration.

Reading from a copy of the transcript prepared by the impeachment inquiry staff, the

Continued on Page 26, Column 1

SCHEEL IS ELECTED PRESIDENT IN BONN

Coalition Proves Strength in First-Ballot Victory — Bitterness Dissipates

By CRAIG R. WHITNEY
Special to The New York Times

BONN, May 15—Walter Scheel was elected to the ceremonial office of the West German presidency today in a demonstration of solidarity between the two governing coalition parties, Mr. Scheel's Free Democrats and the Social Democrats.

The 54-year-old Mr. Scheel, who has been Vice Chancellor and Foreign Minister in the coalition Government since 1969, won a comfortable majority—530 of the 1,036 votes in the presidential electoral college on the first ballot. The fourth President since the formation of the West German Federal Republic in 1949, he is the first to be chosen so easily.

It was clear that despite bickering and fears of a revolt by some Social Democrats because of the resignation of their leader, Willy Brandt, from the chancellorship last week in the wake of a divisive spy scandal, the coalition was holding firmly together. There were only five abstentions and three absences. Mr. Scheel's opponent, Richard von Weizsäcker, received 498 votes, three fewer

Installation in Lisbon

Gen. António de Spínola took office as President of Portugal and named a left-leaning Government promising democracy, at home and in Portuguese Africa. Details on Page 3.

TERROR AT SCHOOL

Soldiers Rush Building as Attempt to Trade Prisoners Fails

By TERENCE SMITH
Special to The New York Times

MAALOT, Israel, May 15—A day of terror ended in this northern town this evening with a savage, 10-minute burst of gunfire and grenade explosions that killed three Arab terrorists and 16 of the high-school students they were holding hostage.

Early this morning, terrorists took command of the school, where about 90 students out on an excursion were sleeping. The three Arabs demanded the release of 20 prisoners held by Israel in return for the lives of the students.

An Israeli attempt to meet the demand failed and, as the deadline set by the guerrillas approached, soldiers rushed the school.

On 26th Independence Day

In the fighting that ensued, besides those killed 70 students were wounded, at least nine seriously. In the morning, as the day's terror began, a family of three was cut down by the Arab guerrillas as they entered the town. One soldier was also killed.

It was one of the bloodiest terrorist incidents in Israel's troubled history and it came on the 26th anniversary of the nation's independence.

After the decision to rush the school had been made, soldiers in bullet-proof vests surrounded the three-story building while snipers trained their sights on its shallow horizontal windows.

The firing broke out suddenly, while an officer with an electric megaphone was still pleading with the guerrillas in Arabic to postpone their 6 P.M. deadline.

Two of the three Arabs were hit by the opening burst of fire. One was apparently killed instantly, but the second had the strength to turn his automatic weapon on the students, spraying the second-story classroom indiscriminately.

Sought to Explode School

The third man tossed two grenades out the windows in an attempt to scatter the attacking soldiers. Then, according to one of the officers, the terrorist raced downstairs toward the entrance of the school where explosive charges had been placed. Before he could detonate them, soldiers shot him.

The screams of the terrified teen-agers could be heard a hundred yards away as the shooting erupted. One girl shrieked over and again, "Up here, he's up here," pointing to the wounded terrorist who was still firing.

Even before the shooting

Continued on Page 18, Column 3

SETBACK IS SEEN IN PEACE EFFORTS

Moves for a Compromise on Israeli-Syrian Troops Are Called Impaired

Special to The New York Times

JERUSALEM, May 15—The terrorist attack at Maalot today forced Secretary of State Henry A. Kissinger to suspend his Middle East peace efforts for one day.

The attack, which occupied the Israeli Cabinet through the day, was denounced by Mr. Kissinger as "this mindless and irrational action." The Secretary made it clear to his aides that he was determined not to let it undermine the progress made so far in this current Middle East negotiating trip.

But the tragic events at Maalot were viewed by both Israeli and American officials as probably having the effect of impairing his efforts to extract any last-minute compromises from either Israel or Syria on disengagement on the Syrian front before his scheduled return to Washington over the weekend.

Mr. Kissinger had been slated to meet with Israeli officials, led by Premier Golda Meir, this morning after an Israeli Cabinet meeting scheduled to discuss Israel's final ideas on disengagement to be conveyed by Mr. Kissinger to Syrian officials.

But this morning, when the dimensions of the terrorist attack became known, Mr. Kissinger put off his plans to leave Israel for Syria, preferring to wait until Mrs. Meir and other Israeli officials could deal with the disengagement problems.

Israeli officials, who spoke from time to time with Mr.

Continued on Page 19, Column 4

Mrs. Meir Pledges Steps To Protect Israeli People

By BERNARD GWERTZMAN
Special to The New York Times

JERUSALEM, May 15—Premier Golda Meir promised a reverse her long-standing policy of not negotiating with terrorists. The Government was prepared to release 23 prisoners in return for the safety of the approximately 90 teen-aged hostages held by three Arab terrorists, the Premier said.

But the deal fell apart, she said, partly out of confusion, when the three terrorists insisted on a code word to begin negotiations. The code word never arrived from abroad for use by the French or Rumanian Ambassadors, who were prepared to begin discussions, she said.

Talking in a firm voice that occasionally faltered, and look-

Israel, she said, will "do everything in its power to cut off the hands that want to harm a child, an adult, a settlement, a town or a village."

Speaking on television, Mrs. Meir went into detail about the "bitter day for all of us" that resulted in the death of three Arab terrorists and 16 teen-aged Israelis in the village of Maalot.

It was clear that despite

Continued on Page 18, Column 5

SANDRA Lee Church graduated from Columbia University (A.B.) yesterday.—Advt.

Nid Nertzberg is President of the Jack Keller Div of WILLCOX & GIBBS WG-AMEX-Advt.

"All the News That's Fit to Print"

The New York Times

LATE CITY EDITION

Weather: Sunny, mild today; cool tonight. Sunny, pleasant tomorrow. Temp. range: today 66-83; Friday 73-93. Highest Temp.-Humi. Index yesterday: 81. Details on Page 62.

VOL. CXXIII..No. 42,546

© 1974 The New York Times Company

NEW YORK, SATURDAY, JULY 20, 1974

15 CENTS

TURKEY LANDS AN ARMED FORCE IN CYPRUS; DROPS PARATROOPERS INTO NICOSIA SECTOR

Doar Urges Committee to Vote for Nixon's Impeachment

5 MAJOR CHARGES

G.O.P. Counsel Backs Appeal to Committee for Senate Trial

By JAMES M. NAUGHTON
Special to The New York Times

WASHINGTON, July 19—The House Judiciary Committee's senior counsels to both the Democrats and Republicans urged the committee today to recommend a Senate trial of President Nixon on one or more of five central impeachment charges.

John M. Doar, the special counsel to the Democrats, told the committee as it began im-

Text of proposed articles of impeachment, Pages 17, 18.

peachment deliberations that he could not remain "indifferent" if President Nixon or any other President committed the "terrible deed of subverting the Constitution."

The special Republican counsel, Albert E. Jenner Jr., endorsed Mr. Doar's conclusions by admonishing the committee to live up to the standards set by the nation's founders.

29 Potential Articles

Mr. Doar submitted to the panel 29 potential articles of impeachment—some drafted by the committee staff and others proposed by committee members—that represented various approaches to the following five fundamental allegations against Mr. Nixon:

¶Obstruction of justice in the Watergate and related scandals.
¶Abuse of Presidential power in dealings with Government agencies.
¶Contempt of Congress and the courts through the defiance of subpoenas for evidence.
¶Failure to adhere to an explicit constitutional duty to "take care that the laws be faithfully executed."
¶Denigration of the Presidency through underpayment of Federal income taxes and use of Federal funds to improve personal property.

Harsh Judgments Suggested

Along with the 29 potential charges against Mr. Nixon, Mr. Doar submitted a thick volume outlining a summary of the inquiry's key findings and suggesting harsh judgments about the President's conduct both before and after the 1972 Watergate burglary. [Page 19.]

The proposed impeachment articles drafted at Mr. Doar's direction contained language accusing the President of "having made it his policy to cover up and conceal responsibility" for the Watergate break-in at Democratic headquarters in June, 1972. Mr. Nixon was said to have furthered the alleged conspiracy through such means

Continued on Page 18, Column 4

Ziegler Condemns A 'Kangaroo Court'

By PHILIP SHABECOFF
Special to The New York Times

SAN CLEMENTE, Calif., July 19—In its harshest attack yet on the House Judiciary Committee, the White House accused the committee's counsel today of conducting a "kangaroo court" and challenged the right of its chief counsel to present articles of impeachment against President Nixon.

Ronald L. Ziegler, the White House press secretary, charged that the committee had made "a total shambles out of what should have been a fair proceeding."

Talking to reporters outside the President's office here, Mr. Ziegler accused the chairman of the committee, Peter W. Rodino Jr. of New Jersey, of "falsely presenting a picture of fairness."

Later, at a news briefing,

Continued on Page 19, Column 5

United Press International

Prince Juan Carlos de Borbón signing Spanish-American declaration in first official act as chief of state. At ceremony was Adm. Horacio Rivero, right, U.S. Ambassador.

House Unit Releases Data On I.T.T. and Milk Affair

Antitrust Suit Inquiry

By E. W. KENWORTHY
Special to The New York Times

WASHINGTON, July 19—The House Judiciary Committee published today voluminous documentation on the tangled web known as "the I.T.T. affair."

But no document substantiated conclusively an allegation that the Nixon Administra-

Excerpts from the committee evidence and White House responses on milk and I.T.T., Pages 12-16.

tion's settlement of an antitrust suit against the International Telephone and Telegraph Corporation was in return for the conglomerate's pledge of up to $400,000 for the Republican National Convention in 1972.

The settlement permitted the corporation to retain the Hartford Fire Insurance Company.

The allegation was at the core of the committee's inquiry as it pursued evidence of impeachable offenses, as it was at the core of the Senate Judiciary Committee's resumed hearings in March-April, 1972, on the nomination of Richard G. Kleindienst to be Attorney General. In the 980 pages of the House committee's volume No. 5 of

Continued on Page 19, Column 1

Price Supports Studied

By WILLIAM ROBBINS
Special to The New York Times

WASHINGTON, July 19—President Nixon disclosed his decision to raise milk-price supports in 1971 after listening to an exposition by John B. Connally on political and economic considerations and on dairy cooperatives' potential for campaign funding, a new transcript released by the House Judiciary Committee showed today.

The President's decision became clear, according to the document, early in a White House discussion on the afternoon of March 23, 1971, after Mr. Connally, then Secretary of the Treasury, had said that Congress would probably raise milk-price supports if the Administration did not and told Mr. Nixon:

"If you do [veto the increase], you've cost yourself the money—you've lost your political advantage."

A short while later, the transcript shows, Mr. Nixon said:

"Under the circumstances, I think the best thing to do is to just uh, relax and enjoy it."

Then, Mr. Nixon, Mr. Connally and other aides then discussed a delay in making a public an-

Continued on Page 19, Column 3

Justices' Ruling on Tapes May Follow Vote by Panel

By WARREN WEAVER Jr.
Special to The New York Times

WASHINGTON, July 19—The Supreme Court may be unable or unwilling to hand down a decision in the Nixon tapes case until after the House Judiciary Committee has voted late next week whether to recommend the impeachment of President Nixon.

Whichever way the Justices decide, their ruling is expected to have a substantial impact on the impeachment proceedings, either upholding the President's unlimited concept of his authority or requiring him to surrender evidence that might further incriminate him and his former colleagues.

The case was argued on July 8, and Court officials said today that a decision could not be expected until next Tuesday at the earliest. One source predicted that the decision might not be handed down next week, which would postpone it until after the Judiciary Committee voting is over.

"I can't exclude that possibility, although I'm not signaling it," Barrett McGurn, the Court information officer, said.

Congressional leaders believe that a Supreme Court ruling

against the President could influence several undecided Republican members of the committee to vote for impeachment. In turn, the number of Republicans who support impeachment at the committee level is expected to have considerable influence on the size of the Republican vote in the House.

Conversely, if the Justices support President Nixon's refusal to surrender 64 more White House tapes to Federal District Judge John J. Sirica and order Mr. Nixon's name stricken from the Watergate cover-up indictment, the decision could stiffen committee

Continued on Page 19, Column 2

NEWS INDEX

FRANCO DELEGATES POWERS AS RULER TO JUAN CARLOS

Gravely III Spanish Leader, 81, Issues Decree That Delegates Authority

By HENRY GINIGER
Special to The New York Times

MADRID, July 19—The ailing Generalissimo Francisco Franco, his condition suddenly worsened, delegated his powers as ruler of Spain today to his designated successor, Prince Juan Carlos de Borbón.

From the clinic where he has been under treatment for phlebitis for 10 days, the 81-year-old chief of state issued a decree that interrupted for the first time his 35 years of dominion over his people, in favor of the 36-year-old heir to a throne that has been vacant since 1931.

The six doctors treating General Franco, after talking at noon of a "setback" caused by "gastric complications," acknowledged tonight that he had vomited blood early this morning. The bulletin at 8:30 P.M. said the bleeding had been checked and that all body functions continued within normal limits. It was believed that anticoagulants, administered to inhibit blood clots in the leg, had caused internal hemorrhaging.

Pio Cabanillas, Minister of Information, said tonight that the news from the general's bedside was satisfactory. He praised the calm of the Spanish people but throughout the day and evening members of the Franco family and dignitaries of the Government indicated their alarm by streaming in general's wife, Carmen, has been staying in a room adjoining his.

General Franco acted under Article 11 of Spain's Organic Laws, which states that in case of absence or illness of the chief of state, the royal heir will assume his duties. But there was a strong feeling in the excited Spanish political world that the end of a long and often bitter era was at hand and that a new chapter in Spanish history was about to open.

Speculation about a possible momentous change, eagerly awaited by some Spaniards, feared by others, had begun the moment General Franco entered the modern hospital named for him in northern Madrid on July 9. There had been frequent meetings between the general, the prince and other officials concerning a temporary delegation of power. But optimistic medical bulletins, backed by photographs published for the first time yes-

Continued on Page 3, Column 4

CONSUMER PRICES UP 1% FOR MONTH

Yearly Increase 11.1%; Rise in Food Slows— Real Earnings Down

By EILEEN SHANAHAN
Special to The New York Times

WASHINGTON, July 19—Consumer prices rose by 1 per cent in June, despite a slowdown in the pace of the rise of food prices, the Labor Department reported today.

The June rise brought the index to a level that was 11.1 per cent higher than in June a year ago.

In the New York-Northeastern New Jersey-Long Island area, prices rose nine-tenths of 1 per cent from the prior month and 10.6 per cent from a year ago, according to the Bureau of Labor Statistics.

The yearly increase was the largest in 27 years, said Herbert Bienstock, regional head of the bureau.

Meat Prices Down

Nationally, although there was a decline in the prices of some food items, particularly meats, the drop was less than is normally expected in June. Thus, the Labor Department's seasonally adjusted statistics, which eliminate the effects of normal seasonal changes in an attempt to focus on basic trends, showed a rise of three-tenths of 1 per cent in food prices.

The food price trend was the best for this year except for April, when seasonally adjusted food prices declined.

The prices of all commodities other than food in the index,

Continued on Page 36, Column 2

Brasco Convicted of Conspiracy To Take Truck-Contract Bribes

By ARNOLD H. LUBASCH

Representative Frank J. Brasco was convicted last night of conspiracy to take bribes to get a Post-Office contract for a Mafia-controlled truck company.

The 41-year-old Brooklyn Democrat, whose first trial on the conspiracy charge resulted in a hung jury, bowed his head but maintained his composure when the guilty verdict was announced at the end of the month-long second trial in Federal District Court here.

His wife, Linda, who sat in the front row of the courtroom throughout the trial, moved quickly to Mr. Brasco's side and put her arms around his shoulders after the jury of five men and seven women reached the verdict following almost eight hours of deliberations.

Judge John M. Cannella set

Oct. 2 for sentencing Mr. Brasco, who faces up to five years in prison and a maximum fine of $10,000.

The short, solidly built Congressman, who served as an assistant district attorney in Brooklyn before he was elected to Congress in 1966, will appeal the verdict, according to his lawyer.

Mr. Brasco declined to comment when asked if he would withdraw from his current race for re-election in the 11th Con-

Continued on Page 11, Column 1

Soyuz Returns Safely

Two Soviet astronauts returned to earth safely after rehearsing docking techniques for next year's Soviet-American space mission. Page 62.

United Press International

Premier Bulent Ecevit announcing invasion in Ankara

U.S. Says Soviet Alerted Seven Airborne Divisions

By JOHN W. FINNEY
Special to The New York Times

WASHINGTON, July 19—Defense Department officials said today that the Soviet Union had put seven airborne divisions on alert.

American officials said that the eventual Soviet military intentions remained unclear and the Administration chose to make no announcement of the Soviet action and ordered no reciprocal alert for American forces.

[In Moscow qualified analysts said that there were indications that the Soviet Union might have placed one division on alert, and probably not more than that.]

As analyzed by Defense Department officials, the Turkish Government was following a deliberate, step-by-step strategy of seeming to indicate a willingness to take military action if no political solution could be reached.

The prevailing Pentagon view, however, was that the Turkish Government was not intent on rushing troops to Cyprus and had little military capability to carry out such action.

Turkey has a small number of amphibious craft, most of those small, open boat not suitable for carrying troops across long stretches of open water. As a result, officials believed Turkish forces would have considerable difficulty mounting an invasion against any resistance from pro-Greek forces on

that detailed the direct involvement of the Greek junta in the Cyprus coup. [Page 8.]

Discussing the Soviet alert, some officials speculated that Moscow was trying to demonstrate its support if Turkey made any move to intervene militarily on Cyprus. According to well-placed officials, there were indications that the Soviet Union had suggested to the Ankara Government that it could count on Soviet support.

Diplomatically, the United States applied pressure today on both the Greek and Turkish Governments in an effort to avoid a military clash between the two Atlantic alliance allies.

Undersecretary of State Joseph Sisco flew into Athens for meetings with Greek civilian and military leaders, and then rushed to Ankara for more talks there.

And in Washington, the State Department announced that Secretary of State Kissinger would meet on Monday with Archbishop Makarios. At the same time, American officials said that the United States Embassy in Athens recently sent a cablegram to Mr. Kissinger

Continued on Page 8, Column 2

3d City Audit Is Believed To Be Most Devastating

By MAURICE CARROLL

Mayor Beame called back yesterday the top team that served him when he was City Controller to try to blunt the impact of still a third audit report from his successor. At City Hall the latest report was said to be "even more devastating" than the first two, which have caused the Mayor profound embarrassment.

The third report deals with the management of $6.7-billion in pension funds. It is due to be made public next week by Controller Harrison J. Goldin, whose aides carefully guarded preliminary draft copies yesterday.

From what the Beame aides have been able to ferret out, the report "comes down hard on bad management," according to one Beame campaign slogan in City Hall.

Proud of his record and well aware of the source of his political reputation, Mr. Beame was upset by the two previous reports, which charged:

¶There was $5.4-million less in a vault holding security deposits from people doing work for the city than the dog-eared handwritten ledgers said should be there. Mr. Goldin

It would say, these sources suggested, that the investment pattern under Mr. Beame had been unimaginative and unproductive and that opportunities to earn money for the retirement funds had been missed.

If so, that will be an ironic comment, because one of Mr. Beame's boasts as Controller was that he had begun exchanging low-yield city bonds held by the pension funds for high-interest stocks, taking a short-term loss on the value change to increase the long-run yield.

Mr. Beame, whose mayoral campaign featured the slogan "If you don't know the buck, you don't know the job," was jolted personally as well as politically by the earlier reports.

would criticize his failure to reconcile city records with bank records by several hundreds of thousands of dollars, would criticize the use of handwritten ledgers—instead of computers—to keep track of investments and would urge that a more seasoned team be put in charge of pension investments.

Continued on Page 32, Column 2

CLASHES REPORTED

Capital's Airport and Northern Port Are Bombed

By NAN ROBERTSON
Special to The New York Times

ANKARA, Turkey, Saturday, July 20—Premier Bulent Ecevit announced today that Turkey had invaded Cyprus by sea and air.

The attack came after intensive diplomatic activity involving officials of Turkey, Britain and the United States had broken down. The crisis grew out of the overthrow Monday of the elected Cypriot Government of Archbishop Makarios by the Greek-officered Cypriote National Guard.

The Turkish Premier, his voice trembling with emotion, announced the invasion after meeting with Under Secretary of State Joseph Sisco of the United States at 2 A.M. today, Ankara time (7 P.M., Friday, New York time). Mr. Sisco had flown here from Athens last night to try to avert war.

Bombing Reported

[Turkish forces strafed and bombed the northern port of Kyrenia and dropped paratroopers into Turkish-Cypriote areas near Nicosia, the capital, Reuters reported.

[Turkish planes bombed Nicosia airport and a Cypriote National Guard camp south of the capital. Other Turkish jets dropped bombs and rockets on a camp of the small Greek army contingent in Cyprus on the western side of Nicosia.

[Machine-gun fire and explosions were heard from many directions around the capital, and Turkish Air Force planes flew overhead.

[The Cyprus radio broadcast an appeal to all Greek Cypriot with weapons to resist the Turkish invaders, and the Turkish Cypriote radio said that a Greek Cypriote gunboat had been sunk off Kyrenia.

[In San Clemente, Calif., President Nixon conferred late last night with Secretary of State Kissinger as soon as he received news that Turkish troops had landed in Cyprus, Reuters reported. The Presidential press secretary, Ronald L. Ziegler, said that "we are following the situation" but made no other comment.]

[The Pentagon ordered the United States carrier Forrestal and other naval vessels toward Cyprus in case American citizens in the area needed to be evacuated, The Associated Press reported.]

Premier Ecevit said that the decision to intervene in Cyprus

Continued on Page 8, Column 1

U.N. Calls Session Today About Cyprus

By Reuters

UNITED NATIONS, N.Y. Saturday, July 20—The Turkish troop landing in Cyprus will top the agenda at a Security Council meeting scheduled for 11 A.M. today.

One Western diplomat predicted a cease-fire all would be the logical first order of business.

The Security Council had been scheduled to meet today to consider a resolution calling for the withdrawal of the Greek Army officers serving with the Cyprus National Guard that toppled the Makarios Government last Monday.

By KATHLEEN TELTSCH
Special to The New York Times

UNITED NATIONS, N.Y., July 19—Archbishop Makarios, the deposed President of Cyprus appealed to the United Nations

Continued on Page 9, Column 4

The New York Times

LATE CITY EDITION

Sunny and pleasant today; fair and seasonable tonight and tomorrow.
Temp. range: today 70-83. Saturday 68-81. Highest Temp.-Hum. Index yesterday 74. Details on Page 51.

SECTION ONE

VOL.CXXIII.. No.42,554   © 1974 The New York Times Company   NEW YORK, SUNDAY, JULY 28, 1974   20c beyond 50-mile zone from New York City, except Long Island. Higher in air delivery cities.   60 CENTS

HOUSE PANEL, 27-11, ASKS IMPEACHMENT OF NIXON FOR OBSTRUCTION OF JUSTICE

TURKS' PROPOSAL RESTORES HOPES AT CYPRUS TALKS

Athens Gets U.S. Assurance of Support for All Efforts for Peaceful Solution

By FLORA LEWIS
Special to The New York Times

GENEVA, July 27—American assurances to Athens and a Turkish compromise proposal revived hope today that the three-nation conference here could reach an agreement on enforcing the cease-fire in Cyprus and open the way for further negotiations.

The conference nearly broke down after its first substantive session yesterday, when the Greek Foreign Minister, George Mavros, said that he could not negotiate while Turkish forces continued advancing in Cyprus.

[On Cyprus, fighting abated as Turkish forces that had advanced to within four miles of the strategic village of Myrtou in the north held their ground and Greek reinforcements moved up from the west. Page 3.]

Turkish, Greek and British experts met late into the night attempting to draft a declaration that would satisfy both Greek requirements for an immediate guaranteed cease-fire and Turkish demands for future political change in Cyprus.

Meeting Put Over

It had been hoped that they would finish in time for their Foreign Ministers to meet tonight and approve and announce the results. But they were still working on a text said to be full of brackets—that is, alternate language without common agreement—at 11 P.M., and the scheduled ministers' session was put over to 11 A.M. tomorrow.

There still seemed to be fair confidence that something would be achieved, nonetheless, and that the conference would not have to break up in failure as was threatened yesterday.

Late last night, the Turkish Foreign Minister, Turan Gunes, presented a proposal combining cease-fire provisions and demands for political talks to Foreign Secretary James Callaghan of Britain, who has been acting as mediator here between Greece and Turkey.

Mr. Callaghan then gave the Turkish proposal to Mr. Mavros, who described it as "a great improvement" and relayed it to Athens.

Meanwhile, Greece's New Premier, Constantine Caramanlis, said that he had received a message and later a telephone call from Secretary of

Continued on Page 4, Column 1

Reinecke Convicted of Lie On I.T.T. Offer to G.O.P.

California Lieutenant Governor Found Guilty Over His Testimony at Hearing on Pledge to Convention in 1972

By E.W. KENWORTHY

WASHINGTON, July 27—Lieut. Gov. Ed Reinecke of California was found guilty by a Federal jury today of lying at a hearing in which the Senate Judiciary Committee delved into a corporation's pledge to help finance the Republican National Convention of 1972.

As Clayton D. Roth, foreman of the jury, said, "We find the defendant guilty," Jean Reinecke, wife of the 50-year-old Lieutenant Governor, gasped and said, "My God, no! No, he's not!"

Later, Mr. Reinecke, a Republican, called the verdict "a gross miscarriage of justice."

James E. Cox, his attorney, said that he would file post-trial motions for dismissal of

the indictment and also for a mistrial. He indicated, without directly saying so, that if these were denied by United States District Court Judge Barrington D. Parker, he would appeal on several grounds after the sentencing.

Sentencing is expected in about six weeks. Meanwhile, Mr. Reinecke will be free on his own recognizance. Conviction for perjury carries a maximum penalty of five years imprisonment or a fine of $2,000, or both, on each count. There was only one count before the jury.

Mr. Reinecke was indicted last April 3 on three counts of having lied to the Senate Judi-

Continued on Page 39, Column 5

Spinola Promises to Free Territories, Starting Now

By Reuters

LISBON, July 27—President António de Spínola today pledged Portugal to the principle of colonial independence and promised to start transferring power immediately to the people of the country's three African territories.

He told the nation in a televised broadcast that he had promulgated a new law permitting Portugal to free Mozambique, Angola and Portuguese Guinea, which since 1933 have been legally part of Portugal herself.

The President gave the most definite assurance so far that Portugal's new leaders, who took power after the coup on April 25, are prepared to accept the idea of outright independence for the African territories, where guerrilla war has raged for 13 years.

President Spínola had originally envisaged granting the overseas territories a wide measure of autonomy under the Portuguese flag — a concept rejected by all the African liberation movements.

The President today hinted that independence would not necessarily apply to all Portugal's colonies.

"We are ready from this moment to initiate the transfer of power to the people of the overseas territories considered suitable for this development, namely Guinea, Angola and Mozambique," he said.

This appeared to indicate that Portugal intended to retain possession of the Cape Verde Islands, strategically situated off the west coast of Africa. Afri-

Continued on Page 16, Column 7

Nation's Cities Fighting to Stem Growth

By GLADWIN HILL

On March 21, the city of St. Petersburg, Fla., adopted an ordinance requiring the last 25,000 people who had settled there to move out.

This extraordinary edict was rescinded only a fortnight later as manifestly unconstitutional and impractical.

But the incident epitomizes rapidly changing attitudes toward community growth. Countless communities around the country, far from welcom-

This is the first of a series of articles on community growth controls.

ing growth in the traditional bigger-is-better vein, now fear they are being overwhelmed by it and are moving hastily to stop it.

Limitations on growth, ranging from population ceilings to moratoriums on building permits, are proliferating by the day. Each place has its own reasons. Water supply and sewage treatment are over-

loaded. Open space or other environmental values are threatened. Taxpayers are outraged at the prospect of big new capital investments needed to provide community services for soaring populations.

But whatever the reasons for growth controls, however logical they may seem on a local basis, collectively they are confronting the nation with a difficult tangle of questions, questions perplexing to the real estate and construction industries, the legal world, civil rights advocates, demographers, planners, politicians and millions of people simply looking for homes. For example:

¶Upward of 50 million peo-

Continued on Page 30, Column 4

NIXON 'CONFIDENT'

Ziegler Sees a Lack of Evidence to Support Any Ouster Move

By PHILIP SHABECOFF
Special to The New York Times

SAN CLEMENTE, Calif., July 27—Ronald L. Ziegler, the White House press secretary, said today after the House Judiciary Committee voted in favor of the first article of impeachment that President Nixon still believed the full House of Representatives would reject any article of impeachment.

"The President remains confident that the full House will recognize that there simply is not the evidence to support his or any other article of impeachment and will not vote to impeach," Mr. Ziegler said in a statement issued here after the committee's vote. "He is confident because he knows he has committed no impeachable offense," the statement added.

Mr. Ziegler expressed similar sentiments at a news briefing earlier today.

No Comment on Debate

Mr. Ziegler said at the news briefing on the lawn of the office complex outside the walls of the President's estate here that neither Mr. Nixon nor his staff would comment on the committee debate on the impeachment articles.

Mr. Ziegler's confidence that any impeachment article would be voted down, he said, "is based on the firm belief that the House of Representatives will exercise its constitutional responsibilities with an open mind."

In response to questions, however, Mr. Ziegler said the White House has not counted votes in the House. He also said the White House would not lobby against the President's impeachment among members of Congress.

Mr. Ziegler told reporters that the President had not been following the House Judiciary

Continued on Page 37, Column 2

GOLDIN SAYS STAFF WAS ORDERED CUT

Contends Mayor Rejected Request for More Help— Cavanagh Disputes Him

By DAVID A. ANDELMAN

Controller Harrison J. Goldin said yesterday that he had asked Mayor Beame two days after taking office last January for an additional 80 staff members because the city's books appeared to be in such bad shape, but that the Mayor had turned down the request and instead ordered the Controller's staff cut by 50.

Deputy Mayor James A. Cavanagh denied in an interview that Mr. Goldin's staff was cut by 50. He said the Controller had asked for additional personnel and had been given authorization to fill 100 vacancies in the department.

Three hours later, Sidney J. Frigand, the Mayor's press secretary, said that Mr. Cavanagh had requested and "did not want to stand on that number — he is just not sure now how many vacancies were involved."

Reorganization Plan

Mr. Goldin added that, within the next month, he would present a comprehensive staff reorganization plan for the Controller's office that would include a larger staff and permit an extensive computerization of the city's books and financial records.

Meanwhile, three separate checks of the city's books were continuing over the weekend, and in many cases temporary summer help and volunteers were being used in a crash effort to find $5.4-million in missing securities and dis-

Continued on Page 17, Column 1

Worst Slump Since '50's Hits City Building Trade

By PAUL GOLDBERGER

New York's building industry finds itself today in its worst crisis since the early nineteen-fifties—and some say since the Depression.

After a construction boom in the city and in the surrounding region that lasted from the nineteen-sixties through the early nineteen-seventies, the industry is now suffering a major setback. The decline strikes a serious blow to New York's traditional role as a center for all aspects of the building industry, from architectural theorizing to nuts-and-bolts construction.

The problem is not limited to New York. Work is down sharply in Boston and on the West Coast, among other areas, and the building boom in Texas and in much of the South, where construction is still at

least moderately brisk, appears to have peaked.

But even though New York's situation is not unique, its long-time role as a center of architectural design work as well as a place of enormous building activity makes the problem all the more severe here.

The following figures indicate the decline:

¶The dollar value of construction projects in the New York area in the first five months of 1974 declined 20 per cent from the 1973 total for the period, from $1.022-billion to $822-million, according to the McGraw-Hill Information Systems Company.

¶There are 15,000 unem-

Continued on Page 42, Column 1

United Press International
Lawrence Hogan, left, Maryland Republican, and Walter Flowers, Alabama Democrat, before they joined majority of House Judiciary Committee voting for impeachment.

Impeachment Article I

Special to The New York Times

WASHINGTON, July 27—Following is the text of Article I of the proposed articles of impeachment:

ARTICLE I

In his conduct of the office of President of the United States, Richard M. Nixon, in violation of his constitutional oath faithfully to execute the office of President of the United States and, to the best of his ability, preserve, protect, and defend the Constitution of the United States, and in violation of his constitutional duty to take care that the laws be faithfully executed, has prevented, obstructed, and impeded the administration of justice, in that:

On June 17, 1972, and prior thereto, agents of the Committee for the Re-election of the President:

Committed unlawful entry of the headquarters of the Democratic National Committee in Washington, District of Columbia, for the purpose of securing political intelligence. Subsequent thereto, Richard M. Nixon, using the powers of his high office, engaged personally and through his subordinates and agents in a course of conduct or plan designed to delay, impede, and obstruct the investigation of such unlawful entry; to cover up, conceal and protect those responsible; and to conceal the existence and scope of other unlawful covert activities.

The means used to implement this course of conduct or plan have included one or more of the following:

[1]

Making or causing to be made false or misleading statements to lawfully authorized investigative officers and employees of the United States.

[2]

Withholding relevant and material evidence or information from lawfully authorized investigative officers and employees of the United States.

[3]

Approving, condoning, acquiescing in, and counseling witnesses with respect to the giving of false or misleading statements to lawfully authorized investigative officers and employees of the United States and false or misleading testimony in duly instituted judicial and Congressional proceedings.

[4]

Interfering or endeavoring to interfere with the conduct of investigations by the Department of Justice of the United States, the Federal Bureau of Investigation, the office of Watergate Special Prosecution Force, and Congressional committees.

[5]

Approving, condoning and acquiescing in the surreptitious payment of substantial sums of money for the purpose of obtaining the silence or influencing the testimony of witnesses, potential witnesses or individuals who participated in such illegal entry and other illegal activities.

[6]

Endeavoring to misuse the Central Intelligence Agency, an agency of the United States.

[7]

Disseminating information received from officers of the Department of Justice of the United States to subjects of investigations conducted by lawfully authorized investigative officers and employees of the United States, for the purpose of aiding and assisting such subjects in their attempts to avoid criminal liability.

[8]

Making false or misleading public statements for the purpose of deceiving the people of the United States into believing that a thorough and complete investigation had been conducted with respect to allegations of misconduct on the part of personnel of the executive branch of the United States and personnel of the Committee for the Re-election of the President, and that there was no involvement of such personnel in such misconduct; or

[9]

Endeavoring to cause prospective defendants, and individuals duly tried and convicted, to expect favored treatment and consideration in return for their silence or false testimony, or rewarding individuals for their silence or false testimony.

In all of this, Richard M. Nixon has acted in a manner contrary to his trust as President and subversive of constitutional government, to the great prejudice of the cause of law and justice and to the manifest injury of the people of the United States.

Wherefore Richard M. Nixon, by such conduct, warrants impeachment and trial, and removal from office.

A HISTORIC CHARGE

6 Republicans Join 21 Democrats in Vote for Resolution

By JAMES M. NAUGHTON
Special to The New York Times

WASHINGTON, July 27—The House Judiciary Committee voted tonight, 27 to 11, to recommend the impeachment of President Nixon on a charge that he personally engaged in "course of conduct" designed to obstruct justice in the Watergate case.

This historic charge, the first to be lodged against a President by a House investi-

Committee Vote, Page 34.
Debate, Pages 34 and 35;

gating body since 1868, set in motion the constitutional process by which Mr. Nixon could ultimately be stripped of his office.

The charge became official when, at 5 minutes and 21 seconds after 7 o'clock tonight, Peter W. Rodino Jr., the committee's Democratic chairman, his head bobbing gently, said "Aye," and ended the committee's decisive roll-call. He then adjourned the deliberations until 10:30 A.M. Monday.

The margin of the vote, with six of the committee's Republicans joining all 21 Democrats in adoption of the resolution, seemed certain to set a pattern for debate in the full House next month on the charge.

The six Republicans who voted for impeachment were Tom Railsback of Illinois, Hamilton Fish Jr. of upstate New York, Lawrence J. Hogan of Maryland, M. Caldwell Butler of Virginia, William S. Cohen of Maine and Harold V. Froehlich of Wisconsin.

Two More Articles

Mr. Nixon would be subjected to a trial by the Senate should a majority of the House vote to approve the article of impeachment, or either of two other articles the Judiciary Committee is expected to debate and, in all likelihood, adopt early next week. Should any one of the charges be proved to the satisfaction of two-thirds of the Senate, the President would be removed from office.

Specifically, the committee charged that the President, in violation of his constitutional oath to uphold the law, "engaged personally and through his subordinates or agents in a course of conduct or plan designed to delay, impede, and obstruct the investigation" of the ill-fated burglary of the Democratic headquarters in the Watergate complex on June 17, 1972.

The article of impeachment listed nine methods by which he was alleged to have carried out the plan to obstruct justice.

They included accusations

Continued on Page 36, Column 1

ARCHAEOLOGY BUFFS! Tour Egypt & Israel with the Experts. 725-7251. Advert.

Steele Nominated by Connecticut G.O.P.

By LAWRENCE FELLOWS
Special to The New York Times

HARTFORD, July 27 — United States Representative Robert H. Steele won a first-ballot victory over three other contenders today to capture the Republican nomination for Governor of Connecticut.

"I feel great, I really feel great," the maverick, 35-year-old Congressman from Vernon said as he made his way through well-wishers backstage at Bushnell Memorial Hall, the convention site.

The convention picked James H. Brannen of Colchester to run against Senator Abraham A. Ribicoff, who is seeking his third sixth-year term in the United States Senate. Mr. Brannen is the first black candidate nominated by either party for the Senate in Connecticut.

Mr. Brannen, a freshman member of the Connecticut House of Representatives, is an airline pilot and a fiery, enthusiastic politician who does not subscribe to the argument that Senator Ribicoff is unbeatable.

"Abe is beaten," Mr. Bran-

Continued on Page 46, Column 1

United Press International
Robert H. Steele on winning gubernatorial nomination

"All the News That's Fit to Print"

The New York Times

LATE CITY EDITION

Weather: Sunny and warm today; fair and mild tonight, tomorrow. Temp. range: today 66-85; Monday 66-85. Highest Temp.-Hum. Index yesterday: 75. Details on Page 66.

VOL. CXXIII..No. 42,563   © 1974 The New York Times Company   NEW YORK, TUESDAY, AUGUST 6, 1974   20c beyond 50-mile radius of New York City, except Long Island. Higher in air delivery cities.   15 CENTS

NIXON ADMITS ORDER TO HALT INQUIRY ON WATERGATE 6 DAYS AFTER BREAK-IN; EXPECTS IMPEACHMENT; SUPPORT EBBS

SENATORS GLOOMY

G.O.P. Leaders See Defense Weakened in Case of Trial

By CHRISTOPHER LYDON
Special to The New York Times

WASHINGTON, Aug. 5—Key Republican Senators said today that President Nixon's latest release of Watergate transcripts would weaken his defense in what they expect may be an expedited Senate trial.

Senator Robert P. Griffin of Michigan, the Republican whip in the Senate, early in the day had called on the President to resign. After Mr. Nixon's announcement about the tapes, the Senator expressed disappointment that the President seemed determined to force a trial in the Senate.

Senator Robert Dole of Kansas said: "I just think he loses. I just think everything is downhill." He spoke while standing with half a dozen colleagues around a television set in the Senate Republican cloakroom to hear the news of further tapes of White House conversations "at variance," in Mr. Nixon's words, "with certain of my previous statements."

'Set of Inconsistencies'

Senator Pete V. Domenici of New Mexico said: "It's another set of inconsistencies. The whole thing weakens the position of the President substantially."

Senator John G. Tower of Texas quoted from the poetry of Greek tragedy: "And now a wave of melancholy tranquility settles over Thebes," he said.

Senator Peter H. Dominick of Colorado called the President's statement "sorrowful news."

The five Republicans were all included among the 34 Senators whom the White House has been counting on as being needed to vote against Mr. Nixon's removal from office. But they and others were saying today that no votes in support of the President could be taken for granted any longer.

Backing Found Dissolving

And while all denied that any nose counts had been taken, Senators in a broad political spectrum observed that Mr. Nixon's backing was dissolving rapidly. One senior Republican observed this morning, before the report of the new tapes was released, that all but a half-dozen of the 43 Republicans in the Senate would heave a sigh of relief if Mr. Nixon decided to resign.

In the Senate, Mr. Nixon's statement was read as giving license to anguished Republicans in the House to vote for impeachment, if only to bring on the Senate trial that the President described as inevitable.

The President's analysis that

Continued on Page 17, Column 5

Senator Robert Dole
"I just think he loses"

Senator Robert P. Griffin
Sadly advises resignation

Rep. Charles E. Wiggins
"Facts . . . have now changed"

Rep. Thomas P. O'Neill Jr.
Forecasts impeachment

Wiggins For Impeachment; Others in G.O.P. Join Him

By DAVID E. ROSENBAUM
Special to The New York Times

WASHINGTON, Aug. 5 — Representative Charles E. Wiggins, President Nixon's strongest defender during the House Judiciary Committee's impeachment proceedings, and many other influential House Republicans announced today that they would vote for impeachment.

Mr. Wiggins, members of the House Republican leadership

Text of Wiggins statement is printed on Page 17.

and one of the leaders of the Southern-conservative bloc in the House expressed a deep sense of disillusionment after the President conceded this afternoon that he had been an early participant in efforts to conceal the facts of the Watergate burglary.

After a day of hurriedly called caucuses and intense whispering in the corridors of the Capitol, Representative Thomas P. O'Neill Jr. of Massachusetts, the House majority leader, predicted that no more than 75 of the 435 Representatives would vote against impeachment.

Mr. O'Neill's assessment went unchallenged by those who had supported the President until today.

Two other Republicans on the Judiciary Committee who had voted against impeachment —Representative Wiley Mayne of Iowa and Representative Joseph J. Maraziti of New Jersey —also said that they would vote for impeachment on the charge of obstruction of justice.

Representative David W. Dennis, an Indiana Republican who supported the President unwaveringly during the impeachment votes, said tonight that, on the basis of the transcripts released by the White House today, "I intend to vote for Article I."

That article accuses Mr. Nixon of complicity in the Watergate cover-up.

Mr. Dennis said it was his impression, during a meeting this afternoon of the 10 Republican members of the Judiciary Committee who supported the President a few days ago on all three articles of impeachment, that "everybody seemed to have pretty much the same idea" about voting in favor of Article I.

He said this included Representatives Charles W. Sandman Jr. of New Jersey, who had

Continued on Page 17, Column 1

Goldin Stands By Charge on Scoppetta

By JOHN DARNTON

Cutting short his vacation abroad to return to his desk yesterday, Harrison J. Goldin promptly stood by his charges that the city's Investigations Commissioner had instructed a civil servant to make entries in city ledgers after the fact.

Mr. Goldin said he would repeat his charge against the

Text of Goldin's statement will be found on Page 40.

Commissioner "anyplace, anywhere," including before a grand jury. "I won't have to be subpoenaed," he said.

At a packed afternoon news conference, which he said he had called to "clear away the smoke screen which has been created," Mr. Goldin made the following points:

¶He defended the "careful and professional work" of the outside auditors who turned up the "discrepancy" of $5.4-million between the amount of securities in a city vault and the amount the ledgers had on record. The auditors, commissioned by Mr. Goldin, issued their report July 14.

¶He attacked as "assumptions and guesswork" the findings of a task force — headed by the Investigations Commissioner, Nicholas Scoppetta, and District Attorney Richard H. Kuh — that said last week it had easily resolved the discrepancy.

¶He said he "absolutely" stood by the charge he had made about Mr. Scoppetta in his letter of resignation to the way in which Mr. Scoppetta handled the public release of the audits on Thursday. Mr. Goldin later said under questioning that the "in-

struction," involving two entries that reconcile $642,000, might not have been made in so many words.

¶He said the entire dispute had been diverted into "side issues" and "personal animosities" and had become "not by my choice, a conflict over the public's right to know."

In another development, a professor of accountancy at Baruch College resigned as a member of the advisory committee that advised Mr. Goldin as a candidate and then drew up the specifications for the outside audits.

The professor, Abraham J. Briloff, objected in his letter of resignation to the way in which Mr. Goldin handled the public release of the audits last Thursday.

Continued on Page 40, Column 3

President's Statement About Disclosure

Special to The New York Times

WASHINGTON, Aug. 5—Following is a statement by President Nixon announcing his decision to make public the transcripts of three recorded conversations with H. R. Haldeman on June 23, 1972:

I have today instructed my attorneys to make available to the House Judiciary Committee, and I am making public, the transcripts of three conversations with H. R. Haldeman on June 23, 1972. I have also turned over the tapes of these conversations to Judge Sirica, as part of the process of my compliance with the Supreme Court ruling.

On April 29, in announcing my decision to make public the original set of White House transcripts, I stated, "as far as what the President personally knew and did with regard to Watergate and the cover-up is concerned, these materials—together with those already made available—will tell it all."

Shortly after that, in May, I made a preliminary review of some of the 64 taped conversations subpoenaed by the special prosecutor.

Among the conversations I listened to at that time were two of those of June 23. Although I recognized that these presented potential problems, I did not inform my staff or my counsel of it, or those arguing my case, nor did I amend my submission to the Judiciary Committee in order to include and reflect it. At the time, I did not realize the extent of the implications which these conversations might now appear to have. As a result, those arguing my case, as well as those passing judgment on the case, did so with information that was incomplete and in some respects erroneous. This was a serious act of omission for which I take full responsibility and which I deeply regret.

At Variance With Certain Statements

Since the Supreme Court's decision 12 days ago, I have ordered my counsel to analyze the 64 tapes, and I have listened to a number of them myself. This process has made it clear that portions of the tapes of these June 23 conversations are at variance with certain of my previous statements. Therefore, I have ordered the transcripts made available immediately to the Judiciary Committee so that they can be reflected in the committee's report, and included in the record to be considered by the House and Senate.

In a formal written statement on May 22 of last year, I said that shortly after the Watergate break-in I became concerned about the possibility that the F.B.I. investigation might lead to the exposure either of unrelated covert activities of the C.I.A. or of sensitive national security matters that the so-called "plumbers" unit at the White House had been working on because of the C.I.A. and plumbers connections of some of those involved. I said that I therefore gave instructions that the F.B.I. should be alerted to coordinate with the C.I.A. and to ensure that the investigation not expose these sensitive national security matters.

That statement was based on my recollection at the time — some 11 months later — plus documentary ma-

terials and relevant public testimony of those involved.

The June 23 tapes clearly show, however, that at the time I gave those instructions I also discussed the political aspects of the situation, and that I was aware of the advantages this course of action would have with respect to limiting possible public exposure of involvement by persons connected with the re-election committee.

My review of the additional tapes has, so far, shown no major inconsistencies with what I have previously submitted. While I have no way at this stage of being certain that there will not be others, I have no reason to believe that there will be. In any case, the tapes in their entirety are now in the process of being furnished to Judge Sirica. He has begun what may be a rather lengthy process of reviewing the tapes, passing on specific claims of executive privilege on portions of them, and forwarding to the special prosecutor those tapes or those portions that are relevant to the Watergate investigation.

Impeachment Virtually Certain

It is highly unlikely that this review will be completed in time for the House debate. It appears at this stage, however, that a House vote of impeachment is, as a practical matter, virtually a foregone conclusion, and that the issue will therefore go to trial in the Senate. In order to ensure that no other significant relevant materials are withheld, I shall voluntarily furnish to the Senate everything from these tapes that Judge Sirica rules should go to the special prosecutor.

I recognize that this additional material I am now furnishing may further damage my case, especially because attention will be drawn separately to it rather than to the evidence in its entirety. In considering its implications, therefore, I urge that two points be borne in mind.

The first of these points is to remember what actually happened as a result of the instructions I gave on June 23. Acting Director Gray of the F.B.I. did coordinate with Director Helms and Deputy Director Walters of the C.I.A. The C.I.A. did undertake an extensive check to see whether any of its covert activities could be compromised by a full F.B.I. investigation of Watergate. Deputy Director Walters then reported back to Mr. Gray, that they would not be compromised. On July 6, when I called Mr. Gray and when he expressed concern about improper attempts to limit his investigation, as the record shows, I told him to press ahead vigorously with his investigation — which he did.

The second point I would urge is that the evidence be looked at in its entirety, and the events be looked at in perspective. Whatever mistakes I made in the handling of Watergate, the basic truth remains that when all the facts were brought to my attention I insisted on a full investigation and prosecution of those guilty. I am firmly convinced that the record, in its entirety, does not justify the extreme step of impeachment and removal of a President. I trust that as the constitutional process goes forward, this perspective will prevail.

REPORT CRITICIZES EMBASSY IN SAIGON

Senate Study Says Mission Adheres Too Closely to South Vietnam's Line

By BERNARD GWERTZMAN
Special to The New York Times

WASHINGTON, Aug. 5 — A staff report issued today by the Senate Foreign Relations Committee criticizes the United States Embassy in Saigon for reports that were described as adhering too closely to the official line of the Saigon Government.

"Over the years," the study said, "the American Embassy in Saigon has acquired a reputation, among both official and unofficial observers, for close identification with the policies of the South Vietnamese Government and for selective reporting. These same tendencies are apparent today."

The 47-page report was prepared by Richard M. Moose and Charles E. Meissner, staff members, after a mission to Indochina from May 12 to June 4.

The report on Vietnam said that unless the big powers apply strong pressure, the South Vietnamese Government and the Communists will fail to reach a political settlement.

"The present military confrontation seems likely to continue," the report said, "with the South Vietnamese unable to expel the North Vietnamese

Continued on Page 4, Column 4

Nixon Ordered That the F.B.I. Be Told: 'Don't Go Any Further Into This Case'

By JOHN M. CREWDSON
Special to The New York Times

WASHINGTON, Aug. 5—Six days after the Watergate break-in, President Nixon, informed that his campaign director had urged the illegal bugging operation, ordered that the Federal Bureau of Investigation be told: "Don't go any further into this case period!"

The remark was made by Mr. Nixon in the Oval Office during a meeting on June 23, 1972, with H. R. Haldeman, then his chief of staff. A transcript of the conversation, recorded at the time, was one of three made public by the President today.

The transcripts of the conversations, all with Mr. Haldeman on June 23, contradict in

detail what the President was saying publicly about his knowledge of Watergate in the summer of 1972 and his later statement of noninvolvement in the cover-up of responsibility for the bugging.

According to the transcript of the recording, which had been withheld by Mr. Nixon from the House Judiciary Committee and the Watergate special prosecutor, Mr. Haldeman began the 90-minute meeting by telling the President that the F.B.I. "is not under control."

The agents, he told the President, had traced five checks that had been deposited two months earlier in the Florida bank account of Bernard L. Barker, one of the five burglars

arrested at the Democratic party's headquarters on June 17, 1972.

He also reported that the unsuccessful bugging and burglary operation had been carried out under "pressure" from John N. Mitchell, the former Attorney General and, at the time, the head of Nixon's re-election effort.

Agrees on Message

When Mr. Haldeman suggested that top officials of the Central Intelligence Agency be directed to tell the F.B.I. to stay out of the investigation of the checks, which had come to Mr. Barker from the Nixon campaign committee, Mr. Nixon replied, "Right, fine."

"You call them," he added. "Play it tough. That's the way they [the Democrats] play it, and that's the way we are going to play it."

For nearly two months after the June 23 conversations, Mr. Haldeman, the President remained silent on the Watergate matter.

Then on Aug. 22, 1972, in the midst of his re-election campaign, Mr. Nixon told reporters that he could say "categorically" that an investigation by John W. Dean 3d, then his counsel, "indicates that no one in the White House staff, no one in this Administration, presently employed, was involved in this very bizarre incident."

"What really hurts in matters of this sort," the President added, "is not the fact that they occur, because overzealous people in campaigns do things that are wrong. What really hurts is if you try to cover it

Continued on Page 16, Column 1

President Considered Resigning But Rejected Idea, Aides Assert

Special to The New York Times

WASHINGTON, Aug. 5—President Nixon seriously considered the possibility of resigning during a meeting at Camp David yesterday, but discarded it at least for the time being, White House officials said today.

In addition, the aides reportedly weighed another option—stepping aside under the 25th Amendment to enable Vice President Ford to succeed him on an interim basis. But that, too, was reportedly rejected.

It was only over the weekend, apparently, that Mr. Nixon's Watergate lawyer, James D. St. Clair, and the President's chief of staff, Gen. Alexander M. Haig Jr., learned

that the contents of the newly disclosed June 23 tape recordings contradicted statements the President had previously made.

Mr. St. Clair, according to a highly reliable authority, advised the President that he would have to correct the record.

In Mr. St. Clair's advice was the implication, although it was not stated, that he would be obliged to resign as his lawyer if the President did not set the record straight.

During the emergency meeting at the Catoctin Mountains in Maryland, Mr. Nixon was said to have received a gloomy

Continued on Page 18, Column 1

Cab Strike Averted

A possible taxi strike was averted last night for at least three days. Page 66.

TAPES RELEASED

President Still Hopeful That the Senate Will Vote for Acquittal

By JOHN HERBERS
Special to The New York Times

WASHINGTON, Aug. 5—In a sharp setback to his fight against impeachment, President Nixon admitted today that six days after the Watergate burglary he ordered a halt to the investigation of the break-in for political as well as national security reasons and that he kept the evidence from his lawyers and supporters on the House Judiciary Committee.

He made the admission in a statement accompanying the

Texts of three conversations appear on Pages 14 and 15.

release of transcripts of three conversations on June 23, 1972, which he said might further damage his case against impeachment. It is "virtually a foregone conclusion," the President added, that the House would vote to impeach him but he said he hoped the Senate would look at all the evidence "in perspective" and vote to acquit him.

G.O.P. Senators Briefed

James D. St. Clair, the President's chief lawyer, briefing Republican Senators on what he called "bad news," said that Mr. Nixon would not resign because the President felt it would be setting a precedent for removing future Presidents from office.

The President disclosed that he had tried to keep the Federal Bureau of Investigation from pursuing an investigation of the source of the money that financed the Watergate break-in. This was widely regarded in Congress as an admission of guilt to the charge of obstructing justice—a criminal offense—made in Article I of the committee's impeachment resolution. It was cited by several former supporters on the Judiciary Committee in announcing that they would now vote for impeachment.

Although Mr. Nixon's motives were not entirely clear, it was evident that in view of the fact that the information was to be made public later in an event, he chose to put his own interpretation on it, as he did in release of the first White House transcripts on April 30.

Use In House Debate

The three transcripts made public today were of conversations with the President's former chief of staff, H. R. Haldeman, six days after the Watergate burglary. They were among those Mr. Nixon has had turned over to Judge John J. Sirica under orders of the Supreme Court.

The President said he was making them public so they could be used by the House in its impeachment debate, tentatively scheduled to begin Aug. 19. He said Judge Sirica was reviewing the first of some 64 conversations and other materials subpoenaed for the trial of some of the Watergate defendants, adding that it was unlikely that the review would be completed in time for the House debate.

"It appears at this stage, however, that a House vote of impeachment is, as a practical

Continued on Page 15, Column 4

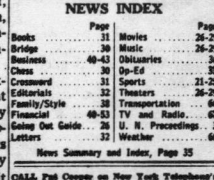

LATE CITY EDITION

"All the News
That's Fit to Print"

Weather: Partly cloudy today; cool
tonight. Fair, pleasant tomorrow.
Temp. range: today 65-78; Thursday
64-85. Highest Temp.-Hum. Index
yesterday: 75. Details on Page 66.

The New York Times

VOL. CXXIII..No. 42,566   © 1974 The New York Times Company   NEW YORK, FRIDAY, AUGUST 9, 1974   20c beyond 50-mile radius of New York City. except Long Island. Higher in air delivery cities   15 CENTS

NIXON RESIGNS

HE URGES A TIME OF 'HEALING';
FORD WILL TAKE OFFICE TODAY

'Sacrifice' Is Praised; Kissinger to Remain

By ANTHONY RIPLEY
Special to The New York Times

WASHINGTON, Aug. 8—
Vice President Ford praised
President Nixon tonight for
"one of the greatest personal
sacrifices for the country and
one of the finest personal decisions on behalf of all of us as
Americans."

Mr. Ford, who will take office as the 38th President at
noon tomorrow, vowed to continue Mr. Nixon's foreign policy
and announced that Secretary
of State Kissinger had agreed
to stay on in the new Administration.

"I pledge to you tonight, as

SPECULATION RIFE ON VICE PRESIDENT

Some Ford Associates Say Selecting a Successor Could Take Weeks

By CHRISTOPHER LYDON
Special to The New York Times

WASHINGTON, Aug. 8 — Po-
tentially the most revealing and
most important decision of
Gerald R. Ford's Presidential
debut — his choice of a successor in the Vice Presidency —
was a much-discussed mystery
here today.

Close friends of Mr. Ford
continued to feed speculation
about more than a dozen possible candidates. But none of
the friends claimed to have
discussed the Vice-Presidential
question with Mr. Ford or to
be speaking for him on it. A
number of Ford associates
thought he might hold off the
decision for days or even weeks.

"Everybody's on tenterhooks
up here," a Senator remarked
this afternoon in a telephone
interview from the Repablican
cloakroom, "but I think they're
wasting their time. It's going to
be a week or two. So far I'd
say he's a loner on this issue."

Former Defense Secretary
Melvin R. Laird, a Ford counselor in the House for more
than a decade, was being
quoted again today as saying he
believes that Nelson A. Rocke-

Continued on Page 4, Column 1

I will pledge to you tomorrow
and in the future, my best efforts in cooperation, leadership
and dedication to what's good
for America and good for the
world," he said.

The Vice President, who
never sought the nation's highest office and disclaimed any
intention of seeking it after Mr.
Nixon's term, will take the oath
of office in a private ceremony
at the White House.

Thus will he become the first
man to serve as President without being chosen by the American people in an election. Tomorrow night he will address
the nation on radio and television. It is expected that he
will speak at 6 P.M.

All day today the signs of
the historic change were in the
air, sensed by the crowds that
gathered along Pennsylvania

*Text of Mr. Ford's remarks
appears on Page 2.*

Avenue near the White House.
Applause rang out from the
crowds when Mr. Ford appeared
briefly.

After watching Mr. Nixon on
television tonight with his family, the Vice President stepped
outside into a slight drizzle at
his suburban split-level home
in nearby Alexandria, Va., to
face television cameras and
photographers assembled in the
street and about 100 cheering
neighbors.

Speaks Outside Home

Speaking without notes or a
prepared text, Mr. Ford pledged
to continue the Nixon foreign
policy and called the Secretary
of State "a very great man"
whom he has known for many
years.

On domestic policy, he said
that he had been "very fortunate in my lifetime" to have
adversaries in Congress but
said that he did not think he
had "a single enemy" there.

President Nixon had cited in
his resignation address his lack
of support in Congress as one
of the major reasons for his
resignation.

Mr. Ford said, "The net result is that I think tomorrow I
can start out working with
Democrats and with Republi-

Continued on Page 4, Column 3

Vice President Ford meeting with newsmen last night
The New York Times/William E. Sauro

President Nixon on TV as he announced his resignation
United Press International

POLITICAL SCENE SHARPLY ALTERED

G.O.P. Prospects Improved, Ford in Good Spot for '76 and Watergate Fades

By R. W. APPLE Jr.
Special to The New York Times

WASHINGTON, Aug. 8—
President Nixon's resignation
drastically altered the American
political landscape.

It improved Republican prospects for the Congressional
elections in November, thrust
Vice President Ford into the
favorite's role for the 1976
Presidential election, ended the
Watergate agony that has
served to bind together the
heterogeneous Democratic party
and removed from the political
stage the man who was the
dominant Republican for the
last 15 years.

In a larger sense, it seemed
to presage an era of more open
government, of more cooperation and less antagonism between Capitol Hill and the
White House and of decline of
the White House staff as an
independent power center.

Lives Are Altered

A kind of "honeymoon" be-
tween the executive and legislative branches was widely
predicted by Congressional
leaders today. Congressmen
who knew Mr. Ford for years
as a Capitol Hill colleague said
that they expected to work
closely with him.

At least in the beginning,
pragmatic conservatism is expected to remain the dominant
ideological tone in the executive
branch.

How that will be translated
into policies, and how those
policies will shape the political
dialogue, will not be clear for
weeks. But experts in the two
fields forecast an essentially
unchanged foreign policy and
a similar, but more carefully
and consistently applied, economic policy.

By his decision, Mr. Nixon

Continued on Page 6, Column 4

Rise and Fall
Appraisal of Nixon Career

By ROBERT B. SEMPLE Jr.

The central question is how
a man who so much could
have lost so much. How could a
public figure who so well per-
ceived the instincts of the majority of his countrymen have
misused the powers and duties
those same countrymen so eagerly ceded him?

The historians will be kept
busy on these questions, but
for those who spent their time
observing Mr. Nixon for the
last six years the answer may
well be found in a phrase he
often applied to himself. "At
bottom," he used to say, "I
am a political man."

By his own description, he
was a man of action rather
than contemplation, a tactician
rather than a theologian, a student of technique who seemed
always impatient with substance, a figure whose exceptional antennae seemed to
dwarf and even hide what lay
at the core.

To his enemies, he was both
manipulative and synthetic; to
his friends, a pragmatist unen-
cumbered by inflexible principles; to those who watched
him, a man who learned to run
before he had learned to walk

and who, on reaching his destination, was not always certain what to do when he got
there—except, perhaps, to keep
going.

That image has only been reinforced and deepened by the
transcripts of three conversations with H. R. Haldeman on
June 23, 1972, six days after the
Watergate break-in, which were
released on Aug. 5, and the edited transcripts of White House
conversations published April
30. Whatever history's judgment
of those tapes, this much was
clear: Faced with mounting evidence of deception and wrongdoing in his own official family,
he sought not to confront the
issue but to manipulate it until
he himself became part of the
deception.

Mr. Nixon used the words "I
am a political man" proudly, as
if to challenge the moralists;
but in the end they became
his epitaph—a possible explanation for both his success and
failure.

For if the words implied the
presence of a talent for finding
opportunities for political prof-

Continued on Page 11, Column 1

JAWORSKI ASSERTS NO DEAL WAS MADE

Says Nixon Did Not Ask for and Was Not Given a Way to Avoid Prosecution

By RICHARD D. LYONS
Special to The New York Times

WASHINGTON, Aug. 8—Leon
Jaworski, the special Watergate prosecutor, said tonight
after President Nixon's resignation speech that no deals had
been either made or offered
that would have given Mr.
Nixon immunity from prosecution on any charges that might
stem from the Watergate scandal.

"There has been no agree-
ment or understanding of any
sort between the President or
his representatives and the special prosecutor relating in any
way to the President's resignation," Mr. Jaworski said in a
statement issued by his office.

Mr. Jaworski's words, plus
the fact that the President made
no mention of the immunity issue in his address to the nation, left open the possibility,
at least for the moment, that
Mr. Nixon might be charged
and stand trial.

No Immunity Sought

Mr. Nixon did not ask for
any immunity assurances from
Mr. Jaworski before the resignation speech, the prosecutor
said, adding that none had been
offered.

As Mr. Jaworski put it, "The
special prosecutor's office was
not asked for any such agreement or understanding and offered none."

"Although I was informed of
the President's decision this
afternoon, my office did not
participate in any way in the
President's decision to resign,"
the statement concluded.

At the same time they spoke
hopefully of the Ford Administration and of moving urgently
to tasks long neglected—ending
the nation's political turmoil
and easing its economic distress.

Earlier today, there were
moves in both houses of Congress to grant Mr. Nixon immunity from prosecution, and

Continued on Page 2, Column 4

The 37th President Is First to Quit Post

By JOHN HERBERS
Special to The New York Times

WASHINGTON, Aug. 8—Richard Milhous Nixon, the 37th
President of the United States,
announced tonight that he
had given up his long and arduous fight to remain in office
and would resign, effective at
noon tomorrow.

At that hour, Gerald Rudolph Ford, whom Mr. Nixon
nominated for Vice President last Oct. 12, will be sworn
in as the 38th President, to serve out the 895 days remaining
in Mr. Nixon's second term.

Less that two years after his landslide re-election
victory, Mr. Nixon, in a conciliatory address on national

Text of the address will be found on Page 2.

television, said that he was leaving not with a sense of
bitterness but with a hope that his departure would start a
"process of healing that is so desperately needed in America."

He spoke of regret for any "injuries" done "in the course
of the events that led to this decision." He acknowledged
that some of his judgments had been wrong.

The 61-year-old Mr. Nixon, appearing calm and resigned
to his fate as a victim of the Watergate scandal, became the
first President in the history of the Republic to resign from
office. Only 10 months earlier Spiro Agnew resigned the
Vice-Presidency.

Speaks of Pain at Yielding Post

Mr. Nixon, speaking from the Oval Office, where his
successor will be sworn in tomorrow, may well have
delivered his most effective speech since the Watergate
scandals began to swamp his Administration in early 1973.

In tone and content, the 15-minute address was in sharp
contrast to his frequently combative language of the past,
especially his first "farewell" appearance—that of 1962, when
he announced he was retiring from politics after losing the
California governorship race and declared that the news
media would not have "Nixon to kick around" anymore.

Yet he spoke tonight of how painful it was for him to
give up the office.

"I would have preferred to carry through to the finish
whatever the personal agony it would have involved, and my
family unanimously urged me to do so," he said.

Puts 'Interests of America First'

"I have never been a quitter," he said. "To leave office
before my term is completed is opposed to every instinct in
my body." But he said that he had decided to put "the
interests of America first."

Conceding that he did not have the votes in Congress to
escape impeachment in the House and conviction in the
Senate, Mr. Nixon said, "To continue to fight through the
months ahead for my personal vindication would almost
totally absorb the time and attention of the President and
the Congress in a period when our entire focus should be
on the great issues of peace abroad and prosperity without
inflation at home."

"Therefore," he continued, "I shall resign the Presidency
effective at noon tomorrow. Vice President Ford will be

Continued on Page 3, Column 1

Only Nixon Is Serene At Sad White House

By PHILIP SHABECOFF
Special to The New York Times

WASHINGTON, Aug. 8—On
his 2,027th and penultimate day
as President of the United
States, with his staff and family
unable to conceal their anguish,
Richard M. Nixon went com-
posedly through the schedule
of a busy President.

He met with his Vice President and the bipartisan leadership of Congress. He appointed
Federal judges, accepted resignations from executive agencies
and signed executive laws.

He vetoed as inflationary an
appropriation bill for the Department of Agriculture and the
Environmental Protection
Agency.

He also announced, over national television, that tomorrow he would resign his high
office.

Mr. Nixon did not loosen his
self control even when he
talked of his "regret" and his
"sadness" at leaving the Presidency. His delivery, with its
familiar half-smiles, did not re-

flect the momentous message
he had for his audience: that
at noon tomorrow he would become the first healthy, living
American President to leave office before his term expired.

At 12:30 this afternoon, the
White House press secretary,
Ronald L. Ziegler, announced
that the President would address the nation at 9 P.M.

Mr. Ziegler did not say what
the speech would be about. He
did not have to. He choked on
his words several times and
was struggling visibly to keep
himself under control as he left
the rostrum of the packed but
hushed briefing room at the
White House.

The young women who work
in the press office went through
the motions of their jobs while
tears streamed down their
faces.

But the President himself, according to his appointments

Continued on Page 3, Column 6

The Other Major News

Wholesale Prices Up

A new upward surge of
farm prices joined a big jump
in industrial prices to produce
the year's largest monthly
increase in the wholesale
price index. The rise for July
was 3.7 per cent, seasonally
adjusted, and 3.9 per cent before adjustment. Page 45.

Election Bill Voted

The House approved by a
vote of 355 to 48 a broad
campaign-finance reform bill.
The measure would set limits
on political contributions, restrict candidate spending and
provide subsidies for Presidential primaries, conventions and elections. The bill
now goes to a House-Senate
conference committee. Page
36.

Cyprus Talks Open

The foreign ministers of
Greece, Turkey and Britain
met in Geneva to try to work
out an effective cease-fire on
Cyprus and to tackle the political problems behind the
fighting there. On Cyprus, acting President

Glafkos Clerides named a
moderate Cabinet stripped of
any militant proponents of
union with Greece.

Mr. Clerides, who will occupy the key posts of Foreign
Affairs and Interior, left for
Athens on his way to Geneva
for the talks on a political
settlement. Page 16.

10 Police Accused

Ten New York City police
sergeants were arrested for
allegedly participating in a
"club" that collected more
than $250,000 over a decade
from legitimate businesses and
illegal rackets operations in
Queens. Page 68.

Meskill Named Judge

Gov. Thomas J. Meskill of
Connecticut was nominated
by President Nixon for a
seat on the Federal bench.
Mr. Meskill, a Republican,
stunned the state Republican
party earlier this year by declining to run for a second
term amid reports that he
had been offered a judgeship.
Page 38.

A Tiny G.O.P. Bastion Feels Loss and Relief

By PRANAY GUPTE
Special to The New York Times

SHELTER ISLAND, L.I., Aug.
8—Six years after he put it on
his car, Evans K. Griffing sadly stripped off his bold, red-let-
tered bumper sticker today—
the one that said "NIXON."

Mr. Griffing felt a sense of
loss. So did hundreds of people
in this conservative community
100 miles east of New York
City.

In 1968 and 1972, Suffolk
County gave Richard M. Nixon
the largest single election plurality of any county in the
United States. Today all that
had changed on Shelter Island.

As the hour of the Presi-
dent's resignation announcement approached, many islanders expressed both a feeling of
hurt at having been "betrayed"
by Mr. Nixon and relief that
he was leaving office.

"We tried to stay by him
till the very end," said Thomas
L. Jernick, the Town Supervisor. "But when he disclosed
on Monday that he had covered

up his role in Watergate, we
couldn't support him any more.
He lied to us, and for a President of the United States to lie
is inexcusable."

"We really believed in Mr.
Nixon" was a phrase used again
and again by dozens of islanders today.

At the same time they spoke
hopefully of the Ford Administration and of moving urgently
to tasks long neglected—ending
the nation's political turmoil
and easing its economic distress.

Shelter Island's 1,800 year-
round residents, most of whom
are registered Republicans.

Only last June interviews
with islanders indicated that
whatever else Watergate had
done, it apparently had not di-
luted Shelter Island's faith in
Mr. Nixon. People said at the
time that they felt the President
was being vilified by the media

Continued on Page 7, Column 6

NEWS INDEX

	Page		Page
About New York	7	Man in the News	8
Art	35	Movies	19-25
Books	29	Music	19-25
Bridge	29	Obituaries	40
Business	43-53	Op-Ed	37
Crossword	29	Sports	27-30
Editorials	36	Theaters	19-25
Family/Style	39	Transportation	66
Financial	43-53	TV and Radio	67
Going Out Guide	22	Weather	66
		News Summary and Index, Page 35	

JOIN the family on the phone. Call Mrs.
Gardner at 796-2100 and reserve your Metropolitan Opera subscription.—ADVT.

The New York Times

LATE CITY EDITION
Weather: Partly sunny today; cool tonight. Partly sunny tomorrow. Temp. range: today 65-78; Friday 66-84. Highest Temp.-Hum. Index yesterday: 78. Details on Page 58.

VOL. CXXIII...No. 42,567   © 1974 The New York Times Company   NEW YORK, SATURDAY, AUGUST 10, 1974   20c beyond 50-mile radius of New York City. except Long Island. Higher in air delivery cities.   15 CENTS

FORD SWORN IN AS PRESIDENT; ASSERTS 'NIGHTMARE IS OVER'

Nixon Bids an Emotional Farewell to Washington

TEARS AT PARTING

Ex-President Warns Against Bitterness and Revenge

By JAMES T. WOOTEN
Special to The New York Times

WASHINGTON, Aug. 9 — Richard M. Nixon, his face wet with tears, bade an emotional farewell to the remnants of his broken Administration today, urging its members to be proud of their record in government and warning them against bitterness, self-pity and revenge.

"Always remember, others may hate you," he told mem-

The text of Nixon's speech is printed on Page 4.

bers of his Cabinet and staff in a final gathering at the White House, "but those who hate you don't win unless you hate them—and then you destroy yourself."

Shortly thereafter, for the last time as President of the United States, he strode up the ramp of the plane that had taken him to the capitals of the world and was flown home to California, where his career in American politics began nearly thirty years ago.

It was 11:35 A.M. here when President Nixon's letter of resignation was delivered to the office of Secretary of State Kissinger. This is what it said:

"Dear Mr. Secretary: I hereby resign the office of President of the United States. Sincerely, Richard Nixon."

Greeted by 5,000

Soon after his departure, while the giant jet was soaring high above the heartland of the country, Gerald R. Ford was sworn in here as the nation's President.

Despite that new status, 5,000 people greeted his arrival in his native state at El Toro Marine Base. They cheered and applauded when, with his wife, Pat, standing nearby, Mr. Nixon stepped to a waiting microphone, squinted into the brilliant midday heat and said, "We're home."

After a few more remarks, a helicopter whisked the former President, Mrs. Nixon, their daughter Tricia and her husband Edward F. Cox, to La Casa Pacifica, the sprawling seaside villa near San Clemente.

Mr. Nixon's day began in the mist and rain of a humid Washington morning, when Manolo Sanchez, his long-time valet, laid out the clothes he would wear during the final hours of

Continued on Page 4, Column 1

Gerald R. Ford takes the Presidential oath, administered by Chief Justice Warren E. Burger. Mrs. Ford attends the White House ceremony.
Associated Press

G.M. to Raise Prices 9.5% On 1975 Cars and Trucks

Special to The New York Times

DETROIT, Aug. 9—The General Motors Corporation announced today that it would raise prices of 1975 model cars and trucks by an average of $480 or 9.5 per cent.

The price increase will include about $130, or 2.5 per cent for government - required pollution control equipment—catalytic converters, while $350, or 7 per cent, will be to cover added labor and material costs, the corporation said.

Mack W. Worden, G.M. vice president, made the announcement in a letter sent to dealers Thursday and released publicly today. G.M. is traditionally the price pace-setter for the auto industry. The increases it sets are expected to be matched by its competitors.

Ford Sending Notices

The Ford Motor Company has already told its dealers it is sending them advanced billing notices of an average 8 per cent increase above the 1974 prices, which is calculated to mean an increase ranging from about $225 to $800, depending on the model.

Chrysler Corporation officials have indicated their price increases will be in the same area.

A Chrysler spokesman said that next week "we are going to begin mailing tentative price bulletins on 1975 trucks.

They will be in the same ball park as the G.M. and Ford increases. But that is as much as we are going to say at the present time."

Mr. Worden, in charge of the G.M. marketing staff, said that "based on past practice we would expect the Bureau of Labor Statistics will recognize "the catalytic converter's added value and not consider it a price increase in their published data."

Mr. Worden told the dealers G.M. recognized the increases were "substantial" but said the corporation had "no alternative in light of rapidly rising labor and material costs over which we have only limited control and the necessity of complying with 1975 emission standards, which have been mandated by the Government."

As for the other auto com-

Continued on Page 36, Column 4

Friedmann Case Ends

The third and last person charged with the 1972 murder of Wolfgang Friedmann, Columbia University law professor, pleaded guilty to robbery last night. The others had earlier pleaded guilty to robbery. As a result, none of those who have admitted robbing the professor will be convicted of murdering him. Page 33.

PAPERS AND TAPES ISSUES IN CAPITAL

Impoundment of Nixon Data in White House Is Urged by Some in Congress

By RICHARD D. LYONS
Special to The New York Times

WASHINGTON, Aug. 9—On the heels of Richard M. Nixon's resignation, some members of Congress were urging impoundment of Presidential documents still in the White House. A few even demanded that the Watergate investigations be continued.

But Representative Peter W. Rodino Jr. said after a morning discussion of whether his House Judiciary Committee should make another attempt to obtain the 147 subpoenaed Presidential tape recordings that "we're not an investigative body."

"Our inquiry is at an end," the New Jersey Democrat said in expressing what seemed to be the feeling of the majority of the membership of both houses of Congress.

Yet the disposition and even ownership of the vast amount of Presidential records, some of which could be used as evidence in forthcoming trials, remained unresolved.

As Representative Jonathan

Continued on Page 7, Column 6

Aide Doubtful That Ford Would Give Nixon Pardon

By LESLEY OELSNER
Special to The New York Times

WASHINGTON, Aug. 9—The new White House press secretary, J. F. terHorst, suggested today that President Ford was not likely to grant a pardon to former President Nixon. The press secretary was asked at a briefing this afternoon about the prospects of a pardon.

He replied that he had not spoken to Mr. Ford about the question directly, but that the President had apparently stated his position on the matter last fall, during the Senate confirmation hearings on his nomination as Vice President.

"I do not think the public would stand for it," Mr. Ford said then.

Mr. Nixon's prospects for avoiding criminal prosecution thus remained in doubt, with the office of the special Watergate prosecutor saying only that a decision on whether to prosecute had not been made.

Mr. Nixon lost whatever immunity from prosecution that he may have had when he resigned today. According to Mr. terHorst, Mr. Nixon did not try to pardon himself before leaving office, nor did he grant pardons to anyone else.

Some Republican members of Congress urged today that Mr. Nixon not be prosecuted, saying that he had already suffered enough. But even among Republicans, the sentiment was not unanimous.

Senator Edward W. Brooke, Republican of Massachusetts, submitted a resolution to the Senate yesterday expressing the "sense" of the Congress

Continued on Page 5, Column 2

4 NAMED TO HELP FORD'S TRANSITION

All on New Panel Served in House—President Vows Open Administration

By JOHN HERBERS
Special to The New York Times

WASHINGTON, Aug. 9—Immediately after he was sworn in today as the nation's 38th President, Gerald R. Ford took control of the Presidency and moved to give it a character and shape different from that of his predecessor, Richard M. Nixon.

After declaring in his inaugural speech that "here the people rule," President Ford named a four-member committee composed of former elected officials to oversee the transition and make recommendations for staff changes.

The four are William W. Scranton, former Governor of Pennsylvania; Donald M. Rumsfeld, Ambassador to the North Atlantic Treaty Organization and a former Republican member of Congress from Illinois; Rogers C. B. Morton, Secretary of the Interior and a former

Continued on Page 5, Column 3

President and Kissinger Confer With the Envoys of 60 Nations

By BERNARD GWERTZMAN
Special to The New York Times

WASHINGTON, Aug. 9—President Ford undertook to convince foreign governments today that he would pursue the same foreign policy objectives that brought wide respect to Richard M. Nixon.

Two hours after taking the oath as President, Mr. Ford, assisted by Secretary of State Kissinger, who will retain his office, began meeting with about 60 envoys—some in groups and some individually—in brief sessions that lasted into the early evening.

The substance of what was said, in general, was a reaffirmation of well-known American policy positions. But Mr.

Ford and Mr. Kissinger believed the exercise to be necessary to emphasize that there would be no significant change during the transition period in which Mr. Ford, who is less experienced in foreign affairs than his predecessor, makes his leadership felt.

Priority was given to a group meeting in the Roosevelt Room of the White House with members of the North Atlantic Treaty Organization. In a pattern followed in the other sessions, Mr. Kissinger and members of his staff met with 13 envoys for about 20 minutes

Continued on Page 6, Column 6

A Plea to Bind Up Watergate Wounds

By MARJORIE HUNTER
Special to The New York Times

WASHINGTON, Aug. 9—Gerald Rudolph Ford became the 38th President of the United States today, declaring that "our long national nightmare is over."

Calling upon the nation to "bind up the internal wounds of Watergate," he said, "Our Constitution works. Our great Republic is a government of laws and not of men. Here the people rule."

And then, his voice filled with emotion, he urged the nation to pray for his predecessor

The text of Ford's address will be found on Page 3.

and friend of a quarter century, Richard Milhous Nixon.

"May our former President, who brought peace to millions, find it for himself," he said.

Mr. Ford assumed the powers of the Presidency at 11:35 A.M., the moment that Mr. Nixon's letter of resignation was handed to Secretary of State Kissinger.

Then, at 12:03 P.M., he was administered the oath of office in the historic East Room of the White House by Chief Justice Warren E. Burger before an overflow crowd of friends, the Cabinet and former Congressional colleagues from both parties.

Wife Holds Bible

It was in that same room, scarcely two hours earlier, that Mr. Nixon said an emotional good-by to his Cabinet and top aides.

Raising his right hand, Mr. Ford rested his left hand on a Bible held by his wife and opened to one of his favorite passages, the fifth and sixth verses of the third chapter of Proverbs: "Trust in the Lord with all thine heart; and lean not unto thine own understanding. In all thy ways acknowledge Him, and He shall direct thy paths."

Then, in a firm voice, he took the oath of office: "I, Gerald R. Ford, do solemnly swear that I will faithfully execute the office of President of the United States and will to the best of my ability preserve, protect and defend the

Constitution of the United States."

As the heavy applause ended, the 61-year-old President began perhaps the most moving speech of his career. Speaking in his flat, Middle Western tone, but with what appeared to be a new sense of self-assurance, he said that he was assuming the Presidency under circumstances never before experienced by Americans.

Minds Are Troubled

"This is an hour of history that troubles our minds and hurts our hearts," he said.

"Therefore," he continued, "I feel it is my first duty to make an unprecedented compact with my countrymen. Not an inaugural address, not a fireside chat, not a campaign speech. Just a little straight talk among friends. I intend it to be the first of many."

As the first American to assume the office after the resignation of a President, Mr. Ford said that he was "acutely aware that you have not elected me as your President by your ballots."

"So I ask you to confirm me as your President with your prayers," he added.

He declared that he had not gained office by secret promises, that he had not campaigned either for the Presidency or the Vice-Presidency.

"I have not subscribed to any partisan platform," he said. "I am indebted to no man and only to one woman, my dear wife."

This was reminiscent of his earlier "I am my own man," a declaration that he repeated frequently in recent months as he sought to remain loyal to Mr. Nixon and at the same time hold himself above the spreading taint of the Watergate affair.

He said that while he had not sought the responsibility, he would not shirk it. He said that those who nominated him and confirmed him just eight months ago as Vice President were his friends from both parties.

"It is only fitting then that I

Continued on Page 3, Column 1

Gains of Watergate

Positive and Hopeful Results Found As the Transition Is Made Smoothly

By CLIFTON DANIEL

WASHINGTON, Aug. 9—Watergate has now joined Teapot Dome, Credit Mobilier and the Whisky Ring in the lexicon of political infamy. Yet, in millions of minds it **News** also symbolizes **Analysis** the finest hour of American democracy. A President has been deposed, but the Republic endures. Its institutions have survived, and some are saying they have been strengthened as well. Even the Presidency, which Richard M. Nixon professed to be so anxious to protect, shows no signs of debility. The man in the White House is as powerful today as he was yesterday, although his name has changed from Nixon to Ford.

He is just as powerful, although, as the new President said today, he is "acutely aware" that he was not elected by the votes of the people, whereas his predecessor had the largest popular majority in history.

Under the United States

Constitution, removal of the President requires drastic surgery, not just a shift in the political balance, as it does in the parliamentary democracies.

However, the surgery performed on the American Government this week, while agonizing and painful, has done a minimum of visible damage to the body politic.

Mr. Nixon himself has said that one way to judge a country is to see how it effects a transfer of power. Today's transfer was effected without missing a heartbeat.

"Our Constitution works," President Ford proclaimed, after taking the oath of office. "Here the people rule."

"All in all," William P.

Continued on Page 7, Column 3

President Nixon at ceremony where he bade his Cabinet and staff good-by. At left is his daughter Julie Eisenhower.
The New York Times/Mike Lien

"All the News That's Fit to Print"

The New York Times

LATE CITY EDITION
Weather: Warm, partly sunny today; partly cloudy tonight, tomorrow. Temp. range: today 62-78; Sunday 58-77. Highest Temp.-Hum. Index yesterday: 72. Details on Page 66.

VOL.CXXIII..No. 42,597   © 1974 The New York Times Company   NEW YORK, MONDAY, SEPTEMBER 9, 1974   Higher in air delivery cities.   20 CENTS

FORD GIVES PARDON TO NIXON, WHO REGRETS 'MY MISTAKES'

U.S.-Bound Plane With 88 Crashes in Sea Off Greece

All on T.W.A. Flight From Tel Aviv Are Believed Dead—Wreckage Is Sighted

By The Associated Press

ATHENS, Sept. 8 — A Trans World Airlines jet bound for the United States with 88 persons aboard crashed today in the stormy Ionian Sea off Greece. The Greek Civil Aviation Authority said there appeared to be no survivors.

T.W.A. said that the Boeing 707 fell from an overcast sky after the pilot reported that an engine had failed.

Flight 841 originated in Tel Aviv, stopped in Athens and was scheduled to make stops in Rome and New York.

The airline's Tel Aviv office said 49 passengers boarded

the plane there for Rome and the United States. They included 17 Americans, including a baby, 13 Japanese, four Italians, four French, three Indians, two Iranians, two Israelis, two Sri Lankans, an Australian and a Canadian.

The nationalities of 30 other passengers and the nine crew members were not immediately known. [Reuters reported a total of 37 Americans aboard.]

[In Beirut, it was reported that a Palestinian youth organization said it had placed a guerrilla aboard the plane with a bomb. In New York, however, a spokesman for T.W.A. said sabotage was "highly unlikely."]

"All that can be seen by our overflying planes are remnants of the wreckage and bodies floating on the surface," said a Greek aviation official. "The stormy sea in the area is making it difficult for our ships to approach.

"Only when our ships can get nearer will we be able to

Continued on Page 6, Column 1

State Panel Charges City Fails to Pursue Fugitives

By SELWYN RAAB

The State Commission of Investigation disclosed yesterday that the backlog of missing bail jumpers and probation violators in the city had risen during the last three years from 82,000 to 130,000.

After sifting through voluminous police and court records, the commission largely blamed the Police Department's warrant division for the 50 per cent increase since 1971 in unexecuted warrants who fail to appear in court. The police division is primarily responsible for capturing such fugitives.

Sharply criticizing the performance of the division over the last three years, the investigation commission said in a report that it had found that warrant officers rarely worked at night or on weekends and that a typical attempt to track down a fugitive consisted of no more than one or two visits to an often fictitious home address given by the suspect.

The commission described the problem of fugitives here as "critical to the public safety" and called for a major reorganization of the warrant division.

"At the present time the people of New York City are unnecessarily subjected to the risk of grave harm from known criminals because of ineffective warrant enforcement," the commission declared in its report.

In response to the findings, Police Commissioner Michael J. Codd said he was "concerned" by the growing backlog, and he hinted there might be a reorganization of the warrant division.

He also announced the assignment of First Deputy Com

Continued on Page 21, Column 1

CANDIDATES SKIRT LAW ON FINANCING

Evidence Shows Big Money Played a Major Role—Voting Is Tomorrow

By FRANK LYNN

Big money—from family for tunes and large contributions—played a major role in the Democratic primary campaigns despite new state and Federal

Ballot and candidate list appear on Page 28.

campaign-finance laws that were supposed to have reduced its influence.

The question of how much money was spent and where it came from was being discussed as the primary campaigns drew to a close. The polls will be open tomorrow in the city from 6 A.M. to 9 P.M. and in the rest of the state from noon to 9 P.M.

Interviews with campaign aides and campaign financial reports show that there was considerable evidence of circumventing of the new laws in fact and in spirit, possible unrecorded cash contributions and spending and even "laundering" of campaign contribu

Continued on Page 28, Column 1

'PAIN' EXPRESSED

Ex-President Cites His Sorrow at the Way He Handled Watergate

By EVERETT R. HOLLES

SAN CLEMENTE, Calif., Sept. 8—President Ford's pardon for Richard M. Nixon evoked today from the former President an expression of "regret and pain at the anguish my mistakes over Watergate have caused the nation and the Presidency."

Within 10 minutes after the Presidential pardon was announced in Washington, Mr. Nixon's statement was released at his Casa Pacifica estate, citing his sorrow at allowing Watergate to become "a national tragedy."

"That the way I tried to deal with Watergate was the wrong way is the burden I shall bear .or every day of the life that is left in me," he said.

Hopes Burden Is Lifted

In a subsequent statement, given in response to reporters' questions, an aide quoted Mr. Nixon as saying that, in gratefully accepting the Presidential pardon, he hoped Mr. Ford's "compassionate act would contribute to lifting the burden of Watergate from our country."

When the Nixon statement was released by his adviser and former White House press secretary, Ronald L. Ziegler, Mr. and Mrs. Nixon were already on the way to a new haven of seclusion away from the heavily guarded Casa Pacifica.

They left at 7 A.M., Pacific Coast time, in a large black limousine accompanied by Secret Service agents and Mr. Nixon's military aide,. Lieut. Col. Jack Brennan, reportedly for the Palm Desert estate of Walter H. Annenberg, Ambassador to Britain.

A close friend of the Nixons said the former President planned to play golf on the Annenberg private 18-hole course.

[In New York, Mr. Nixon's daughter, Julie Nixon Eisenhower, said that her father had gone to the Annenberg estate "for a rest." The Associated Press reported.]

Mr. Ziegler and Mr. Nixon's appointments secretary, Stephen

Continued on Page 24, Column 1

Richard M. Nixon in a photo made earlier this year

The Statement by Nixon

I have been informed that President Ford has granted me a full and absolute pardon for any charges which may be brought against me for actions taken during the time I was the President of the United States. In accepting this pardon, I hope that his compassionate act will contribute to lifting the burden of Watergate from our country.

Here in California, my perspective on Watergate is quite different than it was while I was embattled in the midst of the controversy while I was still subject to the unrelenting daily demand of the Presidency itself.

Looking back on what is still in my mind a complex and confusing maze of events, decisions, pressures, and personalities, one thing I can see clearly now is that I was wrong in not acting more decisively and more forthrightly in dealing with Watergate, particularly when it reached the stage of judicial proceedings and grew from a political scandal into a national tragedy.

No words can describe the depths of my regret and pain at the anguish my mistakes over Watergate have caused the nation and the Presidency, a nation I so deeply love and an institution I so greatly respect.

I know that many fair-minded people believe that my motivation and actions in the Watergate affair were intentionally self-serving and illegal. I now understand how my own mistakes and misjudgments have contributed to that belief and seemed to support it. This burden is the heaviest one of all to bear.

That the way I tried to deal with Watergate was the wrong way is a burden I shall bear for every day of the life that is left to me.

Jaworski Won't Challenge Pardon, Spokesman Says

By JOHN M. CREWDSON
Special to The New York Times

WASHINGTON, Sept. 8 — Leon Jaworski, the Watergate special prosecutor, apparently has no plans to challenge the validity of the unconditional pardon that President Ford bestowed today on Richard M. Nixon, according to a spokesman for Mr. Jaworski.

The special prosecutor "accepts the decision," said John Barker, the spokesman. "He thinks it's within the President's power to do it. His feeling is that the President is exercising his lawful power, and he accepts it."

Mr. Barker added that Mr. Jaworski had not been consulted in advance on the decision by either Mr. Ford or White House lawyers, and learned of the President's position less than an hour before it was announced.

Some lawyers, including Sen

ator Edmund S. Muskie, Democrat of Maine, questioned the legal and constitutional validity of a Presidential pardon conferred before an indictment had been brought or a conviction obtained.

"It could be challenged," declared Mr. Muskie, adding "there are those who say that it ought to be challenged, lest the precedent be established in an undesirable way."

But the remarks by Mr. Barker and by other lawyers familiar with the Watergate prosecutions indicated strongly that Mr. Jaworski was little inclined to test the pardon by seeking to indict Mr. Nixon, which one authority described as "the way to do it."

The principal Watergate grand jury voted earlier this

Continued on Page 25, Column 6

Some Mixed Reactions in Foley Square

By PAUL L. MONTGOMERY

A few hours after President Ford's pardon of his predecessor was announced yesterday, Mr. and Mrs. Wilson Wainwright of Olean, N.Y., were strolling in Foley Square in lower Manhattan, looking at the public buildings.

"It's going to make a lot of people mad, but I can see why he did it," Mr. Wainwright said. "It wouldn't look right to the rest of the world to have a President of the United States in jail."

Mr. Wainwright, on a late-summer vacation, was asked if he had any doubts about former President Richard M. Nixon's guilt.

"None that I can see," his wife, Judy, replied. "I guess

some people would say it would have been better to pardon him after the courts decided."

Nearby, at 100 Centre Street, the afternoon session of the arraignment part of Criminal Court was about to begin. In the dingy, crowded room, lawyers and policemen, and defendants and their families lounged on the oak benches, waiting for the judge to return from lunch.

"Seriously, though, it's outrageous," he continued. "You get a lady here who's going to jail for stealing a blouse, or some guy on assault because he got tired of living with the rats and hit somebody. And here's one of the biggest plun

Continued on Page 25, Column 6

concept of equal justice under law."

"How about all the young men who refused to serve in an illegal, immoral and vicious war?" Mr. Mayerson asked. "Is he going to pardon them, too? It's like Peter was saying, maybe they should give Nixon a pardon if he does 18 months of alternate service."

Mr. Mayerson surveyed the room.

Hal Mayerson and Peter Davis of the Legal Aid Society, which represents indigent defendants, had been discussing the pardon during the break.

"It's a bit unseemly to pardon someone before they're prosecuted," Mr. Davis said. "It doesn't do much for the

Knievel Safe as Rocket Falls Into Snake Canyon

By JON NORDHEIMER
Special to The New York Times

TWIN FALLS, Idaho, Sept. 8 —Evel Knievel failed today in an attempt to rocket 1,600 feet across the Snake River Canyon when a tail parachute deployed prematurely on the take-off of his vehicle.

The vehicle, which Mr. Knievel calls the Sky-Cycle X-2, went streaking to about 1,000 feet above the river before floating into the canyon to make a nose-down crash landing on a rocky bank at the river's edge.

Mr. Knievel was pulled from the craft several minutes later by a rescue team. He had superficial cuts and scrapes of the face and legs.

The flight aborted almost as soon as steam exploded from a rear nozzle of the 13-foot-long craft and propelled it along a 108-foot launching track aimed at the cloudless sky.

A drogue parachute designed to slow the rocket at an altitude of 2,800 feet deployed while the vehicle was still on the ramp, whipping in a blast of steam.

Once the vehicle lifted off the ramp, it turned belly up and the main chute, attached to the drogue, was automatically deployed at about 1,000 feet.

A large crowd along the canyon's south rim gasped as a 15-mile-an-hour wind blew the vehicle back toward them, rocking gently in the air nose-down like a red, white and blue Christmas ornament.

For several seconds, it appeared that Mr. Knievel, who could be seen struggling inside the open cockpit, might crash into the crowd on the rim of the canyon.

But the vehicle dropped onto boulder-strewn ledge, bounced twice on its journey and came to rest about 20 feet from the water's edge.

The vehicle was obscured from sight from the plateau 540 feet above, and some cries of anguish were heard in the crowd when there was no sign of the stuntman.

But a helicopter picked him

Continued on Page 58, Column 5

Chris Evert Beaten

Evonne Goolagong of Australia defeated Chris Evert in the semifinals of the United States Open tennis at Forest Hills, Queens, yesterday, 6-0, 6-7, 6-3, and will meet Billie Jean King in the final today. Details, Page 45.

Associated Press
President Ford speaking at the White House yesterday

Proclamation of Pardon

Richard Nixon became the thirty-seventh President of the United States on January 20, 1969, and was re-elected in 1972 for a second term by the electors of forty-nine of the fifty states. His term in office continued until his resignation on August 9, 1974.

Pursuant to resolutions of the House of Representatives, its Committee on the Judiciary conducted an inquiry and investigation on the impeachment of the President extending over more than eight months. The hearings of the committee and its deliberations, which received wide national publicity over television, radio, and in printed media, resulted in votes adverse to Richard Nixon on recommended Articles of Impeachment.

As a result of certain acts or omissions occurring before his resignation from the office of President, Richard Nixon has become liable to possible indictment and trial for offenses against the United States. Whether or not he shall be so prosecuted depends on findings of the appropriate grand jury and on the discretion of the authorized prosecutor. Should an indictment ensue, the accused shall then be entitled to a fair trial by an impartial jury, as guaranteed to every individual by the Constitution.

It is believed that a trial of Richard Nixon, if it became necessary, could not fairly begin until a year or more has elapsed. In the meantime, the tranquility to which this nation has been restored by the events of recent weeks could be irreparably lost by .the prospects of bringing to trial a former President of the United States. The prospects of such trial will involve prolonged and divisive debate over the propriety of exposing to further punishment and degradation a man who has already paid the unprecedented penalty of relinquishing the highest elective office in the United States.

NOW, THEREFORE, I, Gerald R. Ford, President of the United States, pursuant to the pardon power conferred upon me by Article II, Section 2, of the Constitution, have granted and by these presents do grant a full, free, and absolute pardon unto Richard Nixon for all offenses against the United States which he, Richard Nixon, has committed or may have committed or taken part in during the period from January 20, 1969, through August 9, 1974.

IN WITNESS WHEREOF, I have hereunto set my hand this 8th day of September in the year of our Lord nineteen hundred seventy-four, and of the independence of the United States of America the 199th.

Nixon Tapes Must Be Kept 3 Years for Use in Court

By R. W. APPLE Jr.
Special to The New York Times

WASHINGTON, Sept. 8 — Richard M. Nixon and the Ford Administration have reached an agreement under which the former President will ultimately be permitted to destroy the White House tape recordings that led to his downfall.

The agreement, announced

today by the White House, also provides that all of Mr. Nixon's Presidential papers and tapes will be preserved for three years for possible use in court cases arising out of the Watergate scandals.

Mr. Nixon signed the agreement in San Clemente, Calif., on Friday; it was countersigned yesterday by Arthur F. Sampson, head of the General Services Administration.

Philip W. Buchen, counsel for President Ford, said at a White House briefing this afternoon that Mr. Ford instructed him about 10 days ago to resolve the controversy over the White House files so the Administration would not find itself "enmeshed for a long time" in jurisdictional disputes.

Although Mr. Buchen denied

Continued on Page 26, Column 1

NO CONDITIONS SET

Action Taken to Spare Nation and Ex-Chief, President Asserts

By JOHN HERBERS
Special to The New York Times

WASHINGTON, Sept. 8— President Ford granted former President Richard M. Nixon an unconditional pardon today for all Federal crimes that he "committed or may have committed or taken part in" while in office, an act Mr. Ford said was intended to spare Mr. Nixon and the nation further punishment in the Watergate scandals.

Mr. Nixon, in San Clemente, Calif., accepted the pardon, which exempts him from indictment and trial for, among

Text of the Ford statement is printed on Page 24.

other things, his role in the cover-up of the Watergate burglary. He issued a statement saying that he could now see he was "wrong in not acting more decisively and more forthrightly in dealing with Watergate."

Philip W. Buchen, the White House counsel, who advised Mr. Ford on the legal aspects of the pardon, said the "act of mercy" on the President's part was done without making any demands on Mr. Nixon and without asking the advice of the Watergate special prosecutor, Leon Jaworski, who had the legal responsibility to prosecute the case.

Reaction to the pardon was sharply divided, but not entirely along party lines. Most Democrats who commented voiced varying degrees of disapproval and dismay, while most Republican comment backed President Ford.

However, Senators Edward W. Brooke of Massachusetts and Jacob K. Javits of New York disagreed with the action. [Page 25.]

Dangers Seen in Delay

Mr. Buchen said that, at the President's request, he had asked Mr. Jaworski how long it would be, in the event Mr. Nixon was indicted, before he could be brought to trial and that Mr. Jaworski had replied it would be at least nine months or more, because of the enormous amount of publicity the charges against Mr. Nixon had received when the House Judiciary Committee recommended impeachment.

This was one reason Mr. Ford cited for granting the pardon, saying that he had concluded that "many months and perhaps more years will have to pass before Richard Nixon could obtain a fair trial by jury in any jurisdiction of the United States under governing decisions of the Supreme Court."

"During this long period of delay and potential litigation, ugly passions would again be aroused, our people would

Continued on Page 24, Column 4

terHorst Quits Post To Protest Pardon

Special to The New York Times

WASHINGTON, Sept. 8—J. F. terHorst, whose appointment as White House press secretary was the first in President Ford's new Administration, resigned tonight in what he said was a protest over the granting of an unconditional pardon to former President Richard Nixon.

In a statement released by the White House tonight, Mr. Ford said that he deeply regretted Mr. terHorst's decision.

"I understand his position," the statement said. "I appreciate the fact that good people will differ with me on this very difficult decision. However, it is my judgment that it is in

Continued on Page 26, Column 1

The New York Times

LATE CITY EDITION

Weather: Sunny, warmer today; cold tonight. Chance of rain tomorrow. Temperature range: today 31-47; Thursday 29-38. Details on Page 74.

VOL. CXXIV .. No. 42,699   © 1974 The New York Times Company   NEW YORK, FRIDAY, DECEMBER 20, 1974   Price higher in air delivery cities.   20 CENTS

ROCKEFELLER SWORN IN AS VICE PRESIDENT AFTER CONFIRMATION BY HOUSE, 287 TO 128

Congress Votes $1-Billion For Jobs for Unemployed

By DAVID E. ROSENBAUM
Special to The New York Times

WASHINGTON, Dec. 19 — The House and Senate gave final approval tonight to legislation appropriating $1-billion for jobs for the unemployed next year.

The money was part of a $5-billion appropriations bill that also allocates money for increased unemployment compensation.

President Ford supports the measure and is considered certain to sign it.

It was estimated that the measure would provide 100,000 jobs nationwide at an average salary of $7,500.

More than $2-billion would become available for unemployment compensation, with the exact amount depending on the number of persons out of work next year.

Under the bill, $875-million would be distributed to states and communities to provide public service jobs for the unemployed in such areas as health, education, recreation and sanitation.

The measure specified that $125-million would be distributed through the Economic Development Administration to stimulate public works projects in depressed areas.

Based on the September unemployment statistics and an appropriation of $1-billion, the Labor Department calculated that New York State would get $107-million, of which New York City would get $61-million; New Jersey would get $48-million, and Connecticut $18-million. [Page 4.]

The Senate had authorized $4-billion and the House $2-billion for the public service jobs program. But the authorization figures merely set ceilings on the amount of money that might be made available. The appropriation determines the amount available to be spent.

Meanwhile, today, the Democrats on the House Ways and Means Committee, which has jurisdiction over many of the important economic measures to be considered next year, created six subcommittees and appointed six chairmen.

It was the first time the panel formed subcommittees since 1957.

The committee Democrats de-

Continued on Page 10, Column 2

Cuomo Selected by Carey As His Secretary of State

By FRANCIS X. CLINES

Governor-elect Hugh L. Carey announced yesterday that Mario M. Cuomo, a longtime friend, would be appointed Secretary of State, and that Raymond T. Schuler, the incumbent Secretary of Transportation, would be retained in the new administration, which takes office Jan. 1.

Mr. Cuomo, who ran unsuccessfully this year for the Democratic nomination for Lieutenant Governor, will have the responsibilities of his post expanded to include special advisory and trouble-shooting duties, Mr. Carey announced. These include the inquiry into nursing home abuses Mr. Carey charged him with earlier this week, plus executive responsibilities in programs for judicial selection, income disclosure for public officials and the current review of the New York City Charter.

Commissioner Schuler, like Mr. Cuomo, is a Democrat. He has 18 years of career service in the state bureaucracy and was appointed Commissioner two years ago by former Gov. Nelson A. Rockefeller. Under his control, the transportation agency has started to shed its traditional highway-oriented direction and to stress the need for mass transit.

Mr. Cuomo, who is 42 years old, practices law in Brooklyn and lives in Queens with his wife, Matilda, and five children. He is also a law professor at St. John's University Law School. He had been reported concerned about moving to Albany and yesterday he said that in the light of the expanded role being created for Secretary

Mario M. Cuomo

of State, he was not sure whether he would be living upstate. The Department of State, which has headquarters in Albany, oversees the licensing and registration procedures for professions and technical jobs.

Mr. Cuomo said the Governor-elect had emphasized that the post—which politicians in recent years had come to consider a Governor's symbolic Italian-American chamberlain—would not be "an ethnic position."

Mr. Cuomo first came to pub-

Continued on Page 25, Column 2

Man, 98, Strangled In Brooklyn Robbery

By JOSEPH B. TREASTER

A 98-year-old former yeshiva principal was choked to death with his yarmulke early yesterday morning by thieves who climbed into his ground-floor apartment in the Crown Heights section of Brooklyn as he slept, the police said.

The victim, Nathan Friedler, who was described by neighbors as "a nice, quiet old man," was found tied on his bed, spreadeagled with neckties to the four corner posts. He was slugged by his daughter, Mrs. Sigmund Schwartz, as she brought him breakfast at about 8 A.M. from her own apartment in the same building at 899 Montgomery Street. The skull cap had been

Continued on Page 74, Column 4

CITY AND UNIONS SEEK RETIREMENT ON ELECTIVE BASIS

510 Workers Who Were to Be Let Go Today Get a Month's Reprieve

By FRED FERRETTI

The city and a group of leaders representing the municipal unions agreed yesterday to seek voluntary retirements of city employes aged 63 to 70 to save the jobs of 860 younger employes. The latter are scheduled to be dismissed in the budget-cutting layoffs recently announced by Mayor Beame.

The agreement is an alternative to an earlier plan, which would have forced the retirement of 860 older Civil Service employes to save the jobs of the younger employes — a plan that on Wednesday was declared illegal by the United States Secretary of Labor, Peter J. Brennan.

First Deputy Mayor James Cavanagh, in announcing the alternative, said that to give prospective volunteers, 510 employes scheduled to be dismissed today would get a month's reprieve.

The 510 represented part of the first wave of 1,510 municipal layoffs announced by Mr. Beame on Nov. 22 in an effort to decrease the deficit in the city's $11.1-billion budget.

The Second Wave

On Dec. 11 the Mayor called for the discharge of 6,425 more city employes, consisting of 2,200 permanent Civil Service workers, 1,525 appointed provisionals and 2,700 workers aged 65 or older who the Mayor said would not receive renewals of their work extensions and would have to retire by next June 30. In the group of 2,200 were teachers, policemen, firemen and sanitation workers and 350 other permanent Civil Service employes.

The 350, like the first group of 510, are in the New York City Employes Retirement System, one of the city's five pension programs. It was these 860 employes, mostly young members of minority groups and women, who were scheduled to be dismissed and on whom a week's effort was expended in attempts to save their jobs.

After Victor Gotbaum, executive director of the 110,000-member District 37, American Federation of State, County and Municipal Employes, and other union leaders denounced the dismissals, the Mayor met with them and announced a plan to

Continued on Page 25, Column 1

Nominee Takes His Oath On the Old Family Bible

By RICHARD L. MADDEN
Special to The New York Times

WASHINGTON, Dec. 19—In a simple but well-organized ceremony in the Senate chamber, Nelson A. Rockefeller held a black family Bible in his left hand tonight and took the oath of office as Vice President.

The oath was administered by Chief Justice Warren E. Burger amid a blaze of lights to accommodate television cameras, the first time they had been allowed in the room. It brought the 66-year-old Mr. Rockefeller within a heartbeat of the Presidency, a job he had

been denied three times by the Republican party.

The Bible was the same one that Mr. Rockefeller had used four times when he was sworn in at Albany as Governor of New York, and in it was a note from his father, John D. Rockefeller, Jr., which said:

"This was my mother's Bible, which always lay on the table in the library at 4 West 54th Street, New York. April 1, 1946."

The 25-minute ceremony was a combination of a solemn oath, a brief speech of gratitude, formal expressions of good wishes from Senate leaders and finally hearty applause and handshakes from Representatives who had confirmed Mr. Rockefeller's nomination two hours earlier and from Senators who had done the same last week, as well as some who had

Mr. Rockefeller, wearing a dark blue suit, blue-and-white-striped shirt and dark blue tie, stumbled briefly as he took the first step down to the well of the Senate on entering the chamber. But he recovered his balance quickly, grinned and waved as he strode toward the

Continued on Page 17, Column 1

6 SUGAR REFINERS INDICTED BY JURY

Price - Fixing Conspiracies Alleged in Three Markets in West and Midwest

By HENRY WEINSTEIN
Special to The New York Times

SAN FRANCISCO, Dec. 19—Six major sugar refining companies were indicted today by a Federal Grand Jury on charges of illegal price fixing after an 18-month investigation.

The companies indicted were the Great Western Sugar Company of Denver, the American Crystal Sugar Company, formerly of Denver; the Holly Sugar Corporation of Colorado Springs, Colo.; California and Hawaiian Sugar Company of San Francisco; the Amalgamated Sugar Company of Ogden, Utah; and the Union Sugar Division of the Consolidated Foods Corporation of Chicago. Also named as civil defendants were the National Sugar Beet Growers Federation of Greeley, Colo.; and Utah-Idaho Sugar Company of Salt Lake City, Utah.

The indictments and three companion civil antitrust suits covered acts allegedly committed through the end of 1972. Since then sugar prices have soared, and Robert J. Staal, assistant United States Attorney, stated here today that "the current pricing practices of the sugar industry are still under investigation."

Last month the staff of the Council on Wage and Price Stability said the United States sugar industry had "reaped very large windfall gains" this year from rapidly increasing sugar prices. Mr. Staal declined to state whether a grand jury

Continued on Page 62, Column 4

Nelson A. Rockefeller being sworn in as Vice President last night by Chief Justice Warren E. Burger. In background from left are Senators Hugh Scott, Jacob K. Javits, Robert C. Byrd, James L. Buckley and Howard W. Cannon.

The New York Times/George Tames

Outlook for Rockefeller

Long Experience in Running Things Is Expected to Reinforce President

By R. W. APPLE Jr.
Special to The New York Times

WASHINGTON, Dec. 19—Even before Nelson A. Rockefeller was sworn into office, the Washington sharpshooters were reminding him that the principal assignment of most Vice Presidents has been to stay reasonably healthy. In his whimsy for today, for example, Art Buchwald wrote of the Vice President who had to pretend he was the March of Dimes poster child's father just to get into the President's office.

News Analysis

But the fact is that Mr. Rockefeller has the best chance of anyone who has held the Vice-Presidency in recent times to make a real impact on government and politics, despite all the continuing constraints of the No. 2 job.

First, Mr. Rockefeller himself brings to the job a depth of executive experience—years and years of running things, not just talking about them—that is unmatched in this century. He is by disposition and

Continued on Page 17, Column 1

TEN ECONOMISTS FAVOR STIMULUS

Group Meets With Ford's Top Advisers — Details of Some Views Differ

By EDWIN L. DALE Jr.
Special to The New York Times

WASHINGTON, Dec. 19—Government stimulus for the sliding economy was reported favored by a group of 10 leading private economists at an unpublicized meeting at the White House today.

Participants at the meeting declined to discuss individual views in detail. However, some of the views are well known. But one participant did say, "I can't think of anyone who didn't favor stimulus in some form." The group's members, however, were reported to have differed on numerous important details, including the type of stimulus and how large it should be.

President Ford was not present, but nearly all his chief economic advisers were. Alan Greenspan, chairman of the Council of Economic Advisers, presided.

According to reports, the Government members mainly listened and asked questions and made no attempt to achieve a consensus. Mr. Greenspan had previously pledged to solicit

Continued on Page 54, Column 1

Export Bank Credit Curbs Are Said to Anger Moscow

By BERNARD GWERTZMAN
Special to The New York Times

WASHINGTON, Dec. 19—The Soviet Union has followed up yesterday's disavowal of a deal on emigration for trade benefits with a private denunciation of Congressional adoption of a ceiling on Export-Import Bank credits to Moscow.

According to State Department officials, Ambassador Anatoly F. Dobrynin told Secretary of State Kissinger yesterday that Moscow was angry at what it regarded as the failure of the United States to live up to its side of détente.

Without stating whether the Soviet Union would step up emigration in return for the modest trade benefits approved by Congress, Mr. Dobrynin reportedly was caustic in his complaints, particularly about the credit limitation.

Some officials said that because the additional credits—a ceiling of $300-million over four years, limited to $75-million-a year—were lower than Moscow had expected, there was some question whether the Kremlin would go ahead with the informal arrangement to ease emigration restrictions in return for trade concessions. Despite the Soviet denial, the officials insist that such an arrangement exists.

The consensus was that it

Continued on Page 13, Column 1

City's Fire Alarm Boxes Are Called Undependable

By JOHN DARNTON

The city's fire-alarm boxes, connected to a deteriorating network of cables laid more than half a century ago, are becoming dangerously unreliable, according to Fire Department dispatchers, maintenance men and fire fighters.

While some of the old mechanical "pull" boxes have failed in recent months, the new voice-alarm boxes that are replacing them at the rate of 60 a month have developed technological problems of their own. All of these Emergency Response System boxes installed in the city so far—over 1,000—will be replaced by their manufacturer because they were found to "transmit themselves" during electrical storms.

The scope of the fire-box problem, as the city enters its heavy fire-fatality season, is indicated by the aftereffects of one severe ice storm a year ago. The storm knocked out 2,500 of the department's 15,840 street and building boxes. Most

of them were in Queens and many were out of service for weeks.

Since the storm of Dec. 17, 1973, "silent sentries"—alarm boxes that do not work—have been implicated in at least two deaths here so far.

The problem appears most severe in Queens, where aerial cables that have lost their insulation come into contact with tree branches, sometimes grounding entire circuits. In Queens, some circuits carry as many as 80 boxes, contrary to the generally accepted standard of allowing 20 to 30 boxes on a circuit.

But the problem appears in the other boroughs, such as

Continued on Page 38, Column 1

NEWS INDEX

BACKPACKER MAGAZINE $5.00 for a one-year subscription. Send check to Dept. 6151, 28 West 44 St., New York 10036. Advt.

By LINDA CHARLTON
Special to The New York Times

WASHINGTON, Dec. 19 — Nelson Aldrich Rockefeller was sworn in tonight as the 41st Vice President of the United States.

He was sworn in by Chief Justice Warren E. Burger in a televised ceremony in the Senate chamber.

Mr. Rockefeller became Vice President one day short of four months after his nomination by President Ford. He was escorted to the Senate by Mr. Ford.

Transcript of the ceremony appears on Page 16.

Members of Mr. Rockefeller's family, Congress, the Cabinet and New York State dignitaries were among those who witnessed the ceremony.

He took the oath of office with his hand on a family Bible at 10:12 P.M.

The former New York Governor, only the second man to become Vice President without a public vote, took office after the House completed Congressional approval of his nomination by a vote of 287 to 128. The Senate approved him by a vote of 90 to 7 last week.

Ford Is Pleased

Immediately after the confirmation vote, the White House issued the following statement by President Ford:

"I am delighted that Nelson Rockefeller has been duly confirmed today to be the 41st Vice President of the United States. I congratulate him and look forward to his participation and assistance in the Administration. I commend the House of Representatives for its confirmation vote today, and the Senate for its vote earlier. Members of the 93d Congress have rendered a service to the nation by filling the constitutional office of the Vice President before adjournment. All Americans will benefit from the distinguished and devoted public service of the new Vice President."

Oath and Speech

At just past 10:11 P.M., Mr. Rockefeller raised his right hand to take the oath: "I, Nelson Aldrich Rockefeller, do solemnly swear that I will support and defend the Constitution of the United States . . . ."

When the applause had subsided, Mr. Rockefeller read a short speech to the crowded chamber illuminated by five banks of television lights.

"I feel," he said, "a great sense of gratitude for the privilege of serving the country I love."

He went on to thank all those involved in his nomination—the President, Congress, Betty Ford for "her great warmth and her courage."

"And if you'll forgive me for a personal note, my love and

Continued on Page 16, Column 1

Publisher Suspends Luciano Paperback

By NICHOLAS GAGE

New American Library is suspending its plans to publish a paperback edition of "The Last Testament of Lucky Luciano," for which it was going to pay $800,000, according to a company spokesman.

The spokesman, Harold Rosenthal, said the decision was reached following a meeting Wednesday with executives of Little, Brown & Co., the book's primary publisher.

The New York Times disclosed last Tuesday that an examination of the sources and documents concerning Mr. Luciano and more than 20 interviews, produced information that questioned the publisher's

Continued on Page 29, Column 7

Watergate Argument

The chief prosecutor at the Watergate cover-up trial began his final argument to the jury yesterday after 46 days of testimony. The prosecutor, James F. Neal, mocked and scorned the five defendants. Page 18.

United Press International

The New York Times

LATE CITY EDITION

Weather: Milder with rain likely today, tonight. Clearing tomorrow. Temperature range: today 40-51; Tuesday 36-49. Details on Page 93.

VOL. CXXIV....No. 42,788   © 1975 The New York Times Company   NEW YORK, WEDNESDAY, MARCH 19, 1975   Price higher in air delivery cities.   20 CENTS

Vietnam Refugees Stream From Highlands to Coast

100,000 Said to Be Using Only Road Left as the Cities Are Deserted and Military Facilities Are Blown Up

By MALCOLM W. BROWNE
Special to The New York Times

SAIGON, South Vietnam, Wednesday, March 19—A vast exodus of refugees from South Vietnam's Central Highlands is under way, with rear-guard troops blowing up military installations and civilian stragglers burning down their houses.

According to one estimate, 100,000 people—farmers, businessmen, montagnard tribesmen and soldiers—were strung out for 140 miles along the sole open road to the safety of the seacoast last night.

Behind them, Communist forces were poised to occupy a huge economically important area they had never before entirely . conquered, even during the final days of the French Indochina War.

The exodus from the highlands began with the fall of the key town of Ban Me Thuot to Communist forces last week but became a flood after a decision by the Saigon Govern-

ment to move forces out of the area.

Last night, the Saigon Government spokesman, Lieut. Col. Le Trung Hien, repeated earlier denials that the Government was abandoning the Central Highlands, but conceded that "for tactical reasons" some ground forces were withdrawing, and that all aircraft based at the large Pleiku base had been flown off.

He also said that some Government forces were still holding out in Ban Me Thuot.

Reached by telephone, the North Vietnamese military spokesman, Maj. Nguyen Phuong Nam, asserted, however, that Ban Me Thuot had been completely under Communist control since last week.

"You may be interested to know," he said, "that on Sunday a meeting was held in the middle of the city at which Dang Chung Thi, vice president

Continued on Page 19, Column 1

HANOI DRIVE SEEN TO BISECT SOUTH

A Push From Highlands to Sea Expected in Shift to Conventional War

By DREW MIDDLETON

North Vietnamese forces, continuing to occupy territory in the Central Highlands abandoned by retreating South Vietnamese troops, have entered what United States military sources regard as the second phase of an offensive designed to cut South Vietnam in half.

The American sources said that the North Vietnamese forces were moving toward South Vietnam's seacoast yesterday.

The South Vietnamese command has identified elements of 15 North Vietnamese divisions in the fighting, which Pentagon sources said was now a conventional war in which guerrilla and local forces are playing little or no part.

South Vietnamese forces recently engaged around the important highland city of Ban Me Thuot were reported to have fallen back to within 60 miles of the seacoast, apparently in an effort to hold Route 1,

Continued on Page 18, Column 4

OIL DEPLETION AID IS VOTED FOR MANY

Senate, 47-41, Acts to Keep Allowance for All but Largest Companies

By EILEEN SHANAHAN
Special to The New York Times

WASHINGTON, March 18—The Senate voted today to keep the oil depletion allowance in effect for all but a small number of the nation's largest oil companies.

By a vote of 47 to 41 the Senate amended the tax-cut bill that was passed by the House last month to add major exceptions to the essentially complete repeal of the depletion allowance that the House had approved.

Whereas the House version had been expected to add about $2.5-billion to the Federal taxes paid by oil producers this year, the Senate version would reduce that amount to about $1.3-billion by exempting permanently from repeal all but 124 of the nation's 10,000 oil producers.

The exemption, which was sponsored by Senator Lloyd Bentsen, Democrat of Texas, was considerably wider than

Continued on Page 23, Column 1

NEW OFFER MADE IN DOCTOR STRIKE; REJECTION IS SEEN

Counteroffer Is Expected on Issue of Physicians' Hours —A.M.A. Backs Internes

By PETER KIHSS

A new offer to striking physicians was made yesterday by the League of Voluntary Hospitals, but the union of internes and residents indicated it would reject the offer and make a counterproposal.

The league's offer came on the second day of a strike that has affected 21 hospitals here.

The management offer, which came after Federal mediators had arranged the resumption of negotiations, presumably was directed to the demand of the Committee of Internes and Residents for a reduction in duty schedules to 80 hours a week from periods doctors say run as long as 100 hours.

At 9:30 last night, Dr. Richard A. Knutson, president of the union, issued a statement saying it had studied the new offer for two hours, and added that "it is apparent" that the union "will submit a counter-proposal to the league."

Then the committee reconvened for further consideration of the proposal.

Statement a Surprise

Members of the doctors union were surprised and gratified by a statement from the two top officers of the usually conservative American Medical Association that "in important respects, it is a strike for better patient care."

Dr. Richard E. Palmer of Alexandria, Va., chairman of the A.M.A. board of trustees, and Dr. Malcolm C. Todd of Long Beach, Calif., president, said in their statement in Chicago:

"When a physician has to work 50 hours straight or 100 hours in a week, it is not only tough on him or her, it is also a threat to the quality of care the patient is receiving."

This drew an immediate rejoinder from Dr. S. David Pomrinse, director of the 1,300-bed Mount Sinai, the largest hospital struck here, who said the statement showed "ignorance of the rules" of the A.M.A.'s own requirements on educational residences and was "a naked power play for future additional members" from the strikers' ranks.

In their statement, Dr. Palmer and Dr. Todd said:

"The A.M.A. does not believe a physician has a right to strike against a patient. It is evident that the Committee of

Continued on Page 93, Column 1

F.B.I. HARASSED A LEFTIST PARTY

Documents Show 10-Year Campaign of Disruption of Socialist Workers

By NICHOLAS M. HORROCK
Special to The New York Times

WASHINGTON, March 18—The Federal Bureau of Investigation harassed the Socialist Workers party for a decade with efforts to have members dismissed from their jobs, with leaks to news media of unsavory items about their personal lives and attempts to encourage police agencies to press petty prosecutions, newly released bureau documents show.

As a result of a court order in a civil suit brought in Federal District Court in New York, the F.B.I. was compelled last week to release 3,138 pages of internal documents to the party and its youth arm, the Young Socialist Alliance.

A Large Disclosure

It is one of the largest disclosures of internal F.B.I. workings in the history of the bureau and probably the most revealing set of documents since the theft of F.B.I. documents in Media, Pa., in 1971, laying bare bureau operations in Pennsylvania. The papers were made available to The New York Times today.

The documents have also been made available to the Senate Select Committee on Intelligence headed by Senator Frank Church, Democrat of Idaho, a Socialist Workers source confirmed.

The carton of papers sketched 31 years of bureau attention to the Socialist Workers party that included detailed investigations of virtually every office

Continued on Page 31, Column 1

House Again Votes Strip Mining Curb

By BEN A. FRANKLIN
Special to The New York Times

WASHINGTON, March 18—The House of Representatives voted 333 to 86 tonight for a tough strip mine control bill similar to one that President Ford vetoed last December as too restrictive on surface-mined coal production.

The majority in today's House vote on the environmental reform measure was greater than last July when the similar bill was passed 291 to 81.

Last week a somewhat weaker bill with only minor differences from the House version cleared the Senate by a vote of 84 to 13. The differences in the two versions are expected to be compromised quickly in a con-

Continued on Page 26, Column 1

C.I.A. SALVAGE SHIP BROUGHT UP PART OF SOVIET SUB LOST IN 1968, FAILED TO RAISE ATOM MISSILES

The Glomar Explorer, which was used in 1974 to salvage part of a Soviet submarine from the Pacific Ocean

Summa Corporation

A nuclear-powered Russian missile submarine of type that sank in the Pacific in 1968

Associated Press

Portuguese Regime Bans 3 Parties From Elections

By HENRY GINIGER
Special to The New York Times

LISBON, March 18 — Portugal's military rulers announced today that the Christian Democratic party and two militant extreme left-wing groups would not be permitted to participate in the forthcoming elections.

A major effect of the decision was to strengthen the hand of the Communist party, which had to contend with strong competition on its left among workers, peasants and students. The party is expected to increase its influence even more when a new Government, now being formed, is announced shortly with the addition of some Communist allies.

In announcing the ban, the High Council of the Revolution, formed last week after the military said it had crushed a rightwing coup attempt, accused all three parties of employing and stirring violence and of showing "disrespect" for the program of the armed forces.

The banning of the Christian Democrats, a relatively new center-right party with a large following in rural areas, left only one conservative group in the election.

The elections are now scheduled for April 12, but the Ministry of Information indicated they may be postponed until April 25, the first anniversary of the 1974 coup that over-

threw the authoritarian Government of Premier Marcello Caetano. The ministry cited "technical difficulties" for the possible delay.

One of the banned leftist parties, a Maoist-oriented group known as the Movement for the Reorganization of the Portuguese Proletariat, reacted strongly to the decision with a rally in Lisbon's main square, the Rossio, followed by a march on the main Government seat, the São Bento Palace.

Some 4,000 young militants denounced fascism and "social

Continued on Page 7, Column 1

High Court Restricts Censorship of Plays

By WARREN WEAVER Jr.
Special to The New York Times

WASHINGTON, March 18—The Supreme Court extended today to theatrical productions the same kind of constitutional protection against advance censorship and prohibition that newspapers, books and motion pictures have had.

The high court ruled that a city-operated theater cannot, sight unseen, bar a musical from its stage as obscene without observing certain safeguards to help insure fair treatment for the producers of the show.

Dividing 5 to 4, the Justices held that the refusal by directors of a Chattanooga municipal theater to permit a road

Continued on Page 14, Column 4

HUGHES BUILT SHIP

Bodies of 70 Russians Were Found in Craft and Buried at Sea

By SEYMOUR HERSH
Special to The New York Times

WASHINGTON, March 18—The Central Intelligence Agency financed the construction of a multimillion-dollar deep-sea salvage vessel and used it in an unsuccessful effort last summer to recover hydrogen-warhead missiles and codes from a sunken Soviet nuclear submarine in the Pacific Ocean, according to high Government officials.

The salvage vessel, constructed under disguise for the C.I.A. by Howard R. Hughes, the reclusive billionaire industrialist, did successfully recover about one-third of the submarine, the officials said, but the portion raised from the ocean bottom did not include either the ship's missiles or its code room.

Instead, the Government officials said, the C.I.A.-led expedition recovered the forward section of the ship containing the bodies of more than 70 Soviet seamen and officers who went down with the vessel when she mysteriously exploded and sank in 1968 in more than three miles of water.

Burial Ceremonies

The Soviet submariners were buried at sea in military ceremonies that were filmed and recorded by C.I.A. technicians.

Although thousands of scientists and workmen had security clearance for the program, known as Project Jennifer, the submarine salvage operation remained one of the Nixon and Ford Administrations' closest secrets.

The Jennifer operation had provoked extended debate inside the United States intelligence community since the C.I.A. proposal to build the salvage vessel, first underwent high-level evaluation in the early nineteen-seventies.

Critics Cite Cost

Critics of the program have said that the value of the information that could be gained from what they depict as outmoded code books and outmoded missiles did not justify either the high cost of the operation or its potential for jeopardizing the United States Soviet détente.

The program's defenders, who include William E. Colby, the Director of Central Intelligence, have said that the successful recovery of the whole sub marine would have been the biggest single intelligence coup in history.

They argue that even a 1968 code book would give the Government's signal experts a chance to evaluate all of the Soviet submarine communications that were in existence then and perhaps for years before the ship sank.

New Mission Proposed

Recovery of the missiles also would help provide standards for judging the existing analysis of such weapons as compiled from the precise scrutiny of aerial photographs taken by satellites, Government experts have maintained.

In recent weeks, Mr. Colby has formally asked Secretary of State Kissinger for permission to stage another attempt next summer to salvage the rest of the submarine, which reportedly is lying in nearly 17,000 feet of water about 750 miles northwest of Oahu, Hawaii.

Mr. Kissinger, who serves as head of the 40 Committee, the secret Government panel that reviews and finances all intelligence operations, supported the efforts of the C.I.A. to keep the salvage program secret until a decision could

Continued on Page 52, Column 1

BRITISH YES VOTE ON MARKET URGED

Cabinet Splits on the Issue but Recommends Staying in Economic Community

By ALVIN SHUSTER
Special to The New York Times

LONDON, March 18 — The Government decided today to recommend to the British people that they vote in a referendum this summer to remain in the European Economic Community.

The decision, announced by Prime Minister Harold Wilson in the House of Commons, came after his Cabinet had split deeply on the issue.

Of 23 ministers at a four-hour meeting seven argued that it was time for Britain to withdraw from the nine-nation bloc.

Despite widespread predictions that a Cabinet majority would favor remaining in the Economic Community, or Common Market, Mr. Wilson's appearance generated a sense of drama, with members crowding into the chamber to hear the announcement.

"Her Majesty's Government have decided to recommend to the British people to vote for staying in the Community," Mr. Wilson said at the outset of a rambling speech that reviewed Britain's efforts to win a relaxation in the terms of her membership.

The decision was cheered by members of the Conservative party but was largely greeted in silence by Mr. Wilson's colleagues in the Labor party. The

Continued on Page 2, Column 4

ONASSIS IS BURIED ON SKORPIOS: Jacqueline Kennedy Onassis and her son, John F. Kennedy Jr., at the service conducted by the Rev. Zavitsanos Apostolous, the Greek Orthodox priest from nearby Nidri, Greece, for Aristotle Onassis yesterday. Page 56.

Associated Press

"All the News
That's Fit to Print"

The New York Times

LATE CITY EDITION

Weather: Sunny, milder today; cool tonight. Chance of rain tomorrow. Temperature range: today 43-64; Wednesday 42-60. Details, Page 78.

VOL. CXXIV..No. 42,817   © 1975 The New York Times Company   NEW YORK, THURSDAY, APRIL 17, 1975   Price higher in air delivery cities.   20 CENTS

PHNOM PENH SURRENDERS TO REBEL FORCES AFTER OFFER OF A CEASE-FIRE IS REJECTED

Saigon Peril Grows as Troops Near Xuan Loc Fall Back

S.E.C. Says Northrop Kept $30-Million Secret Fund

By EILEEN SHANAHAN
Special to The New York Times

WASHINGTON, April 16 — The Securities and Exchange Commission filed suit today accusing the Northrop Corporation of maintaining a secret fund of $30-million for political and other purposes, at least some of them illegal.

The company immediately announced that it had agreed to settlement of the suit.

The alleged fund was the largest that any company has so far been accused of maintaining for such purposes and far exceeded the $1.2-million that Northrop had previously admitted maintaining as an illegal fund from which political contributions were made.

Northrop, a relatively small company in the aerospace industry, has specialized in making jet fighters. Its F-5 has been used in as many as 17 air forces. In 1972 its total assets were some $409.9-million. The industry's leader, Boeing

Company, has assets of more than $2-billion.

The suit, similar to ones filed recently by the S.E.C. against such companies as the Gulf Oil Corporation, the United Brands Company and the Phillips Petroleum Company, formally accused Northrop only of statutory violations over which the S.E.C. has jurisdiction. These are confined to charges that the companies failed to make proper disclosure in their reports to stockholders and to the Government of what they were doing with significant sums of money.

Northrop, Thomas V. Jones, its board chairman, and James Allen, former vice president and board member who retired in December, were all named as defendants in the suit filed in United States District Court here.

The S.E.C.'s complaint also

Continued on Page 56, Column 1

EXTRA TAX SOUGHT TO AID DOWNTOWN

Business Group Backs City Plan to Assess Area for Civic Improvements

By PAUL GOLDBERGER

The Downtown-Lower Manhattan Association, an influential organization of businessmen and civic leaders, has approved a city plan for a special real estate tax in lower Manhattan to pay for such urban amenities as pedestrian malls and park areas and to raise planning funds for new projects, such as the now-stalled Manhattan Landing.

The special assessment, which would raise the tax by approximately $1.25 per $1,000 of assessed valuation, would be limited to a five-year period and would apply in a district from river to river bordered on the north by either Chambers Street or Canal Street. It is expected to yield $3-million to $4-million annually.

The plan, developed by the city's Office of Lower Manhattan Planning, was called a "persuasive vote of confidence in lower Manhattan" yesterday by Mayor Beame, who said he "strongly supports this imaginative and sound approach."

Mr. Beame said the

Continued on Page 30, Column 3

Business Leaders Assert Recession Nears a Low Point

By MICHAEL C. JENSEN

Even as the nation suffers from some of the grimmest economic conditions since the nineteen-forties, a number of industrialists and businessmen across the country say they are convinced that the current recession is reaching its low point.

"The worst that can happen already has," said Malcolm Baldrige, chairman of the Scovill Manufacturing Company in Waterbury, Conn. "Most businessmen are still very concerned with the present recession, but we've seen the beginning of the end."

In Washington yesterday the Department of Commerce, reporting on new home-building and individual income levels in March, found that the pace of the business downturn was slowing but disclosed no indication of an upturn. [Page 57.]

Reginald H. Jones, chairman of the General Electric Company, agreed that the rate of decline in the economy had clearly slackened. "We should reach bottom by the end of the second quarter, or the early part of the third quarter," he added.

The businessmen's views were sought in a canvass of a dozen executives in major

Continued on Page 63, Column 3

BIEN HOA POUNDED

South Vietnam Force Abandons Port City of Phan Rang

By MALCOLM W. BROWNE
Special to The New York Times

SAIGON, South Vietnam, Thursday, April 17 — Government units holding the approaches to the devastated city of Xuan Loc, 38 miles northeast of here, were falling back yesterday as the military situation for Saigon appeared to worsen.

A thousand shells again fell on Xuan Loc, where resistance continued, but many Government troops were also pulling back with crowds of refugees from the fighting.

Communist gunners firing at Bien Hoa air base, 15 miles northeast of Saigon, seriously disrupted fighter-bomber traffic.

In a further blow to Saigon, the enclave held by Government forces at the port city of Phan Rang, 170 miles northeast of the capital, was abandoned.

Thus the military situation for the Government appeared markedly worse tonight than it any time since the central part of the country was yielded to the Communist forces two weeks ago.

Enemy Reinforcements Sent

The North Vietnamese have been rushing fresh divisions from central Vietnam to the fighting northeast of Saigon, and there are indications that some of these forces are now in combat.

Several days ago, long-barrelled 122-mm. artillery with a range of 15 miles, about equal to that of the Communists' 130-mm. gun, was brought to bear on Bien Hoa as well as on Xuan Loc and the surrounding area.

In barrages yesterday, about 60 shells fell on or near the Bien Hoa air base. A Government spokesman, reporting that two persons had been killed, conceded that air traffic had been hampered by damage from the shelling and from the explosion two nights ago of a large bomb storage dump. That blast apparently was set off by a commando attack.

The Bien Hoa air base is the main remaining center of Government air operations against the Communists.

The Communists' 122-mm. guns and other heavy artillery

Continued on Page 20, Column 1

Radhakrishnan Dies

Sarvepalli Radhakrishnan, the philosopher and former President of India, died in Madras at 86. Page 42.

Insurgents manning a 105-mm. howitzer in an attack on Cambodian Government forces in positions around Phnom Penh, according to the caption with this photograph. It was radioed from Peking and relayed from Warsaw.

Associated Press

FORD ASSERTS U.S. HAS FAILED SAIGON

Says Commitments on Aid Were Not Met, Creating a 'Tragic Situation'

By PHILIP SHABECOFF
Special to The New York Times

WASHINGTON, April 16—President Ford said today that the failure of the United States to meet its commitments to Saigon had created "this present tragic situation" in South Vietnam.

Responding to questions at the annual convention of the American Society of Newspaper Editors, the President compared the United States behavior toward its South Vietnamese ally unfavorably with what he characterized as the fidelity of Moscow and Peking to Hanoi.

He said that this country had promised Saigon when the Paris peace accords were signed in January, 1973, that it would supply replacement war materiel to South Vietnam. He said he assumed that the Soviet Union and China had made similar commitments to North Vietnam.

"It appears that they have maintained that commitment," the President said. "Unfortunately the United States did not carry out its commitment in the supplying of military

Continued on Page 20, Column 4

Reporter's Notebook: Cambodia

The following dispatch by Sydney H. Schanberg accompanied his account of the battle for Phnom Penh.

Special to The New York Times

PHNOM PENH, Cambodia, April 16—Last night, with this city facing imminent capture by the insurgents who surround it, the National Bank of Cambodia sent a cablegram to the Irving Trust Company in New York, asking the American bank, where it presumably has dollar credits, to confirm that it was carrying out an earlier order to pay $1-million to Marshal Lon Nol. The earlier order was sent by letter on April 1, the

day that the marshal, Cambodia's former President, went into exile under American prodding.

Perhaps the marshal was worried that if Phnom Penh fell to the insurgents before the transaction was confirmed, he would never get the money.

How did the marshal come by the money? It was always rumored here that he was deeply corrupt and had used American aid to build large bank accounts abroad. But no one could ever pin it down. Maybe Irving Trust can shed some light now.

In any case, it was only

one of the many peculiar things that have happened here in the last few days as the insurgents closed in. Here are a few of them.

It is possible that people in the outside world imagine us hunkered down in bunkers, praying as shells fall all around us. Sometimes, near a front line, things do get hairy, and even in Phnom Penh, as this is being written, the sounds of shelling are fierce just outside the southern gates of the city. But there have always been oases. Two nights ago, near the hotel's

Continued on Page 18, Column 5

U.S. Considers Corridor To Evacuate Vietnamese

By DAVID E. ROSENBAUM
Special to The New York Times

WASHINGTON, April 16—Gen. Frederick C. Weyand, the Army Chief of Staff, told a Senate committee today that the Pentagon was considering establishing a corridor from Saigon to the sea to evacuate tens of thousands of Vietnamese.

Creation of such a corridor, one of several evacuation plans being considered, could involve a major commitment of American forces.

Pentagon officials said that, under hostile conditions, at least one Marine division—about 20,000 men — plus air power from Navy carriers would be required to protect the corridor.

At the same time, State Department officials said that the United States was expected to announce tomorrow that 980 Cambodian refugees would be

admitted as temporary residents. [Page 18.]

Meanwhile, the rift between President Ford and Congress over aid to South Vietnam and the evacuation of Americans widened.

The President rejected as inadequate a Congressional plan that would give him $200-million for emergency assistance and restricted authority to use troops for evacuation purposes.

Members of the Senate Foreign Relations Committee said they had been misled about the rate at which Americans were being evacuated and put off, at least until tomorrow, further action on legislation.

An accommodation over the amount of money to be made available still appeared pos-

Continued on Page 20, Column 6

Soviet Politburo Drops Shelepin, Formerly a Contender for Power

By CHRISTOPHER S. WREN
Special to The New York Times

MOSCOW, April 16—Aleksandr N. Shelepin, who once figured as a prominent contender for the authority assumed by Leonid I. Brezhnev, was removed from the Communist party's ruling Politburo today.

The departure of the 56-year-old trade union chief was viewed here as strengthening Mr. Brezhnev's power by eliminating a long-standing and younger rival in anticipation of the 25th congress of the Communist party.

The meeting of the Central Committee that eliminated Mr. Shelepin today scheduled the congress for Feb. 24, 1976. The congress, which lays down

long-term policies, is convened every five years.

Mr. Shelepin, who headed the secret police under Nikita S. Khrushchev, attracted Western attention two weeks ago when he was hounded by demonstrators during an official visit to Britain and returned home early. Some Soviet insiders have suggested that Mr. Shelepin was sent to Britain with the knowledge that he would be embarrassed and thus provide a pretext for removal.

While the official press agency Tass, in a one-sentence reference, reported only that

Continued on Page 2, Column 4

VIETCONG DEMAND FULL U.S. PULLOUT

Charge American Military Has 25,000 in Vietnam Disguised as Civilians

By FLORA LEWIS
Special to The New York Times

PARIS, April 16—The representative of the Vietcong's Provisional Revolutionary Government issued a call here today for "immediate and permanent" withdrawal of what he said were 25,000 American military personnel "disguised as civilians" in South Vietnam.

In a series of statements and at a press conference, he said there would be "no difficulty, no obstacle" placed in the way of their departure.

"If the U.S. really wants to save their lives," a statement said, "it should withdraw them totally and immediately."

But Dinh Ba Thi, interim head of the government's mission here, would not respond to efforts by reporters to determine exactly what would happen to Americans and other foreigners if they remained in areas that fell under Vietcong control. He referred only to a previous statement saying their lives and property would be protected if they obeyed "the policy of the revolutionary power."

The statements accused the Ford Administration of advancing plans for evacuations from Vietnam only as a "pretext for renewed American military intervention."

The warning by Defense Secretary James R. Schlesinger that the lives of 200,000 South Vietnamese would be endangered if they remained in their country was denounced as "a pure fabrication" and a "cal-

Continued on Page 20, Column 7

REPORT IS ON RADIO

Government Soldiers Are Directed to Cease Combat

By United Press International

The Cambodian Government surrendered to insurgent forces today, the Cambodian radio announced. The Phnom Penh Government ordered all its troops to stop firing and lay down their arms.

Brig. Gen. Mey Sichan, chief of operations for the Cambodian Government Army, went on the radio and said

Text of cease-fire proposal is printed on Page 18.

soldiers and functionaries should cease all combat and invite the rebels to take power. This announcement was monitored in Saigon.

After his speech a "representative of the insurgent forces" told all Government officers to report to the Information Ministry, site of the radio station, under a white flag of surrender.

"We enter Phnom Penh as conquerors," the insurgents' representative said. "We order the surrender of all officers and officials of the Phnom puppet regime under a white flag."

The rebels' representative said the final victory for the insurgents had come at 9 A.M. (10 P.M., Wednesday, New York time) when insurgent troops seized the Information Ministry. The ministry and its third-story broadcasting studio are in the center of Phnom Penh, about 200 yards from the Phnom Hotel.

There was no initial word on the fate of the foreigners sequestered at the hotel. These included newsmen, a few diplomats and representatives of the International Red Cross and the United Nations.

Truce Was Sought

By SYDNEY H. SCHANBERG
Special to The New York Times

PHNOM PENH, Cambodia, Thursday, April 17 — The Cambodian military Government asked yesterday for an immediate cease-fire from the Cambodian insurgents, who were attacking Phnom Penh from all sides. The Government said it would turn over power to them.

Several hours later, reports from Peking said that Prince Norodom Sihanouk, the nominal leader of the insurgents who is in exile there, had rejected the cease-fire proposal as unacceptable.

The Phnom Penh Government's proposal, which might be described as conditional surrender, had called for a complete transfer of power to the insurgent side under the supervision of the United Nations and representatives of the International Committee of the Red Cross who are now in Phnom Penh.

A second major point among the five in the proposal was a demand for assurances that there would be no reprisals against persons or organizations for their activities during the five-year war.

The cease-fire proposal, which was transmitted through the Red Cross delegation here, came as this suffering city of more than two million, relatively calm until now, began to show signs of collapse.

Throughout the day, the Com-

Continued on Page 18, Column 1

NEWS INDEX

GOLD! Fabulous Scythian Gold from the USSR. Apr. 19, Metropolitan Museum.-Advt.

FUNERAL OF CHIANG KAI-SHEK IS HELD: Members of the family of President Chiang Kai-shek, who died on April 5, beside his coffin as it was closed during the service yesterday on Taiwan. From left: Chiang Hsiao-wu, grandson; Premier Chiang Ching-kuo, son; Mrs. Chiang and Gen. Chiang Wei-kuo, younger son. Page 42.

Associated Press

"All the News That's Fit to Print"

The New York Times

LATE CITY EDITION

Weather: Continued mostly cloudy, cool today, tonight and tomorrow. Temperature range: today 46-58; Tuesday 45-53. Details on Page 81.

VOL. CXXIV...No. 42,830

© 1975 The New York Times Company

NEW YORK, WEDNESDAY, APRIL 30, 1975

Price higher in air delivery cities.

20 CENTS

MINH SURRENDERS, VIETCONG IN SAIGON; 1,000 AMERICANS AND 5,500 VIETNAMESE EVACUATED BY COPTER TO U.S. CARRIERS

U.S., GREECE AGREE TO END HOME PORT FOR THE 6TH FLEET

Air Base of Americans at Athens Is Also Closed, but Some Facilities Remain

By United Press International

ATHENS, April 29 — United States and Greek officials announced today the termination of the home-port arrangement for Sixth Fleet ships at the port of Eleusis near Athens and the closing of the American air base at Athens airport.

The announcement came in a joint statement at the end of a second round of talks on the status of United States military facilities in Greece.

The Greek Government threatened to close all United States bases and it withdrew from the North Atlantic Treaty Organization's military command after the invasion of Cyprus by Turkey last July.

"Certain United States facilities which contribute to Greek defense needs will continue to operate on the Greek Air Force base at Hellenikon," today's statement said.

The statement said that the second phase of the talks, held April 7 to 29 by the two delegations under the United States Embassy Minister, Monteagle Stearns, and Ambassador Petros Kalogeras of Greece also discussed the status of other facilities.

"Agreement is also expected on the elimination, reduction and conservation of other United States facilities in Greece," it said.

The two delegations said that they made progress on the review of the privileges, immunities and exemptions of American personnel in Greece.

The two Governments said

Continued on Page 4, Column 4

G.M.'s Profits Fall

First-quarter profits of General Motors declined 50.8 per cent from the depressed 1974 quarter. Page 53.

HEAVY USERS FACE CON ED INCREASE

P.S.C. Also Orders Cuts for Smaller Consumers

By WILL LISSNER

The state's Public Service Commission ordered the Consolidated Edison Company yesterday to raise its rates for those customers who accounted for the heaviest summer power demands and to cut the rates for customers whose usage did not create excess power demand.

The change — technically a revision of the rate structure approved last November to give the utility $338.7-million more a year — will not mean any extra revenue for the company. Nor will it affect the rates for the great majority of customers, the 2.5 million small residential and commercial users.

Instead, yesterday's order makes revisions in bills that will take less than $20-million from some customers and give it to others, a relatively small amount compared with its total annual billings of $2.10-billion. It affected less than 500,000 of its 2.9 million customers in New York City, Westchester County and part of Nassau County.

But the order was significant because it introduced into energy ratemaking the philosophy that the customers who are responsible for excess costs should be required to bear more

Continued on Page 34, Column 5

LEARN TO SHOPWELL
Advt.

Abram Offers Bills To Curtail Abuses Of Nursing Homes

By ALFONSO A. NARVAEZ

ALBANY, April 29 — Morris B. Abram proposed today a series of changes in the laws governing nursing homes to "deal with the most serious immediate problems" uncovered during his month-long investigation.

The proposals were contained in a package of 11 bills submitted to Governor Carey and legislative leaders by Mr. Abram, head of the Moreland Act Commission investigating the nursing-home industry.

Among other things, Mr. Abram would authorize nursing-home residents to file class-action suits for deprivation of their rights and would entitle them to receive a minimum of 25 per cent of the daily reimbursement rate paid by government regulations for each day of a violation.

[In Washington, Senator Frank Moss, Democrat of Utah and chairman of the long-term care subcommittee of the Special Committee on Aging, introduced a package of 36 bills for nursing home reform. Among them were measures to make long-term care more readily available to all older Americans, improve inspection and enforcement procedures and provide training for nursing-home physicians, nurses,

Continued on Page 81, Column 3

2d Key Met Museum Aide Quits In Dispute Over Hoving Methods

By GRACE GLUECK

With an attack on Thomas P. F. Hoving's administration of the Metropolitan Museum of Art alleging its inability to function "in any way that creates or preserves trust, confidence and decency," Anthony M. Clark, chairman of the museum's department of European paintings, has resigned.

Mr. Clark's resignation, one of several that have occurred among senior curatorial personnel at the museum, is the first open

challenge to Mr. Hoving's administration.

The resignation, effective June 30, follows that of John Walsh, the vice chairman and curator of this key department a month ago. Mr. Clark would not speak for Mr. Walsh, who is abroad, but it is understood that their basic grievances are similar.

"I can't work with or for the present administration at the Met," said Mr. Clark, who had been director of the Minneapolis Institute of Arts for 10 years before his appointment to the Metropolitan in 1973. "I believe that its relation to art has become incidental, wrong and even risky. It's also held on professionals."

In a statement last night, Mr. Hoving said that he was

Continued on Page 24, Column 1

A crewman from an American helicopter helping evacuees to the top of a building in Saigon for flight to a U.S. carrier

United Press International

CAMBODIA ORDERS FOREIGNERS OUT

Planned 250-Mile Road Trip to Border Is Protested by Paris as Debilitating

By FLORA LEWIS

PARIS, April 29 — The French Government said today that the people who have been isolated in its Phnom Penh embassy since the Cambodian Communists took over two weeks ago had been ordered expelled "in the worst possible conditions."

There are 610 refugees in the embassy. They are to be sent out by truck to the town of Poipet on the Thailand border, beginning tomorrow.

Foreign Minister Jean Sauvagnargues told newsmen after having conferred with President Valéry Giscard d'Estaing:

"We fear these extremely precarious evacuation conditions will be beyond the strength of some whose health is poor."

"We continue to insist that the plane that we have held in Vientiane for evacuation of the ill be allowed to land in Phnom Penh."

However, a Foreign Ministry spokesman said that so far there has been no response to

Continued on Page 17, Column 6

74 Saigon Planes Fly 2,000 to Thailand

By DAVID A. ANDELMAN
Special to The New York Times

BANGKOK, Thailand, April 29 — At least 74 South Vietnamese Air Force planes fleeing the country streamed into U Taphao air base in southern Thailand without warning this afternoon.

The pilots and passengers — 2,000 people — requested asylum, American and Thai Foreign Ministry officials said.

About 30 of the planes were F-5 jet fighters and there were reports that at least one had crashed on a highway near the base as it was making its approach.

The planes began arriving at the huge naval and air base on the Gulf of Siam at about the time that the American evacuation of South Vietnam was ending and the planes were still landing as night fell.

The aircraft were said to include C-47 transports and the C-130 cargo planes that the American military has been using to ferry refugees from South Vietnam to Guam and the Philippines. However, all the aircraft were understood to be Vietnam Air Force planes, originally supplied by the United States.

A Thai Foreign Ministry spokesman said that American authorities at U Taphao had been asked to turn over the aircraft to the Thai Government, which would return them to "the new South Vietnamese government." The pilots and passengers, the Thai spokesman said, "must leave Thailand."

"They just landed first and

asked permission afterwards," said an astounded Thai Foreign Ministry official. Other Government sources said that apparently no efforts were made to prevent the planes from landing and no aircraft went up to intercept the fighters as they roared in.

American Embassy officials in Bangkok declined to comment on the Thai request that the planes be returned and their status was unclear. An unresolved question here appeared to be whether the planes were still American property or belonged to whatever government continued in Saigon. The planes could be worth $200-million, one official said.

No details were available on the status of the refugees or

Continued on Page 16, Column 6

FORD UNITY PLEA

President Says That Departure 'Closes a Chapter' for U.S.

By JOHN W. FINNEY
Special to The New York Times

WASHINGTON, April 29 — The United States ended two decades of military involvement in Vietnam today with the evacuation of about 1,000 Americans from Saigon as well as more than 5,500 South Vietnamese.

The emergency helicopter evacuation was ordered last night by President Ford after the Saigon airport was closed

Ford statement and excerpts from Kissinger's, Page 17.

because of Communist rocket and artillery fire. The 1,000 Americans were the last contingent of a force that once numbered more than 500,000.

They were carried by a fleet of 81 American helicopters to carriers in the South China Sea. The helicopters removed the 5,500 South Vietnamese citizens because their lives were presumed to be in danger with a Communist take-over of South Vietnam. Over the last two weeks, a total of about 55,000 South Vietnamese have been removed. Most of them will come to the United States.

Last Marines Evacuated

The helicopter flights ended the United States evacuation of South Vietnam.

The final withdrawal of Americans was completed at 7:52 P.M., about two hours after the White House had announced the evacuation was completed, when 11 marines were taken by helicopter from the roof of the American Embassy in Saigon. Officials said that the marines, the last of a security guard sent in to protect the evacuation, were taken although small-arms fire had broken out around the deserted embassy.

President Ford, in a statement issued by the White House, said the evacuation "closes a chapter in the American experience." In a plea for national unity in the post-Vietnam period, the President said:

"I ask all Americans to close ranks, to avoid recrimination about the past, to look ahead to the many goals we share and to work together on the great tasks that remain to be accomplished."

Appeal by Kissinger

At a news conference, Secretary of State Kissinger appealed to North Vietnam not to storm Saigon by force because the United States believed the new South Vietnamese Govern-

Continued on Page 17, Column 1

DEFENSE ENDS

General Tells His Troops to Turn in Their Weapons

By The Associated Press

SAIGON, South Vietnam, Wednesday, April 30—President Duong Van Minh announced today the unconditional surrender of the Saigon Government and its military forces to the Vietcong.

Columns of South Vietnamese troops pulled out of their defensive positions in the capital and marched to central points to turn in their weapons.

Within two hours, Communist forces began moving into Saigon. A jeep flying the Vietcong flag and carrying eight cheering men in civilian clothes armed with an assortment of weapons drove along the street a block from the United States Embassy compound.

This action followed by hours the ending of the American involvement in Vietnam through the evacuation of most of the approximately 1,000 Americans still here.

In Washington, the White House said that President Ford had "no comment" on the surrender of Saigon, but a White House spokesman said the surrender was considered 'inevitable.' Page 16]

3 Decades of Fighting

The surrender announcement, made in a broadcast to the nation, signaled the end of three decades of fighting. It came 21 years after the 1954 Geneva accords divided Viet-

The text of President Minh's statement is on Page 16.

nam into North and South and a little more than two years after the Vietnam cease-fire agreement was signed in Paris on Jan. 27, 1973. The last American troops left the country in March of that year.

President Minh, who took office on Monday to lead South Vietnam into peace negotiations, said in his brief radio address:

"I believe firmly in reconciliation among Vietnamese to avoid unnecessary shedding of the blood of Vietnamese. For this reason, I ask the soldiers of the Republic of Vietnam to cease hostilities in calm and to stay where they are."

The President also asked the "brother soldiers" of the Vietcong to cease hostilities and added:

"We wait here to meet the Provisional Revolutionary Government of South Vietnam to discuss together a ceremony of orderly transfer of power so as to avoid any unnecessary

Continued on Page 16, Column 1

Saigon Copter Lands on Another In Stampede to U.S. Ship's Deck

By The Associated Press

ABOARD U.S.S. BLUE RIDGE, in South China Sea, April 29 — Scores of South Vietnamese helicopters filled with military men and civilians fled Saigon today and headed out to sea to search for the carriers of the United States Seventh Fleet.

Seven of the helicopters arrived unexpectedly above this vessel carrying Americans and Vietnamese evacuated from South Vietnam. The seven copters made a dash for the helipad at the rear of the ship.

One pilot dropped his helicopter on the blades of another that had just landed and chunks of metal ripped through the air. The top helicopter, with its load of women and children, nearly toppled into the sea, but there were no injuries.

United States sailors heaved the two damaged choppers overboard to clear the landing pad. For the Vietnamese it was a last-ditch chance to survive.

As other Vietnamese helicopters landed their passengers were pulled free. American sailors ripped the doors off the craft to make them sink and the pilots then jettisoned them in the sea to make room for other arrivals circling overhead. Two small craft rescued the swimming pilots.

The American evacuation was reported orderly, although it was delayed several times because of weather and pilot fatigue.

The Blue Ridge is the command and communications vessel of the 40-ship Seventh Fleet armada waiting off the coast of South Vietnam to evacuate Americans and other foreigners

Continued on Page 17, Colum

President Ford and Secretary of State Kissinger returning to White House to resume talks on Vietnam. They had just said good-by to King Hussein of Jordan after visit.

United Press International

WESTCHESTERITES, arise! Move your money to a bank that puts it to work for Westchester. Scarsdale National. Advt.